of

CIVIL LITIGATION

A–Z
of
CIVIL LITIGATION

by

James Pyke, M.A., LL.M.
Solicitor

SWEET & MAXWELL

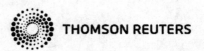

THOMSON REUTERS

First Edition published in 2001

Published in 2013 by Sweet & Maxwell, 100 Avenue Road, London NW3 3PF
part of Thomson Reuters (Professional) UK Limited
(Registered in England & Wales, Company No 1679046.
Registered Office and address for service:
Aldgate House, 33 Aldgate High Street, London EC3N 1DL)

Typeset by Interactive Sciences Ltd, Gloucester
Printed and bound by CPI Group (UK) Ltd, Croydon, CR0 4YY
* For further information on our products and services, visit www.sweetandmaxwell.co.uk

No natural forests were destroyed to make this product;
only farmed timber was used and re-planted.

A CIP catalogue record for this book is available from the British Library.

ISBN 978 0 414 04782 2

Thomson Reuters and the Thomson Reuters logo are trademarks of Thomson Reuters. Sweet &
Maxwell ® is a registered trademark of Thompson Reuters (Professional) UK Limited

Dedication

To the staff of James Pyke & Co, Solicitors of London.

Foreword

The Civil Procedure Rules 1998 came into force on April 26, 1999. Since then, there have been 61 updates to the Rules as at April 1, 2013; and there are still more to follow. It reminds me of the Proverb: "The Law is a bottomless pit".

The idea of the A–Z came from a comment made to me by articled clerks and trainee solicitors that civil procedure is difficult to learn because the provisions are all over the place.

The Civil Procedure Rules 1998 are in a more simplified form. I have gone further by putting into A to Z format, the Rules and the Practice Directions that supplement them; and also the Rules of the Supreme Court 1965 and the County Court Rules 1981 that still apply.

The 60th and 61st updates were released just ahead of the book being sent to press. The publishers kindly gave me the opportunity to deal with the main updates. These being: (i) the amendment to the definition of "overriding objective" so the courts deal with cases justly and at proportionate costs; (ii) increase in the limit of the small claims track (excluding personal injury and housing disrepair claims) from £5,000 to £10,000; and (iii) the revocation of CPR Pt 43 and re-drafting of Pts 44–48 (Costs) and the Practice Directions in support.

James Pyke

Common Abbreviations used in this Book

Civil Procedure Rules 1998	CPR
Practice Direction supplementing a Civil Procedure Rule	PD
Practice Directions about costs supplementing Parts 43 to 48 of the Civil Procedure Rules 1998	Costs PD
Supreme Court Act 1981	SCA
Rules of the Supreme Court 1965	RSC
County Courts Act 1984	CCA
County Court Rules 1981	CCR

A

AARHUS CONVENTION CLAIM

Pt 45 r.45.41

(2) a claim for judicial review of a decision, act or omission all or part of which is subject to the provisions of the UNECE Convention on Access to Information, Public Participation in Decision-Making and Access to Justice in Environmental Matters done at Aarhus, Denmark on June 25, 1998, including a claim which proceeds on the basis that the decision, act or omission, or part of it, is so subject.

Costs limits

Pt 45. r.45.41

(1) [Section VII of Pt 45] provides for the costs which are to be recoverable between the parties in Aarhus Convention claims.
(r. 52.9A makes provision in relation to costs of an appeal.)

Opting out

Pt 45 r.45.42

R. 45.43 to 45.44 do not apply where the claimant—
  (a) has not stated in the claim form that the claim is an Aarhus Convention claim; or
  (b) has stated in the claim form that—
    (i) the claim is not an Aarhus Convention claim, or
    (ii) although the claim is an Aarhus Convention claim, the claimant does not wish those rules to apply.

Limit on costs recoverable from a party in an Aarhus Convention claim

Pt 45 r.45.43

(1) Subject to r. 45.44, a party to an Aarhus Convention claim may not be ordered to pay costs exceeding the amount prescribed in PD 45.
(2) PD 45 may prescribe a different amount for the purpose of para.(1) according to the nature of the claimant.

PD 45 s.VII para.5.1

Where a claimant is ordered to pay costs, the amount specified for the purpose of r. 45.43(1) is—

(a) £5,000 where the claimant is claiming only as an individual and not as, or on behalf of, a business or other legal person;

(b) in all other cases, £10,000.

PD 45 s.VII para.5.2

Where a defendant is ordered to pay costs, the amount specified for the purpose of r. 45.43(1) is £35,000.

Challenging whether the claim is an Aarhus Convention claim

Pt 45 r.45.44

(1) If the claimant has stated in the claim form that the claim is an Aarhus Convention claim, r.45.43 will apply unless—

(a) the defendant has in the acknowledgment of service filed in accordance with r. 54.8—

(i) denied that the claim is an Aarhus Convention claim; and

(ii) set out the defendant's grounds for such denial; and

(b) the court has determined that the claim is not an Aarhus Convention claim.

(2) Where the defendant argues that the claim is not an Aarhus Convention claim, the court will determine that issue at the earliest opportunity.

(3) In any proceedings to determine whether the claim is an Aarhus Convention claim—

(a) if the court holds that the claim is not an Aarhus Convention claim, it will normally make no order for costs in relation to those proceedings;

(b) if the court holds that the claim is an Aarhus Convention claim, it will normally order the defendant to pay the claimant's costs of those proceedings on the indemnity basis, and that order may be enforced notwithstanding that this would increase the costs payable by the defendant beyond the amount prescribed in PD 45.

See **Judicial review.**

ABANDONED CLAIM WHERE DEFAULT JUDGMENT SET ASIDE

Pt 16 r.13.6

Where—

(a) the claimant claimed a remedy in addition to one specified in r.12.4(1) (claims in respect of which the claimant may obtain default judgment by filing a request);

(b) the claimant abandoned his claim for that remedy in order to obtain default judgment on request in accordance with r.12.4(3); and

(c) that default judgment is set aside under this Part,

the abandoned claim is restored when the default judgment is set aside.

ABUSE OF PROCESS

Pt 3 r.3.4

(2) The court may **strike out** a **statement of case** if it appears to the court—

(b) that the statement of case is an abuse of the court's process or is otherwise likely to obstruct the just disposal of the proceedings.

ACCELERATED POSSESSION CLAIMS

Pt 55 r.55.11

(1) The claimant may bring a possession claim under this section of this Part where—
   (a) the claim is brought under s.21 of the 1988 Act to recover possession of residential property let under an assured shorthold tenancy; and
   (b) subject to r.55.12(2), all the conditions listed in r.55.12(1) are satisfied.
(2) The claim must be started in the county court for the district in which the property is situated.

(By virtue of s.20B of the 1988 Act, a demoted assured shorthold tenancy is an assured shorthold tenancy).

Conditions

Pt 55 r.55.12

(1) The conditions referred to in r.55.11(1)(b) are that—
   (a) the tenancy and any agreement for the tenancy were entered into on or after January 15, 1989;
   (b) the only purpose of the claim is to recover possession of the property and no other claim is made;
   (c) the tenancy did not immediately follow an assured tenancy which was not an assured shorthold tenancy;
   (d) the tenancy fulfilled the conditions provided by ss.19A or 20(1)(a) to (c) of the 1988 Act;
   (e) the tenancy—
       (i) was the subject of a written agreement;
       (ii) arises by virtue of s.5 of the 1988 Act but follows a tenancy that was the subject of a written agreement; or
       (iii) relates to the same or substantially the same property let to the same tenant and on the same terms (though not necessarily as to rent or duration) as a tenancy which was the subject of a written agreement; and
   (f) a notice in accordance with s.21(1) or 21(4) of the 1988 Act was given to the tenant in writing.
(2) If the tenancy is a demoted assured shorthold tenancy, only the conditions in para.(1)(b) and (f) need be satisfied.

Claim Form

Pt 55 r.55.13

(1) The claim form must—
   (a) be in the form set out in PD 55A; and
   (b) (i) contain such information; and
       (ii) be accompanied by such documents, as are required by that form.
(2) All relevant sections of the form must be completed.
(3) The court will serve the claim form by first class post (or an alternative service which provides for delivery on the next working day).

Defence

Pt 55 r.55.14

(1) A defendant who wishes to—
    (a) oppose the claim; or
    (b) seek a postponement of possession in accordance with r.55.18,
    must file his defence within 14 days after service of the claim form.
(2) The defence should be in the form set out in PD 55A.

Claim referred to judge

Pt 55 r 55.15

(1) On receipt of the defence the court will—
    (a) send a copy to the claimant; and
    (b) refer the claim and defence to a judge.
(2) Where the period set out in r.55.14 has expired without the defendant filing a defence—
    (a) the claimant may file a written request for an order for possession; and
    (b) the court will refer that request to a judge.
(3) Where the defence is received after the period set out in r.55.14 has expired but before a request is filed in accordance with para.(2), para.(1) will still apply.
(4) Where—
    (a) the period set out in r.55.14 has expired without the defendant filing a defence; and
    (b) the claimant has not made a request for an order for possession under para.(2) within three months after the expiry of the period set out in r.55.14,
    the claim will be stayed.

Consideration of the claim

Pt 55 r.55.16

(1) After considering the claim and any defence, the judge will—
    (a) make an order for possession under r.55.17;
    (b) where he is not satisfied as to any of the matters set out in para.(2)—
        (i) direct that a date be fixed for a hearing; and
        (ii) give any appropriate case management directions; or
    (c) strike out the claim if the claim form discloses no reasonable grounds for bringing the claim.
(2) The matters referred to in para.(1)(b) are that—
    (a) the claim form was served; and
    (b) the claimant has established that he is entitled to recover possession under s.21 of the 1988 Act against the defendant.
(3) The court will give all parties not less than 14 days' notice of a hearing fixed under para.(1)(b)(i).
(4) Where a claim is struck out under para.(1)(c)—
    (a) the court will serve its reasons for striking out the claim with the order; and
    (b) the claimant may apply to restore the claim within 28 days after the date the order was served on him.

Possession order

Pt 55 r.55.17

Except where r.55.16(1)(b) or (c) apply, the judge will make an order for possession without requiring the attendance of the parties.

Postponement of possession

Pt 55 r.55.18

(1) Where the defendant seeks postponement of possession on the ground of exceptional hardship under s.89 of the Housing Act 1980 the judge may direct a hearing of that issue.
(2) Where the judge directs a hearing under para.(1)—
    (a) the hearing must be held before the date on which possession is to be given up; and
    (b) the judge will direct how many days' notice the parties must be given of that hearing.
(3) Where the judge is satisfied, on a hearing directed under para.(1), that exceptional hardship would be caused by requiring possession to be given up by the date in the order of possession, he may vary the date on which possession must be given up.

PD 55A para.8.1

If the judge is satisfied as to the matters set out in r.55.16(2), he will make an order for possession in accordance with r.55.17, whether or not the defendant seeks a postponement of possession on the ground of exceptional hardship under s.89 of the Housing Act 1980.

PD 55A para.8.2

In a claim in which the judge is satisfied that the defendant has shown exceptional hardship, he will only postpone possession without directing a hearing under r.55.18(1) if—
(1) he considers that possession should be given up six weeks after the date of the order or, if the defendant has requested postponement to an earlier date, on that date; and
(2) the claimant indicated on his claim form that he would be content for the court to make such an order without a hearing.

PD 55A para.8.3

In all other cases if the defendant seeks a postponement of possession under s.89 of the Housing Act 1980, the judge will direct a hearing under r.55.18(1).

PD 55A para.8.4

If, at that hearing, the judge is satisfied that exceptional hardship would be caused by requiring possession to be given up by the date in the order of possession, he may vary that order under r.55.18(3) so that possession is to be given up at a later date. That later date may be no later than six weeks after the making of the order for possession on the papers (see s.89 of the Housing Act 1980).

Application to set aside or vary

Pt 55, r.55.19

The court may
   (a) on application by a party within 14 days of service of the order; or
   (b) of its own initiative,
set aside or vary any order made under r.55.17.
See also **Possession claims**.

ACCESS TO NEIGHBOURING LAND ACT 1992

PD 56 para.11.1

The claimant must use the **Part 8 procedure**.

PD 56 para.11.2

The claim form must set out:
   (1) details of the dominant and servient land involved and whether the dominant land includes or consists of residential property;
   (2) the work required;
   (3) why entry to the servient land is required with plans (if applicable);
   (4) the names and addresses of the persons who will carry out the work;
   (5) the proposed date when the work will be carried out; and
   (6) what (if any) provision has been made by way of insurance in the event of possible injury to persons or damage to property arising out of the proposed work.

PD 56 para.11.3

The owner and occupier of the servient land must be defendants to the claim.

ACCOUNTS AND INQUIRIES

PD 24 para.6

If a remedy sought by a claimant in his claim form includes, or necessarily involves, taking an account or making an inquiry, an application can be made under Pt 24 [**summary judgment**] by any party to the proceedings for an order directing any necessary accounts or inquiries to be taken or made.

PD 40A para.1.1

Where the court orders any account to be taken or any inquiry to be made, it may, by the same or a subsequent order, give directions as to the manner in which the account is to be taken and verified or the inquiry is to be conducted.

PD 40A para.1.2

In particular, the court may direct that in taking an account, the relevant books of account shall be evidence of their contents but that any party may take such objections to the contents as he may think fit.

PD 40A para.1.3

Any party may apply to the court in accordance with CPR Pt 23 for directions as to the taking of an account or the conduct of an inquiry or for the variation of directions already made.

PD 40A para.1.4

Every direction for the taking of an account or the making of an inquiry shall be numbered in the order so that, as far as possible, each distinct account and inquiry is given its own separate number.

Verifying the account

PD 40A para.2

Subject to any order to the contrary:
    (1) the accounting party must make out his account and verify it by an affidavit or witness statement to which the account is exhibited,
    (2) the accounting party must file the account with the court and at the same time notify the other parties that he has done so and of the filing of any affidavit or witness statement verifying or supporting the account.

Objections

PD 40A para.3.1

Any party who wishes to contend:
    (a) that an accounting party has received more than the amount shown by the account to have been received, or
    (b) that the accounting party should be treated as having received more than he has actually received, or
    (c) that any item in the account is erroneous in respect of amount, or
    (d) that in any other respect the account is inaccurate, must, unless the court directs otherwise, give written notice to the accounting party of his objections.

PD 40A para.3.2

The written notice referred to in para.3.1 must, so far as the objecting party is able to do so:
    (a) state the amount by which it is contended that the account understates the amount received by the accounting party,
    (b) state the amount which it is contended that the accounting party should be treated as having received in addition to the amount he actually received,
    (c) specify the respects in which it is contended that the account is inaccurate, and
    (d) in each case, give the grounds on which the contention is made.

PD 40A para.3.3

The contents of the written notice must, unless the notice contains a statement of truth, be verified by either an affidavit or a witness statement to which the notice is an exhibit.
(Part 22 and PD 22 contain provisions about **statements of truth**).

Allowances

PD 40A para.4

In taking any account all just allowances shall be made without any express direction to that effect.

Management of proceedings

PD 40A para.5

The court may at any stage in the taking of an account or in the course of an inquiry direct a hearing in order to resolve an issue that has arisen and for that purpose may order that points of claim and points of defence be served and give any necessary directions.

Delay

PD 40A para.6.1

If it appears to the court that there is undue delay in the taking of any account or the progress of any inquiry the court may require the accounting party or the party with the conduct of the inquiry, as the case may be, to explain the delay and may then make such order for the management of the proceedings (including a stay) and for costs as the circumstances may require.

PD 40A para.6.2

The directions the court may give under para.6.1 include a direction that the Official Solicitor take over the conduct of the proceedings and directions providing for the payment of the Official Solicitor's costs.

Distribution

PD 40A para.7

Where some of the persons entitled to share in a fund are known but there is, or is likely to be, difficulty or delay in ascertaining other persons so entitled, the court may direct, or allow, immediate payment of their shares to the known persons without reserving any part of those shares to meet the subsequent costs of ascertaining the other persons.

Guardian's accounts

PD 40A para.8

The accounts of a person appointed guardian of the property of a child (defined in CPR r.21.1(2)) must be verified and approved in such manner as the court may direct.

See also **Guardian's account**.

Accounts and inquiries to be conducted before master or district judge

PD 40A para.9

Unless the court orders otherwise, an account or inquiry will be taken or made—
    (1) by a Master or district judge, if the proceedings are in the High Court; and
    (2) by a district judge, if the proceedings are in a county court.

Advertisements

PD 40A para.10

The court may—
    (1) direct any necessary advertisement; and
    (2) fix the time within which the advertisement should require a reply.

Examination of claims

PD 40A para.11.1

Where the court orders an account of debts or other liabilities to be taken, it may direct any party, within a specified time, to—
    (1) examine the claims of persons claiming to be owed money out of the estate or fund in question.
    (2) determine, so far as he is able, which of them are valid; and
    (3) file written evidence—
        (a) stating his findings and his reasons for them; and
        (b) listing any other debts which are or may be owed out of the estate or fund.

PD 40A para.11.2

Where the court orders an inquiry for next of kin or other unascertained claimants to an estate or fund, it may direct any party, within a specified time, to—
    (1) examine the claims that are made;
    (2) determine, so far as he is able, which of them are valid; and
    (3) file written evidence stating his findings and his reasons for them.

PD 40A para.11.3

If the personal representatives or trustees concerned are not the parties directed by the court to examine claims, the court may direct them to join with the party directed to examine claims in producing the written evidence required by this rule.

Consideration of claims by the court

PD 40A para.12

For the purpose of considering a claim the court may—
    (1) direct it to be investigated in any manner;

    (2) direct the person making the claim to give further details of it; and
    (3) direct that person to—
        (a) file written evidence; or
        (b) attend court to give evidence,
    to support his claim.

Notice of decision

PD 40A para.13

If—
    (1) the court has allowed or disallowed any claim or part of a claim; and
    (2) the person making the claim was not present when the decision was made,
the court will serve on that person a notice informing him of its decision.

See **Interest**.

ACKNOWLEDGMENT OF RECEIPT

Possession claims online

PD 55B para.6.5

When an online claim form is received, an acknowledgment of receipt will automatically be sent to the claimant. The acknowledgment does not constitute notice that the claim form has been issued or served.

PD 55B para.7.3

When an online defence form is received, an acknowledgment of receipt will automatically be sent to the defendant. The acknowledgment does not constitute notice that the defence has been served.

PD 55B para.11.3

When an online application form is received, an acknowledgment of receipt will automatically be sent to the applicant. The acknowledgment does not constitute a notice that the online application form has been issued or served.

ACKNOWLEDGMENT OF SERVICE

Pt 10 r.10.1

    (1) This Part deals with the procedure for filing an acknowledgment of service.
    (2) Where the claimant uses the procedure set out in Pt 8 (alternative procedure for claims) this Part applies subject to the modifications set out in r.8.3.
    (3) A defendant may file an acknowledgment of service if—
        (a) he is unable to file a defence within the period specified in r.15.4; or
        (b) he wishes to dispute the court's jurisdiction.
(Part 11 sets out the procedure for disputing the court's jurisdiction)

Consequence of not filing an acknowledgment of service

Pt 10 r.10.2

If—
   (a) a defendant fails to file an acknowledgment of service within the period specified in r.10.3; and
   (b) does not within that period file a defence in accordance with Pt 15 or serve or file an admission in accordance with Pt 14, the claimant may obtain default judgment if Pt 12 allows it.

Period for filing an acknowledgment of service

Pt 10 r.10.3

   (1) The general rule is that the period for filing an acknowledgment of service is—
      (a) where the defendant is served with a claim form which states that particulars of claim are to follow, 14 days after service of the particulars of claim; and
      (b) in any other case, 14 days after service of the claim form.
   (2) The general rule is subject to the following rules—
      (a) rule 6.35 (which specifies how the period for filing an acknowledgment of service is calculated where the claim form is served out of the jurisdiction under rr.6.32 or 6.33);
      (b) rule 6.12(3) (which requires the court to specify the period for responding to the particulars of claim when it makes an order under that rule); and
      (c) rule 6.37(5) (which requires the court to specify the period within which the defendant may file an acknowledgment of service calculated by reference to PD 6B when it makes an order giving permission to serve a claim form out of the jurisdiction).

Notice to claimant that defendant has filed an acknowledgment of service

Pt 10 r.10.4

On receipt of an acknowledgment of service, the court must notify the claimant in writing.

Contents of acknowledgment of service

Pt 10 r.10.5

   (1) An acknowledgment of service must—
      (a) be signed by the defendant or the defendant's legal representative; and
      (b) include the defendants' address for service.
(Rule 6.23 makes provision in relation to addresses for service).
(Rule 19.8A modifies this Part where a notice of claim is served under that rule to bind a person not a party to the claim).

Form of acknowledgment of service

PD 10 para.10.2

A defendant who wishes to acknowledge service of a claim should do so by using Form N9.

PD 10 para.5.1

The defendant's name should be set out in full on the acknowledgment of service.

PD 10 para.5.2

Where the defendant's name has been incorrectly set out in the claim form, it should be correctly set out on the acknowledgment of service followed by the words 'described as' and the incorrect name.

PD 10 para.5.3

If two or more defendants to a claim acknowledge service of a claim through the same legal representative at the same time, only one acknowledgment of service need be used.

Address for service

PD 110 para.3.1

The defendant must include in the acknowledgment of service an address for the service of document.

PD 10 para.3.2

Where the defendant is represented by a **legal representative** and the legal representative has signed the acknowledgment of service form, the address must be the legal representative's business address; otherwise the address for service that is given should be as set out in r.6.23.

See **Service of documents**.

Signing the acknowledgment of service

PD 10, para.4.1

An acknowledgment of service must be signed by the defendant or by his legal representative.

Amendment or withdrawal of acknowledgment of service

PD 10 para.5.4

An acknowledgment of service may be amended or withdrawn only with the permission of the court.

PD 10 para.5.5

An application for permission under para.5.4 must be made in accordance with Pt 23 and supported by evidence.
(Paragraph 8.2 of PD 6A contains provisions about service by the court on the claimant of any notice of funding filed with an acknowledgment of service).

Judgment against a state in default of acknowledgment of service

PD 10 para.40.10

(1) Where the claimant obtains default judgment under Pt 12 on a claim against a State where the defendant has failed to file an acknowledgment of service, the judgment does not take effect until two months after service on the State of—
   (a) a copy of the judgment; and
   (b) a copy of the evidence in support of the application for permission to enter default judgment (unless the evidence has already been served on the State in accordance with an order made under Pt 12).
(2) In this rule, 'State' has the meaning given by s.14 of the State Immunity Act 1978.

Disputing the court's jurisdiction

See **Jurisdiction**.

Failure to acknowledge service in a probate claim

Pt 57 r.57.10

(1) A default judgment cannot be obtained in a **Probate claim**.

See also **Acknowledgment of service—Pt 8 Procedure, Child, Protected party, Commercial Court, Company, Inheritance (Provision for Family and Dependants) Act 1975, Landlord and Tenant claims, Mercantile courts,** and **Partnership**.

ACKNOWLEDGMENT OF SERVICE—PT 8 PROCEDURE

Pt 8 r.8.3

(1) The defendant must—
   (a) file an acknowledgment of service in the relevant practice form not more than 14 days after service of the claim form; and
   (b) serve the acknowledgment of service on the claimant and any other party.
(2) The acknowledgment of service must state—
   (a) whether the defendant contests the claim; and
   (b) if the defendant seeks a different remedy from that set out in the claim form, what that remedy is.
(3) The following rules of Pt 10 (acknowledgment of service) apply—
   (a) rule 10.3(2) (exceptions to the period for filing an acknowledgment of service); and

(b) rule 10.5 (contents of acknowledgment of service).

See also **Acknowledgment of service**.

Consequence of not filing an acknowledgment of service

Pt 8 r.8.4

(1) This rule applies where—
   (a) the defendant has failed to file an acknowledgment of service; and
   (b) the time period for doing so has expired.
(2) The defendant may attend the hearing of the claim but may not take part in the hearing unless the court gives permission.

ACQUISITION ORDER

See **Landlord and Tenant Act 1987**.

ACQUITTAL

See **Quashing of an acquittal**.

ADDITION OF PARTY

See **Parties**.

ADDITIONAL CLAIMS

Pt 20 r.20.2

(2) Any claim other than the claim by the claimant against the defendant; and
   (b) unless the context requires otherwise, references to a claimant or defendant include a party bringing or defending an additional claim.

Pt 20 r.20.1

The purpose of [Pt 20] is to enable counterclaims and other additional claims to be managed in the most convenient and effective manner.

Pt 20 r.20.2

(1) [Part 20] applies to—
   (a) a counterclaim by a defendant against the claimant or against the claimant and some other person;
   (b) an additional claim by a defendant against any person (whether or not already a party) for contribution or indemnity or some other remedy; and

    (c) where an additional claim has been made against a person who is not already a party, any additional claim made by that person against any other person (whether or not already a party).

PD 20 para.3

The CPR apply generally to additional claims as if they were claims. Parties should be aware that the provisions relating to failure to respond to a claim will apply.

Application of these rules to additional claims

Pt 20 r.20.3

    (1) An additional claim shall be treated as if it were a claim for the purposes of these rules, except as provided by this Part.
    (2) The following rules do not apply to additional claims—
        (a) Rules 7.5 and 7.6 (time within which a claim form may be served);
        (b) Rule 16.3(5) (statement of value where claim to be issued in the High Court); and
        (c) Part 26 (case management—preliminary stage).
    (3) Part 12 (default judgment) applies to a counterclaim but not to other additional claims.
    (4) Part 14 (admissions) applies to a counterclaim, but only—
        (a) Rule 14.1(1) and 14.1(2) (which provide that a party may admit the truth of another party's case in writing); and
        (b) Rule 14.3 (admission by notice in writing—application for judgment),
    apply to other additional claims.

Defendant's counterclaim against the claimant

Pt 20 r.20.4

    (1) A defendant may make a counterclaim against a claimant by filing particulars of the counterclaim.
    (2) A defendant may make a counterclaim against a claimant—
        (a) without the court's permission if he files it with his defence; or
        (b) at any other time with the court's permission.
(Part 15 makes provision for a defence to a claim and applies to a defence to a counterclaim by virtue of r.20.3).
    (3) Part 10 (acknowledgment of service) does not apply to a claimant who wishes to defend a counterclaim.

Counterclaim against a person other than the claimant

Pt 20 r.20.5

    (1) A defendant who wishes to counterclaim against a person other than the claimant must apply to the court for an order that that person be added as an additional party.
    (2) An application for an order under para.(1) may be made without notice unless the court directs otherwise.

(3) Where the court makes an order under para.(1), it will give directions as to the management of the case.

Defendant's additional claim for contribution or indemnity from another party

Pt 20 r.20.6

(1) A defendant who has filed an acknowledgment of service or a defence may make an additional claim for contribution or indemnity against a person who is already a party to the proceedings by—
 (a) filing a notice containing a statement of the nature and grounds of his additional claim; and
 (b) serving the notice on that party.
(2) A defendant may file and serve a notice under this rule—
 (a) without the court's permission, if he files and serves it—
  (i) with his defence; or
  (ii) if his additional claim for contribution or indemnity is against a party added to the claim later, within 28 days after that party files his defence; or
 (b) at any other time with the court's permission.

Procedure for making any other additional claim

Pt 20 r.20.7

(1) This rule applies to any additional claim except—
 (a) a counterclaim only against an existing party; and
 (b) a claim for contribution or indemnity made in accordance with r.20.6.
(2) An additional claim is made when the court issues the appropriate claim form.
(Rule 7.2(2) provides that a claim form is issued on the date entered on the form by the court)
(3) A defendant may make an additional claim—
 (a) without the court's permission if the additional claim is issued before or at the same time as he files his defence;
 (b) at any other time with the court's permission.
(Rule 15.4 sets out the period for filing a defence).
(4) Particulars of an additional claim must be contained in or served with the additional claim.
(5) An application for permission to make an additional claim may be made without notice, unless the court directs otherwise.

Service of claim form

Pt 20 r.20.8

(1) Where an additional claim may be made without the court's permission, any claim form must—
 (a) in the case of a counterclaim against an additional party only, be served on every other party when a copy of the defence is served;
 (b) in the case of any other additional claim, be served on the person against whom it is made within 14 days after the date on which the additional claim is issued by the court.

(2) Paragraph (1) does not apply to a claim for contribution or indemnity made in accordance with r.20.6.

(3) Where the court gives permission to make an additional claim it will at the same time give directions as to its service.

Matters relevant to question of whether an additional claim should be separate from the claim

Pt 20 r.20.9

(1) This rule applies where the court is considering whether to—
   (a) permit an additional claim to be made;
   (b) dismiss an additional claim; or
   (c) require an additional claim to be dealt with separately from the claim by the claimant against the defendant.
(Rule 3.1(2)(e) and (j) deal respectively with the court's power to order that part of proceedings be dealt with as separate proceedings and to decide the order in which issues are to be tried).
(2) The matters to which the court may have regard include—
   (a) the connection between the additional claim and the claim made by the claimant against the defendant;
   (b) whether the additional claimant is seeking substantially the same remedy which some other party is claiming from him; and
   (c) whether the additional claimant wants the court to decide any question connected with the subject matter of the proceedings—
      (i) not only between existing parties but also between existing parties and a person not already a party; or
      (ii) against an existing party not only in a capacity in which he is already a party but also in some further capacity.

Effect of service of an additional claim

Pt 20 r.20.10

(1) A person on whom an additional claim is served becomes a party to the proceedings if he is not a party already.

(2) When an additional claim is served on an existing party for the purpose of requiring the court to decide a question against that party in a further capacity, that party also becomes a party in the further capacity specified in the additional claim.

Special provisions relating to default judgment on an additional claim other than a counterclaim or a contribution or indemnity notice

Pt 20 r.20.11

(1) This rule applies if—
   (a) the additional claim is not—
      (i) a counterclaim; or
      (ii) a claim by a defendant for contribution or indemnity against another defendant under r.20.6; and

   (b) the party against whom an additional claim is made fails to file an acknowledgment of service or defence in respect of the additional claim.

(2) The party against whom the additional claim is made—

   (a) is deemed to admit the additional claim, and is bound by any judgment or decision in the proceedings in so far as it is relevant to any matter arising in the additional claim;

   (b) subject to para.(3), if default judgment under Pt 12 is given against the additional claimant, the additional claimant may obtain judgment in respect of the additional claim by filing a request in the relevant practice form.

(3) An additional claimant may not enter judgment under para.(2)(b) without the court's permission if—

   (a) he has not satisfied the default judgment which has been given against him; or

   (b) he wishes to obtain judgment for any remedy other than a contribution or indemnity.

(4) An application for the court's permission under para.(3) may be made without notice unless the court directs otherwise.

(5) The court may at any time set aside or vary a judgment entered under para.(2)(b).

Procedural steps on service of an additional claim form on a non-party

Pt 20 r.20.12

(1) Where an additional claim form is served on a person who is not already a party it must be accompanied by—

   (a) a form for defending the claim;

   (b) a form for admitting the claim;

   (c) a form for acknowledging service; and

   (d) a copy of—

      (i) every statement of case which has already been served in the proceedings; and

      (ii) such other documents as the court may direct.

(2) A copy of the additional claim form must be served on every existing party.

Case management where a defence to an additional claim is filed

Pt 20 para.13

(1) Where a defence is filed to an additional claim the court must consider the future conduct of the proceedings and give appropriate directions.

(2) In giving directions under para.(1) the court must ensure that, so far as practicable, the original claim and all additional claims are managed together.

(Part 66 contains provisions about counterclaims and other Pt 20 claims in relation to proceedings by or against the Crown).

Cases where court's permission to make an additional claim is required

PD 20 para.1.1

Rules 20.4(2)(b), 20.5(1) and 20.7(3)(b) set out the circumstances in which the court's permission will be needed for making an additional claim.

PD 20 para.1.2

Where an application is made for permission to make an additional claim the application notice should be filed together with a copy of the proposed additional claim.

Applications for permission to issue an additional claim

PD 20 para.2.1

An application for permission to make an additional claim must be supported by evidence stating:
  (1) the stage which the proceedings have reached,
  (2) the nature of the additional claim to be made or details of the question or issue which needs to be decided,
  (3) a summary of the facts on which the additional claim is based, and
  (4) the name and address of any proposed additional party.
(For further information regarding evidence see PD 32).

PD 20 para.2.2

Where delay has been a factor contributing to the need to apply for permission to make an additional claim an explanation of the delay should be given in evidence.

PD 20 para.2.3

Where possible the applicant should provide a timetable of the proceedings to date.

PD 20 para.2.4

Rules 20.5(2) and 20.7(5) allow applications to be made to the court without notice unless the court directs otherwise.

Statement of truth

PD 20 para.4.1

The contents of an additional claim should be verified by a statement of truth. Part 22 requires a statement of case to be verified by a statement of truth.

PD 20 para.4.2

The form of the statement of truth should be as required by para.2.1 of PD 22.

PD 20 para.4.3

Attention is drawn to r.32.14 which sets out the consequences of verifying a statement of case containing a false statement without an honest belief in its truth.

Case management where there is a defence to an additional claim

PD 20 para.5.1

Where the defendant to an additional claim files a defence, other than to a counterclaim, the court will arrange a hearing to consider case management of the additional claim. This will normally be at the same time as a case management hearing for the original claim and any other additional claims.

PD 20 para.5.2

The court will give notice of the hearing to each party likely to be affected by any order made at the hearing.

PD 20 para.5.3

At the hearing the court may:
  (1) treat the hearing as a summary judgment hearing,
  (2) order that the additional claim be dismissed,
  (3) give directions about the way any claim, question or issue set out in or arising from the additional claim should be dealt with,
  (4) give directions as to the part, if any, the additional defendant will take at the trial of the claim,
  (5) give directions about the extent to which the additional defendant is to be bound by any judgment or decision to be made in the claim.

PD 20 para.,5.4

The court may make any of the Orders in rr.5.3(1) to (5) either before or after any judgment in the claim has been entered by the claimant against the defendant.

Form of counterclaim

PD 20 para.6.1

Where a defendant to a claim serves a counterclaim, the defence and counterclaim should normally form one document with the counterclaim following on from the defence.

PD 20 para.6.2

Where a claimant serves a reply and a defence to counterclaim, the reply and the defence to counterclaim should normally form one document with the defence to counterclaim following on from the reply.

Titles of proceedings where there are additional claims

PD 20 para.7.1

Paragraph 4 of PD 7A contains directions regarding the title to proceedings.

PD 20 para.7.2

Where there are additional claims which add parties, the title to the proceedings should comprise a list of all parties describing each by giving them a single identification. Subject to para.7.11, this identification should be used throughout.

PD 20 para.7.3

Claimants and defendants in the original claim should always be referred to as such in the title to the proceedings, even if they subsequently acquire an additional procedural status.

PD 20 para.7.4

Additional parties should be referred to in the title to the proceedings in accordance with the order in which they are joined to the proceedings, for example 'Third Party' or 'Fourth Party', whatever their actual procedural status.
Examples:
  (a) If the defendant makes an additional claim against a single additional party, the additional party should be referred to in the title as 'Third Party'.
  (b) If the defendant makes separate additional claims against two additional parties, the additional parties should be referred to in the title as 'Third Party' and 'Fourth Party'.
  (c) If the defendant makes a counterclaim against the claimant and an additional party, the claimant should remain as 'Claimant' and the additional party should be referred to in the title as 'Third Party'.
  (d) If the Third Party in example (b) makes an additional claim against a further additional party, that additional party should be referred to in the title as 'Fifth Party'.

PD 20 para.7.5

If an additional claim is brought against more than one party jointly, they should be referred to in the title to the proceedings as, for example, 'First Named Third Party' and 'Second Named Third Party'.

PD 20 para.7.6

In group litigation, the court should give directions about the designation of parties.

PD 20 para.7.7

All parties should co-operate to ensure that two parties each making additional claims do not attribute the same nominal status to more than one party.

PD 20 para.7.8

In proceedings with numerous parties, the court will if necessary give directions as to the preparation and updating of a list of parties giving their roles in the claim and each additional claim.

PD 20 para.7.9

If an additional party ceases to be a party to the proceedings, for example because the claim against that party is discontinued or dismissed, all other additional parties should retain their existing nominal status.

PD 20 para.7.10

In proceedings where there are additional parties, the description of all statements of case or other similar documents should clearly identify the nature of the document with reference to each relevant party.

Examples:

  (e) In example (a), the defendant's additional claim should be headed 'Defendant's Additional Claim against Third Party' and the Third Party's defence to it should be headed 'Third Party's Defence to Defendant's Additional Claim'.

  (f) In example (c), the defendant's counterclaim should be headed 'Defendant's Counterclaim against Claimant and Third Party' and the Third Party's defence to it should be headed 'Third Party's defence to Defendant's Counterclaim'.

PD 20 para.7.11

In proceedings where there are Fourth or subsequent parties, additional parties should be referred to in the text of statements of case or other similar documents by name, suitably abbreviated if appropriate. If parties have similar names, suitable distinguishing abbreviations should be used.

ADDRESS FOR SERVICE

Address for service to be given after proceedings are started

Pt 6 r.6.23

  (1) A party to proceedings must give an address at which that party may be served with documents relating to those proceedings. The address must include a full **postcode** or its equivalent in any EEA state (if applicable) unless the court orders otherwise.

  (2) Except where any other rule or PD makes different provision, a party's address for service must be—

    (a) The business address either within the UK or any other EEA state of a solicitor acting for the party to be served; or

    (b) the business address in any EEA state of a European Lawyer nominated to accept service of documents; or

    (c) where there is no solicitor acting for the party or no European Lawyer nominated to accept service of documents—

      (i) an address within the UK at which the party resides or carries on business; or

      (ii) an address within any other EEA state at which the party resides or carries on business.

  (3) Where none of subparas (2)(a), (b) or (c) applies, the party must give an address for service within the UK.

(Part 42 contains provisions about change of solicitor. Rule 42.1 provides that where a party gives the business address of a solicitor as that party's address for service, that solicitor will be considered to be acting for the party until the provisions of Pt 42 are complied with.)

  (4) Subject to the provisions of s.IV of this Part (where applicable), any document to be served in proceedings must be sent or transmitted to, or left at, the party's address for service under para.(2) or (3) unless it is to be served personally or the court orders otherwise.

  (5) Where, in accordance with PD 6A, a party indicates or is deemed to have indicated that they will accept service by fax, the fax number given by that party must be at the address for service.

(6) Where a party indicates in accordance with PD 6A that they will accept service by electronic means other than fax, the e-mail address or electronic identification given by that party will be deemed to be at the address for service.

(7) In proceedings by or against the Crown, service of any document in the proceedings on the Crown must be effected in the same manner prescribed in r.6.10 as if the document were a claim form.

(8) This rule does not apply where an order made by the court under r.6.27 (service by an alternative method or at an alternative place) specifies where a document may be served.

Change of address for service

P6 r.6.24

Where the address for service of a party changes, that party must give notice in writing of the change as soon as it has taken place to the court and every other party.

Address in claim form

PD 16 para.2.2

The claim form must include an address at which the claimant resides or carries on business. This paragraph applies even though the claimant's address for service is the business address of his solicitor.

PD 16 para.2.3

Where the defendant is an individual, the claimant should (if he is able to do so) include in the claim form an address at which the defendant resides or carries on business. This paragraph applies even though the defendant's solicitors have agreed to accept service on the defendant's behalf.

PD 16 para.2.4

Any address which is provided for the purpose of these provisions must include a postcode or its equivalent in any EEA state (if applicable), unless the court orders otherwise.

PD 16 para.2.5

If the claim form does not show a full address, including postcode, at which the claimant(s) and defendant(s) reside or carry on business, the claim form will be issued but will be retained by the court and will not be served until the claimant has supplied a full address, including postcode, or the court has dispensed with the requirement to do so. The court will notify the claimant.

Address for service in acknowledgment of service

PD10 para.3.1

The defendant must include in the acknowledgment of service an address for the service of documents.

Legal representative acting for defendant

PD 10 para.3.2

Where the defendant is represented by a **legal representative** and the legal representative has signed the acknowledgment of service form, the address must be the legal representative's business address; otherwise the address for service that is given should be as set out in r.6.23.

New address for service where order made solicitor has ceased to act

PD 42 para.5.1

Where the court has made an order under r.42.3 that a solicitor has ceased to act or under r.42.4 declaring that a solicitor has ceased to be the solicitor for a party, the party for whom the solicitor was acting must give a new address for service to comply with rr.6.23(1) and 6.24.
(Rule 6.23(2)(a) provides that a party must give an address for service within the UK or where a solicitor is acting for a party, an address for service either in the UK or any other EEA state).
(Until such time as a new address for service is given r.6.9 will apply).

Possession claims online

PD 55B para.5.1

A claim may be started online if inter alia—
  (3A) the claimant has an address for service in the UK.
   (4) the defendant has an address for service in England and Wales; and
   (5) the claimant is able to provide a postcode for the property.

See **Possession claims online**.

Production centre

PD 7C para.2.3

The Centre will not issue inter alia the following types of claim—
   (7) a claim where the claimant's address for service as it appears on the claim form is not in the UK.
  (7A) a claim where the defendant's address for service as it appears on the claim form is not in England and Wales.

See also **Service of documents**.

ADMINISTRATION ACTIONS

See **Administration of estates and trusts**.

ADMINISTRATION OF ESTATES AND TRUSTS

Pt 64 r.64.1

(1) [Part 64] contains rules—
    (a) in section 1, about claims relating to—
        (i) the administration of estates of deceased persons, and
        (ii) trusts.
(2) In this Part and PD s 64A and 64B, where appropriate, references to trustees include executors and administrators.
(3) All proceedings in the High Court to which this Part applies must be brought in the Chancery Division.

Claims

Pt 64 r.64.2

[Section I of Pt 64] applies to claims—
    (a) for the court to determine any question arising in—
        (i) the administration of the estate of a deceased person; or
        (ii) the execution of a trust;
    (b) for an order for the administration of the estate of a deceased person, or the execution of a trust, to be carried out under the direction of the court ('an administration order');
    (c) under the Variation of Trusts Act 1958; or
    (d) under s.48 of the **Administration of Justice Act 1985**.

Examples of claims under r.64.2(a)

PD 64A para.1

The following are examples of the types of claims which may be made under r.64.2(a)—
    (1) a claim for the determination of any of the following questions—
        (a) any question as to who is included in any class of persons having—
            (i) a claim against the estate of a deceased person;
            (ii) a beneficial interest in the estate of such a person; or
            (iii) a beneficial interest in any property subject to a trust;
        (b) any question as to the rights or interests of any person claiming—
            (i) to be a creditor of the estate of a deceased person;
            (ii) to be entitled under a will or on the intestacy of a deceased person; or
            (iii) to be beneficially entitled under a trust;
    (2) a claim for any of the following remedies—
        (a) an order requiring a trustee—
            (i) to provide and, if necessary, verify accounts;
            (ii) to pay into court money which he holds in that capacity; or
            (iii) to do or not to do any particular act;
        (b) an order approving any sale, purchase, compromise or other transaction by a trustee (whether administrative or dispositive); or
        (c) an order directing any act to be done which the court could order to be done if the estate or trust in question were being administered or executed under the direction of the court.

Determining certain claims under r.64.2(a) without a hearing

PD 64A para.1A.1

Where a claim is made by a trustee for a remedy within paragraph 1(2)(b) (including a case where the remedy sought is approval of a transaction affected by conflict of interests or duties), the court may be requested to determine the claim without a hearing.

PD 64A para.1A.2

The claim form in such a case may be issued in accordance with r.8.2A (Issue of claim form without naming defendants), and no separate application for permission under r.8.2A need be made.

PD 64A para.1A.3

The claim form must be accompanied by—
  (a) a witness statement setting out the material facts justifying determination without a hearing and in particular—
    (i) identifying those affected by the remedy sought and
    (ii) detailing any consultation of those so affected and the result of that consultation;
  (b) the advice of a lawyer having a 10-year High Court qualification within the meaning of s.71 of the Courts and Legal Services Act 1990 on the merits of the claim;
  (c) a draft order for the remedy sought;
  (d) a statement of costs.

PD 64A para.1A.4

If the court considers that the case does not require an oral hearing, it will proceed to consider the claim on the papers.

PD 64A para.1A.5

If the court considers that an oral hearing is required, it will give appropriate directions.

PD 64A para.1A.6

If the court considers it appropriate, it will make the order sought and may direct that the claimant must—
  (a) serve notice of the order on the interested parties in accordance with r.19.8A, and
  (b) file a certificate of service within seven days of doing so.

Administration orders—r.64.2(b)

PD 64A para.3.1

The court will only make an administration order if it considers that the issues between the parties cannot properly be resolved in any other way.

PD 64A para.3.2

If, in a claim for an administration order, the claimant alleges that the trustees have not provided proper accounts, the court may—
(1) stay the proceedings for a specified period, and order them to file and serve proper accounts within that period; or
(2) if necessary to prevent proceedings by other creditors or persons claiming to be entitled to the estate or fund, make an administration order and include in it an order that no such proceedings are to be taken without the court's permission.

PD 64A para.3.3

Where an administration order has been made in relation to the estate of a deceased person, and a claim is made against the estate by any person who is not a party to the proceedings—
(1) no party other than the executors or administrators of the estate may take part in any proceedings relating to the claim without the permission of the court; and
(2) the court may direct or permit any other party to take part in the proceedings, on such terms as to costs or otherwise as it thinks fit.

PD 64A para.3.4

Where an order is made for the sale of any property vested in trustees, those persons shall have the conduct of the sale unless the court directs otherwise.

Applications under the Variation of Trusts Act 1958—r.64.2(c)

PD 64A para.4.1

Where children or unborn beneficiaries will be affected by a proposed arrangement under the Act, the evidence filed in support of the application must—
(1) show that their litigation friends or the trustees support the arrangements as being in the interests of the children or unborn beneficiaries; and
(2) unless para.4.3 applies or the court Orders otherwise, be accompanied by a written opinion to this effect by the advocate who will appear on the hearing of the application.

PD 64A para.4.2

A written opinion filed under para.4.1(2) must—
(1) if it is given on formal instructions, be accompanied by a copy of those instructions; or
(2) otherwise, state fully the basis on which it is given.

PD 64A para.4.3

No written opinion needs to be filed in support of an application to approve an arrangement under s.1(1)(d) of the Act (discretionary interests under protective trusts).

PD 64A para.4.4

Where the interests of two or more children, or two or more of the children and unborn beneficiaries, are similar, only a single written opinion needs to be filed.

Prospective costs orders

PD 64A para.6.1

These paragraphs are about the costs of applications under r.64.2(a).

PD 64A para.6.2

Where trustees have power to agree to pay the costs of a party to such an application, and exercise such a power, r.48.3 applies. In such a case, an order is not required and the trustees are entitled to recover out of the trust fund any costs which they pay pursuant to the agreement made in the exercise of such power.

PD 64A para.6.3

Where the trustees do not have, or decide not to exercise, a power to make such an agreement, the trustees or the party concerned may apply to the court at any stage of proceedings for an order that the costs of any party (including the costs of the trustees) shall be paid out of the fund (a 'prospective costs order').

PD 64A para.6.4

The court, on an application for a prospective costs order, may—
  (a) in the case of the trustees' costs, authorise the trustees to raise and meet such costs out of the fund;
  (b) in the case of the costs of any other party, authorise or direct the trustees to pay such costs (or any part of them, or the costs incurred up to a particular time) out of the trust fund to be assessed, if not agreed by the trustees, on the indemnity basis or, if the court directs, on the standard basis, and to make payments from time to time on account of such costs. A model form of order is annexed to this PD .

PD 64A para.6.5

The court will always consider whether it is possible to deal with the application for a prospective costs order on paper without a hearing and in an ordinary case would expect to be able to do so. The trustees must consider whether a hearing is needed for any reason. If they consider that it is they should say so and explain why in their evidence. If any party to the application referred to in para.6.1 above (or any other person interested in the trust fund) considers that a hearing is necessary (for instance because he wishes to oppose the making of a prospective costs order) this should be stated, and the reasons explained, in his evidence, if any, or otherwise in a letter to the court.

PD 64A para.6.6

If the court would be minded to refuse the application on a consideration of the papers alone, the parties will be notified and given the opportunity, within a stated time, to ask for a hearing.

PD 64A para.6.7

The evidence in support of an application for a prospective costs order should be given by witness statement. The trustees and the applicant (if different) must ensure full disclosure of the relevant matters to show that the case is one which falls within the category of case where a prospective costs order can properly be made.

PD 64A para.6.8

The model form of order is designed for use in the more straightforward cases, where a question needs to be determined which has arisen in the administration of the trust, whether the claimants are the trustees or a beneficiary. The form may be adapted for use in less straightforward cases, in particular where the proceedings are hostile, but special factors may also have to be reflected in the terms of the order in such a case.

Claim form

Pt 64 r.64.3

A claim to which this Section applies must be made by issuing a Pt 8 claim form.

PD 64B para.2

If confidentiality of the directions sought is important (for example, where the directions relate to actual or proposed litigation with a third party who could find out what directions the trustees are seeking through access to the claim form under CPR r.5.4) the statement of the remedy sought, for the purposes of CPR r.8.2(b), may be expressed in general terms. The trustees must, in that case, state specifically in the evidence what it is that they seek to be allowed to do.

Parties

Pt 64 r.64.4

 (1) In a claim to which this Section applies, other than an application under s.48 of the Administration of Justice Act 1985—
  (a) all the trustees must be parties;
  (b) if the claim is made by trustees, any of them who does not consent to being a claimant must be made a defendant; and
  (c) the claimant may make parties to the claim any persons with an interest in or claim against the estate, or an interest under the trust, who it is appropriate to make parties having regard to the nature of the order sought.
 (2) In addition, in a claim under the Variation of Trusts Act 1958, unless the court directs otherwise any person who—
  (a) created the trust; or
  (b) provided property for the purposes of the trust,
  must, if still alive, be made a party to the claim.
  (The court may, under r.19.2, order additional persons to be made parties to a claim).

Proceedings in private

PD 64B para.3

The proceedings will in the first instance be listed in private (see para.1.5 of PD 39A and r.39.2(3)(f)). Accordingly the order made, as well as the other documents among the court records (apart from a claim form which has been served), will not be open to inspection by third parties without the court's permission (r.5.4(2)). If the matter is disposed of without a hearing, the order made will be expressed to have been made in private.

Joining defendants or giving notice to those interested

PD 64B para.4.1

Rule 64.4(1)(c) deals with the joining of beneficiaries as defendants. Often, especially in the case of a private trust, it will be clear that some, and which, beneficiaries need to be joined as defendants. Sometimes, if there are only two views of the appropriate course, and one is advocated by one beneficiary who will be joined, it may not be necessary for other beneficiaries to be joined since the trustees may be able to present the other arguments. Equally, in the case of pension trust, it may not be necessary for a member of every possible different class of beneficiaries to be joined.

PD 64B para.4.2

In some cases the court may be able to assess whether or not to give the directions sought, or what directions to give, without hearing from any party other than the trustees. If the trustees consider that their case is in that category they may apply to the court to issue the claim form without naming any defendants under r.8.2A. They must apply to the court before the claim form is issued (r.8.2A(2)) and include a copy of the claim form that they propose to issue (r.8.2A(3)(b)).

PD 64B para.4.3

In other cases the trustees may know that beneficiaries need to be joined as defendants, or to be given notice, but may be in doubt as to which. Examples could include a case concerning a pension scheme with many beneficiaries and a number of different categories of interest, especially if they may be differently affected by the action for which directions are sought, or a private trust with a large class of discretionary beneficiaries. In those cases the trustees may apply to issue the claim form without naming any defendants under r.8.2A. The application may be combined with an application to the court for directions as to which persons to join as parties or to give notice to under r.19.8A.

PD 64B para.4.4

In the case of a charitable trust the Attorney General is always the appropriate defendant, and almost always the only one.

Case management directions

PD 64B para.5.1

The claim will be referred to the master or district judge once a defendant has acknowledged service, or otherwise on expiry of the period for acknowledgment of service, (or, if no defendant is named, as soon as the claimants' evidence has been filed) to consider directions for the management of the case. Such directions may be given without a hearing in some cases; these might include directions as to parties or as to notice of proceedings, as mentioned in para.4 above.

Applications by trustees for directions

PD 64A para.2

A separate PD contains guidance about applications by trustees for directions [PD 64B].

Joining defendants or giving notice to those interested

PD 64B para.4.1

Rule 64.4(1)(c) deals with the joining of beneficiaries as defendants. Often, especially in the case of a private trust, it will be clear that some, and which, beneficiaries need to be joined as defendants. Sometimes, if there are only two views of the appropriate course, and one is advocated by one beneficiary who will be joined, it may not be necessary for other beneficiaries to be joined since the trustees may be able to present the other arguments. Equally, in the case of pension trust, it may not be necessary for a member of every possible different class of beneficiaries to be joined.

PD 64B para.4.2

In some cases the court may be able to assess whether or not to give the directions sought, or what directions to give, without hearing from any party other than the trustees. If the trustees consider that their case is in that category they may apply to the court to issue the claim form without naming any defendants under r.8.2A. They must apply to the court before the claim form is issued (r.8.2A(2)) and include a copy of the claim form that they propose to issue (r.8.2A(3)(b)).

PD 64B para.4.3

In other cases the trustees may know that beneficiaries need to be joined as defendants, or to be given notice, but may be in doubt as to which. Examples could include a case concerning a pension scheme with many beneficiaries and a number of different categories of interest, especially if they may be differently affected by the action for which directions are sought, or a private trust with a large class of discretionary beneficiaries. In those cases the trustees may apply to issue the claim form without naming any defendants under r.8.2A. The application may be combined with an application to the court for directions as to which persons to join as parties or to give notice to under r.19.8A.

PD 64B para.4.4

In the case of a charitable trust the Attorney General is always the appropriate defendant, and almost always the only one.

Case management directions

PD 64B para.5.1

The claim will be referred to the master or district judge once a defendant has acknowledged service, or otherwise on expiry of the period for acknowledgment of service, (or, if no defendant is named, as soon as the claimants' evidence has been filed) to consider directions for the management of the case. Such directions may be given without a hearing in some cases; these might include directions as to parties or as to notice of proceedings, as mentioned in para.4 above.

Proceeding without a hearing

PD 64B para.6.1

(1) The court will dispose of the application without a hearing if it considers that to do so will save time or expense, and that a hearing is not necessary. The trustees must therefore consider whether a hearing is not necessary and, if so, explain why in their evidence.

(2) When considering whether to hold a hearing, the court will take into account any dispute between the parties as to directions, but will not necessarily direct a hearing for that reason alone.

(3) If a defendant considers that a hearing is needed, and that the need is noty sufficiently explained in the trustees' evidence, that defendant should so state in evidence, giving reasons why.

PD 64B para.6.2

Where the court deals with an application without a hearing, it will in any order give the parties an opportunity within a stated time to apply to vary or discharge the order at an oral hearing.

PD 64B para.6.3

In charity cases, the master or district judge may deal with the case without a hearing on the basis of a letter by or on behalf of the Attorney-General that sets out his attitude to the application.

Evidence

PD 64B para.7.1

The trustees' evidence should be given by witness statement. In order to ensure that, if directions are given, the trustees are properly protected by the order, they must ensure full disclosure of relevant matters, even if the case is to proceed with the participation of beneficiaries as defendants.

PD 64B para.7.2

Applications for directions whether or not to take or defend or pursue litigation should be supported by evidence of the following matters—

(1) The advice of an appropriately qualified lawyer as to the prospects of success;

(2) An estimate in summary form of—

    (a) the value or other significance to the trust estate of the issues in the proceedings;

    (b) the costs likely to be incurred by the trustees in the proceedings, by reference ot the principal stages in the proceedings; and

    (c) the costs of other parties to the proceedings for which, if unsuccessful, the trustees may be exposed to liability;

(3) any known facts concerning the means of other parties to the proceedings; and

(4) any other factors relevant to th court's decision whether to give the directions sought.

PD 64B para.7.3

References in [PD 64B] to an appropriately qualified lawyer mean one whose qualifications and experience are appropriate to the circumstances of the case. The qualifications should be stated. If the advice is given on formal instructions, the instructions should always be put in evidence as well, so that the court can see the basis on which the advice was given. If it is not, the advice must state fully the basis on which it is given.

PD 64B para.7.5

On an application for directions about actual or possible litigation the evidence should also state whether (i) the PD (Pre-Action Conduct) or any relevant Pre-Action Protocol has been complied with; and (ii) the trustees have proposed or undertaken, or intend to propose, mediation by ADR, and (in each case) if not why not.

PD 64B para.7.6

If a beneficiary of the trust is a party to the litigation about which directions are sought, with an interest opposed to that of the trustees, that beneficiary should be a defendant to the trustees' application, but any material which would be privileged as regards that beneficiary in the litigation should be put in evidence as exhibits to the trustees' witness statement, and should not be served on the beneficiary. However if the trustees' representatives consider that no harm would be done by the disclosure of all or some part of the material, then that material should be served on that defendant. That defendant may also be excluded from part of the hearing, including that which is devoted to discussion of the material withheld.

Consultation with beneficiaries

PD 64B para.7.7

The evidence must explain what, if any, consultation there has been with beneficiaries, and with what result. In preparation for an application for directions in respect of litigation, the following guidance is to be followed:

(1) If the trust is a private trust where the beneficiaries principally concerned are not numerous and are all or mainly adult, identified and traceable, the trustees will be expected to have canvassed with all the adult beneficiaries the proposed or possible courses of action before applying for directions.

(2) If it is a private trust with a larger number of beneficiaries, including those not yet born or identified, or children, it is likely that there will nevertheless be some adult beneficiaries principally concerned, with whom the trustees must consult.

(3) In relation to a charitable trust the trustees must have consulted the Attorney-General, through the Treasury Solicitor, as well as the Charity Commissioners whose consent to the application will have been needed under s.33 of the Charities Act 1993.

(4) In relation to a pension trust, unless the members are very few in number, no particular steps by way of consultation with beneficiaries (including, where relevant, employers) or their representatives are required in preparation for the application, though the trustees' evidence should describe any consultation that has in fact taken place. If no consultation has taken place, the court could in some cases direct that meetings of one or more classes of beneficiaries be held to consider the subject matter of the application, possibly as a preliminary to deciding whether a member of a particular class ought to be joined as a defendant, though in a case concerning actual or proposed litigation, steps would need to be considered to protect privileged material from too wide disclosure.

PD 64B para.7.8

(1) If the court gives directions allowing the trustees to take, defend or pursue litigation it may do so up to a particular stage in the litigation, requiring the trustees, before they carry on beyond that point, to renew their application to the court. What stage that should

be will depend on the likely management of the litigation under the CPR. If the application is to be renewed after disclosure of documents, and disclosed documents need to be shown to the court, it may be necessary to obtain permission to do this from the court in which the other litigation is proceeding.

PD 64B para.7.9

In a case of urgency, such as where a limitation period or period for service of proceedings is about to expire, the court may be able to give directions on a summary consideration of the evidence to cover the steps which need to be taken urgently, but limiting those directions so that the application needs to be renewed on fuller consideration at an early stage.

PD 64B para.7.10

In any application for directions where a child is a defendant, the court will expect to have put before it the instructions to and advice of an appropriately qualified lawyer as to the benefits and disadvantages of the proposed, and any other relevant, course of action from the point of view of the child beneficiary.

PD 64B para.7.11

The master or district judge may give the directions sought though, if the directions relate to actual or proposed litigation, only if it is a plain case, and therefore the master or district judge may think it appropriate to give the directions without a hearing: see PD 2B, para 4.1 and para.5.1(e), and see also para.6 above. Otherwise the case will be referred to the judge.

PD 64B para.7.12

Where a hearing takes place, if the advice of a lawyer has been put in evidence in accordance with paras 7.2 or 7.10, that lawyer should if possible appear on the hearing.

ADMINISTRATION OF JUSTICE ACT 1985

Pt 64 r.64.2

[Section I of Pt 64] applies to claims—
    (d) under s.48 of the Administration of Justice Act 1985.

See **Administration of estates and trusts**.

Applications under s.48 of the 1985 Act

PD 65 para.5

A Pt 8 claim form for an application by trustees under s.48 of the Administration of Justice Act 1985 (power of High Court to authorise action to be taken in reliance on legal opinion) may be issued without naming a defendant, under r.8.2A. No separate application for permission under r.8.2A need be made.

ADMINISTRATION ORDER

Exercise of powers by district judge

CCR Ord.3 r.1

Any powers conferred on the court by Pt VI of the Act, s.4 of the Attachment of Earnings Act 1971 or this order may be exercised by the district judge or, in the circumstances mentioned in this order, by the court officer.

Request and list of creditors

CCR Ord.39 r.2

(1) A debtor who desires to obtain an administration order under Pt VI of the Act shall file a request in that behalf in the court for the district in which he resides or carries on business.
(2) Where on his examination under CPR Pt 71, or otherwise, a debtor furnishes to the court on oath a list of his creditors and the amounts which he owes to them respectively and sufficient particulars of his resources and needs, the court may proceed as if the debtor had filed a request under para.(1).
(3) Where a debtor is ordered to furnish a list under s.4(1)(b) of the said Act of 1971, then, unless otherwise directed, the list shall be filed within 14 days after the making of the order.

Verification on oath

CCR Ord.3 r.3

The statements in the request mentioned in r.2(1) and the list mentioned in r.2(3) shall be verified by the debtor on oath.

Orders made by the court officer

CCR Ord.39 r.5

(1) The question whether an administration order should be made, and the terms of such an order, may be decided by the court officer in accordance with the provisions of this rule.
(2) On the filing of a request or list under r.2, the court officer may, if he considers that the debtor's means are sufficient to discharge in full and within a reasonable period the total amount of the debts included in the list, determine the amount and frequency of the payments to be made under such an order ('the proposed rate') and—
    (a) notify the debtor of the proposed rate requiring him to give written reasons for any objection he may have to the proposed rate within 14 days of service of notification upon him;
    (b) send to each creditor mentioned in the list provided by the debtor a copy of the debtor's request or of the list together with the proposed rate;

(c) require any such creditor to give written reasons for any objection he may have to the making of an administration order within 14 days of service of the documents mentioned in sub-paragraph (b) upon him.

Objections under subpara.(c) may be to the making of an order, to the proposed rate or to the inclusion of a particular debt in the order.

(3) Where no objection under para.(2)(a) or (c) is received within the time stated, the court officer may make an administration order providing for payment in full of the total amount of the debts included in the list.

(4) Where the debtor or a creditor notifies the court of any objection within the time stated, the court officer shall fix a day for a hearing at which the district judge will decide whether an administration order should be made and the court officer shall give not less than 14 days' notice of the day so fixed to the debtor and to each creditor mentioned in the list provided by the debtor.

(5) Where the court officer is unable to fix a rate under para.(2) (whether because he considers that the debtor's means are insufficient or otherwise), he shall refer the request to the district judge.

(6) Where the district judge considers that he is able to do so without the attendance of the parties, he may fix the proposed rate providing for payment of the debts included in the list in full or to such extent and within such a period as appears practicable in the circumstances of the case.

(7) Where the proposed rate is fixed under para.(6), paras (2) to (4) shall apply with the necessary modifications as if the rate had been fixed by the court officer.

(8) Where the district judge does not fix the proposed rate under para.(6), he shall direct the court officer to fix a day for a hearing at which the district judge will decide whether an administration order should be made and the court officer shall give not less than 14 days' notice of the day so fixed to the debtor and to each creditor mentioned in the list provided by the debtor.

(9) Where an administration order is made under para.(3), the court officer may exercise the power of the court under s.5 of the Attachment of Earnings Act 1971 to make an attachment of earnings order to secure the payments required by the administration order.

Notice of objection by creditor

CCR Ord.39 r.6

(1) Any creditor to whom notice has been given under r.5(8) and who objects to any debt included in the list furnished by the debtor shall, not less than seven days before the day of hearing, give notice of his objection, stating the grounds thereof, to the court officer, to the debtor and to the creditor to whose debt he objects.

(2) Except with the permission of the court, no creditor may object to a debt unless he has given notice of his objection under para.(1).

Procedure on day of hearing

CCR Ord.39 r.7

On the day of the hearing—

(a) any creditor, whether or not he is mentioned in the list furnished by the debtor, may attend and prove his debt or, subject to r.6, object to any debt included in that list;

(b) every debt included in that list shall be taken to be proved unless it is objected to by a creditor or disallowed by the court or required by the court to be supported by evidence;

(c) any creditor whose debt is required by the court to be supported by evidence shall prove his debt;

(d) the court may adjourn proof of any debt and, if it does so, may either adjourn consideration of the question whether an administration order should be made or proceed to determine the question, in which case, if an administration order is made, the debt, when proved, shall be added to the debts scheduled to the order;

(e) any creditor whose debt is admitted or proved, and, with the permission of the court, any creditor the proof of whose debt has been adjourned, shall be entitled to be heard and to adduce evidence on the question whether an administration order should be made and, if so, in what terms.

Direction for order to be subject to review

CCR Ord.39 r. 8

(1) The court may, on making an administration order or at any subsequent time, direct that the order shall be subject to review at such time or at such intervals as the court may specify.

(2) Where the court has directed that an administration order shall be subject to review, the court officer shall give to the debtor and to every creditor who appeared when the order was made not less than seven days' notice of any day appointed for such a review.

(3) Nothing in this rule shall require the court officer to fix a day for a review under r.13A.

Service of order

CCR Ord.39 r.9

Where an administration order is made, the court officer shall send a copy to—

(a) the debtor;

(b) every creditor whose name was included in the list furnished by the debtor;

(c) any other creditor who has proved his debt; and

(d) every other court in which, to the knowledge of the district judge, judgment has been obtained against the debtor or proceedings are pending in respect of any debt scheduled to the order.

Subsequent objection by creditor

CCR Ord.39 r.10

(1) After an administration order has been made, a creditor who has not received notice under r.5 and who wishes to object to a debt scheduled to the order, or to the manner in which payment is directed to be made by instalments, shall give notice to the court officer of his objection and of the grounds thereof.

(2) On receipt of such notice the court shall consider the objection and may—

(a) allow it;

(b) dismiss it; or

(c) adjourn it for hearing on notice being given to such persons and on such terms as to security for costs or otherwise as the court thinks fit.

(3) Without prejudice to the generality of para.(2), the court may dismiss an objection if it is not satisfied that the creditor gave notice of it within a reasonable time of his becoming aware of the administration order.

Subsequent proof by creditor

CCR Ord.39 r.11

(1) Any creditor whose debt is not scheduled to an administration order, and any person who after the date of the order became a creditor of the debtor, shall, if he wishes to prove his debt, send particulars of his claim to the court officer, who shall give notice of it to the debtor and to every creditor whose debt is so scheduled.
(2) If neither the debtor nor any creditor gives notice to the court officer, within seven days after receipt of notice under para.(1), that he objects to the claim, then, unless it is required by the court to be supported by evidence, the claim shall be taken to be proved.
(3) If the debtor or a creditor gives notice of objection within the said period of seven days or the court requires the claim to be supported by evidence, the court officer shall fix a day for consideration of the claim and give notice of it to the debtor, the creditor by whom the claim was made and the creditor, if any, making the objection, and on the hearing the court may either disallow the claim or allow it in whole or in part.
(4) If a claim is taken to be proved under para.(2) or allowed under para.(3), the debt shall be added to the schedule to the order and a copy of the order shall then be sent to the creditor by whom the claim was made.

Permission to present bankruptcy petition

CCR Ord.39 r.12

An application by a creditor under s.112(4) of the [County Court Act 1984] for permission to present or join in a bankruptcy petition shall be made on notice to the debtor in accordance with [Pt 23], but the court may, if it thinks fit, order that notice be given to any other creditor whose debt is scheduled to the administration order.

Conduct of order

CCR Ord.39 r.13

(1) The court manager or such other officer of the court as the court making an administration order shall from time to time appoint shall have the conduct of the order and shall take all proper steps to enforce the order (including exercising the power of the court under s.5 of the Attachment of Earnings Act 1971 to make an attachment of earnings order to secure payments required by the administration order) or to bring to the attention of the court any matter which may make it desirable to review the order.
(2) Without prejudice to s.115 of the [County Court Act 1984], any creditor whose debt is scheduled to the order may, with the permission of the court, take proceedings to enforce the order.
(3) The debtor or, with the permission of the court, any such creditor may apply to the court to review the order.

(4) When on a matter being brought to its attention under para.(1) the court so directs or the debtor or a creditor applies for the review of an administration order, r.8(2) shall apply as if the order were subject to review under that rule.

(5) Nothing in this rule shall require the court officer to fix a day for a review under r.13A.

Review by court officer in default of payment

CCR Ord.39 r.13A

(1) Where it appears that the debtor is failing to make payments in accordance with the order, the court officer shall (either of his own initiative or on the application of a creditor whose debt is scheduled to the administration order) send a notice to the debtor—

(a) informing him of the amounts which are outstanding; and

(b) requiring him (within 14 days of service of the notice upon him) to—

    (i) make the payments as required by the order; or

    (ii) explain his reasons for failing to make the payments; and

    (iii) make a proposal for payment of the amounts outstanding; or

    (iv) make a request to vary the order.

(2) If the debtor does not comply with para.(1)(b) within the time stated, the court officer shall revoke the administration order.

(3) The court officer shall refer a notice given by a debtor under para.(1)(b)(ii), (iii) or (iv) to the district judge who may—

(a) without requiring the attendance of the parties—

    (i) revoke the administration order or vary it so as to provide for payment of the debts included in the order in full or to such extent and within such a period as appears practicable in the circumstances of the case; or

    (ii) suspend the operation of the administration order for such time and on such terms as he thinks fit; or

(b) require the court officer to fix a day for the review of the administration order and to give to the debtor and to every creditor whose debt is scheduled to the administration order not less than eight days' notice of the day so fixed.

(4) Any party affected by an order made under para.(2) or (3)(a) may, within 14 days of service of the order on him and giving his reasons, apply on notice for the district judge to consider the matter afresh and the court officer shall fix a day for the hearing of the application before the district judge and give to the debtor and to every creditor whose debt is scheduled to the administration order not less than eight days' notice of the day so fixed.

(5) On hearing an application under para.(4), the district judge may confirm the order or set it aside and make such new order as he thinks fit and the order so made shall be entered in the records of the court.

Review of order

CCR Ord.39 r.14

(1) On the review of an administration order the court may—

(a) if satisfied that the debtor is unable from any cause to pay any instalment due under the order, suspend the operation of the order for such time and on such terms as it thinks fit;

(b) if satisfied that there has been a material change in any relevant circumstances since the order was made, vary any provision of the order made by virtue of s.112(6) of the [County Court Act 1984];

    (c) if satisfied that the debtor has failed without reasonable cause to comply with any provision of the order or that it is otherwise just and expedient to do so, revoke the order, either forthwith or on failure to comply with any condition specified by the court; or

    (d) make an attachment of earnings order to secure the payments required by the administration order or vary or discharge any such attachment of earnings order already made.

(2) The court officer shall send a copy of any order varying or revoking an administration order to the debtor, to every creditor whose debt is scheduled to the administration order and, if the administration order is revoked, to any other court to which a copy of the administration order was sent pursuant to r.9.

Discharge of attachment of earnings order

CCR Ord.39 r.16

On the revocation of an administration order any attachment of earnings order made to secure the payments required by the administration order shall be discharged.

Declaration of dividends

CCR Ord.39 r.17

(1) The officer having the conduct of an administration order shall from time to time declare dividends and distribute them among the creditors entitled to them.

(2) When a dividend is declared, notice shall be sent by the officer to each of the creditors.

Creditors to rank equally

CCR Ord.39 r.18

All creditors scheduled under s.113(d) of the [County Court Act 1984] before an administration order is superseded under s.117(2) of the Act shall rank equally in proportion to the amount of their debts subject to the priority given by the said para.(d) to those scheduled as having been creditors before the date of the order, but no payment made to any creditor by way of dividend or otherwise shall be disturbed by reason of any subsequent proof by any creditor under the said para.(d).

Change of debtor's address

CCR Ord.39 r.19

(1) A debtor who changes his residence shall forthwith inform the court of his new address.

(2) Where the debtor becomes resident in the district of another court, the court in which the administration order is being conducted may transfer the proceedings to that other court.

ADMINISTRATIVE COURT

Types of cases

The Administrative Court deals with:
  Judicial review—of decisions of inferior courts and tribunals, public bodies and persons
  exercising a public function. Criminal cases may arise from decisions of magistrates' courts
  or the Crown Court when it is acting in its appellate capacity.
  Statutory appeals and applications—the right given by certain statutes to challenge decisions
  of, e.g. Ministers, Local Government, Tribunals.
  Appeals by way of case stated—appeals against decisions of magistrates' courts and the
  Crown Court (predominantly criminal cases).
  Applications for **habeas corpus.**
  Applications for **committal** for contempt.
  Applications for an order preventing a **vexatious litigant** from instituting or continuing
  proceedings without the leave of a judge.
  Applications under the Coroners Act 1988 (**Coroners Court**).
Some matters are required by statute or rules of Court to be heard by a Divisional Court (i.e. a
court of two or more judges):
  Applications for committal for contempt where the contempt (a) is committed in connection
  with (i) proceedings before a Q.B. Divisional Court, (ii) criminal proceedings (except where
  it is in the face of the court or disobedience to an order), (iii) proceedings in an inferior court
  or (b) is committed otherwise than in any proceedings
  Appeals from the Law Society Disciplinary Tribunal (**Solicitor**). Such appeals are heard by a
  three judge court unless the Lord Chief Justice otherwise directs. By convention these appeals
  are heard by a Court presided over by the Lord Chief Justice
  Applications under s.13 of the Coroners Act 1988 (with fiat of the Attorney General)
  Applications for vexatious litigant orders under s.42 of the Senior Courts Act 1981
  Applications relating to parliamentary and local government elections under the Representa-
  tion of the People Acts (unless exercisable by a single judge by express statutory provi-
  sion).
Others can be and usually are heard by a **Divisional Court**:
  Applications for **judicial review** in a criminal cause or matter.
  Applications for leave to apply for judicial review in a criminal cause or matter, after refusal
  by a single judge (whether on paper or after oral argument).
  Appeals by way of case stated in a criminal cause or matter, whether from the Crown Court
  or from a magistrates court.
The remaining matters in the Administrative Court List will generally be heard by a single
judge.

Venue

PD 54D para.1.1

[PD 54D] concerns the place in which a claim before the Administrative Court should be started
and administered and the venue at which it will be determined.

PD 54D para.1.2

This PD is intended to facilitate access to justice by enabling cases to be administered and
determined in the most appropriate location. To achieve this purpose it provides flexibility in
relation to where claims are to be administered and enables claims to be transferred to different
venues.

PD 54D, para.2.1

The claim form in proceedings in the Administrative Court may be issued at the Administrative Court Office of the High Court at—
  (1) the Royal Courts of Justice in London; or
  (2) at the District Registry of the High Court at Birmingham, Cardiff, Leeds, or Manchester unless the claim is one of the excepted classes of claim set out in para.3 of [PD 54D] which may only be started and determined at the Royal Courts of Justice in London.

PD 54D para.2.2

Any claim started in Birmingham will normally be determined at a court in the Midland region (geographically covering the area of the Midland Circuit); in Cardiff in Wales; in Leeds in the North-Eastern Region (geographically covering the area of the North Eastern Circuit); in London at the Royal Courts of Justice; and in Manchester, in the North-Western Region (geographically covering the Northern Circuit).

Excepted classes of claim

PD 54D para.3.1

The excepted classes of claim referred to in para.2.1(2) are—
  (1) proceedings to which Pt 76 or Pt 79 applies, and for the avoidance of doubt—
    (a) proceedings relating to control orders (within the meaning of Pt 76);
    (b) financial restrictions proceedings (within the meaning of Pt 79);
    (c) proceedings relating to terrorism or alleged terrorists (where that is a relevant feature of the claim); and
    (d) proceedings in which a special advocate is or is to be instructed;
  (2) proceedings to which RSC Ord.115 [Confiscation and Forfeiture in connection with Criminal Proceedings] applies;
  (3) proceedings under the Proceeds of Crime Act 2002;
  (4) appeals to the Administrative Court under the Extradition Act 2003;
  (5) proceedings which must be heard by a Divisional Court; and
  (6) proceedings relating to the discipline of solicitors.

PD 54D para.3.2

If a claim form is issued at an Administrative Court office other than in London and includes one of the excepted classes of claim, the proceedings will be transferred to London.

Assignment to another venue

PD 54D para.5.1

The proceedings may be transferred from the office at which the claim form was issued to another office. Such transfer is a judicial act.

PD 54D para.5.2

The general expectation is that proceedings will be administered and determined in the region with which the claimant has the closest connection, subject to the following considerations as applicable—
  (1) any reason expressed by any party for preferring a particular venue;

(2) the region in which the defendant, or any relevant office or department of the defendant, is based;

(3) the region in which the claimant's legal representatives are based;

(4) the ease and cost of travel to a hearing;

(5) the availability and suitability of alternative means of attending a hearing (for example, by videolink);

(6) the extent and nature of media interest in the proceedings in any particular locality;

(7) the time within which it is appropriate for the proceedings to be determined;

(8) whether it is desirable to administer or determine the claim in another region in the light of the volume of claims issued at, and the capacity, resources and workload of, the court at which it is issued;

(9) whether the claim raises issues sufficiently similar to those in another outstanding claim to make it desirable that it should be determined together with, or immediately following, that other claim; and

(10) whether the claim raises devolution issues and for that reason whether it should more appropriately be determined in London or Cardiff.

PD 54D para.5.3

(1) When an urgent application is made under paras 4.1 or 4.2, this will not by itself decide the venue for the further administration or determination of the claim.

(2) The court dealing with the urgent application may direct that the case be assigned to a particular venue.

(3) When an urgent application is made under para.4.2, and the court does not make a direction under subpara.(2), the claim will be assigned in the first place to London but may be reassigned to another venue at a later date.

PD 54D para.5.4

The court may on an application by a party or of its own initiative direct that the claim be determined in a region other than that of the venue in which the claim is currently assigned. The considerations in para.5.2 apply.

PD 54D para.5.5

Once assigned to a venue, the proceedings will be both administered from that venue and determined by a judge of the Administrative Court at a suitable court within that region, or, if the venue is in London, at the Royal Courts of Justice. The choice of which court (of those within the region which are identified by the Presiding Judge of the circuit suitable for such hearing) will be decided, subject to availability, by the considerations in para.5.2.

PD 54D para.5.6

When giving directions under r.54 10, the court may direct that proceedings be reassigned to another region for hearing (applying the considerations in para.5.2). If no such direction is given, the claim will be heard in the same region as that in which the permission application was determined (whether on paper or at a hearing).

Urgent applications

PD 54D para.4.1

During the hours when the court is open, where an urgent application needs to be made to the Administrative Court outside London, the application must be made to the judge designated to deal with such applications in the relevant district registry.

PD 54D para.4.2

Any urgent application to the Administrative Court during the hours when the court is closed, must be made to the duty out of hours High Court judge (tel: 020 7947 6000).

ADMIRALTY AND COMMERCIAL COURT

See **Admiralty claims**, **Admiralty and Commercial Courts Guide**, and **Commercial Court**.

ADMIRALTY AND COMMERCIAL COURTS GUIDE

The Guide is intended to promote the efficient conduct of litigation in the Admiralty and Commercial Courts. It does not provide a complete blueprint for litigation and should be seen as providing guidance to be adopted flexibly and adapted to the exigencies of the particular case. It should not be understood to override in any way the CPR or PD made under them, or as fettering the discretion of the judges.

Proceedings in the Commercial Court are governed by the CPR and PD. CPR Pat 58 and its associated PD deal specifically with the Commercial Court. Part 61 deals with the Admiralty Court and Part 62 deals with arbitration applications.

The administrative office for the Admiralty Court and the Commercial Court is the Admiralty and Commercial Registry, 7 Rolls Building, Fetter Lane, London EC4A 1NL. The Commercial Court Listing office is located at the same address.

ADMIRALTY CLAIMS

Pt 61 r.61.1

    (1) [Part 61] applies to admiralty claims.
    (2) In this Part—
        (a) 'admiralty claim' means a claim within the Admiralty jurisdiction of the High Court as set out in s.20 of the Supreme Court Act 1981;
        (c) 'claim in rem' means a claim in an admiralty action in rem;
        (f) 'salvage claim' means a claim—
            (i) for or in the nature of salvage;
            (ii) for special compensation under Article 14 of Schedule 11 to the Merchant Shipping Act 1995;
            (iii) for the apportionment of salvage; and
            (iv) arising out of or connected with any contract for salvage services;
        (g) 'caution against arrest' means a caution entered in the Register under r.61.7;
        (h) 'caution against release' means a caution entered in the Register under r.61.8;
    (3) Part 58 (Commercial Court) applies to claims in the Admiralty Court except where this Part provides otherwise.
    (4) The Registrar [means the Queen's Bench Master with responsibility for Admiralty claims has all the powers of the Admiralty judge except where a rule or [PD] provides otherwise.

PD 61 para.1.1

[PD 58] also applies to Admiralty claims except where it is inconsistent with Pt 61 or this PD.

Admiralty claims

P61 r.61.2

(1) The following claims must be started in the Admiralty Court [of the Queen's Bench Division of the High Court of Justice]—
   (a) a claim—
     (i) in rem;
     (ii) for damage done by a ship [includes any vessel used in navigation];
     (iii) concerning the ownership of a ship;
     (iv) under the Merchant Shipping Act 1995;
     (v) for loss of life or personal injury specified in s.20(2)(f) of the Supreme Court Act 1981;
     (vi) by a master or member of a crew for wages;
     (vii) in the nature of towage; or
     (viii) in the nature of pilotage;
   (b) a collision claim [a claim within s.20(3)(b) of the Supreme Court Act 1981];
   (c) a limitation claim [a claim under the Merchant Shipping Act 19952 for the limitation of liability in connection with a ship or other property]; or
   (d) a salvage claim.
(2) Any other admiralty claim may be started in the Admiralty Court.
(3) Rule 30.5 applies to claims in the Admiralty Court except that the Admiralty Court may order the transfer of a claim to—
   (a) the Commercial list;
   (b) a Mercantile Court;
   (c) the Mercantile list at the Central London County Court; or
   (d) any other appropriate court.

Case management

PD 61 para.2.1

After a claim form is issued the Registrar will issue a direction in writing stating—
   (1) whether the claim will remain in the Admiralty Court or be transferred to another court; and
   (2) if the claim remains in the Admiralty Court—
     (a) whether it will be dealt with by—
       (i) the Admiralty judge; or
       (ii) the Registrar; and
     (b) whether the trial will be in London or elsewhere.

PD 61 para.2.2

In making these directions the Registrar will have regard to—
   (1) the nature of the issues and the sums in dispute; and
   (2) the criteria set in r.26.8 so far as they are applicable.

PD 61 para.2.3

Where the Registrar directs that the claim will be dealt with by the Admiralty judge, case management directions will be given and any case management conference or pre-trial review will be heard by the Admiralty judge.

Claims in rem

Pt 61 r.61.3

(1) This r.applies to claims in rem.
(2) A claim in rem is started by the issue of an in rem claim form as set out in PD 61.
(3) Subject to r.61.4, the particulars of claim must—
    (a) be contained in or served with the claim form; or
    (b) be served on the defendant by the claimant within 75 days after service of the claim form.
(4) An acknowledgment of service must be filed within 14 days after service of the claim form.
(5) The claim form must be served—
    (a) in accordance with PD 61; and
    (b) within 12 months after the date of issue and rr.7.5 and 7.6 are modified accordingly.
(6) If a claim form has been issued (whether served or not), any person who wishes to defend the claim may file an acknowledgment of service.

PD 61 para.3.1

A claim form in rem must be in Form ADM1.

PD 61 para.3.2

The claimant in a claim in rem may be named or may be described, but if not named in the claim form must identify himself by name if requested to do so by any other party.

PD 61 para.3.3

The defendant must be described in the claim form.

PD 61 para.3.4

The acknowledgment of service must be in Form ADM2. The person who acknowledges service must identify himself by name.

PD 61 para.3.5

The period for acknowledging service under r.61.3(4) applies irrespective of whether the claim form contains particulars of claim.

PD 61 para.3.6

A claim form in rem may be served in the following ways:
(1) on the property against which the claim is brought by fixing a copy of the claim form—
    (a) on the outside of the property in a position which may reasonably be expected to be seen; or
    (b) where the property is freight, either—
        (i) on the cargo in respect of which the freight was earned; or
        (ii) on the ship on which the cargo was carried;

(2) if the property to be served is in the custody of a person who will not permit access to it, by leaving a copy of the claim form with that person;

(3) where the property has been sold by the Marshal, by filing the claim form at the court;

(4) where there is a notice against arrest, on the person named in the notice as being authorised to accept service;

(5) on any solicitor authorised to accept service;

(6) in accordance with any agreement providing for service of proceedings; or

(7) in any other manner as the court may direct under r.6.15 provided that the property against which the claim is brought or part of it is within the jurisdiction of the court.

PD 61 para.3.7

In claims where the property—
(1) is to be arrested; or
(2) is already under arrest in current proceedings,
the [Admiralty] Marshal will serve the in rem claim form if the claimant requests the court to do so.

PD 61 para.3.8

In all other cases in rem claim forms must be served by the claimant.

PD 61 para.3.9

Where the defendants are described and not named on the claim form (for example as 'the Owners of the Ship X'), any acknowledgment of service in addition to stating that description must also state the full names of the persons acknowledging service and the nature of their ownership.

PD 61 para.3.10

After the acknowledgment of service has been filed, the claim will follow the procedure applicable to a claim proceeding in the Commercial list except that the claimant is allowed 75 days to serve the particulars of claim.

PD 61 para.3.11

A defendant who files an acknowledgment of service to an in rem claim does not lose any right he may have to dispute the jurisdiction of the court (see r.10.1(3)(b) and Part 11).

PD 61 para.3.12

Any person who pays the prescribed fee may, during office hours, search for, inspect and take a copy of any claim form in rem whether or not it has been served.

Security in claim in rem

Pt 61 r.61.6

(1) This rule applies if, in a claim in rem, security has been given to—
(a) obtain the release of property under arrest; or

    (b) prevent the arrest of property.
(2) The court may order that the—
    (a) amount of security be reduced and may stay the claim until the order is complied with; or
    (b) claimant may arrest or re-arrest the property proceeded against to obtain further security.
(3) The court may not make an order under para.(2)(b) if the total security to be provided would exceed the value of the property at the time—
    (a) of the original arrest; or
    (b) security was first given (if the property was not arrested).

Collision claims

Pt 61 r.61.4

(1) [P61] applies to collision claims.
(2) A claim form need not contain or be followed by particulars of claim and r.7.4 does not apply.
(3) An acknowledgment of service must be filed.
(4) A party who wishes to dispute the court's jurisdiction must make an application under Pt 11 within two months after filing his acknowledgment of service.
(5) Every party must—
    (a) within two months after the defendant files the acknowledgment of service; or
    (b) where the defendant applies under Pt 11, within 2 months after the defendant files the further acknowledgment of service,
    file at the court a completed collision statement of case in the form specified in [PD 61].
(6) A collision statement of case must be—
    (a) in the form set out in PD 61; and
    (b) verified by a statement of truth.
(7) A claim form in a collision claim may not be served out of the jurisdiction unless—
    (a) the case falls within s.22(2)(a), (b) or (c) of the Supreme Court Act 1981; or
    (b) the defendant has submitted to or agreed to submit to the jurisdiction; and
    the court gives permission in accordance with s.IV of Pt 6.
(8) Where permission to serve a claim form out of the jurisdiction is given, the court will specify the period within which the defendant may file an acknowledgment of service and, where appropriate, a collision statement of case.
(9) Where, in a collision claim in rem ('the original claim')—
    (a) (i) a **Pt 20 claim**; or
        (ii) a cross claim in rem
        arising out of the same collision or occurrence is made; and
    (b) (i) the party bringing the original claim has caused the arrest of a ship or has obtained security in order to prevent such arrest; and
        (ii) the party bringing the Pt 20 claim or cross claim is unable to arrest a ship or otherwise obtain security,
    the party bringing the Pt 20 claim or cross claim may apply to the court to stay the original claim until sufficient security is given to satisfy any judgment that may be given in favour of that party.
(10) The consequences set out in para.(11) apply where a party to a claim to establish liability for a collision claim (other than a claim for loss of life or personal injury)—
    (a) makes an offer to settle in the form set out in para.(12) not less than 21 days before the start of the trial;
    (b) that offer is not accepted; and
    (c) the maker of the offer obtains at trial an apportionment equal to or more favourable than his offer.

(11) Where para.(10) applies the parties will, unless the court considers it unjust, be entitled to the following costs—
    (a) the maker of the offer will be entitled to—
        (i) all his costs from 21 days after the offer was made; and
        (ii) his costs before then in the percentage to which he would have been entitled had the offer been accepted; and
    (b) all other parties to whom the offer was made—
        (i) will be entitled to their costs up to 21 days after the offer was made in the percentage to which they would have been entitled had the offer been accepted; but
        (ii) will not be entitled to their costs thereafter.
(12) An offer under para.(10) must be in writing and must contain—
    (a) an offer to settle liability at stated percentages;
    (b) an offer to pay costs in accordance with the same percentages;
    (c) a term that the offer remain open for 21 days after the date it is made; and
    (d) a term that, unless the court orders otherwise, on expiry of that period the offer remains open on the same terms except that the offeree should pay all the costs from that date until acceptance.

PD 61 para.4.1

A collision statement of case must be in Form ADM3.

PD 61 para.4.2

A collision statement of case must contain—
    (1) in Pt 1 of the form, answers to the questions set out in that Part; and
    (2) in Pt 2 of the form, a statement—
        (a) of any other facts and matters on which the party filing the collision statement of case relies;
        (b) of all allegations of negligence or other fault which the party filing the collision statement of case makes; and
        (c) of the remedy which the party filing the collision statement of case claims.

PD 61 para.4.3

When he files his collision statement of case each party must give notice to every other party that he has done so.

PD 61 para.4.4

Within 14 days after the last collision statement of case is filed each party must serve a copy of his collision statement of case on every other party.

PD 61 para.4.5

Before the coming into force of Pt 61, a collision statement of case was known as a Preliminary Act and the law relating to Preliminary Acts will continue to apply to collision statements of case

Arrest

Pt 61 r.61.5

(1) In a claim in rem—
  (a) a claimant; and
  (b) a judgment creditor
  may apply to have the property proceeded against arrested.
(2) [PD 61] sets out the procedure for applying for arrest.
(3) A party making an application for arrest must—
  (a) request a search to be made in the Register [means the Register of cautions against arrest and release which is open to inspection as provided by [PD 61]] before the warrant is issued to determine whether there is a caution against arrest in force with respect to that property; and
  (b) file a declaration in the form set out in PD 61.
(4) A warrant of arrest may not be issued as of right in the case of property in respect of which the beneficial ownership, as a result of a sale or disposal by any court in any jurisdiction exercising admiralty jurisdiction in rem, has changed since the claim form was issued.
(5) A warrant of arrest may not be issued against a ship owned by a State where by any convention or treaty, the UK has undertaken to minimise the possibility of arrest of ships of that State until—
  (a) notice in the form set out in PD 61 has been served on a consular officer at the consular office of that State in London or the port at which it is intended to arrest the ship; and
  (b) a copy of that notice is attached to any declaration under para.(3)(b).
(6) Except—
  (a) with the permission of the court; or
  (b) where notice has been given under para.(5),
  a warrant of arrest may not be issued in a claim in rem against a foreign ship belonging to a port of a State in respect of which an order in council has been made under s.4 of the Consular Relations Act 1968, until the expiration of two weeks from appropriate notice to the consul.
(7) A warrant of arrest is valid for 12 months but may only be executed if the claim form—
  (a) has been served; or
  (b) remains valid for service at the date of execution.
(8) Property may only be arrested by the Marshal or his substitute.
(9) Property under arrest—
  (a) may not be moved unless the court orders otherwise; and
  (b) may be immobilised or prevented from sailing in such manner as the Marshal may consider appropriate.
(10) Where an in rem claim form has been issued and security sought, any person who has filed an acknowledgment of service may apply for an order specifying the amount and form of security to be provided.

PD 61 para.5.1

An application for arrest must be—
  (1) in Form ADM4 (which must also contain an undertaking); and
  (2) accompanied by a declaration in form ADM5.

PD 61 para.5.2

When it receives an application for arrest that complies with the rules and the PD the court will issue an arrest warrant.

PD 61 para.5.3

The declaration required by r.61.5(3)(b) must be verified by a statement of truth and must state—
- (1) in every claim—
  - (a) the nature of the claim or counterclaim and that it has not been satisfied and if it arises in connection with a ship, the name of that ship;
  - (b) the nature of the property to be arrested and, if the property is a ship, the name of the ship and her port of registry; and
  - (c) the amount of the security sought, if any.
- (2) in a claim against a ship by virtue of s.21(4) of the Senior Courts Act 1981—
  - (a) the name of the person who would be liable on the claim if it were not commenced in rem;
  - (b) that the person referred to in sub-paragraph (a) was, when the right to bring the claim arose—
    - (i) the owner or charterer of; or
    - (ii) in possession or in control of,

    the ship in connection with which the claim arose; and
  - (c) that at the time the claim form was issued the person referred to in sub-paragraph (a) was either—
    - (i) the beneficial owner of all the shares in the ship in respect of which the warrant is required; or
    - (ii) the charterer of it under a charter by demise;
- (3) in the cases set out in rr.61.5 (5) and (6) that the relevant notice has been sent or served, as appropriate; and
- (4) in the case of a claim in respect of liability incurred under s.153 of the Merchant Shipping Act 1995, the facts relied on as establishing that the court is not prevented from considering the claim by reason of s.166(2) of that Act.

The notice required by r.61.5(5)(a) must be in Form ADM6.

PD 61 para.5.5

Property is arrested—
- (1) by service on it of an arrest warrant in form ADM9 in the manner set out at para.3.6(1); or
- (2) where it is not reasonably practicable to serve the warrant, by service of a notice of the issue of the warrant—
  - (a) in the manner set out in para.3.6(1) on the property; or
  - (b) by giving notice to those in charge of the property.

PD 61 para.5.6

When property is arrested the Registrar will issue standard directions in Form ADM10.

PD 61 para.5.7

The Marshal does not insure property under arrest.

Cautions against arrest

Pt 61 r.61.7

- (1) Any person may file a request for a caution against arrest.
- (2) When a request under para.(1) is filed the court will enter the caution in the Register if the request is in the form set out in PD 61 and—

    (a) the person filing the request undertakes—
        (i) to file an acknowledgment of service; and
        (ii) to give sufficient security to satisfy the claim with interest and costs; or
    (b) where the person filing the request has constituted a limitation fund in accordance with art.11 of the Convention on Limitation of Liability for Maritime Claims 1976 he—
        (i) states that such a fund has been constituted; and
        (ii) undertakes that the claimant will acknowledge service of the claim form by which any claim may be begun against the property described in the request.
(3) A caution against arrest—
    (a) is valid for 12 months after the date it is entered in the Register; but
    (b) may be renewed for a further 12 months by filing a further request.
(4) Paragraphs (1) and (2) apply to a further request under para.(3)(b).
(5) Property may be arrested if a caution against arrest has been entered in the Register but the court may order that—
    (a) the arrest be discharged; and
    (b) the party procuring the arrest pays compensation to the owner of or other persons interested in the arrested property.

PD 61 para.6.1

The entry of a caution against arrest is not treated as a submission to the jurisdiction of the court.

PD 61 para.6.2

The request for a caution against arrest must be in Form ADM7.

PD 61 para.6.3

On the filing of such a request, a caution against arrest will be entered in the Register.

PD 61 para.6.4

The Register is open for inspection when the Admiralty and Commercial Registry is open.

Release and cautions against release

Pt 61 r.61.8

(1) Where property is under arrest—
    (a) an in rem claim form may be served upon it; and
    (b) it may be arrested by any other person claiming to have an in rem claim against it.
(2) Any person who—
    (a) claims to have an in rem right against any property under arrest; and
    (b) wishes to be given notice of any application in respect of that property or its proceeds of sale,
may file a request for a caution against release in the form set out in PD 61.
(3) When a request under para.(2) is filed, a caution against release will be entered in the Register.
(4) Property will be released from arrest if—
    (a) it is sold by the court;
    (b) the court orders release on an application made by any party;

    (c)   (i) the arresting party; and

        (ii) all persons who have entered cautions against release

      file a request for release in the form set out in PD 61; or

    (d) any party files—

        (i) a request for release in the form set out in PD 61 (containing an undertaking); and

        (ii) consents to the release of the arresting party and all persons who have entered cautions against release.

(5) Where the release of any property is delayed by the entry of a caution against release under this rule any person who has an interest in the property may apply for an order that the person who entered the caution pay damages for losses suffered by the applicant because of the delay.

(6) The court may not make an order under para.(5) if satisfied that there was good reason to—

    (a) request the entry of; and

    (b) maintain

the caution.

(7) Any person—

    (a) interested in property under arrest or in the proceeds of sale of such property; or

    (b) whose interests are affected by any order sought or made,

may be made a party to any claim in rem against the property or proceeds of sale.

(8) Where—

    (a)   (i) a ship is not under arrest but cargo on board her is; or

        (ii) a ship is under arrest but cargo on board her is not; and

    (b) persons interested in the ship or cargo wish to discharge the cargo,

they may, without being made parties, request the Marshal to authorise steps to discharge the cargo.

(9) If—

    (a) the Marshal considers a request under para.(8) reasonable; and

    (b) the applicant gives an undertaking in writing acceptable to the Marshal to pay—

        (i) his fees; and

        (ii) all expenses to be incurred by him or on his behalf on demand,

the Marshal will apply to the court for an order to permit the discharge of the cargo.

(10) Where persons interested in the ship or cargo are unable or unwilling to give an undertaking as referred to in para.(9)(b), they may—

    (a) be made parties to the claim; and

    (b) apply to the court for an order for—

        (i) discharge of the cargo; and

        (ii) directions as to the fees and expenses of the Marshal with regard to the discharge and storage of the cargo.

PD 61 para.7.1

The request for a caution against release must be in Form ADM11.

PD 61 para.7.2

On the filing of such a request, a caution against release will be entered in the Register.

PD 61 para.7.3

The Register is open for inspection when the Admiralty and Commercial Registry is open.

PD 61 para.7.4

A request for release under r.61.8(4)(c) and (d) must be in Form ADM12.

PD 61 para.7.5

A withdrawal of a caution against release must be in form ADM12A.

Judgment in default

Pt 61 r.61.9

(1) In a claim in rem (other than a collision claim) the claimant may obtain judgment in default of—
  (a) an acknowledgment of service only if—
    (i) the defendant has not filed an acknowledgment of service; and
    (ii) the time for doing so set out in r.61.3(4) has expired; and
  (b) defence only if—
    (i) a defence has not been filed; and
    (ii) the relevant time limit for doing so has expired.
(2) In a collision claim, a party who has filed a collision statement of case within the time specified by r.61.4(5) may obtain judgment in default of a collision statement of case only if—
  (a) the party against whom judgment is sought has not filed a collision statement of case; and
  (b) the time for doing so set out in r.61.4(5) has expired.
(3) An application for judgment in default—
  (a) under para.(1) or para.(2) in an in rem claim must be made by filing—
    (i) an application notice as set out in PD 61;
    (ii) a certificate proving service of the claim form; and
    (iii) evidence proving the claim to the satisfaction of the court; and
  (b) under para.(2) in any other claim must be made in accordance with Pt 12 with any necessary modifications.
(4) An application notice seeking judgment in default and, unless the court orders otherwise, all evidence in support, must be served on all persons who have entered cautions against release on the Register.
(5) The court may set aside or vary any judgment in default entered under this rule.
(6) The claimant may apply to the court for judgment against a party at whose instance a notice against arrest was entered where—
  (a) the claim form has been served on that party;
  (b) the sum claimed in the claim form does not exceed the amount specified in the undertaking given by that party in accordance with r.61.7(2)(a)(ii) and
  (c) that party has not fulfilled that undertaking within 14 days after service on him of the claim form.

PD 61 para.8.1

An application notice for judgment in default must be in Form ADM13.

Sale by the court, priorities and payment out

Pt 61 r.61.10

(1) An application for an order for the survey, appraisement or sale of a ship may be made in a claim in rem at any stage by any party.
(2) If the court makes an order for sale, it may—

       (a) set a time within which notice of claims against the proceeds of sale must be filed; and

       (b) the time and manner in which such notice must be advertised.

(3) Any party with a judgment against the property or proceeds of sale may at any time after the time referred to in para.(2) apply to the court for the determination of priorities.

(4) An application notice under para.(3) must be served on all persons who have filed a claim against the property.

(5) Payment out of the proceeds of sale will be made only to judgment creditors and—

       (a) in accordance with the determination of priorities; or

       (b) as the court orders.

PD 61 para.9.1

Any application to the court concerning—

(1) the sale of the property under arrest; or

(2) the proceeds of sale of property sold by the court will be heard in public and the application notice served on—

       (a) all parties to the claim;

       (b) all persons who have requested cautions against release with regard to the property or the proceeds of sale; and

       (c) the Marshal.

PD 61 para.9.2

Unless the court orders otherwise an order for sale will be in Form ADM14.

PD 61 para.9.3

An order for sale before judgment may only be made by the Admiralty judge.

PD 61 para.9.4

Unless the Admiralty judge orders otherwise, a determination of priorities may only be made by the Admiralty judge.

PD 61 para.9.5

When—

(1) proceeds of sale are paid into court by the Marshal; and

(2) such proceeds are in a foreign currency,

the funds will be placed on one day call interest bearing account unless the court orders otherwise.

PD 61 para.9.6

Unless made at the same time as an application for sale, or other prior application, an application to place foreign currency on longer term deposit may be made to the Registrar.

PD 61 para.9.7

Notice of the placement of foreign currency in an interest bearing account must be given to all parties interested in the fund by the party who made the application under para.9.6.

PD 61 para.9.8

Any interested party who wishes to object to the mode of investment of foreign currency paid into court may apply to the Registrar for directions.

Limitation claims

Pt 61 r.61.11

(1) This rule applies to limitation claims.
(2) A claim is started by the issue of a limitation claim form as set out in PD 61.
(3) The—
    (a) claimant; and
    (b) at least one defendant
    must be named in the claim form, but all other defendants may be described.
(4) The claim form—
    (a) must be served on all named defendants and any other defendant who requests service upon him; and
    (b) may be served on any other defendant.
(5) The claim form may not be served out of the jurisdiction unless—
    (a) the claim falls within s.22(2)(a), (b) or (c) of the Supreme Court Act 19816;
    (b) the defendant has submitted to or agreed to submit to the jurisdiction of the court; or
    (c) the Admiralty Court has jurisdiction over the claim under any applicable Convention; and
    the court grants permission in accordance with s.IV of Pt 6.
(6) An acknowledgment of service is not required.
(7) Every defendant upon whom a claim form is served must—
    (a) within 28 days of service file—
        (i) a defence; or
        (ii) a notice that the defendant admits the right of the claimant to limit liability; or
    (b) if the defendant wishes to—
        (i) dispute the jurisdiction of the court; or
        (ii) argue that the court should not exercise its jurisdiction,
    file within 14 days of service (or where the claim form is served out of the jurisdiction, within the time specified in r.6.35) an acknowledgment of service as set out in [PD 61].
(8) If a defendant files an acknowledgment of service under para.(7)(b) he will be treated as having accepted that the court has jurisdiction to hear the claim unless he applies under Pt 11 within 14 days after filing the acknowledgment of service.
(9) Where one or more named defendants admits the right to limit—
    (a) the claimant may apply for a restricted limitation decree in the form set out in [PD 61]; and
    (b) the court will issue a decree in the form set out in PD 61 limiting liability only against those named defendants who have admitted the claimant's right to limit liability.
(10) A restricted limitation decree—
    (a) may be obtained against any named defendant who fails to file a defence within the time specified for doing so; and
    (b) need not be advertised, but a copy must be served on the defendants to whom it applies.
(11) Where all the defendants upon whom the claim form has been served admit the claimant's right to limit liability—
    (a) the claimant may apply to the Admiralty Registrar for a general limitation decree in the form set out in [PD 61]; and

      (b) the court will issue a limitation decree.

(12) Where one or more of the defendants upon whom the claim form has been served do not admit the claimant's right to limit, the claimant may apply for a general limitation decree in the form set out in [PD 61].

(13) When a limitation decree is granted the court—
      (a) may—
          (i) order that any proceedings relating to any claim arising out of the occurrence be stayed;
          (ii) order the claimant to establish a limitation fund if one has not been established or make such other arrangements for payment of claims against which liability is limited; or
          (iii) if the decree is a restricted limitation decree, distribute the limitation fund; and
      (b) will, if the decree is a general limitation decree, give directions as to advertisement of the decree and set a time within which notice of claims against the fund must be filed or an application made to set aside the decree.

(14) When the court grants a general limitation decree the claimant must—
      (a) advertise it in such manner and within such time as the court directs; and
      (b) file—
          (i) a declaration that the decree has been advertised in accordance with para.(a); and
          (ii) copies of the advertisements.

(15) No later than the time set in the decree for filing claims, each of the defendants who wishes to assert a claim must file and serve his statement of case on—
      (a) the limiting party; and
      (b) all other defendants except where the court orders otherwise.

(16) Any person other than a defendant upon whom the claim form has been served may apply to the court within the time fixed in the decree to have a general limitation decree set aside.

(17) An application under para.(16) must be supported by a declaration—
      (a) stating that the applicant has a claim against the claimant arising out of the occurrence; and
      (b) setting out grounds for contending that the claimant is not entitled to the decree, either in the amount of limitation or at all.

(18) The claimant may constitute a limitation fund by making a payment into court.

(19) A limitation fund may be established before or after a limitation claim has been started.

(20) If a limitation claim is not commenced within 75 days after the date the fund was established—
      (a) the fund will lapse; and
      (b) all money in court (including interest) will be repaid to the person who made the payment into court.

(21) Money paid into court under para.(18) will not be paid out except under an order of the court.

(22) A limitation claim for—
      (a) a restricted decree may be brought by counterclaim; and
      (b) a general decree may only be brought by counterclaim with the permission of the court.

PD 61 para.10.1

The claim form in a limitation claim must be—
    (1) in Form ADM15; and
    (2) accompanied by a declaration—
      (a) setting out the facts upon which the claimant relies; and

     (b) stating the names and addresses (if known) of all persons who, to the knowledge of
        the claimant, have claims against him in respect of the occurrence to which the claim
        relates (other than named defendants),
verified by a statement of truth.

PD 61 para.10.2

A defence to a limitation claim must be in Form ADM16A.

PD 61 para.10.3

A notice admitting the right of the claimant to limit liability in a limitation claim must be in Form
ADM18.

PD 61 para.10.4

An acknowledgment of service in a limitation claim must be in Form ADM16B.

PD 61 para.10.5

An application for a restricted limitation decree must be in Form ADM17 and the decree issued
by the court on such an application must be in Form ADM18.

PD 61 para.10.6

An application for a general limitation decree must be in Form ADM17A.

PD 61 para.10.7

Where—
     (1) the right to limit is not admitted; and
     (2) the claimant seeks a general limitation decree in form ADM17A.
the claimant must, within seven days after the date of the filing of the defence of the defendant
last served or the expiry of the time for doing so, apply for an appointment before the Registrar
for a case management conference.

PD 61 para.10.8

On an application under r.61.11(12) the Registrar may—
     (1) grant a general limitation decree; or
     (2) if he does not grant a decree—
         (a) order service of a defence;
         (b) order disclosure by the claimant; or
         (c) make such other case management directions as may be appropriate.

PD 61 para.10.9

The fact that a limitation fund has lapsed under r.61.11(20)(a) does not prevent the establishment
of a new fund.

PD 61 para.10.10

Where a limitation fund is established, it must be—
  (1) the sterling equivalent of the number of special drawing rights to which [the claimant] claims to be entitled to limit his liability under the Merchant Shipping Act 1995; together with
  (2) interest from the date of the occurrence giving rise to his liability to the date of payment into court.

PD 61 para.10.11

Where the claimant does not know the sterling equivalent referred to in paragraph 10.10(1) on the date of payment into court he may—
  (1) calculate it on the basis of the latest available published sterling equivalent of a special drawing right as fixed by the International Monetary Fund; and
  (2) in the event of the sterling equivalent of a special drawing right on the date of payment into court being different from that used for calculating the amount of that payment into court the claimant may—
      (a) make up any deficiency by making a further payment into court which, if made within 14 days after the payment into court, will be treated, except for the purpose of the rules relating to the accrual of interest on money paid into court, as if made on the date of that payment into court; or
      (b) apply to the court for payment out of any excess amount (together with any interest accrued) paid into court.

PD 61 para.10.12

An application under para.10.11(2)(b)—
  (1) may be made without notice to any party; and
  (2) must be supported by evidence proving, to the satisfaction of the court, the sterling equivalent of the appropriate number of special drawing rights on the date of payment into court.

PD 61 para.10.13

The claimant must give notice in writing to any named defendant of—
  (1) any payment into court specifying—
      (a) the date of the payment in;
      (b) the amount paid in;
      (c) the amount and rate of interest included; and
      (d) the period to which it relates; and
  (2) any excess amount (and interest) paid out to him under para.10.11(2)(b).

PD 61 para.10.14

A claim against the fund must be in Form ADM20.

PD 61 para.10.15

A defendant's statement of case filed and served in accordance with r.61.11(15) must contain particulars of the defendant's claim.

PD 61 para.10.16

Any defendant who is unable to file and serve a statement of case in accordance with r.61.11(15) and para.10.15 must file a declaration, verified by a statement of truth, in Form ADM21 stating the reason for his inability.

PD 61 para.10.17

No later than seven days after the time for filing claims [or declarations], the Registrar will fix a date for a case management conference at which directions will be given for the further conduct of the proceedings.

PD 61 para.10.18

Nothing in r.61.11 prevents limitation being relied on by way of defence.

Stay of proceedings

Pt 61 r.61.12

Where the court orders a stay of any claim in rem—
    (a) any property under arrest in the claim remains under arrest; and
    (b) any security representing the property remains in force,
unless the court orders otherwise.

See also **Assessors**.

Proceeding against or concerning the International Oil Pollution Compensation Fund 1992 and the International Oil pollution Supplementary Fund

PD 61 para.11.1

For the purposes of s.177 of the Merchant Shipping Act 1995 ('the Act'), the Fund may be given notice of proceedings by any party to a claim against an owner or guarantor in respect of liability under s.153 of the Act by that person serving a notice in writing on the Fund together with copies of the claim form and any statements of case served in the claim.

PD 61 para.11.2

Notice given to the Fund under para.11.1 shall be deemed to have been given to the Supplementary Fund.

PD 61 para.11.3

The Fund or the Supplementary Fund may intervene in any claim to which para.11.1 applies, (whether or not served with the notice), by serving notice of intervention on the—
    (1) owner;
    (2) guarantor; and
    (3) court.

PD 61 para.11.4

Where a judgment is given against—
(1) the Fund in any claim under s.175 of the Act;
(2) the Supplementary Fund in any claim under s.176A of the Act, the Registrar will arrange for a stamped copy of the judgment to be sent by post to—
    (a) the Fund (where para.(1) applies);
    (b) the Supplementary Fund (where para.(2) applies).

PD 61 para.11.5

Notice to the Registrar of the matters set out in—
(1) section 176(3)(b) of the Act in proceedings under s.175; or
(2) section 176B(2)(b) of the Act in proceedings under s.176A, must be given in writing and sent to the court by—
    (a) the Fund (where para.(1) applies);
    (b) the Supplementary Fund (where para.(2) applies).

Other claims

PD 61 para.12.1

This section applies to Admiralty claims which, before the coming into force of Pt 61, would have been called claims in personam. Subject to the provisions of Pt 61 and [PD 61] relating to limitation claims and to collision claims, the following provisions apply to such claims.

PD 61 para.12.2

All such claims will proceed in accordance with Pt 58 (Commercial Court).

PD 61 para.12.3

The claim form must be in Form ADM1A and must be served by the claimant.

PD 61 para.12.4

The claimant may be named or may be described, but if not named in the claim form must identify himself by name if requested to do so by any other party.

PD 61 para.12.5

The defendant must be named in the claim form.

PD 61 para.12.6

Any person who files a defence must identify himself by name in the defence.

References to the registrar

PD 61 para.13.1

The court may at any stage in the claim refer any question or issue for determination by the Registrar (a 'reference').

PD 61 para.13.2

Unless the court orders otherwise, where a reference has been ordered—
   (1) if particulars of claim have not already been served, the claimant must file and serve
       particulars of claim on all other parties within 14 days after the date of the order; and
   (2) any party opposing the claim must file a defence to the claim within 14 days after service
       of the particulars of claim on him.

PD 61 para.13.3

Within seven days after the defence is filed, the claimant must apply for an appointment before
the Registrar for a case management conference.

Undertakings

PD 61 para.14.1

Where, in [Pt 61] or [PD 61] any undertaking to the Marshal is required it must be given—
   (1) in writing and to his satisfaction; or
   (2) in accordance with such other arrangements as he may require.

PD 61 para.14.2

Where any party is dissatisfied with a direction given by the Marshal in this respect he may apply
to the Registrar for a ruling.

Appeals under the Merchant Shipping Act 1995

PD 52D para.4.1

Appeals are to be heard in the Queen's Bench Division.

PD 52D para.25.1

   (1) This paragraph applies to appeals under the Merchant Shipping Act 1995 and for this
       purpose a re-hearing and an application under s.61 of the Merchant Shipping Act 1995
       are treated as appeals.
   (2) The appellant must file any report to the Secretary of State containing the decision from
       which the appeal is brought with the appellant's notice.
   (3) Where a re-hearing by the High Court is ordered under ss.64 or 269 of the Merchant
       Shipping Act 1995, the Secretary of State must give reasonable notice to the parties
       whom he considers to be affected by the re-hearing.

Levying execution on certain days

PD RSC Ord.46 para.1.2

[Not levying execution on a Sunday, Good Friday or Christmas Day] does not apply to an
Admiralty claim in rem.

ADMISSIONS

P9 r.9.2

When **particulars of claim** are served on a defendant, the defendant may—
  (a) file or serve an admission in accordance with Pt 14;
  (b) file a **defence** in accordance with Pt 15,
(or do both, if he admits only part of the claim); or
  (c) file an **acknowledgment of service** in accordance with Pt 10.

PD 14 para.1.1

  (1) Rules 14.1, 14.1A and 14.2 deal with the manner in which a defendant may make an admission of a claim or part of a claim.
  (2) Rule 14.1A makes provision about admissions made before commencement of a claim. It applies only to admissions made after April 6, 2007, and only in proceedings to which one of the following pre-action protocols apply—
    (a) the **Pre-action Protocol for Personal Injury claims**;
    (b) the **Pre-action Protocol for the resolution of Clinical disputes**; or
    (c) the **Pre-action Protocol for Disease and illness claims**.
(The Pre-action Protocol for Personal Injury claims states that it is primarily designed for certain types of personal injury claim with a value of less than the fast track limit. But, para.2.2 of the protocol indicates that it generally applies to all claims which include a claim for personal injury).

PD 14 para.1.2

Rules 14.3, 14.4, 14.5, 14.6 and 14.7 set out how judgment may be obtained on a written admission.

Admissions made after commencement of proceedings

Pt 14 r.14.1

  (1) A party may admit the truth of the whole or any part of another party's case.
  (2) He may do this by giving notice in writing (such as in a statement of case or by letter).
  (3) Where the only remedy which the claimant is seeking is the payment of money, the defendant may also make an admission in accordance with—
    (a) rule 14.4 (admission of whole claim for specified amount of money);
    (b) rule 14.5 (admission of part of claim for specified amount of money);
    (c) rule 14.6 (admission of liability to pay whole of claim for unspecified amount of money); or
    (d) rule r.14.7 (admission of liability to pay claim for unspecified amount of money where defendant offers a sum in satisfaction of the claim).
  (4) Where the defendant makes an admission as mentioned in para.(3), the claimant has a right to enter judgment except where-
    (a) the defendant is a **child** or **protected party**; or
    (b) the claimant is a child or protected party and the admission is made under rr.14.5 or 14.7.
(Rule 21.10 provides that, where a claim is made by or on behalf of a child or protected party or against a child or protected party, no settlement, compromise or payment shall be valid, so far as it relates to that person's claim, without the approval of the court)

(5) The permission of the court is required to amend or withdraw an admission.
(Rule 3.1(3) provides that the court may attach conditions when it makes an order).

Admissions made before commencement of proceedings

Pt 14 r.14.1A

(1) A person may, by giving notice in writing, admit the truth of the whole or any part of another party's case before commencement of proceedings (a 'pre-action admission').
(2) Paragraphs (3) to (5) of this rule apply to a pre-action admission made in the types of proceedings listed at para.1.1(2) of [PD] 14 if one of the following conditions is met—
   (a) it is made after the party making it has received a letter before claim in accordance with the [PD] (Pre-Action Conduct) or any relevant pre-action protocol; or
   (b) it is made before such letter before claim has been received, but it is stated to be made under Pt 14.
(3) A person may, by giving notice in writing, withdraw a pre-action admission—
   (a) before commencement of proceedings, if the person to whom the admission was made agrees;
   (b) after commencement of proceedings, if all parties to the proceedings consent or with the permission of the court.
(4) After commencement of proceedings—
   (a) any party may apply for judgment on the pre-action admission; and
   (b) the party who made the pre-action admission may apply to withdraw it.
(5) An application to withdraw a pre-action admission or to enter judgment on such an admission—
   (a) must be made in accordance with Pt 23;
   (b) may be made as a cross-application.

Forms

PD 14 para.2.1

When particulars of claim are served on a defendant the forms for responding to the claim that will accompany them will include a form1 for making an admission.

PD 14 para.2.2

If the defendant is requesting time to pay he should complete as fully as possible the statement of means contained in the admission form, or otherwise give in writing the same details of his means as could have been given in the admission form.

Period for making an admission

Pt 14 r.14.2

(1) The period for returning an admission under r.14.4 or for filing it under rr.14.5, 14.6 or 14.7 is—
   (a) where the defendant is served with a claim form which states that particulars of claim will follow, 14 days after service of the particulars; and

   (b) in any other case, 14 days after service of the claim form.
(2) Paragraph (1) is subject to the following rules—
   (a) rule 6.35 (which specifies how the period for filing or returning an admission is
       calculated where the claim form is served out of the jurisdiction under rr.6.32 or
       6.33); and
   (b) rule 6.12(3) (which requires the court to specify the period for responding to the
       particulars of claim when it makes an order under that rule).
(3) A defendant may return an admission under r.14.4 or file it under rr.14.5, 14.6 or 14.7
    after the end of the period for returning or filing it specified in para.(1) if the claimant has
    not obtained default judgment under Pt 12.
(4) If he does so, this Part shall apply as if he had made the admission within that period.

Returning or filing the admission

PD 14 para.3.1

If the defendant wishes to make an admission in respect of the whole of a claim for a specified
amount of money, the admission form or other written notice of the admission should be
completed and returned to the claimant within 14 days of service of the particulars of claim.

PD 14 para.3.2

If the defendant wishes to make an admission in respect of a part of a claim for a specified
amount of money, or in respect of a claim for an unspecified amount of money, the admission
form or other written notice of admission should be completed and filed with the court within 14
days of service of the particulars of claim.

PD 14 para.3.3

The defendant may also file a defence under r.15.2.

Admission by notice in writing—application for judgment

Pt 14 r.14.3

(1) Where a party makes an admission under r.14.1(2) (admission by notice in writing), any
    other party may apply for judgment on the admission.
(2) Judgment shall be such judgment as it appears to the court that the applicant is entitled
    to on the admission.

Admission of whole of claim for specified amount of money

Pt 14 r.14.4

(1) This rule applies where—
   (a) the only remedy which the claimant is seeking is the payment of a specified amount
       of money; and
   (b) the defendant admits the whole of the claim.
(2) The defendant may admit the claim by returning to the claimant an admission in the
    relevant practice form.

(3) The claimant may obtain judgment by filing a request in the relevant practice form and, if he does so—
   (a) if the defendant has not requested time to pay, the procedure in paras (4) to (6) will apply;
   (b) if the defendant has requested time to pay, the procedure in r.14.9 will apply.
(4) The claimant may specify in his request for judgment—
   (a) the date by which the whole of the judgment debt is to be paid; or
   (b) the times and rate at which it is to be paid by instalments.
(5) On receipt of the request for judgment the court will enter judgment.
(6) Judgment will be for the amount of the claim (less any payments made) and costs—
   (a) to be paid by the date or at the rate specified in the request for judgment; or
   (b) if none is specified, immediately.

(Rule 14.14 deals with the circumstances in which judgment under this rule may include interest).

Admission of part of a claim for a specified amount of money

Pt 14 r.14.5

(1) This rule applies where—
   (a) the only remedy which the claimant is seeking is the payment of a specified amount of money; and
   (b) the defendant admits part of the claim.
(2) The defendant may admit part of the claim by filing an admission in the relevant practice form.
(3) On receipt of the admission, the court will serve a notice on the claimant requiring him to return the notice stating that—
   (a) he accepts the amount admitted in satisfaction of the claim;
   (b) he does not accept the amount admitted by the defendant and wishes the proceedings to continue; or
   (c) if the defendant has requested time to pay, he accepts the amount admitted in satisfaction of the claim, but not the defendant's proposals as to payment.
(4) The claimant must—
   (a) file the notice; and
   (b) serve a copy on the defendant,
   within 14 days after it is served on him.
(5) If the claimant does not file the notice within 14 days after it is served on him, the claim is stayed until he files the notice.
(6) If the claimant accepts the amount admitted in satisfaction of the claim, he may obtain judgment by filing a request in the relevant practice form and, if he does so—
   (a) if the defendant has not requested time to pay, the procedure in paras (7) to (9) will apply;
   (b) if the defendant has requested time to pay, the procedure in r.14.9 will apply.
(7) The claimant may specify in his request for judgment—
   (a) the date by which the whole of the judgment debt is to be paid; or
   (b) the time and rate at which it is to be paid by instalments.
(8) On receipt of the request for judgment, the court will enter judgment.
(9) Judgment will be for the amount admitted (less any payments made) and costs—
   (a) to be paid by the date or at the rate specified in the request for judgment; or
   (b) if none is specified, immediately.

(If the claimant files notice under para.(3) that he wishes the proceedings to continue, the procedure which then follows is set out in Pt 26).

Admission of liability to pay whole of claim for unspecified amount of money

Pt 14 r.14.6

(1) This rule applies where—
 (a) the only remedy which the claimant is seeking is the payment of money;
 (b) the amount of the claim is not specified; and
 (c) the defendant admits liability but does not offer to pay a specified amount of money in satisfaction of the claim.
(2) The defendant may admit the claim by filing an admission in the relevant practice form.
(3) On receipt of the admission, the court will serve a copy on the claimant.
(4) The claimant may obtain judgment by filing a request in the relevant practice form.
(5) If the claimant does not file a request for judgment within 14 days after service of the admission on him, the claim is stayed until he files the request.
(6) On receipt of the request for judgment the court will enter judgment.
(7) Judgment will be for an amount to be decided by the court and costs.

Admission of liability to pay claim for unspecified amount of money where defendant offers a sum in satisfaction of the claim

Pt 14 r.14.7

(1) This rule applies where—
 (a) the only remedy which the claimant is seeking is the payment of money;
 (b) the amount of the claim is not specified; and
 (c) the defendant—
  (i) admits liability; and
  (ii) offers to pay a specified amount of money in satisfaction of the claim.
(2) The defendant may admit the claim by filing an admission in the relevant practice form.
(3) On receipt of the admission, the court will serve a notice on the claimant requiring him to return the notice stating whether or not he accepts the amount in satisfaction of the claim.
(4) If the claimant does not file the notice within 14 days after it is served on him, the claim is stayed until he files the notice.
(5) If the claimant accepts the offer he may obtain judgment by filing a request in the relevant practice form and if he does so—
 (a) if the defendant has not requested time to pay, the procedure in paras (6) to (8) will apply;
 (b) if the defendant has requested time to pay, the procedure in r.14.9 will apply.
(6) The claimant may specify in his request for judgment—
 (a) the date by which the whole of the judgment debt is to be paid; or
 (b) the times and rate at which it is to be paid by instalments.
(7) On receipt of the request for judgment, the court will enter judgment.
(8) Judgment will be for the amount offered by the defendant (less any payments made) and costs—
 (a) to be paid on the date or at the rate specified in the request for judgment; or
 (b) if none is specified, immediately.
(9) If the claimant does not accept the amount offered by the defendant, he may obtain judgment by filing a request in the relevant practice form.
(10) Judgment under para.(9) will be for an amount to be decided by the court and costs.

Automatic transfer

Pt 14 r.14.7A

If—
  (a) a claimant files a request for judgment for an amount of money to be decided by the court in accordance with rr.14.6 or 14.7; and
  (b) the claim is a **designated money claim**,
the court will transfer the claim to the preferred court.

Allocation of claims in relation to outstanding matters

Pt 14 r.14.8

Where the court enters judgment under rr.14.6 or 14.7 for an amount to be decided by the court it will—
  (a) give any directions it considers appropriate; and
  (b) if it considers it appropriate, allocate the case.

Request for time to pay

Pt 14 r.14.9

  (1) A defendant who makes an admission under rr.14.4, 14.5 or 14.7 (admission relating to a claim for a specified amount of money or offering to pay a specified amount of money) may make a request for time to pay.
  (2) A request for time to pay is a proposal about the date of payment or a proposal to pay by instalments at the times and rate specified in the request.
  (3) The defendant's request for time to pay must be served or filed (as the case may be) with his admission.
  (4) If the claimant accepts the defendant's request, he may obtain judgment by filing a request in the relevant practice form.
  (5) On receipt of the request for judgment, the court will enter judgment.
  (6) Judgment will be—
    (a) where r.14.4 applies, for the amount of the claim (less any payments made) and costs;
    (b) where r.14.5 applies, for the amount admitted (less any payments made) and costs; or
    (c) where r.14.7 applies, for the amount offered by the defendant (less any payments made) and costs; and
    (in all cases) will be for payment at the time and rate specified in the defendant's request for time to pay.
    (Rule 14.10 sets out the procedure to be followed if the claimant does not accept the defendant's request for time to pay).

PD 14 para.4.1

A defendant who makes an admission in respect of a claim for a specified sum of money or offers to pay a sum of money in respect of a claim for an unspecified sum may, in the admission form, make a request for time to pay.

PD 14 para.4.2

If the claimant accepts the defendant's request, he may obtain judgment by filing a request for judgment contained in Form N225A, the court will then enter judgment for payment at the time and rate specified in the defendant's request.

PD 14 para.4.3

If the claimant does not accept the request for time to pay, he should file notice to that effect by completing Form N225A, the court will then enter judgment for the amount of the admission (less any payments made) at a time and rate of payment decided by the court (see r.14.10).

Determination of rate of payment

Pt 14 r.14.10

(1) This rule applies where the defendant makes a request for time to pay under r.14.9.
(2) If the claimant does not accept the defendant's proposals for payment, he must file a notice in the relevant practice form.
(3) Where the defendant's admission was served direct on the claimant, a copy of the admission and the request for time to pay must be filed with the claimant's notice.
(4) When the court receives the claimant's notice, it will enter judgment for the amount admitted (less any payments made) to be paid at the time and rate of payment determined by the court.

Determination of rate of payment by court officer

Pt 14 r.14.11

(1) A court officer may exercise the powers of the court under r.14.10(4) where the amount outstanding (including costs) is not more than £50,000.
(2) Where a court officer is to determine the time and rate of payment, he must do so without a hearing.

Determination of rate of payment by judge

Pt 14 r.14.12

(1) Where a judge is to determine the time and rate of payment, he may do so without a hearing.
(2) Where a judge is to determine the time and rate of payment at a hearing, the proceedings will be transferred automatically to the defendant's home court if—
    (a) the only claim is for a specified amount of money;
    (b) the defendant is an individual;
    (c) the claim has not been transferred to another defendant's home court;
    (d) the claim was not started in the defendant's home court; and
    (e) the claim was not started in a specialist list.
(2A) Where the judge is to determine the time and rate of payment at a hearing, the proceedings will be transferred automatically to the preferred court if—

(a) the only claim is for a specified amount of money;
(b) the claim is a designated money claim;
(c) the defendant is not an individual; and
(d) the claim has not been transferred to another court.
(3) If there is to be a hearing to determine the time and rate of payment, the court will give each party at least seven days' notice of the hearing.

Determining the rate of payment

PD 14 para.5.1

In deciding the time and rate of payment the court will take into account:
(1) the defendant's statement of means set out in the admission form or in any other written notice of the admission filed,
(2) the claimant's objections to the defendant's request set out in the claimant's notice7, and
(3) any other relevant factors.

PD 14 para.5.2

The time and rate of payment may be decided:
(1) by a judge with or without a hearing, or
(2) by a court officer without a hearing provided that—
(a) the only claim is for a specified sum of money, and
(b) the amount outstanding is not more than £50,000 (including costs).

PD 14 para.5.3

Where a decision has been made without a hearing whether by a court officer or by a judge, either party may apply for the decision to be re-determined by a judge.

PD 14 para.5.4

If the decision was made by a court officer the re-determination may take place without a hearing, unless a hearing is requested in the application notice.

PD 14 para.5.5

If the decision was made by a judge the re-determination must be made at a hearing unless the parties otherwise agree.

PD 14 para.5.6

Rule 14.13(2) describes how to apply for a re-determination.

Varying the rate of payment

PD 14 para.6.1

Either party may, on account of a change in circumstances since the date of the decision (or **re-determination** as the case may be) apply to vary the time and rate of payment of instalments still remaining unpaid.

PD 14 para.6.2

An application to vary under para.6.1 above should be made in accordance with Pt 23.

Withdrawing an admission

PD 14 para.7.1

An admission made under Pt 14 may be withdrawn with the court's permission.

PD 14 para.7.2

In deciding whether to give permission for an admission to be withdrawn, the court will have regard to all the circumstances of the case, including—
  (a) the grounds upon which the applicant seeks to withdraw the admission including whether or not new evidence has come to light which was not available at the time the admission was made;
  (b) the conduct of the parties, including any conduct which led the party making the admission to do so;
  (c) the prejudice that may be caused to any person if the admission is withdrawn;
  (d) the prejudice that may be caused to any person if the application is refused;
  (e) the stage in the proceedings at which the application to withdraw is made, in particular in relation to the date or period fixed for trial;
  (f) the prospects of success (if the admission is withdrawn) of the claim or part of the claim in relation to which the offer was made; and
  (g) the interests of the administration of justice.

See **Commercial Court**, **Interest**, **Mercantile Courts**, and **RTA Protocol**.

ADOPTION PROCEEDINGS

Pt 2 r.2.1(2)

The CPR do not apply to these proceedings except to the extent that they are applied by s.66 of the Adoption Act 1976 or s.141(c) of the Adoption and Children Act 2002.

ADR

Alternative dispute resolution.

ADVOCATE

Pt 46 r.46.1

A person exercising a right of audience as a representative of, or on behalf of, a party.

AFFIDAVIT

Glossary

A written, sworn statement of evidence.

PD 32 para.1.7

An affidavit, where referred to in the CPR or a PD, also means an **affirmation** unless the context requires otherwise.

Form of affidavit

Pt 32 para.32.16

An affidavit must comply with the requirements set out in [PD 32].

Heading

PD 32, para.3.1

The affidavit should be headed with the title of the proceedings (see para.4 of PD 7A and para.7 of PD 20); where the proceedings are between several parties with the same status it is sufficient to identify the parties as follows: Number:

A.B. (and others)   Claimants/Applicants
C.D. (and others)   Defendants/Respondents (as appropriate)

PD 32 para.3.2

At the top right hand corner of the first page (and on the backsheet) there should be clearly written:
  (1) the party on whose behalf it is made,
  (2) the initials and surname of the deponent,
  (3) the number of the affidavit in relation to that deponent,
  (4) the identifying initials and number of each exhibit referred to, and
  (5) the date sworn.

Body of affidavit

PD 32 para.4.1

The affidavit must, if practicable, be in the deponent's own words, the affidavit should be expressed in the first person and the **deponent** should:
  (1) commence 'I (full names) of (address) state on oath . . . ',
  (2) if giving evidence in his professional, business or other occupational capacity, give the address at which he works in (1) above, the position he holds and the name of his firm or employer,

(3) give his occupation or, if he has none, his description, and
(4) state if he is a party to the proceedings or employed by a party to the proceedings, if it be the case.

PD 32 para.4.2

An affidavit must indicate:
(1) which of the statements in it are made from the deponent's own knowledge and which are matters of information or belief, and
(2) the source for any matters of information or belief.

PD 32 para.4.3

Where a deponent:
(1) refers to an exhibit or exhibits, he should state 'there is now shown to me marked '. . . ' the (description of exhibit)', and
(2) makes more than one affidavit (to which there are exhibits) in the same proceedings, the numbering of the exhibits should run consecutively throughout and not start again with each affidavit.

Format of affidavits

PD 32 para.6.1

An affidavit should:
(1) be produced on durable quality A4 paper with a 3.5cm margin,
(2) be fully legible and should normally be typed on one side of the paper only,
(3) where possible, be bound securely in a manner which would not hamper filing, or otherwise each page should be endorsed with the case number and should bear the initials of the deponent and of the person before whom it was sworn,
(4) have the pages numbered consecutively as a separate document (or as one of several documents contained in a file),
(5) be divided into numbered paragraphs,
(6) have all numbers, including dates, expressed in figures, and
(7) give the reference to any document or documents mentioned either in the margin or in bold text in the body of the affidavit.

PD 32, para.6.2

It is usually convenient for an affidavit to follow the chronological sequence of events or matters dealt with; each paragraph of an affidavit should as far as possible be confined to a distinct portion of the subject.

Inability of deponent to read or sign affidavit

PD 32 para.7.1

Where an affidavit is sworn by a person who is unable to read or sign it, the person before whom the affidavit is sworn must certify in the jurat that:
(1) he read the affidavit to the deponent,
(2) the deponent appeared to understand it, and

(3) the deponent signed or made his mark, in his presence.

PD 32 para.7.2

If that certificate is not included in the jurat, the affidavit may not be used in evidence unless the court is satisfied that it was read to the deponent and that he appeared to understand it. Two versions of the form of jurat with the certificate are set out at Annex 1 to this PD.

Alterations to affidavits

PD 32 para.8.1

Any alteration to an affidavit must be initialled by both the deponent and the person before whom the affidavit was sworn.

PD 32 para.8.2

An affidavit which contains an alteration that has not been initialled may be filed or used in evidence only with the permission of the court.

Who may administer oaths and take affidavits

PD 32 para.9.2

An affidavit must be sworn before a person independent of the parties or their representatives.
See also **Oaths**.

Filing of affidavits

PD 32 para.10.1

If the court directs that an affidavit is to be filed, it must be filed in the court or Division, or Office or Registry of the court or Division where the action in which it was or is to be used, is proceeding or will proceed.

Foreign language

PD 32 para.10.2

Where an affidavit is in a foreign language:
  (1) the party wishing to rely on it—
      (a) must have it translated, and
      (b) must file the foreign language affidavit with the court, and
  (2) the translator must make and file with the court an affidavit verifying the translation and exhibiting both the translation and a copy of the foreign language affidavit

Affidavit made outside the jurisdiction

PD 32 para.32.17

A person may make an affidavit outside the jurisdiction in accordance with—
  (a) [Part 32]; or
  (b) the law of the place where he makes the affidavit.

Defects in affidavits, witness statements and exhibits

PD 32 para.25.1

Where:
  (1) an affidavit, or
  (2) a witness statement, or
  (3) an exhibit to either an affidavit or a witness statement,
does not comply with Pt 32 or [PD 32] in relation to its form, the court may refuse to admit it as evidence and may refuse to allow the costs arising from its preparation.

PD 32 para.25.2

Permission to file a defective affidavit or witness statement or to use a defective exhibit may be obtained from a judge in the court where the case is proceeding.

See also **Affidavit evidence**, **Exhibit**, **Affirmation**, and **Jurat**.

AFFIDAVIT EVIDENCE

Pt 32 r.32.15

  (1) Evidence must be given by affidavit instead of or in addition to a witness statement if this is required by the court, a provision contained in any other rule, a PD or any other enactment.
  (2) Nothing in these rules prevents a witness giving evidence by affidavit at a hearing other than the trial if he chooses to do so in a case where para.(1) does not apply, but the party putting forward the affidavit may not recover the additional cost of making it from any other party unless the court orders otherwise.

PD 32 r.1.5

If a party believes that sworn evidence is required by a court in another jurisdiction for any purpose connected with the proceedings, he may apply to the court for a direction that evidence shall be given only by affidavit on any pre-trial applications.

PD 32 r.1.6

The court may give a direction under r.32.15 that evidence shall be given by affidavit instead of or in addition to a witness statement or statement of case:
  (1) on its own initiative, or

(2) after any party has applied to the court for such a direction.

PD 32 r.1.7

An affidavit, where referred to in the CPR or a PD, also means an affirmation unless the context requires otherwise.

When affidavit must be used

PD 32 para.1.4

Affidavits must be used as evidence in the following instances:
(1) where sworn evidence is required by an enactment, rule, Order or PD,
(2) in any application for a search order, a freezing injunction, or an order requiring an occupier to permit another to enter his land.

See **Contempt of court**.

AFFIDAVIT OF SERVICE

Affidavit of service has been replaced by **certificate of service**.

AFFIRMATION

PD 32 para.16

All provisions in [PD 32] or any other PD relating to **affidavits** apply to affirmations with the following exceptions:
(1) the deponent should commence 'I (name) of (address) do solemnly and sincerely affirm . . . ', and
(2) in the jurat the word 'sworn' is replaced by the word 'affirmed'.

AGGRAVATED DAMAGES

Glossary

Additional damages which the court may award as compensation for the defendant's objectionable behaviour.

AGREED COSTS

Procedure where costs are agreed

Pt 47 r.47.10

(1) If the paying party and the receiving party agree the amount of costs, either party may apply for a costs certificate (either interim or final) in the amount agreed.

(2) An application for a certificate under para.(1) must be made to the court which would be the venue for detailed assessment proceedings under r.47.4.

PD 47 para.9.1

Where the parties have agreed terms as to the issue of a costs certificate (either interim or final) they should apply under r.40.6 (**Consent judgments and orders**) for an order that a certificate be issued in terms set out in the application. Such an application may be dealt with by a court officer, who may issue the certificate.

PD 47 para.9.2

Where in the course of proceedings the receiving party claims that the paying party has agreed to pay costs but that he will neither pay those costs nor join in a consent application under para.9.1, the receiving party may apply under Pt 23 (General Rules about Applications for Court Orders) for a certificate either interim or final [costs certificate] to be issued.

PD 47 para.9.3

Nothing in r.47.10 prevents parties who seek a judgment or order by consent from including in the draft a term that a party shall pay to another party a specified sum in respect of costs.

PD 47 para.9.4

(1) The receiving party may discontinue the detailed assessment proceedings in accordance with Pt 38 (**Discontinuance**).
(2) Where the receiving party discontinues the detailed assessment proceedings before a detailed assessment hearing has been requested, the paying party may apply to the appropriate office for an order about the costs of the detailed assessment proceedings.
(3) Where a detailed assessment hearing has been requested the receiving party may not discontinue unless the court gives permission.
(4) A bill of costs may be withdrawn by consent whether or not a detailed assessment hearing has been requested.

See **Final costs certificate** and **Interim costs certificate**.

AGRICULTURAL HOLDINGS ACT 1986

Enforcement of order imposing penalty

CCR Ord.44 r.4

(1) When taking any proceedings for the enforcement in a county court of an Order under s.27 of the Agricultural Holdings Act 1986, the party in whose favour the Order was made shall file—
(a) a certified copy of the order; and
(b) a certificate specifying the amount due under the order and stating whether any previous proceedings have been taken for its enforcement and, if so, the nature of the proceedings and their result.
(2) Where it is desired to enforce the order by warrant of execution, the proceedings may be taken in any court in the district of which execution is to be levied.

See also **Agricultural Land Tribunal**.

AGRICULTURAL LAND TRIBUNAL

Reference of question of law by Agriculture Land Tribunal

PD 52D para.18.1

(1) A question of law referred to the High Court by an Agricultural Land Tribunal under s.6 of the Agriculture (Miscellaneous Provisions) Act 1954 shall be referred by way of case stated by the Tribunal.

(2) Where the proceedings before the tribunal arose on an application under s.11 of the Agricultural Holdings Act 1986, an—
  (a) application notice for an order under s. 6 that the tribunal refers a question of law to the court; and
  (b) appellant's notice by which an appellant seeks the court's determination on a question of law,
  must be served on the authority having power to enforce the statutory requirement specified in the notice in addition to every other party to those proceedings and on the secretary of the tribunal.

(3) Where, in accordance with para.(2), a notice is served on the authority mentioned in that paragraph, that authority may attend the appeal hearing and make representations to the court.

See **Farmer**.

ALL PROCEEDINGS ORDER

Senior Courts Act 1981 s.42(1A)

An order which has the combined effect of [civil proceedings order and criminal proceedings order, which is an order that (a) no information shall be laid before a justice of the peace by the person against whom the order is made and (b) no application for leave to prefer a bill of indictment shall be made by him] without the leave of the High Court.
See **Vexatious litigants**.

ALLOCATION

Pt 26 r.26.5

(1) The court will allocate the claim to a track—
  (a) when every defendant has filed an **allocation questionnaire**, or
  (b) when the period for filing the allocation questionnaires has expired,
  whichever is the sooner, unless it has—
   (i) stayed the proceedings under r.26.4; or
  (ii) dispensed with the need for allocation questionnaires.
(Rules 12.7 and 14.8 provide for the court to allocate a claim to a track where the claimant obtains default judgment on request or judgment on admission for an amount to be decided by the court)
(2) If the court has stayed the proceedings under r.26.4, it will allocate the claim to a track at the end of the period of the stay.
(3) Before deciding the track to which to allocate proceedings or deciding whether to give directions for an allocation hearing to be fixed, the court may order a party to provide further information about his case.

(4) The court may hold an allocation hearing if it thinks it is necessary.

(5) If a party fails to file an allocation questionnaire, the court may give any direction it considers appropriate.

PD 26 para.12.3

(1) If, when the court makes a relevant order—
    (a) the claim has not previously been allocated to a track; and
    (b) the financial value of the claim (determined in accordance with Pt 26) is such that the claim would, if defended be allocated to the small claims track,
the court will normally allocate it to that track.

(2) Where para.(1)(b) does not apply, the court will not normally allocate the claim to a track (other than the small claims track) unless—
    (a) the amount payable appears to be genuinely disputed on substantial grounds; or
    (b) the dispute is not suitable to be dealt with at a disposal hearing.

(3) Rule 26.8 sets out the matters relevant to allocation to a track.

Court's general approach

PD 26 para.4.1

The [CPR] lay down the overriding objective, the powers and duties of the court and the factors to which it must have regard in exercising them. The court will expect to exercise its powers as far as possible in co-operation with the parties and their legal representatives so as to deal with the case justly in accordance with that objective.

Allocation to track

PD 26 para.4.2

(1) In most cases the court will expect to have enough information from the statements of case and allocation questionnaires to be able to allocate the claim to a track and to give case management directions.

(2) If the court does not have enough information to allocate the claim it will generally make an order under r.26.5(3) requiring one or more parties to provide further information within 14 days.

(3) Where there has been no allocation hearing the notice of allocation will be in Forms N154 (fast track), N155 (multi-track) or N157–160 (small claims).

(4) (a) The general rule is that the court will give brief reasons for its allocation decision, and these will be set out in the notice of allocation.
    (b) The general rule does not apply where all the allocation questionnaires which have been filed have expressed the wish for the claim to be allocated to the track to which the court has allocated it

(5) Paragraph 6 of this PD deals with allocation hearings and para.7 deals with allocation principles.

(6) Paragraph 11 of this PD deals with re-allocation.

PD 26 para.4.3

The [PD s] supplementing Pts 27, 28 and 29 contain further information about the giving of case management directions at the allocation stage.

General rule for allocation

Pt 26 r.26.7

(1) In considering whether to allocate a claim to the normal track for that claim under r.26.6, the court will have regard to the matters mentioned in r.26.8(1).

(2) The court will allocate a claim which has no financial value to the track which it considers most suitable having regard to the matters mentioned in r.26.8(1).

(3) The court will not allocate proceedings to a track if the financial value of the claim, assessed by the court under r.26.8, exceeds the limit for that track unless all the parties consent to the allocation of the claim to that track.

(4) The court will not allocate a claim to the small claims track, if it includes a claim by a tenant of residential premises against his landlord for a remedy in respect of harassment or unlawful eviction.

Matters relevant to allocation to a track

Pt 26 r.26.8

(1) When deciding the track for a claim, the matters to which the court shall have regard include—
(a) the financial value, if any, of the claim;
(b) the nature of the remedy sought;
(c) the likely complexity of the facts, law or evidence;
(d) the number of parties or likely parties;
(e) the value of any counterclaim or other Pt 20 claim and the complexity of any matters relating to it;
(f) the amount of oral evidence which may be required;
(g) the importance of the claim to persons who are not parties to the proceedings;
(h) the views expressed by the parties; and
(i) the circumstances of the parties.

(2) It is for the court to assess the financial value of a claim and in doing so it will disregard—
(a) any amount not in dispute;
(b) any claim for interest;
(c) costs; and
(d) any contributory negligence.

(3) Where—
(a) two or more claimants have started a claim against the same defendant using the same claim form; and
(b) each claimant has a claim against the defendant separate from the other claimants, the court will consider the claim of each claimant separately when it assesses financial value under para.(1).

Objective

PD 26 para.7.2

The object of this paragraph is to explain what will be the court's general approach to some of the matters set out in r.26.8.

PD 26 para.7.3

"The financial value of the claim"

    (1) Rule 26.8(2) provides that it is for the court to assess the financial value of a claim.
    (2) Where the court believes that the amount the claimant is seeking exceeds what he may reasonably be expected to recover it may make an order under r.26.5(3) directing the claimant to justify the amount.

PD 26 para.7.4

"Any amount not in dispute"

In deciding, for the purposes of r.26.8(2), whether an amount is in dispute the court will apply the following general principles:
    (1) Any amount for which the defendant does not admit liability is in dispute,
    (2) Any sum in respect of an item forming part of the claim for which judgment has been entered (for example a summary judgment) is not in dispute,
    (3) Any specific sum claimed as a distinct item and which the defendant admits he is liable to pay is not in dispute,
    (4) Any sum offered by the defendant which has been accepted by the claimant in satisfaction of any item which forms a distinct part of the claim is not in dispute.
It follows from these provisions that if, in relation to a claim the value of which is above the small claims track limit of £10,000, the defendant makes, before allocation, an admission that reduces the amount in dispute to a figure below £10,000 (see CPR Pt 14), the normal track for the claim will be the small claims track. As to recovery of pre-allocation costs, the claimant can, before allocation, apply for judgment with costs on the amount of the claim that has been admitted (see CPR r.14.3 but see also para.15.1(3) of the Costs PD supplementing Pts 43 to 48 under which the court has a discretion to allow pre-allocation costs).

PD 26 para.7.5

"The views expressed by the parties"

The court will treat these views as an important factor, but the allocation decision is one for the court, to be taken in the light of all the circumstances, and the court will not be bound by any agreement or common view of the parties.

PD 26 para.7.6

"The circumstances of the parties"

See para.8.

"the value of any counterclaim or other Part 20 claim".

PD 26 para.7.7

Where the case involves more than one money claim (for example where there is a Pt 20 claim or there is more than one claimant each making separate claims) the court will not generally aggregate the claims. Instead it will generally regard the largest of them as determining the financial value of the claims.

Notice of allocation

Pt 26 r.26.9

(1) When it has allocated a claim to a track, the court will serve notice of allocation on every party.
(2) When the court serves notice of allocation on a party, it will also serve—
    (a) a copy of the allocation questionnaires filed by the other parties; and
    (b) a copy of any further information provided by another party about his case (whether by order or not).

(Rule 26.5 provides that the court may, before allocating proceedings, order a party to provide further information about his case).

Hearings before allocation

PD 26 para.2.4

Where a court hearing takes place (for example on an application for an interim injunction or for summary judgment under Pt 24) before the claim is allocated to a track, the court may at that hearing:
    (1) dispense with the need for the parties to file allocation questionnaires, treat the hearing as an allocation hearing, make an order for allocation and give directions for case management, or
    (2) fix a date for allocation questionnaires to be filed and give other directions.

See **Automatic transfer, Allocation hearing, Case management, Directions questionnaire, Fast track, Multi-track, Small claims track, Judgments and orders, Jury trial, Re-allocation to a different track, Stay, Summary assessment,** and **Summary judgment.**

ALLOCATION HEARING

PD 26 para.6.1

The court will only hold an allocation hearing on its own initiative if it considers that it is necessary to do so.

Procedure

PD 64A para.6.2

Where the court orders an allocation hearing to take place:
    (1) it will give the parties at least seven days' notice of the hearing in Form N153, and
    (2) Form N153 will give a brief explanation of the decision to order the hearing.

Power to treat another hearing as an allocation hearing

PD 64A para.6.3

Where the court may treat another hearing as an allocation hearing it does not need to give notice to any party that it proposes to do so.

PD 64A para.6.4

The notice of allocation after an allocation hearing will be in Forms N154, N155 or N157.

Representation

PD 64A para.6.5

A **legal representative** who attends an allocation hearing should, if possible, be the person responsible for the case and must in any event be familiar with the case, be able to provide the court with the information it is likely to need to take its decisions about allocation and case management, and have sufficient authority to deal with any issues that are likely to arise.

Sanctions

PD 64A para.6.6

(1) This paragraph sets out the sanctions that the court will usually impose for default in connection with the allocation procedure, but the court may make a different order.

(2) (a) Where an allocation hearing takes place because a party has failed to file an allocation questionnaire or to provide further information which the court has ordered, the court will usually order that party to pay on the indemnity basis the costs of any other party who has attended the hearing, summarily assess the amount of those costs, and order them to be paid forthwith or within a stated period.

   (b) The court may order that if the party does not pay those costs within the time stated his statement of case will be struck out.

(3) Where a party whose default has led to a fixing of an allocation hearing is still in default and does not attend the hearing the court will usually make an order specifying the steps he is required to take and providing that unless he takes them within a stated time his statement of case will be struck out.

See also **Allocation** and **Directions questionnaire**.

ALLOCATION QUESTIONNAIRE

From April 1, 2013, re-named **Directions questionnaire.**

ALTERNATIVE DISPUTE RESOLUTION

Glossary

Collective description of methods of resolving disputes otherwise than through the normal trial process.

Court's duty to manage cases

Pt 1 r.1.4

(1) The court must further the overriding objective by actively managing cases.

(2) Active case management includes—

(e) encouraging the parties to use an alternative dispute resolution procedure if the court considers that appropriate and facilitating the use of such procedure.

Determining the amount to be paid under a judgment or order

(1) When the court makes a **relevant order** it will give directions, which may include—
(d) staying the claim while the parties try to settle the case by alternative dispute resolution or other means.

Multi-track

Directions on allocation

PD 29 para.4.10

(9) in such cases as the court thinks appropriate, the court may give directions requiring the parties to consider ADR. Such directions may be, for example, in the following terms:

The parties shall by [date] consider whether the case is capable of resolution by ADR. If any party considers that the case is unsuitable for resolution by ADR, that party shall be prepared to justify that decision at the conclusion of the trial, should the judge consider that such means of resolution were appropriate, when he is considering the appropriate costs order to make.

The party considering the case unsuitable for ADR shall, not less than 28 days before the commencement of the trial, file with the court a witness statement without prejudice save as to costs, giving reasons upon which they rely for saying that the case was unsuitable.

Pre-action protocols

[The various Pre-action Protocols suggest ADR. The Professional Negligence Pre-action Protocol, states:]

The parties should consider whether some form of alternative dispute resolution procedure would be more suitable than litigation, and if so, endeavour to agree which form to adopt. Both the claimant and professional may be required by the court to provide evidence that alternative means of resolving their dispute were considered. The courts take the view that litigation should be a last resort, and that claims should not be issued prematurely when a settlement is still actively being explored. Parties are warned that if the protocol is not followed (including this paragraph) then the court must have regard to such conduct when determining costs.

It is not practicable in this protocol to address in detail how the parties might decide which method to adopt to resolve their particular dispute. However, summarised below are some of the options for resolving disputes without litigation:

Discussion and negotiation

Early neutral evaluation by an independent third party (for example, a lawyer experienced in the field of professional negligence or an individual experienced in the subject matter of the claim).

Mediation—a form of facilitated negotiation assisted by an independent neutral party.

The Legal Services Commission has published a booklet on "Alternatives to Court", CLS Direct Information Leaflet 23 *http://www.clsdirect.org.uk/legalhelp/leaflet23.jsp*, which lists a number of organisations that provide alternative dispute resolution services.

It is expressly recognised that no party can or should be forced to mediate or enter into any form of ADR.

ALTERNATIVE METHOD OF SERVICE

See **Service of documents**.

ALTERNATIVE PROCEDURE FOR CLAIMS

See **Pt 8 procedure**.

ANTI-SOCIAL BEHAVIOUR ORDERS UNDER THE CRIME AND DISORDER ACT 1998

Pt 65 r.65.21

(1) [Section IV of Part 65] applies to applications in proceedings in a county court under sub-ss.(2), (3) or (3B) of s.1B of the Crime and Disorder Act 1998 by a relevant authority, and to applications for interim orders under s.1D of that Act.

Application where the relevant authority is a party in principal proceedings

Pt 65 r.65.22

(1) Subject to para.(2)—
   (a) where the relevant authority] [has same meaning as in s.1(1A) of the [Crime and Disorder Act 1998] is the claimant in the principal proceedings, an application under s.1B(2) of the 1998 Act for an order under s.1B(4) of the 1998 Act must be made in the claim form; and
   (b) where the relevant authority is a defendant in the principal proceedings [means any proceedings in a county court], an application for an order must be made by application notice which must be filed with the defence.
(2) Where the relevant authority becomes aware of the circumstances that lead it to apply for an order after its claim is issued or its defence filed, the application must be made by application notice as soon as possible thereafter.
(3) Where the application is made by application notice, it should normally be made on notice to the person against whom the order is sought.

Application by a relevant authority to join a person to the principal proceedings

Pt 65 r.65.23

(1) An application under s.1B(3B) of the 1998 Act by a relevant authority which is a party to the principal proceedings to join a person to the principal proceedings must be made—

(a) in accordance with s.I of Pt 19;

(b) in the same application notice as the application for an order under s.1B(4) of the 1998 Act against the person; and

(c) as soon as possible after the relevant authority considers that the criteria in section 1B(3A) of the 1998 Act are met.

(2) The application notice must contain—

(a) the relevant authority's reasons for claiming that the person's anti-social acts are material in relation to the principal proceedings; and

(b) details of the anti-social acts alleged.

(3) The application should normally be made on notice to the person against whom the order is sought.

Application where the relevant authority is not party in principal proceedings

Pt 65 r.65.24

(1) Where the relevant authority is not a party to the principal proceedings—

(a) an application under s.1B(3) of the 1998 Act to be made a party must be made in accordance with s.I of Pt 19; and

(b) the application to be made a party and the application for an order under s.1B(4) of the 1998 Act must be made in the same application notice.

(2) The applications—

(a) must be made as soon as possible after the authority becomes aware of the principal proceedings; and

(b) should normally be made on notice to the person against whom the order is sought.

Evidence

Pt 65 r.65.25

An application for an order under s.1B(4) of the 1998 Act must be accompanied by written evidence, which must include evidence that s.1E of the 1998 Act has been complied with.

Application for an interim order

Pt 65 r.65.26

(1) An application for an interim order under s.1D of the 1998 Act must be made in accordance with Pt 25.

(2) The application should normally be made—

(a) in the claim form or application notice seeking the order; and

(b) on notice to the person against whom the order is sought.

ANTON PILLER ORDER

See **Search order**.

APPEALS

Pt 52 r.52.1

(1) The rules in [Pt 52] apply to appeals to—
   (a) the civil division of the Court of Appeal;
   (b) the High Court; and
   (c) a county court.
(2) This Pt does not apply to an appeal in detailed assessment proceedings against a decision of an authorised court officer [**appeals from an authorised court officer in detailed assessment proceedings**].
(3) In [Pt 52]—
   (a) 'appeal' includes an appeal by way of case stated;
   (b) 'appeal court' means the court to which an appeal is made;
   (c) 'lower court' means the court, tribunal or other person or body from whose decision an appeal is brought;
   (d) 'appellant' means a person who brings or seeks to bring an appeal;
   (e) 'respondent' means—
      (i) a person other than the appellant who was a party to the proceedings in the lower court and who is affected by the appeal; and
      (ii) a person who is permitted by the appeal court to be a party to the appeal; and
   (f) 'appeal notice' means an appellant's or respondent's notice.
(4) [Pt 52] is subject to any rule, enactment or PD which sets out special provisions with regard to any particular category of appeal.

Pt 52 r.52.2

All parties to an appeal must comply with PDs 52A to 52E.

PD52A para.2.1

[PD52A] apply to all appeals to which Pt 52 applies.

PD 52A para.2.2

Pt 52 complements the provisions of ss.54 to 57 of the Access to Justice Act 1999 and provides a uniform procedure for appeals in the county courts and the High Court and a modified procedure for the Civil Division of the Court of Appeal. Pt 52 does not apply to—
   (a) family proceedings in the High Court or county courts but does apply to appeals to the Court of Appeal from decisions made in family proceedings with such modifications as may be required;
   (b) appeals in detailed assessment proceedings against the decision of an authorised court officer.

Destinations of appeal

PD 52A para.3.1

Section 56 of the Access to Justice Act 1999 enables the Lord Chancellor by Order to specify the destinations of appeal in different cases. The Access to Justice Act 1999 (Destination of Appeals) Order 2000, SI 2000/1071 made under s.56, specifies the general destinations of appeal which apply subject to any statutory provision to the contrary. The destinations of appeal provided by that Order are explained in the following paras. of this section of [PD 52A].

PD 52A paras 3.3 and 3.5

The court or judge to which an appeal is to be made (subject to obtaining any necessary permission) is set out in the tables below—
Table 1 deals with appeals in proceedings other than family and insolvency proceedings;
Table 2 deals with appeals in insolvency proceedings; and
Table 3 deals with appeals in family proceedings which may be heard in the Family Division and to which the CPR may apply.
The proceedings to which this table applies include proceedings under the Inheritance (Provision for Family and Dependants) Act 1975 and proceedings under the Trusts of Land and Appointment of Trustees Act 1996.

PD 52A para.3.5

The destinations in the Tables set out whether [it is interim decision or **final decision**].

Permission

Pt 52 r.52.3

(1) An appellant or respondent requires permission to appeal—
  (a) where the appeal is from a decision of a judge in a county court or the High Court, except where the appeal is against—
    (i) a **committal order**;
    (ii) a refusal to grant **habeas corpus**; or
    (iii) a secure accommodation order made under s.25 of the Children Act 1989; or
  (b) as provided by PD 52.
(Other enactments may provide that permission is required for particular appeals)
(2) An application for permission to appeal may be made—
  (a) to the lower court at the hearing at which the decision to be appealed was made; or
  (b) to the appeal court in an appeal notice.
(R.52.4 sets out the time limits for filing an appellant's notice at the appeal court. R. 52.5 sets out the time limits for filing a respondent's notice at the appeal court. Any application for permission to appeal to the appeal court must be made in the appeal notice (see rr. 52.4(1) and 52.5(3))
(R.52.13(1) provides that permission is required from the Court of Appeal for all appeals to that court from a decision of a county court or the High Court which was itself made on appeal)
(3) Where the lower court refuses an application for permission to appeal, a further application for permission to appeal may be made to the appeal court.
(4) Subject to para.(4A), where the appeal court, without a hearing, refuses permission to appeal, the person seeking permission may request the decision to be reconsidered at a hearing.
(4A) (a) Where a judge of the Court of Appeal or of the High Court, a Designated Civil Judge or a Specialist Circuit Judge refuses permission to appeal without a hearing and considers that the application is totally without merit, the judge may make an order that the person seeking permission may not request the decision to be reconsidered at a hearing.
  (b) For the purposes of subpara.(a) "Specialist Circuit Judge" means a patents county court judge and any circuit judge in any county court nominated to hear cases in the Mercantile, Chancery or Technology and Construction Court lists.

(4B) R. 3.3(5) will not apply to an order that the person seeking permission may not request the decision to be reconsidered at a hearing made under para. (4A).

(5) A request under para. (4) must be filed within 7 days after service of the notice that permission has been refused.

(6) Permission to appeal may be given only where—

    (a) the court considers that the appeal would have a real prospect of success; or

    (b) there is some other compelling reason why the appeal should be heard.

(7) An order giving permission may—

    (a) limit the issues to be heard; and

    (b) be made subject to conditions.

(R. 3.1(3) also provides that the court may make an order subject to conditions)

(R. 25.15 provides for the court to order **security for costs** of an appeal)

Where to apply for permission

PD 52A para.4.1

An application for permission to appeal may be made—

    (a) to the lower court at the hearing at which the decision to be appealed against is given (in which case the lower court may adjourn the hearing to give a party an opportunity to apply for permission to appeal); or

    (b) where the lower court refuses permission to appeal or where no application is made to the lower court, to the appeal court in accordance with r. 52.4.

Form

PD 52A para.4.2

An application for permission to appeal to the appeal court must be made using an appellant's notice (form N161 or N164 (**small claims track**)).

Appeals from Masters and district judges of High Court

PD 52A para.4.3

In relation to appeals from Masters or district judges of the High Court: appeals, applications for permission and any other applications in the appeal may be heard and directions in the appeal may be given by a High Court Judge or by any person authorised under s.9 of the Senior Courts Act 1981 to act as a judge of the High Court.

Where the lower court is a county court

PD 52A para.4.4

Where the lower court is a county court—

    (a) subject to para.(2), appeals and applications for permission to appeal will be heard by a High Court Judge or by a person authorised under paras (1), (2) or (4) of the Table in s.9(1) of the Senior Courts Act 1981 to act as a judge of the High Court;

(b) an appeal or application for permission to appeal from the decision of a recorder may be heard by a Designated Civil Judge who is authorised under para.(5) of the Table in s.9(1) of the Senior Courts Act 1981 to act as a judge of the High Court; and

(c) other applications in the appeal may be heard and directions in the appeal may be given either by a High Court Judge or by any person authorised under s.9 of the Senior Courts Act 1981 to act as a judge of the High Court.

PD 52A para.4.5

The Designated Civil Judge in consultation with the Presiding Judge has responsibility for allocating appeals from decisions of district judges to circuit judges.

Appeal in relation to case management decision

PD 52A para.4.6

Where the application is for permission to appeal from a case management decision, the court dealing with the application may take into account whether—

(a) the issue is of sufficient significance to justify the costs of an appeal;

(b) the procedural consequences of an appeal (e.g. loss of trial date) outweigh the significance of the case management decision;

(c) it would be more convenient to determine the issue at or after trial.

Case management decisions include decisions made under r. 3.1(2) and decisions about disclosure, filing of witness statements or experts' reports, directions about the timetable of the claim, adding a party to a claim and security for costs.

Second appeal

PD 52A para.4.7

An application for permission to appeal from a decision of the High Court or a county court which was itself made on appeal is a second appeal and must be made to the Court of Appeal. If permission to appeal is granted the appeal will be heard by the Court of Appeal.

Appellant's notice

Pt 52 r.52.4

(1) Where the appellant seeks permission from the appeal court it must be requested in the appellant's notice.

(2) The appellant must file the appellant's notice at the appeal court within—

(a) such period as may be directed by the lower court (which may be longer or shorter than the period referred to in sub-para.(b)); or

(b) where the court makes no such direction, 21 days after the date of the decision of the lower court that the appellant wishes to appeal.

(3) Subject to para.(4) and unless the appeal court orders otherwise, an appellant's notice must be served on each respondent—

(a) as soon as practicable; and

(b) in any event not later than 7 days,

after it is filed.

(4) Where an appellant seeks permission to appeal against a decision to refuse to grant an interim injunction under s.41 of the Policing and Crime Act 2009 the appellant is not required to serve the appellant's notice on the respondent.

Amendment of appeal notice

Pt 52 r.52.8

An appeal notice may not be amended without the permission of the appeal court.

Variation of time

Pt 52 r.52.6

(1) An application to vary the time limit for filing an appeal notice must be made to the appeal court.
(2) The parties may not agree to extend any date or time limit set by—
  (a) these Rules;
  (b) PD 52; or
  (c) an order of the appeal court or the lower court.

(R.3.1(2)(a) provides that the court may extend or shorten the time for compliance with any rule, PD or court order (even if an application for extension is made after the time for compliance has expired))
(R. 3.1(2)(b) provides that the court may adjourn or bring forward a hearing)

Filing appellant's notice in wrong court

PD 52A para.3.9

(1) Where a party attempts to file an appellant's notice in a court which does not have jurisdiction to issue the notice, a court officer may notify that party in writing that the appeal court does not have jurisdiction in respect of the notice.
(2) Before notifying a person under para.(1) the court officer must confer—
  (a) with a judge of the appeal court; or
  (b) where the Court of Appeal is the appeal court, with a court officer who exercises the jurisdiction of that Court under r. 52.16.
(3) Where a court officer, in the Court of Appeal, notifies a person under para.(1), r. 52.16(5) and (6) shall not apply.

Filing appellant's notice in wrong court

PD 52A para.3.9

(1) Where a party attempts to file an appellant's notice in a court which does not have jurisdiction to issue the notice, a court officer may notify that party in writing that the appeal court does not have jurisdiction in respect of the notice.
(2) Before notifying a person under para.(1) the court officer must confer—

(a) with a judge of the appeal court; or

(b) where the Court of Appeal is the appeal court, with a court officer who exercises the jurisdiction of that Court under r. 52.16.

(3) Where a court officer, in the Court of Appeal, notifies a person under para. (1), r.52.16(5) and (6) shall not apply.

Striking outappeal notices and setting aside or imposing conditions on permission to appeal

Pt 52 r.52.9

(1) The appeal court may—
   (a) strike out the whole or part of an appeal notice;
   (b) set aside permission to appeal in whole or in part;
   (c) impose or vary conditions upon which an appeal may be brought.
(2) The court will only exercise its powers under para.(1) where there is a compelling reason for doing so.
(3) Where a party was present at the hearing at which permission was given he may not subsequently apply for an order that the court exercise its powers under sub-paras (1)(b) or (1)(c).

Respondent's notice

Pt 52 r.52.5

(1) A respondent may file and serve a respondent's notice.
(2) A respondent who—
   (a) is seeking permission to appeal from the appeal court; or
   (b) wishes to ask the appeal court to uphold the order of the lower court for reasons different from or additional to those given by the lower court,
   must file a respondent's notice.
(3) Where the respondent seeks permission from the appeal court it must be requested in the respondent's notice.
(4) A respondent's notice must be filed within—
   (a) such period as may be directed by the lower court; or
   (b) where the court makes no such direction, 14 days after the date in para. (5).
(5) The date referred to in para. (4) is—
   (a) the date the respondent is served with the appellant's notice where—
      (i) permission to appeal was given by the lower court; or
      (ii) permission to appeal is not required;
   (b) the date the respondent is served with notification that the appeal court has given the appellant permission to appeal; or
   (c) the date the respondent is served with notification that the application for permission to appeal and the appeal itself are to be heard together.
(6) Unless the appeal court orders otherwise a respondent's notice must be served on the appellant and any other respondent—
   (a) as soon as practicable; and
   (b) in any event not later than 7 days,
   after it is filed.
(7) This rule does not apply where r. 52.4(4) applies.

Stay

Pt 52 r.52.7

Unless—
  (a) the appeal court or the lower court orders otherwise; or
  (b) the appeal is from the Immigration and Asylum Chamber of the Upper Tribunal,
an appeal shall not operate as a stay of any order or decision of the lower court.

Dismissal of applications or appeals by consent

PD 52A para.6.1

An appellant who does not wish to pursue an application or appeal may request the appeal court to dismiss the application or the appeal. If such a request is granted it will usually be subject to an order that the appellant pays the costs of the application or appeal.

Allowing unopposed appeals or applications on paper

PD 52A para.6.4

The appeal court will not normally make an order allowing an appeal unless satisfied that the decision of the lower court was wrong or unjust because of a serious procedural or other irregularity. The appeal court may, however, set aside or vary the order of the lower court by consent and without determining the merits of the appeal if it is satisfied that there are good and sufficient reasons for so doing. Where the appeal court is requested by all parties to allow an application or an appeal the court may consider the request on the papers. The request should set out the relevant history of the proceedings and the matters relied on as justifying the order and be accompanied by a draft order.

Disposal of applications and appeals involving children or protected parties

PD 52A para.6.5

Where one of the parties is a child or protected party, any disposal of an application or the appeal requires the court's approval. A draft order signed by the parties' solicitors should be sent to the appeal court, together with an opinion from the advocate acting on behalf of the child or protected party and, in the case of a protected party, any relevant documents prepared for the Court of Protection.

Appeal court's powers

Pt 52 r.52.10

  (1) In relation to an appeal the appeal court has all the powers of the lower court.
(R. 52.1(4) provides that this Part is subject to any enactment that sets out special provisions with regard to any particular category of appeal—where such an enactment gives a statutory power

to a tribunal, person or other body it may be the case that the appeal court may not exercise that power on an appeal)

    (2) The appeal court has power to—

        (a) affirm, set aside or vary any order or judgment made or given by the lower court;

        (b) refer any claim or issue for determination by the lower court;

        (c) order a new trial or hearing;

        (d) make orders for the payment of interest;

        (e) make a costs order.

    (3) In an appeal from a claim tried with a jury the Court of Appeal may, instead of ordering a new trial—

        (a) make an order for damages; or

        (b) vary an award of damages made by the jury.

    (4) The appeal court may exercise its powers in relation to the whole or part of an order of the lower court.

(Pt 3 contains general rules about the court's case management powers)

    (5) If the appeal court—

        (a) refuses an application for permission to appeal;

        (b) strikes out an appellant's notice; or

        (c) dismisses an appeal,

    and it considers that the application, the appellant's notice or the appeal is totally without merit, the provisions of para.(6) must be complied with.

    (6) Where para.(5) applies—

        (a) the court's order must record the fact that it considers the application, the appellant's notice or the appeal to be totally without merit; and

        (b) the court must at the same time consider whether it is appropriate to make a civil restraint order.

Hearing of appeals

Pt 52 r.52.11

    (1) Every appeal will be limited to a review of the decision of the lower court unless–

        (a) a PD makes different provision for a particular category of appeal; or

        (b) he court considers that in the circumstances of an individual appeal it would be in the interests of justice to hold a re-hearing.

    (2) Unless it orders otherwise, the appeal court will not receive—

        (a) oral evidence; or

        (b) evidence which was not before the lower court.

    (3) The appeal court will allow an appeal where the decision of the lower court wa—

        (a) wrong; or

        (b) unjust because of a serious procedural or other irregularity in the proceedings in the lower court.

    (4) The appeal court may draw any inference of fact which it considers justified on the evidence.

    (5) At the hearing of the appeal a party may not rely on a matter not contained in his appeal notice unless the appeal court gives permission.

Non-disclosure of Pt 36 offers and payments

Pt 52.12

    (1) The fact that a Pt 36 offer or payment into court has been made must not be disclosed to any judge of the appeal court who is to hear or determine—

    (a) an application for permission to appeal; or
    (b) an appeal,
    until all questions (other than costs) have been determined.
 (2) Paragraph (1) does not apply if the **Pt 36 offer** or **payment into court** is relevant to the
     substance of the appeal.
 (3) Paragraph (1) does not prevent disclosure in any application in the appeal proceedings if
     disclosure of the fact that a Pt 36 offer or payment into court has been made is properly
     relevant to the matter to be decided.
(R. 36.3 has the effect that a Pt 36 offer made in proceedings at first instance will not have
consequences in any appeal proceedings. Therefore, a fresh Pt 36 offer needs to be made in
appeal proceedings. However, r. 52.12 applies to a Pt 36 offer whether made in the original
proceedings or in the appeal.)

PD 52A para.6.2

If the appellant wishes to have the application or appeal dismissed without costs, his request must
be accompanied by a letter signed by the respondent stating that the respondent so consents.

PD 52A para.6.3

Where a settlement has been reached disposing of the application or appeal, the parties may
make a joint request to the court for the application or appeal to be dismissed by consent. If the
request is granted the application or appeal will be dismissed.

Transitional provisions

PD 52A para.8.1

[PD 52A] and PDs 52B, 52C, 52D and 52E [came] into force on October 1, 2012 and [apply]
to all appeals where—
    (a) the appeal notice was filed; or
    (b) permission to appeal was given
on or after that date.

PD 52A para.8.2

The appeal court may at any time direct that, in relation to any appeal, one or more of PDs 52A,
52B, 52C, 52D or 52E shall apply irrespective of the date on which the appeal notice was filed
or permission to appeal was given.

See also **Appeals by way of case stated, Appeals from an authorised court officer in detailed
assessment proceedings, Appeals in the county court and High Court, Appeals to the Court
of Appeal, Citation of authorities, Court bundle, Final decision, Reopening of final appeals,
Skeleton arguments, Specific appeals, Statutory appeals,** and **Tribunals and Inquiries Act
1992**.

APPEALS BY WAY OF CASE STATED

PD 52E para.1.1

An appeal by case stated is an appeal to a superior court on the basis of a set of facts specified
by the inferior court for the superior court to make a decision on the application of the law to
those facts.

PD 52E para.1.2

(1) This section applies where, under any enactment—
    (a) an appeal lies to the court by way of case stated; or
    (b) a question of law may be referred to the court by way of case stated.
(2) This section is subject to any provision governing a specific category of appeal in any enactment or PD 52A, 52B or 52D.

Case stated by Crown Court or Magistrates' Court

Application to state a case

PD 52E para.2.1

The procedure for applying to the Crown Court or a Magistrates' Court to have a case stated for the opinion of the High Court is set out in the Criminal Procedure Rules.

Filing of appellant's notice

PD 52E para.2.2

An appellant must file the appellant's notice at the appeal court within 10 days of the date of the case stated by the court.

Documents to be lodged

PD 52E para.2.3

The appellant must lodge the following documents with the appellant's notice—
    (a) the stated case;
    (b) a copy of the judgment, order or decision in respect of which the case has been stated; and
    (c) where the judgment, order or decision in respect of which the case has been stated was itself given or made on appeal, a copy of the judgment, order or decision appealed from.

Service of appellant's notice

PD 52E para.2.4

The appellant must serve the appellant's notice and accompanying documents on all respondents within four days after they are filed or lodged at the appeal court.

Case stated by Minister, Government Department, Tribunal or other person

Application to state a case

PD 52E para.3.1

The procedure for applying to a Minister, Government department, tribunal or other person ('Minister or tribunal, etc.') to have a case stated for the opinion of the court may be set out in—
  (a) the enactment which provides for the right of appeal; or
  (b) any rules of procedure relating to the Minister or tribunal, etc.

Signing of stated case by Minister or tribunal, etc.

PD 52E para.3.2

  (1) A case stated by a tribunal must be signed by—
      (a) the chairman or president (where there is one); or
      (b) in any other instance, by the member or members, of the tribunal.
  (2) A case stated by any other person must be signed by that person or by a person authorised to do so.

Service of stated case by Minister or tribunal, etc.

PD 52E para.3.3

The Minister or tribunal etc. must serve the stated case on—
  (a) the party who requested it; or
  (b) the party as a result of whose application to the court the case was stated.

PD 52E para.3.4

Where an enactment provides that a Minister or tribunal, etc. may state a case or refer a question of law to the court by way of case stated without a request being made, the Minister or tribunal, etc. must—
  (a) serve the stated case on those parties that the Minister or tribunal, etc. considers appropriate and on any other party who may be affected by the decision of the court; and
  (b) give notice to every other party to the proceedings that the stated case has been served on the party named and on the date specified in the notice.

Filing and service of appellant's notice

PD 52E para.3.5

The party on whom the stated case was served must file the appellant's notice and the stated case at the appeal court and serve copies of the notice and stated case on—
  (a) the Minister or tribunal, etc. who stated the case; and
  (b) every party to the proceedings to which the stated case relates, within four days after the stated case was served on that party.

PD 52E para.3.6

Where para.3.4 applies the Minister or tribunal, etc. must—
(a) file an appellant's notice and the stated case at the appeal court; and
(b) serve copies of those documents on the persons served under para.3.4 within 14 days after stating the case.

PD 52E para.3.7

Where—
(a) a stated case has been served by the Minister or tribunal, etc. in accordance with para.3.3; and
(b) the party on whom the stated case was served does not file an appellant's notice in accordance with para.3.5,
any other party may file an appellant's notice with the stated case at the appeal court and serve a copy of the notice and the case on the persons listed in para.3.5 within the period of time set out in para.3.8.

PD 52E para.3.8

The period of time referred to in para.3.7 is 14 days from the last day on which the party on whom the stated case was served may file an appellant's notice in accordance with para.3.5.

Amendment of stated case

PD 52E para.3.9

The court may amend the stated case or order it to be returned to the Minister or tribunal etc. for amendment and may draw inferences of fact from the facts stated in the case.

Right of Minister or Government department to be heard on the appeal

PD 52E para.3.10

Where the case is stated by a Minister or government department, that Minister or department, as the case may be, is entitled to appear on the appeal and to make representations to the court.

Application for order to state a case

PD 52E para.3.11

An application to the court for an order requiring a minister or tribunal, etc. to state a case for the decision of the court, or to refer a question of law to the court by way of case stated must be made to the court, which would be the appeal court if the case were stated.

PD 52E para.3.12

An application to the court for an order directing a Minister or tribunal, etc. to—
  (a) state a case for determination by the court; or
  (b) refer a question of law to the court by way of case stated, must be made in accordance with Part 23.

PD 52E para.3.13

The application notice must contain—
  (a) the grounds of the application;
  (b) the question of law on which it is sought to have the case stated; and
  (c) any reasons given by the Minister or tribunal, etc. for the refusal to state a case.

PD 52E para.3.14

The application notice must be filed at the appeal court and served on—
  (a) the Minister, department, secretary of the tribunal or other person as the case may be; and
  (b) every party to the proceedings to which the application relates, within 14 days after the appellant receives notice of the refusal of his request to state a case.

APPEALS FROM AN AUTHORISED COURT OFFICER IN DETAILED ASSESSMENT PROCEEDINGS

Right to appeal

Pt 47 r.47.21

  (1) Any party to detailed assessment proceedings may appeal against a decision of an authorised court officer in those proceedings.
  (2) For the purposes of this section, a LSC funded client or an assisted person is not a party to detailed assessment proceedings.
(Part 52 sets out general rules about appeals).

Court to hear appeal

Pt 47 r.47.22

An appeal against a decision of an authorised court officer is to a costs judge or a district judge of the High Court.

Appeal procedure

Pt 47 r.47.23

  (1) The appellant must file an appeal notice within 21 days after the date of the decision he wishes to appeal against.

(2) On receipt of the appeal notice, the court will—
    (a) serve a copy of the notice on the parties to the detailed assessment proceedings; and
    (b) give notice of the appeal hearing to those parties.

Powers of the court on appeal

Pt 47 r.47.24

On an appeal from an authorised court officer the court will—
    (a) re-hear the proceedings which gave rise to the decision appealed against; and
    (b) make any order and give any directions as it considers appropriate.

PD 47 para.20.1

This Section relates only to appeals from authorised court officers in detailed assessment proceedings. All other appeals arising out of detailed assessment proceedings (and arising out of summary assessments) are dealt with in accordance with Pt 52 and PDs 52A–52E. The destination of appeals is dealt with in accordance with the Access to Justice Act 1999 (Destination of Appeals) Order 2000.

PD 47 para.20.2

In respect of appeals from authorised court officers, there is no requirement to obtain permission, or to seek written reasons.

PD 47 para.20.3

The appellant must file a notice which should be in Form N161 (an appellant's notice).

PD 47 para.20.4

The appeal will be heard by a costs judge or a district judge of the High Court, and is a re-hearing.

PD 47 para.20.5

The appellant's notice should, if possible, be accompanied by a suitable record of the judgment appealed against. Where reasons given for the decision have been officially recorded by the court an approved transcript of that record should accompany the notice. Where there is no official record the following documents will be acceptable—
    (a) the officer's comments written on the bill;
    (b) advocates' notes of the reasons agreed by the respondent if possible and approved by the authorised court officer.

PD 47 para.20.6

Where the appellant is not able to obtain a suitable record of the authorised court officer's decision within the time in which the appellant's notice must be filed, the appellant's notice must still be completed to the best of the appellant's ability. It may however be amended subsequently with the permission of the costs judge or district judge hearing the appeal.

APPEALS IN THE COUNTY COURTS AND HIGH COURT

Application

PD 52B para.1.1

[PD 52B] applies to—
  (a) appeals within a county court (from a District Judge to a Circuit Judge);
  (b) appeals from a county court to the High Court; and
  (c) appeals within the High Court (from a Master, a District Judge sitting in a District Registry, a Registrar in Bankruptcy, a Registrar of the Companies Court, a Costs Judge or an officer of the High Court to a judge of the High Court).

Venue for appeals and filling of notices and applications

PD 52B para.2.1

Appeals within a county court, appeals from a county court and appeals within the High Court to a judge of the High Court must be brought in the appropriate appeal centre and all other notices (including any respondent's notice) and applications must be filed at that appeal centre. The venue for an appeal within a county court will be determined by the Designated Civil Judge and may be different from the appeal centre.

PD 52B para.2.2

[Table A and Table B at the end of [PD 52B] set out the Appeal Centres for each circuit.

Extending time in which to appeal

PD 52B para.3.1

A party may apply to the lower court for an extension of time in which to file an appellant's notice. The application must be made at the same time as the appellant applies to the lower court for permission to appeal.

PD 52B para.3.2

Where the time for filing an appellant's notice has expired, the appellant must include an application for an extension of time within the appellant's notice (form N161 or, in respect of a small claim, form N164) stating the reason for the delay and the steps taken prior to making the application.

PD 52B para.3.3

The court may make an order granting or refusing an extension of time and may do so with or without a hearing. If an order is made without a hearing, any party seeking to set aside or vary the order may apply, within 14 days of service of the order, for a hearing.

Initiating an appeal

PD 52B para.4.1

An appellant's notice (Form N161 or, in respect of a small claim, Form N164) must be filed and served in all cases. The appellant's notice must be accompanied by the appropriate fee or, if appropriate, a fee remission application or certificate.

PD 52B para.4.2

Documents to be filed with the appellant's notice: The appellant must file with the appellant's notice—
(a) three copies of the appellant's notice and one additional copy for each respondent;
(b) a copy of the sealed order under appeal;
(c) where an application was made to the lower court for permission to appeal, a copy of any order granting or refusing permission to appeal together with a copy of the reasons, if any, for allowing or refusing permission to appeal; and
(d) grounds of appeal, which must be set out on a separate sheet attached to the appellant's notice and must set out, in simple language, clearly and concisely, why the order of the lower court was wrong or unjust because of a serious procedural or other irregularity (r. 52.11(3)).

PD 52B para.4.3

Applications in the appeal: Any application to be made in the appeal (for example, for a stay of the order of the lower court, or for an extension of time) should be included within the appellant's notice. Where the applicant qualifies for fee remission, any application for a transcript of the judgment of the lower court at public expense should be made within the appellant's notice.

Case managing the appeal; orders of the court

PD 52B para.5.1

The appeal court may make orders for the case management of an appeal.

PD 52B para.5.2

When making a case management order, the court may dispense with any requirements of or directions made in this PD.

Conduct of the appeal

PD 52B para.6.1

Service of appellant's notice on the respondent: The appellant must file a certificate of service of the appellant's notice with the court as soon as practicable after service.

PD 52B para.6.2

Transcript of the judgment of the lower court or other record of reasons: Except where the claim has been allocated to the small claims track, the appellant must obtain a transcript or other record of reasons of the lower court as follows—
  (a) where the judgment has been officially recorded, the appellant must apply for an approved transcript as soon as possible and, in any event, within 7 days of the filing of the appellant's notice;
  (b) where the judgment under appeal has been handed down in writing, the appellant must obtain and retain a copy of the written judgment;
  (c) in any other case, the appellant must cause a note of the judgment under appeal to be made and typed. The parties to the appeal should agree the note, which should then be sent to the judge of the lower court for approval. The parties and their advocates have a duty to make, and to co-operate in agreeing, a note of the judgment.

Determination of applications

PD 52B para.7.1

Applications made in the appeal, including applications for permission to appeal under r. 52.3(2)(a) or r. 52.5(3), may be determined with or without a hearing.

PD 52B para.7.2

Where the court refuses an application for permission to appeal without a hearing, the appellant (or, where appropriate, the respondent) may request the application to be reconsidered at a hearing.

PD 52B para.7.3

Where the court determines any other application without hearing the respondent (including an application for permission to bring the appeal out of time) any party affected by the determination may apply to have the order set aside or varied.

PD 52B para.7.4

Any request or application made under this section must be made within 7 days of service of notification of the determination upon the person making the application. Where any such request or application is made—
  (a) a copy of the request or application must be served on all other parties at the same time; and
  (b) the court will give directions for the determination of the application.

Hearings

PD 52B para.8.1

Attendance at permission hearings: Where a respondent to an appeal or cross-appeal attends the hearing of an application for permission to appeal, costs will not be awarded to the respondent unless—

(a) the court has ordered or requested attendance by the respondent;

(b) the court has ordered that the appeal be listed at the same time as the determination of other applications;

(c) the court has ordered that the hearing of the appeal will follow the hearing of the application if permission is granted; or

(d) the court considers it just, in all the circumstances, to award costs to the respondent.

PD 52B para.8.2

Respondent's documents: A respondent who has been served with an appeal bundle and who considers that relevant documents have been omitted may file and serve on all parties a respondent's supplemental appeal bundle containing copies of other relevant documents. The supplemental appeal bundle must be filed and served as soon as practicable after service of the appeal bundle, but in any event not less than seven days before the hearing.

See also **Court bundles, Skeleton arguments, Specific appeals**, and **Transcript**.

APPEALS TO THE COURT OF APPEAL

PD 52C para.1

In [PD52C]—

'appeal notice' means either an appellant's notice in form N161 or a respondent's notice in form N162 ;

'appellant's notice' means an appeal notice filed by an appellant and a 'respondent's notice' means an appeal notice filed by a respondent;

'hearing date' means the date on which the appeal is listed to be heard, including a 'floating' date over two or more days;

'listing window notification' means the letter sent by the Civil Appeals Office in accordance with [Timetable Pt 1—see below] notifying the parties of the window within which the appeal is likely to be heard; and 'date of the listing window notification' means the date of such letter;

'replacement skeleton argument' means a skeleton argument which has been amended in order to include cross references to the appeal bundle and is lodged and served in accordance with the Timetable Pt 2—see below].

PD 52C para.2

The court may make such directions as the case may require and such directions will prevail over any provision of this practice direction.

Filing the Appellant's Notice and accompanying documents

PD 52C para.3

(1) An appellant's notice (Form N161) must be filed and served in all cases. The appellant's notice must be accompanied by the appropriate fee or, if appropriate, a fee remission certificate.

(2) The appellant's notice and accompanying documents must be filed in the Civil Appeals Office Registry, Room E307, Royal Courts of Justice, Strand, London, WC2A 2LL.

(3) At the same time as filing an appellant's notice, the appellant must provide for the use of the court three copies of the appellant's notice and one copy of each of the following—

    (a) the sealed order or tribunal determination being appealed;

    (b) any order granting or refusing permission to appeal, together with a copy of the judge's or tribunal's reasons for granting or refusing permission to appeal;

    (c) any witness statements or affidavits relied on in support of any application included in the appellant's notice;

    (d) in cases where the decision of the lower court was itself made on appeal, the first order, the reasons given by the judge who made it, and the appellant's notice of appeal against that order;

    (e) in a claim for judicial review or a statutory appeal, the original decision which was the subject of the application to the lower court;

    (f) the order allocating the case to a track (if any);

    (g) the appellant's skeleton argument in support of the appeal;

    (h) the approved transcript of the judgment.

(4) The appellant must also provide to the court one copy of the appellant's notice for each respondent for sealing by the court and return to the appellant for service.

(5) Where the appellant applies for permission to appeal, additional documents are required: see [below].

Extension of time for filing appellant's notice

PD 52C para.4

(1) Where the time for filing an appellant's notice has expired, the appellant must—

    (a) file the appellant's notice; and

    (b) include in that appellant's notice an application for an extension of time.

(2) The appellant's notice must state the reason for the delay and the steps taken prior to the application being made.

(3) Where the appellant's notice includes an application for an extension of time and permission to appeal has been given or is not required, the respondent has the right to oppose that application and to be heard at any hearing of that application. In respect of any application to extend time—

    (a) The respondent must—

        (i) be served with a copy of any evidence filed in support of the application; and

        (ii) inform the court in writing of any objections to the grant of the extension of time within 7 days of being served with the appellant's notice.

    (b) A respondent who unreasonably opposes an application for an extension of time may be ordered to pay the costs of the application.

    (c) An application for an extension of time will normally be determined without a hearing unless the court directs otherwise.

Grounds of Appeal

PD 52C para.5

(1) The grounds of appeal must identify as concisely as possible the respects in which the judgment of the court below is—

    (a) wrong; or

    (b) unjust because of a serious procedural or other irregularity,

as required by r. 52.11(3).

(2) The reasons why the decision under appeal is wrong or unjust must not be included in the grounds of appeal and must be confined to the skeleton argument.

Non-availability of documents

PD 52C para.6

If the appellant is unable to provide any of the necessary documents in time, the appellant must complete the appeal notice on the basis of the available documents. The notice may be amended subsequently with the permission of the court.

Service of appellant's notice on the respondent

PD 52C para.7.1

The Civil Appeals Office will not serve documents. Where service is required by the Rules or [PD 52C], it must be effected by the parties.

PD 52C para.7.2

The evidence in support of any application made in an appellant's notice must be filed and served with the appellant's notice.

PD 52C para.7.3

An application for an order to dispense with service of the appellant's notice under r. 6.28 must be made in the appeal notice or, thereafter, by application notice under Pt 23.

Respondent's notice

PD 52C para.8

(1) A respondent who seeks to appeal against any part of the order made by the court below must file an appeal notice.
(2) A respondent who seeks a variation of the order of the lower court must file an appeal notice and must obtain permission to appeal.
(3) A respondent who seeks to contend that the order of the court below should be upheld for reasons other than those given by that court must file a respondent's notice.
(4) The notice may be amended subsequently with the permission of the court.

Applications within respondent's notice

PD 52C para.11

(1) A respondent may include an application within a respondent's notice.
(2) The parties must consider whether it would be more convenient for any application to be listed with the appeal or whether the application needs to be considered in advance.
(3) Where parties consider that the time estimate for the appeal will be affected by listing the application with the appeal, they must inform the court without delay.

Time limits

Pt 52 r.52.5

(4) A respondent's notice must be filed within—
    (a) such period as may be directed by the lower court; or
    (b) where the court makes no such direction, 14 days after the date in para.(5).
(5) The date referred to in para.(4) is—
    (a) the date the respondent is served with the appellant's notice where—
        (i) permission to appeal was given by the lower court; or
        (ii) permission to appeal is not required;
    (b) the date the respondent is served with notification that the appeal court has given the appellant permission to appeal; or
    (c) the date the respondent is served with notification that the application for permission to appeal and the appeal itself are to be heard together.

PD 52C para.12

Where an extension of time is required, the respondent must apply in the respondent's notice and explain the delay.

Skeleton argument to be lodged with the respondent's notice

PD 52C para.9

A respondent who files a respondent's notice must, within 14 days of filing the notice, lodge a **skeleton argument** with the court and serve a copy of the skeleton argument on every other party to the appeal.

Respondent's skeleton argument (where no respondent's notice filed)

PD 52C para.13

(1) In all cases where the respondent is legally represented and proposes to address the court, the respondent must lodge and serve a skeleton argument.
(2) A respondent's skeleton argument must be lodged and served in accordance with [Timetable Pt 1—see below].

Documents to be filed with respondent's notice

PD 52C para.10

The respondent must file the following documents with the respondent's notice—
    (a) two additional copies of the respondent's notice for the court; and
    (b) one copy each for the appellant and any other respondents.

Procedure where permission to appeal is sought from the Court of Appeal

Documents for use on an application for permission

PD 52C para.14

(1) Within 14 days of filing the appeal notice the appellant must lodge a bundle containing only those documents which are necessary for the court to determine that application.
(2) The bundle of documents must—
  (a) be paginated and in chronological order;
  (b) contain an index at the front.

Determination of applications for permission to appeal

PD 52C para.15

(1) Applications for permission to appeal will generally be considered by the court without a hearing in the first instance. The court will notify the parties of the decision and the reasons for it.
(2) If permission is refused the appellant is entitled to have the decision reconsidered at an oral hearing, except where r. 52.3(4A) (applications totally without merit) applies. The hearing may be before the same judge.
(3) A request for the decision to be reconsidered at an oral hearing must be filed within seven days after service of the letter giving notice that permission has been refused. A copy of the request must be served by the appellant on the respondent at the same time.

Permission hearing

PD 52C para.16

(1) Where an appellant who is represented makes a request for a decision to be reconsidered at an oral hearing, the appellant's advocate must at least 4 days before the hearing file a brief written statement—
  (a) informing the court and the respondent of the points which are to be raised at the hearing; and
  (b) setting out the reasons why permission should be granted notwithstanding the reasons given for the refusal of permission.
(2) The court will notify the respondent of the hearing but the respondent is not expected to attend unless the court so directs.
(3) If the court directs the respondent to attend the permission hearing, the appellant must supply the respondent with a copy of the skeleton argument and any documents to which the appellant intends to refer.

Limited permission

Pt 52 r.52.3

(7) An order giving permission may—
  (a) limit the issues to be heard; and

(b) be made subject to conditions.

PD 52C para.18

(1) If, under r. 52.3(7), the court grants permission to appeal on some issues only, it will—
   (a) refuse permission on any remaining issues; or
   (b) adjourn the application in respect of those issues to the hearing of the appeal.
(2) If the court adjourns the application under sub-para. (1)(b), the appellant must inform the court and the respondent in writing, within 14 days after the date of the court's order, whether the appellant intends to pursue the application. If the appellant intends to pursue the application, the parties must include in any time estimate for the appeal hearing an allowance for the adjourned application.
(3) If the court refuses permission to appeal on the remaining issues without a hearing and the applicant wishes to have that decision reconsidered at an oral hearing, the time limit in r. 52.3(5) applies. Any application for an extension of this time should be made promptly. When hearing the appeal on the issues for which permission has been given the court will not normally grant an application to extend time in relation to the remaining issues.

Respondent need not take any action when served with an appellant's notice

PD 52C para.19

Unless the court directs otherwise, a respondent need not take any action when served with an appellant's notice until notified that permission to appeal has been granted.

Respondent's costs of permission applications

PD 52C para.20

(1) In most cases an application for permission to appeal will be determined without the need for the respondent to file submissions or attend a hearing. In such circumstances an order for costs will not normally be made in favour of a respondent who voluntarily makes submissions or attends a hearing.
(2) If the court directs the respondent to file submissions or attend a hearing, it will normally award costs to the respondent if permission is refused.

Timetable

PD 52C para.21

The timetable for the conduct of an appeal after the date of the listing window notification is set out [in two Timetables as follows]—

Timetable Pt 1—Listing window notification to lodging bundle

Timetable Pt 2—Steps to be taken once hearing date fixed: lodging bundles, supplemental skeletons and bundle of authorities

Management of the appeal

Listing and hear-by dates

PD 52C para.22

The hear-by date is the last day of the listing window.

Appeal Questionnaire

PD 52C para.23

The appellant must complete and file the Appeal Questionnaire and serve it on the respondent within 14 days after the date of the listing window notification.

Time estimates

PD 52C para.24

If the respondent disagrees with the appellant's time estimate, the respondent must inform the court within seven days of service of the Appeal Questionnaire. In the absence of such notification the respondent will be deemed to have accepted the appellant's time estimate.

Multiple Appeals

PD 52C para.25

(1) If two or more appeals are pending in the same or related proceedings, the parties must seek directions as to whether they should be heard together or consecutively by the same judges.
(2) Whether appeals are heard together or consecutively, the parties must attempt to agree a single appeal bundle or set of bundles for all the appeals and seek directions if they are unable to do so.

Expedition

PD 52C para.26

(1) The court may direct that the hearing of an appeal be expedited.
(2) The court will deal with requests for expedition without a hearing. Requests for expedition must be made by letter setting out succinctly the grounds on which expedition is sought. The letter (or, if time is particularly short, email) must be marked for the immediate attention of the court and copied to the other parties to the appeal.
(3) If an expedited appeal hearing is required as a matter of extreme urgency, the Civil Appeals Office must be informed as soon as possible. If necessary, parties or their legal representatives should call the Royal Courts of Justice switchboard on 020 7947 6000 and ask a member of the security staff to contact the Duty Judge.

(4) An expedited hearing will be listed at the convenience of the court and not according to the availability of counsel.

Bundles and amendment

Bundle of documents

PD 52C para.27

(1) The appellant must lodge an appeal bundle which must contain only those documents relevant to the appeal. The bundle must—
   (a) be paginated and in chronological order;
   (b) contain an index at the front.
(2) Documents relevant to the appeal: Subject to any order made by the court, the following documents must be included in the appeal bundle—
   (a) a copy of the appellant's notice;
   (b) a copy of any respondent's notice;
   (c) a copy of any appellant's or respondent's skeleton argument;
   (d) a copy of the order under appeal;
   (e) a copy of the order of the lower court granting or refusing permission to appeal together with a copy of the judge's reasons, if any, for granting or refusing permission;
   (f) a copy of any order allocating the case to a track;
   (g) the approved transcript of the judgment of the lower court (except in appeals in cases which were allocated to the small claims track but subject to any order of the court).
(3) Documents which may be included: The following documents should also be considered for inclusion in the appeal bundle but should be included only where relevant to the appeal—
   (a) **statements of case**;
   (b) **application notices**;
   (c) other orders made in the case;
   (d) a chronology of relevant events;
   (e) **witness statements** made in support of any application made in the appellant's notice;
   (f) other witness statements;
   (g) other documents which the appellant or respondent consider relevant to the appeal.
(4) Bundles not to include originals: Unless otherwise directed, the appeal bundle should not include original material such as original documents, photographs and recorded media. Such material should be provided to the court, if necessary, at the hearing.
(5) Destruction of bundles: Bundles lodged with the court will not be returned to the parties but will be destroyed in the confidential waste system at the conclusion of the proceedings and without further notification.

Bundle of authorities

PD 52C para.29

(1) After consultation with any opposing advocate, the appellant's advocate must file a bundle containing photocopies of the authorities upon which each party will rely at the hearing.

(2) The most authoritative report of each authority must be used in accordance with the PD on Citation of Authorities (2012) and must have the relevant passages marked by a vertical line in the margin.

(3) Photocopies of authorities should not be in landscape format and the type should not be reduced in size.

(4) The bundle should not—
   (a) include authorities for propositions not in dispute; or
   (b) contain more than 10 authorities unless the issues in the appeal justify more extensive citation.

(5) A bundle of authorities must bear a certificate by the advocates responsible for arguing the case that the requirements of sub-paras (2) to (4) of this paragraph have been complied with in respect of each authority included.

Amendment of appeal notice

Pt 52 r.52.8

An appeal notice may not be amended without the permission of the appeal court.

PD 52C para.30

(1) An appeal notice may not be amended without the permission of the court.

(2) An application for permission to amend made before permission to appeal has been considered will normally be determined without a hearing.

(3) An application for permission to amend (after permission to appeal has been granted) and any submissions in opposition will normally be dealt with at the hearing unless that would cause unnecessary expense or delay, in which case a request should be made for the application to amend to be heard in advance.

(4) Legal representatives must—
   (a) inform the court at the time they make the application if the existing time estimate is affected by the proposed amendment; and
   (b) attempt to agree any revised time estimate no later than seven days after service of the application.

See also **Appeals, Immigration and Asylum**, and **LSC funded client**.

APPELLANT

Pt 52 r.52.1

(3)(d) A person who brings or seeks to bring an appeal.

APPLICANT

A person who makes an application.

APPLICATION

Pt 23 r.23.2

(1) The general rule is that an application must be made to the court where the claim was started.
(2) If a claim has been transferred to another court since it was started, an application must be made to the court to which the claim has been transferred.
(3) If the parties have been notified of a fixed date for the trial, an application must be made to the court where the trial is to take place.
(4) Subject to para.(4A), if an an application is made before a claim has been started, it must be made to the court where it is likely that the claim to which the application relates will be started unless there is good reason to make the application to a different court.
(4A) If—
    (a) application is made before a claim has been started; and
    (b) the claim is a **designated money claim**;
    the application may be made in any county court.
(5) If an application is made after proceedings to enforce judgment have begun, it must be made to any court which is dealing with the enforcement of the judgment unless any rule or PD provides otherwise.

PD 23 para.5

All applications made before a claim is commenced should be made under Pt 23 of the [CPR]. Attention is drawn in particular to r.23.2(4).

PD 23 para.2.2

On receipt of an application notice containing a request for a hearing the court will notify the applicant of the time and date for the hearing of the application.

PD 23 para.2.3

On receipt of an application notice containing a request that the application be dealt with without a hearing, the application notice will be sent to a Master or district judge so that he may decide whether the application is suitable for consideration without a hearing.

PD 23 para.2.4

Where the Master or district judge agrees that the application is suitable for consideration without a hearing, the court will so inform the applicant and the respondent and may give directions for the filing of evidence. (Rules 23.9 and 23.10 enable a party to apply for an order made without a hearing to be set aside or varied.)

PD 23 para.2.5

Where the Master or district judge does not agree that the application is suitable for consideration without a hearing, the court will notify the applicant and the respondent of the time, date and place for the hearing of the application and may at the same time give directions as to the filing of evidence.

PD 23 para.2.6

If the application is intended to be made to a judge, the application notice should so state. In that case, paras 2.3, 2.4 and 2.5 will apply as though references to the Master or district judge were references to a judge.

PD 23 para.2.7

Every application should be made as soon as it becomes apparent that it is necessary or desirable to make it.

PD 23A para.2.8

Applications should wherever possible be made so that they can be considered at any other hearing for which a date has already been fixed or for which a date is about to be fixed. This is particularly so in relation to case management conferences, allocation and listing hearings and pre-trial reviews fixed by the court.

PD 23A para.2.9

The parties must anticipate that at any hearing the court may wish to review the conduct of the case as a whole and give any necessary case management directions. They should be ready to assist the court in doing so and to answer questions the court may ask for this purpose.

PD 23A para.2.10

Where a date for a hearing has been fixed and a party wishes to make an application at that hearing but he does not have sufficient time to serve an application notice he should inform the other party and the court (if possible in writing) as soon as he can of the nature of the application and the reason for it. He should then make the application orally at the hearing.

Giving notice of an application

PD 23A para.4.1

Unless the court otherwise directs or para.3 or para.4.1A of [PD 23] applies the application notice must be served as soon as practicable after it has been issued and, if there is to be a hearing, at least three days before the hearing date (r.23.7(1)(b)).

PD 23A para.4.2

Where an application notice should be served but there is not sufficient **time** to do so, informal notification of the application should be given unless the circumstances of the application require secrecy.

Applications without service of application notice

PD 23A para.3

An application may be made without serving an **application notice** only:
    (1) where there is exceptional urgency,

(2) where the overriding objective is best furthered by doing so,
(3) by consent of all parties,
(4) with the permission of the court,
(5) where para.2.10 above applies, or
(6) where a court order, rule or PD permits.

Dismissal of totally without merit applications

PD 23 para.1

If the court dismisses an application (including an application for permission to appeal or for permission to apply for judicial review) and it considers that the application is totally without merit—
(a) the court's order must record that fact; and
(b) the court must at the same time consider whether it is appropriate to make a civil restraint order.

See **Telephone hearings**.

Reference to a judge

Pt 23 r.1

A Master or district judge may refer to a judge any matter which he thinks should properly be decided by a judge, and the judge may either dispose of the matter or refer it back to the Master or district judge.

Video conferencing

PD 23A para.7

Where the parties to a matter wish to use **video conferencing** facilities, and those facilities are available in the relevant court, they should apply to the Master or district judge for directions.

Note of proceedings

PD 23A para.8

The procedural judge should keep, either by way of a note or a tape recording, brief details of all proceedings before him, including the dates of the proceedings and a short statement of the decision taken at each hearing.

Evidence

PD 23A para.9.1

The requirement for evidence in certain types of applications is set out in some of the rules and practice directions. Where there is no specific requirement to provide evidence it should be borne in mind that, as a practical matter, the court will often need to be satisfied by evidence of the facts that are relied on in support of or for opposing the application.

PD 23A para.9.2

The court may give directions for the filing of evidence in support of or opposing a particular application. The court may also give directions for the filing of evidence in relation to any hearing that it fixes on its own initiative. The directions may specify the form that evidence is to take and when it is to be served.

PD 23A para.9.3

Where it is intended to rely on evidence which is not contained in the application itself, the evidence, if it has not already been served, should be served with the application.

PD 23A para.9.4

Where a respondent to an application wishes to rely on evidence which has not yet been served he should serve it as soon as possible and in any event in accordance with any directions the court may have given.

PD 23A para.9.5

If it is necessary for the applicant to serve any evidence in reply it should be served as soon as possible and in any event in accordance with any directions the court may have given.

PD 23A para.9.6

Evidence must be filed with the court as well as served on the parties. Exhibits should not be filed unless the court otherwise directs.

PD 23A para.9.7

The contents of an application notice may be used as evidence (otherwise than at trial) provided the contents have been verified by a statement of truth.

Consent orders

PD 23A para.10.1

R.40.6 sets out the circumstances where an agreed judgment or order may be entered and sealed.

PD 23A para.10.2

Where all parties affected by an order have written to the court consenting to the making of the order a draft of which has been filed with the court, the court will treat the draft as having been signed in accordance with r.40.6(7).

PD 23A para.10.3

Where a consent order must be made by a judge (i.e. r.40.6(2) does not apply) the order must be drawn so that the judge's name and judicial title can be inserted.

PD 23A para.10.4

The parties to an application for a consent order must ensure that they provide the court with any material it needs to be satisfied that it is appropriate to make the order. Subject to any rule or PD a letter will generally be acceptable for this purpose.

PD 23A para.10.5

Where a judgment or order has been agreed in respect of an application or claim where a hearing date has been fixed, the parties must inform the court immediately. (Note that parties are reminded that under rr.28.4 and 29.5 the case management timetable cannot be varied by written agreement of the parties.)

Other applications considered without a hearing

PD 23A para.11.1

Where r.23.8(b) applies the parties should so inform the court in writing and each should confirm that all evidence and other material on which he relies has been disclosed to the other parties to the application.

PD 23A para.11.2

Where r. 23.8(c) applies the court will treat the application as if it were proposing to make an order on its own initiative.

Applications to stay claim where related criminal proceedings

PD 23A para.11A.1

An application for the stay of civil proceedings pending the determination of related criminal proceedings may be made by any party to the civil proceedings or by the prosecutor or any defendant in the criminal proceedings.

PD 23A para.11A.2

Every party to the civil proceedings must, unless he is the applicant, be made a respondent to the application.

PD 23A para.11A.3

The evidence in support of the application must contain an estimate of the expected duration of the stay and must identify the respects in which the continuance of the civil proceedings may prejudice the criminal trial.

PD 23A para.11A.4

In order to make an application under para.11A.1, it is not necessary for the prosecutor or defendant in the criminal proceedings to be joined as a party to the civil proceedings.

Miscellaneous

PD 23A para.12.1

Except in the most simple application the applicant should bring to any hearing a draft of the order sought. If the case is proceeding in the Royal Courts of Justice and the order is unusually long or complex it should also be supplied on disk for use by the court office.

PD 23A para.12.2

Where r.23.11 applies, the power to re-list the application in r.23.11(2) is in addition to any other powers of the court with regard to the order (for example to set aside, vary, discharge or suspend the order).

Costs

PD 23A para.13.1

Attention is drawn to the Costs PD and, in particular, to the court's power to make a summary assessment of costs.

PD 23A para.13.2

Attention is also drawn to r.44.13(i) which provides that if an order makes no mention of costs, none are payable in respect of the proceedings to which it relates.

APPLICATION NOTICE

Pt 23 r.23.1

A document in which the applicant states his intention to seek a court order.

Content of an application notice

Pt 23 r.23.6

An application notice must state—
  (a) what order the applicant is seeking; and
  (b) briefly, why the applicant is seeking the order.
(Part 22 requires an application notice to be verified by a statement of truth if the applicant wishes to rely on matters set out in his application notice as evidence).

PD 23A para.2.1

An application notice must, in addition to the matters set out in r.23.6, be signed and include:
    (1) the title of the claim,
    (2) the reference number of the claim,
    (3) the full name of the applicant,
    (4) where the applicant is not already a party, his address for service, including a postcode. Postcode information may be obtained from *http://www.royalmail.com* (Accessed November 21, 2012) or the Royal Mail Address Management Guide, and
    (5) either a request for a hearing or a request that the application be dealt with without a hearing.
(Practice Form N244 may be used).

Filing of application notice

Pt 23 r.23.3

    (1) The general rule is that an applicant must file an application notice.
    (2) An applicant may make an application without filing an application notice if—
        (a) this is permitted by a rule or practice direction; or
        (b) the court dispenses with the requirement for an application notice.

Service

Pt 23 r.23.4

    (1) The general rule is that a copy of the application notice must be served on each respondent.
    (2) An application may be made without serving a copy of the application notice if this is permitted by—
        (a) a rule; (b) a [PD]; or (c) a court order.

Time when an application is made

Pt 23 r.23.5

Where an application must be made within a specified time, it is so made if the application notice is received by the court within that time.

Applications which may be dealt with without a hearing

Pt 23 r.23.8

The court may deal with an application without a hearing if—
    (a) the parties agree as to the terms of the order sought;
    (b) the parties agree that the court should dispose of the application without a hearing, or
    (c) the court does not consider that a hearing would be appropriate.

Service of application where application made without notice

Pt 23 r.23.9

(1) This rule applies where the court has disposed of an application which it permitted to be made without service of a copy of the application notice.

(2) Where the court makes an order, whether granting or dismissing the application, a copy of the application notice and any evidence in support must, unless the court orders otherwise, be served with the order on any party or other person—
(a) against whom the order was made; and
(b) against whom the order was sought.

(3) The order must contain a statement of the right to make an application to set aside(GL) or vary the order under r.23.10.

Application to set aside or vary order made without notice

Pt 23 r.23.10

(1) A person who was not served with a copy of the application notice before an order was made under r.23.9, may apply to have the order set aside or varied.

(2) An application under this rule must be made within seven days after the date on which the order was served on the person making the application.

Power of the court to proceed in the absence of a party

Pt 23 r.23.11

(1) Where the applicant or any respondent fails to attend the hearing of an application, the court may proceed in his absence.

(2) Where—
(a) the applicant or any respondent fails to attend the hearing of an application; and
(b) the court makes an order at the hearing,
the court may, on application or of its own initiative, re-list the application.
(Part 40 deals with service of orders).

Pt 23A r.23.7

(1) A copy of the application notice—
(a) must be served as soon as practicable after it is filed; and
(b) except where another time limit is specified in these rules or a PD, must in any event be served at least three days before the court is to deal with the application.

(2) If a copy of the application notice is to be served by the court, the applicant must, when he files the application notice, file a copy of any written evidence in support.

(3) When a copy of an application notice is served it must be accompanied by—
(a) a copy of any written evidence in support; and
(b) a copy of any draft order which the applicant has attached to his application.

(4) If—
(a) an application notice is served; but
(b) the period of notice is shorter than the period required by these rules or a PD,
the court may direct that, in the circumstances of the case, sufficient notice has been given and hear the application.

(5) This rule does not require written evidence—
    (a) to be filed if it has already been filed; or
    (b) to be served on a party on whom it has already been served.
(Part 6 contains the general rules about service of documents including who must serve a copy of the application notice).

PD 23A para.4.1

Unless the court otherwise directs or para.3 or para.4.1A of this PD applies the application notice must be served as soon as practicable after it has been issued and, if there is to be a hearing, at least three days before the hearing date (r.23.7(1)(b)).

PD 23A para.4.1A

Where there is to be a telephone hearing the application notice must be served as soon as practicable after it has been issued and in any event at least five days before the date of the hearing.

PD 23 para.4.2

Where an application notice should be served but there is not sufficient time to do so, informal notification of the application should be given unless the circumstances of the application require secrecy.
(Rule 2.8 explains how to calculate periods of time expressed in terms of days).

See **Application** and **Telephone hearings**.

APPOINTEE

Remuneration of appointee

PD Insolvency Proceedings, para.20.1.1

[Part V of PD IP] applies to any remuneration application made under the Act [means the Insolvency Act 1986 and includes the Act as applied to limited liability partnerships by the Limited Liability Partnerships Regulations 2001 or to any other person or body by virtue of the Act or any other legislation] or the Insolvency R.s.

Objective and guiding principles

PD IP para.20.2.1

The objective of [Part V] is to ensure that the remuneration of an appointee which is fixed and approved by the court is fair, reasonable and commensurate with the nature and extent of the work properly undertaken by the appointee in any given case and is fixed and approved by a process which is consistent and predictable.

PD IP para.20.2.2

[Part V] sets out below are the guiding principles by reference to which remuneration applications are to be considered both by applicants, in the preparation and presentation of their application, and by the court determining such applications.

APPROPRIATELY QUALIFIED LAWYER

Applications to the court for directions by trustees in relation to administration of trusts

PD 64B para.7.3

References in [PD 64B] to an appropriately qualified lawyer mean one whose qualifications and experience are appropriate to the circumstances of the case. The qualifications should be stated. If the advice is given on formal instructions, the instructions should always be put in evidence as well, so that the court can see the basis on which the advice was given. If it is not, the advice must state fully the basis on which it is given.

ARBITRATION

A term no longer used for small claims.

ARBITRATION CLAIMS BEFORE THE ARBITRATION ACT 1996

Pt 62 r.62.11

(1) [Section II of Pt 62] contains rules about arbitration claims to which the old law applies.

ARBITRATION CLAIMS UNDER THE ARBITRATION ACT 1996

Pt 62 r.62.1

(3) Part 58 (Commercial Court) applies to arbitration claims in the Commercial Court, Pt 59 (Mercantile Court) applies to arbitration claims in the Mercantile Court and Pt 60 (Technology and Construction Court claims) applies to arbitration claims in the Technology and Construction Court, except where Pt 62] provides otherwise.

Pt 62 r.62.2

(1) In this section of [Pt 62] 'arbitration claim' means—
    (a) any application to the court under the [the Arbitration Act 1996];
    (b) a claim to determine—
       (i) whether there is a valid arbitration agreement;
      (ii) whether an arbitration tribunal is properly constituted; or
    what matters have been submitted to arbitration in accordance with an arbitration agreement;
    (c) a claim to declare that an award by an arbitral tribunal is not binding on a party; and
    (d) any other application affecting—
       (i) arbitration proceedings (whether started or not); or

    (ii) an arbitration agreement.

(2) This Section of [Pt 62] does not apply to an arbitration claim to which ss.II [rules about arbitration claims to which the old law applies] or III [all arbitration enforcement proceedings other than by a claim on the award] of [Pt 62] apply.

Starting the claim

Pt 62 r.62.3

(1) Except where para.(2) applies an arbitration claim must be started by the issue of an arbitration claim form in accordance with the Pt 8 procedure.

(2) An application under s.9 of the [Arbitration Act 1996] to stay legal proceedings must be made by application notice to the court dealing with those proceedings.

(3) The courts in which an arbitration claim may be started are set out in PD 62.

(4) Rule 30.5 applies with the modification that a judge of the Technology and Construction Court may transfer the claim to any other court or specialist list.

PD 62 para.2.1

An arbitration claim under the [Arbitration Act 1996] (other than under s.9) must be started in accordance with the High Court and County Courts (Allocation of Arbitration Proceedings) Order 1996 by the issue of an arbitration claim form.

PD 62 para.2.2

An arbitration claim form must be substantially in the form set out in Appendix A to this PD.

PD 62 para.2.3

Subject to para.2.1, an arbitration claim form—

(1) may be issued at the courts set out in column 1 of the table below and will be entered in the list set out against that court in column 2;

(2) relating to a landlord and tenant or partnership dispute must be issued in the Chancery Division of the High Court.

Court	List
Admiralty and Commercial Registry at the Royal Courts of Justice, London	Commercial list
Technology and Construction Court Registry, St. Dunstan's House, London	TCC list
District Registry of the High Court (where mercantile court established)	Mercantile list
District Registry of the High Court (where arbitration claim form marked 'Technology and Construction Court' in top right hand corner)	TCC list

PD 62 para.2.3A

An arbitration claim form must, in the case of an appeal, or application for permission to appeal, from a judge-arbitrator, be issued in the Civil Division of the Court of Appeal. The judge hearing the application may adjourn the matter for oral argument before two judges of that court.

Arbitration claim form

Pt 62 r.62.4

(1) An arbitration claim form must—
    (a) include a concise statement of—
        (i) the remedy claimed; and
        (ii) any questions on which the claimant seeks the decision of the court;
    (b) give details of any arbitration award challenged by the claimant, identifying which part or parts of the award are challenged and specifying the grounds for the challenge;
    (c) show that any statutory requirements have been met;
    (d) specify under which section of the 1996 Act the claim is made;
    (e) identify against which (if any) defendants a costs order is sought; and
    (f) specify either—
        (i) the persons on whom the arbitration claim form is to be served, stating their role in the arbitration and whether they are defendants; or
        (ii) that the claim is made without notice under s.44(3) of the 1996 Act and the grounds relied on.
(2) Unless the court orders otherwise an arbitration claim form must be served on the defendant within one month from the date of issue and rr.7.5 and 7.6 are modified accordingly.
(3) Where the claimant applies for an order under s.12 of the 1996 Act (extension of time for beginning arbitral proceedings or other dispute resolution procedures), he may include in his arbitration claim form an alternative application for a declaration that such an order is not needed.

Service

PD 62 para.3.1

The court may exercise its powers under r.6.15 to permit service of an arbitration claim form at the address of a party's solicitor or representative acting for that party in the arbitration.

PD 62 para.3.2

Where the arbitration claim form is served by the claimant he must file a certificate of service within seven days of service of the arbitration claim form.
(Rule 6.17 specifies what a **certificate of service** must show).

Service out of the jurisdiction

Pt 62 r.62.5

(1) The court may give permission to serve an arbitration claim form out of the jurisdiction if—

    (a) the claimant seeks to—
        (i) challenge; or
        (ii) appeal on a question of law arising out of,
        an arbitration award made within the jurisdiction;
(The place where an award is treated as made is determined by s.53 of the 1996 Act).
    (b) the claim is for an order under s.44 of the 1996 Act; or
    (c) the claimant—
        (i) seeks some other remedy or requires a question to be decided by the court affecting an arbitration (whether started or not), an arbitration agreement or an arbitration award; and
        (ii) the seat of the arbitration is or will be within the jurisdiction or the conditions in s.2(4) of the 1996 Act are satisfied.
  (2) An application for permission under para.(1) must be supported by written evidence—
    (a) stating the grounds on which the application is made; and
    (b) showing in what place or country the person to be served is, or probably may be found.
  (3) Rules 6.40 to 6.46 apply to the service of an arbitration claim form under para.(1).
  (4) An order giving permission to serve an arbitration claim form out of the jurisdiction must specify the period within which the defendant may file an acknowledgment of service.

Acknowledgment of service or making representations by arbitrator or ACAS

PD 62 para.4.1

Where—
  (1) an arbitrator; or
  (2) ACAS (in a claim under the 1996 Act as applied with modifications by the ACAS Arbitration Scheme (England and Wales) Order 2001)
is sent a copy of an arbitration claim form (including an arbitration claim form sent under r.62.6(2)), that arbitrator or ACAS (as the case may be) may—
    (a) apply to be made a defendant; or
    (b) make representations to the court under para.4.3.

PD 62 para.4.2

An application under para.4.1(2)(a) to be made a defendant—
  (1) must be served on the claimant; but
  (2) need not be served on any other party.

PD 62 para.4.3

An arbitrator or ACAS may make representations by filing written evidence or in writing to the court.

Supply of documents from court records

PD 62 para.5.1

An arbitration claim form may only be inspected with the permission of the court.

Notice

Pt 62 r.62.6

(1) Where an arbitration claim is made under ss.24, 28 or 56 of the 1996 Act, each arbitrator must be a defendant.

(2) Where notice must be given to an arbitrator or any other person it may be given by sending him a copy of—
   (a) the arbitration claim form; and
   (b) any written evidence in support.

(3) Where the 1996 Act requires an application to the court to be made on notice to any other party to the arbitration, that notice must be given by making that party a defendant.

Case management

Pt 62 r.62.7

(1) Part 26 and any other rule that requires a party to file an allocation questionnaire does not apply.

(2) Arbitration claims are allocated to the multi-track.

(3) Part 29 does not apply.

(4) The automatic directions set out in PD 62 apply unless the court orders otherwise.

PD 62 para.6.1

The following directions apply unless the court orders otherwise.

PD 62 para.6.2

A defendant who wishes to rely on evidence before the court must file and serve his written evidence—

(1) within 21 days after the date by which he was required to acknowledge service; or,

(2) where a defendant is not required to file an acknowledgement of service, within 21 days after service of the arbitration claim form.

PD 62 para.6.3

A claimant who wishes to rely on evidence in reply to written evidence filed under para.6.2 must file and serve his written evidence within seven days after service of the defendant's evidence.

PD 62 para.6.4

Agreed indexed and paginated bundles of all the evidence and other documents to be used at the hearing must be prepared by the claimant.

PD 62 para.6.5

Not later than five days before the hearing date estimates for the length of the hearing must be filed together with a complete set of the documents to be used.

PD 62 para.6.6

Not later than two days before the hearing date the claimant must file and serve—
  (1) a chronology of the relevant events cross-referenced to the bundle of documents;
  (2) (where necessary) a list of the persons involved; and
  (3) a skeleton argument which lists succinctly—
      (a) the issues which arise for decision;
      (b) the grounds of relief (or opposing relief) to be relied upon;
      (c) the submissions of fact to be made with the references to the evidence; and
      (d) the submissions of law with references to the relevant authorities.

PD 62 para.6.7

Not later than the day before the hearing date the defendant must file and serve a skeleton argument which lists succinctly—
  (1) the issues which arise for decision;
  (2) the grounds of relief (or opposing relief) to be relied upon;
  (3) the submissions of fact to be made with the references to the evidence; and
  (4) the submissions of law with references to the relevant authorities.

Interim remedies

PD 62 para.8.1

An application for an interim remedy under s.44 of the 1996 Act must be made in an arbitration claim form.

Applications under ss.32 and 45 of the 1996 Act

PD 62 para.9.1

This paragraph applies to arbitration claims for the determination of—
  (1) a question as to the substantive jurisdiction of the arbitral tribunal under s.32 of the 1996 Act; and
  (2) a preliminary point of law under s.45 of the 1996 Act.

PD 62 para.9.2

Where an arbitration claim is made without the agreement in writing of all the other parties to the arbitral proceedings but with the permission of the arbitral tribunal, the written evidence or witness statements filed by the parties must set out any evidence relied on by the parties in support of their contention that the court should, or should not, consider the claim.

PD 62 para.9.3

As soon as practicable after the written evidence is filed, the court will decide whether or not it should consider the claim and, unless the court otherwise directs, will so decide without a hearing.

Decisions without a hearing

PD 62 para.10.1

Having regard to the overriding objective the court may decide particular issues without a hearing. For example, as set out in para.9.3, the question whether the court is satisfied as to the matters set out in s.32(2)(b) or s.45(2)(b) of the 1996 Act.

PD 62 para.10.2

The court will generally decide whether to extend the time limit under s.70(3) of the 1996 Act without a hearing. Where the court makes an order extending the time limit, the defendant must file his written evidence within 21 days from service of the order.

Stay of legal proceedings

Pt 62 r.62.8

(1) An application notice seeking a stay of legal proceedings under s.9 of the 1996 Act must be served on all parties to those proceedings who have given an address for service.

(2) A copy of an application notice under para.(1) must be served on any other party to the legal proceedings (whether or not he is within the jurisdiction) who has not given an address for service, at—

    (a) his last known address; or

    (b) a place where it is likely to come to his attention.

(3) Where a question arises as to whether—

    (a) an arbitration agreement has been concluded; or

    (b) the dispute which is the subject-matter of the proceedings falls within the terms of such an agreement,

the court may decide that question or give directions to enable it to be decided and may order the proceedings to be stayed pending its decision.

Variation of time

Pt 62 r.62.9

(1) The court may vary the period of 28 days fixed by s.70(3) of the 1996 Act for—

    (a) challenging the award under ss.67 or 68 of the Act; and

    (b) appealing against an award under s.69 of the Act.

(2) An application for an order under para.(1) may be made without notice being served on any other party before the period of 28 days expires.

(3) After the period of 28 days has expired—

    (a) an application for an order extending time under para.(1) must—

        (i) be made in the arbitration claim form; and

        (ii) state the grounds on which the application is made;

    (b) any defendant may file written evidence opposing the extension of time within seven days after service of the arbitration claim form; and

    (c) if the court extends the period of 28 days, each defendant's time for acknowledging service and serving evidence shall start to run as if the arbitration claim form had been served on the date when the court's order is served on that defendant.

PD 62 para.11.1

An application for an order under r.62.9(1)—
(1) before the period of 28 days has expired, must be made in a Pt 23 application notice; and
(2) after the period of 28 days has expired, must be set out in a separately identified part in the arbitration claim form.

Hearings

Pt 62 r.62.10

(1) The court may order that an arbitration claim be heard either in public or in private.
(2) Rule 39.2 does not apply.
(3) Subject to any order made under para.(1)—
  (a) the determination of—
    (i) a preliminary point of law under s.45 of the 1996 Act; or
    (ii) an appeal under s.69 of the 1996 Act on a question of law arising out of an award,
  will be heard in public; and
  (b) all other arbitration claims will be heard in private.
(4) Paragraph (3)(a) does not apply to—
  (a) the preliminary question of whether the court is satisfied of the matters set out in s.45(2)(b); or
  (b) an application for permission to appeal under s.69(2)(b).

Applications for permission to appeal

PD 62 para.12.1

Where a party seeks permission to appeal to the court on a question of law arising out of an arbitration award, the arbitration claim form must, in addition to complying with r.62.4(1)—
(1) identify the question of law;
(2) state the grounds (but not the argument) on which the party challenges the award and contends that permission should be given;
(3) be accompanied by a **skeleton argument** in support of the application in accordance with para.12.2; and
(4) append the award.

PD 62 para.12.2

Subject to para.12.3, the skeleton argument—
(1) must be printed in 12 point font, with 1.5 line spacing;
(2) should not exceed 15 pages in length; and
(3) must contain an estimate of how long the court is likely to need to deal with the application on the papers.

PD 62 para.12.3

If the skeleton argument exceeds 15 pages in length the author must write to the court explaining why that is necessary.

PD 62 para.12.4

Written evidence may be filed in support of the application only if it is necessary to show (insofar as that is not apparent from the award itself)—
  (1) that the determination of the question raised by the appeal will substantially affect the rights of one or more of the parties;
  (2) that the question is one which the tribunal was asked to determine;
  (3) that the question is one of general public importance;
  (4) that it is just and proper in all the circumstances for the court to determine the question raised by the appeal.
Any such evidence must be filed and served with the arbitration claim form.

PD 62 para.12.5

Unless there is a dispute whether the question raised by the appeal is one which the tribunal was asked to determine, no arbitration documents may be put before the court other than—
  (1) the award; and
  (2) any document (such as the contract or the relevant parts thereof) which is referred to in the award and which the court needs to read to determine a question of law arising out of the award.
A respondent who wishes to oppose an application for permission to appeal must file a respondent's notice which—
  (1) sets out the grounds (but not the argument) on which the respondent opposes the application; and
  (2) states whether the respondent wishes to contend that the award should be upheld for reasons not expressed (or not fully expressed) in the award and, if so, states those reasons (but not the argument).

PD 62 para.12.7

The respondent's notice must be filed and served within 21 days after the date on which the respondent was required to acknowledge service and must be accompanied by a skeleton argument in support which complies with para.12.2 above.

PD 62 para.12.8

Written evidence in opposition to the application should be filed only if it complies with the requirements of para.12.4 above. Any such evidence must be filed and served with the respondent's notice.

PD 62 para.12.9

The applicant may file and serve evidence or argument in reply only if it is necessary to do so. Any such evidence or argument must be as brief as possible and must be filed and served within seven days after service of the respondent's notice.

PD 62 para.12.10

If either party wishes to invite the court to consider arbitration documents [means documents adduced in or produced for the purposes of the arbitration] other than those specified in para.12.5 above the counsel or solicitor responsible for settling the application documents must write to the court explaining why that is necessary.

PD 62 para.12.11

If a party or its representative fails to comply with the requirements of paras 12.1 to 12.9 the court may penalise that party or representative in costs.

PD 62 para.12.12

The court will normally determine applications for permission to appeal without an oral hearing but may direct otherwise, particularly with a view to saving time (including court time) or costs.

PD 62 para.12.13

Where the court considers that an oral hearing is required, it may give such further directions as are necessary.

PD 62 para.12.14

Where the court refuses an application for permission to appeal without an oral hearing, it will provide brief reasons.

PD 62 para.12.15

The bundle for the hearing of any appeal should contain only the claim form, the respondent's notice, the arbitration documents referred to in para.12.5, the order granting permission to appeal and the skeleton arguments.

See **Witness**.

ARBITRATION ENFORCEMENT PROCEEDINGS

Pt 62 r.62.17

[Section III of Part 62] applies to all arbitration enforcement proceedings other than by a claim on the award.

Enforcement of awards

Pt 62 r.62.18

(1) An application for permission under—
  (a) section 66 of the [Arbitration Act] 1996;
  (b) section 101 of the 1996 Act;
  (c) section 26 of the [Arbitration Act] 1950; or
  (d) section 3(1)(a) of the [Arbitration Act] 1975,
  to enforce an award in the same manner as a judgment or order may be made without notice in an arbitration claim form.
(2) The court may specify parties to the arbitration on whom the arbitration claim form must be served.

(3) The parties on whom the arbitration claim form is served must acknowledge service and the enforcement proceedings will continue as if they were an arbitration claim under s.I of this Part.

(4) With the permission of the court the arbitration claim form may be served out of the jurisdiction irrespective of where the award is, or is treated as, made.

(5) Where the applicant applies to enforce an agreed award within the meaning of s. 51(2) of the 1996 Act—

   (a) the arbitration claim form must state that the award is an agreed award; and

   (b) any order made by the court must also contain such a statement.

(6) An application for permission must be supported by written evidence—

   (a) exhibiting—

      (i) where the application is made under s.66 of the 1996 Act or under s.26 of the 1950 Act, the arbitration agreement and the original award (or copies);

      (ii) where the application is under s.101 of the 1996 Act, the documents required to be produced by s.102 of that Act; or

      (iii) where the application is under s.3(1)(a) of the 1975 Act, the documents required to be produced by s.4 of that Act;

   (b) stating the name and the usual or last known place of residence or business of the claimant and of the person against whom it is sought to enforce the award; and

   (c) stating either—

      (i) that the award has not been complied with; or

      (ii) the extent to which it has not been complied with at the date of the application.

(7) An order giving permission must—

   (a) be drawn up by the claimant; and

   (b) be served on the defendant by—

      (i) delivering a copy to him personally; or

      (ii) sending a copy to him at his usual or last known place of residence or business.

(8) An order giving permission may be served out of the jurisdiction—

   (a) without permission; and

   (b) in accordance with rr. 6.40 to 6.46 as if the order were an arbitration claim form.

(9) Within 14 days after service of the order or, if the order is to be served out of the jurisdiction, within such other period as the court may set—

   (a) the defendant may apply to set aside the order; and

   (b) the award must not be enforced until after—

      (i) the end of that period; or

      (ii) any application made by the defendant within that period has been finally disposed of.

(10) The order must contain a statement of—

   (a) the right to make an application to set the order aside; and

   (b) the restrictions on enforcement under r.62.18(9)(b).

(11) Where a body corporate is a party any reference in this rule to place of residence or business shall have effect as if the reference were to the registered or principal address of the body corporate

Registration in high court of foreign awards

Pt 62 r.62.20

(1) Where—

   (a) an award is made in proceedings on an arbitration in any part of a British overseas territory or other territory to which Pt I of the Foreign Judgments (Reciprocal Enforcement) Act 1933 ('the 1933 Act') extends;

(b) Part II of the Administration of Justice Act 1920 extended to that part immediately before Pt I of the 1933 Act was extended to that part; and

(c) an award has, under the law in force in the place where it was made, become enforceable in the same manner as a judgment given by a court in that place,

Rules 74.1 to 74.7 and 74.9 apply in relation to the award as they apply in relation to a judgment given by the court subject to the modifications in para.(2).

(2) The modifications referred to in para.(1) are as follows—

(a) for references to the State of origin are substituted references to the place where the award was made; and

(b) the written evidence required by r.74.4 must state (in addition to the matters required by that r.) that to the best of the information or belief of the maker of the statement the award has, under the law in force in the place where it was made, become enforceable in the same manner as a judgment given by a court in that place.

Registration of awards under the Arbitration (International Investment Disputes) Act 1966

Pt 62 r.62.21

(1) In this rule—

(c) 'the Convention' means the Convention on the settlement of investment disputes between States and nationals of other States which was opened for signature in Washington on 18th March 1965;

(d) 'judgment creditor'; and

(e) 'judgment debtor' means the other party to the award.

(2) Subject to the provisions of this rule, the following provisions of Pt 74 apply with such modifications as may be necessary in relation to an award [means an award under the Convention] as they apply in relation to a judgment to which Pt I of the Foreign Judgments (Reciprocal Enforcement) Act 1933 applies—

(a) rule 74.1;

(b) rule 74.3;

(c) rule 74.4(1),(2)(a)–(d) and (4);

(d) rule 74.6 (except para.(3)(c)–(e)); and

(e) rule 74.9(2).

(3) An application to have an award registered in the High Court under s.1 of the [Arbitration (International Investment Disputes) Act 1966 must be made in accordance with the Pt 8 procedure.

(4) The written evidence required by r.74.4 in support of an application for registration must—

(a) exhibit the award certified under the Convention instead of the judgment (or a copy of it); and

(b) in addition to stating the matters referred to in r.74.4(2)(a) to (d) state whether—

(i) at the date of the application the enforcement of the award has been stayed (provisionally or otherwise) under the Convention; and

(ii) any, and if so what, application has been made under the Convention, which, if granted, might result in a stay of the enforcement of the award.

(5) Where, on granting permission to register an award or an application made by the judgment debtor after an award has been registered, the court considers—

(a) that the enforcement of the award has been stayed (whether provisionally or otherwise) under the Convention; or

(b) that an application has been made under the Convention which, if granted, might result in a stay of the enforcement of the award,

the court may stay the enforcement of the award for such time as it considers appropriate.

See **Interest**.

ARCHITECTS ACT 1997

Appeals against decisions affecting registration

PD 52D para.19.1

(1) This paragraph applies to an appeal to the High Court under s.22 of the Architects Act 1997.
(2) Every appeal to which this paragraph applies must be supported by written evidence and, if the court so orders, oral evidence and will be by way of re-hearing.
(3) The appellant must file the appellant's notice within 28 days after the decision that the appellant wishes to appeal.
(4) [The respondent is the Architects' Registration Council of the UK and the person to be served with the appellant's notice is the registrar of the Council].

ARMED FORCES

Service on members of armed forces

PD 6A para.5.1

The provisions that apply to service on members of the regular forces (within the meaning of the Armed Forces Act 2006) are annexed to [PD 6A].

ASSESSORS

Pt 35 r.35.15

(1) This rule applies where the court appoints one or more persons under s.70 of the Senior Courts Act 1981 or s.63 of the County Courts Act 1984 as an assessor.
(2) An assessor will assist the court in dealing with a matter in which the assessor has skill and experience.
(3) An assessor will take such part in the proceedings as the court may direct and in particular the court may direct an assessor to—
  (a) prepare a report for the court on any matter at issue in the proceedings; and
  (b) attend the whole or any part of the trial to advise the court on any such matter.
(4) If an assessor prepares a report for the court before the trial has begun—
  (a) the court will send a copy to each of the parties; and
  (b) the parties may use it at trial.
(5) The remuneration to be paid to an assessor is to be determined by the court and will form part of the costs of the proceedings.
(6) The court may order any party to deposit in the court office a specified sum in respect of an assessor's fees and, where it does so, the assessor will not be asked to act until the sum has been deposited.
(7) Paragraphs (5) and (6) do not apply where the remuneration of the assessor is to be paid out of money provided by Parliament.

PD 35 para.10.1

An assessor may be appointed to assist the court under r.35.15. Not less than 21 days before making any such appointment, the court will notify each party in writing of the name of the proposed assessor, of the matter in respect of which the assistance of the assessor will be sought and of the qualifications of the assessor to give that assistance.

PD 35 para.10.2

Where any person has been proposed for appointment as an assessor, any party may object to that person either personally or in respect of that person's qualification.

PD 35 para.10.3

Any such objection must be made in writing and filed with the court within seven days of receipt of the notification referred to in para.10.1 and will be taken into account by the court in deciding whether or not to make the appointment.

PD 35 para.10.4

Copies of any report prepared by the assessor will be sent to each of the parties but the assessor will not give oral evidence or be open to cross-examination or questioning.

Admiralty claims

Pt 61 r.61.13

The court may sit with assessors when hearing—
    (a) collision claims; or
    (b) other claims involving issues of navigation or seamanship, and
the parties will not be permitted to call expert witnesses unless the court orders otherwise.

Small claims

Pt 27 r.27.2

    (1) (e) [The appointment of assessors does not apply to the small claims track].

ASSISTED PERSON

Pt 43 r.43(1)

    (h) An assisted person within the statutory provisions relating to legal aid.

See also **LSC funded client.**

ASSURED SHORTHOLD TENANCY

See **Accelerated possession claims.**

ASSURED TENANCY

See **Possession claims**.

ASYLUM AND IMMIGRATION

See **Immigration and Asylum**.

ATTACHMENT OF EARNINGS

CCR Ord.27 r.1

(1) In this Order—
'the Act of 1971' means the Attachment of Earnings Act and, unless the context otherwise requires, expressions used in that Act have the same meanings as in that Act.

Index of orders

CCR Ord.27 r.2

(1) The court officer of every court shall keep a nominal index of the debtors residing within the district of his court in respect of whom there are in force attachment of earnings Orders which have been made by that court or of which the court officer has received notice from another court.
(2) Where a debtor in respect of whom a court has made an attachment of earnings order resides within the district of another court, the court officer of the first-mentioned court shall send a copy of the order to the court officer of the other court for entry in his index.
(3) The court officer shall, on the request of any person having a judgment or rder against a person believed to be residing within the district of the court, cause a search to be made in the index of the court and issue a certificate of the result of the search.

Appropriate court

CCR Ord.27 r.3

(1) Subject to paras (2) and (3), an application for an attachment of earnings order may be made to the court for the district in which the debtor resides.
(2) If the debtor does not reside within England or Wales, or the creditor does not know where he resides, the application may be made to the court in which, or for the district in which, the judgment or order sought to be enforced was obtained.
(3) Where the creditor applies for attachment of earnings Orders in respect of two or more debtors jointly liable under a judgment or order, the application may be made to the court for the district in which any of the debtors resides, so however that if the judgment or order was given or made by any such court, the application shall be made to that court.

Mode of applying

CCR Ord.27 r.4

(1) A judgment creditor who desires to apply for an attachment of earnings order shall file his application certifying the amount of money remaining due under the judgment or order and that the whole or part of any instalment due remains unpaid and, where it is sought to enforce an order of a magistrates' court—
   (a) a certified copy of the order; and
   (b) a witness statement or affidavit verifying the amount due under the order or, if payments under the order are required to be made to the justices' chief executive for the magistrates' court, a certificate by that chief executive to the same effect.

(2) On the filing of the documents mentioned in para.(1) the court officer shall, where the order to be enforced is a maintenance order, fix a day for the hearing of the application.

Service and reply

CCR Ord.27 r.5

(1) Notice of the application together with a form of reply in the appropriate form, shall be served on the debtor in the manner set out in CPR r.6.20.

(2) The debtor shall, within eight days after service on him of the documents mentioned in para.(1), file a reply in the form provided, and the instruction to that effect in the notice to the debtor shall constitute a requirement imposed by virtue of s.14(4) of the Act of 1971. Provided that no proceedings shall be taken for an offence alleged to have been committed under s.23(2)(c) or (f) of the Act of 1971 in relation to the requirement unless the said documents have been served on the debtor personally or the court is satisfied that they came to his knowledge in sufficient time for him to comply with the requirement.

(2A) Nothing in para.(2) shall require a defendant to file a reply if, within the period of time mentioned in that paragraph, he pays to the judgment creditor the money remaining due under the judgment or order and, where such payment is made, the judgment creditor shall so inform the court officer.

(3) On receipt of a reply the court officer shall send a copy to the applicant.

Notice to employer

CCR Ord.27 r.6

Without prejudice to the powers conferred by s.14(1) of the Act of 1971, the court officer may, at any stage of the proceedings, send to any person appearing to have the debtor in his employment a notice requesting him to give to the court, within such period as may be specified in the notice, a statement of the debtor's earnings and anticipated earnings with such particulars as may be so specified.

Attachment of earnings order

CCR Ord.27 r.7

(1) On receipt of the debtor's reply, the court officer may, if he has sufficient information to do so, make an attachment of earnings order and a copy of the order shall be sent to the parties and to the debtor's employer.

(2) Where an order is made under para.(1), the judgment creditor or the debtor may, within 14 days of service of the order on him and giving his reasons, apply on notice for the order to be re-considered and the court officer shall fix a day for the hearing of the application and give to the judgment creditor and the debtor not less than two days' notice of the day so fixed.

(3) On hearing an application under para.(2), the district judge may confirm the order or set it aside and make such new order as he thinks fit and the order so made shall be entered in the records of the court.

(4) Where an order is not made under para.(1), the court officer shall refer the application to the district judge who shall, if he considers that he has sufficient information to do so without the attendance of the parties, determine the application.

(5) Where the district judge does not determine the application under para.(4), he shall direct that a day be fixed for the hearing of the application whereupon the court officer shall fix such a day and give to the judgment creditor and the debtor not less than eight days' notice of the day so fixed.

(6) Where an order is made under para.(4), the judgment creditor or the debtor may, within 14 days of service of the order on him and giving his reasons, apply on notice for the order to be re-considered; and the court officer shall fix a day for the hearing of the application and give to the judgment creditor and the debtor not less than two days' notice of the day so fixed.

(7) On hearing an application under paragraph (6), the district judge may confirm the order or set it aside and make such new order as he thinks fit and the order so made shall be entered in the records of the court.

(8) If the creditor does not appear at the hearing of the application under para.(5) but—
   (a) the court has received a witness statement or affidavit of evidence from him; or
   (b) the creditor requests the court in writing to proceed in his absence, the court may proceed to hear the application and to make an order thereon.

(9) An attachment of earnings order may be made to secure the payment of a judgment debt if the debt is—
   (a) of not less than £50; or
   (b) for the amount remaining payable under a judgment for a sum of not less than £50.

Failure by debtor

CCR Ord.27 r.7A

(1) If the debtor has failed to comply with r.5(2) or to make payment to the judgment creditor, the court officer may issue an order under s.14(1) of the Act of 1971 which shall—
   (a) be indorsed with or incorporate a notice warning the debtor of the consequences of disobedience to the order;
   (b) be served on the debtor personally; and
   (c) direct that any payments made thereafter shall be paid into the court and not direct to the judgment creditor.

(2) Without prejudice to r.16, if the person served with an order made pursuant to para.(1) fails to obey it or to file a statement of his means or to make payment, the court officer shall issue a notice calling on that person to show good reason why he should not be imprisoned and any such notice shall be served on the debtor personally not less than five days before the hearing.

(3) Ord.29 r.1 shall apply, with the necessary modifications and with the substitution of references to the district judge for references to the judge, where a notice is issued under paras (2) or (4) of that rule.

(4) In this rule 'statement of means' means a statement given under s.14(1) of the Act of 1971.

Suspended committal order

CCR Ord.27 r.7B

(1) If the debtor fails to attend at an adjourned hearing of an application for an attachment of earnings order and a committal order is made, the judge or district judge may direct that the committal order shall be suspended so long as the debtor attends at the time and place specified in the committal order and paras (2), (4) and (5) of Ord.28 r.7 shall apply, with the necessary modifications, where such a direction is given as they apply where a direction is given under para.(1) of that rule.

(2) Where a committal order is suspended under para.(1) and the debtor fails to attend at the time and place specified under para.(1), a certificate to that effect given by the court officer shall be sufficient authority for the issue of a warrant of committal.

Costs

CCR Ord.27 r.9

(1) Where costs are allowed to the judgment creditor on an application for an attachment of earnings order, there may be allowed—
   (a) a charge of a solicitor for attending the hearing and, if the court so directs, for serving the application;
   (b) if the court certifies that the case is fit for counsel, a fee to counsel; and
   (c) the court fee on the issue of the application.

(2) For the purpose of para.(1)(a) a solicitor who has prepared on behalf of the judgment creditor a witness statement or affidavit or request under r.7(8) shall be treated as having attended the hearing.

(3) The costs may be fixed and allowed without detailed assessment under CPR Pt 47.

Contents and service of order

CCR Ord.27 r.10

(1) An attachment of earnings order shall contain such of the following particulars relating to the debtor as are known to the court, namely—
   (a) his full name and address;
   (b) his place of work; and
   (c) the nature of his work and his works number, if any,
   and those particulars shall be the prescribed particulars for the purposes of s.6(3) of the Act of 1971.

(2) An attachment of earnings order and any order varying or discharging such an order shall be served on the debtor and on the person to whom the order is directed, and CPR Pt 6 and CPR rr 40.4 and 40.5 shall apply with the further modification that where the order is directed to a corporation which has requested the court that any communication relating to the debtor or to the class of persons to whom he belongs shall be directed to the corporation at a particular address, service may, if the district judge thinks fit, be effected on the corporation at that address.

(3) Where an attachment of earnings order is made to enforce a judgment or order of the High Court or a magistrates' court, a copy of the attachment of earnings order and of any order discharging it shall be sent by the court officer of the county court to the court officer of the High Court, or, as the case may be, the justices' chief executive for the magistrates' court.

Application to determine whether particular payments are earnings

CCR Ord.27 r.11

An application to the court under s.16 of the Act of 1971 to determine whether payments to the debtor of a particular class or description are earnings for the purpose of an attachment of earnings order may be made to the district judge in writing and the court officer shall thereupon fix a date and time for the hearing of the application by the court and give notice thereof to the persons mentioned in the said s.16(2)(a), (b) and (c).

Notice of cesser

CCR Ord.27 r.12

Where an attachment of earnings order ceases to have effect under s.8(4) of the Act of 1971, the court officer of the court in which the matter is proceeding shall give notice of the cesser to the person to whom the order was directed.

Variation and discharge by court of own motion

CCR Ord.27 r.13

(1) Subject to para.(9), the powers conferred by s.9(1) of the Act of 1971 may be exercised by the court of its own motion in the circumstances mentioned in the following paragraphs.

(2) Where it appears to the court that a person served with an attachment of earnings order directed to him has not the debtor in his employment, the court may discharge the order.

(3) Where an attachment of earnings order which has lapsed under s.9(4) of the Act of 1971 is again directed to a person who appears to the court to have the debtor in his employment, the court may make such consequential variations in the order as it thinks fit.

(4) Where, after making an attachment of earnings order, the court makes or is notified of the making of another such order in respect of the same debtor which is not to secure the payment of a judgment debt or payments under an administration order, the court may discharge or vary the first-mentioned order having regard to the priority accorded to the other order by para.8 of Sch.3 to the Act of 1971.

(5) Where, after making an attachment of earnings order, the court makes an order under s.4(1)(b) of the Act of 1971 (see *http://www.justice.gov.uk/courts/procedure-rules/civil/ sched_ccr/ccrorder27*) or makes an administration order, the court may discharge the attachment of earnings order or, if it exercises the power conferred by s.5(3) of the said Act, may vary the order in such manner as it thinks fit.

(6) On making a consolidated attachment of earnings order the court may discharge any earlier attachment of earnings order made to secure the payment of a judgment debt by the same debtor.

(7) Where it appears to the court that a bankruptcy order has been made against a person in respect of whom an attachment of earnings order is in force to secure the payment of a judgment debt, the court may discharge the attachment of earnings order.

(8) Where an attachment of earnings order has been made to secure the payment of a judgment debt and the court grants permission to issue execution for the recovery of the debt, the court may discharge the order.

(9) Before varying or discharging an attachment of earnings order of its own motion under any of the foregoing paragraphs of this rule, the court shall, unless it thinks it unnecessary in the circumstances to do so, give the debtor and the person on whose application the order was made an opportunity of being heard on the question whether the order should be varied or discharged, and for that purpose the court officer may give them notice of a date, time and place at which the question will be considered.

Transfer of attachment order

CCR Ord.27 r.14

(1) Where the court by which the question of making a consolidated attachment order falls to be considered is not the court by which any attachment of earnings order has been made to secure the payment of a judgment debt by the debtor, the district judge of the last-mentioned court shall, at the request of the district judge of the first-mentioned court, transfer to that court the matter in which the attachment of earnings order was made.

(2) Without prejudice to para.(1), if in the opinion of the judge or district judge of any court by which an attachment of earnings order has been made, the matter could more conveniently proceed in some other court, whether by reason of the debtor having become resident in the district of that court or otherwise, he may order the matter to be transferred to that court.

(3) The court to which proceedings arising out of an attachment of earnings are transferred under this rule shall have the same jurisdiction in relation to the order as if it has been made by that court.

Exercise of power to obtain statement of earnings etc.

CCR Ord.27 r.15

(1) An Order under s.14(1) of the Act of 1971 shall be indorsed with or incorporate a notice warning the person to whom it is directed of the consequences of disobedience to the order and shall be served on him personally.

(2) Ord.34 r.2, shall apply, with the necessary modifications, in relation to any penalty for failure to comply with an order under the said s.14(1) or, subject to the proviso to r.5(2), any penalty for failure to comply with a requirement mentioned in that rule, as it applies in relation to a fine under s.55 of the County Courts Act 1984.

Offences

CCR Ord.27 r.16

(1) Where it is alleged that a person has committed any offence mentioned in s.23(2)(a), (b), (d), (e) or (f) of the Act of 1971 in relation to proceedings in, or to an attachment of earnings order made by, a county court, the district judge shall, unless it is decided to proceed against the alleged offender summarily, issue a summons calling upon him to show cause why he should not be punished for the alleged offence.

The summons shall be served on the alleged offender personally not less than 14 days before the return day.

(2) Ord.34 rr.3 and 4, shall apply, with the necessary modifications, to proceedings for an offence under s.23(2) of the Act of 1971 as they apply to proceedings for offences under

the County Courts Act 1984 (*http://www.justice.gov.uk/courts/procedure-rules/civil/ sched_ccr/ccrorder27*—Accessed November 21, 2012).

Consolidated attachment of earnings orders

Cases in which consolidated order may be made

CCR Ord.27 r.18

Subject to the provisions of rr.19 to 21, the court may make a consolidated attachment order where—
- (a) two or more attachment of earnings Orders are in force to secure the payment of judgment debts by the same debtor; or
- (b) on an application for an attachment of earnings order to secure the payment of a judgment debt, or for a consolidated attachment order to secure the payment of two or more judgment debts, it appears to the court that an attachment of earnings order is already in force to secure the payment of a judgment debt by the same debtor.

Application for consolidated order

CCR Ord. 27 r.19

- (1) An application for a consolidated attachment order may be made—
  - (a) by the debtor in respect of whom the order is sought; or
  - (b) by any person who has obtained or is entitled to apply for an attachment of earnings order to secure the payment of a judgment debt by that debtor.
- (2) An application under para.(1) may be made in the proceedings in which any attachment of earnings order (other than a priority order) is in force and rr. 3, 4 and 5 of this order shall not apply.
- (3) Where the judgment which it is sought to enforce was not given by the court which made the attachment of earnings order, the judgment shall be automatically transferred to the court which made the attachment of earnings order.
- (3A) An application under para.(1)(b) shall certify the amount of money remaining due under the judgment or order and that the whole or part of any instalment due remains unpaid.
- (3B) Where an application for a consolidated attachment of earnings order is made, the court officer shall—
  - (a) notify any party who may be affected by the application of its terms; and
  - (b) require him to notify the court in writing, within 14 days of service of notification upon him, giving his reasons for any objection he may have to the granting of the application.
- (3C) If notice of any objection is not given within the time stated, the court officer shall make a consolidated attachment of earnings order.
- (3D) If any party objects to the making of a consolidated attachment of earnings order, the court officer shall refer the application to the district judge who may grant the application after considering the objection made and the reasons given.
- (3E) In the foregoing paragraphs of this rule, a party affected by the application means—
  - (a) where the application is made by the debtor, the creditor in the proceedings in which the application is made and any other creditor who has obtained an attachment of earnings order which is in force to secure the payment of a judgment debt by the debtor;

    (b) where the application is made by the judgment creditor, the debtor and every person who, to the knowledge of the applicant, has obtained an attachment of earnings order which is in force to secure the payment of a judgment debt by the debtor.

(4) A person to whom two or more attachment of earnings Orders are directed to secure the payment of judgment debts by the same debtor may request the court in writing to make a consolidated attachment order to secure the payment of those debts, and on receipt of such a request paras (3B) to (3E) shall apply, with the necessary modifications, as if the request were an application by the judgment creditor.

Making of consolidated order by court of its own motion

CCR Ord.27 r.20

Where an application is made for an attachment of earnings order to secure the payment of a judgment debt by a debtor in respect of whom an attachment of earnings order is already in force to secure the payment of another judgment debt and no application is made for a consolidated attachment order, the court officer may make such an order of his own motion after giving all persons concerned an opportunity of submitting written objections.

Extension of consolidated order

CCR Ord.27 r.21

(1) Where a consolidated attachment order is in force to secure the payment of two or more judgment debts, any creditor to whom another judgment debt is owed by the same judgment debtor may apply to the court by which the order was made for it to be extended so as to secure the payment of that debt as well as the first-mentioned debts and, if the application is granted, the court may either vary the order accordingly or may discharge it and make a new consolidated attachment order to secure payment of all the aforesaid judgment debts.

(2) An application under this rule shall be treated for the purposes of rr.19 and 20 as an application for a consolidated attachment order.

Payments under consolidated order

CCR Ord.27 r.22

Instead of complying with s.13 of the Act of 1971, a court officer who receives payments made to him in compliance with a consolidated attachment order shall, after deducting such court fees, if any, in respect of proceedings for or arising out of the order as are deductible from those payments, deal with the sums paid as he would if they had been paid by the debtor to satisfy the relevant adjudications in proportion to the amounts payable thereunder, and for that purpose dividends may from time to time be declared and distributed among the creditors entitled thereto.

Exercise of powers by district judge

CCR Ord.39 r.1

Any powers conferred on the court by Pt VI of the Act, s.4 of the Attachment of Earnings Act 1971 or this Order may be exercised by the district judge or, in the circumstances mentioned in this order, by the court officer.

Committal

PD 2B para.8.3

A District Judge may only make an order committing a person to prison or attach a power of arrest to an injunction or remand a person where an enactment authorises this [see s.23 of the Attachment of Earnings Act 1971 and the relevant rules].

See **Maintenance order.**

AUTHORISED COURT OFFICER

Pt 44 r.44.1(1)

> (1) (c) [In the Costs Rules]
>   (d) any officer of—
>   (i) a county court;
>   (ii) a district registry;
>   (iii) the Principal Registry of the Family Division; or
>   (iv) the Costs Office,
>   whom the Lord Chancellor has authorised to assess costs.

See **Appeals from an authorised court officer in detailed assessment proceedings.**

Powers of an authorised court officer

Pt 47 r.47.3

> (1) An authorised court officer has all the powers of the court when making a **detailed assessment**, except—
>   (a) power to make a **wasted costs** order as defined in r.48.7;
>   (b) power to make an order under—
>   (i) rule 44.14 (powers in relation to **misconduct**);
>   (ii) rule r.47.8 (sanction for delay in commencing detailed assessment proceedings);
>   (iii) paragraph (2) (objection to detailed assessment by authorised court officer); and
>   (c) power to make a detailed assessment of costs payable to a solicitor by his client, unless the costs are being assessed under r.48.5 (costs where money is payable to a **child** or **protected party**).
> (2) Where a party objects to the detailed assessment of costs being made by an authorised court officer, the court may order it to be made by a costs judge or a district judge.
> (The Costs PD sets out the relevant procedure)

Costs PD para.30.1

> (1) The court officers authorised by the Lord Chancellor to assess costs in the Costs Office and the Principal Registry of the Family Division are authorised to deal with claims for costs not exceeding £30,000 (excluding VAT) in the case of senior executive officers, or their equivalent, and £75,000 (excluding VAT) in the case of principal officers.

(2) In calculating whether or not a bill of costs is within the authorised amounts, the figure to be taken into account is the total claim for costs including any additional liability.

(3) Where the receiving party, paying party and any other party to the detailed assessment proceedings who has served points of dispute are agreed that the assessment should not be made by an authorised court officer, the receiving party should so inform the court when requesting a hearing date. The court will then list the hearing before a costs judge or a district judge.

(4) In any other case a party who objects to the assessment being made by an authorised court officer must make an application to the costs judge or district judge under Pt 23 (General Rules about Applications for Court Orders) setting out the reasons for the objection and if sufficient reason is shown the court will direct that the bill be assessed by a costs judge or district judge.

See **Detailed assessment**.

AUTHORISED LITIGATOR

Courts and Legal Services Act 1990 s.119(1)

Any person (including a solicitor) who has the right to conduct litigation granted by an authorised body in accordance with the provisions of the 1990 Act.

AUTHORISED PERSON

PD 22 r.3A.2

An authorised person is a person able to administer oaths and take affidavits but need not be independent of the parties or their representatives.

AUTOMATIC STRIKING OUT

See **Strike out**.

AUTOMATIC TRANSFER

Pt 26 r.26.2

This rule applies where r.26.2A [automatic transfer of **designated money claims**]

(1) This rule applies to proceedings where—
   (a) the claim is for a specified amount of money;
   (b) the claim was commenced in a court which is not the **defendant's home court**;
   (c) the claim has not been transferred to another defendant's home court; and
   (d) the defendant is an individual.

(2) This rule does not apply where the claim was commenced in a **specialist list**.

(3) Where this rule applies, the court will transfer the proceedings to the defendant's home court when a defence is filed, unless para.(4) applies.

(4) Where the claimant notifies the court under r.15.10 or r.14.5 that he wishes the proceedings to continue, the court will transfer the proceedings to the defendant's home court when it receives that notification from the claimant.

(Rule 15.10 deals with a claimant's notice where the defence is that money claimed has been paid).

(Rule 14.5 sets out the procedure where the defendant admits part of a claim for a specified amount of money).

    (5) Where—

        (a) the claim is against two or more defendants with different home courts; and

        (b) the defendant whose defence is filed first is an individual,

    proceedings are to be transferred under this rule to the home court of that defendant.

    (6) The time when a claim is automatically transferred under this rule may be varied by a PD in respect of claims issued by the Production Centre.

(Rule 7.10 makes provision for the **Production Centre**)

Automatic transfer of designated money claims

Pt 26 r.26.2A

    (1) This rule applies where the claim is a designated money claim.

    (2) If at any time before the service of a notice by the court under r.26.3(1A) a proper officer considers that the claim should be referred to a judge for directions the proper office may transfer the proceedings to the preferred court.

    (3) Subject to para.(5), if the defendant is an individual and the claim is for a specified sum of money, the court will, at the relevant time, transfer the claim to the defendant's home court (save that where there are two or more defendants, one or more of whom are individuals the court will transfer the claim to the home court of the defendant who first files his defence.

    (4) Subject to para.(5) in any other claim to which this rule applies, the court will at the relevant time transfer the claim to the preferred court.

    (5) If a defendant under para.(3) or a claimant under para.(4) has specified a court other than the preferred court on their **allocation questionnaire**, the court will transfer the claim to that court.

    (6) The relevant time for the purpose of this rule is when—

        (a) all parties have filed their allocation questionnaire; or

        (b) the period for filing questionnaires has expired,

    whichever occurs first save that where allocation questionnaires are not required the relevant time is the time prescribed for filing the defence.

AWARDS

Interest on awards

Pt 62 r.62.19

    (1) Where an applicant seeks to enforce an award of interest the whole or any part of which relates to a period after the date of the award, he must file a statement giving the following particulars—

        (a) whether simple or compound interest was awarded;

        (b) the date from which interest was awarded;

        (c) where rests were provided for, specifying them;

        (d) the rate of interest awarded; and

        (e) a calculation showing—

           (i) the total amount claimed up to the date of the statement; and

           (ii) any sum which will become due on a daily basis.

(2) A statement under para.(1) must be filed whenever the amount of interest has to be quantified for the purpose of—
 (a) obtaining a judgment or order under s.66 of the 1996 Act (enforcement of the award); or
 (b) enforcing such a judgment or order.

Registration in high court of foreign awards

Pt 62 r.62.20

(1) Where—
 (a) an award is made in proceedings on an arbitration in any part of a British overseas territory or other territory to which Pt I of the Foreign Judgments (Reciprocal Enforcement) Act 1933 ('the 1933 Act') extends;
 (b) Part II of the Administration of Justice Act 1920 extended to that part immediately before Pt I of the 1933 Act was extended to that Part; and
 (c) an award has, under the law in force in the place where it was made, become enforceable in the same manner as a judgment given by a court in that place, Rules 74.1 to 74.7 and 74.9 apply in relation to the award as they apply in relation to a judgment given by the court subject to the modifications in para.(2).
(2) The modifications referred to in para.(1) are as follows—
 (a) for references to the State of origin are substituted references to the place where the award was made; and
 (b) the written evidence required by r.74.4 must state (in addition to the matters required by that rule) that to the best of the information or belief of the maker of the statement the award has, under the law in force in the place where it was made, become enforceable in the same manner as a judgment given by a court in that place.

Registration of awards under the Arbitration (International Investment Disputes) Act 1966

Pt 62 r.62.21

(1) In this rule—
 (c) 'the Convention' means the Convention on the settlement of investment disputes between States and nationals of other States which was opened for signature in Washington on 18th March 1965;
(2) Subject to the provisions of this rule, the following provisions of Pt 74 apply with such modifications as may be necessary in relation to an award [means an award under the Convention] as they apply in relation to a judgment to which Pt I of the Foreign Judgments (Reciprocal Enforcement) Act 1933 applies—
 (a) rule 74.1 [enforcement in England and Wales of judgments of foreign courts];
 (b) rule 74.3 [applications for registration];
 (c) rule 74.4(1), (2)(a) to (d), and (4)[evidence in support];
 (d) rule 74.6 (except para.(3)(c) to (e))[registration orders]; and
 (e) rule 74.9(2)[enforcement].
(3) An application to have an award registered in the High Court under s.1 of the [Arbitration (International Investment Disputes) Act 1966Act] must be made in accordance with the Pt 8 procedure.
(4) The written evidence required by r.74.4 in support of an application for registration must—

    (a) exhibit the award certified under the Convention instead of the judgment (or a copy of it); and

    (b) in addition to stating the matters referred to in r.74.4(2)(a) to (d) state whether—

        (i) at the date of the application the enforcement of the award has been stayed (provisionally or otherwise) under the Convention; and

        (ii) any, and if so what, application has been made under the Convention, which, if granted, might result in a stay of the enforcement of the award.

(5) Where, on granting permission to register an award or an application made by the judgment debtor after an award has been registered, the court considers—

    (a) that the enforcement of the award has been stayed (whether provisionally or otherwise) under the Convention; or

    (b) that an application has been made under the Convention which, if granted, might result in a stay of the enforcement of the award,

the court may stay the enforcement of the award for such time as it considers appropriate

Pt 62 r.16.1

Awards ordered to be registered under the 1966 Act and particulars will be entered in the Register kept for that purpose at the Admiralty and Commercial Registry.

See also **Arbitration claims under the Arbitration Act 1996.**

B

BAIL

RSC Ord.79 r.9

(1) Subject to the provisions of this rule, every application to the High Court in respect of bail in any criminal proceeding—
   (a) where the defendant is in custody, must be made by claim form to a judge to show cause why the defendant should not be granted bail;
   (b) where the defendant has been admitted to bail, must be made by claim form to a judge to show cause why the variation in the arrangements for bail proposed by the applicant should not be made.

(2) Subject to para.(5), the claim form (in Form No.97 or 97A in PD 4) must, at least 24 hours before the day named therein for the hearing, be served—
   (a) where the application was made by the defendant, on the prosecutor and on the Director of Public Prosecutions, if the prosecution is being carried on by him;
   (b) where the application was made by the prosecutor or a constable under s.3(8) of the Bail Act 1976 on the defendant.

(3) Subject to para.(5), every application must be supported by witness statement or affidavit.

(4) Where a defendant in custody who desires to apply for bail is unable through lack of means to instruct a solicitor, he may give notice in writing to the court stating his desire to apply for bail and requesting that the Official Solicitor shall act for him in the application, and the court may assign the Official Solicitor to act for the applicant accordingly.

(5) Where the Official Solicitor has been so assigned the court may dispense with the requirements of paras (1) to (3) and deal with the application in a summary manner.

(6) Where the court grants the defendant bail, the order must be in Form No.98 in PD 4 and a copy of the order shall be transmitted forthwith—
   (a) where the proceedings in respect of the defendant have been transferred to the Crown Court for trial or where the defendant has been committed to the Crown Court to be sentenced or otherwise dealt with, to the appropriate officer of the Crown Court;
   (b) in any other case, to the justices' chief executive for the court which committed the defendant.

(6A) The recognisance of any surety required as a condition of bail granted as aforesaid may, where the defendant is in a prison or other place of detention, be entered into before the governor or keeper of the prison or place as well as before the persons specified in s.8(4) of the Bail Act 1976.

(6B) Where under s.3(5) or (6) of the Bail Act 1976 the court imposes a requirement to be complied with before a person's release on bail, it may give directions as to the manner in which and the person or persons before whom the requirement may be complied with.

(7) A person who in pursuance of an order for the grant of bail made by the court under this rule proposes to enter into a recognisance or give security must, unless the court otherwise directs, give notice (in Form No.100 in PD 4) to the prosecutor at least 24 hours before he enters into the recognisance or complies with the requirements as aforesaid.

(8) Where in pursuance of such an order as aforesaid a recognisance is entered into or requirement complied with before any person, it shall be the duty of that person to cause

the recognisance or, as the case may be, a statement of the requirement complied with to be transmitted forthwith—

(a) where the proceedings in respect of the defendant have been transferred to the Crown Court for trial or where the defendant has been committed to the Crown Court to be sentenced or otherwise dealt with, to the appropriate officer of the Crown Court;

(b) in any other case, to the justices' chief executive for the court which committed the defendant,

and a copy of such recognisance or statement shall at the same time be sent to the governor or keeper of the prison or other place of detention in which the defendant is detained, unless the recognisance was entered into or the requirement complied with before such governor or keeper.

(10) An order varying the arrangements under which the defendant has been granted bail shall be in Form 98A in PD 4 and a copy of the order shall be transmitted forthwith—

(a) where the proceedings in respect of the defendant have been transferred to the Crown Court for trial or where the defendant has been committed to the Crown Court to be sentenced or otherwise dealt with, to the appropriate officer of the Crown Court;

(b) in any other case, to the justices' chief executive for the court which committed the defendant.

(11) Where in pursuance of an order of the High Court or the Crown Court a person is released on bail in any criminal proceeding pending the determination of an appeal to the High Court or the Supreme Court or an application for a quashing order, then, upon the abandonment of the appeal or application, or upon the decision of the High Court or the Supreme Court being given, any justice (being a justice acting for the same petty sessions area as the magistrates' court by which that person was convicted or sentenced) may issue process for enforcing the decision in respect of which such appeal or application was brought or, as the case may be, the decision of the High Court or the Supreme Court.

(12) If an applicant to the High Court in any criminal proceedings is refused bail, the applicant shall not be entitled to make a fresh application for bail to any other judge or to a Divisional Court.

(13) The record required by s.5 of the Bail Act to be made by the High Court shall be made by including in the file relating to the case in question a copy of the relevant order of the Court and shall contain the particulars set out in Form No.98 or 98A in PD 4, whichever is appropriate, except that in the case of a decision to withhold bail the record shall be made by inserting a statement of the decision on the court's copy of the relevant claim form and including it in the file relating to the case in question.

(14) In the case of a person whose return or surrender is sought under the Extradition Act 1989, this rule shall apply as if references to the defendant were references to that person and references to the prosecutor were references to the state seeking the return or surrender of that person.

Estreat of recognisances

RSC Ord.79 r.8

(1) No recognisance acknowledged in or removed into the Queen's Bench Division shall be estreated without the order of a judge.

(2) Every application to estreat a recognisance in the Queen's Bench Division must be made by claim form and will be heard by a judge and must be supported by a witness statement or affidavit showing in what manner the breach has been committed and proving that the claim form was duly served.

(2A) When it issues the claim form the court will fix a date for the hearing of the application.

(3) A claim form under this rule must be served at least two clear days before the day named therein for the hearing.

(4) On the hearing of the application the judge may, and if requested by any party shall, direct any issue of fact in dispute to be tried by a jury.

(5) If it appears to the judge that a default has been made in performing the conditions of the recognisance, the judge may order the recognisance to be estreated.

Release of appellant on bail

RSC Ord.109 r.3

(1) Where, in the case of an appeal under s.13 of the Administration of Justice Act 1960, to a Divisional Court or to the Supreme Court from a Divisional Court, the appellant is in custody, the High Court may order his release on his giving security (whether by recognisance, with or without sureties, or otherwise and for such reasonable sum as the court may fix) for his appearance, within 10 days after the judgment of the Divisional Court or, as the case may be, of the Supreme Court, on the appeal before the court from whose order or decision the appeal is brought unless the order or decision is reversed by that judgment.

(2) Ord.79 r.9(1) to (6) and (8) shall apply in relation to an application to the High Court for bail pending an appeal under the said s.13 to which this r.applies, and to the admission of a person to bail in pursuance of an order made on the application, as they apply in relation to an application to that court for bail in criminal proceedings, and to the admission of a person to bail in pursuance of an order made on the application, but with the substitution, for references to the defendant, of references to the appellant, and, for references to the prosecutor, of references to the court officer of the court from whose order or decision the appeal is brought and to the parties to the proceedings in that court who are directly affected by the appeal.

Release of appellant on bail by the court of appeal

RSC Ord.109 r.4

(1) Where, in the case of an appeal under s.13 of the Administration of Justice Act 1960, to the Court of Appeal or to the Supreme Court from the Court of Appeal, the appellant is in custody, the Court of Appeal may order his release on his giving security (whether by recognisance, with or without sureties, or otherwise and for such reasonable sum as that court may fix) for his appearance within 10 days after the judgment of the Court of Appeal or, as the case may be, of the Supreme Court on the appeal shall have been given, before the court from whose order of decision the appeal is brought unless the order or decision is reversed by that judgment.

(2) An application for the release of a person under para.(1) pending an appeal to the Court of Appeal or the Supreme Court under the said s.13 must be made in accordance with CPR Pt 23, and the application notice must, at least 24 hours before the day named therein for the hearing, be served on the court from whose order or decision the appeal is brought and on all parties to the proceedings in that court who are directly affected by the appeal.

(3) Ord.79 rr.9 (6), (6A) and (8) shall apply in relation to the grant of bail under this rule by the Court of Appeal in a case of criminal contempt of court as they apply in relation to the grant of bail in criminal proceedings by the High Court, but with the substitution for references to a judge of references to the Court of Appeal and for references to the defendant of references to the appellant.

(4) When granting bail under this rule in a case of civil contempt of court, the Court of Appeal may order that the recognisance or other security to be given by the appellant or the recognisance of any surety shall be given before any person authorised by virtue of

s.119 (1) of the Magistrates' Courts Act to take a recognisance where a magistrates' court having power to take it has, instead of taking it, fixed the amount in which the principal and his sureties, if any, are to be bound. An order by the Court of Appeal granting bail is aforesaid must be in Form 98 in PD 4 with the necessary adaptations.

(5) Where in pursuance of an order of the Court of Appeal under para.(4) of this rule a recognisance is entered into or other security given before any person, it shall be the duty of that person to cause the recognisance of the appellant or any surety or, as the case may be, a statement of the other security given, to be transmitted forthwith to the justices' chief executive for the court which committed the appellant; and a copy of such recognisance or statement shall at the same time be sent to the governor or keeper of the prison or other place of detention in which the appellant is detained, unless the recognisance or security was given before such governor or keeper.

(6) The powers conferred on the Court of Appeal by paras (1), (3) and (4) of this rule may be exercised by a single judge.

See also **Drinking banning order**, **Housing Act 1996 injunction**, and **Quashing of an acquittal**.

BANK HOLIDAY

Pt 6 r.6.2

A bank holiday under the Banking and Financial Dealings Act 1971 in the part of the United Kingdom where service is to take place.

BANKRUPTCY

See **Bankruptcy Court**, **Bankruptcy Petition**, **Insolvency proceedings**, **Personal insolvency**, **Statutory demand**, and **Validation order**.

BANKRUPTCY COURT

The Bankruptcy Court deals with all bankruptcy petitions which may be presented in the London insolvency district.

Creditors and debtors' petitions below the value of £50,000 and £100,000 respectively are dealt with as county court matter. For this purpose the Central London County Court sits at the Thomas More Building, Royal Courts of Justice, where petitions will continue to be issued and heard.

There are cases where, notwithstanding these monetary limits, the proceedings will continue to be presented in the High Court:

(a) where the bankruptcy petition is being presented against a member of a partnership being wound up by the High Court in London;

(b) where the debtor is not resident in England and Wales and has not carried on business or resided in England and Wales in the 6 months before the presentation of the petition; and

(c) where the petitioner is unable to determine the debtor's place of residence and place of business.

(d) Applications to set aside statutory demands.

(e) Post-bankruptcy applications, the purpose of which is to obtain information about or achieve realisation of the bankrupt's assets.

(f) Public examinations and applications for the suspension of the bankrupt's discharge period.

(g) Applications for permission to act as director where the applicant is an undischarged bankrupt.

BANKRUPTCY PETITION

Listing of petitions

PD Insolvency Proceedings para.14.1.1

All petitions presented will be listed under the name of the debtor unless the court directs otherwise.

Content of petitions

PD IP para.14.2.1

The attention of practitioners is drawn to the following points—
(1) A creditor's petition does not require dating, signing or witnessing but must be verified in accordance with r.6.12.
(2) In the heading it is only necessary to recite the debtor's name, e.g. Re John William Smith or Re JW Smith (Male). Any alias or trading name will appear in the body of the petition.

PD IP para.14.2.2

Where the petition is based solely on a statutory demand, only the debt claimed in the demand may be included in the petition.

PD IP para.14.2.3

The attention of practitioners is also drawn to rr.6.7 and 6.8, and in particular to r.6.8(1) where the 'aggregate sum' is made up of a number of debts.

PD IP para.14.2.4

The date of service of the statutory demand should be recited as follows—
(1) In the case of personal service, the date of service as set out in the certificate of service should be recited and whether service is effected before/after 17.00 on Monday to Friday or at any time on a Saturday or a Sunday.
(2) In the case of substituted service (other than by advertisement), the date alleged in the certificate of service should be recited.
(3) In the strictly limited case of service by advertisement under r.6.3, the date to be alleged is the date of the advertisement's appearance or, as the case may be, its first appearance (see rr 6.3(3) and 6.11(8)).

Searches

PD IP para.14.3.1

The petitioning creditor [means the person seeking recognition or enforcement of an award]shall, before presenting a petition, conduct a search for petitions presented against the debtor in the previous 18 months (a) in the Royal Courts of Justice, (b) in the Central London County Court and (c) in any county court which he believes is or was within that period the debtor's own county court within the meaning of r.6.9A(3) and shall include the certificate [set out in this paragraph] at the end of the petition.

Deposit

PD IP para.14.4.1

The deposit will be taken by the court and forwarded to the Official Receiver. In the Royal Courts of Justice the petition fee and deposit should be paid in the Fee Room, which will record the receipt and will impress two entries on the original petition, one in respect of the court fee and the other in respect of the deposit. In a District Registry or a county court, the petition fee and deposit should be handed to the duly authorised officer of the court's staff who will record its receipt.

PD IP para.14.4.2

In all cases cheque(s) for the whole amount should be made payable to 'HM Courts and Tribunals Service' or 'HMCTS'.

Certificates of continuing debt and of notice of adjournment

PD IP para.14.5.1

On the hearing of a petition where a bankruptcy order is sought, in order to satisfy the court that the debt on which the petition is founded has not been paid or secured or compounded for the court will normally accept as sufficient a certificate signed by the person representing the petitioning creditor in the form [set out in this paragraph].

PD IP para.14.5.2

For convenience, in the Royal Courts of Justice this certificate is incorporated in the attendance sheet for the parties to complete when they come to court and which is filed after the hearing. A fresh certificate will be required on each adjourned hearing.

PD IP para.14.5.3

On any adjourned hearing of a petition where a bankruptcy order is sought, in order to satisfy the court that the petitioner has complied with r.6.29, the petitioner will be required to file evidence of the date on which, manner in which and address to which notice of the making of the order of adjournment and of the venue for the adjourned hearing has been sent to—
  (1) the debtor, and
  (2) any creditor who has given notice under r.6.23 but was not present at the hearing when the order for adjournment was made or was present at the hearing but the date of the adjourned hearing was not fixed at that hearing. For convenience, in the Royal Courts of Justice this certificate is incorporated in the attendance sheet [set out in this papragraph] for the parties to complete when they come to court and which is filed after the hearing.
A fresh certificate will be required on each adjourned hearing.

Extension of hearing date of petition

PD IP para.14.6.1

Late applications for extension of hearing dates under r.6.28, and failure to attend on the listed hearing of a petition, will be dealt with as follows—
  (1) If an application is submitted less than two clear working days before the hearing date (for example, later than Monday for Thursday, or Wednesday for Monday) the costs of the application will not be allowed under r.6.28(3).
  (2) If the petition has not been served and no extension has been granted by the time fixed for the hearing of the petition, and if no one attends for the hearing, the petition may be dismissed or re-listed for hearing about 21 days later. The court will notify the petitioning creditor's solicitors (or the petitioning creditor in person), and any known supporting or opposing creditors or their solicitors, of the new date and times. Written evidence should then be filed on behalf of the petitioning creditor explaining fully the reasons for the failure to apply for an extension or to appear at the hearing, and (if appropriate) giving reasons why the petition should not be dismissed.
  (3) On the re-listed hearing the court may dismiss the petition if not satisfied it should be adjourned or a further extension granted.

PD IP para.14.6.2

All applications for an extension should include a statement of the date fixed for the hearing of the petition.

PD IP para.14.6.3

The petitioning creditor should contact the court (by solicitors or in person) on or before the hearing date to ascertain whether the application has reached the file and been dealt with. It should not be assumed that an extension will be granted.

Substituted service of bankruptcy petitions

PD IP para.14.7.1

In most cases evidence that the steps set out in para.13.3.4 have been taken will suffice to justify an order for substituted service of a bankruptcy petition.

See **Administration order, Bankruptcy Court, Insolvency proceedings, Personal insolvency, Statutory demand**, and **Validation order**.

BARRISTER

See **Counsel**.

BASE COSTS

Costs PD para.43.2

(2.2) Costs other than the amount of any **additional liability**.

BASE RATE

Glossary

The interest rate set by the Bank of England which is used as the basis for other banks' rates.

BILL OF COSTS

Form and content

[PD 47 paras 5.7 to 5.22 sets out in detail the form and content of a bill of costs.]

Electronic copy of bill of costs

PD 47 para.5.6

Where—
   (a) the bill of costs is capable of being copied electronically; and
   (b) before the detailed assessment hearing,
a paying party requests an electronic copy of the bill, the receiving party must supply the paying party with a copy in its native format (for example, in Excel or an equivalent) free of charge not more than seven days after receipt of the request.

BILLS OF SALE

Applications under s.14 of the Bills of Sale Act 1878

PD 8A para.10A.1

This paragraph applies to an application under s.14 of the Bills of Sale Act 1878 for an order to rectify an omission or mis-statement in relation to the registration, or renewal of the registration, of a bill of sale—
   (1) by inserting in the register the true name, residence or occupation of a person; or
   (2) by extending the time for registration of the bill of sale or an affidavit of its renewal.

PD 8A para.10A.2

The application must be made—
   (1) by claim form under Pt 8; or
   (2) by witness statement.

PD 8A para.10A.3

Where the application is made by witness statement—
   (1) Part 23 applies to the application;
   (2) the witness statement constitutes the application notice under that Part;
   (3) the witness statement does not need to be served on any other person; and
   (4) the application will normally be dealt with without a hearing.

PD 8A para.10A.4

The application must set out—
    (1) the particulars of the bill of sale and of the omission or mis-statement; and
    (2) the grounds on which the application is made.

PD 8A para.10A.5

The application must be made to a Master of the Queen's Bench Division and accompanied by payment of the prescribed fee.

Applications under s.15 of the Bills of Sale Act 1878

PD 8A para.11.1

This paragraph applies where an application is made under s.15 of the Bills of Sale Act 1878 for an order that a memorandum of satisfaction be written on a registered copy of a bill of sale.

PD 8A para.11.2

If the person entitled to the benefit of the bill of sale has not consented to the satisfaction, the claim form—
    (1) must be served on that person; and
    (2) must be supported by evidence that the debt (if any) for which the bill of sale was made has been satisfied or discharged.

PD 8A para.11.3

If the person entitled to the benefit of the bill of sale has consented to the satisfaction, the application may be made by—
    (1) claim form under Pt 8; or
    (2) witness statement.

PD 8A para.11.4

Where para.11.3 applies and the application is made by Pt 8 claim form, the claim form—
    (1) must contain details of the consent;
    (2) must be supported by a witness statement by a person who witnessed the consent verifying the signature on it; and
    (3) must not be served on any person other than the person entitled to the benefit of the bill of sale.

PD 8A para.11.5

Where para.11.3 applies and the application is made by witness statement—
    (1) Part 23 will apply to the application;
    (2) the witness statement will constitute the application notice under that Part;
    (3) the witness statement does not need to be served on any other person; and
    (4) the application will normally be dealt with without a hearing.

Applications under s.16 of the Bills of Sale Act 1878

PD 8A para.11A.1

This paragraph applies to an application under s.16 of the Bills of Sale Act 1878 for a search of the bills of sale register and for a certificate of the results of the search.

PD 8A para.11A.2

The application must be made—
- (1) by claim form under Pt 8; or
- (2) by written request.

PD 8A para.11A.3

The application must give sufficient information to enable the relevant bill of sale to be identified.

PD 8A para.11A.4

The application must be made to a Master of the Queen's Bench Division and accompanied by payment of the prescribed fee.

BLOOD TESTS IN DETERMINING PATERNITY

PD 23B para.1.1

In this section—
- (2) 'direction' means a direction under s.20(1) of the [Family Law Reform Act 1969] made in any proceedings in which a person's parentage falls to be determined;
- (3) 'responsible adult' means—
  - (a) in relation to a person under 16 to whom subpara.(b) does not apply, the person having care and control of him;
  - (b) in relation to a person who lacks capacity (within the meaning of the Mental Capacity Act 2005) to give his consent to tests—
    - (i) a person having power under that Act to give consent on his behalf; or

PD 23B para.1.2

Where an application is made for a direction in respect of a person who either—
- (a) is under 16; or
- (b) lacks capacity (within the meaning of the Mental Capacity Act 2005) to give his consent to the tests,

the application notice must state the name and address of the responsible adult.

PD 23B para.1.3

Unless the court orders otherwise—
- (1) the court will serve a copy of the application notice on every party to the proceedings other than the applicant; and

(2) the applicant must serve a copy of the application notice personally on any other person who would be directed to give samples[means bodily samples within the meaning of s.25 of the Act] and, where para.1.2 applies, on the responsible adult.

PD 23B para.1.4

Unless the court orders otherwise, where the court gives a direction—
(1) the court will serve a copy of the direction on every party to the proceedings;
(2) the applicant must serve a copy of the direction personally on any other person directed to give samples and, where para.1.2 applies, on the responsible adult; and
(3) further consideration of the proceedings shall be adjourned until the court receives a report of the tests [means scientific tests within the meaning of s.25 of the Act] carried out or samples taken.

PD 23B para.1.5

When the court receives the report of the tests carried out or samples taken, the court officer shall send a copy of the report to—
(1) every party to the proceedings;
(2) the responsible adult where para.1.2 applies; and
(3) every other person directed to give samples.

BRITISH ISLANDS ORDER

RSC Ord.115 r.24

(f) a Scottish order, a Northern Ireland order or an Islands order as defined in para.12 of Sch.4 of the Drug Trafficking Act 1994.

BUDGET

Glossary

An estimate of the reasonable and proportionate costs (including disbursements) which a party intends to incur in the proceedings.

BUILDING DISPUTES

Small claims track

PD 27 Appendix A

Information and documentation the court usually needs in the case of building disputes, repairs, goods sold and similar contractual claims (where the information or document is available):
Any written contract; photographs; any plans; a list of works complained of; a list of any outstanding works; any relevant estimate, invoice or receipt including any relating to repairs to each of the defects; invoices for work done or goods supplied; estimates for work to be completed; a valuation of work done to date.

BUNDLE OF AUTHORITIES

Court of Appeal

PD 52 para.15.11

(1) Once the parties have been notified of the date fixed for the hearing, the appellant's advocate must, after consultation with his opponent, file a bundle containing photocopies of the authorities upon which each side will rely at the hearing.
(2) The bundle of authorities should, in general—
   (a) have the relevant passages of the authorities marked;
   (b) not include authorities for propositions not in dispute; and
   (c) not contain more than 10 authorities unless the scale of the appeal warrants more extensive citation.
(3) The bundle of authorities must be filed—
   (a) at least seven days before the hearing; or
   (b) where the period of notice of the hearing is less than seven days, immediately.
(4) If, through some oversight, a party intends, during the hearing, to refer to other authorities the parties may agree a second agreed bundle. The appellant's advocate must file this bundle at least 48 hours before the hearing commences.
(5) A bundle of authorities must bear a certification by the advocates responsible for arguing the case that the requirements of subparas (3) to (5) of para.5.10 have been complied with in respect of each authority included.

BUNDLE OF DOCUMENTS

See **Trial bundles**.

BUSINESS DAY

P6 r.6.2

(b) Any day except Saturday, Sunday, a bank holiday, Good Friday or Christmas Day.

BUSINESS NAME

Persons carrying on business in another name

PD 7A para.5C.1

This paragraph applies where—
   (1) a claim is brought against an individual;
   (2) that individual carries on a business within the jurisdiction (even if not personally within the jurisdiction); and
   (3) that business is carried on in a name other than that individual's own name ('the business name').

PD 7A para.5C.2

The claim may be brought against the business name as if it were the name of a partnership.

C

CCR

Pt 50 r.50(4)

County Court Rules 1981. A provision previously contained in the CCR and unless otherwise stated in the Schedules, to the CPR or the relevant PDs, applies only in the county court.

CPR

Pt 1 r.1.1(1)

The Civil Procedure Rules 1998 came into force on April 26, 1999. As at October 1, 2012, there have been 59 updates.

Pt 1 r.1.1

    (1) These rules are a new procedural code with the **overriding objective** of enabling the court to deal with cases justly.

Application of the CPR

Pt 2 r.2.1

    (1) Subject to para.(2), these rules apply to all proceedings in—
        (a) county courts;
        (b) the High Court; and
        (c) the Civil Division of the Court of Appeal.
    (2) These rules do not apply to proceedings of the kinds specified in the first column of the following table (proceedings for which rules may be made under the enactments specified in the second column) except to the extent that they are applied to those proceedings by another enactment—

	Proceedings	Enactments
1.	Insolvency proceedings	Insolvency Act 1986 ss.411 and 412
2.	Non-contentious or common form probate proceedings	Supreme Court Act 1981 s.127

	Proceedings	Enactments
3.	Proceedings in the High Court when acting as a Prize Court	Prize Courts Act 1894 s.3
4.	Proceedings before the Court of Protection	Mental Capacity Act 2005 s.51
5.	Family proceedings	Matrimonial and Family Proceedings Act 1984 s.40
6.	Adoption proceedings	Adoption Act 1976 s.66 or Adoption and Children Act 2002 s.141(c)
7.	Election petitions in the High Court	Representation of the People Act 1983 s.182

Error in procedure

Pt 3 r.3.10

Where there has been an error of procedure such as a failure to comply with a rule or PD—
  (a) the error does not invalidate any step taken in the proceedings unless the court so orders; and
  (b) the court may make an order to remedy the error.

CALDERBANK LETTER

See **Part 36 offer.**

CASE ALLOCATION

See **Allocation.**

CASE MANAGEMENT

Pt 1 r.1.4

  (1) The court must further the **overriding objective** by actively managing cases.
  (2) Active case management includes—
    (a) encouraging the parties to co-operate with each other in the conduct of the proceedings;
    (b) identifying the issues at an early stage;
    (c) deciding promptly which issues need full investigation and trial and accordingly disposing summarily of the others;
    (d) deciding the order in which issues are to be resolved;
    (e) encouraging the parties to use an alternative dispute resolution procedure if the court considers that appropriate and facilitating the use of such procedure;

(f) helping the parties to settle the whole or part of the case;

(g) fixing timetables or otherwise controlling the progress of the case;

(h) considering whether the likely benefits of taking a particular step justify the cost of taking it;

(i) dealing with as many aspects of the case as it can on the same occasion;

(j) dealing with the case without the parties needing to attend at court;

(k) making use of technology; and

(l) giving directions to ensure that the trial of a case proceeds quickly and efficiently.

Court's discretion as to where it deals with cases

Pt 2 r.2.7

The court may deal with a case at any place that it considers appropriate.

Court's general powers of management

Pt 3 r.3.1

(1) The list of powers in this rule is in addition to any powers given to the court by any other rule or PD or by any other enactment or any powers it may otherwise have.

(2) Except where these rules provide otherwise, the court may—

(a) extend or shorten the time for compliance with any rule, PD or court order (even if an application for extension is made after the time for compliance has expired);

(b) adjourn or bring forward a hearing;

(c) require a party or a party's legal representative to attend the court;

(d) hold a hearing and receive evidence by telephone or by using any other method of direct oral communication;

(e) direct that part of any proceedings (such as a counterclaim) be dealt with as separate proceedings;

(f) stay the whole or part of any proceedings or judgment either generally or until a specified date or event;

(g) consolidate proceedings;

(h) try two or more claims on the same occasion;

(i) direct a separate trial of any issue;

(j) decide the order in which issues are to be tried;

(k) exclude an issue from consideration;

(l) dismiss or give judgment on a claim after a decision on a preliminary issue;

(ll) order any party to file and serve an estimate of costs;

(m) take any other step or make any other order for the purpose of managing the case and furthering the overriding objective.

(3) When the court makes an order, it may—

(a) make it subject to conditions, including a condition to pay a sum of money into court; and

(b) specify the consequence of failure to comply with the order or a condition.

(4) Where the court gives directions it will take into account whether or not a party has complied with the PD (Pre-Action Conduct) and any relevant pre-action protocol.

(5) The court may order a party to pay a sum of money into court if that party has, without good reason, failed to comply with a rule, PD or a relevant pre-action protocol.

(6) When exercising its power under para.(5) the court must have regard to—

(a) the amount in dispute; and

(b) the costs which the parties have incurred or which they may incur.

(6A) Where a party pays money into court following an order under para.(3) or (5), the money shall be security for any sum payable by that party to any other party in the proceedings.

(7) A power of the court under these rules to make an order includes a power to vary or revoke the order.

(8) The court may contact the parties from time to time in order to monitor compliance with directions. The parties must respond promptly to any such enquiries from the court.

Court's power to make order of its own initiative

Pt 3 r.3.3

(1) Except where a rule or some other enactment provides otherwise, the court may exercise its powers on an application or of its own initiative.

(Part 23 sets out the procedure for making an application).

(2) Where the court proposes to make an order of its own initiative—
  (a) it may give any person likely to be affected by the order an opportunity to make representations; and
  (b) where it does so it must specify the time by and the manner in which the representations must be made.

(3) Where the court proposes—
  (a) to make an order of its own initiative; and
  (b) to hold a hearing to decide whether to make the order,
  it must give each party likely to be affected by the order at least three days' notice of the hearing.

(4) The court may make an order of its own initiative, without hearing the parties or giving them an opportunity to make representations.

(5) Where the court has made an order under para.(4)—
  (a) a party affected by the order may apply to have it set aside, varied or stayed; and
  (b) the order must contain a statement of the right to make such an application.

(6) An application under para.(5)(a) must be made—
  (a) within such period as may be specified by the court; or
  (b) if the court does not specify a period, not more than seven days after the date on which the order was served on the party making the application.

(7) If the court of its own initiative strikes out a statement of case or dismisses an application, (including an application for permission to appeal or for permission to apply for judicial review) and it considers that the claim or application is totally without merit—
  (a) the court's order must record that fact; and
  (b) the court must at the same time consider whether it is appropriate to make a civil restraint order.

CASE MANAGEMENT CONFERENCE

Multi-track

PD 29 para.5.1

The court will at any case management conference—
  (1) review the steps which the parties have taken in the preparation of the case, and in particular their compliance with any directions that the court may have given,

    (2) decide and give directions about the steps which are to be taken to secure the progress of the claim in accordance with the overriding objective, and

    (3) ensure as far as it can that all agreements that can be reached between the parties about the matters in issue and the conduct of the claim are made and recorded.

PD 29 para.5.2

    (1) Rule 29.3(2) provides that where a party has a legal representative, a representative familiar with the case and with sufficient authority to deal with any issues that are likely to arise must attend case management conferences and pre-trial reviews.

    (2) That person should be someone who is personally involved in the conduct of the case, and who has the authority and information to deal with any matter which may reasonably be expected to be dealt with at such a hearing, including the fixing of the timetable, the identification of issues and matters of evidence.

    (3) Where the inadequacy of the person attending or of his instructions leads to the adjournment of a hearing, the court will expect to make a wasted costs order.

PD 29 para.5.3

The topics the court will consider at a case management conference are likely to include:

    (1) whether the claimant has made clear the claim he is bringing, in particular the amount he is claiming, so that the other party can understand the case he has to meet,

    (2) whether any amendments are required to the claim, a statement of case or any other document,

    (3) what disclosure of documents, if any, is necessary,

    (4) what expert evidence is reasonably required in accordance with r.35.1 and how and when that evidence should be obtained and disclosed,

    (5) what factual evidence should be disclosed,

    (6) what arrangements should be made about the giving of clarification or further information and the putting of questions to experts, and

    (7) whether it will be just and will save costs to order a split trial or the trial of one or more preliminary issues.

PD 29 para.5.4

In all cases the court will set a timetable for the steps it decides are necessary to be taken. These steps may include the holding of a case management conference or a pre-trial review, and the court will be alert to perform its duty to fix a trial date or period as soon as it can.

PD 29 para.5.5

    (1) The court will not at this stage give permission to use expert evidence unless it can identify each expert by name or field in its order and say whether his evidence is to be given orally or by the use of his report.

    (2) A party who obtains expert evidence before obtaining a direction about it does so at his own risk as to costs, except where he obtained the evidence in compliance with a pre-action protocol.

PD 29 para.5.6

To assist the court, the parties and their legal advisers should:

    (1) ensure that all documents that the court is likely to ask to see (including witness statements and experts' reports) are brought to the hearing,

    (2) consider whether the parties should attend,

(3) consider whether a **case summary** will be useful, and

(4) consider what orders each wishes to be made and give notice of them to the other parties.

PD 29 para.5.8

(1) Where a party wishes to obtain an order not routinely made at a case management conference and believes that his application will be opposed, he should issue and serve the application in time for it to be heard at the case management conference.

(2) If the time allowed for the case management conference is likely to be insufficient for the application to be heard he should inform the court at once so that a fresh date can be fixed.

(3) A costs sanction may be imposed on a party who fails to comply with subpara.(1) or (2).

PD 29 para.5.9

At a case management conference the court may also consider whether the case ought to be tried by a High Court judge or by a judge who specialises in that type of claim and how that question will be decided. In that case the claim may need to be transferred to another court.

See **Technology and Construction Court claims**.

CASE MEMORANDUM

PD 58 para.10.8

A short and uncontroversial summary of what the case is about and of its material case history case management tracks.

CASE SUMMARY

Multi-track

PD 29 para.5.7

(1) A case summary:
   (a) should be designed to assist the court to understand and deal with the questions before it,
   (b) should set out a brief chronology of the claim, the issues of fact which are agreed or in dispute and the evidence needed to decide them,
   (c) should not normally exceed 500 words in length, and
   (d) should be prepared by the claimant and agreed with the other parties if possible.

CENTRAL OFFICE OF THE HIGH COURT

PD 2A para.1

The Central Office [is] divided into such departments, and the business performed in the Central Office shall be distributed among the departments in such manner, as is set out in the **Queen's Bench Division Guide**.

CERTIFICATE OF SERVICE

Pt 6 r.6.29

Where a rule, PD or court order requires a certificate of service, the certificate must state the details required by the following table

	Method of Service	Details to be certified
1.	Personal service	Date and time of personal service.
2.	First class post, document exchange or other service which provides for delivery on the next business day	Date of posting, or leaving with, delivering to or collection by the relevant service provider.
3.	Delivery of document to or leaving it at a permitted place	Date and time of when the document was delivered to or left at the permitted place.
4.	Fax	Date and time of completion of the transmission.
5.	Other electronic method	Date and time of sending the e-mail or other electronic transmission.
6.	Alternative method or place permitted by the court	As required by the court.

Certificate of service where claimant serves the claim form

Pt 6 r.6.17

(2) Where the claimant serves the claim form, the claimant—
   (a) must file a certificate of service within 21 days of service of the particulars of claim, unless all the defendants to the proceedings have filed acknowledgments of service within that time; and
   (b) may not obtain judgment in default under Pt 12 unless a certificate of service has been filed.
(3) The certificate of service must state—
   (a) where rr.6.7 [Service on a solicitor or European Lawyer within the UK or in any other EEA state], 6.8 [Service of the claim form where before service the defendant gives an address at which the defendant may be served], 6.9 [Service of the claim form where the defendant does not give an address at which the defendant may be served] or 6.10 [Service of the claim on the Crown] applies, the category of address at which the claimant believes the claim form has been served; and
   (b) the details set out in the following Table.

	Method of service	Details to be certified
1.	Personal service	Date of personal service.
2.	First class post, document exchange or other service which provides for delivery on the next business day	Date of posting, or
		leaving with, delivering to or collection by the relevant service provider.
3.	Delivery of document to or leaving it at a permitted place	Date when the document was delivered to or left at the permitted place.
4.	Fax	Date of completion of the transmission.
5.	Other electronic method	Date of sending the e-mail or other electronic transmission.
6.	Alternative method or place	As required by the court.

PD 6A para.7.1

Where, pursuant to r.6.17(2), the claimant files a certificate of service, the claimant is not required to and should not file—
(1) a further copy of the claim form with the certificate of service; and
(2) a further copy of—
(a) the particulars of claim (where not included in the claim form); or
(b) any document attached to the particulars of claim,
with the certificate of service where that document has already been filed with the court.
(Rule 7.4 requires the claimant to file a copy of the particulars of claim (where served separately from the claim form) within seven days of service on the defendant.)

Statement of truth

Pt 22 r.22.1

(1) The following [document] must be verified by a statement of truth—
(f) a certificate of service.

Supply of documents from court records

PD 5A para.4.2A

A party to proceedings may, unless the court orders otherwise, obtain from the records of the court a copy of—

(e) a certificate of service, other than a certificate of service of an application notice or order in relation to a type of application mentioned in subpara.(h)(i) or (ii);

See also **Service of documents**.

CERTIFICATE OF SUITABILITY

PD 21 para.2.2

A person who wishes to become a litigation friend without a court order pursuant to r.21.5(3) must file a certificate of suitability in Practice Form N235—
  (a) stating that he consents to act,
  (b) stating that he knows or believes that the [claimant] [defendant] [is a child][lacks capacity to conduct the proceedings],
  (c) in the case of a protected party, stating the grounds of his belief and, if his belief is based upon medical opinion or the opinion of another suitably qualified expert, attaching any relevant document to the certificate,
  (d) stating that he can fairly and competently conduct proceedings on behalf of the child or protected party and has no interest adverse to that of the child or protected party, and
  (e) where the child or protected party is a claimant, undertaking to pay any costs which the child or protected party may be ordered to pay in relation to the proceedings, subject to any right he may have to be repaid from the assets of the child or protected party.

PD 21 para.2.3

The certificate of suitability must be verified by a **statement of truth**.

See **Litigation friend**.

CERTIORARI

See **Quashing order**.

CHANCEL REPAIRS ACT 1932

PD 56 para.12.1

The claimant in a claim to recover the sum required to put a chancel in proper repair must use the Pt 8 procedure.

PD 56 para.12.2

A notice to repair under s.2 of the Chancel Repairs Act 1932 must—
  (1) state—
    (a) the responsible authority by whom the notice is given;
    (b) the chancel alleged to be in need of repair;
    (c) the repairs alleged to be necessary; and
    (d) the grounds on which the person to whom the notice is addressed is alleged to be liable to repair the chancel; and
  (2) call upon the person to whom the notice is addressed to put the chancel in proper repair.

PD 56 para.12.3

The notice must be served in accordance with Pt 6.

See **Service of documents**.

CHANCERY DISTRICT REGISTRIES

There are Chancery district registries at Birmingham, Bristol, Caernarfon, Cardiff, Leeds, Liverpool, Manchester, Mold, Newcastle upon Tyne, and Preston.

CHANCERY DIVISION

The Chancery Division is one of the three divisions of the High Court of Justice. The areas of work that it deals with are business and property related disputes, competition, general chancery claims, patents claims, intellectual property claims, companies claims, insolvency claims, trust claims, probate claims and appeals to the High Court, Chancery Division from the lower court.

The head of the Chancery Division is the Chancellor of the High Court.

CHANCERY GUIDE

This guide provides additional practical information not already contained in the CPR or the PDs supplementing them.

This guide does not have the status of a PD. So it does not have the force of law. But failure to comply with this guide may influence the way in which the court exercises its powers under the CPR, including the making of adverse costs orders. In case of any conflict between this guide and a rule or PD, the rule or PD prevails.

CHANCERY MASTERS' PRACTICE FORMS

PD 4 para 4.1

Practice Forms that were previously known as Chancery Masters' Practice Forms.

PD 4 para.4.2

Where a rule permits, a party intending to use a witness statement as an alternative to an affidavit should amend any form in this Table to be used in connection with that rule so that 'witness statement' replaces 'affidavit' wherever it appears in the form.

PD 4 para.4.3

These forms are reproduced in the Appendix to the Chancery's Bench Guide, in practitioners' text books and on Her Majesty's Courts and Tribunals Service website.

CHANCERY PROCEEDINGS

PD 2B para.5.1

In proceedings in the Chancery Division, a Master or a district judge may not deal with the following without the consent of the Chancellor of the High Court—

- (a) approving compromises (other than applications under the Inheritance (Provision for Family and Dependants) Act 1975) (i) on behalf of a person under disability where that person's interest in a fund, or if there is no fund, the maximum amount of the claim, exceeds £100,000 and (ii) on behalf of absent, unborn and unascertained persons;
- (b) making declarations, except in plain cases;
- (c) making final orders under s.1(1) of the Variation of Trusts Act 1958, except for the removal of protective trusts where the interest of the principal beneficiary has not failed or determined;
- (d) where the proceedings are brought by a Pt 8 claim form, seeking determination of any question of law or as to the construction of a document which is raised by the claim form;
- (e) giving permission to executors, administrators and trustees to bring or defend proceedings or to continue the prosecution or defence of proceedings, and granting an indemnity for costs out of the trust estate, except in plain cases;
- (f) granting an indemnity for costs out of the assets of a company on the application of minority shareholders bringing a derivative action, except in plain cases;
- (g) making an order for rectification, except for—
    - (i) rectification of the register under the Land Registration Act 1925; or
    - (ii) alteration or rectification of the register under the Land Registration Act 2002, in plain cases;
- (h) making orders to vacate entries in the register under the Land Charges Act 1972, except in plain cases;
- (i) making final orders on applications under s.19 of the Leasehold Reform Act 1967, s.48 of the Administration of Justice Act 1985 and ss.21 and 25 of the Law of Property Act 1969;
- (j) making final orders under the Landlord and Tenant Acts 1927 and 1954, except (i) by consent, and (ii) orders for interim rents under ss.24A to 24D of the 1954 Act;
- (k) making orders in proceedings in the Patents Court except—
    - (i) orders by way of settlement, except settlement of procedural disputes;
    - (ii) applications for extension of time;
    - (iii) applications for permission to serve out of the jurisdiction;
    - (iv) applications for security for costs;
    - (v) other matters as directed by a judge of the court; and
    - (vi) enforcement of money judgments.

PD 2B para.5.2

A Master or District Judge may only give directions for early trial after consulting the Judge in charge of the relevant list.

PD 2B para.5.3

Where a winding-up order has been made against a company, any proceedings against the company by or on behalf of debenture holders may be dealt with, at the Royal Courts of Justice, by a Registrar and, in a District Registry with insolvency jurisdiction, by a District Judge.

CHANGE OF PARTIES

See **Parties**.

CHANGE OF SOLICITORS

See **Solicitor**.

CHARGING ORDER

Pt 73 r.73.2

This section applies to an application by a judgment creditor for a charging order under—
- (a) section 1 of the [Charging Orders Act 1979]; or
- (b) regulation 50 of the [Council Tax (Administration & Enforcement) Regulations 1992].

Application for charging order

Pt 73 r.73.3

(1) An application for a charging order may be made without notice.
(2) An application for a charging order must be issued in the court which made the judgment or order which it is sought to enforce, unless—
    (a) the proceedings have since been transferred to a different court, in which case the application must be issued in that court;
    (b) the application is made under the 1992 Regulations, in which event it must be issued in the county court for the district in which the relevant dwelling (as defined in reg.50(3)(b) of those Regulations) is situated;
    (c) the application is for a charging order over an interest in a fund in court, in which event it must be issued in the court in which the claim relating to that fund is or was proceeding;
    (d) the application is to enforce a judgment or order of the High Court and it is required by s.1(2) of the 1979 Act to be made to a county court; or
    (e) the application is to enforce a judgment in Northampton County Court in respect of a designated money claim, in which event the application must be in accordance with s.2 of [PD] 70.
(3) Subject to para.(2), a judgment creditor may apply for a single charging order in respect of more than one judgment or order against the same debtor.
(4) The application notice must—
    (a) (i) be in the form; and
        (ii) contain the information,
        required by [PD 73] ; and
    (b) be verified by a statement of truth.

Application notice

PD 73 para.1.1

An application for a charging order must be made by filing an application notice in Practice Form N379 if the application relates to land, or N380 if the application relates to securities.

PD 73 para.1.2

The application notice must contain the following information—
    (1) the name and address of the judgment debtor;

(2) details of the judgment or order sought to be enforced;

(3) the amount of money remaining due under the judgment or order;

(4) if the judgment debt is payable by instalments, the amount of any instalments which have fallen due and remain unpaid;

(5) if the judgment creditor knows of the existence of any other creditors of the judgment debtor, their names and (if known) their addresses;

(6) identification of the asset or assets which it is intended to charge;

(7) details of the judgment debtor's interest in the asset; and

(8) the names and addresses of the persons on whom an interim charging order must be served under r.73.5(1).

PD 73 para.1.3

A judgment creditor may apply in a single application notice for charging orders over more than one asset, but if the court makes interim charging orders over more than one asset, it will draw up a separate order relating to each asset.

Interim charging order

Pt 73 r.73.4

(1) An application for a charging order will initially be dealt with by a judge without a hearing.

(2) The judge may make an order (an 'interim charging order')—

    (a) imposing a charge over the judgment debtor's interest in the asset to which the application relates; and

    (b) fixing a hearing to consider whether to make a final charging order as provided by r.73.8(2)(a).

Jurisdiction

PD 73 para.2

The jurisdiction of the High Court and the county court to make charging orders is set out in s.1(2) of the 1979 Act.

Transfer

PD 73 para.3

The court may, on an application by a judgment debtor who wishes to oppose an application for a charging order, transfer it to the court for the district where the judgment debtor resides or carries on business, or to another court.

Service of interim order

Pt 73 r.73.5

(1) Copies of the interim charging order, the application notice and any documents filed in support of it must, not less than 21 days before the hearing, be served on the following persons—

(a) the judgment debtor;

(b) such other creditors as the court directs;

(c) if the order relates to an interest under a trust, on such of the trustees as the court directs;

(d) if the interest charged is in securities other than securities held in court, then—

    (i) in the case of stock for which the Bank of England keeps the register, the Bank of England;

    (ii) in the case of government stock to which (i) does not apply, the keeper of the register;

    (iii) in the case of stock of any body incorporated within England and Wales, that body;

    (iv) in the case of stock of any body incorporated outside England and Wales or of any state or territory outside the UK, which is registered in a register kept in England and Wales, the keeper of that register;

    (v) in the case of units of any unit trust in respect of which a register of the unit holders is kept in England and Wales, the keeper of that register; and

(e) if the interest charged is in funds in court, the Accountant General at the Court Funds Office.

(2) If the judgment creditor serves the order, he must either—

(a) file a certificate of service not less than 2 days before the hearing; or

(b) produce a certificate of service at the hearing.

effect of interim order in relation to securities.

Pt 73 r.73.6

(1) If a judgment debtor disposes of his interest in any securities, while they are subject to an interim charging order which has been served on him, that disposition shall not, so long as that order remains in force, be valid as against the judgment creditor.

(2) A person served under r.73.5(1)(d) with an interim charging order relating to securities must not, unless the court gives permission—

(a) permit any transfer of any of the securities; or

(b) pay any dividend, interest or redemption payment relating to them.

(3) If a person acts in breach of para.(2), he will be liable to pay to the judgment creditor—

(a) the value of the securities transferred or the amount of the payment made (as the case may be); or

(b) if less, the amount necessary to satisfy the debt in relation to which the interim charging order was made.

Effect of interim order in relation to funds in court

Pt 73 r.73.7

If a judgment debtor disposes of his interest in funds in court while they are subject to an interim charging order which has been served on him and on the Accountant General in accordance with r.73.5(1), that disposition shall not, so long as that order remains in force, be valid as against the judgment creditor.

Further consideration of the application

Pt 73 r.73.8

(1) If any person objects to the court making a final charging order, he must—

(a) file; and

(b) serve on the applicant;
written evidence stating the grounds of his objections, not less than seven days before the hearing.
(2) At the hearing the court may—
    (a) make a final charging order confirming that the charge imposed by the interim charging order shall continue, with or without modification;
    (b) discharge the interim charging order and dismiss the application;
    (c) decide any issues in dispute between the parties, or between any of the parties and any other person who objects to the court making a final charging order; or
    (d) direct a trial of any such issues, and if necessary give directions.
(3) If the court makes a final charging order which charges securities other than securities held in court, the order will include a stop notice unless the court otherwise orders.
(Section III of this Part contains provisions about stop notices).
(4) Any order made at the hearing must be served on all the persons on whom the interim charging order was required to be served.

Discharge or variation of order

Pt 73 r.73.9

(1) Any application to discharge or vary a charging order must be made to the court which made the charging order.
(Section 3(5) of the 1979 Act and reg.51(4) of the 1992 Regulations provide that the court may at any time, on the application of the debtor, or of any person interested in any property to which the order relates, or (where the 1992 Regulations apply) of the authority, make an order discharging or varying the charging order).
(2) The court may direct that—
    (a) any interested person should be joined as a party to such an application; or
    (b) the application should be served on any such person.
(3) An order discharging or varying a charging order must be served on all the persons on whom the charging order was required to be served.

Enforcement of charging order by sale

Pt 73 r.73.10

(1) Subject to the provisions of any enactment, the court may, upon a claim by a person who has obtained a charging order over an interest in property, order the sale of the property to enforce the charging order.
(2) A claim for an order for sale under this rule should be made to the court which made the charging order, unless that court does not have jurisdiction to make an order for sale.
(A claim under this rule is a proceeding for the enforcement of a charge, and s.23(c) of the County Courts Act 1984 provides the extent of the county court's jurisdiction to hear and determine such proceedings).
(3) The claimant must use the Pt 8 procedure.
(4) A copy of the charging order must be filed with the claim form.
(5) The claimant's written evidence must include the information required by PD 73.

PD 73 para.4.1

A county court has jurisdiction to determine a claim under r.73.10 for the enforcement of a charging order if the amount owing under the charge does not exceed the county court limit.

PD 73 para.4.2

A claim in the High Court for an order for sale of land to enforce a charging order must be started in Chancery Chambers at the Royal Courts of Justice, or a Chancery district registry.
(There are Chancery district registries at Birmingham, Bristol, Caernarfon, Cardiff, Leeds, Liverpool, Manchester, Mold, Newcastle upon Tyne and Preston).

PD 73 para.4.3

The written evidence in support of a claim under r.73.10 must—
  (1) identify the charging order and the property sought to be sold;
  (2) state the amount in respect of which the charge was imposed and the amount due at the date of issue of the claim;
  (3) verify, so far as known, the debtor's title to the property charged;
  (4) state, so far as the claimant is able to identify—
      (a) the names and addresses of any other creditors who have a prior charge or other security over the property; and
      (b) the amount owed to each such creditor; and
  (5) give an estimate of the price which would be obtained on sale of the property.
  (6) if the claim relates to land, give details of every person who to the best of the claimant's knowledge is in possession of the property; and
  (7) if the claim relates to residential property—
      (a) state whether—
          (i) a land charge of Class F; or
          (ii) a notice under s.31(10) of the Family Law Act 1996, or under any provision of an Act which preceded that section,
      has been registered; and
      (b) if so, state—
          (i) on whose behalf the land charge or notice has been registered; and
          (ii) that the claimant will serve notice of the claim on that person.

PD 73 para.4.4

The claimant must take all reasonable steps to obtain the information required by para.4.3(4) before issuing the claim.

PD 73 para.4.5

Sample forms of orders for sale are set out in Appendix A to this PD for guidance. These are not prescribed forms of order and they may be adapted or varied by the court to meet the requirements of individual cases.

See **Partnership**.

CHARITY

Charity proceedings

Pt 64 r.64.5

  (1) [Section III of Part 64] applies to Charity proceedings [which has the same meaning as in s.33(8) of the Charities Act 1993].

Application for permission to take charity proceedings

Pt 64 r.64.6

(1) An application to the High Court under s.33(5) of the [Charities Act 1993] for permission to start charity proceedings must be made within 21 days after the refusal by the [Charity Commissioners for England and Wales] of an order authorising proceedings.

(2) The application must be made by issuing a Pt 8 claim form, which must contain the information specified in PD 64A.

(3) The Commissioners must be made defendants to the claim, but the claim form need not be served on them or on any other person.

(4) The judge considering the application may direct the Commissioners to file a written statement of their reasons for their decision.

(5) The court will serve on the applicant a copy of any statement filed under para.(4).

(6) The judge may either—
   (a) give permission without a hearing; or
   (b) fix a hearing.

PD 64A para.9.1

The claim form for an application under s.33(5) of the Act must state—
(1) the name, address and description of the applicant;
(2) details of the proceedings which he wishes to take;
(3) the date of the Commissioners' refusal to grant an order authorising the taking of proceedings;
(4) the grounds on which the applicant alleges that it is a proper case for taking proceedings; and
(5) if the application is made with the consent of any other party to the proposed proceedings, that fact.

PD 64A para.9.2

If the Commissioners have given reasons for refusing to grant an order, a copy of their reasons must be filed with the claim form.

Role of Attorney-General

PD 64A para.7

The Attorney General is a necessary party to all charity proceedings, other than any commenced by the Charity Commissioners, and must be joined as a defendant if he is not a claimant.

Service on charity commissioners or Attorney-General

PD 64A para.8

Any document required or authorised to be served on the Commissioners or the Attorney General must be served on the Treasury Solicitor in accordance with para.2.1 of PD 66.

CHILD

Pt 2 r.2.3

'Child' has the meaning given by r.21.1(2).

Pt 21 r.21.1

(2) A person under 18.

PD 21 para.1.2

In proceedings where one of the parties is a child, where—
  (1) the child has a litigation friend, the child should be referred to in the title to the proceedings as 'A.B. (a child by C.D. his litigation friend)'; or
  (2) the child is conducting the proceedings on his own behalf, the child should be referred to in the title as 'A.B. (a child)'.

Service on children and protected parties

Pt 6 r.6.25

(1) An application for an order appointing a **litigation friend** where a child or **protected party** has no litigation friend must be served in accordance with r.21.8(1) and (2).
(2) Any other document which would otherwise be served on a child or a protected party must be served on the litigation friend conducting the proceedings on behalf of the child or protected party.
(3) The court may make an order permitting a document to be served on the child or protected party or on some person other than the person specified in r.21.8 or para.(2).
(4) An application for an order under para.(3) may be made without notice.
(5) The court may order that, although a document has been sent or given to someone other than the person specified in r.21.8 or para.(2), the document is to be treated as if it had been properly served.
(6) This rule does not apply where the court has made an order under r.21.2(3) allowing a child to conduct proceedings without a litigation friend.

Service of the claim form on children and protected parties

Pt 6 r.6.13

(1) Where the defendant is a child who is not also a protected party, the claim form must be served on—
  (a) one of the child's parents or guardians; or
  (b) if there is no parent or guardian, an adult with whom the child resides or in whose care the child is.
(2) Where the defendant is a protected party, the claim form must be served on—
  (a) one of the following persons with authority in relation to the protected party as—
    (i) the attorney under a registered enduring power of attorney;
    (ii) the donee of a lasting power of attorney; or
    (iii) the deputy appointed by the Court of Protection; or

   (b) if there is no such person, an adult with whom the protected party resides or in whose care the protected party is.

   (3) Any reference in this section to a defendant or a party to be served includes the person to be served with the claim form on behalf of a child or protected party under paras (1) or (2).

   (4) The court may make an order permitting a claim form to be served on a child or protected party, or on a person other than the person specified in paras (1) or (2).

   (5) An application for an order under para.(4) may be made without notice.

   (6) The court may order that, although a claim form has been sent or given to someone other than the person specified in paras (1) or (2), it is to be treated as if it had been properly served.

   (7) This rule does not apply where the court has made an order under r.21.2(3) allowing a child to conduct proceedings without a litigation friend.

(Part 21 contains rules about the appointment of a litigation friend and 'child' and 'protected party' have the same meaning as in r.21.1).

Control of money recovered by or on behalf of a child or protected party

Pt 21 r.21.11

   (1) Where in any proceedings—
     (a) money is recovered by or on behalf of or for the benefit of a child or protected party; or
     (b) money paid into court is accepted by or on behalf of a child or protected party,
the money will be dealt with in accordance with directions given by the court under this rule and not otherwise.

   (2) Directions given under this rule may provide that the money shall be wholly or partly paid into court and invested or otherwise dealt with.

   (3) Where money is recovered by or on behalf of a protected party or money paid into court is accepted by or on behalf of a protected party, before giving directions in accordance with this rule, the court will first consider whether the protected party is a protected beneficiary.

PD 21 para.8.1

When giving directions under r.21.11, the court—
   (1) may direct the money to be paid into court for investment,
   (2) may direct that certain sums be paid direct to the child or protected beneficiary, his litigation friend or his legal representative for the immediate benefit of the child or protected beneficiary or for expenses incurred on his behalf, and
   (3) may direct that the application in respect of the investment of the money be transferred to a local district registry.

PD 21 para.8.2

The court will consider the general aims to be achieved for the money in court (the fund) by investment and will give directions as to the type of investment.

PD 21 para.8.3

Where a child also lacks capacity to manage and control any money recovered by him or on his behalf in the proceedings, and is likely to remain so on reaching full age, his fund should be administered as a protected beneficiary's fund.

PD 21 para.8.4

Where a child or protected beneficiary is in receipt of publicly funded legal services the fund will be subject to a first charge under s.10 of the Access to Justice Act (statutory charge) and an order for the investment of money on the child's or protected beneficiary's behalf must contain a direction to that effect.

Transfer of control of money in court

Pt 30 r.30.7

The court may order that control of any money held by it under r.21.11 (control of money recovered by or on behalf of a child or protected party) be transferred to another court if that court would be more convenient.

Investment on behalf of a child

PD 21 para.9.1

At the hearing of an application for the approval of a settlement or compromise the litigation friend or his legal representative must provide, in addition to the information required by paras 5 and 6—
    (1) a CFO Form 320 (initial application for investment of damages) for completion by the judge hearing the application; and
    (2) any evidence or information which the litigation friend wishes the court to consider in relation to the investment of the award for damages.

PD 21 para.9.2

Following the hearing in para.9.1, the court will forward to the Court Funds Office a request for investment decision (Form 212) and the Public Trustee's investment managers will make the appropriate investment.

PD 21 para.9.3

Where an award for damages for a child is made at trial, unless para.9.7 applies, the trial judge will—
    (1) direct the money to be paid into court and placed into the special investment account until further investment directions have been given by the court;
    (2) direct the litigation friend to make an application to a Master or district judge for further investment directions; and
    (3) give such other directions as the trial judge thinks fit, including a direction that the hearing of the application for further investment directions will be fixed for a date within 28 days from the date of the trial.

PD 21 para.9.4

The application under para.9.3(2) must be made by filing with the court—
    (1) a completed CFO Form 320; and
    (2) any evidence or information which the litigation friend wishes the court to consider in relation to the investment of the award for damages.

PD 21 para.9.5

The application must be sent in proceedings in the Royal Courts of Justice to the Masters' Support Unit (Room E16) at the Royal Courts of Justice.

PD 21 para.9.6

If the application required by para.9.3(2) is not made to the court, the money paid into court in accordance with para.9.3(1) will remain in the special investment account subject to any further order of the court or para.9.8.

PD 21 para.9.7

If the money to be invested is very small the court may order it to be paid direct to the litigation friend to be put into a building society account (or similar) for the child's use.

PD 21 para.9.8

If the money is invested in court, it must be paid out to the child on application when he reaches full age.

Apportionment under the Fatal Accidents Act 1976

PD 21 para.1.3

A settlement of a claim by a child includes an agreement on a sum to be apportioned to a dependent child under the Fatal Accidents Act 1976.

PD 21 para.7.1

A judgment on or settlement in respect of a claim under the Fatal Accidents Act 1976 must be apportioned between the persons by or on whose behalf the claim has been brought.

PD 21 para.7.2

Where a claim is brought on behalf of a dependent child or children, any settlement (including an agreement on a sum to be apportioned to a dependent child under the Fatal Accidents Act 1976) must be approved by the court.

PD 21 para.7.3

The money apportioned to any dependent child must be invested on the child's behalf in accordance with rr.21.10 and 21.11 and paras 8 and 9 below.

PD 21 para.7.4

In order to approve an apportionment of money to a dependent child, the court will require the following information:
  (1) the matters set out in paras 5.1(2) and (3), and
  (2) in respect of the deceased—

    (a) where death was caused by an accident, the matters set out in paras 5.1(6)(a), (b) and
       (c), and
    (b) his future loss of earnings, and
  (3) the extent and nature of the dependency.

Payment out of funds in court

PD 21 para.13.1

Applications to a Master or district judge
  (1) for payment out of money from the fund for the benefit of the child, or
  (2) to vary an investment strategy,
may be dealt with without a hearing unless the court directs otherwise.

PD 21 para.13.2

When the child reaches full age—
  (1) where his fund in court is a sum of money, it will be paid out to him on application;
    or
  (2) where his fund is in the form of investments other than money (for example shares or unit
    trusts), the investments will on application be
    (a) sold and the proceeds of sale paid out to him; or
    (b) transferred into his name.

PD 21 para.13.3

Where the fund is administered by the Court of Protection, any payment out of money from that
fund must be in accordance with any decision or order of the Court of Protection.

PD 21 para.13.4

If an application is required for the payment out of money from a fund administered by the Court
of Protection, that application must be made to the Court of Protection.

See **Payment out of court**.

Anti-social behaviour and harassment

*Application for an injunction against a child under the Policing and Crime Act
2009*

PD 65 para.1A.1

  (1) Attention is drawn to the provisions of Pt 21 and its practice direction: in particular to the
    requirement for a child to have a **litigation friend** unless the court makes an order under
    r.21.2(3), and the procedure for appointment of a litigation friend. The Official Solicitor
    may be invited to act as litigation friend where there is no other willing and suitable
    person.
  (2) When an application for an injunction is made without notice in accordance with
    r.65.43(4)[injunction under the Policing and Crime Act 2009] and the court grants

permission for the application to be heard without the child having a litigation friend, the court will consider whether to direct the applicant to—

(a) make an application for a litigation friend at the earliest opportunity after the child is served with the injunction;

(b) ensure that the terms of the injunction and the consequences resulting from any breach of those terms are explained to the child at the time the injunction is served;

(c) ensure that an appropriate and responsible adult is present at the time the injunction is served;

(d) file a **witness statement** confirming compliance with any such directions.

Part 8 procedure

PD 8A para.3.1

The types of claim for which the Pt 8 procedure may be used include—

(1) a claim by or against a child or protected party, as defined in r.21.1(2), which has been settled before the commencement of proceedings and the sole purpose of the claim is to obtain the approval of the court to the settlement.

RTA Protocol—Stage 3

PD 8B para.1.1

[PD 8B] sets out the procedure ('the Stage 3 Procedure') for a claim where—

(2) (a) the claimant is a child;

(b) a settlement has been agreed by the parties at the end of Stage 2 of the RTA Protocol; and

(c) the approval of the court is required in relation to the settlement in accordance with r.21.10(2).

PD 8B para.1.2

A claim under [PD 8B] must be started in a county court and will normally be heard by a district judge.

Settlement at Stage 2 where the claimant is a child

PD 8B para.12.1

Paragraphs 12.2 to 12.5 apply where—

(1) the claimant is a child;

(2) there is a settlement at Stage 2 of the RTA Protocol; and

(3) an application is made to the court to approve the settlement.

PD 8B para.12.2

Where the settlement is approved at the settlement hearing the court will order the costs to be paid in accordance with r.45.33(2).

PD 8B para.12.3

Where the settlement is not approved at the first settlement hearing and the court orders a second settlement hearing at which the settlement is approved, the court will order the costs to be paid in accordance with r.45.33(4) to (6).

PD 8B para.12.4

Where the settlement is not approved at the first settlement hearing and the court orders that the claim is not suitable to be determined under the Stage 3 Procedure, the court will order costs to be paid in accordance with r.45.35 and will give directions.

PD 8B para.12.5

Where the settlement is not approved at the second settlement hearing the claim will no longer continue under the Stage 3 Procedure and the court will give directions.

Settlement at Stage 3 where the claimant is a child

PD 8B para.13.1

Paragraphs 13.2 and 13.3 apply where—
    (1) the claimant is a child;
    (2) there is a settlement after proceedings have started under the Stage 3 Procedure; and
    (3) an application is made to the court to approve the settlement.

PD 8B para.13.2

Where the settlement is approved at the settlement hearing the court will order the costs to be paid in accordance with r.45.34(2).

PD 8B para.13.3

Where the settlement is not approved at the settlement hearing the court will order the claim to proceed to a Stage 3 hearing.

See also **Appeals**, **Pre-action protocols**.

Costs where money is payable by or to a child or protected party

Pt 48 r.48.5

    (1) This rule applies to any proceedings where a party is a child or protected party and—
        (a) money is ordered or agreed to be paid to, or for the benefit of, that party; or
        (b) money is ordered to be paid by him or on his behalf.
('Child' and 'protected party' have the same meaning as in r.21.1(2)
    (2) The general rule is that—
        (a) the court must order a detailed assessment of the costs payable by, or out of money belonging to, any party who is a child or protected party; and
        (b) on an assessment under para.(a), the court must also assess any costs payable to that party in the proceedings, unless—

(i) the court has issued a default costs certificate in relation to those costs under r.47.11; or

(ii) the costs are payable in proceedings to which s.II or s.VI of Pt 45 applies.

(3) The court need not order detailed assessment of costs in the circumstances set out in the Costs PD.

(4) Where—

(a) a claimant is a child or protected party; and

(b) a detailed assessment has taken place under paragraph (2)(a), the only amount payable by the child or protected party is the amount which the court certifies as payable.

(This rule applies to a counterclaim by or on behalf of a child or protected party by virtue of r.20.3).

Costs PD para.51.1

The circumstances in which the court need not order the assessment of costs under r.48.5(3) are as follows:

(a) where there is no need to do so to protect the interests of the child or protected party or his estate;

(b) where another party has agreed to pay a specified sum in respect of the costs of the child or protected party and the solicitor acting for the child or protected party has waived the right to claim further costs;

(c) where the court has decided the costs payable to the child or protected party by way of summary assessment and the solicitor acting for the child or protected party has waived the right to claim further costs;

(d) where an insurer or other person is liable to discharge the costs which the child or protected party would otherwise be liable to pay to his solicitor and the court is satisfied that the insurer or other person is financially able to discharge those costs.

See **Compromise**, **Guardian**, **Guardian's account**, and **Litigation friend**.

CHIROPRACTORS

See **Health care professionals**.

CIRCUIT JUDGE

See **Judge**.

CITATION OF AUTHORITIES

PD Citation of Authorities (2012)

This PD was issued in order to clarify the practice and procedure governing the citation of authorities and applies throughout the Senior Courts of England and Wales, including the Crown Court, in county courts and in magistrates' courts.

When authority is cited, whether in written or oral submissions, the following practice should be followed:

Where a judgment is reported in the Official Law Reports (A.C., Q.B., Ch., Fam.) published by the Incorporated Council of Law Reporting for England and Wales, that report must be cited. These are the most authoritative reports; they contain a summary of the argument. Other series of reports and official transcripts of judgment may only be used when a case is not reported in the Official Law Reports.

If a judgment is not (or not yet) reported in the Official Law Reports but it is reported in the Weekly Law Reports (W.L.R.) or the All England Law Reports (All E.R.) that report should be cited. If the case is reported in both the W.L.R. and the All E.R. either report may properly be cited.

If a judgment is not reported in the Official Law Reports, the W.L.R, or the All E.R., but it is reported in any of the authoritative specialist series of reports which contain a headnote and are made by individuals holding a Senior Courts qualification (for the purposes of s.115 of the Courts and Legal Services Act 1990), the specialist report should be cited.

Where a judgment is not reported in any of the reports referred to in paragraphs [6]–[8] above, but is reported in other reports, they may be cited.

Where a judgment has not been reported, reference may be made to the official transcript if that is available, not the handed-down text of the judgment, as this may have been subject to late revision after the text was handed down. Official transcripts may be obtained from, for instance, BAILLI (*http://www.bailii.org/*). An unreported case should not usually be cited unless it contains a relevant statement of legal principle not found in reported authority.

Occasions arise when one report is fuller than another, or when there are discrepancies between reports. On such occasions, the practice outlined above need not be followed, but the court should be given a brief explanation as to why this course is being taken, and the alternative references should be given.

If a judgment under appeal has been reported before the hearing but after skeleton arguments have been filed with the court, and counsel wish to argue from the published report rather than from the official transcript, the court should be provided with photocopies of the report for the use of the court.

Judgments reported in any series of reports, including those of the Incorporated Council of Law Reporting, should be provided either by way of a photocopy of the published report or by way of a copy of a reproduction of the judgment in electronic form that has been authorised by the publisher of the relevant series, but in any event: (1) the report must be presented to the court in an easily legible form (a 12-point font is preferred but a 10- or 11-point font is acceptable), and (2) the advocate presenting the report is satisfied that it has not been reproduced in a garbled form from the data source. In any case of doubt the court will rely on the printed text of the report (unless the editor of the report has certified that an electronic version is more accurate because it corrects an error contained in an earlier printed text of the report).

Citation of Authorities Human Rights

PD 39A para.8.1

If it is necessary for a party to give evidence at a hearing of an authority referred to in s. 2 of the Human Rights Act 1998—
  (1) the authority to be cited should be an authoritative and complete report; and
  (2) the party must give to the court and any other party a list of the authorities he intends to cite and copies of the reports not less than three days before the hearing.
(s.2(1) of the Human Rights Act 1998 requires the court to take into account the authorities listed there)
  (3) Copies of the complete original texts issued by the European Court and Commission either paper based or from the Court's judgment database (HUDOC), which is available on the Internet, may be used.

CIVIL APPEAL LIST

The Civil Appeals List of the Court of Appeal is divided as follows:
  The applications list—applications for permission to appeal and other applications.

The appeals list—appeals where permission to appeal has been given or where an appeal lies without permission being required where a hearing date is fixed in advance. (Appeals in this list which require special listing arrangements will be assigned to the special fixtures list).

The expedited list—appeals or applications where the Court of Appeal has directed an expedited hearing. The current practice of the Court of Appeal is summarised in *Unilever Plc v Chefaro Proprietaries Ltd (Practice Note)* [1995]1 W.L.R. 243.

The stand-out list—Appeals or applications which, for good reason, are not at present ready to proceed and have been stood out by judicial direction.

The second fixtures list—if an appeal is designated as a 'second fixture' it means that a hearing date is arranged in advance on the express basis that the list is fully booked for the period in question and therefore the case will be heard only if a suitable gap occurs in the list.

The short-warned list—appeals which the court considers may be prepared for the hearing by an advocate other than the one originally instructed with a half day's notice, or such other period as the court may direct.

CIVIL EVIDENCE ACT 1972

See **Foreign law**.

CIVIL EVIDENCE ACT 1995

See **Hearsay evidence**.

CIVIL JURISDICTION AND JUDGMENTS ACT 1982

Service out of jurisdiction where permission is required

PD 6B para.3.1

The claimant may serve a claim form out of the jurisdiction with the permission of the court under r.6.36 where—
(5) A claim is made for an interim remedy under s.25(1) of the Civil Jurisdiction and Judgments Act 1982.

See **Enforcement in England and Wales of judgments of foreign courts**, **Default judgment**, and **Service of documents**.

CIVIL PARTNERSHIP

Default judgment

Pt 12 r.12.10

The claimant must make an application in accordance with Pt 23 where—
(a)(ii) the claim is a claim in tort by one civil partner against the other.

Pt 12 r.12.11

(2) Any evidence relied on by the claimant in support of his application need not be served on a party who has failed to file an acknowledgment of service.

(3) An application for a default judgment on a claim in tort civil partners must be supported by evidence.

Dissolution or nullity

See **Appeals to the Court of Appeal**.

CIVIL PROCEDURE ACT 1979

An Act that amended the law about civil procedure in England and Wales.

CIVIL PROCEDURE RULES 1998

See **CPR**.

CIVIL PROCEEDINGS ORDER

Senior Courts Act 1981 s.42(1A)

An order that—

(a) no civil proceedings shall without the leave of the High Court be instituted in any court by the person against whom the order is made;

(b) any civil proceedings instituted by him in any court before the making of the order shall not be continued by him without the leave of the High Court; and

(c) no application (other than one for leave under this section) shall be made by him, in any civil proceedings in n any court by any person, without the leave of the High Court.

Senior Courts Act 1981 s.42

(3) Leave for the institution or continuance of, or for the making of an application in, any civil] proceedings by a person who is the subject of an order for the time being in force under subs.(1) shall not be given unless the High Court is satisfied that the proceedings or application are not an abuse of the process of the court in question and that there are reasonable grounds for the proceedings or application.

(3A) Leave for the laying of an information or for an application for leave to pref

(4) No appeal shall lie from a decision of the High Court refusing leave [required by virtue of this section].

(5) A copy of any order made under subs.(1) shall be published in the *London Gazette*.

See **Vexatious litigants**.

CIVIL RECOVERY PROCEEDINGS

PD—Civil Recovery Proceedings para.1.1

Section I of [PD CRP] contains general provisions about proceedings in the High Court under Pts 5 and 8 of the Proceeds of Crime Act 2002 and Pt 5 of the Proceeds of Crime Act 2002 (External Requests and Orders) Order 2005 ["Order in Council"].

Venue

PD CRP para.2.1

Except as otherwise provided in para.2.2, an application made to the High Court under Pt 5 or Pt 8 of the Act or Pt 5 of the Order in Council must be made in the Administrative Court.

PD CRP para.2.2

A claim for a recovery order must be started in the Central Office of the Queen's Bench Division. Where a claim for a recovery order has been issued, any interim proceedings preserving the property which is the subject of the claim will be transferred to the Central Office of the Queen's Bench Division.

PD CRP para.2.3

The preceding paragraph does not limit the power of the High Court to transfer claims or applications to or from the Central Office of the Queen's Bench Division, Administrative Court, Chancery Division or specialist list of the High Court.

See also **Pseudonyms**.

Part 5 of the Proceeds of Crime Act 2002 or Pt 5 of the Order in Council

Claim for a Recovery Order

PD CRP para.4.1

A claim by the enforcement authority for a recovery Order must be made using the CPR Pt 8 procedure.

PD CRP para.4.2

In a claim for a recovery order based on an external order, the claim must include an application to register the external Order.

PD CRP para.4.3

The claim form must—
    (1) identify the property in relation to which a recovery order is sought;
    (2) state, in relation to each item or description of property—

    (a) whether the property is alleged to be recoverable property or associated property; and

    (b) either—

        (i) who is alleged to hold the property; or

        (ii) where the enforcement authority is unable to identify who holds the property, the steps that have been taken to try to establish their identity;

(3) set out the matters relied upon in support of the claim;

(4) give details of the person nominated by the enforcement authority to act as trustee for civil recovery in accordance with s.267 of the Act or art.178 of the Order in Council; and

(5) in a claim which includes an application to register an external order, be accompanied by a copy of the external Order.

PD CRP para.4.4

The evidence in support of the claim must include the signed, written consent of the person nominated by the enforcement authority to act as trustee for civil recovery if appointed by the court.

PD CRP para.4.5

In a claim which includes an application to register an external order, where—

(1) the sum specified in the external order is expressed in a currency other than sterling; and

(2) there are not funds held in the UK in the currency in which the sum specified is expressed sufficient to satisfy the external order,

the claim form, or particulars of claim if served subsequently, must state the sterling equivalent of the sum specified.

(Article 145(2) of the Order in Council provides that the sterling equivalent is to be calculated in accordance with the exchange rate prevailing at end of the day on which the external order is made).

Applications

PD CRP para.5.1

An application for a property freezing order, an interim receiving order or a management receiving order must be made—

(1) to a High Court judge; and

(2) in accordance with CPR Pt 23.

PD CRP para.5.2

CPR r.23.10(2) and s.I of CPR Pt 25 do not apply to applications for property freezing Orders, interim receiving orders and management receiving Orders.

PD CRP para.5.3

The application may be made without notice in the circumstances set out in—

(1) section 245A(3) of the Act and art.147(3) of the Order in Council (in the case of an application for a property freezing Order);

(2) section 246(3) of the Act and art.151(3) of the Order in Council (in the case of an application for an interim receiving Order); or

(3) section 245E of the Act and the Order in Council (in the case of an application for a management receiving Order).

PD CRP para.5.4

An application for a property freezing Order must be supported by written evidence which must—
(1) set out the grounds on which the order is sought; and
(2) give details of each item or description of property in respect of which the order is sought, including
   (a) an estimate of the value of the property; and
   (b) the additional information referred to in para.5.5(2).

PD CRP para.5.5

CPR Pt 69 (court's power to appoint a receiver) and PD 69 apply to an application for an interim receiving order with the following modifications—
(1) Paragraph 2.1 of PD 69 does not apply;
(2) the enforcement authority's written evidence must, in addition to the matters required by para.4.1 of that PD, also state in relation to each item or description of property in respect of which the order is sought—
   (a) whether the property is alleged to be—
      (i) recoverable property; or
      (ii) associated property,
      and the facts relied upon in support of that allegation; and
   (b) in the case of any associated property—
      (i) who is believed to hold the property; or
      (ii) if the enforcement authority is unable to establish who holds the property, the steps that have been taken to establish their identity; and
(3) the enforcement authority's written evidence must always identify a nominee and include the information in para.4.2 of that PD.

PD CRP para.5.5A

Paragraph 2.1 of PD 69 does not apply to an application for a management receiving order.

PD CRP para.5.6

Where an application is made for an interim receiving order or management receiving order, a draft of the order which is sought must be filed with the application notice. This should if possible also be supplied to the court in an electronic form compatible with the word processing software used by the court.

Property freezing order or interim receiving order made before commencement of claim for recovery order

PD CRP para.5A

A property freezing order or interim receiving order which is made before a claim for a recovery order has been commenced will—
(1) specify a period within which the enforcement authority must either start the claim or apply for the continuation of the order while he carries out his investigation; and

(2) provide that the order will be set aside if the enforcement authority does not start the claim or apply for its continuation before the end of that period.

Exclusions when making property freezing order or interim receiving order

PD CRP para.5B.1

When the court makes a property freezing order or interim receiving order on an application without notice, it will normally make an initial exclusion from the order for the purpose of enabling the respondent to meet his reasonable legal costs so that he may—
(1) take advice in relation to the order;
(2) prepare a statement of assets in accordance with para.7A.3; and
(3) if so advised, apply for the order to be varied or set aside.
The total amount specified in the initial exclusion will not normally exceed £3,000.

PD CRP para.5B.2

When it makes a property freezing order or interim receiving order before a claim for a recovery order has been commenced, the court may also make an exclusion to enable the respondent to meet his reasonable legal costs so that (for example) when the claim is commenced—
(1) he may file an acknowledgment of service and any written evidence on which he intends to rely; or
(2) he may apply for a further exclusion for the purpose of enabling him to meet his reasonable costs of the proceedings.

PD CRP para.5B.3

Paragraph 7A contains general provisions about exclusions made for the purpose of enabling a person to meet his reasonable legal costs.

Interim receiving order or management receiving order: application for directions

PD CRP para.6.1

An application for directions as to the exercise of the functions of—
(1) the interim receiver under s.251 of the Act or art.156 of the Order in Council; or
(2) the management receiver under s.245G of the Act or under the Order in Council, may be made at any time by—
(a) the interim receiver or management receiver, as appropriate;
(b) any party to the proceedings; and
(c) any person affected by any action taken, or proposed to be taken, by the interim receiver or management receiver.

PD CRP para.6.2

The application must always be made by application notice, which must be served on—
(1) the interim receiver or management receiver, as appropriate, (unless he is the applicant);
(2) every party to the proceedings; and
(3) any other person who may be interested in the application.

Application to vary or set aside an Order

PD CRP para.7.1

An application to vary or set aside a property freezing Order, an interim receiving Order or a management receiving order (including an application for, or relating to, an exclusion from the order) may be made at any time by—
(1) the enforcement authority; or
(2) any person affected by the order.

PD CRP para.7.2

Unless the court otherwise directs or exceptional circumstances apply, a copy of the application notice must be served on—
(1) every party to the proceedings;
(2) in the case of an application to vary or set aside an interim receiving order or management receiving order, the interim receiver or management receiver (as appropriate); and
(3) any other person who may be affected by the court's decision.

PD CRP para.7.3

The evidence in support of an application for an exclusion from a property freezing order or interim receiving order for the purpose of enabling a person to meet his reasonable legal costs must—
(1) contain full details of the stage or stages in civil recovery proceedings in respect of which the costs in question have been or will be incurred;
(2) include an estimate of the costs which the person has incurred and will incur in relation to each stage to which the application relates, substantially in the form illustrated in Precedent H in the Schedule of Costs Precedents annexed to the Costs PD ;
(3) include a statement of assets containing the information set out in para.7A.3 (unless the person has previously filed such a statement in the same civil recovery proceedings and there has been no material change in the facts set out in that statement);
(4) where the court has previously made an exclusion in respect of any stage to which the application relates, explain why the person's costs will exceed the amount specified in the exclusion for that stage; and
(5) state whether the terms of the exclusion have been agreed with the enforcement authority.

Exclusions for the purpose of meeting legal costs: general provisions

PD CRP para.7A.1

Subject to para.7A.2, when the court makes an order or gives directions in civil recovery proceedings it will at the same time consider whether it is appropriate to make or vary an exclusion for the purpose of enabling any person affected by the order or directions to meet his reasonable legal costs.

PD CRP para.7A.2

The court will not make an exclusion for the purpose of enabling a person to meet his reasonable legal costs, other than an exclusion to meet the costs of taking any of the steps referred to in para.5B.1, unless that person has made and filed a statement of assets.

PD CRP para.7A.3

A statement of assets is a witness statement which sets out all the property which the maker of the statement owns, holds or controls, or in which he has an interest, giving the value, location and details of all such property. Information given in a statement of assets under this PD will be used only for the purpose of the civil recovery proceedings.

PD CRP para.7A.4

The court—
    (1) will not make an exclusion for the purpose of enabling a person to meet his reasonable legal costs (including an initial exclusion under para.5B.1); and
    (2) may set aside any exclusion which it has made for that purpose or reduce any amount specified in such an exclusion,
if it is satisfied that the person has property to which the property freezing Order or interim receiving Order does not apply from which he may meet those costs.

PD CRP para.7A.5

The court will normally refer to a costs judge any question relating to the amount which an exclusion should allow for reasonable legal costs in respect of proceedings or a stage in proceedings.

PD CRP para.7A.6

Attention is drawn to s.245C of the Act and art.149 of the Order in Council (in relation to exclusions from property freezing orders) and to s.252 of the Act and art.157 of the Order in Council (in relation to exclusions from interim receiving orders). An exclusion for the purpose of enabling a person to meet his reasonable legal costs must be made subject to the 'required conditions' specified in Pt 2 of the Regulations.

PD CRP para.7A.7

An exclusion made for the purpose of enabling a person to meet his reasonable legal costs will specify—
    (1) the stage or stages in civil recovery proceedings to which it relates;
    (2) the maximum amount which may be released in respect of legal costs for each specified stage; and
    (3) the total amount which may be released in respect of legal costs pursuant to the exclusion.

PD CRP para.7A.8

A person who becomes aware that his legal costs—
    (1) in relation to any stage in civil recovery proceedings have exceeded or will exceed the maximum amount specified in the exclusion for that stage; or
    (2) in relation to all the stages to which the exclusion relates have exceeded or will exceed the total amount that may be released pursuant to the exclusion,
should apply for a further exclusion or a variation of the existing exclusion as soon as reasonably practicable.

Assessment of costs where recovery order is made

PD CRP para.7B.1

Where the court—
(1) makes a recovery order in respect of property which was the subject of a property freezing Order or interim receiving Order; and
(2) had made an exclusion from the property freezing order or interim receiving order for the purpose of enabling a person to meet his reasonable legal costs,
the recovery order will make provision under s.266(8A) of the Act or art.177(10) of the Order in Council (as appropriate) for the payment of those costs.

PD CRP para.7B.2

Where the court makes a recovery order which provides for the payment of a person's reasonable legal costs in respect of civil recovery proceedings, it will at the same time order the detailed assessment of those costs. Parts 4 and 5 of the Regulations CPR Pt 47 and s.49A of the Costs PD apply to a detailed assessment pursuant to such an order.

Registers

PD CRP para.7C

There will be kept in the Central Office of the Senior Courts at the Royal Courts of Justice, under the direction of the Senior Master, a register of external orders which the High Court has ordered to be registered.

Civil recovery investigations and detained cash investigations

PD CRP para.8.1

An application for an order or warrant under Pt 8 of the Act in connection with a civil recovery investigation or (where applicable) a detained cash investigation must be made—
(1) to a High Court judge;
(2) by filing an application notice.

PD CRP para.8.2

The application may be made without notice.

Confidentiality of court documents

PD CRP para.9.1

CPR rr.5.4, 5.4B and 5.4C do not apply to an application under Pt 8 of the Act, and paras 9.2 and 9.3 below have effect in its place.

PD CRP para.9.2

When an application is issued, the court file will be marked 'Not for disclosure' and, unless a High Court judge grants permission, the court records relating to the application (including the application notice, documents filed in support, and any order or warrant that is made) will not be made available by the court for any person to inspect or copy, either before or after the hearing of the application.

PD CRP para.9.3

An application for permission under para.9.2 must be made on notice to the appropriate officer in accordance with CPR Pt 23.
(CPR r.23.7(1) requires a copy of the application notice to be served as soon as practicable after it is filed, and in any event at least three days before the court is to deal with the application.)

Application notice and evidence

PD CRP para.10.1

The application must be supported by written evidence, which must be filed with the application notice.

PD CRP para.10.2

The evidence must set out all the matters on which the appropriate officer relies in support of the application, including any matters required to be stated by the relevant sections of the Act, and all material facts of which the court should be made aware.

PD CRP para.10.3

There must also be filed with the application notice a draft of the order sought. This should if possible also be supplied to the court on disk in a form compatible with the word processing software used by the court.

Hearing of the application

PD CRP para.11.1

The application will be heard and determined in private, unless the judge hearing it directs otherwise.

Variation or discharge of order or warrant

PD CRP para.12.1

An application to vary or discharge an order or warrant may be made by—
    (1) the appropriate officer; or

(2) any person affected by the order or warrant.

PD CRP para.12.2

An application under para.12.1 to stop an order or warrant from being executed must be made immediately upon it being served.

PD CRP para.12.3

A person applying to vary or discharge a warrant must first inform the appropriate officer that he is making the application.

PD CRP para.12.4

The application should be made to the judge who made the order or issued the warrant or, if he is not available, to another High Court judge.

Production Order

PD CRP para.13.1

The application notice must name as a respondent the person believed to be in possession or control of the material in relation to which a production Order is sought.

PD CRP para.13.2

The application notice must specify—
    (1) whether the application is for an order under paras (a) or (b) of s.345(4) of the Act;
    (2) the material, or description of material, in relation to which the order is sought; and
    (3) the person who is believed to be in possession or control of the material.

PD CRP para.13.3

An application under s.347 of the Act for an order to grant entry may be made either—
    (1) together with an application for a production order; or
    (2) by separate application, after a production order has been made.

PD CRP para.13.4

An application notice for an order to grant entry must—
    (1) specify the premises in relation to which the order is sought; and
    (2) be supported by written evidence explaining why the order is needed.

PD CRP para.13.5

A production order, or an order to grant entry, must contain a statement of the right of any person affected by the order to apply to vary or discharge the order.

Search and seizure warrant

PD CRP para.14.1

The application notice should name as the respondent the occupier of the premises to be subject to the warrant, if known.

PD CRP para.14.2

The evidence in support of the application must state—
  (1) the matters relied on by the appropriate officer to show that one of the requirements in s.352(6) of the Act for the issue of a warrant is satisfied;
  (2) details of the premises to be subject to the warrant, and of the possible occupier or occupiers of those premises;
  (3) the name and position of the member of the staff of the appropriate officer who it is intended will execute the warrant.

PD CRP para.14.3

There must be filed with the application notice drafts of—
  (1) the warrant; and
  (2) a written undertaking by the person who is to execute the warrant to comply with para.13.8 of this PD.

PD CRP para.14.4

A search and seizure warrant must—
  (1) specify the statutory power under which it is issued and, unless the court orders otherwise, give an indication of the nature of the investigation in respect of which it is issued;
  (2) state the address or other identification of the premises to be subject to the warrant;
  (3) state the name of the member of the staff of the appropriate officer who is authorised to execute the warrant;
  (4) set out the action which the warrant authorises the person executing it to take under the relevant sections of the Act;
  (5) give the date on which the warrant is issued;
  (6) include a statement that the warrant continues in force until the end of the period of one month beginning with the day on which it is issued;
  (7) contain a statement of the right of any person affected by the order to apply to discharge or vary the order.

PD CRP para.14.5

An example of a search and seizure warrant is annexed to this PD. This example may be modified as appropriate in any particular case.

PD CRP para.14.6

Rule 40.2 applies to a search and seizure warrant.
(CPR r.40.2 requires every judgment or order to state the name and judicial title of the person making it, to bear the date on which it is given or made, and to be sealed by the court).

PD CRP para.14.7

Upon the issue of a warrant the court will provide to the appropriate officer—
   (1) the sealed warrant; and
   (2) a copy of it for service on the occupier or person in charge of the premises subject to the
       warrant.

PD CRP para.14.8

A person attending premises to execute a warrant must, if the premises are occupied produce the
warrant on arrival at the premises, and as soon as possible thereafter personally serve a copy of
the warrant and an explanatory notice on the occupier or the person appearing to him to be in
charge of the premises.

PD CRP para.14.9

The person executing the warrant must also comply with any order which the court may make
for service of any other documents relating to the application.

Disclosure Order

PD CRP para.15.1

The application notice should normally name as respondents the persons on whom the appropriate officer intends to serve notices under the disclosure order sought.

PD CRP para.15.2

A disclosure order must—
   (1) give an indication of the nature of the investigation for the purposes of which the order
       is made;
   (2) set out the action which the order authorises the appropriate officer to take in accordance
       with s.357(4) of the Act;
   (3) contain a statement of—
       (a) the offences relating to disclosure orders under s.359 of the Act; and
       (b) the right of any person affected by the order to apply to discharge or vary the
           Order.

PD CRP para.15.3

Where, pursuant to a disclosure order, the appropriate officer gives to any person a notice under
s.357(4) of the Act, he must also at the same time serve on that person a copy of the disclosure
order.

Customer Information Order

PD CRP para.16.1

The application notice should normally (unless it is impracticable to do so because they are too
numerous) name as respondents the financial institution or institutions to which it is proposed
that an order should apply.

PD CRP para.16.2

A customer information order must—
    (1) specify the financial institution, or description of financial institutions, to which it applies;
    (2) state the name of the person in relation to whom customer information is to be given, and any other details to identify that person;
    (3) contain a statement of—
        (a) the offences relating to disclosure orders under s.366 of the Act; and
        (b) the right of any person affected by the order to apply to discharge or vary the Order.

PD CRP para.16.3

Where, pursuant to a customer information order, the appropriate officer gives to a financial institution a notice to provide customer information, he must also at the same time serve a copy of the order on that institution.

Account Monitoring Order

PD CRP para.17.1

The application notice must name as a respondent the financial institution against which an account monitoring order is sought.

PD CRP para.17.2

The application notice must—
    (1) state the matters required by s.370(2) and (3) of the Act; and
    (2) give details of—
        (a) the person whose account or accounts the application relates to;
        (b) each account or description of accounts in relation to which the order is sought, including if known the number of each account and the branch at which it is held;
        (c) the information sought about the account or accounts;
        (d) the period for which the order is sought;
        (e) the manner in which, and the frequency with which, it is proposed that the financial institution should provide account information during that period.

PD CRP para.17.3

An account monitoring order must contain a statement of the right of any person affected by the order to apply to vary or discharge the order.

CIVIL RESTRAINT ORDERS

Pt 2 r.2.3(1)

'Civil restraint order' means an order restraining a party—
    (a) from making any further applications in current proceedings (a **limited civil restraint order**);

   (b) from issuing certain claims or making certain applications in specified courts (an **extended civil restraint order**); or

   (c) from issuing any claim or making any application in specified courts (a **general civil restraint order**).

Power of the court to make civil restraint orders

Pt 3 para.3.11

A [PD] may set out—
   (a) the circumstances in which the court has the power to make a civil restraint order against a party to proceedings;
   (b) the procedure where a party applies for a civil restraint order against another party; and
   (c) the consequences of the court making a civil restraint order.

PD 3C para.1

[PD 3C] applies where the court is considering whether to make—
   (a) a limited civil restraint order;
   (b) an extended civil restraint order; or
   (c) a general civil restraint order,
against a party who has issued claims or made applications which are totally without merit.
Rules 3.3(7), 3.4(6) and 23.12 provide that where a statement of case or application is struck out or dismissed and is totally without merit, the court order must specify that fact and the court must consider whether to make a civil restraint order. Rule 52.10(6) makes similar provision where the appeal court refuses an application for permission to appeal, strikes out an appellant's notice or dismisses an appeal.

PD 3C para.5.1

The other party or parties to the proceedings may apply for any civil restraint order.

PD 3C para.5.2

An application under para.5.1 must be made using the Pt 23 procedure unless the court otherwise directs and the application must specify which type of civil restraint order is sought.

PD 3C para.5.3

Examples of a limited civil restraint order, an extended civil restraint order and a general civil restraint order are annexed to this PD. These examples may be modified as appropriate in any particular case.

CLAIM

The word is not defined in the CPR but usually means the case in question or cause of action.

CLAIM FOR PERSONAL INJURIES

See **Personal injuries claim** and **Pre-action protocols**.

CLAIM FORM

PD 7A para.3.1

A claimant must use Practice Form N1 or Practice Form N208 (the Pt 8 claim form) to start a claim (but see paras 3.2 and 3.4 below).

PD 7A para.3.2

R.7.9 deals with fixed date claims and R.7.10 deals with Production Centre for the value of claims; there are separate PDs supplementing r.7.9 and r.7.10.

PD 7A para.3.4

Other PDs may require special practise forms to be used to commence particular types of proceedings, or proceedings in particular courts.

Right to use one claim form to start two or more claims

Pt 7 r.7.3

A claimant may use a single claim form to start all claims which can be conveniently disposed of in the same proceedings.

Contents of the claim form

Pt 16 r.16.2

(1) The claim form must—
    (a) contain a concise statement of the nature of the claim;
    (b) specify the remedy which the claimant seeks;
    (c) where the claimant is making a claim for money, contain a statement of value in accordance with r.16.3;
    (cc) where the claimant's only claim is for a specified sum, contain a statement of the interest accrued on that sum; and
    (d) contain such other matters as may be set out in a PD.
(1A) In civil proceedings against the Crown, as defined in r.66.1(2), the claim form must also contain—
    (a) the names of the government departments and officers of the Crown concerned; and
    (b) brief details of the circumstances in which it is alleged that the liability of the Crown arose.
(2) If the particulars of claim specified in r.16.4 are not contained in, or are not served with the claim form, the claimant must state on the claim form that the particulars of claim will follow.

(3) If the claimant is claiming in a representative capacity, the claim form must state what that capacity is.

(4) If the defendant is sued in a representative capacity, the claim form must state what that capacity is.

(5) The court may grant any remedy to which the claimant is entitled even if that remedy is not specified in the claim form.

(Part 22 requires a claim form to be verified by a statement of truth).

(The Costs PD sets out the information about a funding arrangement to be provided with the statement of case where the defendant intends to seek to recover an additional liability)

PD 16 para.2.1

Rule 16.2 refers to matters which the claim form must contain. Where the claim is for money, the claim form must also contain the statement of value referred to in r.16.3.

PD 16 para.2.2

The claim form must include an address at which the claimant resides or carries on business. This paragraph applies even though the claimant's address for service is the business address of his solicitor.

PD 16 para.2.3

Where the defendant is an individual, the claimant should (if he is able to do so) include in the claim form an address at which the defendant resides or carries on business. This paragraph applies even though the defendant's solicitors have agreed to accept service on the defendant's behalf.

PD 16 para.2.4

Any address which is provided for the purpose of these provisions must include a postcode or its equivalent in any EEA state (if applicable), unless the court orders otherwise. Postcode information for the UK may be obtained from *http://www.royalmail.com* (Accessed November 21, 2012) or the Royal Mail Address Management Guide.

PD 16 para.2.5

If the claim form does not show a full address, including postcode, at which the claimant(s) and defendant(s) reside or carry on business, the claim form will be issued but will be retained by the court and will not be served until the claimant has supplied a full address, including postcode, or the court has dispensed with the requirement to do so. The court will notify the claimant.

PD 16 para.2.6

The claim form must be headed with the title of the proceedings, including the full name of each party. The full name means, in each case where it is known:

    (a) in the case of an individual, his full unabbreviated name and title by which he is known;

    (b) in the case of an individual carrying on business in a name other than his own name, the full unabbreviated name of the individual, together with the title by which he is known, and the full trading name (for example, John Smith 'trading as' or 'T/as' 'JS Autos');

    (c) in the case of a partnership (other than a limited liability partnership (LLP))—

        (i) where partners are being sued in the name of the partnership, the full name by which the partnership is known, together with the words '(A Firm)'; or

      (ii) where partners are being sued as individuals, the full unabbreviated name of each
           partner and the title by which he is known;
  (d) in the case of a company or limited liability partnership registered in England and Wales,
      the full registered name, including suffix (plc, limited, LLP, etc), if any;
  (e) in the case of any other company or corporation, the full name by which it is known,
      including suffix where appropriate.
(For information about how and where a claim may be started see Part 7 and PD 7A).)

PD 7A para.3.3

If a claimant wishes the claim to proceed under Pt 8, or if the claim is required to proceed under
Pt 8, the claim form should so state. Otherwise the claim will proceed under Pt 7. But note that
in respect of claims in specialist proceedings (listed in CPR Pt 49) and claims brought under the
RSC or CCR set out in the Schedule to the CPR (see CPR Pt 50) the CPR will apply only to the
extent that they are not inconsistent with the rules and PDs that expressly apply to those
claims.

PD 7A para.3.5

Where a claim form to be served out of the jurisdiction is one which the court has power to deal
with—
  (a) under the Civil Jurisdiction and Judgments Act 1982; and
  (b) the Judgments Regulation (which has the same meaning as in r.6.31(d)),
the claim form must, pursuant to r.6.34, be filed and served with the notice referred to in that rule
and para.2.1 of PD 6B.

PD 7A para.3.6

If a claim for damages or for an unspecified sum is started in the High Court, the claim form
must:
  (1) state that the claimant expects to recover more than £25,000 (or £50,000 or more if the
      claim is for personal injuries) or
  (2) state that some enactment provides that the claim may only be commenced in the High
      Court and specify that enactment or
  (3) state that the claim is to be in one of the specialist High Court lists (see CPR Pts 49 and
      58–62) and specify that list.

PD 7A para.3.7

If the contents of a claim form commencing specialist proceedings comply with the requirements
of the specialist list in question the claim form will also satisfy para.3.6 above.

PD 7A para.3.8

If a claim for damages for personal injuries is started in the county court, the claim form must
state whether or not the claimant expects to recover more than £1000 in respect of pain, suffering
and loss of amenity.

PD 7A para.3.9

If a claim for housing disrepair which includes a claim for an order requiring repairs or other
work to be carried out by the landlord is started in the county court, the claim form must
state:

(1) whether or not the cost of the repairs or other work is estimated to be more than £1000, and

(2) whether or not the claimant expects to recover more than £1000 in respect of any claim for damages.

If either of the amounts mentioned in (1) and (2) is more than £1000, the small claims track will not be the normal track for that claim.

(Section 19 of the Costs PD supplementing Pts 43 to 48 contains details of the information required to be filed with a claim form to comply with r.44.15 (providing information about funding arrangements)).

Application by defendant for service of claim form

Pt 7 r.7.7

(1) Where a claim form has been issued against a defendant, but has not yet been served on him, the defendant may serve a notice on the claimant requiring him to serve the claim form or discontinue the claim within a period specified in the notice.

(2) The period specified in a notice served under para.(1) must be at least 14 days after service of the notice.

(3) If the claimant fails to comply with the notice, the court may, on the application of the defendant—
(a) dismiss the claim; or
(b) make any other order it thinks just.

Form for defence, etc. must be served with particulars of claim

Pt 7 r.7.8

(1) When particulars of claim are served on a defendant, whether they are contained in the claim form, served with it or served subsequently, they must be accompanied by—
(a) a form for defending the claim;
(b) a form for admitting the claim; and
(c) a form for acknowledging service.

(2) Where the claimant is using the procedure set out in Pt 8 (alternative procedure for claims)—
(a) paragraph (1) does not apply; and
(b) a form for acknowledging service must accompany the claim form.

Title of proceedings

PD 7A para.4.1

The claim form and every other statement of case, must be headed with the title of the proceedings. The title should state:
(1) the number of proceedings,
(2) the court or Division in which they are proceeding,
(3) the full name of each party,
(4) each party's status in the proceedings (i.e. claimant/defendant).

PD 16 para.2.6

The claim form must be headed with the title of the proceedings, including the full name of each party. The full name means, in each case where it is known:
   (a) in the case of an individual, his full unabbreviated name and title by which he is known;
   (b) in the case of an individual carrying on business in a name other than his own name, the full unabbreviated name of the individual, together with the title by which he is known, and the full trading name (for example, John Smith 'trading as' or 'T/as' 'JS Autos');
   (c) in the case of a partnership (other than a limited liability partnership (LLP))—
       (i) where partners are being sued in the name of the partnership, the full name by which the partnership is known, together with the words '(A Firm)'; or
       (ii) where partners are being sued as individuals, the full unabbreviated name of each partner and the title by which he is known;
   (d) in the case of a company or limited liability partnership registered in England and Wales, the full registered name, including suffix (Plc, Ltd, LLP, etc.), if any;
   (e) in the case of any other company or corporation, the full name by which it is known, including suffix where appropriate.

PD 7A para.4.2

Where there is more than one claimant and/or more than one defendant, the parties should be described in the title as follows:
AB
CD
EF   Claimants
and
GH
IJ
KL   Defendants

CLAIMANT

Pt 2 r.2.3(1)

A person who makes a claim.

Addition or substitution of claimant

PD 19A para.2.1

Where an application is made to the court to add or to substitute a new party to the proceedings as claimant, the party applying must file:
   (1) the application notice,
   (2) the proposed amended claim form and particulars of claim, and
   (3) the signed, written consent of the new claimant to be so added or substituted.

PD 19A para.2.2

Where the court makes an order adding or substituting a party as claimant but the signed, written consent of the new claimant has not been filed:

(1) the order, and
(2) the addition or substitution of the new party as claimant,
will not take effect until the signed, written consent of the new claimant is filed.

PD 19A para.2.3

Where the court has made an order adding or substituting a new claimant, the court may direct:
(1) a copy of the order to be served on every party to the proceedings and any other person affected by the order,
(2) copies of the statements of case and of documents referred to in any statement of case to be served on the new party,
(3) the party who made the application to file within 14 days an amended claim form and particulars of claim.

See also **Parties**.

CLAIMANT'S/DEFENDANT'S COSTS IN CASE/ APPLICATION

Pt 44 s.1(4) para.4.2

If the party in whose favour the costs order is made is awarded costs at the end the proceedings, that party is entitled to his costs of the part of the proceedings to which the order relates. If any other party is awarded costs at the end of the proceedings, the party in whose favour the final costs order is made is not liable to pay the costs of any other party in respect of the part of the proceedings to which the order relates

CLEAR DAYS

See **Month**.

CLINICAL DISPUTES

See **Pre-action protocols**.

CLINICAL NEGLIGENCE CLAIMS

PD 16 para.9.3

In clinical negligence claims, the words 'clinical negligence' should be inserted at the top of every **statement of case**.

Recovery of Costs insurance premiums

PD 48 para.4.1

Section 46 of the Legal Aid, Sentencing and Punishment of Offenders Act 2012 enables the Lord Chancellor by regulations to provide that a costs order may include provision requiring the payment of an amount in respect of all or part of the premium of a costs insurance policy, where—

(a) the order is made in favour of a party to clinical negligence proceedings of a prescribed description;
(b) the party has taken out a costs insurance policy insuring against the risk of incurring a liability to pay for one or more expert reports in respect of clinical negligence in connection with the proceedings (or against that risk and other risks);
(c) the policy is of a prescribed description; and
(d) the policy states how much of the premium relates to the liability to pay for such an expert report or reports, and the amount to be paid is in respect of that part of the premium.

PD 48 para.4.2

The regulations made under the power are the Recovery of Costs Insurance Premiums in Clinical Negligence Proceedings Regulations 2013. The regulations relate only to clinical negligence cases where a costs insurance policy is taken out on or after April 1, 2013, so the provisions in force in the CPR prior to April 1, 2013 relating to funding arrangements will not apply.

See **Pre-action protocol for the resolution of clinical disputes.**

COMMERCIAL CLAIM

Pt 58 r.58.1

(2) In Pt 58 and PD 58, 'commercial claim' means any claim arising out of the transaction of trade and commerce and includes any claim relating to—

(a) a business document or contract;
(b) the export or import of goods;
(c) the carriage of goods by land, sea, air or pipeline;
(d) the exploitation of oil and gas reserves or other natural resources;
(e) insurance and re-insurance;
(f) banking and financial services;
(g) the operation of markets and exchanges;
(h) the purchase and sale of commodities;
(i) the construction of ships;
(j) business agency; and
(k) arbitration.

See **Commercial Court.**

COMMERCIAL COURT

Pt 58 r.58.1

(1) [Part 58] applies to claims in the Commercial Court of the Queen's Bench Division.

See **Commercial claim.**

PD 58 para.1.1

[PD 58] applies to commercial claims proceeding in the commercial list of the Queen's Bench Division. It supersedes all previous PDs and practice statements in the Commercial Court.

PD 58 para.1.2

All proceedings in the commercial list, including any appeal from a judgment, order or decision of a master or district judge before the proceedings were transferred to the Commercial Court, will be heard or determined by a Commercial Court judge, except that—
1. (1) another judge of the Queen's Bench Division or Chancery Division may hear urgent applications if no Commercial Court judge is available; and
2. (2) unless the court otherwise Orders, any application relating to the enforcement of a Commercial Court judgment or order for the payment of money will be dealt with by a master of the Queen's Bench Division or a district judge.

PD 58 para.1.3

Provisions in other PDs which refer to a master or district judge are to be read, in relation to claims in the commercial list, as if they referred to a Commercial Court judge.

PD 58 para.1.4

The Admiralty and Commercial Registry in the Royal Courts of Justice is the administrative office of the court for all proceedings in the commercial list.

Specialist list

Pt 58 r.58.2

(1) The commercial list is a specialist list for claims proceeding in the Commercial Court.
(2) One of the judges of the Commercial Court shall be in charge of the commercial list.

Application of the Civil Procedure Rules

Pt 58 r.58.3

These rules and their PDs apply to claims in the commercial list unless this Part or a PD provides otherwise

Applications before proceedings are issued

PD 58 para.3.1

A party who intends to bring a claim in the commercial list must make any application before the claim form is issued to a Commercial Court judge.

PD 58 para.3.2

The written evidence in support of such an application must state that the claimant intends to bring proceedings in the commercial list.

PD 58 para.3.3

If the Commercial Court judge hearing the application considers that the proceedings should not be brought in the commercial list, he may adjourn the application to be heard by a master or by a judge who is not a Commercial Court judge.

Transferring proceedings to or from the Commercial Court

PD 58 para.4.1

If an application is made to a court other than the Commercial Court to transfer proceedings to the commercial list, the other court may—
    (1) adjourn the application to be heard by a Commercial Court judge; or
    (2) dismiss the application.

PD 58 para.4.2

If the Commercial Court orders proceedings to be transferred to the commercial list—
    (1) it will order them to be transferred to the Royal Courts of Justice; and
    (2) it may give case management directions.

PD 58 para.4.3

An application by a defendant, including a Pt 20 defendant, for an order transferring proceedings from the commercial list should be made promptly and normally not later than the first case management conference.

PD 58 para.4.4

A party applying to the Commercial Court to transfer a claim to the commercial list must give notice of the application to the court in which the claim is proceeding, and the Commercial Court will not make an order for transfer until it is satisfied that such notice has been given.

Proceedings in the commercial list

Pt 58 r.58.4

    (1) A **commercial claim** may be started in the commercial list.
    (2) Rule 30.5 applies to claims in the commercial list, except that a Commercial Court judge
        may order a claim to be transferred to any other specialist list.
(Rule 30.5(3) provides that an application for the transfer of proceedings to or from a specialist list must be made to a judge dealing with claims in that list).

Starting proceedings in the Commercial Court

PD 58 para.2.1

Claims in the Commercial Court must be issued in the Admiralty and Commercial Registry.

PD 58 para.2.2

When the Registry is closed, a request to issue a claim form may be made by fax, using the procedure set out in Appendix A to this PD. If a request is made which complies with that procedure, the claim form is issued when the fax is received by the Registry.

PD 58 para.2.3

The claim form must be marked in the top right hand corner 'Queen's Bench Division, Commercial Court'.

PD 58 para.2.4

A claimant starting proceedings in the commercial list, other than an arbitration claim, must use practice form N1(CC) for Pt 7 claims or practice N208(CC) for Pt 8 claims.

Claim form and particulars of claim

Pt 58 r.58.5

(1) If, in a Pt 7 claim, particulars of claim are not contained in or served with the claim form—
  (a) the claim form must state that, if an acknowledgment of service is filed which indicates an intention to defend the claim, particulars of claim will follow;
  (b) when the claim form is served, it must be accompanied by the documents specified in r.7.8(1);
  (c) the claimant must serve particulars of claim within 28 days of the filing of an acknowledgment of service which indicates an intention to defend; and
  (d) rule 7.4(2) does not apply.
(2) A statement of value is not required to be included in the claim form.
(3) If the claimant is claiming interest, he must—
  (a) include a statement to that effect; and
  (b) give the details set out in r.16.4(2),
  in both the claim form and the particulars of claim.

Acknowledgment of service

Pt 58 r.58.6

(1) A defendant must file an acknowledgment of service in every case.
(2) Unless para.(3) applies, the period for filing an acknowledgment of service is 14 days after service of the claim form.
(3) Where the claim form is served out of the jurisdiction, or on the agent of a defendant who is overseas, the time periods provided by rr.6.12(3), 6.35 and 6.37(5) apply after service of the claim form.

PD 58 para.5.1

For Pt 7 claims, a defendant must file an acknowledgment of service using Practice Form N9 (CC).

PD 58 para.5.2

For Pt 8 claims, a defendant must file an acknowledgment of service using Practice Form N210 (CC).

Admissions

Pt 58 r.58.9

(1) Rule 14.5 does not apply to claims in the commercial list.
(2) If the defendant admits part of a claim for a specified amount of money, the claimant may apply under r.14.3 for judgment on the admission.
(3) Rule 14.14(1) applies with the modification that paragraph (a) shall be read as if it referred to the claim form instead of the particulars of claim.

Defence and reply

Pt 58 r.58.10

(1) Part 15 (defence and reply) applies to claims in the commercial list with the modification to r.15.8 that the claimant must—
(a) file any reply to a defence; and
(b) serve it on all other parties,
within 21 days after service of the defence.
(2) Rule 6.35 (in relation to the period for filing a defence where the claim form is served out of the jurisdiction) applies to claims in the commercial list, except that if the particulars of claim are served after the defendant has filed an acknowledgment of service the period for filing a defence is 28 days from service of the particulars of claim.

Statements of case

Pt 58 r.58.11

The court may at any time before or after the issue of the claim form order a claim in the commercial list to proceed without the filing or service of statements of case.

Part 8 claims

Pt 58 r.58.12

Part 8 applies to claims in the commercial list, with the modification that a defendant to a Pt 8 claim who wishes to rely on written evidence must file and serve it within 28 days after filing an acknowledgment of service.

Case management

Pt 58 r.58.13

(1) All proceedings in the commercial list are treated as being allocated to the multi-track and Pt 26 does not apply.

(2) The following parts only of Pt 29 apply—
   (a) rule 29.3(2) (legal representative to attend case management conferences and pre-trial reviews);
   (b) rule 29.5 (variation of case management timetable) with the exception of r.29.5(1)(c).
(3) As soon as practicable the court will hold a case management conference which must be fixed in accordance with PD 58.
(4) At the case management conference or at any hearing at which the parties are represented the court may give such directions for the management of the case as it considers appropriate.

PD 58 para.10.1

The following parts only of PD 29 apply—
   (1) paragraph 5 (case management conferences), excluding para.5.9 and modified so far as is made necessary by other specific provisions of this PD; and
   (2) paragraph 7 (failure to comply with case management directions).

PD 58 para.10.2

If the proceedings are started in the commercial list, the claimant must apply for a case management conference—
   (a) for a Pt 7 claim, within 14 days of the date when all defendants who intend to file and serve a defence have done so; and
   (b) for a Pt 8 claim, within 14 days of the date when all defendants who intend to serve evidence have done so.

PD 58 para.10.3

If the proceedings are transferred to the commercial list, the claimant must apply for a case management conference within 14 days of the date of the order transferring them, unless the judge held, or gave directions for, a case management conference when he made the order transferring the proceedings.

PD 58 para.10.4

Any party may, at a time earlier than that provided in paras 10.2 or 10.3, apply in writing to the court to fix a case management conference.

PD 58 para.10.5

If the claimant does not make an application in accordance with paras 10.2 or 10.3, any other party may apply for a case management conference.

PD 58 para.10.6

The court may fix a case management conference at any time on its own initiative. If it does so, the court will give at least seven days notice to the parties, unless there are compelling reasons for a shorter period of notice.

PD 58 para.10.7

Not less than seven days before a case management conference, each party must file and serve—

(1) a completed case management information sheet; and

(2) an application notice for any order which that party intends to seek at the case management conference, other than directions referred to in the case management information sheet.

PD 58 para.10.8

Unless the court Orders otherwise, the claimant, in consultation with the other parties, must prepare—

(1) a case memorandum, containing a short and uncontroversial summary of what the case is about and of its material case history;

(2) a list of issues, with a section listing important matters which are not in dispute; and

(3) a case management bundle containing—

(a) the claim form;

(b) all statements of case (excluding schedules), except that, if a summary of a statement of case has been filed, the bundle should contain the summary, and not the full statement of case;

(c) the case memorandum;

(d) the list of issues;

(e) the case management information sheets and, if a pre-trial timetable has been agreed or ordered, that timetable;

(f) the principal orders of the court; and

(g) any agreement in writing made by the parties as to disclosure,

and provide copies of the case management bundle for the court and the other parties at least 7 days before the first case management conference or any earlier hearing at which the court may give case management directions.

PD 58 para.10.9

The claimant, in consultation with the other parties, must revise and update the documents referred to in para.10.8 appropriately as the case proceeds. This must include making all necessary revisions and additions at least seven days before any subsequent hearing at which the court may give case management directions.

Case management where there is a Part 20 claim

PD 58 para.12.

Paragraph 5 of PD 20 applies, except that, unless the court otherwise orders, the court will give case management directions for Part 20 claims at the same case management conferences as it gives directions for the main claim.

Disclosure—ships papers

Pt 58 r.58.14

(1) If, in proceedings relating to a marine insurance policy, the underwriters apply for specific disclosure under r.31.12, the court may—

(a) order a party to produce all the ships papers; and

(b) require that party to use his best endeavours to obtain and disclose documents which are not or have not been in his control.

(2) An order under this rule may be made at any stage of the proceedings and on such terms, if any, as to staying the proceedings or otherwise, as the court thinks fit.

Judgments and orders

Pt 58 r.58.15

(1) Except for orders made by the court on its own initiative and unless the court orders otherwise, every judgment or order will be drawn up by the parties, and r.40.3 is modified accordingly.
(2) An application for a consent order must include a draft of the proposed order signed on behalf of all the parties to whom it relates.
(3) Rule 40.6 (**consent judgments and orders**) does not apply.

PD 58 para.14.1

An application for a consent order must include a draft of the proposed order signed on behalf of all parties to whom it relates (see para.10.4 of PD 23A).

PD 58 para.14.2

Judgments and orders are generally drawn up by the parties (see r.58.15). The parties are not therefore required to supply draft Orders on disk (see para.12.1 of PD 23A).

Variation of time limits

PD 58 para.7.1

If the parties, in accordance with r.2.11, agree in writing to vary a time limit, the claimant must notify the court in writing, giving brief written reasons for the agreed variation.

PD 58 para.7.2

The court may make an order overriding an agreement by the parties varying a time limit.

Amendments

PD 58 para.8

Paragraph 2.2 of PD 17 is modified so that amendments to a statement of case must show the original text, unless the court orders otherwise.

Service of documents

PD 58 para.9

Unless the court orders otherwise, the Commercial Court will not serve documents or orders and service must be effected by the parties.

Pre-trial review

PD 58 para.11.1

At any pre-trial review or case management hearing, the court will ensure that case management directions have been complied with and give any further directions for the trial that are necessary.

PD 58 para.11.2

Advocates who are to represent the parties at the trial should represent them at the pre-trial review and any case management hearing at which arrangements for the trial are to be discussed.

PD 58 para.11.3

Before the pre-trial review, the parties must discuss and, if possible, agree a draft written timetable for the trial.

PD 58 para.11.4

The claimant must file a copy of the draft timetable for the trial at least two days before the hearing of the pre-trial review. Any parts of the timetable which are not agreed must be identified and short explanations of the disagreement must be given.

PD 58 para.11.5

At the pre-trial review, the court will set a timetable for the trial, unless a timetable has already been fixed or the court considers that it would be inappropriate to do so or appropriate to do so at a later time.

Evidence for applications

PD 58 para.13.1

The general requirement is that, unless the court orders otherwise—
  (1) evidence in support of an application must be filed and served with the application (see r.23.7(3));
  (2) evidence in answer must be filed and served within 14 days after the application is served; and
  (3) evidence in reply must be filed and served within seven days of the service of evidence in answer.

PD 58 para.13.2

In any case in which the application is likely to require an oral hearing of more than half a day the periods set out in paras 13.1(2) and (3) will be 28 days and 14 days respectively.

PD 58 para.13.3

If the date fixed for the hearing of an application means that the times in paras 13.1(2) and (3) cannot both be achieved, the evidence must be filed and served—

(1) as soon as possible; and

(2) in sufficient time to ensure that the application may fairly proceed on the date fixed.

PD 58 para.13.4

The parties may, in accordance with r.2.11, agree different periods from those in paras 13.1(2) and (3) provided that the agreement does not affect the date fixed for the hearing of the application.

See also **Default judgment** and **Jurisdiction**.

COMMERCIAL COURT GUIDE

See **Admiralty and Commercial Courts Guide**.

COMMON COSTS

Pt 44 para.4.2

    (b)   (i) Costs incurred in relation to the GLO issues;

          (ii) individual costs incurred in a claim while it is proceeding as a test claim, and

         (iii) costs incurred by the lead solicitor in administering the group litigation.

COMMON FORM PROBATE PROCEEDINGS

PD 57 para.1.2

The rules and procedure relating to non-contentious probate proceedings (also known as 'common form') are the Non-Contentious Probate Rules 1987 as amended.

See **Non-contentious probate proceedings** and **Court documents**.

COMMONHOLD AND LEASEHOLD REFORM ACT 2002

Transfer to Leasehold Valuation Tribunal

PD 56 para.15.1

If a question is ordered to be transferred to a leasehold valuation tribunal for determination under para.3 of Sch.12 to the Commonhold and Leasehold Reform Act 2002, the court will—

    (1) send notice of the transfer to all parties to the claim; and

    (2) send to the leasehold valuation tribunal—

        (a) the order of transfer; and

        (b) all documents filed in the claim relating to the question.

(Paragraph 15.1 applies to proceedings in England but does not apply to proceedings in Wales).

COMMONS REGISTRATION ACT 1965

The claimant must use the **Part 8 procedure**, and applications under s.14 of the Commons Registration Act 1965 brought in the Chancery Division.

COMMUNITY DESIGN COURTS

PD 63 para.15.1

The Patents Court and the patents county court at the Central London County Court are the designated Community design courts under art.80(5) of Council Regulation (EC) 6/2002.

COMMUNITY JUDGMENT

See **European Community judgments**.

COMMUNITY LEGAL SERVICE (COSTS) REGULATIONS 2000

Costs PD para.22.1

In [Costs PD]:
'order for costs to be determined' means an order for costs to which s.11 of the Access to Justice Act 1999 applies under which the amount of costs payable by the LSC funded client is to be determined by a costs judge or district judge under s.23 of this PD.
'order specifying the costs payable' means an order for costs to which s.11 of the Act applies and which specifies the amount which the LSC funded client is to pay.
'full costs' means, where an order to which s.11 of the Act applies is made against a LSC funded client, the amount of costs which that person would, had cost protection not applied, have been ordered to pay.
'determination proceedings' means proceedings to which paras 22.1 to 22.10 apply.
'Section 11(1) costs order' means an order for costs to be determined or an order specifying the costs payable other than an order specifying the costs payable which was made in determination proceedings.
'statement of resources' means:
   (1) a statement, verified by a statement of truth, made by a party to proceedings setting out:
     (a) his income and capital and financial commitments during the previous year and, if applicable, those of his partner;
     (b) his estimated future financial resources and expectations and, if applicable, those of his partner ('partner' is defined in para.21.4, above);
     (c) a declaration that he and, if applicable, his partner, has not deliberately foregone or deprived himself of any resources or expectations;
     (d) particulars of any application for funding made by him in connection with the proceedings; and,
     (e) any other facts relevant to the determination of his resources; or
   (2) a statement, verified by a statement of truth, made by a client receiving funded services, setting out the information provided by the client under reg.6 of the Community Legal Service (Financial) Regulations 2000, and stating that there has been no significant change in the client's financial circumstances since the date on which the information was provided or, as the case may be, details of any such change.

'Regional Director' means any Regional Director appointed by the LSC and any member of his staff authorised to act on his behalf.

Costs PD para.22.2

Regulations 8 to 13 of the Community Legal Service (Costs) Regulations 2000 as amended set out the procedure for seeking costs against a funded client and the LSC. The effect of these Regulations is set out in this section and the next section of this PD.

Costs PD para.22.3

As from June 5, 2000, regs 9 to13 of the Community Legal Service (Costs) Regulations 2000 as amended also apply to certificates issued under the Legal Aid Act 1988 where costs against the assisted person fall to be assessed under reg.124 of the Civil Legal Aid (General) Regulations 1989. In this section and the next section of this PD the expression 'LSC funded client' includes an assisted person (defined in r.43.2).

Costs PD para.22.4

Regulation 8 of the Community Legal Service (Costs) Regulations 2000 as amended provides that a party intending to seek an order for costs against a LSC funded client may at any time file and serve on the LSC funded client a statement of resources. If that statement is served seven or more days before a date fixed for a hearing at which an order for costs may be made, the LSC funded client must also make a statement of resources and produce it at the hearing.

Costs PD para.22.5

If the court decides to make an order for costs against a LSC funded client to whom cost protection applies it may either:
 (1) make an order for costs to be determined, or
 (2) make an order specifying the costs payable.

Costs PD para.22.6

If the court makes an order for costs to be determined it may also:
 (1) state the amount of full costs, or
 (2) make findings of facts, e.g. concerning the conduct of all the parties which are to be taken into account by the court in the subsequent determination proceedings.

Costs PD para.22.7

The court will not make an order specifying the costs payable unless:
 (1) it considers that it has sufficient information before it to decide what amount is a reasonable amount for the LSC funded client to pay in accordance with s.11 of the Act, and
 (2) either
  (a) the order also states the amount of full costs, or
  (b) the court considers that it has sufficient information before it to decide what amount is a reasonable amount for the LSC funded client to pay in accordance with s.11 of the Act and is satisfied that, if it were to determine the full costs at that time, they would exceed the amounts specified in the order.

Costs PD para.22.8

Where an order specifying the costs payable is made and the LSC funded client does not have cost protection in respect of all of the costs awarded in that order, the order must identify the sum payable (if any) in respect of which the LSC funded client has cost protection and the sum payable (if any) in respect of which he does not have cost protection.

Costs PD para.22.9

The court cannot make an order under regs 8 to 13 of the Community Legal Service (Costs) Regulations 2000 as amended except in proceedings to which the next section of this PD applies.

Costs PD para.23.1

[S.3 of Costs PD] deals with
   (1) proceedings subsequent to the making of an order for costs to be determined,
   (2) variations in the amount stated in an order specifying the amount of costs payable and
   (3) the late determination of costs under an order for costs to be determined;
   (4) appeals in respect of determination.

Costs PD para.23.2

In this section of this PD 'appropriate court office' means:
   (1) the district registry or county court in which the case was being dealt with when the s.11(1) order was made, or to which it has subsequently been transferred; or
   (2) in all other cases, the Costs Office.

Costs PD para.23.2A

   (1) This paragraph applies where the appropriate office is any of the following county courts:
       Barnet, Bow, Brentford, Bromley, Central London, Clerkenwell and Shoreditch, Croydon, Edmonton, Ilford, Kingston, Lambeth, Mayors and City of London, Romford, Uxbridge, Wandsworth, West London, Willesden and Woolwich.
   (2) Where this para. applies:
       (i) a receiving party seeking an order specifying costs payable by an LSC funded client and/or by the Legal Services Commission under this section must file his application in the Costs Office and, for all purposes relating to that application, the Costs Office will be treated as the appropriate office in that case; and
       (ii) unless an order is made transferring the application to the Costs Office as part of the High Court, an appeal from any decision made by a costs judge shall lie to the Designated Civil Judge for the London Group of County Courts or such judge as he shall nominate. The appeal notice and any other relevant papers should be lodged at the Central London Civil Justice Centre.

Costs PD para.23.3

   (1) A receiving party seeking an order specifying costs payable by an LSC funded client and/ or by the LSC may within three months of an order for costs to be determined, file in the appropriate court office an application in Form N244 accompanied by
       (a) the receiving party's bill of costs (unless the full costs have already been determined);

    (b) the receiving party's statement of resources (unless the court is determining an application against a costs order against the LSC and the costs were not incurred in the court of first instance); and

    (c) if the receiving party intends to seek costs against the LSC, written notice to that effect.

  (2) If the LSC funded client's liability has already been determined and is less than the full costs, the application will be for costs against the LSC only. If the LSC funded client's liability has not yet been determined, the receiving party must indicate if costs will be sought against the LSC if the funded client's liability is determined as less than the full costs.

(The LSC funded client's certificate will contain the addresses of the LSC funded client, his solicitor, and the relevant Regional Office of the LSC).

Costs PD para.23.4

The receiving party must file the above documents in the appropriate court office and (where relevant) serve copies on the LSC funded client and the Regional Director. In respect of applications for funded services made before December 3, 2001 a failure to file a request within the three month time limit specified in reg.10(2) is an absolute bar to the making of a costs order against the LSC. Where the application for funded services was made on or after December 3, 2001 the court does have power to extend the three month time limit, but only if the applicant can show good reason for the delay.

Costs PD para.23.5

On being served with the application, the LSC funded client must respond by filing a statement of resources and serving a copy of it on the receiving party (and the Regional Director where relevant) within 21 days. The LSC funded client may also file and serve written points disputing the bill within the same time limit. (Under r.3.1 the court may extend or shorten this time limit).

Costs PD para.23.6

If the LSC funded client fails to file a statement of resources without good reason, the court will determine his liability (and the amount of full costs if relevant) and need not hold an oral hearing for such determination.

Costs PD para.23.7

When the LSC funded client files a statement or the 21 day period for doing so expires, the court will fix a hearing date and give the relevant parties at least 14 days notice. The court may fix a hearing without waiting for the expiry of the 21 day period if the application is made only against the LSC.

Costs PD para.23.8

Determination proceedings will be listed for hearing before a costs judge or district judge. The determination of the liability on the LSC funded client will be listed as a private hearing.

Costs PD para.23.9

Where the LSC funded client does not have cost protection in respect of all of the costs awarded, the order made by the costs judge or district judge must in addition to specifying the costs payable, identify the full costs in respect of which cost protection applies and the full costs in respect of which cost protection does not apply.

Costs PD para.23.10

The Regional Director may appear at any hearing at which a costs order may be made against the LSC. Instead of appearing, he may file a written statement at court and serve a copy on the receiving party. The written statement should be filed and a copy served, not less than seven days before the hearing.

Variation of an order specifying the costs payable

Costs PD para.23.11

(1) This paragraph applies where the amount stated in an order specifying the costs payable plus the amount ordered to be paid by the LSC is less than the full costs to which cost protection applies.

(2) The receiving party may apply to the court for a variation of the amount which the LSC funded client is required to pay on the ground that there has been a significant change in the client's circumstances since the date of the order.

Costs PD para.23.12

On an application under para.23.11, where the order specifying the costs payable does not state the full costs:

(1) the receiving party must file with his application the receiving party's statement of resources and bill of costs and copies of these documents should be served with the application.

(2) The LSC funded client must respond to the application by making a statement of resources which must be filed at court and served on the receiving party within 21 days thereafter. The LSC funded client may also file and serve written points disputing the bill within the same time limit.

(3) The court will, when determining the application assess the full costs identifying any part of them to which cost protection does apply and any part of them to which cost protection does not apply.

Costs PD para.23.13

On an application under para.23.11 the order specifying the costs payable may be varied as the court thinks fit. That variation must not increase:

(1) the amount of any costs ordered to be paid by the LSC, and

(2) the amount payable by the LSC funded client,

to a sum which is greater than the amount of the full costs plus the costs of the application.

Costs PD para.23.14

(1) Where an order for costs to be determined has been made but the receiving party has not applied, within the three month time limit under para.23.2, the receiving party may apply on any of the following grounds for a determination of the amount which the funded client is required to pay:

(a) there has been a significant change in the funded client's circumstances since the date of the order for costs to be determined; or

    (b) material additional information about the funded client's financial resources is available which could not with reasonable diligence have been obtained by the receiving party at the relevant time; or

    (c) there were other good reasons for the failure by the receiving party to make an application within the time limit.

(2) An application for costs payable by the LSC cannot be made under this paragraph.

Costs PD para.23.15

(1) Where the receiving party has received funded services in relation to the proceedings, the LSC may make an application under paras 23.11 and 23.14 above.

(2) In respect of an application under para.23.11 made by the LSC, the LSC must file and serve copies of the documents described in para.23.12(1).

Costs PD para.23.16

An application under paras 23.11, 23.14 and 23.15 must be commenced before the expiration of six years from the date on which the court made the order specifying the costs payable, or (as the case may be) the order for costs to be determined.

Costs PD para.23.17

Applications under paras 23.11, 23.14 and 23.15 should be made in the appropriate court office and should be made in Form N244 to be listed for a hearing before a costs judge or district judge.

Appeals

Costs PD para.23.18

(1) Save as mentioned above any determination made under regs 9 or 10 of the Costs Regulations is final (reg.11(1)). Any party with a financial interest in the assessment of the full costs, other than a funded party, may appeal against that assessment in accordance with CPR Pt 52 (reg.11(2) and CPR r.47.20).

(2) The receiving party or the Commission may appeal on a point of law against the making of a costs order against the Commission, against the amount of costs the Commission is required to pay or against the court's refusal to make such an order (reg.11(4)).

COMPANIES ACTS 1985 AND 2006

Pt 49 r.49

[The CPR] apply to proceedings under—
    (a) the Companies Act 1985;
    (b) the Companies Act 2006; and
    (c) other legislation relating to companies and limited liability partnerships,
subject to the provision of [PD 49A and 49B] which applies to those proceedings.

PD 49A para.2

[PD 49A] applies to proceedings under—
    (a) the 1985 Act;

(b) the 2006 Act (except proceedings under Ch.1 of Pt 11 or Pt 30 of that Act);
(c) section 59 of the CJPA;
(d) Articles 22, 25 and 26 of the EC Regulation;
(e) Part VII FSMA; and
(f) the Cross-Border Mergers Regulations.
(Part 19 and PD 19C contain provisions about proceedings under Ch.1 of Pt 11 of the 2006 Act (derivative claims)).

Title of documents

PD 49A para.4

(1) The claim form in proceedings under the 1985 Act, the 2006 Act . . . and any application, affidavit, witness statement, notice or other document in such proceedings, must be entitled 'In the matter of [the name of the company in question] and in the matter of [the relevant law]', where '[the relevant law]' means 'the Companies Act 1985', 'the Companies Act 2006' . . . , as the case may be.
(2) Where a company changes its name in the course of proceedings, the title must be altered by—
  (a) substituting the new name for the old; and
  (b) inserting the old name in brackets at the end of the title.

Starting proceedings and notification of application made

PD 49A para.5

(1) Proceedings to which [PD 49A] applies must be started by a Pt 8 claim form—
  (a) unless a provision of this or another PD provides otherwise, but
  (b) subject to any modification of that procedure by this or any other PD.
(2) The claim form—
  (a) will, where issued in the High Court, be issued out of the Companies Court or a Chancery district registry; or
  (b) will, where issued in a county court, be issued out of a county court office.
(3) Where this PD requires a party to proceedings to notify another person of an application, such notification must, unless the court orders otherwise, be given by sending to that other person a copy of the claim form as soon as reasonably practicable after the claim form has been issued.

Company generally to be made a party to a claim under the 2006 Act

PD 49A para.7

(1) Where in a claim under the 2006 Act the company concerned is not the claimant, the company is to be made a defendant to the claim unless—
  (a) any other enactment, the CPR or this or another PD makes a different provision; or
  (b) the court orders otherwise.
(2) Where an application is made in the course of proceedings to which the company is or is required to be a defendant, the company must be made a respondent to the application unless—

    (a) any other enactment, the CPR or this or another PD makes a different provision;
    or
    (b) the court orders otherwise.

Applications under s.169 (director's right to protest against removal)

PD 49A para.8

    (1) This paragraph applies to an application for an order under s.169(5).
    (2) The claimant must notify the director concerned of the application.

Applications under s.244 (disclosure under court order of protected information)

PD 49A para.9

    (1) This paragraph applies to an application for an order under s.244.
    (2) The claimant must notify the director concerned of the application.

Applications under s.295 (application not to circulate members' statement) or s.317 (application not to circulate members' statement)

PD 49A para.10

    (1) This paragraph applies to an application for an order under ss.295 or 317.
    (2) The claimant must notify each member who requested the circulation of the relevant
    statement of the application.

Proceedings under s.370 (Unauthorised donations—enforcement of directors' liabilities by shareholder action)

PD 49A para.11

Proceedings to enforce a director's liability under s.370 must be started by a Pt 7 claim form.

Proceedings under s.456 (application in respect of defective accounts or directors' report)

PD 49A para.12

    (1) This paragraph applies to an application for a declaration under s.456(1).
    (2) The claimant must notify any former director who was a director at the time of the
    approval of the annual accounts or directors' report of the application.

Proceedings under ss.511, 514, 515 or 518 (representations or statements made by the auditor)

PD 49A para.13.

(1) This paragraph applies to an application for an order under ss.511(6), 514(7), 515(7) or 518(9).
(2) The claimant must notify the auditor of the application.

Proceedings under s.527 (members' powers to require website publication of audit concerns)

PD 49A para.14

(1) This paragraph applies to an application for an order under s.527(5).
(2) The claimant must, unless the court orders otherwise, notify each member who requested a statement to be placed on the website of the application.

Proceedings under Pts 26 and 27 of the 2006 Act (applications to sanction a compromise or arrangement)

PD 49A para.15

(1) This paragraph applies to an application for an order under Pts 26 and 27 of the 2006 Act to sanction a compromise or arrangement.
(2) Where the application is made by the company concerned, or by a liquidator or administrator of the company, there need be no defendant to the claim unless the court so orders.
(3) The claim form must be supported by written evidence, including—
    (a) statutory information about the company; and
    (b) the terms of the proposed compromise or arrangement.
(4) The claim form must seek—
    (a) directions for convening a meeting of creditors or members or both, as the case requires;
    (b) the sanction of the court to the compromise or arrangement, if it is approved at the meeting or meetings, and a direction for a further hearing for that purpose; and
    (c) a direction that the claimant files a copy of a report to the court by the chairman of the meeting or of each meeting.

Proceedings under s.955 (takeovers—enforcement by the court)

PD 49A para.16

Proceedings for an order under s.955 must be started by a Pt 7 claim form.

PD 49A para.17

Proceedings to recover compensation under s.968(6) must be started by a Pt 7 claim form.

Applications under s.1132 (production and inspection of documents where offence suspected)

PD 49A para.18

(a) This paragraph applies to an application for an order under s.1132.
(b) No notice need be given to any person against whom the order is sought.

Reduction of capital—evidence

PD 49A para.27

In the case of an application to confirm a reduction in capital, if any shares were issued otherwise than for cash—
    (a) for any shares so issued on or after January 1, 1901, it is sufficient to set out in the, application the extent to which the shares are, or are treated as being, paid up; and
    (b) for any shares so issued between September 1, 1867 and December 31, 1900, the application must also show that the requirement as to the filing of the relevant contract with the Registrar of Joint Stock Companies in s.25 of the Companies Act 1867 was complied with.

Service of documents

PD 49A para.28

The parties are responsible for service of documents in proceedings to which this PD applies.

COMPANIES COURT

The Bankruptcy and Companies Court is part of the Chancery Division of the High Court.
    The Companies Court deals with:
    Company winding up petitions;
    Post-winding up applications, the purpose of which is to obtain information about or achieve realisations of company assets;
    Petitions for the approval of the reduction in the capital or share premium account of companies;
    A wide range of final applications relating to companies, such as:
    Applications to restore to the register
    To register charges out of time
    Applications for permission to bring proceedings
    Applications appealing a liquidator's rejection of proof
    A range of interlocutory applications such as the pre-trial management of unfair prejudice petitions
    Applications by the secretary of State for Trade and Industry and the Official Receiver for the disqualification of unfit company directors
    Applications for permission to act as a director following the making of such an order.

COMPANY

Acknowledgment of service

PD 10 para.4.2

Where the defendant is a company or other corporation, a person holding a senior position in the company or corporation may sign the acknowledgment of service on the defendant's behalf, but must state the position he holds.

PD 10 para.4.3

Each of the following persons is a person holding a senior position:
  (1) in respect of a registered company or corporation, a director, the treasurer, secretary, chief executive, manager or other officer of the company or corporation, and
  (2) in respect of a corporation which is not a registered company, in addition to those persons set out in (1), the mayor, chairman, president, town clerk or similar officer of the corporation.

Claim form

PD 16 para.2.6

The claim form must be headed with the title of the proceedings, including the full name of each party. The full name means, in each case where it is known:
  (d) in the case of a company or limited liability partnership registered in England and Wales, the full registered name, including suffix (Plc, Ltd, LLP, etc.), if any;
  (e) in the case of any other company or corporation, the full name by which it is known, including suffix where appropriate.

Personal service on a company or other corporation

PD 6A para.6.1

Personal service on a registered company or corporation in accordance with r.6.5(3) is effected by leaving a document with a person holding a senior position.

PD 6A para.6.2

Each of the following persons is a person holding a senior position—
  (1) in respect of a registered company or corporation, a director, the treasurer, the secretary of the company or corporation, the chief executive, a manager or other officer of the company or corporation.

Representation at trial of companies or other corporations

PD 39 r.39.6

A company or other corporation may be represented at trial by an employee if—
  (a) the employee has been authorised by the company or corporation to appear at trial on its behalf; and

(b) the court gives permission.

Statements of truth

PD 22 para.3.4

Where a document is to be verified on behalf of a company or other corporation, subject to para.3.7 below, the statement of truth must be signed by a person holding a senior position in the company or corporation. That person must state the office or position held.

PD 22 para.3.5

Each of the following persons is a person holding a senior position:
  In respect of a registered company or corporation, a director, the treasurer, secretary, chief executive, manager or other officer of the company or corporation.

PD 22 para.3.11

The word "manager" will be construed in the context of the phrase "a person holding a senior position" which it is used to define. The court will consider the size of the company and the size and nature of the claim. It would expect the manager signing the statement of truth to have personal knowledge of the content of the document or to be responsible for managing those who have that knowledge of the content. A small company may not have a manager, apart from the directors, who holds a senior position. A large company will have many such managers. In a larger company with specialist claims, insurance or legal departments the statement may be signed by the manager of such a department if he or she is responsible for handling the claim or managing the staff handling it.

COMPANY INSOLVENCY

Administrations

PD IP para.10.1

In the absence of special circumstances, an application for the extension of an administration should be made not less than one month before the end of the administration. The evidence in support of any later application must explain why the application is being made late. The court will consider whether any part of the costs should be disallowed where an application is made less than one month before the end of the administration.

Winding-up petitions

PD IP para.11.1

Before presenting a winding-up petition the creditor must conduct a search to ensure that no petition is already pending. Save in exceptional circumstances a second winding up petition should not be presented whilst a prior petition is pending. A petitioner who presents his own petition while another petition is pending does so at risk as to costs.

PD IP para.11.2

Every creditor's winding-up petition must (in the case of a company) contain the following—
 (1) the full name and address of the petitioner;
 (2) the name and number of the company in respect of which a winding up order is sought;
 (3) the date of incorporation of the company and the Companies Act or Acts under which it was incorporated;
 (4) the address of the company's registered office;
 (5) a statement of the nominal capital of the company, the manner in which its shares are divided up and the amount of the capital paid up or credited as paid up;
 (6) brief details of the principal objects for which the company was established followed, where appropriate, by the words 'and other objects stated in the memorandum of association of the company';
 (7) details of the basis on which it is contended that the company is insolvent including, where a debt is relied on, sufficient particulars of the debt (the amount, nature and approximate date(s) on which it was incurred) to enable the company and the court to identify the debt;
 (8) a statement that the company is insolvent and unable to pay its debts;
 (9) a statement that for the reasons set out in the evidence verifying the petition the EC Regulation on Insolvency Proceedings either applies or does not and if the former whether the proceedings will be main, territorial or secondary proceedings;
 (10) the statement that, 'In the circumstances it is just and equitable that the company be wound up under the provisions of the Insolvency Act 1986';
 (11) a prayer that the company be wound up, for such other order as the court thinks fit and any other specific relief sought.
Similar information (so far as is appropriate) should be given where the petition is presented against a partnership.

PD IP para.11.3

The statement of truth verifying the petition in accordance with r.4.12 should be made no more than ten business days before the date of issue of the petition.

PD IP para.11.4

Where the company to be wound up has been struck off the register, the petition should state that fact and include as part of the relief sought an order that it be restored to the register. Save where the petition has been presented by a Minister of the Crown or a government department, evidence of service on the Treasury Solicitor or the Solicitor for the affairs of the Duchy of Lancaster (as appropriate) should be filed exhibiting the bona vacantia waiver letter.

Errors in petitions

PD IP para.11.6.1

Applications for permission to amend errors in petitions which are discovered after a winding up order has been made should be made to the member of court staff in charge of the winding up list in the Royal Courts of Justice or to a District Judge in any other court.

PD IP para.11.6.2

Where the error is an error in the name of the company, the member of court staff in charge of the winding up list in the Royal Courts of Justice or a District Judge in any other court may make any necessary amendments to ensure that the winding up order is drawn up with the correct name of the company inserted. If there is any doubt, e.g. where there might be another company in existence which could be confused with the company to be wound up, the member of court staff in charge of the winding up list will refer the application to a Registrar at the Royal Courts of Justice and a District Judge may refer it to a Judge.

PD IP para.11.6.3

Where it is discovered that the company has been struck off the Register of Companies prior to the winding up order being made, the matter must be restored to the list as soon as possible to enable an order for the restoration of the name to be made as well as the order to wind up.

Gazetting of the petition

PD IP para.11.5.1

[Insolvency Rules], r.4.11 must be complied with (unless waived by the court): it is designed to ensure that the class remedy of winding up by the court is made available to all creditors, and is not used as a means of putting improper pressure on the company to pay the petitioner's debt or costs. Failure to comply with the rule, without good reason accepted by the court, may lead to the summary dismissal of the petition on the return date (r.4.11(6)) or to the court depriving the petitioner of the costs of the hearing. If the court, in its discretion, grants an adjournment, this will usually be on terms that notice of the petition is gazetted or otherwise given in accordance with the rule in due time for the adjourned hearing. No further adjournment for the purpose of gazetting will normally be granted.

PD IP para.11.5.2

Copies of every notice gazetted in connection with a winding up petition, or where this is not practicable a description of the form and content of the notice, must be lodged with the court as soon as possible after publication and in any event not later than five business days before the hearing of the petition. This direction applies even if the notice is defective in any way (e.g. is published on a date not in accordance with the Insolvency Rules, or omits or misprints some important words) or if the petitioner decides not to pursue the petition (e.g. on receiving payment).

Rescission of a winding up order

PD IP para.11.7.1

An application to rescind a winding up order must be made by application.

PD IP para.11.7.2

The application should normally be made within five business days after the date on which the order was made ([Insolvency Rules], r.7.47(4)) failing which it should include an application to extend time. Notice of any such application must be given to the petitioning creditor, any supporting or opposing creditor and the Official Receiver.

PD IP para.11.7.3

Applications will only be entertained if made (a) by a creditor, or (b) by a contributory, or (c) by the company jointly with a creditor or with a contributory. The application must be supported by a witness statement which should include details of assets and liabilities and (where appropriate) reasons for any failure to apply within five business days.

PD IP para.11.7.4

In the case of an unsuccessful application the costs of the petitioning creditor, any supporting creditors and of the Official Receiver will normally be ordered to be paid by the creditor or the contributory making or joining in the application. The reason for this is that if the costs of an unsuccessful application are made payable by the company, they fall unfairly on the general body of creditors.

Validation orders

PD IP para.11.8.1

A company against which a winding up petition has been presented may apply to the court after presentation of the petition for relief from the effects of s.127(1) of the Act by seeking an order that a disposition or dispositions of its property, including payments out of its bank account (whether such account is in credit or overdrawn), shall not be void in the event of a winding up order being made on the hearing of the petition (a validation order).

PD IP para.11.8.2

An application for a validation order should generally be made to the Registrar. An application should be made to the Judge only if: (a) it is urgent and no Registrar is available to hear it; or (b) it is complex or raises new or controversial points of law; or (c) it is estimated to last longer than 30 minutes.

PD IP para.11.8.3

Save in exceptional circumstances, notice of the making of the application should be given to: (a) the petitioning creditor; (b) any person entitled to receive a copy of the petition pursuant to [Insolvency Rules], r.4.10; (c) any creditor who has given notice to the petitioner of his intention to appear on the hearing of the petition pursuant to r.4.16; and (d) any creditor who has been substituted as petitioner pursuant to r.4.19.

PD IP para.11.8.4

The application should be supported by a witness statement which, save in exceptional circumstances, should be made by a director or officer of the company who is intimately acquainted with the company's affairs and financial circumstances. If appropriate, supporting evidence in the form of a witness statement from the company's accountant should also be produced.

PD IP para.11.8.5

The extent and contents of the evidence will vary according to the circumstances and the nature of the relief sought, but in the majority of cases it should include, as a minimum, the following information—

(1) when and to whom notice has been given in accordance with para.11.8.3 above;
(2) the company's registered office;
(3) the company's nominal and paid up capital;
(4) brief details of the circumstances leading to presentation of the petition;
(5) how the company became aware of presentation of the petition;
(6) whether the petition debt is admitted or disputed and, if the latter, brief details of the basis on which the debt is disputed;
(7) full details of the company's financial position including details of its assets (including details of any security and the amount(s) secured) and liabilities, which should be supported, as far as possible, by documentary evidence, e.g. the latest filed accounts, any draft audited accounts, management accounts or estimated statement of affairs;
(8) a cash flow forecast and profit and loss projection for the period for which the order is sought;
(9) details of the dispositions or payments in respect of which an order is sought;
(10) the reasons relied on in support of the need for such dispositions or payments to be made;
(11) any other information relevant to the exercise of the court's discretion;
(12) details of any consents obtained from the persons mentioned in para.11.8.3 above (supported by documentary evidence where appropriate);
(13) details of any relevant bank account, including its number and the address and sort code of the bank at which such account is held.

PD IP para.11.8.6

Where an application is made urgently to enable payments to be made which are essential to continued trading (e.g. wages) and it is not possible to assemble all the evidence listed above, the court may consider granting limited relief for a short period, but there should be sufficient evidence to satisfy the court that the interests of creditors are unlikely to be prejudiced.

PD IP para.11.8.7

Where the application involves a disposition of property the court will need details of the property (including its title number if the property is land) and to be satisfied that any proposed disposal will be at a proper value. Accordingly, an independent valuation should be obtained and exhibited to the evidence.

PD IP para.11.8.8

The court will need to be satisfied by credible evidence either that the company is solvent and able to pay its debts as they fall due or that a particular transaction or series of transactions in respect of which the order is sought will be beneficial to or will not prejudice the interests of all the unsecured creditors as a class (*Denney v John Hudson & Co Ltd* [1992] B.C.L.C. 901; *Re Fairway Graphics Ltd* [1991] B.C.L.C. 468).

PD IP para.11.8.9

A draft of the order sought should be attached to the application.

PD IP para.11.8.10

Similar considerations to those set out above are likely to apply to applications seeking ratification of a transaction or payment after the making of a winding-up order.

Applications

PD IP para.12.1

In accordance with [Insolvency Rules], r.13.2(2), in the Royal Courts of Justice the member of court staff in charge of the winding up list has been authorised to deal with applications—
   (1) to extend or abridge time prescribed by the Insolvency Rules in connection with winding up (r.4.3);
   (2) for permission to withdraw a winding up petition (r.4.15);
   (3) for the substitution of a petitioner (r.4.19);
   (4) by the Official Receiver for limited disclosure of a statement of affairs (r.4.35);
   (5) by the Official Receiver for relief from duties imposed upon him by the Insolvency Rules (r.4.47);
   (6) by the Official Receiver for permission to give notice of a meeting by advertisement only (r.4.59);
   (7) to transfer proceedings from the High Court (Royal Courts of Justice) to a county court after the making of a winding-up order (r.7.11).

PD IP para.12.2

In District Registries or a county court such applications must be made to a District Judge.

Order under s.127 of the Insolvency Act 1986

PD 49B para.1

Attention is drawn to the undesirability of asking as a matter of course for a winding up order as an alternative to an order under s.994 of the Companies Act 2006. The petition should not ask for a winding up order unless that is the remedy which the petitioner prefers or it is thought that it may be the only remedy to which the petitioner is entitled.

PD 49B paras 2 and 7

Whenever a winding up order is asked for in a contributory's petition, the petition must state whether the petitioner consents or objects to an order under s.127 of the Insolvency Act 1986 ('a s.127 order') in the standard form [set out in para.7 of PD 49B, which form may be departed from where the circumstances of the case require]. If he objects, the written evidence in support must contain a short statement of his reasons.

PD 49B para.3

If the petitioner objects to a s.127 order in the standard form but consents to such an order in a modified form, the petition must set out in the form of order to which he consents, and the written evidence in support must contain a short statement of his reasons for seeking the modification.

PD 49B para.4

If the petition contains a statement that the petitioner consents to a s.127 order, whether in the standard or a modified form, but the petitioner changes his mind before the first hearing of the petition, he must notify the respondents and may apply on notice to a Judge for an order directing that no s.127 order or a modified order only (as the case may be) shall be made by the Registrar, but validating dispositions made without notice of the order made by the Judge.

PD 49B para.5

If the petition contains a statement that the petitioner consents to a s.127 order, whether in the standard or a modified form, the Registrar shall without further enquiry make an order in such form at the first hearing unless an order to the contrary has been made by the Judge in the meantime.

PD 49B para.6

If the petition contains a statement that the petitioner objects to a s.127 order in the standard form, the company may apply (in the case of urgency, without notice) to the Judge for an order.

See also **Winding up proceedings**.

COMPETITION ACT 1998

Application for a warrant under the Act

PD Application for a warrant under the Competition Act para.1.1

PD AWCA para.1.2

In relation to an application for a warrant [under ss.28, 28A, 62, 62A, 63, 65G or 65H of the Act] by a regulator entitled pursuant to s.54 and Sch.10 of the Act to exercise the functions of the OFT, references to the OFT shall be interpreted as referring to that regulator.

Application for a warrant

PD AWCA para.2.1

An application by the [Office of Fair Trading] for a warrant must be made to a High Court judge using the **Part 8 procedure** as modified by [PD AWCA].

PD AWCA para.2.2

The application should be made to a judge of the Chancery Division at the Royal Courts of Justice (if available).

PD AWCA para.2.3

The application is made without notice and the claim form may be issued without naming a defendant. Rules 8.1(3), 8.3, 8.4, 8.5(2)–(6), 8.6(1), 8.7 and 8.8 do not apply.

Confidentiality of court documents

PD AWCA para.3.1

The court will not effect service of any claim form, warrant, or other document filed or issued in an application to which [PD AWCA] applies, except in accordance with an order of the judge hearing the application.

PD AWCA para.3.2

CPR rr.5.4, 5.4B and 5.4C do not apply, and paras 3.3 and 3.4 have effect in its place.

PD AWCA para.3.3

When a claim form is issued the court file will be marked 'Not for disclosure' and, unless a High Court judge grants permission, the court records relating to the application (including the claim form and documents filed in support and any warrant or order that is issued) will not be made available by the court for any person to inspect or copy, either before or after the hearing of the application.

PD AWCA para.3.4

An application for permission under para.3.3 must be made on notice to the OFT in accordance with Pt 23.
(Rule 23.7(1) requires a copy of the application notice to be served as soon as practicable after it is filed, and in any event at least three days before the court is to deal with the application).

Contents of claim form, affidavit and documents in support

PD AWCA para.4.1

The claim form must state—
  (1) the section of the [Competition Act 1998] under which the OFT is applying for a warrant;
  (2) the address or other identification of the premises to be subject to the warrant; and
  (3) the anticipated date or dates for the execution of the warrant.

PD AWCA para.4.2

The application must be supported by affidavit evidence, which must be filed with the claim form.

PD AWCA para.4.3

The evidence must set out all the matters on which the OFT relies in support of the application, including all material facts of which the court should be made aware. In particular it must state—
  (1) the subject matter (i.e. the nature of the suspected infringement of the Chs I or II prohibitions in the Act, or of arts 81 or 82 of the Treaty establishing the European Community) and purpose of the investigation to which the application relates;

(2) the identity of the undertaking or undertakings suspected to have committed the infringement;

(3) the grounds for applying for the issue of the warrant and the facts relied upon in support;

(4) details of the premises to be subject to the warrant and of the possible occupier or occupiers of those premises;

(5) the connection between the premises and the undertaking or undertakings suspected to have committed the infringement;

(6) the name and position of the officer [of the OFT] who it is intended will be the named officer [the person identified in a warrant as the principal officer in charge of executing that warrant, and includes a named authorised officer under s.63 of the Act];

(7) if it is intended that the warrant may pursuant to a relevant provision of the Act authorise any person (other than an officer or a Commission official [a person authorised by the Commission for any of the purposes set out in ss.62(10), 62A(12) or 63(10) of the Act]) to accompany the named officer in executing the warrant, the name and job title of each such person and the reason why it is intended that he may accompany the named officer.

PD AWCA para.4.4

There must be exhibited to an affidavit in support of the application—

(1) the written authorisation of the OFT containing the names of—
    (a) the officer who it is intended will be the named officer;
    (b) the other persons who it is intended may accompany him in executing the warrant; and

(2) in the case of an application under ss.62, 62A or 63 of the Act, if it is intended that Commission officials will accompany the named officer in executing the warrant, the written authorisations of the [European Commission] containing the names of the Commission officials.

PD AWCA para.4.5

There must also be filed with the claim form—

(1) drafts of—
    (a) the warrant; and
    (b) an explanatory note to be produced and served with it; and

(2) the written undertaking by the named officer required by para.6.2 of this PD .

(Examples of forms of warrant under ss.28 and 62 of the Act, and explanatory notes to be produced and served with them, are annexed to this PD. These forms and notes should be used with appropriate modifications in applications for warrants under other sections of the Act).

PD AWCA para.4.6

If possible the draft warrant and explanatory note should also be supplied to the court on disk in a form compatible with the word processing software used by the court.

Listing

PD AWCA para.5

The application will be listed by the court on any published list of cases as 'An application by D'.

Hearing of the application

PD AWCA para.6.1

An application for a warrant will be heard and determined in private, unless the judge hearing it directs otherwise.

PD AWCA para.6.2

The court will not issue a warrant unless there has been filed a written undertaking, signed by the named officer, to comply with para.8.1 of this PD.

Warrant

PD AWCA para.7.1

The warrant must—
- (1) contain the information required by ss.29(1), 64(1) or 65I(1) of the Act;
- (2) state the address or other identification of the premises to be subject to the warrant;
- (3) state the names of—
    - (a) the named officer; and
    - (b) any other officers, Commission officials or other persons who may accompany him in executing the warrant;
- (4) set out the action which the warrant authorises the persons executing it to take under the relevant section of the Act;
- (5) give the date on which the warrant is issued;
- (6) include a statement that the warrant continues in force until the end of the period of one month beginning with the day on which it issued; and
- (7) state that the named officer has given the undertaking required by para.6.2.

PD AWCA para.7.2

Rule 40.2 applies to a warrant.
(Rule 40.2 requires every judgment or order to state the name and judicial title of the person making it, to bear the date on which it is given or made, and to be sealed by the court.)

PD AWCA para.7.3

Upon the issue of a warrant the court will provide to the OFT—
- (1) the sealed warrant and sealed explanatory note; and
- (2) a copy of the sealed warrant and sealed explanatory note for service on the occupier or person in charge of the premises subject to the warrant.

Execution of warrant

PD AWCA para.8.1

A named officer attending premises to execute a warrant must, if the premises are occupied—
- (1) produce the warrant and an explanatory note on arrival at the premises; and
- (2) as soon as possible thereafter personally serve a copy of the warrant and the explanatory note on the occupier or person appearing to him to be in charge of the premises.

PD AWCA para.8.2

The named officer must also comply with any order which the court may make for service of any other documents relating to the application.

PD AWCA para.8.3

Unless the court otherwise orders—
   (1) the initial production of a warrant and entry to premises under the authority of the warrant must take place between 9.30 and 17.30 Monday to Friday; but
   (2) once persons named in the warrant have entered premises under the authority of a warrant, they may, whilst the warrant remains in force—
   (a) remain on the premises; or
   (b) re-enter the premises to continue executing the warrant,
   outside those times.

PD AWCA para.8.4

If the persons executing a warrant propose to remove any items from the premises pursuant to the warrant they must, unless it is impracticable—
   (1) make a list of all the items to be removed;
   (2) supply a copy of the list to the occupier or person appearing to be in charge of the premises; and
   (3) give that person a reasonable opportunity to check the list before removing any of the items.

Application to vary or discharge warrant

PD AWCA para.9.1

The occupier or person in charge of premises in relation to which a warrant has been issued may apply to vary or discharge the warrant.

PD AWCA para.9.2

An application under para.9.1 to stop a warrant from being executed must be made immdiately upon the warrant being served.

PD AWCA para.9.3

A person applying to vary or discharge a warrant must first inform the named officer that he is making the application.

PD AWCA para.9.4

The application should be made to the judge who issued the warrant, or, if he is not available, to another High Court judge.

Application under s.59 of the Criminal Justice and Police Act 2001

PD AWCA para.10.1

Attention is drawn to s.59 of the Criminal Justice and Police Act 2001, which makes provision about applications relating to property seized in the exercise of the powers conferred by (among other provisions) s.28(2) of the Act.

PD AWCA para.10.2

An application under s.59—
    (1) must be made by application notice in accordance with CPR Pt 23; and
    (2) should be made to a judge of the Chancery Division at the Royal Courts of Justice (if available).

Claims relating to the application of arts 81 and 82 of the EC Treaty and Chapters I and II of Pt I of the Competition Act 1998

PD—Competition Law—Claims relating to the application of arts 81 and 82 of the EC Treaty and Chs I and II of Pt I of the Competition Act 1998 para.1.1

This PD applies to any claim relating to the application of—
    (a) Article 81 or art.82 of the Treaty establishing the European Community; or
    (b) Chapter I or Ch.II of Pt I of the Competition Act 1998.

Venue

PD—CL para.2.1

A claim to which this PD applies—
    (a) must be commenced in the High Court at the Royal Courts of Justice; and
    (b) will be assigned to the Chancery Division, unless it comes within the scope of r.58.1(2), in which case it will be assigned to the Commercial Court of the Queen's Bench Division.

PD—CL para.2.2

Any party whose statement of case raises an issue relating to the application of arts 81 or 82 of the Treaty [establishing the European Community], or Chs I or II of Pt I of the [Competition Act 1998], must—
    (a) state that fact in his statement of case; and
    (b) apply for the proceedings to be transferred to the Chancery Division at the Royal Courts of Justice, if they have not been commenced there, or in the Commercial or Admiralty Courts; or
    (c) apply for the transfer of the proceedings to the Commercial Court, in accordance with rr.58.4(2) and 30.5(3). If such application is refused, the proceedings must be transferred to the Chancery Division of the High Court at the Royal Courts of Justice.

PD—CL para.2.3

Rule 30.8 provides that where proceedings are taking place in the Queen's Bench Division (other than proceedings in the Commercial or Admiralty Courts), a district registry of the High Court or a county court, the court must transfer the proceedings to the Chancery Division at the Royal Courts of Justice if the statement of case raises an issue relating to the application of arts 81 or 82, or Chs I or II. However, if any such proceedings which have been commenced in the Queen's Bench Division or a Mercantile Court fall within the scope of r.58.1(2), any party to those proceedings may apply for the transfer of the proceedings to the Commercial Court, in accordance with rr.58.4(2) and 30.5(3). If the application is refused, the proceedings must be transferred to the Chancery Division of the High Court at the Royal Courts of Justice.

PD—CL para.2.4

Where proceedings are commenced in or transferred to the Chancery Division at the Royal Courts of Justice in accordance with this paragraph, that court may transfer the proceedings or any part of the proceedings to another court if—
   (a) the issue relating to the application of arts 81 or 82, or Chs I or II, has been resolved; or
   (b) the judge considers that the proceedings or part of the proceedings to be transferred does not involve any issue relating to the application of arts 81 or 82, or Chs I or II.
(Rule 30.3 sets out the matters to which the court must have regard when considering whether to make a transfer order).

Notice of proceedings

PD—CL para.3

Any party whose statement of case raises or deals with an issue relating to the application of arts 81 or 82, or Chs I or II, must serve a copy of the statement of case on the Office of Fair Trading at the same time as it is served on the other parties to the claim (addressed to the Director of Competition Policy Co-ordination, Office of Fair Trading, Fleetbank House, 2–6 Salisbury Square, London EC4Y 8JX).

Case management

PD—CL para.4.1

Attention is drawn to the provisions of art.15.3 of the Competition Regulation [8 [means Council Regulation (EC) No 1/2003 of December 16, 2002 on the implementation of the rules on competition laid down in arts 81 and 82 of the Treaty] as a national competition authority of the UK]] (co-operation with national courts), which entitles competition authorities and the [European Commission] to submit written observations to national courts on issues relating to the application of arts 81 or 82 and, with the permission of the court in question, to submit oral observations to the court.

PD—CL para.4.1A

A national competition authority [means the Office of Fair Trading and any other person or body designated pursuant to art.35 of the Competition Regulation] may also make written observations to the court, or apply for permission to make oral observations, on issues relating to the application of Chs I or II.

PD—CL para.4.2

If a national competition authority or the Commission intends to make written observations to the court, it must give notice of its intention to do so by letter to Chancery Chambers at the Royal

Courts of Justice (including the claim number and addressed to the Court Manager, Room TM 6.06, Royal Courts of Justice, Strand, London WC2A 2LL) at the earliest reasonable opportunity.

PD—CL para.4.3

An application by a national competition authority or the Commission for permission to make oral representations at the hearing of a claim must be made by letter to Chancery Chambers (including the claim number and addressed to the Court Manager, Room TM 6.06, Royal Courts of Justice, Strand, London WC2A 2LL) at the earliest reasonable opportunity, identifying the claim and indicating why the applicant wishes to make oral representations.

PD—CL para.4.4

If a national competition authority or the Commission files a notice under para.4.2 or an application under para.4.3, it must at the same time serve a copy of the notice or application on every party to the claim.

PD—CL para.4.5

Any request by a national competition authority or the Commission for the court to send it any documents relating to a claim should be made at the same time as filing a notice under para.4.2 or an application under para.4.3.

PD—CL para.4.6

Where the court receives a notice under para.4.2 it may give case management directions to the national competition authority or the Commission, including directions about the date by which any written observations are to be filed.

PD—CL para.4.7

The court will serve on every party to the claim a copy of any directions given or order made—
  (a) on an application under para.4.3; or
  (b) under para.4.6.

PD—CL para.4.

In any claim to which this PD applies, the court shall direct a pre-trial review to take place shortly before the trial, if possible before the judge who will be conducting the trial.

Avoidance of conflict with commission decisions

PD—CL para.5.1

In relation to claims which raise an issue relating to the application of arts 81 or 82 of the Treaty, attention is drawn to the provisions of art.16 of the Competition Regulation (uniform application of Community competition law).

PD—CL para.5.2

Every party to such a claim, and any national competition authority which has been served with a copy of a party's statement of case, is under a duty to notify the court at any stage of the proceedings if they are aware that—
   (a) the Commission has adopted, or is contemplating adopting, a decision in relation to proceedings which it has initiated; and
   (b) the decision referred to in (a) above has or would have legal effects in relation to the particular agreement, decision or practice in issue before the court.

PD—CL para.5.3

Where the court is aware that the Commission is contemplating adopting a decision as mentioned in para.5.2(a), it shall consider whether to stay the claim pending the Commission's decision.

Judgments

PD—CL para.6

Where any judgment is given which decides on the application of art.81 or art.82 of the Treaty, the judge shall direct that a copy of the transcript of the judgment shall be sent to the Commission.

   Judgments may be sent to the Commission electronically to comp-amicus@cec.eu.int or by post to the European Commission—DG Competition, B–1049, Brussels.

Statement of case

PD 16 para.14

A party who wishes to rely on a finding of the Office of Fair Trading as provided by s.58 of the Competition Act 1998 must include in his statement of case a statement to that effect and identify the Office's finding on which he seeks to rely.

Transfer of competition law claims

Pt 30 r.30.8

   (1) This rule applies if, in any proceedings in the Queen's Bench Division, (other than proceedings in the Commercial or Admiralty Courts) a district registry of the High Court or a county court, a party's statement of case raises an issue relating to the application of—
      (a) Article 81 or art.82 of the Treaty establishing the European Community; or
      (b) Chapter I or II of Pt I of the Competition Act 1998;
   (2) Rules 30.2 and 30.3 do not apply.
   (3) The court must transfer the proceedings to the Chancery Division of the High Court at the Royal Courts of Justice.
   (4) If any such proceedings which have been commenced in the Queen's Bench Division or a Mercantile Court fall within the scope of r.58.1(2), any party to those proceedings may apply for the transfer of the proceedings to the Commercial Court, in accordance with

r.58.4(2) and r.30.5(3). If the application is refused, the proceedings must be transferred to the Chancery Division of the High Court at the Royal Courts of Justice.

See also **Competition Appeal Tribunal**.

COMPENSATION RECOVERY PAYMENTS

Final judgment

Adjustment of final judgment figure in respect of compensation recovery payments

PD 40B para.5.1

In a final judgment where some or all of the damages awarded—
  (1) fall under the heads of damage set out in column 1 of Sch.2 to the Social Security (Recovery of Benefits) Act 1997 in respect of recoverable benefits received by the claimant set out in column 2 of that Schedule; and
  (2) where the defendant has paid to the Secretary of State the recoverable benefits in accordance with the certificate (as defined in r.36.15(1)(e)),
there will be stated in the preamble to the judgment or order the amount awarded under each head of damage and the amount by which it has been reduced in accordance with s.8 of and Sch.2 to the 1997 Act.

PD 40B para.5.1A

Where damages are awarded in a case where a lump sum payment (to be construed in accordance with s.1A of the 1997 Act) has been made to a dependant, then s.15 of the 1997 Act (as modified by Sch.1 to the Social Security (Recovery of Benefits)(Lump Sum Payments) Regulations 2008 sets out what the court order must contain.

PD 40B para.5.2

The judgment or order should then provide for entry of judgment and payment of the balance.

See **Interim payment**.

COMPETITION APPEAL TRIBUNAL

Appeal from Competition Appeal Tribunal

PD 52D para.8.1

  (1) Where the appellant applies for permission to appeal at the hearing at which the decision is delivered by the tribunal and—
    (a) permission is given; or
    (b) permission is refused and the appellant wishes to make an application to the Court of Appeal for permission to appeal,

the appellant's notice must be filed at the Court of Appeal within 14 days after the date of that hearing.

(2) Where the appellant applies in writing to the Registrar of the tribunal for permission to appeal and—

    (a) permission is given; or

    (b) permission is refused and the appellant wishes to make an application to the Court of Appeal for permission to appeal,

the appellant's notice must be filed at the Court of Appeal within 14 days after the date of receipt of the tribunal's decision on permission.

(3) Where the appellant does not make an application to the tribunal for permission to appeal, but wishes to make an application to the Court of Appeal for permission, the appellant's notice must be filed at the Court of Appeal within 14 days after the end of the period within which he may make a written application to the Registrar of the tribunal.

Transfer from the High Court or a county court to the Competition Appeal Tribunal under s.16(4) of the Enterprise Act 2002

PD 30 para.8.3

The High Court or a county court may pursuant to s.16(4) of the [Enterprise Act 2002], on its own initiative or on application by the claimant or defendant, order the transfer of any part of the proceedings before it, which relates to a claim to which s.47A of the 1998 Act applies, to the [Competition Appeal Tribunal].

PD 30 para.8.4

When considering whether to make an order under para.8.3 the court shall take into account whether—

(1) there is a similar claim under s.47A of the [Competition Act 1998] based on the same infringement currently before the CAT;

(2) the CAT has previously made a decision on a similar claim under s.47A of the 1998 Act based on the same infringement; or

(3) the CAT has developed considerable expertise by previously dealing with a significant number of cases arising from the same or similar infringements.

PD 30 para.8.5

Where the court orders a transfer under paragraph 8.3 it will immediately—

(1) send to the CAT—

    (a) a notice of the transfer containing the name of the case; and

    (b) all papers relating to the case; and

(2) notify the parties of the transfer.

PD 30 para.8.6

An appeal against a transfer order made under para.8.3 must be brought in the court which made the transfer order.

Transfer from the Competition Appeal Tribunal to the High Court under s.16(5) of the Enterprise Act 2002

PD 30 para.8.7

Where the [Competition Appeal Tribunal] pursuant to s.16(5) of the [Enterprise Act 2002] directs transfer of a claim made in proceedings under s.47A of the [Competition Act 1998] to the High Court, the claim should be transferred to the Chancery Division of the High Court at the Royal Courts of Justice.

PD 30 para.8.8

As soon as a claim has been transferred under para.8.7, the High Court must—
    (1) allocate a case number; and
    (2) list the case for a case management hearing before a judge.

PD 30 para.8.9

A party to a claim which has been transferred under para.8.7 may apply to transfer it to the Commercial Court if it otherwise falls within the scope of r.58.2(1), in accordance with the procedure set out in rr.58.4(2) and 30.5(3).

COMPLETED BILL OF COSTS

Pt 47 r.47.16

    (1) A bill calculated to show the amount due following the detailed assessment of the costs.

COMPROMISE

Child or protected party

Compromise, etc. by or on behalf of a child or protected party

Pt 21 r.21.10

    (1) Where a claim is made—
        (a) by or on behalf of a **child** or **protected party**; or
        (b) against a child or protected party,
    no settlement, compromise or payment (including any voluntary interim payment) and no acceptance of money paid into court shall be valid, so far as it relates to the claim by, on behalf of or against the child or protected party, without the approval of the court.
    (2) Where—
        (a) before proceedings in which a claim is made by or on behalf of, or against, a child or protected party (whether alone or with any other person) are begun, an agreement is reached for the settlement of the claim; and
        (b) the sole purpose of proceedings is to obtain the approval of the court to a settlement or compromise of the claim,
    the claim must—

     (i) be made using the procedure set out in Part 8 (alternative procedure for claims); and

     (ii) include a request to the court for approval of the settlement or compromise.

(3) In proceedings to which s.II or s.VI of Pt 45 applies, the court will not make an order for detailed assessment of the costs payable to the child or protected party but will assess the costs in the manner set out in that section.

(Rule 48.5 contains provisions about costs where money is payable to a child or protected party).

Settlement or compromise by or on behalf of a child or protected party before the issue of proceedings

PD 21 para.5.1

Where a claim by or on behalf of a child or protected party has been dealt with by agreement before the issue of proceedings and only the approval of the court to the agreement is sought, the claim must, in addition to containing the details of the claim and satisfying the requirements of r.21.10(2), include the following—

  (1) subject to para.5.3, the terms of the settlement or compromise or have attached to it a draft consent order in Practice Form N292;

  (2) details of whether and to what extent the defendant admits liability;

  (3) the age and occupation (if any) of the child or protected party;

  (4) the litigation friend's approval of the proposed settlement or compromise,

  (5) a copy of any financial advice relating to the proposed settlement; and

  (6) in a personal injury case arising from an accident—

     (a) details of the circumstances of the accident,

     (b) any medical reports,

     (c) where appropriate, a schedule of any past and future expenses and losses claimed and any other relevant information relating to the personal injury as set out in PD 16 (statements of case), and

     (d) where considerations of liability are raised—

       (i) any evidence or reports in any criminal proceedings or in an inquest, and

       (ii) details of any prosecution brought.

PD 21 para.5.2

  (1) An opinion on the merits of the settlement or compromise given by counsel or solicitor acting for the child or protected party must, except in very clear cases, be obtained.

  (2) A copy of the opinion and, unless the instructions on which it was given are sufficiently set out in it, a copy of the instructions, must be supplied to the court.

PD 21 para.5.3

Where in any personal injury case a claim for damages for future pecuniary loss is settled, the provisions in paras 5.4 and 5.5 must in addition be complied with.

PD 21 para.5.4

The court must be satisfied that the parties have considered whether the damages should wholly or partly take the form of periodical payments.

PD 21 para.5.5

Where the settlement includes provision for periodical payments, the claim must—
    (1) set out the terms of the settlement or compromise; or
    (2) have attached to it a draft consent order,
which must satisfy the requirements of rr.41.8 and 41.9 as appropriate.

PD 21 para.5.6

Applications for the approval of a settlement or compromise will normally be heard by—
    (1) a Master or a district judge in proceedings involving a child; and
    (2) a Master, designated civil judge or his nominee in proceedings involving a protected party.
(For information about provisional damages claims see Part 41 and PD 41A).

Settlement or compromise by or on behalf of a child or protected party after proceedings have been issued

PD 21 para.6.1

Where in any personal injury case a claim for damages for future pecuniary loss, by or on behalf of a child or protected party, is dealt with by agreement after proceedings have been issued, an application must be made for the court's approval of the agreement.

PD 21 para.6.2

The court must be satisfied that the parties have considered whether the damages should wholly or partly take the form of periodical payments.

PD 21 para.6.3

Where the settlement includes provision for periodical payments, an application under para.6.1 must—
    (1) set out the terms of the settlement or compromise; or
    (2) have attached to it a draft consent order,
which must satisfy the requirements of rr.41.8 and 41.9 as appropriate.

PD 21, para.6.4

The court must be supplied with—
    (1) an opinion on the merits of the settlement or compromise given by counsel or solicitor acting for the child or protected party, except in very clear cases; and
    (2) a copy of any financial advice.

PD 21 para.6.5

Applications for the approval of a settlement or compromise, except at the trial, will normally be heard by—
    (1) a Master or a district judge in proceedings involving a child; and

(2) a Master, designated civil judge or his nominee in proceedings involving a protected party.

See also **Pre-action protocols**.

Companies

Applications to sanction a compromise or arrangement

PD 49A para.15

(1) This paragraph applies to an application for an order under Pts 26 and 27 of the Companies Act 2006 to sanction a compromise or arrangement.
(2) Where the application is made by the company concerned, or by a liquidator or administrator of the company, there need be no defendant to the claim unless the court so orders.
(3) The claim form must be supported by written evidence, including—
   (a) statutory information about the company; and
   (b) the terms of the proposed compromise or arrangement.
(4) The claim form must seek—
   (a) directions for convening a meeting of creditors or members or both, as the case requires;
   (b) the sanction of the court to the compromise or arrangement, if it is approved at the meeting or meetings, and a direction for a further hearing for that purpose; and
   (c) a direction that the claimant files a copy of a report to the court by the chairman of the meeting or of each meeting.

Transfer of proceedings for enforcement

Pt 70 r.70.3

(1) A judgment creditor wishing to enforce a High Court judgment or order in a county court must apply to the High Court for an order transferring the proceedings to that county court.

PD 70 para.2.1

Subject to s.II of [PD70][automatic transfer of proceedings in designated money claims], if a judgment creditor is required by a rule or practice direction to enforce a judgment or order of one county court in a different county court, he must first make a request in writing to the court in which the case is proceeding to transfer the proceedings to that other court.

PD 70 para.2.2

Subject to s.II of [PD70], on receipt of such a request, a court officer will transfer the proceedings to the other court unless a judge orders otherwise.

PD 70 para.2.3

The court will give notice of the transfer to all the parties.

PD 70 para.2.4

When the proceedings have been transferred, the parties must take any further steps in the proceedings in the court to which they have been transferred, unless a rule or PD provides otherwise.

Enforcement of judgment or order by or against non-party

Pt 70 r.70.4

If a judgment or order is given or made in favour of or against a person who is not a party to proceedings, it may be enforced by or against that person by the same methods as if he were a party.

Enforcement of decisions of bodies other than the High Court and county courts and compromises enforceable by enactment

Pt 70 r.70.5

(1) This rule applies, subject to para.(2), where an enactment provides that—
    (a) a decision of a court, tribunal, body or person other than the High Court or a county court; or
    (b) a compromise,
    may be enforced as if it were a court order or that any sum of money payable under that decision or compromise may be recoverable as if payable under a court order.
(2) This rule does not apply to—
    (a) any judgment to which Pt 74 applies;
    (b) arbitration awards;
    (c) any order to which [RSC Ord] 115 applies; or
    (d) proceedings to which Pt 75 (traffic enforcement) applies.
(2A) Unless para.(3) applies, a party may enforce the decision or compromise by applying for a specific method of enforcement under [Pts] 71 to 73, Schedule 1 RSC [Ord] 45 to 47 and 52 and Schedule 2 CCR [Ord] 25 to 29 and must—
    (a) file with the court a copy of the decision or compromise being enforced; and
    (b) provide the court with the information required by PD 70.
(3) If an enactment provides that a decision or compromise is enforceable or a sum of money is recoverable if a court so orders, an application for such an order must be made in accordance with para.(4) to (7A) of this rule.
(4) The application—
    (a) may, unless [para.(4A)] applies, be made without notice; and
    (b) must be made to the court for the district where the person against whom the order is sought, resides or carries on business, unless the court otherwise orders.
(4A) Where a compromise requires a person to whom a sum of money is payable under the compromise to do anything in addition to discontinuing or not starting proceedings ('a conditional compromise'), an application under [para] (4) must be made on notice.
(5) The application notice must—
    (a) be in the form; and
    (b) contain the information
    required by PD 70.
(6) A copy of the decision or compromise must be filed with the application notice.
(7) An application other than in relation to a conditional compromise may be dealt with by a court officer without a hearing.

(7A) Where an application relates to a conditional compromise, the respondent may oppose it by filing a response within 14 days of service of the application notice and if the respondent—
    (a) does not file a response within the time allowed, the court will make the order; or
    (b) files a response within the time allowed, the court will make such order as appears appropriate.
  (8) If an enactment provides that a decision or compromise may be enforced in the same manner as an order of the High Court if it is registered, any application to the High Court for registration must be made in accordance with PD70.

PD 70 para.4.1

The information referred to in r. 70.5(2A) must—
    (a) be included in [PF] N322B or, where para. 4.1A applies, in the [PF] required by para. 4.1A(2);
    (b) specify the statutory provision under which enforcement or the recovery of a sum of money is sought;
    (c) state the name and address of the person against whom enforcement or recovery is sought;
    (d) where the decision or compromise requires that person to pay a sum of money, state the amount which remains unpaid; and
    (e) confirm that, where a sum of money is being recovered pursuant to a compromise, the compromise is not a conditional compromise.

PD 70 para.4.1A

  (1) This paragraph applies where—
    (a) either—
      (i) the decision to be enforced is a decision of an employment tribunal in England and Wales; or
      (ii) the application is for the recovery of a compromise sum under s. 19A(3) of the Employment Tribunals Act 1996; and
    (b) the party seeking to enforce the decision wishes to enforce by way of a writ offieri facias
  (2) The practice form which is to be used is—
    (a) where para.(1)(a)(i) applies, [PF] N471;
    (b) where para. (1)(a)(ii) applies, [PF] N471A.

PD 70 para.4.2

Application under r. 70.5(3) for an order to enforce a decision or compromise must be made by filing an application notice in [PF] N322A.

PD 70 para.4.3

The application notice must state—
    (a) the name and address of the person against whom the order is sought;
    (b) how much remains unpaid or what obligation remains to be performed; and
    (c) where the application relates to a conditional compromise, details of what under the compromise the applicant is required to do and has done under the compromise in addition to discontinuing or not starting proceedings.

PD 70 para.4.4

Where—
  (a) the application relates to a conditional compromise; and
  (b) the application notice is served by the applicant on the respondent, the applicant must file a certificate of service with the court within seven days of service of the application notice.

CONCURRENT WARRANTS

CCR Ord.26 r.4

Two or more warrants of execution may be issued concurrently for execution in different districts, but—
  (a) no more shall be levied under all the warrants together than is authorised to be levied under one of them; and
  (b) the costs of more than one such warrant shall not be allowed against the debtor except by order of the court.

CONDITIONAL ORDER

PD 24 para.5.2

A conditional order is an order which requires a party:
  (1) to pay a sum of money into court, or
  (2) to take a specified step in relation to his claim or defence, as the case may be, and provides that that party's claim will be dismissed or his statement of case will be struck out if he does not comply.
(Note—the court will not follow its former practice of granting leave to a defendant to defend a claim, whether conditionally or unconditionally).

CONDUCT MONEY

See **Depositions** and **Witness summons**.

CONFISCATION AND FORFEITURE IN CONNECTION WITH CRIMINAL PROCEEDINGS

Drug Trafficking Act 1994 and Criminal Justice (International Co-operation) Act 1990

RSC Ord.115 r.1

  (2) Expressions used in this Part of this Order which are used in the Act have the same meanings in this Part of this order as in the Act and include any extended meaning given by the Criminal Justice (Confiscation) (Northern Ireland) Order 1990.

Assignment of proceedings

RSC Ord.115 r.2

Subject to r.12, the jurisdiction of the High Court under the [Drug Trafficking Act 1994] shall be exercised by a judge of the Chancery Division or of the Queen's Bench Division.

Title of proceedings

RSC Ord.115 r.2A

An application made in accordance with CPR Pt 23, or a claim form issued in relation to proceedings under this Part of this order shall be entitled in the matter of the defendant, naming him, and in the matter of the Act, and all subsequent documents in the matter shall be so entitled.

Application for confiscation order

RSC Ord.115 r.2B

(1) An application by the prosecutor for a confiscation order under s.19 shall be made in accordance with CPR Pt 23 where there have been proceedings against the defendant in the High Court, and shall otherwise be made by the issue of a claim form.
(2) The application shall be supported by a witness statement or affidavit giving full particulars of the following matters—
    (a) the grounds for believing that the defendant has died or absconded;
    (b) the date or approximate date on which the defendant died or absconded;
    (c) where the application is made under s.19(2), the offence or offences of which the defendant was convicted, and the date and place of conviction;
    (d) where the application is made under s.19(4), the proceedings which have been initiated against the defendant (including particulars of the offence and the date and place of institution of those proceedings); and
    (e) where the defendant is alleged to have absconded, the steps taken to contact him.
(3) The prosecutor's statement under s.11 shall be exhibited to the witness statement or affidavit and shall include the following particulars—
    (a) the name of the defendant;
    (b) the name of the person by whom the statement is given;
    (c) such information known to the prosecutor as is relevant to the determination whether the defendant has benefited from drug trafficking and to the assessment of the value of his proceeds of drug trafficking.
(4) Unless the court otherwise orders, a witness statement or affidavit under para.(2) may contain statements of information and belief, with their sources and grounds.
(5) The application and the witness statement or affidavit in support shall be served not less than seven days before the date fixed for the hearing of the application on—
    (a) the defendant (or on the personal representatives of a deceased defendant);
    (b) any person who the prosecutor reasonably believes is likely to be affected by the making of a confiscation order; and
    (c) the receiver, where one has been appointed in the matter.

Application for restraint order or charging order

RSC Ord.115 r.3

(1) An application for a restraint order under s.26 or for a charging order under s.27 (to either of which may be joined an application for the appointment of a receiver) may be made by the prosecutor by the issue of a claim form notice of which need not be served on any other party.

(2) An application under para.(1) shall be supported by a witness statement or affidavit, which shall—

    (a) give the grounds for the application; and

    (b) to the best of the witness's ability, give full particulars of the realisable property in respect of which the order is sought and specify the person or persons holding such property.

(3) Unless the court otherwise directs, a witness statement or affidavit under para.(2) may contain statements of information or belief with the sources and grounds thereof.

Restraint Order and Charging Order

RSC Ord.115 r.4

(1) A restraint order may be made subject to conditions and exceptions, including but not limited to conditions relating to the indemnifying of third parties against expenses incurred in complying with the order, and exceptions relating to living expenses and legal expenses of the defendant, but the prosecutor shall not be required to give an undertaking to abide by any order as to damages sustained by the defendant as a result of the restraint order.

(2) Unless the court otherwise directs, a restraint order made where notice of it has not been served on any person shall have effect until a day which shall be fixed for the hearing where all parties may attend on the application and a charging order shall be an order to show cause, imposing the charge until such day.

(3) Where a restraint order is made the prosecutor shall serve copies of the order and of the witness statement or affidavit in support on the defendant and on all other named persons restrained by the order and shall notify all other persons or bodies affected by the order of its terms.

(4) Where a charging order is made the prosecutor shall serve copies of the order and of the witness statement or affidavit in support on the defendant and, where the property to which the order relates is held by another person, on that person and shall serve a copy of the order on such of the persons or bodies specified in CPR r.73.5(1)(c) to (e) as shall be appropriate.

Discharge or variation of Order

RSC Ord.115 r.5

(1) Any person or body on whom a restraint order or a charging order is served or who is notified of such an order may make an application in accordance with CPR Pt 23 to discharge or vary the order.

(2) The application notice and any witness statement or affidavit in support shall be lodged with the court and served on the prosecutor and, where he is not the applicant, on the defendant, not less than two clear days before the date fixed for the hearing of the application.

(3) Upon the court being notified that proceedings for the offences have been concluded or that the amount, payment of which is secured by a charging order has been paid into court, any restraint order or charging order, as the case may be, shall be discharged.

(4) The court may also discharge a restraint order or a charging order upon receiving notice from the prosecutor that it is no longer appropriate for the restraint order or the charging order to remain in place.

Further application by prosecutor

RSC Ord.115 r.6

(1) Where a restraint order or a charging order has been made the prosecutor may apply by an application in accordance with CPR Pt 23 with notice or, where the case is one of urgency or the giving of notice would cause a reasonable apprehension of dissipation of assets, without notice—
   (a) to vary such order; or
   (b) for a restraint order or a charging order in respect of other realisable property; or
   (c) for the appointment of a receiver.

(2) An application under para.(1) shall be supported by a witness statement or affidavit which, where the application is for a restraint order or a charging order, shall to the best of the witness's ability give full particulars of the realisable property in respect of which the order is sought and specify the person or persons holding such property.

(3) The application and witness statement or affidavit in support shall be lodged with the court and served on the defendant and, where one has been appointed in the matter, on the receiver, not less than two clear days before the date fixed for the hearing of the application.

(4) Rule 4(3) and (4) shall apply to the service of restraint orders and charging orders respectively made under this rule on persons other than the defendant.

Form of restraint Order

PD RSC 115 para.2

An example of a restraint order is set out in Appendix 1 to [PD RSC]. This example may be modified as appropriate in any particular case.

Amount under restraint

PD RSC 115 para.3.1

A restraint order may, where appropriate, apply to—
   (1) all of the defendant's realisable property;
   (2) the defendant's realisable property up to a specified value; or
   (3) one or more particular specified assets.

PD RSC 115 para.3.2

Where—
   (1) a confiscation order or forfeiture order has already been made against the defendant in a particular amount; or

(2) the prosecutor is able to make a reasonably accurate estimate of the amount of any confiscation order or forfeiture order that might be made against him,

and, in either case, it is clear that the defendant's realisable property is greater in value than the amount or estimated amount of that order, the court will normally limit the application of the restraint order in accordance with para.3.1(2) or (3).

PD RSC 115 para.3.3

In such cases the prosecutor's draft order should normally either include an appropriate financial limit or specify the particular assets to which the order should apply.

Living expenses and legal fees

PD RSC 115 para.4

A restraint order will normally, unless it is clear that a person restrained has sufficient assets which are not subject to the order, include an exception to the order permitting that person to spend assets—

(1) in the case of an individual, for reasonable living expenses; and

(2) in the case of either an individual or a company, to pay reasonable legal fees so that they may take advice in relation to the order and if so advised apply for its variation or discharge.

Restraint Orders against third parties

PD RSC 115 para.5.1

Where a restraint order applies to property held in the name of a person other than the defendant—

(1) the order must be addressed to that person in addition to the defendant; and

(2) in applying for the order, the prosecutor must consider the guidance given in the matter of *G (restraint order)* [2001] EWHC Admin 606.

PD RSC 115 para.5.2

Examples of additional persons to whom an order must, where appropriate, be addressed include—

(1) a person who has a joint bank account with the defendant;

(2) in proceedings under the 1988 Act or the 1994 Act, a person to whom the defendant is alleged to have made a gift which may be treated as realisable property of the defendant under the provisions of the relevant Act; or

(3) a company, where the prosecutor alleges that assets apparently belonging to the company are in reality those of the defendant.

PD RSC 115 para.5.3

However, an order should not normally be addressed—

(1) to a bank with whom a defendant has an account; or

(2) to the business name of a defendant who carries on an unincorporated business (such business not being a separate legal entity from the defendant).

Restraint Orders against businesses

PD RSC 115 para.6

If an application for a restraint order is made against a company, partnership or individual apparently carrying on a legitimate business—
- (1) the court will take into account the interests of the employees, creditors and customers of the business and, in the case of a company, any shareholders other than the defendant, before making an order which would or might prevent the business from being continued; and
- (2) any restraint order made against that person will normally contain an exception enabling it to deal with its assets in the ordinary course of business.

Duration of order made on application without notice—rules 4(2) and 27(2)

PD RSC Ord.115 para.7.1

RSC Ord.115 rr.4(2) and 27(2) provide that, unless the court otherwise directs, a restraint order made without notice shall have effect until a day which shall be fixed for a further hearing where all parties may attend ('the return date').

PD RSC Ord.115 para.7.2

Where a return date is fixed, it will normally be no more than 14 days after the date of the order.

PD RSC Ord.115 para.7.3

Where no return date is fixed, the court will always include in the order a provision giving the defendant or anyone affected by the order permission to apply to vary or discharge the order (see paragraph 14 of the sample form of order).

Receivers

RSC Ord.115 r.8

- (1) Subject to the provisions of this rule, the provisions of CPR Pt 69 shall apply where a receiver is appointed in pursuance of a **charging order** or under ss.26 or 29.
- (2) Where the receiver proposed to be appointed has been appointed receiver in other proceedings under the Act, it shall not be necessary for a witness statement or affidavit of fitness to be sworn or for the receiver to give security, unless the court otherwise orders.
- (3) Where a receiver has fully paid the amount payable under the confiscation order and any sums remain in his hands, he shall make an application to the court for directions in accordance with CPR Pt 23, as to the distribution of such sums.
- (4) An application under para.(3) shall be served with any evidence in support not less than seven days before the date fixed for the hearing of the application on—
  - (a) the defendant; and
  - (b) any other person who held property realised by the receiver.
- (5) A receiver may apply for an order to discharge him from his office by making an application in accordance with CPR Pt 23, which shall be served, together with any

evidence in support, on all persons affected by his appointment not less than seven days before the day fixed for the hearing of the application.

Appointment of receiver

PD RSC Ord.115 para.8.1

CPR Pt 69, and PD 69, apply to the appointment of a receiver under the 1988,1994 or 2000 Act, subject to the provisions of RSC Ord.115 r.8 and r.23(e) where applicable.

PD RSC Ord.115 para.8.2

In particular, CPR r.69.7, and para.9 of PD 69, apply in relation to the remuneration of the receiver.

PD RSC Ord.115 para.8.3

Where no confiscation or forfeiture order has been made—
(1) an application for the appointment of a receiver should not be made without notice, unless the application is urgent or there is some other good reason for not giving notice to the defendant; and
(2) if the application is made without notice, the prosecutor's written evidence should explain the reasons for doing so.

PD RSC 115 para.8.4

Where the court appoints a receiver on an application without notice in the circumstances set out in para.8.3, the order will normally limit the receiver's powers to manage, deal with or sell property (other than with the defendant's consent) to the extent that is shown to be urgently necessary. If the receiver seeks further powers, he should apply on notice for further directions.

Certificate of inadequacy

RSC Ord.115 r.9

(1) The defendant or a receiver appointed under ss.26 or 29 or in pursuance of a charging order may apply in accordance with CPR Pt 23 for a certificate under s.17(1).
(2) An application under para.(1) shall be served with any supporting evidence not less than seven days before the date fixed for the hearing of the application on the prosecutor and, as the case may be, on either the defendant or the receiver (where one has been appointed).

Certificate under section 16

RSC Ord.115 r.9A

An application under s.16(2) (increase in realisable property) shall be served with any supporting evidence not less than seven days before the date fixed for the hearing of the application on the defendant and, as the case may be, on either the prosecutor or (where one has been appointed in the matter) on the receiver.

Compensation

RSC Ord.115 r.10

An application for an order under s.18 shall be made in accordance with CPR Pt 23, which shall be served, with any supporting evidence, on the person alleged to be in default and on the relevant authority under s.18(5) not less than seven days before the date fixed for the hearing of the application.

Disclosure of information

RSC Ord.115 r.11

(1) An application by the prosecutor under s.59 shall be made in accordance with CPR Pt 23 and the application notice shall state the nature of the order sought and whether material sought to be disclosed is to be disclosed to a receiver appointed under ss.26 or 29 or in pursuance of a charging order or to a person mentioned in s.59(8).
(2) The application notice and witness statement or affidavit in support shall be served on the authorised Government Department in accordance with Ord.77, r.4 not less than seven days before the date fixed for the hearing of the application.
(3) The witness statement or affidavit in support of an application under para.(1) shall state the grounds for believing that the conditions in s.59(4) and, if appropriate, s.59(7) are fulfilled.

Compensation for, discharge and variation of confiscation order

RSC Ord.115 r.11A

(1) An application under ss.21, 22 or 23 shall be made in accordance with CPR Pt 23 which, together with any evidence in support, shall be lodged with the court and served on the prosecutor not less than seven days before the day fixed for the hearing of the application.
(2) Notice shall also be served on any receiver appointed in pursuance of a charging order or under ss.26 or 29.
(3) An application for an order under s.22 shall be supported by a witness statement or affidavit giving details of—
   (a) the confiscation order made under s.19(4);
   (b) the acquittal of the defendant;
   (c) the realisable property held by the defendant; and
   (d) the loss suffered by the applicant as a result of the confiscation order.
(4) An application for an order under s.23 shall be supported by a witness statement or affidavit giving details of—
   (a) the confiscation order made under s.19(4);
   (b) the date on which the defendant ceased to be an absconder;
   (c) the date on which proceedings against the defendant were instituted and a summary of the steps taken in the proceedings since then; and
   (d) any indication given by the prosecutor that he does not intend to proceed against the defendant.

(5) An application made under s.21 shall be supported by a witness statement or affidavit giving details of—
  (a) the confiscation order made under s.19(4);
  (b) the circumstances in which the defendant ceased to be an absconder; and
  (c) the amounts referred to in s.21(2).

(6) Where an application is made for an order under ss.23(3) or 24(2)(b), the witness statement or affidavit shall also include—
  (a) details of the realisable property to which the application relates; and
  (b) details of the loss suffered by the applicant as a result of the confiscation order.

(7) Unless the court otherwise orders, a witness statement or affidavit under paras (3) to (6) may contain statements of information and belief, with the sources and grounds thereof.

Exercise of powers under ss.37 and 40

RSC Ord.115 r.12

The powers conferred on the High Court by ss.37 and 40 may be exercised by a judge or a Master of the Queen's Bench Division.

Application for registration

RSC Ord.115 r.13

An application for registration of an order specified in an Order in Council made under s.37 or of an external confiscation order under s.40(1) must be made in accordance with CPR Pt 23, and may be made without notice.

Evidence in support of application under s.37

RSC Ord.115 r.14

An application for registration of an order specified in an Order in Council made under s.37 must be made in accordance with CPR Pt 23, and be supported by a witness statement or affidavit—
  (i) exhibiting the order or a certified copy thereof; and
  (ii) stating, to the best of the witness's knowledge, particulars of what property the person against whom the order was made holds in England and Wales, giving the source of the witness's knowledge.

Evidence in support of application under s.40(1)

RSC Ord.115 r.15

(1) An application for registration of an external confiscation order must be made in accordance with CPR Pt 23, and be supported by a witness statement or affidavit—
  (a) exhibiting the order or a verified or certified or otherwise duly authenticated copy thereof and, where the order is not in the English language, a translation thereof into

English certified by a notary public or authenticated by witness statement or affidavit; and

(b) stating—

    (i) that the order is in force and is not subject to appeal;

    (ii) where the person against whom the order was made did not appear in the proceedings, that he received notice thereof in sufficient time to enable him to defend them;

    (iii) in the case of money, either that at the date of the application the sum payable under the order has not been paid or the amount which remains unpaid, as may be appropriate, or, in the case of other property, the property which has not been recovered; and

    (iv) to the best of the witness's knowledge, particulars of what property the person against whom the order was made holds in England and Wales, giving the source of the witness's knowledge.

(2) Unless the court otherwise directs, a witness statement or affidavit for the purposes of this rule may contain statements of information or belief with the sources and grounds thereof.

Register of Orders

RSC Ord.115 r.16

(1) There will be kept in the Central Office at the Royal Courts of Justice in London under the direction of the Master of the Administrative Court a register of the orders registered under the Act.

(2) There shall be included in such register particulars of any variation or setting aside of a registration and of any execution issued on a registered order.

Notice of registration

RSC Ord.115 r.17

(1) Notice of the registration of an order must be served on the person against whom it was obtained by delivering it to that person personally or by sending it to that person's usual or last known address or place of business or in such other manner as the court may direct.

(2) Permission is not required to serve such a notice out of the jurisdiction and CPR rr.6.40, 6.42 and 6.46 apply in relation to such a notice as they apply in relation to a claim form.

Application to vary or set aside registration

RSC Ord.115 r.18

An application made in accordance with CPR Pt 23 by the person against whom an order was made to vary or set aside the registration of an order must be made to a judge and be supported by witness statement or affidavit.

Enforcement of Order

RSC Ord.115 r.19

If an application is made under r.18, an order shall not be enforced until after such application is determined.

Variation, satisfaction and discharge of registered Order

RSC Ord.115 r.20

Upon the court being notified by the applicant for registration that an order which has been registered has been varied, satisfied or discharged, particulars of the variation, satisfaction or discharge, as the case may be, shall be entered in the register.

Rules to have effect subject to orders in council

RSC Ord.115 r.21

Rules 12 to 20 shall have effect subject to the provisions of the Order in Council made under s.37 or, as the case may be, of the Order in Council made under s.39.

Criminal Justice (International Co-operation) Act 1990: external forfeiture Orders

RSC Ord.115 r.21A

The provisions of this Part of this order shall, with such modifications as are necessary and subject to the provisions of any Order in Council made under s.9 of the Criminal Justice (International Co-operation) Act 1990, apply to proceedings for the registration and enforcement of external forfeiture orders as they apply to such proceedings in relation to external confiscation orders.

For the purposes of this rule, an external forfeiture order is an order made by a court in a country or territory outside the UK which is enforceable in the UK by virtue of any such Order in Council.

See also **Realisation of property** and **Receiver**.

Part VI of the Criminal Justice Act 1988

RSC Ord.115 r.22

(2) Expressions which are used in this Part of this order which are used in the 1988 Act have the same meanings in this Part of this order as in the 1988 Act and include any extended meaning given by the Criminal Justice (Confiscation) (Northern Ireland) Order 1990.

Application of Pt I of Ord.115

RSC Ord.115 r.23

Part I of Ord.115 (except r.11) shall apply for the purposes of proceedings under Pt VI of the [Criminal Justice Act 1988] with the necessary modifications and, in particular—

(a) references to drug trafficking offences and to drug trafficking shall be construed as references to offences to which Pt VI of the 1988 Act applies and to committing such an offence;

(b) references to the Drug Trafficking Act 1994 shall be construed as references to the 1988 Act and references to ss.5(2), 26, 27, 29, 30(2), 17(1), 18, 18(5), 39 and 40 of the 1994 Act shall be construed as references to ss.73(6), 77, 78, 80, 81, 81(1), 83(1), 89, 89(5), 96 and 97 of the 1988 Act, respectively;

(c) rule 3(2) shall have effect as if the following sub-paragraphs were substituted for subparas (a) and (b)—

   (a) state, as the case may be, either that proceedings have been instituted against the defendant for an offence to which Pt VI of the 1988 Act applies (giving particulars of the offence) and that they have not been concluded or that, whether by the laying of an information or otherwise, a person is to be charged with such an offence;

   (b) state, as the case may be, either that a confiscation order has been made or the grounds for believing that such an order may be made;

(d) rule 7 (3) shall have effect as if the words 'certificate issued by a magistrates' court or the Crown Court' were substituted for the words 'certificate issued by the Crown Court';

(e) rule 8 shall have effect as if the following paragraph were added at the end—

   (6) Where a receiver applies in accordance with CPR Pt 23 for the variation of a confiscation order, the application notice shall be served, with any supporting evidence, on the defendant and any other person who may be affected by the making of an order under s.83 of the 1988 Act, not less than seven days before the date fixed for the hearing of the application.

(f) rule 11 shall apply with the necessary modifications where an application is made under s.93J of the 1988 Act for disclosure of information held by government departments.

Terrorism Act 2000

RSC Ord.115 r.24

In this Part of this Order—

(c) 'the prosecutor' means the person with conduct of proceedings which have been instituted in England and Wales for an offence under any of ss.15 to 18 of the Act, or the person who the High Court is satisfied will have the conduct of any proceedings for such an offence;

(d) 'domestic freezing order certificate' means a certificate made by the High Court under para.11B of Sch.4 in relation to property in a country other than the UK;

(e) 'Overseas Freezing Order' means an order made in accordance with para.11D of Sch.4 in relation to property in the UK;

(f) 'British Islands order' means a Scottish order, a Northern Ireland order or an Islands order as defined in para.12 of Sch.4; and

(g) other expressions used have the same meanings as they have in Sch.4 to the Act.

Assignment of proceedings

RSC Ord.115 r.25

(1) Subject to para.(2), the jurisdiction of the High Court under the [Terrorism Act 2000] shall be exercised by a judge of the Queen's Bench Division or of the Chancery Division.

(2) The jurisdiction conferred on the High Court by para.13 of Sch.4 may also be exercised by a Master of the Queen's Bench Division.

Application for restraint order and domestic freezing order certificate

RSC Ord.115 r.26

(1) An application for a restraint order and, where relevant, a domestic freezing order certificate under paras 5 and 11B of Sch.4 may be made by the prosecutor by a claim form, which need not be served on any person.

(2) An application under para.(1) shall be supported by a witness statement or affidavit, which shall—

    (a) state, as the case may be, either—

        (i) that proceedings have been instituted against a person for an offence under any of ss.15 to 18 of the Act and that they have not been concluded; or

        (ii) that a criminal investigation has been started in England and Wales with regard to such an offence,

    and in either case give details of the alleged or suspected offence and of the defendant's involvement;

    (b) where proceedings have been instituted, state, as the case may be, that a forfeiture order has been made in the proceedings or the grounds for believing that such an order may be made;

    (ba) where proceedings have not been instituted—

        (i) indicate the state of progress of the investigation and when it is anticipated that a decision will be taken on whether to institute proceedings against the defendant;

        (ii) state the grounds for believing that a forfeiture order may be made in any proceedings against the defendant; and

        (iii) verify that the prosecutor is to have the conduct of any such proceedings;

    (c) to the best of the witness's ability, give full particulars of the property in respect of which the restraint order and, where relevant, the domestic freezing order certificate is sought and specify the person or persons holding such property and any other persons having an interest in it.

(2A) An applicant who seeks a domestic freezing order certificate must—

    (a) prepare a draft of the certificate in accordance with para.11B of Sch.4; and

    (b) attach it to the application for the restraint order under para.(1).

(3) A claim form under para.(1) shall be entitled in the matter of the defendant, naming him, and in the matter of the Act, and all subsequent documents in the matter shall be so entitled.

(4) Unless the court otherwise directs, a witness statement or affidavit under para.(2) may contain statements of information or belief with the sources and grounds thereof.

Restraint Order

RSC Ord.115 r.27

(1) A restraint order may be made subject to conditions and exceptions, including but not limited to conditions relating to the indemnifying of third parties against expenses incurred in complying with the order, and exceptions relating to living expenses and legal expenses of the defendant, but the prosecutor shall not be required to give an undertaking to abide by any order as to damages sustained by the defendant as a result of the restraint order.

(2) Unless the court otherwise directs, a restraint order made without notice of the application for it being served on any person shall have effect until a day which shall be fixed for the hearing where all parties may attend on the application.

(3) Where a restraint order is made the prosecutor shall serve copies of the order and unless the court otherwise orders, of the witness statement or affidavit in support on the defendant and on all other persons affected by the order.

(4) Where a domestic freezing order certificate is made it must be served with the copies of the restraint order as provided for in para.(3).

Form of domestic freezing order certificate

PD RSC 115 para.9

An example of a domestic freezing order certificate is set out in the Annex to Council Framework Decision 2003/577/JHA of July 22, 2003 on the execution in the European Union of orders freezing property or evidence.

Discharge or variation of a restraint order and a domestic freezing order certificate

RSC Ord.115 r.28

(1) Subject to para.(2), an application to discharge or vary a restraint order shall be made in accordance with CPR Pt 23.

(2) Where the case is one of urgency, an application under this rule by the prosecutor may be made without notice.

(3) The application and any witness statement or affidavit in support shall be lodged with the court and, where the application is made in accordance with CPR Pt 23 the application notice shall be served on the following persons (other than the applicant)—
(a) the prosecutor;
(b) the defendant; and
(c) all other persons restrained or otherwise affected by the restraint order;
not less than two clear days before the date fixed for the hearing of the application.

(4) Where a restraint Order has been made and has not been discharged, the prosecutor shall notify the court when proceedings for the offence have been concluded, and the court shall thereupon discharge the restraint Order.

(5) Where an Order is made discharging or varying a restraint order, the applicant shall serve copies of the order of discharge or variation on all persons restrained by the earlier order and shall notify all other persons affected of the terms of the order of discharge or variation.

(6) A reference in this rule to a restraint Order also applies, where relevant, to a domestic freezing order certificate.

(7) Where an order is made under para.(5) which discharges or varies a domestic freezing order certificate the applicant must notify the court or authority in accordance with para.11C of Sch. 4.

Compensation in relation to a restraint Order, domestic freezing Order certificate or forfeiture Order

RSC Ord.115 r.29

An application for an order under paras 9 or 10 of Sch.4 shall be made in accordance with CPR Pt 23, and the application notice, shall be served, with any supporting evidence, on the person alleged to be in default and on the person or body by whom compensation, if ordered, will be payable under paras 9(6) or 10(4) not less than seven days before the date fixed for the hearing of the application.

Application for registration of a British Islands Order

RSC Ord.115 r.28.30

An application for registration of a British Islands order under para.13(4) of Sch.4 must be made in accordance with CPR Pt 23 and may be made without notice.

RSC Ord.115 r.31

(1) An application for registration of a British Islands order must be supported by a witness statement or affidavit—
    (a) exhibiting the order or a certified copy thereof; and
    (b) which shall, to the best of the witness's ability, give particulars of such property in respect of which the order was made as is in England and Wales, and specify the person or persons holding such property.
(2) Unless the court otherwise directs, a witness statement or affidavit for the purposes of this rule may contain statements of information or belief with the sources and grounds thereof.

Register of all Orders registered under the Act

RSC Ord.115 r.32

(1) There will be kept in the Central Office at the Royal Courts of Justice in London under the direction of the Master of the Administrative Court a register of the orders registered under the Act.
(2) There shall be included in such register particulars of any variation or setting aside of a registration, and of any execution issued on a registered order.

Notice of registration of a British Islands Order

RSC Ord.115 r.33

(1) Notice of the registration of a British Islands order must be served on the person or persons holding the property referred to in r.31(1)(b) and any other persons appearing to have an interest in that property.
(2) Permission is not required to serve such a notice out of the jurisdiction and CPR rr. 6.40, 6.42 and 6.46 apply in relation to such a notice as they apply in relation to a claim form.

Application to vary or cancel registration of a British Islands Order

RSC Ord.115 r.34

An application to vary or cancel the registration of a British Islands Order must be made to a judge in accordance with CPR Pt 23 and be supported by a witness statement or affidavit.
   This rule does not apply to a variation or cancellation under r.36.

Enforcement of a British Islands Order

RSC Ord.115 r.35

(2) If an application is made under r.34, an order shall not be enforced until after such application is determined.

(3) This rule does not apply to the taking of steps under paras 7 or 8 of Sch.4, as applied by para.13(6) of that Schedule.

Variation and cancellation of registration of a British Islands Order

RSC Ord.115 r.36

If effect has been given (whether in England or Wales or elsewhere) to a British Islands Order, or if the order has been varied or discharged by the court by which it was made, the applicant for registration shall inform the court and—

(a) if such effect has been given in respect of all the money or other property to which the order applies, or if the order has been discharged by the court by which it was made, registration of the order shall be cancelled;

(b) if such effect has been given in respect of only part of the money or other property, or if the order has been varied by the court by which it was made, registration of the order shall be varied accordingly.

Giving effect to an Overseas Freezing Order—consideration by the court

RSC Ord.115 r.36A

(1) Save in exceptional circumstances the court will consider an Overseas Freezing Order the next business day after receipt of a copy of that order from the Secretary of State.

(2) In any event the court will consider the order within five business days of receipt of it.

(3) The court will not make an order giving effect to an Overseas Freezing Order unless it is satisfied that the Director of Public Prosecutions has had the opportunity to make representations to the court in writing or at a hearing.

(4) 'Business day' has the same meaning as in CPR r.6.2.

Giving effect to an Overseas Freezing Order—registration

RSC Ord.115 r.36B

Where the court makes an order to give effect to an Overseas Freezing Order the court will register that order in accordance with r.32.

Notice of registration of an Overseas Freezing Order

RSC Ord.115 r.36C

Where the court gives effect to an Overseas Freezing Order it will order the Director of Public Prosecutions to serve notice of registration of the order on any persons affected by it.

Application to cancel the registration of, or vary, an Overseas Freezing Order

RSC Ord.115 r.36D

An application under para.11G(4) of Sch.4 by the Director of Public Prosecutions or any person affected by an Overseas Freezing Order must be made to the court in accordance with CPR Pt 23.

International Criminal Court Act 2001: Fines, Forfeitures and Reparation Orders

RSC Ord.115 r.37

In this Part of this Order—
    (c) "an order of the ICC" means—
        (i) a fine or forfeiture ordered by the ICC; or
        (ii) an order by the ICC against a person convicted by the ICC specifying a reparation to, or in respect of, a victim.

Registration of ICC Orders for enforcement

RSC Ord.115 r.38

    (1) An application to the High Court to register an order of the ICC for enforcement, or to vary or set aside the registration of an order, may be made to a judge or a Master of the Queen's Bench Division.
    (2) Rule 13 and rr.15 to 20 in Pt I of this Order shall, with such modifications as are necessary and subject to the provisions of any regulations made under s.49 of the [International Criminal Court Act 2001], apply to the registration for enforcement of an order of the [International Criminal Court] as they apply to the registration of an External Confiscation Order.

CONSENT JUDGMENTS AND ORDERS

Pt 40 r.40.6

    (1) This rule applies where all the parties agree the terms in which a judgment should be given or an order should be made.
    (2) A **court officer** may enter and seal an agreed judgment or order if—
        (a) the judgment or order is listed in para.(3);
        (b) none of the parties is a **litigant in person**; and
        (c) the approval of the court is not required by these rules, a PD or any enactment before an agreed order can be made.
    (3) The judgments and orders referred to in para.(2) are—
        (a) a judgment or order for—
            (i) the payment of an amount of money (including a judgment or order for damages or the value of goods to be decided by the court); or
            (ii) the delivery up of goods with or without the option of paying the value of the goods or the agreed value.

    (b) an order for—
        (i) the dismissal of any proceedings, wholly or in part;
        (ii) the stay of proceedings on agreed terms, disposing of the proceedings, whether those terms are recorded in a schedule to the order or elsewhere;
        (iii) the stay of enforcement of a judgment, either unconditionally or on condition that the money due under the judgment is paid by instalments specified in the order;
        (iv) the setting aside under Pt 13 of a default judgment which has not been satisfied;
        (v) the payment out of money which has been paid into court;
        (vi) the discharge from liability of any party;
        (vii) the payment, assessment or waiver of costs, or such other provision for costs as may be agreed.
(4) R.40.3 (drawing up and filing of judgments and orders) applies to judgments and orders entered and sealedby a court officer under para.(2) as it applies to other judgments and orders.
(5) Where para.(2) does not apply, any party may apply for a judgment or order in the terms agreed.
(6) The court may deal with an application under para.(5) without a hearing.
(7) Where this rule applies—
    (a) the order which is agreed by the parties must be drawn up in the terms agreed;
    (b) it must be expressed as being 'By Consent';
    (c) it must be signed by the **legal representative** acting for each of the parties to whom the order relates or, where para.(5) applies, by the party if he is a **litigant in person**.

PD 40B para.3.1

Rule 40.6(3) sets out the types of consent judgments and orders which may be entered and sealed by a court officer. The court officer may do so in those cases provided that:
    (1) none of the parties is a litigant in person, and
    (2) the approval of the court is not required by the rules, a PD or any enactment.

PD 40B para.3.2

If a consent order filed for sealing appears to be unclear or incorrect the court officer may refer it to a judge for consideration.

PD 40B para.3.3

Where a consent judgment or order does not come within the provisions of r.40.6(2):
    (1) an application notice requesting a judgment or order in the agreed terms should be filed with the draft judgment or order to be entered or sealed, and
    (2) the draft judgment or order must be drawn so that the judge's name and judicial title can be inserted.

PD 40B para.3.4

A consent judgment or order must:
    (1) be drawn up in the terms agreed,
    (2) bear on it the words 'By Consent', and
    (3) be signed by
        (a) solicitors or counsel acting for each of the parties to the order, or
        (b) where a party is a litigant in person, the litigant.

PD 40B para.3.5

Where the parties draw up a consent order in the form of a stay of proceedings on agreed terms, disposing of the, and where the terms are recorded in a schedule to the order, any direction for:
  (1) payment of money out of court, or
  (2) payment and assessment of costs
should be contained in the body of the order and not in the schedule.

Consent Orders

PD 23A para.10.1

Rule 40.6 sets out the circumstances where an agreed judgment or order may be entered and sealed.

PD 23A para.10.2

Where all parties affected by an order have written to the court consenting to the making of the order a draft of which has been filed with the court, the court will treat the draft as having been signed in accordance with r.40.6(7).

PD 23A para.10.3

Where a consent order must be made by a judge (i.e. r.40.6(2) does not apply) the Order must be drawn so that the judge's name and judicial title can be inserted.

PD 23A para.10.4

The parties to an application for a consent order must ensure that they provide the court with any material it needs to be satisfied that it is appropriate to make the Order. Subject to any rule or PD a letter will generally be acceptable for this purpose.

PD 23A para.10.5

Where a judgment or order has been agreed in respect of an application or claim where a hearing date has been fixed, the parties must inform the court immediately. (Note that parties are reminded that under rr. 28.4 and 29.5 the case management timetable cannot be varied by written agreement of the parties).

Appeals

Dismissal of applications or appeals by consent

PD 52A para.6.1

An appellant who does not wish to pursue an application or an appeal may request the appeal court to dismiss the application or appeal. Such a request must contain a statement that the appellant is not a child or protected party and that the appeal or application is not from a decision of the Court of Protection. If such a request is granted it will usually be on the basis that the appellant pays the costs of the application or appeal.

PD 52A para.6.2

If the appellant wishes to have the application or appeal dismissed without costs, his request must be accompanied by a letter signed by the respondent stating that the respondent consents.

PD 52A para.6.3

Where a settlement has been reached disposing of the application or appeal, the parties may make a joint request to the court for the application or appeal to be dismissed. If the request is granted the application or appeal would be dismissed.

Provisional damages

PD 41A para.4.1

An application to give effect to a consent order for **provisional damages** should be made in accordance with CPR Pt 23. If the claimant is a child or protected the approval of the court must also be sought and the application for approval will normally be dealt with at a hearing.

PD 41A para.4.2

The order should be in the form of a consent judgment and should contain:
   (1) the matters set out in para.2.1(1) to (3) above, and
   (2) a direction as to the documents to be preserved as the case file documents, which will
       normally be
       (a) the consent judgment,
       (b) any **statements of case**,
       (c) an agreed statement of facts, and
       (d) any agreed medical report(s).

PD 41A para.4.3

The claimant or his **legal representative** must lodge the case file documents in the court office where the proceedings are taking place for inclusion in the court file. The court file should be endorsed as in para.3.3(2) above, and the case file documents preserved as in para.3.3(3) above.

CONSENT ORDERS

See **Consent judgments and orders**.

CONSOLIDATED ATTACHMENT OF EARNINGS

See **Attachment of earnings**.

CONSTRUCTION AND ENGINEERING DISPUTES

See **Pre-action Protocols.**

Pre-action Protocol for construction and engineering disputes

This Pre-Action Protocol applies to all construction and engineering disputes (including professional negligence claims against architects, engineers and quantity surveyors).

The general aim of this Protocol is to ensure that before court proceedings commence:

    (i) the claimant and the defendant have provided sufficient information for each party to know the nature of the other's case;

    (ii) each party has had an opportunity to consider the other's case, and to accept or reject all or any part of the case made against him at the earliest possible stage;

    (iii) there is more pre-action contact between the parties;

    (iv) better and earlier exchange of information occurs;

    (v) there is better pre-action investigation by the parties;

    (vi) the parties have met formally on at least one occasion with a view to defining and agreeing the issues between them; and exploring possible ways by which the claim may be resolved;

    (vii) the parties are in a position where they may be able to settle cases early and fairly without recourse to litigation; and

    (viii) proceedings will be conducted efficiently if litigation does become necessary.

Exceptions

A claimant shall not be required to comply with this Protocol before commencing proceedings to the extent that the proposed proceedings (i) are for the enforcement of the decision of an adjudicator to whom a dispute has been referred pursuant to s.108 of the Housing Grants, Construction and Regeneration Act 1996 ('the 1996 Act'), (ii) include a claim for interim injunctive relief, (iii) will be the subject of a claim for summary judgment pursuant to Pt 24 of the Civil Procedure Rules, or (iv) relate to the same or substantially the same issues as have been the subject of recent adjudication under the 1996 Act, or some other formal alternative dispute resolution procedure.

See **Technology and Construction Court claims.**

CONSUMER CREDIT CLAIMS

Default judgment

Pt 12 r.12.2

A claimant may not obtain a **default judgment—**

    (a) on a claim for delivery of goods subject to an agreement regulated by the Consumer Credit Act 1974.

Possession claims

Particulars of claim

PD 55A para.2.5

If the claim is a possession claim by a mortgagee, the particulars of claim must also set out:
  (4) whether or not the loan which is secured by the mortgage is a regulated consumer credit agreement and, if so, specify the date on which any notice required by ss.76 or 87 of the Consumer Credit Act 1974 was given;
  (5) if appropriate details that show the property is not one to which s.141 of the Consumer Credit Act 1974 applies.

Time Order

PD 55A para.7.1

Any application by the defendant for a time order under s.129 of the Consumer Credit Act 1974 may be made:
  (1) in his defence; or
  (2) by application notice in the proceedings.

See **Possession claims**.

Unfair relationships—Consumer Credit Act 2006

PD 7B para.2.1

A claimant must use the Consumer Credit Act procedure where he makes a claim under a provision of the [Consumer Credit Act 2006] to which para.3 of this PD applies.

PD 7B para.2.2

Where a claimant is using the Consumer Credit Act procedure the CPR are modified to the extent that they are inconsistent with the procedure set out in this PD.

PD 7B para.2.3

The court may at any stage order the claim to continue as if the claimant had not used the Consumer Credit Act procedure, and if it does so the court may give any directions it considers appropriate.

PD 7B para.2.4

This PD also sets out matters which must be included in the particulars of claim in certain types of claim, and restrictions on where certain types of claim may be started.

Provisions of the Consumer Credit Act 2006

PD 7B para.3.1

Subject to paras 3.2 and 3.3 [of PD 7B] applies to claims made under the following provisions of the [Consumer Credit Act 2006]:

(1) s.141 (claim by the creditor to enforce regulated agreement relating to goods etc);

(2) s.129 (claim by debtor or hirer for a time order);

(3) s.90 (creditor's claim for an order for recovery of protected goods);

(4) s.92(1) (creditor's or owner's claim to enter premises to take possession of goods);

(5) s.140B(2)(a) (debtor's or surety's application for an order relating to an unfair relationship);

(6) creditor's or owner's claim for a court order to enforce a regulated agreement relating to goods or money where the court order is required by—

(a) s.65(1) (improperly executed agreement),

(b) s.86(2) (death of debtor or hirer where agreement is partly secured or unsecured),

(c) s.111(2) (default notice, etc. not served on surety),

(d) s.124(1) or (2) (taking of a negotiable instrument in breach of terms of s.123), or

(e) s.105(7)(a) or (b) (security not expressed in writing, or improperly executed).

PD 7B para.3.2

This PD does not apply to any claim made under the provisions listed in para.3.1 above if that claim relates to the recovery of land.

PD 7B para.3.3

This PD also does not apply to a claim made by the creditor under s.141 of the Act to enforce a regulated agreement where the agreement relates only to money. Such a claim must be started by the issue of a Pt 7 claim form.

Restrictions on where to start some Consumer Credit Act claims

PD 7B para.4.1

Where the claim includes a claim to recover goods to which a regulated hire purchase agreement or conditional sale agreement relates, it may only be started in the county court for the district in which the debtor, or one of the debtors:

(1) resides or carries on business, or

(2) resided or carried on business at the date when the defendant last made a payment under the agreement.

PD 7B para.4.2

In any other claim to recover goods, the claim may only be started in the court for the district:

(1) in which the defendant, or one of the defendants, resides or carries on business, or

(2) in which the goods are situated.

PD 7B para.4.3

A claim of a debtor or hirer for an order under s.129(1)(b) or 129(1)(ba) of the Act (a time order) may only be started in the court where the claimant resides or carries on business.
(Costs r.45.1(2)(b) allows the claimant to recover fixed costs in certain circumstances where such a claim is made).
(Paragraph 7 sets out the matters the claimant must include in his particulars of claim where he is using the Consumer Credit Act procedure).

Consumer Credit Act procedure

PD 7B para.5.1

In the types of claim to which para.3 applies the court will fix a hearing date on the issue of the claim form.

PD 7B para.5.2

The particulars of claim must be served with the **claim form**.

PD 7B para.5.3

Where a claimant is using the Consumer Credit Act procedure, the defendant to the claim is not required to:
(1) serve an acknowledgment of service, or
(2) file a defence, although he may choose to do so.

PD 7B para.5.4

Where a defendant intends to defend a claim, his defence should be filed within 14 days of service of the particulars of claim. If the defendant fails to file a defence within this period, but later relies on it, the court may take such a failure into account as a factor when deciding what order to make about costs.

PD 7B para.5.5

Part 12 (default judgment) does not apply where the claimant is using the Consumer Credit Act procedure.

PD 7B para.5.6

Each party must be given at least 28 days' notice of the hearing date.

PD 7B para.5.7

Where the claimant serves the claim form, he must serve notice of the hearing date at the same time, unless the hearing date is specified in the claim form.

Powers of the court at the hearing

PD 7B para.6.1

On the hearing date the court may dispose of the claim.

PD 7B para.6.2

If the court does not dispose of the claim on the hearing date:
(1) if the defendant has filed a defence, the court will:
   (a) allocate the claim to a track and give directions about the management of the case, or
   (b) give directions to enable it to allocate the claim to a track,
(2) if the defendant has not filed a defence, the court may make any order or give any direction it considers appropriate.

PD 7B para.6.3

Rule 26.5 (3) to (5) and rr.26.6 to 26.10 apply to the allocation of a claim under paragraph 6.2.

Matters which must be included in the particulars of claim

PD 7B para.7.1

Where the Consumer Credit Act procedure is used, the claimant must state in his particulars of claim that the claim is a Consumer Credit Act claim.

PD 7B para.7.2

A claimant making a claim for the delivery of goods to enforce a hire purchase agreement or conditional sale agreement which is:
(1) a regulated agreement for the recovery of goods, and
(2) let to a person other than a company or other corporation, must also state (in this order) in his particulars of claim:
   (a) the date of the agreement,
   (b) the parties to the agreement,
   (c) the number or other identification of the agreement (with enough information to allow the debtor to identify the agreement),
   (d) where the claimant was not one of the original parties to the agreement, the means by which the rights and duties of the creditor passed to him,
   (e) the place where the agreement was signed by the defendant (if known),
   (f) the goods claimed,
   (g) the total price of the goods,
   (h) the paid up sum,
   (i) the unpaid balance of the total price,
   (j) whether a default notice or a notice under s.76(1) or s.88(1) of the Act has been served on the defendant, and, if it has, the date and the method of service,
   (k) the date on which the right to demand delivery of the goods accrued,
   (l) the amount (if any) claimed as an alternative to the delivery of goods, and
   (m) the amount (if any) claimed in addition to—
      (i) the delivery of the goods, or

(ii) any claim under sub-para.(l) above with the grounds of each such claim.

PD 7B para.7.3

A claimant who is a debtor or hirer making a claim for an order under s.129(1)(b) or 129(1)(ba) of the Act (a time order) must state (in the following order) in the particulars of claim:
  (1) the date of the agreement,
  (2) the parties to the agreement,
  (3) the number or other means of identifying the agreement,
  (4) details of any sureties,
  (5) if the defendant is not one of the original parties to the agreement then the name of the original party to the agreement,
  (6) the names and addresses of the persons intended to be served with the claim form,
  (7) the place where the claimant signed the agreement,
  (8) details of the notice served by the creditor or owner giving rise to the claim for the time order,
  (9) the total unpaid balance the claimant admits is due under the agreement, and—
      (a) the amount of any arrears (if known), and
      (b) the amount and frequency of the payments specified in the agreement,
  (10) the claimant's proposals for payments of any arrears and of future instalments together with details of his means;
  (11) where the claim relates to a breach of the agreement other than for the payment of money the claimant's proposals for remedying it.

PD 7B para.7.3A

A claimant who is a debtor or hirer making a claim for an order under s.129(1)(ba) of the Act must attach to the particulars of claim a copy of the notice served on the creditor or owner under s.129A(1)(a) of the Act.

PD 7B para.7.4

  (1) This paragraph applies where a claimant is required to obtain a court order to enforce a regulated agreement by:
      (a) section 65(1) (improperly executed agreement),
      (b) section 105(7)(a) or (b) (security not expressed in writing, or improperly executed),
      (c) section 111(2) (default notice etc. not served on surety),
      (d) section 124(1) or (2) (taking of a negotiable instrument in breach of terms of s.123), or
      (e) section 86(2) of the Act (death of debtor or hirer where agreement is partly secured or unsecured).
  (2) The claimant must state in his particulars of claim what the circumstances are that require him to obtain a court order for enforcement.

See **Hire purchase claims**.

CONTEMPT OF COURT

Appeals

PD 52D para.9.1

In an appeal under s.13 of the Administration of Justice Act 1960 (appeals in cases of contempt of court), the appellant must serve the appellant's notice on the court or the Upper Tribunal from whose order or decision the appeal is brought in addition to the persons to be served under r.52.4(3) and in accordance with that rule.

See also **False statement, False disclosure statement, Penalty recording of proceedings, Writ of sequestration**.

Pt 81 r.81.1

(1) [Pt 81] sets out the procedure in respect of—
    (a) contempt of court; and
    (b) the penal, contempt and disciplinary provisions of the [CCA 1984].
(2) So far as applicable, and with the necessary modifications, this Part applies in relation to an order requiring a person—
    (a) guilty of contempt of court; or
    (b) punishable by virtue of any enactment as if that person had been guilty of contempt of the High Court,
to pay a fine or to give security for good behaviour, as it applies in relation to an order of committal.
(3) Unless otherwise stated, this Pt applies to procedure in the Court of Appeal, the High Court and county courts.

Saving for other powers

Pt 81 r.81.2

(1) [Pt 81] is concerned only with procedure and does not itself confer upon the court the power to make an order for—
    (a) committal;
    (b) sequestration; or
    (c) the imposition of a fine in respect of contempt of court.
(2) Nothing in this Part affects the power of the court to make an order requiring a person—
    (a) guilty of contempt of court; or
    (b) punishable by virtue of any enactment as if that person had been guilty of contempt of the High Court,
to pay a fine or to give security for good behaviour.
(3) Nothing in this Pt affects any statutory or inherent power of the court to make a committal order of its own initiative against a person guilty of contempt of court.

I Committal for breach of a judgment, order or undertaking to do or abstain from doing an act

Enforcement of judgment, order or undertaking to do or abstain from doing an act

Pt 81 r.81.4

(1) If a person—
    (a) required by a judgment or order to do an act does not do it within the time fixed by the judgment or order; or
    (b) disobeys a judgment or order not to do an act,
then, subject to the Debtors Acts 1869 and 1878 and to the provisions of these Rules, the judgment or order may be enforced by an order for committal.

(2) If the time fixed by the judgment or order for doing an act has been varied by a subsequent order or agreement of the parties under r. 2.11, then references in para.(1)(a) to the time fixed are references to the time fixed by that subsequent order or agreement.

(3) If the person referred to in para.(1) is a company or other corporation, the committal order may be made against any director or other officer of that company or corporation.

(4) So far as applicable, and with the necessary modifications, this Section applies to undertakings given by a party as it applies to judgments or orders.

(R. 81.17(3) and (4) make provision for cases in which both this Section and s.6 (Committal for making a false statement of truth or disclosure statement) may be relevant.)

(5) If a judgment or order requires a person to deliver goods or pay their value—
    (a) the judgment or order may not be enforced by a committal order under para.(1);
    (b) the person entitled to enforce the judgment or order may apply to the court for an order requiring that the goods be delivered within a specified time; and
    (c) where the court grants such an order, that order may be enforced under para.(1).

Requirement for service of a copy of the judgment or order and time for service

Pt 81 r.81.5

(1) Unless the court dispenses with service under r.81.8, a judgment or order may not be enforced under r.81.4 unless a copy of it has been served on the person required to do or not do the act in question, and in the case of a judgment or order requiring a person to do an act—
    (a) the copy has been served before the end of the time fixed for doing the act, together with a copy of any order fixing that time;
    (b) where the time for doing the act has been varied by a subsequent order or agreement under r.2.11, a copy of that subsequent order or agreement has also been served; and
    (c) where the judgment or order was made under r.81.4(5), or was made pursuant to an earlier judgment or order requiring the act to be done, a copy of the earlier judgment or order has also been served.

(2) Where the person referred to in para.(1) is a company or other corporation, a copy of the judgment or order must also be served on the respondent before the end of the time fixed for doing the act.

(3) Copies of the judgment or order and any orders or agreements fixing or varying the time for doing an act must be served in accordance with r.81.6 or 81.7, or in accordance with an order for alternative service made under r. 81.8(2)(b).

Method of service—Copies of judgments or orders

Pt 81 r.81.6

Subject to r.81.7 and 81.8, copies of judgments or orders and any orders or agreements fixing or varying the time for doing an act must be served personally.

Method of service—Copies of undertakings

Pt 81 r.81.7

(1) Subject to para.(2) and r.81.8, a copy of any document recording an undertaking will be delivered by the court to the person who gave the undertaking—

  (a) by handing to that person a copy of the document before that person leaves the court building;
  (b) by posting a copy to that person at the residence or place of business of that person where this is known; or
  (c) by posting a copy to that person's solicitor.
  (2) If delivery cannot be effected in accordance with para.(1), the court officer will deliver a copy of the document to the party for whose benefit the undertaking was given and that party must serve it personally on the person who gave the undertaking as soon as practicable.
  (3) Where the person referred to in para.(1) is a company or other corporation, a copy of the judgment or order must also be served on the respondent.

Dispensation with personal service

Pt 81 r.81.8

  (1) In the case of a judgment or order requiring a person not to do an act, the court may dispense with service of a copy of the judgment or order in accordance with r. 81.5 to 81.7 if it is satisfied that the person has had notice of it—
  (a) by being present when the judgment or order was given or made; or
  (b) by being notified of its terms by telephone, email or otherwise.
  (2) In the case of any judgment or order the court may—
  (a) dispense with service under r. 81.5 to 81.7 if the court thinks it just to do so; or
  (b) make an order in respect of service by an alternative method or at an alternative place.

Requirement for a penal notice on judgments and orders

Pt 81 r.81.9

  (1) Subject to para.(2), a judgment or order to do or not do an act may not be enforced under r.81.4 unless there is prominently displayed, on the front of the copy of the judgment or order served in accordance with this Section, a warning to the person required to do or not do the act in question that disobedience to the order would be a contempt of court punishable by imprisonment, a fine or sequestration of assets.
  (2) An undertaking to do or not do an act which is contained in a judgment or order may be enforced under r.81.4 notwithstanding that the judgment or order does not contain the warning described in para.(1).
(Paras 2.1 to 2.4 of [PD 81] and form N117 contain provisions about penal notices and warnings in relation to undertakings.)

Form of penal notice

PD 81 para.1

A judgment or order which restrains a party from doing an act or requires an act to be done must, if disobedience is to be dealt with by proceedings for contempt of court, have a penal notice endorsed on it as follows (or in words to substantially the same effect)—

> "If you the within—named [ ] do not comply with this order you may be held to be in contempt of court and imprisoned or fined, or your assets may be seized."

Undertakings

PD 81 para.2.1

The provisions of para.8.1 of [PD 40B—Judgments and orders that supplements [Pt 40] apply to an order which contains an undertaking by a party to do or not do an act, subject to para.2.2 below.
(Para.8.1 of PD 40B contains provisions about specifying the time within which acts must be done.)

PD 81 para.2.2

The court may decline to—
    (1) accept an undertaking; and
    (2) deal with disobedience in respect of an undertaking by contempt of court proceedings,
unless the party giving the undertaking has made a signed statement to the effect that that party understands the terms of the undertaking and the consequences of failure to comply with it.

PD 81 para.2.3

The statement may be endorsed on the order containing the undertaking or may be filed in a separate document such as a letter.

PD 81 para.2.4

Where the order containing an undertaking is made in a county court, form N117 may be used.

How to make the committal application

Pt 81 r.81.10

    (1) A committal application is made by an application notice under Pt 23 in the proceedings in which the judgment or order was made or the undertaking was given.
    (2) Where the committal application is made against a person who is not an existing party to the proceedings, it is made against that person by an application notice under Pt 23.
    (3) The application notice must—
        (a) set out in full the grounds on which the committal application is made and must identify, separately and numerically, each alleged act of contempt including, if known, the date of each of the alleged acts; and
        (b) be supported by one or more affidavits containing all the evidence relied upon.
    (4) Subject to para.(5), the application notice and the evidence in support must be served personally on the respondent.
    (5) The court may—
        (a) dispense with service under para.(4) if it considers it just to do so; or
        (b) make an order in respect of service by an alternative method or at an alternative place.

III Committal for interference with the due administration of justice

Pt 81 r.81.12

(1) This section regulates committal applications in relation to interference with the due administration of justice in connection with proceedings—
    (a) in the High Court;
    (b) in a Divisional Court;
    (c) in the Court of Appeal;
    (d) in an inferior court (which includes a county court); or
    (e) which are criminal proceedings,
    except where the contempt is committed in the face of the court or consists of disobedience to an order of the court or a breach of an undertaking to the court.
(2) This Section also regulates committal applications otherwise than in connection with any proceedings.
(3) A committal application under this Section may not be made without the permission of the court.
(The procedure for applying for permission to make a committal application is set out in rule 81.14.)
(R.81.17(5) and (6) make provision for cases in which both this Section and s.6 (Committal for making a false statement of truth or disclosure statement) may be relevant.)

Court to which application for permission under this Section is to be made

Pt 81 r.81.13

(1) Where contempt of court is committed in connection with any proceedings—
    (a) in the High Court (other than proceedings in a Divisional Court), the application for permission may be made only to a single judge of the Division of the High Court in which the proceedings were commenced or to which they have subsequently been transferred;
    (b) in a Divisional Court, the application for permission may be made only to a single judge of the Queen's Bench Division;
    (c) in the Court of Appeal, the application for permission may be made only to a Divisional Court of the Queen's Bench Division;
    (d) in an inferior court, the application for permission may be made only to a single judge of the Queen's Bench Division; and
    (e) which are criminal proceedings, the application for permission may be made only to a Divisional Court of the Queen's Bench Division.
(2) Where contempt of court is committed otherwise than in connection with any proceedings, the application for permission may be made only to the Administrative Court.

Application for permission (High Court, Divisional Court or Administrative Court)

Pt 81 r.81.14

(1) The application for permission to make a committal application must be made by a Part 8 claim form which must include or be accompanied by—
    (a) a detailed statement of the applicant's grounds for bringing the committal application; and
    (b) an affidavit setting out the facts and exhibiting all documents relied upon.

(2) The claim form and the documents referred to in para. (1) must be served personally on the respondent unless the court otherwise directs.

(3) Within 14 days of service on the respondent of the claim form, the respondent—
  (a) must file and serve an acknowledgment of service; and
  (b) may file and serve evidence.

(4) The court will consider the application for permission at an oral hearing, unless it considers that such a hearing is not appropriate.

(5) If the respondent intends to appear at the permission hearing referred to in para.(4), the respondent must give 7 days' notice in writing of such intention to the court and any other party and at the same time provide a written summary of the submissions which the respondent proposes to make.

(6) Where permission to proceed is given, the court may give such directions as it thinks fit, and may—
  (a) transfer the proceedings to another court; or
  (b) direct that the application be listed for hearing before a single judge or a Divisional Court.

IV Certifications by any court, tribunal etc to the High Court under any enactment; and applications to the High Court under s.336 of the Charities Act 2011

Certifications of conduct, and applications under s.336 of the Charities Act 2011, to the High Court under this section

Pt 81 r.81.15

(1) This section applies where, by virtue of any enactment, the High Court has power to punish or take steps for the punishment of any person charged with having done or omitted to do anything in relation to a court, tribunal or person which, if it had been an act or omission in relation to the High Court, would have been a contempt of that court.

(2) Subject to para.(3), an order under this Section may be made by a single judge of the Administrative Court.

(3) An order made on an application under section 336 of the Charities Act 2011('a section 336 application') may be made only by a single judge of the Chancery Division.

(4) The certification or s. 336 application, as appropriate, must be in the form annexed to PD 81 at Annex A, and include or be accompanied by—
  (a) a detailed statement of the grounds for the certification or s. 336 application;
  (b) any written evidence relied upon; and
  (c) any other documents required for the disposal of the certification or s.336 application.

(5) Subject to para.(6), the certification or s.336 application, accompanied by the other documents referred to in para.(4), must be served personally on the respondent.

(6) The court may—
  (a) dispense with service under para. (5) if it thinks it just to do so; or
  (b) make an order in respect of service by an alternative method or at an alternative place.

(7) Within 14 days of service on the respondent of the certification or s. 336 application, the respondent—
  (a) must file and serve an acknowledgment of service in the form annexed to PD 81 at Annex B; and
  (b) may file and serve evidence.

PD 81 para.3

Section 4 of Pt 81 contains rules in relation to statutory powers of the High Court to commit any person for contempt in respect of anything done or not done in relation to a court, tribunal or person. The statutory powers include—
(1) s.336 of the Charities Act 2011;
(2) ss.436 and 453C of the Companies Act 1985;
(3) para.8 of Schedule 6 to the Data Protection Act 1998; and
(4) ss.18, 161 and 232 of the Financial Services and Markets Act 2000.

PD 81 para.4.1

Where the committal proceedings relate to a contempt in the face of the court the matters referred to in para.4.3 should be given particular attention. Normally, it will be appropriate to defer consideration of the respondent's actions and behaviour to allow the respondent time to reflect on what has occurred. The time needed for the following procedures should allow such a period of reflection.

PD 81 para.4.2

A Pt 8 claim form and an application notice are not required for contempt falling under s. 5 of Pt 81, but other provisions of this PD should be applied, as necessary, or adapted to the circumstances.

PD 81 para.4.3

The judge should—
(1) tell the respondent of the possible penalty that the respondent faces;
(2) inform the respondent in detail, and preferably in writing, of the actions and behaviour of the respondent which have given rise to the committal application;
(3) if the judge considers that an apology would remove the need for the committal application, tell the respondent;
(4) have regard to the need for the respondent to be—
    (a) allowed a reasonable time for responding to the committal application, including, if necessary, preparing a defence;
    (b) made aware of the availability of assistance from the Community Legal Service and how to contact the Service;
    (c) given the opportunity, if unrepresented, to obtain legal advice;
    (d) if unable to understand English, allowed to make arrangements, seeking the court's assistance if necessary, for an interpreter to attend the hearing; and
    (e) brought back before the court for the committal application to be heard within a reasonable time;
(5) allow the respondent an opportunity to—
    (a) apologise to the court;
    (b) explain the respondent's actions and behaviour; and
    (c) if the contempt is proved, to address the court on the penalty to be imposed on the respondent; and
(6) where appropriate, nominate a suitable person to give the respondent the information. (It is likely to be appropriate to nominate a person where the effective communication of information by the judge to the respondent was not possible when the incident occurred.)

PD 81 para.4.4

If there is a risk of the appearance of bias, the judge should ask another judge to hear the committal application.

PD 81 para.4.5

Where the committal application is to be heard by another judge, a written statement by the judge before whom the actions and behaviour of the respondent which have given rise to the committal application took place may be admitted as evidence of those actions and behaviour.

V Contempt in the face of the court

Committal for contempt in the face of the court

Pt 81 r.81.16

Where—
    (a) contempt has occurred in the face of the court; and
    (b) that court has power to commit for contempt,
the court may deal with the matter of its own initiative and give such directions as it thinks fit for the disposal of the matter.

VI Committal for making a false statement of truth (r.32.14) or disclosure statement (r.31.23)

Pt 81 r.81.17

    (1) This section contains rules about committal applications in relation to making, or causing to be made—
        (a) a false statement in a document verified by a statement of truth; or
        (b) a false disclosure statement,
    without an honest belief in its truth.
    (2) Where the committal application relates only to a false statement of truth or disclosure statement, this Section applies.
    (3) Where the committal application relates to both—
        (a) a false statement of truth or disclosure statement; and
        (b) breach of a judgment, order or undertaking to do or abstain from doing an act,
        s.2 (Committal for breach of a judgment, order or undertaking to do or abstain from doing an act) applies, but subject to para.(4).
    (4) To the extent that a committal application referred to in para.(3) relates to a false statement of truth or disclosure statement—
        (a) the applicant must obtain the permission of the court in accordance with r.81.18; or
        (b) the court may direct that the matter be referred to the Attorney General with a request that the Attorney General consider whether to bring proceedings for contempt of court.
    (5) Where the committal application relates to both
        (a) a false statement of truth or disclosure statement; and
        (b) other interference with the due administration of justice,
        s.3 (Committal for interference with the due administration of justice) applies, but subject to para.(6).
    (6) To the extent that a committal application referred to in para.(5) relates to a false statement of truth or disclosure statement, the court may direct that the matter be referred to the Attorney General with a request that the Attorney General consider whether to bring proceedings for contempt of court.

VII Committal application in relation to a false statement of truth or disclosure statement

Pt 81 r.81.18

(1) A committal application in relation to a false statement of truth or disclosure statement in connection with proceedings in the High Court, a Divisional Court or the Court of Appeal, may be made only—
  (a) with the permission of the court dealing with the proceedings in which the false statement or disclosure statement was made; or
  (b) by the Attorney General.
(2) Where permission is required under para.(1)(a), r. 81.14 applies as if the reference in that rule to a Pt 8 claim form were a reference to a Pt 23 application notice and the references to the claim form were references to the Pt 23 application notice.
(3) A committal application in relation to a false statement of truth or disclosure statement in connection with proceedings in a county court may be made only—
  (a) with the permission of a single judge of the Queen's Bench Division; or
  (b) by the Attorney General.
(4) Where permission is required under para.(3)(a) r. 81.14 applies without the modifications referred to in para.(2).
  (Under r.81.14(6)(b), the court granting permission may direct that the application be listed for hearing before a single judge or a Divisional Court.)
(5) The court may direct that the matter be referred to the Attorney General with a request that the Attorney General consider whether to bring proceedings for contempt of court.
(6) Where the committal application is made by the Attorney General, the application may be made to a single judge or a Divisional Court of the Queen's Bench Division.

PD 81 para.5.1

R.81.18(1)(b) and 81.18(3)(b) provide that a committal application may be made by the Attorney General. However, the Attorney General prefers a request that comes from the court to one made direct by a party to the proceedings in which the alleged contempt occurred without prior consideration by the court. A request to the Attorney General is not a way of appealing against, or reviewing, the decision of the judge.

PD 81 para.5.2

Where the permission of the court is sought under r. 81.18(1)(a) or 81.18(3)(a) so that r. 81.14 is applied by r. 81.18(2) or 81.18(4), the affidavit evidence in support of the application must—
  (1) identify the statement said to be false;
  (2) explain—
    (a) why it is false; and
    (b) why the maker knew the statement to be false at the time it was made; and
  (3) explain why contempt proceedings would be appropriate in the light of the overriding objective in Pt 1.

PD 81 para.5.3

The court may—
  (1) exercise any of its powers under the rules (including the power to give directions under r. 81.14(6));

(2) initiate steps to consider if there is a contempt of court and, where there is, to punish it; or

(3) as provided by r. 81.18(5), direct that the matter be referred to the Attorney General with a request to consider whether to bring proceedings for contempt of court.

PD 81 para.5.4

A request to the Attorney General to consider whether to bring proceedings for contempt of court must be made in writing and sent to the Attorney General's Office at 20 Victoria Street, London, SW1H 0NF.

PD 81 para.5.5

A request to the Attorney General must be accompanied by a copy of any order directing that the matter be referred to the Attorney General and must—

(1) identify the statement said to be false;
(2) explain—
  (a) why it is false; and
  (b) why the maker knew the statement to be false at the time it was made; and
(3) explain why contempt proceedings would be appropriate in the light of the overriding objective in Pt 1.

PD 81 para.5.6

Once the applicant receives the result of the request to the Attorney General, the applicant must send a copy of it to the court that will deal with the committal application, and the court will give such directions as it sees fit.

PD 81 para.5.7

The rules do not change the law of contempt or introduce new categories of contempt. A person applying to commence such proceedings should consider whether the incident complained of does amount to contempt of court and whether such proceedings would further the overriding objective in Pt 1.

VIII General rules about committal applications, orders for committal and writs of sequestration

PD 81 para.8.1

Subject to para.8.2, this s. of the PD applies in relation to all matters covered by Pt 81.

PD 81 para.8.2

Where there is a conflict between the provisions in this s. of the PD and specific provisions elsewhere in this PD or in Pt 81, the specific provisions prevail.

Human rights

PD 81 para.9

In all cases the Convention rights of those involved should particularly be borne in mind. It should be noted that the standard of proof, having regard to the possibility that a person may be sent to prison, is that the allegation be proved beyond reasonable doubt.
(Section 1 of the Human Rights Act 1998 defines "the Convention rights".)

Court to which applications should be made and levels of judiciary

PD 81 para.10.1

A committal application or an application for permission to make a committal application—
  (1) may be made in a county court if the alleged contempt is a contempt which a county
  (2) must otherwise be made in the High Court.

PD 81 para.10.2

Except where under an enactment a Master or district judge has power to make a committal order, a committal order can only be made—
  (1) in High Court proceedings, by a High Court Judge or a person authorised to act as such; or
  (2) in county court proceedings, by a Circuit Judge or a person authorised to act as such.

PD 81 para.10.3

Paragraph 10.4 applies in relation to proceedings in any court (the first court) where the judge or judges exercising the jurisdiction of the first court are deemed to constitute a court of the High Court by virtue of an enactment.

PD 81 para.10.4

The reference in para.10.2(1) to a High Court Judge will be construed as a reference to a judge of the first court.

General rules about applications: applications which cannot be made without permission

PD 81 para.11

If the committal application is one which cannot be made without permission—
  (1) the permission may only be granted by a judge who would have power to hear the committal application if permission were granted;
  (2) the date on which and the name of the judge by whom the requisite permission was granted must be stated on the claim form or application notice by which the committal application is commenced;
  (3) the claim form or application notice may not be issued or filed until the requisite permission has been granted; and
  (4) r.23.9 and 23.10 do not apply.

General rules about applications: applications by claim form

PD 81 para.12

If the application for permission to make a committal application or the committal application is commenced by the issue of a claim form—
  (1) Pt 8 will apply—
     (a) subject to the provisions of Pt 81 and [PD 81], in particular sub-paras 2–4;
     (b) as though references to 'claimant' were references to the applicant; and
     (c) as though references to 'defendant' were references to the respondent;
  (2) an amendment to the claim form may be made with the permission of the court but not otherwise;
  (3) r. 8.4 does not apply; and
  (4) the claim form must contain a prominent notice stating the possible consequences of the court making a committal order and of the respondent not attending the hearing. A form of notice which may be used is annexed to [PD 81] at Annex 3.

General rules about applications: applications by application notice

PD 81 para.13.1

Where the application is made by application notice, the application notice must state that the application is made in the proceedings in question, and its title and reference number must correspond with the title and reference number of those proceedings.

PD 81 para.13.2

If the application for permission to make a committal application or the committal application is commenced by the filing of an application notice—
  (1) Pt 23 will apply subject to the provisions of Pt 81 and [PD 81], in particular sub-paras 2–4;
  (2) an amendment to the application notice may be made with the permission of the court but not otherwise;
  (3) the court may not dispose of the application without a hearing; and
  (4) the application notice must contain a prominent notice stating the possible consequences of the court making a committal order and of the respondent not attending the hearing. A form of notice which may be used is annexed to [PD 81] at Annex 3.

Evidence and information

PD 81 para.14.1

Written evidence in support of or in opposition to a committal application must be given by affidavit.

PD 81 para.14.2

Written evidence served in support of or in opposition to a committal application must, unless the court otherwise directs, be filed.

PD 81 para.14.3

The following rules do not apply to committal applications—
(1) r. 35.7 (Court's power to direct that evidence is to be given by a single joint expert);
(2) r. 35.8 (Instructions to single joint expert); and
(3) r. 35.9 (Power of court to direct a party to provide information).

PD 81 para.14.4

An order under r. 18.1 (Obtaining further information) may not be made against a respondent to a committal application.

Striking out, procedural defects and discontinuance

PD 81 para.16.1

On application by the respondent or on its own initiative, the court may strike out a committal application if it appears to the court—
(1) that the application and the evidence served in support of it disclose no reasonable ground for alleging that the respondent is guilty of a contempt of court;
(2) that the application is an abuse of the court's process or, if made in existing proceedings, is otherwise likely to obstruct the just disposal of those proceedings; or
(3) that there has been a failure to comply with a rule, practice direction or court order.

PD 81 para.16.2

The court may waive any procedural defect in the commencement or conduct of a committal application if satisfied that no injustice has been caused to the respondent by the defect.

PD 81 para.16.3

A committal application may not be discontinued without the permission of the court.

General rules about committal applications, orders for committal and writs of sequestration

Hearing

Pt 81 r.81.28

(1) Unless the court hearing the committal application or application for sequestration otherwise permits, the applicant may not rely on—
    (a) any grounds other than—
        (i) those set out in the claim form or application notice; or
        (ii) in relation to a committal application under s. 3 or 4, the statement of grounds required by rule 81.14(1)(a) (where not included in the claim form) or 81.15(4)(a); or
    (b) any evidence unless it has been served in accordance with the relevant Section of [Pt 81] or [PD81].
(2) At the hearing, the respondent is entitled—

     (a) to give oral evidence, whether or not the respondent has filed or served written evidence, and, if doing so, may be cross-examined; and

     (b) with the permission of the court, to call a witness to give oral evidence whether or not the witness has made an affidavit or witness statement.

(3) The court may require or permit any party or other person (other than the respondent) to give oral evidence at the hearing.

(4) The court may give directions requiring the attendance for cross-examination of a witness who has given written evidence.

(5) If the court hearing an application in private decides to make a committal order against the respondent, it will in public state—

     (a) the name of the respondent;

     (b) in general terms, the nature of the contempt of court in respect of which the committal order is being made; and

     (c) the length of the period of the committal order.

       (r.39.2 contains provisions about hearings in private.)

(6) Where a committal order is made in the absence of the respondent, the court may on its own initiative fix a date and time when the respondent is to be brought before the court.

PD 81 para.15.1

When issuing or filing the claim form or application notice for a committal application, the applicant must obtain from the court a date for the hearing of the committal application.

PD 81 para.15.2

Unless the court otherwise directs, the hearing date of a committal application must not be less than 14 days after service of the claim form or application notice on the respondent. The hearing date must be specified in the claim form or application notice or in a Notice of Hearing attached to and served with the claim form or application notice.

PD 81 para.15.3

Paragraphs 15.1 and 15.2 apply to certifications of conduct and applications under s. 336 of the Charities Act 2011 ('s. 336 application') referred to in Section 4 of [Pt 81] as if references to the claim form or application notice were references to the certification or s.336 application.

    The definition of 'applicant' in r.81.3 includes a person who makes a committal application by way of certification or s.336 application.

PD 81 para.15.4

The court may on the hearing date—

     (1) give case management directions with a view to a hearing of the committal application on a future date; or

     (2) if the committal application is ready to be heard, proceed to hear it.

PD 81 para.15.5

In dealing with any committal application, the court will have regard to the need for the respondent to have details of the alleged acts of contempt and the opportunity to respond to the committal application.

PD 81 para.15.6

The court will also have regard to the need for the respondent to be—
  (1) allowed a reasonable time for responding to the committal application including, if necessary, preparing a defence;
  (2) made aware of the availability of assistance from the Community Legal Service and how to contact the Service;
  (3) given the opportunity, if unrepresented, to obtain legal advice; and
  (4) if unable to understand English, allowed to make arrangements, seeking the assistance of the court if necessary, for an interpreter to attend the hearing.

Power to suspend execution of a committal order

Pt 81 r.81.29

  (1) The court making the committal order may also order that its execution will be suspended for such period or on such terms or conditions as it may specify.
  (2) Unless the court otherwise directs, the applicant must serve on the respondent a copy of any order made under para.(1).

Warrant of committal

Pt 81 r.81.30

  (1) If a committal order is made, the order will be for the issue of a warrant of committal.
  (2) Unless the court orders otherwise—
      (a) a copy of the committal order must be served on the respondent either before or at the time of the execution of the warrant of committal; or
      (b) where the warrant of committal has been signed by the judge, the committal order may be served on the respondent at any time within 36 hours after the execution of the warrant.
  (3) Without further order of the court, a warrant of committal must not be enforced more than two years after the date on which the warrant is issued.

Discharge of a person in custody

Pt 81 r.81.31

  (1) A person committed to prison for contempt of court may apply to the court to be discharged.
  (2) The application must—
      (a) be in writing and attested by the governor of the prison (or any other officer of the prison not below the rank of principal officer);
      (b) show that the person committed to prison for contempt has purged, or wishes to purge, the contempt; and
      (c) be served on the person (if any) at whose instance the warrant of committal was issued at least one day before the application is made.
  (3) Paragraph (2) does not apply to—

    (a) a warrant of committal to which CCR Ord 27 r. 8, or CCR Ord 28 rr.4 or 14 relates; or

    (b) an application made by the Official Solicitor acting with official authority for the discharge of a person in custody.

(4) If the committal order is made in a county court and—

    (a) does not direct that any application for discharge must be made to a judge; or

    (b) was made by a district judge under s.118 of the [CCA]1984,

the application for discharge may be made to a district judge.

(5) If the committal order is made in the High Court, the application for discharge may be made to a single judge of the Division in which the committal order was made.

IX Penal, contempt and disciplinary provisions under the County Courts Act 1984

Pt 81 r.81.33

(1) This Section applies to county courts only and contains rules in relation to the penal, contempt and disciplinary provisions of the [CCA] 1984.

Offences under ss.14, 92 or 118 of the [CCA 1984]

Pt 81 r.81.34

(1) This rule applies where it is alleged that any person has committed an offence—

    (a) under s.14 of the Act, by assaulting an officer of the court acting in the execution of the officer's duties;

    (b) under s.92 of the Act, by rescuing or attempting to rescue any goods seized in execution; or

    (c) under s.118 of the Act, by wilfully insulting a judge, juror, witness or any officer of the court or by wilfully interrupting the proceedings of a county court or otherwise misbehaving in court,

and the alleged offender has not been taken into custody and brought before the court.

(2) The court will issue a summons, which must be served on the alleged offender personally not less than seven days before the day of the hearing stated in the summons.

(3) r.81.30 applies, with the necessary modifications, where an order is made under s.14, 92 or 118 of the Act committing a person to prison.

Offences under s.124 of the [CCA 1984]

Pt 81 r.81.35

Where a complaint is made against an officer of the court under s.124 of the Act for having lost the opportunity of levying execution, the court will issue a summons, which must be served on the alleged offender personally not less than seven days before the day of the hearing stated in the summons.

Notice to give evidence before or after a fine is imposed under s.55 of the [CCA 1984]

Pt 81 r.81.36

(1) Before or after imposing a fine on any person under s.55 of the Act for disobeying a witness summons or refusing to be sworn or give evidence, the court may direct that notice be given to that person in accordance with para.(2).

(2) The notice must state that if the recipient of the notice can demonstrate any reason why a fine should not be or should not have been imposed, that person may give evidence—

(a) by witness statement, affidavit or otherwise; and

(b) on a day named in the notice.

Non-payment of fine

Pt 81 r.81.37

(1) If a fine is not paid in accordance with the order imposing it, the court officer will, as soon as reasonably possible, report the matter to a judge.

(2) Where by an order imposing a fine—

(a) the amount of the fine is directed to be paid by instalments; and

(b) default is made in the payment of any instalment,

the same proceedings may be taken as if default had been made in payment of the whole of the fine.

(3) If the court makes an order for payment of a fine to be enforced by warrant of execution, the order will be treated as an application to the court for the issue of the warrant at the time when the order was made.

Repayment of fine

Pt 81 r.81.38

If a person pays a fine and later gives evidence to satisfy the court that, if the evidence had been given earlier, no fine or a smaller fine would have been imposed, the court may order the whole or part of the fine to be repaid.

See **Appeals to the Court of Appeal** and **Writ of sequestration**.

CONTENTIOUS PROBATE PROCEEDINGS

See **Probate claim**.

CONTRACT

Costs payable pursuant to a contract

Pt 48 r.48.3

(1) Where the court assesses (whether by the summary or detailed procedure) costs which are payable by the paying party to the receiving party under the terms of a contract, the

costs payable under those terms are, unless the contract expressly provides otherwise, to be presumed to be costs which—
  (a) have been reasonably incurred; and
  (b) are reasonable in amount, and the court will assess them accordingly.
(The Costs PD sets out circumstances where the court may order otherwise).
  (2) This rule does not apply where the contract is between a solicitor and his client.

Costs PD para.50.1

Where the court is assessing costs payable under a contract, it may make an order that all or part of the costs payable under the contract shall be disallowed if it is satisfied by the paying party that costs have been unreasonably incurred or are unreasonable in amount.

Costs PD para.50.2

Rule 48.3 only applies if the court is assessing costs payable under a contract. It does not—
  (1) require the court to make an assessment of such costs; or
  (2) require a mortgagee to apply for an order for those costs that he has a contractual right to recover out of the mortgage funds.

Costs PD para.50.3

The following principles apply to costs relating to a mortgage—
  (1) An order for the payment of costs of proceedings by one party to another is always a discretionary order: s.51 of the Senior Courts Act 1981.
  (2) Where there is a contractual right to the costs the discretion should ordinarily be exercised so as to reflect that contractual right.
  (3) The power of the court to disallow a mortgagee's costs sought to be added to the mortgage security is a power that does not derive from s.51, but from the power of the courts of equity to fix the terms on which redemption will be allowed.
  (4) A decision by a court to refuse costs in whole or in part to a mortgagee litigant may be—
    (a) a decision in the exercise of the s.51 discretion;
    (b) a decision in the exercise of the power to fix the terms on which redemption will be allowed;
    (c) a decision as to the extent of a mortgagee's contractual right to add his costs to the security; or
    (d) a combination of two or more of these things.
    The statements of case in the proceedings or the submissions made to the court may indicate which of the decisions has been made.
  (5) A mortgagee is not to be deprived of a contractual or equitable right to add costs to the security merely by reason of an order for payment of costs made without reference to the mortgagee's contractual or equitable rights, and without any adjudication as to whether or not the mortgagee should be deprived of those costs.

Costs PD para.50.4

  (1) Where the contract entitles a mortgagee to—
    (a) add the costs of litigation relating to the mortgage to the sum secured by it;
    (b) require a mortgagor to pay those costs, or
    (c) both,
    the mortgagor may make an application for the court to direct that an account of the mortgagee's costs be taken.
(Rule 25.1(1)(n) provides that the court may direct that a party file an account).

(2) The mortgagor may then dispute an amount in the mortgagee's account on the basis that it has been unreasonably incurred or is unreasonable in amount.

(3) Where a mortgagor disputes an amount, the court may make an order that the disputed costs are assessed under r.48.3.

Service of documents

Service of the claim form by contractually agreed method

Pt 6 r.6.11

(1) Where—
    (a) a contract contains a term providing that, in the event of a claim being started in relation to the contract, the claim form may be served by a method or at a place specified in the contract; and
    (b) a claim solely in respect of that contract is started,
the claim form may, subject to para.(2), be served on the defendant by the method or at the place specified in the contract.

(2) Where in accordance with the contract the claim form is to be served out of the jurisdiction, it may be served—
    (a) if permission to serve it out of the jurisdiction has been granted under r.6.36; or
    (b) without permission under rr.6.32 or 6.33.

Service of the claim form relating to a contract on an agent of a principal who is out of the jurisdiction

Pt 6 r.6.12

(1) The court may, on application, permit a claim form relating to a contract to be served on the defendant's agent where—
    (a) the defendant is out of the jurisdiction;
    (b) the contract to which the claim relates was entered into within the jurisdiction with or through the defendant's agent; and
    (c) at the time of the application either the agent's authority has not been terminated or the agent is still in business relations with the defendant.

(2) An application under this rule—
    (a) must be supported by evidence setting out—
        (i) details of the contract and that it was entered into within the jurisdiction or through an agent who is within the jurisdiction;
        (ii) that the principal for whom the agent is acting was, at the time the contract was entered into and is at the time of the application, out of the jurisdiction; and
        (iii) why service out of the jurisdiction cannot be effected; and
    (b) may be made without notice.

(3) An order under this rule must state the period within which the defendant must respond to the particulars of claim.

(4) Where the court makes an order under this rule—
    (a) a copy of the application notice and the order must be served with the claim form on the agent; and
    (b) unless the court orders otherwise, the claimant must send to the defendant a copy of the application notice, the order and the claim form.

(5) This rule does not exclude the court's power under r.6.15 (service by an alternative method or at an alternative place).

CONTRIBUTION

Glossary

A right of someone to recover from a third person all or part of the amount which he himself is liable to pay.

See **Additional claims**.

CONTRIBUTION CLAIM

See **Indemnity basis**.

CONTROL OF MISLEADING ADVERTISEMENTS REGULATIONS 1988

See **Fair Trading Act 1973**.

CONVENTION TERRITORY

Pt 12 r.12.11(6)

(b) The territory or territories of any Contracting State, as defined by s.1(3) of the Civil Jurisdiction and Judgments Act 1982, to which the Brussels Conventions or **Lugano Convention** apply.

Service of the claim form on a defendant in a convention territory within Europe or a Member State

Pt 6 r.6.35

(3) Where the claimant serves the claim form on a defendant in a Convention territory within Europe or a Member State under r.6.33, the period—
    (a) for filing an acknowledgment of service or admission, is 21 days after service of the particulars of claim; or
    (b) for filing a defence is—
        (i) 21 days after service of the particulars of claim; or
        (ii) where the defendant files an acknowledgment of service, 35 days after service of the particulars of claim.

Service of the claim form on a defendant in a convention territory outside Europe

P6 r.6.35

(4) Where the claimant serves the claim form on a defendant in a Convention territory outside Europe under r.6.33, the period—

(a) for filing an acknowledgment of service or admission, is 31 days after service of the particulars of claim; or

(b) for filing a defence is—

    (i) 31 days after service of the particulars of claim; or

    (ii) where the defendant files an acknowledgment of service, 45 days after service of the particulars of claim.

CONVEYANCING COUNSEL

Appointed under s.131 of the Supreme Court Act 1981.

Fees payable to conveyancing counsel appointed by the court to assist it

Costs PD para.8.8

(1) Where the court refers any matter to the conveyancing counsel of the court the fees payable to counsel in respect of the work done or to be done will be assessed by the court in accordance with r.44.3.

(2) An appeal from a decision of the court in respect of the fees of such counsel will be dealt with under the general r.s as to appeals set out in Part 52. If the appeal is against the decision of an authorised court officer, it will be dealt with in accordance with rr.47.20 to 47.23.

Reference to conveyancing counsel

Pt 40 r.40.18

(1) The court may direct conveyancing counsel to investigate and prepare a report on the title of any land or to draft any document.

(2) The court may take the report on title into account when it decides the issue in question.

(Provisions dealing with the fees payable to conveyancing counsel are set out in the Costs PD).

PD 40D para.6.1

When the court refers a matter under r.40.18, the court may specify a particular conveyancing counsel.

PD 40D para.6.2

If the court does not specify a particular conveyancing counsel, references will be distributed among conveyancing counsel in accordance with arrangements made by the Chief Chancery Master.

PD 40D para.6.3

Notice of every reference under r.40.18 must be given to the Chief Chancery Master.

PD 40D para.6.4

The court will send a copy of the Order, together with all other necessary documents, to conveyancing counsel.

PD 40D para.6.5

A court order sent to conveyancing counsel under para.6.4 will be sufficient authority for him to prepare his report or draft the document.

PD 40D para.6.6

    (1) An objection under r.40.19 to a report on title prepared by conveyancing counsel must be made by application notice.
    (2) The application notice must state—
       (a) the matters the applicant objects to; and
       (b) the reason for the objection.

Party may object to report

Pt 40 r.40.19

    (1) Any party to the proceedings may object to the report on title prepared by conveyancing counsel.
    (2) Where there is an objection, the issue will be referred to a judge for determination.
(Part 23 contains general rules about making an application).

COPYRIGHT

See **Intellectual property claims**.

CORE BUNDLE

See **Court bundles**.

CORONERS COURT

Applications under s.13 of the Coroners Act 1988

PD 8A para.19.1

An application under s.13 of the Coroners Act 1988 is heard and determined by a Divisional Court.

PD 8A para.19.2

The application must, unless made by the Attorney General, be accompanied by the Attorney General's fiat.

PD 8A para.19.3

The [Pt 8] claim form must—
    (1) state the grounds for the application;
    (2) be filed at the Administrative Court; and

(3) be served upon all persons directly affected by the application within six weeks of the grant of the Attorney General's fiat.

See also **Part 8 claim form** and **Part 8 procedure**.

CORPORATION

See **Company**.

COSTS

Pt 44 r.44.1

(1) Includes fees, charges, disbursements, expenses, remuneration, reimbursement allowed to a **litigant in person** under r.46.5, and any fee or reward charged by a **lay representative** for acting on behalf of a party in proceedings allocated to the **small claims track**.

(2) The costs to which Pts 44–47 apply include—
    (a) the following costs where those costs may be assessed by the court—
        (i) costs of proceedings before an arbitrator or umpire;
        (ii) costs of proceedings before a tribunal or other statutory body; and
        (iii) costs payable by a client to their **legal representative**; and
    (b) costs which are payable by one party to another party under the terms of a contract, where the court makes an order for an assessment of those costs.

(3) Where advocacy or litigation services are provided to a clients under a conditional fee agreement, costs are recoverable under Pts 44–47 notwithstanding that the client is liable to pay the legal representative's fees and expenses only to the extent that sums are recovered in respect of the proceedings, whether by way of costs or otherwise.

Court's discretion and circumstances to be taken into account when exercising its discretion as to costs

Pt 44 r.44.2

(1) The court has discretion as to—
    (a) whether costs are payable by one party to another;
    (b) the amount of those costs; and
    (c) when they are to be paid.

(2) If the court decides to make an order about costs—
    (a) the general rule is that the unsuccessful party will be ordered to pay the costs of the successful party; but
    (b) the court may make a different order.

(3) The general rule does not apply to the following proceedings—
    (a) proceedings in the Court of Appeal on an application or appeal made in connection with proceedings in the Family Division; or
    (b) proceedings in the Court of Appeal from a judgment, direction, decision or order given or made in probate proceedings or family proceedings.

(4) In deciding what order (if any) to make about costs, the court must have regard to all the circumstances, including—
    (a) the conduct of all the parties;
    (b) whether a party has succeeded on part of his case, even if he has not been wholly successful; and

    (c) any payment into court or admissible offer to settle made by a party which is drawn to the court's attention, and which is not an offer to which costs consequences under Pt 36 apply.

(5) The conduct of the parties includes—

    (a) conduct before, as well as during, the proceedings and in particular the extent to which the parties followed the PD (Pre-Action Conduct) or any relevant Pre-Action Protocol;

    (b) whether it was reasonable for a party to raise, pursue or contest a particular allegation or issue;

    (c) the manner in which a party has pursued or defended his case or a particular allegation or issue; and

    (d) whether a claimant who has succeeded in his claim, in whole or in part, exaggerated his claim.

(6) The orders which the court may make under this rule include an order that a party must pay—

    (a) a proportion of another party's costs;

    (b) a stated amount in respect of another party's costs;

    (c) costs from or until a certain date only;

    (d) costs incurred before proceedings have begun;

    (e) costs relating to particular steps taken in the proceedings;

    (f) costs relating only to a distinct part of the proceedings; and

    (g) interest on costs from or until a certain date, including a date before judgment.

(7) Where the court would otherwise consider making an order under para.(6)(f), it must instead, if practicable, make an order under para.(6)(a) or (c).

(8) Where the court has ordered a party to pay costs, it may order an amount to be paid on account before the costs are assessed.

PD 44 para.4.2

The court may make an order about costs at any stage in a case.

Basis of assessment

Pt 44 r.44.4

(1) Where the court is to assess the amount of costs (whether by summary or detailed assessment) it will assess those costs—

    (a) on the **standard basis**; or

    (b) on the **indemnity basis**,

but the court will not in either case allow costs which have been unreasonably incurred or are unreasonable in amount.

(R.44.5 sets out how the court decides the amount of costs payable under a **contract**)

(2) Where the amount of costs is to be assessed on the standard basis, the court will—

    (a) only allow costs which are proportionate to the matters in issue; and

    (b) resolve any doubt which it may have as to whether costs were reasonably incurred or reasonable and proportionate in amount in favour of the paying party.

(Factors which the court may take into account are set out in r.44.4).

(3) Where the amount of costs is to be assessed on the indemnity basis, the court will resolve any doubt which it may have as to whether costs were reasonably incurred or were reasonable in amount in favour of the receiving party.

(4) Where—

    (a) the court makes an order about costs without indicating the basis on which the costs are to be assessed; or

    (b) the court makes an order for costs to be assessed on a basis other than the standard basis or the indemnity basis, the costs will be assessed on the standard basis.

(6) Where the amount of a solicitor's remuneration in respect of non-contentious business is regulated by any general orders made under the Solicitors Act 1974 (*http://www.justice .gov.uk/courts/procedure-rules/civil/rules/part44*—Accessed November 22, 2012) " the amount of the costs to be allowed in respect of any such business which falls to be assessed by the court will be decided in accordance with those general orders rather than this rule and r.44.4.

(7) Paragraphs 2(a) and (5) do not apply in relation to cases commenced before April 1, 2013 and in relation to such cases, r.44.4(2)(a) as it was in force immediately before April 1, 2013 will apply instead.

Factors to be taken into account in deciding the amount of costs

Pt 44 r.44.4

(1) The court is to have regard to all the circumstances in deciding whether costs were—
    (a) if it is assessing costs on the standard basis—
        (i) proportionately and reasonably incurred; or
        (ii) were proportionate and reasonable in amount, or
    (b) if it is assessing costs on the indemnity basis—
        (i) unreasonably incurred; or
        (ii) unreasonable in amount.
(2) In particular the court must give effect to any orders which have already been made.
(3) The court must also have regard to—
    (a) the conduct of all the parties, including in particular—
        (i) conduct before, as well as during, the proceedings; and
        (ii) the efforts made, if any, before and during the proceedings in order to try to resolve the dispute;
    (b) the amount or value of any money or property involved;
    (c) the importance of the matter to all the parties;
    (d) the particular complexity of the matter or the difficulty or novelty of the questions raised;
    (e) the skill, effort, specialised knowledge and responsibility involved;
    (f) the time spent on the case; and
    (g) the place where and the circumstances in which work or any part of it was done.
    (h) the receiving party's last approved or agreed budget.
(Rule 35.4(4) gives the court power to limit the amount that a party may recover with regard to the fees and expenses of an expert).

See also **Contract**.

Procedure for assessing costs

Pt 44 r.44.6

Where the court orders a party to pay costs to another party (other than **fixed costs**) it may either—
    (a) make a summary assessment of the costs; or
    (b) order detailed assessment of the costs by a costs officer,
unless any rule, PD or other enactment provides otherwise.
(PD 44—General rules about costs sets out the factors which will affect the court's decision under para.(1).)
    (4) A party may recover the fixed costs specified in Part 45 in accordance with that Part.

PD 44 para.8.1

Subject to para.8.3, where the court does not order fixed costs (or no fixed costs are provided for) the amount of costs payable will be assessed by the court. R. 44.6 allows the court making an order about costs either—
(a) to make a summary assessment of the amount of the costs; or
(b) to order the amount to be decided in accordance with Pt 47 (a detailed assessment).

PD 44 para.8.2

An order for costs will be treated as an order for the amount of costs to be decided by a detailed assessment unless the order otherwise provides.

PD 44 para.8.3

Where a party is entitled to costs some of which are fixed costs and some of which are not, the court will assess those costs which are not fixed. For example, the court will assess the disbursements payable in accordance with rr. 45.12 or 45.19. The decision whether such assessment should be summary or detailed will be made in accordance with paras 9.1 to 9.10 of [the Costs PD].

Cases where costs orders deemed to have been made

Pt 44 r.44.9

(1) Subject to para.(2), where a right to costs arises under—
    (a) r. 3.7 (defendant's right to costs where claim struck out for non-payment of fees);
    (b) rr. 36.10(1) or (2) (claimant's entitlement to costs where a Pt 36 offer is accepted);
    (d) r. 38.6 (defendant's right to costs where claimant discontinues),
    a costs order will be deemed to have been made on the standard basis.
(2) Paragraph 1(b) does not apply where a **Part 36 offer** is accepted before the commencement of proceedings.
(3) Where such an order is deemed to be made in favour of a party with **pro bono** representation, that party may apply for an order under s.194(3) of the Legal Services Act 2007.
(4) Interest payable pursuant to s.17 of the Judgments Act 1838 or s.74 of the County Courts Act 1984 on the costs deemed to have been ordered under para.(1) shall begin to run from the date on which the event which gave rise to the entitlement to costs occurred.

Where the court makes no order for costs

Pt 44 r.10

(1) Where the court makes an order which does not mention costs—
    (a) subject to paras (2) and (3), the general rule is that no party is entitled—

      (i) to costs; or
     (ii) to seek an order under s.194(3) of the Legal Services Act 2007 in relation to that order; but
  (b) this does not affect any entitlement of a party to recover costs out of a fund held by that party as trustee or personal representative, or under any lease, mortgage or other security.
(2) Where the court makes—
  (a) an order granting permission to appeal;
  (b) an order granting permission to apply for judicial review; or
  (c) any other order or direction sought by a party on an application without notice, and its order does not mention costs,
  it will be deemed to include an order for applicant's costs in the case.
(3) Any party affected by a deemed order for costs under para.(2) may apply at any time to vary the order.
(4) The court hearing an appeal may, unless it dismisses the appeal, make orders about the costs of the proceedings giving rise to the appeal as well as the costs of the appeal.
(5) Subject to any order made by the transferring court, where proceedings are transferred from one court to another, the court to which they are transferred may deal with all the costs, including the costs before the transfer.

Court's powers in relation to misconduct

Pt 44 r.11

(1) The court may make an order under this rule where—
  (a) a party or that party's legal representative, in connection with a summary or detailed assessment, fails to comply with a rule, practice direction or court order; or
  (b) it appears to the court that the conduct of a party or that party's legal representative, before or during the proceedings or in the assessment proceedings, was unreasonable or improper.

Set off

Pt 44 r.44.12

(1) Where a party entitled to costs is also liable to pay costs, the court may assess the costs which that party is liable to pay and either—
  (a) set off the amount assessed against the amount the party is entitled to be paid and direct that party to pay any balance; or
  (b) delay the issue of a certificate for the costs to which the party is entitled until the party has paid the amount which that party is liable to pay.

Time for complying with an Order for costs

Pt 44 r.44.7

A party must comply with an order for the payment of costs within 14 days of—
  (a) the date of the judgment or order if it states the amount of those costs;
  (b) if the amount of those costs (or part of them) is decided later in accordance with Pt 47, the date of the certificate which states the amount; or

(c) in either case, such later date as the court may specify.
(Part 47 sets out the procedure for detailed assessment of costs).

COSTS CAPPING

Pt 3 r.3.19

(1) A costs capping order is an order limiting the amount of future costs (including disbursements) which a party may recover pursuant to an order for costs subsequently made.
(2) In this rule, 'future costs' means costs incurred in respect of work done after the date of the costs capping order but excluding the amount of any additional liability.
(3) This rule does not apply to protective costs orders.
(4) A costs capping order may be in respect of—
    (a) the whole litigation; or
    (b) any issues which are ordered to be tried separately.
(5) The court may at any stage of proceedings make a costs capping order against all or any of the parties, if—
    (a) it is in the interests of justice to do so;
    (b) there is a substantial risk that without such an order costs will be disproportionately incurred; and
    (c) it is not satisfied that the risk in subpara.(b) can be adequately controlled by—
        (i) case management directions or orders made under this Part; and
        (ii) detailed assessment of costs.
(6) In considering whether to exercise its discretion under this rule, the court will consider all the circumstances of the case, including—
    (a) whether there is a substantial imbalance between the financial position of the parties;
    (b) whether the costs of determining the amount of the cap are likely to be proportionate to the overall costs of the litigation;
    (c) the stage which the proceedings have reached; and
    (d) the costs which have been incurred to date and the future costs.
(7) A costs capping order, once made, will limit the costs recoverable by the party subject to the order unless a party successfully applies to vary the order. No such variation will be made unless—
    (a) there has been a material and substantial change of circumstances since the date when the order was made; or
    (b) there is some other compelling reason why a variation should be made.

Application for a costs capping order

PD 3F para.1.1

The court will make a costs capping order only in exceptional circumstances.

PD 3F para.1.2

An application for a costs capping order must be made as soon as possible, preferably before or at the first case management hearing or shortly afterwards. The stage which the proceedings have reached at the time of the application will be one of the factors the court will consider when deciding whether to make a costs capping order.

Pt 3 r.3.20

(1) An application for a costs capping order must be made on notice in accordance with Pt 23.
(2) The application notice must—
    (a) set out—
        (i) whether the costs capping order is in respect of the whole of the litigation or a particular issue which is ordered to be tried separately; and
        (ii) why a costs capping order should be made; and
    (b) be accompanied by a budget setting out—
        (i) the costs (and disbursements) incurred by the applicant to date; and
        (ii) the costs (and disbursements) which the applicant is likely to incur in the future conduct of the proceedings.
(3) The court may give directions for the determination of the application and such directions may—
    (a) direct any party to the proceedings—
        (i) to file a schedule of costs in the form set out in para.3 of PD 3F—Costs capping;
        (ii) to file written submissions on all or any part of the issues arising;
    (b) fix the date and time estimate of the hearing of the application;
    (c) indicate whether the judge hearing the application will sit with an assessor at the hearing of the application; and
    (d) include any further directions as the court sees fit.

Costs budget

PD 3F para.2

The budget required by r.3.20 must be in the form of Precedent H annexed to this Practice Direction.

Schedule of costs

PD 3F para.3

The schedule of costs referred to in r. 3.20(3)—
    (a) must set out—
        (i) each sub-heading as it appears in the applicant's budget (column 1);
        (ii) alongside each sub-heading, the amount claimed by the applicant in the applicant's budget (column 2); and
        (iii) alongside the figures referred to in subpara.(ii) the amount that the respondent proposes should be allowed under each sub-heading (column 3); and
    (b) must be supported by a statement of truth.

Assessing the quantum of the costs cap

PD 3F para.4.1

When assessing the quantum of a costs cap, the court will take into account the factors detailed in r.44.5 and the relevant provisions supporting that rule in the Practice Direction supplementing

Pt 44. When considering a party's budget of the costs they are likely to incur in the future conduct of the proceedings, the court may also take into account a reasonable allowance on costs for contingencies.

Application to vary a costs capping order

Pt 3 r.3.21

An application to vary a costs capping order must be made by application notice pursuant to Pt 23.

Costs capping orders in relation to trust funds

PD 3F para.5.1

'Trust fund' means property which is the subject of a trust, and includes the estate of a deceased person.

PD 3F para.5.2

[Section II of PD 3F] contains additional provisions to enable—
  (a) the parties to consider whether to apply for; and
  (b) the court to consider whether to make of its own initiative,
a costs capping order in proceedings relating to trust funds.

PD 3F para.5.3

[Section II of PD 3F] supplements rr.3.19 to 3.21 and s.I of [PD 3F].

PD 3F para.5.4

Any party to such proceedings who intends to apply for an order for the payment of costs out of the trust fund must file and serve on all other parties written notice of that intention together with a budget of the costs likely to be incurred by that party.

PD 3F para.5.5

The documents mentioned in para.5.4 must be filed and served—
  (a) in a Pt 7 claim, with the first statement of case; and
  (b) in a Pt 8 claim, with the evidence (or, if a defendant does not intend to serve and file evidence, with the acknowledgement of service).

PD 3F para.5.6

When proceedings first come before the court for directions the court may make a costs capping order of its own initiative whether or not any party has applied for such an order.

COSTS CERTIFICATE

See **Final costs certificate** and **Interim costs certificate**.

COSTS HERE AND BELOW

PD 44 s.1(4) para.4.2

The party in whose favour the costs order is made is entitled not only to his costs in respect of the proceedings in which the court makes the order but also to his costs of the proceedings in any lower court. In the case of an appeal from a Divisional Court the party is not entitled to any costs incurred in any court below the Divisional Court.

COSTS IN ANY EVENT

PD 44 s.1(4) para.4.2

The party in whose favour the order is made is entitled to the costs in respect of the part of the proceedings to which the order relates, whatever other costs orders are made in the proceedings.

COSTS IN THE APPLICATION

PD 44 para.4.2

The party in whose favour the court makes an order for costs at the end of the proceedings is entitled to his costs of the part of the proceedings to which the order relates.

COSTS IN THE CASE

PD 44 para.4.2

The party in whose favour the court makes an order for costs at the end of the proceedings is entitled to his costs of the part of the proceedings to which the order relates.

COSTS JUDGE

Pt 44 r.44.1(1)

(b) A taxing master of the Senior Courts.

See also **Costs officer**.

COSTS MANAGEMENT

Pt 3 r.3.12

(1) [Section 1 of Pt 3] and PD 3E apply to all **multi-track** cases commenced on or after April 1, 2013 in—
   (a) a county court; or
   (b) the Chancery Division or Queen's Bench Division of the High Court (except the Admiralty and Commercial Courts),
   (c) unless the proceedings are the subject of fixed costs or scale costs or the court otherwise orders. This Section and PD 3E shall apply to any other proceedings (including applications) where the court so orders.
(2) The purpose of costs management is that the court should manage both the steps to be taken and the costs to be incurred by the parties to any proceedings so as to further the **overriding objective**.

Filing and exchanging budgets

Pt 3 r.3.13

Unless the court otherwise orders, all parties except litigants in person must file and exchange budgets as required by the rules or as the court otherwise directs. Each party must do so by the date specified in the notice served under r.26.3(1) or, if no such date is specified, seven days before the first case management conference.

Budget format

Unless the court otherwise orders, a budget must be in the form of Precedent H annexed to [PD 3E]. It must be in landscape format with an easily legible typeface. In substantial cases, the court may direct that budgets be limited initially to part only of the proceedings and subsequently extended to cover the whole proceedings. A budget must be dated and verified by a statement of truth signed by a senior legal representative of the party. In cases where a party's budgeted costs do not exceed £25,000, there is no obligation on that party to complete more than the first page of Precedent H.
(The wording for a statement of truth verifying a budget is set out in PD 22.)

Failure to file a budget

Pt 3 r.3.14

Unless the court otherwise orders, any party which fails to file a budget despite being required to do so will be treated as having filed a budget comprising only the applicable court fees.

Costs management orders

Pt 3 r.3.15

(1) In addition to exercising its other powers, the court may manage the costs to be incurred by any party in any proceedings.

(2) The court may at any time make a 'costs management order'. By such order the court will—
   (a) record the extent to which the budgets are agreed between the parties;
   (b) in respect of budgets or parts of budgets which are not agreed, record the court's approval after making appropriate revisions.
(3) If a costs management order has been made, the court will thereafter control the parties' budgets in respect of recoverable costs.

PD 3E para.2.1

If the court makes a costs management order under r.3.15, the following paragraphs apply.

PD 3E para.2

Save in exceptional circumstances—
   (1) the recoverable costs of initially completing Precedent H shall not exceed the higher of £1,000 or 1 per cent of the approved budget;
   (2) All other recoverable costs of the budgeting and costs management process shall not exceed 2 per cent of the approved budget.

PD 3E para.2.3

If the budgets or parts of the budgets are agreed between all parties, the court will record the extent of such agreement. In so far as the budgets are not agreed, the court will review them and, after making any appropriate revisions, record its approval of those budgets. The court's approval will relate only to the total figures for each phase of the proceedings, although in the course of its review the court may have regard to the constituent elements of each total figure. When reviewing budgets, the court will not undertake a detailed assessment in advance, but rather will consider whether the budgeted costs fall within the range of reasonable and proportionate costs.

PD 3E para.2.4

As part of the costs management process the court may not approve costs incurred before the date of any budget. The court may, however, record its comments on those costs and should take those costs into account when considering the reasonableness and proportionality of all subsequent costs.

PD 3E para.2.5

The court may set a timetable or give other directions for future reviews of budgets.

PD 3E para.2.6

Each party shall revise its budget in respect of future costs upwards or downwards, if significant developments in the litigation warrant such revisions. Such amended budgets shall be submitted to the other parties for agreement. In default of agreement, the amended budgets shall be submitted to the court, together with a note of (a) the changes made and the reasons for those changes and (b) the objections of any other party. The court may approve, vary or disapprove the revisions, having regard to any significant developments which have occurred since the date when the previous budget was approved or agreed.

PD 3E para.2.7

After its budget has been approved, each party shall re-file and re-serve the budget in the form approved with re-cast figures, annexed to the order approving it.

PD 3E para.2.8

A **litigant in person**, even though not required to prepare a budget, shall nevertheless be provided with a copy of the budget of any other party.

PD 3E para.2.9

If interim applications are made which, reasonably, were not included in a budget, then the costs of such interim applications shall be treated as additional to the approved budgets.

Costs budgets

PD 44 para.3.1

In any case where the parties have filed budgets in accordance with PD 3E but the court has not made a costs management order under r.3.15, the provisions of this subsection shall apply.

PD 44 para.3.2

If there is a difference of 20 per cent or more between the costs claimed by a receiving party on detailed assessment and the costs shown in a budget filed by that party, the receiving party must provide a statement of the reasons for the difference with the bill of costs.

PD 44 para.3.3

If a paying party—
 (a) claims to have reasonably relied on a budget filed by a receiving party; or
 (b) wishes to rely upon the costs shown in the budget in order to dispute the reasonableness
   or proportionality of the costs claimed,
the paying party must serve a statement setting out the case in this regard in that party's points of dispute.

PD 44 para.3.4

On an assessment of the costs of a party, the court will have regard to the last approved or agreed budget, and may have regard to any other budget previously filed by that party, or by any other party in the same proceedings. Such other budgets may be taken into account when assessing the reasonableness and proportionality of any costs claimed.

PD 44 para.3.5

Subject to para.3.4, paras 3.6 and 3.7 apply where there is a difference of 20 per cent or more between the costs claimed by a receiving party and the costs shown in a budget filed by that party.

PD 44 para.3.6

Where it appears to the court that the paying party reasonably relied on the budget, the court may restrict the recoverable costs to such sum as is reasonable for the paying party to pay in the light of that reliance, notwithstanding that such sum is less than the amount of costs reasonably and proportionately incurred by the receiving party.

PD 44 para.3.7

Where it appears to the court that the receiving party has not provided a satisfactory explanation for that difference, the court may regard the difference between the costs claimed and the costs shown in the budget as evidence that the costs claimed are unreasonable or disproportionate.

Costs management conferences

Pt 3 r.3.16

(1) Any hearing which is convened solely for the purpose of costs management (for example, to approve a revised budget) is referred to as a 'costs management Conference'.
(2) Where practicable, costs management conferences should be conducted by telephone or in writing.

Court to have regard to budgets and to take account of costs

Pt 3 r.3.17

(1) When making any case management decision, the court will have regard to any available budgets of the parties and will take into account the costs involved in each procedural step.
(2) Paragraph (1) applies whether or not the court has made a costs management order.

Assessing costs on the standard basis where a costs management order has been made

Pt 3 r.3.18

In any case where a costs management order has been made, when assessing costs on the standard basis, the court will—
(a) have regard to the receiving party's last approved or agreed budget for each phase of the proceedings; and
(b) not depart from such approved or agreed budget unless satisfied that there is good reason to do so.
(Attention is drawn to r.44.3(2)(a) and r.44.3(5), which concern proportionality of costs.)

COSTS MANAGEMENT IN MERCANTILE COURTS AND TECHNOLOGY AND CONSTRUCTION COURTS SCHEME

PD 51G para.1.1

[PDG] provided for a pilot scheme (Costs Management in Mercantile Courts and Technology and Construction Courts Scheme) to—
(1) operate from October 1, 2011 to March 31, 2013;
(2) operated in all Mercantile Courts and Technology and Construction Courts; and
(3) applied to proceedings in which the first case management conference is heard on or after October 1, 2011.

COSTS OF AND CAUSED BY

Costs PD para.4.2

Where, for example, the court makes this order on an application to amend a statement of case, the party in whose favour the costs order is made is entitled to the costs of preparing for and attending the application and the costs of any consequential amendment to his own statement of case.

COSTS OFFICE

PT 44 r.44.1(1)

The Senior Courts Costs Office.

COSTS OFFICER

Pt 44 r.44.1

    (c) (i) a costs judge;
         (ii) a district judge; and
        (iii) an **authorised court officer**.

COSTS PAYABLE PURSUANT TO A CONTRACT

Pt 44 r.44.5

  (1) Subject to paras (2)–(4), where the court assesses (whether by the summary or detailed procedure) costs which are payable by the paying party to the receiving party under the terms of a contract, the costs payable under those terms are, unless the contract expressly provides otherwise, to be presumed to be costs which—
    (a) have been reasonably incurred; and
    (b) are reasonable in amount,
    and the court will assess them accordingly.
  (2) The presumptions in para.(1) are rebuttable. PD 44—General rules sets out circumstances where the court may order otherwise.
  (3) Paragraph (1) does not apply where the contract is between a solicitor and client.

PD 44 para.7.1

R. 44.5 only applies if the court is assessing costs payable under a contract. It does not—
    (a) require the court to make an assessment of such costs; or
    (b) require a mortgagee to apply for an order for those costs where there is a contractual right to recover out of the mortgage funds.

Costs relating to a mortgage

PD 44 para.7.2

(1) The following principles apply to costs relating to a mortgage.
(2) An order for the payment of costs of proceedings by one party to another is always a discretionary order: s. 51 of the Senior Courts Act 1981 ('the s.51 discretion').
(3) Where there is a contractual right to the costs, the discretion should ordinarily be exercised so as to reflect that contractual right.
(4) The power of the court to disallow a mortgagee's costs sought to be added to the mortgage security is a power that does not derive from s.51, but from the power of the courts of equity to fix the terms on which redemption will be allowed.
(5) A decision by a court to refuse costs in whole or in part to a mortgagee may be—
   (a) a decision in the exercise of the s.51 discretion;
   (b) a decision in the exercise of the power to fix the terms on which redemption will be allowed;
   (c) a decision as to the extent of a mortgagee's contractual right to add the mortgagee's costs to the security; or
   (d) a combination of two or more of these things.
(6) A mortgagee is not to be deprived of a contractual or equitable right to add costs to the security merely by reason of an order for payment of costs made without reference to the mortgagee's contractual or equitable rights, and without any adjudication as to whether or not the mortgagee should be deprived of those costs.

PD 44 para.7.3

(1) Where the contract entitles a mortgagee to—
   (a) add the costs of litigation relating to the mortgage to the sum secured by it; or
   (b) require a mortgagor to pay those costs,
   the mortgagor may make an application for the court to direct that an account of the mortgagee's costs be taken.
(R. 25.1(1)(n) provides that the court may direct that a party file an account.)
(2) The mortgagor may then dispute an amount in the mortgagee's account on the basis that it has been unreasonably incurred or is unreasonable in amount.
(3) Where a mortgagor disputes an amount, the court may make an order that the disputed costs are assessed under r. 44.5.

COSTS-ONLY PROCEEDINGS

Pt 46 r.46.14

(1) This rule applies where—
   (a) the parties to a dispute have reached an agreement on all issues (including which party is to pay the costs) which is made or confirmed in writing; but
   (b) they have failed to agree the amount of those costs; and
   (c) no proceedings have been started.
(2) Where this rule applies, the procedure set out in this rule must be followed.
(3) Proceedings under this rule are commenced by issuing a claim form in accordance with Pt 8.
(4) The claim form must contain or be accompanied by the agreement or confirmation.
(5) In proceedings to which this rule applies the court may make an order for the payment of costs the amount of which is to be determined by assessment and/or, where appropriate, for the payment of fixed costs.

(6) Where this rule applies but the procedure set out in this rule has not been followed by a party—
   (a) that party will not be allowed costs greater than those that would have been allowed to that party had the procedure been followed; and
   (b) the court may award the other party the costs of the proceedings up to the point where an order for the payment of costs is made.
(7) R. 44.5 (amount of costs where costs are payable pursuant to a **contract**) does not apply to claims started under the procedure in this rule.

PD 46 para.9.1

A claim form under r.46.14 should not be issued in the High Court unless the dispute to which the agreement relates was of such a value or type that had proceedings been begun they would have been commenced in the High Court.

PD 46 para.9.2

Claim form which is to be issued in the High Court at the Royal Courts of Justice will be issued in the Costs Office.

PD 46 para.9.3

Attention is drawn to r.8.2 (in particular to para.(b)(ii)) and to r.44.12A(3). The claim form must:
   (1) identify the claim or dispute to which the agreement to pay costs relates;
   (2) state the date and terms of the agreement on which the claimant relies;
   (3) set out or have attached to it a draft of the order which the claimant seeks;
   (4) state the amount of the costs claimed.

PD 46 para.9.5

The evidence to be filed and served with the claim form under r.8.5 must include copies of the documents on which the claimant relies to prove the defendant's agreement to pay costs.

PD 46 para.9.6

A costs judge or a district judge has jurisdiction to hear and decide any issue which may arise in a claim issued under this rule irrespective of the amount of the costs claimed or of the value of the claim to which the agreement to pay costs relates. A costs officer may make an order by consent under para.9.8, or an order dismissing a claim under para.9.8 below.

PD 46 para.9.7

When the time for filing the defendant's acknowledgement of service has expired, the claimant may by letter request the court to make an order in the terms of his claim, unless the defendant has filed an acknowledgement of service stating that he intends to contest the claim or to seek a different order.

PD 46 para.9.8

Rule 40.6 applies where an order is to be made by consent. An order may be made by consent in terms which differ from those set out in the claim form.

PD 46 para.9.9

Where costs are ordered to be assessed, the general rule is that this should be by detailed assessment. However when an order is made under this rule following a hearing and the court is in a position to summarily assess costs it should generally do so.

PD 46 para.9.10

If the defendant opposes the claim the defendant must file a witness statement in accordance with r. 8.5(3). The court will then give directions including, if appropriate, a direction that the claim shall continue as if it were a Pt 7 claim. A claim is not treated as opposed merely because the defendant disputes the amount of the claim for costs.

PD 46 para.9.11

A claim issued under this rule may be dealt with without being allocated to a track. R. 8.9 does not apply to claims issued under this rule.

PD 46 para.9.12

Where there are other issues nothing in r. 46.14 prevents a person from issuing a claim form under Pt 7 or Pt 8 to sue on an agreement made in settlement of a dispute where that agreement makes provision for costs, nor from claiming in that case an order for costs or a specified sum in respect of costs but the 'costs only' procedure in r. 46.14 must be used where the sole issue is the amount of costs.

COSTS PD

PD about costs supplementing Pts 44–48 of the CPR.

COSTS PRACTICE DIRECTION

See **Costs PD**.

COSTS RESERVED

PD 44 para.4.2

The decision about costs is deferred to a later occasion, but if no later order is made the costs will be costs in the case.

COSTS RULES

Costs PD r.43.1

Part 43 contains definitions and interpretation of certain matters set out in the rules about costs contained in Pts 44 to 48.

Part 44 contains general rules about costs;

Part 45 deals with fixed costs;

Part 46 deals with Costs–special cases;

Part 47 deals with procedure for detailed assessment of costs and default provisions; and

Part 48 deals with Pt 2 of the Legal Aid, Sentencing and Punishment of Offenders Act 2012 relating to civil litigation funding and costs: transition provisions in relation to pre-commencement funding arrangements (rr.15 and 16 of the Schedule to the CPR).

SCHEDULE OF COSTS PRECEDENTS

A   Model form of bill of costs
B: Model form of bill of costs (detailed assessment of additional liability only)
C: Model form of bill of costs (payable by Defendant and the LSC)
D: Model form of bill of costs (alternative form, single column for amounts claimed, separate parts for costs payable by the LSC only)
E: Legal Aid/ LSC Schedule of Costs
F: Certificates for inclusion in bill of costs
G: Points of Dispute and Reply
H: Costs Budget
J: Solicitors Act 1974: Part 8 claim form under Part III of the Act
K: Solicitors Act 1974: order for delivery of bill
L: Solicitors Act 1974: order for detailed assessment (client)
M: Solicitors Act 1974: order for detailed assessment (solicitors)
P: Solicitors Act 1974: breakdown of costs

COSTS THROWN AWAY

PD 44 para.4.2

Where, for example, a judgment or order is set aside, the party in whose favour the costs order is made is entitled to the costs which have been incurred as a consequence. This includes the costs of—

(1) preparing for and attending any hearing at which the judgment or order which has been set aside was made;

(2) preparing for and attending any hearing to set aside the judgment or order in question;

(3) preparing for and attending any hearing at which the court orders the proceedings or the part in question to be adjourned.

COUNSEL

PD 44 para.5.1

(1) When making an order for costs the court may state an opinion as to whether or not the hearing was fit for the attendance of one or more counsel, and, if it does so, the court conducting a detailed assessment of those costs will have regard to the opinion stated.

(2) The court will generally express an opinion only where—

    (a) the paying party asks it to do so;

    (b) more than one counsel appeared for a party; or

(c) the court wishes to record its opinion that the case was not fit for the attendance of counsel.

PD 44 para.5.2

(1) Where the court refers any matter to the conveyancing counsel of the court the fees payable to counsel in respect of the work done or to be done will be assessed by the court in accordance with r. 44.2.
(2) An appeal from a decision of the court in respect of the fees of such counsel will be dealt with under the general rules as to appeals set out in Pt 52. If the appeal is against the decision of an authorised court officer, it will be dealt with in accordance with rr. 47.22 to 47.24.

COUNTERCLAIM

Glossary

A claim brought by a defendant in response to the claimant's claim, which is included in the same proceedings as the claimant's claim.

Crown

Pt 66 r.66.4

(1) In a claim by the Crown for taxes, duties or penalties, the defendant cannot make a counterclaim or other **Part 20 claim** or raise a defence of **set-off**.
(2) In any other claim by the Crown, the defendant cannot make a counterclaim or other Pt 20 claim or raise a defence of set-off which is based on a claim for repayment of taxes, duties or penalties.
(3) In proceedings by or against the Crown in the name of the Attorney General, no counterclaim or other Pt 20 claim can be made or defence of set-off raised without the permission of the court.
(4) In proceedings by or against the Crown in the name of a government department, no counterclaim or other Pt 20 claim can be made or defence of set-off raised without the permission of the court unless the subject-matter relates to that government department.

Possession claims online

PD 55B para.7.1

A defendant wishing to file—
(2) a counterclaim (to be filed together with a defence) to a claim which has been issued through the PCOL system, may, instead of filing a written form, do so by—
   (a) completing the relevant online form at the PCOL website; and
   (b) if the defendant is making a counterclaim, paying the appropriate fee electronically at the PCOL website or by some other means approved by Her Majesty's Courts and Tribunals Service.

See **Additional claims**, **Judgments and orders**, and **Probate claim**.

COUNTY COURTS ACT 1984

A consolidating Act relating to county courts.

COUNTY COURT PROVISIONAL ASSESSMENT PILOT SCHEME

PD 51E para.1

[PD 51E] was made under r.51.2. It provided for a pilot scheme (the County Court Provisional Assessment Pilot Scheme) to—
- (1) operate from October 1, 2010 to September 30, 2012;
- (2) operate in the Leeds, York and Scarborough County Courts;
- (3) applied to detailed assessment proceedings—
    - (a) which were commenced on or after October 1, 2010; and
    - (b) in which the base costs claimed are £25,000 or less.

COUNTY COURT RULES 1981

A code of procedure for the county courts which have been in operation since September 1, 1981 and been mostly replaced by the **CPR**.

COURT

Pt 2 r.2.3(3)

(3) Where the context requires, means a reference to a particular county court, a district registry, or the Royal Courts of Justice.

COURT BUNDLES

Appeals in the county courts and the High Court

PD 52B para.6.3

Appeal bundle: As soon as practicable, but in any event within 35 days of the filing of the appellant's notice, the appellant must file an appeal bundle which must contain only those documents relevant to the appeal. The appeal bundle must be paginated and indexed.

PD 52B para.6.4

Documents relevant to the appeal:
- (1) Subject to any order made by the court, the following documents must be included in the appeal bundle—
    - (a) a copy of the appellant's notice;
    - (b) a copy of any respondent's notice;
    - (c) a copy of any appellant's or respondent's skeleton argument;

(d) a copy of the order under appeal;

(e) a copy of the order of the lower court granting or refusing permission to appeal together with a copy of the judge's reasons, if any, for granting or refusing permission;

(f) a copy of any order allocating the case to a track;

(g) a transcript of the judgment of the lower court or other record of reasons (except in appeals in cases which were allocated to the small claims track and subject to any order of the court).

(2) The following documents should also be considered for inclusion in the appeal bundle but should be included only where relevant to the appeal—

(a) statements of case;

(b) application notices;

(c) other orders made in the case;

(d) a chronology of relevant events;

(e) witness statements made in support of any application made in the appellant's notice;

(f) other witness statements;

(g) any other documents which any party considers would assist the appeal court.

PD 52B para.6.5

Service of the appeal bundle: A copy of the appeal bundle must be served on each respondent—

(a) where permission to appeal was granted by the lower court, at the same time as filing the appeal bundle;

(b) where the appeal court has granted permission to appeal, as soon as practicable after notification and in any event within 14 days of the grant of permission;

(c) where the appeal court directs that the application for permission to appeal is to be heard on the same occasion as the appeal, as soon as practicable and in any event within 14 days after notification of the hearing date.

PD 52B para.6.6

Late documents: Any relevant document which is obtained or created after the appeal bundle has been filed (for example a respondent's notice or a skeleton argument) should be added to the appeal bundle as soon as practicable and, in any event, no less than 7 days before the hearing of the appeal or any application.

Court of Appeal

PD 52C para.27(5)

Bundles lodged with the court will not be returned to the parties but will be destroyed in the confidential waste system at the conclusion of the proceedings and without further notification.

PD 52C para.2.7

(1) The appellant must lodge an appeal bundle which must contain only those documents relevant to the appeal. The bundle must—

(a) be paginated and in chronological order;

(b) contain an index at the front.

(2) Documents relevant to the appeal: Subject to any order made by the court, the following documents must be included in the appeal bundle—
  (a) a copy of the appellant's notice;
  (b) a copy of any respondent's notice;
  (c) a copy of any appellant's or respondent's skeleton argument;
  (d) a copy of the order under appeal;
  (e) a copy of the order of the lower court granting or refusing permission to appeal together with a copy of the judge's reasons, if any, for granting or refusing permission;
  (f) a copy of any order allocating the case to a track;
  (g) the approved transcript of the judgment of the lower court (except in appeals in cases which were allocated to the small claims track but subject to any order of the court).
(3) Documents which may be included: The following documents should also be considered for inclusion in the appeal bundle but should be included only where relevant to the appeal—
  (a) statements of case;
  (b) application notices;
  (c) other orders made in the case;
  (d) a chronology of relevant events;
  (e) witness statements made in support of any application made in the appellant's notice;
  (f) other witness statements;
  (g) other documents which the appellant or respondent consider relevant to the appeal.
(4) Bundles not to include originals: Unless otherwise directed, the appeal bundle should not include original material such as original documents, photographs and recorded media. Such material should be provided to the court, if necessary, at the hearing.

COURT DOCUMENTS

Pt 5 r.5.1

[Part 5] contains general provisions about—
  (a) documents used in court proceedings; and
  (b) the obligations of a court officer in relation to those documents.

See also **Signing of documents**.

Documents for filing at court

PD 5A para.5.1

The date on which a document was filed at court must be recorded on the document. This may be done by a seal or a receipt stamp.

PD 5A para.5.2

Particulars of the date of delivery at a court office of any document for filing and the title of the proceedings in which the document is filed shall be entered in court records, on the court file or on a computer kept in the court office for the purpose. Except where a document has been delivered at the court office through the post, the time of delivery should also be recorded.

PD 5A para.2.2

Every document prepared by a party for filing or use at the court must—
(1) Unless the nature of the document renders it impracticable, be on A4 paper of durable quality having a margin, not less than 3.5cm wide,
(2) be fully legible and should normally be typed,
(3) where possible be bound securely in a manner which would not hamper filing or otherwise each page should be endorsed with the case number,
(4) have the pages numbered consecutively,
(5) be divided into numbered paragraphs,
(6) have all numbers, including dates, expressed as figures, and
(7) give in the margin the reference of every document mentioned that has already been filed.

PD 5A para.2.3

A document which is a copy produced by a colour photostat machine or other similar device may be filed at the court office provided that the coloured date seal of the court is not reproduced on the copy.

PD 5A para.5.4

Where the court orders any document to be lodged in court, the document must, unless otherwise directed, be deposited in the office of that court.

PD 5A para.5.5

A document filed, lodged or held in any court office shall not be taken out of that office without the permission of the court unless the document is to be sent to the office of another court (for example under CPR Pt 30 (Transfer)), except in accordance with CPR r.39.7 (impounded documents) or in accordance with para.5.6 below.

PD 5A para.5.6

(1) Where a document filed, lodged or held in a court office is required to be produced to any court, tribunal or arbitrator, the document may be produced by sending it by registered post (together with a certificate as in para.5.6(8)(b)) to the court, tribunal or arbitrator in accordance with the provisions of this paragraph.
(2) Any court, tribunal or arbitrator or any party requiring any document filed, lodged or held in any court office to be produced must apply to that court office by sending a completed request ([see] para.5.6 (8)(a)), stamped with the prescribed fee.
(3) On receipt of the request the court officer will submit the same to a Master in the Royal Courts of Justice or to a District Judge elsewhere, who may direct that the request be complied with. Before giving a direction the Master or District Judge may require to be satisfied that the request is made in good faith and that the document is required to be produced for the reasons stated. The Master or District Judge giving the direction may also direct that, before the document is sent, an official copy of it is made and filed in the court office at the expense of the party requiring the document to be produced.
(4) On the direction of the Master or District Judge the court officer shall send the document by registered post addressed to the court, Tribunal or arbitrator, with:
   (a) an envelope stamped and addressed for use in returning the document to the court office from which it was sent;
   (b) a certificate [see para.5.6(8)(b)];
   (c) a covering letter describing the document, stating at whose request and for what purpose it is sent, referring to this paragraph of the PD and containing a request that

the document be returned to the court office from which it was sent in the enclosed envelope as soon as the Court or Tribunal no longer requires it.

(5) It shall be the duty of the court, tribunal or arbitrator to whom the document was sent to keep it in safe custody, and to return it by registered post to the court office from which it was sent, as soon as the court, tribunal or arbitrator no longer requires it.

(6) In each court office a record shall be kept of each document sent and the date on which it was sent and the court, tribunal or arbitrator to whom it was sent and the date of its return. It shall be the duty of the court officer who has signed the certificate referred to in para.5.6(8)(b) below to ensure that the document is returned within a reasonable time and to make inquiries and report to the Master or District Judge who has given the direction under para.(3) above if the document is not returned, so that steps may be taken to secure its return.

(7) Notwithstanding the preceding paragraphs, the Master or District Judge may direct a court officer to attend the court, tribunal or arbitrator for the purpose of producing the document.

Preparation of documents

Pt 5 r.5.2

(1) Where under these rules, a document is to be prepared by the court, the document may be prepared by the party whose document it is, unless—
 (a) a court officer otherwise directs; or
 (b) it is a document to which—
  (ii) CCR Ord.25 r.8(9) (reissue of warrant where condition upon which warrant was suspended has not been complied with); or
  (iii) CCR Ord.28 r.11(1) (issue of warrant of committal),
  applies.

(2) Nothing in this rule shall require a court officer to accept a document which is illegible, has not been duly authorised, or is unsatisfactory for some other similar reason.

Supply of documents to Attorney General from court records

Pt 5 r.5.4A

(1) The Attorney General may search for, inspect and take a copy of any documents within a court file for the purpose of preparing an application or considering whether to make an application under s.42 of the Supreme Court Act 1981 or s.33 of the Employment Tribunals Act 1996 (restriction of vexatious proceedings).

(2) The Attorney-General must, when exercising the right under para.(1)—
 (a) pay any prescribed fee; and
 (b) file a written request, which must—
  (i) confirm that the request is for the purpose of preparing an application or considering whether to make an application mentioned in para.(1); and
  (ii) name the person who would be the subject of the application.

Supply of documents to a party from court records

Pt 5 r.5.4B

(1) A party to proceedings may, unless the court orders otherwise, obtain from the records of the court a copy of any document listed in para.4.2A of PD 5A.

(2) A party to proceedings may, if the court gives permission, obtain from the records of the court a copy of any other document filed by a party or communication between the court and a party or another person.

PD 5A para.4.5

Rule 5.4B allows a person who is a party to proceedings to obtain copies of documents from court records. A person is a party to proceedings who has been named as a party on a statement of case irrespective of whether they have been served with that statement of case.

Supply of documents to new parties

PD 5A para.3.1

Where a party is joined to existing proceedings, the party joined shall be entitled to require the party joining him to supply, without charge, copies of all statements of case, written evidence and any documents appended or exhibited to them which have been served in the proceedings by or upon the joining party which relate to any issues between the joining party and the party joined, and copies of all orders made in those proceedings. The documents must be supplied within 48 hours after a written request for them is received.

PD 5A para.3.2

If the party joined is not supplied with copies of the documents requested under para.3.1 within 48 hours, he may apply under Pt 23 for an order that they be supplied.

PD 5A para.3.3

The party by whom a copy is supplied under para.3.1 or, if he is acting by a solicitor, his solicitor, shall be responsible for it being a true copy.

Supply of documents to a non-party from court records

Pt 5 r.5.4C

(1) The general rule is that a person who is not a party to proceedings may obtain from the court records a copy of—
   (a) a statement of case, but not any documents filed with or attached to the statement of case, or intended by the party whose statement it is to be served with it;
   (b) a judgment or order given or made in public (whether made at a hearing or without a hearing), subject to para.(1B).
(1A) Where a non-party seeks to obtain a copy of a statement of case filed before October 2, 2006—
   (a) this rule does not apply; and
   (b) the rules of court relating to access by a non-party to statements of case in force immediately before October 2, 2006 apply as if they had not been revoked.

(The rules relating to access by a non-party to statements of case in force immediately before October 2, 2006 were contained in the former rr.5.4(5) to 5.4(9). PD 5A sets out the relevant provisions as they applied to statements of case).

(1B) No document—

    (a) relating to an application under r.78.24(1) [Making a mediation settlement enforceable] for a mediation settlement enforcement order;

    (b) annexed to a **mediation settlement enforcement order** made under r.78.24(5);

    (c) relating to an application under r.78.26(1) or otherwise for disclosure or inspection of mediation evidence; or

    (d) annexed to an order for disclosure or inspection made under r.78.26 or otherwise, may be inspected without the court's permission.

(2) A non-party may, if the court gives permission, obtain from the records of the court a copy of any other document filed by a party, or communication between the court and a party or another person.

(3) A non-party may obtain a copy of a statement of case or judgment or order under para.(1) only if—

    (a) where there is one defendant, the defendant has filed an acknowledgment of service or a defence;

    (b) where there is more than one defendant, either—

        (i) all the defendants have filed an acknowledgment of service or a defence;

        (ii) at least one defendant has filed an acknowledgment of service or a defence, and the court gives permission;

    (c) the claim has been listed for a hearing; or

    (d) judgment has been entered in the claim.

(4) The court may, on the application of a party or of any person identified in a statement of case—

    (a) order that a non-party may not obtain a copy of a statement of case under para.(1);

    (b) restrict the persons or classes of persons who may obtain a copy of a statement of case;

    (c) order that persons or classes of persons may only obtain a copy of a statement of case if it is edited in accordance with the directions of the court; or

    (d) make such other order as it thinks fit.

(5) A person wishing to apply for an order under para.(4) must file an application notice in accordance with Pt 23.

(6) Where the court makes an order under para.(4), a non-party who wishes to obtain a copy of the statement of case, or to obtain an unedited copy of the statement of case, may apply on notice to the party or person identified in the statement of case who requested the order, for permission.

Supply of documents from court records—statements of case filed before October 2, 2006

PD 5A para.4A.1

Rule 5.4C(1A) provides that the rules of court relating to access by a non-party to statements of case in force immediately before October 2, 2006 apply to statements of case filed before that date as if they had not been revoked. For ease of reference, those rules are set out in the following paragraphs [paras 4A.2 to 4.4 of PD 5A].

See also **Enrolment of deeds**, **Fax or other electronic means**, **Register of claims**, and **Signing of documents**.

COURT FEES

Civil Proceedings Fees (Amendment) Order 2011 came into force on April 4, 2011; and for convenience this Order replaces the entire schedule of fees payable in civil proceedings in the Court of Appeal, High Court and county courts.

Sanctions for non-payment of certain fees

Pt 3 r.3.7

    (1) This rule applies where—
        (a) an **allocation questionnaire** or a pre-trial check list (listing questionnaire) is filed without payment of the fee specified by the relevant Fees Order;
        (b) the court dispenses with the need for an allocation questionnaire or a pre-trial check list or both;
        (c) these rules do not require an allocation questionnaire or a pre-trial check list to be filed in relation to the claim in question;
        (d) the court has made an order giving permission to proceed with a claim for judicial review; or
        (e) the fee payable for a hearing specified by the relevant Fees Order is not paid.
(Rule 26.3 provides for the court to dispense with the need for an allocation questionnaire and rr.28.5 and 29.6 provide for the court to dispense with the need for a pre-trial check list).
(Rule 54.12 provides for the service of the order giving permission to proceed with a claim for judicial review).
    (2) The court will serve a notice on the claimant requiring payment of the fee specified in the relevant Fees Order if, at the time the fee is due, the claimant has not paid it or made an application for full or part remission.
    (3) The notice will specify the date by which the claimant must pay the fee.
    (4) If the claimant does not—
        (a) pay the fee; or
        (b) make an application for full or part remission of the fee,
        by the date specified in the notice—
        (i) the claim will automatically be struck out without further order of the court; and
        (ii) the claimant will be liable for the costs which the defendant has incurred unless the court orders otherwise.
(Rule 44.12 provides for the basis of assessment where a right to costs arises under this rule and contains provisions about when a costs order is deemed to have been made and applying for an order under s.194(3) of the Legal Services Act 2007.
    (5) Where an application for—
        (a) full or part remission of a fee is refused, the court will serve notice on the claimant requiring payment of the full fee by the date specified in the notice; or
        (b) part remission of a fee is granted, the court will serve notice on the claimant requiring payment of the balance of the fee by the date specified in the notice; and
    (6) If the claimant does not pay the fee by the date specified in the notice—
        (a) the claim will automatically be struck out without further order of the court; and
        (b) the claimant will be liable for the costs which the defendant has incurred unless the court orders otherwise.
    (7) If—
        (a) a claimant applies to have the claim reinstated; and
        (b) the court grants relief,
        the relief will be conditional on the claimant either paying the fee or filing evidence of full or part remission of the fee within the period specified in para.(8).
    (8) The period referred to in para.(7) is—
        (a) if the order granting relief is made at a hearing at which the claimant is present or represented, two days from the date of the order;

(b) in any other case, seven days from the date of service of the order on the claimant.

PD 3B para.1

If a claim is struck out under r.3.7, the court will send notice that it has been struck out to the
defendant.

PD 3B para.2

The notice will also explain the effect of r.25.11. This provides that any interim injunction will
cease to have effect 14 days after the date the claim is struck out under r.3.7. Paragraph (2)
provides that if the claimant applies to reinstate the claim before the interim injunction ceases to
have effect, the injunction will continue until the hearing of the application unless the court
orders otherwise. If the claimant makes such an application, the defendant will be given notice
in the ordinary way under r.23.4.

PD 3B para.3.7A

(1) This rule applies where—
    (a) a defendant files a counterclaim without—
        (i) payment of the fee specified by the relevant Fees Order; or
        (ii) making an application for full or part remission of the fee; or
    (b) the proceedings continue on the counterclaim alone and—
        (i) an allocation questionnaire or a pre-trial check list (listing questionnaire) is filed
            without payment of the fee specified by the relevant Fees Order;
        (ii) the court dispenses with the need for an allocation questionnaire or a pre-trial
            check list or both;
        (iii) these rules do not require an allocation questionnaire or a pre-trial checklist to
            be filed in relation to the claim in question; or
        (iv) the fee payable for a hearing specified by the relevant Fees Order is not paid.
(2) The court will serve a notice on the defendant requiring payment of the fee specified in
    the relevant Fees Order if, at the time the fee is due, the defendant has not paid it or made
    an application for full or part remission.
(3) The notice will specify the date by which the defendant must pay the fee.
(4) If the defendant does not—
    (a) pay the fee; or
    (b) make an application for full or part remission of the fee,
    by the date specified in the notice, the counterclaim will automatically be struck out
    without further order of the court.
(5) Where an application for—
    (a) full or part remission of a fee is refused, the court will serve notice on the defendant
        requiring payment of the full fee by the date specified in the notice; or
    (b) part remission of a fee is granted, the court will serve notice on the defendant
        requiring payment of the balance of the fee by the date specified in the notice.
(6) If the defendant does not pay the fee by the date specified in the notice, the counterclaim
    will automatically be struck out without further order of the court.
(7) If—
    (a) the defendant applies to have the counterclaim reinstated; and
    (b) the court grants relief,
    the relief will be conditional on the defendant either paying the fee or filing evidence of
    full or part remission of the fee within the period specified in para.(8).
(8) The period referred to in para.(7) is—
    (a) if the order granting relief is made at a hearing at which the defendant is present or
        represented, two days from the date of the order;

(b) in any other case, seven days from the date of service of the order on the defendant.

Sanctions for dishonouring cheque

Pt 3 r.3.7B

(1) This rule applies where any fee is paid by cheque and that cheque is subsequently dishonoured.
(2) The court will serve a notice on the paying party requiring payment of the fee which will specify the date by which the fee must be paid.
(3) If the fee is not paid by the date specified in the notice—
   (a) where the fee is payable by the claimant, the claim will automatically be struck out without further order of the court;
   (b) where the fee is payable by the defendant, the defence will automatically be struck out without further order of the court,
   and the paying party shall be liable for the costs which any other party has incurred unless the court orders otherwise.
(Rule 44.12 provides for the basis of assessment where a right to costs arises under this rule).
(4) If—
   (a) the paying party applies to have the claim or defence reinstated; and
   (b) the court grants relief,
   the relief shall be conditional on that party paying the fee within the period specified in para.(5).
(5) The period referred to in para.(4) is—
   (a) if the order granting relief is made at a hearing at which the paying party is present or represented, two days from the date of the order;
   (b) in any other case, seven days from the date of service of the order on the paying party.
(6) For the purposes of this rule, 'claimant' includes a Pt 20 claimant and 'claim form' includes a Pt 20 claim.

COURT OF PROTECTION

Pt 2 r.2.1(2)

The CPR do not apply to these proceedings except to the extent that they are applied by s.51 of the Mental Capacity Act 2005.

Appeal from the Court of Protection

PD 52D para.10.1

(1) In this paragraph—
   (a) 'P' means a person who lacks, or who is alleged to lack, capacity within the meaning of the Mental Capacity Act 2005 to make a decision or decisions in relation to any matter that is subject to an order of the Court of Protection;
   (b) 'the person effecting notification' means—
      (i) the appellant;
      (ii) an agent duly appointed by the appellant; or

        (iii) such other person as the Court of Protection may direct,

    (c) 'final order' means a decision of the Court of Appeal that finally determines the appeal proceedings before it.

  (2) Where P is not a party to the proceedings, unless the Court of Appeal directs otherwise, the person effecting notification must notify P—

    (a) that an appellant's notice has been filed with the Court of Appeal and—

        (i) who the appellant is;

        (ii) what final order the appellant is seeking;

        (iii) what will happen if the Court of Appeal makes the final order sought by the appellant; and

        (iv) that P may apply under r.52.12A by letter for permission to file evidence or make representations at the appeal hearing;

    (b) of the final order, the effect of the final order and what steps P can take in relation to it; and

    (c) of such other events and documents as the Court of Appeal may direct.

(Paragraphs 17.7 to 17.11 of this PD contain provisions on how a third party can apply for permission to file evidence or make representations at an appeal hearing).

  (3) The person effecting notification must provide P with the information specified in sub-para.(2)—

    (a) within 14 days of the date on which the appellant's notice was filed with the Court of Appeal;

    (b) within 14 days of the date on which the final order was made; or

    (c) within such time as the Court of Appeal may direct,

as the case may be.

  (4) The person effecting notification must provide P in person with the information specified in sub-para.(2) in a way that is appropriate to P's circumstances (for example, using simple language, visual aids or any other appropriate means).

  (5) Where P is to be notified as to—

    (a) the existence or effect of a document other than the appellant's notice or final order; or

    (b) the taking place of an event,

the person effecting notification must explain to P—

    (i) in the case of a document, what the document is and what effect, if any, it has; or

    (ii) in the case of an event, what the event is and its relevance to P.

  (6) The person effecting notification must, within seven days of notifying P, file a certificate of notification (Form N165) which certifies—

    (a) the date on which P was notified; and

    (b) that P was notified in accordance with this paragraph.

  (7) Where the person effecting notification has not notified P in accordance with this paragraph, he must file with the Court of Appeal a certificate of non-notification (Form N165) stating the reason why notification has not been effected.

  (8) Where the person effecting notification must file a certificate of non-notification with the Court of Appeal, he must file the certificate within the following time limits—

    (a) where P is to be notified in accordance with subpara.(2)(a) (appellant's notice), within 21 days of the appellant's notice being filed with the Court of Appeal;

    (b) where P is to be notified in accordance with subpara.(2)(b) (final order), within 21 days of the final order being made by the Court of Appeal; or

    (c) where P is to be notified of such other events and documents as may be directed by the Court of Appeal, within such time as the Court of Appeal directs.

  (9) The appellant or such other person as the Court of Appeal may direct may apply to the Court of Appeal seeking an order—

    (a) dispensing with the requirement to comply with the provisions of this paragraph; or

    (b) requiring some other person to comply with the provisions of this paragraph.

  (10) An application made under subpara.(9) may be made in the appellant's notice or by Pt 23 application notice.

(Paragraph 12 contains provisions about the dismissal of applications or appeals by consent. Paragraph 13 contains provisions about allowing unopposed appeals or applications on paper and procedures for consent orders and agreements to pay periodical payments involving a child or protected party or in appeals to the Court of Appeal from a decision of the Court of Protection).

See also **Protected party**.

COURT OFFICER

Pt 2 r.2.3(1)

A member of the court staff.

Pt 2 r.2.5

(1) Where these rules require or permit the court to perform an act of a formal or administrative character, that act may be performed by a court officer.
(2) A requirement that a court officer carry out any act at the request of a party is subject to the payment of any fee required by a fees order for the carrying out of that act.

Court officer's power to refer to a judge

Pt 3 r.3.2

Where a step is to be taken by a court officer—
(a) the court officer may consult a judge before taking that step;
(b) the step may be taken by a judge instead of the court officer.

COURT ORDER

See **Judgments and orders**.

COURT SEAL

See **Seal**.

COURT SITTINGS

Court of Appeal and the High Court

PD 39B para.1.1

(1) The sittings of the Court of Appeal and of the High Court shall be four in every year, that is to say
(a) the Michaelmas sittings which shall begin on October 1 and end on December 21;

(b) the Hilary sittings which shall begin on January 11 and end on the Wednesday before Easter Sunday;

(c) the Easter sittings which, subject to subpara.(3), shall begin on the second Tuesday after Easter Sunday and end on the Friday before the spring holiday; and

(d) the Trinity sittings which shall begin on the second Tuesday after the spring holiday and end on July 31.

(2) In the above paragraph 'spring holiday' means the bank holiday falling on the last Monday in May or any day appointed instead of that day under s.1(2) of the Banking and Financial Dealings Act 1971.

See **Vacations**.

COURT STAFF

See **Court officer**.

CPR ERROR OF PROCEDURE

See **Judgments and orders**.

CRIME AND DISORDER ACT 1998

See **Anti-social behaviour orders**.

CRIMINAL JUSTICE ACT 1988

See **Confiscation and forfeiture in connection with criminal proceedings**.

CRIMINAL JUSTICE AND POLICE ACT 2001

[PD 49A] applies to proceedings under—

(c) s.59 of the [Criminal Justice and Police Act 2001][application for the return of the whole or a part of the seized property].

Applications under s.59 of the CJPA

PD 49A para.26

(1) In subparas (2) to (8)—
(b) references to a relevant interest in property have the same meaning as in s.59 of the CJPA.

(2) This paragraph applies to applications under s.59 in respect of property seized in exercise of the power conferred by s.448(3) of the 1985 Act (including any additional powers of seizure conferred by s.50 that are exercisable by reference to that power).

(3) The application must be supported by evidence—

    (a) that the claimant has a relevant interest in the property to which the application relates; and

    (b) in the case of an application under s.59(2), that one or more of the grounds set out in s.59(3) is satisfied in relation to the property.

(4) Where the claimant has a relevant interest in the property, the defendants to the claim are to be—

    (a) the person in possession of the property; and

    (b) any other person who appears to have a relevant interest in the property.

(5) Where the claimant is in possession of the property, the defendants are to be—

    (a) the person from whom the property was seized; and

    (b) any other person who appears to have a relevant interest in the property.

(6) In the case of an application for the return of seized property, the claimant must serve a copy of the claim form and the claimant's evidence in support of it on the person specified, by the notice given under s.52 when the property was seized, as the person to whom notice of such an application should be given.

(7) If the claimant knows the identity of the person who seized the property, the claimant must also notify that person of the application.

(8) When the court issues the claim form it will fix a date for the hearing.

CRIMINAL PROCEDURE AND INVESTIGATIONS ACT 1996

See **Quashing of an acquittal**.

CROSS-BORDER MERGERS REGULATIONS

[PD 49A] applies to proceedings under—

    (f) the Cross-Border Mergers Regulations.

Applications under the Cross-Border Mergers Regulations

PD 49A para.22

(1) In this paragraph and paras 23 to 25 a reference to a regulation by number is a reference to the regulation so numbered in the Cross-Border Mergers Regulations.

(2) Any document that is filed with the court must, if not in English, be accompanied by a translation of that document into English—

    (a) certified by a notary public or other qualified person; or

    (b) accompanied by written evidence confirming that the translation is accurate.

Application for approval of pre-merger requirements

PD 49A para.23

(1) This paragraph applies to an application under reg.6.

(2) There need be no defendant to the application.

(3) The application must—

    (a) set out the pre-merger acts and formalities required by regs 7 to 10 and 12 to 15 applicable to the applicant company; and

    (b) be accompanied by evidence that those acts and formalities have been completed properly.

(4) Where an application under reg.11 to summon a meeting of creditors has been made, the court will not determine the application under reg.6 to approve the pre-merger requirements until the result of the meeting is known.

(5) Where the court makes an order certifying that all pre-merger acts and formalities have been completed properly, the applicant must draw up the order and file it no later than seven days after the date on which the order was made so that it can be sealed by the court. The court will seal and return the order to the applicant within 15 days of receipt.

Application for appointment of independent expert or to summon a meeting of members or creditors

PD 49A para.24

(1) This paragraph applies to—
    (a) an application for the appointment of an independent expert under reg.9;
    (b) an application under reg.11 for an order to summon a meeting of members or creditors or both.

(2) The application must be made—
    (a) where the application is made at the same time as or after the application for approval of the pre-merger acts and formalities under reg.6 has been filed with the court, by application notice pursuant to Pt 23; or
    (b) where no application under reg.6 has been made, by a Pt 8 claim form.

(3) The application (whether by claim form or application notice, as the case may be) must be accompanied by evidence in support of the application.

Application for the approval of the completion of the merger

PD 49A para.25

(1) This paragraph applies to an application under reg.16.

(2) The application must be made by a Pt 8 claim form.

(3) There need be no defendant to the application.

(4) The claim form must be accompanied by—
    (a) the documents referred to in reg.16(1)(b), (c) and (e);
    (b) where appropriate, evidence that reg.16(1)(f) has been complied with; and
    (c) such other evidence as may be required to enable the court to decide the application.

(5) Where the court makes an order under regulation 16 approving the merger, it will fix a date on which the consequences of the merger are to take effect.

Title of documents

PD 49A para.4

(1) The claim form in proceedings under the Companies (Cross-Border Merger) Regulations 2007 and any application, affidavit, witness statement, notice or other document in such proceedings, must be entitled 'In the matter of [the name of the company in question] and

in the matter of [the relevant law]', where '[the relevant law]' means 'the Companies (Cross-Border Merger) Regulations 2007'.

(2) Where a company changes its name in the course of proceedings, the title must be altered by—

(a) substituting the new name for the old; and

(b) inserting the old name in brackets at the end of the title.

CROSS EXAMINATION

Glossary

Questioning of a witness by a party other than the party who called the witness.

Order for cross-examination

Pt 32 r.32.7

(1) Where, at a hearing other than the trial, evidence is given in writing, any party may apply to the court for permission to cross-examine the person giving the evidence.

(2) If the court gives permission under para.(1) but the person in question does not attend as required by the order, his evidence may not be used unless the court gives permission.

Experts

Instructions

PD 35 para.5

Cross-examination of experts on the contents of their instructions will not be allowed unless the court permits it (or unless the party who gave the instructions consents). Before it gives permission the court must be satisfied that there are reasonable grounds to consider that the statement in the report of the substance of the instructions is inaccurate or incomplete. If the court is so satisfied, it will allow the cross-examination where it appears to be in the interests of justice.

Mediation evidence of certain cross-border disputes

Pt 78 r.78.27

(1) This rule applies where a party wishes to obtain mediation evidence from a mediator or mediation administrator by—

(b) cross-examination with permission of the court under rr.32.7 or 33.4 (hearsay);

(2) When applying for a witness summons, permission under rr.32.7 or 33.4, the party must provide the court with evidence that—

(a) all parties to the mediation agree to the obtaining of the mediation evidence;

(b) obtaining the mediation evidence is necessary for overriding considerations of public policy, in accordance with art.7(1)(a) of the Mediation Directive; or

(c) the disclosure or inspection of the mediation settlement is necessary to implement or enforce the mediation settlement agreement.

(3) When considering a request for permission under rr.32.7 or 33.4 the court may invite any person, whether or not a party, to make representations.

(4) This rule does not apply to proceedings in England and Wales that have been allocated to the small claims track.

(5) Where this rule applies, Pts 31 to 34 apply to the extent they are consistent with this rule.

P78 r.78.28

Where a party wishes to rely on mediation evidence in proceedings that are allocated to the small claims track, that party must inform the court immediately.

Witness statement

Pt 32 r.32.11

Where a witness is called to give evidence at trial, he may be cross-examined on his witness statement whether or not the statement or any part of it was referred to during the witness's evidence in chief.

See **Freezing Order.**

CROWN

Pt 66 r.66.1

(1) This Part contains rules for civil proceedings by or against the Crown, and other civil proceedings to which the Crown is a party.

(2) In this Part—

(b) 'civil proceedings by the Crown' means the civil proceedings described in s.23(1) of the Act, but excluding the proceedings described in s.23(3);

(c) 'civil proceedings against the Crown' means the civil proceedings described in s.23(2) of the Act, but excluding the proceedings described in s.23(3);

(d) 'civil proceedings to which the Crown is a party' has the same meaning as it has for the purposes of Pts III and IV of the Act by virtue of s.38(4).

Application of the CPR

Pt 66 r.66.2

These rules and their PDs apply to civil proceedings by or against the Crown and to other civil proceedings to which the Crown is a party unless this Part, a PD or any other enactment provides otherwise.

Action on behalf of the crown

Pt 66 r.66.3

(1) Where by reason of a rule, PD or court order the Crown is permitted or required—

(a) to make a witness statement,

(b) to swear an affidavit,

(c) to verify a document by a statement of truth;

(d) to make a disclosure statement; or

(e) to discharge any other procedural obligation,

that function shall be performed by an appropriate officer acting on behalf of the Crown.

(2) The court may if necessary nominate an appropriate officer.

Service of documents

PD 66 para.2.1

In civil proceedings by or against the Crown, documents required to be served on the Crown must be served in accordance with rr.6.10 or 6.23(7).

(The list published under s.17 of the Crown Proceedings Act 1947 of the solicitors acting for the different government departments on whom service is to be effected, and of their addresses is annexed to [PD 6]).

Service of the claim form in proceedings against the crown

Pt 6 r.6.10

In proceedings against the Crown—

(a) service on the Attorney General must be effected on the Treasury Solicitor; and

(b) service on a government department must be effected on the solicitor acting for that department [see list published].

Address for service to be given after proceedings are started

Pt 6 r.6.23

(7) In proceedings by or against the Crown, service of any document in the proceedings on the Crown must be effected in the same manner prescribed in r.6.10 as if the document were a claim form.

Revenue matters

Pt 66 r.66.5

(1) This rule sets out the procedure under s.14 of the [Crown Proceedings Act 1947] which allows the Crown to make summary applications in the High Court in certain revenue matters.

(2) The application must be made in the High Court using the Pt 8 procedure.

(3) The title of the claim form must clearly identify the matters which give rise to the application.

Claim form

Contents of claim form

Pt 16 r.16.2

(1A) In civil proceedings against the Crown, as defined in r.66.1(2), the claim form must also contain—
(a) the names of the government departments and officers of the Crown concerned; and
(b) brief details of the circumstances in which it is alleged that the liability of the Crown arose.

Default judgment

Pt 12 r.12.4

(4) In civil proceedings against the Crown, as defined in r.66.1(2), a request for a **default judgment** must be considered by a Master or district judge, who must in particular be satisfied that the claim form and particulars of claim have been properly served on the Crown in accordance with s.18 of the Crown Proceedings Act 1947 and r.6.10 [see above].

Enforcement against the Crown

Pt 66 r.66.6

(1) The following rules do not apply to any order against the Crown—
(a) Part 69 to 73 [Receiver; Enforcement of judgments and Orders; Orders to obtain information from judgment debtors; Third Party Debt Orders, Charging Orders, Stop Orders and Stop notices];
(b) RSC Ords 45 to 47 and 52 [Enforcement of judgments and orders; Writs of execution; Writs of fi fa; Committal];
(c) CCR Ords 25 to 29 [Enforcement of judgments and orders; Warrants of execution, delivery and possession; Attachment of earnings; Judgment summonses; Committal for breach of undertaking or order].
(2) In para.(1), 'order against the Crown' means any judgment or order against the Crown, a government department, or an officer of the Crown as such, made—
(a) in civil proceedings by or against the Crown;
(b) in proceedings in the Administrative Court;
(c) in connection with an arbitration to which the Crown is a party; or
(d) in other civil proceedings to which the Crown is a party.
(3) An application under s.25(1) of the Act for a separate certificate of costs payable to the applicant may be made without notice.

Money due from the Crown

Pt 66 r.66.7

(1) None of the following Orders—
(a) a **Third Party Debt Order** under Pt 72;

    (b) an Order for the appointment of a receiver under Pt 69; or

    (c) an Order for the appointment of a sequestrator under RSC Ord.45,

    may be made or have effect in respect of any money due from the Crown.

(2) In para.(1), 'money due from the Crown' includes money accruing due, and money alleged to be due or accruing due.

(3) An application for an order under s.27 of the Act—

    (a) restraining a person from receiving money payable to him by the Crown; and

    (b) directing payment of the money to the applicant or another person,

        may be made under Pt 23.

(4) The application must be supported by written evidence setting out the facts on which it is based, and in particular identifying the debt from the Crown.

(5) Where the debt from the Crown is money in a National Savings Bank account, the witness must if possible identify the number of the account and the name and address of the branch where it is held.

(6) Notice of the application, with a copy of the written evidence, must be served—

    (a) on the Crown, and

    (b) on the person to be restrained,

    at least seven days before the hearing.

(7) Rule 72.8 applies to an application under this rule as it applies to an application under rule r.72.2 for a Third Party Debt Order, except that the court will not have the power to order enforcement to issue against the Crown.

Summary judgment

Pt 24 r.24.4

(1A) In civil proceedings against the Crown, as defined in r.66.1(2), a claimant may not apply for **summary judgment** until after expiry of the period for filing a defence specified in r.15.4.

Transfer

PD 66 para.1.1

Rule 30.3(2) sets out the circumstances to which the court must have regard when considering whether to make an order under ss.40(2), 41(1) or 42(2) of the County Courts Act 1984 (transfer between the High Court and County Court), r.30.2(1) (transfer between county courts) or r.30.2(4) (transfer between the Royal Courts of Justice and the district registries).

Venue

PD 66 para.1.2

From time to time the Attorney General will publish a note concerning the organisation of the Government Legal Service and matters relevant to the venue of Crown proceedings, for the assistance of practitioners and judges. When considering questions of venue under r.30.3(2), the court should have regard to the Attorney General's note in addition to all the other circumstances of the case.

See also **Counterclaim**.

D

DAMAGES

Glossary

A sum of money awarded by the court as compensation to the claimant.

See also **Aggravated damages**, **Exemplary damages**, and **Provisional damages**.

Assessment of damages in county court

PD 2B para.11.1

A District Judge has jurisdiction to hear the following:
  (c) the assessment of damages or other sum due to a party under a judgment without any
      financial limit.

Assessments of damages in the High Court

PD 2B para.4.2

A Master or a District Judge may assess the damages or sum due to a party under a judgment
without limit as to the amount.

Fatal Accidents Act 1976 and the Law Reform (Miscellaneous Provisions) Act 1934

Pt 41 r.41.3A

  (1) Where—
      (a) a claim includes claims arising under—
          (i) the Fatal Accidents Act 1976; and
          (ii) the Law Reform (Miscellaneous Provisions) Act 1934; and
      (b) a single sum of money is ordered or agreed to be paid in satisfaction of the
          claims,
      the court will apportion the money between the different claims.
  (2) Where, in an action in which a claim under the Fatal Accidents Act 1976 is made by or
      on behalf of more than one person, a single sum of money is ordered or agreed to be paid
      in satisfaction of the claim, the court will apportion it between the persons entitled to
      it.
  (3) Unless it has already been apportioned by the court, a jury or agreement between the
      parties, the court will apportion money under paras (1) and (2)—

(a) when it gives directions under r.21.11 (control of money received by a **child** or patient); or

(b) if r.21.11 does not apply, on application by one of the parties in accordance with Pt 23.

RTA Protocol

Application to the court to determine the amount of damages

PD 8B para.5.1

An application to the court to determine the amount of damages must be started by a claim form.

PD 8B para.5.2

The claim form must state—

(1) that the claimant has followed the procedure set out in the **RTA Protocol**;

(2) the date when the Court Proceedings Pack (Pt A and Pt B) Form was sent to the defendant. (This provision does not apply where the claimant is a child and the application is for a settlement hearing);

(3) whether the claimant wants the claim to be determined by the court on the papers (except where a party is a child) or at a Stage 3 hearing;

(4) where the claimant seeks a settlement hearing or a Stage 3 hearing, the dates which the claimant requests should be avoided; and

(5) the value of the claim.

See also **Damages Act 1996**.

DAMAGES ACT 1996

Pt 41 r.41.4

(1) [Section II of Pt 41] contains rules about the exercise of the court's powers under s.2(1) of the Damages Act 1996 to order that all or part of an award of damages in respect of personal injury is to take the form of periodical payments.

Statement of case

Pt 41 r.41.5

(1) In a claim for **damages for personal injury**, each party in its statement of case may state whether it considers periodical payments [means periodical payments under s.2(1) of the 1996 Act] or a lump sum is the more appropriate form for all or part of an award of damages and where such statement is given must provide relevant particulars of the circumstances which are relied on.

(2) Where a statement under para.(1) is not given, the court may order a party to make such a statement.

(3) Where the court considers that a statement of case contains insufficient particulars under para.(1), the court may order a party to provide such further particulars as it considers appropriate.

Court's indication to parties

Pt 41 r.41.6

The court shall consider and indicate to the parties as soon as practicable whether periodical payments or a lump sum is likely to be the more appropriate form for all or part of an award of damages [meaning damages for future pecuniary loss].

Factors to be taken into account

Pt 41 r.41.7

When considering—
   (a) its indication as to whether periodical payments or a lump sum is likely to be the more appropriate form for all or part of an award of damages under r.41.6; or
   (b) whether to make an order under s.2(1)(a) of the 1996 Act,
the court shall have regard to all the circumstances of the case and in particular the form of award which best meets the claimant's needs, having regard to the factors set out in PD 41B.

PD 41B para.1

The factors which the court shall have regard to under r.41.7 include—
   (1) the scale of the annual payments taking into account any deduction for contributory negligence;
   (2) the form of award preferred by the claimant including—
      (a) the reasons for the claimant's preference; and
      (b) the nature of any financial advice received by the claimant when considering the form of award; and
   (3) the form of award preferred by the defendant including the reasons for the defendant's preference.

Award

Pt 41 r.41.8

   (1) Where the court awards damages in the form of periodical payments, the order must specify—
      (a) the annual amount awarded, how each payment is to be made during the year and at what intervals;
      (b) the amount awarded for future—
         (i) loss of earnings and other income; and
         (ii) care and medical costs and other recurring or capital costs;
      (c) that the claimant's annual future pecuniary losses, as assessed by the court, are to be paid for the duration of the claimant's life, or such other period as the court orders; and
      (d) that the amount of the payments shall vary annually by reference to the retail prices index, unless the court orders otherwise under s.2(9) of the 1996 Act.
   (3) Where an amount awarded under para.(1)(b) is to increase or decrease on a certain date, the order must also specify—
      (a) the date on which the increase or decrease will take effect; and
      (b) the amount of the increase or decrease at current value.

(4) Where damages for substantial capital purchases are awarded under para.(1)(b)(ii), the order must also specify—
(a) the amount of the payments at current value;
(b) when the payments are to be made; and
(c) that the amount of the payments shall be adjusted by reference to the retail prices index, unless the court orders otherwise under s.2(9) of the 1996 Act.

PD 41B para.2.1

An order may be made under r.41.8(2) where a dependant would have had a claim under s.1 of the Fatal Accidents Act 1974 if the claimant had died at the time of the accident.

PD 41B para.2.2

Examples of circumstances which might lead the court to order an increase or decrease under r.41.8(3) are where the court determines that—
(1) the claimant's condition will change leading to an increase or reduction in his or her need to incur care, medical or other recurring or capital costs;
(2) gratuitous carers will no longer continue to provide care;
(3) the claimant's educational circumstances will change;
(4) the claimant would have received a promotional increase in pay;
(5) the claimant will cease earning.

Continuity of payment

Pt 41 r.41.9

(1) An order for periodical payments shall specify that the payments must be funded in accordance with s.2(4) of the 1996 Act, unless the court orders an alternative method of funding.
(2) Before ordering an alternative method of funding, the court must be satisfied that—
(a) the continuity of payment under the order is reasonably secure; and
(b) the criteria set out in PD 41B are met.
(3) An order under para.(2) must specify the alternative method of funding.

PD 41B para.3

Before ordering an alternative method of funding under r.41.9(1), the court must be satisfied that the following criteria are met—
(1) that a method of funding provided for under s.2(4) of the 1996 Act is not possible or there are good reasons to justify an alternative method of funding;
(2) that the proposed method of funding can be maintained for the duration of the award or for the proposed duration of the method of funding; and
(3) that the proposed method of funding will meet the level of payment ordered by the court.

Assignment or charge

Pt 41 r.41.10

Where the court under s.2(6)(a) of the 1996 Act is satisfied that special circumstances make an assignment or charge of periodical payments necessary, it shall, in deciding whether or not to approve the assignment or charge, also have regard to the factors set out in PD 41B.

PD 41B para.4

The factors which the court shall have regard to under r.41.10 include—
  (1) whether the capitalised value of the assignment or charge represents value for money;
  (2) whether the assignment or charge is in the claimant's best interests, taking into account whether these interests can be met in some other way; and
  (3) how the claimant will be financially supported following the assignment or charge.

Variation

PD 41B para.5

The Damages (Variation of Periodical Payments) Order 2005 sets out provisions which enable the court in certain circumstances to provide in an order for periodical payments that it may be varied.

Settlement

PD 41B para.6

Where the parties settle a claim to which r.36.5 applies, any consent order, whether made under r.40.6 or on an application under Pt 23, must satisfy the requirements of rr.41.8 and 41.9.

Settlement or compromise on behalf of child or protected party

PD 41B para.7

Where a claim for damages for personal injury is made by or on behalf of a child or protected party and is settled prior to the start of proceedings or before trial, the provisions of PD 21 must be complied with.

See **Damages** and **Fatal accident claim**.

DAMAGES-BASED AGREEMENT

Glossary

A damages-based agreement is an agreement which complies with the provisions of the Damage-Based Agreements Regulations 2013.

Award of costs where there is a damages-based agreement

PD 44 r.44.18

  (1) The fact that a party has entered into a damages-based agreement will not affect the making of any order for costs which otherwise would be made in favour of that party.

(2) Where costs are to be assessed in favour of a party who has entered into a damages-based agreement—

(a) the party's recoverable costs will be assessed in accordance with r.44.3; and

(b) the party may not recover by way of costs more than the total amount payable by that party under the damages-based agreement for legal services provided under that agreement.

DAMAGES FOR PERSONAL INJURIES

Pt 26 r.26.6

(2) Damages claimed as compensation for pain, suffering and loss of amenity and does not include any other damages which are claimed.

DATE FOR COMPLIANCE

Pt 2 r.2.9

(1) Where the court gives a judgment, order or direction which imposes a time limit for doing any act, the last date for compliance must, wherever practicable—

(a) be expressed as a calendar date; and

(b) include the time of day by which the act must be done.

(2) Where the date by which an act must be done is inserted in any document, the date must, wherever practicable, be expressed as a calendar date.

DAY

See **Clear days**.

DECEASED PARTY

Pt 19 r.19.8

(1) Where a person who had an interest in a claim has died and that person has no personal representative the court may order—

(a) the claim to proceed in the absence of a person representing the estate of the deceased; or

(b) a person to be appointed to represent the estate of the deceased.

(2) Where a defendant against whom a claim could have been brought has died and—

(a) a grant of probate or administration has been made, the claim must be brought against the persons who are the personal representatives of the deceased;

(b) a grant of probate or administration has not been made—

(i) the claim must be brought against 'the estate of' the deceased; and

(ii) the claimant must apply to the court for an order appointing a person to represent the estate of the deceased in the claim.

(3) A claim shall be treated as having been brought against 'the estate of' the deceased in accordance with para.(2)(b)(i) where—

(a) the claim is brought against the 'personal representatives' of the deceased but a grant of probate or administration has not been made; or

   (b) the person against whom the claim was brought was dead when the claim was started.
(4) Before making an order under this rule, the court may direct notice of the application to be given to any other person with an interest in the claim.
(5) Where an order has been made under paras (1) or (2)(b)(ii) any judgment or order made or given in the claim is binding on the estate of the deceased.

DECLARATORY JUDGMENTS

Pt 40 para.40.20

The court may make binding declarations whether or not any other remedy is claimed.

DEDUCTIBLE AMOUNTS

Pt 36 r.15(1)(d)

   (i) Any benefits by the amount of which damages are to be reduced in accordance with s.8 of, and Sch.2 to the 1997 Act ('deductible benefits'); and
  (ii) any lump sum payment by the amount of which damages are to be reduced in accordance with reg.12 of the 2008 Regulations ('deductible lump sum payments').

DEED POLL

Enrolment of deed in which a child's name is to be changed

PD 5A para.6.1

   (1) Any deed or document which by virtue of any enactment is required or authorised to be enrolled in the Senior Courts may be enrolled in the Central Office of the High Court.
   (2) Attention is drawn to the Enrolment of Deeds (Change of Name) Regulations 1994 which are reproduced in the Appendix to this PD.

PD 5A para.6.2

The following paragraph of the PD describes the practice to be followed in any case in which a child's name is to be changed and to which the 1994 Regulations apply.

PD 5A para.6.3

   (1) Where a person has by any order of the High Court, County Court or Family Proceedings Court been given parental responsibility for a child and applies to the Central Office, Filing Department, for the enrolment of a deed poll to change the surname (family name) of a child who is under the age of 18 years (unless a child who is or has been married or has formed a civil partnership), the application must be supported by the production of the consent in writing of every other person having parental responsibility.
   (2) In the absence of that consent, the application will be adjourned generally unless and until permission is given in the proceedings, in which the said order was made, to change the surname of the child and the permission is produced to the central office.

(3) Where an application is made to the central office by a person who has not been given parental responsibility for a child by any order of the High Court, County Court or Family Proceedings Court for the enrolment of a Deed Poll to change the surname of the child who is under the age of 18 years (unless the child is or has been married or has formed a civil partnership), permission of the court to enrol the deed will be granted if the consent in writing of every person having parental responsibility is produced or if the person (or, if more than one, persons) having parental responsibility is dead or overseas or despite the exercise of reasonable diligence it has not been possible to find him or her for other good reason.

(4) In cases of doubt the Senior Master or, in his absence, the Practice Master will refer the matter to the Master of the Rolls.

(5) In the absence of any of the conditions specified above the Senior Master or the Master of the Rolls, as the case may be, may refer the matter to the Official Solicitor for investigation and report.

DEEDS OF ARRANGEMENT

PD 8A para.12A.1

This paragraph applies to an application under s.7 of the Deeds of Arrangement Act 1914 for an order to rectify an omission or mis-statement in relation to the registration of a deed of arrangement—

(1) by inserting in the register the true name, residence or description of a person; or

(2) by extending the time for registration.

PD 8A para.12A.2

The application must be made—

(1) by claim form under Pt 8; or

(2) by witness statement.

PD 8A para.12A.3

Where the application is made by witness statement—

(1) Part 23 applies to the application;

(2) the witness statement constitutes the application notice under that Part;

(3) the witness statement does not need to be served on any other person; and

(4) the application will normally be dealt with without a hearing.

PD 8A para.12A.4

The application must set out—

(1) the particulars of the deed of arrangement and of the omission or mis-statement; and

(2) the grounds on which the application is made.

PD 8A para.12A.5

The application must be made to a Master of the Queen's Bench Division and accompanied by payment of the prescribed fee.

DEEMED DATE OF SERVICE

See **Service of documents**.

DEEMED ORDER FOR COSTS

Pt 44 r.44.13

(1) Where the court makes an order which does not mention costs—
  (a) subject to paras (1A) and (1B), the general rule is that no party is entitled—
    (i) to costs; or
    (ii) to seek an order under s.194(3) of the Legal Services Act 2007,
    in relation to that order; but
  (b) this does not affect any entitlement of a party to recover costs out of a fund held by that party as trustee or personal representative, or pursuant to any lease, mortgage or other security.
(1A) Where the court makes—
  (a) an order granting permission to appeal;
  (b) an order granting permission to apply for judicial review; or
  (c) any other order or direction sought by a party on an application without notice,
  and its order does not mention costs, it will be deemed to include an order for applicant's costs in the case.
(1B) Any party affected by a deemed order for costs under para.(1A) may apply at any time to vary the order.
(2) The court hearing an appeal may, unless it dismisses the appeal, make orders about the costs of the proceedings giving rise to the appeal as well as the costs of the appeal.
(3) Where proceedings are transferred from one court to another, the court to which they are transferred may deal with all the costs, including the costs before the transfer.
(4) Paragraph (3) is subject to any order of the court which ordered the transfer.

DEFAMATION

See **Defamation claims**.

DEFAMATION CLAIMS

Pre-action protocol for defamation

The Pre-Action Protocol for Claims in Defamation is intended to encourage exchange of information between parties at an early stage and to provide a clear framework within which parties to a claim in defamation, acting in good faith, can explore the early and appropriate resolution of that claim.

There are important features which distinguish defamation claims from other areas of civil litigation, and these must be borne in mind when both applying, and reviewing the application of, the Pre-Action Protocol. In particular, time is always 'of the essence' in defamation claims; the limitation period is (uniquely) only one year, and almost invariably, a claimant will be seeking an immediate correction and/or apology as part of the process of restoring his/her reputation.

This Protocol aims to set out a code of good practice which parties should follow when litigation is being considered.

It encourages early communication of a claim.

It aims to encourage both parties to disclose sufficient information to enable each to understand the other's case and to promote the prospect of early resolution.

It sets a timetable for the exchange of information relevant to the dispute.

It sets standards for the content of correspondence.

It identifies options which either party might adopt to encourage settlement of the claim.

Should a claim proceed to litigation, the extent to which the protocol has been followed both in practice and in spirit by the parties will assist the Court in dealing with liability for costs and making other Orders.

Letters of claim and responses sent pursuant to this Protocol are not intended to have the same status as a Statement of Case in proceedings.

It aims to keep the costs of resolving disputes subject to this protocol proportionate.

Sources of information

Pt 53 r.53.3

Unless the court orders otherwise, a party will not be required to provide further information about the identity of the defendant's sources of information.
(Part 18 provides for requests for further information).

Statements of case

PD 53 para.2.1

Statements of case should be confined to the information necessary to inform the other party of the nature of the case he has to meet. Such information should be set out concisely and in a manner proportionate to the subject matter of the claim.

PD 53 para.2.2

(1) In a claim for libel the publication the subject of the claim must be identified in the claim form.
(2) In a claim for slander the claim form must so far as possible contain the words complained of, and identify the person to whom they were spoken and when.

PD 53 para.2.3

(1) The claimant must specify in the particulars of claim the defamatory meaning which he alleges that the words or matters complained of conveyed, both
 (a) as to their natural and ordinary meaning; and
 (b) as to any innuendo meaning (that is a meaning alleged to be conveyed to some person by reason of knowing facts extraneous to the words complained of).
(2) In the case of an innuendo meaning, the claimant must also identify the relevant extraneous facts.

PD 53 para.2.4

In a claim for slander the precise words used and the names of the persons to whom they were spoken and when must, so far as possible, be set out in the particulars of claim, if not already contained in the claim form.

PD 53 para.2.5

Where a defendant alleges that the words complained of are true he must—
 (1) specify the defamatory meanings he seeks to justify; and

(2) give details of the matters on which he relies in support of that allegation.

PD 53 para.2.6

Where a defendant alleges that the words complained of are fair comment on a matter of public interest he must—
(1) specify the defamatory meaning he seeks to defend as fair comment on a matter of public interest; and
(2) give details of the matters on which he relies in support of that allegation.

PD 53 para.2.7

Where a defendant alleges that the words complained of were published on a privileged occasion he must specify the circumstances he relies on in support of that contention.

PD 53 para.2.8

Where a defendant alleges that the words complained of are true, or are fair comment on a matter of public interest, the claimant must serve a reply specifically admitting or denying the allegation and giving the facts on which he relies.

PD 53 para.2.9

If the defendant contends that any of the words or matters are fair comment on a matter of public interest, or were published on a privileged occasion, and the claimant intends to allege that the defendant acted with malice, the claimant must serve a reply giving details of the facts or matters relied on.

PD 53 para.2.10

(1) A claimant must give full details of the facts and matters on which he relies in support of his claim for damages.
(2) Where a claimant seeks aggravated or exemplary damages he must provide the information specified in r.16.4(1)(c).

PD 53 para.2.11

A defendant who relies on an offer to make amends under s.2 of the Defamation Act 1996, as his defence must—
(1) state in his defence—
(a) that he is relying on the offer in accordance with s.4(2) of the Defamation Act 1996; and
(b) that it has not been withdrawn by him or been accepted, and
(2) attach a copy of the offer he made with his defence.

Offer to make amends

PD 53 para.3.1

Sections 2 to 4 of the Defamation Act 1996 make provision for a person who has made a statement which is alleged to be defamatory to make an offer to make amends. Section 3 provides for the court to assist in the process of making amends.

PD 53 para.3.2

A claim under s.3 of the Defamation Act 1996 made other than in existing proceedings may be made under CPR Pt 8—
    (1) where the parties agree on the steps to make amends, and the sole purpose of the claim is for the court to make an order under s.3(3) for an order that the offer be fulfilled; or
    (2) where the parties do not agree—
        (a) on the steps to be taken by way of correction, apology and publication (see s.3(4));
        (b) on the amount to be paid by way of compensation (see s.3(5)); or
        (c) on the amount to be paid by way of costs (see s.3(6)).
(Applications in existing proceedings made under s.3 of the Defamation Act 1996 must be made in accordance with CPR Pt 23).

PD 53 para.3.3

    (1) A claim or application under s.3 of the Defamation Act 1996 must be supported by written evidence.
    (2) The evidence referred to in para.(1) must include—
        (a) a copy of the offer of amends;
        (b) details of the steps taken to fulfil the offer of amends;
        (c) a copy of the text of any correction and apology;
        (d) details of the publication of the correction and apology;
        (e) a statement of the amount of any sum paid as compensation;
        (f) a statement of the amount of any sum paid for costs;
        (g) why the offer is unsatisfactory.
    (3) Where any step specified in s.2(4) of the Defamation Act 1996 has not been taken, then the evidence referred to in para.(2)(c) to (f) must state what steps are proposed by the party to fulfil the offer of amends and the date or dates on which each step will be fulfilled and, if none, that no proposal has been made to take that step.

Ruling on meaning

PD 53 para.4.1

At any time the court may decide—
    (1) whether a statement complained of is capable of having any meaning attributed to it in a statement of case;
    (2) whether the statement is capable of being defamatory of the claimant;
    (3) whether the statement is capable of bearing any other meaning defamatory of the claimant.

PD 53 para.4.2

An application for a ruling on meaning may be made at any time after the service of particulars of claim. Such an application should be made promptly.
(This provision disapplies for these applications the usual time restriction on making applications in r.24.4.1).

PD 53 para.4.3

Where an application is made for a ruling on meaning, the application notice must state that it is an application for a ruling on meaning made in accordance with this PD.

PD 53 para.4.4

The application notice or the evidence contained or referred to in it, or served with it, must identify precisely the statement, and the meaning attributed to it, that the court is being asked to consider.
(Rule 3.3 applies where the court exercises its powers on its own initiative).
(Following a ruling on meaning the court may exercise its power under r.3.4).
(Section 7 of the Defamation Act 1996 applies to rulings on meaning)

Summary disposal under the Defamation Act 1996

Pt 53 r.53.2

(1) This rule provides for summary disposal in accordance with the Defamation Act 1996.
(2) In proceedings for summary disposal under ss.8 and 9 of the Act, rr.24.4 (procedure), 24.5 (evidence) and 24.6 (directions) apply.
(3) An application for summary judgment under Pt 24 may not be made if—
  (a) an application has been made for summary disposal in accordance with the Act, and that application has not been disposed of; or
  (b) summary relief has been granted on an application for summary disposal under the Act.
(4) The court may on any application for summary disposal direct the defendant to elect whether or not to make an offer to make amends under s.2 of the Act.
(5) When it makes a direction under para.(4), the court will specify the time by which and the manner in which—
  (a) the election is to be made; and
  (b) notification of it is to be given to the court and the other parties.

PD 53 para.5.1

Where an application is made for summary disposal, the application notice must state—
  (1) that it is an application for summary disposal made in accordance with s.8 of the Defamation Act 1996.
  (2) the matters set out in para.2(3) of PD 24; and
  (3) whether or not the defendant has made an offer to make amends under s.2 of the Act and whether or not it has been withdrawn.

PD 53 para.5.2

An application for summary disposal may be made at any time after the service of particulars of claim.
(This provision disapplies for these applications the usual time restriction on making applications in r.24.4.1).

PD 53 para.5.3

(1) This paragraph applies where—
  (a) the court has ordered the defendant in defamation proceedings to agree and publish a correction and apology as summary relief under s.8(2) of the Defamation Act 1996; and
  (b) the parties are unable to agree its content within the time specified in the Order.

(2) Where the court grants this type of summary relief under the Act, the order will specify the date by which the parties should reach agreement about the content, time, manner, form and place of publication of the correction and apology.

(3) Where the parties cannot agree the content of the correction and apology by the date specified in the order, then the claimant must prepare a summary of the judgment given by the court and serve it on all the other parties within 3 days following the date specified in the Order.

(4) Where the parties cannot agree the summary of the judgment prepared by the claimant they must within three days of receiving the summary—

  (a) file with the court and serve on all the other parties a copy of the summary showing the revisions they wish to make to it; and

  (b) apply to the court for the court to settle the summary.

(5) The court will then itself settle the summary and the judge who delivered the judgment being summarised will normally do this.

Summary disposal

PD 53 para.5.1

Where an application is made for summary disposal, the application notice must state—

  (1) that it is an application for summary disposal made in accordance with s.8 of the Defamation Act 1996.

  (2) the matters set out in para.2(3) of PD 24; and

  (3) whether or not the defendant has made an offer to make amends under s.2 of the Act and whether or not it has been withdrawn.

PD 53 para.5.2

An application for summary disposal may be made at any time after the service of particulars of claim.

(This provision disapplies for these applications the usual time restriction on making applications in r.24.4.1).

PD 53 para.5.3

  (1) This paragraph applies where—

  (a) the court has ordered the defendant in defamation proceedings to agree and publish a correction and apology as summary relief under s.8(2) of the Defamation Act 1996; and

  (b) the parties are unable to agree its content within the time specified in the Order.

  (2) Where the court grants this type of summary relief under the Act, the order will specify the date by which the parties should reach agreement about the content, time, manner, form and place of publication of the correction and apology.

  (3) Where the parties cannot agree the content of the correction and apology by the date specified in the order, then the claimant must prepare a summary of the judgment given by the court and serve it on all the other parties within 3 days following the date specified in the Order.

  (4) Where the parties cannot agree the summary of the judgment prepared by the claimant they must within three days of receiving the summary—

  (a) file with the court and serve on all the other parties a copy of the summary showing the revisions they wish to make to it; and

  (b) apply to the court for the court to settle the summary.

  (5) The court will then itself settle the summary and the judge who delivered the judgment being summarised will normally do this.

Statements in open court

PD 53 para.6.1

This paragraph only applies where a party wishes to accept a Pt 36 offer or other offer of settlement in relation to a claim for—
- (1) libel;
- (2) slander;
- (3) malicious falsehood;
- (4) misuse of private or confidential information.

PD 53 para.6.2

A party may apply for permission to make a statement in open court before or after he accepts the Pt 36 offer in accordance with r.36.9(1) or other offer to settle the claim.

PD 53 para.6.3

The statement that the applicant wishes to make must be submitted for the approval of the court and must accompany the notice of application.

PD 53 para.6.4

The court may postpone the time for making the statement if other claims relating to the subject matter of the statement are still proceeding.
(**Applications** must be made in accordance with Pt 23).

DEFAMATION PROCEEDINGS COSTS MANAGEMENT SCHEME

PD 51D para.1.1

[PD 51D] [provided] for a pilot scheme (the Defamation Proceedings Costs Management Scheme) to—
- (1) operate from October 1, 2011 to March 31, 2013.
- (2) operate in the Royal Courts of Justice and the District Registry at Manchester;
- (3) apply to proceedings in which the claim was started on or after October 1, 2009.
(Rule 30.2(4) enables cases issued at other district registries to be transferred to London or Manchester if those court centres are more appropriate).

PD 51D para.1.2

The Defamation Proceedings Costs Management Scheme [applied] to proceedings which included allegations of—
- (1) libel;
- (2) slander; and/or
- (3) malicious falsehood.

DEFAULT COSTS CERTIFICATE

Pt 47 r.47.11

(1) Where the receiving party is permitted by r.47.9 to obtain a default costs certificate, that party does so by filing a request in the relevant practice form.

(2) A default costs certificate will include an order to pay the costs to which it relates.

(3) Where a receiving party obtains a default costs certificate, the costs payable to that party for the commencement of detailed assessment proceedings will be the sum set out in the Costs PD.

(4) A receiving party who obtains a default costs certificate in detailed assessment proceedings pursuant to an order under s.194(3) of the Legal Services Act 2007 must send a copy of the default costs certificate to the prescribed charity.

PD 47 para.10.1

(1) A request for the issue of a default costs certificate must be made in Form N254 and must be signed by the receiving party or his solicitor.

(2) The request must be accompanied by a copy of the document giving the right to detailed assessment and must be filed at the appropriate office. (Paragraph 13.3 below identifies the appropriate documents.)

PD 47 para.10.2

A default costs certificate will be in Form N255.

PD 47 para.10.3

Attention is drawn to rr.40.3 (Drawing up and Filing of Judgments and orders) and 40.4 (Service of Judgments and orders) which apply to the preparation and service of a default costs certificate. The receiving party will be treated as having permission to draw up a default costs certificate by virtue of this PD.

PD 47 para.10.4

The issue of a default costs certificate does not prohibit, govern or affect any detailed assessment of the same costs which are payable out of the Community Legal Service Fund or by the Lord Chancellor under Pt 1 of the Legal Aid, Sentencing and Punishment of Offenders Act 2012.

PD 47 para.10.5

An application for an order staying enforcement of a default costs certificate may be made either—

(1) to a costs judge or district judge of the court office which issued the certificate; or

(2) to the court (if different) which has general jurisdiction to enforce the certificate.

PD 47 para.10.6

Proceedings for enforcement of default costs certificates may not be issued in the Costs Office.

Fixed costs on the issue of a default costs certificate

PD 47 para.10.7

Unless para.1.2 of PD 45 (Fixed costs in small claims) applies or unless the court orders otherwise, the fixed costs to be included in a default costs certificate are £80 plus a sum equal to any appropriate court fee payable on the issue of the certificate.

PD 47 para.10.8

The fixed costs included in a certificate must not exceed the maximum sum specified for costs and court fee in the notice of commencement.

Setting aside default costs certificate

Pt 47 r.47.12

(1) The court will set aside a default costs certificate if the receiving party was not entitled to it.
(2) In any other case, the court may set aside or vary a default costs certificate if it appears to the court that there is some good reason why the detailed assessment proceedings should continue.
(3) (PD 47 contains further details about the procedure for setting aside a default costs certificate and the matters which the court must take into account.)

Where the court sets aside or varies a default costs certificate in detailed assessment proceedings pursuant to an order under s.194(3) of the Legal Services Act 2007, the receiving party must send a copy of the order setting aside or varying the default costs certificate to the prescribed charity.

PD 47 para.11.1

A court officer may set aside a default costs certificate at the request of the receiving party under r.47.12. A costs judge or a district judge will make any other order or give any directions under this rule.

PD 47 para.11.2

(1) An application for an order under r.47.12(2) to set aside or vary a default costs certificate must be supported by evidence.
(2) In deciding whether to set aside or vary a certificate under r.47.12(2) the matters to which the court must have regard include whether the party seeking the order made the application promptly.
(3) As a general rule a default costs certificate will be set aside under r.47.12(2) only if the applicant shows a good reason for the court to do so and if he files with his application a copy of the bill and a copy of the default costs certificate, and a draft of the points of dispute he proposes to serve if his application is granted.

PD 47 para.11.3

(1) Attention is drawn to r.3.1(3) (which enables the court when making an order to make it subject to conditions) and to r.44.2(8) (which enables the court to order a party whom it has ordered to pay costs to pay an amount on account before the costs are assessed).

(2) A costs judge or a district judge may exercise the power of the court to make an order under r.44.3(8) although he did not make the order about costs which led to the issue of the default costs certificate.

DEFAULT JUDGMENT

Pt 12 r.12.1

Judgment without trial where a defendant—
   (a) has failed to file an **acknowledgment of service**; or
   (b) has failed to file a **defence**.

PD 13 para.1.1

For this purpose a defence includes any document purporting to be a defence.

PD 12 para.5.1

On all applications to which [PD 12] applies, other than those referred to in paras 4.3 and 4.4, notice should be given in accordance with Pt 23 (notice of application).

Obtaining default judgment

PD 12 para.2.1

Rules 12.4(1) and 12.9(1) describe the claims in respect of which a default judgment may be obtained by filing a request in the appropriate[**PF**].

PD 12 para.2.2

A default judgment on:
   (1) the claims referred to in rr.12.9(1)(b) and 12.10, and
   (2) claims other than those described in r.12.4(1),
can only be obtained if an application for default judgment is made and cannot be obtained by filing a request.

PD 12 para.2.3

The following are some of the types of claim which require an application for a default judgment:
   (1) against children and protected parties,
   (2) for costs (other than fixed costs) only,
   (3) by one spouse or civil partner against the other on a claim in tort,
   (4) for delivery up of goods where the defendant will not be allowed the alternative of paying their value; and
   (6) against persons or organisations who enjoy immunity from civil jurisdiction under the provisions of the International Organisations Acts 1968 and 1981.

Claims in which default judgment may not be obtained

Pt 12 r.12.2

PD 12 para.1.1

A claimant may not obtain a default judgment—
- (a) on a claim for delivery of goods subject to an agreement regulated by the **Consumer Credit** Act 1974;
- (b) where he uses the procedure set out in Pt 8 (alternative procedure for claims); or
- (c) in any other case where a PD provides that the claimant may not obtain default judgment.

For this purpose a defence includes any document purporting to be a defence.

PD 12 para.1.2

A claimant may not obtain a default judgment under Pt 12 (notwithstanding that no acknowledgment of service or defence has been filed) if:
- (1) the procedure set out in Pt 8 (Alternative Procedure for Claims) is being used, or
- (2) the claim is for delivery of goods subject to an agreement regulated by the Consumer Credit Act 1974, or

PD 12 para.1.3

Other rules and PD provide that default judgment under Pt 12 cannot be obtained in particular types of proceedings. Examples are:
- (1) admiralty proceedings;
- (2) **arbitration proceedings**;
- (3) **contentious probate proceedings**;
- (4) claims for **provisional damages**;
- (5) **possession claims**.

Conditions to be satisfied

Pt 12 r.12.3

- (1) The claimant may obtain judgment in default of an acknowledgment of service only if—
    - (a) the defendant has not filed an acknowledgment of service or a defence to the claim (or any part of the claim); and
    - (b) the relevant time for doing so has expired.
- (2) Judgment in default of defence may be obtained only—
    - (a) where an acknowlegement of service has been filed but a defence has not been filed;
    - (b) in a counterclaim made under r.20.4, where a defence has not been filed,
    and, in either case, the relevant time limit for doing so has expired.

(Rule 20.4 makes general provision for a defendant's counterclaim against a claimant, and r.20.4(3) provides that Pt 10 (acknowledgement of service) does not apply to a counterclaim made under that rule).
- (3) The claimant may not obtain a default judgment if—
    - (a) the defendant has applied—
        - (i) to have the claimant's **statement of case** struck out under r.3.4; or

      (ii) for **summary judgment** under Pt 24,

    and, in either case, that application has not been disposed of;

  (b) the defendant has satisfied the whole claim (including any claim for costs) on which the claimant is seeking judgment; or

  (c)   (i) the claimant is seeking judgment on a claim for money; and

      (ii) the defendant has filed or served on the claimant an admission under r.14.4 or 14.7 (admission of liability to pay all of the money claimed) together with a request for time to pay.

(Part 14 sets out the procedure where a defendant admits a money claim and asks for time to pay).

(Rule 6.17 provides that, where the claim form is served by the claimant, the claimant may not obtain default judgment unless a certificate of service has been filed).

(Article 19(1) of the Service Regulation (which has the same meaning as in r.6.31(e)) applies in relation to judgment in default where the claim form is served in accordance with that Regulation).

Procedure for obtaining default judgment

Pt 12 r.12.4

  (1) Subject to para.(2), a claimant may obtain a default judgment by filing a request in the relevant practice form where the claim is for—

    (a) a specified amount of money;

    (b) an amount of money to be decided by the court;

    (c) delivery of goods where the claim form gives the defendant the alternative of paying their value; or

    (d) any combination of these remedies.

  (2) The claimant must make an application in accordance with Pt 23 if he wishes to obtain a default judgment—

    (a) on a claim which consists of or includes a claim for any other remedy; or

    (b) where r.12.9 or r.12.10 so provides,

    and where the defendant is an individual, the claimant must provide the defendant's date of birth (if known) in Pt C of the application notice.

  (3) Where a claimant—

    (a) claims any other remedy in his claim form in addition to those specified in para.(1); but

    (b) abandons that claim in his request for judgment,

    he may still obtain a default judgment by filing a request under para.(1).

See **Crown**.

PD 12 para.2.2

A default judgment on:

  (1) the claims referred to in rr.12.9(1)(b) and 12.10, and

  (2) claims other than those described in r.12.4(1),

can only be obtained if an application for default judgment is made and cannot be obtained by filing a request.

PD 12 para.2.3

The following are some of the types of claim which require an application for a default judgment:

  (1) against children and protected parties,

(2) for costs (other than fixed costs) only,

(3) by one spouse or civil partner against the other on a claim in tort,

(4) for delivery up of goods where the defendant will not be allowed the alternative of paying their value; and

(6) against persons or organisations who enjoy immunity from civil jurisdiction under the provisions of the International Organisations Acts 1968 and 1981.

Nature of judgment where default judgment obtained by filing a request

Pt 12 r.12.5

(1) Where the claim is for a specified sum of money, the claimant may specify in a request filed under r.12.4(1)—

(a) the date by which the whole of the judgment debt is to be paid; or

(b) the times and rate at which it is to be paid by instalments.

(2) Except where para.(4) applies, a default judgment on a claim for a specified amount of money obtained on the filing of a request, will be judgment for the amount of the claim (less any payments made) and costs—

(a) to be paid by the date or at the rate specified in the request for judgment; or

(b) if none is specified, immediately.

(**Interest** may be included in a default judgment obtained by filing a request if the conditions set out in r.12.6 are satisfied).

(Rule 45.4 provides for **fixed costs** on the entry of a default judgment).

(3) Where the claim is for an unspecified amount of money a default judgment obtained on the filing of a request will be for an amount to be decided by the court and costs.

(4) Where the claim is for **delivery of goods** and the claim form gives the defendant the alternative of paying their value, a default judgment obtained on the filing of a request will be judgment requiring the defendant to—

(a) deliver the goods or (if he does not do so) pay the value of the goods as decided by the court (less any payments made); and

(b) pay costs.

(Rule 12.7 sets out the procedure for deciding the amount of a judgment or the value of the goods).

(5) The claimant's right to enter judgment requiring the defendant to deliver goods is subject to r.40.14 (judgment in favour of certain part owners relating to the detention of goods).

PD 12 para.3.1

Requests for default judgment:

(1) in respect of a claim for a specified amount of money or for the delivery of goods where the defendant will be given the alternative of paying a specified sum representing their value, or for fixed costs only, must be in Form N205A or N225, and

(2) in respect of a claim where an amount of money (including an amount representing the value of goods) is to be decided by the court, must be in Form N205B or N227.

PD 12 para.3.2

The forms require the claimant to provide the date of birth (if known) of the defendant where the defendant is an individual.

Automatic transfer

Pt 12 r.12.5A

If—
(a) a claimant files a request for judgment which includes an amount of money to be decided by the court in accordance with rr.12.4 and 12.5; and
(b) the claim is a designated money claim,
the court will transfer the claim to the preferred court upon receipt of the request for judgment.

Procedure for deciding an amount or value

Pt 12 r.12.7

(1) This rule applies where the claimant obtains a default judgment on the filing of a request under r.12.4(1) and judgment is for—
(a) an amount of money to be decided by the court;
(b) the value of goods to be decided by the court; or
(c) an amount of interest to be decided by the court.
(2) Where the court enters judgment it will—
(a) give any directions it considers appropriate; and
(b) if it considers it appropriate, allocate the case.

Claim against more than one defendant

Pt 12 r.12.8

(1) A claimant may obtain a default judgment on request under this Part on a claim for money or a claim for delivery of goods against one of two or more defendants, and proceed with his claim against the other defendants.
(2) Where a claimant applies for a default judgment against one of two or more defendants—
(a) if the claim can be dealt with separately from the claim against the other defendants—
(i) the court may enter a default judgment against that defendant; and
(ii) the claimant may continue the proceedings against the other defendants;
(b) if the claim cannot be dealt with separately from the claim against the other defendants—
(i) the court will not enter default judgment against that defendant; and
(ii) the court must deal with the application at the same time as it disposes of the claim against the other defendants.
(3) A claimant may not enforce against one of two or more defendants any judgment obtained under this Part for possession of land or for delivery of goods unless—
(a) he has obtained a judgment for possession or delivery (whether or not obtained under this Part) against all the defendants to the claim; or
(b) the court gives permission.

Procedure for obtaining a default judgment for costs only

Pt 12 r.12.9

(1) Where a claimant wishes to obtain a default judgment for costs only—
    (a) if the claim is for fixed costs, he may obtain it by filing a request in the relevant practice form;
    (b) if the claim is for any other type of costs, he must make an application in accordance with Pt 23.
(2) Where an application is made under this rule for costs only, judgment shall be for an amount to be decided by the court.

(Part 45 sets out when a claimant is entitled to fixed costs).

Default judgment obtained by making an application

Pt 12 r.12.10

The claimant must make an application in accordance with Pt 23 where—
    (a) the claim is—
        (i) a claim against a child or protected party; or
        (ii) a claim in tort by one spouse or **civil partner** against the other.
    (b) the claimant wishes to obtain a default judgment where the defendant has failed to file an acknowledgment of service—
        (i) against a defendant who has been served with the claim out of the jurisdiction under rr.6.32(1), 6.33(1) or 6.33(2); (service where permission of the court is not required under the Civil Jurisdiction and Judgments Act 1982);
        (ii) against a defendant domiciled in Scotland or Northern Ireland or in any other Convention territory or Member State;
        (iii) against a **State**;
        (iv) against a diplomatic agent who enjoys immunity from civil jurisdiction by virtue of the Diplomatic Privileges Act 1964; or
        (v) against persons or organisations who enjoy immunity from civil jurisdiction pursuant to the provisions of the International Organisations Acts 1968 and 1981.

Supplementary provisions where applications for default judgment are made

Pt 12 r.12.11

(1) Where the claimant makes an application for a default judgment, judgment shall be such judgment as it appears to the court that the claimant is entitled to on his statement of case.
(2) Any evidence relied on by the claimant in support of his application need not be served on a party who has failed to file an acknowledgment of service.
(3) An application for a default judgment on a claim against a child or protected party or a claim in tort between spouses or civil partners must be supported by evidence.
(4) An application for a default judgment may be made without notice if—
    (a) the claim under the Civil Jurisdiction and Judgments Act 1982 or the **Lugano Convention** or the **Judgments Regulation**, was served in accordance with rr. 6.32(1), 6.33(1) or 6.33(2) as appropriate;
    (b) the defendant has failed to file an acknowledgment of service; and
    (c) notice does not need to be given under any other provision of these rules.

(5) Where an application is made against a State for a default judgment where the defendant has failed to file an acknowledgment of service—

    (a) the application may be made without notice, but the court hearing the application may direct that a copy of the **application notice** be served on the State;

    (b) if the court—

        (i) grants the application; or

        (ii) directs that a copy of the application notice be served on the State,

    the judgment or application notice (and the evidence in support) may be served out of the jurisdiction without any further order;

    (c) where para.(5)(b) permits a judgment or an application notice to be served out of the jurisdiction, the procedure for serving the judgment or the application notice is the same as for serving a claim form under s.III of Pt 6 except where an alternative method of service has been agreed under s.12(6) of the State Immunity Act 1978.

(6) For the purposes of this rule and r.12.10—

    (a) 'domicile' is to be determined—

        (i) in relation to a Convention territory, in accordance with ss.41 to 46 of the Civil Jurisdiction and Judgments Act 1982;

        (ii) in relation to a Member State, in accordance with the Judgments Regulation and paras 9 to 12 of Sch.1 to the Civil Jurisdiction and Judgments Order 2001;

    (b) 'Convention territory' means the territory or territories of any Contracting State, as defined by s.1(3) of the Civil Jurisdiction and Judgments Act 1982, to which the Brussels Conventions or Lugano Convention apply;

    (d) 'Diplomatic agent' has the meaning given by art.1(e) of Sch.1 to the Diplomatic Privileges Act 1964.

Evidence

PD 12 para.4.1

Both on a request and on an application for default judgment the court must be satisfied that:

    (1) the particulars of claim have been served on the defendant (a certificate of service on the court file will be sufficient evidence),

    (2) either the defendant has not filed an acknowledgment of service or has not filed a defence and that in either case the relevant period for doing so has expired,

    (3) the defendant has not satisfied the claim, and

    (4) the defendant has not returned an admission to the claimant under r.14.4 or filed an admission with the court under r.14.6.

PD 12 para.4.2

On an application against a **child** or **protected party**:

    (1) a litigation friend to act on behalf of the child or protected party must be appointed by the court before judgment can be obtained, and

    (2) the claimant must satisfy the court by evidence that he is entitled to the judgment claimed.

PD 12 para.4.3

On an application where the defendant was served with the claim either:

    (1) outside the jurisdiction without leave under the Civil Jurisdiction and Judgments Act 1982, or the Lugano Convention or the Judgments Regulation, or

    (2) within the jurisdiction but when domiciled in Scotland or Northern Ireland or in any other Convention territory or Member State,

and the defendant has not acknowledged service, the evidence must establish that:

(a) the claim is one that the court has power to hear and decide,

(b) no other court has exclusive jurisdiction under the Act or the Lugano Convention or Judgments Regulation to hear and decide the claim, and

(c) the claim has been properly served in accordance with art.20 of Sch.1 to the Act, art.26 of the Lugano Convention, para.15 of Sch.4 to the Act, or art.26 of the Judgments Regulation.

PD 12 para.4.4

On an application against a State the evidence must:

(1) set out the grounds of the application,

(2) establish the facts proving that the State is excepted from the immunity conferred by s.1 of the State Immunity Act 1978,

(3) establish that the claim was sent through the Foreign and Commonwealth Office to the Ministry of Foreign Affairs of the State or, where the State has agreed to another form of service, that the claim was served in the manner agreed; and

(4) establish that the time for acknowledging service (which is extended to two months by s.12(2) of the Act when the claim is sent through the Foreign and Commonwealth Office to the Ministry of Foreign Affairs of the State) has expired.

(See r.40.8 for when default judgment against a State takes effect).

PD 12 para.4.5

Evidence in support of an application referred to in paras 4.3 and 4.4 above must be by **affidavit**.

PD 12 para.4.6

On an application for judgment for delivery up of goods where the defendant will not be given the alternative of paying their value, the evidence must identify the goods and state where the claimant believes the goods to be situated and why their specific delivery up is sought.

Additional claim other than a counterclaim or a contribution or indemnity notice

Pt 20 r.20.11

(1) This rule applies if—

    (a) the **additional claim** is not—

        (i) a **counterclaim**; or

        (ii) a claim by a defendant for **contribution** or **indemnity** against another defendant under r.20.6; and

    (b) the party against whom an additional claim is made fails to file an acknowledgment of service or defence in respect of the additional claim.

(2) The party against whom the additional claim is made—

    (a) is deemed to admit the additional claim, and is bound by any judgment or decision in the proceedings in so far as it is relevant to any matter arising in the additional claim;

    (b) subject to para.(3), if default judgment under Pt 12 is given against the additional claimant, the additional claimant may obtain judgment in respect of the additional claim by filing a request in the relevant practice form.

(3) An additional claimant may not enter judgment under paragraph (2)(b) without the court's permission if—

(a) he has not satisfied the default judgment which has been given against him; or

(b) he wishes to obtain judgment for any remedy other than a contribution or indemnity.

(4) An application for the court's permission under para.(3) may be made without notice unless the court directs otherwise.

(5) The court may at any time set aside or vary a judgment entered under para.(2)(b).

Commercial court

Pt 58 r.58.8

(1) If, in a Pt 7 claim in the commercial list, a defendant fails to file an acknowledgment of service, the claimant need not serve particulars of claim before he may obtain or apply for default judgment in accordance with Pt 12.

(2) Rule 12.6(1) applies with the modification that para.(a) shall be read as if it referred to the claim form instead of the particulars of claim.

PD 58 para.6

The PDs supplementing Pts 12 and 14 apply with the following modifications—

(1) Paragraph 4.1(1) of PD 12 is to be read as referring to the service of the claim form; and

(2) the references to 'particulars of claim' in paras 2.1, 3.1 and 3.2 of PD 14 are to be read as referring to the claim form.

Judgment against a state in default of acknowledgment of service

Pt 40 r.40.10

(1) Where the claimant obtains default judgment under Pt 12 on a claim against a State where the defendant has failed to file an acknowledgment of service, the judgment does not take effect until two months after service on the **State** of—

(a) a copy of the judgment; and

(b) a copy of the evidence in support of the application for permission to enter default judgment (unless the evidence has already been served on the State in accordance with an order made under Pt 12).

Setting aside or varying default judgment

Pt 13 r.13.1

The rules in this Part set out the procedure for setting aside or varying judgment entered under Pt 12 (default judgment).

(CCR Ord.22 r.10 sets out the procedure for varying the rate at which a judgment debt must be paid).

Cases where the court must set aside judgment entered under Pt 12

Pt 13 r.13.2

The court must **set aside** a judgment entered under Pt 12 if judgment was wrongly entered because—
    (a) in the case of a judgment in default of an acknowledgment of service, any of the conditions in r.12.3(1) and 12.3(3) was not satisfied;
    (b) in the case of a judgment in default of a defence, any of the conditions in r.12.3(2) and 12.3(3) was not satisfied; or
    (c) the whole of the claim was satisfied before judgment was entered.

Cases where the court may set aside or vary judgment entered under Pt 12

Pt 13 r.13.3

    (1) In any other case, the court may set aside or vary a judgment entered under Pt 12 if—
        (a) the defendant has a real prospect of successfully defending the claim; or
        (b) it appears to the court that there is some other good reason why—
            (i) the judgment should be set aside or varied; or
            (ii) the defendant should be allowed to defend the claim.
    (2) In considering whether to set aside or vary a judgment entered under Pt 12, the matters to which the court must have regard include whether the person seeking to set aside the judgment made an application to do so promptly.
(Rule 3.1(3) provides that the court may attach conditions when it makes an order).
(Article 19(4) of the Service Regulation (which has the same meaning as in r.6.31(e)) applies to applications to appeal a judgment in default when the time limit for appealing has expired).

Procedure

Pt 13 r.13.4

    (1) Where—
        (a) the claim is for a specified amount of money;
        (b) the judgment was obtained in a court which is not the defendant's home court;
        (c) the claim has not been transferred to another defendant's home; and
        (d) the defendant is an individual,
    the court will transfer an application by a defendant under this Part to set aside or vary judgment to the **defendant's home court**.
    (1B) Where—
        (a) the claim is for a specified amount of money;
        (b) the claim is a designated money claim;
        (c) the claim has not been transferred to another court; and
        (d) the defendant is not an individual,
    the court will transfer an application by a defendant under this Part to set aside or vary the judgment to the preferred court.
    (2) Paragraph (1) does not apply where the claim was commenced in a specialist list.
    (3) An application under r.13.3 (cases where the court may set aside or vary judgment) must be supported by evidence.

See **Abandoned claim where default judgment set aside, Foreign currency, Interest,** and **Mercantile Courts.**

DEFENCE

Pt 15 r.15.1

PD 15 para.1.1

[Part 15] does not apply where the claimant uses the [**Part 8 procedure**].

PD 15 para.1.2

In relation to **specialist proceedings** (see Pt 49) in respect of which special provisions for defence and reply are made by the rules and PDs applicable to those claims, the provisions of Part 15 apply only to the extent that they are not inconsistent with those rules and PDs.

PD 15 para.1.3

Form N9B (specified amount) or N9D (unspecified amount or non-money claims) may be used for the purpose of defence and is included in the response pack served on the defendant with the particulars of claim

Content of defence

Pt 16 r.16.5

(1) In his defence, the defendant must state—
   (a) which of the allegations in the particulars of claim he denies;
   (b) which allegations he is unable to admit or deny, but which he requires the claimant to prove; and
   (c) which allegations he admits.
(2) Where the defendant denies an allegation—
   (a) he must state his reasons for doing so; and
   (b) if he intends to put forward a different version of events from that given by the claimant, he must state his own version.
(3) A defendant who—
   (a) fails to deal with an allegation; but
   (b) has set out in his defence the nature of his case in relation to the issue to which that allegation is relevant,
   shall be taken to require that allegation to be proved.
(4) Where the claim includes a money claim, a defendant shall be taken to require that any allegation relating to the amount of money claimed be proved unless he expressly admits the allegation.
(5) Subject to paras (3) and (4), a defendant who fails to deal with an allegation shall be taken to admit that allegation.
(6) If the defendant disputes the claimant's statement of value under r.16.3 he must—
   (a) state why he disputes it; and
   (b) if he is able, give his own statement of the value of the claim.
(7) If the defendant is defending in a representative capacity, he must state what that capacity is.

(8) If the defendant has not filed an acknowledgment of service under Pt 10, the defendant must give an address for service.

(Part 22 requires a defence to be verified by a **statement of truth**).

(Rule 6.23 makes provision in relation to **addresses for service**).

Limitation period

PD 16 para.13.1

The defendant must give details of the expiry of any relevant limitation period relied on.

PD 16 para.13.2

Defence of tender

See **Defence of tender before claim**.

Points of law

PD 16 para.13.3

A party may:
    (1) refer in his statement of case to any point of law on which his claim or defence, as the case may be, is based,
    (2) give in his statement of case the name of any witness he proposes to call, and
    (3) attach to or serve with this statement of case a copy of any document which he considers is necessary to his claim or defence, as the case may be (including any expert's report to be filed in accordance with Pt 35).

(The Costs PD supplementing Pts 43 to 48 contains details of the information required to be filed with certain statements of case to comply with r.44.15 (providing information about funding arrangements)).

Competition Act 1998

PD 16 para.14

A party who wishes to rely on a finding of the Office of Fair Trading as provided by s.58 of the Competition Act 1998 must include in his statement of case a statement to that effect and identify the Office's finding on which he seeks to rely.

Human rights

See **Human rights**.

Filing a defence

Pt 15 r.15.2

A defendant who wishes to defend all or part of a claim must file a defence.

(Part 14 contains further provisions which apply where the defendant admits a claim).

Consequence of not filing a defence

Pt 15 r.15.3

If a defendant fails to file a defence, the claimant may obtain default judgment if Pt 12 allows it.

Period for filing a defence

Pt 15 r.15.4

(1) The general r.is that the period for filing a defence is—
    (a) 14 days after service of the particulars of claim; or
    (b) if the defendant files an acknowledgment of service under Pt 10, 28 days after service of the particulars of claim.

(Rule 7.4 provides for the particulars of claim to be contained in or served with the claim form or served within 14 days of service of the claim form).

(2) The general rule is subject to the following rules—
    (a) rule 6.35 (which specifies how the period for filing a defence is calculated where the claim form is served out of the jurisdiction under r.6.32 or 6.33);
    (b) rule 11 (which provides that, where the defendant makes an application disputing the court's jurisdiction, the defendant need not file a defence before the hearing);
    (c) rule 24.4(2) (which provides that, if the claimant applies for summary judgment before the defendant has filed a defence, the defendant need not file a defence before the summary judgment hearing); and
    (d) rule 6.12(3) (which requires the court to specify the period for responding to the particulars of claim when it makes an order under that rule).

Agreement extending the period for filing a defence

Pt 15 r.15.5

(1) The defendant and the claimant may agree that the period for filing a defence specified in r.15.4 shall be extended by up to 28 days.
(2) Where the defendant and the claimant agree to extend the period for filing a defence, the defendant must notify the court in writing.

Service of copy of defence

Pt 15 r.15.6

A copy of the defence must be served on every other party.
(Part 16 sets out what a defence must contain).
(The Costs PD sets out the information about a funding arrangement to be provided with the defence where the defendant intends to seek to recover an additional liability).
(Paragraph 8.2 of PD 6A contains provisions about service by the court on the claimant of any acknowledgment of service that has been filed by the defendant or any notice of funding that has been filed.)

Stay

PD 15 para.3.3

Where a claim has been stayed under rr.15.10(3) [claimant's notice where defence is that money claimed has been paid] or 15.11(1) any party may apply for the stay to be lifted.

PD 15 para.3.4

The application should be made in accordance with Pt 23 and should give the reason for the applicant's delay in proceeding with or responding to the claim.

Claim stayed if it is not defended or admitted

Pt 15 r.15.11

  (1) Where—
      (a) at least six months have expired since the end of the period for filing a defence specified in r.15.4;
      (b) no defendant has served or filed an admission or filed a defence or counterclaim; and
      (c) the claimant has not entered or applied for judgment under Pt 12 (default judgment), or Pt 24 (summary judgment),
      the claim shall be stayed.
  (2) Where a claim is stayed under this rule any party may apply for the stay to be lifted.

Statement of truth

PD 16 para.2.1

Part 22 requires a defence to be verified by a statement of truth.

PD 16 para.2.2

The form of the statement of truth is as follows:
  '[I believe][the defendant believes] that the facts stated in this defence are true.'

PD 16 para.2.3

Attention is drawn to r.32.14 which sets out the consequences of verifying a statement of case containing a false statement without an honest belief in its truth.

Counterclaim

Pt 15 r.15.7

Part 20 applies to a defendant who wishes to make a **counterclaim**.

PD 15 para.3.1

Where a defendant to a claim serves a **counterclaim** under Pt 20, the defence and counterclaim should normally form one document with the counterclaim following on from the defence.

Reply and defence to counterclaim

PD 15 para.3.2

Where a claimant serves a reply and a defence to counterclaim, the reply and defence to counterclaim should normally form one document with the defence to counterclaim following on from the reply.

PD 15 para.3.2A

Rule 15.8(a) provides that a claimant must file any reply with his **allocation questionnaire**. Where the date by which he must file his allocation questionnaire is later than the date by which he must file his defence to counterclaim (because the time for filing the allocation questionnaire under r.26.3(6) is more than 14 days after the date on which it is deemed to be served), the court will normally order that the defence to counterclaim must be filed by the same date as the reply. Where the court does not make such an order the reply and defence to counterclaim may form separate documents.

PD 18 r.15.8

If a claimant files a reply to the defence, he must—
  (a) file this reply when he files his **allocation questionnaire**; and
  (b) serve his reply on the parties at the same time as he files it.

Production centre

PD 7C para.5.3

  (1) This paragraph applies where a Centre user has started a claim in the Northampton County Court and the defendant has filed a defence to the claim or to part of the claim.
  (2) On the filing of the defence the officer will serve a notice on the Centre user requiring the Centre user to state within 28 days whether the claim is to proceed.
  (3) If the Centre user does not notify the officer within the time specified in the notice that the claim is to proceed, the claim will be stayed, and the officer will notify the parties accordingly.
  (4) The proceedings will not be transferred as provided by para.1.3(2)(e) until the Centre user notifies the officer that the claim is to continue.

See also **Personal injury claims**.

Possession claims online

PD 55B para.7.1

A defendant wishing to file—
  (1) a defence; or

   (2) a counterclaim (to be filed together with a defence) to a claim which has been issued
      through the PCOL system, may, instead of filing a written form, do so by—
      (a) completing the relevant online form at the PCOL website; and
      (b) if the defendant is making a counterclaim, paying the appropriate fee electronically
         at the PCOL website or by some other means approved by Her Majesty's Courts and
         Tribunal Service.

PD 55B para.7.2

Where a defendant files a defence by completing the relevant online form, he must not send the court a hard copy.

PD 55B para.7.3

When an online defence form is received, an acknowledgment of receipt will automatically be sent to the defendant. The acknowledgment does not constitute notice that the defence has been served.

PD 55B para.7.4

The online defence form will be treated as being filed—
   (1) on the day the court receives it, if it receives it before 16.00 on a working day; and
   (2) otherwise, on the next working day after the court receives the online defence form.

PD 55B para.7.5

A defence is filed when the online defence form is received by the court's computer system. The court will keep a record, by electronic or other means, of when online defence forms are received.

See also **Additional claims**, **Defence of set-off**, **Defence of tender before claim** and **Defence that money claimed has been paid**, and **stay**.

DEFENCE OF SET-OFF

Pt 16 r.16.6

Where a defendant—
   (a) contends he is entitled to money from the claimant; and
   (b) relies on this as a defence to the whole or part of the claim,
the contention may be included in the defence and set off against the claim, whether or not it is also a Pt 20 claim.

See **Crown proceedings**.

DEFENCE OF TENDER BEFORE CLAIM

Glossary

A defence that, before the claimant started proceedings, the defendant unconditionally offered to the claimant the amount due or, if no specified amount is claimed, an amount sufficient to satisfy the claim.

Pt 37 r.37.2

(1) Where a defendant wishes to rely on a defence of tender before claim he must make a payment into court of the amount he says was tendered.
(2) If the defendant does not make a payment in accordance with para.(1), the defence of tender before claim will not be available to him until he does so.

PD 37 para.1.1

Except where para.1.2 applies, a party paying money into court under an order or in support of a defence of tender before claim must—
(1) send to the Court Funds Office—
  (a) the payment, usually a cheque made payable to the Accountant General of the Senior Courts;
  (b) a sealed copy of the order or a copy of the defence; and
  (c) a completed Court Funds Office Form 100;
(2) serve a copy of the Form 100 on each other party; and
(3) file at the court—
  (a) a copy of the Form 100; and
  (b) a certificate of service confirming service of a copy of that form on each party served.

PD 37 para.1.2

Instead of complying with para.1.1(1), a litigant in person without a current account may, in a claim proceeding in a county court or District Registry, make a payment into court by—
(1) lodging the payment in cash with the court; and
(2) giving the court a completed Court Funds Office Form 100.

DEFENCE THAT MONEY CLAIMED HAS BEEN PAID

Pt 15 r.15.10

(1) Where—
  (a) the only claim (apart from a claim for costs and interest) is for a specified amount of money; and
  (b) the defendant states in his defence that he has paid to the claimant the amount claimed,
  the court will send notice to the claimant requiring him to state in writing whether he wishes the proceedings to continue.
(2) When the claimant responds, he must serve a copy of his response on the defendant.
(3) If the claimant fails to respond under this rule within 28 days after service of the court's notice on him the claim shall be stayed.
(4) Where a claim is stayed under this rule any party may apply for the stay to be lifted.
(If the claimant files notice under this r.that he wishes the proceedings to continue, the procedure which then follows is set out in Pt 26).

DEFENDANT

Pt 2 r.2.3(1)

A person against whom a claim is made.

Addition or substitution of defendant

PD 19A para.3.1

The CPR apply to a new defendant who has been added or substituted as they apply to any other defendant (see in particular the provisions of Pts 9, 10, 11 and 15).

PD 19A para.3.2

Where the court has made an order adding or substituting a defendant whether on its own initiative or on an application, the court may direct:
    (1) the claimant to file with the court within 14 days (or as ordered) an amended claim form and particulars of claim for the court file,
    (2) a copy of the order to be served on all parties to the proceedings and any other person affected by it,
    (3) the amended claim form and particulars of claim, forms for admitting, defending and acknowledging the claim and copies of the statements of case and any other documents referred to in any statement of case to be served on the new defendant.
    (4) unless the court orders otherwise, the amended claim form and particulars of claim to be served on any other defendants.

PD 19A para.3.3

A new defendant does not become a party to the proceedings until the amended claim form has been served on him.

See also **Parties**.

Additional claim

PD 20 para.7.3

Claimants and defendants in the original claim should always be referred to as such in the title to the proceedings, even if they subsequently acquire an additional procedural status.

See also **Acknowledgement of service**.

DEFENDANT'S HOME COURT

Pt 2 r.2.3(1)

    (a) If the claim is proceeding in a county court, the county court for the district in which the defendant resides or carries on business; and
    (b) if the claim is proceeding in the High Court, the district registry for the district in which the defendant resides or carries on business or, where there is no such district registry, the Royal Courts of Justice;
(Rule 6.23 provides for a party to give an address for service).

DELIVERY OF GOODS

Enforcement of judgment for delivery of goods

RSC Ord.45 r.4

    (1) Subject to the provisions of these rules, a judgment or order for the delivery of any goods which does not give a person against whom the judgment is given or order made the

alternative of paying the assessed value of the goods may be enforced by one or more of the following means, that is to say—

    (a) writ of delivery to recover the goods without alternative provision for recovery of the assessed value thereof (hereafter in this rule referred to as a 'writ of specific delivery');

    (b) in a case in which r.81.4 applies, an order of committal;

    (c) in a case in which r.81.20 applies, writ of sequestration.

(2) Subject to the provisions of these rules, a judgment or order for the delivery of any goods or payment of their assessed value may be enforced by one or more of the following means, that is to say—

    (a) writ of delivery to recover the goods or their assessed value;

    (b) by order of the court, writ of specific delivery;

    (c) in a case in which r.81.20 applies, writ of sequestration.

An application for an order under subpara.(b) shall be made in accordance with CPR Pt 23, which must be served on the defendant against whom the judgment or order sought to be enforced was given or made.

(3) A writ of specific delivery, and a writ of delivery to recover any goods or their assessed value, may include provision for enforcing the payment of any money adjudged or ordered to be paid by the judgment or order which is to be enforced by the writ.

(4) A judgment or order for the payment of the assessed value of any goods may be enforced by the same means as any other judgment or order for the payment of money.

DELIVERY UP ORDER

PD 25A para.8.1

The following provisions apply to orders, other than search orders, for delivery up or preservation of evidence or property where it is likely that such an order will be executed at the premises of the respondent or a third party.

PD 25A para.8.2

In such cases the court shall consider whether to include in the order for the benefit or protection of the parties similar provisions to those specified above in relation to injunctions and search orders.

Default judgment

PD 12 para.4.6

On an application for judgment for delivery up of goods where the defendant will not be given the alternative of paying their value, the evidence must identify the goods and state where the claimant believes the goods to be situated and why their specific delivery up is sought.

DEMOTED TENANCY

Pt 55 r.55.1(g) and Pt 65 r.65.11(2)(b)

A tenancy created by virtue of a demotion order.

See **Demotion claim**.

DEMOTION CLAIM

Pt 65 r.65.11

(1) [Section III of Pt 65] applies to—
(a) [a **demotion order**];
(aa) [a **suspension order**); and
(b) proceedings relating to a tenancy created by virtue of a demotion order.

Demotion claims or suspension claims made in the alternative to possession claims

Pt 65 r.65.12

Where a demotion order or suspension order (or both) is claimed in the alternative to a possession order, the claimant must use the Pt 55 procedure and s.I of Pt 55 applies, except that the claim must be made in the county court for the district in which the property to which the claim relates is situated.
(Suspension claims may be made in England, but may not be made in Wales).

Other demotion or suspension claims

Pt 65 r.65.13

Where a demotion claim or suspension claim (or both) is made other than in a possession claim, rr.65.14 to 65.19 apply.

PD 65 para.6.1

Demotion or suspension claims, other than those made in the alternative to possession claims, must be made in the county court for the district in which the property to which the claim relates is situated.

PD 65 para.6.2

The claimant must use the appropriate claim form and particulars of claim form set out in Table 1 to PD 4. The defence must be in Form N11D as appropriate.

PD 65 para.6.3

The claimant's evidence should include details of the conduct alleged, and any other matters relied upon.

Starting a demotion or suspension claim

Pt 65 r.65.14

(1) The claim must be made in the county court for the district in which the property to which the claim relates is situated.

(2) the claim form and form of defence sent with it must be in the forms set out in PD 65.

(Part 16 and PD 65 provide details about the contents of the particulars of claim).

Particulars of claim

Pt 65 r.65.15

The particulars of claim must be filed and served with the claim form.

PD 65 para.5.1

If the claim relates to residential property let on a tenancy and if the claim includes a demotion claim, the particulars of claim must—

(1) state whether the demotion claim is a claim under s.82A(2) of the 1985 Act or under s.6A(2) of the 1988 Act;
(2) state whether the claimant is a local housing authority, a housing action trust, a registered social landlord or a private registered provider of social housing;
(3) provide details of any statement of express terms of the tenancy served on the tenant under s.82A(7) of the 1985 Act or under s.6A(10) of the 1988 Act, as applicable; and
(4) state details of the conduct alleged.

PD 65 para.7.1

In a demotion claim the particulars of claim must—

(1) state whether the demotion claim in a claim under s.82A(2) of the 1985 Act or under s.6A(2) of the 1988 Act;
(2) state whether the claimant is a local housing authority, a housing action trust, a registered social landlord or a private registered provider of social housing;
(3) identify the property to which the claim relates;
(4) provide the following details about the tenancy to which the demotion claim relates—
   (a) the parties to the tenancy;
   (b) the period of the tenancy;
   (c) the amount of the rent;
   (d) the dates on which the rent is payable; and
   (e) any statement of express terms of the tenancy served on the tenant under s.82A(7) of the 1985 Act or under s.6A(10) of the 1988 Act, as applicable; and
(5) state details of the conduct alleged.

Defendant's response

Pt 65 r.65.17

(1) an acknowledgement of service is not required and Pt 10 does not apply.
(2) where the defendant does not file a defence within the time specified in r.15.4 he may take part in any hearing but the court may take his failure to do so into account when deciding what order to make about costs.
(3) Part 12 (**default judgment**) does not apply.

Hearing date

Pt 65 r.65.16

   (1) the court will fix a date for the hearing when it issues the claim form.
   (2) the hearing date will be not less than 28 days from the date of issue of the claim form.
   (3) the standard period between the issue of the claim form and the hearing will be not more than eight weeks.
   (4) the defendant must be served with the claim form and the particulars of claim not less than 21 days before the hearing date.

Rule 3.1(2)(a) provides that the court may extend or shorten the time for compliance with any rule and r.3.1(2)(b) provides that the court may adjourn or bring forward a hearing).

PD 65 para.8.1

The court may use its powers under rr.3.1(2)(a) and (b) to shorten the time periods set out in rr.65.16(2), (3) and (4).

PD 65 para.8.2

Particular consideration should be given to the exercise of this power if—
   (1) the defendant, or a person for whom the defendant is responsible, has assaulted or threatened to assault—
      (a) the claimant;
      (b) a member of the claimant's staff; or
      (c) another resident in the locality;
   (2) there are reasonable grounds for fearing such an assault; or
   (3) the defendant, or a person for whom the defendant is responsible, has caused serious damage or threatened to cause serious damage to the property or to the home or property of another resident in the locality.

PD 65 para.8.3

Where para.8.2 applies but the case cannot be determined at the first hearing fixed under r.65.16, the court will consider what steps are needed to finally determine the case as quickly as reasonably practicable.

Hearing

Pt 65 r.65.18

   (1) At the hearing fixed in accordance with r.65.16(1) or at any adjournment of that hearing the court may—
      (a) decide the claim; or
      (b) give case management directions.
   (2) where the claim is genuinely disputed on grounds which appear to be substantial, case management directions given under para.(1)(b) will include the allocation of the claim to a track or directions to enable it to be allocated.
   (3) except where—
      (a) the claim is allocated to the fast track or the multi-track; or
      (b) the court directs otherwise,

any fact that needs to be proved by the evidence of witnesses at a hearing referred to in para.(1) may be proved by evidence in writing.

(Rule 32.2(1) sets out the general rule about evidence. Rule 32.2(2) provides that r.32.2(1) is subject to any provision to the contrary).

(4) all witness statements must be filed and served at least two days before the hearing.

(5) where the claimant serves the claim form and particulars of claim, the claimant must produce at the hearing a certificate of service of those documents and r.6.17(2)(a) does not apply.

PD 65 para.9.1

Attention is drawn to r.65.18(3). Each party should wherever possible include all the evidence he wishes to present in his statement of case, verified by a statement of truth.

PD 65 para.9.2

The claimant's evidence should include details of the conduct to which s.153A or 153B of the 1996 Act applies and in respect of which the claim is made.

PD 65 para.9.3

If—

(1) the maker of a witness statement does not attend a hearing; and

(2) the other party disputes material evidence contained in the statement,

the court will normally adjourn the hearing so that oral evidence can be given.

Allocation

Pt 65 r.65.19

When the court decides the track for the claim, the matters to which it shall have regard include—

(a) the matters set out in r.26.8; and

(b) the nature and extent of the conduct alleged.

proceedings relating to demoted tenancies.

Pt 65 r.65.20

A PD may make provision about proceedings relating to demoted tenancies.

Proceedings for the possession of a demoted tenancy

PD 65 para.10.1

Proceedings against a tenant of a demoted tenancy for possession must be brought under the procedure in Pt 55 (**Possession claims**).

Proceedings in relation to a written statement of demoted tenancy terms

PD 65 para.11.1

Proceedings as to whether a statement supplied in pursuance to s.143M(4)(b) of the 1996 Act (written statement of certain terms of tenancy) is accurate must be brought under the procedure in Pt 8.

Recovery of costs

PD 65 para.12.1

Attention is drawn to s.143N(4) of the 1996 Act which provides that if a person takes proceedings under Ch.1A of the 1996 Act in the High Court which he could have taken in the county court, he is not entitled to recover any costs.

Trials and assessments of damages

PD 2B para.11.1

A District Judge has jurisdiction to hear the following:
    (b) proceedings for the recovery of land, proceedings under s.82A(2) of the Housing Act 1985 or s. 6A(2) of the Housing Act 1988 (demotion claims) or proceedings in a county court under Ch.1A of the Housing Act 1996 (demoted tenancies).

Venue

PD 59A para.1.9

Where the claim form includes a demotion claim, the claim must be started in the county court for the district in which the land is situated.

DEMOTION ORDER

Pt 55 r.55.1(f) and Pt 65.11(10(a)

A claim made by a landlord for an order under s.82A of the Housing Act 1985 or s.6A of the Housing Act 1988.

DENTISTS

See **Health care professionals**.

DEPONENT

PD 32 para.2

A deponent is a person who gives evidence by affidavit or affirmation.

DEPOSITIONS

Evidence by deposition

Pt 34 r.34.8

   (1) A party may apply for an order for a person to be examined before the hearing takes place.
   (2) A person from whom evidence is to be obtained following an order under this rule is referred to as a 'deponent' and the evidence is referred to as a 'deposition'.
   (3) An order under this rule shall be for a deponent to be examined on oath before—
      (a) a judge;
      (b) an examiner of the court; or
      (c) such other person as the court appoints.
(Rule 34.15 makes provision for the appointment of examiners of the court).
   (4) The order may require the production of any document which the court considers is necessary for the purposes of the examination.
   (5) The order must state the date, time and place of the examination.
   (6) At the time of service of the order the deponent must be offered or paid—
      (a) a sum reasonably sufficient to cover his expenses in travelling to and from the place of examination; and
      (b) such sum by way of compensation for loss of time as may be specified in PD 34A.
   (7) Where the court makes an order for a deposition to be taken, it may also order the party who obtained the order to serve a witness statement or witness summary in relation to the evidence to be given by the person to be examined.
(Pt 32 contains the general rules about witness statements and witness summaries).

See also **Examiner of the court**.

Conduct of examination

Pt 34 r.34.9

   (1) Subject to any directions contained in the order for examination, the examination must be conducted in the same way as if the witness were giving evidence at a trial.
   (2) If all the parties are present, the examiner may conduct the examination of a person not named in the order for examination if all the parties and the person to be examined consent.
   (3) The examiner may conduct the examination in private if he considers it appropriate to do so.
   (4) The examiner must ensure that the evidence given by the witness is recorded in full.
   (5) The examiner must send a copy of the deposition—
      (a) to the person who obtained the order for the examination of the witness; and
      (b) to the court where the case is proceeding.

(6) The party who obtained the order must send each of the other parties a copy of the deposition which he receives from the examiner.

Use of deposition at a hearing

Pt 34 r.34.11

(1) A deposition ordered under r.34.8 may be given in evidence at a hearing unless the court orders otherwise.
(2) A party intending to put in evidence a deposition at a hearing must serve notice of his intention to do so on every other party.
(3) He must serve the notice at least 21 days before the day fixed for the hearing.
(4) The court may require a deponent to attend the hearing and give evidence orally.
(5) Where a deposition is given in evidence at trial, it shall be treated as if it were a witness statement for the purposes of r.32.13 (availability of witness statements for inspection).

Restrictions on subsequent use of deposition taken for the purpose of any hearing except the trial

Pt 34 r.34.12

(1) Where the court orders a party to be examined about his or any other assets for the purpose of any hearing except the trial, the deposition may be used only for the purpose of the proceedings in which the order was made.
(2) However, it may be used for some other purpose—
    (a) by the party who was examined;
    (b) if the party who was examined agrees; or
    (c) if the court gives permission.

Deposition to be taken in England and Wales for use as evidence in proceedings in courts in England and Wales

PD 34A para.4.1

A party may apply for an order for a person to be examined on oath before:
    (1) a judge, (2) an examiner of the court, or (3) such other person as the court may appoint.

PD 34A para.4.2

The party who obtains an order for the examination of a deponent before an examiner of the court must:
    (1) apply to the Foreign Process Section of the Masters' Secretary's Department at the Royal Courts of Justice for the allocation of an examiner,
    (2) when allocated, provide the examiner with copies of all documents in the proceedings necessary to inform the examiner of the issues, and
    (3) pay the deponent a sum to cover his travelling expenses to and from the examination and compensation for his loss of time.

PD 34A para.4.3

In ensuring that the deponent's evidence is recorded in full, the court or the examiner may permit it to be recorded on audiotape or videotape, but the depositionmust always be recorded in writing by him or by a competent shorthand writer or stenographer.

PD 34A para.4.4

If the deposition is not recorded word for word, it must contain, as nearly as may be, the statement of the deponent; the examiner may record word for word any particular questions and answers which appear to him to have special importance.

PD 34A para.4.5

If a deponent objects to answering any question or where any objection is taken to any question, the examiner must:
  (1) record in the deposition or a document attached to it—
     (a) the question,
     (b) the nature of and grounds for the objection, and
     (c) any answer given, and
  (2) give his opinion as to the validity of the objection and must record it in the deposition or a document attached to it.
The court will decide as to the validity of the objection and any question of costs arising from it.

PD 34A para.4.6

Documents and exhibits must:
  (1) have an identifying number or letter marked on them by the examiner, and
  (2) be preserved by the party or his legal representative who obtained the order for the examination, or as the court or the examiner may direct.

PD 34A para.4.7

The examiner may put any question to the deponent as to:
  (1) the meaning of any of his answers, or
  (2) any matter arising in the course of the examination.

PD 34A para.4.8

Where a deponent:
  (1) fails to attend the examination, or
  (2) refuses to:
     (a) be sworn, or
     (b) answer any lawful question, or
     (c) produce any document,
the examiner will sign a certificate of such failure or refusal and may include in his certificate any comment as to the conduct of the deponent or of any person attending the examination.

PD 34A para.4.9

The party who obtained the order for the examination must file the certificate with the court and may apply for an order that the deponent attend for examination or as may be. The application may be made without notice.

PD 34A para.4.10

The court will make such order on the application as it thinks fit including an order for the deponent to pay any costs resulting from his failure or refusal.

PD 34A para.4.11

A deponent who wilfully refuses to obey an order made against him under Pt 34 may be proceeded against for contempt of court.

PD 34A para.4.12

A deposition must:
    (1) be signed by the examiner,
    (2) have any amendments to it initialled by the examiner and the deponent,
    (3) be endorsed by the examiner with—
        (a) a statement of the time occupied by the examination, and
        (b) a record of any refusal by the deponent to sign the deposition and of his reasons for not doing so, and
    (4) be sent by the examiner to the court where the proceedings are taking place for filing on the court file.

Depositions to be taken abroad for use as evidence in proceedings before courts in England and Wales (where the taking of evidence regulation does not apply)

Where a person to be examined is out of the jurisdiction—letter of request

Pt 34 r.34.13

    (1) This rule applies where a party wishes to take a deposition from a person who is—
        (a) out of the jurisdiction; and
        (b) not in a Regulation State within the meaning of s.III of [Pt 34].
  (1A) The High Court may order the issue of a letter of request to the judicial authorities of the country in which the proposed deponent is.
    (2) A letter of request is a request to a judicial authority to take the evidence of that person, or arrange for it to be taken.
    (3) The High Court may make an order under this rule in relation to county court proceedings.
    (4) If the government of a country allows a person appointed by the High Court to examine a person in that country, the High Court may make an order appointing a special examiner for that purpose.
    (5) A person may be examined under this rule on oath or affirmation or in accordance with any procedure permitted in the country in which the examination is to take place.
    (6) If the High Court makes an order for the issue of a letter of request, the party who sought the order must file—
        (a) the following documents and, except where para.(7) applies, a translation of them—
            (i) a draft letter of request;
            (ii) a statement of the issues relevant to the proceedings;
            (iii) a list of questions or the subject matter of questions to be put to the person to be examined; and
        (b) an undertaking to be responsible for the Secretary of State's expenses.
    (7) There is no need to file a translation if—

    (a) English is one of the official languages of the country where the examination is to
        take place; or
    (b) a PD has specified that country as a country where no translation is necessary.

Letter of request—proceeds of Crime Act 2002

Pt 34 r.34.13A

(1) This rule applies where a party to existing or contemplated proceedings in—
    (a) the High Court; or
    (b) a magistrates' court,
    under Pt 5 of the Proceeds of Crime Act 2002 (civil recovery of the proceeds, etc. of
    unlawful conduct) wishes to take a deposition from a person who is out of the juris-
    diction.
(2) The High Court may, on the application of such a party, order the issue of a letter of
    request to the judicial authorities of the country in which the proposed deponent is.
(3) Paragraphs (4) to (7) of r.34.13 shall apply irrespective of where the proposed deponent
    is, and r.34.23 shall not apply in cases where the proposed deponent is in a Regulation
    State within the meaning of s.III of this Part.

PD 34B para.5.1

Where a party wishes to take a deposition from a person outside the jurisdiction, the High Court
may order the issue of a letter of request to the judicial authorities of the country in which the
proposed deponent is.

PD 34B para.5.2

An application for an order referred to in para.5.1 should be made by application notice in
accordance with Pt 23.

PD 34B para.5.3

The documents which a party applying for an order for the issue of a letter of request must file
with his application notice are set out in r.34.13(6). They are as follows:
(1) a draft letter of request in the form set out in Annex A to this practice direction,
(2) a statement of the issues relevant to the proceedings,
(3) a list of questions or the subject matter of questions to be put to the proposed depo-
    nent,
(4) a translation of the documents in (1), (2) and (3) above, unless the proposed deponent is
    in a country of which English is an official language, and
(5) an undertaking to be responsible for the expenses of the Secretary of State.
In addition to the documents listed above the party applying for the order must file a draft
order.

PD 34B para.5.4

The above documents should be filed with the Masters' Secretary in Room E214, Royal Courts
of Justice, Strand, London WC2A 2LL.

PD 34B para.5.5

The application will be dealt with by the Senior Master of the Queen's Bench Division of the
High Court who will, if appropriate, sign the letter of request.

PD 34B para.5.6

Attention is drawn to the provisions of r.23.10 (application to vary or discharge an order made without notice).

PD 34B para.5.7

If parties are in doubt as to whether a translation under para.5.3(4) above is required, they should seek guidance from the Foreign Process Section of the Masters' Secretary's Department.

PD 34B para.5.8

A special examiner appointed under r.34.13(4) may be the British Consul or the Consul-General or his deputy in the country where the evidence is to be taken if:
- (1) there is in respect of that country a Civil Procedure Convention providing for the taking of evidence in that country for the assistance of proceedings in the High Court or other court in this country, or
- (2) with the consent of the Secretary of State.

PD 34B para.5.9

The provisions of paras 4.1 to 4.12 above apply to the depositions referred to in this paragraph.

See **Examiner of the court** and **Foreign courts.**

DERIVATIVE CLAIM

Pt 19 r.19.9

- (1) [Part 19]—
  - (a) applies to a derivative claim (where a company, other body corporate or trade union is alleged to be entitled to claim a remedy, and a claim is made by a member of it for it to be given that remedy), whether under Ch.1 of Pt 11 of the Companies Act 2006 or otherwise; but
  - (b) does not apply to a claim made pursuant to an order under s.996 of that Act.
- (2) A derivative claim must be started by a claim form.
- (3) The company, body corporate or trade union for the benefit of which a remedy is sought must be made a defendant to the claim.
- (4) After the issue of the claim form, the claimant must not take any further step in the proceedings without the permission of the court, other than –
  - (a) a step permitted or required by r.19.9A or 19.9C; or
  - (b) making an urgent application for interim relief.
  - [PD 19 also] —
  - (a) applies to—
    - (i) derivative claims, whether under Ch.1 of Pt 11 of the Companies Act 2006 or otherwise; and
    - (ii) applications for permission to continue or take over such claims; but
  - (b) does not apply to claims in pursuance of an order under s.996 of that Act.

Claim form

PD 19C para.2

(1) A claim form must be headed 'Derivative claim'.
(2) If the claimant seeks an order that the defendant company or other body concerned indemnify the claimant against liability for costs incurred in the permission application or the claim, this should be stated in the permission application or claim form or both, as the case requires.

Derivative claims under Ch.1 of Pt 11 of the Companies Act 2006—application for permission

Pt 19 r.19.9A

(2) When the claim form for a derivative claim is issued, the claimant must file—
    (a) an application notice under Pt 23 for permission to continue the claim; and
    (b) the written evidence on which the claimant relies in support of the permission application.
(3) The claimant must not make the company a respondent to the permission application.
(4) Subject to para.(7), the claimant must notify the company [the company for the benefit of which the derivative claim is brought] of the claim and permission application by sending to the company as soon as reasonably practicable after the claim form is issued—
    (a) a notice in the form set out in PD 19C, and to which is attached a copy of the provisions of the [Companies Act 2006] required by that form;
    (b) copies of the claim form and the particulars of claim;
    (c) the application notice; and
    (d) a copy of the evidence filed by the claimant in support of the permission application [means an application referred to in ss.261(1), 262(2) or 264(2) of the Companies Act 2006].
(5) The claimant may send the notice and documents required by para.(4) to the company by any method permitted by Pt 6 as if the notice and documents were being served on the company.
(6) The claimant must file a witness statement confirming that the claimant has notified the company in accordance with para.(4).
(7) Where notifying the company of the permission application would be likely to frustrate some party of the remedy sought, the court may, on application by the claimant, order that the company need not be notified for such period after the issue of the claim form as the court directs.
(8) An application under para.(7) may be made without notice.
(9) Where the court dismisses the claimant's permission application without a hearing, the court will notify the claimant and (unless the court orders otherwise) the company of that decision.
(10) The claimant may ask for an oral hearing to reconsider the decision to dismiss the permission application, but the claimant—
    (a) must make the request to the court in writing within seven days of being notified of the decision; and
    (b) must notify the company in writing, as soon as reasonably practicable, of that request unless the court orders otherwise.
(11) Where the court dismisses the permission application at a hearing pursuant to para.(10), it will notify the claimant and the company of its decision.
(12) Where the court does not dismiss the application under s.261(2) of the Act, the court will—

(a) order that the company and any other appropriate party must be made respondents to the permission application; and

(b) give directions for the service on the company and any other appropriate party of the application notice and the claim form.

Application for order delaying notice

PD 19C para.3

If the applicant seeks an order under r.19.9A(7) delaying notice to the defendant company or other body concerned, the applicant must also—

(a) state in the application notice the reasons for the application; and

(b) file with it any written evidence in support of the application.

Form to be sent to defendant company or other body

PD 19C para.4

The form required by r.19.9A(4)(a) to be sent to the defendant company or other body is set out at the end of this PD. There are separate versions of the form for claims involving a company, and claims involving a body corporate of another kind or a trade union.

Early intervention by the company

PD 19C para.5

The decision whether the claimant's evidence discloses a prima facie case will normally be made without submissions from or (in the case of an oral hearing to reconsider such a decision reached pursuant to r.19.9A(9)) attendance by the company. If without invitation from the court the company volunteers a submission or attendance, the company will not normally be allowed any costs of that submission or attendance.

(Sections 261, 262 and 264 of the Companies Act 2006 contain provisions about disclosing a prima facie case in applications to continue a derivative claim).

Derivative claims under Ch.1 of Pt 11 of the Companies Act 2006—members of companies taking over claims by companies or other members

Pt 19 r.19.9B

(1) This rule applies to proceedings under ss.262(1) or 264(1) of the Companies Act 2006.

(2) The application for permission must be made by an application notice in accordance with Pt 23.

(3) Rule 19.9A (except for paras (1), (2) and (4)(b) of that rule, and para.(12)(b) so far as it applies to the claim form) applies to an application under this rule and references to the claimant in r.19.9A are to be read as references to the person who seeks to take over the claim.

Other bodies corporate and trade unions

Pt 19 r.19.9C

(1) This rule sets out the procedure where—
  (a) either—
    (i) a body corporate to which Ch.1 of Pt 11 of the Companies Act 2006 does not apply; or
    (ii) a trade union,
  is alleged to be entitled to a remedy; and
  (b) either—
    (i) a claim is made by a member for it to be given that remedy; or
    (ii) a member of the body corporate or trade union seeks to take over a claim already started, by the body corporate or trade union or one or more of its members, for it to be given that remedy.
(2) The member who starts, or seeks to take over, the claim must apply to the court for permission to continue the claim.
(3) The application for permission must be made by an application notice in accordance with Pt 23.
(4) The procedure for applications in relation to companies under ss.261, 262 or 264 (as the case requires) of the Companies Act 2006 applies to the permission application as if the body corporate or trade union were a company.
(5) Rules 19.9A (except for para.(1) of that rule) and 19.9B apply to the permission application as if the body corporate or trade union were a company.

Derivative claims arising in the course of other proceedings

Pt 19 r.19.9D

If a derivative claim (except such a claim in pursuance of an order under s.996 of the Companies Act 2006) arises in the course of other proceedings—
  (a) in the case of a derivative claim under Ch.1 of Pt 11 of that Act, r.19.9A or 19.9B applies, as the case requires; and
  (b) in any other case, r.19.9C applies.

Costs

Pt 19 r.19.9E

The court may order the company, body corporate or trade union for the benefit of which a derivative claim is brought to indemnify the claimant against liability for costs incurred in the permission application or in the derivative claim or both.

Discontinuance and settlement

Pt 19 r.19.9F

Where the court has given permission to continue a derivative claim, the court may order that the claim may not be discontinued, settled or compromised without the permission of the court.

PD 19C para.7

As a condition of granting permission to continue or take over a derivative claim, the court may order that the claim is not to be discontinued, settled or compromised without the court's permission. Such a condition may be appropriate where any future proposal to discontinue or settle might not come to the attention of members who might have an interest in taking over the claim.

PD 19 para.1

Hearing of applications

PD 19C para.6

(1) Where a permission application to which this PD applies is made in the High Court it will be assigned to the Chancery Division and decided by a High Court judge.
(2) Where such an application is made in a county court it will be decided by a circuit judge.

DESIGN RIGHTS

See **Intellectual property claims**.

DESIGNATED CIVIL JUDGES

Senior civil judges to each civil trial centre. They have particular responsibility for promoting an effective and consistent approach to case management by the judicial teams.

DESIGNATED MONEY CLAIM

Pt 2 r.2.3(1)

Any claim which —
(a) is started in a county court under Pt 7 [of CPR];
(b) is only a claim for either or both a specified amount of money or an unspecified amount of money; and
(c) is not a claim for which special procedures are provided in the [CPR].

DESIGNATIONS UNDER THE TERRORIST ASSET-FREEZING ETC ACT 2010

Pt 79 r.79.14A

[Section 3 of Pt 79] applies to an appeal under s.26 of the [Terrorist Asset-Freezing etc Act 2010] (appeals to the court in relation to designations) in relation to designations and variations, revocation and renewal, of those designations.

Modification of Pt 52 (Appeals)

Pt 79 r.79.14B

(1) Part 52 (appeals) applies to an appeal under s.26 of the 2010 Act subject to—
    (a) Rule 79.2;
    (b) Section 4 of [Pt 79]; and
    (c) the modifications set out in para.(2).
(2) Rule 52.2 (parties to comply with PD 52A–52E) apply, but the parties are not required to comply with paras 6.3–6.6 of PD 52B.

Appellant's notice

Pt 79 r.79.14C

(1) The appellant's notice must set out the details of—
    (a) the interim or final designation;
    (b) how the appellant is affected by the interim or final designation; and
    (c) the grounds of the appeal.
(2) The appellant must file and serve the following documents with the appellant's notice—
    (a) a copy of the written notice of the interim or final designation; and
    (b) any evidence, including witness statements in support of the appeal.
(PD 52 contains details about the filing and service of the appellant's notice for statutory appeals).

Appeals to the Court of Appeal

Pt 79 r.79.14D

(1) Part 52 (appeals) applies to an appeal to the Court of Appeal against an order of the High Court under this section subject to—
    (a) Rule 79.2;
    (b) Section 4 of [Pt 79]; and
    (c) Paragraph (2) of this rule.
(2) The appellant must serve a copy of the appellant's notice on any special advocate.

General provisions

See **Financial restrictions proceedings.**

DETAILED ASSESSMENT

Pt 44 r.44.1(1)

The procedure by which the amount of costs is decided by a **costs officer** in accordance with Pt 47.

PD 47 para.5.1

Precedents A, B, C and D in the Schedule of Costs Precedents annexed to PD 47 are model forms of bills of costs to be used for detailed assessments.

Appeals from authorised court officers

See **Authorised court officer**.

Commencement of detailed assessment proceedings

Pt 47 r.47.6

  (1) Detailed assessment proceedings are commenced by the receiving party serving on the paying party—
     (a) notice of commencement in [Form N252]; and
     (b) a copy of the bill of costs.
  (2) The receiving party must also serve a copy of the notice of commencement and the bill on any other relevant persons specified in the PD 47.
  (3) A person on whom a copy of the notice of commencement is served under para.(2) is a party to the detailed assessment proceedings (in addition to the paying party and the receiving party).
(PD 47 deals with—
other documents which the party must file when requesting detailed assessment;
the court's powers where it considers that a hearing may be necessary;
the form of a bill; and
the length of notice which will be given if a hearing date is fixed.)

Relevant person

PD 47 para.5.5

  (1) For the purposes of r. 47.6(2) a 'relevant person' means:
     (a) any person who has taken part in the proceedings which gave rise to the assessment and who is directly liable under an order for costs made against him;
     (b) any person who has given to the receiving party notice in writing that he has a financial interest in the outcome of the assessment and wishes to be a party accordingly;
     (c) any other person whom the court orders to be treated as such.
  (2) Where a party is unsure whether a person is or is not a relevant person, that party may apply to the appropriate office for directions.
  (3) The court will generally not make an order that the person in respect of whom the application is made will be treated as a relevant person, unless within a specified time he

applies to the court to be joined as a party to the assessment proceedings in accordance with Part 19 (Parties and Group Litigation).

Costs PD para.32.9

(1) This paragraph applies where the notice of commencement is to be served outside England and Wales.
(2) The date to be inserted in the notice of commencement for the paying party to send points of dispute is a date (not less than 21 days from the date of service of the notice) which must be calculated by reference to s.IV of Pt 6 as if the notice were a claim form and as if the date to be inserted was the date for the filing of a defence.

Period for commencing detailed assessment proceedings

Pt 47 r.47.7

The following table shows the period for commencing detailed assessment proceedings.

Source of right to detailed assessment	Time by which detailed assessment proceedings must be commenced
Judgment, direction, order, award or other determination	Three months after the date of the judgment etc. Where detailed assessment is stayed pending an appeal, three months after the date of the order lifting the stay
Discontinuance under Pt 38	Three months after the date of service of notice of discontinuance under r.38.3; or three months after the date of the dismissal of application to set the notice of discontinuance aside under r.38.4
Acceptance of an offer to settle under Pt 36	Three months after the date when the right to costs arose

PD 47 para.6.1

The time for commencing the detailed assessment proceedings may be extended or shortened either by agreement (r. 2.11) or by the court (r. 3.1(2)(a)). Any application is to the appropriate office.

PD 47 para.6.2

The detailed assessment proceedings are commenced by service of the documents referred to. Permission to commence assessment proceedings out of time is not required.

Sanction for delay in commencing detailed assessment proceedings

Pt 47 r.47.8

(1) Where the receiving party fails to commence detailed assessment proceedings within the period specified—

(a) in r.47.7; or

(b) by any direction of the court,

the paying party may apply for an order requiring the receiving party to commence detailed assessment proceedings within such time as the court may specify.

(2) On an application under para.(1), the court may direct that, unless the receiving party commences detailed assessment proceedings within the time specified by the court, all or part of the costs to which the receiving party would otherwise be entitled will be disallowed.

(3) If—

(a) the paying party has not made an application in accordance with para.(1); and

(b) the receiving party commences the proceedings later than the period specified in r.47.7,

the court may disallow all or part of the interest otherwise payable to the receiving party under—

 (i) section 17 of the Judgments Act 1838; or

(ii) section 74 of the County Courts Act 1984,

but must not impose any other sanction except in accordance with r.44.14 (powers in relation to misconduct).

(4) Where the costs to be assessed in a detailed assessment are payable out of the Community Legal Service Fund, this rule applies as if the receiving party were the solicitor to whom the costs are payable and the paying party were the Legal Services Commission.

PD 47 para.7

An application for an order under r.47.8 must be made in writing and be issued in the appropriate office. The application notice must be served at least seven days before the hearing.

Hearing

Pt 47 r.47.14

(1) Where points of dispute are served in accordance with [Pt 47], the receiving party must file a request for a detailed assessment hearing within three months of the expiry of the period for commencing detailed assessment proceedings as specified—

(a) in r.47.7; or

(b) by any direction of the court.

(2) Where the receiving party fails to file a request in accordance with para.(2), the paying party may apply for an order requiring the receiving party to file the request within such time as the court may specify.

(3) On an application under para.(2), the court may direct that, unless the receiving party requests a detailed assessment hearing within the time specified by the court, all or part of the costs to which the receiving party would otherwise be entitled will be disallowed.

(4) If—

(a) the paying party has not made an application in accordance with para.(2); and

(b) the receiving party files a request for a detailed assessment hearing later than the period specified in para.(1),

the court may disallow all or part of the interest otherwise payable to the receiving party under—

 (i) section 17 of the Judgments Act 1838; or

(ii) section 74 of the County Courts Act 1984,

but will not impose any other sanction except in accordance with r.44.11 (powers in relation to misconduct).

(5) No party other than—
    (a) the receiving party;
    (b) the paying party; and
    (c) any party who has served points of dispute under r.47.9,
    may be heard at the detailed assessment hearing unless the court gives permission.
(6) Only items specified in the points of dispute may be raised at the hearing, unless the court gives permission.
(PD 47 specifies other documents which must be filed with the request for hearing and the length of notice which the court will give when it fixes a hearing date).

PD 47 para.13

The time for requesting a detailed assessment hearing is within three months of the expiry of the period for commencing detailed assessment proceedings.

PD 47 para.13.1

The request for a detailed assessment hearing must be in Form N258. The request must be accompanied by the [papers in support of the bill of costs as set out in paras 13.2–13.3].

PD 47 para.13.4

On receipt of the request for a detailed assessment hearing the court will fix a date for the hearing, or, if the costs officer so decides, will give directions or fix a date for a preliminary appointment.

PD 47 para.13.6

The court will give at least 14 days' notice of the time and place of the detailed assessment hearing to every person named in the statement referred to in para.13.2(j) above.

PD 47 para.13.7

If either party wishes to make an application in the detailed assessment proceedings the provisions of Pt 23 (General Rules about Applications for Court Orders) apply.

PD 47 para.13.8

(1) This paragraph deals with the procedure to be adopted where a date has been given by the court for a detailed assessment hearing and
    (a) the detailed assessment proceedings are settled; or
    (b) a party to the detailed assessment proceedings wishes to apply to vary the date which the court has fixed; or
    (c) the parties to the detailed assessment proceedings agree about changes they wish to make to any direction given for the management of the detailed assessment proceedings.
(2) If detailed assessment proceedings are settled, the receiving party must give notice of that fact to the court immediately, preferably by fax.
(3) A party who wishes to apply to vary a direction must do so in accordance with Pt 23 (General Rules about Applications for Court Orders).
(4) If the parties agree about changes they wish to make to any direction given for the management of the detailed assessment proceedings—

(a) they must apply to the court for an order by consent; and

(b) they must file a draft of the directions sought and an agreed statement of the reasons why the variation is sought; and

(c) the court may make an order in the agreed terms or in other terms without a hearing, but it may direct that a hearing is to be listed.

PD 47 para.13.10

(1) If a party wishes to vary his bill of costs, points of dispute or a reply, an amended or supplementary document must be filed with the court and copies of it must be served on all other relevant parties.

(2) Permission is not required to vary a bill of costs, points of dispute or a reply but the court may disallow the variation or permit it only upon conditions, including conditions as to the payment of any costs caused or wasted by the variation.

PD 47 para.13.12

Unless the court directs otherwise the receiving party must file with the court the papers in support of the bill not less than seven days before the date for the detailed assessment hearing and not more than 14 days before that date.

PD 47 para.13.13

The court may direct the receiving party to produce any document which in the opinion of the court is necessary to enable it to reach its decision. These documents will in the first instance be produced to the court, but the court may ask the receiving party to elect whether to disclose the particular document to the paying party in order to rely on the contents of the document, or whether to decline disclosure and instead rely on other evidence.

PD 47 para.13.14

Once the detailed assessment hearing has ended it is the responsibility of the receiving party to remove the papers filed in support of the bill.

Provisional assessment

Pt 47 r. 47.15

(1) This rule applies to any detailed assessment proceedings commenced in the High Court or a county court on or after April 1, 2013 in which the costs claimed are the amount set out in para.14.1 of the practice direction supplementing [Pt 47], or less.

(2) In proceedings to which this rule applies, the parties must comply with the procedure set out in Pt 47 as modified by para.14 PD 47.

(3) The court will undertake a provisional assessment of the receiving party's costs on receipt of Form N258 and the relevant supporting documents specified in PD 47.

(4) The provisional assessment will be based on the information contained in the bill and supporting papers and the contentions set out in Precedent G (the points of dispute and any reply).

(5) The court will not award more than £1,500 to any party in respect of the costs of the provisional assessment.

(6) The court may at any time decide that the matter is unsuitable for a provisional assessment and may give directions for the matter to be listed for hearing. The matter will then proceed under r.47.14 without modification.

(7) When a provisional assessment has been carried out, the court will send a copy of the bill, as provisionally assessed, to each party with a notice stating that any party who wishes to challenge any aspect of the provisional assessment must, within 21 days of the receipt of the notice, file and serve on all other parties a written request for an oral hearing. If no such request is filed and served within that period, the provisional assessment shall be binding upon the parties, save in exceptional circumstances.

(8) The written request referred to in para.(7) must—

    (a) identify the item or items in the court's provisional assessment which are sought to be reviewed at the hearing; and

    (b) provide a time estimate for the hearing.

(9) The court then will fix a date for the hearing and give at least 14 days' notice of the time and place of the hearing to all parties.

(10) Any party which has requested an oral hearing, will pay the costs of and incidental to that hearing unless—

    (a) it achieves an adjustment in its own favour by 20 per cent or more of the sum provisionally assessed; or

    (b) the court otherwise orders.

PD 47 para.14.1

The amount of costs referred to in r. 47.15(1) is £75,000.

PD 47 para.14.2

The following provisions of Pt 47 and this Practice Direction will apply to cases falling within r. 47.15—

    (1) rr. 47.1, 47.2, 47.4 to 47.13, 47.14 (except paras (6) and (7)), 47.16, 47.17, 47.20 and 47.21; and

    (2) paras 1, 2, 4 to 12, 13 (with the exception of paras 13.4 to 13.7, 13.9, 13.11 and 13.14), 15, and 16, of [PD 47].

PD 47 para.14.3

In cases falling within r. 47.15, when the receiving party files a request for a detailed assessment hearing, that party must file—

    (a) the request in Form N258;

    (b) the documents set out at paras 8.3 and 13.2 of [PD 47];

    (c) an additional copy of the bill, including a statement of the costs claimed in respect of the detailed assessment drawn on the assumption that there will not be an oral hearing following the provisional assessment;

    (d) the offers made (those marked "without prejudice save as to costs" or made under Pt 36 must be contained in a sealed envelope, marked 'Pt 36 or similar offers', but not indicating which party or parties have made them);

    (e) completed Precedent G (points of dispute and any reply).

PD 47 para.14.4

    (1) On receipt of the request for detailed assessment and the supporting papers, the court will use its best endeavours to undertake a provisional assessment within six weeks. No party will be permitted to attend the provisional assessment.

    (2) Once the provisional assessment has been carried out the court will return Precedent G (the points of dispute and any reply) with the court's decisions noted upon it. Within 14 days of receipt of Precedent G the parties must agree the total sum due to the receiving party on the basis of the court's decisions. If the parties are unable to agree the arithmetic,

they must refer the dispute back to the court for a decision on the basis of written submissions.

PD 47 para.14.5

When considering whether to depart from the order indicated by r. 47.15(10) the court will take into account the conduct of the parties and any offers made.

PD 47 para.14.6

If a party wishes to be heard only as to the order made in respect of the costs of the initial provisional assessment, the court will invite each side to make written submissions and the matter will be finally determined without a hearing. The court will decide what if any order for costs to make in respect of this procedure.

Liability for costs of detailed assessment proceedings

Pt 47 r.47.20

(1) The receiving party is entitled to the costs of the detailed assessment proceedings except where—
   (a) the provisions of any Act, any of these rules or any relevant PD provide otherwise; or
   (b) the court makes some other order in relation to all or part of the costs of the detailed assessment proceedings.
(2) Paragraph (1) does not apply where the receiving party has **pro bono representation** in the detailed assessment proceedings but that party may apply for an order in respect of that representation under s.194(3) of the Legal Services Act 2007.
(3) In deciding whether to make some other order, the court must have regard to all the circumstances, including—
   (a) the conduct of all the parties;
   (b) the amount, if any, by which the bill of costs has been reduced; and
   (c) whether it was reasonable for a party to claim the costs of a particular item or to dispute that item.
(4) The provisions of Pt 36 apply to the costs of detailed assessment proceedings with the following modifications—
   (a) 'claimant' refers to 'receiving party' and 'defendant' refers to 'paying party';
   (b) 'trial' refers to 'detailed assessment hearing';
   (c) in r. 36.9(5), at the end insert 'or, where the Part 36 offer is made in respect of the detailed assessment proceedings, after the commencement of the detailed assessment hearing.';
   (d) for r. 36.11(7) substitute 'If the accepted sum is not paid within 14 days or such other period as has been agreed the offeree may apply for a final costs certificate for the unpaid sum.';
   (e) a reference to 'judgment being entered' is to the completion of the detailed assessment, and references to a 'judgment' being advantageous or otherwise are to the outcome of the detailed assessment.

Offers to settle under Pt 36 or otherwise

PD 47 para.19

Where an offer to settle is made, whether under Pt 36 or otherwise, it should specify whether or not it is intended to be inclusive of the cost of preparation of the bill, interest and VAT. Unless the offer states otherwise it will be treated as being inclusive of these.

Claims to withhold disclosure of a document

Pt 47 r.47.3

> (1) An authorised court officer has all the powers of the court when making a detailed assessment, except—
>> (a) power to make a **wasted costs order** as defined in r. 48.7;
>> (b) power to make an order under—
>>> (i) r. 44.14 (powers in relation to misconduct);
>>> (ii) r. 47.8 (sanction for delay in commencing detailed assessment proceedings);
>>> (iii) para. (2) (objection to detailed assessment by authorised court officer); and
>> (c) power to make a detailed assessment of costs payable to a solicitor by his client, unless the costs are being assessed under r. 48.5 (costs where money is payable to a **child** or **protected party**).
> (2) Where a party objects to the detailed assessment of costs being made by an authorised court officer, the court may order it to be made by a costs judge or a district judge.

Appeal

Costs PD para.47.2

In respect of appeals from authorised court officers, there is no requirement to obtain permission, or to seek written reasons.

Costs PD para.48.1

The appellant must file a notice which should be in Form N161 (an appellant's notice).

Costs PD para.48.2

The appeal will be heard by a costs judge or a district judge of the High Court, and is a re-hearing.

Costs PD para.48.3

The appellant's notice should, if possible, be accompanied by a suitable record of the judgment appealed against. Where reasons given for the decision have been officially recorded by the court an approved transcript of that record should accompany the notice. Photocopies will not be accepted for this purpose. Where there is no official record the following documents will be acceptable:
> (1) The officer's comments written on the bill.
> (2) Advocates' notes of the reasons agreed by the respondent if possible and approved by the authorised court officer.

When the appellant was unrepresented before the authorised court officer, it is the duty of any advocate for the respondent to make his own note of the reasons promptly available, free of charge to the appellant where there is no official record or if the court so directs. Where the appellant was represented before the authorised court officer, it is the duty of his/her own former advocate to make his/her notes available. The appellant should submit the note of the reasons to the costs judge or district judge hearing the appeal.

Costs PD para.48.4

The appellant may not be able to obtain a suitable record of the authorised court officer's decision within the time in which the appellant's notice must be filed. In such cases, the appellant's notice must still be completed to the best of the appellant's ability. It may however be amended subsequently with the permission of the costs judge or district judge hearing the appeal.

Pt 31 r.31.19

(1) A person may apply, without notice, for an order permitting him to withhold disclosure of a document on the ground that disclosure would damage the public interest.
(2) Unless the court orders otherwise, an order of the court under para.(1)—
   (a) must not be served on any other person; and
   (b) must not be open to inspection by any person.

Time when detailed assessment may be carried out

Pt 47 r.47.1

The general rule is that the costs of any proceedings or any part of the proceedings are not to be assessed by the detailed procedure until the conclusion of the proceedings but the court may order them to be assessed immediately.

PD 47 para.1.1

(1) For the purposes of r. 47.1, proceedings are concluded when the court has finally determined the matters in issue in the claim, whether or not there is an appeal, or made an award of **provisional damages** under Pt 41.

PD 47 para.1.2

The court may order or the parties may agree in writing that, although the proceedings are continuing, they will nevertheless be treated as concluded.

PD 47 para.1.3

A party who is served with a notice of commencement (see para.5.2 below) may apply to a costs judge or a district judge to determine whether the party who served it is entitled to commence detailed assessment proceedings. On hearing such an application the orders which the court may make include: an order allowing the detailed assessment proceedings to continue, or an order setting aside the notice of commencement.

PD 47 para.1.4

A costs judge or a district judge may make an order allowing detailed assessment proceedings to be commenced where there is no realistic prospect of the claim continuing.

No stay of detailed assessment where there is an appeal

Pt 47 r.47.2

Detailed assessment is not stayed pending an appeal unless the court so orders.

Costs PD para.29.1

> 2. An application to stay the detailed assessment of costs pending an appeal may be made to the court whose order is being appealed or to the court who will hear the appeal.

Venue

Pt 47 para.47.4

> (1) All applications and requests in detailed assessment proceedings must be made to or filed at the appropriate office.
>
> (PD 47 sets out the meaning of 'appropriate office' in any particular case)
>
> (2) The court may direct that the appropriate office is to be the Costs Office.
> (3) A county court may direct that another county court is to be the appropriate office.
> (4) A direction under para.(3) may be made without proceedings being transferred to that court.
>
> (Rule 30.2 makes provision for any county court to transfer the proceedings to another county court for detailed assessment of costs).

PD 47 para.4.1

> For the purposes of r.47.4(1) the 'appropriate office' means:
>
> (a) the district registry or county court in which the case was being dealt with when the judgment or order was made or the event occurred which gave rise to the right to assessment, or to which it has subsequently been transferred;
> (b) where a tribunal, person or other body makes an order for the detailed assessment of costs, a county court (subject to para.31.1A(1)); or
> (c) in all other cases, including Court of Appeal cases, the Costs Office.

Costs PD para.31.1A

> (1) This paragraph applies where the appropriate office is any of the following county courts:
>
> Barnet, Bow, Brentford, Bromley, Central London, Clerkenwell and Shoreditch, Croydon, Edmonton, Ilford, Kingston, Lambeth, Mayors and City of London, Romford, Uxbridge, Wandsworth, West London, Willesden and Woolwich.
>
> (2) Where this paragraph applies:
>
> (a) the receiving party must file any request for a detailed assessment hearing in the Costs Office and, for all purposes relating to that detailed assessment (other than the issue of default costs certificates and applications to set aside default costs certificates), the Costs Office will be treated as the appropriate office in that case;
> (b) default costs certificates should be issued and applications to set aside default costs certificates should be issued and heard in the relevant county court; and
> (c) unless an order is made under r.47.4(2) directing that the Costs Office as part of the High Court shall be the appropriate office, an appeal from any decision made by a costs judge shall lie to the Designated Civil Judge for the London Group of County Courts or such judge as he shall nominate. The appeal notice and any other relevant papers should be lodged at the Central London Civil Justice Centre.

PD 47 para.4.3

> (1) A direction under r.47.4(2) or (3) specifying a particular court, registry or office as the appropriate office may be given on application or on the court's own initiative.

(2) Unless the Costs Office is the appropriate office for the purposes of r.47.4(1) an order directing that an assessment is to take place at the Costs Office will be made only if it is appropriate to do so having regard to the size of the bill of costs, the difficulty of the issues involved, the likely length of the hearing, the cost to the parties and any other relevant matter.

See also **Agreed costs**, **Costs**, **Bill of costs**, **Default costs certificate**, **Litigants in person**, **LSC funded client**, **Points of dispute**, and **Solicitor**.

DETENTION OF GOODS

Judgment in favour of certain part owners

Pt 40 r.40.14

(2) Where—
(a) a **part owner** makes a claim relating to the detention of the goods; and
(b) the claim is not based on a right to possession,
any judgment or order given or made in respect of the claim is to be for the payment of damages only, unless the claimant had the written authority of every other part owner of the goods to make the claim on his behalf as well as for himself.
(3) This rule applies notwithstanding anything in subs.(3) of s.3 of the Torts (Interference with Goods) Act 1977, but does not affect the remedies and jurisdiction mentioned in subs.(8) of that section.

DEVOLUTION ISSUES

PD DI para.1

Has the same meaning as in para.1 Sch.9 to the Government of Wales Act 2006 para.1 Sch.10 to the Northern Ireland Act 1998; and para.1 Sch.6 to the Scotland Act 1998.

PD DI para.2.1

[PD Devolution Issues] supplements the provisions dealing with devolution issues in the [Government of Wales Act 2006, Northern Ireland Act 1998 and Scotland Act 1998. It deals specifically with the position if a devolution issue arises under the [Government of Wales Act 2006]. If a devolution issue arises under the [Northern Ireland Act 1998] or the [Scotland Act 1998] the procedure laid down in [PD Devolution Issues] should be adapted as required.

Civil proceedings in the county courts and the High Court

PD DI para.16.1

A party wishing to raise a devolution issue must specify in the claim form, or if he is a defendant, in the defence (or written evidence filed with the acknowledgement of service in a Part 8 claim) that the claim raises a devolution issue and the relevant provisions of the [Government of Wales Act 1998].

PD DI para.16.2

The particulars of claim or defence if the devolution issue is raised by the defendant (or written evidence filed with the acknowledgement of service in a Part 8 claim) must contain the facts and circumstances and points of law on the basis of which it is alleged that a devolution issue arises in sufficient detail to enable PD the court to determine whether a devolution issue arises in the proceedings.

PD DI para.16.3

Whether or not the allocation rules apply, if a question is raised during the proceedings that might be a devolution issue, then a directions hearing must take place and the matter must be referred to a circuit judge (in county court actions) or a High Court judge (in High Court actions) for determination as to whether a devolution issue arises and for further directions.

PD DI para.16.4

If a party fails to specify in the appropriate document that a devolution issue arises but that party subsequently wishes to raise a devolution issue, that party must seek the permission of the court.

PD DI para.16.5

Where any party has specified that a devolution issue arises, no default judgment can be obtained.

Judicial review

PD 54A para.5.4

Where the claimant intends to raise a devolution issue, the claim form must:
  (1) specify that the applicant wishes to raise a devolution issue and identify the relevant provisions of the Government of Wales Act 2006, the Northern Ireland Act 1998 or the Scotland Act 1998; and
  (2) contain a summary of the facts, circumstances and points of law on the basis of which it is alleged that a devolution issue arises.

DILAPIDATIONS PROTOCOL

See **Pre-action Protocols**.

DIPLOMATIC AGENT

Pt 12 r.12.11(6)

For the purpose of obtaining default judgment—
  (d) 'Diplomatic agent' has the meaning given by Article 1(e) of Schedule 1 to the Diplomatic Privileges Act 1964.

DIRECTIONS

Court of Appeal

PD 52 para.15.10

To ensure that all requests for directions are centrally monitored and correctly allocated, all requests for directions or rulings (whether relating to listing or any other matters) should be made to the Civil Appeals Office. Those seeking directions or rulings must not approach the supervising Lord Justice either directly, or via his or her clerk.

Part 8 procedure

PD 8A para.4.1

Part 7 and PD 7A contain a number of rules and directions applicable to all claims, including those to which Pt 8 applies. Those rules and directions should be applied where appropriate.

PD 8A para.6.1

The court may give directions immediately a Pt 8 claim form is issued either on the application of a party or on its own initiative. The directions may include fixing a hearing date where—
   (1) there is no dispute, such as in child and protected party settlements; or
   (2) where there may be a dispute, but a hearing date could conveniently be given.

PD 8A para.6.1

The court may give directions immediately a Part 8 claim form is issued either on the application of a party or on its own initiative. The directions may include fixing a hearing date where—
   (1) there is no dispute, such as in child and protected party settlements; or
   (2) where there may be a dispute, but a hearing date could conveniently be given.

PD 8A para.6.2

Where the court does not fix a hearing date when the claim form is issued, it will give directions for the disposal of the claim as soon as practicable after the defendant has acknowledged service of the claim form or, as the case may be, after the period for acknowledging service has expired.

PD 8A para.6.3

Certain applications may not require a hearing.

PD 8A para.6.4

The court may convene a directions hearing before giving directions.

Fast track

Pt 28 r.28.2

(1) When it allocates a case to the fast track, the court will give directions for the management of the case and set a timetable for the steps to be taken between the giving of the directions and the trial.

Pt 28 r.28.3

(1) The matters to be dealt with by directions under r.28.2(1) include—
   (a) disclosure of documents;
   (b) service of witness statements; and
   (c) expert evidence.
(2) If the court decides not to direct standard disclosure, it may—
   (a) direct that no disclosure take place; or
   (b) specify the documents or the classes of documents which the parties must disclose.
(Rule 31.6 explains what is meant by standard disclosure).
(Rule 26.6(5) deals with limitations in relation to expert evidence and the likely length of trial in fast track cases).

Pt 28 r.28.6

(1) As soon as practicable after the date specified for filing a completed pre-trial check list the court will—
   (a) fix the date for the trial (or, if it has already done so, confirm that date);
   (b) give any directions for the trial, including a trial timetable, which it considers appropriate; and
   (c) specify any further steps that need to be taken before trial.
(2) The court will give the parties at least three weeks' notice of the date of the trial unless, in exceptional circumstances, the court directs that shorter notice will be given.

Directions on allocation

PD 28 para.3.1

Attention is drawn to the court's duty under r.28.2(2) to set a case management timetable and to fix a trial date or a trial period, and to the matters which are to be dealt with by directions under r.28.3(1).

PD 28 para.3.2

The court will seek to tailor its directions to the needs of the case and the steps of which it is aware that the parties have already taken to prepare the case. In particular it will have regard to the extent to which PD (Pre-Action Conduct) or any pre-action protocol has or (as the case may be) has not been complied with.

PD 28 para.3.3

At this stage the court's first concern will be to ensure that the issues between the parties be identified and that the necessary evidence is prepared and disclosed.

PD 28 para.3.4

The court may have regard to any document filed by a party with his allocation questionnaire containing further information provided that the document states either that its contents have been agreed with every other party or that it has been served on every other party and when it was served.

PD 28 para.3.5

If:
    (1) the parties have filed agreed directions for the management of the case, and
    (2) the court considers that the proposals are suitable,
it may approve them and give directions in the terms proposed.

PD 28 para.3.6

    (1) To obtain the court's approval the agreed directions must:
        (a) set out a timetable by reference to calendar dates for the taking of steps for the preparation of the case,
        (b) include a date or a period (the trial period) when it is proposed that the trial will take place,
        (c) include provision about disclosure of documents, and
        (d) include provision about both factual and expert evidence.
    (2) The latest proposed date for the trial or the end of the trial period must be not later than 30 weeks from the date the directions order is made.
    (3) The trial period must not be longer than three weeks.
    (4) The provision in (1)(c) above may:
        (a) limit disclosure to standard disclosure between all parties or to less than that, and/ or
        (b) direct that disclosure will take place by the supply of copy documents without a list, but it must in that case either direct that the parties must serve a disclosure statement with the copies or record that they have agreed to disclose in that way without such a statement.
    (5) The provision in (1)(d) may be to the effect that no expert evidence is required.

PD 28 para.3.7

Directions agreed by the parties should also where appropriate contain provisions about:
    (1) the filing of any reply or amended statement of case that may be required,
    (2) dates for the service of requests for further information under PD 18 and questions to experts under r.35.6 and when they are to be dealt with,
    (3) the disclosure of evidence,
    (4) the use of a single joint expert, or in cases where the use of a single expert has not been agreed the exchange and agreement of expert evidence (including whether exchange is to be simultaneous or sequential) and without prejudice discussions of the experts.

PD 28 para.3.8

If the court does not approve the agreed directions filed by the parties but decides that it will give directions on its own initiative without a hearing, it will take them into account in deciding what directions to give.

PD 28 para.3.9

Where the court is to give directions on its own initiative and it is not aware of any steps taken by the parties other than the service of statements of case, its general approach will be:
(1) to give directions for the filing and service of any further information required to clarify either party's case,
(2) to direct standard disclosure between the parties,
(3) to direct the disclosure of witness statements by way of simultaneous exchange,
(4) to give directions for a single joint expert unless there is good reason not to do so,
(5) in cases where directions for a single expert are not given:
   (a) to direct disclosure of experts' reports by way of simultaneous exchange, and
   (b) if experts' reports are not agreed, to direct a discussion between the experts for the purpose set out in r.35.12(1) and the preparation of a report under r.35.12(3).

PD 28 para.3.10

(1) If it appears to the court that the claim is one which will be allocated to the fast track but that it cannot properly give directions on its own initiative or approve agreed directions that have been filed, the court may either:
   (a) allocate the claim to the fast track, fix a trial date or trial period and direct that a case management hearing is to be listed and give directions at that hearing, or
   (b) direct that an allocation hearing is to be listed and give directions at that hearing.
(2) In either case the hearing will be listed as promptly as possible.

PD 28 para.3.11

Where the court is proposing on its own initiative to make an order under r.35.15 (which gives the court power to appoint an assessor), the court must, unless the parties have consented in writing to the order, list a directions hearing.

Variation of directions

PD 28 para.4.1

This paragraph deals with the procedure to be adopted:
(1) where a party is dissatisfied with a direction given by the court,
(2) where the parties agree about changes they wish made to the directions given, or
(3) where a party wishes to apply to vary a direction.

PD 28 para.4.2

(1) It is essential that any party who wishes to have a direction varied takes steps to do so as soon as possible.
(2) The court will assume for the purposes of any later application that a party who did not appeal and who made no application to vary within 14 days of service of the order containing the directions was content that they were correct in the circumstances then exist

PD 28 para.4.3

(1) Where a party is dissatisfied with a direction given or other order made by the court he may appeal or apply to the court for it to reconsider its decision.

(2) He should appeal if the direction was given or the order was made at a hearing at which he was present or represented, or of which he had due notice.
(3) In any other case he should apply to the court to reconsider its decision.
(4) If an application is made for the court to reconsider its decision:
    (a) it will usually be heard by the judge who gave the directions or another judge of the same level,
    (b) the court will give all parties at least three days notice of the hearing, and
    (c) the court may confirm its decision or make a different order.

PD 28 para.4.4

Where there has been a change in the circumstances since the order was made the court may set aside or vary any direction it has given. It may do so on application or on its own initiative.

PD 28 para.4.5

Where the parties agree about changes to be made to the directions given:
(1) If r.2.11 (variation by agreement of a date set by the court for doing any act other than those stated in the note to that rule) or r.31.5, 31.10(8) or 31.13 (agreements about disclosure) applied the parties need not file the written agreement.
(2) (a) In any other case the parties must apply for an order by consent.
    (b) The parties must file a draft of the order sought and an agreed statement of the reasons why the variation is sought.
    (c) The court may make an order in the agreed terms or in other terms without a hearing, but it may direct that a hearing is to be listed.

Failure to comply with case management directions

PD 28 para.5.1

Where a party has failed to comply with a direction given by the court any other party may apply for an order to enforce compliance or for a sanction to be imposed or both of these.

PD 28 para.5.2

The party entitled to apply for such an order must do so without delay but should first warn the other party of his intention to do so.

PD 28 para.5.3

The court may take any such delay into account when it decides whether to make an order imposing a sanction or whether to grant relief from a sanction imposed by the rules or any PD.

PD 28 para.5.4

(1) The court will not allow a failure to comply with directions to lead to the postponement of the trial unless the circumstances of the case are exceptional.
(2) If it is practicable to do so the court will exercise its powers in a manner that enables the case to come on for trial on the date or within the period previously set.
(3) In particular the court will assess what steps each party should take to prepare the case for trial, direct that those steps are taken in the shortest possible time and impose a

sanction for non-compliance. Such a sanction may, for example, deprive a party of the right to raise or contest an issue or to rely on evidence to which the direction relates.

(4) Where it appears that one or more issues are or can be made ready for trial at the time fixed while others cannot, the court may direct that the trial will proceed on the issues which are or will then be ready, and order that no costs will be allowed for any later trial of the remaining issues or that those costs will be paid by the party in default.

(5) Where the court has no option but to postpone the trial it will do so for the shortest possible time and will give directions for the taking of the necessary steps in the meantime as rapidly as possible.

(6) Litigants and lawyers must be in no doubt that the court will regard the postponement of a trial as an order of last resort. The court may exercise its power to require a party as well as his legal representative to attend court at a hearing where such an order is to be sought.

Directions the court will give on listing

PD 28 para.7.1

Directions the court must give:

(1) The court must confirm or fix the trial date, specify the place of trial and give a time estimate. The trial date must be fixed and the case listed on the footing that the hearing will end on the same calendar day as that on which it commenced.

(2) The court will serve a notice of hearing on the parties at least three weeks before the hearing unless they agree to accept shorter notice or the court authorises shorter service under r.28.6(2), and

(3) The notice of hearing will be in Form N172.

PD 28 para.7.2

Other directions:

(1) The parties should seek to agree directions and may file the proposed order. The court may make an order in those terms or it may make a different order.

(2) Agreed directions should include provision about:
   (a) evidence,
   (b) a trial timetable and time estimate,
   (c) the preparation of a **trial bundle**,
   (d) any other matter needed to prepare the case for trial.

(3) The court will include such of these provisions as are appropriate in any order that it may make, whether or not the parties have filed agreed directions.

(4) (a) A direction giving permission to use expert evidence will say whether it gives permission for oral evidence or reports or both and will name the experts concerned.
   (b) The court will not make a direction giving permission for an expert to give oral evidence unless it believes it is necessary in the interests of justice to do so.
   (c) Where no 'without prejudice' meeting or other discussion between experts has taken place the court may grant that permission conditionally on such a discussion taking place and a report being filed before the trial.

PD 28 para.7.3

The principles set out in para.4 of this PD about the variation of directions apply also to directions given at this stage.

Multi-track

Pt 29 r.29.2

(1) When it allocates a case to the multi-track, the court will—
    (a) give directions for the management of the case and set a timetable for the steps to be taken between the giving of directions and the trial.

PD 29 para.4.2

The court will seek to tailor its directions to the needs of the case and the steps which the parties have already taken to prepare the case of which it is aware. In particular it will have regard to the extent to which PD (Pre-Action Conduct) or any pre-action protocol has or (as the case may be) has not been complied with.

PD 29 para 4.5

On the allocation of a claim to the multi-track the court will consider whether it is desirable or necessary to hold a case management conference straight away, or whether it is appropriate instead to give directions on its own initiative.

PD 29 para 4.6

The parties and their advisers are encouraged to try to agree directions and to take advantage of r.29.4 which provides that if:
    (1) the parties agree proposals for the management of the proceedings (including a proposed trial date or period in which the trial is to take place), and
    (2) the court considers that the proposals are suitable,
it may approve them without a hearing and give directions in the terms proposed.

PD 29 para 4.7

(1) To obtain the court's approval the agreed directions must—
    (a) set out a timetable by reference to calendar dates for the taking of steps for the preparation of the case,
    (b) include a date or a period (the trial period) when it is proposed that the trial will take place,
    (c) include provision about disclosure of documents, and
    (d) include provision about both factual and expert evidence.
(2) The court will scrutinise the timetable carefully and in particular will be concerned to see that any proposed date or period for the trial and (if provided for) for a case management conference is no later than is reasonably necessary.
(3) The provision in (1)(c) above may—
    (a) limit disclosure to standard disclosure or less than that, and/or
    (b) direct that disclosure will take place by the supply of copy documents without a list, but it must in that case say either that the parties must serve a disclosure statement with the copies or that they have agreed to disclose in that way without such a statement.
(4) The provision in (1)(d) about expert evidence may be to the effect that none is required.

PD 29 para 4.8

Directions agreed by the parties should also where appropriate contain provisions about:
    (1) the filing of any reply or amended statement of case that may be required,

(2) dates for the service of requests for further information under PD 18 and of questions to experts under r.35.6 and by when they are to be dealt with,

(3) the disclosure of evidence,

(4) the use of a **single joint expert**, or in cases where it is not agreed, the exchange of expert evidence (including whether exchange is to be simultaneous or sequential) and without prejudice discussions between experts.

PD 29 para.4.9

If the court does not approve the agreed directions filed by the parties but decides that it will give directions of its own initiative without fixing a case management conference, it will take them into account in deciding what directions to give.

PD 29 para.4.10

Where the court is to give directions on its own initiative without holding a case management conference and it is not aware of any steps taken by the parties other than the exchange of statements of case, its general approach will be:

(1) to give directions for the filing and service of any further information required to clarify either party's case,

(4) to give directions for a single joint expert on any appropriate issue unless there is a good reason not to do so,

(5) unless para.4.11 (below) applies, to direct disclosure of experts' reports by way of simultaneous exchange on those issues where a single joint expert is not directed,

(6) if experts' reports are not agreed, to direct a discussion between experts for the purpose set out in r.35.12(1) and the preparation of a statement under r.35.12(3),

(7) to list a case management conference to take place after the date for compliance with those directions,

(8) to specify a trial period; and

(9) in such cases as the court thinks appropriate, the court may give directions requiring the parties to consider ADR.

PD 29 para.4.11

If it appears that expert evidence will be required both on issues of liability and on the amount of damages, the court may direct that the exchange of those reports that relate to liability will be exchanged simultaneously but that those relating to the amount of damages will be exchanged sequentially.

PD 29 para.4.12

(1) If it appears to the court that it cannot properly give directions on its own initiative and no agreed directions have been filed which it can approve, the court will direct a case management conference to be listed.

(2) The conference will be listed as promptly as possible.

PD 29 para.9.2

(1) The parties should seek to agree directions and may file an agreed order. The court may make an order in those terms or it may make a different order.

(2) Agreed directions should include provision about:

(a) evidence especially expert evidence,

(b) a trial timetable and time estimate,

(c) the preparation of a trial bundle, and

(d) any other matter needed to prepare the case for trial.
(3) The court will include such of these provisions as are appropriate in any order that it may make, whether or not the parties have filed agreed directions.
(4) Unless a direction doing so has been given before, a direction giving permission to use expert evidence will say whether it gives permission to use oral evidence or reports or both and will name the experts concerned.

PD 29 para.9.3

The principles set out in para.6 of this PD about variation of directions applies equally to directions given at this stage.

Status

Failure to comply

PD 29 para.7.1

Where a party fails to comply with a direction given by the court any other party may apply for an order that he must do so or for a sanction to be imposed or both of these.

PD 29 para.7.2

The party entitled to apply for such an order must do so without delay but should first warn the other party of his intention to do so.

PD 29 para.7.3

The court may take any such delay into account when it decides whether to make an order imposing a sanction or to grant relief from a sanction imposed by the rules or any other PD.

PD 29 para.7.4

(1) The court will not allow a failure to comply with directions to lead to the postponement of the trial unless the circumstances are exceptional.
(2) If it is practical to do so the court will exercise its powers in a manner that enables the case to come on for trial on the date or within the period previously set.
(3) In particular the court will assess what steps each party should take to prepare the case for trial, direct that those steps are taken in the shortest possible time and impose a sanction for non-compliance. Such a sanction may, for example, deprive a party of the right to raise or contest an issue or to rely on evidence to which the direction relates.
(4) Where it appears that one or more issues are or can be made ready for trial at the time fixed while others cannot, the court may direct that the trial will proceed on the issues which are then ready, and direct that no costs will be allowed for any later trial of the remaining issues or that those costs will be paid by the party in default.
(5) Where the court has no option but to postpone the trial it will do so for the shortest possible time and will give directions for the taking of the necessary steps in the meantime as rapidly as possible.

Variation of directions

PD 29 para.6.1

This paragraph deals with the procedure to be adopted:
(1) where a party is dissatisfied with a direction given by the court,
(2) where the parties have agreed about changes they wish made to the directions given, or
(3) where a party wishes to apply to vary a direction.

PD 29 para.6.2

(1) It is essential that any party who wishes to have a direction varied takes steps to do so as soon as possible.
(2) The court will assume for the purposes of any later application that a party who did not appeal, and who made no application to vary within 14 days of service of the order containing the directions, was content that they were correct in the circumstances then existing.

PD 29 para.6.3

(1) Where a party is dissatisfied with a direction given or other order made by the court he may appeal or apply to the court for it to reconsider its decision.
(2) Unless para.6.4 applies, a party should appeal if the direction was given or the order was made at a hearing at which he was present, or of which he had due notice.
(3) In any other case he should apply to the court to reconsider its decision.
(4) If an application is made for the court to reconsider its decision:
   (a) it will usually be heard by the judge who gave the directions or another judge of the same level,
   (b) the court will give all parties at least three days notice of the hearing, and
   (c) the court may confirm its directions or make a different order.

PD 29 para.6.4

Where there has been a change in the circumstances since the order was made the court may set aside or vary a direction it has given. It may do so on application or on its own initiative.

PD 29 para.6.5

Where the parties agree about changes they wish made to the directions given:
(1) If r.2.11 (variation by agreement of a date set by the court for doing any act other than those stated in the note to that rule) or r.31.5, 31.10(8) or 31.13 (agreements about disclosure) applies the parties need not file the written agreement.
(2) (a) In any other case the parties must apply for an order by consent.
   (b) The parties must file a draft of the order sought and an agreed statement of the reasons why the variation is sought.
   (c) The court may make an order in the agreed terms or in other terms without a hearing, but it may direct that a hearing is to be listed.

Power of court to control evidence

Pt 32 r.32.1

(1) The court may control the evidence by giving directions as to—
   (a) the issues on which it requires evidence;

(b) the nature of the evidence which it requires to decide those issues; and

(c) the way in which the evidence is to be placed before the court.

(2) The court may use its power under this rule to exclude evidence that would otherwise be admissible.

(3) The court may limit cross-examination.

Small claims track

Pt 27 r.27.4

(1) After allocation the court will—

   (a) give standard directions and fix a date for the final hearing;

   (b) give special directions and fix a date for the final hearing;

   (c) give special directions and direct that the court will consider what further directions are to be given no later than 28 days after the date the special directions were given;

(3) In this rule—

   (a) 'standard directions' means—

      (i) a direction that each party shall, at least 14 days before the date fixed for the final hearing, file and serve on every other party copies of all documents (including any expert's report) on which he intends to rely at the hearing; and

      (ii) any other standard directions set out in PD 27; and

   (b) 'special directions' means directions given in addition to or instead of the standard directions.

Case management directions

PD 27 para.2.1

Rule 27.4 explains how directions will be given, and r.27.6 contains provisions about the holding of a preliminary hearing and the court's powers at such a hearing.

PD 27 para.2.2

Appendix A sets out details of the case that the court usually needs in the type of case described. Appendix B sets out the Standard Directions that the court may give. Appendix C sets out Special Directions that the court may give.

PD 27 para.2.3

Before allocating the claim to the small claims track and giving directions for a hearing the court may require a party to give further information about that party's case.

PD 27 para.2.4

A party may ask the court to give particular directions about the conduct of the case.

Power of court to add to, vary or revoke directions

Pt 27 r.27.7

The court may add to, vary or revoke directions.

DIRECTIONS QUESTIONNAIRE

Until April 1, 2013 this was named Allocation questionnaire.

Pt 26 r.26.3

   (1) If a defendant files a defence—
     (a) a court officer will—
       (i) provisionally decide the track which appears to be most suitable for the claim;
         and
       (ii) serve on each party a notice of proposed allocation; and
     (b) the notice of proposed allocation will—
       (i) specify any matter to be complied with by the date specified in the notice;
       (ii) require the parties to file a completed directions questionnaire and serve copies on all other parties;
       (iii) state the address of the court or the court office to which the directions questionnaire must be returned;
       (iv) inform the parties how to obtain the directions questionnaire; and
       (v) if a case appears suitable for allocation to the fast track or multi-track, require the parties to file proposed directions by the date specified in the notice.
  (1B) The court will always serve on any unrepresented party the appropriate directions questionnaire.
   (2) Where there are two or more defendants and at least one of them files a defence, the court will serve a notice under paragraph (1)—
     (a) when all the defendants have filed a defence; or
     (b) when the period for the filing of the last defence has expired, whichever is the sooner.
(Rule 15.4 specifies the period for filing a defence)
   (3) If proceedings are automatically transferred under rule 26.2 or rule 26.2A the court in which the proceedings have been commenced—
     (a) will serve the notice of proposed allocation before the proceedings are transferred; and
     (b) will not transfer the proceedings until all parties have complied with the notice or the time for doing so has expired.
   (4) If rule 15.10 or rule 14.5 applies, the court will not serve a notice under rule 26.3(1) until the claimant has filed a notice requiring the proceedings to continue.
   (6) If a notice is served under rule 26.3(1)—
     (a) each party must file at court, and serve on all other parties, the documents required by the notice by no later than the date specified in it; and
     (b) the date specified will be—
       (i) if the notice relates to the small claims track, at least 14 days; or
       (ii) if the notice relates to the fast track or multi-track, at least 28 days, after the date when it is deemed to be served on the party in question.
  (6A) The date for complying with a notice served under rule 26.3(1) may not be varied by agreement between the parties.
   (7) The time when the court serves a directions questionnaire under this rule may be varied by a PD in respect of claims issued by the Production Centre.

(7A) If a claim is a designated money claim and a party does not comply with the notice served under rule 26.3(1) by the date specified—

    (a) the court will serve a further notice on that party, requiring them to comply within 7 days; and

    (b) if that party fails to comply with the notice served under subparagraph (a), the party's statement of case will be struck out without further order of the court.

(8) If a claim is not a designated money claim and a party does not comply with the notice served under rule 26.3(1) by the date specified, the court will make such order as it considers appropriate, including—

    (a) an order for directions;

    (b) an order striking out the claim;

    (c) an order striking out the defence and entering judgment; or

    (d) listing the case for a case management conference.

(9) Where an order has been made under r.26.3(7A)(b) or r.26.3(8) a party who was in default will not normally be entitled to an order for the costs of any application to set aside or vary that order nor of attending any case management conference and will, unless the court thinks it unjust to do so, be ordered to pay the costs that the default caused to any other party.

(Rule 7.10 makes provision for the Production Centre.)

(Rules 6.14 and 6.26 specify when a document is deemed to be served.)

DIRECTOR'S DISQUALIFICATION PROCEEDINGS

See **Disqualification proceedings.**

DISABILITY

See **Child** and **Protected party**.

DISABILITY DISCRIMINATION

See **Discrimination proceedings**.

DISBURSEMENTS

Disbursements not classified as such for VAT purposes

PD 44 para.2.10

(1) Legal representatives often make payments to third parties for the supply of goods or services where no VAT was chargeable on the supply by the third party: for example, the cost of meals taken and travel costs. The question whether legal representatives should include VAT in respect of these payments when invoicing their clients or in claims for costs between litigants should be decided in accordance with this Direction and with the criteria set out in the VAT Guide (Notice 700).

(2) Payments to third parties which are normally treated as part of the legal representative's overheads (for example, postage costs and telephone costs) will not be treated as disbursements. The third party supply should be included as part of the costs of the legal representatives' legal services and VAT must be added to the total bill charged to the client.

(3) Disputes may arise in respect of payments made to a third party which the legal representative shows as disbursements in the invoice delivered to the receiving party. Some payments, although correctly described as disbursements for some purposes, are not classified as disbursements for VAT purposes. Items not classified as disbursements for VAT purposes must be shown as part of the services provided by the legal representative and, therefore, VAT must be added in respect of them whether or not VAT was chargeable on the supply by the third party.

(4) Guidance as to the circumstances in which disbursements may or may not be classified as disbursements for VAT purposes is given in the VAT Guide (Notice 700, para.25.1). One of the key issues is whether the third party supply (i) was made to the legal representative (and therefore subsumed in the onward supply of legal services), or (ii) was made direct to the receiving party (the third party having no right to demand payment from the legal representative, who makes the payment only as agent for the receiving party).

(5) Examples of payments under sub-para.(4)(a) are: travelling expenses, such as an airline ticket, and subsistence expenses, such as the cost of meals, where the person travelling and receiving the meals is the legal representative. The supplies by the airline and the restaurant are supplies to the legal representative, not to the client.

(6) Payments under sub-para.(4)(b) are classified as disbursements for VAT purposes and, therefore, the legal representative need not add VAT in respect of them. Simple examples are payments by a legal representative of court fees and payment of fees to an expert witness.

Road traffic accidents—fixed recoverable costs in costs-only proceedings

PD 45 para.2.10

If the parties agree the amount of the fixed recoverable costs and the only dispute is as to the payment of, or amount of, a disbursement, then proceedings should be issued under r.46.14.

See also **Road traffic accidents**.

DISCLOSURE OF DOCUMENTS

Meaning of disclosure

Pt 31 r.31.2

A party discloses a document by stating that the document exists or has existed.

Meaning of document

Pt 31 r.31.4

In this Part—
'document' means anything in which information of any description is recorded; and
'copy', in relation to a document, means anything onto which information recorded in the document has been copied, by whatever means and whether directly or indirectly.

Disclosure and inspection of documents

Pt 31 r.31.1

(1) Part [31] sets out rules about the disclosure and **inspection of documents**.
(2) This Part applies to all claims except a claim on the **small claims track**.

See also **Standard disclosure**.

Duty of disclosure limited to documents which are or have been in a party's control

Pt 31 r.31.8

(1) A party's duty to disclose documents is limited to documents which are or have been in his control.
(2) For this purpose a party has or has had a document in his control if—
   (a) it is or was in his physical possession;
   (b) he has or has had a right to possession of it; or
   (c) he has or has had a right to inspect or take copies of it.

Disclosure of copies

Pt 31 r.31.9

(1) A party need not disclose more than one copy of a document.
(2) A copy of a document that contains a modification, obliteration or other marking or feature—
   (a) on which a party intends to rely; or
   (b) which adversely affects his own case or another party's case or supports another party's case;
   shall be treated as a separate document.

Duty of disclosure continues during proceedings

Pt 31 r.31.11

(1) Any duty of disclosure continues until the proceedings are concluded.
(2) If documents to which that duty extends come to a party's notice at any time during the proceedings, he must immediately notify every other party.

Disclosure in stages

Pt 31 r.31.13

The parties may agree in writing, or the court may direct, that disclosure or inspection or both shall take place in stages.

Orders for disclosure against a person not a party

Pt 31 r.31.17

(1) This rule applies where an application is made to the court under any Act for disclosure by a person who is not a party to the proceedings.

(2) The application must be supported by evidence.

(3) The court may make an order under this rule only where—

(a) the documents of which disclosure is sought are likely to support the case of the applicant or adversely affect the case of one of the other parties to the proceedings; and

(b) disclosure is necessary in order to dispose fairly of the claim or to save costs.

(4) An Order under this rule must—

(a) specify the documents or the classes of documents which the respondent must disclose; and

(b) require the respondent, when making disclosure, to specify any of those documents—

(i) which are no longer in his control; or

(ii) in respect of which he claims a right or duty to withhold inspection.

(5) Such an Order may—

(a) require the respondent to indicate what has happened to any documents which are no longer in his control; and

(b) specify the time and place for disclosure and inspection.

Rule 78.26 contains rules in relation to the disclosure and inspection of evidence arising out of mediation of certain cross-border disputes.)

Rules not to limit other powers of the court to order disclosure

Pt 31 r.31.18

Rules 31.16 and 31.17 do not limit any other power which the court may have to order—

(a) disclosure before proceedings have started; and

(b) disclosure against a person who is not a party to proceedings.

Subsequent use of disclosed documents and completed Electronic Documents Questionnaires

Pt 31 r.31.22

(1) A party to whom a document has been disclosed may use the document only for the purpose of the proceedings in which it is disclosed, except where—

(a) the document has been read to or by the court, or referred to, at a hearing which has been held in public;

(b) the court gives permission; or

(c) the party who disclosed the document and the person to whom the document belongs agree.

(2) The court may make an order restricting or prohibiting the use of a document which has been disclosed, even where the document has been read to or by the court, or referred to, at a hearing which has been held in public.

(3) An application for such an order may be made—

(a) by a party; or

(b) by any person to whom the document belongs.

(4) For the purpose of this rule, an Electronic Documents Questionnaire which has been completed and served by another party pursuant to PD 31B is to be treated as if it is a document which has been disclosed.

Consequence of failure to disclose documents or permit inspection

Pt 31 r.31.21

A party may not rely on any document which he fails to disclose or in respect of which he fails to permit inspection unless the court gives permission.

Subsequent use of disclosed documents and completed electronic documents questionnaires

Pt 31 r.31.22

(1) A party to whom a document has been disclosed may use the document only for the purpose of the proceedings in which it is disclosed, except where—
    (a) the document has been read to or by the court, or referred to, at a hearing which has been held in public;
    (b) the court gives permission; or
    (c) the party who disclosed the document and the person to whom the document belongs agree.
(2) The court may make an order restricting or prohibiting the use of a document which has been disclosed, even where the document has been read to or by the court, or referred to, at a hearing which has been held in public.
(3) An application for such an order may be made—
    (a) by a party; or
    (b) by any person to whom the document belongs.
(4) For the purpose of this rule, an Electronic Documents Questionnaire which has been completed and served by another party pursuant to PD 31B is to be treated as if it is a document which has been disclosed.

See also **Specific disclosure and inspection**.

Disclosure before proceedings start

Pt 31 r.31.16

(1) This rule applies where an application is made to the court under any Act for disclosure before proceedings have started.
(2) The application must be supported by evidence.
(3) The court may make an order under this rule only where—
    (a) the respondent is likely to be a party to subsequent proceedings;
    (b) the applicant is also likely to be a party to those proceedings;
    (c) if proceedings had started, the respondent's duty by way of standard disclosure, set out in r.31.6, would extend to the documents or classes of documents of which the applicant seeks disclosure; and
    (d) disclosure before proceedings have started is desirable in order to—
        (i) dispose fairly of the anticipated proceedings;

       (ii) assist the dispute to be resolved without proceedings; or

       (iii) save costs.

  (4) An order under this rule must—

     (a) specify the documents or the classes of documents which the respondent must disclose; and

     (b) require him, when making disclosure, to specify any of those documents—

       (i) which are no longer in his control; or

       (ii) in respect of which he claims a right or duty to withhold inspection.

  (5) Such an order may—

     (a) require the respondent to indicate what has happened to any documents which are no longer in his control; and

     (b) specify the time and place for disclosure and inspection.

(Rule 78.26 contains rules in relation to the disclosure and inspection of evidence arising out of mediation of certain cross-border disputes.)

Consequence of failure to disclose expert's report

Pt 35 r.35.13

A party who fails to disclose an expert's report may not use the report at the trial or call the expert to give evidence orally unless the court gives permission.

Use by one party of expert's report disclosed by another

Pt 35 r.35.11

Where a party has disclosed an expert's report, any party may use that expert's report as evidence at the trial.

Financial restrictions decisions and designation under the Terrorist Asset-Freezing etc. Act 2010

Pt 79 r.79.22

Part 31 (disclosure and inspection of documents) do not apply to any proceedings to which [Financial restrictions decisions and designation under the Terrorist Asset-Freezing etc. Act 2010] applies.

See also **Disclosure statement, Electronic disclosure, European procedures, False disclosure statement, Inspection of documents, List of documents, Specific disclosure and inspection,** and **Standard disclosure.**

DISCLOSURE STATEMENT

Pt 31 r.31.10

  (6) A disclosure statement is a statement made by the party disclosing the documents—

     (a) setting out the extent of the search that has been made to locate documents which he is required to disclose;

(b) certifying that he understands the duty to disclose documents; and

(c) certifying that to the best of his knowledge he has carried out that duty.

(7) Where the party making the disclosure statement is a company, firm, association or other organisation, the statement must also—

(a) identify the person making the statement; and

(b) explain why he is considered an appropriate person to make the statement.

(8) The parties may agree in writing—

(a) to disclose documents without making a list; and

(b) to disclose documents without the disclosing party making a disclosure statement.

(9) A disclosure statement may be made by a person who is not a party where this is permitted by a relevant PD.

PD 31A para.4.1

A list of documents must (unless r.31.10(8)(b) applies) contain a disclosure statement complying with r.31.10. The form of disclosure statement is set out in the Annex to this PD.

PD 31A para.4.2

The disclosure statement should:

(1) expressly state that the disclosing party believes the extent of the search to have been reasonable in all the circumstances, and

(2) in setting out the extent of the search (see r.31.10(6)) draw attention to any particular limitations on the extent of the search which were adopted for proportionality reasons and give the reasons why the limitations were adopted, e.g. the difficulty or expense that a search not subject to those limitations would have entailed or the marginal relevance of categories of documents omitted from the search.

PD 31A para.4.3

Where r.31.10(7) applies, the details given in the disclosure statement about the person making the statement must include his name and address and the office or position he holds in the disclosing party or the basis upon which he makes the statement on behalf of the party.

PD 31A para.4.4

If the disclosing party has a **legal representative** acting for him, the legal representative must endeavour to ensure that the person making the disclosure statement (whether the disclosing party or, in a case to which r.31.10(7) applies, some other person) understands the duty of disclosure under Pt 31.

PD 31A para.4.5

If the disclosing party wishes to claim that he has a right or duty to withhold a document, or part of a document, in his list of documents from inspection (see r.31.19(3)), he must state in writing:

(1) that he has such a right or duty, and

(2) the grounds on which he claims that right or duty.

PD 31A para.4.6

The statement referred to in para.4.5 above should normally be included in the disclosure statement and must indicate the document, or part of a document, to which the claim relates.

PD 31A para.4.7

An insurer or the Motor Insurers' Bureau may sign a disclosure statement on behalf of a party where the insurer or the Motor Insurers' Bureau has a financial interest in the result of proceedings brought wholly or partially by or against that party. Rule 31.10(7) and para.4.3 above shall apply to the insurer or the Motor Insurers' Bureau making such a statement.

See **False disclosure statement.**

DISCONTINUANCE

Pt 38 r.38.1

(1) The rules in this Part set out the procedure by which a claimant may discontinue all or part of a claim.
(2) A claimant who—
    (a) claims more than one remedy; and
    (b) subsequently abandons his claim to one or more of the remedies but continues with his claim for the other remedies,
is not treated as discontinuing all or part of a claim for the purposes of this Part.
(The procedure for amending a statement of case, set out in Pt 17, applies where a claimant abandons a claim for a particular remedy but wishes to continue with his claim for other remedies).

Right to discontinue claim

Pt 38 r.38.2

(1) A claimant may discontinue all or part of a claim at any time.
(2) However—
    (a) a claimant must obtain the permission of the court if he wishes to discontinue all or part of a claim in relation to which—
        (i) the court has granted an interim injunction; or
        (ii) any party has given an undertaking to the court;
    (b) where the claimant has received an interim payment in relation to a claim (whether voluntarily or pursuant to an order under Pt 25), he may discontinue that claim only if—
        (i) the defendant who made the interim payment consents in writing; or
        (ii) the court gives permission;
    (c) where there is more than one claimant, a claimant may not discontinue unless—
        (i) every other claimant consents in writing; or
        (ii) the court gives permission.
(3) Where there is more than one defendant, the claimant may discontinue all or part of a claim against all or any of the defendants.

Procedure for discontinuing

Pt 38 r.38.3

(1) To discontinue a claim or part of a claim, a claimant must—
    (a) file a notice of discontinuance; and

(b) serve a copy of it on every other party to the proceedings.
(2) The claimant must state in the notice of discontinuance which he files that he has served notice of discontinuance on every other party to the proceedings.
(3) Where the claimant needs the consent of some other party, a copy of the necessary consent must be attached to the notice of discontinuance.
(4) Where there is more than one defendant, the notice of discontinuance must specify against which defendants the claim is discontinued.

Right to apply to have notice of discontinuance set aside

Pt 38 r.38.4

(1) Where the claimant discontinues under r.38.2(1) the defendant may apply to have the notice of discontinuance set aside.
(2) The defendant may not make an application under this rule more than 28 days after the date when the notice of discontinuance was served on him.

When discontinuance takes effect where permission of the court is not needed

Pt 38 r.38.5

(1) Discontinuance against any defendant takes effect on the date when notice of discontinuance is served on him under r.38.3(1).
(2) Subject to r.38.4, the proceedings are brought to an end as against him on that date.
(3) However, this does not affect proceedings to deal with any question of costs.

Liability for costs

Pt 38 r.38.6

(1) Unless the court orders otherwise, a claimant who discontinues is liable for the costs which a defendant against whom the claimant discontinues incurred on or before the date on which notice of discontinuance was served on the defendant.
(2) If proceedings are only partly discontinued—
    (a) the claimant is liable under para.(1) for costs relating only to the part of the proceedings which he is discontinuing; and
    (b) unless the court orders otherwise, the costs which the claimant is liable to pay must not be assessed until the conclusion of the rest of the proceedings.
(3) This rule does not apply to claims allocated to the small claims track.
(Rule 44.12 provides for the basis of assessment where the right to costs arises on discontinuance and contains provisions about when a costs order is deemed to have been made and applying for an order under s 194(3) of the Legal Services Act 2007).

Discontinuance and subsequent proceedings

Pt 38 r.38.7

A claimant who discontinues a claim needs the permission of the court to make another claim against the same defendant if—

(a) he discontinued the claim after the defendant filed a defence; and
(b) the other claim arises out of facts which are the same or substantially the same as those relating to the discontinued claim.

Stay of remainder of partly discontinued proceedings where costs not paid

Pt 38 r.38.8

(1) This rule applies where—
    (a) proceedings are partly discontinued;
    (b) a claimant is liable to—
        (i) pay costs under r.38.6; or
        (ii) make a payment pursuant to an order under s.194(3) of the Legal Services Act 2007; and
    (c) the claimant fails to pay those costs or make the payment within 14 days of—
        (i) the date on which the parties agreed the sum payable by the claimant; or
        (ii) the date on which the court ordered the costs to be paid or the payment to be made.
(2) Where this rule applies, the court may stay the remainder of the proceedings until the claimant pays the whole of the costs which the claimant is liable to pay under r.38.6 or makes the payment pursuant to an order under s.194(3) of the Legal Services Act 2007.

(Rules 44.3C and 44.12 contain provisions about applying for an order under s.194(3) of the Legal Services Act 2007).

DISCOVERY OF DOCUMENTS

See **Disclosure of documents**.

DISCRIMINATION PROCEEDINGS

PD—Proceedings under enactments relating to Discrimination, para.1.1

This PD applies to certain county court proceedings under the enactments defined in para.1.2.

PD—Discrimination, para.1.2

    (a) Sex Discrimination Act 1975;
    (b) Race Relations Act 1976;
    (c) Disability Discrimination Act 1995;
    (d) Equality Act 2006;
    (e) Employment Equality (Religion or Belief) Regulations 2003;
    (f) Employment Equality (Sexual Orientation) Regulations 2003;
    (g) Employment Equality (Age) Regulations 2006;
    (h) Equality Act (Sexual Orientation) Regulations 2007.
(2) Where it applies to proceedings under the [Race Relations Act 1976], 'court' means a designated county court under s.67(1) of that Act.

Commission to be given notice of claims

PD—Discrimination para.2.1

This paragraph applies to claims under—
- (a) section 66 of the [Sex Discrimination Act 1975];
- (b) section 57 of the [Race Relations Act 1976];
- (c) section 25 of the [Disability Discrimination Act 1995];
- (d) section 66 of the [Equality Act 2006];
- (e) regulation 39 of the [Employment Equality (Age) Regulations 2006];
- (f) regulation 31 of the [Employment Equality (Religion or Belief) Regulations 2003];
- (g) regulation 31 of the [the Employment Equality (Sexual Orientation) Regulations 2003]; or
- (h) regulation 20 of the [Equality Act (Sexual Orientation) Regulations 2007].

PD—Discrimination para.2.2

When a claim to which this paragraph applies is commenced, the claimant must—
- (a) give notice of the commencement of the proceedings to the Commission [for Equality and Human Rights];
- (b) file a copy of that notice.

Assessors

PD—Discrimination para.3

Rule 35.15 has effect in relation to an **assessor** who is to be appointed in proceedings under s.66(1) of the 1975 Act.

Admissibility of evidence

PD—Discrimination para.4.1

This paragraph applies where a claimant in a claim alleging discrimination has questioned the defendant under—
- (a) section 74 of the [Sex Discrimination Act 1975];
- (b) section 65 of the [Race Relations Act 1976];
- (c) section 56 of the [Disability Discrimination Act 1995];
- (d) regulation 41 of the Age Regulations [means the Employment Equality (Age) Regulations 2006];
- (e) regulation 33 of the Religion or Belief Regulations; or
- (f) regulation 33 of the Sexual Orientation Regulations 2003;
- (g) section 70 of the 2006 Act; or
- (h) regulation 24 of the Sexual Orientation Regulations 2007.

PD—Discrimination para.4.2

Either party may apply to the court to determine whether the question or any reply is admissible under that section.
(Part 23 contains general rules about making applications).

PD—Discrimination para.4.3

Rule 3.4 (power to strike out a statement of case) applies to the question and any answer as it applies to a statement of case.

Exclusion of persons from certain proceedings

PD—Discrimination para.5.1

In a claim—
  (1) brought under s.66(1) of the 1975 Act;
  (2) brought under s.57(1) of the 1976 Act;
  (3) alleging discrimination under the 1995 Act;
  (4) brought under s.66 of the 2006 Act; or
  (5) brought under reg.20 of the Sexual Orientation Regulations 2007,
    the court may, where it considers it expedient in the interests of **national security**—
    (a) exclude from all or part of the proceedings—
        (i) the claimant;
        (ii) the claimant's representatives; or
        (iii) any assessors
(Section 67(4) of the 1976 Act allows an assessor to be appointed in proceedings under that Act);
    (b) permit a claimant or representative to make a statement to the court before the start of the proceedings (or the part of the proceedings) from which he is excluded; or
    (c) take steps to keep secret all or part of the reasons for its decision in the claim.

PD—Discrimination para.5.2

In this paragraph, a **'special advocate'** means a person appointed under—
  (1) section 66B(2) of the 1975 Act;
  (2) section 67A(2) of the 1976 Act;
  (3) section 59A(2) of the 1995 Act;
  (4) section 71(2) of the 2006 Act to represent the claimant; and
  (5) regulation 25(2) of the Sexual Orientation Regulations 2007.

PD—Discrimination para.5.3

In proceedings to which this paragraph refers, where the claimant or his representatives have been excluded from all or part of the proceedings—
  (a) the court will inform the Attorney-General of the proceedings; and
  (b) the Attorney-General may appoint a special advocate to represent the claimant in respect of those parts of the proceedings from which he or his representative have been excluded.

PD—Discrimination para.5.4

In exercise of its powers under para.5.1(c), the court may order the special advocate not to communicate (directly or indirectly) with any persons (including the excluded claimant)—
  (a) on any matter discussed or referred to; or
  (b) with regard to any material disclosed,
during or with reference to any part of the proceedings from which the claimant or his representative are excluded.

PD—Discrimination para.5.5

Where the court makes an order referred to in para.5.4 (or any similar order), the special advocate may apply to the court for directions enabling him to seek instructions from, or otherwise to communicate with an excluded person.

Expenses of commission

PD—Discrimination para.6.1

This paragraph applies where the Commission has, in respect of a claim, provided a claimant with assistance under s.28 of the 2006 Act.

PD—Discrimination para.6.2

If the Commission claim a charge for expenses incurred by it in providing such assistance, it must give notice of the claim to—
  (a) the court; and
  (b) the claimant,
within 14 days of determination of the proceedings.

PD—Discrimination para.6.3

If notice is given to the court under para.6.2—
  (a) money paid into court for the benefit of the claimant that relates to costs and expenses must not be paid out unless this is permitted by an order of the court; and
  (b) the court may order the expenses incurred by the Commission to be assessed as if they were costs payable by the claimant to his own solicitor for work done in connection with the proceedings.

PD—Discrimination para.6.4

The court may either—
  (a) make a summary assessment of the expenses; or
  (b) order detailed assessment of the expenses by a costs officer.

DISEASE AND ILLNESS CLAIMS

See **Pre-action protocols**.

DISPOSAL OF CLAIMS

See **Summary judgment**.

DISPUTING THE COURT'S JURISDICTION

See **Jurisdiction**.

DIVISIONAL COURT

Part of the Queen's Bench Division of the High Court.

Some matters are required by statute or rules of Court to be heard by a Divisional Court (ie a court of two or more judges):

1. Applications for committal for contempt where the contempt (a) is committed in connection with (i) proceedings before a QB Divisional Court, (ii) criminal proceedings (except where it is in the face of the court or disobedience to an order), (iii) proceedings in an inferior court or (b) is committed otherwise than in any proceedings
2. Appeals from the Law Society Disciplinary Tribunal. Such appeals are heard by a three judge court unless the Lord Chief Justice otherwise directs. By convention these appeals are heard by a Court presided over by the Lord Chief Justice
3. Applications under s.13 of the Coroners Act 1988 (with fiat of the Attorney General)
4. Applications for **vexatious litigant** orders under s.42 of the Senior Courts Act 1981
5. Applications relating to parliamentary and local government elections under the Representation of the People Acts (unless exercisable by a single judge by express statutory provision).

Others can be and usually are heard by a Divisional Court:

1. Applications for judicial review in a criminal cause or matter;
2. Applications for leave to apply for judicial review in a criminal cause or matter, after refusal by a single judge (whether on paper or after oral argument);
3. Appeals by way of case stated in a criminal cause or matter, whether from the Crown Court or from a magistrates court.

DIVORCE

Appeal against decree nisi of divorce or nullity of marriage or conditional dissolution or nullity order in relation to civil partnership

PD 52D para.6.1

(1) The appellant must file the appellant's notice at the Court of Appeal within 28 days after the date on which the decree was pronounced or conditional order made.
(2) The appellant must file the following documents with the appellant's notice—
    (a) the decree or conditional order; and
    (b) a certificate of service of the appellant's notice.
(3) The appellant's notice must be served on the appropriate district judge (see sub-para.(6)) in addition to the persons to be served under r.52.4(3) and in accordance with that rule.
(4) The lower court may not alter the time limits for filing of the appeal notices.
(5) Where an appellant intends to apply to the Court of Appeal for an extension of time for serving or filing the appellant's notice he must give notice of that intention to the appropriate district judge (see subpara.6) before the application is made.
(6) In this paragraph 'the appropriate district judge' means, where the lower court is—
    (a) a county court, the district judge of that court;
    (b) a district registry, the district judge of that registry;
    (c) the Principal Registry of the Family Division, the senior district judge of that division.

DOCUMENT

Pt 31 r.31.4

In [Part 31][**disclosure of documents**]—
  'document' means anything in which information of any description is recorded; and
  'copy', in relation to a document, means anything onto which information recorded in the
  document has been copied, by whatever means and whether directly or indirectly.

See also **Electronic disclosure**.

DOCUMENT EXCHANGE

Pt 6 r.6.3

  (1) A claim form may be served by any of the following methods—
  (b) document exchange in accordance with PD 6A

P6 r.6.20(b)

  (1) A document may be served by any of the following methods—
  (b) document in accordance with PD 6A.

PD 6A para.2.1

Service by document exchange (DX) may take place only where—
  (1) the address at which the party is to be served includes a numbered box at a DX, or
  (2) the writing paper of the party who is to be served or of the solicitor acting for that party
    sets out a DX box number, and
  (3) the party or the solicitor acting for that party has not indicated in writing that they are
    unwilling to accept service by DX.

PD 6A para.3.1

Service DX is effected by—
  (1) placing the document in a post box.

See **Service of documents**.

DOMICILE

Pt 12 r.12.11(6)(a)

  (a) determined—
    (i) in relation to a Convention territory, in accordance with ss.41 to 46 of the Civil
       Jurisdiction and Judgments Act 1982;
    (ii) in relation to a Member State, in accordance with the Judgments Regulation and
       paras 9 to 12 of Sch.1 to the Civil Jurisdiction and Judgments Order 2001.

DRINKING BANNING ORDER

Pt 65 r.65.31

(1) [Section VI of Pt 65] applies to applications in proceedings in a county court under sub-ss.(2), (3) or (5) of s.4 of the Violent Crime Reduction Act 2006 by a relevant authority, and to applications for interim orders under s.9 of that Act.

Application where the relevant authority is a party in principal proceedings

Pt 65 r.65.32

(1) Subject to para.(2)—
   (a) where the relevant authority [has the same meaning as in s.14(1) of the 2006 Act] is the claimant in the principal proceedings [means any proceedings in a county court], an application under s.4(2) of the 2006 Act for an order under s.4(7) of the [Violent Crime Reduction Act 2006] must be made in the claim form; and
   (b) where the relevant authority is a defendant in the principal proceedings, an application for an order must be made by application notice which must be filed with the defence.
(2) Where the relevant authority becomes aware of the circumstances that lead it to apply for an order after its claim is issued or its defence filed, the application must be made by application notice as soon as possible thereafter.
(3) Where the application is made by application notice, it should normally be made on notice to the person against whom the order is sought.

Application where the relevant authority is not a party in principal proceedings

Pt 65 r.65.33

(1) Where the relevant authority is not a party to the principal proceedings—
   (a) an application under s.4(3) of the 2006 Act to be made a party must be made in accordance with s.I of Pt 19; and
   (b) the application to be made a party and the application for an order under s.4(7) of the 2006 Act must be made in the same application notice.
(2) The applications—
   (a) must be made as soon as possible after the relevant authority becomes aware of the principal proceedings; and
   (b) should normally be made on notice to the person against whom the order is sought.

Application by a relevant authority to join a person to the principal proceedings

Pt 65 r.65.34

(1) An application under s.4(5) of the 2006 Act by a relevant authority which is a party to the principal proceedings to join a person to the principal proceedings must be made—

  (a) in accordance with s.I of Pt 19;
  (b) in the same application notice as the application for an order under s.4(7) of the 2006
      Act against the person; and
  (c) as soon as possible after the relevant authority considers that the criteria in s.4(4) of
      the 2006 Act are met.
(2) The application notice must contain—
  (a) the relevant authority's reasons for claiming that the person's conduct is material in
      relation to the principal proceedings; and
  (b) details of the conduct alleged.
(3) The application should normally be made on notice to the person against whom the order
    is sought.

PD 65 para.15.2

An application by a relevant authority under s.4(5) of the 2006 Act to join a person to the
principal proceedings may only be made against a person aged 18 or over.

Evidence

Pt 65 r.65.35

An application for an order under s.4(7) of the 2006 Act must be accompanied by written
evidence, which must include evidence that s.4(6) of the 2006 Act has been complied with.

Application for an interim order

Pt 65 r.65.36

(1) An application for an interim order under s.9 of the 2006 Act must be made in
    accordance with Pt 25.
(2) The application should normally be made—
  (a) in the claim form or application notice seeking the order; and
  (b) on notice to the person against whom the order is sought.
(3) An application for an interim order may be—
  (a) made without a copy of the application notice being served on the person against
      whom the order is sought;
  (b) heard in the absence of the person against whom the order is sought,
  with the permission of the court.

Service of an order under ss.4(7) or 9 of the 2006 Act

PD 65 para.15.1

An order under s.4(7) or an interim order under s.9 of the 2006 Act must be served personally
on the defendant.

Bail application

PD 65 para.4A.1

The following paragraphs of s.I of [PD 65] apply in relation to an application for bail by a person arrested under a power of arrest attached to an injunction under s.27 of the 2006 Act—
    (1) paragraph 3.1(1), as if a reference to Ch.III of Pt V of the Housing Act 1996 was a reference to s.27 of the 2006 Act;
    (2) paragraph 3.2; and
    (3) paragraph 3.3.

Remand for medical examination and report

PD 65 para.4A.2

Paragraph 4.1 of s.I of [PD 65] applies in relation to s.27 of the 2006 Act, as if a reference in para.4.1 to s.156(4) of the Housing Act 1996 was a reference to s.27(11) of the 2006 Act.

Allocation of case

PD 2B para.8.1A

A District Judge has jurisdiction to make an order under—
    (3) sections 4 or 9 of the Violent Crime Reduction Act 2006 (**drinking banning orders**).

See **Housing Act 1996 Injunction**.

DRUG TRAFFICKING ACT 1994

See **Confiscation and forfeiture**.

DX

See **Document exchange**.

E

E-MAIL

Communications and documents which may be sent by e-mail

PD 5B para.3.1

Subject to para.3.2, a party to a claim in a specified court may send a specified document to the court by e-mail.
- (1) a specified court is a court or court office which has published an e-mail address for the filing of documents on Her Majesty's Courts and Tribunals Service website; and
- (2) a specified document is a document listed on Her Majesty's Courts and Tribunals Service website as a document that may be sent to or filed in that court by e-mail.

PD 5B para.3.2

Subject to para.3.2A, a party must not use e-mail to take any step in a claim for which a fee is payable.

PD 5B para.3.2A

A party may make an application using e-mail in the Preston Combined Court, where he is permitted to do so by PREMA (Preston E-mail Application Service) User Guide and Protocols.

PD 5B para.3.3

Subject to para.3.3A and para.15.1A of Practice Direction 52, if—
- (a) a fee is payable on the filing of a particular document; and
- (b) a party purports to file that document by e-mail,
the court shall treat the document as not having been filed.

PD 5B para.3.3A

A party may file by e-mail an application notice in the Preston Combined Court where permitted to do so by PREMA (Preston E-mail Application Service) User Guide and Protocols.
(Paragraph 15.1A of PD 52 provides for filing by e-mail an appeal notice or application notice in proceedings in the Court of Appeal, Civil Division).
(Rules 6.3(1)(d) and 6.20(1)(d) permit service by e-mail in accordance with the relevant practice direction. Rule 6.23(6) and para.4 of PD 6A set out the circumstances in which a party may serve a document by e-mail).

Technical specifications of e-mail

PD 5B para.4.1

The e-mail message must contain the name, telephone number and e-mail address of the sender and should be in plain text or rich text format rather than HTML.

PD 5B para.4.2

Correspondence and documents may be sent as either text in the body of the e-mail, or as attachments, except as mentioned in para.4.3.

PD 5B para.4.3

Documents required to be in a practice form must be sent in that form as attachments.

PD 5B para.4.4

Court forms may be downloaded from Her Majesty's Courts and Tribunals Service website.

PD 5B para.4.5

Attachments must be sent in a format supported by the software used by the specified
Court to which it is sent. The format or formats which may be used in sending attachments to a particular specified court are listed in Her Majesty's Courts and Tribunals Service website.

PD 5B para.4.6

An attachment which is sent to a specified court in a format not listed on Her Majesty's Courts and Tribunals Service website as appropriate for the court will be treated as not having been received by the court.

PD 5B para.4.7

The length of attachments and total size of e-mail must not exceed the maximum which
A particular specified court has indicated that it can accept. This information is listed on Her Majesty's Courts and Tribunals Service website.

PD 5B para.4.8

Where proceedings have been commenced, the subject line of the e-mail must contain the following information—
   (1) the case number;
   (2) the parties' names (abbreviated if necessary); and
   (3) the date and time of any hearing to which the e-mail relates.

E-mail guidance

September 2012

What you can file by e-mail

You are responsible for the security of the information you are sending and therefore you must assess its sensitivity and whether e-mail is a secure enough method of communication.

If you are filing a document by e-mail that contains a statement of truth you are reminded that you should retain the document containing the original signature. The version of the document which is filed by e-mail must satisfy one of the following requirements:

(a) the name of the person who has signed the statement of truth is typed underneath the statement:

or

(b) the person who has signed the statement of truth has applied a facsimile of his signature to the statement in the document by mechanical means; or (c) the document that is filed is a scanned version of the document containing the signed original statement of truth.

Below is a list of the work that will be accepted by the court if filed by e-mail in accordance with PD 5B.

Pre-trial check list (listing questionnaire), provided that no fee is payable by the party filing the check list (N170)

Allocation questionnaire, provided that no fee is payable by the party filing the questionnaire; (N150)

Particulars of claim (after filing of claim form)

Request for judgment in default under r.12.4(1) or for judgment upon admission under r.14.4(3), 14.5(6), 14.6(4) or 14.7(5) (N225)

Acknowledgement of service (N9)

Claimant's response to notice of admission under r.14.5(3) or r.14.7(3); (N225A)

Claimant's response to notice under r.15.10, where defence is that money claimed has been paid (N236)

Defence, provided that no counterclaim is made (N9B)

Notice of discontinuance, provided that the claimant does not require permission to discontinue, and is not required to attach to the notice the consent of another party (N279)

Reply to defence

Re-issue/amend process, no hearing (provided that no fee is payable) (N446)

Re-issue/amend process, hearing (provided that no fee is payable) (N446)

Claimant/Defendant List of Documents (provided documents comply with 3.5 of PD 5B) (N265)

Notice of Admission (ROG) (N228)

Admission of Liability (unspecified amount) (N226)

Amended Defence

Part Admission not accepted (N225A)

Intention to proceed with states paid defence

Request for Interlocutory Judgment (provided that no fee is payable) (N277)

Notice of acceptance and request for payment (N243A)

Application to claimant to vary judgment (N294)

Request for Certificate of Judgment (N293A)

Notice by solicitor of acting (N434)

Certificate of service (N215)

Statement of witness (provided the document is no more than 10 pages and the total size of the e-mail does not exceed 2Mb as set out in 3.5 of PD 5B)

Claimant/Defendant List of Documents (provided documents comply with 3.5 of PD 5B) (N265)

Experts Reports
Notice of change of address
Notice of change of solicitor
List of documents (265)
Skeleton arguments/case summaries
Draft judgments/orders and editorial suggestions for them
Any document which the court has specifically directed to be filed by e mail

You may also correspond with the court by e-mail, making general enquiries about the progress of a case, or providing information to the court, for example:

Information for the bailiff

Confirmation of appointments
Listing information such as dates to avoid
Chasing up replies

If you choose to send a document to the court via e-mail please do not send again via fax or post.

What you cannot file by e-mail

A party, save for public law proceedings issued by a Local Authority, must not use e-mail to take any step in a claim which requires a fee to be paid. If a party sends a document by e-mail for which a fee is payable upon filing, the document will be treated as not having been filed.

Anything in Insolvency or Adoption proceedings
Anything that does not meet the requirements of PD 5B.

What the court can send via e-mail

Generally the courts will only use e-mail for limited correspondence including requests for availability dates for hearings, issues concerning reports and general enquiries on specific proceedings. Where technology allows courts will endeavour to send out court orders via e-mail however at this time our systems do not generally allow us to place the court seal on system generated orders and therefore use of this will be limited.

Which address to send e-mails
E-mail addresses for courts are displayed on Courtfinder.

If you case is being handled at an HMCTS Business Centre the relevant e-mail contacts will be communicated to you on issue of proceedings at the centre and should be used whilst proceedings remain with the Business Centre.

Do not use personal e-mail addresses for court staff or judiciary, including legal advisers unless the judge or legal adviser has directed or a local protocol is in place. Please ensure the business e-mail address of the hearing centre concerned is also copied into the correspondence in any event.

Form and content of e-mails

When you e-mail the court the subject line of your mail must contain (in the following order):

The claim number
The title of the claim (abbreviated if necessary)

The subject matter (e.g. defence)

If relating to a hearing the date and time of hearing

The judge or legal advisers name, where the correspondence/document is for their attention

Your message should also contain the name, telephone number and e-mail address of the sender. If you e-mail us we will normally send any reply to you by e-mail.

Correspondence and documents may be sent as either text or attachments. Where there is a practice form, it must be sent in that form by attachment.

Attachments must be in one of the following formats and the complete e-mail (including any attachment(s)) must not exceed 10Mb.

Document file types

Rich Text Format files (.rtf)

Plain/Formatted Text files (.txt)

Hypertext documents files (.htm)

Microsoft Word viewer/reader files (.doc) minimum Word '97 format

Adobe Acrobat files (.pdf) minimum viewer version 4

Spreadsheet file types

Hypertext document files (.htm)

Delimited files (.csv)

Presentation file types

Hypertext document files (.htm)

General and compressed file types

Zipped (Compressed) files (.zip, .gz, .tgz, .tar)

Graphics file types

Joint Photographic Experts Group (ISO 10918) files (.jpg)

Vector graphics file types

Scalable Vector Graphics files (.svg)

What the court will do with your e-mail

The court will check your e-mail and either respond to your enquiry or, where further action is required, will confirm in due course:

(a) that your document has been accepted, and

(b) the date of filing

The date of filing will normally be the date of receipt unless the time of receipt is recorded as after 16.00 in which case the date of filing will be the next day the court office is open.

If your e-mail does not comply with the requirements of the Practice Direction you will be sent a reply stating that it has been rejected and the reasons why.

The court will, where possible, reply to you electronically, although for the present orders of the court will generally be despatched by post as they are not currently produced in electronic form.

Points to remember

This guide does not replace the PD 5B.

when you file documents by e-mail you must still comply with any rule or Practice Direction requiring the document to be served on any other person.

There is nothing in the PD 5B that requires any person to accept service of a document by e-mail.

Where a time limit applies it is the parties responsibility to ensure that the document is filed in time.

Warning

E-mail is not a secure medium. Any message or reply to your message could be intercepted and read by someone else. Please bear this in mind when deciding whether to send an e-mail.

If you require any assistance or have an enquiry regarding the e-mail service please contact the appropriate court or Business Centre.

CJS Secure E-mail Service (CJSM)

If you are a solicitor and have any doubts about the sensitivity of the contents that you intend to e-mail then you should consider signing up to CJS Secure E-mail (CJSM). This is a service currently provided by MOJ ICT.

CJSM is currently free for civil solicitors to sign up to and use, and allows users to securely send and receive information up to and including data that attracts a security marking of restricted. It is not available to the general public.

E-mails transmitted via the gsi network and other equivalent secure Government networks, can send and receive from CJSM accounts.

Service by electronic means

PD 6A para.4.1

Subject to the provisions of r. 6.23(5) and (6), where a document is to be served by fax or other electronic means—
  (1) the party who is to be served or the solicitor acting for that party must previously have indicated in writing to the party serving—
      (a) that the party to be served or the solicitor is willing to accept service by fax or other electronic means; and
      (b) the fax number, e-mail address or other electronic identification to which it must be sent; and
  (2) the following are to be taken as sufficient written indications for the purposes of para. 4.1(1)—
      (b) an e-mail address set out on the writing paper of the solicitor acting for the party to be served but only where it is stated that the e-mail address may be used for service; or
      (c) e-mail address or electronic identification set out on a statement of case or a response to a claim filed with the court.

PD 6A para.4.2

Where a party intends to serve a document by electronic means (other than by fax) that party must first ask the party who is to be served whether there are any limitations to the recipient's agreement to accept service by such means (for example, the format in which documents are to be sent and the maximum size of attachments that may be received).

PD 6A para.4.3

Where a document is served by electronic means, the party serving the document need not in addition send or deliver a hard copy.

Pt 6 r.6.23

(5) Where, in accordance with PD 6A, a party indicates or is deemed to have indicated that they will accept service by fax, the fax number given by that party must be at the address for service.

(6) Where a party indicates in accordance with PD 6A that they will accept service by electronic means other than fax, the e-mail address or electronic identification given by that party will be deemed to be at the address for service.

ESCP

See **European small claims procedure**.

EARLY NEUTRAL EVALUATION

PD—Pre-Action Conduct

An independent person or body, for example a lawyer or an expert in the subject, gives an opinion on the merits of a dispute.

EC REGULATIONS

Means Council Regulation (EC) No.2157/2001 October 8, 2001 on the statute for a European Company (SE).

[PD 49A] applies to proceedings under—
(d) Articles 22, 25 and 26 of the EC Regulation;

Applications under the EC Regulation—art.25

PD 49A para.19

(1) In this paragraph and paras 20 and 21—
   (a) a reference to an Article by number is a reference to the Article so numbered in the EC Regulation; and
   (b) 'SE' means a European public limited-liability company (Societas Europaea) within the meaning of the EC Regulation.
(1A) Any document that is filed with the court must, if not in English, be accompanied by a translation of that document into English—
   (a) certified by a notary public or other qualified person; or
   (b) accompanied by written evidence confirming that the translation is accurate.
(2) An application for a certificate under art.25(2) —
   (a) must set out the pre-merger acts and formalities applicable to the applicant company;
   (b) must be accompanied by evidence that those acts and formalities have been completed; and
   (c) must be accompanied by copies of—
      (i) the draft terms of merger, as provided for in art.20;
      (ii) the entry in the *London Gazette* containing the particulars specified in art.21;
      (iii) a directors' report;

   (iv) an expert's report; and
    (v) the resolution of the applicant company approving the draft terms of merger in accordance with art.23.
 (3) In para.(2)(c)—
 'directors' report' in relation to a company means a report by the directors of the company containing the information required by s.908 of the 2006 Act;
 'expert's report' in relation to a company means a report to the members of the company drawn up in accordance with—
  (a) Section 909 of the 2006 Act; or
  (b) Article 22.
 (4) There need be no defendant to the application.

Applications under the EC Regulation—art.22 (appointment of an independent expert)

PD 49A para.20

 (1) An application under art.22 for the appointment of an independent expert must be made—
  (a) where the application is made at the same time as or after the application under art.25(2) for the approval of the pre-merger acts and formalities has been filed with the court, by application notice pursuant to Pt 23; or
  (b) where no application under art.25(2) has been made, by a Pt 8 claim form.
 (2) The application (whether by a claim form or application notice, as the case may be) must be accompanied by evidence in support of the application.

Applications under the EC Regulation—art.26

PD 49A para.21

 (1) Where under art.26(2) a merging company is required to submit a certificate to the High Court, that company must, if no other merging company has begun proceedings under art.26, start such proceedings by way of a Pt 8 claim form.
 (2) There need be no defendant to the claim.
 (3) The claim form—
  (a) must name the SE and all of the merging companies;
  (b) must be accompanied by the documents referred to in subpara.(5); and
  (c) must be served on each of the other merging companies.
 (4) Where under art.26(2) a merging company is required to submit a certificate to the High Court, and proceedings under art.26 have already been begun, the company—
  (a) must, not more than 14 days after service on it of the claim form, file an acknowledgment of service and serve it on each of the other merging companies; and
  (b) must file the documents, in relation to each merging company, referred to in subpara.(5) within the time limit specified in art.26(2), and serve copies of them on each of the other merging companies.
 (5) The documents in relation to each merging company are—
  (a) the certificate issued under art.25(2) in respect of the company;
  (b) a copy of the draft terms of merger approved by the company;
  (c) evidence that arrangements for employee involvement have been determined by the company pursuant to Council Directive 2001/86/EC October 8, 2001 supplementing the Statute for a European company with regard to the involvement of employees; and

(d) evidence that the SE has been formed in accordance with art.26(4).

Title of documents

PD 49A para.4

(1) The claim form in proceedings under the ... EC Regulation and any application, affidavit, witness statement, notice or other document in such proceedings, must be entitled 'In the matter of [the name of the company in question] and in the matter of [the relevant law]', where '[the relevant law]' means 'Council Regulation (EC) No 2157/2001 of October 8, 2001 on the Statute for a European Company (SE)' . . . .

(2) Where a company changes its name in the course of proceedings, the title must be altered by—

(a) substituting the new name for the old; and

(b) inserting the old name in brackets at the end of the title.

ELECTION PETITIONS IN THE HIGH COURT

Pt 2 r.2.1(2)

The CPR do not apply to these proceedings except to the extent that they are applied by s.182 of the Representation of the People Act 1983.

ELECTRONIC APPLICATIONS

PD 55B para.11.5

When the court receives an online application form it shall—

(1) serve a copy of the online application endorsed with the date of the hearing by post on the claimant at least two clear days before the hearing; and

(2) send the defendant notice of service and confirmation of the date of the hearing by post; provided that

(3) where either party has provided the court with an e-mail address for service, service of the application and/or the notice of service and confirmation of the hearing date may be effected by electronic means.

ELECTRONIC DISCLOSURE

PD 31B para.2

The purpose of [PD 31B] is to encourage and assist the parties to reach agreement in relation to the disclosure of **Electronic Documents** in a proportionate and cost-effective manner.

PD 31B para.3

Unless the court orders otherwise, this PD only applies to proceedings that are (or are likely to be) allocated to the **multi-track**.

PD 31B para.4

Unless the court orders otherwise, this PD only applies to proceedings started on or after October 1, 2010. Paragraph 2A.2 to 2A.5 of PD 31A in force immediately before that date continues to apply to proceedings started before that date.

PD 31B para.5

In PD [31B]—
(1) 'Data Sampling' means the process of checking data by identifying and checking representative individual documents;
(2) 'Disclosure Data' means data relating to disclosed documents, including for example the type of document, the date of the document, the names of the author or sender and the recipient, and the party disclosing the document;
(4) 'Electronic Image' means an electronic representation of a paper document;
(7) 'Metadata' is data about data. In the case of an Electronic Document, Metadata is typically embedded information about the document which is not readily accessible once the Native Electronic Document has been converted into an Electronic Image or paper document. It may include (for example) the date and time of creation or modification of a word-processing file, or the author and the date and time of sending an e-mail. Metadata may be created automatically by a computer system or manually by a user;
(8) 'Native Electronic Document' or 'Native Format' means an Electronic Document stored in the original form in which it was created by a computer software program; and
(9) 'Optical Character Recognition (OCR)' means the computer-facilitated recognition of printed or written text characters in an Electronic Image in which the text-based contents cannot be searched electronically.

See **Keyword search**.

Meaning of document

Pt 31 r.31.4

'document' means anything in which information of any description is recorded.

PD 31B para.1

[The above definition of 'document'] extends to **Electronic Documents**.

Disclosure of electronic documents

PD 31B, para.6

When considering disclosure of Electronic Documents, the parties and their legal representatives should bear in mind the following general principles—
(1) Electronic documents should be managed efficiently in order to minimise the cost incurred;
(2) technology should be used in order to ensure that document management activities are undertaken efficiently and effectively;
(3) disclosure should be given in a manner which gives effect to the overriding objective;

(4) Electronic documents should generally be made available for inspection in a form which allows the party receiving the documents the same ability to access, search, review and display the documents as the party giving disclosure; and

(5) disclosure of Electronic documents which are of no relevance to the proceedings may place an excessive burden in time and cost on the party to whom disclosure is given.

Preservation of documents

PD 31B para.7

As soon as litigation is contemplated, the parties' **legal representatives** must notify their clients of the need to preserve disclosable documents. The documents to be preserved include Electronic Documents which would otherwise be deleted in accordance with a document retention policy or otherwise deleted in the Ordinary course of business.

Discussions between the parties before the first case management conference in relation to the use of technology and disclosure

PD 31B para.8

The parties and their legal representatives must, before the first case management conference, discuss the use of technology in the management of Electronic Documents and the conduct of proceedings, in particular for the purpose of—

(1) creating lists of documents to be disclosed;

(2) giving disclosure by providing documents and information regarding documents in electronic format; and

(3) presenting documents and other material to the court at the trial.

PD 31B para.9

The parties and their legal representatives must also, before the first case management conference, discuss the disclosure of Electronic Documents. In some cases (for example heavy and complex cases) it may be appropriate to begin discussions before proceedings are commenced. The discussions should include (where appropriate) the following matters—

(1) the categories of electronic documents within the parties' control, the computer systems, electronic devices and media on which any relevant documents may be held, storage systems and document retention policies;

(2) the scope of the reasonable search for electronic documents required by r.31.7;

(3) the tools and techniques (if any) which should be considered to reduce the burden and cost of disclosure of electronic documents, including—

(a) limiting disclosure of documents or certain categories of documents to particular date ranges, to particular custodians of documents, or to particular types of documents;

(b) the use of agreed keyword searches;

(c) the use of agreed software tools;

(d) the methods to be used to identify duplicate documents;

(e) the use of data sampling;

(f) the methods to be used to identify privileged documents and other non-disclosable documents, to redact documents (where redaction is appropriate), and for dealing with privileged or other documents which have been inadvertently disclosed; and

(g) the use of a staged approach to the disclosure of electronic documents;

(4) the preservation of electronic documents, with a view to preventing loss of such documents before the trial;

(5) the exchange of data relating to electronic documents in an agreed electronic format using agreed fields;

(6) the formats in which electronic documents are to be provided on inspection and the methods to be used;

(7) the basis of charging for or sharing the cost of the provision of electronic documents, and whether any arrangements for charging or sharing of costs are final or are subject to re-allocation in accordance with any order for costs subsequently made; and

(8) whether it would be appropriate to use the services of a neutral electronic repository for storage of electronic documents.

Preparation for the first case management conference

PD 31B para.14

The documents submitted to the court in advance of the first case management conference should include a summary of the matters on which the parties agree in relation to the disclosure of electronic documents and a summary of the matters on which they disagree.

PD 31B para.15

If the parties indicate that they have been unable to reach agreement in relation to the disclosure of electronic documents and that no agreement is likely, the court will give written directions in relation to disclosure or order a separate hearing in relation to disclosure. When doing so, the court will consider making an order that the parties must complete and exchange all or any part of the Electronic Documents Questionnaire within 14 days or such other period as the court may direct.

PD 31B para.16

The person signing the Electronic Documents Questionnaire should attend the first case management conference, and any subsequent hearing at which disclosure is likely to be considered.

Where the parties are unable to reach an appropriate agreement in relation to the disclosure of electronic documents

PD 31B para.17

If at any time it becomes apparent that the parties are unable to reach agreement in relation to the disclosure of electronic documents, the parties should seek directions from the court at the earliest practical date.

PD 31B para.18

If the court considers that the parties' agreement in relation to the disclosure of electronic documents is inappropriate or insufficient, the court will give directions in relation to disclosure. When doing so, the court will consider making an order that the parties must complete and exchange all or any part of the Electronic Documents Questionnaire within 14 days or such other period as the court may direct.

PD 31B para.19

If a party gives disclosure of electronic documents without first discussing with other parties how to plan and manage such disclosure, the court may require that party to carry out further searches for documents or to repeat other steps which that party has already carried out.

Reasonable search

PD 31B para.20

The extent of the reasonable search required by r.31.7 for the purposes of standard disclosure is affected by the existence of electronic documents. The extent of the search which must be made will depend on the circumstances of the case including, in particular, the factors referred to in r.31.7(2). The parties should bear in mind that the overriding objective includes dealing with the case in ways which are proportionate.

PD 31B para.21

The factors that may be relevant in deciding the reasonableness of a search for electronic documents include (but are not limited to) the following—
(1) the number of documents involved;
(2) the nature and complexity of the proceedings;
(3) the ease and expense of retrieval of any particular document. This includes:
    (a) the accessibility of electronic documents including e-mail communications on computer systems, servers, back-up systems and other electronic devices or media that may contain such documents taking into account alterations or developments in hardware or software systems used by the disclosing party and/or available to enable access to such documents;
    (b) the location of relevant electronic documents, data, computer systems, servers, back-up systems and other electronic devices or media that may contain such documents;
    (c) the likelihood of locating relevant data;
    (d) the cost of recovering any electronic documents;
    (e) the cost of disclosing and providing inspection of any relevant electronic documents; and
    (f) the likelihood that electronic documents will be materially altered in the course of recovery, disclosure or inspection;
(4) the availability of documents or contents of documents from other sources; and
(5) the significance of any document which is likely to be located during the search.

PD 31B para.22

Depending on the circumstances, it may be reasonable to search all of the parties' electronic storage systems, or to search only some part of those systems. For example, it may be reasonable to decide not to search for documents coming into existence before a particular date, or to limit the search to documents in a particular place or places, or to documents falling into particular categories.

PD 31B para.23

In some cases a staged approach may be appropriate, with disclosure initially being given of limited categories of documents. Those categories may subsequently be extended or limited depending on the results initially obtained.

PD 31B para.24

The primary source of disclosure of electronic documents is normally reasonably accessible data. A party requesting under r.31.12 specific disclosure of electronic documents which are not reasonably accessible must demonstrate that the relevance and materiality justify the cost and burden of retrieving and producing it.

Disclosure of metadata

PD 31B para.28

Where copies of disclosed documents are provided in Native Format in accordance with para.33 below, some metadata will be disclosed with each document. A party requesting disclosure of additional metadata or forensic image copies of disclosed documents (for example in relation to a dispute concerning authenticity) must demonstrate that the relevance and materiality of the requested metadata justify the cost and burden of producing that metadata.

PD 31B para.29

Parties using document management or litigation support systems should be alert to the possibility that metadata or other useful information relating to documents may not be stored with the documents.

Lists of documents

PD 31B para.30

If a party is giving disclosure of electronic documents, para.3 of PD 31A is to be read subject to the following—
  (1) Form N265 may be amended to accommodate the sub-paragraphs which follow;
  (2) a list of documents may by agreement between the parties be an electronic file in .csv (comma-separated values) or other agreed format;
  (3) documents may be listed otherwise than in date order where a different order would be more convenient;
  (4) save where otherwise agreed or ordered, documents should be listed individually if a party already possesses data relating to the document (for example, type of document and date of creation) which make this possible (so that as far as possible each document may be given a unique reference number);
  (5) a party should be consistent in the way in which documents are listed;
  (6) consistent column headings should be repeated on each page of the list on which documents are listed, where the software used for preparing the list enables this to be carried out automatically; and
  (7) the disclosure list number used in any supplemental list of documents should be unique and should run sequentially from the last number used in the previous list.

Disclosure data in electronic form

PD 31B para.31

Where a party provides another party with Disclosure Data in electronic form, the following provisions will apply unless the parties agree or the court directs otherwise—

(1) Disclosure Data should be set out in a single, continuous table or spreadsheet, each separate column containing exclusively one of the following types of Disclosure Data—
   (a) disclosure list number (sequential)
   (b) date
   (c) document type
   (d) author/sender
   (e) recipient
   (f) disclosure list number of any parent or covering document;
(2) other than for disclosure list numbers, blank entries are permissible and preferred if there is no relevant Disclosure Data (that is, the field should be left blank rather than state 'Undated');
(3) dates should be set out in the alphanumeric form '01 Jan 2010'; and
(4) Disclosure Data should be set out in a consistent manner.

Electronic copies of disclosed documents

PD 31B para.32

The parties should co-operate at an early stage about the format in which electronic documents are to be provided on inspection. In the case of difficulty or disagreement, the matter should be referred to the court for directions at the earliest practical date, if possible at the first case management conference.

PD 31B para.33

Save where otherwise agreed or ordered, electronic copies of disclosed documents should be provided in their Native Format, in a manner which preserves metadata relating to the date of creation of each document.

PD 31B para.34

A party should provide any available searchable OCR versions of Electronic Documents with the original. A party may however choose not to provide OCR versions of documents which have been redacted. If OCR versions are provided, they are provided on an 'as is' basis, with no assurance to the other party that the OCR versions are complete or accurate.

PD 31B para.35

(1) Subject to sub-para.(2) below, if a party is providing in electronic form copies of disclosed documents and wishes to redact or otherwise make alterations to a document or documents, then—
   (a) the party redacting or altering the document must inform the other party in accordance with r.31.19 that redacted or altered versions are being supplied; and
   (b) the party redacting or altering the document must ensure that the original unredacted and unaltered version is preserved, so that it remains available to be inspected if required.
(2) Sub-paragraph (1) above does not apply where the only alteration made to the document is an alteration to the metadata as a result of the ordinary process of copying and/or accessing the document. Sub-paragraph (1) does apply to the alteration or suppression of metadata in other situations.

Specialised technology

PD 31B para.36

If electronic documents are best accessed using technology which is not readily available to the party entitled to disclosure, and that party reasonably requires additional inspection facilities, the party making disclosure shall co-operate in making available to the other party such reasonable additional inspection facilities as may be appropriate in order to afford inspection in accordance with r.31.3.

Subsequent use of disclosed documents and completed Electronic Documents Questionnaires

See **Disclosure of documents**.

ELECTRONIC DOCUMENT

PD 31B para.5

    (2) Any document held in electronic form. It includes, for example, e-mail and other electronic communications such as text messages and voicemail, word-processed documents and databases, and documents stored on portable devices such as memory sticks and mobile phones. In addition to documents that are readily accessible from computer systems and other electronic devices and media, it includes documents that are stored on servers and back-up systems and documents that have been deleted. It also includes Metadata and other embedded data which is not typically visible on screen or a print out.

See **Electronic disclosure**.

ELECTRONIC DOCUMENTS QUESTIONNAIRE

PD 31B para.10

In some cases the parties may find it helpful to exchange the Electronic Documents Questionnaire in order to provide information to each other in relation to the scope, extent and most suitable format for disclosure of electronic xocuments in the proceedings.

PD 31B para.11

The answers to the Electronic Documents Questionnaire must be verified by a statement of truth.

PD 31B para.12

Answers to the Electronic Documents Questionnaire will only be available for inspection by non-parties if permission is given under r.5.4C(2).

PD 31B para.13

[*See* Schedule to PD 31 for Electronic Documents Questionnaire form]

ELECTRONIC MEANS

See **E-mail** and **Fax and other electronic means**.

ELECTRONIC WORKING SCHEME

PD [5C] provided for a scheme of electronic working by which—
  (a) proceedings could be started and all subsequent steps taken electronically; and
  (b) proceedings which had not been started electronically, could be continued electronically after documents in paper format in those proceedings had been converted to an electronic format by means of a scanning procedure by the Court and the proceedings would then continue under the scheme as if they had been started electronically.
This Scheme has been abolished.

EMPLOYMENT EQUALITY (AGE) REGULATIONS 2006

See **Discrimination proceedings**.

EMPLOYMENT EQUALITY (RELIGION OR BELIEF) REGULATIONS 2003

See **Discrimination proceedings**.

EMPLOYMENT EQUALITY (SEXUAL ORIENTATION) REGULATIONS 2003

See **Discrimination proceedings**.

EMPLOYMENT TRIBUNALS

Appeal from tribunal

PD 52 para.22.6E

  (1) This paragraph applies to an appeal from a tribunal constituted under s.1 of the Employment Tribunals Act 1996.
  (2) The appellant must file the appellant's notice at the High Court within 42 days after the date of the decision of the tribunal.
  (3) The appellant must serve the appellant's notice on the secretary of the tribunal.

ENERGY ACT 2008

See **Town and Country Planning**.

ENFORCEMENT IN FOREIGN COUNTRIES OF JUDGMENTS OF THE HIGH COURT AND COUNTY COURTS

Application for a certified copy of a judgment

Pt 74 r.74.12

(1) This section applies to applications—
  (a) to the High Court under s.10 of the [Administration of Justice Act 1920];
  (b) to the High Court or to a county court under s.10 of the [Foreign Judgments (Reciprocal Enforcement) Act 1933];
  (c) to the High Court or to a county court under s.12 of the [Civil Jurisdiction and Judgments Act 1982]; or
  (d) to the High Court or to a county court under art.54 of the Judgments Regulation or under art.54 of the Lugano Convention.
(2) A judgment creditor who wishes to enforce in a foreign country a judgment obtained in the High Court or in a county court must apply for a certified copy of the judgment.
The application may be made without notice.

PD 74A para.4.2

[The application] must be made—
  (1) in the case of a judgment given in the Chancery Division or the Queen's Bench Division of the High Court, to a Master, Registrar or district judge;
  (2) in the case of a judgment given in the Family Division of the High Court, to a district judge of that Division;
  (3) in the case of a county court judgment, to a district judge.

PD 74A para.4.4

[The **application** must be made in accordance with Pt 23].

PD 74A para.7.1

In an application by a judgment creditor under r.74.12 for the enforcement abroad of a High Court judgment, the certified copy of the judgment will be an office copy, and will be accompanied by a certificate signed by a judge. The judgment and certificate will be sealed with the Seal of the Senior Courts.

PD 74A para.7.2

In an application by a judgment creditor under r.74.12 for the enforcement abroad of a county court judgment, the certified copy will be a sealed copy, and will be accompanied by a certificate signed by a judge.

PD 74A para.7.3

In applications under the 1920, 1933 or 1982 Acts, the certificate will be in Form 110, and will have annexed to it a copy of the claim form by which the proceedings were begun.

PD 74A para.7.4

In an application under the Judgments Regulation, the certificate will be in the form of Annex V to the regulation.

PD 74A para.7.5

In an application under the Lugano Convention, the certificate will be in the form of Annex V to the convention.

Evidence in support

Pt 74 r.74.13

(1) The application must be supported by written evidence exhibiting copies of—
    (a) the claim form in the proceedings in which judgment was given;
    (b) evidence that it was served on the defendant;
    (c) the statements of case; and
    (d) where relevant, a document showing that for those proceedings the applicant was an assisted person or an LSC funded client, as defined in r.43.2(1)(h) and (i).
(2) The written evidence must—
    (a) identify the grounds on which the judgment was obtained;
    (b) state whether the defendant objected to the jurisdiction and, if he did, the grounds of his objection;
    (c) show that the judgment—
        (i) has been served in accordance with Pt 6 and r.40.4, and
        (ii) is not subject to a stay of execution;
    (d) state—
        (i) the date on which the time for appealing expired or will expire;
        (ii) whether an appeal notice has been filed;
        (iii) the status of any application for permission to appeal; and
        (iv) whether an appeal is pending;
    (e) state whether the judgment provides for the payment of a sum of money, and if so, the amount in respect of which it remains unsatisfied;
    (f) state whether interest is recoverable on the judgment, and if so, either—
        (i) the amount of interest which has accrued up to the date of the application, or
        (ii) the rate of interest, the date from which it is recoverable, and the date on which it ceases to accrue.
(2) The judgment debtor shall, as soon as practicable, serve a copy of any order made under the Article on—
    (a) all other parties to the proceedings and any other person affected by the order; and
    (b) any court in which enforcement proceedings are pending in England and Wales;
    and the order will not have effect on any person until it has been served in accordance with this rule and they have received it.

ENFORCEMENT IN THE HIGH COURT OF A COUNTY COURT JUDGMENT OR ORDER

CCR Ord.25 r.13

(1) Where the judgment creditor makes a request for a certificate of judgment under Ord.22 r.8(1) for the purpose of enforcing the judgment or order in the High Court—

   (a) by execution against goods; or

   (b) where the judgement or order to be enforced is an order for possession of land made in a possession claim against trespassers,

the grant of a certificate by the court shall take effect as an order to transfer the proceedings to the High Court and the transfer shall have effect on the grant of that certificate.

(2) On the transfer of proceedings in accordance with para.(1), the court shall give notice to the debtor or the person against whom the possession order was made that the proceedings have been transferred and shall make an entry of that fact in the records of his court.

(3) In a case where a request for a certificate of judgment is made under Ord.22 r.8(1) for the purpose of enforcing a judgment or order in the High Court and—

   (a) an application for a variation in the date or rate of payment of money due under a judgment or order;

   (b) an application under either CPR r.39.3(3) or CPR r.13.4;

   (c) a request for an administration order; or

   (d) an application for a stay of execution under s.88 of the Act, is pending,

the request for the certificate shall not be dealt with until those proceedings are determined.

ENFORCEMENT OF A JUDGMENT OR ORDER OF ONE COUNTY COURT IN A DIFFERENT COUNTY COURT

PD 70 para.2.1

Subject to s.II of [PD 70—designated money claims], if a judgment creditor is required by a rule or PD to enforce a judgment or order of one county court in a different county court, he must first make a request in writing to the court in which the case is proceeding to transfer the proceedings to that other court.

PD 70 para.2.2

Subject to s.II of [PD 70—designated money claims], on receipt of such a request, a court officer will transfer the proceedings to the other court unless a judge orders otherwise.

PD 70 para.2.3

The court will give notice of the transfer to all the parties.

PD 70 para.2.4

When the proceedings have been transferred, the parties must take any further steps in the proceedings in the court to which they have been transferred, unless a rule or PD provides otherwise.

(Part 52 and PD 52 provide to which court or judge an appeal against the judgment or order, or an application for permission to appeal, must be made).

ENFORCEMENT OF AWARD

See **Enforcement of decisions of bodies other than the High Court and County Courts and compromises enforceable by enactment.**

ENFORCEMENT OF DECISIONS OF BODIES OTHER THAN THE HIGH COURT AND COUNTY COURTS AND COMPROMISES ENFORCEABLE BY ENACTMENT

Pt 70 r.70.5

(1) This rule applies, subject to para.(2), where an enactment provides that—
    (a) a decision of a court, tribunal, body or person other than the High Court or a county court; or
    (b) a compromise,
may be enforced as if it were a court order or that any sum of money payable under that decision or compromise may be recoverable as if payable under a court order.

(2) This rule does not apply to—
    (a) any judgment to which Pt 74 applies;
    (b) arbitration awards;
    (c) any order to which RSC Ord.115 applies; or
    (d) proceedings to which Pt 75 (**traffic enforcement**) applies.

(2A) Unless para.(3) applies, a party may enforce the decision or compromise by applying for a specific method of enforcement under Pts 71 to 73, Sch.1 RSC Ords 45 to 47 and 52 and Sch.2 CCR Ords 25 to 29 and must—
    (a) file with the court a copy of the decision or compromise being enforced; and
    (b) provide the court with the information required by PD 70.

(3) If an enactment provides that a decision or compromise is enforceable or a sum of money is recoverable if a court so orders, an application for such an order must be made in accordance with paras (4) to (7A) of this rule.

(4) The application—
    (a) may, unless para.(4A) applies, be made without notice; and
    (b) must be made to the court for the district where the person against whom the order is sought, resides or carries on business, unless the court otherwise orders.

(4A) Where a compromise requires a person to whom a sum of money is payable under the compromise to do anything in addition to discontinuing or not starting proceedings ('a conditional compromise'), an application under para.(4) must be made on notice.

(5) The application notice must—
    (a) be in the form; and
    (b) contain the information
required by PD 70.

(6) A copy of the decision or compromise must be filed with the application notice.

(7) An application other than in relation to a conditional compromise may be dealt with by a court officer without a hearing.

(7A) Where an application relates to a conditional compromise, the respondent may oppose it by filing a response within 14 days of service of the application notice and if the respondent—
    (a) does not file a response within the time allowed, the court will make the order; or
    (b) files a response within the time allowed, the court will make such order as appears appropriate.

(8) If an enactment provides that a decision or compromise may be enforced in the same manner as an order of the High Court if it is registered, any application to the High Court for registration must be made in accordance with PD 70.

PD 70 para.4.1

The information referred to in r.70.5(2A) must—
  (a) be included in Practice Form N322B or, where para.4.1A applies, in the practice form required by para.4.1A(2);

   (b) specify the statutory provision under which enforcement or the recovery of a sum of money is sought;
   (c) state the name and address of the person against whom enforcement or recovery is sought;
   (d) where the decision or compromise requires that person to pay a sum of money, state the amount which remains unpaid; and
   (e) confirm that, where a sum of money is being recovered pursuant to a compromise, the compromise is not a conditional compromise.

PD 70 para.4.1A

   (1) This paragraph applies where—
      (a) either—
         (i) the decision to be enforced is a decision of an employment tribunal in England and Wales; or
         (ii) the application is for the recovery of a compromise sum under s.19A(3) of the Employment Tribunals Act 1996; and
      (b) the party seeking to enforce the decision wishes to enforce by way of a writ of fiera facias.
   (2) The practice form which is to be used is—
      (a) where para.(1)(a)(i) applies, Practice Form N471;
      (b) where para.(1)(a)(ii) applies, Practice Form N471A.

PD 70 para.4.2

An application under r.70.5(3) for an order to enforce a decision or compromise must be made by filing an application notice in Practice Form N322A.

PD 70 para.4.3

The application notice must state—
   (a) the name and address of the person against whom the order is sought;
   (b) how much remains unpaid or what obligation remains to be performed; and
   (c) where the application relates to a conditional compromise, details of what under the compromise the applicant is required to do and has done under the compromise in addition to discontinuing or not starting proceedings.

PD 70 para.4.4

Where—
   (a) the application relates to a conditional compromise; and
   (b) the application notice is served by the applicant on the respondent,
the applicant must file a certificate of service with the court within seven days of service of the application notice.

Decisions for enforcement in the High Court

PD 70 para.5.1

An application to the High Court under an enactment to register a decision for enforcement must be made in writing to the head clerk of the Action Department at the Royal Courts of Justice, Strand, London WC2A 2LL.

PD 70 para.5.2

The application must—
(1) specify the statutory provision under which the application is made;
(2) state the name and address of the person against whom it is sought to enforce the decision;
(3) if the decision requires that person to pay a sum of money, state the amount which remains unpaid.

Court may order act to be done at expense of disobedient party

RSC Ord.45 r.8

If a mandatory order, an injunction or a judgment or order for the specific performance of a contract is not complied with, then, without prejudice to its powers under s.39 of the Act and its powers to punish the disobedient party for contempt, the court may direct that the act required to be done may, so far as practicable, be done by the party by whom the order or judgment was obtained or some other person appointed by the court, at the cost of the disobedient party, and upon the act being done the expenses incurred may be ascertained in such manner as the court may direct and execution may issue against the disobedient party for the amount so ascertained and for costs.

ENFORCEMENT OF JUDGMENT FOR DELIVERY OF GOODS

See **Delivery of goods**.

ENFORCEMENT OF JUDGMENTS AND ORDERS

Pt 70 r.70.1

(1) [Part 70] contains general rules about enforcement of judgments and orders.
(Rules about specific methods of enforcement are contained in Pts 71 to 73, Sch.1 RSC Ords 45 to 47 and 52 and Sch.2 CCR Ords 25 to 29)
(2) In this Part and in Pts 71 to 73—
(c) 'judgment or order' includes an award which the court has—
(i) registered for enforcement;
(ii) ordered to be enforced; or
(iii) given permission to enforce
as if it were a judgment or order of the court, and in relation to such an award, 'the court which made the judgment or order' means the court which registered the award or made such an order; and
(d) 'judgment or order for the payment of money' includes a judgment or order for the payment of costs, but does not include a judgment or order for the payment of money into court.

See **Interest** and **Partnership**.

Methods of enforcing judgments or orders

Pt 70, r.70.2

(1) PD 70 sets out methods of enforcing judgments or orders for the payment of money.
(2) A judgment creditor [a person who has obtained or is entitled to enforce a judgment or order] may, except where an enactment, rule or PD provides otherwise—
    (a) use any method of enforcement which is available; and
    (b) use more than one method of enforcement, either at the same time or one after another.

PD 70 para.1.1

A judgment creditor may enforce a judgment or order for the payment of money by any of the following methods:
    (1) a **writ of fieri facias** or **warrant of execution** (see RSC Orders 46 and 47 and CCR Order 26);
    (2) a **Third Party Debt Order** (see Pt 72);
    (3) a **charging order, stop order** or **stop notice** (see Pt 73);
    (4) in a county court, an **attachment of earnings** order (see CCR Ord.27);
    (5) the appointment of a **receiver** (see Pt 69).

PD 70 para.1.2

In addition the court may make the following orders against a judgment debtor [a person against whom a judgment or order was given or made]—
    (1) an order of **committal**, but only if permitted by—
        (a) a rule; and
        (b) the Debtors Acts 1869 and 1878
(See RSC Ord.45 r.5 and CCR Ord.28. PD RSC Ord.52 and CCR Ord.29 applies to an application for committal of a judgment debtor); and
    (2) in the High Court, a **writ of sequestration**, but only if permitted by RSC Ord.45 r.5.

PD 70 para.1.3

The enforcement of a judgment or order may be affected by—
    (1) the enactments relating to **insolvency**; and
    (2) county court **administration orders**.

Effect of setting aside judgment or order

Pt 70 r.70.6

If a judgment or order is set aside, any enforcement of the judgment or order shall cease to have effect unless the court otherwise orders.

Payment of debt after issue of enforcement proceedings

PD 70 para.7.1

If a judgment debt or part of it is paid—
    (1) after the judgment creditor has issued any application or request to enforce it; but

(2) before—
    (a) any writ or warrant has been executed; or
    (b) in any other case, the date fixed for the hearing of the application;
    the judgment creditor must, unless para.7.2 applies, immediately notify the court in writing.

PD 70 para.7.2

If a judgment debt or part of it is paid after the judgment creditor has applied to the High Court for a writ of execution, para.7.1 does not apply, and the judgment creditor must instead immediately notify the relevant enforcement officer in writing.

County court

Description of parties

CCR Ord.25 r.6

Where the name or address of the judgment creditor or the debtor as given in the request for the issue of a warrant of execution or delivery, judgment summons or warrant of committal differs from his name or address in the judgment or order sought to be enforced and the judgment creditor satisfies the court officer that the name or address as given in the request is applicable to the person concerned, the judgment creditor or the debtor, as the case may be, shall be described in the warrant or judgment summons as 'C.D. of [name and address as given in the request] suing [or sued] as A.D. of [name and address in the judgment or order]'.

Recording and giving information as to warrants and orders

CCR Ord.25 r.7

(1) Subject to para.(1A), every district judge by whom a warrant or order is issued or received for execution shall from time to time state in the records of his court what has been done in the execution of the warrant or order.
(1A) Where a warrant of execution issued by a court ('the home court') is sent to another court for execution ('the foreign court'), para.(1) shall not apply to the district judge of the home court, but when such a warrant is returned to the home court under para.(7), the court officer of the home court shall state in the records of his court what has been done in the execution of the warrant or order.
(2) If the warrant or order has not been executed within one month from the date of its issue or receipt by him, the court officer of the court responsible for its execution shall, at the end of that month and every subsequent month during which the warrant remains outstanding, send notice of the reason for non-execution to the judgment creditor and, if the warrant or order was received from another court, to that court.
(3) The district judge responsible for executing a warrant or order shall give such information respecting it as may reasonably be required by the judgment creditor and, if the warrant or order was received by him from another court, by the district judge of that court.
(4) Where money is received in pursuance of a warrant of execution or committal sent by one court to another court, the foreign court shall, subject to para.(5) and to s.346 of the Insolvency Act 1986 and s.326 of the Companies Act 1948, send the money to the judgment creditor in the manner prescribed by the Court Funds Rules 1987 and, where

the money is received in pursuance of a warrant of committal, make a return to the home court.

(5) Where interpleader proceedings are pending, the court shall not proceed in accordance with para.(4) until the interpleader proceedings are determined and the district judge shall then make a return showing how the money is to be disposed of and, if any money is payable to the judgment creditor, the court shall proceed in accordance with para.(4).

(6) Where a warrant of committal has been received from another court, the foreign court shall, on the execution of the warrant, send notice thereof to the home court.

(7) Where a warrant of execution has been received from another court, either—
  (a) on the execution of the warrant; or
  (b) if the warrant is not executed—
     (i) on the making of a final return to the warrant; or
     (ii) on suspension of the warrant under r.8 (suspension of judgment or execution) or Ord.26, r.10 (withdrawal and suspension of warrant at creditor's request),
the foreign court shall return the warrant to the home court.

Suspension of judgment or execution

CCR Ord.25 r.8

(1) The power of the court to suspend or stay a judgment or order or to stay execution of any warrant may be exercised by the district judge or, in the case of the power to stay execution of a warrant of execution and in accordance with the provisions of this rule, by the court officer.

(2) An application by the debtor to stay execution of a warrant of execution shall be in the appropriate form stating the proposed terms, the grounds on which it is made and including a signed statement of the debtor's means.

(3) Where the debtor makes an application under para.(2), the court shall—
  (a) send the judgment creditor a copy of the debtor's application (and statement of means); and
  (b) require the creditor to notify the court in writing, within 14 days of service of notification upon him, giving his reasons for any objection he may have to the granting of the application.

(4) If the judgment creditor does not notify the court of any objection within the time stated, the court officer may make an order suspending the warrant on terms of payment.

(5) Upon receipt of a notice by the judgment creditor under para.(3)(b), the court officer may, if the judgment creditor objects only to the terms offered, determine the date and rate of payment and make an order suspending the warrant on terms of payment.

(6) Any party affected by an order made under para.(5) may, within 14 days of service of the order on him and giving his reasons, apply on notice for the order to be reconsidered and the court shall fix a day for the hearing of the application before the district judge and give to the judgment creditor and the debtor not less than 8 days' notice of the day so fixed.

(7) On hearing an application under para.(6), the district judge may confirm the order or set it aside and make such new order as he thinks fit and the order so made shall be entered in the records of the court.

(8) Where the judgment creditor states in his notice under para.(3)(b) that he wishes the bailiff to proceed to execute the warrant, the court shall fix a day for a hearing before the district judge of the debtor's application and give to the judgment creditor and to the debtor not less than two days' notice of the day so fixed.

(9) Subject to any directions given by the district judge, where a warrant of execution has been suspended, it may be re-issued on the judgment creditor's filing a request showing that any condition subject to which the warrant was suspended has not been complied with.

(10) Where an order is made by the district judge suspending a warrant of execution, the debtor may be ordered to pay the costs of the warrant and any fees or expenses incurred before its suspension and the order may authorise the sale of a sufficient portion of any goods seized to cover such costs, fees and expenses and the expenses of sale.

Transfer to High Court for enforcement

CCR Ord.25, r.13

(1) Where the judgment creditor makes a request for a certificate of judgment under Ord.22 r.8(1) for the purpose of enforcing the judgment or order in the High Court—
   (a) by execution against goods; or
   (b) where the judgement or order to be enforced is an order for possession of land made in a possession claim against trespassers,
   the grant of a certificate by the court shall take effect as an order to transfer the proceedings to the High Court and the transfer shall have effect on the grant of that certificate.
(2) On the transfer of proceedings in accordance with para.(1), the court shall give notice to the debtor or the person against whom the possession order was made that the proceedings have been transferred and shall make an entry of that fact in the records of his court.
(3) In a case where a request for a certificate of judgment is made under Ord.22, r.8(1) for the purpose of enforcing a judgment or order in the High Court and—
   (a) an application for a variation in the date or rate of payment of money due under a judgment or order;
   (b) an application under either CPR r.39.3(3) or CPR r.13.4;
   (c) a request for an administration order; or
   (d) an application for a stay of execution under s.88 of the Act, is pending,
   the request for the certificate shall not be dealt with until those proceedings are determined.

Orders to obtain information from judgment debtors

Pt 71 r.71.1

This Part contains rules which provide for a judgment debtor to be required to attend court to provide information, for the purpose of enabling a judgment creditor to enforce a judgment or order against him.

Order to attend court

Pt 71 r.71.2

(1) A judgment creditor may apply for an order requiring—
   (a) a judgment debtor; or
   (b) if a judgment debtor is a company or other corporation, an officer of that body,
   to attend court to provide information about—
   (i) the judgment debtor's means; or
   (ii) any other matter about which information is needed to enforce a judgment or order.

(2) An application under para.(1)—
    (a) may be made without notice; and
    (b) must be issued in the court which made the judgment or order which it is sought to enforce except that—
        (i) if the proceedings have since been transferred to a different court, it must be issued in that court; or
        (ii) subject to subpara.(b)(i), if it is to enforce a judgment made in Northampton County Court in respect of a **designated money claim**, it must be issued in accordance with s.2 of PD 70.
(3) The application notice must—
    (a) be in the form; and
    (b) contain the information
    required by PD 71.
(4) An application under para.(1) may be dealt with by a court officer without a hearing.
(5) If the application notice complies with para.(3), an order to attend court will be issued in the terms of para.(6).
(6) A person served with an order issued under this rule must—
    (a) attend court at the time and place specified in the order;
    (b) when he does so, produce at court documents in his control which are described in the order; and
    (c) answer on oath such questions as the court may require.
(7) An order under this r.will contain a notice in the following terms—

"You must obey this order. If you do not, you may be sent to prison for contempt of court."

PD 71 para.1.1

An application by a judgment creditor under r.71.2(1) must be made by filing an application notice in Practice Form N316 if the application is to question an individual judgment debtor, or N316A if the application is to question an officer of a company or other corporation.

PD 71 para.1.2

The application notice must—
(1) state the name and address of the judgment debtor;
(2) identify the judgment or order which the judgment creditor is seeking to enforce;
(3) if the application is to enforce a judgment or order for the payment of money, state the amount presently owed by the judgment debtor under the judgment or order;
(4) if the judgment debtor is a company or other corporation, state—
    (a) the name and address of the officer of that body whom the judgment creditor wishes to be ordered to attend court; and
    (b) his position in the company;
(5) if the judgment creditor wishes the questioning to be conducted before a judge, state this and give his reasons;
(6) if the judgment creditor wishes the judgment debtor (or other person to be questioned) to be ordered to produce specific documents at court, identify those documents; and
(7) if the application is to enforce a judgment or order which is not for the payment of money, identify the matters about which the judgment creditor wishes the judgment debtor (or officer of the judgment debtor) to be questioned.

PD 71 para.1.3

The court officer considering the application notice—
(1) may, in any appropriate case, refer it to a judge (r.3.2); and
(2) will refer it to a judge for consideration, if the judgment creditor requests the judgment debtor (or officer of the judgment debtor) to be questioned before a judge.

PD 71 para.2.1

The order will provide for the judgment debtor (or other person to be questioned) to attend the county court for the district in which he resides or carries on business, unless a judge decides otherwise.

PD 71 para.2.2

The order will provide for questioning to take place before a judge only if the judge considering the request decides that there are compelling reasons to make such an order.

Service of Order

Pt 71 r.71.3

(1) An order to attend court must, unless the court otherwise orders, be served personally on the person ordered to attend court not less than 14 days before the hearing.
(2) If the order is to be served by the judgment creditor, he must inform the court not less than seven days before the date of the hearing if he has been unable to serve it.

PD 71 para.3

Service of an order to attend court for questioning may be carried out by—
(a) the judgment creditor (or someone acting on the judgment creditor's behalf)
(b) a High Court enforcement officer; or
(c) a county court bailiff.

Travelling expenses

Pt 71 r.71.4

(1) A person ordered to attend court may, within seven days of being served with the order, ask the judgment creditor to pay him a sum reasonably sufficient to cover his travelling expenses to and from court.
(2) The judgment creditor must pay such a sum if requested.

Judgment creditor's affidavit

Pt 71 r.71.5

(1) The judgment creditor must file an affidavit or affidavits—
(a) by the person who served the order (unless it was served by the court) giving details of how and when it was served;
(b) stating either that—
(i) the person ordered to attend court has not requested payment of his travelling expenses; or
(ii) the judgment creditor has paid a sum in accordance with such a request; and
(c) stating how much of the judgment debt remains unpaid.
(2) The judgment creditor must either—

(a) file the affidavit or affidavits not less than two days before the hearing; or

(b) produce it or them at the hearing.

Conduct of the hearing

Pt 71 r.71.6

(1) The person ordered to attend court will be questioned on oath.

(2) The questioning will be carried out by a court officer unless the court has ordered that the hearing shall be before a judge.

(3) The judgment creditor or his representative—

    (a) may attend and ask questions where the questioning takes place before a court officer; and

    (b) must attend and conduct the questioning if the hearing is before a judge.

PD 71 para.4.1

The court officer will ask a standard series of questions, as set out in the forms in Appendices A and B to this PD. The form in Appendix A will be used if the person being questioned is the judgment debtor, and the form in Appendix B will be used if the person is an officer of a company or other corporation.

PD 71 para.4.2

The judgment creditor or his representative may either—

(1) attend court and ask questions himself; or

(2) request the court officer to ask additional questions, by attaching a list of proposed additional questions to his application notice.

PD 71 para.4.3

The court officer will—

(1) make a written record of the evidence given, unless the proceedings are tape recorded;

(2) at the end of the questioning, read the record of evidence to the person being questioned and ask him to sign it; and

(3) if the person refuses to sign it, note that refusal on the record of evidence.

PD 71 para.5.1

Where the hearing takes places before a judge, the questioning will be conducted by the judgment creditor or his representative, and the standard questions in the forms in Appendices A and B will not be used.

PD 71 para.5.2

The proceedings will be tape recorded and the court will not make a written record of the evidence.

Adjournment of the hearing

Pt 71 r.71.7

If the hearing is adjourned, the court will give directions as to the manner in which notice of the new hearing is to be served on the judgment debtor.

Failure to comply with order

Pt 71 r.71.8

(1) If a person against whom an order has been made under r.71.2—
    (a) fails to attend court;
    (b) refuses at the hearing to take the oath or to answer any question; or
    (c) otherwise fails to comply with the order,
    the court will refer the matter to a High Court judge or circuit judge.
(2) That judge may, subject to paragraphs (3) and (4), make a committal order against the person.
(3) A committal order for failing to attend court may not be made unless the judgment creditor has complied with rr.71.4 and 71.5.
(4) If a committal order is made, the judge will direct that—
    (a) the order shall be suspended provided that the person—
        (i) attends court at a time and place specified in the order; and
        (ii) complies with all the terms of that order and the original order; and
    (b) if the person fails to comply with any term on which the committal order is suspended, he shall be brought before a judge to consider whether the committal order should be discharged.

PD 71 para.6

If a judge or court officer refers to a High Court judge or circuit judge the failure of a judgment debtor to comply with an order under r.71.2, he shall certify in writing the respect in which the judgment debtor failed to comply with the order.

PD 71 para.7.1

A committal order will be suspended provided that the person attends court at a time and place specified in the order (r.71.8(4)(a)(i)). The appointment specified will be—
(1) before a judge, if—
    (a) the original order under r.71.2 was to attend before a judge; or
    (b) the judge making the suspended committal order so directs; and
(2) otherwise, before a court officer.

PD 71 para.7.2

Rule 71.3 and para 3 of this PD (service of order), and r.71.5(1)(a) and (2) (affidavit of service), apply with the necessary changes to a suspended committal order as they do to an order to attend court.

PD 71 para.8.1

If—
(1) the judgment debtor fails to attend court at the time and place specified in the suspended committal order; and

(2) it appears to the judge or court officer that the judgment debtor has been duly served with the order,

the judge or court officer will certify in writing the debtor's failure to attend.

PD 71 para.8.2

If the judgment debtor fails to comply with any other term on which the committal order was suspended, the judge or court officer will certify in writing the non-compliance and set out details of it.

PD 71 para.8.3

A warrant to bring the judgment debtor before a judge may be issued on the basis of a certificate under para.8.1 or 8.2.

PD 71 para.8.4

The hearing under r.71.8(4)(b) may take place before a master or district judge.

PD 71 para.8.5

At the hearing the judge will discharge the committal order unless he is satisfied beyond reasonable doubt that—
(1) the judgment debtor has failed to comply with—
   (a) the original order to attend court; and
   (b) the terms on which the committal order was suspended; and
(2) both orders have been duly served on the judgment debtor.

PD 71 para.8.6

If the judge decides that the committal order should not be discharged, a warrant of committal shall be issued immediately.

See **Non-parties**.

ENFORCEMENT IN A COUNTY COURT OF A HIGH COURT JUDGMENT OR ORDER

Pt 70 r.70.3

(1) A judgment creditor wishing to enforce a High Court judgment or order in a county court must apply to the High Court for an order transferring the proceedings to that county court.
(2) A PD may make provisions about the transfer of proceedings for enforcement.

PD 70 para.3.1

If a judgment creditor wishes to enforce a High Court judgment or order in a county court, he must file the following documents in the county court with his application notice or request for enforcement—
(1) a copy of the judgment or order;

(2) a certificate verifying the amount due under the judgment or order;

(3) if a writ of execution has previously been issued in the High Court to enforce the judgment or order, a copy of the relevant enforcement officer's return to the writ; and

(4) a copy of the order transferring the proceedings to the county court.

PD 70 para.3.2

In this paragraph and para.7—

(1) 'enforcement officer' means an individual who is authorised to act as an enforcement officer under the Courts Act 2003; and

(2) 'relevant enforcement officer' means—

(a) in relation to a writ of execution which is directed to a single enforcement officer, that officer;

(b) in relation to a writ of execution which is directed to two or more enforcement officers, the officer to whom the writ is allocated.

ENFORCEMENT IN ENGLAND AND WALES OF JUDGMENTS OF FOREIGN COURTS

Pt 74 r.74.2

(1) In this section—

(a) 'Contracting State' has the meaning given in s.1(3) of the [Civil Jurisdiction and Judgments Act 1982];

(b) 'Regulation State' means a Member State;

(c) 'judgment' means, subject to any other enactment, any judgment given by a foreign court or tribunal, whatever the judgment may be called, and includes

(i) a decree;

(ii) an order;

(iii) a decision;

(iv) a writ of execution; and

(v) the determination of costs by an officer of the court;

(d) 'State of origin', in relation to any judgment, means the State in which that judgment was given.

(2) For the purposes of this section, 'domicile' is to be determined—

(a) in an application under the 1982 Act or the Lugano Convention, in accordance with ss.41 to 46 that Act;

(b) in an application under the Judgments Regulation, in accordance with paras 9 to 12 of Sch.1 to the Civil Jurisdiction and Judgments Order 2001.

PD 74A para.2

In r.74.2(1)(c), the definition of 'judgment' is 'subject to any other enactment'. Such provisions include—

(1) section 9(1) of the [Administration of Justice Act 1920], which limits enforcement under that Act to judgments of superior courts;

(2) section 1(1) of the Foreign Judgments (Reciprocal Enforcement) Act 1933, which limits enforcement under that Act to judgments of those courts specified in the relevant Order in Council;

(3) section 1(2) of the 1933 Act, which limits enforcement under that Act to money judgments.

Applications for registration

Pt 74 r.74.3

(1) This section provides rules about applications under—
   (a) section 9 of the [Administration of Justice Act 1920], in respect of judgments to which Pt II of that Act applies;
   (b) section 2 of the [Foreign Judgments (Reciprocal Enforcement) Act 1933], in respect of judgments to which Pt I of that Act applies;
   (c) section 4 of the [Civil Jurisdiction and Judgments Act 1982]; and
   (d) the Judgments Regulation [means Council Regulation (EC) No.44/2001 of December 22, 2000 on jurisdiction and the recognition and enforcement of judgments in civil and commercial matters, as amended from time to time and as applied by the Agreement made on October 19, 2005 between the European Community and the Kingdom of Denmark on jurisdiction and the recognition and enforcement of judgments in civil and commercial matters]; and
   (e) the **Lugano Convention**,
   for the registration of foreign judgments for enforcement in England and Wales.
(2) Applications—
   (a) must be made to the High Court; and
   (b) may be made without notice.

PD 74A para.4.1

Applications for the registration for enforcement in England and Wales of—
   (1) foreign judgments under r.74.3;
are assigned to the Queen's Bench Division and may be heard by a Master.

PD 74A para.4.4

[The **application** must be made in accordance with Pt 23].

Evidence in support

Pt 74 r.74.4

(1) An application for registration of a judgment under the 1920, 1933 or 1982 Acts must be supported by written evidence exhibiting—
   (a) the judgment or a verified or certified or otherwise authenticated copy of it; and
   (b) where the judgment is not in English, a translation of it into English—
      (i) certified by a notary public or other qualified person; or
      (ii) accompanied by written evidence confirming that the translation is accurate.
(2) The written evidence in support of the application must state—
   (a) the name of the judgment creditor and his address for service within the jurisdiction;
   (b) the name of the judgment debtor and his address or place of business, if known;
   (c) the grounds on which the judgment creditor is entitled to enforce the judgment;
   (d) in the case of a money judgment, the amount in respect of which it remains unsatisfied; and
   (e) where interest is recoverable on the judgment under the law of the State of origin—
      (i) the amount of interest which has accrued up to the date of the application, or

      (ii) the rate of interest, the date from which it is recoverable, and the date on which it ceases to accrue.

(3) Written evidence in support of an application under the 1920 Act must also state that the judgment is not a judgment—

  (a) which under s.9 of that Act may not be ordered to be registered; or

  (b) to which s.5 of the Protection of Trading Interests Act 1980 applies.

(4) Written evidence in support of an application under the 1933 Act must also—

  (a) state that the judgment is a money judgment;

  (b) confirm that it can be enforced by execution in the State of origin;

  (c) confirm that the registration could not be set aside under s.4 of that Act;

  (d) confirm that the judgment is not a judgment to which s.5 of the Protection of Trading Interests Act 1980 applies;

  (e) where the judgment contains different provisions, some but not all of which can be registered for enforcement, set out those provisions in respect of which it is sought to register the judgment; and

  (f) be accompanied by any further evidence as to—

    (i) the enforceability of the judgment in the State of origin, and

    (ii) the law of that State under which any interest has become due under the judgment,

which may be required under the relevant Order in Council extending Pt I of the 1933 Act to that State.

(5) Written evidence in support of an application under the 1982 Act must also exhibit—

  (a) documents which show that, under the law of the State of origin, the judgment is enforceable on the judgment debtor and has been served;

  (b) in the case of a judgment in default, a document which establishes that the party in default was served with the document instituting the proceedings or with an equivalent document; and

  (c) where appropriate, a document showing that the judgment creditor is in receipt of legal aid in the State of origin.

(6) An application for registration under the Judgments Regulation or the Lugano Convention must, in addition to the evidence required by that Regulation or that Convention, be supported by the evidence required by paras (1)(b) and (2)(e) of this rule.

Evidence in support: r.74.4(6)

PD 74A para.6.1

Where a judgment is to be recognised or enforced in a regulation state, the Judgments Regulation applies.

PD 74A para.6.2

As a consequence of art.38(2) of the Judgments Regulation, the provisions in Ch.III of that regulation relating to declaring judgments enforceable are the equivalent, in the UK, of provisions relating to registering judgments for enforcement.

PD 74A para.6.3

Chapter III of, and Annex V to, the Judgments Regulation are annexed to [PD 74A]. They were originally published in the official languages of the European Community in the Official Journal of the European Communities by the Office for Official Publications of the European Communities.

PD 74A para.6.4

Sections 2 and 3 of Ch.III of the Judgments Regulation (in particular arts 40, 53, 54 and 55, and Annex V) set out the evidence needed in support of an application.

PD 74A para.6.5

The Judgments Regulation is supplemented by the Civil Jurisdiction and Judgments Order 2001 (SI 2001/3929). The Order also makes amendments, in respect of that regulation, to the Civil Jurisdiction and Judgments Act 1982.

Evidence in support of application: rule 74(4)

PD 74A para.6A.1

Where a judgment is to be recognised or enforced in a Contracting State which is a State bound by the Lugano Convention, that Convention applies.

PD 74A para.6A.2

As a consequence of art.38(2) of the Lugano Convention the provisions of Title III of that Convention relating to declaring judgments enforceable are the equivalent, in the UK, of provisions relating to registering judgments for enforcement.

PD 74A para.6A.3

Title III of, and Annex V to, the Lugano Convention are annexed to [PD 74A]. They were originally published in the official languages of the European Community in the Official Journal of the European Communities by the Office for Official Publications of the European Communities.

PD 74A para.6A.4

Sections 2 and 3 of Title III of the Lugano Convention (in particular arts 40, 53, 54 and Annex V) set out the evidence needed in support of an application.

PD 74A 6A.5

The Civil Jurisdiction and Judgments (England and Wales and Northern Ireland) Regulations 2009 make amendments to the Civil Jurisdiction and Judgments Act 1982 in respect of the Lugano Convention.

Security for costs

Pt 74 r.74.5

(1) Subject to paras (2) and (3), s.II of Pt 25 applies to an application for security for the costs of—
(a) the application for registration;

(b) any proceedings brought to set aside the registration; and

(c) any appeal against the granting of the registration

as if the judgment creditor were a claimant.

(2) A judgment creditor making an application under the 1982 Act or the Lugano Convention, the Judgments Regulation may not be required to give security solely on the ground that he is resident out of the jurisdiction.

(3) Paragraph (1) does not apply to an application under the 1933 Act where the relevant Order in Council otherwise provides.

Registration orders

Pt 74 r.74.6

(1) An order granting permission to register a judgment ('a registration order') must be drawn up by the judgment creditor and served on the judgment debtor—

(a) by delivering it to the judgment debtor personally;

(b) by any of the methods of service permitted under the Companies Act 2006; or

(c) in such other manner as the court may direct.

(2) Permission is not required to serve a registration order out of the jurisdiction, and rr.6.40, 6.42, 6.43 and 6.46 apply to such an order as they apply to a claim form.

(3) A registration order must state—

(a) full particulars of the judgment registered;

(b) the name of the judgment creditor and his address for service within the jurisdiction;

(c) the right of the judgment debtor—

(i) in the case of registration following an application under the 1920 or the 1933 Act, to apply to have the registration set aside;

(ii) in the case of registration following an application under the 1982 Act the Lugano Convention, or the Judgments Regulation, to appeal against the registration order;

(d) the period within which such an application or appeal may be made; and

(e) that no measures of enforcement will be taken before the end of that period, other than measures ordered by the court to preserve the property of the judgment debtor.

Applications to set aside registration

Pt 74 r.74.7

(1) An application to set aside registration under the 1920 or the 1933 Act must be made within the period set out in the registration order.

(2) The court may extend that period, but an application for such an extension must be made before the end of the period as originally fixed or as subsequently extended.

(3) The court hearing the application may order any issue between the judgment creditor and the judgment debtor to be tried.

PD 74A para.4.4

[The application must be made in accordance with Pt 23].

Appeals

Pt 74 r.74.8

(1) An appeal against the granting or the refusal of registration under the 1982 Act or the Lugano Convention or the Judgments Regulation must be made in accordance with Pt 52, subject to the following provisions of this rule.

(2) Permission is not required—
   (a) to appeal; or
   (b) to put in evidence.

(3) If—
   (a) the judgment debtor is not domiciled within a Contracting State or a Regulation State, as the case may be, and
   (b) an application to extend the time for appealing is made within two months of service of the registration order
   the court may extend the period for filing an appellant's notice against the order granting registration, but not on grounds of distance.

(4) The appellant's notice must be served—
   (a) where the appeal is against the granting of registration, within—
      (i) one month; or
      (ii) where service is to be effected on a party not domiciled within the jurisdiction, two months of service of the registration order;
   (b) where the appeal is against the refusal of registration, within one month of the decision on the application for registration.

Enforcement

Pt 74 r.74.9

(1) No steps may be taken to enforce a judgment—
   (a) before the end of the period specified in accordance with r.74.6(3)(d), or that period as extended by the court; or
   (b) where there is an application under r.74.7 or an appeal under r.74.8, until the application or appeal has been determined.

(2) Any party wishing to enforce a judgment must file evidence of the service on the judgment debtor of—
   (a) the registration order; and
   (b) any other relevant order of the court.

(3) Nothing in this rule prevents the court from making orders to preserve the property of the judgment debtor pending final determination of any issue relating to the enforcement of the judgment.

Recognition

Pt 74 r.74.10

(1) Registration of a judgment serves as a decision that the judgment is recognised for the purposes of the 1982 Act, the Lugano Convention and the Judgments Regulation.

(2) An application for recognition of a judgment is governed by the same rules as an application for registration of a judgment under the 1982 Act, the Lugano Convention or the Judgments Regulation, except that r.74.4(5)(a) and (c) does not apply.

Authentic instruments and court settlements

Pt 74 r.74.11

The rules governing the registration of judgments under the 1982 Act, the Lugano Convention or the Judgments Regulation apply as appropriate and with any necessary modifications for the enforcement of—
  (a) authentic instruments which are subject to—
      (i) article 50 of Sch.3C to the 1982 Act;
      (ii) article 57 of the Lugano Convention; and
      (iii) article 57 of the Judgments Regulation; and
  (b) court settlements which are subject to—
      (i) article 51 of Sch.1 to the 1982 Act;
      (ii) article 58 of the Lugano Convention; and
      (iii) article 58 of the Judgments Regulation.

See also **European Community judgments** and **European Enforcement Order**.

ENFORCEMENT OF JUDGMENT FOR POSSESSION OF LAND

High Court

RSC Ord.45 r.3

  (1) Subject to the provisions of these rules, a judgment or order for the giving of possession of land may be enforced by one or more of the following means, that is to say—
      (a) **writ of possession**;
      (b) in a case in which r.5 applies, an order of **committal**;
      (c) in a case in which r.81.20 applies, **writ of sequestration**.
  (2) A writ of possession to enforce a judgment or order for the giving of possession of any land shall not be issued without the permission of the court except where the judgment or order was given or made in proceedings by a mortgagee or mortgagor or by any person having the right to foreclose or redeem any mortgage, being proceedings in which there is a claim for—
      (a) payment of moneys secured by the mortgage;
      (b) sale of the mortgaged property;
      (c) foreclosure;
      (d) delivery of possession (whether before or after foreclosure or without foreclosure) to the mortgagee by the mortgagor or by any person who is alleged to be in possession of the property;
      (e) redemption;
      (f) reconveyance of the land or its release from the security; or
      (g) delivery of possession by the mortgagee.
  (2A) In para.(2) 'mortgage' includes a legal or equitable mortgage and a legal or equitable charge, and reference to a mortgagor, a mortgagee and mortgaged land is to be interpreted accordingly.
  (3) Such permission as is referred to in para.(2) shall not be granted unless it is shown—
      (a) that every person in actual possession of the whole or any part of the land has received such notice of the proceedings as appears to the court sufficient to enable him to apply to the court for any relief to which he may be entitled; and
      (b) if the operation of the judgment or order is suspended by subs.(2) of s.16 of the **Landlord and Tenant Act, 1954**, that the applicant has not received notice in writing

from the tenant that he desires that the provisions of paras (a) and (b) of that subsection shall have effect.

(4) A writ of possession may include provision for enforcing the payment of any money adjudged or ordered to be paid by the judgment or order which is to be enforced by the writ.

See **Writ of possession**.

ENFORCEMENT OF UNITED KINGDOM JUDGMENTS IN OTHER PARTS OF THE UNITED KINGDOM

Pt 74 r.74.14

In [s.III of Pt 74]—
(a) 'money provision' means a provision for the payment of one or more sums of money in a judgment whose enforcement is governed by s.18 of, and Sch.6 to, the [Civil Jurisdiction and Judgments Act 1982]; and
(b) 'non-money provision' means a provision for any relief or remedy not requiring payment of a sum of money in a judgment whose enforcement is governed by s.18 of, and Sch.7 to, the 1982 Act.

Registration of money judgments in the High Court

Pt 74 r.74.15

(1) This rule applies to applications to the High Court under para.5 of Sch.6 to the 1982 Act for the registration of a certificate for the enforcement of the money provisions of a judgment—
(a) which has been given by a court in another part of the UK, and
(b) to which s.18 of that Act applies.
(2) The certificate must within six months of the date of its issue be filed in the Central Office of the Senior Courts, together with a copy certified by written evidence to be a true copy.

PD 74A para.8.1

A certificate of a money judgment of a court in Scotland or Northern Ireland must be filed for enforcement under r.74.15(2) in the Action Department of the Central Office of the Senior Courts, Royal Courts of Justice, Strand, London WC2A 2LL. The copy will be sealed by a court officer before being returned to the applicant.

PD 74A para.4.4

[The application must be made in accordance with Pt 23].

Registration of non-money judgments in the High Court

PD 74A para.4.1

Applications for the registration for enforcement in England and Wales of—
(2) judgments of courts in Scotland or Northern Ireland;
are assigned to the Queen's Bench Division and may be heard by a Master.

Pt 74 r.74.16

(1) This rule applies to applications to the High Court under para.5 of Sch.7 to the 1982 Act for the registration for enforcement of the non-money provisions of a judgment—
    (a) which has been given by a court in another part of the UK, and
    (b) to which s.18 of that Act applies.
(2) An application under para.(1) may be made without notice.
(3) An application under para.(1) must be accompanied
    (a) by a certified copy of the judgment issued under Sch.7 to the 1982 Act; and
    (b) by a certificate, issued not more than six months before the date of the application, stating that the conditions set out in para.3 of Sch.7 are satisfied in relation to the judgment.
(4) Rule 74.6 applies to judgments registered under Sch.7 to the 1982 Act as it applies to judgments registered under s.4 of that Act.
(5) Rule 74.7 applies to applications to set aside the registration of a judgment under para.9 of Sch.7 to the 1982 Act as it applies to applications to set aside registrations under the 1920 and 1933 Acts.

PD 74A para.4.1

Applications for the registration for enforcement in England and Wales of—
    (1) judgments of courts in Scotland or Northern Ireland;
are assigned to the Queen's Bench Division and may be heard by a Master.

Certificates of High Court and county court money judgments

Pt 74 r.74.17

(1) This rule applies to applications under para.2 of Sch.6 to the 1982 Act for a certificate to enable the money provisions of a judgment of the High Court or of a county court to be enforced in another part of the UK.
(2) The judgment creditor may apply for a certificate by filing at the court where the judgment was given or has been entered written evidence stating—
    (a) the name and address of the judgment creditor and, if known, of the judgment debtor;
    (b) the sums payable and unsatisfied under the money provisions of the judgment;
    (c) where interest is recoverable on the judgment, either—
        (i) the amount of interest which has accrued up to the date of the application, or
        (ii) the rate of interest, the date from which it is recoverable, and the date on which it ceases to accrue;
    (d) that the judgment is not stayed;
    (e) the date on which the time for appealing expired or will expire;
    (f) whether an appeal notice has been filed;
    (g) the status of any application for permission to appeal; and
    (h) whether an appeal is pending.

PD 74A para.8.2

A certificate issued under r.74.17 for the enforcement in Scotland or Northern Ireland of a money judgment of the High Court or of a county court will be in Form 111.

Certified copies of High Court and county court non-money judgments

PD 74A para.4.3

[An application] must be made—
1. (1) in the case of a judgment given in the Chancery Division or the Queen's Bench Division of the High Court, to a Master, Registrar or district judge;
2. (2) in the case of a judgment given in the Family Division of the High Court, to a district judge of that Division;
3. (3) in the case of a county court judgment, to a district judge.

Pt 74 r.74.18

(1) This rule applies to applications under para.2 of Sch.7 to the 1982 Act for a certified copy of a judgment of the High Court or of a county court to which s.18 of the Act applies and which contains non-money provisions for enforcement in another part of the UK.
(2) An application under para.(1) may be made without notice.
(3) The applicant may apply for a certified copy of a judgment by filing at the court where the judgment was given or has been entered written evidence stating—
   (a) full particulars of the judgment;
   (b) the name and address of the judgment creditor and, if known, of the judgment debtor;
   (c) that the judgment is not stayed;
   (d) the date on which the time for appealing expired or will expire;
   (e) whether an appeal notice has been filed;
   (f) the status of any application for permission to appeal; and
   (g) whether an appeal is pending.

PD 74A para.4.3

[An application] must be made—
1. (1) in the case of a judgment given in the Chancery Division or the Queen's Bench Division of the High Court, to a Master, Registrar or district judge;
2. (2) in the case of a judgment given in the Family Division of the High Court, to a district judge of that Division;
3. (3) in the case of a county court judgment, to a district judge.

PD 74A para.8.3

In an application by a judgment creditor under r.74.18 for the enforcement in Scotland or Northern Ireland of a non-money judgment of the High Court or of a county court, the certified copy of the judgment will be a sealed copy to which will be annexed a certificate in Form 112.

Applications under the 1933 Act

PD 74A para.5

Foreign judgments are enforceable in England and Wales under the [Foreign Judgments (Reciprocal Enforcement) Act 1933] where there is an agreement on the reciprocal enforcement of judgments between the UK and the country in which the judgment was given. Such an agreement may contain particular provisions governing the enforcement of judgments (for example limiting the categories of judgments which are enforceable, or the courts whose judgments are enforceable). Any such specific limitations will be listed in the Order in Council giving effect in the UK to the agreement in question, and the rules in s.I of Pt 74 will take effect subject to such limitations.

ENFORCEMENT UNDER THE MERCHANT SHIPPING (LINER CONFERENCES) ACT 1982

PD 74A para.10

The Merchant Shipping (Liner Conferences) Act 1982 ('the Act') contains provisions for the settlement of disputes between liner conferences, shipping lines and shippers. This section of [PD 74A] deals with the enforcement by the High Court under s.9 of the Act of recommendations of conciliators, and determinations and awards of costs.

Exercise of powers under the Act

PD 74A para.11

The powers of the High Court under the Act are exercised by the Commercial Court.

Applications for registration

PD 74A para.12.1

An application under s.9 of the Act for the registration of a recommendation, determination or award is made under Pt 23.

PD 74A para.12.2

An application for the registration of a recommendation must be supported by written evidence exhibiting—
    (1) a verified or certified or otherwise authenticated copy of—
        (a) the recommendation;
        (b) the reasons for it; and
        (c) the record of settlement,
    (2) where any of those documents is not in English, a translation of it into English—
        (a) certified by a notary public or other qualified person; or
        (b) accompanied by written evidence confirming that the translation is accurate; and
    (3) copies of the acceptance of the recommendation by the parties on whom it is binding, or otherwise verifying the acceptance where it is not in writing.

PD 74A para.12.3

The evidence in support of the application must—
    (1) give particulars of the failure to implement the recommendation; and
    (2) confirm that none of the grounds which would render it unenforceable is applicable.

PD 74A para.12.4

An application for the registration of a determination of costs or an award of costs must be supported by written evidence—
(1) exhibiting a verified or certified or otherwise authenticated copy of the recommendation or other document containing the determination or award; and
(2) stating that the costs have not been paid.

Order for registration

PD 74A para.13.1

The applicant must draw up the order giving permission to register the recommendation, determination or award.

PD 74A para.13.2

The order must include a provision that the reasonable costs of the registration should be assessed.

Register of recommendations

PD 74A para.14.

There will be kept in the Admiralty and Commercial Registry at the Royal Courts of Justice, under the direction of the Senior Master, a register of the recommendations, determinations and awards ordered to be registered under s.9 of the Act, with particulars of enforcement.

ENGINEERING DISPUTES

See **Construction and engineering disputes**.

ENROLMENT OF DEEDS

PD 5A para.6.1

(1) Any deed or document which by virtue of any enactment is required or authorised to be enrolled in the Senior Courts may be enrolled in the Central Office of the High Court.
(2) Attention is drawn to the Enrolment of Deeds (Change of Name) Regulations 1994 which are reproduced in the Appendix to this PD.

PD 5A para.6.2

The following paragraph of the PD describes the practice to be followed in any case in which a child's name is to be changed and to which the 1994 Regulations apply.

PD 5A para.6.3

(1) Where a person has by any order of the High Court, county court or Family Proceedings Court been given parental responsibility for a child and applies to the Central Office, Filing Department, for the enrolment of a Deed Poll to change the surname (family name) of a child who is under the age of 18 years (unless a child who is or has been married or has formed a civil partnership), the application must be supported by the production of the consent in writing of every other person having parental responsibility.

(2) In the absence of that consent, the application will be adjourned generally unless and until permission is given in the proceedings, in which the said order was made, to change the surname of the child and the permission is produced to the Central Office.

(3) Where an application is made to the Central Office by a person who has not been given parental responsibility for a child by any order of the High Court, County Court or Family Proceedings Court for the enrolment of a Deed Poll to change the surname of the child who is under the age of 18 years (unless the child is or has been married or has formed a civil partnership), permission of the Court to enrol the Deed will be granted if the consent in writing of every person having parental responsibility is produced or if the person (or, if more than one, persons) having parental responsibility is dead or overseas or despite the exercise of reasonable diligence it has not been possible to find him or her for other good reason.

(4) In cases of doubt the Senior Master or, in his absence, the Practice Master will refer the matter to the Master of the Rolls.

(5) In the absence of any of the conditions specified above the Senior Master or the Master of the Rolls, as the case may be, may refer the matter to the Official Solicitor for investigation and report.

ENTERPRISE ACT 2002

Application for a warrant

PD Application for a warrant under the Enterprise Act 2002 para.2.1

An application by the OFT [Office of Fair Trading] for a warrant [under s.194 of the Act] must be made to a High Court judge using the Part 8 procedure as modified by this PD.

PD AWEA para.2.2

The application must be made to a judge of the Chancery Division at the Royal Courts of Justice.

PD AWEA para.2.3

The application is made without notice and the claim form may be issued without naming a defendant. Rules 8.1(3), 8.3, 8.4, 8.5(2)–(6), 8.6(1), 8.7 and 8.8 do not apply.

Confidentiality of court documents

PD AWEA para.3.1

The court will not serve any claim form, warrant, or other document filed or issued in an application to which this PD applies, except in accordance with an order of the judge hearing the application.

PD AWEA para.3.2

CPR rules 5.4(2), 5.4B and 5.4C do not apply, and paras 3.3 and 3.4 have effect in their place.

PD AWEA para.3.3

When a claim form is issued the court file will be marked 'Not for disclosure' and, unless a High Court judge grants permission, the court records relating to the application (including the claim form and documents filed in support and any warrant or order that is issued) will not be made available by the court for any person to inspect or copy, either before or after the hearing of the application.

PD AWEA para.3.4

An application for permission under para.3.3 must be made on notice to the OFT in accordance with Pt 23.
(Rule 23.7(1) requires a copy of the application notice to be served as soon as practicable after it is filed, and in any event at least three days before the court is to deal with the application).

Contents of claim form, affidavit and documents in support

PD AWEA para.4.1

The claim form must state—
    (1) that the OFT is applying for a warrant under s.194 of the Act;
    (2) the address or other identification of the premises to be subject to the warrant; and
    (3) the anticipated date or dates for the execution of the warrant.

PD AWEA para.4.2

The application must be supported by affidavit evidence, which must be filed with the claim form.

PD AWEA para.4.3

The evidence must set out all the matters on which the OFT relies in support of the application, including all material facts of which the court should be made aware. In particular it must state—
    (1) the subject matter (i.e. the nature of the suspected offence under s.188 of the Act) and purpose of the investigation to which the application relates;
    (2) the identity of the person or persons suspected to have committed the offence;
    (3) the grounds for applying for the issue of the warrant and the facts relied upon in support;
    (4) details of the premises to be subject to the warrant and of the possible occupier or occupiers of those premises;
    (5) the connection between the premises and the person or persons suspected to have committed the offence;
    (6) the name and position of the officer who it is intended will be the named officer;
    (7) the name and position of the officer or officers who it is intended will accompany the named officer;

(8) if it is intended that the named officer is to be a person who is not an officer and who has been authorised by the OFT pursuant to s.195(1) of the Act to exercise on its behalf all or any of the powers conferred by s.194 of the Act and to act as the named officer, the name and job title of such person and the reason why it is intended that he may act as the named officer and exercise the relevant powers conferred by s.194 of the Act;

(9) if it is intended that the warrant may pursuant to s.194(4) of the Act authorise any person (other than an officer) to accompany the named officer in executing the warrant, the name and job title of each such person and the reason why it is intended that he may accompany the named officer; and

(10) if it is intended that any competent person who is not an officer will be authorised by the OFT pursuant to s.195(1) to exercise on its behalf all or any of the powers conferred by s.194, the name and job title of each such person and the reason why it is intended that he may exercise such powers.

PD AWEA para.4.4

There must be exhibited to an affidavit in support of the application the written authorisation of the OFT containing the names of all persons falling within the categories described at sub-paras (6) to (10) of para.4.3 above.

PD AWEA para.4.5

There must also be filed with the claim form—
(1) a draft of the warrant;
(2) the Notice [of the powers to search premises and the rights of occupiers] to be produced and served with it; and
(3) the written undertaking by the named officer required by para.6.2 of this PD.
(An example of the form of a warrant under s.194 of the Act, and the Notice to be produced and served with it, are annexed to this PD).

PD AWEA para.4.6

If possible the draft warrant and the Notice should also be supplied to the court on disk or electronically in a form compatible with the word processing software used by the court.

Listing

PD AWEA para.5.

The application will be listed by the court on any published list of cases as 'An application by [D]'.

Hearing of the application

PD AWEA para.6.1

An application for a warrant will be heard and determined in private, unless the judge hearing it directs otherwise.

PD AWEA para.6.2

The court will not issue a warrant unless there has been filed a written undertaking, signed by the named officer, to comply with para.8.1 of this PD.

Warrant

PD AWEA para.7.1

The warrant must—
  (1) state the address or other identification of the premises to be subject to the warrant;
  (2) state the names of—
    (a) the named officer; and
    (b) any other officers or other persons who may accompany him in executing the warrant;
  (3) set out the action which the warrant authorises the persons executing it to take under s.194 of the Act;
  (4) give the date on which the warrant is issued; and
  (5) state that the named officer has given the undertaking required by para.6.2.

PD AWEA para.7.2

Rule 40.2 applies to a warrant.
(Rule 40.2 requires every judgment or order to state the name and judicial title of the person making it, to bear the date on which it is given or made, and to be sealed by the court).

PD AWEA para.7.3

Upon the issue of a warrant the court will provide to the OFT—
  (1) the sealed warrant and the Notice; and
  (2) a copy of the sealed warrant and the Notice for service on the occupier or person in charge of the premises subject to the warrant.

Execution of warrant

PD AWEA para.8.1

A named officer attending premises to execute a warrant must, if the premises are occupied—
  (1) produce the warrant and Notice immediately upon arrival at the premises to the occupier or any other person entitled to grant access to the premises, explaining the authority under which entry is sought; and
  (2) as soon as possible after his arrival at the premises, personally serve a copy of the warrant and Notice on the occupier or person appearing to him to be in charge of the premises.

The named officer is not required to serve the warrant and Notice personally if he reasonably believes this would frustrate the object of the search or endanger officers or other people.

PD AWEA para.8.2

If the occupier is not present, the named officer shall leave copies of the warrant and Notice of the powers to search premises and of the rights of occupiers in a prominent place on the premises or appropriate part of the premises, recording the name of the named officer in charge of the search and the date and time of the search, unless the named officer reasonably believes recording or disclosing his name might put him in danger.

PD AWEA para.8.3

The named officer must also comply with any order which the court may make for service of any other documents relating to the application.

PD AWEA para.8.4

Unless the court otherwise orders—
    (1) the initial production of a warrant and entry to premises under the authority of the warrant must take place at a reasonable hour, unless this might frustrate the purpose of the search; but
    (2) once persons named in the warrant have entered premises under the authority of a warrant, they may, whilst the warrant remains in force—
        (a) remain on the premises; or
        (b) re-enter the premises to continue executing the warrant.

PD AWEA para.8.5

If the persons executing a warrant propose to remove any items from the premises pursuant to the warrant they must, unless it is impracticable—
    (1) make a list of all the items to be removed;
    (2) supply a copy of the list to the occupier or person appearing to be in charge of the premises; and
    (3) give that person a reasonable opportunity to check the list before removing any of the items.

Application to vary or discharge warrant

PD AWEA para.9.1

The occupier or person in charge of premises in relation to which a warrant has been issued may apply to vary or discharge the warrant.

PD AWEA para.9.2

An application under para.9.1 to stop a warrant from being executed must be made immediately upon the warrant being served.

PD AWEA para.9.3

A person applying to vary or discharge a warrant must first inform the named officer that he is making the application.

PD AWEA para.9.4

The application should be made to the judge who issued the warrant, or, if he is not available, to another judge of the Chancery Division.

Expiry of the warrant

PD AWEA para.10

The warrant will expire one month after the date on which it is issued.

Application under s.59 of the Criminal Justice and Police Act 2001

PD AWEA para.11

Attention is drawn to s.59 of the Criminal Justice and Police Act 2001, which makes provision about applications relating to property seized in the exercise of the powers conferred by (among other provisions) s.194(2) of the Act.

See **Competition Appeal Tribunal.**

ENVIRONMENTAL CONTROL PROCEEDINGS

EQUALITY ACT 2006

See **Discrimination proceedings.**

EQUALITY ACT (SEXUAL ORIENTATION) REGULATIONS 2007

See **Discrimination proceedings.**

EQUALITY PROCEEDINGS

PD—Proceedings under enactments relating to equality para.1.1.

This PD applies to certain county court proceedings under the enactments defined in paragraph PD—PEE para.1.2.
    (1) Equality Act 2006;
    (2) Equality Act 2010.

PD—PEE para.1.3

For proceedings which relate to conduct before October 1, 2010, the PD on Proceedings Under Enactments Relating to **Discrimination** applies.

Commission to be given notice of claims

PD—PEE para.2

When a claim under s.114 of the [Equality Act 2010] is commenced, the claimant must give notice of the commencement of the proceedings to the Commission [Equality and Human Rights] and file a copy of that notice.

Assessors

PD—PEE para.3

Rule 35.15 has effect in relation to an **assessor** who is to be appointed in proceedings under s.114 (7) of the 2010 Act.

Exclusion of persons from certain proceedings

PD—PEE para.4.1

In a claim brought under s.114 of the 2010 Act the court may, where it considers it expedient in the interests of national security—
    (a) exclude from all or part of the proceedings—
        (i) the claimant;
       (ii) a representative of the claimant;
      (iii) an assessor;
    (b) permit a claimant or representative who has been excluded to make a statement to the court before the commencement of the proceedings, or the part of the proceedings, to which the exclusion relates;
    (c) take steps to keep secret all or part of the reasons for its decision in the claim.

PD—PEE para.4.2

In this paragraph, a 'special advocate' means a person appointed under s.117(5) of the 2010 Act.

PD—PEE para.4.3

In proceedings to which this paragraph refers, where the claimant or a representative of the claimant has been excluded from all or part of the proceedings—
    (a) the court will inform the Attorney General of the proceedings; and
    (b) the Attorney General may appoint a special advocate to represent the interests of a claimant in, or in any part of, proceedings to which an exclusion under para.4.1 relates.

PD—PEE para.4.4

In exercise of its powers under para.4.1(c), the court may order the special advocate not to communicate (directly or indirectly) with any person (including the excluded claimant)—
    (a) on any matter discussed or referred to; or
    (b) with regard to any material disclosed,
during or with reference to any part of the proceedings to which an exclusion under para.4.1 relates.

PD—PEE para.4.5

Where the court makes an order referred to in para.4.4 (or any similar order), the special advocate may apply for permission to seek instructions from, or otherwise to communicate with an excluded person and the court may make directions for that purpose.

Expenses of commission

PD—PEE para.5.1

This paragraph applies where the Commission has, in respect of a claim, provided a claimant with assistance under s.28 of the Equality Act 2006.

PD—PEE para.5.2

If the Commission claims a charge for expenses incurred by it in providing such assistance, it must give notice of the claim to—
  (a) the court; and
  (b) the claimant,
within 14 days of determination of the proceedings.

PD—PEE para.5.3

If notice is given to the court under para.5.2—
  (a) money paid into court for the benefit of the claimant that relates to costs and expenses must not be paid out unless this is permitted by an order of the court; and
  (b) the court may order the expenses incurred by the Commission to be assessed and paid as if they were costs payable by claimant to own solicitor.

PD—PEE para.5.4

The court may either—
  (a) make a summary assessment of the expenses; or
  (b) order detailed assessment of the expenses by a costs officer.

EQUITABLE EXECUTION

See **Receiver**.

EURATOM INSPECTION ORDER

Pt 74 r.74.19

  (b) An order made by the President of the European Court, or a decision of the Commission of the European Communities, under art.81 of the Euratom Treaty.

Registration and enforcement

Pt 74 r.74.26

(1) Rules 74.20, 74.21(1), and 74.22(1) and (2), which apply to the registration of a Community judgment, also apply to the registration of a Euratom inspection order but with the necessary modifications.
(2) An application under art.6 of the European Communities (Enforcement of Community Judgments) Order 1972 to give effect to a Euratom inspection order may be made on written evidence, and—
   (a) where the matter is urgent, without notice;
   (b) otherwise, by claim form.

EUROPEAN COMMUNITIES (SERVICES OF LAWYERS) ORDER 1978

Annex 2 of PD 6A para.4.

The provisions of this Order shall have effect for the purpose of enabling a European lawyer to pursue his professional activities in any part of the UK by providing, under the conditions specified in or permitted by the Directive, services otherwise reserved to advocates, barristers and solicitors.

EUROPEAN COMMUNITY JUDGMENTS

Enforcement in England and Wales

PD 74A para.9.1

Enforcement of Community judgments and of **Euratom inspection orders** is governed by the European Communities (Enforcement of Community Judgments) Order 1972.

PD 74A para 9.2

The Treaty establishing the European Community is the Treaty establishing the European Economic Community (Rome, 1957); relevant amendments are made by the Treaty of Amsterdam (1997, Cm.3780).

PD 74A para.9.3

The text of the Protocol of June 3, 1971 on the interpretation by the European Court of the Convention of September 27, 1968 on Jurisdiction and the Enforcement of Judgments in Civil and Commercial Matters is set out in Sch.2 to the Civil Jurisdiction and Judgments Act 1982.

PD 74A para.9.4

The text of the Protocol of December 19, 1988 on the interpretation by the European Court of the Convention of June 19, 1980 on the Law applicable to Contractual Obligations is set out in Sch.3 to the Contracts (Applicable Law) Act 1990. After the commencement on December 17,

2009 of EC Regulation 593/2008 ('the Rome I Regulation') this Convention and Protocol will only apply to contracts concluded before that date.

Pt 74 r.74.19

In this section—
- (a) 'Community judgment' means any judgment, decision or order which is enforceable under—
    - (i) article 244 or 256 of the Treaty establishing the European Community;
    - (ii) article 18, 159 or 164 of the Euratom Treaty;
    - (iii) article 44 or 92 of the ECSC Treaty;
    - (iv) article 82 of Council Regulation (EC) 40/94 of December 20, 1993 on the Community trade mark; or
    - (v) article 71 of Council Regulation (EC) 6/2002 of December 12, 2001 on Community designs;

Application for registration of a community judgment

Pt 74 r.74.20

An application to the High Court for the registration of a Community judgment may be made without notice.

PD 74A para.4.1

Applications for the registration for enforcement in England and Wales of—
    (3) [Community judgments]
are assigned to the Queen's Bench Division and may be heard by a Master.

Evidence in support

Pt 74 r.74.21

- (1) An application for registration must be supported by written evidence exhibiting—
    - (a) the Community judgment and the order for its enforcement, or an authenticated copy; and
    - (b) where the judgment is not in English, a translation of it into English—
        - (i) certified by a notary public or other qualified person; or
        - (ii) accompanied by written evidence confirming that the translation is accurate.
- (2) Where the application is for registration of a Community judgment which is a money judgment, the evidence must state—
    - (a) the name of the judgment creditor and his address for service within the jurisdiction;
    - (b) the name of the judgment debtor and his address or place of business, if known;
    - (c) the amount in respect of which the judgment is unsatisfied; and
    - (d) that the European Court [means the Court of Justice of the European Communities] has not suspended enforcement of the judgment.

Registration orders

Pt 74 r.74.22

(1) A copy of the order granting permission to register a Community judgment ('the registration order') must be served on every person against whom the judgment was given.

(2) The registration order must state the name and address for service of the person who applied for registration, and must exhibit—
    (a) a copy of the registered Community judgment; and
    (b) a copy of the order for its enforcement.

(3) In the case of a Community judgment which is a money judgment, the registration order must also state the right of the judgment debtor to apply within 28 days for the variation or cancellation of the registration under r.74.23.

Application to vary or cancel registration

Pt 74 r.74.23

(1) An application to vary or cancel the registration of a Community judgment which is a money judgment on the ground that at the date of registration the judgment had been partly or wholly satisfied must be made within 28 days of the date on which the registration order was served on the judgment debtor.

(2) The application must be supported by written evidence.

Enforcement

Pt 74 r.74.24

No steps may be taken to enforce a Community judgment which is a money judgment—
    (a) before the end of the period specified in accordance with r.74.23(1); or
    (b) where an application is made under that rule, until it has been determined.

Application for registration of suspension order

Pt 74 r.74.25

(1) Where the European Court has made an order that the enforcement of a registered Community judgment should be suspended, an application for the registration of that order in the High Court is made by filing a copy of the order in the Central Office of the Senior Courts.

(2) The application may be made without notice.

EUROPEAN CONVENTION ON HUMAN RIGHTS

Pt 33 r.33.9

(1) This rule applies where a claim is—
    (a) for a remedy under s.7 of the Human Rights Act 1998 in respect of a judicial act which is alleged to have infringed the claimant's art.5 Convention rights; and

    (b) based on a finding by a court or tribunal that the claimant's Convention rights have
        been infringed.
  (2) The court hearing the claim—
    (a) may proceed on the basis of the finding of that other court or tribunal that there has
        been an infringement but it is not required to do so, and
    (b) may reach its own conclusion in the light of that finding and of the evidence heard
        by that other court or tribunal.

Committal applications

PD 81 para.9

In all cases the convention rights of those involved should particularly be borne in mind. It
should be noted that the burden of proof, having regard to the possibility that a person may be
sent to prison, is that the allegation be proved beyond reasonable doubt.
(Section 1 of the Human Rights Act defines 'the Convention rights').

Hearings

PD 39A para.1.4A

The judge should also have regard to art.6(1) of the European Convention on Human Rights.
This requires that, in general, court hearings are to be held in public, but the press and public may
be excluded in the circumstances specified in that Article. Article 6(1) will usually be relevant,
for example, where a party applies for a hearing which would normally be held in public to be
held in private as well as where a hearing would normally be held in private. The judge may need
to consider whether the case is within any of the exceptions permitted by art.6(1).

Judgments and orders

PD 40B para.14.4

On any application or appeal concerning—
    (i) a **committal** order;
   (ii) a refusal to grant **habeas corpus** or
  (iii) a secure accommodation order made under s.25 of the Children Act 1989,
if the court ordering the release of the person concludes that his Convention rights have been
infringed by the making of the order to which the application or appeal relates, the judgment or
order should so state. If the court does not do so, that failure will not prevent another court from
deciding the matter.

EUROPEAN COURT

Pt 68 r.68.1

  (b) 'the European Court' means the Court of Justice of the European Communities.

References to the European Court

Pt 68 r.68.1

In [Pt 68]—
   (a) 'the court' means the court making the order;
   (c) 'order' means an order referring a question to the European Court for a preliminary ruling
        under
           (i) article 234 of the Treaty establishing the European Community;
          (ii) article 150 of the Euratom Treaty;
         (iii) article 41 of the ECSC Treaty;
          (iv) the Protocol of June 3, 1971 on the interpretation by the European Court of the
                Convention of September 27, 1968 on Jurisdiction and the Enforcement of Judg-
                ments in Civil and Commercial Matters; or
           (v) the Protocol of December 19, 1988 on the interpretation by the European Court of the
                Convention of June 19, 1980 on the Law applicable to Contractual Obligations;
                and
   (d) 'reference' means a request to the European Court for a preliminary ruling.

Making of order

Pt 68 r.68.2

   (1) An order may be made at any stage of the proceedings—
        (a) by the court of its own initiative; or
        (b) on an application by a party in accordance with Pt 23.
   (2) An order may not be made—
        (a) in the High Court, by a Master or district judge;
        (b) in a county court, by a district judge.
   (3) The reference, which must contain the information required by Practice Direction 68,
        must be set out in a schedule to the order, and the court may give directions on the
        preparation of the schedule.

Wording of references

PD 68 para.1.1

Where the court intends to refer a question to the European Court it may direct the parties to
produce a draft of the reference but responsibility for the terms of the reference lies with the court
making the reference and not with the parties.

PD 68 para.1.2

The reference should identify as clearly and succinctly as possible the question on which the
court seeks the ruling of the European Court. In choosing the wording of the reference, it should
be remembered that it will need to be translated into many other languages.

PD 68 para.1.3

The court will incorporate the reference as a schedule to its order. The schedule must—
   (1) give the full name of the referring court;

(2) identify the parties;

(3) summarise the nature and history of the proceedings, including the salient facts, indicating whether these are proved or admitted or assumed;

(4) set out the relevant rules of national law;

(5) summarise the relevant contentions of the parties;

(6) explain why a ruling of the European Court is sought;

(7) identify the provisions of Community law which the European Court is being requested to interpret;

(8) state the question on which a ruling of the European Court is sought; and

(9) state any opinion on the answer to the question that may have been expressed by the court in the course of delivering judgment.

PD 68 para.1.4

If some of these matters are conveniently set out in a judgment, the relevant passages should be summarised succinctly. If it is not possible to produce such a summary, only those passages that contain information of the kind referred to in para.1.3 should be cited.

PD 68 para.1.5

The reference should not exceed 20 pages in length.

Request to apply the urgent preliminary ruling procedure

Pt 68 r.68.2A

Any request by the court to the European Court that the preliminary ruling be dealt with under its urgent preliminary ruling procedure must be made in a document separate from the order or in a covering letter.

PD 68 para.1A.1

The request to the European Court to apply its urgent preliminary ruling procedure must set out—

(1) the matters of fact and law which establish the urgency;

(2) the reasons why the urgent preliminary ruling procedure applies; and

(3) in so far as possible, the court's view on the answer to the question referred to the European Court for a preliminary ruling.

Transmission to the European Court

Pt 68 r.68.3

(1) The Senior Master will send a copy of—

(a) the order; and

(b) where relevant, any request to apply the urgent preliminary ruling procedure

to the Registrar of the European Court.

(2) Where an order is made by a county court, a court officer will send a copy of it to the Senior Master for onward transmission to the European Court.

(3) Unless the court orders otherwise, the Senior Master will not send a copy of the order to the European Court until—

  (a) the time for appealing against the order has expired; or
  (b) any application for permission to appeal has been refused, or any appeal has been determined.

PD 68 para.2.1

The order containing the reference, and where relevant any request to the European Court to apply its urgent preliminary ruling procedure, must be sent to the Senior Master, Room E101, Queen's Bench Division, Royal Courts of Justice, Strand, London, WC2A 2LL, for onward transmission to the European Court.

PD 68 para.2.2

The relevant court file must also be sent to the Senior Master at the above address.

Stay of proceedings

Pt 68 r.68.4

Where an order is made, unless the court orders otherwise the proceedings will be stayed until the European Court has given a preliminary ruling on the question referred to it.

Wording of references

PD 68 para.1.1

Where the court intends to refer a question to the European Court it may direct the parties to produce a draft of the reference but responsibility for the terms of the reference lies with the court making the reference and not with the parties.

PD 68 para.1.2

The reference should identify as clearly and succinctly as possible the question on which the court seeks the ruling of the European Court. In choosing the wording of the reference, it should be remembered that it will need to be translated into many other languages.

PD 68 para.1.3

The court will incorporate the reference as a schedule to its order. The schedule must—
  (1) give the full name of the referring court;
  (2) identify the parties;
  (3) summarise the nature and history of the proceedings, including the salient facts, indicating whether these are proved or admitted or assumed;
  (4) set out the relevant rules of national law;
  (5) summarise the relevant contentions of the parties;
  (6) explain why a ruling of the European Court is sought;
  (7) identify the provisions of Community law which the European Court is being requested to interpret;
  (8) state the question on which a ruling of the European Court is sought; and
  (9) state any opinion on the answer to the question that may have been expressed by the court in the course of delivering judgment.

PD 68 para.1.4

If some of these matters are conveniently set out in a judgment, the relevant passages should be summarised succinctly. If it is not possible to produce such a summary, only those passages that contain information of the kind referred to in para.1.3 should be cited.

PD 68 para.1.5

The reference should not exceed 20 pages in length.

Request to apply the urgent preliminary ruling procedure

PD 68 para.1A.1

The request to the European Court to apply its urgent preliminary ruling procedure must set out—
   (1) the matters of fact and law which establish the urgency;
   (2) the reasons why the urgent preliminary ruling procedure applies; and
   (3) in so far as possible, the court's view on the answer to the question referred to the European Court for a preliminary ruling.

Transmission to the European Court

PD 68 para.2.1

The order containing the reference, and where relevant any request to the European Court to apply its urgent preliminary ruling procedure, must be sent to the Senior Master, Room E101, Queen's Bench Division, Royal Courts of Justice, Strand, London, WC2A 2LL, for onward transmission to the European Court.

PD 68 para.2.2

The relevant court file must also be sent to the Senior Master at the above address.

European Court information note

PD 68 para.3

There are annexed to [PD 68]—
   (1) an Information Note issued by the European Court; and
   (2) a supplement to the Information Note following the implementation of the urgent ruling procedure applicable to references concerning the area of freedom, security and justice.

See also **Mediation settlement enforcement orders**.

EUROPEAN COURT OF JUSTICE

See **European Court**.

EUROPEAN ECONOMIC AREA STATES

See **Service of documents**.

EUROPEAN ENFORCEMENT ORDER

Pt 74 r.74.28(1)

In [s.V of Pt 7]—
  (a) European Enforcement Regulation].

Pt 74 r.74.27

  (1) In this section—
    (c) 'judgment', 'authentic instrument', 'member state of origin', 'member state of
       enforcement', and 'court of origin' have the meanings given by art.4 of the EEO
       Regulation; and
    (d) 'Regulation State' has the same meaning as 'Member State' in the EEO Regulation
       that is all Member States except Denmark.

Council regulation

PD 74B para.1.1

Certification and enforcement of European Enforcement Orders is governed by Council Regulation (EC) No 805/2004 creating a European Enforcement order for uncontested claims.

PD 74B para.1.2

The EEO Regulation [has the meaning given in European Enforcement Orders Regulations] is
annexed to [PD 74B. It was originally published in the official languages of the European
Community in the Official Journal of the European Communities by the Office for Official
Publications of the European Communities.

PD 74B para.1.3

A claim that does not meet the requirements of the EEO Regulation, or which the judgment
creditor does not wish to enforce using the EEO Regulation, may be enforceable using another
method of enforcement.

Certification of judgments of the courts of England and Wales

Pt 74 r.74.28

An application for an EEO certificate must be made by filing the relevant practice form in
accordance with art.6 of the EEO Regulation.

PD 74B para.1

An application under r.74.28 for a certificate of a High Court or county court judgment for enforcement in another Regulation State must be made using Form N219 or Form N219A—
(1) in the case of a judgment given in the Chancery or Queen's Bench Division of the High Court, or in a district registry, to a Master, Registrar or district judge; or
(2) in the case of a county court judgment, to a district judge.

PD 74B para.2.2

Where the application is granted, the court will send the EEO certificate and a sealed copy of the judgment to the person making the application. Where the court refuses the application, the court will give reasons for the refusal and may give further directions.

Applications for a certificate of lack or limitation of enforceability

Pt 74 r.74.29

An application under art.6(2) of the EEO Regulation for a certificate indicating the lack or limitation of enforceability of an EEO certificate must be made to the court of origin by application in accordance with Pt 23.
An application under art.10 of the EEO Regulation for rectification or withdrawal of an EEO certificate must be made to the court of origin and may be made by application in accordance with Pt 23.

PD 74B para.3.1

An application must be supported by written evidence in support of the grounds on which the judgment has ceased to be enforceable or its enforceability has been suspended or limited.

Applications for rectification or withdrawal

Pt 74 r.74.30

An application under art.10 of the EEO Regulation for rectification or withdrawal of an EEO certificate must be made to the court of origin and may be made by application in accordance with Pt 23.

PD 74B para.4.1

An application must be supported by written evidence in support of the grounds on which it is contended that the EEO should be rectified or withdrawn.

Enforcement of European enforcement orders in England and Wales

Pt 74 r.74.31

(1) A person seeking to enforce an EEO in England and Wales must lodge at the court in which enforcement proceedings are to be brought the documents required by art.20 of the EEO Regulation.

(2) Where a person applies to enforce an EEO expressed in a foreign currency, the application must contain a certificate of the sterling equivalent of the judgment sum at the close of business on the date nearest preceding the date of the application.

(Part 70 contains further rules about enforcement).

Refusal of enforcement

Pt 74 r.74.32

(1) An application under art.21 of the EEO Regulation that the court should refuse to enforce an EEO must be made by application in accordance with Pt 23 to the court in which the EEO is being enforced.

(2) The judgment debtor must, as soon as practicable, serve copies of any order made under art.21(1) on—
   (a) all other parties to the proceedings and any other person affected by the order ('the affected persons'); and
   (b) any court in which enforcement proceedings are pending in England and Wales ('the relevant courts').

(3) Upon service of the order on the affected persons, all enforcement proceedings under the EEO in the relevant courts will cease.

PD 74B para.6.1

An application must be accompanied by an official copy of the earlier judgment, any other documents relied upon and any translations required by the EEO Regulation and supported by written evidence showing—

(1) why the earlier judgment is irreconcilable with the judgment which the judgment creditor is seeking to enforce; and

(2) why the irreconcilability was not, and could not have been, raised as an objection in the proceedings in the court of origin.

Stay of or limitation on enforcement

Pt 74 r.74.33

(1) Where an EEO certificate has been lodged and the judgment debtor applies to stay or limit the enforcement proceedings under art.23 of the EEO Regulation, such application must be made in accordance with Pt 23 to the court in which the EEO is being enforced.

(2) The judgment debtor shall, as soon as practicable, serve a copy of any order made under the Article on—
   (a) all other parties to the proceedings and any other person affected by the order; and
   (b) any court in which enforcement proceedings are pending in England and Wales,
   and the order will not have effect on any person until it has been served in accordance with this rule and they have received it.

PD 74B para.7.1

Unless the court orders otherwise, an application must be accompanied by evidence of the application in the court of origin, including—

    (1) the application (or equivalent foreign process) or a copy of the application (or equivalent foreign process) certified by an appropriate officer of the court of origin; and

    (2) where that document is not in English, a translation of it into English—

        (a) certified by a notary public or person qualified to certify a translation in the Member State of the court of origin under Article 20(2)(c) of the EEO Regulation; or

        (b) accompanied by written evidence confirming that the translation is accurate.

PD 74B para.7.2

The written evidence in support of the application must state—

    (1) that an application has been brought in the member state of origin;

    (2) the nature of that application; and

    (3) the date on which the application was filed, the state of the proceedings and the date by which it is believed that the application will be determined.

Enforcement of European orders for payment

Pt 74 r.78.9

    (1) A person seeking to enforce an EOP in England and Wales must file at the court in which enforcement proceedings are to be brought the documents required by art.21 of the EOP Regulation.

    (2) Where a person applies to enforce an EOP expressed in a foreign currency, the application must contain a certificate of the sterling equivalent of the judgment sum at the close of business on the date nearest preceding the date of the application.

(Parts 70 to 74 contain further rules about enforcement).

Refusal of enforcement

Pt 74 r.78.10

    (1) An application under art.22 of the EOP Regulation that the court should refuse to enforce an EOP must be made in accordance with Pt 23 to the court in which the EOP is being enforced.

    (2) The judgment debtor must, as soon as practicable, serve copies of any order made under art.22 on—

        (a) all other parties to the proceedings and any other person affected by the order ('the affected persons'); and

        (b) any court in which enforcement proceedings of the EOP are pending in England and Wales ('the relevant courts').

    (3) Upon service of the order on the affected persons, all enforcement proceedings of the EOP in the relevant courts will cease.

Stay of or limitation on enforcement

Pt 74 r.78.11

    (1) Where the defendant has sought a review and also applies for a stay of or limitation on enforcement in accordance with art.23 of the EOP Regulation, such application must be made in accordance with Pt 23 to the court in which the EOP is being enforced.

(2) The defendant must, as soon as practicable, serve a copy of any order made under art.23 on—
  (a) all other parties to the proceedings and any other person affected by the order; and
  (b) any court in which enforcement proceedings are pending in England and Wales,
  and the order will not have effect on any person until it has been served in accordance with this rule and they have received it.

EUROPEAN LAWYER

Pt 6 r.6.2

(e) Has the meaning set out in art.2 of the European Communities (Services of Lawyers) Ord. 1978 (SI 1978/1910) [which is set out in Annex 2 of PD 6A].

Service of the claim form in specified circumstances within the EEA

Pt 6 r.6.7(3)

Subject to r.6.5(1) and the provisions of s.IV of [Pt 6], and except where any other rule or PD makes different provision, where—
  (a) the defendant has given in writing the business address of a European Lawyer in any EEA state as an address at which the defendant may be served with the claim form; or
  (b) a European Lawyer in any EEA state has notified the claimant in writing that the European Lawyer is instructed by the defendant to accept service of the claim form on behalf of the defendant at a business address of the European Lawyer,
the claim form must be served at the business address of that European Lawyer.

Service of documents other than the claim form in specified circumstances within the EEA

See **Service of documents**.

EUROPEAN ORDERS FOR PAYMENT PROCEDURE

Pt 78 r.78.2

(f) "European order for payment" means an order for payment made by a court under art.12(1) of the EOP Regulation.

Pt 78 r.78.2

(1) This section applies to applications for European orders for payment and other related proceedings under Regulation (EC) No.1896/2006 of the European Parliament and of the Council of December 12, 2006 creating a European order for payment procedure.

EOP applications made to a court in England and Wales

Application for a European Order for payment

Pt 78 r.78.3

Where a declaration provided by the claimant under art.7(3) of the EOP Regulation contains any deliberate false statement, r.32.14 applies as if the EOP application form A were verified by a statement of truth.
(An EOP application is made in accordance with the EOP Regulation and in particular art.7 of that regulation).

PD 78 para.2.1

An EOP application form A [means the Application for a European order for payment form A, annexed to the EOP Regulation at Annex I to that Regulation] must be—
    (1) completed in English or accompanied by a translation into English; and
    (2) filed at court in person or by post.

PD 78 para.2.2

An EOP application made to the High Court will be assigned to the Queen's Bench Division, but that will not prevent the application being transferred where appropriate.

Filing documents at court other than the EOP application form A

PD 78 para.3

Documents other than the EOP application form A that are filed at or sent to the court in the EOP proceedings, including statements of opposition, may be filed, in addition to by post or in person, by—
    (1) fax; or
    (2) other electronic means where the facilities are available.

Service

PD 78 para.4

Where the EOP Regulation is silent on service, the Service Regulation and the Civil Procedure Rules apply as appropriate.

Completion or rectification of the EOP application form A

PD 78 para.5.1

Article 9 of the EOP Regulation makes provision for the completion or rectification of the EOP application form A within a specified time.

PD 78 para.5.2

The time specified for the purposes of art.9 will normally be within 30 days of the date of the request by the court to complete or rectify the EOP application form A (using form B annexed to the EOP Regulation).

Withdrawal of EOP application

Pt 78 r.78.4

    (1) At any stage before a statement of opposition [means a statement of opposition filed in accordance with art.16 of the EOP Regulation is filed, the claimant may notify the court that the claimant no longer wishes to proceed with the claim.

    (2) Where the claimant notifies the court in accordance with para.(1)—
        (a) the court will notify the defendant that the application has been withdrawn; and
        (b) no order as to costs will be made.

Transfer of proceedings where an eop application has been opposed

Pt 78 r.78.5

    (1) Where a statement of opposition is filed in accordance with art.16 of the EOP Regulation and the claimant has not opposed the transfer of the matter—
        (a) the EOP application will be treated as if it had been started as a claim under Pt 7 and the EOP application form A will be treated as a Pt 7 claim form including particulars of claim; and
        (b) thereafter, these rules apply with necessary modifications and subject to this rr.78.6 and 78.7.

    (2) When the court notifies the claimant in accordance with art.17(3) of the EOP Regulation the court will also—
        (a) notify the claimant—
            (i) that the EOP application form A is now treated as a Pt 7 claim form including particulars of claim; and
            (ii) of the time within which the defendant must respond under r.78.6; and
        (b) notify the defendant—
            (i) that a statement of opposition has been received;
            (ii) that the application will not continue under Part 78;
            (iii) that the application has been transferred under article 17 of the EOP Regulation;
            (iv) that the EOP application form A is now treated as a Pt 7 claim form including particulars of claim; and
            (v) of the time within which the defendant must respond under r.78.6.

Filing of acknowledgment of service and defence where an EOP application is transferred under article 17 of the EOP Regulation

Pt 78 r.78.6

    (1) The defendant must file a defence within 30 days of the date of the notice issued by the court under r.78.5(2)(b).

(2) If the defendant wishes to dispute the court's jurisdiction, the defendant must instead—
  (a) file an acknowledgment of service within the period specified in para.(1); and
  (b) make an application under Pt 11 within the period specified in that Part.
(3) Where this rule applies, the following rules do not apply—
  (a) rule 10.1(3)[a defendant may file an acknowledgment of service if he is unable to file a defence within the period specified in r.15.4; or he wishes to dispute the court's jurisdiction];
  (b) rule 10.3 [period for filing an acknowledgment of service]; and
  (c) rule 15.4(1)[period for filing a defence].

Default judgment

Pt 78 r.78.7

(1) If—
  (a) the defendant fails to file an acknowledgment of service within the period specified in r.78.6(2)(a); and
  (b) does not within that period—
    (i) file a defence in accordance with Pt 15 (except r.15.4(1)) and r.78.6(1); or
    (ii) file an admission in accordance with Pt 14,
  the claimant may obtain default judgment if Pt 12 allows it.
(2) Where this rule applies, r.10.2 does not apply.

Review in exceptional cases

Pt 78 r.78.8

An application for a review under art.20 of the EOP Regulation must be made in accordance with Pt 23.

Enforcement of European Orders for payment in England and Wales

Pt 78 r.78.9

(1) A person seeking to enforce an EOP in England and Wales must file at the court in which enforcement proceedings are to be brought the documents required by art.21 of the EOP Regulation.
(2) Where a person applies to enforce an EOP expressed in a foreign currency, the application must contain a certificate of the sterling equivalent of the judgment sum at the close of business on the date nearest preceding the date of the application.
(Parts 70 to 74 contain further rules about enforcement).

PD 78 para.7.1

When an EOP is filed at the High Court or county court in which enforcement proceedings are to be brought, it will be assigned a case number.

PD 78 para.7.2

A copy of a document will satisfy the conditions necessary to establish its authenticity if it is an official copy of the court of origin [meaning given by art.5(4) of the EOP Regulation].

PD 78 para.7.3

If judgment is set aside in the court of origin, the judgment creditor must notify all courts in which enforcement proceedings are pending in England and Wales under the EOP as soon as reasonably practicable after the order is served on the judgment creditor. Notification may be by any means available including fax, e-mail, post or telephone.

Refusal of enforcement

Pt 78 r.78.10

(1) An application under art.22 of the EOP Regulation that the court should refuse to enforce an EOP must be made in accordance with Pt 23 to the court in which the EOP is being enforced.
(2) The judgment debtor must, as soon as practicable, serve copies of any order made under art.22 on—
   (a) all other parties to the proceedings and any other person affected by the order ('the affected persons'); and
   (b) any court in which enforcement proceedings of the EOP are pending in England and Wales ('the relevant courts').
(3) Upon service of the order on the affected persons, all enforcement proceedings of the EOP in the relevant courts will cease.

PD 78 para.8.1

An application must be accompanied by an official copy of the earlier judgment, any other documents relied upon and any translations required by the EOP Regulation.

PD 78 para.8.2

Where the applicant relies on art.22(1) of the EOP Regulation, the application must be supported by written evidence showing—
(1) why the earlier judgment is irreconcilable with the judgment which the claimant is seeking to enforce; and
(2) why the irreconcilability was not, and could not have been, raised as an objection in the proceedings in the court of origin.

PD 78 para.8.3

Where the applicant relies on art.22(2), the application must be supported by written evidence of the extent to which the defendant has paid the claimant the amount awarded in the EOP.

Stay of or limitation on enforcement

Pt 78 r.78.11

(1) Where the defendant has sought a review and also applies for a stay of or limitation on enforcement in accordance with art.23 of the EOP Regulation, such application must be made in accordance with Pt 23 to the court in which the EOP is being enforced.

(2) The defendant must, as soon as practicable, serve a copy of any order made under art.23 on—

(a) all other parties to the proceedings and any other person affected by the order; and

(b) any court in which enforcement proceedings are pending in England and Wales, and the order will not have effect on any person until it has been served in accordance with this rule and they have received it.

PD 78 para.9.1

Unless the court orders otherwise, an application must be accompanied by evidence of the review application in the court of origin, including—

(1) the review application or a copy of the review application certified by an appropriate officer of the court of origin; and

(2) where that document is not in English, a translation of it into English.

PD 78 para.9.2

The written evidence in support of the application must state—

(1) that a review application has been brought in the Member State of origin;

(2) the nature of that review application; and

(3) the date on which the review application was filed, the stage the application has reached and the date by which it is believed that the application will be determined.

EUROPEAN PROCEDURES

PD 78 r.78.1

(1) Section I contains rules about **European orders for payment** made under Regulation (EC) No.1896/2006 of the European Parliament and of the Council of December 12, 2006 creating a European order for payment procedure.

(2) Section II contains rules about the **European small claims procedure** under Regulation (EC) No.861/2007 of the European Parliament and of the Council of July 11, 2007 establishing a European small claims procedure.

(2A) Section III contains rules about **mediated cross-border disputes** that are subject to Directive 2008/52/EC of the European Parliament and of the Council of May 21, 2008 on certain aspects of mediation in civil and commercial matters.

(3) In this Part—

(a) unless otherwise stated, a reference to an Annex is to an Annex to PD 78; and

(b) 'Service Regulation' means Regulation (EC) 1393/2007 on service, within the same meaning as r.6.31(e).

(4) Except where—

(a) the EOP Regulation (which has the same meaning as in r.78.2(2)(a));

(b) the ESCP Regulation (which has the same meaning as in r.78.12(2)(a)); or

(c) the Service Regulation

makes different provisions about the certification or verification of translations, every translation required by this Part or such regulation must be accompanied by a statement by the person making it that it is a correct translation. The statement must include that person's name, address and qualifications for making the translation.

PD 78 para.1.1

EOP applications are primarily governed by the EOP Regulation. Where the EOP Regulation is silent, the Civil Procedure Rules apply with necessary modifications.

EUROPEAN SMALL CLAIMS PROCEDURE

Pt 78 r.78.12(2)

(c) 'ESCP' means the European small claims procedure established by the ESCP Regulation [means Regulation (EC) No.861/2007 of the European Parliament and of the Council of July 11, 2007 establishing a European small claims procedure. A copy of the ESCP Regulation can be found at Annex 2].

Pt 78 r.78.12

(1) [Section II of Pt 78] applies to the European small claims procedure under Regulation (EC) No 861/2007 of the European Parliament and of the Council of July 11, 2007 establishing a European small claims procedure.

PD 78 para.9.1

Unless the court orders otherwise, an application must be accompanied by evidence of the review application in the court of origin, including—
(1) the review application or a copy of the review application certified by an appropriate officer of the court of origin; and
(2) where that document is not in English, a translation of it into English.

PD 78 para.9.2

The written evidence in support of the application must state—
(1) that a review application has been brought in the Member State [has the meaning given by art.2(3) of the ESCP Regulation] of origin;
(2) the nature of that review application; and
(3) the date on which the review application was filed, the stage the application has reached and the date by which it is believed that the application will be determined.

ESCP Regulation and application of the Civil Procedure Rules

PD 78 para.10

Claims under the ESCP are primarily governed by the ESCP Regulation. Where the ESCP Regulation is silent, the Civil Procedure Rules apply with necessary modifications. In particular, Pt 52 applies to any appeals.

ESCP claims made in a court in England and Wales

Filing an ESCP claim form

Pt 78 r.78.13

Where a declaration provided by the claimant in the ESCP claim form [means the claim form completed and filed in the ESCP] contains any deliberate false statement, r.32.14 applies as if the ESCP claim form were verified by a statement of truth.
(An ESCP claim form is completed and filed in accordance with the ESCP Regulation, in particular art.4(1), and in accordance with this paragraph).

Oral hearing under art.8 of the ESCP Regulation

PD 78 para.17.1

Attention is drawn to art.5(1) of the ESCP Regulation, which sets out limitations on when oral hearings may be held.

PD 78 para.17.2

Where an oral hearing is to be held, it will normally take place by telephone or video conference.

Applications under Pt 23

PD 78 para.18.1

Where an application is made under s.II of Pt 78 there will not normally be an oral hearing.

PD 78 para.18.2

Where an oral hearing is to be held, it will normally take place by telephone or video conference

Allocation of ESCP claims

PD 78 r.78.14

(1) ESCP claims are treated as if they were allocated to the small claims track.
(2) Part 27 applies, except r.27.14.

PD 78 para.13.1

Rule 78.14(1) provides that ESCP claims are treated as if they were allocated to the small claims track. However, r.78.14(2) disapplies r.27.14 on costs because recital 29 to the ESCP Regulation contains different provisions on costs.

PD 78 para.13.2

Rule 26.6(1) (scope of the small claims track) is also disapplied because art.2(1) of the ESCP Regulation has a different financial limit.

Filing documents at court other than the ESCP claim form

PD 78 para.14

Documents other than the ESCP claim form that are filed at or sent to the court in the ESCP proceedings, including the defendant's response [means the response to the ESCP claim form], may be filed, in addition to by post or in person, by—
    (1) fax; or
    (2) other electronic means where the facilities are available.

Service

PD 78 para.15

Where the ESCP Regulation is silent on service, the Service Regulation and the Civil Procedure Rules apply as appropriate.

Transfer of proceedings where the claim is outside the scope of the ESCP Regulation—art.4(3) of the ESCP Regulation

Pt 78 r.78.15

    (1) Where the court identifies that the claim is outside the scope of the ESCP Regulation, the court will notify the claimant of this in a transfer of proceedings notice.
    (2) If the claimant wishes to withdraw the claim, the claimant must notify the court of this within 21 days of the date of the transfer of proceedings notice.
    (3) Where the claimant has notified the court in accordance with para.(2), the claim is automatically withdrawn.
    (4) Where the claimant has not notified the court in accordance with para.(2) and the claim is instead to be transferred under art.4(3) of the ESCP Regulation—
        (a) the claim will be treated as if it had been started as a claim under Pt 7 and the ESCP claim form will be treated as a Pt 7 claim form including particulars of claim; and
        (b) thereafter, these rules apply with necessary modifications and subject to this rule, and the court will notify the claimant of the transfer and its effect.

Defendant's response

Pt 78 r.78.16

Where a declaration provided by the defendant in the defendant's response contains any deliberate false statement, r.32.14 applies as if the defendant's response were verified by a statement of truth.
(The defendant's response is made in accordance with the ESCP Regulation and in particular art.5(3) of the ESCP Regulation).

Transfer of proceedings where the defendant claims that the non-monetary claim exceeds the limit set in art.2(1) of the ESCP Regulation—art.5(5) of the ESCP Regulation

Pt 78 r.78.17

(1) This rule applies where, under art.5(5) of the ESCP Regulation, the defendant claims that the value of a non-monetary claim exceeds the limit in art.2(1) of the ESCP Regulation.

(2) When the court dispatches the defendant's response to the claimant, it will—
   (a) notify the claimant that the court is considering whether the claim is outside the scope of the ESCP Regulation in a consideration of transfer notice; and
   (b) send a copy of the notice to the defendant.

(3) If the claimant wishes to withdraw the claim in the event that the court decides that the claim is outside the scope of the ESCP Regulation the claimant must notify the court and the defendant of this within 21 days of the date of the consideration of transfer notice.

(4) The court will notify the defendant as well as the claimant of its decision whether the claim is outside the scope of the ESCP Regulation.

(Article 5(5) of the ESCP Regulation provides that the court shall decide within 30 days of dispatching the defendant's response to the claimant, whether the claim is within the scope of the ESCP Regulation).

(5) If the court decides that the claim is outside the scope of the ESCP Regulation and the claimant has notified the court and defendant in accordance with para.(3), the claim is automatically withdrawn.

(6) If the court decides that the claim is outside the scope of the ESCP Regulation and the claimant has not notified the court and defendant in accordance with para.(3)—
   (a) the claim will be treated as if it had been started as a claim under Pt 7 and the ESCP claim form will be treated as a Pt 7 claim form including particulars of claim;
   (b) the defendant's response will be treated as a defence; and
   (c) thereafter, these rules apply with necessary modifications and subject to this rule, and the court will notify the parties.

(7) This rule applies to an ESCP counterclaim as if the counterclaim were an ESCP claim.

PD 78 para.16.1

Rule 78.17(7) applies to counterclaims as if the counterclaim were an ESCP claim because the second paragraph of art.5(7) of the ESCP Regulation applies certain provisions about claims in the ESCP Regulation, including art.5(5), to ESCP counterclaims.

PD 78 para.16.2

Attention is also drawn to the first paragraph of art.5(7) of the ESCP Regulation (transfer of claim and counterclaim in certain circumstances).

Transfer of proceedings where the ESCP counterclaim exceeds the limit set in art.2(1) of the ESCP Regulation—art.5(7) of the ESCP Regulation

Pt 78 r.78.18

(1) Where the ESCP counterclaim [has the meaning given to counterclaim by recital 16 of the ESCP Regulation] exceeds the limit set in art.2(1) of the ESCP Regulation, the court will—

     (a) notify the defendant of this in a transfer of proceedings notice; and

     (b) send a copy of the notice to the claimant,

    when the court dispatches the defendant's response to the claimant.

(2) If the defendant wishes to withdraw the ESCP counterclaim, the defendant must notify the court and the claimant of this within 21 days of the date of the transfer of proceedings notice.

(3) If the defendant notifies the court and claimant under para.(2), the ESCP counterclaim is automatically withdrawn.

(4) If the defendant does not notify the court and claimant in accordance with para.(2)—

     (a) the claim will be treated as if it had been started as a claim under Pt 7 and the ESCP claim form will be treated as a Pt 7 claim form including particulars of claim;

     (b) the defendant's response and ESCP counterclaim are to be treated as the defence and counterclaim; and

     (c) thereafter, these rules apply with necessary modifications and subject to this rule, and the court will notify the parties.

Review of judgment

Pt 78 r.78.19

An application for a review under art.18 of the ESCP Regulation must be made in accordance with Pt 23.

Enforcement of an ESCP judgment in England and Wales

Pt 78 r.78.20

(1) A person seeking to enforce an ESCP judgment [means a judgment given in the ESCP] in England and Wales must file at the court in which enforcement proceedings are to be brought the documents required by art.21 of the ESCP Regulation.

(2) Where a person applies to enforce an ESCP judgment expressed in a foreign currency, the application must contain a certificate of the sterling equivalent of the judgment sum at the close of business on the date nearest preceding the date of the application.

(Parts 70 to 74 contain further rules about enforcement).

PD 78 para.19.1

When an ESCP judgment is filed at the High Court or county court in which enforcement proceedings are to be brought, it will be assigned a case number.

PD 78 para.19.2

A copy of a document will satisfy the conditions necessary to establish its authenticity if it is an official copy of the courts of the Member State of judgment.

PD 78 para.19.3

If judgment is set aside in the Member State of judgment [Member State in which the ESCP judgment is given], the judgment creditor must notify all courts in which proceedings are pending in England and Wales to enforce the ESCP judgment as soon as reasonably practicable after the order is served on the judgment creditor. Notification may be by any means available including fax, e-mail, post or telephone.

Refusal of enforcement

Pt 78 r.78.21

(1) An application under art.22 of the ESCP Regulation that the court should refuse to enforce an ESCP judgment must be made in accordance with Pt 23 to the court in which the ESCP judgment is being enforced.
(2) The judgment debtor must, as soon as practicable, serve copies of any order made under art.22 on—
    (a) all other parties to the proceedings and any other person affected by the order ('the affected persons'); and
    (b) any court in which enforcement proceedings are pending in England and Wales ('the relevant courts').
(3) Upon service of the order on the affected persons, all enforcement proceedings of the ESCP judgment in the relevant courts will cease.

PD 78 para.20.1

An application must be accompanied by an official copy of the earlier judgment, any other documents relied upon and any translations required by the ESCP Regulation.

PD 78 para.20.2

The application must be supported by written evidence showing—
    (1) why the earlier judgment is irreconcilable with the judgment which the claimant is seeking to enforce; and
    (2) why the irreconcilability was not, and could not have been, raised as an objection in the proceedings in the Member State of judgment.

Stay of or limitation on enforcement

PD 78 r.78.22

(1) An application by the defendant under art.23 of the ESCP Regulation must be made in accordance with Pt 23 to the court in which the ESCP judgment is being enforced.
(2) The defendant must, as soon as practicable, serve a copy of any order made under art.23 on—
    (a) all other parties to the proceedings and any other person affected by the order; and
    (b) any court in which enforcement proceedings are pending in England and Wales,
    and the order will not have effect on any person until it has been served in accordance with this rule and they have received it.

PD 78 para.21.1

This paragraph applies where a defendant makes an application under art.23 of the ESCP Regulation in circumstances where—
    (1) an application for review has been made under art.18 ('review application'); or

(2) the defendant has challenged the judgment.

PD 78 para.21.2

Unless the court orders otherwise, the application under art.23 must be accompanied by evidence of the review application or challenge in the Member State of judgment. This must include a copy of the document initiating the review application or challenge or a copy of the review application or challenge, certified by an appropriate officer of the court in the Member State of judgment.

PD 78 para.21.3

Where a document is not in English, it must be accompanied by a translation of it into English.

PD 78 para.21.4

The written evidence in support of the application must state—
(1) that a review application or challenge has been brought in the Member State of judgment;
(2) the nature of that review application or challenge; and
(3) the date on which the review application or challenge was filed, the state of the proceedings and the date by which it is believed that the application or challenge will be determined.

EVIDENCE

Pt 32 r.32.1

(1) The court may control the evidence by giving directions as to—
(a) the issues on which it requires evidence;
(b) the nature of the evidence which it requires to decide those issues; and
(c) the way in which the evidence is to be placed before the court.
(2) The court may use its power under this rule to exclude evidence that would otherwise be admissible.
(3) The court may limit cross-examination.

EVIDENCE IN CHIEF

Glossary

The evidence given by a witness for the party who called him

EVIDENCE OF WITNESS

PD 32 para.1.1

Rule 32.2 sets out how evidence is to be given and facts are to be proved

PD 32 para.32.2

(1) The general rule is that any fact which needs to be proved by the evidence of witnesses is to be proved—
  (a) at **trial**, by their oral evidence given in public; and
  (b) at any other hearing, by their evidence in writing.
(2) This is subject—
  (a) to any provision to the contrary contained in [the CPR] or elsewhere; or
  (b) to any order of the court.

Evidence in proceedings other than at trial

Pt 32 para.32.6

(1) Subject to para.(2), the general rule is that evidence at hearings other than the trial is to be by **witness statement** unless the court, a PD or any other enactment requires otherwise.
(2) At hearings other than the trial, a party may, rely on the matters set out in—
  (a) his **statement of case**; or
  (b) his **application notice**, if the statement of case or application notice is verified by a **statement of truth**.

PD 32 para.1.2

Evidence at a hearing other than the trial should normally be given by witness evidence statement). However a witness may give evidence by **affidavit** if he wishes to do so.

PD 32 para.1.3

Statements of case and application noticesmay also be used as evidence provided that their contents have been verified by a statement of truth.

PD 32 para.1.4

Affidavits must be used as evidence in the following instances:
  (1) where sworn evidence is required by an enactment, rule, order or PD and
  (2) in any application for a search order, a freezing injunction, or an order requiring an occupier to permit another to enter his land.

See **Deposition**.

PD 32 para.1.5

If a party believes that sworn evidence is required by a court in another jurisdiction for any purpose connected with the proceedings, he may apply to the court for a direction that evidence shall be given only by affidavit on any pre-trial applications.

PD 32 para.1.6

The court may give a direction under r.32.15 [**affidavit evidence**] that evidence shall be given by affidavit instead of or in addition to a witness statement or statement of case:

(1) on its own initiative, or

(2) after any party has applied to the court for such a direction.

EXAMINER OF THE COURT

Pt 34 r.34.15

(1) The Lord Chancellor shall appoint persons to be examiners of the court.

(2) The persons appointed shall be barristers or solicitor-advocates who have been practising for a period of not less than three years.

(3) The Lord Chancellor may revoke an appointment at any time.

Fees and expenses

Pt 34 r.34.14

(1) An examiner of the court may charge a fee for the examination.

(2) He need not send the deposition to the court unless the fee is paid.

(3) The examiner's fees and expenses must be paid by the party who obtained the order for examination.

(4) If the fees and expenses due to an examiner are not paid within a reasonable time, he may report that fact to the court.

(5) The court may order the party who obtained the order for examination to deposit in the court office a specified sum in respect of the examiner's fees and, where it does so, the examiner will not be asked to act until the sum has been deposited.

(6) An order under this rule does not affect any decision as to the party who is ultimately to bear the costs of the examination.

PD 34B para.1.1

[PD 34B] sets out—

(1) how to calculate the fees an examiner of the court may charge; and

(2) the expenses he may recover.

PD 34B para.1.2

The party who obtained the order for the examination must pay the fees and expenses of the examiner.

Examination fee

PD 34B para.2.1

An examiner may charge an hourly rate for each hour (or part of an hour) that he is engaged in examining the witness.

PD 34B para.2.2

The hourly rate is to be calculated by reference to the formula set out in para.3 of PD 34B].

Single fee chargeable on making the appointment for examination

PD 34B para.4.1

An examiner of court is also entitled to charge a single fee of twice the hourly rate (calculated in accordance with para.3 above) as 'the appointment fee' when the appointment for the examination is made.

PD 34B para.4.2

The examiner is entitled to retain the appointment fee where the witness fails to attend on the date and time arranged.

PD 34B para.4.3

Where the examiner fails to attend on the date and time arranged he may not charge a further appointment fee for arranging a subsequent appointment.
(The examiner need not send the deposition to the court until his fees are paid—see CPR r.34.14 (2)).

Examiner's expenses

PD 34B para.5.1

The examiner of court is also entitled to recover the following expenses—
    (1) all reasonable travelling expenses;
    (2) any other expenses reasonably incurred; and
    (3) subject to para.5.2, any reasonable charge for the room where the examination takes place.

PD 34B para.5.2

No expenses may be recovered under subpara.(3) above if the examination takes place at the examiner's usual business address.

Attendance before examiner

Judgment summons

CCR Ord.28 r.4

    (1) Order 27 rr.7B and 8, shall apply, with the necessary modifications, to an order made under s.110(1) of the [County Court Act 1984] for the attendance of the debtor at an adjourned hearing of a judgment summons as they apply to an order made under s.23(1) of the Attachment of Earnings Act 1971 for the attendance of the debtor at an adjourned hearing of an application for an attachment of earnings order.
  (1A) An order made under s.110(1) of the [1984] Act must be served personally on the judgment debtor.
  (1B) Copies of—
      (a) the judgment summons; and

(b) the written evidence,

must be served with the order.

(2) At the time of service of the order there shall be paid or tendered to the debtor a sum reasonably sufficient to cover his expenses in travelling to and from the court, unless such a sum was paid to him at the time of service of the judgment summons.

Witness

Pt 34 r.34.10

(1) If a person served with an order to attend before an examiner—
  (a) fails to attend; or
  (b) refuses to be sworn for the purpose of the examination or to answer any lawful question or produce any document at the examination,
  a certificate of his failure or refusal, signed by the examiner, must be filed by the party requiring the deposition.
(2) On the certificate being filed, the party requiring the deposition may apply to the court for an order requiring that person to attend or to be sworn or to answer any question or produce any document, as the case may be.
(3) An application for an order under this rule may be made without notice.
(4) The court may order the person against whom an order is made under this rule to pay any costs resulting from his failure or refusal.

See also **Deposition**.

EXECUTION

See **Warrant of execution**, and **Writ of fi fa**.

EXEMPLARY DAMAGES

Glossary

Damages which go beyond compensating for actual loss and are awarded to show the court's disapproval of the defendant's behaviour.

EXHIBIT

Manner of exhibiting documents

PD 32 para.11.1

A document used in conjunction with an affidavit should be:
(1) produced to and verified by the deponent, and remain separate from the affidavit, and
(2) identified by a declaration of the person before whom the affidavit was sworn.

PD 32 para.11.2

The declaration should be headed with the name of the proceedings in the same way as the affidavit.

EXHIBIT 514

PD 32 para.11.3

The first page of each exhibit should be marked:
    (1) as in para.3.2 above, and
    (2) with the exhibit mark referred to in the affidavit.

Letters

PD 32 para.12.1

Copies of individual letters should be collected together and exhibited in a bundle or bundles. They should be arranged in chronological order with the earliest at the top, and firmly secured.

PD 32 para.12.2

When a bundle of correspondence is exhibited, the exhibit should have a front page attached stating that the bundle consists of original letters and copies. They should be arranged and secured as above and numbered consecutively.

Other documents

PD 32 para.13.1

Photocopies instead of original documents may be exhibited provided the originals are made available for inspection by the other parties before the hearing and by the judge at the hearing.

PD 32 para.13.2

Court documents must not be exhibited (official copies of such documents prove themselves).

PD 32 para.13.3

Where an exhibit contains more than one document, a front page should be attached setting out a list of the documents contained in the exhibit; the list should contain the dates of the documents.

PD 32 para.15.1

Where an exhibit contains more than one document:
    (1) the bundle should not be stapled but should be securely fastened in a way that does not hinder the reading of the documents, and
    (2) the pages should be numbered consecutively at bottom centre.

Exhibits other than documents

PD 32 para.14.1

Items other than documents should be clearly marked with an exhibit number or letter in such a manner that the mark cannot become detached from the exhibit.

PD 32 para.14.2

Small items may be placed in a container and the container appropriately marked.

General provisions

PD 32 para.15.2

Every page of an exhibit should be clearly legible; typed copies of illegible documents should be included, paginated with 'a' numbers.

PD 32 para.15.3

Where affidavits and exhibits have become numerous, they should be put into separate bundles and the pages numbered consecutively throughout.

PD 32 para.15.4

Where on account of their bulk the service of exhibits or copies of exhibits on the other parties would be difficult or impracticable, the directions of the court should be sought as to arrangements for bringing the exhibits to the attention of the other parties and as to their custody pending trial.

Exhibits at trial

PD 39A para.7

Exhibits which are handed in and proved during the course of the trial should be recorded on an exhibit list and kept in the custody of the court until the conclusion of the trial, unless the judge directs otherwise. At the conclusion of the trial it is the parties' responsibility to obtain the return of those exhibits which they handed in and to preserve them for the period in which any appeal may take place.

EX PARTE

Without notice.

EXPERT

Pt 35 r.35.2

(1) Reference to a person who has been instructed to give or prepare expert evidence for the purpose of proceedings.

Overriding duty to the court

Pt 35 r.35.3

(1) It is the duty of experts to help the court on matters within their expertise.
(2) This duty overrides any obligation to the person from whom experts have received instructions or by whom they are paid.

PD 35 para.2.2

Experts should assist the court by providing objective, unbiased opinions on matters within their expertise, and should not assume the role of an advocate.

PD 35 para.2.3

Experts should consider all material facts, including those which might detract from their opinions.

PD 35 para.2.4

Experts should make it clear—
(a) when a question or issue falls outside their expertise; and
(b) when they are not able to reach a definite opinion, for example because they have insufficient information.

PD 35 para.2.5

If, after producing a report, an expert's view changes on any material matter, such change of view should be communicated to all the parties without delay, and when appropriate to the court.

Court's power to restrict expert evidence

Pt 35 r.35.4

(1) No party may call an expert or put in evidence an expert's report without the court's permission.
(2) When parties apply for permission they must provide an estimate of the costs of the proposed address and identify—
   (a) the field in which expert evidence is required and the issues which the expert evidence will address; and
   (b) where practicable, the name of the proposed expert.
(3) If permission is granted it shall be in relation only to the expert named or the field identified under para.(2). The order granting permission may specify the issues which the expert evidence should address.
(3A) Where a claim has been allocated to the small claims track or the fast track, if permission is given for expert evidence, it will normally be given for evidence from only one expert on a particular issue.
(Paragraph 7 of PD 35 sets out some of the circumstances the court will consider when deciding whether expert evidence should be given by a single joint expert).

(4) The court may limit the amount of a party's expert's fees and expenses that may be recovered from any other party.

See **Single joint expert.**

EXPERT EVIDENCE

PD 35 para.1

Part 35 is intended to limit the use of oral expert evidence to that which is reasonably required. In addition, where possible, matters requiring expert evidence should be dealt with by only one expert. Experts and those instructing them are expected to have regard to the guidance contained in the Protocol for the Instruction of Experts to give Evidence in Civil Claims annexed to [PD 35]. (Further guidance on experts is contained in Annex C to the PD (Pre-Action Conduct)).

Pt 35 r.35.1

Expert evidence shall be restricted to that which is reasonably required to resolve the proceedings.

PD 35 para.2.1

Expert evidence should be the independent product of the expert uninfluenced by the pressures of litigation.

Concurrent expert evidence

PD 35 para.11.1

At any stage in the proceedings the court may direct that some or all of the experts from like disciplines shall give their evidence concurrently. The following procedure shall then apply.

PD 35 para.11.2

The court may direct that the parties agree an agenda for the taking of concurrent evidence, based upon the areas of disagreement identified in the experts' joint statements made pursuant to r. 35.12.

PD 35 para.11.3

At the appropriate time the relevant experts will each take the oath or affirm. Unless the court orders otherwise, the experts will then address the items on the agenda in the manner set out in para.11.4.

PD 35 para.11.4

In relation to each issue on the agenda, and subject to the judge's discretion to modify the procedure–
(1) the judge may initiate the discussion by asking the experts, in turn, for their views. Once an expert has expressed a view the judge may ask questions about it. At one or more appropriate stages when questioning a particular expert, the judge may invite the other expert to comment or to ask that expert's own questions of the first expert;

(2) after the process set out in (1) has been completed for all the experts, the parties' representatives may ask questions of them. While such questioning may be designed to test the correctness of an expert's view, or seek clarification of it, it should not cover ground which has been fully explored already. In general a full cross-examination or re-examination is neither necessary nor appropriate; and

(3) after the process set out in (2) has been completed, the judge may summarise the experts' different positions on the issue and ask them to confirm or correct that summary.

General requirement for expert evidence to be given in a written report

Pt 35 r.35.5

(1) Expert evidence is to be given in a written report unless the court directs otherwise.

(2) If a claim is on the **small claims** track or the **fast track**, the court will not direct an expert to attend a hearing unless it is necessary to do so in the interests of justice.

Form and content of an expert's report

Pt 35 r.35.10

(1) An expert's report must comply with the requirements set out in PD 35.

(2) At the end of an expert's report there must be a statement that the expert understands and has complied with their duty to the court.

(3) The expert's report must state the substance of all material instructions, whether written or oral, on the basis of which the report was written.

(4) The instructions referred to in para.(3) shall not be privileged against disclosure but the court will not, in relation to those instructions—

(a) order disclosure of any specific document; or

(b) permit any questioning in court, other than by the party who instructed the expert, unless it is satisfied that there are reasonable grounds to consider the statement of instructions given under para.(3) to be inaccurate or incomplete.

PD 35 para.3.1

An expert's report should be addressed to the court and not to the party from whom the expert has received instructions.

PD 35 para.3.2

An expert's report must:

(1) give details of the expert's qualifications;

(2) give details of any literature or other material which has been relied on in making the report;

(3) contain a statement setting out the substance of all facts and instructions which are material to the opinions expressed in the report or upon which those opinions are based;

(4) make clear which of the facts stated in the report are within the expert's own knowledge;

(5) say who carried out any examination, measurement, test or experiment which the expert has used for the report, give the qualifications of that person, and say whether or not the test or experiment has been carried out under the expert's supervision;

(6) where there is a range of opinion on the matters dealt with in the report—
  (a) summarise the range of opinions; and
  (b) give reasons for the expert's own opinion;
(7) contain a summary of the conclusions reached;
(8) if the expert is not able to give an opinion without qualification, state the qualification; and
(9) contain a statement that the expert—
  (a) understands their duty to the court, and has complied with that duty; and
  (b) is aware of the requirements of Pt 35, this PD and the Protocol for Instruction of Experts to give Evidence in Civil Claims.

PD 35 para.3.3

An expert's report must be verified by a statement of truth in the following form—

> "I confirm that I have made clear which facts and matters referred to in this report are within my own knowledge and which are not. Those that are within my own knowledge I confirm to be true. The opinions I have expressed represent my true and complete professional opinions on the matters to which they refer".

(Part 22 deals with statements of truth. Rule 32.14 sets out the consequences of verifying a document containing a false statement without an honest belief in its truth).

Power of court to direct a party to provide information

Pt 35 r.35.9

Where a party has access to information which is not reasonably available to another party, the court may direct the party who has access to the information to—
  (a) prepare and file a document recording the information; and
  (b) serve a copy of that document on the other party.

Information

PD 35 para.4

Under r.35.9 the court may direct a party with access to information, which is not reasonably available to another party to serve on that other party a document, which records the information. The document served must include sufficient details of all the facts, tests, experiments and assumptions which underlie any part of the information to enable the party on whom it is served to make, or to obtain, a proper interpretation of the information and an assessment of its significance.

Instructions

See **Cross examination**.

Questions to experts

Pt 35 r.35.6

(1) A party may put written questions about an expert's report (which must be proportionate) to—

      (a) an expert instructed by another party; or

      (b) a **single joint expert** appointed under r.35.7.

  (2) Written questions under para.(1)—

      (a) may be put once only;

      (b) must be put within 28 days of service of the expert's report; and

      (c) must be for the purpose only of clarification of the report,

        unless in any case—

          (i) the court gives permission; or

          (ii) the other party agrees.

  (3) An expert's answers to questions put in accordance with para.(1) shall be treated as part of the expert's report.

  (4) Where—

      (a) a party has put a written question to an expert instructed by another party; and

      (b) the expert does not answer that question,

      the court may make one or both of the following orders in relation to the party who instructed the expert—

          (i) that the party may not rely on the evidence of that expert; or

          (ii) that the party may not recover the fees and expenses of that expert from any other party.

PD 35 para.6.1

Where a party sends a written question or questions under r.35.6 direct to an expert, a copy of the questions must, at the same time, be sent to the other party or parties.

PD 35 para.6.2

The party or parties instructing the expert must pay any fees charged by that expert for answering questions put under r.35.6. This does not affect any decision of the court as to the party who is ultimately to bear the expert's fees.

Orders

PD 35 para.8

Where an order requires an act to be done by an expert, or otherwise affects an expert, the party instructing that expert must serve a copy of the order on the expert. The claimant must serve the order on a single joint expert.

Discussions between experts

Pt 35 r.35.12

  (1) The court may, at any stage, direct a discussion between experts for the purpose of requiring the experts to—

      (a) identify and discuss the expert issues in the proceedings; and

      (b) where possible, reach an agreed opinion on those issues.

  (2) The court may specify the issues which the experts must discuss.

  (3) The court may direct that following a discussion between the experts they must prepare a statement for the court setting out those issues on which—

      (a) they agree; and

(b) they disagree, with a summary of their reasons for disagreeing.
(4) The content of the discussion between the experts shall not be referred to at the trial unless the parties agree.
(5) Where experts reach agreement on an issue during their discussions, the agreement shall not bind the parties unless the parties expressly agree to be bound by the agreement.

PD 35 para.9.1

Unless directed by the court discussions between experts are not mandatory. Parties must consider, with their experts, at an early stage, whether there is likely to be any useful purpose in holding an experts' discussion and if so when.

PD 35 para.9.2

The purpose of discussions between experts is not for experts to settle cases but to agree and narrow issues and in particular to identify:
  (i) the extent of the agreement between them;
 (ii) the points of and short reasons for any disagreement;
(iii) action, if any, which may be taken to resolve any outstanding points of disagreement; and
(iv) any further material issues not raised and the extent to which these issues are agreed.

PD 35 para.9.3

Where the experts are to meet, the parties must discuss and if possible agree whether an agenda is necessary, and if so attempt to agree one that helps the experts to focus on the issues which need to be discussed. The agenda must not be in the form of leading questions or hostile in tone.

PD 35 para.9.4

Unless ordered by the court, or agreed by all parties, and the experts, neither the parties nor their legal representatives may attend experts discussions.

PD 35 para.9.5

If the legal representatives do attend—
  (i) they should not normally intervene in the discussion, except to answer questions put to them by the experts or to advise on the law; and
 (ii) the experts may if they so wish hold part of their discussions in the absence of the legal representatives.

PD 35 para.9.6

A statement must be prepared by the experts dealing with paras 9.2(i)–(iv) above. Individual copies of the statements must be signed by the experts at the conclusion of the discussion, or as soon thereafter as practicable, and in any event within seven days. Copies of the statements must be provided to the parties no later than 14 days after signing.

PD 35 para.9.7

Experts must give their own opinions to assist the court and do not require the authority of the parties to sign a joint statement.

PD 35 para.9.8

If an expert significantly alters an opinion, the joint statement must include a note or addendum by that expert explaining the change of opinion.

Use by one party of expert's report disclosed by another

Pt 35 r.35.11

Where a party has disclosed an expert's report, any party may use that expert's report as evidence at the trial.

Consequence of failure to disclose expert's report

Pt 35 r.35.13

A party who fails to disclose an expert's report may not use the report at the trial or call the expert to give evidence orally unless the court gives permission.

Expert's right to ask court for directions

Pt 35 r.35.14

(1) Experts may file written requests for directions for the purpose of assisting them in carrying out their functions.
(2) Experts must, unless the court orders otherwise, provide copies of the proposed requests for directions under para.(1)—
   (a) to the party instructing them, at least seven days before they file the requests; and
   (b) to all other parties, at least four days before they file them.
(3) The court, when it gives directions, may also direct that a party be served with a copy of the directions.

Use by one party of expert's report disclosed by another

Pt 35 r.35.11

Where a party has disclosed an expert's report, any party may use that expert's report as evidence at the trial.

See **Cross examination, Disclosure of documents, Expert, Inspection of documents, Pre-action conduct, Single joint expert** and **Small claims track**.

EXPERT REPORT

See **Expert evidence.**

F

FAILURE TO ATTEND HEARING

Hearing other than trial

See **Application**.

Trial

See **Trial.**

FAIR TRADING ACT 1973

Trials and assessments of damages

PD 2B para.11.1

A District Judge has jurisdiction to hear the following:
(a) (vi) under ss.35, 38 or 40 of the Fair Trading Act 1973.

FALSE DISCLOSURE STATEMENT

Pt 31 r.31.23(1)

Proceedings for **contempt of court** may be brought against a person if he makes, or causes to be made, a false disclosure, without an honest belief in its truth.

See **Disclosure of statement**.

FALSE STATEMENT

Pt 32 r.32.14

(1) Proceedings for **contempt of court** may be brought against a person if he makes, or causes to be made, a false statement in a document verified by a **statement of truth** without an honest belief in its truth.
(2) Proceedings under this rule may be brought only—
(a) by the Attorney General; or
(b) with the permission of the court.

FAMILY DIVISION

The Family Division is one of the three Divisions of the High Court of Justice.

The Family Division of the High Court has jurisdiction to deal with all matrimonial matters, the Children Act 1989 and the Child Abduction and Custody Act 1985. It also deals with matters relating to Pt IV of the Family Law Act 1996 (Family Homes and Domestic Violence), Adoption, Inheritance Act 1975 applications and Probate and Court of Protection work.

Family Procedure Rules Pt 2 r.2.1

(1) Unless the context otherwise requires, the Family Procedure Rules apply to family proceedings in—
   (a) the High Court;
   (b) a county court; and
   (c) a magistrates' court.
(2) Nothing [in the Family Procedure Rules] is to be construed as—
   (a) purporting to apply to proceedings in a magistrates' court which are not family proceedings within the meaning of s.65 of the Magistrates' Courts Act 1980, or
   (b) conferring upon a magistrate a function which a magistrate is not permitted by statute to perform.

FAMILY LAW REFORM ACT 1969

See **Blood tests in determining paternity**.

FAMILY PROVISION

See **Inheritance claims**.

FARMER

Execution against farmer

CCR Ord.26 r.3

If after the issue of a warrant of execution the district judge for the district in which the warrant is to be executed has reason to believe that the debtor is a farmer, the execution creditor shall, if so required by the district judge, furnish him with an official certificate, dated not more than three days beforehand, of the result of a search at the Land Registry as to the existence of any charge registered against the debtor under the Agricultural Credits Act 1928.

See also **Agricultural Land Tribunal**.

FAST TRACK

Pt 28 r.28.1

[Part 28] contains general provisions about management of cases allocated to the fast track and applies only to cases allocated to that track.

Allocation

Pt 26 r.26.6

(4) Subject to para.(5), the fast track is the normal track for any claim—
    (a) for which the **small claims track** is not the normal track; and
    (b) which has a value—
        (i) for proceedings issued on or after April 6, 2009, of not more than £25,000; and
        (ii) for proceedings issued before April 6, 2009, of not more than £15,000.
(5) The fast track is the normal track for the claims referred to in para.(4) only if the court considers that—
    (a) the trial is likely to last for no longer than one day; and
    (b) oral expert evidence at trial will be limited to-
        (i) one expert per party in relation to any expert field; and
        (ii) expert evidence in two expert fields.

PD 26 para.9.1

(1) Where the court is to decide whether to allocate to the fast track or the **multi-track** a claim for which the normal track is the fast track, it will allocate the claim to the fast track unless it believes that it cannot be dealt with justly on that track.
(2) The court will, in particular, take into account the limits likely to be placed on disclosure, the extent to which expert evidence may be necessary and whether the trial is likely to last more than a day.
(3) (a) When it is considering the likely length of the trial the court will regard a day as being a period of five hours, and will consider whether that is likely to be sufficient time for the case to be heard.
    (b) The court will also take into account the case management directions (including the fixing of a trial timetable) that are likely to be given and the court's powers to control evidence and to limit cross-examination.
    (c) The possibility that a trial might last longer than one day is not necessarily a conclusive reason for the court to allocate or to re-allocate a claim to the multi-track.
    (d) A claim may be allocated to the fast track or ordered to remain on that track although there is to be a split trial.
    (e) Where the case involves a counterclaim or other Pt 20 claim that will be tried with the claim and as a result the trial will last more than a day, the court may not allocate it to the fast track.

PD 26 para.9.2

(1) Directions for the case management of claims which have been allocated to the fast track will be given at the allocation stage or at the listing stage (in either case with or without a hearing) or at both, and if necessary at other times. The trial judge may, at or before the trial, give directions for its conduct.
(2) PD 28 contains further provisions and contains standard directions which the court may give.

Variation of case management timetable

Pt 28 r.28.4

(1) A party must apply to the court if he wishes to vary the date which the court has fixed for—

(a) the return of a pre-trial check list under r.28.5;
(b) the trial; or
(c) the trial period.
(2) Any date set by the court or these rules for doing any act may not be varied by the parties if the variation would make it necessary to vary any of the dates mentioned in para.(1).

(Rule 2.11 allows the parties to vary a date by written agreement except where the rules provide otherwise or the court orders otherwise [**Time**]).

Conduct of trial

Pt 28 r.28.7

Unless the trial judge otherwise directs, the trial will be conducted in accordance with any order previously made.

Case management

PD 28 para.2.1

Case management of cases allocated to the fast track will generally be by directions given at two stages in the case:
(1) at allocation to the track, and
(2) on the filing of pre-trial check lists (listing questionnaires).

PD 28 para.2.2

The court will seek whenever possible to give directions at those stages only and to do so without the need for a hearing to take place. It will expect to do so with the co-operation of the parties.

PD 28 para.2.3

The court will however hold a hearing to give directions whenever it appears necessary or desirable to do so, and where this happens because of the default of a party or his legal representative it will usually impose a sanction.

PD 28 para.2.4

The court may give directions at any hearing on the application of a party or on its own initiative.

PD 28 para.2.5

When any hearing has been fixed it is the duty of the parties to consider what directions the court should be asked to give and to make any application that may be appropriate to be dealt with at that hearing.

PD 28 para.2.6

When the court fixes a hearing to give directions it will give the parties at least 3 days notice of the hearing.

PD 28 para.2.8

Where a party needs to apply for a direction of a kind not included in the case management timetable which has been set (for example to amend his statement of case or for further information to be given by another party) he must do so as soon as possible so as to minimise the need to change that timetable.

PD 28 para.2.9

Courts will make arrangements to ensure that applications and other hearings are listed promptly to avoid delay in the conduct of cases.

Timetable

PD 28 para.3.12

The Table set out below contains a typical timetable the court may give for the preparation of the case.

Disclosure	4 weeks
Exchange of witness statements	10 weeks
Exchange of experts' reports	14 weeks
Sending of pre-trial check lists (listing questionnaires) by the court	20 weeks
Filing of completed pre-trial check lists	22 weeks
Hearing	30 weeks

These periods will run from the date of the notice of allocation.

PD 28 para.3.13

(1) Where it considers that some or all of the steps in that timetable are not necessary the court may omit them and direct an earlier trial.

(2) This may happen where the court is informed that Practice Direction (Pre-Action Conduct) or any pre-action protocol has been complied with or that steps which it would otherwise order to be taken have already been taken.

(3) It may also happen where an application (for example for summary judgment or for an injunction) has been heard before allocation and little or no further preparation is required. In such a case the court may dispense with the need for a pre-trial check list.

Trial

PD 28 para.8.1

The trial will normally take place at the court where the case is being managed, but it may be at another court if it is appropriate having regard to the needs of the parties and the availability of court resources.

PD 28 para.8.2

The judge will generally have read the papers in the trial bundle and may dispense with an opening address.

PD 28 para.8.3

The judge may confirm or vary any timetable given previously, or if none has been given set his own.

PD 28 para.8.4

Attention is drawn to the provisions in Pt 32 and the following parts of the rules about evidence, and in particular—
    (1) to r.32.1 (court's power to control evidence and to restrict cross-examination), and
    (2) to r.32.5(2) (witness statements to stand as evidence in chief).

PD 28 para.8.5

At the conclusion of the trial the judge will normally summarily assess the costs of the claim in accordance with r.44.7 and Pt 46 (fast track trial costs). Attention is drawn to the steps the [PDs] about costs requires the parties to take.

PD 28 para.8.6

Where a trial is not finished on the day for which it is listed the judge will normally sit on the next court day to complete it.

Appendix

[The Appendix contains the Fast Track Standard Directions, which deals with the following matters:
    Further Statements of Case
    Requests for Further Information
    Disclosure of Documents
    Witnesses of Fact
    Expert Evidence
    Questions to Experts
    Requests for clarification or further Information
    Documents to be filed with Pre-trial Check Lists
    Dates for filing Pre-trial Check Lists and the Trial
    Directions following filing of Pre-trial Check List
    Expert evidence

Trial timetable
Trial Bundle and Case summary
Settlement]

See also **Directions**, **Listing hearing**, **Listing questionnaire**, and **Standard directions**.

FAST TRACK COSTS

Pt 46 r.46.11

(1) Part 45 (**fast track trial costs**) contain special rules about—
   (a) liability for costs;
   (b) the amount of costs which the court may award; and
   (c) the procedure for assessing costs.
(2) Once a claim is allocated to a particular track, those special rules shall apply to the period before, as well as after, allocation except where the court or a PD provides otherwise.

FAST TRACK TRIAL COSTS

Pt 45 r.45.37

(1) [Section VI of P45] deals with the amount of costs which the court may award as the costs of an advocate for preparing for and appearing at the trial of a claim in the fast track.
(2) For the purposes of [s.VI of P45] —
   "advocate" means a person exercising a right of audience as a representative of, or on behalf of, a party;
   "fast track trial costs" means the costs of a party's advocate for preparing for and appearing at the trial, but does not include—
    (i) any other disbursements; or
    (ii) any value added tax payable on the fees of a party's advocate; and
   "trial" includes a hearing where the court decides an amount of money or the value of goods following a judgment under Pt 12 (**default judgment**) or Pt 14 (**admissions**) but does not include—
    (i) the hearing of an application for **summary judgment** under Pt 24; or
    (ii) the court's approval of a settlement or other compromise under r. 21.10.

PD 45 para.4.1

Section VI of Pt 45 applies to the costs of an advocate for preparing for and appearing at the trial of a claim in the fast track.

PD 45 para.4.2

It applies only where, at the date of the trial, the claim is allocated to the fast track. It does not apply in any other case, irrespective of the final value of the claim.

PD 45 para.4.3

In particular it does not apply to a disposal hearing at which the amount to be paid under a judgment or order is decided by the court (see para.12.4 of PD 26).

Cases which settle before trial

Costs PD para.26.4

Attention is drawn to r.44.10 (limitation on amount court may award where a claim allocated to the fast track settles before trial (fast track costs).

Amount of fast track trial costs

Pt 45 r.45.38

(1) Table 9 shows the amount of fast track trial costs which the court may award (whether by summary or detailed assessment).
(2) The court may not award more or less than the amount shown in the table except where—
    (a) it decides not to award any fast track trial costs; or
    (b) rule 46.3 [power to award more or less than the amount of fast track trial costs] applies,
but the court may apportion the amount awarded between the parties to reflect their respective degrees of success on the issues at trial.
(3) Where the only claim is for the payment of money—
    (a) for the purpose of quantifying fast track trial costs awarded to a claimant, the value of the claim is the total amount of the judgment excluding—
        (i) interest and costs; and
        (ii) any reduction made for contributory negligence.
    (b) for the purpose of quantifying fast track trial costs awarded to a defendant, the value of the claim is—
        (i) the amount specified in the claim form (excluding interest and costs);
        (ii) if no amount is specified, the maximum amount which the claimant reasonably expected to recover according to the statement of value included in the claim form under r.16.3; or
        (iii) more than £15,000, if the claim form states that the claimant cannot reasonably say how much is likely to be recovered.
(4) Where the claim is only for a remedy other than the payment of money the value of the claim is deemed to be more than £3,000 but not more than £10,000, unless the court orders otherwise.
(5) Where the claim includes both a claim for the payment of money and for a remedy other than the payment of money, the value of the claim is deemed to be the higher of—
    (a) the value of the money claim decided in accordance with para.(3); or
    (b) the deemed value of the other remedy decided in accordance with para.(4),
unless the court orders otherwise.
(6) Where—
    (a) a defendant has made a counterclaim against the claimant;
    (b) the counterclaim has a higher value than the claim; and
    (c) the claimant succeeds at trial both on the claim and the counterclaim,

for the purpose of quantifying fast track trial costs awarded to the claimant, the value of the claim is the value of the defendant's counterclaim calculated in accordance with this rule.

Power to award more or less than the amount of fast track trial costs

Pt 45 r.45.39

(1) This rule sets out when a court may award—
    (a) an additional amount to the amount of fast track trial costs shown in the table in r.46.2(1); and
    (b) less than those amounts.
(2) If—
    (a) in addition to the advocate, a party's legal representative attends the trial;
    (b) the court considers that it was necessary for a legal representative to attend to assist the advocate; and
    (c) the court awards fast track trial costs to that party,
the court may award an additional £345 in respect of the legal representative's attendance at the trial.
(2A) The court may in addition award a sum representing an additional liability.
(The requirements to provide information about a funding arrangement where a party wishes to recover any additional liability under a funding arrangement are set out in the Costs PD).
(3) If the court considers that it is necessary to direct a separate trial of an issue then the court may award an additional amount in respect of the separate trial but that amount is limited in accordance with para.(4) of this rule.
(4) The additional amount the court may award under para.3 must not exceed two-thirds of the amount payable for that claim, subject to a minimum award of £485.
(5) Where the party to whom fast track trial costs are to be awarded is a litigant in person, the court will award—
    (a) if the litigant in person can prove financial loss, two-thirds of the amount that would otherwise be awarded; or
    (b) if the litigant in person fails to prove financial loss, an amount in respect of the time spent reasonably doing the work at the rate specified in the Costs PD.
(6) Where a defendant has made a counterclaim against the claimant, and—
    (a) the claimant has succeeded on his claim; and
    (b) the defendant has succeeded on his counterclaim,
the court will quantify the amount of the award of fast track trial costs to which—
    (i) but for the counterclaim, the claimant would be entitled for succeeding on his claim; and
    (ii) but for the claim, the defendant would be entitled for succeeding on his counterclaim,
and make one award of the difference, if any, to the party entitled to the higher award of costs.
(7) Where the court considers that the party to whom fast track trial costs are to be awarded has behaved unreasonably or improperly during the trial, it may award that party an amount less than would otherwise be payable for that claim, as it considers appropriate.
(8) Where the court considers that the party who is to pay the fast track trial costs has behaved improperly during the trial the court may award such additional amount to the other party as it considers appropriate.

See **Litigant in person**.

Fast track trial costs where there is more than one claimant or defendant

Pt 45 r.45.40

(1) Where the same advocate is acting for more than one party—
    (a) the court may make only one award in respect of fast track trial costs payable to that advocate; and
    (b) the parties for whom the advocate is acting are jointly entitled to any fast track trial costs awarded by the court.
(2) Where—
    (a) the same advocate is acting for more than one claimant; and
    (b) each claimant has a separate claim against the defendant,
the value of the claim, for the purpose of quantifying the award in respect of fast track trial costs is to be ascertained in accordance with para.(3).
(3) The value of the claim in the circumstances mentioned in para.(2) is—
    (a) where the only claim of each claimant is for the payment of money—
        (i) if the award of fast track trial costs is in favour of the claimants, the total amount of the judgment made in favour of all the claimants jointly represented; or
        (ii) if the award is in favour of the defendant, the total amount claimed by the claimants,
    and in either case, quantified in accordance with r.46.2(3);
    (b) where the only claim of each claimant is for a remedy other than the payment of money, deemed to be more than £3,000 but not more than £10,000; and
    (c) where claims of the claimants include both a claim for the payment of money and for a remedy other than the payment of money, deemed to be—
        (i) more than £3,000 but not more than £10,000; or
        (ii) if greater, the value of the money claims calculated in accordance with sub paragraph (a) above.
(4) Where—
    (a) there is more than one defendant; and
    (b) any or all of the defendants are separately represented,
the court may award fast track trial costs to each party who is separately represented.
(5) Where—
    (a) there is more than one claimant; and
    (b) a single defendant,
the court may make only one award to the defendant of fast track trial costs, for which the claimants are jointly and severally liable (See *http://www.justice.gov.uk/courts/proce dure-rules/civil/glossary*—Accessed November 21, 2012).
(6) For the purpose of quantifying the fast track trial costs awarded to the single defendant under para.(5), the value of the claim is to be calculated in accordance with para.(3) of this Rule.

Cases which settle before trial

Limitation on amount court may allow where a claim allocated to the Fast Track settles before trial

Pt 46 r.46.12

(1) Where the court—
    (a) assesses costs in relation to a claim which—
        (i) has been allocated to the fast track; and
        (ii) settles before the start of the trial; and

(b) is considering the amount of costs to be allowed in respect of a party's advocate for preparing for the trial,

it may not allow, in respect of those advocate's costs, an amount that exceeds the amount of fast track trial costs which would have been payable in relation to the claim had the trial taken place.

(2) When deciding the amount to be allowed in respect of the advocate's costs, the court shall have regard to—
  (a) when the claim was settled; and
  (b) when the court was notified that the claim had settled.

(3) In this rule, 'advocate' and 'fast track trial costs' have the meanings given to them by Pt 45 s.VI.

FATAL ACCIDENT CLAIM

Particulars of claim

PD 16 para.5.1

In a fatal accident claim the claimant must state in his particulars of claim:
  (1) that it is brought under the Fatal Accidents Act 1976,
  (2) the dependants on whose behalf the claim is made,
  (3) the date of birth of each dependant, and
  (4) details of the nature of the dependency claim.

PD 16 para.5.2

A fatal accident claim may include a claim for damages for bereavement.

Law Reform (Miscellaneous Provisions) Act 1934

PD 16 para.5.3

In a fatal accident claim the claimant may also bring a claim under the Law Reform (Miscellaneous Provisions) Act 1934 on behalf of the estate of the deceased.
(For information on apportionment under the Law Reform (Miscellaneous Provisions) Act 1934 and the Fatal Accidents Act 1976 or between dependants see Pt 37 and PD 37).

Periodical payments under the Damages Act 1996

PD 41B para.2.1

An order may be made under r.41.8(2) [where the court orders that any part of the award shall continue after the claimant's death, for the benefit of the claimant's dependants, the order must also specify the relevant amount and duration of the payments and how each payment is to be made during the year and at what intervals] where a dependant would have had a claim under s.1 of the Fatal Accidents Act 1976 if the claimant had died at the time of the accident.

See also **Child** and **Personal injury claims**.

FAX OR OTHER ELECTRONIC MEANS

Fling at court by fax

PD 5A para.5.3

(1) Subject to para.(6) below, a party may file a document at court by sending it by facsimile ('fax').
(2) Where a party files a document by fax, he must not send a hard copy in addition.
(3) A party filing a document by fax should be aware that the document is not filed at court until it is delivered by the court's fax machine, whatever time it is shown to have been transmitted from the party's machine.
(4) The time of delivery of the faxed document will be recorded on it in accordance with para.5.2.
(5) It remains the responsibility of the party to ensure that the document is delivered to the court in time.
(6) If a fax is delivered after 16.00 it will be treated as filed on the next day the court office is open.
(7) If a fax relates to a hearing, the date and time of the hearing should be prominently displayed.
(8) Fax should not be used to send letters or documents of a routine or non-urgent nature.
(9) Fax should not be used, except in an unavoidable emergency, to deliver:
    (a) a document which attracts a fee;
    (c) a document relating to a hearing less than two hours ahead;
    (d) trial bundles or skeleton arguments.
(10) Where (9)(a) or (b) applies, the fax should give an explanation for the emergency and include an undertaking that the fee or money has been dispatched that day by post or will be paid at the court office counter the following business day.
(11) Where courts have several fax machines, each allocated to an individual section, fax messages should only be sent to the machine of the section for which the message is intended.

Address for service and service by fax

Pt 6 r.6.23

(5) Where, in accordance with PD 6A, a party indicates or is deemed to have indicated that they will accept service by fax, the fax number given by that party must be at the address for service.

PD 6A para.4.1

Subject to the provisions of r.6.23(5) and (6) [where a party indicates in accordance with PD 6A that they will accept service by electronic means other than fax, the e-mail address or electronic identification given by that party will be deemed to be at the address for service], where a document is to be served by fax or other electronic means—
    (1) the party who is to be served or the solicitor acting for that party must previously have indicated in writing to the party serving—
        (a) that the party to be served or the solicitor is willing to accept service by fax or other electronic means; and
        (b) the fax number, e-mail address or other electronic identification to which it must be sent; and

(2) the following are to be taken as sufficient written indications for the purposes of para.4.1(1)—

    (a) a fax number set out on the writing paper of the solicitor acting for the party to be served;

    (b) an e-mail address set out on the writing paper of the solicitor acting for the party to be served but only where it is stated that the e-mail address may be used for service; or

    (c) a fax number, e-mail address or electronic identification set out on a statement of case or a response to a claim filed with the court.

PD 6A para.4.2

Where a party intends to serve a document by electronic means (other than by fax) that party must first ask the party who is to be served whether there are any limitations to the recipient's agreement to accept service by such means (for example, the format in which documents are to be sent and the maximum size of attachments that may be received).

PD 6A para.4.3

Where a document is served by electronic means, the party serving the document need not in addition send or deliver a hard copy.

See also **Court documents**, **E-mail**, and **Service of documents**.

FEEDER COURT

Multi-track

PD 26 para.10(2)

    (4) The following sub-paragraphs apply to a claim which is issued in or automatically transferred to a court which is not a Civil Trial Centre. Such a court is referred to as a 'feeder court'.

    (5) Where a judge sitting at a feeder court decides, on the basis of the allocation questionnaires and any other documents filed by the parties, that the claim should be dealt with on the multi-track he will normally make an order:

        (a) allocating the claim to that track,

        (b) giving case management directions, and

        (c) transferring the claim to a Civil Trial Centre.

    (6) If he decides that an allocation hearing or some pre-allocation hearing is to take place (for example to strike out a statement of case under Pt 3 of the rules) that hearing will take place at the feeder court.

    (7) If, before allocation, a hearing takes place at a feeder court and in exercising his powers under para.2.4(1) above the judge allocates the claim to the multi-track, he will also normally make an order transferring the claim to a Civil Trial Centre.

    (8) A judge sitting at a feeder court may, rather than making an allocation order himself, transfer the claim to a Civil Trial Centre for the decision about allocation to be taken there.

See also **Multi-track**.

FEES

See **Court fees**.

FEES ORDER

See **Court fees**.

FIDUCIARY CAPACITY

Detailed assessment procedure where costs are payable out of a fund other than the community legal service fund or by the Lord Chancellor under Pt 1 of the Legal Aid, Sentencing and Punishment of Offenders Act 2012

PD 47 para.18.2

A person has a financial interest in the outcome of the assessment if the assessment will or may affect the amount of money or property to which that person is or may become entitled out of the fund. Where an interest in the fund is itself held by a trustee for the benefit of some other person, that trustee will be treated as the person having such a financial interest unless it is not appropriate to do so. 'Trustee' includes a personal representative, receiver or any other person acting in a fiduciary capacity.

FIERA FACIAS

See **Writ of fieri facias**.

FILING

Pt 2 r.2.3(1)

In relation to a document, means delivering it, by post or otherwise, to the court office.

Documents for filing at court

PD 5 para.5.1

The date on which a document was filed at court must be recorded on the document. This may be done by a seal or a receipt stamp.

PD 5 para.5.2

Particulars of the date of delivery at a court office of any document for filing and the title of the proceedings in which the document is filed shall be entered in court records, on the court file or on a computer kept in the court office for the purpose. Except where a document has been delivered at the court office through the post, the time of delivery should also be recorded.

FINAL COSTS CERTIFICATE

Procedure for detailed assessment of costs

Pt 47 r.47.17

(1) In this rule a 'completed bill' means a bill calculated to show the amount due following the detailed assessment of the costs.

(2) The period for filing the completed is 14 days after the end of the detailed assessment hearing.

(3) When a completed bill is filed the court will issue a final costs certificate and serve it on the parties to the detailed assessment proceedings.

(4) Paragraph (3) is subject to any order made by the court that a certificate is not to be issued until other costs have been paid.

(5) A final costs certificate will include an order to pay the costs to which it relates, unless the court orders otherwise.

(PD 47 deals with the form of a final costs certificate.)

(6) Where the court issues a final costs certificate in detailed assessment proceedings pursuant to an order under s.194(3) of the Legal Services Act 2007, the receiving party must send a copy of the final costs certificate to the prescribed charity.

PD 47 para.16.1

At the detailed assessment hearing the court will indicate any disallowance or reduction in the sums claimed in the bill of costs by making an appropriate note on the bill.

PD 47 para.16.2

The receiving party must, in order to complete the bill after the detailed assessment hearing make clear the correct figures agreed or allowed in respect of each item and must re-calculate the summary of the bill appropriately.

PD 47 para.16.3

The completed bill of costs must be filed with the court no later than 14 days after the detailed assessment hearing.

PD 47 para.16.4

At the same time as filing the completed bill of costs, the party whose bill it is must also produce receipted fee notes and receipted accounts in respect of all disbursements except those covered by a certificate in Precedent F(5) in the Schedule of Costs Precedents annexed to [PD 47].

PD 47 para.16.5

No final costs certificate will be issued until all relevant court fees payable on the assessment of costs have been paid.

PD 47 para.16.6

If the receiving party fails to file a completed bill in accordance with r. 47.16 the paying party may make an application under Pt 23 seeking an appropriate order under r. 3.1 (The court's general powers of management).

PD 47 para.16.7

A final costs certificate will show:
  (a) the amount of any costs which have been agreed between the parties or which have been
      allowed on detailed assessment;
  (b) where applicable the amount agreed or allowed in respect of VAT on such costs.
This provision is subject to any contrary provision made by the statutory provisions relating to
costs payable out of the Community Legal Service Fund or by the Lord Chancellor under Pt 1
of the Legal Aid, Sentencing and Punishment of Offenders Act 2012.

PD 47 para.16.8

A final costs certificate will include disbursements in respect of the fees of counsel only if
receipted fee notes or accounts in respect of those disbursements have been produced to the court
and only to the extent indicated by those receipts.

PD 47 para.16.9

Where the certificate relates to costs payable between parties a separate certificate will be issued
for each party entitled to costs.

PD 47 para.16.10

Form N257 is a model form of interim costs certificate and Form N256 is a model form of final
costs certificate.

PD 47 para.16.11

An application for an order staying enforcement of an interim costs certificate or final costs
certificate may be made either:
  (1) to a costs judge or district judge of the court office which issued the certificate; or
  (2) to the court (if different) which has general jurisdiction to enforce the certificate.

PD 47 para.16.12

An interim or final costs certificate may be enforced as if it were a judgment for the payment of
an amount of money. However, proceedings for the enforcement of interim costs certificates or
final costs certificates may not be issued in the Costs Office.

FINAL DECISION

Appeals

PD 52A para.3.6

A decision of a court that would finally determine (subject to any possible appeal or detailed
assessment of costs) the entire proceedings whichever way the court decided the issues before it.
Decisions made on an application to strike-out or for summary judgment are not final decisions
for the purpose of determining the appropriate route of appeal (art.1 of the Access to Justice Act
1999 (Destination of Appeals) Order 2000). Accordingly:
  (1) a case management decision;

(2) the grant or refusal of interim relief;

(3) a summary judgment;

(4) a striking out,

are not final decisions for this purpose.

PD 52A para.3.7

A decision of a court is to be treated as a final decision for routes of appeal purposes where it:

(1) is made at the conclusion of part of a hearing or trial which has been split into parts; and

(2) would, if it had been made at the conclusion of that hearing or trial, have been a final decision.

Accordingly, a judgment on liability at the end of a split trial is a 'final decision' for this purpose and the judgment at the conclusion of the assessment of damages following a judgment on liability is also a 'final decision' for this purpose.

PD 52A para.3.8

(1) The following are examples of final decisions—

a judgment on liability at the end of a split trial;

judgment at the conclusion of an assessment of damages following a judgment on liability.

(2) The following are examples of decisions that are not final—

a case management decision (within the meaning of para.4.6 [include decisions made under r. 3.1(2) (list of powers in addition to any powers given to the court by any other rule or PD or by any other enactment or any powers it may otherwise have) and decisions about disclosure, filing of witness statements or experts' reports, directions about the timetable of the claim, adding a party to a claim and security for costs]);

a grant or refusal of interim relief;

summary judgment;

striking out a claim or statement of case;

a summary or detailed assessment of costs;

an order for the enforcement of a final decision.

See **Appeals**.

FINAL REMEDY

Small claims track

Pt 27 r.27.3

The court may grant any final remedy in relation to a small claim which it could grant if the proceedings were on the fast track or the multi-track.

FINANCIAL RESTRICTIONS PROCEEDINGS

Pt 79 r.79.1(c)

[Under the Counter-Terrorism Act 2008 and the Terrorist Asset-Freezing etc Act 2010] "financial restrictions proceedings" means—

(i) financial restrictions proceedings within the meaning of s.65 of the 2008 Act; and
(ii) proceedings in the High Court on an application under s.27 of the 2010 Act, or on a claim arising from any matter to which such an application relates.

Title of documents

PD 49A para.4

(1) The claim form in proceedings under the [Companies Act 1985], the [Companies Act 2006], Part VII [Financial Services and Markets Act 2000], the [Council Regulation (EC) No. 2157/2001 of 8 October 2001 on the Statute for a European Company (SE] or the [Companies (Cross-Border Mergers) Regulations 2007], and any application, affidavit, witness statement, notice or other document in such proceedings, must be entitled 'In the matter of [the name of the company in question] and in the matter of [the relevant law]', where '[the relevant law]' means 'the Companies Act 1985', 'the Companies Act 2006', 'Part VII of the Financial Services and Markets Act 2000', 'Council Regulation (EC) No 2157/2001 of 8 October 2001 on the Statute for a European Company (SE)' or 'the Companies (Cross-Border Merger) Regulations 2007', as the case may be.
(2) Where a company changes its name in the course of proceedings, the title must be altered by—
   (a) substituting the new name for the old; and
   (b) inserting the old name in brackets at the end of the title.

Application to set aside financial restrictions decisions under the 2008 Act and the 2010 Act

Pt 79 r.79.3

[Section 2 of Part 79] applies to an application to set aside a financial restrictions decision under s.63(2) of the 2008 Act or s.27(2) of the 2010 Act.

Applications to set aside a financial restrictions decision

Pt 79 r.79.5

(1) An application to set aside a financial restrictions decision must be made pursuant to Pt 8, as modified by this Part, and subject to para.(2).
(2) The following rules do not apply to an application under this section—
   (a) rule 8.1(3);
   (b) rule 8.2A (issue of claim form without naming defendants);
   (c) rule 8.4 (consequence of not filing an acknowledgment of service);
   (d) rule 8.5 (filing and serving written evidence);
   (e) rule 8.6 (evidence—general); and
   (f) rule 8.8 (defendant objects to use of Pt 8).

Pt 79 r.79.6

(1) An application to set aside a financial restrictions decision must be started by a claim form.
(2) The claim form must set out—

    (a) the details of the financial restrictions decision;

    (b) details of how the claimant is affected by the financial restrictions decision; and

    (c) the grounds on which the claimant seeks to set aside the decision.

(3) The claimant must file with the claim form—

    (a) a copy of—

       (i) the written notice of the relevant financial restrictions decision made by the Treasury; or

      (ii) where relevant, any direction, order or licence made under Sch.7 to the 2008 Act or any freezing order made under Pt 2 of the Anti-terrorism, Crime and Security Act; and

    (b) any evidence, including witness statements, on which the claimant relies at that stage.

Service of the claim form and accompanying documents

Pt 79 r.79.8

The court will—

    (a) serve on the Treasury and any special advocate (if one has been appointed)—

       (i) the claim form; and

      (ii) the documents specified in r.79.6(3); and

    (b) send to all parties and any special advocate a notice of the directions hearing date (where such date is not endorsed on the claim form).

Acknowledgment of service

Pt 79 r.79.9

Where a special advocate has been appointed, the Treasury must serve on that special advocate a copy of the acknowledgment of service filed under r.8.3.

Directions hearing

Pt 79 r.79.7

(1) When the court issues the claim form it will fix a date for a directions hearing.

(2) Unless the court directs otherwise, the directions hearing will be not less than 14 days but not more than 28 days after the date of issue of the claim form.

Pt 79 r.79.10

At the directions hearing the court may give case management directions, in particular—

    (a) for the holding of a further hearing to determine the application;

    (b) fixing a date, time and place for the further hearing at which the parties, their legal representatives (if any) and any special advocate can be present; and

    (c) as to the order in which, and the time within which, the following are to be filed and served—

       (i) any response to the application to be filed and served by the Treasury under r.79.11(1), (2) and (4);

      (ii) any application to be made under r.79.11(5);

    (iii) any information to be filed and served by the Treasury pursuant to an Order under r.79.11(7);

    (iv) any evidence to be filed and served by the claimant under r.79.12(1);

    (v) any evidence to be filed and served by the Treasury under r.79.12(2);

    (vi) any application by the Treasury under r.79.11(3), 79.11(8) or 79.12(3); and

    (vii) any further evidence, including witness statements, written submissions or skeleton arguments, to be filed and served by the parties and any special advocate.

Response by the treasury

Pt 79 r.79.11

(1) Where the Treasury intend to oppose the application to set aside the financial restrictions decision, they must file with the court—
    (a) the grounds for contesting the application; and
    (b) any relevant evidence of which they are aware at that stage.

(2) Unless the Treasury object to the grounds and evidence in para.(1) being disclosed to the claimant and the claimant's legal representative, the Treasury must serve a copy of the grounds and evidence on the claimant at the same time as filing the grounds.

(3) Where the Treasury object to the grounds and evidence in para.(1) being disclosed to the claimant and the claimant's legal representative, the Treasury must make an application in accordance with r.79.25.

(4) Where a special advocate has been appointed, the Treasury must serve on that special advocate a copy of the grounds and evidence filed under para.(1).

(5) The claimant and any special advocate may apply to the court for an order directing the Treasury to file and serve further information about the Treasury's grounds filed under para.(1)(a).

(6) The application under para.(5) must set out—
    (a) what information is sought; and
    (b) why the information sought is necessary for the determination of the application to set aside the financial restrictions decision.

(7) The court may make an order on an application under para.(5) where it considers that the information sought is—
    (a) necessary for the determination of the application to set aside the financial restrictions decision; and
    (b) may be provided without disproportionate cost, time or effort.

(8) Where the Treasury object to serving on the claimant and the claimant's legal representative the information sought under para.(5), the Treasury must make an application in accordance with r.79.25 [application to withholdclosed material].

Filing and service of evidence

Pt 79 r.79.12

(1) Where the claimant wishes to rely on evidence in support of the application to set aside the financial restrictions decision and—
    (a) such evidence was not filed with the court with the claim form; or
    (b) such evidence was filed with the court with the claim form but the claimant wishes to rely on further evidence,
the claimant must file and serve that evidence, including any witness statement, on the Treasury and any special advocate.

(2) Where the claimant serves evidence in support of the application, the Treasury must file and serve, subject to para.(3), any further evidence, including any witness statement, on the claimant and any special advocate.

(3) Where the Treasury seek to withhold disclosure of any closed material from the claimant and the claimant's legal representative, the Treasury must make an application in accordance with r.79.25.

(4) The Treasury must serve any closed material upon the special advocate.

(5) The parties and, where relevant, any special advocate must file and serve any further evidence, including witness statements, written submissions or skeleton arguments as directed by the court.

General provisions

Pt 79 r.79.15

[Section 5 of Pt 79] applies to all proceedings specified in rule in ss.2 [financial restrictions proceedings] and 3 [**designations**] of [Pt 79].

Where to make an application

Pt 79 r.79.15A

An application under s.2 and an appeal under s.3 of this Part must be started and heard in the Administrative Court.

Notification of hearing

Pt 79 r.79.16

Unless the court orders otherwise, the court will serve any notice of the date, time and place fixed for a hearing on—
  (a) every party, whether or not a party is entitled to attend that hearing; and
  (b) if one has been appointed for the purposes of the proceedings, the special advocate or those instructing the special advocate.

Hearings

Pt 79 r.79.17

(1) All proceedings to which ss.2 or 3 of [Pt 79] applies must be determined at a hearing except where—
  (a) the claimant withdraws the claim or application;
  (b) the Treasury consent to the claim or application being allowed;
  (c) the appellant withdraws the appeal against a decision of the Treasury or the High Court;
  (d) the respondent to the appeal consents to the appeal being allowed; or
  (e) the parties agree to a determination without a hearing.

(2) Where the court considers it necessary for a party other than the Treasury and that party's legal representative to be excluded from a hearing or part of a hearing in order to secure that information is not disclosed contrary to the public interest, the court will—

    (a) direct accordingly; and

    (b) conduct the hearing, or that part of it from which the party and that party's legal representative are excluded, in private but attended by a special advocate to represent the interests of the excluded party.

Appointment of a special advocate

Pt 79 r.79.18

(1) Subject to para.(2), the Treasury must immediately give notice of the proceedings to the Attorney General—

    (a) upon being served with any claim form, application notice or appeal notice; or

    (b) where the Treasury intend to file an appeal notice,

in proceedings to which ss.2 or 3 of this Part applies.

(2) Paragraph (1) applies unless—

    (a) the Treasury do not intend to—

        (i) oppose the claim, application or appeal; or

        (ii) apply for permission to withhold closed material from a party and that party's legal representative; or

    (b) a special advocate has already been appointed to represent the interests of a party other than the Treasury and that special advocate is not prevented from communicating with that party by virtue of r.79.20.

(3) Where any proceedings to which ss.2 or 3 of this Part applies are pending but no special advocate has been appointed, any party may request the Attorney General to appoint a special advocate.

Function of a special advocate

Pt 79 r.79.19

The function of a special advocate is to represent the interests of a party other than the Treasury by, for example—

    (a) making submissions to the court at any hearing from which the party and that party's legal representative are excluded;

    (b) adducing evidence and cross-examining witnesses at such a hearing;

    (c) making applications to the court or seeking directions from the court where necessary; and

    (d) making written submissions to the court.

Special advocate: communicating about proceedings

Pt 79 r.79.20

(1) The special advocate may communicate with the specially represented party or that party's legal representative at any time before the Treasury serve closed material on the special advocate.

(2) After the Treasury serve closed material on the special advocate, the special advocate must not communicate with any person about any matter connected with the proceedings,

except in accordance with para.(3) or a direction of the court pursuant to a request under para.(4).

(3) The special advocate may, without directions from the court, communicate about the proceedings with—

    (a) the court;

    (b) the Treasury and any persons acting for them;

    (c) the Attorney General and any persons acting for the Attorney General; and

    (d) any other person, except for—

        (i) the specially represented party and that party's legal representative; and

        (ii) any other party to the proceedings (other than the Treasury) and that party's legal representative,

    with whom it is necessary for administrative purposes for the special advocate to communicate about matters not connected with the substance of the proceedings.

(4) The special advocate may request directions from the court authorising the special advocate to communicate with the specially represented party or that party's legal representative or with any other person.

(5) Where the special advocate makes a request for directions under para.(4)—

    (a) the court will notify the Treasury of the request; and

    (b) the Treasury must, within a period specified by the court, file and serve on the special advocate notice of any objection which they have to the proposed communication, or to the form in which it is proposed to be made.

(6) Paragraph (2) does not prohibit the specially represented party from communicating with the special advocate after the Treasury have served closed material on the special advocate as mentioned in para.(1), but—

    (a) that party may only communicate with the special advocate through a legal representative in writing; and

    (b) the special advocate must not reply to the communication other than in accordance with directions given by the court, except that the special advocate may without such directions send a written acknowledgment of receipt to the specially represented party's legal representative.

Consideration of the Treasury's objection

Pt 79 r.79.21

(1) Where the Treasury object under r.79.20(5)(b) to a proposed communication by the special advocate the court will fix a hearing for the Treasury and the special advocate to make oral representations, unless—

    (a) the special advocate gives notice to the court that the special advocate does not challenge the objection;

    (b) the court—

        (i) has previously considered an objection under r.79.20(5)(b) to the same or substantially the same communication; and

        (ii) is satisfied that it would be just to uphold or dismiss that objection without a hearing; or

    (c) the Treasury and the special advocate consent to the court deciding the issue without a hearing.

(2) If the special advocate does not challenge the objection, the special advocate must give notice of that fact to the court and to the Treasury—

    (a) within 14 days after the Treasury serve on the special advocate a notice under r.79.20(5)(b); or

    (b) within such other period as the court may direct.

(3) Where the court fixes a hearing under para.(1)—

    (a) the special advocate may file with the court and serve on the Treasury a reply to the Treasury's objection;

(b) the Treasury may file with the court and serve on the special advocate a response to the special advocate's reply; and

(c) the Treasury and the special advocate must file with the court at least seven days before the hearing a schedule identifying the issues which cannot be agreed between them and which must—

(i) give brief reasons for their contentions on each issue in dispute; and

(ii) set out any proposals for the court to resolve the issues in dispute.

(4) A hearing under this rule must take place in the absence of the specially represented party and that party's legal representative.

Modification of the general rules of evidence and disclosure

Pt 79 r.79.22

(1) Part 31 (disclosure and inspection of documents), Pt 32 (evidence) and Pt 33 (miscellaneous rules about evidence) do not apply to any proceedings to which ss.2 or 3 of this Part applies.

(2) Subject to the other rules in ss.2 and 3 and this section of this Part and to any directions of the court, the evidence of a witness may be given either—

(a) orally before the court; or

(b) in a witness statement.

(3) The court may also receive evidence in documentary or any other form.

(4) A party is entitled to adduce evidence and to cross-examine witnesses during any part of a hearing from which a party and that party's legal representative are not excluded.

(4A) A special advocate is entitled to adduce evidence and to cross-examine witnesses

(5) The court may require a witness to give evidence on oath or by affirmation.

Search for, filing of and service of material

Pt 79 r.79.23

(1) A party (the disclosing party) must—

(a) make a reasonable search for material relevant to the matters under consideration in the proceedings to which ss.2 or 3 of this Part applies; and

(b) file and serve on the other party and any special advocate material other than closed material—

(i) on which the disclosing party relies;

(ii) which adversely affects the disclosing party's case; or

(iv) which supports the other party's case.

(2) The factors relevant in deciding the reasonableness of a search under para.(1)(a) include—

(a) the amount of material involved;

(b) the nature and complexity of the proceedings;

(c) whether the material is in the control of the party making the search;

(d) the ease and expense of retrieval of any material; and

(e) the significance of any material which is likely to be located during the search.

(3) The duty to search for, file and serve material under para.(1) continues until the proceedings to which ss.2 or 3 of this Part applies have been determined.

(4) Where material, other than closed material, to which the duty under para.(1) extends comes to a party's attention before the proceedings to which ss.2 or 3 of this Part applies have been determined, that party must immediately—

(a) file it with the court;

(b) serve it on the other party; and

(c) serve it on any special advocate.

Redacted material

Pt 79 r.79.24

Where the Treasury serve on another party any evidence (including a witness statement) or material which has been redacted on grounds other than those of legal professional privilege, the Treasury must—
(a) notify the party that the evidence or material has been redacted and on what grounds it has been redacted;
(b) file the evidence or material with the court in an unredacted form together with an explanation of the redaction.

Application to withhold closed material

Pt 79 r.79.25

(1) The Treasury—
   (a) must apply to the court for permission to withhold closed material from another party and that party's legal representative in accordance with this rule; and
   (b) may not rely on closed material at a hearing unless a special advocate has been appointed and attends the hearing to represent the interests of that party.
(2) The Treasury must file with the court and serve, at such time as the court directs, on the special advocate—
   (a) the closed material;
   (b) a statement of the reasons for withholding that material from the specially represented party; and
   (c) if the Treasury consider it possible to summarise that material without disclosing information contrary to the public interest, a summary of that material in a form which can be served on the specially represented party or that party's legal representative.
(3) Where the Treasury serve on the special advocate any closed material which has been redacted on grounds other than those of legal professional privilege—
   (a) the Treasury must file with the court the material in an unredacted form together with an explanation of the redactions; and
   (b) the court will give a direction to the Treasury as to what may be redacted and what, if any, must be served on the special advocate in an unredacted form.
(4) The Treasury may at any time amend or supplement material filed under this rule, but only with—
   (a) the agreement of the special advocate; or
   (b) the permission of the court.

Consideration of the Treasury's application

Pt 79 r.79.26

(1) Where the Treasury apply in accordance with r.79.25 for permission to withhold closed material the court will fix a hearing for the Treasury and the special advocate to make oral representations, unless—

    (a) the special advocate gives notice to the court that the special advocate does not challenge the application;

    (b) the court—

        (i) has previously considered an application for permission to withhold the same or substantially the same material; and

        (ii) is satisfied that it would be just to give permission without a hearing; or

    (c) the Treasury and the special advocate consent to the court deciding the issue without a hearing.

  (2) If the special advocate does not challenge the application, the special advocate must give notice of that fact to the court and to the Treasury—

    (a) within 14 days after the Treasury serve on the special advocate the material under r.79.25(2); or

    (b) within such other period as the court may direct.

  (3) Where the court fixes a hearing under para.(1)—

    (a) the special advocate may file with the court and serve on the Treasury a reply to the Treasury's application;

    (b) the Treasury may file with the court and serve on the special advocate a response to the special advocate's reply; and

    (c) the Treasury and the special advocate must file with the court at least 7 days before the hearing a schedule identifying the issues which cannot be agreed between them and which must—

        (i) give brief reasons for their contentions on each issue in dispute; and

        (ii) set out any proposals for the court to resolve the issues in dispute.

  (4) A hearing under this rule must take place in the absence of the specially represented party and that party's legal representative.

  (5) The court will give permission to the Treasury to withhold closed material where it considers that disclosure of that material would be contrary to the public interest.

  (6) Where the court gives permission to the Treasury to withhold closed material, the court will—

    (a) consider whether to direct the Treasury to serve a summary of that material on the specially represented party or that party's legal representative; but

    (b) ensure that such a summary does not contain material, the disclosure of which would be contrary to the public interest.

  (7) Where the court does not give permission to the Treasury to withhold closed material from, or directs the Treasury to serve a summary of that material on, the specially represented party or that party's legal representative—

    (a) the Treasury are not required to serve that material or summary; but

    (b) if they do not do so, at a hearing on notice, the court may—

        (i) where it considers that the material or anything that is required to be summarised might adversely affect the Treasury's case or supports the case of the specially represented party, direct that the Treasury must not rely on such material in their case, or must make such concessions or take such other steps, as the court may specify; or

        (ii) in any other case, direct that the Treasury do not rely on the material or (as the case may be) on that which is required to be summarised.

Failure to comply with directions

Pt 79 r.79.27

  (1) Where a party or special advocate fails to comply with a direction of the court, the court may serve on that party or the special advocate a notice which states—

    (a) the respect in which that party or special advocate has failed to comply with the direction;

(b) a time limit for complying with the direction; and

(c) that the court may proceed to determine the proceedings before it, on the material available to it, if the party or special advocate fails to comply with the relevant direction within the time specified.

(2) Where a party or special advocate fails to comply with such a notice, the court may proceed in accordance with para.(1)(c).

Judgments

Pt 79 r.79.28

(1) When the court gives judgment in any proceedings to which ss.2 or 3 of this Part applies, it may withhold all or some of its reasons if and to the extent that it is not possible to give reasons without disclosing information contrary to the public interest.

(2) Where the judgment of the court does not include the full reasons for its decision, the court will serve on the Treasury and the special advocate a separate written judgment including those reasons.

(3) Where the court serves a separate written judgment under para.(2), the special advocate may apply to the court to amend that judgment and the judgment under para.(1) on the grounds that the separate written judgment under para.(2) contains material not in the judgment under para.(1) the disclosure of which would not be contrary to the public interest.

(4) The special advocate must serve a copy of the application under para.(3) on the Treasury.

(5) The court will give the special advocate and the Treasury an opportunity to file written submissions and may determine the application with or without a hearing.

Application by treasury for reconsideration of order, direction or judgment

Pt 79 r.79.29

(1) This rule applies where the court proposes, in any proceedings to which ss.2 or 3 of this Part applies, to serve on a party other than the Treasury—

(a) notice of any order or direction made or given in the absence of the Treasury; or

(b) any written judgment.

(2) Before the court serves any such notice or judgment on a party other than the Treasury, it will first serve notice on the Treasury of its intention to do so.

(3) The Treasury may, within five days of being served with notice under para.(2), apply to the court to reconsider the terms of the order or direction or to review the terms of the proposed judgment if they consider—

(a) their compliance with the order or direction; or

(b) the notification to another party of any matter contained in the judgment, order or direction,

would cause information to be disclosed contrary to the public interest.

(4) Where the Treasury make an application under para.(3), they must at the same time serve on a special advocate, if one has been appointed—

(a) a copy of the application;

(b) a copy of the relevant document referred to in para.(1)(a) or (b); and

(c) a copy of the notice served on the Treasury pursuant to para.(2).

(5) If a special advocate has been appointed, r.79.26 (except for paras (6) and (7)) will apply with any necessary modifications to the consideration of an application under para.(3) of this rule.

(6) The court will not serve notice on a party other than the Treasury as mentioned in para.(1) before the time for the Treasury to make an application under para.(3) has expired.

Supply of court documents

Pt 79 r.79.30

Unless the court directs otherwise, r.5.4 (Register of Claims), r.5.4B (Supply of documents from court records—a party) and r.5.4C (Supply of documents from court records—a non-party) do not apply to any proceedings to which ss.2 or 3 of this Part applies or to any document relating to such proceedings.

Appeals to Court of Appeal

Pt 79 r.79.13

Part 52 (appeals) applies to an appeal to the Court of Appeal against an order of the High Court in financial restrictions proceedings, subject to—
 (a) Rule 79.2; and
 (b) Section 4 of this Part.

Service of appellant's notice on special advocate

Pt 79 r.79.14

The appellant must serve a copy of the appellant's notice on any special advocate.

See **Designations under the Terrorist Asset-freezing etc Act 2012** and **Notification orders under the Counter-Terrorism Act 2008**.

FINANCIAL SERVICES AND MARKETS ACT 2000

PD 8A para.21.1

This paragraph applies to proceedings in the High Court under the [Act].

PD 8A para.2

Proceedings in the High Court under the Act (other than applications for a mandatory order) and actions for damages for breach of a statutory duty imposed by the Act shall be assigned to the Chancery Division.

PD 8A para.21.3

Such proceedings and actions must be begun by [Pt 8] claim form (except for applications by petition by the Financial Services Authority under s.367 of the Act).

PD 8A para.21.4

The Financial Services Authority may make representations to the court where there is a question about the meaning of any rule or other instrument made by, or with the approval or consent of, the Financial Services Authority.

See also **Part 8 claim form** and **Part 8 procedure**.

FINE

Notice to show cause before or after fine under s.55 of the act

CCR Ord.34 r.2

Before or after imposing a fine on any person under s.55 of the Act for disobeying a **witness summons** or refusing to be sworn or give evidence, the judge may direct the court officer to give to that person notice that if he has any cause to show why a fine should not be or should not have been imposed on him, he may show cause in person or by witness statement or affidavit or otherwise on a day named in the notice, and the judge after considering the cause shown may make such order as he thinks fit.

Non-payment of fine

CCR Ord.34 r.3

(1) If a fine is not paid in accordance with the order imposing it, the court officer shall forthwith report the matter to the judge.
(2) Where, by an order imposing a fine, the amount of the fine is directed to be paid by instalments and default is made in the payment of any instalment, the same proceedings may be taken as if default had been made in payment of the whole of the fine.
(3) If the judge makes an order for payment of a fine to be enforced by warrant of execution, the order shall be treated as an application made to the district judge for the issue of the warrant at the time when the order was received by him.

Repayment of fine

CCR Ord.34 r.4

If, after a fine has been paid, the person on whom it was imposed shows cause sufficient to satisfy the judge that, if it had been shown at an earlier date, he would not have imposed a fine or would have imposed a smaller fine or would not have ordered payment to be enforced, the judge may order the fine or any part thereof to be repaid.

Registration of international criminal courtorders [including fine] for enforcement

RSC Ord.115 r.38

(1) An application to the High Court to register an order of the ICC for enforcement, or to vary or set aside the registration of an order, may be made to a judge or a Master of the Queen's Bench Division.

(2) Rule 13 and rr.15 to 20 in Part I of [RSC Order 115] shall, with such modifications as are necessary and subject to the provisions of any regulations made under s.49 of [International Criminal Court Act 2001], apply to the registration for enforcement of an order of the ICC as they apply to the registration of an external confiscation order.

See also **Contempt of court**.

FIRM

See **Claim form**.

FIXED COSTS

Pt 44 r.44.1(1)

Costs the amounts of which are fixed by [CPR] whether or not the court has a discretion to allow some other or no amount, and include—
  (i) the amounts which are to be allowed in respect of **legal representatives**' charges in the circumstances set out in s.I of Pt 45;
 (ii) fixed recoverable costs calculated in accordance with r.45.11;
 (iii) the additional costs allowed by r.45.18;
 (iv) fixed costs determined under r.45.21;
  (v) costs fixed by rr.45.37 and 45.38.
[Section 1 of Pt 45 sets out the fixed costs which are allowed in respect of legal representatives' charges, unless the court orders otherwise, in claims listed in r.45.1(2).
Paragraphs 1.1 and 1.2 of PD 45 deals with fixed costs in small claims and para.1.3 deals with claims in which Pt 45 does not apply.]

See also **Disbursements** and **Road traffic accidents**.

FOREIGN COURTS

Evidence for foreign courts

Pt 34 r.34.16

(1) [Section II of Pt 34] applies to an application for an order under the [Evidence (Proceedings in Other Jurisdictions) Act 1975] for evidence to be obtained, other than an application made as a result of a request by a court in another Regulation State.
(2) In this section—
   (b) 'Regulation State' [has the same meaning as 'Member State' in the Taking of Evidence Regulation, that is all Member States except Denmark].

Application for order

Pt 34 r.34.17

An application for an order under the 1975 Act for evidence to be obtained—
  (a) must be—

(i) made to the High Court;
(ii) supported by written evidence; and
(iii) accompanied by the request as a result of which the application is made, and where appropriate, a translation of the request into English; and
(b) may be made without notice.

Examination

Pt 34 r.34.18

(1) The court may order an examination to be taken before—
    (a) any fit and proper person nominated by the person applying for the order;
    (b) an examiner of the court; or
    (c) any other person whom the court considers suitable.
(2) Unless the court orders otherwise—
    (a) the examination will be taken as provided by r.34.9; and
    (b) rule 34.10 applies.
(3) The court may make an order under r.34.14 for payment of the fees and expenses of the examination.

Dealing with deposition

Pt 34 r.34.19

(1) The examiner must send the deposition of the witness to the Senior Master unless the court orders otherwise.
(2) The Senior Master will—
    (a) give a certificate sealed with the seal of the Senior Courts for use out of the jurisdiction identifying the following documents—
        (i) the request;
        (ii) the order of the court for examination; and
        (iii) the deposition of the witness; and
    (b) send the certificate and the documents referred to in para.(a) to—
        (i) the Secretary of State; or
        (ii) where the request was sent to the Senior Master by another person in accordance with a Civil Procedure Convention, to that other person,
    for transmission to the court or tribunal requesting the examination.

Claim to privilege

Pt 34 r.34.20

(1) This rule applies where—
    (a) a witness claims to be exempt from giving evidence on the ground specified in s.3(1)(b) of the 1975 Act; and
    (b) That claim is not supported or conceded as referred to in s.3(2) of that Act.
(2) The examiner may require the witness to give the evidence which he claims to be exempt from giving.
(3) Where the examiner does not require the witness to give that evidence, the court may order the witness to do so.

(4) An application for an order under para.(3) may be made by the person who obtained the order under s.2 of the 1975 Act.

(5) Where such evidence is taken—
(a) it must be contained in a document separate from the remainder of the deposition;
(b) the examiner will send to the Senior Master—
    (i) the deposition; and
    (ii) a signed statement setting out the claim to be exempt and the ground on which it was made;

(6) On receipt of the statement referred to in para.(5)(b)(ii), the Senior Master will—
(a) retain the document containing the part of the witness's evidence to which the claim to be exempt relates; and
(b) send the statement and a request to determine that claim to the foreign court or tribunal together with the documents referred to in r.34.17.

(7) The Senior Master will—
(a) if the claim to be exempt is rejected by the foreign court or tribunal, send the document referred to in para.(5)(a) to that court or tribunal;
(b) if the claim is upheld, send the document to the witness; and
(c) in either case, notify the witness and person who obtained the order under s.2 of the foreign court or tribunal's decision.

Definitions to be taken on in England and Wales for use as evidence in proceedings before courts abroad pursuant to letters of request (where the Taking of Evidence does not apply)

PD 34A para.6.2

The Evidence (Proceedings in Other Jurisdictions) Act 1975 applies to these depositions.

PD 34A para.6.3

The written evidence supporting an application under r.34.17 (which should be made by application notice—see Pt 23) must include or exhibit—
(1) a statement of the issues relevant to the proceedings;
(2) a list of questions or the subject matter of questions to be put to the proposed deponent;
(3) a draft order; and
(4) a translation of the documents in (1) and (2) into English, if necessary.

PD 34A para.6.4

(1) The Senior Master will send to the Treasury Solicitor any request—
(a) forwarded by the Secretary of State with a recommendation that effect should be given to the request without requiring an application to be made; or
(b) received by him in pursuance of a Civil Procedure Convention providing for the taking of evidence of any person in England and Wales to assist a court or tribunal in a foreign country where no person is named in the document as the applicant.

(2) In relation to such a request, the Treasury Solicitor may, with the consent of the Treasury—
(a) apply for an order under the 1975 Act; and
(b) take such other steps as are necessary to give effect to the request.

PD 34A para.6.5

The order for the deponent to attend and be examined together with the evidence upon which the order was made must be served on the deponent.

PD 34A para.6.6

Attention is drawn to the provisions of r.23.10 (application to vary or discharge an order made without notice).

PD 34A para.6.7

Arrangements for the examination to take place at a specified time and place before an **examiner of the court** or such other person as the court may appoint shall be made by the applicant for the order and approved by the Senior Master.

PD 34A para.6.8

The provisions of paras 4.2 to 4.12 apply to the depositions referred to in this paragraph, except that the examiner must send the deposition to the Senior Master.

Order under the 1975 Act as applied by the Patents Act 1977

Pt 34 r.34.21

Where an order is made for the examination of witnesses under s.1 of the 1975 Act as applied by s.92 of the Patents Act 1977 the court may permit an officer of the European Patent Office to—
  (a) attend the examination and examine the witnesses; or
  (b) request the court or the examiner before whom the examination takes place to put specified questions to them.

Taking of evidence—Member States of the European Union

Evidence of person in Member States of the European Union

Pt 34 r.34.22

In this section—
  (a) 'designated court' has the meaning given in PD 34A;
  (b) 'Regulation State' has the same meaning as 'Member State' in the Taking of Evidence Regulation, that is all Member States except Denmark;
  (c) 'the Taking of Evidence Regulation' means Council Regulation (EC) No.1206/2001 of May 28, 2001 on co-operation between the courts of the Member States in the taking of evidence in civil and commercial matters.

Where a person to be examined is in another regulation state

Pt 34 r.34.23

  (1) Subject to r.34.13A, this rule applies where a party wishes to take a deposition from a person who is in another Regulation State-

    (a) outside the jurisdiction; and

    (b) in a Regulation State.

(2) The court may order the issue of a request to a designated court ('the requested court') in the Regulation State in which the proposed deponent is.

(3) If the court makes an order for the issue of a request, the party who sought the order must file—

    (a) a draft Form A as set out in the annex to the Taking of Evidence Regulation (request for the taking of evidence);

    (b) except where para.(4) applies, a translation of the form;

    (c) an undertaking to be responsible for costs sought by the requested court in relation to—

        (i) fees paid to experts and interpreters; and

        (ii) where requested by that party, the use of special procedures or communications technology; and

    (d) an undertaking to be responsible for the court's expenses.

(4) There is no need to file a translation if—

    (a) English is one of the official languages of the Regulation State where the examination is to take place; or

    (b) the Regulation State has indicated, in accordance with the Taking of Evidence Regulation, that English is a language which it will accept.

(5) Where art.17 of the Taking of Evidence Regulation (direct taking of evidence by the requested court) allows evidence to be taken directly in another Regulation State, the court may make an order for the submission of a request in accordance with that article.

(6) If the court makes an order for the submission of a request under para.(5), the party who sought the order must file—

    (a) a draft Form I as set out in the annex to the Taking of Evidence Regulation (request for direct taking of evidence);

    (b) except where para.(4) applies, a translation of the form; and

    (c) an undertaking to be responsible for the court's expenses.

Taking of evidence regulation

PD 34A para.7.1

Where evidence is to be taken—

    (a) from a person in another Member State of the European Union for use as evidence in proceedings before courts in England and Wales; or

    (b) from a person in England and Wales for use as evidence in proceedings before a court in another Member State, Council Regulation (EC) No 1206/2001 of 28 May 2001 on co-operation between the courts of the Member States in the taking of evidence in civil or commercial matters ('the Taking of Evidence Regulation') applies.

PD 34A para.7.2

The Taking of Evidence Regulation is annexed to [PD 34B] as Annex B.

PD 34A para.7.3

The Taking of Evidence Regulation does not apply to Denmark. In relation to Denmark, therefore, r.34.13 and s.II of Pt 34 will continue to apply.

(Article 21(1) of the Taking of Evidence Regulation provides that the Regulation prevails over other provisions contained in bilateral or multilateral agreements or arrangements concluded by the Member States and in particular the Hague Convention of March 1, 1954 on Civil Procedure and the Hague Convention of March 18, 1970 on the Taking of Evidence Abroad in Civil or Commercial Matters).

Originally published in the official languages of the European Community in the Official Journal of the European Communities by the Office for Official Publications of the European Communities.

Meaning of 'designated court'

PD 34A para.8.1

In accordance with the Taking of Evidence Regulation, each Regulation State has prepared a list of courts competent to take evidence in accordance with the Regulation indicating the territorial and, where appropriate, special jurisdiction of those courts.

PD 34A para.8.2

Where Pt 34, s.III refers to a 'designated court' in relation to another Regulation State, the reference is to the court, referred to in the list of competent courts of that State, which is appropriate to the application in hand.

PD 34A para.8.3

Where the reference is to the 'designated court' in England and Wales, the reference is to the appropriate competent court in the jurisdiction. The designated courts for England and Wales are listed in Annex C to this practice direction.

Central body

PD 34A para.9.1

The Taking of Evidence Regulation stipulates that each Regulation State must nominate a Central Body responsible for—
   (a) supplying information to courts;
   (b) seeking solutions to any difficulties which may arise in respect of a request; and
   (c) forwarding, in exceptional cases, at the request of a requesting court, a request to the competent court.

PD 34A para.9.2

The UK has nominated the Senior Master, Queen's Bench Division, to be the Central Body for England and Wales.

PD 34A para.9.3

The Senior Master, as Central Body, has been designated responsible for taking decisions on requests pursuant to art.17 of the regulation. Article 17 allows a court to submit a request to the Central Body or a designated competent authority in another Regulation State to take evidence directly in that State.

Evidence to be taken in England and Wales for use in another regulation state

Pt 34 r.34.24

(1) This rule applies where a court in another Regulation State ('the requesting court') issues a request for evidence to be taken from a person who is in the jurisdiction.
(2) An application for an order for evidence to be taken—
    (a) must be made to a designated court;
    (b) must be accompanied by—
        (i) the form of request for the taking of evidence as a result of which the application is made; and
        (ii) where appropriate, a translation of the form of request; and
    (c) may be made without notice.
(3) Rule 34.18(1) and (2) apply.
(4) The examiner must send—
    (a) the deposition to the court for transmission to the requesting court; and
    (b) a copy of the deposition to the person who obtained the order for evidence to be taken.

PD 34A para.11.1

Where a designated court in England and Wales receives a request to take evidence from a court in a Regulation State, the court will send the request to the Treasury Solicitor.

PD 34A para.11.2

On receipt of the request, the Treasury Solicitor may, with the consent of the Treasury, apply for an order under r.34.24.

PD 34A para.11.3

In application to the court for an order must be accompanied by the Form of request to take evidence and any accompanying documents, translated if required under para.11.4.

PD 34A para.11.4

The UK has indicated that, in addition to English, it will accept French as a language in which documents may be submitted. Where the form or request and any accompanying documents are received in French they will be translated into English by the Treasury Solicitor.

PD 34A para.1.5

The order for the deponent to attend and be examined together with the evidence on which the order was made must be served on the deponent.

PD 34A para.11.6

Arrangements for the examination to take place at a specified time and place shall be made by the Treasury Solicitor and approved by the court.

PD 34A para.11.7

The court shall send details of the arrangements for the examination to such of
    (a) the parties and, if any, their representatives; or

(b) the representatives of the foreign court,

who have indicated, in accordance with the Taking of Evidence Regulation, that they wish to be present at the examination.

PD 34A para.11.8

The provisions of paras 4.3 to 4.12 apply to the depositions referred to in this paragraph.

Evidence to be taken in another regulation state for use in England and Wales

PD 34A para.10.1

Where a person wishes to take a deposition from a person in another Regulation State, the court where the proceedings are taking place may order the issue of a request to the designated court in the Regulation State (r.34.23(2)). The form of request is prescribed as Form A in the Taking of Evidence Regulation.

PD 34A para.10.2

An application to the court for an order under r.34.23(2) should be made by application notice in accordance with Pt 23.

PD 34A para.10.3

Rule 34.23(3) provides that the party applying for the order must file a draft form of request in the prescribed form. Where completion of the form requires attachments or documents to accompany the form, these must also be filed.

PD 34A para.10.4

If the court grants an order under r.34.23 (2), it will send the form of request directly to the designated court.

PD 34A para.10.5

Where the taking of evidence requires the use of an expert, the designated court may require a deposit in advance towards the costs of that expert. The party who obtained the order is responsible for the payment of any such deposit which should be deposited with the court for onward transmission. Under the provisions of the Taking of Evidence Regulation, the designated court is not required to execute the request until such payment is received.

PD 34A para.10.6

Article 17 permits the court where proceedings are taking place to take evidence directly from a deponent in another Regulation State if the conditions of the article are satisfied. Direct taking of evidence can only take place if evidence is given voluntarily without the need for coercive measures. Rule 34.23(5) provides for the court to make an order for the submission of a request to take evidence directly. The form of request is Form I annexed to the Taking of Evidence Regulation and r.34.23(6) makes provision for a draft of this form to be filed by the party seeking the order. An application for an order under r.34.23(5) should be by application notice in accordance with Pt 23.

PD 34A para.10.7

Attention is drawn to the provisions of r.23.10 (application to vary or discharge an order made without notice).

Judgment summons

CCR Ord.28 r.12

Where, after a warrant of committal has been sent to a foreign court for execution but before the debtor is lodged in prison, the home court is notified that an amount which is less than the sum on payment of which the debtor is to be discharged has been paid, the home court shall send notice of the payment to the foreign court.

FOREIGN COURT JUDGMENTS

See **European Community judgments**.

FOREIGN CURRENCY

European enforcement orders

Pt 74 r.74.31

(2) Where a person applies to enforce an EEO expressed in a foreign currency, the application must contain a certificate of the sterling equivalent of the judgment sum at the close of business on the date nearest preceding the date of the application.

Default judgment

PD 12 para.5.2

Where default judgment is given on a claim for a sum of money enforced in a foreign curency, the judgment should be for the amount of the foreign currency with the addition of "or the sterling equivalent at the time of payment."

Judgment and order

PD 40B para.10

Where judgment is ordered to be entered in a foreign currency, the order should be in the following form:

"It is ordered that the defendant pay the claimant (state the sum in the foreign currency) or the Sterling equivalent at the time of payment."

Mediation settlement enforcement orders

Pt 78 r.78.25

(1) Where a person applies to enforce a mediation settlement enforcement order which is expressed in a foreign currency, the application must contain a certificate of the sterling equivalent of the sum remaining due under the order at the close of business on the day before the date of the application.

Particulars of claim

PD 16 para.9.1

Where a claim is for a sum of money expressed in a foreign currency it must expressly state:
    (1) that the claim is for payment in a specified foreign currency,
    (2) why it is for payment in that currency,
    (3) the Sterling equivalent of the sum at the date of the claim, and
    (4) the source of the exchange rate relied on to calculate the Sterling equivalent.

FOREIGN LAW

Evidence of finding on question of foreign law

Pt 33 r.33.7

(1) This rule sets out the procedure which must be followed by a party who intends to put in evidence a finding on a question of foreign law by virtue of s.4(2) of the Civil Evidence Act 1972.
(2) He must give any other party notice of his intention.
(3) He must give the notice—
    (a) if there are to be witness statements, not later than the latest date for serving them; or
    (b) otherwise, not less than 21 days before the hearing at which he proposes to put the finding in evidence.
(4) The notice must—
    (a) specify the question on which the finding was made; and
    (b) enclose a copy of a document where it is reported or recorded.

FOREIGN LIMITATION PERIODS ACT 1984

See **Limitation period**.

FORMS

Pt 4 r.4

(1) The forms set out in a PD shall be used in the cases to which they apply.
(2) A form may be varied by the court or a party if the variation is required by the circumstances of a particular case.

(3) A form must not be varied so as to leave out any information or guidance which the form gives to the recipient.

(4) Where these rules require a form to be sent by the court or by a party for another party to use, it must be sent without any variation except such as is required by the circumstances of the particular case.

(5) Where the court or a party produces a form shown in a PD with the words 'Royal Arms', the form must include a replica of the Royal Arms at the head of the first page.

PD 4 para.1.1

PD [4] lists the forms to be used in civil proceedings on or after April 26,1999, when the CPR came into force.

PD 4 para.1.2

The forms may be modified as the circumstances require, provided that all essential information, especially information or guidance which the form gives to the recipient, is included.

PD 4 para.1.3

[PD 4] contains three tables—
Table 1 lists forms required by CPR Parts 1–81.
Table 2 lists High Court forms in use before April 26, 1999 which have remained in use on or after that date (see paragraph 4 below).
Table 3 lists county court forms in use before April 26, 1999 that will remain in use on or after that date (see para.5 below).

PD 4 para.1.4

Former prescribed forms are shown as 'No 00'. The former practice forms where they are appropriate for use in either the Chancery or Queen's Bench Division (or where no specific form is available for use in the county court, in that court also) are prefixed 'PF' followed by the number. Where the form is used mainly in the Chancery or Queen's Bench Division, the suffix CH or QB follows the form number.

Other forms

PD 4 para.2.1

Other forms may be authorised by PDs. For example the forms relating to Pt 61 Admiralty claims are authorised by, and annexed to, PD 61.

Table 1

PD 4 para.3.1

This table lists the forms that are referred to and required by rules or PDs supplementing particular Parts of the CPR. A PD and its paragraphs are abbreviated by reference to the Part of the CPR which it supplements and the relevant paragraph of the PD, for example PD 34 para.1.2. For ease of reference, forms required for claims in the Commercial Court, Technology and Construction Court and for Admiralty claims and Arbitration claims, are separately listed.

PD 4 para.3.2

These are Court Funds Office forms referred to in Pt 37. These are not listed below. They are Form 100 (Request for Lodgment (General)), Form 201 (Request for payment out of money in court to satisfy a Part 36 offer) and Form 202 (Notice of Defendant's consent to payment out of money in court to satisfy a Part 36 offer). It should also be noted that use of Form N242A—Offer to settle—Pt 36, referred to in para.1.1 of PD 36A and in the Table below, is not mandatory.

Table 2

Practice Forms

PD 4 para.4.1

This Table lists the Practice Forms that may be used under this PD. It contains forms that were previously—
Prescribed Forms contained in Appendix A to the rules of the Supreme Court 1965.
Queen's Bench Masters' Practice Forms.
Chancery Masters' Practice Forms.

Table 3

PD 4 para.5.1

This Table lists county court forms in use before April 26, 1999 that have continued to be used on or after that date.

PD 4 para.5.2

Where a rule permits, a party intending to use a witness statement as an alternative to an affidavit should amend any form in this Table to be used in connection with that rule so that 'witness statement' replaces 'affidavit' wherever it appears in the form.

PD 4 para.4.2

Where a rule permits, a party intending to use a witness statement as an alternative to an affidavit should amend any form in this Table to be used in connection with that rule so that 'witness statement' replaces 'affidavit' wherever it appears in the form.

PD 4 para 4.3

The forms in this list are reproduced in an Appendix to the Chancery and Queen's Bench Guides, in practitioners' text books and on Her Majesty's Courts and Tribunals Service website.

FORTHWITH

Ps *Refson & Co Ltd v Saggers* [1984] 3 All E.R. 111.
As soon as practicable

FREEZING ORDER

See **Freezing injunction**.

FREEZING INJUNCTION

Cross examination of deponents about assets

High Court

PD 2B para.7

Where the court has made a freezing order under r.25.1(f) and has ordered a person to make a witness statement or affidavit about his assets and to be cross-examined on its contents, unless the Judge directs otherwise, the cross-examination will take place before a Master or a District Judge, or if the Master or District Judge directs, before an examiner of the Court.

County court

PD 2B para.12

To the extent that a county court has power to make a freezing order, paragraph 7 [of PD 2B] applies as appropriate.

Orders to restrain disposal of assets worldwide and within England and Wales

PD 25A para.6.1

An example of a Freezing Injunction is annexed to [PD 25A]. This give details of costs, communication with the Court, exceptions to the order, variation and discharge of the order and the undertakings given to the Court by the applicant.

PD 25A para.6.2

This example may be modified as appropriate in any particular case. In particular, the court may, if it considers it appropriate, require the applicant's solicitors, as well as the applicant, to give undertakings.

See also **Interim injunction** and **Interim remedies**.

FUNDING ARRANGEMENT

Pt 43 r.43.2(1)

   (k) An arrangement where a person has—
      (i) entered into a conditional fee agreement or a collective conditional fee agreement which provides for a success fee within the meaning of s.58(2) of the Courts and Legal Services Act 1990;

    (ii) taken out an insurance policy to which s.29 of the Access to Justice Act 1999 (recovery of insurance premiums by way of costs) applies; or

   (iii) made an agreement with a membership organisation to meet that person's legal costs.

Costs orders relating to funding arrangements

Pt 44 r.44.3A

(1) The court will not assess any **additional liability** until the conclusion of the proceedings, or the part of the proceedings, to which the funding arrangement relates.

(2) At the conclusion of the proceedings, or the part of the proceedings, to which the funding arrangement relates the court may—

   (a) make a summary assessment of all the costs, including any additional liability;

   (b) make an order for detailed assessment of the additional liability but make a summary assessment of the other costs; or

   (c) make an order for detailed assessment of all the costs.

(Part 47 sets out the procedure for the detailed assessment of costs).

Costs PD para.9.1

Under an order for payment of 'costs' the costs payable will include an additional liability incurred under a funding arrangement.

Costs PD para.9.2

(1) If before the conclusion of the proceedings the court carries out a summary assessment of the base costs it may identify separately the amount allowed in respect of: solicitors' charges; counsels' fees; other disbursements; and any value added tax (VAT). (Sections 13 and 14 of this PD deal with summary assessment).

(2) If an order for the base costs of a previous application or hearing did not identify separately the amounts allowed for solicitor's charges, counsel's fees and other disbursements, a court which later makes an assessment of an additional liability may apportion the base costs previously ordered.

Limits on recovery under funding arrangements

Pt 44 r.44.3B

(1) Unless the court orders otherwise, a party may not recover as an additional liability—

   (a) any proportion of the percentage increase relating to the cost to the legal representative of the postponement of the payment of his fees and expenses;

   (b) any provision made by a membership organisation which exceeds the likely cost to that party of the premium of an insurance policy against the risk of incurring a liability to pay the costs of other parties to the proceedings;

   (c) any additional liability for any period during which that party failed to provide information about a funding arrangement in accordance with a rule, PD or court order;

   (d) any percentage increase where that party has failed to comply with—

     (i) a requirement in the Costs PD; or

     (ii) a court order,

to disclose in any assessment proceedings the reasons for setting the percentage increase at the level stated in the conditional fee agreement;

(e) any insurance premium where that party has failed to provide information about the insurance policy in question by the time required by a rule, PD or court order.

(Paragraph 9.3 of the PD (Pre-Action Conduct) provides that a party must inform any other party as soon as possible about a funding arrangement entered into before the start of proceedings.)

(2) This rule does not apply in an assessment under r.48.9 (assessment of a solicitor's bill to his client).

(Rule 3.9 sets out the circumstances the court will consider on an application for relief from a sanction for failure to comply with any rule, PD or court order).

Costs PD para.10.1

In a case to which r.44.3B(1)(c) or (d) applies the party in default may apply for relief from the sanction. He should do so as quickly as possible after he becomes aware of the default. An application, supported by evidence, should be made under Pt 23 to a costs judge or district judge of the court which is dealing with the case. (Attention is drawn to rr.3.8 and 3.9 which deal with sanctions and relief from sanctions).

Costs PD para.10.2

Where the amount of any percentage increase recoverable by counsel may be affected by the outcome of the application, the solicitor issuing the application must serve on counsel a copy of the application notice and notice of the hearing as soon as practicable and in any event at least two days before the hearing. Counsel may make written submissions or may attend and make oral submissions at the hearing. (Paragraph 1.4 contains definitions of the terms 'counsel' and 'solicitor').

Providing information about funding arrangements

Pt 44 r.44.15

(1) A party who seeks to recover an additional liability must provide information about the funding arrangement to the court and to other parties as required by a rule, PD or court order.

(2) Where the funding arrangement has changed, and the information a party has previously provided in accordance with para.(1) is no longer accurate, that party must file notice of the change and serve it on all other parties within seven days.

(3) Where para.(2) applies, and a party has already filed—

(a) an allocation questionnaire; or

(b) a pre-trial check list (listing questionnaire)

he must file and serve a new estimate of costs with the notice.

(Rule 44.3B sets out situations where a party will not recover a sum representing any additional liability).

Costs PD para.19.1

(1) A party who wishes to claim an additional liability in respect of a funding arrangement must give any other party information about that claim if he is to recover the additional liability. There is no requirement to specify the amount of the additional liability separately nor to state how it is calculated until it falls to be assessed. That principle is reflected in rr.44.3A and 44.15, in the following paragraphs and in ss.6, 13, 14 and 31 of

this PD. Section 6 deals with estimates of costs, ss.13 and 14 deal with summary assessment and s.31 deals with detailed assessment.

(2) In the following paragraphs a party who has entered into a funding arrangement is treated as a person who intends to recover a sum representing an additional liability by way of costs.

(3) Attention is drawn to para.57.9 of this PD which sets out time limits for the provision of information where a funding arrangement is entered into between March 31 and July 2, 2000 and proceedings relevant to that arrangement are commenced before July 3, 2000.

Method of giving information

Costs PD para.19.2

(1) In this paragraph, 'claim form' includes petition and application notice, and the notice of funding to be filed or served is a notice containing the information set out in Form N251.

(2) (a) A claimant who has entered into a funding arrangement before starting the proceedings to which it relates must provide information to the court by filing the notice when he issues the claim form.

    (b) He must provide information to every other party by serving the notice. If he serves the claim form himself he must serve the notice with the claim form. If the court is to serve the claim form, the court will also serve the notice if the claimant provides it with sufficient copies for service.

(3) A defendant who has entered into a funding arrangement before filing any document

    (a) must provide information to the court by filing notice with his first document. A 'first document' may be an acknowledgement of service, a defence, or any other document, such as an application to set aside a default judgment.

    (b) must provide information to every party by serving notice. If he serves his first document himself he must serve the notice with that document. If the court is to serve his first document the court will also serve the notice if the defendant provides it with sufficient copies for service.

(4) In all other circumstances a party must file and serve notice within seven days of entering into the funding arrangement concerned.

(PD (Pre-Action Conduct) provides that a party must inform any other party as soon as possible about a funding arrangement entered into prior to the start of proceedings).

Notice of change of information

Costs PD para.19.3

(1) Rule 44.15 imposes a duty on a party to give notice of change if the information he has previously provided is no longer accurate. To comply he must file and serve notice containing the information set out in Form N251. Rule 44.15(3) may impose other duties in relation to new estimates of costs.

(2) Further notification need not be provided where a party has already given notice:

    (a) that he has entered into a conditional fee agreement with a legal representative and during the currency of that agreement either of them enters into another such agreement with an additional legal representative; or

    (b) of some insurance cover, unless that cover is cancelled or unless new cover is taken out with a different insurer.

(3) Part 6 applies to the service of notices.

(4) The notice must be signed by the party or by his legal representative.

Information which must be provided

Costs PD para.19.4

(1) Unless the court otherwise Orders, a party who is required to supply information about a funding arrangement must state whether he has—

entered into a conditional fee agreement which provides for a success fee within the meaning of s.58(2) of the Courts and Legal Services Act 1990;

taken out an insurance policy to which s.29 of the Access to Justice Act 1999 applies;

made an arrangement with a body which is prescribed for the purpose of s.30 of that Act;

or more than one of these.

(2) Where the funding arrangement is a conditional fee agreement, the party must state the date of the agreement and identify the claim or claims to which it relates (including Pt 20 claims if any).

(3) Where the funding arrangement is an insurance policy, the party must—

(a) state the name and address of the insurer, the policy number and the date of the policy and identify the claim or claims to which it relates (including Pt 20 claims if any);

(b) state the level of cover provided by the insurance; and

(c) state whether the insurance premiums are staged and, if so, the points at which an increased premium is payable.

(4) Where the funding arrangement is by way of an arrangement with a relevant body the party must state the name of the body and set out the date and terms of the undertaking it has given and must identify the claim or claims to which it relates (including Pt 20 claims if any).

(5) Where a party has entered into more than one funding arrangement in respect of a claim, for example a conditional fee agreement and an insurance policy, a single notice containing the information set out in Form N251 may contain the required information about both or all of them (see *http://www.justice.gov.uk/courts/procedure-rules/civil/ forms*—Accessed November 21, 2012).

Costs PD para.19.5

Where the court makes a **Group Litigation order**, the court may give directions as to the extent to which individual parties should provide information in accordance with r.44.15. (Part 19 deals with Group Litigation Orders).

Transitional provision

Costs PD para.19.6

The amendments to the parenthesis below para.19.2 and to para.19.4(3) do not apply where the funding arrangement was entered into before October 1, 2009 and the parenthesis below para.19.2 and para.19.4(3) in force immediately before that date will continue to apply to that funding arrangement as if those amendments had not been made.

FUNDS IN COURT

Applications relating to funds in court

PD 37 para.2.1

This paragraph applies to an application relating to money or securities which have been paid into court other than an application for the payment out of the money or securities (for example, an application for money to be invested, or for payment of interest to any person).

PD 37 para.2.2

An application—
  (1) must be made in accordance with Pt 23; and
  (2) may be made without notice, but the court may direct notice to be served on any person.
(Where money paid into court is accepted by or on behalf of a **child** or **protected party**, r.21.11(1)(b) provides that the money shall be dealt with in accordance with directions given by the court under that rule and not otherwise. Paragraphs 8 to 13 of PD 21 make further provision about how the money may be dealt with).

See also **Charging order**.

FURTHER AND BETTER PARTICULARS

See **Further information**.

FURTHER DAMAGES

Application for further damages

Pt 41 r.41.3

  (1) The claimant may not make an application for further damages after the end of the period specified under r.41.2(2), or such period as extended by the court.
  (2) Only one application for further damages may be made in respect of each disease or type of deterioration specified in the award of provisional damages.
  (3) The claimant must give at least 28 days' written notice to the defendant of his intention to apply for further damages.
  (4) If the claimant knows—
    (a) that the defendant is insured in respect of the claim; and
    (b) the identity of the defendant's insurers,
    he must also give at least 28 days' written notice to the insurers.
  (5) Within 21 days after the end of the 28 day notice period referred to in paras (3) and (4), the claimant must apply for directions.

FURTHER INFORMATION

Pt 18 r.18.1

  (1) The court may at any time order a party to—
    (a) clarify any matter which is in dispute in the proceedings; or

    (b) give additional information in relation to any such matter,

    whether or not the matter is contained or referred to in a statement of case.

  (2) Paragraph (1) is subject to any rule of law to the contrary.

  (3) Where the court makes an order under para.(1), the party against whom it is made must—

    (a) file his response; and

    (b) serve it on the other parties,

    within the time specified by the court.

(Part 22 requires a response to be verified by a **statement of truth**).

(Part 53 (**defamation**) restricts requirements for providing further information about sources of information in defamation claims).

Preliminary request for further information or clarification

PD 18 para.1.1

Before making an application to the court for an order under Pt 18, the party seeking clarification or information (the first party) should first serve on the party from whom it is sought (the second party) a written request for that clarification or information (a Request) stating a date by which the response to the Request should be served. The date must allow the second party a reasonable time to respond.

PD 18 para.1.2

A Request should be concise and strictly confined to matters which are reasonably necessary and proportionate to enable the first party to prepare his own case or to understand the case he has to meet.

PD 18 para.1.3

Requests must be made as far as possible in a single comprehensive document and not piece-meal.

PD 18 para.1.4

A request may be made by letter if the text of the Request is brief and the reply is likely to be brief; otherwise the Request should be made in a separate document.

PD 18 para.1.5

If a Request is made in a letter, the letter should, in order to distinguish it from any other that might routinely be written in the course of a case,

  (1) state that it contains a request made under Pt 18, and

  (2) deal with no matters other than the Request.

PD 18 para.1.6

  (1) A Request (whether made by letter or in a separate document) must—

    (a) be headed with the name of the court and the title and number of the claim,

    (b) in its heading state that it is a request made under Pt 18, identify the first party and the second party and state the date on which it is made,

    (c) set out in a separate numbered paragraph each request for information or clarification,

    (d) where a request relates to a document, identify that document and (if relevant) the paragraph or words to which it relates,

    (e) state the date by which the first party expects a response to the request.

(2) (a) A request which is not in the form of a letter may, if convenient, be prepared in such a way that the response may be given on the same document.

    (b) To do this the numbered paragraphs of the Request should appear on the left hand half of each sheet so that the paragraphs of the response may then appear on the right.

    (c) Where a Request is prepared in this form an extra copy should be served for the use of the second party.

PD 18 para.1.7

Subject to the provisions of r.6.23(5) and (6) and paras 4.1 to 4.3 of PD 6A, a request should be served by e-mail if reasonably practicable.

Responding to a request

PD 18 para.2.1

A response to a Request must be in writing, dated and signed by the second party or his legal representative.

PD 18 para.2.2

(1) Where the request is made in a letter the second party may give his response in a letter or in a formal reply.

(2) Such a letter should identify itself as a response to the request and deal with no other matters than the response.

PD 18 para.2.3

(1) Unless the request is in the format described in para.1.6(2) and the second party uses the document supplied for the purpose, a response must:

    (a) be headed with the name of the court and the title and number of the claim,

    (b) in its heading identify itself as a response to that request,

    (c) repeat the text of each separate paragraph of the Request and set out under each paragraph the response to it,

    (d) refer to and have attached to it a copy of any document not already in the possession of the first party which forms part of the response.

(2) A second or supplementary response to a request must identify itself as such in its heading.

PD 18 para.2.4

The second party must when he serves his response on the first party serve on every other party and file with the court a copy of the Request and of his response.

Statements of truth

PD 18 para.3

Attention is drawn to Pt 22 and to the definition of a statement of case in Pt 2 of the rules; a response should be verified by a statement of truth.

General matters

PD 18 para.4.1

(1) If the second party objects to complying with the Request or part of it or is unable to do so at all or within the time stated in the Request he must inform the first party promptly and in any event within that time.
(2) He may do so in a letter or in a separate document (a formal response), but in either case he must give reasons and, where relevant, give a date by which he expects to be able to comply.

PD 18 para.4.2

(1) There is no need for a second party to apply to the court if he objects to a request or is unable to comply with it at all or within the stated time. He need only comply with para.4.1(1) above.
(2) Where a second party considers that a request can only be complied with at disproportionate expense and objects to comply for that reason he should say so in his reply and explain briefly why he has taken that view.

Applications for orders

PD 18 para.5.2

An **application notice** for an order under Pt 18 should set out or have attached to it the text of the order sought and in particular should specify the matter or matters in respect of which the clarification or information is sought.

PD 18 para.5.3

(1) If a request under para.1 for the information or clarification has not been made, the application notice should, in addition, explain why not.
(2) If a request for clarification or information has been made, the application notice or the evidence in support should describe the response, if any.

PD 18 para.5.4

Both the first party and the second party should consider whether evidence in support of or in opposition to the application is required.

PD 18 para.5.5

(1) Where the second party has made no response to a request served on him, the first party need not serve the application notice on the second party, and the court may deal with the application without a hearing.

(2) Sub-paragraph (1) above only applies if at least 14 days have passed since the request was served and the time stated in it for a response has expired.

PD 18 para.5.6

Unless para.5.5 applies the application notice must be served on the second party and on all other parties to the claim.

PD 18 para.5.7

An order made under Pt 18 must be served on all parties to the claim.

Restriction on the use of further information

P18 r.18.2

The court may direct that information provided by a party to another party (whether given voluntarily or following an order made under r.18.1) must not be used for any purpose except for that of the proceedings in which it is given.

Costs

PD 18 para.5.8

(1) Attention is drawn to the Costs PD and in particular the court's power to make **a summary assessment** of costs.
(2) Attention is also drawn to r.44.13(1) which provides that the general rule is that if an order does not mention costs no party is entitled to costs relating to that order.

Small claims

Pt 27 para.27.2

(1) The following [Part] of these rules do not apply to small claims—
  (f) Subject to paragraph (3), Part 18 (further information);
(3) The court of its own initiative may order a party to provide further information if it considers it appropriate to do so.

PD 27 para.2.3

Before allocating the claim to the small claims track and giving directions for a hearing the court may require a party to give further information about that party's case.

See **Traffic enforcement**.

G

GARNISHEE ORDER

Replaced by **Third Party Debt Order**.

GENERAL CIVIL RESTRAINT ORDERS

PD 3C para.4.1

A general civil restraint order may be made by—
    (1) a judge of the Court of Appeal;
    (2) a judge of the High Court; or
    (3) a designated civil judge or his appointed deputy in a county court,
where the party against whom the order is made persists in issuing claims or making applications which are totally without merit, in circumstances where an extended civil restraint order would not be sufficient or appropriate.

PD 3C para.4.2

Unless the court otherwise Orders, where the court makes a general civil restraint order, the party against whom the order is made—
    (1) will be restrained from issuing any claim or making any application in—
        (a) any court if the order has been made by a judge of the Court of Appeal;
        (b) the High Court or any county court if the order has been made by a judge of the High Court; or
        (c) any county court identified in the order if the order has been made by a designated civil judge or his appointed deputy,
      without first obtaining the permission of a judge identified in the order;
    (2) may apply for amendment or discharge of the order provided he has first obtained the permission of a judge identified in the order; and
    (3) may apply for permission to appeal the order and if permission is granted, may appeal the order.

PD 3C para.4.3

Where a party who is subject to a general civil restraint order—
    (1) issues a claim or makes an application in a court identified in the order without first obtaining the permission of a judge identified in the order, the claim or application will automatically be struck out or dismissed—
        (a) without the judge having to make any further order; and
        (b) without the need for the other party to respond to it;
    (2) repeatedly makes applications for permission pursuant to that order which are totally without merit, the court may direct that if the party makes any further application for permission which is totally without merit, the decision to dismiss that application will be final and there will be no right of appeal, unless the judge who refused permission grants permission to appeal.

PD 3C para.4.4

A party who is subject to a general civil restraint order may not make an application for permission under paras 4.2(1) or 4.2(2) without first serving notice of the application on the other party in accordance with para.4.5.

PD 3C para.4.5

A notice under para.4.4 must—
    (1) set out the nature and grounds of the application; and
    (2) provide the other party with at least seven days within which to respond.

PD 3C para.4.6

An application for permission under paras 4.2(1) or 4.2(2)—
    (1) must be made in writing;
    (2) must include the other party's written response, if any, to the notice served under para.4.4; and
    (3) will be determined without a hearing.

PD 3C para.4.7

An order under para.4.3(2) may only be made by—
    (1) a Court of Appeal judge;
    (2) a High Court judge; or
    (3) a designated civil judge or his appointed deputy.

PD 3C para.4.8

Where a party makes an application for permission under paras 4.2(1) or 4.2(2) and permission is refused, any application for permission to appeal—
    (1) must be made in writing; and
    (2) will be determined without a hearing.

PD 3C para.4.9

A general civil restraint order—
    (1) will be made for a specified period not exceeding two years;
    (2) must identify the courts in which the party against whom the order is made is restrained from issuing claims or making applications; and
    (3) must identify the judge or judges to whom an application for permission under paras 4.2(1), 4.2(2) or 4.8 should be made.

PD 3C para.4.10

The court may extend the duration of a general civil restraint order, if it considers it appropriate to do so, but it must not be extended for a period greater than two years on any given occasion.

PD 3C para.4.11

If he considers that it would be appropriate to make a general civil restraint order—
    (1) a master or a district judge in a district registry of the High Court must transfer the proceedings to a High Court judge; and

    (2) a circuit judge or a district judge in a county court must transfer the proceedings to the designated civil judge.

See also **Civil restraint orders.**

GLO

PD 19B, para.1

[PD 19B] deals with group litigation where the multiple parties are claimants. Section III of Pt 19 [rr.19.10 to 19.15] also applies where the multiple parties are defendants. The court will give such directions in such a case as are appropriate.

Group litigation order

Pt 19 r.19.11

    (1) The court may make a GLO where there are or are likely to be a number of claims giving rise to the **GLO issues.**
    (2) A GLO must—
        (a) contain directions about the establishment of a register (the 'group register') on which the claims managed under the GLO will be entered;
        (b) specify the GLO issues which will identify the claims to be managed as a group under the GLO; and
        (c) specify the court (the 'management court') which will manage the claims on the group register.
    (3) A GLO may—
        (a) in relation to claims which raise one or more of the GLO issues—
            (i) direct their transfer to the management court;
            (ii) order their stay until further order; and
            (iii) direct their entry on the group register;
        (b) direct that from a specified date claims which raise one or more of the GLO issues should be started in the management court and entered on the group register; and
        (c) give directions for publicising the GLO.

Effect of the GLO

Pt 19 r.19.12

    (1) Where a judgment or order is given or made in a claim on the group register in relation to one or more GLO issues—
        (a) that judgment or order is binding on the parties to all other claims that are on the group register at the time the judgment is given or the order is made unless the court orders otherwise; and
        (b) the court may give directions as to the extent to which that judgment or order is binding on the parties to any claim which is subsequently entered on the group register.
    (2) Unless para.(3) applies, any party who is adversely affected by a judgment or order which is binding on him may seek permission to appeal the order.
    (3) A party to a claim which was entered on the group register after a judgment or order which is binding on him was given or made may not—

(a) apply for the judgment or order to be set aside, varied or stayed; or
(b) appeal the judgment or order,
but may apply to the court for an order that the judgment or order is not binding on him.
(4) Unless the court orders otherwise, disclosure of any document relating to the GLO issues by a party to a claim on the group register is disclosure of that document to all parties to claims—
(a) on the group register; and
(b) which are subsequently entered on the group register.

Case management

Pt 19 r.19.13

Directions given by the management court may include directions—
(a) varying the GLO issues;
(b) providing for one or more claims on the group register to proceed as test claims;
(c) appointing the solicitor of one or more parties to be the lead solicitor for the claimants or defendants;
(d) specifying the details to be included in a statement of case in order to show that the criteria for entry of the claim on the group register have been met;
(e) specifying a date after which no claim may be added to the group register unless the court gives permission; and
(f) for the entry of any particular claim which meets one or more of the GLO issues on the group register.
(Part 3 contains general provisions about the case management powers of the court).

Test claims

Pt 19 r.19.15

(1) Where a direction has been given for a claim on the group register to proceed as a test claim and that claim is settled, the management court may order that another claim on the group register be substituted as the test claim.
(2) Where an order is made under para.(1), any order made in the test claim before the date of substitution is binding on the substituted claim unless the court orders otherwise.

Preliminary steps

PD 19B para.2.1

Before applying for a Group Litigation order ('GLO') the solicitor acting for the proposed applicant should consult the Law Society's Multi Party Action Information Service in order to obtain information about other cases giving rise to the proposed GLO issues.

PD 19B para.2.2

It will often be convenient for the claimants' solicitors to form a Solicitors' Group and to choose one of their number to take the lead in applying for the GLO and in litigating the GLO issues.

The lead solicitor's role and relationship with the other members of the Solicitors' Group should be carefully defined in writing and will be subject to any directions given by the court under CPR r.19.13(c).

PD 19B para.2.3

In considering whether to apply for a GLO, the applicant should consider whether any other order would be more appropriate. In particular he should consider whether, in the circumstances of the case, it would be more appropriate for—
(1) the claims to be consolidated; or
(2) the rules in s.II of Pt 19 (representative parties) to be used.

Application for a GLO

PD 19B para.3.1

An application for a GLO must be made in accordance with CPR Pt 23, may be made at any time before or after any relevant claims have been issued and may be made either by a claimant or by a defendant.

PD 19B para.3.2

The following information should be included in the application notice or in written evidence filed in support of the application:
(1) a summary of the nature of the litigation;
(2) the number and nature of claims already issued;
(3) the number of parties likely to be involved;
(4) the common issues of fact or law (the 'GLO issues') that are likely to arise in the litigation; and
(5) whether there are any matters that distinguish smaller groups of claims within the wider group.

PD 19B para.3.3

A GLO may not be made—
(1) in the Queen's Bench Division, without the consent of the Lord Chief Justice,
(2) in the Chancery Division, without the consent of the Vice-Chancellor, or
(3) in a county court, without the consent of the Head of Civil Justice.

PD 19B para.3.4

The court to which the application for a GLO is made will, if minded to make the GLO, send to the Lord Chief Justice, the Vice-Chancellor, or the Head of Civil Justice, as appropriate—
(1) a copy of the application notice,
(2) a copy of any relevant written evidence, and
(3) a written statement as to why a GLO is considered to be desirable.
These steps may be taken either before or after a hearing of the application.

High Court

London

PD 19B para.3.5

The application for the GLO should be made to the Senior Master in the Queen's Bench Division or the Chief Chancery Master in the Chancery Division. For claims that are proceeding or are likely to proceed in a specialist list, the application should be made to the senior judge of that list.

Outside London

PD 19B para.3.6

Outside London, the application should be made to a Presiding Judge or a Chancery Supervising Judge of the Circuit in which the District Registry which has issued the application notice is situated.

County courts

PD 19B para.3.7

The application should be made to the Designated Civil Judge for the area in which the county court which has issued the application notice is situated.

PD 19B para.3.8

The applicant for a GLO should request the relevant court to refer the application notice to the judge by whom the application will be heard as soon as possible after the application notice has been issued. This is to enable the judge to consider whether to follow the practice set out in para.3.4 above prior to the hearing of the application.

PD 19B para.3.9

The directions under paras 3.5, 3.6 and 3.7 above do not prevent the judges referred to from making arrangements for other judges to hear applications for GLOs when they themselves are unavailable.

GLO made by court of its own initiative

PD 19B para.4

Subject to obtaining the appropriate consent referred to in para.3.3 and the procedure set out in para.3.4, the court may make a GLO of its own initiative.
(CPR r.3.3 deals with the procedure that applies when a court proposes to make an order of its own initiative).

Contents of GLO

PD 19B para.5

CPR r.19.11(2) and (3) set out rules relating to the contents of GLOs.

Allocation to track

PD 19B para.7

Once a GLO has been made and unless the management court directs otherwise:
  (1) every claim in a case entered on the group register will be automatically allocated, or re-allocated (as the case may be), to the multi-track;
  (2) any case management directions that have already been given in any such case otherwise than by the management court will be set aside; and
  (3) any hearing date already fixed otherwise than for the purposes of the group litigation will be vacated.

Managing judge

PD 19B para.8

A judge ('the managing judge') will be appointed for the purpose of the GLO as soon as possible. He will assume overall responsibility fo the management of the claims and will generally hear the GLO issues. A Master or a District Judge may be appointed to deal with procedural matters, which he will do in accordance with any directions given by the managing judge. A costs judge may be appointed and may be invited to attend case management hearings.

Claims to be started in management court

PD 19B para.9.1

The management court may order that as from a specified date all claims that raise one or more of the GLO issues shall be started in the management court.

PD 19B para.9.2

Failure to comply with an order made under para.9.1 will not invalidate the commencement of the claim but the claim should be transferred to the management court and details entered on the Group Register as soon as possible. Any party to the claim may apply to the management court for an order under CPR r.19.14 removing the case from the Register or, as the case may be, for an order that details of the case be not entered on the Register.

Transfer

PD 19B para.10

Where the management court is a county court and a claim raising one or more of the GLO issues is proceeding in the High Court, an order transferring the case to the management court and directing the details of the case to be entered on the Group Register can only be made in the High Court.

Publicising the GLO

PD 19B para.11

After a GLO has been made, a copy of the GLO should be supplied—
  (1) to the Law Society, 113 Chancery Lane, London WC2A 1PL; and
  (2) to the Senior Master, Queen's Bench Division, Royal Courts of Justice, Strand, London WC2A 2LL.

Case management

PD 19B para.12.1

The management court may give case management directions at the time the GLO is made or subsequently. Directions given at a case management hearing will generally be binding on all claims that are subsequently entered on the Group Register (see CPR r.19.12(1)).

PD 19B para.12.2

Any application to vary the terms of the GLO must be made to the management court.

PD 19B para.12.3

The management court may direct that one or more of the claims are to proceed as test claims.

PD 19B para.12.4

The management court may give directions about how the costs of resolving common issues or the costs of claims proceeding as test claims are to be borne or shared as between the claimants on the Group Register.

Cut-off dates

PD 19B para.13

The management court may specify a date after which no claim may be added to the group register unless the court gives permission. An early cut-off date may be appropriate in the case of 'instant disasters' (such as transport accidents). In the case of consumer claims, and particularly pharmaceutical claims, it may be necessary to delay the ordering of a cut-off date.

Statements of case

PD 19B para.14.1

The management court may direct that the GLO claimants serve 'Group Particulars of Claim' which set out the various claims of all the claimants on the group register at the time the particulars are filed. Such particulars of claim will usually contain—

(1) general allegations relating to all claims; and

(2) a schedule containing entries relating to each individual claim specifying which of the general allegations are relied on and any specific facts relevant to the claimant.

PD 19B para.14.2

The directions given under para.14.1 should include directions as to whether the group particulars should be verified by a statement or statements of truth and, if so, by whom.

PD 19B para.14.3

The specific facts relating to each claimant on the group register may be obtained by the use of a questionnaire. Where this is proposed, the management court should be asked to approve the questionnaire. The management court may direct that the questionnaires completed by individual claimants take the place of the schedule referred to in para.14.1(2).

PD 19B para.14.4

The management court may also give directions about the form that particulars of claim relating to claims which are to be entered on the group register should take.

Trial

PD 19B para.15.1

The management court may give directions—

(1) for the trial of common issues; and

(2) for the trial of individual issues.

PD 19B para.15.2

Common issues and test claims will normally be tried at the management court. Individual issues may be directed to be tried at other courts whose locality is convenient for the parties.

Costs

PD 19B para.16.2

Where the court has made an order about costs in relation to any application or hearing which involved both—

(1) one or more of the GLO issues; and

(2) an issue or issues relevant only to individual claims;

and the court has not directed the proportion of the costs that is to relate to common costs and the proportion that is to relate to individual costs in accordance with r.48.6A(5), the costs judge will make a decision as to the relevant proportions at or before the commencement of the detailed assessment of costs.

Pt 46 r.46.6

(1) This rule applied where the court has made a [GLO].

(2) In this rule—

    (a) 'individual costs' means costs incurred in relation to an individual claim on the group register;

(3) Unless the court orders otherwise, any order for **common costs** against group litigants imposes on each group litigant several liability for an equal proportion of those common costs.

(4) The general rule is that where a group litigant is the paying party, he will, in addition to any costs he is liable to pay to the receiving party, be liable for—
    (a) the individual costs of his claim; and
    (b) an equal proportion, together with all the other group litigants, of the common costs.

(5) Where the court makes an order about costs in relation to any application or hearing which involved—
    (a) one or more GLO issues; and
    (b) issues relevant only to individual claims,
the court will direct the proportion of the costs that is to relate to common costs and the proportion that is to relate to individual costs.

(6) Where common costs have been incurred before a claim is entered on the group register, the court may order the group litigant to be liable for a proportion of those costs.

(7) Where a claim is removed from the group register, the court may make an order for costs in that claim which includes a proportion of the common costs incurred up to the date on which the claim is removed from the group register.

PD 19B para.16.2

Where the court has made an order about costs in relation to any application or hearing which involved both—
    (1) one or more of the GLO issues; and
    (2) an issue or issues relevant only to individual claims;
and the court has not directed the proportion of the costs that is to relate to common costs and the proportion that is to relate to individual costs in accordance with r.48.6A(5), the costs judge will make a decision as to the relevant proportions at or before the commencement of the detailed assessment of costs.

Titles of proceedings where there are additional claims

PD 20 para.7.6

In group litigation, the court should give directions about the designation of parties.

GLO ISSUES

Pt 19 r.19.10

Common or related issues of fact or law.

GLOSSARY

Pt 2 r.2.2

(1) The glossary at the end of [CPR] is a guide to the meaning of certain legal expressions used in the rules, but is not to be taken as giving those expressions any meaning in the rules which they do not have in the law generally.

GOODS

See **Delivery of goods**, **Detention of goods** and **Wrongful intereference with goods**.

GOVERNMENT LEGAL SERVICE

PD 66 Annex 1

The Government Legal Service (GLS) has the responsibility for advising the Government about its legal affairs and has the conduct of civil litigation on its behalf. The Treasury Solicitor conducts this litigation for the majority of Government Departments but lawyers in HM Revenue and Customs, the Department for the Environment, Food and Rural Affairs and the Department for Work and Pensions (which also acts for the Department of Health and the Food Standards Agency) have the conduct of litigation for their Departments. All Government litigation lawyers are based in the London with the exception of HM Revenue and Customs, whose personal injury lawyers are in Manchester. A full list of addresses for service is annexed to the PD accompanying Pt 66 of the CPR.

GROUP LITIGANT

   (c) A claimant or defendant, as the case may be, whose claim is entered on the group register.

GROUP LITIGATION ORDER

Pt 19 r.19.10

A Group Litigation Order ('GLO') means an order made under r.19.11 to provide for the case management of claims which give rise to common or related issues of fact or law (the 'GLO issues').

See **GLO**.

GROUP REGISTER

PD 19B para.6.1

Once a GLO has been made a group register will be established on which will be entered such details as the court may direct of the cases which are to be subject to the GLO.

PD 19B para.6.1A

A claim must be issued before it can be entered on a group register.

PD 19B para.6.2

An application for details of a case to be entered on a group register may be made by any party to the case.

PD 19B para.6.3

An order for details of the case to be entered on the group register will not be made unless the case gives rise to at least one of the GLO issues.

PD 19B para.6.4

The court, if it is not satisfied that a case can be conveniently case managed with the other cases on the group register, or if it is satisfied that the entry of the case on the group register would adversely affect the case management of the other cases, may refuse to allow details of the case to be entered on the group register, or order their removal from the register if already entered, although the case gives rise to one or more of the group issues.

PD 19B para.6.5

The Group Register will normally be maintained by and kept at the court but the court may direct this to be done by the solicitor for one of the parties to a case entered on the register.

PD 19B para.6.6

(1) Rules 5.4 (Register of Claims), 5.4B (Supply of documents from court records—a party) and 5.4C (supply of documents from court records—a non-party) apply where the register is maintained by the court. A party to a claim on the group register may request documents relating to any other claim on the group register in accordance with r.5.4 as if he were a party to those proceedings.
(2) Where the register is maintained by a solicitor, any person may inspect the Group Register during normal business hours and upon giving reasonable notice to the solicitor; the solicitor may charge a fee not exceeding the fee prescribed for a search at the court office.

Removal from the register

Pt 19 r.19.14

(1) A party to a claim entered on the group register may apply to the management court for the claim to be removed from the register.
(2) If the management court orders the claim to be removed from the register it may give directions about the future management of the claim.

GUARDIAN

Appointment of a guardian of a child's estate

Pt 21 r.21.13

(1) The court may appoint the Official Solicitor to be a guardian of a child's estate where—
   (a) money is paid into court on behalf of the child in accordance with directions given under r.21.11 (control of money received by a child or protected party);
   (b) the Criminal Injuries Compensation Authority notifies the court that it has made or intends to make an award to the child;

    (c) a court or tribunal outside England and Wales notifies the court that it has ordered or intends to order that money be paid to the child;

    (d) the child is absolutely entitled to the proceeds of a pension fund; or

    (e) in any other case, such an appointment seems desirable to the court.

(2) The court may not appoint the Official Solicitor under this rule unless—

    (a) the persons with parental responsibility (within the meaning of s.3 of the Children Act 1989) agree; or

    (b) the court considers that their agreement can be dispensed with.

(3) The Official Solicitor's appointment may continue only until the child reaches 18.

GUARDIAN'S ACCOUNT

Pt 21 r.12

Paragraph 8 of PD 40A deals with the approval of the accounts of a guardian of assets of a child.

PD 40A para.8

The accounts of a person appointed guardian of the property of a child must be verified and approved in such manner as the court may direct.

GUARDIAN AD LITEM

See **Litigation friend**.

H

HABEAS CORPUS

Application for writ of habeas corpus ad subjiciendum

RSC Ord.54 r.1

(1) Subject to r.11, an application for a writ of habeas corpus ad subjiciendum shall be made to a judge in court, except that—
   (a) it shall be made to a Divisional Court of the Queen's Bench Division if the court so directs;
   (b) it may be made to a judge otherwise than in court at any time when no judge is sitting in court; and
   (c) any application on behalf of a child must be made in the first instance to a judge otherwise than in court.
(2) An application for such writ may be made without notice being served on any other party and, subject to para.(3) must be supported by a witness statement or affidavit by the person restrained showing that it is made at his instance and setting out the nature of the restraint. (3) Where the person restrained is unable for any reason to make the witness statement or affidavit required by para.(2) the witness statement or affidavit may be made by some other person on his behalf and that witness statement or affidavit must state that the person restrained is unable to make the witness statement or affidavit himself and for what reason.

Power of court to whom application made without notice being served on any other party

RSC Ord.54 r.2

(1) The court or judge to whom an application under r.1 is made without notice being served on any other party may make an order forthwith for the writ to issue, or may—
   (a) where the application is made to a judge otherwise than in court, direct the issue of a claim form seeking the writ, or that an application therefor be made by claim form to a Divisional Court or to a judge in court;
   (b) where the application is made to a judge in court, adjourn the application so that notice thereof may be given, or direct that an application be made by claim form to a Divisional Court;
   (c) where the application is made to a Divisional Court, adjourn the application so that notice thereof may be given.
(2) The claim form must be served on the person against whom the issue of the writ is sought and on such other persons as the court or judge may direct, and, unless the court or judge otherwise directs, there must be at least 8 clear days between the service of the claim form and the date named therein for the hearing of the application.

Administrative Court

PD RSC 54 para.6.1

When the court directs that an application is to be made by claim form under—
    (1) rule 2(1) (powers of court to whom application made under r. 1); or
    (2) rule 4(2) (power of court where application made in criminal proceedings)
the application must be entered in the Administrative Court List in accordance with PD (Crown Office List) 1987 1 W.L.R. 232; [1987] 1 All E.R. 368.

Copies of witness statements or affidavits to be supplied

RSC Ord.54 r.3

Every party to an application under r.1 must supply to every other party on demand and on payment of the proper charges copies of the witness statements or affidavits which he proposes to use at the hearing of the application.

Power to order release of person restrained

RSC Ord.54 r.4

    (1) Without prejudice to r.2(1), the court or judge hearing an application for a writ of habeas corpus ad subjiciendum may in its or his discretion order that the person restrained be released, and such order shall be a sufficient warrant to any governor of a prison, constable or other person for the release of the person under restraint.
    (2) Where such an application in criminal proceedings is heard by a judge and the judge does not order the release of the person restrained, he shall direct that the application be made by claim form to a Divisional Court of the Queen's Bench Division.

Directions as to return to writ

RSC Ord.54 r.5

Where a writ of habeas corpus ad subjiciendum is ordered to issue, the court or judge by whom the order is made shall give directions as to the court or judge before whom, and the date on which, the writ is returnable.

Service of writ and notice

RSC Ord.54 r.6

    (1) Subject to paras (2) and (3), a writ of habeas corpus ad subjiciendum must be served personally on the person to whom it is directed.
    (2) If it is not possible to serve such writ personally, or if it is directed to a governor of a prison or other public official, it must be served by leaving it with a servant or agent of the person to whom the writ is directed at the place where the person restrained is confined or restrained.

(3) If the writ is directed to more than one person, the writ must be served in manner provided by this rule on the person first named in the writ, and copies must be served on each of the other persons in the same manner as the writ.

(4) There must be served with the writ a notice (in Form No. 90 in PD 4) stating the court or judge before whom and the date on which the person restrained is to be brought and that in default of obedience proceedings for committal of the party disobeying will be taken.

PD RSC 54 para.5.1

The party seeking the writ must serve—
(1) the claim form in accordance with r. 2.2; and
(2) the writ of habeas corpus ad subjiciendum and notice in Form 90, as modified, in accordance with rule 6.

(R.6.3 provides that the court will normally serve a document which it has issued or prepared.)

Return to the writ

RSC Ord.54 r.7

(1) The return to a writ of habeas corpus ad subjiciendum must be indorsed on or annexed to the writ and must state all the causes of the detainer of the person restrained.

(2) The return may be amended, or another return substituted therefor, by permission of the court or judge before whom the writ is returnable.

Procedure at hearing of writ

RSC Ord.54 r.8

When a return to a writ of habeas corpus ad subjiciendum is made, the return shall first be read, and motion then made for discharging or remanding the person restrained or amending or quashing the return, and where that person is brought up in accordance with the writ, his counsel shall be heard first, then the counsel for the Crown, and then one counsel for the person restrained in reply.

Form of writ

RSC Ord.54 r.10

A writ of habeas corpus must be in Form Nos 89, 91 or 92 in PD 4, whichever is appropriate.

Form to be used where court directs claim form to be used

PD RSC 45 para.3.1

Where the court directs that an application be made by claim form, under—
(1) r. 2 (on hearing application under rule 1); or

(2) r. 4(2) (application in criminal proceedings ordered to be made to Divisional Court of the Queen's Bench Division),
the claimant must use Form 87 modified in accordance with the guidance set out in PD 4 [Forms].

Form to be used for Notice of adjourned application directed by court

PD RSC 54 para.4.1

Where the court directs under r.2(1)(c) that an application made under r.1 is adjourned to allow for service of notice of the application, such notice must be given in modified Form 88.

Applications relative to the custody, etc. of child

RSC Ord.54 r.11

An application by a parent or guardian of a child for a writ of habeas corpus ad subjiciendum relative to the custody, care or control of the child must be made in the Family Division, and this order shall accordingly apply to such applications with the appropriate modifications.

Writ of habeas corpus ad testificandum or or habeas corpus ad respondendum

Bringing up prisoner to give evidence, etc.

RSC Ord.54 r.9

(1) An application for a writ of habeas corpus ad testificandum or of habeas corpus ad respondendum must be made on witness statement or affidavit to a judge.
(2) An application for an order to bring up a prisoner, otherwise than by writ of habeas corpus, to give evidence in any proceedings, civil or criminal, before any court, tribunal or justice, must be made on witness statement or affidavit to a judge.

HAGUE CONVENTION

Pt 6 r.6.31

Convention on the service abroad of judicial and extrajudicial documents in civil or commercial matters signed at the Hague on November 15, 1965.

HANSARD EXTRACTS

For reference to extracts from Hansards in support of any argument—see *Pepper v Hart* [1993] A.C. 593; [1992] 3 W.L.R.1032, and *Pickstone v Freemans Plc* [1989] A.C. 66; [1988] C.M.L.R. 221 HL.

HARASSMENT

See **Protection from Harassment Act 1997.**

HARDSHIP PAYMENT ORDER

Arrangements for debtors in hardship

Pt 72 r.72.7

(1) If—
   (a) a judgment debtor is an individual;
   (b) he is prevented from withdrawing money from his account with a bank or building society as a result of an interim Third Party Debt Order; and
   (c) he or his family is suffering hardship in meeting rdinary living expenses as a result,

   the court may, on an application by the judgment debtor, make an order permitting the bank or building society to make a payment or payments out of the account ('a hardship payment order').

(2) An application for a hardship payment order may be made—
   (a) in High Court proceedings, at the Royal Courts of Justice or to any district registry; and
   (b) in county court proceedings, to any county court.

(3) A judgment debtor may only apply to one court for a hardship payment order.

(4) An application notice seeking a hardship payment order must—
   (a) include detailed evidence explaining why the judgment debtor needs a payment of the amount requested; and
   (b) be verified by a statement of truth.

(5) Unless the court orders otherwise, the application notice——
   (a) must be served on the judgment creditor at least two days before the hearing; but
   (b) does not need to be served on the third party.

(6) A hardship payment order may—
   (a) permit the third party to make one or more payments out of the account; and
   (b) specify to whom the payments may be made.

Applications for hardship payment orders

PD 72 para.5.1

The court will treat an application for a hardship payment order as being made—
   (1) in the proceedings in which the interim Third Party Debt Order was made; and
   (2) under the same claim number,
regardless of where the judgment debtor makes the application.

PD 72 para.5.2

An application for a hardship payment order will be dealt with by the court to which it is made.

PD 72 para.5.3

If the application is made to a different court from that dealing with the application for a Third Party Debt Order—

(1) the application for a Third Party Debt Order will not be transferred; but
(2) the court dealing with that application will send copies of—
    (a) the application notice; and
    (b) the interim Third Party Debt Order
to the court hearing the application for a hardship payment order

PD 72 para.5.4

Rule 72.7(3) requires an application for a hardship payment order to be served on the judgment creditor at least two days before the court is to deal with the application, unless the court orders otherwise. In cases of exceptional urgency the judgment debtor may apply for a hardship payment order without notice to the judgment creditor and a judge will decide whether to—
(1) deal with the application without it being served on the judgment creditor; or
(2) direct it to be served.

PD 72 para.5.5

If the judge decides to deal with the application without it being served on the judgment creditor, where possible he will normally—
(1) direct that the judgment creditor be informed of the application; and
(2) give him the opportunity to make representations,
by telephone, fax or other appropriate method of communication.

PD 72 para.5.6

The evidence filed by a judgment debtor in support of an application for a hardship payment order should include documentary evidence, for example (if appropriate) bank statements, wage slips and mortgage statements, to prove his financial position and need for the payment.

See also **Third Party Debt Orders**.

HEALTH CARE PROFESSIONALS

Appeals against decisions affecting registration

PD 52D para.19.1

(1) This paragraph applies to an appeal to the High Court under—
    (a) section 22 of the Architects Act 1997;
    (b) section 31 of the Chiropractors Act 1994;
    (c) section 29 or section 44 of the Dentists Act 1984;
    (d) article 38 of the Health Professions Order 2001;
    (e) section 40 of the Medical Act 1983;
    (f) section 82(3) and 83(2) of the Medicines Act 1968;
    (g) section 12 of the Nurses, Midwives and Health Visitors Act 1997;
    (h) article 38 of the Nursing and Midwifery Order 2001;
    (i) section 23 of the Opticians Act 1989;
    (j) section 31 of the Osteopaths Act 1993;
    (k) section 10 of the Pharmacy Act 1954;
    (l) article 58 of the Pharmacy Order 2010.

(2) Every appeal to which this paragraph applies must be supported by written evidence and, if the court so orders, oral evidence and will be by way of re-hearing.

(3) The appellant must file the appellant's notice within 28 days after the decision that the appellant wishes to appeal.

(4) In the case of an appeal under an enactment specified in column 1 of the following table, the persons to be made respondents are the persons specified in relation to that enactment in column 2 of the table and the person to be served with the appellant's notice is the Registrar of the relevant Council.

1	2	3
Enactment	Respondents	Person to be served
Architects Act 1997 s.22	The Architects' Registration Council of the United Kingdom	The Registrar of the Society
Chiropractors Act 1994 s.31	The General Chiropractic Council	The Registrar of the Council
Dentists Act 1984 ss.29 and 44	The General Dental Council	The Registrar of the Society
Health Professions Order 2001 art.38	The Health Professions Council	The Registrar of the Council
Medical Act 1983 s.40	The General Medical Council	The Registrar of the Council
Medicines Act 1968 ss.82(3) and 83(2)	The Pharmaceutical Society of Great Britain	The Registrar of the Council
Nurses, Midwives and Health Visitors Act 1997 s.12; Nursing and Midwifery Order 2001 art.38	The Nursing and Midwifery Council	The Registrar of the Council
Opticians Act 1989 s.23	The General Optical Council	The Registrar of the Council
Osteopaths Act 1993 s.31	The General Osteopathic Council	The Registrar of the Council
Pharmacy Act 1954 s.10	The Royal Pharmaceutical Society of Great Britain	The Registrar of the Council
Pharmacy Order 2010 art.58	The General Pharmaceutical Council	The Registrar of the Council

HEALTH RECORDS

See **Medical records**.

HEARING

Pt 39 r.39.1

In this Part, reference to a hearing includes a reference to the trial.

PD 39A para.1.4

The decision as to whether to hold a hearing in public or in private must be made by the judge conducting the hearing having regard to any representations which may have been made to him.

PD 39A para.1.4A

The judge should also have regard to art.6(1) of the European Convention on Human Rights. This requires that, in general, court hearings are to be held in public, but the press and public may be excluded in the circumstances specified in that Article. Article 6(1) will usually be relevant, for example, where a party applies for a hearing which would normally be held in public to be held in private as well as where a hearing would normally be held in private. The judge may need to consider whether the case is within any of the exceptions permitted by art.6(1).

PD 39A para.1.14

References to hearings being in public or private or in a judge's room contained in the civil procedure rules (including the rules of the supreme court and the county court rules scheduled to Pt 50) and the PDs which supplement them do not restrict any existing rights of audience or confer any new rights of audience in respect of applications or proceedings which under the rules previously in force would have been heard in court or in chambers respectively.

PD 39A para.1.9

If the court or judge's room in which the proceedings are taking place has a sign on the door indicating that the proceedings are private, members of the public who are not parties to the proceedings will not be admitted unless the court permits.

PD 39A para.1.10

Where there is no such sign on the door of the court or judge's room, members of the public will be admitted where practicable. The judge may, if he thinks it appropriate, adjourn the proceedings to a larger room or court.

PD 39A para.1.8

Nothing in this PD prevents a judge ordering that a hearing taking place in public shall continue in private, or vice-versa.

Public hearing

Pt 39 r.39.2

(1) The general rule is that a hearing is to be in public.
(2) The requirement for a hearing to be in public does not require the court to make special arrangements for accommodating members of the public.

PD 39A para.1.11

When a hearing takes place in public, members of the public may obtain a transcript of any judgment given or a copy of any order made, subject to payment of the appropriate fee.

Private hearing

Pt 39 r.39.2

    (3) A hearing, or any part of it, may be in private if—
        (a) publicity would defeat the object of the hearing;
        (b) it involves matters relating to national security;
        (c) it involves confidential information (including information relating to personal finan-
            cial matters) and publicity would damage that confidentiality;
        (d) a private hearing is necessary to protect the interests of any **child** or **protected
            party**;
        (e) it is a hearing of an application made without notice and it would be unjust to any
            respondent for there to be a public hearing;
        (f) it involves uncontentious matters arising in the administration of trusts or in the
            administration of a deceased person's estate; or
        (g) the court considers this to be necessary, in the interests of justice.
    (4) The court may order that the identity of any party or witness must not be disclosed if it
        considers non-disclosure necessary in order to protect the interests of that party or
        witness.

PD 39A para.1.5

The hearings set out below shall in the first instance be listed by the court as hearings in private under r.39.2(3)(c), namely:
    (1) a claim by a mortgagee against one or more individuals for an order for possession of
        land,
    (2) a claim by a landlord against one or more tenants or former tenants for the repossession
        of a dwelling house based on the non-payment of rent,
    (3) an application to suspend a warrant of execution or a warrant of possession or to stay
        execution where the court is being invited to consider the ability of a party to make
        payments to another party,
    (4) a redetermination under r.14.13 or an application to vary or suspend the payment of a
        judgment debt by instalments,
    (5) an application for a charging order (including an application to enforce a charging order),
        Third Party Debt Order, attachment of earnings order, administration order, or the
        appointment of a receiver,
    (6) an order to attend court for questioning,
    (7) the determination of the liability of an LSC funded client under regs 9 and 10 of the
        Community Legal Service (Costs) Regulations 2000, or of an assisted person's liability
        for costs under reg.127 of the Civil Legal Aid (General) Regulations 1989,
    (8) an application for security for costs to be provided by a claimant who is a company or
        a limited liability partnership in the circumstances set out in r.25.13(2)(c),
    (9) proceedings brought under the Consumer Credit Act 1974, the Inheritance (Provision for
        Family and Dependants) Act 1975 or the Protection from Harassment Act 1997,
   (10) an application by a trustee or personal representative for directions as to bringing or
        defending legal proceedings.

PD 39A para.1.6

Rule 39.2(3)(d) states that a hearing may be in private where it involves the interests of a child or protected party. This includes the approval of a compromise or settlement on behalf of a child or protected party or an application for the payment of money out of court to such a person.

PD 39A para.1.7

Attention is drawn to para.5.1 of PD 27 (relating to the hearing of claims in the small claims track), which provides that the judge may decide to hold a small claim hearing in private if the parties agree or if a ground mentioned in r.39.2(3) applies. A hearing of a small claim in premises other than the court will not be a hearing in public.

PD 39A para.1.7A

Attention is drawn to para.24.5(8) of PD 52, which provides that an appeal to a county court against certain decisions under the Representation of the People Act 1983 is to be heard in private unless the court Orders otherwise. Attention is also drawn to para.24.5(9) of that PD, which provides that an appeal to the Court of Appeal against such a decision of a county court may be heard in private if the Court of Appeal so orders.

PD 39A para.1.12

When a judgment is given or an order is made in private, if any member of the public who is not a party to the proceedings seeks a transcript of the judgment or a copy of the order, he must seek the leave of the judge who gave the judgment or made the order.

PD 39A para.1.13

A judgment or order given or made in private, when drawn up, must have clearly marked in the title:

'Before [title and name of judge] sitting in Private'

PD 39A para.1.15

Where the court lists a hearing of a claim by a mortgagee for an order for possession of land under para.1.5(1) above to be in private, any fact which needs to be proved by the evidence of witnesses may be proved by evidence in writing.
(CPR r.32.2 sets out the general rule as to how evidence is to be given and facts are to be proved.)

Failure to attend the trial

Pt 39 r.39.3

(1) The court may proceed with a trial in the absence of a party but—
    (a) if no party attends the trial, it may strike out the whole of the proceedings;
    (b) if the claimant does not attend, it may strike out his claim and any defence to counterclaim; and
    (c) if a defendant does not attend, it may strike out his defence or counterclaim (or both).

(2) Where the court strikes out proceedings, or any part of them, under this rule, it may subsequently restore the proceedings, or that part.

(3) Where a party does not attend and the court gives judgment or makes an order against him, the party who failed to attend may apply for the judgment or order to be set aside.

(4) An application under para.(2) or para.(3) must be supported by evidence.

(5) Where an application is made under para.(2) or (3) by a party who failed to attend the trial, the court may grant the application only if the applicant—

(a) acted promptly when he found out that the court had exercised its power to strike out or to enter judgment or make an order against him;

(b) had a good reason for not attending the trial; and

(c) has a reasonable prospect of success at the trial.

PD 39A para.2.1

Rule 39.3 sets out the consequences of a party's failure to attend the trial.

PD 39A para.2.2

The court may proceed with a trial in the absence of a party. In the absence of:

(1) the defendant, the claimant may—

(a) prove his claim at trial and obtain judgment on his claim and for costs, and

(b) seek the striking out of any counterclaim,

(2) the claimant, the defendant may—

(a) prove any counterclaim at trial and obtain judgment on his counterclaim and for costs, and

(b) seek the striking out of the claim, or

(3) both parties, the court may strike out the whole of the proceedings.

PD 39A para.2.3

Where the court has struck out proceedings, or any part of them, on the failure of a party to attend, that party may apply in accordance with Pt 23 for the proceedings, or that part of them, to be restored and for any judgment given against that party to be set aside.

PD 39A para.2.4

The application referred to in para.2.3 above must be supported by evidence giving reasons for the failure to attend court and stating when the applicant found out about the order

Timetable for trial

Pt 39 r.39.4

When the court sets a timetable for a trial in accordance with r.28.6 (fixing or confirming the trial date and giving directions—fast track) or r.29.8 (setting a trial timetable and fixing or confirming the trial date or week—multi-track) it will do so in consultation with the parties.

Settlement or discontinuance after the trial date is fixed

PD 39A para.4.1

Where:
  (1) an offer to settle a claim is accepted,
  (2) or a settlement is reached, or
  (3) a claim is discontinued, which disposes of the whole of a claim for which a date or 'window' has been fixed for the trial, the parties must ensure that the listing officer for the trial court is notified immediately.

PD 39A para.4.2

If an order is drawn up giving effect to the settlement or discontinuance, a copy of the sealed order should be filed with the listing officer.

Representation at hearings

PD 39A para.5.1

At any hearing, a written statement containing the following information should be provided for the court:
  (1) the name and address of each advocate,
  (2) his qualification or entitlement to act as an advocate, and
  (3) the party for whom he so acts.

PD 39A para.5.2

Where a party is a company or other corporation and is to be represented at a hearing by an employee the written statement should contain the following additional information:
  (1) The full name of the company or corporation as stated in its certificate of registration.
  (2) The registered number of the company or corporation.
  (3) The position or office in the company or corporation held by the representative.
  (4) The date on which and manner in which the representative was authorised to act for the company or corporation, e.g. _____ 19____: written authority from managing director; or _____ 19____: Board resolution dated _____ 19____ .

PD 39A para.5.3

Rule 39.6 is intended to enable a company or other corporation to represent itself as a litigant in person. Permission under r.39.6(b) should therefore be given by the court unless there is some particular and sufficient reason why it should be withheld. In considering whether to grant permission the matters to be taken into account include the complexity of the issues and the experience and position in the company or corporation of the proposed representative.

PD 39A para.5.4

Permission under r.39.6(b) should be obtained in advance of the hearing from, preferably, the judge who is to hear the case, but may, if it is for any reason impracticable or inconvenient to do so, be obtained from any judge by whom the case could be heard.

PD 39A para.5.5

The permission may be obtained informally and without notice to the other parties. The judge who gives the permission should record in writing that he has done so and supply a copy to the company or corporation in question and to any other party who asks for one.

PD 39A para.5.6

Permission should not normally be granted under r.39.6:
(a) in jury trials;
(b) in contempt proceedings.

See also **Exhibit, Impounded documents, Recording of proceedings, Transcript**, and **Trial bundle**.

HEARSAY

Pt 33 r.33.1

(a) A statement made, otherwise than by a person while giving oral evidence in proceedings, which is tendered as evidence of the matters stated; and
(b) references to hearsay include hearsay of whatever degree.

HEARSAY EVIDENCE

Notice of intention to rely on hearsay evidence

Pt 33 r.33.2

(1) Where a party intends to rely on **hearsay evidence** at trial and either—
 (a) that evidence is to be given by a witness giving oral evidence; or
 (b) that evidence is contained in a witness statement of a person who is not being called to give oral evidence;
 that party complies with s.2(1)(a) of the Civil Evidence Act 1995 serving a witness statement on the other parties in accordance with the court's order.
(2) Where para.(1)(b) applies, the party intending to rely on the hearsay evidence must, when he serves the witness statement—
 (a) inform the other parties that the witness is not being called to give oral evidence; and
 (b) give the reason why the witness will not be called.
(3) In all other cases where a party intends to rely on hearsay evidence at trial, that party complies with s.2(1)(a) of the Civil Evidence Act 1995 by serving a notice on the other parties which—
 (a) identifies the hearsay evidence;
 (b) states that the party serving the notice proposes to rely on the hearsay evidence at trial; and
 (c) gives the reason why the witness will not be called.
(4) The party proposing to rely on the hearsay evidence must—
 (a) serve the notice no later than the latest date for serving witness statements; and

(b) if the hearsay evidence is to be in a document, supply a copy to any party who requests him to do so.

Circumstances in which notice of intention to rely on hearsay evidence is not required

Pt 33 r.33.3

Section 2(1) of the Civil Evidence Act 1995 (duty to give notice of intention to rely on hearsay evidence) does not apply—
  (a) to evidence at hearings other than trials;
  (aa) to an affidavit or witness statement which is to be used at trial but which does not contain hearsay evidence;
  (b) to a statement which a party to a probate action wishes to put in evidence and which is alleged to have been made by the person whose estate is the subject of the proceedings; or
  (c) where the requirement is excluded by a PD.

Power to call witness for cross-examination on hearsay evidence

Pt 33 r.33.4

  (1) Where a party—
    (a) proposes to rely on hearsay evidence; and
    (b) does not propose to call the person who made the original statement to give oral evidence,
    the court may, on the application of any other party, permit that party to call the maker of the statement to be cross-examined on the contents of the statement.
  (2) An application for permission to cross-examine under this rule must be made not more than 14 days after the day on which a notice of intention to rely on the hearsay evidence was served on the applicant.

Credibility

Pt 33 r.33.5

  (1) Where a party—
    (a) proposes to rely on hearsay evidence; but
    (b) does not propose to call the person who made the original statement to give oral evidence; and
    (c) another party wishes to call evidence to attack the credibility of the person who made the statement,
    the party who so wishes must give notice of his intention to the party who proposes to give the hearsay statement in evidence.
  (2) A party must give notice under para.(1) not more than 14 days after the day on which a hearsay notice relating to the hearsay evidence was served on him.

HIGHWAY TRIPPING CLAIM

Pre-action Protocol for personal injury claims

2.3
This Protocol is primarily designed for [cases such as] tripping and slipping which include an element of personal injury with a value of less than the fast track limit and which are likely to be allocated to that track.

See **Pre-action protocols**.

HIRE PURCHASE CLAIMS

Particulars of claim

PD 16 para.6.1

Where the claim is for the delivery of goods let under a hire-purchase agreement or conditional sale agreement to a person other than a company or other corporation, the claimant must state in the particulars of claim:
  (1) the date of the agreement,
  (2) the parties to the agreement,
  (3) the number or other identification of the agreement,
  (4) where the claimant was not one of the original parties to the agreement, the means by which the rights and duties of the creditor passed to him,
  (5) whether the agreement is a regulated agreement, and if it is not a regulated agreement, the reason why,
  (6) the place where the agreement was signed by the defendant,
  (7) the goods claimed,
  (8) the total price of the goods,
  (9) the paid-up sum,
  (10) the unpaid balance of the total price,
  (11) whether a default notice or a notice under ss.76(1) or 98(1) of the Consumer Credit Act 1974 has been served on the defendant, and if it has, the date and method of service,
  (12) the date when the right to demand delivery of the goods accrued,
  (13) the amount (if any) claimed as an alternative to the delivery of goods, and
  (14) the amount (if any) claimed in addition to—
        (a) the delivery of the goods, or
        (b) any claim under (13) above,
        With the grounds of each claim.
(if the agreement is a regulated agreement the procedure set out in PD 7b should be used).

PD 16 para.6.2

Where the claim is not for the delivery of goods, the claimant must state in his particulars of claim:
  (1) the matters set out in para.6.1(1) to (6) above,
  (2) the goods let under the agreement,
  (3) the amount of the total price,
  (4) the paid-up sum,
  (5) the amount (if any) claimed as being due and unpaid in respect of any instalment or instalments of the total price, and
  (6) the nature and amount of any other claim and how it arises.

PD 16 para.7.6

In a claim issued in the High Court relating to a consumer credit agreement, the particulars of claim must contain a statement that the action is not one to which s.141 of the Consumer Credit Act 1974 applies.

See also **Consumer credit claims**.

HOLDING DEFENCE

P3 rr.3.3 and 3.4

PD 3A para.1.6(1)

A holding defence may be struck out.

HOME COURT

Pt 2 r.2.3

   (1) (a) If the claim is proceeding in a county court, the county court for the district in which the defendant resides or carries on business; and
       (b) if the claim is proceeding in the High Court, the district registry for the district in which the defendant resides or carries on business or, where there is no such district registry, the Royal Courts of Justice.
(Rule 6.23 provides for a party to give an address for service).

HOME PURCHASE PLAN

Pre-Action Protocol for Possession claims based on Mortgage or Home Plan.

4.1(2)
A method of purchasing a property by way of a sale and lease arrangement that does not require the payment of interest.

See also **Mortgage claims**.

HOSPITAL MEDICAL REPORTS

See **Pre-action protocols**.

HOUSING ACT 1988

See **Demotion Order**.

HOUSING ACT 1996

See **Housing Act 1996 Injunction**.

HOUSING ACT 1996 INJUNCTION

Pt 65 r.65.2

(1) This section applies to applications for an injunction and other related proceedings under Ch.III of Pt V of the Housing Act 1996 (injunctions against anti-social behaviour).

Applications for an injunction

Pt 65 r.65.3

(1) An application for an injunction under Ch.III of Pt V of the [Housing Act1996] shall be subject to the Pt 8 procedure as modified by this rule and PD 65.
(2) The application must be—
   (a) made by a claim form in accordance with PD 65;
   (b) commenced in the court for the district in which the defendant resides or the conduct complained of occurred; and
   (c) supported by a witness statement which must be filed with the claim form.
(3) The claim form must state—
   (a) the matters required by r.8.2; and
   (b) the terms of the injunction applied for.
(4) An application under this rule may be made without notice and where such an application without notice is made—
   (a) the witness statement in support of the application must state the reasons why notice has not been given; and
   (b) the following rules do not apply—
      (i) 8.3 [acknowledgment of service];
      (ii) 8.4 [consequence of not filing an acknowledgment of service];
      (iii) 8.5(2) to (6) [the claimant's evidence must be served on the defendant with the claim form; a defendant who wishes to rely on written evidence must file it when he files his acknowledgment of service andserve a copy of his evidence on the other parties; and the claimant may, within 14 days of service of the defendant's evidence on him, file further written evidence in reply and serve a copy of his evidence on the other parties];
      (iv) 8.6(1) [no written evidence may be relied on at the hearing of the claim unless it has been served in accordance with r.8.5 or the court gives permission].
      (v) 8.7 [Pt 20 claims]; and
      (vi) 8.8 [procedure where defendant objects to use of the Pt 8 procedure].
(5) In every application made on notice, the application notice must be served, together with a copy of the witness statement, by the claimant on the defendant personally.
(6) An application made on notice may be listed for hearing before the expiry of the time for the defendant to file an acknowledgement of service under r.8.3, and in such a case—
   (a) the claimant must serve the application notice and witness statement on the defendant not less than two days before the hearing; and
   (b) the defendant may take part in the hearing whether or not he has filed an acknowledgment of service.

Issuing the claim

PD 65 para.1

An application for an injunction under Ch.III of Pt V of the [Housing Act 1996] or Pt 4 of the Policing and Crime Act 2009] must be made by Form N16A and for the purposes of applying Practice Direction 8A to applications under s.I or s.VIII of Pt 65, Form N16A shall be treated as the Pt 8 claim form.

Hearings

PD 65 para.1.2

Unless the court otherwise orders, an application on notice for an injunction under r.65.43 [injunction under Pt 4 of the Policing and Crime Act 2009] or any other hearing requiring the respondent's attendance must be heard at one of the following county courts—
  (a) Birmingham
  (b) Bradford
  (c) Bristol
  (d) Cardiff
  (e) Croydon
  (f) Leicester
  (g) Liverpool
  (h) Manchester
  (i) Newcastle
  (j) Nottingham
  (k) Peterborough
  (l) Portsmouth
  (m) Preston
  (n) Sheffield
  (o) West London.
(Attention is drawn to the statutory guidance on listing for hearings. These hearings will take place in courts which have been identified as having suitable facilities if special measures are needed for potential witnesses or security).

Injunction containing provisions to which a power of arrest is attached

Pt 65 r.65.4

  (1) In this rule 'relevant provision' means a provision of an injunction to which a power of arrest is attached.
(Section 153C(3) and 153D(4) of the 1996 Act confer powers to attach a power of arrest to an injunction).
  (2) Where an injunction contains one or more relevant provisions—
      (a) each relevant provision must be set out in a separate paragraph of the injunction; and
      (b) subject to para.(3), the claimant must deliver a copy of the relevant provisions to any police station for the area where the conduct occurred.
  (3) Where the injunction has been granted without notice, the claimant must not deliver a copy of the relevant provisions to any police station for the area where the conduct occurred before the defendant has been served with the injunction containing the relevant provisions.

(4) Where an order is made varying or discharging any relevant provision, the claimant must—
  (a) immediately inform the police station to which a copy of the relevant provisions was delivered under para.(2)(b); and
  (b) deliver a copy of the order to any police station so informed.

Application for warrant of arrest under s.155(3) of the 1996 Act

Pt 65 r.65.5

(1) An application for a warrant of arrest under s.155(3) of the 1996 Act must be made in accordance with Pt 23 and may be made without notice.
(2) An applicant for a warrant of arrest under s.155(3) of the 1996 Act must—
  (a) file an affidavit setting out grounds for the application with the application notice; or
  (b) give oral evidence as to the grounds for the application at the hearing.

Warrant of arrest on an application under s.155(3) of the 1996 Act or s.44(2) of the 2009 Act

PD 65 para.2.1

In accordance with s.155(4) of the 1996 Act and s.44(3) of the 2009 Act, a warrant of arrest on an application under s.155(3) of the 1996 Act or s.44(2) of the 2009 Act shall not be issued unless—
(1) the application is substantiated on oath; and
(2) in any proceedings under the 1996 Act the judge has reasonable grounds for believing that the defendant has failed to comply with the injunction.

Proceedings following arrest

Pt 65 r.65.6

(1) This rule applies where a person is arrested pursuant to—
  (a) a power of arrest attached to a provision of an injunction; or
  (b) a warrant of arrest.
(2) The judge before whom a person is brought following his arrest may—
  (a) deal with the matter; or
  (b) adjourn the proceedings.
(3) Where the proceedings are adjourned the judge may remand the arrested person in accordance with s.155(2)(b) or (5) of the 1996 Act.
(4) Where the proceedings are adjourned and the arrested person is released—
  (a) the matter must be dealt with (whether by the same or another judge) within 28 days of the date on which the arrested person appears in court; and
  (b) the arrested person must be given not less than two days' notice of the hearing.
(5) An application notice seeking the committal for contempt of court of the arrested person may be issued even if the arrested person is not dealt with within the period mentioned in para.(4)(a).
(6) Sections 2 and 8 of Pt 81 shall apply where an application is made in a county court to commit a person for breach of an injunction, as if references in these rules to the judge included references to a district judge.

(For applications for the discharge of a person committed to prison for contempt of court see r.81.31 and 81.32).

Bail application

PD 65 para.3.1

An application for bail by a person arrested under—
    (1) a power of arrest attached to an injunction under Ch.III of Pt V of the 1996 Act or Pt 4 of the 2009 Act; or
    (2) a warrant of arrest issued on an application under s.155(3) of the 1996 Act or Pt 4 of the 2009 Act,
may be made either orally or in an application notice.

PD 65 para.3.2

An application notice seeking bail must contain—
    (1) the full name of the person making the application;
    (2) the address of the place where the person making the application is detained at the time when the application is made;
    (3) the address where the person making the application would reside if that person were to be granted bail;
    (4) the amount of the recognisance in which that person would agree to be bound; and
    (5) the grounds on which the application is made and, where previous application has been refused, full details of any change in circumstances which has occurred since that refusal.

PD 65 para.3.3

A copy of the application notice must be served on the person who obtained the injunction.

Remand for medical examination and report

PD 65 para.4.1

Section 156(4) of the 1996 Act and s.45(5) of the 2009 Act provides that the judge has power to make an order under s.35 of the Mental Health Act 1983 in certain circumstances. If he does so attention is drawn to s.35(8) of that Act, which provides that a person remanded to hospital under that section may obtain at his own expense an independent report on his mental condition from a registered medical practitioner chosen by him and apply to the court on the basis of it for his remand to be terminated under s.35(7).

See also **Injunctions under the Policing and Crime Act 2009**.

HOUSING ACT 2004

See **Landlord and tenant claims**.

HOUSING DISREPAIR CLAIMS

(a) A disrepair claim is a civil claim arising from the condition of residential premises and may include a related personal injury claim. It does not include disrepair claims which originate as counterclaims or set-offs in other proceedings.

(b) The types of claim which this Protocol is intended to cover include those brought under Section 11 of the Landlord and Tenant Act 1985, Section 4 of the Defective Premises Act 1972, common law nuisance and negligence, and those brought under the express terms of a tenancy agreement or lease. It does not cover claims brought under Section 82 of the Environmental Protection Act 1990 (which are heard in the Magistrates' Court).

(c) This Protocol covers claims by any person with a disrepair claim as referred to in paragraphs (a) and (b) above, including tenants, lessees and members of the tenant's family. The use of the term 'tenant' in this Protocol is intended to cover all such people.

See **Pre-action protocols**.

HOUSING GRANTS, CONSTRUCTION AND REGENERATION ACT 1996

See **Technology and Construction Court claims**.

HUMAN RIGHTS

Allocation

PD 2B para.7A

A deputy High Court Judge, a Master or District Judge may not try—
(1) a case in a claim made in respect of a judicial act under the Human Rights Act 1998, or
(2) a claim for a declaration of incompatibility in accordance with s.4 of the Human Rights Act 1998.

PD 2B para.5

A district judge may not try a case in which an allegation of indirect discrimination is made against a public authority that would, if the court finds that it occurred, be unlawful under s.19B of the Race Relations Act 1976.

Citation of authorities

PD 39A r.8.1

If it is necessary for a party to give evidence at a hearing of an authority referred to in s.2 of the Human Rights Act 1998—
(1) the authority to be cited should be an authoritative and complete report; and
(2) the party must give to the court and any other party a list of the authorities he intends to cite and copies of the reports not less than three days before the hearing.

(Section 2(1) of the Human Rights Act 1998 requires the court to take into account the authorities listed there).

    (3) Copies of the complete original texts issued by the European Court and Commission either paper based or from the Court's judgment database (HUDOC), which is available on the Internet, may be used.

Declaration of incompatibility

Pt 19 r.19.4A

    (1) The court may not make a declaration of incompatibility in accordance with s.4 of the Human Rights Act 1998 unless 21 days' notice, or such other period of notice as the court directs, has been given to the Crown.

    (2) Where notice has been given to the Crown a Minister, or other person permitted by that Act, shall be joined as a party on giving notice to the court.

(Only courts specified in s.4 of the Human Rights Act 1998 can make a declaration of incompatibility).

Evidence

Pt 33 r.33.9

    (1) This rule applies where a claim is—
        (a) for a remedy under s.7 of the Human Rights Act 1998 in respect of a judicial act which is alleged to have infringed the claimant's art.5 Convention rights; and
        (b) based on a finding by a court or tribunal that the claimant's Convention rights have been infringed.

    (2) The court hearing the claim—
        (a) may proceed on the basis of the finding of that other court or tribunal that there has been an infringement but it is not required to do so, and
        (b) may reach its own conclusion in the light of that finding and of the evidence heard by that other court or tribunal.

Starting proceedings

Pt 7 r.7.11

    (1) A claim under s.7(1)(a) of the Human Rights Act 1998 in respect of a judicial act may be brought only in the High Court.

    (2) Any other claim under s.7(1)(a) of that Act may be brought in any court.

Statement of case

PD 16 para.15.1

A party who seeks to rely on any provision of or right arising under the Human Rights Act 1998 or seeks a remedy available under that Act—

    (1) must state that fact in his **statement of case**; and

(2) must in his statement of case—
    (a) give precise details of the Convention right which it is alleged has been infringed and details of the alleged infringement;
    (b) specify the relief sought;
    (c) state if the relief sought includes—
        (i) a declaration of incompatibility in accordance with s.4 of that Act, or
        (ii) damages in respect of a judicial act to which s.9(3) of that Act applies;
    (d) where the relief sought includes a declaration of incompatibility in accordance with s.4 of that Act, give precise details of the legislative provision alleged to be incompatible and details of the alleged incompatibility;
    (e) where the claim is founded on a finding of unlawfulness by another court or tribunal, give details of the finding; and
    (f) where the claim is founded on a judicial act which is alleged to have infringed a Convention right of the party as provided by s.9 of the Human Rights Act 1998, the judicial act complained of and the court or tribunal which is alleged to have made it.
(PD 19A provides for notice to be given and parties joined in the circumstances referred to in (c), (d) and (f)).

PD 16 para.15.2

A party who seeks to amend his statement of case to include the matters referred to in para.15.1 must, unless the court orders otherwise, do so as soon as possible.

Crown

PD 19A para.6.1

Where a party has included in his **statement of case**—
    (1) a claim for a declaration of incompatibility in accordance with s.4 of the Human Rights Act 1998, or
    (2) an issue for the court to decide which may lead to the court considering making a declaration,
then the court may at any time consider whether notice should be given to the Crown as required by that Act and give directions for the content and service of the notice. The rule allows a period of 21 days before the court will make the declaration but the court may vary this period of time.

PD 19A para.6.2

The court will normally consider the issues and give the directions referred to in para.6.1 at the case management conference.

PD 19A para.6.3

Where a party amends his statement of case to include any matter referred to in para.6.1, then the court will consider whether notice should be given to the Crown and give directions for the content and service of the notice.
(PD 16 requires a party to include issues under the Human Rights Act 1998 in his statement of case).

PD 19A para.6.4

(1) The notice given under r.19.4A must be served on the person named in the list published under s.17 of the Crown Proceedings Act 1947.

(The list, made by the Minister for the Civil Service, is annexed to PD 66)

    (2) The notice will be in the form directed by the court but will normally include the directions given by the court and all the statements of case in the claim. The notice will also be served on all the parties.

    (3) The court may require the parties to assist in the preparation of the notice.

    (4) In the circumstances described in the National Assembly for Wales (Transfer of Functions) (No.2) Order 2000 the notice must also be served on the National Assembly for Wales.

(Section 5(3) of the Human Rights Act 1998 provides that the Crown may give notice that it intends to become a party at any stage in the proceedings once notice has been given).

PD 19A para.6.5

Unless the court orders otherwise, the Minister or other person permitted by the Human Rights Act 1998 to be joined as a party must, if he wishes to be joined, give notice of his intention to be joined as a party to the court and every other party. Where the Minister has nominated a person to be joined as a party the notice must be accompanied by the written nomination.

(Section 5(2)(a) of the Human Rights Act 1998 permits a person nominated by a Minister of the Crown to be joined as a party. The nomination may be signed on behalf of the Minister).

Judicial acts

PD 19A para.6.6

(1) The procedure in paras 6.1 to 6.5 also applies where a claim is made under ss.7(1)(a) and 9(3) of the Human Rights Act 1998 for damages in respect of a judicial act.

    (2) Notice must be given to the Lord Chancellor and should be served on the Treasury Solicitor on his behalf, except where the judicial act is of a Court-Martial when the appropriate person is the Secretary of State for Defence and the notice must be served on the Treasury Solicitor on his behalf.

    (3) The notice will also give details of the judicial act, which is the subject of the claim for damages, and of the court or tribunal that made it.

(Section 9(4) of the Human Rights Act 1998 provides that no award of damages may be made against the Crown as provided for in s.9(3) unless the appropriate person is joined the proceedings. The appropriate person is the Minister responsible for the court concerned or a person or department nominated by him (s.9(5) of the Act)).

Pt 19 r.19.4A

(3) Where a claim is made under [s.9 of the Human Rights Act 1998] for damages in respect of a judicial Act—

    (a) that claim must be set out in the statement of case or the appeal notice; and

    (b) notice must be given to the Crown.

    (4) Where para.(3) applies and the appropriate person has not applied to be joined as a party within 21 days, or such other period as the court directs, after the notice is served, the court may join the appropriate person as a party.

Judicial review

PD 54A para.5.3

Where the claimant is seeking to raise any issue under the Human Rights Act 1998, or seeks a remedy available under that Act, the claim form must include the information required by para.15 of PD 16.

Statements of case

PD 16 para.15.1

A party who seeks to rely on any provision of or right arising under the Human Rights Act 1998 or seeks a remedy available under that Act—
    (1) must state that fact in his statement of case; and
    (2) must in his statement of case—
        (a) give precise details of the Convention right which it is alleged has been infringed and details of the alleged infringement;
        (b) specify the relief sought;
        (c) state if the relief sought includes—
            (i) a declaration of incompatibility in accordance with s.4 of that Act, or
            (ii) damages in respect of a judicial act to which s.9(3) of that Act applies;
        (d) where the relief sought includes a declaration of incompatibility in accordance with s.4 of that Act, give precise details of the legislative provision alleged to be incompatible and details of the alleged incompatibility;
        (e) where the claim is founded on a finding of unlawfulness by another court or tribunal, give details of the finding; and
        (f) where the claim is founded on a judicial act which is alleged to have infringed a Convention right of the party as provided by s.9 of the Human Rights Act 1998, the judicial act complained of and the court or tribunal which is alleged to have made it.
(PD 19A provides for notice to be given and parties joined in the circumstances referred to in (c), (d) and (f)).

Amendment of statement of case

PD 16 para.15.2

A party who seeks to amend his statement of case to include the matters referred to in para.15.1 must, unless the court orders otherwise, do so as soon as possible.

Venue for claim

Pt 7 r.7.11

    (1) A claim under s.7(1)(a) of the Human Rights Act 1998 in respect of a judicial act may be brought only in the High Court.
    (2) Any other claim under s.7(1)(a) of that Act may be brought in any court.

See also **Transfer of proceedings**.

I

IMMIGRATION AND ASYLUM

Appeals from the Upper Tribunal Immigration and Asylum Chamber

Bundle of documents

PD 52C para.28

    (1) In an appeal from the Immigration and Asylum Chamber of the Upper Tribunal (other than an appeal relating to a claim for judicial review)—
        (a) the Immigration and Asylum Chamber of the Upper Tribunal, upon request, shall send to the Civil Appeals Office copies of the documents which were before the relevant Tribunal when it considered the appeal;
        (b) the appellant is not required to file an appeal bundle;
        (c) the appellant must file with the appellant's notice the documents specified in paragraphs 4(3)(a) to (e) and (g) of [PD52C].

Appeal from Special Immigration Appeals Commission

Appeal to the Court of Appeal

PD 52D para.17.1

    (1) An application for permission to appeal to the Court of Appeal must first be made to the Special Immigration Appeals Commission pursuant section 7(2) of the Special Immigration Appeals Commission Act 1997 and para.27 of the SIAC (Procedure) Rules 2003 (as amended).
    (2) The appellant's notice must be filed at the Court of Appeal within 21 days of the date on which the Special Immigration Appeals Commission's decision granting or refusing permission to appeal to the Court of Appeal is given.

Appeals under the Extradition Act 2003

Appeals to the High Court

PD 52D para.21.1

    (2) Appeals to the High Court under the [Extradition Act 2003] must be started in the Administrative Court of the Queen's Bench Division at the Royal Courts of Justice in London.
    (3) Where an appeal is brought under section 26 or 28 of the Act—
        (a) the appellant's notice must be filed and served before the expiry of 7 days, starting with the day on which the order is made;

(b) the appellant must endorse the appellant's notice with the date of the person's arrest;

(c) the High Court must begin to hear the substantive appeal within 40 days of the person's arrest; and

(d) the appellant must serve a copy of the appellant's notice on the Crown Prosecution Service, if they are not a party to the appeal, in addition to the persons to be served under rule 52.4(3) and in accordance with that rule.

(4) The High Court may extend the period of 40 days under sub-paragraph (3)(c) if it believes it to be in the interests of justice to do so.

(5) Where an appeal is brought under section 103 of the Act, the appellant's notice must be filed and served before the expiry of 14 days, starting with the day on which the Secretary of State informs the person under section 100(1) or (4) of the Act that an order has made in respect of the person.

(6) Where an appeal is brought under section 105 of the Act, the appellant's notice must be filed and served before the expiry of 14 days, starting with the day on which the order for discharge is made.

(7) Where an appeal is brought under section 108 of the Act the appellant's notice must be filed and served before the expiry of 14 days, starting with the day on which the Secretary of State informs the person that an order for extradition has been made.

(8) Where an appeal is brought under section 110 of the Act the appellant's notice must be filed and served before the expiry of 14 days, starting with the day on which the Secretary of State informs the person acting on behalf of a category 2 territory, as defined in section 69 of the Act, of the order for discharge.

(Section 69 of the Act provides that a category 2 territory is that designated for the purposes of Part 2 of the Act.)

(9) Subject to sub-paragraph (10), where an appeal is brought under section 103, 105, 108 or 110 of the Act, the High Court must begin to hear the substantive appeal within 76 days of the appellant's notice being filed.

(10) Where an appeal is brought under section 103 of the Act before the Secretary of State has decided whether the person is to be extradited—

(a) the period of 76 days does not start until the day on which the Secretary of State informs the person of the decision; and

(b) the Secretary of State must, as soon as practicable after the person has been informed of the decision, inform the High Court—

(i) of the decision; and

(ii) of the date on which the person was informed of the decision.

(11) The High Court may extend the period of 76 days if it believes it to be in the interests of justice to do so.

(12) Where an appeal is brought under section 103, 105, 108 or 110 of the Act, the appellant must serve a copy of the appellant's notice on—

(a) the Crown Prosecution Service; and

(b) the Home Office,

if they are not a party to the appeal, in addition to the persons to be served under rule 52.4(3) and in accordance with that rule.

Appeal under Pt II of the Immigration and Asylum Act 1999 (carriers' liability)

Appeal to county court

PD 52D para.29.1

(1) A person appealing to a county court under s.35A or s.40B of the Immigration and Asylum Act 1999 against a decision by the Secretary of State to impose a penalty under

s.32 or a charge under s.40 of the Act must, subject to sub-paragraph (2), file the appellant's notice within 28 days after receiving the penalty notice or charge notice.

(2) Where the appellant has given notice of objection to the Secretary of State under s.35(4) or s.40A(3) of the Act within the time prescribed for doing so, the appellant must file the appellant's notice within 28 days after receiving notice of the Secretary of State's decision in response to the notice of objection.

(3) Ss.35A and 40B of the Act provide that any appeal under those sections shall be a re-hearing of the Secretary of State's decision to impose a penalty or charge, and therefore r.52.11(1) does not apply.

Judicial review of decisions of the Upper Tribunal

Pt 54 r.54.7A

(1) This rule applies where an application is made, following refusal by the Upper Tribunal of permission to appeal against a decision of the First Tier Tribunal, for judicial review—
   (a) of the decision of the Upper Tribunal refusing permission to appeal; or
   (b) which relates to the decision of the First Tier Tribunal which was the subject of the application for permission to appeal.

(2) Where this rule applies—
   (a) the application may not include any other claim, whether against the Upper Tribunal or not; and
   (b) any such other claim must be the subject of a separate application.

(3) The claim form and the supporting documents required by para.(4) must be filed no later than 16 days after the date on which notice of the Upper Tribunal's decision was sent to the applicant.

(4) The supporting documents are—
   (a) the decision of the Upper Tribunal to which the application relates, an any document giving reason for the decision;
   (b) the grounds of appeal to the Upper Tribunal and any documents which were sent with them;
   (c) the decision of the First Tier Tribunal, the application to that Tribunal for permission to appeal and its reasons for refusing permission; and
   (d) any other documents essential to the claim.

(5) The claim form and supporting documents must be served on the Upper Tribunal and any other Interested party no later than 7 days after the date of issue.

(6) The Upper Tribunal and any person served with the claim form who wishes to take part in the proceedings for judicial review must, no later than 21 days after service of the claim form, file and serve on the applicant and any other party an acknowledgment of service in the relevant PD form.

(7) The court will give permission to proceed only if it considers—
   (a) that there is an arguable case, which has a reasonable prospect of success, that both the decision of the Upper Tribunal refusing permission to appeal and the decision of the First Tier Tribunal against which permission to appeal was sought are wrong in law; and
      (i) the claim raises an important point of principle or practice; or
      (ii) there is some other compelling reason to hear it.

(8) If the application for permission is refused on paper without an oral hearing, r.54.12(3) (request for reconsideration at a hearing) does not apply.

(9) If permission to apply for judicial review is granted—
   (a) if the Upper Tribunal or any interested party wishes there to be a hearing of the substantive application, it must make its request for such a hearing no later than 14 days after service of the order granting permission; and
   (b) if no request for a hearing is made within that period, the court will make a final order quashing the refusal of permission without a further hearing.

(10) The power to make a final order under para.(9)(b) may be exercised by the Master of the Crown Office or a Master of the Administrative Court.

Appeals under s.11 of the UK Borders Act 2007

Appeals to the county court

PD 52 r.24.7

(1) A person appealing to a county court under s.11 of the UK Borders Act 2007 ('the Act') against a decision by the Secretary of State to impose a penalty under s.9(1) of the Act, must, subject to para.(2), file the appellant's notice within 28 days after receiving the penalty notice.
(2) Where the appellant has given notice of objection to the Secretary of State under s.10 of the Act within the time prescribed for doing so, the appellant's notice must be filed within 28 days after receiving notice of the Secretary of State's decision in response to the notice of objection.

Judicial review of the Upper Tribunal

Pt 54 and 54.7A

Service of claim form

Pt 54 r.54.7

The claim form must be served on—
(a) the defendant; and
(b) unless the court otherwise directs, any person the claimant considers to be an interested party,
within seven days after the date of issue.

PD 54A para.6.1

The Administrative Court will not serve documents and service must be effected by the parties.

PD 54A para.6.2

Where the defendant or interested party to the claim for judicial review is—
the Immigration and Asylum Chamber of the First-tier Tribunal, the address for service of the claim form is Official Correspondence Unit, PO Box 6987, Leicester, LE1 6ZX or fax: 0116 249 4240.

Judicial review of decisions of the Upper Tribunal

54.7A

(1) This rule applies where an application is made, following refusal by the Upper Tribunal of permission to appeal against a decision of the First Tier Tribunal, for judicial review—

    (a) of the decision of the Upper Tribunal refusing permission to appeal; or

    (b) which relates to the decision of the First Tier Tribunal which was the subject of the application for permission to appeal.

(2) Where this rule applies—

    (a) the application may not include any other claim, whether against the Upper Tribunal or not; and

    (b) any such other claim must be the subject of a separate application.

(3) The claim form and the supporting documents required by paragraph (4) must be filed no later than 16 days after the date on which notice of the Upper Tribunal's decision was sent to the applicant.

(4) The supporting documents are—

    (a) the decision of the Upper Tribunal to which the application relates, and any document giving reasons for the decision;

    (b) the grounds of appeal to the Upper Tribunal and any documents which were sent with them;

    (c) the decision of the First Tier Tribunal, the application to that Tribunal for permission to appeal and its reasons for refusing permission; and

    (d) any other documents essential to the claim.

(5) The claim form and supporting documents must be served on the Upper Tribunal and any other interested party no later than 7 days after the date of issue.

(6) The Upper Tribunal and any person served with the claim form who wishes to take part in the proceedings for judicial review must, no later than 21 days after service of the claim form, file and serve on the applicant and any other party an acknowledgment of service in the relevant practice form.

(7) The court will give permission to proceed only if it considers—

    (a) that there is an arguable case, which has a reasonable prospect of success, that both the decision of the Upper Tribunal refusing permission to appeal and the decision of the First Tier Tribunal against which permission to appeal was sought are wrong in law; and

    (b) that either—

        (i) the claim raises an important point of principle or practice; or

        (ii) there is some other compelling reason to hear it.

(8) If the application for permission is refused on paper without an oral hearing, rule 54.12(3) (request for reconsideration at a hearing) does not apply.

(9) If permission to apply for judicial review is granted—

    (a) if the Upper Tribunal or any interested party wishes there to be a hearing of the substantive application, it must make its request for such a hearing no later than 14 days after service of the order granting permission; and

    (b) if no request for a hearing is made within that period, the court will make a final order quashing the refusal of permission without a further hearing.

(10) The power to make a final order under paragraph (9)(b) may be exercised by the Master of the Crown Office or a Master of the Administrative Court.

Applications for permission to apply for judicial review to challenge removal

PD 54A para.18.1

    [s.II of PD 54A]—

    (a) a person has been served with a copy of directions for his removal from the UK by the UK Border Agency of the Home Office and notified that this section applies; and

    (b) that person makes an application for permission to apply for judicial review before his removal takes effect.

(2) This section does not prevent a person from applying for judicial review after he has been removed.

(3) The requirements contained in this section are additional to those contained elsewhere in [PD 54A].

PD 54A para.18.2

(1) A person who makes an application for permission to apply for judicial review must file a claim form and a copy at court, and the claim form must—
  (a) indicate on its face that this section of [PD 54A] applies; and
  (b) be accompanied by—
    (i) a copy of the removal directions and the decision to which the application relates; and
    (ii) any document served with the removal directions including any document which contains the UK Border Agency's factual summary of the case; and
  (c) contain or be accompanied by the detailed statement of the claimant's grounds for bringing the claim for judicial review; or
  (d) if the claimant is unable to comply with para.(b) or (c), contain or be accompanied by a statement of the reasons why.
(2) The claimant must, immediately upon issue of the claim, send copies of the issued claim form and accompanying documents to the address specified by the UK Border Agency.
(Rule 54.7 also requires the defendant to be served with the claim form within seven days of the date of issue. Rule 6.10 provides that service on a Government Department must be effected on the solicitor acting for that Department, which in the case of the UK Border Agency is the Treasury Solicitor. The address for the Treasury Solicitor may be found in the Annex to Pt 66 of these Rules).

PD 54A para.18.3

Where the claimant has not complied with para.18.2(1)(b) or (c) and has provided reasons why he is unable to comply, and the court has issued the claim form, the Administrative Court—
  (a) will refer the matter to a Judge for consideration as soon as practicable; and
  (b) will notify the parties that it has done so.

PD 54A para.18.4

If, upon a refusal to grant permission to apply for judicial review, the Court indicates that the application is clearly without merit, that indication will be included in the order refusing permission.

IMPOUNDED DOCUMENTS

P39 r.39.7

(1) Documents impounded by order of the court must not be released from the custody of the court except in compliance—
  (a) with a court order; or
  (b) with a written request made by a Law Officer or the Director of Public Prosecutions.
(2) A document released from the custody of the court under para.(1)(b) must be released into the custody of the person who requested it.
(3) Documents impounded by order of the court, while in the custody of the court, may not be inspected except by a person authorised to do so by a court order.

IN HOUSE LEGAL REPRESENTATIVE

Statement of truth

PD 22 para.3.11

A legal representative employed by a party may sign a **statement of truth**. However a person who is not a solicitor, barrister or other authorised litigator, but who is employed by the company and is managed by such a person, is not employed by that person and so cannot sign a statement of truth. (This is unlike the employee of a solicitor in private practice who would come within the definition of legal representative.) However such a person may be a manager and able to sign the statement on behalf of the company in that capacity.

INDEMNITY

Glossary

A right of someone to recover from a third party the whole amount which he himself is liable to pay.

See **Additional claims**.

INDEMNITY BASIS

Pt 44 r.44.3

    (3) Where the amount of costs is to be assessed on the indemnity basis, the court will resolve any doubt which it may have as to whether costs were reasonably incurred or were reasonable in amount in favour of the receiving party.

PD 44 para.6.1

If costs are awarded on the indemnity basis, the court assessing costs will disallow any costs—
    (a) which it finds to have been unreasonably incurred; or
    (b) which it considers to be unreasonable in amount.

INDEX OF ORDERS

Attachment of earnings orders

CCR Ord.27 r.2

    (1) The court officer of every court shall keep a nominal index of the debtors residing within the district of his court in respect of whom there are in force attachment of earnings orders which have been made by that court or of which the court officer has received notice from another court.
    (2) Where a debtor in respect of whom a court has made an attachment of earnings order resides within the district of another court, the court officer of the first-mentioned court

shall send a copy of the order to the court officer of the other court for entry in his index.

(3) The court officer shall, on the request of any person having a judgment or order against a person believed to be residing within the district of the court, cause a search to be made in the index of the court and issue a certificate of the result of the search.

INFERIOR COURT OR TRIBUNAL

Pt 34 r.34.4

(3) Any court or tribunal that does not have power to issue a **witness summons** in relation to proceedings before it.

INHERITANCE CLAIMS

See **Probate claim**.

INHERITANCE (PROVISION FOR FAMILY AND DEPENDANTS) ACT 1975

Proceedings in the High Court

Pt 57 r.57.15

(1) Proceedings in the High Court under the [1975] Act shall be issued in either—
(a) the Chancery Division; or
(b) the Family Division.
(2) The Civil Procedure Rules apply to proceedings under the Act which are brought in the Family Division, except that the provisions of the Family Proceedings Rules 1991 relating to the drawing up and service of orders apply instead of the provisions in Pt 40 and PD 40B.

Procedure for claims under s.1 of the Act

Pt 57 para.57.16

(1) A claim under s.1 of the Act must be made by issuing a claim form in accordance with Pt 8.
(2) Rule 8.3 (acknowledgment of service) and r.8.5 (filing and serving written evidence) apply as modified by paras (3) to (5) of this Rule.
(3) The written evidence filed and served by the claimant with the claim form must have exhibited to it an official copy of—
(a) the grant of probate or letters of administration in respect of the deceased's estate; and
(b) every testamentary document in respect of which probate or letters of administration were granted.
(4) Subject to para.(4A), the time within which a defendant must file and serve—
(a) an acknowledgment of service; and

      (b) any written evidence,

      is not more than 21 days after service of the claim form on him.

  (4A) If the claim form is served out of the jurisdiction under rr.6.32 or 6.33, the period for filing an acknowledgment of service and any written evidence is seven days longer than the relevant period specified in r.6.35 or PD 6B.

   (5) A defendant who is a personal representative of the deceased must file and serve written evidence, which must include the information required by PD 57.

[See Annex to PD 57 for a form of witness statement or affidavit about testamentary documents].

Acknowledgment of service by personal representative

PD 57 para.15

Where a defendant who is a personal representative wishes to remain neutral in relation to the claim, and agrees to abide by any decision which the court may make, he should state this in Section A of the acknowledgment of service form.

Written evidence of personal representative

PD 57 para.16

The written evidence filed by a defendant who is a personal representative must state to the best of that person's ability—

   (1) full details of the value of the deceased's net estate, as defined in s.25(1) of the Act;

   (2) the person or classes of persons beneficially interested in the estate, and—

      (a) the names and (unless they are parties to the claim) addresses of all living beneficiaries; and

      (b) the value of their interests in the estate so far as they are known.

   (3) whether any living beneficiary (and if so, naming him) is a child or a person who lacks capacity (within the meaning of the Mental Capacity Act 2005); and

   (4) any facts which might affect the exercise of the court's powers under the Act.

Separate representation of claimants

PD 57 para.17

If a claim is made jointly by two or more claimants, and it later appears that any of the claimants have a conflict of interests—

   (1) any claimant may choose to be represented at any hearing by separate solicitors or counsel, or may appear in person; and

   (2) if the court considers that claimants who are represented by the same solicitors or counsel ought to be separately represented, it may adjourn the application until they are.

Production of the grant

PD 57 para.18.1

On the hearing of a claim the personal representative must produce to the court the original grant of representation to the deceased's estate.

PD 57 para.18.2

If the court makes an order under the Act, the original grant (together with a sealed copy of the order) must be sent to the Principal Registry of the Family Division for a memorandum of the order to be endorsed on or permanently annexed to the grant in accordance with s.19(3) of the Act.

PD 57 para.18.3

Every final order embodying terms of compromise made in proceedings under the Act, whether made with or without a hearing, must contain a direction that a memorandum of the order shall be endorsed on or permanently annexed to the probate or letters of administration and a copy of the order shall be sent to the Principal Registry of the Family Division with the relevant grant of probate or letters of administration for endorsement.

Hearings

Pt 39 r.39.2(3)(c)

(c) it involves confidential information (including information relating to personal financial matters) and publicity would damage that confidentiality;

PD 39A para.1.5(9)

The hearings shall in the first instance be listed by the court as hearings in private under r.39.2(3)(c) [it involves confidential information (including information relating to personal financial matters) and publicity would damage that confidentiality].

INHERITANCE TAX 1984

Appeal under s.222 of the Inheritance Tax Act 1984

PD 52D para.5.1

Any appeal to the High Court shall be heard in the Chancery Division.

PD 52 para.23.3

(1) This paragraph applies to appeals to the High Court under s.222(3) of the Inheritance Tax Act 1984 (the '1984 Act') and reg.8(3) of the Stamp Duty Reserve Tax Regulations 1986 (the '1986 Regulations').
(2) The appellant's notice must—
   (a) state the date on which the Commissioners for HM Revenue and Customs (the 'Board') gave notice to the appellant under s.221 of the 1984 Act or reg.6 of the 1986 Regulations of the determination that is the subject of the appeal;
   (b) state the date on which the appellant gave to the Board notice of appeal under s.222(1) of the 1984 Act or reg.8(1) of the 1986 Regulations and, if notice was not given within the time permitted, whether the Board or the Special Commissioners have given their consent to the appeal being brought out of time, and, if they have, the date they gave their consent; and

(c) either state that the appellant and the Board have agreed that the appeal may be to the High Court or contain an application for permission to appeal to the High Court.

(3) The appellant must file the following documents with the appellant's notice—

(a) Two copies of the notice referred to in para.2(a);

(b) Two copies of the notice of appeal (under s.222(1) of the 1984 Act or reg.8(1) of the 1986 Regulations) referred to in para.2(b); and

(c) where the appellant's notice contains an application for permission to appeal, written evidence setting out the grounds on which it is alleged that the matters to be decided on the appeal are likely to be substantially confined to questions of law.

(4) The appellant must—

(a) file the appellant's notice at the court; and

(b) serve the appellant's notice on the Board,

within 30 days of the date on which the appellant gave to the Board notice of appeal under s.222(1) of the 1984 Act or reg.8(1) of the 1986 Regulations or, if the Board or the Special Commissioners have given consent to the appeal being brought out of time, within 30 days of the date on which such consent was given.

(5) The court will set a date for the hearing of not less than 40 days from the date that the appellant's notice was filed.

(6) Where the appellant's notice contains an application for permission to appeal—

(a) a copy of the written evidence filed in accordance with para.(3)(c) must be served on the Board with the appellant's notice; and

(b) the Board—

(i) may file written evidence; and

(ii) if it does so, must serve a copy of that evidence on the appellant,

within 30 days after service of the written evidence under para.(6)(a).

(7) The appellant may not rely on any grounds of appeal not specified in the notice referred to in para.(2)(b) on the hearing of the appeal without the permission of the court.

INJUNCTIONS

Glossary

A court order prohibiting a person from doing something or requiring a person to do something.

See also **Freezing injunction**, **Interim injunction**, and **Search orders**.

INJUNCTIONS AGAINST ANTI-SOCIAL BEHAVIOUR

See **Housing Act 1996 injunctions**.

INJUNCTIONS UNDER THE POLICING AND CRIME ACT 2009

Pt 65 r.65.42

(1) [Section VIII of Pt 65] applies to applications for an injunction and other related proceedings under Pt 4 of the Policing and Crime Act 2009 (Injunctions: gang-related violence).

Applications for an injunction

Pt 65 r.65.43

(1) An application for an injunction under Pt 4 of the [Policing and Crime Act 2009] is subject to the Pt 8 procedure as modified by this rule and PD 65.

(2) The application must be—
  (a) made by a claim form in accordance with PD 65;
  (b) commenced in the court for the district in which the defendant resides or the conduct complained of occurred; and
  (c) supported by a witness statement which must be filed with the claim form.

(3) The claim form must state—
  (a) the matters required by r.8.2; and
  (b) the terms of the injunction applied for.

(4) An application under this rule may be made without notice and where such an application without notice is made—
  (a) the witness statement in support of the application must state the reasons why notice has not been given; and
  (b) the following rules do not apply—
    (i) 8.3 [acknowledgment of service];
    (ii) 8.4 [consequence of not filing an acknowledgment of service];
    (iii) 8.5(2) to (6)[the claimant's evidence must be served on the defendant with the claim form; a defendant who wishes to rely on written evidence must file it when he files his acknowledgment of service andserve a copy of his evidence on the other parties; and the claimant may, within 14 days of service of the defendant's evidence on him, file further written evidence in reply and serve a copy of his evidence on the other parties];
    (iv) 8.6(1) [no written evidence may be relied on at the hearing of the claim unless it has been served in accordance with r.8.5 or the court gives permission].
    (v) 8.7 [Pt 20 claims]; and
    (vi) 8.8 [procedure where defendant objects to use of the Pt 8 procedure].

(5) In every application made on notice, the application notice must be served, together with a copy of the witness statement, by the claimant on the defendant personally.

(6) An application made on notice may be listed for hearing before the expiry of the time for the defendant to file an acknowledgement of service under r.8.3, and in such a case—
  (a) the claimant must serve the application notice and witness statement on the defendant not less than two days before the hearing; and
  (b) the defendant may take part in the hearing whether or not the defendant has filed an acknowledgment of service.

Issuing the claim

PD 65 para.1.1

An application for an injunction under [Pt 4 of the 2009 Act] must be made by form N16A and for the purposes of applying PD 8A to applications under [s. VIII of Pt 65], form N16A shall be treated as the **Pt 8 claim form**.

Injunction containing provisions to which a power of arrest is attached

Pt 65 r.65.44

(1) In this rule 'relevant provision' means a provision of an injunction to which a power of arrest is attached.

(Section 36(6) and (7) and ss.40(3) and 41(4) of the 2009 Act confer powers to attach a power of arrest to an injunction).

    (2) Where an injunction contains one or more relevant provisions—

        (a) each relevant provision must be set out in a separate paragraph of the injunction; and

        (b) subject to para.(3), the claimant must deliver a copy of the relevant provisions to any police station for the area where the conduct occurred.

    (3) Where the injunction has been granted without notice, the claimant must not deliver a copy of the relevant provisions to any police station for the area where the conduct occurred before the defendant has been served with the injunction containing the relevant provisions.

    (4) Where an order is made varying or discharging any relevant provision, the claimant must—

        (a) immediately inform the police station to which a copy of the relevant provisions was delivered under para.(2)(b); and

        (b) deliver a copy of the order to any police station so informed.

Application to vary or discharge an injunction

Pt 65 r.65.45

    (1) An application to vary or discharge an injunction under s.42(1)(b) of the 2009 Act must be made in accordance with Pt 23.

    (2) An application by the claimant to vary or discharge the injunction under s.42(1)(b) of the 2009 Act may be made without notice.

    (3) If an application under this rule is made without giving notice, the application notice must state the reasons why notice has not been given.

Applications for a power of arrest to be attached to any provision of an injunction

Pt 65 r.65.49

    (1) An application under ss.34 or 39 of the 2009 Act which includes an application for a power of arrest to be attached to any provision of an injunction must be made in the proceedings seeking the injunction by—

        (a) the claim form; or

        (b) an application under Pt 23.

    (2) Every application must be supported by written evidence.

    (3) Every application made on notice must be served personally, together with a copy of the written evidence, by the applicant on the person against whom the injunction is sought not less than two days before the hearing.

(Attention is drawn to r.25.3(3)—applications without notice.)

Application for warrant of arrest under s.44(2) of the 2009 Act

Pt 65 r.65.46

    (1) An application for a warrant of arrest under s.44(2) of the 2009 Act must be made in accordance with Pt 23 and may be made without notice.

(2) An applicant for a warrant of arrest under s. 44(2) of the 2009 Act must—
   (a) file an affidavit setting out grounds for the application with the application notice; or
   (b) give oral evidence of the grounds for the application at the hearing.
(3) Where in accordance with subpara.(2)(b), oral evidence is given, the applicant must produce a written record of that evidence which must be served on the person arrested at the time of the arrest.

PD 65 para.2.1

In accordance with [s.44(3) of the 2009 Act], a warrant of arrest on an application under [s.44(2) of the 2009 Act] shall not be issued unless—
   (1) the application is substantiated on oath.

Proceedings following arrest under the 2009 Act

Pt 65 r.65.47

(1) This rule applies where a person is arrested pursuant to—
   (a) a power of arrest attached to a provision of an injunction; or
   (b) a warrant of arrest.
(2) The judge before whom a person is brought following his arrest may—
   (a) deal with the matter; or
   (b) adjourn the proceedings.
(3) If proceedings under ss.43 or 44 of the 2009 Act are adjourned and the arrested person is released—
   (a) the matter must be dealt with (whether by the same or another judge) within 28 days of the date on which the arrested person appears in court; and
   (b) the arrested person must be given not less than two days' notice of the hearing.
(4) An application notice seeking the committal for contempt of court of the arrested person may be issued even if the arrested person is not dealt with within the period in sub-para.(3)(a).
(5) CCR Ord.29 r.1 applies where an application is made in a county court to commit a person for breach of an injunction as if references in that rule to the judge include references to a district judge.
(For applications in the High Court for the discharge of a person committed to prison for contempt of court see RSC Ord.52 r.8. For such applications in the county court see CCR Ord.29 r.3).

See also **Child** and **Recognisance**.

INQUIRIES

See **Accounts and inquiries**, **Interim remedies**, and **Summary judgment**.

INSOLVENCY PROCEEDINGS

PD Insolvency Proceedings para.1.1

(6) 'Insolvency proceedings' means—
   (a) any proceedings under the Act [means the Insolvency Act 1986 and includes the Act as applied to limited liability partnerships by the Limited Liability Partnerships

Regulations 2001 or to any other person or body by virtue of the Act or any other legislation], the Insolvency Rules, the Administration of Insolvent Estates of Deceased Persons Order 1986, the Insolvent Partnerships Order 1994 or the Limited Liability Partnerships Regulations 2001;
  (b) any proceedings under the EC Regulation on Insolvency Proceedings or the Cross-Border Insolvency Regulations 2006.

Pt 2 r.2.1(2)

The CPR do not apply to these proceedings except to the extent that they are applied by ss.411 and 412 of the Insolvency Act 1986.

Coming into force

PD IP para.2.1

[PD IP] [came] into force on February 12, 2012 and [replaced all previous PDs, Practice Statements and Practice Notes relating to insolvency proceedings].

Distribution of business

PD IP para.3.1

As a general rule all petitions and applications (except those listed in paras 3.2 and 3.3 below) should be listed for initial hearing before a Registrar in accordance with r.7.6A(2) and (3).

PD IP para.3.2

The following applications relating to insolvent companies [include a limited liability partnership] should always be listed before a Judge—
  (1) applications for committal for contempt;
  (2) applications for an administration order;
  (3) applications for an injunction;
  (4) applications for the appointment of a provisional liquidator;
  (5) interim applications and applications for directions or case management after any proceedings have been referred or adjourned to the Judge (except where liberty to apply to the Registrar has been given).

PD IP para.3.3

The following applications relating to insolvent individuals should always be listed before a Judge—
  (1) applications for committal for contempt;
  (2) applications for an injunction;
  (3) interim applications and applications for directions or case management after any proceedings have been referred or adjourned to the Judge (except where liberty to apply to the Registrar has been given).

PD IP para.3.4

When deciding whether to hear proceedings or to refer or adjourn them to the Judge, the Registrar should have regard to the following factors—

(1) the complexity of the proceedings;
(2) whether the proceedings raise new or controversial points of law;
(3) the likely date and length of the hearing;
(4) public interest in the proceedings.

Court documents

PD IP para.4.1

All insolvency proceedings should be commenced and applications in proceedings should be made using the forms prescribed by the Act, the Insolvency Rules or other legislation under which the same is or are brought or made and/or should contain the information prescribed by the Act, the Insolvency Rules or other legislation.

PD IP paras 4.2 and 4.3

Every court document in insolvency proceedings under Pts I to VII and Pts IX to XI of the Act shall be headed [in the format set out in these paragraphs].

Evidence

PD IP para.5.1

Subject to the provisions of r.7.9 or any other provisions or directions as to the form in which evidence should be given, written evidence in insolvency proceedings must be given by witness statement.

Service of court documents in insolvency proceedings

PD IP para.6.1

Except where the Insolvency Rules otherwise provide, CPR Pt 6 applies to the service of court documents both within and out of the jurisdiction as modified by this PD or as the court may otherwise direct.

PD IP para.6.2

Except where the Insolvency Rules otherwise provide or as may be required under the Service Regulation, service of documents in insolvency proceedings will be the responsibility of the parties and will not be undertaken by the court.

PD IP para.6.3

A document which, pursuant to r.12A.16(3)(b), is treated as a claim form, is deemed to have been served on the date specified in CPR Pt 6.14, and any other document is deemed to have been served on the date specified in CPR Pt 6.26, unless the court otherwise directs.

PD IP para.6.4

Except as provided below, service out of the jurisdiction of an application which is to be treated as a claim form under r.12A.16(3) requires the permission of the court.

PD IP para.6.5

An application which is to be treated as a claim form under r.12A.16(3) may be served out of the jurisdiction without the permission of the court if—
    (1) the application is by an office-holder appointed in insolvency proceedings in respect of a company with its centre of main interests within the jurisdiction exercising a statutory power under the Act, and the person to be served is to be served within the EU; or
    (2) it is a copy of an application, being served on a member State liquidator.

PD IP para.6.6

An application for permission to serve out of the jurisdiction must be supported by a witness statement setting out—
    (1) the nature of the claim or application and the relief sought;
    (2) that the applicant believes that the claim has a reasonable prospect of success; and
    (3) the address of the person to be served or, if not known, in what place or country that person is, or is likely, to be found.

PD IP para.6.7

CPR rr.6.36 and 6.37(1) and (2) do not apply in insolvency proceedings.

Jurisdiction

PD IP para.7.1

Where CPR r.2.4 provides for the court to perform any act, that act may be performed by a Registrar.

Drawing up of orders

PD IP para.8.1

The court will draw up all orders except orders on the application of the Official Receiver or for which the Treasury Solicitor is responsible or where the court otherwise directs.

Urgent applications

PD IP para.9.1

In the Royal Courts of Justice the Registrars (and in other courts exercising insolvency jurisdiction the District Judges) operate urgent applications lists for urgent and time-critical applications and may be available to hear urgent applications at other times. Parties asking for an application to be dealt with in the urgent applications lists or urgently at any other time must complete the certificate [set out in this paragraph of PD].

Appeals

PD IP para.19.1

An appeal from a decision of a county court (whether made by a District Judge, a Recorder or a Circuit Judge) or of a Registrar in insolvency proceedings lies to a Judge of the High Court.

PD IP para.19.2

An appeal from a decision of a Judge of the High Court, whether at first instance or on appeal, lies to the Court of Appeal.

PD IP para.19.3

A first appeal, whether under paras 19.1 or 19.2 above, is subject to the permission requirements of CPR Pt 52 r.3.

PD IP para.19.4

An appeal from a decision of a Judge of the High Court which was made on a first appeal requires the permission of the Court of Appeal.

Filing appeals

PD IP para.19.5.1

An appeal from a decision of a Registrar must be filed at the Royal Courts of Justice in London.

PD IP para.19.5.2

An appeal from a decision of a District Judge sitting in a district registry of the High Court may be filed—
(1) at the Royal Courts of Justice in London; or
(2) in that district registry.

PD IP para.19.6

The court centres at which appeals from decisions of county courts on any particular Circuit must be filed, managed and heard (unless the appeal court otherwise orders) are as follows—
Midland Circuit: Birmingham
North Eastern Circuit: Leeds or Newcastle upon Tyne
Northern Circuit: Manchester or Liverpool
Wales Circuit: Cardiff, Caernarfon or Mold
Western Circuit: Bristol
South Eastern Circuit: Royal Courts of Justice.

PD IP para.19.7

Where the lower court is a county court—
  (1) an appeal or application for permission to appeal from a decision of a District Judge will be heard or considered by a High Court Judge or by any person authorised under s.9 of the Senior Courts Act 1981 to act as a judge of the High Court in the Chancery Division;
  (2) an appeal or application for permission to appeal from a decision of a Recorder or a Circuit Judge will be heard or considered by a High Court Judge or by a person authorised under paras (1), (2) or (4) of the table in s.9(1) of the Senior Courts Act 1981 to act as a judge of the High Court in the Chancery Division;
  (3) other applications in any appeal or application for permission to appeal may be heard or considered and directions may be given by a High Court Judge or by any person authorised under s.9 of the Senior Courts Act 1981 to act as a judge of the High Court in the Chancery Division.

PD IP para.19.8

In the case of appeals from decisions of Registrars or District Judges in the High Court, appeals, applications for permission to appeal and other applications may be heard or considered and directions may be given by a High Court Judge or by any person authorised under s.9 of the Senior Courts Act 1981 to act as a judge of the High Court in the Chancery Division.

PD IP para.19.9.1

CPR Pt 52 and ss.I and IV of PD 52 and its forms shall, as appropriate, apply to appeals in insolvency proceedings, save as provided below.

PD IP para.19.9.2

Paragraphs 8.2 to 8.8, 8.13, 8.14 and 8A.1 of PD 52 shall not apply, and para.8.9 shall apply with the exclusion of the last sentence.

See also **Bankruptcy, Bankruptcy Court, Company insolvency, Part 8 procedure, Personal insolvency, Statutory demand, Validation order, Warrant of execution**, and **Winding up proceedings**.

INSPECTION OF DOCUMENTS

Documents referred to in statements of case, etc.

Pt 31 r.31.14

  (1) A party may inspect a document mentioned in—
      (a) a **statement of case**;
      (b) a **witness statement**;
      (c) a **witness summary**; or
      (d) an **affidavit**.

Documents mentioned in expert's report

PD 31A r.7.1

If a party wishes to inspect documents referred to in the **expert report** of another party, before issuing an application he should request inspection of the documents informally, and inspection should be provided by agreement unless the request is unreasonable.

Application for inspection

Pt 33 r.35.10

    (2) Subject to r.35.10(4) [which makes provision in relation to instructions referred to in an expert's report], a party may apply for an order for inspection of any document mentioned in an expert's report which has not already been disclosed in the proceedings.

PD 31A para.7.1

If a party wishes to inspect documents referred to in the expert report of another party, before issuing an application he should request inspection of the documents informally, and inspection should be provided by agreement unless the request is unreasonable.

PD 31A para.7.2

Where an expert report refers to a large number or volume of documents and it would be burdensome to copy or collate them, the court will only order inspection of such documents if it is satisfied that it is necessary for the just disposal of the proceedings and the party cannot reasonably obtain the documents from another source.

Claim to withhold inspection of a document

Pt 31 r.31.19

    (3) A person who wishes to claim that he has a right or a duty to withhold inspection of a document, or part of a document, must state in writing—
        (a) that he has such a right or duty; and
        (b) the grounds on which he claims that right or duty.
    (4) The statement referred to in para.(3) must be made—
        (a) in the list in which the document is disclosed; or
        (b) if there is no list, to the person wishing to inspect the document.
    (5) A party may apply to the court to decide whether a claim made under para.(3) should be upheld.
    (6) For the purpose of deciding an application under para.(1) (application to withhold disclosure) or para.(3) (claim to withhold inspection) the court may—
        (a) require the person seeking to inspection of a document to produce that document to the court; and
        (b) invite any person, whether or not a party, to make representations.
    (7) An application under para.(5) must be supported by evidence.

(8) This Part does not affect any rule of law which permits or requires a document to be withheld from disclosure or inspection on the ground that its disclosure or inspection would damage the public interest.

Inspection in stages

Pt 31 r.31.13

The parties may agree in writing, or the court may direct, that disclosure or inspection or both shall take place in stages.

Specific inspection

Pt 31 r.31.12

(1) The court may make an order for specific disclosure or specific inspection.
(2) An order for specific disclosure is an order that a party must do one or more of the following things—
(3) An order for specific inspection is an order that a party permit inspection of a document referred to in r. 31.3(2) [see above].

(R. 78.26 contains rules in relation to the disclosure and inspection of evidence arising out of mediation of certain cross-border disputes.)

Inspection and copying of documents

Pt 31 r.31.15

Where a party has a right to inspect a document—
(a) that party must give the party who disclosed the document written notice of his wish to inspect it;
(b) the party who disclosed the document must permit inspection not more than 7 days after the date on which he received the notice; and
(c) that party may request a copy of the document and, if he also undertakes to pay reasonable copying costs, the party who disclosed the document must supply him with a copy not more than seven days after the date on which he received the request.

Restriction on use of a privileged document inspection of which has been inadvertently allowed

Pt 31 r.31.20

Where a party inadvertently allows a privileged document to be inspected, the party who has inspected the document may use it or its contents only with the permission of the court.

Consequence of failure to permit inspection

Pt 31 r.31.21

A party may not rely on any document which he fails to disclose or in respect of which he fails to permit inspection unless the court gives permission.

Right of inspection of a disclosed document

Pt 31 r.31.3

(1) A party to whom a document has been disclosed has a right to inspect that document except where—
    (a) the document is no longer in the control of the party who disclosed it;
    (b) the party disclosing the document has a right or a duty to withhold inspection of it;
    (c) paragraph (2) applies; or
    (d) rule 78.26 applies.
(2) Where a party considers that it would be disproportionate to the issues in the case to permit inspection of documents within a category or class of document disclosed under r.31.6(b) [standard disclosure]—
    (a) he is not required to permit inspection of documents within that category or class; but
    (b) he must state in his disclosure statement that inspection of those documents will not be permitted on the grounds that to do so would be disproportionate.

Supply of documents to a non-party from court records

Pt 5 r.5.4C

(1B) No document—
    (a) relating to an application under r.78.24(1) for a mediation settlement enforcement order;
    (b) annexed to a mediation settlement enforcement order made under r.78.24(5);
    (c) relating to an application under r.78.26(1) or otherwise for disclosure or inspection of mediation evidence; or
    (d) annexed to an order for disclosure or inspection made under r.78.26 or otherwise,
may be inspected without the court's permission.

Witness statements for inspection

Pt 32 r.32.13

(1) A witness statement which stands as evidence in chief is open to inspection during the course of the trial unless the court otherwise directs.
(2) Any person may ask for a direction that a witness statement is not open to inspection.
(3) The court will not make a direction under para.(2) unless it is satisfied that a witness statement should not be open to inspection because of—
    (a) the interests of justice;
    (b) the public interest;
    (c) the nature of any expert medical evidence in the statement;
    (d) the nature of any confidential information (including information relating to personal financial matters) in the statement; or
    (e) the need to protect the interests of any child or protected party.
(4) The court may exclude from inspection words or passages in the statement.

INTELLECTUAL PROPERTY CLAIMS

Pt 63 r.63.1

(1) Part [63] applies to all intellectual property claims including—
  (a) registered intellectual property rights such as—
    (i) patents; (ii) registered designs; and (iii) registered trade marks; and
  (b) unregistered intellectual property rights such as—
    (i) copyright; (ii) design right; (iii) the right to prevent passing off; and (iv) the other rights set out in PD 63.

(2) In this Part—
  (j) 'the register' means whichever of the following registers is appropriate—
    (i) patents maintained by the Comptroller under s.32 of the 1977 Act;
    (ii) designs maintained by the registrar under s.17 of the Registered Designs Act 1949;
    (iii) Trade marks maintained by the registrar under s.63 of the 1994 Act;
    (iv) Community trade marks maintained by the Office for Harmonisation in the Internal Market under art.83 of Council Regulation (EC) No.40/94;
    (v) Community designs maintained by the Office for Harmonisation in the Internal Market under art.72 of Council Regulation (EC) No.6/2002; and
    (vi) Plant varieties maintained by the Controller under reg.12 of the Plant Breeders' Rights Regulations 1998; and
  (k) 'the registrar' means—
    (i) the registrar of trade marks; or (ii) the registrar of registered designs, whichever is appropriate.

Allocation

Pt 63 r.63.1

(3) Claims to which this Part applies are allocated to the **Multi-track**.

Registered trade marks and other intellectual property rights

Pt 63 r.63.13

Claims relating to matters arising out of the 1994 Act and other intellectual property rights set out in PD 63 must be started in—
  (a) the Chancery Division;
  (b) a patents county court; or
  (c) save as set out in PD 63, a county court where there is also a Chancery District Registry.

Service of documents and participation by the Comptroller

Pt 63 r.63.14

(1) Subject to para.(2), Pt 6 applies to service of a claim form and any document in any proceedings under this Part.
(2) A claim form relating to a registered right may be served—

    (a) on a party who has registered the right at the address for service given for that right in the UK Patent Office register, provided the address is within the UK; or

    (b) in accordance with rr.6.32(1), 6.33(1) or 6.33(2) on a party who has registered the right at the address for service given for that right in the appropriate register at—

        (i) the UK Patent Office; or

        (ii) the Office for Harmonisation in the Internal Market.

(3) Where a party seeks any remedy (whether by claim form, counterclaim or application notice), which would if granted affect an entry in any UK Patent Office register, that party must serve on the Comptroller or registrar—

    (a) the claim form, counterclaim or application notice;

    (b) any other statement of case where relevant (including any amended statement of case); and

Participation by the comptroller

Pt 63 r.63.15

Where the documents set out in r.63.14(3) are served, the Comptroller or registrar—

    (a) may take part in proceedings; and

    (b) need not serve a defence or other statement of case unless the court orders otherwise.

Appeals from decisions of the comptroller or the registrar

Pt 63 r.63.16

    (1) Part 52 applies to appeals from decisions of the Comptroller and the registrar.

    (2) Appeals about patents must be made to the Patents Court, and other appeals to the Chancery Division.

    (3) Where Pt 52 requires a document to be served, it must also be served on the Comptroller or registrar, as appropriate.

Reference to the court by an appointed person

PD 63 para.25.1

This paragraph applies where a person appointed by the Lord Chancellor to hear and decide appeals under s.77 of the 1994 Act, refers an appeal to the Chancery Division under s.76(3) of the 1994 Act.

PD 63 para.25.2

The appellant must file a claim form seeking the court's determination of the appeal within 14 days of receiving notification of the decision to refer.

PD 63 para.25.3

The appeal will be deemed to have been abandoned if the appellant does not file a claim form within the period prescribed by para.25.2.

PD 63 para.25.4

The period prescribed under para.25.2 may be extended by—
(1) the person appointed by the Lord Chancellor; or
(2) the court
where the appellant so applies, even if such application is not made until after the expiration of that period.

Costs

PD 63 para.26.1

Where the court makes an order for delivery up or destruction of infringing goods, or articles designed or adapted to make such goods, the person against whom the order is made must pay the costs of complying with that order unless the court orders otherwise.

PD 63 para.26.2

Where the court finds that an intellectual property right has been infringed, the court may, at the request of the applicant, order appropriate measures for the dissemination and publication of the judgment to be taken at the expense of the infringer.

See also **Patents County Court**, **Patents and registered designs**, **Registered trade marks and other intellectual property rights**.

INTER PARTES

With notice.

INTEREST

Arbitration awards

Pt 62 r.62.19

(1) Where an applicant seeks to enforce an award of interest the whole or any part of which relates to a period after the date of the award, he must file a statement giving the following particulars—
   (a) whether simple or compound interest was awarded;
   (b) the date from which interest was awarded;
   (c) where rests were provided for, specifying them;
   (d) the rate of interest awarded; and
   (e) a calculation showing—
       (i) the total amount claimed up to the date of the statement; and
       (ii) any sum which will become due on a daily basis.
(2) A statement under para.(1) must be filed whenever the amount of interest has to be quantified for the purpose of—
   (a) obtaining a judgment or order under s.66 of the 1996 Act (enforcement of the award); or

(b) enforcing such a judgment or order.

Claim form

Pt 16 r.16.2

(1) The claim form must—
(cc) where the claimant's only claim is for a specified sum, contain a statement of the interest accrued on that sum.

Costs Order

Pt 44 r.44.12

(2) Interest payable pursuant to s.17 of the Judgments Act 1838 or s.74 of the County Courts Act 1984 on the costs deemed to have been ordered under para.(1) shall begin to run from the date on which the event which gave rise to the entitlement to costs occurred.

Debts of a deceased person

PD 40A para.14

(1) Where an account of the debts of a deceased person is directed by any judgment, unless the deceased's estate is insolvent or the court orders otherwise, interest shall be allowed—
(a) on any debt which carries interest, at the rate it carries, and
(b) on any other debt, from the date of the judgment, at the rate payable on judgment debts at that date.
(2) Where interest on a debt is allowed under paragraph (1)(b), it shall be paid out of any assets of the estate which remain after payment of—
(a) any costs of the proceedings directed to be paid out of the estate;
(b) all the debts which have been established; and
(c) the interest on such of those debts as by law carry interest.
(3) For the purpose of this rule—
(a) 'debt' includes funeral, testamentary or administration expenses; and
(b) in relation to any expenses incurred after the judgment, para.(1)(b) applies as if, instead of the date of the judgment, it referred to the date when the expenses became payable.

Default judgment

Pt 12 r.12.6

(1) A default judgment on a claim for a specified amount of money obtained on the filing of a request may include the amount of interest claimed to the date of judgment if—
(a) the particulars of claim include the details required by r.16.4;
(b) where interest is claimed under s.35A of the Supreme Court Act 1981 or s.69 of the County Courts Act 1984, the rate is no higher than the rate of interest payable on judgment debts at the date when the claim form was issued; and

(c) the claimant's request for judgment includes a calculation of the interest claimed for the period from the date up to which interest was stated to be calculated in the claim form to the date of the request for judgment.

(2) In any case where para.(1) does not apply, judgment will be for an amount of interest to be decided by the court.

Judgment debts

Pt 40 r.40.8

(1) Where interest is payable on a judgment pursuant to s.17 of the Judgments Act 1838 or s.74 of the County Courts Act 1984, the interest shall begin to run from the date that judgment is given unless—
(a) a r. in another Part or a PD makes different provision; or
(b) the court orders otherwise.

(2) The court may order that interest shall begin to run from a date before the date that judgment is given.

Interest on High Court judgment debts

Judgments Act 1838 s.17

(1) Every judgment debt shall carry interest at the rate of 8 pounds per centum per annum from such time as shall be prescribed by rules of court until the same shall be satisfied, and such interest may be levied under a writ of execution on such judgment.

(2) Rules of court may provide for the court to disallow all or part of any interest otherwise payable under subsection (1).

Interest on county court judgment debts

CCA 1984 s.74

(1) The Lord Chancellor may by order provide that any sums to which this subsection applies shall carry interest at such rate and between such times as may be prescribed by the order.

(2) The sums to which subs.(1) applies are—
(a) sums payable under judgments or orders given or made in a county court, including sums payable by instalments; and
(b) sums which by virtue of any enactment are, if the county court so orders, recoverable as if payable under an order of that court, and in respect of which the county court has so ordered.

(3) The payment of interest due under subs.(1) shall be enforceable as a sum payable under the judgment or order.

(4) The power conferred by subs.(1) includes power—
(a) to specify the descriptions of judgment or order in respect of which interest shall be payable;
(b) to provide that interest shall be payable only on sums exceeding a specified amount;
(c) to make provision for the manner in which and the periods by reference to which the interest is to be calculated and paid;

    (d) to provide that any enactment shall or shall not apply in relation to interest payable under subs.(1) or shall apply to it with such modifications as may be specified in the order; and

    (e) to make such incidental or supplementary provisions as the Lord Chancellor considers appropriate.

  (5) Without prejudice to the generality of subs.(4), an order under subs.(1) may provide that the rate of interest shall be the rate specified in s.17 of **the Judgments Act 1838** as that enactment has effect from time to time.

(5A) The power conferred by subs.(1) includes power to make provision enabling a county court to order that the rate of interest applicable to a sum expressed in a currency other than sterling shall be such rate as the court thinks fit (instead of the rate otherwise applicable)

  (6) The power to make an order under subs.(1) shall be exercisable by statutory instrument.

[The current rate of interest is the same as in the High Court, i.e. 8 per cent per annum [since April 1, 1993]].

Enforcement proceedings

PD 70 para.6

If a judgment creditor is claiming interest on a judgment debt, he must include in his application or request to issue enforcement proceedings in relation to that judgment details of—

  (1) the amount of interest claimed and the sum on which it is claimed;

  (2) the dates from and to which interest has accrued; and

  (3) the rate of interest which has been applied and, where more than one rate of interest has been applied, the relevant dates and rates.

Legacies

PD 40A para.15

Where an account of legacies is directed by any judgment, then, subject to—

  (a) any directions contained in the will or codicil in question; and

  (b) any order made by the court,

interest shall be allowed on each legacy at the basic rate payable for the time being on funds in court or at such other rate as the court shall direct, beginning one year after the testator's death.

Part 36 offer

Pt 36 r.36

  (3) A Pt 36 offer which offers to pay or offers to accept a sum of money will be treated as inclusive of all interest until—

    (a) the date on which the period stated under r.36.2(2)(c) expires; or

    (b) if r.36.2(3) applies, a date 21 days after the date the offer was made.

INTERIM COSTS CERTIFICATE

Pt 47 r.47.16

   (1) The court may at any time after the receiving party has filed a request for a detailed assessment hearing—
      (a) issue an interim costs certificate for such sum as it considers appropriate;
      (b) amend or cancel an interim certificate.
   (2) An interim certificate will include an order to pay the costs to which it relates, unless the court orders otherwise.
   (3) The court may order the costs certified in an interim certificate to be paid into court.
   (4) Where the court—
      (a) issues an interim costs certificate; or
      (b) amends or cancels an interim certificate,
   in detailed assessment proceedings pursuant to an order under s.194(3) of the Legal Services Act 2007, the receiving party must send a copy of the interim costs certificate or the order amending or cancelling the interim costs certificate to the prescribed charity.

Power to issue an interim certificate

PD 47 para.15

A party wishing to apply for an interim certificate may do so by making an application in accordance with Pt 23.

INTERIM DECLARATION

Pt 25 r.25.1

   (1) (b) The court may grant an interim declaration.

INTERIM INJUNCTION

Injunction

Glossary

A court order prohibiting a person from doing something or requiring a person to do something.

Pt 25 r.25.1

   (1) The court may grant the following interim remedies—
      (a) an interim injunction.
   (4) The court may grant an interim remedy whether or not there has been a claim for a final remedy of that kind.

Jurisdiction

PD 25A para.1.1

High Court Judges and any other Judge duly authorised may grant '**search orders**' and '**freezing injunctions**'.

PD 25A para.1.2

In a case in the High Court, Masters and district judges have the power to grant injunctions:
   (1) by consent,
   (2) in connection with charging orders and appointments of receivers,
   (3) in aid of execution of judgments.

PD 25A para.1.3

In any other case any judge who has jurisdiction to conduct the trial of the action has the power to grant an injunction in that action.

PD 25A para.1.4

A Master or district judge has the power to vary or discharge an injunction granted by any Judge with the consent of all the parties.

Making an application

PD 25A para.2.1

The application notice must state:
   (1) the order sought, and
   (2) the date, time and place of the hearing.

PD 25A para.2.2

The application notice and evidence in support must be served as soon as practicable after issue and in any event not less than 3 days before the court is due to hear the application.

PD 25A para.2.3

Where the court is to serve, sufficient copies of the application notice and evidence in support for the court and for each respondent should be filed for issue and service.

PD 25A para.2.4

Whenever possible a draft of the order sought should be filed with the application notice and a disk containing the draft should also be available to the court in a format compatible with the word processing software used by the court. This will enable the court officer to arrange for any amendments to be incorporated and for the speedy preparation and sealing of the order.

Evidence

PD 25A para.3.1

Applications for search orders and freezing injunctions must be supported by affidavit evidence.

PD 25A para.3.2

Applications for other interim injunctions must be supported by evidence set out in either:
- (1) a witness statement, or
- (2) a statement of case provided that it is verified by a statement of truth; or
- (3) the application provided that it is verified by a statement of truth,
    unless the court, an Act, a rule or a PD requires evidence by affidavit.

PD 25A para.3.3

The evidence must set out the facts on which the applicant relies for the claim being made against the respondent, including all material facts of which the court should be made aware.

PD 25A para.3.4

Where an application is made without notice to the respondent, the evidence must also set out why notice was not given.
(See Pt 32 and PD 32 for information about evidence).

Urgent applications and applications without notice

PD 25A para.4.1

These fall into two categories:
- (1) applications where a claim form has already been issued, and
- (2) applications where a claim form has not yet been issued,
and, in both cases, where notice of the application has not been given to the respondent.

PD 25A para.4.2

These applications are normally dealt with at a court hearing but cases of extreme urgency may be dealt with by telephone.

PD 25A para.4.3

Applications dealt with at a court hearing after issue of a claim form:
- (1) the application notice, evidence in support and a draft order (as in para.2.4 above) should be filed with the court two hours before the hearing wherever possible,
- (2) if an application is made before the application notice has been issued, a draft order (as in para.2.4 above) should be provided at the hearing, and the application notice and evidence in support must be filed with the court on the same or next working day or as ordered by the court, and
- (3) except in cases where secrecy is essential, the applicant should take steps to notify the respondent informally of the application.

PD 25A para.4.4

Applications made before the issue of a claim form:
  (1) in addition to the provisions set out at para.4.3 above, unless the court Orders otherwise, either the applicant must undertake to the court to issue a claim form immediately or the court will give directions for the commencement of the claim.
  (2) where possible the claim form should be served with the order for the injunction,
  (3) an order made before the issue of a claim form should state in the title after the names of the applicant and respondent 'the Claimant and Defendant in an Intended Action'.

Orders for injunctions

PD 25A para.5.1

Any order for an injunction, unless the court Orders otherwise, must contain:
  (1) an undertaking by the applicant to the court to pay any damages which the respondent sustains which the court considers the applicant should pay.
  (2) if made without notice to any other party, an undertaking by the applicant to the court to serve on the respondent the application notice, evidence in support and any order made as soon as practicable,
  (3) if made without notice to any other party, a return date for a further hearing at which the other party can be present,
  (4) if made before filing the application notice, an undertaking to file and pay the appropriate fee on the same or next working day, and
  (5) if made before issue of a claim form—
      (a) an undertaking to issue and pay the appropriate fee on the same or next working day, or
      (b) directions for the commencement of the claim.

PD 25A para.5.1A

When the court makes an order for an injunction, it should consider whether to require an undertaking by the applicant to pay any damages sustained by a person other than the respondent, including another party to the proceedings or any other person who may suffer loss as a consequence of the order.

PD 25A para.5.2

An order for an injunction made in the presence of all parties to be bound by it or made at a hearing of which they have had notice, may state that it is effective until trial or further order.

PD 25A para.5.3

Any order for an injunction must set out clearly what the respondent must do or not do.

Injunctions against third parties

PD 25A para.9.1

The following provisions apply to orders which will affect a person other than the applicant or respondent, who:

(1) did not attend the hearing at which the order was made; and

(2) is served with the order.

PD 25A para.9.2

Where such a person served with the order requests—

(1) a copy of any materials read by the judge, including material prepared after the hearing at the direction of the judge or in compliance with the order; or

(2) a note of the hearing,

the applicant, or his legal representative, must comply promptly with the request, unless the court orders otherwise.

Interim injunction to cease if claim is stayed

Pt 25 r.25.10

If—

(a) the court has granted an interim injunction other than a freezing injunction; and

(b) the claim is stayed other than by agreement between the parties,

the interim injunction shall be set aside unless the court Orders that it should continue to have effect even though the claim is stayed.

Interim injunction to cease after 14 days if claim struck out

Pt 25 r.25.11

(1) If—

(a) the court has granted an interim injunction; and

(b) the claim is struck out under r.3.7 (sanctions for non-payment of certain fees),

the interim injunction shall cease to have effect 14 days after the date that the claim is struck out unless para.(2) applies.

(2) If the claimant applies to reinstate the claim before the interim injunction ceases to have effect under para.(1), the injunction shall continue until the hearing of the application unless the court orders otherwise.

Application for an Interim Anti-social Behaviour Order under the Crime and Disorder Act 1998

Pt 65 r.65.26

(1) An application for an interim order under s.1D of the 1998 Act must be made in accordance with Pt 25.

(2) The application should normally be made—

(a) in the claim form or application notice seeking the order; and

(b) on notice to the person against whom the order is sought.

See **Freezing injunction**, **Interim remedies**, **Search order**, and **Telephone hearings**.

INTERIM PAYMENT

Pt 25 r.25.1(1)

(k) An order (referred to as an order for interim payment) under r.25.6 for payment by a defendant on account of any damages, debt or other sum (except costs) which the court may hold the defendant liable to pay.

Pt 25 r.25.6

(1) The claimant may not apply for an order for an interim payment before the end of the period for filing an acknowledgment of service applicable to the defendant against whom the application is made.

(R.10.3 sets out the period for filing an **acknowledgment of service**).

(2) The claimant may make more than one application for an order for an interim payment.

(3) A copy of an application notice for an order for an interim payment must—
   (a) be served at least 14 days before the hearing of the application; and
   (b) be supported by evidence.

(4) If the respondent to an application for an order for an interim payment wishes to rely on written evidence at the hearing, he must—
   (a) file the written evidence; and
   (b) serve copies on every other party to the application,
   at least seven days before the hearing of the application.

(5) If the applicant wishes to rely on written evidence in reply, he must—
   (a) file the written evidence; and
   (b) serve a copy on the respondent,
   at least three days before the hearing of the application.

(6) This rule does not require written evidence—
   (a) to be filed if it has already been filed; or
   (b) to be served on a party on whom it has already been served.

(7) The court may order an interim payment in one sum or in instalments.

(Part 23 contains general rules about applications).

PD 25B para.2A.2

If the Guidance on the application for interim payment shows that the account is bound to result in a payment to the applicant the count will, before making an order for interim payment, order that the liable party pay to the applicant "the amount shown by the account to be due."

Conditions to be satisfied and matters to be taken into account

Pt 25 r.25.7

(1) The court may only make an order for an interim payment where any of the following conditions are satisfied—
   (a) the defendant against whom the order is sought has admitted liability to pay damages or some other sum of money to the claimant;
   (b) the claimant has obtained judgment against that defendant for damages to be assessed or for a sum of money (other than costs) to be assessed;
   (c) it is satisfied that, if the claim went to trial, the claimant would obtain judgment for a substantial amount of money (other than costs) against the defendant from whom

he is seeking an order for an interim payment whether or not that defendant is the only defendant or one of a number of defendants to the claim;

(d) the following conditions are satisfied—

    (i) the claimant is seeking an order for possession of land (whether or not any other order is also sought); and

    (ii) the court is satisfied that, if the case went to trial, the defendant would be held liable (even if the claim for possession fails) to pay the claimant a sum of money for the defendant's occupation and use of the land while the claim for possession was pending; or

(e) in a claim in which there are two or more defendants and the order is sought against any one or more of those defendants, the following conditions are satisfied—

    (i) the court is satisfied that, if the claim went to trial, the claimant would obtain judgment for a substantial amount of money (other than costs) against at least one of the defendants (but the court cannot determine which); and

    (ii) all the defendants are either—

        (a) a defendant that is insured in respect of the claim;

        (b) a defendant whose liability will be met by an insurer under s.151 of the Road Traffic Act 1988 or an insurer acting under the Motor Insurers Bureau Agreement, or the Motor Insurers Bureau where it is acting itself; or

        (c) a defendant that is a public body.

(4) The court must not order an interim payment of more than a reasonable proportion of the likely amount of the final judgment.

(5) The court must take into account—

    (a) contributory negligence; and

    (b) any relevant set-off or counterclaim.

Evidence

PD 25B para.2.1

An application for an interim payment of damages must be supported by evidence dealing with the following:

(1) the sum of money sought by way of an interim payment,

(2) the items or matters in respect of which the interim payment is sought,

(3) the sum of money for which final judgment is likely to be given,

(4) the reasons for believing that the conditions set out in r.25.7 are satisfied,

(5) any other relevant matters,

(6) in claims for personal injuries, details of special damages and past and future loss, and

(7) in a claim under the Fatal Accidents Act 1976, details of the person(s) on whose behalf the claim is made and the nature of the claim.

PD 25B para 2.2

Any documents in support of the application should be exhibited, including, in personal injuries claims, the medical report(s).

PD 25B para 2.3

If a respondent to an application for an interim payment wishes to rely on written evidence at the hearing he must comply with the provisions of r.25.6(4).

PD 25B para 2.4

If the applicant wishes to rely on written evidence in reply he must comply with the provisions of r.25.6(5).

Powers of court where it has made an order for interim payment

Pt 25 r.25.8

(1) Where a defendant has been ordered to make an interim payment, or has in fact made an interim payment (whether voluntarily or under an order), the court may make an order to adjust the interim payment.

(2) The court may in particular—
    (a) order all or part of the interim payment to be repaid;
    (b) vary or discharge the order for the interim payment;
    (c) order a defendant to reimburse, either wholly or partly, another defendant who has made an interim payment.

(3) The court may make an order under para.(2)(c) only if—
    (a) the defendant to be reimbursed made the interim payment in relation to a claim in respect of which he has made a claim against the other defendant for a contribution, indemnity or other remedy; and
    (b) where the claim or part to which the interim payment relates has not been discontinued or disposed of, the circumstances are such that the court could make an order for interim payment under r.25.7.

(4) The court may make an order under this rule without an application by any party if it makes the order when it disposes of the claim or any part of it.

(5) Where—
    (a) a defendant has made an interim payment; and
    (b) the amount of the payment is more than his total liability under the final judgment or order,
    the court may award him interest on the overpaid amount from the date when he made the interim payment.

Instalments

PD 25B para.3

Where an interim payment is to be paid in instalments the order should set out:
    (1) the total amount of the payment,
    (2) the amount of each instalment,
    (3) the number of instalments and the date on which each is to be paid, and
    (4) to whom the payment should be made.

Adjustment of final judgment figure

PD 25B para.5.1

In this paragraph 'judgment' means:
    (1) any order to pay a sum of money,
    (2) a final award of damages,

(3) an assessment of damages.

PD 25B para.5.2 and PD 40B para.6.1

In a final judgment where an interim payment has previously been made which is less than the total amount awarded by the judge, the order should set out in a preamble:
(1) the total amount awarded by the judge, and
(2) the amounts and dates of the interim payment(s).

PD 25B para.5.3 and PD 40B para.6.2

The total amount awarded by the judge should then be reduced by the total amount of any interim payments, and an order made for entry of judgment and payment of the balance.

PD 25B para.5.4 and PD 40B para.6.3

In a final judgment where an interim payment has previously been made which is more than the total amount awarded by the judge, the order should set out in a preamble:
(1) the total amount awarded by the judge, and
(2) the amounts and dates of the interim payment(s).

PD 25B para.5.5 and PD 40B para.6.4

An order should then be made for repayment, reimbursement, variation or discharge under r.25.8(2) and for interest on an overpayment under r.25.8(5).

Compensation recovery payments

PD 25B para.4.1

Where in a claim for personal injuries there is an application for an interim payment of damages—
(1) which is other than by consent;
(2) which either—
    (i) falls under the heads of damage set out in column 1 of Schedule 2 to the Social Security (Recovery of Benefits) Act 1997 ('the 1997 Act') in respect of recoverable benefits received by the claimant set out in column 2 of that Schedule; or
    (ii) includes damages in respect of a disease for which a lump sum payment within the definition in s.1A(2) of the 1997 Act has been, or is likely to be made; and
(3) where the defendant is liable to pay a recoverable amount (as defined in r.36.15(1)(c)) to the Secretary of State,
the defendant should obtain from the Secretary of State a certificate (as defined in r.36.15(1)(e)).

PD 25B para.4.2

A copy of the certificate must be filed at the hearing of the application for an interim payment.

PD 25B para.4.3

The order will set out the deductible amount (as defined in r.36.15(1)(d)).

PD 25B para.4.4

The payment made to the claimant will be the net amount but the interim payment for the purposes of para.5 below will be the gross amount.

Restriction on disclosure of an interim payment

Pt 25 r.25.9

The fact that a defendant has made an interim payment, whether voluntarily or by court order, shall not be disclosed to the trial judge until all questions of liability and the amount of money to be awarded have been decided unless the defendant agrees.

Voluntary payment to child or protected person

PD 25B para.1.2

The permission of the court must be obtained before making a voluntary interim payment in respect of a claim by a **child** or **protected party**.

See also **Interim remedy**.

INTERIM POSSESSION ORDER

Pt 55 r.55.20

(1) This section of [Pt 55] applies where the claimant seeks an Interim Possession order [IPO].
(3) Where this section requires an act to be done within a specified number of hours, r.2.8(4) [Where the specified period (a) is five days or less; and (b) includes (i) a Saturday or Sunday; or (ii) a Bank Holiday, Christmas Day or Good Friday, that day does not count] does not apply.

Conditions for IPO application

Pt 55 r.55.21

(1) An application for an IPO may be made where the following conditions are satisfied—
(a) the only claim made is a possession claim against trespassers for the recovery of premises [has the same meaning as in s.12 of the Criminal Law Act 1977];
(b) the claimant—
(i) has an immediate right to possession of the premises; and

    (ii) has had such a right throughout the period of alleged unlawful occupation; and

  (c) the claim is made within 28 days of the date on which the claimant first knew, or ought reasonably to have known, that the defendant (or any of the defendants), was in occupation.

(2) An application for an IPO may not be made against a defendant who entered or remained on the premises with the consent of a person who, at the time consent was given, had an immediate right to possession of the premises.

Application

Pt 55 r.55.22

(1) Rules 55.3(1) [The claim must be started in the county court for the district in which the land is situated unless para.(2) applies or an enactment provides otherwise] and (4) [Where, in a possession claim against trespassers, the claimant does not know the name of a person in occupation or possession of the land, the claim must be brought against 'persons unknown' in addition to any named defendants] apply to the claim.

(2) The claim form and the defendant's form of witness statement must be in the form set out in PD 55A.

(3) When he files his claim form, the claimant must also file—
  (a) an application notice in the form set out in PD 55A; and
  (b) written evidence.

(4) The written evidence must be given—
  (a) by the claimant personally; or
  (b) where the claimant is a body corporate, by a duly authorised officer.

(Rule 22.1(6)(b) provides that the statement of truth must be signed by the maker of the witness statement).

(5) The court will—
  (a) issue—
    (i) the claim form; and
    (ii) the application for the IPO; and
  (b) set a date for the hearing of the application.

(6) The hearing of the application will be as soon as practicable but not less than 3 days after the date of issue.

Service

Pt 55 r.55.23

(1) Within 24 hours of the issue of the application, the claimant must serve on the defendant—
  (a) the claim form;
  (b) the application notice together with the written evidence in support; and
  (c) a blank form for the defendant's witness statement (as set out in PD 55A) which must be attached to the application notice.

(2) The claimant must serve the documents listed in para.(1) in accordance with r.55.6(a).

(3) At or before the hearing the claimant must file a certificate of service in relation to the documents listed in para.(1) and r.6.17(2)(a) does not apply.

Defendant's response

Pt 55 r.55.24

    (1) At any time before the hearing the defendant may file a witness statement in response to the application.

    (2) The witness statement should be in the form set out in PD 55A.

Hearing of the application

Pt 55 r.55.25

    (1) In deciding whether to grant an IPO, the court will have regard to whether the claimant has given, or is prepared to give, the following undertakings in support of his application—

        (a) if, after an IPO is made, the court decides that the claimant was not entitled to the order to—

            (i) reinstate the defendant if so ordered by the court; and

            (ii) pay such damages as the court may order; and

        (b) before the claim for possession is finally decided, not to—

            (i) damage the premises;

            (ii) grant a right of occupation to any other person; and

            (iii) damage or dispose of any of the defendant's property.

    (2) The court will make an IPO if—

        (a) the claimant has—

            (i) filed a certificate of service of the documents referred to in r.55.23(1); or

            (ii) proved service of those documents to the satisfaction of the court; and

        (b) the court considers that—

            (i) the conditions set out in r.55.21(1) are satisfied; and

            (ii) any undertakings given by the claimant as a condition of making the order are adequate.

    (3) An IPO will be in the form set out in PD 55A and will require the defendant to vacate the premises specified in the claim form within 24 hours of the service of the order.

    (4) On making an IPO the court will set a date for the hearing of the claim for possession which will be not less than 7 days after the date on which the IPO is made.

    (5) Where the court does not make an IPO—

        (a) the court will set a date for the hearing of the claim;

        (b) the court may give directions for the future conduct of the claim; and

        (c) subject to such directions, the claim shall proceed in accordance with s.I of this Part.

Service and enforcement of the IPO

Pt 55 r.55.26

    (1) An IPO must be served within 48 hours after it is sealed.

    (2) The claimant must serve the IPO on the defendant together with copies of

        (a) the claim form; and

        (b) the written evidence in support, in accordance with r.55.6(a).

    (3) CCR Ord.26 r.17 does not apply to the enforcement of an IPO.

(4) If an IPO is not served within the time limit specified by this rule, the claimant may apply to the court for directions for the claim for possession to continue under s.I of this Part.

After IPO made

Pt 55 r.55.27

(1) Before the date for the hearing of the claim, the claimant must file a certificate of service in relation to the documents specified in r.55.26(2).
(2) The IPO will expire on the date of the hearing of the claim.
(3) At the hearing the court may make any order it considers appropriate and may, in particular—
    (a) make a final order for possession;
    (b) dismiss the claim for possession;
    (c) give directions for the claim for possession to continue under s.I of this Part; or
    (d) enforce any of the claimant's undertakings.
(4) Unless the court directs otherwise, the claimant must serve any order or directions in accordance with r.55.6(a).
(5) CCR Ord.24 r.6 applies to the enforcement of a final order for possession.

Application to set aside IPO

Pt 55 r.55.28

(1) If the defendant has left the premises, he may apply on grounds of urgency for the IPO to be set aside before the date of the hearing of the claim.
(2) An application under para.(1) must be supported by a witness statement.
(3) On receipt of the application, the court will give directions as to—
    (a) the date for the hearing; and
    (b) the period of notice, if any, to be given to the claimant and the method of service of any such notice.
(4) No application to set aside an IPO may be made under r.39.3.
(5) Where no notice is required under para.(3)(b), the only matters to be dealt with at the hearing of the application to set aside are whether—
    (a) the IPO should be set aside; and
    (b) any undertaking to re-instate the defendant should be enforced,
and all other matters will be dealt with at the hearing of the claim.
(6) The court will serve on all the parties—
    (a) a copy of the order made under para.(5); and
    (b) where no notice was required under para.(3)(b), a copy of the defendant's application to set aside and the witness statement in support.
(7) Where notice is required under para.(3)(b), the court may treat the hearing of the application to set aside as the hearing of the claim.

PD 55A para.9.1

The claim form must be in Form N5, the application notice seeking the interim possession order must be in Form N130 and the defendant's witness statement must be in Form N133.

PD 55A para.9.2

The IPO will be in Form N134 (annexed to this PD).

See also **Possession claims**.

INTERIM REMEDIES

Pt 25 r.25.1

(1) The court may grant the following interim remedies—
   (a) an **interim injunction**;
   (b) an **interim declaration**;
   (c) an order—
      (i) for the detention, custody or preservation of relevant property;
      (ii) for the inspection of relevant property;
      (iii) for the taking of a sample of relevant property;
      (iv) for the carrying out of an experiment on or with relevant property;
      (v) for the sale of relevant property which is of a perishable nature or which for any other good reason it is desirable to sell quickly; and
      (vi) for the payment of income from relevant property until a claim is decided;
   (d) an order authorising a person to enter any land or building in the possession of a party to the proceedings for the purposes of carrying out an order under subpara.(c);
   (e) an order under s.4 of the Torts (Interference with Goods) Act 1977 to deliver up goods;
   (f) an order (referred to as a '**freezing injunction**')—
      (i) restraining a party from removing from the jurisdiction assets located there; or
      (ii) restraining a party from dealing with any assets whether located within the jurisdiction or not;
   (g) an order directing a party to provide information about the location of relevant property or assets or to provide information about relevant property or assets which are or may be the subject of an application for a freezing injunction;
   (h) an order (referred to as a 'search order') under s.7 of the Civil Procedure Act 1997 (order requiring a party to admit another party to premises for the purpose of preserving evidence, etc.);
   (i) an order under s.33 of the Supreme Court Act 1981 or s.52 of the County Courts Act 1984 (order for disclosure of documents or inspection of property before a claim has been made);
   (j) an order under s.34 of the Supreme Court Act 1981 or s.53 of the County Courts Act 1984 (order in certain proceedings for disclosure of documents or inspection of property against a non-party);
   (k) an order (referred to as an order for interim payment) under r.25.6 for payment by a defendant on account of any damages, debt or other sum (except costs) which the court may hold the defendant liable to pay;
   (l) an order for a specified fund to be paid into court or otherwise secured, where there is a dispute over a party's right to the fund;
   (m) an order permitting a party seeking to recover personal property to pay money into court pending the outcome of the proceedings and directing that, if he does so, the property shall be given up to him;
   (n) an order directing a party to prepare and file accounts relating to the dispute;
   (o) an order directing any account to be taken or inquiry to be made by the court; and
   (p) an order under art.9 of Council Directive (EC) 2004/48 on the enforcement of intellectual property rights (order in intellectual property proceedings making the continuation of an alleged infringement subject to the lodging of guarantees).

(Rule 34.2 provides for the court to issue a **witness summons** requiring a witness to produce documents to the court at the hearing or on such date as the court may direct).

    (2) In para.(1)(c) and (g), 'relevant property' means property (including land) which is the subject of a claim or as to which any question may arise on a claim.

    (3) The fact that a particular kind of interim remedy is not listed in para.(1) does not affect any power that the court may have to grant that remedy.

    (4) The court may grant an interim remedy whether or not there has been a claim for a final remedy of that kind.

Time when an order for an interim remedy may be made

Pt 25 r.25.2

    (1) An order for an interim remedy may be made at any time, including—
        (a) before proceedings are started; and
        (b) after judgment has been given.
(Rule 7.2 provides that proceedings are started when the court issues a claim form).

    (2) However—
        (a) Paragraph (1) is subject to any rule, PD or other enactment which provides otherwise;
        (b) the court may grant an interim remedy before a claim has been made only if—
            (i) the matter is urgent; or
            (ii) it is otherwise desirable to do so in the interests of justice; and
        (c) unless the court otherwise orders, a defendant may not apply for any of the orders listed in r.25.1(1) before he has filed either an acknowledgment of service or a defence.
(Part 10 provides for filing an **acknowledgment of service** and Pt 15 for **filing** a **defence**).

    (3) Where it grants an interim remedy before a claim has been commenced, the court should give directions requiring a claim to be commenced.

    (4) In particular, the court need not direct that a claim be commenced where the application is made under s.33 of the Supreme Court Act 1981 or s.52 of the County Courts Act 1984 (order for disclosure, inspection etc. before commencement of a claim).

How to apply for an interim remedy

Pt 25 r.25.3

    (1) The court may grant an interim remedy on an application made without notice if it appears to the court that there are good reasons for not giving notice.

    (2) An application for an interim remedy must be supported by evidence, unless the court orders otherwise.

    (3) If the applicant makes an application without giving notice, the evidence in support of the application must state the reasons why notice has not been given.
(Part 3 lists general powers of the court).
(Part 23 contains general rules about making an application).

Application for an interim remedy where there is no related claim

Pt 25 r.25.4

    (1) This rule applies where a party wishes to apply for an interim remedy but—
        (a) the remedy is sought in relation to proceedings which are taking place, or will take place, outside the jurisdiction; or

(b) the application is made under s.33 of the Supreme Court Act 1981 or s.52 of the County Courts Act 1984 (order for disclosure, inspection etc. before commencement) before a claim has been commenced.
(2) An application under this rule must be made in accordance with the general rules about applications contained in Pt 23.
(The following provisions are also relevant—
Rule 25.5 (inspection of property before commencement or against a non-party)
Rule 31.16 (orders for disclosure of documents before proceedings start)
Rule 31.17 (orders for disclosure of documents against a person not a party)

Inspection of property before commencement or against a non-party

Pt 25 r.25.5

(1) This rule applies where a person makes an application under—
(a) section 33(1) of the Supreme Court Act 1981 or s.52(1) of the County Courts Act 1984 (inspection etc. of property before commencement);
(b) section 34(3) of the Supreme Court Act 1981 or s.53(3) of the County Courts Act 1984 (inspection, etc. of property against a non-party).
(2) The evidence in support of such an application must show, if practicable by reference to any statement of case prepared in relation to the proceedings or anticipated proceedings, that the property—
(a) is or may become the subject matter of such proceedings; or
(b) is relevant to the issues that will arise in relation to such proceedings.
(3) A copy of the **application notice** and a copy of the evidence in support must be served on—
(a) the person against whom the order is sought; and
(b) in relation to an application under s.34(3) of the Supreme Court Act 1981 or s.53(3) of the County Courts Act 1984, every party to the proceedings other than the applicant.

See also **Interim imjunction**.

INTERLOCUTORY REMEDY

See **Interim remedy**.

INTERPLEADER PROCEEDINGS

High Court

Entitlement to relief by way of interpleader

RSC Ord.17 r.1

(1) Where—
(a) a person is under a liability in respect of a debt or in respect of any money, goods or chattels and he is, or expects to be, sued for or in respect of that debt or money or those goods or chattels by two or more persons making adverse claims thereto; or

(b) claim is made to any money, goods or chattels taken or intended to be taken by a sheriff in execution under any process, or to the proceeds or value of any such goods or chattels, by a person other than the person against whom the process is issued, the person under liability as mentioned in sub-para.(a) or (subject to r.2) the sheriff, may apply to the court for relief by way of interpleader.

(2) References in this Order to a sheriff shall be construed as including references to—

   (a) an individual authorised to act as an enforcement officer under the Courts Act 2003; and

   (b) any other officer charged with the execution of process by or under the authority of the High Court.

Claim to goods, etc. taken in execution

RSC Ord.17 r.2

(1) Any person making a claim to or in respect of any money, goods or chattels taken or intended to be taken in execution under process of the court, or to the proceeds or value of any such goods or chattels, must give notice of his claim to the sheriff charged with the execution of the process and must include in his notice a statement of his address, and that address shall be his address for service.

(2) On receipt of a claim made under this rule the sheriff must forthwith give notice thereof to the execution creditor and the execution creditor must, within seven days after receiving the notice, give notice to the sheriff informing him whether he admits or disputes the claim. An execution creditor who gives notice in accordance with this paragraph admitting a claim shall only be liable to the sheriff for any fees and expenses incurred by the sheriff before receipt of that notice.

(3) Where—

   (a) the sheriff receives a notice from an execution creditor under para.(2) disputing a claim, or the execution creditor fails, within the period mentioned in that paragraph, to give the required notice; and

   (b) the claim made under this rule is not withdrawn, the sheriff may apply to the court for relief under this order.

(4) A sheriff who receives a notice from an execution creditor under paragraph (2) admitting a claim made under this rule shall withdraw from possession of the money, goods or chattels claimed and may apply to the court for relief under this order of the following kind, that is to say, an order restraining the bringing of a claim against him for or in respect of his having taken possession of that money or those goods or chattels.

Claim in respect of goods protected from seizure

RSC Ord.17 r.2A

(1) Where a judgment debtor whose goods have been seized, or are intended to be seized, by a sheriff under a writ of execution claims that such goods are not liable to execution by virtue of s.138(3A) of the Act, he must within five days of the seizure give notice in writing to the sheriff identifying all those goods in respect of which he makes such a claim and the grounds of such claim in respect of each item.

(2) Upon receipt of a notice of claim under para.(1), the sheriff must forthwith give notice thereof to the execution creditor and to any person who has made a claim to, or in respect of, the goods under r.2(1) and the execution creditor and any person who has made claim must, within seven days of receipt of such notice, inform the sheriff in writing whether he admits or disputes the judgment debtor's claim in respect of each item.

(3) The sheriff shall withdraw from possession of any goods in respect of which the judgment debtor's claim is admitted or if the execution creditor or any person claiming

under r.2(1) fails to notify him in accordance with para.(2) and the sheriff shall so inform the parties in writing.

(4) Where the sheriff receives notice from—
   (a) the execution creditor; or
   (b) any such person to whom notice was given under para.(2), that the claim or any part thereof is disputed, he must forthwith seek the directions of the court and may include therein an application for an order restraining the bringing of any claim against him for, or in respect of, his having seized any of those goods or his having failed so to do.

(5) The sheriff's application for directions under para.(4) shall be made by an application in accordance with CPR Pt 23 and, on the hearing of the application, the court may—
   (a) determine the judgment debtor's claim summarily; or
   (b) give such directions for the determination of any issue raised by such claim as may be just.

(6) A Master and a district judge of a district registry shall have power to make an order of the kind referred to in para.(4) and the reference to Master shall be construed in accordance with r.4.

Mode of application

RSC Ord.17 r.3

(1) An application for relief under this order must be made by claim form unless made in an existing claim, in which case it must be made by accordance with CPR Pt 23.

(2) Where the applicant is a sheriff who has withdrawn from possession of money, goods or chattels taken in execution and who is applying for relief under r.2(4) the claim form must be served on any person who made a claim under that rule to or in respect of that money or those goods or chattels, and that person may attend the hearing of the application.

(4) Subject to para.(5) a claim form or application notice under this rule must be supported by evidence that the applicant—
   (a) claims no interest in the subject-matter in dispute other than for charges or costs;
   (b) does not collude with any of the claimants to that subject-matter; and
   (c) is willing to pay or transfer that subject-matter into court or to dispose of it as the court may direct.

(5) Where the applicant is a sheriff, he shall not provide such evidence as is referred to in para.(4) unless directed by the court to do so.

(6) Any person who makes a claim under r.2 and who is served with a claim form under this rule shall within 14 days serve on the execution creditor and the sheriff a witness statement or affidavit specifying any money and describing any goods and chattels claimed and setting out the grounds upon which such claim is based.

(7) Where the applicant is a sheriff a claim form under this rule must give notice of the requirement in para.(6).

To whom sheriff may apply for relief

RSC Ord.17 r.4

An application to the court for relief under this order may, if the applicant is a sheriff, be made—
   (a) where the claim in question is proceeding in the Royal Courts of Justice, to a Master or, if the execution to which the application relates has been or is to be levied in the district of a District Registry, either to a Master or to the district judge of that Registry;

(b) where the claim in question is proceeding in a District Registry, to the district judge of that Registry or, if such execution has been or is to be levied in the district of some other District Registry or outside the district of any District Registry, either to the said district judge or to the district judge of that other registry or to a Master as the case may be.

Where the claim in question is proceeding in the Admiralty Court or the Family Division, references in this rule to a Master shall be construed as references to the Admiralty Registrar or to a Registrar of that Division.

Powers of court hearing claim

RSC Ord.17 r.5

(1) Where on the hearing of a claim under this order all the persons by whom adverse claims to the subject-matter in dispute (hereafter in this Order referred to as 'the interpleader claimants') appear, the court may order—
   (a) that any interpleader claimant be made a defendant in any claim pending with respect to the subject-matter in dispute in substitution for or in addition to the applicant for relief under this order; or
   (b) that an issue between the interpleader claimants be stated and tried and may direct which of the interpleader claimants is to be claimant and which defendant.
(2) Where—
   (a) the applicant under this order is a sheriff;
   (b) all the interpleader claimants consent or any of them so requests; or
   (c) the question at issue between the interpleader claimants is a question of law and the facts are not in dispute,
   the court may summarily determine the question at issue between the interpleader claimants and make an order accordingly on such terms as may be just.
(3) Where an interpleader claimant, having been duly served with a claim form under this order, does not appear at the hearing or, having appeared, fails or refuses to comply with an order made in the proceedings, the court may make an order declaring the interpleader claimant, and all persons claiming under him, for ever barred from prosecuting his claim against the applicant for such relief and all persons claiming under him, but such an order shall not affect the rights of the interpleader claimants as between themselves.

Power to order sale of goods taken in execution

RSC Ord.17 r.6

Where an application for relief under this order is made by a sheriff who has taken possession of any goods or chattels in execution under any process, and an interpleader claimant alleges that he is entitled, under a bill of sale or otherwise, to the goods or chattels by way of security for debt, the court may order those goods or chattels or any part thereof to be sold and may direct that the proceeds of sale be applied in such manner and on such terms as may be just and as may be specified in the order.

Power to stay proceedings

RSC Ord.17 r.7

Where a defendant to a claim applies for relief under this Order in the claim, the court may by order stay all further proceedings in the claim.

Other powers

RSC Ord.17 r.8

(1) Subject to the foregoing rules of this Order, the court may in or for the purposes of any interpleader proceedings make such order as to costs or any other matter as it thinks just.

(2) Where the interpleader claimant fails to appear at the hearing, the Court may direct that the sheriff's and execution creditor's costs shall be assesed by a master or, where the hearing was heard in a district registry, by a district judge of that registry and the following CPR rules shall apply—

    (a) 44.4 (basis of assessment);

    (b) 44.5 (factors to be taken into account in deciding the amount of costs);

    (c) 48.4 (limitations on court's power to award costs in favour of trustee or personal representative); and

    (d) 48.6 (litigants in person).

(3) Where the claim in question is proceeding in the Admiralty Court or the Family Division, references in this rule to a Master shall be construed as references to the Admiralty Register or to a Registrar of that Division.

One order in several proceedings

RSC Ord.17 r.9

Where the Court considers it necessary or expedient to make an order in any interpleader proceedings in several proceedings pending in several Divisions, or before different judges of the same Division, the court may make such an order; and the order shall be entitled in all those causes or matters and shall be binding on all the parties to them.

Disclosure

RSC Ord.17 r.10

CPR Pts 31 and 18 shall, with the necessary modifications, apply in relation to an interpleader issue as they apply in relation to any other proceedings.

Trial of interpleader issue

RSC Ord.17 r.11

(1) CPR Pt 39 shall, with the necessary modifications, apply to the trial of an interpleader issue as it applies to the trial of a claim.

(2) The court by whom an interpleader issue is tried may give such judgment or make such order as finally to dispose of all questions arising in the interpleader proceedings.

County court—under execution

Notice of claim

CCR Ord.33 r.1

(A1) In this Part of this order 'the interpleader claimant' means any person making a claim to or in respect of goods seized in execution or the proceeds or value thereof and 'the interpleader claim' means that claim.

(1) The interpleader claimant shall deliver to the bailiff holding the warrant of execution, or file in the office of the court for the district in which the goods were seized, notice of his claim stating—

    (a) the grounds of the interpleader claim or, in the case of a claim for rent, the particulars required by s.102(2) of the Act; and

    (b) the interpleader claimant's full name and address.

(2) On receipt of an interpleader claim made under this rule, the court shall—

    (a) send notice thereof to the execution creditor; and

    (b) except where the interpleader claim is to the proceeds or value of the goods, send to the interpleader claimant a notice requiring him to make a deposit or give security in accordance with s.100 of the Act.

Reply to interpleader claim

CCR Ord.33 r.2

(1) Within four days after receiving notice of an interpleader claim under r.1(2) the execution creditor shall give notice to the court informing him whether he admits or disputes the interpleader claim or requests the district judge to withdraw from possession of the goods or money claimed.

(2) If, within the period aforesaid, the execution creditor gives notice to the court admitting the interpleader claim or requesting the district judge to withdraw from possession of the goods or money claimed, the execution creditor shall not be liable to the district judge for any fees or expenses incurred after receipt of the notice.

Order protecting district judge

CCR Ord.33 r.3

Where the execution creditor gives the court such a notice as is mentioned in r.2(2), the district judge shall withdraw from possession of the goods or money claimed and may apply to the judge, on notice to the interpleader claimant, for an order restraining the bringing of a claim against the district judge for or in respect of his having taken possession of the goods or money and on the hearing of the application the judge may make such order as may be just.

Issue of interpleader proceedings

CCR Ord.33 r.4

(1) Where the execution creditor gives notice under r.2(1) disputing an interpleader claim made under r.1 or fails, within the period mentioned in r.2(1), to give the notice required by that rule, the district judge shall, unless the interpleader claim is withdrawn, issue an interpleader notice to the execution creditor and the interpleader claimant.

(2) On the issue of an interpleader notice under para.(1) the court officer shall enter the proceedings in the records of the court, fix a day for the hearing by the judge and prepare sufficient copies of the notice for service under this rule.

(3) Subject to para.(4) the notice shall be served on the execution creditor and the interpleader claimant in the manner set out in CPR r.6.20.

(4) Service shall be effected not less than 14 days before the return day.

Claim for damages

CCR Ord.33 r.5

Where in interpleader proceedings under an execution the interpleader claimant claims from the execution creditor or the district judge, or the execution creditor claims from the district judge, damages arising or capable of arising out of the execution—

(a) the party claiming damages shall, within eight days after service of the notice on him under r.4(3), give notice of this claim to the court and to any other party against whom the claim is made, stating the amount and the grounds of the claim; and

(b) the party from whom damages are claimed may pay money into court in satisfaction of the claim as if the interpleader proceedings were a claim brought in accordance with CPR Pt 7 by the person making the claim.

County court—otherwise than under execution

Application for relief

CCR Ord.33 r.6

(1) Where a person (in this Part of this order called 'the applicant') is under a liability in respect of a debt or any money or goods and he is, or expects to be, sued for or in respect of the debt, money or goods by two or more persons making adverse claims thereto ('the interpleader claimants'), he may apply to the court, in accordance with these rules, for relief by way of interpleader.

(2) The application shall be made to the court in which the claim is pending against the applicant or, if no claim is pending against him, to the court in which he might be sued.

(3) The application shall be made by filing a witness statement or affidavit showing that—

(a) the applicant claims no interest in the subject-matter in dispute other than for charges or costs;

(b) the applicant does not collude with any of the interpleader claimants; and

(c) the applicant is willing to pay or transfer the subject-matter into court or to dispose of it as the court may direct,

together with as many copies of the witness statement or affidavit as there are interpleader claimants.

Relief in pending claim

CCR Ord.33 r.7

Where the applicant is a defendant in a pending claim—

(a) the witness statement or affidavit and copies required by r.6(3) shall be filed within 14 days after service on him of the claim form;

(b) the return day of the application shall be a day fixed for the pre-trial review of the claim including the interpleader proceedings and, if a day has already been fixed for the pre-trial review or hearing of the claim, the court shall, if necessary, postpone it;

(c) the interpleader claimant, the applicant and the claimant in the claim shall be given notice of the application, which shall be prepared by the court together with sufficient copies for service;

(d) the notice to the interpleader claimant shall be served on him, together with a copy of the witness statement or affidavit filed under r.6(3) and of the claim form and particulars of claim in the claim, not less than 21 days before the return day in the same manner as an interpleader notice in accordance with r.4(3);

(e) the notices to the applicant and the claimant shall be sent to them by the court and the notice to the claimant shall be accompanied by a copy of the said witness statement or affidavit.

Relief otherwise than in pending claim

CCR Ord.33 r.8

Where the applicant is not a defendant in a pending claim—

(a) the court shall enter the proceedings in the records of the court;

(b) the court shall fix a day for the pre-trial review or, if the court so directs, a day for the hearing of the proceedings and shall prepare and issue an interpleader notice, together with sufficient copies for service;

(c) the notice together with a copy of the witness statement or affidavit filed under r.6(3), shall be served on each of the claimants not less than 21 days before the return day in the same manner as an interpleader notice to be served under r.4(3); and

(d) the court shall deliver or send a notice of issue to the applicant.

Payment into court, etc.

CCR Ord.33. r.9

Before or after the court officer proceeds under rr.7 or 8 the district judge may direct the applicant to bring the subject-matter of the proceedings into court, or to dispose of it in such manner as the district judge thinks fit, to abide the order of the court.

Reply by interpleader claimant

CCR Ord.33 r.10

(1) An interpleader claimant shall, within 14 days after service on him of the notice under r.7(c) or the interpleader notice under r.8(c), file—

(a) a notice that he makes no interpleader claim; or

(b) particulars stating the grounds of his interpleader claim to the subject-matter, together in either case with sufficient copies for service under para.(2).

(2) The court shall send to each of the other parties a copy of any notice or particulars filed under para.(1).

(3) The court may, if it thinks fit, hear the proceedings although no notice or particulars have been filed.

Order barring interpleader claim, etc.

CCR Ord.33 r.11

(1) Where an interpleader claimant does not appear on any day fixed for a pre-trial review or the hearing of interpleader proceedings, or fails or refuses to comply with an order made in the proceedings, the court may make an order barring his interpleader claim.

(2) If, where the applicant is a defendant in a pending claim, the claimant does not appear on any day fixed for a pre-trial review or the hearing of the interpleader proceedings, the claim including the interpleader proceedings may be struck out.

(3) In any other case where a day is fixed for the hearing of interpleader proceedings, the court shall hear and determine the proceedings and give judgment finally determining the rights and claims of the parties.

(4) Where the court makes an order barring the interpleader claim of an interpleader claimant, the order shall declare the interpleader claimant, and all persons claiming under him, forever barred from prosecuting his interpleader claim against the applicant and all persons claiming under him, but unless the interpleader claimant has filed a notice under r.10 that he makes no interpleader claim, such an order shall not affect the rights of the interpleader claimants as between themselves.

INTERPRETERS

Deaf and hearing impaired litigants

Her Majesty's Courts & Tribunals Service will meet the reasonable costs of interpreters for deaf and hearing-impaired litigants for hearings in civil proceedings.

If the deaf person wants such a friend or relative to interpret, he/she will need to ask for permission from the Judge. The Judge must be satisfied that the friend or relative can exactly interpret what is being said to the court and what the court is saying to the deaf person.

Unless the relative or friend has a recognised qualification in relaying information between deaf and hearing people, it may be better to use a qualified interpreter. The friend or relative may still be able to attend and provide support, but permission should be sought from the Judge first.

If an interpreter is needed, the court will make arrangements for an interpreter to attend.

Welsh language

PD relating to the use of the Welsh language in cases in the civil courts in Wales, para.5.1.

Whenever an interpreter is needed to translate evidence from English to Welsh or from Welsh to English, the Court Manager in whose court the case is to be heard will take steps to secure the attendance of an interpreter whose name is included in the list of approved court.

(As soon as it is known that the Welsh language is to be used at a hearing details should be provided to HMCTS' Welsh Language Unit by e-mailing *welsh.language.unit.manager @hmcts.gsi.gov.uk* who will arrange a Welsh interpeter. HMCTS is responsible for paying the interpreter's fees).

INTERVENTION IN SOLICITOR'S OFFICE

Proceedings under Sch.1 to the Solicitors Act 1974

Pt 67 r.67.4

(1) Proceedings in the High Court under Schedule 1 to the Act must be brought—
    (a) in the Chancery Division; and
    (b) by Pt 8 claim form, unless para.(4) below applies.

(2) The heading of the claim form must state that the claim relates to a solicitor and is made under Sch.1 to the Act.

(3) Where proceedings are brought under paras 6(4) or 9(8) of Sch.1 to the Act, the court will give directions and fix a date for the hearing immediately upon issuing the claim form.

(4) If the court has made an order under Sch.1 to the Act, any subsequent application for an order under that Schedule which has the same parties may be made by a Pt 23 application in the same proceedings.

(5) The table [in Pt 67] sets out who must be made a defendant to each type of application under Sch.1.

(6) At any time after the Law Society has issued an application for an order under para.5 of Sch.1 to the Act, the court may, on an application by the Society—
    (a) make an interim order under that paragraph to have effect until the hearing of the application; and
    (b) order the defendant, if he objects to the order being continued at the hearing, to file and serve written evidence showing cause why the order should not be continued.

IRREGULAR JUDGMENT

See **Default judgment**.

J

JOINDER OF PARTIES

Pt 19 r.19.1

Any number of claimants or defendants may be joined as parties to a claim.

JOINT ENTITLEMENT TO REMEDY

Provisions applicable where two or more persons are jointly entitled to a remedy

Pt 1 r.19.3

(1) Where a claimant claims a remedy to which some other person is jointly entitled with him, all persons jointly entitled to the remedy must be parties unless the court orders otherwise.
(2) If any person does not agree to be a claimant, he must be made a defendant, unless the court Orders otherwise.
(3) This rule does not apply in probate proceedings.

JOINT LIABILITY

Glossary

Parties who are jointly liable share a single liability and each party can be held liable for the whole of it.
See also **Several liability**.

JUDGE

Pt 2 r.2.3(1)

Unless the context otherwise requires, a judge, Master or district judge or a person authorised to act as such.

Power of judge, master or district judge to perform functions of the court

Pt 2 r.2.4

Where these rules provide for the court to perform any act then, except where an enactment, rule or PD provides otherwise, that act may be performed—
  (a) in relation to proceedings in the High Court, by any judge, Master or district judge of that Court; and
  (b) in relation to proceedings in a county court, by any judge or district judge.

PD 2B para.1.1

Rule 2.4 provides that Judges, Masters and District Judges may exercise any function of the court except where an enactment, rule or PD provides otherwise. This PD sets out the matters over which Masters and District Judges do not have jurisdiction or which they may deal with only on certain conditions. It does not affect jurisdiction conferred by other enactments. Reference should also be made to other relevant PDs (e.g. Pt 24, para.3 and Pt 26, paras 12.1–10). References to Circuit Judges include Recorders and Assistant Recorders and references to Masters and District Judges include Deputies.

PD 2B para.1.2

Wherever a Master or District Judge has jurisdiction, he may refer the matter to a Judge instead of dealing with it himself.

High Court

Injunctions

PD 2B para.2.1

Search orders (r.25.1(1)(h)), freezing orders (r.25.1(1)(f)), an ancillary order under r.25.1(1)(g) and orders authorising a person to enter land to recover, inspect or sample property (r.25.1(1)(d)) may only be made by a Judge.

PD 2B para.2.2

Except where paras 2.3 and 2.4 apply, injunctions and orders relating to injunctions, including orders for specific performance where these involve an injunction, must be made by a Judge.

PD 2B para.2.3

A Master or a District Judge may only make an injunction:
  (a) in terms agreed by the parties;
  (b) in connection with or ancillary to a charging order;
  (c) in connection with or ancillary to an order appointing a receiver by way of equitable execution; or
  (d) in proceedings under r.66.7 (order restraining person from receiving sum due from the Crown).

PD 2B para.2.4

A Master or District Judge may make an order varying or discharging an injunction or undertaking given to the court if all parties to the proceedings have consented to the variation or discharge.

Other pre-trial orders and interim remedies

PD 2B para.3.1

A Master or District Judge may not make orders or grant interim remedies:
  (a) relating to the liberty of the subject;
  (b) relating to criminal proceedings or matters except procedural applications in appeals to the High Court (including appeals by case stated) under any enactment;
  (c) relating to a claim for judicial review, except that interim applications in claims for judicial review may be made to Masters of the Queen's Bench Division.
  (d) relating to appeals from Masters or District Judges;
  (e) in appeals against costs assessment under Pts 43 to 48, except on an appeal under r.47.20 against the decision of an authorised court officer.
  (f) in applications under s.42 of the Senior Courts Act 1981 by a person subject to a Civil or a Criminal or an All Proceedings order (vexatious litigant) for permission to start or continue proceedings.
  (g) in applications under s.139 of the Mental Health Act 1983 for permission to bring proceedings against a person.

Trials and assessments of damages

PD 2B para.4.1

A Master or District Judge may, subject to any PD, try a case which is treated as being allocated to the multi-track because it is proceeding under Pt 8 (see r.8.9(c)). He may try a case which has been allocated to the multi-track under Pt 26 only with the consent of the parties. Restrictions on the trial jurisdiction of Masters and District Judges do not prevent them from hearing applications for summary judgment or, if the parties consent, for the determination of a preliminary issue.

PD 2B para.4.2

A Master or a District Judge may assess the damages or sum due to a party under a judgment without limit as to the amount.

Family proceedings

PD 2B para.3.2

[PD 2] is not concerned with Family proceedings. It is also not concerned with proceedings in the Family Division except to the extent that such proceedings can be dealt with in the Chancery Division or the Family Division, e.g. proceedings under the Inheritance (Provision for Family and Dependants) Act 1975 or under s.14 of the Trusts of Land and Appointment of Trustees Act

1996. District Judges (including District Judges of the Principal Registry of the Family Division) have jurisdiction to hear such proceedings, subject to any Direction given by the President of the Family Division.

Chancery proceedings

PD 2B para.5.1

In proceedings in the Chancery Division, a Master or a district judge may not deal with the following without the consent of the Chancellor of the High Court—
- (a) approving compromises (other than applications under the Inheritance (Provision for Family and Dependants) Act 1975) (i) on behalf of a person under disability where that person's interest in a fund, or if there is no fund, the maximum amount of the claim, exceeds £100,000 and (ii) on behalf of absent, unborn and unascertained persons;
- (b) making declarations, except in plain cases;
- (c) making final orders under s.1(1) of the Variation of Trusts Act 1958, except for the removal of protective trusts where the interest of the principal beneficiary has not failed or determined;
- (d) where the proceedings are brought by a Part 8 claim form, seeking determination of any question of law or as to the construction of a document which is raised by the claim form;
- (e) giving permission to executors, administrators and trustees to bring or defend proceedings or to continue the prosecution or defence of proceedings, and granting an indemnity for costs out of the trust estate, except in plain cases;
- (f) granting an indemnity for costs out of the assets of a company on the application of minority shareholders bringing a derivative action, except in plain cases;
- (g) making an order for rectification, except for—
  - (i) rectification of the register under the Land Registration Act 1925; or
  - (ii) alteration or rectification of the register under the Land Registration Act 2002, in plain cases;
- (h) making orders to vacate entries in the register under the Land Charges Act 1972, except in plain cases;
- (i) making final orders on applications under s.19 of the Leasehold Reform Act 1967, s.48 of the Administration of Justice Act 1985 and ss.21 and 25 of the Law of Property Act 1969;
- (j) making final orders under the Landlord and Tenant Acts 1927 and 1954, except (i) by consent, and (ii) orders for interim rents under ss.24A to 24D of the 1954 Act;
- (k) making orders in proceedings in the Patents Court except—
  - (i) orders by way of settlement, except settlement of procedural disputes;
  - (ii) applications for extension of time;
  - (iii) applications for permission to serve out of the jurisdiction;
  - (iv) applications for security for costs;
  - (v) other matters as directed by a judge of the court; and
  - (vi) enforcement of money judgments.

PD 2B para.5.2

A Master or District Judge may only give directions for early trial after consulting the Judge in charge of the relevant list.

PD 2B para.5.3

Where a winding-up order has been made against a company, any proceedings against the company by or on behalf of debenture holders may be dealt with, at the Royal Courts of Justice, by a Registrar and, in a District Registry with insolvency jurisdiction, by a District Judge.

Assignment of claims to masters and transfer between masters

PD 2B para.6.1

The Senior Master, and the Chief Master will make arrangements for proceedings to be assigned to individual Masters. They may vary such arrangements generally or in particular cases, for example, by transferring a case from a Master to whom it had been assigned to another Master.

PD 2B para.6.2

The fact that a case has been assigned to a particular Master does not prevent another Master from dealing with that case if circumstances require, whether at the request of the assigned Master or otherwise.

Freezing orders: cross examination of deponents about assets

PD 2B para.7

Where the court has made a freezing order under r.25.1(f) and has ordered a person to make a witness statement or affidavit about his assets and to be cross-examined on its contents, unless the Judge directs otherwise, the cross-examination will take place before a Master or a District Judge, or if the Master or District Judge directs, before an examiner of the Court.

Human rights

PD 2B para.7A

A deputy High Court Judge, a Master or District Judge may not try—
  (1) a case in a claim made in respect of a judicial act under the Human Rights Act 1998, or
  (2) a claim for a declaration of incompatibility in accordance with s.4 of the Human Rights Act 1998.

County courts

Injunctions, anti-social behaviour orders and committal

PD 2B para.8.1

Injunctions which a county court has jurisdiction to make may only be made by a Circuit Judge, except:
  (a) where the injunction is to be made in proceedings which a District Judge otherwise has jurisdiction to hear (see para.11.1 below);
  (b) where the injunction is sought in a money claim which has not yet been allocated to a track and the amount claimed does not exceed the fast track financial limit;
  (c) in the circumstances provided by para.2.3;
  (d) where the injunction is to be made under any of the following provisions—
    (i) section 153A, 153B or 153D of the Housing Act 1996;

    (ii) section 3 of the Protection from Harassment Act 1997; or

    (iii) sections 34, 40 or 41 of the Policing and Crime Act 2009.

PD 2B para.8.1A

A District Judge has jurisdiction to make an order under—

    (1) section 1B or 1D of the Crime and Disorder Act 1998 (anti-social behaviour);

    (2) section 26A, 26B or 26C of the Anti-social Behaviour Act 2003 (parenting Orders); and

    (3) section 4 or 9 of the Violent Crime Reduction Act 2006 (**drinking banning Orders**).

PD 2B para.8.2

A District Judge may make orders varying or discharging injunctions in the circumstances provided by para.2.4.

PD 2B para 8.3

A District Judge may only make an order committing a person to prison or attach a power of arrest to an injunction or remand a person where an enactment authorises this: see s.23 of the Attachment of Earnings Act 1971, ss.14 and 118 of the County Courts Act 1984, ss.153C, 153D and ss.154–158 of and Sch.15 to the Housing Act 1996, ss.36, 40–45 and 48 of and Sch.5 to the Policing and Crime Act 2009, and the relevant rules.

Homelessness appeals

PD 2B para.9

A District Judge may not hear appeals under s.204 or s.204A of the Housing Act 1996.

Other pre-trial orders and interim remedies

PD 2B para.10.1

In addition to the restrictions on jurisdiction mentioned at paras 8.1–3, para.3.1(d) and (e) above applies.

Trials and assessments of damages

PD 2B para.11.1

A District Judge has jurisdiction to hear the following:

    (a) any claim which has been allocated to the small claims track or fast track or which is treated as being allocated to the multi-track under r.8.9(c) and the Table at section B of PD 8A, except claims:

        (i) under Pt I of the Landlord and Tenant Act 1927;

        (ii) for a new tenancy under s.24 or for the termination of a tenancy under s.29(2) of the Landlord and Tenant Act 1954;

        (iii) for an order under ss.38 or 40 of the Landlord and Tenant Act 1987;

(iv) under paras 26 or 27 of Sch.11 to or s.27 of the Agricultural Holdings Act 1986;
(v) under s.45(2) of the Matrimonial Causes Act 1973 for a declaration of legitimation by virtue of the Legitimacy Act 1976;
(vi) under ss.35, 38 or 40 of the Fair Trading Act 1973; or
(vii) under Pt II of the Mental Health Act 1983.
(b) proceedings for the recovery of land, proceedings under s.82A(2) of the Housing Act 1985 or s.6A(2) of the Housing Act 1988 (demotion claims) or proceedings in a county court under Ch.1A of the Housing Act 1996 (demoted tenancies);
(c) the assessment of damages or other sum due to a party under a judgment without any financial limit;
(d) with the permission of the Designated Civil Judge in respect of that case, any other proceedings.

PD 2B para.11.2

A case allocated to the small claims track may only be assigned to a Circuit Judge to hear with his consent.

Freezing orders: cross examination of deponents about assets

PD 2B para.12

To the extent that a county court has power to make a freezing order, para.7 applies as appropriate.

Distribution of business between circuit judge and district judge

PD 2B para.13

Where both the Circuit Judge and the District Judge have jurisdiction in respect of any proceedings, the exercise of jurisdiction by the District Judge is subject to any arrangements made by the Designated Civil Judge for the proper distribution of business between Circuit Judges and District Judges.

PD 2B para.14.1

In district registries of the High Court and in the county court, the Designated Civil Judge may make arrangements for proceedings to be assigned to individual District Judges. He may vary such arrangements generally or in particular cases.

PD 2B para 14.2

The fact that a case has been assigned to a particular District Judge does not prevent another District Judge from dealing with the case if the circumstances require.

Human rights

PD 2B para.15

A district judge may not try a case in which an allegation of indirect discrimination is made against a public authority that would, if the court finds that it occurred, be unlawful under s.19B of the Race Relations Act 1976.

Welsh language

Role of the liaison judge

PD relating to use of Welsh language in civil courts in Wales, para.7.1

If any question or difficulty arises concerning the implementation of this PD, contact should in the first place be made with the Liaison Judge for the Welsh language.

JUDGMENT CREDITOR

Pt 70 r.70.1

    (a) A person who has obtained or is entitled to enforce a judgment or order.

JUDGMENT DEBTOR

Pt 70 r.70.1

    (b) A person against whom a judgment or order was given or made.

JUDGMENTS ACT 1838

Judgment debts to carry interest

Section 17
    (1) Every judgment debt shall carry interest at the rate of 8 pounds per centum per annum from such time as shall be prescribed by rules of court until the same shall be satisfied, and such interest may be levied under a writ of execution on such judgment.
    (2) Rules of court may provide for the court to disallow all or part of any interest otherwise payable under subs.(1).

JUDGMENTS REGULATION

Pt 6 r.6.31

    (c) Council Regulation (EC) No.44/2001 of December 22, 2000 on jurisdiction and the recognition and enforcement of judgments in civil and commercial matters, as amended from time to time and as applied by the Agreement made on October 19, 2005 between the European Community and the Kingdom of Denmark on jurisdiction and the recognition and enforcement of judgments in civil and commercial matters.

JUDGMENT SUMMONS

Application for judgment summons

CCR Ord.28 r.1

(1) An application for the issue of a judgment summons may be made to the court for the district in which the debtor resides or carries on business or, if the summons is to issue against two or more persons jointly liable under the judgment or order sought to be enforced, in the court for the district in which any of the debtors resides or carries on business.

(2) The judgment creditor shall make his application by filing a request in that behalf certifying the amount of money remaining due under the judgment or order, the amount in respect of which the judgment summons is to issue and that the whole or part of any instalment due remains unpaid.

(3) The judgment creditor must file with the request all written evidence on which he intends to rely.

Mode of service

CCR Ord.28 r.2

(1) Subject to para.(2), a judgment summons shall be served personally on every debtor against whom it is issued.

(2) Where the judgment creditor or the judgment creditor's solicitor gives a certificate for postal service in respect of a debtor residing or carrying on business within the district of the court, the judgment summons will, unless the district judge otherwise directs, be served on that debtor by the court sending it to the debtor by first-class post at the address stated in the request for the judgment summons and, unless the contrary is shown, the date of service is deemed to be the seventh day after the date on which the judgment summons was sent to the debtor.

(3) Where a judgment summons has been served on a debtor in accordance with para.(2), no order of commitment shall be made against him unless—
   (a) he appears at the hearing; or
   (b) it is made under s.110(2) of the Act.

(4) The written evidence on which the judgment creditor intends to rely must be served with the judgment summons.

Time for service

CCR Ord.28 r.3

(1) The judgment summons and written evidence must be served not less than 14 days before the day fixed for the hearing.

(2) A notice of non-service will be sent pursuant to CPR r.6.18 in respect of a judgment summons which has been sent by post under r.2(2) and has been returned to the court undelivered.

(3) CPR rr.7.5 and 7.6 apply, with the necessary modifications, to a judgment summons as they apply to a claim form.

Enforcement of debtor's attendance

CCR Ord.28 r.4

    (1) Order 27, rr.7B and 8, shall apply, with the necessary modifications, to an order made under s.110(1) of the Act for the attendance of the debtor at an adjourned hearing of a judgment summons as they apply to an order made under s.23(1) of the Attachment of Earnings Act 1971 for the attendance of the debtor at an adjourned hearing of an application for an attachment of earnings order.

  (1A) An order made under s.110(1) of the Act must be served personally on the judgment debtor.

  (1B) Copies of—
      (a) the judgment summons; and
      (b) the written evidence,
    must be served with the order.

    (2) At the time of service of the order there shall be paid or tendered to the debtor a sum reasonably sufficient to cover his expenses in travelling to and from the court, unless such a sum was paid to him at the time of service of the judgment summons.

Evidence

CCR Ord.28 r.5

    (1) No person may be committed on an application for a judgment summons unless-
      (a) the order is made under s.110(2) of the Act; or
      (b) the judgment creditor proves that the debtor—
         (i) has or has had since the date of the judgment or order the means to pay the sum in respect of which he has made default; and
        (ii) has refused or neglected or refuses or neglects to pay that sum.

    (2) The debtor may not be compelled to give evidence.

Suspension of committal order

CCR Ord.28 r.7

    (1) If on the hearing of a judgment summons a committal order is made, the judge may direct execution of the order to be suspended to enable the debtor to pay the amount due.

    (2) A note of any direction given under para.(1) shall be entered in the records of the court and notice of the suspended committal order shall be sent to the debtor.

    (3) Where a judgment summons is issued in respect of one or more but not all of the instalments payable under a judgment or order for payment by instalments and a committal order is made and suspended under para.(1), the judgment or order shall, unless the judge otherwise orders, be suspended for so long as the execution of the committal order is suspended.

    (4) Where execution of a committal order is suspended under para.(1) and the debtor subsequently desires to apply for a further suspension, the debtor shall attend at or write to the court office and apply for the suspension he desires, stating the reasons for his inability to comply with the terms of the original suspension, and the court shall fix a day for the hearing of the application by the judge and give at least three days' notice thereof to the judgment creditor and the debtor.

    (5) The district judge may suspend execution of the committal order pending the hearing of an application under para.(4).

New order on judgment summons

Rule 8

(1) Where on the hearing of a judgment summons, the judge makes a new order for payment of the amount of the judgment debt remaining unpaid, there shall be included in the amount payable under the order for the purpose of any enforcement proceedings, otherwise than by judgment summons, any amount in respect of which a committal order has already been made and the debtor imprisoned.

(2) No judgment summons under the new order shall include any amount in respect of which the debtor was imprisoned before the new order was made, and any amount subsequently paid shall be appropriated in the first instance to the amount due under the new order.

Notification of order on judgment of High Court

CCR Ord.28 r.9

(1) Notice of the result of the hearing of a judgment summons on a judgment or order of the High Court shall be sent by the county court to the High Court.

(2) If a committal order or a new order for payment is made on the hearing, the office copy of the judgment or order filed in the county court shall be deemed to be a judgment or order of the court in which the judgment summons is heard.

Costs on judgment summons

CCR Ord.28 r.10

(1) No costs shall be allowed to the judgment creditor on the hearing of a judgment summons unless—
   (a) a committal order is made; or
   (b) the sum in respect of which the judgment summons was issued is paid before the hearing.

(2) Where costs are allowed to the judgment creditor,
   (a) there may be allowed—
      (i) a charge of the judgment creditor's solicitor for attending the hearing and, if the judge so directs, for serving the judgment summons;
      (ii) a fee to counsel if the court certifies that the case is fit for counsel;
      (iii) any travelling expenses paid to the debtor, and
      (iv) the court fee on the issue of the judgment summons;
   (b) the costs may be fixed and allowed without detailed assessment under CPR Pt 47.

Issue of warrant of committal

CCR Ord.28 r.11

(1) A judgment creditor desiring a warrant to be issued pursuant to a committal order shall file a request in that behalf.

(2) Where two or more debtors are to be committed in respect of the same judgment or order, a separate warrant of committal shall be issued for each of them.

(3) Where a warrant of committal is sent to a foreign court for execution, that court shall indorse on it a notice as to the effect of s.122(3) of the Act addressed to the governor of the prison of that court.

Notification to foreign court of part payment before debtor lodged in prison

CCR Ord.28 r.12

Where, after a warrant of committal has been sent to a foreign court for execution but before the debtor is lodged in prison, the home court is notified that an amount which is less than the sum on payment of which the debtor is to be discharged has been paid, the home court shall send notice of the payment to the foreign court.

Payment after debtor lodged in prison

CCR Ord.28 r.13

(1) Where, after the debtor has been lodged in prison under a warrant of committal, payment is made of the sum on payment of which the debtor is to be discharged, then—
  (a) if the payment is made to the court responsible for the execution of the warrant, the court officer shall make and sign a certificate of payment and send it by post or otherwise to the gaoler;
  (b) if the payment is made to the court which issued the warrant of committal after the warrant has been sent to a foreign court for execution, the home court shall send notice of the payment to the foreign court, and the court officer at the foreign court shall make and sign a certificate of payment and send it by post or otherwise to the gaoler;
  (c) if the payment is made to the gaoler, he shall sign a certificate of payment and send the amount to the court which made the committal order.
(2) Where, after the debtor has been lodged in prison under a warrant of committal, payment is made of an amount less than the sum on payment of which the debtor is to be discharged, then subject to para.(3), para.(1)(a) and (b) shall apply with the substitution of references to a notice of payment for the references to a certificate of payment and para.(1)(c) shall apply with the omission of the requirement to make and sign a certificate of payment.
(3) Where, after the making of a payment to which para.(2) relates, the balance of the sum on payment of which the debtor is to be discharged is paid, para.(1) shall apply without the modifications mentioned in para.(2).

Discharge of debtor otherwise than on payment

CCR Ord.28 r.14

(1) Where the judgment creditor lodges with the district judge a request that a debtor lodged in prison under a warrant of committal may be discharged from custody, the district judge shall make an order for the discharge of the debtor in respect of the warrant of committal and the court shall send the gaoler a certificate of discharge.
(2) Where a debtor who has been lodged in prison under a warrant of committal desires to apply for his discharge under s.121 of the Act, the application shall be made to the judge in writing and without notice showing the reasons why the debtor alleges that he is unable to pay the sum in respect of which he has been committed and ought to be

discharged and stating any offer which he desires to make as to the terms on which his discharge is to be ordered, and Ord.27 r.8(3) and (4), shall apply, with the necessary modifications, as it applies to an application by a debtor for his discharge from custody under s.23(7) of the Attachment of Earnings Act 1971.

(3) If in a case to which para.(2) relates the debtor is ordered to be discharged from custody on terms which include liability to re-arrest if the terms are not complied with, the judge may, on the application of the judgment creditor if the terms are not complied with, order the debtor to be re-arrested and imprisoned for such part of the term of imprisonment as remained unserved at the time of discharge.

(4) Where an order is made under para.(3), a duplicate warrant of committal shall be issued, indorsed with a certificate signed by the court officer as to the order of the judge.

JUDGMENTS AND ORDERS

Pt 40 r.40.1

[Section I of Pt 40] sets out rules about judgments and orders which apply except where any other of these rules or a PD makes a different provision in relation to the judgment or order in question.

Pt 40 r.40.2

(1) Every judgment or order must state the name and judicial title of the person who made it, unless it is—
  (a) default judgment entered under r.12.4(1) (entry of default judgment where judgment is entered by a court officer) or a default costs certificate obtained under r.47.11;
  (b) judgment entered under rr.14.4, 14.5, 14.6, 14.7 and 14.9 (entry of judgment on admission where judgment is entered by a court officer);
  (c) a consent order under r.40.6(2) (consent orders made by court officers);
  (d) an order made by a court officer under r.70.5 (orders to enforce awards as if payable under a court order); or
  (e) an order made by a court officer under r.71.2 (orders to obtain information from judgment debtors).

(2) Every judgment or order must—
  (a) bear the date on which it is given or made; and
  (b) be sealed by the court.

(3) Paragraph (4) applies where a party applies for permission to appeal against a judgment or order at the hearing at which the judgment or order was made.

(4) Where this paragraph applies, the judgment or order shall state—
  (a) whether or not the judgment or order is final;
  (b) whether an appeal lies from the judgment or order and, if so, to which appeal court;
  (c) whether the court gives permission to appeal; and
  (d) if not, the appropriate appeal court to which any further application for permission may be made.

(Paragraph 4.3B of PD 52 deals with the court's power to adjourn a hearing where a judgment or order is handed down and no application for permission to appeal is made at that hearing)

Drawing up and filing of judgments and orders

Pt 40 r.40.3

(1) Except as is provided at para.(4) below or by any PD, every judgment or order will be drawn up by the court unless—

    (a) the court orders a party to draw it up;

    (b) a party, with the permission of the court, agrees to draw it up;

    (c) the court dispenses with the need to draw it up; or

    (d) it is a consent order under r.40.6.

(2) The court may direct that—

    (a) a judgment or an order drawn up by a party must be checked by the court before it is sealed; or

    (b) before a judgment or an order is drawn up by the court, the parties must file an agreed statement of its terms.

(3) Where a judgment or an order is to be drawn up by a party—

    (a) he must file it no later than seven days after the date on which the court ordered or permitted him to draw it up so that it can be sealed by the court; and

    (b) if he fails to file it within that period, any other party may draw it up and file it.

(4) Except for orders made by the court of its own initiative and unless the court otherwise orders, every judgment or order made in claims proceeding in the Queen's Bench Division at the Royal Courts of Justice, other than in the Administrative Court, will be drawn up by the parties, and r.40.3 is modified accordingly.

PD 40B para.1.2

A party who has been ordered or given permission to draw up an order must file it for sealing within seven days of being ordered or permitted to do so. If he fails to do so, any other party may draw it up and file it.

PD 40B para.1.3

If the court directs that a judgment or order which is being drawn up by a party must be checked by the court before it is sealed, the party responsible must file the draft within seven days of the date the order was made with a request that the draft be checked before it is sealed.

PD 40B para.1.4

If the court directs the parties to file an agreed statement of terms of an order which the court is to draw up, the parties must do so no later than seven days from the date the order was made, unless the court directs otherwise.

PD 40B para.1.5

If the court requires the terms of an order which is being drawn up by the court to be agreed by the parties the court may direct that a copy of the draft order is to be sent to all the parties:

    (1) for their agreement to be endorsed on it and returned to the court before the order is sealed, or

    (2) with notice of an appointment to attend before the court to agree the terms of the order.

PD 40B para.2.1

Where a judgment or order directs any deed or document to be prepared, executed or signed, the order will state:

    (1) the person who is to prepare the deed or document, and

    (2) if the deed or document is to be approved, the person who is to approve it.

PD 40B para.2.2

If the parties are unable to agree the form of the deed or document, any party may apply in accordance with Pt 23 for the form of the deed or document to be settled.

PD 40B para.2.3

In such case the judge may:
  (1) settle the deed or document himself, or
  (2) refer it to
      (a) a master, or
      (b) a district judge, or
      (c) a **conveyancing counsel** of the Senior Courts to settle.

Service of judgments and orders

Pt 40 r.40.4

  (1) Where a judgment or an order has been drawn up by a party and is to be served by the court—
      (a) the party who drew it up must file a copy to be retained at court and sufficient copies for service on him and on the other parties; and
      (b) once it has been sealed, the court must serve a copy of it on each party to the proceedings.
  (2) Unless the court directs otherwise, any order made otherwise than at trial must be served on—
      (a) the applicant and the respondent; and
      (b) any other person on whom the court orders it to be served.
(Rule 6.21 sets out who is to serve a document other than the claim form).

Power to require judgment or order to be served on a party as well as his solicitor

Pt 40 r.40.5

Where the party on whom a judgment or order is to be served is acting by a solicitor, the court may order the judgment or order to be served on the party as well as on his solicitor.

Time from which interest begins to run

Pt 40 r.40.8

  (1) Where interest is payable on a judgment pursuant to s.17 of the Judgments Act 1838 or s.74 of the County Courts Act 1984, the interest shall begin to run from the date that judgment is given unless—
      (a) a rule in another Part or a PD makes different provision; or
      (b) the court orders otherwise.
  (2) The court may order that interest shall begin to run from a date before the date that judgment is given.

Who may apply to set aside or vary a judgment or order

Pt 40 r.40.9

A person who is not a party but who is directly affected by a judgment or order may apply to have the judgment or order set aside or varied.

Judgment against a state in default of acknowledgment of service

Pt 40 r.40.10

(1) Where the claimant obtains default judgment under Pt 12 on a claim against a State where the defendant has failed to file an acknowledgment of service, the judgment does not take effect until two months after service on the State of—
 (a) a copy of the judgment; and
 (b) a copy of the evidence in support of the application for permission to enter default judgment (unless the evidence has already been served on the State [has the meaning given by s.14 of the State Immunity Act 1978] in accordance with an order made under Pt 12).

Time for complying with a judgment or order

Pt 40 r.40.11

A party must comply with a judgment or order for the payment of an amount of money (including costs) within 14 days of the date of the judgment or order, unless—
 (a) the judgment or order specifies a different date for compliance (including specifying payment by instalments);
 (b) any of these rules specifies a different date for compliance; or
 (c) the court has stayed the proceedings or judgment.
(Parts 12 and 14 specify different dates for complying with certain default judgments and judgments on admissions).

Correction of errors in judgments and orders

Pt 40 r.40.12

(1) The court may at any time correct an accidental slip or omission in a judgment or order.
(2) A party may apply for a correction without notice.

PD 40B para.4.1

Where a judgment or order contains an accidental slip or omission a party may apply for it to be corrected.

PD 40B para.4.2

The application notice (which may be an informal document such as a letter) should describe the error and set out the correction required. An application may be dealt with without a hearing:

(1) where the applicant so requests,

(2) with the consent of the parties, or

(3) where the court does not consider that a hearing would be appropriate.

PD 40B para.4.3

The judge may deal with the application without notice if the slip or omission is obvious or may direct notice of the application to be given to the other party or parties.

PD 40B para.4.4

If the application is opposed it should, if practicable, be listed for hearing before the judge who gave the judgment or made the order.

PD 40B para.4.5

The court has an inherent power to vary its own orders to make the meaning and intention of the court clear.

Cases where court gives judgment both on claim and counterclaim

Pt 40 r.40.13

(1) This rule applies where the court gives judgment for specified amounts both for the claimant on his claim and against the claimant on a counterclaim.

(2) If there is a balance in favour of one of the parties, it may order the party whose judgment is for the lesser amount to pay the balance.

(3) In a case to which this rule applies, the court may make a separate order as to costs against each party.

Statement as to service of a claim form

PD 40B para.7.1

Where a party to proceedings which have gone to trial requires a statement to be included in the judgment as to where, and by what means the claim form issued in those proceedings was served, application should made to the trial judge when judgment is given.

PD 40B para.7.2

If the judge so orders, the statement will be included in a preamble to the judgment as entered.

Orders requiring an act to be done

PD 40B para.8.1

An order which requires an act to be done (other than a judgment or order for the payment of an amount of money) must specify the time within which the act should be done.

PD 40B para.8.2

The consequences of failure to do an act within the time specified may be set out in the order. In this case the wording of the following examples suitably adapted must be used:
  (1) Unless the [claimant][defendant] serves his list of documents by 16.00 on Friday, January 22, 1999 his [claim][defence] will be struck out and judgment entered for the [defendent][claimant], or
  (2) Unless the [claimant][defendant] serves his list of documents within 14 days of service of this order his [claim][defence] will be struck out and judgment entered for the [defendant][claimant].
Example (1) should be used wherever possible.

Non-compliance with a judgment or order

PD 40B para.9.1

An order which restrains a party from doing an act or requires an act to be done should, if disobedience is to be dealt with by an application to bring contempt of court proceedings, have a penal notice endorsed on it as follows:

If you the within-named [ ] do not comply with this order you may be held to be in contempt of court and imprisoned or fined, or [in the case of a company or corporation] your assets may be seized.

PD 40B para.9.2

The provisions of para.8.1 above also apply to an order which contains an undertaking by a party to do or not do an act, subject to para.9.3 below.

PD 40B para.9.3

The court has the power to decline to:
  (1) accept an undertaking, and
  (2) deal with disobedience in respect of an undertaking by contempt of court proceedings, unless the party giving the undertaking has made a signed statement to the effect that he understands the terms of his undertaking and the consequences of failure to comply with it.

PD 40B para.9.4

The statement may be endorsed on the [court copy of the] order containing the undertaking or may be filed in a separate document such as a letter.

Costs

PD 40B para.11.1

Attention is drawn to the Costs PD and, in particular, to the court's power to make a summary assessment of costs and the provisions relating to interest in detailed assessment proceedings.

PD 40B para.11.2

Attention is also drawn to costs r.44.13(1) which provides that if an order makes no mention of costs, none are payable in respect of the proceedings to which it relates.

Judgments paid by instalments

PD 40B para.12

Where a judgment is to be paid by instalments, the judgment should set out:
  (1) the total amount of the judgment,
  (2) the amount of each instalment,
  (3) the number of instalments and the date on which each is to be paid, and
  (4) to whom the instalments should be paid.

Order to make an Order of the Supreme Court an Order of the High Court

PD 40B para.13.1

Application may be made in accordance with Pt 23 for an order to make an order of the Supreme Court an order of the High Court. The application should be made to the procedural judge of the Division, District Registry or court in which the proceedings are taking place and may be made without notice unless the court directs otherwise.

PD 40B para.13.2

The application must be supported by the following evidence:
  (1) details of the order which was the subject of the appeal to the Supreme Court,
  (2) details of the order of the Supreme Court, with a copy annexed, and
  (3) a copy annexed of the certificate of the Registrar of the Supreme Court of the assessment of the costs of the appeal to the Supreme Court in the sum of £.......................

PD 40B para.13.3

The order to make an order of the Supreme Court an order of the High Court should be in Form No.PF68.

Examples of forms of trial judgment

PD 40B para.14.1

The following general forms may be used;
  (1) judgment after trial before judge without jury—Form No.45,
  (2) judgment after trial before judge with jury—Form No.46,
  (3) judgment after trial before a Master or district judge—Form No.47,
  (4) judgment after trial before a judge of the Technology and Construction court—Form No.47 but with any necessary modifications.

PD 40B para.14.2

A trial judgment should, in addition to the matters set out in paras 5, 6 and 7 above, have the following matters set out in a preamble:
    (1) the questions put to a jury and their answers to those questions,
    (2) the findings of a jury and whether unanimous or by a majority,
    (3) any order made during the course of the trial concerning the use of evidence,
    (4) any matters that were agreed between the parties prior to or during the course of the trial in respect of
        (a) liability,
        (b) contribution,
        (c) the amount of the damages or part of the damages, and
    (5) the findings of the judge in respect of each head of damage in a personal injury case.

PD 40B para.14.3

Form No.49 should be used for a trial judgment against an Estate.
    The forms referred to in this PD are listed in PD 4.

PD 40B para.14.4

On any application or appeal concerning—
    (i) a committal order;
    (ii) a refusal to grant habeas corpus or
    (iii) a secure accommodation order made under s.25 of the Children Act 1989,
if the court ordering the release of the person concludes that his Convention rights have been infringed by the making of the order to which the application or appeal relates, the judgment or order should so state. If the court does not do so, that failure will not prevent another court from deciding the matter.

When judgment or Order takes effect

Pt 40 r.40.7

    (1) A judgment or order takes effect from the day when it is given or made, or such later date as the court may specify.
    (2) This rule applies to all judgments and orders except those to which r.40.10 (judgment against a State) applies.

Power to make judgements binding on non-parties

Pt 19 r.19.8A

    (1) This rule applies to any claim relating to—
        (a) the estate of a deceased person;
        (b) property subject to a trust; or
        (c) the sale of any property.
    (2) The court may at any time direct that notice of—
        (a) the claim; or

(b) any judgment or order given in the claim,

be served on any person who is not a party but who is or may be affected by it.

(3) An application under this rule—

    (a) may be made without notice; and

    (b) must be supported by written evidence which includes the reasons why the person to be served should be bound by the judgment in the claim.

(4) Unless the court orders otherwise—

    (a) a notice of a claim or of a judgment or order under this rule must be—

        (i) in the form required by the practice direction;

        (ii) issued by the court; and

        (iii) accompanied by a form of acknowledgment of service with any necessary modifications;

    (b) a notice of a claim must also be accompanied by—

        (i) a copy of the claim form; and

        (ii) such other statements of case, witness statements or affidavits as the court may direct; and

    (c) a notice of a judgment or order must also be accompanied by a copy of the judgment or order.

(5) If a person served with notice of a claim files an acknowledgment of service of the notice within 14 days he will become a party to the claim.

(6) If a person served with notice of a claim does not acknowledge service of the notice he will be bound by any judgment given in the claim as if he were a party.

(7) If, after service of a notice of a claim on a person, the claim form is amended so as substantially to alter the relief claimed, the court may direct that a judgment shall not bind that person unless a further notice, together with a copy of the amended claim form, is served on him.

(8) Any person served with a notice of a judgment or order under this rule—

    (a) shall be bound by the judgment or order as if he had been a party to the claim; but

    (b) may, provided he acknowledges service—

        (i) within 28 days after the notice is served on him, apply to the court to set aside or vary the judgment or order; and

        (ii) take part in any proceedings relating to the judgment or order.

(9) The following rules of Part 10 (acknowledgment of service) apply—

    (a) rule 10.4; and

    (b) rule 10.5, subject to the modification that references to the defendant are to be read as references to the person served with the notice.

(10) A notice under this rule is issued on the date entered on the notice by the court.

Obtaining copy of judgment

PD 5A para.4.2A

A party to proceedings may, unless the court orders otherwise, obtain from the records of the court a copy of—

    (j) a judgment or order given or made in public (whether made at a hearing or without a hearing).

See **Accounts and inquiries, Compensation recovery payments, Consent judgments and orders, Conveyancing counsel, Declaratory judgments, Detention of goods, Foreign currency, Interim payment, Provisional damages, Reserved judgment, Strike out,** and **Undertaking.**

JUDICIAL REVIEW

PD 54A para.1.1

In addition to Pt 54 and this practice direction attention is drawn to s.31 of the Senior Courts Act 1981; and the Human Rights Act 1998.

PD 54A para.2.1

Part 54 claims for judicial review are dealt with in the Administrative Court.

See also **Administrative Court**.

Pt 54 r.54.1

(1) [Part 54] contains rules about judicial review.
(2) In this section—
    (a) a 'claim for judicial review' means a claim to review the lawfulness of—
        (i) an enactment; or
        (ii) a decision, action or failure to act in relation to the exercise of a public function.
    (e) 'the judicial review procedure' means the Pt 8 procedure as modified by this section;
    (f) 'interested party' means; and
(Rule 8.1(6)(b) provides that a rule or PD may, in relation to a specified type of proceedings, disapply or modify any of the rules set out in Pt 8 as they apply to those proceedings)

Pt 54 r.54.2

The judicial review procedure must be used in a claim for judicial review where the claimant is seeking—
    (a) a mandatory order; (b) a prohibiting order; (c) a **quashing order**; or (d) an **injunction** under s.30 of the Supreme Court Act 1981 (restraining a person from acting in any office in which he is not entitled to act).

Pt 54 r.54.3

(1) The judicial review procedure may be used in a claim for judicial review where the claimant is seeking—
    (a) a declaration; or
    (b) an injunction.
(Section 31(2) of the Supreme Court Act 1981 sets out the circumstances in which the court [means the High Court, unless otherwise stated] may grant a declaration or injunction in a claim for judicial review).
(Where the claimant is seeking a declaration or injunction in addition to one of the remedies listed in r.54.2, the judicial review procedure must be used).
    (2) A claim for judicial review may include a claim for damages, restitution or the recovery of a sum due but may not seek such a remedy alone.
(Section 31(4) of the Supreme Court Act sets out the circumstances in which the court may award damages, restitution or the recovery of a sum due on a claim for judicial review)

Court

PD 54A para.2.1

Part 54 claims for judicial review are dealt with in the Administrative Court.

Permission required

Pt 54 r.54.4

The court's permission to proceed is required in a claim for judicial review whether started under [CPT 54] or transferred to the Administrative Court.

PD 54A para.8.4

The court will generally, in the first instance, consider the question of permission without a hearing.

Permission given

Pt 54 r.54.10

(1) Where permission to proceed is given the court may also give directions.
(2) Directions under para.(1) may include—
    (a) a stay of proceedings to which the claim relates;
    (b) directions requiring the proceedings to be heard by a Divisional Court.

PD 54A para.8.1

Case management directions under r.54.10(1) may include directions about serving the claim form and any evidence on other persons.

PD 54A para.8.2

Where a claim is made under the Human Rights Act 1998, a direction may be made for giving notice to the Crown or joining the Crown as a party. Attention is drawn to r.19.4A and para.6 of PD 19A.

Permission decision without a hearing

Pt 54 r.54.12

(1) This rule applies where the court, without a hearing—
    (a) refuses permission to proceed; or
    (b) gives permission to proceed—
        (i) subject to conditions; or
        (ii) on certain grounds only.
(2) The court will serve its reasons for making the decision when it serves the order giving or refusing permission in accordance with r.54.11.
(3) The claimant may not appeal but may request the decision to be reconsidered at a hearing.
(4) A request under para.(3) must be filed within seven days after service of the reasons under para.(2).
(5) The claimant, defendant and any other person who has filed an acknowledgment of service will be given at least two days' notice of the hearing date.
(6) The court may give directions requiring the proceedings to be heard by a Divisional Court.

PD 54A para.8.4

The court will generally, in the first instance, consider the question of permission without a hearing.

Time limit for filing claim form

Pt 54 r.54.5

(1) The claim form must be filed—
    (a) promptly; and
    (b) in any event not later than three months after the grounds to make the claim first arose.
(2) The time limit in this rule may not be extended by agreement between the parties.
(3) This rule does not apply when any other enactment specifies a shorter time limit for making the claim for judicial review.

PD 54 para.4.1

Where the claim is for a quashing order in respect of a judgment, order or conviction, the date when the grounds to make the claim first arose, for the purposes of r.54.5(1)(b), is the date of that judgment, order or conviction.

Claim form

Pt 54 r.54.6

(1) In addition to the matters set out in r.8.2 (contents of the claim form) the claimant must also state—
    (a) the name and address of any person he considers to be an interested party [any person (other than the claimant and defendant) who is directly affected by the claim];
    (b) that he is requesting permission to proceed with a claim for judicial review; and
    (c) any remedy (including any interim remedy) he is claiming; and
    (d) where appropriate, the grounds on which it is contended that the claim is an **Aarhus Convention claim**.

(Part 25 sets out how to apply for an interim remedy).
The claim form must be accompanied by the documents required by PD 54A.

PD 54A para.5.1

Where the claim for judicial review relates to proceedings in a court or tribunal, any other parties to those proceedings must be named in the claim form as interested parties under r.54.6(1)(a) (and therefore served with the claim form under r.54.7(b)).

PD 54A para.5.2

For example, in a claim by a defendant in a criminal case in the Magistrates or Crown Court for judicial review of a decision in that case, the prosecution must always be named as an interested party.

PD 54A para.5.6

The claim form must include or be accompanied by—
  (1) a detailed statement of the claimant's grounds for bringing the claim for judicial review;
  (2) a statement of the facts relied on;
  (3) any application to extend the time limit for filing the claim form;
  (4) any application for directions.

PD 54A para.5.7

In addition, the claim form must be accompanied by
  (1) any written evidence in support of the claim or application to extend time;
  (2) a copy of any order that the claimant seeks to have quashed;
  (3) where the claim for judicial review relates to a decision of a court or tribunal, an approved copy of the reasons for reaching that decision;
  (4) copies of any documents on which the claimant proposes to rely;
  (5) copies of any relevant statutory material; and
  (6) a list of essential documents for advance reading by the court (with page references to the passages relied on).

PD 54A para.5.8

Where it is not possible to file all the above documents, the claimant must indicate which documents have not been filed and the reasons why they are not currently available.

Service of claim form

Pt 54 r.54.7

The claim form must be served on—
  (a) the defendant; and
  (b) unless the court otherwise directs, any person the claimant considers to be an interested party,
within seven days after the date of issue.

PD 54A para.6.1

Except as required by rr.54.11 or 54.12(2), the Administrative Court will not serve documents and service must be effected by the parties.

PD 54A para.6.2

Where the defendant or interested party to the claim for judicial review is—
  (a) the Immigration and Asylum Chamber of the First-tier Tribunal, the address for service of the claim form is Official Correspondence Unit, PO Box 6987, Leicester, LE1 6ZX or fax number 0116 249 4240;
  (b) the Crown, service of the claim form must be effected on the solicitor acting for the relevant government department as if the proceedings were civil proceedings as defined in the Crown Proceedings Act 1947.

(PD 66 gives the list published under s.17 of the Crown Proceedings Act 1947 of the solicitors acting in civil proceedings (as defined in that Act) for the different government departments on whom service is to be effected, and of their addresses).
(Part 6 contains provisions about the service of claim forms).

Acknowledgment of service

Pt 54 r.54.8

(1) Any person served with the claim form who wishes to take part in the judicial review must file an acknowledgment of service in the relevant practice form in accordance with the following provisions of this rule.
(2) Any acknowledgment of service must be—
    (a) filed not more than 21 days after service of the claim form; and
    (b) served on—
        (i) the claimant; and
        (ii) subject to any direction under r.54.7(b), any other person named in the claim form,
    as soon as practicable and, in any event, not later than seven days after it is filed.
(3) The time limits under this rule may not be extended by agreement between the parties.
(4) The acknowledgment of service—
    (a) must—
        (i) where the person filing it intends to contest the claim, set out a summary of his grounds for doing so; and
        (ii) state the name and address of any person the person filing it considers to be an interested party; and
    (b) may include or be accompanied by an application for directions.
(5) Rule 10.3(2) does not apply.

PD 54A para.7.1

Attention is drawn to r.8.3(2) and the relevant PD and to r.10.5.

Failure to file acknowledgment of service

Pt 54 r.54.9

(1) Where a person served with the claim form has failed to file an acknowledgment of service in accordance with r.54.8, he—
    (a) may not take part in a hearing to decide whether permission should be given unless the court allows him to do so; but
    (b) provided he complies with r.54.14 or any other direction of the court regarding the filing and service of—
        (i) detailed grounds for contesting the claim or supporting it on additional grounds; and
        (ii) any written evidence,
    may take part in the hearing of the judicial review.
(2) Where that person takes part in the hearing of the judicial review, the court may take his failure to file an acknowledgment of service into account when deciding what order to make about costs.
(3) Rule 8.4 does not apply.

Service of order giving or refusing permission

Pt 54 r.54.11

The court will serve—
   (a) the order giving or refusing permission; and
   (b) any directions,
      on—
         (i) the claimant;
         (ii) the defendant; and
         (iii) any other person who filed an acknowledgment of service.

PD 54A para.9.1

An order refusing permission or giving it subject to conditions or on certain grounds only must set out or be accompanied by the court's reasons for coming to that decision.

Defendant, etc. may not apply to set aside

Pt 54 r.54.13

Neither the defendant nor any other person served with the claim form may apply to set aside an order giving permission to proceed.

Response

Pt 54 r.54.14

   (1) A defendant and any other person served with the claim form who wishes to contest the claim or support it on additional grounds must file and serve—
      (a) detailed grounds for contesting the claim or supporting it on additional grounds; and
      (b) any written evidence,
      within 35 days after service of the order giving permission.
   (2) The following rules do not apply—
      (a) Rule 8.5(3) and 8.5(4) (defendant to file and serve written evidence at the same time as acknowledgment of service); and
      (b) Rule 8.5(5) and 8.5(6) (claimant to file and serve any reply within 14 days).

PD 54A para.10.1

Where the party filing the detailed grounds intends to rely on documents not already filed, he must file a paginated bundle of those documents when he files the detailed grounds.

Where claimant seeks to rely on additional grounds

Pt 54 r.54.15

The court's permission is required if a claimant seeks to rely on grounds other than those for which he has been given permission to proceed.

PD 54A para.11.1

Where the claimant intends to apply to rely on additional grounds at the hearing of the claim for judicial review, he must give notice to the court and to any other person served with the claim form no later than seven clear days before the hearing (or the warned date where appropriate).

Evidence

Pt 54 r.54.16

(1) Rule 8.6 (1) does not apply.
(2) No written evidence may be relied on unless—
    (a) it has been served in accordance with any—
        (i) rule under this section; or
        (ii) direction of the court; or
        (iii) the court gives permission.

PD 54A para.12.1

Disclosure is not required unless the court orders otherwise.

Court's powers to hear any person

Pt 54 r.4.17

(1) Any person may apply for permission—
    (a) to file evidence; or
    (b) make representations at the hearing of the judicial review.
(2) An application under para.(1) should be made promptly.

PD 54A para.13.1

Where all the parties consent, the court may deal with an application under r.54.17 without a hearing.

PD 54A para.13.2

Where the court gives permission for a person to file evidence or make representations at the hearing of the claim for judicial review, it may do so on conditions and may give case management directions.

PD 54A para.13.3

An application for permission should be made by letter to the Administrative Court office, identifying the claim, explaining who the applicant is and indicating why and in what form the applicant wants to participate in the hearing.

PD 54A para.13.4

If the applicant is seeking a prospective order as to costs, the letter should say what kind of order and on what grounds.

PD 54A para.13.5

Applications to intervene must be made at the earliest reasonable opportunity, since it will usually be essential not to delay the hearing.

Judicial review may be decided without a hearing

Pt 54 r.54.18

The court may decide the claim for judicial review without a hearing where all the parties agree.

Court's powers in respect of quashing orders

Pt 54 r.54.19

(1) This rule applies where the court makes a quashing order in respect of the decision to which the claim relates.
(2) The court may—
    (a) (i) remit the matter to the decision-maker; and
         (ii) direct it to reconsider the matter and reach a decision in accordance with the judgment of the court; or
    (b) in so far as any enactment permits, substitute its own decision for the decision to which the claim relates.
(Section 31 of the Supreme Court Act 1981 enables the High Court, subject to certain conditions, to substitute its own decision for the decision in question).

Transfer

Pt 54 r.54.20

The court may
    (a) order a claim to continue as if it had not been started under this section; and
    (b) where it does so, give directions about the future management of the claim.
(Part 30 (transfer) applies to transfers to and from the Administrative Court).

PD 54A para.14.1

Attention is drawn to r.30.5 [transfer between Divisions and to and from a specialist list].

PD 54A para.14.2

In deciding whether a claim is suitable for transfer to the Administrative Court, the court will consider whether it raises issues of public law to which Pt 54 should apply.

Skeleton arguments

PD 54A para.15.1

The claimant must file and serve a skeleton argument not less than 21 working days before the date of the hearing of the judicial review (or the warned date).

PD 54A para.15.2

The defendant and any other party wishing to make representations at the hearing of the judicial review must file and serve a skeleton argument not less than 14 working days before the date of the hearing of the judicial review (or the warned date).

PD 54A para.15.3

Skeleton arguments must contain:
    (1) a time estimate for the complete hearing, including delivery of judgment;
    (2) a list of issues;
    (3) a list of the legal points to be taken (together with any relevant authorities with page references to the passages relied on);
    (4) a chronology of events (with page references to the bundle of documents (see para. 16.1);
    (5) a list of essential documents for the advance reading of the court (with page references to the passages relied on) (if different from that filed with the claim form) and a time estimate for that reading; and
    (6) a list of persons referred to.

Bundle of documents to be filed

PD 54A para.16.1

The claimant must file a paginated and indexed bundle of all relevant documents required for the hearing of the judicial review when he files his skeleton argument.

PD 54A para.16.2

The bundle must also include those documents required by the defendant and any other party who is to make representations at the hearing.

Bundle of documents

PD 54A para.5.9

The claimant must file two copies of a paginated and indexed bundle containing all the documents referred to in paras 5.6 and 5.7.

PD 54A para.5.10

Attention is drawn to rr.8.5(1) [the claimant must file any written evidence on which he intends to rely when he files his claim form] and 8.5(7) [claimant may rely on the matters set out in his claim form as evidence under this rule if the claim form is verified by a statement of truth].

Agreed final order

PD 54A para.17.1

If the parties agree about the final order to be made in a claim for judicial review, the claimant must file at the court a document (with two copies) signed by all the parties setting out the terms of the proposed agreed order together with a short statement of the matters relied on as justifying the proposed agreed order and copies of any authorities or statutory provisions relied on.

PD 54A para.17.2

The court will consider the documents referred to in para.17.1 and will make the order if satisfied that the order should be made.

PD 54A para.17.3

If the court is not satisfied that the order should be made, a hearing date will be set.

PD 54A para.17.4

Where the agreement relates to an order for costs only, the parties need only file a document signed by all the parties setting out the terms of the proposed order.

See **Appeals**, **Devolution issues**, **Human rights**, **Immigration and asylum**, **Judge**, **Pre-action protocols**, **Quash orders**, and **Sanctions**

JUDICIAL REVIEW APPEALS

Pt 52 r.52.15

  (1) Where permission to apply for judicial review has been refused at a hearing in the High Court, the person seeking that permission may apply to the Court of Appeal for permission to appeal.
  (2) An application in accordance with para.(1) must be made within seven days of the decision of the High Court to refuse to give permission to apply for judicial review.
  (3) On an application under para.(1), the Court of Appeal may, instead of giving permission to appeal, give permission to apply for judicial review.
  (4) Where the Court of Appeal gives permission to apply for judicial review in accordance with para.(3), the case will proceed in the High Court unless the Court of Appeal Orders otherwise.

JURAT

PD 32 para.5.1

The jurat of an affidavit is a statement set out at the end of the document which authenticates the affidavit.

PD 32 para.5.2

It must:
(1) be signed by all deponents,
(2) be completed and signed by the person before whom the affidavit was sworn whose name and qualification must be printed beneath his signature,
(3) contain the full address of the person before whom the affidavit was sworn, and
(4) follow immediately on from the text and not be put on a separate page.

JURISDICTION

Pt 3 r.2.3(1)

Unless the context requires otherwise, England and Wales and any part of the territorial waters of the UK adjoining England and Wales.

Disputing the court's jurisdiction

Pt 11 r.11

(1) A defendant who wishes to—
    (a) dispute the court's jurisdiction to try the claim; or
    (b) argue that the court should not exercise its jurisdiction
    may apply to the court for an order declaring that it has no such jurisdiction or should not exercise any jurisdiction which it may have.
(2) A defendant who wishes to make such an application must first file **an acknowledgment of service** in accordance with Pt 10.
(3) A defendant who files an acknowledgment of service does not, by doing so, lose any right that he may have to dispute the court's jurisdiction.
(4) An application under this rule must—
    (a) be made within 14 days after filing an acknowledgment of service; and
    (b) be supported by evidence.
(5) If the defendant—
    (a) files an acknowledgment of service; and
    (b) does not make such an application within the period specified in para.(4),
    he is to be treated as having accepted that the court has jurisdiction to try the claim.
(6) An order containing a declaration that the court has no jurisdiction or will not exercise its jurisdiction may also make further provision including—
    (a) setting aside the claim form;
    (b) setting aside service of the claim form;
    (c) discharging any order made before the claim was commenced or before the claim form was served; and
    (d) staying the proceedings.
(7) If on an application under this rule the court does not make a declaration—
    (a) the acknowledgment of service shall cease to have effect;
    (b) the defendant may file a further acknowledgment of service within 14 days or such other period as the court may direct; and
    (c) the court shall give directions as to the filing and service of the defence in a claim under Pt 7 or the filing of evidence in a claim under Pt 8 in the event that a further acknowledgment of service is filed.
(8) If the defendant files a further acknowledgment of service in accordance with para.(7)(b) he shall be treated as having accepted that the court has jurisdiction to try the claim.

(9) If a defendant makes an application under this rule, he must file and serve his written evidence in support with the application notice, but he need not before the hearing of the application file—
   (a) in a Pt 7 claim, a defence; or
   (b) in a Pt 8 claim, any other written evidence.

Commercial Court

Pt 58 r.58.7

(1) Part 11 [disputing the court's jurisdiction] applies to claims in the commercial list with the modifications set out in this rule.
(2) An application under r.11(1) [to the court for an order declaring that it has no such jurisdiction or should not exercise any jurisdiction which it may have] must be made within 28 days after filing an acknowledgment of service.
(3) If the defendant files an acknowledgment of service indicating an intention to dispute the court's jurisdiction, the claimant need not serve particulars of claim before the hearing of the application.

Mercantile courts

Pt 59 r.59.6

(1) Part 11 [disputing the court's jurisdiction] applies to mercantile claims with the modifications set out in this rule.
(2) An application under r.11(1) [to the court for an order declaring that it has no such jurisdiction or should not exercise any jurisdiction which it may have] must be made within 28 days after filing an acknowledgment of service.
(3) If the defendant files an acknowledgment of service indicating an intention to dispute the court's jurisdiction, the claimant need not serve particulars of claim before the hearing of the application.

Jurisdiction regarding appeals

PD 52A para.3.9

(1) Where an applicant attempts to file an appellant's notice and the appeal court does not have jurisdiction to issue the notice, a court officer may notify the applicant in writing that the appeal court does not have jurisdiction in respect of the notice.
(2) Before notifying a person under para.(1) the court officer must confer—
   (a) with a judge of the appeal court; or,
   (b) where the Court of Appeal, Civil Division is the appeal court, with a court officer who exercises the jurisdiction of that Court under r.52.16.
(3) Where a court officer in the Court of Appeal, Civil Division notifies a person under para.(1), r.52.16(5) shall not apply.

JURY TRIAL

Pt 26 r.26.11

An application for a claim to be tried with a jury must be made within 28 days of service of the defence.

High Court

Supreme Court Act 1981 s.69

(1) Where, on the application of any party to an action to be tried in the Queen's Bench Division, the court is satisfied that there is in issue—
(a) a charge of fraud against that party; or
(b) a claim in respect of libel, slander, malicious prosecution or false imprisonment; or
(c) any question or issue of a kind prescribed for the purposes of this paragraph,
the action shall be tried with a jury, unless the court is of opinion that the trial requires any prolonged examination of documents or accounts or any scientific or local investigation which cannot conveniently be made with a jury.
(2) An application under subs.(1) must be made not later than such time before the trial as may be prescribed.
(3) An action to be tried in the Queen's Bench Division which does not by virtue of subs.(1) fall to be tried with a jury shall be tried without a jury unless the court in its discretion orders it to be tried with a jury.
(4) Nothing in subs.(1) to (3) shall affect the power of the court to order, in accordance with rules of court, that different questions of fact arising in any action be tried by different modes of trial; and where any such order is made, subs.(1) shall have effect only as respects questions relating to any such charge, claim, question or issue as is mentioned in that subsection.
(5) Where for the purpose of disposing of any action or other matter which is being tried in the High Court by a judge with a jury it is necessary to ascertain the law of any other country which is applicable to the facts of the case, any question as to the effect of the evidence given with respect to that law shall, instead of being submitted to the jury, be decided by the judge alone.

County courts

County Court Act 1984 s.66

(1) In the following proceedings in a county court the trial shall be without a jury—
(a) Admiralty proceedings;
(b) proceedings arising—
(i) under Pts I, II or III of the Rent (Agriculture) Act 1976, or
(ii) under any provision of the Rent Act 1977 other than a provision contained in Pt V, ss.103 to 106 or Part IX, or
(iii) under Pt I of the Protection from Eviction Act 1977; or
(iv) under Pt I of the Housing Act 1988
(c) any appeal to the county court under the Housing Act 1985.
(2) In all other proceedings in a county court the trial shall be without a jury unless the court otherwise orders on an application made in that behalf by any party to the proceeings in such manner and within such time before the trial as may be prescribed.
(3) Where, on any such application, the court is satisfied that there is in issue—
(a) a charge of fraud against the party making the application; or
(b) a claim in respect of libel, slander, malicious prosecution or false imprisonment; or
(c) any question or issue of a kind prescribed for the purposes of this paragraph,
the action shall be tried with a jury, unless the court is of opinion that the trial requires any prolonged examination of documents or accounts or any scientific or local investigation which cannot conveniently be made with a jury.

(4) There shall be payable, in respect of the trial with a jury of proceedings in a county court, such fees as may be prescribed by an order under section 92 of the Courts Act 2003 (fees).

Juror

See **Welsh language**.

K

KEYWORD SEARCH

PD 31B para.5(6)

A software-aided search for words across the text of an **Electronic Document**.

Keyword and other automated searches

PD 31B para.25

It may be reasonable to search for Electronic Documents by means of Keyword Searches or other automated methods of searching if a full review of each and every document would be unreasonable.

PD 31B para.26

However, it will often be insufficient to use simple Keyword Searches or other automated methods of searching alone. The injudicious use of Keyword Searches and other automated search techniques—
  (1) may result in failure to find important documents which ought to be disclosed, and/or
  (2) may find excessive quantities of irrelevant documents, which if disclosed would place an excessive burden in time and cost on the party to whom disclosure is given.

PD 31B para.27

The parties should consider supplementing Keyword Searches and other automated searches with additional techniques such as individually reviewing certain documents or categories of documents (for example important documents generated by key personnel) and taking such other steps as may be required in order to justify the selection to the court.

KNOWLEDGE

Affidavit

PD 32 para.4.2

An **affidavit** must indicate:
  (1) which of the statements in it are made from the deponent's own knowledge and which are matters of information or belief, and
  (2) the source for any matters of information or belief.

L

LAND

Power to order sale, etc.

Pt 40 r.40.16

In any proceedings relating to land, the court may order the land, or part of it, to be—
    (a) sold; (b) mortgaged; (c) exchanged; or (d) partitioned.

Power to order delivery up of possession, etc.

Pt 40 r.40.17

Where the court has made an order under r.40.16, it may order any party to deliver up to the purchaser or any other person—
    (a) possession of the land; (b) receipt of rents or profits relating to it; or (c) both.

Directions about the sale, etc.

PD 40D para.2

Where the court has made an order under r.40.16 it may give any other directions it considers appropriate for giving effect to the order. In particular the court may give directions—
    (1) appointing a party or other person to conduct the sale;
    (2) for obtaining evidence of the value of the land;
    (3) as to the manner of sale;
    (4) settling the particulars and conditions of the sale;
    (5) fixing a minimum or reserve price;
    (6) as to the fees and expenses to be allowed to an auctioneer or estate agent;
    (7) for the purchase money to be paid:
        (a) into court;
        (b) to trustees; or
        (c) to any other person;
    (8) for the result of a sale to be certified;
    (9) under r.40.18.

Application for permission to bid

PD 40D para.3.1

Where—
    (1) the court has made an order under r.40.16 for land to be sold; and

(2) a party wishes to bid for the land,
he should apply to the court for permission to do so.

PD 40D para.3.2

An application for permission to bid must be made before the sale takes place.

PD 40D para.3.3

If the court gives permission to all the parties to bid, it may appoint an independent person to conduct the sale.

PD 40D para.3.4

'Bid' in this paragraph includes submitting a tender or other offer to buy.

Certifying sale result

PD 40D para.4.1

If—
    (1) the court has directed the purchase money to be paid into court; or
    (2) the court has directed that the result of the sale be certified,
the result of the sale must be certified by the person having conduct of the sale.

PD 40D para.4.2

Unless the court directs otherwise, the certificate must give details of
    (1) the amount of the purchase price;
    (2) the amount of the fees and expenses payable to any auctioneer or estate agent;
    (3) the amount of any other expenses of the sale;
    (4) the net amount received in respect of the sale;
and must be verified by a statement of truth.

PD 40D para.4.3

The certificate must be filed
    (1) if the proceedings are being dealt with in the Royal Courts of Justice, in Chancery Chambers;
    (2) if the proceedings are being dealt with anywhere else, in the court where the proceedings are being dealt with.

Fees and expenses of auctioneers and estate agents

PD 40D para.5.1

    (1) Where the court has ordered the sale of land under r.40.16, auctioneer's and estate agent's charges may, unless the court orders otherwise, include
        (a) commission;
        (b) fees for valuation of the land;

(c) charges for advertising the land;

(d) other expenses and disbursements but not charges for surveys.

(2) The court's authorisation is required for charges relating to surveys.

PD 40D para.5.2

If the total amount of the auctioneer's and estate agent's charges authorised under para.5.1(1)—

(1) does not exceed 2.5 per cent of the sale price; and

(2) does not exceed the rate of commission that that agent would normally charge on a sole agency basis

the charges may, unless the court Orders otherwise and subject to para.5.3(3) and (4), be met by deduction of the amount of the charges from the proceeds of sale without the need for any further authorisation from the court.

PD 40D para.5.3

If—

(1) a charge made by an auctioneer or estate agent (whether in respect of fees or expenses or both) is not authorised under para.5.1(1);

(2) the total amount of the charges so authorised exceeds the limits set out in para.5.2;

(3) the land is sold in lots or by valuation; or

(4) the sale is of investment property, business property or farm property

an application must be made to the court for approval of the fees and expenses to be allowed.

PD 40D para.5.4

An application under para.5.3 may be made by any party or, if he is not a party, by the person having conduct of the sale, and may be made either before or after the sale has taken place.

Application to the court where land subject to an incumbrance

PD 40D para.1.1

In this paragraph 'incumbrance' has the same meaning as it has in s.205(1) of the Law of Property Act 1925.

PD 40D para.1.2

Where land subject to any incumbrance is sold or exchanged any party to the sale or exchange may apply to the court for a direction under s.50 of the Law of Property Act 1925 (discharge of incumbrances by the court on sales or exchanges).

PD 40D para.1.3

The directions a court may give on such an application include a direction for the payment into court of a sum of money that the court considers sufficient to meet—

(1) the value of the incumbrance; and

(2) further costs, expenses and interest that may become due on or in respect of the incumbrance.

(Section 50(1) of the Law of Property Act 1925 contains provisions relating to the calculation of these amounts).

PD 40D para.1.4

Where a payment into court has been made in accordance with a direction under s.50(1) the court may—
    (1) declare the land to be freed from the incumbrance; and
    (2) make any order it considers appropriate for giving effect to an order made under r.40.16 or relating to the money in court and the income thereof.

PD 40D para.1.5

An application under s.50 should—
    (1) if made in existing proceedings, be made in accordance with CPR Pt 23;
    (2) otherwise, be made by claim form under CPR Pt 8.

See **Conveyancing counsel**.

LAND REGISTRATION ACTS 1925 AND 2002

Allocation of cases to levels of judiciary

See **Judge**.

Appeals to High Court

PD 52D para.5.1

Any appeal to the High Court, and any case stated or question referred for the opinion of that court under [Land Registration Acts 1925 and 2002] shall be heard in the Chancery Division.

Appeal against a decision of the adjudicator under s.111 of the Land Registration Act 2002

PD 52D para.24.1

    (1) A person who is aggrieved by a decision of the adjudicator and who wishes to appeal that decision must obtain permission to appeal.
    (2) The appellant must serve on the adjudicator a copy of the appeal court's decision on a request for permission to appeal as soon as reasonably practicable and in any event within 14 days of receipt by the appellant of the decision on permission.
    (3) The appellant must serve on the adjudicator and the Chief Land Registrar a copy of any order by the appeal court to stay a decision of the adjudicator pending the outcome of the appeal as soon as reasonably practicable and in any event within 14 days of receipt by the appellant of the appeal court's order to stay.
    (4) The appellant must serve on the adjudicator and the Chief Land Registrar a copy of the appeal court's decision on the appeal as soon as reasonably practicable and in any event within 14 days of receipt by the appellant of the appeal court's decision.

LANDLORD AND TENANT ACT 1927

Claim for compensation for improvements under Pt I of the 1927 Act

Claim form

PD 56 para.2

The claim form must include details of:
(1) the nature of the claim or the matter to be determined;
(2) the property to which the claim relates;
(3) the nature of the business carried on at the property;
(4) particulars of the lease or agreement for the tenancy including:
    (a) the names and addresses of the parties to the lease or agreement;
    (b) its duration;
    (c) the rent payable;
    (d) details of any assignment or other devolution of the lease or agreement;
(5) the date and mode of termination of the tenancy;
(6) if the claimant has left the property, the date on which he did so;
(7) particulars of the improvement or proposed improvement to which the claim relates; and
(8) if the claim is for payment of compensation, the amount claimed.

PD 56 para.5.3

The court will fix a date for a hearing when it issues the claim form.

Defendant

PD 56 para.5.4

The claimant's immediate landlord must be a defendant to the claim.

PD 56 para.5.5

The defendant must immediately serve a copy of the claim form and any document served with it and of his acknowledgment of service on his immediate landlord. If the person so served is not the freeholder, he must serve a copy of these documents on his landlord and so on from landlord to landlord.

Evidence

PD 56 para.5.6

Evidence need not be filed—with the claim form or acknowledgment of service.

Certification under s.3 of the 1927 Act

PD 56 para.5.7

If the court intends to certify under s.3 of the 1927 Act that an improvement is a proper improvement or has been duly executed, it shall do so by way of an order.

Compensation under ss.1 or 8 of the 1927 Act

PD 56 para.5.8

A claim under s.1(1) or 8(1) of the 1927 Act must be in writing, signed by the claimant, his solicitor or agent and include details of—
  (1) the name and address of the claimant and of the landlord against whom the claim is made;
  (2) the property to which the claim relates;
  (3) the nature of the business carried on at the property;
  (4) a concise statement of the nature of the claim;
  (5) particulars of the improvement, including the date when it was completed and costs; and
  (6) the amount claimed.

PD 56 para.5.9

A mesne landlord must immediately serve a copy of the claim on his immediate superior landlord. If the person so served is not the freeholder, he must serve a copy of the document on his landlord and so on from landlord to landlord.
(Paragraphs 5.8 and 5.9 provide the procedure for making claims under ss.1(1) and 8(1) of the 1927 Act—these 'claims' do not, at this stage, relate to proceedings before the court).
See also **Landlord and tenant claims**.

LANDLORD AND TENANT ACT 1954

Claims for a new tenancy under s.24 and for the termination of a tenancy under s.29(2) of the Landlord and Tenant Act 1954

Pt 56 r.56.3

  (1) This rule applies to a claim for a new [business] tenancy under s.24 and to a claim for the termination of a tenancy under s.29(2) of the 1954 Act.
  (2) In this rule—
  'an unopposed claim' means a claim for a new tenancy under s.24 of the 1954 Act in circumstances where the grant of a new tenancy is not opposed;
  (c) 'an opposed claim' means a claim for—
  (i) a new tenancy under s.24 of the 1954 Act in circumstances where the grant of a new tenancy is opposed; or
  (ii) the termination of a tenancy under s.29(2) of the 1954 Act.
  (3) Where the claim is an unopposed claim—
  (a) the claimant must use the Pt 8 procedure, but the following rules do not apply—
  (i) rule 8.5 [filing written evidence]; and

      (ii) rule 8.6 [no written evidence may be relied on at the hearing of the claim unless it has been served in accordance with r.8.5; or the court gives permission];
the court will give directions about the future management of the claim following receipt of the acknowledgment of service.

(4) Where the claim is an opposed claim the claimant must use the Pt 7 procedure.

Claims for a new tenancy under s.24 and termination of a tenancy under s.29(2) of the 1954 Act

PD 56 para.3.1

This paragraph applies to a claim for a new tenancy under s.24 and termination of a tenancy under s.29(2) of the 1954 Act where r.56.3 applies and in this paragraph—

(1) 'an unopposed claim' means a claim for a new tenancy under s.24 of the 1954 Act in circumstances where the grant of a new tenancy is not opposed;

(2) 'an opposed claim' means a claim for—

    (a) a new tenancy under s.24 of the 1954 Act in circumstances where the grant of a new tenancy is opposed; or

    (b) the termination of a tenancy under s.29(2) of the 1954 Act; and

(3) 'grounds of opposition' means—

    (a) the grounds specified in s.30(1) of the 1954 Act on which a landlord may oppose an application for a new tenancy under s.24(1) of the 1954 Act or make an application under s.29(2) of the 1954 Act; or

    (b) any other basis on which the landlord asserts that a new tenancy ought not to be granted.

Precedence of claim forms where there is more than one application to the court under s.24(1) or s.29(2) of the 1954 Act

PD 56 para.3.2

Where more than one application to the court under s.24(1) or s.29(2) of the 1954 Act is made, the following provisions shall apply—

(1) once an application to the court under s.24(1) of the 1954 Act has been served on a defendant, no further application to the court in respect of the same tenancy whether under s.24(1) or s.29(2) of the 1954 Act may be served by that defendant without the permission of the court;

(2) if more than one application to the court under s.24(1) of the 1954 Act in respect of the same tenancy is served on the same day, any landlord's application shall stand stayed until further order of the court;

(3) if applications to the court under both s.24(1) and s.29(2) of the 1954 Act in respect of the same tenancy are served on the same day, any tenant's application shall stand stayed until further order of the court; and

(4) if a defendant is served with an application under s.29(2) of the 1954 Act ('the s.29(2) application') which was issued at a time when an application to the court had already been made by that defendant in respect of the same tenancy under s.24(1) of the 1954 Act ('the section 24(1) application'), the service of the s.29(2) application shall be deemed to be a notice under r.7.7 requiring service or discontinuance of the s.24(1) application within a period of 14 days after the service of the s.29(2) application.

Defendant where the claimant is the tenant making a claim for a new tenancy under s.24 of the 1954 Act

PD 56 para.3.3

Where a claim for a new tenancy under s.24 of the 1954 Act is made by a tenant, the person who, in relation to the claimant's current tenancy, is the landlord as defined in s.44 of the 1954 Act must be a defendant.

Contents of the claim form in all cases

PD 56 para.3.4

The claim form must contain details of—
  (1) the property to which the claim relates;
  (2) the particulars of the current tenancy (including date, parties and duration), the current rent (if not the original rent) and the date and method of termination;
  (3) every notice or request given or made under ss.25 or 26 of the 1954 Act; and
  (4) the expiry date of—
      (a) the statutory period under s.29A(2) of the 1954 Act; or
      (b) any agreed extended period made under s.29B(1) or 29B(2) of the 1954 Act.

Claim form where the claimant is the tenant making a claim for a new tenancy under s.24 of the 1954 Act

PD 56 para.3.5

Where the claimant is the tenant making a claim for a new tenancy under s.24 of the 1954 Act, in addition to the details specified in para.3.4, the claim form must contain details of—
  (1) the nature of the business carried on at the property;
  (2) whether the claimant relies on ss.23(1A), 41 or 42 of the 1954 Act and, if so, the basis on which he does so;
  (3) whether the claimant relies on s.31A of the 1954 Act and, if so, the basis on which he does so;
  (4) whether any, and if so what part, of the property comprised in the tenancy is occupied neither by the claimant nor by a person employed by the claimant for the purpose of the claimant's business;
  (5) the claimant's proposed terms of the new tenancy; and
  (6) the name and address of—
      (a) anyone known to the claimant who has an interest in the reversion in the property (whether immediate or in not more than 15 years) on the termination of the claimant's current tenancy and who is likely to be affected by the grant of a new tenancy; or
      (b) if the claimant does not know of anyone specified by subpara.(6)(a), anyone who has a freehold interest in the property.

PD 56 para.3.6

The claim form must be served on the persons referred to in para.3.5(6)(a) or (b) as appropriate.

Claim form where the claimant is the landlord making a claim for a new tenancy under s.24 of the 1954 Act

PD 56 para.3.7

Where the claimant is the landlord making a claim for a new tenancy under s.24 of the 1954 Act, in addition to the details specified in para.3.4, the claim form must contain details of—
  (1) the claimant's proposed terms of the new tenancy;
  (2) whether the claimant is aware that the defendant's tenancy is one to which s.32(2) of the 1954 Act applies and, if so, whether the claimant requires that any new tenancy shall be a tenancy of the whole of the property comprised in the defendant's current tenancy or just of the holding as defined by s.23(3) of the 1954 Act; and
  (3) the name and address of—
      (a) anyone known to the claimant who has an interest in the reversion in the property (whether immediate or in not more than 15 years) on the termination of the claimant's current tenancy and who is likely to be affected by the grant of a new tenancy; or
      (b) if the claimant does not know of anyone specified by subpara.(3)(a), anyone who has a freehold interest in the property.

PD 56 para.3.8

The claim form must be served on the persons referred to in para.3.7(3)(a) or (b) as appropriate.

Claim form where the claimant is the landlord making an application for the termination of a tenancy under s.29(2) of the 1954 Act

PD 56 para.3.9

Where the claimant is the landlord making an application for the termination of a tenancy under s.29(2) of the 1954 Act, in addition to the details specified in para.3.4, the claim form must contain—
  (1) the claimant's grounds of opposition;
  (2) full details of those grounds of opposition; and
  (3) the terms of a new tenancy that the claimant proposes in the event that his claim fails.

Acknowledgment of service where the claim is an unopposed claim and where the claimant is the tenant

PD 56 para.3.10

Where the claim is an unopposed claim and the claimant is the tenant, the acknowledgment of service is to be in Form N210 and must state with particulars—
  (1) whether, if a new tenancy is granted, the defendant objects to any of the terms proposed by the claimant and if so—
      (a) the terms to which he objects; and
      (b) the terms that he proposes in so far as they differ from those proposed by the claimant;

(2) whether the defendant is a tenant under a lease having less than 15 years unexpired at the date of the termination of the claimant's current tenancy and, if so, the name and address of any person who, to the knowledge of the defendant, has an interest in the reversion in the property expectant (whether immediate or in not more than 15 years from that date) on the termination of the defendant's tenancy;

(3) the name and address of any person having an interest in the property who is likely to be affected by the grant of a new tenancy; and

(4) if the claimant's current tenancy is one to which s.32(2) of the 1954 Act applies, whether the defendant requires that any new tenancy shall be a tenancy of the whole of the property comprised in the claimant's current tenancy.

Acknowledgment of service where the claim is an unopposed claim and the claimant is the landlord

PD 56 para.3.11

Where the claim is an unopposed claim and the claimant is the landlord, the acknowledgment of service is to be in Form N210 and must state with particulars—

(1) the nature of the business carried on at the property;

(2) if the defendant relies on ss.23(1A), 41 or 42 of the 1954 Act, the basis on which he does so;

(3) whether any, and if so what part, of the property comprised in the tenancy is occupied neither by the defendant nor by a person employed by the defendant for the purpose of the defendant's business;

(4) the name and address of—

  (a) anyone known to the defendant who has an interest in the reversion in the property (whether immediate or in not more than 15 years) on the termination of the defendant's current tenancy and who is likely to be affected by the grant of a new tenancy; or

  (b) if the defendant does not know of anyone specified by subpara.(4)(a), anyone who has a freehold interest in the property; and

(5) whether, if a new tenancy is granted, the defendant objects to any of the terms proposed by the claimant and, if so—

  (a) the terms to which he objects; and

  (b) the terms that he proposes in so far as they differ from those proposed by the claimant.

Acknowledgment of service and defence where the claim is an opposed claim and where the claimant is the tenant

PD 56 para.3.12

Where the claim is an opposed claim and the claimant is the tenant—

(1) the acknowledgment of service is to be in form N9; and

(2) in his defence the defendant must state with particulars—

  (a) the defendant's grounds of opposition;

  (b) full details of those grounds of opposition;

  (c) whether, if a new tenancy is granted, the defendant objects to any of the terms proposed by the claimant and if so—

   (i) the terms to which he objects; and

   (ii) the terms that he proposes in so far as they differ from those proposed by the claimant;

(d) whether the defendant is a tenant under a lease having less than 15 years unexpired at the date of the termination of the claimant's current tenancy and, if so, the name and address of any person who, to the knowledge of the defendant, has an interest in the reversion in the property expectant (whether immediately or in not more than 15 years from that date) on the termination of the defendant's tenancy;

(e) the name and address of any person having an interest in the property who is likely to be affected by the grant of a new tenancy; and

(f) if the claimant's current tenancy is one to which s.32(2) of the 1954 Act applies, whether the defendant requires that any new tenancy shall be a tenancy of the whole of the property comprised in the claimant's current tenancy.

Acknowledgment of service and defence where the claimant is the landlord making an application for the termination of a tenancy under s.29(2) of the 1954 Act

PD 56 para.3.13

Where the claim is an opposed claim and the claimant is the landlord—
  (1) the acknowledgment of service is to be in Form N9; and
  (2) in his defence the defendant must state with particulars—
     (a) whether the defendant relies on ss.23(1A), 41 or 42 of the 1954 Act and, if so, the basis on which he does so;
     (b) whether the defendant relies on s.31A of the 1954 Act and, if so, the basis on which he does so; and
     (c) the terms of the new tenancy that the defendant would propose in the event that the claimant's claim to terminate the current tenancy fails.

Evidence in an unopposed claim

PD 56 para.3.14

Where the claim is an unopposed claim, no evidence need be filed unless and until the court directs it to be filed.

Evidence in an opposed claim

PD 56 para.3.15

Where the claim is an opposed claim, evidence (including expert evidence) must be filed by the parties as the court directs and the landlord shall be required to file his evidence first.

Grounds of opposition to be tried as a preliminary issue

PD 56 para.3.16

Unless in the circumstances of the case it is unreasonable to do so, any grounds of opposition shall be tried as a preliminary issue.

Applications for interim rent under ss.24A–24D of the 1954 Act

PD 56 para.3.17

Where proceedings have already been commenced for the grant of a new tenancy or the termination of an existing tenancy, the claim for interim rent under s.24A of the 1954 Act shall be made in those proceedings by—
(1) the claim form;
(2) the acknowledgment of service or defence; or
(3) an application on notice under Pt 23.

PD 56 para.18

Any application under s.24D(3) of the 1954 Act shall be made by an application on notice under Pt 23 in the original proceedings.

PD 56 para.3.19

Where no other proceedings have been commenced for the grant of a new tenancy or termination of an existing tenancy or where such proceedings have been disposed of, an application for interim rent under s.24A of the 1954 Act shall be made under the procedure in Pt 8 and the claim form shall include details of—
(1) the property to which the claim relates;
(2) the particulars of the relevant tenancy (including date, parties and duration) and the current rent (if not the original rent);
(3) every notice or request given or made under ss.25 or 26 of the 1954 Act;
(4) if the relevant tenancy has terminated, the date and mode of termination; and
(5) if the relevant tenancy has been terminated and the landlord has granted a new tenancy of the property to the tenant—
(a) particulars of the new tenancy (including date, parties and duration) and the rent; and
(b) in a case where s.24C(2) of the 1954 Act applies but the claimant seeks a different rent under s.24C(3) of that Act, particulars and matters on which the claimant relies as satisfying s.24C(3).

Other claims under Pt II of the 1954 Act

PD 56 para.4.1

The mesne landlord to whose consent a claim for the determination of any question arising under para.4(3) of Sch.6 to the 1954 Act shall be made a defendant to the claim.

PD 56 para.4.2

If any dispute as to the rateable value of any holding has been referred under s.37(5) of the 1954 Act to the Commissioners for HM Revenue and Customs for decision by a valuation officer, any document purporting to be a statement of the valuation officer of his decision is admissible as evidence of the matters contained in it.

See also **Landlord and tenant claims.**

LANDLORD AND TENANT ACT 1985

Transfer to Leasehold Valuation Tribunal

PD 56 para.6.1

If a question is ordered to be transferred to a leasehold valuation tribunal for determination under s.31C of the [Landlord and Tenant Act 1985] the court will:
    (1) send notice of the transfer to all parties to the claim; and
    (2) send to the Leasehold Valuation Tribunal:
        (a) copies certified by the district judge of all entries in the records of the court relating to the question;
        (b) the order of transfer; and
        (c) all documents filed in the claim relating to the question.
(Paragraph 6.1 no longer applies to proceedings in England but continues to apply to proceedings in Wales).
See also **Landlord and tenant claims**.

LANDLORD AND TENANT ACT 1987

Claim to enforce obligation under Pt I of the 1987 Act

PD 56 para.7.1

A copy of the notice served under s.19(2)(a) of the 1987 Act must accompany the claim form seeking an order under s.19(1) of that Act.

Claim for Acquisition Order under s.28 of the 1987 Act

Claim form

PD 56 para.8.2

The claim form must:
    (1) identify the property to which the claim relates and give details to show that s.25 of the 1987 Act applies;
    (2) give details of the claimants to show that they constitute the requisite majority of qualifying tenants;
    (3) state the names and addresses of the claimants and of the landlord of the property, or, if the landlord cannot be found or his identity ascertained, the steps taken to find him or ascertain his identity;
    (4) state the name and address of:
        (a) the person nominated by the claimants for the purposes of Part III of the 1987 Act; and
        (b) every person known to the claimants who is likely to be affected by the application, including (but not limited to), the other tenants of flats contained in the property (whether or not they could have made a claim), any mortgagee or superior landlord of the landlord, and any tenants' association (within the meaning of s.29 of the 1985 Act); and
    (5) state the grounds of the claim.

Notice under section 27

PD 56 para.8.3

A copy of the notice served on the landlord under s.27 of the 1987 Act must accompany the claim form unless the court has dispensed with the requirement to serve a notice under s.27(3) of the 1987 Act.

Defendants

PD 56 para.8.4

The landlord of the property (and the nominated person, if he is not a claimant) must be defendants.

Service

PD 56 para.8.5

A copy of the claim form must be served on each of the persons named by the claimant under para.8.2(4)(b) together with a notice that he may apply to be made a party.

Payment into court by nominated person

PD 56 para.8.6

If the nominated person pays money into court in accordance with an order under s.33(1) of the 1987 Act, he must file a copy of the certificate of the surveyor selected under s.33(2)(a) of that Act.

Claim for an order varying leases under the 1987 Act

PD 56 para.9.1

This para.[9] applies to a claim for an order under s.38 or s.40 of the 1987 Act.

Claim form

PD 56 para.9.2

The claim form must state:
   (1) the name and address of the claimant and of the other current parties to the lease or leases to which the claim relates;
   (2) the date of the lease or leases, the property to which they relate, any relevant terms and the variation sought;

(3) the name and address of every person known to the claimant who is likely to be affected by the claim, including (but not limited to), the other tenants of flats contained in premises of which the relevant property forms a part, any previous parties to the lease, any mortgagee or superior landlord of the landlord, any mortgagee of the claimant and any tenants' association (within the meaning of s.29 of the 1985 Act); and

(4) the grounds of the claim.

Defendants

PD 56 para.9.3

The other current parties to the lease must be defendants.

Service

PD 56 para.9.4

A copy of the claim form must be served on each of the persons named under para.9.2(3).

PD 56 para.9.5

If the defendant knows of or has reason to believe that another person or persons are likely to be affected by the variation, he must serve a copy of the claim form on those persons, together with a notice that they may apply to be made a party.

Defendant's application to vary other leases

PD 56 para.9.6

If a defendant wishes to apply to vary other leases under s.36 of the 1987 Act:

(1) he must make the application in his acknowledgment of service;

(2) paragraphs 9.2 to 9.5 apply as if the defendant were the claimant; and

(3) Part 20 does not apply.

(Paragraphs 9.1–9.6 no longer apply to proceedings in England but continue to apply to proceedings in Wales).

Service of documents in claims under the 1987 Act

PD 56 para.10.1

All documents must be served by the parties.

PD 56 para.10.2

If a notice is to be served in or before a claim under the 1987 Act, it must be served—

(1) in accordance with s.54, and

(2) in the case of service on a landlord, at the address given under s.48(1).

See also **Landlord and tenant claims.**

LANDLORD AND TENANT CLAIMS

Pt 56 r.56.1

(1) In [s.I of Pt 56, which deals with landlord and tenanct claims] 'landlord and tenant claim' means a claim under—
   (a) the **Landlord and Tenant Act 1927**;
   (b) the **Leasehold Property (Repairs) Act 1938**;
   (c) the **Landlord and Tenant Act 1954**;
   (d) the **Landlord and Tenant Act 1985**;
   (e) the **Landlord and Tenant Act 1987**; or
   (f) section 214 of the Housing Act 2004 [proceedings relating to tenancy deposits].

Starting the claim

Pt 56 r.56.2

(1) The claim must be started in the county court for the district in which the land is situated unless para.(2) applies or an enactment provides otherwise.
(2) Unless an enactment provides otherwise, the claim may be started in the High Court if the claimant files with the claim form a certificate stating the reasons for bringing the claim in that court verified by a statement of truth in accordance with r.22.1(1).
(3) PD 56 refers to circumstances which may justify starting the claim in the High Court.

PD 56 para.2.1

Subject to para.2.1A, the claimant in a landlord and tenant claim must use the Pt 8 procedure as modified by Pt 56 and [PD 56].

PD 56 para.2.1A

Where the landlord and tenant claim is a claim for—
   (1) a new tenancy under s.24 of the 1954 Act in circumstances where the grant of a new tenancy is opposed; or
   (2) the termination of a tenancy under s.29(2) of the 1954 Act,
the claimant must use the Pt 7 procedure as modified by Pt 56 and this PD.

PD 56 para.2.2

Except where the county court does not have jurisdiction , landlord and tenant claims should normally be brought in the county court. Only exceptional circumstances justify starting a claim in the High Court.

PD 56 para.2.3

If a claimant starts a claim in the High Court and the court decides that it should have been started in the county court, the court will normally either strike the claim out or transfer it to the county court on its own initiative. This is likely to result in delay and the court will normally disallow the costs of starting the claim in the High Court and of any transfer.

Starting claim in the High Court

PD 56 para.2.4

Circumstances which may, in an appropriate case, justify starting a claim in the High Court are if—
    (1) there are complicated disputes of fact; or
    (2) there are points of law of general importance.

PD 56 para.2.5

The value of the property and the amount of any financial claim may be relevant circumstances, but these factors alone will not normally justify starting the claim in the High Court.

PD 56 para.2.6

A landlord and tenant claim started in the High Court must be brought in the Chancery Division.

See also **Possession claims** and **Possession claims online**.

LANDS TRIBUNAL

Appeal from Lands Tribunal

PD 52 para.21.9

The appellant must file the appellant's notice at the Court of Appeal within 28 days after the date of the decision of the tribunal.

LAW OF PROPERTY ACT 1922

Pt 52 r.52.18

An appeal lies to the High Court against a decision of the Secretary of State under para.16 of Sch.15 to the Law of Property Act 1922.

PD 52D para.5.1

Any appeal to the High Court, and any case stated or question referred for the opinion of that court under [para.16 of Sch.15 to the Law of Property Act 1922] shall be heard in the Chancery Division.

LAW OF PROPERTY ACT 1969

PD 8A para.9.4

Proceedings under ss.21 or 25 of the Law of Property Act 1969 are assigned to the Chancery Division.

LAW REFORM (MISCELLANEOUS PROVISIONS) ACT 1934

See **Damages** and **Fatal Accident claim**.

LAW SOCIETY

Appeals from decisions of the Law Society to the High Court

See **Solicitors Disciplinary Tribunal**.

LAWYER

Small claims track

Representation at a hearing

PD 27 para.3.1

In this paragraph:
    (1) a lawyer means a barrister, a solicitor or a legal executive employed by a solicitor.

LAY REPRESENTATIVE

Small claims track

Representation at a hearing

PD 27 para.3.1

In this paragraph:
    (2) a lay representative means any person other than a **lawyer**.

PD 27 para.3.2

    (1) A party may present his own case at a hearing or a lawyer or lay representative may present it for him.
    (2) The Lay Representatives (Right of Audience) Order 1999 provides that a lay representative may not exercise any right of audience:
        (a) where his client does not attend the hearing;
        (b) at any stage after judgment; or
        (c) on any appeal brought against any decision made by the district judge in the proceedings.
    (3) However the court, exercising its general discretion to hear anybody, may hear a lay representative even in circumstances excluded by the Order.
    (4) Any of its officers or employees may represent a corporate party.

LEASEHOLD PROPERTY (REPAIRS) ACT 1938

See **Landlord and tenant claims**.

LEASEHOLD REFORM ACT 1967

PD 56 para.6

An application made to the High Court under ss.19 or 27 shall be assigned to the Chancery Division.

PD 56 para.13.2

If a tenant of a house and premises wishes to pay money into court under ss.11(4), 13(1) or 13(3)[of Leasehold Reform Act 1967]—
  (1) he must file in the office of the appropriate court an application notice containing or accompanied by evidence stating—
      (a) the reasons for the payment into court,
      (b) the house and premises to which the payment relates;
      (c) the name and address of the landlord; and
      (d) so far as they are known to the tenant, the name and address of every person who is or may be interested in or entitled to the money;
  (2) on the filing of the witness statement the tenant must pay the money into court and the court will send notice of the payment to the landlord and every person whose name and address are given in the witness statement;
  (3) any subsequent payment into court by the landlord under s.11(4) must be made to the credit of the same account as the payment into court by the tenant and subparas (1) and (2) will apply to the landlord as if he were a tenant; and
  (4) the appropriate court for the purposes of paragraph (a) is the county court for the district in which the property is situated or, if the payment into court is made by reason of a notice under s.13(3), any other county court as specified in the notice.

PD 56 para.13.3

If an order is made transferring an application to a leasehold valuation tribunal under s.21(3), the court will:
  (1) send notice of the transfer to all parties to the application; and
  (2) send to the tribunal copies of the order of transfer and all documents filed in the proceedings.
(Paragraph 13.3 no longer applies to proceedings in England but continues to apply to proceedings in Wales).

PD 56 para.13.4

A claim under ss.17 or 18 for an order for possession of a house and premises must be made in accordance with Pt 55.

PD 56 para.13.5

In a claim under ss.17 or 18 Leasehold Reform Act 1967, the defendant must:
  (1) immediately after being served with the claim form, serve on every person in occupation of the property or part of it under an immediate or derivative sub-tenancy, a notice

informing him of the claim and of his right under para.3(4) of Sch.2 take part in the hearing of the claim with the permission of the court; and

(2) within 14 days after being served with the claim form, file a defence stating the ground, if any, on which he intends to oppose the claim and giving particulars of every such sub-tenancy.

Allocation to level of judiciary

PD 2B para.5.1

In proceedings in the Chancery Division, a Master or a district judge may not deal with the following without the consent of the Chancellor of the High Court—

(i) making final orders on applications under s.19 of the Leasehold Reform Act 1967.

LEASEHOLD REFORM, HOUSING AND URBAN DEVELOPMENT ACT 1993

PD 56 para.14.2

If a claim is made under s.23(1) [of Leasehold Reform, Housing and Urban Development Act 1993] by a person other than the reversioner:

(1) on the issue of [Pt 8] claim form, the claimant must send a copy to the reversioner; and

(2) the claimant must promptly inform the reversioner either:

(a) of the court's decision; or

(b) that the claim has been withdrawn.

PD 56 para.14.3

Where an application is made under s.26(1) or (2) or s.50(1) or (2):

(1) it must be made by the issue of a claim form in accordance with the Pt 8 procedure which need not be served on any other party; and

(2) the court may grant or refuse the application or give directions for its future conduct, including the addition as defendants of such persons as appear to have an interest in it.

PD 56 para.14.4

An application under s.26(3) must be made by the issue of a claim form in accordance with the Pt 8 procedure and:

(1) the claimants must serve the claim form on any person who they know or have reason to believe is a relevant landlord, giving particulars of the claim and the hearing date and informing that person of his right to be joined as a party to the claim;

(2) the landlord whom it is sought to appoint as the reversioner must be a defendant, and must file an acknowledgment of service;

(3) a person on whom notice is served under para.(1) must be joined as a defendant to the claim if he gives notice in writing to the court of his wish to be added as a party, and the court will notify all other parties of the addition.

PD 56 para.14.5

If a person wishes to pay money into court under s.27(3), s.51(3) or para.4 of Sch.8 [of Leasehold Reform, Housing and Urban Development Act 1993]—
(1) he must file in the office of the appropriate court an application notice containing or accompanied by evidence stating—
(a) the reasons for the payment into court,
(b) the interest or interests in the property to which the payment relates or where the payment into court is made under s.51(3), the flat to which it relates;
(c) details of any vesting order;
(d) the name and address of the landlord; and
(e) so far as they are known to the tenant, the name and address of every person who is or may be interested in or entitled to the money;
(2) on the filing of the witness statement the money must be paid into court and the court will send notice of the payment to the landlord and every person whose name and address are given in the witness statement;
(3) any subsequent payment into court by the landlord must be made to the credit of the same account as the earlier payment into court;
(4) the appropriate court for the purposes of para.(1) is—
(a) where a vesting order has been made, the county court that made the order; or
(b) where no such order has been made, the county court in whose district the property is situated.

PD 56 para.14.6

If an order is made transferring an application to a leasehold valuation tribunal under s.91(4) [of the Leasehold Reform, Housing and Urban Development Act 1993], the court will:
(1) send notice of the transfer to all parties to the application; and
(2) send to the tribunal copies of the order of transfer and all documents filed in the proceedings.
(Paragraph 14.6 no longer applies to proceedings in England but continues to apply to proceedings in Wales).

PD 56 para.14.7

If a relevant landlord acts independently under Sch.1, para.7 [of the Leasehold Reform, Housing and Urban Development Act 1993], he is entitled to require any party to claims under the 1993 Act (as described in para.7(1)(b) of Sch.1) to supply him, on payment of the reasonable costs of copying, with copies of all documents which that party has served on the other parties to the claim.
See **Commonhold and Leasehold Reform Act 2002**.

LEASEHOLD VALUATION TRIBUNAL

See **Commonhold and Leasehold Reform Act 2002** and **Landlord and Tenant Act 1985**.

LEAVE OF COURT

Permission of the court.

LEGAL AID

Pt 44.1(1)

Civil legal services made available under arrangements made for the purposes of Pt 1 of the Legal Aid, Sentencing and Punishment of Offenders Act 2012.

See **LSC funded client**.

Production centre

PD 7C r.2.3

The [Production] Centre will not issue any of the following types of claim—
　(6) a claim where the claimant is a legally assisted person within the meaning of the Legal Aid Act 1988.

LEGAL COMMISSION SERVICES

References by the Legal Services Commission to High Court

PD 54C para.1.1

[PD 54C] applies where the Legal Services Commission ('the Commission') refers to the High Court a question that arises on a review of a decision about an individual's financial eligibility for a representation order in criminal proceedings under the Criminal Defence Service (Financial Eligibility) Regulations 2006.

PD 54C para.1.2

A reference of a question by the Legal Services Commission must be made to the Administrative Court.

PD 54C para.1.3

Part 52 does not apply to a review under this paragraph.

PD 54C para.1.4

The Commission must—
　(a) file at the court—
　　(i) the individual's applications for a representation order and for a review, and any supporting documents;
　　(ii) a copy of the question on which the court's decision is sought; and
　　(iii) a statement of the Commission's observations on the question; and
　(b) serve a copy of the question and the statement on the individual.

PD 54C para.1.5

The individual may file representations on the question at the court within seven days after service on him of the copy of the question and the statement.

PD 54C para.1.6

The question will be decided without a hearing unless the court directs otherwise.

LEGAL REPRESENTATIVE

Pt 2 r.2.3(1)

(a) barrister; (b) solicitor; (c) solicitor's employee; (d) manager of a body recognised under s.9 of the Administration of Justice Act 19851; or (e) person who, for the purposes of the Legal Services Act 2007, is an authorised person in relation to an activity which constitutes the conduct of litigation (within the meaning of that Act), who has been instructed to act for a party in relation to proceedings.

LEGITIMACY ACT 1976

Allocation

PD 2B para.11.1

A District Judge has jurisdiction to hear the following:
  (v) under s.45(2) of the Matrimonial Causes Act 1973 for a declaration of legitimation by virtue of the Legitimacy Act 1976.

LIBEL

See **Defamation claims**.

LIMITATION PERIOD

Adding or substituting parties after the end of a relevant limitation period

Pt 19 r.19.5

  (1) This rule applies to a change of parties after the end of a period of limitation under—
      (a) the Limitation Act 1980;
      (b) the Foreign Limitation Periods Act 1984; or
      (c) any other enactment which allows such a change, or under which such a change is allowed.
  (2) The court may add or substitute a party only if—
      (a) the relevant limitation period was current when the proceedings were started; and
      (b) the addition or substitution is necessary.
  (3) The addition or substitution of a party is necessary only if the court is satisfied that—
      (a) the new party is to be substituted for a party who was named in the claim form in mistake for the new party;
      (b) the claim cannot properly be carried on by or against the original party unless the new party is added or substituted as claimant or defendant; or

(c) the original party has died or had a bankruptcy order made against him and his interest or liability has passed to the new party.

(4) In addition, in a claim for personal injuries the court may add or substitute a party where it directs that—

    (a) (i) section 11 (special time limit for claims for personal injuries); or

        (ii) section 12 (special time limit for claims under fatal accidents legislation), of the Limitation Act 1980 shall not apply to the claim by or against the new party; or

    (b) the issue of whether those sections apply shall be determined at trial.

Amendments to statements of case after the end of a relevant limitation period

Pt 17 r.17.4

(1) This rule applies where—

    (a) a party applies to amend his statement of case in one of the ways mentioned in this rule; and

    (b) a period of limitation has expired under—

        (i) the Limitation Act 1980;

        (ii) the Foreign Limitation Periods Act 1984; or

        (iii) any other enactment which allows such an amendment, or under which such an amendment is allowed.

(2) The court may allow an amendment whose effect will be to add or substitute a new claim, but only if the new claim arises out of the same facts or substantially the same facts as a claim in respect of which the party applying for permission has already claimed a remedy in the proceedings.

(3) The court may allow an amendment to correct a mistake as to the name of a party, but only where the mistake was genuine and not one which would cause reasonable doubt as to the identity of the party in question.

(4) The court may allow an amendment to alter the capacity in which a party claims if the new capacity is one which that party had when the proceedings started or has since acquired.

Money claim online

PD 7E para.5.4

When the court issues a claim form following the submission of an online claim form, the claim is 'brought' for the purposes of the Limitation Act 1980 and any other enactment on the date on which the online claim form is received by the court's computer system. The court will keep a record, by electronic or other means, of when online claim forms are received.

Possession claim online

PD 55B para.6.6

When the court issues a claim form following the submission of an online claim form, the claim is 'brought' for the purposes of the Limitation Act 1980 and any other enactment on the date on which the online claim form is received by the court's computer system. The court will keep a record, by electronic or other means, of when online claim forms are received.

Start of proceedings

PD 7A para.5.1

Proceedings are started when the court issues a claim form at the request of the claimant (see r.7.2) but where the claim form as issued was received in the court office on a date earlier than the date on which it was issued by the court, the claim is 'brought' for the purposes of the Limitation Act 1980 and any other relevant statute on that earlier date.

Housing repair

Pre-action Protocol for Housing disrepair cases, para.3.4

The procedures in this Protocol do not extend statutory limitation periods. If a limitation period is about to expire, the tenant may need to issue proceedings immediately unless the landlord confirms that they will not rely on limitation as a defence in subsequent proceedings.
(See para.4.8 for guidance about the limitation period, and para.4.10 for a definition of 'limitation period').
   Alternatively the tenant can ask the landlord to agree to extend the limitation period.

PPHDC para.4.8

   (a) In cases where the limitation period will shortly expire, the tenant should ask in the first letter for an extension of the limitation period. The extension requested should be only so long as is necessary to avoid the cost of starting court proceedings.
   (b) It will be for the court to decide whether refusal to grant the request is reasonable and whether any sanctions, including costs orders, are appropriate.

Pre-action conduct

PD Pre-action conduct para.9.5

There are statutory time limits for starting proceedings ('the limitation period'). If a claimant starts a claim after the limitation period applicable to that type of claim has expired the defendant will be entitled to use that as a defence to the claim.

PD PC para.9.6

In certain instances compliance may not be possible before the expiry of the limitation period. If, for any reason, proceedings are started before the parties have complied, they should seek to agree to apply to the court for an order to stay (i.e. suspend) the proceedings while the parties take steps to comply.

Road traffic accidents—low value personal injury claims

PD 8B para.16.1

Where compliance with the RTA Protocol is not possible before the expiry of a limitation period the claimant may start proceedings in accordance with para.16.2.

PD 8B para.16.2

The claimant must—
  (1) start proceedings under this PD; and
  (2) state on the claim form that—
    (a) the claim is for damages; and
    (b) a stay of proceedings is sought in order to comply with the RTA Protocol.

PD 8B para.16.3

The claimant must send to the defendant the claim form together with the order imposing the stay.

PD 8B para.16.5

Where—
  (1) a stay is granted by the court;
  (2) the parties have complied with the RTA Protocol; and
  (3) the claimant wishes to start the Stage 3 Procedure,
the claimant must make an application to the court to lift the stay and request directions.

PD 8B para.16.6

Where the court orders that the stay be lifted—
  (1) the provisions of this PD will apply; and
  (2) the claimant must—
    (a) amend the claim form in accordance with para.5.2; and
    (b) file the documents in para.6.1.

Construction and engineering disputes

Pre-Action Protocol for Construction and Engineering Disputes para.6.

If by reason of complying with any part of this protocol a claimant's claim may be time-barred under any provision of the Limitation Act 1980, or any other legislation which imposes a time limit for bringing an action, the claimant may commence proceedings without complying with this Protocol. In such circumstances, a claimant who commences proceedings without complying with all, or any part, of this Protocol must apply to the court on notice for directions as to the timetable and form of procedure to be adopted, at the same time as he requests the court to issue proceedings. The court will consider whether to order a stay of the whole or part of the proceedings pending compliance with this Protocol.

LIMITED CIVIL RESTRAINT ORDER

Pt 2 r.2.3(1)

An order restraining a party from making any further applications in current proceedings.

PD 3C para.2.1

A limited civil restraint order may be made by a judge of any court where a party has made 2 or more applications which are totally without merit.

PD 3C para.2.2

Where the court makes a limited civil restraint order, the party against whom the order is made—
  (1) will be restrained from making any further applications in the proceedings in which the order is made without first obtaining the permission of a judge identified in the order;
  (2) may apply for amendment or discharge of the order provided he has first obtained the permission of a judge identified in the order; and
  (3) may apply for permission to appeal the order and if permission is granted, may appeal the order.

PD 3C para.2.3

Where a party who is subject to a limited civil restraint order—
  (1) makes a further application in the proceedings in which the order is made without first obtaining the permission of a judge identified in the order, such application will automatically be dismissed—
    (a) without the judge having to make any further order; and
    (b) without the need for the other party to respond to it;
  (2) repeatedly makes applications for permission pursuant to that order which are totally without merit, the court may direct that if the party makes any further application for permission which is totally without merit, the decision to dismiss the application will be final and there will be no right of appeal, unless the judge who refused permission grants permission to appeal.

PD 3C para.2.4

A party who is subject to a limited civil restraint order may not make an application for permission under para.2.2(1) or 2.2(2) without first serving notice of the application on the other party in accordance with para.2.5.

PD 3C para.2.5

A notice under para.2.4 must—
  (1) set out the nature and grounds of the application; and
  (2) provide the other party with at least seven days within which to respond.

PD 3C para.2.6

An application for permission under para.2.2(1) or 2.2(2)—
  (1) must be made in writing;
  (2) must include the other party's written response, if any, to the notice served under para.2.4; and
  (3) will be determined without a hearing.

PD 3C para.2.7

An order under para.2.3(2) may only be made by—
  (1) a Court of Appeal judge;
  (2) a High Court judge or master; or
  (3) a designated civil judge or his appointed deputy.

PD 3C para.2.8

Where a party makes an application for permission under para.2.2(1) or 2.2(2) and permission is refused, any application for permission to appeal—
(1) must be made in writing; and
(2) will be determined without a hearing.

PD 3C para.2.9

A limited civil restraint order—
(1) is limited to the particular proceedings in which it is made;
(2) will remain in effect for the duration of the proceedings in which it is made, unless the court otherwise Orders; and
(3) must identify the judge or judges to whom an application for permission under paras 2.2(1), 2.2(2) or 2.8 should be made.

PD 3C para.5.1

The other party or parties to the proceedings may apply for any civil restraint order.

PD 3C para.5.2

An application under para.5.1 must be made using the Pt 23 procedure unless the court otherwise directs and the application must specify which type of civil restraint order is sought.

PD 3C para.5.3

Example of a limited civil restraint order annexed to this PD. The example may be modified as appropriate in any particular case.

See also **Civil restraint orders**.

LIMITED LIABILITY PARTNERSHIP

Service of the claim form in the jurisdiction or in specified circumstances within the EEA

Pt 6 r.6.3

(3) A limited liability partnership may be served—
  (a) by any method permitted under [Pt 6][**service of documents**]; or
  (b) by any of the methods of service permitted under the Companies Act 2006 as applied with modification by regulations made under the Limited Liability Partnerships Act 2000.

Service of documents other than the claim form in the UK or in specified circumstances within the EEA

Pt 6 r.6.20

(3) A limited liability partnership may be served—
  (a) by any method permitted under this Part; or

(b) by any of the methods of service permitted under the Companies Act 2006 as applied
    with modification by regulations made under the Limited Liability Partnerships Act
    2000.

See **Hearing**.

Application of PD 49A to certain proceedings in relation to limited liability partnerships

PD 49A para.3.

[PD 49A] applies to proceedings under the Companies Act 1985 and the Companies Act 2006
as applied to limited liability partnerships by regulations made under the Limited Liability
Partnerships Act 2000.

LIQUIDATED SUM

Glossary

Specified sum of money.

LIST

Glossary

Cases are allocated to different lists depending on the subject matter of the case. The lists are
used for administrative purposes and may also have their own procedures and judges.

LIST OF DOCUMENTS

Pt 31 r.31.10

PD 31A para.3.1

(1) The procedure for **standard disclosure** is as follows.
(2) Each party must make and serve on every other party, a list of documents in the relevant
    practice form [Form N265].
(3) The list must identify the documents in a convenient order and manner and as concisely
    as possible.
(4) The list must indicate—
    (a) those documents in respect of which the party claims a right or duty to withhold
        inspection; and
    (b) (i) those documents which are no longer in the party's control; and
        (ii) what has happened to those documents.
(Rule 31.19(3) and (4) require a statement in the list of documents relating to any documents
inspection of which a person claims he has a right or duty to withhold)
(5) The list must include a **disclosure statement**.

PD 31A para.3.2

In order to comply with r.31.10(3) it will normally be necessary to list the documents in date order, to number them consecutively and to give each a concise description (e.g. letter, claimant to defendant). Where there is a large number of documents all falling into a particular category the disclosing party may list those documents as a category rather than individually, e.g. 50 bank statements relating to account number.......at.........Bank,...........20 .. to...........20 ..; or, 35 letters passing between..........and.........between.........20......... and .. 20 . . .

PD 31A para.3.3

The obligations imposed by an order for disclosure will continue until the proceedings come to an end. If, after a list of documents has been prepared and served, the existence of further documents to which the order applies comes to the attention of the disclosing party, the party must prepare and serve a supplemental list.

Pt 31 r.31.10

(8) The parties may agree in writing—
(a) to disclose documents without making a list; and
(b) to disclose documents without the disclosing party making a disclosure statement.

See also **Electronic document**.

LISTING DIRECTIONS

See **Fast track** and **Multi-track**.

LISTING HEARING

Fast track

Pt 28 r.5

(4) If—
(c) the court considers that a hearing is necessary to enable it to decide what directions to give in order to complete preparation of the case for trial,
the court may give such directions as it thinks appropriate.

PD 28 para.6.3

Where the judge decides to hold a hearing under r.28.5(4) the court will fix a date which is as early as possible and the parties will be given at least three days' notice of the date.
The notice of such a hearing will be in Form N153.

Multi-track

Pt 29 r.29.6

(4) If—
(c) the court considers that a hearing is necessary to enable it to decide what directions to give in order to complete preparation of the case for trial,

the court may give such directions as it thinks appropriate.

PD 29 para.8.4

Where the court decides to hold a hearing under r.29.6(4) the court will fix a date which is as early as possible and the parties will be given at least three days notice of the date.

PD 29 para.8.5

Where the court decides to hold a pre-trial review (whether or not this is in addition to a hearing under r.29.6(4)) the court will give the parties at least seven days notice of the date.

LISTING QUESTIONNAIRE

Fast track

Pt 28 r.28.5

(1) The court will send the parties a pre-trial check list (listing questionnaire) for completion and return by the date specified in the notice of allocation unless it considers that the claim can proceed to trial without the need for a pre-trial check list.
(2) The date specified for filing a pre-trial check list will not be more than eight weeks before the trial date or the beginning of the trial period.
(3) If no party files the completed pre-trial checklist by the date specified, the court will order that unless a completed pre-trial checklist is filed within seven days from service of that order, the claim, defence and any counterclaim will be struck out without further order of the court.
(4) If—
   (a) a party files a completed pre-trial checklist but another party does not;
   (b) a party has failed to give all the information requested by the pre-trial checklist; or
   (c) the court considers that a hearing is necessary to enable it to decide what directions to give in order to complete preparation of the case for trial,
   the court may give such directions as it thinks appropriate.

PD 28 para.6.1

(1) The pre-trial check list (listing questionnaire) will be in Form N170.
(2) Unless it has dispensed with pre-trial check lists, the court will send Forms N170 and N171 (Notice of date for return of the pre-trial check list) to each party no later than two weeks before the date specified in the notice of allocation or in any later direction of the court for the return of the completed check lists.
(3) When all the pre-trial check lists have been filed or when the time for filing them has expired and where a party has filed a pre-trial checklist but another party has not done so, the file will be placed before a judge for his directions.
(4) Although the rules do not require the parties to exchange copies of the check lists before they are filed they are encouraged to do so to avoid the court being given conflicting or incomplete information.

Attention is drawn to the Costs PD s.6, which requires a costs estimate to be filed and served at the same time as the pre-trial check list is filed.

PD 28 para.6.2

Attention is drawn to r.28.6(1) (which sets out the court's duty at the pre-trial check list stage) and to r.28.5(4) (which sets out circumstances in which the court may decide to hold a hearing).

PD 28 para.6.3

Where the judge decides to hold a hearing under r.28.5(4) the court will fix a date which is as early as possible and the parties will be given at least three days' notice of the date.
   The notice of such a hearing will be in Form N153.

PD 28 para.6.4

The court's general approach will be as set out in the following paragraphs. The court may however decide to make other orders, and in particular the court will take into account the steps, if any, which the parties have taken to prepare the case for trial.

PD 28 para.6.5

(1) Where no party files a pre-trial checklist the court will order that unless a completed pre-trial checklist is filed within seven days from service of that order, the claim, defence and any counterclaim will be struck out without further order of the court.
(2) Where a party files a pre-trial check list but another party does not do so, the court normally will give directions. These will usually fix or confirm the trial date and provide for steps to be taken to prepare the case for trial.

Multi-track

Pt 29 r.29.6

(1) The court will send the parties a pre-trial check list (listing questionnaire) for completion and return by the date specified in directions given under r.29.2(3) unless it considers that the claim can proceed to trial without the need for a pre-trial check list.
(2) Each party must file the completed pre-trial check list by the date specified by the court.
(3) If no party files the completed pre-trial checklist by the date specified, the court will order that unless a completed pre-trial checklist is filed within seven days from service of that order, the claim, defence and any counterclaim will be struck out without further order of the court.
(4) If—
    (a) a party files a completed pre-trial checklist but another party does not;
    (b) a party has failed to give all the information requested by the pre-trial checklist; or
    (c) the court considers that a hearing is necessary to enable it to decide what directions to give in order to complete preparation of the case for trial, the court may give such directions as it thinks appropriate.

PD 29 para.8.1

(1) The pre-trial check list (listing questionnaire) will be in Form N170.
(2) Unless it dispenses with pre-trial check lists and orders an early trial on a fixed date, the court will specify the date for filing completed pre-trial check lists when it fixes the trial date or trial period under r.29.2(2).

(3) The date for filing the completed pre-trial check list will be not later than eight weeks before the trial date or the start of the trial period.

(4) The court will serve the pre-trial check lists on the parties at least 14 days before that date.

(5) Although the rules do not require the parties to exchange copies of the check lists before they are filed they are encouraged to do so to avoid the court being given conflicting or incomplete information.

(6) The file will be placed before a judge for his directions when all the check lists have been filed or when the time for filing them has expired and where a party has filed a checklist but another party has not done so.

PD 29 para.8.2

The court's general approach will be as set out in the following paragraphs. The court may however decide to make other orders, and in particular the court will take into account the steps, if any, of which it is aware which the parties have taken to prepare the case for trial.

PD 29 para.8.3

(1) Where no party files a pre-trial checklist the court will order that unless a completed pre-trial checklist is filed within seven days from service of that order, the claim, defence and any counterclaim will be struck out without further order of the court.

(2) Where a party files a pre-trial check list but another party (the defaulting party) does not do so, the court will fix a hearing under r.29.6(4). Whether or not the defaulting party attends the hearing, the court will normally fix or confirm the trial date and make other orders about the steps to be taken to prepare the case for trial.

PD 29 para.8.4

Where the court decides to hold a hearing under r.29.6(4) the court will fix a date which is as early as possible and the parties will be given at least three days notice of the date.

PD 29 para.8.5

Where the court decides to hold a pre-trial review (whether or not this is in addition to a hearing under r.29.6(4)) the court will give the parties at least seven days notice of the date.

LITIGANT IN PERSON

Pt 46 r.46.5

(6) For the purposes of this rule, a litigant in person includes—

(a) a company or other corporation which is acting without a **legal representative**; and

(b) any of the following who acts in person (except where any such person is represented by a firm in which that person is a partner)—

(i) a barrister;

(ii) a solicitor;

(iii) a solicitor's employee;

(iv) a manager of a body recognised under s. 9 of the Administration of Justice Act 1985; or

(v) a person who, for the purposes of the [Legal Services Act 2007], is an authorised person in relation to an activity which constitutes the conduct of litigation (within the meaning of that Act).

Pt 46 r.46.5

(1) This rule applies where the court orders (whether by **summary assessment** or **detailed assessment**) that the costs of a litigant in person are to be paid by any other person.
(2) The costs allowed under this rule will not exceed, except in the case of a disbursement, two-thirds of the amount which would have been allowed if the litigant in person had been represented by a **legal representative**.
(3) The litigant in person shall be allowed—
    (a) costs for the same categories of—
        (i) work; and
        (ii) disbursements,
    which would have been allowed if the work had been done or the disbursements had been made by a legal representative on the litigant in person's behalf;
    (b) the payments reasonably made by the litigant in person for legal services relating to the conduct of the proceedings; and
    (c) the costs of obtaining expert assistance in assessing the costs claim.
(4) The amount of costs to be allowed to the litigant in person for any item of work claimed will be—
    (a) where the litigant can prove financial loss, the amount that the litigant can prove to have been lost for time reasonably spent on doing the work; or
    (b) where the litigant cannot prove financial loss, an amount for the time reasonably spent on doing the work at the rate set out in PD 46.
(5) A litigant who is allowed costs for attending at court to conduct the case is not entitled to a witness allowance in respect of such attendance in addition to those costs.

PD 46 para.3.1

In order to qualify as an expert for the purpose of r. 46.5(3)(c) (expert assistance in connection with assessing the claim for costs), the person in question must be a—
(a) barrister;
(b) solicitor;
(c) Fellow of the Institute of Legal Executives;
(d) Fellow of the Association of Costs Lawyers;
(e) law costs draftsman who is a member of the Academy of Experts;
(f) law costs draftsman who is a member of the Expert Witness Institute.

PD 46 para.3.2

Where a self-represented litigant wishes to prove that the litigant has suffered financial loss, the litigant should produce to the court any written evidence relied on to support that claim, and serve a copy of that evidence on any party against whom the litigant seeks costs at least 24 hours before the hearing at which the question may be decided.

PD 46 para.3.3

A self-represented litigant who commences detailed assessment proceedings under r. 47.5 should serve copies of that written evidence with the notice of commencement.

PD 46 para.3.4

The amount, which may be allowed to a self-represented litigant under r. 45.39(5)(b) and r. 46.5(4)(b), is £18 per hour.

Fast track trial costs

Pt 45 r.45.39

    (5) Where the party to whom fast track trial costs are to be awarded is a litigant in person, the court will award—
        (a) if the litigant in person can prove financial loss, two-thirds of the amount that would otherwise be awarded; or
        (b) if the **litigant in person** fails to prove financial loss, an amount in respect of the time spent reasonably doing the work at the rate specified in the PD 46.

Value added tax

PD 44 para.2.12

Where a litigant acts in person, that litigant is not treated for the purposes of VAT as having supplied services and therefore no VAT is chargeable in respect of work done by that litigant (even where, for example, that litigant is a solicitor or other legal representative). Consequently in such circumstances a bill of costs should not claim any VAT.

PD 44 para.2.5

Where the receiving party is a litigant in person who is claiming VAT, evidence to support the claim (such as a letter from HMRC) must be produced at the hearing at which the costs are assessed.

Court of Appeal

Skeleton arguments and litigant in person

PD 52 para.5.9

    (3) An appellant who is not represented need not file a skeleton argument but is encouraged to do so since this will be helpful to the court.

See also **McKenzie friend** and **Vexatious litigants**.

LITIGATION

A court case or court proceedings. The taking of legal action by someone.

LITIGATION FRIEND

Pt 21 r.21.1

(1) [Part 21]–
  (a) contains special provisions which apply in proceedings involving children and protected parties;
  (b) sets out how a person becomes a litigation friend; and
  (c) does not apply to proceedings under Pt 75 where one of the parties to the proceedings is a **child**.

PD 21 para.2.1

A person may become a litigation friend—
  (a) without a court order under r.21.5, or
  (b) by a court order under r.21.6.

Requirement for a litigation friend in proceedings by or against children and protected parties

Pt 21 r.21.2

(1) A **protected party** must have a litigation friend to conduct proceedings on his behalf.
(2) A child must have a litigation friend to conduct proceedings on his behalf unless the court makes an order under para.(3).
(3) The court may make an order permitting a child to conduct proceedings without a litigation friend.
(4) An application for an order under para.(3)—
  (a) may be made by the child;
  (b) if the child already has a litigation friend, must be made on notice to the litigation friend; and
  (c) if the child has no litigation friend, may be made without notice.
(5) Where—
  (a) the court has made an order under para.(3); and
  (b) it subsequently appears to the court that it is desirable for a litigation friend to conduct the proceedings on behalf of the child,
  the court may appoint a person to be the child's litigation friend.

Stage of proceedings at which a litigation friend becomes necessary

Pt 21 r.21.3

(1) This rule does not apply where the court has made an order under r.21.2(3).
(2) A person may not, without the permission of the court—
  (a) make an application against a child or protected party before proceedings have started; or
  (b) take any step in proceedings except—
    (i) issuing and serving a claim form; or
    (ii) applying for the appointment of a litigation friend under r.21.6,
  until the child or protected party has a litigation friend.

(3) If during proceedings a party lacks capacity to continue to conduct proceedings, no party may take any further step in the proceedings without the permission of the court until the protected party has a litigation friend.

(4) Any step taken before a child or protected party has a litigation friend has no effect unless the court orders otherwise.

Who may be a litigation friend without a court order

Pt 21 r.21.4

(1) This rule does not apply if the court has appointed a person to be a litigation friend.

(2) A deputy appointed by the Court of Protection under the [Mental Capacity Act 2005] with power to conduct proceedings on the protected party's behalf is entitled to be the litigation friend of the protected party in any proceedings to which his power extends.

(3) If nobody has been appointed by the court or, in the case of a protected party, has been appointed as a deputy as set out in para.(2), a person may act as a litigation friend if he—

(a) can fairly and competently conduct proceedings on behalf of the child or protected party;

(b) has no interest adverse to that of the child or protected party; and

(c) where the child or protected party is a claimant, undertakes to pay any costs which the child or protected party may be ordered to pay in relation to the proceedings, subject to any right he may have to be repaid from the assets of the child or protected party.

Becoming a litigation friend without a court order

Pt 21 r.21.5

(1) If the court has not appointed a litigation friend, a person who wishes to act as a litigation friend must follow the procedure set out in this rule.

(2) A deputy appointed by the Court of Protection under the 2005 Act with power to conduct proceedings on the protected party's behalf must file an **official copy** of the order of the Court of Protection which confers his power to act either—

(a) where the deputy is to act as a litigation friend for a claimant, at the time the claim is made; or

(b) where the deputy is to act as a litigation friend for a defendant, at the time when he first takes a step in the proceedings on behalf of the defendant.

(3) Any other person must file a **certificate of suitability** stating that he satisfies the conditions specified in r.21.4(3) either—

(a) where the person is to act as a litigation friend for a claimant, at the time when the claim is made; or

(b) where the person is to act as a litigation friend for a defendant, at the time when he first takes a step in the proceedings on behalf of the defendant.

(4) The litigation friend must—

(a) serve the certificate of suitability on every person on whom, in accordance with r.6.13 (service on a parent, guardian, etc.) the claim form should be served; and

(b) file a certificate of service when filing the certificate of suitability.

(Rules 6.17 and 6.29 set out the details to be contained in a certificate of service).

PD 21 para.2.2

A person who wishes to become a litigation friend without a court order pursuant to r.21.5(3) must file [inter alia]—

    (e) where the child or protected party is a claimant, undertaking to pay any costs which the child or protected party may be ordered to pay in relation to the proceedings, subject to any right he may have to be repaid from the assets of the child or protected party.

PD 21 para.2.4

The litigation friend is not required to serve the document referred to in para.2.2(c) when he serves a certificate of suitability on the person to be served under r.21.5(4)(a).

Certificate of suitability

PD 21 para.2.3

The certificate of suitability must be verified by a **statement of truth**.

Becoming a litigation friend by court order

Pt 21 r.21.6

    (1) The court may make an order appointing a litigation friend.
    (2) An application for an order appointing a litigation friend may be made by—
        (a) a person who wishes to be the litigation friend; or
        (b) a party.
    (3) Where—
        (a) a person makes a claim against a child or protected party;
        (b) the child or protected party has no litigation friend;
        (c) the court has not made an order under r.21.2(3) (order that a child can conduct proceedings without a litigation friend); and
        (d) either—
            (i) someone who is not entitled to be a litigation friend files a defence; or
            (ii) the claimant wishes to take some step in the proceedings,
    the claimant must apply to the court for an order appointing a litigation friend for the child or protected party.
    (4) An application for an order appointing a litigation friend must be supported by evidence.
    (5) The court may not appoint a litigation friend under this rule unless it is satisfied that the person to be appointed satisfies the conditions in r.21.4(3).

Pt 21 r.21.9

    (4) On an application for an order under r.21.6, the court may appoint the person proposed or any other person who satisfies the conditions specified in r.21.4(3).

PD 21 para.3.2

An application must be made in accordance with Pt 23 and must be supported by evidence.

PD 21 para.3.3

The evidence in support must satisfy the court that the proposed litigation friend—
  (1) consents to act,
  (2) can fairly and competently conduct proceedings on behalf of the child or protected party,
  (3) has no interest adverse to that of the child or protected party, and
  (4) where the child or protected party is a claimant, undertakes to pay any costs which the child or protected party may be ordered to pay in relation to the proceedings, subject to any right he may have to be repaid from the assets of the child or protected party.

PD 21 para.3.4

Where it is sought to appoint the **Official Solicitor** as the litigation friend, provision must be made for payment of his charges.

Court's power to change a litigation friend and to prevent person acting as a litigation friend

Pt 21 r.21.7

  (1) The court may—
      (a) direct that a person may not act as a litigation friend;
      (b) terminate a litigation friend's appointment; or
      (c) appoint a new litigation friend in substitution for an existing one.
  (2) An application for an order under para.(1) must be supported by evidence.
  (3) The court may not appoint a litigation friend under this rule unless it is satisfied that the person to be appointed satisfies the conditions in r.21.4(3).

Pt 21 r.21.9

  (4) On an application for an order under r.21.7, the court may appoint the person proposed or any other person who satisfies the conditions specified in r.21.4(3).

Service

Pt 21 r.21.8

  (1) An application for an order under r.21.6 or 21.7 must be served on every person on whom, in accordance with r.6.13 (service on parent, guardian etc.), the claim form must be served.
  (2) Where an application for an order under r.21.6 is in respect of a protected party, the application must also be served on the protected party unless the court orders otherwise.
  (3) An application for an order under r.21.7 must also be served on—
      (a) the person who is the litigation friend, or who is purporting to act as the litigation friend, when the application is made; and
      (b) the person who it is proposed should be the litigation friend, if he is not the applicant.

Procedure where appointment of a litigation friend ceases

Pt 21 r.21.9

(1) When a child who is not a protected party reaches the age of 18, the litigation friend's appointment ceases.

(2) Where a protected party regains or acquires capacity to conduct the proceedings, the litigation friend's appointment continues until it is ended by court order.

(3) An application for an order under para.(2) may be made by—
   (a) the former protected party;
   (b) the litigation friend; or
   (c) a party.

(4) The child or protected party in respect of whom the appointment to act has ceased must serve notice on the other parties—
   (a) stating that the appointment of his litigation friend to act has ceased;
   (b) giving his address for service; and
   (c) stating whether or not he intends to carry on the proceedings.

(5) If the child or protected party does not serve the notice required by para.(4) within 28 days after the day on which the appointment of the litigation friend ceases the court may, on application, **strike out** any claim brought by or defence raised by the child or protected party.

(6) The liability of a litigation friend for costs continues until—
   (a) the person in respect of whom his appointment to act has ceased serves the notice referred to in para.(4); or
   (b) the litigation friend serves notice on the parties that his appointment to act has ceased.

PD 21 para.4.1

Rule 21.9 deals with the situation where the need for a litigation friend comes to an end during the proceedings because either—
   (1) a child who is not also a protected party reaches the age of 18 (full age) during the proceedings, or
   (2) a protected party regains or acquires capacity to conduct the proceedings.

PD 21 para.4.2

A child on reaching full age must serve on the other parties to the proceedings and file with the court a notice—
   (1) stating that he has reached full age,
   (2) stating that his litigation friend's appointment has ceased,
   (3) giving an address for service, and
   (4) stating whether or not he intends to carry on with or continue to defend the proceedings.

PD 21 para.4.3

If the notice states that the child intends to carry on with or continue to defend the proceedings he must subsequently be described in the proceedings as 'A.B. (formerly a child but now of full age)'.

PD 21 para.4.4

Whether or not a child having reached full age serves a notice in accordance with r.21.9(4) and para.4.2 above, a litigation friend may, at any time after the child has reached full age, serve a notice on the other parties that his appointment has ceased.

PD 21 para.4.5

Where a protected party regains or acquires capacity to conduct the proceedings, an application under r.21.9(3) must be made for an order under r.21.9(2) that the litigation friend's appointment has ceased.

PD 21 para.4.6

The application must be supported by the following evidence—
    (1) a medical report or other suitably qualified expert's report indicating that the protected party has regained or acquired capacity to conduct the proceedings,
    (2) a copy of any relevant order or declaration of the Court of Protection, and
    (3) if the application is made by the protected party, a statement whether or not he intends to carry on with or continue to defend the proceedings.

PD 21 para.4.7

An order under r.21.9(2) must be served on the other parties to the proceedings. The former protected party must file with the court a notice—
    (1) stating that his litigation friend's appointment has ceased,
    (2) giving an address for service, and
    (3) stating whether or not he intends to carry on with or continue to defend the proceedings.

Expenses incurred by a litigation friend

Pt 21 r.21.12

    (1) In proceedings to which r.21.11 [Control of money recovered by or on behalf of a child or protected party] applies, a litigation friend who incurs expenses on behalf of a child or protected party in any proceedings is entitled on application to recover the amount paid or payable out of any money recovered or paid into court to the extent that it—
        (a) has been reasonably incurred; and
        (b) is reasonable in amount.
    (2) Expenses may include all or part of—
        (a) a premium in respect of a costs insurance policy (as defined by s.58(c)(5) of the Courts and Legal Services Act 1990); or
        (b) interest on a loan taken out to pay a premium in respect of a costs insurance policy or other recoverable disbursement.
    (3) No application may be made under the rule for expenses that—
        (a) are of a type that may be recoverable on an assessment of costs payable by or out of money belonging to a child or protected party; but
        (b) are disallowed in whole or in part on such an assessment.
(Expenses which are also 'costs' as defined in r.44.1(1)(a) are dealt with under r.46.4(2).)
    (4) In deciding whether the expenses were reasonably incurred and reasonable in amount, the court will have regard to all the circumstances of the case including the factors set out in r.44.4(3).
    (5) When the court is considering the factors to be taken into account in assessing the reasonableness of the expenses, it will have regard to the facts and circumstances as they reasonably appeared to the litigation friend or to the child's or protected party's legal representative when the expense was incurred.
    (6) Where the claim is settled or compromised, or judgment is given, on terms that an amount not exceeding £5,000 is paid to the child or protected party, the total amount the

litigation friend may recover under para.(1) must not exceed 25 per cent of the sum so agreed or awarded, unless the court directs otherwise. Such total amount must not exceed 50 per cent of the sum so agreed or awarded.

Appointment of a guardian of a child's estate

Pt 21 21.13

(1) The court may appoint the Official Solicitor to be a guardian of a child's estate where—
    (a) money is paid into court on behalf of the child in accordance with directions given under rule 21.11 (control of money received by a child or protected party);
    (b) the Criminal Injuries Compensation Authority notifies the court that it has made or intends to make an award to the child;
    (c) a court or tribunal outside England and Wales notifies the court that it has ordered or intends to order that money be paid to the child;
    (d) the child is absolutely entitled to the proceeds of a pension fund; or
    (e) in any other case, such an appointment seems desirable to the court.
(2) The court may not appoint the Official Solicitor under this rule unless—
    (a) the persons with parental responsibility (within the meaning of s.3 of the Children Act 1989 agree; or
    (b) the court considers that their agreement can be dispensed with.
(3) The Official Solicitor's appointment may continue only until the child reaches 18.

PD 21 para.11.1

A litigation friend may make a claim for expenses under r.21.12(1)—
(1) where the court has ordered an assessment of costs under r.48.5(2), at the detailed assessment hearing;
(2) where the litigation friend's expenses are not of a type which would be recoverable as costs on an assessment of costs between the parties, to the Master or district judge at the hearing to approve the settlement or compromise under Pt 21 (the Master or district judge may adjourn the matter to the costs judge); or
(3) where an assessment of costs under Pt 48.5(2) is not required, and no approval under Pt 21 is necessary, by a Pt 23 application supported by a witness statement to a costs judge or district judge as appropriate.

PD 21 para.11.2

In all circumstances, the litigation friend must support a claim for expenses by filing a witness statement setting out—
(1) the nature and amount of the expense; and
(2) the reason the expense was incurred.

Title of proceedings

PD 21 para.1.1

In proceedings where one of the parties is a protected party, the protected party should be referred to in the title to the proceedings as 'A.B. (a protected party by C.D. his litigation friend)'.

PD 21 para.1.2

In proceedings where one of the parties is a child, where—
  (1) the child has a litigation friend, the child should be referred to in the title to the proceedings as 'A.B. (a child by C.D. his litigation friend)'; or
  (2) the child is conducting the proceedings on his own behalf, the child should be referred to in the title as 'A.B. (a child)'.

LLOYD'S NAME

The procedure for personal representatives who wish to apply to the court for permission to distribute the estate of as deceased Lloyd's Name following the decision in *Re Yorke (Deceased)* [1997] 4 All E.R. 907.

LODGING

Filing.

LONDON MERCANTILE COURT

PD 59 para.1.2

  (2) the Commercial Court of the Queen's Bench Division at the Royal Courts of Justice (called 'The London Mercantile Court').

LSC FUNDED CLIENT

Detailed assessment procedure for costs of a LSC funded client or an assisted person where costs are payable out of the community legal service fund

Detailed assessment procedure where costs are payable out of the community legal service fund

Pt 47 r.47.18

  (1) Where the court is to assess costs of a LSC funded client or an assisted person which are payable out of the Community Legal Services Fund, that person's solicitor may commence detailed assessment proceedings by filing a request in the relevant practice form.
  (2) A request under para.(1) must be filed within three months after the date when the right to detailed assessment arose.
  (3) The solicitor must also serve a copy of the request for detailed assessment on the LSC funded client or the assisted person, if notice of that person's interest has been given to the court in accordance with community legal service or legal aid regulations.
  (4) Where the solicitor has certified that the LSC funded client or that person wishes to attend an assessment hearing, the court will, on receipt of the request for assessment, fix a date for the assessment hearing.

(5) Where para.(3) does not apply, the court will, on receipt of the request for assessment provisionally assess the costs without the attendance of the solicitor, unless it considers that a hearing is necessary.

(6) After the court has provisionally assessed the bill, it will return the bill to the solicitor.

(7) The court will fix a date for an assessment hearing if the solicitor informs the court, within 14 days after he receives the provisionally assessed bill, that he wants the court to hold such a hearing.

PD 47 para.17.1

The time for requesting a detailed assessment under r.47.17 is within three months after the date when the right to detailed assessment arose.

PD 47 para.17.2

(1) The request for a detailed assessment of costs must be in Form N258A [and accompanied by copy of the bill of costs and documents listed in para.17.2(1)].

PD 47 para.17.3

Where the court has provisionally assessed a bill of costs it will send to the legal representation a notice, in Form N253 annexed to PD 47 together with the bill itself. The legal representative should, if the provisional assessment is to be accepted, then complete the bill.

PD 47 para.17.4

If the solicitor whose bill it is, or any other party wishes to make an application in the detailed assessment proceedings, the provisions of Pt 23 [**application**] applies.

PD 47 para.17.5

It is the responsibility of the legal representative to complete the bill by entering in the bill the correct figures allowed in respect of each item, recalculating the summary of the bill appropriately and completing the Community Legal Service assessment certificate (Form EX80A). [PD 47 paras 17.6 to 17.11 deal with the filing of a legal aid/LSC schedule where costs are payable by the Legal Services Commission or Lord Chancellor at prescribed rates.]

Detailed assessment procedure where costs are payable out of a fund other than the community legal service fund or by the Lord Chancellor under Pt 1 of the Legal Aid, Sentencing and Punishment of Offenders Act 2012

PD 47 para.47.19

(1) Where the court is to assess costs which are payable out of a fund other than the Community Legal Service Fund, the receiving party may commence detailed assessment proceedings by filing a request in the relevant practice form.

(2) A request under para.(1) must be filed within three months after the date when the right to detailed assessment arose.

(3) The court may direct that the party seeking assessment serve a copy of the request on any person who has a financial interest in the outcome of the assessment.

(4) The court will, on receipt of the request for assessment, provisionally assess the costs without the attendance of the receiving party, unless the court considers that a hearing is necessary.
(5) After the court has provisionally assessed the bill, it will return the bill to the receiving party.
(6) The court will fix a date for an assessment hearing if the receiving party informs the court, within 14 days after receiving the provisionally assessed bill, that the receiving party wants the court to hold such a hearing.

PD 47 para.18.1

R. 47.19 enables the court to direct under r. 47.19(3) that the receiving party must serve a copy of the request for assessment and copies of the documents which accompany it, on any person who has a financial interest in the outcome of the assessment.

PD 47 para.18.2

A person has a financial interest in the outcome of the assessment if the assessment will or may affect the amount of money or property to which that person is or may become entitled out of the fund. Where an interest in the fund is itself held by a trustee for the benefit of some other person, that trustee will be treated as the person having such a financial interest unless it is not appropriate to do so. 'Trustee' includes a personal representative, receiver or any other person acting in a fiduciary capacity.

PD 47 para.18.3

The request for a detailed assessment of costs out of the fund should be in Form N258B, be accompanied by the documents set out at paras 17.2(1) (a)–(e) and the following—
(a) a statement signed by the receiving party giving his name, address for service, reference, telephone number,
(b) a statement of the postal address of any person who has a financial interest in the outcome of the assessment; and
(c) if a person having a financial interest is a child or protected party, a statement to that effect.

PD 47 para.18.4

The court will decide, having regard to the amount of the bill, the size of the fund and the number of persons who have a financial interest, which of those persons should be served and may give directions about service and about the hearing. The court may dispense with service on all or some of those persons.

PD 47 para.18.5

Where the court makes an order dispensing with service on all such persons it may proceed at once to make a provisional assessment, or, if it decides that a hearing is necessary, give appropriate directions. Before deciding whether a hearing is necessary, the court may require the receiving party to provide further information relating to the bill.

PD 47 para.18.6

(1) The court will send the provisionally assessed bill to the receiving party with a notice in Form N253. If the receiving party is legally represented the legal representative should, if the provisional assessment is to be accepted, then complete the bill.

(2) The court will fix a date for a detailed assessment hearing, if the receiving party informs the court within 14 days after receiving the notice in Form N253, that the receiving party wants the court to hold such a hearing.

PD 47 para.18.7

The court will give at least 14 days notice of the time and place of the hearing to the receiving party and to any person who has a financial and who has been served with a copy of the request for assessment.

PD 47 para.18.8

If any party or any person who has a financial interest wishes to make an application in the detailed assessment proceedings, the provisions of Pt 23 (General Rules about Applications for Court Orders) apply.

PD 47 para.18.9

If the receiving party is legally represented the legal representative must complete the bill by inserting the correct figures in respect of each item and must recalculate the summary of the bill.

Appellant in receipt of services funded by the Legal Services Commission applying for permission to appeal

PD 52C para.17

Where the appellant is in receipt of services funded by the Legal Services Commission (or legally aided) and permission to appeal has been refused by the appeal court without a hearing, the appellant must send a copy of the reasons the appeal court gave for refusing permission to the relevant office of the Legal Services Commission as soon as it has been received from the court. The court will require confirmation that this has been done if a hearing is requested to re-consider the question of permission.

See also **Legal Aid**.

LUGANO CONVENTION

(f) Convention on jurisdiction and the recognition and enforcement of judgments in civil and commercial matters, between the European Community and the Republic of Iceland, the Kingdom of Norway, the Swiss Confederation and the Kingdom of Denmark and signed by the European Community on October 30, 2007.

M

MAINTENANCE ORDER

Attachment of Earnings Order

CCR Ord.27 r.17

(1) [CCR Ord.27] shall apply in relation to maintenance payments as they apply in relation to a judgment debt, subject to the following paragraphs.

(2) An application for an attachment of earnings order to secure payments under a maintenance order made by a county court shall be made to that county court.

(3) Any application under s.32 of the Matrimonial Causes Act 1973 for permission to enforce the payment of arrears which became due more than 12 months before the application for an attachment of earnings order shall be made in that application.

(3A) Notice of the application together with a form of reply in the appropriate form, shall be served on the debtor in the manner set out in CPR r.6.20. (3B) Service of the notice shall be effected not less than 21 days before the hearing, but service may be effected at any time before the hearing on the applicant satisfying the court by witness statement or affidavit that the respondent is about to remove from his address for service. (3C) Rule 5(2A) shall not apply.

(4) An application by the debtor for an attachment of earnings order to secure payments under a maintenance order may be made on the making of the maintenance order or an order varying the maintenance order, and rr.4 and 5 shall not apply.

(5) Rule 7 shall have effect as if for paras (1) to (8) there were substituted the following paragraph—(1) An application for an attachment of earnings order may be heard and determined by the district judge, who shall hear the application in private.'

(6) Rule 9 shall apply as if for the reference to the amount payable under the relevant adjudication there were substituted a reference to the arrears due under the related maintenance order.

(7) Where an attachment of earnings order made by the High Court designates the court officer of a county court as the collecting officer, that officer shall, on receipt of a certified copy of the order from the court officer of the High Court, send to the person to whom the order is directed a notice as to the mode of payment.

(8) Where an attachment of earnings order made by a county court to secure payments under a maintenance order ceases to have effect and—
   (a) the related maintenance order was made by that court; or
   (b) the related maintenance order was an order of the High Court and—
      (i) the court officer of the county court has received notice of the cessation from the court officer of the High Court; or
      (ii) a committal order has been made in the county court for the enforcement of the related maintenance order,
   the court officer of the county court shall give notice of the cessation to the person to whom the attachment of earnings order was directed.

(9) Where an attachment of earnings order has been made by a county court to secure payments under a maintenance order, notice under s.10(2) of the Act of 1971 to the

debtor and to the person to whom the district judge is required to pay sums received under the order shall be in the form provided for that purpose, and if the debtor wishes to request the court to discharge the attachment of earnings order or to vary it otherwise than by making the appropriate variation, he shall apply to the court, within 14 days after the date of the notice, for the remedy desired.

(10) Rule 13 shall have effect as if for paras (4) to (7) there were substituted the following paragraph—

"(4) Where it appears to the court by which an attachment of earnings order has been made that the related maintenance order has ceased to have effect, whether by virtue of the terms of the maintenance order or under section 28 of the Matrimonial Causes Act 1973 or otherwise, the court may discharge or vary the attachment of earnings order."

CCR Ord.27 r.8

(1) An order made under s.23(1) of the Act of 1971 for the attendance of the debtor at an adjourned hearing of an application for an attachment of earnings order to secure payments under a maintenance order shall—
   (a) be served on the debtor personally not less than five days before the day fixed for the adjourned hearing; and
   (b) direct that any payments made thereafter shall be paid into the court and not direct to the judgment creditor.

(2) An application by a debtor for the revocation of an order committing him to prison and, if he is already in custody, for his discharge under subs.(7) of the said s.23 shall be made to the judge or district judge in writing without notice to any other party showing the reasons for the debtor's failure to attend the court or his refusal to be sworn or to give evidence, as the case may be, and containing an undertaking by the debtor to attend the court or to be sworn or to give evidence when next ordered or required to do so.

(3) The application shall, if the debtor has already been lodged in prison, be attested by the governor of the prison (or any other officer of the prison not below the rank of principal officer) and in any other case be made on witness statement or affidavit.

(4) Before dealing with the application the judge or district judge may, if he thinks fit, cause notice to be given to the judgment creditor that the application has been made and of a day and hour when he may attend and be heard.

See also **Attachment of Earnings**.

MALICIOUS FALSEHOOD

See **Defamation claims**.

MAREVA INJUNCTIONS

See **Freezing injunction**.

MARITIME CLAIMS

Admiralty claims.

MCKENZIE FRIEND

A litigant in person may be assisted at a hearing by another person, often referred to as a McKenzie friend (*McKenzie v McKenzie* [1971] P 33). The litigant must be present at the hearing.

If the hearing is in private, it is a matter of discretion for the court whether such an assistant is allowed to attend the hearing. Guideline is found in *Family Division's Practice Note (Family Courts: Mackenzie Friends) (No 2)* [2008] 1 W.L.R. 2757.

MEDIATED CROSS-BORDER DISPUTES

Pt 78 r.78.23

(1) This section applies to mediated cross-border disputes that are subject to Directive 2008/52/EC of the European Parliament and of the Council of May 21, 2008 on certain aspects of mediation in civil and commercial matters.

(2) In this section—

'Mediation Directive' means Directive 2008/52/EC of the European Parliament and of the Council of May 21, 2008 on certain aspects of mediation in civil and commercial matters. A copy of the Directive can be found at Annex 3;

'cross-border dispute' has the meaning given by art.2 of the Mediation Directive;

'mediation' has the meaning given by art.3(a) of the Mediation Directive]

'mediation settlement enforcement order' means an order made under r.78.24(5);

'mediator' has the meaning given by art.3(b) of the Mediation Directive; and

'relevant dispute' means a cross-border dispute that is subject to the Mediation Directive.

MEDICAL RECORDS

Obtaining the health records

Pre-action Protocol for the resolution of Clinical Disputes (PRCD) para.3.7

Any request for records by the patient or their adviser should—

provide sufficient information to alert the healthcare provider where an adverse outcome has been serious or had serious consequences;

be as specific as possible about the records which are required.

PRCD para.3.8

Requests for copies of the patient's clinical records should be made using the Law Society and Department of Health approved standard forms (enclosed at Annex B), adapted as necessary.

PRCD para.3.9

The copy records should be provided within 40 days of the request and for a cost not exceeding the charges permissible under the Access to Health Records Act 1990 (currently a maximum of £10 plus photocopying and postage).

PRCD para.3.10

In the rare circumstances that the healthcare provider is in difficulty in complying with the request within 40 days, the problem should be explained quickly and details given of what is being done to resolve it.

PRCD para.3.11

It will not be practicable for healthcare providers to investigate in detail each case when records are requested. but healthcare providers should adopt a policy on which cases will be investigated (see para.3.5 on clinical governance and adverse outcome reporting).

PRCD para.3.12

If the healthcare provider fails to provide the health records within 40 days, the patient or their adviser can then apply to the court for an order for pre-action disclosure. The new Civil Procedure Rules should make pre-action applications to the court easier. The court will also have the power to impose costs sanctions for unreasonable delay in providing records.

PRCD para.3.13

If either the patient or the healthcare provider considers additional health records are required from a third party, in the first instance these should be requested by or through the patient. Third party healthcare providers are expected to co-operate. The Civil Procedure Rules will enable patients and healthcare providers to apply to the court for pre-action disclosure by third parties.

MEDIATION EVIDENCE

Disclosure or inspection

Pt 78 r.78.26

(1) Where a person seeks disclosure or inspection of mediation evidence [means evidence arising out of or in connection with a mediation process] that is in the control of a mediator or mediation administrator, that person must apply—
   (a) where there are existing proceedings in England and Wales, by an application made in accordance with Pt 23; and
   (b) where there are no existing proceedings in England and Wales, by the Pt 8 procedure.
(2) Where the application is made—
   (a) under para.(1)(a), the mediator or mediation administrator who has control of the mediation evidence must be named as a respondent to the application and must be served with a copy of the application notice; and
   (b) under para.(1)(b), the mediator or mediation administrator [means a person involved in the administration of the mediation process] who has control of the mediation evidence must be made a party to the claim.
(3) Evidence in support of the application under para.(1)(a) or (1)(b) must include evidence that—
   (a) all parties to the mediation agree to the disclosure or inspection of the mediation evidence;
   (b) disclosure or inspection of the mediation evidence is necessary for overriding considerations of public policy, in accordance with art.7(1)(a) of the Mediation Directive; or
   (c) disclosure or inspection of the mediation settlement is necessary to implement or enforce the mediation settlement agreement.
(4) This rule does not apply to proceedings in England and Wales that have been allocated to the small claims track.

(5) Where this rule applies, Pts 31 to 34 apply to the extent they are consistent with this rule.

Witnesses and depositions

Pt 78 r.78.27

(1) This rule applies where a party wishes to obtain mediation evidence from a mediator or mediation administrator by—
    (a) a witness summons;
    (b) cross-examination with permission of the court under rr.32.7 or 33.4;
    (c) an order under r.34.8 (evidence by deposition);
    (d) an order under r.34.10 (enforcing attendance of witness);
    (e) an order under r.34.11(4) (deponent's evidence to be given orally); or
    (f) an order under r.34.13(1A) (order for the issue of a letter of request).
(2) When applying for a witness summons, permission under rr.32.7 or 33.4 or an order under rr.34.8, 34.10, 34.11(4) or 34.13(1A), the party must provide the court with evidence that—
    (a) all parties to the mediation agree to the obtaining of the mediation evidence;
    (b) obtaining the mediation evidence is necessary for overriding considerations of public policy, in accordance with art.7(1)(a) of the Mediation Directive; or
    (c) the disclosure or inspection of the mediation settlement is necessary to implement or enforce the mediation settlement agreement.
(3) When considering a request for a witness summons, permission under rr.32.7 or 33.4 or an order under rr.34.8, 34.10, 34.11(4) or 34.13(1A), the court may invite any person, whether or not a party, to make representations.
(4) This rule does not apply to proceedings in England and Wales that have been allocated to the small claims track.
(5) Where this rule applies, Pts 31 to 34 apply to the extent they are consistent with this rule.

Small claims

Pt 78 r.78.28

Where a party wishes to rely on mediation evidence in proceedings that are allocated to the small claims track, that party must inform the

MEDIATION SETTLEMENT ENFORCEMENT ORDERS

Pt 78 r.78.24

(1) Where the parties, or one of them with the explicit consent of the others, wish to apply for a mediation settlement [means the content of a written agreement resulting from mediation of a relevant dispute] to be made enforceable, the parties or party may apply—
    (a) where there are existing proceedings in England and Wales, by an application made in accordance with Pt 23; or
    (b) where there are no existing proceedings in England and Wales, by the Pt 8 procedure as modified by this rule and PD 78—European Procedures.

(2) Where r.78.24(1)(b) applies, rr.8.3 to 8.8 will not apply.

(3) The mediation settlement agreement [a written agreement resulting from mediation of a relevant dispute] must be annexed to the application notice or claim form when it is filed.

(4) Except to the extent that para.(7) applies, the parties must file any evidence of explicit consent to the application under para.(1) when the parties file the application or claim form.

(5) Subject to para.(6), where an application is made under para.(1), the court will make an order making the mediation settlement enforceable.

(6) The court will not make an order under para.(5) unless the court has evidence that each of the parties to the mediation settlement agreement has given explicit consent to the application for the order.

(7) Where a party to the mediation settlement agreement—
   (a) has agreed in the mediation settlement agreement that a mediation settlement enforcement order should be made in respect of that mediation settlement;
   (b) is a party to the application under para.(1); or
   (c) has written to the court consenting to the application for the mediation settlement enforcement order,
   that party is deemed to have given explicit consent to the application for the mediation settlement enforcement order.

(8) An application under para.(1) will be dealt with without a hearing, unless the court otherwise directs.

PD 78 para.22.1

Where an application for a mediation settlement enforcement order is made under r.78.24(1)(a) in accordance with Pt 23, a copy of the application notice, mediation settlement agreement and evidence of explicit consent must be served on all parties to the mediation settlement agreement who are not also parties to the application.

PD 78 para.22.2

Where an application for a mediation settlement enforcement order is made under r.78.24(1)(b) by the Pt 8 procedure—
   (1) the claim form may be issued without naming a defendant; and
   (2) a copy of the claim form, mediation settlement agreement and evidence of explicit consent must be served on all parties to the mediation settlement agreement who are not also parties to the application.

PD 78 para.22.3

No document relating to an application for a mediation settlement enforcement order may be inspected by a person who is not a party to the proceedings under r.5.4C without the permission of the court.

PD 78 para.22.4

Where the application is supported by evidence of explicit consent to the application by a party to the mediation settlement agreement, the evidence must be in English or accompanied by a translation into English.

PD 78 para.22.5

Where a party to the mediation settlement agreement writes to the court consenting to the making of the mediation settlement enforcement order, the correspondence must be in English or accompanied by a translation into English.

PD 78 para.22.6

Where the parties to pending proceedings agree to apply for a mediation settlement enforcement order, they must inform the court immediately.
(Parts 70 to 74 contain further rules about enforcement).

See **Foreign currency**.

MEDICAL NEGLIGENCE

See **Pre-action protocols**.

MENTAL HEALTH ACT 1983

PD 8A para.18.2

The [Pt 8] claim form must be filed—
   (1) in the court for the district in which the patient's place of residence [means, in relation to a patient who is receiving treatment as an in-patient in a hospital or other institution, that hospital or institution] is situated; or
   (2) in the case of an application under s.30, in the court that made the order under s.29 [of the Mental Health Act 1983] which the application seeks to discharge or vary.

PD 8A para.18.3

Where an application is made under s.29 for an order that the functions of the nearest relative of the patient are to be exercisable by some other person—
   (1) the nearest relative must be made a respondent, unless—
      (a) the application is made on the grounds that the patient has no nearest relative or that it is not reasonably practicable to ascertain whether he has a nearest relative; or
      (b) the court orders otherwise; and
   (2) the court may order that any other person shall be made a respondent.

PD 8A para.18.4

Subject to para.18.5, the court may accept as evidence of the facts relied upon in support of the application, any report made—
   (1) by a medical practitioner; or
   (2) by any of the following acting in the course of their official duties—
      (a) a probation officer;
      (b) an officer of a local authority;
      (c) an officer of a voluntary body exercising statutory functions on behalf of a local authority; or
      (d) an officer of a hospital manager [the manager of a hospital as defined in s.145(1) of the Mental Health Act 1983]

PD 8A para.18.5

The respondent must be informed of the substance of any part of the report dealing with his fitness or conduct that the court considers to be material to the determination of the claim.

PD 8A para.18.6

An application under Pt II [of the Mental Health Act 1983] shall be heard in private unless the court orders otherwise.

PD 8A para.18.7

The judge may, for the purpose of determining the application, interview the patient. The interview may take place in the presence of, or separately from, the parties. The interview may be conducted elsewhere than at the court. Alternatively, the judge may direct the district judge to interview the patient and report to the judge in writing.

See also **Part 8 claim form** and **Part 8 procedure.**

MERCANTILE CLAIMS

Pt 59 r.59.1(3)

(b) A claim proceeding in a **Mercantile Courts**.

MERCANTILE COURTS

PD 59 para.1.2

Mercantile Courts are established in—
    (1) the following district registries of the High Court—Birmingham, Bristol, Cardiff, Chester, Leeds, Liverpool, Manchester, Mold and Newcastle upon Tyne; and
    (2) the Commercial Court of the Queen's Bench Division at the Royal Courts of Justice (called 'The London Mercantile Court').

Pt 59 r.59.1

(1) [P59] applies to claims in Mercantile Courts.
(2) A claim may only be started in a Mercantile Court if it—
    (a) relates to a commercial or business matter in a broad sense; and
    (b) is not required to proceed in the Chancery Division or in another specialist list.

PD 59 para.1.3

All mercantile claims will be heard or determined by a Mercantile judge, except that—
    (1) an application may be heard and determined by any other judge who, if the claim were not a mercantile claim, would have jurisdiction to determine it, if—
    (a) the application is urgent and no Mercantile judge is available to hear it; or
    (b) a Mercantile judge directs it to be heard by another judge; and
    (2) unless the court otherwise Orders, all proceedings for the enforcement of a Mercantile Court judgment or order for the payment of money will be dealt with by a district judge.

PD 59 para.1.4

Provisions in other PDs which refer to a master or district judge are to be read, in relation to mercantile claims, as if they referred to a Mercantile judge.

Application of the CPR

Pt 59 r.59.2

[CPR] and their PDs apply to mercantile claims unless this Part or a PD provides otherwise.

Transfer of proceedings

Pt 59 r.59.3

Rule 30.5 applies with the modifications that—
    (a) a Mercantile judge may transfer a mercantile claim to another Mercantile Court; and
    (b) a Commercial Court judge may transfer a claim from the Commercial Court to a
        Mercantile Court.
(Rule 30.5(3) provides that an application for the transfer of proceedings to or from a specialist
list must be made to a judge dealing with claims in that list).

Transfer of proceedings to or from a Mercantile Court

PD 59 para.4.1

If a claim which has not been issued in a Mercantile Court is suitable to continue as a mercantile
claim—
    (1) any party wishing the claim to be transferred to a Mercantile Court may make an
        application for transfer to the court to which transfer is sought;
    (2) if all parties consent to the transfer, the application may be made by letter to the
        mercantile listing officer of the court to which transfer is sought, stating why the case is
        suitable to be transferred to that court and enclosing the written consents of the parties,
        the claim form and statements of case.

PD 59 para.4.2

If an application for transfer is made to a court which does not have power to make the order,
that court may—
    (1) adjourn the application to be heard by a Mercantile judge; or
    (2) dismiss the application.

PD 59 para.4.3

A Mercantile judge may make an order under r.59.3 of his own initiative.

Claim form and particulars of claim

Pt 59 r.59.4

    (1) If particulars of claim are not contained in or served with the claim form—
        (a) the claim form must state that, if an acknowledgment of service is filed which
            indicates an intention to defend the claim, particulars of claim will follow;

    (b) when the claim form is served, it must be accompanied by the documents specified in r.7.8(1);

    (c) the claimant must serve particulars of claim within 28 days of the filing of an acknowledgment of service which indicates an intention to defend; and

    (d) r.7.4(2) does not apply.

(2) If the claimant is claiming interest, he must—

    (a) include a statement to that effect; and

    (b) give the details set out in r.16.4(2),

in both the claim form and the particulars of claim.

(3) Rules 12.6(1)(a) and 14.14(1)(a) apply with the modification that references to the particulars of claim shall be read as if they referred to the claim form.

Acknowledgment of service

Pt 59 r.59.5

(1) A defendant must file an acknowledgment of service in every case.

(2) Unless para.(3) applies, the period for filing an acknowledgment of service is 14 days after service of the claim form.

(3) Where the claim form is served out of the jurisdiction, or on the agent of a defendant who is overseas, the time periods provided by rr.6.12(3), 6.35 and 6.37(5) apply after service of the claim form.

Default judgment

Pt 59 r.59.7

(1) Part 12 applies to mercantile claims, except that rr.12.10 and 12.11 apply as modified by paras (2) and (3) of this rule.

(2) If, in a Pt 7 claim—

    (a) the claim form has been served but no particulars of claim have been served; and

    (b) the defendant has failed to file an acknowledgment of service,

the claimant must make an application if he wishes to obtain a default judgment.

(3) The application may be made without notice, but the court may direct it to be served on the defendant.

PD 59 para.5

The PD s supplementing Pt 12 apply with the following modification—

(1) paragraph 4.1(1) of PD 12 is to be read as referring to the service of the claim form.

Admissions

Pt 59 r.59.8

(1) Rule 14.5 does not apply to mercantile claims.

(2) If the defendant admits part of a claim for a specified amount of money, the claimant may apply under r.14.3 for judgment on the admission.

PD 59 para.5

The PD supplementing Pt 14 apply with the following modification—
    (2) the references to 'particulars of claim' in paras 2.1, 3.1 and 3.2 of PD 14 are to be read as referring to the claim form.

Defence and reply

Pt 59 r.59.9

    (1) Part 15 (Defence and Reply) applies to mercantile claims with the modification to r.15.8 that the claimant must—
        (a) file any reply to a defence; and
        (b) serve it on all other parties,
    within 21 days after service of the defence.
    (2) Rule 6.35 (in relation to the period for filing a defence where the claim form is served out of the jurisdiction) applies to mercantile claims, except that if the particulars of claim are served after the defendant has filed an acknowledgment of service the period for filing a defence is 28 days from service of the particulars of claim.

Statements of case

Pt 59 r.59.10

The court may at any time before or after issue of the claim form order a mercantile claim to proceed without the filing or service of statements of case.

Case management

Pt 59 r.59.5

    (1) All mercantile claims are treated as being allocated to the multi-track, and Pt 26 does not apply.
    (2) The following parts only of Pt 29 apply—
        (a) rule 29.3(2) (appropriate legal representative to attend case management conferences and pre-trial reviews); and
        (b) rule 29.5 (variation of case management timetable) with the exception of r.29.5(1)(c).
    (3) As soon as practicable the court will hold a case management conference which must be fixed in accordance with PD 59
    (4) At the case management conference or at any hearing at which the parties are represented the court may give such directions for the management of the case as it considers appropriate.

Judgments and orders

Pt 59 r.59.12

    (1) Except for orders made by the court of its own initiative and unless the court otherwise orders every judgment or order will be drawn up by the parties, and r.40.3 is modified accordingly.

(2) An application for a consent order must include a draft of the proposed order signed on behalf of all the parties to whom it relates.

(3) Rule 40.6 (consent judgments and orders) does not apply.

PD 59 para.11.1

After any hearing the claimant must draw up a draft order, unless the decision was made on the application of another party in which case that party must do so.

PD 59 para.11.2

A draft order must be submitted by the party responsible for drawing it up within three clear days of the decision, with sufficient copies for each party and for one to be retained by the court.

PD 59 para.11.3

The sealed orders will be returned to the party submitting them, who will be responsible for serving the order on the other parties.

PD 59 para.11.4

Orders must be dated with the date of the decision, except for consent orders submitted for approval, which must be left undated.

Starting proceedings in a Mercantile Court

PD 59 para.2.1

A claim should only be started in a Mercantile Court if it will benefit from the expertise of a Mercantile judge.

PD 59 para.2.2

The claim form must be marked in the top right hand corner 'Queen's Bench Division, _____ District Registry, Mercantile Court' or 'Queen's Bench Division, The London Mercantile Court' as appropriate.

Applications before proceedings are issued

PD 59 para.3.1

A party who intends to bring a claim in a Mercantile Court must make any application before the claim form is issued to a judge of that court.

PD 59 para.3.2

The written evidence in support of such an application should show why the claim is suitable to proceed as a mercantile claim.

Variation of time limits by agreement

PD 59 para.6.1

If the parties, in accordance with r.2.11, agree in writing to vary a time limit, the claimant must notify the court in writing, giving brief written reasons for the agreed variation.

PD 59 para.6.2

The court may make an order overriding an agreement by the parties varying a time limit.

Case management

PD 59 para.7.1

The following parts only of PD 29 apply—
    (1) paragraph 5 (case management conferences), excluding para.5.9 and modified so far as is made necessary by other specific provisions of this PD; and
    (2) paragraph 7 (failure to comply with case management directions).

PD 59 para.7.2

If proceedings are started in a Mercantile Court, the claimant must apply for a case management conference—
    (1) for a Pt 7 claim, within 14 days of the date when all defendants who intend to file and serve a defence have done so; and
    (2) for a Pt 8 claim, within 14 days of the date when all defendants who intend to serve evidence have done so.

PD 59 para.7.3

If proceedings are transferred to a Mercantile Court, the claimant must apply for a case management conference within 14 days of receiving an acknowledgment of the transfer from the receiving court, unless the judge held, or gave directions for, a case management conference when he made the order transferring the proceedings.

PD 59 para.7.4

Any party may, at a time earlier than that provided in paras 7.2 or 7.3, apply in writing to the court to fix a case management conference.

PD 59 para.7.5

If the claimant does not make an application in accordance with paras 7.2 or 7.3, any other party may apply for a case management conference.

PD 59 para.7.6

The court may fix a case management conference at any time on its own initiative. If it does so, the court will give at least seven days notice to the parties, unless there are compelling reasons for a shorter period of notice.

PD 59 para.7.7

Not less than seven days before a case management conference—
  (1) each party shall file and serve—
      (a) a case management information sheet substantially in the form set out at Appendix A to this PD ; and
      (b) an application notice for any order which that party intends to seek at the case management conference, other than directions referred to in the case management information sheet; and
  (2) the claimant (or other party applying for the conference) shall in addition file and serve—
      (a) a case management file containing—
          — the claim form;
          — the statements of case (excluding schedules of more than 15 pages);
          — any orders already made;
          — the case management information sheets; and
          — a short list of the principal issues to be prepared by the claimant; and
      (b) a draft order substantially in the form set out at Appendix B to this PD, setting out the directions which that party thinks appropriate.

PD 59 para.7.8

In appropriate cases—
  (1) the parties may, not less than seven days before the date fixed for the case management conference, submit agreed directions for the approval of the judge;
  (2) the judge will then either—
      (a) make the directions proposed; or
      (b) make them with alterations; or
      (c) require the case management conference to proceed; but
  (3) the parties must assume that the conference will proceed until informed to the contrary.

PD 59 para.7.9

If the parties submit agreed directions and the judge makes them with alterations, any party objecting to the alterations may, within seven days of receiving the order containing the directions, apply to the court for the directions to be varied.

PD 59 para.7.10

The directions given at the case management conference—
  (1) will normally cover all steps in the case through to trial, including the fixing of a trial date or window, or directions for the taking of steps to fix the trial date or window; and
  (2) may include the fixing of a progress monitoring date or dates, and make provision for the court to be informed as to the progress of the case at the date or dates fixed.

PD 59 para.7.11

If the court fixes a progress monitoring date, it may after that date fix a further case management conference or a pre-trial review on its own initiative if—
  (1) no or insufficient information is provided by the parties; or
  (2) it is appropriate in view of the information provided.

Pre-trial review and questionnaire

PD 59 para.8.1

The court may order a pre-trial review at any time.

PD 59 para.8.2

Each party must file and serve a completed pre-trial check list substantially in the form set out in Appendix C to [PD 59]—
  (1) if a pre-trial review has been ordered, not less than seven days before the date of the review; or
  (2) if no pre-trial review has been ordered, not less than six weeks before the trial date.

PD 59 para.8.3

When pre-trial check lists are filed under para.8.2(2)—
  (1) the judge will consider them and decide whether to order a pre-trial review; and
  (2) if he does not order a pre-trial review, he may on his own initiative give directions for the further preparation of the case or as to the conduct of the trial.

PD 59 para.8.4

At a pre-trial review—
  (1) the parties should if possible be represented by the advocates who will be appearing at the trial;
  (2) any representatives appearing must be fully informed and authorised for the purposes of the review; and
  (3) the court will give such directions for the conduct of the trial as it sees fit.

Applications

Evidence

PD 59 para.9.1

The general requirement is that, unless the court orders otherwise—
  (1) evidence in support of an application must be filed and served with the application: see r.23.7(3);
  (2) evidence in answer must be filed and served within 14 days after the application is served;
  (3) evidence in reply must be filed and served within seven days of the service of the evidence in answer.

PD 59 para.9.2

In any case in which the application is likely to require an oral hearing of more than half a day the periods set out in para.9.1(2) and (3) will be 28 days and 14 days respectively.

PD 59 para.9.3

If the date fixed for the hearing of the application means that the times in para.9.1(2) and (3) cannot both be achieved, the evidence must be filed and served—

(1) as soon as possible; and
(2) in sufficient time to ensure that the application may fairly proceed on the date fixed.

PD 59 para.9.4

The parties may, in accordance with r.2.11, agree different periods from those provided above, provided that the agreement does not affect the ability to proceed on the date fixed for the hearing of the application.

Files for applications

PD 59 para.10

Before the hearing of any application, the applicant must—
(1) provide to the court and each other party an appropriate indexed file for the application with consecutively numbered pages; and
(2) attach to the file an estimate of the reading time required by the judge.

See **Jurisdiction**.

MERCHANT SHIPPING (LINER CONFERENCES) ACT 1982

PD 74A para.10

The Merchant Shipping (Liner Conferences) Act 1982 ('the Act') contains provisions for the settlement of disputes between liner conferences, shipping lines and shippers. This section of PD [74A] deals with the enforcement by the High Court under s.9 of the Act of recommendations of conciliators, and determinations and awards of costs.

Exercise of powers under the Act

PD 74A para.11

The powers of the High Court under the Act are exercised by the Commercial Court.

Applications for registration

PD 74A para.12.1

An application under s.9 of the Act for the registration of a recommendation, determination or award is made under Pt 23.

PD 74A para.12.2

An application for the registration of a recommendation must be supported by written evidence exhibiting—
(1) a verified or certified or otherwise authenticated copy of—

(a) the recommendation;
(b) the reasons for it; and
(c) the record of settlement;
(2) where any of those documents is not in English, a translation of it into English—
    (a) certified by a notary public or other qualified person; or
    (b) accompanied by written evidence confirming that the translation is accurate; and
(3) copies of the acceptance of the recommendation by the parties on whom it is binding, or otherwise verifying the acceptance where it is not in writing.

PD 74A para.12.3

The evidence in support of the application must—
(1) give particulars of the failure to implement the recommendation; and
(2) confirm that none of the grounds which would render it unenforceable is applicable.

PD 74A para.12.4

An application for the registration of a determination of costs or an award of costs must be supported by written evidence—
(1) exhibiting a verified or certified or otherwise authenticated copy of the recommendation or other document containing the determination or award; and
(2) stating that the costs have not been paid.

Order for registration

PD 74A para.13.1

The applicant must draw up the order giving permission to register the recommendation, determination or award.

PD 74A para.13.2

The order must include a provision that the reasonable costs of the registration should be assessed.

Register of recommendations

PD 74A para.14

There will be kept in the Admiralty and Commercial Registry at the Royal Courts of Justice, under the direction of the Senior Master, a register of the recommendations, determinations and awards ordered to be registered under s.9 of the Act, with particulars of enforcement.

MESOTHELIOMA

PD 3D para.1

[PD 3D] applies to claims for compensation for mesothelioma.

Definitions

PD 3D para.2

In this PD—
'show cause procedure' means (without prejudice to the court's general case management powers in Pt 3 of the CPR) the procedure set out in para.6;
'outline submissions showing cause' means an outline or skeleton argument of the defendant's case within the show cause procedure; and
'standard interim payment' means the standard payment in respect of interim damages, and (if appropriate) interim costs and disbursements as determined from time to time by the Head of Civil Justice. The amount of this payment is currently £50,000.

Starting proceedings

PD 3D para.3.1

The claim form and every statement of case must be marked with the title 'Living Mesothelioma Claim' or 'Fatal Mesothelioma Claim' as appropriate.

PD 3D para.3.2

In order for the court to adopt the show cause procedure in the first case management conference, the claimant must file and serve any witness statements about liability (as are available)—
    (1) either—
        (a) at the same time as filing and serving the claim form and (where appropriate) the particulars of claim; or
        (b) as soon as possible after filing and serving the claim form and (where appropriate) the particulars of claim; and
    (2) in any event not less than seven days before the case management conference.

PD 3D para.3.3

Any witness statement about liability must identify as far as is possible—
    (1) the alleged victim's employment history and history of exposure to asbestos;
    (2) the identity of any employer where exposure to asbestos of the alleged victim is alleged;
    (3) details of any self employment in which the alleged victim may have been exposed; and
    (4) details of all claims made and payments received under the Pneumoconiosis etc. (Workers' Compensation) Act 1979.

PD 3D para.3.4

The claimant must also attach to the claim form—
    (1) a work history from HM Revenue and Customs (where available); and
    (2) any pre-action letter of claim.

Claimants with severely limited life expectancy

PD 3D para.4.1

Where the claimant believes that the claim is particularly urgent then on issue of the claim form, the claimant—
  (1) may request in writing that the court file is placed immediately before a judge nominated to manage such cases in order to fix a case management conference; and
  (2) must explain in writing to the court why the claim is urgent.

PD 3D para.4.2

Where the court decides that the claim is urgent (and notwithstanding that a claim has not yet been served or a defence has not yet been filed) it will—
  (1) fix the date for the case management conference to take place within a short period of time; and
  (2) give directions as to the date by which the claimant must serve the claim form if it has not been served already.

Fixing the case management conference for other claims

PD 3D para.5.1

Where para.4 does not apply and—
  (1) a defence is filed by the defendant or one of the defendants (where there is more than one); or
  (2) the claimant has obtained a default judgment,
the court file will be referred to a judge nominated to manage such cases and the judge will give directions for the date of the case management conference.

PD 3D para.5.2

Claims marked 'Living Mesothelioma Claim' will be given priority when fixing a case management conference.

Show cause procedure

PD 3D para.6.1

The show cause procedure is a requirement by the court, of its own initiative and usually on a 'costs in the case' basis, for the defendant to identify the evidence and legal arguments that give the defendant a real prospect of success on any or all issues of liability. The court will use this procedure for the resolution of mesothelioma claims.

PD 3D para.6.2

At the first case management conference, unless there is good reason not to do so, the defendant should be prepared to show cause why—
  (1) a judgment on liability should not be entered against the defendant; and
  (2) a standard interim payment on account of damages and (if appropriate) costs and disbursements should not be made by the defendant by a specified date.

PD 3D para.6.3

At the first case management conference if liability remains in issue the court will normally order that the defendant show cause within a further given period.

PD 3D para.6.4

The order requiring the defendant to show cause within a further given period will direct—
  (1) that the defendant file and serve on the claimant by a specified date outline submissions showing cause and—
    (a) if the outline submissions are not filed and served by a specified date, judgment, for a sum to be determined by the court, will be entered against the defendant without the need for any further order and the defendant will be ordered to make a standard interim payment by a specified date; or
    (b) if the outline submissions are filed and served by the specified date, the claim will be listed for a show cause hearing; or
  (2) that the defendant show cause at a hearing on a date fixed by the court.

PD 3D para.6.5

At the first case management conference the court will—
  (1) fix the date or trial window for the determination of damages and give any other case management directions as appropriate where the defendant admits liability or judgment is entered;
  (2) fix the date or trial window for the determination of damages and give any other case management directions as appropriate where an order to show cause under para.6.3 has been made (if the defendant subsequently shows cause then the determination date or trial window may be utilised for the trial of any issue); or
  (3) in cases in which there is to be a trial on liability, give directions including the date or window for the trial.

PD 3D para.6.6

Where the defendant fails to show cause on some issues, the court will normally enter judgment on those issues.

PD 3D para.6.7

Where the defendant fails to show cause on all issues, the court will enter judgment for a sum to be determined and will normally order that a standard interim payment be made.

PD 3D para.6.8

Where the defendant succeeds in showing cause on some or all issues, the court will order a trial of those issues. The court may also require the issue of quantum or apportionment (as appropriate) to be dealt with at the trial provided that it does not delay the date for the fixing of the trial.

Setting the trial date

PD 3D para.7.1

In Living Mesothelioma Claims the date of the determination of damages or the trial will generally not be more than 16 weeks following service of the claim form.

PD 3D para.7.2

In Fatal Mesothelioma Claims the hearing date may be more than 16 weeks following service of the claim form.

Taking evidence by deposition

PD 3D para.8

Any party who for good reason wishes evidence to be taken by deposition may apply to the court at any time for such an order. However, the court will normally expect that such a request is made at a case management conference. The order will include a direction for the recording of such evidence on DVD and for the provision of a transcript. The parties must also be prepared to arrange for the provision of equipment to view the DVD by the court.
(Part 34 contains provisions for evidence to be taken by deposition).

Compliance with Pre-action Protocols

PD 3D para.9

In Living Mesothelioma Claims the court may decide not to require strict adherence **to PD (Pre-Action Conduct)** and any relevant pre-action protocol.

Pre-action Protocol for disease and illness claims

para.2.7

In a terminal disease claim with short life expectancy, for instance where a claimant has a disease such as mesothelioma, the time scale of the Protocol is likely to be too long. In such a claim, the claimant may not be able to follow the Protocol and the defendant would be expected to treat the claim with urgency including any request for an interim payment.

para.2.8

In a claim for mesothelioma, additional provisions apply, which are set out in Annex C of this Protocol.

See also **Disease and illness claims**.

MINES (WORKING FACILITIES AND SUPPORT) ACT 1966

PD 8A para.9.4

Application under the Mines (Working Facilities and Support) Act 1966 must be brought in the Chancery Division.

PD 8A para.15.2

This paragraph applies where the Secretary of State refers an application to the High Court under any provision of the Act.

PD 8A para.15.3

The Secretary of State must—
  (1) file a reference signed by him or a person authorised to sign on his behalf in the Chancery Division of the High Court;
  (2) file, along with the reference, any documents and plans deposited with him by the applicant in support of his application; and
  (3) within three days of filing the reference, give notice to the applicant that the reference has been filed.

PD 8A para.15.4

Within 10 days of receiving the notice referred to in para.15.3(3), the applicant must issue a claim form.

PD 8A para.15.5

The claim form—
  (1) must identify the application under the Act and the remedy sought; and
  (2) need not be served on any other party.

PD 8A para.15.6

Within seven days of the claim form being issued, the applicant must—
  (1) apply for the claim to be listed for a hearing before a Master; and
  (2) give notice of the hearing date to the Secretary of State.

PD 8A para.15.7

The applicant must, not less than two days before the date fixed for a hearing, file at court—
  (1) a witness statement in support of the claim, giving details of all persons known to the applicant to be interested in, or affected by, the application; and
  (2) a draft of any proposed advertisement or notice of the application.

PD 8A para.15.8

At the hearing, the Master will—
  (1) fix a date by which any notice of objection under para.15.9 must be filed;
  (2) fix a date for a further hearing of the claim; and
  (3) give directions about—
    (a) any advertisement that is to be inserted or notice of the application and hearing date that is to be given; and
    (b) what persons are to be served with a copy of the application or any other document in the proceedings.

PD 8A para.15.9

Any person who wishes to oppose the application must, within the time fixed by the court under para.15.8, serve notice of objection on the applicant, stating—

    (a) his name and address;
    (b) the name and address of his solicitor, if any;
    (c) the grounds of his objection;
    (d) any alternative method for effecting the objects of the application that he alleges may be used; and
    (e) the facts on which he relies.

PD 8A para.15.10

Any document that is required to be served on the person who has given notice of objection ('the objector') may be served by posting it to the following address—
    (1) where the notice of objection gives the name and address of a solicitor, to the solicitor;
    (2) in any other case, to the objector at the address stated in the notice of objection.

PD 8A para.15.11

The objector may appear, or be represented at any further hearing, and may take such part in the proceedings as the court allows.

PD 8A para.15.12

The applicant must, not less than two days before the date set for the further hearing, file at court—
    (1) any notices of objection served on him;
    (2) a list of objectors, together with—
        (a) their names and addresses;
        (b) the names and addresses of their solicitors, if any; and
        (c) a summary of their respective grounds of objection.

PD 8A para.15.13

If the objector does not appear, or is not represented, at the further hearing—
    (1) his notice of objection will have no effect; and
    (2) he will not be entitled to take any further part in the proceedings unless the court orders otherwise.

PD 8A para.15.14

At the further hearing, the court will—
    (1) give directions about the future conduct of the claim, including—
        (a) any further information the applicant is required to give in relation to any of the grounds or facts relied on in support of the application;
        (b) any further information the objector is required to give in relation to any of the grounds or facts relied on in opposition to the application;
        (c) whether the applicant may serve a reply to any notice of objection;
        (d) whether any particular fact should be proved by a witness statement;
        (e) whether any statements of case or points of claim or defence are to be served; and
    (2) adjourn the claim for hearing before a judge.

MINOR

See **Child**.

MISCONDUCT

Misconduct in connection with summary or detailed assessment

Pt 44 para.44.14

(1) The court may make an order under this rule where—
    (a) a party or his legal representative, in connection with a summary or detailed assessment, fails to comply with a rule, PD or court order; or
    (b) it appears to the court that the conduct of a party or his legal representative, before or during the proceedings which gave rise to the assessment proceedings, was unreasonable or improper.
(2) Where para.(1) applies, the court may—
    (a) disallow all or part of the costs which are being assessed; or
    (b) order the party at fault or his legal representative to pay costs which he has caused any other party to incur.
(3) Where—
    (a) the court makes an order under para.(2) against a legally represented party; and
    (b) the party is not present when the order is made,
the party's solicitor must notify his client in writing of the order no later than seven days after the solicitor receives notice of the order.

Costs PD para.18.1

Before making an order under r.44.14 the court must give the party or legal representative in question a reasonable opportunity to attend a hearing to give reasons why it should not make such an order.

Costs PD para.18.2

Conduct before or during the proceedings which gave rise to the assessment which is unreasonable or improper includes steps which are calculated to prevent or inhibit the court from furthering the overriding objective.

Costs PD para.18.3

Although r.44.14(3) does not specify any sanction for breach of the obligation imposed by the r.the court may, either in the order under para.(2) or in a subsequent order, require the solicitor to produce to the court evidence that he took reasonable steps to comply with the obligation.

See also **Wasted costs order**.

MOBILE HOMES ACT 1983

Starting the claim

PD 55A para.55.3

A claim under paras 4, 5 or 6 of Pt I of Sch.1 to the Mobile Homes Act 1983 may be brought using the procedure set out in s.I of Pt 55 if the claim is started in the same claim form as a claim enforcing the rights referred to in s.3(1)(b) of the Caravan Sites Act 1968 (which, by virtue of r.55.2(1) must be brought under s.I of Pt 55).

See **Possession claims**.

MODELS

See **Plans**.

MONEY CLAIM ONLINE

PD 7A para.4A.1

In an designated money claims, Practice Form N1 must be sent to County Court Money Claims Centre, PO Box 527, M5 0BY. The claims will then be issued in Northampton County Court.

PD 7A para.4A.2

In proceedings referred to in para.4A.1, the claimant must specify the preferred court Form N1.

PD 7E para.1.1

[PD 7E] provides for a scheme in which, in the circumstances set out in this PD, a request for a claim form to be issued and other specified documents may be filed electronically ('Money Claim Online').

PD 7E para.1.2

PD [7E] enables claimants—
    (1) to start certain types of county court claims by requesting the issue of a claim form electronically via Her Majesty's Courts and Tribunals Service website; and
    (2) where a claim has been started electronically—
        (a) to file electronically a request for—
            (i) judgment in default;
            (ii) judgment on acceptance of an admission of the whole of the amount claimed; or
            (iii) the issue of a warrant of execution; and
        (b) to view an electronic record of the progress of the claim.

PD 7E para.1.3

PD [7E] also enables defendants—
    (1) to file electronically—
        (a) an acknowledgment of service;
        (b) a part admission;
        (c) a defence; or
        (d) a counterclaim (if filed together with a defence); and
    (2) to view an electronic record of the progress of the claim.

PD 7E para.1.4

Claims started using Money Claim Online will be issued by Northampton County Court and will proceed in that court unless they are transferred to another court. The address for filing any document, application or request (other than one which is filed electronically in accordance with this PD) is Northampton County Court, St Katharine's House, 21–27 St Katharine's Street, Northampton, NN1 2LH, DX 702885 Northampton 7, fax: 0845 6015889.

Security

PD 7E para.2

Her Majesty's Courts and Tribunals Service will take such measures as it thinks fit to ensure the security of steps taken or information stored electronically. These may include requiring users of Money Claim Online—
  (1) to enter a customer identification and password;
  (2) to provide personal information for identification purposes; and
  (3) to comply with any other security measures,
before taking any of the steps mentioned in paras 1.2 or 1.3.

Fees

PD 7E para.3.1

Where this PD provides for a fee to be paid electronically, it may be paid by—
  (1) credit card;
  (2) debit card; or
  (3) any other method which Her Majesty's Courts and Tribunals Service may permit.

PD 7E para.3.2

A step may only be taken using Money Claim Online on payment of the prescribed fee. The Civil Proceedings Fees Order provides that a party may, in certain circumstances, be entitled to a remission or part remission of a fee prescribed by that Order. Her Majesty's Courts and Tribunals Service website contains guidance as to when this entitlement might arise.

PD 7E para.3.3

A claimant who wishes to apply for a remission or part remission of fees must not use Money Claim Online and must file the claim form at a court office.

Types of claims which may be started using Money Claim Online

PD 7E para.4

A claim may be started using Money Claim Online if it meets all the following conditions—
  (1) the only remedy claimed is a specified amount of money—
    (a) less than £100,000 (excluding any interest or costs claimed); and
    (b) in sterling;

(2) the procedure under Pt 7 is used;
(3) the claimant is not—
    (a) a child or protected party; or
    (b) funded by the Legal Services Commission;
(3A) the claimant's address for service is within the UK;
(4) the claim is against—
    (a) a single defendant; or
    (b) two defendants, if the claim is for a single amount against each of them;
(5) the defendant is not—
    (a) the Crown; or
    (b) a person known to be a **child** or **protected party**; and
(6) the defendant's address for service is within England and Wales.

Starting a claim

PD 7E para.5.1

A claimant may request the issue of a claim form by—
(1) completing and sending an online claim form; and
(2) electronically paying the appropriate issue fee,
via Her Majesty's Courts and Tribunals Service website.

PD 7E para.5.2

Detailed particulars of claim must either be—
(1) included in the online claim form but must be limited in size to not more than 1080 characters (including spaces); or
(2) served and filed by the claimant separately from the claim form in accordance with para.6 but the claimant must—
    (a) state that detailed particulars of claim will follow; and
    (b) include a brief summary of the claim,
in the online claim form in the section headed 'particulars of claim'.

PD 7E para.5.2A

The requirement in para.7.3 of PD 16 for documents to be attached to the particulars of contract claims does not apply to claims started using an online claim form, unless the particulars of claim are served separately in accordance with para.5.2 of this PD.

PD 7E para.5.3

When an online claim form is received by the Money Claim Online website, an acknowledgment of receipt will automatically be sent to the claimant. The acknowledgment of receipt does not constitute a notice that the claim form has been issued.

PD 7E para.5.4

When the court issues a claim form following the submission of an online claim form, the claim is 'brought' for the purposes of the Limitation Act 1980 and any other enactment on the date on which the online claim form is received by the court's computer system. The court will keep a record, by electronic or other means, of when online claim forms are received.

PD 7E para.5.5

When the court issues a claim form, it will—
    (1) serve a printed version of the claim form on the defendant; and
    (2) send the claimant notice of issue.

PD 7E para.5.6

The claim form will have printed on it a unique customer identification number or a password by which the defendant may access details of the claim on Her Majesty's Courts and Tribunals Service website.

PD 7E para.5.7

The claim form will be deemed to be served on the fifth day after the claim was issued irrespective of whether that day is a business day or not. 'Business day' has the same meaning as in r.6.2(b).

Particulars of claim and certificate of service

PD 7E para.6.1

Where the particulars of claim are served by the claimant separately from the claim form pursuant to para.5.2(2), the claimant must—
    (1) serve the particulars of claim in accordance with r.7.4(1)(b); and
    (2) file a certificate of service in Form N215 at Northampton County Court within 14 days of service of the particulars of claim on the defendant.

PD 7E para.6.2

The certificate of service may be filed at the court by sending Form N215 by e-mail to *mcolaos@hmcourts-service.gsi.gov.uk*. However, the subject line to the e-mail must contain the claim number.

PD 7E para.6.3

The claimant must file the particulars of claim at the court to which the proceedings are transferred under paras 12.1 or 12.2 within seven days of service of the notice of transfer by the court.

PD 7E para.6.4

Where the proceedings are not transferred under paras 12.1 or 12.2 and remain at Northampton County Court, the claimant is not required to file the particulars of claim at that court unless ordered to do so.

Online response

PD 7E para.7.1

A defendant wishing to file—
    (1) an acknowledgment of service of the claim form under Pt 10;

    (2) a part admission under r.14.5;

    (3) a defence under Pt 15; or

    (4) a counterclaim (to be filed together with a defence),

may, instead of filing a written form, do so by completing and sending the relevant online form at *http://www.justice.gov.uk/about/hmcts/* (Accessed November 22, 2012).

PD 7E para.7.2

Where a defendant files an online form—

    (1) a hard copy must not be sent in addition;

    (2) the form is not filed until it is received by the court, whatever time it is shown to have been sent;

    (3) an online form received after 16.00 will be treated as filed on the next day the court office is open; and

    (4) where a time limit applies, it remains the responsibility of the defendant to ensure that the online form is filed in time.

Counterclaim

PD 7E para.8

Where a counterclaim is filed using an online form, any fee payable must be paid to the court to which the claim is transferred under paras 12.1 or 12.2.

Statement of truth

PD 7E para.9.1

Part 22 requires any statement of case to be verified by a statement of truth. This applies to all online forms.

PD 7E para.9.2

The statement of truth in an online statement of case must be in the form—

    '[I believe][The claimant believes] that the facts stated in this claim form are true.'; or

    '[I believe][The defendant believes] that the facts stated in this defence are true.',

as appropriate.

PD 7E para.9.3

Attention is drawn to—

    (1) paragraph 3 of PD 22, which provides who may sign a statement of truth; and

    (2) rule 32.14, which sets out the consequences of making, or causing to be made, a false statement in a document verified by a statement of truth, without an honest belief in its truth.

Signature

PD 7E para.10

Any provision of the CPR which requires a document to be signed by any person is satisfied by that person entering their name on an online form.

Request for judgment or issue of warrant

PD 7E para.11.1

If, in a claim started using Money Claim Online—
  (1) the claimant wishes to apply for judgment in default in accordance with Pt 12; or
  (2) the defendant has filed or served an admission of the whole of the claim in accordance with r.14.4,
the claimant may request judgment to be entered in default or on the admission (as the case may be) by completing and sending an online request form at *http://www.justice.gov.uk/about/hmcts/* (Accessed November 15, 2012).

PD 7E para.11.2

Where—
  (1) judgment has been entered following a request under para.11.1; and
  (2) the claimant is entitled to the issue of a warrant of execution without requiring the permission of the court,
the claimant may request the issue of a warrant of execution by—
  (a) completing and sending an online request form; and
  (b) electronically paying the appropriate fee,
at *http://www.justice.gov.uk/about/hmcts/* (Accessed November 22, 2012).
(Ord.26 of the County Court Rules ('CCR') contains rules about warrants of execution. Among other matters, CCR Ord.26 r.1 contains restrictions on when a warrant of execution may be issued if the court has made an order for payment of a sum of money by instalments, and CCR Ord.26 r.5 sets out certain circumstances in which a warrant of execution may not be issued without the permission of the court.)

PD 7E para.11.3

A request under para.11.1 or 11.2 will be treated as being filed—
  (1) on the day the court receives the request, if it receives it before 9.00 on a working day (which is any day on which the court is open); and
  (2) otherwise, on the next working day after the court receives the request.

Transfer of claim

PD 7E para.12.1

Where the defendant is an individual and Northampton County Court is not their home court, the court will transfer the claim to the defendant's home court—
  (1) under r.13.4, if the defendant applies to set aside or vary judgment;
  (2) under r.14.12, if there is to be a hearing for a judge to determine the time and rate of payment;
  (3) under r.26.2, if a defence is filed to all or part of the claim; or
  (4) if either party makes an application which cannot be dealt with without a hearing.

PD 7E para.12.2

Where the defendant is not an individual, if—
  (1) the claimant's address for service on the claim form is not within the district of Northampton County Court; and

(2) one of the events mentioned in para.12.1 arises,
the court will transfer the claim to the county court for the district in which the claimant's address
for service on the claim form is situated.

Viewing the case record

PD 7E para.13.1

A facility will be provided for parties or their legal representatives to view an electronic record
of the status of claims started using Money Claim Online.

PD 7E para.13.2

The record of each claim will be reviewed and, if necessary, updated at least once each day until
the claim is transferred from Northampton County Court.

MONTH

Pt 2 r.2.10

Where 'month' occurs in any judgment, order, direction or other document, it means a calendar
month.

MORTGAGE

Pt 55 r.55.1

(c) Includes a legal or equitable mortgage and a legal or equitable charge and 'mortgagee' is
to be interpreted accordingly.

MORTGAGE ACTIONS

See **Mortgage claims**.

MORTGAGE CLAIMS

Particulars of claim

PD 55A para.2.5

If the claim is a possession claim by a mortgagee, the particulars of claim must also set out:
(1) if the claim relates to residential property whether:
(a) a land charge of Class F has been registered under s.2(7) of the Matrimonial Homes
Act 1967;

    (b) a notice registered under ss.2(8) or 8(3) of the Matrimonial Homes Act 1983 has been entered and on whose behalf; or

    (c) a notice under s.31(10) of the Family Law Act 1996 has been registered and on whose behalf; and

if so, that the claimant will serve notice of the claim on the persons on whose behalf the land charge is registered or the notice or caution entered.

(2) the state of the mortgage account by including:

    (a) the amount of:

      (i) the advance;

      (ii) any periodic repayment; and

      (iii) any payment of interest required to be made;

    (b) the amount which would have to be paid (after taking into account any adjustment for early settlement) in order to redeem the mortgage at a stated date not more than 14 days after the claim started specifying the amount of solicitor's costs and administration charges which would be payable;

    (c) if the loan which is secured by the mortgage is a regulated consumer credit agreement, the total amount outstanding under the terms of the mortgage; and

    (d) the rate of interest payable:

      (i) at the commencement of the mortgage;

      (ii) immediately before any arrears referred to in para.(3) accrued;

      (iii) at the commencement of the proceedings.

(3) if the claim is brought because of failure to pay the periodic payments when due:

    (a) in schedule form, the dates and amounts of all payments due and payments made under the mortgage agreement or mortgage deed for a period of two years immediately preceding the date of issue, or if the first date of default occurred less than two years before the date of issue from the first date of default and a running total of the arrears;

    (b) give details of:

      (i) any other payments required to be made as a term of the mortgage (such as for insurance premiums, legal costs, default interest, penalties, administrative or other charges);

      (ii) any other sums claimed and stating the nature and amount of each such charge; and

      (iii) whether any of these payments is in arrears and whether or not it is included in the amount of any periodic payment.

(4) whether or not the loan which is secured by the mortgage is a regulated consumer credit agreement and, if so, specify the date on which any notice required by ss.76 or 87 of the Consumer Credit Act 1974 was given;

(5) if appropriate details that show the property is not one to which s.141 of the Consumer Credit Act 1974 applies;

(6) any relevant information about the defendant's circumstances, in particular:

    (a) whether the defendant is in receipt of social security benefits; and

    (b) whether any payments are made on his behalf directly to the claimant under the Social Security Contributions and Benefits Act 1992;

(7) give details of any tenancy entered into between the mortgagor and mortgagee (including any notices served); and

(8) state any previous steps which the claimant has taken to recover the money secured by the mortgage or the mortgaged property and, in the case of court proceedings, state:

    (a) the dates when the claim started and concluded; and

    (b) the dates and terms of any orders made.

PD 55A para.2.5A

If the claimant wishes to rely on a history of arrears which is longer than two years, he should state this in his particulars and exhibit a full (or longer) schedule to a **witness statement**.

Possession claims relating to mortgaged residential property

Pt 55 r.55.10

(1) This rule applies where a mortgagee seeks possession of land which consists of or includes residential property.

(2) Within five days of receiving notification of the date of the hearing by the court, the claimant must send a notice to—

    (a) the property, addressed to 'the tenant or the occupier';

    (b) the housing department of the local authority within which the property is located; and

    (c) any registered proprietor (other than the claimant) of a registered charge over the property.

(3) The notice referred to in para.(2)(a) must—

    (a) state that a possession claim for the property has started;

    (b) show the name and address of the claimant, the defendant and the court which issued the claim form; and

    (c) give details of the hearing.

(3A) The notice referred to in para.2(b) must contain the information in para.(3) and must state the full address of the property.

(4) The claimant must produce at the hearing—

    (a) a copy of the notices; and

    (b) evidence that they have been sent.

(4A) An unauthorised tenant of residential property may apply to the court for the order for possession to be suspended.

MOTION

Judge's application.

MOTOR INSURERS' BUREAU

Pre-action Protocol for low value Personal injury claims in Road Traffic Accidents, para.4.4

[Pre-action Protocol for low value Personal Injury claims in Road Traffic Accidents] does not apply to a claim—

    (3) made to the MIB pursuant to the Untraced Drivers' Agreement 2003 or any subsequent or supplementary Untraced Drivers' Agreements.

PJICRTA para.6.13

Where no insurer is identified and the claim falls to be dealt with by the MIB or its agents the CNF [Claim Notification Form] response must be completed and sent to the claimant within 30 days.

PJICRTA para.6.14

Where the MIB passes the claim to an insurer to act on its behalf, that insurer must notify the claimant of that fact. There is no extension to the time period in para.6.13.

See **Interim payment**.

MULTI-TRACK

Pt 26 r.26.6

(6) The multi-track is the normal track for any claim for which the **small claims track** or the **fast track** is not the normal track.

Pt 29 r.29.1

[Part 29] contains general provisions about management of cases allocated to the multi-track and applies only to cases allocated to that track.

Allocation and case management

PD 26 para.10.1

Paragraph 10.2 does not apply—
(1) a claim for possession of land in the county court or a demotion claim whether in the alternative to a possession claim or under Pt 65;
(2) any claim which is being dealt with at the Royal Courts of Justice.

PD 26 para.10.2

(1) The case management of a claim which is allocated to the multi-track will normally be dealt with at a Civil Trial Centre.
(2) In the case of a claim to which any of Pts 49 or 58–62 apply, case management must be dealt with at a Civil Trial Centre. Subparagraphs (4) to (10) do not apply to such a claim. The claim will be allocated to the multi-track irrespective of its value, and must be transferred to a Civil Trial Centre for allocation and case management if not already there.
(3) Where a claim is issued in or automatically transferred to a Civil Trial Centre it will be allocated and managed at that court.
(4) The following sub-paragraphs apply to a claim which is issued in or automatically transferred to a court which is not a Civil Trial Centre. Such a court is referred to as a 'feeder court'.
(5) Where a judge sitting at a feeder court decides, on the basis of the allocation questionnaires and any other documents filed by the parties, that the claim should be dealt with on the multi-track he will normally make an order:
(a) allocating the claim to that track,
(b) giving case management directions, and
(c) transferring the claim to a Civil Trial Centre.
(6) If he decides that an allocation hearing or some pre-allocation hearing is to take place (for example to strike out a statement of case under Pt 3 of the rules) that hearing will take place at the feeder court.
(7) If, before allocation, a hearing takes place at a feeder court and in exercising his powers under para.2.4(1) above the judge allocates the claim to the multi-track, he will also normally make an order transferring the claim to a Civil Trial Centre.
(8) A judge sitting at a feeder court may, rather than making an allocation order himself, transfer the claim to a Civil Trial Centre for the decision about allocation to be taken there.
(9) When, following an order for transfer, the file is received at the Civil Trial Centre, a judge sitting at that Centre will consider it and give any further directions that appear necessary or desirable.

(10) Where there is reason to believe that more than one case management conference may be needed and the parties or their legal advisers are located inconveniently far from the Civil Trial Centre, a judge sitting at a feeder court may, with the agreement of the Designated Civil Judge and notwithstanding the allocation of the case to the multi-track, decide that in the particular circumstances of the case it should not be transferred to a Civil Trial Centre, but should be case managed for the time being at the feeder court.

(11) A Designated Civil Judge may at any time make an order transferring a claim from a feeder court to a Civil Trial Centre and he may do so irrespective of the track, if any, to which it has been allocated. He may also permit a feeder court to keep for trial a claim or (subject to review from time to time) a category of claims. Any such permisson should take into account the ability of the feeder court in relation to the Civil Trial Centre to provide suitable and effective trial within an appropriate trial period.

(12) No order will be made by a feeder court fixing a date for a hearing at a Civil Trial Centre unless that date has been given or confirmed by a judge or listing officer of that Centre.

PD 26 para.10.3

[Pt 29] and PD 29 set out the procedure [for case management] to be adopted.

Case management—general provisions

Pt 29 r.29.2

(1) When it allocates a case to the multi-track, the court will—
    (a) give directions for the management of the case and set a timetable for the steps to be taken between the giving of directions and the trial; or
    (b) fix—
        (i) a case management conference; or
        (ii) a pre-trial review,
        or both, and give such other directions relating to the management of the case as it sees fit.

(2) The court will fix the trial date or the period in which the trial is to take place as soon as practicable.

(3) When the court fixes the trial date or the trial period under para.(2), it will—
    (a) give notice to the parties of the date or period; and
    (b) specify the date by which the parties must file a pre-trial check list.

PD 29 para.3.1

(1) Case management of a claim which is proceeding at the Royal Courts of Justice will be undertaken there.

(2) (a) Case management of any other claim which has been allocated to the multi-track will normally be undertaken at a Civil Trial Centre.
    (b) [PD] 26 provides for what will happen in the case of a claim which is issued in or transferred to a court which is not a Civil Trial Centre.

PD 29 para.3.2

The hallmarks of the multi-track are:
(1) the ability of the court to deal with cases of widely differing values and complexity, and
(2) the flexibility given to the court in the way it will manage a case in a way appropriate to its particular needs.

PD 29 para.3.3

(1) On allocating a claim to the multi-track the court may give directions without a hearing, including fixing a trial date or a period in which the trial will take place,

(2) Alternatively, whether or not it fixes a trial date or period, it may either—

(a) give directions for certain steps to be taken and fix a date for a case management conference or a pre-trial review to take place after they have been taken, or

(b) fix a date for a case management conference.

(3) Attention is drawn to r.29.2(2) which requires the court to fix a trial date or period as soon as practicable.

PD 29 para.3.4

The court may give or vary directions at any hearing which may take place on the application of a party or of its own initiative.

PD 29 para.3.5

When any hearing has been fixed it is the duty of the parties to consider what directions the court should be asked to give and to make any application that may be appropriate to be dealt with then.

PD 29 para.3.6

The court will hold a hearing to give directions whenever it appears necessary or desirable to do so, and where this happens because of the default of a party or his legal representative it will usually impose a sanction.

PD 29 para.3.7

When the court fixes a hearing to give directions it will give the parties at least three days' notice of the hearing unless r.29.7 applies (seven days' notice to be given in the case of a pre-trial review).

PD 29 para.3.8

Where a party needs to apply for a direction of a kind not included in the case management timetable which has been set (for example to amend his statement of case or for further information to be given by another party) he must do so as soon as possible so as to minimise the need to change that timetable.

PD 29 para.3.9

Courts will make arrangements to ensure that applications and other hearings are listed promptly to avoid delay in the conduct of cases.

PD 29 para.3.10

(1) Case management will generally be dealt with by—

(a) a Master in cases proceeding in the Royal Courts of Justice,

(b) a district judge in cases proceeding in a District Registry of the High Court, and

(c) a district judge or a Circuit Judge in cases proceeding in a county court.

(2) A Master or a district judge may consult and seek the directions of a judge of a higher level about any aspect of case management.

(3) A member of the court staff who is dealing with the listing of a hearing may seek the directions of any judge about any aspect of that listing.

Consideration of periodical payments

PD 29 para.3A

Attention is drawn to PD 41B supplementing Pt 41 and in particular to the direction that in a personal injury claim the court should consider and indicate to the parties as soon as practicable whether periodical payments or a lump sum is likely to be the more appropriate form for all or part of an award of damages for future pecuniary loss.

See also **Transfer of proceedings.**

Case management in the High Court of Justice

PD 29 para.2.2

This part of [PD 29] applies to claims begun by claim form issued in the Central Office or Chancery Chambers in the Royal Courts of Justice.

PD 29 r.2.2

A claim with an estimated value of less than £50,000 will generally, unless:
   (a) it is required by an enactment to be tried in the High Court,
   (b) it falls within a specialist list, or
   (c) it falls within one of the categories specified in para.2.6 below or is otherwise within the criteria of art.7(5) of the High Court and County Courts Jurisdiction Order 1991,
be transferred to a county court.

PD 29 r.2.3

Paragraph 2.2 is without prejudice to the power of the court in accordance with Pt 30 to transfer to a county court a claim with an estimated value that exceeds £50,000.

PD 29 r.2.4

The decision to transfer may be made at any stage in the proceedings but should, subject to para.2.5, be made as soon as possible and in any event not later than the date for the filing of pre-trial check lists (listing questionnaires).

PD 29 r.2.5

If an application is made under r.3.4 (striking out) or under Pt 24 (summary judgment) or under Pt 25 (interim remedies), it will usually be convenient for the application to be dealt with before a decision to transfer is taken.

Case management conference and pre-trial review

Pt 29 r.29.3

(1) The court may fix—
   (a) a case management conference; or
   (b) a pre-trial review, at any time after the claim has been allocated.
(2) If a party has a legal representative, a representative—
   (a) familiar with the case; and
   (b) with sufficient authority to deal with any issues that are likely to arise, must attend case management conferences and pre-trial reviews.
(Rule 3.1(2)(c) provides that the court may require a party to attend the court).

Directions on allocation

PD 29 para.4.1

Attention is drawn to the court's duties under r.29.2.

PD 29 para.4.3

At this stage the court's first concern will be to ensure that the issues between the parties are identified and that the necessary evidence is prepared and disclosed.

PD 29 para.4.4

The court may have regard to any document filed by a party with his allocation questionnaire containing further information, provided that the document states either that its contents has been agreed with every other party or that it has been served on every other party, and when it was served.

PD 29 para.4.5

On the allocation of a claim to the multi-track the court will consider whether it is desirable or necessary to hold a case management conference straight away, or whether it is appropriate instead to give directions on its own initiative.

PD 29 para.4.6

The parties and their advisers are encouraged to try to agree directions and to take advantage of r.29.4 which provides that if:
   (1) the parties agree proposals for the management of the proceedings (including a proposed trial date or period in which the trial is to take place), and
   (2) the court considers that the proposals are suitable,
it may approve them without a hearing and give directions in the terms proposed.

PD 29 para.4.7

(1) To obtain the court's approval the agreed directions must—
   (a) set out a timetable by reference to calendar dates for the taking of steps for the preparation of the case,

    (b) include a date or a period (the trial period) when it is proposed that the trial will take place,

    (c) include provision about disclosure of documents, and

    (d) include provision about both factual and expert evidence.

(2) The court will scrutinise the timetable carefully and in particular will be concerned to see that any proposed date or period for the trial and (if provided for) for a case management conference is no later than is reasonably necessary.

(3) The provision in (1)(c) above may—

    (a) limit disclosure to standard disclosure or less than that, and/or

    (b) direct that disclosure will take place by the supply of copy documents without a list, but it must in that case say either that the parties must serve a disclosure statement with the copies or that they have agreed to disclose in that way without such a statement.

(4) The provision in (1)(d) about expert evidence may be to the effect that none is required.

PD 29 para.4.8

Directions agreed by the parties should also where appropriate contain provisions about:

(1) the filing of any reply or amended statement of case that may be required,

(2) dates for the service of requests for further information under PD 18 and of questions to experts under r.35.6 and by when they are to be dealt with,

(3) the disclosure of evidence,

(4) the use of a single joint expert, or in cases where it is not agreed, the exchange of expert evidence (including whether exchange is to be simultaneous or sequential) and without prejudice discussions between experts.

(See paras 6, 7 and 9 of PD 35).

PD 29 para.4.9

If the court does not approve the agreed directions filed by the parties but decides that it will give directions of its own initiative without fixing a case management conference, it will take them into account in deciding what directions to give.

PD 29 para.4.10

Where the court is to give directions on its own initiative without holding a case management conference and it is not aware of any steps taken by the parties other than the exchange of statements of case, its general approach will be:

(1) to give directions for the filing and service of any further information required to clarify either party's case,

(2) to direct standard disclosure between the parties,

(3) to direct the disclosure of witness statements by way of simultaneous exchange,

(4) to give directions for a single joint expert on any appropriate issue unless there is a good reason not to do so,

(5) unless para.4.11 (below) applies, to direct disclosure of experts' reports by way of simultaneous exchange on those issues where a single joint expert is not directed,

(6) if experts' reports are not agreed, to direct a discussion between experts for the purpose set out in r.35.12(1) and the preparation of a statement under r.35.12(3),

(7) to list a case management conference to take place after the date for compliance with those directions,

(8) to specify a trial period.

PD 29 para.4.11

If it appears that expert evidence will be required both on issues of liability and on the amount of damages, the court may direct that the exchange of those reports that relate to liability will be exchanged simultaneously but that those relating to the amount of damages will be exchanged sequentially.

PD 29 para.4.12

(1) If it appears to the court that it cannot properly give directions on its own initiative and no agreed directions have been filed which it can approve, the court will direct a case management conference to be listed.
(2) The conference will be listed as promptly as possible.

PD 29 para.4.13

Where the court is proposing on its own initiative to make an order under r.35.7 (which gives the court power to direct that evidence on a particular issue is to be given by a single expert) or under r.35.15 (which gives the court power to appoint an assessor), the court must, unless the parties have consented in writing to the order, list a case management conference.

Directions the court will give on listing

Directions the court must give

PD 29 para.9.1

The court must fix the trial date or week, give a time estimate and fix the place of trial.

Other directions

PD 29 para.9.2

(1) The parties should seek to agree directions and may file an agreed order. The court may make an order in those terms or it may make a different order.
(2) Agreed directions should include provision about:
    (a) evidence especially expert evidence,
    (b) a trial timetable and time estimate,
    (c) the preparation of a trial bundle, and
    (d) any other matter needed to prepare the case for trial.
(3) The court will include such of these provisions as are appropriate in any order that it may make, whether or not the parties have filed agreed directions.
(4) Unless a direction doing so has been given before, a direction giving permission to use expert evidence will say whether it gives permission to use oral evidence or reports or both and will name the experts concerned.

PD 29 para.9.3

The principles set out in para.6 of [PD 29] about variation of directions applies equally to directions given at this stage.

Steps taken by the parties

Pt 29 r.29.4

If—
  (a) the parties agree proposals for the management of the proceedings (including a proposed trial date or period in which the trial is to take place); and
  (b) the court considers that the proposals are suitable,
it may approve them without a hearing and give directions in the terms proposed.

Failure to comply with case management directions

PD 29 para.7.1

Where a party fails to comply with a direction given by the court any other party may apply for an order that he must do so or for a sanction to be imposed or both of these.

PD 29 para.7.2

The party entitled to apply for such an order must do so without delay but should first warn the other party of his intention to do so.

PD 29 para.7.3

The court may take any such delay into account when it decides whether to make an order imposing a sanction or to grant relief from a sanction imposed by the rules or any other practice direction.

PD 29 para.7.4

  (1) The court will not allow a failure to comply with directions to lead to the postponement of the trial unless the circumstances are exceptional.
  (2) If it is practical to do so the court will exercise its powers in a manner that enables the case to come on for trial on the date or within the period previously set.
  (3) In particular the court will assess what steps each party should take to prepare the case for trial, direct that those steps are taken in the shortest possible time and impose a sanction for non-compliance. Such a sanction may, for example, deprive a party of the right to raise or contest an issue or to rely on evidence to which the direction relates.
  (4) Where it appears that one or more issues are or can be made ready for trial at the time fixed while others cannot, the court may direct that the trial will proceed on the issues which are then ready, and direct that no costs will be allowed for any later trial of the remaining issues or that those costs will be paid by the party in default.
  (5) Where the court has no option but to postpone the trial it will do so for the shortest possible time and will give directions for the taking of the necessary steps in the meantime as rapidly as possible.
  (6) Litigants and lawyers must be in no doubt that the court will regard the postponement of a trial as an order of last resort. Where it appears inevitable the court may exercise its power to require a party as well as his legal representative to attend court at the hearing where such an order is to be sought.
  (7) The court will not postpone any other hearing without a very good reason, and for that purpose the failure of a party to comply on time with directions previously given will not be treated as a good reason.

Variation of case management timetable

Pt 29 r.29.5

    (1) A party must apply to the court if he wishes to vary the date which the court has fixed
        for—
        (a) a case management conference;
        (b) a pre-trial review;
        (c) the return of a pre-trial check list under r.29.6;
        (d) the trial; or
        (e) the trial period.
    (2) Any date set by the court or these rules for doing any act may not be varied by the parties
        if the variation would make it necessary to vary any of the dates mentioned in
        para.(1).
(Rule 2.11 allows the parties to vary a date by written agreement except where the rules provide
otherwise or the court orders otherwise).

Pre-trial review

Pt 29 r.29.7

If, on receipt of the parties' pre-trial check lists, the court decides—
    (a) to hold a pre-trial review; or
    (b) to cancel a pre-trial review which has already been fixed,
it will serve notice of its decision at least seven days before the date fixed for the hearing or, as
the case may be, the cancelled hearing.

Setting a trial timetable and fixing or confirming the trial date or week

Pt 29 r.29.8

As soon as practicable after—
    (a) each party has filed a completed pre-trial check list;
    (b) the court has held a listing hearing under r.29.6(3); or
    (c) the court has held a pre-trial review under r.29.7,
the court will—
      (i) set a timetable for the trial unless a timetable has already been fixed, or the court considers
        that it would be inappropriate to do so;
      (ii) fix the date for the trial or the week within which the trial is to begin (or, if it has already
        done so, confirm that date); and
     (iii) notify the parties of the trial timetable (where one is fixed under this rule) and the date or
        trial period.

Case management in the High Court of Justice

PD 29 r.2.1

This part of [PD 29] applies to claims begun by claim form issued in the Central Office or
Chancery Chambers in the Royal Courts of Justice.

PD 29 r.2.2

A claim with an estimated value of less than £50,000 will generally, unless:
  (a) it is required by an enactment to be tried in the High Court,
  (b) it falls within a specialist list, or
  (c) it falls within one of the categories specified in para.2.6 below or is otherwise within the
      criteria of art.7(5) of the High Court and County Courts Jurisdiction Order 1991,
be transferred to a county court.

PD 29 r.2.3

Paragraph 2.2 is without prejudice to the power of the court in accordance with Pt 30 to transfer
to a county court a claim with an estimated value that exceeds £50,000.

PD 29 r.2.4

The decision to transfer may be made at any stage in the proceedings but should, subject to
para.2.5, be made as soon as possible and in any event not later than the date for the filing of pre-
trial check lists (listing questionnaires).

PD 29 r.2.5

If an application is made under r.3.4 (striking out) or under Pt 24 (summary judgment) or under
Pt 25 (interim remedies), it will usually be convenient for the application to be dealt with before
a decision to transfer is taken.

PD 29 r.2.6

Each party should state in his allocation questionnaire whether he considers the claim should be
managed and tried at the Royal Courts of Justice and, if so, why. Claims suitable for trial in the
Royal Courts of Justice include:
  (1) professional negligence claims,
  (2) Fatal Accident Act claims,
  (3) fraud or undue influence claims,
  (4) defamation claims,
  (5) claims for malicious prosecution or false imprisonment,
  (6) claims against the police,
  (7) contentious probate claims.
Such claims may fall within the criteria of article 7(5) of the High Court and County Courts
Jurisdiction Order 1991.

Variation of directions

PD 29 para.6.1

This paragraph deals with the procedure to be adopted:
  (1) where a party is dissatisfied with a direction given by the court,
  (2) where the parties have agreed about changes they wish made to the directions given,
      or
  (3) where a party wishes to apply to vary a direction.

PD 29 para.6.2

(1) It is essential that any party who wishes to have a direction varied takes steps to do so as soon as possible.
(2) The court will assume for the purposes of any later application that a party who did not appeal, and who made no application to vary within 14 days of service of the order containing the directions, was content that they were correct in the circumstances then existing.

PD 29 para.6.3

(1) Where a party is dissatisfied with a direction given or other order made by the court he may appeal or apply to the court for it to reconsider its decision.
(2) Unless para.6.4 applies, a party should appeal if the direction was given or the order was made at a hearing at which he was present, or of which he had due notice.
(3) In any other case he should apply to the court to reconsider its decision.
(4) If an application is made for the court to reconsider its decision:
    (a) it will usually be heard by the judge who gave the directions or another judge of the same level,
    (b) the court will give all parties at least three days notice of the hearing, and
    (c) the court may confirm its directions or make a different order.

PD 29 para.6.4

Where there has been a change in the circumstances since the order was made the court may set aside or vary a direction it has given. It may do so on application or on its own initiative.

PD 29 para.6.5

Where the parties agree about changes they wish made to the directions given:
(1) If r.2.11 (variation by agreement of a date set by the court for doing any act other than those stated in the note to that rule) or r.31.5, 31.10(8) or 31.13 (agreements about disclosure) applies the parties need not file the written agreement.
(2) (a) In any other case the parties must apply for an order by consent.
    (b) The parties must file a draft of the order sought and an agreed statement of the reasons why the variation is sought.
    (c) The court may make an order in the agreed terms or in other terms without a hearing, but it may direct that a hearing is to be listed.

Conduct of trial

Pt 29 r.29.9

Unless the trial judge otherwise directs, the trial will be conducted in accordance with any order previously made.

Trial

PD 29 para.10.1

The trial will normally take place at a Civil Trial Centre but it may be at another court if it is appropriate having regard to the needs of the parties and the availability of court resources.

PD 29, para.10.2

The judge will generally have read the papers in the trial bundle and may dispense with an opening address.

PD 29 para.10.3

The judge may confirm or vary any timetable given previously, or if none has been given set his own.

PD 29 para.10.4

Attention is drawn to the provisions in Pt 32 and the following parts of the rules about evidence, and in particular:
   (1) to r.32.1 (court's power to control evidence and to restrict cross-examination), and
   (2) to r.32.5(2) statements and reports to stand as evidence in chief.

PD 29 para.10.5

In an appropriate case the judge may summarily assess costs in accordance with r.44.7. Attention is drawn to the practice directions about costs and the steps the parties are required to take.

PD 29 para.10.6

Once the trial of a multi-track claim has begun, the judge will normally sit on consecutive court days until it has been concluded.

See also **Alternative dispute resolution**, **Case management conference**, **Case summary**, **Directions**, **Listing hearing**, **Listing questionnaire**, and **Place of trial**.

MULTIPLE CLAIMANTS

See **Group litigation order**.

MULTIPLE CLAIMS

See **Default judgment**.

N

"N" FORMS

PD 4 para.3.1

Table [1 of PD 4] lists the forms that are referred to and required by rules or PDs supplementing particular Parts of the CPR.

NATIONAL CREDITOR CODE

PD 7C para.1.1

The number or reference allotted to a [Production] Centre user by the officer.

NATIONAL DEBT ACT 1870

Applications in proceedings under s.55 of the National Debt Act 1870

PD 23B para.2.1

Where a claim is brought under s.55 of the National Debt Act 1870, the claimant must apply to the court for directions about giving notice of the claim.

PD 23B para.2.2

The court may—
- (a) direct that notice of the proceedings shall be given by advertisement or by such other method as appropriate; or
- (b) dispense with notice.

NATIONAL INSURANCE CONTRIBUTIONS

See **Revenue and customs**.

NATIONAL SECURITY

Exclusion of persons from certain proceedings

PD Proceedings under enactments relating to Discrimination para.5.1

In a claim—
- (1) brought under s.66(1) of the [Sex Discrimination Act 1975];

    (2) brought under s.57(1) of the [Race Relations Act 1976];

    (3) alleging discrimination under the [Disability Discrimination Act 1995];

    (4) brought under s.66 of the [Equality Act 2006]; or

    (5) brought under reg.20 of the Sexual Orientation Regulations 2007,

the court may, where it considers it expedient in the interests of national security—

    (a) exclude from all or part of the proceedings—

        (i) the claimant;

        (ii) the claimant's representatives; or

        (iii) any assessors

(Section 67(4) of the 1976 Act allows an assessor to be appointed in proceedings under that Act);

    (b) permit a claimant or representative to make a statement to the court before the start of the proceedings (or the part of the proceedings) from which he is excluded; or

    (c) take steps to keep secret all or part of the reasons for its decision in the claim.

PD Discrimination para.5.2

In this paragraph, a 'special advocate' means a person appointed under—

    (1) section 66B(2) of the 1975 Act;

    (2) section 67A(2) of the 1976 Act;

    (3) section 59A(2) of the 1995 Act;

    (4) section 71(2) of the 2006 Act to represent the claimant; and

    (5) regulation 25(2) of the Sexual Orientation Regulations 2007.

PD Discrimination para.5.3

In proceedings to which this paragraph refers, where the claimant or his representatives have been excluded from all or part of the proceedings—

    (a) the court will inform the Attorney-General of the proceedings; and

    (b) the Attorney-General may appoint a special advocate to represent the claimant in respect of those parts of the proceedings from which he or his representative have been excluded.

PD Discrimination para.5.4

In exercise of its powers under para.5.1(c), the court may order the special advocate not to communicate (directly or indirectly) with any persons (including the excluded claimant)—

    (a) on any matter discussed or referred to; or

    (b) with regard to any material disclosed,

during or with reference to any part of the proceedings from which the claimant or his representative are excluded.

PD Discrimination para.5.5

Where the court makes an order referred to in para.5.4 (or any similar order), the special advocate may apply to the court for directions enabling him to seek instructions from, or otherwise to communicate with an excluded person.

NEGLIGENCE

See **Disease and illness claims**, **Personal injury claims**, and **Pre-action protocols**.

NEIGHBOURING LAND

See **Access to Neighbouring Land Act 1992**.

NEXT FRIEND

See **Litigation friend**.

NON-CONTENTIOUS PROBATE PROCEEDINGS

Pt 2 r.2.1(2)

The CPR do not apply to these proceedings except to the extent that they are applied by s.127 of the Supreme Court Act 1981.

NON-DISCLOSURE INJUNCTIONS INFORMATION COLLECTION PILOT SCHEME

PD 40F para.1

This PD provides for a scheme for the recording, and transmission to the Ministry of Justice for analysis, of certain data in relation to injunctions prohibiting publication of private or confidential information. The purpose of the scheme is to enable the Ministry of Justice to collate and publish, in anonymised form, information about applications for injunctions where s.12 of the Human Rights Act 1998 is engaged.

PD 40F para.2

This scheme applies in any civil proceedings in the High Court or Court of Appeal in which the court considers an application for an injunction prohibiting the publication of private or confidential information, the continuation of such an injunction, or an appeal against the grant or refusal of such an injunction. The scheme does not apply to proceedings to which the Family Procedure Rules 2010 apply, to immigration or asylum proceedings, to proceedings which raise issues of national security or to proceedings to which Pt 21 applies.

PD 40F para.3

An injunction to which this PD applies is called a 'Non-disclosure injunction'.

PD 40F para.4

Except where a direction under paragraph 6 is made, following the hearing of an application for a non-disclosure injunction or any appeal against the grant or refusal of any such injunction the judge will record the following information in the form attached in the Annex (the information)—
    (a) the claim or application number;
    (b) whether the hearing was of—
        (i) an application for an interim injunction;

    (ii) an application for an extension or variation of an interim injunction;
    (iii) an application for a final injunction; or
    (iv) an appeal against the grant or refusal of an interim or final injunction.
  (c) whether the hearing was on notice, or without notice to—
    (i) the defendant; or
    (ii) any third party liable to be affected by the order.
  (d) whether the parties consented to the order;
  (e) whether any derogations from the principle of open justice were sought, and if so—
    (i) what they were;
    (ii) whether they were granted;
    (iii) if granted, whether with the parties' consent.

PD 40F para.5

Derogations from the principle of open justice include, but are not limited to—
  (a) an order that the hearing be held wholly or partly in private;
  (b) an order that the names of one or more of the parties not be disclosed;
  (c) an order that access to documents on the court file be restricted (under r.5.4C or the inherent jurisdiction);
  (d) an order that the provision of documents to third parties be restricted (under PD 25A, para.9.2); and
  (e) an order prohibiting disclosure of the existence of the proceedings or the order.

PD 40F para.6

Subject to any express direction to the contrary in the order, any order made by the court on an application for a non-disclosure injunction or appeal from the grant or refusal of such an injunction shall be deemed to include a provision giving permission to a court officer to transmit the information to the Chief Statistician in the Ministry of Justice in order for it to be analysed and published in such form as does not enable the public identification of the parties to any proceedings.

PD 40F para.7

If, in exceptional circumstances, the judge makes any direction under para.6, the judge shall report that fact, and the nature of any derogation from open justice contained in the non-disclosure injunction to the Master of the Rolls. The Master of the Rolls is, following consultation with the judge, entitled to transmit such information as he sees fit to the Chief Statistician to enable publication by the Ministry of Justice of the bare fact that an injunction of that type had been made.

PD 40F para.8

Once completed the form in the Annex [to this PD] will be sent by a court officer to the Chief Statistician in the Ministry of Justice.

NON-FUNDED PARTY

Costs PD para.21.17

A party to proceedings who has not received LSC funded services in relation to these proceedings under a legal aid certificate or a certificate issued under the LSC Funding Code other than a certificate which has been revoked.

NON-PARTIES

Enforcement of judgment or order by or against non-party

Pt 70 r.70.4

If a judgment or order is given or made in favour of or against a person who is not a party to proceedings, it may be enforced by or against that person by the same methods as if he were a party.

Inspection of property against a non-party

See **Interim remedies**.

Pre-commencement disclosure and orders for disclosure against a person who is not a party

Pt 46 r.46.1

    (1) This paragraph applies where a person applies—
        (a) for an order under—
            (i) section 33 of the Supreme Court Act 1981; or
            (ii) section 52 of the County Courts Act 1984,
        (which give the court powers exercisable before commencement of proceedings); or
        (b) for an order under—
            (i) section 34 of the Supreme Court Act 1981; or
            (ii) section 53 of the County Courts Act 1984,
        (which give the court power to make an order against a non-party for disclosure of documents, inspection of property etc.).
    (2) The general rule is that the court will award the person against whom the order is sought his costs—
        (a) of the application; and
        (b) of complying with any order made on the application.
    (3) The court may however make a different order, having regard to all the circumstances, including—
        (a) the extent to which it was reasonable for the person against whom the order was sought to oppose the application; and
        (b) whether the parties to the application have complied with any relevant pre-action protocol.

See also **Additional claim**, **Court documents**, **Interim remedies**, and **Service of documents**.

Costs orders in favour of or against non-parties

Pt 46 r.46.2

    (1) Where the court is considering whether to exercise its power under s.51 of the Senior Courts Act 1981 (costs are in the discretion of the court) to make a costs order in favour of or against a person who is not a party to proceedings, that person must—

     (a) be added as a party to the proceedings for the purposes of costs only; and

     (b) be given a reasonable opportunity to attend a hearing at which the court will consider the matter further.

(2) This rule does not apply—

     (a) where the court is considering whether to—

          (i) make an order against the Lord Chancellor in proceedings in which the Lord Chancellor has provided legal aid to a party to the proceedings;

          (ii) make a **wasted costs order** (as defined in r. 46.8); and

     (b) in proceedings to which r. 46.1 applies (pre-commencement disclosure and orders for disclosure against a person who is not a party).

Service of an additional claim form on a non-party

See **Additional claims**.

Service of application notice on a non-party to the proceedings

See **Service of documents**.

Supply of documents to a non-party from court records

See **Court documents**.

NOTARIAL ACTS AND INSTRUMENTS

Pt 32 r.32.20

A notarial act or instrument may be received in evidence without further proof as duly authenticated in accordance with the requirements of law unless the contrary is proved.

NOTICE TO ADMIT FACTS

Pt 32 r.32.18

(1) A party may serve notice on another party requiring him to admit the facts, or the part of the case of the serving party, specified in the notice.

(2) A notice to admit facts must be served no later than 21 days before the trial.

(3) Where the other party makes any admission in response to the notice, the admission may be used against him only—

     (a) in the proceedings in which the notice to admit is served; and

     (b) by the party who served the notice.

(4) The court may allow a party to amend or withdraw any admission made by him on such terms as it thinks just.

NOTICE TO ADMIT OR PRODUCE DOCUMENTS

PD 32 r.32.19

(1) A party shall be deemed to admit the authenticity of a document disclosed to him under Pt 31 (disclosure and inspection of documents) unless he serves notice that he wishes the document to be proved at trial.

(2) A notice to prove a document must be served—
   (a) by the latest date for serving witness statements; or
   (b) within seven days of disclosure of the document, whichever is later.

NOTIFICATION ORDERS UNDER THE COUNTER-TERRORISM ACT 2008

Applications for a notification order

Pt 79 r.79.31

(1) An application for a notification order under Sch.4 to the 2008 Act must be made in accordance with Pt 8.

(2) Where the defendant wishes to serve a notice under para.2(4) of Sch.4 to the 2008 Act, the defendant must file and serve the notice with an acknowledgment of service not more than 14 days after service of the claim form.

NULLITY

See **Divorce**.

NULLITY OF MARRIAGE

See **Divorce**.

NURSES, MIDWIVES AND HEALTH VISITORS

See **Health care professionals**.

O

OVERRIDING OBJECTIVE

Pt 1 r.1.1

(1) These Rules are a new procedural code with the overriding objective of enabling the court to deal with cases justly and at proportionate cost.

(2) Dealing with a case justly and at proportionate cost includes, so far as is practicable—

    (a) ensuring that the parties are on an equal footing;

    (b) saving expense;

    (c) dealing with the case in ways which are proportionate—

        (i) to the amount of money involved;

        (ii) to the importance of the case;

        (iii) to the complexity of the issues; and

        (iv) to the financial position of each party;

    (d) ensuring that it is dealt with expeditiously and fairly;

    (e) allotting to it an appropriate share of the court's resources, while taking into account the need to allot resources to other cases;

    (f) enforcing compliance with rules, PDs and orders.

P

PD

Practice Direction supplementing a rule of the **CPR**.

PF

See **Practice form**.

PARENTING ORDERS

Pt 65 r.65.37

(1) [Section VII of Pt 65] applies in relation to applications for parenting orders under ss.26A and 26B of the Anti-social Behaviour Act 2003 by a relevant authority.

Applications for parenting orders

Pt 65 r.65.38

(1) Subject to para.(2)—
   (a) where the relevant authority [has the same meaning as in s.26C of the 2003 Act] is the claimant in the proceedings, an application for an order under s.26A or 26B of the 2003 Act must be made in the claim form; and
   (b) where the relevant authority is a defendant in the proceedings, an application for such an order must be made by application notice which must be filed with the defence.
(2) Where the relevant authority becomes aware of the circumstances that lead it to apply for an order after its claim is issued or its defence filed, the application must be made by application notice as soon as possible thereafter.
(3) Where the application is made by application notice, it must normally be made on notice to the person against whom the order is sought.

PD 65 para.16.1

Where the applicant is a registered social landlord or a private registered provider of social housing, the application must be supported by evidence that the relevant local authority has been consulted in accordance with s.26B(8) of the 2003 Act.

PD 65 para.16.2

An order under s.26A or 26B of the 2003 Act must be served personally on the defendant.

PD 65 para.16.3

An application by a relevant authority under s.26C(3) of the 2003 Act to join a person to the proceedings may only be made against a person aged 18 or over.

Applications by the relevant authority to be joined to proceedings

Pt 65 r.65.39

(1) Where the relevant authority is not a party to the proceedings—
   (a) an application under s.26C(2) of the 2003 Act to be made a party must be made in accordance with s.I of Pt 19; and
   (b) the application to be made a party and the application for an order under s.26A or 26B of the 2003 Act must be made in the same application notice.
(2) The applications—
   (a) must be made as soon as possible after the relevant authority becomes aware of the proceedings; and
   (b) must normally be made on notice to the person against whom the order is sought.

Applications by the relevant authority to join a parent to proceedings

Pt 65 r.65.40

(1) An application under s.26C(3) of the 2003 Act by a relevant authority which is a party to the proceedings to join a parent to those proceedings must be made—
   (a) in the same application notice as the application for an order under section 26A or 26B of the 2003 Act; and
   (b) as soon as possible after the relevant authority considers that the grounds for the application are met.
(2) Rule 19.2 does not apply in relation to an application made by a relevant authority under s.26C(3) of the 2003 Act to join a parent to the proceedings.
(3) The application notice must contain—
   (a) the relevant authority's reasons for claiming the anti-social behaviour of the child or young person is material in relation to the proceedings; and
   (b) details of the behaviour alleged.
(4) The application must normally be made on notice to the person against whom the order is sought.

Evidence

Pt 65 r.65.41

An application under s.26A, 26B or 26C of the 2003 Act must be accompanied by written evidence.

PARENTING ORDERS UNDER THE ANTI-SOCIAL BEHAVIOUR ACT 2003

See **Parenting orders**.

PARKING PENALTIES UNDER THE ROAD TRAFFIC ACT 1991

See **Traffic enforcement**.

PART OWNER

Pt 40 r.40.14

(1) One of two or more persons who have an interest in the same goods.

PART 8 CLAIM FORM

Pt 8 r.8.2

Where the claimant uses the Pt 8 procedure the claim form must state—
  (a) that [Pt 8] applies;
  (b) (i) the question which the claimant wants the court to decide; or
      (ii) the remedy which the claimant is seeking and the legal basis for the claim to that remedy;
  (c) if the claim is being made under an enactment, what that enactment is;
  (d) if the claimant is claiming in a representative capacity, what that capacity is; and
  (e) if the defendant is sued in a representative capacity, what that capacity is.
(Pt 22 provides for the claim form to be verified by a statement of truth).
(R.7.5 provides for service of the claim form).
(The Costs PD sets out the information about a funding arrangement to be provided with the claim form where the claimant intends to seek to recover an additional liability)
('Funding arrangement' and 'additional liability' are defined in r.43.2).

Issue of claim form without naming defendants

Pt 8 r.8.2A

(1) A PD may set out circumstances in which a claim form may be issued under this Part without naming a defendant.
(2) The PD may set out those cases in which an application for permission must be made by application notice before the claim form is issued.
(3) The application notice for permission—
    (a) need not be served on any other person; and
    (b) must be accompanied by a copy of the claim form that the applicant proposes to issue.
(4) Where the court gives permission it will give directions about the future management of the claim.

PART 8 PROCEDURE

Types of claim in which part 8 procedure may be followed

Pt 8 r.8.1

(1) The Pt 8 procedure is the procedure set out in this Part.
(2) A claimant may use the Pt 8 procedure where—
    (a) he seeks the court's decision on a question which is unlikely to involve a substantial dispute of fact; or
    (b) paragraph (6) applies.
(3) The court may at any stage order the claim to continue as if the claimant had not used the Pt 8 procedure and, if it does so, the court may give any directions it considers appropriate.
(4) Paragraph (2) does not apply if a PD provides that the Pt 8 procedure may not be used in relation to the type of claim in question.
(5) Where the claimant uses the Part 8 procedure he may not obtain default judgment under Pt 12.
(6) A rule or PD may, in relation to a specified type of proceedings—
    (a) require or permit the use of the Pt 8 procedure; and
    (b) disapply or modify any of the rules set out in this Part as they apply to those proceedings.

(Rule 8.9 provides for other modifications to the general rules where the Pt 8 procedure is being used).
(Part 78 provides procedures for European Orders for payment and for the European small claims procedure. It also provides procedures for applications for mediation settlement enforcement Orders in relation to certain cross-border disputes).

PD 8A para.3.1

The types of claim for which the Pt 8 procedure may be used include—
(1) a claim by or against a child or protected party, as defined in r.21.1(2), which has been settled before the commencement of proceedings and the sole purpose of the claim is to obtain the approval of the court to the settlement; or
(2) a claim for provisional damages which has been settled before the commencement of proceedings and the sole purpose of the claim is to obtain a consent judgment.

PD 8A para.3.2

(1) The Pt 8 procedure must be used for those claims, petitions and applications listed in the table in Section B [of PD 8A].
(2) Where a claim is listed in the Table in section B and is identified as a claim to which particular provisions of section C [Special provisions] apply, the Pt 8 procedure shall apply subject to the additions and modifications set out in the relevant paragraphs in section C [Special provision].

PD 8A para.3.3

The Pt 8 procedure must also be used for any claim or application in relation to which an Act, rule or PD provides that the claim or application is brought by originating summons, originating motion or originating application.

PD 8A para.3.4

Where it appears to a court officer that a claimant is using the Part 8 procedure inappropriately, he may refer the claim to a judge for the judge to consider the point.

PD 8A para.3.5

The court may at any stage order the claim to continue as if the claimant had not used the Pt 8 procedure and, if it does so, the court will allocate the claim to a track and give such directions as it considers appropriate.

Issuing the claim

PD 8A para.4.2

Where a claimant uses the Part 8 procedure, the claim form (practice Form N208) should be used and must state the matters set out in r.8.2 **[Part 8 claim form]** and, if r.8.1(6) applies, must comply with the requirements of the rule or PD in question. In particular, the claim form must state that Pt 8 applies; a Pt 8 claim form means a claim form which so states.
(The Costs PD supplementing Pts 43 to 48 contains details of the information required to be filed with a claim form to comply with r.44.15 (providing information about funding arrangements)).

Responding to the claim

PD 8A para.5.1

The provisions of Pt 15 (defence and reply) do not apply where the claim form is a Part 8 claim form.

PD 8A para.5.2

Where a defendant who wishes to respond to a Pt 8 claim form is required to file an acknowledgment of service, that acknowledgment of service should be in PF N210.

PD 8A para.5.3

Where a defendant objects to the use of the Pt 8 procedure, and his statement of reasons includes matters of evidence, the acknowledgment of service must be verified by a **statement of truth**.

Managing the claim

See **Directions.**

Evidence

Pt 8 r.8.6

> (1) No written evidence may be relied on at the hearing of the claim unless—
>   (a) it has been served in accordance with r.8.5; or

(b) the court gives permission.

(2) The court may require or permit a party to give oral evidence at the hearing.

(3) The court may give directions requiring the attendance for cross-examination of a witness who has given written evidence.

(Rule 32.1 contains a general power for the court to control evidence).

Filing and serving written evidence

Pt 8 r.8.5

(1) The claimant must file any written evidence on which he intends to rely when he files his claim form.

(2) The claimant's evidence must be served on the defendant with the claim form.

(3) A defendant who wishes to rely on written evidence must file it when he files his acknowledgment of service.

(4) If he does so, he must also, at the same time, serve a copy of his evidence on the other parties.

(5) The claimant may, within 14 days of service of the defendant's evidence on him, file further written evidence in reply.

(6) If he does so, he must also, within the same time limit, serve a copy of his evidence on the other parties.

(7) The claimant may rely on the matters set out in his claim form as evidence under this rule if the claim form is verified by a statement of truth.

PD 8A para.7.1

A claimant must file the written evidence on which he relies when his Pt 8 claim form is issued (unless the evidence is contained in the claim form itself).

PD 8A para.7.2

Evidence will normally be in the form of a witness statement or an affidavit but a claimant may rely on the matters set out in his claim form provided that it has been verified by a statement of truth.

(For information about (1) statements of truth see Pt 22 and PD 22, and (2) written evidence see Pt 32 and PD 32).

PD 8A para.7.3

A defendant wishing to rely on written evidence, must file it with his acknowledgment of service.

PD 8A para.7.4

A party may apply to the court for an extension of time to serve and file evidence under r.8.5 or for permission to serve and file additional evidence under r.8.6(1).

(For information about applications see Pt 23 and PD 23A).

PD 8A para.7.5

(1) The parties may, subject to the following provisions, agree in writing on an extension of time for serving and filing evidence under r.8.5(3) or r.8.5(5).

(2) An agreement extending time for a defendant to file evidence under r.8.5(3)—

    (a) must be filed by the defendant at the same time as he files his acknowledgement of service; and

    (b) must not extend time by more than 14 days after the defendant files his acknowledgement of service.

(3) An agreement extending time for a claimant to file evidence in reply under r.8.5(5) must not extend time to more than 28 days after service of the defendant's evidence on the claimant.

Hearing

PD 8A para.8.1

The court may on the hearing date—

    (1) proceed to hear the case and dispose of the claim;

    (2) give case management directions.

PD 8A para.8.2

Case management directions may include the specific allocation of a case to a track.

PD 8A para.8.3

CPR r.26.5(3) to (5) and rr.26.6 to 26.10 apply to the allocation of a claim under para.8.2.

Part 20 claims

Pt 8 r.8.7

Where the Pt 8 procedure is used, Pt 20 (counterclaims and other additional claims) applies except that a party may not make a Pt 20 claim (as defined by r.20.2) without the court's permission.

Procedure where defendant objects to use of the Part 8 procedure

Pt 8 r.8.8

(1) Where the defendant contends that the Prt 8 procedure should not be used because—

    (a) there is a substantial dispute of fact; and

    (b) the use of the Pt 8 procedure is not required or permitted by a rule or PD,

    he must state his reasons when he files his acknowledgment of service.

(Rule 8.5 requires a defendant who wishes to rely on written evidence to file it when he files his acknowledgment of service).

(2) When the court receives the acknowledgment of service and any written evidence it will give directions as to the future management of the case.

(Rule 8.1(3) allows the court to make an order that the claim continue as if the claimant had not used the Pt 8 procedure)

Modifications to the general rules

Pt 8 r.8.9

Where the Pt 8 procedure is followed—
  (a) provision is made in this Part for the matters which must be stated in the claim form and the defendant is not required to file a defence and therefore—
     (i) Part 16 (statements of case) does not apply;
     (ii) Part 15 (defence and reply) does not apply;
     (iii) any time limit in these rules which prevents the parties from taking a step before a defence is filed does not apply;
     (iv) the requirement under r.7.8 to serve on the defendant a form for defending the claim does not apply;
  (b) the claimant may not obtain judgment by request on an admission and therefore—
     (i) rules 14.4 to 14.7 do not apply; and
     (ii) the requirement under r.7.8 to serve on the defendant a form for admitting the claim does not apply; and
  (c) the claim shall be treated as allocated to the multi-track and therefore Pt 26 does not apply.

Terminology

PD 8A para.1.1

In [PD 8A], 'Schedule rules' means provisions contained in the Schedules to the CPR, which were previously contained in the Rules of the Supreme Court (1965) or the County Court Rules (1981).

See **Part 8 claim form**.

Claims and applications that must be made under Pt 8

PD 8A para.9.1

The claimant must use the Pt 8 procedure if the claim is listed in the Table [in PD 8A].

PD 8A para.9.3

Some of the claims and applications listed in the [said] table [in PD 8A] are dealt with in the Schedule Rules [RSC Ord and CCR Ord\, and those rules modify the Pt 8 procedure. A cross-reference to the relevant Schedule Rule is contained in the [said] table.

PD 8A para.9.4

For applications that may or must be brought in the High Court, where no other rule or PD assigns the application to a Division of the court, the [said] table [in PD 8A] specifies the Division to which the application is assigned.

Special provisions

PD 8A para.10.1

The following special provisions apply to the applications [listed below].

Applications under ss.14 and 15 of the Bills of Sale Act 1878

See **Bills of Sale**.

Application under the Public Trustee Act 1906

See **Public Trustee Act 1906**.

Applications by the Secretary of State under the Representation of the People Acts

[The procedures for application for the detailed assessment of a returning officer's account and other proceedings under the Acts are set out in PD 8A, para.17.2 to para.17.8 and 17A.1.

Application under s.2(3) of the Public Order Act 1936

PD 8A para.13.1

The Attorney General may determine the persons who should be made defendants to an application under s.2(3) of the Public Order Act 1936.

PD 8A para.13.2

If the court directs an inquiry under s.2(3), it may appoint the Official Solicitor to represent any interests it considers are not sufficiently represented and ought to be represented.

Proceedings under s.1 of the Railway and Canal Commission (Abolition) Act 1949

PD 8A para.14.1

Paragraphs 15.3 to 15.14 [of Pt 8] apply, with appropriate modifications, to proceedings in which jurisdiction has been conferred on the High Court by s.1 of the Railway and Canal Commission (Abolition) Act 1949, except to the extent that—
    (1) an Act;
    (2) a rule;
    (3) a PD,
provides otherwise.

Application under the Mines (Working Facilities and Support) Act 1966

PD 8A para.15.1

[Where] the Secretary of State refers an application to the High Court under any provision of the Act, the procedure is set out in PD 8A para.15.3].

Applications under art.10 of the Mortgaging of Aircraft Order 1972

PD 8A para.15A.1

This paragraph applies to an application under art.10 of the Mortgaging of Aircraft Order 1972 for an order to amend the Register of Aircraft Mortgages.

PD 8A para.15A.2

The application must be made by claim form under Pt 8.

PD 8A para.15A.3

Every person (other than the claimant) who appears in the register as mortgagor or mortgagee of the aircraft concerned must be made a defendant to the claim.

PD 8A para.15A.4

A copy of the claim form must be sent to the Civil Aviation Authority.

PD 8A para.15A.5

The application will be assigned to the Chancery Division.

PD 8A para.15A.6

The Civil Aviation Authority is entitled to be heard in the proceedings.

Applications under s.344 of the Insolvency Act 1986 for registration of assignments of book debts

PD 8A para.15B.1

This paragraph applies to an application under s.344 of the Insolvency Act 1986 to register an assignment of book debts.

PD 8A para.15B.2

The application must be made—
    (1) by claim form under Pt 8; or
    (2) by witness statement.

PD 8A para.15B.3

The application must be made to a Master of the Queen's Bench Division and accompanied by payment of the prescribed fee.

PD 8A para.15B.4

Where the application is made by witness statement—
(1) Part 23 applies to the application;
(2) the witness statement constitutes the application notice under that Part;
(3) the witness statement does not need to be served on any other person; and
(4) the application will normally be dealt with without a hearing.

PD 8A para.15B.5

The application—
(1) must have exhibited to it a true copy of the assignment and of every schedule to it;
(2) must set out the particulars of the assignment and the parties to it; and
(3) must verify the date and time of the execution of the assignment, and its execution in the presence of a witness.

PD 8A para.15B.6

Upon the court being satisfied, the documents so exhibited will be filed and the particulars of the assignment and of the parties to it entered in the register.

Application for injunction to prevent environmental harm or unlicensed activities

PD 8A para.20.1

This paragraph relates to applications under—
(1) sections 187B or 214A of the Town and Country Planning Act 1990;
(2) section 44A of the Planning (Listed Buildings and Conservation Areas) Act 1990;
(3) section 26AA of the Planning (Hazardous Substances) Act 1990; or
(4) sections 12 or 26 of the Energy Act 2008.

PD 8A para.20.2

An injunction may be granted under those sections against a person whose identity is unknown to the applicant.

PD 8A para.20.3

In this paragraph, an injunction refers to an injunction under one of those sections and 'the defendant' is the person against whom the injunction is sought.

PD 8A para.20.4

In the [Pt 8] claim form, the applicant must describe the defendant by reference to—
(1) a photograph;
(2) a thing belonging to or in the possession of the defendant; or
(3) any other evidence.

PD 8A para.20.5

The description of the defendant under para.20.4 must be sufficiently clear to enable the defendant to be served with the proceedings.

(The court has power under Pt 6 to dispense with service or make an order permitting service by an alternative method or at an alternative place).

PD 8A para.20.6

The application must be accompanied by a witness statement. The witness statement must state—
  (1) that the applicant was unable to ascertain the defendant's identity within the time reasonably available to him;
  (2) the steps taken by him to ascertain the defendant's identity;
  (3) the means by which the defendant has been described in the claim form; and
  (4) that the description is the best the applicant is able to provide.

PD 8A para.20.7

When the court issues the claim form it will—
  (1) fix a date for the hearing; and
  (2) prepare a notice of the hearing date for each party.

PD 8A para.20.8

The claim form must be served not less than 21 days before the hearing date.

PD 8A para.20.9

Where the claimant serves the claim form, he must serve notice of the hearing date at the same time, unless the hearing date is specified in the claim form.
(CPR r.3.1(2)(a) and (b) provide for the court to extend or shorten the time for compliance with any rule or PD, and to adjourn or bring forward a hearing)

PD 8A para.20.10

The court may on the hearing date—
  (1) proceed to hear the case and dispose of the claim; or
  (2) give case management directions.

See also **Acknowledgment of service, Child, Coroners Court, Financial Services and Markets Act 2000, Mental Health Act 1983, Quashing of an aquittal**, and **Vexatious litigants**.

Application to quash certain orders, schemes, etc.

PD 8A para.22.1

This paragraph applies where the High Court has jurisdiction under any enactment, on the application of any person to quash or prohibit any—
  (1) order, scheme, certificate or plan of;
  (2) amendment or approval of a plan of;
  (3) decision of;
  (4) action on the part of,
a Minister or government department.

[Paragraphs 22.2 to 22.11 of PD8A set out the procedure.]

PART 20 CLAIM

Claims under [Pt 20] were formerly known as 'Part 20 claims'. As a result of the amendments to Pt 20, introduced by Civil Procedure (Amendment No.4) Rules 2005, they are now called **'additional claims'**.

However, they are described as 'Part 20 claims' on a number of court forms. For the present, some of those forms will continue to refer to Pt 20 claims. These references should be construed as being additional claims under this Part. Any reference to a Pt 20 claimant or a Pt 20 defendant means a claimant or defendant in an additional claim under this Part.

PART 36 OFFER

Pt 36 r.36.A1

(1) [Part 36] contains rules about—
   (a) offers to settle; and
   (b) the consequences where an offer to settle is made in accordance with this Part.
(2) Section I of this Part contains rules about offers to settle other than where s.II applies.
(3) Section II of this Part contains rules about offers to settle where the parties have followed the **Pre-Action protocols**.

Section I of Pt 36

Pt 36 r.36.1

(1) This Section does not apply to an offer to settle to which Section II of this Part [RTA Protocol offers to settle] applies.
(2) Nothing in this Section prevents a party making an offer to settle in whatever way he chooses, but if the offer is not made in accordance with r.36.2, it will not have the consequences specified in rr.36.10, 36.11 and 36.14.
(Rule 44.3 requires the court to consider an offer to settle that does not have the costs consequences set out in this Section in deciding what order to make about costs)

Form and content of a Pt 36 offer

Pt 36 r.36.2

(1) An offer to settle which is made in accordance with this rule is called a Pt 36 offer.
(2) A Pt 36 offer must—
   (a) be in writing;
   (b) state on its face that it is intended to have the consequences of s.I of Pt 36;
   (c) specify a period of not less than 21 days within which the defendant will be liable for the claimant's costs in accordance with r.36.10 if the offer is accepted;
   (d) state whether it relates to the whole of the claim or to part of it or to an issue that arises in it and if so to which part or issue; and
   (e) state whether it takes into account any counterclaim.
(Rule 36.7 makes provision for when a Pt 36 offer is made).
(3) Rule 36.2(2)(c) does not apply if the offer is made less than 21 days before the start of the trial.
(4) In appropriate cases, a Pt 36 offer must contain such further information as is required by r.36.5 (Personal injury claims for future pecuniary loss), r.36.6 (Offer to settle a claim for provisional damages), and r.36.15 (Deduction of benefits).

(5) An offeror may make a Pt 36 offer solely in relation to liability.

PD 36A para.1.1

A Pt 36 offer may be made using Form N242A.

PD 36A para.11.2

Where a Pt 36 offer, notice of acceptance or notice of withdrawal or change of terms is to be served on a party who is legally represented, the document to be served must be served on the legal representative.

General provisions

Pt 36 r.36.3

(1) In [Pt 36]—
    (a) the party who makes an offer is the 'offeror';
    (b) the party to whom an offer is made is the 'offeree'; and
    (c) 'the relevant period' means—
        (i) in the case of an offer made not less than 21 days before trial, the period stated under r.36.2(2)(c) or such longer period as the parties agree;
        (ii) otherwise, the period up to end of the trial or such other period as the court has determined.
(2) A Pt 36 offer—
    (a) may be made at any time, including before the commencement of proceedings; and
    (b) may be made in appeal proceedings.
(3) A Pt 36 offer which offers to pay or offers to accept a sum of money will be treated as inclusive of all interest until—
    (a) the date on which the period stated under r.36.2(2)(c) expires; or
    (b) if r.36.2(3) applies, a date 21 days after the date the offer was made.
(4) A Pt 36 offer shall have the consequences set out in this section only in relation to the costs of the proceedings in respect of which it is made, and not in relation to the costs of any appeal from the final decision in those proceedings.
(5) Before expiry of the relevant period, a Pt 36 offer may be withdrawn or its terms changed to be less advantageous to the offeree, only if the court gives permission.
(6) After expiry of the relevant period and provided that the offeree has not previously served notice of acceptance, the offeror may withdraw the offer or change its terms to be less advantageous to the offeree without the permission of the court.
(7) The offeror does so by serving written notice of the withdrawal or change of terms on the offeree.
(Rule 36.14(6) deals with the costs consequences following judgment of an offer that is withdrawn)

Application for permission to withdraw a Pt 36 offer

PD 36A para.2.1

Rule 36.3(4) provides that before expiry of the relevant period a Pt 36 offer may only be withdrawn or its terms changed to be less advantageous to the offeree with the permission of the court.

PD 36A para.2.2

The permission of the court must be sought—
   (1) by making an application under Pt 23, which must be dealt with by a judge other than the judge (if any) allocated in advance to conduct the trial, unless the parties agree that such judge may hear the application;
   (2) at a trial or other hearing, provided that it is not to the trial judge or to the judge (if any) allocated in advance to conduct the trial, unless the parties agree that such judge may hear the application.

Defendants' offers

Pt 36 para.36.4

   (1) Subject to r.36.5(3) and r.36.6(1), a Pt 36 offer by a defendant to pay a sum of money in settlement of a claim must be an offer to pay a single sum of money.
   (2) But, an offer that includes an offer to pay all or part of the sum, if accepted, at a date later than 14 days following the date of acceptance will not be treated as a Pt 36 offer unless the offeree accepts the offer.

Personal injury claims for future pecuniary loss

Pt 36 para.36.5

   (1) This rule applies to a claim for damages for personal injury which is or includes a claim for future pecuniary loss.
   (2) An offer to settle such a claim will not have the consequences set out in rr.36.10, 36.11 and 36.14 unless it is made by way of a Pt 36 offer under this rule.
   (3) A Pt 36 offer to which this rule applies may contain an offer to pay, or an offer to accept—
      (a) the whole or part of the damages for future pecuniary loss in the form of—
         (i) a lump sum; or
         (ii) periodical payments; or
         (iii) both a lump sum and periodical payments;
      (b) the whole or part of any other damages in the form of a lump sum.
   (4) A Pt 36 offer to which this rule applies—
      (a) must state the amount of any offer to pay the whole or part of any damages in the form of a lump sum;
      (b) may state—
         (i) what part of the lump sum, if any, relates to damages for future pecuniary loss; and
         (ii) what part relates to other damages to be accepted in the form of a lump sum;
      (c) must state what part of the offer relates to damages for future pecuniary loss to be paid or accepted in the form of periodical payments and must specify—
         (i) the amount and duration of the periodical payments;
         (ii) the amount of any payments for substantial capital purchases and when they are to be made; and
         (iii) that each amount is to vary by reference to the retail prices index (or to some other named index, or that it is not to vary by reference to any index); and
      (d) must state either that any damages which take the form of periodical payments will be funded in a way which ensures that the continuity of payment is reasonably secure

in accordance with s.2(4) of the Damages Act 1996 or how such damages are to be paid and how the continuity of their payment is to be secured.

(5) Rule 36.4 applies to the extent that a Pt 36 offer by a defendant under this rule includes an offer to pay all or part of any damages in the form of a lump sum.

(6) Where the offeror makes a Pt 36 offer to which this rule applies and which offers to pay or to accept damages in the form of both a lump sum and periodical payments, the offeree may only give notice of acceptance of the offer as a whole.

(7) If the offeree accepts a Pt 36 offer which includes payment of any part of the damages in the form of periodical payments, the claimant must, within seven days of the date of acceptance, apply to the court for an order for an award of damages in the form of periodical payments under r.41.8.

(PD 41B contains information about periodical payments under the Damages Act 1996)

Time when a Pt 36 offer is made

Pt 36 para.36.7

(1) A Pt 36 offer is made when it is served on the offeree.

(2) A change in the terms of a t 36 offer will be effective when notice of the change is served on the offeree.

(Rule 36.3 makes provision about when permission is required to change the terms of an offer to make it less advantageous to the offeree).

Clarification of a Pt 36 offer

Pt 36 para.36.8

(1) The offeree may, within seven days of a Pt 36 offer being made, request the offeror to clarify the offer.

(2) If the offeror does not give the clarification requested under para.(1) within seven days of receiving the request, the offeree may, unless the trial has started, apply for an order that he does so.

(Part 23 contains provisions about making an application to the court).

(3) If the court makes an order under para.(2), it must specify the date when the Pt 36 offer is to be treated as having been made.

Acceptance of a Pt 36 offer

Pt 36 para.36.9

(1) A Part 36 offer is accepted by serving written notice of the acceptance on the offeror.

(2) Subject to r.36.9(3), a Pt 36 offer may be accepted at any time (whether or not the offeree has subsequently made a different offer) unless the offeror serves notice of withdrawal on the offeree.

(Rule 21.10 deals with compromise, etc. by or on behalf of a child or protected party).

(3) The court's permission is required to accept a Pt 36 offer where—

    (a) rule 36.12(4) applies;

    (b) rule 36.15(3)(b) applies, the relevant period has expired and further deductible amounts have been paid to the claimant since the date of the offer;

    (c) an apportionment is required under r.41.3A; or

        (d) the trial has started.
(Rule 36.12 deals with offers by some but not all of multiple defendants).
(Rule 36.15 defines 'deductible amounts').
(Rule 41.3A requires an apportionment in proceedings under the Fatal Accidents Act 1976 (Fatal accident claims) and Law Reform (Miscellaneous Provisions) Act 1934).

> (4) Where the court gives permission under para.(3), unless all the parties have agreed costs, the court will make an order dealing with costs, and may order that the costs consequences set out in r.36.10 will apply.
> (5) Unless the parties agree, a Pt 36 offer may not be accepted after the end of the trial but before judgment is handed down.

PD 36A para.3.1

Where a Pt 36 offer is accepted in accordance with r.36.9(1) the notice of acceptance must be served on the offeror and filed with the court where the case is proceeding.

PD 36A para.3.2

Where the court's permission is required to accept a Pt 36 offer, the permission of the court must be sought—

> (1) by making an application under Pt 23, which must be dealt with by a judge other than the judge (if any) allocated in advance to conduct the trial, unless the parties agree that such judge may hear the application;
> (2) at a trial or other hearing, provided that it is not to the trial judge or to the judge (if any) allocated in advance to conduct the trial, unless the parties agree that such judge may hear the application.

PD 36A para.3.3

Where r.36.9(3)(b) applies, the application for permission to accept the offer must—

> (1) state
>> (a) the net amount offered in the Pt 36 offer;
>> (b) the deductible amounts that had accrued at the date the offer was made;
>> (c) the deductible amounts that have subsequently accrued; and
> (2) be accompanied by a copy of the current certificate.

Costs consequences of acceptance of a Pt 36 offer

Pt 36 para.36.10

> (1) Subject to para.(2) and para.(4)(a), where a Pt 36 offer is accepted within the relevant period the claimant will be entitled to the costs of the proceedings up to the date on which notice of acceptance was served on the offeror.
> (2) Where—
>> (a) a defendant's Pt 36 offer relates to part only of the claim; and
>> (b) at the time of serving notice of acceptance within the relevant period the claimant abandons the balance of the claim,
> the claimant will be entitled to the costs of the proceedings up to the date of serving notice of acceptance unless the court orders otherwise.
> (3) Costs under paras (1) and (2) of this rule will be assessed on the standard basis if the amount of costs is not agreed.

(Rule 44.4(2) explains the standard basis for assessment of costs).
(Rule 44.12 contains provisions about when a costs order is deemed to have been made and applying for an order under s.194(3) of the Legal Services Act 2007).

(4) Where—
    (a) a Pt 36 offer that was made less than 21 days before the start of trial is accepted; or
    (b) a Pt 36 offer is accepted after expiry of the relevant period,
    if the parties do not agree the liability for costs, the court will make an order as to costs.

(5) Where para.(4)(b) applies, unless the court Orders otherwise—
    (a) the claimant will be entitled to the costs of the proceedings up to the date on which the relevant period expired; and
    (b) the offeree will be liable for the offeror's costs for the period from the date of expiry of the relevant period to the date of acceptance.

(6) The claimant's costs include any costs incurred in dealing with the defendant's counter-claim if the Pt 36 offer states that it takes into account the counterclaim.

Effect of acceptance of a Pt 36 offer

Pt 36 para.36.11

(1) If a Pt 36 offer is accepted, the claim will be stayed.
(2) In the case of acceptance of a Pt 36 offer which relates to the whole claim the stay will be upon the terms of the offer.
(3) If a Pt 36 offer which relates to part only of the claim is accepted—
    (a) the claim will be stayed as to that part upon the terms of the offer; and
    (b) subject to r.36.10(2), unless the parties have agreed costs, the liability for costs shall be decided by the court.
(4) If the approval of the court is required before a settlement can be binding, any stay which would otherwise arise on the acceptance of a Pt 36 offer will take effect only when that approval has been given.
(5) Any stay arising under this rule will not affect the power of the court—
    (a) to enforce the terms of a Pt 36 offer;
    (b) to deal with any question of costs (including interest on costs) relating to the pro-ceedings.
(6) Unless the parties agree otherwise in writing, where a Pt 36 offer by a defendant that is or that includes an offer to pay a single sum of money is accepted, that sum must be paid to the offeree within 14 days of the date of—
    (a) acceptance; or
    (b) the order when the court makes an order under r.41.2 (order for an award of provisional damages) or r.41.8 (order for an award of periodical payments), unless the court orders otherwise.
(7) If the accepted sum is not paid within 14 days or such other period as has been agreed the offeree may enter judgment for the unpaid sum.
(8) Where—
    (a) a Pt 36 offer (or part of a Pt 36 offer) which is not an offer to which para.(6) applies is accepted; and
    (b) a party alleges that the other party has not honoured the terms of the offer,
    that party may apply to enforce the terms of the offer without the need for a new claim.

Acceptance of a Pt 36 offer made by one or more, but not all, defendants

Pt 36 para.36.12

(1) This rule applies where the claimant wishes to accept a Pt 36 offer made by one or more, but not all, of a number of defendants.

(2) If the defendants are sued jointly or in the alternative, the claimant may accept the offer if—
   (a) he discontinues his claim against those defendants who have not made the offer; and
   (b) those defendants give written consent to the acceptance of the offer.
(3) If the claimant alleges that the defendants have a several liability to him, the claimant may—
   (a) accept the offer; and
   (b) continue with his claims against the other defendants if he is entitled to do so.
(4) In all other cases the claimant must apply to the court for an order permitting him to accept the Pt 36 offer.

Restriction on disclosure of a Pt 36 offer

Pt 36 para.36.13

(1) A Pt 36 offer will be treated as 'without prejudice except as to costs'.
(2) The fact that a Pt 36 offer has been made must not be communicated to the trial judge or to the judge (if any) allocated in advance to conduct the trial until the case has been decided.
(3) Paragraph (2) does not apply—
   (a) where the defence of tender before claim has been raised;
   (b) where the proceedings have been stayed under r.36.11 following acceptance of a Pt 36 offer; or
   (c) where the offeror and the offeree agree in writing that it should not apply.

Costs consequences following judgment

Pt 36 para.36.14

(1) This rule applies where upon judgment being entered—
   (a) a claimant fails to obtain a judgment more advantageous than a defendant's Pt 36 offer; or
   (b) judgment against the defendant is at least as advantageous to the claimant as the proposals contained in a claimant's Pt 36 offer.
(1A) For the purposes of para.(1), in relation to any money claim or money element of a claim, 'more advantageous' means better in money terms by any amount, however small, and 'at least as advantageous' shall be construed accordingly.
(2) Subject to para.(6), where r.36.14(1)(a) applies, the court will, unless it considers it unjust to do so, order that the defendant is entitled to—
   (a) his costs from the date on which the relevant period expired; and
   (b) interest on those costs.
(3) Subject to para.(6), where r.36.14(1)(b) applies, the court will, unless it considers it unjust to do so, order that the claimant is entitled to—
   (a) interest on the whole or part of any sum of money (excluding interest) awarded at a rate not exceeding 10 per cent above base rate for some or all of the period starting with the date on which the relevant period expired;
   (b) his costs on the indemnity basis from the date on which the relevant period expired; and
   (c) interest on those costs at a rate not exceeding 10 per cent above base rate.
(4) In considering whether it would be unjust to make the Orders referred to in paras (2) and (3) above, the court will take into account all the circumstances of the case including—

(a) the terms of any Pt 36 offer;

(b) the stage in the proceedings when any Pt 36 offer was made, including in particular how long before the trial started the offer was made;

(c) the information available to the parties at the time when the Pt 36 offer was made; and

(d) the conduct of the parties with regard to the giving or refusing to give information for the purposes of enabling the offer to be made or evaluated.

(5) Where the court awards interest under this rule and also awards interest on the same sum and for the same period under any other power, the total rate of interest may not exceed 10 per cent above base rate.

(6) Paragraphs (2) and (3) of this rule do not apply to a Pt 36 offer—

(a) that has been withdrawn;

(b) that has been changed so that its terms are less advantageous to the offeree, and the offeree has beaten the less advantageous offer;

(c) made less than 21 days before trial, unless the court has abridged the relevant period.

(Rule 44.3 requires the court to consider an offer to settle that does not have the costs consequences set out in this Section in deciding what order to make about costs).

Deduction of benefits and lump sum payments

Pt 36 para.36.15

(1) In this rule and r.36.9—

(a) 'the 1997 Act' means the Social Security (Recovery of Benefits) Act 1997;

(b) 'the 2008 Regulations' means the Social Security (Recovery of Benefits)(Lump Sum Payments) Regulations 2008;

(c) 'recoverable amount' means—

(i) 'recoverable benefits' as defined in s.1(4)(c) of the 1997 Act; and

(ii) 'recoverable lump sum payments' as defined in reg.4 of the 2008 Regulations;

(d) 'deductible amount' means—

(i) any benefits by the amount of which damages are to be reduced in accordance with s.8 of, and Sch.2 to the 1997 Act ('deductible benefits'); and

(ii) any lump sum payment by the amount of which damages are to be reduced in accordance with reg.12 of the 2008 Regulations ('deductible lump sum payments'); and

(e) 'certificate'—

(i) in relation to recoverable benefits is construed in accordance with the provisions of the 1997 Act; and

(ii) in relation to recoverable lump sum payments has the meaning given in s.29 of the 1997 Act as applied by reg.2 of, and modified by Sch.1 to the 2008 Regulations.

(2) This rule applies where a payment to a claimant following acceptance of a Pt 36 offer would be a compensation payment as defined in s.1(4)(b) or 1A(5)(b) of the 1997 Act.

(3) A defendant who makes a Pt 36 offer should state either—

(a) that the offer is made without regard to any liability for recoverable amounts; or

(b) that it is intended to include any deductible amounts.

(4) Where para.(3)(b) applies, paras (5) to (9) of this rule will apply to the Pt 36 offer.

(5) Before making the Pt 36 offer, the offeror must apply for a certificate.

(6) Subject to para.(7), the Pt 36 offer must state—

(a) the amount of gross compensation;

(b) the name and amount of any deductible amount by which the gross amount is reduced; and

(c) the net amount of compensation.

(7) If at the time the offeror makes the Pt 36 offer, the offeror has applied for, but has not received a certificate, the offeror must clarify the offer by stating the matters referred to in paras (6)(b) and (6)(c) not more than seven days after receipt of the certificate.

(8) For the purposes of r.36.14(1)(a), a claimant fails to recover more than any sum offered (including a lump sum offered under r.36.5) if the claimant fails upon judgment being entered to recover a sum, once deductible amounts identified in the judgment have been deducted, greater than the net amount stated under para.(6)(c).

(Section 15(2) of the 1997 Act provides that the court must specify the compensation payment attributable to each head of damage. Schedule 1 to the 2008 Regulations modifies s.15 of the 1997 Act in relation to lump sum payments and provides that the court must specify the compensation payment attributable to each or any dependant who has received a lump sum payment).

(9) Where—
(a) further deductible amounts have accrued since the Pt 36 offer was made; and
(b) the court gives permission to accept the Pt 36 offer,
the court may direct that the amount of the offer payable to the offeree shall be reduced by a sum equivalent to the deductible amounts paid to the claimant since the date of the offer.

(Rule 36.9(3)(b) states that permission is required to accept an offer where the relevant period has expired and further deductible amounts have been paid to the claimant

Offers and payments made before April 6, 2007

From April 6, 2007, new rules came into force concerning offers to settle, and Pt 36, as it was in force immediately before April 6, 2007, was substituted by a new Pt 36. Rule 7 of the Civil Procedure (Amendment No.3) Rules 2006 that brought those new rules into force and replaced the previous rules contained some provisions that dealt with how the rules are to apply to offers and payments into court made before April 6, 2007. PD 36B explains how those provisions will operate.

See **Compromise**, **Pre-action protocols**, and **Damages**.

PART 36 PAYMENT

See **Part 36 offer** and **Payment into court**.

PARTICULARS OF CLAIM

Pt 7 r.7.4

(1) Particulars of claim must—
(a) be contained in or served with the claim form; or
(b) subject to para.(2) be served on the defendant by the claimant within 14 days after service of the claim form.

(2) Particulars of claim must be served on the defendant no later than the latest time for serving a claim form.

(Rule 7.5 sets out the latest time for serving a claim form).

(3) Where the claimant serves particulars of claim separately from the claim form in accordance with para.(1)(b), the claimant must, within seven days of service on the defendant, file a copy of the particulars except where—

(a) paragraph 5.2(4) of PD 7C applies; or

(b) paragraph 6.4 of PD 7E applies.

(Part 16 sets out what the particulars of claim must include).

(Part 22 requires particulars of claim to be verified by a statement of truth).

PD 7A para.6.1

Where the claimant does not include the particulars of claim in the claim form, they may be served separately:

(1) either at the same time as the claim form, or

(2) within 14 days after service of the claim form provided that the service of the particulars of claim is within four months after the date of issue of the claim form (or six months where the claim form is to be served out of the jurisdiction).

PD 7A para.6.2

If the particulars of claim are not included in or have not been served with the claim form, the claim form must contain a statement that particulars of claim will follow.

(These paragraphs do not apply where the Pt 8 procedure is being used. For information on matters to be included in the claim form or the particulars of claim, see Pt 16 (statements of case) and PD 16).

Pt 16 para.16.1

Part [16] does not apply where the claimant uses the procedure set out in Pt 8 (alternative procedure for claims).

Contents of the particulars of claim

Pt 16 para.16.4

(1) Particulars of claim must include—

(a) a concise statement of the facts on which the claimant relies;

(b) if the claimant is seeking **interest**, a statement to that effect and the details set out in para.(2);

(c) if the claimant is seeking **aggravated damages** or **exemplary damages**, a statement to that effect and his grounds for claiming them;

(d) if the claimant is seeking **provisional damages**, a statement to that effect and his grounds for claiming them; and

(e) such other matters as may be set out in a PD.

(2) If the claimant is seeking **interest** he must—

(a) state whether he is doing so—

(i) under the terms of a contract;

(ii) under an enactment and if so which; or

(iii) on some other basis and if so what that basis is; and

(b) if the claim is for a specified amount of money, state—

(i) the percentage rate at which interest is claimed;

(ii) the date from which it is claimed;

(iii) the date to which it is calculated, which must not be later than the date on which the claim form is issued;

(iv) the total amount of interest claimed to the date of calculation; and

(v) the daily rate at which interest accrues after that date.

(Part 22 requires particulars of claim to be verified by a **statement of truth**)

PD 16 para.3.1

If practicable, the particulars of claim should be set out in the **claim form**.

PD 16 para.3.2

Where the claimant does not include the particulars of claim in the claim form, particulars of claim may be served separately:
(1) either at the same time as the claim form, or
(2) within 14 days after service of the claim form provided that the service of the particulars of claim is not later than four months from the date of issue of the claim form (or six months where the claim form is to be served out of the jurisdiction).

PD 16 para.3.3

If the particulars of claim are not included in or have not been served with the claim form, the claim form must also contain a statement that particulars of claim will follow.

PD 16, para.3.4

Particulars of claim which are not included in the claim form must be verified by a statement of truth, the form of which is as follows:
'[I believe][the claimant believes] that the facts stated in these particulars of claim are true.'

PD 16 para.3.5

Attention is drawn to r.32.14 which sets out the consequences of verifying a statement of case containing a **false statement** without an honest belief in its truth.

PD 16 para.3.6

The full particulars of claim must include:
(1) the matters set out in r.16.4, and
(2) where appropriate, the matters set out in PDs relating to specific types of claims.

PD 16 para.3.7

Attention is drawn to the provisions of r.16.4(2) in respect of a claim for interest.

PD 16 para.3.8

Particulars of claim served separately from the claim form must also contain:
(1) the name of the court in which the claim is proceeding,
(2) the claim number,
(3) the title of the proceedings, and
(4) the claimant's address for service.

Other matters to be included in particulars of claim

PD 16 para.7.1

Where a claim is made for an injunction or declaration in respect of or relating to any land or the possession, occupation, use or enjoyment of any land the particulars of claim must:

(1) state whether or not the injunction or declaration relates to residential premises, and

(2) identify the land (by reference to a plan where necessary).

PD 16 para.7.2

Where a claim is brought to enforce a right to recover possession of goods the particulars of claim must contain a statement showing the value of the goods.

PD 16 para.7.3

Where a claim is based upon a written agreement:

(1) a copy of the contract or documents constituting the agreement should be attached to or served with the particulars of claim and the original(s) should be available at the hearing, and

(2) any general conditions of sale incorporated in the contract should also be attached (but where the contract is or the documents constituting the agreement are bulky this PD is complied with by attaching or serving only the relevant parts of the contract or documents).

PD 16 para.7.4

Where a claim is based upon an oral agreement, the particulars of claim should set out the contractual words used and state by whom, to whom, when and where they were spoken.

PD 16 para.7.5

Where a claim is based upon an agreement by conduct, the particulars of claim must specify the conduct relied on and state by whom, when and where the acts constituting the conduct were done.

PD 16 para.7.6

In a claim issued in the High Court relating to a Consumer Credit Agreement, the particulars of claim must contain a statement that the action is not one to which s.141 of the Consumer Credit Act 1974 applies.

Matters which must be specifically set out in the particulars of claim if relied on

PD 16 para.8.1

A claimant who wishes to rely on evidence:

(1) under s.11 of the Civil Evidence Act 1968 of a conviction of an offence, or

(2) under s.12 of the above-mentioned Act of a finding or adjudication of adultery or paternity, must include in his particulars of claim a statement to that effect and give the following details:

(1) the type of conviction, finding or adjudication and its date,

(2) the court or Court-Martial which made the conviction, finding or adjudication, and

(3) the issue in the claim to which it relates.

PD 16 para.8.2

The claimant must specifically set out the following matters in his particulars of claim where he wishes to rely on them in support of his claim:
    (1) any allegation of fraud,
    (2) the fact of any illegality,
    (3) details of any misrepresentation,
    (4) details of all breaches of trust,
    (5) notice or knowledge of a fact,
    (6) details of unsoundness of mind or undue influence,
    (7) details of wilful default, and
    (8) any facts relating to mitigation of loss or damage.

See also **Child, Fatal accident claim, Foreign currency, Hire purchase claim, Human rights, Personal injuries claim**, and **Provisional damages**.

PD 16 para.9.2

A subsequent statement of case must not contradict or be inconsistent with an earlier one; for example a reply to a defence must not bring in a new claim. Where new matters have come to light the appropriate course may be to seek the court's permission to amend the statement of case.

PARTIES

Pt 19 r.19.1

Any number of claimants or defendants may be joined as parties to a claim.

Addition and substitution of parties

Pt 19 r.19.2

    (1) This rule applies where a party is to be added or substituted except where the case falls within r.19.5 (special provisions about changing parties after the end of a relevant limitation period).
    (2) The court may order a person to be added as a new party if—
        (a) it is desirable to add the new party so that the court can resolve all the matters in dispute in the proceedings; or
        (b) there is an issue involving the new party and an existing party which is connected to the matters in dispute in the proceedings, and it is desirable to add the new party so that the court can resolve that issue.
    (3) The court may order any person to cease to be a party if it is not desirable for that person to be a party to the proceedings.
    (4) The court may order a new party to be substituted for an existing one if—
        (a) the existing party's interest or liability has passed to the new party; and
        (b) it is desirable to substitute the new party so that the court can resolve the matters in dispute in the proceedings.

Procedure for adding and substituting parties

Pt 19 r.19.4

(1) The court's permission is required to remove, add or substitute a party, unless the claim form has not been served.

(2) An application for permission under para.(1) may be made by—
(a) an existing party; or
(b) a person who wishes to become a party.

(3) An application for an order under r.19.2(4) (substitution of a new party where existing party's interest or liability has passed)—
(a) may be made without notice; and
(b) must be supported by evidence.

(4) Nobody may be added or substituted as a claimant unless—
(a) he has given his consent in writing; and
(b) that consent has been filed with the court.

(4A) The Commissioners for HM Revenue and Customs may be added as a party to proceedings only if they consent in writing.

(5) An order for the removal, addition or substitution of a party must be served on—
(a) all parties to the proceedings; and
(b) any other person affected by the order.

(6) When the court makes an order for the removal, addition or substitution of a party, it may give consequential directions about—
(a) filing and serving the claim form on any new defendant;
(b) serving relevant documents on the new party; and
(c) the management of the proceedings.

PD 19A para.1.1

Parties may be removed, added or substituted in existing proceedings either on the court's own initiative or on the application of either an existing party or a person who wishes to become a party.

PD 19A para.1.2

The application may be dealt with without a hearing where all the existing parties and the proposed new party are in agreement.

PD 19A para.1.3

The application to add or substitute a new party should be supported by evidence setting out the proposed new party's interest in or connection with the claim.

PD 19A para.1.4

The application notice should be filed in accordance with r.23.3 and, unless the application is made under r.19.2(4) be served in accordance with r.23.4.

PD 19A para.1.5

An order giving permission to amend will, unless the court orders otherwise, be drawn up. It will be served by the court unless the parties wish to serve it or the court orders them to do so.

Addition or substitution of claimant

PD 19A para.2.1

Where an application is made to the court to add or to substitute a new party to the proceedings as claimant, the party applying must file:
  (1) the application notice,
  (2) the proposed amended claim form and particulars of claim, and
  (3) the signed, written consent of the new claimant to be so added or substituted.

PD 19A para.2.2

Where the court makes an order adding or substituting a party as claimant but the signed, written consent of the new claimant has not been filed:
  (1) the order, and
  (2) the addition or substitution of the new party as claimant,
     will not take effect until the signed, written consent of the new claimant is filed.

PD 19A para.2.3

Where the court has made an order adding or substituting a new claimant, the court may direct:
  (1) a copy of the order to be served on every party to the proceedings and any other person affected by the order,
  (2) copies of the statements of case and of documents referred to in any statement of case to be served on the new party,
  (3) the party who made the application to file within 14 days an amended claim form and particulars of claim.

Addition or substitution of defendant

PD 19A para.3.1

The Civil Procedure Rules apply to a new defendant who has been added or substituted as they apply to any other defendant (see in particular the provisions of Pts 9, 10, 11 and 15).

PD 19A para.3.2

Where the court has made an order adding or substituting a defendant whether on its own initiative or on an application, the court may direct:
  (1) the claimant to file with the court within 14 days (or as ordered) an amended claim form and particulars of claim for the court file,
  (2) a copy of the order to be served on all parties to the proceedings and any other person affected by it,
  (3) the amended claim form and particulars of claim, forms for admitting, defending and acknowledging the claim and copies of the statements of case and any other documents referred to in any statement of case to be served on the new defendant.
  (4) unless the court orders otherwise, the amended claim form and particulars of claim to be served on any other defendants.

PD 19A para.3.3

A new defendant does not become a party to the proceedings until the amended claim form has been served on him.

Power of the court to proceed in the absence of a party

Pt 23 r.23.11

(1) Where the applicant or any respondent fails to attend the hearing of an application, the court may proceed in his absence.
(2) Where—
(a) the applicant or any respondent fails to attend the hearing of an application; and
(b) the court makes an order at the hearing,
the court may, on application or of its own initiative, re-list the application.
(Part 40 deals with service of orders).

Provisions applicable where two or more persons are jointly entitled to a remedy

Pt 19 r.19.3

(1) Where a claimant claims a remedy to which some other person is jointly entitled with him, all persons jointly entitled to the remedy must be parties unless the court orders otherwise.
(2) If any person does not agree to be a claimant, he must be made a defendant, unless the court orders otherwise.
(3) This rule does not apply in probate proceedings.

Removal of party

PD 19A para.4

Where the court makes an order for the removal of a party from the proceedings:
(1) the claimant must file with the court an amended claim form and particulars of claim, and
(2) a copy of the order must be served on every party to the proceedings and on any other person affected by the order.

Death

Pt 19 r.19.8

(1) Where a person who had an interest in a claim has died and that person has no personal representative the court may order—
(a) the claim to proceed in the absence of a person representing the estate of the deceased; or
(b) a person to be appointed to represent the estate of the deceased.
(2) Where a defendant against whom a claim could have been brought has died and—
(a) a grant of probate or administration has been made, the claim must be brought against the persons who are the personal representatives of the deceased;
(b) a grant of probate or administration has not been made—
(i) the claim must be brought against 'the estate of' the deceased; and
(ii) the claimant must apply to the court for an order appointing a person to represent the estate of the deceased in the claim.

(3) A claim shall be treated as having been brought against 'the estate of' the deceased in accordance with para.(2)(b)(i) where—
   (a) the claim is brought against the 'personal representatives' of the deceased but a grant of probate or administration has not been made; or
   (b) the person against whom the claim was brought was dead when the claim was started.
(4) Before making an order under this rule, the court may direct notice of the application to be given to any other person with an interest in the claim.
(5) Where an order has been made under paras (1) or (2)(b)(ii) any judgment or order made or given in the claim is binding on the estate of the deceased.

Transfer of interest or liability

PD 19A para.5.1

Where the interest or liability of an existing party has passed to some other person, application should be made to the court to add or substitute that person.

PD 19A para.5.2

The application must be supported by evidence showing the stage the proceedings have reached and what change has occurred to cause the transfer of interest or liability.
(For information about making amendments generally, see PD 17).

See **Human rights**, **Limitation period**, and **Wrongful interference with goods**.

PARTNERS

See **Partnership**.

PARTNERSHIP

Claims by and against partnerships within the jurisdiction

PD 7A para.5A.1

Paragraphs 5A and 5B apply to claims that are brought by or against two or more persons who—
   (1) were partners; and
   (2) carried on that partnership business within the jurisdiction, at the time when the cause of action accrued.

PD 7A para.5A.2

For the purposes of this paragraph, 'partners' includes persons claiming to be entitled as partners and persons alleged to be partners.

PD 7A para.5A.3

Where that partnership has a name, unless it is inappropriate to do so, claims must be brought in or against the name under which that partnership carried on business at the time the cause of action accrued.

Acknowledgment of service

PD 10 para.4.4

Where a claim is brought against a partnership—
  (1) service must be acknowledged in the name of the partnership on behalf of all persons who were partners at the time when the cause of action accrued; and
  (2) the acknowledgment of service may be signed by any of those partners, or by any person authorised by any of those partners to sign it.

Applications for orders against partnership property for a partner's separate judgment debt

PD 73 para.6.1

This paragraph relates to orders made under s.23 of the Partnership Act 1890.

PD 73 para.6.2

The following applications must be made in accordance with Pt 23—
  (1) an application for an order under s.23 of the 1890 Act made by a judgment creditor of a partner;
  (2) an application for any order by a partner of the judgment debtor in consequence of any application made by the judgment creditor under s.23.

PD 73 para.6.3

The powers conferred on a judge by s.23 may be exercised by—
  (1) a Master;
  (2) the Admiralty Registrar; or
  (3) a district judge.

PD 73 para.6.4

Every application notice filed under this paragraph by a judgment creditor, and every order made following such an application, must be served on the judgment debtor and on any of the other partners that are within the jurisdiction.

PD 73 para.6.5

Every application notice filed under this paragraph by a partner of a judgment debtor, and every order made following such an application, must be served—
  (1) on the judgment creditor and the judgment debtor; and
  (2) on the other partners of the judgment debtor who are not joined in the application and who are within the jurisdiction.

PD 73 para.6.6

An application notice or order served under this paragraph on one or more, but not all, of the partners of a partnership shall be deemed to have been served on all the partners of that partnership.

Applications for orders made under s.23 of the Partnership Act 1890

PD 73 para.6.1

This paragraph relates to orders made under s.23 of the Partnership Act 1890 ("Section 23").

PD 73 para.6.2

The following applications must be made in accordance with Part 23—
  (1) an application for an order under s.23 of the 1890 Act made by a judgment creditor of a partner;
  (2) an application for any order by a partner of the judgment debtor in consequence of any application made by the judgment creditor under s.23.

PD 73 para.6.3

The powers conferred on a judge by s.23 may be exercised by—
  (1) a Master;
  (2) the Admiralty Registrar; or
  (3) a district judge.

PD 73 para.6.4

Every application notice filed under this paragraph by a judgment creditor, and every order made following such an application, must be served on the judgment debtor and on any of the other partners that are within the jurisdiction.

PD 73 para.6.5

Every application notice filed under this paragraph by a partner of a judgment debtor, and every order made following such an application, must be served—
  (1) on the judgment creditor and the judgment debtor; and
  (2) on the other partners of the judgment debtor who are not joined in the application and who are within the jurisdiction.

PD 73 para.6.6

An application notice or order served under this paragraph on one or more, but not all, of the partners of a partnership shall be deemed to have been served on all the partners of that partnership.

Attachment of debts owed by a partnership

Charging Order

PD 73 para.4A.1

A charging order or interim charging order may be made against any property, within the jurisdiction, belonging to a judgment debtor that is a partnership.

PD 73 para.4A.2

For the purposes of r.73.5(1)(a) (service of the interim order), the specified documents must be served on—
    (1) a member of the partnership within the jurisdiction;
    (2) a person authorised by a partner; or
    (3) some other person having the control or management of the partnership business.

PD 73 para.4A.3

Where an order requires a partnership to appear before the court, it will be sufficient for a partner to appear before the court.

Claim form

PD 16 para.2.6

The claim form must be headed with the title of the proceedings, including the full name of each party. The full name means, in each case where it is known:
    (c) in the case of a partnership (other than a limited liability partnership (LLP))—
        (i) where partners are being sued in the name of the partnership, the full name by which the partnership is known, together with the words '(A Firm)'; or
        (ii) where partners are being sued as individuals, the full unabbreviated name of each partner and the title by which he is known.

Enforcing a judgment or order against a partnership

PD 70 para.6A.1

A judgment or order made against a partnership may be enforced against any property of the partnership within the jurisdiction.

PD 70 para.6A.2

Subject to para.6A.3, a judgment or order made against a partnership may be enforced against any person who is not a limited partner and who—
    (1) acknowledged service of the claim form as a partner;
    (2) having been served as a partner with the claim form, failed to acknowledge service of it;
    (3) admitted in his statement of case that he is or was a partner at a material time; or
    (4) was found by the court to have been a partner at a material time.

PD 70 para.6A.3

A judgment or order made against a partnership may not be enforced against a limited partner or a member of the partnership who was ordinarily resident outside the jurisdiction when the claim form was issued unless that partner or member—
(1) acknowledged service of the claim form as a partner;
(2) was served within the jurisdiction with the claim form as a partner; or
(3) was served out of the jurisdiction with the claim form, as a partner, with the permission of the court given under s.IV of Pt 6.

PD 70 para.6A.4

A judgment creditor wishing to enforce a judgment or order against a person in circumstances not set out in paras 6A.2 or 6A.3 must apply to the court for permission to enforce the judgment or order.

Statement of truth

PD 22 para.3.6

Where the document is to be verified on behalf of a partnership, those who may sign the statement of truth are:
(1) any of the partners, or
(2) a person having the control or management of the partnership business.

Third Party Debt Order

Attachment of debts owed by a partnership

PD 72 para.3A.1

This paragraph relates to debts due or accruing due to a judgment creditor from a partnership.

PD 72 para.3A.2

An interim Third Party Debt Order under r.72.4(2) relating to such debts must be served on—
(1) a member of the partnership within the jurisdiction;
(2) a person authorised by a partner; or
(3) some other person having the control or management of the partnership business.

PD 72 para.3A.3

Where an order made under r.72.4(2) requires a partnership to appear before the court, it will be sufficient for a partner to appear before the court.

Partnership membership statements

PD 7A para.5B.1

A written statement of the names and last known places of residence of all the persons who were partners in the partnership at the time when the cause of action accrued, being the date specified for this purpose in accordance with para.5B.3.

PD 7A para.5B.2

If the partners are requested to provide a copy of a partnership membership statement by any party to a claim, the partners must do so within 14 days of receipt of the request.

PD 7A para.5B.3

In that request the party seeking a copy of a partnership membership statement must specify the date when the relevant cause of action accrued.

PATENT

Pt 63 r.63.1

    (e) A patent under the 1977 Act or a supplementary protection certificate granted by the Patent Office under art.10(1) of Council Regulation (EEC) No.1768/92 or of Regulation (EC) No.1610/96 of the European Parliament and the Council and includes any application for a patent or supplementary protection certificate.

See **Intellectual property claims**.

PATENTS AND REGISTERED DESIGNS

Pt 63 r.63.2

    (1) This section applies to—
        (a) any claim under—
            (i) the [Patents Act 1977];
            (ii) the Registered Designs Act 1949;
            (iii) the Defence Contracts Act 1958; and
        (b) any claim relating to—
            (i) Community registered designs;
            (ii) semiconductor topography rights; or
            (iii) plant varieties.
    (2) Claims to which this section applies must be started in—
        (a) the Patents Court; or
        (b) a patents county court.

Specialist list

Pt 63 r.63.3

Claims in the Patents Court and a patents county court form specialist lists for the purpose of r.30.5.

Starting the claim

Pt 63 r.63.5

Claims to which this Section applies must be started—
(a) by a Pt 7 claim form; or
(b) in existing proceedings under Pt 20.

PD 63 para.3.1

A claim form to which this Section applies must—
(a) be marked 'Chancery Division Patents Court' or 'Patents County Court' as the case may be, in the top right hand corner below the title of the court, and
(b) state the number of any patent or registered design to which the claim relates.

Claim for infringement or challenge to validity of a patent or registered design

Pt 63 r.63.6

A statement of case in a claim for infringement or a claim in which the validity of a patent or registered design is challenged must contain particulars as set out in PD 63.

PD 63 para.4.1

In a claim for infringement of a patent—
(1) the statement of case must—
(a) show which of the claims in the specification of the patent are alleged to be infringed; and
(b) give at least one example of each type of infringement alleged; and
(2) a copy of each document referred to in the statement of case, and where necessary a translation of the document, must be served with the statement of case.

PD 63 para.4.2

Where the validity of a patent or registered design is challenged—
(1) the statement of case must contain particulars of—
(a) the remedy sought; and
(b) the issues except those relating to validity of the patent or registered design;
(2) the statement of case must have a separate document attached to and forming part of it headed 'Grounds of Invalidity' which must—
(a) specify the grounds on which validity of the patent or registered design is challenged; and
(b) include particulars that will clearly define every issue (including any challenge to any claimed priority date) which it is intended to raise; and
(3) a copy of each document referred to in the Grounds of Invalidity, and where necessary a translation of the document, must be served with the Grounds of Invalidity.

PD 63 para.4.3

Where in an application in which the validity of a patent or a registered design is challenged, the Grounds of Invalidity include an allegation—

(1) that the invention is not a patentable invention because it is not new or does not include an inventive step, the particulars must specify details of the matter in the state of the art relied on, as set out in para.4.4;
(2) that the specification of the patent does not disclose the invention clearly enough and completely enough for it to be performed by a person skilled in the art, the particulars must state, if appropriate, which examples of the invention cannot be made to work and in which respects they do not work or do not work as described in the specification; or
(3) that the registered design is not new or lacks individual character, the particulars must specify details of any prior design relied on, as set out in para.4.4.

PD 63 para.4.4

The details required under paras 4.3(1) and 4.3(3) are—
(1) in the case of matter or a design made available to the public by written description, the date on which and the means by which it was so made available, unless this is clear from the fact of the matter; and
(2) in the case of matter or a design made available to the public by use—
    (a) the date or dates of such use;
    (b) the name of all persons making such use;
    (c) the place of such use;
    (d) any written material which identifies such use;
    (e) the existence and location of any apparatus employed in such use; and
    (f) all facts and matters relied on to establish that such matter was made available to the public.

PD 63 para.4.5

In any proceedings in which the validity of a patent is challenged, where a party alleges that machinery or apparatus was used before the priority date of the claim the court may order inspection of that machinery or apparatus.

PD 63 para.4.6

If the validity of a patent is challenged on the ground that the invention did not involve an inventive step, a party who wishes to rely on the commercial success of the patent must state in the statement of case the grounds on which that party so relies.

Defence and reply

Pt 63 r.63.7

Part 15 applies with the modification—
(a) to r.15.4(1)(b) that in a claim for infringement under r.63.6, the period for filing a defence where the defendant files an acknowledgment of service under Pt 10 is 42 days after service of the particulars of claim;
(b) that where r.15.4(2) provides for a longer period to file a defence than in r.63.7(a), then the period of time in r.15.4(2) will apply; and
(c) to r.15.8 that the claimant must—
    (i) file any reply to a defence; and
    (ii) serve it on all other parties,
    within 21 days of service of the defence.

Case management

Pt 63 r.63.8

(1) Parties do not need to file an allocation questionnaire.
(2) The following provisions only of Pt 29 apply—
    (a) rule 29.3(2) (legal representatives to attend case management conferences);
    (b) rule 29.4 (the court's approval of agreed proposals for the management of proceedings); and
    (c) rule 29.5 (variation of case management timetable) with the exception of para.(1)(b) and (c).
(3) As soon as practicable the court will hold a case management conference which must be fixed in accordance with PD 63.

PD 63 para.5.1

The following paragraphs only of PD 29 apply—
(1) paragraph 5 (case management conferences)
    (a) excluding para.5.9; and
    (b) modified so far as is made necessary by other specific provisions of this PD ; and
(2) paragraph 7 (failure to comply with case management directions).

PD 63 para.5.2

Case management will be dealt with by—
(1) a judge of the Patents Court, a patents judge or a Master, but
(2) a Master may only deal with the following matters—
    (a) orders by way of settlement, except settlement of procedural disputes;
    (b) applications for extension of time;
    (c) applications for permission to serve out of the jurisdiction;
    (d) applications for security for costs;
    (e) other matters as directed by a judge of the court; and
    (f) enforcement of money judgments.

PD 63 para.5.3

The claimant must apply for a case management conference within 14 days of the date when all defendants who intend to file and serve a defence have done so.

PD 63 para.5.4

Where the claim has been transferred, the claimant must apply for a case management conference within 14 days of the date of the order transferring the claim, unless the court held or gave directions for a case management conference when it made the order transferring the claim.

PD 63 para.5.5

Any party may, at a time earlier than that provided in paras 5.3 and 5.4, apply in writing to the court to fix a case management conference.

PD 63 para.5.6

If the claimant does not make an application in accordance with paras 5.3 and 5.4, any other party may apply for a case management conference.

PD 63 para.5.7

The court may fix a case management conference at any time on its own initiative.

PD 63 para.5.8

Not less than four days before a case management conference, each party must file and serve an application notice for any order which that party intends to seek at the case management conference.

PD 63 para.5.9

Unless the court orders otherwise, the claimant, or the party who makes an application under para.5.6, in consultation with the other parties, must prepare a case management bundle containing—
  (1) the claim form;
  (2) all other statements of case (excluding schedules), except that, if a summary of a statement of case has been filed, the bundle must contain the summary, and not the full statement of case;
  (3) a pre-trial timetable, if one has been agreed or ordered;
  (4) the principal orders of the court; and
  (5) any agreement in writing made by the parties as to disclosure,
and provide copies of the case management bundle for the court and the other parties at least 4 days before the first case management conference or any earlier hearing at which the court may give case management directions.

PD 63 para.5.10

At the case management conference the court may direct that—
  (1) a scientific adviser under s.70(3) of the Senior Courts Act 1981 or under s.63(1) of the County Courts Act 1984 be appointed; and
  (2) a document setting out basic undisputed technology should be prepared.
(Rule 35.15 applies to scientific advisers).

PD 63 para.5.11

Where a trial date has not been fixed by the court, a party may apply for a trial date by filing a certificate which must—
  (1) state the estimated length of the trial, agreed if possible by all parties;
  (2) detail the time required for the judge to consider the documents;
  (3) identify the area of technology; and
  (4) assess the complexity of the technical issues involved by indicating the complexity on a scale of 1 to 5 (with 1 being the least and 5 the most complex).

PD 63 para.5.12

The claimant, in consultation with the other parties, must revise and uPD ate the documents, referred to in para.5.9 appropriately as the case proceeds. This must include making all necessary revisions and additions at least seven days before any subsequent hearing at which the court may give case management directions.

Disclosure and inspection

Pt 63 r.63.9

Part 31 is modified to the extent set out in PD 63.

PD 63 para.6.1

Standard disclosure does not require the disclosure of documents that relate to—
   (1) the infringement of a patent by a product or process where—
      (a) not less than 21 days before the date for service of a list of documents the defendant notifies the claimant and any other party of the defendant's intention to serve—
         (i) full particulars of the product or process alleged to infringe; and
         (ii) any necessary drawings or other illustrations; and
      (b) on or before the date for service the defendant serves on the claimant and any other party the documents referred to in para.6.1(1)(a);
   (2) any ground on which the validity of a patent is put in issue, except documents which came into existence within the period—
      (a) beginning two years before the earliest claimed priority date; and
      (b) ending two years after that date; and
   (3) the issue of commercial success.

PD 63 para.6.2

The particulars served under para.6.1(1)(b) must be accompanied by a signed written statement which must state that the person making the statement—
   (1) is personally acquainted with the facts to which the particulars relate;
   (2) verifies that the particulars are a true and complete description of the product or process alleged to infringe; and
   (3) understands that he or she may be required to attend court in order to be cross-examined on the contents of the particulars.

PD 63 para.6.3

Where the issue of commercial success arises, the patentee must, within such time limit as the court may direct, serve a schedule containing—
   (1) where the commercial success relates to an article or product—
      (a) an identification of the article or product (for example by product code number) which the patentee asserts has been made in accordance with the claims of the patent;
      (b) a summary by convenient periods of sales of any such article or product;
      (c) a summary for the equivalent periods of sales, if any, of any equivalent prior article or product marketed before the article or product in subpara.(a); and
      (d) a summary by convenient periods of any expenditure on advertising and promotion which supported the marketing of the articles or products in subparas (a) and (c); or
   (2) where the commercial success relates to the use of a process—
      (a) an identification of the process which the patentee asserts has been used in accordance with the claims of the patent;
      (b) a summary by convenient periods of the revenue received from the use of such process;
      (c) a summary for the equivalent periods of the revenues, if any, received from the use of any equivalent prior art process; and

    (d) a summary by convenient periods of any expenditure which supported the use of the
        process in subparas (a) and (c).

Experiments

PD 63 para.7.1

A party seeking to establish any fact by experimental proof conducted for the purpose of
litigation must, at least 21 days before service of the application notice for directions under
para.7.3, or within such other time as the court may direct, serve on all parties a notice—
    (1) stating the facts which the party seeks to establish; and
    (2) giving full particulars of the experiments proposed to establish them.

PD 63 para.7.2

A party served with a notice under para.7.1—
    (1) must within 21 days after such service, serve on the other party a notice stating whether
        or not each fact is admitted; and
    (2) may request the opportunity to inspect a repetition of all or a number of the experiments
        identified in the notice served under para.7.1.

PD 63 para.7.3

Where any fact which a party seeks to establish by experimental proof is not admitted, that party
must apply to the court for permission and directions by application notice.

Use of models or apparatus

PD 63 para.8.1

A party that intends to rely on any model or apparatus must apply to the court for directions at
the first case management conference.

Time estimates for trial, trial bundle, reading guide and detailed trial timetable

PD 63 para.9.1

Not less than one week before the beginning of the trial, each party must inform the court in
writing of the estimated length of its—
    (1) oral submissions;
    (2) examination in chief, if any, of its own witnesses; and
    (3) cross-examination of witnesses of any other party.

PD 63 para.9.2

At least four days before the date fixed for the trial, the claimant must file—
    (1) the trial bundle;
    (2) a reading guide for the judge; and
    (3) a detailed trial timetable which should be agreed, if possible.

PD 63 para.9.3

The reading guide filed under para.9.2 must—
    (1) be short and, if possible, agreed;
    (2) set out the issues, the parts of the documents that need to be read on each issue and the most convenient order in which they should be read;
    (3) identify the relevant passages in text books and cases, if appropriate; and
    (4) not contain argument.

Application to amend a patent specification in existing proceedings

Pt 63 r.63.10

    (1) An application under s.75 of the 1977 Act for permission to amend the specification of a patent by the proprietor of the patent must be made by application notice.
    (2) The application notice must—
      (a) give particulars of—
        (i) the proposed amendment sought; and
        (ii) the grounds upon which the amendment is sought;
      (b) state whether the applicant will contend that the claims prior to the amendment are valid; and
      (c) be served by the applicant on all parties and the Comptroller within seven days of it being filed.
    (3) The application notice must, if it is reasonably possible, be served on the Comptroller electronically.
    (4) Unless the court otherwise orders, the Comptroller will, as soon as practicable, advertise the application to amend in the journal.
    (5) The advertisement will state that any person may apply to the Comptroller for a copy of the application notice.
    (6) Within 14 days of the first appearance of the advertisement any person who wishes to oppose the application must file and serve on all parties and the Comptroller a notice opposing the application which must include the grounds relied on.
    (7) Within 28 days of the first appearance of the advertisement the applicant must apply to the court for directions.
    (8) Unless the court otherwise orders, the applicant must within seven days serve on the Comptroller any order of the court on the application.
    (9) In this rule 'the journal' means the journal published pursuant to rules under s.123(6) of the 1977 Act.

Pt 63 r.10.1

Where the application notice is served on the Comptroller electronically under r.63.10(3), the applicant must comply with any requirements for the sending of electronic communications to the Comptroller.

PD 63 para.10.2

Not later than two days before the first hearing date the applicant, the Comptroller if wishing to be heard, the parties to the proceedings and any other opponent, must file and serve a document stating the directions sought.

Court's determination of question or application

Pt 63 r.63.11

(1) This rule applies where the Comptroller—
   (a) declines to deal with a question under ss.8(7), 12(2), 37(8) or 61(5) of the 1977 Act;
   (b) declines to deal with an application under s.40(5) of the 1977 Act; or
   (c) certifies under s.72(7)(b) of the 1977 Act that the court should determine the question whether a patent should be revoked.
(2) Any person seeking the court's determination of that question or application must start a claim for that purpose within 14 days of receiving notification of the Comptroller's decision.
(3) A person who fails to start a claim within the time prescribed by r.63.11(2) will be deemed to have abandoned the reference or application.
(4) A party may apply to the Comptroller or the court to extend the period for starting a claim prescribed by r.63.11(2) even where the application is made after expiration of that period.

Application by employee for compensation

Pt 63 r.63.12

(1) An application by an employee for compensation under s.40(1) or (2) of the 1977 Act must be made—
   (a) in a claim form; and
   (b) within the period prescribed by paras (2), (3) and (4).
(2) The prescribed period begins on the date of the grant of the patent and ends 1 year after the patent has ceased to have effect.
(3) Where the patent has ceased to have effect as a result of failure to pay renewal fees, the prescribed period continues as if the patent has remained continuously in effect provided that—
   (a) the renewal fee and any additional fee are paid in accordance with s.25(4) of the 1977 Act; or
   (b) restoration is ordered by the Comptroller following an application under s.28 of the 1977 Act.
(4) Where restoration is refused by the Comptroller following an application under s.28 of the 1977 Act, the prescribed period will end one year after the patent has ceased to have effect or six months after the date of refusal, whichever is the later.

PD 63 para.12.1

Where an employee applies for compensation under s.40(1) or (2) of the 1977 Act, the court will at the case management conference give directions as to—
   (1) the manner in which the evidence, including any accounts of expenditure and receipts relating to the claim, is to be given at the hearing of the claim and if written evidence is to be given, specify the period within which witness statements must be filed; and
   (2) the provision to the claimant by the defendant or a person deputed by the defendant, of reasonable facilities for inspecting and taking extracts from the accounts by which the defendant proposes to verify the accounts in subpara.(1) or from which those accounts have been derived.

Communication of information to the European Patent Office

PD 63 para.13.1

The court may authorise the communication of any such information in the court files as the court thinks fit to—
(1) the European Patent Office; or
(2) the competent authority of any country which is a party to the European Patent Convention.

PD 63 para.13.2

Before authorising the communication of information under para.13.1, the court will permit any party who may be affected by the disclosure to make representations, in writing or otherwise, on the question of whether the information should be disclosed.

Order affecting entry in the register of patents or designs

PD 63 para.14.1

Where any order of the court affects the validity of an entry in the register, the party in whose favour the order is made, must serve a copy of such order on the Comptroller within 14 days.

PD 63 para.14.2

Where the order is in favour of more than one party, a copy of the order must be served by such party as the court directs.

PD 63 para.15.2

Where a counterclaim is filed at the **Community design court**, for a declaration of invalidity of a registered Community design, the Community design court will inform the Office for Harmonisation in the Internal Market of the date on which the counterclaim was filed, in accordance with art.86(2) of Council Regulation (EC) 6/2002.

PD 63 para.15.3

On filing a counterclaim under para.15.2, the party filing it must inform the Community design court in writing that it is a counterclaim to which para.15.2 applies and that the Office for Harmonisation in the Internal Market needs to be informed of the date on which the counterclaim was filed.

PD 63 para.15.4

Where a Community design court has given a judgment which has become final on a counterclaim for a declaration of invalidity of a registered Community design, the Community design court will send a copy of the judgment to the Office for Harmonisation in the Internal Market, in accordance with art.86(4) of Council Regulation (EC) 6/2002.

PD 63 para.15.5

The party in whose favour judgment is given under para.15.4 must inform the Community design court at the time of judgment that para.15.4 applies and that the Office for Harmonisation in the Internal Market needs to be sent a copy of the judgment.

PATENTS COUNTY COURT

Pt 63 r.63.1

(g) A county court designated as a patents county court under s.287(1) of the 1988 Act.

Pt 63 r.63.17

[Part 63] as modified by this Section, applies to claims started in or transferred to a patents county court.

PD 63 para.27.1

Except as provided for in para.27.2 this PD, as modified by this section, applies to claims in a patents county court.

PD 63 para.27.2

Paragraphs 5.10 to 9.1 and para.9.2(3) **[patents and registered designs]** do not apply to a claim in a patents county court.

Claims for infringement or challenge to validity

PD 63 para.28.1

Paragraph 4.2(2) **[patents and registered designs]** is modified so that the grounds for invalidity must be included in the statement of case and not in a separate document.

Transfer of proceedings to or from a patents county court

Pt 63 r.63.18

When considering whether to transfer proceedings to or from a patents county court, the court will have regard to the provisions of PD 30.

PD 30 para.9.1

When deciding whether to order a transfer of proceedings to or from a patents county court the court will consider whether—
  (1) a party can only afford to bring or defend the claim in a patents county court; and
  (2) the claim is appropriate to be determined by a patents county court having regard in particular to—

    (a) the value of the claim (including the value of an injunction);
    (b) the complexity of the issues; and
    (c) the estimated length of the trial.

PD 30 para.9.2

Where the court orders proceedings to be transferred to or from a patents county court it may—
    (1) specify terms for such a transfer; and
    (2) award reduced or no costs where it allows the claimant to withdraw the claim.

Scale costs for claims

[Section IV, rr.45.30 to 45.32 of Pt 45 and Costs PD s.IV, paras 3.1 to 3.3 apply to claims in a patents county court.]

Patents judge

Pt 63 r.63.1

    (h) A person nominated under s.291(1) of the 1988 Act as the patents judge of a patents county court.

Pt 63 r.63.19

    (1) Subject to para.(2), proceedings in a patents county court will be dealt with by the patents judge of that court.
    (2) When a matter needs to be dealt with urgently and it is not practicable or appropriate for the patents judge to deal with it, the matter may be dealt with by another judge with appropriate specialist experience nominated by the Chancellor of the High Court.

Statements of case

Pt 63 r.63.20

    (1) Part 16 applies with the modification that a statement of case must set out concisely all the facts and arguments upon which the party serving it relies.
    (2) The particulars of claim must state whether the claimant has complied with para.7.1(1) and Annex A (para.2) of the PD (Pre-Action Conduct).

Statement of truth

Pt 63 r.63.21

Part 22 applies with the modification that the statement of truth verifying a statement of case must be signed by a person with knowledge of the facts alleged, or if no one person has knowledge of all the facts, by persons who between them have knowledge of all the facts alleged.

Defence and reply

Pt 63 r.63.22

(1) Rule 63.7 does not apply and Pt 15 applies with the following modifications.
(2) Where the particulars of claim contain a confirmation in accordance with r.63.20(2), the period for filing a defence is 42 days after service of the particulars of claim unless r.15.4(2) provides for a longer period to do so.
(3) Where the particulars of claim do not contain a confirmation in accordance with r.63.20(2), the period for filing a defence is 70 days after service of the particulars of claim.
(4) Where the claimant files a reply to a defence it must be filed and served on all other parties within 28 days of service of the defence.
(5) Where the defendant files a reply to a defence to a counterclaim it must be filed and served on all other parties within 14 days of service of the defence to the counterclaim.
(6) The periods in this rule may only be extended by order of the court and for good reason.

Case management

Pt 63 r.63.23

(1) At the first case management conference after those defendants who intend to file and serve a defence have done so, the court will identify the issues and decide whether to make an order in accordance with para.29.1 of PD 63.
(2) Save in exceptional circumstances the court will not consider an application by a party to submit material in addition to that ordered under para.(1).
(3) The court may determine the claim on the papers where all parties consent.

PD 63 para.29.1

At the case management conference referred to in r.63.23 the court may order any of the following—
(1) specific disclosure;
(2) a product or process description (or a supplementary product or process description where one has already been provided);
(3) experiments;
(4) witness statements;
(5) experts' reports;
(6) cross examination at trial;
(7) written submissions or skeleton arguments.

PD 63 para.29.2

The court will make an order under para.29.1 only—
(1) in relation to specific and identified issues; and
(2) if the court is satisfied that the benefit of the further material in terms of its value in resolving those issues appears likely to justify the cost of producing and dealing with it.

Disclosure and inspection

Pt 63 r.63.24

(1) Rule 63.9 does not apply.
(2) Part 31 applies save that the provisions on standard disclosure do not apply.

Applications

Pt 63 r.63.25

(1) Part 23 applies with the modifications set out in this rule.
(2) Except at the case management conference provided for in r.63.23(1), a respondent to an application must file and serve on all relevant parties a response within five days of the service of the application notice.
(3) The court will deal with an application without a hearing unless the court considers it necessary to hold a hearing.
(4) An application to transfer the claim to the High Court or to stay proceedings must be made before or at the case management conference provided for in r.63.23(1).
(5) The court will consider an application to transfer the claim later in the proceedings only where there are exceptional circumstances.

PD 63 para.30.1

Where the court considers that a hearing is necessary under r.63.25(3) the court will conduct a hearing by telephone or video conference in accordance with paras 6.2 to 7 of PD 23A unless it considers that a hearing in person would be more cost effective for the parties or is otherwise necessary in the interests of justice.

Costs

Pt 63 r.63.26

(1) Subject to para.(2), the court will reserve the costs of an application to the conclusion of the trial when they will be subject to summary assessment.
(2) Where a party has behaved unreasonably the court will make an order for costs at the conclusion of the hearing.
(3) Where the court makes a summary assessment of costs, it will do so in accordance with s.VII of Pt 45.

Determination of the claim

PD 63 para.31.1

Where possible, the court will determine the claim solely on the basis of the parties' statements of case and oral submissions.

PD 63 para.31.2

The court will set the timetable for the trial and will, so far as appropriate, allocate equal time to the parties. Cross-examination will be strictly controlled by the court. The court will endeavour to ensure that the trial lasts no more than two days.

PATENTS COURT

(f) The Patents Court of the High Court constituted as part of the Chancery Division by s.6(1) of the Senior Courts Act 1981.

PATENTS COURT GUIDE

This Guide applies to the Patents County Court . It is written for all users of the Patents County Court, whether a litigant in person or a specialist IP litigator.

The Guide aims to help users and potential users of the Patents County Court by explaining how the procedures will operate, providing guidelines where appropriate and dealing with various practical aspects of proceedings before the Patents County Court.

The Guide cannot be wholly comprehensive of all issues which may arise before the Patents County Court. In circumstances which are not covered by this guide, reference may be made to the Patents Court Guide and the Chancery Guide.

PATERNITY

See **Blood tests in determining paternity**.

PATIENT

See **Protected party**.

PAYMENT INTO COURT

Money paid into court under a court order

Pt 37 r.37.1

A party who makes a payment into court under a court order must—
(a) serve notice of the payment on every other party; and
(b) in relation to each such notice, file a certificate of service.
money paid into court where defendant wishes to rely on a defence of tender before claim

Pt 37 r.37.2

(1) Where a defendant wishes to rely on a defence of tender before claim he must make a payment into court of the amount he says was tendered.
(2) If the defendant does not make a payment in accordance with para.(1), the defence of tender before claim will not be available to him until he does so.

Payment into court under enactments

Pt 37 r.37.4

A PD may set out special provisions with regard to payments into court under various enactments.

See also **Payment out of court**.

Payment into court under an order, etc.

PD 37 para.1.1

Except where para.1.2 applies, a party paying money into court under an order or in support of a defence of tender before claim must—
  (1) send to the Court Funds Office—
    (a) the payment, usually a cheque made payable to the Accountant General of the Senior Courts;
    (b) a sealed copy of the order or a copy of the defence; and
    (c) a completed Court Funds Office Form 100;
  (2) serve a copy of the Form 100 on each other party; and
  (3) file at the court—
    (a) a copy of the Form 100; and
    (b) a certificate of service confirming service of a copy of that form on each party served.

PD 37 para.1.2

Instead of complying with para.1.1(1), a litigant in person without a current account may, in a claim proceeding in a county court or District Registry, make a payment into court by—
  (1) lodging the payment in cash with the court; and
  (2) giving the court a completed Court Funds Office Form 100.

Payment into court by life assurance company

PD 37 para.4.1

A company wishing to make a payment into court under the Life Assurance Companies (Payment into Court) Act 1896 ('the 1896 Act') must file a witness statement or an affidavit setting out—
  (1) a short description of the policy under which money is payable;
  (2) a statement of the persons entitled under the policy, including their names and addresses so far as known to the company;
  (3) a short statement of—
    (a) the notices received by the company making any claim to the money assured, or withdrawing any such claim;
    (b) the dates of receipt of such notices; and
    (c) the names and addresses of the persons by whom they were given;
  (4) a statement that, in the opinion of the board of directors of the company, no sufficient discharge can be obtained for the money which is payable, other than by paying it into court under the 1896 Act;

   (5) a statement that the company agrees to comply with any order or direction the court may
       make—
       (a) to pay any further sum into court; or
       (b) to pay any costs;
   (6) an undertaking by the company to immediately send to the Accountant General at the
       Court Funds Office any notice of claim received by the company after the witness
       statement or affidavit has been filed, together with a letter referring to the Court Funds
       Office reference number; and
   (7) the company's address for service.

PD 37 para.4.2

The witness statement or affidavit must be filed at—
   (1) Chancery Chambers at the Royal Courts of Justice, or
   (2) a Chancery district registry of the High Court.

PD 37 para.4.3

The company must not deduct from the money payable by it under the policy any costs of the
payment into court, except for any court fee.

PD 37 para.4.4

If the company is a party to any proceedings issued in relation to the policy or the money assured
by it, it may not make a payment into court under the 1896 Act without the permission of the
court in those proceedings.

PD 37 para.4.5

If a company pays money into court under the 1896 Act, unless the court orders otherwise it must
immediately serve notice of the payment on every person who is entitled under the policy or has
made a claim to the money assured.

Payment into court under Trustee Act 1925

PD 37 para.6.1

A trustee wishing to make a payment into court under s.63 of the Trustee Act 1925 must file a
witness statement or an affidavit setting out—
   (1) a short description of—
       (a) the trust; and
       (b) the instrument creating the trust, or the circumstances in which the trust arose;
   (2) the names of the persons interested in or entitled to the money or securities to be paid into
       court, with their address so far as known to him;
   (3) a statement that he agrees to answer any inquiries which the court may make or direct
       relating to the application of the money or securities; and
   (4) his address for service.

PD 37 para.6.2

The witness statement or affidavit must be filed at—
   (1) Chancery Chambers at the Royal Courts of Justice;

(2) a Chancery district registry of the High Court; or

(3) a county court.

PD 37 para.6.3

If a trustee pays money or securities into court, unless the court Orders otherwise he must immediately serve notice of the payment into court on every person interested in or entitled to the money or securities.

Payment into court by nominated person under the Landlord and Tenant Act 1987

PD 56 para.8.6

If the nominated person pays money into court in accordance with an order under s.33(1) of the 1987 Act, he must file a copy of the certificate of the surveyor selected under s.33(2)(a) of that Act.

See **Funds in court**, **Payment out of court**, and **Vehicular Access Across Common and Other Land (England) Regulations 2002**.

PAYMENT OUT OF COURT

Payment out of money paid into court

Pt 37 r.37.3

(1) Money paid into court under a court order or in support of a **defence of tender before claim** may not be paid out without the court's permission except where—

(a) a Pt 36 offer is accepted without needing the permission of the court; and

(b) the defendant agrees that a sum paid into court by him should be used to satisfy the offer (in whole or in part).

(R.36.9 sets out when the court's permission is required to accept a Pt 36 offer).

PD 37 para.3.2

Permission may be obtained by making an application in accordance with Pt 23. The **application notice** must state the grounds on which the order for payment out is sought. Evidence of any facts on which the applicant relies may also be necessary.

PD 37 para.3.3

Where the court gives permission under r.37.3, it will include a direction for the payment out of any money in court, including any **interest** accrued.

PD 37 para.3.4

Where permission is not required to take money out of court, the requesting party should file a request for payment in Court Funds Office Form 201 with the Court Funds Office, accompanied by a statement that the defendant agrees that the money should be used to satisfy the Pt 36 offer in Court Funds Office Form 202.

(Paragraph 3.6 of PD 36B provides that a defendant who made a Pt 36 payment before April 6, 2007, and whose Pt 36 offer underlying the payment is accepted without requiring the permission of the court, is not required to file Form 202).

PD 37 para.3.5

The request for payment should contain the following details—
- (1) where the party receiving the payment is legally represented—
  - (a) the name, business address and reference of the legal representative; and
  - (b) the name of the bank and the sort code number, the title of the account and the account number where the payment is to be transmitted;
- (2) where the party is acting in person—
  - (a) his name and address; and
  - (b) his bank account details as in para.(1)(b) above; and
- (3) whether the party receiving the payment is, or has been, in receipt of services funded by the Legal Services Commission as part of the Community Legal Service.

Interest

PD 37 para.3.6

Where para.3.4 applies, interest accruing up to the date of acceptance will be paid to the defendant.
(Rule 20.2 provides that in these rules references to a claimant or defendant include a party bringing or defending an additional claim).

Payment by cheque

PD 37 para.3.7

Subject to para.3.8, if a party does not wish the payment to be transmitted into his bank account or if he does not have a bank account, he may send a written request to the Accountant-General for the payment to be made to him by cheque.

Payee

PD 37 para.3.8

Where a party seeking payment out of court has provided the necessary information, the payment—
- (1) where a party is legally represented, must be made to the legal representative;
- (2) if the party is not legally represented but has given notice under para.3.5(3), must be made to the Legal Services Commission.

Payment out of money paid into court by life assurance company

PD 37 para.5.1

Any application for the payment out of money which has been paid into court under the 1896 Act must be made in accordance with para.3 of this PD.

PD 37 para.5.2

The application must be served on—
  (1) every person stated in the written evidence of the company which made the payment to be entitled to or to have an interest in the money;
  (2) any other person who has given notice of a claim to the money; and
  (3) the company which made the payment, if an application is being made for costs against it, but not otherwise.

Payment out of funds paid into court under Trustee Act 1925

PD 37 para.7.1

An application for the payment out of any money or securities paid into court under s.63 of the Trustee Act 1925 must be made in accordance with para.3 of this practice direction.

PD 37 para.7.2

The application may be made without notice, but the court may direct notice to be served on any person.

See **Child**.

PENALTY

See **False disclosure statement** and **False statement**.

PERCENTAGE INCREASE

Pt 43 r.43.2(1)

  (l) 'percentage increase' means the percentage by which the amount of a legal representative's fee can be increased in accordance with a conditional fee agreement which provides for a success fee.

PERSON UNDER DISABILITY

See **Protected party**.

PERSONAL INJURIES

Pt 2 r.2.3

Includes any disease and any impairment of a person's physical or mental condition.

PERSONAL INJURIES CLAIM

Defence

PD 16 para.12.1

Where the claim is for personal injuries and the claimant has attached a medical report in respect of his alleged injuries, the defendant should:
  (1) state in his defence whether he—
      (a) agrees,
      (b) disputes, or
      (c) neither agrees nor disputes but has no knowledge of,
      the matters contained in the medical report,
  (2) where he disputes any part of the medical report, give in his defence his reasons for doing so, and
  (3) where he has obtained his own medical report on which he intends to rely, attach it to his defence.

PD 16 para.12.2

Where the claim is for personal injuries and the claimant has included a schedule of past and future expenses and losses, the defendant should include in or attach to his defence a counter-schedule stating:
  (1) which of those items he—
      (a) agrees,
      (b) disputes, or
      (c) neither agrees nor disputes but has no knowledge of, and
  (2) where any items are disputed, supplying alternative figures where appropriate.

PERSONAL INJURY CLAIMS

See also **Pre-action protocols** and **Provisional damages**.

PERSONAL INSOLVENCY

See **Appointee, Bankruptcy Court, Bankruptcy petition, Insolvency proceedings, Statutory demand**, and **Validation order**.

PERSONAL REPRESENTATIVE

Lmitation on court's power to order costs

Pt 46 r.46.3

  (1) This rule applies where—
      (a) a person is or has been a party to any proceedings in the capacity of trustee or personal representative; and
      (b) r.44.5 [amount of costs where costs are payable pursuant to a **contract**] does not apply.

(2) The general rule is that he is entitled to be paid the costs of those proceedings, insofar as they are not recovered from or paid by any other person, out of the relevant trust fund or estate.

(3) Where he is entitled to be paid any of those costs out of the fund or estate, those costs will be assessed on the indemnity basis.

PD 46 para.1.1

A trustee or personal representative is entitled to an indemnity out of the relevant trust fund or estate for costs properly incurred depends. Whether costs were properly incurred depends on all the circumstances of the case including whether the trustee or personal representative ('the trustee')—

(a) obtained directions from the court before bringing or defending the proceedings;

(2) acted in the interests of the fund or estate or in substance for a benefit other than that of the estate, including the trustee's own; and

(3) acted in some way unreasonably in bringing or defending, or in the conduct of, the proceedings.

PD 46 para.1.2

The trustee is not to be taken to have acted in substance for a benefit other than that of the fund by reason only that the trustee has defended a claim in which relief is sought against him personally.

Substitution and removal of personal representatives

Pt 57 r.57.13

(1) This section [of P57] contains rules about claims and applications for substitution or removal of a personal representative.

PD 57 para.12

This section of [PD 57] applies to claims and applications for substitution or removal of a personal representative. If substitution or removal of a personal representative is sought by application in existing proceedings, this section shall apply with references to the claim, claim form and claimant being read as if they referred to the application, application notice and applicant respectively.

Pt 57 r.57.13

(2) Claims under this section must be brought in the High Court and are assigned to the Chancery Division.

(Section 50 of the Administration of Justice Act 1985 gives the High Court power to appoint a substitute for, or to remove, a personal representative).

(3) Every personal representative of the estate shall be joined as a party.

(4) PD 57 makes provision for lodging the grant of probate or letters of administration in a claim under this section.

(5) If substitution or removal of a personal representative is sought by application in existing proceedings, this rule shall apply with references to claims being read as if they referred to applications.

Production of the grant

PD 57 para.14.1

On the hearing of the claim the personal representative must produce to the Court the grant of representation to the deceased's estate.

PD 57 para.14.2

If an order is made substituting or removing the personal representative, the grant (together with a sealed copy of the order) must be sent to and remain in the custody of the Principal Registry of the Family Division until a memorandum of the order has been endorsed on or permanently annexed to the grant.

PD 57 para.14.3

Where the claim is to substitute or remove an executor and the claim is made before a grant of probate has been issued, paras 14.1 and 14.2 do not apply. Where in such a case an order is made substituting or removing an executor a sealed copy of the order must be sent to the Principal Registry of the Family Division where it will be recorded and retained pending any application for a grant. An order sent to the Principal Registry in accordance with this paragraph must be accompanied by a note of the full name and date of death of the deceased, if it is not apparent on the face of the order.

Starting the claim

PD 57 para.13.1

The claim form must be accompanied by—
  (1) either—
      (a) a sealed or certified copy of the grant of probate or letters of administration, or
      (b) where the claim is to substitute or remove an executor and is made before a grant of probate has been issued, the original or, if the original is not available, a copy of the will; and
  (2) written evidence containing the grounds of the claim and the following information so far as it is known to the claimant—
      (a) brief details of the property comprised in the estate, with an approximate estimate of its capital value and any income that is received from it;
      (b) brief details of the liabilities of the estate;
      (c) the names and addresses of the persons who are in possession of the documents relating to the estate;
      (d) the names of the beneficiaries and their respective interests in the estate; and
      (e) the name, address and occupation of any proposed substituted personal representative.

PD 57 para.13.2

If the claim is for the appointment of a substituted personal representative, the claim form must be accompanied by—
  (1) a signed or (in the case of the Public Trustee or a corporation) sealed consent to act; and

(2) written evidence as to the fitness of the proposed substituted personal representative, if an individual, to act.

See also **Discontinuance** and **Probate claim**.

PERSONAL SERVICE

See **Service of documents**.

PERSONS CARRYING ON BUSINESS IN ANOTHER NAME

PD 7A para.5C.1

This paragraph applies where—
(1) a claim is brought against an individual;
(2) that individual carries on a business within the jurisdiction (even if not personally within the jurisdiction); and
(3) that business is carried on in a name other than that individual's own name ('the business name').

PD 7A para.5C.2

The claim may be brought against the business name as if it were the name of a partnership.

PETITION

Claim form.

PHARMACISTS

See **Health care professionals**.

PHOTOGRAPHS

See **Plans**.

PILOT SCHEMES

Pt 51 r.51.2

PDs may modify or disapply any provision of [CPR]—
(a) for specified periods; and
(b) in relation to proceedings in specified courts,
during the operation of pilot schemes for assessing the use of new practices and procedures in connection with proceedings.

See **County Court Provisional Assessment Pilot Scheme**, **Defamation Proceedings Costs Management Scheme**, and **Non-disclosure Injunctions Information Collection Pilot Scheme**.

PLACE OF TRIAL

Pt 30 r.30.6

The court may specify the place (for instance, a particular county court) where the trial or some other hearing in any proceedings is to be held and may do so without ordering the proceedings to be transferred.

High Court and County Courts Jurisdiction Order 1991

This Order make arrangements for the distribution of proceedings between the High Court and the county courts.

Articles 4 to 8 provide criteria for determining where proceedings are to be commenced and tried and where judgments are to be enforced.

In particular, actions in respect of personal injuries must be commenced in a county court unless the claim is worth £50,000 or more (art.5) and certain proceedings under the Local Government Finance Act 1982 must be commenced in the High Court (art.6).

The Order provides (art.7) that actions worth less than £25,000 must normally be tried in a county court, and those worth £50,000 or more must normally be tried in the High Court, with those in between going either way, subject to the criteria laid down in art.7(5) for determining which level of court is the more appropriate for a particular case.

The value of an action for the purposes of these provisions as to commencement and trial is defined by arts 9 and 10.

For enforcement, art.8 provides that county court judgments for the payment of a sum of money of £5,000 or more must be enforced in the High Court, and may be enforced in the High Court if they are for £2,000 or more. Below that they must be enforced in a county court.

The Order does not affect family or Admiralty proceedings.

Multi-track

PD 29 para.2.6

Each party should state in his allocation questionnaire whether he considers the claim should be managed and tried at the Royal Courts of Justice and, if so, why. Claims suitable for trial in the Royal Courts of Justice include:

(1) professional negligence claims,
(2) Fatal Accident Act claims,
(3) fraud or undue influence claims,
(4) defamation claims,
(5) claims for malicious prosecution or false imprisonment,
(6) claims against the police,
(7) contentious probate claims.

Such claims may fall within the criteria of art.7(5) of the High Court and County Courts Jurisdiction Order 1991.

See **Administrative Court** and **Trial**.

PLAINTIFF

See **Claimant**.

PLANS

Use of plans, photographs and models as evidence

Pt 33 r.33.6

(1) This rule applies to evidence (such as a plan, photograph or model) which is not—
  (a) contained in a witness statement, affidavit or expert's report;
  (b) to be given orally at trial; or
  (c) evidence of which prior notice must be given under r.33.2.
(2) This rule includes documents which may be received in evidence without further proof under s.9 of the Civil Evidence Act 1995.
(3) Unless the court Orders otherwise the evidence shall not be receivable at a trial unless the party intending to put it in evidence has given notice to the other parties in accordance with this rule.
(4) Where the party intends to use the evidence as evidence of any fact then, except where para.(6) applies, he must give notice not later than the latest date for serving witness statements.
(5) He must give notice at least 21 days before the hearing at which he proposes to put in the evidence, if—
  (a) there are not to be witness statements; or
  (b) he intends to put in the evidence solely in order to disprove an allegation made in a witness statement.
(6) Where the evidence forms part of expert evidence, he must give notice when the expert's report is served on the other party.
(7) Where the evidence is being produced to the court for any reason other than as part of factual or expert evidence, he must give notice at least 21 days before the hearing at which he proposes to put in the evidence.
(8) Where a party has given notice that he intends to put in the evidence, he must give every other party an opportunity to inspect it and to agree to its admission without further proof.

PLEADING

See **Statement of truth**.

POINTS OF DISPUTE

Pt 47 r.47.9

(1) The paying party and any other party to the detailed assessment proceedings may dispute any item in the bill of costs by serving points of dispute on—
  (a) the receiving party; and
  (b) every other party to the detailed assessment proceedings.
(2) The period for serving points of dispute is 21 days after the date of service of the notice of commencement.

(3) If a party serves points of dispute after the period set out in para.(2), he may not be heard further in the detailed assessment proceedings unless the court gives permission.

(4) The receiving party may file a request for a **default costs certificate** if—
 (a) the period set out in para.(2) for serving points of dispute has expired; and
 (b) the receiving party has not been served with any points of dispute.

(5) If any party (including the paying party) serves points of dispute before the issue of a default costs certificate the court may not issue the default costs certificate.

PD 47 para.8.1

Subject to para.8.3, where the court does not order fixed costs (or no fixed costs are provided for) the amount of costs payable will be assessed by the court. R. 44.6 allows the court making an order about costs either—
 (a) to make a summary assessment of the amount of the costs; or
 (b) to order the amount to be decided in accordance with Part 47 (a detailed assessment).

PD 47 para.8.2

An order for costs will be treated as an order for the amount of costs to be decided by a detailed assessment unless the order otherwise provides.

PD 47 para.8.3

Where a party is entitled to costs some of which are fixed costs and some of which are not, the court will assess those costs which are not fixed. For example, the court will assess the disbursements payable in accordance with rr. 45.12 or 45.19. The decision whether such assessment should be summary or detailed will be made in accordance with paras. 9.1 to 9.10 of [PD 47].

Optional reply

Pt 47 r.47.13

(1) Where any party to the detailed assessment proceedings serves points of dispute, the receiving party may serve a reply on the other parties to the assessment proceedings.

(2) He may do so within 21 days after service on him of the points of dispute to which his reply relates.

PD 47 para.12.1

A reply served by the receiving party under Rule 47.13 must be limited to points of principle and concessions only. It must not contain general denials, specific denials or standard form responses.

PD 47 para.12.2

Whenever practicable, the reply must be set out in the form of Precedent G.

POSSESSION CLAIMS

Pt 55 r.55.1

In [Pt 55]—
  (a) 'a possession claim' means a claim for the recovery of possession of land (including buildings or parts of buildings);
  (c) 'mortgage' includes a legal or equitable mortgage and a legal or equitable charge and 'mortgagee' is to be interpreted accordingly;
  (f) 'a demotion claim' means a claim made by a landlord for an order under s.82A of the 1985 Act or s.6A of the 1988 Act ('a demotion order');
  (g) 'a demoted tenancy' means a tenancy created by virtue of a demotion order; and
  (h) 'a suspension claim' means a claim made by a landlord judgesfor an order under s.121A of the 1985 Act.

Pt 55 r.55.2

  (1) The procedure set out in this section of this Part must be used where the claim includes—
      (a) a possession claim brought by a—
          (i) landlord (or former landlord);
          (ii) mortgagee; or
          (iii) licensor (or former licensor); or
      (c) a claim by a tenant seeking relief from forfeiture.
(Where a demotion claim or a suspension claim (or both) is made in the same claim form in which a possession claim is started, this section of this Part applies as modified by r.65.12. Where the claim is a demotion claim or a suspension claim only, or a suspension claim made in addition to a demotion claim, s.III of Pt 65 applies).
  (2) This section of this Part—
      (a) is subject to any enactment or PD which sets out special provisions with regard to any particular category of claim;
      (b) does not apply where the claimant uses the procedure set out in s.II of this Part [accelerated possession claims]; and
      (c) does not apply where the claimant seeks an interim possession order under s.III of this Part except where the court orders otherwise or that section so provides.

Starting the claim

Pt 55 r.55.3

  (1) The claim must be started in the county court for the district in which the land is situated unless para.(2) applies or an enactment provides otherwise.
  (2) The claim may be started in the High Court if the claimant files with his claim form a certificate stating the reasons for bringing the claim in that court verified by a statement of truth in accordance with r.22.1(1).
  (3) PD 55A refers to circumstances which may justify starting the claim in the High Court.
  (5) The claim form and form of defence sent with it must be in the forms set out in PD 55A.

PD 55A para.1.1

Except where the county court does not have jurisdiction, possession claims should normally be brought in the county court. Only exceptional circumstances justify starting a claim in the High Court.

PD 55A para.1.2

If a claimant starts a claim in the High Court and the court decides that it should have been started in the county court, the court will normally either strike the claim out or transfer it to the county court on its own initiative. This is likely to result in delay and the court will normally disallow the costs of starting the claim in the High Court and of any transfer.

PD 55A para.1.3

Circumstances which may, in an appropriate case, justify starting a claim in the High Court are if—
(1) there are complicated disputes of fact;
(2) there are points of law of general importance; or
(3) the claim is against trespassers and there is a substantial risk of public disturbance or of serious harm to persons or property which properly require immediate determination.

PD 55A para.1.4

The value of the property and the amount of any financial claim may be relevant circumstances, but these factors alone will not normally justify starting the claim in the High Court.

PD 55A para.1.5

The claimant must use the appropriate claim form and particulars of claim form set out in Table 1 to PD 4. The defence must be in Forms N11, N11B, N11M or N11R, as appropriate.

PD 55A para.1.6

High Court claims for the possession of land subject to a mortgage will be assigned to the Chancery Division.

PD 55A para.1.7

A claim which is not a possession claim may be brought under the procedure set out in s.I of Pt 55 if it is started in the same claim form as a possession claim which, by virtue of r.55.2(1) must be brought in accordance with that section.
(Rule 7.3 provides that a claimant may use a single claim form to start all claims which can be conveniently disposed of in the same proceedings).

PD 55A para.1.8

For example a claim under paras 4, 5 or 6 of Pt I of Sch.1 to the Mobile Homes Act 1983 may be brought using the procedure set out in s.I of Pt 55 if the claim is started in the same claim form as a claim enforcing the rights referred to in s.3(1)(b) of the Caravan Sites Act 1968 (which, by virtue of r.55.2(1) must be brought under s.I of Pt 55).

PD 55A para.1.9

Where the claim form includes a **demotion claim**, the claim must be started in the county court for the district in which the land is situated.

Particulars of claim

Pt 55 r.55.4

The particulars of claim must be filed and served with the claim form.
(Part 16 and PD 55A provide details about the contents of the particulars of claim).

PD 55A para.2.1

In a possession claim the particulars of claim must:
  (1) identify the land to which the claim relates;
  (2) state whether the claim relates to residential property;
  (3) state the ground on which possession is claimed;
  (4) give full details about any mortgage or tenancy agreement; and
  (5) give details of every person who, to the best of the claimant's knowledge, is in possession
      of the property.

Residential property let on a tenancy

PD 55A para.2.2

Paragraphs 2.3 to 2.4B apply if the claim relates to residential property let on a tenancy.

PD 55A para.2.3

If the claim includes a claim for non-payment of rent the particulars of claim must set out:
  (1) the amount due at the start of the proceedings;
  (2) in schedule form, the dates and amounts of all payments due and payments made under
      the tenancy agreement for a period of two years immediately preceding the date of issue,
      or if the first date of default occurred less than two years before the date of issue from
      the first date of default and a running total of the arrears;
  (3) the daily rate of any rent and interest;
  (4) any previous steps taken to recover the arrears of rent with full details of any court
      proceedings; and
  (5) any relevant information about the defendant's circumstances, in particular:
      (a) whether the defendant is in receipt of social security benefits; and
      (b) whether any payments are made on his behalf directly to the claimant under the
          Social Security Contributions and Benefits Act 1992.

PD 55A para.2.3A

If the claimant wishes to rely on a history of arrears which is longer than two years, he should
state this in his particulars and exhibit a full (or longer) schedule to a witness statement.

PD 55A para.2.4

If the claimant knows of any person (including a mortgagee) entitled to claim relief against
forfeiture as underlessee under s.146(4) of the Law of Property Act 1925 (or in accordance with
s.38 of the Senior Courts Act 1981, or s.138(9C) of the County Courts Act 1984):
  (1) the particulars of claim must state the name and address of that person; and
  (2) the claimant must file a copy of the particulars of claim for service on him.

PD 55A para.2.4A

If the claim for possession relates to the conduct of the tenant, the particulars of claim must state details of the conduct alleged.

PD 55A para.2.4B

If the possession claim relies on a statutory ground or grounds for possession, the particulars of claim must specify the ground or grounds relied on.

PD 55A para.2.5A

If the claimant wishes to rely on a history of arrears which is longer than two years, he should state this in his particulars and exhibit a full (or longer) schedule to a witness statement.

See also **Mortgage claims** and **Trespasser**.

Possession claim in relation to a demoted tenancy by a housing action trust or a local housing authority

PD 55A para.2.7

If the claim is a possession claim under s.143D of the Housing Act 1996 (possession claim in relation to a demoted tenancy where the landlord is a housing action trust or a local housing authority), the particulars of claim must have attached to them a copy of the notice to the tenant served under s.143E of the 1996 Act.

Hearing date

Pt 55 r.55.5

    (1) The court will fix a date for the hearing when it issues the claim form.
    (3) In all other possession claims—
       (a) the hearing date will be not less than 28 days from the date of issue of the claim form;
       (b) the standard period between the issue of the claim form and the hearing will be not more than eight weeks; and
       (c) the defendant must be served with the claim form and particulars of claim not less than 21 days before the hearing date.
(Rule 3.1(2)(a) provides that the court may extend or shorten the time for compliance with any rule).

PD 55A para.3.1

The court may exercise its powers under rr.3.1(2)(a) and (b) to shorten the time periods set out in rr.55.5(2) and (3).

PD 55A para.3.2

Particular consideration should be given to the exercise of this power if:
    (1) the defendant, or a person for whom the defendant is responsible, has assaulted or threatened to assault:

(a) the claimant;

(b) a member of the claimant's staff; or

(c) another resident in the locality;

(2) there are reasonable grounds for fearing such an assault; or

(3) the defendant, or a person for whom the defendant is responsible, has caused serious damage or threatened to cause serious damage to the property or to the home or property of another resident in the locality.

PD 55A para.3.3

Where para.3.2 applies but the case cannot be determined at the first hearing fixed under r.55.5, the court will consider what steps are needed to finally determine the case as quickly as reasonably practicable.

Defendant's response

Pt 55 r.55.7

(1) An acknowledgment of service is not required and Pt 10 does not apply.

(3) Where, in any other possession claim, the defendant does not file a defence within the time specified in r.15.4, he may take part in any hearing but the court may take his failure to do so into account when deciding what order to make about costs.

(4) Part 12 (default judgment) does not apply in a claim to which this Part applies.

Hearing

Pt 55 r.55.8

(1) At the hearing fixed in accordance with r.55.5(1) or at any adjournment of that hearing, the court may—

(a) decide the claim; or

(b) give case management directions.

(2) Where the claim is genuinely disputed on grounds which appear to be substantial, case management directions given under para.(1)(b) will include the allocation of the claim to a track or directions to enable it to be allocated.

(3) Except where—

(a) the claim is allocated to the fast track or the multi-track; or

(b) the court orders otherwise,

any fact that needs to be proved by the evidence of witnesses at a hearing referred to in para.(1) may be proved by evidence in writing.

(Rule 32.2(1) sets out the general rule about evidence. Rule 32.2(2) provides that r.32.2(1) is subject to any provision to the contrary).

(4) Subject to para.(5), all witness statements must be filed and served at least two days before the hearing.

(6) Where the claimant serves the claim form and particulars of claim, the claimant must produce at the hearing a certificate of service of those documents and r.6.17(2)(a) does not apply.

PD 55A para.5.1

Attention is drawn to r.55.8(3). Each party should wherever possible include all the evidence he wishes to present in his statement of case, verified by a statement of truth.

PD 55A para.5.2

If relevant the claimant's evidence should include the amount of any rent or mortgage arrears and interest on those arrears. These amounts should, if possible, be up to date to the date of the hearing (if necessary by specifying a daily rate of arrears and interest). However, r.55.8(4) does not prevent such evidence being brought up to date orally or in writing on the day of the hearing if necessary.

PD 55A para.5.3

If relevant the defendant should give evidence of:
    (1) the amount of any outstanding social security or housing benefit payments relevant to rent or mortgage arrears; and
    (2) the status of:
        (a) any claims for social security or housing benefit about which a decision has not yet been made; and
        (b) any applications to appeal or review a social security or housing benefit decision where that appeal or review has not yet concluded.

PD 55A para.5.4

If:
    (1) the maker of a witness statement does not attend a hearing; and
    (2) the other party disputes material evidence contained in his statement,
the court will normally adjourn the hearing so that oral evidence can be given.

PD 55A para.5.5

The claimant must bring two completed copies of Form N123 to the hearing.

Allocation

Pt 55 r.55.9

    (1) When the court decides the track for a possession claim, the matters to which it shall have regard include—
        (a) the matters set out in r.26.8 as modified by the relevant PD;
        (b) the amount of any arrears of rent or mortgage instalments;
        (c) the importance to the defendant of retaining possession of the land;
        (d) the importance of vacant possession to the claimant; and
        (e) if applicable, the alleged conduct of the defendant.
    (2) The court will only allocate possession claims to the small claims track if all the parties agree.
    (3) Where a possession claim has been allocated to the small claims track the claim shall be treated, for the purposes of costs, as if it were proceeding on the fast track except that trial costs shall be in the discretion of the court and shall not exceed the amount that would be recoverable under r.46.2 (amount of fast track costs) if the value of the claim were up to £3,000.
    (4) Where all the parties agree the court may, when it allocates the claim, order that r.27.14 (costs on the small claims track) applies and, where it does so, para.(3) does not apply.

Possession claims relating to mortgaged residential property

Pt 55 r.55.10

    (1) This rule applies where a mortgagee seeks possession of land which consists of or includes residential property.

    (2) Within five days of receiving notification of the date of the hearing by the court, the claimant must send a notice to—

        (a) the property, addressed to 'the tenant or the occupier';

        (b) the housing department of the local authority within which the property is located; and

        (c) any registered proprietor (other than the claimant) of a registered charge over the property.

    (3) The notice referred to in para.(2)(a) must—

        (a) state that a possession claim for the property has started;

        (b) show the name and address of the claimant, the defendant and the court which issued the claim form; and

        (c) give details of the hearing.

    (3A) The notice referred to in paragraph 2(b) must contain the information in para. (3) and must state the full address of the property.

    (4) The claimant must produce at the hearing—

        (a) a copy of the notices; and

        (b) evidence that they have been sent.

    (4A) An unauthorised tenant of residential property may apply to the court for the order for possession to be suspended.

Consumer Credit Act claims relating to the recovery of land

PD 55A para.7.1

Any application by the defendant for a time order under s.129 of the [Consumer Credit Act 1974] may be made:

    (1) in his defence; or

    (2) by application notice in the proceedings.

Enforcement of charging order by sale

PD 55A para.7.2

A party seeking to enforce a **charging order** by sale should follow the procedure set out in r.73.10 and the Pt 55 procedure [possession claims] should not be used.

Orders fixing a date for possession

PD 55A para.10.1

This paragraph applies where the court has made an order postponing the date for possession under s.85(2)(b) of the Housing Act 1985 (secure tenancies) or under s.9(2)(b) of the Housing Act 1988 (assured tenancies).

PD 55A para.10.2

If the defendant fails to comply with any of the terms of the order which relate to payment, the claimant, after following the procedure set out in para.10.3, may apply for an order fixing the date upon which the defendant has to give up possession of the property. Unless the court further postpones the date for possession, the defendant will be required to give up possession on that date.

PD 55A para.10.3

At least 14 days and not more than three months before applying for an order under para.10.2, the claimant must give written notice to the defendant in accordance with para.10.4.

PD 55A para.10.4

The notice referred to in para.10.3 must—
  (1) state that the claimant intends to apply for an order fixing the date upon which the defendant is to give up possession of the property;
  (2) record the current arrears and state how the defendant has failed to comply with the order referred to in para.10.1 (by reference to a statement of the rent account enclosed with the notice);
  (3) request that the defendant reply to the claimant within seven days, agreeing or disputing the stated arrears; and
  (4) inform the defendant of his right to apply to the court—
       (a) for a further postponement of the date for possession; or
       (b) to stay or suspend enforcement.

PD 55A para.10.5

In his reply to the notice, the defendant must—
  (1) where he disputes the stated arrears, provide details of payments or credits made;
  (2) where he agrees the stated arrears, explain why payments have not been made.

PD 55A para.10.6

An application for an order under para.10.2 must be made by filing an application notice in accordance with Pt 23. The application notice must state whether or not there is any outstanding claim by the defendant for housing benefit.

PD 55A para.10.7

The claimant must file the following documents with the application notice—
  (1) a copy of the notice referred to in para.10.3;
  (2) a copy of the defendant's reply, if any, to the notice and any relevant subsequent correspondence between the claimant and the defendant;
  (3) a statement of the rent account showing—
       (a) the arrears that have accrued since the first failure to pay in accordance with the order referred to in para.10.2; or
       (b) the arrears that have accrued during the period of two years immediately preceding the date of the application notice, where the first such failure to pay occurs more than two years before that date.

PD 55A para.10.8

Rules 23.7 (service of a copy of an application notice) and 23.10 (right to set aside or vary an order made without service of the application notice) and paras 2.3, 2.4 and 2.5 of PD 23A (dealing with applications without a hearing) do not apply to an application under this section.

PD 55A para.10.9

On being filed, the application will be referred to the District Judge who—
  (1) will normally determine the application without a hearing by fixing the date for possession as the next working day; but
  (2) if he considers that a hearing is necessary—
      (a) will fix a date for the application to be heard; and
      (b) direct service of the application notice and supporting evidence on the defendant.

PD 55A para.10.10

The court does not have jurisdiction to review a decision that it was reasonable to make an order for possession.

See also **Accelerated possession claims**, **Interim possession order**, **Possession claims online**, **Pre-action protocols**, and **Trespassers**.

POSSESSION CLAIMS BASED ON MORTGAGE OR HOME PURCHASE PLAN ARREARS IN RESPECT OF RESIDENTIAL PROPERTY

See **Pre-action protocols**.

POSSESSION CLAIMS BASED ON RENT ARREARS

See **Pre-action protocols**.

POSSESSION CLAIMS ONLINE

Electronic issue of certain possession claims

Pt 55 r.55.10A

  (1) A PD may make provision for a claimant to start certain types of possession claim in certain courts by requesting the issue of a claim form electronically.
  (2) The PD may, in particular—
      (a) provide that only particular provisions apply in specific courts;
      (b) specify—
          (i) the type of possession claim which may be issued electronically;
          (ii) the conditions that a claim must meet before it may be issued electronically;
      (c) specify the court where the claim may be issued;
      (d) enable the parties to make certain applications or take further steps in relation to the claim electronically;

(e) specify the requirements that must be fulfilled in relation to such applications or steps;

(f) enable the parties to correspond electronically with the court about the claim;

(g) specify the requirements that must be fulfilled in relation to electronic correspondence;

(h) provide how any fee payable on the filing of any document is to be paid where the document is filed electronically.

(3) The PD may disapply or modify these rules as appropriate in relation to possession claims started electronically.

PD 55B para.1.1

[PD 55B] provides for a scheme ('Possession Claims Online') to operate in specified county courts—

(1) enabling claimants and their representatives to start certain possession claims under CPR Pt 55 by requesting the issue of a claim form electronically via the PCOL website; and

(2) where a claim has been started electronically, enabling the claimant or defendant and their representatives to take further steps in the claim electronically as specified below.

PD 55B para.1.2

In this PD —

(1) 'PCOL website' means the website which may be accessed via the Business Link website, and through which Possession Claims Online will operate; and

(2) 'specified court' means a county court specified on the PCOL website as one in which Possession Claims Online is available.

Information on the PCOL website

PD 55B para.2.1

The PCOL website contains further details and guidance about the operation of Possession Claims Online.

PD 55B para.2.2

In particular the PCOL website sets out—

(1) the specified courts; and

(2) the dates from which Possession Claims Online will be available in each specified court.

PD 55B para.2.3

The operation of Possession Claims Online in any specified court may be restricted to taking certain of the steps specified in this PD, and in such cases the PCOL website will set out the steps which may be taken using Possession Claims Online in that specified court.

Security

PD 55B para.3.1

Her Majesty's Courts Service will take such measures as it thinks fit to ensure the security of steps taken or information stored electronically. These may include requiring users of Possession Claims Online—
  (1) to enter a customer identification number or password;
  (2) to provide personal information for identification purposes; and
  (3) to comply with any other security measures,
before taking any step online.

Fees

PD 55B para.4.1

A step may only be taken using Possession Claims Online on payment of the prescribed fee where a fee is payable. Where this PD provides for a fee to be paid electronically, it may be paid by—
  (1) credit card;
  (2) debit card; or
  (3) any other method which Her Majesty's Courts and Tribunals Service may permit.

PD 55B para.4.2

A defendant who wishes to claim exemption from payment of fees must do so through an organisation approved by Her Majesty's Courts and Tribunals Service before taking any step using PCOL which attracts a fee. If satisfied that the defendant is entitled to fee exemption, the organisation will submit the fee exemption form through the PCOL website to Her Majesty's Courts Service. The defendant may then use PCOL to take such a step.
(Her Majesty's Courts and Tribunals Service website contains guidance as to when the entitlement to claim an exemption from payment of fees arises. The PCOL website will contain a list of organisations through which the defendant may claim an exemption from fees).

Claims which may be started using possession claims online

PD 55B para.5.1

A claim may be started online if—
  (1) it is brought under s.I of Pt 55;
  (2) it includes a possession claim for residential property by—
      (a) a landlord against a tenant, solely on the ground of arrears of rent (but not a claim for forfeiture of a lease); or
      (b) a mortgagee against a mortgagor, solely on the ground of default in the payment of sums due under a mortgage,
      relating to land within the district of a specified court;
  (3) it does not include a claim for any other remedy except for payment of arrears of rent or money due under a mortgage, interest and costs;
  (3A) the claimant has an address for service in the UK;
  (4) the defendant has an address for service in England and Wales; and
  (5) the claimant is able to provide a postcode for the property.

PD 55B para.5.2

A claim must not be started online if a defendant is known to be a child or protected party.

Starting a claim

PD 55B para.6.1

A claimant may request the issue of a claim form by—
(1) completing an online claim form at the PCOL website;
(2) paying the appropriate issue fee electronically at the PCOL website or by some other means approved by Her Majesty's Courts and Tribunals Service.

PD 55B para.6.2

The particulars of claim must be included in the online claim form and may not be filed separately. It is not necessary to file a copy of the tenancy agreement, mortgage deed or mortgage agreement with the particulars of claim.

PD 55B para.6.2A

In the case of a possession claim for residential property that relies on a statutory ground or grounds for possession, the claimant must specify, in s.4(a) of the online claim form, the ground or grounds relied on.

PD 55B para.6.3

Subject to paras 6.3A and 6.3B, the particulars of claim must include a history of the rent or mortgage account, in schedule form setting out—
(1) the dates and amounts of all payments due and payments made under the tenancy agreement, mortgage deed or mortgage agreement either from the first date of default if that date occurred less than two years before the date of issue or for a period of two years immediately preceding the date of issue; and
(2) a running total of the arrears.

PD 55B para.6.3A

Paragraph 6.3B applies where the claimant has, before commencing proceedings, provided the defendant in schedule form with—
(1) details of the dates and amounts of all payments due and payments made under the tenancy agreement, mortgage deed or mortgage account—
    (a) for a period of two years immediately preceding the date of commencing proceedings; or
    (b) if the first date of default occurred less than two years before that date, from the first date of default; and
(2) a running total of the arrears.

PD 55B para.6.3B

Where this paragraph applies the claimant may, in place of the information required by para.6.3, include in his particulars of claim a summary only of the arrears containing at least the following information—

(1) The amount of arrears as stated in the notice of seeking possession served under either s.83 of the Housing Act 1985 or s.8 of the Housing Act 1988, or at the date of the claimant's letter before action, as appropriate;

(2) the dates and amounts of the last three payments in cleared funds made by the defendant or, if less than three payments have been made, the dates and amounts of all payments made;

(3) the arrears at the date of issue, assuming that no further payments are made by the defendant.

PD 55B para.6.3C

Where the particulars of claim include a summary only of the arrears the claimant must—

(1) serve on the defendant not more than seven days after the date of issue, a full, up-to-date arrears history containing at least the information required by para.6.3; and

(2) either—

    (a) make a witness statement confirming that he has complied with subpara.(1) or (2) of para.6.3A as appropriate, and including or exhibiting the full arrears history; or

    (b) verify by way of oral evidence at the hearing that he has complied with subpara.(1) or (2) of para.6.3A as appropriate and also produce and verify the full arrears history.

(Rule 55.8(4) requires all witness statements to be filed and served at least two days before the hearing).

PD 55B para.6.4

If the claimant wishes to rely on a history of arrears which is longer than two years, he should state this in his particulars and exhibit a full (or longer) schedule to a witness statement.

PD 55B para.6.5

When an online claim form is received, an acknowledgment of receipt will automatically be sent to the claimant. The acknowledgment does not constitute notice that the claim form has been issued or served.

PD 55B para.6.6

When the court issues a claim form following the submission of an online claim form, the claim is 'brought' for the purposes of the Limitation Act 1980 and any other enactment on the date on which the online claim form is received by the court's computer system. The court will keep a record, by electronic or other means, of when online claim forms are received.

PD 55B para.6.7

When the court issues a claim form it will—

(1) serve a printed version of the claim form and a defence form on the defendant; and

(2) send the claimant notice of issue by post or, where the claimant has supplied an e-mail address, by electronic means.

PD 55B para.6.8

The claim shall be deemed to be served on the fifth day after the claim was issued irrespective of whether that day is a business day or not.

PD 55B para.6.9

Where the period of time within which a defence must be filed ends on a day when the court is closed, the defendant may file his defence on the next day that the court is open.

PD 55B para.6.10

The claim form shall have printed on it a unique customer identification number or a password by which the defendant may access the claim on the PCOL website.

PD 55B para.6.11

PCOL will issue the proceedings in the appropriate county court by reference to the post code provided by the claimant and that court shall have jurisdiction to hear and determine the claim and to carry out enforcement of any judgment irrespective of whether the property is within or outside the jurisdiction of that court.
(CPR r.30.2(1) authorises proceedings to be transferred from one county court to another).

Defence

PD 55B para.7.1

A defendant wishing to file—
    (1) a defence; or
    (2) a counterclaim (to be filed together with a defence) to a claim which has been issued
        through the PCOL system,
may, instead of filing a written form, do so by—
    (a) completing the relevant online form at the PCOL website; and
    (b) if the defendant is making a counterclaim, paying the appropriate fee electronically at the
        PCOL website or by some other means approved by Her Majesty's Courts and Tribunals
        Service.

PD 55B para.7.2

Where a defendant files a defence by completing the relevant online form, he must not send the court a hard copy.

PD 55B para.7.3

When an online defence form is received, an acknowledgment of receipt will automatically be sent to the defendant. The acknowledgment does not constitute notice that the defence has been served.

PD 55B para.7.4

The online defence form will be treated as being filed—
    (1) on the day the court receives it, if it receives it before 16.00 on a working day; and
    (2) otherwise, on the next working day after the court receives the online defence form.

PD 55B para.7.5

A defence is filed when the online defence form is received by the court's computer system. The court will keep a record, by electronic or other means, of when online defence forms are received.

Statement of truth

PD 55B para.8.1

CPR Pt 22 requires any statement of case to be verified by a statement of truth. This applies to any online claims and defences and application notices.

PD 55B para.8.2

CPR Pt 22 also requires that if an applicant wishes to rely on matters set out in his application notice as evidence, the application notice must be verified by a statement of truth. This applies to any application notice completed online that contains matters on which the applicant wishes to rely as evidence.

PD 55B para.8.3

Attention is drawn to—
  (1) paragraph 2 of PD 22, which stipulates the form of the statement of truth; and
  (2) paragraph 3 of PD 22, which provides who may sign a statement of truth; and
  (3) CPR r.32.14, which sets out the consequences of making, or causing to be made, a false statement in a document verified by a statement of truth, without an honest belief in its truth.

Communication with the court electronically by the messaging service

PD 55B para.10.1

If the PCOL website specifies that a court accepts electronic communications relating to claims brought using Possession Claims Online the parties may communicate with the court using the messaging service facility, available on the PCOL website ('the messaging service').

PD 55B para.10.2

The messaging service is for brief and straightforward communications only. The PCOL website contains a list of examples of when it will not be appropriate to use the messaging service.

PD 55B para.10.3

Parties must not send to the court forms or attachments via the messaging service.

PD 55B para.10.4

The court shall treat any forms or attachments sent via the messaging service as not having been filed or received.

PD 55B para.10.5

The court will normally reply via the messaging service where—
  (1) the response is to a message transmitted via the messaging service; and
  (2) the sender has provided an e-mail address.

Electronic applications

PD 55B para.11.1

Certain applications in relation to a possession claim started online may be made electronically ('online applications'). An online application may be made if a form for that application is published on the PCOL website ('online application form') and the application is made at least five clear days before the hearing.

PD 55B para.11.2

If a claim for possession has been started online and a party wishes to make an online application, he may do so by—
(1) completing the appropriate online application form at the PCOL website; and
(2) paying the appropriate fee electronically at the PCOL website or by some other means approved by Her Majesty's Courts and Tribunals Service.

PD 55B para.11.3

When an online application form is received, an acknowledgment of receipt will automatically be sent to the applicant. The acknowledgment does not constitute a notice that the online application form has been issued or served.

PD 55B para.11.4

Where an application must be made within a specified time, it is so made if the online application form is received by the court's computer system within that time. The court will keep a record, by electronic or other means, of when online application forms are received.

PD 55B para.11.5

When the court receives an online application form it shall—
(1) serve a copy of the online application endorsed with the date of the hearing by post on the claimant at least two clear days before the hearing; and
(2) send the defendant notice of service and confirmation of the date of the hearing by post; provided that
(3) where either party has provided the court with an e-mail address for service, service of the application and/or the notice of service and confirmation of the hearing date may be effected by electronic means.

Request for issue of warrant

PD 55B para.12.1

Where—
(1) the court has made an order for possession in a claim started online; and
(2) the claimant is entitled to the issue of a warrant of possession without requiring the permission of the court
the claimant may request the issue of a warrant by completing an online request form at the PCOL website and paying the appropriate fee electronically at the PCOL website or by some other means approved by Her Majesty's Courts and Tribunals Service.

PD 55B para.12.2

A request under para. 12.1 will be treated as being filed—
  (1) on the day the court receives the request, if it receives it before 4 p.m. on a working day; and
  (2) otherwise, on the next working day after the court receives the request.
(CCR Ord 26 r. 5 sets out certain circumstances in which a warrant of execution may not be issued without the permission of the court. CCR Ord. 26 r. 17(6) applies r. 5 of that Order with necessary modifications to a warrant of possession.)

Application to suspend warrant of possession

PD 55B para.13.1

Where the court has issued a warrant of possession, the defendant may apply electronically for the suspension of the warrant, provided that:
  (1) the application is made at least five clear days before the appointment for possession; and
  (2) the defendant is not prevented from making such an application without the permission of the court.

PD 55B para.13.2

The defendant may apply electronically for the suspension of the warrant, by—
  (1) completing an online application for suspension at the PCOL website; and
  (2) paying the appropriate fee electronically at the PCOL website or by some other means approved by Her Majesty's Courts and Tribunals Service.

PD 55B para.13.3

When an online application for suspension is received, an acknowledgment of receipt will automatically be sent to the defendant. The acknowledgment does not constitute a notice that the online application for suspension has been served.

PD 55B para.13.4

Where an application must be made within a specified time, it is so made if the online application for suspension is received by the court's computer system within that time. The court will keep a record, by electronic or other means, of when online applications for suspension are received.

PD 55B para.13.5

When the court receives an online application for suspension it shall—
  (1) serve a copy of the online application for suspension endorsed with the date of the hearing by post on the claimant at least two clear days before the hearing; and
  (2) send the defendant notice of service and confirmation of the date of the hearing by post; provided that
  (3) where either party has provided the court with an e-mail address for service, service of the application and/or the notice of service and confirmation of the hearing date may be effected by electronic means.

Viewing the case record

PD 55B para.14.1

A facility will be provided on the PCOL website for parties or their representatives to view—
  (1) an electronic record of the status of claims started online, which will be reviewed and, if necessary, updated at least once each day; and
  (2) all information relating to the case that has been filed by the parties electronically.

PD 55B para.14.2

In addition, where the PCOL website specifies that the court has the facility to provide viewing of such information by electronic means, the parties or their representatives may view the following information electronically—
  (1) court orders made in relation to the case; and
  (2) details of progress on enforcement and subsequent Orders made.

See also **Electronic applications** and **Signature**.

POSTAL SERVICES ACT 2000

Pt 19 r.19.7B

  (1) An application under s.92 of the Postal Services Act 2000 for permission to bring proceedings in the name of the sender or addressee of a postal packet or his personal representative is made in accordance with Pt 8.
  (2) A copy of the application notice must be served on the universal service provider and on the person in whose name the applicant seeks to bring the proceedings.

POSTCODE

PD 16 para.2.4

Any address which is provided for the purpose of [statement of case] must include a postcode or its equivalent in any EEA state (if applicable), unless the court orders otherwise. Postcode information for the UK may be obtained from *http://www.royalmail.com/* (Accessed November 20, 2012) or the Royal Mail Address Management Guide.

POST-JUDGMENT INTEREST

See **Interest**.

PRACTICE FORM

Glossary

Form to be used for a particular purpose in proceedings, the form and purpose being specified by a PD.

PRACTICE MASTER

PD 2A para.2.2

One of the Masters of the Queen's Bench Division present at the Central Office on every day on which the office is open for the purpose of superintending the business performed there and giving any directions which may be required on questions of practice and procedure.

PRE-ACTION CONDUCT

Aims

PD-PAC para.1.1

The aims of [PD—Pre-Action Conduct] are to—
(1) enable parties to settle the issue between them without the need to start proceedings (that is, a court claim); and
(2) support the efficient management by the court and the parties of proceedings that cannot be avoided.

PD—PAC para.1.2

These aims are to be achieved by encouraging the parties to—
(1) exchange information about the issue, and
(2) consider using a form of Alternative Dispute Resolution ('ADR').

PD—PAC para.2.1

This PD describes the conduct the court will normally expect of the prospective parties prior to the start of proceedings.

PD—PAC para.2.2

There are some types of application where the principles in this PD clearly cannot or should not apply. These include, but are not limited to, for example—
(1) applications for an order where the parties have agreed between them the terms of the court order to be sought ('consent orders');
(2) applications for an order where there is no other party for the applicant to engage with;
(3) most applications for directions by a trustee or other fiduciary;
(4) applications where telling the other potential party in advance would defeat the purpose of the application (for example, an application for an order to freeze assets).

PD—PAC para.2.3

Section II deals with the approach of the court in exercising its powers in relation to pre-action conduct. Subject to para.2.2, it applies in relation to all types of proceedings including those governed by the pre-action protocols that have been approved by the Head of Civil Justice and which are listed in para.5.2 of this PD.

PD—PAC para.2.4

Section III deals with principles governing the conduct of the parties in cases which are not subject to a pre-action protocol.

PD—PAC para.2.5

Section III of this PD is supplemented by two annexes aimed at different types of claimant.
 (1) Annex A sets out detailed guidance on a pre-action procedure that is likely to satisfy the court in most circumstances where no pre-action protocol or other formal pre-action procedure applies. It is intended as a guide for parties, particularly those without legal representation, in straightforward claims that are likely to be disputed. It is not intended to apply to debt claims where it is not disputed that the money is owed and where the claimant follows a statutory or other formal pre-action procedure.
 (2) Annex B sets out some specific requirements that apply where the claimant is a business and the defendant is an individual. The requirements may be complied with at any time between the claimant first intimating the possibility of court proceedings and the claimant's letter before claim.

PD—PAC para.2.6

Section IV contains requirements that apply to all cases including those subject to the pre-action protocols (unless a relevant pre-action protocol contains a different provision). It is supplemented by Annex C, which sets out guidance on instructing experts.

Compliance

PD—PAC para.4.1

The CPR enable the court to take into account the extent of the parties' compliance with this PD or a relevant pre-action protocol (see para.5.2) when giving directions for the management of claims (see CPR rr.3.1(4) and (5) and 3.9(1)(e)) and when making orders about who should pay costs (see CPR r.44.3(5)(a)).

PD—PAC para.4.2

The court will expect the parties to have complied with this PD or any relevant pre-action protocol. The court may ask the parties to explain what steps were taken to comply prior to the start of the claim. Where there has been a failure of compliance by a party the court may ask that party to provide an explanation.

Assessment of compliance

PD—PAC para.4.3

When considering compliance the court will—
 (1) be concerned about whether the parties have complied in substance with the relevant principles and requirements and is not likely to be concerned with minor or technical shortcomings;
 (2) consider the proportionality of the steps taken compared to the size and importance of the matter;

(3) take account of the urgency of the matter. Where a matter is urgent (for example, an application for an injunction) the court will expect the parties to comply only to the extent that it is reasonable to do so. (Paras 9.5 and 9.6 of this PD concern urgency caused by limitation periods).

Examples of non-compliance

PD—PAC para.4.4

The court may decide that there has been a failure of compliance by a party because, for example, that party has—
(1) not provided sufficient information to enable the other party to understand the issues;
(2) not acted within a time limit set out in a relevant pre-action protocol, or, where no specific time limit applies, within a reasonable period;
(3) unreasonably refused to consider ADR (para.8 in Pt III of this PD and the pre-action protocols all contain similar provisions about ADR); or
(4) without good reason, not disclosed documents requested to be disclosed.

Sanctions for non-compliance

PD—PAC para.4.5

The court will look at the overall effect of non-compliance on the other party when deciding whether to impose sanctions.

PD—PAC para.4.6

If, in the opinion of the court, there has been non-compliance, the sanctions which the court may impose include—
(1) staying (that is suspending) the proceedings until steps which ought to have been taken have been taken;
(2) an order that the party at fault pays the costs, or part of the costs, of the other party or parties (this may include an order under r.27.14(2)(g) in cases allocated to the small claims track);
(3) an order that the party at fault pays those costs on an indemnity basis (r.44.4(3) sets out the definition of the assessment of costs on an indemnity basis);
(4) if the party at fault is the claimant in whose favour an order for the payment of a sum of money is subsequently made, an order that the claimant is deprived of interest on all or part of that sum, and/or that interest is awarded at a lower rate than would otherwise have been awarded;
(5) if the party at fault is a defendant, and an order for the payment of a sum of money is subsequently made in favour of the claimant, an order that the defendant pay interest on all or part of that sum at a higher rate, not exceeding 10% above base rate, than would otherwise have been awarded.

Commencement of pre-action protocols

PD—PAC para.5.1

When considering compliance, the court will take account of a relevant pre-action protocol if the proceedings were started after the relevant pre-action protocol came into force.

PD—PAC para.6.1

The principles that should govern the conduct of the parties are that, unless the circumstances make it inappropriate, before starting proceedings the parties should—
  (1) exchange sufficient information about the matter to allow them to understand each other's position and make informed decisions about settlement and how to proceed;
  (2) make appropriate attempts to resolve the matter without starting proceedings, and in particular consider the use of an appropriate form of ADR in order to do so.

PD—PAC para.6.2

The parties should act in a reasonable and proportionate manner in all dealings with one another. In particular, the costs incurred in complying should be proportionate to the complexity of the matter and any money at stake. The parties must not use this PD as a tactical device to secure an unfair advantage for one party or to generate unnecessary costs.

Exchanging information before starting proceedings

PD—PAC para.7.1

Before starting proceedings—
  (1) the claimant should set out the details of the matter in writing by sending a letter before claim to the defendant. This letter before claim is not the start of proceedings; and
  (2) the defendant should give a full written response within a reasonable period, preceded, if appropriate, by a written acknowledgment of the letter before claim.

PD—PAC para.7.2

A 'reasonable period of time' will vary depending on the matter. As a general guide—
  (1) the defendant should send a letter of acknowledgment within 14 days of receipt of the letter before claim (if a full response has not been sent within that period);
  (2) where the matter is straightforward, for example an undisputed debt, then a full response should normally be provided within 14 days;
  (3) where a matter requires the involvement of an insurer or other third party or where there are issues about evidence, then a full response should normally be provided within 30 days;
  (4) where the matter is particularly complex, for example requiring specialist advice, then a period of longer than 30 days may be appropriate;
  (5) a period of longer than 90 days in which to provide a full response will only be considered reasonable in exceptional circumstances.

PD—PAC para.7.3

Annex A sets out detailed guidance on a pre-action procedure that is likely to satisfy the court in most circumstances where no pre-action protocol applies and where the claimant does not follow any statutory or other formal pre-action procedure.

PD—PAC para.7.4

Annex B sets out the specific information that should be provided in a debt claim by a claimant who is a business against a defendant who is an individual.

Alternative dispute resolution

PD—PAC para.8.1

Starting proceedings should usually be a step of last resort, and proceedings should not normally be started when a settlement is still actively being explored. Although ADR is not compulsory, the parties should consider whether some form of ADR procedure might enable them to settle the matter without starting proceedings. The court may require evidence that the parties considered some form of ADR (see para.4.4(3)).

PD—PAC para.8.2

It is not practicable in this PD to address in detail how the parties might decide to resolve a matter. However, some of the options for resolving a matter without starting proceedings are—

(1) discussion and negotiation;
(2) mediation (a form of negotiation with the help of an independent person or body);
(3) early neutral evaluation (where an independent person or body, for example a lawyer or an expert in the subject, gives an opinion on the merits of a dispute); or
(4) arbitration (where an independent person or body makes a binding decision), many types of business are members of arbitration schemes for resolving disputes with consumers.

PD—PAC para.8.3

The Legal Services Commission has published a booklet on 'Alternatives to Court', CLS Direct Information Leaflet 23 (*http://www.legalservices.gov.uk/public/help/legal_leaflets.asp*—Accessed November 15, 2012) which lists a number of organisations that provide alternative dispute resolution services. The National Mediation Helpline on 0845 603 0809 or at *http://www.civilmediation.justice.gov.uk/*—Accessed on November 15, 2012—can provide information about mediation.

PD—PAC para.8.4

The parties should continue to consider the possibility of reaching a settlement at all times. This still applies after proceedings have been started, up to and during any trial or final hearing.

Specific provisions

PD—PAC para.9.1

The following requirements (including Annex C) apply in all cases except where a relevant preaction protocol contains its own provisions about the topic.

Disclosure

PD—PAC para.9.2

[In all cases except where a relevant pre-action protocol contains its own provisions] documents provided by one party to another in the course of complying with this PD or any relevant preaction protocol must not be used for any purpose other than resolving the matter, unless the disclosing party agrees in writing.

Information about funding arrangements

PD—PAC para.9.3

[In all cases except where a relevant pre-action protocol contains its own provisions] where a party enters into a funding arrangement within the meaning of r.43.2(1)(k), that party must inform the other parties about this arrangement as soon as possible and in any event either within seven days of entering into the funding arrangement concerned or, where a claimant enters into a funding arrangement before sending a letter before claim, in the letter before claim. (CPR r.44.3B(1)(c) provides that a party may not recover certain additional costs where information about a funding arrangement was not provided).

Pre-action behaviour not covered by approved protocol

PD—PAC para.6.1

The principles that should govern the conduct of the parties are that, unless the circumstances make it inappropriate, before starting proceedings the parties should—
(1) exchange sufficient information about the matter to allow them to understand each other's position and make informed decisions about settlement and how to proceed;
(2) make appropriate attempts to resolve the matter without starting proceedings, and in particular consider the use of an appropriate form of ADR in order to do so.

PD—PAC para.6.2

The parties should act in a reasonable and proportionate manner in all dealings with one another. In particular, the costs incurred in complying should be proportionate to the complexity of the matter and any money at stake. The parties must not use this PD as a tactical device to secure an unfair advantage for one party or to generate unnecessary costs.

Exchanging information before starting proceedings

PD—PAC para.7.1

Before starting proceedings—
(1) the claimant should set out the details of the matter in writing by sending a letter before claim to the defendant. This letter before claim is not the start of proceedings; and
(2) the defendant should give a full written response within a reasonable period, preceded, if appropriate, by a written acknowledgment of the letter before claim.

PD—PAC para.7.2

A 'reasonable period of time' will vary depending on the matter. As a general guide—
(1) the defendant should send a letter of acknowledgment within 14 days of receipt of the letter before claim (if a full response has not been sent within that period);
(2) where the matter is straightforward, for example an undisputed debt, then a full response should normally be provided within 14 days;

(3) where a matter requires the involvement of an insurer or other third party or where there are issues about evidence, then a full response should normally be provided within 30 days;

(4) where the matter is particularly complex, for example requiring specialist advice, then a period of longer than 30 days may be appropriate;

(5) a period of longer than 90 days in which to provide a full response will only be considered reasonable in exceptional circumstances.

PD—PAC para.7.3

Annex A sets out detailed guidance on a pre-action procedure that is likely to satisfy the court in most circumstances where no pre-action protocol applies and where the claimant does not follow any statutory or other formal pre-action procedure.

PD—PAC para.7.4

Annex B sets out the specific information that should be provided in a debt claim by a claimant who is a business against a defendant who is an individual.

Alternative dispute resolution

PD—PAC para.8.1

Starting proceedings should usually be a step of last resort, and proceedings should not normally be started when a settlement is still actively being explored. Although ADR is not compulsory, the parties should consider whether some form of ADR procedure might enable them to settle the matter without starting proceedings. The court may require evidence that the parties considered some form of ADR (see para.4.4(3)).

PD—PAC para.8.2

It is not practicable in this PD to address in detail how the parties might decide to resolve a matter. However, some of the options for resolving a matter without starting proceedings are—

(1) discussion and negotiation;

(2) mediation (a form of negotiation with the help of an independent person or body);

(3) early neutral evaluation (where an independent person or body, for example a lawyer or an expert in the subject, gives an opinion on the merits of a dispute); or

(4) arbitration (where an independent person or body makes a binding decision), many types of business are members of arbitration schemes for resolving disputes with consumers.

PD—PAC para.8.3

The Legal Services Commission has published a booklet on "Alternatives to Court", CLS Direct Information Leaflet 23 (*http://www.legalservices.gov.uk/public/help/legal_leaflets.asp*—Accessed November 15, 2012) which lists a number of organisations that provide alternative dispute resolution services. The National Mediation Helpline on 0845 603 0809 or at *http://www.civilmediation.justice.gov.uk/*—Accessed on November 15, 2012—can provide information about mediation.

PD—PAC para.8.4

The parties should continue to consider the possibility of reaching a settlement at all times. This still applies after proceedings have been started, up to and during any trial or final hearing.

Experts

PD—PAC para.9.4

[In all cases except where a relevant pre-action protocol contains its own provisions] where the evidence of an expert is necessary the parties should consider how best to minimise expense. Guidance on instructing experts can be found in Annex C.

Limitation periods

PD—PAC para.9.5

[In all cases except where a relevant pre-action protocol contains its own provisions] there are statutory time limits for starting proceedings ('the limitation period'). If a claimant starts a claim after the limitation period applicable to that type of claim has expired the defendant will be entitled to use that as a defence to the claim.

PD—PAC para.9.6

[In all cases except where a relevant pre-action protocol contains its own provisions] in certain instances compliance may not be possible before the expiry of the limitation period. If, for any reason, proceedings are started before the parties have complied, they should seek to agree to apply to the court for an order to stay (i.e. suspend) the proceedings while the parties take steps to comply.

Notifying the court

PD—PAC para.9.7

[In all cases except where a relevant pre-action protocol contains its own provisions] where proceedings are started the claimant should state in the claim form or the particulars of claim whether they have complied with ss.III and IV of this PD or any relevant protocol.

Transitional provision

PD—PAC para.9.8

[In all cases except where a relevant pre-action protocol contains its own provisions] the amendments to para.9.3 do not apply to a funding arrangement entered into before October 1, 2009 and para.9.3 in force immediately before that date will continue to apply to that funding arrangement as if para.9.3 had not been amended.

Summary judgment

PD 24 para.2

(7) Where the claimant has failed to comply with PD (Pre-Action Conduct) or any relevant pre-action protocol, an action for summary judgment will not normally be entertained before the defence has been filed or, alternatively, the time for doing so has expired.

PRE-ACTION PROTOCOLS

Glossary

Statements of best practice about pre-action conduct which have been approved by the Head of Civil Justice and are listed in PD [**Pre-action Conduct**].

Commencement of Pre-action Protocol

Pre-Action Protocol	Came into force
Personal Injury	April 26, 1999
Clinical Disputes	April 26, 1999
Construction and Engineering	October 2, 2000
Defamation	October 2, 2000
Professional Negligence	July 16, 2001
Judicial Review	March 4, 2002
Disease and Illness	December 8, 2003
Housing Disrepair	December 8, 2003
Possession Claims based on rent arrears	October 2, 2006
Possession Claims based on Mortgage Arrears etc.	November 19, 2008
Low value Personal Injury claims in Road Traffic accidents	April 30, 2010
Dilapidations (commercial property)	January 1, 2012

Pre-action Protocol for the resolution of Clinical Disputes

This protocol is not a comprehensive code governing all the steps in clinical disputes. Rather it attempts to set out a code of good practice which parties should follow when litigation might be a possibility.

The commitments section of the protocol summarises the guiding principles which healthcare providers and patients and their advisers are invited to endorse when dealing with patient dissatisfaction with treatment and its outcome, and with potential complaints and claims.

Protocol steps

The steps section sets out in a more prescriptive form, a recommended sequence of actions to be followed if litigation is a prospect

The steps of this protocol which follow have been kept deliberately simple. An illustration of the likely sequence of events in a number of healthcare situations is at Annex A [of the protocol].

Pre-action Protocol for Construction and Engineering Dispute

This Pre-Action Protocol applies to all construction and engineering disputes (including professional negligence claims against architects, engineers and quantity surveyors).

Exceptions

A claimant shall not be required to comply with this Protocol before commencing proceedings to the extent that the proposed proceedings (i) are for the enforcement of the decision of an adjudicator to whom a dispute has been referred pursuant to s. 108 of the Housing Grants, Construction and Regeneration Act 1996 ('the 1996 Act'), (ii) include a claim for interim injunctive relief, (iii) will be the subject of a claim for summary judgment pursuant to Pt 24, or (iv) relate to the same or substantially the same issues as have been the subject of recent adjudication under the 1996 Act, or some other formal alternative dispute resolution procedure.

General Aim

The general aim of this Protocol is to ensure that before court proceedings commence:
  (i) the claimant and the defendant have provided sufficient information for each party to know the nature of the other's case;
 (ii) each party has had an opportunity to consider the other's case, and to accept or reject all or any part of the case made against him at the earliest possible stage;
(iii) there is more pre-action contact between the parties;
 (iv) better and earlier exchange of information occurs;
  (v) there is better pre-action investigation by the parties;
 (vi) the parties have met formally on at least one occasion with a view to defining and agreeing the issues between them; and exploring possible ways by which the claim may be resolved;
(vii) the parties are in a position where they may be able to settle cases early and fairly without recourse to litigation; and
(viii) proceedings will be conducted efficiently if litigation does become necessary.

See **Construction and Engineering Disputes**.

Pre-action Protocol for Defamation

Aims of the Protocol

This protocol aims to set out a code of good practice which parties should follow when litigation is being considered.
It encourages early communication of a claim.
It aims to encourage both parties to disclose sufficient information to enable each to understand the other's case and to promote the prospect of early resolution.
It sets a timetable for the exchange of information relevant to the dispute.

It sets standards for the content of correspondence.

It identifies options which either party might adopt to encourage settlement of the claim.

Should a claim proceed to litigation, the extent to which the protocol has been followed both in practice and in spirit by the parties will assist the Court in dealing with liability for costs and making other Orders.

Letters of claim and responses sent pursuant to this Protocol are not intended to have the same status as a Statement of Case in proceedings.

It aims to keep the costs of resolving disputes subject to this protocol proportionate.

See **Defamation claims**.

Pre-action Protocol for claims for damages in relation to the physical state of Commercial Property at termination of a tenancy (the "Dilapidations Protocol")

This protocol applies to commercial property situated in England and Wales. It relates to claims for damages for dilapidations against tenants at the termination of a tenancy. These are generally referred to as terminal dilapidations claims. There is a separate Pre-Action Protocol for Housing Disrepair cases.

This protocol sets out conduct that the court would normally expect prospective parties to follow prior to the commencement of proceedings. It establishes a reasonable process and timetable for the exchange of information relevant to a dispute, sets standards for the content and quality of schedules and Quantified Demands and, in particular, the conduct of pre-action negotiations.

If the landlord or tenant does not seek professional advice from a surveyor they should still, in so far as reasonably possible, fully comply with the terms of this protocol. In this protocol "surveyor" is intended to encompass reference to any other suitably qualified person.

This protocol does not define "dilapidations", "repair", "reinstatement "or "redecoration". Work to property which may be required will depend on the contractual terms of the lease and any other relevant documents.

Where the court considers non-compliance, and the sanctions to impose where it has occurred, it will, amongst other things, be concerned about whether the parties have complied in substance with the relevant principles and requirements and is not likely to be concerned with minor or technical shortcomings (see paras 4.3–4.5 of the Practice Direction on Pre-Action Conduct).

General Aim

The protoco's objectives are:
- to encourage the exchange of early and full information about the dispute;
- to enable the parties to avoid litigation by agreeing a settlement of the dispute before proceedings are commenced; and
- to support the efficient management of proceedings where litigation cannot be avoided.

A flow chart is attached at Annex A [of the protocol], which shows each of the stages that the parties are expected to undertake before the commencement of proceedings.

Pre-action Protocol for Disease and Illness claims

This protocol is intended to apply to all personal injury claims where the injury is not as the result of an accident but takes the form of an illness or disease.

This protocol covers disease claims which are likely to be complex and frequently not suitable for fast-track procedures even though they may fall within fast-track limits. Disease for the purpose of this protocol primarily covers any illness physical or psychological, any disorder, ailment, affliction, complaint, malady, or derangement other than a physical or psychological injury solely caused by an accident or other similar single event.

In appropriate cases it may be agreed between the parties that this protocol can be applied rather than the Pre-Action Protocol for Personal Injury Claims where a single event occurs but causes a disease or illness.

This protocol is not limited to diseases occurring in the workplace but will embrace diseases occurring in other situations for example through occupation of premises or the use of products. It is not intended to cover those cases, which are dealt with as a "group" or "class" action.

The "cards on the table" approach advocated by the Pre-Action Protocol for Personal Injury Claims is equally appropriate to disease claims. The spirit of that protocol and of the clinical negligence protocol is followed here, in accordance with the sense of the civil justice reforms.

The timetable and the arrangements for disclosing documents and obtaining expert evidence may need to be varied to suit the circumstances of the case. If a party considers the detail of the protocol to be inappropriate they should communicate their reasons to all of the parties at that stage. If proceedings are subsequently issued, the court will expect an explanation as to why the protocol has not been followed, or has been varied.

In a terminal disease claim with short life expectancy, for instance where a claimant has a disease such as mesothelioma, the time scale of the protocol is likely to be too long. In such a claim, the claimant may not be able to follow the protocol and the defendant would be expected to treat the claim with urgency including any request for an interim payment.

In a claim for mesothelioma, additional provisions apply, which are set out in Annex C of this protocol.

Alternative dispute resolution

The parties should consider whether some form of alternative dispute resolution procedure would be more suitable than litigation, and if so, endeavour to agree which form to adopt. Both the claimant and defendant may be required by the court to provide evidence that alternative means of resolving their dispute were considered. The courts take the view that litigation should be a last resort, and that claims should not be issued prematurely when a settlement is still actively being explored. Parties are warned that if the protocol is not followed (including this paragraph) then the court must have regard to such conduct when determining costs.

It is not practicable in this protocol to address in detail how the parties might decide which method to adopt to resolve their particular dispute. However, summarised below are some of the options for resolving disputes without litigation:

Discussion and negotiation.

- Early neutral evaluation by an independent third party (for example, a lawyer experienced in the field of disease or illness, or an individual experienced in the subject matter of the claim).
- Mediation—a form of facilitated negotiation assisted by an independent neutral party.
- Arbitration (where an independent person or body makes a binding decision).

The Legal Services Commission has published a booklet on "Alternatives to Court", CLS Direct Information Leaflet (*http://www.communitylegaladvice.org.uk/media/808/FD/leaflet23e.pdf*), which lists a number of organisations that provide alternative dispute resolution services.

It is expressly recognised that no party can or should be forced to mediate or enter into any form of ADR, but the parties should continue to consider the possibility of reaching a settlement at all times.

General aims

The general aims of the protocol are—
- to resolve as many disputes as possible without litigation; and
- where a claim cannot be resolved, to identify the relevant issues which remain in dispute.

Pre-action Protocol for Housing Disrepair cases

Aims of the protocol

The specific aims of this Protocol are—
- to avoid unnecessary litigation,
- to promote the speedy and appropriate carrying out of any repairs which are the landlord's responsibility,
- to ensure that tenants receive any compensation to which they are entitled as speedily as possible,
- to promote good pre-litigation practice, including the early exchange of information and to give guidance about the instruction of experts, and
- to keep the costs of resolving disputes down.

Definitions

For the purposes of this protocol:
(a) A disrepair claim is a civil claim arising from the condition of residential premises and may include a related personal injury claim. It does not include disrepair claims which originate as counterclaims or set-offs in other proceedings.
(b) The types of claim which this Protocol is intended to cover include those brought under s.11 of the Landlord and Tenant Act 1985, s.4 of the Defective Premises Act 1972, common law nuisance and negligence, and those brought under the express terms of a tenancy agreement or lease. It does not cover claims brought under s.82 of the Environmental Protection Act 1990 (which are heard in the Magistrates' Court).
(c) This protocol covers claims by any person with a disrepair claim as referred to in paras (a) and (b) above, including tenants, lessees and members of the tenant's family. The use of the term 'tenant' in this protocol is intended to cover all such people.

Pre-action protocol for Judicial Review

This Protocol applies to proceedings within England and Wales only. It does not affect the time limit specified by r.54.5(1) of CPR which requires that any claim form in an application for judicial review must be filed promptly and in any event not later than three months after the grounds to make the claim first arose.

Judicial review allows people with a sufficient interest in a decision or action by a public body to ask a judge to review the lawfulness of:
- an enactment;
- or a decision, action or failure to act in relation to the exercise of a public function.

Judicial review may be used where there is no right of appeal or where all avenues of appeal have been exhausted.

The parties should consider whether some form of alternative dispute resolution procedure would be more suitable than litigation, and if so, endeavour to agree which form to adopt. Both the claimant and defendant may be required by the court to provide evidence that alternative means of resolving their dispute were considered. The courts take the view that litigation should be a last resort, and that claims should not be issued prematurely when a settlement is still actively being explored. Parties are warned that if the protocol is not followed (including this paragraph) then the court must have regard to such conduct when determining costs. However, parties should also note that a claim for judicial review "must be filed promptly and in any event not later than three months after the grounds to make the claim first arose".

It is expressly recognised that no party can or should be forced to mediate or enter into any form of ADR.

This Protocol sets out a code of good practice and contains the steps which parties should generally follow before making a claim for judicial review.

This protocol does not impose a greater obligation on a public body to disclose documents or give reasons for its decision than that already provided for in statute or common law. However, where the court considers that a public body should have provided relevant documents and/or information, particularly where this failure is a breach of a statutory or common law requirement, it may impose sanctions.

This Protocol will not be appropriate where the defendant does not have the legal power to change the decision being challenged, for example decisions issued by tribunals such as the Asylum and Immigration Tribunal.

This Protocol will not be appropriate in urgent cases, for example, when directions have been set, or are in force, for the claimant's removal from the UK, or where there is an urgent need for an interim order to compel a public body to act where it has unlawfully refused to do so (for example, the failure of a local housing authority to secure interim accommodation for a homeless claimant) a claim should be made immediately. A letter before claim will not stop the implementation of a disputed decision in all instances.

All claimants will need to satisfy themselves whether they should follow the protocol, depending upon the circumstances of his or her case. Where the use of the protocol is appropriate, the court will normally expect all parties to have complied with it and will take into account compliance or non-compliance when giving directions for case management of proceedings or when making orders for costs. However, even in emergency cases, it is good practice to fax to the defendant the draft Claim Form which the claimant intends to issue. A claimant is also normally required to notify a defendant when an interim mandatory order is being sought.

Pre-action protocol for Low Value Personal Injury Claims in Road Traffic Accidents

This Protocol describes the behaviour the court will normally expect of the parties prior to the start of proceedings where a claimant claims damages valued at no more than £10,000 as a result of a personal injury sustained by that person in a road traffic accident [an accident resulting in bodily injury to any person caused by, or arising out of, the use of a motor vehicle on a road or other public place in England and Wales unless the injury was caused wholly or in part by a breach by the defendant of one or more of the relevant statutory provisions as defined by s.53 of the Health and Safety at Work etc Act 1974].

The aim of this Protocol is to ensure that—
(1) the defendant pays damages and costs using the process set out in the Protocol without the need for the claimant to start proceedings;
(2) damages are paid within a reasonable time; and
(3) the claimant's **legal representative** receives the fixed costs at the end of each stage in this Protocol.

This Protocol applies where—
(1) a claim for damages arises from a road traffic accident occurring on or after 30th April 2010;
(2) the claim includes damages in respect of personal injury;
(3) the claimant values the claim at not more than £10,000 on a full liability basis including pecuniary losses but excluding interest ("the upper limit"); and

(4) if proceedings were started the small claims track would not be the normal track for that claim.

(Paragraphs 1.1(6) and 4.3 state the damages that are excluded for the purposes of valuing the claim under para.4.1.)

(R.26.6 provides that the small claims track is not the normal track where the value of any claim for damages for personal injuries (defined as compensation for pain, suffering and loss of amenity) is more than £1,000.)

4.2

This Protocol ceases to apply to a claim where, at any stage, the claimant notifies the defendant that the claim has now been revalued at more than the upper limit.

4.3

A claim may include vehicle related damages but these are excluded for the purposes of valuing the claim under para.4.1.

This Protocol does not apply to a claim—
(1) in respect of a breach of duty owed to a road user by a person who is not a road user;
(2) made to the MIB pursuant to the Untraced Drivers' Agreement 2003 or any subsequent or supplementary Untraced Drivers' Agreements;
(3) where the claimant or defendant is—
    (a) deceased; or
    (b) a protected party as defined in r.21.1(2)(d);
(4) where the claimant is bankrupt; or
(5) where the defendant's vehicle is registered outside the United Kingdom.

The fixed costs in r.45.29 apply in relation to a claimant only where a claimant has a legal representative.

Pre-action protocol for Personal Injury claims

The Protocol has been kept deliberately simple to promote ease of use and general acceptability.

The notes of guidance which follows relate particularly to issues which arose during the piloting of the protocol.

This Protocol is intended to apply to all claims which include a claim for personal injury (except those claims covered by the Clinical Disputes and Disease and Illness Protocols) and to the entirety of those claims: not only to the personal injury element of a claim which also includes, for instance, property damage.

This Protocol is primarily designed for those road traffic, tripping and slipping and accident at work cases which include an element of personal injury with a value of less than the fast track limit and which are likely to be allocated to that track. This is because time will be of the essence, after proceedings are issued, especially for the defendant, if a case is to be ready for trial within 30 weeks of allocation. Also, proportionality of work and costs to the value of what is in dispute is particularly important in lower value claims. For some claims within the value "scope" of the fast track some flexibility in the timescale of the protocol may be necessary.

However, the "cards on the table" approach advocated by the Protocol is equally appropriate to higher value claims. The spirit, if not the letter of the Protocol, should still be followed for multi-track type claims. In accordance with the sense of the civil justice reforms, the court will expect to see the spirit of reasonable pre-action behaviour applied in all cases, regardless of the existence of a specific protocol. In particular with regard to personal injury cases with a value of more than the fast track limit, to avoid the necessity of proceedings parties are expected to comply with the Protocol as far as possible, e.g. in respect of letters before action, exchanging information and documents and agreeing experts.

The timetable and the arrangements for disclosing documents and obtaining expert evidence may need to be varied to suit the circumstances of the case. Where one or both parties consider the detail of the Protocol is not appropriate to the case, and proceedings are subsequently issued, the court will expect an explanation as to why the protocol has not been followed, or has been varied.

Pre-action protocol for Possession Claims based on Mortgage or Home Purchase Plan Arrears in respect of residential property

This Protocol describes the behaviour the court will normally expect of the parties prior to the start of certain possession claim (see below).

This Protocol does not alter the parties' rights and obligations.

It is in the interests of the parties that mortgage payments or payments under home purchase plans are made promptly and that difficulties are resolved wherever possible without court proceedings. However in some cases an order for possession may be in the interest of both the lender and the borrower.

The aims of this Protocol are to—

(1) ensure that a lender or home purchase plan provider (in this Protocol collectively referred to as 'the lender') and a borrower or home purchase plan customer (in this Protocol collectively referred to as 'the borrower') act fairly and reasonably with each other in resolving any matter concerning mortgage or home purchase plan arrears; and

(2) encourage more pre-action contact between the lender and the borrower in an effort to seek agreement between the parties, and where this cannot be reached, to enable efficient use of the court's time and resources.

Where either party is required to communicate and provide information to the other, reasonable steps should be taken to do so in a way that is clear, fair and not misleading. If the lender is aware that the borrower may have difficulties in reading or understanding the information provided, the lender should take reasonable steps to ensure that information is communicated in a way that the borrower can understand.

This Protocol applies to arrears on—

(1) first charge residential mortgages and home purchase plans regulated by the Financial Services Authority under the Financial Services and Markets Act 2000;

(2) second charge mortgages over residential property and other secured loans regulated under the Consumer Credit Act 1974 on residential property; and

(3) unregulated residential mortgages.

Where a potential claim includes a money claim and a claim for possession this protocol applies to both.

Warrant of possession

CCR Ord.26 r.17

(1) A judgment or order for the recovery of land shall be enforceable by warrant of possession.

(2) Without prejudice to para.(3A), the person applying for a warrant of possession must file a certificate that the land which is subject of the judgment or order has not been vacated.

(2A) When applying for a warrant of possession of a dwelling-house subject to a mortgage, the claimant must certify that notice has been given in accordance with the Dwelling Houses (Execution of Possession Orders by Mortgagees) Regulations 2010.

Pre-action Protocol for Possession claims based on Rent Arrears

This protocol applies to residential possession claims by social landlords (such as local author-ities, Registered Social Landlords and Housing Action Trusts) and private registered providers of social housing which are based solely on claims for rent arrears. The protocol does not apply to claims in respect of long leases or to claims for possession where there is no security of tenure.

The protocol reflects the guidance on good practice given to social landlords and private registered providers in the collection of rent arrears. It recognises that it is in the interests of both landlords and tenants to ensure that rent is paid promptly and to ensure that difficulties are resolved wherever possible without court proceedings.

Its aim is to encourage more pre-action contact between landlords and tenants and to enable court time to be used more effectively.

Courts should take into account whether this protocol has been followed when considering what orders to make. Registered Social Landlords, private registered providers of social housing and local authorities should also comply with guidance issued from time to time by the Housing Corporation and the Department for Communities and Local Government.

Pre-action Protocol for Professional Negligence

This protocol merges the two protocols previously produced by the Solicitors Indemnity Fund (SIF) and claims against professionals (CAP).

This protocol is designed to apply when a claimant wishes to claim against a professional (other than construction professionals and healthcare providers) as a result of that professional's alleged negligence or equivalent breach of contract or breach of fiduciary duty. Although these claims will be the usual situation in which the protocol will be used, there may be other claims for which the protocol could be appropriate.

The aim of this protocol is to establish a framework in which there is an early exchange of information so that the claim can be fully investigated and, if possible, resolved without the need for litigation. This includes:

(a) ensuring that the parties are on an equal footing;
(b) saving expense;
(c) dealing with the dispute in ways which are proportionate;
   (i) to the amount of money involved,
   (ii) to the importance of the case,
   (iii) to the complexity of the issues,
   (iv) to the financial position of each party, and
(d) ensuring that it is dealt with expeditiously and fairly.

This protocol is not intended to replace other forms of pre-action dispute resolution (such as internal complaints procedures, the Surveyors and Valuers Arbitration Scheme, etc.). Where such procedures are available, parties are encouraged to consider whether they should be used. If, however, these other procedures are used and fail to resolve the dispute, the protocol should be used before litigation is started, adapting it where appropriate.

The courts will be able to treat the standards set in this protocol as the normal reasonable approach. If litigation is started, it will be for the court to decide whether sanctions should be imposed as a result of substantial non-compliance with a protocol. Guidance on the courts' likely approach is given in the Protocols Practice Direction. The court is likely to disregard minor departures from this protocol and so should the parties as between themselves.

Both in operating the timetable and in requesting and providing information during the protocol period, the parties are expected to act reasonably, in line with the court's expectations of them.

See also **Pre-action conduct**.

PRE-CLAIM DISCLOSURE

Pt 31 r.31.16

(1) This rule applies where an application is made to the court under any Act for disclosure before proceedings have started.
(2) The application must be supported by evidence.
(3) The court may make an order under this rule only where—
    (a) the respondent is likely to be a party to subsequent proceedings;
    (b) the applicant is also likely to be a party to those proceedings;
    (c) if proceedings had started, the respondent's duty by way of standard disclosure, set out in r.31.6, would extend to the documents or classes of documents of which the applicant seeks disclosure; and
    (d) disclosure before proceedings have started is desirable in order to—
        (i) dispose fairly of the anticipated proceedings;
        (ii) assist the dispute to be resolved without proceedings; or
        (iii) save costs.
(4) An order under this rule must—
    (a) specify the documents or the classes of documents which the respondent must disclose; and
    (b) require him, when making disclosure, to specify any of those documents—
        (i) which are no longer in his control; or
        (ii) in respect of which he claims a right or duty to withhold inspection.
(5) Such an order may—
    (a) require the respondent to indicate what has happened to any documents which are no longer in his control; and
    (b) specify the time and place for disclosure and inspection.
(Rule 78.26 contains rules in relation to the disclosure and inspection of evidence arising out of mediation of certain cross-border disputes).

PD—Pre-Action Conduct para.9.2

Documents provided by one party to another in the course of complying with this PD or any relevant Pre-Action Protocol must not be used for any purpose other than resolving the matter, unless the disclosing party agrees in writing.

PREVENTION OF TERRORISM ACT 2005

Pt 76 r.76.1

(1) This Part contains rules about—
    (a) control order proceedings in the High Court; and
    (b) appeals to the Court of Appeal against an order of the High Court in such proceedings.
(2) In the case of proceedings brought by virtue of s.11(2) of the Act, the rules in this Part shall apply with any modification which the court considers necessary
(3) In this Part—
    (a) 'the Act' means the Prevention of Terrorism Act 2005;
    (b) 'closed material' means any relevant material that the Secretary of State objects to disclosing to a relevant party;
    (c) 'control order proceedings' has the same meaning as in s.11(6) of the Act;
    (d) 'controlled person', has the same meaning as in s.15(1) of the Act;
    (e) 'legal representative' is to be construed in accordance with para.11 of the Schedule to the Act;

    (f) 'open material' means any relevant material that the Secretary of State does not object to disclosing to a relevant party;

    (h) 'relevant material' has the same meaning as in para.4(5) of the Schedule to the Act;

    (i) 'relevant party' has the same meaning as in para.11 of the Schedule to the Act;

    (j) 'special advocate' means a person appointed under para.7 of the Schedule to the Act.

(4) For the purposes of this Part, disclosure is contrary to the public interest if it is made contrary to the interests of national security, the international relations of the UK, the detection and prevention of crime, or in any other circumstances where disclosure is likely to harm the public interest.

Modification to the overriding objective

Pt 76 r.76.2

(1) Where this Part applies, the overriding objective in Pt 1, and so far as relevant any other rule, must be read and given effect in a way which is compatible with the duty set out in para.(2).

(2) The court must ensure that information is not disclosed contrary to the public interest.

(3) Subject to para.(2), the court must satisfy itself that the material available to it enables it properly to determine proceedings.

High Court relating to derogating control orders

Pt 76 r.76.3

(1) This section of this Part contains rules about applications relating to derogating control orders.

(2) Part 23 does not apply to an application made under this section of this Part.

Applications for the making of a derogating control order

Pt 76 r.76.4

An application for the making of a derogating control order under s.4(1) of the Act must be made by the Secretary of State by filing with the court—

    (a) a statement of reasons to support the application for—

        (i) making such an order, and

        (ii) imposing each of the obligations to be imposed by that order;

    (b) all relevant material;

    (c) any written submissions; and

    (d) a draft of the order sought.

Directions for a full hearing on notice

Pt 76 r.76.5

(1) When the court makes a derogating control order under s.4(3) of the Act it must—

    (a) immediately fix a date, time and place for a further hearing at which the controlled person, his legal representative and a special advocate (if one has been appointed) can be present; and

    (b) unless the court otherwise directs, that date must be no later than seven days from the date that the order is made.

(2) At the hearing referred to in para.(1)(a) the court must give directions—

    (a) for the holding of a full hearing under s.4(1)(b) of the Act to determine whether to confirm the control order (with or without modifications) or to revoke it; and

    (b) specifying the date and time by which the parties and special advocate must file and serve any written evidence or written submissions in accordance with r.76.30.

(3) When giving directions under para.(2), the court must have regard to the need to expedite the full hearing.

Applications on notice

Pt 76 r.76.6

(1) An application under s.4(9) for the renewal, or under s.7(4) of the Act, for the revocation of a control order or for the modification of obligations imposed by such an order, must be made in accordance with this rule.

(2) An application by the Secretary of State must be made by—

    (a) filing with the court—

        (i) a statement of reasons to support the application,

        (ii) all relevant material,

        (iii) any written submissions, and

        (iv) a draft of the order sought; and

    (b) serving on the controlled person or his legal representative any open material.

(3) An application by the controlled person must be made by filing with the court and serving on the Secretary of State—

    (a) a statement of reasons to support the application;

    (b) any written evidence upon which he relies;

    (c) any written submissions; and

    (d) where appropriate, a draft of the order sought.

(4) If the controlled person wishes to oppose an application made under this rule, he must as soon as practicable file with the court, and serve on the Secretary of State, any written evidence and any written submissions upon which he relies.

(5) If the Secretary of State wishes to oppose an application made under this rule, he must as soon as practicable—

    (a) file with the court—

        (i) all relevant material, and

        (ii) any written submissions; and

    (b) serve on the controlled person any open material.

(Attention is drawn to r.76.18 relating to the address for issuing proceedings in the High Court. Rules 76.28 and 76.29 will apply where any closed material is filed by the Secretary of State).

Application for permission and reference of and appeal relating to non-derogating control orders

Pt 76 r.76.7

This section of this Part contains rules about—

    (a) applications under s.3(1)(a) of the Act (application for permission to make a non-derogating control order);

(b) references under s.3(3) of the Act (reference of a non-derogating control order made without permission); and

(c) appeals to the High Court under section 10 of the Act (appeals relating to non-derogating control orders).

Application for permission to make non-derogating control order

Pt 76 r.76.8

An application under s.3(1)(a) for permission to make a non-derogating control order must be made by the Secretary of State by filing with the court—

(a) a statement of reasons to support the application;

(b) all relevant material;

(c) any written submissions; and

(d) the proposed control order.

References under s.3(3) of the Act

Pt 76 r.76.9

(1) This rule applies where the Secretary of State makes a reference under s.3(3) of the Act (reference of a non-derogating control order).

(2) The Secretary of State must promptly file with the court—

(a) a statement of the reasons for—

(i) making the control order,

(ii) imposing the obligations imposed by that order;

(b) all relevant material; and

(c) any written submissions.

Directions for hearing on application for permission or on a reference

Pt 76 r.76.10

(1) This rule applies where the court gives directions under s.3(2)(c) or (6)(b) or (c) of the Act.

(2) The court must immediately—

(a) fix a date, time and place for a further hearing at which the controlled person, his legal representative and a special advocate (if one has been appointed) can be present; and

(b) unless the court otherwise directs—

(i) in the case of directions given under s.3(2)(c), that date must be no later than 7 days from the date on which the notice of the terms of the control order is delivered to the controlled person in accordance with s.7(8) of the Act; or

(ii) in the case of directions given under s.3(6)(b) or (c), that date must be seven days from the date on which the court's determination on the reference is made.

(3) At the hearing referred to in para.(2), the court must give directions—

(a) for a hearing under s.3(10); and

(b) specifying the date and time by which the parties and special advocate must file and serve any written evidence or written submissions in accordance with r.76.30.

(4) When giving directions under para.(3), the court must have regard to the need to expedite that hearing.

(Rules 76.28 and 76.29 will apply where any closed material is filed by the Secretary of State).

Appeals under s.10 of the Act

Pt 76 r.76.11

This rule and rr.76.12 to 76.15 apply to an appeal under s.10 of the Act (appeals relating to a non-derogating control order).

Modification of Pt 52 (appeals)

Pt 76 r.76.12

(1) Part 52 (appeals) applies to an appeal under s.10 of the Act, subject to—
   (a) r.76.2;
   (b) the rules in s.5 of this Part; and
   (c) the modifications set out in paras (2) and (3) of this rule.
(2) The following rules do not apply to appeals under s.10 of the Act—
   (a) r.52.3 (permission);
   (b) r.52.4 (appellant's notice);
   (c) r.52.5 (respondent's notice); and
   (d) r.52.11 (hearing of appeals).
(3) R.52.2 (all parties to comply with PD 52) applies, but the parties shall not be required to comply with paras 5.6, 5.6A, 5.7, 5.9 and 5.10 of that PD.

Notice of appeal

Pt 76 r.76.13

(1) The controlled person must give notice of appeal by—
   (a) filing it with the court; and
   (b) serving a copy of the notice and any accompanying documents on the Secretary of State.
(2) The notice of appeal must—
   (a) set out the grounds of the appeal; and
   (b) state the name and address of—
      (i) the controlled person, and
      (ii) any legal representative of that person.
(3) A notice of appeal may include an application for an order under r.76.19 requiring anonymity.
(4) The notice of appeal must be filed with—
   (a) a copy of the order that is the subject of the appeal;
   (b) a copy of the Secretary of State's decision on an application for the revocation of the control order, or for the modification of an obligation imposed by such an order.

(Attention is drawn to r.76.18 relating to the address for issuing proceedings in the High Court).

Time limit for appealing

Pt 76 r.76.14

(1) Subject to para.(2), the controlled person must give notice of appeal no later than 28 days after receiving—
  (a) the notice setting out the terms of the order, renewal or modification that is the subject of the appeal; or
  (b) notice of the decision by the Secretary of State on an application for the revocation of the control order, or for the modification of an obligation imposed by such an order.
(2) In a case where the Secretary of State has failed to determine an application for the revocation of the control order, or for the modification of an obligation imposed by such an order, the controlled person must file the notice of appeal—
  (a) no earlier than 28 days; and
  (b) no later than 42 days;
  after the date the application was made.

Secretary of State's reply

Pt 76 r.76.15

(1) If the Secretary of State wishes to oppose an appeal made under s.10 of the Act, he must no later than 14 days after he is served with the notice of appeal—
  (a) file with the court—
    (i) all relevant material, and
    (ii) any written submissions; and
  (b) serve on the controlled person any open material.

Appeals to the Court of Appeal

Modification of Pt 52 (Appeals)

Pt 76 r.76.16

(1) Part 52 (appeals) applies to an appeal to the Court of Appeal against an order of the High Court in control order proceedings, subject to—
  (a) rule 76.2;
  (b) the rules in s.5 of this Part; and
  (c) paragraphs (2) and (3) of this rule.
(2) The following rules do not apply to appeals to the Court of Appeal—
  (a) rule 52.4(1) (appellant's notice); and
  (b) rule 52.5 (respondent's notice); but
  the provisions of rr.76.13 and 76.15 shall apply with appropriate modifications.
(3) Rule 52.2 (all parties to comply with PDs 52A to 52E) apply, but the parties shall not be required to comply with paras 6.3 to 6.6 of PD 52B and para.28 of PD 52C.
This section of this Part applies to—
  (a) control order proceedings in the High Court; and
  (b) appeals to the Court of Appeal against an order of the High Court in such proceedings.

Address for issuing proceedings in the High Court

Pt 76 r.76.18

Any control order proceedings must be issued at the Administrative Court Office, Room C315, Royal Courts of Justice, Strand, London, WC2A 2LL.

Applications for anonymity

Pt 76 r.76.19

(1) The controlled person or the Secretary of State may apply for an order requiring the anonymity of the controlled person.
(2) An application under para.(1) may be made at any time, irrespective of whether any control order proceedings have been commenced.
(3) An application may be made without notice to the other party.
(4) References in this rule—
    (a) to an order requiring anonymity for the controlled person are to be construed in accordance with para.5(3) of the Schedule to the Act; and
    (b) to the controlled person, in relation to a time before the control order has been made, are to be construed in accordance with para.5(4) of the Schedule to the Act.

Notification of hearing

Pt 76 r.76.20

Unless the court orders otherwise, it must serve notice of the date, time and place fixed for any hearing on—
    (a) every party, whether or not entitled to attend that hearing; and
    (b) if one has been appointed for the purposes of the hearing, the special advocate or those instructing him.

Hearings

Pt 76 r.76.21

(1) The following proceedings must be determined at a hearing—
    (a) a hearing pursuant to directions given under s.4(1)(b) of the Act (derogating control orders);
    (b) a hearing pursuant to directions given under ss.3(2)(c) or (6)(b) or (c) of the Act (non-derogating control orders);
    (c) an appeal under s.10 of the Act (appeal relating to a non-derogating control order);
    (d) an appeal to the Court of Appeal from an order of the High Court made in any of the above proceedings; and
    (e) a hearing under r.76.29(2) (consideration of Secretary of State's objection).
(2) Paragraph (1)(c) and (d) do not apply where—
    (a) the appeal is withdrawn by the controlled person;
    (b) the Secretary of State consents to the appeal being allowed; or

(c) the controlled person is outside the UK or it is impracticable to give him notice of a hearing and, in either case, he is unrepresented.

Hearings in private

Pt 76 r.76.22

(1) If the court considers it necessary for any relevant party and his legal representative to be excluded from a hearing or part of a hearing in order to secure that information is not disclosed contrary to the public interest, it must—
  (a) direct accordingly; and
  (b) conduct the hearing, or that part of it from which the relevant party and his legal representative are excluded, in private.
(2) The court may conduct a hearing or part of a hearing in private for any other good reason.

Appointment of a special advocate

Pt 76 r.76.23

(1) Subject to para.(2), the Secretary of State must immediately give notice of the proceedings to the Attorney General upon—
  (a) making an application under s.4(1) of the Act (relating to a derogating control order);
  (b) making an application under s.3(1)(a) of the Act (application for permission to make a non-derogating control order);
  (c) making a reference under s.3(3) of the Act (reference of a non-derogating control order made without permission); or
  (d) being served with a copy of any application, claim, or notice of appeal in proceedings to which this Part applies.
(2) Paragraph (1) applies unless—
  (a) the Secretary of State does not intend to—
    (i) oppose the appeal or application; or
    (ii) withhold closed material from a relevant party; or
  (b) a special advocate has already been appointed to represent the interests of the relevant party in the proceedings and that special advocate is not prevented from communicating with that party by virtue of r.76.25.
(3) Where notice is given to the Attorney General under para.(1), the Attorney General may appoint a special advocate to represent the interests of the relevant party in the proceedings.
(4) Where any proceedings to which this Part apply are pending but no special advocate has been appointed, a relevant party or the Secretary of State may request the Attorney General to appoint a special advocate.

Functions of special advocate

Pt 76 r.76.24

The functions of a special advocate are to represent the interests of a relevant party by—
  (a) making submissions to the court at any hearings from which the relevant party and his legal representatives are excluded;

(b) adducing evidence and cross-examining witnesses at any such hearings; and

(c) making written submissions to the court.

Special advocate: communicating about proceedings

Pt 76 r.76.25

(1) The special advocate may communicate with the relevant party or his legal representative at any time before the Secretary of State serves closed material on him.

(2) After the Secretary of State serves closed material on the special advocate, the special advocate must not communicate with any person about any matter connected with the proceedings, except in accordance with para.(3) or a direction of the court pursuant to a request under para.(4).

(3) The special advocate may, without directions from the court, communicate about the proceedings with—

(a) the court;

(b) the Secretary of State, or any person acting for him;

(c) the Attorney General, or any person acting for him; or

(d) any other person, except for the relevant party or his legal representative, with whom it is necessary for administrative purposes for him to communicate about matters not connected with the substance of the proceedings.

(4) The special advocate may request directions from the court authorising him to communicate with the relevant party or his legal representative or with any other person.

(5) Where the special advocate makes a request for directions under para.(4)—

(a) the court must notify the Secretary of State of the request; and

(b) the Secretary of State must, within a period specified by the court, file with the court and serve on the special advocate notice of any objection which he has to the proposed communication, or to the form in which it is proposed to be made.

(6) Paragraph (2) does not prohibit the relevant party from communicating with the special advocate after the Secretary of State has served material on him as mentioned in para.(1), but—

(a) the relevant party may only communicate with the special advocate through a legal representative in writing; and

(b) the special advocate must not reply to the communication other than in accordance with directions of the court, except that he may without such directions send a written acknowledgment of receipt to the legal representative of the relevant party.

Modification of the general rules of evidence and disclosure

Pt 76 r.76.26

(1) Part 31 (disclosure and inspection of documents), Pt 32 (evidence) and Pt 33 (miscellaneous rules about evidence) do not apply to any proceedings to which this Pt applies.

(2) Subject to the other rules in this Part, the evidence of a witness may be given either—

(a) orally, before the court; or

(b) in writing, in which case it shall be given in such manner and at such time as the court directs.

(3) The court may also receive evidence in documentary or any other form.

(4) The court may receive evidence that would not, but for this rule, be admissible in a court of law.

(5) Every party shall be entitled to adduce evidence and to cross-examine witnesses during any part of a hearing from which he and his legal representative are not excluded.

(5A) A special advocate shall be entitled to adduce evidence and to cross-examine witnesses.

(6) The court may require a witness to give evidence on oath.

Filing and service of relevant material

Pt 76 r.76.27

The Secretary of State is required to make a reasonable search for relevant material and to file and serve that material in accordance with the rules in this Part.

Closed material

Pt 76 r.76.28

(1) The Secretary of State—
    (a) must apply to the court for permission to withhold closed material from a relevant party or his legal representative in accordance with this rule; and
    (b) may not rely on closed material at a hearing on notice unless a special advocate has been appointed to represent the interests of the relevant party.

(2) The Secretary of State must file with the court and serve, at such time as the court directs, on the special advocate—
    (a) the closed material;
    (b) a statement of his reasons for withholding that material from the relevant party; and
    (c) if he considers it possible to summarise that material without disclosing information contrary to the public interest, a summary of that material in a form which can be served on the relevant party.

(3) The Secretary of State may at any time amend or supplement material filed under this rule, but only with—
    (a) the agreement of the special advocate; or
    (b) the permission of the court.

Consideration of Secretary of State's objection

Pt 76 r.76.29

(1) This rule applies where the Secretary of State has—
    (a) objected under r.76.25(5)(b) to a proposed communication by the special advocate; or
    (b) applied under r.76.28 for permission to withhold closed material.

(2) The court must fix a hearing for the Secretary of State and the special advocate to make oral representations, unless—
    (a) the special advocate gives notice to the court that he does not challenge the objection or application;
    (b) the court has previously considered—
        (i) an objection under r.76.25(5)(b) to the same or substantially the same communication, or
        (ii) an application under r.76.28(1) for permission to withhold the same or substantially the same material, and

is satisfied that it would be just to uphold that objection or to give permission without a hearing; or

  (c) the Secretary of State and the special advocate consent to the court deciding the issue without a hearing.

(3) If the special advocate does not challenge the objection or the application, he must give notice of that fact to the court and the Secretary of State within 14 days, or such other period as the court may direct, after the Secretary of State serves on him a notice under r.76.25(5)(b) or material under r.76.28(2).

(4) Where the court fixes a hearing under this rule, the Secretary of State and the special advocate must before the hearing file with the court a schedule identifying the issues which cannot be agreed between them, which must—

  (a) list the items or issues in dispute;

  (b) give brief reasons for their contentions on each; and

  (c) set out any proposals for the court to resolve the issues in contention.

(5) A hearing under this rule shall take place in the absence of the relevant party and his legal representative.

(6) Where the court gives permission to the Secretary of State to withhold closed material, the court must—

  (a) consider whether to direct the Secretary of State to serve a summary of that material on the relevant party or his legal representative; but

  (b) ensure that no such summary contains information or other material the disclosure of which would be contrary to the public interest.

(7) Where the court has not given permission to the Secretary of State to withhold closed material from, or has directed the Secretary of State to serve a summary of that material on, a relevant party or his legal representative—

  (a) the Secretary of State shall not be required to serve that material or summary; but

  (b) if he does not do so, at a hearing on notice the court may—

    (i) if it considers that the material or anything that is required to be summarised might be of assistance to the relevant party in relation to a matter under consideration by the court, direct that the matter be withdrawn from its consideration, and

    (ii) in any other case, direct that the Secretary of State shall not rely in the proceedings on that material or (as the case may be) on what is required to be summarised.

(8) The court must give permission to the Secretary of State to withhold closed material where it considers that the disclosure of that material would be contrary to the public interest.

Order of filing and serving material and written submissions

Pt 76 r.76.30

Subject to any directions given by the court, the parties must file and serve any material and written submissions, and the special advocate must file and serve any written submissions, in the following order—

  (a) the Secretary of State must file with the court all relevant material;

  (b) the Secretary of State must serve on

    (i) the relevant party or his legal representative; and

    (ii) the special advocate (as soon as one is appointed) or those instructing him,

  any open material;

  (c) the relevant party must file with the court and serve on the Secretary of State and special advocate (if one is appointed) or those instructing him any written evidence which he wishes the court to take into account at the hearing;

  (d) the Secretary of State must file with the court any further relevant material;

(e) the Secretary of State must serve on—
    (i) the relevant party or his legal representative, and
    (ii) the special advocate (as soon as one is appointed) or those instructing him,
    any open material filed with the court under para. (d);
(f) the Secretary of State must serve on the special advocate (if one has been appointed) any closed material;
(g) the parties and the special advocate (if one has been appointed) must file and serve any written submissions as directed by the court.

(Rules 76.28 and 76.29 will apply where any closed material is filed by the Secretary of State).

Failure to comply with directions

Pt 76 r.76.31

(1) Where a party or the special advocate fails to comply with a direction of the court, the court may serve on him a notice which states—
    (a) the respect in which he has failed to comply with the direction;
    (b) a time limit for complying with the direction; and
    (c) that the court may proceed to determine the proceedings before it, on the material available to it, if the party or the special advocate fails to comply with the relevant direction within the time specified.
(2) Where a party or special advocate fails to comply with such a notice, the court may proceed in accordance with para.(1)(c).

Judgments

Pt 76 r.76.32

(1) When the court gives judgment in any proceedings to which this Part applies, it may withhold any or part of its reasons if and to the extent that it is not possible to give reasons without disclosing information contrary to the public interest.
(2) Where the judgment of the court does not include the full reasons for its decision, the court must serve on the Secretary of State and the special advocate a separate written judgment including those reasons.

Application by Secretary of State for reconsideration of decision

Pt 76 r.76.33

(1) This rule applies where the court proposes, in any proceedings to which this Part applies, to serve notice on a relevant party of any—
    (a) order or direction made or given in the absence of the Secretary of State; or
    (b) any judgment.
(2) Before the court serves any such notice on the relevant party, it must first serve notice on the Secretary of State of its intention to do so.
(3) The Secretary of State may, within five days of being served with notice under para.(2), apply to the court to reconsider the terms of the order or direction or to review the terms of the proposed judgment if he considers that—
    (a) his compliance with the order or direction; or

   (b) the notification to the relevant party of any matter contained in the judgment, order
       or direction;
   would cause information to be disclosed contrary to the public interest.
(4) Where the Secretary of State makes an application under para.(3), he must at the same
    time serve on the special advocate, if one has been appointed—
   (a) a copy of the application; and
   (b) a copy of the notice served on the Secretary of State pursuant to para.(2).
(5) Rule 76.29 (except for paras (6) and (7)) shall, if a special advocate has been appointed,
    apply with any necessary modifications to the consideration of an application under
    para.(3) of this rule.
(6) The court must not serve notice on the relevant party as mentioned in para.(1) before the
    time for the Secretary of State to make an application under para.(3) has expired.

Supply of court documents

Pt 76 r.76.34

Unless the court otherwise directs, r.5.4 (Register of Claims), r.5.4B (Supply of documents from
court records—a party) and r.5.4C (Supply of documents from court records—a non-party) do
not apply to any proceedings to which this Part applies.

PRIVATE HEARING

Previously referred to as "in Chambers".

See **Hearing**.

PRIVILEGE

Glossary

The right of a party to refuse to disclose a document, produce a document or to refuse to answer
questions on the ground of some special interest recognised by law.

PRIZE COURT

Proceedings in the High Court when acting as a Prize Court.

Pt 2 r.2.1(2)

The CPR do not apply to these proceedings except to the extent that they are applied by s.3 of
the Prize Courts Act 1894.

PROBATE CLAIM

Pt 57 r.57.1

   (a) A claim for—
       (i) the grant of probate of the will, or letters of administration of the estate, of a deceased
           person;

(ii) the revocation of such a grant; or

(iii) a decree pronouncing for or against the validity of an alleged will;

not being a claim which is non-contentious (or common form) probate business.

PD 57 para.1.2

The rules and procedure relating to non-contentious probate proceedings (also known as 'common form') are the Non-Contentious Probate Rules 1987 as amended.

Pt 57 r.2

(2) Probate claims in the High Court are assigned to the Chancery Division.

(3) Probate claims in the county court must only be brought in—

(a) a county court where there is also a Chancery district registry; or

(b) the Central London County Court.

(4) All probate claims are allotted to the multi-track.

Start of a probate claim

Pt 57 r.57.3

A probate claim must be commenced—

(a) in the relevant office; and

(b) using the procedure in Pt 7.

PD 57 para.2.1

A claim form and all subsequent court documents relating to a probate claim must be marked at the top 'In the estate of [name] deceased (Probate)'.

PD 57 para.2.2

The claim form must be issued out of—

(1) Chancery Chambers at the Royal Courts of Justice; or

(2) one of the Chancery district registries; or

(3) if the claim is suitable to be heard in the county court—

(a) a county court in a place where there is also a Chancery district registry; or

(b) the Central London County Court.

There are Chancery district registries at Birmingham, Bristol, Caernarfon, Cardiff, Leeds, Liverpool, Manchester, Mold, Newcastle upon Tyne and Preston.

(Section 32 of the County Courts Act 1984 identifies which probate claims may be heard in a county court).

PD 57 para.2.3

When the claim form is issued, the relevant office will send a notice to Leeds District Probate Registry, Coronet House, Queen Street, Leeds, LS1 2BA, DX 26451 Leeds (Park Square), tel: 0113 243 1505, requesting that all testamentary documents, grants of representation and other relevant documents currently held at any probate registry are sent to the relevant office.

PD 57 para.2.4

The commencement of a probate claim will, unless a court otherwise directs, prevent any grant of probate or letters of administration being made until the probate claim has been disposed of.
(Rule 45 of the Non-Contentious Probate Rules 1987 makes provision for notice of the probate claim to be given, and s.117 of the Senior Courts Act 1981 for the grant of letters of administration pending the determination of a probate claim. Paragraph 8 of this PD makes provision about an application for such a grant).

Acknowledgment of service and defence

Pt 57 r.57.4

(1) A defendant who is served with a claim form must file an acknowledgment of service.
(2) Subject to para.(3), the period for filing an acknowledgment of service is—
   (a) if the defendant is served with a claim form which states that particulars of claim are to follow, 28 days after service of the particulars of claim; and
   (b) in any other case, 28 days after service of the claim form.
(3) If the claim form is served out of the jurisdiction under r.6.32 or 6.33, the period for filing an acknowledgment of service is 14 days longer than the relevant period specified in r.6.35 or PD 6B.
(4) Rule 15(4) (which provides the period for filing a defence) applies as if the words 'under Part 10' were omitted from r.15.4(1)(b).

Appeals to the Court of Appeal

PD 52C para.3

(3) At the same time as filing an appellant's notice, the appellant must provide for the use of the court three copies of the appellant's notice and one copy of each of the following—
(h) the approved transcript of the judgment.

Appeals in the county court and the High Court

PD 52B para.6.2

Transcript of the judgment of the lower court or other record of reasons: Except where the claim has been allocated to the small claims track, the appellant must obtain a transcript or other record of reasons of the lower court as follows
   (a) where the judgment has been officially recorded, the appellant must apply for an approved transcript as soon as possible and, in any event, within 7 days of the filing of the appellant's notice;
   (b) where the judgment under appeal has been handed down in writing, the appellant must obtain and retain a copy of the written judgment;
   (c) in any other case, the appellant must cause a note of the judgment under appeal to be made and typed. The parties to the appeal should agree the note, which should then be sent to

the judge of the lower court for approval. The parties and their advocates have a duty to make, and to co-operate in agreeing, a note of the judgment.

Testamentary documents and filing of evidence about testamentary documents

Pt 57 r.57.5

(1) Any testamentary document of the deceased person in the possession or control of any party must be lodged with the court.

(2) Unless the court directs otherwise, the testamentary documents must be lodged in the relevant office—
   (a) by the claimant when the claim form is issued; and
   (b) by a defendant when he acknowledges service.

(3) The claimant and every defendant who acknowledges service of the claim form must in written evidence—
   (a) describe any testamentary document of the deceased of which he has any knowledge or, if he does not know of any such testamentary document, state that fact, and
   (b) if any testamentary document of which he has knowledge is not in his possession or under his control, give the name and address of the person in whose possession or under whose control it is or, if he does not know the name or address of that person, state that fact.

(A specimen form for the written evidence about testamentary documents is annexed to PD 57).

(4) Unless the court directs otherwise, the written evidence required by para.(3) must be filed in the relevant office—
   (a) by the claimant, when the claim form is issued; and
   (b) by a defendant when he acknowledges service.

(5) Except with the permission of the court, a party shall not be allowed to inspect the testamentary documents or written evidence lodged or filed by any other party until he himself has lodged his testamentary documents and filed his evidence.

(7) The provisions of paras (2) and (4) may be modified by a PD under this Part.

PD 57 para.3.1

Unless the court orders otherwise, if a testamentary document is held by the court (whether it was lodged by a party or it was previously held at a probate registry) when the claim has been disposed of the court will send it to the Leeds District Probate Registry.

PD 57 para.3.2

The written evidence about testamentary documents required by this Part—
(1) should be in the form annexed to this PD; and
(2) must be signed by the party personally and not by his solicitor or other representative (except that if the party is a child or protected party the written evidence must be signed by his litigation friend).

PD 57 para.3.3

In a case in which there is urgent need to commence a probate claim (for example, in order to be able to apply immediately for the appointment of an administrator pending the determination of the claim) and it is not possible for the claimant to lodge the testamentary documents or to file the evidence about testamentary documents in the relevant office at the same time as the claim form is to be issued, the court may direct that the claimant shall be allowed to issue the claim form upon his giving an undertaking to the court to lodge the documents and file the evidence within such time as the court shall specify.

Revocation of existing grant

Pt 57 r.57.6

(1) In a probate claim which seeks the revocation of a grant of probate or letters of administration every person who is entitled, or claims to be entitled, to administer the estate under that grant must be made a party to the claim.
(2) If the claimant is the person to whom the grant was made, he must lodge the probate or letters of administration in the relevant office when the claim form is issued.
(3) If a defendant has the probate or letters of administration under his control, he must lodge it in the relevant office when he acknowledges service.
(4) Paragraphs (2) and (3) do not apply where the grant has already been lodged at the court, which in this paragraph includes the Principal Registry of the Family Division or a district probate registry.

Contents of statements of case

Pt 57 r.57.7

(1) The claim form must contain a statement of the nature of the interest of the claimant and of each defendant in the estate.
(2) If a party disputes another party's interest in the estate he must state this in his statement of case and set out his reasons.
(3) Any party who contends that at the time when a will was executed the testator did not know of and approve its contents must give particulars of the facts and matters relied on.
(4) Any party who wishes to contend that—
    (a) a will was not duly executed;
    (b) at the time of the execution of a will the testator lacked testamentary capacity; or
    (c) the execution of a will was obtained by undue influence or fraud,
    must set out the contention specifically and give particulars of the facts and matters relied on.
(5) (a) A defendant may give notice in his defence that he does not raise any positive case, but insists on the will being proved in solemn form and, for that purpose, will cross-examine the witnesses who attested the will.
    (b) If a defendant gives such a notice, the court will not make an order for costs against him unless it considers that there was no reasonable ground for opposing the will.

Counterclaim

Pt 57 r.57.8

(1) A defendant who contends that he has any claim or is entitled to any remedy relating to the grant of probate of the will, or letters of administration of the estate, of the deceased person must serve a counterclaim making that contention.
(2) If the claimant fails to serve particulars of claim within the time allowed, the defendant may, with the permission of the court, serve a counterclaim and the probate claim shall then proceed as if the counterclaim were the particulars of claim.

Probate counterclaim in other proceedings

Pt 57 r.57.9

(1) In this rule 'probate counterclaim' means a counterclaim in any claim other than a probate claim by which the defendant claims any such remedy as is mentioned in r.57.1(2)(a).
(2) Subject to the following paragraphs of this rule, this Part shall apply with the necessary modifications to a probate counterclaim as it applies to a probate claim.
(3) A probate counterclaim must contain a statement of the nature of the interest of each of the parties in the estate of the deceased to which the probate counterclaim relates.
(4) Unless an application notice is issued within seven days after the service of a probate counterclaim for an order under r.3.1(2)(e) or 3.4 for the probate counterclaim to be dealt with in separate proceedings or to be struck out, and the application is granted, the court shall order the transfer of the proceedings to either—
  (a) the Chancery Division (if it is not already assigned to that Division) and to either the Royal Courts of Justice or a Chancery district registry (if it is not already proceeding in one of those places); or
  (b) if the county court has jurisdiction, to a county court where there is also a Chancery district registry or the Central London County Court.
(5) If an order is made that a probate counterclaim be dealt with in separate proceedings, the order shall order the transfer of the probate counterclaim as required under para.(4).

Failure to acknowledge service or to file a defence

Pt 57 r.57.10

(1) A default judgment cannot be obtained in a probate claim and r.10.2 and Pt 12 do not apply.
(2) If any of several defendants fails to acknowledge service the claimant may—
  (a) after the time for acknowledging service has expired; and
  (b) upon filing written evidence of service of the claim form and (if no particulars of claim were contained in or served with the claim form) the particulars of claim on that defendant;
  proceed with the probate claim as if that defendant had acknowledged service.
(3) If no defendant acknowledges service or files a defence then, unless on the application of the claimant the court orders the claim to be discontinued, the claimant may, after the time for acknowledging service or for filing a defence (as the case may be) has expired, apply to the court for an order that the claim is to proceed to trial.
(4) When making an application under para.(3) the claimant must file written evidence of service of the claim form and (if no particulars of claim were contained in or served with the claim form) the particulars of claim on each of the defendants.
(5) Where the court makes an order under para.(3), it may direct that the claim be tried on written evidence.

Rectification of Wills

PD 57 para.57.12

(1) This Section contains rules about claims for the rectification of a will.
(Section 20 of the Administration of Justice Act 1982provides for rectification of a will. Additional provisions are contained in rule 55 of the **Non-Contentious Probate Rules 1987**).

(2) Every personal representative of the estate shall be joined as a party.

Lodging the grant

PD 57 para.10.1

If the claimant is the person to whom the grant was made in respect of the will of which rectification is sought, he must, unless the court orders otherwise, lodge the probate or letters of administration with the will annexed with the court when the claim form is issued.

PD 57 para.10.2

If a defendant has the probate or letters of administration in his possession or under his control, he must, unless the court orders otherwise, lodge it in the relevant office within 14 days after the service of the claim form on him.

Orders

PD 57 para.11

A copy of every order made for the rectification of a will shall be sent to the Principal Registry of the Family Division for filing, and a memorandum of the order shall be endorsed on, or permanently annexed to, the grant under which the estate is administered.

Case management

PD 57 para.4

In giving case management directions in a probate claim the court will give consideration to the questions—
    (1) whether any person who may be affected by the claim and who is not joined as a party should be joined as a party or given notice of the claim, whether under r.19.8A [power to make judgments binding on non-parties] otherwise; and
    (2) whether to make a representation order under r.19.6 [representative parties with interest] or r.19.7 [representation of interested persons who cannot be ascertained etc.]

Summary judgment

PD 57 para.5.1

If an order pronouncing for a will in solemn form is sought on an application for summary judgment, the evidence in support of the application must include written evidence proving due execution of the will.

PD 57 para.5.2

If a defendant has given notice in his defence under r.57.7(5) that he raises no positive case but—
    (1) he insists that the will be proved in solemn form; and

(2) for that purpose he will cross-examine the witnesses who attested the will;
any application by the claimant for summary judgment is subject to the right of that defendant to require those witnesses to attend court for cross-examination.

Settlement of a probate claim

PD 57 para.6.1

If at any time the parties agree to settle a probate claim, the court may—
  (1) order the trial of the claim on written evidence, which will lead to a grant in solemn form;
  (2) order that the claim be discontinued or dismissed under r.57.11, which will lead to a grant in common form; or
  (3) pronounce for or against the validity of one or more wills under s.49 of the Administration of Justice Act 1985.
(For a form of order which is also applicable to discontinuance and which may be adapted as appropriate, see Practice Form CH38).
(Section 49 of the Administration of Justice Act 1985 permits a probate claim to be compromised without a trial if every 'relevant beneficiary', as defined in that section, has consented to the proposed order. It is only available in the High Court).

PD 57 para.6.2

Applications under s.49 of the Administration of Justice Act 1985 may be heard by a master or district judge and must be supported by written evidence identifying the relevant beneficiaries and exhibiting the written consent of each of them. The written evidence of testamentary documents required by r.57.5 will still be necessary.

Application for an order to bring in a will, etc.

PD 57 para.7.1

Any party applying for an order under s.122 of the Senior Courts Act 1981 ('the 1981 Act') must serve the application notice on the person against whom the order is sought.
(Section 122 of the 1981 Act empowers the court to order a person to attend court for examination, and to answer questions and bring in documents, if there are reasonable grounds for believing that such person has knowledge of a testamentary document. Rule 50(1) of the Non-Contentious Probate Rules 1987 makes similar provision where a probate claim has not been commenced).

PD 57 para.7.2

An application for the issue of a witness summons under s.123 of the 1981 Act—
  (1) may be made without notice; and
  (2) must be supported by written evidence setting out the grounds of the application.
(Section 123 of the 1981 Act empowers the court, where it appears that any person has in his possession, custody or power a testamentary document, to issue a witness summons ordering such person to bring in that document. Rule 50(2) of the Non-Contentious Probate Rules makes similar provision where a probate claim has not been commenced).

PD 57 para.7.3

An application under ss.122 or 123 of the 1981 Act should be made to a master or district judge.

PD 57 para.7.4

A person against whom a witness summons is issued under s.123 of the 1981 Act who denies that the testamentary document referred to in the witness summons is in his possession or under his control may file written evidence to that effect.

Administration pending the determination of a probate claim

PD 57 para.8.1

An application under s.117 of the Senior Courts Act 1981 for an order for the grant of administration pending the determination of a probate claim should be made by application notice in the probate claim.

PD 57 para.8.2

If an order for a grant of administration is made under s.117 of the 1981 Act—
  (1) Rules 69.4 to 69.7 shall apply as if the administrator were a receiver appointed by the court;
  (2) if the court allows the administrator remuneration under r.69.7, it may make an order under s.117(3) of the 1981 Act assigning the remuneration out of the estate of the deceased; and
  (3) every application relating to the conduct of the administration shall be made by application notice in the probate claim.

PD 57 para.8.3

An order under s.117 may be made by a master or district judge.

PD 57 para.8.4

If an order is made under s.117 an application for the grant of letters of administration should be made to the Principal Registry of the Family Division, First Avenue House, 42–49 High Holborn, London WC1V 6NP.

PD 57 para.8.5

The appointment of an administrator to whom letters of administration are granted following an order under s.117 will cease automatically when a final order in the probate claim is made but will continue pending any appeal.

See also **Discontinuance**.

PRO BONO REPRESENTATION

Costs order

Pt 46 r.46.7

  (2) Where the court makes an order under s.194(3) of the [Legal Services Act 2007]—
    (a) the court may order the payment to the prescribed charity of a sum no greater than the costs specified in Pt 45 to which the party with pro bono representation would

have been entitled in accordance with that Part and in respect of that representation had it not been provided free of charge; or

(b) where Pt 45 does not apply, the court may determine the amount of the payment (other than a sum equivalent to fixed costs) to be made by the paying party to the prescribed charity by—

    (i) making a **summary assessment**; or

    (ii) making an order for **detailed assessment**,

of a sum equivalent to all or part of the costs the paying party would have been ordered to pay to the party with pro bono representation in respect of that representation had it not been provided free of charge.

(3) Where the court makes an order under s.194(3) of the 2007 Act, the order must specify that the payment by the paying party must be made to the prescribed charity.

(4) The receiving party must send a copy of the order to the prescribed charity within seven days of receipt of the order.

(5) Where the court considers making or makes an order under s.194(3) of the 2007 Act, Pts 44–47 apply, where appropriate, with the following modifications—

(a) references to 'costs orders', 'orders about costs' or 'orders for the payment of costs' are to be read, unless otherwise stated, as if they refer to an order under s.194(3);

(b) references to 'costs' are to be read, as if they referred to a sum equivalent to the costs that would have been claimed by, incurred by or awarded to the party with pro bono representation in respect of that representation had it not been provided free of charge; and

(c) references to 'receiving party' are to be read, as meaning a party who has pro bono representation and who would have been entitled to be paid costs in respect of that representation had it not been provided free of charge.

PD 46 para.4.1

Where an order under s.194(3) of the Legal Services Act 2007 is sought, the party who has pro bono representation must prepare, file and serve a written statement of the sum equivalent to the costs that party would have claimed for that legal representation had it not been provided free of charge.

Value added tax

PD 44 para.14

Where an order is made under s.194(3) of the Legal Services Act 2007 any bill presented for agreement or assessment pursuant to that order must not include a claim for VAT.

PRODUCTION CENTRE

Pt 7 r.7.10

(1) There shall be a Production Centre for the issue of claim forms and other related matters.

(2) PD 7C makes provision for—

(a) which claimants may use the Production Centre;

(b) the type of claims which the Production Centre may issue;

(c) the functions which are to be discharged by the Production Centre;

(d) the place where the Production Centre is to be located; and

(e) other related matters.

(3) PD 7C may disapply or modify these rules as appropriate in relation to claims issued by the Production Centre.

PD 7C para.1.1

In [PD 7C]—
'the Centre' means the Production Centre;
'Centre user' means a person who is for the time being permitted to start a claim through the Centre, and includes a legal representative acting for such a person;
'officer' means the court officer in charge of the Centre or another officer of the Centre acting on the former's behalf;
'national creditor code' means the number or reference allotted to a Centre user by the officer;
'Code of Practice' means any code of practice which may at any time be issued by Her Majesty's Courts and Tribunals Service relating to the discharge by the Centre of its functions and the way in which a Centre user is to conduct business with the Centre; and
'data' means any information which is required to be given to the court or which is to be contained in any document to be sent to the court or to any party.

PD 7C para.1.2

For any purpose connected with the exercise of its functions, the Centre will be treated as part of the office of the court whose name appears on the claim form to which the functions relate, or in whose name the claim form is requested to be issued, and the officer will be treated as an officer of that court.

PD 7C para.1.3

(1) The functions of the Centre include the provision of a facility which, through the use of information technology, enables a Centre user to have claim forms issued and served, whether or not those claim forms are to be treated as issued in the Northampton County Court or in another county court.

(2) If a Centre user files claim forms in the name of Northampton County Court, the functions of the Centre also include—
  (a) the handling of defences and admissions;
  (b) the entry of judgment in default, on admission, on acceptance, or on determination;
  (c) the registration of judgments;
  (d) the issue of warrants of execution;
  (e) where the defendant is an individual, the transfer to the defendant's home court of any case that is to continue following the filing of a defence or where a hearing is required before judgment; or, where the defendant is not an individual, the transfer to the court for the area of the claimant's, or where legally represented, the claimant's legal representative's address; and
  (f) the transfer to the defendant's home court of any case for the questioning of the defendant pursuant to an order for information under Pt 71 or where enforcement of a judgment (other than by **warrant of execution**, **charging order** or **Third Party Debt Order**) is to follow.

PD 7C para.1.4

(1) Where the officer is to take any step, any rule or PD which requires a document to be filed before such step is taken will be treated as complied with if the data which that document would contain are delivered to the Centre in computer readable form in accordance with the Code of Practice.

(2) Data relating to more than one case may be included in a single document or delivery of data.

(3) Rules 6.4(3) and 6.21(4)(copies of documents to be served by the court) do not apply to any document which is to be produced by electronic means from data supplied by a Centre user.

(3A) The requirement in para.7.3 of PD 16 for documents to be attached to the particulars of contract claims does not apply to claims to be issued by the Centre, unless the particulars of claim are served separately in accordance with para.5.2 of this PD.

(4) PD 22 is modified as follows—

    (a) a single statement of truth may accompany each batch of requests to issue claim forms and may be in electronic form;

    (b) the form of such a statement must be: 'I believe that the facts stated in the attached claim forms are true.'; and

    (c) the signature of the appropriate person (as to which see para.3 of PD 22) may be in electronic form.

Claims which may not be issued through the centre

PD 7C para.2.1

The Centre will not issue any claim form which is to be issued in the High Court.

PD 7C para.2.2

The Centre will only issue a claim form if the claim is for a specified sum of money less than £100,000.

PD 7C para.2.3

The Centre will not issue any of the following types of claim—

(1) a claim against more than two defendants;

(2) a claim against two defendants where a different sum is claimed against each of them;

(3) a claim against the Crown;

(4) a claim for an amount in a foreign currency;

(5) a claim where either party is known to be a child or protected party within Pt 21;

(6) a claim where the claimant is a legally assisted person within the meaning of the Legal Aid Act 1988;

(7) a claim where the claimant's address for service as it appears on the claim form is not the UK.

(7A) a claim where the defendant's address for service as it appears on the claim form is not the UK.

(8) a claim which is to be issued under Pt 8.

Centre users

PD 7C para.3.1

Only a Centre user may start or conduct claims through the Centre.

PD 7C para.3.2

The officer may permit any person to be a Centre user.

PD 7C para.3.3

The officer may withdraw the permission for any person to be a Centre user.

PD 7C para.3.4

A Centre user must comply with the provisions of the Code of Practice in dealing with the Centre.

PD 7C para.3.5

The officer will allot a national creditor code to each Centre user.

Other modifications to the CPR

Powers of the officer to make orders

PD 7C para.5.1

The officer may make the following orders—
   (1) an order to set aside a default judgment where, after that judgment has been entered, the claim form is returned by the Post Office as undelivered;
   (2) an order to set aside a judgment on application by a Centre user;
   (3) an order to transfer a case to another county court for enforcement or for a judgment debtor to attend court for questioning pursuant to an order for information under CPR PT 71.

Filing separate particulars of claim

PD 7C para.5.2

   (1) Subject to the sub-paragraphs below, the claimant may serve and file particulars of claim separately from the claim form but the claimant must in the claim form—
      (a) state that the particulars of claim will follow; and
      (b) include a brief summary of the claim.
   (2) Where the claimant serves the particulars of claim separately from the claim form pursuant to sub-para. (1), the claimant must—
      (a) serve the particulars of claim in accordance with r. 7.4(1)(b); and
      (b) file a certificate of service in form N215 at the Centre within 14 days of service of the particulars of claim on the defendant.
   (3) The claimant must file the particulars of claim at the court to which the proceedings are transferred under para.1.3(2)(e) within 7 days of service of the notice of transfer.
   (4) Where the proceedings are not transferred under para.1.3(2)(e) and remain at the Centre, the claimant is not required to file the particulars of claim unless ordered to do so.

Procedure on the filing of a defence

PD 7C para.5.3

(1) This paragraph applies where a Centre user has started a claim in the Northampton County Court and the defendant has filed a defence to the claim or to part of the claim.
(2) On the filing of the defence the officer will serve a notice on the Centre user requiring the Centre user to state within 28 days whether the claim is to proceed.
(3) If the Centre user does not notify the officer within the time specified in the notice that the claim is to proceed, the claim will be stayed, and the officer will notify the parties accordingly.
(4) The proceedings will not be transferred as provided by para.1.3(2)(e) until the Centre user notifies the officer that the claim is to continue.

PROFESSIONAL NEGLIGENCE

See **Pre-action protocols**.

PROFESSIONAL NEGLIGENCE CLAIMS

Pre-Action Protocol for Professional Negligence

This Protocol is designed to apply when a cwishes to claim against a professional (other than construction professionals and healthcare providers) as a result of that professional's alleged negligence or equivalent breach of contract or breach of fiduciary duty. Although these claims will be the usual situation in which the protocol will be used, there may be other claims for which the Protocol could be appropriate. For a more detailed explanation of the scope of the Protocol, there is a Guidance Note.

This Protocol is not intended to replace other forms of Pre-Action Dispute Resolution (such as internal complaints procedures, the Surveyors and Valuers Arbitration Scheme, etc.). Where such procedures are available, parties are encouraged to consider whether they should be used. If, however, these other procedures are used and fail to resolve the dispute, the protocol should be used before litigation is started, adapting it where appropriate.

The courts will be able to treat the standards set in this Protocol as the normal reasonable approach. If litigation is started, it will be for the court to decide whether sanctions should be imposed as a result of substantial non-compliance with a protocol. Guidance on the courts' likely approach is given in the Protocols PD. The court is likely to disregard minor departures from this protocol and so should the parties as between themselves.

Both in operating the timetable and in requesting and providing information during the protocol period, the parties are expected to act reasonably, in line with the court's expectations of them.

PROHIBITION

See **Charging order**, **Stop order** and **Stop notice**.

PROSPECTIVE COSTS ORDERS

See **Administration of estates and trusts**.

PROTECTED BENEFICIARY

Pt 21 r.21.1

A protected party who lacks capacity to manage and control any money recovered by him or on his behalf or for his benefit in the proceedings.

Investment on behalf of a protected beneficiary

PD 21 para.10.1

The Court of Protection has jurisdiction to make decisions in the best interests of a protected beneficiary. Fees may be charged for the administration of funds and these must be provided for in any settlement.

PD 21 para.10.2

Where the sum to be administered for the benefit of the protected beneficiary is—
- (1) £ 30,000 or more, unless a person with authority as—
    - (a) the attorney under a registered enduring power of attorney;
    - (b) the donee of a lasting power of attorney; or
    - (c) the deputy appointed by the Court of Protection,
    to administer or manage the protected beneficiary's financial affairs has been appointed, the order approving the settlement will contain a direction to the litigation friend to apply to the Court of Protection for the appointment of a deputy, after which the fund will be dealt with as directed by the Court of Protection; or
- (2) under £30,000, it may be retained in court and invested in the same way as the fund of a child.

PD 21 para.10.3

A form of order transferring the fund to the Court of Protection is set out in Practice Form N292.

PD 21 para.10.4

In order for the Court Funds Office to release a fund which is subject to the statutory charge, the litigation friend or his legal representative or the person with authority referred to in para.10.2(1) must provide the appropriate regional office of the Legal Services Commission with an undertaking in respect of a sum to cover their costs, following which the regional office will advise the Court Funds Office in writing of that sum, enabling them to transfer the balance to the Court of Protection on receipt of a CFO Form 200 payment schedule authorised by the court.

PD 21 para.10.5

The CFO Form 200 should be completed and presented to the court where the settlement or trial took place for authorisation, subject to paras 10.6 and 10.7.

PD 21 para.10.6

Where the settlement took place in the Royal Courts of Justice the CFO form 200 must be completed and presented for authorisation—

(1) on behalf of a child, in the Masters' Support Unit, room E105, and
(2) on behalf of a protected beneficiary, in the Judgment and Orders Section in the Action Department, room E17.

PD 21 para.10.7

Where the trial took place in the Royal Courts of Justice, the CFO Form 200 is completed and authorised by the court officer.

PROTECTED PARTY

A party, or an intended party, who lacks capacity to conduct the proceedings.

Requirement for a litigation friend in proceedings by or against protected parties

Pt 21 r.21.2(1)

A protected party must have a **litigation friend** to conduct proceedings on his behalf.

PD 21 para.1.1

In proceedings where one of the parties is a protected party, the protected party should be referred to in the title to the proceedings as 'A.B. (a protected party by C.D. his litigation friend)'.

See also **Child, Guardian, Guardian's account** and **Litigation friend**.

PROTECTION FROM HARASSMENT ACT 1997

Pt 65 r.65.27

[Section V of Part 65] applies to proceedings under s.3 of the Protection from Harassment Act 1997.

Claims under s.3 of the 1997 Act

Pt 65 r.65.28

A claim under section 3 of the 1997 Act—
(a) shall be subject to the Part 8 procedure; and
(b) must be commenced—
  (i) if in the High Court, in the Queen's Bench Division;
  (ii) if in the county court, in the court for the district in which the defendant resides or carries on business or the court for the district in which the claimant resides or carries on business.

Applications for issue of a warrant of arrest under s.3(3) of the 1997 Act

Pt 65 r.65.29

(1) An application for a warrant of arrest under s.3(3) of the 1997 Act—
    (a) must be made in accordance with Pt 23; and
    (b) may be made without notice.
(2) The application notice must be supported by affidavit evidence which must—
    (a) set out the grounds for the application;
    (b) state whether the claimant has informed the police of the conduct of the defendant as described in the affidavit; and
    (c) state whether, to the claimant's knowledge, criminal proceedings are being pursued.

Warrant of arrest on application under s.3(3) of the 1997 Act

PD 65 para.14.1

In accordance with s.3(5) of the 1997 Act, a warrant of arrest on an application under s.3(3) of that Act may only be issued if—
(1) the application is substantiated on oath; and
(2) the judge has reasonable grounds for believing that the defendant has done anything which he is prohibited from doing by the injunction.

Proceedings following arrest

Pt 65 r.65.30

(1) The judge before whom a person is brought following his arrest may—
    (a) deal with the matter; or
    (b) adjourn the proceedings.
(2) Where the proceedings are adjourned and the arrested person is released—
    (a) the matter must be dealt with (whether by the same or another judge) within 28 days of the date on which the arrested person appears in court; and
    (b) the arrested person must be given not less than two days' notice of the hearing.

Allocation

PD 2B para.8.1(d)

Injunctions which a county court has jurisdiction to make may only be made by a Circuit Judge, except:
    (ii) section 3 of the Protection from Harassment Act 1997.

Hearings

PD 39A para.1.5

The hearing set out below shall in the first instance be listed by the court as hearing in private under r.39.2(3)(c), namely:

(9) proceedings brought under the Protection from Harassment Act 1997.

PROVISIONAL ASSESSMENT

Pt 47 r.47.15

(1) This rule applies to any detailed assessment proceedings commenced in the High Court or a county court on or after April 1, 2013 in which the costs claimed are the amount set out in para.14.1 of [PD47], or less.

(2) In proceedings to which this rule applies, the parties must comply with the procedure set out in Pt 47 as modified by para.14 of PD 47.

(3) The court will undertake a provisional assessment of the receiving party's costs on receipt of Form N258 and the relevant supporting documents specified in PD 47.

(4) The provisional assessment will be based on the information contained in the bill and supporting papers and the contentions set out in Precedent G (the points of dispute and any reply).

(5) The court will not award more than £1,500 to any party in respect of the costs of the provisional assessment.

(6) The court may at any time decide that the matter is unsuitable for a provisional assessment and may give directions for the matter to be listed for hearing. The matter will then proceed under r. 47.14 without modification.

(7) When a provisional assessment has been carried out, the court will send a copy of the bill, as provisionally assessed, to each party with a notice stating that any party who wishes to challenge any aspect of the provisional assessment must, within 21 days of the receipt of the notice, file and serve on all other parties a written request for an oral hearing. If no such request is filed and served within that period, the provisional assessment shall be binding upon the parties, save in exceptional circumstances.

(8) The written request referred to in para.(7) must—
    (a) identify the item or items in the court's provisional assessment which are sought to be reviewed at the hearing; and
    (b) provide a time estimate for the hearing.

(9) The court then will fix a date for the hearing and give at least 14 days' notice of the time and place of the hearing to all parties.

(10) Any party which has requested an oral hearing, will pay the costs of and incidental to that hearing unless—
    (a) it achieves an adjustment in its own favour by 20 per cent or more of the sum provisionally assessed; or
    (b) the court otherwise orders.

PD 47 para.14.1

The amount of costs referred to in r. 47.15(1) is £75,000.

PD 47 para.14.2

The following provisions of Pt 47 and this Practice Direction will apply to cases falling within r. 47.15—
    (1) rr. 47.1, 47.2, 47.4 to 47.13, 47.14 (except paras (6) and (7)), 47.16, 47.17, 47.20 and 47.21; and
    (2) paras 1, 2, 4 to 12, 13 (with the exception of paras 13.4 to 13.7, 13.9, 13.11 and 13.14), 15, and 16, of PD 47].

PD 47 para.14.3

In cases falling within r. 47.15, when the receiving party files a request for a detailed assessment hearing, that party must file—
  (a) the request in Form N258;
  (b) the documents set out at paras 8.3 and 13.2 of [PD 47];
  (c) an additional copy of the bill, including a statement of the costs claimed in respect of the detailed assessment drawn on the assumption that there will not be an oral hearing following the provisional assessment;
  (d) the offers made (those marked 'without prejudice save as to costs' or made under Pt 36 must be contained in a sealed envelope, marked 'Part 36 or similar offers', but not indicating which party or parties have made them);
  (e) completed Precedent G (points of dispute and any reply).

PD 47 para.14.4

  (1) On receipt of the request for detailed assessment and the supporting papers, the court will use its best endeavours to undertake a provisional assessment within six weeks. No party will be permitted to attend the provisional assessment.
  (2) Once the provisional assessment has been carried out the court will return Precedent G (the points of dispute and any reply) with the court's decisions noted upon it. Within 14 days of receipt of Precedent G the parties must agree the total sum due to the receiving party on the basis of the court's decisions. If the parties are unable to agree the arithmetic, they must refer the dispute back to the court for a decision on the basis of written submissions.

PD 47 para.14.5

When considering whether to depart from the order indicated by r. 47.15(10) the court will take into account the conduct of the parties and any offers made.

PD 47 para.14.6

If a party wishes to be heard only as to the order made in respect of the costs of the initial provisional assessment, the court will invite each side to make written submissions and the matter will be finally determined without a hearing. The court will decide what if any order for costs to make in respect of this procedure.

PROVISIONAL DAMAGES

Award of provisional damages

Pt 41 r.41.1

  (c) An award of damages for personal injuries under which—
      (i) damages are assessed on the assumption referred to in [s.32A of the Supreme Court Act 1981] or [s.51 of the County Courts Act 1984] that the injured person will not develop the disease or suffer the deterioration; and
      (ii) the injured person is entitled to apply for **further damages** at a future date if he develops the disease or suffers the deterioration.

Pt 41 r.41.2

(1) The court may make an order for an award of provisional damages if—
    (a) the particulars of claim include a claim for provisional damages; and
    (b) the court is satisfied that SCA s.32A or CCA s.51 applies.
(2) An order for an award of provisional damages—
    (a) must specify the disease or type of deterioration in respect of which an application may be made at a future date;
    (b) must specify the period within which such an application may be made; and
    (c) may be made in respect of more than one disease or type of deterioration and may, in respect of each disease or type of deterioration, specify a different period within which a subsequent application may be made.
(3) The claimant may make more than one application to extend the period specified under para.(2)(b) or (2)(c).

Judgment for an award of provisional damages

PD 41A para.2.1

When giving judgment at trial the judge will:
(1) specify the disease or type of deterioration, or diseases or types of deterioration, which
    (a) for the purpose of the award of immediate damages it has been assumed will not occur, and
    (b) will entitle the claimant to further damages if it or they do occur at a future date.
(2) give an award of immediate damages,
(3) specify the period or periods within which an application for further damages may be made in respect of each disease or type of deterioration, and
(4) direct what documents are to be filed and preserved as the case file in support of any application for further damages.

PD 41A para.2.2

The claimant may make an application or applications to extend the periods referred to in para.2.1(3) above.

PD 41A para.2.3

A period specified under para.2.1(3) may be expressed as being for the duration of the life of the claimant.

PD 41A para.2.4

The documents to be preserved as the case file ('the case file documents') referred to in para.2.1(4) will be set out in a schedule to the judgment as entered.

PD 41A para.2.5

Causation of any further damages within the scope of the order shall be determined when any application for further damages is made.

PD 41A para.2.6

A form for a provisional damages judgment is set out in the Annex to this PD.

Case file

PD 41A para.3.1

The case file documents must be preserved until the expiry of the period or periods specified or of any extension of them.

PD 41A para.3.2

The case file documents will normally include:
  (1) the judgment as entered,
  (2) the statements of case,
  (3) a transcript of the judge's oral judgment,
  (4) all medical reports relied on, and
  (5) a transcript of any parts of the claimant's own evidence which the judge considers necessary.

PD 41A para.3.3

The associate/court clerk will:
  (1) ensure that the case file documents are provided by the parties where necesary and filed on the court file,
  (2) endorse the court file
      (a) to the effect that it contains the case file documents, and
      (b) with the period during which the case file documents must be preserved, and
  (3) preserve the case file documents in the court office where the proceedings took place.

PD 41A para.3.4

Any subsequent order:
  (1) extending the period within which an application for further damages may be made, or
  (2) of the Court of Appeal discharging or varying the provisions of the original judgment or of any subsequent order under subpara.(1) above,
will become one of the case file documents and must be preserved accordingly and any variation of the period within which an application for further damages may be made should be endorsed on the court file containing the case file documents.

PD 41A para.3.5

On an application to extend the periods referred to in para.2.1(3) above a current medical report should be filed.

PD 41A para.3.6

Legal representatives are reminded that it is their duty to preserve their own case file.

Consent orders

PD 41A para.4.1

An application to give effect to a consent order for provisional damages should be made in accordance with CPR Pt 23. If the claimant is a child or protected party the approval of the court must also be sought and the application for approval will normally be dealt with at a hearing.

PD 41A para.4.2

The order should be in the form of a consent judgment and should contain:
   (1) the matters set out in para.2.1(1) to (3) above, and
   (2) a direction as to the documents to be preserved as the case file documents, which will normally be
      (a) the consent judgment,
      (b) any statements of case,
      (c) an agreed statement of facts, and
      (d) any agreed medical report(s).

PD 41A para.4.3

The claimant or his legal representative must lodge the case file documents in the court office where the proceedings are taking place for inclusion in the court file. The court file should be endorsed as in para.3.3(2) above, and the case file documents preserved as in para.3.3(3) above.

Default judgment

PD 41A para.5.1

Where a defendant:
   (1) fails to file an acknowledgment of service in accordance with CPR Pt 10, and
   (2) fails to file a defence in accordance with CPR Pt 15,
within the time specified for doing so, the claimant may not, unless he abandons his claim for provisional damages, enter judgment in default but should make an application in accordance with CPR Pt 23 for directions.

PD 41A para.5.2

The Master or district judge will normally direct the following issues to be decided:
   (1) whether the claim is an appropriate one for an award of provisional damages and if so, on what terms, and
   (2) the amount of immediate damages.

PD 41A para.5.3

If the judge makes an award of provisional damages, the provisions of paragraph 3 above apply.

Particulars of claim

PD 16 para.4.4

In a provisional damages claim the claimant must state in his particulars of claim:
   (1) that he is seeking an award of provisional damages under either s.32A of the Senior Courts Act 1981 or s.51 of the County Courts Act 1984,
   (2) that there is a chance that at some future time the claimant will develop some serious disease or suffer some serious deterioration in his physical or mental condition, and
   (3) specify the disease or type of deterioration in respect of which an application may be made at a future date.

Offer to settle a claim for provisional damages

Pt 36 r.36.6

   (1) An offeror may make a Pt 36 offer in respect of a claim which includes a claim for provisional damages.
   (2) Where he does so, the Pt 36 offer must specify whether or not the offeror is proposing that the settlement shall include an award of provisional damages.
   (3) Where the offeror is offering to agree to the making of an award of provisional damages the Pt 36 offer must also state—
       (a) that the sum offered is in satisfaction of the claim for damages on the assumption that the injured person will not develop the disease or suffer the type of deterioration specified in the offer;
       (b) that the offer is subject to the condition that the claimant must make any claim for further damages within a limited period; and
       (c) what that period is.
   (4) Rule 36.4 applies to the extent that a Pt 36 offer by a defendant includes an offer to agree to the making of an award of provisional damages.
   (5) If the offeree accepts the Pt 36 offer, the claimant must, within seven days of the date of acceptance, apply to the court for an order for an award of provisional damages under r.41.2.

PSEUDONYMS

Civil Recovery Proceedings PD para.3.1

If a member of the staff of the relevant Director gives written or oral evidence in any proceedings using a pseudonym in accordance with section 449 or section 449A of the [Proceeds of Crime Act 2002] Act—
   (1) the court must be informed that the witness is using a pseudonym; and
   (2) a certificate under s.449(3) or 449A(3) (as appropriate) of the Act must be filed or produced.

PUBLIC HEARING

See **Hearing**.

PUBLIC KIOSK SERVICE

PD 5C para.16.1

A version of the electronic court file allowing access only to those documents which are available to non-parties pursuant to r.5.4C(1) or 5.4C(1A) and subject to r.5.4C(4) will be made through a public kiosk service.
(Part 5 contains provisions about access to court documents by non-parties).

PD 5C para.16.2

Persons wishing to obtain copies of documents available to non-parties—
  (1) may select the documents they require using the computer facilities provided by the public kiosk service; and
  (2) must pay the appropriate fee.

PD 5C para.16.3

Electronic copies of the documents will be sent by e-mail to an address supplied by the person applying for copies.

See **Electronic working scheme**.

PUBLIC ORDER ACT 1936

Application under s.2(3)

PD 8A para.9.4

[Applications under s.2(3) are assigned to the Chancery Division.]

PD 8A para.13.1

The Attorney General may determine the persons who should be made defendants to an application under s.2(3) of the Public Order Act 1936.

PD 8A para.13.2

If the court directs an inquiry under s.2(3), it may appoint the Official Solicitor to represent any interests it considers are not sufficiently represented and ought to be represented.

PUBLIC TRUSTEE ACT 1906

PD 8A para.12.1

An application under the Public Trustee Act 1906 must be made—
  (1) where no proceedings have been issued, by a Pt 8 claim;
  (2) in existing proceedings, by a Pt 23 application.

PD 8A para.12.2

Without prejudice to ss.10(2) and 13(7) of the Public Trustee Act 1906, the jurisdiction of the High Court under the Act is exercised by a single judge of the Chancery Division sitting in private.

Q

QOCS

Qualified one-way costs shifting.

QUALIFIED ONE-WAY COSTS SHIFTING

Pt 44 r.44.13

(1) [Section II of Pt 44] applies to proceedings which include a claim for damages—
(a) for personal injuries;
(b) under the Fatal Accidents Act 1976; or
(c) which arises out of death or personal injury and survives for the benefit of an estate by virtue of s.1(1) of the Law Reform (Miscellaneous Provisions) Act 1934, but does not apply to applications pursuant to s.33 of the Senior Courts Act 1981 or s.52 of the County Courts Act 1984 (applications for pre-action disclosure), or where r.44.17 applies.
(2) In this Section, 'claimant' means a person bringing a claim to which this Section applies or an estate on behalf of which such a claim is brought, and includes a person making a counterclaim or an additional claim.

Effect of qualified one-way costs shifting

Pt 44 r.44.14

(1) Subject to rr.44.15 and 44.16, orders for costs made against a claimant may be enforced without the permission of the court but only to the extent that the aggregate amount in money terms of such orders does not exceed the aggregate amount in money terms of any orders for damages and interest made in favour of the claimant have been concluded and the costs have been assessed or agreed.
(3) An order for costs which is enforced only to the extent permitted by para.(1) shall not be treated as an unsatisfied or outstanding judgment for the purposes of any court record.

Exceptions to qualified one-way costs shifting where permission not required

Pt 44 r.44.15

Orders for costs made against the claimant may be enforced to the full extent of such orders without the permission of the court where the proceedings have been struck out on the grounds that—
(a) the claimant has disclosed no reasonable grounds for bringing the proceedings;
(b) the proceedings are an abuse of the court's process; or
(c) the conduct of—

    (i) the claimant; or
    (ii) a person acting on the claimant's behalf and with the claimant's knowledge of such
        conduct,
is likely to obstruct the just disposal of the proceedings.

Exceptions to qualified one-way costs shifting where permission required

Pt 44 r.44.16

(1) Orders for costs made against the claimant may be enforced to the full extent of such
orders with the permission of the court where the claim is found on the balance of
probabilities to be fundamentally dishonest.

(2) Orders for costs made against the claimant may be enforced up to the full extent of such
orders with the permission of the court, and to the extent that it considers just,
where—
    (a) the proceedings include a claim which is made for the financial benefit of a person
other than the claimant or a dependant within the meaning of s.1(3) of the Fatal
Accidents Act 1976 (other than a claim in respect of the gratuitous provision of care,
earnings paid by an employer or medical expenses); or
    (b) a claim is made for the benefit of the claimant other than a claim to which this Section
applies.

(3) Where para.(2)(a) applies, the court may, subject to r.46.2, make an order for costs
against a person, other than the claimant, for whose financial benefit the whole or part of
the claim was made.

PD 44 para.12.2

Examples of claims made for the financial benefit of a person other than the claimant or a
dependant within the meaning of s.1(3) of the Fatal Accidents Act 1976 within the meaning of
r.44.16(2) are subrogated claims and claims for credit hire.

PD 44 para.12.3

'Gratuitous provision of care' within the meaning of r.44.16(2)(a) includes the provision of
personal services rendered gratuitously by persons such as relatives and friends for things such
as personal care, domestic assistance, childminding, home maintenance and decorating, garden-
ing and chauffeuring.

PD 44 para.12.4

In a case to which r.44.16(1) applies (fundamentally dishonest claims)—
    (a) the court will normally direct that issues arising out of an allegation that the claim is
fundamentally dishonest be determined at the trial;
    (b) where the proceedings have been settled, the court will not, save in exceptional circum-
stances, order that issues arising out of an allegation that the claim was fundamentally
dishonest be determined in those proceedings;
    (c) where the claimant has served a notice of discontinuance, the court may direct that issues
arising out of an allegation that the claim was fundamentally dishonest be determined
notwithstanding that the notice has not been set aside pursuant to r.38.4;
    (d) the court may, as it thinks fair and just, determine the costs attributable to the claim having
been found to be fundamentally dishonest.

PD 44 para.12.5

The court has power to make an order for costs against a person other than the claimant under s.51(3) of the Senior Courts Act 1981 and r.46.2. In a case to which r.44.16(2)(a) applies (claims for the benefit of others)—

  (a) the court will usually order any person other than the claimant for whose financial benefit such a claim was made to pay all the costs of the proceedings or the costs attributable to the issues to which r.44.16(2)(a) applies, or may exceptionally make such an order permitting the enforcement of such an order for costs against the claimant.
  (b) the court may, as it thinks fair and just, determine the costs attributable to claims for the financial benefit of persons other than the claimant.

PD 44 para.12.6

In proceedings to which r. 44.16 applies, the court will normally order the claimant or, as the case may be, the person for whose benefit a claim was made to pay costs notwithstanding that the aggregate amount in money terms of such orders exceeds the aggregate amount in money terms of any orders for damages, interest and costs made in favour of the claimant.

PD 44 para.12.7

Assessments of costs may be on a standard or indemnity basis and may be subject to a summary or detailed assessment.

Transitional provision

PD 44 r.44.17

[Section II of Pt 44] does not apply to proceedings where the claimant has entered into a pre-commencement funding arrangement (as defined in r.48.2).

QUASH ORDERS, SCHEMES, ETC. OF A MINISTER OR GOVERNMENT DEPARTMENT

PD 8A para.22.1

This paragraph applies where the High Court has jurisdiction under any enactment, on the application of any person to quash or prohibit any—
  (1) order, scheme, certificate or plan of;
  (2) amendment or approval of a plan of;
  (3) decision of;
  (4) action on the part of,
a Minister or government department.

PD 8A para.22.2

The jurisdiction shall be exercisable by a single judge of the Queen's Bench Division.

PD 8A para.22.3

The claim form must be filed at the Administrative Court and served within the time limited by the relevant enactment for making the application. PD 54D applies to applications under this paragraph.

PD 8A para.22.4

Subject to para.22.6, the claim form must be served on the appropriate Minister or government department [means the Minister of the Crown or government department (1) by whom the order, scheme, certificate, plan, amendment, approval or decision in question was or may be made, authorised, confirmed, approved or given; (2) on whose part the action in question was or may be taken] and on the person indicated in the [Table set out in this paragraph].

PD 8A para.22.6

Where the application relates to an order made under the Road Traffic Regulation Act 1984, the claim form must be served—
  (1) if the order was made by a Minister of the Crown, on that Minister;
  (2) if the order was made by a local authority with the consent, or following a direction, of a Minister of the Crown, on that authority and also on that Minister;
  (3) in any other case, on the local authority by whom the order was made.

PD 8A para.22.7
Evidence at the hearing of an application under this paragraph is by witness statement.

PD 8A para.22.8

The applicant must—
  (1) file a witness statement in support of the application in the Administrative Court within 14 days after service of the claim form; and
  (2) serve a copy of the witness statement and of any exhibit on the respondent at the time of filing.

PD 8A para.22.9

The respondent must—
  (1) file any witness statement in opposition to the application in the Administrative Court within 21 days after service on him of the applicant's witness statement; and
  (2) serve a copy of his witness statement and of any exhibit on the applicant at the time of filing.

PD 8A para.22.10

A party must, when filing a witness statement, file a further copy of the witness statement, including exhibits, for the use of the court.

PD 8A para.22.11

Unless the court otherwise orders, the application will not be heard earlier than 14 days after the time for filing a witness statement by the respondent has expired.

See also **Quashing order.**

QUASHING OF AN ACQUITTAL

Pt 77 r.77.6

(1) This section contains rules about applications to quash an acquittal under s.54(3) of the Criminal Procedure and Investigations Act 1996 and applies in relation to acquittals in respect of offences alleged to have been committed on or after April 15, 1997.

(2) An application made under this section may be made only by the individual or body which acted as prosecutor in the proceedings which led to the acquittal.

(3) In this section—

   (b) 'acquitted person' means a person whose acquittal of an offence is the subject of a certification under s.54(2) of the 1996 Act, and 'acquittal' means the acquittal of that person of that offence;

   (c) 'magistrates' court' has the same meaning as in s.148 of the Magistrates' Courts Act 1980; and

   (d) 'record of court proceedings' means—
      (i) where the proceedings took place in the Crown Court, a transcript of the evidence; or
      (ii) where the proceedings took place in a magistrates' court, a transcript of the evidence if there is one and if not a note of the evidence made by the justices' clerk,

in the proceedings which led to the conviction for the administration of justice offence referred to in s.54(1)(b) of the 1996 Act or, as the case may be, the proceedings which led to the acquittal.

Time limit for making the application

Pt 77 r.77.7

(1) An application for an order quashing an acquittal under s.54(3) of the [Criminal Procedure and Investigations Act 1996] shall not be made later than 28 days after—
   (a) the expiry of the period allowed for—
      (i) appealing (whether by case stated or otherwise); or
      (ii) making an application for permission to appeal,
      against the conviction referred to in s.54(1)(b) of the 1996 Act; or
   (b) where an appeal notice is filed or an application for permission to appeal against that conviction is made, the determination of the appeal or application for permission to appeal.

(2) For the purpose of subpara.(1)(b), 'determination' includes abandonment within the meaning of rr.63.8 and 65.13 of the Criminal Procedure Rules 2010 or, as the case may be, r.11 of the Crown Court Rules 1982.

Where to make the application

Pt 77 r.77.8

(1) The jurisdiction of the High Court under s.54(3) of the 1996 Act may be exercised by a Divisional Court or a single judge of the High Court.

(2) The application must be made to the Administrative Court which will direct whether the application should be dealt with by a Divisional Court or a single judge of the High Court.

How to make the application

Pt 77 r.77.9

(1) The application must be made by filing a claim form pursuant to Pt 8.

(2) The claimant must file with the claim form—

    (a) a witness statement which deals with the conditions in s.55(1), (2) and (4) of the 1996 Act and which exhibits any relevant documents (which may include a copy of any record of court proceedings); and

    (b) a copy of the certification under s.54(2) of the 1996 Act.

Notice to acquitted person

Pt 77 r.77.10

(1) Within seven days of the claim form being issued by the court, the claimant must serve on the defendant (the acquitted person) a copy of the claim form and the documents which accompanied it.

(2) The documents referred to in para.(1) must be accompanied by a notice informing the defendant that—

    (a) the result of the application may be the making of an order by the High Court quashing the acquittal; and

    (b) the defendant must, if wishing to respond to the application, file—

        (i) within 14 days of service of the claim form an acknowledgment of service; and

        (ii) within 28 days of service of the claim form any witness statement on which the defendant wishes to rely.

(3) The claimant must file as soon as practicable after service of the notice on the defendant a certificate of service together with a copy of the notice.

Response to the application

Pt 77 r.77.11

(1) The defendant must, if wishing to respond to the application, file—

    (a) an acknowledgment of service within 14 days of service of the claim form under r.77.10; and

    (b) a witness statement which—

        (i) deals with the conditions in s.55(1), (2) and (4) of the 1996 Act; and

        (ii) exhibits any relevant documents (which may include a copy of any record of court proceedings),

    within 28 days of service of the claim form under r.77.10.

(2) The defendant must serve the documents in para.(1) on the claimant within seven days of filing them with the court.

(3) Rule 8.5(3) does not apply.

Further evidence

Pt 77 r.77.12

(1) The claimant may, not later than 10 days after the expiry of the period allowed in r.77.11(1), apply without notice for permission to file further evidence.

(2) Any order granting permission to file further evidence will specify the period within which that further evidence is to be filed.

(3) The claimant must serve a copy of the further evidence on the defendant within four days of filing that further evidence.

(4) Rule 8.5(5) and 8.5(6) do not apply.

Determination of the application to quash an acquittal (general provisions)

Pt 77 r.77.13

(1) The application to quash an acquittal will be determined without a hearing unless the court, of its own initiative or on the application by a party, orders otherwise.

(2) The determination of the application to quash an acquittal will not be made, and any hearing of the application (if ordered) will not take place, before the expiry of—

    (a) 10 days after the expiry of the period allowed under r.77.11(1); or

    (b) 10 days after the expiry of the period allowed by any order made under r.77.12(2).

(3) The court will serve notice of any order made on the application to quash an acquittal on the parties and where the court before which the acquittal or conviction occurred was—

    (a) a magistrates' court, on the designated officer; or

    (b) the Crown Court, on the appropriate officer of the Crown Court sitting at the place where the acquittal or conviction occurred.

Application for a hearing to determine the application to quash an acquittal

Pt 77 r.77.14

(1) An application for a hearing under r.77.13(1) must—

    (a) be made no later than seven days after the expiry of the period allowed—

        (i) under r.77.11(1); or

        (ii) by any order made under r.77.12(2); and

    (b) state whether a hearing is requested in order for a witness for the other party to attend to be cross-examined and, if so, the reasons for wishing the witness to attend.

(2) The party applying for a hearing must—

    (a) serve a copy of the application notice on the other party within four days of filing it with the court; and

    (b) file a certificate of service.

(3) The party served with an application for a hearing must file any representations within five days of service of the application notice.

(4) Subject to para.(5), the court will not determine an application for a hearing unless a certificate of service has been filed pursuant to subpara.(2)(b) and—

    (a) representations have been filed under para.(3); or

    (b) the period for filing representations under para.(3) has expired.

(5) Where—

    (a) no certificate of service has been filed; and

    (b) no representations under para.(3) have been received after the expiry of seven days from the date of filing the application,

the court may dismiss the application for a hearing.

Hearing to determine the application to quash an acquittal

Pt 77 r.77.15

Where a hearing is ordered, the court—
  (a) may order a witness to attend to be cross-examined—
      (i) of its own initiative; or
      (ii) on a without notice application by a party; and
  (b) will serve a notice on all parties setting out—
      (i) the date, time and place of the hearing; and
      (ii) the details of any witness ordered to attend for cross-examination.

Bail

RSC Ord.79 r.9

  (11) Where in pursuance of an order of the High Court or the Crown Court a person is
       released on bail in any criminal proceeding pending the determination of an appeal to the
       High Court or the Supreme Court or an application for a quashing order, then, upon the
       abandonment of the appeal or application, or upon the decision of the High Court or the
       Supreme Court being given, any justice (being a justice acting for the same petty sessions
       area as the magistrates' court by which that person was convicted or sentenced) may
       issue process for enforcing the decision in respect of which such appeal or application
       was brought or, as the case may be, the decision of the High Court or the Supreme
       Court.

QUASHING ORDER

Judicial review

Court's powers in respect of quashing orders

Pt 54 r.54.19

  (1) This rule applies where the court makes a quashing order in respect of the decision to
      which the claim relates.
  (2) The court may—
      (a) (i) remit the matter to the decision-maker; and
           (ii) direct it to reconsider the matter and reach a decision in accordance with the
                judgment of the court; or
      (b) in so far as any enactment permits, substitute its own decision for the decision to
          which the claim relates.
(Section 31 of the Supreme Court Act 1981 enables the High Court, subject to certain conditions,
to substitute its own decision for the decision in question).

See also **Quash orders, schemes, etc. of a minister or government department.**

QUEEN'S BENCH DIVISION

The Queen's Bench Division is one of the three divisions of the High Court, together with the
Chancery Division and Family Division

Outside London, the work of the Queen's Bench Division is administered in provincial offices known as District Registries. In London, the work is administered in the Central Office at the Royal Courts of Justice.

The work of the Queen's Bench Division is (with certain exceptions) governed by the CPR. The Administrative Court, the Admiralty Court, the Commercial Court and the Technology and Construction Court are all part of the Queen's Bench Division. However, each does specialised work requiring a distinct procedure that to some extent modifies the CPR. For that reason each has an individual Part of the CPR, its own PD and (except for the Administrative Court) its own Guide. The work of the Queen's Bench Division consists mainly of claims for—

Damages in respect of personal injury, negligence, breach of contract, libel and slander (defamation), other tortious acts, breach of statutory duty.

Non-payment of a debt, and possession of land or property.

Proceedings retained to be dealt with in the Central Office of the Queen's Bench Division will almost invariably be multi-track claims.

In many types of claim—for example claims in respect of negligence by solicitors, account-ants, etc. or claims for possession of land—the claimant has a choice whether to bring the claim in the Queen's Bench Division or in the Chancery Division. However, there are certain matters that may be brought only in the Queen's Bench Division, namely:

High Court Enforcement Officer's interpleader proceedings.

Applications for the enrolment of deeds.

Registration of foreign judgments under the Civil Jurisdictions and Judgments Act 1982 or the European Regulation.

Applications for bail in criminal proceedings.

Applications under the Administration of Justice Act 1920 and the Foreign Judg-ments (Reciprocal Enforcement) Act 1933 and European Regulations.

Registration and satisfaction of Bills of Sale.

Election Petitions.

Applications for orders to obtain evidence for foreign courts.

QUEEN'S BENCH DIVISION GUIDE

The Guide must be read with the CPR and the supporting PDs. The Guide does not have the force of law, but parties using the Queen's Bench Division will be expected to act in accordance with this Guide. Further guidance as to the practice of the Queen's Bench Division may be obtained from the Practice Master.

It is assumed throughout the Guide that the litigant intends to proceed in the Royal Courts of Justice. For all essential purposes, though, the Guide is equally applicable to the work of the District Registries, which deal with the work of the Queen's Bench Division outside London, but it should be borne in mind that there are some differences.

QUEEN'S BENCH MASTERS' PRACTICE FORMS

PD 4 para.4.1

Practice Forms that were previously known as Queen's Bench Masters' Practice Forms.

PD 4 para.4.2

These forms are reproduced in the Appendix to the Queen's Bench Guide, in practitioners' text books and on Her Majesty's Courts and Tribunals Service website.

PD 4 para.4.2

Where a rule permits, a party intending to use a witness statement as an alternative to an affidavit should amend any form in this Table to be used in connection with that rule so that 'witness statement' replaces 'affidavit' wherever it appears in the form.

R

RACE RELATIONS

See **Discrimination proceedings**.

RE-ALLOCATION TO A DIFFERENT TRACK

Pt 26 r.26.10

The court may subsequently re-allocate a claim to a different track.

PD 26 para.11.1

(1) Where a party is dissatisfied with an order made allocating the claim to a track he may appeal or apply to the court to re-allocate the claim.
(2) He should appeal if the order was made at a hearing at which he was present or represented, or of which he was given due notice.
(3) In any other case he should apply to the court to re-allocate the claim.

PD 26 para.11.2

Where there has been a change in the circumstances since an order was made allocating the claim to a track the court may re-allocate the claim. It may do so on application or on its own initiative.

Costs

Pt 26 r.26.10

(1) Any costs orders made before a claim is allocated will not be affected by allocation.
(2) Where—
   (a) a claim is allocated to a track; and
   (b) the court subsequently re-allocates that claim to a different track,
   then unless the court orders otherwise, any special rules about costs applying—
   (i) to the first track, will apply to the claim up to the date of re-allocation; and
   (ii) to the second track, will apply from the date of re-allocation.
(3) Where the court is assessing costs on the standard basis of a claim which concluded without being allocated to a track, it may restrict those costs to costs that would have been allowed on the track to which the claim would have been allocated if allocation had taken place.

PD 46 para.8.1

Before re-allocating a claim from the small claims track to another track the court must decide whether any party is to pay costs to the date of the order to re-allocate in accordance with the rules about costs contained in Pt 27. If it decides to make such an order the court will make a summary assessment of those costs in accordance with that Part.

Small claims track

Re-allocation of a claim from the small claims track to another track

Pt 27 r.27.15

Where a claim is allocated to the small claims track and subsequently re-allocated to another track, r.27.14 (**costs on the small claims track**) will cease to apply after the claim has been re-allocated and the fast track or multi-track costs rules will apply from the date of re-allocation.

RE-DETERMINATION

Pt 14 r.14.13

  (1) Where—
    (a) a court officer has determined the time and rate of payment under r.14.11 [**admission**]; or
    (b) a judge has determined the time and rate of payment under r.14.12 [**admission**] without a hearing,
  either party may apply for the decision to be re-determined by a judge.
  (2) An application for re-determination must be made within 14 days after service of the determination on the applicant.
  (3) Where an application for re-determination is made, the proceedings will be transferred to the defendant's home court if—
    (a) the only claim (apart from a claim for interest or costs) is for a specified amount of money;
    (b) the defendant is an individual;
    (c) the claim has not been transferred to another defendant's home court;
    (d) the claim was not started in the defendant's home court; and
    (e) the claim was not started in a specialist list.
  (3A) Where an application for re-determination is made the proceedings will be transferred to the preferred court if—
    (a) the only claim (apart from a claim for interest or costs) is for a specified amount of money;
    (b) the claim is a **designated money claim**;
    (c) the defendant is not an individual; and
    (d) the claim has not been transferred to another court.

RE-HEARING

Small claims track

Setting judgment aside and re-hearing

Pt 27 r.27.11

  (1) A party—
    (a) who was neither present nor represented at the hearing of the claim; and
    (b) who has not given written notice to the court under r.27.9(1)[notice by party for decision to be made in his absence],
  may apply for an order that a judgment under [Pt 27] shall be set aside and the claim re-heard.

(2) A party who applies for an order setting aside a judgment under this rule must make the application not more than 14 days after the day on which notice of the judgment was served on him.

(3) The court may grant an application under para.(2) only if the applicant—

(a) had a good reason for not attending or being represented at the hearing or giving written notice to the court under r.27.9(1); and

(b) has a reasonable prospect of success at the hearing.

(4) If a judgment is set aside—

(a) the court must fix a new hearing for the claim; and

(b) the hearing may take place immediately after the hearing of the application to set the judgment aside and may be dealt with by the judge who set aside the judgment.

(5) A party may not apply to set a judgment under this rule if the court dealt with the claim without a hearing under r.27.10 [court may, if all parties agree, deal with the claim without a hearing].

REALISATION OF PROPERTY

Confiscation and forfeiture in connection with criminal proceedings

RSC Ord.115 r.7

(1) An application by the prosecutor under s.29 [of the Drug Trafficking Act 1994] shall, where there have been proceedings against the defendant in the High Court, be made by an application in accordance with CPR Pt 23 and shall otherwise be made by the issue of a claim form.

(2) The application notice or claim form, as the case may be, shall be served with the evidence in support not less than seven days before the date fixed for the hearing of the application or claim on—

(a) the defendant;

(b) any person holding any interest in the realisable property to which the application relates; and

(c) the receiver, where one has been appointed in the matter.

(3) The application shall be supported by a witness statement or affidavit, which shall, to the best of the witness's ability, give full particulars of the realisable property to which it relates and specify the person or persons holding such property, and a copy of the confiscation order, of any certificate issued by the Crown Court under s.5(2) and of any charging order made in the matter shall be exhibited to such witness statement or affidavit.

(4) The Court may, on an application under s.29—

(a) exercise the power conferred by s.30(2) to direct the making of payments by a receiver;

(b) give directions in respect of the property interests to which the application relates; and

(c) make declarations in respect of those interests.

See **Confiscation and forfeiture in connection with criminal proceedings**.

RECEIVER

PD 69 para.1.1

The court's powers to appoint a receiver are set out in—

(1) section 37 of the Senior Courts Act 1981 (powers of the High Court with respect to injunctions and receivers);

(2) section 38 of the County Courts Act 1984 (remedies available in county courts); and

(3) section 107 of the County Courts Act 1984 (receivers by way of equitable execution).

PD 69 r.69.1

(1) [PD 69] contains provisions about the court's power to appoint a receiver [includes a manager].

PD 69 r.69.2

(1) The court may appoint a receiver—
    (a) before proceedings have started;
    (b) in existing proceedings; or
    (c) on or after judgment.
(2) A receiver must be an individual.
(3) The court may at any time—
    (a) terminate the appointment of a receiver; and
    (b) appoint another receiver in his place.

Applications before proceedings are started

PD 69 para.2.1

The court will normally only consider an application for the appointment of a receiver before proceedings are started after notice of the application has been served.

PD 69 para.2.2

Rule 25.2(2) [Time when an order for an interim remedy may be made] contains provisions about the grant of an order before proceedings are started.

Application for the appointment of a receiver

PD 69 r.69.3

An application for the appointment of a receiver—
    (a) may be made without notice ; and
    (b) must be supported by written evidence.

PD 69 para.4.1

The written evidence in support of an application for the appointment of a receiver must—
    (1) explain the reasons why the appointment is required;
    (2) give details of the property which it is proposed that the receiver should get in or manage, including estimates of—
        (a) the value of the property; and
        (b) the amount of income it is likely to produce;
    (3) if the application is to appoint a receiver by way of equitable execution, give details of—
        (a) the judgment which the applicant is seeking to enforce;

(b) the extent to which the debtor has failed to comply with the judgment;

(c) the result of any steps already taken to enforce the judgment; and

(d) why the judgment cannot be enforced by any other method; and

(4) if the applicant is asking the court to allow the receiver to act—

(a) without giving security; or

(b) before he has given security or satisfied the court that he has security in place,

explain the reasons why that is necessary.

PD 69 para.4.2

In addition, the written evidence should normally identify an individual whom the court is to be asked to appoint as receiver ('the nominee'), and should—

(1) state the name, address and position of the nominee;

(2) include written evidence by a person who knows the nominee, stating that he believes the nominee is a suitable person to be appointed as receiver, and the basis of that belief; and

(3) be accompanied by written consent, signed by the nominee, to act as receiver if appointed.

PD 69 para.4.3

If the applicant does not nominate a person to be appointed as receiver, or if the court decides not to appoint the nominee, the court may—

(1) order that a suitable person be appointed as receiver; and

(2) direct any party to nominate a suitable individual to be appointed.

PD 69 para.4.4

A party directed to nominate a person to be appointed as receiver must file written evidence containing the information required by para.4.2 and accompanied by the written consent of the nominee.

Related injunctions

PD 69 para.3.1

If a person applies at the same time for—

(1) the appointment of a receiver; and

(2) a related injunction,

he must use the same claim form or application notice for both applications.

PD 69 para.3.2

PD 2B sets out who may grant injunctions. Among other things, it provides that a Master or a District Judge may grant an injunction related to an order appointing a receiver by way of equitable execution.

Service of order appointing receiver

Pt 69 r.69.4

An order appointing a receiver must be served by the party who applied for it on—

(a) the person appointed as receiver;

(b) unless the court orders otherwise, every other party to the proceedings; and

(c) such other persons as the court may direct.

Appointment of receiver to enforce a judgment

PD 69 para.5

Where a judgment creditor applies for the appointment of a receiver as a method of enforcing a judgment, in considering whether to make the appointment the court will have regard to—

(1) the amount claimed by the judgment creditor;

(2) the amount likely to be obtained by the receiver; and

(3) the probable costs of his appointment.

Court's directions

PD 69 para.6.1

The court may give directions to the receiver when it appoints him or at any time afterwards.

PD 69 para.6.2

The court will normally, when it appoints a receiver, give directions in relation to security—see para.7 below.

PD 69 para.6.3

Other matters about which the court may give directions include—

(1) whether, and on what basis, the receiver is to be remunerated for carrying out his functions;

(2) the preparation and service of accounts—see r.69.8(1) and para.10 below;

(3) the payment of money into court; and

(4) authorising the receiver to carry on an activity or incur an expense.

Receiver's application for directions

Pt 69 r.69.6

(1) The receiver may apply to the court at any time for directions to assist him in carrying out his function as a receiver.

(2) The court, when it gives directions, may also direct the receiver to serve on any person

(a) the directions; and

(b) the application for directions.

PD 69 para.8.1

An application by a receiver for directions may be made by filing an application notice in accordance with Pt 23.

PD 69 para.8.2

If the directions sought by the receiver are unlikely to be contentious or important to the parties, he may make the application by letter, and the court may reply by letter. In such cases the receiver need not serve his letter or the court's reply on the parties, unless the court orders him to do so.

PD 69 para.8.3

Where a receiver applies for directions by letter, the court may direct him to file and serve an application notice.

Security

PD 69 r.69.5

(1) The court may direct that before a receiver begins to act or within a specified time he must either—
    (a) give such security as the court may determine; or
    (b) file and serve on all parties to the proceedings evidence that he already has in force sufficient security,
    to cover his liability for his acts and omissions as a receiver.
(2) The court may terminate the appointment of the receiver if he fails to—
    (a) give the security; or
    (b) satisfy the court as to the security he has in force,
    by the date specified.

PD 69 para.7.1

An order appointing a receiver will normally specify the date by which the receiver must—
    (1) give security; or
    (2) file and serve evidence to satisfy the court that he already has security in force.

PD 69 para.7.2

Unless the court directs otherwise, security will be given—
    (1) if the receiver is an authorised insolvency practitioner, by the bond provided by him under the Insolvency Practitioner Regulations 1990 or the Insolvency Practitioners Regulations 2005 extended to cover appointment as a court appointed receiver; or
    (2) in any other case, by a guarantee.

PD 69 para.7.3

Where the court has given directions about giving security, then either—
    (1) written evidence of the bond, the sufficiency of its cover and that it includes appointment as a court appointed receiver must be filed at court; or
    (2) a guarantee should be prepared in a form, and entered into with a clearing bank or insurance company, approved by the court.

Accounts

Pt 69 r.69.8

(1) The court may order a receiver to prepare and serve accounts.
(PD 69 contains provisions about directions for the preparation and service of accounts).
    (2) A party served with such accounts may apply for an order permitting him to inspect any document in the possession of the receiver relevant to those accounts.
    (3) Any party may, within 14 days of being served with the accounts, serve notice on the receiver—
        (a) specifying any item in the accounts to which he objects;
        (b) giving the reason for such objection; and
        (c) requiring the receiver, within 14 days of receipt of the notice, either—
            (i) to notify all the parties who were served with the accounts that he accepts the objection; or
            (ii) if he does not accept the objection, to apply for an examination of the accounts in relation to the contested item.
    (4) When the receiver applies for the examination of the accounts he must at the same time file—
        (a) the accounts; and
        (b) a copy of the notice served on him under this rule.
    (5) If the receiver fails to comply with para.(3)(c) of this rule, any party may apply to the court for an examination of the accounts in relation to the contested item.
    (6) At the conclusion of its examination of the accounts the court will certify the result.
(PD 40A provides for inquiries into accounts).

PD 69 r.10.1

When the court gives directions under r.69.8(1) for the receiver to prepare and serve accounts, it may—
    (1) direct the receiver to prepare and serve accounts either by a specified date or at specified intervals; and
    (2) specify the persons on whom he must serve the accounts.

PD 69 para.10.2

A party should not apply for an order under r.69.8(2) permitting him to inspect documents in the possession of the receiver, without first asking the receiver to permit such inspection without an order.

PD 69 para.10.3

Where the court makes an order under r.69.8(2), it will normally direct that the receiver must—
    (1) permit inspection within seven days after being served with the order; and
    (2) provide a copy of any documents the subject of the order within seven days after receiving a request for a copy from the party permitted to inspect them, provided that party has undertaken to pay the reasonable cost of making and providing the copy.

Non-compliance by receiver

Pt 69 r.69.9

(1) If a receiver fails to comply with any rule, PD or direction of the court the court may order him to attend a hearing to explain his non-compliance.

(2) At the hearing the court may make any order it considers appropriate, including—
   (a) terminating the appointment of the receiver;
   (b) reducing the receiver's remuneration or disallowing it altogether; and
   (c) ordering the receiver to pay the costs of any party.
(3) Where—
   (a) the court has ordered a receiver to pay a sum of money into court; and
   (b) the receiver has failed to do so,
   the court may order him to pay interest on that sum for the time he is in default at such rate as it considers appropriate.

Discharge of receiver

Pt 69 r.69.10

(1) A receiver or any party may apply for the receiver to be discharged on completion of his duties.
(2) The application notice must be served on the persons who were required under r.69.4 to be served with the order appointing the receiver.

Order discharging or terminating appointment of receiver

Pt 69 r.69.11

(1) An order discharging or terminating the appointment of a receiver may—
   (a) require him to pay into court any money held by him; or
   (b) specify the person to whom he must pay any money or transfer any assets still in his possession; and
   (c) make provision for the discharge or cancellation of any guarantee given by the receiver as security.
(2) The order must be served on the persons who were required under r.69.4 to be served with the order appointing the receiver.

Crown

Pt 66 para.66.7(1)

(b) [No] order for the appointment of a receiver under Part 69 may be made or have effect in respect of any money due [includes money accruing due, and money alleged to be due or accruing due] from the Crown.

See also **Receiver's remuneration**.

RECEIVER'S REMUNERATION

Pt 69 r.69.7

(1) A receiver may only charge for his services if the court—
   (a) so directs; and

(b) specifies the basis on which the receiver is to be remunerated.

(2) The court may specify—

    (a) who is to be responsible for paying the receiver; and

    (b) the fund or property from which the receiver is to recover his remuneration.

(3) If the court directs that the amount of a receiver's remuneration is to be determined by the court—

    (a) the receiver may not recover any remuneration for his services without a determination by the court; and

    (b) the receiver or any party may apply at any time for such a determination to take place.

(4) Unless the court orders otherwise, in determining the remuneration of a receiver the court shall award such sum as is reasonable and proportionate in all the circumstances and which takes into account—

    (a) the time properly given by him and his staff to the receivership;

    (b) the complexity of the receivership;

    (c) any responsibility of an exceptional kind or degree which falls on the receiver in consequence of the receivership;

    (d) the effectiveness with which the receiver appears to be carrying out, or to have carried out, his duties; and

    (e) the value and nature of the subject matter of the receivership.

(5) The court may refer the determination of a receiver's remuneration to a costs judge.

PD 69 para.9.1

A receiver may only charge for his services if the court gives directions permitting it and specifying how the remuneration is to be determined.

PD 69 para.9.2

The court will normally determine the amount of the receiver's remuneration on the basis of the criteria in r.69.7(4). Parts 43 to 48 (costs) do not apply to the determination of the remuneration of a receiver.

PD 69 para.9.3

Unless the court orders otherwise, the receiver will only be paid or be able to recover his remuneration after the amount of it has been determined.

PD 69 para.9.4

An application by a receiver for the amount of his remuneration to be determined must be supported by—

(1) written evidence showing—

    (a) on what basis the remuneration is claimed; and

    (b) that it is justified and in accordance with this Part; and

(2) a certificate signed by the receiver that he considers that the remuneration he claims is reasonable and proportionate.

PD 69 para.9.5

The court may, before determining the amount of a receiver's remuneration—

(1) require the receiver to provide further information in support of his claim; and

(2) appoint an assessor under r.35.15 to assist the court.

PD 69 para.9.6

Paragraphs 9.1 to 9.5 do not apply to expenses incurred by a receiver in carrying out his functions. These are accounted for as part of his account for the assets he has recovered, and not dealt with as part of the determination of his remuneration.

RECEIVING PARTY

Pt 43 r.43.2

A party entitled to be paid costs.

RECOGNISANCE

Pt 65 r.65.7

(1) Where, in accordance with para.2(2)(b) of Sch.15 to the [Housing Act 1996], the court fixes the amount of any recognisance with a view to it being taken subsequently, the recognisance may be taken by—
(a) a judge;
(b) a justice of the peace;
(c) a justices' clerk;
(d) a police officer of the rank of inspector or above or in charge of a police station; or
(e) where the arrested person is in his custody, the governor or keeper of a prison,
with the same consequences as if it had been entered into before the court.
(2) The person having custody of an applicant for bail must release him if satisfied that the required recognisances have been taken.

RECONSIDERATION

Application by secretary of state for reconsideration of decision

Pt 76 r.76.33

(1) This rule applies where the court proposes, in any proceedings to which [Part 76][control order proceedings in the High Court and (b) appeals to the Court of Appeal against an order of the High Court in such proceedings] applies, to serve notice on a relevant party of any—
(a) order or direction made or given in the absence of the Secretary of State; or
(b) any judgment.
(2) Before the court serves any such notice on the relevant party, it must first serve notice on the Secretary of State of its intention to do so.
(3) The Secretary of State may, within five days of being served with notice under para.(2), apply to the court to reconsider the terms of the order or direction or to review the terms of the proposed judgment if he considers that—
(a) his compliance with the order or direction; or
(b) the notification to the relevant party of any matter contained in the judgment, order or direction;
would cause information to be disclosed contrary to the public interest.
(4) Where the Secretary of State makes an application under para.(3), he must at the same time serve on the special advocate, if one has been appointed—

(a) a copy of the application; and

(b) a copy of the notice served on the Secretary of State pursuant to para.(2).

(5) Rule 76.29 (except for paras (6) and (7)) [consideration of Secretary of State's objection] shall, if a special advocate has been appointed, apply with any necessary modifications to the consideration of an application under para.(3) of this rule.

(6) The court must not serve notice on the relevant party as mentioned in para.(1) before the time for the Secretary of State to make an application under para.(3) has expired.

See **Financial restrictions proceedings.**

RECORDING OF PROCEEDINGS

PD 39A para.6.1

At any hearing, whether in the High Court or a county court, the proceedings will be tape recorded unless the judge directs otherwise.

PD 39A para.6.2

No party or member of the public may use unofficial recording equipment in any court or judge's room without the permission of the court. To do so without permission constitutes a contempt of court.

PD 39A para.6.3

Any party or person may require a transcript or transcripts of the recording of any hearing to be supplied to him, upon payment of the charges authorised by any scheme in force for the making of the recording or the transcript.

PD 39A para.6.4

Where the person requiring the transcript or transcripts is not a party to the proceedings and the hearing or any part of it was held in private under CPR r.39.2, para.6.3 does not apply unless the court so orders.

PD 39A para.6.5

Attention is drawn to para.7.9 of the Court of Appeal (Civil Division) Practice Direction which deals with the provision of transcripts for use in the Court of Appeal at public expense. [Attention is drawn to s.9 of the Contempt of Court Act 1981 (which deals with the unauthorised use of tape recorders in court) and to the PD ([1981] 1 W.L.R. 1526) which relates to it].

RECOVERY OF BENEFITS

Claim form

Statement of value to be included in the claim form

Pt 16 r.16.3

(1) This rule applies where the claimant is making a claim for money.

(2) The claimant must, in the claim form, state—

    (d) that the defendant may be liable to pay an amount of money which the court awards
to the claimant to the Secretary of State for Social Security under section 6 of the
Social Security (Recovery of Benefits) Act 1997.

RECOVERY OF LAND

See **Enforcement of judgment for possession of land** and **Possession claims**.

RECTIFICATION OF WILLS

See **Probate claim.**

REGISTER OF CLAIMS

Pt 5 r.5.4

    (1) A court or court office may keep a publicly accessible register of claims which have been
issued out of that court or court office.
    (2) Any person who pays the prescribed fee may, during office hours, search any available
register of claims.
(PD 5A contains details of available registers).

PD 5A para.4.1

Registers of claims which have been issued are available for inspection at the following offices
of the High Court at the Royal Courts of Justice:
    (1) the Central Office of the Queen's Bench Division;
    (2) Chancery Chambers;
    (3) the Admiralty and Commercial Court Registry.

PD 5A para.4.2

No registers of claims are at present available for inspection in county courts or in district
registries or other offices of the High Court.

REGISTERED TRADE MARKS AND OTHER
INTELLECTUAL PROPERTY RIGHTS

Allocation

Pt 63 r.63.13

Claims relating to matters arising out of the [Trade Marks Act 1994] and other intellectual
property rights set out in PD 63 must be started in—
    (a) the Chancery Division;
    (b) a patents county court; or
    (c) [a county court where there is also a **Chancery District Registry** excluding Caernarfon,
Mold and Preston].

PD 63 para.16.1

Other intellectual property rights

The other intellectual property rights referred to in r.63.13 are—
  (1) copyright;
  (2) rights in performances;
  (3) rights conferred under Pt VII of the [Copyright, Designs and Patents Act 1988];
  (4) design right;
  (5) Community design right;
  (6) association rights;
  (7) moral rights;
  (8) database rights;
  (9) unauthorised decryption rights;
  (10) hallmarks;
  (11) technical trade secrets litigation;
  (12) passing off;
  (13) protected designations of origin, protected geographical indications and traditional speciality guarantees;
  (14) registered trade marks; and
  (15) Community trade marks.

Starting the claim

PD 63 para.17.1

Except for claims started in a patents county court, a claim form to which s.II of Pt 63 applies must be marked in the top right hand corner 'Intellectual Property' below the title of the court in which it is issued.

PD 63 para.17.2

In the case of claims concerning registered trade marks and Community trade marks, the claim form must state the registration number of any trade mark to which the claim relates.

Reference to the court by the registrar or the comptroller

PD 63 para.18.1

This paragraph applies where—
  (1) an application is made to the registrar under the [Trade Marks Act 1994] and the registrar refers the application to the court; or
  (2) a reference is made to the [Comptroller General of Patents, Designs and Trade Marks] under s.246 of the 1988 Act and the Comptroller refers the whole proceedings or a particular question or issue to the court under s.251(1) of that Act.

PD 63 para.18.2

Where para.18.1 applies, the applicant under the 1994 Act or the person making the reference under s.246 of the 1988 Act, as the case may be, must start a claim seeking the court's determination of the reference within 14 days of receiving notification of the decision to refer.

PD 63 para.18.3

If the person referred to in para.18.2 does not start a claim within the period prescribed by that paragraph, that person will be deemed to have abandoned the reference.

PD 63 para.18.4

The period prescribed under para.18.2 may be extended by—
  (1) the registrar or the Comptroller as the case may be; or
  (2) the court
where a party so applies, even if the application is not made until after the expiration of that period.

Application to the court under s.19 of the Trade Marks Act 1994

PD 63 para.19.1

Where an application is made under s.19 of the 1994 Act, the applicant must serve the claim form or application notice on all identifiable persons having an interest in the goods, materials or articles within the meaning of s.19 of the 1994 Act.

Order affecting entry in the register of trade marks

PD 63 para.20.1

Where any order of the court affects the validity of an entry in the register, the provisions of paras 14.1 and 14.2 apply.

European community trade marks

PD 63 para.21.1

The Chancery Division, the patents county court at the Central London County Court and the county courts where there is also a Chancery district registry, except Caernarfon, Mold and Preston, are designated Community trade mark courts for the purposes of art.91(1) of Council Regulation (EC) 40/94.

PD 63 para.21.2

Where a counterclaim is filed at the Community trade mark court, for revocation or for a declaration of invalidity of a Community trade mark, the Community trade mark court will inform the Office for Harmonisation in the Internal Market of the date on which the counterclaim was filed, in accordance with art.96(4) of Council Regulation (EC) 40/94.

PD 63 para.21.3

On filing a counterclaim under para.21.2, the party filing it must inform the Community trade mark court in writing that it is a counterclaim to which para.21.2 applies and that the Office for Harmonisation in the Internal Market needs to be informed of the date on which the counterclaim was filed.

PD 63 para.21.4

Where the Community trade mark court has given a judgment which has become final on a counterclaim for revocation or for a declaration of invalidity of a Community trade mark, the Community trade mark court will send a copy of the judgment to the Office for Harmonisation in the Internal Market, in accordance with art.96(6) of Council Regulation (EC) 40/94.

PD 63 para.21.5

The party in whose favour judgment is given under para.21.4 must inform the Community trade mark court at the time of judgment that para.21.4 applies and that the Office for Harmonisation in the Internal Market needs to be sent a copy of the judgment.

Claim for additional damages under s.97(2), s.191J(2) or s.229(3) of the Copyright, Designs and Patents Act 1988

PD 63 para.22.1

Where a claimant seeks to recover additional damages under s.97(2), s.191J(2) or s.229(3) of the 1988 Act, the particulars of claim must include—
    (1) a statement to that effect; and
    (2) the grounds for claiming them.

Application for delivery up or forfeiture under the Copyright, Designs and Patents Act 1988

PD 63 para.23.1

An applicant who applies under ss.99, 114, 195, 204, 230 or 231 of the 1988 Act for delivery up or forfeiture must serve—
    (1) the claim form; or
    (2) application notice, where appropriate,
on all identifiable persons who have an interest in the goods, material or articles within the meaning of ss.114, 204 or 231 of the 1988 Act.

Association rights

PD 63 para.24.1

Where an application is made under regulations made under s.7 of the Olympic Symbol etc (Protection) Act 1995, the applicant must serve the claim form or application notice on all identifiable persons having an interest in the goods, materials or articles within the meaning of the regulations.

REGISTERS OF CERTIFICATES

See **Register of foreign judgments.**

REGISTERS OF FOREIGN JUDGMENTS

PD 74A para.3

There will be kept in the Central Office of the Senior Courts at the Royal Courts of Justice, under the direction of the Senior Master—
  (1) registers of foreign judgments ordered by the High Court to be enforced following applications under—
    (a) section 9 of the [Administration of Justice Act 1920];
    (b) section 2 of the Foreing Judgments (Reciprocol Enforcement) Act 1933;
    (c) section 4 of the 1Civil Jurisdiction and Judgments Act 1982;
    (d) the **Judgments Regulation**; or
    (e) the **Lugano Convention**.
  (2) registers of certificates issued for the enforcement in foreign countries of High Court judgments under the 1920, 1933 and 1982 Acts, and under art.54 of the Judgments Regulation and art.54 of the Lugano Convention;
  (3) a register of certificates filed in the Central Office of the High Court under r.74.15(2) for the enforcement of money judgments given by the courts of Scotland or Northern Ireland;
  (4) a register of certificates issued under r.74.16(3) for the enforcement of non-money judgments given by the courts of Scotland or Northern Ireland;
  (5) registers of certificates issued under rr.74.17 and 74.18 for the enforcement of High Court judgments in Scotland or Northern Ireland under Sch.6 or Sch.7 to the 1982 Act; and
  (6) a register of Community judgments and Euratom inspection orders ordered to be registered under art.3 of the European Communities (Enforcement of Community Judgments) Order 1972.

RELIEF FROM SANCTIONS

Pt 3 r.3.9

  (1) On an application for relief from any sanction imposed for a failure to comply with any rule, PD or court order, the court will consider all the circumstances of the case, so as to enable it to deal justly with the application, including the need—
    (a) for litigation to be conducted efficiently and at proportionate cost;
    (b) to enforce compliance with rules, PDs and orders;
    (c) whether the failure to comply was intentional;
    (d) whether there is a good explanation for the failure;
    (e) the extent to which the party in default has complied with other rules, PD, court order and any relevant preaction protocol;
    (f) whether the failure to comply was caused by the party or his legal representative;
    (g) whether the trial date or the likely trial date can still be met if relief is granted;
    (h) the effect which the failure to comply had on each party; and
    (i) the effect which the granting of relief would have on each party.

(2) An application for relief must be supported by evidence.

REOPENING OF FINAL APPEALS

Pt 52 para.52.17

(1) The Court of Appeal or the High Court will not reopen a final determination of any appeal unless—
    (a) it is necessary to do so in order to avoid real injustice;
    (b) the circumstances are exceptional and make it appropriate to reopen the appeal; and
    (c) there is no alternative effective remedy.
(2) In paras (1), (3), (4) and (6), "appeal" includes an application for permission to appeal.
(3) This rule does not apply to appeals to a county court.
(4) Permission is needed to make an application under this rule to reopen a final determination of an appeal even in cases where under r. 52.3(1) permission was not needed for the original appeal.
(5) There is no right to an oral hearing of an application for permission unless, exceptionally, the judge so directs.
(6) The judge will not grant permission without directing the application to be served on the other party to the original appeal and giving him an opportunity to make representations.
(7) There is no right of appeal or review from the decision of the judge on the application for permission, which is final.
(8) The procedure for making an application for permission is set out in PD52 [A and C].

REPLY TO DEFENCE

Pt 15 r.15.8

If a claimant files a reply to the defence, he must—
    (a) file his reply when he files his **allocation questionnaire; and**
    (b) serve his reply on the other parties at the same time as he files it.

PD 15 para.3.2

Where a claimant serves a reply and a defence to counterclaim, the reply and defence to counterclaim should normally form one document with the defence to counterclaim following on from the reply.

PD 15 para.3.2A

Rule 15.8(a) provides that a claimant must file any reply with his allocation questionnaire. Where the date by which he must file his allocation questionnaire is later than the date by which he must file his defence to counterclaim (because the time for filing the allocation questionnaire under r.26.3(6) is more than 14 days after the date on which it is deemed to be served), the court will normally order that the defence to counterclaim must be filed by the same date as the reply. where the court does not make such an order the reply and defence to counterclaim may form separate documents

Statement of case after a reply to be filed

Pt 15 r.15.9

A party may not file or serve any statement of case after a reply without the permission of the court.

Commercial court

Pt 58 r.58.10

(1) Part 15 (defence and reply) applies to claims in the **Commercial List** with the modification to r.15.8 that the claimant must—
(a) file any reply to a defence; and
(b) serve it on all other parties,
within 21 days after service of the defence

Mercantile courts

Pt 59 r.59.9

(1) Part 15 (Defence and Reply) applies to **mercantile claims** with the modification to r.15.8 that the claimant must—
(a) file any reply to a defence; and
(b) serve it on all other parties,
within 21 days after service of the defence.

Technology and construction court claims

Pt 60 r.60.5

Part 15 (Defence and Reply) applies to **TCC claims** with the modification to r.15.8 that the claimant must—
(a) file any reply to a defence; and
(b) serve it on all other parties;
within 21 days after service of the defence.

REPRESENTATION OF THE PEOPLE ACT 1983

PD 52D para.31.1

(1) This paragraph applies in relation to an appeal against a decision of a registration officer, being a decision referred to in s.56(1) of the Representation of the People Act 1983 ('the Act').
(2) Where a person ('the appellant') has given notice of such an appeal in accordance with the relevant requirements of s.56, and of the regulations made under s.53 ('the Regulations'), of the Act, the registration officer must, within seven days after he receives the notice, forward—

(a) the notice; and
(b) the statement required by the regulations,
by post to the county court.
(3) The respondents to the appeal will be—
    (a) the registration officer; and
    (b) if the decision of the registration officer was given in favour of any other person than the appellant, that other person.
(4) On the hearing of the appeal—
    (a) the statement forwarded to the court by the registration officer, and any document containing information submitted to the court by the registration officer pursuant to the Regulations, are admissible as evidence of the facts stated in them; and
    (b) the court—
        (i) may draw any inference of fact that the registration officer might have drawn; and
        (ii) may give any decision and make any order that the registration officer ought to have given or made.
(5) A respondent to an appeal (other than the registration officer) is not liable for nor entitled to costs, unless he appears before the court in support of the registration officer's decision.
(6) Rule 52.4, and paras 5, 6 and 7 of this PD , do not apply to an appeal to which this paragraph applies.

Special provision in relation to anonymous entries in the register

PD 52D para.31.2

(1) In this paragraph—
'anonymous entry' has the meaning given by s.9B(4) of the Representation of the People Act 1983;
'appeal notice' means the notice required by reg.32 of the Representation of the People (England and Wales) Regulations 2001.
(2) This paragraph applies to an appeal to a county court to which para.24.4 applies if a party to the appeal is a person—
    (a) whose entry in the register is an anonymous entry; or
    (b) who has applied for such an entry.
(3) This paragraph also applies to an appeal to the Court of Appeal from a decision of a county court in an appeal to which para.24.4 applies.
(4) The appellant may indicate in his appeal notice that he has applied for an anonymous entry, or that his entry in the register is an anonymous entry.
(5) The respondent or any other person who applies to become a party to the proceedings may indicate in a respondent's notice or an application to join the proceedings that his entry in the register is an anonymous entry, or that he has applied for an anonymous entry.
(6) Where the appellant gives such an indication in his appeal notice, the court will refer the matter to a district judge for directions about the further conduct of the proceedings, and, in particular, directions about how the matter should be listed in the court list.
(7) Where the court otherwise becomes aware that a party to the appeal is a person referred to in subpara. (2), the court will give notice to the parties that no further step is to be taken until the court has given any necessary directions for the further conduct of the matter.
(8) In the case of proceedings in a county court, the hearing will be in private unless the court orders otherwise.
(9) In the case of proceedings in the Court of Appeal, the hearing may be in private if the court so orders.

Appeals selected as test cases

PD 52D para.31.3

(1) Where two or more appeals to which para.24.4 applies involve the same point of law, the court may direct that one appeal ('the test-case appeal') is to be heard first as a test case.
(2) The court will send a notice of the direction to each party to all of those appeals.
(3) Where any party to an appeal other than the test-case appeal gives notice to the court, within seven days after the notice is served on him, that he desires the appeal to which he is a party to be heard—
    (a) the court will hear that appeal after the test-case appeal is disposed of;
    (b) the court will give the parties to that appeal notice of the day on which it will be heard; and
    (c) the party who gave the notice is not entitled to receive any costs of the separate hearing of that appeal unless the judge otherwise orders.
(4) Where no notice is given under subpara.(3) within the period limited by that paragraph—
    (a) the decision on the test-case appeal binds the parties to each of the other appeals;
    (b) without further hearing, the court will make, in each other appeal, an order similar to the order in the test-case appeal; and
    (c) the party to each other appeal who is in the same interest as the unsuccessful party to the selected appeal is liable for the costs of the test-case appeal in the same manner and to the same extent as the unsuccessful party to that appeal and an order directing him to pay such costs may be made and enforced accordingly.
(5) Subpara.(4)(a) does not affect the right to appeal to the Court of Appeal of any party to an appeal other than the test-case appeal.

REPRESENTATIVE CAPACITY

See **Legal aid**.

REPRESENTATIVE PARTIES

Representative parties with same interest

Pt 19 r.19.6

(1) Where more than one person has the same interest in a claim—
    (a) the claim may be begun; or
    (b) the court may order that the claim be continued,
by or against one or more of the persons who have the same interest as representatives of any other persons who have that interest.
(2) The court may direct that a person may not act as a representative.
(3) Any party may apply to the court for an order under para.(2).
(4) Unless the court otherwise directs any judgment or order given in a claim in which a party is acting as a representative under this rule—
    (a) is binding on all persons represented in the claim; but
    (b) may only be enforced by or against a person who is not a party to the claim with the permission of the court.
(5) This rule does not apply to a claim to which r.19.7 [representation of interested persons who cannot be ascertained etc.] applies.

Representation of interested persons who cannot be ascertained etc.

Pt 19 r.19.7

(1) This rule applies to claims about—
   (a) the estate of a deceased person;
   (b) property subject to a trust; or
   (c) the meaning of a document, including a statute.
(2) The court may make an order appointing a person to represent any other person or persons in the claim where the person or persons to be represented—
   (a) are unborn;
   (b) cannot be found;
   (c) cannot easily be ascertained; or
   (d) are a class of persons who have the same interest in a claim and—
      (i) one or more members of that class are within subparas (a), (b) or (c); or
      (ii) to appoint a representative would further the overriding objective.
(3) An application for an order under para.(2)—
   (a) may be made by—
      (i) any person who seeks to be appointed under the order; or
      (ii) any party to the claim; and
   (b) may be made at any time before or after the claim has started.
(4) An application notice for an order under para.(2) must be served on—
   (a) all parties to the claim, if the claim has started;
   (b) the person sought to be appointed, if that person is not the applicant or a party to the claim; and
   (c) any other person as directed by the court.
(5) The court's approval is required to settle a claim in which a party is acting as a representative under this rule.
(6) The court may approve a settlement where it is satisfied that the settlement is for the benefit of all the represented persons.
(7) Unless the court otherwise directs, any judgment or order given in a claim in which a party is acting as a representative under this rule—
   (a) is binding on all persons represented in the claim; but
   (b) may only be enforced by or against a person who is not a party to the claim with the permission of the court.

Representation of beneficiaries by trustees, etc.

Pt 19 r.19.7A

(1) A claim may be brought by or against trustees, executors or administrators in that capacity without adding as parties any persons who have a beneficial interest in the trust or estate ('the beneficiaries').
(2) Any judgment or order given or made in the claim is binding on the beneficiaries unless the court orders otherwise in the same or other proceedings.

See **Judgments and orders, Parties, Personal representative** and **Postal Services Act 2000**.

RESERVED JUDGMENT

PD 40E para.1.1

[PD 40E] applies to all reserved judgments which the court intends to hand down in writing.

Availability of reserved judgments before handing down

PD 40E para.2.1

Where judgment is to be reserved the judge (or Presiding Judge) may, at the conclusion of the hearing, invite the views of the parties' legal representatives as to the arrangements made for the handing down of the judgment.

PD 40E para.2.2

Unless the court directs otherwise, the following provisions of this paragraph apply where the judge or Presiding Judge is satisfied that the judgment will attract no special degree of confidentiality or sensitivity.

PD 40E para.2.3

The court will provide a copy of the draft judgment to the parties' legal representatives by 16.00 on the second working day [any day on which the relevant court office is open] before handing down, or at such other time as the court may direct.

PD 40E para.2.4

A copy of the draft judgment may be supplied, in confidence, to the parties provided that—
  (a) neither the draft judgment nor its substance is disclosed to any other person or used in the public domain; and
  (b) no action is taken (other than internally) in response to the draft judgment, before the judgment is handed down.

PD 40E para.2.5

Where a copy of the draft judgment is supplied to a party's legal representatives in electronic form, they may supply a copy to that party in the same form.

PD 40E para.2.6

If a party to whom a copy of the draft judgment is supplied under para.2.4 is a partnership, company, government department, local authority or other organisation of a similar nature, additional copies may be distributed in confidence within the organisation, provided that all reasonable steps are taken to preserve its confidential nature and the requirements of para.2.4 are adhered to.

PD 40E para.2.7

If the parties or their legal representatives are in any doubt about the persons to whom copies of the draft judgment may be distributed they should enquire of the judge or Presiding Judge.

PD 40E para.2.8

Any breach of the obligations or restrictions under para.2.4 or failure to take all reasonable steps under para.2.6 may be treated as contempt of court.

PD 40E para.2.9

The case will be listed for judgment, and judgment handed down at the appropriate time.

Corrections to the draft judgment

PD 40E para.3.1

Unless the parties or their legal representatives are told otherwise when the draft judgment is circulated, any proposed corrections to the draft judgment should be sent to the clerk of the judge who prepared the draft with a copy to any other party.

Orders consequential on judgment

PD 40E para.4.1

Following the circulation of the draft judgment the parties or their legal representatives must seek to agree orders consequential upon the judgment.

PD 40E para.4.2

In respect of any draft agreed order the parties must—
(a) fax or e-mail a copy to the clerk to the judge or Presiding Judge (together with any proposed corrections or amendments to the draft judgment); and
(b) file four copies (with completed backsheets) in the relevant court office [office of the court in which judgment is to be given], by 12 noon on the working day before handing down.

PD 40E para.4.3

A copy of a draft order must bear the case reference, the date of handing down and the name of the judge or Presiding Judge.

PD 40E para.4.4

Where a party wishes to apply for an order consequential on the judgment the application must be made by filing written submissions with the clerk to the judge or Presiding Judge by 12 noon on the working day before handing down.

PD 40E para.4.5

Unless the court orders otherwise—
(a) where judgment is to be given by an appeal court (which has the same meaning as in r.52.1(3)(b)), the application will be determined without a hearing; and
(b) where judgment is to be given by any other court, the application will be determined at a hearing.

Attendance at handing down

PD 40E para.5.1

If there is not to be an oral hearing of an application for an order consequential on judgment—
  (a) the parties' advocates need not attend on the handing down of judgment; and
  (b) the judgment may be handed down by a judge sitting alone.

PD 40E para.5.2

Where para.5.1(a) applies but an advocate does attend the handing down of judgment, the court may if it considers such attendance unnecessary, disallow the costs of the attendance.

RESPONDENT

Pt 23 r.23.1

  (a) the person against whom the order is sought; and
  (b) such other person as the court may direct.

REVENUE AND CUSTOMS

PD 7D para.1.1

PD [7D] applies to claims by HM Revenue and Customs for the recovery of—
  (a) Income Tax,
  (b) Corporation Tax,
  (c) Capital Gains Tax,
  (d) Interest, penalties and surcharges on Income Tax, Corporation Tax or Capital Gains Tax which by virtue of s.69 of the Taxes Management Act 1970 are to be treated as if they are taxes due and payable,
  (e) National Insurance Contributions and interest, penalties and surcharges thereon,
  (f) student loan repayments deducted by and recoverable from an employer under Pt IV of the Education (Student Loans) (Repayment) Regulations 2000 (SI 2000/944),
  (g) Value added tax and interest and surcharges thereon,
  (h) Insurance premium tax and interest and penalties thereon,
  (i) Stamp duty land tax and interest and penalties thereon,
  (j) the following environmental taxes—
      (i) landfill tax and interest and penalties thereon,
      (ii) aggregates levy and interest and penalties thereon, and
      (iii) climate change levy and interest and penalties thereon,
  (k) the following duties of customs and excise—
      (i) amusement machine licence duty and penalties thereon,
      (ii) air passenger duty and interest and penalties thereon,
      (iii) beer duty and penalties thereon,
      (iv) bingo duty and penalties thereon,
      (v) cider and perry duty,
      (vi) excise and spirits duty,
      (vii) excise wine duty,
      (viii) gaming duty and penalties thereon,

   (ix) general betting duty,
   (x) lottery duty and penalties thereon,
   (xi) REDS (registered excise dealers and shippers) duty,
   (xii) road fuel duty and penalties thereon,
   (xiii) tobacco duty, and
   (xiv) wine and made-wine duty.

Fixed costs

Pt 45 r.45.33

(1) Section V [of Pt 45] sets out the amounts which, unless the court orders otherwise, are to be allowed in respect of HM Revenue and Customs charges in the cases to which [s.V] applies.

(4) s.V [of Pt 45] applies where the only claim is a claim conducted by an HMRC Officer in the county court for recovery of a debt and the Commissioners obtain judgment on the claim.

(5) Any appropriate court fee will be allowed in addition to the costs set out in [s.V of Pt 45].

(6) The claim form may include a claim for fixed commencement costs.

Procedure

PD 7D para.2.1

If a defence is filed, the court will fix a date for the hearing.

PD 7D para.2.2

Part 26 (Case management—preliminary stage) apart from CPR r.26.2 (automatic transfer) does not apply to claims to which this PD applies.

At the hearing

PD 7D para.3.1

On the hearing date the court may dispose of the claim.
(Section 25A(1) and (2) of the Commissioners for Revenue and Customs Act 2005 ('the 2005 Act') provides that a certificate of an officer of Revenue and Customs that, to the best of that officer's knowledge and belief, a sum payable to the Commissioners under or by virtue of an enactment or by virtue of a contract settlement (within the meaning of s.25(6) of the 2005 Act) has not been paid, is sufficient evidence that the sum mentioned in the certificate is unpaid).

PD 7D para.3.2

But exceptionally, if the court does not dispose of the claim on the hearing date it may give case management directions, which may, if the defendant has filed a defence, include allocating the case.

Amount of fixed commencement costs in a county court claim for the recovery of money

Pt 45 r.45.34

The amount of fixed commencement costs in a claim to which r.45.45.33 applies—
  (a) shall be calculated by reference to Table 7 [of Pt 45]; and
  (b) the amount claimed in the claim form is to be used for determining which claim band in Table 7 applies.

Costs on entry of judgment in a county court claim for recovery of money

Pt 45 r.35

Where—
  (a) An HMRC Officer has claimed fixed commencement costs under r.45.34; and
  (b) judgment is entered in a claim to which r.45.44 applies the amount to be included in the judgment for HMRC charges [the fixed costs set out in Tables 7 and 8 of Pt 45] is the total of—
      (i) the fixed commencement costs; and
      (ii) the amount in Table 10 [of Pt 45] relevant to the value of the claim.

When the defendant is only liable for fixed commencement costs

Pt 45 r.47

Where—
  (a) the only claim is for a specified sum of money; and
  (b) the defendant pays the money claimed within 14 days after service of the particulars of claim, together with the fixed commencement costs stated in the claim form,
the defendant is not liable for any further costs unless the court orders otherwise.

ROAD TRAFFIC ACCIDENTS

Fixed recoverable costs

Pt 45 r.45.9

  (1) Subject to para.(3) s.II of Pt 45 [and the Costs PD s.II paras 2.1 to 2.10] set out the costs which are to be allowed in—
      (a) proceedings to which r. 46.14(1) applies (costs-only proceedings); or
      (b) proceedings for approval of a settlement or compromise under r. 21.10(2),
      in cases to which [s.II] applies.
  (2) [Section II of Pt 45] applies where—
      (a) the dispute arises from a road traffic accident occurring on or after October 6, 2003;
      (b) the agreed damages include damages in respect of personal injury, damage to property, or both;
      (c) the total value of the agreed damages does not exceed £10,000; and

    (d) if a claim had been issued for the amount of the agreed damages, the small claims track would not have been the normal track for that claim.

(3) [Section II of Pt 45] does not apply where—

    (a) the claimant is a **litigant in person**; or

    (b) Section III of [Pt 45] [**Pre-Action Protocol for Low Value Personal Injury Claims in Road Traffic Acidents**] applies.

(4) In [s.II of Pt 45] —

"road traffic accident" means an accident resulting in bodily injury to any person or damage to property caused by, or arising out of, the use of a motor vehicle on a road or other public place in England and Wales;

"motor vehicle" means a mechanically propelled vehicle intended for use on roads; and

"road" means any highway and any other road to which the public has access and includes bridges over which a road passes.

Disbursements

Pt 45 r.45.12

(1) The court—

    (a) may allow a claim for a disbursement of a type mentioned in para.(2); but

    (b) will not allow a claim for any other type of disbursement.

(2) The disbursements referred to in para.(1) are—

    (a) the cost of obtaining—

        (i) medical records;

        (ii) a medical report;

        (iii) a police report;

        (iv) an engineer's report; or

        (v) a search of the records of the Driver Vehicle Licensing Authority;

    (b) where they are necessarily incurred by reason of one or more of the claimants being a **child** or **protected party** as defined in Pt 21—

        (i) fees payable for instructing counsel; or

        (ii) court fees payable on an application to the court; or

    (c) any other disbursement that has arisen due to a particular feature of the dispute.

ROYAL ARMS

Pt 4 r.4

(5) Where the court or a party produces a form shown in a PD with the words 'Royal Arms', the form must include a replica of the Royal Arms at the head of the first page.

RSC

Pt 50 r.50(3)

(3) A provision previously contained in the rules of the Supreme Court 1965.

RTA PROTOCOL

See **Pre-action protocols**.

S

SALE OF LAND BY COURT ORDER

See **Land**.

SANCTIONS

Sanctions for non-compliance

PD—Pre-action conduct

4.5
The court will look at the overall effect of non-compliance on the other party when deciding whether to impose sanctions.
4.6
If, in the opinion of the court, there has been non-compliance, the sanctions which the court may impose include—
  (1) staying (that is suspending) the proceedings until steps which ought to have been taken have been taken;
  (2) an order that the party at fault pays the costs, or part of the costs, of the other party or parties (this may include an order under r.27.14(2)(g) in cases allocated to the small claims track);
  (3) an order that the party at fault pays those costs on an indemnity basis (r.44.4(3) sets out the definition of the assessment of costs on an indemnity basis);
  (4) if the party at fault is the claimant in whose favour an order for the payment of a sum of money is subsequently made, an order that the claimant is deprived of interest on all or part of that sum, and/or that interest is awarded at a lower rate than would otherwise have been awarded;
  (5) if the party at fault is a defendant, and an order for the payment of a sum of money is subsequently made in favour of the claimant, an order that the defendant pay interest on all or part of that sum at a higher rate, not exceeding 10% above base rate, than would otherwise have been awarded

Sanctions for non-payment of certain fees

Pt 3 r.3.7

  (1) This rule applies where—
    (a) an **allocation questionnaire** or a pre-trial check list (listing questionnaire) is filed without payment of the fee specified by the relevant Fees order;
    (b) the court dispenses with the need for an allocation questionnaire or a pre-trial check list or both;
    (c) these rules do not require an allocation questionnaire or a pre-trial check list to be filed in relation to the claim in question;

(d) the court has made an order giving permission to proceed with a claim for judicial review; or

(e) the fee payable for a hearing specified by the relevant Fees order is not paid.

(Rule 26.3 provides for the court to dispense with the need for an allocation questionnaire and rr.28.5 and 29.6 provide for the court to dispense with the need for a pre-trial check list).

(Rule 54.12 provides for the service of the order giving permission to proceed with a claim for judicial review).

(2) The court will serve a notice on the claimant requiring payment of the fee specified in the relevant Fees order if, at the time the fee is due, the claimant has not paid it or made an application for full or part remission.

(3) The notice will specify the date by which the claimant must pay the fee.

(4) If the claimant does not—
   (a) pay the fee; or
   (b) make an application for full or part remission of the fee,
   by the date specified in the notice—
    (i) the claim will automatically be struck out without further order of the court; and
    (ii) the claimant will be liable for the costs which the defendant has incurred unless the court orders otherwise.

(Rule 44.12 provides for the basis of assessment where a right to costs arises under this rule and contains provisions about when a costs order is deemed to have been made and applying for an Order under s.194(3) of the Legal Services Act 2007.

(5) Where an application for—
   (a) full or part remission of a fee is refused, the court will serve notice on the claimant requiring payment of the full fee by the date specified in the notice; or
   (b) part remission of a fee is granted, the court will serve notice on the claimant requiring payment of the balance of the fee by the date specified in the notice.'; and

(6) If the claimant does not pay the fee by the date specified in the notice—
   (a) the claim will automatically be struck out without further order of the court; and
   (b) the claimant will be liable for the costs which the defendant has incurred unless the court orders otherwise.

(7) If—
   (a) a claimant applies to have the claim reinstated; and
   (b) the court grants relief,
   the relief will be conditional on the claimant either paying the fee or filing evidence of full or part remission of the fee within the period specified in para.(8).

(8) The period referred to in para.(7) is—
   (a) if the order granting relief is made at a hearing at which the claimant is present or represented, two days from the date of the order;
   (b) in any other case, seven days from the date of service of the order on the claimant.

Pt 3 r.3.7A

(1) This r. applies where—
   (a) a defendant files a counterclaim without—
    (i) payment of the fee specified by the relevant Fees order; or
    (ii) making an application for full or part remission of the fee; or
   (b) the proceedings continue on the counterclaim alone and—
    (i) an allocation questionnaire or a pre-trial check list (listing questionnaire) is filed without payment of the fee specified by the relevant Fees Order;
    (ii) the court dispenses with the need for an allocation questionnaire or a pre-trial check list or both;
    (iii) these rules do not require an allocation questionnaire or a pre-trial checklist to be filed in relation to the claim in question; or
    (iv) the fee payable for a hearing specified by the relevant Fees order is not paid.

(2) The court will serve a notice on the defendant requiring payment of the fee specified in the relevant Fees order if, at the time the fee is due, the defendant has not paid it or made an application for full or part remission.

(3) The notice will specify the date by which the defendant must pay the fee.

(4) If the defendant does not—
  (a) pay the fee; or
  (b) make an application for full or part remission of the fee,
  by the date specified in the notice, the counterclaim will automatically be struck out without further order of the court.

(5) Where an application for—
  (a) full or part remission of a fee is refused, the court will serve notice on the defendant requiring payment of the full fee by the date specified in the notice; or
  (b) part remission of a fee is granted, the court will serve notice on the defendant requiring payment of the balance of the fee by the date specified in the notice.

(6) If the defendant does not pay the fee by the date specified in the notice, the counterclaim will automatically be struck out without further order of the court.

(7) If—
  (a) the defendant applies to have the counterclaim reinstated; and
  (b) the court grants relief,
  the relief will be conditional on the defendant either paying the fee or filing evidence of full or part remission of the fee within the period specified in para.(8).

(8) The period referred to in para.(7) is—
  (a) if the order granting relief is made at a hearing at which the defendant is present or represented, two days from the date of the order;
  (b) in any other case, seven days from the date of service of the order on the defendant.

PD 3B para.1

If a claim is struck out under r.3.7, the court will send notice that it has been struck out to the defendant.

PD 3B para.2

The notice will also explain the effect of r.25.11. This provides that any interim injunction will cease to have effect 14 days after the date the claim is struck out under r.3.7. Paragraph (2) provides that if the claimant applies to reinstate the claim before the interim injunction ceases to have effect, the injunction will continue until the hearing of the application unless the court orders otherwise. If the claimant makes such an application, the defendant will be given notice in the ordinary way under r.23.4.

Sanctions for dishonouring cheque

Pt 3 r.3.7B

(1) This rule applies where any fee is paid by cheque and that cheque is subsequently dishonoured.

(2) The court will serve a notice on the paying party requiring payment of the fee which will specify the date by which the fee must be paid.

(3) If the fee is not paid by the date specified in the notice—
  (a) where the fee is payable by the claimant, the claim will automatically be struck out without further order of the court;
  (b) where the fee is payable by the defendant, the defence will automatically be struck out without further order of the court,

and the paying party shall be liable for the costs which any other party has incurred unless the court orders otherwise.

(r.44.12 provides for the basis of assessment where a right to costs arises under this rule).

(4) If—

(a) the paying party applies to have the claim or defence reinstated; and

(b) the court grants relief,

the relief shall be conditional on that party paying the fee within the period specified in para.(5).

(5) The period referred to in para.(4) is—

(a) if the order granting relief is made at a hearing at which the paying party is present or represented, two days from the date of the order;

(b) in any other case, seven days from the date of service of the order on the paying party.

(6) For the purposes of this rule, 'claimant' includes a Pt 20 claimant and 'claim form' includes a Pt 20 claim.

Sanctions have effect unless defaulting party obtains relief

Pt 3 r.3.8

(1) Where a party has failed to comply with a rule, PD or court order, any sanction for failure to comply imposed by the rule, PD or court order has effect unless the party in default applies for and obtains relief from the sanction.

(Rule 3.9 sets out the circumstances which the court may consider on an application to grant relief from a sanction).

(2) Where the sanction is the payment of costs, the party in default may only obtain relief by appealing against the order for costs.

(3) Where a rule, PD or court order—

(a) requires a party to do something within a specified time, and

(b) specifies the consequence of failure to comply,

the time for doing the act in question may not be extended by agreement between the parties.

Relief from sanctions

Pt 3 r.3.9

(1) On an application for relief from any sanction imposed for a failure to comply with any rule, PD or court order the court will consider all the circumstances including—

(a) the interests of the administration of justice;

(b) whether the application for relief has been made promptly;

(c) whether the failure to comply was intentional;

(d) whether there is a good explanation for the failure;

(e) the extent to which the party in default has complied with other rules, PD s, court orders and any relevant preaction protocols;

(f) whether the failure to comply was caused by the party or his legal representative;

(g) whether the trial date or the likely trial date can still be met if relief is granted;

(h) the effect which the failure to comply had on each party; and

(i) the effect which the granting of relief would have on each party.

(2) An application for relief must be supported by evidence.

SCOTT SCHEDULE

Where there are several items in issue between the parties, as to liability or amount or both, for example in a building contractor's claim or in a scheduleof dilapidations served under s.146 of the Law of Property Act 1925, it is common practice for a document called a "Scott Schedule" to be prepared.

The Scott Schedule is divided into columns, providing in separate columns for the consecutive numbering of the items, the full description of each item, the contention of each party against each item as to liability or amount or both, and finally a column for the use of the court.

SEAL

Glossary

A seal is a mark which the court puts on a document to indicate that the document has been issued by the court.

Court documents to be sealed

Pt 2 r.2.6

(1) The court must seal the following documents on issue—
   (a) the claim form; and
   (b) any other document which a rule or PD requires it to seal.
(2) The court may place the seal on the document—
   (a) by hand; or
   (b) by printing a facsimile of the seal on the document whether electronically or otherwise.
(3) A document purporting to bear the court's seal shall be admissible in evidence without further proof.

SEARCH ORDER

Pt 25 r.25.1

(1) The court may grant the following interim remedies—
   (h) a [search order] under s.7 of the Civil Procedure Act 1997 (order requiring a party to admit another party to premises for the purpose of preserving evidence etc.).
(4) The court may grant an interim remedy whether or not there has been a claim for a final remedy of that kind.

Supervising solicitor

PD 25A para.7.2

The Supervising Solicitor must be experienced in the operation of search Orders. A Supervising Solicitor may be contacted either through the Law Society or, for the London area, through the London Solicitors Litigation Association.

PD 25A para.7.6

The Supervising Solicitor must not be an employee or member of the applicant's firm of solicitors.

PD 25A para.7.7

If the court orders that the order need not be served by the Supervising Solicitor, the reason for so ordering must be set out in the order.

Evidence

PD 25A para.7.3

(1) the affidavit must state the name, firm and its address, and experience of the Supervising Solicitor, also the address of the premises and whether it is a private or business address, and
(2) the affidavit must disclose very fully the reason the order is sought, including the probability that relevant material would disappear if the order were not made.

Service

PD 25A para.7.4

(1) the order must be served personally by the Supervising Solicitor, unless the court otherwise Orders, and must be accompanied by the evidence in support and any documents capable of being copied,
(2) confidential exhibits need not be served but they must be made available for inspection by the respondent in the presence of the applicant's solicitors while the order is carried out and afterwards be retained by the respondent's solicitors on their undertaking not to permit the respondent—
    (a) to see them or copies of them except in their presence, and
    (b) to make or take away any note or record of them,
(3) the Supervising Solicitor may be accompanied only by the persons mentioned in the order,
(4) the Supervising Solicitor must explain the terms and effect of the order to the respondent in everyday language and advise him—
    (a) of his right to take legal advice and to apply to vary or discharge the order; and
    (b) that he may be entitled to avail himself of—
        (i) legal professional privilege; and
        (ii) the privilege against self-incrimination.

(5) where the Supervising Solicitor is a man and the respondent is likely to be an unaccompanied woman, at least one other person named in the order must be a woman and must accompany the Supervising Solicitor, and

(6) the order may only be served between 9.30 and 17.30 Monday to Friday unless the court otherwise orders.

Search and custody of materials

PD 25A para.7.5

(1) no material shall be removed unless clearly covered by the terms of the order,

(2) the premises must not be searched and no items shall be removed from them except in the presence of the respondent or a person who appears to be a responsible employee of the respondent,

(3) where copies of documents are sought, the documents should be retained for no more than two days before return to the owner,

(4) where material in dispute is removed pending trial, the applicant's solicitors should place it in the custody of the respondent's solicitors on their undertaking to retain it in safekeeping and to produce it to the court when required,

(5) in appropriate cases the applicant should insure the material retained in the respondent's solicitors' custody,

(6) the Supervising Solicitor must make a list of all material removed from the premises and supply a copy of the list to the respondent,

(7) no material shall be removed from the premises until the respondent has had reasonable time to check the list,

(8) if any of the listed items exists only in computer readable form, the respondent must immediately give the applicant's solicitors effective access to the computers, with all necessary passwords, to enable them to be searched, and cause the listed items to be printed out,

(9) the applicant must take all reasonable steps to ensure that no damage is done to any computer or data,

(10) the applicant and his representatives may not themselves search the respondent's computers unless they have sufficient expertise to do so without damaging the respondent's system,

(11) the Supervising Solicitor shall provide a report on the carrying out of the order to the applicant's solicitors,

(12) as soon as the report is received the applicant's solicitors shall—
(a) serve a copy of it on the respondent, and
(b) file a copy of it with the court, and

(13) where the Supervising Solicitor is satisfied that full compliance with para.7.5(7) and (8) above is impracticable, he may permit the search to proceed and items to be removed without compliance with the impracticable requirements.

General

PD 25A para.7.8

The search order must not be carried out at the same time as a police search warrant.

PD 25A para.7.9

There is no privilege against self incrimination in—

(1) Intellectual Property cases in respect of a 'related offence' or for the recovery of a 'related penalty' as defined in s.72 of the Senior Courts Act 1981;

(2) proceedings for the recovery or administration of any property, for the execution of a trust or for an account of any property or dealings with property, in relation to—

    (a) an offence under the Theft Act 1968 (see s.31 of the Theft Act); or

    (b) an offence under the Fraud Act 2006 (see s.13 of the Fraud Act 2006) or a related offence within the meaning given by s.13(4) of that Act—that is, conspiracy to defraud or any other offence involving any form of fraudulent conduct or purpose; or

(3) proceedings in which a court is hearing an application for an order under Pt IV or Pt V of the Children Act 1989 (see s.98 of the Children Act 1989).

However, the privilege may still be claimed in relation to material or information required to be disclosed by an order, as regards potential criminal proceedings outside those statutory provisions.

PD 25A para.7.10

Applications in intellectual property cases should be made in the Chancery Division.

PD 25A para.7.11

An example of a Search order is annexed to [PD 25A]. This example may be modified as appropriate in any particular case.

See also **Interim injunction**.

SECURITY FOR COSTS

Pt 25 r.25.12

(1) A defendant to any claim may apply under this section of this part for security for his costs of the proceedings.

(Pt 3 provides for the court to order payment of sums into court in other circumstances. R.20.3 provides for this section of this part to apply to Pt 20 claims).

(2) An application for security for costs must be supported by written evidence.

(3) Where the court makes an order for security for costs, it will—

    (a) determine the amount of security; and

    (b) direct—

        (i) the manner in which; and

        (ii) the time within which

    the security must be given.

Conditions to be satisfied

Pt 25 r.25.13

(1) The court may make an order for security for costs under r.25.12 if—

    (a) it is satisfied, having regard to all the circumstances of the case, that it is just to make such an order; and

    (b) (i) one or more of the conditions in para.(2) applies, or

        (ii) an enactment permits the court to require security for costs.

(2) The conditions are—

    (a) the claimant is—

> (i) resident out of the jurisdiction; but
>
> (ii) not resident in a Brussels Contracting State, a State bound by the Lugano Convention or a Regulation State, as defined in s.1(3) of the Civil Jurisdiction and Judgments Act 1982;
>
> (c) the claimant is a company or other body (whether incorporated inside or outside Great Britain) and there is reason to believe that it will be unable to pay the defendant's costs if ordered to do so;
>
> (d) the claimant has changed his address since the claim was commenced with a view to evading the consequences of the litigation;
>
> (e) the claimant failed to give his address in the claim form, or gave an incorrect address in that form;
>
> (f) the claimant is acting as a nominal claimant, other than as a representative claimant under Pt 19, and there is reason to believe that he will be unable to pay the defendant's costs if ordered to do so;
>
> (g) the claimant has taken steps in relation to his assets that would make it difficult to enforce an order for costs against him.

(Rule 3.4 allows the court to strike out a statement of case and Pt 24 for it to give summary judgment).

Security for costs other than from the claimant

Pt 25 r.25.14

> (1) The defendant may seek an order against someone other than the claimant, and the court may make an order for security for costs against that person if—
>
> (a) it is satisfied, having regard to all the circumstances of the case, that it is just to make such an order; and
>
> (b) one or more of the conditions in para.(2) applies.
>
> (2) The conditions are that the person—
>
> (a) has assigned the right to the claim to the claimant with a view to avoiding the possibility of a costs order being made against him; or
>
> (b) has contributed or agreed to contribute to the claimant's costs in return for a share of any money or property which the claimant may recover in the proceedings; and
>
> is a person against whom a costs order may be made.

(Rule 48.2 makes provision for costs orders against non-parties).

Security for costs for enforcement in England and Wales of judgments of foreign courts

Pt 74 r.74.5

> (1) Subject to paras (2) and (3), s.II of Pt 25 [see above] applies to an application for security for the costs of—
>
> (a) the application for registration;
>
> (b) any proceedings brought to set aside the registration; and
>
> (c) any appeal against the granting of the registration
>
> as if the judgment creditor were a claimant.
>
> (2) A judgment creditor making an application under the 1982 Act or the Lugano Convention, the Judgments Regulation may not be required to give security solely on the ground that he is resident out of the jurisdiction.
>
> (3) Paragraph (1) does not apply to an application under the 1933 Act where the relevant Order in Council otherwise provides.

Security for costs of an appeal

Pt 25 r.25.15

(1) The court may order security for costs of an appeal against—
   (a) an appellant;
   (b) a respondent who also appeals,
   on the same grounds as it may order security for costs against a claimant under this Part.
(2) The court may also make an order under para.(1) where the appellant, or the respondent who also appeals, is a limited company and there is reason to believe it will be unable to pay the costs of the other parties to the appeal should its appeal be unsuccessful.

Security from receiver

Pt 69 r.69.5

(1) The court may direct that before a receiver begins to act or within a specified time he must either—
   (a) give such security as the court may determine; or
   (b) file and serve on all parties to the proceedings evidence that he already has in force sufficient security,
   to cover his liability for his acts and omissions as a receiver.
(2) The court may terminate the appointment of the receiver if he fails to—
   (a) give the security; or
   (b) satisfy the court as to the security he has in force,
   by the date specified.

SENIOR COURTS

Senior Courts Act 1981 s.1

(1) The Senior Courts of England and Wales shall consist of the Court of Appeal, the High Court of Justice and the Crown Court, each having such jurisdiction as is conferred on it by or under this or any other Act.
(2) The Lord Chancellor shall be president of the Senior Courts.

SERIOUS CRIME PREVENTION ORDERS

Pt 77 r.77.1A

In this section—
   (b) 'SCPO' means a serious crime prevention order under ss.1 or 9 of the [Serious Crime Act 2007].

Application for a SCPO

Pt 77 r.77.2

An application under s.8 of the for a SCPO must be started in accordance with Pt 8 as modified by PD 77.

Applications by third parties to make representations and applications to vary or discharge a SCPO made by the High Court.

Pt 77 r.77.3

An application under—
  (a) section 9 of the 2007 Act; or
  (b) section 17 or 18 of the 2007 Act to vary or discharge a SCPO made by the High Court,
must be made in accordance with Pt 23 as modified by PD 77.

Application to vary or discharge a SCPO made by the crown court

Pt 77 r.77.4

An application under ss.17 or 18 of the 2007 Act to vary or discharge a SCPO made by the Crown Court must be started in accordance with Pt 8.

Where to make an application

Pt 77 r.77.5

Applications under this Part must be made to the Queen's Bench Division of the High Court in one of the courts set out in PD 77.

PD 77 para.4.1

An application for a SCPO or relating to a SCPO must be started and heard in the Queen's Bench Division of the High Court at—
  (a) the Royal Courts of Justice; or
  (b) at one of the following district registries—
      (i) Cardiff;
      (ii) Birmingham;
      (iii) Bristol;
      (iv) Leeds;
      (v) Manchester
      (vi) Newcastle; or
      (vii) Nottingham.

See also **Appeals to the Court of Appeal** and **Housing Act 1996 injunction.**

Claim form

PD 77 para.1.1

An application for a SCPO must be started by way of a Pt 8 claim form, although the court may decide during the proceedings that it would be more appropriate to continue the proceedings in accordance with Pt 7.
(Rule 8.1(3) allows the court to make an order that the claim continue as if the claimant had not used the Pt 8 procedure).

PD 77 para.1.2

The claim form must—
(1) identify which provisions of s.2(1) of the 2007 Act the applicant relies on and under each provision identified, set out the details of the allegations that the respondent has been involved in serious crime (whether in England and Wales or elsewhere);
(2) set out the applicant's grounds for contending that the proposed terms of the SCPO are appropriate for the purpose of protecting the public in accordance with s.1(3) of the 2007 Act; and
(3) include details of any third party whom the applicant believes is likely to be significantly adversely affected by the SCPO and the nature of that adverse effect.

PD 77 para.1.3

The claim form must be accompanied by a draft of the SCPO for which the application is made. The terms of the draft SCPO must include any proposed dates, including those upon which the applicant proposes that the SCPO should come into force and cease to be in force.

PD 77 para.r.4

Where it is alleged that the respondent has committed a serious offence, the claim form must be accompanied by evidence that the respondent has been convicted of the offence. Where a certificate of conviction can be obtained, this must be put in evidence.

PD 77 para.1.5

Where it is alleged that the respondent has been convicted of an offence in another jurisdiction, the applicant must put in evidence—
(a) a document from the appropriate public authority in the jurisdiction concerned certifying that the respondent has after due process of law been convicted of the offence; and
(b) where the document is not in English, a translation of that document into English—
(i) certified by a notary public or other qualified person; or
(ii) accompanied by written evidence confirming that the translation is accurate.

Applications by third parties to make representations

PD 77 para.2.1

The evidence in support of an application made under s.9 of the 2007 Act must contain details of why the third party believes the proposed order would be likely to have a significant adverse effect on that third party.

Application to vary or discharge a SCPO

PD 77 para.3.1

The application notice or claim form must contain—
(1) where the applicant is the person who is the subject of the SCPO, details of the change of circumstances affecting the SCPO;

(2) where the applicant seeks to vary the SCPO, any grounds advanced by the applicant for contending that the terms of the SCPO as varied would protect the public in accordance with s.17(1) of the 2007 Act;

(2A) where the applicant for the SCPO seeks to vary the SCPO—

   (a) details of any third party whom the applicant believes is likely to be significantly adversely affected by the proposed variation to the SCPO; and

   (b) details of the nature of that adverse effect;

(3) where the applicant seeks to vary the SCPO and is a third party or the person who is the subject of the SCPO—

   (a) particulars of why the applicant believes the applicant is significantly adversely affected by the SCPO;

   (b) particulars of how condition A or B in s.17 of the 2007 Act is met; and

   (c) particulars relied upon to establish that the purpose of the application is not to make the SCPO more onerous on the person who is the subject of the order; and

(4) where the application is for the discharge of the SCPO and the applicant is a third party or the person who is the subject of the SCPO, particulars of—

   (a) why the applicant believes the applicant is significantly adversely affected by the SCPO; and

   (b) how condition A or B in s.18 of the 2007 Act is met.

PD 77 para.3.2

Where the application is to vary or discharge a SCPO made by the Crown Court, the claim form must be accompanied by a copy of the SCPO made by the Crown Court.

SERVICE OF DOCUMENTS

Glossary

Steps required by rules of court to bring documents used in court proceedings to a person's attention.

Service of the claim form in the jurisdiction or in specified circumstances within the Methods of service

Pt 6 r.6.3

(1) A claim form may (subject to s.IV [Service of the claim form and other documents out of the jurisdiction] of [Pt 6] and the rules in this section relating to service out of the jurisdiction on solicitors, European Lawyers and parties) be served by any of the following methods—

   (a) personal service in **accordance with r.6.5;**

   (b) **first class post, document exchange** or other service which provides for delivery on the next business day, in accordance with PD 6A;

   (c) leaving it at a place specified in rr.6.7, 6.8, 6.9 or 6.10;

   (d) **fax** or other means of electronic communication in accordance with PD 6A; or

   (e) any method authorised by the court under r.6.15.

See **Charity, Claim form, Company,** and **Limited Liability Partnership.**

Who is to serve the claim form

Pt 6 r.6.4

(1) Subject to s.IV [Service of the claim form and other documents out of the jurisdiction] of [Pt 6] and the rules in this section relating to service out of the jurisdiction on solicitors, European Lawyers and parties, the court will serve the claim form except where—
  (a) a rule or PD provides that the claimant must serve it;
  (b) the claimant notifies the court that the claimant wishes to serve it; or
  (c) the court orders or directs otherwise.
(2) Where the court is to serve the claim form, it is for the court to decide which method of service is to be used.
(3) Where the court is to serve the claim form, the claimant must, in addition to filing a copy for the court, provide a copy for each defendant to be served.
(4) Where the court has sent—
  (a) a notification of outcome of postal service to the claimant in accordance with r.6.18; or
  (b) a notification of non-service by a bailiff in accordance with r.6.19,
  the court will not try to serve the claim form again.

Personal service

Pt 6 r.6.5

(1) Where required by another Part, any other enactment, a PD or a court order, a claim form must be served personally.
(2) In other cases, a claim form may be served personally except—
  (a) where r.6.7 [Service on a solicitor or European Lawyer within the United Kingdom or in any other EEA state] applies; or
  (b) in any proceedings against the Crown.
(Part 54 contains provisions about **judicial review** claims and Part 66 contains provisions about **Crown proceedings**.)
(3) A claim form is served personally on—
  (a) an individual by leaving it with that individual;
  (b) a company or other corporation by leaving it with a person holding a senior position within the company or corporation; or
  (c) a partnership (where partners are being sued in the name of their firm) by leaving it with—
    (i) a partner; or
    (ii) a person who, at the time of service, has the control or management of the partnership business at its principal place of business.
(PD 6A sets out the meaning of 'senior position'.)

Where to serve the claim form—general provisions

Pt 6 r.6.6

(1) The claim form must be served within the jurisdiction except where rr.6.7(2), 6.7(3) or 6.11 applies or as provided by s.IV [Service of the claim form and other documents out of the jurisdiction] of [Part 6].

(2) The claimant must include in the claim form an address at which the defendant may be served. That address must include a full **postcode** or its equivalent in any EEA state (if applicable), unless the court orders otherwise.

(3) Paragraph (2) does not apply where an order made by the court under r.6.15 (service by an alternative method or at an alternative place) specifies the place or method of service of the claim form.

Service on European lawyer within the United Kingdom or in any other EEA state

Pt 6 r.6.7

(3) **European Lawyer** in any EEA state: Subject to r.6.5(1) and the provisions of s. IV of this Part, and except where any other rule or PD makes different provision, where—

    (a) the defendant has given in writing the business address of a European Lawyer in any EEA state as an address at which the defendant may be served with the claim form; or

    (b) a European Lawyer in any EEA state has notified the claimant in writing that the European Lawyer is instructed by the defendant to accept service of the claim form on behalf of the defendant at a business address of the European Lawyer,

the claim form must be served at the business address of that European Lawyer.

(For Production Centre Claims see para.2.3(7A) of PD 7C; for Money Claims Online see para.4(6) of PD 7E; and for Possession Claims Online see para.5.1(4) of PD 55B).

Service on Solicitor

See **Solicitor**.

Service of the claim form where before service the defendant gives an address at which the defendant may be served

Pt 6 r.6.8

Subject to rr.6.5(1) and 6.7 and the provisions of s.IV of this Part, and except where any other rule or PD makes different provision—

    (a) the defendant may be served with the claim form at an address at which the defendant resides or carries on business within the UK or any other EEA state and which the defendant has given for the purpose of being served with the proceedings; or

    (b) in any claim by a tenant against a landlord, the claim form may be served at an address given by the landlord under s.48 of the Landlord and Tenant Act 1987.

(For Production Centre Claims see para.2.3(7A) of PD 7C; for Money Claims Online see para.4(6) of PD 7E; and for Possession Claims Online see para.5.1(4) of PD 55B.)

(For service out of the jurisdiction see rr.6.40 to 6.47).

Service of the claim form where the defendant does not give an address at which the defendant may be served

Pt 6 r.6.9

(1) This rule applies where—

    (a) rule 6.5(1) (personal service);

    (b) rule 6.7 (service of claim form on solicitor or European Lawyer); and

    (c) rule 6.8 (defendant gives address at which the defendant may be served),

    do not apply and the claimant does not wish to effect personal service under r.6.5(2).

(2) Subject to paras (3) to (6), the claim form must be served on the defendant at the place shown in the following table.

Nature of defendant to be served	
1. Individual	Usual or last known residence.
2. Individual being sued in the name of a business	Usual or last known residence of the individual; or principal or last known place of business.
3. Individual being sued in the business name of a partnership	Usual or last known residence of the individual; or principal or last known place of business of the partnership.
4. Limited liability partnership	Principal office of the partnership; or any place of business of the partnership within the jurisdiction which has a real connection with the claim.
5. Corporation (other than a company) incorporated in England and Wales	Principal office of the corporation; or any place within the jurisdiction where the corporation carries on its activities and which has a real connection with the claim.
6. Company registered in England and Wales	Principal office of the company; or any place of business of the company within the jurisdiction which has a real connection with the claim.
7. Any other company or corporation	Any place within the jurisdiction where the corporation carries on its activities; or any place of business of the company within the jurisdiction.

(3) Where a claimant has reason to believe that the address of the defendant referred to in entries 1, 2 or 3 in the Table in para.(2) is an address at which the defendant no longer resides or carries on business, the claimant must take reasonable steps to ascertain the address of the defendant's current residence or place of business ('current address').

(4) Where, having taken the reasonable steps required by para.(3), the claimant—

    (a) ascertains the defendant's current address, the claim form must be served at that address; or

    (b) is unable to ascertain the defendant's current address, the claimant must consider whether there is—

        (i) an alternative place where; or

        (ii) an alternative method by which,

    service may be effected.

(5) If, under para.(4)(b), there is such a place where or a method by which service may be effected, the claimant must make an application under r.6.15.

(6) Where para.(3) applies, the claimant may serve on the defendant's usual or last known address in accordance with the table in para.(2) where the claimant—

    (a) cannot ascertain the defendant's current residence or place of business; and

    (b) cannot ascertain an alternative place or an alternative method under para.(4)(b).

Service of the claim form in proceedings against the Crown

See **Crown proceedings**.

Service of the claim form by contractually agreed method or claim form relating to a contract on an agent of a principal who is out of the jurisdiction

See **Contract**.

Deemed service

Pt 6 r.6.14

A claim form served within the UK in accordance with this Part is deemed to be served on the second business day after completion of the relevant step under r.7.5(1).

Service of the claim form by an alternative method or at an alternative place

Pt 6 r.6.15

(1) Where it appears to the court that there is a good reason to authorise service by a method or at a place not otherwise permitted by this Part, the court may make an order permitting service by an alternative method or at an alternative place.
(2) On an application under this rule, the court may order that steps already taken to bring the claim form to the attention of the defendant by an alternative method or at an alternative place is good service.
(3) An application for an order under this rule—
    (a) must be supported by evidence; and
    (b) may be made without notice.
(4) An order under this rule must specify—
    (a) the method or place of service;
    (b) the date on which the claim form is deemed served; and
    (c) the period for—
        (i) filing an acknowledgment of service;
        (ii) filing an admission; or
        (iii) filing a defence.

PD 6A para.9.1

Where an application for an order under r.6.15 is made before the document is served, the application must be supported by evidence stating—
(1) the reason why an order is sought;
(2) what alternative method or place is proposed, and
(3) why the applicant believes that the document is likely to reach the person to be served by the method or at the place proposed.

PD 6A para.9.2

Where the application for an order is made after the applicant has taken steps to bring the document to the attention of the person to be served by an alternative method or at an alternative place, the application must be supported by evidence stating—

(1) the reason why the order is sought;

(2) what alternative method or alternative place was used;

(3) when the alternative method or place was used; and

(4) why the applicant believes that the document is likely to have reached the person to be served by the alternative method or at the alternative place.

PD 6A para.9.3

Examples—

(1) an application to serve by posting or delivering to an address of a person who knows the other party must be supported by evidence that if posted or delivered to that address, the document is likely to be brought to the attention of the other party;

(2) an application to serve by sending a SMS text message or leaving a voicemail message at a particular telephone number saying where the document is must be accompanied by evidence that the person serving the document has taken, or will take, appropriate steps to ensure that the party being served is using that telephone number and is likely to receive the message; and

(3) an application to serve by e-mail to a company (where para.4.1 does not apply) must be supported by evidence that the e-mail address to which the document will be sent is one which is likely to come to the attention of a person holding a senior position in that company.

Power of court to dispense with service of the claim form

Pt 6 r.6.16

(1) The court may dispense with service of a claim form in exceptional circumstances.

(2) An application for an order to dispense with service may be made at any time and—

(a) must be supported by evidence; and

(b) may be made without notice.

Notice and certificate of service relating to the claim form

Pt 6 r.6.17

(1) Where the court serves a claim form, the court will send to the claimant a notice which will include the date on which the claim form is deemed served under r.6.14.

Notification of outcome of postal service by the court

Pt 6 r.6.18

(1) Where—

(a) the court serves the claim form by post; and

(b) the claim form is returned to the court,

the court will send notification to the claimant that the claim form has been returned.

(2) The claim form will be deemed to be served unless the address for the defendant on the claim form is not the relevant address for the purpose of rr.6.7 to 6.10.

Notice of non-service by bailiff

Pt 6 r.6.19

Where—
(a) the court bailiff is to serve a claim form; and
(b) the bailiff is unable to serve it on the defendant,
the court will send notification to the claimant.

Service of documents other than the claim form in the UK or in specified circumstances within the EEA

Methods of service

Pt 6 r.6.20

(1) Subject to s.IV [Service of the claim form and other documents out of the jurisdiction] of [Part 6] and the rules in this section relating to service out of the jurisdiction on solicitors, European Lawyers and parties, a document may be served by any of the following methods—
(a) personal service, in accordance with r.6.22;
(b) first class post, document exchange or other service which provides for delivery on the next business day, in accordance with PD 6A;
(c) leaving it at a place specified in r.6.23;
(d) fax or other means of electronic communication in accordance with PD 6A; or
(e) any method authorised by the court under r.6.27.
(2) A company may be served—
(a) by any method permitted under this Part; or
(b) by any of the methods of service permitted under the Companies Act 2006.
(3) A limited liability partnership may be served—
(a) by any method permitted under this Part; or
(b) by any of the methods of service permitted under the Companies Act 2006 as applied with modification by regulations made under the Limited Liability Partnerships Act 2000.

Who is to serve

Pt 6 r.6.21

(1) Subject to s.IV of this Part and the rules in this section relating to service out of the jurisdiction on solicitors, European Lawyers and parties, a party to proceedings will serve a document which that party has prepared except where—
(a) a rule or PD provides that the court will serve the document; or
(b) the court orders otherwise.

(2) The court will serve a document which it has prepared except where—
   (a) a rule or PD provides that a party must serve the document;
   (b) the party on whose behalf the document is to be served notifies the court that the party wishes to serve it; or
   (c) the court orders otherwise.
(3) Where the court is to serve a document, it is for the court to decide which method of service is to be used.
(4) Where the court is to serve a document prepared by a party, that party must provide a copy for the court and for each party to be served.

PD 6A para.8.1

Where the court serves a document in accordance with rr.6.4 or 6.21(2), the method will normally be first class post.

PD 6A para.8.2

Where the court serves a claim form, delivers a defence to a claimant or notifies a claimant that the defendant has filed an acknowledgment of service, the court will also serve or deliver a copy of any notice of funding that has been filed, if—
   (1) it was filed at the same time as the claim form, defence or acknowledgment of service, and
   (2) copies of it were provided for service.
(Rule 44.15 deals with the provision of information about funding arrangements.)

Personal service

Pt 6 r.6.22

(1) Where required by another Part, any other enactment, a PD or a court order, a document must be served personally.
(2) In other cases, a document may be served personally except—
   (a) where the party to be served has given an address for service under r.6.23; or
   (b) in any proceedings by or against the Crown.
(3) A document may be served personally as if the document were a claim form in accordance with r.6.5(3).
(For service out of the jurisdiction see rr.6.40 to 6.47).

Address for service to be given after proceedings are started

Pt 6 r.6.23

(1) A party to proceedings must give an address at which that party may be served with documents relating to those proceedings. The address must include a full postcode or its equivalent in any EEA state (if applicable) unless the court orders otherwise.

(2) Except where any other rule or PD makes different provision, a party's address for service must be—

    (a) the business address either within the UK or any other EEA state of a solicitor acting for the party to be served; or

    (b) the business address in any EEA state of a European Lawyer nominated to accept service of documents; or

    (c) where there is no solicitor acting for the party or no European Lawyer nominated to accept service of documents—

        (i) an address within the UK at which the party resides or carries on business; or

        (ii) an address within any other EEA state at which the party resides or carries on business.

(3) Where none of subparas (2)(a), (b) or (c) applies, the party must give an address for service within the UK.

(Part 42 contains provisions about change of solicitor. Rule 42.1 provides that where a party gives the business address of a solicitor as that party's address for service, that solicitor will be considered to be acting for the party until the provisions of Pt 42 are complied with).

(4) Subject to the provisions of s.IV of this Part (where applicable), any document to be served in proceedings must be sent or transmitted to, or left at, the party's address for service under para.(2) or (3) unless it is to be served personally or the court orders otherwise.

(5) Where, in accordance with PD 6A, a party indicates or is deemed to have indicated that they will accept service by fax, the fax number given by that party must be at the address for service.

(6) Where a party indicates in accordance with PD 6A that they will accept service by electronic means other than fax, the e-mail address or electronic identification given by that party will be deemed to be at the address for service.

(8) This rule does not apply where an order made by the court under r.6.27 (service by an alternative method or at an alternative place) specifies where a document may be served.

(For service out of the jurisdiction see rr.6.40 to 6.47.)

See also **Crown**, **Production centre**, **Limitation period**, and **Possession claims online**.

Change of address for service

Pt 6 r.6.24

Where the address for service of a party changes, that party must give notice in writing of the change as soon as it has taken place to the court and every other party.

Deemed service

Pt 6 r.6.26

A document, other than a claim form, served within the UK in accordance with these rules or any relevant PD is deemed to be served on the day shown in the following table—

Method of service	Deemed date of service
1. First class post (or other service which provides for delivery on the next business day)	The second day after it was posted, left with, delivered to or collected by the relevant service provider provided that day is a business day; or if not, the next business day after that day.
2. Document exchange	The second day after it was left with, delivered to or collected by the relevant service provider provided that day is a business day; or if not, the next business day after that day.
3. Delivering the document to or leaving it at a permitted address	If it is delivered to or left at the permitted address on a business day before 4.30p.m., on that day; or in any other case, on the next business day after that day.
4. Fax	If the transmission of the fax is completed on a business day before 16.30 on that day; or in any other case, on the next business day after the day on which it was transmitted.
5. Other electronic method	If the e-mail or other electronic transmission is sent on a business day before 16.30, on that day; or in any other case, on the next business day after the day on which it was sent.

(Paragraphs 10.1 to 10.7 of PD 6A contain examples of how the date of deemed service is calculated).

PD 6A para.10.1

Rule 6.26 contains provisions about deemed service of a document other than a claim form. Examples of how deemed service is calculated are set out below.

PD 6A para.10.2

Example 1

Where the document is posted (by first class post) on a Monday (a business day), the day of deemed service is the following Wednesday (a business day).

PD 6A para.10.3

Example 2

Where the document is left in a numbered box at the DX on a Friday (a business day), the day of deemed service is the following Monday (a business day).

PD 6A para.10.4

Example 3

Where the document is sent by fax on a Saturday and the transmission of that fax is completed by 16.30 on that day, the day of deemed service is the following Monday (a business day).

PD 6A para.10.5

Example 4

Where the document is served personally before 16.30 on a Sunday, the day of deemed service is the next day (Monday, a business day).

PD 6A para.10.6

Example 5

Where the document is delivered to a permitted address after 16.30 on the Thursday (a business day) before Good Friday, the day of deemed service is the following Tuesday (a business day) as the Monday is a bank holiday.

PD 6A para.10.7

Example 6

Where the document is posted (by first class post) on a bank holiday Monday, the day of deemed service is the following Wednesday (a business day).

Service by an alternative method or at an alternative place

Pt 6 r.6.27

Rule 6.15 applies to any document in the proceedings as it applies to a claim form and reference to the defendant in that rule is modified accordingly.

Power to dispense with service

Pt 6 r.6.28

(1) The court may dispense with service of any document which is to be served in the proceedings.
(2) An application for an order to dispense with service must be supported by evidence and may be made without notice.

Service by document exchange

See **Document exchange**.

Service effected by post, an alternative service provider or DX

PD 6A para.3.1

Service by post, DX or other service which provides for delivery on the next business day is effected by—
  (1) placing the document in a post box;
  (2) leaving the document with or delivering the document to the relevant service provider; or
  (3) having the document collected by the relevant service provider.

See **Certificate of service, Child**, and **Fax or other electronic means**.

SERVICE OF DOCUMENTS FROM FOREIGN COURTS OR TRIBUNALS

Pt 6 r.6.48

Section [V of Pt 6] —
  (a) applies to the service in England and Wales of any document in connection with civil or commercial proceedings in a foreign court or tribunal; but
  (b) does not apply where the **Service Regulation** applies.

Request for service

Pt 6 r.6.50

The Senior Master will serve a document to which section [V of Part 6] applies upon receipt of—
  (a) a written request for service—
    (i) where the foreign court or tribunal [a court or tribunal in a country outside of the UK] is in a convention country, from a consular or other authority of that country; or
    (ii) from the Secretary of State for Foreign and Commonwealth Affairs, with a recommendation that service should be effected;
  (b) a translation of that request into English;
  (c) two copies of the document to be served; and
  (d) unless the foreign court or tribunal certifies that the person to be served understands the language of the document, two copies of a translation of it into English.

Method of service

Pt 6 r.6.51

The Senior Master will determine the method of service.

After service

Pt 6 r.6.52

(1) Where service of a document has been effected by a process server [(i) a process server appointed by the Lord Chancellor to serve documents to which this Section applies, or (ii) the process server's agent] , the process server must—
    (a) send to the Senior Master a copy of the document, and
        (i) proof of service; or
        (ii) a statement why the document could not be served; and
    (b) if the Senior Master directs, specify the costs incurred in serving or attempting to serve the document.
(2) The Senior Master will send to the person who requested service—
    (a) a certificate, sealed with the seal of the Senior Courts for use out of the jurisdiction, stating—
        (i) when and how the document was served or the reason why it has not been served; and
        (ii) where appropriate, an amount certified by a costs judge to be the costs of serving or attempting to serve the document; and
    (b) a copy of the document.

SERVICE OF DOCUMENTS OUT OF THE JURISDICTION

Pt 6 r.6.30

Section [IV of Pt 6] contains rules about—
    (a) service of the claim form and other documents out of the **jurisdiction**;
    (b) when the permission of the court is required and how to obtain that permission; and
    (c) the procedure for service.

Scotland and Northern Ireland

Service of the claim form where the permission of the court is not required

Pt 6 r.6.32

(1) The claimant may serve the claim form on a defendant in Scotland or Northern Ireland where each claim made against the defendant to be served and included in the claim form is a claim which the court has power to determine under the [Civil Jurisdiction and Judgments Act 1982] and—
    (a) no proceedings between the parties concerning the same claim are pending in the courts of any other part of the UK; and
    (b) (i) the defendant is domiciled in the UK;
        (ii) the proceedings are within para.11 of Sch.4 to the 1982 Act; or
        (iii) the defendant is a party to an agreement conferring jurisdiction, within para.12 of Sch.4 to the 1982 Act.
(2) The claimant may serve the claim form on a defendant in Scotland or Northern Ireland where each claim made against the defendant to be served and included in the claim form is a claim which the court has power to determine under any enactment other than the 1982 Act notwithstanding that—
    (a) the person against whom the claim is made is not within the jurisdiction; or

    (b) the facts giving rise to the claim did not occur within the jurisdiction.

Service out of the UK

Service of the claim form where the permission of the court is not required

Pt 6 r.6.33

  (1) The claimant may serve the claim form on the defendant out of the UK where each claim against the defendant to be served and included in the claim form is a claim which the court has power to determine under the 1982 Act or the **Lugano Convention** and—

    (a) no proceedings between the parties concerning the same claim are pending in the courts of any other part of the |UK or any other Convention territory [the territory or territories of any Contracting State to which the Brussels or Lugano Conventions (as defined in section 1(1) of the 1982 Act) apply]; and

    (b) (i) the defendant is domiciled in the UK or in any Convention territory;

        (ii) the proceedings are within art.16 of Sch.1 to the 1982 Act or art.22 of the Lugano Convention; or

        (iii) the defendant is a party to an agreement conferring jurisdiction, within art.17 of Sch.1 to the 1982 Act or art.23 of the Lugano Convention.

  (2) The claimant may serve the claim form on a defendant out of the UK where each claim made against the defendant to be served and included in the claim form is a claim which the court has power to determine under the **Judgments Regulation** and—

    (a) no proceedings between the parties concerning the same claim are pending in the courts of any other part of the UK or any other Member State; and

    (b) (i) the defendant is domiciled in the UK or in any Member State;

        (ii) the proceedings are within art.22 of the Judgments Regulation; or

        (iii) the defendant is a party to an agreement conferring jurisdiction, within art.23 of the Judgments Regulation.

  (3) The claimant may serve the claim form on a defendant out of the UK where each claim made against the defendant to be served and included in the claim form is a claim which the court has power to determine other than under the 1982 Act or the Lugano Convention or the Judgments Regulation, notwithstanding that—

    (a) the person against whom the claim is made is not within the jurisdiction; or

    (b) the facts giving rise to the claim did not occur within the jurisdiction.

Notice of statement of grounds where the permission of the court is not required for service

Pt 6 r.6.34

  (1) Where the claimant intends to serve a claim form on a defendant under rr.6.32 or 6.33, the claimant must—

    (a) file with the claim form a notice containing a statement of the grounds on which the claimant is entitled to serve the claim form out of the jurisdiction; and

    (b) serve a copy of that notice with the claim form.

  (2) Where the claimant fails to file with the claim form a copy of the notice referred to in para.(1)(a), the claim form may only be served—

    (a) once the claimant files the notice; or

    (b) if the court gives permission.

2.1

Where r.6.34 applies, the claimant must file Practice Form N510 when filing the claim form
Period for responding to the claim form where permission was not required for service

Pt 6 r.6.35

(1) This rule sets out the period for—
    (a) filing an acknowledgment of service;
    (b) filing an admission; or
    (c) filing a defence,
    where a claim form has been served out of the jurisdiction under rr.6.32 or 6.33.
(Part 10 contains rules about acknowledgments of service, Pt 14 contains rules about admissions
and Pt 15 contains rules about defences).

Service of the claim form on a defendant in Scotland or Northern Ireland

Pt 6 r.6.35

(2) Where the claimant serves on a defendant in Scotland or Northern Ireland under r.6.32,
the period—
    (a) for filing an acknowledgment of service or admission is 21 days after service of the
particulars of claim; or
    (b) for filing a defence is—
        (i) 21 days after service of the particulars of claim; or
        (ii) where the defendant files an acknowledgment of service, 35 days after service
of the particulars of claim.
(Part 7 provides that particulars of claim must be contained in or served with the claim form or
served separately on the defendant within 14 days after service of the claim form).

Service of the claim form on a defendant in a convention territory within Europe or a Member State

Pt 6 r.6.35

(3) Where the claimant serves the claim form on a defendant in a Convention territory within
Europe or a Member State under r.6.33, the period—
    (a) for filing an acknowledgment of service or admission, is 21 days after service of the
particulars of claim; or
    (b) for filing a defence is—
        (i) 21 days after service of the particulars of claim; or
        (ii) where the defendant files an acknowledgment of service, 35 days after service
of the particulars of claim.

Service of the claim form on a defendant in a Convention territory outside Europe

Pt 6 r.6.35

(4) Where the claimant serves the claim form on a defendant in a Convention territory
outside Europe under r.6.33, the period—

(a) for filing an acknowledgment of service or admission, is 31 days after service of the particulars of claim; or

(b) for filing a defence is—

   (i) 31 days after service of the particulars of claim; or

   (ii) where the defendant files an acknowledgment of service, 45 days after service of the particulars of claim.

Service on a defendant elsewhere

Pt 6 r.6.35

(5) Where the claimant serves the claim form under r.6.33 in a country not referred to in paras (3) or (4), the period for responding to the claim form is set out in PD 6B.

PD 6B para.6.1

Where r.6.35(5) applies, the periods within which the defendant must—

(1) file an acknowledgment of service;

(2) file or serve an admission; or

(3) file a defence,

will be calculated in accordance with paras 6.3, 6.4 or 6.5.

PD 6B para.6.2

Where the court grants permission to serve a claim form out of the jurisdiction the court will determine in accordance with paras 6.3, 6.4 or 6.5 the periods within which the defendant must—

(1) file an acknowledgment of service;

(2) file or serve an admission; or

(3) file a defence.

(Rule 6.37(5)(a) provides that when giving permission to serve a claim form out of the jurisdiction the court will specify the period within which the defendant may respond to the claim form).

PD 6B para.6.3

The period for filing an acknowledgment of service under Pt 10 or for filing or serving an admission under Pt 14 is the number of days listed in the Table after service of the particulars of claim.

PD 6B para.6.4

The period for filing a defence under Pt 15 is—

(1) the number of days listed in the Table after service of the particulars of claim; or

(2) where the defendant has filed an acknowledgment of service, the number of days listed in the Table plus an additional 14 days after the service of the particulars of claim.

PD 6B para.6.5

Under the State Immunity Act 1978, where a State is served, the period permitted under paras 6.3 and 6.4 for filing an acknowledgment of service or defence or for filing or serving an admission does not begin to run until two months after the date on which the State is served.

PD 6B para.6.6

Where particulars of claim are served out of the jurisdiction any statement as to the period for responding to the claim contained in any of the forms required by r.7.8 to accompany the particulars of claim must specify the period prescribed under r.6.35 or by the order permitting service out of the jurisdiction under r.6.37(5).

Service of the claim form where the permission of the court is required

Pt 6 r.6.36

In any proceedings to which rr.6.32 or 6.33 does not apply, the claimant may serve a claim form out of the jurisdiction with the permission of the court if any of the grounds set out in para.3.1 of PD 6B apply.

PD 6B para.3.1

The claimant may serve a claim form out of the jurisdiction with the permission of the court under r.6.36 where—

General grounds

(1) A claim is made for a remedy against a person domiciled within the jurisdiction.
(2) A claim is made for an injunction ordering the defendant to do or refrain from doing an act within the jurisdiction.
(3) A claim is made against a person ('the defendant') on whom the claim form has been or will be served (otherwise than in reliance on this paragraph) and—
   (a) there is between the claimant and the defendant a real issue which it is reasonable for the court to try; and
   (b) the claimant wishes to serve the claim form on another person who is a necessary or proper party to that claim.
(4) A claim is an additional claim under Pt 20 and the person to be served is a necessary or proper party to the claim or additional claim.

Claims for interim remedies

(5) A claim is made for an interim remedy under s.25(1) of the Civil Jurisdiction and Judgments Act 1982.

Claims in relation to contracts

(6) A claim is made in respect of a contract where the contract—
   (a) was made within the jurisdiction;
   (b) was made by or through an agent trading or residing within the jurisdiction;
   (c) is governed by English law; or
   (d) contains a term to the effect that the court shall have jurisdiction to determine any claim in respect of the contract.
(7) A claim is made in respect of a breach of contract committed within the jurisdiction.

(8) A claim is made for a declaration that no contract exists where, if the contract was found to exist, it would comply with the conditions set out in para.(6).

Claims in tort

(9) A claim is made in tort where
   (a) damage was sustained within the jurisdiction; or
   (b) the damage sustained resulted from an act committed within the jurisdiction.

Enforcement

(10) A claim is made to enforce any judgment or arbitral award.

Claims about property within the jurisdiction

(11) The whole subject matter of a claim relates to property located within the jurisdiction.

Claims about trusts etc.

(12) A claim is made for any remedy which might be obtained in proceedings to execute the trusts of a written instrument where—
   (a) the trusts ought to be executed according to English law; and
   (b) the person on whom the claim form is to be served is a trustee of the trusts.
(13) A claim is made for any remedy which might be obtained in proceedings for the administration of the estate of a person who died domiciled within the jurisdiction.
(14) A probate claim or a claim for the rectification of a will.
(15) A claim is made for a remedy against the defendant as constructive trustee where the defendant's alleged liability arises out of acts committed within the jurisdiction.
(16) A claim is made for restitution where the defendant's alleged liability arises out of acts committed within the jurisdiction.

Claims by HM Revenue and Customs

(17) A claim is made by the Commissioners for HM Revenue and Customs relating to duties or taxes against a defendant not domiciled in Scotland or Northern Ireland.

Claim for costs order in favour of or against third parties

(18) A claim is made by a party to proceedings for an order that the court exercise its power under s.51 of the Senior Courts Act 1981 to make a costs order in favour of or against a person who is not a party to those proceedings.
(Rule 48.2 sets out the procedure where the court is considering whether to exercise its discretion to make a costs order in favour of or against a non-party.)

Admiralty claims

(19) A claim is—
  (a) in the nature of salvage and any part of the services took place within the jurisdiction; or
  (b) to enforce a claim under ss.153, 154,175 or 176A of the Merchant Shipping Act 1995.

Claims under various enactments

(20) A claim is made—
  (a) under an enactment which allows proceedings to be brought and those proceedings are not covered by any of the other grounds referred to in this paragraph; or
  (b) under the Directive of the Council of the European Communities dated March 15, 1976 No.76/308/EEC, where service is to be effected in a Member State of the European Union.

Application for permission to serve the claim form out of the jurisdiction

Pt 6 r.6.37

(1) An application for permission under r.6.36 must set out—
  (a) which ground in para.3.1 of PD 6B is relied on;
  (b) that the claimant believes that the claim has a reasonable prospect of success; and
  (c) the defendant's address or, if not known, in what place the defendant is, or is likely, to be found.
(2) Where the application is made in respect of a claim referred to in para.3.1(3) of PD 6B, the application must also state the grounds on which the claimant believes that there is between the claimant and the defendant a real issue which it is reasonable for the court to try.
(3) The court will not give permission unless satisfied that England and Wales is the proper place in which to bring the claim.
(4) In particular, where—
  (a) the application is for permission to serve a claim form in Scotland or Northern Ireland; and
  (b) it appears to the court that the claimant may also be entitled to a remedy in Scotland or Northern Ireland, the court, in deciding whether to give permission, will—
    (i) compare the cost and convenience of proceeding there or in the jurisdiction; and
    (ii) (where relevant) have regard to the powers and jurisdiction of the Sheriff court in Scotland or the county courts or courts of summary jurisdiction in Northern Ireland.
(5) Where the court gives permission to serve a claim form out of the jurisdiction—
  (a) it will specify the periods within which the defendant may—
    (i) file an acknowledgment of service;
    (ii) file or serve an admission;
    (iii) file a defence; or
    (iv) file any other response or document required by a rule in another Part, any other enactment or a PD ; and
  (b) it may—
    (i) give directions about the method of service; and
    (ii) give permission for other documents in the proceedings to be served out of the jurisdiction.

(The periods referred to in paras (5)(a)(i), (ii) and (iii) are those specified in the Table in PD 6B).

Service of documents other than the claim form—permission

Pt 6 r.6.38

(1) Unless paras (2) or (3) applies, where the permission of the court is required for the claimant to serve the claim form out of the jurisdiction, the claimant must obtain permission to serve any other document in the proceedings out of the jurisdiction.

(2) Where—

    (a) the court gives permission for a claim form to be served on a defendant out of the jurisdiction; and

    (b) the claim form states that particulars of claim are to follow,

the permission of the court is not required to serve the particulars of claim.

(3) The permission of the court is not required if a party has given an address for service in Scotland or Northern Ireland.

Service of application notice on a non-party to the proceedings

Pt 6 r.6.39

(1) Where an application notice is to be served out of the jurisdiction on a person who is not a party to the proceedings rr.6.35 and 6.37(5)(a)(i), (ii) and (iii) do not apply.

(2) Where an application is served out of the jurisdiction on a person who is not a party to the proceedings, that person may make an application to the court under Pt 11 as if that person were a defendant, but r.11(2) does not apply.

(Part 11 contains provisions about disputing the court's **jurisdiction**).

Methods of service—general provisions

Pt 6 r.6.40

(1) This rule contains general provisions about the method of service of a claim form or other document on a party out of the jurisdiction.

Where service is to be effected on a party in Scotland or Northern Ireland

(2) Where a party serves a claim form or other document on a party in Scotland or Northern Ireland, it must be served by a method permitted by s.II (and references to 'jurisdiction' in that Section are modified accordingly) or s.III of this Part and r.6.23(4) applies.

Where service is to be effected on a party out of the UK

(3) Where a party wishes to serve a claim form or other document on a party out of the UK, it may be served—

    (a) by any method provided for by—

      (i) rule 6.41 (service in accordance with the **Service Regulation**);

      (ii) rule 6.42 (service through foreign governments, judicial authorities and British Consular authorities); or

      (iii) rule 6.44 (service of claim form or other document on a State);

  (b) by any method permitted by a Civil Procedure Convention [the Brussels and Lugano Conventions (as defined in s.1(1) of the 1982 Act) and any other Convention (including the Hague Convention) entered into by the UK regarding service out of the jurisdiction] or Treaty; or

  (c) by any other method permitted by the law of the country in which it is to be served.

  (4) Nothing in para.(3) or in any court order authorises or requires any person to do anything which is contrary to the law of the country where the claim form or other document is to be served.

(The texts of the Civil Procedure Treaties which the UK has entered into may be found on the Foreign and Commonwealth Office website).

Service in accordance with the service regulation

Pt 6 r.6.41

  (1) This rule applies where a party wishes to serve the claim form or other document in accordance with the Service Regulation.

  (2) The party must file—

    (a) the claim form or other document;

    (b) any translation; and

    (c) any other documents required by the Service Regulation.

  (3) When a party files the documents referred to in para.(2), the court officer will forward the relevant documents to the Senior Master.

  (4) Rule 6.47 does not apply to this rule.

(The Service Regulation is annexed to PD 6B).

(Article 20(1) of the Service Regulation provides that the Regulation prevails over other provisions contained in any other agreement or arrangement concluded by Member States. The Regulation does not apply to service in EEA states that are not member states of the EU).

Service through foreign governments, judicial authorities and British Consular authorities

Pt 6 r.6.42

  (1) Where a party wishes to serve a claim form or any other document in any country which is a party to a Civil Procedure Convention or Treaty providing for service in that country, it may be served—

    (a) through the authority designated under the Hague Convention [Convention on the service abroad of judicial and extrajudicial documents in civil or commercial matters signed at the Hague on November 15, 1965] or any other Civil Procedure Convention or Treaty (where relevant) in respect of that country; or

    (b) if the law of that country permits—

      (i) through the judicial authorities of that country, or

      (ii) through a British Consular authority in that country (subject to any provisions of the applicable convention about the nationality of persons who may be served by such a method).

(2) Where a party wishes to serve a claim form or any other document in any country with respect to which there is no Civil Procedure Convention or Treaty providing for service in that country, the claim form or other document may be served, if the law of that country so permits—

    (a) through the government of that country, where that government is willing to serve it; or

    (b) through a British Consular authority in that country.

(3) Where a party wishes to serve the claim form or other document in—

    (a) any Commonwealth State [a state listed in Sch.3 to the British Nationality Act 1981] which is not a party to the Hague Convention or is such a party but HM Government has not declared acceptance of its accession to the Convention;

    (b) the Isle of Man or the Channel Islands; or

    (c) any British overseas territory,

the methods of service permitted by paras (1)(b) and (2) are not available and the party or the party's agent must effect service direct, unless PD 6B provides otherwise.

(A list of British overseas territories is reproduced in para.5.2 of PD 6B.)

Procedure where service is to be through foreign governments, judicial authorities and British Consular authorities

Pt 6 r.6.43

(1) This rule applies where a party wishes to serve a claim form or any other document under r.6.42(1) or 6.42(2).

(2) Where this rule applies, that party must file—

    (a) a request for service of the claim form or other document specifying one or more of the methods in r.6.42(1) or 6.42(2);

    (b) a copy of the claim form or other document;

    (c) any other documents or copies of documents required by PD 6B; and

    (d) any translation required under r.6.45.

(3) Where a party files the documents specified in para.(2), the court officer will—

    (a) seal the copy of the claim form or other document; and

    (b) forward the documents to the Senior Master.

(4) The Senior Master will send documents forwarded under this rule—

    (a) where the claim form or other document is being served through the authority designated under the Hague Convention or any other Civil Procedure Convention or Treaty, to that authority; or

    (b) in any other case, to the Foreign and Commonwealth Office with a request that it arranges for the claim form or other document to be served.

(5) An official certificate which—

    (a) states that the method requested under para.(2)(a) has been performed and the date of such performance;

    (b) states, where more than one method is requested under para.(2)(a), which method was used; and

    (c) is made by—

        (i) a British Consular authority in the country where the method requested under para.(2)(a) was performed;

        (ii) the government or judicial authorities in that country; or

        (iii) the authority designated in respect of that country under the a Civil Procedure Convention or Treaty,

    is evidence of the facts stated in the certificate.

(6) A document purporting to be an official certificate under para.(5) is to be treated as such a certificate, unless it is proved not to be.

PD 6B para.4.1

A party must provide the following documents for each party to be served out of the jurisdiction—
  (1) a copy of the particulars of claim if not already contained in or served with the claim form and any other relevant documents;
  (2) a duplicate of the claim form, a duplicate of the particulars of claim (if not already contained in or served with the claim form), copies of any documents accompanying the claim form and copies of any other relevant documents;
  (3) forms for responding to the claim; and
  (4) any translation required under r.6.45 in duplicate.

PD 6B para.4.2

Some countries require legalisation of the document to be served and some require a formal letter of request which must be signed by the Senior Master. Any queries on this should be addressed to the Foreign Process Section (Room E02) at the Royal Courts of Justice.

Undertaking to be responsible for expenses

Pt 6 r.6.46

Every request for service filed under r.6.43 (service through foreign governments, judicial authorities etc.) or r.6.44 (service of claim form or other document on a State) must contain an undertaking by the person making the request—
  (a) to be responsible for all expenses incurred by the Foreign and Commonwealth Office or foreign judicial authority; and
  (b) to pay those expenses to the Foreign and Commonwealth Office or foreign judicial authority on being informed of the amount.

Proof of service before obtaining judgment

Pt 6 r.6.47

Where—
  (a) a hearing is fixed when the claim form is issued;
  (b) the claim form is served on a defendant out of the jurisdiction; and
  (c) that defendant does not appear at the hearing,
the claimant may not obtain judgment against the defendant until the claimant files written evidence that the claim form has been duly served in accordance with this Part.

State

Service of claim form or other document on a state

Pt 6 r.6.44

  (1) This rule applies where a party wishes to serve the claim form or other document on a State [has the meaning given by s.14 of the State Immunity Act 1978].

(3) The party must file in the Central Office of the Royal Courts of Justice—
    (a) a request for service to be arranged by the Foreign and Commonwealth Office;
    (b) a copy of the claim form or other document; and
    (c) any translation required under r.6.45.
(4) The Senior Master will send the documents filed under this rule to the Foreign and Commonwealth Office with a request that it arranges for them to be served.
(5) An official certificate by the Foreign and Commonwealth Office stating that a claim form or other document has been duly served on a specified date in accordance with a request made under this rule is evidence of that fact.
(6) A document purporting to be such a certificate is to be treated as such a certificate, unless it is proved not to be.
(7) Where—
    (a) section 12(6) of the State Immunity Act 1978 applies; and
    (b) the State has agreed to a method of service other than through the Foreign and Commonwealth Office,
    the claim form or other document may be served either by the method agreed or in accordance with this rule.
(Section 12(6) of the State Immunity Act 1978 provides that s.12(1) enables the service of a claim form or other document in a manner to which the State has agreed.)

Service in a Commonwealth state or British overseas territory

PD 6B para.5.1

The judicial authorities of certain Commonwealth States which are not a party to the Hague Convention require service to be in accordance with r.6.42(1)(b)(i) and not 6.42(3). A list of such countries can be obtained from the Foreign Process Section (Room E02) at the Royal Courts of Justice.

PD 6B para.5.2

The list of British overseas territories is contained in Sch.6 to the British Nationality Act 1981. For ease of reference, these are [listed in para.5.2 of PD 6B].

Period for responding to an application notice

PD 6B para.7.1

Where an application notice is served out of the jurisdiction, the period for responding is seven days less than the number of days listed in the Table [in PD 6B] .

Translation of claim form or other document

Pt 6 r.6.45

(1) Except where para.(4) or (5) applies, every copy of the claim form or other document filed under rr.6.43 (service through foreign governments, judicial authorities etc.) or 6.44

(service of claim form or other document on a State) must be accompanied by a translation of the claim form or other document.

(2) The translation must be—

(a) in the official language of the country in which it is to be served; or

(b) if there is more than one official language of that country, in any official language which is appropriate to the place in the country where the claim form or other document is to be served.

(3) Every translation filed under this rule must be accompanied by a statement by the person making it that it is a correct translation, and the statement must include that person's name, address and qualifications for making the translation.

(4) A party is not required to file a translation of a claim form or other document filed under r.6.43 (service through foreign governments, judicial authorities etc.) where the claim form or other document is to be served—

(a) in a country of which English is an official language; or

(b) on a British citizen (within the meaning of the British Nationality Act 1981, unless a Civil Procedure Convention or Treaty requires a translation.

(5) A party is not required to file a translation of a claim form or other document filed under r.6.44 (service of claim form or other document on a State) where English is an official language of the State in which the claim form or other document is to be served.

(The Service Regulation contains provisions about the translation of documents).

Further information

PD 6B para.7.2

Further information concerning service out of the jurisdiction can be obtained from the Foreign Process Section, Room E02, Royal Courts of Justice, Strand, London WC2A 2LL (tel: 020 7947 6691).

SERVICE REGULATION

Pt 6 r.6.31

(e) Regulation (EC) No. 1393/2007 of the European Parliament and of the Council of November 13, 2007 on the service in the Member States of judicial and extrajudicial documents in civil or commercial matters (service of documents), and repealing Council Regulation (EC) No. 1348/2000, as amended from time to time and as applied by the Agreement made on October 19, 2005 between the European Community and the Kingdom of Denmark on the service of judicial and extrajudicial documents on civil and commercial matters.

SET ASIDE

Glossary

Cancelling a judgment or order or a step taken by a party in the proceedings.

SET OFF

Set off of cross-judgment

CCR Ord.22 r.11

(1) An application under s.72 of the [County Courts Act 1984] for permission to set off any sums, including costs, payable under several judgments or orders each of which was obtained in a county court shall be made in accordance with this rule.

(2) Where the judgments or orders have been obtained in the same county court, the application may be made to that court on the day when the last judgment or order is obtained, if both parties are present, and in any other case shall be made on notice.

(3) Where the judgments or orders have been obtained in different county courts, the application may be made to either of them on notice, and notice shall be given to the other court.

(4) The district judge of the court to which the application is made and the district judge of any other court to which notice is given under para.(3) shall forthwith stay execution on any judgment or order in his court to which the application relates and any money paid into court under the judgment or order shall be retained until the application has been disposed of.

(5) The application may be heard and determined by the court and any order giving permission shall direct how any money paid into court is to be dealt with.

(6) Where the judgments or orders have been obtained in different courts, the court in which an order giving permission is made shall send a copy of the order to the other court, which shall deal with any money paid into that court in accordance with the order.

(7) The court officer or, as the case may be, each of the court officers affected shall enter satisfaction in the records of his court for any sums ordered to be set off, and execution or other process for the enforcement of any judgment or order not wholly satisfied shall issue only for the balance remaining payable.

(8) Where an order is made by the High Court giving permission to set off sums payable under several judgments and orders obtained respectively in the High Court and a county court, the court officer of the county court shall, on receipt of a copy of the order, proceed in accordance with para.(7).

See also **Crown** and **Defence of set off.**

SETTING ASIDE DEFAULT JUDGMENT

See **Default judgment**.

SETTING ASIDE SUMMARY JUDGMENT

See **Summary judgment**.

SETTLEMENT

See **Compromise**.

SEVERAL LIABILITY

Glossary

A person who is severally liable with others may remain liable for the whole claim even where judgment has been obtained against the others.

SEX DISCRIMINATION ACT 1975

See **Discrimination proceedings**.

SIGNATURE

Signature of documents by mechanical means

Pt 5 r.5.3

Where any of these rules or any PD requires a document to be signed, that requirement shall be satisfied if the signature is printed by computer or other mechanical means.

PD 5 para.1

Where, under r.5.3, a replica signature is printed electronically or by other mechanical means on any document, the name of the person whose signature is printed must also be printed so that the person may be identified. This paragraph does not apply to claim forms issued through the Claims Production Centre.

Money claim online

PD 7E para.10

Any provision of the CPR which requires a document to be signed by any person is satisfied by that person entering their name on an online form.

Possession claims online

PD 55B para.9.1

Any provision of the CPR which requires a document to be signed by any person is satisfied by that person entering his name on an online form.

SIGNING OF DOCUMENTS

PD 5A para.2.1

Statements of case and other documents drafted by a **legal representative** should bear his/her **signature** and if they are drafted by a legal representative as a member or employee of a firm they should be signed in the name of the firm.

See also **Acknowledgment of service** and **Statement of truth**.

SINGLE JOINT EXPERT

Pt 35 r.35.2

(2) An expert instructed to prepare a report for the court on behalf of two or more of the parties (including the claimant) to the proceedings.

PD 35 para.7

When considering whether to give permission for the parties to rely on expert evidence and whether that evidence should be from a **single joint expert** the court will take into account all the circumstances in particular, whether:
(a) it is proportionate to have separate experts for each party on a particular issue with reference to—
  (i) the amount in dispute;
  (ii) the importance to the parties; and
  (iii) the complexity of the issue;
(b) the instruction of a single joint expert is likely to assist the parties and the court to resolve the issue more speedily and in a more cost-effective way than separately instructed experts;
(c) expert evidence is to be given on the issue of liability, causation or quantum;
(d) the expert evidence falls within a substantially established area of knowledge which is unlikely to be in dispute or there is likely to be a range of expert opinion;
(e) a party has already instructed an expert on the issue in question and whether or not that was done in compliance with any PD or relevant pre-action protocol;
(f) questions put in accordance with r.35.6 are likely to remove the need for the other party to instruct an expert if one party has already instructed an expert;
(g) questions put to a single joint expert may not conclusively deal with all issues that may require testing prior to trial;
(h) a conference may be required with the legal representatives, experts and other witnesses which may make instruction of a single joint expert impractical; and
(i) a claim to privilege makes the instruction of any expert as a single joint expert inappropriate.

Court's power to direct that evidence is to be given by a single joint expert

Pt 35 r.35.7

(1) Where two or more parties wish to submit expert evidence on a particular issue, the court may direct that the evidence on that issue is to be given by a single joint expert.
(2) Where the parties who wish to submit the evidence ('the relevant parties') cannot agree who should be the single joint expert, the court may—
  (a) select the expert from a list prepared or identified by the relevant parties; or
  (b) direct that the expert be selected in such other manner as the court may direct.

Instructions to a single joint expert

Pt 35 r.35.8

(1) Where the court gives a direction under r.35.7 for a single joint expert to be used, any relevant party may give instructions to the expert.

(2) When a party gives instructions to the expert that party must, at the same time, send a copy to the other relevant parties.

(3) The court may give directions about—

(a) the payment of the expert's fees and expenses; and

(b) any inspection, examination or experiments which the expert wishes to carry out.

(4) The court may, before an expert is instructed—

(a) limit the amount that can be paid by way of fees and expenses to the expert; and

(b) direct that some or all of the relevant parties pay that amount into court.

(5) Unless the court otherwise directs, the relevant parties are jointly and severally liable(GL) for the payment of the expert's fees and expenses.

See **Expert** and **Expert evidence**.

SITTING IN CHAMBERS

Sitting in private.

SKELETON ARGUMENTS

Appeals

PD 52A para.5.1

(1) The purpose of a skeleton argument is to assist the court by setting out as concisely as practicable the arguments upon which a party intends to rely.

(2) A skeleton argument must—

be concise;

both define and confine the areas of controversy;

be set out in numbered paragraphs;

be cross-referenced to any relevant document in the bundle;

be self-contained and not incorporate by reference material from previous skeleton arguments;

not include extensive quotations from documents or authorities.

(3) Documents to be relied on must be identified.

(4) Where it is necessary to refer to an authority, a skeleton argument must—

(a) state the proposition of law the authority demonstrates; and

(b) identify the parts of the authority that support the proposition.

If more than one authority is cited in support of a given proposition, the skeleton argument must briefly state why.

(5) The cost of preparing a skeleton argument which—

(a) does not comply with the requirements set out in this paragraph; or

(b) was not filed within the time limits provided by this Practice Direction (or any further time granted by the court),

will not be allowed on assessment except as directed by the court.

PD 52A para.5.2

The appellant should consider what other information the appeal court will need. This may include a list of persons who feature in the case or glossaries of technical terms. A chronology of relevant events will be necessary in most appeals.

PD 52A para.5.3

Any statement of costs must show the amount claimed for the skeleton argument separately.

Appeals in the county court and High Court

PD 52B para.8.3

Subject to any order of the court, the parties to the appeal should file and serve skeleton arguments only where—
   (a) the complexity of the issues of fact or law in the appeal justify them; or
   (b) skeleton arguments would assist the court in respects not readily apparent from the papers in the appeal

Appeals to Court of Appeal

PD 52C para.31

   (1) Any skeleton argument [must]—
      (a) not normally exceed 25 pages (excluding front sheets and back sheets);
      (b) be printed on A4 paper in not less than 12 point font and 1.5 line spacing.
   (2) Where an appellant has filed a skeleton argument in support of an application for permission to appeal, the same skeleton argument may be relied upon in the appeal or the appellant may file an appeal skeleton argument.
   (3) At the hearing the court may refuse to hear argument on a point not included in a skeleton argument filed within the prescribed time.
   (4) The court may disallow the cost of preparing an appeal skeleton argument which does not comply with these requirements or was not filed within the prescribed time.

Supplementary skeleton arguments

PD 52C para.32

   (1) A party may file a supplementary skeleton argument only where strictly necessary and only with the permission of the court.
   (2) If a party wishes to rely on a supplementary skeleton argument, it must be lodged and served as soon as practicable. It must be accompanied by a request for permission setting out the reasons why a supplementary skeleton argument is necessary and why it could not reasonably have been lodged earlier.
   (3) Only exceptionally will the court allow the use of a supplementary skeleton argument if lodged later than 7 days before the hearing.

Judicial review

PD 54A para.15.1

The claimant must file and serve a skeleton argument not less than 21 working days before the date of the hearing of the judicial review (or the warned date).

PD 54A para.15.2

The defendant and any other party wishing to make representations at the hearing of the judicial review must file and serve a skeleton argument not less than 14 working days before the date of the hearing of the judicial review (or the warned date).

PD 54A para.15.3

Skeleton arguments must contain:
  (1) a time estimate for the complete hearing, including delivery of judgment;
  (2) a list of issues;
  (3) a list of the legal points to be taken (together with any relevant authorities with page references to the passages relied on);
  (4) a chronology of events (with page references to the bundle of documents (see para.16.1);
  (5) a list of essential documents for the advance reading of the court (with page references to the passages relied on) (if different from that filed with the claim form) and a time estimate for that reading; and
  (6) a list of persons referred to.

Arbitration

PD 62 para.12.2

Subject to para.12.3, the skeleton argument—
  (1) must be printed in 12 point font, with 1.5 line spacing;
  (2) should not exceed 15 pages in length; and
  (3) must contain an estimate of how long the court is likely to need to deal with the application on the papers.

PD 62 para.12.3

If the skeleton argument exceeds 15 pages in length the author must write to the court explaining why that is necessary.

SLANDER

See **Defamation**.

SLIP RULE

Errors.

See **Judgments and orders**.

SMALL CLAIMS TRACK

Pt 26 r.26.6

  (1) The small claims track is the normal track for—
      (a) any claim for personal injuries where—

> > > (i) the value of the claim is not more than £10,000; and
> > > (ii) the value of any claim for damages for personal injuries is not more than £1,000;
> > (b) any claim which includes a claim by a tenant of residential premises against a landlord where—
> > > (i) the tenant is seeking an order requiring the landlord to carry out repairs or other work to the premises (whether or not the tenant is also seeking some other remedy);
> > > (ii) the cost of the repairs or other work to the premises is estimated to be not more than £1,000; and
> > > (iii) the value of any other claim for damages is not more than £1,000.
> (2) For the purposes of para.(1) 'damages for personal injuries' means damages claimed as compensation for pain, suffering and loss of amenity and does not include any other damages which are claimed.
> (3) Subject to para.(1), the small claims track is the normal track for any claim which has a value of not more than £10,000.

Pt 26 r.26.7

> (4) The court will not allocate a claim to the small claims track, if it includes a claim by a tenant of residential premises against his landlord for a remedy in respect of harassment or unlawful eviction.

Pt 27 r.27.1

> (1) [Part 27]—
> > (a) sets out the special procedure for dealing with claims which have been allocated to the small claims track under Pt 26; and
> > (b) limits the amount of costs that can be recovered in respect of a claim which has been allocated to the small claims track.
> (2) A claim being dealt with under this Part is called a small claim.

Allocation

PD 26 para.8.1

> (1) (a) The small claims track is intended to provide a proportionate procedure by which most straightforward claims with a financial value of not more than £10,000 can be decided, without the need for substantial pre-hearing preparation and the formalities of a traditional trial, and without incurring large legal costs. (Rule 26.6 provides for a lower financial value in certain types of case).
> > (b) The procedure laid down in Pt 27 for the preparation of the case and the conduct of the hearing are designed to make it possible for a litigant to conduct his own case without legal representation if he wishes.
> > (c) Cases generally suitable for the small claims track will include consumer disputes, accident claims, disputes about the ownership of goods and most disputes between a landlord and tenant other than opposed claims under Pt 56, disputed claims for possession under Pt 55 and **demotion claims** whether in the alternative to possession claims or under Pt 65.
> > (d) A case involving a disputed allegation of dishonesty will not usually be suitable for the small claims track.
> (2) Rule 26.7(3) and r.27.14(5).

(a) These rules allow the parties to consent to the allocation to the small claims track of a claim the value of which is above the limits mentioned in r.26.6(2) and, in that event, the rules make provision about costs.

(b) The court will not allocate such a claim to the small claims track, notwithstanding that the parties have consented to the allocation, unless it is satisfied that it is suitable for that track.

(c) The court will not normally allow more than one day for the hearing of such a claim.

(d) The court will give case management directions to ensure that the case is dealt with in as short a time as possible. These may include directions of a kind that are not usually given in small claim cases, for example, for **Scott Schedules**.

Extent to which other parts apply

Pt 27 r.27.2

(1) The following Parts of these rules do not apply to small claims—
   (a) Part 25 (**interim remedies**) except as it relates to interim injunctions;
   (b) Part 31 (**disclosure and inspection**);
   (c) Part 32 (**evidence**) except r.32.1 (power of court to control evidence);
   (d) Part 33 (miscellaneous rules about evidence);
   (e) Part 35 (**experts** and **assessors**) except rr.35.1 (duty to restrict expert evidence), 35.3 (experts—overriding duty to the court), 35.7 (court's power to direct that evidence is to be given by single joint expert) and 35.8 (instructions to a single joint expert);
   (f) Subject to para.(3), Pt 18 (further information);
   (g) Part 36 (**offers to settle**); and
   (h) Part 39 (**hearing**) except r.39.2 (general rule—hearing to be in public).
(2) The other Parts of these rules apply to small claims except to the extent that a rule limits such application.
(3) The court of its own initiative may order a party to provide further information if it considers it appropriate to do so.

Case management directions

PD 26 para.8.2

(1) Directions for case management of claims allocated to the small claims track will generally be given by the court on allocation.

PD 27 para.2.2

Appendix A [of PD 27] sets out details of the case that the court usually needs in the type of case described. Appendix B sets out the Standard Directions that the court may give. Appendix C sets out Special Directions that the court may give.

PD 27 para.2.3

Before allocating the claim to the Small Claims Track and giving directions for a hearing the court may require a party to give further information about that party's case.

PD 27 para.2.4

A party may ask the court to give particular directions about the conduct of the case.

Preparation for the hearing

Pt 27 r.27.4

(1) After allocation the court will—
    (a) give **standard directions** and fix a date for the final hearing;
    (b) give **special directions**
    and fix a date for the final hearing;
    (c) give special directions and direct that the court will consider what further directions are to be given no later than 28 days after the date the special directions were given;
    (d) fix a date for a preliminary hearing under r.27.6; or
    (e) give notice that it proposes to deal with the claim without a hearing under r.27.10 and invite the parties to notify the court by a specified date if they agree the proposal.
(2) The court will—
    (a) give the parties at least 21 days' notice of the date fixed for the final hearing, unless the parties agree to accept less notice; and (b) inform them of the amount of time allowed for the final hearing.

PD 27 para.2.5

In deciding whether to make an order for exchange of **witness statements** the court will have regard to the following—
    (a) whether either or both the parties are represented;
    (b) the amount in dispute in the proceedings;
    (c) the nature of the matters in dispute;
    (d) whether the need for any party to clarify his case can better be dealt with by an order under para.2.3;
    (e) the need for the parties to have access to justice without undue formality, cost or delay.

Power of court to add to, vary or revoke directions

Pt 27 r.27.7

The court may add to, vary or revoke directions.

Experts

Pt 27 r.27.5

No expert may give evidence, whether written or oral, at a hearing without the permission of the court.

Preliminary hearing

Pt 27 r.27.6

(1) The court may hold a preliminary hearing for the consideration of the claim, but only—
  (a) where—
    (i) it considers that special directions, as defined in r.27.4, are needed to ensure a fair hearing; and
    (ii) it appears necessary for a party to attend at court to ensure that he understands what he must do to comply with the special directions; or
  (b) to enable it to dispose of the claim on the basis that one or other of the parties has no real prospect of success at a final hearing; or
  (c) to enable it to strike out a statement of case or part of a statement of case on the basis that the statement of case, or the part to be struck out, discloses no reasonable grounds for bringing or defending the claim.
(2) When considering whether or not to hold a preliminary hearing, the court must have regard to the desirability of limiting the expense to the parties of attending court.
(3) Where the court decides to hold a preliminary hearing, it will give the parties at least 14 days' notice of the date of the hearing.
(4) The court may treat the preliminary hearing as the final hearing of the claim if all the parties agree.
(5) At or after the preliminary hearing the court will—
  (a) fix the date of the final hearing (if it has not been fixed already) and give the parties at least 21 days' notice of the date fixed unless the parties agree to accept less notice;
  (b) inform them of the amount of time allowed for the final hearing; and
  (c) give any appropriate directions.

Representation at a hearing

PD 27 para.3.1

In this paragraph:
  (1) a lawyer means a barrister, a solicitor or a legal executive employed by a solicitor, and
  (2) a lay representative means any other person.

PD 27 para.3.2

(1) A party may present his own case at a hearing or a lawyer or lay representative may present it for him.
(2) The Lay Representatives (Right of Audience) Order 1999 provides that a lay representative may not exercise any right of audience
  (a) where his client does not attend the hearing;
  (b) at any stage after judgment; or
  (c) on any appeal brought against any decision made by the district judge in the proceedings.
(3) However the court, exercising its general discretion to hear anybody, may hear a lay representative even in circumstances excluded by the Order.
(4) Any of its officers or employees may represent a corporate party.

Small claim hearing

PD 27 para.4.1

(1) The general rule is that a small claim hearing will be in public.
(2) The judge may decide to hold it in private if:
    (a) the parties agree, or
    (b) a ground mentioned in r.39.2(3) applies.
(3) A hearing or part of a hearing which takes place other than at the court, for example at the home or business premises of a party, will not be in public.

PD 27 para.4.2

A hearing that takes place at the court will generally be in the judge's room but it may take place in a courtroom.

Conduct of the hearing

Pt 27 r.27.8

(1) The court may adopt any method of proceeding at a hearing that it considers to be fair.
(2) Hearings will be informal.
(3) The strict rules of evidence do not apply.
(4) The court need not take evidence on oath.
(5) The court may limit cross-examination.
(6) The court must give reasons for its decision.

PD 27 para.4.3

Rule 27.8 allows the court to adopt any method of proceeding that it considers to be fair and to limit cross-examination. The judge may in particular:
(1) ask questions of any witness himself before allowing any other person to do so,
(2) ask questions of all or any of the witnesses himself before allowing any other person to ask questions of any witnesses,
(3) refuse to allow cross-examination of any witness until all the witnesses have given evidence in chief,
(4) limit cross-examination of a witness to a fixed time or to a particular subject or issue, or both.

Recording evidence and the giving of reasons

PD 27 para.5.1

A hearing that takes place at the court will be tape recorded by the court. A party may obtain a transcript of such a recording on payment of the proper transcriber's charges.

PD 7 para.5.2

Attention is drawn to s.9 of the Contempt of Court Act 1981 (which deals with the unauthorised use of tape recorders in court) and to the PD ([1981] 1 W.L.R. 1526) which relates to it.

PD 27 para.5.3

(1) The judge may give reasons for his judgment as briefly and simply as the nature of the case allows.

(2) He will normally do so orally at the hearing, but he may give them later at a hearing either orally or in writing.

PD 27 para.5.4

Where the judge decides the case without a hearing under r.27.10 or a party who has given notice under r.27.9(1) does not attend the hearing, the judge will prepare a note of his reasons and the court will send a copy to each party.

PD 27 para.5.5

Nothing in [PD 27] affects the duty of a judge at the request of a party to make a note of the matters referred to in s.80 of the County Courts Act 1984.

Non-attendance of parties at a final hearing

Pt 27 r.27.9

(1) If a party who does not attend a final hearing—
   (a) has given written notice to the court and the other party at least seven days before the hearing date that he will not attend;
   (b) has served on the other party at least seven days before the hearing date any other documents which he has filed with the court; and
   (c) has, in his written notice, requested the court to decide the claim in his absence and has confirmed his compliance with paras (a) and (b) above,
   the court will take into account that party's statement of case and any other documents he has filed and served when it decides the claim.

(2) If a claimant does not—
   (a) attend the hearing; and
   (b) give the notice referred to in para.(1),
   the court may strike out the claim.

(3) If—
   (a) a defendant does not—
       (i) attend the hearing; or
       (ii) give the notice referred to in para.(1); and
   (b) the claimant either—
       (i) does attend the hearing; or
       (ii) gives the notice referred to in para.(1),
   the court may decide the claim on the basis of the evidence of the claimant alone.

(3) If neither party attends or gives the notice referred to in para.(1), the court may strike out the claim and any defence and counterclaim.

PD 27 para.6.1

Attention is drawn to r.27.9 (which enables a party to give notice that he will not attend a final hearing and sets out the effect of his giving such notice and of not doing so), and to para.3 above.

PD 27 para.6.2

Nothing in those provisions affects the general power of the court to adjourn a hearing, for example where a party who wishes to attend a hearing on the date fixed cannot do so for a good reason.

Disposal without a hearing

Pt 27 r.27.10

The court may, if all parties agree, deal with the claim without a hearing.

Appeals

PD 27 para.8.1

Part 52 deals with **appeals** and attention is drawn to that Part and PD 52.

PD 27 para.8.A

An appellant's notice in small claims must be filed and served in Form N164.

PD 27 para.8.2

Where the court dealt with the claim to which the appellant is a party:
   (1) under r.27.10 without a hearing; or
   (2) in his absence because he gave notice under r.27.9 requesting the court to decide the claim in his absence,
an application for permission to appeal must be made to the appeal court.

PD 27 para.8.3

Where an appeal is allowed the appeal court will, if possible, dispose of the case at the same time without referring the claim to the lower court or ordering a new hearing. It may do so without hearing further evidence.

Judges

PD 27 para.1

The functions of the court described in Pt 27 which are to be carried out by a judge will generally be carried out by a district judge but may be carried out by a Circuit Judge.

Appendices to PD 27

Appendix A

Information and documentation the court usually needs in particular types of case
  Road accident cases (where the information or documentation is available)

Building disputes, repairs, goods sold and similar contractual claims (where the information or documentation is available)

Landlord and tenant claims (where the information or documentation is available)

Breach of duty cases (negligence, deficient professional services and the like)

Appendix B

Standard directions

Appendix C

Special directions

See also **Final remedy**, **Re-allocation to a different track**, **Re-hearing**, and **Small claims track costs**.

SMALL CLAIMS TRACK COSTS

Pt 46 r.46.11

(1) Part 27 (small claims) and Part 46 (**fast track trial costs**) contain special rules about—

(a) liability for costs;

(b) the amount of costs which the court may award; and

(c) the procedure for assessing costs.

(2) Once a claim is allocated to a particular track, those special rules shall apply to the period before, as well as after, allocation except where the court or a PD provides otherwise.

PD 46 para.7.1

(1) Before a claim is allocated to either the small claims track or the fast track the court is not restricted by any of the special rules that apply to that track but see para.8.2 below.

(2) Where a claim has been so allocated, the special rules which relate to that track will apply to work done before as well as after allocation save to the extent (if any) that an order for costs in respect of that work was made before allocation.

(3) Where a claim, issued for a sum in excess of the normal financial scope of the small claims track, is allocated to that track only because an admission of part of the claim by the defendant reduces the amount in dispute to a sum within the normal scope of that track; on entering judgment for the admitted part before allocation of the balance of the claim the court may allow costs in respect of the proceedings down to that date.

PD 46 para.8.2

Where a settlement is reached or a Pt 36 offer accepted in a case which has not been allocated but would, if allocated, have been suitable for allocation to the small claims track, r. 46.13

enables the court to allow only small claims track costs in accordance with r. 27.14. This power is not exercisable if the costs are to be paid on the indemnity basis.

PD 27 para.7.1

Attention is drawn to r.27.14 which contains provisions about the costs which may be ordered to be paid by one party to another.

PD 27 para.7.2

The amount which a party may be ordered to pay under r.27.14(2)(b) (for legal advice and assistance in claims including an injunction or specific performance) is a sum not exceeding £260.

PD 27 para.7.3

The amounts which a party may be ordered to pay under r.27.14(3)(c) (loss of earnings) and (d) (experts' fees) are:
  (1) for the loss of earnings or loss of leave of each party or witness due to attending a hearing or staying away from home for the purpose of attending a hearing, a sum not exceeding £90 per day for each person, and
  (2) for experts' fees, a sum not exceeding £750 for each expert.
(As to recovery of pre-allocation costs in a case in which an admission by the defendant has reduced the amount in dispute to a figure below £10,000, reference should be made to para.7.4 of PD 26 and to para.15.1(3) of the Costs PD).

Pt 27 r.27.14

  (1) This rule applies to any case which has been allocated to the small claims track.
(Rules 44.9 and 44.11 make provision in relation to orders for costs made before a claim has been allocated to the small claims track).
  (2) The court may not order a party to pay a sum to another party in respect of that other party's costs, fees and expenses, including those relating to an appeal, except—
    (a) the fixed costs attributable to issuing the claim which—
      (i) are payable under Pt 45; or
      (ii) would be payable under Pt 45 if that Part applied to the claim;
    (b) in proceedings which included a claim for an injunction or an order for specific performance a sum not exceeding the amount specified in PD 27 for legal advice and assistance relating to that claim;
    (c) any court fees paid by that other party;
    (d) expenses which a party or witness has reasonably incurred in travelling to and from a hearing or in staying away from home for the purposes of attending a hearing;
    (e) a sum not exceeding the amount specified in PD 27 for any loss of earnings or loss of leave by a party or witness due to attending a hearing or to staying away from home for the purposes of attending a hearing;
    (f) a sum not exceeding the amount specified in PD 27 for an expert's fees;
    (g) such further costs as the court may assess by the summary procedure and order to be paid by a party who has behaved unreasonably; and
    (h) the Stage 1 and, where relevant, the Stage 2 fixed costs in r.45.29 where—
      (i) the claim was within the scope of the Pre-Action Protocol for Low Value Personal Injury Claims in Road Traffic Accidents ('the RTA Protocol');
      (ii) the claimant reasonably believed that the claim was valued at more than the small claims track limit in accordance with para.4.1(4) of the RTA Protocol; and

    (iii) the defendant admitted liability under the process set out in the RTA Protocol; but

    (iv) the defendant did not pay those Stage 1 and, where relevant, Stage 2 fixed costs; and

    (v) in an appeal, the cost of any approved transcript reasonably incurred.

(3) A party's rejection of an offer in settlement will not of itself constitute unreasonable behaviour under para.(2)(g) but the court may take it into consideration when it is applying the unreasonableness test.

(4) The limits on costs imposed by this rule also apply to any fee or reward for acting on behalf of a party to the proceedings charged by a person exercising a right of audience by virtue of an order under s.11 of the Courts and Legal Services Act 1990 (a lay representative).

Fixed costs in small claims

Costs PD para.24.1

Under r.27.14 the costs which can be awarded to a claimant in a small claims track case include the fixed costs payable under Pt 45 attributable to issuing the claim.

Costs PD para.24.2

Those fixed costs shall be the sum of
    (a) the fixed commencement costs calculated in accordance with Table 1 of r.45.2 and;
    (b) the appropriate court fee or fees paid by the claimant.

Costs on the small claims track and fast track

Pt 44 r.44.9

(1) Pt 27 (small claims) and Pt 46 (fast track trial costs) contain special rules about—
    (a) liability for costs;
    (b) the amount of costs which the court may award; and
    (c) the procedure for assessing costs.

(2) Once a claim is allocated to a particular track, those special rules shall apply to the period before, as well as after, allocation except where the court or a practice direction provides otherwise.

Costs PD para.15.1

(1) Before a claim is allocated to one of those tracks the court is not restricted by any of the special rules that apply to that track.

(2) Where a claim has been allocated to one of those tracks, the special rules which relate to that track will apply to work done before as well as after allocation save to the extent (if any) that an order for costs in respect of that work was made before allocation.

(3) (i) This paragraph applies where a claim, issued for a sum in excess of the normal financial scope of the small claims track, is allocated to that track only because an admission of part of the claim by the defendant reduces the amount in dispute to a sum within the normal scope of that track.

   (ii) On entering judgment for the admitted part before allocation of the balance of the claim the court may allow costs in respect of the proceedings down to that date.

PD 26 para.7.4

"any amount not in dispute"

In deciding, for the purposes of r.26.8(2) [Matters relevant to allocation to a track], whether an amount is in dispute the court will apply the following general principles:
   (1) Any amount for which the defendant does not admit liability is in dispute,
   (2) Any sum in respect of an item forming part of the claim for which judgment has been entered (for example a summary judgment) is not in dispute,
   (3) Any specific sum claimed as a distinct item and which the defendant admits he is liable to pay is not in dispute,
   (4) Any sum offered by the defendant which has been accepted by the claimant in satisfaction of any item which forms a distinct part of the claim is not in dispute.
It follows from these provisions that if, in relation to a claim the value of which is above the small claims track limit of £5,000, the defendant makes, before allocation, an admission that reduces the amount in dispute to a figure below £5,000 (see Pt 14), the normal track for the claim will be the small claims track. As to recovery of pre-allocation costs, the claimant can, before allocation, apply for judgment with costs on the amount of the claim that has been admitted (see r.14.3 but see also para.15.1(3) of the Costs PD supplementing Pts 43 to 48 under which the court has a discretion to allow pre-allocation costs).

Costs following allocation and re-allocation

Pt 44 r.44.11

   (1) Any costs orders made before a claim is allocated will not be affected by allocation.
   (2) Where—
      (a) a claim is allocated to a track; and
      (b) the court subsequently re-allocates that claim to a different track,
         then unless the court orders otherwise, any special rules about costs applying—
            (i) to the first track, will apply to the claim up to the date of re-allocation; and
            (ii) to the second track, will apply from the date of re-allocation.
(Pt 26 deals with the allocation and re-allocation of claims between tracks)

Costs PD para.16.1

This paragraph applies where the court is about to make an order to re-allocate a claim from the small claims track to another track.

Costs PD para.16.2

Before making the order to re-allocate the claim, the court must decide whether any party is to pay costs to any other party down to the date of the order to re-allocate in accordance with the rules about costs contained in Pt 27 (The Small Claims Track).

Costs PD para.16.3

If it decides to make such an order about costs, the court will make a summary assessment of those costs in accordance with that Part.

SOLICITOR

Acting for a party

Pt 42 r.42.1

Where the **address for service** of a party is the business address of his solicitor, the solicitor will be considered to be acting for that party until the provisions of [Pt 42] have been complied with.

PD 42 para.1.2

Subject to r.42.2(6) (where the certificate of a **LSC funded client** or **assisted person** is revoked or discharged), where a party has changed his solicitor or intends to act in person, the former solicitor will be considered to be the party's solicitor unless or until:
    (1) a notice of the change is
        (a) filed with the court, and
        (b) served on every other party, or
    (2) the court makes an order under r.42.3 and the order is served on every other party.
The notice should not be filed until every other party has been served.

Acting as advocate only

PD 42 para.1.3

A solicitor appointed to represent a party only as an advocate at a hearing will not be considered to be acting for that party within the meaning of Pt 42.

Change of address for service

PD 42 para.2.3

In addition, where a party or solicitor changes his address for service, a notice of that change should be filed and served on every party.

Notice of change of solicitor

Pt 42 r.42.2

    (1) This rule applies where—
        (a) a party for whom a solicitor is acting wants to change his solicitor;
        (b) a party, after having conducted the claim in person, appoints a solicitor to act on his behalf (except where the solicitor is appointed only to act as an advocate for a hearing); or
        (c) a party, after having conducted the claim by a solicitor, intends to act in person.
    (2) Where this rule applies, the party or his solicitor (where one is acting) must—
        (a) file notice of the change; and
        (b) serve notice of the change on every other party and, where para.(1)(a) or (c) applies, on the former solicitor.

(3) The notice must state the party's new address for service.

(4) The notice filed at court must state that notice has been served as required by para.(2)(b).

(5) Subject to para.(6), where a party has changed his solicitor or intends to act in person, the former solicitor will be considered to be the party's solicitor unless and until—

    (a) notice is filed and served in accordance with para.(2); or

    (b) the court makes an order under r.42.3 and the order is served as required by para.(3) of that rule.

LSC funded client or assisted person

Pt 42 r.42.2

(6) Where the certificate [in the case of a LSC funded client, a certificate issued under the Funding Code (approved under s.9 of the Access to Justice Act 1999), or in the case of an assisted person, a certificate within the meaning of the Civil Legal Aid (General) Regulations 1989] of a LSC funded client or an assisted person is revoked or discharged—

    (a) the solicitor who acted for that person will cease to be the solicitor acting in the case as soon as his retainer is determined—

        (i) under reg.4 of the Community Legal Service (Costs) Regulations 2000

        (ii) under reg.83 of the Civil Legal Aid (General) Regulations 1989

    (b) if that person wishes to continue—

        (i) where he appoints a solicitor to act on his behalf, para.(2) will apply as if he had previously conducted the claim in person; and

        (ii) where he wants to act in person, he must give an **address for service**.

PD 42 para.2.2

A notice of the change giving the last known address of the former assisted person must also be filed and served on every party where, under r.42.2(6):

(1) the certificate of a LSC funded client or assisted person is revoked or discharged,

(2) the solicitor who acted for that person ceased to act on determination of his retainer under reg.83 of those regulations, and

(3) the LSC funded client or the assisted person wishes either to act in person or appoint another solicitor to act on his behalf.

Party acting in person

PD 42 para.2.4

A party who, having conducted a claim by a solicitor, intends to act in person must give in the notice an address for service that is within the UK.

PD 42 para.2.5

Practice Form N434 should be used to give notice of any change. The notice should be filed in the court office in which the claim is proceeding.

PD 42 para.2.6

Where the claim is proceeding in the High Court the notice should be filed either in the appropriate District Registry or if the claim is proceeding in the Royal Courts of Justice, as follows;
  (1) a claim proceeding in the Queen's Bench Division—in the Action Department of the Central Office,
  (2) a claim proceeding in the Chancery Division—in Chancery Chambers,
  (3) a claim proceeding in the Administrative Court—in the Administrative Court office;
  (4) a claim proceeding in the Admiralty and Commercial Registry—in the Admiralty and Commercial Registry, and
  (5) a claim proceeding in the Technology and Construction Court—in the Registry of the Technology and Construction Court.

PD 42 para.2.7

Where the claim is the subject of an appeal to the Court of Appeal, the notice should also be filed in the Civil Appeals Office.
(The Costs PD supplementing Pts 43 to 48 contains details of the information required to be included when the funding arrangements for the claim change).

Order that a solicitor has ceased to act

Pt 42 r.42.3

  (1) A solicitor may apply for an order declaring that he has ceased to be the solicitor acting for a party.
  (2) Where an application is made under this rule—
    (a) notice of the application must be given to the party for whom the solicitor is acting, unless the court directs otherwise; and
    (b) the application must be supported by evidence.
  (3) Where the court makes an order that a solicitor has ceased to act—
    (a) a copy of the order must be served on every party to the proceedings; and
    (b) if it is served by a party or the solicitor, the party or the solicitor (as the case may be) must file a certificate of service.

PD 42 para.3.1

A solicitor may apply under r.42.3 for an order declaring that he has ceased to be the solicitor acting for a party.

PD 42 para.3.2

The application should be made in accordance with Pt 23 and must be supported by evidence. Unless the court directs otherwise the application notice must be served on the party.

PD 42 para.3.3

An order made under r.42.3 must be served on every party and takes effect when it is served. Where the order is not served by the court, the person serving must file a certificate of service in practice Form N215.

Removal of solicitor who has ceased to act on application of another party

Pt 42 r.42.4

(1) Where—
    (a) a solicitor who has acted for a party—
        (i) has died;
        (ii) has become bankrupt;
        (iii) has ceased to practice; or
        (iv) cannot be found; and
    (b) the party has not given notice of a change of solicitor or notice of intention to act in person as required by r.42.2(2),
    any other party may apply for an order declaring that the solicitor has ceased to be the solicitor acting for the other party in the case.
(2) Where an application is made under this rule, notice of the application must be given to the party to whose solicitor the application relates unless the court directs otherwise.
(3) Where the court makes an order made under this rule—
    (a) a copy of the order must be served on every other party to the proceedings; and
    (b) where it is served by a party, that party must file a certificate of service.

PD 42 para.4.1

Rule 42.4 sets out circumstances in which any other party may apply for an order declaring that a solicitor has ceased to be the solicitor acting for another party in the proceedings.

PD 42 para.4.2

The application should be made in accordance with Pt 23 and must be supported by evidence. Unless the court directs otherwise the application notice must be served on the party to whose solicitor the application relates.

PD 42 para.4.3

An order made under r.42.4 must be served on every other party to the proceedings. Where the order is not served by the court, the person serving must file a certificate of service in Practice Form N215.

New address for service following change of solicitor pursuant to court order

PD 42 para.5.1

Where the court has made an order under r.42.3 that a solicitor has ceased to act or under r.42.4 declaring that a solicitor has ceased to be the solicitor for a party, the party for whom the solicitor was acting must give a new address for service to comply with rr.6.23(1) and 6.24.
(Rule 6.23(2)(a) provides that a party must give an address for service within the UK or where a solicitor is acting for a party, an address for service either in the UK or any other EEA state.)
(Until such time as a new address for service is given r.6.9 will apply).

Proceedings relating to solicitors

Pt 67 r.67.1

(1) Part [67] contains rules about the following types of proceedings relating to solicitors—

    (a) proceedings to obtain an order for a solicitor to deliver a bill or cash account and proceedings in relation to money or papers received by a solicitor (r.67.2);

    (b) proceedings under Pt III of the Solicitors Act 1974 relating to the remuneration of solicitors (r.67.3); and

    (c) proceedings under Sch.1 to the Solicitors Act 1974 arising out of the Law Society's intervention in a solicitor's practice (r.67.4).

(Part 48 and s.56 of the Costs PD contain provisions about the procedure and basis for the detailed assessment of **solicitor and client costs** under Part III of the Act).

(PD 52 contains provisions about Appeals to the High Court from the **Solicitors Disciplinary Tribunal** under s.49 of the Act).

PD 67 para.1

[PD 67] applies to proceedings under r.67.2 [power to order solicitor to deliver cash account etc.] and to the following types of claim under r.67.3 and Pt III [remuneration of solicitors] of the Solicitors Act 1974 ('the Act'):

(1) an application under s.57(5) of the Act for a costs officer to enquire into the facts and certify whether a **non-contentious business agreement** should be set aside or the amount payable under it reduced;

(2) a claim under s.61(1) of the Act for the court to enforce or set aside a **contentious business agreement** and determine questions as to its validity and effect;

(3) a claim by a client under s.61(3) of the Act for a costs officer to examine a contentious business agreement as to its fairness and reasonableness;

(4) where the amount agreed under a contentious business agreement has been paid, a claim under s.61(5) of the Act for the agreement to be re-opened and the costs assessed;

(5) proceedings under s.62 of the Act for the examination of a contentious business agreement, where the client makes the agreement as a representative of a person whose property will be chargeable with the amount payable;

(6) proceedings under s.63 of the Act where, after some business has been done under a contentious business agreement, but before the solicitor has wholly performed it:

    (a) the solicitor dies or becomes incapable of acting; or

    (b) the client changes solicitor;

(7) where an action is commenced on a gross sum bill, an application under section 64(3) of the Act for an order that the bill be assessed;

(8) a claim under s.68 of the Act for the delivery by a solicitor of a bill of costs and for the delivery up of, or otherwise in relation to, any documents;

(9) an application under s.69 of the Act for an order that the solicitor be at liberty to commence an action to recover his costs within one month of delivery of the bill;

(10) a claim under s.70(1) of the Act, by the party chargeable with the solicitor's bill, for an order that the bill be assessed and that no action be taken on the bill until the assessment is completed;

(11) a claim under s.70(2) of the Act, by either party, for an order that the bill be assessed and that no action be commenced or continued on the bill until the assessment is completed;

(12) a claim under s.70(3) of the Act, by the party chargeable with the bill, for detailed assessment showing special circumstances;

(13) a claim under s.71(1) of the Act, by a person other than the party chargeable with the bill, for detailed assessment;

(14) a claim under s.71(3) of the Act, by any person interested in any property out of which a trustee, executor or administrator has paid or is entitled to pay a solicitor's bill, for **detailed assessment**; and

(15) a claim by a solicitor under s.73 of the Act for a **charging order**.

Power to order solicitor to deliver cash account etc.

Pt 67 r.67.2

(1) Where the relationship of solicitor and client exists or has existed, the orders which the court may make against the solicitor, on the application of the client or his personal representatives, include any of the following—
 (a) to deliver a bill or cash account;
 (b) to pay or deliver up any money or securities;
 (c) to deliver a list of the moneys or securities which the solicitor has in his possession or control on behalf of the applicant;
 (d) to pay into or lodge in court any such money or securities.
(2) An application for an order under this rule must be made—
 (a) by Pt 8 claim form; or
 (b) if the application is made in existing proceedings, by application notice in accordance with Pt 23.
(3) If the solicitor alleges that he has a claim for costs against the applicant, the court may make an order for—
 (a) the detailed assessment and payment of those costs; and
 (b) securing the payment of the costs, or protecting any solicitor's lien.

Pt 67 r.67.3

Remuneration of solicitor—proceedings under Pt III of the Act

(1) A claim for an order under Pt III of the Act for the assessment of costs payable to a solicitor by his client—
 (a) which—
  (i) relates to contentious business done in a county court; and
  (ii) is within the financial limit of the county court's jurisdiction specified in s.69(3) of the Act.
 may be made in that county court;
 (b) in every other case, must be made in the High Court.
(Rule 30.2 makes provision for any county court to transfer the proceedings to another county court for detailed assessment of costs).
(Provisions about the venue for detailed assessment proceedings are contained in r.47.4 and s.31 of the Costs PD).
(2) A claim for an order under Pt III of the Act must be made—
 (a) by Pt 8 claim form; or
 (b) if the claim is made in existing proceedings, by application notice in accordance with Pt 23.
(A model form of claim form is annexed to the Costs PD)
(3) A claim in the High Court under Pt III of the Act may be determined by—
 (a) a High Court judge;
 (b) a Master, a costs judge or a district judge of the Principal Registry of the Family Division; or
 (c) a district judge, if the costs are for—
  (i) contentious business done in proceedings in the district registry of which he is the district judge;

(ii) contentious business done in proceedings in a county court within the district of that district registry; or

(iii) non-contentious business.

General provisions for certain proceedings under the Solicitors Act 1974

PD 67 para.1

[PD 67] applies to proceedings under r.67.2 [power to order solicitor to deliver cash account etc.] and to the following types of claim under r.67.3 and Pt III [remuneration of solicitors] of the Solicitors Act 1974 ('the Act'):

(1) an application under s.57(5) of the Act for a costs officer to enquire into the facts and certify whether a non-contentious business agreement should be set aside or the amount payable under it reduced;

(2) a claim under s.61(1) of the Act for the court to enforce or set aside a contentious business agreement and determine questions as to its validity and effect;

(3) a claim by a client under s.61(3) of the Act for a costs officer to examine a contentious business agreement as to its fairness and reasonableness;

(4) where the amount agreed under a contentious business agreement has been paid, a claim under s.61(5) of the Act for the agreement to be re-opened and the costs assessed;

(5) proceedings under s.62 of the Act for the examination of a contentious business agreement, where the client makes the agreement as a representative of a person whose property will be chargeable with the amount payable;

(6) proceedings under s.63 of the Act where, after some business has been done under a contentious business agreement, but before the solicitor has wholly performed it:
(a) the solicitor dies or becomes incapable of acting; or
(b) the client changes solicitor;

(7) where an action is commenced on a gross sum bill, an application under section 64(3) of the Act for an order that the bill be assessed;

(8) a claim under s.68 of the Act for the delivery by a solicitor of a bill of costs and for the delivery up of, or otherwise in relation to, any documents;

(9) an application under s.69 of the Act for an order that the solicitor be at liberty to commence an action to recover his costs within one month of delivery of the bill;

(10) a claim under s.70(1) of the Act, by the party chargeable with the solicitor's bill, for an order that the bill be assessed and that no action be taken on the bill until the assessment is completed;

(11) a claim under s.70(2) of the Act, by either party, for an order that the bill be assessed and that no action be commenced or continued on the bill until the assessment is completed;

(12) a claim under s.70(3) of the Act, by the party chargeable with the bill, for detailed assessment showing special circumstances;

(13) a claim under s.71(1) of the Act, by a person other than the party chargeable with the bill, for detailed assessment;

(14) a claim under s.71(3) of the Act, by any person interested in any property out of which a trustee, executor or administrator has paid or is entitled to pay a solicitor's bill, for detailed assessment; and

(15) a claim by a solicitor under s.73 of the Act for a charging order.

PD 67 para.2.1

Where a claim to which this PD applies is made by Pt 8 claim form in the High Court in London—

(1) if the claim is of a type referred to in paras 1(1) to (5), it must be issued in the Costs Office;

(2) in any other case, the claim may be issued in the Costs Office.

PD 67 para.2.2

A claim which is made by Pt 8 claim form in a district registry or by Pt 23 application notice in existing High Court proceedings may be referred to the Costs Office.

PD 67 para.2.2A

Where a claim under ss.70 or 71 of the Act is made by Pt 8 claim form is used.

PD 67 para.2.3

The Costs Office, the court will fix a date for the hearing of the claim when the claim form is issued.

PD 67 para.3.1

Rule 67.3(3) makes provision about jurisdiction to determine claims under Pt III of the Act [remuneration of solicitors].

PD 67 para.3.2

Claims for any of the orders listed in para.1 should normally be made to a Master, costs judge or district judge. Only exceptional circumstances will justify making the claim directly to a High Court Judge.

PD 67 para.3.3

Paragraph 1 of PD 23A sets out the circumstances in which a matter may be referred to a judge.

PD 67 para.5

Unless the court orders otherwise, an order in proceedings in the Costs Office to which this PD applies shall be drawn up and served by the party who made the relevant claim or application.

Evidence in proceedings for order for detailed assessment

PD 67 para.4

Where a Pt 8 claim is brought for an order for the detailed assessment of a solicitor's bill of costs, the parties are not required to comply with r.8.5 [filing and serving written evidence] unless:
(1) the claim will be contested; or
(2) the court directs that the parties should comply with r.8.5.

See **Intervention in solicitor's office.**

Drawing up and service of orders

PD 67 para.5

Unless the court orders otherwise, an order in proceedings in the Court Offices to which [PD 67—Proceedings relating to Solicitors] applies shall be drawn up and served by the party who made the relevant claim or application.

Service of documents within the jurisdiction

Pt 6 r.6.7

(1) Subject to r.6.5(1)[requirement by another Part of CPR, any other enactment, a PD or a court order, a claim form must be served personally], where—
  (a) the defendant has given in writing the business address within the jurisdiction of a solicitor as an address at which the defendant may be served with the claim form; or
  (b) a solicitor acting for the defendant has notified the claimant in writing that the solicitor is instructed by the defendant to accept service of the claim form on behalf of the defendant at a business address within the jurisdiction,
  the claim form must be served at the business address of that solicitor.
('Solicitor' has the extended meaning set out in r.6.2(d)[includes any other person who, for the purposes of the Legal Services Act 2007, is an authorised person in relation to an activity which constitutes the conduct of litigation (within the meaning of that Act).]

SOLICITOR AND CLIENT COSTS

Basis of detailed assessment of solicitor and client costs

PD 46 para.46.9

(1) This rule applies to every assessment of a solicitor's bill to his client except a bill which is to be paid out of the Community Legal Service Fund under the Legal Aid Act 1988 or the Access to Justice Act 1999; and
(2) Section 74(3) of the Solicitors Act 1974(a) applies unless the solicitor and client have entered into a written agreement which expressly permits payment to the solicitor of an amount of costs greater than that which the client could have recovered from another party to the proceedings.
(3) Subject to para.(2), costs are to be assessed on the **indemnity basis** but are to be presumed—
  (a) to have been reasonably incurred if they were incurred with the express or implied approval of the client;
  (b) to be reasonable in amount if their amount was expressly or impliedly approved by the client;
  (c) to have been unreasonably incurred if—
    (i) they are of an unusual nature or amount; and
    (ii) the solicitor did not tell his client that as a result he might not recover all of them from the other party.
(4) Where the court is considering a percentage increase, on the application of the client, the court will have regard to all the relevant factors as they reasonably appeared to the solicitor or counsel when the conditional fee agreement [agreement enforceable under

s.58 of the Courts and Legal Services Act 1990 at the date on which that agreement was entered into or varied] was entered into or varied.

PD 46 para.6.1

A client and his solicitor may agree whatever terms they consider appropriate about the payment of the solicitor's charges for his services. If however, the costs are of an unusual nature (either in amount or in the type of costs incurred) those costs will be presumed to have been unreasonably incurred unless the solicitor satisfies the court that he informed the client that they were unusual and, where the costs relate to litigation, that he informed the client they might not be allowed on an assessment of costs between the parties. That information must have been given to the client before the costs were incurred.

PD 46 para.6.2

(1) Costs as between a solicitor and client are assessed on the **indemnity basis**. The presumptions in r.46.9(3) are rebuttable.

PD 46 para.6.3

If a party fails to comply with the requirements of r. 46.10 concerning the service of a breakdown of costs or points of dispute, any other party may apply to the court in which the detailed assessment hearing should take place for an order requiring compliance. If the court makes such an order, it may—
(a) make it subject to conditions including a condition to pay a sum of money into court; and
(b) specify the consequence of failure to comply with the order or a condition.

PD 46 para.6.4

The procedure for obtaining an order under Pt III of the Solicitors Act 1974 is by a Pt 8 claim, as modified by r. 67.3 and PD 67. Precedent J of the Schedule of Costs Precedents is a model form of claim form. The application must be accompanied by the bill or bills in respect of which assessment is sought, and, if the claim concerns a conditional fee agreement, a copy of that agreement. If the original bill is not available a copy will suffice.

PD 46 para.6.5

Model forms of order, which the court may make, are set out in Precedents K, L and M of the Schedule of Costs Precedents.

PD 46 para.6.6

The breakdown of costs referred to in r. 46.10 is a document which contains the following information—
(a) details of the work done under each of the bills sent for assessment; and
(b) in applications under s.70 of the Solicitors Act 1974, a cash account showing money received by the solicitor to the credit of the client and sums paid out of that money on behalf of the client but not payments out which were made in satisfaction of the bill or of any items which are claimed in the bill.

PD 46 para.6.7

Precedent P of the Schedule of Costs Precedents is a model form of breakdown of costs. A party who is required to serve a breakdown of costs must also serve—

  (a) copies of the fee notes of counsel and of any expert in respect of fees claimed in the breakdown, and
  (b) written evidence as to any other disbursement which is claimed in the breakdown and which exceeds £250.

PD 46 para.6.8

The provisions relating to **default costs certificate**s (r. 47.11) do not apply to cases to which r. 46.10 applies.

PD 46 para.6.9

The time for requesting a detailed assessment hearing is within three months after the date of the order for the costs to be assessed.

PD 46 para.6.10

The form of request for a hearing date must be in Form N258C. The request must be accompanied by copies of—
  (a) the order sending the bill or bills for assessment;
  (b) the bill or bills sent for assessment;
  (c) the solicitor's breakdown of costs and any invoices or accounts served with that breakdown;
  (d) a copy of the points of dispute;
  (e) a copy of any replies served;
  (f) a statement signed by the party filing the request or that party's legal representative giving the names and addresses for service of all parties to the proceedings.

PD 46 para.6.11

The request must include the estimated length of hearing.

PD 46 para.6.12

On receipt of the request the court will fix a date for the hearing, or will give directions.

PD 46 para.6.13

The court will give at least 14 days notice of the time and place of the detailed assessment hearing.

PD 46 para.6.14

Unless the court gives permission, only the solicitor whose bill it is and parties who have served.
Points of dispute may be heard and only items specified in the points of dispute may be raised.

PD 46 para.6.15

If a party wishes to vary that party's breakdown of costs, points of dispute or reply, an amended or supplementary document must be filed with the court and copies of it must be served on all other relevant parties. Permission is not required to vary a breakdown of costs, points of dispute or a reply but the court may disallow the variation or permit it only upon conditions, including conditions as to the payment of any costs caused or wasted by the variation.

PD 46 para.6.16

Unless the court directs otherwise the solicitor must file with the court the papers in support of the bill not less than seven days before the date for the detailed assessment hearing and not more than 14 days before that date.

PD 46 para.6.17

Once the detailed assessment hearing has ended it is the responsibility of the legal representative appearing for the solicitor or, as the case may be, the solicitor in person to remove the papers filed in support of the bill.

PD 46 para.6.18

If, in the course of a detailed assessment hearing of a solicitor's bill to that solicitor's client, it appears to the court that in any event the solicitor will be liable in connection with that bill to pay money to the client, it may issue an interim certificate specifying an amount which in its opinion is payable by the solicitor to the client.

PD 46 para.6.19

After the detailed assessment hearing is concluded the court will—
- (a) complete the court copy of the bill so as to show the amount allowed;
- (b) determine the result of the cash account;
- (c) award the costs of the detailed assessment hearing in accordance with s.70(8) of the Solicitors Act 1974; and
- (d) issue a **final costs certificate**.

SOLICITORS DISCIPLINARY TRIBUNAL

Appeals from decisions of the Law Society and Solicitors Disciplinary Tribunal to the High Court

PD 52D para.27.1

- (1) This paragraph applies to appeals from the Law Society or the Solicitors Disciplinary Tribunal ('the Tribunal') to the High Court under the Solicitors Act 1974, the Administration of Justice Act 1985, the Courts and Legal Services Act 1990, the European Communities (Lawyer's Practice) Regulations 2000 or the European Communities (Recognition of Professional Qualifications) Regulations 2007.
- (2) The appellant must file the appellant's notice in the **Administrative Court**.
- (3) Unless the court orders otherwise, serve the appellant's notice on—
  - (a) every party to the proceedings before the Tribunal; and
  - (b) the Law Society.

SOLICITOR'S UNDERTAKING

Solicitors Act 1974 s.50(2)

County Court Act 1984 s.142

The court may enforce a solicitor's undertaking by committal order against the solicitor.

High Court

The basis of enforcing a solicitor's undertaking in the High Court is that the solicitor is an officer of the court.

County court

The basis of enforcing a solicitor's undertaking in the county court as a result of s.142 of the County Court Act 1984.

Pt 81 r.81.11

(1) The applicant must obtain permission from the court before making a committal application under this rule.
(2) The application for permission must be made by filing an application notice under Pt 23.
(3) The application for permission must be supported by an affidavit setting out—
    (a) the name, description and address of the respondent; and
    (b) the grounds on which the committal order is sought.
(4) The application for permission may be made without notice.
(5) R. 23.9 [Service of application where application made without notice] and r.23.10 [Application to set aside or vary order made without notice] do not apply.
(6) Unless the applicant makes the committal application within 14 days after permission has been granted under this rule, the permission will lapse.

SPECIAL DIRECTIONS

Small claims track

Pt 27 r.27.4

(1) After allocation the court will—
    (b) give special directions and fix a date for the final hearing;
    (c) give special directions and direct that the court will consider what further directions are to be given no later than 28 days after the date the special directions were given.

PD 27 para.2.2

Appendix C of PD 27 sets out Special Directions that the court may give.

SPECIALIST LISTS

Pt 2 r.2.3(2)

A list that has been designated as such by a rule or PD.

These lists are in the Commercial Court of the Queen's Bench Division, Technology and Construction Court, the Patents Court, and a county court specified in PD 60 [Technology and Construction Court claims].

Commercial list

Pt 58 r.58.2

(1) The commercial list is a specialist list for claims proceeding in the Commercial Court.
(2) One of the judges of the Commercial Court shall be in charge of the commercial list.

Patents Court

Pt 63 r.63.3

Claims in the Patents Court and a patents county court form specialist lists for the purpose of r.30.5.

Technology and Construction Court

Pt 60 r.60.2

(1) TCC claims form a specialist list.
(2) A judge will be appointed to be the judge in charge of the TCC specialist list.

Transfer to and from a specialist list

Pt 30 r.30.5

(2) A judge dealing with claims in a specialist list may order proceedings to be transferred to or from that list.
(3) An application for the transfer of proceedings to or from a specialist list must be made to a judge dealing with claims in that list.

SPECIFIC APPEALS

PD 52D para.1.1

PD 52D applies to [appeals which are subject to special provision], but not to **appeals by way of case stated** (to which PD 52E applies).

Provisions about specific appeals

PD 52D para.4.1

[s.IV of PD52D] sets out special provisions about the appeals listed in the Table [in para.5.1]. This Section is not exhaustive and does not create, amend or remove any right of appeal.

PD 52D para.4.2

Pt 52 applies to all appeals to which [s.IV] applies subject to any special provisions set out in this Section.

PD 52D para.4.3

Where any of the provisions in [s.IV] provide for documents to be filed at the appeal court, these documents are in addition to any documents required under Pt 52 or PD 52B or 52C.

Routes of appeal

PD 52D para.2.1

In [PD52D], the court to which an appeal lies is prescribed by statute.

Appeals to Court of Appeal

Appeals relating to the application of arts 101 and 102 of the Treaty on the Functioning of the European Union and Chapters I and II of Pt I of the Competition Act 1998

PD 52D para.7.1

(1) This paragraph applies to any appeal to the Court of Appeal relating to the application of—
  (a) Article 101 or Article 102 of the Treaty on the Functioning of the European Union; or
  (b) Chapter I or Chapter II of Part I of the Competition Act 1998.
(2) In this paragraph—
  (c) 'the Competition Regulation' means Council Regulation (EC) No. 1/2003 of 16 December 2002 on the implementation of the rules on competition laid down in Articles 81 and 82 of the Treaty establishing the European Community (as amended in consequence of the Treaty on the Functioning of the European Union);
  (d) 'national competition authority' means—
    (i) the Office of Fair Trading; and
    (ii) any other person or body designated pursuant to Article 35 of the Competition Regulation as a national competition authority of the United Kingdom;
  (e) 'the Treaty' means the Treaty on the Functioning of the European Union.
(3) Any party whose appeal notice raises an issue relating to the application of Article 101 or 102 of the [Treaty on the Functioning of the European Union], or Chapter I or II of Part I of the [Competition Act 1998], must—
  (a) state that fact in the appeal notice; and

    (b) serve a copy of the appeal notice on the Office of Fair Trading at the same time as it is served on the other party to the appeal (addressed to the Director of Competition Policy Co-ordination, Office of Fair Trading, Fleetbank House, 2–6 Salisbury Square, London EC4Y 8JX).

 (4) Attention is drawn to the provisions of article 15.3 of the Competition Regulation, which entitles competition authorities and the [European Commission] to submit written observations to national courts on issues relating to the application of Article 101 or 102 and, with the permission of the court in question, to submit oral observations to the court.

 (5) A national competition authority may also make written observations to the Court of Appeal, or apply for permission to make oral observations, on issues relating to the application of Chapter I or II.

 (6) If a national competition authority or the Commission intends to make written observations to the Court of Appeal, it must give notice of its intention to do so by letter to the Civil Appeals Office at the earliest opportunity.

 (7) An application by a national competition authority or the Commission for permission to make oral representations at the hearing of an appeal must be made by letter to the Civil Appeals Office at the earliest opportunity, identifying the appeal and indicating why the applicant wishes to make oral representations.

 (8) If a national competition authority or the Commission files a notice under sub-para.(6) or an application under sub-para.(7), it must at the same time serve a copy of the notice or application on every party to the appeal.

 (9) Any request by a national competition authority or the Commission for the court to send it any documents relating to an appeal should be made at the same time as filing a notice under sub-para.(6) or an application under sub-para.(7).

(10) When the Court of Appeal receives a notice under sub-para.(6) it may give case management directions to the national competition authority or the Commission, including directions about the date by which any written observations are to be filed.

(11) The Court of Appeal will serve on every party to the appeal a copy of any directions given or order made—
    (a) on an application under sub-para.(7); or
    (b) under sub-para.(10).

(12) Every party to an appeal which raises an issue relating to the application of Article 101 or 102, and any national competition authority which has been served with a copy of a party's appeal notice, is under a duty to notify the Court of Appeal at any stage of the appeal if they are aware that—
    (a) the Commission has adopted, or is contemplating adopting, a decision in relation to proceedings which it has initiated; and
    (b) the decision referred to in (a) above has or would have legal effects in relation to the particular agreement, decision or practice in issue before the court.

(13) Where the Court of Appeal is aware that the Commission is contemplating adopting a decision as mentioned in sub-para.(12)(a), it shall consider whether to stay the appeal pending the Commission's decision.

(14) Where any judgment is given which decides on the application of Article 101 or 102, the court shall direct that a copy of the transcript of the judgment shall be sent to the Commission. Judgments may be sent to the Commission electronically to comp-amicus@cec.eu.int or by post to the European Commission DG Competition, B-1049, Brussels.

Appeals in cases of contempt of court (s.13 Administration of Justice Act 1960)

PD 52D para.9.1

In an appeal under s.13 of the Administration of Justice Act 1960 (appeals in cases of contempt of court), the appellant must serve the appellant's notice on the court or the Upper Tribunal from whose order or decision the appeal is brought in addition to the persons to be served under rule 52.4(3) and in accordance with that rule.

Appeal from Employment Appeal Tribunal

PD 52D para.11.1

(1) This paragraph applies to an appeal to the Court of Appeal from the Employment Appeal Tribunal (EAT) under section 37 of the Employment Tribunals Act 1996.
(2) If an application for permission to appeal to the Court of Appeal is refused by the EAT or is not made, then such an application must be made to the Court of Appeal within 21 days of the date of the sealed order of the EAT.
(3) An application for extension of time for filing an appellant's notice may be entertained by the EAT but such applications should normally be made to the Court of Appeal.

Immigration and Asylum Appeals

PD 52D para.12.1

The provisions of para.28 of PD 52C (bundle of documents in immigration appeals and asylum appeals) apply to appeals from the Upper Tribunal Immigration and Asylum Chamber.

Appeal from Patents Court on appeal from Comptroller

PD 52D para.13.1

Where the appeal is from a decision of the Patents Court which was itself made on an appeal from a decision of the Comptroller-General of Patents, Designs and Trade Marks, the appellant must serve the appellant's notice on the Comptroller in addition to the persons to be served under r. 52.4(3) and in accordance with that rule.

Appeal against order for revocation of patent

PD 52D para.14.1

(1) This paragraph applies where an appeal lies to the Court of Appeal from an order for the revocation of a patent.
(2) The appellant must serve the appellant's notice on the Comptroller-General of Patents, Designs and Trade Marks (the 'Comptroller') in addition to the persons to be served under r. 52.4(3) and in accordance with that rule.
(3) Where, before the appeal hearing, the respondent decides not to oppose the appeal or not to attend the appeal hearing, the respondent must immediately serve notice of that decision on—
   (a) the Comptroller; and
   (b) the appellant.
(4) Where the respondent serves a notice in accordance with sub-para. (3), copies of the following documents must also be served on the Comptroller with that notice—
   (a) the petition;

    (b) any statements of claim;
    (c) any written evidence filed in the claim.
(5) Within 14 days after receiving the notice in accordance with sub-para. (3), the Comp-
    troller must serve on the appellant a notice stating an intention to attend the appeal
    hearing or otherwise.
(6) The Comptroller may attend the appeal hearing and oppose the appeal—
    (a) in any case where notice has been given under paragraph (5) of the intention to
        attend; and
    (b) in any other case (including, in particular, a case where the respondent withdraws his
        opposition to the appeal during the hearing) if the Court of Appeal so directs or
        permits.

Appeal from Proscribed Organisations Appeal Commission

PD 52D para.15.1

The appellant's notice must be filed at the Court of Appeal within 14 days after the date when
the Proscribed Organisations Appeal Commission—
    (a) granted; or
    (b) where s.6(2)(b) of the Terrorism Act 2000 applies, refused permission to appeal.

Appeals in relation to serious crime prevention orders

PD 52D para.16.1

(1) This paragraph applies to an appeal under s.23(1) of the Serious Crime Act 2007 or s.16
    of the Senior Courts Act 1981 in relation to a serious crime prevention order and is
    made.
(2) The appellant must serve the appellant92s notice on any person who made representa-
    tions in the proceedings by virtue of s.9(1), (2) or (3) of the Serious Crime Act 2007 in
    addition to the persons to be served under r. 52.4(3) and in accordance with that rule.

See also **Competition Appeal Tribunal**, **Court of Protection**, **Divorce**, and **Immigration and
Asylum**.

Special provisions applying to the Court of Appeal

Second appeals to the Court

Pt 52 r.52.13

(1) Permission is required from the Court of Appeal for any appeal to that court from a
    decision of a county court or the High Court which was itself made on appeal.
(2) The Court of Appeal will not give permission unless it considers that—
    (a) the appeal would raise an important point of principle or practice; or
    (b) there is some other compelling reason for the Court of Appeal to hear it.

Assignment of appeals to the Court of Appeal

Pt 52 r.52.14

(1) Where the court from or to which an appeal is made or from which permission to appeal is sought ('the relevant court') considers that—
　(a) an appeal which is to be heard by a county court or the High Court would raise an important point of principle or practice; or
　(b) there is some other compelling reason for the Court of Appeal to hear it,
the relevant court may order the appeal to be transferred to the Court of Appeal.
(The Master of the Rolls has the power to direct that an appeal which would be heard by a county court or the High Court should be heard instead by the Court of Appeal—see s.57 of the Access to Justice Act 1999).
(2) The Master of the Rolls or the Court of Appeal may remit an appeal to the court in which the original appeal was or would have been brought.

Judicial review appeals

Pt 52 r.52.15

(1) Where permission to apply for judicial review has been refused at a hearing in the High Court, the person seeking that permission may apply to the Court of Appeal for permission to appeal.
(1A) Where permission to apply for judicial review of a decision of the Upper Tribunal has been refused by the High Court—
　(a) The applicant may apply to the Court of Appeal for permission to appeal;
　(b) The application will be determined on paper without an oral hearing.
(2) An application in accordance with paras (1) or (1A) must be made within seven days of the decision of the High Court to refuse to give permission to apply for judicial review.
(3) On an application under para.(1), the Court of Appeal may, instead of giving permission to appeal, give permission to apply for judicial review.
(4) Where the Court of Appeal gives permission to apply for judicial review in accordance with para.(3), the case will proceed in the High Court unless the Court of Appeal orders otherwise.

Who may exercise the powers of the Court of Appeal

Pt 52 r.52.16

(1) A court officer assigned to the Civil Appeals Office who is—
　(a) a barrister; or
　(b) a solicitor
may exercise the jurisdiction of the Court of Appeal with regard to the matters set out in para.(2) with the consent of the Master of the Rolls.
(2) The matters referred to in para.(1) are—
　(a) any matter incidental to any proceedings in the Court of Appeal;
　(b) any other matter where there is no substantial dispute between the parties; and
　(c) the dismissal of an appeal or application where a party has failed to comply with any order, rule or PD.
(3) A court officer may not decide an application for—
　(a) permission to appeal;

    (b) bail pending an appeal;

    (c) an injunction;

    (d) a stay of any proceedings, other than a temporary stay of any order or decision of the lower court over a period when the Court of Appeal is not sitting or cannot conveniently be convened.

(4) Decisions of a court officer may be made without a hearing.

(5) A party may request any decision of a court officer to be reviewed by the Court of Appeal.

(6) At the request of a party, a hearing will be held to reconsider a decision of—

    (a) a single judge; or

    (b) a court officer,

made without a hearing.

(6A) A request under para.(5) or (6) must be filed within seven days after the party is served with notice of the decision.

(7) A single judge may refer any matter for a decision by a court consisting of two or more judges.

(s.54(6) of the Supreme Court Act 1981 provides that there is no appeal from the decision of a single judge on an application for permission to appeal.)

(s.58(2) of the Supreme Court Act 1981 provides that there is no appeal to the Supreme Court from decisions of the Court of Appeal that—

    (a) are taken by a single judge or any officer or member of staff of that court in proceedings incidental to any cause or matter pending before the civil division of that court; and

    (b) do not involve the determination of an appeal or of an application for permission to appeal.

and which may be called into question by rules of court. rr. 52.16(5) and (6) provide the procedure for the calling into question of such decisions.)

See also **Appeals, Reopening of final appeals, Specific appeals**, and **Statutory appeals**.

Appeals to the High Court

Appeals under reg.74 of the European Public Limited-Liability Company Regulations 2004

PD 52D para.20.1

(1) In this paragraph—

    (c) 'SE' means a European public limited-liability company (Societas Europaea) within the meaning of art.1 of the EC Regulation.

(2) This paragraph applies to appeals under reg.74 of the [European Public Limited-Liability Company Regulations 2004] against the opposition—

    (a) of the Secretary of State or national financial supervisory authority to the transfer of the registered office of an SE under art.8(14) of the [Council Regulation (EC) No 2157/2001 of 8 October 2001 on the Statute for a European company (SE)]; and

    (b) of the Secretary of State to the participation by a company in the formation of an SE by merger under art.19 of the EC Regulation.

(3) Where an SE seeks to appeal against the opposition of the national financial supervisory authority to the transfer of its registered office under art.8(14) of the EC Regulation, it must serve the appellant's notice on both the national financial supervisory authority and the Secretary of State.

(4) The appellant's notice must contain an application for permission to appeal.

(5) The appeal will be a review of the decision of the Secretary of State and not a re-hearing. The grounds of review are set out in reg.74(2) of the 2004 Regulations.

(6) The appeal will be heard by a High Court judge.

Appeals affecting industrial and provident societies, etc.

PD 52D para.22.1

(1) This paragraph applies to all appeals under—
   (a) the Friendly Societies Act 1974;
   (b) the Friendly Societies Act 1992 and;
   (c) the Industrial and Provident Societies Act 1965.
(2) At any stage on an appeal, the court may—
   (a) direct that the appellant's notice be served on any person;
   (b) direct that notice be given by advertisement or otherwise of—
      (i) the bringing of the appeal;
      (ii) the nature of the appeal; and
      (iii) the time when the appeal will or is likely to be heard; or
   (c) give such other directions as it thinks proper to enable any person interested in—
      (i) the society, trade union, alleged trade union or industrial assurance company; or
      (ii) the subject matter of the appeal, to appear and be heard at the appeal hearing.

Appeals under reg.8(3) of the Stamp Duty Reserve Tax Regulations 1986

PD 52D para.23.1

[Para.23.1 of PD 52D also] applies to appeals to the High Court under reg.8(3) of the Stamp Duty Reserve Tax Regulations 1986.

See **Inheritance Tax Act 1984**.

Appeals under s.289(6) of the Town and Country Planning Act 1990 and s.65(5) of the Planning (Listed Buildings and Conservation Areas) Act 1990

PD 52D para.26.1

(1) An application for permission to appeal to the High Court under s.289 of the Town and Country Planning Act 1990 ('the TCP Act') or s. 65 of the Planning (Listed Buildings and Conservation Areas) Act 1990 ('the PLBCA Act') must be made within 28 days after notice of the decision is given to the applicant.
(2) The application—
   (a) must be in writing and must set out the reasons why permission should be granted; and
   (b) if the time for applying has expired, must include an application to extend the time for applying, and must set out the reasons why the application was not made within that time.
(3) The applicant must, before filing the application, serve a copy of it on the persons referred to in sub-para.(12) with the draft appellant's notice and a copy of the witness statement or affidavit to be filed with the application.
(4) The applicant must file the application in the Administrative Court Office with—

    (a) a copy of the decision being appealed;

    (b) a draft appellant's notice;

    (c) a witness statement or affidavit verifying any facts relied on; and

    (d) a witness statement or affidavit giving the name and address of, and the place and date of service on, each person who has been served with the application. If any person who ought to be served has not been served, the witness statement or affidavit must state that fact and the reason why the person was not served.

(5) An application will be heard—

    (a) by a single judge; and

    (b) unless the court otherwise orders, not less than 21 days after it was filed at the Administrative Court Office.

(6) PD 54D applies to applications and appeals under this para.

(7) Any person served with the application is entitled to appear and be heard.

(8) Any respondent who intends to use a **witness statement** or **affidavit** at the hearing—

    (a) must file it in the Administrative Court Office; and

    (b) must serve a copy on the applicant as soon as is practicable and in any event, unless the court otherwise allows, at least two days before the hearing.

(9) The court may allow the applicant to use a further witness statement or affidavit.

(10) Where on the hearing of an application the court is of the opinion that a person who ought to have been served has not been served, the court may adjourn the hearing, on such terms as it directs, in order that the application may be served on that person.

(11) Where the court grants permission—

    (a) it may impose terms as to costs and as to giving security;

    (b) it may give directions; and

    (c) the relevant appellant's notice must be served and filed within seven days of the grant.

(12) The persons to be served with the appellant's notice are—

    (a) the Secretary of State;

    (b) the local planning authority who served the notice or gave the decision, as the case may be, or, where the appeal is brought by that authority, the appellant or applicant in the proceedings in which the decision appealed against was given;

    (c) in the case of an appeal brought by virtue of s.289(1) of the TCP Act or s.65(1) of the PLBCA Act, any other person having an interest in the land to which the notice relates; and

    (d) in the case of an appeal brought by virtue of s.289(2) of the TCP Act, any other person on whom the notice to which those proceedings related was served.

(13) The appeal will be heard and determined by a single judge unless the court directs that the matter be heard and determined by a Divisional Court.

(14) The court may remit the matter to the Secretary of State to the extent necessary to enable the Secretary of State to provide the court with such further information in connection with the matter as the court may direct.

(15) Where the court is of the opinion that the decision appealed against was erroneous in point of law, it will not set aside or vary that decision but will remit the matter to the Secretary of State for re-hearing and determination in accordance with the opinion of the court.

(16) The court may give directions as to the exercise, until an appeal brought by virtue of s.289(1) of the TCP Act is finally concluded and any re-hearing and determination by the Secretary of State has taken place, of the power to serve, and institute proceedings (including criminal proceedings) concerning—

    (a) a stop notice under s.183 of that Act; and

    (b) a breach of condition notice under s.187A of that Act.

See also **Admiralty claims, Agricultural Land Tribunal, Architects Act 1997, Health care professionals, Immigration and Asylum, Inheritance Tax 1984, Land Registration Acts 1925 and 2002, Law of Property Act 1922 and 1969**, and **Solicitors Disciplinary Tribunal**.

Appeals to the county court

Appeals under ss.204 and 204A of the Housing Act 1996

PD 52D para.28.1

(1) An appellant should include appeals under s.204 and s.204A of the Housing Act 1996 in one appellant's notice.

(2) If it is not possible to do so (for example because an urgent application under s.204A is required) the appeals may be included in separate appellant's notices.

(3) An appeal under s.204A may include an application for an order under s.204A(4)(a) requiring the authority to secure that accommodation is available for the applicant's occupation.

(4) If, exceptionally, the court makes an order under s.204A(4)(a) without notice, the appellant's notice must be served on the authority together with the order. Such an order will normally require the authority to secure that accommodation is available until a hearing date when the authority can make representations as to whether the order under s.204A(4)(a) should be continued.

(5) Unless the court orders otherwise—

    (a) the appellant shall file and serve its proposed case management directions for the appeal together with the appellant's notice;

    (b) the respondent shall within 14 days thereafter either agree those directions or file and serve alternative proposed directions;

    (c) within 14 days after service of the appellant's notice the respondent must disclose any documents relevant to the decision under appeal, in so far as not previously disclosed;

    (d) within 14 days after receipt of any documents disclosed under sub-paragraph (c) the appellant may make any amendments to its grounds of appeal which arise out of those documents.

Local Government (Miscellaneous Provisions) Act 1976

PD 52D para.30.1

Where one of the grounds upon which an appeal against a notice under ss.21, 23 or 35 of the Local Government (Miscellaneous Provisions) Act 1976 is brought is that—

    (a) it would have been fairer to serve the notice on another person; or

    (b) that it would be reasonable for the whole or part of the expenses to which the appeal relates to be paid by some other person,

that person must be made a respondent to the appeal, unless the court, on application of the appellant made without notice, otherwise directs.

See also **Immigration and asylum** and **Representation of the People Act 1983**.

SPECIFIC DISCLOSURE AND INSPECTION

Pt 31 r.31.12

(1) The court may make an order for specific disclosure or specific inspection.

(2) An order for specific disclosure is an order that a party must do one or more of the following things—

    (a) disclose documents or classes of documents specified in the order;
    (b) carry out a search to the extent stated in the order;
    (c) disclose any documents located as a result of that search.
  (3) An order for specific inspection is an order that a party permit inspection of a document referred to in r.31.3(2).

(Rule 31.3(2) allows a party to state in his **disclosure statement** that he will not permit inspection of a document on the grounds that it would be disproportionate to do so).

(Rule 78.26 contains rules in relation to the disclosure and inspection of evidence arising out of mediation of certain cross-border disputes).

PD 31A para.5.1

If a party believes that the disclosure of documents given by a disclosing party is inadequate he may make an application for an order for specific disclosure (see r.31.12).

PD 31A para.5.2

The application notice must specify the order that the applicant intends to ask the court to make and must be supported by evidence (see r.31.12(2) which describes the orders the court may make).

PD 31A para.5.3

The grounds on which the order is sought may be set out in the application notice itself but if not there set out must be set out in the evidence filed in support of the application.

PD 31A para.5.4

In deciding whether or not to make an order for specific disclosure the court will take into account all the circumstances of the case and, in particular, the overriding objective described in Pt 1. But if the court concludes that the party from whom specific disclosure is sought has failed adequately to comply with the obligations imposed by an order for disclosure (whether by failing to make a sufficient search for documents or otherwise) the court will usually make such order as is necessary to ensure that those obligations are properly complied with.

PD 31A para.5.5

An order for specific disclosure may in an appropriate case direct a party to—
  (1) carry out a search for any documents which it is reasonable to suppose may contain information which may—
    (a) enable the party applying for disclosure either to advance his own case or to damage that of the party giving disclosure; or
    (b) lead to a train of enquiry which has either of those consequences; and
  (2) disclose any documents found as a result of that search.

SPECIFIC PERFORMANCE

PD 24 para.7.1

  (1) If a remedy sought by a claimant in his claim form includes a claim—
    (a) for specific performance of an agreement (whether in writing or not) for the sale, purchase, exchange, mortgage or charge of any property, or for the grant or assignment of a lease or tenancy of any property, with or without an alternative claim for damages, or

    (b) for rescission of such an agreement, or
    (c) for the forfeiture or return of any deposit made under such an agreement,
    the claimant may apply under Pt 24 for [summary] judgment.
(3) The claimant may do so at any time after the claim form has been served, whether or not the defendant has acknowledged service of the claim form, whether or not the time for acknowledging service has expired and whether or not any particulars of claim have been served.

PD 24 para.7.2

The application notice by which an application under para.7.1 is made must have attached to it the text of the order sought by the claimant.

PD 24 para.7.3

The application notice and a copy of every affidavit or witness statement in support and of any exhibit referred to therein must be served on the defendant not less than four days before the hearing of the application. (Note—the four days replaces for these applications the 14 days specified in r.24.4(3). Rule 24.5 cannot, therefore apply).
(This paragraph replaces RSC Ord.86 rr.1 and 2 but applies to county court proceedings as well as to High Court proceedings).

SPLIT TRIAL

Pt 3 r.3.1

    (2) Except where these rules provide otherwise, the court may—
      (i) direct a separate trial of any issue.

Fast track

PD 26 para.9.1(3)

    (d) A claim may be allocated to the fast track or ordered to remain on that track although there is to be a split trial.

Multi-track

PD 29 para.5.3

    (7) whether it will be just and will save costs to order a split trial or the trial of one or more preliminary issues.

STANDARD BASIS

Costs

Pt 44 r.44.3

    (2) Where the amount of costs is to be assessed on the standard basis, the court will—
      (a) only allow costs which are proportionate to the matters in issue; and

(b) resolve any doubt which it may have as to whether costs were reasonably incurred or reasonable and proportionate in amount in favour of the paying party.

PD 44 para.6.2

If costs are awarded on the standard basis, the court assessing costs will disallow any costs—
(a) which it finds to have been unreasonably incurred;
(b) which it considers to be unreasonable in amount;
(c) which it considers to have been disproportionately incurred or to be disproportionate in amount; or
(d) about which it has doubts as to whether they were reasonably or proportionately incurred, or whether they are reasonable and proportionate in amount.

See **Indemnity basis**.

STANDARD DIRECTIONS

Small claims track

Pt 27 r.27.4

(3) In [P27 r.27.4]—
  (a) 'standard directions' means—
    (i) a direction that each party shall, at least 14 days before the date fixed for the final hearing, file and serve on every other party copies of all documents (including any expert's report) on which he intends to rely at the hearing; and
    (ii) any other standard directions set out in PD 27.

Pt 27 r.27.4

(1) After allocation the court will—
  (a) give standard directions and fix a date for the final hearing.

Fast track

PD 28 para.2.7

Appendix A of PD 28 contains forms of directions. When making an order the court will as far as possible base its order on those forms. Agreed directions which the parties file and invite the court to make should also be based on those forms.

Mercantile Court

PD 59 Annex

Annex B of PD 59 contains the Standard Directions in Mercantile Court.

STANDARD DISCLOSURE

Pt 31 r.31.6

Standard disclosure requires a party to disclose only—
  (a) the documents on which he relies; and
  (b) the documents which—
      (i) adversely affect his own case;
      (ii) adversely affect another party's case; or
      (iii) support another party's case; and
  (c) the documents which he is required to disclose by a relevant practice direction.

Pt 31 r.31.5

In all claims to which r.31.5(2) does not apply
  (1) An order to give disclosure is an order to give standard disclosure unless the court directs otherwise.
  (2) The court may dispense with or limit standard disclosure.
  (3) The parties may agree in writing to dispense with or to limit standard disclosure.
  (4) Unless the court otherwise orders, paras (3)–(8) apply to all multi-track claims, other than those which include a claim for personal injuries.
  (5) Not less than 14 days before the first case management conference each party must file and serve a report verified by a statement of truth, which—
      (a) describes briefly what documents exist or may exist that are or may be relevant to the matters in issue in the case;
      (b) describes where and with whom those documents are or may be located;
      (c) in the case of electronic documents, describes how those documents are stored;
      (d) estimates the broad range of costs that could be involved in giving standard disclosure in the case, including the costs of searching for and disclosing any electronically stored documents; and
      (e) states which of the directions under paras (7) or (8) are to be sought.
  (6) In cases where the Electronic Documents Questionnaire has been exchanged, the Questionnaire should be filed with the report required by para.(3).
  (7) Not less than seven days before the first case management conference, and on any other occasion as the court may direct, the parties must, at a meeting or by telephone, discuss and seek to agree a proposal in relation to disclosure that meets the overriding objective.
  (8) If—
      (a) the parties agree proposals for the scope of disclosure; and
      (b) the court considers that the proposals are appropriate in all the circumstances, the court may approve them without a hearing and give directions in the terms proposed.
  (9) At the first or any subsequent case management conference, the court will decide, having regard to the overriding objective and the need to limit disclosure to that which is necessary to deal with the case justly, which of the following orders to make in relation to disclosure—
      (a) an order dispensing with disclosure;
      (b) an order that a party disclose the documents on which it relies, and at the same time request any specific disclosure it requires from any other party;
      (c) an order that directs, where practicable, the disclosure to be given by each party on an issue by issue basis;
      (d) an order that each party disclose any documents which it is reasonable to suppose may contain information which enables that party to advance its own case or to damage that of any other party, or which leads to an enquiry which has either of those consequences;

      (e) an order that a party give standard disclosure;

      (f) any other order in relation to disclosure that the court considers appropriate.

(10) The court may at any point give directions as to how disclosure is to be given, and in particular—

      (a) what searches are to be undertaken, of where, for what, in respect of which time periods and by whom and the extent of any search for electronically stored documents;

      (b) whether lists of documents are required;

      (c) how and when the disclosure statement is to be given;

      (d) in what format documents are to be disclosed (and whether any identification is required);

      (e) what is required in relation to documents that once existed but no longer exist; and

      (f) whether disclosure shall take place in stages.

(11) To the extent that the documents to be disclosed are electronic, the provisions of PD 31B—Disclosure of Electronic Documents will apply in addition to paras (3)–(8).

PD 31A para.1.1

The normal order for disclosure will be an order that the parties give standard disclosure.

PD 31A para.1.2

In order to give standard disclosure the disclosing party must make a reasonable search for documents falling within the paragraphs of r.31.6.

PD 31A para.1.3

Having made the search the disclosing party must (unless r.31.10(8) applies) make a list of the documents of whose existence the party is aware that fall within those paragraphs and which are or have been in the party's control (see r.31.8).

PD 31A para.1.4

The obligations imposed by an order for standard disclosure may be dispensed with or limited either by the court or by written agreement between the parties. Any such written agreement should be lodged with the court.

Duty of search

PD 31A para.31.7

(1) When giving standard disclosure, a party is required to make a reasonable search for documents falling within r.31.6(b) or (c).

(2) The factors relevant in deciding the reasonableness of a search include the following—

      (a) the number of documents involved;

      (b) the nature and complexity of the proceedings;

      (c) the ease and expense of retrieval of any particular document; and

      (d) the significance of any document which is likely to be located during the search.

(3) Where a party has not searched for a category or class of document on the grounds that to do so would be unreasonable, he must state this in his disclosure statement and identify the category or class of document.

(Rule 31.10 makes provision for a **disclosure statement**).

PD 31A para.2

The extent of the search which must be made will depend upon the circumstances of the case including, in particular, the factors referred to in r.31.7(2). The parties should bear in mind the overriding principle of proportionality (see r.1.1(2)(c)). It may, for example, be reasonable to decide not to search for documents coming into existence before some particular date, or to limit the search to documents in some particular place or places, or to documents falling into particular categories.

Procedure for standard disclosure

Pt 31 r.31.10

(1) The procedure for standard disclosure is as follows.
(2) Each party must make and serve on every other party, a **list of documents** in the relevant practice form.

See also **Document, Specific disclosure and inspection, Electronic disclosure, Fast track, List of documents**, and **Multi-track.**

START OF PROCEEDINGS

Pt 7 r.7.2

(1) Proceedings are started when the court issues a claim form at the request of the claimant.
(2) A claim form is issued on the date entered on the form by the court.

PD 7A para.1

Subject to the following provisions of [PD 7A], proceedings which both the High Court and the county courts have jurisdiction to deal with may be started in the High Court or in a county court.

PD 7A para.5.1

Proceedings are started when the court issues a claim form at the request of the claimant but where the claim form as issued was received in the court office on a date earlier than the date on which it was issued by the court, the claim is "brought" for the purposes of the Limitation Act 1980 and any other relevant statute on that earlier date.

PD 7A para.5.2

The date on which the claim form was received by the court will be recorded by a date stamp either on the claim form held on the court file or on the letter that accompanied the claim form when it was received by the court.

PD 7A para.5.3

An enquiry as to the date on which the claim form was received by the court should be directed to a court officer.

Limitation period

PD 7A para.5.1

Proceedings are started when the court issues a claim form at the request of the claimant but where the claim form as issued was received in the court office on a date earlier than the date on which it was issued by the court, the claim is 'brought' for the purposes of the Limitation Act 1980 and any other relevant statute on that earlier date.

PD 7A para.5.4

Parties proposing to start a claim which is approaching the expiry of the limitation period should recognise the potential importance of establishing the date the claim form was received by the court and should themselves make arrangements to record the date.

Deceased defendant

PD 7A para.5.5

Where it is sought to start proceedings against the estate of a deceased defendant where probate or letters of administration have not been granted, the claimant should issue the claim against 'the personal representatives of A.B. deceased'. The claimant should then, before the expiry of the period for service of the claim form, apply to the court for the appointment of a person to represent the estate of the deceased.

See also **Venue**.

STATE

Pt 40 r.40.10

(3) 'State' has the meaning given by s.14 of the State Immunity Act 1978.

See **Default judgment** and **Service of documents**.

STATEMENT OF TRUTH

Documents to be verified by a statement of truth

Pt 22 r.22.1

(1) The following documents must be verified by a statement of truth—
(a) a **statement of case**;

    (b) a response complying with an order under r.18.1 to provide **further information**;

    (c) a **witness statement**;

    (d) an **acknowledgement of service** in a claim begun by way of the Part 8 procedure;

    (e) a certificate stating the reasons for bringing a possession claim or a landlord and tenant claim in the High Court in accordance with rr.55.3(2) and 56.2(2);

    (f) a **certificate of service**; and

    (g) any other document where a rule or PD requires.

(2) Where a statement of case is amended, the amendments must be verified by a statement of truth unless the court orders otherwise.

(Part 17 provides for amendments to statements of case).

(3) If an applicant wishes to rely on matters set out in his **application notice** as evidence, the application notice must be verified by a statement of truth.

(4) Subject to para.(5), a statement of truth is a statement that—

    (a) the party putting forward the document;

    (b) in the case of a witness statement, the maker of the witness statement; or

    (c) in the case of a certificate of service, the person who signs the certificate,

believes the facts stated in the document are true.

(5) If a party is conducting proceedings with a litigation friend, the statement of truth in—

    (a) a statement of case;

    (b) a response; or

    (c) an application notice,

is a statement that the litigation friend believes the facts stated in the document being verified are true.

(6) The statement of truth must be signed by—

    (a) in the case of a statement of case, a response or an application—

        (i) the party or **litigation friend**; or

        (ii) the **legal representative** on behalf of the party or litigation friend; and

    (b) in the case of a witness statement, the maker of the statement.

(7) A statement of truth which is not contained in the document which it verifies, must clearly identify that document.

(8) A statement of truth in a statement of case may be made by—

    (a) a person who is not a party; or

    (b) by two parties jointly,

where this is permitted by a relevant PD.

PD 22 para.1.2

If an applicant wishes to rely on matters set out in his application notice as evidence, the application notice must be verified by a statement of truth.

PD 22 para.1.3

An expert's report should also be verified by a statement of truth. For the form of the statement of truth verifying an expert's report (which differs from that set out below) see PD 35.

PD 22 para.1.4

In addition, the following documents must be verified by a statement of truth:

(1) an **application notice** for—

    (a) a **Third Party Debt Order** (r.72.3),

    (b) a **Hardship Payment Order** (r.72.7), or

    (c) a **Charging Order** (r.73.3);

    (2) a notice of objections to an account being taken by the court, unless verified by an affidavit or witness statement;

    (3) a schedule or counter-schedule of expenses and losses in a personal injury claim, and any amendments to such a schedule or counter-schedule, whether or not they are contained in a statement of case.

PD 22 para.1.5

The statement of truth may be contained in the document it verifies or it may be in a separate document served subsequently, in which case it must identify the document to which it relates.

PD 22 para.1.6

Where the form to be used includes a jurat for the content to be verified by an affidavit then a statement of truth is not required in addition.

Form of the statement of truth

PD 22 para.2.1

The form of the statement of truth verifying a statement of case, a response, an application notice or a notice of objections should be as follows:

> '[I believe][the (claimant or as may be) believes] that the facts stated in this [name document being verified] are true.'

PD 22 para.2.2

The form of the statement of truth verifying a witness statement should be as follows:

> 'I believe that the facts stated in this witness statement are true.'

PD 22 para.2.3

Where the statement of truth is contained in a separate document, the document containing the statement of truth must be headed with the title of the proceedings and the claim number. The document being verified should be identified in the statement of truth as follows:

    (1) claim form: 'the claim form issued on [date]',

    (2) particulars of claim: 'the particulars of claim issued on [date]',

    (3) statement of case: 'the [defence or as may be] served on the [name of party] on [date]',

    (4) application notice: 'the application notice issued on [date] for [set out the remedy sought]',

    (5) witness statement: 'the witness statement filed on [date] or served on [party] on [date]'.

Failure to verify a statement of case

Pt 22 r.22.2

    (1) If a party fails to verify his statement of case by a statement of truth—

       (a) the statement of case shall remain effective unless struck out; but

(b) the party may not rely on the statement of case as evidence of any of the matters set out in it.

(2) The court may strike out a statement of case which is not verified by a statement of truth.

(3) Any party may apply for an order under para.(2).

Failure to verify a witness statement

Pt 22 r.22.3

If the maker of a witness statement fails to verify the witness statement by a statement of truth the court may direct that it shall not be admissible as evidence.

Power of the court to require a document to be verified

Pt 22 r.22.4

(1) The court may order a person who has failed to verify a document in accordance with r.22.1 to verify the document.

(2) Any party may apply for an order under para.(1).

Who may sign the statement of truth

PD 22 para.3.1

In a statement of case, a response or an application notice, the statement of truth must be signed by:

(1) the party or his litigation friend, or

(2) the legal representative of the party or litigation friend.

PD 22 para.3.2

A statement of truth verifying a witness statement must be signed by the witness.

PD 22 para.3.3

A statement of truth verifying a notice of objections to an account must be signed by the objecting party or his legal representative.

PD 22 para.3.4

Where a document is to be verified on behalf of a company or other corporation, subject to para.3.7 below, the statement of truth must be signed by a person holding a senior position in the company or corporation. That person must state the office or position held.

PD 22 para.3.5

Each of the following persons is a person holding a senior position:

(1) in respect of a registered company or corporation, a director, the treasurer, secretary, chief executive, manager or other officer of the company or corporation, and

(2) in respect of a corporation which is not a registered company, in addition to those persons set out in (1), the mayor, chairman, president or town clerk or other similar officer of the corporation.

PD 22 para.3.6

Where the document is to be verified on behalf of a partnership, those who may sign the statement of truth are:
(1) any of the partners, or
(2) a person having the control or management of the partnership business.

PD 22 para.3.6A

An insurer or the Motor Insurers' Bureau may sign a statement of truth in a statement of case on behalf of a party where the insurer or the Motor Insurers' Bureau has a financial interest in the result of proceedings brought wholly or partially by or against that party.

PD 22 para.3.6B

If insurers are conducting proceedings on behalf of many claimants or defendants a statement of truth in a statement of case may be signed by a senior person responsible for the case at a lead insurer, but—
(1) the person signing must specify the capacity in which he signs;
(2) the statement of truth must be a statement that the lead insurer believes that the facts stated in the document are true; and
(3) the court may order that a statement of truth also be signed by one or more of the parties.

PD 22 para.3.7

Where a party is legally represented, the legal representative may sign the statement of truth on his behalf. The statement signed by the legal representative will refer to the client's belief, not his own. In signing he must state the capacity in which he signs and the name of his firm where appropriate.

PD 22 para.3.8

Where a legal representative has signed a statement of truth, his signature will be taken by the court as his statement:
(1) that the client on whose behalf he has signed had authorised him to do so,
(2) that before signing he had explained to the client that in signing the statement of truth he would be confirming the client's belief that the facts stated in the document were true, and
(3) that before signing he had informed the client of the possible consequences to the client if it should subsequently appear that the client did not have an honest belief in the truth of those facts (see r.32.14).

PD 22 para.3.9

The individual who signs a statement of truth must print his full name clearly beneath his signature.

PD 22 para.3.10

A legal representative who signs a statement of truth must sign in his own name and not that of his firm or employer.

The following are examples of the possible application of this PD describing who may sign a statement of truth verifying statements in documents other than a witness statement. These are only examples and not an indication of how a court might apply the PD to a specific situation.

Managing Agent: An agent who manages property or investments for the party cannot sign a statement of truth. It must be signed by the party or by the legal representative of the party.

Trusts: Where some or all of the trustees comprise a single party one, some or all of the trustees comprising the party may sign a statement of truth. The legal representative of the trustees may sign it.

Insurers and the Motor Insurers' Bureau: If an insurer has a financial interest in a claim involving its insured then, if the insured is the party, the insurer may sign a statement of truth in a statement of case for the insured party. Paragraphs 3.4 and 3.5 apply to the insurer if it is a company. The claims manager employed by the insurer responsible for handling the insurance claim or managing the staff handling the claim may sign the statement of truth for the insurer (see next example). The position for the Motor Insurers' Bureau is similar.

Companies: Paras 3.4 and 3.5 apply. The word manager will be construed in the context of the phrase 'a person holding a senior position' which it is used to define. The court will consider the size of the company and the size and nature of the claim. It would expect the manager signing the statement of truth to have personal knowledge of the content of the document or to be responsible for managing those who have that knowledge of the content. A small company may not have a manager, apart from the directors, who holds a senior position. A large company will have many such managers. In a larger company with specialist claims, insurance or legal departments the statement may be signed by the manager of such a department if he or she is responsible for handling the claim or managing the staff handling it.

In-house legal representatives: Legal representative is defined in r.2.3(1). A legal representative employed by a party may sign a statement of truth. However a person who is not a solicitor, barrister or other authorised litigator, but who is employed by the company and is managed by such a person, is not employed by that person and so cannot sign a statement of truth. (This is unlike the employee of a solicitor in private practice who would come within the definition of legal representative). However such a person may be a manager and able to sign the statement on behalf of the company in that capacity.

Inability to persons to read or sign documents to be verified by a statement of truth

PD 22 para.3A.1

Where a document containing a statement of truth is to be signed by a person who is unable to read or sign the document, it must contain a certificate made by an authorised person.

PD 22 para.3A.2

An authorised person is a person able to administer oaths and take affidavits but need not be independent of the parties or their representatives.

PD 22 para.3A.3

The authorised person must certify:
    (1) that the document has been read to the person signing it;

(2) that that person appeared to understand it and approved its content as accurate;

(3) that the declaration of truth has been read to that person;

(4) that that person appeared to understand the declaration and the consequences of making a false declaration; and

(5) that that person signed or made his mark in the presence of the authorised person.

PD 22 para.3A.4

The form of the certificate is set out at Annex 1 to [PD 22].

Power of the court to require a document to be verified

Pt 22 r.22.4

(1) The court may order a person who has failed to verify a document in accordance with rule 22.1 to verify the document.

(2) Any party may apply for an order under paragraph (1).

Consequences of failure to verify

PD 22 para.4.1

If a statement of case is not verified by a statement of truth, the statement of case will remain effective unless it is struck out, but a party may not rely on the contents of a statement of case as evidence until it has been verified by a statement of truth.

PD 22 para.4.2

Any party may apply to the court for an order that unless within such period as the court may specify the statement of case is verified by the service of a statement of truth, the statement of case will be struck out.

PD 22 para.4.3

The usual order for the costs of an application referred to in para.4.2 will be that the costs be paid by the party who had failed to verify in any event and forthwith.

See **False statement** and **Witness statement**.

STATEMENT OF VALUE

Claim form

Pt 16 r.16.3

(1) This rule applies where the claimant is making a claim for money.

(2) The claimant must, in the claim form, state—

(a) the amount of money claimed;

    (b) that the claimant expects to recover—
        (i) not more than (£10,000);
       (ii) more than (£10,000) but not more than £25,000; or
      (iii) more than £25,000; or
    (c) that the claimant cannot say how much is likely to be recovered.
(3) In a claim for personal injuries, the claimant must also state in the claim form whether the amount which the claimant expects to recover as general damages for pain, suffering and loss of amenity is—
    (a) not more than £1,000; or
    (b) more than £1,000.
(4) In a claim which includes a claim by a tenant of residential premises against a landlord where the tenant is seeking an order requiring the landlord to carry out repairs or other work to the premises, the claimant must also state in the claim form—
    (a) whether the estimated costs of those repairs or other work is—
        (i) not more than £1,000; or
       (ii) more than £1,000; and
    (b) whether the value of any other claim for damages is—
        (i) not more than £1,000; or
       (ii) more than £1,000.
(5) If the claim form is to be issued in the High Court it must, where this rule applies—
    (a) state that the claimant expects to recover more than £25,000;
    (b) state that some other enactment provides that the claim may be commenced only in the High Court and specify that enactment;
    (c) if the claim is a claim for personal injuries state that the claimant expects to recover £50,000 or more; or
    (d) state that the claim is to be in one of the specialist High Court lists and state which list.
(6) When calculating how much the claimant expects to recover, the claimant must disregard any possibility—
    (a) that the court may make an award of—
        (i) interest;
       (ii) costs;
    (b) that the court may make a finding of contributory negligence;
    (c) that the defendant may make a counterclaim or that the defence may include a set-off; or
    (d) that the defendant may be liable to pay an amount of money which the court awards to the claimant to the Secretary of State for Social Security under s.6 of the Social Security (Recovery of Benefits) Act 1997.
(7) The statement of value in the claim form does not limit the power of the court to give judgment for the amount which it finds the claimant is entitled to.

STATEMENTS OF CASE

Pt 2 r.2.3(1)

    (a) Means a **claim form, particulars of claim** where these are not included in a claim form, **defence, Part 20 claim**, or reply to defence; and
    (b) includes any **further information** given in relation to them voluntarily or by court order under r.18.1.

PD 16 para.1.4

If exceptionally a statement of case exceeds 25 pages (excluding schedules) an appropriate short summary must also be filed and served.

PD 16 para.9.2

A subsequent statement of case must not contradict or be inconsistent with an earlier one; for example a reply to a defence must not bring in a new claim. Where new matters have come to light the appropriate course may be to seek the court's permission to amend the statement of case.

Special provisions about statements of case

PD 16 para.1.2

Where special provisions about statements of case are made by the rules and PDs applying to particular types of proceedings, the provisions of Pt 16 and of this PD apply only to the extent that they are not inconsistent with those rules and PDs.

PD 16 para.1.3

Examples of types of proceedings with special provisions about statements of case include—
    (1) **defamation claims** (Pt 53);
    (2) **possession claims** (Pt 55); and
    (3) **probate claims** (Pt 57).

Amendments to statements of case before service

Pt 17 r.17.1

    (1) A party may amend his statement of case at any time before it has been served on any other party.
    (2) If his statement of case has been served, a party may amend it only—
        (a) with the written consent of all the other parties; or
        (b) with the permission of the court.
    (3) If a statement of case has been served, an application to amend it by removing, adding or substituting a party must be made in accordance with r.19.4.
(Part 22 requires amendments to a statement of case to be verified by a statement of truth unless the court orders otherwise).

Power of court to disallow amendments made without permission

Pt 17 r.17.2

    (1) If a party has amended his statement of case where permission of the court was not required, the court may disallow the amendment.
    (2) A party may apply to the court for an order under para.(1) within 14 days of service of a copy of the amended statement of case on him.

Amendments to statements of case with the permission of the court

Pt 17 r.17.3

    (1) Where the court gives permission for a party to amend his statement of case, it may give directions as to—

    (a) amendments to be made to any other statement of case; and
    (b) service of any amended statement of case.
  (2) The power of the court to give permission under this rule is subject to—
    (a) rule 19.1 (change of parties—general);
    (b) rule 19.4 (special provisions about adding or substituting parties after the end of a relevant limitation period; and
    (c) rule 17.4 (amendments of statement of case after the end of a relevant limitation period).

PD 17 para.1.1

[An] application [to amend] may be dealt with at a hearing or, if r.23.8 applies, without a hearing.

PD 17 para.1.2

When making an application to amend a statement of case, the applicant should file with the court:
  (1) the application notice, and
  (2) a copy of the statement of case with the proposed amendments.

PD 17 para.1.3

Where permission to amend has been given, the applicant should within 14 days of the date of the order, or within such other period as the court may direct, file with the court the amended statement of case.

PD 17 para.1.4

If the substance of the statement of case is changed by reason of the amendment, the statement of case should be re-verified by a statement of truth.

PD 17 para.1.5

A copy of the order and the amended statement of case should be served on every party to the proceedings, unless the court orders otherwise.

Amendments to statements of case after the end of a relevant limitation period

Pt 17 r.17.4

  (1) This rule applies where—
    (a) a party applies to amend his statement of case in one of the ways mentioned in this rule; and
    (b) a period of limitation has expired under—
      (i) the Limitation Act 1980;
      (ii) the Foreign Limitation Periods Act 1984; or
      (iii) any other enactment which allows such an amendment, or under which such an amendment is allowed.
  (2) The court may allow an amendment whose effect will be to add or substitute a new claim, but only if the new claim arises out of the same facts or substantially the same facts as

a claim in respect of which the party applying for permission has already claimed a remedy in the proceedings.

(3) The court may allow an amendment to correct a mistake as to the name of a party, but only where the mistake was genuine and not one which would cause reasonable doubt as to the identity of the party in question.

(4) The court may allow an amendment to alter the capacity in which a party claims if the new capacity is one which that party had when the proceedings started or has since acquired.

(Rule 19.5 specifies the circumstances in which the court may allow a new party to be added or substituted after the end of a relevant limitation period.

Amended statement of case

PD 17 para.2.1

[An] amended statement of case and the court copy of it should be endorsed as follows:

(1) where the court's permission was required:

Amended [Particulars of Claim or as may be] by Order of [Master....................][District Judge.................... or as may be] dated......................

(2) Where the court's permission was not required:

Amended [Particulars of Claim or as may be] under CPR [r.17.1(1) or (2)(a)] dated........................

PD 17 para.2.2

The statement of case in its amended form need not show the original text. However, where the court thinks it desirable for both the original text and the amendments to be shown, the court may direct that the amendments should be shown either:

(1) by coloured amendments, either manuscript or computer generated, or

(2) by use of a numerical code in a monochrome computer generated document.

PD 17 para.2.3

Where colour is used, the text to be deleted should be struck through in colour and any text replacing it should be inserted or underlined in the same colour.

PD 17 para.2.4

The order of colours to be used for successive amendments is: (1) red, (2) green, (3) violet and (4) yellow.

Power to dispense with statements of case

Pt 16 r.16.8

If a claim form has been—

(a) issued in accordance with r.7.2 [how to start proceedings]; and

(b) served in accordance with r.7.5 [service of a claim form],

the court may make an order that the claim will continue without any other statement of case.

Part 8 procedure

Pt 16 r.16.1

The provisions of Pt 16 do not apply to claims in respect of which the Pt 8 procedure is being used.

See **Commercial Court, Defamation claims, Mercantile Courts, Patents County Court, Personal injury claims, Statement of truth,** and **Strike out**.

STATEMENT OF COSTS

Summary assessment

Costs PD para.13.5

(1) It is the duty of the parties and their legal representatives to assist the judge in making a summary assessment of costs in any case to which para.13.2 above [general rule is that the court should make a summary assessment of the costs] applies, in accordance with the following paragraphs.
(2) Each party who intends to claim costs must prepare a written statement of those costs showing separately in the form of a schedule:
    (a) the number of hours to be claimed,
    (b) the hourly rate to be claimed,
    (c) the grade of fee earner;
    (d) the amount and nature of any disbursement to be claimed, other than counsel's fee for appearing at the hearing,
    (e) the amount of solicitor's costs to be claimed for attending or appearing at the hearing,
    (f) the fees of counsel to be claimed in respect of the hearing, and
    (g) any value added tax (VAT) to be claimed on these amounts.
(3) The statement of costs should follow as closely as possible Form N260 and must be signed by the party or the party's legal representative. Where a litigant is an assisted person or is a LSC funded client or is represented by a solicitor in the litigant's employment the statement of costs need not include the certificate appended at the end of Form N260.
(4) The statement of costs must be filed at court and copies of it must be served on any party against whom an order for payment of those costs is intended to be sought. The statement of costs must be filed and the copies of it must be served as soon as possible and in any event—
    (a) for a fast track trial, not less than two days before the trial; and
    (b) for all other hearings, not less than 24 hours before the time fixed for the hearing.
(5) Where the litigant is or may be entitled to claim an additional liability the statement filed and served need not reveal the amount of that liability.

STATUTORY APPEALS

PD 52D para.1.1

[PD52D] applies to all statutory appeals, but not to **appeals by way of case stated** (to which PD 52E applies).

PD 52D para.3.1

[s.III of PD52D] contains general provisions about statutory appeals. For where this PD or a statute makes additional special provision see **[Specific appeals]**.

PD 52D para.3.2

Where any of the provisions in this s. provide for documents to be filed at the appeal court, those documents are in addition to any documents required under Pt 52 or PD 52B or 52C.

Applications by third parties

Pt 52 r.52.12A

    (1) In a statutory appeal, any person may apply for permission—
        (a) to file evidence; or
        (b) to make representations at the appeal hearing.
    (2) An application under para.(1) must be made promptly.

PD 52D para.3.7

Where all the parties consent, the court may deal with an application under r. 52.12A without a hearing.

    An application for permission must be made by letter to the relevant court office, identifying the appeal, explaining who the applicant is and indicating why and in what form the applicant wants to participate in the hearing.

PD 52D para.3.8

If the applicant is seeking a prospective order as to costs, the letter must say what kind of order and on what grounds.

Route of appeal

PD 52D para.2.1

The court to which an appeal lies is prescribed by statute.

Service of appellant's notice

Pt 52 r.52.4(3)

    (3) [Unless the appeal court orders otherwise], an appellant's notice must be served on each respondent—
        (a) as soon as practicable; and
        (b) in any event not later than seven days,
    after it is filed.

PD 52D para.3.4

(1) The appellant must serve the appellant's notice on the respondent and on the chairman of the tribunal, Minister of State, government department or other person from whose decision the appeal is brought.

(2) In the case of an appeal from the decision of a tribunal that has no chairman or member who acts as a chairman, the appellant's notice must be served on the member (or members if more than one) of the tribunal.

Variation of time

Pt 52 r.52.6

(1) An application to vary the time limit for filing an appeal notice must be made to the appeal court.

(2) The parties may not agree to extend any date or time limit set by—

(a) these Rules;

(b) PD 52; or

(c) an order of the appeal court or the lower court.

(R. 3.1(2)(a) provides that the court may extend or shorten the time for compliance with any rule, PD or court order (even if an application for extension is made after the time for compliance has expired))

(R. 3.1(2)(b) provides that the court may adjourn or bring forward a hearing)

PD 52D para.3.5

Where any statute prescribes a period within which an appeal must be filed then, unless the statute otherwise provides, the appeal court may not extend that period.

Appeals under the Law of Property Act 1922

Pt 52 r.52.18

An appeal lies to the High Court against a decision of the Secretary of State under para.16 of Sch. 15 to the Law of Property Act 1922.

Appeals under certain planning legislation

Pt 52 r.52.20

(1) Where the Secretary of State has given a decision in proceedings on an appeal under Pt VII of the Town and Country Planning Act 1990 against an enforcement notice—

(a) the appellant;

(b) the local planning authority; or

(c) another person having an interest in the land to which the notice relates,

may appeal to the High Court against the decision on a point of law.

(2) Where the Secretary of State has given a decision in proceedings on an appeal under Pt VIII of that Act against a notice under s. 207 of that Act—

(a) the appellant;

    (b) the local planning authority; or
    (c) any person (other than the appellant) on whom the notice was served,
    may appeal to the High Court against the decision on a point of law.
(3) Where the Secretary of State has given a decision in proceedings on an appeal under s. 39 of the Planning (Listed Buildings and Conservation Areas) Act 1990 against a listed building enforcement notice—
    (a) the appellant;
    (b) the local planning authority; or
    (c) any other person having an interest in the land to which the notice relates,
    may appeal to the High Court against the decision on a point of law.

See also **Immigration and asylum** and **Tribunals and Inquiries Act 1992**.

STATUTORY DEMAND

Deemed date of service

IPPD para.13.1

A statutory demand is deemed to be served on the date applicable to the method of service set out in CPR Pt 6.26 unless the statutory demand is advertised in which case it is deemed served on the date of the appearance of the advertisement pursuant to r.6.3.

Service abroad of statutory demand

IPPD para.13.2.1

A statutory demand is not a document issued by the court. Permission to serve out of the jurisdiction is not, therefore, required.

IPPD para.13.2.2

Rule 6.3(2) ('Requirements as to service') applies to service of the statutory demand whether within or out of the jurisdiction.

IPPD para.13.2.3

A creditor wishing to serve a statutory demand out of the jurisdiction in a foreign country with which a civil procedure convention has been made (including the Hague Convention) may and, if the assistance of a British Consul is desired, must adopt the procedure prescribed by CPR Pts 6.42 and 6.43. In the case of any doubt whether the country is a 'convention country', enquiries should be made of the Queen's Bench Masters' Secretary Department, Room E216, Royal Courts of Justice.

IPPD para.13.2.4

In all other cases, service of the demand must be effected by private arrangement in accordance with r.6.3(2) and local foreign law.

IPPD para.13.2.5

When a statutory demand is to be served out of the jurisdiction, the time limits of 21 days and 18 days respectively referred to in the demand must be amended as provided in the next paragraph. For this purpose reference should be made to the table set out in the PD supplementing s.IV of CPR Pt 6.

IPPD para.13.2.6

A creditor should amend the statutory demand as follows—
  (1) for any reference to 18 days there must be substituted the appropriate number of days set out in the table plus four days;
  (2) for any reference to 21 days there must be substituted the appropriate number of days in the table plus seven days.

IPPD para.13.2.7

Attention is drawn to the fact that in all forms of the statutory demand Figures 18 and 21 occur in more than one place.

Substituted service of statutory demands

IPPD para.13.3.1

The creditor is under an obligation to do all that is reasonable to bring the statutory demand to the debtor's attention and, if practicable, to cause personal service to be effected (r.6.3(2)).

IPPD para.13.3.2

In the circumstances set out in r.6.3(3) the demand may instead be advertised. As there is no statutory form of advertisement, the court will accept an advertisement in the form [set out in para.13.3.2].

IPPD para.13.3.3

Where personal service is not effected or the demand is not advertised in the limited circumstances permitted by r.6.3(3), substituted service is permitted, but the creditor must have taken all those steps which would justify the court making an order for substituted service of a petition. The steps to be taken to obtain an order for substituted service of a petition are set out below. Failure to comply with these requirements may result in the court declining to issue the petition (r.6.11(9)) or dismissing it.

IPPD para.13.3.4

In most cases, evidence of the following steps will suffice to justify acceptance for presentation of a petition where the statutory demand has been served by substituted service (or to justify making an order for substituted service of a petition)—
  (1) One personal call at the residence and place of business of the debtor where both are known or at either of such places as is known. Where it is known that the debtor has more than one residential or business address, personal calls should be made at all the addresses.

(2) Should the creditor fail to effect personal service, a first class prepaid letter should be written to the debtor referring to the call(s), the purpose of the same and the failure to meet the debtor, adding that a further call will be made for the same purpose on the [day] of [month] 20[ ] at [ ] hours at [place]. At least two business days' notice should be given of the appointment and copies of the letter sent to all known addresses of the debtor. The appointment letter should also state that:

(a) in the event of the time and place not being convenient, the debtor should propose some other time and place reasonably convenient for the purpose;

(b) (In the case of a statutory demand) if the debtor fails to keep the appointment the creditor proposes to serve the debtor by [advertisement] [post] [insertion through a letter box] or as the case may be, and that, in the event of a bankruptcy petition being presented, the court will be asked to treat such service as service of the demand on the debtor;

(c) (In the case of a petition) if the debtor fails to keep the appointment, application will be made to the Court for an order for substituted service either by advertisement, or in such other manner as the court may think fit.

(3) When attending any appointment made by letter, inquiry should be made as to whether the debtor has received all letters left for him. If the debtor is away, inquiry should also be made as to whether or not letters are being forwarded to an address within the jurisdiction (England and Wales) or elsewhere.

(4) If the debtor is represented by a solicitor, an attempt should be made to arrange an appointment for personal service through such solicitor. The Insolvency Rules enable a solicitor to accept service of a statutory demand on behalf of his client but there is no similar provision in respect of service of a bankruptcy petition.

(5) The certificate of service of a statutory demand filed pursuant to r.6.11 should deal with all the above matters including all relevant facts as to the debtor's whereabouts and whether the appointment letter(s) have been returned. It should also set out the reasons for the belief that the debtor resides at the relevant address or works at the relevant place of business and whether, so far as is known, the debtor is represented by a solicitor.

Setting aside a statutory demand

IPPD para.13.4.1

The application (Form 6.4) and witness statement in support (Form 6.5) exhibiting a copy of the statutory demand must be filed in court within 18 days of service of the statutory demand on the debtor. Where service is effected by advertisement the period of 18 days is calculated from the date of the first appearance of the advertisement. Three copies of each document must be lodged with the application to enable the court to serve notice of the hearing date on the applicant, the creditor and the person named in Pt B of the statutory demand.

IPPD para.13.4.2

Where copies of the documents are not lodged with the application, any order of the Registrar fixing a venue is conditional upon copies of the documents being lodged on the next business day after the Registrar's order otherwise the application will be deemed to have been dismissed.

IPPD para.13.4.3

Where the debt claimed in the statutory demand is based on a judgment, order, liability order, costs certificate, tax assessment or decision of a tribunal, the court will not at this stage inquire into the validity of the debt nor, as a general rule, will it adjourn the application to await the result of an application to set aside the judgment, order decision, costs certificate or any appeal.

IPPD para.13.4.4

Where the debtor (a) claims to have a counterclaim, set-off or cross demand (whether or not he could have raised it in the action in which the judgment or order was obtained) which equals or exceeds the amount of the debt or debts specified in the statutory demand or (b) disputes the debt (not being a debt subject to a judgment, order, liability order, costs certificate or tax assessment) the court will normally set aside the statutory demand if, in its opinion, on the evidence there is a genuine triable issue.

IPPD para.13.4.5

A debtor who wishes to apply to set aside a statutory demand after the expiration of 18 days from the date of service of the statutory demand must apply for an extension of time within which to apply. If the applicant wishes to apply for an injunction to restrain presentation of a petition the application must be made to the Judge. Paragraphs 1 and 2 of Form 6.5 (witness statement in support of application to set aside statutory demand) should be used in support of the application for an extension of time with the [additional paragraphs set out in para.13.4.5].

See **Bankruptcy Court**, **Bankruptcy petition**, **Insolvency proceedings**, **Statutory demand**, and **Validation order**.

STATUTORY INTEREST

See **Interest**.

STAY

Glossary

A stay imposes a halt on proceedings, apart from taking any steps allowed by the rules or the terms of the stay. Proceedings can be continued if a stay is lifted.

Admiralty claims

Pt 61 r.61.12

Where the court orders a stay of any claim in rem—
    (a) any property under arrest in the claim remains under arrest; and
    (b) any security representing the property remains in force,
unless the court orders otherwise.

Arbitration claims

Pt 62 r.62.8

    (1) An application notice seeking a stay of legal proceedings under s.9 of the 1996 Act must be served on all parties to those proceedings who have given an address for service.
    (2) A copy of an application notice under para.(1) must be served on any other party to the legal proceedings (whether or not he is within the jurisdiction) who has not given an address for service, at—

(a) his last known address; or

(b) a place where it is likely to come to his attention.

(3) Where a question arises as to whether—

(a) an arbitration agreement has been concluded; or

(b) the dispute which is the subject-matter of the proceedings falls within the terms of such an agreement,

the court may decide that question or give directions to enable it to be decided and may order the proceedings to be stayed pending its decision.

Attempt to settle the case

Pt 26 r.26.4

(1) A party may, when filing the completed allocation questionnaire, make a written request for the proceedings to be stayed while the parties try to settle the case by alternative dispute resolution or other means.

(2) Where—

(a) all parties request a stay under para.(1); or

(b) the court, of its own initiative, considers that such a stay would be appropriate,

the court will direct that the proceedings , either in whole or in part, be stayed for one month, or for such specified period as it considers appropriate.

(3) The court may extend the stay until such date or for such specified period as it considers appropriate.

(4) Where the court stays the proceedings under this rule, the claimant must tell the court if a settlement is reached.

(5) If the claimant does not tell the court by the end of the period of the stay that a settlement has been reached, the court will give such directions as to the management of the case as it considers appropriate.

Extending the stay

Pt 26 r.3.1

(1) (a) The court will generally accept a letter from any party or from the solicitor for any party as an application to extend the stay under r.26.4.

(b) The letter should—

(i) confirm that the application is made with the agreement of all parties, and

(ii) explain the steps being taken and identify any mediator or expert assisting with the process.

(2) (a) An order extending the stay must be made by a judge.

(b) The extension will generally be for no more than four weeks unless clear reasons are given to justify a longer time.

(3) More than one extension of the stay may be granted.

Position at the end of the stay if no settlement is reached

PD 26 para.3.2

(1) At the end of the stay the file will be referred to a judge for his directions.

(2) He will consider whether to allocate the claim to a track and what other directions to give, or may require any party to give further information or fix an allocation hearing.

PD 26 para.3.3

Any party may apply for a stay to be lifted.

Position where settlement is reached during a stay

PD 26 para.3.4

Where the whole of the proceedings are settled during a stay, the taking of any of the following steps will be treated as an application for the stay to be lifted:
- (1) an application for a consent order (in any form) to give effect to the settlement,
- (2) an application for the approval of a settlement where a party is a person under a disability,
- (3) giving notice of acceptance of money paid into court in satisfaction of the claim or applying for money in court to be paid out.

Criminal proceedings

PD 23A para.11A.1

An application for the stay of civil proceedings pending the determination of related criminal proceedings may be made by any party to the civil proceedings or by the prosecutor or any defendant in the criminal proceedings.

PD 23A para.11A.2

Every party to the civil proceedings must, unless he is the applicant, be made a respondent to the application.

PD 23A para.11A.3

The evidence in support of the application must contain an estimate of the expected duration of the stay and must identify the respects in which the continuance of the civil proceedings may prejudice the criminal trial.

PD 23A para.11A.4

In order to make an application under para.11A.1, it is not necessary for the prosecutor or defendant in the criminal proceedings to be joined as a party to the civil proceedings.

Detailed assessment

Pt 47 r.47.2

Detailed assessment is not stayed pending an appeal unless the court so orders.

Costs PD para.29.1

> (1) Rule 47.2 provides that detailed assessment is not stayed pending an appeal unless the court so orders.
> (2) An application to stay the detailed assessment of costs pending an appeal may be made to the court whose order is being appealed or to the court who will hear the appeal.

Enforcement of judgments and orders

RSC Ord.45 r.11

Without prejudice to Ord.47 r.1, a party against whom a judgment has been given or an order made may apply to the court for a stay of execution of the judgment or order or other relief on the ground of matters which have occurred since the date of the judgment or order, and the court may by order grant such relief, and on such terms, as it thinks just.

European court

Pt 68 r.68.4

Where an order is made, unless the court orders otherwise the proceedings will be stayed until the European Court has given a preliminary ruling on the question referred to it.

Appeals

Pt 52 r.52.7

Unless—
> (a) the appeal court or the lower court orders otherwise; or
> (b) the appeal is from the Immigration and Asylum Chamber of the Upper Tribunal,
>   an appeal shall not operate as a stay of any order or decision of the lower court.

Claim stayed if it is not defended or admitted

Pt 15 r.15.11

> (1) Where—
>   (a) at least six months have expired since the end of the period for filing a defence specified in r.15.4;
>   (b) no defendant has served or filed an admission or filed a defence or counterclaim; and
>   (c) the claimant has not entered or applied for judgment under Pt 12 (default judgment), or Pt 24 (summary judgment),
>   the claim shall be stayed.
> (2) Where a claim is stayed under this rule any party may apply for the stay to be lifted.

Partly discontinued proceedings where costs not paid

Pt 38 r.38.8

(1) This rule applies where—
    (a) proceedings are partly discontinued;
    (b) a claimant is liable to—
        (i) pay costs under r.38.6; or
        (ii) make a payment pursuant to an order under s.194(3) of the Legal Services Act 2007; and
    (c) the claimant fails to pay those costs or make the payment within 14 days of—
        (i) the date on which the parties agreed the sum payable by the claimant; or
        (ii) the date on which the court ordered the costs to be paid or the payment to be made.
(2) Where this rule applies, the court may stay the remainder of the proceedings until the claimant pays the whole of the costs which the claimant is liable to pay under r.38.6 or makes the payment pursuant to an order under s.194(3) of the Legal Services Act 2007.

(Rules 44.3C and 44.12 contain provisions about applying for an order under s.194(3) of the Legal Services Act 2007).

Interpleader

RSC Ord.17 r.7

Where a defendant to a claim applies for relief under this Order in the claim, the court may by order stay all further proceedings in the claim.

Reference to European Court

Pt 68 r.68.4

Where an order is made, unless the court orders otherwise the proceedings will be stayed until the European Court has given a preliminary ruling on the question referred to it.

Writ of fieri facias

RSC Ord.47 r.1

(1) Where a judgment is given or an order made for the payment by any person of money, and the court is satisfied, on an application made at the time of the judgment or order, or at any time thereafter, by the judgment debtor or other party liable to execution—
    (a) that there are special circumstances which render it inexpedient to enforce the judgment or order; or
    (b) that the applicant is unable from any cause to pay the money,
    then, notwithstanding anything in rr.2 or 3, the court may by order stay the execution of the judgment or order by writ of fieri facias either absolutely or for such period and subject to such conditions as the court thinks fit.
(2) An application under this rule, if not made at the time the judgment is given or order made, must be made in accordance with CPR Pt 23 and may be so made notwithstanding

that the party liable to execution did not acknowledge service of the claim form or serve a defence or take any previous part in the proceedings.

(3) The grounds on which an application under this rule is made must be set out in the application notice and be supported by a witness statement or affidavit made by or on behalf of the applicant substantiating the said grounds and, in particular, where such application is made on the grounds of the applicant's inability to pay, disclosing his income, the nature and value of any property of his and the amount of any other liabilities of his.

(4) The application notice and a copy of the supporting witness statement or affidavit must, not less than four clear days before the hearing, be served on the party entitled to enforce the judgment or order.

(5) An order staying execution under this rule may be varied or revoked by a subsequent order.

European Court

Pt 68 r.68.4

Where an order is made, unless the court orders otherwise the proceedings will be stayed until the European Court has given a preliminary ruling on the question referred to it.

STOP NOTICE

PD 73 para.73.16

In this section—

(a) 'stop notice' means a notice issued by the court which requires a person or body not to take, in relation to securities specified in the notice, any of the steps listed in s.5(5) of the 1979 Act, without first giving notice to the person who obtained the notice; and

(b) 'securities' does not include securities held in court.

PD 73 para.5

A sample form of stop notice is set out in Appendix B to [PD 73].

Request for stop notice

Pt 73 r.73.17

(1) The High Court may, on the request of any person claiming to be beneficially entitled to an interest in securities, issue a stop notice.

(A stop notice may also be included in a final charging order, by either the High Court or a county court, under r.73.8(3).)

(2) A request for a stop notice must be made by filing—

(a) a draft stop notice; and

(b) written evidence which—

(i) identifies the securities in question;

(ii) describes the applicant's interest in the securities; and

(iii) gives an address for service for the applicant.

(A sample form of stop notice is annexed to PD 73.)

(3) If a court officer considers that the request complies with para.(2), he will issue a stop notice.
(4) The applicant must serve copies of the stop notice and his written evidence on the person to whom the stop notice is addressed.

Effect of stop notice

Pt 73 r.73.18

(1) A stop notice—
    (a) takes effect when it is served in accordance with r.73.17(4); and
    (b) remains in force unless it is withdrawn or discharged in accordance with r.73.20 or 73.21.
(2) While a stop notice is in force, the person on whom it is served—
    (a) must not—
        (i) register a transfer of the securities described in the notice; or
        (ii) take any other step restrained by the notice,
    without first giving 14 days' notice to the person who obtained the stop notice; but
    (b) must not, by reason only of the notice, refuse to register a transfer or to take any other step, after he has given 14 days' notice under para.(2)(a) and that period has expired.

Amendment of stop notice

Pt 73 r.73.19

(1) If any securities are incorrectly described in a stop notice which has been obtained and served in accordance with r.73.17, the applicant may request an amended stop notice in accordance with that rule.
(2) The amended stop notice takes effect when it is served.

Withdrawal of stop notice

Pt 73 r.73.20

(1) A person who has obtained a stop notice may withdraw it by serving a request for its withdrawal on—
    (a) the person or body on whom the stop notice was served; and
    (b) the court which issued the stop notice.
(2) The request must be signed by the person who obtained the stop notice, and his signature must be witnessed by a practising solicitor.

Discharge or variation of stop notice

Pt 73 r.73.21

(1) The court may, on the application of any person claiming to be beneficially entitled to an interest in the securities to which a stop notice relates, make an order discharging or varying the notice.

(2) An application to discharge or vary a stop notice must be made to the court which issued the notice.

(3) The application notice must be served on the person who obtained the stop notice.

See **Partnership**.

STOP ORDER

Pt 73 r.73.11

An order of the High Court not to take, in relation to funds in court or securities specified in the order, any of the steps listed in s.5(5) of the 1979 Act.

Application for stop order

Pt 73 r.73.12

(1) The High Court may make—
    (a) a stop order relating to funds in court, on the application of any person—
        (i) who has a mortgage or charge on the interest of any person in the funds; or
        (ii) to whom that interest has been assigned; or
        (iii) who is a judgment creditor of the person entitled to that interest; or
    (b) a stop order relating to securities other than securities held in court, on the application of any person claiming to be beneficially entitled to an interest in the securities.

(2) An application for a stop order must be made—
    (a) by application notice in existing proceedings; or
    (b) by Pt 8 claim form if there are no existing proceedings in the High Court.

(3) The application notice or claim form must be served on—
    (a) every person whose interest may be affected by the order applied for; and
    (b) either—
        (i) the Accountant General at the Court Funds Office, if the application relates to funds in court; or
        (ii) the person specified in r.73.5(1)(d), if the application relates to securities other than securities held in court.

Stop order relating to funds in court

Pt 73 r.73.13

A stop order relating to funds in court shall prohibit the transfer, sale, delivery out, payment or other dealing with—
    (a) the funds or any part of them; or
    (b) any income on the funds.

Stop order relating to securities

Pt 73 r.73.14

(1) A stop order relating to securities other than securities held in court may prohibit all or any of the following steps—

    (a) the registration of any transfer of the securities;
    (b) the making of any payment by way of dividend, interest or otherwise in respect of the securities; and
    (c) in the case of units of a unit trust, any acquisition of or other dealing with the units by any person or body exercising functions under the trust.
(2) The order shall specify—
    (a) the securities to which it relates;
    (b) the name in which the securities stand;
    (c) the steps which may not be taken; and
    (d) whether the prohibition applies to the securities only or to the dividends or interest as well.

Variation or discharge of order

Pt 73 r.73.15

(1) The court may, on the application of any person claiming to have a beneficial interest in the funds or securities to which a stop order relates, make an order discharging or varying the order.
(2) An application notice seeking the variation or discharge of a stop order must be served on the person who obtained the order.

STRIKE OUT

Glossary

The court ordering written material to be deleted so that it may no longer be relied upon.

Statement of case

PD 3A para.4.2

Where a judge at a hearing strikes out all or part of a party's statement of case he may enter such judgment for the other party as that party appears entitled to.

Judgment without trial after striking out

Pt 3 r.3.5

(1) This rule applies where—
    (a) the court makes an order which includes a term that the **statement of case** of a party shall be struck out if the party does not comply with the order; and
    (b) the party against whom the order was made does not comply with it.
(2) A party may obtain judgment with costs by filing a request for judgment if—
    (a) the order referred to in para.(1)(a) relates to the whole of a statement of case; and
    (b) where the party wishing to obtain judgment is the claimant, the claim is for—
        (i) a specified amount of money;
        (ii) an amount of money to be decided by the court;

(iii) delivery of goods where the claim form gives the defendant the alternative of paying their value; or

(iv) any combination of these remedies.

(3) Where judgment is obtained under this rule in a case to which para.(2)(b)(iii) applies, it will be judgment requiring the defendant to deliver goods, or (if he does not do so) pay the value of the goods as decided by the court (less any payments made).

(4) The request must state that the right to enter judgment has arisen because the court's order has not been complied with.

(5) A party must make an application in accordance with Pt 23 if he wishes to obtain judgment under this rule in a case to which para.(2) does not apply.

Setting aside judgment entered after striking out

Pt 3 r.3.6

(1) A party against whom the court has entered judgment under r.3.5 may apply to the court to set the judgment aside.

(2) An application under para.(1) must be made not more than 14 days after the judgment has been served on the party making the application.

(3) If the right to enter judgment had not arisen at the time when judgment was entered, the court must set aside the judgment.

(4) If the application to set aside is made for any other reason, r.3.9 (relief from sanctions) shall apply.

Power to strike out a statement of case

Pt 1 r.1.4

(1) The court must further the overriding objective by actively managing cases.

(2) Active case management includes—

(c) deciding promptly which issues need full investigation and trial and accordingly disposing summarily of the others.

Pt 3 r.3.4

(1) In this rule and r.3.5 [Judgment without trial after striking out], reference to a statement of case includes reference to part of a statement of case.

(2) The court may strike out a statement of case if it appears to the court—

(a) that the statement of case discloses no reasonable grounds for bringing or defending the claim;

(b) that the statement of case is an abuse of the court's process or is otherwise likely to obstruct the just disposal of the proceedings; or

(c) that there has been a failure to comply with a rule, PD or court order.

(3) When the court strikes out a statement of case it may make any consequential order it considers appropriate.

(4) Where—

(a) the court has struck out a claimant's statement of case;

(b) the claimant has been ordered to pay costs to the defendant; and

(c) before the claimant pays those costs, he starts another claim against the same defendant, arising out of facts which are the same or substantially the same as those relating to the claim in which the statement of case was struck out, the court may, on the application of the defendant, stay that other claim until the costs of the first claim have been paid.

(5) Paragraph (2) does not limit any other power of the court to strike out a statement of case.

(6) If the court strikes out a claimant's statement of case and it considers that the claim is totally without merit—

    (a) the court's order must record that fact; and

    (b) the court must at the same time consider whether it is appropriate to make a civil restraint order.

PD 3A para.1.2

The rules give the court two distinct powers which may be used to achieve this. Rule 3.4 enables the court to strike out the whole or part of a statement of case which discloses no reasonable grounds for bringing or defending a claim (r.3.4(2)(a)), or which is an abuse of the process of the court or otherwise likely to obstruct the just disposal of the proceedings (r.3.4(2)(b)). Rule 24.2 enables the court to give **summary judgment** against a claimant or defendant where that party has no real prospect of succeeding on his claim or defence. Both those powers may be exercised on an application by a party or on the court's own initiative.

PD 3A para.1.3

[PD 3A] sets out the procedure a party should follow if he wishes to make an application for an order under r.3.4.

PD 3A para.1.4

The following are examples of cases where the court may conclude that particulars of claim (whether contained in a claim form or filed separately) fall within r.3.4(2)(a):

(1) those which set out no facts indicating what the claim is about, for example 'Money owed £5000',

(2) those which are incoherent and make no sense,

(3) those which contain a coherent set of facts but those facts, even if true, do not disclose any legally recognisable claim against the defendant.

PD 3A para.1.5

A claim may fall within r.3.4(2)(b) where it is vexatious, scurrilous or obviously ill-founded.

PD 3A para.1.6

A defence may fall within r.3.4(2)(a) where:

(1) it consists of a bare denial or otherwise sets out no coherent statement of facts, or

(2) the facts it sets out, while coherent, would not even if true amount in law to a defence to the claim.

PD 3A para.1.7

A party may believe he can show without a trial that an opponent's case has no real prospect of success on the facts, or that the case is bound to succeed or fail, as the case may be, because of a point of law (including the construction of a document). In such a case the party concerned may make an application under r.3.4 or Pt 24 (or both) as he thinks appropriate.

PD 3A para.1.8

The examples set out above are intended only as illustrations.

PD 3A para.1.9

Where a rule, PD or order states 'shall be struck out or dismissed' or 'will be struck out or dismissed' this means that the striking out or dismissal will be automatic and that no further order of the court is required.

PD 3A para.4.1

The court may exercise its powers under r.3.4(2)(a) or (b) on application or on its own initiative at any time.

PD 3A para.4.2

Where a judge at a hearing strikes out all or part of a party's statement of case he may enter such judgment for the other party as that party appears entitled to.

Claims which appear to fall within r.3.4(2)(a) or (b)

PD 3A para.2.1

If a court officer is asked to issue a claim form which he believes may fall within r.3.4(2)(a) or (b) he should issue it, but may then consult a judge (under r.3.2) before returning the claim form to the claimant or taking any other step to serve the defendant. The judge may on his own initiative make an immediate order designed to ensure that the claim is disposed of or (as the case may be) proceeds in a way that accords with the rules.

PD 3A para.2.3

The judge may allow the claimant a hearing before deciding whether to make such an order.

PD 3A para.2.4

Orders the judge may make include:
  (1) an order that the claim be stayed until further order,
  (2) an order that the claim form be retained by the court and not served until the stay is lifted,
  (3) an order that no application by the claimant to lift the stay be heard unless he files such further documents (for example a witness statement or an amended claim form or particulars of claim) as may be specified in the order.

PD 3A para.2.5

Where the judge makes any such order or, subsequently, an order lifting the stay he may give directions about the service on the defendant of the order and any other documents on the court file.

PD 3A para.2.6

The fact that a judge allows a claim referred to him by a court officer to proceed does not prejudice the right of any party to apply for any order against the claimant.

Defences which appear to fall within r.3.4(2)(a) or (b)

PD 3A para.3.1

A court officer may similarly consult a judge about any document filed which purports to be a defence and which he believes may fall within r.3.4(2)(a) or (b).

PD 3A para.3.2

If the judge decides that the document falls within r.3.4(2)(a) or (b) he may on his own initiative make an order striking it out. Where he does so he may extend the time for the defendant to file a proper defence.

PD 3A para.3.3

The judge may allow the defendant a hearing before deciding whether to make such an order.

PD 3A para.3.4

Alternatively the judge may make an order under r.18.1 requiring the defendant within a stated time to clarify his defence or to give additional information about it. The order may provide that the defence will be struck out if the defendant does not comply.

PD 3A para.3.5

The fact that a judge does not strike out a defence on his own initiative does not prejudice the right of the claimant to apply for any order against the defendant.

Applications for orders under r.3.4(2)

PD 3A para.5.1

Attention is drawn to Pt 23 (General Rules about Applications) and to PD 23A. The PD requires all applications to be made as soon as possible and before allocation if possible.

PD 3A para.5.2

While many applications under r.3.4(2) can be made without evidence in support, the applicant should consider whether facts need to be proved and, if so, whether evidence in support should be filed and served.

Allocation questionnaire

PD 26 para.2.5

(1) If no party files an allocation questionnaire within the time specified by Form N152, the court will order that unless an allocation questionnaire is filed within seven days from

service of that order, the claim, defence and any counterclaim will be struck out without further order of the court.

Committal application

PD 81 para.16.1

On application by the respondent or on its own initiative, the court may strike out a committal application if it appears to the court:
(1) that the committal application and the evidence served in support of it disclose no reasonable ground for alleging that the respondent is guilty of a contempt of court;
(2) that the committal application is an abuse of the court's process or, if made in existing proceedings, is otherwise likely to obstruct the just disposal of those proceedings; or
(3) that there has been a failure to comply with a rule, PD or court order.

Statement of case

Pt 3 r.3.4

(1) In this rule and r.3.5 [judgment without trial after striking out], reference to a statement of case includes reference to part of a statement of case.
(2) The court may strike out a statement of case if it appears to the court—
   (a) that the statement of case discloses no reasonable grounds for bringing or defending the claim;
   (b) that the statement of case is an abuse of the court's process or is otherwise likely to obstruct the just disposal of the proceedings; or
   (c) that there has been a failure to comply with a rule, PD or court order.
(3) When the court strikes out a statement of case it may make any consequential order it considers appropriate.
(4) Where—
   (a) the court has struck out a claimant's statement of case;
   (b) the claimant has been ordered to pay costs to the defendant; and
   (c) before the claimant pays those costs, he starts another claim against the same defendant, arising out of facts which are the same or substantially the same as those relating to the claim in which the statement of case was struck out,
the court may, on the application of the defendant, stay that other claim until the costs of the first claim have been paid.
(5) Paragraph (2) does not limit any other power of the court to strike out a statement of case.
(6) If the court strikes out a claimant's statement of case and it considers that the claim is totally without merit—
   (a) the court's order must record that fact; and
   (b) the court must at the same time consider whether it is appropriate to make a civil restraint order.

PD 3A para.1.2

The rules give the court two distinct powers which may be used to achieve this. Rule 3.4 enables the court to strike out the whole or part of a statement of case which discloses no reasonable grounds for bringing or defending a claim (r.3.4(2)(a)), or which is an abuse of the process of the court or otherwise likely to obstruct the just disposal of the proceedings (r.3.4(2)(b)). Rule 24.2 enables the court to give summary judgment against a claimant or defendant where that party has no real prospect of succeeding on his claim or defence. Both those powers may be exercised on an application by a party or on the court's own initiative.

PD 3A para.1.4

The following are examples of cases where the court may conclude that particulars of claim (whether contained in a claim form or filed separately) fall within r.3.4(2)(a):
  (1) those which set out no facts indicating what the claim is about, for example 'Money owed £5000',
  (2) those which are incoherent and make no sense,
  (3) those which contain a coherent set of facts but those facts, even if true, do not disclose any legally recognisable claim against the defendant.

PD 3A para.1.6

A defence may fall within r.3.4(2)(a) where:
  (1) it consists of a bare denial or otherwise sets out no coherent statement of facts, or
  (2) the facts it sets out, while coherent, would not even if true amount in law to a defence to the claim.

PD 3A para.1.7

A party may believe he can show without a trial that an opponent's case has no real prospect of success on the facts, or that the case is bound to succeed or fail, as the case may be, because of a point of law (including the construction of a document). In such a case the party concerned may make an application under r.3.4 or Pt 24 (or both) as he thinks appropriate.

PD 3A para.1.8

The examples set out above are intended only as illustrations.

PD 3A para.1.9

Where a rule, PD or order states 'shall be struck out or dismissed' or 'will be struck out or dismissed' this means that the striking out or dismissal will be automatic and that no further order of the court is required.

Claims which appear to fall within r.3.4(2)(a) or (b)

PD 3A para.2.1

If a court officer is asked to issue a claim form which he believes may fall within r.3.4(2)(a) or (b) he should issue it, but may then consult a judge (under r.3.2) before returning the claim form to the claimant or taking any other step to serve the defendant. The judge may on his own initiative make an immediate order designed to ensure that the claim is disposed of or (as the case may be) proceeds in a way that accords with the rules.

PD 3A para.2.3

The judge may allow the claimant a hearing before deciding whether to make such an order.

PD 3A para.2.4

Orders the judge may make include:
   (1) an order that the claim be stayed until further order,
   (2) an order that the claim form be retained by the court and not served until the stay is lifted,
   (3) an order that no application by the claimant to lift the stay be heard unless he files such further documents (for example a witness statement or an amended claim form or particulars of claim) as may be specified in the order.

PD 3A para.2.5

Where the judge makes any such order or, subsequently, an order lifting the stay he may give directions about the service on the defendant of the order and any other documents on the court file.

PD 3A para.2.6

The fact that a judge allows a claim referred to him by a court officer to proceed does not prejudice the right of any party to apply for any order against the claimant.

Defences which appear to fall within r.3.4(2)(a) or (b)

PD 3A para.3.1

A court officer may similarly consult a judge about any document filed which purports to be a defence and which he believes may fall within r.3.4(2)(a) or (b).

PD 3A para.3.2

If the judge decides that the document falls within r.3.4(2)(a) or (b) he may on his own initiative make an order striking it out. Where he does so he may extend the time for the defendant to file a proper defence.

PD 3A para.3.3

The judge may allow the defendant a hearing before deciding whether to make such an order.

PD 3A para.3.4

Alternatively the judge may make an order under r.18.1 requiring the defendant within a stated time to clarify his defence or to give additional information about it. The order may provide that the defence will be struck out if the defendant does not comply.

PD 3A para.4.1

The court may exercise its powers under r.3.4(2)(a) or (b) on application or on its own initiative at any time.

PD 3A para.4.2

Where a judge at a hearing strikes out all or part of a party's statement of case he may enter such judgment for the other party as that party appears entitled to.

PD 3A para.3.5

The fact that a judge does not strike out a defence on his own initiative does not prejudice the right of the claimant to apply for any order against the defendant.

Applications for orders under r.3.4(2)

PD 3A para.5.1

Attention is drawn to Pt 23 (General Rules about Applications) and to PD 23A. The PD requires all applications to be made as soon as possible and before allocation if possible.

PD 3A para.5.2

While many applications under r.3.4(2) can be made without evidence in support, the applicant should consider whether facts need to be proved and, if so, whether evidence in support should be filed and served.

See also **Appeal** and **Court fees**.

STUDENT LOAN REPAYMENTS

See **Revenue and Customs**.

SUBPOENA

See **Witness summons**.

SUBSTITUTED SERVICE

See **Service of documents**.

SUMMARY ASSESSMENT

Pt 44 r.44.1(1)

The procedure whereby costs are assessed by the judge who has heard the case or application.

When the court should consider whether to make a summary assessment

PD 44 para.9.1

Whenever a court makes an order about costs which does not provide only for fixed costs to be paid the court should consider whether to make a summary assessment of costs.

Timing of summary assessment

PD 44 para.9.2

The general rule is that the court should make a summary assessment of the costs—
  (a) at the conclusion of the trial of a case which has been dealt with on the fast track, in which case the order will deal with the costs of the whole claim; and
  (b) at the conclusion of any other hearing, which has lasted not more than one day, in which case the order will deal with the costs of the application or matter to which the hearing related. If this hearing disposes of the claim, the order may deal with the costs of the whole claim,
unless there is good reason not to do so, for example where the paying party shows substantial grounds for disputing the sum claimed for costs that cannot be dealt with summarily.

Summary assessment of mortgagee's costs

PD 44 para.9.3

The general rule in para.9.2 does not apply to a mortgagee's costs incurred in mortgage possession proceedings or other proceedings relating to a mortgage unless the mortgagee asks the court to make an order for the mortgagee's costs to be paid by another party.
(Paragraphs 7.2 and 7.3 deal in more detail with costs relating to mortgages.)

Consent orders

PD 44 para.9.4

Where an application has been made and the parties to the application agree an order by consent without any party attending, the parties should seek to agree a figure for costs to be inserted in the consent order or agree that there should be no order for costs.

Duty of parties and legal representatives

PD 44 para.9.5

  (1) It is the duty of the parties and their legal representatives to assist the judge in making a summary assessment of costs in any case to which para.9.2 above applies, in accordance with the following subparas.
  (2) Each party who intends to claim costs must prepare a written statement of those costs showing separately in the form of a schedule—

(a) the number of hours to be claimed;

(b) the hourly rate to be claimed;

(c) the grade of fee earner;

(d) the amount and nature of any disbursement to be claimed, other than counsel's fee for appearing at the hearing;

(e) the amount of legal representative's costs to be claimed for attending or appearing at the hearing;

(f) counsel's fees; and

(g) any VAT to be claimed on these amounts.

(3) The statement of costs should follow as closely as possible Form N260 and must be signed by the party or the party's legal representative. Where a party is—

(a) an assisted person;

(b) a LSC funded client;

(c) a person for whom civil legal services (within the meaning of Pt 1 of the Legal Aid, Sentencing and Punishment of Offenders Act 2012) are provided under arrangements made for the purposes of that Part of that Act; or

(d) represented by a person in the party's employment,

the statement of costs need not include the certificate appended at the end of Form N260.

(4) The statement of costs must be filed at court and copies of it must be served on any party against whom an order for payment of those costs is intended to be sought as soon as possible and in any event—

(a) for a fast track trial, not less than two days before the trial; and

(b) for all other hearings, not less than 24 hours before the time fixed for the hearing.

PD 44 para.9.6

The failure by a party, without reasonable excuse, to comply with para.9.5 will be taken into account by the court in deciding what order to make about the costs of the claim, hearing or application, and about the costs of any further hearing or detailed assessment hearing that may be necessary as a result of that failure.

No summary assessment by a costs officer

PD 44 para.9.7

The court awarding costs cannot make an order for a summary assessment of costs by a costs officer. If a summary assessment of costs is appropriate but the court awarding costs is unable to do so on the day, the court may give directions as to a further hearing before the same judge.

Assisted persons. etc.

PD 44 para.9.8

The court will not make a summary assessment of the costs of a receiving party who is an assisted person or LSC funded client or who is a person for whom civil legal services (within the meaning of Pt 1 of the Legal Aid, Sentencing and Punishment of Offenders Act 2012) are provided under arrangements made for the purposes of that Part of that Act.

Children or protected parties

PD 44 para.9.9

    (1) The court will not make a summary assessment of the costs of a receiving party who is a child or protected party within the meaning of Pt 21 unless the legal representative acting for the child or protected party has waived the right to further costs (see PD 46 para.2.1).

    (2) The court may make a summary assessment of costs payable by a child or protected party.

Disproportionate or unreasonable costs

PD 44 para.9.10

The court will not give its approval to disproportionate or unreasonable costs. When the amount of the costs to be paid has been agreed between the parties the order for costs must state that the order is by consent.

SUMMARY DISPOSAL

PD 26 para.5.1

Part of the court's duty of active case management is the summary disposal of issues which do not need full investigation and trial (r.1.4(2)(c)).

PD 26 para.5.2

The court's powers to make orders to dispose of issues in that way include:
    (a) under r.3.4, striking out a statement of case, or part of a statement of case, and
    (b) under Pt 24, giving **summary judgment** where a claimant or a defendant has no reasonable prospect of success.
The court may use these powers on an application or on its own initiative. PD 24 contains further information.

PD 26 para.5.3

    (1) A party intending to make such an application should do so before or when filing his allocation questionnaire.

    (2) Where a party makes an application for such an order before a claim has been allocated to a track the court will not normally allocate the claim before the hearing of the application.

    (3) Where a party files an allocation questionnaire stating that he intends to make such an application but has not done so, the judge will usually direct that an allocation hearing is listed.

    (4) The application may be heard at that allocation hearing if the application notice has been issued and served in sufficient time.

PD 26 para.5.4

    (1) This paragraph applies where the court proposes to make such an order of its own initiative.

(2) The court will not allocate the claim to a track but instead it will either:

    (a) fix a hearing, giving the parties at least 14 days' notice of the date of the hearing and of the issues which it is proposed that the court will decide, or

    (b) make an order directing a party to take the steps described in the order within a stated time and specifying the consequence of not taking those steps.

PD 26 para.5.5

Where the court decides at the hearing of an application or a hearing fixed under para.5.4(2)(a) that the claim (or part of the claim) is to continue it may:

    (1) treat that hearing as an allocation hearing, allocate the claim and give case management directions, or

    (2) give other directions.

See also **Defamation claims** and **Summary judgment**.

SUMMARY JUDGMENT

Applications for summary judgment

Pt 24 r.24.1

[Pt 24] sets out a procedure by which the court may decide a claim or a particular issue without a trial. Attention is drawn to that Part and to PD 24.

PD 24 para.1.1

Attention is drawn to Pt 24 itself and to:

    Pt 3 [court's case management powers] , in particular r.3.1(3) [make order subject to conditions, including a condition to pay a sum of money into court; and specify the consequence of failure to comply with the order or a condition] and (5) [order a party to pay a sum of money into court if that party has, without good reason, failed to comply with a rule, PD or a relevant pre-action protocol],

    Pt 22 [statement of truth], Pt 23 [general rules about applications for cour orders], in particular r.23.6 [an application notice must state what order the applicant is seeking; and briefly, why the applicant is seeking the order].

    Pt 32 [evidence], in particular r.32.6(2) [at hearings other than the trial, a party may, rely on the matters set out in his statement of case; or his application notice, if the statement of case or application notice is verified by a statement of truth].

PD 24 para.1.3

An application for summary judgment under r.24.2 may be based on:

    (1) a point of law (including a question of construction of a document),

    (2) the evidence which can reasonably be expected to be available at trial or the lack of it, or

    (3) a combination of these.

PD 24 para.1.4

R.24.4(1) deals with the stage in the proceedings at which an application under Pt 24 can be made (but see para.7.1 below).

Procedure for making an application

Pt 24 r.24.4

(1) A claimant may not apply for summary judgment until the defendant against whom the application is made has filed—
(a) an **acknowledgement of service**; or
(b) a **defence**,
unless—
(i) the court gives permission; or
(ii) a PD provides otherwise.
(2) If a claimant applies for summary judgment before a defendant against whom the application is made has filed a defence, that defendant need not file a defence before the hearing.
(3) Where a summary judgment hearing is fixed, the respondent (or the parties where the hearing is fixed of the court's own initiative) must be given at least 14 days' notice of—
(a) the date fixed for the hearing; and
(b) the issues which it is proposed that the court will decide at the hearing.
(4) A PD may provide for a different period of notice to be given.
(Pt 23 contains the general rules about how to make an application).
(R.3.3 applies where the court exercises its powers of its own initiative).

PD 24 para.2

(1) Attention is drawn to rr.24.4(3) and 23.6 [an **application notice** must state what order the applicant is seeking; and briefly, why the applicant is seeking the order].
(2) The application notice must include a statement that it is an application for summary judgment made under Pt 24.
(3) The application notice or the evidence contained or referred to in it or served with it must—
(a) identify concisely any point of law or provision in a document on which the applicant relies, and/or
(b) state that it is made because the applicant believes that on the evidence the respondent has no real prospect of succeeding on the claim or issue or (as the case may be) of successfully defending the claim or issue to which the application relates,
and in either case state that the applicant knows of no other reason why the disposal of the claim or issue should await trial.
(4) Unless the application notice itself contains all the evidence (if any) on which the applicant relies, the application notice should identify the written evidence on which the applicant relies. This does not affect the applicant's right to file further evidence under r.24.5(2).
(5) The application notice should draw the attention of the respondent to r.24.5(1).
(6) Where the claimant has failed to comply with PD (Pre-Action Conduct) or any relevant pre-action protocol, an action for summary judgment will not normally be entertained before the defence has been filed or, alternatively, the time for doing so has expired.

Grounds for summary judgment

Pt 24 r.24.2

The court may give summary judgment against a claimant or defendant on the whole of a claim [includes a part of a claim and an issue on which the claim in whole or part depends] or on a particular issue if—

(a) it considers that—
    (i) that claimant has no real prospect of succeeding on the claim or issue; or
    (ii) that defendant has no real prospect of successfully defending the claim or issue; and
(b) there is no other compelling reason why the case or issue should be disposed of at a trial.

(R.3.4 makes provision for the court to strike out a statement of case or part of a statement of case if it appears that it discloses no reasonable grounds for bringing or defending a claim).

Types of proceedings in which summary judgment is available

Pt 24 r.24.3

(1) The court may give summary judgment against a claimant in any type of proceedings.
(2) The court may give summary judgment against a defendant in any type of proceedings except—
    (a) proceedings for possession of residential premises against—
        (i) a mortgagor; or
        (ii) a tenant or a person holding over after the end of his tenancy whose occupancy is protected within the meaning of the Rent Act 1977 or the Housing Act 1988 and;
    (b) proceedings for an admiralty claim in rem.

Evidence for the purposes of a summary judgment hearing

Pt 24 r.24.5

(1) If the respondent to an application for summary judgment wishes to rely on written evidence at the hearing, he must—
    (a) file the written evidence; and
    (b) serve copies on every other party to the application,
at least seven days before the summary judgment hearing.
(2) If the applicant wishes to rely on written evidence in reply, he must—
    (a) file the written evidence; and
    (b) serve a copy on the respondent,
at least three days before the summary judgment hearing.
(3) Where a summary judgment hearing is fixed by the court of its own initiative—
    (a) any party who wishes to rely on written evidence at the hearing must—
        (i) file the written evidence; and
        (ii) unless the court orders otherwise, serve copies on every other party to the proceedings,
    at least seven days before the date of the hearing;
    (b) any party who wishes to rely on written evidence at the hearing in reply to any other party's written evidence must—
        (i) file the written evidence in reply; and
        (ii) unless the court orders otherwise serve copies on every other party to the proceedings,
    at least three days before the date of the hearing.
(4) This rule does not require written evidence—
    (a) to be filed if it has already been filed; or
    (b) to be served on a party on whom it has already been served.

Court's powers when it determines a summary judgment application

Pt 24 r.24.6

When the court determines a summary judgment application it may—
- (a) give directions as to the filing and service of a defence;
- (b) give further directions about the management of the case.

(R. 3.1(3) provides that the court may attach conditions when it makes an order).

Hearing

PD 24 para.3

(1) The hearing of the application will normally take place before a Master or a district judge.
(2) The Master or district judge may direct that the application be heard by a High Court Judge (if the case is in the High Court) or a circuit judge (if the case is in a county court).

Court's approach to orders that it may make

PD 24 para.4

Where it appears to the court possible that a claim or defence may succeed but improbable that it will do so, the court may make a conditional order.

PD 24 para.5.1

The orders the court may make on an application under Pt 24 include:
(1) judgment on the claim,
(2) the striking out or dismissal of the claim,
(3) the dismissal of the application,
(4) a conditional order.

PD 24 para.5.2

A conditional order is an order which requires a party:
(1) to pay a sum of money into court, or
(2) to take a specified step in relation to his claim or defence, as the case may be, and provides that that party's claim will be dismissed or his statement of case will be struck out if he does not comply.

(Note—the court will not follow its former practice of granting leave to a defendant to defend a claim, whether conditionally or unconditionally).

Setting aside order for summary judgment

PD 24 para.8.1

If an order for summary judgment is made against a respondent who does not appear at the hearing of the application, the respondent may apply for the order to be set aside or varied (see also r.23.11).

PD 24 para.8.2

On the hearing of an application under para.8.1 the court may make such order as it thinks just.

Case management

PD 24 para.10

Where the court dismisses the application or makes an order that does not completely dispose of the claim, the court will give case management directions as to the future conduct of the case.

Case management following defence to an additional claim

PD 20 para.5.1

Where the defendant to an additional claim files a defence, other than to a counterclaim, the court will arrange a hearing to consider case management of the additional claim. This will normally be at the same time as a case management hearing for the original claim and any other additional claims.

PD 20 para.5.2

The court will give notice of the hearing to each party likely to be affected by any order made at the hearing.

PD 20 para.5.3

At the hearing the court may:
    (1) treat the hearing as a summary judgment hearing.

Costs

PD 24 para.9.1

Attention is drawn to Pt 45 (**fixed costs**).

PD 24 para.9.2

Attention is drawn to the Costs PD and in particular to the court's power to make a **summary assessment** of costs.

PD 24 para.9.3

Attention is also drawn to r.44.13(1) which provides that if an order does not mention costs no party is entitled to costs relating to that order.

Probate

PD 57 para.5.1

If an order pronouncing for a will in solemn form is sought on an application for summary judgment, the evidence in support of the application must include written evidence proving due execution of the will.

PD 20 para.5.2

If a defendant has given notice in his defence under r.57.7(5) that he raises no positive case but—
    (1) he insists that the will be proved in solemn form; and
    (2) for that purpose he will cross-examine the witnesses who attested the will;
any application by the claimant for summary judgment is subject to the right of that defendant to require those witnesses to attend court for cross-examination.

See **Defamation claims** and **Specific performance**.

SUMMONS

Application.

SUPREME COURT

In October 2009, the Supreme Court replaced the Appellate Committee of the House of Lords as the highest court in the United Kingdom.
    The 12 Justices of the Supreme Court are now explicitly separate from both Government and Parliament.
    The Court hears appeals on arguable points of law of the greatest public importance, for the whole of the United Kingdom in civil cases, and for England, Wales and Northern Ireland in criminal cases.
    Additionally, it hears cases on devolution matters under the Scotland Act 1998, the Northern Ireland Act 1988 and the Government of Wales Act 2006. This jurisdiction was transferred to the Supreme Court from the Judicial Committee of the Privy Council.
    The Court's website address is *http://www.supremecourt.gov.uk*.

SUPREME COURT ACT 1981

An Act to consolidate with amendments the Supreme Court of Judicature (Consolidation) Act 1925 and other enactments relating to theSenior Courts in England and Wales and the administration of justice therein.

SUPREME COURT ORDER

PD 40B para.13.1

Application may be made in accordance with Pt 23 for an order to make an order of the Supreme Court an order of the High Court. The application should be made to the procedural judge of the

Division, District Registry or court in which the proceedings are taking place and may be made without notice unless the court directs otherwise.

PD 40B para.13.2

The application must be supported by the following evidence:
(1) details of the order which was the subject of the appeal to the Supreme Court,
(2) details of the order of the Supreme Court, with a copy annexed, and
(3) a copy annexed of the certificate of the Registrar of the Supreme Court of the assessment of the costs of the appeal to the Supreme Court in the sum of £ ... ...

PD 40B para.13.3

The order to make an order of the Supreme Court an order of the High Court should be in Form PF68.

SUSPENSION CLAIM

Right to buy

Pt 55 r.55.1

(h) A claim made by a landlord for an order under s.121A of the [Housing Act 1985][order suspending right to buy because of anti-social behaviour].

SUSPENSION CLAIMS MADE IN THE ALTERNATIVE TO POSSESSION CLAIMS

PD 65 para.5A.1

If the claim relates to a residential property let on a tenancy and if the claim includes a suspension claim, the particulars of claim must—
(1) state that the suspension claim is a claim under s.121A of the 1985 Act;
(2) state which of the bodies the claimant's interest belongs to in order to comply with the landlord condition under s.80 of the 1985 Act;
(3) state details of the conduct alleged; and
(4) explain why it is reasonable to make the suspension order, having regard in particular to the factors set out in s.121A(4) of the 1985 Act.

Particulars of claim

PD 65 para.7.2

In a suspension claim, the particulars of claim must—
(1) state that the suspension claim is a claim under s.121A of the 1985 Act;
(2) state which of the bodies the claimant's interest belongs to in order to comply with the landlord condition under s.80 of the 1985 Act;
(3) identify the property to which the claim relates;
(4) state details of the conduct alleged; and

(5) explain why it is reasonable to make the order, having regard in particular to the factors set out in s.121A(4) of the 1985 Act.

See also **Demotion claim**.

SUSPENSION ORDER

Pt 65 r.65.11

(aa) Claims by a landlord for an order under s.121a of the Housing Act 1985.

T

TAPE RECORDERS IN COURT

Section 9 of the Contempt of Court Act 1981 deals with the unauthorised use of tape recorders in court; and the PD ([1981] 1 W.L.R. 1526) relates to it.

TAXATION OF COSTS

Costs PD para.3.8

In any order of the court (whether made before or after April 26, 1999) the word 'taxation' will be taken to mean 'detailed assessment' and the words 'to be taxed' will be taken to mean 'to be decided by detailed assessment' unless in either case the context otherwise requires.

TAXES

See **Revenue and Customs**.

TAXING MASTER OF THE SENIOR COURTS

Costs judge.

TCC JUDGE

Pt 60 r.60.1

(c) Any judge authorised to hear TCC claims.

TECHNOLOGY AND CONSTRUCTION COURT CLAIMS

Pt 60 r.60.1

(1) [Pt 60] applies to Technology and Construction Court claims ('TCC claims').
(2) In this Part and PD 60—
    (a) 'TCC claim' means a claim which—
        (i) satisfies the requirements of para.(3); and
        (ii) has been issued in or transferred into the specialist list for such claims;
    (b) 'Technology and Construction Court' means any court in which TCC claims are dealt with in accordance with this Part or PD 60; and

(3) A claim may be brought as a TCC claim if—
    (a) it involves issues or questions which are technically complex; or
    (b) a trial by a TCC judge is desirable.
(PD 60 gives examples of types of claims which it may be appropriate to bring as TCC claims).
    (4) TCC claims include all official referees' business referred to in s.68(1)(a) of the Supreme Court Act 1981.
    (5) TCC claims will be dealt with:
        (a) in a Technology and Construction Court; and
        (b) by a TCC judge, unless—
            (i) this Part or PD 60 permits otherwise, or
            (ii) a TCC judge directs otherwise.

PD 60 para.2.1

The following are examples of the types of claim which it may be appropriate to bring as TCC claims—
    (a) building or other construction disputes, including claims for the enforcement of the decisions of adjudicators under the Housing Grants, Construction and Regeneration Act 1996;
    (b) engineering disputes;
    (c) claims by and against engineers, architects, surveyors, accountants and other specialised advisers relating to the services they provide;
    (d) claims by and against local authorities relating to their statutory duties concerning the development of land or the construction of buildings;
    (e) claims relating to the design, supply and installation of computers, computer software and related network systems;
    (f) claims relating to the quality of goods sold or hired, and work done, materials supplied or services rendered;
    (g) claims between landlord and tenant for breach of a repairing covenant;
    (h) claims between neighbours, owners and occupiers of land in trespass, nuisance etc;
    (i) claims relating to the environment (for example, pollution cases);
    (j) claims arising out of fires;
    (k) claims involving taking of accounts where these are complicated; and
    (l) challenges to decisions of arbitrators in construction and engineering disputes including applications for permission to appeal and appeals.

PD 60 para.2.2

A claim given as an example in para.2.1 will not be suitable for this specialist list unless it demonstrates the characteristics in r.60.1(3). Similarly, the examples are not exhaustive and other types of claim may be appropriate to this specialist list.

PD 60 para.3.1

TCC claims must be issued in the High Court or in a county court specified in this PD.

PD 60 para.3.2

The claim form must be marked in the top right hand corner 'Technology and Construction Court' below the words 'The High Court, Queen's Bench Division' or 'The _____ County Court'.

PD 60 para.3.3

TCC claims brought in the High Court outside London may be issued in any district registry, but it is preferable that wherever possible they should be issued in one of the following district registries, in which a TCC judge will usually be available—
Birmingham, Bristol, Cardiff, Chester, Exeter, Leeds, Liverpool, Manchester, Mold, Newcastle upon Tyne and Nottingham.

PD 60 para.3.4

The county courts in which a TCC claim may be issued are the following—
Birmingham, Bristol, Cardiff, Central London, Chester, Exeter, Leeds, Liverpool, Manchester, Mold, Newcastle upon Tyne and Nottingham.

Specialist list

Pt 60 r.60.2

(1) TCC claims form a specialist list.
(2) A judge will be appointed to be the judge in charge of the TCC specialist list.

Applications

PD 60 para.7.1

An application should normally be made to the assigned TCC judge. If the assigned TCC judge is not available, or the court gives permission, the application may be made to another TCC judge.

PD 60 para.7.2

If an application is urgent and there is no TCC judge available to deal with it, the application may be made to any judge who, if the claim were not a TCC claim, would be authorised to deal with the application.

Application of the Civil Procedure Rules

Pt 60 r.60.3

These rules and their PD s apply to TCC claims unless [Part 60] or a PD provides otherwise.

Applications before proceedings are issued

PD 60 para.4.1

A party who intends to issue a TCC claim must make any application before the claim form is issued to a TCC judge.

PD 60 para.4.2

The written evidence in support of such an application must state that the proposed claim is a TCC claim.

Assignment of claim to a TCC judge

PD 60 para.6.1

When a TCC claim is issued or an order is made transferring a claim to the TCC specialist list, the court will assign the claim to a named TCC judge ('the assigned TCC judge') who will have the primary responsibility for the case management of that claim.

PD 60 para.6.2

All documents relating to the claim must be marked in similar manner to the claim form with the words 'Technology and Construction Court' and the name of the assigned TCC judge.

Issuing a TCC claim

Pt 60 r.60.4

A TCC claim must be issued in—
  (a) the High Court in London;
  (b) a district registry of the High Court; or
  (c) a county court specified in PD 60.

Reply

Pt 60 r.60.5

Part 15 (Defence and Reply) applies to TCC claims with the modification to r.15.8 that the claimant must—
  (a) file any reply to a defence; and
  (b) serve it on all other parties;
within 21 days after service of the defence.

Case management

Pt 60 r.60.6

  (1) All TCC claims are treated as being allocated to the multi-track and Pt 26 does not apply.
  (2) Part 29 and PD 29 apply to the case management of TCC claims, except where they are varied by or inconsistent with PD 60.

Case management conference

PD 60 para.8.1

The court will fix a case management conference within 14 days of the earliest of these events—
  (1) the filing of an acknowledgment of service;
  (2) the filing of a defence; or
  (3) the date of an order transferring the claim to a TCC.

PD 60 para.8.2

When the court notifies the parties of the date and time of the case management conference, it will at the same time send each party a case management information sheet and a case management directions form.
(The case management information sheet and the case management directions form are in the form set out in Appendices A and B to [PD 60]).

PD 60 para.8.3

Not less than two days before the case management conference, each party must file and serve on all other parties—
  (1) completed copies of the case management information sheet and case management directions form; and
  (2) an application notice for any order which that party intends to seek at the case management conference, other than directions referred to in the case management directions form.

PD 60 para.8.4

The parties are encouraged to agree directions to propose to the court by reference to the case management directions form.

PD 60 para.8.5

If any party fails to file or serve the case management information sheet and the case management directions form by the date specified, the court may—
  (1) impose such sanction as it sees fit; and
  (2) either proceed with or adjourn the case management conference.

PD 60 para.8.6

The directions given at the case management conference will normally include the fixing of dates for—
  (1) any further case management conferences;
  (2) a pre-trial review;
  (3) the trial of any preliminary issues that it orders to be tried; and
  (4) the trial.

Judgments and orders

Pt 60 r.60.7

(1) Except for orders made by the court of its own initiative and unless the court otherwise orders, every judgment or order made in claims proceeding in the Technology and Construction Court will be drawn up by the parties, and r.40.3 is modified accordingly.
(2) An application for a consent order must include a draft of the proposed order signed on behalf of all the parties to whom it relates.
(3) Rule 40.6 (consent judgments and orders) does not apply.

Pre-trial review

PD 60 para.9.1

When the court fixes the date for a pre-trial review it will send each party a pre-trial review questionnaire.
(The pre-trial review questionnaire is in the form set out in Appendix C to [PD 60]).

PD 60 para.9.2

Each party must file and serve on all other parties completed copies of the questionnaire not less than two days before the date fixed for the pre-trial review.

PD 60 para.9.3

The parties are encouraged to agree directions to propose to the court.

PD 60, para.9.4

If any party fails to return or exchange the questionnaire by the date specified the court may—
(1) impose such sanction as it sees fit; and
(2) either proceed with or adjourn the pre-trial review.

PD 60 para.9.5

At the pre-trial review, the court will give such directions for the conduct of the trial as it sees fit.

Listing

PD 60 para.10

The provisions about listing questionnaires and listing in Pt 29 and PD 29 do not apply to TCC claims.

Trial

PD 60 para.11.1

Whenever possible the trial of a claim will be heard by the assigned TCC judge.

PD 60 para.11.2

A TCC claim may be tried at any place where there is a TCC judge available to try the claim.

Transfer of proceedings

PD 60 para.5.1

Where no TCC judge is available to deal with a claim which has been issued in a High Court District Registry or one of the county courts listed in para.3.4 above, the claim may be transferred—
- (1) if it has been issued in a District Registry, to another District Registry or to the High Court in London; or
- (2) if it has been issued in a county court, to another county court where a TCC judge would be available.

PD 60 para.5.2

Paragraph 5.1 is without prejudice to the court's general powers to transfer proceedings under Pt 30.
(Rule 30.5(3) provides that an application for the transfer of proceedings to or from a specialist list must be made to a judge dealing with claims in that list).

PD 60 para.5.3

A party applying to a TCC judge to transfer a claim to the TCC specialist list must give notice of the application to the court in which the claim is proceeding, and a TCC judge will not make an order for transfer until he is satisfied that such notice has been given.

See **Pilot schemes**.

TECHNOLOGY AND CONSTRUCTION COURT GUIDE

The Technology and Construction Court Guide is intended to provide straightforward, practical guidance on the conduct of litigation in the TCC. Whilst it is intended to be comprehensive, it naturally concentrates on the most important aspects of such litigation. It therefore cannot cover all the procedural points that may arise. It does, however, describe the main elements of the practice that is likely to be followed in most TCC cases. This Guide does not and cannot add to or amend the CPR or the relevant PD s. The purpose and function of this Guide is to explain how the substantive law, rules and PD s are applied in the TCC and cannot affect their proper interpretation and effect: see *Secretary of State for Communities and Local Government v Bovale* [2009] 1 W.L.R. 2274, [36].

TELEPHONE HEARINGS

Giving notice of an application

PD 23A para.4.1A

Where there is to be a telephone hearing the application notice must be served as soon as practicable after it has been issued and in any event at least five days before the date of the hearing.

PD 23A para.4.2

Where an application notice should be served but there is not sufficient time to do so, informal notification of the application should be given unless the circumstances of the application require secrecy.

PD 23A para.6.2

Subject to para.6.3, at a telephone conference enabled court [means a district registry of the High Court or a county court, in which telephone conferencing facilities are available] the following hearings will be conducted by telephone unless the court otherwise orders—
  (a) **allocation hearings**;
  (b) **listing hearings**; and
  (c) **interim applications**, **case management conferences** and **pre-trial reviews** with a time estimate of no more than one hour.

PD 23A para.6.3

Paragraph 6.2 does not apply where—
  (a) the hearing is of an application made without notice to the other party;
  (b) all the parties are unrepresented; or
  (c) more than four parties wish to make representations at the hearing (for this purpose where two or more parties are represented by the same person, they are to be treated as one party).

PD 23A para.6.4

A request for a direction that a hearing under para.6.2 should not be conducted by telephone—
  (a) must be made at least seven days before the hearing or such shorter time as the court may permit; and
  (b) may be made by letter,
and the court shall determine such request without requiring the attendance of the parties.

PD 23A para.6.5

The court may order that an application, or part of an application, to which para.6.2 does not apply be dealt with by a telephone hearing. The court may make such order—
  (a) of its own initiative; or
  (b) at the request of the parties.

PD 23A para.6.6

The applicant should indicate on his application notice if he seeks a court order under para.6.5. Where he has not done so but nevertheless wishes to seek an order, the request should be made as early as possible.

PD 23A para.6.7

An order under para.6.5 will not normally be made unless every party entitled to be given notice of the application and to be heard at the hearing has consented to the order.

PD 23A para.6.8

If the court makes an order under para.6.5 it will give any directions necessary for the telephone hearing.

Conduct of the telephone hearing

PD 23A para.6.9

No party, or representative of a party, to an application being heard by telephone may attend the judge in person while the application is being heard unless every other party to the application has agreed that he may do so.

PD 23A para.6.10

If an application is to be heard by telephone the following directions will apply, subject to any direction to the contrary—
  (1) The designated legal representative [means the applicant's legal representative (if any), or the legal representative of such other party as the court directs to arrange the telephone hearing] is responsible for arranging the telephone conference for precisely the time fixed by the court. The telecommunications provider used must be one of the approved panel of service providers (see Her Majesty's Courts and Tribunals Service website).
  (2) The designated legal representative must tell the operator the telephone numbers of all those participating in the conference call and the sequence in which they are to be called.
  (3) It is the responsibility of the designated legal representative to ascertain from all the other parties whether they have instructed counsel and, if so, the identity of counsel, and whether the legal representative and counsel will be on the same or different telephone numbers.
  (4) The sequence in which they are to be called will be—
    (a) the designated legal representative and (if on a different number) his counsel;
    (b) the legal representative (and counsel) for all other parties; and
    (c) the judge.
  (5) Each speaker is to remain on the line after being called by the operator setting up the conference call. The call shall be connected at least 10 minutes before the time fixed for the hearing.
  (6) When the judge has been connected the designated legal representative (or his counsel) will introduce the parties in the usual way.
  (7) If the use of a 'speakerphone' by any party causes the judge or any other party any difficulty in hearing what is said the judge may require that party to use a hand held telephone.

(8) The telephone charges debited to the account of the party initiating the conference call will be treated as part of the costs of the application.

Documents

PD 23A para.6.11

Where a document is required to be filed and served the party or the designated legal representative must do so no later than 16.00 at least two days before the hearing.

PD 23A para.6.12

A case summary and draft order must be filed and served in—
(a) multi-track cases; and
(b) small and fast track cases if the court so directs.

PD 23A para.6.13

Any other document upon which a party seeks to rely must be filed and served in accordance with the period specified in para.6.11.

Interim injunction

PD 25A para.4.5

Applications made by telephone:
(1) where it is not possible to arrange a hearing, application can be made between 10.00 and 17.00 weekdays by telephoning the Royal Courts of Justice on 020 7947 6000 and asking to be put in contact with a High Court Judge of the appropriate Division available to deal with an emergency application in a High Court matter. The appropriate district registry may also be contacted by telephone. In county court proceedings, the appropriate county court should be contacted,
(2) where an application is made outside those hours the applicant should either—
  (a) telephone the Royal Courts of Justice on 020 7947 6000 where he will be put in contact with the clerk to the appropriate duty judge in the High Court (or the appropriate area Circuit Judge where known), or
  (b) the Urgent Court Business Officer of the appropriate Circuit who will contact the local duty judge,
(3) where the facility is available it is likely that the judge will require a draft order to be faxed to him,
(4) the application notice and evidence in support must be filed with the court on the same or next working day or as ordered, together with two copies of the order for sealing,
(5) injunctions will be heard by telephone only where the applicant is acting by counsel or solicitors.

See **Time**.

THIRD PARTY CLAIMS

Additional claims.

THIRD PARTY DEBT ORDERS

Pt 72 r.72.1

(1) This Part contains rules which provide for a **judgment creditor** to obtain an order for the payment to him of money which a third party who is within the jurisdiction owes to the judgment debtor.

(2) In this Part, 'bank or building society' includes any person carrying on a business in the course of which he lawfully accepts deposits in the UK.

Pt 72 r.72.2

(1) Upon the application of a judgment creditor, the court may make an order (a 'final Third Party Debt Order') requiring a third party to pay to the judgment creditor—

    (a) the amount of any debt due or accruing due to the judgment debtor from the third party; or

    (b) so much of that debt as is sufficient to satisfy the judgment debt and the judgment creditor's costs of the application.

(2) The court will not make an order under para.1 without first making an order (an 'interim Third Party Debt Order') as provided by r.72.4(2).

(3) In deciding whether money standing to the credit of the judgment debtor in an account to which s.40 of the Supreme Court Act 1981 or s.108 of the County Courts Act 1984 relates may be made the subject of a Third Party Debt Order, any condition applying to the account that a receipt for money deposited in the account must be produced before any money is withdrawn will be disregarded.

(Section 40(3) of the Supreme Court Act 1981 and s.108(3) of the County Courts Act 1984 contain a list of other conditions applying to accounts that will also be disregarded.)

Application for Third Party Debt Order

Pt 72 r.72.3

(1) An application for a Third Party Debt Order—

    (a) may be made without notice; and

    (b) (i) must be issued in the court which made the judgment or order which it is sought to enforce; except that

        (ii) if the proceedings have since been transferred to a different court, it must be issued in that court.

(2) The application notice must—

    (a) (i) be in the form; and

        (ii) contain the information

    required by PD 72; and

    (b) be verified by a statement of truth.

PD 72 para.1.1

An application for a Third Party Debt Order must be made by filing an application notice in Practice Form N349.

PD 72 para.1.2

The application notice must contain the following information—

    (1) the name and address of the judgment debtor;

(2) details of the judgment or order sought to be enforced;

(3) the amount of money remaining due under the judgment or order;

(4) if the judgment debt is payable by instalments, the amount of any instalments which have fallen due and remain unpaid;

(5) the name and address of the third party;

(6) if the third party is a bank or building society—

    (a) its name and the address of the branch at which the judgment debtor's account is believed to be held; and

    (b) the account number;

    or, if the judgment creditor does not know all or part of this information, that fact;

(7) confirmation that to the best of the judgment creditor's knowledge or belief the third party—

    (a) is within the jurisdiction; and

    (b) owes money to or holds money to the credit of the judgment debtor;

(8) if the judgment creditor knows or believes that any person other than the judgment debtor has any claim to the money owed by the third party—

    (a) his name and (if known) his address; and

    (b) such information as is known to the judgment creditor about his claim;

(9) details of any other applications for Third Party Debt Orders issued by the judgment creditor in respect of the same judgment debt; and

(10) the sources or grounds of the judgment creditor's knowledge or belief of the matters referred to in (7), (8) and (9).

PD 72 para.1.3

The court will not grant speculative applications for Third Party Debt Orders, and will only make an interim Third Party Debt Order against a bank or building society if the judgment creditor's application notice contains evidence to substantiate his belief that the judgment debtor has an account with the bank or building society in question.

Interim Third Party Debt Order

Pt 72 r.72.4

(1) An application for a Third Party Debt Order will initially be dealt with by a judge without a hearing.

(2) The judge may make an interim Third Party Debt Order—

    (a) fixing a hearing to consider whether to make a final Third Party Debt Order; and

    (b) directing that until that hearing the third party must not make any payment which reduces the amount he owes the judgment debtor to less than the amount specified in the order.

(3) An interim Third Party Debt Order will specify the amount of money which the third party must retain, which will be the total of—

    (a) the amount of money remaining due to the judgment creditor under the judgment or order; and

    (b) an amount for the judgment creditor's fixed costs of the application, as specified in PD 72.

(4) An interim Third Party Debt Order becomes binding on a third party when it is served on him.

(5) The date of the hearing to consider the application shall be not less than 28 days after the interim Third Party Debt Order is made.

PD 72 para.2

An interim Third Party Debt Order will specify the amount of money which the third party must retain (r.72.4(3)). This will include, in respect of the judgment creditor's fixed costs of the application, the amount which would be allowed to the judgment creditor under r.45.6 if the whole balance of the judgment debt were recovered.

Service of Interim Order

Pt 72 r.72.5

(1) Copies of an interim Third Party Debt Order, the application notice and any documents filed in support of it must be served—
    (a) on the third party, not less than 21 days before the date fixed for the hearing; and
    (b) on the judgment debtor not less than—
        (i) seven days after a copy has been served on the third party; and
        (ii) seven days before the date fixed for the hearing.
(2) If the judgment creditor serves the order, he must either—
    (a) file a certificate of service not less than two days before the hearing; or
    (b) produce a certificate of service at the hearing.

Obligations of third parties served with interim order

Pt 72 r.72.6

(1) A bank or building society served with an interim Third Party Debt Order must carry out a search to identify all accounts held with it by the judgment debtor.
(2) The bank or building society must disclose to the court and the creditor within seven days of being served with the order, in respect of each account held by the judgment debtor—
    (a) the number of the account;
    (b) whether the account is in credit; and
    (c) if the account is in credit—
        (i) whether the balance of the account is sufficient to cover the amount specified in the order;
        (ii) the amount of the balance at the date it was served with the order, if it is less than the amount specified in the order; and
        (iii) whether the bank or building society asserts any right to the money in the account, whether pursuant to a right of set-off or otherwise, and if so giving details of the grounds for that assertion.
(3) If—
    (a) the judgment debtor does not hold an account with the bank or building society; or
    (b) the bank or building society is unable to comply with the order for any other reason (for example, because it has more than one account holder whose details match the information contained in the order, and cannot identify which account the order applies to),
the bank or building society must inform the court and the judgment creditor of that fact within seven days of being served with the order.
(4) Any third party other than a bank or building society served with an interim Third Party Debt Order must notify the court and the judgment creditor in writing within seven days of being served with the order, if he claims—

    (a) not to owe any money to the judgment debtor; or
    (b) to owe less than the amount specified in the order.

PD 72 para.3.1

A bank or building society served with an interim Third Party Debt Order is only required by r.72.6, unless the order states otherwise—

    (1) to retain money in accounts held solely by the judgment debtor (or, if there are joint judgment debtors, accounts held jointly by them or solely by either or any of them); and
    (2) to search for and disclose information about such accounts.

PD 72 para.3.2

The bank or building society is not required, for example, to retain money in, or disclose information about—

    (1) accounts in the joint names of the judgment debtor and another person; or
    (2) if the interim order has been made against a firm, accounts in the names of individual members of that firm.

Transfer

PD 72 para.4

The court may, on an application by a judgment debtor who wishes to oppose an application for a Third Party Debt Order, transfer it to the court for the district where the judgment debtor resides or carries on business, or to another court.

Further consideration of the application

Pt 72 r.72.8

    (1) If the judgment debtor or the third party objects to the court making a final Third Party Debt Order, he must file and serve written evidence stating the grounds for his objections.
    (2) If the judgment debtor or the third party knows or believes that a person other than the judgment debtor has any claim to the money specified in the interim order, he must file and serve written evidence stating his knowledge of that matter.
    (3) If—
        (a) the third party has given notice under r.72.6 that he does not owe any money to the judgment debtor, or that the amount which he owes is less than the amount specified in the interim order; and
        (b) the judgment creditor wishes to dispute this,
    the judgment creditor must file and serve written evidence setting out the grounds on which he disputes the third party's case.
    (4) Written evidence under paras (1), (2) or (3) must be filed and served on each other party as soon as possible, and in any event not less than three days before the hearing.
    (5) If the court is notified that some person other than the judgment debtor may have a claim to the money specified in the interim order, it will serve on that person notice of the application and the hearing.
    (6) At the hearing the court may—

(a) make a final Third Party Debt Order;
(b) discharge the interim Third Party Debt Order and dismiss the application;
(c) decide any issues in dispute between the parties, or between any of the parties and any other person who has a claim to the money specified in the interim order; or
(d) direct a trial of any such issues, and if necessary give directions.

Effect of final Third Party Debt Order

Pt 72 r.72.9

(1) A final Third Party Debt Order shall be enforceable as an order to pay money.
(2) If—
(a) the third party pays money to the judgment creditor in compliance with a Third Party Debt Order; or
(b) the order is enforced against him,
the third party shall, to the extent of the amount paid by him or realised by enforcement against him, be discharged from his debt to the judgment debtor.
(3) Paragraph (2) applies even if the Third Party Debt Order, or the original judgment or order against the judgment debtor, is later set aside.

Money in court

Pt 72 r.72.10

(1) If money is standing to the credit of the judgment debtor in court—
(a) the judgment creditor may not apply for a Third Party Debt Order in respect of that money; but
(b) he may apply for an order that the money in court, or so much of it as is sufficient to satisfy the judgment or order and the costs of the application, be paid to him.
(2) An application notice seeking an order under this rule must be served on—
(a) the judgment debtor; and
(b) the Accountant General at the Court Funds Office.
(3) If an application notice has been issued under this rule, the money in court must not be paid out until the application has been disposed of.

Costs

Pt 72 r.72.11

If the judgment creditor is awarded costs on an application for an order under rr.72.2 or 72.10—
(a) he shall, unless the court otherwise directs, retain those costs out of the money recovered by him under the order; and
(b) the costs shall be deemed to be paid first out of the money he recovers, in priority to the judgment debt.

Final orders relating to building society accounts

PD 72 para.6

A final Third Party Debt Order will not require a payment which would reduce to less than £1 the amount in a judgment debtor's account with a building society or credit union.

See also **Hardship payment order** and **Partnership**.

TIME

Pt 2 r.2.8

(1) This rule shows how to calculate any period of time for doing any act which is specified—
    (a) by these rules;
    (b) by a PD; or
    (c) by a judgment or order of the court.
(2) A period of time expressed as a number of days shall be computed as clear days.
(3) In this rule 'clear days' means that in computing the number of days—
    (a) the day on which the period begins; and
    (b) if the end of the period is defined by reference to an event, the day on which that event occurs
    are not included.

Examples

    (i) Notice of an application must be served at least three days before the hearing.
    An application is to be heard on Friday October 20.
    The last date for service is Monday October 16.
    (ii) The court is to fix a date for a hearing.
    The hearing must be at least 28 days after the date of notice.
    If the court gives notice of the date of the hearing on October 1, the earliest date for the hearing is October 30.
    (iii) Particulars of claim must be served within 14 days of service of the claim form.
    The claim form is served on October 2.
    The last day for service of the particulars of claim is October 16.

(4) Where the specified period—
    (a) is five days or less; and
    (b) includes—
      (i) a Saturday or Sunday; or
      (ii) a Bank Holiday, Christmas Day or Good Friday,
    that day does not count.

Example

    Notice of an application must be served at least three days before the hearing.
    An application is to be heard on Monday October 20.

The last date for service is Tuesday October 14.

(5) Subject to the provisions of PD 5C, when the period specified—

(a) by these rules or a PD ; or

(b) by any judgment or court order,

for doing any act at the court office ends on a day on which the office is closed, that act shall be in time if done on the next day on which the court office is open.

Dates for compliance to be calendar dates and to include time of day

Pt 2 r.2.9

(1) Where the court gives a judgment, order or direction which imposes a time limit for doing any act, the last date for compliance must, wherever practicable—

(a) be expressed as a calendar date; and

(b) include the time of day by which the act must be done.

(2) Where the date by which an act must be done is inserted in any document, the date must, wherever practicable, be expressed as a calendar date.

Variation of time limits

Time limits may be varied by parties

Pt 2 r.2.11

Unless these rules or a PD provide otherwise or the court orders otherwise, the time specified by a rule or by the court for a person to do any act may be varied by the written agreement of the parties.

Commercial Court

PD 58 para.7.1

If the parties, in accordance with r.2.11, agree in writing to vary a time limit, the claimant must notify the court in writing, giving brief written reasons for the agreed variation.

PD 58 para.7.2

The court may make an order overriding an agreement by the parties varying a time limit.

Time limits which may not be varied by parties

Pt 3 r.3.8(3)

(3) Where a rule, PD or court order—

(a) requires a party to do something within a specified time, and

(b) specifies the consequence of failure to comply,

the time for doing the act in question may not be extended by agreement between the parties.

Fast track—variation of case management timetable

Pt 28 r.28.4

  (1) A party must apply to the court if he wishes to vary the date which the court has fixed for—
     (a) the return of a pre-trial check list under r.28.5;
     (b) the trial; or
     (c) the trial period.
  (2) Any date set by the court or these rules for doing any act may not be varied by the parties if the variation would make it necessary to vary any of the dates mentioned in para.(1).

Multi-track—variation of case management timetable

Pt 29 para.29.5

  (1) A party must apply to the court if he wishes to vary the date which the court has fixed for—
     (a) a case management conference;
     (b) a pre-trial review;
     (c) the return of a pre-trial check list under r.29.6;
     (d) the trial; or
     (e) the trial period.
  (2) Any date set by the court or these rules for doing any act may not be varied by the parties if the variation would make it necessary to vary any of the dates mentioned in para.(1).

Court of Appeal

Pt 52 r.52.6

  (1) An application to vary the time limit for filing an appeal notice must be made to the appeal court.
  (2) The parties may not agree to extend any date or time limit set by—
     (a) these rules;
     (b) PD 52; or
     (c) an order of the appeal court or the lower court.

(Rule 3.1(2)(a) provides that the court may extend or shorten the time for compliance with any rule, PD or court order (even if an application for extension is made after the time for compliance has expired)).

(Rule 3.1(2)(b) provides that the court may adjourn or bring forward a hearing).

See **Month**.

TO BE TAXED

To be decided by **detailed assessment**.

TOWN AND COUNTRY PLANNING

PD 8A para.9.4

[Applications are assigned to the Queen's Bench Division.]

Application for injunction to prevent environmental harm or unlicensed activities

PD 8A para.20.1

This paragraph relates to applications under—
    (1) section 187B or 214A of the Town and Country Planning Act 1990;
    (2) section 44A of the Planning (Listed Buildings and Conservation Areas) Act 1990;
    (3) section 26AA of the Planning (Hazardous Substances) Act 1990; or
    (4) section 12 or 26 of the Energy Act 2008.

PD 8A para.20.2

An injunction may be granted under those sections against a person whose identity is unknown to the applicant.

PD 8A para.20.3

In this paragraph, an injunction refers to an injunction under one of those sections and 'the defendant' is the person against whom the injunction is sought.

PD 8A para.20.4

In the claim form, the applicant must describe the defendant by reference to—
    (1) a photograph;
    (2) a thing belonging to or in the possession of the defendant; or
    (3) any other evidence.

PD 8A para.5

The description of the defendant under para.20.4 must be sufficiently clear to enable the defendant to be served with the proceedings.
(The court has power under Pt 6 to dispense with service or make an order permitting service by an alternative method or at an alternative place).

PD 8A para.20.6

The application must be accompanied by a witness statement. The witness statement must state—
    (1) that the applicant was unable to ascertain the defendant's identity within the time reasonably available to him;
    (2) the steps taken by him to ascertain the defendant's identity;
    (3) the means by which the defendant has been described in the claim form; and
    (4) that the description is the best the applicant is able to provide.

PD 8A para.20.7

When the court issues the claim form it will—
  (1) fix a date for the hearing; and
  (2) prepare a notice of the hearing date for each party.

PD 8A para.20.8

The claim form must be served not less than 21 days before the hearing date.

PD 8A para.20.9

Where the claimant serves the claim form, he must serve notice of the hearing date at the same time, unless the hearing date is specified in the claim form.
(CPR rr.3.1(2)(a) and (b) provide for the court to extend or shorten the time for compliance with any rule or PD, and to adjourn or bring forward a hearing)

PD 8A para.20.10

The court may on the hearing date—
  (1) proceed to hear the case and dispose of the claim; or
  (2) give case management directions.

See **Part 8 procedure**.

TRADE MARK MATTERS

See **Registered trade marks and other intellectual property rights.**

TRADE UNION AND LABOUR RELATIONS CONSOLIDATIONS ACT 1992

See **Derivative claim**.

TRAFFIC ENFORCEMENT

Pt 75 r.75.1

  (1) [PD] 75 para.1.2—
      (a) sets out the proceedings to which [Pt 75] applies[increased penalty charges and increased fixed penalties]; and
      (b) may apply this Part with modifications in relation to any particular category of those proceedings.
(Rule 21.1(1)(c) provides that Pt 21 (children and protected parties) does not apply to proceedings under this Part where one of the parties is a **child**).
  (2) In this Part—
      (b) 'no relevant return to the warrant' means that—
          (i) the bailiff has been unable to seize goods because the bailiff has been denied access to premises occupied by the defendant or because the goods have been removed from those premises;

> > (ii) any goods seized under a warrant of execution are insufficient to satisfy the debt and the cost of execution; or
> > (iii) the goods are insufficient to cover the cost of their removal and sale;
> (d) 'relevant period', in relation to any particular case, means—
> > (i) the period allowed for serving a statutory declaration or witness statement under any enactment which applies to that case; or
> > (ii) where an enactment permits the court to extend that period, the period as extended;
> (e) 'specified debts' means the debts specified in art.2 of the [Enforcement of Road Traffic Debts Order 1993] or treated as so specified by any other enactment; and

Traffic enforcement centre

Pt 75 r.75.2

(1) Proceedings to which this Part applies must be started in the [Traffic Enforcement Centre].
(2) For any purpose connected with the exercise of the Centre's functions—
> (a) the Centre is deemed to be part of the office of the court whose name appears on the documents to which the functions relate or in whose name the documents are issued; and
> (b) any officer of the Centre, in exercising its functions, is deemed to act as an officer of that court.

PD 75 para.2.1

All claims to which Pt 75 applies must be started in the Traffic Enforcement Centre ('the Centre') at Northampton County Court.

Request

Pt 75 r.75.3

The authority entitled to recover amounts due under the enactments referred to in PD 75 para.1.2 must file a request in the appropriate form scheduling the amount claimed to be due [meaning a parking charge certificate and fixed penaty notice issued under the enactments listed in PD 75 para.1.3(2)].
(2) The authority must, in that request or in another manner approved by the court officer
> (a) certify—
> > (i) that 14 days have elapsed since service of the notice of the amount due;
> > (ii) the date of such service;
> > (iii) the number of the notice of the amount due; and
> > (iv) that the amount due remains unpaid;
> (b) specify the grounds (whether by reference to the appropriate code or otherwise), as stated in the notice, on which the authority claims to be entitled to claim that amount; and
> (c) state—
> > (i) the name, title and address of the respondent [the person on whom the notice of the amount due was served or the person (other than an authority) by whom the amount due under an adjudication is payable];
> > (ii) the registration number of the vehicle concerned;
> > (iii) the authority's address for service;

    (iv) the court fee; and
    (v) such other matters as required by PD 75.
(3) On receipt of a request that meets the requirements of paras (1) and (2), the court officer
    will order that the amount due may be recovered as if it were payable under a county
    court order by registering the request and returning it to the authority.
(4) On receipt of a registered request the authority may draw up the order and must—
    (a) insert in the order the date by which the respondent must either—
        (i) comply with the order; or
        (ii) file a statutory declaration or witness statement; and
    (b) attach to the order a form of statutory declaration or witness statement for the
        respondent's use.
(5) The authority must serve in accordance with Pt 6 the order (and the form of statutory
    declaration or witness statement) on the respondent within 15 days of the date on which
    the request is registered by the court.

PD 75 para.3.1

Where an order in respect of amounts payable by a person other than an authority under an
adjudication pursuant to—
    (a) section 73 of the 1991 Act;
    (b) the Representations and Appeals (England) Regulations;
    (c) the Representations and Appeals (Wales) Regulations; or
    (d) the Schedule to the Road User Charging Regulations, is sought, r.75.3 applies with the
        necessary modifications and, in addition, the request must—
        (i) state the date on which the adjudication was made;
        (ii) provide details of the order made on the adjudication; and
        (iii) certify the amount awarded by way of costs and that the amount remains unpaid.

Service of order

PD 75 para.3A.1

Rule 75.3(5) requires the authority to serve the order within 15 days of the date on which the
request is registered with the court. For clarity, the respondent must be served within 15 days and
attention is drawn to the provisions of Pt 6, particularly the provisions relating to deemed
service.

Application for longer period for filing of statutory declaration or witness statement

PD 75 para.5.1

Paragraphs 5.2 to 5.5 apply where the respondent applies for an order allowing a longer period
than 21 days to serve—
    (1) a statutory declaration pursuant to [the Acts and regulations listed in PD 75, par-
        a,5.1(1).
    (2) a witness statement pursuant to [the regulations listed in PD 75, para.5.1(2)]

PD 75 para.5.2

The respondent must send to the Centre—
    (1) a completed application notice (Form PE 2 may be used for applications relating to
        statutory declarations and Form TE 7 may be used for applications relating to witness
        statements); and

(2) a completed—
    (a) statutory declaration in Form PE 3; or
    (b) witness statement in Form TE 9.
(The Forms can be obtained from the Centre at Northampton County Court, Bulk Centre, 21/27 St. Katharine's Street, Northampton NN1 2LH. (Tel: 08457 045007)).

PD 75 para.5.3

The court will serve a copy of the application notice and a copy of the statutory declaration or witness statement on the authority that obtained the court order seeking representations on the application.

PD 75 para.5.4

A court officer will deal with the application without a hearing. The matter will not be dealt with until at least 14 days after the date on which the application notice and statutory declaration or witness statement were served on the authority.

PD 75 para.5.5

If the proceedings have been transferred to another court the Centre will transfer the application to that court.

PD 75 para.5.6

Paragraphs 5.3 to 5.5 do not apply where the court receives an application notice that is accompanied by a statutory declaration that is invalid by virtue of para.8(2A) of Sch.6 to the 1991 Act as inserted by s.15 of the 2003 Act.

Electronic delivery of documents

Pt 75 r.75.4

(1) Where the authority is required to file any document other than the request, that requirement is satisfied if the information which would be contained in the document is delivered in computer-readable form.
(2) For the purposes of para.(1), information which would be contained in a document relating to one case may be combined with information of the same nature relating to another case.
(3) Where a document is required to be produced, that requirement will be satisfied if a copy of the document is produced from computer records.

Functions of court officer

Pt 75 r.75.5

PD 75 sets out the circumstances in which a court officer may exercise the functions of the court.

PD 75 para.4.1

A court officer may exercise the functions of the district judge [under the Acts and regulations listed in PD 75, para.4.1(1) and the court under the regulations listed in PD 75, para.4.1(2).

PD 75 para.6.1

Where any order is made by a court officer it will contain a statement of the right of either party to request a review of the decision by a district judge.

PD 75 para.6.3

Attention is drawn to the limited powers of a district judge where a request is made to review an order of a court officer refusing an application for further time for filing a statutory declaration or witness statement. Any review of that order by a district judge will only be a review of the decision to refuse the application for further time for filing a statutory declaration or witness statement. The review will not be a review of the validity of the notice of the amount due or any order within the meaning of para.1.3(3) of this PD.

Review of decision of court officer

Pt 75 r.75.5A

(1) Any party may request any decision of a court officer to be reviewed by a district judge.
(2) Such a request must be made within 14 days of service of the decision.
(3) Unless—
     (a) the party requesting the review requests an oral hearing; or
     (b) the court orders an oral hearing,
     a request for a review under para.(2) will be dealt with without an oral hearing.

Hearing

PD 75 para.7.1

When a hearing is to be held, the proceedings will be transferred to the county court for the district in which the respondent's address is situated. This transfer is only for the purposes of holding the hearing and serving any orders made as a result of the hearing.

PD 75 para.7.2

The respondent's address is the address for service shown on the application notice or, if more than one, the latest application notice.

PD 75 para.7.3

The court where the hearing is held will serve any orders made as a result of the hearing before returning the papers to the Centre, or, if the proceedings have been transferred, to the court where the proceedings have been transferred.

PD 75 para 7.4

Evidence at any hearing may be given orally or by witness statement.

Enforcement of orders

Pt 75 r.75.6

Subject to the [Enforcement of Road Traffic Debts Order 1993] and this rule the following rules apply to the enforcement of specified debts—Parts 70 to 73 [Enforcement of judgments and orders, Orders to obtain information from judgment debtors, Third Party Debt Orders, charging orders, stop orders and stop notices]; CCR Ord.25 r.1; CCR Ord.26 r.5; and CCR Ord.27 rr.1 to 7, 7A, 7B, 9 to 16 and 18 to 22.
(Rule 30.2 provides for the transfer between courts in order to enforce a judgment).

Warrant of execution

Pt 75 r.75.7

(1) An authority seeking the issue of a warrant of execution must file a request—
    (a) certifying the amount remaining due under the order;
    (b) specifying the date of service of the order on the respondent; and
    (c) certifying that the relevant period has elapsed.
(2) The court will seal the request and return it to the authority.
(3) Within seven days of the sealing of the request the authority must prepare the warrant in the appropriate form.
(4) No payment under a warrant will be made to the court.
(5) For the purposes of execution a warrant will be valid for 12 months beginning with the date of its issue.
(6) An authority may not renew a warrant issued in accordance with this Part beyond the 12 month validity period but, subject to para.(7), an authority may request the reissue of a warrant during the 12 month validity period.
(7) Where the address of the respondent has changed since the issue of the warrant, the authority may request the reissue of the warrant by filing a request—
    (a) specifying the new address of the respondent;
    (b) providing evidence that the new address for the respondent does relate to the respondent named in the order and against whom enforcement is sought; and
    (c) certifying that the amount due under the order remains unpaid.
(8) Where the court is satisfied that the new address of the respondent given in the request for the reissue of the warrant relates to the respondent named in the order, it will seal the request and return it to the authority.
(9) The authority must prepare the reissued warrant in the appropriate form within seven days of the sealing of the request to reissue.
(10) A reissued warrant will only be valid for the remainder of the 12 month period beginning with the date it was originally issued.

Applications to suspend a warrant of execution

PD 75 para.8.1

Where—
    (1) the respondent makes an application under para.5; and

(2) before that application is determined, a warrant of execution is issued,
the local authority must suspend enforcement of the warrant of execution until the application for
an extension order is determined.
(Rule 75.8(b) provides that, where a court order is deemed to have been revoked following the
filing of a statutory declaration or witness statement, any execution issued on the order will cease
to have effect).

Revocation of order

Pt 75 r.75.8

Where, in accordance with any enactment, an order is deemed to have been revoked following
the filing of a statutory declaration or a witness statement—
  (a) the court will serve a copy of the statutory declaration or witness statement on the
      authority;
  (b) any execution issued on the order will cease to have effect; and
  (c) if appropriate, the authority must inform any bailiff instructed to levy execution of the
      withdrawal of the warrant as soon as possible.

Transfer for enforcement

Pt 75 r.75.9

Where the authority requests the transfer of proceedings to another county court for enforcement,
the request must—
  (a) where the authority has not attempted to enforce by execution, give the reason why no
      such attempt was made;
  (b) certify that there has been no relevant return to the warrant of execution;
  (c) specify the date of service of the order on the respondent; and
  (d) certify that the relevant period has elapsed.

Further information required

Pt 75 r.75.10

An application for—
  (a) an attachment of earnings order;
  (b) an order to obtain information from a debtor;
  (c) a Third Party Debt Order; or
  (d) a charging order,
must, in addition to the requirements of Pts 71, 72 or 73 or CCR Ord.27—
    (i) where the authority has not attempted to enforce by execution, give the reason why no
        such attempt was made;
   (ii) certify that there has been no relevant return to the warrant of execution
  (iii) specify the date of service of the order on the respondent; and
   (iv) certify that the relevant period has elapsed.

Combining requests

Pt 75 r.75.11

Where the court officer allows, the authority may combine information relating to different orders against the same respondent in any request or application made under rr.75.9 or 75.10.

TRANSCRIPT

PD 39A para.6.3

Any party or person may require a transcript or transcripts of the recording of any hearing to be supplied to him, upon payment of the charges authorised by any scheme in force for the making of the recording or the transcript.

PD 39A para.6.4

Where the person requiring the transcript or transcripts is not a party to the proceedings and the hearing or any part of it was held in private under CPR r.39.2, para.6.3 does not apply unless the court so orders.

Appeals

Appeals to the Court of Appeal

PD 52C para.3

    (3) At the same time as filing an appellant's notice, the appellant must provide for the use of the court three copies of the appellant's notice and one copy of each of the following—
    (h) the approved transcript of the judgment.

Appeals in the county court and the High Court

PD 52B para.6.2

Transcript of the judgment of the lower court or other record of reasons: Except where the claim has been allocated to the small claims track, the appellant must obtain a transcript or other record of reasons of the lower court as follows—
    (a) where the judgment has been officially recorded, the appellant must apply for an approved transcript as soon as possible and, in any event, within 7 days of the filing of the appellant's notice;
    (b) where the judgment under appeal has been handed down in writing, the appellant must obtain and retain a copy of the written judgment;
    (c) in any other case, the appellant must cause a note of the judgment under appeal to be made and typed. The parties to the appeal should agree the note, which should then be sent to the judge of the lower court for approval. The parties and their advocates have a duty to make, and to co-operate in agreeing, a note of the judgment.

TRANSFER BETWEEN COUNTY COURTS

Pt 30 r.30.2

(1) A county court may order proceedings before that court, or any part of them (such as a counterclaim or an application made in the proceedings), to be transferred to another county court if it is satisfied that—
    (a) an order should be made having regard to the criteria in r. 30.3 [see below]; or
    (b) proceedings for—
        (i) the detailed assessment of costs; or
        (ii) the enforcement of a judgment or order,
could be more conveniently or fairly taken in that other county court.
(2) If proceedings have been started in the wrong county court, a judge of the county court may order that the proceedings—
    (a) be transferred to the county court in which they ought to have been started;
    (b) continue in the county court in which they have been started; or
    (c) be struck out.
(3) An application for an order under para. (1) or (2) must be made to the county court where the claim is proceeding.

(7) Where some enactment, other than these Rules, requires proceedings to be started in a particular county court, neither paras (1) nor (2) give the court power to order proceedings to be transferred to a county court which is not the court in which they should have been started or to order them to continue in the wrong court.

Transfer between Divisions of High Court and to and from a specialist list

Pt 30 r.30.5

(1) The High Court may order proceedings in any Division of the High Court to be transferred to another Division.
(2) A judge dealing with claims in a specialist list may order proceedings to be transferred to or from that list.
(3) An application for the transfer of proceedings to or from a specialist list must be made to a judge dealing with claims in that list.

TRANSFER OF PROCEEDINGS

Criteria for a transfer order

Pt 30 r.30.3

(1) Paragraph (2) sets out the matters to which the court must have regard when considering whether to make an order under—
    (a) sections 40(2), 41(1) or 42(2) of the County Courts Act 1984 (transfer between the High Court and a county court);
    (b) rule 30.2(1) (transfer between county courts); or
    (c) r.30.2(4) (transfer between the Royal Courts of Justice and the district registries).
(2) The matters to which the court must have regard include—
    (a) the financial value of the claim and the amount in dispute, if different;

(b) whether it would be more convenient or fair for hearings (including the trial) to be held in some other court;

(c) the availability of a judge specialising in the type of claim in question;

(d) whether the facts, legal issues, remedies or procedures involved are simple or complex;

(e) the importance of the outcome of the claim to the public in general;

(f) the facilities available to the court at which the claim is being dealt with, particularly in relation to—

    (i) any disabilities of a party or potential witness;

    (ii) any special measures needed for potential witnesses; or

    (iii) security;

(g) whether the making of a declaration of incompatibility under s.4 of the **Human Rights** Act 1998 has arisen or may arise;

(h) in the case of civil proceedings by or against the Crown, as defined in r.66.1(2), the location of the relevant government department or officers of the Crown and, where appropriate, any relevant public interest that the matter should be tried in London.

PD 30 para.7

A transfer should only be made on the basis of the criterion in r.30.3(2)(g) where there is a real prospect that a declaration of incompatibility will be made.

Procedure

Pt 30 r.30.4

(1) Where the court orders proceedings to be transferred, the court from which they are to be transferred must give notice of the transfer to all the parties.

(2) An order made before the transfer of the proceedings shall not be affected by the order to transfer.

Value of a case and transfer

PD 30 para.1

In addition to the criteria set out in r.30.3(2) attention is drawn to the financial limits set out in the High Court and County Courts Jurisdiction Order 1991, as amended.

PD 30 para.2

Attention is also drawn to para.2 of the PD 29 [case management in the Royal Courts of Justice].

PD 30 para.4.1

Where an order for transfer has been made the transferring court will immediately send notice of the transfer to the receiving court. The notice will contain:

(1) the name of the case, and

(2) the number of the case.

PD 30 para.4.2

At the same time as the transferring court notifies the receiving court it will also notify the parties of the transfer under r.30.4(1).

Date of transfer

PD 30 para.3

Where the court orders proceedings to be transferred, the order will take effect from the date it is made by the court.

Power to specify place where hearings are to be held

Pt 30 r.30.6

The court may specify the place (for instance, a particular county court) where the trial or some other hearing in any proceedings is to be held and may do so without ordering the proceedings to be transferred.

Appeal against order of transfer

PD 30 para.5.1

Where a district judge orders proceedings to be transferred and both the transferring and receiving courts are county courts, any appeal against that order should be made in the receiving court.

PD 30 para.5.2

The receiving court may, if it is more convenient for the parties, remit the appeal to the transferring court to be dealt with there.

Applications to set aside

PD 30 para.6.1

Where a party may apply to set aside an order for transfer (e.g. under r.23.10) the application should be made to the court which made the order.

PD 30 para.6.2

Such **application** should be made in accordance with Pt 23 of the rules and PD 23A.

See **Child**.

TRANSFER WITHIN THE HIGH COURT

Pt 30 r.30.2

> (4) The High Court may, having regard to the criteria in r.30.3 [see below], order proceedings in the Royal Courts of Justice or a district registry, or any part of such proceedings (such as a counterclaim or an application made in the proceedings), to be transferred—
>
> (a) from the Royal Courts of Justice to a district registry; or
>
> (b) from a district registry to the Royal Courts of Justice or to another district registry.
>
> (5) A district registry may order proceedings before it for the detailed assessment of costs to be transferred to another district registry if it is satisfied that the proceedings could be more conveniently or fairly taken in that other district registry.
>
> (6) An application for an order under para.(4) or (5) must, if the claim is proceeding in a district registry, be made to that registry.
>
> (7) Where some enactment, other than these Rules, requires proceedings to be started in a particular county court, neither paragraphs (1) nor (2) give the court power to order proceedings to be transferred to a county court which is not the court in which they should have been started or to order them to continue in the wrong court.
>
> (8) Probate proceedings may only be transferred under para.(4) to the Chancery Division at the Royal Courts of Justice or to one of the Chancery district registries.

TRESPASSER

Possession claim against trespassers

Pt 55 r.55.1

> (b) 'a possession claim against trespassers' means a claim for the recovery of land which the claimant alleges is occupied only by a person or persons who entered or remained on the land without the consent of a person entitled to possession of that land but does not include a claim against a tenant or sub-tenant whether his tenancy has been terminated or not.

Pt 55 r.55.2

> (1) The procedure set out in [s.I of Pt 55] must be used where the claim includes—
> (b) a possession claim against trespassers.

Starting the claim

Pt 55 r.55.3

> (1) The claim must be started in the county court for the district in which the land is situated unless para.(2) applies or an enactment provides otherwise.
>
> (2) The claim may be started in the High Court if the claimant files with his claim form a certificate stating the reasons for bringing the claim in that court verified by a statement of truth in accordance with r.22.1(1).

PD 55A para.1.3

Circumstances which may, in an appropriate case, justify starting a claim in the High Court are if—

(1) there are complicated disputes of fact;

(2) there are points of law of general importance; or

(3) the claim is against trespassers and there is a substantial risk of public disturbance or of serious harm to persons or property which properly require immediate determination.

Pt 55 r.55.3

(4) Where, in a possession claim against trespassers, the claimant does not know the name of a person in occupation or possession of the land, the claim must be brought against 'persons unknown' in addition to any named defendants.

(5) The claim form and form of defence sent with it must be in the forms set out in PD 55A.

Particulars of claim

Pt 55 r.55.4

The particulars of claim must be filed and served with the claim form.
(Part 16 and PD 55A provide details about the contents of the particulars of claim).

PD 55A para.2.6

If the claim is a possession claim against trespassers, the particulars of claim must state the claimant's interest in the land or the basis of his right to claim possession and the circumstances in which it has been occupied without licence or consent.

Hearing date

Pt 55 r.55.5

(1) The court will fix a date for the hearing when it issues the claim form.

(2) In a possession claim against trespassers the defendant must be served with the claim form, particulars of claim and any witness statements—
    (a) in the case of residential property, not less than five days; and
    (b) in the case of other land, not less than two days,
    before the hearing date.

(R.3.1(2)(a) provides that the court may extend or shorten the time for compliance with any rule).

PD 55A para.3.1

The court may exercise its powers under rr.3.1(2)(a) and (b) to shorten the time periods set out in r.55.5(2) and (3).

PD 55A para.3.2

Particular consideration should be given to the exercise of this power if:

(1) the defendant, or a person for whom the defendant is responsible, has assaulted or threatened to assault:
    (a) the claimant;

    (b) a member of the claimant's staff; or

    (c) another resident in the locality;

(2) there are reasonable grounds for fearing such an assault; or

(3) the defendant, or a person for whom the defendant is responsible, has caused serious damage or threatened to cause serious damage to the property or to the home or property of another resident in the locality.

PD 55A para.3.3

Where para.3.2 applies but the case cannot be determined at the first hearing fixed under r.55.5, the court will consider what steps are needed to finally determine the case as quickly as reasonably practicable.

Service of claims against trespassers

Pt 55 r.55.6

Where, in a possession claim against trespassers, the claim has been issued against 'persons unknown', the claim form, particulars of claim and any witness statements must be served on those persons by—

    (a) (i) attaching copies of the claim form, particulars of claim and any witness statements to the main door or some other part of the land so that they are clearly visible; and

        (ii) if practicable, inserting copies of those documents in a sealed transparent envelope addressed to 'the occupiers' through the letter box; or

    (b) placing stakes in the land in places where they are clearly visible and attaching to each stake copies of the claim form, particulars of claim and any witness statements in a sealed transparent envelope addressed to 'the occupiers'.

PD 55A para.4.1

If the claim form is to be served by the court and in accordance with r.55.6(b) the claimant must provide sufficient stakes and transparent envelopes.

Defendant's response

Pt 55 r.55.7

(1) An acknowledgment of service is not required and Pt 10 does not apply.

(2) In a possession claim against trespassers r.15.2 [which requires a defendant who wishes to defend all or part of a claim to file a defence] does not apply and the defendant need not file a defence.

(4) Part 12 (default judgment) does not apply in a claim to which this Part applies.

Hearing

Pt 55 r.55.8

(1) At the hearing fixed in accordance with r.55.5(1) or at any adjournment of that hearing, the court may—

    (a) decide the claim; or

    (b) give case management directions.

(2) Where the claim is genuinely disputed on grounds which appear to be substantial, case management directions given under para.(1)(b) will include the allocation of the claim to a track or directions to enable it to be allocated.

(3) Except where—

    (a) the claim is allocated to the fast track or the multi-track; or

    (b) the court orders otherwise,

    any fact that needs to be proved by the evidence of witnesses at a hearing referred to in para.(1) may be proved by evidence in writing.

(5) In a possession claim against trespassers all witness statements on which the claimant intends to rely must be filed and served with the claim form.

(6) Where the claimant serves the claim form and particulars of claim, the claimant must produce at the hearing a certificate of service of those documents and r.6.17(2)(a) does not apply.

PD 55A para.5.1

Attention is drawn to r.55.8(3). Each party should wherever possible include all the evidence he wishes to present in his statement of case, verified by a statement of truth.

PD 55A para.5.4

If:

    (1) the maker of a witness statement does not attend a hearing; and

    (2) the other party disputes material evidence contained in his statement,

the court will normally adjourn the hearing so that oral evidence can be given.

PD 55A para.5.5

The claimant must bring two completed copies of Form N123 to the hearing.

Allocation

Pt 55 r.55.9

(1) When the court decides the track for a possession claim, the matters to which it shall have regard include—

    (a) the matters set out in r.26.8 as modified by the relevant PD;

    (c) the importance to the defendant of retaining possession of the land;

    (d) the importance of vacant possession to the claimant; and

    (e) if applicable, the alleged conduct of the defendant.

(2) The court will only allocate possession claims to the small claims track if all the parties agree.

(3) Where a possession claim has been allocated to the small claims track the claim shall be treated, for the purposes of costs, as if it were proceeding on the fast track except that trial costs shall be in the discretion of the court and shall not exceed the amount that would be recoverable under r.46.2 (amount of fast track costs) if the value of the claim were up to £3,000.

(4) Where all the parties agree the court may, when it allocates the claim, order that r.27.14 (costs on the small claims track) applies and, where it does so, para.(3) does not apply.

See also **Possession claims.**

TRIAL

See **Hearing**.

TRIAL BUNDLES

Agreed bundles for hearings

PD 32 para.27.1

The court may give directions requiring the parties to use their best endeavours to agree a bundle or bundles of documents for use at any hearing.

PD 32 para.27.2

All documents contained in bundles which have been agreed for use at a hearing shall be admissible at that hearing as evidence of their contents, unless—
    (1) the court orders otherwise; or
    (2) a party gives written notice of objection to the admissibility of particular documents.

Bundles of documents for hearings and trial

Pt 39 r.39.5

    (1) Unless the court orders otherwise, the claimant must file a trial bundle containing documents required by—
        (a) a relevant PD; and
        (b) any court order.
    (2) The claimant must file the trial bundle not more than seven days and not less than three days before the start of the trial.

PD 39A para.3.1

Unless the court orders otherwise, the claimant must file the trial bundle not more than seven days and not less than three days before the start of the trial.

PD 39A para.3.2

Unless the court orders otherwise, the trial bundle should include a copy of:
    (1) the claim form and all statements of case,
    (2) a **case summary** and/or chronology where appropriate,
    (3) requests for **further information** and responses to the requests,
    (4) all **witness statements** to be relied on as evidence,
    (5) any **witness summaries**,
    (6) any notices of intention to rely on hearsay evidence under r.32.2,
    (7) any notices of intention to rely on evidence (such as a plan, photograph etc.) under r.33.6 which is not—
        (a) contained in a witness statement, affidavit or experts report,
        (b) being given orally at trial,
        (c) **hearsay evidence** under r.33.2,

(8) any medical reports and responses to them,
(9) any experts' reports and responses to them,
(10) any order giving directions as to the conduct of the trial, and
(11) any other necessary documents.

PD 39A para.3.3

The originals of the documents contained in the trial bundle, together with copies of any other court orders should be available at the trial.

PD 39A para.3.4

The preparation and production of the trial bundle, even where it is delegated to another person, is the responsibility of the legal who has conduct of the claim on behalf of the claimant.

PD 39A para.3.5

The trial bundle should be paginated (continuously) throughout, and indexed with a description of each document and the page number. Where the total number of pages is more than 100, numbered dividers should be placed at intervals between groups of documents.

PD 39A para.3.6

The bundle should normally be contained in a ring binder or lever arch file. Where more than one bundle is supplied, they should be clearly distinguishable, for example, by different colours or letters. If there are numerous bundles, a core bundle should be prepared containing the core documents essential to the proceedings, with references to the supplementary documents in the other bundles.

PD 39A para.3.7

For convenience, experts' reports may be contained in a separate bundle and cross referenced in the main bundle.

PD 39A para.3.8

If a document to be included in the trial bundle is illegible, a typed copy should be included in the bundle next to it, suitably cross-referenced.

PD 39A para.3.8

The contents of the trial bundle should be agreed where possible. The parties should also agree where possible:
(1) that the documents contained in the bundle are authentic even if not disclosed under Pt 31, and
(2) that documents in the bundle may be treated as evidence of the facts stated in them even if a notice under the Civil Evidence Act 1995 has not been served.
Where it is not possible to agree the contents of the bundle, a summary of the points on which the parties are unable to agree should be included.

PD 39A para.3.10

The party filing the trial bundle should supply identical bundles to all the parties to the proceedings and for the use of the witnesses.

Fast track

Standard Directions

PD 28 Appendix

The claimant shall lodge an indexed bundle of documents contained in a ring binder and with each page clearly numbered at the court not more than seven days and not less than three days before the start of the trial.

[A case summary (which should not exceed 250 words) outlining the matters still in issue, and referring where appropriate to the relevant documents shall be included in the bundle for the assistance of the judge in reading the papers before the trial].

[The parties shall seek to agree the contents of the trial bundle and the case summary]

See **Judicial review.**

TRIBUNALS AND INQUIRIES ACT 1992

Pt 52 r.52.19

    (1) A person who was a party to proceedings before a tribunal referred to in s.11(1) of the Tribunals and Inquiries Act 1992 and is dissatisfied in point of law with the decision of the tribunal may appeal to the High Court.

    (2) The tribunal may, of its own initiative or at the request of a party to the proceedings before it, state, in the form of a special case for the decision of the High Court, a question of law arising in the course of the proceedings.

Appeals from certain tribunals

Section 11 of Act

    (1) Subject to subsection (2), if any party to proceedings before any tribunal specified in paragraph 8, 15(a) or (d), 16, 24, 26, 31, 33(b), 37, 40A, 44 or 45 of Schedule 1 [of the Act] is dissatisfied in point of law with a decision of the tribunal he may, according as rules of court may provide, either appeal from the tribunal to the High Court or require the tribunal to state and sign a case for the opinion of the High Court.

    (2) This section shall not apply in relation to proceedings before employment tribunals which arise under or by virtue of any of the enactments mentioned in s.21(1) of the Employment Tribunals Act 1996.

TRUSTEE

Limitation on court's power to order costs

See **Personal representative.**

TRUSTEE ACT 1925

See **Payment into court** and **Payment out of court.**

U

UNDERTAKING

Admiralty claims

PD 61 para.14.1

Where, in [Pt 61] or [PD 61], any undertaking to the Marshal is required it must be given—
  (1) in writing and to his satisfaction; or
  (2) in accordance with such other arrangements as he may require.

PD 61 para.14.2

Where any party is dissatisfied with a direction given by the Marshal in this respect he may apply to the Registrar for a ruling.

Discontinuance of claim

Pt 38 r.38.2

  (1) A claimant may discontinue all or part of a claim at any time.
  (2) However—
      (a) a claimant must obtain the permission of the court if he wishes to discontinue all or part of a claim in relation to which—
          (ii) any party has given an undertaking to the court.

Insolvency proceedings

See **Bankruptcy**.

Solicitor's undertaking

See **Solicitor**.

Injunction orders

PD 25A para.5.1

Any order for an injunction, unless the court orders otherwise, must contain:
  (1) an undertaking by the applicant to the court to pay any damages which the respondent sustains which the court considers the applicant should pay.

(2) if made without notice to any other party, an undertaking by the applicant to the court to serve on the respondent the application notice, evidence in support and any order made as soon as practicable,

(4) if made before filing the application notice, an undertaking to file and pay the appropriate fee on the same or next working day, and

(5) if made before issue of a claim form—

    (a) an undertaking to issue and pay the appropriate fee on the same or next working day.

PD 25A para.5.1A

When the court makes an order for an injunction, it should consider whether to require an undertaking by the applicant to pay any damages sustained by a person other than the respondent, including another party to the proceedings or any other person who may suffer loss as a consequence of the order.

PD 40B para.9.2

The provisions of [PD 40B], para.8.1 also apply to an order which contains an undertaking by a party to do or not do an act, subject to para.9.3 below.

[Para.8.1 provides that an order which requires an act to be done (other than a judgment or order for the payment of an amount of money) must specify the time within which the act should be done]

PD 40B para.9.3

The court has the power to decline to:

(1) accept an undertaking, and

(2) deal with disobedience in respect of an undertaking by contempt of court proceedings, unless the party giving the undertaking has made a signed statement to the effect that he understands the terms of his undertaking and the consequences of failure to comply with it.

PD 40B para.9.4

The statement may be endorsed on the [court copy of the] order containing the undertaking or may be filed in a separate document such as a letter.

Non-compliance with undertaking

PD 40B para.9.1

An order which restrains a party from doing an act or requires an act to be done should, if disobedience is to be dealt with by an application to bring contempt of court proceedings, have a penal notice endorsed on it as follows:

    If you the within-named [ ] do not comply with this order you may be held to be in contempt of court and imprisoned or fined, or [in the case of a company or corporation] your assets may be seized.

Committal for breach of undertaking in county court

CCR Ord.29 r.1

(1) Where a person required by a judgment or order to do an act refuses or neglects to do it within the time fixed by the judgment or order or any subsequent order, or where a person disobeys a judgment or order requiring him to abstain from doing an act, then, subject to the Debtors Acts 1869 and 1878 and to the provisions of these rules, the judgment or order may be enforced, by order of the judge, by a committal order against that person or, if that person is a body corporate, against any director or other officer of the body.

(2) Subject to paras (6) and (7), a judgment or order shall not be enforced under para.(1) unless—

'(2) A copy of the document recording the undertaking shall be delivered by the court officer to the party giving the undertaking—

    (a) by handing a copy of the document to him before he leaves the court building; or

    (b) where his place of residence is known, by posting a copy to him at his place of residence; or

    (c) through his solicitor,'

(3) Where a judgment or order enforceable by committal order under para.(1) has been given or made, the court officer shall, if the judgment or order is in the nature of an injunction, at the time when the judgment or order is drawn up, and in any other case on the request of the judgment creditor, issue a copy of the judgment or order, indorsed with or incorporating a notice as to the consequences of disobedience, for service in accordance with para.(2).

(4) If the person served with the judgment or order fails to obey it, the judgment creditor may issue a claim form or, as the case may be, an application notice seeking the committal for contempt of court of that person and subject to para.(7), the claim form or application notice shall be served on him personally.

(4A) The claim form or application notice (as the case may be) shall—

    (a) identify the provisions of the injunction or undertaking which it is alleged have been disobeyed or broken;

    (b) list the ways in which it is alleged that the injunction has been disobeyed or the undertaking has been broken;

    (c) be supported by an affidavit stating the grounds on which the application is made, and unless service is dispensed with under para.(7), a copy of the affidavit shall be served with the claim form or application notice.

(5) If a committal order is made, the order shall be for the issue of a warrant of committal and, unless the judge otherwise orders—

    (a) a copy of the order shall be served on the person to be committed either before or at the time of the execution of the warrant; or

    (b) where the warrant has been signed by the judge, the order for issue of the warrant may be served on the person to be committed at any time within 36 hours after the execution of the warrant.

(5A) A warrant of committal shall not, without further order of the court, be enforced more than two years after the date on which the warrant is issued.

(7) Without prejudice to its powers under Pt 6 of the CPR, the court may dispense with service of a claim form or application notice under para.(4) if the court thinks it just to do so.

(8) Where service of the claim form or application notice has been dispensed with under para.(7) and a committal order is made in the absence of the respondent, the judge may on his own initiative fix a date and time when the person to be committed is to be brought before him or before the court.

See also **Committal** and **Litigation friend**.

Service of document abroad or on a state

Pt 6 r.6.46

Every request for service filed under r.6.43 (service through foreign governments, judicial authorities, etc.) or r.6.44 (service of claim form or other document on a State) must contain an undertaking by the person making the request—
- (a) to be responsible for all expenses incurred by the Foreign and Commonwealth Office or foreign judicial authority; and
- (b) to pay those expenses to the Foreign and Commonwealth Office or foreign judicial authority on being informed of the amount.

Service of document on members of HM Forces

PD 6A Annex

As a first step, the claimant's legal representative will need to find out where the member is serving, if this is not already known. For this purpose the claimant's legal representative should write to the appropriate officer of the Ministry of Defence. The letter of enquiry must contain an undertaking by the legal representative that, if the address is given, it will be used solely for the purpose of issuing and serving documents in the proceedings and that so far as is possible the legal representative will disclose the address only to the court and not to the claimant or to any other person or body. A legal representative in the service of a public authority or private company must undertake that the address will be used solely for the purpose of issuing and serving documents in the proceedings and that the address will not be disclosed so far as is possible to any other part of the legal representative's employing organisation or to any other person but only to the court. Normally on receipt of the required information and undertaking the appropriate office will give the service address.

See also **Admiralty and Commercial Court** and **Solicitor**.

UNITED STATES AIR FORCE MEMBERS

Pt 6 r.5.1

The provisions that apply to service members of the United States Air Force are annexed to PD 6A.

UNLIQUIDATED SUM

Unspecified sum of money.

UNTRACED DRIVERS' AGREEMENT 2003

Pre-Action Protocol for Low Value Personal Injury Claims in Road Traffic Accidents Protocol does not apply to a claim made to the MIB pursuant to the Untraced Drivers' Agreement 2003 or any subsequent or supplementary Untraced Drivers' Agreements.

V

VACATIONS

Divisional court

RSC Ord.64 r.4

Proceedings which require to be immediately or promptly heard and which by virtue of the following provisions must be brought in a Divisional Court may, in vacation, be brought before a single judge:
(a) RSC Ord.52, rr.1(2) and 3(1) (**Committal**).

High Court

PD 39B para.2.1

(1) One or more judges of each Division of the High Court shall sit in vacation on such days as the senior judge of that Division may from time to time direct, to hear such cases, claims, matters or applications as require to be immediately or promptly heard and to hear other cases, claims, matters or applications if the senior judge of that Division determines that sittings are necessary for that purpose.
(2) Any party to a claim or matter may at any time apply to the Court for an order that such claim or matter be heard in vacation and, if the Court is satisfied that the claim or matter requires to be immediately or promptly heard, it may make an order accordingly and fix a date for the hearing.
(3) Any judge of the High Court may hear such other cases, claims, matters or applications in vacation as the Court may direct.

PD 39B para.2.2

The directions in para.3.1 shall not apply in relation to the trial or hearing of cases, claims, matters or applications outside the Royal Courts of Justice but the senior Presiding Judge of each Circuit, with the concurrence of the Senior Presiding Judge, and the Vice-Chancellor of the County Palatine of Lancaster and the Chancery Supervising Judge for Birmingham, Bristol and Cardiff, with the concurrence of the Vice-Chancellor, may make such arrangements for vacation sittings in the courts for which they are respectively responsible as they think desirable.

PD 39B para.2.3

(1) Subject to the discretion of the Judge, any appeal and any application normally made to a Judge may be made in the month of September.
(2) In the month of August, save with the permission of a Judge or under arrangements for vacation sittings in courts outside the Royal Courts of Justice, appeals to a Judge will be limited to the matters set out in para.3.5 below, and only applications of real urgency will

be dealt with, for example urgent applications in respect of injunctions or for possession under RSC Ord.113 (Sch.1 to the CPR).

(3) It is desirable, where this is practical, that applications or appeals are submitted to a Master, District Judge or Judge prior to the hearing of the application or appeal so that they can be marked 'fit for August' or 'fit for vacation.' If they are so marked, then normally the Judge will be prepared to hear the application or appeal in August, if marked 'fit for August' or in September if marked 'fit for vacation'. A request to have the papers so marked should normally be made in writing, shortly setting out the nature of the application or appeal and the reasons why it should be dealt with in August or in September, as the case may be.

Chancery Masters

PD 39B para.2.4

There is no distinction between term time and vacation so far as business before the Chancery Masters is concerned. The Masters will deal with all types of business throughout the year, and when a Master is on holiday his list will normally be taken by a Deputy Master.

Queen's Bench Masters

PD 39B para.2.5

(1) An application notice may, without permission, be issued returnable before a Master in the month of August for any of the following purposes:
to set aside a claim form or particulars of claim, or service of a claim form or particulars of claim;
to set aside judgment;
for stay of execution;
for any order by consent;
for judgment or permission to enter judgment;
for approval of settlements or for interim payment;
for relief from forfeiture;
for charging order;
for garnishee order;
for appointment or discharge of a receiver;
for relief by way of interpleader by a sheriff or High Court enforcement officer;
for transfer to a county court or for trial by Master;
for time where time is running in the month of August;
(2) In any case of urgency any other type of application notice (that is other than those for the purposes in (1) above), may, with the permission of a Master be issued returnable before a Master during the month of August.

VALIDATION ORDER

PD IP para.14.8.1

A person against whom a bankruptcy petition has been presented ('the debtor') may apply to the court after presentation of the petition for relief from the effects of s.284(1)–(3) of the Act by seeking an order that any disposition of his assets or payment made out of his funds, including any bank account (whether it is in credit or overdrawn) shall not be void in the event of a bankruptcy order being made on the petition (a 'validation order').

PD IP para.14.8.2

Save in exceptional circumstances, notice of the making of the application should be given to (a) the petitioning creditor(s) or other petitioner, (b) any creditor who has given notice to the petitioner of his intention to appear on the hearing of the petition pursuant to r.6.23 1986, (c) any creditor who has been substituted as petitioner pursuant to r.6.30 of the Insolvency Rules 1986 and (d) any creditor who has carriage of the petition pursuant to r.6.31 of the Insolvency Rules 1986.

PD IP para.14.8.3

The application should be supported by a witness statement which, save in exceptional circumstances, should be made by the debtor. If appropriate, supporting evidence in the form of a witness statement from the debtor's accountant should also be produced.

PD IP para.14.8.4

The extent and contents of the evidence will vary according to the circumstances and the nature of the relief sought, but in a case where the debtor is trading or carrying on business it should include, as a minimum, the following information—
   (1) when and to whom notice has been given in accordance with para.14.8.2 above;
   (2) brief details of the circumstances leading to presentation of the petition;
   (3) how the debtor became aware of the presentation of the petition;
   (4) whether the petition debt is admitted or disputed and, if the latter, brief details of the basis on which the debt is disputed;
   (5) full details of the debtor's financial position including details of his assets (including details of any security and the amount(s) secured) and liabilities, which should be supported, as far as possible, by documentary evidence, e.g. accounts, draft accounts, management accounts or estimated statement of affairs;
   (6) a cash flow forecast and profit and loss projection for the period for which the order is sought;
   (7) details of the dispositions or payments in respect of which an order is sought;
   (8) the reasons relied on in support of the need for such dispositions or payments to be made;
   (9) any other information relevant to the exercise of the court's discretion;
   (10) details of any consents obtained from the persons mentioned in para.14.8.2 above (supported by documentary evidence where appropriate);
   (11) details of any relevant bank account, including its number and the address and sort code of the bank at which such account is held.

PD IP para.14.8.5

Where an application is made urgently to enable payments to be made which are essential to continued trading (e.g. wages) and it is not possible to assemble all the evidence listed above, the court may consider granting limited relief for a short period, but there must be sufficient evidence to satisfy the court that the interests of creditors are unlikely to be prejudiced.

PD IP para.14.8.6

Where the debtor is not trading or carrying on business and the application relates only to a proposed sale, mortgage or re-mortgage of the debtor's home evidence of the following will generally suffice—

(1) when and to whom notice has been given in accordance with para.14.8.2 above;
(2) whether the petition debt is admitted or disputed and, if the latter, brief details of the basis on which the debt is disputed;
(3) details of the property to be sold, mortgaged or re-mortgaged (including its title number);
(4) the value of the property and the proposed sale price, or details of the mortgage or re-mortgage;
(5) details of any existing mortgages or charges on the property and redemption figures;
(6) the costs of sale (e.g. solicitors' or agents' costs);
(7) how and by whom any net proceeds of sale (or sums coming into the debtor's hands as a result of any mortgage or re-mortgage) are to be held pending the final hearing of the petition;
(8) any other information relevant to the exercise of the court's discretion;
(9) details of any consents obtained from the persons mentioned in para.14.8.2 above (supported by documentary evidence where appropriate).

PD IP para.14.8.7

Whether or not the debtor is trading or carrying on business, where the application involves a disposition of property the court will need to be satisfied that any proposed disposal will be at a proper value. Accordingly an independent valuation should be obtained and exhibited to the evidence.

PD IP para.14.8.8

The court will need to be satisfied by credible evidence that the debtor is solvent and able to pay his debts as they fall due or that a particular transaction or series of transactions in respect of which the order is sought will be beneficial to or will not prejudice the interests of all the unsecured creditors as a class (*Denney v John Hudson & Co Ltd* [1992] B.C.L.C. 901; [1992] B.C.C. 503, CA; *Re Fairway Graphics Ltd* [1991] B.C.L.C. 468).

PD IP para.14.8.9

A draft of the order sought should be attached to the application.

PD IP para.14.8.10

Similar considerations to those set out above are likely to apply to applications seeking ratification of a transaction or payment after the making of a bankruptcy order.

See **Bankruptcy Court**, **Bankruptcy Petition**, **Insolvency proceedings**, **Personal Insolvency**, and **Statutory demand.**

VALUE ADDED TAX

Appeal from Value Added Tax and Duties Tribunal

PD 52 para.23.8

(1) A party to proceedings before a Value Added Tax and Duties Tribunal who is dissatisfied in point of law with a decision of the tribunal may appeal under s.11(1) of the Tribunals and Inquiries Act 1992 to the High Court.

(2) The appellant must file the appellant's notice—
   (a) where the appeal is made following the refusal of the Value Added Tax and Duties Tribunal to grant a certificate under art.2(b) of the Value Added Tax and Duties Tribunal Appeals Order 1986, within 28 days from the date of the release of the decision containing the refusal;
   (b) in all other cases within 56 days after the date of the decision or determination that the appellant wishes to appeal.

See **Tribunals and Inquiries Act 1992.**

Apportionment

PD 44 para.2.9

Subject to paras 2.7 and 2.8, all bills of costs, fees and disbursements on which VAT is included must be divided into separate parts so as to show work done before, on and after the date or dates from which any change in the rate of VAT takes effect. Where, however, a lump sum charge is made for work which spans a period during which there has been a change in VAT rates, and paras 2.7 and 2.8 above do not apply, reference should be made to paras 30.7 or 30.8 of the VAT Guide (Notice 700)(or any revised edition of that notice) published by HMRC, a copy of which should be in the possession of every registered trader. If necessary, the lump sum should be apportioned. The totals of profit costs and disbursements in each part must be carried separately to the summary.

Change in VAT rate

PD 44 para.2.10

Should there be a change in the rate between the conclusion of a detailed assessment and the issue of the final costs certificate, any interested party may apply for the detailed assessment to be varied so as to take account of any increase or reduction in the amount of tax payable. Once the final costs certificate has been issued, no variation under this para. will be permitted.

Entitlement to VAT on costs

PD 44 para.2.3

VAT should not be included in a claim for costs if the receiving party is able to recover the VAT as input tax. Where the receiving party is able to obtain credit from HMRC for a proportion of the VAT as input tax, only that proportion which is not eligible for credit should be included in the claim for costs.

PD 44 para.2.4

The receiving party has responsibility for ensuring that VAT is claimed only when the receiving party is unable to recover the VAT or a proportion thereof as input tax.

PD 44 para.2.5

Where there is a dispute as to whether VAT is properly claimed the receiving party must provide a certificate signed by the solicitors or the auditors of the receiving party substantially in the form illustrated in Precedent F in the Schedule of Costs Precedents annexed to PD 47.

PD 44 para.2.6

Where there is a dispute as to whether any service in respect of which a charge is proposed to be made in the bill is **zero rated** or exempt from VAT, reference should be made to HMRC and its view obtained and made known at the hearing at which the costs are assessed. Such enquiry should be made by the receiving party. In the case of a bill from a solicitor to the solicitor's legal representative's own client, such enquiry should be made by the client.

Form of Bill of Costs where VAT rate changes

PD 44 para.2.7

Where there is a change in the rate of VAT, suppliers of goods and services are entitled by ss.88(1) and 88(2) of the VAT Act 1994 in most circumstances to elect whether the new or the old rate of VAT should apply to a supply where the basic and actual tax points span a period during which the rate changed.

PD 44 para.2.8

It will be assumed, unless a contrary indication is given in writing, that an election to take advantage of the provisions mentioned in para.2.7 and to charge VAT at the lower rate has been made. In any case in which an election to charge at the lower rate is not made, such a decision must be justified to the court assessing the costs.

Government departments

PD 44 para.2.13

On an assessment between parties, where costs are being paid to a Government Department in respect of services rendered by its legal staff, VAT should not be added.

VAT registration number

Costs PD para.5.2

The number allocated by HMRC to every person registered under the Value Added Tax Act 1983 (except a Government Department) must appear in a prominent place at the head of every statement, bill of costs, fee sheet, account or voucher on which VAT is being included as part of a claim for costs.

See **Disbursements, Litigant in person**, and **Pro bono representation**.

Disbursements not classified as such for VAT purposes

Costs PD para.5.11

(1) Legal representatives often make payments to third parties for the supply of goods or services where no VAT was chargeable on the supply by the third party: for example, the cost of meals taken and travel costs. The question whether legal representatives should include VAT in respect of these payments when invoicing their clients or in claims for costs between litigants should be decided in accordance with this Direction and with the

criteria set out in the VAT Guide (Notice 700) published by HM Revenue and Customs.

(2) Payments to third parties which are normally treated as part of the legal representative's overheads (for example, postage costs and telephone costs) will not be treated as disbursements. The third party supply should be included as part of the costs of the legal representatives' legal services and VAT must be added to the total bill charged to the client.

(3) Disputes may arise in respect of payments made to a third party which the legal representative shows as disbursements in the invoice delivered to the receiving party. Some payments, although correctly described as disbursements for some purposes, are not classified as disbursements for VAT purposes. Items not classified as disbursements for VAT purposes must be shown as part of the services provided by the legal representative and, therefore, VAT must be added in respect of them whether or not VAT was chargeable on the supply by the third party.

(4) Guidance as to the circumstances in which disbursements may or may not be classified as disbursements for VAT purposes is given in the VAT Guide (Notice 700, para.25.1). One of the key issues is whether the third party supply (i) was made to the legal representative (and therefore subsumed in the onward supply of legal services), or (ii) was made direct to the receiving party (the third party having no right to demand payment from the legal representative, who makes the payment only as agent for the receiving party).

(5) Examples of payments under (i) are: travelling expenses, such as an airline ticket, and subsistence expenses, such as the cost of meals, where the person travelling and receiving the meals is the legal representative. The supplies by the airline and the restaurant are supplies to the legal representative, not to the client.

(6) Payments under (ii) are classified as disbursements for VAT purposes and, therefore, the legal representative need not add VAT in respect of them. Simple examples are payments by a legal representative of court fees and payment of fees to an expert witness.

Legal aid/LSC certificate

Value added tax

Costs PD para.5.13

(1) VAT will be payable in respect of every supply made pursuant to a legal aid/LSC certificate where—
   (a) the person making the supply is a taxable person; and
   (b) the assisted person/LSC funded client—
      (i) belongs in the UK or another member state of the European Union; and
      (ii) is a private individual or receives the supply for non-business purposes.

(2) Where the assisted person/LSC funded client belongs outside the European Union, VAT is generally not payable unless the supply relates to land in the UK.

(3) For the purpose of subparas (1) and (2), the place where a person belongs is determined by s.9 of the Value Added Tax Act 1994.

(4) Where the assisted person/LSC funded client is registered for VAT and the legal services paid for by the LSC are in connection with that person's business, the VAT on those services will be payable by the LSC only.

Costs PD para.5.14

Any summary of costs payable by the LSC must be drawn so as to show the total VAT on Counsel's fees as a separate item from the VAT on other disbursements and the VAT on profit costs.

See also **Litigant in person** and **Zero rated**.

VARIATION OF TRUSTS ACT 1958

Pt 64 r.64.2

[s.1 of Pt 64] applies to claims—
  (c) under the Variation of Trusts Act 1958.

Allocation of cases

PD 2B para.5.1

In proceedings in the Chancery Division, a Master or a district judge may not deal with the following without the consent of the Chancellor of the High Court—
  (c) making final orders under s.1(1) of the Variation of Trusts Act 1958, except for the removal of protective trusts where the interest of the principal beneficiary has not failed or determined.

Applications under the Act

PD 64A para.4.1

Where children or unborn beneficiaries will be affected by a proposed arrangement under the Act, the evidence filed in support of the application must—
  (1) show that their litigation friends or the trustees support the arrangements as being in the interests of the children or unborn beneficiaries; and
  (2) unless para.4.3 applies or the court orders otherwise, be accompanied by a written opinion to this effect by the advocate who will appear on the hearing of the application.

PD 64A para.4.2

A written opinion filed under para.4.1(2) must—
  (1) if it is given on formal instructions, be accompanied by a copy of those instructions; or
  (2) otherwise, state fully the basis on which it is given.

PD 64A para.4.3

No written opinion needs to be filed in support of an application to approve an arrangement under s.1(1)(d) of the Act (discretionary interests under protective trusts).

PD 64A para.4.4

Where the interests of two or more children, or two or more of the children and unborn beneficiaries, are similar, only a single written opinion needs to be filed.

Hearing

PD 39A para.1.5

The hearings set out below shall in the first instance be listed by the court as hearings in private under r.39.2(3)(c), namely:

(10) an application by a trustee or personal representative for directions as to bringing or defending legal proceedings.

Parties to claim

Pt 64 r.64.4

(1) In a claim [under the Variation of Trusts Act 1958]—
    (a) all the trustees must be parties;
    (b) if the claim is made by trustees, any of them who does not consent to being a claimant must be made a defendant; and
    (c) the claimant may make parties to the claim any persons with an interest in or claim against the estate, or an interest under the trust, who it is appropriate to make parties having regard to the nature of the order sought.
(2) In addition, in a claim under the Variation of Trusts Act 1958, unless the court directs otherwise any person who—
    (a) created the trust; or
    (b) provided property for the purposes of the trust,
    must, if still alive, be made a party to the claim.
(The court may, under r.19.2, order additional persons to be made parties to a claim).

VEHICULAR ACCESS ACROSS COMMON AND OTHER LAND (ENGLAND) REGULATIONS 2002

Payment into court

PD 37 para.8.2

Where the applicant wishes to pay money into a county court under reg.14 [he must file a witness statement or an affidavit when he lodges the money].

PD 37 para.8.3

The witness statement or affidavit must—
    (1) state briefly why the applicant is making the payment into court; and
    (2) be accompanied by copies of—
        (a) the notice served under reg.6;
        (b) any counter-notice served under reg.8;
        (c) any amended notice or counter-notice served under reg.9;
        (d) any determination of the Lands Tribunal of a matter referred to it under reg.10; and
        (e) any determination of the value of the premises by a chartered surveyor following the service of a valuation notice under reg.12.

PD 37 para.8.4

If an applicant pays money into court under reg.14 [of Vehicular Access Across Common and Other Land (England) Regulations 2002], he must immediately serve notice of the payment and a copy of the witness statement or affidavit on the land owner.

PD 37 para.8.5

Payment out of court

An application for payment out of the money must be made in accordance with [PD 37, para.3].

See **Payment out of court**.

VENUE

Court's discretion

Pt 2 r.2.7

The court may deal with a case at any place that it considers appropriate.

Where to start proceedings

PD 7A para.2.1

Proceedings (whether for damages or for a specified sum) may not be started in the High Court unless the value of the claim is more than £25,000.

PD 7A para.2.2

Proceedings which include a claim for damages in respect of personal injuries must not be started in the High Court unless the value of the claim is £50,000 or more (para.9 of the High Court and County Courts Jurisdiction Order 1991 (SI 1991/724 as amended) describes how the value of a claim is to be determined).

PD 7A para.2.3

A claim must be issued in the High Court or a county court if an enactment so requires.

PD 7A para.2.4

Subject to paras 2.1 and 2.2 above, a claim should be started in the High Court if by reason of:
  (1) the financial value of the claim and the amount in dispute, and/or
  (2) the complexity of the facts, legal issues, remedies or procedures involved, and/or
  (3) the importance of the outcome of the claim to the public in general,
       the claimant believes that the claim ought to be dealt with by a High Court judge.
(CPR Pt 30 and PD 30 contain provisions relating to the transfer to the county court of proceedings started in the High Court and vice-versa).

PD 7A para.2.5

A claim relating to Chancery business (which includes any of the matters specified in para.1 of Sch.1 to the Senior Courts Act 1981) may, subject to any enactment, rule or PD , be dealt with

in the High Court or in a county court. The claim form should, if issued in the High Court, be marked in the top right hand corner 'Chancery Division' and, if issued in the county court, be marked 'Chancery Business'.
(For the equity jurisdiction of county courts, see s.23 of the County Courts Act 1984).

PD 7A para.2.6

A claim relating to any of the matters specified in subparas (a) and (b) of para.2 of Sch.1 to the Senior Courts Act 1981 must be dealt with in the High Court and will be assigned to the Queen's Bench Division.

PD 7A para.2.7

PD s applying to particular types of proceedings, or to proceedings in particular courts, will contain provisions relating to the commencement and conduct of those proceedings.

PD 7A para.2.8

A claim in the High Court for which a **jury trial** is directed will, if not already being dealt with in the Queen's Bench Division, be transferred to that Division.

PD 7A para.2.9

The following proceedings may not be started in a county court unless the parties have agreed otherwise in writing:
- (1) a claim for damages or other remedy for libel or slander, and
- (2) a claim in which the title to any toll, fair, market or franchise is in question.

PD 7A para.2.10

- (1) The normal rules apply in deciding in which court and specialist list a claim that includes issues under the Human Rights Act 1998 should be started. They also apply in deciding which procedure to use to start the claim; this Part or CPR Pt 8 or CPR Pt 54 (**judicial review**).
- (2) The exception is a claim for damages in respect of a judicial act, which should be commenced in the High Court. If the claim is made in a notice of appeal then it will be dealt with according to the normal rules governing where that appeal is heard.

(A county court cannot make a declaration of incompatibility in accordance with s.4 of the Human Rights Act 1998. Legislation may direct that such a claim is to be brought before a specified tribunal).

Designated money claim

PD 7A para.4A.1

In all designated money claims, practice Form N1 must be sent to County Court Money Claims Centre PO Box 527, M5 0BY. The claim will then be issued in Northampton County Court.

PD 7A para.4A.2

In proceedings referred to in para.4A.1, the claimant must specify the preferred court on practice Form N1.

See also **Start of proceedings**.

VEXATIOUS LITIGANTS

Application under s.42 of the Senior Courts Act 1981

PD 8A para.16.1

An application under s.42 of the Senior Courts Act 1981 [Restriction of vexatious legal proceedings] is heard and determined by a Divisional Court.

PD 8A para.16.2

The [Part 8] claim form must be filed at the Administrative Court and—
    (1) be accompanied by a witness statement in support; and
    (2) be served on the person against whom the order is sought.

Permission to begin or continue proceedings by a vexatious litigant

PD 3A para.7.1

This PD applies where a '**civil proceedings order**' or an '**all proceedings order**' (as respectively defined under s.42(1A) of the Senior Courts Act 1981) is in force against a person ('the litigant').

PD 3A para.7.2

An application by the litigant for permission to begin or continue, or to make any application in, any civil proceedings shall be made by application notice issued in the High Court and signed by the litigant.

PD 3A para.7.3

The application notice must state:
    (1) the title and reference number of the proceedings in which the civil proceedings order or the all proceedings order, as the case may be, was made,
    (2) the full name of the litigant and his address,
    (3) the order the applicant is seeking, and
    (4) briefly, why the applicant is seeking the order.

PD 3A para.7.4

The application notice must be filed together with any written evidence on which the litigant relies in support of his application.

PD 3A para.7.5

Either in the application notice or in written evidence filed in support of the application, the previous occasions on which the litigant made an application for permission under s.42(1A) of the said Act must be listed.

PD 3A para.7.6

The application notice, together with any written evidence, will be placed before a High Court judge who may:
  (1) without the attendance of the applicant make an order giving the permission sought;
  (2) give directions for further written evidence to be supplied by the litigant before an order is made on the application;
  (3) make an order dismissing the application without a hearing; or
  (4) give directions for the hearing of the application.

PD 3A para.7.7

Directions given under para.7.6(4) may include an order that the application notice be served on the Attorney General and on any person against whom the litigant desires to bring the proceedings for which permission is being sought.

PD 3A para.7.8

Any order made under paras 6 or 7 will be served on the litigant at the address given in the application notice. CPR Pt 6 will apply.

PD 3A para.7.9

A person may apply to set aside the grant of permission if:
  (1) the permission allowed the litigant to bring or continue proceedings against that person or to make any application against him, and
  (2) the permission was granted other than at a hearing of which that person was given notice under para.7.

PD 3A para.7.10

Any application under para.7.9 must be made in accordance with CPR Pt 23.

VIDEO CONFERENCING

PD 23A para.7

Where the parties to a matter wish to use **video conferencing** facilities, and those facilities are available in the relevant court, they should apply to the Master or district judge for directions.

Guidance

PD 32 para.29.1

Guidance on the use of video conferencing in the civil courts is set out at Annex 3 to [PD 32].
  A list of the sites which are available for video conferencing can be found on Her Majesty's Courts and Tribunals Service website.

VIDEO LINK EVIDENCE

Pt 1 rr.1.4(1) and (2)(k)

The court may further the **overriding objective** by actively managing cases. This includes making use of technology.

Pt 32 r.32.3

The court may allow a witness to give evidence through a video link or by other means.

VIOLENT CRIME REDUCTION ACT 2006

See **Drinking banning order**.

W

WARRANT OF DELIVERY

CCR Ord.26 r.16

(1) Except where an Act or rule provides otherwise, a judgment or order for the delivery of any goods shall be enforceable by warrant of delivery in accordance with this rule.

(2) If the judgment or order does not give the person against whom it was given or made the alternative of paying the value of the goods, it may be enforced by a warrant of specific delivery, that is to say, a warrant to recover the goods without alternative provision for recovery of their value.

(3) If the judgment or order is for the delivery of the goods or payment of their value, it may be enforced by a warrant of delivery to recover the goods or their value.

(4) Where a warrant of delivery is issued, the judgment creditor shall be entitled, by the same or a separate warrant, to execution against the debtor's goods for any money payable under the judgment or order which is to be enforced by the warrant of delivery.

(4A) Where a judgment or order is given or made for the delivery of goods or payment of their value and a warrant is issued to recover the goods or their value, money paid into court under the warrant shall be appropriated first to any sum of money and costs awarded.

(5) The foregoing provisions of this order, so far as applicable, shall have effect, with the necessary modifications, in relation to warrants of delivery as they have effect in relation to warrants of execution.

Saving for enforcement by committal

CCR Ord.26 r.18

Nothing in rr.16 or 17 [warrant of possession] shall prejudice any power to enforce a judgment or order for the delivery of goods or the recovery of land by an order of committal.

WARRANT OF EXECUTION

CCR Ord.26 r.1

(1) A judgment creditor desiring a warrant of execution to be issued shall file a request in that behalf certifying—
   (a) the amount remaining due under the judgment or order; and
   (b) where the order made is for payment of a sum of money by instalments—
      (i) that the whole or part of any instalment due remains unpaid; and
      (ii) the amount for which the warrant is to be issued.

(1A) The court officer shall discharge the functions—
   (a) under s.85(2) of the [County Court Act 1984] of issuing a warrant of execution;
   (b) under s.85(3) of the Act of entering in the record mentioned in that subsection and on the warrant the precise time of the making of the application to issue the warrant; and

     (c) under s.103(1) of the Act of sending the warrant of execution to another county court.

(2) Where the court has made an order for payment of a sum of money by instalments and default has been made in payment of such an instalment, a warrant of execution may be issued for the whole of the said sum of money and costs then remaining unpaid or, subject to para.(3), for such part as the judgment creditor may request, not being in the latter case less than £50 or the amount of one monthly instalment or, as the case may be, four weekly instalments, whichever is the greater.

(3) In any case to which para.(2) applies no warrant shall be issued unless at the time when it is issued—

     (a) the whole or part of an instalment which has already become due remains unpaid; and

     (b) any warrant previously issued for part of the said sum of money and costs has expired or has been satisfied or abandoned.

(4) Where a warrant is issued for the whole or part of the said sum of money and costs, the court officer shall, unless the district judge responsible for execution of the warrant directs otherwise, send a warning notice to the person against whom the warrant is issued and, where such a notice is sent, the warrant shall not be levied until seven days thereafter.

(5) Where judgment is given or an order made for payment otherwise than by instalments of a sum of money and costs to be assessed in accordance with CPR Pt 47 (detailed assessment procedure) and default is made in payment of the sum of money before the costs have been assessed, a warrant of execution may issue for recovery of the sum of money and a separate warrant may issue subsequently for the recovery of the costs if default is made in payment of them.

Execution of High Court judgment

CCR Ord.26 r.2

(1) Where it is desired to enforce by warrant of execution a judgment or order of the High Court, or a judgment, order, decree or award which is or has become enforceable as if it were a judgment of the High Court, the request referred to in r.1(1) may be filed in any court in the district of which execution is to be levied.

(2) Subject to Ord.25 r.9(5), any restriction imposed by these rules on the issue of execution shall apply as if the judgment, order, decree or award were a judgment or order of the county court, but permission to issue execution shall not be required if permission has already been given by the High Court.

(3) Notice of the issue of the warrant shall be sent by the county court to the High Court.

Concurrent warrants

CCR Ord.26 r.4

Two or more warrants of execution may be issued concurrently for execution in different districts, but—

     (a) no more shall be levied under all the warrants together than is authorised to be levied under one of them; and

     (b) the costs of more than one such warrant shall not be allowed against the debtor except by order of the court.

Permission to issue certain warrants

CCR Ord.26 r.5

(1) A warrant of execution shall not issue without the permission of the court where—
   (a) six years or more have elapsed since the date of the judgment or order;
   (b) any change has taken place, whether by death or otherwise in the parties entitled to enforce the judgment or order or liable to have it enforced against them;
   (c) the judgment or order is against the assets of a deceased person coming into the hands of his executors or administrators after the date of the judgment or order and it is sought to issue execution against such assets; or
   (d) any goods to be seized under a warrant of execution are in the hands of a receiver appointed by a court.

(2) An application for permission shall be supported by a witness statement or affidavit establishing the applicant's right to relief and may be made without notice being served on any other party in the first instance but the court may direct the application notice to be served on such persons as it thinks fit.

(3) Where, by reason of one and the same event, a person seeks permission under para.(1)(b) to enforce more judgments or orders than one, he may make one application only, specifying in a schedule all the judgments or orders in respect of which it is made, and if the application notice is directed to be served on any person, it need set out only such part of the application as affects him.

(4) Paragraph (1) is without prejudice to any enactment, rule or direction by virtue of which a person is required to obtain the permission of the court for the issue of a warrant or to proceed to execution or otherwise to the enforcement of a judgment or order.

Duration and renewal of warrant

CCR Ord.26 r.6

(1) A warrant of execution shall, for the purpose of execution, be valid in the first instance for 12 months beginning with the date of its issue, but if not wholly executed, it may be renewed from time to time, by order of the court, for a period of 12 months at any one time, beginning with the day next following that on which it would otherwise expire, if an application for renewal is made before that day or such later day (if any) as the court may allow.

(2) A note of any such renewal shall be indorsed on the warrant and it shall be entitled to priority according to the time of its original issue or, where appropriate, its receipt by the district judge responsible for its execution.

Levying execution on certain days

PD RSC Ord.46 and CCR Ord.26 para.1.1

Unless the Court orders otherwise, a writ of execution or a warrant of execution to enforce a judgment or order must not be executed on a Sunday, Good Friday or Christmas Day.

PD RSC Ord.46 and CCR Ord.26 para.1.2

Paragraph 1.1 does not apply to an Admiralty **claim in rem**.

Notice on levy

CCR Ord.26 r.7

Any bailiff upon levying execution shall deliver to the debtor or leave at the place where execution is levied a notice of the warrant.

Bankruptcy or winding up of debtor

CCR Ord.26 r.8

(1) Where the district judge responsible for the execution of a warrant is required by any provision of the Insolvency Act 1986 or any other enactment relating to insolvency to retain the proceeds of sale of goods sold under the warrant or money paid in order to avoid a sale, the court shall, as soon as practicable after the sale or the receipt of the money, send notice to the execution creditor and, if the warrant issued out of another court, to that court.

(2) Where the district judge responsible for the execution of a warrant—

    (a) receives notice that a bankruptcy order has been made against the debtor or, if the debtor is a company, that a provisional liquidator has been appointed or that an order has been made or a resolution passed for the winding up of the company; and

    (b) withdraws from possession of goods seized or pays over to the official receiver or trustee in bankruptcy or, if the debtor is a company, to the liquidator the proceeds of sale of goods sold under the warrant or money paid in order to avoid a sale or seized or received in part satisfaction of the warrant,

    the court shall send notice to the execution creditor and, if the warrant issued out of another court, to that court.

(2) Where the court officer of a court to which a warrant issued out of another court has been sent for execution receives any such notice as is referred to in para.(2)(a) after he has sent to the home court any money seized or received in part satisfaction of the warrant, he shall forward the notice to that court.

Withdrawal and suspension of warrant at creditor's request

CCR Ord.26 r.10

(1) Where an execution creditor requests the district judge responsible for executing a warrant to withdraw from possession, he shall, subject to the following paragraphs of this rule, be treated as having abandoned the execution, and the court shall mark the warrant as withdrawn by request of the execution creditor.

(2) Where the request is made in consequence of a claim having been made under Ord.33 r.1, to goods seized under the warrant, the execution shall be treated as being abandoned in respect only of the goods claimed.

(3) If the district judge responsible for executing a warrant is requested by the execution creditor to suspend it in pursuance of an arrangement between him and the debtor, the court shall mark the warrant as suspended by request of the execution creditor and the execution creditor may subsequently apply to the district judge holding the warrant for it to be re-issued and, if he does so, the application shall be deemed for the purpose of s.85(3) of the Act to be an application to issue the warrant.

(4) Nothing in this rule shall prejudice any right of the execution creditor to apply for the issue of a fresh warrant or shall authorise the re-issue of a warrant which has been withdrawn or has expired or has been superseded by the issue of a fresh warrant.

Suspension of part warrant

CCR Ord.26 r.11

Where a warrant issued for part of a sum of money and costs payable under a judgment or order is suspended on payment of instalments, the judgment or order shall, unless the court otherwise directs, be treated as suspended on those terms as respects the whole of the sum of money and costs then remaining unpaid.

Inventory and notice where goods removed

CCR Ord.26 r.12

(1) Where goods seized in execution are removed, the court shall forthwith deliver or send to the debtor a sufficient inventory of the goods removed and shall, not less than four days before the time fixed for the sale, give him notice of the time and place at which the goods will be sold.
(2) The inventory and notice shall be given to the debtor by delivering them to him personally or by sending them to him by post at his place of residence or, if his place of residence is not known, by leaving them for him, or sending them to him by post, at the place from which the goods were removed.

Account of sale

CCR Ord.26 r.13

Where goods are sold under an execution, the court shall furnish the debtor with a detailed account in writing of the sale and of the application of the proceeds.

Notification to foreign court of payment made

CCR Ord.26 r.14

Where, after a warrant has been sent to a foreign court for execution but before a final return has been made to the warrant, the home court is notified of a payment made in respect of the sum for which the warrant is issued, the home court shall send notice of the payment to the foreign court.

Order for private sale

CCR Ord.26 r.15

(1) Subject to para.(6), an order of the court under s.97 of the Act that a sale under an execution may be made otherwise than by public auction may be made on the application of the execution creditor or the debtor or the district judge responsible for the execution of the warrant.
(2) Where he is not the applicant for an order under this rule, the district judge responsible for the execution of the warrant shall, on the demand of the applicant, furnish him with

a list containing the name and address of every execution creditor under any other warrant or writ of execution against the goods of the debtor of which the district judge has notice, and where the district judge is the applicant, he shall prepare such a list.

(3) Not less than four days before the day fixed for the hearing of the application, the applicant shall give notice of the application to each of the other persons by whom the application might have been made and to every person named in the list referred to in para.(2).

(4) The applicant shall produce the list to the court on the hearing of the application.

(5) Every person to whom notice of the application was given may attend and be heard on the hearing of the application.

(6) Where the district judge responsible for the execution of the warrant is the district judge by whom it was issued and he has no notice of any other warrant or writ of execution against the goods of the debtor, an order under this rule may be made by the court of its own motion with the consent of the execution creditor and the debtor or after giving them an opportunity of being heard.

See **Civil recovery proceedings**, **Competition Act 1998**, **Enterprise Act 2002**, **Judgments and orders**, **Farmer**, **Possession claims online**, **Traffic enforcement**, and **Writ of fi fa**.

WARRANT OF POSSESSION

CCR Ord.26 r.17

(1) A judgment or order for the recovery of land shall be enforceable by warrant of possession.

(2) Without prejudice to para.(3A), the person applying for a warrant of possession must file a certificate that the land which is subject of the judgment or order has not been vacated.

(2A) When applying for a warrant of possession of a dwelling-house subject to a mortgage, the claimant must certify that notice has been given in accordance with the Dwelling Houses (Execution of Possession Orders by Mortgagees) Regulations 2010 [These Regulations, which extend to England and Wales, provide for a notice of execution of possession order to be given at all residential properties where the mortgage lender is seeking to execute a possession order against the borrower].

(3) Where a warrant of possession is issued, the judgment creditor shall be entitled, by the same or a separate warrant, to execution against the debtor's goods for any money payable under the judgment or order which is to be enforced by the warrant of possession.

(3A) In a case to which para.(3) applies or where an order for possession has been suspended on terms as to payment of a sum of money by instalments, the judgment creditor shall in his request certify—

(a) the amount of money remaining due under the judgment or order; and

(b) that the whole or part of any instalment due remains unpaid.

(6) Rules 5 and 6 shall apply, with the necessary modifications, in relation to a warrant of possession and any further warrant in aid of such a warrant as they apply in relation to a warrant of execution.

Saving for enforcement by committal

CCR Ord.26 r.18

Nothing in rr.16 [**warrant of delivery**] or 17 [**warrant of possession**] shall prejudice any power to enforce a judgment or order for the delivery of goods or the recovery of land by an order of committal.

WARRANT OF RESTITUTION

CCR Ord.26 r.17

(4) A warrant of restitution may be issued, with the permission of the court, in aid of any warrant of possession.

(5) An application for permission under para.(4) may be made without notice being served on any other party and shall be supported by evidence of wrongful re-entry into possession following the execution of the warrant of possession and of such further facts as would, in the High Court, enable the judgment creditor to have a writ of restitution issued.

WASTED COSTS ORDER

Supreme Court Act 1981 s.51(7)

[Wasted costs are] any costs incurred by a party—
as a result of any improper, unreasonable or negligent act or omission on the part of any legal or other representative or any employee of such a representative; or which, in the light of any such act or omission occurring after they were incurred, the court considers it is unreasonable to expect that party to pay.

PD 46 para.5.1

A wasted costs order is an order—
(1) that the legal representative pay a specified sum in respect of costs to a party; or
(2) for costs relating to a specified sum or items of work to be disallowed.

Supreme Court Act 1981 s.51(6)

In any proceedings in—
the Civil Division of the Court of Appeal;
the High Court; and
any county court.
the court may (i) disallow; or (b) order the legal or other representative concerned to meet the whole of any wasted costs or such part of them as may be determined.

Personal liability of legal representatives for costs

Pt 46 r.46.8

(1) This rule applies where the court is considering whether to make an order under s.51(6) of the Supreme Court Act (court's power to disallow or (as the case may be) order a **legal representative** to meet 'wasted costs').

(2) The court will give the legal representative a reasonable opportunity to make written submissions or, if the legal representative prefers, to attend a hearing before it makes such an order.

(3) When the court makes a wasted costs order, it will—
(a) specify the amount to be disallowed or paid; or
(b) direct a costs judge or a district judge to decide the amount of costs to be disallowed or paid.

(4) The court may direct that notice must be given to the legal representative's client, in such manner as the court may direct—
   (a) of any proceedings under this rule; or
   (b) of any order made under it against his legal representative.

PD 46 para.5.2

Such orders can be made at any stage in the proceedings up to and including the proceedings relating to the **detailed assessment** of costs. In general, applications for wasted costs are best left until after the end of the trial.

PD 46 para.5.3

The court may make a wasted costs order against a legal representative on its own initiative.

PD 46 para.5.4

A party may apply for a wasted costs order—
   (a) by filing an application notice in accordance with Pt 23; or
   (b) by making an application orally in the course of any hearing.

PD 46 para.5.5

It is appropriate for the court to make a wasted costs order against a legal representative, only if—
   (1) the legal representative has acted improperly, unreasonably or negligently;
   (2) the legal representative's conduct has caused a party to incur unnecessary costs, or has meant that costs incurred by a party prior to the improper, unreasonable or negligent act or omission have been wasted; and
   (3) it is just in all the circumstances to order the legal representative to compensate that party for the whole or part of those costs.

PD 46 para.5.6

The court will give directions about the procedure that will be followed in each case in order to ensure that the issues are dealt with in a way which is fair and as simple and summary as the circumstances permit.

PD 46 para.5.7

As a general rule the court will consider whether to make a wasted costs order in two stages—
   (a) in the first stage, the court must be satisfied—
      (i) that it has before it evidence or other material which, if unanswered, would be likely to lead to a wasted costs order being made; and
      (ii) the wasted costs proceedings are justified notwithstanding the likely costs involved.
   (b) at the second stage (even if the court is satisfied under para.(1)) the court will consider, after giving the legal representative an opportunity to make a wasted costs order in accordance with para.5.5 above.

PD 46 para.5.8

The court may proceed to the second stage described in para.5.7 without first adjourning the hearing if it is satisfied that the legal representative has already had a reasonable opportunity to make representations.

PD 46 para.5.9

On an application for a wasted costs order under Pt 23 the application notice and any evidence in support must identify—
  (1) what the legal representative is alleged to have done or failed to do; and
  (2) the costs that the legal representative may be ordered to pay or which are sought against the legal representative.

Solicitor's duty to notify client

Pt 44 r.44.8

Where—
  (a) the court makes a costs order against a legally represented party; and
  (b) the party is not present when the order is made,
the party's solicitor must notify his client in writing of the costs order no later than seven days after the solicitor receives notice of the order.

WEBSITES

Citizens Advice website at *http://www.citizensadvice.org.uk* (Accessed November 20, 2012)
Community Legal Advice (formerly Community Legal Services Direct) website at *http://www.legalservices.gov.uk/civil.asp*
Court of Appeal, Civil Division website at *http://www.justice.gov.uk/courts/rcj-rolls-building/court-of-appeal/civil-division*
Her Majesty's Courts and Tribunals website at *http://www.hmcourts-service.com/*
Legal Services Commission website at *http://www.legalservices.gov.uk/*
National Debtline website at *http://www.nationaldebtline.co.uk/*

WELSH LANGUAGE

PD relating to the use of the Welsh Language, para.1.1

This PD applies to civil proceedings in courts in Wales.

PD WL para.1.2

The existing practice of conducting a hearing entirely in the Welsh language on an ad hoc basis and without notice will continue to apply when all parties and witnesses directly involved at the time consent to the proceedings being so conducted.

PD WL para.1.3

In every case in which it is possible that the Welsh language may be used by any party or witness [or in any document which may be placed before the court], the parties or their legal representatives must inform the court of that fact so that appropriate arrangements can be made for the management and listing of the case.

PD WL para.1.4

If costs are incurred as a result of a party failing to comply with this direction, a costs order may be made against him or his legal representative.

PD WL para.1.5

Where a case is tried with a jury, the law does not permit the selection of jurors in a manner which enables the court to discover whether a juror does or does not speak Welsh or to secure a jury whose members are bilingual to try a case in which the Welsh language may be used.

Allocation questionnaire

PD WL para.2.1

In any proceedings in which a party is required to complete an allocation questionnaire, he must include details relating to the possible use of Welsh i.e. details of any person wishing to give oral evidence in Welsh and of any documents in Welsh (e.g. documents to be disclosed under Pt 31 or witness statements) which that party expects to use.

PD WL para.2.2

A party must include the details mentioned in para.(2.1) in the allocation questionnaire even if he has already informed the court of the possible use of Welsh in accordance with the provisions of s.1 above.

Case management

PD WL para.3.1

At any interlocutory hearing, the court will take the opportunity to consider whether it should give case management directions. To assist the court, a party or his legal representative should draw the court's attention to the possibility of Welsh being used in the proceedings, even where he has already done so in compliance with other provisions of this direction.

PD WL para.3.2

In any case where a party is required to complete a pre-trial check list (listing questionnaire) and has already intimated the intention to use Welsh, he should confirm the intended use of Welsh in the pre-trial check list and provide any details which have not been set out in the allocation questionnaire.

Listing by the court

PD WL para.4.1

The diary manager, in consultation with the Designated Civil Judge, will ensure that a case in which the Welsh language is to be used is listed:
  (a) wherever practicable before a Welsh speaking judge; and
  (b) where translation facilities are needed, at a court with simultaneous translation facilities.

Witnesses and jurors

PD WL para.6.1

When each witness is called, the court officer administering the oath or affirmation will inform the witness that he or she may be sworn or may affirm in Welsh or English as he or she wishes.

PD WL para.6.2

Where a case is tried with a jury, the court officer swearing in the jury will inform the jurors in open court that each juror may take the oath or may affirm in Welsh or English as he or she wishes.

Role of the liaison judge

PD WL para.7.1

If any question or difficulty arises concerning the implementation of this PD, contact should in the first place be made with the Liaison Judge for the Welsh language.

See **Interpreters**.

WILLS

Lodging the grant

PD 57 para.10.1

The claimant is the person to whom the grant was made in respect of the will of which rectification is sought, he must, unless the court orders otherwise, lodge the probate or letters of administration with the Will annexed with the court when the claim form is issued.

PD 57 para.10.2

Unless the court orders otherwise, lodge it in the relevant office within 14 days after the service of the claim form on him.

Orders

PD 57 para.11

A copy of every order made for the rectification of a Will shall be sent to the Principal Registry of the Family Division for filing, and a memorandum of the order shall be endorsed on, or permanently annexed to, the grant under which the estate is administered.

See **Probate claim**.

WINDING UP PROCEEDINGS

Applications in insolvency relating to companies (and to insolvent partnerships) are governed by the Insolvency Rules 1986 (as amended), Insolvency Rules 1986 and PD Insolvency Proceedings.

Central registry of winding up petitions

Chancery Guide para.20.19

When a winding up petition is presented to either the Companies Court, a Chancery District Registry or a county court having jurisdiction, particulars including the name of the company and the petitioner's solicitors are entered in a computerised register. This is called the "Central Registry of Winding Up Petitions". It may be searched by personal attendance at the Companies Court general office, or by tel: 020 7947 7328.

See also **Company insolvency** and **Warrant of execution**.

Applications

PD IP para.12.

(1) In accordance with r.13.2(2), in the Royal Courts of Justice the member of court staff in charge of the winding up list has been authorised to deal with applications—
   (i) to extend or abridge time prescribed by the Insolvency Rules in connection with winding up (r.4.3);
   (ii) for permission to withdraw a winding up petition (r.4.15);
   (iii) for the substitution of a petitioner (r.4.19);
   (iv) by the Official Receiver for limited disclosure of a statement of affairs (r.4.35);
   (v) by the Official Receiver for relief from duties imposed upon him by the Insolvency Rules (r.4.47);
   (vi) by the Official Receiver for permission to give notice of a meeting by advertisement only (r.4.59);
   (vii) to transfer proceedings from the High Court (Royal Courts of Justice) to a county court after the making of a winding-up order (r.7.11).

PD IP para.12.2

In District Registries or a county court such applications must be made to a District Judge.

WITHOUT PREJUDICE

Glossary

Negotiations with a view to a settlement are usually conducted "without prejudice", which means that the circumstances in which the content of those negotiations may be revealed to the court are very restricted.

WITNESS

Disability

Pt 30 r.30.3

> (2) The matters to which the court must have regard [when considering whether to make an order transferring a claim from one court to another] include—
>> (f) the facilities available to the court at which the claim is being dealt with, particularly in relation to —
>>> (i) any disabilities of a party or potential witness.

See **Hearsay evidence**, **Welsh language**, **Witness evidence**, **Witness statement**, and **Witness summons**.

WITNESS EVIDENCE

Pt 32 r.32.2

> (1) The general rule is that any fact which needs to be proved by the evidence of witnesses is to be proved—
>> (a) at trial, by their oral evidence given in public; and
>> (b) at any other hearing, by their evidence in writing.
> (2) This is subject—
>> (a) to any provision to the contrary contained in these rules or elsewhere; or
>> (b) to any order of the court.
> (3) The court may give directions—
>> (a) identifying or limiting the issues to which factual evidence may be directed;
>> (b) identifying the witnesses who may be called or whose evidence may be read; or
>> (c) limiting the length or format of witness statements.

See **Evidence**.

WITNESS STATEMENT

Pt 32 r.32.4

> (1) A witness statement is a written statement signed by a person which contains the evidence which that person would be allowed to give orally.
> (2) The court will order a party to serve on the other parties any witness statement of the oral evidence which the party serving the statement intends to rely on in relation to any issues of fact to be decided at the trial.

(3) The court may give directions as to—
  (a) the order in which witness statements are to be served; and
  (b) whether or not the witness statements are to be filed.

Use at trial of witness statements which have been served

Pt 32 r.32.5

(1) If—
  (a) a party has served a witness statement; and
  (b) he wishes to rely at trial on the evidence of the witness who made the statement,
  he must call the witness to give oral evidence unless the court Orders otherwise or he puts the statement in as hearsay evidence.
(Part 33 contains provisions about hearsay evidence).
  (2) Where a witness is called to give oral evidence under para.(1), his witness statement shall stand as his evidence in chief unless the court orders otherwise.
  (3) A witness giving oral evidence at trial may with the permission of the court—
  (a) amplify his witness statement; and
  (b) give evidence in relation to new matters which have arisen since the witness statement was served on the other parties.
  (4) The court will give permission under para.(3) only if it considers that there is good reason not to confine the evidence of the witness to the contents of his witness statement.
  (5) If a party who has served a witness statement does not—
  (a) call the witness to give evidence at trial; or
  (b) put the witness statement in as hearsay evidence, any other party may put the witness statement in as hearsay evidence.

Consequence of failure to serve witness statement or summary

Pt 32 r.32.10

If a witness statement or a witness summary for use at trial is not served in respect of an intended witness within the time specified by the court, then the witness may not be called to give oral evidence unless the court gives permission.

Cross-examination on a witness statement

Pt 32 r.32.11

Where a witness is called to give evidence at trial, he may be cross-examined on his witness statement whether or not the statement or any part of it was referred to during the witness's evidence in chief.

Use of witness statements for other purposes

Pt 32 r.32.12

(1) Except as provided by this rule, a witness statement may be used only for the purpose of the proceedings in which it is served.

(2) Paragraph (1) does not apply if and to the extent that—
    (a) the witness gives consent in writing to some other use of it;
    (b) the court gives permission for some other use; or
    (c) the witness statement has been put in evidence at a hearing held in public.

Availability of witness statements for inspection

Pt 32 r.32.13

(1) A witness statement which stands as evidence in chief is open to inspection during the course of the trial unless the court otherwise directs.
(2) Any person may ask for a direction that a witness statement is not open to inspection.
(3) The court will not make a direction under para.(2) unless it is satisfied that a witness statement should not be open to inspection because of—
    (a) the interests of justice;
    (b) the public interest;
    (c) the nature of any expert medical evidence in the statement;
    (d) the nature of any confidential information (including information relating to personal financial matters) in the statement; or
    (e) the need to protect the interests of any child or protected party.
(4) The court may exclude from inspection words or passages in the statement.

Heading of witness statement

PD 32 para.17.1

The witness statement should be headed with the title of the proceedings (see para.4 of PD 7A and para.7 of PD 20); where the proceedings are between several parties with the same status it is sufficient to identify the parties as follows:

    Number:

A.B. (and others)	Claimants/Applicants
C.D. (and others)	Defendants/Respondents
(as appropriate)	

PD 32 para.17.2

At the top right hand corner of the first page there should be clearly written:
    (1) the party on whose behalf it is made,
    (2) the initials and surname of the witness,
    (3) the number of the statement in relation to that witness,
    (4) the identifying initials and number of each exhibit referred to, and
    (5) the date the statement was made.

Body of witness statement

PD 32 para.18.1

The witness statement must, if practicable, be in the intended witness's own words, the statement should be expressed in the first person and should also state:
    (1) the full name of the witness,

(2) his place of residence or, if he is making the statement in his professional, business or other occupational capacity, the address at which he works, the position he holds and the name of his firm or employer,

(3) his occupation, or if he has none, his description, and

(4) the fact that he is a party to the proceedings or is the employee of such a party if it be the case.

PD 32 para.18.2

A witness statement must indicate:

(1) which of the statements in it are made from the witness's own knowledge and which are matters of information or belief, and

(2) the source for any matters of information or belief.

PD 32 para.18.3

An exhibit used in conjunction with a witness statement should be verified and identified by the witness and remain separate from the witness statement.

PD 32 para.18.4

Where a witness refers to an exhibit or exhibits, he should state "I refer to the (description of exhibit) marked ' . . . ' ".

PD 32 para.18.5

The provisions of paras 11.3 to 15.4 (exhibits) apply similarly to witness statements as they do to affidavits.

PD 32 para.18.6

Where a witness makes more than one witness statement to which there are exhibits, in the same proceedings, the numbering of the exhibits should run consecutively throughout and not start again with each witness statement.

Format of witness statement

PD 32 para.19.1

A witness statement should:

(1) be produced on durable quality A4 paper with a 3.5cm margin,

(2) be fully legible and should normally be typed on one side of the paper only,

(3) where possible, be bound securely in a manner which would not hamper filing, or otherwise each page should be endorsed with the case number and should bear the initials of the witness,

(4) have the pages numbered consecutively as a separate statement (or as one of several statements contained in a file),

(5) be divided into numbered paragraphs,

(6) have all numbers, including dates, expressed in figures, and

(7) give the reference to any document or documents mentioned either in the margin or in bold text in the body of the statement.

PD 32 para.19.2

It is usually convenient for a witness statement to follow the chronological sequence of the events or matters dealt with, each paragraph of a witness statement should as far as possible be confined to a distinct portion of the subject.

Statement of truth

PD 32 para.20.1

A witness statement is the equivalent of the oral evidence which that witness would, if called, give in evidence; it must include a statement by the intended witness that he believes the facts in it are true.

PD 32 para.20.2

To verify a witness statement the statement of truth is as follows:

"I believe that the facts stated in this witness statement are true".

PD 32 para.20.3

Attention is drawn to r.32.14 which sets out the consequences of verifying a witness statement containing a false statement without an honest belief in its truth.
(Paragraph 3A of PD 22 sets out the procedure to be followed where the person who should sign a document which is verified by a statement of truth is unable to read or sign the document).

Failure to verify a witness statement

Pt 22 r.22.3

If the maker of a witness statement fails to verify the witness statement by a statement of truth the court may direct that it shall not be admissible as evidence.

Alterations to witness statements

PD 32 para.22.1

Any alteration to a witness statement must be initialled by the person making the statement or by the authorised person where appropriate (see para.21).

PD 32 para.22.2

A witness statement which contains an alteration that has not been initialled may be used in evidence only with the permission of the court.

Filing of witness statements

PD 32 para.23.1

If the court directs that a witness statement is to be filed, it must be filed in the court or Division, or Office or Registry of the court or Division where the action in which it was or is to be used, is proceeding or will proceed.

PD 32 para.23.2

Where the court has directed that a witness statement in a foreign language is to be filed:
  (1) the party wishing to rely on it must—
    (a) have it translated, and
    (b) file the foreign language witness statement with the court, and
  (2) the translator must make and file with the court an affidavit verifying the translation and exhibiting both the translation and a copy of the foreign language witness statement.

Certificate of court officer

PD 32 para.24.1

Where the court has ordered that a witness statement is not to be open to inspection by the public or that words or passages in the statement are not to be open to the court officer will so certify on the statement and make any deletions directed by the court under r.32.13(4).

Defects

PD 32 para.25.1

Where:
  (2) a **witness statement,** or
  (3) an **exhibit** to either an affidavit or a witness statement,
does not comply with Pt 32 or this PD in relation to its form, the court may refuse to admit it as evidence and may refuse to allow the costs arising from its preparation.

PD 32 para.25.2

Permission to file a defective affidavit or witness statement or to use a defective exhibit may be obtained from a judge in the court where the case is proceeding.

Small claims track

PD 27 para.2.5

In deciding whether to make an order for exchange of witness statements the court will have regard to the following—
  (a) whether either or both the parties are represented;
  (b) the amount in dispute in the proceedings;

   (c) the nature of the matters in dispute;

   (d) whether the need for any party to clarify his case can better be dealt with by an order under para.2.3;

   (e) the need for the parties to have access to justice without undue formality, cost or delay.

See also **False statement** and **Witness statement.**

WITNESS SUMMARY

Pt 32 r.32.9

(1) A party who—
   (a) is required to serve a witness statement for use at trial; but
   (b) is unable to obtain one, may apply, without notice, for permission to serve a witness summary instead.

(2) A witness summary is a summary of—
   (a) the evidence, if known, which would otherwise be included in a witness statement; or
   (b) if the evidence is not known, the matters about which the party serving the witness summary proposes to question the witness.

(3) Unless the court Orders otherwise, a witness summary must include the name and address of the intended witness.

(4) Unless the court Orders otherwise, a witness summary must be served within the period in which a witness statement would have had to be served.

(5) Where a party serves a witness summary, so far as practicable rr.32.4 (requirement to serve witness statements for use at trial), 32.5(3) (amplifying witness statements), and 32.8 (form of witness statement) shall apply to the summary.

See also **False statement** and **Witness statement.**

WITNESS SUMMONS

Court

Pt 34 r.34.2

(1) A witness summons is a document issued by the court requiring a witness to—
   (a) attend court to give evidence; or
   (b) produce documents to the court.

(2) A witness summons must be in the relevant practice form.

(3) There must be a separate witness summons for each witness.

(4) A witness summons may require a witness to produce documents to the court either—
   (a) on the date fixed for a hearing; or
   (b) on such date as the court may direct.

(5) The only documents that a summons under this rule can require a person to produce before a hearing are documents which that person could be required to produce at the hearing.

Issue of a witness summons

Pt 34 r.34.3

(1) A witness summons is issued on the date entered on the summons by the court.
(2) A party must obtain permission from the court where he wishes to—
    (a) have a summons issued less than seven days before the date of the trial;
    (b) have a summons issued for a witness to attend court to give evidence or to produce documents on any date except the date fixed for the trial; or
    (c) have a summons issued for a witness to attend court to give evidence or to produce documents at any hearing except the trial.
(3) A witness summons must be issued by—
    (a) the court where the case is proceeding; or
    (b) the court where the hearing in question will be held.
(4) The court may set aside or vary a witness summons issued under this rule.

PD 34A para.1.1

A witness summons may require a witness to:
    (1) attend court to give evidence,
    (2) produce documents to the court, or
    (3) both,
on either a date fixed for the hearing or such date as the court may direct.

PD 34A para 1.2

Two copies of the witness summons should be filed with the court for sealing, one of which will be retained on the court file.

PD 34A para.1.3

A mistake in the name or address of a person named in a witness summons may be corrected if the summons has not been served.

PD 34A para.1.4

The corrected summons must be re-sealed by the court and marked 'amended and re-sealed'.

Witness summons in aid of inferior court or of tribunal

Pt 34 r.34.4

(1) The court may issue a witness summons in aid of an inferior court or of a tribunal.
(2) The court which issued the witness summons under this rule may set it aside.
(3) In this rule, 'inferior court or tribunal' means any court or tribunal that does not have power to issue a witness summons in relation to proceedings before it.

Time for serving a witness summons

Pt 34 r.34.5

(1) The general rule is that a witness summons is binding if it is served at least seven days before the date on which the witness is required to attend before the court or tribunal.

(2) The court may direct that a witness summons shall be binding although it will be served less than seven days before the date on which the witness is required to attend before the court or tribunal.

(3) A witness summons which is—

(a) served in accordance with this rule; and

(b) requires the witness to attend court to give evidence,

is binding until the conclusion of the hearing at which the attendance of the witness is required.

Who is to serve a witness summons

Pt 34 r.34.6

(1) A witness summons is to be served by the court unless the party on whose behalf it is issued indicates in writing, when he asks the court to issue the summons, that he wishes to serve it himself.

(2) Where the court is to serve the witness summons, the party on whose behalf it is issued must deposit, in the court office, the money to be paid or offered to the witness under r.34.7.

Travelling expenses and compensation for loss of time

Pt 34 r.34.7

At the time of service of a witness summons the witness must be offered or paid—

(a) a sum reasonably sufficient to cover his expenses in travelling to and from the court; and

(b) such sum by way of compensation for loss of time as may be specified in PD 34A.

PD 34A para.3.1

When a witness is served with a witness summons he must be offered a sum to cover his travelling expenses to and from the court and compensation for his loss of time.

PD 34A para.3.2

If the witness summons is to be served by the court, the party issuing the summons must deposit with the court:

(1) a sum sufficient to pay for the witness's expenses in travelling to the court and in returning to his home or place of work, and

(2) a sum in respect of the period during which earnings or benefit are lost, or such lesser sum as it may be proved that the witness will lose as a result of his attendance at court in answer to the witness summons.

PD 34A para.3.3

The sum referred to in 3.2(2) is to be based on the sums payable to witnesses attending the Crown Court.

PD 34A para.3.4

Where the party issuing the witness summons wishes to serve it himself, he must:
(1) notify the court in writing that he wishes to do so, and
(2) at the time of service offer the witness the sums mentioned in para. 3.2 above

Arbitration

Securing the attendance of witnesses

PD 62 para.7.1

A party to arbitral proceedings being conducted in England or Wales who wishes to rely on s.43 of the 1996 Act to secure the attendance of a witness must apply for a witness summons in accordance with Pt 34.

PD 62 para.7.2

If the attendance of the witness is required within the district of a district registry, the application may be made at that registry.

PD 62 para.7.3

A witness summons will not be issued until the applicant files written evidence showing that the application is made with—
(1) the permission of the tribunal; or
(2) the agreement of the other parties.

Court or tribunal who cannot issue a witness summons

PD 34A para.2.1

A witness summons may be issued in the High Court or a county court in aid of a court or tribunal which does not have the power to issue a witness summons in relation to the proceedings before it.

PD 34A para.2.2

A witness summons referred to in para.2.1 may be set aside by the court which issued it.

PD 34A para.2.3

An application to set aside a witness summons referred to in para.2.1 will be heard:
(1) in the High Court by a Master at the Royal Courts of Justice or by a district judge in a District Registry, and
(2) in a county court by a district judge.

PD 34A para.2.4

Unless the court otherwise directs, the applicant must give at least 2 days' notice to the party who issued the witness summons of the application, which will normally be dealt with at a hearing.

WRIT

See **Claim form**.

WRIT OF EXECUTION

RSC Ord.46 r.1

In this order, unless the context otherwise requires, 'writ of execution' includes a writ of fieri facias, a writ of possession, a writ of delivery, a writ of sequestration and any further writ in aid of any of the aforementioned writs.

When permission to issue any writ of execution is necessary

RSC Ord.46, r.2

(1) A writ of execution to enforce a judgment or order may not issue without the permission of the court in the following cases, that is to say—
   (a) where six years ormore have elapsed since the date of the judgment or order;
   (b) where any change has taken place, whether by death or otherwise, in the parties entitled or liable to execution under the judgment or order;
   (c) where the judgment or order is against the assets of a deceased person coming to the hands of his executors or administrators after the date of the judgment or order, and it is sought to issue execution against such assets;
   (d) where under the judgment or order any person is entitled to a remedy subject to the fulfilment of any condition which it is alleged has been fulfilled;
   (e) where any goods sought to be seized under a writ of execution are in the hands of a receiver appointed by the court or a sequestrator.
(2) Paragraph (1) is without prejudice to s.2 of the Reserve and Auxiliary Forces (Protection of Civil Interests) Act 1951, or any other enactment or rule by virtue of which a person is required to obtain the permission of the court for the issue of a writ of execution or to proceed to execution on or otherwise to the enforcement of a judgment or order.
(3) Where the court grants permission, whether under this rule or otherwise, for the issue of a writ of execution and the writ is not issued within one year after the date of the order granting such permission, the order shall cease to have effect, without prejudice, however, to the making of a fresh order.

Permission required for issue of writ in aid of other writ

RSC Ord.46 r. 3

A writ of execution in aid of any other writ of execution shall not issue without the permission of the court.

Application for permission to issue writ

RSC Ord.46 r.4

(1) An application for permission to issue a writ of execution may be made in accordance with CPR Pt 23 but the application notice need not be served on the respondent unless the court directs.

(2) Such an application must be supported by a witness statement or affidavit—

    (a) identifying the judgment or order to which the application relates and, if the judgment or order is for the payment of money, stating the amount originally due thereunder and the amount due thereunder at the date the application notice is filed;

    (b) stating, where the case falls within r.2(1)(a), the reasons for the delay in enforcing the judgment or order;

    (c) stating, where the case falls within r.2(1)(b), the change which has taken place in the parties entitled or liable to execution since the date of the judgment or order;

    (d) stating, where the case falls within r.2(1)(c) or (d), that a demand to satisfy the judgment or order was made on the person liable to satisfy it and that he has refused or failed to do so;

    (e) giving such other information as is necessary to satisfy the court that the applicant is entitled to proceed to execution on the judgment or order in question and that the person against whom it is sought to issue execution is liable to execution on it.

(3) The court hearing such application may grant permission in accordance with the application or may order that any issue or question, a decision on which is necessary to determine the rights of the parties, be tried in any manner in which any question of fact or law arising in proceedings may be tried and, in either case, may impose such terms as to costs or otherwise as it thinks just.

Issue of writ of execution

RSC Ord.46 r.6

(1) Issue of a writ of execution takes place on its being sealed by a court officer of the appropriate office.

(2) Before such a writ is issued, a praecipe for its issue must be filed.

(3) The praecipe must be signed by or on behalf of the solicitor of the person entitled to execution or, if that person is acting in person, by him.

(4) No such writ shall be sealed unless at the time of the tender thereof for sealing—

    (a) the person tendering it produces—

        (i) the judgment or order on which the writ is to issue, or an office copy thereof;

        (ii) where the writ may not issue without the permission of the court, the order granting such permission or evidence of the granting of it;

        (iii) where judgment on failure to acknowledge service has been entered against a State, as defined in s.14 of the State Immunity Act 1978, evidence that the State has been served in accordance with CPR r.40.10 and that the judgment has taken effect; and

    (b) the court officer authorised to seal it is satisfied that the period, if any, specified in the judgment or order for the payment of any money or the doing of any other act thereunder has expired.

(5) Every writ of execution shall bear the date of the day on which it is issued.

(6) In this rule 'the appropriate office' means—

    (a) where the proceedings in which execution is to issue are in a District Registry, that Registry;

    (b) where the proceedings are in the Principal Registry of the Family Division, that Registry;

   (c) where the proceedings are Admiralty proceedings or commercial proceedings which are not in a District Registry, the Admiralty and Commercial Registry;

  (ca) where the proceedings are in the Chancery Division, Chancery Chambers;

   (d) in any other case, the Central Office of the Senior Courts.

Duration and renewal of writ of execution

RSC Ord.46 r.8

(1) For the purpose of execution, a writ of execution is valid in the first instance for 12 months beginning with the date of its issue.

(2) Where a writ has not been wholly executed the court may by order extend the validity of the writ from time to time for a period of 12 months at any one time beginning with the day on which the order is made, if an application for extension is made to the court before the day next following that on which the writ would otherwise expire or such later day, if any, as the court may allow.

(3) Before a writ the validity of which had been extended under para.(2) is executed either the writ must be sealed with the seal of the office out of which it was issued showing the date on which the order extending its validity was made or the applicant for the order must serve a notice (in Form No.71 in PD 4) sealed as aforesaid, on the sheriff to whom the writ is directed or the relevant enforcement officer informing him of the making of the order and the date thereof.

(4) The priority of a writ, the validity of which has been extended under this rule, shall be determined by reference to the date on which it was originally delivered to the sheriff or relevant enforcement officer.

(5) The production of a writ of execution, or of such a notice as is mentioned in para.(3) purporting in either case to be sealed as mentioned in that paragraph, shall be evidence that the validity of that writ, or, as the case may be, of the writ referred to in that notice, has been extended under para.(2).

(6) If, during the validity of a writ of execution, an interpleader summons is issued in relation to an execution under that writ, the validity of the writ shall be extended until the expiry of 12 months from the conclusion of the interpleader proceedings.

Return to writ of execution

RSC Ord.46 r.9

(1) Any party at whose instance or against whom a writ of execution was issued may serve a notice on the sheriff to whom the writ was directed or the relevant enforcement officer requiring him, within such time as may be specified in the notice, to indorse on the writ a statement of the manner in which he has executed it and to send to that party a copy of the statement.

(2) If a sheriff or enforcement officer on whom such a notice is served fails to comply with it the party by whom it was served may apply to the court for an order directing the sheriff or enforcement officer to comply with the notice.

Levying execution on certain days

PD RSC Ord.46 para.1.1

Unless the court orders otherwise, a writ of execution or a warrant of execution to enforce a judgment or order must not be executed on a Sunday, Good Friday or Christmas Day.

PD RSC Ord.46 para.1.2

Paragraph 1.1 does not apply to an Admiralty **claim in rem**.

See **Warrant of execution** and **Writ of sequestration**.

WRIT OF FI FA

Form of writ

RSC Ord.45 r.12

(1) A writ of fieri facias must be in such of the Forms Nos 53 to 63 in PD 4 as is appropriate in the particular case. (3) A writ of possession must be in Form No.66 or 66A in PD 4, whichever is appropriate.

Power to stay execution by writ of fieri facias

RSC Ord.47 r.1

(1) Where a judgment is given or an order made for the payment by any person of money, and the court is satisfied, on an application made at the time of the judgment or order, or at any time thereafter, by the judgment debtor or other party liable to execution—
   (a) that there are special circumstances which render it inexpedient to enforce the judgment or order; or
   (b) that the applicant is unable from any cause to pay the money,
   then, notwithstanding anything in rr.2 or 3, the court may by order stay the execution of the judgment or order by writ of fieri facias either absolutely or for such period and subject to such conditions as the court thinks fit.
(2) An application under this rule, if not made at the time the judgment is given or order made, must be made in accordance with CPR Pt 23 and may be so made notwithstanding that the party liable to execution did not acknowledge service of the claim form or serve a defence or take any previous part in the proceedings.
(3) The grounds on which an application under this rule is made must be set out in the application notice and be supported by a witness statement or affidavit made by or on behalf of the applicant substantiating the said grounds and, in particular, where such application is made on the grounds of the applicant's inability to pay, disclosing his income, the nature and value of any property of his and the amount of any other liabilities of his.
(4) The application notice and a copy of the supporting witness statement or affidavit must, not less than four clear days before the hearing, be served on the party entitled to enforce the judgment or order.
(5) An order staying execution under this rule may be varied or revoked by a subsequent order.

Separate writs to enforce payment of costs, etc.

RSC Ord.47 r.3

(1) Where only the payment of money, together with costs to be assessed in accordance with CPR Pt 47 (detailed costs assessment), is adjudged or ordered, then, if when the money

becomes payable under the judgment or order the costs have not been assessed, the party entitled to enforce that judgment or order may issue a writ of fieri facias to enforce payment of the sum (other than for costs) adjudged or ordered and, not less than 8 days after the issue of that writ, he may issue a second writ to enforce payment of the assessed costs.

(2) A party entitled to enforce a judgment or order for the delivery of possession of any property (other than money) may, if he so elects, issue a separate writ of fieri facias to enforce payment of any damages or costs awarded to him by that judgment or order.

No expenses of execution in certain cases

RSC Ord.47 r.4

Where a judgment or order is for less than £600 and does not entitle the claimant to costs against the person against whom the writ of fieri facias to enforce the judgment or order is issued, the writ may not authorise the sheriff or enforcement officer to whom it is directed to levy any fees, poundage or other costs of execution.

Writ of fieri facias de bonis ecclesiasticis, etc.

RSC Ord.47 r.5

(1) Where it appears upon the return of any writ of fieri facias that the person against whom the writ was issued has no goods or chattels in the county of the sheriffs to whom the writ was directed or the district of the relevant enforcement officer but that he is the incumbent of a benefice named in the return, then, after the writ and return have been filed, the party by whom the writ of fieri facias was issued may issue a writ of fieri facias de bonis ecclesiasticis or a writ of sequestrari de bonis ecclesiasticis directed to the bishop of the diocese within which that benefice is.

(2) Any such writ must be delivered to the bishop to be executed by him.

(3) Only such fees for the execution of any such writ shall be taken by or allowed to the bishop or any diocesan officer as are for the time being authorised by or under any enactment, including any measure of the General Synod.

Order for sale otherwise than by auction

RSC Ord.47 r.6

(1) An order of the court under para.10 of Sch.7 to the Courts Act 2003 that a sale of goods seized under an execution may be made otherwise than by public auction may be made on the application of—

(a) the person at whose instance the writ of execution under which the sale is to be made was issued;

(b) the person against whom that writ was issued (in this rule referred to as 'the judgment debtor');

(c) if the writ was directed to a sheriff, that sheriff; and

(d) if the writ was directed to one or more enforcement officers, the relevant enforcement officer.

(2) Such an application must be made in accordance with CPR Pt 23 and the application notice must contain a short statement of the grounds of the application.

   (3) Where the applicant for an order under this rule is not the sheriff or enforcement officer, the sheriff or enforcement officer must, on the demand of the applicant, send to the applicant a list stating—

     (a) whether he has notice of the issue of another writ or writs of execution against the goods of the judgment debtor; and

     (b) so far as is known to him, the name and address of every creditor who has obtained the issue of another such writ of execution,

   and where the sheriff or enforcement officer is the applicant, he must prepare such a list.

   (4) Not less than four clear days before the hearing the applicant must serve the application notice on each of the other persons by whom the application might have been made and on every person named in the list under para.(3).

   (5) Service of the application notice on a person named in the list under para.(3) is notice to him for the purpose of para.10(3) of Sch.7 to the Courts Act 2003.

(Paragraph 10(3) provides that if the person who seized the goods has notice of another execution or other executions, the court must not consider an application for leave to sell privately until the notice prescribed by Civil Procedure Rules has been given to the other execution creditor or creditors)

   (6) The applicant must produce the list under para.(3) to the court on the hearing of the application.

   (7) Every person on whom the application notice was served may attend and be heard on the hearing of the application.

Notice of seizure

RSC Ord.45 r.2

When first executing a writ of fieri facias, the Sheriff or his officer or the relevant enforcement officer shall deliver to the debtor or leave at each place where execution is levied a notice in Form No.55 in PD 4 informing the debtor of the execution.

Matters occurring after judgment: stay of execution, etc.

RSC Ord.45 r.11

Without prejudice to Ord.47 r.1, a party against whom a judgment has been given or an order made may apply to the court for a stay of execution of the judgment or order or other relief on the ground of matters which have occurred since the date of the judgment or order, and the court may by order grant such relief, and on such terms, as it thinks just.

WRIT OF FIERI FACIAS

See **Writ of fi fa**.

WRIT OF POSSESSION

Form of writ

RSC Ord.45 r.12

   (3) A writ of possession must be in Form No.66 or 66A in PD 4, whichever is appropriate.

Mirjam Sprau
Kolyma nach dem GULAG

Mirjam Sprau

Kolyma nach dem GULAG

—

Entstalinisierung im Magadaner Gebiet 1953–1960

DE GRUYTER
OLDENBOURG

Das vorliegende Buch ist eine überarbeitete Fassung meiner Dissertationsschrift. Die Promotion erfolgte an der Universität Bremen, das Prüfungskolloquium fand am 24.11.2015 statt. Gutachter waren Prof. Dr. Wolfgang Eichwede und Prof. Dr. Susanne Schattenberg. Eine Übersicht über die Änderungen von der eingereichten zur veröffentlichten Fassung kann in der Geschäftsstelle des Promotionsausschusses der Universität Bremen eingesehen werden.

ISBN 978-3-11-055555-4
e-ISBN (PDF) 978-3-11-055787-9
e-ISBN (EPUB) 978-3-11-055572-1

Library of Congress Cataloging-in-Publication Data
A CIP catalog record for this book has been applied for at the Library of Congress.

Bibliografische Information der Deutschen Nationalbibliothek
Die Deutsche Nationalbibliothek verzeichnet diese Publikation in der Deutschen Nationalbibliografie; detaillierte bibliografische Daten sind im Internet über http://dnb.dnb.de abrufbar.

© 2018 Walter de Gruyter GmbH, Berlin/Boston
Umschlagabbildung: Magadanskaja Pravda, 1. Januar 1959
Druck und Bindung: CPI books GmbH, Leck
♾ Gedruckt auf säurefreiem Papier

Printed in Germany

www.degruyter.com

Vorwort

Die Arbeit an der vorliegenden Dissertation zog sich hin. Sie wurde unterbrochen durch die Geburt dreier Kinder, ein Archivreferendariat und meine Arbeit beim Bundesarchiv. Dass ich das Buch dennoch schreiben konnte und dabei so viel Freude hatte, verdanke ich vielen Menschen und Institutionen.

Wolfgang Eichwede, als Doktorvater, und Galina Ivanova, als meine russische Doktormutter, haben die Arbeit mit großem Interesse begleitet und mich mit lebendigen Diskussionen ermuntert. Ihnen gegenüber empfinde ich Hochachtung und große Dankbarkeit. Durch ein Stipendium der Prof. Dr. Adolf Schmidtmann Stiftung der Universität Marburg konnte ich zur Forschungsreise nach Magadan aufbrechen, ein Promotionsstipendium der Studienstiftung des deutschen Volkes ermöglichte mir die Arbeit an der Dissertation. Viele Menschen der Studienstiftung haben mich begleitet und unterstützt. In Magadan hat mich Anatolij Širokov in seine Familie und den Kreis seiner Doktoranden aufgenommen. Durch ihn konnte ich das Magadaner Leben, Zeitzeugen und eine ganze Reihe lokaler Historiker kennenlernen – der ganzen Familie und dem Freundeskreis möchte ich für ihre große Gastfreundschaft danken. Die Mitarbeiterinnen des Magadaner Staatsarchivs und der lokalen Puschkin-Bibliothek haben meine Arbeit engagiert gefördert. Ihnen gilt, ebenso wie den Mitarbeiterinnen der Moskauer Archive, mein besonderer Dank. Die Zeitung *Magadanskaja Pravda* hat mir mit Publikationsgenehmigungen sehr geholfen. Gabriele Jaroschka und Florian Ruppenstein vom Verlag De Gruyter Oldenbourg danke ich für ihr Interesse und die umsichtige Betreuung. In großer Verbundenheit sende ich einen Dank an das Moskauer Sacharow-Zentrum und seinen ehemaligen Leiter Jurij Samodurov, durch den der Kontakt nach Magadan zustande kam. Pavel Grebenjuk gilt mein herzlicher Dank für den intensiven Gedankenaustausch zwischen Magadan und Frankfurt.

Unzählige Anregungen, Hinweise und Korrekturen verdanke ich einer Reihe von Menschen – Gabriel Superfin, Ulrike Huhn und Nikolay Mitrokhin von der Forschungsstelle Osteuropa an der Universität Bremen, Wolfgang Kissel, Delia González de Reufels, Aleksej Zacharčenko, Klaus Gestwa, Marc Elie, Sören Urbansky, dem Zeitzeugen und Autor Peter Demant † (Vernon Kress), Henrik Halbleib, Gregor Schaab, Christine Tries und Gunnar Wendt. Ralf, Johanna, Maria und David Sprau sei von Herzen gedankt – für Nachsicht und Geduld.

Frankfurt, den 15. Februar 2018   Mirjam Sprau

https://doi.org/10.1515/9783110557879-001

Inhalt

Anhang

1 Einleitung

1.1 Thema und Fragestellung

Die Begriffe „Kolyma" und „Magadan" sind zum Sinnbild stalinistischer Lager geworden. „Magadan" ist die Hauptstadt, „Kolyma" der größte Fluss einer Region im äußersten Nordosten der Sowjetunion / der Russischen Föderation – gelegentlich spricht man vom „Kolymaer Gebiet", fast immer aber von „der Kolyma" als Ortsbezeichnung.[1] Die Kolyma gilt als „Extrempol der Grausamkeit"[2] – durch die klimatischen Extreme des Gebietes, seine naturräumlichen Bedingungen, seine Abgeschiedenheit und die Gewalt des Lagersystems. Im Stalinismus hatte die Region einen machtpolitischen Sonderstatus – sie bestand fast nur aus Lagern, Häftlinge wurden zur Förderung der reichen Rohstoffvorkommen, v. a. des Goldes, gezwungen. Bekannt wurden Kolyma und Magadan durch die Erzählungen des ehemaligen Häftlings Varlam Šalamov und die Erinnerungen von Evgenija Ginzburg an ihre Lagerhaft.[3] Der Tod Stalins und die folgende Entstalinisierung veränderten das Gesicht der Region, seine politische und soziale Struktur, seine Wirtschaftsweise. Durch die Gründung des Magadaner Gebietes (*Magadanskaja oblast'*) am 3. Dezember 1953 wurde der Sonderstatus aufgegeben, in der Folge wurden die Lager schrittweise aufgelöst und die Produktion auf freie Arbeitskräfte umgestellt.

Geographisch betrachtet wird die Region im Norden durch das Nordmeer und im Süden durch das Ochotskische Meer begrenzt; sie reicht im Westen bis an die Region Jakutien und im Osten bis zur Beringstraße, im südöstlichen Teil zählt auch der Norden der Halbinsel Kamtschatka dazu. Bis zur Auflösung der Sowjetunion im Jahr 1991 und der Reorganisation der Verwaltungsgebiete gehörte auch der nationale Kreis Tschukotka (*Čukotskij nacional'nyj okrug*) im äußersten nordöstlichen Zipfel der UdSSR zum Magadaner Gebiet, er ist daher ebenfalls Gegenstand dieser Arbeit. Das Gebiet ist ausgesprochen rohstoffreich, neben Zinn, Wolfram, Kobalt und Uran sind v. a die gewaltigen Goldvorkommen zu nennen. Das Land wird traditionell von verschiedenen, zahlenmäßig kleinen Ethnien bewohnt, den Čukčen, Yupik, Ėvenen u. a., die noch in der sowjetischen Periode fast ausschließlich von Rentierzucht und Fischfang lebten. Das Territorium ist zum größten Teil von Permafrost bedeckt, bei dem die Erde unterhalb von 30 cm dauerhaft gefroren ist; der Winter dauert neun Monate und die durchschnittliche Jahrestemperatur liegt bei 10° C unter Null (im Winter werden Temperaturen von bis zu -60° C gemessen). Ein „sonderbarer Planet –

---

1 Offiziell wird das Gebiet als „Severo-Vostok" bezeichnet, als „Nordosten", gelegentlich aber auch als „Dal'nyj Sever", als „Ferner Norden", in Anlehnung an die Nachbarregion „Ferner Osten". Zu der Verwendung der unterschiedlichen Begriffe „Kolyma" und „Magadan" siehe Gogoleva, Leksemy.
2 So die Herausgeber des Themenheftes „Das Lager schreiben" der Zeitschrift OSTEUROPA in Rekurs auf Varlam Šalamov. Vgl. Sapper/Weichsel/Hutterer, Bollwerk, S. 5.
3 Schalamow, Erzählungen sowie Ginsburg, Marschroute; Ginsburg, Gratwanderung.

https://doi.org/10.1515/9783110557879-002

hier herrscht zwölf Monate Winter, der Rest ist Sommer", so lautete einer der bekanntesten Häftlingssprüche über das Gebiet. Der südliche Teil der Region ist hauptsächlich von Taiga bedeckt, der nördliche und östliche Teil von Tundra. Die Landschaft ist durch steile Gebirgsketten mit über 2.000 Metern Höhe geprägt. Durch die tiefen Täler, die die Gebirgsketten durchschneiden, wehen sehr starke Monsunwinde. Die großen Flüsse, am bekanntesten die Kolyma und die Indigirka mit ihren breiten Strombecken und zahlreichen Nebenflüssen, münden fast alle ins Nordpolarmeer. Im Stalinismus war die Region nur während weniger Sommermonate über das Meer und nur sehr eingeschränkt per Flugzeug erreichbar. Keine Autostraße führte dorthin, was den „Inselcharakter" des Lagersystems im Archipel GULAG noch einmal verstärkte. Die infrastrukturelle Anbindung ist bis heute schwierig, dies reflektiert die Bezeichnung „*materik*", „Kontinent" oder „Festland", die in Magadan noch immer für die zentralen Teile der Russischen Föderation benutzt wird.

Bis zu Stalins Tod im Jahr 1953 war dieses Gebiet durchdrungen von einem der größten stalinistischen Lagerkomplexe. Die Region beherrschte der MVD („Ministerstvo Vnutrennich Del – Ministerium des Innern") bzw. seine Vorgängerorganisation NKVD, der politische Staatsschutz, der zur Bekämpfung „innerer Feinde", ihrer Inhaftierung, Verbannung oder Erschießung und zur Ausbeutung von Häftlingsarbeit in riesigen Zwangsarbeitsprojekten eingesetzt wurde. Die Kolyma unterstand bis Ende des Jahres 1953 einer Hauptverwaltung des MVD, dem Kombinat „Dal'stroj" (Fern-Bau), das die enormen Rohstoffvorkommen, v. a das Gold des Nordostens, ausbeutete. Als Stellvertreter des jeweiligen Chefs des NKVD/MVD herrschte der Leiter von Dal'-stroj in Personalunion über das Lagersystem, den Industriekomplex und zugleich über die gesamte Region.[4] Diese stalinistische Herrschafts- und Wirtschaftsstruktur wird, nach Galina Ivanova, als „Lager-Industrieller Komplex" bezeichnet.[5] Die institutionellen Strukturen der Gewalt erzeugten an den Rändern der Sowjetunion – an der Kolyma, aber auch in den Gebieten von Norilsk und Workuta – machtpolitische Subsysteme, die mit den zivilen Organen der sowjetischen Partei- und Staatsführung in keiner Verbindung standen. Die Lagergebiete waren abgeschnitten von den üblichen Entscheidungsstrukturen, sie unterstanden einem eigenen System der Geheimhaltung, wurden durch eigene Infrastrukturen versorgt und hatten eigene Rechtsstrukturen. So war auch der Einfluss des ZK der KPdSU auf die Situation im Nordosten extrem begrenzt. Dal'stroj unterstand unmittelbar dem Chef des NKVD/MVD, der wiederum nur Stalin gegenüber verpflichtet war. Treffend hat der Historiker David Nordlander Dal'stroj als das „liebste Kind des NKVD"[6] bezeichnet.

Das Gebiet war durchzogen von zahlreichen Lagerabteilungen und Hunderten einzelner Lagerpunkte des Lagerkomplexes *Sevvostlag* („Severo-Vostočnyj ispravi-

---

4 Ausführlich zu Geschichte und Struktur von Dal'stroj siehe Kapitel 2.
5 Ivanova spielt damit auf den „Militär-Industriellen Komplex" späterer Jahre an. Vgl. Ivanova, Istorija, S. 242–250. Das Handbuch „Sistema ispravitel'no-trudovych lagerej" spricht dagegen von „Lager-Industrie-Komplexen", vgl. Smirnov, Sistema lagerej, S. 46.
6 Nordlander, Stanovlenie ėkonomiki, S. 239.

tel'no-trudovoj lager' – Nordöstliches Besserungs- und Arbeitslager"). Seit 1948 existierte zudem das *Berlag* („Beregovoj lager'" – das sogenannte „Uferlager") als Teil der „Sonderlager", einer eigenen Lagerstruktur in der Sowjetunion, in der sogenannte „politische Häftlinge" unter besonders unmenschlichen Bedingungen leben und arbeiten mussten. Strukturell betrachtet waren *Sevvostlag* und *Berlag* nicht Teil der Lagerhauptverwaltung GULAG; der Begriff „GULAG" wird in dieser Arbeit dennoch verwendet – als Chiffre für das stalinistische Haft- und Lagersystem.

An der Kolyma waren Häftlinge die Arbeitskräftebasis der Region, die einzelnen Lagerabteilungen waren jeweils direkt mit einer Industrieeinheit des Kombinates Dal'stroj verzahnt. Die Präsenz des GULAG reichte jedoch noch sehr viel weiter. Das nordöstliche Industrie- und Lagersystem war mehr als ein Instrument zur Inhaftierung und Ausbeutung von Häftlingen in einer Region, an der Kolyma war es seit 1931 Methode der Raumeroberung und lokales Herrschaftssystem der Sowjetunion. Der Herrschaftsbereich von Dal'stroj dehnte sich immer weiter aus; wann immer in benachbarten Gebieten reiche Rohstoffvorkommen (neben Gold auch Zinn, Kobalt, Wolfram und Uran) gefunden wurden, inkorporierte das Kombinat diese Territorien in seinen Machtbereich, bis es schließlich mit ca. 3 Mio. km^2 etwa ein Siebtel des Territoriums der Sowjetunion umfasste.

Lager waren die der Kolyma eigene Normalität, und strukturell bildeten sie dort bis zu Stalins Tod das Rückgrat der sowjetischen Herrschaft, Verwaltung und Wirtschaft. Die praktischen Konsequenzen dieser Politik kommen in der Erinnerung eines ehemaligen Kolyma-Häftlings, Abraham Dück, anschaulich zum Ausdruck, wenn er schildert, dass an der Kolyma auf spezielle Häftlingskleidung verzichtet wurde:

> Unsere [Häftlings-]Kleider waren nicht mehr scheckig, wie früher. Man brauchte die Sklaven nicht mehr von der Zivilbevölkerung zu unterscheiden. Die gab es einfach nicht. Es gab Aufseher und Wachposten in Militäruniform und Sklaven in hässlichen Steppanzügen.[7]

Dal'stroj hatte als Industriekombinat die Aufgabe, durch Zwangsarbeiter den enormen Rohstoffreichtum des Territoriums auszubeuten. Während es damit in den ersten Jahren seit 1931 sehr erfolgreich war, gingen die Förderzahlen seit Ende des Zweiten Weltkrieges kontinuierlich zurück. Dieser Rückgang weitete sich zu Beginn der 1950er Jahre zu einer schweren Krise aus, die im Zusammenhang mit einer unionsweiten Krise der sowjetischen Lagerwirtschaft jener Jahre gesehen werden muss.[8] An der Kolyma sanken die Förderzahlen dramatisch, zugleich geriet die Situation in den Lagern durch die Verlegung zahlreicher berufskrimineller Häftlinge zunehmend außer Kontrolle. Banden kämpften um die Oberhand in den Lagerpunkten, Schwerkriminelle terrorisierten ihre Mithäftlinge. Doch unter der Ägide Stalins wurde die Kon-

---

[7] Dück, Erinnerungen, S. 357.
[8] Zur ökonomischen Krise des GULAG siehe Ivanova, Istorija, S. 355–385 sowie Borodkin/Gregory/Khlevnjuk, Ėkonomika; Gregory/Lazarev, Forced Labor.

struktion Dal'stroj und die auf Zwangsarbeit beruhende Wirtschaft nicht in Frage gestellt.

Als der Diktator am 5. März 1953 starb, stimmte die verbleibende Führung bezüglich des Reformbedarfs des stalinistischen Repressionsapparates überein.[9] Neue Terrorwellen, die Stalin kurz vor seinem Tod initiiert hatte, bedrohten zunehmend die Führungselite selbst, die ökonomische Krise des GULAG-Systems war nicht mehr zu übersehen – Zwangsarbeit und Massenrepression wurden als dysfunktional und ineffektiv eingeschätzt. „Politik musste", so die treffende Formulierung Manfred Hildermeiers, „wieder an die Stelle von Gewalt treten"[10].

Stalins Nachfolger stellten wenige Tage später die fingierten Verfahren gegen die sogenannte „Ärzteverschwörung" und antisemitische Kampagnen ein und verboten offiziell die Folter bei Verhören. Der als „Stalins Henker" titulierte Lavrentij Berija vereinigte den Geheimdienst MGB und den MVD zu einer Behörde und machte sich selbst zu deren machtvollem Chef. Mit dem Ziel, die bestehenden ökonomischen Belastungen für den MVD zu reduzieren, verfügte Berija die Ausgliederung kostenintensiver, auf Zwangsarbeit basierender Kombinate aus dem MVD. Er verfügte zudem die Aufhebung der Verbannung für die auf Anweisung Stalins während des Zweiten Weltkrieges deportierten Ethnien und veranlasste nur wenige Wochen nach Stalins Tod eine weitreichende Amnestie. Etwa 1,2 Mio Menschen wurden in der Folge ihre weiteren Haftstrafen erlassen, sie konnten Lager und Gefängnisse verlassen.[11]

Machtpolitisch hatten sich die Mitglieder des Präsidiums des ZK, neben Berija sind v. a. Georgij Malenkov, Nikolaj Bulganin, Vjačeslav Molotov und Nikita Chruščev zu nennen, zwar auf eine „kollektive Führung" geeinigt. Aber die zunehmende Machtfülle des MVD und seine Ambitionen wurden dem als besonders grausam geltenden Berija zum Verhängnis. In einer von Chruščev initiierten, schnellen Aktion ließen seine Kollegen Berija im Juli 1953 verhaften. Auf dem zu seiner Anklage inszenierten Juli-Plenum des ZK der KPdSU wurde Berija u. a. für die „Aufwiegelung der Nationen" (den Volksaufstand vom 17. Juni in der DDR) verantwortlich gemacht und in stalinistischer Manier zum „Volksfeind" erklärt. Das ZK der KPdSU forderte auf dem Plenum die Entmilitarisierung des MVD, eine Beschneidung seiner Macht und eine stärkere Kontrolle durch Parteiorgane.[12] Berija selbst wurde im Dezember 1953 erschossen; er was das letzte sowjetische Mitglied des Präsidiums des ZK der KPdSU, das von seinen Kollegen ermordet wurde.[13]

---

9 Zur Lage im ZK der KPdSU unmittelbar nach dem Tod Stalins siehe Medvedev/Medvedev, Neizvestnyj Stalin, S. 40 f. sowie Chlevnjuk, Politbjuro CK VKP (b) i Sovet Ministrov, S. 101.

10 Hildermeier, Sowjetunion, S. 757.

11 Vgl. Gorlizki/Khlevniuk, Cold Peace, S. 132; Khlevnyuk, Economy of the OGPU, S. 54 sowie zur Amnestie Werth, L'amnistie.

12 Vgl. Fall Berija, S. 106–109. Zur folgenden Schwächung des MVD-Apparates nach dem Sommer 1953 siehe Lejbovič, Reforma, S. 104–105; zum innerparteilichen Kampf im Jahr 1953 siehe Žukov, Bor'ba.

13 Vgl. Hildermeier, Sowjetunion, S. 760.

Diese unionsweiten Veränderungen beeinflussten die Situation an der Kolyma nachhaltig: Nur wenige Tage nach Stalins Tod wurde Dal'stroj aus dem MVD herausgelöst und in ein gewöhnliches Produktionsministerium, das Ministerium für Metallwirtschaft, überführt. Die Führungsriege des Kombinats, bislang Offiziere des MVD, verlor daraufhin ihren exklusiven Status und ihre Privilegien. Nach der Amnestie konnten etwa 80.000 Häftlinge die Lager des *Sevvostlag* verlassen, die Produktion stand in der Folge an vielen Orten still. Nach dem Juli-Plenum drängte das ZK der KPdSU auf Einfluss auf die bislang ganz dem MVD unterstellten Lagergebiete. Zum ersten Mal besuchten ZK-Mitglieder die Kolyma, sie drängten auf einen neuen Status des Gebietes, auf eine Beschneidung des MVD-Einflusses und eine neue administrative und machtpolitische Struktur der Region.

Am 3. Dezember 1953 gründete die sowjetische Führung in der Region von Dal'stroj das „Magadaner Gebiet" als neue administrativ-territoriale Verwaltungseinheit. Dieser Akt beendete die Alleinherrschaft des MVD und integrierte die Region in die institutionellen Bezüge und Infrastrukturen der zentralen Teile der Sowjetunion. In Abhängigkeit vom ZK der KPdSU wurde ein Gebietsparteikomitee unter Führung Tichon Ababkovs und ein Gebietsexekutivkomitee mit Pavel Afanas'ev an der Spitze als neue politische Leitung eingesetzt. Ivan Mitrakov blieb Chef von Dal'stroj, nun ein Kombinat des zivilen Ministeriums für Metallwirtschaft.

Analog zu den Entwicklungen in der gesamten Union wurden in den folgenden Jahren die Lager weitgehend aufgelöst, sehr viele Menschen entlassen. Die Veränderungen waren jedoch noch viel weitreichender – so umfassend das Gebiet bis 1953 von den Strukturen der MVD-Herrschaft und dem Lager-Industriellen Komplex Dal'stroj beherrscht war, so vielschichtig waren auch die Folgen des Wandels. Was bedeutete also Entstalinisierung in einer Region, in der das Lager die Normalität war? Welche Herrschaftsstrukturen entwickelten sich anstelle der Leitung durch den MVD, wer übernahm die Arbeiten, die bislang von Zwangsarbeitern geleistet wurden? Welche sozialen Auswirkungen hatte der Abbau des Lagerkomplexes? Was geschah mit den bestehenden Lagerinfrastrukturen, was mit den Bereichen, die administrativ und wirtschaftlich vom Lager abhängig waren, ohne unmittelbar zu ihm zu gehören?

Eine Analyse der Entstalinisierung an der Kolyma kann somit nicht allein das Lagersystem, seine strukturelle Verortung, die Situation in den Lagern und die Lage der entlassenen Häftlinge in den Blick nehmen. Der Blick muss vielmehr geweitet werden für die Folgen, die das Ende des Terrors für die gesamte Region hatte. Dies hat zugleich eine unionsweite Bedeutung: Das Gebiet von Dal'stroj hatte durch die umfassende Macht des MVD zwar einen Sonderstatus, zugleich aber waren hier stalinistische Lagerstrukturen besonders verdichtet. Was in der ganzen Sowjetunion für alle Betriebe, Kombinate und Infrastrukturprojekte des MVD galt, war an der Kolyma auf ein riesiges Territorium ausgeweitet worden. In der stalinistischen Sowjetunion waren Lager nicht nur Leidensorte an der Peripherie, an denen Menschen ohne Rückkehrmöglichkeit dahinsiechten oder brutal ermordet wurden – das GULAG-System und der MVD waren ökonomische und machtpolitische Schwergewichte. Den GULAG aufzulösen bedeutete dementsprechend den Bruch mit einer machtpolitischen, ökonomischen und administrativen Grundkonstante des stalinistischen Systems, er brachte die Auflösung einer regelrechten sowjetischen Parallelwelt. Auf diese Perspektive muss man sich einlassen, wenn man die Veränderungen der Entstalinisierung in einer Lager-Region erkunden will.[14]

Die Auflösung des GULAG-Systems ist ein Kernelement sowjetischer Entstalinisierung. Entstalinisierung ist ein westlicher Begriff, der bereits in den 1950er Jahren verwandt wurde – als Epochenbezeichnung und als wertendes Label der Reformen. Neben dem neutraleren Begriff „Poststalinismus", der rein chronologisch verwendet wird, werden unter „Entstalinisierung" alle Reformen subsumiert, die auf eine Veränderung des stalinistischen Systems abzielten – unabhängig von den Intentionen und der Motivation der Reformer. So werden in dieser Arbeit, rekurrierend auf die Thesen Stephan Merls, auch die Reformen des Geheimdienstchefs Berija zur Entstalinisierung gezählt, die zwar auf eine Stärkung des MVD ausgerichtet waren, zugleich aber mit Grundkonstanten des stalinistischen Lagersystems brachen.[15]

Der Titel der Erzählung „Tauwetter" von Il'ja Ėrenburg ist zum Synonym für die kulturpolitischen Liberalisierungen der Entstalinisierung geworden. Im angelsächsischen Kontext wird er häufig auf die gesamte poststalinistische Epoche angewendet, während in der Russischen Föderation bislang schlicht von der „Ära Chruščev" die Rede war, entsprechend der sowjetischen Epocheneinteilung nach ihrem jeweiligen obersten Parteiführer.[16] Erst in letzter Zeit wird auch dort der Begriff „Entstalinisierung" populärer. Als Höhepunkt der Entstalinisierung gilt die Abrechnung des Ersten Parteisekretärs Chruščev mit dem Personenkult Stalins. In seiner vierstündigen „Geheimrede" hinter verschlossenen Türen im Anschluss an den 20. Parteitag im Februar 1956 charakterisierte er vor den anwesenden Delegierten Stalin als kaltblütigen Mörder. Chruščev benannte offen stalinistische Verbrechen, u. a. die Ermordung Sergej Kirovs, die Schauprozesse, die durch Folter an Genossen erpressten „Geständnisse", die Verbrechen an der Führungsriege der sowjetischen Armee am Vorabend des Zweiten Weltkrieges. Seine Enthüllungen waren in der damaligen Sowjetunion eine Sensation, die Rede verbreitete sich schnell im ganzen Land.[17]

Infolge des 20. Parteitages kam es zu einer ersten Welle von Rehabilitationen, die jedoch bald darauf wieder begrenzt wurden. Unter Wiederbelebung des Schlagwortes „sozialistische Gesetzlichkeit" ging die schrittweise Auflösung des GULAG-Systems mit der Überprüfung und Abschaffung der gravierendsten sowjetischen Rechtsbrüche

---

14 Donald Filtzer hat mit Nachdruck auf die Notwendigkeit einer solchen Untersuchung aus Sicht der Arbeitskräfte und der sowjetischen Unternehmen hingewiesen. Vgl. Filtzer, From Mobilized to Free, S. 159.

15 Vgl. Merl, Political Communication, S. 68.

16 Vgl. Zubkova, Malenkov i Chruščev, S. 103; Daycock, Pattern, S. 2.

17 Die „Geheimrede" konnte in den 1950er Jahren nur im westlichen Ausland publiziert werden. In der Sowjetunion wurde sie erst zur Zeit der Perestrojka veröffentlicht. Vgl. Izvestija ZK KPSS (1989), H. 3, S. 128–170.

einher.[18] Sogenannte „Revisionskommissionen" reisten an die Lagerorte und überprüften die Verfahren „politischer Häftlinge", von denen eine große Zahl daraufhin entlassen wurde.[19] Lager für „politische" und kriminelle Häftlinge gab es auch weiterhin, bis zum Ende der UdSSR. Aber das System der massenhaften Verhaftung ganz unterschiedlicher Bevölkerungsgruppen mit dem Ziel ihrer wirtschaftlichen Ausbeutung in gewaltigen Industrieprojekten kam nach 1953 an sein Ende: „[...] The Gulag evolved from a gigantic and omnipresent repressive machine into an agency of narrowly limited purposes, designed to inhibit public disorder and political opposition."[20]

Der 20. Parteitag hatte durch seine Abrechnung mit dem „Personenkult" Stalins, durch den Bruch mit dem Schweigen über stalinistische Verbrechen und Opfer und durch das folgende Ende des GULAG-Systems weitreichende Folgen – auf die sowjetische Kulturpolitik, auf das Verhältnis zur Bevölkerung, auf die Satellitenstaaten des Warschauer Paktes und auf unzählige Einzelschicksale. Die Reformen der Entstalinisierung blieben jedoch nicht auf den 20. Parteitag beschränkt. Nach ersten Maßnahmen unmittelbar nach Stalins Tod beschloss Chruščev, der sich seit der Niederschlagung eines Putschversuchs im Jahre 1957 als unumstrittener Herrscher durchgesetzt hatte, Veränderungen in der Agrarpolitik, der Bildung und der Wirtschaftsstruktur der Sowjetunion. Unter seiner Führung wurden erste sozialpolitische Maßnahmen eingeführt und ein großes Wohnungsbauprogramm initiiert. Er modernisierte und reaktivierte den Parteiapparat und setzte große Wirtschaftsreformen um.

All diese Veränderungen hatten erheblichen Einfluss auf das Magadaner Gebiet, das seit 1953 in die gewöhnlichen administrativen und machtpolitischen Strukturen der Sowjetunion integriert wurde – sich also an ein System anpasste, das selbst weitreichenden Veränderungen unterlag.

Seit Gründung des Magadaner Gebietes im Dezember 1953 führten die neuen Verhältnisse zu einer Konfrontation der vom ZK der KPdSU eingesetzten Leitung mit den alteingesessenen Offizieren von Dal'stroj. Dieser regionale Machtkampf wird in der vorliegenden Arbeit vor dem Hintergrund der Bestrebungen des ZK der KPdSU analysiert, ihren umfassenden Führungs- und Kontrollanspruch auf die bislang vom MVD beherrschten Lagergebiete auszudehnen und sich zugleich gegenüber den Machtansprüchen der Industrieministerien durchzusetzen. Die unionsweite Aufwertung der regionalen Parteistrukturen unter Chruščev spielte dabei der lokalen Führungsriege um Ababkov und Afanas'ev in die Hände. Die Einführung der Volkswirtschaftsräte im Juni 1957, mit der Chruščev die Industrieministerien auflöste, führte im Magadaner Gebiet zur Aufgabe von Dal'stroj. Dadurch wurden Parteiinstitutionen oberste Führungs- und Kontrollinstanzen, während zugleich die regionale Wirtschaftsleitung eine maßgebliche Position behielt und den allumfassenden Machtan-

---

18 Siehe zur Bedeutung des Terminus „sozialistische Gesetzlichkeit" in der Entstalinisierung Luchterhandt, Justiz sowie Gill, Symbols, S. 171 f.
19 Vgl. Kokurin/Petrov, GULAG, S. 443; Hardy, Campaign, S. 92. Ausführlich zu den Entlassungswellen siehe Elie, Khrushchev's Gulag sowie Elie, Amnistiés et réhabilités; Elie, Unmögliche Rehabilitation.
20 Elie, Khrushchev's Gulag, S. 132.

spruch der Parteistrukturen immer wieder in Frage stellte. Aus regionaler Perspektive leistet die vorliegende Arbeit einen Beitrag zur Forschungsdebatte um die Machtverhältnisse in der Entstalinisierung, die Entstehung neuer politischer Netzwerke sowie die politische Bedeutung der Wirtschaftsreformen und verortet sie in der alltäglichen Führungspraxis einer lokalen Parteileitung.

Im Stalinismus hatte die fast 25-jährige Alleinherrschaft von Dal'stroj nicht nur eine spezifische Ordnung, eine bestimmte Herrschaftsform geschaffen, sie brachte auch eine eigene Führung mit einem eigenen Selbstverständnis und einer eigenen Symbolpolitik hervor, die ganz auf den NKVD/MVD bezogen war. Die neue politische Führung, die als Vertreter der Organe von Partei und Staat nach Magadan kam und in ihrem Selbstverständnis und ihrer Karriere ganz auf das ZK der KPdSU ausgerichtet war, wollte seit ihrer Ankunft die Dal'stroj-Offiziere nicht nur politisch verdrängen, sondern auch symbolisch den nordöstlichen Raum besetzen. Dazu übernahm sie die Zeitungen der Region, gründete einen eigenen Verlag und installierte infolgedessen eine nordöstliche Heimatkunde, die Teil des Aufbauprogramms der Region war und zugleich aus der sowjetunionweiten Aufwertung regionaler Identitätsbildung in den 1950er Jahren resultierte. Das Magadaner Gebiet wurde als lebenswert und aufregend, die neue Leitung als fürsorglich und kompetent inszeniert. Diese Repräsentationsstrategien offenbaren das Bewusstsein für die Notwendigkeit propagandistischer Anstrengungen gegenüber einer Bevölkerung, die nach Auflösung der Lager auf einmal zum Bleiben bzw. zum Kommen überredet werden musste. Denn seit 1953 war eine der wichtigsten Fragen der Leitung, wie die bisherige Zwangsarbeit ersetzt werden sollte: Wer sollte zu den Holzwannen für das Goldwaschen greifen, wer die Gruben mit Spaten ausheben oder die goldhaltigen Berge sprengen? Woher sollten Spezialisten mit neuen Methoden des Abbaus kommen?

Das Magadaner Gebiet war in den 1950er Jahren eines von mehreren Gebieten und Baustellen, wie z. B. das „Neuland" in der Kasachischen SSR, die Donbass-Region, die Baikal-Amur-Magistrale und die sogenannten Großbauten, die mit Mobilisierungskampagnen Arbeiter zum Zuzug bewegen wollten.[21] Zudem gab es noch immer einen zunächst hohen, dann schnell sinkenden Anteil an Zwangsarbeitern. Die Bevölkerung, die mit einer neu entstehenden sozialen Infrastruktur, mit Boni und höheren Löhnen in die Region gelockt oder zum Bleiben animiert werden sollte, war ausgesprochen instabil und inhomogen. Entlassene Häftlinge, Vertragsarbeiter, „junge Spezialisten" und Komsomolzen prägten das Bild der Bevölkerung. Junge Frauen kamen in die Region, sehr viele Kinder wurden geboren. Die Suche nach neuen Arbeitskräften setzte in der Region erhebliche sozialpolitische Anstrengungen in Gang, denn zu den Hauptmerkmalen von Dal'stroj zählte auch die Abwesenheit einer zivilen sozialen Infrastruktur.

---

21 Vgl. Filtzer, From Mobilized to Free; Tromly, Soviet Intelligentsia; Grützmacher, Baikal-Amur-Magistrale; Pohl, Tselinograd; Pohl, Virgin Lands; Mc Cauley, Soviet Agriculture; Gestwa, Stalinsche Großbauten.

Das sozialpolitische Aufbauprogramm entsprang den Bemühungen der Parteiführung, den Sonderstatus der Region aufzugeben und der verheerenden Folgen des Abbruchs bisher bestehender Versorgungsstrukturen Herr zu werden. Die unionsweiten Modernisierungs- und Urbanisierungstendenzen, die sich in den 1950er Jahren erheblich verstärkten[22], trugen ein Übriges zu einer Veränderung des Magadaner Gebietes bei. Die Verbindung zwischen der Auflösung der Lager und den Reformen der Entstalinisierung offenbart sich hier anschaulich in der Neugestaltung von Siedlungen, der Errichtung von wissenschaftlichen Instituten, aber auch in sich allmählich abzeichnenden Reformen von Arbeitsbedingungen und lang anhaltenden Debatten über Löhne, spezielle Boni und Vergünstigungen für Arbeiter im Hohen Norden der Sowjetunion.[23] Der Blick auf die Lebens- und Arbeitsbedingungen der Bevölkerung wird im Zuge dieser Analyse nicht nur deren konkrete Lage mit den Proklamationen der sowjetischen Führung kontrastieren, sondern auch nach den Folgen dieser Facette der Entstalinisierungspolitik für die Legitimität der neuen Herrschaftsverhältnisse fragen.

Im Bereich der Industriestrukturen führte die Auflösung des Lagersystems zu einer weitreichenden Umstellung der regionalen Wirtschaft. Mechanisierte Produktionsformen, der Ausbau geologischer Untersuchungen sowie die Entwicklung einer lokalen Industrie zur rudimentären Versorgung der Region zählten ebenso dazu wie die Notwendigkeit, das Gebiet an die unionsweiten Infrastruktur- und Handelswege anzuschließen.[24] Die Schaffung lokaler Forschungseinrichtungen zur Unterstützung der wirtschaftlichen Entwicklung profitierte vom unionsweiten Ausbau von Wissenschaft und Forschung, der auch den Hohen Norden einbezog.[25]

Aus der Perspektive des Magadaner Gebietes wird gezeigt, welche Dynamiken die Reformen der Entstalinisierung auslösten, welche intendierten und nicht-intendierten Folgen sich für Struktur und Bevölkerung ergaben. Zu fragen ist dabei auch, ob die Region lediglich Objekt politischer und ökonomischer Entscheidungen gewesen ist, oder ob die Veränderungen in Magadan (und in anderen lagergeprägten Regionen der Sowjetunion) auch einen Veränderungsschub für das machtpolitische Zentrum in Moskau bedeuteten.

Die vorliegende Arbeit knüpft zudem an einen Bereich der GULAG-Forschung an, der sich mit den Grundlagen von Zwangsarbeit und stalinistischen Industriestrukturen auseinandersetzt und nach den ökonomischen und politischen Hintergründen

---

22 Vgl. Bohn, Minsk; Bohn, Sozialistische Stadt.

23 Vgl. Filtzer, Soviet Workers; Filtzer, From Mobilized to Free; Burton, Detoxification; Jo, Trade Unions; Gregory, Political Economy.

24 Zur Aufwertung von Leichtindustrie und Verbraucherkonsum siehe Merl, Anspruch und Realität; Ivanova, Na poroge, Filtzer, Soviet Workers; Zhuk, Popular Culture; Merl, Konsum.

25 Vgl. zur Erschließung des sowjetischen Nordens Forsyth, Peoples of Siberia; Slezkine, Arctic Mirrors; Josephson, Soviet Arctic; Simakov/Gončarov, Akademičeskaja nauka. Siehe zur Aufwertung von Wissenschaft und Fachkonferenzen in der Entstalinisierung Tromly, Soviet Intelligentsia; Beyrau, Intelligenz; Autio-Sarasmo, Challenge; Schröder, Lebendige Verbindung.

dieser gewaltvollen Produktionsweise fragt.[26] Hier ermöglichen neue regionale Daten zu Produktionsleistungen vor und nach 1953 einen konkreten Vergleich der ökonomischen Effektivität von Zwangsarbeit in einem System wie Dal'stroj mit einer mechanisierten Industriestruktur.

Der zeitliche Rahmen liegt in den Jahren zwischen 1953 und 1960. In vielen lokalen Berichten und Statistiken galt der Zeitraum 1954 bis 1960 als eine Berichtseinheit, bei der das erste Jahr nach der Gebietsgründung und das Ende der 1950er Jahre als Eckpunkte gewählt wurden. Sicherlich spielte dabei auch die Einführung des Siebenjahrplans im Jahr 1959 eine Rolle, der den bisherigen Fünfjahrplan ersetzte; häufig wurde das Jahr 1959 als Kontrollziffer noch in den Betrachtungszeitraum des alten Fünfjahrplans (bei statistischen Darstellungen) miteinbezogen. Da sich diese Arbeit intensiv mit der ökonomischen Position des Kombinats Dal'stroj / dem Volkswirtschaftsrat vor und nach 1953 auseinandersetzt, hatte die Wahl des zeitlichen Rahmens zudem den Vorteil, auf komplizierte Umrechnungen nach der Währungsreform von 1961 verzichten zu können. Aber auch inhaltlich ergab die Analyse der Quellen, dass die wichtigsten politischen und ökonomischen Umbrüche Ende der 1950er Jahre abgeschlossen waren oder sich zumindest eine klar erkennbare Richtung abzeichnete.

1.2 Forschungsstand

Westliche Historiker haben die Entstalinisierung lange Zeit v. a. mit der Wertung „Ambivalenz" versehen.[27] Demnach standen die Entwicklungen nach 1953 in einem Spannungsverhältnis zwischen Reformen, die auf eine Beseitigung der dysfunktionalen Elemente des Stalinismus abzielten und den stalinistischen Grundlagen des Systems, die nicht angegriffen wurden.[28] Susanne Schattenberg bezeichnet diese historische Wertung der Chruščev'schen Politik anschaulich als „Zick-Zack-Kurs-Theorie", an der sie das Versäumnis bemängelt, „Liberalisierung und Sozialkontrolle, Entstalinisierung und stalinistische Normen und Werte als sich gegenseitig bedingend

---

26 Vgl. Khlevnyuk, Economy of the Gulag; Khlevnyuk, Economy of the OGPU; Borodkin/Gregory/Khlevniuk, Ėkonomika; Craveri, Forced Labour; Kraveri/Khlevnyuk, Krizis ėkonomiki MVD; Gregory/Lazarev, Forced Labor; Linden, Forced Labour; Ivanova, Istorija; Stettner, Archipel Gulag.

27 Auch in der theoretischen Verarbeitung der Entstalinisierung, ob aus totalitaristischer, moderner oder postmoderner Sicht, war diese Wertung lange vorherrschend, wie Christiana Christova in ihrer Studie zu Deutungen der poststalinistischen Sowjetunion zeigen kann. Vgl. Christova, Deutungen, S. 5 f.

28 Die ältere Literatur lässt sich am besten über den Artikel Stephan Merls im Handbuch der Geschichte Russlands erschließen. Vgl. Merl, Reformen. Die wichtigsten Dokumentensammlungen zur Entstalinisierungs-Periode sind: Fursenko, Černovye protokol'nye zapisi; Fursenko, Postanovlenija 1954–1958; Fursenko, Postanovlenija 1959–1964; Afanas'ev, Apparat CK KPSS; Afanas'ev, Ideologičeskie komissii; Afiani, Apparat CK KPSS i kul'tura; Artizov, Chruščev 1964; Ajmermacher, Doklad Chruščeva sowie die Dokumentenbände Artizov, Reabilitacija, Tom I und II.

beziehungsweise als Folgen ein und derselben Entwicklung"[29] zu betrachten. Seit einigen Jahren steht die Entstalinisierung erneut im Fokus der Forschung, die nunmehr traditionelle Untersuchungsgegenstände einer Neubewertung auf der Grundlage eines breiteren Quellenzugangs unterzieht. Die neuen Forschungen öffnen den Blick auf eine Sowjetunion, die zu dieser Zeit in fast allen Lebensbereichen fundamentalen Veränderungen ausgesetzt war.

Die GULAG-Forschung bezieht nun verstärkt das Ende der stalinistischen Lagerstrukturen in den 1950er Jahren mit ein und löst sich so von der bisherigen Konzentration auf die 1930er und 1940er Jahre.[30] Dies ermöglichen auch Studien, die sich mit Lagern in einzelnen Regionen oder zur Durchführung spezieller Industrieprojekte beschäftigen; in ihnen wird auch die Auflösung der jeweiligen Lager untersucht.[31] Ein weiterer Zweig der Forschung konzentriert sich auf die letzte Phase des GULAG, auf eine Analyse der Motive, die zur Auflösung von Lagerkomplexen und schließlich zum Ende des GULAG-Systems führten, auf die Aufstände in den Lagern, den Ablauf der Entlassungswellen, ihre machtpolitischen Hintergründe und Strategien.[32] Neben einer älteren Arbeit von van Goudoever zur Rehabilitationspolitik der 1950er Jahre[33] haben zudem in jüngster Zeit eine ganze Reihe von Autoren die Situation ehemaliger Häftlinge und ihr Verhältnis zur Mehrheitsgesellschaft, in die sie „zurückkehrten", untersucht. Dazu zählen u. a. Nanci Adler, Marc Elie und Meinhard Stark. Sie fragen nach den konkreten Umständen der Entlassungen, nach dem individuell sehr unterschiedlichen rechtlichen Status, nach formalen Vorgaben zur Arbeitsplatz- und Wohnraumsuche, nach Möglichkeiten einer Rehabilitierung, nach der schwierigen Identitätssuche nach Terror und Lagerhaft.[34] Miriam Dobson beschreibt die unheimlichen Reaktionen der sowjetischen Bevölkerung auf „Rückkehrer", das Wiederauf-

---

29 So Schattenberg in ihrer Beurteilung der Monographie „Cold Summer" über die GULAG-Heimkehrer und deren Einfluss auf die Reformpolitik der Chruščev-Ära von Miriam Dobson. Schattenberg, Von Chruščev zu Gorbačev, S. 276.

30 Vgl. Ivanova, Istorija; Barnes, Death and Redemption; Applebaum, Gulag. Auch die Editionen zur Geschichte des GULAG folgen diesem weiteren Zeitrahmen, vgl. die mehrbändige Reihe Istorija stalinskogo Gulaga, Moskau 2004.

31 Vgl. Gestwa, Stalinsche Großbauten; Hedeler, Ökonomik; Barenberg, Gulag Town; Hedeler/Stark, Grab in der Steppe; Barnes, Gulag in the Karaganda Region; Joyce, Karelia; Klause, Klang des Gulag sowie der Dokumentenband von Hedeler, KARLAG.

32 Vgl. Elie, Revisionskommissionen; Elie, Khrushchev's Gulag; Elie, Verbrecherbanden; Barenberg, Vorkuta; Hardy, Campaign; Tikhonov, The End; Barnes, Uprising; Hedeler, Rote Sklaven; Craveri, Strikes; Craveri, Kengirskoe vosstanie; Kozlov, Vosstanija; Zacharčenko, K raspadu ėkonomiki prinuditel'nogo truda.

33 Vgl. Van Goudoever, Rehabilitationen.

34 Vgl. Adler, Gulag Survivor; Adler, Life; Adler, Enduring Repression; Adler, Faith; Stark, Die Gezeichneten; Elie, Les anciens détenus; Barenberg, Gulag Town; Merridale, Night of Stone; Toker, Return from Archipelago; Fieseler, Amnestien; Round, Marginalised; Round, Surviving the Gulag; Cohen, Victims Return; Sprau, Petitionen. Die wichtigste Quellenedition zu diesem Thema ist Artizov, Reabilitacija, Tom I -III. Die Mitarbeiter des oral-history Projektes „The Whisperers" haben bei ihren Untersuchungen auch die 1950er Jahre miteinbezogen. Vgl. Figes, Whisperers.

leben von Feindbildern und die große Verunsicherung, die die Auflösung der Lager für die Bevölkerung bedeutete.[35]

In den Bereichen Politik, Wirtschaft und Sozialsystem dringt die aktuelle Forschung tiefer in die Hintergründe der sich wandelnden Herrschaft und einzelner Reformen ein. Yoram Gorlizki, Alexander Titov, Graeme Gill und Nikolaj Mitrochin setzen sich intensiv mit den machtpolitischen Veränderungen im Präsidium des ZK der KPdSU und den obersten sowjetischen Verwaltungsstrukturen auseinander, sie fragen nach Interessengruppen, Netzwerken und den Hintergründen des Machtkampfes in der obersten Führungsriege nach Stalins Tod.[36] Die einschneidenden ökonomischen Veränderungen, wie die Gründung der Volkswirtschaftsräte, die in der älteren Literatur zumeist nur konstatiert werden, rücken v. a. Nataliya Kibita und Viktor Mercalov in den Fokus ihrer Forschung.[37]

Mit Blick auf die Bevölkerung können neuere Forschungen, allen voran die einschlägige Studie Galina Ivanovas, zeigen, dass die Sozialpolitik, die im allgemeinen Bewusstsein bislang mit der Brežnev-Ära verbunden war, bereits als ein wesentlicher Teil der Entstalinisierung, im Sinne einer paternalistischen Hinwendung zum Menschen, verstanden werden muss.[38] Die Folgen, die sich daraus für das unmittelbare Leben ergaben, werden in umfangreichen Studien zum Wohnungsbauprogramm (Mark Smith), zur Urbanisierung (Thomas Bohn) sowie zur Rentenversorgung (Lukas Mücke) beschrieben.[39]

Ein weiterer Kreis der Forschung widmet sich intensiv der Symbolpolitik jener Jahre. Dabei untersuchen Graeme Gill und Pavel Kolář die politische Kommunikation jener Jahre, die wichtige Rückschlüsse auf die Dynamik zwischen „Herrschenden" und „Beherrschten" ermöglicht.[40] Dazu gehört die weitere Auseinandersetzung mit der Geheimrede Chruščevs und ihre Bedeutung für die Entstehung von Formen von Öf-

---

35 Vgl. Dobson, Cold Summer.
36 Zu den Machtverhältnissen in der Entstalinisierung siehe Gill, Question of Reformability; Gill/Pitty, Power; Titov, Central Committee; Mitrokhin, Political Clans; Gorlizki, Party Revivalism; Gorlizki, Anti-Ministerialism; Gorlizki, Political Reform; Gorlizki, Structures of Trust; Gorlizki/Khlevniuk, Cold Peace; Žukov, Bor'ba; Lejbovič, Reforma; Zubkova, Malenkov i Chruščv; Knight, Beria; Thatcher, Khrushchev; Tompson, Khrushchev; Tompson, Leadership Transition; Titov, Central Committee; Pauling, Diener des Plenums; Schröder, Lebendige Verbindung; Solomon, Soviet Politicians; Merl, Political Communication; Conyngham, Industrial Management.
37 Vgl. Mercalov, Reforma chozjajstvennogo upravlenija; Kibita, Sovnarkhoz Reform; Kibita, Moscow-Kiev; Kibita, Alternative Version. Zur Einführung der Volkswirtschaftsräte und der wirtschaftlichen Entwicklung der Sowjetunion unter Chruščev siehe außerdem Vasiliev; Failings; Hanson, Rise and Fall sowie Kruglov, Chozjajstvennaja reforma.
38 Vgl. Ivanova, Na poroge; Ivanova, Question of Honour; Merl, Konsum; Zubkova, Marginaly; Smith, Khrushchev's Promise; Smith, Khrushchev; Attwood, Housing; Varga-Harris, Socialist Contract; Bittner, Appeals; Davies/Ilic, From Khrushchev to Khrushchev; Reid, Utopia; Tromly, Soviet Intelligentsia.
39 Vgl. Smith, Property; Bohn, Minsk; Mücke, Altersrentenversorgung.
40 Siehe zur symbolischen Legitimation sowjetischer Herrschaft zur Zeit der Entstalinisierung Kolář, Poststalinismus; Gill, Symbols; Yurchak, Was Forever; Kusber, Herrscherbild; Merl, Political Communication; Markwick, Thaws; Thatcher, Khrushchev; Pavlenko, Soviet Myth; Wolfe, Soviet Journalism.

fentlichkeit in den Arbeiten von Polly Jones, Susanne Schattenberg und Cynthia Hooper.[41] Zur Symbolpolitik der Jahre nach Stalins Tod ist der Aufstieg der *kraevedenie* zu rechnen, der Entwicklung spezifisch regionaler Identitäten, die mit den machtpolitischen Veränderungen in den Beziehungen zwischen „Zentrum" und „Region" einhergehen; sie werden von Emily Johnson, Catherine Evtuhov und Victoria Donovan untersucht.[42]

Vor allem der englischsprachigen Historiographie kommt das Verdienst zu, eine große Bandbreite kulturgeschichtlicher Fragestellungen in die Debatte einzubringen. Die britische Historikerin Miriam Dobson hat in ihrer Analyse der Forschungslandschaft alltagsgeschichtliche Fragestellungen, Dissens und Devianz sowie die Reaktionen der Bevölkerung auf die Reformen als die aktuell wichtigsten Forschungsaspekte herausgearbeitet.[43] Tatsächlich sind die Forschungstätigkeiten hier besonders rege. Im Fokus stehen die Reaktionen auf den 20. Parteitag, Untersuchungen zur öffentlichen Meinung und zu den Auswirkungen dieser neuen Politik auf die kulturelle Dimension des Zusammenlebens der Menschen, auf Sphären von Privatheit und Öffentlichkeit, auf eine veränderte Wahrnehmung von Kindheit und Jugend, auf Veränderungen im Alltag, auf Mode, Musik und Kunst.[44] Ein Teil der Forschung weist auch auf neue Unterdrückungs- und Verhaftungswellen unter Chruščev hin, die den repressiven Umgang mit Ansätzen von Protest oder Devianz belegen.[45] Dieser differenzierende Blick auf die Entstalinisierung führt mitunter auch zur Infragestellung der scharfen Epochengliederung in eine Zeit vor und nach 1953. Es ist das Verdienst einer Reihe von Studien, dass sie in ihrem jeweiligen Untersuchungsbereich Kontinuitäten zwischen Spätstalinismus und Entstalinisierung aufzeigen und darauf aufmerksam machen, dass die Vorstellung von einem abrupten Politikwechsel nach dem 5. März 1953 falsche Vorstellungen weckt – so beispielsweise Mark Smith für die großen Wohnungsbauprogramme, Juliane Fürst in ihrer Studie zur Jugend der Nachkriegszeit, Benjamin Tromlys Studie zu sowjetischen Universitäten und Ulrike Huhn für den Bereich orthodoxer Glaubenspraktiken.[46]

Neben den hier genannten Monographien lassen sich die mittlerweile breit gefächerten Forschungstätigkeiten am besten über eine ganze Reihe von Sammelbänden verfolgen, die auch von einer regen Konferenztätigkeit zur Chruščev-Ära in den letzten

---

41 Vgl. Jones, Secret Speech; Jones, De-Mythologising; Schattenberg, Secret speech; Kusber, Herrscherbild; Hooper, New Soviet future sowie für die ältere Forschung Naumov, Geheimrede.

42 Vgl. Evtuhov, Voices; Johnson, Kraevedenie; Donovan, Kraevedenie Revival.

43 Vgl. Dobson, Post-Stalin Era.

44 Vgl. Zhuk, Popular Culture; Lebina, Povsednevnost'; Bittner, Many Lives; Reid, Kitchen; Field, Private Life; Dobson, Cold Summer; Jones, Myth; Meridale, Night of Stone; Kozlov, Readers; Smith, Moscow 1956; Einax, Entstalinisierung auf Weißrussisch; Hasanli, National Identity.

45 Vgl. Kozlov/Fitzpatrick/Mironenko, Sedition; Kozlov/Mironenko, Kramola; Kozlov, Mass Uprisings; Hornsby, Protest; Kulavig, Dissident; LaPierre, Devianz.

46 Vgl. Smith, Property; Tromly, Soviet Intelligentsia; Fürst, Last Generation; Huhn, Eigensinn. Mit Blick auf die gesamte Sowjetunion hatten dies bereits Elena Zubkova sowie Yoram Gorlizki und Oleg Khlevniuk betont. Vgl. Zubkova, Poslevoenne obščestvo; Gorlizki/Khlevniuk, Cold Peace, S. 166 f.

Jahren künden. Dazu zählt zuallererst der Band „De-Stalinization Reconsidered" von Thomas Bohn, Rayk Einax und Michel Abeßer, der vor allem einen herausragenden systematisierenden historiographischen Überblick über die aktuelle Forschungslandschaft bietet, „Nikita Khrushchev" von William Taubman, Sergei Khrushchev und Sergei Gleason (bereits aus dem Jahr 2000) sowie die Bände „Khrushchev in the Kremlin" und „Soviet State and Society under Khrushchev" von Jeremy Smith und Melanie Ilic.[47] In jüngster Zeit erschienen sind die Beiträge der russischen Konferenz „Posle Stalina" aus dem Jahr 2015.[48] Stärker kulturwissenschaftlich ausgerichtet sind die etwas älteren Sammelbände „Women in the Khrushchev Era" von Melanie Ilic, Susan Reid und Lynne Attwood sowie „The Dilemmas of De-Stalinization" von Polly Jones; das Themenheft „The Relaunch of the Soviet Project" der „Slavonic and East European Review" von Juliane Fürst, Polly Jones und Susan Morrisey sowie der Band „The Thaw" von Denis Kozlov und Eleonory Gilburd aus dem Jahr 2013.[49] Eine systematisierende Gesamtschau, die diese Ergebnisse aufgreift und zu einer Gesamtdarstellung zusammenfügt, steht bislang noch aus.

Verallgemeinernd lässt sich sagen, dass die neue Forschung nicht nur das Wissen über die Reformen nach Stalins Tod erweitert. Vielmehr stellt sie an diese Reformen ganz neue Fragen, bricht dabei mit den gängigen Dichotomien von „Anspruch und Realität", „Reform und Beharrungskräften des Systems" und arbeitet die Dynamiken der Veränderungen, ihre vielschichtigen Folgen und die Reaktionen der Bevölkerung heraus.

Mit Blick auf die neuesten Forschungstendenzen hat Stefan Plaggenborg jüngst die Notwendigkeit herausgestellt, die Reformen der Entstalinisierung analytisch vom Ende des Terrors zu trennen. Zwar sei das Ende von GULAG und Terror „the most striking difference between Stalinism and post-Stalinism", analytisch betrachtet hätte dies jedoch die stalinistischen Strukturen nicht grundsätzlich in Frage gestellt:

> [...] we should admit that the rejection of terror as a means of conducting politics after 1953 was not related to the question of enduring Stalinist structures. It certainly did not mean the abolition of brutal and sometimes terroristic methods as an option for the government and organs of state security. Neither did it mean that the Stalinists who became post-Stalinists in 1953, and who continued to govern the Soviet Union until the middle of the 1980s, were 'structurally' humanized. It meant only that they *decided* [Hervorhebung im Original – M. S.] to stop employing Stalinist methods of terror, whilst many other aspects of Stalinism continued.[50]

In Bezug auf das Ende des Terrors wird hier die traditionelle Wertung „Ambivalenz" wiedereingeführt. Entsprechend dieser Sichtweise wurde der Terror zwar eingestellt,

---

47 Vgl. Bohn/Einax/Abeßer, De-Stalinization; Taubman/Khrushchev/Gleason, Khrushchev; Ilic/Smith, Soviet State; Ilic/Smith, Khrushchev in the Kremlin.
48 Vgl. Posle Stalina.
49 Vgl. Ilic/Reid/Attwood, Women; Jones, De-Stalinization; Fürst/Jones/Morrisey, Relaunch; Kozlov/Gilburd, Thaw.
50 Plaggenborg, Under Repair, S. 46 f.

auf die stalinistischen Strukturen habe dies jedoch keinen Einfluss gehabt. Dies suggeriert eine „unsichtbare" Trennlinie zwischen stalinistischen Grundfesten und neuen Freiheiten, entlang derer sich die sowjetische Führung hin- und herbewegte, als habe sie nach Bedarf in den alten oder den neuen Instrumentenkasten gegriffen, etwas Sozialpolitik dosiert oder bei Bedarf neue Repressionswellen durchgesetzt. Dabei geraten der dynamische Charakter der Veränderungen aus dem Blick, die vielfach nicht-intendierten Folgen und die Auswirkungen, die das Ende des Terrors langfristig auf die sowjetische Führung selbst hatte. Den GULAG aufzulösen, die Folter einzustellen, die massenhafte Zwangsarbeit aufzugeben, all dies berührte Kerne des stalinistischen Systems. Langfristig führte dies – und hier ist Jörg Baberowski in seiner weiteren Perspektive zuzustimmen[51] – tatsächlich zu einer Befriedung des sowjetischen Systems. Die poststalinistische Sowjetunion war viel mehr als „Stalinismus minus Terror".

Das große Verdienst der aktuell so regen Entstalinisierungsforschung ist ja gerade, die Dynamiken der Entstalinisierung herauszuarbeiten. Indem die neue Forschung mit den gängigen Dichotomien bricht, kann sie im Bereich der Struktur-, Wirtschafts- und Sozialpolitik, vor allem aber bei den vielfältigen kulturwissenschaftlichen Fragestellungen, den Blick für die neue Qualität öffnen, welche die Veränderungen der Chruščev-Periode mit sich brachten. Diese Sichtweise hat sich mit Blick auf die strukturelle Bedeutung der Abschaffung des Terrors noch nicht durchgesetzt.

Tatsächlich stehen die Forschungen zu den Reformen der Entstalinisierung unverbunden neben der großen Zahl von Arbeiten, die sich mit den Lagerauflösungen und dem Ende des GULAG-Systems beschäftigen. In den Debatten um die Reformen der Entstalinisierung spielen die Lagerauflösungen meist keine Rolle. Zwar wird das Ende des Terrors konstatiert, seine Interdependenz zu der entstehenden Sozialpolitik, den ökonomischen Reformen und den machtpolitischen Veränderungen aber kaum betrachtet. Umgekehrt fokussieren sich die Arbeiten, die sich mit den Lagerstrukturen und ihrer Auflösung in den 1950er Jahren beschäftigen, sehr stark auf die MVD-Strukturen, auf die Situation an den Orten der Haft, auf die Lage entlassener Häftlinge. Obwohl mit Blick auf das GULAG-System in der neueren Forschung gerade betont wird, wie weit die Strukturen der Lager in die zivilen Sphären hineinreichten und wie unzureichend die Vorstellung vom „Archipel GULAG" ist[52], wurde die strukturelle und ökonomische Bedeutung der Auflösung der Lager für die Entstalinisierung bislang nur unzureichend untersucht. Damit wird die Forschung nicht nur der fundamentalen Bedeutung der Lager für ganze Regionen unzureichend gerecht, sie verengt so auch die notwendige Analyse der Perspektive der damaligen Akteure. Denn für sie waren die Lager kein ideologisches oder moralisches, sondern ein infrastrukturelles, öko-

---

51 Vgl. Baberowski, Wege aus der Gewalt, S. 414.
52 Dies betonen die Herausgeber des Sonderheftes „The Soviet Gulag: New Research and New Interpretations" der Zeitschrift Kritika. Siehe dort auch Khlevniuk, Gulag and Non-Gulag sowie Shearer, Archipelago.

nomisches und machtpolitisches Problem. Die vorliegende Arbeit will die Interdependenzen zwischen Entstalinisierung und „EntGULAGisierung" mit Blick auf eine spezielle Region herausarbeiten, „das Lager" in die Debatten um die poststalinistischen Reformen der 1950er Jahre zurückbringen.

Dazu wird jedoch keine regionale Verortung unionsweiter Entwicklungen angestrebt, wie es Rayk Einax in seiner Geschichte der belorussischen Sowjetrepublik anschaulich leistet.[53] Dementsprechend wird in der vorliegenden Arbeit nicht gefragt, ob sich die Sputnik-Begeisterung auch an der Kolyma zeigte, wie der Putschversuch gegen Chruščev aufgenommen oder ob die Aufstände in Polen und Ungarn auch eine Auswirkung auf die Entwicklung im Nordosten hatten – es geht nicht darum, gesetzte Linien der politischen Ereignisgeschichte vor Ort nachzuvollziehen.

Um den vielfältigen Veränderungen, die die Entstalinisierung im Magadaner Gebiet mit sich brachte, gerecht zu werden, bewegt sich diese Arbeit zwischen einer Struktur-, Wirtschafts-, Sozial- und Kulturgeschichte der Region. Die Mehrschichtigkeit der Transformation wird durch „Tiefenbohrungen" offengelegt – in Anweisungen der Finanzverwaltung des Ministeriums für Metallwirtschaft, in den Stenogrammprotokollen von Beratungen über einzelne Baustellen, auf denen Häftlinge und freie Arbeitskräfte arbeiteten, in Berichten über die Lage des Psychiatrischen Krankenhauses und zu den Perspektivplänen der Akademie der Wissenschaften, in Erinnerungen entlassener Häftlinge, in statistischen Angaben über die neuesten Ergebnisse von Schwimmbaggern, im Petitionswesen zu miserablen Wohnverhältnissen und an vielen anderen Stellen, die auf den ersten Blick nicht mit dem Lagerthema assoziiert werden. So wird am Magadaner Beispiel ein Einblick in die weitreichenden Folgen der Lagerauflösungen geboten, der die Dynamik der Abschaffung des Terrors aufzeigen kann.

Um das Ausmaß der Veränderungen in der Entstalinisierung erfassen zu können, bedarf es einer genauen Kenntnis der stalinistischen Epoche. Die Arbeit beginnt daher mit einer Darstellung der Jahre bis 1953, die in dieser Form bisher nicht vorliegt. Denn obwohl die Herrschaftsform des MVD an der Kolyma eine Ausnahmestellung im Rahmen stalinistischer Zwangsarbeiterprojekte einnahm, hat die westliche Forschung den Nordosten bisher kaum zur Kenntnis genommen. Eine Ausnahme bilden die Arbeiten des amerikanischen Historikers David Nordlander, der sich jedoch auf die Gründung von Dal'stroj und die ersten Jahre des Kombinats konzentriert.[54] Die große Bekanntheit der Regionsbezeichnung – dank der Erinnerungen von Ginzburg und Šalamov – sorgte dafür, dass „die Kolyma" und „Magadan" immer wieder als Synonyme für sowjetische Lagerorte verwendet wurden, allerdings meist ohne dezidierte historische oder geographische Kenntnisse. Robert Conquest kommt dabei das Ver-

---

53 Vgl. Einax, Entstalinisierung auf Weißrussisch.
54 Vgl. Nordlander, Magadan; Nordlander, Stanovlenie ėkonomika; Nordlander, Gulag Capital; Nordlander, Evolution.

dienst zu, eine breite Öffentlichkeit bereits 1978 auf das Lagergebiet aufmerksam gemacht zu haben.[55]

Aufgrund des Forschungsdesiderats zu Dal'stroj in der westlichen Historiographie wird in dieser Arbeit in erster Linie auf die Arbeiten regionaler Historiker zurückgegriffen, die sich auf lokale Archive stützen. Ende der 1990er und zu Beginn der 2000er Jahre begann eine Gruppe junger Historiker um Anatolij Širokov, sich intensiv mit der stalinistischen Geschichte der eigenen Region auseinanderzusetzen. Während Širokov selbst zuletzt im Jahr 2014 eine systematisierende Gesamtschau auf Dal'stroj vorgelegt hat,[56] widmen sich seine jüngeren Kollegen meist einzelnen Industriezweigen oder speziellen Infrastrukturprogrammen. Mitunter konzentrieren sich diese Arbeiten weitgehend auf die Auswertung statistischer Daten.[57] Stärker auf die Geschichte des Lagerkomplexes bezogen bleiben die Arbeiten älterer Kollegen, die sich dabei um den Abdruck wichtiger Dokumente verdient gemacht haben.[58] Eine hervoragende Analyse eines wichtigen Bereiches des Kolymaer Lagerlebens bietet Inna Klause mit ihrer 2014 erschienenen Studie zu Musikern in sowjetischen Lagern.[59] Für die poststalinistische Epoche der Region liegt bislang eine Studie des Historikers Pavel Grebenjuk vor, die 2007 erschien. Grebenjuk bietet mit seinem Blick auf die Jahre 1953 bis 1964 eine anschauliche Darstellung. Methodisch beschränkt er sich zwar weitgehend auf die Auswertung von Sitzungsprotokollen, er greift aber auch auf Ergebnisse von Zeitzeugenbefragungen zur Untermauerung seiner Thesen zurück. Das große Verdienst seiner Studie besteht darin, diese Selbstdarstellungen des damaligen Magadaner Führungspersonals den Lesern zugänglich zu machen und damit die machtpolitischen Veränderungen nach 1953 lebendig werden zu lassen.[60]

---

55 Vgl. Conquest, Kolyma. Conquest ging von völlig übertriebenen Häftlingszahlen aus. Er spricht von durchschnittlich etwa 500.000 Häftlingen pro Jahr und insgesamt von mindestens 2,5 Mio. Toten. Diese Zahlenangaben sind mit dem damals fehlenden Archivzugang zu erklären, sie trugen in der Folge aber verstärkend zu dem besonderen „Ruf" der Lager im sowjetischen Nordosten bei. Vgl. Conquest, Great Terror, S. 325 sowie die ausführliche Diskussion dieser Zahlen in Conquest, Kolyma, S. 216 ff.

56 Vgl. Širokov, Dal'stroj v social'no-ėkonomičeskom razvitii.

57 Darauf verweisen schon die Titel der Arbeiten von V. G. Zeljak, S. M Rajzman, A. F. Pozdnjakov und M. V. Tret'jakov – „5 Metalle von Dal'stroj", „Industrielle Erschließung des Nordostens", „Besonderheiten des Straßenbaus" u. a. Eine Ausnahme bildet hierbei die Historikerin Šulubina, die sich ganz auf den Lagerkomplex *Sevvostlag* konzentriert sowie die Gesamtdarstellung von Mel'nikov, Repressivno-proizvodstvennaja struktura.

58 Siehe vor allem die Arbeiten von I. D. Bacaev; A. G. Kozlov und D. I. Rajzman sowie Panikarov, Kolyma.

59 Vgl. Klause, Klang des Gulag.

60 Vgl. Grebenjuk, Kolymskij led. In jüngster Zeit hat Pavel Grebenjuk seine Forschungen wieder aufgegriffen und mehrere Veröffentlichungen zu sozialen und kulturwissenschaftlichen Aspekten des poststalinistischen Magadaner Gebietes vorgelegt. Vgl. Grebenjuk, Ėkonomičeskaja effektivnost'; Grebenjuk, Smechovaja praktika; Grebenjuk, Narodnoe obrazovanie; Grebenjuk, Vovlečenie rassochinskoj kočevoj gruppy; Grebenjuk, Kul'turnaja politika.

1.3 Die „Sowjetisierung" des Magadaner Gebietes: Militärische versus zivile Herrschaft

Die Region war bis zur Gründung des Magadaner Gebietes im Dezember 1953 dem militärischen Sektor der Sowjetunion zugeordnet. Mit der Gebietsgründung wurde sie in den zivilen Sektor überführt. „Militärisch" und „zivil" sind die Schlüsselbegriffe, mit denen die herrschaftspolitischen Unterschiede zwischen stalinistischer und poststalinistischer Raumeroberung gegeneinander abgegrenzt werden können. Die Hintergründe dieser Begriffe sollen im Folgenden erläutert werden:

Der NKVD/MVD, der durch seine Hauptabteilung Dal'stroj bis zum Dezember 1953 die Region vollständig beherrschte, war eine para-militärische Organisation. Im Selbstverständnis der sowjetischen Führung war der NKVD/MVD nicht an den Grenzen zum kapitalistischen Ausland tätig, sondern an der „inneren Front", im Kampf gegen „innere Feinde", die die Union in ebensolchem Maße zu bedrohen schienen wie ein ausländischer Aggressor. Die Wurzeln dieses Selbstverständnisses reichen weit zurück: In der Zeit unmittelbar nach der Oktoberrevolution ging die VČK (eine Vorgängerorganisation des NKVD) bereits als militärische Einheit gegen die Feinde der neuen Sowjetmacht vor, sie verstand sich als „Kampforgan der Diktatur des Proletariats", im Sinne eines „Kampfes gegen die Konterrevolution".[61] Sie führte einen „inneren Krieg", den „Roten Terror" gegen Abweichler, angebliche „gefährliche Propaganda" und Verleumdung der Sowjetmacht.

Die Mitarbeiter des MVD und seiner Vorgängerorganisation wurden nach militärischen Prinzipien ausgebildet und geführt, sie waren „Truppen" mit militärischen Rängen. Nach dem Vorbild der Roten Armee herrschte eine besonders straffe und streng hierarchische Organisation; die ausgegebenen Direktiven hatten durch ihren Charakter als „militärische Befehle" absolute Dringlichkeit; sich ihnen zu widersetzen oder sie nicht auszuführen wurde als „militärisches Vergehen" geahndet. Revolutionäre Tribunale ersetzten als eine Art „Kriegsgerichte" in den eigenen Bereichen die regulären juristischen Strukturen.[62] Außerdem unterlagen alle Angelegenheiten und Aufgaben des NKVD, die internen Abläufe, aber auch die Zwangsarbeiterprojekte, der Bau ganzer Städte, Kanäle und die Erschließung riesiger Gebiete einer besonderen Geheimhaltung. Die militärische Organisation ermöglichte zugleich den Anschluss an exklusive Versorgungswege und an eine eigene Infrastruktur, die parallel zu zivilen Verkehrsstrukturen existierte.

Die Ausbeutung von Häftlingen in großen Zwangsarbeitsprojekten und die Gewinnung von Rohstoffen wurden als militärische Aufgabe verstanden. Seit der Übernahme des NKVD durch Berija 1938 erhielt die Lagerwirtschaft der Sowjetunion

---

61 Siehe zu den Anfängen der staatlichen Unterdrückung von juristisch nicht eindeutig definierbaren „Feinden der neuen Sowjetmacht" Ivanova, Istorija, S. 95 f.
62 Vgl. Ivanova, Istorija, S. 100 f. Zum militärischen Charakter von Dal'stroj vgl. Širokov, Organizacionnye formy, S. 67; Bacaev, Osobennosti, S. 33; Roščupkin/Bubnis, K voprosu ob administrativnom ustrojstve, S. 70; Zeljak, Osobennosti razvitija, S. 91.

„einen planmäßigen, groß angelegten und deutlich ausgeprägt militär-industriellen Charakter"[63]. Auch die Natur wurde dieser militärischen Logik unterworfen: Ein bislang nicht erschlossenes Gebiet galt als „zu erobern". In Dal'stroj wurden die natürlichen Ressourcen durch den Einsatz von Stoßarbeitern „erstürmt", Goldfelder wurden „bezwungen", indem alle Kräfte ohne Rücksicht auf Verluste auf ein bestimmtes Gebiet „geworfen" wurden.[64]

Dal'stroj war für den NKVD/MVD eine der wichtigsten industriellen „Fronten". Kein anderes Zwangsarbeiterprojekt war in ähnlichem Maße militärischen Strukturen und einer streng hierarchischen, militärischen Führungsweise unterworfen, wie es in Dal'stroj angesichts der Abgeschiedenheit der Region und der Bedeutung der Goldförderung gewesen ist. Die Konzeption und euphemistische Bezeichnung von Dal'-stroj als „Industriekombinat" oder, wie es Stalin ausgedrückt hatte, als „Kombinat besonderen Typs"[65] verstärkte diese Abschottung noch.

Die Gründung des Magadaner Gebietes löste die Region auf einen Schlag formal aus den militärischen Strukturen des MVD und überführte sie in den „zivilen" Bereich der Sowjetunion, ohne dass damit eine unmittelbare „Zivilisierung" im Sinne einer „Humanisierung" einherging. Die Gebietsgründung war der erste Schritt – eine Angleichung an die Infrastrukturen und sozialen Systeme in anderen sowjetischen Regionen folgte. Politisch bedeutete diese Übertragung in den zivilen Sektor das Ende der besonderen Herrschaftsform, die Dal'stroj unter der Ägide des MVD geprägt hatte.

In vielerlei Hinsicht erinnert der Aufbau ziviler Strukturen im Nordosten, die Errichtung der Herrschaft der KPdSU und die Einrichtung ziviler Infrastrukturen in seinem Ausmaß an den Aufbau sowjetischer Herrschaft in den besetzten osteuropäischen Staaten. E. A. Rees beschreibt die in diesen vollzogene „Sowjetisierung" als Errichtung eines spezifisch sowjetischen Systems mit den ihm inhärenten institutionellen Strukturen und Praktiken, das ökonomische, politische, soziale und kulturelle Untersysteme umfasste, und dem besondere Herrschaftsmethoden zu eigen waren. Ausgebildet in den 1920er Jahren, habe es mit einigen Veränderungen bis 1985 bestanden.[66] Diese Struktur und Praxis wurde an der Kolyma zwischen 1917 und 1953 nicht errichtet, was Robert Conquest treffend als Abwesenheit „sowjetischer Normalität" beschreibt: „In all this vast area, the normal Soviet administration did not

---

63 Ivanova, Istorija, S. 242.
64 Zu der militärischen Arbeitsweise in der Produktion siehe Zeljak, Osobennosti razvitija, S. 91. Siehe zum Naturverständnis im Stalinismus Gestwa, Besitzergreifen. Magadaner Historiker haben für die Vernichtung des Naturraumes schon früh mit dem Begriff „Ökozid" gearbeitet, vgl. Širokov/Ètlis, Sovetskij period, S. 15. Ausführlicher zu diesem Begriff siehe Gestwa, Stalinsche Großbauten, S. 552–555.
65 Vgl. Sovetskaja Kolyma, 23. Februar 1940.
66 Vgl. Rees, Introduction, S. 1 ff. In Ergänzung zu der üblichen Fokussierung der Forschung auf die Nachkriegsgeschichte widmet sich Dietrich Beyrau in seiner Studie zur Sowjetisierung Ostmitteleuropas dezidiert den Jahren seit Stalins Tod. Vgl. Beyrau, Brutkasten. Siehe zur Sowjetisierung Osteuropas das Themenheft der Zeitschrift Jahrbücher für Geschichte Osteuropas 64 (2016), H. 3, „Reframing Postwar Sovietization. Power, Conflict, and Accomodation", hg. von Sören Urbansky und Felix Ackermann sowie Apor/Apor/Rees, Sovietization.

operate, and Dalstroy itself was in charge of all the activities of government."[67] Man kann daher durchaus von einer „zivilen Sowjetisierung" im Zuge der Entstalinisierung sprechen, die einen strukturellen Umbruch zur Ära der quasi-militärischen Eroberungsideologie und -praxis bedeutete, um den Strukturaufbau zu illustrieren.

Auch Zeitzeugen haben sich des Bildes von der fehlenden Sowjetisierung bedient, wenn sie hervorheben, dass vor 1953 an der Kolyma *die sowjetische Macht* nicht geherrscht habe. So antwortete die Lagerleitung einer Häftlingsgruppe in Tschukotka, die angesichts von entsetzlichen Lebensbedingungen und Erschießungen nach der „sowjetischen Macht" fragte: „Ja, die sowjetische Macht gibt es hier nicht, hier gibt es die Macht der Berge und der Staatsanwalt ist ein weißer Bär."[68] Generalmajor Derevjanko, Lagerkommandant des *Sevvostlag*, soll Häftlingen, die die Bucht von Magadan erreichten, entgegengeschleudert haben: „Sträflinge! Dies ist die Kolyma! Das Gesetz ist jenes der Taiga, und der öffentliche Ankläger ist der Bär!"[69]

Natürlich war es die „sowjetische Macht", die Erschießungen in Tschukotka anordnete oder sie wissend duldete, natürlich war es die sowjetische Institution NKVD/MVD, die Menschen unter diesen klimatischen Bedingungen zur Arbeit zwang – Dal'stroj war ein Kernelement sowjetisch-stalinistischer Ausbeutung und Unterdrückung. Die Unterstellung einer gesamten Region unter die militärische Leitung des NKVD/MVD hatte jedoch im Rahmen der sowjetischen Diktatur besondere Konsequenzen, die mit der „Macht von Bergen und Taiga" und „dem Bär" in der Rolle des Staatsanwalts veranschaulicht werden sollten. Sie bedeutete die Abwesenheit des gewohnten und als gegeben akzeptierten sowjetischen Bezugsrahmens.[70] Und damit war nicht nur die Entrechtung der Menschen infolge ihres Häftlingsstatus gemeint. Es gab an der Kolyma nicht ein „Lager" in einer ansonsten gewöhnlichen Region, die militärische Struktur des Lagers bestimmte das gesamte Gebiet, das Gebiet wurde als „ein Lager" verwaltet und beherrscht. Dies reichte von militärischen Transportmitteln über die Krankenversorgung, über Handelsstrukturen bis zur völligen Abwesenheit ziviler Staatsanwälte. In dem oben geschilderten Sinne verstand man die Region als „nicht sowjetisch", weil eine zivile sowjetische Macht tatsächlich nicht existierte. Das Sprechen von einer „zivilen Sowjetisierung" unter den Bedingungen der Entstalinisierung soll daher nicht als moralische Wertung verstanden werden, sondern verdeutlichen, dass der institutionelle, infrastrukturelle und soziale Aufbau ziviler Strukturen, der nach 1953 einsetzte, strukturell an die Auflösung der Lager und ihrer

---

67 Conquest, Kolyma, S. 40.

68 GARF f. R-7523, op. 58, d. 432, l. 12–13, hier l. 12.

69 Vgl. die Erinnerungen des ehemaligen rumänischen Häftlings Michael Solomon sowie des bekannten Chirurgen Jurij Viktorovič Šapiro, der von 1954 bis 1958 an der Kolyma praktizierte. Solomon, Magadan, S. 137 sowie Šapiro, Vospominanija.

70 Der Kolymaer Slogan erinnert dabei an den höhnischen „Gruß", mit dem Häftlinge in einem der ersten großen Lager der Sowjetunion, dem Solowezker Sonderlager, von der Lagerleitung und den Wachen bedacht wurden: „Zdes' vlast' ne sovetskaja, a solovetskaja" – „Hier ist die Macht nicht sowjetisch, sondern solovetisch".

Herrschaftssysteme geknüpft war. Der Begriff von der „Sowjetisierung" der Region wird hier zur Beschreibung der Abschaffung eines Sonderstatus dienen.

1.4 Militärische versus zivile Herrschaft: Von der Kolonie zur Provinz?

Die „Sowjetisierung" der Kolyma führte auch zur Veränderung ihres Status in den sowjetischen Zentrum-Peripherie-Beziehungen. Die Bedeutung, die dem Raum vor und nach Stalins Tod zugewiesen wurde, die infrastrukturellen und institutionellen Maßnahmen, die zu seiner Eroberung ergriffen wurden und die kulturellen Zuschreibungen, die das Gebiet erfuhr, sind zentrale Untersuchungskategorien der vorliegenden Arbeit. Damit einher geht auch die Suche nach angemessenen Begrifflichkeiten, die den unterschiedlichen Status der Region – vor wie nach 1953 – beschreiben können.

Für die stalinistische Epoche wird mitunter von der Kolyma als „Kolonie" gesprochen. In der aktuellen GULAG-Forschung wird dieser Begriff häufiger auf die Eroberung ferner Räume durch die Gründung von Lagern angewandt, so z. B. von Judith Pallot für die Region Perm.[71] Der Historiker Paul Gregory bezieht sich auf den Sprachgebrauch des NKVD, der selbst von der „Kolonisierung peripherer Gebiete" sprach, wenn er für den GULAG konstatiert: „The history of the Gulag is the history of the colonization and industrial exploitation of the remote regions of the state."[72]

Der Magadaner Historiker Anatolij Širokov versteht die Existenz des stalinistischen Kombinats Dal'stroj als eine „strafende Form der Kolonisation" und zeigt die Lager an der Kolyma als eine Art „extreme Variante" im Rahmen der sibirischen Erschließung. Širokov bezieht sich dabei explizit auf eine sibirische Historikerschule, die die Eroberung und Ausbeutung des sibirischen und fernöstlichen Teils Russlands als „Innere Kolonisation" und damit als Landnahme eines im Kern zum russischen Imperium gehörenden Territoriums betrachtet.[73] Für Širokov ist Dal'stroj die Erweiterung dieser Eroberungsstrategie mit besonders repressiven Mitteln. Auch die deutsche Historikerin Eva-Maria Stolberg betrachtet die Kolyma als „Kolonie". Sie integriert die Region in ihr Konzept einer Binnenkolonisation Sibiriens, den Nordosten des Kontinents und die Halbinsel Tschukotka betrachtet sie als östlichsten Teil Sibiriens.[74]

---

71 Vgl. Pallot, Forced Labour for Forestry; Viola, Stalin's Empire; Khili, Nasledie GULAGa.

72 Gregory, Introduction, S. 4.

73 Vgl. Širokov, Organizacionnye formy kolonizacii. A. G. Kozlov reagiert kritisch auf diesen Kolonisationsbegriff, vgl. Kozlov, Kombinat osobogo tipa, S. 11 f. Siehe für eine Analyse der Historikerschule Frank, Innere Kolonisation; Stolberg, Raumerschließungsprozesse sowie Kusber, Mastering the Imperial Space.

74 Vgl. Stolberg, Wilder Osten, S. 325. Dittmar Dahlmann hat in seiner umfassenden Sibirien-Monographie die Bezeichnung „Sibirien" als Zuschreibung an den gesamten Raum östlich des Urals aufgefasst, dessen geographische Grenzen jeweils historisch unterschiedlich gefasst wurden. Mit Verweis

„Der GULag im Nordosten", so Stolberg, ist für sie, ebenso wie für Širokov, die „repressivste Form" dieser Kolonisation. Sie vermisst in der bisherigen Forschung die zentrale Rolle des GULAG als Kolonialisierungselement in Sibirien:

> Die Tatsache, dass der ‚Archipel GULag' nicht im europäischen Russland errichtet wurde, sondern sich über die unwirtlichen Weiten Sibiriens erstreckte, zeigt, dass das stalinistische Regime mittels ‚antizivilisatorischer Maßnahmen' dort eine ‚Zivilisation' aufbauen wollte, wo ‚Wildnis' herrschte.[75]

Die Eroberung des Nordostens mit Hilfe von Lagerstrukturen, die punktuelle Ausbeutung des rohstoffreichen Gebietes und die Unterdrückung der dort lebenden Ethnien lassen sich tatsächlich anschaulich als „Kolonisierung" beschreiben. Problematisch ist jedoch die Betrachtung als Binnen-Kolonisation, weil sie den bislang fast unberührten und von einer Vielzahl anderer Ethnien bewohnten Nordosten Asiens als Teil des russischen Imperiums versteht, ohne sich einer Diskussion über die territoriale Lage „Russlands" zu stellen. Erobert und kolonisiert wurde eigentlich bislang „fremdes" Territorium.

Unpassend ist zudem Stolbergs Versuch, die Eroberung durch Dal'stroj in ihre Vorstellung von einer sowjetischen *frontier* einzubinden. Wie eine ganze Reihe von Historikern, die sich mit der sowjetischen Geschichte Sibiriens auseinandersetzen, rekurriert auch Stolberg auf das Konzept des US-amerikanischen Historikers Frederick J. Turner, der *frontier* als eine imaginierte Grenze zwischen „Zivilisation" und „Wildnis" versteht, die im Laufe von Erschließungsmaßnahmen immer weiter verschoben wird.[76] Für Stolberg ist diese sowjetische *frontier* in ihrer „repressivsten Form" durch Dal'stroj bis an die Beringstraße verschoben worden, bis „Sibirien" vollständig in den Machtbereich der Sowjetunion inkorporiert war.

Das Bild von der *frontier* weckt hier falsche Vorstellungen. Tatsächlich verhinderte gerade der Lager-Industrielle Komplex Dal'stroj eine Aufnahme der Region in die zivile Struktur der Sowjetunion. Ganz bewusst sollte die Region nicht dauerhaft besiedelt und erschlossen werden, sie galt ausschließlich als auszubeutendes Territorium, das administrativ und machtpolitisch als ein exterritorialer Bereich behandelt wurde.

Die Auflösung der Lager hat die Beziehungen zwischen dem Moskauer Zentrum und der nordöstlichen Region in ihren Grundfesten verändert. Durch die Gründung der *oblast'*, des Magadaner Gebietes, wurde die Region formal in die Struktur der

---

auf diese Zuschreibungen verwendet Dahlmann den Begriff „Sibirien" auch für die geographischen Regionen des Fernen Ostens und des Nordostens. Vgl. Dahlmann, Sibirien, S. 19 f.

75 Stolberg, Wilder Osten, S. 324.

76 Vgl. Stolberg, Frontiers, S. 14. Siehe auch Baberowski, Suche nach Eindeutigkeit; Grützmacher, Baikal-Amur-Magistrale, S. 401 f. Siehe ebenso Grützmacher, Young Men; Frank, Innere Kolonisation; Häfner, Frontier; Bassin, Turner; Daly, „Wild East" sowie Khodarkovsky, Steppe Frontier. Klaus Gestwa spricht bei den von ihm betrachteten „Großbauten des Kommunismus" von einer „spezifisch sowjetischen Frontier-Mentalität". Gestwa, Technologische Kolonisation, S. 79.

Sowjetunion eingebunden. David Shearer hat in seiner Analyse der Erschließung Westsibiriens in den 1930er Jahren auf die fundamentale Bedeutung hingewiesen, die die unterschiedliche administrative Struktur einer Region für ihren Status im Rahmen des sowjetischen Systems hatte. Ein „Gebiet" (*oblast'*) sei dabei eine relativ kleine administrative Einheit gewesen, gekennzeichnet durch eine gute Kommunikations- und Transportinfrastruktur, im Unterschied zu einem „Distrikt" (*kraj*), was meist eine unerschlossene und unterentwickelte Grenzregion war. Shearer schildert die Reorganisation des Distrikts Westsibirien in das Nowosibirsker Gebiet in den 1930er Jahren als Endpunkt einer ökonomischen und administrativen Assimilation an die Zentren der Sowjetunion.[77] Diesen Gedanken aufgreifend, wird für die nordöstliche Region gefragt, ob die Gründung des Magadaner Gebietes die Aufgabe der Kolonisierung bedeutete, ob die sowjetische *frontier* schließlich nach 1953 bis an die Beringstraße verschoben wurde, und ob sich so ein gleichberechtigtes Gebiet, eine typische „sowjetische Provinz" ausbildete.

„Provinz" wurde und wird in Russland / der Sowjetunion allgemein für alle Gebiete verwendet, die nicht zu Moskau oder St. Petersburg / Leningrad zählen. Der Begriff der Provinz hat auch eine kulturelle Dimension. Walter Sperling beschreibt, mit Blick auf das 19. Jahrhundert, die Erschaffung des Begriffes „Provinz" als wirkmächtigen Topos durch die Bildungseliten des 19. Jahrhunderts, als „Tropen der Rückständigkeit", die dazu dienten, „die kulturell eigenständigen und ökonomisch lebendigen Randgebiete zu unterwerfen und abhängig zu machen"[78]. Die vermeintliche „Rückständigkeit" der Provinz steht in der vorliegenden Darstellung nicht im Fokus, vielmehr soll das Sprechen von der „sowjetischen Provinz", die „Gleichheit" sowjetischer Peripherien verdeutlichen, die vor dem diktatorischen Kontext alle in ein festes Hierarchiegefüge mit dem übermächtigen Zentrum eingebunden waren und in denen dadurch ökonomische und soziale Verhältnisse geschaffen wurden, die sich ähnelten. „Die Provinz ist überall"[79] formuliert Sperling treffend.

Pragmatischer gehen die Herausgeber des Bandes „Stalinismus in der Provinz" mit dem Begriff um. Sie grenzen „Provinz" lediglich als „Gebiete" und „Regionen" (hier: oblast' und kraj) von einer „höchsten Ebene", dem „Moskauer Zentrum" ab.[80] Auch wenn das Wesen der „sowjetischen Provinz" damit nicht beschrieben wird, machen Binner, Bonwetsch und Junge doch auf ein wichtiges Charakteristikum aufmerksam. Für sie ist „Provinz" eine eigenständige Verwaltungseinheit, in der die Kompetenzen der regionalen Leitung durch die Übergriffe des Zentrums zwar immer bedroht sind, die aber grundsätzlich in Verwaltung, Wirtschaft und bei den sozialen Verhältnissen eine lokale Zuständigkeit besitzt.

Bei der Untersuchung der Position des Nordostens im hierarchischen System der Sowjetunion nach 1953 wird hier zu fragen sein, ob die Überführung des Gebietes in

---

77 Vgl. Shearer, Soviet Frontier, S. 160 f.
78 Sperling, Provinz, S. 27 f. Vgl. auch Schattenberg, Korrupte Provinz, S. 63 f.
79 Sperling, Provinz, S. 30.
80 Vgl. Binner/Bonwetsch/Junge, Operativer Befehl, S. 13 f.

den zivilen Sektor, ob seine „Sowjetisierung" im Zuge der Abschaffung des Sonder-status und der Gründung des Magadaner Gebietes zur Entstehung einer regelrechten „sowjetischen Provinz" geführt hat.

1.5 Quellengrundlage und Gliederung

Die vorliegende Arbeit stützt sich zum überwiegenden Teil auf Quellen der lokalen politischen und wirtschaftlichen Führung seit 1953. Ihre Korrespondenz mit dem Präsidium des ZK der KPdSU und dem Ministerrat in Moskau in Form von Berichten und Bitten bzw. Erlassen und Weisungen, Statistiken und Darstellungen der einzelnen Abteilungen der regionalen Partei- und Staatsleitung (der Abteilungen für Führung, Agitation und Propaganda, Industrie, Infrastruktur, Handel und Kultur) ebenso wie Berichte aus den einzelnen Bezirken waren wesentliche Quellen. Hinzu kamen Sit-zungsprotokolle sowie Eingaben und Petitionen der lokalen Bevölkerung. Für die einzelnen Themenaspekte war zusätzlich die umfangreiche Korrespondenz mit Mi-nisterien und sowjetunionweiten Organisationen in Moskau (den entsprechenden Industrieministerien, dem MVD, Handelsorganisationen, Wissenschaftsorganisatio-nen etc.) von Bedeutung. Ausgewertet wurden auch Akten des Industriekombinats Dal'stroj bzw. ab 1957 des Magadaner Volkswirtschaftsrates – seine Buchführung und Rechenschaftsberichte, Statistiken, längerfristige Planungsunterlagen, Korrespon-denzen mit dem MVD bzw. den entsprechenden Industrieministerien oder dem ZK der KPdSU ebenso wie mit der politischen Leitung in der Region. Fast alle diese Quellen wurden für die vorliegende Studie erstmalig erschlossen und ausgewertet.

Hinzu kamen zu einem geringeren Teil Akten aus der Zeit des Kombinats Dal'stroj vor 1953, da hier auf die Arbeiten der lokalen Historiker zurückgegriffen werden konnte. Die konkrete Quellenauswahl war auch von ihrer Zugänglichkeit abhängig. Der Studie gingen zwei Forschungsreisen nach Magadan voraus. Im ehemaligen Parteiarchiv der Region, das zur Zeit der Recherchen die Bezeichnung *Centr Chranenie Sovremennoj Dokumentacii Magadanskoj oblasti* – CCHSDMO (Aufbewahrungszen-trum für moderne Dokumentation des Magadaner Gebietes) trug, war eine Nutzung erst im zweiten Anlauf und selbst dann nur sehr eingeschränkt möglich. Zur Zeit des Forschungsaufenthaltes stand dieses Archiv selbst einigen regionalen Historikern nicht offen.[81] Dieses Manko konnte jedoch durch die hervorragenden Zugangsmög-lichkeiten im Staatsarchiv des Magadaner Gebietes – *Gosudarstvennyj Archiv Maga-danskoj Oblasti* – GAMO aufgefangen werden. Sehr viele klassifizierte Akten wurden unmittelbar für die vorliegende Studie freigegeben. So konnte auch der schlechtere Zugang zum ehemaligen Parteiarchiv zum Teil kompensiert werden, da zahlreiche Schriftstücke an Partei- *und* Staatsorgane gerichtet waren bzw. Kopien zirkulierten.

---

[81] Die Forschungsreisen fanden im Jahr 2006 statt. Zu den damaligen Arbeitsbedingungen in den Magadaner Archiven siehe meine Darstellung in Urbansky, Auf in die Provinz.

Die guten Arbeitsmöglichkeiten und die Unterstützung der dortigen Archivmitarbeiter trugen maßgeblich zum Gelingen der Forschungsaufenthalte bei.[82]

Auch die Überlieferung in den Moskauer Archiven konnte Lücken, die durch den eingeschränkten Zugang zu regionalen Parteidokumenten drohten, schließen. Von großer Bedeutung war die Überlieferung in den beiden ehemaligen Parteiarchiven RGANI und RGASPI. Sehr wichtig waren auch die Unterlagen der beiden Industrieministerien, denen das Kombinat Dal'stroj nach dem März 1953 unterstellt war, sowie die klassifizierten Sonderbestände zu Dal'stroj. Diese Unterlagen konnten, wie auch der Bestand des Finanzministeriums der UdSSR, im Russischen Staatsarchiv für Wirtschaft (RGAĖ) eingesehen werden. Hinzu kamen Unterlagen von territorial-administrativer Bedeutung aus dem Bestand des Obersten Sowjets der UdSSR sowie die Wirtschaftsunterlagen des MVD für die Überlieferung zu Dal'stroj bis Ende des Jahres 1953. Dieses Schriftgut konnte im Staatsarchiv der Russischen Föderation (GARF) genutzt werden.

Neben den Archivdokumenten wurde für diese Studie eine Vielzahl weiterer Quellen herangezogen. Dazu zählen zum einen Erinnerungen von Überlebenden der nordöstlichen Lager sowie literarische Verarbeitungen, die zwar nur am Rande Eingang in diese Arbeit gefunden haben, die aber wesentliche Überlegungen angeregt haben.[83] An erster Stelle ist hier Varlam Šalamov zu nennen, dessen Literatur den Leser schonungslos mit der Lagerwelt konfrontiert. Seine Arbeiten haben im Zuge einer Neuübersetzung ins Deutsche in den vergangenen Jahren endlich die notwendige Aufmerksamkeit erfahren.[84]

Zum anderen stützt sich die vorliegende Studie auf eine große Zahl von Texten, die in den 1950er Jahren veröffentlicht worden sind und die für eine Analyse der Selbstrepräsentation der lokalen Führung eingesetzt wurden. Dazu zählt u. a. die wichtigste Tageszeitung der Region, die *Magadanskaja Pravda*, deren Jahrgänge 1953 bis 1960 vollständig ausgewertet wurden. Hinzu kamen weitere lokale Zeitungen so-

---

82 Inzwischen sind die beiden Archive (CCHSDMO und GAMO) zu einem Archiv, GAMO, vereint worden. Die Parteidokumente werden durch ein „P" bei der Benennung des Bestandes gekennzeichnet. In Magadan existiert auch ein Archiv des FSB, der Nachfolgeorganisation des MVD. In diesem Archiv, in dem besonders aussagekräftige und wertvolle Unterlagen zur Herrschaft des MVD in der Region vermutet werden, hat bisher nur eine lokale Historikerin (Svetlana Šulubina) zu einer sehr begrenzten Thematik arbeiten können – allen anderen lokalen Historikern blieb der Zugang bislang verwehrt.

83 Vgl. Schalamow, Erzählungen; Bardach/Gleeson, Wolf; Sobolev, Pis'ma s Kolymy; Solomon, Magadan; Dück, Erinnerungen; Ginsburg, Gratwanderung; Olickaja, Vospominanija; Kress, Parochoda; Lipper, Elf Jahre; Meta, Žertvy Kolymy; Adamova-Sliozberg, Put'; Kuz'mina, Ja pomnju; Steinberger, Berlin – Moskau – Kolyma; Vilenskij, Osvencim bez pečej; Vilenskij, Dodnes' tjagoteet; Vilenskij, Est' vsjudu svet sowie der Al'manach *Volja*.

84 Die Neuerscheinungen wurden begleitet von einer Reihe von Veranstaltungen zu Varlam Šalamov sowie von einem Themenheft der Zeitschrift OSTEUROPA. Vgl. Sapper/Weichsel/Hutterer, Lager schreiben; Thun-Hohenstein, Poetik der Unerbittlichkeit; Kissel, Überlebenswissen; Kissel, Pluto, nicht Orpheus; Kissel, Gulag und Autofiktion; Kissel, Sentenz; Jurgenson, Šalamovs Erzählungen; Ryklin, Verfluchter Orden; Schmid, Nicht-Literatur; Städtke, Sturz der Idole.

wie eine große Zahl von Publikationen die aus einem in den 1950er Jahren gegründeten Magadaner Verlag stammen, der sich der Verbreitung von Heimatkunde, historischen Abhandlungen zur Geschichte der Region sowie der Darstellung einzelner Bezirke oder Industriebereiche widmete. Eine wichtige Rolle spielten dabei Rückblicke der Parteileitung auf die ersten Jahre der Region seit 1953. Diese Literatur konnte in der Magadaner wissenschaftlichen Puschkin-Bibliothek und in der Bibliothek der Russländischen Akademie der Wissenschaften, INION, in Moskau ausgewertet werden.

Die Studie beginnt mit einem historischen Exkurs, in dem summarisch die Entwicklung der stalinistischen Eroberung des Nordostens vorgestellt wird. Damit wird hier eine Forschungslücke geschlossen; zugleich hat dieser historische Vorlauf wesentliche Bedeutung für ein Verständnis der poststalinistischen Strategien und Verhältnisse. Wann immer nötig, werden auch an weiteren Stellen der Arbeit historische Exkurse, z. B. zur industriellen Entwicklung der Region, eingeflochten.

In drei Kapiteln werden die Veränderungen des Magadaner Gebietes in der Entstalinisierung untersucht. Nach Einleitung und historischem Überblick fokussiert sich Kapitel 3 auf den machtpolitischen Wandel, auf den Aufbau einer zivilen regionalen Leitung und den Machtkampf mit der Führung von Dal'stroj. Kapitel 4 veranschaulicht die Strategien der zentralen und lokalen Führung, die Goldförderung ohne Zwangsarbeit zu mechanisieren und zu effektivieren und dem Magadaner Gebiet ein umfassenderes industrielles Profil zu geben. Im sich anschließenden Kapitel (Kapitel 5) werden die sozialen Realitäten des Magadaner Gebiets vor dem Hintergrund der sozialpolitischen Reformen jener Jahre dargestellt und mit den Repräsentationen der neuen Herrschaft kontrastiert. Das abschließende Resümee fasst die weitreichenden Folgen der Veränderungen nach Stalins Tod für das Magadaner Gebiet zusammen und ordnet die Bedeutung der Lagerauflösung in die Dynamiken der unionsweiten Entstalinisierung ein (Kapitel 6).[85]

Auf die Verwendung von russischen Begriffen wird in dieser Arbeit zugunsten einer besseren Lesbarkeit weitgehend verzichtet. Wann immer möglich werden Übersetzungen geboten, bei ihrer Erstverwendung wird die Originalbezeichnung mitaufgenommen. So ist hier vom Magadaner Gebiet (*Magadanskaja oblast'*), vom Ten'kinsker Bezirk (*Ten'kinskij rajon*), dem Chabarowsker Distrikt (*Chabarovskij kraj*) oder dem Nationalen Kreis Tschukotka (*Čukotskij nacional'nyj okrug*) die Rede, ebenso vom Gebietsparteikomitee (*obkom*) und dem Gebietsexekutivkomitee (*oblispolkom*). Lediglich weithin bekannte Begriffe wie „RSFSR" oder „GULAG" werden mit den üblichen sowjetischen Akronymen angegeben. Russische Begriffe und Organisationsbe-

---

85 Die Erarbeitung dieser Dissertation wurde von einigen Publikationen begleitet, in denen Teilergebnisse der Arbeit bereits vorgestellt worden sind. Vgl. Sprau, Kolyma und Magadan; Sprau, Entstalinisierung verortet; Sprau, Diktaturüberwindung; Sprau, Gold; Sprau, Magadanskaja pressa.

zeichnungen werden in der Arbeit kursiv gesetzt, eine Ausnahme bildet die Bezeichnung „Dal'stroj" aufgrund der Häufigkeit ihrer Verwendung.

2 Historische Verortung: Stalinismus im Nordosten

Schon seit der Oktoberrevolution existierten im Nordosten keine der in anderen sowjetischen Regionen üblichen Herrschafts- und Verwaltungsstrukturen. Die sowjetische Macht trat nur in Form von sogenannten „Revolutionären Komitees" in Erscheinung, eine Herrschaftsform, die in der Sowjetunion nach dem Bürgerkrieg grundsätzlich aufgegeben worden war. Zusätzlich existierten fünf „kul'tbazy", die in einem Teil des Gebietes eine rudimentäre medizinische und kulturelle Versorgung der indigenen Bevölkerung ermöglichen sollten.[1] Aufgrund der enormen Ausdehnung des Gebietes und durch das Fehlen einer sozialen Gruppe, die als Vertreter der sowjetischen Macht hätte fungieren können, wurde die Region tatsächlich aber nur in ganz geringem Maße kontrolliert. So konnten noch in den 1920er Jahren amerikanische Firmen unkontrolliert Handel mit der indigenen Bevölkerung treiben.

Zu Beginn der 1930er Jahre änderte sich die Haltung der sowjetischen Führung gegenüber dem Nordosten. Die entlegene Region wurde Objekt einer Politik, die die Ausbeutung natürlicher Ressourcen in schwer zugänglichen Gebieten auf der Grundlage von Zwangsarbeit zum Ziel hatte. Damit einher ging eine veränderte Einstellung zu sowjetischen Häftlingen: Wurde die von ihnen geleistete Arbeit seit der Oktoberrevolution als Strafmaßnahme verstanden, so rückte nun das ökonomische Potential von Zwangsarbeit in den Vordergrund.[2] Zum ersten Mal sollte der Einsatz von Häftlingen eine wirklich tragende Rolle für die sowjetische Volkswirtschaft spielen. Bereits seit 1925 wurden der OGPU („Ob"edinėnnoe Gosudarstvennoe Političeskoe Upravlenie – Vereinigte staatliche politische Verwaltung"), eine der Vorgängerorganisationen des MVD, in einigen wenigen, streng geheimen Dokumenten wirtschaftliche Aufgaben übertragen.[3] Damit waren die Weichen gestellt für die Verbindung von naturräumlicher Ausbeutung mit einer Einrichtung, die eigentlich für innenpolitische und geheimdienstliche Fragen verantwortlich zeichnete und zur

---

1 Nordlander vergleicht die *kul'tbazy* mit Missionseinrichtungen der orthodoxen Kirche im Norden des Russischen Reiches. Vgl. Nordlander, Origins, S. 793. Für eine sowjetische Beschreibung dieser Institution siehe Nefedova/Bubnis, O podgotovke nacional'nych kadrov. In Magadan haben lokale Historiker in den späten 1980er Jahren häufiger versucht, die Errichtung der *kul'tbazy* als positive Episode in der ansonsten von Gewalt geprägten Geschichte ihrer Region zu beschreiben. Vgl. beispielsweise Kozlov, Svetloe načalo, S. 8. Die sogenannten „Revolutionären Komitees" (*Revkomy*) der Bürgerkriegszeit behielten in der Region ihre außerordentliche Machtfülle, obwohl seit 1923 in den Nachbarregionen die üblichen Partei- und Sowjetstrukturen bestanden. Vgl. Žicharev, V bor'be; Gun'ko/Galin, Iz istorii sozdanija, S. 17; Roščupkin/Bubnis, K voprosu ob administrativnom ustrojstve, S. 69; Žicharev, Očerki, S. 174 f. sowie Širokov, Dal'stroj, S. 30 f. Zur Geschichte der Region im Kontext der Eroberung Sibiriens von den ersten Expeditionen bis zum Stalinismus siehe Dahlmann, Sibirien.
2 Vgl. zur Debatte um die Ausrichtung des GULAG Gregory, Introduction.
3 Ivanova verweist auf einen streng geheimen Bericht vom 10. November 1925 an Dzeržinskij, der einen Vorschlag zur Verlegung von Häftlingen in wirtschaftlich interessante Gebiete und eine ausführliche Beschreibung der entsprechenden Regionen (an der Mündung des Jenissei, im heutigen Kasachstan u. a.) enthielt. Vgl. Ivanova, Istorija, S. 226 f.

https://doi.org/10.1515/9783110557879-003

Unterdrückung sogenannter „innerer Feinde" eingesetzt wurde. Der Vorsitzende der OGPU, F. È. Dzeržinskij trieb diese Entwicklung von Anfang an voran.

Am 11. Juli 1929 erließ der Rat der Volkskommissare der UdSSR (auf der Grundlage einer Entscheidung des Politbüros) eine grundlegende Verordnung über die Verwendung von Häftlingsarbeit. Die OGPU wurde beauftragt, das bestehende sowjetische Lagersystem zu erweitern und neue Lager in Sibirien, im Norden, im Fernen Osten und in anderen entlegenen Gebieten einzurichten. Nach Ansicht des Volkskommissars für Justiz der RSFSR sollten die Lager durch die „billige Arbeitskraft von Häftlingen" zu „Pionieren der Besiedelung neuer Gebiete" werden; die Frage nach der Versorgung und infrastrukturellen Entwicklung dieser Regionen sei daher zweitrangig. Dementsprechend entstand in den Jahren zwischen 1929 und 1931 auf dem Territorium der UdSSR ein ganzes Netz an Lagern, die bereits bei ihrer Gründung eine klar gekennzeichnete wirtschaftliche Ausrichtung (Lager für Baumaßnahmen, zur Kohleförderung, für den Holzschlag etc.) besaßen.[4]

In diesem Rahmen richtete sich der Blick der sowjetischen Führung auch auf den Nordosten und die dortigen enormen Goldvorkommen, die Expeditionen Ende der 1920er entdeckt hatten.[5] Gold war für den Außenhandel der Sowjetunion von entscheidender Bedeutung. Es konnte als Devisenbringer zur Anschaffung von schweren Geräten und ausländischer Technik eingesetzt werden, die die Sowjetunion während der forcierten Industrialisierung zu Beginn der 1930er Jahre dringend benötigte.[6] Hinzu kam das Bedürfnis, das bisher administrativ kaum erschlossene und nur ausgesprochen dünn besiedelte Gebiet, dem jedoch aufgrund seiner Randlage auch eine wichtige außenpolitische Bedeutung zukam, in stärkerem Maße zu durchdringen.[7]

Die Bedingungen für eine Eroberung des nordöstlichen Raumes durch die neu konzipierte Lagerstruktur waren in den Augen der sowjetischen Herrschaft somit ausgesprochen günstig. Seit dem Sommer 1931 erarbeitete eine Kommission des Politbüros, der G. K. Ordžonikidze, V. V. Kujbyšev und Ja. È. Rudzutak angehörten,

---

4 Vgl. Ivanova, Istorija, S. 228. Zu der Erschließung des sowjetischen Nordens auf Grundlage von Lagern siehe Josephson, Soviet Arctic, S. 422.

5 Diese Expeditionen waren Teil großer geologischer Untersuchungen in vielen Gebieten der UdSSR Ende der 1920er und zu Beginn der 1930er Jahre. Die Sowjetführung hoffte dabei auf Rohstoffe für die einsetzenden Industrialisierungskampagnen und auf wertvolle Metalle für den Ankauf von Devisen. Im Nordosten hatte eine Expedition unter der Leitung des berühmten Geologen Ju. A. Bilibin Goldfelder am oberen Flusslauf der Kolyma entdeckt; eine weitere Expedition im Jahr 1930 bestätigte den enormen Goldgehalt. Aus dieser Zeit stammt auch der weit verbreitete Ausdruck von der „goldenen Kolyma". Unter dem Dach der Aktiengesellschaft *Sojuzzoloto* begann man bereits 1930 mit ersten Förderarbeiten. Vgl. Širokov, Dal'stroj, S. 39–45. Kozlov schildert ausführlich die geologischen Expeditionen einzelner Personen und kleiner Gruppen seit 1908 in der Region. Vgl. Kozlov, Geologorazvedočnye raboty.

6 Zur Rolle des Goldhandels für die Sowjetunion siehe Zeljak, Osobennosti razvitija, S. 100; Širokov, Politika, S. 448.

7 Zu den Zielen der sowjetischen Führung im Nordosten siehe Bacaev, Osobennosti, S. 30 f.; Nikolaev, K voprosy izučenija, S. 31; Širokov, Dal'stroj, S. 47 f.; Kozlov, Kombinat osobogo tipa, S. 16.

konkrete Vorschläge für einen entsprechenden organisatorischen Aufbau.[8] Stalin verfolgte von Anfang an persönlich die Planungen – er favorisierte den Aufbau eines gewaltigen industriellen Kombinats und wandte sich gegen Bestrebungen, lokale Organisationen mit den Aufgaben zu betrauen. Der Diktator traf auch im Folgenden alle wesentlichen Entscheidungen und war über die Entwicklungen an der Kolyma sehr genau informiert.[9]

Der Maßgabe Stalins folgend beschloss das Politbüro am 11. November 1931 in seiner Verordnung „Über die Kolyma" die Einrichtung eines Industriekombinats mit der Kurzbezeichnung *Dal'stroj* im Rahmen des Rates für Arbeit und Verteidigung der UdSSR (STO). Dal'stroj wurde direkt dem ZK VKP (b) unterstellt, die Aufsicht und Kontrolle über das Kombinat führte G. G. Jagoda als stellvertretender Vorsitzender der OGPU. Der gesamte Prozess der Kombinatsgründung unterlag strengster Geheimhaltung.[10]

Im Falle des Nordostens entschied sich die sowjetische Führung nicht nur für die Gründung eines ökonomisch ausgerichteten Lagerkomplexes, sondern für ein Industriekombinat, in dem die beiden Bereiche Wirtschaft und Lager auf das Engste miteinander verzahnt waren.[11] Zugleich war Dal'stroj von Anfang an auch für die administrativ-politische Verwaltung der Region zuständig.[12] Ende des Jahres 1931 erließ die oberste Sowjetführung vergleichbare Verordnungen über die Gebiete am Jenissei und in Workuta, die sich in den folgenden Jahren zu ähnlichen Lagergebieten entwickelten.[13]

---

8 Vgl. Kokurin/Morukov, Stalinskie strojki, S. 368. Širokov verweist darauf, dass Vorschläge zur Errichtung eines großen Kombinats zur Durchdringung der Region Kolyma im Oktober 1931 auch in den Partei- und Sowjetstrukturen des Dal'nevostočner Distrikts geäußert wurden. Vgl. Širokov, Organizacionnye formy, S. 55.

9 Vgl. Nordlander, Gulag Capital, S. 79. Siehe zur Rolle Stalins an der Kolyma ebenso Applebaum, Gulag, S. 87.

10 Vgl. den Abdruck der Verordnung des ZK der KPdSU in Kokurin/Petrov, GULAG, S. 72. Der STO war eine Organisation für militärische Fragen und industrielle Entwicklung. Er war zwar eine unabhängige Organisation, seine Mitglieder wurden jedoch vom Rat der Volkskommissare ernannt. Sein Vorsitzender war zu dieser Zeit V. M. Molotov. Formal trat dieser Beschluss erst durch die Verordnung des STO am 13. November 1931 in Kraft, in der die exakte Bezeichnung des Kombinats und organisatorische Details festgeschrieben wurden. Vgl. den Abdruck der Verordnung in Stalinskie Strojki, S. 419–420, hier S. 419. Nach der Abschaffung des STO der UdSSR im April 1937 wurde Dal'stroj an den ökonomischen Rat des Rates der Volkskommissare der UdSSR übergeben. Vgl. Kozlov, Kombinat osobogo tipa, S. 18.

11 So war Dal'stroj für die Finanzierung von Transport, Bewachung und Versorgung der Häftlinge und ihrer Verwaltung verantwortlich. Vgl. Šulubina, Sevvostlaga, S. 72.

12 Unterstützt wurde diese Konstruktion durch das „Komitee des Nordens", das 1931 die Gründung von Kombinaten für die Erschließung des sowjetischen Nordens grundsätzlich befürwortete, um eine einheitliche Leitung und wirtschaftliche Durchdringung der großen Gebiete zu ermöglichen. Allerdings verband das Komitee damit die Hoffnung auf eine vollwertige Entwicklung und Erschließung der Region zugunsten der indigenen Völker. Vgl. Širokov, Organizacionnye formy, S. 54.

13 Vgl. Ivanova, Istorija, S. 228.

Die Ausbeutung der Zwangsarbeiter wurde im Nordosten mit Gründung des Lagerkomplexes *Sevvostlag* durch die OGPU am 1. April 1932 institutionalisiert.[14] Die Bezeichnung „Lagerkomplex" ist ein historischer Begriff. Dabei handelte es sich um eine organisatorische Einheit, wie das *Sevvostlag*, die eine Reihe von Lagerabteilungen für verschiedene Aufgaben umfasste. Lagerabteilungen wiederum bestanden aus vielen einzelnen Lagerpunkten, die am ehesten heute verbreiteten Vorstellungen eines „Lagers" entsprechen.[15] Bis zu seiner Auflösung 1957 sind insgesamt etwa 880.000 Menschen in den Lagerpunkten des *Sevvostlag* inhaftiert gewesen.[16] Daneben gab es seit 1948 auf dem Gebiet von Dal'stroj die Lager des *Berlag*, in dem ausschließlich sogenannte „politische Häftlinge" (Personen, denen staatsfeindliche Aktivitäten wie Spionage, antisowjetische Propaganda etc. zur Last gelegt wurden) unter besonders schweren Bedingungen inhaftiert waren. Das *Berlag* war Teil der „besonderen Lager" und unterstand unmittelbar dem MVD. „Besondere Lager" gab es in der Sowjetunion seit 1948, sie dienten der verschärften Inhaftierung und Ausbeutung als „politisch" geltender Häftlinge in extrem unwirtlichen Gegenden. Jährlich waren zwischen 1948 und 1954 ca. 20.000 Menschen im *Berlag* inhaftiert.[17] Unter den Inhaftierten von *Sevvostlag* und *Berlag* waren auch Häftlinge anderer Staatsangehörigkeit, darunter Mitglieder der kommunistischen Internationale, Menschen, die während des Krieges in die Sowjetunion geflohen waren sowie einige japanische Kriegsgefangene.[18] An der

---

14 Vgl. den Abdruck dieses Befehls in Kokurin/Petrov, GULAG, S. 226.

15 Vgl. zur Verwendung des Begriffes „Lager" in den Quellen Smirnov, Sistema lagerej, S. 78. Wenn in dieser Arbeit vom sowjetischen „Lagersystem" die Rede ist, dann ist damit nicht eine organisatorische Einheit, sondern generell die politische und wirtschaftliche Struktur der Sowjetunion gemeint, in deren Rahmen Menschen in verschiedenen Formen von Lagern festgehalten wurden. Dazu zählen auch alle weiteren Formen wie Kolonien, Verbannung oder die Freiheitsberaubung von sogenannten „Sondersiedlern". Vgl. die erweiterte Bedeutung des Akronyms GULAG, die Anne Applebaum für den „Entire Soviet Slave-Labor Complex" verwendet. Applebaum, Introduction, S. VIII.

16 Kozlov nennt die Gesamtzahl von 876.043 Menschen. Vgl. Kozlov, Kombinat osobogo tipa, S. 28. Ebenso wie in Bezug auf das gesamte Lagersystem der Sowjetunion unterlagen die in der Literatur genannten Häftlingszahlen für den Lagerkomplex *Sevvostlag* im Laufe der Zeit großen Veränderungen. Diese standen v. a. im Zusammenhang mit dem erst in den letzten Jahren möglichen Archivzugang für Historiker. Die Geschichte der Historiographie dieser Häftlingszahlen für den Nordosten zeichnet Kozlov nach. Vgl. Kozlov, Čislennosti zaključennych. In dieser Arbeit werden die Zahlen von Bacaev verwendet, der sich zum einen sehr detailliert mit verschiedenen Häftlingsgruppen sowie mit An- und Abreisen auseinandergesetzt hat. Zum anderen stimmen seine Zahlen mit den Daten des Handbuchs Smirnov, Sistema lagerej überein. Siehe zu den genauen Häftlingszahlen in den einzelnen Jahren, zu An- und Abtransporten Bacaev, Kolymskaja grjada, S. 50; Bacaev, Osobennosti, S. 63 sowie S. 73 ff. und Il'ina, Dinamika, S. 52.

17 Insgesamt gab es in der Sowjetunion 12 „besondere Lager" (das nordöstliche *Berlag* war das Lager Nr. 5). Vgl. Širokov, Osobyj lager', S. 85 f.; Kozlov, Osobyj lager'. Leider liegt keine Gesamtzahl aller Häftlinge des *Berlag* vor. Das *Berlag* wurde im Sommer 1954 als organisatorische Einheit aufgelöst, seine Häftlinge in Lagerabteilungen des *Sevvostlag*, getrennt von anderen Häftlingsgruppen, untergebracht. Vgl. Smirnov, Sistema lagerej, S. 60. Vgl. zur Auflösung aller Sonderlager Hedeler, Widerstand im Gulag, S. 354 sowie Hardy, Campaign, S. 94.

18 Vgl. die Darstellung vieler derartiger Schicksale in Rajzman, Inostrancy-Nevol'niki.

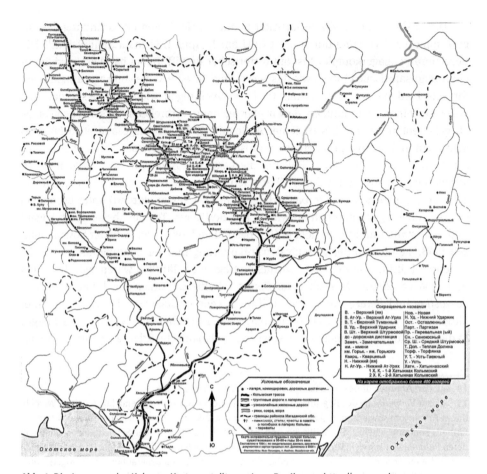

Abb. 1 Die Lager an der Kolyma. Karte erstellt von Ivan Panikarov, http://www.gulagmuseum.org

Kolyma wurden die Häftlinge zum Abbau von Gold, später auch von Zinn, Uran und weiteren Metallen gezwungen, schufteten in der Nebenindustrie und bei Bauarbeiten.[19]

Zum Direktor von Dal'stroj ernannte der STO, in Bestätigung einer Verordnung des Politbüros, am 14. November 1931 Ėduard Petrovič Berzin.[20] Nach Angaben von Nordlander traf Stalin persönlich diese Wahl. Er entschied sich damit für einen Veteranen der Čeka – GPU, der aus Lettland stammte und seit 1926 Leiter des Višersker Lagers (das zu den berüchtigten Lagern der Solovkij-Inseln zählte) gewesen war.[21]

---

19 Zum Lagerkomplex *Sevvostlag* siehe Šulubina, Sistema Sevvostlaga. Eine Karte aller Lagerpunkte des *Sevvostlag* und des *Berlag* zu einem bestimmten Zeitpunkt existiert nicht. Abbildung 1 zeigt eine von Ivan Panikarov erarbeitete Karte der Lager im Hauptgebiet der Goldförderung an der Kolyma.
20 Vgl. den Abdruck der Verordnung in Stalinskie Strojki, S. 420.
21 Zur Biographie des ersten Direktors von Dal'stroj siehe Širokov, Politika, S. 70 sowie Nordlander, Gulag Capital, S. 797; Nordlander, Evolution, S. 650 und 652 sowie Verkina/Kozlov, Novye dannye. In

Einen Eindruck von den schweren Lebens- und Arbeitsbedingungen, denen in die Häftlinge in den ersten Jahren seit Gründung von Dal'stroj ausgesetzt waren, vermittelt die Darstellung Michael Solomons, ein ehemaliger rumänischer Häftling an der Kolyma:

> Die Kommunisten wußten immer, daß sie das erforderliche Rohmaterial [für die Industrialisierung des Landes – M. S.] besaßen: Gold und Eisen, Uran und Blei, Bauxit und Zinn. Sagenhafte Vorkommen lagen in den sibirischen Bergen vergraben. Es war ein Wettlauf mit der Zeit, und die Bolschewisten waren entschlossen ihn zu gewinnen. Als erstes markierten ihre Vermessungstrupps die Adern auf Karten. Dann schickte man schubweise Häftlinge als Bergleute hinaus. Oft hatten sie kaum mehr als ihre bloßen Hände. Ein Trupp Sträflinge traf irgendwo in der schneebedeckten Taiga ein, man gab ihnen Schaufeln, Äxte, Eisenstangen und befahl ihnen, Bäume zu fällen und sich Baracken zu bauen. Die Baracken mußten sie allerdings nachts errichten, denn der Tag gehörte ihren Herren. So lebten sie, schliefen im Schnee und aßen auch draußen, bis es ihnen gelang, sich in ihrer „Freizeit" ein primitives Dach überm Kopf zu schaffen. Jene, die starben, wurden durch neue ersetzt. Wer die Norm nicht erfüllte, wurde erschossen. Ob Krieg oder nicht, die Arbeit ging pausenlos weiter.[22]

Im Jahr 1938 erhielten Dal'stroj und das *Sevvostlag* eine neue strukturelle Gliederung, die den Sonderstatus der Region noch einmal stärkte und die Phase der administrativen Organisation abschloss. Zu dieser Zeit geschaffene Strukturen blieben bis zu Stalins Tod im März 1953 im Wesentlichen unangetastet. Hintergrund der Reorganisation von 1938 bildete der deutliche Machtanstieg des NKVD (seit 1934 war die bisherige OGPU zu einem Volkskommissariat, dem Narodnyj Komissariat Vnutrennich Del – Volkskommissariat des Innern umstrukturiert worden) zur Zeit des sogenannten „Großen Terrors" und sein Ausbau zu einer der größten wirtschaftlichen Behörden der Sowjetunion. Damit wurde Zwangsarbeit endgültig zu einer der tragenden Säulen der sowjetischen Wirtschaft. Alle großen Zwangsarbeitsprojekte, die bisher von der OGPU-NKVD lediglich kontrolliert worden waren, wurden nun unmittelbar in die Struktur des NKVD integriert.[23]

Der lokalen Umstrukturierung von Dal'stroj ging die Verhaftung der bisherigen Führungsriege des Kombinats um Berzin voraus. Fast alle Angehörigen der ersten Führungsgruppe wurden erschossen oder starben im Zuge der Verhöre.[24] Auf ihre

---

seinem Aufsatz schildert Nordlander detailliert die biographischen Hintergründe, Ziele, Karrieren und Netzwerke Berzins und des weiteren Führungspersonals von Dal'stroj in den 1930er Jahren.

22 Solomon, Magadan, S. 157 f.

23 Im Frühjahr 1938 gab es in der UdSSR bereits 33 Lagerwirtschaftskomplexe im Rahmen des GULAG. Der GULAG wurde, wie es seine Mitarbeiter selbst ausdrückten, zu einem „riesigen Kombinat". Dies ging mit einem deutlichen Anstieg der Häftlingszahlen und einer allgemeinen Verlängerung der Haftdauer einher. Vgl. Ivanova, Istorija, S. 242.

24 Berzin selbst „gestand" im Verhör des Apparats des NKVD seine angebliche Teilnahme an einer Verschwörung, an der u. a. auch Rudzutak und Jagoda selbst teilgenommen haben sollten. Vgl. Širokov, Dal'stroj, S. 75. Er wurde am 1. August 1938 erschossen. Seine Rehabilitation erfolgte 1956, nach Chruščevs Geheimrede. Vgl. Nordlander, Evolution, S. 655.

Positionen brachte Ežov, der Nachfolger Jagodas, seine eigenen Leute.[25] Seit Dezember 1937 herrschte K. A. Pavlov über Dal'stroj, Chef über das *Sevvostlag* wurde S. N. Garanin.[26]

Nach Beschluss des Rates der Volkskommissare wurde Dal'stroj am 4. März 1938 dem NKVD unterstellt und zu einer seiner „Hauptverwaltungen" (*glavk*) ernannt.[27] Damit einher ging auch eine Umbenennung des Kombinats, wobei die Abkürzung „Dal'stroj" erhalten blieb. Nun lautete die Bezeichnung dieser Organisation „Glavnoe Upravlenie Stroitel'stva Dal'nego Severa (Dal'stroj) – GUSDS NKVD SSSR".[28] Mit diesem Schritt verlor der Lagerkomplex *Sevvostlag* seinen bisherigen Status; er wurde als eine Produktionsverwaltung unmittelbar in die Struktur von Dal'stroj aufgenommen.[29] Die Bezeichnung „Lager" hatte für den NKVD eine erweiterte Bedeutung; in seinen Direktiven bezeichnete er die gesamte Hauptverwaltung Dal'stroj nun als „Lager": „Dal'stroj ist ein Lager, in das nicht die Ordnungen übertragen werden dürfen, die für territoriale Organe [gemeint sind die regulären Organe von Partei und Sowjets – M. S.] aufgestellt wurden."[30]

---

25 Zu den Personalveränderungen in Dal'stroj nach der Überstellung in den NKVD siehe Grebenjuk, Rukovodjaščie kadry Dal'stroja, S. 86 ff.

26 Vgl. Nordlander, Evolution, S. 656. Unter Pavlov verschärfte sich der lokale „Große Terror" – eine lokal modifizierte *Trojka*, bei der der Leiter von Dal'stroj die Position des Parteivertreters besetzte (in Ermangelung eines Parteisekretärs im Rahmen des Sonderstatus von Dal'stroj), verhaftete und erschoss bis zum Frühjahr 1939 etwa 8.000 Häftlinge und freie Arbeiter. Die lokalen Terrormaßnahmen wurden – in Anlehnung an die Bezeichnung „Ešovščina" – als „Garaninščina" bezeichnet, da sich der Leiter des *Sevvostlag* Garanin durch besondere Grausamkeit „auszeichnete". Vgl. die ausführliche Darstellung dieser Zeit und die Rolle der einzelnen politischen Figuren bei Nordlander, Evolution, S. 656 ff.; Kozlov, Iz istorii kolymskich lagerej, S. 130; Conquest, Kolyma, S. 51; Lipper, Elf Jahre, S. 96 f. Die hier genannte Zahlenangabe von etwa 8.000 betroffenen Personen wurde entnommen aus Bacaev, Formy i metody, S. 78. Ein Teil der Repressionen wurde dabei von sogenannten „Meergrenzsoldatentruppen" ausgeübt, die seit 1932 gegen angeblich aktive kapitalistische Geheimdienste (v. a. der Japaner) und ihre Verbündeten auf Seiten der lokalen Bevölkerung des Nordostens aktiv waren. Diesen Verfolgungen fielen in der Mehrheit Angehörige der indigenen Völker zum Opfer. Siehe zur Geschichte dieser Organisation und ihrer Repressionspolitik Rajzman, Operativnaja rabota. V. A. Il'ina schildert ein weiteres Beispiel der gnadenlosen Verfolgung Indigener als angebliche „Volksfeinde", die zu einem massiven Bevölkerungsverlust führte, da die Rentiere verfolgter Familienangehöriger gänzlich konfisziert wurden. Vgl. Il'nia, Dinamika, S. 51.

27 Grundsätzlich wurde eine „Glavnoe upravlenie", eine „Hauptverwaltung" eines Volkskommissariats / Wirtschaftsministeriums (und als solches fungierte das NKVD schließlich seit dieser Zeit) als „glavk" bezeichnet. Ihr unterstand die Leitung des entsprechenden Wirtschaftsbereiches, die entsprechenden Betriebe oder Kombinate waren ihr rechenschaftspflichtig. Vgl. das Stichwort *Glavnoe upravlenie*, in: Bol'šaja Sovetskaja Ėnciklopedia, Band 6, Moskau 1975, S. 153.

28 Vgl. Širokov, Dal'stroj, S. 76. Siehe auch den Befehl von Ežov, der die entsprechende Verordnung des SNK SSSR vom 4. März 1938 über die Struktur des GUS DS NKVD SSSR am 9. Juni 1938 offiziell für den NKVD bestätigte. Abgedruckt in Kokurin/Petrov, GULAG, S. 248. Diese Unterordnung unter den NKVD/MVD bestand bis 1953. Vgl. Širokov, Severo-Vostok, S. 23.

29 Vgl. Šulubina, Sistema Sevvostlaga, S. 18.

30 Zitiert nach Bacaev, Osobennosti, S. 33.

Parallel zu dieser Reorganisation wurden bis 1940 eine ganze Reihe weiterer Giganten der Lagerwirtschaft zu Hauptverwaltungen des NKVD (z. B. *Enisejstroj*) ernannt.[31] Auf den ersten Blick waren sie damit der Lagerhauptverwaltung GULAG gleichgestellt, die ebenfalls eine *glavk* des NKVD war. Tatsächlich waren die strukturellen Verknüpfungen jedoch komplizierter, da der Lagerkomplex *Sevvostlag* durch die Zuteilung von Häftlingen und Material nach wie vor von der Hauptverwaltung der Lager (GULAG) abhängig blieb und der GULAG durch seine Direktiven theoretisch Einfluss auf das Regime im *Sevvostlag* nehmen konnte.[32]

Die Überführung von Dal'stroj in den NKVD bedingte, dass der militärische Charakter des Zwangsarbeitsprojektes noch deutlicher zutage trat. Zwar waren Berzin und die Moskauer Führung auch bisher bereits bestrebt gewesen, die Administration des Kombinats analog zu Strukturen in der Armee zu organisieren[33], nun aber wurde Dal'stroj endgültig zu einer Hauptabteilung einer militärischen Einrichtung. Der Lagerkomplex *Sevvostlag* und das Industriekombinat wurden unter dieser militärischen Leitung noch fester aneinander gebunden, es entstand jene Organisationsstruktur, die Ivanova als „Lager-Industrieller Komplex" bezeichnet hat und für die Dal'stroj als Prototyp gelten kann.

In der Roten Armee trug der Kommandant in Personalunion gegenüber der Kommunistischen Partei und der sowjetischen Regierung die Verantwortung sowohl für die militärische Bereitschaft als auch für den politisch-moralischen Zustand der Truppe.[34] In Dal'stroj wurde diese Einzelleitung, die sogenannte *edinonačalie*, auf die Verhältnisse in der Lagerwirtschaft übertragen. Dementsprechend stand an der Spitze von Dal'stroj seit 1939 nicht mehr ein ziviler Direktor, sondern ein „načal'nik", ein Führer mit einem militärischen Rang, dessen Befehle unbedingten Gehorsam verlangten und dem sich zu widersetzen mit einem Verfahren vor einem Militärtribunal geahndet wurde. Dieser militärische Führer war zugleich auch Bevollmächtigter des

---

31 Vgl. Ertz, Lagernaja sistema. Zudem wurde eine größere Zahl kleinerer und größerer Zwangsarbeiterprojekte, die bisher gewöhnlichen Produktionsministerien unterstanden hatten, dem NKVD unterstellt – aber nicht zu eigenständigen Hauptverwaltungen ernannt. Für eine Beschreibung einiger dieser Projekte siehe Ivanova, Istorija, S. 242f.

32 Die Kompetenzverteilung innerhalb des NKVD/MVD unterlag im Laufe der Jahre zahlreichen Veränderungen und war immer wieder Gegenstand von Streitigkeiten. Der GULAG war aber grundsätzlich für die Zusammenstellung der Häftlingskontingente und für das Lagerregime des *Sevvostlag* verantwortlich. Vgl. Kozlov, Lagernaja sistema, S. 173; Širokov, Organizacionnye formy, S. 64. Anders als von Anne Applebaum dargestellt, waren die Lager an der Kolyma bis zu Stalins Tod niemals unmittelbar Teil der Hauptverwaltung der Lager, GULAG. Vgl. Applebaum, Gulag, S. 87.

33 Berzin wehrte sich zwischen 1932 und 1938 immer wieder vehement gegen Bestrebungen von Parteimitgliedern zum Aufbau regulärer Parteiorganisationen und setzte sich in Moskau persönlich für die Ausweitung des Sonderstatus der Region ein. So äußerte er sich schon 1937: „Meine persönliche Meinung ist, dass an der Kolyma eine Parteiorganisation in Form einer militärischen Organisation benötigt wird – die große Masse der Arbeitskräfte sind Häftlinge". Zitiert nach Širokov, Organizacionnye formy, S. 62f.

34 Vgl. das Stichwort *edinonačalie*, in: Bol'šaja Sovetskaja Ènciklopedija, Band 9, Moskau 1972, S. 67–68.

Chabarowsker Exekutivkomitees (formal zählte das Territorium von Dal'stroj zum Chabarowsker Distrikt[35]) und der Chabarowsker Parteileitung.[36] Innerhalb des Kombinats übernahm eine kleine, unbedeutende Einheit, die administrativ-zivile Abteilung (AGO), die Leitung aller Angelegenheiten der freien Bevölkerung.[37] Freie Arbeitskräfte hatte es zu allen Zeiten in Dal'stroj gegeben. Zu einem hohen Anteil handelte es sich dabei um entlassene Häftlinge, denen in vielen Fällen streng verboten wurde, das Gebiet nach Ende ihrer Haftzeit zu verlassen. Das Kombinat wollte auf diese Weise den Verlust erfahrener Arbeitskräfte verhindern. Hinzu kamen Vertragsarbeiter, die sich für eine Arbeit in Dal'stroj hatten anwerben lassen. Die militärischen Strukturen der Region und die unerbittliche Härte, mit der das Kombinat auch freien Arbeitern begegnete, führten zu einem permanenten Mangel an Facharbeitern.

Der Kombinatsleiter war in der Region für alle politischen Aufgaben verantwortlich, die in anderen Gebieten der Sowjetunion durch Partei- und Sowjetstrukturen verwaltet wurden. Er war in Personalunion Chef über das Industriekombinat, den Lagerkomplex, die freie Bevölkerung und das gesamte Territorium. Der Kombinatsleiter war nur Ežov bzw. den weiteren NKVD/MVD-Leitern und Stalin persönlich verantwortlich und unterlag ihnen gegenüber der militärischen Meldepflicht. Stalin ließ sich über alle Entwicklungen in Dal'stroj ausführlich informieren, er traf auch weiterhin die wichtigsten Entscheidungen persönlich.[38]

Von anderen staatlichen Einrichtungen und Organisationen war Dal'stroj vollkommen unabhängig, es verfügte über eigene Versorgungssysteme und eine eigene Flotte. Auf dem Gebiet von Dal'stroj gab es ein eigenes Rechtssystem mit Militärtribunalen anstelle von gewöhnlichen Gerichten. Alle Aspekte der Hauptverwaltung unterlagen besonderer Geheimhaltung; eine Zusammenarbeit mit anderen Organisationen in der Region war untersagt.[39] Auch finanziell hatte Dal'stroj einen Sonder-

---

35 Bis zum 20. Oktober 1938 gehörte das Gebiet zu dem riesigen Dal'nevostočner Distrikt, der dann in einen Primorsker und den Chabarowsker Distrikt geteilt wurde. Vgl. Kozlov, U istokov, S. 28.

36 Zwar gab es bei Gründung des Kombinats drei Bezirke, die sich als „nationale Bezirke" auf die indigenen Völker der Region bezogen. In allen weiteren Gebieten, die im Laufe der Zeit Dal'stroj zugeordnet wurden, wurden jedoch keine Bezirke mehr eingerichtet. Vgl. Verkina/Kozlov, Nacional'nye rajony Kolymy, S. 73–80 sowie Čistjakov, Desjatiletie, S. 42.

37 Diese Abteilung wurde auch zur Leitung aller Aspekte des Lebens der indigenen Bevölkerung bestimmt, v. a. für ihre gewaltsame Kollektivierung. Vgl. Širokov, Dal'stroj, S. 138 f.

38 Vgl. zu der militärischen Struktur von Dal'stroj Širokov, Organizacionnye formy, S. 67; Širokov, Politika, S. 448–450; Bacaev, Osobennosti, S. 33, Roščupkin/Bubnis, K voprosu ob administrativnom ustrojstve, S. 70, Zeljak, Osobennosti razvitija, S. 91. Mitrochin kontrastiert anschaulich die persönlichen Beziehungen Stalins zu einer ganzen Reihe ihm loyaler Funktionäre für bestimmte Aufgaben mit der Gestaltung von machtpolitischen Strukturen auf der Basis politischer Clans unter Chruščev. Vgl. Mitrokhin, Political Clans, S. 26 f.

39 Sämtliche Bereiche des Wirtschaftskomplexes und des Lagers unterlagen von Anfang an einer absoluten Geheimhaltungspflicht. Dies beinhaltete alle Befehle und Verordnungen, Berichte aus Magadan (die nur durch spezielle Eilkuriere des NKVD übermittelt wurden) sowie Informationen über das Gebiet (Karten, Statistiken, Lagebeschreibungen etc.). Ebenso wurden auch die geförderten Rohstoffe ausschließlich mit speziellen Kurieren und geheimen Transportmitteln ins Zentrum gebracht.

status – das Kombinat konnte nahezu unbegrenzt staatliche Mittel anfordern und war zeitweise sogar von Steuern und Abgaben befreit.[40]

Zur Beschreibung dieser Sonderstellung des Kombinats sprechen Magadaner Historiker von Dal'stroj als einem „Staat im Staat"[41]. Diese Beschreibung soll dazu dienen, die Abkapselung des nordöstlichen Gebietes, seine geschlossenen Versorgungssysteme und seine Herrschaftsform, unabhängig von zivilen staatlichen Strukturen, zu charakterisieren. Sie ist jedoch unpassend, wenn sie zugleich ein Netz fester Institutionen und normierter Staatsstrukturen impliziert. An der Kolyma handelte es sich keineswegs um eine permanent durchherrschte Zone, tatsächlich war „Herrschaft" nur punktuell greifbar. Das Interesse an einem Punkt auf der Karte war rein ökonomisch definiert und konnte jederzeit versiegen. Dal'stroj war darauf angelegt, seine militärischen Versorgungs- und Befehlsstrukturen zur Bewältigung kurzfristiger, hochintensiver Produktionsanstrengungen im aktuell reichhaltigsten Goldgebiet einzusetzen und sich dabei hauptsächlich mobiler Lagerpunkte zu bedienen.

So war Dal'stroj nicht nur ein Industrieprojekt in einer Region, das Kombinat bestimmte die Herrschaftsform des gesamten Gebietes. Der Lager-Industrielle Komplex war für die sowjetische Führung eine Raumeroberungsstrategie. Seine Gebietsgrenzen wurden nicht anhand administrativer Grenzen (wie Distrikt oder Gebiet) gezogen, sondern unterlagen wirtschaftlichen Kriterien. In den Jahren seit 1931 dehnte sich der Herrschaftsbereich von Dal'stroj immer weiter aus. Wann immer reiche Rohstoffvorkommen (neben Gold auch Zinn, Kobalt, Wolfram und Uran) in angrenzenden Gebieten gefunden wurden, inkorporierte Dal'stroj diese Territorien in seinen Machtbereich. 1951 hatte das Kombinat seine größte Ausdehnung erreicht, es umfasste ca. 3 Mio. km^2.[42]

Zudem war eine Reise in das Gebiet ohne eine besondere Genehmigung durch den NKVD unmöglich. Vgl. Kozlov, Kombinat osobogo tipa, S. 21; Nikolaev, K voprosy izučenija, S. 31; Širokov, Dal'stroj, S. 55f.

40 Vgl. Širokov, Dal'stroj v social'no-ėkonomičeskom razvitii, S. 49.

41 Vgl. Širokov, Severo-Vostok, S. 25. Širokov greift dabei auf eine Formulierung Ivanovas zurück, die die Behörde GULAG als „Staat im Staat" bezeichnet hat. Vgl. Ivanova, Gosudarstvo v gosudarstve. Anne Applebaum spricht dagegen von einem „country within a country, almost a separate civilization", womit sie stärker eine kulturwissenschaftliche Blickrichtung einnimmt, die auf die dem GULAG eigene Sprache, Gesetze, Moralvorstellungen etc. verweist. Vgl. Applebaum, Gulag, S. XVI. Magadaner Historiker haben immer wieder versucht, mit Definitionen die Besonderheit dieser Strukturen zu beschreiben. Der Wirtschaftswissenschaftler S. V. Slavin hat sich zu Beginn der 1960er Jahre ausführlicher mit der Geschichte von Dal'stroj auseinandergesetzt. Er beschreibt den Industriekomplex mit Blick auf seinen administrativen Sonderstatus als „integrales Kombinat", ohne jedoch auf den Lagerkomplex, die tausendfache Zwangsarbeit und den Terror der NKVD-Hauptverwaltung einzugehen. Vgl. Slavin, Promyšlennoe osvoenie. Mitte der 1990er Jahre blickte der Historiker A. N. Piljasov schon deutlich kritischer auf die Ausnahmestellung des Kombinats und beschrieb Dal'stroj als „Superorganisation", ohne damit jedoch den militärischen Charakter dieser Einrichtung und die massenhafte Zwangsarbeit wirklich offenzulegen. Vgl. Piljasov, Zakonomernosti.

42 1939 wurde die Halbinsel Tschukotka in die Struktur des Kombinats aufgenommen. Nach Angaben des Leiters von Dal'stroj umfasste sein Territorium im März 1953 sogar mehr als 3,5 Mio. km^2. Siehe zu

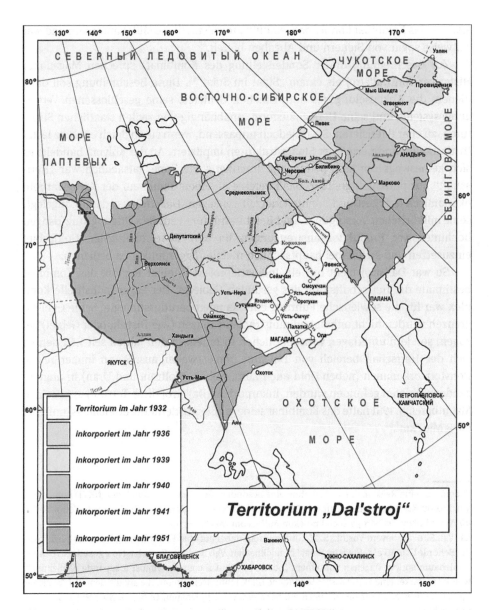

Abb. 2 Territorium von Dal'stroj. Karte erstellt von Alglus, CC BY-SA 3.0

Der militärische Sonderstatus des Kombinats hatte im Laufe der Jahre auch dazu geführt, dass sich in seinem Innern eine besondere Leitungsmentalität herausbildete. Die Region wurde von den sogenannten *Dal'stroevcy* beherrscht, einer Kaste von Of-

den Grenzen des Territoriums Smirnov, Spravočnik, S. 117 sowie zu den Angaben von Mitrakov Kozlov, Lagernaja sistema, S. 175.

fizieren des MVD, die über Jahre ohne die üblichen Personalrotationen die Geschäfte und Angelegenheiten des Kombinats beherrschte.[43] Auch die riesige Entfernung von den zentralen Teilen der Union und die langwierigen Transport- und Kommunikationswege bestärkten diese Gruppe, an deren Spitze zuletzt Mitrakov stand, in ihrer Selbstherrlichkeit. Persönliche Bereicherung, Korruption und Vetternwirtschaft waren an der Tagesordnung; sie hatten sich als informelle Arrangements an die formalen Strukturen angelagert und diese schließlich vollständig durchdrungen.[44] Die enormen finanziellen Mittel des Kombinats und der unbedingte Befehl zur Einhaltung der Produktionspläne führten zugleich zu gewaltigen Verschwendungen und einer zum Teil grotesken Misswirtschaft.[45]

Die Taiga wurde immer wieder als Sinnbild für die Rechtlosigkeit und Schutzlosigkeit der Untergebenen dieser Offizierskaste herangezogen. Wer aus den hölzernen Baracken floh, kam im Eis ums Leben, wer eine Waffe trug, war Herr eines kleinen Imperiums.[46] Diese Mentalität setzte sich in der Hierarchie nach unten fort. Jeder Lagerpunkt- und Produktionsleiter betrachtete das jeweilige Gebiet als sein Reich. Übergriffe durch Wachmannschaften, Leitungskader und kriminelle Häftlinge, die Marc Elie und Manuela Putz zutreffend als „Berufsverbrecher" bezeichnen und die in den Lagern die übrigen Häftlinge terrorisierten[47], waren an der Tagesordnung. Häftlinge waren der Willkür der Wachen, der Führung eines Lagerpunktes und den Banden schwerkrimineller Häftlinge schutzlos ausgeliefert; für sie gab es „da draußen" nicht einmal mehr eine wahrnehmbare Struktur der Sowjetunion, die ihnen als Folie hätte dienen können, um den Grad ihrer Entrechtung zu ermessen. Weibliche wie männliche Häftlinge fielen Vergewaltigungen, Folter und Mord zum Opfer. Im Schutz der Taiga drohte den Tätern kaum jemals eine Aufklärung. Der weiteren Verrohung des Personals, das in der Regel über eine kaum nennenswerte Bildung verfügte und das meist nach Dal'stroj strafversetzt worden war, waren kaum Schranken gesetzt.[48]

---

43 Nach den Angaben von Grebenjuk habe Stalin persönlich verlangt, im Fall der Dal'strojer Kader eine Ausnahme von dem System der permanenten Versetzungen und Säuberungen zu machen. Vgl. Grebenjuk, Kolymskij led, S. 42.

44 So z. B. im Bereich der Flugzeugflotte, vgl. RGAĖ f. 9163, op. 6, d. 12, l. 100, bei der Kaderauswahl, vgl. RGAĖ f. 9163, op. 6, d. 11, l. 139 und bei der Festlegung von „persönlichen Gehältern", die auf der Grundlage von persönlichen Beurteilungen der Kombinatsleitung und einer Sonderentscheidung des MVD festgelegt wurden. Vgl. RGAĖ f. 9163, op. 6, d. 11, l. 142 sowie die Akte zur Auszahlung von Sondergehältern in GARF f. R-9401, op. 4, d. 1627.

45 Ausführlich dazu siehe das Kapitel 4.3.1.

46 Eine der wenigen zugänglichen Erinnerungen eines Lagermitarbeiters stammt von Fyodor Mochulsky, der zwischen 1940 und 1946 in Pechorlag, einem Lagerkomplex im westlichen Teil des sowjetischen Nordens, angestellt war und der NKVD-Mitarbeiter, Wachen und Kader aus seiner damaligen Perspektive beschreibt. Vg. Mochulsky, Gulag Boss.

47 Elie, Verbrecherbanden; Putz, Berufsverbrecher.

48 Das Phänomen der fehlenden Kontrolle der obersten Lagerleitung über die Verhältnisse in einzelnen Lagerpunkten beschreibt Golfo Alexopoulos anschaulich anhand einer Untersuchungskommission des MVD im Lagerkomplex Petchorlag. Vgl. Alexopoulos, Torture Memo.

In wirtschaftlicher Hinsicht waren die ersten Jahre seit Gründung des Kombinats der Schaffung einer grundlegenden Infrastruktur gewidmet, um die Fördergebiete an der Kolyma mit dem Hafen von Magadan zu verbinden. Bereits 1937 verzeichnete die Leitung erste Erfolge beim Abbau der enorm goldhaltigen Erde und schon im Jahr 1940 wurde mit 80 Tonnen chemisch reinen Goldes ein absolutes Rekordergebnis erzielt; Dal'stroj war zu den wichtigsten Goldfördergebieten der Welt aufgestiegen. In den Kriegsjahren kam der Rohstoffförderung im Nordosten eine besondere Bedeutung zu, da die Sowjetunion auf Valuta aus dem Goldverkauf zur Anschaffung schweren Kriegsgeräts dringend angewiesen war. Die Einstufung als besonders kriegswichtige Produktion sowie amerikanische Lieferungen durch Lend-Lease-Verträge sorgten dafür, dass die Versorgung Dal'strojs auch in den Kriegsjahren nicht abriss und noch recht hohe Golderträge erzielt werden konnten.[49] Im Spätstalinismus erlebte die Rohstoffförderung einen kontinuierlichen Rückgang, der sich Ende der 1940er und zu Beginn der 1950er Jahre zu einer schweren Krise des Kombinats ausweitete. Diese war bedingt durch einen Rückgang des Goldgehaltes; die Fördergebiete, in denen das Gold in besonders gut zugänglichen Erdschichten lagerte, schienen erschöpft. Zudem veränderte sich im Zuge einer allgemeinen ökonomischen Krise der sowjetischen Zwangsarbeitswirtschaft die Position des Kombinats. Einerseits musste es mit einer deutlichen Beschneidung seiner bislang fast unbegrenzten Mittel kämpfen, andererseits veränderte sich sein Bestand an Zwangsarbeitern dramatisch. Der GULAG sandte nun zu einem hohen Prozentsatz schwerkriminelle Häftlinge (Personen verurteilt wegen Mord, schwerer Körperverletzung etc.), die die Arbeit in vielen Fällen verweigerten, sowie alte und kranke Häftlinge nach Dal'stroj, um auf diese Weise die zentralen Lager der Union zu entlasten. Die beiden Teile der Einzelleitung waren zunehmend konkurrierenden Aufgaben unterworfen.

Kurz vor Stalins Tod sah sich Dal'stroj nicht nur einem dramatischen Rückgang der Förderzahlen bei einer finanziellen und strukturellen Verschlechterung seiner Position ausgesetzt, auch die Lage in den Lagern und Siedlungen war an vielen Stellen außer Kontrolle geraten. Die schlechte Versorgung führte zu einem gewaltigen Anstieg der Todesrate.[50] Zahlreiche Banden krimineller Häftlinge und Mitglieder nationaler Gruppierungen kämpften um die Oberhand in Lagerpunkten, sie führten, unter erheblichem Waffeneinsatz, regelrechte Kriege gegeneinander, die Zahl der Fluchtversuche stieg kontinuierlich. Andere Häftlinge waren der unvorstellbaren Gewalt dieser vollkommen verrohten Gruppen, die oftmals mit der Leitung in den Lagerpunkten kooperierten, schutzlos ausgeliefert. Die schlechte Versorgung und die geringe Dichte an Wachmannschaften gerade in besonders weit entfernten Lagerpunkten machte

---

49 Ausführlich zur wirtschaftlichen Entwicklung des Kombinats und zu den verschiedenen industriellen Bereichen siehe Kapitel 4.1.
50 Vgl. Kozlov, Lagernaja sistema, S. 158. Siehe ebenso die ausführliche Beschreibung bei Bacaev, Osobennosti, S. 134. Bacaev weist auch darauf hin, dass durch die – regelwidrige – Zusammenlegung männlicher und weiblicher Häftlinge die Zahl der Syphilis-Erkrankungen unter den Häftlingen, aber auch unter freien Arbeitskräften dramatisch zunahm. Vgl. Bacaev, Osobennosti, S. 136.

eine Isolierung der verschiedenen Häftlingsgruppen unmöglich; in einigen Gebieten wagten sich selbst bewaffnete Wachen nicht mehr in die Häftlingsbaracken. In den Weiten der Taiga setzten viele Lagerpunkte auf die „Selbstbewachung" durch kriminelle Häftlinge, eine klar umrissene Lagerzone gab es häufig nicht.[51] Die mangelnden Sicherheitsanlagen und Stacheldrähte sorgten für eine Durchdringung des gesamten Gebietes mit Lagerpunkten und Häftlingen, Übergriffe krimineller Häftlinge weiteten sich auch auf Siedlungen freier Arbeiter aus. „Das Lager" war in der Region von Dal'stroj omnipräsent und Gewalt allgegenwärtig.[52]

Im Jahr 1952 kam es zu einer Strukturreform, nach der Dal'stroj auch nominell in ein riesiges Lager verwandelt wurde.[53] Die neue Struktur trug nun den Titel „Hauptverwaltung der Lager und des Bauwesens des Fernen Nordens" („Glavnoe Upravlenie Lagerej i Stroitel'stva Dal'nevo Severa (GULSDS MVD SSSR)"). Hinter dieser Veränderung stand der Versuch, die Einzelleitung zu stärken und der Bedeutung der Zwangsarbeit für das Kombinat Rechnung zu tragen. Dementsprechend forderte der stellv. Leiter von Dal'stroj, Generalleutnant G. S. Žukov: „Wenn man unsere Entfernung vom ‚Festland' berücksichtigt, brauchen wir mehr [an Zwangsarbeitern – M. S.], als es irgendwo sonst gibt, wir müssen unseren eigenen kleinen GULAG haben."[54] Fragen der administrativen Gliederung von Dal'stroj waren jedoch nicht geeignet, den Lager-Industriellen Komplex aus seiner strukturellen Schieflage herauszuführen. Schließlich war die sowjetische Führung nach wie vor nicht willens, die Produktionsanforderungen an das Kombinat zugunsten einer besseren Versorgung der Lagerpunkte zurückzunehmen.

Alle Prämissen der regionalen stalinistischen Produktionsweise – Extensivität, Zwangsarbeit und die militärische Sonderstellung des Kombinats – gerieten in der spätstalinistischen Krise der sowjetischen Lagerwirtschaft unter erheblichen Druck. Dennoch standen diese spezifischen Bedingungen nicht zur Disposition. Unter der persönlichen Aufsicht Stalins war die Metallförderung im nordöstlichsten Teil der Sowjetunion für die sowjetische Führung nur in Form eines Lager-Industriellen Komplexes denkbar. Für den Historiker Nordlander hat sich Stalin mit dem Kombinat ein „monument to his rule" geschaffen; eine Organisation, mit der er seine Vorstellungen von Raumeroberung beispielhaft umsetzte.[55]

---

51 Im Jahr 1952 stieg die Kriminalität im Vergleich zum Vorjahr um 44 % an. Vgl. Bacaev, Dejatel'nost' organov, S. 224. Siehe zum Begriff der „Zone" in stalinistischen Lagern Applebaum, Gulag, S. XXIX.
52 Vgl. die Berichte von Betroffenen und Augenzeugen bei Bacaev, Obostrenie, S. 197.
53 Vgl. den Abdruck der neuen Struktur entsprechend des Befehls des MVD der UdSSR vom 26. Mai 1952, in Stalinskie Strojki, S. 418 f. Gegen diese neue Struktur regte sich Widerstand aus dem GULAG. Vgl. den Brief des Leiters des GULAG Dolgich, in Kozlov, Lagernaja sistema, S. 173.
54 Mitrakov hat in einem Brief an Berija im März 1953 diese Forderung noch einmal erklärt. Ihm sei es damals darum gegangen, die lokale Verwaltung des MVD abzuschaffen und die operative Überwachung der Lager unmittelbar Dal'stroj zu übertragen. Vgl. Kozlov, Lagernaja sistema, S. 172.
55 Vgl. Nordlander, Gulag Capital, S. 798 ff.

3 Erobern und Verwalten

3.1 1953: der Lager-Industrielle Komplex wankt

3.1.1 Berijas Strukturreformen

Die erste Statusveränderung des Lager-Industriellen Komplexes Dal'stroj betraf seine Unterordnung unter den MVD. Fast unmittelbar nach Stalins Tod vereinigte Berija den Geheimdienst MGB und den MVD zu einer Behörde. In seiner neuen Position als Chef des MVD begann Berija mit einer Restrukturierung, die auf eine Trennung der wirtschaftlichen Funktionen des Ministeriums von Haftsystem und Miliz abzielte.[1] Am 18. März wurden eine ganze Reihe Lager-Industrieller Komplexe (darunter Dal'stroj), diverse Industriekombinate und Bauprojekte, die sich auf Zwangsarbeit stützten, aus dem MVD herausgelöst und gewöhnlichen, zivilen Produktionsministerien unterstellt.[2] Zwangsarbeit wurde damit keineswegs in Frage gestellt, Berija wollte durch die Abspaltung enorm verlustreicher Wirtschaftsprojekte eine schnelle ökonomische Entlastung des MVD erreichen; das Ministerium verlor damit automatisch seine Stellung als wichtigste Wirtschaftsbehörde der Sowjetunion.[3]

Hintergrund dieser Maßnahme war eine schwere Krise der sowjetischen Lagerwirtschaft, die bereits seit Ende der 1940er Jahre andauerte. Die lagergeprägte Wirtschaftsweise hatte sich insgesamt als ineffektiv und ausgesprochen verlustreich erwiesen. Die Kosten für die Lager und die Aufrechterhaltung des riesigen Geheimapparates waren im Vergleich zu den wirtschaftlichen Ergebnissen der Kombinate enorm hoch, zudem gab es in den Lagerpunkten eine große Zahl nicht arbeitsfähiger Häftlinge und Zwangsarbeiter, die ihre Arbeitsnormen nicht erfüllen konnten.

Auch das Kombinat Dal'stroj war Teil dieser systemischen Krise der Lagerwirtschaft, zugleich hatten die regionalen Schwierigkeiten spezifische Ursachen. In wirtschaftlicher Hinsicht litt das Kombinat an einem seit 1949 anhaltenden Rückgang der Goldförderung, während die Kosten für die Rohstoffgewinnung permanent stiegen.[4] Zudem drifteten die beiden Teile des Lager-Industriellen Komplexes, Produktion und Lager, immer weiter auseinander, da die wirtschaftlichen Anforderungen an das

---

1 Vgl. Elie, Khrushchev's Gulag, S.110.
2 Vgl. Smirnov, Sistema lagerej, S. 58; Zacharčenko, K raspadu ėkonomiki prinuditel'nogo truda, S. 300 f.
3 Vgl. zur Diskussion um die Hintergründe dieser Maßnahme Gorlizki/Khlevniuk, Cold Peace, S. 132. Auch für die damaligen lokalen Akteure war dieser Hintergrund evident, so z. B. für den stellvertretenden Leiter von Dal'stroj, Čuguev, der diesen Schritt im April 1953 als „Befreiung des MVD von produktiv-wirtschaftlichen Tätigkeiten" bezeichnete. Vgl. GAMO f. R-23, op. 1, d. 4681, l. 274. Ausführlicher zu den weiteren wirtschaftlichen Veränderungen im MVD im Frühjahr 1953 siehe Khlevnyuk, Economy of the OGPU, S. 54.
4 Siehe dazu ausführlich das Kapitel 4.1.

https://doi.org/10.1515/9783110557879-004

Kombinat in Widerspruch zu den Aufgaben des Lagerkomplexes als Strafvollzugsorgan gerieten: Im Spätstalinismus betrachtete die sowjetische Führung die Abgeschiedenheit von Dal'stroj als Möglichkeit, das *Sevvostlag* als Auffanglager für nicht arbeitsfähige und schwerkriminelle Häftlinge aus allen Teilen der Sowjetunion zu nutzen, wodurch es dem Kombinat an einsatzfähigen Arbeitskräften mangelte.[5]

Mit der Herauslösung des Kombinats aus seinem Ministerium befreite Berija den MVD von der riesigen finanziellen Belastung durch Dal'stroj und von einem schwer zu kontrollierenden Gebiet. Zugleich wurde mit dieser Maßnahme zum ersten Mal der Sonderstatus der Region eingedämmt. Seit dem 18. März 1953 war Dal'stroj – gemeinsam mit weiteren Giganten der Lagerwirtschaft – als eine Hauptverwaltung dem Ministerium für Metallindustrie der UdSSR (Ministerstvo Metallurgičeskoj Promyšlennosti – MMP) unterstellt, ab dem 21. Januar 1954 dann dem Ministerium für Buntmetalle der UdSSR (Ministerstvo Cvetnoj Metallurgii – MCM), das aus dem MMP hervorging.[6] Entsprechend seiner Geheimhaltungsstufe gelangte Dal'stroj nicht in den allgemeinen Bestand des Ministeriums, sondern in eine Sonderverwaltung.[7]

Das Kombinat verlor damit auf einen Schlag seine exklusive Stellung als eine Hauptverwaltung des MVD, die Lieferungen der von ihm benötigten Waren und Materialien wurden nicht mehr im Rahmen der militärischen Versorgungskreise des MVD bedient. Zudem bewirkte die Zuordnung zu einem gewöhnlichen Ministerium eine gewisse Öffnung – ein ziviles Ministerium erhielt, zunächst noch in begrenztem Maße, Einblick in die Verhältnisse des Nordostens und übertrug seine bürokratischen Standards auf die Region. Gleichzeitig mühte sich Dal'stroj darum, die Kenntnisse des

---

5 Stalins Tod verhinderte die eigentlich geplante Erweiterung des Lagersystems *Sevvostlag* durch die Schaffung weiterer Lagerabteilungen für schwerkriminelle Häftlinge aus anderen Lagergebieten. Diese Pläne wurden nach dem 5. März 1953 ad acta gelegt. Vgl. Bacaev, Kolymskij Gulag, S. 78.

6 Vgl. Kokurin/Pozarov, Novyj kurs, S. 142. Die konkrete Übergabe an das MMP erfolgte am 3. April 1953. Vgl. den Übergabeakt – unterzeichnet vom stellv. Innenminister und dem Minister für Metallindustrie, Tevosjan – in GAMO f. R-23, op. 1, d. 4677, l. 1–28. Dieser Akt enthält ausführliche Angaben über sämtliche zu übergebende wirtschaftliche Anlagen und Einrichtungen des Kombinats, über Häftlinge und freie Arbeitskräfte. Ausführliche Anlagen widmen sich außerdem den für Dal'stroj festgesetzten Privilegien der Kombinatsmitarbeiter (l. 105–112), den wissenschaftlichen Einrichtungen (l. 113–115) sowie den Transporteinrichtungen von Dal'stroj (l. 118–120). Siehe zu der Übergabe auch die Akten des Finanzministeriums in RGAÈ f. 7733, op. 42, d. 192, l. 37–39 sowie des MVD in GARF f. R-9401, op. 4, d. 1620, l. 213 sowie 306–307. Die Bezeichnung von Dal'stroj lautete nun: „Hauptverwaltung für die Bauwirtschaft des Fernen Nordens des Ministeriums für Metallindustrie der UdSSR (GUS DS MMP SSSR – Dal'stroj)". Zu der Übergabe an das MMP siehe den Akt in GAMO f. R-23, op. 1, d. 5610, l. 7–15.

7 Das zivile Produktionsministerium für Metalle unterlag im Laufe der Jahre, wie üblich in der Sowjetunion, einer ganzen Reihe von Reorganisationen. Seit 1950 bis zum 15. März 1953 fungierte es unter der Bezeichnung „unionsweites MCM der UdSSR"; vom 15. März 1953 (möglicherweise im Zusammenhang mit der Aufnahme der Lagerwirtschaften) bis zum 8. Februar 1954 existierte es als „MMP der UdSSR", um dann ab dem Februar 1954 als „MCM der UdSSR (sojuzno-respublikanskoe)" organisiert zu sein, bis zur Auflösung aller Produktionsministerien im Mai 1957 im Vorfeld der Einführung der Volkswirtschaftsräte. Eine Konstante des Ministeriums war Lomako, der viele Jahr lang entweder als Minister oder als stellv. Minister der jeweiligen Ministerien fungierte.

neuen Ministeriums über die genauen Verhältnisse in der Region so gering wie möglich zu halten.[8] Mit der Übertragung in ein ziviles Ministerium wurden auch die bisher fast unbeschränkten Mittel des Kombinats beschnitten. Das MMP verweigerte die Finanzierung einiger bereits projektierter und noch unter dem MVD beschlossener Baumaßnahmen und begründete seine Ablehnung mit ökonomischen Schwierigkeiten.[9]

Der Lagerkomplex *Sevvostlag* verlor im Zuge dessen seine relative Unabhängigkeit als eine direkte Unterabteilung des Kombinats Dal'stroj, er wurde in die Hauptverwaltung für Lager (GULAG) integriert, die wiederum selbst am 28. März 1953 dem Justizministerium unterstellt wurde[10], aber seit dem 21. Januar 1954 wieder dem MVD unterstand.[11] Die Lagerabteilungen des eigenständigen *Berlag* wurden am 28. März 1953 zunächst der Hauptverwaltung für Gefängnisse des MVD der UdSSR unterstellt, seit dem 8. Februar 1954 waren sie schließlich auch Teil des GULAG des MVD der UdSSR.[12]

Durch diese Neuzuordnungen unterstanden Lager und Produktion auf einmal unterschiedlichen Ministerien. Anders als in anderen Lagerkomplexen bedeutete dies jedoch nicht die Aufgabe der militärischen Einzelleitung. Vielmehr hatte sich der Minister für Metallindustrie, Tevosjan, bereits im April 1953 beim Vorsitzenden des Ministerrates Malenkov für ihre Beibehaltung in Dal'stroj und Norilsk (das ebenfalls dem MMP unterstand) starkgemacht. Die Einzelleitung sei unter den extremen klimatischen und geographischen Bedingungen, im Angesicht des Mangels an Infrastruktur und Kommunikationsmitteln unbedingt notwendig, um eine „maximale operative Manövrierfähigkeit von Arbeitskräften und materiellen Ressourcen" zu ermöglichen.[13] Der Ministerrat entsprach in der Folge der Bitte Tevosjans: Die Errichtung des Lagerkomplexes *Sevvostlag* im Rahmen des Justizministeriums erfolgte unter

---

8 Vgl. die Beschwerde des Leiters für Baumaßnahmen der Sonderabteilung im MMP über mangelnde Auskünfte aus Dal'stroj. Diese Beschwerde zeigt zugleich die hohen formalen und bürokratischen Vorgaben des neuen Ministeriums in RGAĖ f. 9163, op. 6, d. 15, l. 83–85.

9 Vgl. den Bericht aus der Planungsabteilung von Dal'stroj an das ZK der KPdSU in GAMO f. P-21, op. 5, d. 685, l. 1–20, hier l. 1.

10 Vgl. Kokurin/Petrov, GULAG, S. 792. Eine Verordnung des Ministerrates der UdSSR vom 31. August 1953 übertrug dem Justizministerium das Recht zur Neugründung des *Sevvostlag* im Rahmen seiner GULAG-Strukturen. Am 8. September 1953 erließ das Justizministerium die entsprechende Verordnung zur Gründung der „Verwaltung der nordöstlichen Besserungs- und Arbeitslager des GULAG des Justizministeriums der UdSSR" („Upravlenie Severo-Vostočnyi ispravitel'no-trudovymi lagerjami GULAGa MJu SSSR"). Vgl. die Verordnung in GAMO f. R-23ss, op. 1, d. 344, l. 207.

11 Vgl. Kokurin/Petrov, GULAG, S. 372–373. Die sowjetische Führung war durch die Aufstände in diversen Lagergebieten im Sommer 1953 zu der Ansicht gelangt, dass das Justizministerium nicht in der Lage sei, mit den Schwierigkeiten innerhalb des GULAG umzugehen. Vgl. Petrov, Karatel'naja Sistema, S. 466 f. Zu den Reorganisationen siehe ausführlich Hedeler, Ökonomik, S. 217 f.

12 Vgl. die entsprechende Verfügung des MVD der UdSSR vom 6. Mai 1953 in Smirnov, Sistema lagerej, S. 120. *Berlag* wurde am 25. Juni 1954 schließlich ganz aufgelöst, seine Lagerabteilungen und die verbliebenen Häftlinge an das *Sevvostlag* übergeben. Vgl. Kozlov, Lagernaja sistema, S. 179.

13 Schreiben von Tevosjan an Malenkov vom 23. April 1953 in GAMO f. R-23, op. 1, d. 312, l. 222–223.

Beibehaltung der bisher bestehenden Ordnung, wonach der Leiter von Dal'stroj gleichzeitig der Leiter des Lagersystems und die Leiter der einzelnen Betriebe gleichzeitig die Leiter der entsprechenden Lagerabteilungen waren.[14] Mit dieser Sonderregelung war eine Art von „Zwischenkonstruktion" geschaffen worden, da ein Bereich der Einzelleitung einem anderen Ministerium zugeordnet war als der andere.[15] Nach Darstellung von Širokov war geplant, die Einzelleitung in der Region noch ein bis zwei Jahre aufrechtzuerhalten; faktisch bestand sie jedoch bis zur Auflösung des *Sevvostlag* im August 1957 fort.[16]

Die wechselseitigen Verpflichtungen zwischen Lager und Produktion, v. a. die Bereitstellung von Zwangsarbeitern und deren Versorgung, wurde nun durch Verträge geregelt, die zwischen dem MMP bzw. dem MCM und dem MVD geschlossen wurden.[17] Grundlage dafür waren Standardverträge, wie sie im GULAG für alle zivilen Ministerien, die Zwangsarbeiter ausbeuteten, entwickelt worden waren.[18] In der Realität von Dal'stroj herrschte über die praktische Ausgestaltung dieser Verträge große Verwirrung, da unter den Bedingungen der Einzelleitung bisher kein Produktionsleiter exakte Vorausplanungen des Arbeitskräftebedarfs angestellt hatte.[19] Während durch die Beibehaltung der Einzelleitung Mitrakov nach wie vor als Leiter des Lagerkomplexes fungierte, wurden die Gestaltung der Lager, die Bedingungen und Bewachung der Häftlinge sowie die Isolierung bestimmter Häftlingsgruppen der Aufsicht des GULAG unterstellt.[20] Die Leiter des *Sevvostlag* sprachen daher von einer lediglich „platoni-

---

14 Vgl. die Anordnung des Ministerrats in GAMO f. R-23ss, op. 1, d. 344, l. 207. Dementsprechend erteilte nun der Leiter einer Hauptverwaltung des Ministeriums für Metallindustrie der Lagerverwaltung Befehle. Zur Beibehaltung der Einzelleitung in einigen großen Industriekomplexen vgl. Elie, Khrushchev's Gulag, S. 111.

15 Dal'stroj war nicht das einzige Kombinat, in dem die Einzelleitung beibehalten wurde. Vgl. Smirnov, Sistema lagerej, S. 59.

16 Die Bezeichnung des Leiters des *Sevvostlag* lautete daher: Načal'nik USVITLa MJu pri DS MMP SSSR. Vgl. Širokov, Politika, S. 433. Im August 1957 wurde das *Sevvostlag* als Einheit des GULAG aufgelöst; die noch bestehenden Lagerabteilungen unterstanden nun unmittelbar dem MVD der RSFSR. Vgl. Širokov, Politika, S. 434.

17 Vgl. GAMO f. R-23, op. 1, d. 345, l. 274.

18 Musterverträge aus dem Jahr 1956 und 1962 finden sich in GAMO f. R-23, op. 1, d. 5844, l. 20 – 35 (aus dem Jahr 1956) sowie GAMO f. R-137sč, op. 1b, d. 152, l. 93 – 104 (aus dem Jahr 1962). Siehe auch den strengen Erlass Mitrakovs an alle Wirtschaftseinrichtungen, diese Verträge mit den Lagerabteilungen zu schließen und die entsprechenden Verpflichtungen einzuhalten. GAMO f. R-23, op. 1, d. 5844, l. 76 – 81, hier l. 76. Siehe zu der unionsweiten Praxis dieser Verträge Ertz, Lagernaja sistema, S. 117.

19 Vgl. die Beschwerden bei einer Abschlussdiskussion der Ergebnisse einer Kommission des GULAG im Januar 1954 in GAMO f. R-23, op. 1, d. 5207, l. 13 – 54, hier l. 19 f. Zu den Diskussionen über die Details dieser Verträge siehe den Schriftverkehr zwischen dem MCM, Dal'stroj und dem MVD in GAMO f. R-23, op. 1, d. 5610, l. 36 sowie GAMO f. R-23sč, op. 1, d. 458, l. 39. Die strittigen Fragen kreisten dabei v. a. um die Finanzierung.

20 Der GULAG war nun für die Organisation und Kontrolle von Inhaftierung, Bewachung und Versorgung der Häftlinge zuständig. Vgl. Ertz, Lagernaja sistema, S. 118. So wurde auch die Versorgung von Dal'stroj und dem *Sevvostlag* unabhängig voneinander organisiert. Vgl. GAMO f. R-146, op. 1, d. 47, l. 90 – 93.

schen Einzelleitung", die nicht mehr in der Lage sei, entscheidende Fragen des Lagerkomplexes zu bestimmen, zumal sich die Finanzierung des *Sevvostlag* unter der Leitung des GULAG erheblich verschlechtert habe.[21] Eine Kommission des GULAG, die zum ersten Mal im Jahr 1953 das *Sevvostlag* überprüfte, stellte dem Lagerkomplex in allen Fragen der Lagergestaltung ein schlechtes Zeugnis aus.[22] Der Leiter einer Lagerabteilung stellte daraufhin fest:

> Die Regelverletzungen in der Lagergestaltung [bezüglich der Standards des GULAG – M. S.] wurden nicht in den vergangenen zwei Jahren hervorgerufen, sondern sind das Ergebnis der ganzen historischen Entwicklung von Dal'stroj. Bei uns unterliegen 60 bis 70 % der Lager der Abschreibung, nach allen Forderungen des GULAG müssten sie schnellstmöglich geschlossen werden.[23]

Gegenüber dem GULAG verteidigten Mitrakov und sein Stellvertreter für das Lager die besonderen Bedingungen des Kombinats, in dem man „das Lager nicht allein als Lager" sehen dürfe. Die „Janusköpfigkeit der Einzelleitung", die sowohl dem Lagerkomplex als auch den Anforderungen der Produktion gerecht werden müsse, bestimme die besonderen Bedingungen des Kombinats Dal'stroj, denen auch der GULAG mit seinen Anforderungen Rechnung tragen müsse.[24] Die schematische Übertragung der Standards des GULAG auf das Lagersystem *Sevvostlag*, bei Hygienevorschriften, der Größe der Lagerbaracken und der Versorgung der Häftlinge, löste bei den einzelnen Leitern von Lagerabteilungen des *Sevvostlag* nur Spott aus. So schilderte der Leiter der medizinischen Abteilung des *Sevvostlag* die Reaktion seiner Leute auf die Kommission des GULAG folgendermaßen: „Als ich ihnen gesagt habe, dass wir laut GULAG für die Häftlinge unbedingt auch frisches Fleisch und frisches Gemüse vorsehen müssen, um den Skorbut zu verhindern, haben sie mich mit Hohn übergossen."[25]

Faktisch aber war die Leitung von Dal'stroj von nun an „zwei Herren" mit ihren jeweiligen Ansprüchen an das Kombinat verpflichtet – den Anforderungen des MMP an Planerfüllung und effektive Wirtschaftslenkung und den Regelungen des Justizministeriums für Inhaftierung und die Gestaltung des Lagerkomplexes.

---

21 Vgl. GAMO f. R-23, op. 1, d. 5207, l. 13 – 54, hier l. 16. Zur Finanzierung des *Sevvostlag* im Rahmen des GULAG siehe l. 26 f.

22 Obwohl die Behörde GULAG bei der Zuteilung von Häftlingen und Materialien sowie bei der Gestaltung der Lagerabteilungen in all den Jahren Einfluss auf das *Sevvostlag* gehabt hatte, war das Lagersystem weitgehend autark verwaltet worden. Zu der Abgrenzung zwischen dem GULAG und Dal'stroj siehe Bacaev, Kolymskaja grjada, S. 54 f.; Širokov, Organizacionnye formy, S. 64. Die Kompetenzverteilung innerhalb des NKVD/MVD unterlag im Laufe der Jahre zahlreichen Veränderungen und war immer wieder Gegenstand von Streitigkeiten. Vgl. Kozlov, Lagernaja sistema, S. 173.

23 GAMO f. R-23, op. 1, d. 5207, l. 13 – 54, hier l. 16.

24 Vgl. GAMO f. R-23, op. 1, d. 5207, l. 13 – 54, hier l. 17. Diese Ansicht wurde von allen Leitern des *Sevvostlag* unterstützt.

25 GAMO f. R-23, op. 1, d. 5207, l. 13 – 54, hier l. 33.

Die Kader von Dal'stroj hatten durch die Neuzuordnung von Kombinat und Lagersystem nicht nur mit strukturellen Einschränkungen, sondern auch persönlich mit erheblichen materiellen Einbußen zu kämpfen. In seiner Doppelfunktion als Leiter von Dal'stroj und Stellvertreter Berijas bezog Mitrakov bis zum 18. März 1953 ein monatliches Grundgehalt von 8.000 Rubel plus Sonderzulagen von etwa 5.000 Rubel. Nach der Übergabe von Dal'stroj an das MMP und dem damit einhergehenden Verlust seines Postens als stellvertretender Innenminister wurde Mitrakovs Grundgehalt auf 5.000 Rubel abgesenkt, ein Teil der Sonderzulagen zu seinem militärischen Rang wurden gestrichen. Daneben drohte der Verlust seiner kostenlosen Privatwohnung und Datscha – eine Vergünstigung, die dem jeweiligen Chef von Dal'stroj seit Gründung des Kombinats garantiert gewesen war.[26]

Nicht besser erging es seinen Offizieren, die als Mitarbeiter des MVD bis zum März 1953 allesamt nach Militärrängen vergütet worden waren. Die militärischen Bezüge plus Boni und Prämien sowie die zu erwartenden Pensionen überstiegen die Gehälter und Vergünstigungen von Mitarbeitern ziviler Ministerien deutlich. Nach der Ausgliederung von Dal'stroj und der offiziellen Abkommandierung der Offiziere verweigerte jedoch das MVD jede Verantwortung für diesen Personenkreis. Im MMP gab es aber keine militärischen Ränge und auch die bestehenden Vergünstigungen für Mitarbeiter des Ministeriums im Hohen Norden wurden nicht automatisch auf die bisherigen Dal'stroj-Offiziere übertragen, wodurch ihnen eine radikale Schlechterstellung drohte. An der Kolyma, wie auch in anderen betroffenen Lagergebieten, erhob sich ein Sturm der Entrüstung. Die etwa 1.700 Offiziere von Dal'stroj reagierten mit Protestschreiben an lokale und unionsweite Behörden, teilweise stellten sie einfach ihre Arbeit ein.[27]

Vor allem ging es bei diesen Vergünstigungen um die spezielle Form der Rentenberechnung, die den Offizieren in Dal'stroj durch den MVD gewährt worden war und bei der ein Dienstjahr wie zwei Arbeitsjahre gezählt wurde. Da der harte Kern der Offiziere, die *Dal'strojevcy*, im Schnitt vor etwa 10 bis 15 Jahren unter dem Leiter Nikišov in das Kombinat eingetreten und dort zum Offizier ernannt worden war, hatte

---

26 Vgl. die Gehaltsübersicht für Mitrakov und frühere Leiter von Dal'stroj in RGAĖ f. 9163, op. 6, d. 13, l. 30–31. Ob Mitrakov (und seinen Nachfolgern) die Wohnung auch weiterhin zur Verfügung gestellt wurde, ist nicht bekannt. Der Minister für Buntmetalle, Lomako, stellte jedoch im Mai 1954 einen dementsprechenden Antrag beim Ministerrat, offensichtlich kam es darauf an, Mitrakov bei Laune zu halten. Vgl. ebd., l. 123.

27 Der stellv. Leiter der Politischen Abteilung von Dal'stroj, Šmygin, sprach in einem Bericht an Chruščev davon, dass die Offiziere von Dal'stroj nun sogar schlechter gestellt seien „als in Dal'stroj arbeitende Sondersiedler und ehemalige Häftlinge", da jenen die Vergünstigungen des Ministeriums für Metallindustrie zur Verfügung stünden. Vgl. RGANI f. 5, op. 27, d. 117, l. 179–181ob., Zitat l. 181. Ganz ähnliche Probleme schilderte auch Kuščinskij, der stellvertretende Leiter der Politischen Verwaltung von „Glavzoloto", einem goldfördernden Kombinat, das ebenfalls aus dem MVD in das MMP übergeben worden war. In seinem Schreiben an das Präsidium des ZK der KPdSU ging Kuščinskij vor allem auf die Bedeutung der Schaffung neuer materieller Anreize für Offiziere ein. RGANI f. 5, op. 27, d. 117, l. 177–178ob.

dieser Personenkreis auf einen baldigen Pensionsbeginn gehofft. Trotz eines Beschlusses des Ministerrates zur Beibehaltung dieser Regelungen weigerte sich das zuständige Ministerium für Sozialfürsorge der RSFSR, die im MVD übliche Form der Rentenberechnung durchzuführen.[28]

Der russlanddeutsche Mennonit und ehemalige Häftling des *Berlag*, Abraham Dück, berichtet in seinen Erinnerungen von der Situation zweier solcher Offiziere, die er im Spätsommer 1953 nach seiner Entlassung in Magadan wiedertraf und die er beide aus dem Lager kannte:

> Und dann kam er [ein Major – M. S.] mit der Sprache raus, wie ich es erwartet hatte. Trunkener Mund verrät des Herzens Grund. Nach Stalins Tod habe sich alles sehr verändert. Er sei aus dem Dienst entlassen. Sein Eifer hatte ihm nichts genützt. Deshalb sei er damals im Lager auch barsch gewesen. Er war als Inspektor ins Frauenlager geschickt worden, weil der Obrigkeit über viele Intrigen berichtet wurde, womöglich von den Offiziersfrauen. Aber er war den Ränken nicht gewachsen. Ohne Beruf sei es jetzt schwer, eine gut bezahlte Arbeit zu finden. In der Bergbaufachschule mache er jetzt eine Ausbildung. Wir verabschiedeten uns friedlich. Später hatte ich noch eine ähnliche Begegnung. Ganz zufällig auf dem Trödelmarkt. Es war der Sergeant Pupko, der am letzten Tag meiner Haft auch eine wichtige Rolle gespielt hatte. Er verkaufte Birkenbesen fürs Dampfbad. Wo waren seine stolze Haltung und die von den Frauen der Wäscherei immer aufs peinlichste geplättete Uniform geblieben? Er sah ziemlich heruntergekommen aus. [..] Ich verließ den Markt. Pupko war in derselben Lage wie auch der Major. Verabschiedet, ohne Beruf, und zudem wohl auch nur mit einer sehr dürftigen Dorfschulbildung.[29]

Eine gewisse Klärung des Status der Offiziere erreichte der Ministerrat schließlich im Mai 1954. Die Abkommandierung der Offiziere und Sergeanten aus dem MVD in zivile Ministerien und Einrichtungen wurde unionsweit aufgehoben und die betreffenden Personen in die Reserve des Verteidigungsministeriums versetzt, was ihnen die erneute Anerkennung ihrer militärischen Ränge (nun in der Reserve) ermöglichte.[30] Ob diesen Personen eine Rente ausgezahlt wurde, hing vom Stand ihres Rentenanspruchs zum Zeitpunkt der Versetzung in die Reserve ab. Gleichzeitig konnten sie nun als übliche Mitarbeiter ziviler Ministerien eingestuft und entsprechend entlohnt werden und dabei die in diesen Ministerien üblichen Vergünstigungen beziehen.

Schwierigkeiten und Unklarheiten bestanden jedoch auch weiterhin. So hatten die Offiziere der Lagerabteilungen, die als Mitarbeiter des *Sevvostlag* dem GULAG unterstanden, bei ihren Pensionsberechnungen keine Probleme und waren dadurch gegenüber den Offizieren des Dal'stroj im Vorteil. Denn das Offizierskorps des GULAG hatte bei der Übergabe an das Justizministerium die Vorgaben für Pensionszahlungen

---

28 Vgl. RGANI f. 5, op. 27, d. 117, l. 180.
29 Dück, Erinnerungen, S. 433. Ich danke Julia Landau herzlich für den Hinweis auf die Biographie Abraham Dücks und seine Erinnerungen.
30 Vgl. die Verordnung des Ministerrates vom 14. Mai 1954 in GAMO f. R-23, op. 1, d. 5207, l. 114–115.

weitgehend behalten können bzw. unterstand seit dem 21. Januar 1954 ja bereits wieder dem MVD.[31]

Mit Blick auf Dal'stroj zeigt sich, dass die ministeriellen Neuzuordnungen bisher bestehende Widersprüche zwischen Lager und Produktion verschärften, da unterschiedliche Ministerien nun verschiedene Ansprüche an die Teilbereiche der Einzelleitung formulierten. Zudem vergrößerte sich der Kreis der an der Lage im Nordosten beteiligten Institutionen und Personen, während zugleich die lokale Leitung an Machtfülle und persönlichem Status einbüßte. Der Sonderstatus der Region hatte bereits wenige Tage nach Stalins Tod Risse bekommen.

3.1.2 Die Amnestie vom 27. März

Die Herauslösung des Kombinats aus dem MVD rüttelte von politischer und administrativer Seite an wichtigen Pfeilern des Dal'stroj'schen Sonderstatus. Sehr viel heftiger waren jedoch die Erschütterungen, die von Veränderungen im Lagerkomplex *Sevvostlag* durch die große Amnestie ausgingen. Am 27. März 1953 wurden auf Betreiben Berijas unionsweit etwa 1,2 Mio. Menschen amnestiert und konnten in den folgenden Monaten sowjetische Lager verlassen.[32] Dabei handelte es sich zum einen um Häftlinge, die nicht oder nur eingeschränkt in der Lage waren zu arbeiten (schwangere Frauen und Frauen mit kleineren Kindern, Minderjährige, alte Menschen und Invaliden). Zum anderen kamen Personen frei, die zu Haftstrafen von bis zu fünf

---

31 Der Ministerrat der UdSSR hatte in einer Anordnung vom 4. April 1953 verfügt, die Pensionsregelungen sämtlicher Dienstränge des GULAG bei der Übergabe aus dem MVD in das Justizministerium beizubehalten. Vgl. GAMO f. R-23, op. 1, d. 4656, l. 110–111.

32 Vgl. zu der Zahlenangabe Werth, L'amnistie, S. 212. Aleksei Tikhonov nennt die Zahl von mehr als 1,5 Mio. Menschen. Tikhonov, The End, S. 72. Nach Angaben des Justizministers K. P. Goršenin änderte sich darüber hinaus der rechtliche Status von mehr als 2,6 Mio. Häftlingen, v. a. da durch die Amnestie ihre Haftzeit reduziert wurde. Außerdem hoben die Organe des MVD, der Staatsanwaltschaft und der Gerichte Anklagen gegen etwa 524.000 Menschen auf, die zum Zeitpunkt der Amnestie verhaftet worden waren bzw. stellten das Verfahren ein oder reduzierten das angesetzte Strafmaß um die Hälfte. Aus Arbeitskolonien wurden zusätzlich 24.600 Minderjährige entlassen, bzw. ihre Haftstrafen wurden halbiert, aus Gefängnissen kamen 75.600 und aus den Verbannungsorten etwa 8.000 Personen frei. Vgl. den Bericht des Justizministers K. P. Goršenin, in Auszügen abgedruckt in Kokurin/Morukov, Struktura i kadry. Stat'ja dvadcat' vtoraja, S. 100 f. Der Amnestieerlass selbst trat am 27. März 1953 in Kraft, einen Tag später wurde er auf der ersten Seite der *Pravda* und der *Izvestija* veröffentlicht. Dabei handelte es sich um eine bemerkenswerte Ausnahme mit propagandistischem Hintergrund, denn den GULAG betreffende Erlasse wurden ansonsten niemals der Öffentlichkeit zugänglich gemacht. Vgl. die Beschreibung der Veröffentlichung in Kokurin/Morukov, Struktura i kadry. Stat'ja dvadcat' vtoraja, S. 100. Genauere Bestimmungen zur Ausführung der Amnestie erließen das Justiz- und das Innenministerium in Zusammenarbeit mit der Generalstaatsanwaltschaft der UdSSR. Vgl. das Dekret vom 28. März 1953, abgedruckt in Artizov, Reabilitacija Tom I, S. 16–18, hier S. 17.

Jahren verurteilt worden waren, und Personen, die wegen Amts- und Wirtschaftsvergehen in Haft saßen.[33]

Ausgenommen waren somit Häftlinge mit längeren Haftstrafen sowie alle als „politische Häftlinge" Geltenden. Aus diesem Grund betraf die Amnestie auch nicht das System der Sonderlager, zu dem das *Berlag* an der Kolyma zählte.[34] Aber aus den Lagerpunkten des *Sevvostlag* kam eine große Zahl von Häftlingen frei.[35] Bis zum 1. Dezember 1953 wurden etwa 78.000 Häftlinge entlassen, bei etwa einem Viertel sorgte die Amnestie dafür, dass das reguläre Ende ihrer Haftzeit nun auch zu ihrer tatsächlichen Entlassung führte.[36]

Die Amnestie löste durch die Entlassung von zu kürzeren Haftstrafen verurteilten Personen einen enormen Arbeitskräftemangel aus. Neben Häftlingen konnten auch Sondersiedler und ein Teil der zwangsweise an die Region gebundenen Arbeiter das Kombinat verlassen, so dass dem Kombinat durch die Amnestie rund 84.400 Zwangsarbeiter verlorengingen, das waren 35,8 % aller Arbeitskräfte.[37] Zusätzlich dazu stieg die Entlassung freier Arbeitskräfte sprunghaft an, denn eine ganze Reihe von Arbeitern und Wachmannschaften mussten aufgrund der Verkleinerung des Häftlingskontingents freigestellt werden.[38]

Die Ziele Berijas, die ihn zur Initiierung dieser Amnestie veranlassten, sind, soweit es die zugänglichen Quellen erkennen lassen, recht gut aufgearbeitet. Während er

---

33 Daneben wurde bestimmten Häftlingsgruppen ihre Haftstrafe um die Hälfte verkürzt bzw. ihnen die verbleibenden 50 % ihrer Haftzeit erlassen.

34 Personen, die aus „politischen Motiven" zu weniger als fünf Jahren Haft verurteilt worden waren, wurden ebenfalls nach dieser Amnestie entlassen – dabei handelte es sich jedoch um einen sehr kleinen Kreis von Häftlingen.

35 Am 1. April 1953 waren im *Sevvostlag* etwa 145.600 Menschen inhaftiert. Hinzu kamen ca. 8.000 Sondersiedler (*specposelency*), mehr als 5.000 Verbannte, über 17.000 „freie" Personen, die mit Arbeitsverträgen zwangsweise an Dal'stroj gebunden waren, und ca. 47.000 ehemalige Häftlinge, die die Region noch nicht verlassen durften. All diese Menschen waren in den diversen Abteilungen und Punkten des Lagerkomplexes untergebracht. Verbannte Personen waren Entlassene des *Berlag*, die auch nach Verbüßung ihrer Haftstrafe „auf ewig" zum Verbleib in Dal'stroj gezwungen wurden. Menschen, die aufgrund besonderer Arbeitsleistungen (*začety*) vorzeitig freigekommen waren, mussten die Hälfte ihrer eingesparten Haftzeit als „freie" Lohnarbeiter in Dal'stroj abarbeiten. Zum Vergleich: Die Zahl der im eigentlichen Sinne freien Arbeitskräfte in Dal'stroj betrug zu dieser Zeit 66.300 Personen. Vgl. die statistischen Angaben in GAMO f. 23, op. 1, d. 1809, l. 47.

36 Vgl. Bacaev, Amnistija, S. 204. Auch in den folgenden Jahren konnten Häftlinge aufgrund der Amnestie das *Sevvostlag* vorzeitig verlassen, da ihnen durch diesen Erlass ihre Haftzeit verkürzt worden war.

37 Vgl. Bacaev, Amnistija, S. 205 sowie die Angaben zu den Arbeitskräftezahlen an das MMP, GAMO f. R-23, op. 1, d. 1809, l. 1.

38 1953 wurden 41.200 freie Arbeitskräfte und Wachmannschaften entlassen, im Jahr 1952 waren es nur 19.700. Zahlenangaben nach einer streng geheimen Tabelle über die Fluktuation freier Arbeitskräfte in Dal'stroj, GAMO f. R-23sč, op. 1, d. 503, l. 155. Vgl. den Erlass des Justizministers zur Entlassung von Mitarbeitern vom 22. April 1953 in GAMO f. R-23, op. 1, d. 4656, 98 ff. sowie die entsprechende Direktive der Dal'stroj-Leitung, die allerdings die Entlassung freier Fachkräfte grundsätzlich verbot, GAMO f. R-23, op. 1, d. 4686, l. 102 f.

durch die Verschiebung unrentabler Zwangsarbeiterprojekte in zivile Ministerien den ihm unterstellten MVD von finanziellen Belastungen befreien wollte, so zielte „seine Amnestie" darauf ab, Zwangsarbeit insgesamt effektiver zu gestalten. Man erhoffte sich eine Senkung der enormen Kosten des Lagersystems durch die Entlassung von Menschen, die als „politisch unbedenklich" galten und als Zwangsarbeiter nicht eingesetzt werden konnten.[39] Mit der Amnestie sollte das sowjetische Lagersystem nicht etwa angegriffen, sondern im Gegenteil dadurch gestärkt werden, dass die wirtschaftliche Bedeutung der Zwangsarbeit betont wurde, die Rolle der Lager als Repressionsinstrument bei kleineren Vergehen sollte hingegen sinken. Verhaftungen, Prozesse und Inhaftierungen der angeblichen „politischen Gegner" blieben davon unberührt.[40]

In Dal'stroj hatte Berijas Amnestie jedoch den vollkommen gegenteiligen Effekt. Die seit Anfang der 1950er Jahre bestehende wirtschaftliche Krise des Kombinats erlebte 1953 einen neuen Höhepunkt. Lager und Produktion drifteten immer weiter auseinander. Das *Sevvostlag* war zur Entlassung vieler Zehntausender Menschen gezwungen, obwohl die Zwangsarbeiter für die Planerfüllung eigentlich unentbehrlich waren. Die Goldförderung sank immer weiter, die Kosten der Förderung stiegen unablässig.[41] Bereits im April und Mai 1953 wurde die Metallförderung in diversen Gruben eingestellt, Produktionsstätten verkleinert, die ihnen zugeordneten Lagerpunkte zusammengelegt oder aufgegeben.[42] Besonders schwer war die Lage im Bereich der Zinnförderung, da dort fast die Hälfte aller Häftlinge der Amnestie unterlag.[43] Auch in den weniger von Entlassungen betroffenen Teilen des Kombinats zeigten sich die Auswirkungen. Die Amnestie desorganisierte die gesamte Produktion von Dal'stroj, da die Arbeitskräfte aufgrund der Entlassungen sehr ungleich über die einzelnen

---

39 Diese Einschätzung stützt sich hauptsächlich auf einen Brief Berijas an das Präsidium des ZK der KPdSU, in dem er auf die Notwendigkeit einer dauerhaften Verkleinerung des Häftlingsbestandes verweist. Die von ihm vorgeschlagene Amnestie sollte zu einer schnellen Entlassung einer großen Zahl Inhaftierter führen, eine Veränderung des Strafgesetzbuches ein erneutes Anwachsen der Lager verhindern. Vgl. das Schreiben Berijas vom 26. März 1953, abgedruckt in Naumov/Sigačev, Berija, S. 20. Zu den Hintergründen der Amnestie siehe Elie, Revisionskommissionen; Elie, Amnistiés et réhabilités; Werth, L' amnistie; Hedeler, Ökonomik, S. 218 ff.

40 So wurden, parallel zu den Entlassungen, im Jahr 1953 knapp 463.400 Personen neu in sowjetische Lager verbracht. Vgl. die Übersicht über Häftlingsbewegungen in Lagern und Kolonien in Kokurin/ Petrov, GULAG, S. 435.

41 Aufgrund dieser gestiegenen Selbstkosten bat das MMP Malenkov um die Erlaubnis, die Arbeitszeit in den Fördermonaten von Juni bis August um zwei Stunden heraufzusetzen. Vgl. RGAÈ f. 7733, op. 42, d. 1048, l. 209.

42 So beispielsweise in den Gruben „Central'nyj", „Kontrand'ja", „Udarnik" und Čelban'ja" der südlichen Bergbauverwaltung. Vgl. Bacaev, Amnistija, S. 205. Für die Lage in der nördlichen Wirtschaftsverwaltung vgl. den Befehl zur Zusammenlegung von Gruben in RGAÈ f. 9163, op. 6, d. 12, l. 20.

43 Die Produktion wurde noch einmal dadurch behindert, dass in den Sommermonaten die verbliebenen Häftlinge in großer Zahl zu Verladearbeiten eingesetzt werden mussten, weil die Zinnförderung v. a. im nordöstlichen Teil von Dal'stroj lag und die dortigen Häfen nur eine kurze Zeit im Jahr überhaupt eisfrei waren. Vgl. GAMO f. R-23, op. 1, d. 1809, l. 3–4.

Produktionsfelder verteilt waren. Allein in den ersten acht Monaten des Jahres 1953 gab es für 11.288 Personen (Zwangsarbeiter und freie Arbeitskräfte) an ihrem Aufenthaltsort keine Arbeit; 2.990 Häftlinge wurden nicht eingesetzt, weil nach dem Verbot der „Selbstbewachung" (ausgewählte Häftlinge bewachen ihre Mithäftlinge) im Zuge der Amnestie die Wachmannschaften in den Produktionsbereichen nicht ausreichten.[44] Hinzu kamen vermehrt Fälle von Arbeitsverweigerung, die auf den gestiegenen Hoffnungen der Häftlinge auf weitere Entlassungen beruhten.[45] Dal'stroj mangelte es schlagartig an mehr als 7.000 Fachkräften, wie Schlosser oder Sprengmeister, die z. T. in Dal'stroj ausgebildet worden waren und nun von der Amnestie profitierten.[46]

Obwohl der Ministerrat über die wirtschaftliche Lage des Kombinats unterrichtet war, kam es zu keiner Veränderung der Planziffern für das Jahr 1953.[47] Die Kombinatsleitung musste daher kurzfristig nach Lösungen suchen. Mitrakov reagierte auf die Entlassung einer so großen Zahl von Häftlingen reflexhaft mit der Bestellung neuer Zwangsarbeiter. Beim Justizministerium verlangte er 50.000 neue Häftlinge und 50 Mio. Rubel für ihren Transport in die Region; tatsächlich wurden lediglich 16.000 neue Häftlinge nach Dal'stroj gebracht.[48] Unter ihnen waren, wie bereits in den Jahren zuvor, viele schwerkriminelle Häftlinge (verurteilt wegen Mord, schwerer Körperverletzung etc.) aus anderen Lagergebieten der Sowjetunion, die in den allermeisten Fällen die Arbeit grundsätzlich verweigerten. Trotz der schweren wirtschaftlichen Lage von Dal'stroj betrachtete der GULAG das Gebiet noch immer als „Sammelpunkt" besonders gefährlicher, krimineller Häftlinge. Unter den im Jahr 1953 neu ankommenden Häftlingen waren auch etwa 1.260 Überlebende des Häftlingsaufstandes in Norilsk, die in das Lager *Berlag* gebracht wurden. Auf dem Weg dorthin hatten sie versucht über das Meer in Richtung Alaska zu entkommen. Von der Parteileitung des Magadaner Gebietes wurde diese Personengruppe später für den Kriminalitätsanstieg mitverantwortlich gemacht.[49]

---

44 Vgl. Kozlov, Sevvostlag, S. 127. Aufgrund der großen Schwierigkeiten mit fehlenden Wachmannschaften erlaubte daraufhin ein Erlass des Justizministeriums der UdSSR vom 18. Mai 1953 die Wiedereinführung der „Selbstbewachung". Vgl. Bacaev, Amnistija, S. 206 f.

45 So gab es Gruben, in denen lediglich 59 %, zum Teil auch nur 49 oder 37 % der Häftlinge des zugeordneten Lagerpunktes an der Arbeit beteiligt waren. Vgl. Bacaev, Amnistija, S. 206 f.

46 Vgl. die Angabe zum 1. November 1953 in GAMO f. R-23, op. 1, d. 1809, l. 54. Dabei handelte es sich um ein generelles Problem in Lagerkomplexen des GULAG. Der GULAG bat den Ministerrat um Finanzmittel zur Weiterbildung von Häftlingen, da durch die Amnestie eine erhebliche Zahl von Fachkräften verlorengegangen sei. Vgl. GARF f. R-9401, op. 4, d. 1783, l. 40.

47 Vgl. Bacaev, Amnistija, S. 205.

48 Vgl. GAMO f. R-23, op. 1, d. 1809, l. 5 sowie l. 9. Weiterhin fuhr man mit der Praxis fort, sogenannte „politische Häftlinge" aus anderen Lagerkomplexen in das Sonderlager *Berlag* zu verlegen. Vgl. Kozlov, Osobyj lager', S. 87.

49 Vgl. den Bericht des Ersten Parteisekretärs des Gebietes, Ababkov, an das ZK der KPdSU vom 14. Juni 1954 in GAMO f. P-21, op. 5, d. 759, l. 1–10, hier l. 3. Der ehemalige rumänische Häftling Solomon schildert die Ankunft der Norilsker Überlebenden unter extremen Sicherheitsvorkehrungen. Solomon,

Unter den chaotischen Bedingungen nach der Amnestie nahm die Gewalt, die in den Lagern herrschte und die von den Lagern auf Siedlungen freier Arbeitskräfte übergriff, bisher unbekannte Ausmaße an. Nach Angabe des MVD wurden im Jahr 1953 und in der ersten Jahreshälfte 1954 107 Häftlinge durch ihre Mitinsassen getötet.[50] Mitglieder von Lagerbanden stahlen wichtige Produktionsanlagen, zerstörten die Lagerinfrastruktur und gingen gegen Lageradministrationen vor, was diese wiederum mit brutalem Waffeneinsatz beantworteten. Die Zahl der Fluchtversuche stieg immer weiter, kriminelle Häftlinge überfielen Siedlungen, beraubten und vergewaltigten die Bevölkerung. An diesen Formen erratischer Gewalt hatten auch bewaffnete Wachen einen Anteil, die nicht selten mit den kriminellen Häftlingsbanden gemeinsame Sache machten.[51]

Der Versuch, schwerkriminelle Häftlinge zu isolieren, auf einzelne Produktions-verwaltungen aufzuteilen und immer wieder umzugruppieren, sorgte jedoch nur für eine weitere Destabilisierung des Wirtschaftsprozesses und war aufgrund des Mangels an Lagerinfrastruktur oft kaum möglich.[52] Trotz dieser Erfahrungen forderte Mitrakov auch weiterhin die Versendung von Zwangsarbeitern nach Dal'stroj; in den kommenden zwei Jahren sollten noch einmal 40.000 Häftlinge für die Kolyma bereitgestellt werden.[53]

Da für die Kombinatsleitung aber eine ausreichende „Lieferung" neuer Zwangs-arbeiter nicht abzusehen war, erklärte Mitrakov die Bindung der Amnestierten an Dal'stroj zum wichtigsten Ziel des Kombinats. Es galt, die unter die Amnestie fallenden Personen so lange wie möglich in den Gruben festzuhalten, um sie noch in der Fördersaison des Jahres 1953 einsetzen zu können. Parallel dazu wurde Druck auf Amnestierte, und dabei in besonderem Maße auf ausgebildete Arbeiter und Fach-kräfte, ausgeübt, um sie zum Abschluss von individuellen Verträgen mit Dal'stroj zu bewegen.[54] Noch während sie in Lagerhaft saßen, sollten jene Menschen zu einem freiwilligen Verbleib auf dieser grausamen Insel überredet werden. Dabei spielten der

---

Magadan, S. 265. Steven Barnes berichtet, dass ebenso Überlebende des Kengir-Aufstandes an die Kolyma gebracht wurden. Vgl. Barnes, Death and Redemption, S. 230.

50 Vgl. GAMO f. P-21, op. 5, d. 759, l. 5.

51 Allein in einem Monat des Jahres 1953 registrierte die innere Abteilung von Dal'stroj 96 Verbrechen und Verstöße gegen die Disziplinarordnung, die von bewaffneten Wachen in einem einzigen Gebiet verübt worden waren. Dazu zählten Mord, unerlaubte Verwendung der Waffe, Verkehr mit weiblichen Häftlingen, Trunkenheit etc. Vgl. GAMO f. R-23, op. 1, d. 4696, l. 60 – 64 (ausführlicher Bericht mit vielen Einzelfallschilderungen). Siehe auch Bacaev, Amnistija, S. 208. Berichte über derartige Gewalttaten in der Region erreichten in Form von Beschwerden auch das Präsidium des Obersten Sowjet in Moskau. Vgl. GARF f. R-7523, op. 58, d. 432, l. 2 – 8.

52 Vgl. Kozlov, Sevvostlag, S. 127 f. Zu dem Mangel an geeigneten Gefängnissen, Wachanlagen und Isolatoren vgl. GAMO f. P-21, op. 5, d. 759, l. 4.

53 Vgl. GAMO f. R-23, op. 1, d. 1809, l. 5 sowie l. 9.

54 Die Anwerbung von ausgebildeten Arbeitern und Fachleuten wurde zur persönlichen Aufgabe aller Funktionäre erklärt, Plakate in den Lagern und Proklamationen auf speziellen Versammlungen ver-kündeten die versprochenen Vergünstigungen. Vgl. GAMO f. R-23, op. 1, d. 4115, l. 196 – 202.

Kombinatsleitung die große Entfernung der Region zu den zentralen Teilen der Union und die ungewissen Zukunftsaussichten der Amnestierten in die Hände. Die unmenschlichen Umstände bei ihrer Entlassung und dem Transport taten schließlich ihr Übriges:

Erst einmal mussten alle zu amnestierenden Häftlinge, die in mehreren Hunderten Lagerpunkten auf einem Gebiet von über 3 Mio. km² inhaftiert waren, erfasst, tatsächlich entlassen und dann unter den extremen klimatischen Bedingungen (im März-April herrscht im Nordosten noch Winter) aus dem Gebiet verbracht werden.[55] Immer wieder kam es dazu, dass Häftlinge, die eigentlich der Amnestie unterlagen, überhaupt nicht entlassen, sondern nur in andere Fördergebiete verbracht wurden, weil es dort an Arbeitskräften mangelte.[56]

Der Transport der etwa 80.000 Amnestierten aus allen Winkeln des Gebietes, über Flüsse und Meere – die nur kurze Zeit im Jahr überhaupt eisfrei sind – bedeutete für Dal'stroj, zusätzlich zur einsetzenden Fördersaison ab Mai 1953, eine gewaltige organisatorische Aufgabe. Die Betroffenen hatten unter chaotischen Verhältnissen, den monatelangen Transporten und der miserablen Versorgung zu leiden, bis sie endlich Teile des „Festlandes" – die westlichen Gebiete Jakutiens, v. a. aber die Häfen des Chabarowsker Distrikts – erreichen konnten. Dort waren sie, mit Zehntausenden weiterer Häftlinge aus anderen Lagergebieten des Fernen Ostens, zum Warten auf völlig überfüllte Züge gezwungen. Amnestierte schwerkriminelle Häftlinge wurden kaum von den übrigen isoliert, so dass die Mehrheit Überfällen und gewaltvollen Bandenkriegen schutzlos ausgeliefert war.[57]

Entsprechend den allgemeinen Verordnungen aus Moskau sollten die Amnestierten mit Reisegeld, Bekleidung, ihren Entlassungspapieren, Pässen und Fahrscheinen ausgestattet werden, die Massenabfahrten sowie die medizinische Betreuung der vielen Menschen sollten in Zusammenarbeit von MVD und Miliz organisiert werden.[58] Näheres für die Lage vor Ort regelte eine Reihe von Erlassen und Befehlen

---

55 Alle Personen, die aus den Lagern nördlich des Polarkreises entlassen wurden, brachte man mit Einsetzen der eisfreien Periode per Schiff zu den Häfen Wanino und Nachodka. Die in der Nähe von Jakutien befindlichen Häftlinge wurden über die jakutische ASSR entlassen. Alle übrigen Amnestierten verbrachte man der Reihe nach in die Stadt Magadan. Vgl. Bacaev, Amnistija, S. 204.

56 Vgl. die strenge Rüge dieser Vorfälle durch die Leitung von Dal'stroj in RGAĖ, f. 9163, op. 6, d. 11, l. 294 f. Die Kritik der Kombinatsleitung bezog sich allerdings nicht auf die unrechtmäßige Inhaftierung von Amnestierten, sondern lediglich auf die erheblichen Kosten, die Dal'stroj durch diese sinnlosen Transporte entstanden seien. In einem weiteren Schreiben an alle Wirtschaftsabteilungen forderte Mitrakov ihre Leiter auf, die Akten sämtlicher Häftlinge noch einmal zu überprüfen und bis zum 25. Juni 1953 die zu amnestierenden Personen zu entlassen. Vgl. GAMO f. R-23, op. 1, d. 4686, l. 54 f.

57 Einer der Staatsanwälte, die 1954 in das Gebiet versetzt wurden, Ivan Pantjuchin, schildert in seinen Erinnerungen, dass die Lage in den großen Häfen derart außer Kontrolle geriet, dass der Verteidigungsminister der UdSSR in das Gebiet gerufen wurde. Vgl. Pantjuchin, Zapiski, S. 83.

58 Anordnung des Innenministers, des Justizministers und der Generalstaatsanwaltschaft der UdSSR „Über die Art und Weise der Ausführung des Erlasses des Präsidiums des Obersten Sowjet vom 27. März 1953 ,Über die Amnestie'." Abgedruckt in Artizov, Reabilitacija Tom I, S. 16 – 18, hier S. 18.

der leitenden Kader von Dal'stroj.[59] Tatsächlich wurden immer wieder die notwendigen Entlassungspapiere nicht ausgestellt, Wertgegenstände und Finanzmittel der Amnestierten widerrechtlich einbehalten. Trotz anderslautender Verordnungen transportierte man verfeindete Häftlingsgruppen gemeinsam, was zu brutalen Übergriffen und Schlägereien führte.

Aus der gesamten Sowjetunion berichteten sowjetische Bürger von einem erheblichen Kriminalitätsanstieg durch die Amnestie. Nach ihren Angaben überfielen entlassene Häftlinge auf besonders brutale Weise Siedlungen freier Arbeiter, stahlen, vergewaltigten, prügelten und mordeten. Das Phänomen ist allgemein als „Kalter Sommer des Jahres 53" bekannt und fungierte als Folie für einen sehr bekannten sowjetischen Film aus dem Jahr 1987.[60] Hintergrund der Berichte über den erheblichen Gewaltanstieg sind Tausende Briefe, in denen sich Bürger der Sowjetunion bei verschiedenen staatlichen Stellen und der Parteiführung über die Verhältnisse vor Ort beklagten. Diese Petitionen berichteten jedoch nicht nur von ungeheurer Gewalt, sie sind selbst von gewaltvoller Sprache geprägt. Die Petenten forderten ein massives Vorgehen staatlicher Stellen, drakonische, zum Teil ausgesprochen brutale körperliche Strafen und eine erneute Inhaftierung der entsprechenden Personen.[61] In der Forschung ist in den letzten Jahren eine angeregte Diskussion über die Interpretation dieser Briefe geführt worden, über ihren Wahrheitsgehalt ebenso wie über die Intentionen ihrer Autoren und die sich daraus ergebenden Konsequenzen für eine Beurteilung gesellschaftlicher Stimmungen nach dem Tode Stalins.[62]

---

59 Vgl. GAMO f. R-23, op. 1, d. 4115, l. 196 – 202.

60 Der Film mit dem bekannten Schauspieler Anatolij Papanov wurde 1989 mit dem Staatspreis der UdSSR ausgezeichnet.

61 Siehe z. B. die entsprechenden Schreiben an den Obersten Sowjet der Sowjetunion in GARF, f. R-7523, op. 58, d. 164 sowie d. 423, l. 10 – 26 (aus dem Jahr 1953); GARF, f. R-7523, op. 75, d. 1569, d. 1581 u. d. 1582 (aus den Jahren 1955 und 1956). Für Berichte aus der Region Kolyma siehe GARF f. R-7523, op. 75, d. 1569 l. 106 ff. Eine gänzlich andere Reaktion war in den ersten Tagen nach dem Amnestieerlass zu beobachten: Beim Obersten Sowjet gingen eine erhebliche Zahl von Dankschreiben und Glückwünschen ein, die von Amnestierten, ihren Angehörigen oder anderen betroffenen Bürgern stammten. In ihrer Mehrheit waren sie persönlich an den Vorsitzenden des Präsidiums, Kliment Vorošilov, gerichtet. Ihm galt der Dank und die Bewunderung für ein besonderes Zeichen der Humanität. Falls sich Berija durch den von ihm initiierten Erlass eine Verbesserung seines öffentlichen Ansehens erhofft hatte, wie in der Forschung vermutet wird, so erwies sich diese Strategie offensichtlich nicht als erfolgreich. Als Autor des Erlasses wurde der Vorsitzende des zwar als volksnah geltenden, tatsächlich aber machtlosen Obersten Sowjets angesehen. Vgl. GARF, f. R-7523, op. 58, d. 130, d. 131 und 132. Diese Akten enthalten ausschließlich Dankesbriefe für die Amnestie vom 27. März 1953.

62 Miriam Dobson widmet sich in ihrer entsprechend betitelten Studie „Khrushchev's Cold Summer" ausführlich den gesellschaftlichen Folgen der Amnestie. Vgl. Dobson, Cold Summer, S. 37 ff.; Kozlov, Neizvestnyj SSSR, S. 97 ff.; Elie, Les anciens détenus; Sprau, Petitionen, S. 109. Auch Häftlinge, die nicht unter die Amnestie vom März 1953 gefallen waren, meldeten sich zu Wort. Diese Personen, wie Evgenija Ginzburg, die aus politischen Gründen verurteilt worden waren, nahmen die Amnestie mit Verbitterung auf. Ginzburg betrachtete die Entlassenen ausschließlich als „Gauner" und „Diebe", die nicht entlassen werden sollten. Vgl. Ginsburg, Gratwanderung, S. 427 sowie den Brief des zu 25 Jahren

Der Kriminalitätsanstieg in der Region Kolyma war in jedem Fall real. Neben den Übergriffen in den Lagern berichtete der UMVD seit Mitte April 1953 von einer deutlichen Zunahme von Wohnungseinbrüchen und Plünderungen in der Hauptstadt Magadan.[63]

Die verheerenden Umstände bei der Freilassung und dem Rücktransport der Entlassenen sorgten mit dafür, dass etwa 18.500 Amnestierte einen Vertrag zum weiteren Verbleib in Dal'stroj abschlossen. Er beinhaltete die Übertragung der Privilegien von Dal'stroj-Mitarbeitern auf die Amnestierten. Weitergehende Vergünstigungen – finanzielle Unterstützungen, der kostenlose Zuzug von Angehörigen etc. – wurden nur bei einem Vertrag mit längerer Laufzeit gewährt.[64] Tatsächlich hatte sich aber die Hälfte der neuen „freien" Dal'stroj-Arbeiter lediglich für eine Zeit zwischen sechs Monaten und einem Jahr verpflichtet. Zudem fiel die Anwerbung auch in absoluten Zahlen viel geringer aus als geplant; Mitrakov hatte mit einer Bindung von 25–30.000 Amnestierten an das Kombinat gerechnet. An den schrecklichen Lebensbedingungen für einfache freie Arbeiter änderte sich jedoch nichts. Amnestierte Vertragsarbeiter lebten in ihrer großen Mehrheit in den gleichen Lagerbaracken wie vor ihrer Entlassung.[65] Auch die ihnen zustehenden Gelder von insgesamt 140 Mio. Rubel (zu ihrer Versorgung, dem Transport ihrer Familien an die Kolyma etc.) wurden nicht oder nur zum Teil gezahlt. Folglich verließ ein großer Teil der amnestierten Vertragsarbeiter nach Erfüllung ihrer Verträge die Region.[66]

Für eine dauerhafte Lösung des Arbeitskräftemangels war die Anwerbung von Entlassenen also ungeeignet.[67] Auf diese Weise gelangte der weitreichende Einsatz von freien Arbeitskräften in der Metallförderung auf die Tagesordnung. Diskutiert wurde, freie Vertragsarbeiter in den zentralen Teilen der Union anzuwerben und mit besonderen Vergünstigungen und höheren Löhnen nach Dal'stroj zu locken. Mitrakov wandte sich gegenüber Chruščev und Malenkov entschieden gegen dieses Modell und berief sich auf die vollkommen unzureichende soziale Infrastruktur in der Region.[68] Für ihn waren die schlechten Lebensbedingungen der bereits in Dal'stroj lebenden

---

Haft verurteilten Häftlings Levickij aus dem Lager „Maglag", GAMO f. R-23, op. 1, d. 4696, l. 187–195 (Memorandum zur Stimmung unter den Häftlingen), hier l. 191 f.

63 Vgl. den Bericht des stellv. Leiters von Dal'stroj, Čuguev, an den Leiter des UMVD in GAMO f. R-23, op. 1, d. 4115, l. 268. Siehe die Zusammenstellung diverser Berichte in Bacaev, Obostrenie, S. 197.

64 Grundlage bildeten Verordnungen des Ministerrates und des Ministeriums für Metallindustrie. Vgl. GAMO f. R-23, op. 1, d. 4115, l. 198 sowie die Verordnungen vom 4. bzw. 13. April 1953 in RGAĖ f. 9163, op. 6, d. 11, l. 156 f. sowie l. 258.

65 Vgl. GAMO f. R-23, op. 1, d. 1809, l. 9.

66 Vgl. Bacaev, Amnistija, S. 205.

67 Zu den Zahlen der Arbeitsverträge siehe GAMO f. R-23, op. 1, d. 1809, l. 47. Vielmehr verließen im Laufe des Jahres 1954 noch einmal etwa 33.000 Personen Dal'stroj – darunter befanden sich Häftlinge, die ihre Haftzeit regulär abgesessen hatten, etwa 7.000 Menschen, die noch unter den Amnestieerlass fielen, sowie die Gruppe der Amnestierten, deren kurze Arbeitsverträge mit Dal'stroj 1954 ausliefen. Vgl. Bacaev, Amnistija, S. 205.

68 Siehe sein Schreiben an Chruščev und Malenkov in GAMO f. R-23sč, op. 1, d. 328, l. 212.

freien Arbeitskräfte Ausdruck der Tatsache, dass das Kombinat nur als Teil der Lagerwirtschaft denkbar und wirtschaftlich überlebensfähig sei.[69] Bei der Frage der Arbeitskräftebasis sah Mitrakov den gesamten militärischen Sonderstatus und die grundlegende Verbindung zwischen Produktion und Lager in Gefahr. Immer wieder beharrte er auf der bestehenden Struktur von Dal'stroj – „das Lager ist die Voraussetzung für die Erfüllung unseres Produktionsplanes"[70], so Mitrakov gegenüber Vertretern des GULAG.

Dennoch konnten Mitrakov und seine Leute nicht verhindern, dass durch den gewaltigen Arbeitskräftemangel und den Kriminalitätsanstieg nach der Amnestie die Frage nach Arbeitskräften und deren Lebensbedingungen ins Zentrum der wirtschaftlichen Entwicklung der Region rückte. Damit hatte die Amnestie vom 27. März 1953, die in der Forschung allgemein als „Türöffner für das Ende des GULAG" bezeichnet wird, den Sonderstatus der Region Kolyma von Seiten des Lagers in Frage gestellt.

3.1.3 Machtkampf um die Herrschaftsstruktur in der Region

Die nächste Erschütterung des Dal'strojer Sonderstatus ging von machtpolitischen Veränderungen im Moskauer Zentrum aus. Die Verhaftung (und spätere Erschießung) Berijas schwächte den gesamten MVD-Apparat und verringerte seinen politischen Einfluss. Auf dem Juli-Plenum des ZK der KPdSU, das zur Abrechnung mit Berija inszeniert worden war, forderte das ZK eine Beschneidung der Macht des MVD, seine Entmilitarisierung und stärkere Kontrolle durch Parteiorgane.[71]

Diese Forderungen sind vor dem Hintergrund der Verhältnisse im Spätstalinismus – einer Beschneidung der praktischen Macht der Kommunistischen Partei gegenüber einem ausgesprochen aktiven MVD und einer wachsenden Bedeutung des Ministerialsystems – zu sehen. Chruščev warnte auf dem Juli-Plenum massiv vor der drohenden Gefahr eines weiteren Bedeutungsverlusts der obersten Parteiführung und propagierte die Erneuerung der traditionellen bolschewistischen Rolle der Partei als der einzigen Kraft, die in der Lage gewesen sei, „to transcend the narrow departmental perspectives of individual institutions and pursue the interests of society as a whole"[72], um mit

---

69 Vgl. Mitrakovs Schilderungen der schlechten Lebensbedingungen für freie Arbeitskräfte in GAMO f. R-23, op. 1, d. 1809, l. 6. Für die Versorgung der neuen amnestierten Vertragsarbeiter erließ Mitrakov zahlreiche Verordnungen – vgl. GAMO f. R-23, op. 1, d. 4115, l. 199 ff. sowie RGAĖ f. 9163, op. 6, d. 11, l. 156. Finanzmittel des Kombinats für deren Ausführung wurden jedoch nicht zur Verfügung gestellt, vielmehr wandte sich die Leitung von Dal'stroj an das MMP, das jedoch auch keine zusätzlichen Gelder stellte. Vgl. GAMO f. R-23, op. 1, d. 1809, l. 7.

70 Mitrakov bei einer Abschlussdiskussion der Ergebnisse einer Kommission des GULAG im Januar 1954 in GAMO f. R-23, op. 1, d. 5207, l. 13–54, hier l. 52.

71 Vgl. Fall Berija, S. 106–109. Zur Schwächung des MVD-Apparates nach dem Sommer 1953 siehe Lejbovič, Reforma, S. 104–105; zum innerparteilichen Kampf im Jahr 1953 siehe Žukov, Bor'ba.

72 Gorlizki, Political Reform, S. 258.

den Worten von Yoram Gorlizki zu sprechen. Die Beschneidung der führenden Rolle der Partei war der Hauptvorwurf, der auf dem Juli-Plenum gegen Berija erhoben wurde.

Zur gleichen Zeit richtete das Präsidium des ZK der KPdSU seine Aufmerksamkeit zunehmend auf die Situation in den sowjetischen Lagergebieten, die durch die Amnestie und mehrere große Aufstände erschüttert wurden.[73] Das ZK drängte auf Informationen über und Einfluss auf einen Bereich, der bis dato fast völlig dem MVD vorbehalten war. Denn seit Beginn der 1950er Jahre waren die Lager nur noch sehr selten Gegenstand von Sitzungen des ZK-Präsidiums gewesen, der MVD hatte immer weniger Berichte über seine Lagerkomplexe vorgelegt und die gesamte Lagerwirtschaft als seine Hausmacht verstanden.[74]

Im Zuge dessen geriet auch die Lage an der Kolyma in den Fokus der obersten Parteiführung. Bis 1953 war kein einziger Funktionär des Apparates des ZK der KPdSU kontrollierend in Dal'stroj erschienen.[75] Aber seit dem Sommer 1953 bereiste eine Brigade des ZK zahlreiche Gebiete der Region und konsultierte diverse Mitarbeiter und Funktionäre des Kombinats.[76] Vertreter der Parteileitung des Chabarowsker Distrikts, dem die Region von Dal'stroj formal unterstellt war, begleiteten sie und drängten auf eine Ausweitung ihrer Befugnisse auf das nordöstliche Gebiet. Die Kombinatsleitung reagierte auf den Besuch der Brigade mit ausführlichen Selbstdarstellungen, in denen die Leistungen des Kombinats als Ergebnis der straffen Leitung präsentiert und zugleich alle bestehenden Schwierigkeiten verschwiegen wurden.[77] Im Zuge dieser Kontrolle wurden auf Geheiß Mitrakovs große Teile des Kombinatsarchivs vernichtet. Auf diese Weise sollte offensichtlich der Informationsfluss über die bisherigen wirtschaftlichen und persönlichen Verhältnisse in der Region reglementiert werden; der ehemalige Häftling Abraham Dück berichtet in seinen Erinnerungen, dass im Sommer 1953 ein Kesselraum mehrere Tage lang mit den Akten des MVD befeuert wurde.[78]

---

73 Die Aufstände standen im engen Zusammenhang mit der Amnestie und der Entmachtung Berijas. Vgl. Hedeler, Widerstand im Gulag; Hedeler, Rote Sklaven; Barnes, Uprising; Craveri, Strikes; Craveri, Kengirskoe vosstanie; Kozlov, Neizvestnyj SSSR, S. 70–86.

74 Vgl. zu der gestiegenen Aufmerksamkeit, die den Lagern durch das ZK der KPdSU seit dem Frühsommer 1953 zuteil wurden Kozlov, Neizvestnyj SSSR, S. 92 ff. sowie Gorlizki/Khlevniuk, Cold Peace, S. 132.

75 Vgl. Vremja. Sobytija. Ljudi, 1946–1958, S. 10.

76 Vgl. Verkina, Istoričeskaja spravka, S. 2. Von diesen Konsultationen berichtete der beteiligte Inspektor des ZK der KPdSU, A. Švarev, im September 1953 persönlich Chruščev. Er setzte sich im Rahmen dieses Berichtes für einen Häftling ein, den berühmten Geologen Vologdin, auf dessen Schicksal ihn der stellvertretende Direktor des wissenschaftlichen Forschungsinstituts von Dal'stroj, Šilo, aufmerksam gemacht hatte, der Vologdin in seinem Institut einsetzen wollte. Im Folgenden wurde das Urteil gegen Vologdin Ende März 1954 aufgehoben, Vologdin aus der Haft entlassen und als Geologe in Dal'stroj angestellt. Vgl. RGANI f. 5, op. 15, de. 440, l. 142–155.

77 Vgl. GAMO f. R-23, op. 1, d. 4804, l. 64–73 (zu Wirtschaft, Kultur, Bevölkerung, dem Komsomol und weiteren Organisationen), l. 30–33 (zu den zentralen Gebieten der Kolyma).

78 Vgl. Bacaev, Kolymskaja grjada, S. 69; Dück, Erinnerungen, S. 427.

Im Umfeld der Brigade des ZK der KPdSU wurde deutliche Kritik an der Kombinatsleitung laut. Diverse Funktionäre wandten sich in schriftlichen Stellungnahmen an die Partei- und Staatsführung, kritisierten Misswirtschaft und schlechte Lebensbedingungen.[79] Aussprachen über die Ergebnisse des Juli-Plenums des ZK entwickelten sich in der bisherigen Hochburg des MVD zu einer weitreichenden Kritik an der Leitung von Dal'stroj. Die Kritik entzündete sich an den miserablen Lebensbedingungen der freien Arbeitskräfte, die als Ergebnis einer nicht mehr zeitgemäßen Prioritätensetzung verstanden wurden. So äußerte sich Lin'kov, ein Funktionär aus Jansk:

> Im Verlauf der vergangenen Jahre, ja, und auch in diesem Jahr gibt sich die Leitung von Dal'stroj [...] mit Maßnahmen zufrieden, die in unserer Zeit nicht als richtig bezeichnet werden können, anstatt sich tatsächlich mit der Erschließung dieses ausgesprochen reichen Gebietes zu beschäftigen. Die Aufgabe, Zinn um jeden Preis zu kriegen [das Gebiet Jansk war eine wichtige Region der Zinnförderung – M. S.], richtet sich an die gesamte Mannschaft. Ohne zu berücksichtigen, dass die Menschen, die diese großen Aufträge erfüllen sollen, unter ausgesprochen schweren Bedingungen arbeiten und leben, keinen vernünftigen Wohnraum und keine ausreichenden Lebensmittel haben, dass ihre Kinder nichts lernen können, weil es keine Schulen gibt.[80]

Kritische Stimmen gegen die Leitung von Dal'stroj blieben jedoch nicht auf die Lebensbedingungen freier Arbeitskräfte beschränkt, diverse Parteimitglieder, darunter auch Mitglieder der Führungsriege, nutzten die Gelegenheit, grobe Vergehen und Versäumnisse an unterschiedlichen Produktionsstandorten anzuprangern. Wirtschaftliche Fehlentscheidungen, mangelnde Bautätigkeiten und Planungsfehler, die zu hohen Verlusten geführt hätten, wurden en détail dargelegt, der Kombinatsleitung außerdem mangelndes Interesse an den lokalen Verhältnissen vorgeworfen. Die Motivationen der z. T. anonymen Kritiker sind natürlich nicht direkt erkennbar. Sicherlich stand auch der Wunsch nach Verleumdung einzelner Personen hinter diesen Meldungen. Die Berichte vermitteln jedoch häufig den Eindruck, dass damit tatsächlich Missstände aus dem eigenen Arbeitsbereich offengelegt und eine Verbesserung der Verhältnisse erreicht werden sollten.[81]

---

79 Siehe beispielsweise den Bericht eines Ingenieurs an den Minister für Metallindustrie über Pfuschereien, schlechte Arbeitsorganisation und zahlreiche Fälle von Vetternwirtschaft in RGAĖ f. 9163, op. 6, d. 15, l. 136–140. Das oberste Gewerkschaftskomitee von Tschukotka beschwerte sich über die schrecklichen Lebensbedingungen im Kreis; der Minister für Buntmetalle verlangte daraufhin genauere Auskünfte von Mitrakov. Vgl. das Schreiben des stellvertretenden Ministers, Podžajnov, in RGAĖ f. 9163, op. 6, d. 15, l. 197–198. Siehe ebenso das anonyme Schreiben zur Lage des Kombinats in RGAĖ f. 9163, op. 6, d. 14, l. 54–56 sowie die ausführlichen Angaben des Leiters der berghautechnischen Inspektion von Dal'stroj, Solomachin, über mangelnden Arbeitsschutz und schwerwiegende Vergehen im Umgang mit Sprengmaterial in RGANI f. 5, op. 27, d. 122, l. 74–79.

80 GAMO f. R-23, op. 1, d. 4696, l. 231. Ähnliche Beschwerden kamen u. a. aus der Politischen Abteilung der südwestlichen Bergbauverwaltung (l. 238), aus der Bergbauverwaltung Janstroj (l. 238), von einer Pateiversammlung einer geologischen Verwaltung (l. 249) und vom Parteiaktiv des Straßenbaus (l. 242).

81 Auch kamen Fälle von persönlicher Bereicherung zur Sprache. So bei einer Versammlung des Politischen Truppenteils des Indigirsker Lagers. Vgl. GAMO f. R-23, op. 1, d. 4696, l. 235. Aus dem Po-

Die Brisanz der so geäußerten Kritik wird erst vor dem Hintergrund der Dal'strojer Verhältnisse verständlich. Denn die Parteiaktive verbanden ihre Anklagen gegen die Kombinatsleitung mit einer allgemeinen Kritik an der Machtverteilung innerhalb des Kombinats: Nach ihrer Selbstdarstellung wurden sie von der Kombinatsleitung an der Erfüllung ihrer eigentlichen Arbeit gehindert. Weder sei es ihnen möglich, als Parteivertretung die Wirtschaftstätigkeiten des Kombinats zu kontrollieren noch sich für die Lage der freien Arbeitskräfte einzusetzen und eine umfassende Entwicklung der Region zu befördern. Dies stünde im direkten Widerspruch zu den Forderungen und Direktiven des ZK der KPdSU.[82] „Die Leitung des Kombinats und die Politische Verwaltung haben sich selbst in eine solche Lage versetzt, in der eine Kontrolle durch die Partei ausgeschlossen ist"[83], hieß es beispielsweise aus dem Politischen Truppenteil von Jansk. Zudem sei der dringend benötigte Kontakt zu anderen Parteivertretungen außerhalb von Dal'stroj, z. B. zum jakutischen Gebietsparteikomitee, verboten.

Die Kritik an Zuständen innerhalb des Kombinats wurde hier zu einer Kritik am Sonderstatus des gesamten Gebietes erweitert. Die Forderung nach einer Machterweiterung für die Parteivertreter konnte als Voraussetzung einer Verbesserung der Verhältnisse präsentiert werden; zugleich war man in der Lage, sich auf diese Weise der allgemeinen Tendenz des Juli-Plenums anzuschließen.

Die im Sommer 1953 geäußerte Kritik der regionalen Parteivertreter zielte auf die Sonderstellung der Kommunistischen Partei und ihrer Mitglieder im Rahmen der militärischen Einzelleitung in Dal'stroj. Formal war der militärische Führer des Kombinates Bevollmächtigter der Chabarowsker Parteileitung, er hatte alle Vollmachten und war nur dem jeweiligen Chef des NKVD/MVD und Stalin persönlich verantwortlich.[84] Diese Konstruktion bedeutete jedoch keinesfalls, dass die Kommunistische Partei innerhalb von Dal'stroj keine Rolle spielte. Im Gegenteil, der Anteil der Parteimitglieder nahm entsprechend der steigenden Bedeutung des Kombinats im Laufe der Jahre stetig zu.[85] Eine große Zahl an Parteimitgliedern bedeutete jedoch nicht, dass die Leitung des Gebietes wie sonst üblich von Parteigliederungen ausging.

---

litischen Truppenteil des Produktionsstandortes Jansk wurde dabei nicht nur von Fehlern und Schwierigkeiten berichtet, sondern auch ein Katalog mit konkreten Forderungen aufgestellt. Vgl. GAMO f. R-23, op. 1, d. 4696, l. 232. Klagen gab es auch über massive Verschwendungen aufgrund von Fehlentscheidungen der Kombinatsleitung, vgl. l. 244.

82 Vgl. GAMO f. R-23, op. 1, d. 4696, l. 247.

83 GAMO f. R-23, op. 1, d. 4696, l. 237.

84 Vgl. die Beschreibung der militärischen Strukturen in der Einleitung.

85 So betrug er im Jahr 1942 bei den Kadern der Hauptverwaltung 22 %. Vgl. Bacaev, Osobennosti, S. 33. Diese Zahl umfasst Parteimitglieder, Kandidaten der Partei und Mitglieder des Komsomol. Für einen Überblick über die Zahl der Parteimitglieder in den einzelnen Jahren bis 1942 vgl. Kokurin/ Morukov, Stalinskie strojki, S. 458. Während des Krieges wurde eine große Zahl neuer Parteimitglieder aufgenommen; 1948 lag ihre Zahl schon bei mehr als 7.500 Personen, im Sommer 1953 gab es in Dal'stroj bereits etwa 20.000 Parteimitglieder (ohne Komsomol). Siehe die Beschreibung von Dal'stroj im Rahmen des Besuchs der Brigade des ZK der KPdSU vom 31. Juli 1953 in GAMO f. R-23, op. 1, d. 4804, l. 64–73, hier l. 72.

Zwar gab es Parteiaktive als grundständige Parteiorganisationen in allen Produkti-
onsabteilungen.[86] Diese Parteivertretungen verfügten jedoch weder über relevantes
Wissen, noch hatten sie eine irgendwie geartete Entscheidungsgewalt innerhalb des
Kombinats.

Stattdessen unterlag Dal'stroj einer Struktur, die auf Bestrebungen des ZK der
KPdSU Ende der 1930er Jahre zurückging. Innerhalb der Lagerwirtschaft sollten Parteigliederungen eingerichtet werden, die eine besonders umfassende Beherrschung
und Kontrolle ermöglichen konnten. Im Rahmen des GULAG (und entsprechend
ebenso in den einzelnen Lagerkomplexen und Lagerabteilungen) wurden 1937 Parteigliederungen analog zu den Verhältnissen in der Roten Armee eingeführt.[87] So war
auch in Dal'stroj die oberste Truppenleitung der Partei die „Političeskoe upravlenie",
die „Politische Verwaltung". Die Politischen Truppenteile in den einzelnen Bergbau-
verwaltungen und Lagerabteilungen wurden als „Političeskij otdel" bezeichnet, sie
unterstanden der „Politischen Verwaltung" in Magadan.[88]

In der Hierarchie der Hauptverwaltung rangierte die Politische Verwaltung unmittelbar unter dem militärischen Leiter von Dal'stroj; der ebenfalls militärische Be-
fehlshaber („načal'nik") der Politischen Verwaltung fungierte als Stellvertreter der
Kombinatsleitung für politische Arbeit – wiederum in Analogie zu dem Stellvertreter
des Kommandanten für politische Arbeit in der Roten Armee. Damit war selbst eine
gewisse Unabhängigkeit der Parteivertretung gegenüber dem Chef der Hauptverwaltung ausgeschlossen.[89]

Die Politische Verwaltung war eine Nomenklatur des ZK der KPdSU. Sie entschied
viele der wichtigsten Fragen des Kombinats, vor allem war sie für die Kaderpolitik
zuständig, für die Führung der Parteimitglieder, für die politische Arbeit unter den
Offizieren, den militärischen Wachmannschaften und unter der freien Bevölkerung.
Obwohl der Leiter der Politischen Verwaltung bzw. der Politischen Truppenteile unmittelbar vom ZK der KPdSU ernannt wurde, entwickelten sich diese Truppenteile (im
GULAG und ebenso in Dal'stroj) zu einer der wichtigsten Machtbasen des NKVD. Die
Rolle des ZK beschränkte sich mehr und mehr auf eine Bestätigung vorgelegter Per-
sonalvorschläge. Diese Entwicklung folgte der Ernennung Berijas zum Volkskommissar für Inneres (NKVD) und war vor allem seit Beginn der 1940er Jahre spürbar.
Seit dieser Zeit waren die Leiter der Politischen Truppenteile in ihrem Selbstverständnis ganz auf die Unterordnung unter den NKVD/MVD ausgerichtet und verstanden sich als politische Elite der jeweiligen Kombinatsleitung.[90] In ihrer prakti-

---

86 Vgl. zu den grundsätzlich üblichen Parteigliederungen in Wirtschaftseinrichtungen Hough; Fainsod, Soviet Union is Governed, S. 480.
87 Vgl. Petrov, Karatel'naja Sistema, Band 2, S. 134; Hedeler, Ökonomik, S. 17.
88 Vgl. Barnes, Death and Redemption, S. 49 f.
89 Vgl. Širokov, Organizacionnye formy, S. 65; Širokov, Dal'stroj v social'no-ėkonomičeskom razvitii,
S. 71 f.
90 Vgl. Antonov-Ovseenko, Put' naverch, S. 105. In einer seiner Erzählungen hat Šalamov besonders
eindrücklich die Verquickung persönlicher Ambitionen der Dal'strojer Leitung mit der Frage nach den

schen Arbeit waren die Politischen Verwaltungen (und ebenso die Politischen Truppenteile vor Ort) ebenfalls streng militärisch organisiert. Anders als in zivilen Parteiorganisationen, in denen zumindest formal Kritik an der Parteileitung und eine Diskussion von Beschlüssen möglich war, galt der Beschluss des Führers eines Politischen Truppenteils als unumstößlicher Befehl. Den militärischen Charakter der Politischen Verwaltung illustriert das Foto der VII. Parteikonferenz von Dal'stroj im Jahr 1947 (vgl. Abbildung 10, S. 92). Fast alle Anwesenden (ausnahmslos Männer) tragen Uniformen, bei der Veranstaltung scheint es sich mehr um eine Offiziersschulung als um einen Parteitag zu handeln.

Und eben gegen diese Gliederung der Parteiarbeit regte sich nicht erst im Sommer und Herbst 1953 Widerstand an der Kolyma. Von Seiten der Partei hatte es seit Gründung des Kombinats immer wieder Versuche gegeben, den Sonderstatus von Dal'stroj aufzubrechen. Dabei argumentierten die Parteivertreter, wie z. B. bei einer Parteikonferenz Ende 1937, mit einer raumbezogenen Perspektive – der Nordosten wäre durch reguläre Parteiorgane besser zu erschließen und zu verwalten. Der NKVD wies diese Vorschläge mit Verweis auf das Zwangsarbeiterprojekt ab, für ihn war nicht die Erschließung des Raumes, sondern die Effektivität seiner Ausbeutung maßgeblich.[91]

Dementsprechend äußerte sich auch Stalin persönlich, als er mit dem am weitesten gehenden Vorstoß zur Beseitigung der Kolymaer Verhältnisse im Sommer 1939 konfrontiert wurde. Der Vorfall ereignete sich kurz nach Übergabe des Kombinats an den NKVD. Der Leiter der Parteivertretung aus Chabarowsk drängte darauf, die Region von Dal'stroj in den Chabarowsker Distrikt zu inkorporieren. Unterstützt durch die Politische Verwaltung innerhalb des Kombinats erreichte er, dass am 14. Juli 1939 auf Befehl des Präsidiums des Obersten Sowjets der RSFSR tatsächlich ein „Kolymskij okrug" (Kolymaer Kreis) innerhalb des Chabarowsker Distrikts gegründet wurde.[92] Parteimitarbeiter erschienen in Magadan und begannen mit dem Aufbau ziviler Parteigliederungen. Sie entschieden, dem Kombinat „wesensfremde" Aufgaben zu entziehen und aus Dal'stroj eine reine Hauptverwaltung für Bergbau zu machen. Die „organisatorischen Strukturen von Dal'stroj können den neuen Aufgaben für eine allseitige Erschließung der Kolyma nicht gerecht werden"[93], so die Leiter der neuen Parteiorganisation. Sie schlugen vor, Institutionen des Kombinats den zivilen Volkskommissariaten und regulären Organisationen der Sowjetunion zu unterstellen.[94] Diese geradezu umstürzlerischen Vorgänge wurden durch ein persönliches Tele-

---

Einflusssphären von NKVD/MVD und Partei dargestellt. In seiner Erzählung „Ivan Fjodorowitsch" schildert er die Konkurrenz zwischen dem Dal'stroj-Leiter, Nikišov, und dem Leiter der Politischen Verwaltung. Vgl. Schalamow, Linkes Ufer, S. 48–64.

91 Vgl. Širokov, Organizacionnye formy, S. 62f.
92 Vgl. den Abdruck des Befehls in Kozlov, U istokov, S. 28f. Parallel zu diesem Beschluss wurde die Siedlung Magadan, die damals gut 30.000 Einwohner hatte, zur Stadt ernannt.
93 Zitiert nach Roščupkin/Bubnis, K voprosu ob administrativnom ustrojstve, S. 71.
94 Vgl. Chronika partijnoj organizacii, S. 45.

gramm Stalins wenige Tage später beendet, alle neuen Strukturen umgehend aufgelöst.[95] Zur Begründung seines Vorgehens formulierte Stalin verklausuliert: „Dal'stroj ist ein Kombinat besonderen Typs, das unter spezifischen Bedingungen arbeitet; diese Spezifik erfordert besondere Arbeitsbedingungen, eine besondere Disziplin, ein besonderes Regime."[96]

Zehn Jahre später erfolgten weitere Versuche, die ebenfalls von der Chabarowsker Partei- und Sowjetleitung ausgingen und von Parteimitgliedern aus Magadan unterstützt wurden. Vor dem Hintergrund der wirtschaftlichen Schwierigkeiten des Kombinats (die Goldförderung war seit Kriegsende dramatisch gesunken), wurde der damalige Kombinatsleiter Nikišov 1948 angreifbar – Kritik kam dabei aus Moskau, Chabarowsk und Magadan.[97] 1949 wagte sich Chabarowsk noch einmal erfolglos an die Gründung eines „Kolymaer Kreises", 1950 drängte man gegenüber dem ZK der KPdSU und dem Ministerrat der UdSSR sogar auf die Gründung eines selbstständigen Gebietes (bezeichnet als „Kolymaer-Tschukotkaer Gebiet") innerhalb des eigenen Distrikts.[98] In all diesen Fällen verlangte die Chabarowsker Parteileitung eine Ausweitung ihrer Machtbefugnisse nach Norden, Parteimitglieder innerhalb des Kombinats wollten durch die Einschränkung der militärischen Herrschaftsweise ihren eigenen Spielraum erweitern. Im Machtkampf mit dem NKVD/MVD wurde die Partei jeweils zum angeblichen Garanten für die Rechte der freien Bevölkerung, für eine umfassende Entwicklung der Region und für einen kollegialen Führungsstil stilisiert. Zugleich brandmarkten Parteimitglieder die Politische Verwaltung als eine den Parteiprinzipien ferne militärische Abteilung des Kombinats.

Doch bis zu Stalins Tod im März 1953 blieben sämtliche Versuche zur Änderung der Verhältnisse ergebnislos. Erst der Sturz Berijas führte dazu, dass in Moskau eine Ausweitung der Parteikompetenzen auf Lager-Industrielle Komplexe und in Magadan eine Beschneidung der Macht der militärischen Parteileitung möglich wurden. Dem-

---

95 Im Herbst 1939 wurde der damalige Chef von Dal'stroj, K. A. Pavlov, nur zwei Jahre nach seiner Ernennung wieder abberufen. Nach Ansicht des Magadaner Historikers Grebenjuk hat Pavlov sehr wahrscheinlich aufgrund seiner schwachen Position im Streit um die Gründung des Kreises die Region verlassen müssen. Offiziell verließ er Dal'stroj zur Regeneration nach schwerer Krankheit, er kehrte jedoch nie mehr zurück. Vgl. Grebenjuk, Kolymskij led, S. 35. Als Leiter des Kombinats folgte ihm im November I. F. Nikišov, der seit seiner Zeit im Kaukasus zu den Berija-Männern gezählt wurde. Nikišov war selbst Kandidat des ZK der KPdSU. Diese hohe Position innerhalb der Partei hat, so Grebenjuk, die Wahl Stalins beeinflusst. So habe der Diktator sicherstellen wollen, dass die Stellung des Leiters von Dal'stroj auch im Rahmen der Partei die Position des Leiters der Politischen Abteilung überträfe. Dies sei notwendig geworden, da sich die Politische Verwaltung bei der Gründung des Kreises auf die Seite der Chabarowsker Parteileitung gestellt habe. Vgl. Grebenjuk, Kolymskij led, S. 35. Ausführlich zu den ersten Leitern von Dal'stroj siehe auch Nordlander, Evolution, S. 662.
96 Dieses Zitat wurde in der regionalen Tageszeitung *Sovetskaja Kolyma* abgedruckt. Vgl. Sovetskaja Kolyma, 23. Februar 1940. Das vollständige Telegramm findet sich bei Kozlov, U istokov, S. 29.
97 Zitiert nach Rajzman, Osobennosti social'no-ėkonomičeskogo razvitija, S. 170.
98 Vgl. zu den Bestrebungen von 1949 Gun'ko/Galin, Iz istorii sozdanija, S. 18. Zu den Forderungen nach einer Gebietsgründung 1950 siehe Roščupkin/Bubnis, K voprosu ob administrativnom ustrojstve, S. 73.

entsprechend ist die Genese der Parteikritik von 1953 aus dem Juli-Plenum von entscheidender Bedeutung. Auch wenn Kritik an der Herrschaftspraxis in Dal'stroj aus der Region selbst kam, war es doch wiederum die Chabarowsker Parteivertretung, die das ZK der KPdSU Mitte August 1953 um die Einführung von Partei- und Sowjetstrukturen in der Region und auch diesmal wieder um die Gründung eines Gebietes im Rahmen des Chabarowsker Distrikts bat.[99] Nun sollte ein „Magadaner Gebiet" geschaffen werden, mit Bezirkseinteilungen, die sich an der Zahl freier Arbeitskräfte, nicht an der Größe einer Produktionseinheit mit Zwangsarbeitern orientierten.[100]

Die Vertreter von Dal'stroj sprachen sich unter den politischen Gegebenheiten nicht gegen die Gründung eines Gebietes aus. Allerdings drängten sie darauf, den Zuschnitt des neuen administrativen Gebildes mit den Strukturen von Dal'stroj zur Deckung zu bringen. Denn eine Aufsplitterung des Wirkungsbereiches des Kombinats auf eine Vielzahl administrativer Einheiten hätte eine noch größere Schwächung der Position von Dal'stroj bedeutet. Mitrakov meinte:

> Ich denke, ein Gebiet zu gründen, nur für die Gründung eines Gebietes macht keinen Sinn. Im Chabarowsker Distrikt gib es drei Gebiets- und zwei Bezirkskomitees der Partei. Was für eine Wirtschaft wird denn diesem Gebiet zugrunde liegen? Genau diese Frage muss detailliert geprüft werden bei der Gründung eines Gebietes auf dem Territorium von Dal'stroj. [...] Das Magadaner Gebiet wird, wenn man nur die zentralen Territorien in sie aufnimmt, etwa 176.000 Personen umfassen, davon wären nur 120.000 Freie. Bei einer solchen Bevölkerungszahl erscheint mir die Gründung eines Gebietes unzweckmäßig. Ich spreche mich gegen die Gründung mit einer solchen Bevölkerungsgröße aus.[101]

Mitrakov und Bulanov, der Leiter der Politischen Abteilung in Dal'stroj, machten daraufhin konkrete Vorschläge, welche Territorien und Industriezentren in das zu-

---

99 Zitiert nach Gun'ko/Galin, Iz istorii sozdanija, S. 21. Auf der Tagesordnung stand zunächst noch eine Debatte über „die Gründung eines Kolymo-Čukotskischen Gebietes" (namensgleich mit den Forderungen des Chabarowsker Distrikts von 1950). Allerdings setzte sich in der Folge sehr schnell die Bezeichnung „Magadaner Gebiet" durch. Vgl. Bubnis, Iz istorii obrazovanija, S. 43. Bubnis verweist darauf, dass diese Namensänderung auf der Sitzung damit erklärt wurde, die Bedeutung des Čukotsker Kreises in seiner besonderen Rechtsstellung als nationaler Kreis nicht herabsetzen zu wollen. Nach Bubnis begann die Diskussion dieser Frage mit den Mitgliedern der ZK-Brigade am 18. August, Mitrakov hatte jedoch bereits am 12. August von der Gründung eines „Magadaner Gebietes" gesprochen. Vgl. den Abdruck seiner Rede in Verkina/Kozlov, K voprosu ob obrazovanii, S. 116. Es erscheint am wahrscheinlichsten, dass die Änderung der Bezeichnung nicht von den Mitgliedern des Chabarowsker Distrikts ausging, sondern dass diese wichtige Frage von den Mitgliedern des ZK der KPdSU entschieden wurde. Eventuell spielten dabei auch Erwägungen über das negative Image „der Kolyma" eine Rolle und „Magadan" wurde als neutraler empfunden. So bot sich der neuen politischen Leitung die Möglichkeit, sich bereits in der Bezeichnung von der bisherigen Führung abzugrenzen.
100 Das Chabarowsker Distriktparteikomitee schloss dabei von vornherein die Gründung von Bezirken in Gegenden aus, in denen die Zahl der Zwangsarbeiter die der freien Arbeiter überstieg. Beispielsweise kam es daher nicht zur Gründung des Arkagalinsker Bezirks, auf dessen Gebiet es nur ca. 9.000 freie Arbeitskräfte, aber mehr als 10.000 Häftlinge gab. Vgl. Verkina/Kozlov, K voprosu ob obrazovanii, S. 114.
101 So Mitrakov am 12. August 1953. Zitiert nach Verkina/Kozlov, K voprosu ob obrazovanii, S. 116.

künftige Gebiet miteinzuschließen seien.[102] Gleichzeitig wollte Mitrakov der Unterordnung unter den Chabarowsker Distrikt entgehen. Falls sich die Gründung eines Gebietes als unvermeidlich erweise, so Mitrakov auf der Versammlung, dann „sollte dieses Gebiet aus dem Bestand des Chabarowsker Distrikts herausgelöst und der Republik [gemeint ist die RSFSR – M. S.] untergeordnet werden."[103] Angesichts des Verlusts des Sonderstatus wollte Mitrakov offensichtlich retten, was zu retten war, der Region zumindest auch weiterhin die Aufmerksamkeit des Zentrums garantieren und den mächtigen Chabarowsker Bezirk mit seiner großen Parteischule von der Kolyma fernhalten.[104] Ein weiterer Vorstoß aus Dal'stroj, diesmal aus der Politischen Verwaltung, drängte auf die Ausdehnung des neuen Gebietes auf die Regionen, die zwar ökonomisch zu Dal'stroj gehörten, faktisch aber auf dem Territorium der Autonomen Republik Jakutien lagen.[105] Das ZK der KPdSU lehnte schließlich beide Vorschläge, die Gründung des neuen Gebietes im Rahmen des Chabarowsker Distrikts und ihre Erweiterung auf jakutisches Territorium, ab. Am 3. Dezember 1953 wurde das Magadaner Gebiet als eine unmittelbar der Sowjetrepublik RSFSR untergeordnete, neue administrativ-territoriale Einheit gegründet.

Doch bis es zur Gebietsgründung kam, wurden die bestehenden Machtverhältnisse noch einmal auf die Probe gestellt: Im Rahmen einer kritischen Aussprache über das Kombinat und seine Leitung auf einer Sitzung des gesamten Dal'stroj-Parteiaktivs im Oktober 1953 löste der Parteifunktionär S. I. Čmychov einen Skandal aus. Čmychov, der erst seit September 1952 Sekretär der städtischen Parteileitung in Magadan war, griff Mitrakov in einer bis dato unbekannten Schärfe und vor der gesamten Parteiöffentlichkeit an. Er warf ihm eine vorsätzliche Senkung der Metallförderung und eine vollkommen ineffektive Arbeitsweise vor; schließlich beleidigte er den Kombinatschef:

> Es ist daher auch kein Zufall, dass unter den Arbeitern die Redensart von der „Dynastie der Ivans an der Kolyma" die Runde macht. Die Arbeiter sprechen davon, dass wir folgende Leiter hatten: ‚Ivan der Schreckliche – Ivan Fedorovič Nikišov' [Dal'stroj-Leiter von 1939 – 1948], ‚Ivan der Weise – Ivan Grigor'evič Petrenko' [Dal'stroj-Leiter von 1948 – 1950], und jetzt haben wir ‚den Unverständlichen – Ivan Lukič Mitrakov'. [...] Und diese Redensart entbehrt, meiner Meinung nach, nicht ihrer Grundlage. Schwerwiegende Mängel bei der Arbeit der Hauptverwaltung und seines Apparates bezüglich der Wirtschaftsleitung wurden deshalb möglich, weil die Leiter, die Genossen Mitrakov, Bulanov und andere die Lage in Dal'stroj unkritisch beurteilen, sich in ihrer Arbeit nicht auf die kollektive Erfahrung der Parteiorganisationen stützen und weil die Politische Verwaltung – die Genossen Bulanov, Guščin und Šmygin – dienstbeflissen die ‚Autorität' der Leiter

---

102 Vgl. Verkina/Kozlov, K voprosu ob obrazovanii, S. 115.
103 Zitiert nach Bubnis, Iz istorii obrazovanija, S. 47; vgl. Kozlov, U istokov, S. 40.
104 Auf diesen Punkt machte der bekannte Dal'strojer Geologe M. I. Konyčev aufmerksam, der seit 1933 im Kombinat gearbeitet hatte. Er forderte, der Region auch weiterhin eine „zentralisierte Aufmerksamkeit" zukommen zu lassen. Zitiert nach Gun'ko/Galin, Iz istorii sozdanija, S. 22.
105 Vgl. das Schreiben des Leiters der Politischen Verwaltung, Bulanov, vom 8. Oktober 1953 an Chruščev in RGANI f. 5, op. 27, d. 117, l. 157.

von Dal'stroj schützt, ihre falschen Handlungen bei einer ganzen Reihe von Fragen rechtfertigt und so Prinzipienlosigkeit bei der Arbeit gestattet.[106]

Mit der Offenlegung der Redensart von den „drei Ivans der Kolyma" erreichte die Kritik an der Dal'stroj-Leitung eine neue Qualität. Mitrakovs Autorität wurde erheblich untergraben, die Parteiorganisation der Politischen Verwaltung öffentlich als eigentlich „parteifern" gebrandmarkt. Allerdings hatte sich Čmychov in Bezug auf die realen Machtverhältnisse in der Region verschätzt. Die Teilnehmer der Sitzung reagierten uneinheitlich, die Kombinatsleitung übte sofort massiven Druck auf Čmychov aus und verlangte von ihm, die „wahren Ziele" seiner Rede offenzulegen. Unter diesen Bedingungen zog Čmychov seine Beleidigung formal zurück, unter dem Druck der Leitung von Dal'stroj wurde er jedoch aus dem Präsidium der Parteileitung der Stadt Magadan ausgeschlossen. Tatsächlich erhielt Čmychov etwa einen Monat später Unterstützung aus Chabarowsk. Am 11. November beschloss die Chabarowsker Parteileitung eine eigene Verordnung „in der Sache S. I. Čmychov". Darin hieß es:

> Die Genossen Mitrakov und Bulanov sind auf ihr falsches Verhalten im Parteiaktiv hinzuweisen, als der Vorschlag zum Ausschluss Čmychovs [...] geäußert wurde. Es ist ihnen klarzumachen, dass solche Maßnahmen gegenüber Personen, die mit Kritik an Mängeln der Leitung von Dal'stroj auftreten, die Kader nicht richtig erziehen und die Entfaltung von Kritik und Selbstkritik in den Parteiorganisationen von Dal'stroj verhindern.[107]

Kurz vor Gründung des Gebietes zeigt der Skandal um Čmychov die massiv gesunkene Autorität Mitrakovs, der sich nur unter Ausübung erheblichen Drucks einer solchen bisher undenkbaren Beleidigung erwehren und seine Truppe hinter sich scharen konnte. Zugleich demonstrierte Chabarowsk noch einmal sein Interesse an einer Stärkung der Magadaner Parteistrukturen.

Das Jahr 1953 war für die Region Kolyma ein „Türöffner". Unabhängig von Berijas Intention beendeten seine Reformen die inselartige Abkapselung von Dal'stroj. Die Amnestie öffnete die Lagertore für 80.000 Menschen. Sie versetzte damit der Wirtschaft von Dal'stroj einen schweren Schlag, griff die Zwangsarbeit als wichtigste Basis des Lager-Industriellen Komplexes an und verhalf der Diskussion über die Lebensbedingungen der freien Arbeitskräfte zum Auftrieb. Die wirtschaftliche und soziale

---

106 Zitiert nach Kozlov, U istokov, S. 43. Siehe dazu auch Grebenjuk, Kolymskij led, S. 54. Nach Grebenjuk habe Čmychov schon von der Entscheidung des ZK der KPdSU über die Gründung des Gebietes gewusst. Nikišov galt aufgrund seiner extremen Grausamkeit, seines absoluten Machtwillens und seiner langen Herrschaft in Dal'stroj als „der Schreckliche", von dem sich Petrenko als „der Weise" abgrenzte. Nikišovs Frau Gridasova war als Chefin von *Maglag*, einer großen Lagerabteilung, und als Herrin über das Magadaner Theater für ihre Grausamkeit, ihre mangelnde Bildung und ihren enormen Bedarf an Luxusgütern verschrien. Vgl. die Erinnerungen von Lipper, Elf Jahre, S. 101; Varpachovskaja, Kolymskoj Traviaty, S. 73 f. sowie Schalamow, Linkes Ufer, S. 53 ff.
107 Zitiert nach Kozlov, U istokov, S. 44.

Instabilität der Region wirkte als Katalysator für kritische Stimmen, die sich schnell zur Forderung nach einer Änderung der Herrschaftsform verschärften. Die Herrschaft selbst sah sich bedroht, seit März 1953 kämpfte die bisher unangreifbare Leitung von Dal'stroj gegen den Entzug von Boni, Pensionen und Auszeichnungen. Mitrakov erlebte zunächst den Entzug eines Teils seines Gehalts, schließlich wurde er Ende des Jahres öffentlich verhöhnt. Im äußersten Nordosten wurde also in Ansätzen verwirklicht, was das ZK der KPdSU auf dem Juli-Plenum in Moskau und regionale Parteiaktive seit 1938 gefordert hatten: Eine Entmilitarisierung des MVD und eine stärkere Kontrolle durch Parteiorgane.

Es erscheint als relativ wahrscheinlich, dass Chruščev an der Kolyma eine maßgebliche Rolle spielte. Als einer der aktivsten Männer bei der Verhaftung und Verurteilung Berijas kann ihm ein persönliches Interesse am bisherigen Machtbereich des MVD-Chefs unterstellt werden. Zudem fiel der Beschluss über die Gründung des Gebietes und der damit verbundene Aufstieg der Partei zur entscheidenden Macht in eine Phase, in der Chruščev damit begann, Parteivorsitzende in den einzelnen sowjetischen Regionen auszuwechseln und durch ihm genehme Personen zu ersetzen, wozu er in seiner Funktion als Erster Sekretär des ZK der KPdSU seit September 1953 die Möglichkeiten hatte.[108] Alexander Titov beschreibt diesen Schritt nicht nur als eine reine Auswechslung von Personen, vielmehr sei sie mit einer prinzipiellen Hinwendung des Zentralkomitees zu den Regionen, einem „new regional focus"[109] verbunden gewesen, der eine ganze Reihe organisatorischer Veränderungen im Zentralkomitee mit sich brachte. Zudem benutzte Chruščev in dieser Zeit die Stärkung der Parteistrukturen gegenüber den staatlichen Stellen als eine Waffe im Kampf gegen seine innerparteilichen Widersacher, zunächst Berija, später Malenkov.[110]

Peter Solomon attestiert Chruščev in dieser Zeit eine „intense concern with legality", die bei ihm zugleich mit einer „willingness to take on established local interests"[111] einhergegangen sei. In Magadan ließ sich dies mit der Umsetzung der alten Anstrengungen der Partei zur Überwindung der Einheitsleitung von Dal'stroj verbinden. Chruščev war als Erster Sekretär zudem Ansprechpartner für alle Parteiorganisationen und damit auch mit der besonderen Position Politischer Verwaltungen in militärisch geprägten Herrschaftsformen vertraut.[112] Aber auch inhaltlich soll sich Chruščev zur Kolyma geäußert haben. Teilnehmer von Beratungen über die Lage des Kombinats erinnerten sich später an folgenden Ausspruch Chruščevs:

---

108 Vgl. Chlevnjuk, Regional'naja vlast', S. 31; Pauling, Diener des Plenums, S. 643; Gill, Symbols, S. 166.

109 Titov, Central Committee, S. 44.

110 Vgl. Mitrokhin, Political Clans, S. 33; Gorlizki, Party Revivalism, S. 19 ff.

111 Solomon, Soviet Politicians, S. 9 f.

112 Siehe beispielsweise die an ihn gerichtete Petition der Politischen Abteilung des Kombinats „Chakasszoloto", die sich gegen ihre Gängelung durch die Kombinatsleitung wehrte in RGANI f. 5, op. 27, d. 117, l. 142–145.

> Man muss die dunklen Flecken von Magadan und der Kolyma nehmen, man muss mit voller Kraft die Linie unserer Partei, ein normales Leben und eine zivile Bevölkerung durchsetzen.[113]

Ob sich die „dunklen Flecken" mehr auf die ökonomische Krise, die Führungsmethoden des MVD oder die Zwangsarbeit bezogen, führte Chruščev nicht näher aus. Doch muss bezweifelt werden, dass dieser Ausspruch tatsächlich so im Jahr 1953 erfolgte. Mit der Forderung nach Durchsetzung der Politik der Partei, einer Angleichung an die Verhältnisse in den übrigen Teilen der Sowjetunion und der verstärkten Ansiedlung „ziviler Bevölkerung" hätte Chruščev exakt die Leitlinien für die Arbeit der neuen Gebietsleitung vorgegeben. Denkbar ist vielmehr, dass die lokale Parteiführung Chruščev diese Worte zu einem späteren Zeitpunkt in den Mund legte, als er sich als „Entstalinisierer" bereits durchgesetzt hatte – und als diese Worte hervorragend zu der damals herrschenden lokalen Propaganda passten.[114]

3.2 Aufbau des Magadaner Gebietes

Die oberste Parteileitung in Moskau hatte Ende des Jahres 1953, in der Phase des Umbruchs und Machtkampfes, zwei grundsätzliche Interessen an der Kolyma: Die Region sollte sozial und wirtschaftlich stabilisiert werden, zugleich drängte die Parteileitung darauf, in einen bisher dem MVD vorbehaltenen Raum einzudringen und die Macht über ihn zu gewinnen.

Die Intentionen der obersten Sowjetführung waren also auf eine Klärung der Lage der Region, auf ihre Stabilisierung und gleichzeitig auf eine feste Anbindung an die Organe der Partei- und Sowjetstrukturen ausgerichtet. Die Region sollte – Schritt für Schritt – dem zivilen Sektor der Sowjetunion zugeordnet werden. Während sich hinter dieser Neubestimmung eine ganze Reihe fundamentaler Machtkämpfe verbargen, und obwohl mit der Entmilitarisierung der Kolyma zugleich auch die Aufgabe der Lagerwirtschaft verhandelt wurde, verlief die Überstellung in den zivilen Sektor im Rahmen einer sehr formal anmutenden Gebietsreform.

Die Gründung des Gebietes schloss, sozusagen auf Verwaltungswege, eine militärische Einzelleitung ebenso aus wie die militärisch bestellte Politische Verwaltung, die Erweiterung ihrer Grenzen nach den wirtschaftlichen Bedürfnissen des Kombinats und eine finanzielle Mittelvergabe außerhalb der Standards des sowjetischen Finanzministeriums.

Somit benutzte die KPdSU den Aufbau der zivilen staatlichen Strukturen, um über dieses Netz ihren eigenen Machtanspruch durchsetzen zu können. Yoram Gorlizki hat dieses Vorgehen als ein Kennzeichen der Chruščev'schen Politik in den ersten Jahren nach 1953 beschrieben:

---

113 Zitiert nach Grebenjuk, Kolymskij led, S. 58.
114 Zu dieser lokalen Propaganda siehe das Kapitel 5.3.7.

While taking care not to substitute for the functions of the state, Khrushchev underlined the Party's right to intervene in all areals of public life. Such a commitment to interventionism was especially strong in the early phase of Khrushchev's rule, as the new leader dinstinguished himself from his main rival Malenkov by laying particular stress on Party initiatives and Party-based solutions to the main economic and social problems of the day."[115]

Um zu verstehen, welche intendierten und welche nicht-intendierten Veränderungen die Auflösung des Lager-Industriellen Komplexes für die Region mit sich brachte, muss man der inneren Logik dieser Vorgehensweise folgen. Der bisher von einem Lager-Industriellen Komplex besetzte Raum wurde von Grund auf neu vermessen, neu erschlossen, neu verwaltet und regiert. Die Organe der Partei- und Sowjetstrukturen legten über das Territorium das Netz einer zivilen administrativen Territorialeinheit. Die Grenzen des Gebietes und die Binnengrenzen der einzelnen Regionen mit ihren jeweiligen Zentren wurden bestimmt, das Personal der neuen Strukturen ausgewählt, entsprechend ausgebildet und eingesetzt. Ebenso mussten aber auch regionale Infrastrukturen und Institutionen dem unionsweiten Standard angepasst werden. Diese Erschließung und Besetzung des Magadaner Gebietes durch zivile Organe hatte natürlich auch inhaltliche Folgen. Stück für Stück wurde die Region in das Leben des zivilen Sektors der Sowjetunion integriert, Entwicklungen der gesamten Union in Politik, Wirtschaft und bei den sozialen Verhältnissen hatten mehr und mehr einen Einfluss auf das nordöstliche Gebiet.

3.2.1 Das Territorium und seine Repräsentation

Die Gründung des Magadaner Gebietes machte das *Territorium* zum Ausgangspunkt der neuen Strukturen. Bisher hatte die territoriale Basis von Dal'stroj keine machtpolitische Rolle gespielt; sobald ein angrenzendes Gebiet für das Kombinat wirtschaftlich interessant wurde (wie z. B. die großen Gebiete Jakutiens) wurde es einfach in die Dal'strojer Herrschaft inkorporiert. Die wirtschaftliche Nutzung bestimmte zu dieser Zeit auch die territoriale Gliederung. Die Region war in verschiedene Bergbauverwaltungszonen aufgeteilt, die sich an den vorhandenen Förderanlagen oder Energiestationen orientierten, Siedlungen oder Bevölkerungszahlen waren hingegen unerheblich.

Im Gegensatz dazu war durch die Gründung des Magadaner Gebietes das Territorium der neuen Herrschaftseinheit von Anfang an gesetzt. Es war erheblich kleiner als der Wirkungskreis des Kombinats Dal'stroj. Statt mehr als 3 Mio. km^2 im März 1953 umfasste das Magadaner Gebiet nur noch gut 1,2 Mio. km^2 (davon etwa 720.000 km^2 in Tschukotka), allerdings war dies der territorial und ökonomisch zentrale Teil des

---

115 Gorlizki, Political Reform, S. 258.

Gebietes von Dal'stroj.[116] Territoriale Beschneidungen hatte es überall dort gegeben, wo bereits andere administrative Strukturen bestanden, vor allem auf dem Gebiet der Autonomen Republik Jakutien, des Chabarowsker Distrikts und des Kamčatskaer Gebietes. In diesen Gebieten wurden die zuvor durch Dal'stroj entmachteten Organe der lokalen Partei- und Sowjetstrukturen wieder ins Recht gesetzt und übernahmen die Verwaltung.[117] Der Wirtschaftsraum des Kombinats und die politischen Gebiete waren daher nicht mehr kongruent, Dal'stroj musste sich im Folgenden mit verschiedenen administrativen Einheiten und mit unterschiedlichen Leitungsorganen auseinandersetzen.

Die Vorstellung des neuen Magadaner Gebietes war der erste Schritt, den die zivil-administrative Leitung der neuen Partei- und Sowjetorgane zu ihrer Selbstrepräsentation vor Ort nutzte. Sie bediente sich dabei der größten Tageszeitung der Region, die unter der Bezeichnung *Sovetskaja Kolyma* von der Politischen Verwaltung des Kombinats herausgegeben worden war. Auf Anweisung des ZK der KPdSU hatten das Gebietspartei- und Gebietsexekutivkomitee die Zeitung kurze Zeit nach Gründung des Gebietes übernommen, ab dem 20. Januar erschien sie unter dem Titel *Magadanskaja Pravda* als „Organ des Magadaner Gebiets- und Stadtkomitees der KPdSU und des Gebietsexekutivkomitees".[118] Für die Redation der neuen Zeitung wurde speziell

---

116 Das Gebiet reicht bis in den nordöstlichsten Teil der Sowjetunion, auf einer horizontalen Ausdehnung von fast 2.300 km. Die südlichen Gebiete befinden sich auf der Höhe von Leningrad, während die nördlichen Gebiete (z. B. die Wrangelinsel) 500 km nördlich des Polarkreises liegen.

117 Im Falle der jakutischen ASSR handelte es sich um ein Territorium von 1,2 Mio. km², das bisher vollständig von Dal'stroj verwaltet worden war. Im April 1954 wurde – in Analogie zu den Verhältnissen in Magadan – das Gebiet der jakutischen Partei- und Sowjetführung übergeben, ein neuer Bezirk gegründet und die Gehälter der Führung dem unionsweiten Standard angepasst. Vgl. den entsprechenden Antrag aus Jakutsk sowie die Reaktion aus dem ZK der KPdSU in RGANI f. 5, op. 15, d. 471, l. 15–17 bzw. l. 20. Vorstöße zur Ausweitung des Einflusses der Autonomen Republik Jakutien hatte es bereits im Herbst 1953 gegeben, vgl. RGANI f. 5, op. 15, d. 421, l. 42–50. Brief vom 23. September 1953.

118 Zum Beschluss des ZK der KPdSU siehe Chilobočenko, Istoričeskaja chronika, S. 182. Zur Entwicklung des Pressewesens im Nordosten siehe Zlatina, Periodičeskaja pečat' sowie Smolina, Gazetnoj strokoj. Derartige Übernahmen von Publikationsorganen der bisherigen politischen Verwaltungen durch die lokalen Parteiorgane wurden überall dort praktiziert, wo die bisherige außerordentliche Parteiführung aufgegeben wurde; so auch im GULAG des Justizministeriums im Sommer 1953. Innerhalb der Struktur des GULAG zählten die Parteimitglieder bisheriger politischer Abteilungen der Lagerabteilungen, nach der Übergabe von GULAG-Kombinaten an zivile Produktionsministerien, zu den regulären regionalen Parteiorganisationen. Die Zeitungen der bisherigen Politischen Abteilungen wurden in ihrer Aufgabe umgewidmet, sie sollten in Zukunft nur noch zu Agitations- und Propagandazwecken gegenüber den Wachmannschaften eingesetzt werden und nicht mehr über Produktionsinterna berichten. Um diesen Umschwung auch äußerlich kenntlich zu machen, bat der Justizminister der UdSSR das ZK der KPdSU um das Recht zur Umbenennung von Zeitungen. Z. B. sollte die bisherige Zeitung der Politischen Abteilung des Lagerkomplexes von Workuta, die *Zapoljarnaja Kočegarka* in *Poljarnaja Zvezda* umbenannt werden. Vgl. den Brief des Justizministers der UdSSR an das ZK der KPdSU vom 29. August 1953 in RGANI f. 5, op. 16, d. 613, l. 81–83. Die Umbenennungen wurden durch die Propagandaabteilung des ZK der KPdSU gebilligt, vgl. l. 84. Die Politische Abteilung des GULAG bat auch darum, aufgrund der Schließung ganzer Produktionsteile – nach der Amnestie und der Ein-

ausgewähltes Personal nach Magadan gebracht, wie Vladimir Novikov, der unmittlbar nach Abschluss der Fakultät für Journalistik der Moskauer Lomonossow-Universität zur Arbeit bei der *Magadanskaja Pravda* geschickt wurde.[119] Analog dazu gestaltete das Gebietsparteikomitee die bisherigen Zeitungen der Politischen Abteilungen in den einzelnen Wirtschaftsverwaltungszonen im März 1954 zu offiziellen Bezirkszeitungen um.[120]

In einer der ersten Nummern der *Magadanska Pravda* präsentierte sie das Gebiet als eine sowjetische Region wie jede andere. Diesen verblüffenden Eindruck vermittelte die Karte, die die neuen Herausgeber veröffentlichten. Ein absolutes Novum, denn bisher hatte sämtliches Kartenmaterial über das Gebiet von Dal'stroj absoluter Geheimhaltung unterlegen; an keiner Stelle wäre auch nur die Lage einzelner Orte oder von Flüssen genannt worden. Und nun existierte nicht nur der Naturraum in kartographischer Hinsicht, auch einzelne Ortschaften, die wichtigsten Flüsse sowie die Verwaltungsgrenzen zu anderen sowjetischen Territorialeinheiten erhielten gewissermaßen eine offizielle Existenzberechtigung. Ein Spruchband „Magadaner Gebiet" durchzog die Darstellung, der dazugehörige Text und ein Gedicht zelebrierten die Gründung des Magadaner Gebietes, seine territoriale Lage und seine Bevölkerung (vgl. Abbildung 3). Von der Geburt der Region aus Lagern, von der Anwesenheit der vielen Zehntausenden Häftlinge und bewaffneten Truppen war in dieser Darstellung nichts zu spüren. Karte und Text vermittelten den Eindruck einer friedlichen Region, gegliedert durch mehrere große Flüsse und einige Städte oder Siedlungen. Tatsächlich war das Magadaner Gebiet nun grundsätzlich ebenso erreichbar wie jede andere zivile Region der Sowjetunion. Die Publizistin Evgenija Ginzburg, die nach ihrer Haft als Verbannte in Magadan leben musste, berichtet in ihren Erinnerungen von dem völlig überraschenden Besuch ihres Sohnes Vasilij Aksenov in ihrer Magadaner Baracke, nachdem im Frühjahr 1954 die bislang geforderten Einreisegenehmigungen aufge-

---

stellung von Anlagen – einige Zeitungen ganz aufgeben zu dürfen. Dieser Bitte wurde stattgegeben. Vgl. den Brief der Politischen Abteilung des GULAG an das ZK der KPdSU vom 20. Mai 1953 in RGANI f. 5, op. 16, d. 613, l. 59 – 61.

119 Vgl. Novikov, Kolyma ty, S. 3. Novikov übernahm einige Jahre später die Redaktion der neugegründeten Zeitung des Komsomol *Magadanskij Komsomolec*.

120 Insgesamt gab es 14 Zeitungen in den Wirtschaftsverwaltungszonen. Vgl. die Beschreibung im Übergabeakt von Dal'stroj an das MMP in GAMO f. R-23, op. 1, d. 4677, l. 116. Nach dem März 1954 wurde beispielsweise die bisherige Zeitung der Politischen Abteilung der südwestlichen Bergbauverwaltung zu der Bezirkszeitung *Sejmčanskaja Pravda*, als Organ des Srednekanser Bezirkspartei- und Exekutivkomitees. Die Zeitung der Politischen Abteilung der nördlichen Bergbauverwaltung, die zur Bezirkszeitung des Jagodninsker Bezirks wurde, erschien nun unter dem neuen Namen *Severnaja Pravda*. Zeitgleich wurde das bisherige Organ der Politischen Verwaltung von Dal'stroj, der *Bloknot agitatora*, in das Organ der Abteilung für Propaganda und Agitation des neuen Gebietsparteikomitees umgewandelt und fortan über das Budget des Gebietsexekutivkomitees finanziert. Vgl. Chilobočenko, Istoričeskaja chronika, S. 182f.

ОДИН ДЕНЬ НАШЕЙ ОБЛАСТИ

Взгляните на карту! Обширные пространства Дальнего Северо-Востока нашей великой социалистической Родины занимает Магаданская область. На ее территории могли бы свободно разместиться Великобритания, Франция, Ита-

мают, что организация Магаданской области — итог большого и плодотворного труда. Теперь начинается новый этап в истории края, когда Дальний Северо-Восток станет развиваться и процветать еще быстрее.

В теплицах Сеймчанского совхоза появились первые зеленые всходы турнепса.
Неутомимо трудились люди скромных профессий. Кондитер Анна Корсун на Тасканском пищекомбинате готовила

Abb. 3 Magadanskaja Pravda, 7. Februar 1954

hoben worden waren – zumindest Magadan war damit keine geschlossene Stadt mehr.[121]

Tatsächlich verfügte die neue Führung zu dieser Zeit noch nicht einmal über eine vollständige kartographische Abbildung der Region. Große Teile des Raumes waren eigentlich noch weithin unbekannt. Selbst in Dal'stroj fehlten exakte Angaben über den genauen Verlauf einzelner Flüsse, über Gebirgszüge und die Bodenbeschaffenheit, da sich ihre geophysische Kartographie stets nur an den Produktionsnotwendigkeiten orientiert hatte. Erst im Laufe der Jahre nahm eine genaue Karte des Magadaner Gebietes dank der Unterstützung von Kartographen aus Chabarowsk und von Magadaner Geologen feste Konturen an.[122]

Parallel dazu verlief die administrative Gliederung des Gebietes durch Bezirke (*rajony*). Sie ersetzten die bisherigen Bergbauverwaltungszonen von Dal'stroj. In dem

---

121 Vgl. Ginsburg, Gratwanderung, S. 449.
122 Vgl. Na preobražennoj zemle, S. 25 – 26.

Beschluss des Präsidiums des Obersten Sowjets zur Gründung des Magadaner Gebietes vom 3. Dezember 1953 wurden diese Bezirke, neben der Stadt Magadan, bereits als Territorialeinheiten des neuen Gebietes aufgeführt: „Die Bezirke Srednekanskij, Ol'skij, Severo-Ėvenskij, Susumanskij, Ten'kinskij, Jagodninskij und der Čukotsker nationale Kreis (mit den Bezirken Čaunskij, Čukotskij, Anadyr'skij, Markovskij und Vostočno-Tundrovskij)."[123]

Im Grunde war jedoch diese Struktur lediglich am Reißbrett entstanden und orientierte sich nur ansatzweise an den Gegebenheiten der einzelnen Gebiete. Zu einer genaueren Binnengliederung waren bisher weder der Oberste Sowjet der RSFSR noch die neuen Partei- und Sowjetvertreter in der Region in der Lage. An was es der sowjetischen Führung mangelte, waren genaue Kenntnisse über die einzelnen Bezirke, über Bevölkerungszahlen und die soziale Infrastruktur in den Siedlungspunkten. Informationen lagen lediglich über die wirtschaftliche Bedeutung der einzelnen Gebiete vor, und diese auch nur in dem von Dal'stroj erhobenen Rahmen.

Bei der Einteilung der Bezirke waren jedoch genauere Kenntnisse vonnöten. Eine Verwaltung durch Partei- und Sowjetstrukturen musste sich in der Sowjetunion grundsätzlich an Siedlungspunkten orientieren. Das bedeutete, dass nun zum ersten Mal der Infrastruktur der freien Arbeitskräfte und nicht den Wirtschaftsanlagen mit ihren Lagerpunkten eine strukturierende Bedeutung zugewiesen wurde. Die Ortschaften wurden zu Knotenpunkten des Rasters, das die neue Leitung über das Territorium legte.

Bereits am 22. Dezember 1953 wurden daher 22 Bevölkerungspunkte zu der administrativen Kategorie „Arbeitersiedlung" erhoben und acht neue Dorfsowjets gegründet. Begründet wurde die Statuserhöhung dieser Ortschaften mit ihrer Bedeutung für die in ihnen und in ihrer Umgebung lebenden Menschen (Läden, Klubs, Schulen etc.) – die neue Verwaltung musste sich an zivilen Maßstäben orientieren.[124]

---

123 Veröffentlich in Sbornik zakonov, S. 65. Für den Original-Erlass siehe GARF f. R-7523, op. 58, d. 1169, l. 1, für die Verordnung des Präsidiums des Obersten Sowjets der RSFSR vgl. ebd., l. 3. In Magadan wurde der Erlass am 27. Dezember 1953 in der *Sovetskaja Kolyma* veröffentlicht. Bei der Festlegung der Bezirke wurde folgendermaßen verfahren: Die bereits bestehenden „nationalen Bezirke", die in Dal'stroj bisher keine Bedeutung gehabt hatten (die Bezirke Ol'skij, Severo-Ėvenskij und Srednekanskij), wurden direkt in das Gebiet aufgenommen. Zudem schuf die Sowjetführung einen Tag vor der Gründung des Magadaner Gebietes die Bezirke Susumanskij, Ten'kinskij und Jagodninskij (an der Kolyma) sowie den Iul'tinsker Bezirk (Tschukotka) im Rahmen des Chabarowsker Distrikts. Vgl. den Befehl des Präsidium des Obersten Sowjets der RSFSR zur Gründung der Bezirke am 2. Dezember 1953 in GARF f. R-7523, op. 58, d. 1181, l. 177. Es ist davon auszugehen, dass die Gründung der neuen Bezirke noch im Rahmen des Chabarowsker Distrikts erfolgen musste, um zunächst einmal das Territorium administrativ zu bezeichnen, das schließlich zu einer eigenständigen Einheit werden sollte.

124 Dabei wurden auch Personen, die im Umkreis von 80 km der betreffenden Siedlung lebten, als auf sie bezogen genannt. Die Einwohnerzahl der betreffenden Bevölkerungspunkte lag, nach Auskunft der statistischen Abteilung des Obersten Sowjets der RSFSR, zwischen 2.000 und 13.000 Menschen. Die Erhebung zur Arbeitersiedlung hatte auch Auswirkung auf die Bezahlung der dort Beschäftigten, z. B. erhielten Lehrer in einer Arbeitersiedlung ein höheres Gehalt als in einem Dorf. Vgl. GARF f. R-7523, op. 58, d. 1182, l. 12–21. Insgesamt gab es auf dem Territorium des Magadaner Gebietes 26 Bevölke-

Anders sah es in unbekannterem Terrain aus. Um die Gliederung der neuen Bezirke den tatsächlichen Gegebenheiten anpassen zu können, setzte die neue Leitung des Gebietsexekutivkomitees eine Vielzahl von Kommissionen ein, die die einzelnen Bezirke bereisten. Entlang der grob festgelegten neuen Struktur erschlossen sich diese Kommissionen das Territorium, beschrieben die einzelnen Gebiete und erarbeiteten Vorschläge zu ihrer besseren Gliederung. Allein die Anreise war mit erheblichen Schwierigkeiten verbunden, wie P. I. Borisov, ein Teilnehmer schildert:

> Wir sind mit einem Schiff gereist und hatten so die Möglichkeit, die Besonderheiten der lokalen Natur kennenzulernen. Den Hafen von Ėvensk konnten wir gar nicht erreichen, weil er vereist war. Wir mussten unter größten Schwierigkeiten von einer Eisscholle zur anderen springen, um an das Ufer zu gelangen. Die ganze Zeit befürchteten wir, auf unserer Eisscholle ins offene Meer getrieben zu werden. Eine Fahrt zur Peripherie des Magadaner Gebietes ähnelt nun wirklich nicht einer Reise irgendwo in der Gegend von Rjazan oder Kostroma. Diese Entfernungen! Und es gibt keine Straßen. Und die Transportmittel sind auch andere.[125]

Rentierkolchosen mussten oft tagelang in der Tundra gesucht werden. In den einzelnen Gebieten angekommen, wurden die vorhandenen Einrichtungen dokumentiert und die Lage der Siedlungen beschrieben.[126]

An diesen Kommissionen nahmen auch die Mitarbeiter der geologischen Schürfabteilung von Dal'stroj teil, die mit den geologischen und geographischen Gegebenheiten am besten vertraut waren. Die Arbeit der Kommissionen offenbarte,

---

rungspunkte mit dem Status „Arbeitersiedlung" und 76 Dorfsowjets. Die Zahlenangabe zu den Siedlungen nach Sovety, S. 220. Der Unterschied zwischen diesen beiden Bevölkerungspunkten lag v. a. in ihrer wirtschaftlichen Ausrichtung. Um den Status „Arbeitersiedlung (*rabočyj poselok*)" zu erlangen, musste die Siedlung mindestens 3.000 Einwohner haben und diese mussten zu mindestens 85 % in der Industrie beschäftigt sein. „Dorfsowjets" hingegen bezeichneten Siedlungen mit einer eindeutig landwirtschaftlichen Ausrichtung. Statt des Begriffs „Arbeitersiedlung" wird auch die Bezeichnung „Siedlung städtischen Typs (*poselok gorodskogo tipa*)" verwendet, sie wird jedoch in geographischer Hinsicht gebraucht. Vgl. den Befehl des Präsidiums des Obersten Sowjets der RSFSR zu der genannten Statusveränderung in GARF f. R-7523, op. 58, d. 1182, l. 92. Die Leitung des Zentrums Jagodnoe (ca. 6.000 Einwohner) bemühte sich bereits 1954 darum, von der Kategorie „Arbeitersiedlung" in den Rang einer Stadt erhoben zu werden, um eine Reihe finanzieller Vorteile sowie eine gewisse Eigenständigkeit zu erlangen. Bis in die 1960er Jahre blieb jedoch Magadan die einzige Stadt im Nordosten. In den 1960er Jahren wurden jedoch gleich drei Siedlungen zu Städten ernannt: Susuman (1964), Anadyr' (1965) und Pevek (1967). Vgl. Roščupkin/Bubnis, K voprosu ob administrativnom ustrojstve, S. 74. Zu dem Vorstoß aus Jagodnoe siehe GAMO f. R-146, op. 1, d. 38, l. 13 – 15. Tatsächlich hatten die administrativen Veränderungen auch praktische finanzielle Auswirkungen. So führte z. B. die Verlegung von Siedlungspunkten des Korjakser nationalen Kreises in den Severo-Ėvensker Bezirk am 22. Dezember 1953 dazu, dass Kolchosen in ein und demselben Bezirk verschiedenen Boni-Kategorien angehörten (da die alten Boni des Kreises für diese Siedlungen bestehen blieben) und Korjaken und Evenen trotz gleicher Lebensbedingungen durch die sowjetische Macht nicht gleichgestellt waren. Der stellv. Leiter des Gebietsexekutivkomitees bemühte sich daher bereits im März 1954 beim Ministerrat der RSFSR um eine Angleichung. Vgl. GAMO f. R-146, op. 1, d. 53, l. 5.

125 Zitiert nach Na preobražennoj zemle, S. 36 f.
126 Vgl. Na preobražennoj zemle, S. 45 – 47.

dass die am Reißbrett entstandenen Bezirksgrenzen häufig ungünstig verliefen oder sich nicht an den tatsächlichen Verhältnissen der Bevölkerung orientierten. Daher wurden dem Präsidium des Obersten Sowjets der RSFSR schon bald Vorschläge für eine bessere territoriale Gestaltung der einzelnen Bezirke vorgelegt. Den Prozess der Erarbeitung dieser Vorschläge bezeichnete Afanas'ev, der Vorsitzende des Gebiets-exekutivkomitees, als „rajonirovanie" – als „Bezirkung"[127]. Dabei wurden ausführliche Beschreibungen der einzelnen Gebiete angefertigt, Selbst- und Gegendarstellungen von Siedlungen verfasst, immer wieder neue Kommissionen eingesetzt und eine Vielzahl von Bescheinigungen ausgestellt. Bedenkt man, dass die Bevölkerung des Magadaner Gebietes zu diesem Zeitpunkt von einer enormen Instabilität, von permanentem Zu- und Abzug geprägt war, dass darüber hinaus sehr viele Ortschaften fast vollständig von Kommunikation und Infrastruktur abgeschnitten waren, so wird schnell deutlich, mit welchen Schwierigkeiten das Gebietsexekutivkomitee zum einen zu kämpfen hatte, wie groß zum anderen das Bedürfnis war, eine Beherrschung des Gebietes durch eine formalisierte Struktur zu erreichen. Das Unbekannte und Chaotische des Territoriums sollte in standardisierte Vorgaben gepresst werden. Zugleich sollte ein möglichst günstiger administrativer Zuschnitt die politische Arbeit erleichtern.

Die administrativen Veränderungen zielten zum einen auf Systematisierungen. Die Bezeichnungen der Ortschaften sollten vereinheitlicht und die Zugehörigkeit einzelner Orte zu bestimmten Bezirken der vorhandenen Infrastruktur, den Orientierungen der Bevölkerung in praktischen Fragen (etwa bei der Lebensmittelversorgung oder dem Schulbesuch) angepasst werden.[128] Zudem sollten die Bezirke ein eindeutig erkennbares wirtschaftliches Profil erhalten. Dabei schoben sich die Leiter der Exekutivorgane einzelne Siedlungen, Industrieanlagen und Infrastrukturen wie persön-

---

[127] Afanas'ev in einem Schreiben an das Sekretariat des Obersten Sowjets der RSFSR vom September 1954 in GAMO f. R-146, op. 1, d. 36, l. 42–43, hier l. 43. Dieser Prozess der „rajonirovanie", der Neubestimmung von Bezirken und ihren Grenzen fand in sehr vielen Gebieten der Sowjetunion statt. Vor allem an den Rändern der Union, im Hohen Norden oder z. B. in der Kasachischen SSR, dort, wo viele Siedlungen unmittelbar von Rohstofferschließungen abhängig waren, wurden immer wieder neue Arbeitersiedlungen gegründet oder aufgelöst, Bezirksgrenzen verändert, Bezirke geschaffen oder aufgelöst. In den Jahren nach 1953 sind es sehr viele Lagergebiete, in denen sich die administrative Karte der Sowjetunion häufig veränderte – die Regionen Komi, Murmansk, Norilsk u. a. Dies lässt vermuten, dass auch in diesen Gebieten die Aufgabe der lagergeprägten Herrschaftsform mit einem neuen administrativen Zuschnitt einherging. Am 15. Juli 1953 wurde beispielsweise die Arbeitersiedlung Norilsk zur Stadt erklärt (mit direkter Eingliederung in den Krasnojarsker Distrikt). Vgl. den entsprechenden Befehl des Präsidiums des Obersten Sowjets der RSFSR in GARF f. R-7523, op. 58, d. 1180, l. 107. Diese und weitere Akten enthalten eine große Zahl an Verordnungen, die administrative Veränderungen betreffen. Vgl. GARF f. R-7523, op. 58, d. 1180, 1181 und 1182.

[128] So gab es im Magadaner Gebiet beispielsweise zwei Orte mit der Bezeichnung „Arman'". Aufgrund dieser Namensgleichheit wurde der eine Ort Arman' in den falschen Bezirk integriert. Vgl. GAMO f. R-146, op. 1, d. 36, l. 55–57. Es kam immer wieder vor, dass Siedlungen einem anderen als dem eigentlich vorgesehenen Bezirk zugeordnet wurden, um dem Ort einen leichteren Zugang zu Verkehrsknotenpunkten zu ermöglichen. Vgl. Na preobražennoj zemle, S. 28 f.

liches Eigentum zu.[129] So wurde ein halbes Jahr nach der Gebietsgründung, am 16. Juli 1954, ein weiterer Bezirk geschaffen. Der Bezirk Omsukčanskij (mit dem Zentrum Omsukčan) sollte als ein industrieller Bergbaubezirk entstehen, der Bezirk Severo-Ėvenskij, auf dessen Gebiet der neue Bezirk hauptsächlich gebildet wurde, seine landwirtschaftliche Ausrichtung (v. a. Fischfang) festigen.[130]

Grenzveränderungen zwischen den einzelnen Bezirken und auch ihre Neugründung gab es bis in die 1970er Jahre immer wieder, danach nahmen sie deutlich ab, was auf eine Verstetigung des Bestandes verweist. Neben dem Omsukčansker entstand 1954 noch der Uil'tinsker Bezirk, 1957 kamen der Providensker und der Beringovsker Bezirk (alle im Čukotskaer Kreis) hinzu. In Tschukotka gab es in den folgenden Jahren besonders viele Veränderungen, hier war das Territorium noch weniger erschlossen als an der Kolyma.[131]

In den offiziellen regionalen Publikationsorganen ging diese administrative Erschließung mit einer *mentalen* Besetzung einher, die das riesige Gebiet zunehmend als gewöhnlichen, kleinteilig parzellierten sowjetischen Verwaltungsraum erscheinen

---

129 Besonders die Grenze zwischen dem Jagodninsker und dem Srednekansker Bezirk wurde mehrfach verschoben. Häufig ging es dabei darum, Siedlungen und Territorium aus dem Jagodninsker an den Srednekansker Bezirk zu übergeben, da der Jagodninsker Bezirk besonders groß, infrastrukturell aber besonders schlecht erschlossen war. Siehe beispielsweise den Vorstoß aus Jagodnoe vom Januar 1956 in GAMO f. R-146, op. 1, d. 38, l. 29–30. Zu einer Verschiebung im April 1963 siehe GAMO f. R-146, op. 1, d. 38, l. 60–61.

130 Vgl. Na preobražennoj zemle, S. 26. Dort findet sich auch eine Beschreibung der einzelnen Bezirke mit ihrer jeweiligen wirtschaftlichen Ausrichtung. Die ausführliche Begründung des Gebietsexekutivkomitees für die Bitte beim Präsidium des Obersten Sowjets der RSFSR um Gründung des neuen Bezirk Omsukčanskij vom Juni 1954 findet sich in GAMO f. R-146, op. 1, d. 36, l. 33–39. Der entsprechende Antrag an das ZK der KPdSU findet sich in GAMO f. R-146, op. 1, d. 36, l. 7–10.

131 1960 wurde der Bezirk Markovskij aufgelöst, 1961 der Bezirk Vostočnaja Tundra in Bilibinsker Bezirk umbenannt, 1966 der Chasynsker Bezirk und 1973 der Šmidtovsker Bezirk gegründet. Vgl. zu den territorialen Veränderungen in den folgenden Jahren Administrativno-territorial'noe delenie, S. 23 bzw. S. 32 sowie Roščupkin/Bubnis, K voprosu ob administrativnom ustrojstve, S. 74; Na preobražennoj zemle, S. 26. Auch die Grenzen zur Autonomen Republik Jakutien, v. a. die Grenze zwischen Jakutien und Tschukotka, war Gegenstand von Streitigkeiten. Das Magadaner Gebiet erhob im Laufe mehrerer Jahre immer wieder Anspruch auf eine Grenzverschiebung zu seinen Gunsten, bei der die Kolyma zur neuen, quasi natürlichen Grenze werden sollte. Jakutsk lehnte diese Grenzverschiebung mit dem Hinweis auf in diesem Gebiet lebende Jakuten ab. Vorstöße kamen 1957 und 1958 zunächst nur aus Tschukotka, vgl. RGANI f. 5, op. 32, d. 87, l. 34 f. sowie RGANI f. 5, op. 32, d. 146, l. 15, schließlich 1959 und 1960 vom Magadaner Gebietsparteikomitee selbst, vgl. RGANI f. 5, op. 32, d. 146, l. 4–5 sowie l. 11–12. Zur Reaktion aus Jakutsk vgl. RGANI f. 5, op. 32, d. 146, l. 14–15. Ein weiteres Streitthema zwischen Magadan und Jakutsk war der exakte Verlauf der Grenze zwischen dem Bezirk Srednekanskij und der Autonomen Republik Jakutien. Jakutsk übte schließlich im Frühjahr 1955 Druck auf Magadan aus, noch immer fehle eine exakte Karte der Region, die den Grenzverlauf dokumentieren könne. Vgl. das Schreiben des Präsidiums des Obersten Sowjets der Autonomen Republik Jakutien an Afanas'ev vom Frühjahr 1955 in GAMO f. R-146, op. 1, d. 36, l. 77–78. Die Beratungen über die Grenze zwischen Jakutsk und Magadan hatten bereits im September 1954 begonnen. Dabei ging es v. a. um die Kolchose „Svetlaja Žizn'", die administrativ zum Magadaner Gebiet gehörte, obwohl sie eigentlich auf dem Gebiet der Autonomen Republik Jakutien lag. Vgl. GAMO f. R-146, op. 1, d. 36, l. 42–45.

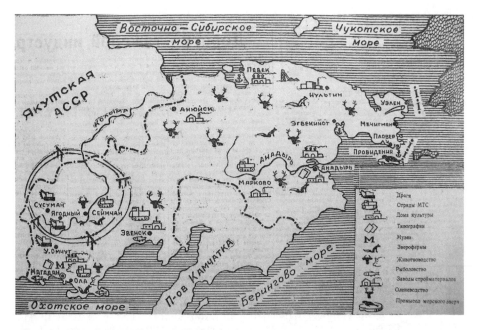

Abb. 4 Magadanskaja Pravda, 8. April 1956

ließ. Deutlich lässt sich das an der Gestaltung der *Magadanskaja Pravda* ablesen. Bereits nach kurzer Zeit hatte sich ihre inhaltliche Gestaltung gegenüber der Vorgänger-Zeitung, der *Sovetskaja Kolyma*, völlig gewandelt. Während bis 1954 lediglich die letzte Seite der Zeitung einen kursorischen Überblick über Entwicklungen in der Region bot, so füllte die Repräsentation des regionalen Raumes seit Mitte der 1950er Jahre fast die gesamte Zeitung. Regionale Themen, die bislang völlig unterrepräsentiert gewesen waren, erschienen in der Tageszeitung *Magadanskaja Pravda* im Rahmen neuer Rubriken – „Ein Tag in unserem Gebiet", „Im Zentrum des Gebiets", „Erzählung über einen Bezirk" etc. –, die in periodischen Abständen wiederkehrten und einzelne Regionen oder Personen porträtierten.

Die Botschaft war eindeutig: Die Organe von Partei und Staat als neue, politische Leitung der Region präsentierten sich in ihrer Verantwortlichkeit für das gesamte Gebiet, für seine wirtschaftliche Entwicklung ebenso wie für seine Infrastruktur, für die in ihm herrschenden Lebensbedingungen und für die Propaganda.[132] Die Karte vom 8. April 1956 (vgl. Abbildung 4) repräsentierte die zunehmende Erschließung des Gebietes.

Nun wurde bereits eine rudimentäre Binnenstruktur vorgeführt: Piktogramme kennzeichneten die wirtschaftlichen Besonderheiten der Gebiete. Die Bezirke er-

---

132 Ausführlicher zu dem Wandel der regionalen Presse siehe Sprau, Magadanskaja pressa.

ЖИЛЫЕ ДОМА, ВОДОПРОВОД, СТАДИОНЫ..:

Я внимательно ознакомился с Директивами XX с'езда КПСС по шестому пятилетнему плану. Перечитывал их неоднократно. И с каждым разом все ярче вырисовывались передо мною величественные картины недалекого будущего.

Многое изменится в нашем Иультинском районе. Правительство отпускает большие средства на культурно-бытовое и жилищное строительство в поселках Иультин, Эгвекинот, Озерный и других. Только в ближайшие два года по одному управлению будут сданы в эксплуатацию около шести тысяч квадратных метров жилой площади и здание детских яслей на 125 мест. Войдет в строй действующих предприятий деревообделочный комбинат по изготовлению столярных изделий и мебели. Будет проложен водопровод. В Эгвекиноте откроется столовая на 150 мест.

Мне, физкультурнику, особенно радостно видеть, как и в нашем поселке, по примеру других городов и рабочих поселков Советского Союза, любовно относятся к физкультуре и спорту. Под спортивный зал отведено одно из лучших помещений поселка. В скором времени приступят к строительству большого спортивного стадиона. Он будет иметь футбольную, теннисную и другие спортивные площадки.

А. БЫКОВ,
токарь.

ЗА ПОЛЯРНЫМ КРУГОМ

Далекий Чаунский район в шестой пятилетке будет всемерно развивать все отрасли народного хозяйства. Повысится благосостояние трудящихся, улучшится культурно-бытовое обслуживание населения. Иной будет жизнь в нашем суровом крае. Приведу несколько примеров. Значительное развитие должно получить сельское хозяйство. Общее поголовье оленей к концу 1960 года возрастет на 25 процентов, а маточное — на 40 процентов. Забой оленей на мясо увеличится в два раза. Товарный выход мяса составит 2.357 центнеров, или на 80 процентов больше, чем было получено в 1955 году.

Abb. 5 Magadanskaja Pravda, 8. April 1956

schienen zusätzlich auf selbstständigen Karten mit kurzen Beschreibungen (vgl. Abbildung 5).

Die neuen Verwaltungseinheiten waren die Konturen der neuen sozialen Infrastruktur. Wie in dem oben abgebildeten Beispiel des Bezirk Iul'tinskij erkennbar, stand im Zentrum der Repräsentation nicht die industrielle Bedeutung eines Gebietes, wie dies in stalinistischen Zeiten üblich gewesen wäre, sondern die Leistungen, die der Bezirk für seine Bevölkerung bereithielt – Wohnhäuser, Wasserleitungen, kulturelle und soziale Angebote.[133]

Selbst Gebiete, die aufgrund ihrer Entfernung real fast vollständig von der Außenwelt abgeschnitten waren, wurden bei dieser Darstellungsform zu festen Punkten auf der Landkarte. Bis an den äußersten nordöstlichen Punkt des Kontinents war die sowjetische Macht vorgedrungen, hatte alles ihrem strukturierenden Zugriff unterworfen, so der Eindruck, den diese Karten vermittelten.

In dieser Darstellungsform war die Gründung des Magadaner Gebiets der entscheidende Wendepunkt der Erschließung. Am 3. Dezember 1953, so die Narration der neuen Leitung, war nicht nur das „Magadaner Gebiet", sondern auch der gesamte Raum des Nordostens geboren worden. Gebiete, die bisher aufgrund der strengen Geheimhaltung quasi nicht existiert hatten, wurden jetzt offiziell legitimiert. Der neue administrative Bezugsrahmen strukturierte das Gebiet, machte es greifbar und beherrschbar.

Diese affirmative kartographische Konstruktion kann, in Anlehnung an Mark Bassin, als Teil eines „geo-ideologischen Konzeptes"[134] verstanden werden, mit dem die neue zivile Leitung ihre Machtansprüche gegenüber der Kombinatsleitung und ihre Zuständigkeit für die freien Arbeitskräfte demonstrieren wollte. Die veröffentlichte Karte war für sie gewissermaßen die „Drucklegung" einer *mental map*, die ihre Raumwahrnehmung repräsentierte und die sie in die Köpfe der alten wie neuen Führung und der Bevölkerung einzeichnen wollte. Der Nordosten wurde in dieser kulturell-politischen Ordnung von sowjetischen Verwaltungsstrukturen strukturiert und begrenzt, zu seiner Repräsentation verwandte man die Bezeichnung „Magadan".[135] Damit distanzierte man sich sowohl von der Bezeichnung „Kolyma", dem Namen des größten Flusses, die zu einer Ortsbezeichnung für die Region der reichsten Goldfelder „an der Kolyma" – „*na Kolyme*" geworden war und die unter der sowjetischen Bevölkerung mit dem Schrecken der Lager verbunden war. Zugleich grenzte man sich aber auch von der Bezeichnung des Kombinats ab, das von seiner Führung auch als Ortsbezeichnung für die gesamte Region verwendet worden war – „im Dal'stroj-Gebiet" – „*na Dal'stroe*".

---

133 Dies war in den folgenden Jahren die allgemeine Linie bei der offiziellen Präsentation von Wirtschaftsdaten. Wann immer möglich, wurden Leistungen der einzelnen Bezirke als Gewinn für die lokale Bevölkerung präsentiert, nicht als Beitrag für die sowjetische Volkswirtschaft. Siehe beispielsweise die Darstellung in Malagin, Ėkonomičeskij rajon (Darstellung der einzelnen Bezirke siehe S. 15 ff.) sowie die Vorstellung der čukotkischen Bezirke in Guščin/Afanas'ev, Čukotskij okrug, S. 55 ff.
134 Auch wenn sich Bassin hier auf ganze Nationen bezieht, kann seine Analyse dieser geo-ideologischen Konzepte auf den Machtkampf in Magadan gewinnbringend angewendet werden. Bassin, Imperialer Raum, S. 381. Siehe auch Dünne, Karte.
135 Ausführlich zur Entstehung von *mental maps* siehe Langenohl, Mental Maps, S. 57 ff.; Hartmann, Konzepte sowie das Themenheft Conrad, Mental Maps.

3.2.2 Neue Organe und ihr Leitungspersonal

3.2.2.1 Personen und Netzwerke

Die wichtigsten Kader der neuen zivilen Leitung waren Ababkov und Afanas'ev. Sie waren beide am 9. Dezember 1953 durch das ZK der KPdSU ernannt worden – Ababkov zum Ersten Sekretär und Kopf des Gebietsparteikomitees (*obkom*), Afanas'ev zum Vorsitzenden des Gebietsexekutivkomitees (*oblispolkom*), dem obersten Gremium der Sowjetstrukturen.[136] Am 21. Dezember 1953 bestätigte das ZK das Büro des neuen Gebietsparteikomitees, einen Tag später folgte die offizielle Annahme des Gebietsexekutivkomitees durch den Obersten Sowjet der RSFSR.[137] Chruščev empfing als Erster Sekretär des ZK der KPdSU Ababkov und Afanas'ev persönlich in Moskau. Er schrieb der neuen Leitung v. a. die Stärkung und Steigerung der Metallförderung ins Stammbuch.[138]

Mit Ababkov und Afanas'ev auf der einen und Mitrakov auf der anderen Seite trafen im Januar 1954 zwei Machtpositionen der stalinistischen Sowjetunion aufeinander, die sich in der Form ihrer Herrschaftsausübung wesentlich unterschieden. Aus dieser Frontstellung entwickelte sich praktisch vom ersten Tag an, nach Ankunft des neuen Personals, ein heftiger Machtkampf, in dem über die Abgrenzung von Zuständigkeiten, über die Rolle politischer und wirtschaftlicher Herrschaft, zugleich aber auch über die Form der Durchdringung des Gebietes gestritten wurde.

Ivan Lukič Mitrakov war seit 1950 Chef des Kombinats. Bis zur Übergabe von Dal'stroj an das MMP im März 1953 war er militärischer Führer der bereits beschriebenen Gruppe der *Dal'strojevcy*, eines Kreises von etwa 2.000 sogenannten „Kolyma-Veteranen", die als Vertreter des MVD die Region, die Metallindustrie und das Lagersystem fest in der Hand hatten. Der oberste Leiter stand an der Spitze einer Kaste, die außergewöhnliche Privilegien genoss und die die Lager häufig zur Produktion ihrer Luxusgüter missbrauchte.[139] Der ehemalige Häftling Abraham Dück, der 1955 als Elektroinstallateur in den als „Rotes Haus" berüchtigten Sitz der Hauptverwaltung von Dal'stroj geschickt worden war, schildert in seinen Erinnerungen das ungläubige Staunen, mit dem er zunächst die Gefängnisse im Keller des Hauses und dann den ersten Stock, den Arbeitsbereich Mitrakovs, betrat:

---

136 Bis zum 10. Januar 1954 sollte sich Ababkov in Magadan einfinden. Vgl. GAMO f. P-21, op. 4, d. 41, l. 2, veröffentlicht in: Archivnyj Otdel, Kalendar' 2003, S. 56.

137 Es folgte kurz danach die Errichtung der entsprechenden Gewerkschaftsstrukturen und des Komsomol. Erst im September 1954 entstand ein Gewerkschaftskomitee in Tschukotka („Čukotskij okružnoj komitet profsjuza"). Vgl. Bubnis, Iz istorii obrazovanija, S. 48 sowie Kur'janova/Uškalov, Iz istorii profsojuznych organizacij, S. 54.

138 In der Darstellung der Magadaner Parteileitung soll Chruščev außerdem die Unterstützung für die indigenen Völker der Region und die Entwicklung der Binnenkommunikation im Gebiet als wichtige Ziele genannt haben. Vgl. Na preobražennoj zemle, S. 34 f. An die Ernennungsprozedur im ZK der KPdSU erinnerte sich Afanas'ev in Vospominanija predsedatelja, S. 223 f.

139 Vgl. Conquest, Kolyma, S. 67 ff.; Solomon, Magadan, S. 227 f.

Abb. 6 Ivan Lukič Mitrakov

[...] Ich sah auch die Luxusräume des Herrschers der Kolyma. Sie befanden sich im ersten Stock. Die Wände, Fußnöden und Decken – alles aus poliertem Holz. Riesige Fenster mit schweren Vorhängen. Nebenan Badezimmer, Toilette, Rauchzimmer, Hausbar. Ein großer, grün bedeckter Schreibtisch. Polstermöbel, mit Knautschleder überzogen. Auch im Traum hätte ich mir solch einen Luxus unserer Herrscher nicht vorstellen können. [...] Und das alles etliche Meter über den Marterzellen.[140]

Mitrakov herrschte auf Grundlage einer militärischen Befehlskette, er unterstand lediglich Berija und Stalin persönlich; sämtliche Parteiorganisationen in der Region waren der Kombinatsleitung untergeordnet. Die wenigen Fotografien, die von dem damaligen Personal der Dal'stroj-Führung existieren, zeigen Mitrakov mit Militärabzeichen, einer typischen Pose der Dal'stroj-Führung, die sich fast ausschließlich in Uniform ablichten ließ.

Mitrakov (1905–1995) war bereits in den 1920er Jahren unter Dzeržinskij Kommissar der OGPU (der Vorgängerorganisation des NKVD/MVD) gewesen. Nach einer Ausbildung am Bergbauinstitut in Moskau und einigen Jahren als stellvertretender Minister für die Baumaterialwirtschaft war Mitrakov seit 1949 Stellvertreter des Innenministers. Seit dem 3. Oktober 1950 fungierte er zusätzlich dazu als Leiter von Dal'stroj; 1952 erhielt er den Lenin-Orden für seinen dortigen Dienst.[141] Seit dem Tode Stalins war seine Position jedoch erheblich geschwächt. Denn mit der Ausgliederung des Kombinats aus dem MVD verlor er mit einem Schlag seine Position als Stellver-

---

140 Dück, Erinnerungen, S. 462 f.
141 Vgl. Kokurin/Morukov, Stalinskie strojki, S. 502.

treter des Innenministers, alle militärischen Ränge und den damit einhergehenden finanziellen Sonderstatus. Die Verhaftung Berijas muss für Mitrakov persönlich eine große Belastung gewesen sein. Im MVD herrschte seit dem Sommer 1953 Unsicherheit und Angst. Nach den Erfahrungen des Stalinismus musste jede Person, die mit einem verhafteten Minister des Inneren bzw. Volkskommissar in Verbindung gebracht wurde, unmittelbar die eigene Verhaftung, Erschießung oder jahrelange Lagerhaft befürchten. Bislang gab es kaum Anhaltspunkte, dass dieses Vorgehen nach der Verhaftung Berijas ein anderes sein sollte als bei dem Ausscheiden von Ežov oder Jagoda.[142] Auch Mitrakov befürchtete wohl, selbst in den Strudel neuer Säuberungen zu geraten. In der Region hatte er zudem bei den Diskussionen um die Gründung des Magadaner Gebietes deutlich an Autorität eingebüßt. Seine Position als Kombinatschef – dem MMP unterstellt – und als Leiter des *Sevvostlag* – dem GULAG und damit dem Justizministerium unterstellt – bedingte des Weiteren eine wachsende Kontrolle seiner Arbeit. Er war zwei Ministerien unterstellt, die begannen, ihren prüfenden Blick auf die Lage an der Kolyma zu richten. Auch seine Offiziere litten unter den unsicheren Verhältnissen. Die frühere Publizistin Evgenija Ginzburg, die nach langjähriger Lagerhaft im Frühjahr 1954 als Verbannte in Magadan lebte, erinnerte sich an die Atmosphäre unter den *Dal'strojevcy*:

> Das Jahr 1954 hatte bei dem allgemeinen Gefuchtel und Gestrampel die Widersacher von gestern auf eine Stufe mit uns gestellt. Jetzt schlugen unsere Herren die Zeitungen genauso beunruhigt auf wie wir, horchten auf bei neuen Meldungen im Radio und bei den Gerüchten, die immer wieder kursierten. Es waren Gerüchte, die vor allem sie betrafen: Dabei ging es um Planstellenkürzungen, die Reorganisation der Ämter, die Beschneidung der in Kolyma üblichen Vergünstigungen, die Kürzung der hohen Gehaltszuschläge. Die Nervosität der Oberen war auf Schritt und Tritt zu spüren. Die etwas Klügeren begriffen, daß ein neuer Wind wehte. Sie behandelten uns [gemeint sind ehemalige Häftlinge und Verbannte – M. S.] betont höflich und zuvorkommend [...], doch viele von ihnen – die hoffnungslos Dummen – benahmen sich weiterhin wie bisher: stur und bösartig.[143]

Ababkov und Afanas'ev traten also im Januar 1954 einem Mann gegenüber, dessen Status in den vergangenen zehn Monaten massiv gelitten hatte. Formal war Mitrakov in der Region jedoch nach wie vor der sogenannte „Einzelleiter", zugleich Chef des *Sevvostlag* und des Kombinats Dal'stroj, Herr über die gesamte lokale Verwaltung, Tausende Häftlinge und freie Arbeitskräfte.

Auch Ababkov und Afanas'ev waren Funktionäre des stalinistischen Systems. Sie hatten ihre jeweiligen politischen Karrieren in den Strukturen der Kommunistischen Partei gemacht, waren fest auf das Herrschaftsverständnis und die Hierarchien der

---

142 Vgl. zu den Verhaftungen und Erschießungen innerhalb des Berija-Clans Mitrokhin, Political Clans, S. 28 sowie S. 32. Der ehemalige Häftling Michael Solomon schildert anschaulich seine Beobachtungen der unmittelbaren Folgen der Verhaftung Berijas an der Kolyma und die Ängste der Lageroffiziere. Vgl. Solomon, Magadan, S. 246–248.
143 Ginsburg, Gratwanderung, S. 447.

Abb. 7 Pavel Jakovlevič Afanas'ev
(GAMO f. P-21 f., op. 1, d. 103)

Partei bezogen. Beide hatten nie in militärischen Strukturen gearbeitet, sie waren auch nicht aktive Teilnehmer des Zweiten Weltkrieges gewesen. Innerhalb der Partei waren sie nach Darstellung Pavel Grebenjuks Anführer zweier Parteigruppierungen, die die neue Führungsgruppe in Magadan dominieren sollten, den „Fernöstlern" aus Chabarowsk und den „Zentrums-Leuten", die in der Mehrzahl mit Swerdlowsk in Verbindung standen.[144] Die „Fernöstler" aus der sowjetischen Region „Ferner Osten" mit der Hauptstadt Chabarowsk waren Leute, die in den Parteiorganen des Fernen Ostens gearbeitet hatten und mit den Bedingungen an der Kolyma und in Tschukotka recht gut vertraut waren.

Pavel Jakovlevič Afanas'ev (1905–1989), der Vorsitzende des neuen Magadaner Gebietsexekutivkomitees, kannte die Region gut, er war seit 1945 im Chabarowsker Distrikt tätig gewesen, seit 1950 in der Position des Stellvertreters des Vorsitzenden des Chabarowsker Distriktexekutivkomitees.

Bereits vor dem Krieg hatte er sich über diverse Posten im Süden der Sowjetunion und in Kasan innerhalb der Kommunistischen Partei langsam nach oben gearbeitet. 1937 bis 1941 war er Leiter einer großen Fabrik für Maschinenbau in der Stadt Murom, was für ihn eine gute Vorbereitung für seine Wirtschaftstätigkeiten im Magadaner Gebiet darstellte. 1945 schloss er die Hochschule für Parteifunktionäre beim ZK der

---

144 Vgl. zu den folgenden Personalbeschreibungen Vospominanija predsedatelja, S. 224–226 sowie Grebenjuk, Kolymskij led, S. 59–67. Siehe zu den Biographien ebenso http://www.az-libr.ru/Persons/ index.shtml (abgerufen am 6. Februar 2018). Zur wachsenden Bedeutung politischer Clans in der Ära Chruščev siehe Mitrokhin, Political Clans.

Abb. 8 Ivan Nikolaevič Kaštanov

KPdSU in Moskau ab und reiste nach Chabarowsk. Während er dort die Karriereleiter immer weiter nach oben stieg, war er Schüler der bekannten Chabarowsker Partei-schule, die ein starkes Netzwerk für alle Funktionäre im dünnbesiedelten Fernen Osten und damit auch für Afanas'evs späteren Magadaner Kreis bildete. Aufgrund seiner Position hatte er die Diskussionen um die Gründung des Magadaner Gebietes und die Positionierung der Dal'strojer Führung aus nächster Nähe mitverfolgen können.[145]

Fast alle seine Mitarbeiter aus Chabarowsk hatte Afanas'ev persönlich ausgewählt und dem ZK der KPdSU vorgeschlagen. Zu seinem Stellvertreter wurde Ivan Petrovič Čistjakov ernannt, ein enger Vertrauter Afanas'evs, der bisher auf Sachalin als In-spektor des Chabarowsker Distriktexekutivkomitees für Volksbildung gearbeitet hatte. Weitere Vertreter Afanas'evs wurden Boris Alekseevič Rogušin, der bereits seit 1932 im Fernen Osten tätig war, sowie der Sekretär des Gebietsexekutivkomitees Georgij Fedorovič Roščupkin, seit 1943 in Chabarowsk. Ebenfalls zur Gruppe um Afanas'ev zu zählen sind Ivan Nikolaevič Kaštanov und Dmitrij Sergeevič Komarovskij, die als Leiter der Abteilung für Propaganda und Agitation bzw. als Leiter der Abteilung für Parteiorgane im neuen Gebietsparteikomitee tätig wurden. Nach Darstellung Gre-

---

145 Zur Biographie Afanas'evs und seiner Zeit im Chabarowsker Distrikt siehe Sergeev, Pervyj pred-sedatel'.

Abb. 9 Tichon Ivanovič Ababkov (GAMO f. P-21, op. 4, d. 41, l. 1)

benjuks einten diese Gruppe enge persönliche Beziehungen und eine sehr gute Kenntnis der politischen, aber auch sozialen und klimatischen Lage an der Kolyma.[146]

Die „Zentrums-Leute" waren in ihrer Mehrzahl von Tichon Ivanovič Ababkov (1908–1984) ausgewählt worden, dem neuen Ersten Parteisekretär des Gebietes. Ababkov hatte in jungen Jahren das Bergbaumetalltechnikum in Swerdlowsk absolviert und danach, sechs Jahre früher als Afanas'ev, die Hochschule für Parteifunktionäre beim ZK der KPdSU in Moskau abgeschlossen. Von dort aus wurde er in die Kasachische SSR gesandt, wo er zunächst als Parteifunktionär für die Buntmetallförderung verantwortlich zeichnete und schließlich von 1947 bis 1952 Erster Sekretär des Gebietsparteikomitees von Karaganda war. Nach Magadan brachte Ababkov somit nicht nur Erfahrungen aus dem Bergbau mit, sondern auch aus der Arbeit in einem Gebiet, das stark von Lagern geprägt war; er war die enge Zusammenarbeit mit dem MVD gewöhnt, so Grebenjuk.[147]

Sein guter Bekannter, V. N. Ferapontov, den Ababkov als seinen persönlichen Vertrauten im Gebietsexekutivkomitees platziert hatte, hatte selbst in den 1940er Jahren eine Zeitlang in einem großen Lagerkomplex Kasachstans, dem „Karlag", gedient. Ebenfalls aus der Kasachischen SSR waren Ababkov V. S. Timofeev (als künftiger zweiter Mann im Gebietsparteikomitee) und N. S. Černobil' vertraut, die er dem ZK der KPdSU für sein Gremium vorschlug. Anders als Timofeev und Černobil' reiste

---

146 Vgl. Grebenjuk, Kolymskij led, S. 61.
147 Vgl. Grebenjuk, Kolymskij led, S. 63.

Ferapontov nicht aus der Kasachischen SSR an, er war seit einiger Zeit bereits Instrukteur der Abteilung für Parteiorgane beim ZK. Ebenfalls aus Moskau kam N. A. Žicharev, ein Absolvent der obersten Parteischule und früherer Mitarbeiter der unionsweiten Zeitung *Pravda*, der zuletzt als Instrukteur der Abteilung für Propaganda und Agitation im ZK gearbeitet hatte und der sich aufgrund seiner historischen Interessen schnell zu einem der wichtigsten Vertreter der Magadaner Heimatkunde entwickelte. Daneben gab es fünf weitere bisherige Mitarbeiter des ZK und der staatlichen Strukturen, die direkt aus Moskau nach Magadan reisten und die im neuen Gebietsparteikomitee und der Redaktion der neuen *Magadanskaja Pravda* unterkamen, darunter eine Frau – E. V. Ivanova, die zur Leiterin der Geheimabteilung des Gebietsparteikomitees ernannt wurde.[148]

Hinzu kam eine große Gruppe von Personen aus ganz verschiedenen Gebieten der Sowjetunion. Aus Dagestan, Gor'kij, Kalinin, Nowgorod und immer wieder aus Swerdlowsk. Grebenjuk beschreibt die Bedeutung Swerdlowsks als mächtiges Netzwerk in den Abteilungen des ZK der KPdSU, zudem waren Kader aus Swerdlowsk aufgrund der dortigen industriellen Ausrichtung auf den Bergbau für den Einsatz in Magadan besonders geeignet.

Für Grebenjuk steht außer Frage, dass die neue Führung des Magadaner Gebietes bereits Teil von Chruščevs strategischen Plänen zur Verbreiterung seiner Machtbasis über regionale Kader der ersten Gebiets- und Distriktsekretäre gewesen sei.[149] 1952 nahm Ababkov für ein Jahr an einem speziellen Kurs für die Leiter von Gebietsparteikomitees des ZK der KPdSU teil. Es ist denkbar, dass Chruščev in dieser Zeit auf Ababkov aufmerksam wurde. Am Ende des Kurses wurde Ababkov sehr schnell zu einem Instrukteur des ZK und kurz danach zum Gebietsparteichef ernannt. Die Quellenlage ist für eine Erhärtung dieser These eigentlich viel zu dürftig; festhalten lässt sich jedoch, dass die persönliche Anbindung der beiden Magadaner Führungspersonen an das ZK der KPdSU von großer Bedeutung war. Ababkov und Afanas'ev hatten ihre Karrieren in den Strukturen der Kommunistischen Partei absolviert und sich in verschiedenen Regionen der Sowjetunion bewiesen, sie waren mit den Herrschaftsstrukturen, ebenso wie mit den praktischen Abläufen zwischen dem Moskauer ZK und der Leitung eines peripheren Gebietes vertraut.

Für Ababkov als Ersten Parteisekretär sprach zudem seine alte Bekanntschaft mit Ju. V. Čuguev, dem Stellvertreter Mitrakovs. Auch Čuguev war Ende der 1930er Jahre in der Nähe von Swerdlowsk tätig gewesen und hatte dort Ababkov kennengelernt. Grebenjuk interpretiert diese frühere Bekanntschaft als Zugeständnis Chruščevs an die Bedürfnisse Mitrakovs, der bei Gründung des Magadaner Gebietes alle Hebel in Bewegung gesetzt hätte, um eine günstige Führung für das Gebiet erhalten zu können.[150]

---

148 Vgl. den Bericht vom 3. Januar 1954 in RGANI f. 5, op. 15, d. 489, l. 13. Abbildung 61 (S. 334) zeigt das damalige Redaktionskollektiv der *Magadanskaja Pravda*.
149 Vgl. Grebenjuk, Kolymskij led, S. 57.
150 Vgl. Grebenjuk, Kolymskij led, S. 64.

Die Wahl der neuen Führungsmannschaft lässt sich so als Kombination aus regionalen Kenntnissen und starker lokaler Parteimacht aus Chabarowsk (Afanas'ev) mit einer Vertrautheit im Umgang mit dem MVD (Ababkov) verstehen. Ababkov machte zudem diesen Job nicht zum ersten Mal, er blickte schließlich bereits auf eine sechsjährige Amtszeit als Erster Sekretär des kasachischen Gebietsparteikomitees zurück. Diverse Mitarbeiter, die direkt aus Abteilungen des ZK der KPdSU stammten, sicherten des Weiteren eine Vertretung der ZK-Strukturen ab.[151]

3.2.2.2 Neue Verwendung für Dal'stroj-Mitarbeiter? Die Bildung politischer Organe

Am 16. Januar 1954 fand die erste Sitzung des Gebietsparteikomitees in Magadan statt. Dem Büro des Komitees gehörten neun Personen an: Ababkov als Erster Sekretär, dem die allgemeine Führung und die Leitung der Parteiorgane oblag, Timofeev als zweiter Sekretär zuständig für die Abteilungen Administration, Wirtschaft, Landwirtschaft und Finanzen, Žicharev als Sekretär für Agitation und Propaganda, Afanas'ev als Vorsitzender des Gebietsexekutivkomitees, N. Ja. Novokreščenov für den Komsomol, Ferapontov als Stellvertreter Afanas'evs, Komarovskij als Leiter der Abteilung der Organe des Gebietsparteikomitees sowie P. I. Romaškov, der als Leiter der Verwaltung des KGB direkt aus Moskau entsandt wurde. All diese Personen waren sozusagen „Externe", kamen mit Ababkov und Afanas'ev und auf Grundlage des Auftrags des ZK der KPdSU nach Magadan. Das einzige Mitglied des Büros, das von Dal'stroj dazustieß, war Mitrakov, der aufgrund seiner Position als Chef der einzigen Wirtschaftseinrichtung des Gebietes quasi per Amt berufen wurde.[152] Mit Einsetzung des Gebietsparteikomitees wurden alle Parteimitglieder in Dal'stroj automatisch dem territorialen Parteiorgan untergeordnet, die Politische Verwaltung von Dal'stroj und alle Politischen Truppenteile in den Industrieverwaltungen dementsprechend aufgelöst.[153]

Schon etwas früher, bereits am 13. Januar 1954, tagte das Gebietsexekutivkomitee unter der Leitung von Afanas'ev das erste Mal, die Sitzung war organisatorischen Fragen gewidmet und legte die Leitungen der Sowjetorgane in den einzelnen Bezirken fest.[154] Die offizielle Formierung dieses neuen Organs ersetzte die bisherige „administrativ-zivile Abteilung" (AGO) von Dal'stroj, die nach einem Befehl von Mitrakov am 18. Januar 1954 aufgelöst wurde.[155] Die bisherigen Mitarbeiter der AGO wurden

---

151 Vgl. die Fotografien von Ababkov und Afanas'ev, die sich, im Gegensatz zu Mitrakov, ganz in ziviler Kleidung präsentierten.

152 Vgl. Chronika partijnoj organizacii, S. 135.

153 Vgl. die offizielle Übergabe der Parteimitglieder von Dal'stroj an das Gebietsparteikomitee in GAMO f. R-23, op. 1, d. 5548, l. 3.

154 Vgl. Na preobražennoj zemle, S. 35.

155 Vgl. GAMO f. 38, op. 1, d. 1, l. 169 – 169ob. Bei der Übergabe der Amtsgeschäfte des AGO an das Gebietsexekutivkomitee bestand Mitrakov darauf, dass alle Akten, die Befehle des MVD enthielten, an

sämtlich zu Mitgliedern des Gebietsexekutivkomitees ernannt.[156] Während allerdings in der AGO lediglich 34 Mitarbeiter beschäftigt gewesen waren, umfasste der Personalbestand des neuen Gebietsexekutivkomitees 350 Personen, analog zu anderen Gebieten der Sowjetunion.[157] Zur Festigung ihrer Position wurde die neue politische Leitung den Mitarbeitern von Dal'stroj formal finanziell gleichgestellt. Im Vergleich zu den zentralen Gebieten der Sowjetunion erhielt das neue Personal der Organe von Partei und Staat ein um 100 % höheres Gehalt, hinzu kamen Zuschläge für die Arbeit im Hohen Norden.[158] Anders als im Fall des Gebietsparteikomitees, in dem sehr hohe Gehälter gezahlt wurden, wurde jedoch das Gehalt der Mitglieder von Exekutivkomitees auf 2.200 Rubel gedeckelt und lag damit zum Teil deutlich unter den „persönlichen Gehältern" einzelner Dal'stroj-Funktionäre.[159]

Für die Infrastruktur der neuen Herrschaft sollte Dal'stroj die Verantwortung tragen. Bis 1955 wurde das Kombinat beauftragt, administrative Gebäude und entsprechende Wohnhäuser in der Hauptstadt und in jedem einzelnen Bezirk zu errichten. Für die erste Zeit wurde Mitrakov verpflichtet, ein Verwaltungsgebäude von

---

das Archiv des Kombinats übergeben werden sollten. Sie befinden sich dementsprechend heute im Archivbestand des Kombinates Dal'stroj, GAMO f. R-23. Vgl. die Anweisung in ebd.

156 Für konkrete Personalübergaben siehe GAMO f. 38, op. 1, d. 1, l. 180 (Befehl von Solovej, dem bisherigen Leiter des AGO, vom 26. Januar 1954).

157 Hieran zeigt sich noch einmal besonders deutlich die minimale Bedeutung, die die „zivile Abteilung" von Dal'stroj hatte; anhand der Personalbögen lässt sich erkennen, dass in ihr v. a. Ehefrauen von Dal'stroj-Funktionären gearbeitet hatten. Vgl. die Übersicht des Leiters der Kaderabteilung des AGO in GAMO f. R-137, op. 1, d. 87, l. 1–2.

158 Bereits am 17. Dezember 1953 beschloss der Ministerrat der UdSSR, alle Boni und besonderen Privilegien der Dal'stroj-Mitarbeiter auf die neuen Funktionäre der Organe von Partei- und Sowjetstrukturen zu übertragen. Die Beibehaltung der bisherigen Gehaltsregelungen sollte auch dann gelten, wenn Einrichtungen, die bisher Dal'stroj unterstanden hatten, an unionsweite zivile Ministerien übergingen oder wenn Einrichtungen und Betriebe im Magadaner Gebiet ganz neu geschaffen wurden. Vgl. die Verordnung „Über Maßnahmen in Verbindung mit der Gründung des Magadaner Gebietes in der RSFSR" (Nr. 2956) in GAMO f. R-23, op. 1, d. 6088, l. 59–60. Damit entsprach der Ministerrat Forderungen, die schon das Chabarowsker Distriktparteikomitee in einem Schreiben an das ZK der KPdSU vom 20. August 1953 erhoben hatte. Vgl. Bubnis, Iz istorii obrazovanija, S. 46.

159 Aufgrund dieser Regelung waren die Gehälter der Mitarbeiter des Gebietsexekutivkomitees auch im Herbst 1954 noch nicht geklärt. Forderungen des Gebietsexekutivkomitees, seine Mitarbeiter mit 4.400 Rubel zu entlohnen, lehnte das Finanzministerium ab, Forderungen des Kreisexekutivkomitees, den Posten des Vorsitzenden der Sowjetorgane in Tschukotka mit 2.600 Rubel zu vergüten, lehnte wiederum das Gebietsexekutivkomitee ab. Vgl. GAMO f. R-146, op. 1, d. 58, l. 29–30. Siehe auch das Schreiben des stellvertretenden Vorsitzenden des Kreisexekutivkomitees in Tschukotka an Afanas'ev vom Juni 1954 in GAMO f. R-146, op. 1, d. 58, l. 14–15. Zum Vergleich: Die Gehälter für die Mitarbeiter von Dal'stroj überstiegen diese Summen deutlich. So erhielt z. B. der Leiter der Janskser Lagerverwaltung und der dortigen Wirtschaftsverwaltung seit dem 1. Januar 1953 ein Gehalt von 6.000 Rubel im Monat, Leiter anderer Wirtschafts- und Lagerverwaltungen 5.000 Rubel, leitende Ingenieure 3.000 Rubel. Diese Summen wurden als „persönliche Gehälter" gezahlt, sie unterlagen also keinen offiziellen Regelungen und konnten vom MVD, auf Vorschlag der Leitung von Dal'stroj, festgelegt werden. Vgl. die Übersicht über die verschiedenen Gehälter in RGAÈ f. 9163, op. 6, d. 11, l. 142 sowie die gesamte Akte zu der Auszahlung von Sondergehältern in GARF f. R-9401, op. 4, d. 1627.

Dal'stroj sowie Wohnungen im Zentrum Magadans zu räumen. Zudem wurde Mitrakov persönlich für den Warentransport verantwortlich gemacht, der die Leitung der Partei- und Sowjetorgane versorgen sollte.[160]

Ababkov und Afanas'ev füllten die neue administrative Gliederung rasch mit Personal. Bereits Anfang Februar bestätigte das Magadaner Gebietsparteikomitee die Büros der Parteileitungen in den einzelnen Bezirken.[161] Schon im Mai 1954 nahmen 272 Delegierte an der ersten Gebiets-Parteikonferenz unter Führung des Gebietspar- teikomitees teil.[162] Ebenfalls im Mai 1954 wurde die Gebietsorganisation des Komso- mol gegründet.[163] In den einzelnen Bezirken waren die jeweiligen Leiter der Partei- und Sowjetstrukturen für das Personal in den Siedlungen verantwortlich. Die Auf- bauphase der Exekutivkomitees wurde in formaler Hinsicht im Februar 1955 mit Wahlen abgeschlossen, bei denen natürlich alle bereits eingesetzten Exekutivkomi- tees bestätigt wurden.[164]

Aber woher kam all das neue Personal? Wo fanden Ababkov und Afanas'ev An- fang 1954 geeignete, ihnen loyale Personen? Die Parteileitung beschrieb die damali- gen Probleme im Rückblick folgendermaßen:

> In dem Gebiet gab es zu dieser Zeit nur sehr wenig Leute, die die ,sowjetische Arbeit', die Arbeit von sowjetischen Organen, kannten. Diese Leute wurden aber dringend benötigt. Was also sollte man tun? Diese Leute in das Gebiet bringen oder sie vor Ort zusammenstellen? Das Gebietspartei- und das Gebietsexekutivkomitee entschieden sich für einen schwierigeren Weg: Sie wählten die Kader vor Ort aus, aus dem Kreis derer, die als erfahrene Arbeiter schon sehr lange im Norden gelebt und in den Apparaten der Industrieverwaltungen von Dal'stroj gearbeitet hatten. Diese Leute wollten sie die Methoden der Arbeit von Partei und Sowjet lehren. Die Kenntnisse der Spezifik des Lebens hier und die Kenntnis der Bedürfnisse der Arbeiter von der Kolyma und in Tschukotka waren in dieser Zeit besonders unentbehrlich.[165]

Faktisch bediente sich also die Leitung des Gebietspartei- und Gebietsexekutivkomi- tees bei „erfahrenem" Dal'stroj-Personal. Dessen Wissen wurde dringend gebraucht. Dieser Vorgehensweise kamen massive Kündigungen durch das Kombinat im Laufe des Jahres 1954 entgegen. Dal'stroj reagierte auf die Herauslösung aus dem MVD sowie

---

160 Vgl. den Befehl des Ministeriums für Metallindustrie vom 23. Dezember 1953, der der praktischen Umsetzung der Verordnung des Ministerrates der UdSSR diente, in GAMO f. P-21, op. 2, d. 2186, l. 1 veröffentlicht in: Archivnyj Otdel, Kalendar' 2003, S. 54–55. Was die finanziellen Mittel betrifft, so wurden dem Gebietsexekutivkomitee für notwendige Transporte, Inventar und Renovierungen im Dezember 1953 2 Mio. Rubel sowie im ersten Halbjahr 1954 noch einmal 5 Mio. Rubel vom Ministerrat der RSFSR zugesprochen.
161 Vgl. Chronika partijnoj organizacii, S. 135f.
162 Vgl. Chronika partijnoj organizacii, S. 137. Siehe zur Atmosphäre auf der Konferenz Grebenjuk, Smechovaja praktika. Kurz danach fand die erste gebietsweite Konferenz der Mitglieder des Komsomol statt. Vgl. Klesova, Sever zovet, S. 55.
163 Zum Aufbau der Komsomolstrukturen in der Region siehe Komsomol Magadanskoj oblasti.
164 Die Wahl aller bestehenden Leiter bestätigte in den Augen der Parteileitung „die Richtigkeit der früheren Auswahl". Vgl. Na preobražennoj zemle, S. 44.
165 Na preobražennoj zemle, S. 35.

auf die erhebliche Verkleinerung seiner Strukturen mit der Aufgabe von Industrieanlagen und Lagern sowie einer Verkleinerung seines Kaderbestandes um 33 %. Dabei trennte sich das Kombinat auch von 189 Verwaltungsleitern, die selbst zuvor einmal inhaftiert gewesen und anscheinend unter den neuen Bedingungen nicht mehr tragbar waren.[166] Anders als in dem obersten Führungsgremium, dem Büro des Gebietsparteikomitees, in dem allein Mitrakov als Vertreter von Dal'stroj saß, waren im Gebietsparteikomitee selbst eine ganze Reihe bislang einflussreicher *Dal'stroevcy* vertreten, die z. T. seit mehreren Jahrzehnten im Dienste des NKVD/MVD an der Kolyma standen. So z. B. der bisherige Leiter des Sekretariats der Politischen Verwaltung von Dal'stroj, A. D. Kuznecov, der zum persönlichen Referenten Ababkovs ernannt wurde, und V. A. Ušakov, der in den Strukturen der Politischen Verwaltung bereits seit 1938 gearbeitet hatte und nun zum Vorsitzenden der Parteikommission des Gebietsparteikomitees gemacht wurde. Auf die Arbeit von Morozov, dem früheren Leiter der Politischen Verwaltung konnte offensichtlich auch nicht verzichtet werden, er fungierte fortan als stellvertretender Leiter der Abteilung für „administrative Organe" (die regionale Abteilung des MVD).[167]

Auch bei einem Blick auf die Bezirke ergibt sich ein differenziertes Bild: Viele Personen, die das Gebietsparteikomitee zu den obersten Leitern einzelner Bezirke ernannte, stammten aus dem Chabarowsker Distrikt, manchmal kamen sie auch aus ganz anderen Gebieten der Sowjetunion. Doch standen an der obersten Spitze der einzelnen Bezirke ebenso Leute, die bereits seit vielen Jahren in Dal'stroj tätig gewesen waren. So wurde beispielsweise A. N. Nikitin zum ersten Bezirksparteisekretär des Srednekanisker Bezirks ernannt, er war seit 1938 Funktionär in der Verwaltung des *Sevvostlag* gewesen; S. V. Markov verdingte sich bereits seit 1932 in der OGPU/NKVD/MVD und seit 1938 in Dal'stroj, ihn machte das Gebietsparteikomitee zum obersten Parteichef des Bezirks Ten'kinskij.[168]

Die Auswahl der Kader für die Bezirksleitungen, die in Zukunft die Verantwortung für die Stabilisierung der Goldförderung und der sozialen Lage vor Ort tragen sollten, wurde nicht dem Zufall überlassen. Ababkov war über die persönlichen Einstellungen des jeweiligen Personals und dessen Verhältnis zur Kommunistischen Partei und dem ZK genau informiert. Bei seinen Entscheidungen konnte sich Ababkov z. B. auf ein umfangreiches streng geheimes Dossier stützen, das ihm im Februar 1954 vom Leiter der Abteilung für Parteiorganisationen des Gebietsparteikomitees übergeben worden war. Es enthielt eine Zusammenstellung aller Diskussionen, die in den einzelnen

---

166 Vgl. den ausführlichen Bericht über die Kaderarbeit von Dal'stroj für das Jahr 1954 in GAMO f. R-23, op. 1, d. 5548, l. 1–43, hier l. 12. Zu den unionsweiten Entlassungen im MVD dieser Jahre siehe Hilger, Grenzen, S. 267.
167 Für eine Reihe weiterer Beispiele dieser Personalkontinuität siehe Grebenjuk, Kolymskij led, S. 69 sowie den ausführlichen Bericht über die Kaderarbeit von Dal'stroj für das Jahr 1954 in GAMO f. R-23, op. 1, d. 5548, l. 1–43, hier l. 4.
168 Vgl. Grebenjuk, Kolymskij led, S. 70 f. sowie für weitere Beispiele GAMO f. R-23, op. 5, d. 5548, l. 1–43, hier l. 4. sowie GAMO f. P-21, op. 5, d. 110, l. 19.

Wirtschaftsverwaltungen über die Ergebnisse des Juli-Plenums im Sommer 1953 geführt worden waren. In diesen Debatten hatten sich die Funktionäre, in einem völlig anderen Kontext und noch ohne die weiteren Entwicklungen in der Region absehen zu können, z. T. sehr deutlich gegen den MVD und für eine Stärkung der Kommunistischen Partei oder für eine Beibehaltung des Status quo ausgesprochen.[169]

Dennoch waren wohl die lokalen Möglichkeiten der Personalauswahl mitunter begrenzt. Denn immer wieder gab es Probleme mit dem militärischen Arbeits- und Kommunikationsstil, der sich über die Jahre unter den *Dal'stroevcy* herausgebildet hatte. Eine Bezirksparteileitung schrieb über die dortigen Dal'stroj-Funktionäre: „erzogen wird nicht mit Agitation und Propaganda, sondern mit dem Stock"[170]. Dagegen setzte man auf eine Art „Erziehungs- und Bildungsprogramm" zugunsten der „Methoden der Arbeit von Partei und Sowjet". Nach der Beschreibung der ehemaligen Gefangenen Evgenija Ginzburg muss es dabei auch um ein Bildungsprogramm im wörtlichen Sinne gegangen sein. Sie unterrichtete in der Zeit nach 1953 eine ganze Reihe von Dal'stroj-Ofizieren, da für jene unter den geänderten Bedingungen die „Anforderungen an die Bildung erhöht worden waren"[171]. Dabei wurde sie immer wieder von ihrem extremen Mangel selbst an einfacher Bildung überrascht.

Die Unterschiede zwischen der militärischen Parteileitung der Politischen Verwaltung von Dal'stroj und der zivilen Magadaner Parteivertretung illustrieren die folgenden Fotos (Abbildung 10 und 11) anschaulich. Sie zeigen zum einen die Delegierten der VII. Parteikonferenz von Dal'stroj aus dem Jahr 1947, zum anderen ein Seminar von Parteisekretären des Magadaner Gebietes aus dem Jahr 1961. Die unterschiedliche Geschlechterverteilung, Körperhaltung und Bekleidung vermitteln einen Eindruck von der je eigenen Atmosphäre der Veranstaltungen, beides Treffen von Mitgliedern der KPdSU.

Wenn in den Bezirken z. T. das alte Personal übernommen wurde, sah es im Fall des Parteikomitees für die Stadt Magadan (*gorkom*) anders aus. Hier war Ababkov sehr an einer bewussten Abgrenzung zu Dal'stroj gelegen.[172] Im Oktober 1954 bat er darum, Parteimitglieder, die auf Veranlassung des ZK der KPdSU mit ihm nach Magadan gekommen waren, durch Kooptation zu Mitgliedern des Stadtparteikomitees machen zu dürfen. Bestimmte Vertrauenspersonen wollte er zum Ersten Sekretär bzw. zu weiteren Sekretären des Stadtkomitees bestimmen. Faktisch forderte Ababkov damit die Entmachtung der alten Parteileitung und die Einsetzung „seines Personals". Begründet wurde sein Vorstoß mit der Notwendigkeit einer „Stärkung der Parteileitung in der Stadt" und der ihr zugrundeliegenden Bedeutung Magadans als neuer Hauptstadt des Gebietes. Das ZK der KPdSU billigte diese Personalentscheidung.[173]

---

169 Vgl. GAMO f. R-23, op. 1, d. 4696.
170 GAMO f. P-23sč, op. 1, d. 458, l. 27.
171 Ginsburg, Gratwanderung, S. 435.
172 Seit Erhebung Magadans zur Stadt im Jahr 1939 gab es dort eine eigene Parteileitung.
173 Vgl. das Schreiben Ababkovs an das Büro des ZK der KPdSU für die RSFSR in RGANI f. 5, op. 32, d. 8, l. 106.

Abb. 10 Delegierte der VII. Parteikonferenz von Dal'stroj, 1947 (GAMO f. P-21f., op. 1, d. 100)

An dieser Stelle kam es Ababkov offensichtlich darauf an, entscheidende Stellen mit seinen Leuten zu besetzen. Auch wenn in den einzelnen Bezirken aus Personalmangel und aufgrund ihrer Kenntnisse nicht auf die bisherigen Leiter verzichtet werden konnte, so war doch die Parteileitung in der Hauptstadt, aufgrund deren Bedeutung als Machtzentrale, als Wohn- und Arbeitsort der gesamten alten und neuen Führungsgruppe und als repräsentatives Aushängeschild für das Gebiet von so großer Bedeutung, dass ihre Mitglieder, ebenso wie im Falle des Gebietsparteikomitees, sorgfältig ausgewählt werden mussten.

Große Personalveränderungen gab es auch im juristischen Bereich. In Dal'stroj hatte es zu keiner Zeit zivile Gerichte gegeben, hier richteten ausschließlich Militärtribunale und die sogenannten Lagersondergerichte.[174] Ab 1954 wurde das zivile Gerichtswesen auf das Magadaner Gebiet übertragen. Ivan Pantjuchin war einer von etwa 40 Staatsanwälten und Untersuchungsrichtern, die im Januar 1954 vom Generalstaatsanwalt der UdSSR für die Arbeit in der Region ausgewählt worden waren. In seinen Erinnerungen schildert er, wie alle bisherigen obersten Staatsanwälte des MVD nach Gründung des Gebiets entlassen, zum Teil auch verhaftet wurden und er selbst

---

174 Lagersondergerichte waren Teil des eigenen Rechtssystems des GULAG, seit 1945 ahndeten sie alle Strafsachen innerhalb der Lager und bei den Arbeitseinsätzen der Häftlinge. Vgl. Ivanova, Lagersondergerichte.

Abb. 11 Seminar von Parteisekretären des Magadaner Gebietes, April 1961 (GAMO f. P-21, op. 1, d. 109)

zunächst zu einem Staatsanwalt für die Inspektion der Lager ernannt wurde.[175] Im Juni 1954 wurde schließlich die Trennung zwischen Staatsanwälten für Lager und für zivile Angelegenheiten aufgehoben; nach Vorschlag des Gebietsparteikomitees ernannte man Pantjuchin daraufhin zum zivilen Staatsanwalt des Bezirkes Omsukčan.[176] Für ihn begann sich unter der Aufsicht der Generalstaatsanwaltschaft nach 1954 das sowjetische Recht und die „sozialistische Gesetzlichkeit"[177] in der Region durchzusetzen:

> An der Kolyma gab es jahrzehntelang nicht nur keine echten Staatsanwälte, sondern überhaupt keine zivilen sowjetischen Einrichtungen, weil in den Händen der lokalen Leitung die gesamte Fülle der Macht, besser gesagt der Autokratie, konzentriert war. Und auf einmal taucht dann ir-

---

175 Vgl. Pantjuchin, Zapiski. Für die 1950er Jahre siehe S. 85 – 141.

176 Zu dieser Zeit wurden neue Gerichtsdistrikte im Gebiet geschaffen. Vgl. die ausführliche Begründung zu der Bitte des Gebietsexekutivkomitees vom 20. Mai 1954 an den Ministerrat der RSFSR in GAMO f. R-146, op. 1, d. 60, l. 18 – 20 (für die Gerichtsdistrikte an der Kolyma), GAMO f. R-146, op. 1, d. 60, l. 16 – 17 (für die Distrikte in Tschukotka).

177 Siehe zur Bedeutung des Terminus „sozialistische Gesetzlichkeit" in der Entstalinisierung Luchterhandt, Justiz sowie Gill, Symbols, S. 171 f.

gend so eine staatsanwaltliche Untersuchung auf. Es kam zu ernsten Konflikten, deren Lösung nicht wenig Zeit und Nerven kostete.[178]

Von diesen Konflikten berichtete auch Ababkov dem ZK der KPdSU. Im Juni 1954, also unmittelbar nach Aufgabe der Trennung zwischen einer Staatsanwaltschaft für Lager und einer Staatsanwaltschaft für zivile Angelegenheiten, hatte das Gebietsparteikomitee eine großangelegte Überprüfung der Lage in *Berlag* und *Sevvostlag* vorgenommen. Abteilungen von Miliz und Staatsanwaltschaft wurden gemeinsam mit einer Brigade des Gebietsparteikomitees in die Lagerabteilungen geschickt. Nach Angaben von Ababkov sei daraufhin die ungesetzliche Praxis eingestellt worden, „Häftlinge als Hausangestellte in den Wohnungen des leitenden Personals von Dal'stroj und den Lagern zu benutzen", zudem würden Untersuchungen „ungesetzlicher Handlungen gegen Häftlinge im Jahr 1952" durchgeführt werden. Im Zuge dieser Brigade wurden in vielen Gebieten Stationen ziviler Milizeinrichtungen gegründet.[179] Vor Ort konnte die Parteileitung auf diese Weise die unionsweite Kampagne zur Stärkung der „sozialistischen Gesetzlichkeit", die mit einem Umbau der Rechtsinstitutionen einherging und die eigentlich auf eine Zurückdrängung des Parteieinflusses abzielte[180], dazu benutzen ihre eigene Position gegenüber der Dal'stroj-Leitung zu stärken.

Personalpolitisch ausgesprochen brisant war die Leitung der sogenannten „grundständigen Parteiorganisationen", die die Partei in allen Betrieben, Bergwerken und Fabriken vertraten. Im Magadaner Gebiet gab es 1954 insgesamt 563 grundständige Parteiorganisationen in Betrieben von Dal'stroj, viele davon waren jedoch zahlenmäßig klein, d. h., sie umfassten weit weniger als 100 Parteimitglieder.[181]

Derart kleine grundständige Parteiorganisationen verfügten über keine hauptamtlichen Parteisekretäre. Zur Zeit der militärischen Einzelleitung in Dal'stroj gab es zur Führung dieser Parteiorganisationen einen sogenannten „Stellvertreter der Produktionsleitung für politische Arbeit", der von den Politischen Truppenteilen ernannt wurde. Unter den zivilen Bedingungen wurden die Leiter der grundständigen Parteiorganisationen in den Betrieben eigentlich von den Parteileitungen der Bezirke vorgeschlagen, auf deren Gebiet sich die Betriebe befanden. Anschließend wurden diese Personen dann vom Parteikollektiv gewählt.

In der Praxis handelte es sich dabei jedoch häufig um ein und denselben Funktionär, der seinen Posten auch weiterhin behielt. Aufgrund der geringen Größe der grundständigen Parteiorganisationen waren diese Personen (insgesamt 82 im Magadaner Gebiet) für ihre Arbeit nicht als hauptamtliche Parteileiter freigestellt und wurden nicht durch die KPdSU entlohnt. Sie fungierten noch immer als Stellvertreter der einzelnen Produktionsleiter (jetzt unter der Bezeichnung „Sekretär") und wurden

---

178 Pantjuchin, Zapiski, S. 116.
179 Ababkov in GAMO f. P-21, op. 5, d. 759, l. 1–10, hier l. 6 f. Ausführlicher zu dieser Untersuchung siehe das Kapitel 3.3.2.
180 Vgl. Gorlizki, Political Reform, S. 258.
181 Vgl. Verkina, Istoričeskaja spravka, S. 5.

auch durch sie bezahlt. Die Leiter mehrerer Bezirksparteikomitees kritisierten diese Position im Jahr 1954 scharf, zumal das Gehalt dieser Stellvertreter sogar über den Bezügen der Mitarbeiter der Bezirksparteikomitees läge. Mit hohen Zahlungen würden so Personen, die außerdem nur über eine ganz geringe Schulbildung verfügten, über Jahre ganz von der Wirtschaftsleitung abhängig gemacht.[182] Vor allem aber entspräche ihre Arbeitsweise nicht dem Standard der Kommunistischen Partei, wie sich beispielsweise der Parteisekretär des Bezirks Jagodninskij, Balakirev, beim Magadaner Gebietsparteikomitee beschwerte:

> Ihr Stil, die Formen und Methoden ihrer Arbeit entsprechen nicht den heutigen Aufgaben, sie sind nicht in der Lage, das Niveau der parteipolitischen Arbeit zu heben. Aufgrund ihrer Abhängigkeit decken sie Unzulänglichkeiten und Fehler der Produktionsleitung nicht auf. Der begonnene organisatorische Umbau der Parteiorgane soll aber doch bis zu Ende geführt und in allen Bereichen endgültig umgesetzt werden.[183]

In den vergangenen Jahren, so Balakirev weiter, hätten die Stellvertreter für die politische Arbeit vollkommen den Führungsstil der Politischen Truppenteile übernommen – sie hätten ohne kollektive Besprechungen, lediglich auf der Grundlage von Befehlen „regiert" und die Anweisungen der mit außergewöhnlicher Machtfülle ausgestatteten Einzelleitung kritiklos umgesetzt: „Außerdem sind viele der Stellvertreter früher ‚politische Offiziere' in der Armee gewesen, sie haben noch nie unter zivilen Bedingungen in Parteiorganisationen gearbeitet."[184]

Zwei Punkte sind hier besonders aufschlussreich: Zunächst offenbart sich sozusagen rückblickend, in welchem Maße sich die militärische Form der Parteileitung zu einem wichtigen Prinzip der allmächtigen Einzelleitung entwickelt hatte, die auch nach Aufgabe der Politischen Verwaltung und unter zivilen Bedingungen in den einzelnen Betrieben noch wirkmächtig war. Außerdem zeugen diese Beschwerden von einem erheblichen Selbstbewusstsein der neuen Bezirksparteiorganisationen. Die einzelnen Sekretäre mussten sich in ihrer Position schon sehr gefestigt gefühlt haben, um Dal'stroj-Parteifunktionäre kollektiv und derart scharf kritisieren zu können. Verstärkend wirkte hier vielleicht auch Neid auf die hohen Gehälter der ehemaligen „Stellvertreter für die politische Arbeit".

Balakirev forderte gegenüber dem Gebietsparteikomitee, hauptamtliche Parteisekretäre zu Leitern der grundständigen Parteiorganisationen zu machen und sie unmittelbar durch die Partei zu entlohnen. Dadurch könnten die betrieblichen Parteiorganisationen tatsächlich zu Organen einer unabhängigen Kontrolle und zu Trägern von Kritik an der Produktionsleitung werden. Von einer solchen Stärkung in der Produktion versprach sich Balakirev eine generelle Aufwertung der Partei im Bezirk

---

182 Das reine Grundgehalt der Stellvertreter läge bei 2.600 Rubel, dazu kämen Aufschläge und Boni. Vgl. GAMO f. P-21, op. 5, d. 520, l. 38.

183 Schreiben von Balakirev vom 29. April 1954, l. 14–15 sowie vom 6. Dezember 1954 in GAMO f. P-21, op. 5, d. 520, l. 1–3.

184 GAMO f. P-21, op. 5, d. 520, l. 2.

Jagodninskij und darüber hinaus einen zivilen Aufbau der Region. Die „Überbleibsel" der alten Machtverhältnisse sollten zunächst bei den Kadern beseitigt werden.[185] Das Gebietsparteikomitee wies Balakirevs Forderungen und ähnliche Bitten anderer Bezirksparteikomitees mit Verweis auf die geringe Zahl an Parteimitgliedern in den Betrieben zurück; hauptamtliche Parteisekretäre seien tatsächlich nur bei ausgesprochen großen Betriebsparteiaktiven vorgesehen.

Veränderungen sollten nicht durch Umstrukturierungen, sondern auf inhaltlicher Ebene herbeigeführt werden. Die eingangs zitierte paradigmatische Formulierung, dass die Kader „die Methoden der Arbeit von Partei und Sowjet gelehrt werden", sollte auch gegenüber den ehemaligen Stellvertretern der Produktionsleiter angewandt werden. Das Gebietsparteikomitee versprach den Bezirksparteileitern, diese Kader in speziellen Schulungskursen entsprechend parteipolitisch zu unterweisen.[186] Die genannten Schulungen fanden auch tatsächlich statt. Mitarbeiter der Partei- und Sowjetstrukturen aus den Bezirken reisten nach Magadan, wurden entsprechend instruiert und propagandistisch „bearbeitet".[187] Sehr viel häufiger zogen jedoch Brigaden des Gebietsparteikomitees in die Siedlungen. Dabei sollten lokale Akteure unterwiesen und regionale Parteikonferenzen überwacht werden, v. a. aber ging es darum, die Lage vor Ort zu erkunden und sich selbst über die Realitäten des Magadaner Gebietes zu unterrichten.[188]

Die Bezirksparteikomitees standen zwischen alten militärischen und neuen zivilen Parteistrukturen unter erheblichem Druck. Neben den problematischen Parteivertretungen in den Betrieben mussten sie mit der Existenz weiterer militärischer Parteistrukturen leben. In den Lagerpunkten des *Sevvostlag* existierten nach wie vor die Politischen Truppenteile, die dem Politischen Truppenteil des GULAG unterstanden. Diese außergewöhnliche Parteivertretung in den Lagern des GULAG war gerade im Oktober 1954 vom ZK der KPdSU noch einmal bestätigt worden. Die Existenz der militärischen Parteivertretungen des *Sevvostlag* zog in den Bezirken von Jakutien Auseinandersetzungen mit dem jakutischen Gebietsparteikomitee über Kompetenzen und Verpflichtungen nach sich.[189] Auch hier zeigten die zivilen Parteivertretungen ein

---

185 Vgl. GAMO f. P-21, op. 5, d. 520, l. 3.

186 Antwort aus dem Gebietsparteikomitee vom 23. August 1954 in GAMO f. P-21, op. 5, d. 520, l. 13. In einem besonders drastischen Fall entschied die regionale Parteileitung, den Stellvertreter für die politische Arbeit zu entlassen. Dabei handelte es sich um einen Stellvertreter in einem Lager, dem Čaun-Čukotsker ITL. Der Stellvertreter S. F. Šmatkov sei bei sexuellen Verhältnissen zwischen bewaffneten Wachen und Häftlingen und bei diversen Übergriffen nicht eingeschritten und halte sich nicht an die Verordnungen des ZK der KPdSU. Vgl. den Bericht der Politischen Abteilung der USVITL GULAGa vom August 1954 in GAMO f. P-21, op. 5, d. 14, l. 179–180.

187 Vgl. Na preobražennoj zemle, S. 42.

188 Siehe als Beispiel den ausführlichen Bericht eines Mitglieds des Gebietsparteikomitees über die Parteikonferenz im Bezirk Anadyr', Bericht vom 20. Juni 1957 in GAMO f. R-146, op. 1, d. 53, l. 64–75.

189 Vgl. das Schreiben des Leiters des Politotdel GULAGa MVD SSSR, Lukojanov, vom 18. Oktober 1954 in RGANI f. 5, op. 32, d. 30, l. 32. Siehe die Beschwerde des Gebietsparteikomitees von Jakutien über die Politischen Truppenteile der Lagerpunkte auf ihrem Territorium. Vgl. das Schreiben des Sekretärs des

neues Selbstbewusstsein gegenüber den militärischen Parteiaktiven. Das jakutische Gebietsparteikomitee bat darum, die Parteivertretungen in den Lagern den territorialen Parteigliederungen zu unterstellen und damit die Kompetenzen der regionalen Parteileitung über die Lager auszuweiten. Militärische Leitungsstrukturen der Partei wurden von territorialen Gliederungen einfach nicht mehr als unumstößlich betrachtet.

Auch die Exekutivkomitees in den Bezirken mussten sich ihre Arbeitsbereiche erkämpfen. Jahrelang fehlten vielerorts die versprochenen Gebäude für die neuen Organe, was Afanas'ev auch dem Desinteresse von Dal'stroj an diesen Bauarbeiten anlastete.[190] Zudem waren die Personaletats, die bereits am 28. Dezember 1953 festgesetzt worden waren und die sich an Muster-Etats des Ministerrates der UdSSR orientierten[191], unter den lokalen Bedingungen völlig unzureichend. 144 zusätzliche Personen forderte Afanas'ev bereits im April 1954 vom Ministerrat der RSFSR, um die Arbeit der Sowjetstrukturen vor Ort bewältigen zu können. Aufgrund der lokalen Verhältnisse seien bewaffnete Wachen für die Exekutivkomitees vonnöten, der Mangel an Telefonverbindungen mache Dienstreisen unentbehrlich, die jedoch aufgrund der schlechten Infrastruktur kostspielig und umständlich seien.[192]

---

jakutischen Gebietsparteikomitees, S. Borisov, an das ZK der KPdSU vom Mai 1955 in RGANI f. 5, op. 32, d. 30, l. 31 u. l. 33. Ausführlich hat Wladislaw Hedeler die Rolle dieser Politabteilungen in zwei Lagerkomplexen, dem „Siblag" und dem „Karlag", analysiert. Vgl. Hedeler, Ökonomik, S. 228–312.

190 Wie im Fall des Omsukčansker Bezirks, in dem das Bezirkspartei- und das Bezirksexekutivkomitee wegen des Mangels an Büroräumen erst einmal in die Räumlichkeiten des aufgelösten Politischen Truppenteils der lokalen Bergbauverwaltung einziehen sollten, vgl. GAMO f. R-146, op. 1, d. 36, l. 33–39, hier l. 36. Doch auch das „Haus der Sowjets" in Magadan war 1956 noch nicht errichtet. Vgl. das Schreiben von Afanas'ev vom 25. Juni 1955 an den Vorsitzenden des Ministerrates der RSFSR, in dem er um die entsprechenden Finanzmittel bat, um das Gebäude wenigstens 1957 in Betrieb nehmen zu können. GAMO f. R-146, op. 1, d. 45, l. 180. Selbst bei der Produktion von Büromöbeln kam es zu erheblichen Engpässen, so der Leiter der Verwaltung für die regionale Wirtschaft in GAMO f. R-146, op. 1, d. 49, l. 40.

191 Die Bestätigung der Magadaner Vorschläge erfolgte durch das Finanzministerium der UdSSR und den Ministerrat der RSFSR. Für das Gebietsexekutivkomitee wurde ein Personaletat von 350 Personen vorgesehen, davon 71 Personen als direkte Mitglieder des Exekutivkomitees. Hinzu kamen Mitglieder der Finanz-, Kultur- und Landwirtschaftsverwaltung. Der Etat sah jedoch keine Abteilungen für schwere Industrie und für Baumaßnahmen vor, diese Verwaltungen lagen nach wie vor bei Dal'stroj. Dem Stadtsowjet wurde ein Personalstand von 69 Personen zugebilligt, den einzelnen Bezirken jeweils 34,5 Stellen. Vgl. die Aufstellung in der Anlage zu dem Schreiben des Finanzministers und des stellv. Vorsitzenden des Ministerrates der RSFSR vom 28. Dezember 1953 in GAMO f. R-146, op. 1, d. 59, l. 1–3. Die bisher bestehenden Personaletats des Magadaner Stadtsowjets und der auch schon bisher bestehenden Bezirksexekutivkomitees wurden annulliert. Vgl. GAMO f. R-146, op. 1, d. 59, l. 3.

192 Vgl. das ausführliche Schreiben Afanas'evs in GAMO f. R-146, op. 1, d. 59, l. 25–28 sowie die genaue Auflistung der einzelnen Zusatzkosten ebd., l. 29–32. Siehe auch das Schreiben Afanas'evs an den Vorsitzenden des Ministerrates der RSFSR vom 20. Januar 1954, in dem er um eine Erweiterung des Personaletats des čukotischen Kreisexekutivkomitees bat, in GAMO f. R-146, op. 1, d. 59, l. 5–9 sowie für den weiteren Schriftwechsel, in dem sich Moskau gegen Erhöhungen aussprach, ebd., l. 64–75.

Insgesamt lässt sich somit feststellen, dass die neuen Herrschaftsstrukturen schnell, v. a. aber formal besetzt wurden. Strukturen wurden aufgebaut, Kommissionen eingesetzt und Posten vergeben, so dass das zivile, administrative Raster eines Gebiets rasch ausgefüllt wurde. Die Gründungen der einzelnen Partei- und Exekutivkomitees konnten ebenso wie Bestätigungen über abgehaltene Sitzungen an die übergeordneten Stellen der RSFSR und der UdSSR gemeldet werden; sie zeigten zugleich den Leitern der Industrieverwaltungen, dass die neue politische Macht in den einzelnen Regionen präsent war.

Die Personalsituation der Partei verbesserte sich in den ersten Jahren nach der Gebietsgründung nur mäßig und war auch ein Problem der Basis. Zwar gab es bei den absoluten Zahlen der Parteimitglieder gegenüber 1954 einen leichten Anstieg um 681 Personen; 1956 hatte die KPdSU im Magadaner Gebiet 12.386 Mitglieder (davon 1.045 Kandidaten). Aber dennoch war die Partei zunächst nicht flächendeckend in allen Lebensbereichen vertreten. Ababkov warf den Parteileitungen der Bezirke vor, neu ankommende Parteimitglieder nur unzureichend zu integrieren und die Kader nicht an die Region zu binden.[193] Die Sekretäre der grundständigen Parteiorganisationen wechselten permanent, 1956 war es mehr als jeder zweite Parteisekretär, der seinen Posten und die Region verließ. Von stabilen Kaderverhältnissen konnte da keine Rede sein, sie folgte der allgemeinen Fluktuation der Magadaner Bevölkerung.[194] Das Gebietsparteikomitee bemühte sich daher, Absolventen der Moskauer und Leningrader Parteihochschulen zu einer Postenübernahme im Magadaner Gebiet zu bewegen.[195]

3.2.3 Infrastrukturen

Infrastrukturen, hier verstanden als Verkehrs- und Kommunikationsmittel, waren für die Besetzung des neuen Herrschaftsraumes von Anfang an von großer praktischer Bedeutung. Zudem spielten sie eine wichtige integrative Rolle.[196] Wie der Blick auf das

---

193 Vgl. GAMO f. P-21, op. 5, d. 110, l. 116.

194 Vgl. den Bericht der Abteilung für Parteiorgane des Gebietsparteikomitees vom Januar 1957 in GAMO f. P-21, op. 5, d. 110, l. 114–116. Zu den Zahlen der Parteimitglieder bei Gründung des Gebietes siehe Chiloböčenko, Istoričeskaja chronika, S. 178.

195 Die endgültige Entscheidung über die Abkommandierung in eine Region lag beim Büro des ZK der KPdSU für die RSFSR, die Magadaner Parteileitung bemühte sich jedoch um eine Werbung für das Gebiet. Siehe die Übersicht über Absolventen der Parteischulen, die im Juni 1958 nach Magadan reisten, im Bericht des Leiters der Abteilung für Parteiorgane des Büros des ZK der KPdSU für die RSFSR in RGANI f. 5, op. 32, d. 123, l. 22–23. Erst im Jahr 1963 konnte Afanas'ev stolz verkünden, in den vergangenen zehn Jahren seien viermal so viele Arbeiter und Kolchosmitglieder in die Partei aufgenommen worden wie in den 25 Jahren der Existenz von Dal'stroj. Magadan war zu dieser Zeit eine der wenigen Städte der Sowjetunion, in denen der Anteil der Parteimitglieder an der Gesamtbevölkerung 10 % ausmachte. Vgl. Grebenjuk, Samoubijstva, S. 215.

196 Fragen der Energieversorgung werden in dieser Arbeit im Kapitel 4 behandelt, das sich der wirtschaftlichen Entwicklung widmet. In den Quellen werden z. T. alle Einrichtungen der „sozialen

neue Personal gezeigt hat, konnte man das Magadaner Gebiet nur beherrschen, wenn man das Territorium bezwang, wenn man die Siedlungen und die Goldfelder erreichte, wenn man Verbindungen auch zu einem Exekutivkomitee im äußersten Osten Tschukotkas aufbauen konnte.[197]

Die Frage nach der Zuordnung von Infrastrukturen war eine Frage der Machtverhältnisse. Die vorhandenen Verkehrs- und Kommunikationsmittel unterstanden dem Kombinat und wurden nicht einfach der neuen politischen Macht zur Verfügung gestellt; die Kombinatsleitung konnte für die Industrie jederzeit Eigenbedarf anmelden. Gebietspartei- und Gebietsexekutivkomitee waren gerade in der ersten Zeit vollkommen von Dal'stroj abhängig.

Zudem waren diese Infrastrukturen von der militärischen Struktur des Lager-Industriellen Komplexes geprägt. So mangelte es an Passagierflugzeugen, weil Häftlinge und einfache Wachmannschaften bislang unter unmenschlichen Bedingungen in unbeheizten Transportflugzeugen befördert wurden. Auch gab es praktisch keine zivilen Kommunikationsmittel, Telefon- oder Telegraphenverbindungen waren für freie Arbeiter fast nie erreichbar. Auch die Vorschriften für Verpackung und Deklaration von Waren unterlagen den strengen Geheimhaltungsregeln eines militärischen Transports.

Der Druck zur Schaffung ziviler Infrastruktur kam daher aus Magadan, aber auch von allen Organisationen und Ministerien der Sowjetunion, die die übrigen sowjetischen Regionen versorgten. Im Auftrag des Ministerrates der UdSSR und der RSFSR drängten sie darauf, die bisherigen Anlagen von Dal'stroj in ihre Verwaltungen aufzunehmen oder ihre eigenen Einrichtungen auf das Magadaner Gebiet auszuweiten, um sie so in das Netz der zivilen Infrastruktur der Union zu integrieren.

Die Angleichung der Magadaner Infrastrukturen an die unionsweiten Strukturen kann zudem nicht isoliert betrachtet werden. Vielmehr muss diese Entwicklung im Rahmen der Anstrengungen der sowjetischen Führung betrachtet werden, die die Erschließung des sowjetischen Nordens, die Entwicklung seiner Infrastruktur, Elektrifizierung, Einrichtung des Postwesens etc. insgesamt seit Mitte der 1950er Jahre vorantrieb. Die extreme Rückständigkeit der arktischen und subarktischen Gebiete resultierte dabei auch aus ihrer bisherigen lagergestützten Ausbeutung; an der Kolyma zeigte sich dies verschärft durch die extreme Abschottung und rein militärische Kontrolle durch Dal'stroj.[198]

Infrastruktur", wie Kindertageseinrichtungen, Internate oder Krankenhäuser, allgemein zu „Infrastrukturen" gezählt. Diese werden jedoch hier unter dem Gesichtspunkt der Lebensbedingungen von freien Arbeitern im Kapitel 5 betrachtet.

197 Infrastrukturen sind in den vergangenen Jahren zu einem wichtigen Forschungsfeld der sowjetischen Kulturgeschichte geworden. Vgl. u. a. Gestwa/Grützmacher, Infrastrukturen; Obertreis, Infrastrukturen; Grützmacher, Baikal-Amur-Magistrale.

198 Vgl. zu diesem Übergang in der Erschließung des sowjetischen Nordens Josephson, Soviet Arctic, S. 435 ff.

3.2.3.1 Kommunikationsmittel

Die Anlagen für Fernmeldetechnik und Radio von Dal'stroj wurden zum 1. Juli 1954 offiziell in das Ministerium für Post- und Fernmeldewesen der UdSSR eingegliedert, worauf das Ministerium eine Magadaner Vertretung „für Post, Telegraph, Telefon und Radio zur allgemeinen [d. h. zur „zivilen" – M. S.] Nutzung" gründete.[199]

Infolge dieser Gründung wurden zum ersten Mal gewöhnliche Briefkästen in Magadan und den größeren Siedlungen aufgehängt, man erhoffte sich einen Ausbau der Postzustellung.[200] Die Versorgung der Bevölkerung mit Radiogeräten sollte sich jetzt ebenso verbessern, außerdem war für die Zeit zwischen 1955 und 1957 die Errichtung eines allgemeinen Telefonnetzes mit 4.000 Anschlüssen geplant. Tatsächlich lässt sich erst Ende der 1950er Jahre eine Steigerung erkennen. Größere Siedlungen besaßen jetzt eine Post- und Telegraphenstation.[201] Auch im Bereich der Printmedien sollte sich die Versorgung verbessern. Die Redaktion der wichtigsten regionalen Zeitung, der *Magandanskaja Pravda*, die Zeitungen der einzelnen Bezirke und die Druckerei unterstellte der Ministerrat im Mai 1954 dem Kulturministerium.[202] Infolgedessen wurden neue Zeitungen gegründet und 1955 auch ein eigener regionaler Verlag (*Magadanskaja Pečat'*), der auf heimatkundliche Themen ausgerichtet war, geschaffen.

Vorrang vor der zivilen Nutzung hatte bei allen Kommunikationsmitteln die Industrie. Ausdrücklich schrieb das Ministerium bei Gründung der Gebietsabteilung fest, dass die Verbindungen zwischen Magadan und den Betrieben nicht unter der Einführung von Fernmeldetechnik zur allgemeinen Nutzung leiden dürften; die Kommunikation zwischen wirtschaftlichen Einrichtungen sei stets an erster Stelle zu gewährleisten.[203] Vielmehr war es eine zusätzliche Aufgabe der neuen Abteilung, den Kontakt zwischen der Leitung in Magadan und den Betrieben vor Ort durch einen neuen Telefonkanal zu stärken. Daneben wurden alle Kommunikationsmittel, die bisher für den Kontakt in den Betrieben benutzt wurden, nicht dem Ministerium

---

199 Der Befehl des Ministeriums für das Post- und Fernmeldewesen geht auf eine spezielle Verordnung des Ministerrates der UdSSR vom 28. Juli 1954 zurück. Vgl. den Abdruck des Befehls in GAMO f. R-146, op. 1, d. 60, l. 30. Ausdrücklich zählten auch die Anlagen von Dal'stroj dazu, die sich auf dem Gebiet von Jakutien befanden.

200 Vgl. die Maßnahmen zu der Verordnung des Ministerrates in GAMO f. R-146, op. 1, d. 6, l. 185–195. Siehe dazu auch den ausführlichen Befehl des Ministers für Buntmetalle an seine Mitarbeiter, an die Leiter einzelner Abteilungen und Verwaltungen und an den Leiter von Dal'stroj, Mitrakov, zur Ausführung der Verordnung des Ministerrates in GAMO f. R-146, op. 1, d. 6, l. 213–230; sowie Roščupkin/Bubnis, K voprosu ob administrativnom ustrojstve, S. 74.

201 Vgl. den Bericht des Leiters der Gebietsabteilung für Post- und Fernmeldewesen vom November 1960 in GAMO f. R-146, op. 1, d. 360, l. 37–41.

202 Vgl. die Liste aller Übergaben in den Anhängen zur Verordnung in RGAĖ f. 9163, op. 6, d. 13, l. 81–101, hier l. 101.

203 Vgl. die Regelungen im Befehl des Ministeriums für das Post- und Fernmeldewesen in GAMO f. R-146, op. 1, d. 60, l. 30. Zu den bisher in Dal'stroj bestehenden Anlagen des Fernmeldewesens siehe den Übergabeakt von Dal'stroj an das MMP in GAMO f. R-23, op. 1, d. 4677, l. 1–28, hier l. 10.

übertragen, sie blieben Teil des Kombinats Dal'stroj, um dessen tägliche Arbeit nicht zu behindern.

3.2.3.2 Verkehrsmittel

Unter den stalinistischen Arbeitsbedingungen in Dal'stroj war eine systematische Erschließung des riesigen Gebietes nicht vorgesehen. Infrastrukturen wurden meist parallel zu den Förderarbeiten errichtet und waren auf die unmittelbaren Bedürfnisse der Industrie ausgerichtet. Auch unter der neuen Gebietsleitung setzte man zunächst bei punktuellen Verbesserungen an.

Eine umfassende verkehrstechnische Erschließung der Region hätte erheblicher Anstrengungen bedurft – nicht nur aufgrund der Größe des Territoriums, sondern v. a. aufgrund des Klimas. Bis auf wenige Gebiete an der Küste musste der Bau von Straßen, Schienen oder Hafenanlagen unter den Bedingungen des ewigen Eises erfolgen, im Sommer verschlammt die obere Erdschicht durch große Hitze und massive Regenfälle. Zudem ist die Region von mehreren gewaltigen Flüssen und Gebirgen durchzogen. Pläne zur Schaffung einer Eisenbahnstrecke als Verbindung zu den zentralen Teilen der Union waren seit Gründung des Kombinats immer wieder aufgelegt worden, bis auf einzelne, sehr kurze Strecken wurden an der Kolyma und in Tschukotka jedoch nie Schienen verlegt.[204] Die Region blieb auf den LKW- und Fährverkehr mit all seinen wetterabhängigen Schwierigkeiten angewiesen. Nach und nach gewann auch der Flugverkehr innerhalb des Gebietes und für die Verbindungen zu anderen Regionen der Union an Bedeutung.[205]

In institutioneller Hinsicht unterstanden alle Fahrzeuge, Reparaturwerkstätten und Autostationen seit dem Sommer 1954 dem Ministerium für Autoverkehr und Straßen der RSFSR.[206] Dazu zählte auch das gesamte Straßennetz des Magadaner Gebietes, das sommers etwa 2.000 km umfasste, im Winter wuchs es durch die Verwendung vereister Flüsse auf etwa 4.000 km an.

Hauptverkehrsachse war und blieb die zentrale „Kolymaer Trasse". Ihr Bau begann unmittelbar nach Gründung des Kombinats 1932 am Hafen von Magadan, über die Leninstraße der Stadt führte sie in den Norden der Region. Die Trasse, auch bezeichnet als „Kolymaer Chaussee", war ein berüchtigtes Symbol des Kolymaer La-

---

204 Zu den wenigen bestehenden Schienenstrecken siehe die Angaben in dem Übergabeakt von Dal'stroj an das MMP in GAMO f. R-23, op. 1, d. 4677, l. 1–28, hier l. 9. Dabei handelte es sich um drei Strecken von jeweils etwa 80 km. Vgl. zu den bisherigen Plänen, die Eisenbahnverbindungen zwischen Kamtschatka und der Baikal-Amur-Linie vorsahen, Širokov, Iz istorii železnodorožnogo stroitel'stva.
205 Die Bedeutung, die der Fährschifffahrt beigemessen wurde, zeigt sich auch daran, dass seit dem März 1954 die Leiter der wichtigsten Seehäfen mit ihren Stellvertretern in das neue Gebietsparteikomitee aufgenommen wurden. Vgl. Širokov, Politika, S. 385.
206 Die Übergabe geht auf die Verordnung des Ministerrates der UdSSR vom 29. Mai 1954 zurück. Vgl. das Schreiben des stellv. Ministers für Autotransport und Chausseen der RSFSR, Savčenkov, an Afanas'ev vom 30. September 1954 in GAMO f. R-146, op. 1, d. 61, l. 46–47.

gersystems, sie war die Schneise, die die Goldförderstätten an der Kolyma mit dem Hafen verband, die Strecke, die die Häftlinge immer weiter vom sowjetischen Festland entfernte, sie „ins Gold" und damit so oft in den Tod führte. Die gesamte Strecke von 2.000 Kilometern musste im Laufe vieler Jahre von Häftlingen errichtet werden, die Trasse war damit der Weg zu den schrecklichen Bergbaustätten und zugleich selbst ein riesiges Zwangsarbeitsprojekt. Unter den Häftlingen war sie als „längste Straße der Welt" verschrien, in allen Häftlingserinnerungen spielt die Kolymaer Trasse eine wichtige Rolle.[207]

Diese Straße war die Lebensader der Region, auf ihr gelangten Häftlinge, alle Maschinen, Lebensmittel und Materialien zu den Industriegebieten. Orte entlang der Trasse waren sehr oft nur nach ihrer Entfernung zum Zentrum Magadan benannt, z. B. „Am Kilometer 47". Zugleich war sie ein lebensgefährlicher Ort, immer wieder blieben LKWs in den riesigen Schneebergen stecken, die Insassen erfroren, Kriminelle überfielen Reisende, raubten Transporter aus.

Die Trasse blieb auch nach 1953 die wichtigste Infrastruktur innerhalb des Gebiets. Bereits 1954 wurde eine Verwaltung für den Automobiltransport gegründet, um den Transport von Passagieren per Bus zu professionalisieren.[208] 1956 machte der Lastwagenverkehr bereits 95 % des gesamten Verkehrs innerhalb des Gebietes aus; es mangelte aber häufig an geeigneten Fahrern.[209] Die Zahl der von Passagieren in Bussen zurückgelegten Kilometer stieg zwischen 1955 und 1959 um ein Drittel.[210] Durch diese Verkehrszunahme und den schlechten Zustand des Straßennetzes kam es zu sehr vielen Unfällen. Das Gebietsexekutivkomitee forderte daher die Einführung einer Verkehrswacht mit einer ständigen Geschwindigkeitskontrolle für die Trasse – die ein paar Jahre später tatsächlich auch eingerichtet wurde.[211]

Parallel zu diesen verkehrspolitischen Maßnahmen, die angesichts der klimatischen und straßenbaulichen Härten dieser Schneise durch die Region etwas hilflos wirken, sollte die Trasse in Reisebeschreibungen und Erzählungen auch ein neues

---

207 Vgl. Conquest, Kolyma, S. 43.

208 Vgl. Na preobražennoj zemle, S. 41. 1954 wurde eine Filiale für Autobusse der Verwaltung für den Automobiltransport gegründet, die zum 1. Januar 1955 in die Verwaltung des Gebietes eingegliedert wurde. Vgl. Širokov, Politika, S. 386.

209 Vgl. den Bericht des Vorsitzenden des Stadtexekutivkomitees an das ZK der KPdSU, eingegangen am 11. Juli 1956 in RGASPI f. 556, op. 21, d. 8, l. 44. Siehe zu den Transportorganisationen auch Širokov, Politika, S. 387.

210 Vgl. Narodnoe chozjajstvo Magadanskoj oblasti, S. 67.

211 Bei der Gebietsgründung gab es etwa 9.000 Autos, die im Jahr 1953 insgesamt 542 Unfälle verursacht hatten, bei denen 92 Menschen starben und über 250 Personen verletzt wurden. Vgl. das entsprechende Schreiben an den Vorsitzenden des Ministerrates der UdSSR, Malenkov, in GAMO f. R-146, op. 1, d. 61, l. 10 – 11. Dennoch nahmen die Unfälle in den folgenden Jahren noch weiter zu, als Ergebnis der deutlichen Zunahme des allgemeinen Straßenverkehrs. Neben dem quantitativen Anstieg waren für die Milizverwaltung auch betrunkene und zum Teil unausgebildete Fahrer Ursache der steigenden Zahl an Unfällen. Vgl. die Beschwerde der Milizverwaltung vom Dezember 1956 bei dem Leiter von Dal'stroj, Čuguev, die dem Kombinat mangelnde Sorgfalt bei der Auswahl ihrer Fahrer vorwarf in GAMO f. R-23sč, op. 1, d. 587, l. 15 – 16.

Abb. 12 Verkehrskontrolle auf der Kolymaer Trasse, Dezember 1958 (RGAKFD Krasnogorsk, 0 – 353430, Fotograf: o.A.)

Image erhalten. Jetzt galt sie als „verbindendes Element" des Gebietes, sie ermöglichte Kontakte, Austausch, Handel, sollte ein menschenfreundliches Bild sowjetischer Infrastrukturprojekte vermitteln. So heißt es in einer Reisebeschreibung:

> Der Autotransport – die wichtigste Verkehrsverbindung im Hohen Norden. Schwere Maschinen vaterländischer Herkunft mit Anhängern – ganze Autozüge – transportieren Tausende Tonnen Fracht; Lebensmittel, Industriewaren, technische Anlagen, Baumaterialien, Brennmaterialien. Zwischen Magadan und den nördlichen Siedlungen kursieren reguläre Passagierbusse. Noch vor kurzem liefen hier, auf unwegsamen Pfaden, nur Rentiergespanne. [...] Industrieanlagen, Goldfelder und Siedlungen entstanden in der tiefen Taiga – und die Trasse hat sie nicht im Stich gelassen. [...] Zu bislang nicht erreichbaren Orten spannt sich die wunderbare Autostraße. Jetzt lenkt eine ganze Armee von Kolymaer Fahrern Tausende Autos über die Straßen des Gebietes. Links und rechts blitzen Siedlungen mit besonderen Namen auf: Atka, Palatka, Staratel'nyj [...].[212]

Noch etwas romantischer lässt Afanas'ev ein junges Mädchen die Straßen des Gebietes beschreiben:

---

212 Danilov, Kraj severnogo sijanija, S. 7 f.

> Die Wege, die hier Trassen heißen, sind ganz lebendig. Es scheint, als würden sie atmen. Durch
> diese Adern fließt das Blut, das diesem erstaunlichen Ende unseres Landes, genannt Kolyma, das
> Leben schenkt.[213]

Im Bereich der See- und Flussschifffahrt herrschte lange Zeit erhebliche Unklarheit
über die institutionelle Zuordnung der einzelnen Teile der bisherigen Dal'strojer
Flotte. Diverse zivile Ministerien waren für verschiedene Bereiche zuständig, die
wichtigsten Häfen unterstanden aufgrund ihrer wirtschaftlichen Bedeutung nach wie
vor Dal'stroj. Da es dem Kombinat jedoch an Mitteln für deren Instandhaltung mangelte, hatte die Leitung von Dal'stroj selbst um eine klare Zuständigkeitsregelung im
Rahmen ziviler Ministerien gebeten. Afanas'ev war es wiederum leid, bei Fragen, die
unmittelbar die Versorgung des Gebietes betrafen, in erheblichem Maße auf das
Kombinat angewiesen zu sein. Infolge dieser Debatte wurden zum 1. Oktober 1957
schließlich alle Häfen und Schiffe dem Ministerium der Meeresflotte der UdSSR unterstellt.[214] Der Umschlag und der Transport von Waren wurden seitdem auf der
Grundlage von Verträgen geregelt.[215]

Auf Anordnung des Vorsitzenden des Ministerrates, Malenkov, sollten bereits seit
Frühjahr 1954 planmäßige Verkehrsverbindungen nach Magadan und Tschukotka
eingerichtet, auf der Strecke Nachodka-Magadan beheizbare Schiffe eingesetzt und
ein Fahrplan aufgestellt werden, der auf eine Kombination von Schifffahrt und an-
schließender Zugverbindung ab Chabarowsk ausgerichtet war. Davon versprach sich
der Ministerrat eine bessere Anbindung der Region an die zentralen Teile der Sowjetunion.[216]

Die Zuordnung des Flugverkehrs erwies sich ebenfalls als schwierig. Erst Anfang
1955 wurde eine eigene Magadaner Luftflotte gegründet, die zunächst der fernöstlichen „Verwaltung der zivilen Luftflotte" in Chabarowsk unterstand, seit Juli 1957 jedoch als selbstständige „nordöstliche Verwaltung der Zivilen Luftflotte (GVF)" existierte.[217] In Tschukotka war hingegen die in Jakutien stationierte Verwaltung der
Polarluftfahrt tätig, was zunächst zu vielen Schwierigkeiten bei der Abgrenzung der

---

213 Afanas'ev, Rossija, S. 112.

214 Vgl. Širokov, Politika, S. 385.

215 Vgl. das Schreiben von Afanas'ev an den Ministerrat der RSFSR vom 11. Dezember 1956 in GAMO f.
R-146, op. 1, d. 61, l. 99–100.

216 Siehe die Maßnahmen, angeordnet von Malenkov, in der „Ausführung der Verordnung des Ministerrates der UdSSR vom 29. Mai 1954" in GAMO f. R-146, op. 1, d. 6, l. 185–195. Siehe dazu auch den
ausführlichen Befehl des Ministers für Buntmetalle zur „Ausführung der Verordnung des Ministerrates" in GAMO f. R-146, op. 1, d. 6, l. 213–230. Vgl. die Angaben zum Schifftransport in dem Übergabeakt
von Dal'stroj an das MMP in GAMO f. R-23, op. 1, d. 4677, l. 1–28, hier l. 8.

217 Die Gründung der Magadaner Verwaltung (im Rahmen des Chabarowsker Distrikts) ging auf eine
Verordnung des Ministerrates der UdSSR vom 22. Februar 1955 zurück. Ebenso wie im Fall der Fernmeldetechnik gehörten zu ihr auch die Gebiete von Jakutien, in denen Dal'stroj tätig war. Die eigenständige Abteilung von GVF hatte Afanas'ev bereits im April 1954 gefordert. Vgl. sein Schreiben an den
Leiter der GVF, Žavoronkov, in GAMO f. R-146, op. 1, d. 61, l. 15–16. Die Gründung der eigenständigen
nordöstlichen Verwaltung erfolgte am 22. Juli 1957. Vgl. Aviacii Severo-Vostoka, S. 66.

Abb. 13 Hafenanlage in der Bucht Nagaeva, Magadan Dezember 1960 (RGAKFD Krasnogorsk, 0 – 370747, Fotograf: B.E. Vdovenko)

beiden Verwaltungen führte.[218] Die Unterordnung unter zivile Ministerien zog auch die Gründung einer Station der zivilen Rettungsflugwacht nach sich.[219]

Nach der Gebietsgründung geriet der Passagiertransport in den Fokus der neuen Organe. Die Zahl der beförderten Personen stieg unmittelbar im Frühjahr 1954 sprunghaft an[220], die Bedingungen dieses Transportes verbesserten sich jedoch erst sehr langsam. Noch Mitte der 1950er Jahre warteten Hunderte Passagiere auf den Flugplätzen von Magadan, Sejmčan oder Anadyr' monatelang auf ein Flugzeug. Wenn sie schließlich einen Platz ergattern konnten, waren die Flugzeuge selbst häufig nur

---

218 Das Gebietsexekutivkomitee wehrte sich immer wieder gegen den Einsatz der Verwaltung für Polarluftfahrt auf dem Territorium des Gebietes, da Absprachen über die Verteilung von Flugzeugen und Brennstoffen nicht eingehalten würden. Außerdem liegen Beschwerden vor, dass die Polarluftfahrtsverwaltung ihre exklusive Stellung schamlos missbrauche, vollkommen überteuerte Tickets verkaufe und die Flugzeuge dazu benutze, vor allem die eigene Verwaltung und ihre Piloten mit Tabak und Alkoholika zu versorgen, während die Bevölkerung einfache Lebensmittel nicht erhalte. Vgl. die Beschwerde von Afanas'ev bei Kaganovič vom 11. September 1954 in GAMO f. R-146, op. 1, d. 61, l. 43 – 45 sowie die Beschwerde von Afanas'ev bei Bulganin vom 31. Oktober 1955 in GAMO f. R-146, op. 1, d. 61, l. 51 – 54. Siehe auch die Beschwerde unmittelbar aus dem Vostočno-Tundrovsker Bezirk in GAMO f. R-146, op. 1, d. 61, l. 18 – 19.
219 Vgl. Aviacii Severo-Vostoka, S. 44.
220 Insgesamt wurden im Jahr 1954 an Arbeitstagen etwa 300 bis 350 Passagiere abgefertigt (dies im Durchschnitt, bezogen auf alle Flugplätze des Gebietes). Siehe den Bericht des Flughafenleiters an das Gebietsexekutivkomitee in GAMO f. R-146, op. 1, d. 61, l. 30 – 31.

В МАГАДАНСКОМ АЭРОПОРТУ

Посадка вакончена, пассажиры уселись в мягкие кресла. Бортпроводница Тамара КУЗЬМЕНКО любезно предлагает пассажирам прохладительные напитки и бутерброды.

Abb. 14 „Im Magadaner Flughafen. Das Boarding ist abgeschlossen, die Passagiere sitzen in weichen Sesseln, die Stewardess bietet freundlich gekühlte Getränke und Butterbrote an", Magadanskaja Pravda, 26. Juni 1956

auf Lastentransporte ausgerichtet, es gab kaum Sitze, geflogen wurde fast immer ohne Heizung. Auf den Flugplätzen gab es, so die vielstimmigen Beschwerden, keinerlei Infrastruktur, weder für die Lagerung und Verladung von Lasten oder die Reinigung der Landebahn noch für die Passagiere. Selbst für Mitarbeiter von Ministerien und Leitungspersonal stand kaum Verpflegung an Bord zur Verfügung.[221] In krassem Widerspruch stand dazu die offizielle Darstellung von Flugreisen auf den Seiten der Zeitung Magadanskaja Pravda (vgl. Abbildung 14).

Trotz der praktischen Schwierigkeiten nahm der Luftverkehr in seiner Bedeutung rasant zu. Waren Flüge von Moskau nach Magadan noch Ende 1953 recht selten, so wurde schon am 10. März 1954 zumindest auf dem Papier ein regulärer Flugplan zwischen Moskau und Magadan aufgenommen; die Flugzeuge benötigten für diese

---

[221] Vgl. die Beschwerde Afanas'evs an den Leiter der Hauptverwaltung für die zivile Luftfahrt vom April 1954 in GAMO f. R-146, op. 1, d. 61, l. 15 – 16, die Beschwerde des Flughafenleiters vom Juni 1954 in GAMO f. R-146, op. 1, d. 61, l. 30 – 31 sowie die Beschwerde von Ababkov und Afanas'ev beim Ministerrat der UdSSR vom 28. Februar 1956 in GAMO f. R-146, op. 1, d. 61, l. 70 – 72. Im November 1957 ging eine erneute Beschwerde aus Magadan beim Ministerrat der RSFSR ein – *Gosplan* und das Finanzministerium der RSFSR würden die benötigten Finanzmittel nicht bereitstellen, so Afanas'ev. Vgl. GAMO f. R-146, op. 1, d. 61, l. 117.

Strecke (mit Zwischenstopps) 48 Stunden.[222] Im Vergleich zum Jahr 1953 verdoppelte sich der Transport von Passagieren 1955, der Lastentransport nahm um das 1,7fache zu. In Bezug auf die Anzahl abgefertigter Passagiere nahm Magadan zu dieser Zeit in der gesamten Sowjetunion den fünften Rang ein, damals wurden von und nach Magadan jedes Jahr etwa 63.000 Personen per Flugzeug transportiert.[223]

Ende der 1950er Jahre entstanden neue Flugrouten, die Magadan auch mit Siedlungen im äußersten Nordosten verbanden.[224] Flüge von und nach Moskau nutzten jetzt die Strecke über den Norden, so dass die Flugzeit auf 14,5 Stunden verkürzt und auch eine Verbindung Moskau–Anadyr' eingerichtet werden konnte.[225] Vollständig etablierte sich das Flugzeug als Verkehrsmittel jedoch erst in den 1960er Jahren, im Zuge einer deutlichen allgemeinen Steigerung des Flugverkehrs in der gesamten Sowjetunion.[226]

3.2.4 Institutionen

Die Gebietsgründung bewirkte formal die Trennung der bisher durch den Sonderstatus verbundenen Machtfelder von Politik und Wirtschaft. Die politische Leitung übernahmen die Organe von Partei- und Sowjetstrukturen, das Kombinat wurde auf die Wirtschaftslenkung beschränkt. Faktisch unterstanden jedoch auch im Frühjahr 1954 noch immer alle wesentlichen Institutionen und Infrastrukturen dem Kombinat Dal'stroj.

Die militärische Sonderstellung des Kombinats hatte auch in institutioneller Hinsicht zu einer fast vollständigen Abkapselung geführt – der Einzelleiter von Dal'stroj herrschte mit militärischer Befehlsgewalt über sämtliche Angelegenheiten der freien Bevölkerung, keine andere Organisation hatte das Recht, sich in die Belange des Kombinats einzumischen.[227] Nach der Gebietsgründung stand die neue Leitung nun also vor der seltsamen Situation, dass sie zwar in Person den neuen Herrschaftsraum besetzt hielt, die wichtigsten politischen Institutionen jedoch noch im-

---

222 Vgl. Aviacii Severo-Vostoka, S. 43.

223 Vgl. einen Bericht von Ababkov an das Büro des ZK der KPdSU für die RSFSR in RGANI f. 5, op. 32, d. 61, l. 144.

224 Vgl. Aviacii Severo-Vostoka, S. 44. Zum Anstieg der Transportzahlen zwischen 1956 und 1959 siehe ebd., S. 46.

225 Vgl. Aviacii Severo-Vostoka, S. 46.

226 1958 wurde beschlossen, den bisher kurz vor der Stadt Magadan befindlichen Flughafen auf ein größeres Gebiet 56 km vor Magadan zu verlegen; 1963 erfolgte dessen Einweihung. Die neue Lage des Flughafens ermöglichte durch eine entsprechende Landebahn die Landung von Flugzeugen bei Nacht und bei schwierigeren Wetterverhältnissen. Vgl. den Beschluss des Gebietsexekutivkomitees zu der Erschließung des Gebietes am 28. November 1958 in GAMO f. R-146, op. 1, d. 138, l. 202, veröffentlicht in: Archivnyj Otdel, Kalendar' 2003, S. 57. Dieser Beschluss basierte auf einer entsprechenden Verordnung des Ministerrates der UdSSR vom 26. Mai 1958.

227 So die Formulierung in dem Erlass zur Gründung von Dal'stroj im November 1931.

mer Dal'stroj untergeordnet waren. Es gab beispielsweise eine Kulturabteilung des Gebietsexekutivkomitees, aber sämtliche Kinos gehörten noch immer zu dem Kombinat.

Die institutionelle Durchdringung der Herrschaftsstrukturen zielte somit darauf ab, dem Kombinat alle „wesensfremden" Aufgaben zu entziehen, es tatsächlich auf die Rolle eines Wirtschaftskombinats zu begrenzen und diese Aufgaben den entsprechenden unionsweiten Organisationen und Ministerien des zivilen sowjetischen Sektors zuzuweisen.

Kern dieses Prozesses waren weitreichende Verordnungen, die am 29. Mai und am 8. Juni 1954 vom Ministerrat der UdSSR (und davon abhängig auch vom Ministerrat der RSFSR) erlassen wurden. In ihnen wurden die neuen Zuständigkeiten der bisherigen Dal'strojer Einrichtungen festgeschrieben. Ministerien und andere sowjetische Organisationen übernahmen die lokalen Institutionen und gründeten ihre Vertretungen in dem Gebiet. Wie bereits beschrieben, gelangten die Anlagen für Fernmeldetechnik und Radio in das Ministerium für Post- und Fernmeldewesen der UdSSR, Teile der Flotte wurden dem Ministerium für Meer- und Flussschifffahrt, sämtliche Straßen und Automobile dem Ministerium für Autowirtschaft der RSFSR unterstellt. Die zivile Luftflotte der UdSSR übernahm die Flugplätze und Flugzeuge von Dal'stroj. Alle Einrichtungen der Kommunalwirtschaft, also die Wasserversorgung der einzelnen Siedlungen, die Badehäuser und eine eventuell bestehende Kanalisation, wurden dem Ministerium für Kommunalwirtschaft zugeordnet, das seinerseits das Gebietsexekutivkomitee bzw. die einzelnen Bezirksexekutivkomitees mit ihrer Leitung beauftragte. Sämtliche Gesundheitseinrichtungen in dem Gebiet wurden dem Ministerium für Gesundheitswesen der RSFSR übertragen. Die bestehenden 104 Gebäude der Grundschulen und die 20 Internate gelangten in die Zuständigkeit des Ministeriums für Volksbildung, Kultureinrichtungen in die Verantwortung des Ministeriums für Kultur der UdSSR bzw. des Ministeriums für Kultur der RSFSR. Die Sovchosen der Region wurden in das Ministerium für Sovchosen der UdSSR eingegliedert usw.[228]

Auf dem Papier unterstanden nun die bisher von einem Lager-Industriellen Komplex beherrschten Institutionen zivilen Ministerien.[229] Dies war ein Prozess von ungeheurem bürokratischen Ausmaß, sowohl die tatsächlichen Übergaben, als auch ihre Vorbereitung. Auf Anordnung des Ministerrates der UdSSR waren an der Erarbeitung der Vorschläge Gebietspartei- und Gebietsexekutivkomitee, das MMP, Dal'stroj, die Behörde *Gosplan* und der Ministerrat der RSFSR beteiligt.[230] Hinzu kamen

---

228 Siehe die Liste aller Übergaben in den Anhängen zur Verordnung in RGAÈ f. 9163, op. 6, d. 13, l. 81–101.

229 Diese Regelung erstreckte sich auf den gesamten Tätigkeitsbereich von Dal'stroj, sie galt ausdrücklich auch für alle bisherigen Dal'stroj-Einrichtungen, die sich in Jakutien befanden. Vgl. RGAÈ f. 9163, op. 6, d. 13, l. 36.

230 Diese Anordnung geht zurück auf die Verordnung des Ministerrates der UdSSR vom 17. Dezember 1953.

diverse Kommissionen der einzelnen Ministerien, die Anschluss an die Strukturen in dem Gebiet erhalten sollten.

Abordnungen der Ministerien, des Ministerrates der RSFSR und von *Gosplan* reisten nach Magadan und diskutierten mit den lokalen Vertretern, welche Einrichtungen, Organisationen und Infrastrukturen von Dal'stroj in welche Ministerien integriert und wie diese Einrichtungen zukünftig unterstützt und ausgebaut werden könnten. Anhand der Korrespondenz zwischen dem ZK der KPdSU und *Gosplan* lässt sich erkennen, dass *Gosplan* in dieser Phase die wichtigsten Entscheidungen über einzelne Zuständigkeitsverschiebungen traf.[231] In Magadan war Afanas'ev in seiner Rolle als Leiter der neuen zivilen Verwaltung für die Ministerien der wichtigste Ansprechpartner.[232]

Dieses lokale Engagement des zentralen staatlichen Apparates muss dabei in den unionsweiten Kontext einer wachsenden Bedeutung der Ministerien in den wichtigsten Endtscheidungsprozessen seit Stalins Tod und bis zu ihrer Ablösung durch die lokalen Volkswirtschaftsräte im Jahr 1957 gesetzt werden.[233] Es war ein ambitionierter Ministerialapparat, der in der industriell so bedeutsamen Region um Einfluss, aber auch um seine Mittel kämpfte. Die Diskussionen waren ausgesprochen kontrovers, kam es doch für alle Seiten darauf an, die jeweiligen Belastungen so gering wie möglich zu halten. Das MCM mühte sich, die künftigen Anforderungen an Dal'stroj zu minimieren. Es befürchtete, dass das Kombinat zu sehr von Bauaufträgen für die neu in der Region tätigen Ministerien und Einrichtungen belastet werden könnte. Zugleich forderte es einen weitgehenden Verbleib von Infrastruktur im Kombinat, um die Wirtschaftstätigkeiten nicht zu behindern.[234]

Der Leiter von Dal'stroj, Mitrakov, verfolgte in den Verhandlungen auch ganz private Interessen. So befürchtete er den Verlust „seines Theaters", des Magadaner Theaters, das bisher über das Dal'strojer Kontor für Filmverleih finanziert worden war und das nun dem Kulturministerium unterstellt werden sollte.[235] Ganz in der Tradition der bisherigen Leiter von Dal'stroj hatte sich Mitrakov das Theater als seine „halb

---

231 Vgl. RGANI f. 5, op. 15, d. 489, l. 159. Vgl. zu den entsprechenden Kommissionen auf Seiten des Gebietspartei- und Gebietsexekutivkomitees, Chronika partijnoj organizacii, S. 135.

232 Vgl. die Anmerkungen des Ministers für Buntmetalle, Lomako, gegenüber dem stellv. Vorsitzenden des Ministerrates der UdSSR, Kosygin, zu den Vorschlägen der Verordnung in RGAÈ f. 9163, op. 6, d. 13, l. 34–42. Siehe als Beispiel für die Vorbereitungen der Verordnung die Vorschläge und Absprachen mit der Hauptverwaltung für zivile Luftfahrt „Aèroflot" in GAMO f. R-146, op. 1, d. 6, l. 209–210 sowie d. 61, l. 15–16.

233 Zu der wachsenden Bedeutung der Ministerien in dieser Zeit siehe Gorlizki, Anti Ministerialism, S. 1291; Conyngham, Industrial Management, S. 103.

234 Vgl. die Anmerkungen des Ministeriums in RGAÈ f. 9163, op. 6, d. 13, l. 39. In einigen Punkten wurde den Bitten des Ministeriums stattgegeben, andere zukünftige Verpflichtungen des Kombinats jedoch festgeschrieben. Beispielsweise hatte sich das MCM gegen die Übergabe der Häfen an das Ministerium für Meer- und Flussflotte gewandt. Vgl. RGAÈ f. 9163, op. 6, d. 13, l. 40–41.

235 Vgl. das Telegramm von Mitrakov an das MCM vom 27. März 1954 sowie der Schriftverkehr zwischen dem MCM und dem Kulturministerium in RGAÈ f. 9163, op. 6, d. 16, l. 4–6.

private" Vergnügungsstätte ausgebaut.[236] Diese Tradition endete nun; Afanas'ev sprach sich in den Debatten für eine zukünftige Finanzierung des Theaters über das Budget des Gebietes aus, damit blieb Mitrakov jeder weitere Einfluss verwehrt.

Zugleich aber ging es bei diesen Umstrukturierungen nicht nur um das Dal'strojer Tafelsilber. Mit einem Schlag befreite sich das Kombinat damit auch von der Verantwortung für eine ganze Reihe kommunaler Aufgaben. Daher waren die diversen Ministerien darum bemüht, das Kombinat zu konkreten Maßnahmen, v. a. zu Bautätigkeiten, verpflichten zu lassen; zudem regelten die Verordnungen Pflichten und Verantwortlichkeiten zwischen dem Gebietsexekutivkomitee, dem MCM und Dal'stroj.

Die tatsächlichen Übergaben erfolgten nach ausgeklügelten Verfahren. Sämtliche existierende Einrichtungen, alles Inventar, jedes Krankenbett, jede kleinste Schulbaracke und jede halbverfallene Garage musste ebenso wie das gesamte Personal dokumentiert und zu einem bestimmten Stichtag in die Bilanz des jeweiligen Ministeriums übertragen werden. Zum Teil mussten dabei neue Verwaltungseinheiten mit eigenem Personal gegründet bzw. bestehende reorganisiert werden.[237] Die Details und konkreten Fragen wurden in speziellen Kommissionen zwischen den jeweiligen Vertretern von Dal'stroj und den Sowjetorganen diskutiert.[238]

Der Übergabeprozess war von zahlreichen Verzögerungen und Unklarheiten geprägt. Gebäude wurden auf dem Papier übertragen, die gar nicht existierten[239], andere Einrichtungen wurden ohne ausreichende Absprachen übergeben. So gelangten z. B. alle Autostraßen Magadans in die Zuständigkeit des städtischen Exekutivkomitees, obwohl mehr als zwei Drittel dieser Straßen von Dal'stroj genutzt wurden. Die unter den klimatischen Bedingungen so wichtige Reinigung und Instandhaltung dieser

---

236 Das Theater spielte für die gesamte Führungsschicht von Dal'stroj eine große Rolle, da das Ensemble immer wieder mit Gastspielen die einzelnen Wirtschaftszonen besuchte. Zu der Bedeutung des Magadaner Theaters und seiner vielen berühmten Schauspieler-, Künstler- und Musiker-Häftlinge siehe Klause, Klang des Gulag sowie die Erinnerungen des Schauspielers Nikolaj Čekarev, in Vremja, Sobytija, Ljudi 1989, H. 16, S. 132–142 sowie Conquest, Kolyma, S. 69.

237 Vgl. die Übergabelisten und die neuen Personalangaben für kommunale Einrichtungen im Magadaner Gebiet in GAMO f. R-146, op. 1, d. 50, l. 28–34.

238 Vgl. beispielsweise die strenge Rüge des Gebietsexekutivkomitees an den Vorsitzenden des Bezirks Ol'skij vom August 1954, die unzureichende Übergabe der lokalen Industrie betreffend in GAMO f. R-146, op. 1, d. 60, l. 5–6. Siehe ebenso die Beschwerde von Dal'stroj gegenüber Afanas'ev vom 9. November 1954 in GAMO f. R-146, op. 1, d. 45, l. 111.

239 Beispielsweise hatte der Ministerrat der UdSSR befohlen, in Magadan ein Autokontor einzurichten. Das Ministerium für Autoverkehr hatte dem Gebiet die geforderte Zahl an LKWs, Taxen und Lastentaxen bereitgestellt (insgesamt 70). Die Autos drohten nun jedoch unter freiem Himmel zu verrosten, weil sich die angebliche Autostation von Dal'stroj, die an das Ministerium übergeben worden war und die das neue Kontor beherbergen sollte, als eine kleine, vollkommen verfallene Autowerkstatt entpuppt hatte. Vgl. den Brief des stellv. Ministers für Autotransport und Chausseestraßen der RSFSR, Savčenkov, an Afanas'ev vom 30. September 1954 in GAMO f. R-146, op. 1, d. 61, l. 46–47.

Straßen wurde nun von beiden Seiten verweigert, was den gesamten Straßenverkehr im Zentrum des Gebietes eine Zeitlang schwer belastete.[240]

Die Aufnahme ehemaliger Dal'stroer Institutionen im zivilen Sektor der Sowjetunion wurde in der Verordnung des Ministerrates der UdSSR nur als erster Schritt, als Voraussetzung weiterer Maßnahmen verstanden. An die Angleichung der institutionellen Verhältnisse sollte sich auch eine *materielle* Angleichung der einzelnen Organisationen anschließen. Wenn z. B. alle Krankenhäuser des Magadaner Gebietes dem Gesundheitsministerium der RSFSR unterstanden, dann sollten auch die Zustände in diesen Krankenhäusern dem festgesetzten Niveau aller Krankenhäuser des Gesundheitsministeriums entsprechen – so die Logik der Verordnungen. Auf diese Weise wurde die Aufgabe der militärischen Herrschaftsform unmittelbar an die Proklamation einer Verbesserung der Verhältnisse geknüpft. Alle an dem Prozess beteiligten Ministerien und Organisationen wurden auf umfangreiche Investitionen in dem Gebiet verpflichtet.

Vom Anspruch dieses Aufbauprogramms zeugen die Titel der Verordnungen des Ministerrates der UdSSR „Über Maßnahmen zur Unterstützung des Magadaner Gebietes beim wirtschaftlichen, kulturell-lebenspraktischen und wohnungsbaumäßigen Aufbau" (vom 29. Mai 1954) sowie „Über Maßnahmen zur Unterstützung der Entwicklung der Landwirtschaft im Magadaner Gebiet" (vom 8. Juni 1954).[241]

Ein solches Maßnahmenpaket erforderte im Vorfeld zunächst eine Analyse der konkreten Lage und eine Bestandsaufnahme der vorhandenen Einrichtungen, wenn man nicht allein auf Beschreibungen von Dal'stroj angewiesen sein wollte.[242] Im Verlauf dieser Arbeit ergab sich ein beständig steigender Mehrbedarf. Afanas'ev schilderte dem Ministerrat der RSFSR, wie auf allen möglichen Gebieten erheblicher Mangel entdeckt wurde, gerade auch in Bereichen, von denen bislang nicht die Rede gewesen sei. So z. B. im bereits existierenden Heimatmuseum, das auf den Standard eines Gebiets-Museums angehoben werden müsste, auch sollten Bibliotheken in den einzelnen Bezirken gegründet werden. Die Gesundheitseinrichtungen bedürften, in noch größerem Maße als veranschlagt, eines Ausbaus. Den dokumentierten Bedarf wollte Afanas'ev nicht nur in die Verordnungen des Ministerrates einfließen lassen, er

---

240 Vgl. das Schreiben von Afanas'ev an den Ministerrat der RSFSR vom 16. März 1955 in GAMO f. R-146, op. 1, d. 50, l. 66 f.

241 Hinzu kamen weitere Verordnungen des Ministerrates der RSFSR, die dazu dienten, die Einhaltung der Verordnungen des Ministerrates der UdSSR zu überwachen.

242 Vgl. beispielsweise die Liste von Dal'stroj vom März 1954 für den Bereich Gesundheitswesen, der alle einzelnen medizinischen Einrichtungen bis zur jeweiligen Bettenzahl auflistete in RGAÈ f. 9163, op. 6, d. 16, l. 9 – 19. Und schließlich enthalten die zahlreichen Anlagen zu den Verordnungen des Ministerrates von UdSSR und RSFSR die genaue Auflistung der einzelnen Betriebe und Einrichtungen, die im Einzelnen an die Organisationen übergeben wurden. Vgl. die Anlagen in GAMO f. R-146, op. 1, d. 6, l. 52 – 53 (Ministerium für die Lebensmittelproduktion), l. 54 – 55 (Ministerium für lokale Industrie und Brennstoffe). Einen Überblick über sämtliche Anlagen liefern die Inhaltsverzeichnisse zu den Verordnungen l. 108 – 109 sowie l. 151 – 152.

forderte vielmehr auch eine Erhöhung des Budgets des Gebietes um weitere 50 Mio. und den personellen Ausbau der Verwaltung des Gebietsexekutivkomitees.[243]

Die Vorschläge, die Ababkov und Afanas'ev dem Vorsitzenden des Ministerrates der UdSSR, Malenkov, und dem Ersten Sekretär des ZK, Chruščev, für das Aufbauprogramm vorlegten, sahen u. a. in den ersten beiden Jahren für den Wohnungsbau 300 Mio., für die soziale Infrastruktur (den Bau von Schulen, Krankenhäusern und Kindertagesstätten) etwa 100 Mio., für die Förderung der lokalen Landwirtschaft 200 Mio. und für den lokalen Handel 70 Mio. Rubel an Investitionen vor.[244]

Neben taktischen Überlegungen zur Generierung zusätzlicher Gelder für die Region belegt der Briefverkehr zwischen Magadan und Moskau und die ausführliche Dokumentation der vorhandenen Institutionen auch das Ausmaß des Mangels. Eine soziale Infrastruktur existierte offenbar so gut wie gar nicht. Die vorhandenen Einrichtungen waren zahlenmäßig viel zu gering, nicht über das gesamte Gebiet verteilt und in einem erbärmlichen Zustand. Anschaulich verdeutlicht dies ein Schreiben, das Ababkov und Afanas'ev als Einleitung ihrer Vorschläge zu den Verordnungen an Malenkov und Chruščev sandten. Darin heißt es:

> Seit der Organisation von Dal'stroj war das Hauptaugenmerk auf die Entwicklung des Bergbaus und der rohstoffverarbeitenden Industrie ausgerichtet. In der gleichen Zeit wurde dem Bau von Einrichtungen für Kultur und Alltag der Menschen nicht die nötige Aufmerksamkeit geschenkt. [...] Mehr als 12.000 Menschen leben in halb gebauten, gerüstartigen Häusern, die kurz vor dem Einsturz stehen und die 1954 abgerissen werden sollen. 7.000 Menschen haben überhaupt keinen Wohnraum. Eine große Zahl von Arbeitern, Fachkräften und Angestellten, die nach Magadan kommen, leben mehrere Monate in sogenannten ‚Transitgebäuden‘, in Baracken aus Moosplatten, die in keiner Weise zum Leben geeignet sind. [...] Die Zahl der Schulkinder stieg zwischen 1940 und 1953 um das Siebenfache, die Zahl der Schulen hingegen nur um das 3,5fache. [...] Die meisten Schulen und Internate verfügen über keine festen Gebäude, sondern sind in Baracken untergebracht. Das Fehlen höherer Schulen verhindert eine dauerhafte Bindung von Kadern an die Region; sie verlassen des Gebiet, sobald ihre Kinder die Mittelschule beendet haben. In der Region herrscht ein gewaltiger Mangel an Kinderbetreuungseinrichtungen, weswegen etwa 1.000 Mütter nicht arbeiten gehen können. [...] Vollkommen unzureichend ist die Gesundheitsversorgung. Die Krankenhäuser sind überfüllt, es mangelt an medizinischem Personal. Unter den Indigenen sind Tuberkulose und Geschlechtskrankheiten immer noch weit verbreitet. [...] Von 166 Arbeitersiedlungen haben nur 14 eine Wasserversorgung. [...] Die Bevölkerung von Tschukotka leidet großen Mangel an Lebensmitteln und Verbrauchsgütern. So wird zum Beispiel Mehl aus den Jahren 1930 bis 1932 angeboten und Öl von 1934; aufgrund fehlender Lagerräume sind diese Lebensmittel verdorben. [...] Wegen der schlechten Lebensbedingungen wollen viele Arbeiter, die einen Vertrag mit Dal'stroj abgeschlossen haben oder aus den Lagern entlassen wurden, nicht dauerhaft in dem Gebiet bleiben. Jedes Jahr verlassen daher etwa 20.000 Menschen die Region; gleichzeitig müssen für die Zufuhr von Kadern jedes Jahr etwa 75 Mio. Rubel ausgegeben werden.[245]

---

243 So sollte zusätzlich eine Abteilung für soziale Fürsorge geschaffen werden. Vgl. das ausführliche Schreiben von Afanas'ev an den Ministerrat der RSFSR zu der gewünschten Budget-Erhöhung vom 26. April 1954 in GAMO f. R-146, op. 1, d. 6, l. 153–162.

244 Vgl. RGANI f. 5, op. 15, d. 489, l. 22.

245 RGANI f. 5, op. 15, d. 489, l. 19–22.

Die Verordnungen selbst griffen eine Vielzahl der lokalen Vorschläge auf und verpflichteten die betreffenden Ministerien, Dal'stroj und das Gebietsexekutivkomitee auf eine ganze Reihe von Maßnahmen zugunsten der freien Bevölkerung: Beschlossen wurde die Verbesserung der Versorgung mit Lebensmitteln und Waren des täglichen Bedarfs, der Bau neuer Gesundheitseinrichtungen in den einzelnen Bezirken und einer Klinik mit Spezialabteilungen in Magadan, die Gründung neuer Schulen, Internate und höherer Bildungseinrichtungen, der Aufbau eines lokalen Verlages, einer Druckerei sowie weiterer kultureller Einrichtungen in den einzelnen Bezirken.[246] Knapp 400 Fachkräfte sollten den erhöhten Personalbedarf in dem Gebiet decken, die entsprechenden Ministerien wurden zur Versetzung von Lehrern, Ärzten, Pflegekräften, Technikern und Agronomen verpflichtet.[247]

Für den geplanten Ausbau des privaten Wohnraums waren verschiedene Maßnahmen, wie die Gründung einer Bauorganisation für zivilen Wohnungsbau und die Vergabe günstiger Kredite für den privaten Hausbau, vorgesehen. Festgesetzt wurden außerdem umfangreiche Maßnahmen zum Ausbau kommunaler Infrastruktur, die Einrichtung von Kanalisationen, zentralen Heizsystemen und Wasserleitungen in den Zentren der Bezirke. Die Hauptstadt Magadan sollte auf der Grundlage eines Generalplans neu strukturiert und konzipiert werden.[248]

Ein Großteil der Maßnahmen war mit Bauarbeiten verbunden. Trotz zahlreicher Proteste von Mitrakov wurde damit fast ausnahmslos Dal'stroj beauftragt. In Ermangelung weiterer regionaler Organisationen verpflichtete man das Kombinat, zusätzlich zu seinen eigentlichen wirtschaftlichen Aufgaben, auf Baumaßnahmen von über 494 Mio. Rubel.[249]

Die Frage, was von all diesen Maßnahmen tatsächlich umgesetzt wurde, lässt sich nur im Einzelfall genau beantworten. Sicher ist, dass durch die Sonderzahlungen an

---

246 Eine Stärkung der lokalen Landwirtschaft war das Ziel der Verordnung des Ministerrats der UdSSR vom 8. Juni 1954: Die wichtigsten Maßnahmen betrafen die Einführung eines einheitlichen Bodenbewirtschaftungssystems, die Gründung von drei Maschinen-Traktoren-Stationen und einer landwirtschaftlichen Basisstation für Technik zur stärkeren Mechanisierung der bisherigen Handarbeit, die Gründung einer Landwirtschaftsschule, die Anwerbung von Fachkräften u. a. Vgl. das Schreiben von Ababkov und Afanas'ev an Malenkov und Chruščev vom 3. Mai 1954 in GAMO f. R-146, op. 1, d. 6, l. 14–19 sowie der von ihnen erarbeitete Entwurf einer Verordnung des Ministerrates der UdSSR in GAMO f. R-146, op. 1, d. 6, l. 9–12. Siehe auch den ausführliche Entwurf einer Verordnung des Ministerrates der RSFSR, in der die einzelnen Ziele und Aufgaben sehr detailliert weitergegeben werden. GAMO f. R-146, op. 1, d. 6, l. 110–122.
247 Vgl. die Auflistung über alle zu entsendenden Facharbeiter in GAMO f. R-146, op. 1, d. 6, l. 148–149.
248 Vgl. die Darstellung des Plans in der lokalen Presse. Magadanskaja Pravda, 21. April 1957, S. 2.
249 Vgl. die Anlage zu der Verordnung des Ministerrates der UdSSR, die eine Auflistung aller von Dal'stroj geforderten Baumaßnahmen (in den Jahren 1954 bis 1956) für das Ministerium für Kommunalwirtschaft, das Kulturministerium, das Ministerium für Autostraßen, für Gesundheitswesen der RSFSR, für Landwirtschaft, Finanzen, Handel etc. enthält, in RGAĖ f. 9163, op. 6, d. 13, l. 74–80. Die Bautätigkeiten wurden entweder von den beauftragenden Ministerien bezahlt oder aus einem Sondertopf von 100 Mio. Rubel für Baumaßnahmen von Dal'stroj gedeckt. Vgl. die Liste der Sonderzahlungen in RGAĖ f. 9163, op. 6, d. 13, l. 103.

die Bauorganisationen von Dal'stroj und durch das Finanzministerium erhebliche Gelder in die Region flossen.[250] Im November 1955 überprüfte die Abteilung für Parteiorgane des ZK der KPdSU die Ausführung der Verordnungen der Ministerräte der UdSSR und RSFSR und musste feststellen, dass viele Maßnahmen von den beteiligten Ministerien nur zum Teil oder noch gar nicht umgesetzt worden waren. Zwischen dem ZK, dem Gebietsexekutivkomitee, Dal'stroj und den entsprechenden Ministerien setzte daraufhin ein reger Schriftverkehr ein, in dem sich die beteiligten Seiten gegenüber dem ZK wechselseitig die Verantwortung für die Mängel zuwiesen. Als Ursache wurden fehlende Gelder und unzureichendes Baumaterial genannt, die Ministerien wären hingegen gegenüber den Baubetrieben zu nachlässig gewesen und hätten Fristen ohne Benachrichtigung der Regierung einfach verlängert.[251]

Ein genauer Blick auf die einzelnen Wirtschaftsabteilungen des Gebietes und die Lebensbedingungen der freien Bevölkerung wird zeigen, dass trotz punktueller Verbesserungen die Auswirkungen der Investitionen erst Ende der 1950er und zu Beginn der 1960er Jahre zu spüren waren. Afanas'ev und Ababkov bemühten sich gegenüber *Gosplan* und dem ZK der KPdSU auch nach dem Erlass der Verordnungen beständig um zusätzliche Finanzspritzen für die Region, um den wachsenden Bedarf zu decken.[252]

Die Bedeutung der Verordnung für den Aufbau des Magadaner Gebietes liegt in ihrer Programmatik. Sie verbindet die Überführung der Magadaner Sonderinstitutionen in den zivilen Sektor der Sowjetunion mit einem großen Aufbauprogramm. Auf diese Weise wird die weitere Entwicklung der Region an die Politik unionsweiter ziviler Ministerien und Einrichtungen gebunden.

Die weitreichenden Verordnungen zur Unterstützung des Magadaner Gebietes hatte der Ministerrat der UdSSR bereits unmittelbar nach der Gebietsgründung im Dezember 1953 angestrengt.[253] Von Anfang an sah die oberste Staatsführung dabei auch für das Kombinat eine neue Rolle vor. Dem Ministerrat kam es nicht nur darauf an, den Sonderstatus von Dal'stroj durch institutionelle Zuordnungen aufzuheben, vielmehr betrachtete er auch eine gewisse Neuorientierung des Kombinats als notwendig. Der Ministerrat forderte das MCM dazu auf, Dal'stroj zu einem anderen Verhältnis zu seinen freien Arbeitskräften zu zwingen. Und dies nicht nur durch konkrete Baumaßnahmen, sondern auch programmatisch, indem das Ministerium verlangte, neben der weiteren Entwicklung der eigentlichen Produktion die Verbesserung der

250 Vgl. Grebenjuk, Kolymskij led, S. 104 f.

251 Vgl. den Bericht des stellv. Leiters der Abteilung für Parteiorgane des Büros des ZK der KPdSU für die RSFSR in RGANI f. 5, op. 32, d. 19, l. 2. Für den Schriftverkehr zu den Mängellisten siehe ebd. l. 14, l. 33, l. 43 l. 57 f., l. 76 – 86 sowie l. 113 – 120. Auf l. 92 – 96 findet sich ein ausführlicher Überblick über die einzelnen Aufgaben der Ministerien und zum Stand ihrer Ausführung.

252 Vgl. den Schriftverkehr zwischen *Gosplan* und dem ZK der KPdSU, in dem die weitergehenden Forderungen aus Magadan diskutiert wurden. Vgl. RGANI f. 5, op. 15, d. 489, l. 160 – 162.

253 Vgl. die Verordnung „Über Maßnahmen in Verbindung mit Gründung des Magadaner Gebietes in der RSFSR" (Nr. 2956) vom 17. Dezember 1953 in GAMO f. R-23, op. 1, d. 6088, l. 59 – 60.

Lebensbedingungen der Arbeitskräfte zu einem Hauptziel des Kombinats zu erheben. Künftig sei es nicht mehr zulässig, Produktionsanlagen zu errichten, ohne für „normale Bedingungen für das Leben und die Arbeit der Werktätigen des Magadaner Gebietes" zu sorgen. Nur so lasse sich die Fluktuation der Arbeitskräfte begrenzen, so der Ministerrat der UdSSR.[254] Auch gegenüber dem nordöstlichen Naturraum wurde das Kombinat zu einer anderen Haltung aufgefordert. Dal'stroj sollte seine Holzbeschaffung in angemessener Weise regeln, an bestimmten Stellen sollte der „Raubbau an den Wäldern" ganz verboten werden.[255]

Damit formulierte der Ministerrat in zwei wichtigen Punkten Aufgaben des Kombinats, hinter denen sich unübersehbar eine Abschwächung der bisher unbegrenzten Verfügungsgewalt des Kombinats und seines hemmungslosen Utilitarismus verbarg. Damit wurde Dal'stroj zu einer Einrichtung, die dem Staat in absoluter Geheimhaltung wertvollste Rohstoffe liefern sollte, die aber zugleich auch für die Herbeischaffung von Kinderkleidung und den Bau von Schulen und Kanalisation verantwortlich gemacht wurde. Diese programmatische Neubestimmung war begleitet von einem massiven Machtverlust, der mit der Gebietsgründung einherging. Zumindest auf dem Papier hatte das Kombinat nicht einmal mehr die Verfügungsgewalt über die Einrichtungen und Institutionen, für die es Sorge tragen sollte.

Die Verordnung des Ministerrates schloss die erste Phase des Gebietsaufbaus ab. Im Juni 1954 herrschten Organe der Partei- und Sowjetstrukturen über ein Territorium, das der administrativen Gliederung der Sowjetunion entsprach. Siedlungen bildeten die Zentren von Bezirken, Verordnungen und Beschlüsse aus Magadan wurden gemäß den Hierarchien des zivilen Sektors an untergebene Organe bis zum Exekutivkomitee eines Dorfes weitergegeben. Zivile Staatsanwälte und Gerichte waren für die Rechtsetzung verantwortlich. Gebietspartei- und Gebietsexekutivkomitee waren nach oben in das Netz an Partei- und Sowjetstrukturen eingebunden, die in das ZK der KPdSU und den Ministerrat der UdSSR mündeten. Ministerien und weitere unionsweite Organisationen trugen, in Absprache mit dem Gebietsexekutivkomitee, die Verantwortung für lokale Einrichtungen sozialer, kommunaler, kultureller und versorgender Infrastruktur. Sie beauftragten das regionale Kombinat mit Bauarbeiten und der Bereitstellung von Energie.

---

254 Siehe den Entwurf der Verordnung des Ministerrates vom Mai 1954 in GAMO f. R-146, op. 1, f. 6, l. 33–51, hier l. 35.
255 Vgl. den Entwurf der Verordnung des Ministerrates vom Mai 1954 in GAMO f. R-146, op. 1, f. 6, l. 33–51, hier l. 36.

3.3 Machtkampf und die neue Machtverteilung

Der australische Historiker Graeme Gill hat in seiner Analyse der politischen Struktur des Stalinismus eine vollständige Unterordnung aller Lebensbereiche unter die politische Sphäre konstatiert:

> Stalinism constituted an historically new form of state: an organizationally integrated structure in which the economic, social, intellectual and cultural spheres of life were coopted into the political and rendered instrumental to the desires of the political elite.[256]

Der NKVD/MVD war zweifellos eine Einrichtung der „politischen Sphäre" der Sowjetunion, wie anders sollte man die tausendfache Verhaftung und Deportation von sogenannten „inneren Feinden" verstehen. Im Sinne Gills trat der NKVD/MVD an der Kolyma jedoch nicht als Vertreter dieser politischen Sphäre auf, sondern in Form seiner Hauptverwaltung Dal'stroj faktisch als reine Wirtschaftsbehörde, die Häftlinge ausschließlich als „billige Arbeitskräfte" wahrnahm und in der alles der erfolgreichen Goldförderung untergeordnet wurde. Hier gab es ebenfalls eine organisatorisch integrierte Struktur, die jedoch ganz auf die ökonomische Sphäre ausgerichtet war. Statt administrativer Gliederungen war die Landkarte der Region in verschiedene Wirtschaftsverwaltungen aufgeteilt, Institutionen und Infrastrukturen waren allein auf die Bedürfnisse der Produktion ausgerichtet, eine Einzelleitung regierte den Lager-Industriellen Komplex, der auch die Parteivertretung in der Region untergeordnet war.

Die Geschichte der nordöstlichen Region seit Gründung des Magadaner Gebietes kann als Herausbildung einer bislang nicht existenten politischen Sphäre interpretiert werden. Dabei ging es nicht nur um einen Kampf der Kader von Partei und Sowjet mit der Leitung von Dal'stroj um Macht und Einfluss, sondern um die grundlegende Entstehung eines eigenständigen Herrschaftsbereichs. Diese „politische Sphäre" musste erst einmal entworfen, Themen mussten besetzt werden. Mehr und mehr wurde durch Infrastrukturen und Institutionen ein Raum des Politischen abgesteckt, der reale Entscheidungs- und Kontrollkompetenzen erhielt.

Der neue Herrschaftsraum sollte jedoch nicht nur einfach die Kontrolle und den Zugriff des ZK der KPdSU in Moskau sichern. Seine Einrichtung war unmittelbar an die geforderte Erhöhung der Rohstoffförderung geknüpft, quasi über die Etablierung einer politischen Sphäre sollte eine Stabilisierung und weitreichende Stärkung der nordöstlichen Wirtschaft erreicht werden. Die politische Leitung schrieb sich dabei selbst eine objektivere Analyse der wirtschaftlichen Entwicklung und auch eine moralische Erneuerung der Führungsebene zu. Folgt man der Argumentation Gills, so wurde in der Entstalinisierung die Form des „state making" des Stalinismus an der Kolyma umgesetzt, der stalinistische Staatsaufbau sozusagen „nachgeholt".

---

256 Gill, Question of Reformability, S. 128 f. In Bezug auf die Wirtschaftsstrukturen im Stalinismus beschreibt dies auch Easter, Reconstructing, S. 61.

Wie aber ging das en détail vonstatten? Konnten Gebietspartei- und Gebietsexekutivkomitee die ihnen von außen verliehene Macht im Inneren des Gebietes tatsächlich umsetzen? Wie gestaltete sich die Abgrenzung von oder die Zusammenarbeit mit den bisherigen Herren der Region, und auf welche Instrumente stützten sich die neuen Akteure? Welches Bild entwarf die neue Leitung dabei von ihrer Herrschaft, wie repräsentierte sie sich? Die folgenden Kapitel beleuchten auf drei unterschiedliche Weisen die Herausbildung dieser politischen Sphäre – den Machtkampf zwischen Dal'stroj und den Kadern von Partei und Staat, die neue politische Leitung zwischen den Anforderungen des Moskauer Zentrums und den Bedingungen an der Peripherie, zwischen realer Lage und propagandistischer Repräsentation sowie die Grenzen der entstandenen politischen Sphäre.

3.3.1 Kompetenzen und Zuständigkeiten der neuen Organe

Die infrastrukturellen und institutionellen Schwierigkeiten des neuen Gebietes waren in administrativer Hinsicht die Probleme des neuen Gebietsexekutivkomitees. Seine Sitzungen waren v. a. Fragen des Alltags gewidmet; für die Teilnehmer an diesen Sitzungen ergab sich ein zunehmend differenzierteres Bild der Lage im Magadaner Gebiet.[257]

Im Gebietsexekutivkomitee lag die Verwaltungszuständigkeit für die vielen neuen Einrichtungen, für die Bereitstellung der notwendigen Strukturen. Dementsprechend entfalteten Afanas'ev und die Abteilungen seines Komitees von Anfang an eine ausgesprochen rege Aktivität: In Hunderten von Schreiben nahm Afanas'ev Kontakt zu Dutzenden beteiligten Ministerien, Organisationen und zum Ministerrat auf. In diesem Prozess geriet Afanas'ev immer wieder in Konflikt mit der Leitung von Dal'stroj. Hintergrund waren die bereits beschriebenen Kompetenzüberschneidungen, v. a. beim infrastrukturellen und institutionellen Aufbau, da sich seit 1954 viele Arbeitsbereiche überlagerten bzw. da eine große Zahl bisheriger Kombinatseinrichtungen in die Zuständigkeit von Afanas'evs Gebietsexekutivkomitee fiel. Zwischen Kombinatsleitung und Gebietsexekutivkomitee wurde zäh um konkrete Einflussbereiche, um einzelne Gebäude und um Gelder gerungen. Dies galt auch für die Vertreter beider Seiten auf der Ebene der Bezirke.

In der Aufbauphase des Magadaner Gebietes kam dem Gebietsexekutivkomitee eine im Rahmen der üblichen Machtverteilung zwischen Partei- und Sowjetorganen ungewöhnlich starke Stellung zu. Hier kann nicht nur davon gesprochen werden, dass die lokale Parteivertretung gewissermaßen durch das Gebietsexekutivkomitee wirkte, wie es Jerry Hough und Merle Fainsod als allgemeine Vorgehensweise regionaler

---

257 Vgl. die Protokolle der Sitzungen der Exekutivkomitees seit dem 19. Januar 1954 in GAMO f. R-146, op. 1, d. 8.

Parteiführung beschreiben.[258] Afanas'ev trat immer wieder selbstständig, mit eigenen Vorschlägen und Ansprüchen auf oder nahm, über die Gliederungen des Gebietsexekutivkomitees, eine vermittelnde Position zwischen verschiedenen Institutionen und der Kombinatsleitung ein.

Die Verwaltungsgliederung des Gebietsexekutivkomitees, seine Personalstärke und auch das wachsende Budget haben in den ersten Jahren diese Position sicherlich begünstigt. Die Vertrautheit Afanas'evs mit der Region, seine langjährige Erfahrung im Fernen Osten und vielleicht auch seine Persönlichkeit – Zeitgenossen beschrieben ihn als energievoll und machtbewusst[259] – haben wohl zur Stärkung seiner Position beigetragen. Seit Mitte der 1950er Jahre kam die von Chruščev betriebene unionsweite Aufwertung der jeweiligen Gebietsexekutivkomitees in ökonomischen und kulturellen Fragen hinzu und stärkte Afanas'ev den Rücken.[260]

Die Aufgaben des Gebietsparteikomitees waren nicht auf die grundsätzliche Verwaltung und den institutionellen Aufbau ausgerichtet, die lokale Parteileitung wirkte entsprechend ihrer Position im sowjetischen Herrschaftssystem auf einer höheren Ebene. Sie war seit 1954 nominell der wichtigste Machtfaktor in der Region, Ababkov die formal mächtigste Person im Magadaner Gebiet.[261] Einem Ersten Parteisekretär und seinem Büro oblag in der Sowjetunion grundsätzlich die gesamte Kaderauswahl, die Führung aller Funktionäre in der Region, die Ernennung der regionalen Staatsanwälte, der Leiter von Schulen, Fabriken, Krankenhäusern etc. Der Erste Sekretär war persönlich für alle wesentlichen politischen und wirtschaftlichen Entscheidungen in der Region verantwortlich, er koordinierte große Infrastrukturmaßnahmen und Bauprojekte, überwachte die industrielle Entwicklung und die Planerfüllung der wichtigsten lokalen Betriebe, kontrollierte die soziale Lage der freien Bevölkerung ebenso wie Stimmungen und Tendenzen unter den Bewohnern des Gebietes – dazu war ihm die lokale Verwaltung des MVD unterstellt.[262]

Von ihrer Stellung im sowjetischen System der Chruščev-Periode aus betrachtet, gab es für eine lokale Parteileitung eigentlich keinen Bereich öffentlichen oder privaten Lebens, der nicht durch sie kontrolliert, überwacht und beherrscht werden konnte.[263] Bei seinem Blick auf die Beherrschung der lokalen Wirtschaftspolitik in der Sowjetunion hat László Csaba die lokale Parteileitung treffend als „Herr im Hause"

---

258 Vgl. Hough; Fainsod, Soviet Union is Governed, S. 501.

259 Vgl die Beurteilungen Afanas'evs, zusammengestellt bei Grebenjuk, Kolymskij led, S. 168 f. sowie in der biographischen Beschreibung Sergeev, Pervyj predsedatel'.

260 Vgl. zu der Stärkung der Sowjets unter Chruščev Gill, Symbols, S. 182.

261 Vgl. Hough; Fainsod, Soviet Union is Governed, S. 497.

262 Vgl. die Aufgabenbeschreibung und regionale Machtverteilung bei Hough; Fainsod, Soviet Union is Governed, S. 501 f.

263 Zur Stärkung der Bedeutung regionaler Parteifunktionäre unter Chruščev siehe Thatcher, Khrushchev, S. 16 f. Zur wachsenden Bedeutung von Parteikonferenzen und Parteitagen siehe Hildermeier, Sowjetunion, S. 773–775.

bezeichnet.[264] Dabei fungierte sie als Bindeglied zwischen dem Moskauer Zentrum, und hier nicht nur dem ZK der KPdSU, sondern auch den wichtigsten staatlichen Stellen wie *Gosplan* oder dem Ministerrat, und der Region. Die Parteileitung musste sicherstellen, dass Moskauer Verordnungen und Direktiven in ihrem Herrschaftsbereich umgesetzt wurden.

Diese Aufgabenbeschreibung galt grundsätzlich auch für den Ersten Magadaner Parteisekretär. Angesichts der historisch gewachsenen Herrschaftsstrukturen in der Region war jedoch ein derartig umfassender Machtanspruch nur bedingt durchsetzbar. Die Institutionen, die eine Kontrolle und Beherrschung der einzelnen Wirtschafts- und Lebensbereiche des Gebietes ermöglichen sollten, die diversen Abteilungen des Partei- und Exekutivkomitees, waren erst im Aufbau begriffen, ihre materielle, zum Teil auch ihre personelle Basis war zunächst sehr dünn. Unter den besonderen infrastrukturellen Bedingungen verfügte Ababkov, und mit ihm auch Afanas'ev, in der ersten Zeit über keine Bauorganisationen, Transportmittel, Lagerhallen oder Hafenanlagen, um seine Ziele überhaupt durchsetzen zu können. Afanas'ev erinnerte sich später an die erste Zeit nach der Gebietsgründung und schilderte ein Beispiel, das für ihn charakteristisch für die damalige Machtverteilung war:

> Im Krankenhaus der Siedlung Debin ging der Kesselraum der Heizung kaputt. In den Krankenzimmern sank die Temperatur auf 4–6 Grad. Hinter den Fenstern – Februar, die Kälte minus 50 Grad. Die Lage ist beunruhigend. Als er gehört hatte, was passiert war, wandte sich der Vorsitzende des Exekutivkomitees schnell an die Leitung von Dal'stroj und bat um Hilfe, weil die Gesundheitsversorgung in Debin noch Dal'stroj unterstand (die lokalen Sowjets hatten es noch nicht geschafft, diesen Bereich zu übernehmen). Die Antwort der Leitung von Dal'stroj war kurz: Jetzt müsst ihr diese Probleme lösen, diese Einrichtung wird ja bald an das Exekutivkomitee übergeben. O weh! Das Exekutivkomitee hatte noch gar keine Renovierungsstation.[265]

Zudem hatte Ababkov, ebenso wie das ZK der KPdSU und die Ministerien in Moskau, zu diesem Zeitpunkt nur einen sehr begrenzten Einblick in die tatsächlichen lokalen Verhältnisse. Ababkov war Chef einer politischen Institution, die gewissermaßen mit einer Verspätung von 23 Jahren gegründet worden war; diese Zeit hatte Dal'stroj ihr in der Region voraus.

Paul Gregory hat sich mit dem Verhältnis zwischen regionaler Parteileitung und der Wirtschaftsführung in sowjetischen Regionen beschäftigt. Er verweist auf die schwierige Stellung der Partei gegenüber einem besonders großen und die Region dominierenden Industriekomplex. Dieser Komplex habe jeweils unmittelbar einem unionsweiten Ministerium unterstanden und sei von dessen Weisungen abhängig gewesen, so dass die offiziellen Kompetenzen der lokalen Parteileitung begrenzt ge-

---

264 Csaba in seinem Kommentar zu Gregory, Institutional Background, S. 46. Zur wachsenden Bedeutung der Parteiorganisationen in Wirtschaftsfragen siehe auch Schröder, Lebendige Verbindung, S. 550–559.

265 Sergeev, Pervyj predsedatel', S. 21.

wesen seien.[266] Ausführlicher haben dieses Machtverhältnis die amerikanischen Politologen Fainsod und Hough beschrieben:

> Party theory may speak about local party dominance of the soviets, but the various departments and administrative offices of the latter institutions are also responsible to ministerial lines of command. If a ministry, working under Central Committee and Council of Ministers directives, issues a decree to its local units, the principle of a centralized party would be destroyed if the various local party organs were permitted to institute their own policies and impose them on the local administrators. Even when the local party organs find that a decision would be possible within existing directives, any significant project or program usually requires financial support and investment and such funds almost always require ministerial approval. A local administrator who disapproves of local party pressure can easily inform his governmental superiors about his reservations.[267]

Die Machtposition des Ersten Parteisekretärs war somit nicht nur aus historischen Gründen, sondern auch strukturell eingeschränkt. Ganz besonders in den Anfangsjahren stärkte die monopolartige Stellung des Kombinats die Wirtschaftsleitung, aber auch das übergeordnete MMP/MCM, in ihren Kompetenzen über relevante Faktoren des lokalen Lebens.

Doch auch Mitrakov stand erheblich unter Druck, seine Machtmittel waren durch die Unterstellung unter zivile Ministerien, die Abgabe einer ganzen Reihe seiner wichtigsten Infrastrukturen und Institutionen an die neue regionale Leitung, den Verlust eines großen Teils seines bisherigen Führungsstabes sowie die Auflösung seiner internen politischen Basis (der Politischen Verwaltung von Dal'stroj) geschrumpft.

3.3.2 Wissen als Machtfaktor

Die Gewinnung internen Wissens über die tatsächlichen Verhältnisse im Kombinat und in der Region war entscheidend für die Stärkung der Position der Partei. Es war der Zugewinn an Informationen, der der allmählichen Machtübernahme der neuen Organe den Boden bereitete. Herrschaft in Dal'stroj war bis zum März 1953 in starkem Maße an die extreme Abschottung des Gebietes durch die hohe militärische Geheimhaltungsstufe gebunden. Der Informationsfluss über sämtliche Aspekte des Lebens an der Kolyma und in Tschukotka war strengstens geregelt; das Selbstverständnis der Dal'stroj-Funktionäre speiste sich zu einem wesentlichen Teil aus ihrem hierarchisch abgestuften exklusiven Wissen über Goldförderung und Lagerpolitik. Kaštanov, der Parteisekretär für Kulturfragen im neuen Magadaner Gebiet erinnerte sich an die erste Zeit nach seiner Ankunft: „Damals war alles geheim, sogar ich, ein

---

266 Vgl. Gregory, Institutional Background, S. 46. Siehe zu dem Verhältnis auch Gregory, Political Economy, S. 180 ff.
267 Hough; Fainsod, Soviet Union is Governed, S. 505 f.

Mitglied des Büros des Gebietsparteikomitees, ein Sekretär, ich habe nichts gewusst – ich, der Sekretär für Kultur."[268]

Auch nach der Gebietsgründung unterlag das Territorium aufgrund seines Status als Grenzregion und wegen der Förderung von Gold und anderen wertvollen Rohstoffen einer besonderen Geheimhaltungsstufe für Infrastruktur und Nachrichtenübertragung.[269] Doch galt dies natürlich nicht für die neue politische Leitung, die Gründung des Magadaner Gebietes war ja gerade Ausdruck des Bestrebens des ZK der KPdSU gewesen, in den inneren Informationskreis über die Lage an der Kolyma vorzustoßen. Nach der Gebietsgründung gelang es der lokalen Parteileitung, im Wesentlichen durch drei Personengruppen, herrschaftsrelevantes Wissen zu generieren:

Im Bereich der Wirtschaft bargen die Berichte des MMP / des MCM sowie von einem neu eingesetzten obersten Kontrolleur für das Magadaner Gebiet und Dal'stroj erhebliche Sprengkraft. Ihre Analysen offenbarten die tatsächlichen wirtschaftlichen Probleme des Kombinats und die riesigen finanziellen Verluste, die das Kombinat für den sowjetischen Staat brachte – ebenso wie das bisherige Ausmaß der Unkenntnis staatlicher Stellen über die Lage in der Region.[270]

Weitere Informationen erhielt das Gebietsparteikomitee nach wie vor auch von unzufriedenem Dal'stroj-Personal. Ein ganzes Dossier lieferte beispielsweise der Leiter der Abteilung für die perspektivische Planung, V. Vasil'ev. Sein Bericht kam auf Bitten von Ababkov zustande, nach einem persönlichen Treffen mit Vasil'ev und einem Inspektor des ZK der der KPdSU. Vasil'ev schilderte ausführlich die wirtschaftlichen Probleme des Kombinats, er fütterte die Parteileitung mit einer großen Zahl wichtiger Informationen über die Machtverteilung zwischen einzelnen Abteilungen von Dal'stroj, über die interne Struktur und diverse Probleme des Kombinats. Vor allem beklagte er das Fehlen einer längerfristigen perspektivischen Planung für das Kombinat, die er sich von der neuen Führung in der Region erhoffte.[271]

---

268 Zitiert nach Grebenjuk, Kolymskij led, S. 235.

269 Dal'stroj unterhielt zu allen Zeiten (wie dann auch der spätere Volkswirtschaftsrat) eine geheime und chiffrierte Abteilung, die 1. Abteilung von Dal'stroj. Ihre Aufgabe bestand darin, alle Staatsgeheimnisse der Bergindustrie und der Metallförderung zu wahren und eine chiffrierte Verbindung zwischen dem Kombinat und den übergeordneten Einrichtungen (Ministerrat der RSFSR, *Gosplan* etc.) sowie den einzelnen Produktionsstätten aufrechtzuerhalten. Auch im Kampf gegen ausländische Nachrichtendienste war es streng verboten, Informationen und Anweisungen, die die Goldförderung, Perspektiven einzelner Gebiete, die Häfen und den Warentransport, aber auch Unfälle und Verbrechen betrafen, über das offene Telefon- und Telegraphennetz weiterzugeben. Vgl. die Angaben zu der ersten Abteilung des Volkswirtschaftsrats und seinem Personal von dem stellv. Leiter des Volkswirtschaftsrats, Berezin, in GAMO f. R-137sč, op. 1b, d. 58, l. 9 – 10 sowie die streng geheime Anordnung über die geheime Informationsübermittlung im Volkswirtschaftsrat vom 6. Juni 1959 von Korolev in GAMO f. R-137sč, op. 1b, d. 177, l. 32 – 33. In dieser Anordnung werden auch Personen, die gegen diese Regelung verstoßen hatten, zur Verantwortung gezogen. Die Anordnung folgt einer Verordnung des Ministerrates der RSFSR vom 16. Mai 1959.

270 Ausführlich zu der wirtschaftlichen Lage des Kombinats und diesen Berichten siehe das Kapitel 4.3.1.

271 Vgl. sein Dossier vom 20. Juni 1954 in GAMO f. P-21, op. 5, d. 685, l. 1 – 20.

Das Gebietsparteikomitee drang drittens mittels eigener Kommissionen und Abteilungen und durch seine Vertretungen in den einzelnen Bezirken auch selbst immer tiefer in die regionalen Verhältnisse ein und ließ sich dabei ausführliche Berichte erstellen.[272] Bereits unmittelbar nach seiner Ankunft wandte sich die lokale Parteileitung der Situation in den Lagern zu. Sie überprüfte die Lage der Häftlinge, ihre Unterbringung sowie Sicherungsmaßnahmen in und außerhalb der Lagerzone; dokumentierte die Gewalt, die von den Lagern auf freie Siedlungen ausging, und beobachtete die Verwendung von Häftlingen als Arbeitskräfte.[273] Auf der Grundlage einzelner Berichte folgte im Juni 1954 eine grundlegende Kontrolle des Lagersystems *Sevvostlag* und des Sonderlagers *Berlag* für das ZK der KPdSU. In dem folgenden Bericht Ababkovs an das ZK hieß es u. a.:

> Das Gebietskomitee der KPdSU hat sich in den vergangenen fünf Monaten systematisch mit den Lagern beschäftigt. So wurde, im Zusammenhang mit der ausgesprochen schweren Lage in den Abteilungen des Čaun-Čukotsker Lagers, nach Beschluss des Büros des Gebietskomitees der KPdSU, eine Brigade des Bezirkskomitees der Partei in die Lager gesandt. [...] Zur Unterstützung wurden Brigaden von operativen Kräften, der Miliz und der Staatsanwaltschaft in das Lager und den Bezirk geschickt, Milizabteilungen für den Bezirk und einzelne Siedlungen wurden gegründet und mit Personal ausgestattet. Im Februar wurde die ungesetzliche Praxis liquidiert, Häftlinge als Hausangestellte in den Wohnungen des leitenden Personals von Dal'stroj und den Lagern zu benutzen. Momentan führen auf Veranlassung des Gebietsparteikomitees die Gebiets- und Militärstaatsanwaltschaften eine Untersuchung ungesetzlicher Handlungen gegen Häftlinge im Jahr 1952 durch.[274]

Mit dieser Untersuchung drang Ababkov in einen der zwei Kernbereiche der noch immer bestehenden Einzelleitung, der Verwaltung von *Sevvostlag* und *Berlag*, vor. Hatte man bei der Überprüfung durch den GULAG im Jahr 1953 noch von einer „fachlichen Zuständigkeit" der Hauptverwaltung für Lager sprechen können, so trat nun die Parteileitung allein durch ihren umfassenden Kontrollanspruch über sämtliche Bereiche des Magadaner Gebietes in Erscheinung und beendete damit die vollkommene Zurückdrängung regionaler Parteileitungen, die den Lageraufbau in allen Gebieten der Sowjetunion strukturell begleitet hatte. Mehr noch, nun fungierte das Gebietsparteikomitee auch als Auftraggeber der Staatsanwaltschaft, der die Wiederherstellung „sozialistischer Gesetzlichkeit", die Überprüfung von Häftlingsakten und das Verbot der jahrelangen Praxis, Häftlinge als persönliche „Haussklaven" zu halten, veranlasste. Auf diese Weise konnte die Parteileitung dem ZK der KPdSU gegenüber Engagement bei der Erfüllung ihres Auftrags zur Stabilisierung der Situation in den Lagern signalisieren, ein deutliches Zeichen ihres umfassenden Macht- und Kon-

---

272 Für weitere Beispiele siehe GAMO f. P-21, op. 5, d. 110, l. 188–196 (Bericht des Leiters der Wirtschaftsabteilung des Gebietsparteikomitees, der auch persönliche Kritik an Mitrakov enthält).
273 Vgl. die Berichte des Gebietsparteikomitees in GAMO f. P-21, op. 5, d. 759 und d. 2. Siehe auch die Protokolle von Diskussionen im Gebietsparteikomitee über die Situation in den Lagern des Gebietes in GAMO f. P-21, op. 5, d. 765, l. 1–16.
274 Ababkov in GAMO f. P-21, op. 5, d. 759, l. 1–10, hier l. 6 f.

trollanspruchs gegenüber Dal'stroj setzen und sich zugleich in puncto Rechtsempfinden und Moral als erneuernde Kraft präsentieren.

Doch auch im zweiten Teil der Einzelleitung, der Industrie, war das Büro von Anfang an aktiv. So zum Beispiel bei der Beurteilung einer der wichtigsten Einrichtungen des Kombinats, des Schürfdienstes von Dal'stroj. Das Gebietsparteikomitee hatte enormes Interesse an einer Kontrolle über diesen perspektivischen Wirtschaftszweig, dessen Prognosen erhebliche Bedeutung für die weitere Existenz von Förderanlagen und ganzen Siedlungen hatten. Der Schürfdienst entschied, wie es Ababkov formulierte, über „die Zukunft des Gebietes"[275]. Aufgrund seiner Bedeutung setzte die Parteileitung bereits Anfang 1954 diverse Kommissionen ein, die einer Überprüfung seiner Arbeit und organisatorischen Verfasstheit dienen sollten. Der Leiter der Abteilung für Wirtschaftsfragen beim Gebietsparteikomitee, Golubev, legte am 12. November 1954 den ersten ausführlichen Bericht vor, der dem geologischen Schürfdienst ein erschütterndes Zeugnis ausstellte: Trotz jahrelanger, enormer Investitionen habe die Planerfüllung des Schürfdienstes in einigen Arbeitsgebieten bei gerade einmal 48 % gelegen.[276] Seine eigentliche Aufgabe habe der Dienst nur vollkommen unzureichend erfüllt, massive Verschwendungen, Leitungsfehler und Unfälle hätten daneben zu Verlusten von vielen Millionen Rubel geführt.

Unterstützung erhielt das Gebietsparteikomitee in seiner Beurteilung vom MCM. Der Dal'stroj vorgesetzte stellvertretende Minister erklärte sich ausdrücklich mit der Beurteilung des Gebietsparteikomitees einverstanden und forderte Dal'stroj immer wieder zu einer Umstellung seiner geologischen Arbeiten auf.

Golubev ging in seinen Analysen noch einen Schritt weiter, er kritisierte in seinem Bericht erhebliche „moralische Missstände" unter den Funktionären. Trinkgelage, entsetzliche Lebensbedingungen der einfachen Arbeiter, Randale und Gewalt in den Siedlungen hätten dem Schürfdienst ein denkbar schlechtes Zeugnis ausgestellt, auf den die Parteileitung einwirken sollte, so Golubev.[277] Im Ergebnis brachten diese Kontrollen einerseits Vorteile für die konkrete Arbeit dieser so wichtigen Abteilung – das Ministerium stützte den Schürfdienst durch zusätzliche Finanzanweisungen im folgenden Jahr.[278] Andererseits bedeuteten sie einen erheblichen Machtzuwachs für die regionale Parteileitung, deren Position im Austausch mit dem MCM gestärkt wurde. Die Leitung des Schürfdienstes, aber auch die oberste Kombinatsleitung in

---

275 So Ababkov in einer Darstellung der Parteiorganisation des Schürfdienstes für das Büro des ZK der KPdSU für die RSFSR in RGANI f. 5, op. 32, d. 61, l. 168. In der Verwaltung des Schürfdienstes arbeiteten 426 Mitarbeiter, insgesamt gab es sieben regionale Schürfdienste in einzelnen Bezirken.
276 In einigen Gebieten liege der Selbstkostenpreis der Arbeiten bei 185 % des Planes. Vgl. GAMO f. P-21, op. 5, d. 14, l. 23–42, hier l. 29.
277 Siehe den ausführlichen Bericht in GAMO f. P-21, op. 5, d. 14, l. 23–42.
278 Vgl. den Brief des stellv. Ministers N. Šemjakin an Ababkov vom Februar 1955, in dem die Vorgehensweise des Ministeriums beschrieben wird, in GAMO f. P-21, op. 5, d. 14, l. 73.

Person von Mitrakov und Kuznecov wurde wegen mangelnder Führung und unzureichender Kontrolle ihrer Abteilung schwer gerügt.[279]

Die Parteileitung drang im Folgenden immer tiefer in die Interna dieser Dal'stroj-Abteilung ein. Ein paar Monate später, im März 1955, legte Golubev erneut einen Bericht über den geologischen Schürfdienst vor. Die Verhältnisse hätten sich im Vergleich zum Herbst 1954 sogar noch verschlechtert, zudem würden die von Dal'stroj erstellten positiven Berichte schlicht nicht den Tatsachen entsprechen und zum Teil auf gefälschten Zahlen beruhen, so Golubev.[280]

Golubevs Bericht deckte außerdem einen „internen Vorgang" von erheblicher Sprengkraft auf – die Veruntreuung von Prämiengeldern und die damit verbundene massive persönliche Bereicherung der Dal'stroj-Spitze. Zunächst betraf dies die Saison 1952–1953, in der 1,4 Mio. Rubel als Prämie für die Entdeckung seltener Rohstoffe ausgeschrieben worden waren. Diese Gelder seien so verteilt worden, dass statt der üblichen 90 % der Prämie lediglich 30 % an die Personen ausgezahlt wurden, die tatsächlich die geologischen Entdeckung gemacht hätten. 70 % der Gelder (statt der gesetzlich vorgeschriebenen 10 %) seien an die Gesamtleitung von Dal'stroj und an die Leitung des Schürfdienstes vergeben worden. Materialien über diese Veruntreuungen habe damals sogar der MVD erhalten, sie seien jedoch von dort mit der Bitte um eine gründlichere Untersuchung nach Magadan zurückgesandt worden. Nachdem die Kombinatsleitung die Vorwürfe als unbegründet zurückgewiesen hatte, habe man den Fall einfach zu den Akten gelegt.

Allerdings beließ es die Kombinatsleitung nicht bei diesem Betrug. Im Jahr 1954, also bereits im Rahmen des Magadaner Gebietes, hätten der erste Geologe von Dal'-stroj, Erofeev, sowie sein Stellvertreter Drabkin, die Unterlagen „noch einmal neu gestempelt", d. h. für exakt die gleiche Fundstelle, für die in der Vergangenheit bereits eine erhebliche Prämie gezahlt worden war, wurde noch einmal eine Prämie, diesmal von mehr als 2 Mio. Rubel, ausgeschrieben (zum Vergleich: der oberste Chef von Dal'stroj erhielt bis zum Jahr 1953 ein Gehalt von monatlich ca. 12.000 Rubel, incl. aller Zulagen).

Dieses Mal wurden die Protokolle über den Fundort der Lagerstätte sogar in der Mehrzahl von Leuten unterschrieben, die nicht einmal Mitglieder der Schürfkommissionen gewesen waren; selbst die angeblichen „aktiven Arbeiter" waren zur

---

279 Das ist insofern von besonderer Bedeutung, weil Mitrakov bereits lange vor der Gebietsgründung den Schürfdienst selbst immer wieder gerügt hatte. Beispielsweise hatte er im April 1953 das ZK der KPdSU gebeten, den Leiter dieser Verwaltung, Caregradskij, wegen Unfähigkeit zu entlassen, was jedoch vertagt worden war. Vgl. RGANI f. 5, op. 27, d. 114, l. 161. Im Juni 1953 hatte Mitrakov dem Schürfdienst wegen schlechter Arbeitsorganisation, mangelnder Planerfüllung und vieler Verschwendungen ein ausgesprochen schlechtes Zeugnis ausgestellt und die Führung schwer gerügt. Vgl. die Revision für das Jahr 1952 und das erste Quartal 1953 in RGAĖ f. 9163, op. 6, d. 12, l. 94–96ob. Das Gebietsparteikomitee machte 1954 Mitrakov persönlich für die Versäumnisse in diesem Teil seines Kombinats verantwortlich.

280 Vgl. GAMO f. P-21, op. 5, d. 14, l. 43–72, hier l. 61.

fraglichen Zeit an anderen Stellen eingesetzt gewesen, so Golubev. Schon an der Gestaltung des Berichts hätte die Leitung von Dal'stroj den Betrug erkennen können, dennoch habe sie eine Untersuchung der Vorgänge abgelehnt. Schließlich seien auch der stellvertretende Leiter von Dal'stroj, Berezin, der stellv. Leiter des Schürfdienstes, Drabkin und einige andere aus der obersten Führungsriege des Kombinats Empfänger der Prämien gewesen. „Offensichtlich", so die ironische Bemerkung Golubevs, „ist der Leitung des Schürfdienstes nicht klar, dass derartige Prämien eigentlich den beteiligten Arbeitern [und Entdeckern – M. S.] gezahlt werden müssen [...] und sie nicht als Einnahmequellen für die Mitarbeiter des Apparates genutzt werden dürfen."[281]

Berichte wie diese haben durch ihren Zugewinn an internen Informationen die Position der lokalen Parteileitung nachdrücklich gestärkt. In diesem Fall wurde ihr auch die Möglichkeit einer persönlichen Diskreditierung der Dal'stroj-Führung geliefert, die sie aber nie öffentlich nutzte – Drabkin und Berezin waren auch in den folgenden Jahren entscheidende Figuren in Dal'stroj bzw. im Volkswirtschaftsrat. Die Parteileitung konnte jedoch stets mit ihrem detaillierten Wissen über persönliche Verhältnisse wuchern und die Vergehen dieser Personen vor 1953 als politisch kompromittierendes Material verwenden, wie es Yoram Gorlizki als neue Möglichkeit unter den Bedingungen poststalinistischer Machtbeziehungen beschreibt.[282]

3.3.3 Neue Herrschafts- und Verwaltungsformen und ihre Repräsentation

Ihre eigene Politik bezeichnete die neue politische Leitung gerne als *osvoenie*, häufig sprach sie in Abgrenzung von Dal'stroj auch von einer „echten osvoenie", um ihren Anspruch auf eine Durchdringung des gesamten sozialen und Naturraumes zu verdeutlichen.[283] Nach einer Definition von Emma Widdis verbirgt sich hinter dem Begriff *osvoenie* im Russischen mehr als das, was der deutsche Begriff „Erschließung" beinhaltet. Für Widdis verkörpert *osvoenie* eine „assimilative attitude toward the periphery"[284]. Genau in diesem Sinne war die Erschließung des Gebietes von Anfang an auf eine enge Anbindung an das machtpolitische Zentrum in Moskau und an die administrativen Verhältnisse in anderen sowjetischen Regionen ausgerichtet. Programmatisch steht dafür der sprechende Titel einer Darstellung des Magadaner Gebietes durch Afanas'ev: „Hier beginnt Russland" sind seine „Skizzen" über das neue Gebiet betitelt.[285] Hierdurch sollten die volle Integration und ihr Status als eine Art

---

281 Der gesamte Bericht an Ababkov in GAMO f. P-21, op. 5, d. 14, l. 43–72, Zitat hier l. 61.
282 Vgl. Gorlizki, Structures of Trust, S. 140.
283 Vor allem Afanas'ev benutzte diesen Begriff häufig. Siehe z. B. seinen Aufsatz Kommunisty sowie den Abdruck einer Rede in: Magadanskaja Pravda, 10. Dezember 1961, S. 2. Vgl. daneben Slavin, Promyšlennoe osvoenie.
284 Widdis, Mobile Perspectives, S. 221.
285 Vgl. Afanas'ev, Rossija.

Vorposten der russischen Sowjetrepublik zum Ausdruck kommen.[286] Magadan sollte nicht mehr als eine „Insel" im Gegensatz zum Festland (*materik*) wahrgenommen werden, sondern als nordöstlicher Außenposten des Imperiums.

Die konkrete Assimilationspolitik gegenüber dieser Peripherie, die sich mit der Erschließung – im Sinne einer *osvoenie* – des Gebietes verband, war dabei an die neue territoriale Gliederung, an den formalen Status der Region geknüpft. Sie war Voraussetzung und infrastruktureller Rahmen für die politische und soziale Angleichung der Region an den allgemeinen unionsweiten Standard. Der Zustand einzelner Ortschaften, die Lage der freien Arbeitskräfte, die Situation in den Lagern, die Verhältnisse bei Infrastruktur oder sozialen Institutionen. In all diesen Punkten wurden Veränderungen dann eingeführt, wenn sie in Bezug auf ihre Stellung im politischen Gefüge der Sowjetunion in den Blickpunkt der Führung gerieten.[287] Dies konnte die Gründung eines Parteikomitees sein, die Ernennung einer Siedlung zum Zentrum eines Bezirkes, die institutionelle Neuanbindung an ein ziviles Ministerium oder die Unterstellung einer Schule unter das Gebietsexekutivkomitee. Auch die Vertreter der einzelnen Bezirke, von Fabriken oder Ortschaften versuchten, ihre Forderungen mit dem jeweiligen neuen Status im Rahmen des Magadaner Gebietes zu rechtfertigen. So auch der Vorsitzende des Exekutivkomitees des Bezirkes Providenskij, N. Charitonov, in seinem Schreiben an das Gebietspartei- und Gebietsexekutivkomitee:

> Jetzt sind schon bald sieben Jahre seit der Gründung des Gebietes vergangen und das vierte Jahr seit der Gründung des Providenser Bezirks, aber die Aufmerksamkeit des Gebietsexekutivkomitees für unsere Angelegenheiten ist immer noch total unbefriedigend.[288]

Materielle und infrastrukturelle Maßstäbe, die für andere Regionen in der Sowjetunion galten, wurden auf der Grundlage der neuen Zuständigkeiten und administrativen Gliederungen auf das Magadaner Gebiet übertragen und die Region zugleich in das Geflecht bürokratischer Strukturen der Sowjetunion miteinbezogen – sie wurde gewissermaßen „sowjetisiert".[289] Dementsprechend ist auch die Beschreibung vom „Staat im Staat", die russische Historiker für Dal'stroj anwenden, in dieser Hinsicht irreführend. Nach außen war das Kombinat zwar ein abgekapseltes Gebilde, das seine Funktionen durch eigene Einrichtungen zu erfüllen wusste, nach innen handelte es

---

286 Diese „Aufzeichnungen" des damaligen Ersten Parteisekretärs des Gebietes erschienen 1967. Vgl. Afanas'ev, Rossija.

287 Dieses Verständnis zeigte sich immer wieder bei der Neugründung von Bezirken. Vgl. für ein derartiges Beispiel aus Tschukotka GAMO f. R-146, op. 1, d. 57, l. 62–67. Eine weitere Abhängigkeit zwischen dem administrativen Staus und der sozialen Lage eines Gebietes zeigt sich auch bei den Gehältern. So war beispielsweise das Gehalt eines Lehrers davon abhängig, ob er in einem Dorf unterrichtete oder in einer Siedlung, die am 22. Dezember 1953 den Status „Arbeitersiedlung" erhalten hatte.

288 GAMO f. R-146, op. 1, d. 442, l. 110–115, hier l. 110.

289 Vgl. Kapitel 1.3.

sich bei Dal'stroj aber keineswegs um einen „Staat" als Verwaltungsgebilde mit entwickelten politischen Verwaltungsstrukturen.

Die vollständige Angleichung ziviler Herrschaftsstrukturen, Hierarchien, Gebietseinteilungen und Infrastrukturen setzte den umfassenden Aufbau bürokratischer Strukturen voraus. Ein Vergleich mit dem westlichsten Gebiet der UdSSR, dem neuen Kaliningrader Gebiet, zeigt dementsprechend viele Parallelen im Programm des administrativen Aufbaus.[290] Per Brodersen macht in seiner umfangreichen Studie zu Kaliningrad jedoch immer wieder auf den Umstand aufmerksam, dass es sich dabei um eine von Moskau vernachlässigte Peripherie handelte, ein Schicksal, das es, so Brodersen, „mit anderen Neuzugängen teilte".[291] Das Magadaner Gebiet wurde hingegen offensichtlich nicht als derart „fremd und nicht dazugehörig"[292] empfunden. Gerade im Vergleich zu den Schwierigkeiten, die Brodersen für das Kaliningrader Gebiet als der westlichsten Region schildert, sticht der Einsatz des Zentrums in Magadan, der östlichsten Region, heraus. Das Magadaner Gebiet war für Moskau in personeller, materieller und infrastruktureller Hinsicht keine gewöhnliche Peripherie. Dies war eine Konstante, die in der stalinistischen Sonderstellung des Kombinats fußte und unter den neuen Bedingungen der einsetzenden Entstalinisierung beibehalten wurde.

Neben den finanziellen Mitteln, die durch die großen Verordnungen zum institutionellen und infrastrukturellen Aufbau in die Region kamen, sind sicherlich die Investitionen, die über das Budget des Gebietsexekutivkomitees in der Region eingesetzt wurden, am stärksten greifbar. Denn die üblichen Zuständigkeiten in der Sowjetunion sahen vor, dass regionale Einrichtungen (wie z. B. Grundschulen) einem entsprechenden Ministerium unterstanden, aber über das Budget des Gebietsexekutivkomitees bzw. Bezirks- oder Stadtexekutivkomitees finanziert und in praktischen Angelegenheiten von der lokalen Partei- und Sowjetverwaltung beaufsichtigt wurden.[293] Die finanzielle Ausstattung der Abteilungen des Gebietsexekutivkomitees stieg zwischen 1954 und 1958 um fast das Doppelte, ihre Zuständigkeiten wuchsen von Jahr zu Jahr.[294] Für die Gestaltung des Herrschaftsraumes war das Signal zur Stärkung der

---

290 Vgl. Hoppe, Königsberg, S. 27 f. Auch Sören Urbansky und Helena Barop ziehen einen Vergleich zwischen einer der östlichsten und der westlichsten sowjetischen Provinz. Sie vergleichen die Sowjetisierung (nach 1945) der beiden bislang feindlichen Territorien, Königsberg und Sachalin. Vgl. Urbansky/Barop, Faint Light.
291 Brodersen, Stadt im Westen, S. 34. Siehe dazu auch Hoppe, Königsberg, S. 86–89.
292 Brodersen, Stadt im Westen, S. 34.
293 Vgl. die Regelung in den Übergabelisten zu der Verordnung in RGAĖ f. 9163, op. 6, d. 13, l. 93 u. 99. Dies betraf im Falle der Schulen natürlich keine inhaltlichen Fragen, wie z. B. die Gestaltung des Lehrplans.
294 Das Budget des Magadaner Gebietes nahm von insgesamt 293,1 Mio. Rubel im Jahr 1954 auf 524,3 Mio. Rubel im Jahr 1958 zu, die Pläne für das Jahr 1959 sahen sogar mehr als eine Verdoppelung gegenüber dem Jahr 1954 vor. Zahlen nach den Budgetangaben des Gebietsexekutivkomitees, vgl. GAMO f. R-146, op. 1, d. 212, l. 157–158. Der Leiter der Finanzabteilung des Gebietsexekutivkomitees spricht in seinem Bericht über die Budgetentwicklung Ende 1955 zwei Ursachen für diese Zunahme an: Zum

neuen Staats- und Parteistrukturen wichtig, das Moskau damit setzte. Die im Rahmen des institutionellen und infrastrukturellen Aufbaus entstehenden lokalen Organisationen entwickelten sich zur machtpolitischen Basis des Gebietspartei- und Gebietsexekutivkomitees; Ababkov und Afanas'ev verfügten vor Ort über immer mehr Instrumente, um ihre eigenen politischen Entscheidungen durchzusetzen, die Abhängigkeit von Dal'stroj-Organisationen sank gewissermaßen auf institutionellem Wege.

In seiner Analyse des Verhältnisses zwischen regionaler Parteileitung und einer die Region dominierenden Wirtschaftseinrichtung hat Paul Gregory einen begrenzten Einfluss der regionalen Parteileitung auf Fragen der lokalen Wirtschaftslenkung konstatiert.[295] Dennoch hätte die regionale Parteileitung grundsätzlich zwei wichtige Möglichkeiten politischer Einflussnahme gehabt: So hätten regionale Parteivertreter ihre Position bei der lokalen Verteilung von Waren und Arbeitskräften politisch gewinnbringend einsetzen und über die Linienstruktur der Partei, durch Stellungnahmen und Anträge, auf das ZK der KPdSU einwirken können.[296]

Diese beiden Wege hat auch die Magadaner Parteileitung beschritten. Gerade bei Transport- und Warenorganisationen stieg die Bedeutung des Gebietsparteikomitees. Zudem konnte es seinen Einfluss dadurch erweitern, dass es die Zuständigkeit für Aufgabenbereiche übernahm, die das Kombinat missachtete oder die es in der Region bislang nicht gegeben hatte. So betrachtete das Gebietsparteikomitee die Sorge um die Lebensbedingungen der Arbeiter als eines seiner wichtigsten Anliegen, ebenso wie die Anwerbung neuer Arbeitskräfte, die Entwicklung einer Leichtindustrie, von Anlagen zur Energieversorgung und zur Verarbeitung der Rohstoffe.

Besonders deutlich zeigt sich die zunehmend führende Rolle des Büros des Gebietsparteikomitees an seiner Mittlerrolle zwischen der Region und dem ZK der KPdSU. Entsprechend der üblichen Vorgehensweise wandte sich auch der Erste Sekretär des Magadaner Gebietes im Falle eines Problems von größerer Tragweite (schlechte Versorgung der Region, Kadermangel u. Ä.) persönlich an ein Mitglied des Präsidiums des ZK der KPdSU oder an eine der entsprechenden Abteilungen des ZK (der Abteilung für Handelsfinanzen und Planorgane, für Agitation und Propaganda u. a.). Ababkov schilderte in einem solchen Vermerk nicht nur die konkrete Situation auf der Basis seiner internen Berichte, sondern bat das ZK der KPdSU zugleich darum, die entsprechende staatliche Stelle (ein Ministerium, *Gosplan*, eine Handelsorgani-

---

einen habe der Ministerrat der RSFSR deutlich höhere Zuwendungen für das Magadaner Gebiet in diversen Bereichen beschlossen und zum anderen seien die eigenen Mehreinnahmen des Gebietes durch die Produktion, den Handel und den Verkauf lokaler Produkte erheblich gestiegen. Vgl. seinen ausführlichen Bericht in GAMO f. R-146, op. 1, d. 108, l. 1–13. Auffällig ist hierbei, dass die Verwaltungskosten des Gebietsexekutivkomitees nicht in einer vergleichbaren Größenordnung stiegen. So betrugen sie 1954 35,8 Mio. Rubel, 1958 waren es 38,8 Mio. Rubel. Der Anteil der Verwaltungskosten am Gesamtbudget ist somit im gleichen Zeitraum dramatisch gesunken.

295 Vgl. für die Magadaner Verhältnisse das Kapitel 3.3.1.

296 Vgl. Gregory, Institutional Background, S. 26 f.

sation o. Ä.) aufzufordern, entsprechend der lokalen Bitte tätig zu werden. Oftmals fügte die lokale Parteileitung sogleich eine Vorlage der eigenen Intentionen bei, die das ZK gegenüber der staatlichen Stelle verwenden sollte (häufig der Entwurf zu einer Verordnung). Die entsprechende Abteilung des ZK der KPdSU holte daraufhin meist Stellungnahmen diverser staatlicher Stellen zu dem Sachverhalt ein, sie konnte aber auch sofort entsprechende Anweisungen erlassen oder staatliche Stellen an die Einhaltung ihrer Verpflichtungen erinnern.

Die Einschätzungen staatlicher Stellen führten mitunter auch dazu, dass das ZK, nach Bericht durch seine Abteilung, eine Entscheidung traf, die nur bedingt den regionalen Intentionen entsprach oder diesen sogar zuwiderlief. So z. B. in Falle eines pädagogischen Institutes, das Ababkov und Afanas'ev 1954 in Magadan aufgrund des massiven Mangels an pädagogischen Kadern in der Region errichten wollten. Ihrem Schreiben an das ZK der KPdSU hatten sie den Entwurf einer Verordnung des Ministerrates der UdSSR beigefügt, in dem bereits die Übergabe eines Gebäudes von Dal'stroj durch das MCM an das Bildungsministerium der RSFSR zugunsten des neuen Instituts eingeplant war. Nach einer Rückfrage des ZK antwortete jedoch das Kombinat der Schulabteilung des ZK, dass Dal'stroj das Gebäude zur eigenen Nutzung benötige, um dort Bergbaufacharbeiter auszubilden. Daraufhin lehnte das ZK der KPdSU das gesamte Vorhaben mit Blick auf die fehlende „materielle Basis" des geplanten Instituts ab.[297] Hier war die Stellung des Kombinats im Jahr 1954, im Rahmen des Ministeriums, noch zu mächtig, wog seine materielle Basis und die Finanzausstattung des Ministeriums schwerer als die formale Richtlinienkompetenz des Büros der Parteileitung. Diese Machtverteilung beschreibt Ian Thatcher als ein allgemeines Kennzeichen der Veränderungen zu Beginn der Herrschaft Chruščevs:

> It was not surprising, that as leader Khrushchev sought to transfer decision-making from central ministries to local party officials. This was not however something that could happen at the stroke of a pen. The central ministries would seek to ignore or subvert Khrushchev's intentions.[298]

Grundsätzlich wurden jedoch die meisten relevanten Angelegenheiten des Gebietes auf die oben beschriebene Weise entschieden; eine Form der Machtausübung, die im Nordosten vollkommen neu war. Das Verfahren war dabei stets das gleiche – das Büro des ZK der KPdSU für die RSFSR funktionierte gewissermaßen als Scharnier für alle institutionellen Prozesse, die mit der Region in Verbindung standen. Dies war nicht auf die Verhandlungen mit unionsweiten Organisationen in Moskau beschränkt,

---

297 Siehe den Schriftwechsel vom November-Dezember 1954 in RGANI f. 5, op. 18, d. 61, l. 31–37.
298 Thatcher, Khrushchev, S. 16, der Bezug nimmt auf Tompson, Khrushchev, S. 189.

sondern betraf auch andere regionale Institutionen, denen gegenüber der Schriftverkehr über das ZK als Druckmittel verwendet wurde.[299]

Eine mächtige Unterstützung erhielt die regionale Parteileitung durch die Errichtung eines Büros für die RSFSR des ZK der KPdSU nach dem 20. Parteitag 1956. Die Errichtung dieses Büros, das bereits einmal für kurze Zeit in den 1930er Jahren existiert hatte, war nach dem Zweiten Weltkrieg immer wieder gefordert, aus Sorge vor einer Ausweitung regionaler Verantwortlichkeiten auf der Ebene der RSFSR von Stalin jedoch wieder abgelehnt worden. Die Einführung des Büros sieht Alexander Titov als Kulminationspunkt der Strategie Chruščevs, das Zentralkomitee sehr viel stärker territorial auszurichten und Verantwortlichkeiten auf der Ebene der Regionen zu erhöhen, wozu die ihm loyal ergebenen Ersten Gebietsparteisekretäre in der Lage gewesen seien:

> In the post-Stalin period the trend towards decentralization of responsibilities was gathering pace and RSFSR matters were high on the agenda. The RSFSR was the only union republic without its own communist party. It therefore lacked a party organ that could take care of the less important issues that in other union republics were dealt with by their CC apparatuses."[300]

Das Büro sollte die Parteistrukturen bei Administration, Wirtschaftslenkung und kulturellem Aufbau in den Regionen der RSFSR unterstützen.[301] Eine mögliche Bedrohung der Macht des zentralen Apparates wurde von Chruščev damit beantwortet, dass er sich selbst zum Vorsitzenden des Büros für die RSFSR machte, um so eine zu große Unabhängigkeit zu verhindern. Durch seine neue Position sowie durch die Tatsache, dass Chruščev diese Organisationseinheit mit einem Teil seines Netzwerkes besetzen konnte, konnte Chruščev die Einführung des Büros zur Stärkung seiner Macht einsetzen. Ebenso wie die spätere Errichtung der Volkswirtschaftsräte stärkte das Büro die regionalen Parteikader in ihren Entscheidungskompetenzen gegenüber dem Apparat der zentralen Parteileitung und den Ministerien, vor Ort unterstützte es Ababkov in seinem Kampf gegen die bisherige Kombinatsleitung.[302]

An einem entscheidenden Punkt für die perspektivische Entwicklung der Goldförderung gelang es der regionalen Parteileitung, eine wirtschaftspolitische Entscheidung des Zentrums positiv für sich zu nutzen. Auf Betreiben des Ministeriums für Geologie und Bodenschätze war die Schürfverwaltung der Region aufgeteilt worden, wobei eine neue Abteilung mit langfristigen Untersuchungen betraut und unmittelbar

---

299 So z. B. häufig in der Korrespondenz mit regionalen Handelsorganisationen, von denen die Führung des Magadaner Gebietes so abhängig war – wie die Organisation *Glavseverotorg*. Siehe den entsprechenden Schriftwechsel in RGANI f. 5, op. 20, d. 154, l. 12–26.

300 Titov, Central Commitee, S. 46.

301 Siehe die Begründung zur Einführung dieses Büros im Bericht des ZK der KPdSU auf dem 20. Parteitag. Zitiert nach Afiani, Akademija nauk v rešenijach Politbjuro, S. 14.

302 Zur Einführung des Büros und seiner organisatorischen Gestaltung siehe Titov, Central Committee, S. 46 f. sowie Pyžikov, Ottepel', S. 103–114.

dem Ministerium unterstellt wurde.[303] Obwohl sich die regionale Parteileitung dadurch in ihrem Führungsanspruch zunächst beschnitten sah, konnte sie diesen Trend langfristig für sich nutzen. Denn ein Teil der lokalen Geologen, die junge und enthusiastische geologische Schürfabteilung des Bezirkes Sejmčan, wagte mit Unterstützung des Ministeriums neue Expeditionen und konnte schon bald von einem Gebiet mit erheblichem Goldgehalt im westlichen Teil Tschukotkas berichten.

Das Gebietsparteikomitee begriff schnell die historische Bedeutung dieses Fundes für die weiteren Perspektiven des Gebietes und für die machtpolitische Stabilisierung seiner Position, die sich daraus gegenüber der Wirtschaftsleitung ergeben konnte. Bereits im November 1957 präsentierte Ababkov dem ZK der KPdSU „grundlegende Veränderungen bei der Bewertung der Rohstoffbasis des Magadaner Gebietes" und versprach die „größten der in der UdSSR in den letzten Jahren eröffneten Gebiete für Goldförderung."[304] Bis zum Jahr 1965 stellte die Magadaner Parteileitung dem ZK einen Mehrertrag von 40 % in Aussicht. Das Zentrum entschied sich daraufhin für eine massive Ausweitung seiner Investitionen im Magadaner Gebiet. Die Geologen keiner anderen Region der Sowjetunion erhielten so große finanzielle und personelle Unterstützung wie die des Magadaner Gebietes, das das Ministerium für Geologie und Bodenschätze als „Valuta-Kraft" des Landes bezeichnete.[305]

Der Parteileitung gelang es durch die pragmatische Anerkennung der Leistungen selbstständig arbeitender Experten, die unter Chruščev gegenüber den als „wirklichkeitsfern" geltenden Entscheidungen der Apparatschiks erheblich aufgewertet wurden[306], sich selbst als die entscheidende wirtschaftspolitische Kraft für die Region zu inszenieren und so im besten Sinne Chruščevs als „mobilizing force in state and society"[307] aufzutreten.

---

303 Zu den genauen Umständen dieser Umstellung siehe das Kapitel 4.3.3.

304 Diese Veränderungen haben Eingang in den neuen Siebenjahrplan (1958 bis 1965) gefunden. Siehe das Schreiben von Ababkov an das ZK der KPdSU vom 10. November 1957 in GAMO f. R-137sč, op. 1b, d. 11, l. 106–109, hier l. 107 f. Die Prognosen bezogen sich nur auf die bereits durch Schürfarbeiten erkundeten Goldvorkommen. Insgesamt vermutete man 1957 Goldvorkommen in der Region von 2.493 Tonnen. Vgl. den Bericht des Gebietsparteikomitees in GAMO f. R-23, op. 1, d. 6088, l. 1–50, hier l. 13. Siehe die Aufforderung des Leiters der Bergbauverwaltung an Čuguev, die entsprechenden Vorarbeiten und Baumaßnahmen in diesem Gebiet voranzutreiben in GAMO f. R-137sč, op. 1b, d. 34, l. 27–28. Zu den weiteren Plänen des Magadaner Volkswirtschaftsrates siehe die Prognose von Korolev über den Goldabbau bis zum Jahre 1970 vom November 1957 in GAMO f. R-137sč, op. 1b, d. 13, l. 21–23.

305 Vgl. die Beschreibung des Vorsizenden der Sektion vom 12. April 1959 in GAMO f. R-137sč, op. 1b, d. 52, l. 47–62, hier l. 62. 1959 waren 7 % aller Arbeiter des Magadaner Gebietes bei den Schürfabteilungen tätig, zudem waren die finanziellen Investitionen für die Geologen so hoch wie in keinem anderen Gebiet der UdSSR. Vgl. Slavin, Promyšlennoe osvoenie, S. 242. Zugleich gingen mit diesen Investitionen Kürzungen in anderen Bereichen einher, so z. B. bei der Kohleförderung, die zugunsten des Goldes stark reduziert wurde. Vgl. Rajzman, SNCH MĖAR, S. 165.

306 Vgl. Ian Thatchers Beschreibung der Rolle von Experten, Thatcher, Khrushchev, S. 23.

307 Titov, Central Commitee, S. 44. Die Experten, denen die lokale Parteileitung ihre wirtschaftspolitische Absicherung verdankte, wurden jedoch nur zeitweise belohnt. Zwar erhielten Ivanov, der junge Leiter der geologischen Schürfabteilung des Bezirkes Sejmčan, und sein Chefgeologe S. M. Abaev für

Auch das Gebietsexekutivkomitee nutzte seine Kanäle, um durch staatliche Stellen im Moskauer Zentrum, z. B. durch die Erarbeitung von Entwürfen zu Verordnungen des Ministerrates der RSFSR durch die Organisation *Gosplan* der RSFSR, seine Forderungen durchzusetzen. Die wichtigste machtpolitische Basis des sowjetischen Zentrums blieb jedoch das Büro des Gebietsparteikomitees, das auch die Moskauer Leitung ständig über die regionale Lage auf dem Laufenden hielt. Im Gebiet selbst diente der Verweis auf grundlegende, unionsweite Entscheidungen des ZK zur Legitimierung der Direktiven der lokalen Parteileitung, z. B. bei der Ausweitung des regionalen Wohnungsbaus.[308]

Für die konkrete machtpolitische Ausgestaltung des Gebietes bedeutete dies, dass sich mit Übergabe der bislang militärischen Institutionen und mit Anschluss der Region an unionsweite Zuständigkeiten der Kreis der an einer konkreten Frage beteiligten Organisationen erheblich erweiterte. Während beispielsweise unter Dal'stroj noch bis Ende 1953 der Leiter einer Wirtschaftsverwaltung die Frage der Krankenversorgung in einer Siedlung unmittelbar durch einen Befehl klären konnte, so waren nach Neuordnung der Institutionen eine Vielzahl von Einrichtungen und Akteuren an einer solchen Frage beteiligt. Bis zur Bewilligung einer neuen Krankenstation mussten seit 1954 alle hierarchischen Ebenen der Sowjetunion abgeschritten werden, zunächst innerhalb des Gebietes – von einer lokalen Sowjetverwaltung über die Abteilung für das Gesundheitswesen der Bezirksleitung bis zum Gebietsexekutivkomitee – anschließend im Austausch mit den entsprechenden Ministerien. Im konkreten Fall der Krankenversorgung bildete eine Verordnung des Ministerrates der UdSSR die Grundlage[309], das Gebietsexekutivkomitee musste sie jedoch in Abstimmung mit dem

---

ihre Entdeckungen den Lenin-Preis. Doch schon im Jahr 1961 wurde ihre Schürfverwaltung in die lokale Verwaltung integriert. Als offizielle Begründung wurde die Bedeutung des neuen Fördergebietes genannt, tatsächlich ging es der politischen Führung aber wohl eher darum, erfolgreiche, aber unbequeme Geologen in ihre Schranken zu verweisen. Ivanov selbst wurde noch im selben Jahr nach Murmansk versetzt. Vgl. Palymskij, Sejmčanskoe RajGRU. Diesen für die weitere industrielle Entwicklung der Region so folgenreichen Fall hat Oleg Kuvaev in seinem Geologen-Roman „Goldsucher" anschaulich porträtiert. In der Figur des Geologen Tschikow meint man Ivanov zu erkennen. Tschikow erhält im Roman, in etwa ebenso wie Ivanov, die Gelder für seine Expeditionen nach Tschukotka nicht von der lokalen Verwaltung Dal'stroj, sondern unmittelbar vom Ministerium für Geologie. Als unionsweite, vom MVD unabhängige Institution war das Ministerium, in dieser Darstellung, bereit, in die Zukunft des Gebietes und damit in die Zukunft der gesamten UdSSR zu investieren, einen Neuanfang zu wagen, geleitet allein vom Engagement der Geologen und nicht von den Machtkämpfen der alten Führung. Siehe zur Geologen-Literatur ausführlicher Kapitel 5.1.5.

308 Vgl. das Schreiben des Sekretärs Timofeev vom 12. September 1957 an die Sekretäre von Stadt-, Bezirk- und Kreisparteikomitees in GAMO f. R-146, op. 1, d. 221, l. 56–57.

309 Die Zahl der Krankenbetten in dem Gebiet sollte um 400 erhöht und die Zahl der Ärzte um insgesamt 135 erweitert werden. Hinzu kam eine Verordnung des Ministerrates der RSFSR, nach der allen indigenen Bevölkerungsgruppen Medikamente ab 1954 kostenlos ausgegeben werden sollten. Vgl. die von Malenkov angeordneten Maßnahmen, zur Umsetzung der Verordnung des Ministerrates in GAMO f. R-146, op. 1, d. 6, l. 185–195 sowie den ausführlichen Befehl des Ministers für Buntmetalle zur Umsetzung in GAMO f. R-146, op. 1, d. 6, l. 213–230.

Finanzministerium (für die Gehälter der neuen Ärzte)[310] und dem Gesundheitsministerium der RSFSR (für die Bereitstellung des Inventars) umsetzen. Schließlich wurden in der Region Dal'stroj und seine entsprechende Wirtschaftsverwaltung beauftragt, die neuen Ärzte mit Wohnraum zu versorgen, eventuell sogar ein neues Gebäude zu errichten und die Räume mit Heizung und elektrischer Energie auszustatten. Der Transport von neuem Personal und Einrichtungen erfolgte in den ersten Jahren ebenfalls über Dal'stroj, später dann mit Hilfe eigener Handelsorganisationen.[311]

Die hier beispielhaft geschilderten Entscheidungswege zeigen einen hohen Grad an institutioneller Vernetzung, der auf der sowjetischen Planwirtschaft und einem gewaltigen bürokratischen Apparat fußte. Bei der institutionellen Ausgestaltung des neuen Herrschaftsraumes war diese Angleichung an die sowjetische Verwaltungsnorm der entscheidende Schritt von der militärischen Kommandowirtschaft der MVD-Hauptabteilung zu einer autoritären bürokratischen Verwaltungsherrschaft unter Führung der Partei.[312] Selbst kleine Entscheidungen zogen aufgrund des materiellen Mangels und durch festgeschriebene Entscheidungsstrukturen eine gewaltige Papierflut, zahlreiche Dokumentationen, Anordnungen, Berichte und Bestellungen nach sich.

Politische Entscheidungen wurden so voraussehbarer, weil sie weniger von persönlichen lokalen Vorlieben und Entscheidungen der Einzelleitung abhingen, sondern vielmehr an Verwaltungsabläufe und Regeln gebunden waren, die unabhängig von der Kolyma aufgestellt worden waren. Sie erforderten Abstimmungen mit republik- und unionsweiten Institutionen, die ohne ein gewisses Maß an Vertrauen in Regelungen und Strukturen nicht auskamen.[313] Dementsprechend verwies Afanas'ev in seinen Anweisungen an untergebene Bezirksstellen häufig auf die Praxis in anderen Gebieten der Sowjetunion und übertrug diese auf die Gegebenheiten in der Region.[314]

Um diese Vernetzung auch verwaltungstechnisch bewältigen zu können, musste in Magadan eine Gebiets-Finanzabteilung sowie ein Kontor für kommunale und landwirtschaftliche Banken eingerichtet werden. Bereits im März 1954 hatte sich Afanas'ev mit der Bitte um eine Verbesserung der finanztechnischen Infrastruktur an Malenkov gewandt. Bis zur Gebietsgründung hatte es in Magadan lediglich eine

---

310 Vgl. die Anordnung an das Finanzministerium in GAMO f. R-146, op. 1, d. 6, l. 185–195.
311 Für entsprechende Dienstleistungen wie Transporte oder die Bereitstellung von Heizmaterial konnte Dal'stroj von ihm festgesetzte Preise verlangen. Vgl. die Regelung in RGAĖ f. 9163, op. 6, d. 13, l. 99.
312 Siehe zur wachsenden Bedeutung der Parteiorganisationen in Wirtschaftsfragen Schröder, Lebendige Verbindung, S. 550–559.
313 Zur Bedeutung des Nexus zwischen „Vertrauen" und „Institutionen" siehe Gorlizki, Structures of Trust, S. 122.
314 Siehe diverse Berichte Afanas'evs in GAMO f. R-146, op. 1, d. 212, l. 35–39 sowie l. 44–46 (aus dem Jahr 1955) und GAMO f. R-146, op. 1, d. 212, l. 74–77 (aus dem Jahr 1958).

einzige Vertretung der staatlichen Bank gegeben. Nun waren jedoch dringend Finanzeinrichtungen vonnöten, die in der Lage waren, die Geldeinnahmen und -ausgaben zahlreicher Institutionen und die Zahlungen diverser Ministerien und Organisationen zu verbuchen, Gelder auszuzahlen und so eine effektive Arbeit zu ermöglichen.[315]

Die wachsende institutionelle Vernetzung der Region hatte viele praktische Konsequenzen: Das Gebiet wurde innerhalb kurzer Zeit Ziel einer großen Gruppe von Dienstreisenden. Zivile Funktionäre kamen von einer Vielzahl von Ministerien, sowjetischen Organisationen und Einrichtungen in die Region, sie verlangten Einblicke in ihre jeweiligen Verantwortungsbereiche. Zugleich strömten Vertreter aus den einzelnen Bezirken nach Magadan, um ihre Anliegen vorzutragen und zu klären. In Ermangelung eines regulären, zivilen Flug- und Fährverkehrs war allerdings die Anreise und dann auch die Unterbringung der Dienstreisenden sehr kompliziert. Selbst in Magadan gab es kein einziges freies Hotel, wie Afanas'ev in einer Beschwerde über Dal'stroj an den Ministerrat der RSFSR äußerte. In dem größten Komplex der Stadt, der als „Hotel" bezeichnet wurde, war seit Jahren die Verwaltung des *Sevvostlag* untergebracht, ein weiteres Hotelgebäude wurde von Dal'stroj-Funktionären zweckentfremdet.[316] Die praktischen Schwierigkeiten, die diese Reisenden mit sich brachten, demonstrieren besonders anschaulich, welch Novum sie selbst darstellten. Die Anwesenheit all dieser Menschen in der Gebietshauptstadt war zugleich ein deutliches Zeichen für die Öffnung, die mit der Angleichung der Region einherging.

Der Anstieg der Dienstreisen war dabei in den 1950er Jahren ein unionsweites Phänomen.[317] Immer mehr Verträge und Beziehungen zwischen einzelnen Unternehmen, aber auch politische Kontrolle und Direktiven wurden durch persönliche Reisen ausgehandelt und überwacht, bis die Kosten für diese Reisen einen Umfang annahmen, der von der sowjetischen Staatsbank als nicht mehr tragbar erachtet

---

315 Vgl. das Schreiben an den Vorsitzenden des Ministerrates der UdSSR, Malenkov, vom 11. März 1954 in GAMO f. R-146, op. 1, d. 60, l. 7. Der Ministerrat der UdSSR hatte in seiner Verordnung vom 29. Mai 1954 dem Finanzministerium die Einrichtung eines Bankkontors und einer Finanzabteilung des Gebietes sowie den Bau entsprechender Gebäude befohlen. Vgl. die ausführlichen Maßnahmen zu der Verordnung des Ministerrates in GAMO f. R-146, op. 1, d. 6, l. 185–195.

316 Von dieser „Zweckentfremdung" des Hotels berichtet auch Robert Conquest, der auf diverse Häftlingserinnerungen rekurriert; vgl. Conquest, Kolyma, S. 74. Vgl. das Schreiben von Afanas'ev an den Vorsitzenden des Ministerrates der RSFSR, Puzanov, in GAMO f. R-146, op. 1, d. 50, l. 2. Afanas'ev bat inständig darum, das Hotel an das Stadtexekutivkomitee zu übergeben. Im Laufe der 1950er Jahre entspannte sich die Lage durch den Neubau von Hotels in Magadan etwas, sie blieb jedoch noch lange Zeit schwierig, da neben den Dienstreisenden auch alle neuankommenden Arbeiter und Funktionäre zunächst nach Magadan reisen mussten und dann von dort aus langsam auf die einzelnen Bezirke verteilt wurden. In den einzelnen Bezirken und Siedlungen blieb die Frage der Unterbringung selbst von leitenden Funktionären auf Dienstreisen auch Ende der 1950er Jahre ein großes Problem.

317 Vgl. die statistischen Angaben in GARF f. A-259, op. 42, d. 5281, l. 73.

wurde.[318] Seit 1954 hatte also auch das Magadaner Gebiet daran Anteil, zumal die schlechten Telefonverbindungen zwischen Magadan und den weit entfernt liegenden Bezirken besonders viele Reisen notwendig machten.

Innerhalb der regionalen Machtstrukturen erhielt das Kombinat einen neuen Platz. Ein aufmerksamer Leser der Tageszeitung *Magadanskaja Pravda* konnte diese Entwicklung schon an der gewandelten Autorenschaft ablesen. Zwischen 1954 und 1957 meldeten sich die Mitarbeiter des Kombinats immer seltener mit eigenen Beiträgen zu Wort. Und wenn sie dies taten, dann sank ihr Anteil an Artikeln, die sich mit allgemein-politischen Themen im Magadaner Gebiet oder der Sowjetunion und mit der gesamten industriellen Entwicklung der Region beschäftigten, rapide ab. Bis 1957 musste sich die Leitung des Kombinats ganz auf Beiträge zu technischen Einzelheiten oder Fragen der Planerfüllung beschränken, alle anderen Themen besetzte das Partei- und das Exekutivkomitee, Vertreter vom Komsomol oder von Gewerkschaften.[319] Der Abdruck von Reden Afanas'evs, Ababkovs und anderer Vertreter der neuen Leitung füllte fortan ganze Seiten der Tageszeitung, ebenso wie ausführliche Berichte über einzelne Veranstaltungen von Partei und Sowjet.[320]

Parallel dazu entwickelte sich Dal'stroj in der praktischen Politik zu einem reinen Industriekombinat, dem Fristen und Finanzen zugewiesen wurden, das sich an Absprachen halten und seine Position zwischen der lokalen Partei- und Sowjetleitung, dem MCM, dem Ministerrat der RSFSR, der UdSSR, unions- und republikweiten Organisationen und dem ZK der KPdSU behaupten musste. Die Beziehungen zwischen dem Gebietsexekutivkomitee, den einzelnen Einrichtungen und den diversen Abteilungen von Dal'stroj wurden entweder durch Anweisungen übergeordneter Stellen geklärt oder sie beruhten auf Verträgen, die die Ansprüche der zivilen Einrichtungen an das Kombinat festlegten.

Verträge waren die neue bürokratische Norm in der Region, mit der Beziehungen zwischen formal gleichgestellten Organisationen geregelt werden sollten.[321] So beispielsweise beim Umschlag und dem Transport von Waren zwischen dem Gebietsexekutivkomitee und Dal'stroj oder bei der so wichtigen Instandhaltung von Straßen.[322] Ebenso bestanden seit 1953 Verträge zwischen der Wirtschaftsleitung und

---

318 Siehe die Übersicht der Staatsbank über Kosten von Dienstreisen an den Ministerrat der UdSSR, auf der Grundlage einer Untersuchung von 107 Industriebetrieben im August 1958 in RGANI f. 5, op. 20, d. 180, l. 106–112.

319 Siehe beispielsweise den Artikel von Berezin, dem stellvertretenden Leiter von Dal'stroj, kurz vor der Auflösung des Kombinats, „Unsere wichtigste Aufgabe", in: Magadanskaja Pravda, 29. Mai 1957, S. 2.

320 Ausführlich zum Wandel von Themen und Autoren in der *Magadanskaja Pravda* siehe Sprau, Magadanskaja pressa.

321 Zur Stärkung organisatorischer Normen und Regularien in der Politik unter Chruščev siehe Gill, Question of Reformability, S. 142.

322 Vgl. das Schreiben von Afanas'ev an den Ministerrat der RSFSR vom 11. Dezember 1956 in GAMO f. R-146, op. 1, d. 61, l. 99–100. Afanas'ev beschreibt dort die Regelungen des Warentransports, für die Autostraßen siehe GAMO f. R-146, op. 1, d. 501, l. 28–34.

Sevvostlag, auf deren Grundlage die einzelnen Produktionsleiter bei nahe gelegenen Lagerpunkten Zwangsarbeiter „entleihen" konnten.[323] Die Notwendigkeit, die Einhaltung bestehender Verträge und Absprachen zu überprüfen sowie bei Fragen des institutionellen Ausgleichs zu schlichten, wurde im Zuge dessen immer offensichtlicher; sie sollte durch eine Ausweitung von Schiedsgerichten ermöglicht werden. Der stellv. Vorsitzende des Gebietsexekutivkomitees, Čistjakov, schilderte die Situation in einem Schreiben an den Leiter der Hauptschiedsgerichtsstelle beim Ministerrat der UdSSR:

> Seit Gründung des Magadaner Gebietes mit ihrem Bestand von 13 Bezirken wuchs das System der Vertragsbeziehungen zwischen staatlichen, gesellschaftlichen und genossenschaftlichen Organisationen. Die Überwachung der Stärkung von vertraglicher und planerischer Disziplin und die Wirtschaftlichkeit der Organisationen liegt bei dem einzigen staatlichen Schiedsgericht im Gebiet, das aus einem einzigen Schiedsrichter besteht.[324]

Die Abteilung des Schiedsgerichts beim Gebietsexekutivkomitee sollte deshalb personell und finanziell erheblich aufgestockt werden, um den Geltungsbereich dieser Behörde ausweiten zu können.

Seit 1954 entwickelte sich im sowjetischen Nordosten allmählich die Herrschaftsstruktur des sowjetischen bürokratischen Verwaltungsregimes, in dem eine Vielzahl von Institutionen und Akteuren ihre Ansprüche und Kompetenzverteilungen miteinander aushandeln mussten.[325] Stefan Plaggenborg hat die Beschreibung des nationalsozialistischen Staates durch Ernst Fraenkel als „Maßnahmen- und Normenstaat" auf den sowjetischen Staat übertragen. Plaggenborg hat dabei v. a. auf die gestiegene Bedeutung des Rechts für das sowjetische System nach Stalins Tod verwiesen, dessen „Janusgesicht" sich als eine Zunahme des Normenstaates, bei Weiterexistenz der Maßnahmen, beschreiben ließe.[326]

Diese Begrifflichkeiten lassen sich gewinnbringend auf die Verhältnisse im sowjetischen Nordosten übertragen, wenn die Verengung auf Veränderungen im Justizwesen aufgebrochen wird. Der neue „Normenstaat" im Magadaner Gebiet kam ohne Maßnahmen nicht aus, aber die elementare Begrenzung der Rechte der neuen politischen Leitung im Vergleich zu der militärischen Einzelleitung von Dal'stroj ist ein entscheidender Unterschied zwischen der Raumeroberung im Stalinismus und während der Entstalinisierung. Die Herrschaftsverhältnisse wurden normierter, bere-

---

[323] Vgl. die Musterverträge aus dem Jahr 1956 in GAMO f. R-23, op. 1, d. 5844, l. 20–35.
[324] Schreiben vom 24. August 1954 in GAMO f. R-146, op. 1, d. 60, l. 47–48.
[325] Vgl. Khlevniuk, Economy sowie, noch immer zutreffend in der Analyse der Machtverhältnisse in einer sowjetischen Provinz, Hough; Fainsod, Soviet Union is Governed, S. 506 f.
[326] Plaggenborg, Experiment, S. 204; vgl. Fraenkel, Doppelstaat sowie Ladwig-Winters, Fraenkel, S. 123–175. Siehe zu der Debatte um die Fraenkel'schen Begrifflichkeiten für ein Verständnis der Sowjetunion Hilger, Grenzen, S. 272 sowie zur Übertragung auf die Verhältnisse in der DDR Huemer, Doppelstaat DDR.

chenbarer, sie begrenzten die Möglichkeiten der Willkür einzelner Kader und von einzelnen Organisationseinheiten.

3.3.4 Offene Auseinandersetzungen und das Ende von Dal'stroj

Auf den Parteikonferenzen des Gebietes und der einzelnen Bezirke tauschten sich Parteifunktionäre intensiv über ihre Schwierigkeiten mit dem Kombinat Dal'stroj in verschiedenen Arbeitsbereichen – bei Baumaßnahmen, fehlender sozialer Infrastruktur, dem schlechten Transportwesen etc. – aus und berichteten ausführlich von ihren jeweiligen Aufgaben. Die Vorwürfe an Dal'stroj betrafen Verzögerungen aus Schludrigkeit, mangelnde Planungen, Desinteresse oder auch offene Feindseligkeiten gegen die neue Leitung. So beschwerte sich der Leiter der Abteilung für Landwirtschaft des Magadaner Gebietsparteikomitees bei Ababkov und Afanas'ev über den Leiter einer Autostation in der Siedlung „Linkes Ufer" an der Kolyma. Dieser Leiter habe seine gesamte Station demontieren lassen, nachdem er von dem Beschluss des Gebietsparteikomitees gehört hatte, diese Station in eine Maschinen-Traktoren-Station des neuen Gebietes zu verwandeln. Ein Telegramm des Bezirksparteikomitees, das den Abbau stoppen sollte, warf er vor den Augen des Vertreters der obersten Parteileitung in den Mülleimer und bemerkte: „Mir hat das Gebietsparteikomitee gar nichts zu befehlen, mein Leiter ist Mitrakov!"[327] Auch die moralische Haltung einzelner Funktionäre und ihre Kaderpolitik wurden debattiert. Zum Teil erstellte das Gebietsparteikomitee auf der Grundlage dieser Sitzungen ganze Dossiers über Dal'stroj („Kritische Anmerkungen der Delegierten an Dal'stroj" oder „Fragen an Dal'stroj") und übergab sie dem Kombinat, z. T. wandten sich die Funktionäre aber auch direkt an Dal'stroj.[328]

Kritik an der Leitung von Dal'stroj wurde in den 1950er Jahren zu einer Art „common sense" unter den lokalen Vertretern von Partei und Sowjet. Der damalige Erste Sekretär des Gebietskomitees des Komsomol, A. D. Bogdanov, erinnert sich an das Verhältnis zum Kombinat: „In dieser Zeit Dal'stroj nicht zu kritisieren ... [wie wäre das seltsam gewesen – M. S.], nur die Faulen haben Dal'stroj nicht kritisiert."[329] Auf verschiedenen Ebenen versuchten sie den Wirtschaftskadern zu drohen – mit einem

---

327 Vgl. den Bericht in GAMO f. R-146, op. 1, d. 7, l. 89–91, hier l. 90.

328 Vgl. das Protokoll der „Kritischen Anmerkungen der Delegierten der zweiten Gebietsparteikonferenz an die Adresse der Hauptverwaltung Dal'stroj des Ministeriums für Buntmetalle" in GAMO f. P-21, op. 5. d. 520, l. 103–115. Siehe beispielhaft auch die an Dal'stroj gerichteten Fragen auf einzelnen Parteikonferenzen in den Bezirken, zusammengestellt vom Gebietsparteikomitee (März 1956) in GAMO f. R-23sč, op. 1, d. 456, l. 2–3 sowie die „Kritischen Anmerkungen und Vorschläge der Delegierten, an die Adresse der Hauptverwaltung Dal'stroj des Ministeriums für Buntmetalle" vom März 1957 in GAMO f. R-23sč, op. 1, d. 458, l. 24–30.

329 Zitiert nach Grebenjuk, Kolymskij led, S. 229. Zur Kritik an Dal'stroj auf der 1. Parteikonferenz im Mai 1954 siehe Grebenjuk, Smechovaja Praktika, S. 324 f.

Hinweis an das ZK der KPdSU, einem Bericht an den Ministerrat oder das entsprechende Ministerium oder auch mit der Einschaltung der Staatsanwaltschaft.[330]

Im Büro des Gebietsparteikomitees trafen mit Mitrakov, Ababkov und Afanas'ev drei Leitungsfiguren aufeinander, die um eine Abgrenzung ihrer jeweiligen Machtkompetenzen und Zuständigkeiten rangen. In ihrer Arbeit waren sie jedoch zugleich auch eng aufeinander bezogen, sie vereinte eine gemeinsame Aufgabe: Sie alle trugen persönlich die Verantwortung für eine Stabilisierung der Goldförderung, für die Herstellung einer gewissen sozialen Ordnung in der Region, für die Schaffung einer neuen, freien Arbeitskräftebasis.[331] Die angespannte Stimmung unter den beteiligten Akteuren schildert der damalige Leiter der Abteilung für Agitation und Propaganda im Gebietsparteikomitee, Ivan Nikolaevič Kaštanov, anschaulich in einem Interview mit dem Magadaner Historiker Grebenjuk:

> Die Sache entwickelte sich schlecht für das Kombinat. Sie haben die Gründung des Gebiets, direkt gesagt, nicht gut aufgenommen – der Leiter von Dal'stroj, Mitrakov, und die alten Kader. Da gab es einen Machtkampf. [...] Erst waren sie [die obersten Funktionäre von Dal'stroj – M. S.] Zar und Gott und militärische Führer, und dann erscheint da das Gebietsparteikomitee, das mehr und mehr wichtige Fragen an sich zieht, ins machtpolitische Zentrum eindringt und sie ausschließt. [...] Dieser Machtkampf war heftig. Zusammenstöße gab es direkt im Büro [des Gebietsparteikomitees – M. S.]. Die Leute konnten sich nicht zurückhalten. Die Partei-Arbeiter haben nicht immer die Wirtschaftsleute verstanden. Wir [die Partei-Leute – M. S.] standen um einiges höher. [...] Die Wirtschaftsleute haben die Partei-Arbeiter wie so einen Überbau wahrgenommen – die Intelligenz, die im Allgemeinen nicht viel versteht, aber versucht zu befehlen.[332]

Das kulturelle Überlegenheitsgefühl, das die Funktionäre des Parteiorgans nach den Erinnerungen von Kaštanov auszeichnete, war Ausdruck ihres prinzipiellen Machtanspruchs, aber auch ihres lokalen Rollenverständnisses, das die „Partei-Arbeiter" gegenüber den Leuten von Dal'stroj als Vertreter der reinen sowjetischen Strukturen und Werte erscheinen ließ. Mit ihnen, so ihre Darstellung, bräche ein völlig neues Kapitel der regionalen Geschichte an, die sowjetische Geschichte des nordöstlichen Raumes zerfalle in eine Epoche vor Gründung des Magadaner Gebietes und eine Zeit danach: „Jetzt beginnt eine neue Etappe in der Geschichte der Region, jetzt, da sich der Ferne Nordosten noch schneller entwickeln und aufblühen wird"[333], so hieß es in der ersten Vorstellung des neuen Gebietes in der Zeitung *Magadanskaja Pravda*. Im Folgenden entstand ein regelrechter Gründungsmythos. Die Jahrestage wurden in der Tageszeitung aufwändig gefeiert. Der „Geburtstag" wurde dabei z. T. mit dem Beginn

---

330 Vgl. beispielsweise die Drohungen in GAMO f. 146, op. 1, d. 47, l. 94–114, hier l. 108.

331 Dementsprechend wandten sie sich bereits kurz nach Gründung des Gebietes in einem gemeinsamen Schreiben an Malenkov und Chruščev und baten um erhöhte finanzielle Mittel für die Aufgaben des Kombinats. Auf diese allgemeine Linie zur weiteren Stärkung der Region konnte man sich offensichtlich einigen. Vgl. ihren Brief vom 18. Februar 1954 in RGANI f. 5, op. 27, d. 233, l. 92–99.

332 Interview, geführt von Grebenjuk im Jahr 2006, vgl. Grebenjuk, Kolymskij led, S. 232 (1. Teil), S. 234 (2. Teil), S. 235 (3. Teil).

333 Magadanskaja Pravda, 7. Februar 1954, S. 1.

Abb. 15a und 15b Magadanskaja Pravda, 1. Januar 1955

des neuen Jahres synchronisiert, was der Erinnerung an die Gebietsgründung einen besonders festlichen Charakter verlieh. Am 1. Januar 1955 beging die *Magadanskaja Pravda* den ersten Geburtstag – unter den Überschriften „Unser Gebiet – ein Jahr!" und „Blühe, nördliches Land".

Die politische Leitung inszenierte eine Sicht auf die Region, die erst unter ihrer Herrschaft zu sich selbst gefunden habe. Sie machte ihre Machtübernahme zum Ausgangspunkt einer neuen Ära. Afanas'ev brachte diese Repräsentation auf den Punkt, wenn er von der Gebietsgründung als der „zweiten Geburt" der Region sprach.[334]

Die Partei trat damit offensiv nicht nur in den Kampf um die Macht, sondern auch um die Deutungshoheit über die Region ein. Sie hatte dabei zwei Adressaten – die bisherige Leitung von Dal'stroj, die in ihrem Machtanspruch beschnitten und auf die Wirtschaftspolitik reduziert, sowie die freie Bevölkerung, die von den positiven Auswirkungen der strukturellen Veränderungen auf ihr persönliches Leben überzeugt werden sollte.

Die Inszenierung von Gründung und Geburt setzte eine Abwertung der vormaligen Herrschaft voraus. Die Kombinatsleitung, die zu ihrem 25-jährigen Bestehen im Jahr 1956 selbst zwei Publikationen herausgab, die die „industriellen Leistungen" von Dal'stroj und seine Perspektiven würdigten, wurde dabei zugleich dem Überkomme-

---

334 Afanas'ev, Rossija, S. 52.

О СЛАВНОМ
трудовом пу-
ти многотысячного
коллектива Даль-
строя подробно и
интересно расска-
зывает выпущен-
ная Магаданским книжным изда-
тельством к 25-летию Дальстроя
книга «Дальстрой». Эта книга пред-

**По поводу одной статьи
в книге „Дальстрой"**

бина создается впечатление, что «ко-
ренные» вопросы мерзлотоведения,
этой молодой еще науки о распро-

много сделавшего для раскрытия
«тайны» Северо-Востока и тем со-
действовавшего работе Дальстроя.

мощности многолетней криолитозоны
данных горных районов впервые
ла установлена Н. В. Губкиным
1944—1946 гг. и впоследствии
тверждена П. Ф. Швецовым.
Явно знакомым кажется и друг
обобщающий вывод А. И. Калаб
на, выделенный жирным шрифто
«Подмерзлотные воды могут бы
получены для водоснабжения кру

Abb. 16 „Zu einen Aufsatz im Buch ‚Dal'stroj'", Magadanskaja Pravda, 17. Mai 1957

ечу промывочному сезону

**ЗАВОДЫ ДАЛЬСТРОЯ
ПЛОХО ВЫПОЛНЯЮТ
ЗАКАЗЫ ГОРНЯКОВ**

Коллективы предприятий Тенькинского
горнопромышленного управления, сорев-
нуясь за досрочное выполнение плана
1956 года, активно готовятся к промывоч-

ного цилиндра. На главной лебедке экска-
ватора № 53-24 местами были перепута-
ны тросовые барабаны. Остались неисправ-
ными реверсы двух других экскаваторов.

Abb. 17 „Die Fabriken von Dal'stroj erfüllen die Aufträge der Bergleute nicht", Magadanskaja Pravda,
1. April 1956

nen zugeschlagen. Ihre Selbstdarstellung wurde in der *Magadanskaja Pravda* kritisch
kommentiert (Abbildung 16).[335]

Mitrakov selbst wurde am 17. Februar 1956 seines Amtes enthoben, sein bisheriger
Stellvertreter Ju. V. Čuguev fungierte fortan als Leiter von Dal'stroj.[336]

Während innerhalb der Organe von Partei und Sowjet Vorbehalte gegenüber
Dal'stroj geäußert wurden, blieb die öffentliche Kritik in der Tageszeitung *Magadanskaja Pravda* noch auf einzelne Bereiche – wie die mangelnde Versorgung der
Bevölkerung – beschränkt.[337] Im Laufe der Zeit wurde sie jedoch immer schärfer;
schon 1955 erschien ein Artikel über das Gebietsparteikomitee, in dem offene, na-
mentliche Kritik an der Leitung des Kombinats, an Mitrakov und Čuguev, geübt
wurde.[338] Seit 1957 wurde das Kombinat allgemein für die „Rückständigkeit" der Region im sozialen und infrastrukturellen Bereich verantwortlich gemacht, seine Arbeitsweise als „fehlerhaft" und nicht mehr „zeitgemäß" gebrandmarkt.

Diese Kritik folgte einer sorgfältigen Sprachregelung, bei der das Kombinat in
keinem Fall grundsätzlich diskreditiert wurde; schließlich baute die neue Leitung

---

335 Vgl. K 25-letiju sowie Gruša, 25 let.

336 Vgl. Kokurin/Morukov, Stalinskie strojki, S. 502.

337 So bereits in dem Artikel „Polnee udovletvorjat' zaprosy naselenija", in: Magadanskaja Pravda,
16. Februar 1954, S. 2.

338 Vgl. „V oblastnom komitete KPSS: O rabote sovchozov i podsobnych chozjajstv Dal'stroja v 1955
godu", in: Magadanskaja Pravda, 28. Oktober 1955, S. 2.

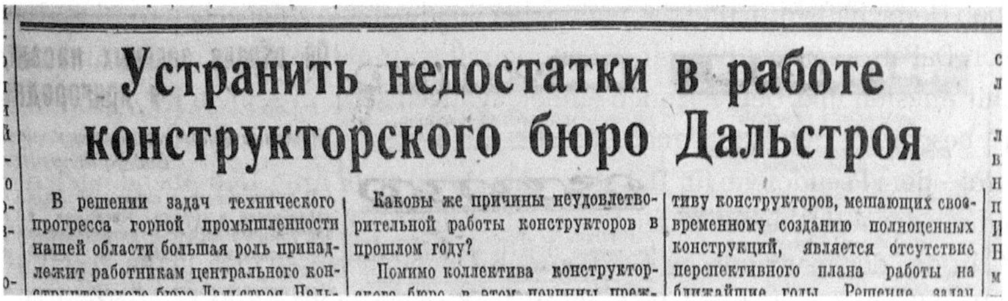

Устранить недостатки в работе конструкторского бюро Дальстроя

В решении задач технического прогресса горной промышленности нашей области большая роль принадлежит работникам центрального кон-

Каковы же причины неудовлетворительной работы конструкторов в прошлом году?

Помимо коллектива конструктор-

тиву конструкторов, мешающих своевременному созданию полноценных конструкций, является отсутствие перспективного плана работы на

Abb. 18 „Unzulänglichkeiten bei der Arbeit des Dal'strojer Konstrukteursbüro beseitigen", Magadanskaja Pravda, 13. Mai 1957

personell und infrastrukturell auf Dal'stroj auf. Damit schloss sich die Magadaner Führung einer neuen Rhetorik an, die für den australischen Historiker Graeme Gill ein wichtiges Element der gewandelten offiziellen Sprachregelung der Entstalinisierung war. Statt der Rede von den „inneren Feinden", mit denen im Stalinismus Personen belegt wurden, die der Sowjetunion „Schaden zufügten" und die deshalb zu „vernichten" seien, dominierte nun die unpersönliche Rede von „Missständen" oder „Defiziten", die auszugleichen wären.[339]

In diesen Tenor verfiel auch Afanas'ev in seiner Darstellung des „kommunistischen Aufbaus" im Nordosten für den Band „10 Jahre". Dort widersprach er einer globalen Verurteilung der Kader von Dal'stroj:

> Aber die Tätigkeit von Dal'stroj, bei all ihren Fehlern, darf man nicht von der Rechnung nehmen. Die Kollektive der Betriebe von Dal'stroj [ganz offensichtlich ist hier nicht von der Kombinatsleitung die Rede – M. S.] haben große Arbeit bei der Umgestaltung des rauen Gebietes geleistet. Die Zeit von Dal'stroj ist ein dunkles Zeitalter [sic!]. Aber selbst unter diesen Bedingungen haben sich die Parteiorganisationen, Kommunisten und Komsomolzen aktiv an der Erschließung des natürlichen Reichtums des Nordostens beteiligt.[340]

Die bisherigen ökonomischen Leistungen des Kombinats präsentierte die neue Führung darum als allgemeine Errungenschaften der sowjetischen Macht im Nordosten, um sie so als „Vorgeschichte" des Gebietes vereinnahmen zu können, ohne zugleich all die Kader zu verurteilen, die auch unter den neuen Verhältnissen im Amt verblieben.[341]

Im Juni 1957 wurde das Kombinat Dal'stroj aufgelöst. Nach dem Ende des Lagersystems *Sevvostlag* im April 1957 waren damit die beiden Kernelemente der stali-

339 Vgl. Gill, Symbols, S. 172.

340 Afanas'ev, Kommunisty, S. 13–14.

341 1961 erschien eine ausführliche historische Darstellung, die die Geschichte von Dal'stroj als eine Abfolge von Parteitagen schilderte und in der alle „Erfolge" von Dal'stroj der Tätigkeit von Kommunisten zugeschrieben wurden. Den Versuchen, reguläre Parteiorganisationen in der Region einzuführen, wurde dabei viel Raum eingeräumt, ebenso wie der Darstellung des Versuchs, 1939 eine zivile administrative Struktur unter Führung der Partei zu gründen. Vgl. Žicharev, Očerki, S. 220 f.

nistischen Herrschaftsform und des regionalen Sonderstatus aufgegeben worden. Das Ende von Dal'stroj musste bei seiner Leitung mit enormer persönlicher Verunsicherung, mit Ängsten und Depressionen einhergegangen sein. In seinem Roman „Goldsucher" beschreibt der Magadaner Geologe Kuvaev den Erlass zur Auflösung von Severstroj – dem Pseudonym für Dal'stroj – als „Ende einer Ära". Den Abend nach der Verkündung der Aufgabe der Bezeichnung „Dal'stroj" schildert er als „Nacht der Infarkte", in der der medizinische Notdienst in Magadan eine ganze Reihe kollabierender Funktionäre zu behandeln hatte.[342] Im Sommer 1957 übertraf die Zahl der Selbstmorde im Magadaner Gebiet noch einmal deutlich die während der gesamten 1950er Jahre erschreckend hohe Rate.[343]

Nach außen hin war jedoch nur sehr verhalten eine Veränderung erkennbar. Auf den Seiten der *Magadanskaja Pravda* zeigte sich die historische Bedeutung dieses Schritts allenfalls an einer ungewöhnlich deutlichen und offen historischen Beurteilung des Kombinats durch seinen Leiter Čuguev:

> Wenn man die Ergebnisse der Tätigkeit von Dal'stroj analysiert, dann wird klar, dass für eine ziemlich kurze historische Zeitspanne, für gerade einmal 25 Jahre, auf dem Gebiet des Nordostens unseres Landes große Schürfarbeiten vorgenommen, gewaltige Industrieanlagen gebaut wurden [...], das heißt alles Notwendige für die Entwicklung des später gegründeten Magadaner Gebietes. Aber bei der Tätigkeit von Dal'stroj gab es auch viele negative Seiten. [...] Einer der grundlegenden Fehler von Dal'stroj war, wie mir scheint, die einseitige Wirtschaftsentwicklung. [...] Der zweite, sehr schwer wiegende Fehler in der Arbeit von Dal'stroj bestand darin, dass es, während es die Aufgaben der Metallförderung erfüllte, [...] dem Staat jedes Jahr große Verluste eintrug und die Selbstkosten seiner Produktion sehr hoch waren.[344]

Čuguev formulierte eine kritische Beurteilung des Kombinats, bekannte schwerwiegende Fehler durch eine „einseitige Wirtschaftsentwicklung" und hohe Belastungen für die sowjetische Volkswirtschaft, er ordnete sogar das Kombinat als eine notwendige Vorstufe gewissermaßen historisch dem neuen Gebiet unter. Tatsächlich aber war die Auflösung des Kombinats nicht allein Ergebnis der neuen Machtverteilung in der Region, sondern vielmehr logische Folge der unionsweiten Einführung der „Volkswirtschaftsräte" (*sovnarchozy*).

Mit dieser großangelegten Wirtschaftsreform beabsichtigte Chruščev im Sommer 1957, die extreme Zentralisierung der stalinistischen Wirtschaftsordnung zu überwinden und zugleich die lokalen Parteifunktionäre in ihrer Leitungs- und Kontrollfunktion über sämtliche Aspekte des Lebens einer Region zu stärken. Für Yoram Gorlizki war die Stärkung der Partei die eigentliche Intention hinter der Reform: „[...] the creation of regional economic councils in 1957 was designed precisely to increase local Party responsibility for industrial production."[345] Die Einführung der Volks-

---

342 Vgl. Kuwajew, Goldsucher, S. 194. Ausführlicher zu Kuvaevs Roman siehe das Kapitel 5.1.5.
343 Vgl. Grebenjuk, Kolymskij led, S. 189.
344 Čuguev, in: Magadanskaja Pravda, 13. Juni 1957, S. 2.
345 Gorlizki, Political Reform, S. 266.

wirtschaftsräte spielte damit Ababkov und Afanas'ev in ihrem Streben nach umfassendem Einfluss im Magadaner Gebiet in die Hände.[346]

Kern der ersten Reformetappe war die Auflösung sämtlicher produktionsbezogener Ministerien und die Neustrukturierung der Wirtschaft nach territorialen Gesichtspunkten. Die Betriebe, Transport- und Versorgungseinrichtungen einer bestimmten Region unterstanden von nun an einem lokalen Leitungsgremium, das unmittelbar dem Ministerrat der RSFSR bzw. der UdSSR verantwortlich war.[347]

Diese Gliederung regionaler Industrie und Landwirtschaft war mit den Strukturen von Dal'stroj nicht vereinbar, da bis 1957 der Wirtschafts- nicht mit dem Herrschaftsraum übereinstimmte. Zum Magadaner Volkswirtschaftsrat (*Magadanskij sovnarchoz*) sollten nun nur noch jene Gruben, Betriebe und Einrichtungen zählen, die innerhalb der Grenzen des Magadaner Gebietes lagen.[348] Alle weiteren Industrieanlagen und Abteilungen, die bislang zum Kombinat Dal'stroj gezählt hatten, wurden

---

346 Die Einführung der Volkswirtschaftsräte geht zurück auf eine Verordnung des Februarplenums des ZK der KPdSU 1957, basierend auf Thesen des Ersten Sekretärs Chruščev. Am 10. Mai 1957 wurde das Gesetz „Über den Umbau der Verwaltung in Industrie und Bauwirtschaft" vom Obersten Sowjet der UdSSR verabschiedet. Vgl. seine Veröffentlichung in Osnovnye zakonodatel'nye akty, S. 10.

347 Mercalov geht in seiner Analyse von drei Etappen der strukturellen Entwicklung der Chruščev'schen Volkswirtschaftsräte aus, wobei die erste Etappe (1957–1959) zu einer weitreichenden Dezentralisierung führte, die in den folgenden Etappen (1959–1962 und 1963–1965) schrittweise wieder zurückgenommen wurde. Mit der Einführung des Obersten Volkswirtschaftsrates (VSNCh) im März 1963 kehrte die Sowjetunion praktisch wieder zu einer zentralen Wirtschaftslenkung zurück. Vgl. Mercalov, Reforma chozjajstvennogo upravlenija, S. 221 f. Zur Einführung der Volkswirtschaftsräte und der wirtschaftlichen Entwicklung der Sowjetunion unter Chruščev siehe außerdem Kibita, Sovnarkhoz Reform; Kibita, Moscow-Kiev; Kibita, Alternative Version; Vasiliev; Failings; Hanson, Rise and Fall, S. 70–97 sowie Kruglov, Chozjajstvennaja reforma.

348 Die ausführliche Bezeichnung lautete „Sovet Narodnogo Chozjajstva Magadanskogo ėkonomičeskogo administrativnogo rajona (SNCH MĖAR)". Die Einrichtung basierte auf der Verordnung des Ministerrates der RSFSR vom 1. Juni 1957. Der Magadaner Volkswirtschaftsrat wurde in zwei Wirtschaftszonen aufgegliedert, den „Kolymo-Magadanskij" und den „Čukotskij" Wirtschaftsbezirk. Vgl. die genaue Beschreibung seiner Struktur in Rajzman, Struktury upravlenija. Siehe auch die 1957 in Magadan veröffentlichte offizielle Beschreibung des neuen Wirtschaftsgebietes Malagin, Ėkonomičeskij rajon. Im Jahr 1958 zählten zum Magadaner Volkswirtschaftsrat 60 Wirtschaftsbetriebe, 17 Transportorganisationen, 27 Schürfabteilungen, 24 Bauorganisationen, mehr als 50 Versorgungseinrichtungen sowie drei wissenschaftliche Institute. Vgl. den Bericht von Korolev über die Ergebnisse des Jahres 1958 in RGAĖ f. 7733, op. 47, d. 538, l. 4. Die ersten Vorschläge zur Struktur des Volkswirtschaftsrates kamen von der lokalen Parteileitung, die angeblich Vorschläge diverser Arbeiterversammlungen aufgriff. Siehe die Beschreibung der Vorgehensweise an das ZK der KPdSU durch Ababkov vom April 1957 in GAMO f. R-23, op. 1, d. 6088, l. 1–50, hier l. 1. Offiziell bestätigt wurde die neue Struktur am 26. Juni 1957 durch den Ministerrat der RSFSR und den Instrukteur der Industrie- und Transportabteilung des Büros des ZK der KPdSU für die RSFSR. Für eine Beschreibung der einzelnen Abteilungen siehe die Anlage des Schreibens von Ababkov in RGANI f. 5, op. 30, d. 201, l. 192–194. Ausführlich dazu, mit einem historischen Rückblick zu Dal'stroj und einer Prognose der Bodenschätze, das Dossier von Ababkov an das ZK, in GAMO f. R-23, op. 1, d. 6088, l. 1–50 sowie l. 54–62.

Abb. 19 „Der Volkswirtschaftsrat beseitigt Verwaltungsbarrieren", Magadanskaja Pravda, 13. Juni 1957

anderen Volkswirtschaftsräten, vor allem dem jakutischen, zugeordnet.[349] Seit 1957 waren also die ökonomische und die politische Sphäre in territorialer Hinsicht deckungsgleich. Die neue Wirtschaftsstruktur wurde von der *Magadanskaja Pravda* ausführlich vorgestellt und illustriert.

Im Bereich der Wirtschaftsleitung kam es, oberflächlich betrachtet, zwar zu keinen wesentlichen Veränderungen. Čuguev fungierte fortan als Vorsitzender des Volkswirtschaftsrates. Doch stärkte die Struktur der sowjetischen Volkswirtschaftsräte deutlich die Kompetenzen der regionalen Parteifunktionäre in ihrer Leitungs- und Kontrollfunktion. Die Leitung des Magadaner Volkswirtschaftsrates musste fortan dem Büro des Gebietsparteikomitees ausführlich Bericht erstatten und sich seinen Entscheidungen unterordnen. Auch die einzelnen Gebietsparteikomitees machten nun Vorschläge zu industriellen Fragen. Der Volkswirtschaftsrat wurde daraufhin aufgefordert, mit ausführlichen Expertisen Stellung zu den Vorschlägen zu beziehen.

---

[349] Bereits 1955 hatte sich das jakutische Gebietsparteikomitee mit dem Vorschlag an das ZK der KPdSU gewandt, Dal'stroj auf zwei Industrieverwaltungen aufzuteilen und so ein eigenes jakutisches Kombinat zu erhalten. Dal'stroj hatte sich heftig gegen diese Abtrennung der Anlagen auf dem Territorium der jakutischen ASSR gewehrt und dabei mit den bereits geleisteten Arbeiten und den großen Perspektiven des Kombinats auf diesem Gebiet argumentiert. Eine territoriale Aufteilung hätte die Metallförderung im Nordosten erheblich geschwächt. Vgl. die ausführliche Stellungnahme Mitrakovs vom 15. März 1955, gerichtet an das ZK der KPdSU in GAMO f. R-23, op. 1, d. 5610, l. 55–64.

Abb. 20 „Struktur des Volkswirtschaftsrates", Magadanskaja Pravda, 13. Juni 1957

Beide Positionen wurden sodann dem Gebietsparteikomitee vorgelegt, das die endgültige Entscheidung traf.[350]

---

[350] Vgl. das Beispiel dieser Vorgehensweise aus dem Bezirk Srednekanskij vom 30. April 1959 in GAMO f. R-137sč, op. 1b, d. 52, l. 19 – 21. Siehe für die gebietsweite Verantwortung der Partei den Bericht des Gebietsparteisekretärs Golubev bei einem Treffen des technisch-wirtschaftlichen Rates des Volkswirtschaftsrates vom 19. August 1958 in GAMO f. R-137, op. 1, d. 59a, l. 51–201, hier l. 192–195.

Abb. 21 „Der Magadaner ökonomische Verwaltungsbezirk", Magadanskaja Pravda, 13. Juni 1957

Die neue administrative Struktur hatte den Organen von Partei und Staat einen Machtbereich geschaffen, der die Wirtschaft der Region dominierte. Dieser machtpolitische Wandel ließ sich auch in den Medien erkennen. Am deutlichsten zeigte es sich im bisherigen Publikationsorgan der Hauptverwaltung von Dal'stroj, der *Kolyma*, das bis zur Auflösung des Kombinats ganz auf Fragen des Bergbaus, auf die Vorstellung von Fördergebieten und auf technische Neuerungen beschränkt geblieben war.[351] 1957 übernahm der Magadaner Volkswirtschaftsrat die Zeitschrift; in seiner ersten

---

Siehe zu den regionalen machtpolitischen Veränderungen nach der Einführung der Volkswirtschaftsräte Hildermeier, Sowjetunion, S. 802 sowie Lejbovič, Reformy, S. 230 f.

351 Die Herauslösung von Dal'stroj aus dem MVD und seine Übergabe in das MMP wurde auf den Seiten der Zeitschrift zunächst gar nicht thematisiert. Erst im November 1954 wurde die Unterstellung unter das MCM in einem Artikel deutlich (Vgl. Kolyma, Nov. 1954, S. 7), ab Januar 1955 wurde diese Zugehörigkeit auch auf dem Titelblatt sichtbar, wenn auch niemals ausdrücklich darauf hingewiesen wurde. Die Zeitschrift trug nun den Titel „Kolyma. Ežemesjačnyj proizvodstvenno-techničeskij bjulleten' Glavnogo upravlenija Dal'stroja MCM SSSR." Bis zu diesem Zeitpunkt ließ sich an der Zeitschrift *Kolyma* nicht erkennen, dass die Hauptverwaltung nicht mehr dem MVD unterstand. Seit 1957 firmierte sie unter dem Titel „Kolyma. Ežemesjačnyj proizvodstvenno-techničeskij bjulleten' Soveta narodnogo chozjajstva Magadanskogo ėkonomičeskogo administrativnogo rajona". Zum Wandel dieser Zeitschrift in den 1950er Jahren siehe ausführlich Sprau, Magadanskaja pressa.

Ausgabe stellte Čuguev den Rat ausführlich vor. Darin präsentierte Čuguev den Volkswirtschaftsrat als einen Teil des gesamten Magadaner Gebietes, als die industrielle Struktur einer größeren politischen Einheit. Ausführlich schilderte Čuguev deutliche Verbesserungen in der Industrie, die erst durch die Gebietsgründung ermöglicht worden seien.[352]

In den folgenden Jahren entwickelte sich die Zeitschrift zum Wirtschaftsorgan der *gesamten* Region; auch kulturelle Entwicklungen, Angaben über die Produktion von Verbrauchsgütern, über die medizinische Versorgung der Bevölkerung etc. wurden nun thematisiert. Zunehmend veröffentlichten auch leitende Parteifunktionäre auf den Seiten der *Kolyma*, im Juni 1958 verfasste ein Sekretär des Gebietsparteikomitees den ersten Leitartikel und im Oktober 1958 kam der neue Erste Parteisekretär, Afanas'ev, auf der Titelseite zu Wort. In seiner Schilderung der regionalen Lage mischten sich wirtschaftliche mit sozial-politischen und kulturellen Fragen; Afanas'ev gab dort auch eine positive Beurteilung des Gebietsparteikomitees durch das Büro des ZK der KPdSU für die RSFSR bekannt. In der Darstellung seiner politischen Linie sprach er sich mit Nachdruck für die Einheit der Organe von Partei, Exekutivkomitee und Volkswirtschaftsrat aus – nicht jedoch ohne ein starkes Plädoyer für die führende Rolle der Partei zu liefern und zugleich die alte Leitung von Dal'stroj zu kritisieren.[353]

Tatsächlich hatte nach Gründung des Magadaner Volkswirtschaftsrates die Partei – und unter ihrer politischen Führung auch die staatlichen Strukturen in der Region – die volle Verantwortung für die Entwicklung der Region. War die neue Führungsmannschaft noch bis 1957 in der Lage, ökonomische Probleme und die schlechten Bedingungen der freien Arbeitskräfte Dal'stroj zur Last zu legen, so musste sie nach der Einführung des Volkswirtschaftsrates nun selbst für diese Schwierigkeiten einstehen. Entsprechend sah sich bereits im Februar 1958 der Erste Parteisekretär, Ababkov, gezwungen, die politische Verantwortung für den schlechten Zustand der Goldförderung übernehmen.

Eine spezielle Kommission des Büros des ZK der KPdSU für die RSFSR, die im Auftrag des ZK Ursachen für die schlechten Wirtschaftsdaten des Magadaner Gebietes untersuchte, hatte Ababkov Unfähigkeit bei der Organisation einer rentablen Wirtschaftsweise vorgeworfen.[354] Sie hatte die Magadaner Staats- und Parteiführung nach Moskau zitiert und sie dort zwar für „große Leistungen" bei der Gebietsgründung und bei der „Beseitigung von Hindernissen der sozialistischen Gesetzlichkeit" gewürdigt, aber in ihren Augen war die Bilanz Ababkovs bei der Erfüllung der Hauptaufgabe – der

352 Die Erfolge der vergangenen vier Jahre zeigte er beispielhaft an der Senkung der Selbstkosten auf. Vgl. Kolyma, Juli 1957, S. 7.

353 Vgl. Kolyma, Oktober 1958.

354 Angeführt wurde die Kommission von dem stellv. Vorsitzenden der Abteilung für Parteiorgane des Büros des ZK der KPdSU für die RSFSR, Sevast'janov. Vgl. seinen Bericht in RGANI f. 5, op. 32, d. 111, l. 29–31. Siehe auch die Beurteilung durch das ZK der KPdSU bei Chlevnjuk, Regional'naja vlast', S. 36.

Frage nach der Zukunft der Goldförderung – katastrophal.[355] Dementsprechend folgte im Februar 1958 seine Abwahl auf der dritten regionalen Parteikonferenz.[356] Dabei wurden dem Ersten Parteisekretär zum Teil wortwörtlich die gleichen Punkte zur Last gelegt, für die die örtliche Parteiführung selbst bisher Dal'stroj kritisiert hatte – dies trifft sogar auf die Zweifel an der moralischen Integrität Ababkovs und auf die Kritik an seinem Führungsstil zu.[357] Die wirtschaftlichen Leiter der Region, Čuguev, Korolev und Berezin, wurden auf der Konferenz zwar ebenfalls kritisiert, ihr persönliches Schicksal jedoch nicht mit den schlechten Wirtschaftsdaten in Verbindung gebracht.[358]

An Stelle Ababkovs wurde, wie häufig in der Sowjetunion, der bisherige Leiter des Gebietsexekutivkomitees, Afanas'ev, zum neuen Ersten Parteisekretär gewählt.[359] Der Anstieg der Goldförderung seit Ende der 1950er Jahre garantierte ihm in der Folge das politische Überleben und eine stabile Herrschaft. Oleg Chlevnjuk und Yoram Gorlizki haben gezeigt, dass regionale Parteichefs in den späten 1950er und 1960er Jahren zu wirklichen starken lokalen Kräften aufsteigen konnten. Afanas'ev wäre hierfür ein besonders prägnantes Beispiel.[360]

3.3.5 Grenzen der politischen Sphäre – der Stellenwert der Wirtschaftsleitung

Auch wenn die neue zivile Gliederung der Region, die Anstrengungen zu einer Angleichung des Gebietes an andere Regionen der Sowjetunion und die Tatsache, dass

---

355 So zumindest die Darstellung der Kritik des ZK der KPdSU durch Afanas'ev, der dies denn auch propagandistisch gegen Ababkov zu wenden wusste. Vgl. Grebenjuk, Kolymskij led, S. 160 f. Grebenjuks Umgang mit den Quellen muss hier kritisiert werden. Er verwendet Afanas'evs Darstellung der Ereignisse wie ein offizielles Protokoll und erzeugt dadurch nachträglich eine unangemessene Dramatisierung der Ereignisse. Insgesamt überdehnt Grebenjuk in seiner Darstellung die Ereignisse auf der 3. Parteikonferenz, er stilisiert sie zu einem regionalen Ergebnis der Ereignisse auf dem 20. Parteitag und zu einer innerparteilichen Entstalinisierungsmaßnahme, bleibt jedoch eine stichhaltige Untermauerung dieser These schuldig. Diese Darstellungsweise ist nicht zuletzt deshalb schwer nachzuvollziehen, weil Chruščev in seiner neuen Rolle als Generalsekretär der Partei im November 1953 persönlich die Entscheidung zugunsten Ababkovs als Erstem Parteisekretär traf.
356 Vgl. den Bericht von Sevast'janov, der im Auftrag des ZK der KPdSU an der Sitzung teilgenommen hatte, RGANI f. 5, op. 32, d. 111, l. 29–31. Für eine offizielle Darstellung der Konferenz siehe Chronika partijnoj organizacii, S. 152.
357 Bericht des stellv. Leiters der Abteilung für Parteiorgane des Büros des ZK der KPdSU für die RSFSR, Sevast'janov, vom 4. März 1958 in RGANI f. 5, op. 32, d. 111, l. 29–31. Die Konferenz fand im Februar 1958 statt. Zu der neuen Mannschaft von Afanas'ev siehe Grebenjuk, Kolymskij led, S. 167.
358 Die Leiter des Volkswirtschaftsrates wurden v. a. für ihre Planungspolitik kritisiert. Vgl. den Bericht in RGANI f. 5, op. 32, d. 111, l. 29–31, hier l. 29.
359 Vorsitzender des Gebietsexekutivkomitees wurde daraufhin T. S. Ivanenko, I. Čistjakov blieb weiterhin Stellvertreter. Vgl. zu dem typischen Karriereschritt des Leiters eines Gebietsexekutivkomitees zum Ersten Sekretär eines Gebietes Hough; Fainsod, Soviet Union is Governed, S. 504.
360 Vgl. Khlevniuk, Regional'naja vlast'; Gorlizki, Too much Trust.

das Gebietsparteikomitee die Verantwortung für die Goldförderung übernahm, den Eindruck vermitteln kann, 1958 hätten die Organe von Partei und Staat die Macht vollständig übernommen, so kann doch zu keinem Zeitpunkt die Rede davon sein, dass Gebietspartei- und Gebietsexekutivkomitee das Gebiet tatsächlich vollständig „durchherrschten". Zu gering war der Grad der infrastrukturellen und institutionellen Erschließung und zu gering waren auch die Möglichkeiten, mit den schwierigen klimatischen Verhältnissen fertig zu werden.[361] Bauwirtschaft, Energieversorgung, Handel und die Verkehrsmittel waren die Achillesferse der neuen Macht und blieben es auch nach Gründung des Magadaner Volkswirtschaftsrates. An diesen Ressourcen mangelte es zu allen Zeiten in den Weiten des Magadaner Gebietes.

Auch in personeller Hinsicht war die Partei Mitte der 1950er Jahre weit davon entfernt, in jeder Siedlung und an allen Produktionsstandorten gut aufgestellt zu sein. Dazu fehlte es nicht nur an Parteivertretern, sondern auch an effektiven Strukturen und an Unabhängigkeit gegenüber den jeweiligen Produktionsleitern. So wurde die Partei oftmals gar nicht als relevanter Ansprechpartner wahrgenommen.[362] Vor allem an der Peripherie hatte sie große Schwierigkeiten, das neue Herrschaftsfeld auszufüllen. Immer wieder gab es Beschwerden, nicht nur über Parteivertreter, sondern auch über einzelne Exekutivorgane. So heißt es 1955 aus Tschukotka, dass in einigen Siedlungen die Exekutivkomitees überhaupt nicht zusammenträten. Der Vorsitzende des Amguêmsker Dorfsowjets, Jasinskij, erscheine z. B. nur am Zahltag, selbst das Exekutivkomitee des gesamten Bezirkes Uil'tinskij bestehe weitgehend formal, der Sekretär Lenskij habe während seiner ganzen Amtszeit noch keine einzige Siedlung besucht.[363] Auch wenn solche Verhältnisse auch anderswo in der Sowjetunion dieser Jahre geherrscht haben mögen, so lagen die Ursachen im Magadaner Gebiet doch in

---

361 Noch im Jahr 1958 bat Afanas'ev das Büro des ZK der KPdSU für die RSFSR darum, die Sitzungen der Bezirksparteikomitees und des Stadtparteikomitees von Magadan aus klimatischen Gründen verschieben zu dürfen. Vgl. das Schreiben von Afanas'ev in RGANI f. 5, op. 32, d. 111, l. 139. Die Abteilung für die Parteiorgane des Büros des ZK der KPdSU für die RSFSR schlug daraufhin vor, in Industriegebieten die Konferenzen im Dezember abzuhalten, in Rentiergebieten im Januar 1959, wenn die Winterwege befestigt seien. Vgl. ebd., l. 141.

362 Vgl. beispielhaft den Bericht des Leiters der Wirtschaftsabteilung des Gebietsparteikomitees, Golubev, über den Zustand der Bezirksparteikomitees in Bezug auf ihre Tätigkeiten bei der Wirtschaftskontrolle. Viel zu selten erschienen die Bezirksvertreter in den einzelnen Siedlungen und an den Produktionsstandorten. Zudem käme es immer noch vor, dass die Leiter von Produktionsabteilungen zugleich auch die Funktion des Leiters der grundständigen Parteiorganisation innehätten – eine unabhängige Kontrolle durch die Partei sei unter diesen Umständen erst gar nicht möglich, so Golubev. Vgl. seinen Bericht in GAMO f. P-21, op. 5, d. 14, l. 70 – 72. Überhaupt wurde den Leitern von Partei und Sowjet auf allen Ebenen immer wieder vorgeworfen, nicht „vor Ort" zu erscheinen, die reale Lage nicht zu kennen. Im Magadaner Gebiet hatte dieser bekannte Vorwurf seinen Ursprung sicher auch in den enormen infrastrukturellen Schwierigkeiten der Region. Die Vertreter von Partei und Staat hatten zum Teil große Schwierigkeiten, zeitnah alle Orte zu erreichen. Vgl. z. B. die Vorwürfe auf Parteiversammlungen im Severo-Évensker und Anadyr'sker Bezirk im November 1957. Vgl. den Bericht an das Gebietsparteikomitee in RGANI f. 5, op. 32, d. 111, l. 168 – 170.

363 Vgl. den Bericht an Afanas'ev in GAMO f. R-146, op. 1, d. 4, l. 55 – 56.

dessen Strukturschwäche und in der mangelnden Kontrolle über ein so großes und schwer zu durchdringendes Territorium.

Doch auch in administrativ-territorialer Hinsicht war das Gebiet noch lange ein brüchiges Gebilde. Davon zeugen nicht nur Neugründungen von Bezirken und Veränderungen ihres territorialen Zuschnitts, die bis in die 1970er Jahre anhielten, sondern auch Diskussionen um die Position des Tschukotkaer nationalen Kreises. Aufgrund seiner Größe, Abgeschiedenheit, der klimatischen und ethnographischen Besonderheiten als Polarregion hatte der Kreis eine Sonderstellung inne – seine Verwaltung war im Vergleich zu einem Bezirk eigenständiger gegenüber der Magadaner Partei- und Staatsführung.

Die Parteivertretung des Kreises nutzte im April 1957 die Beratungen über die Struktur des neuen Volkswirtschaftsrates für den Versuch, sich aus dem Magadaner Gebiet zu lösen. G. Bezrukov, der Sekretär des Čukotsker Kreisparteikomitees, bat Chruščev um die Gründung eines selbstständigen „Čukotkischen Gebietes" in der RSFSR. Für die lokalen Kader brachte die Einführung der Volkswirtschaftsräte die Hoffnung auf ein Ende der mit Dal'stroj begonnenen Unterordnung Tschukotkas unter die Führung in Magadan. Zwischen Magadan und Tschukotka gebe es, so Bezrukov, keinerlei Gemeinsamkeiten, weder kulturell noch klimatisch oder wirtschaftlich.[364] Vielmehr habe die überflüssige Parallelität der Leitung eine vollständige Entwicklung der Region verhindert. Magadan sei gar nicht in der Lage, die lokalen Probleme bei Infrastruktur und Handel oder im Kampf gegen die hohe Kriminalität zu lösen. Von einer administrativen Aufwertung der Region als selbstständiges Gebiet versprach sich die regionale Parteileitung eine bessere Anbindung an das machtpolitische Zentrum in Moskau. So wie 1953 Magadan hegte Tschukotka im Jahr 1957 die Hoffnung, „das Leben des Kreises an das allgemeine Entwicklungstempo des Landes anzunähern".[365] Schließlich erhob Bezrukov sogar die Forderung, aufgrund der Nähe zum kapitalistischen Ausland das gesamte Gebiet einem „Grenzregime" zu unterstellen, Einreisen nur mit Zugangsberechtigungen zu erlauben, Vorbestrafte auszuweisen und noch vorhandene Lager zu schließen.

Die Lebensbedingungen in Tschukotka waren in dieser Zeit tatsächlich erbärmlich; aufgrund der Verlegung schwerkrimineller Häftlinge an die nordöstliche Peri-

---

364 Vgl. RGANI f. 5, op. 32, d. 87, l. 38.
365 Bis zu einer tatsächlichen Lösung des Kreises aus dem Magadaner Gebiet musste Tschukotka jedoch bis 1991 warten. Siehe das Schreiben von Bezrukov vom 12. April 1957 in RGANI f. 5, op. 32, d. 87, l. 33–49, Zitat hier l. 40. Zu seiner persönlichen Motivation für diesen Vorstoß führte Bezrukov aus: „Derjenige, der hier diese Zeilen verfasst, war gezwungen in verschiedenen Gebieten dieses riesigen Territoriums [...] zu einem lebendigen Zeugen und Dulder aller Schwierigkeiten und Unbequemlichkeiten zu werden, die sich in den vergangenen 22 Jahren für die wirtschaftliche Entwicklung dieses Gebietes durch die Entfernung zum Fluss ergeben hatten." RGANI f. 5, op. 32, d. 87, l. 35. Das Büro des ZK der KPdSU für die RSFSR lehnte den Vorstoß aus Tschukotka in seiner Stellungnahme an das ZK der KPdSU rundweg ab. Ebenso positionierte sich auch die Parteiführung in Magadan und Jakutsk. Vgl. das entsprechende Schreiben vom 29. Juni 1957 in RGANI f. 5, op. 32, d. 87, l. 49.

pherie war mangelnde Sicherheit ein großes Problem.[366] Bezrukovs Vorstoß kann daher sicher als geschickter Schachzug verstanden werden – durch einen weitreichenden administrativen Vorschlag sollte das Interesse des Zentrums auf die Region gelenkt werden. Doch darüber hinaus werfen die miserablen Bedingungen in Tschukotka tatsächlich die Frage nach der Sinnhaftigkeit der administrativen Einheit von Tschukotka und Magadan auf. Wenn die Leitung in Magadan bei der Verwaltung und Versorgung der Halbinsel derart versagte, stand die politische Legitimation ihrer Herrschaft über den Wirtschaftsraum zumindest an den Rändern der Region in Frage.

Den Bestrebungen Bezrukovs wurde jedenfalls nicht stattgegeben, das Büro des ZK der KPdSU für die RSFSR sprach sich ebenso wie die Parteileitungen von Magadan und Jakutsk gegen eine Herauslösung der Halbinsel aus dem Magadaner Gebiet aus. Aber die Unterordnung Tschukotkas unter Magadan überlebte das Ende der Sowjetunion nicht. Seit 1991 ist die Halbinsel ein selbstständiger Kreis der Russischen Föderation.

Die Frage der Abgrenzung von politischer und ökonomischer Sphäre blieb auch im Alltag des Gebietes virulent. Im Zentrum stand dabei die Frage nach der Verteilung zwischen kommunalen Aufgaben und der Verantwortung der einzelnen Wirtschaftsbetriebe. Im Vorfeld der Einführung des Magadaner Volkswirtschaftsrates wurde offenbar, dass die Maßnahmen des Jahres 1954 / 1955 bei der Übertragung von Zuständigkeiten bisheriger Dal'stroj-Institutionen an zivile Ministerien keineswegs abgeschlossen worden waren.

Im Jahr 1957 gab es daher noch einmal einen Vorstoß zur Klärung des Status von diversen Einrichtungen – dieser ging jedoch nicht vom Gebietsexekutivkomitee, sondern vom MCM aus. Noch immer gebe es in den Siedlungen und Goldgruben zahlreiche Gebäude, die von der Miliz, der staatlichen Bank, von Klubs, Krankenstationen, Schulen etc. genutzt würden, aber weiterhin der Zuständigkeit von Dal'stroj unterstünden, so Lomako, der Minister für Buntmetalle in einer Beschwerde an den Ministerrat der RSFSR vom April 1957. „All dies", so Lomako, „sorgt für zusätzliche Ausgaben in Dal'stroj und lenkt die Aufmerksamkeit der Betriebe von ihren eigentlichen wirtschaftlichen Aufgaben ab".[367]

Es folgten Verhandlungen zwischen *Gosplan*, dem Ministerium und dem Gebietsexekutivkomitee, infolge derer sich das Gebietsexekutivkomitee zur Aufnahme einzelner Einrichtungen bereit erklärte.[368] Zugleich wandte sich die Sowjetleitung

---

366 Vgl. zur Lage in Tschukotka, vor und hinter dem Stacheldraht, ausführlich Kapitel 5.3.
367 Vgl. das Schreiben Lomakos vom 25. April 1957 an den Ministerrat der RSFSR in GAMO f. R-146, op. 1, d. 50, l. 188.
368 So gelangte beispielsweise das Kulturhaus der nördlichen Bergbauverwaltung in die Zuständigkeit des Exekutivkomitees von Jagodnoe und das Gebäude der südlichen Bergbauverwaltung, in dem die regionale Verwaltung des MVD untergebracht war, in die Zuständigkeit des Exekutivkomitees von Susuman. Vgl. das Schreiben des Gebietsexekutivkomitees an *Gosplan* der RSFSR vom 5. Juni 1957 in GAMO f. R-146, op. 1, d. 50, l. 100 – 102. Zuvor hatte der Ministerrat der RSFSR die Behörde *Gosplan* der

jedoch mit Nachdruck gegen die Übernahme einer großen Zahl kleinerer Einrichtungen, die nicht dem geforderten Standard entsprachen. So wurden z. B. Schulen abgelehnt, bei denen es sich nicht um standardisierte Gebäude, sondern um Baracken handelte; kommunale Einrichtungen (Badehäuser etc.) niedrigen Standards wurden nicht angenommen, weil man ihre sofortige Schließung erwartete, sobald der dazugehörige Betrieb verlagert würde. Eine ganze Reihe von Einrichtungen wurde mit der Begründung zurückgewiesen, sie gehörten unmittelbar zu einzelnen Betrieben und erfüllten keine weitergehenden kommunalen Aufgaben.[369]

Diese Diskussionen begleiteten die lokale Leitung auch weiterhin. Nach dem Sommer 1957 führten der Volkswirtschaftsrat und das Gebietsexekutivkomitee im Auftrag von *Gosplan* die Verhandlungen.[370] Unter dem einheitlichen regionalen Volkswirtschaftsrat kam es jetzt nicht mehr auf die nominelle Zuordnung, sehr wohl aber auf die finanzielle Verantwortung für die einzelnen Einrichtungen an.[371] Auch für *Gosplan* war jedoch kaum zu klären, wo in einer derart auf die Industrie ausgerichteten Region die Grenze zwischen sozialen Einrichtungen eines Betriebes und kommunalen Aufgaben verlaufen sollte.[372]

Größere Siedlungen gewannen, auch wenn sie einstmals als Lagerpunkte gegründet worden waren, mehr und mehr eine Daseinsberechtigung unabhängig von ihrer wirtschaftlichen Bedeutung aufgrund der dort vorhandenen Krankenhäuser, Schulen und Verwaltungseinrichtungen. Aber zahllose kleinere Siedlungspunkte waren in ihrer Existenz nach wie vor von der Industrie abhängig.[373] Wenn die industriellen Anlagen aus wirtschaftlichen Gründen geschlossen wurden, traten die all-

---

RSFSR mit der Klärung dieses Sachverhaltes, im Austausch mit dem Magadaner Gebietsexekutivkomitee, beauftragt. Vgl. das entsprechende Schreiben vom 6. Mai 1957 in GAMO f. R-146, op. 1, d. 50, l. 90.

369 Zur Verdeutlichung des miserablen Zustandes einzelner Einrichtungen hatte das Gebietsexekutivkomitee seinem Schreiben ein Foto beigelegt. Vgl. das Schreiben des Gebietsexekutivkomitees in GAMO f. R-146, op. 1, d. 50, l. 103. Auch sollte die Bauorganisation „Magadanstroj", die bisher dem Gebietsexekutivkomitee unterstanden hatte, in den Volkswirtschaftsrat überführt werden. Anscheinend war sie stark industriell ausgerichtet. Siehe das Schreiben von Čuguev an Afanas'ev und Ababkov vom 20. Juni 1957 in GAMO f. R-146, op. 1, d. 221, l. 39.

370 Vgl. das Schreiben des stellv. Leiters von *Gosplan* der RSFSR an den Ministerrat der RSFSR vom 7. Juni 1957 in GAMO f. R-146, op. 1, d. 50, l. 187.

371 So forderte der Chef des Volkswirtschaftsrats (der bisherige Leiter von Dal'stroj), Čuguev, Ende Juni 1957 die Übergabe weiterer Einrichtungen an Instanzen der lokalen Exekutivkomitees. Vgl. das Schreiben des Volkswirtschaftsrats an das Gebietsexekutivkomitee vom 26. Juni 1957 in GAMO f. R-146, op. 1, d. 50, l. 186.

372 Das zeigt der umfangreiche Schriftverkehr zu den einzelnen Einrichtungen. Siehe als Beispiel die Diskussionen über die Einrichtung einer Basis für den zivilen Bau im Bezirk Ten'kinsk noch im September 1960 in GAMO f. R-146, op. 1, d. 442, 149–152.

373 Diesen Zusammenhang arbeitet E. M. Šeršakova heraus, indem sie für die 1930er bis 1970er Jahre die Bevölkerungsentwicklung in den einzelnen Gebieten in Beziehung zur wirtschaftlichen Entwicklung der jeweiligen Region setzt. Problematisch ist für die Jahre bis 1957 dabei jedoch, dass sie an keiner Stelle deutlich macht, ob sie sich lediglich auf freie Arbeitskräfte oder auch auf die Lagerbevölkerung bezieht. Vgl. Šeršakova, Osobennosti formirovanija naselenija, S. 57 f.

täglichen Probleme einer peripheren sowjetischen Industrieregion besonders sichtbar zutage. Davon berichtete im August 1956 Bol'šemennik, zuständig für die Konservierung einer Goldgrube im Bezirk Jagodninskij. Unter dem Titel „verlassene Siedlung" schilderte er die Zustände in der Ortschaft Stan-Utinyj nach der Schließung der Grube Utinskij, dem bisher wichtigsten Arbeitgeber für die dortige Bevölkerung. 600 Menschen lebten weiterhin in der Siedlung, sie waren mehrheitlich in einer weiteren, kleinen Grube eingesetzt. Zudem gab es in Stan-Utinyj kommunale Einrichtungen, auf die die Bewohner einer benachbarten Siedlung angewiesen waren. Diese waren bisher hauptsächlich von der Produktionsleitung der Grube finanziert worden. Nicht nur fehlte nach der Schließung diese materielle Basis, auch die Sowjetverwaltung zog sich aus dem Siedlungspunkt zurück. Bol'šemennik fragte das Gebietsexekutivkomitee dementsprechend rhetorisch:

> Bedeutet die Schließung der Grube Utinskij etwa, dass in der Siedlung der Grube keine Bewohner zurückbleiben, dass dort kein Krankenhaus, keine Schule, kein Klub und kein Kindergarten gebraucht wird?" [...] Was wird im Winter sein? Mit der Renovierung von Wohngebäuden beschäftigt sich niemand. In den Planungen der Grube Utinskij waren schon für das Jahr 1956 keine Maßnahmen zur Renovierung von Wohnhäusern mehr vorgesehen, war die Frage nicht geklärt, wer die Bevölkerung mit Heizmitteln versorgen soll.[374]

Dieser Fall wurde insofern gelöst, als dass die aufgegebene Grube Utinskij administrativ einfach in die noch bestehende Grube „Pjatiletka" überführt wurde, wodurch die Sorge um die Siedlung Stan-Utinyj direkt auf die Leitung von „Pjatiletka" überging.[375] Auch unter den neuen Bedingungen blieben also in weit entfernten Industriebezirken die Produktionsabteilungen die entscheidenden Versorgungseinrichtungen.

Die Organe von Partei und Staat kämpften in den Weiten des Magadaner Gebietes auch nach ihrer Machtübernahme mit einem Legitimationsproblem des Politischen. Dahinter verbargen sich jedoch nicht nur administrative und infrastrukturelle Schwierigkeiten, die Grenzen des Herrschaftsraums waren auch Ausdruck der spezifischen Interessen des sowjetischen Zentrums an seiner äußersten Peripherie. Das

---

374 GAMO f. R-146, op. 1, d. 53, l. 47–48, hier l. 47 f. Ganz ähnliche Fragen stellte auch der Vorsitzende der Sowjetverwaltung von Srednekansk, nachdem bekannt wurde, dass die südwestliche Bergbauverwaltung von Dal'stroj in diesem Bezirk zum 1. Januar 1955 aufgegeben werden sollte. Vgl. sein Schreiben vom 3. Dezember 1954 an Afanas'ev in GAMO f. R-146, op. 1, d. 50, l. 17–19 sowie die Antwort aus der Finanzabteilung des Gebietes ebd., l. 20.
375 Siehe das Schreiben des Vorsitzenden des Jagodninsker Bezirksexekutivkomitees, Kuz'min, an den stellvertretenden Vorsitzenden des Gebietsexekutivkomitees, Čistjakov, in GAMO f. R-146, op. 1, d. 53, l. 47–48, hier l. 51. Dieser Fall ist von besonderem Interesse, da sich der Leiter von Dal'stroj, M. Gruša, persönlich einschaltete und noch einmal beim Magadaner Gebietsexekutivkomitee intervenierte. Er wies darauf hin, dass die große Bevölkerungsmehrheit der Siedlung eigentlich nicht der Grube „Pjatiletka" zuzuordnen sei, sondern Mitarbeiter einer Lagerverwaltung sei und daher vom *Sevvostlag* betreut werden müsste. Im Folgenden blieb es jedoch dabei, dass die Siedlung durch die Grube „Pjatiletka" versorgt wurde. Vgl. das Schreiben von Gruša an Čistjakov in GAMO f. R-146, op. 1, d. 53, l. 50.

Gebiet sollte die östlichste Grenze sichern, vor allem aber als „Valutazeche"[376] fungieren, also wertvolle Rohstoffe für den Außenhandel der Sowjetunion liefern. Ihre soziale und wirtschaftliche Stabilität war dabei Mittel zum Zweck. Die Lage in einem einzelnen abseits gelegenen Siedlungspunkt fiel dabei nicht ins Gewicht. Mit einer besseren Verfasstheit der Region wollte man die Ausbeutung auch in Zukunft garantieren – die Methoden der Entstalinisierung sollten die stalinistischen Prämissen effektiver umsetzen.

In den 1990er Jahren zeigte sich dann, was diese Ausrichtung unter den Bedingungen des Kapitalismus bedeutete: Als die Staatsbetriebe unrentabel wurden, gab es in weiten Teilen des Gebietes keine Investoren, die unter den bestehenden klimatischen und demographischen Bedingungen die Rohstoffförderung aufrechterhalten wollten.[377] Trotz des nach wie vor vorhandenen Reichtums der Region zog sich die Industrie fast vollständig aus dem Gebiet zurück. Fast zeitgleich lösten sich die Siedlungen auf, Kindergärten und Krankenhäuser schlossen, die Verwaltung wurde abgezogen. Zurück bleiben Geisterstädte, die von der langen Wirkung eines stalinistischen Lager-Industriellen Komplexes in der russischen Peripherie künden.

---

376 So die damals häufig verwendete Bezeichnung. Vgl. Kuwajew, Goldsucher, S. 26. Šilo/Potemkin, Valjutnyj cech; Geroi, S. 4. Die Bezeichnung wurde noch in den 1990er Jahren verwendet. Vgl. Simakov/Gončarov, Akademičeskaja nauka, S. 22.

377 Vgl. zur regionalen Goldförderung seit den 1990er Jahren Gal'ceva, Analiz retrospektivy, S. 209 f. Die Region Tschukotka hat hingegen mit dem Oligarchen Abramovič einen „Sponsor" gefunden, der durch seine Investitionen und soziale Unterstützung mittlerweile zum regelrechten Besitzer der Region geworden ist.

4 Ausbeuten und Erschließen

Wertvolle Rohstoffe, und dabei v. a Gold, zu fördern, war seit 1931 die wichtigste Aufgabe jeder Kolymaer Führung. Die Auflösung der Lager und die politischen Veränderungen im Zuge der Gebietsgründung hatten jedoch erhebliche Auswirkungen auf die Art und Weise der Rohstoffausbeutung. Der Wandel betraf Arbeitskräfte, Arbeitsweisen, Strukturen und Status des Wirtschaftsraumes. Diese Veränderungen sind in ihrer Bedeutung nur vor dem Hintergrund der stalinistischen Industriestrukturen Dal'strojs erkennbar. In einem Exkurs wird daher hier zunächst die strukturelle und wirtschaftliche Entwicklung der Kolymaer Industrie bis 1953 verfolgt. Sodann soll eine Darstellung von Grundzügen der poststalinistischen Wirtschaftsweise einen Überblick über die Charakteristika der 1950er Jahre bieten, bevor die wichtigsten Elemente des Wandels detaillierter betrachtet werden – ihre finanzielle Ausstattung, die Rolle von geologischen Schürfarbeiten und der Wissenschaft und die Herausbildung neuer Industriezweige in der Region. Mit der abschließenden Frage nach der Effektivität von stalinistischer und poststalinistischer Arbeitsweise schließt das Kapitel gewissermaßen den Kreis zu der einleitenden Darstellung von Wirtschaft und Zwangsarbeit in Dal'stroj.

4.1 Gold und Zwangsarbeit in Dal'stroj 1931–1953

In den 25 Jahren seiner Existenz, zwischen 1931 und 1956, förderte das Industriekombinat Dal'stroj 1.187,1 Tonnen chemisch reines Gold und seit 1937 65.300 Tonnen konzentriertes Zinn, daneben Kobalt, Wolfram und Uran.[1] Einen Eindruck von der Masse dieser Förderung kann nur ein Vergleich vermitteln: Eines der weltweit berühmtesten Goldfördergebiete liegt in Kanada, an der Mündung des Flusses Klondike in den Yukon. Seit 1885 wurden im Fluss Yukon bis heute 13.527.555 Feinunzen Gold gewaschen, das sind etwa 421 Tonnen – ein gutes Drittel dessen, was der Nordosten der Sowjetunion in einem Vierteljahrhundert lieferte.[2]

---

1 Zwischen 1941 und 1956 förderte Dal'stroj 2.850 t konzentriertes Wolfram, zwischen 1947 und 1955 397,5 t konzentriertes Kobalt. Zu den Förderzahlen siehe Kozlov, Reorganizacija, S. 46. In der Zeit zwischen 1948 und 1955 wurden in Dal'stroj 135 Tonnen konzentriertes Uran gewonnen. Vgl. Zeljak, Uranodobyvajuščaja otrasl', S. 124. Nach einer Beschreibung des Gebietsparteikomitees im Vorfeld der Gründung des Magadaner Volkswirtschaftsrates für das ZK der KPdSU lieferte Dal'stroj bis 1956 3.000 Tonnen Wolfram (seit 1948) und 398 Tonnen konzentriertes Kobalt (1947–1954). Zudem förderte Dal'stroj in den 25 Jahren seiner Existenz mehr als 10 Mio. Tonnen Kohle. Seit 1932 wurden zur Förderung all dieser Bodenschätze 600 Mio. m³ Erde bearbeitet. Vgl. GAMO f. R-23, op. 1, d. 6088, l. 1–50, hier l. 5.

2 Vgl. Marohn, Anna: „Der zweite Rausch", in: Die Zeit, 21. Juli 2011, S. 19. Seit dem 19. Jahrhundert gibt es Vermutungen, dass sich der Kopf des „Goldenen Kalbes" (Bezeichnung der reichen Goldlagerstätte) in Alaska, der Rumpf jedoch in Tschukotka befindet, dass also diese beiden Lagerstätten durch die

https://doi.org/10.1515/9783110557879-005

Dem enormen Reichtum des Landes und der Flüsse im Gebiet Dal'stroj stand jedoch zunächst das völlige Fehlen jeglicher Infrastruktur gegenüber – alles, was an Straßen, Kraftwerken, Kommunikationswegen, Förderanlagen, Häusern und Häfen benötigt wurde, musste buchstäblich aus dem Boden gestampft werden. Für die Gewinnung von Rohstoffen waren daher von den ersten bis zu den letzten Tagen des Industriekombinats gewaltige Baumaßnahmen nötig, um zumindest den Zugang zu den einzelnen Fördergebieten zu ermöglichen und die notwendigsten technischen Einrichtungen zu schaffen.

Diese Arbeiten wurden durch die geophysikalischen Besonderheiten der Region, den Permafrostboden, das undurchdringliche Gelände, die hohen Gebirge und gewaltigen Flüsse sowie durch den neunmonatigen Winter mit Temperaturen bis unter -60° C erheblich erschwert. Vor diesem Hintergrund erscheinen die Forderungen des Politbüros als besonders extrem, das dem neuen Kombinat bereits für das Jahr 1932 ein Plansoll von 10 Tonnen chemisch reinem Gold diktierte.[3]

Tatsächlich begannen die Arbeiten an der Kolyma, vergleichbar mit anderen Zwangsarbeiterprojekten in dieser Zeit, ohne echte topographische Kenntnisse der Region und ohne eine angemessene Projektierung.[4] Zu einem geringen Teil konnte man auf bereits existierende Förderanlagen des Kombinats „Sojuzzoluto" zurückgreifen. Alles andere musste unter unmenschlichen Bedingungen und fast vollkommen ohne schweres Gerät und technische Anlagen von Grund auf neu errichtet werden.[5] Oberste Priorität hatte dabei stets der Abbau der reichen Goldvorkommen. Die Schaffung von Infrastruktur war auf die Erzielung eines maximalen Goldertrages

---

Beringstraße miteinander verbunden sind. Die größte Goldlagerstätte der Welt, das Witwatersrand-Goldfeld in Südafrika, hat seit 1885 bis heute gut 47.000 Tonnen Gold geliefert. Allerdings lagert das Gold dort in sehr tiefen Erdschichten (bis zu 4 km tief), bedingt also eine ganz andere Abbautechnik, die nur bei einem sehr hohen Goldpreis ökonomisch sinnvoll ist. Vgl. Handley, Witwatersrand Goldfields, S. 1f. Für einen Vergleich mit den Goldförderleistungen im zaristischen Russland und in den 1920er Jahren siehe Mel'nikov, Stranicy istorii, S. 44–47.

3 Vgl. den Abdruck der Verordnung in Stalinskie Strojki, S. 419–420, hier S. 419.

4 Vgl. zur Vorgehensweise in vergleichbaren Industrie- und Bauprojekten Ivanova, Istorja GULAGa, S. 234.

5 Alle Menschen und Materialien wurden per Schiff (der Lufttransport beschränkte sich auf besonders wertvolle Materialien, Gold und hohes Personal) in das Gebiet gebracht. Schiffe konnten allerdings nur von April bis Dezember fahren. Vgl. Navasardov, Transportnoe osvoenie. Häftlinge deportierte man von Transitpunkten im Fernen Osten – den Städten Wanino und Nachodka, in der Nähe der Stadt Chabarowsk bzw. Wladiwostok – zum Hafen an der Bucht Nagaevo bei Magadan. Nach einem häufig monatelangen Aufenthalt in den riesigen Transitlagern (mit bis zu 80.000 Häftlingen) forderte die Überfahrt auf meist sehr unruhiger See in qualvoller Enge bereits viele Opfer, es kam zum Ausbruch von Epidemien, gewaltvollen Übergriffen und Vergewaltigungen. Diese schreckliche Überfahrt, nach monatelanger Zugreise und Wartephase in den Transitlagern, hat zu dem besonderen Ruf von Dal'stroj als „Insel ohne Wiederkehr" beigetragen und Eingang in die Erinnerungsliteratur gefunden. Vgl. Conquest, Kolyma, S. 19ff.; Dück, Erinnerungen, S. 348–356.

ausgerichtet, sie sollte die Goldförderung bestmöglich unterstützen, die Erschließung des Gebietes spielte dabei keine Rolle.[6]

Daher waren die ersten Jahre von Dal'stroj dem Aufbau einer grundlegenden technischen Infrastruktur gewidmet, die Goldförderung blieb in dieser Zeit noch auf recht niedrigem Niveau. Die erste und wichtigste Aufgabe betraf den Straßenbau, um die im Landesinneren gelegenen goldreichen Gebiete und die bereits bestehenden Fördergebiete von *Sojuzzoloto* mit dem Meer und damit mit dem Verkehrssystem der Union zu verbinden.[7] In dieser Zeit entstand der erste Abschnitt der sogenannten „Kolymaer Trasse" (von der Bucht Nagaevo zu den Fördergebieten), die als Symbol der Region Kolyma mit später insgesamt 2.200 km Länge als „längste Straße der Welt" traurige Berühmtheit erlangte.[8] Der Straßenbau erforderte einige große Brücken über den Fluss Kolyma, die ebenfalls in dieser Zeit entstanden. Parallel dazu wurde mit dem Bau der Siedlung und des Hafens Magadan die notwendige Infrastruktur im Süden geschaffen.[9] In Magadan begann man schon 1932 mit der Errichtung erster Häuser, die Siedlung entwickelte sich bald zum administrativen Zentrum von Dal'-stroj.[10]

Im Umkreis der Anlagen zur Goldförderung entstanden Produktionsstätten der Hilfs- und Nebenindustrie wie installierende und instandsetzende Werkstätten und Fabriken.[11] Dazu kam der Bau von einigen größeren Hydroelektrostationen und kleineren regionalen Anlagen zur Energiegewinnung (z. B. Kohlekraftwerke). All dies war jedoch nicht ausreichend, um den enormen Energiebedarf von Dal'stroj auch nur

---

6 Vgl. zu den Prioritäten bei der Erschließung der Region Zeljak, Osobennosti razvitija, S. 91.

7 Vgl. Širokov, Dal'stroj, S. 84. Siehe auch die Darstellung der ersten Dal'strojer Jahre bei Nordlander, Magadan, S. 108 f.

8 Vgl. Širokov, Dal'stroj, S, 133. Širokov beschreibt Pläne zum Ausbau eines Eisenbahnnetzes, das die gesamte Region (in den am weitesten gehenden Vorstellungen bis nach Kamtschatka) mit der Baikal-Amur-Eisenbahnlinie verbinden sollte. Damit sollten sowohl innerregionale Verbindungen verbessert als auch eine Unabhängigkeit von dem unsicheren Transport über das Meer (starker Seegang, Eisbrocken und die als Bedrohung wahrgenommene Aufrüstung der Japaner) erreicht werden. Diese Pläne waren bis 1939 sehr weit fortgeschritten, sie wurden jedoch wegen stark steigender Militärausgaben und einer dadurch entstandenen Umorientierung der Investitionen eingestellt. Auch in den folgenden Jahren kam es nicht mehr zu einer Verbindung der Region mit den zentralen Teilen der Union durch eine Eisenbahnlinie. Vgl. Širokov, Iz istorii železnodorožnogo stroitel'stva.

9 Ivanova führt Magadan neben Komsomolsk, Norilsk, Bratsk und Workuta als Beispiele für Städte an, die in den 1930er Jahren vollkommen durch die Hände von Häftlingen erbaut wurden. Vgl. Ivanova, Istorija, S. 239.

10 Die Siedlung Magadan wurde 1939 zur Stadt ernannt. In Magadan entstand auch eine sehr begrenzte soziale und kulturelle Infrastruktur für die Arbeiter. Wegen des rauen Klimas in der Stadt Magadan, das sich durch enorme Winde und einen sehr kalten Sommer von den extremen Temperaturunterschieden im Landesinneren deutlich abgrenzt, hat man von Anfang an über einen alternativen Standort für das Zentrum von Dal'stroj nachgedacht. Dieser Gedanke wurde 1937 zwar verworfen, derartige Überlegungen tauchten jedoch im Laufe der Jahre immer wieder auf. Vgl. Širokov, Dal'stroj, S. 97.

11 Vgl. Zeljak, Pjat' metallov, S. 101.

annähernd zu decken. Der Mangel musste durch die reine Muskelkraft der Häftlinge ausgeglichen werden.[12]

Grundsätzlich bauten alle Wirtschaftsbereiche auf Zwangsarbeit auf. Häftlinge setzte man bei den körperlich schwersten und gefährlichsten Arbeiten ein. Der ehemalige Häftling Abrahm Dück wurde Ende der 1940er Jahre als Zwangsarbeiter in Dal'stroj eingesetzt. In seinen Erinnerungen beschreibt er die Arbeit in einer der Goldgruben im Winter 1949:

> Und so kam ich in die Förderungsbrigade. Richtiger gesagt, in die Brigade der Lastpferde. Die Grubenwagen wurden von Sklaven befördert. [...] Wir stapfen in die Stollen. Der Brigadier, ein bejahrter, aber noch kräftiger Mann, geht voran. Das Erste, was auffällt, ist der ätzende Geruch von Sprengstoffgasen. Und die völlige Finsternis. Das Gleis führt zum Abbauort. Ein großer Haufen Erz, kurz vorher gesprengt. Das Sprengstoffgas erschwerte das Atmen. Auf dem Boden liegt ein Gummischlauch. Zischend entströmt ihm Pressluft. Das Endstück bewegt sich hin und her wie ein Schlangenkopf. Der Brigadier gibt kurze Anweisungen: das Erz in den Hunt laden und zum Ausgang fahren. Den zischenden Schlangenkopf immer auf den Erzhaufen richten, wo verborgenes Gas lebensgefährlich sein könnte. Zum Ende der Schicht muss der Streb zum Bohren der Sprenglöcher frei sein. [...] Der Stollen war lang, wohl fast einen Kilometer. Stockfinster. Nur die Karbidlampe, vorne an den Wagen angehängt, gab ein spärliches Licht. Wie endlos weit schien die Strecke. Waren wir vielleicht auf der Wendeplatte in ein falsches Gleis abgebogen? Endlich bemerkten wir in der Ferne das weiße Tageslicht der Stollenöffnung. Sehr klein, wie eine Münze. Man konnte kaum glauben, dass es dort Tag war. Wir erreichten die Mündung. Mit voller Brust atmeten wir die frische Luft ein. [...]
>
> Die Schicht ist zu Ende. Müde kriechen die Häftlinge aus den Löchern der Stollen. Aus einer Finsternis in die andere. Eine mörderische Kälte. Im Streb herrscht auch ewiger Frost. Sommers und Winters fast dieselbe Temperatur unter null. Aber doch nicht so unerträglich wie im Freien. Man musste sich mit Pressluft den Staub vom Körper blasen. Ein Bad gab es ja nicht. Aber wer hat schon den Mut, sich dem eiskalten Luftstrom auszusetzen. Da kommen auch die Bohrhauer. [...] Die Kälte ist fast nicht zu ertragen. Die Scheinwerfer durchdringen mit ihrem Licht kaum noch den Frostnebel, der das Gelände bedeckt. Die Bohrhauer, noch verschwitzt von der Arbeit, zittern vor Kälte. Sie schreien: ,Aus dem Stollen sind alle da, macht den Zählappell!' Aber die Posten [...] stehen in ihren neuen, weißen Pelzen am Rande des Geländes wie die Ölgötzen. Die Zeit ist noch nicht abgelaufen.[13]

Häftlinge fungierten aber auch als private „Haussklaven" für einzelne Kommandanten, arbeiteten für die Versorgung der Truppen; hochqualifizierte Häftlinge verwendete man außerdem als ingenieurtechnisches Personal, Buchhalter etc.[14] Daneben wurden Häftlinge, die als besonders „zuverlässig" galten (keine „politischen Häftlinge"), seit Gründung des *Sevvostlag* in bedeutender Zahl zur Arbeit als Wachen herangezogen.[15] Freie Arbeitskräfte hatten in Dal'stroj unterschiedliche Aufgaben, besonders war das Kombinat auf qualifiziertes Fachpersonal angewiesen. Tatsächlich

---

12 Vgl. Širokov, Dal'stroj, S. 135 f.

13 Dück, Erinnerungen, S. 364–371.

14 Zur Häftlingsverwendung vgl. Šulubina, Sistema Sevvostlaga, S. 19.

15 Dabei kam es an der Kolyma zu der einmaligen Situation, dass unter den bewaffneten Wachleuten mehr Häftlinge als Freie waren. Vgl. Bacaev, Kolymskaja grjada, S. 51 f.

machten sie jedoch nur einen sehr geringen Prozentsatz aus. Freie Arbeiter wurden mit einem komplizierten System von Vergünstigungen und Boni angeworben, aufgrund der mitunter schrecklichen Lebensbedingungen war jedoch die Fluktuation unter diesem Personenkreis enorm hoch.[16] Neben Häftlingen und Freien gab es in der Region noch die Gruppe der Sondersiedler, die nur eingeschränkte Rechte besaßen.[17]

In den ersten Jahren war es auf dem Gebiet von Dal'stroj nicht möglich, „Lager" im Sinne fest umgrenzter, vollständig ausgestatteter Zonen auszumachen; Lagerabteilungen waren mobile Einheiten.[18] Mit Beginn der eigentlichen Goldförderung 1935 begann sich dann ein Lagersystem auszuprägen, das auch über feste Lagerpunkte verfügte. Bis zur Auflösung des *Sevvostlag* 1957 existierten jedoch immer auch viele kleinere Lager, die nicht mit festen Wachtürmen und Zäunen umgeben waren; selbst Baracken fehlten immer wieder, Häftlinge schliefen in Erdlöchern oder Zelten. Elinor Lipper, eine deutsche Kommunistin, die nach ihrer Verhaftung im Jahr 1937 in Moskau insgesamt acht Jahre in Lagern an der Kolyma verbrachte, beschreibt diese Lagerformen und ihre Genese aus der spezifischen lokalen Goldförderung:

> Der Goldreichtum an den Flußläufen der Kolyma und der Indigirka ist so groß, daß man vorläufig gar nicht daran denkt, die Goldgruben bis zum Letzten systematisch auszubeuten. Man schöpft den Rahm ab und geht an die Ausbeutung neuer Gruben. Unaufhörlich werden neue Goldgrubenlager eröffnet, die von den Gefangenen um ihrer besonders primitiven Wohnverhältnisse, die meistens in Zelten bestehen, besonders gefürchtet werden. In solchen Lagern kann natürlich weder von Strohsäcken noch von sonstigem Zubehör die Rede sein, die Gefangenen können froh sein, wenn sie eine Decke erwischen, und Tag- und Nachtschicht wechseln sich auf demselben engen Plätzchen auf den Brettern ab, die wie Kistendeckel in drei Etagen aneinandergereiht sind. [...] Zur Zeit der Schneeschmelze, also im Mai, wenn sich alles ringsum in Sümpfe auflöst, sind solche neuen Lager, die abseits von der großen Fahrtstraße [der „Kolymaer Trasse" – M. S.] liegen, und noch nicht über die notwendigen Zufahrtsstraßen verfügen, oft völlig abgeschnitten von der Umwelt und müssen tagelang auf ihre Brotration warten.[19]

---

16 Ende der 1930er Jahre machten qualifizierte Facharbeiter gerade einmal 1 % aller Arbeiter aus. Vgl. Zeljak, Pjat' metallov, S. 86, der den Fachkräften in Dal'stroj eigene Kapitel widmet. Die Infrastruktur für die Arbeiter war von der Bedeutung ihres jeweiligen Produktionsstandortes abhängig. Vielerorts waren der Verelendung unter den extremen klimatischen Bedingungen keine Schranken gesetzt. In großer Enge kam es zu Trinkgelagen, Schlägereien und Übergriffen. Vgl. ausführlich Zeljak, Pjat' metallov, S. 230 ff.

17 Vgl. Bacaev, Kolymskaja grjada, S. 49.

18 Die erste Phase des Lagerregimes wird in der lokalen Historiographie häufig als „liberal" bezeichnet, da sie der Ideologie der Umerziehung („perekovka") folgte. Tatsächlich setzte Berzin auf eine Reihe von besonderen Arbeitsstimuli, mit denen die Erfolge von Dal'stroj eng an das persönliche Schicksal der Häftlinge geknüpft wurde. Vgl. zum Häftlingsregime unter Berzin Širokov, Dal'stroj, S. 110; Nikolaev, K voprosy izučenija, S. 35; Bacaev, Kolymskaja grjada, S. 49 sowie Nordlander, Evolution, S. 650 ff. Ausführlicher zu den verschiedenen Formen der Arbeitsstimulierung siehe Bacaev, Formy i metody, S. 77. Siehe zu der *Perekovka* als Propagandakampagne Ivanova, Istorija, S. 240.

19 Lipper, Elf Jahre, S. 94.

Seit 1935 konnte man von einer wahrnehmbaren Goldförderung sprechen. Die geförderte Menge stieg rasch von 14,5 Tonnen chemisch reinem Gold (1935) auf 51,4 Tonnen im Jahr 1937.[20] Diese so schnelle und deutliche Zunahme wurde schon im gleichen Jahr durch lokale Maßnahmen des „Großen Terrors" abgebremst. Ein Teil der Führungsgruppe um den bisherigen Leiter von Dal'stroj, Berzin, Kreise der technischen Elite und eine große Zahl von Häftlingen und freien Arbeitskräften wurden ermordet, der neue Mann an der Spitze des Kombinats, Pavlov, verschärfte die Lebens- und Arbeitsbedingungen der Häftlinge erheblich.[21]

Kurz darauf erlebte die Kolyma eine andere Auswirkung des sowjetischen „Großen Terrors" – im Rahmen der unionsweiten Verhaftungswellen wurden immer mehr Personen zur Zwangsarbeit nach Dal'stroj geschickt.[22] Dadurch veränderte sich auch die Zusammensetzung der Häftlinge. Ein gutes Drittel waren nun Personen, die aufgrund angeblich „konterrevolutionärer Verbrechen" in den Lagern an der Kolyma einsaßen, darunter viele bekannte Mitglieder oppositioneller Gruppen und ein großer Teil der intellektuellen Elite der Sowjetunion, wie der berühmte Konstrukteur sowjetischer Raketentechnik, Sergej Korolev, die deutsche, in die Sowjetunion emigrierte Kommunistin Trude Richter, der Künster Leonid Vegener oder der Dichter Osip Mandel'štam.[23] Zu Beginn des Jahres 1939 machten die Häftlinge an der Kolyma etwa 10,5 % aller Häftlinge im Machtbereich des sowjetischen NKVD aus.[24] Die wachsende Zahl der Inhaftierten führte zu qualvoller Enge und zu fürchterlichen hygienischen Bedingungen, zugleich stieg die tägliche Arbeitszeit auf bis zu sechzehn Stunden. Über 70 % der Häftlinge waren nicht in der Lage, das unterste Produktionsniveau zu erbringen, und waren infolgedessen schwer unterernährt. In einer Erinnerung an diese Zeit heißt es:

> In den Baracken, in denen früher 40–50 Menschen untergebracht waren, lebten nun 100–120. Kantinen, ausgerichtet auf 1.000 Menschen, verpflegten nun 2.000–2500. Sie gaben das Essen bei 40–50 Grad Kälte durch ein Fensterchen nach draußen. Man hörte auf, die Baracken zu heizen, heißes Wasser wurde nicht ausgegeben. [...] Die Leute begannen zu sterben wie die Fliegen.[25]

---

20 Die beste Übersicht über die Fördermengen in den einzelnen Jahren findet sich in Zeljak, Os-obennosti razvitija, S. 87 f. Siehe zu den Organisationsstrukturen der einzelnen Bau- und Goldförderungsabteilungen innerhalb des Gesamtkomplexes Dal'stroj Kozlov, Reorganizacija, S. 44.

21 Zu den enormen Verlusten bei der technischen Intelligenz und den allgemeinen Arbeitskräften durch die lokalen Terrormaßnahmen siehe Nordlander, Magadan, S. 115 f.

22 Vgl. Nordlander, Stanovlenie ėkonomiki, S. 249.

23 Zu Korolev siehe Golovanov, Korolev; Mick, Wissenschaft, S. 354 sowie Jersak, Rüstungsforschung, S. 176. Zu Mandel'štam und dem polnischen Poeten Bruno Jasienski an der Kolyma siehe Conquest, Kolyma, S. 21. Zu Oppositionellen in den Lagern der Kolyma siehe Rogowin, Partei der Hingerichteten, S. 298.

24 Vgl. Šulubina, Sistema Sevvostlaga, S. 80. Während des Großen Terrors wurden einige Tausend Menschen, die zuvor bereits entlassen worden waren und als sogenannte „Kolonisten" in der Region siedelten, wieder in die Lager eingewiesen. Vgl. Širokov, Dal'stroj, S. 122 sowie S. 128.

25 Zitiert nach Bacaev, Kolymskaja grjada, S. 54. Zu den Haftbedingungen siehe daneben Širokov, Dal'stroj, S. 117 sowie Zeljak, Pjat' metallov, S. 94 f.

Zugleich trafen beständig neue Häftlingstransporte an der Kolyma ein. Unter dem neuen Leiter Nikišov, der seit Ende 1939 über Dal'stroj und das *Sevvostlag* herrschte, hatte das Lagersystem mehr als 176.000 Insassen. Knapp 97 % aller Arbeiter in den Goldgebieten waren Häftlinge. Durch die reine Masse an Arbeitskräften konnte kurzfristig ein extrem hohes Ergebnis erzielt werden – 1940 war das Jahr, in dem Dal'stroj mit 80 Tonnen chemisch reinem Gold die größte Fördermenge per annum erzielte. Ein höheres Ergebnis wurde in den folgenden Jahren nie mehr erreicht. Nun lieferte Dal'stroj fast 50 % des gesamten in der UdSSR gewonnenen Goldes, das Kombinat stieg in den Kreis der weltweit größten Förderkomplexe auf.[26] Umgangssprachlich wurde diese Periode an der Kolyma als „das große Gold" bezeichnet.[27]

Die Leistungen von Dal'stroj im Stalinismus beruhten im Wesentlichen auf drei grundsätzlichen Paradigmen: Alle Arbeit war auf die gnadenlose Ausbeutung eines großen Heeres von Zwangsarbeitern ausgerichtet, die Goldförderung war extensiv und die Versorgung des Kombinats durch das Moskauer Zentrum wurde wie eine militärische Operation betrachtet.

Die extensive, nahezu räuberische Förderung beschränkte sich auf die ergiebigsten Fördergebiete. Dort lagerte das Gold in sehr gut zugänglichen Erdschichten, den sogenannten Goldfeldern, in flach unter der Erdoberfläche verlaufenden Goldgruben oder als Waschgold in Flüssen. Zunächst baute man die reichsten Goldlager ab, dann wandte man sich den Gebieten mit einem mittleren Goldgehalt zu. Nach diesen Arbeiten enthielten die Gruben und Felder sehr wohl noch Gold, der Abbau des verbliebenen Metalls wurde jedoch als ökonomisch ineffektiv eingeschätzt und man warf alle Kräfte auf das nächste reiche Goldlager. In seinem Roman „Goldsucher", der die Geologen der Region verherrlicht, hat Oleg Kuvaev, selbst Geologe, diese Vorgehensweise pointiert als „Abschöpfung der Sahne"[28] bezeichnet. Dabei wurden typische Methoden der stalinistischen Industrialisierung angewandt, wie die Stachanov-Bewegung, der Einsatz von Stoßarbeitern und die blitzartige Verlagerung einer großen Zahl von Häftlingen und freien Arbeitskräften in Gebiete, die drohten den Plan nicht zu erfüllen.[29] Das Tempo der Arbeiten war dabei auch durch die klimatischen Bedingungen vorgegeben. Bedingt durch den langen Winter setzte die Abbausaison auf den Goldfeldern und beim Waschgold erst im Mai ein und musste Ende des Herbstes bereits abgeschlossen sein.

Durch diese Art der Förderung wurden weite Landstriche innerhalb weniger Jahre in regelrechte Mondlandschaften verwandelt, ganze Regionen chemisch verseucht, Flusslandschaften vollkommen zerstört und riesige Waldflächen zur Gewinnung von

26 Vgl. Zeljak, Osobennosti razvitija, S. 87 f.

27 Vgl. das Interview mit einem der berühmtesten Geologen der Kolyma, N. A. Šilo, der die Atmosphäre in den 1930er Jahren anschaulich schildert. Vgl. Šilo, Vse zoloto Kolymy, S. 18.

28 Kuwajew, Goldsucher, S. 26.

29 Vgl. die Beschreibung dieser Aktionen bei Zeljak, Pjat' metallov, S. 72 f.

Brennmaterial abgeholzt.[30] Der Magadaner Historiker Vitalij Zeljak spricht in diesem Zusammenhang zutreffend von der Übertragung des militärischen Leitungsstils auf die Produktionsweise – die Goldfelder wurden regelrecht „gestürmt".[31]

Die Planerfüllung und -übererfüllung stand über allem, und die jeweiligen Leiter des Kombinats gaben den von der staatlichen Leitung ausgeübten Druck an die Leiter der einzelnen Produktionseinheiten weiter. Dabei zählte allein die geförderte Goldmenge im laufenden Jahr. Um diese kurzfristigen Ergebnisse nicht zu gefährden, wurde auf die Errichtung einer dauerhaften Produktionsinfrastruktur verzichtet. Auch alle Lagereinrichtungen und die soziale Infrastruktur für freie Arbeitskräfte waren durch die Einheitsleitung ganz auf die Erfüllung des Produktionsplans ausgerichtet. Der Öffnung oder Schließung von Förderstationen folgte die Einrichtung oder Auflösung des jeweiligen Lagerpunktes, so dass auch in späteren Jahren ständig neue Lagerinfrastruktur und Siedlungen für die freien Arbeitskräfte errichtet werden mussten.[32]

In den folgenden Jahren bedingte die hier beschriebene Ausbeutung der Goldvorkommen immer weiter steigende Anforderungen im Bereich von Erkundungen und Schürfungen. Die geologische Abteilung von Dal'stroj wuchs in ihrer Bedeutung; die Geologen waren vor die Aufgabe gestellt, ständig neue, enorm goldhaltige Regionen zu finden und für den Abbau vorzubereiten.[33] Da die Grenzen des Territoriums ökonomisch definiert waren, war das Kombinat in der Lage, auch neue Felder außerhalb von Dal'stroj einfach in seinen Machtbereich zu integrieren. Dadurch verzichtete man auf aussichtsreiche, aber tiefer im ewigen Eis liegende Goldlager und fast vollständig auf Berg-Gold[34]; dies hätte zwar langfristige Erträge erzielt, kurzfristig stellten derartige Anstrengungen jedoch die Planerfüllung des jeweiligen Jahres in Frage.

Bei der Förderung weiterer Metalle orientierte man sich stets an den Methoden des Goldabbaus. Kein anderer Rohstoff konnte in seiner Bedeutung an das Gold heranreichen. Lediglich Zinn spielte eine größere Rolle; seine Förderung begann im größeren Maßstab im Jahr 1937, als 40,7 Tonnen Zinnkonzentrat gewonnen wurden. Neben Wolfram und Kobalt, denen in Dal'stroj keine derartige Bedeutung zukam, wurde seit 1948 auch Uran gefördert. Zusammen bildeten sie die sogenannten „fünf Metalle von Dal'stroj", faktisch waren jedoch nur zwei bis drei für die Sowjetunion von erheblicher Relevanz.[35] Beim Urabbau, v. a. in der Grube Bugutyčag, herrschten be-

---

30 Erste Arbeiten zur Rekultivierung einzelner Gebiete setzten erst zu Beginn der 1980er Jahre ein. Vgl. Zeljak, Osobennosti razvitija, S. 98.

31 Vgl. Zeljak, Osobennosti razvitija, S. 91.

32 Daneben gab es an zentralen Punkten und wichtigen Siedlungen Lagerpunkte, die über viele Jahre konstant blieben und an die sich übergreifende Lagerinfrastruktur angliederte, wie das große Häftlingskrankenhaus „Linkes Ufer", in dem Šalamov einige Jahre als Feldscher arbeitete.

33 Vgl. Kozlov, Sostojanie geologičeskoj služby.

34 Zeljak beschreibt, dass aus diesem Grund zur Zeit von Dal'stroj mehrere Tausend Tonnen Berg-Gold überhaupt nicht abgebaut wurden. Vgl. Zeljak, Osobennosti razvitija, S. 90.

35 Vgl. zu der leitenden Rolle der Goldförderung Zeljak, Pjat' metallov, S. 82f. Die Förderung von Zinn befreite die Sowjetunion von der Notwendigkeit, dieses Metall unter hohen Kosten im Ausland ein-

sonders entsetzliche Arbeitsbedingungen, da dieses Metall ohne jede Schutzvorrichtung z. T. in einer Tiefe von bis zu 1.000 Metern gefördert wurde. Auch der ehemalige Häftling Abrahm Dück musste eine Zeitlang in der Uranförderung arbeiten. Er beschreibt die dortigen Bedingungen im Rückblick:

> Für die geheimen Urangruben, wohin auch der höchste Lohn keine freien Arbeiter locken konnte, waren die rechtlosen Sklaven die ideale Arbeitskraft. Ein riesiges Bergwerk wurde eröffnet, wohin viele Tausende Häftlinge abtransportiert wurden. Es war die tragisch berühmte Urangrube Budugytschak. [...] Die fast grenzenlose Haft der Sklaven gewährleistete die Geheimhaltung. Aber arbeitsfähig mussten sie sein. Man konnte sie nicht auspowern. Die physische Anstrengung im Abbau war unbeschreiblich. Daher auch die Bedingungen, zwar nicht menschlicher, aber zweckmäßiger, um die Förderung des Urans auf höchstem Niveau zu halten. Der Häftling erlag nicht nach etlichen Wochen oder Monaten der Unterernährung, wie in den Goldgruben, wo er ersetzt wurde. Hier war diese Zeit länger. Aber die Bestrahlung führte unweigerlich zur tödlichen Strahlenkrankheit.[36]

Im Gegensatz zu den Anforderungen war die Technologie, die in Dal'stroj zum Abbau und zur Waschung der Metalle verwandt wurde, stark zurückgeblieben. Dadurch ging eine große Menge Gold verloren, schwerste Arbeiten mussten per Hand erledigt werden und durch eine ineffektive Verwendung der vorhandenen Technik kam es zu ausgesprochen vielen Unfällen.[37] Trotz der primitiven Arbeitsgeräte war diese Vorgehensweise in Dal'stroj so effektiv, da der mittlere Goldgehalt in der Region den Gehalt in anderen Fördergebieten um ein Vielfaches überstieg. In den ersten Jahren gab es in

---

zukaufen. Siehe zu den Fördermengen von Zinn Širokov, Dal'stroj, S. 126. Vgl. zu der Förderung von Wolfram – Zeljak, Pjat' metallov, S. 205 sowie zu Kobalt – Zeljak, Pjat' metallov, S. 208.

36 Dück, Erinnerungen, S. 383. Seit 1946 war der MGB in einem besonders verschärfter Geheimhaltung unterliegenden Projekt auf der Suche nach geeigneten Förderstellen. Trotz zahlreicher Expeditionen erwiesen sich jedoch nur die Regionen Butugyčag und Berendžinskij im Gebiet Kolyma, Čaunskij und Severnoe in Tschukotka und eine Region in Jakutien als aussichtsreich. Auch wenn diese Fundstellen im Weltmaßstab nur einen mäßigen Urangehalt aufwiesen, hatten sie für die Sowjetunion im beginnenden Kalten Krieg eine enorme Bedeutung. Unter Aufwendung erheblicher Investitionen wurden in Dal'stroj zwischen 1948 und 1955 insgesamt etwa 135 Tonnen konzentriertes Uran gefördert. Für die wichtigsten Erlasse zur Uranförderung in Dal'stroj siehe Bacaev, Osobennosti, S. 126–128; Zeljak, Uranodobyvajuščaja otrasl'. Für eine ausführliche Beschreibung des Uranabbaus in Dal'stroj siehe Ioffe/Nesterenko, Volčij kamen'. Hier kommt eine Reihe von Personen zu Wort, die freiwillig beim Uranabbau gearbeitet haben oder als Häftlinge dazu gezwungen wurden.

37 Ein Beispiel für die Primitivität des Arbeitsgerätes ist der Einsatz von hölzernen Trögen, in denen das Gold von Hand gewaschen wurde. Von den 80 Tonnen chemisch reinen Goldes, die 1940 insgesamt erzielt wurden, wurden 18 % auf diese Weise gewonnen. Vgl. Zeljak, Osobennosti razvitija, S. 95. Siehe zu der geringen Effektivität der verwendeten Technik und den enormen Unfallgefahren ebenso Širokov, Dal'stroj, S. 129 sowie Bacaev, Osobennosti, S. 134. Bei seiner Beschreibung der Goldförderung schildert der Kolyma-Überlebende Šalamov eindrucksvoll, mit welchem Enthusiasmus die eigene Produktion von Glühbirnen als Befreiung von „ausländischer Abhängigkeit" gefeiert wurde und wie in einer Goldgrube die Zerstörung einer solchen Glühbirne zum Verlust Tausender Arbeitsstunden führte. Vgl. Schalamow, Linkes Ufer, S. 52. Glühbirnen wurden seit 1941 in einer Glasfabrik in der Nähe von Magadan produziert. Vgl. Malagin, Ėkonomičeskij rajon, S. 100.

Dal'stroj bis zu 36 g Gold pro m³ Erde (im Jahr 1933). Dieser Gehalt sank zwar in den folgenden Jahren, doch noch 1938–1940 betrug er 13,7 g pro m³; in vielen Gruben von *Glavzoloto* waren beispielsweise nur 0,68 g pro m³ vorhanden.[38]

Die Arbeit unter den Prämissen Zwangsarbeit und Extensivität sorgte für ein widersprüchliches Verhältnis des Moskauer Zentrums zu seinem größten Lager-Industriellen Komplex. Das Kombinat hatte nicht nur einen juristischen und politischen, sondern auch einen finanziellen und organisatorischen Sonderstatus. „Viel Metall zu jedem Preis" lautete die Devise, mit der Anträge und Bestellungen von Dal'stroj wie militärische Befehle gehandhabt wurden. Anders als ein gewöhnlicher sowjetischer Betrieb musste das Kombinat seine technischen Anlagen, Maschinen und Materialien nicht einzeln bei verschiedenen Ministerien bestellen und ihre Finanzierung nicht jeweils beantragen, sondern erhielt die benötigten Gelder und Waren unmittelbar bereitgestellt – wie die Leitung einer militärischen Abteilung. Im Laufe der Jahre wurden Dal'stroj auf diese Weise geradezu ungeheuerliche Summen zur Verfügung gestellt.[39] In Moskau existierte eine eigene Vertretung von Dal'stroj („Dal'strojsnab"), deren einzige Aufgabe in der Organisation der Lieferung von technischem Gerät und benötigten Waren für das Kombinat bestand.[40]

Vor diesem Hintergrund überrascht die Primitivität, mit der viele Arbeiten vor Ort durchgeführt wurden. Dieser Widerspruch erklärt sich zum Teil aus der Region selbst: In dem so riesigen und bisher unerschlossenen Gebiet mit großen Gebirgszügen und Flüssen unter den gegebenen extremen klimatischen Bedingungen waren eigentlich sämtliche Lieferungen und Gelder nicht ausreichend – zumal die Fördergebiete häufig wechselten und parallel zum Metallabbau beständig Arbeiten in den Bereichen Energie, Infrastruktur und Bau nötig waren. Außerdem bedeuteten die Lieferungen bei weitem nicht, dass die benötigten Materialien und das technische Gerät auch tatsächlich die Arbeitsstellen erreichten, an denen sie gebraucht wurden. Zudem musste schließlich auch immer Personal vor Ort sein, das in der Lage war, die Geräte sachgemäß zu bedienen und instand zu setzen. Ein ungeheurer finanzieller Schaden entstand dadurch, dass teure Materialien und Geräte im Eis verrotteten oder man Dinge lieferte, die vor Ort gar nicht gebraucht wurden.[41]

Außerdem war Dal'stroj als Zwangsarbeiterprojekt von Anfang auf den massenhaften Einsatz von Häftlingen eingestellt. Für die sowjetische Führung bestand überhaupt nicht die Notwendigkeit, die körperlich schwerste Arbeit von Maschinen verrichten zu lassen. Die Einsicht in die ökonomische Sinnhaftigkeit einer stärkeren

---

38 Vgl. Zeljak, Osobennosti razvitija, S. 90 sowie Bacaev, Dinamika, S. 235. *Glavzoloto* war in den anderen großen goldhaltigen Gebieten der UdSSR tätig, v. a. in Jakutien, in Transbaikalien und am Ural.

39 1956 entwarf das Kombinat einen 15-Jahrplan, der ausführliche Angaben zu seiner bisherigen Geschichte enthält. Demnach hat das Zentrum zwischen 1931 und 1956 insgesamt 13,5 Milliarden Rubel in Dal'stroj investiert. Vgl. GAMO f. R-23, op. 1, d. 5858, l. 3–11, hier l. 3.

40 Vgl. Širokov, Organizacionnye formy, S. 65.

41 Vgl. Zeljak, Pjat' metallov, S. 210 f.

Mechanisierung setzte sich im Wesentlichen erst nach Stalins Tod durch. Zu den Grundbedingungen des Lager-Industriellen Komplexes gehörte es außerdem, dass sich das Interesse der sowjetischen Führung an der Region, gerade auch für Stalin persönlich, auf ihre Bodenschätze beschränkte. Der Nordosten war ein Gebiet, das gnadenlos ausgebeutet werden sollte, die Erfolge der sowjetischen Herrschaft in der Region wurden nur in Tonnen Gold oder Zinn gemessen. Dieser Tonnenideologie folgte auch die Versorgungspolitik, in deren Rahmen Dal'stroj sehr große Spielräume gewährt wurden.

Keineswegs sollte die Kolyma aber zum Empfänger von Hochtechnologie werden. Bemühungen der lokalen Leitung, die Entstehung von Industrieanlagen zu fördern, die über die reine Rohstoffgewinnung hinauswiesen und die eine Entwicklung zu einer vollwertigen Industrieregion erlaubt hätten, wurden von Moskau bewusst unterbunden.[42]

In den Kriegsjahren (1941–1945) veränderten sich die Prämissen des Lager-Industriellen Komplexes.[43] In Bezug auf technische Anlagen und Materialien war Dal'stroj zunehmend von innersowjetischen Warenströmen abgeschnitten, die finanziellen Zuteilungen an das Kombinat wurden deutlich reduziert, und dies obwohl das Kombinat aufgrund seiner Metallförderung als besonders kriegswichtig eingestuft worden war.[44] Zudem stoppten seit Beginn des Krieges sämtliche Häftlingstransporte an die Kolyma.[45] Der Anteil der freien Arbeitskräfte stieg durch Zuzug, aber auch durch Haftentlassungen an. Mitten im Krieg konnten Häftlinge die Lager des *Sevvostlag* verlassen, weil ihnen gestattet wurde, ihre besonderen Arbeitsleistungen auf die Haftzeit anrechnen zu lassen. All diese Personen mussten jedoch in Dal'stroj verbleiben, sie wurden gezwungen, weiterhin als „Freie" im Kombinat zu arbeiten. In vielen Bereichen unterschieden sich ihre Arbeits- und Lebensbedingungen tatsächlich kaum von denen der Häftlinge, sie hatten mit unerbittlichen Arbeitsanforderungen, einer miserablen Versorgung und zahlreichen Repressionen und Verfolgungen zu kämpfen. Auf diese Weise gab es aber zum ersten Mal Förderstellen, in denen ausschließlich freie Arbeiter (bzw. entlassene Häftlinge) tätig waren.[46] In absoluten

---

42 So begann man beispielsweise in Dal'stroj auf eigene Initiative hin mit der Schmelzung des geförderten Zinns. Dies wurde jedoch 1938 von Moskau aus verboten und das Konzentrat in eine Fabrik in Podol'sk gebracht. Nach Zeljak sollte mit diesem Schritt eine komplexere Entwicklung des Nordostens zu einer nicht nur fördernden, sondern auch verarbeitenden Industrieregion verhindert werden. Vgl. Zeljak, Pjat' metallov, S. 80.

43 Grundlegend zur Rolle der Zwangsarbeit im Zweiten Weltkrieg siehe Bacon, Gulag at War.

44 So wurde Dal'stroj gleich mit Beginn des Krieges zu einer harten Ökonomisierung aller Ressourcen, v. a. von Materialien und Brennstoffen, gezwungen. Vgl. Zeljak, Pjat' metallov, S. 110. Für den Historiker Bacaev stellt die enorme Lieferreduktion die Hauptursache für die Senkung der Goldförderung zu Beginn des Krieges dar. Vgl. Bacaev, Osobennosti, S. 109.

45 Šulubina, Sistema Sevvostlaga, S. 22. Seit 1941 wurden auch keine freien Fachleute mehr in den Nordosten gebracht. Vgl. Bacaev, Osobennosti, S. 105.

46 Im Gegensatz zu der Situation von Häftlingen in anderen Lagerkomplexen, die sich im Krieg erheblich verschlechterte, kam es in besonders produktionsintensiven Bereichen zu einer punktuellen

Zahlen lebten Ende des Jahres 1944 etwa 177.200 arbeitende Menschen im Machtbereich von Dal'stroj, davon waren knapp 80.000 Häftlinge – allerdings hatten fast alle „freien Arbeitskräfte" Lagererfahrungen und durften Dal'stroj nicht verlassen.[47]

Dennoch sprechen Magadaner Historiker in Bezug auf die Rohstoffförderung insgesamt von „stabilen Kriegsjahren" – mit einer durchschnittlichen Goldförderung von etwa 72 Tonnen chemisch reinem Gold per Jahr. Die Schwierigkeiten des Kombinats konnten in dieser Zeit auf verschiedenen Wegen ausgeglichen werden. Vor allem lieferte das Gebiet selbst neue Rohstoffe. Allein in den ersten drei Kriegsjahren wurden siebzehn neue, reiche Goldlager erschlossen, weniger effektive Fördergebiete wurden eingestellt, die Nutzung von gut zugänglichem Berg-Gold nahm zu. Hinzu kam eine stark gestiegene Zinnproduktion.[48]

Daneben besserte sich die Versorgung des Kombinats nach einiger Zeit auf unerwartetem Wege – durch amerikanische Lieferungen. Lend-lease-Verträge mit dem kapitalistischen Nachbarn brachten Technik und Verkehrsmittel (v. a. die Planierraupen der Marke Caterpillar), aber auch Kleidungsstücke und Lebensmittel an die Kolyma. Seit 1942 wurden die beiden Häfen im Nordmeer sogar ausschließlich von den Amerikanern versorgt. Der Historiker Bacaev sieht hier die eigentliche Ursache für die relative Stabilität der Kriegsjahre; auch Zeljak verweist auf die amerikanischen Maschinen, die den Mechanisierungsgrad des Kombinats insgesamt deutlich erhöhten.[49]

Verbesserung der Verhältnisse. Vgl. zur Situation der Häftlinge in der Kriegszeit und zu den Entlassungen aufgrund der *začety* (Anrechnung von Arbeitstagen) Širokov, Dal'stroj, S. 140–142; Zeljak, Pjat' metallov, S. 135–138; Bacaev, Kolymskaja Grjada, S. 58; Šulubina, Sistema Sevvostlaga, S. 22; Bacaev, Osobennosti, S. 106–108 sowie Kokurin/Morukov, Stalinskie strojki, S. 537. Zum 1. Oktober 1942 strich man sämtliche Vergünstigungen für freie Arbeiter im Hohen Norden, aufgrund fehlender Häftlingstransporte wurden freie Arbeitskräfte verstärkt in der Metallförderung eingesetzt. Zur Lage der freien Arbeitskräfte siehe Zeljak, Pjat' metallov, S. 126–131; Bacaev, Osobennosti, S. 103.

47 Vgl. Bacaev, Osobennosti, S. 107f. Zu den Zahlen der freien Arbeitskräfte siehe Zeljak, Pjat' metallov, S. 88.

48 Erstmals wurde nun auch Berg-Gold gefördert und der Abbau von Waschgold ausgeweitet. Vgl. Zeljak, Osobennosti razvitija, S. 86. Zwischen 1941 und 1944 wurden 14.400 Tonnen konzentriertes Zinn gefördert, vgl. Zeljak, Pjat' metallov, S. 126. Parallel begann man mit dem Abbau von Wolfram, der von 1941 bis 1944 280 Tonnen umfasste. Für die Förderung all dieser Metalle wurde das Industriekombinat Dal'stroj am 14. Februar 1945 mit dem Orden „Trudovogo Krasnogo Znameni" ausgezeichnet. Vgl. Zeljak, Pjat' metallov, S. 140.

49 Zu den Lieferungen sowie zum Einsatz amerikanischer Technik seit den Kriegsjahren siehe Zeljak, Pjat' metallov, S. 119 sowie Bacaev, Osobennosti, S. 109. In der Erzählung „Lend-Lease" schildert Šalamov, wie begehrt die amerikanischen Lebensmittel und Kleidungsstücke waren; eindrücklich beschreibt er auch die neue Technik. Schalamow, Linkes Ufer, S. 274–284. Die Kriegssituation führte im Mai 1944 zu einem Besuch des amerikanischen Vizepräsidenten Henry A. Wallace (gemeinsam mit einem Vertreter des amerikanischen Office of War Information, O. Lattimore), der sich in grotesker Verkennung der Tatsachen von eilig errichteten „potemkinschen Dörfern" ohne Häftlinge täuschen ließ. In zwei geheimen Telegrammen erstattete Nikišov Berija Bericht über diesen Besuch. Vgl. den Abdruck in Kokurin/Morukov, Stalinskie strojki, S. 464ff. Siehe auch die Beschreibung der Reise bei Wallace, Soviet Asia. Conquest bezeichnet diesen Besuch als eines der „most absurd, and from every point of view, horrifying events in the whole history of the Soviet labour camp system". Conquest,

Kriegswirtschaft in Dal'stroj bedeutete auch eine deutliche Beschleunigung der Arbeiten, bei der die Erstellung der Infrastruktur, die Errichtung einer Energieversorgung und der Abbau des Goldes im hohen Tempo gleichzeitig vollzogen wurde. Diese Arbeitsweise beschreibt ein Arbeiter in seinen Erinnerungen an die Kriegszeit:

> Die Erschließung neuer Gebiete vollzog sich mit dem allergrößten Tempo. Die Abwesenheit von Straßen, Wohnhäusern u. Ä. wurde nicht mehr als unüberwindliche Hürde wahrgenommen. So begann man zum Beispiel erst im Herbst 1941 das Tal von Omčaksk zu erschließen, aber bereits 1942 wurden dort über 21.000 kg chemisch reines Gold gefördert. Der Abbau des Goldes, der Bau und die Organisation der Mine, die Anlegung der Straße – all dies geschah gleichzeitig.[50]

Auf diese Weise konnte trotz der verschärften Bedingungen der Kriegszeit das Niveau der Metallförderung in Dal'stroj annähernd auf dem Höchststand des Jahres 1940 gehalten werden.

Obwohl Stalin persönlich gefordert hatte, das Vorkriegsniveau wieder zu erreichen und zu übertreffen, brach die Goldförderung in Dal'stroj kurz nach Ende des Zweiten Weltkrieges ein.[51] 1946 wurden nur noch 52,2 Tonnen chemisch reines Gold gefördert, in den folgenden beiden Jahren sanken die Erträge auf 41,2 bzw. 43,6 Tonnen. Mit großen finanziellen und geologischen Anstrengungen wurde die Leistung von Dal'stroj im Jahr 1949 noch einmal auf 52,4 Tonnen angehoben, danach war das Kombinat niemals mehr in der Lage, seine wichtigste Kennziffer auf 50 Tonnen zu bringen und blieb damit unter den Ergebnissen des Jahres 1937. Der Einbruch der Förderung in den ersten Jahren nach Kriegsende lässt sich zunächst noch mit dem Abbruch der Lieferungen aus den USA – nach Beginn des Kalten Krieges – und mit der Abreise einer großen Zahl ausgebildeter ehemaliger Häftlinge erklären, die die Produktion während des Krieges bestimmt hatten.[52]

Doch die grundlegenden Ursachen für diesen extremen Einbruch der Förderzahlen im Spätstalinismus sind sehr viel komplexer. Sie sind Teil einer großen strukturellen Krise der sowjetischen Lagerwirtschaft, bei der die auf Zwangsarbeit

---

Kolyma, S. 204. Er beschreibt ausführlich die Folgen und Diskussionen dieses Besuches in den USA in der späteren McCarthy-Ära. Ebd., S. 210 ff. Literarisch hat Šalamov den Besuch von Wallace in seiner Erzählung „Iwan Fjodorowitsch" verarbeitet. In dieser Darstellung erkennt Wallace jedoch den wahren Charakter der Produktionsanlagen. Vgl. Schalamow, Linkes Ufer, S. 48 – 64. Auch Elinor Lipper schildert in ihren Erinnerungen den Besuch von Wallace und Lattimore. Vgl. Lipper, Elf Jahre, S. 234 ff.

50 Zitiert nach Bacaev, Osobennosti, S. 112 f. Zu der spezifischen Produktionsweise im Krieg siehe Zeljak, V gody velikoj otečestvennoj vojny, S. 214.

51 Vgl. Zeljak, Pjat' metallov, S. 151.

52 Vgl. Zeljak, Pjat' metallov, S. 154. Die relative Stabilisierung der Förderzahlen im Jahr 1949 zeigt, dass mit enormem wirtschaftlichen Einsatz eine Verlangsamung des Absinkens der Goldförderung erzielt werden konnte, die jedoch nicht grundsätzlich in der Lage war, die Situation zu ändern. Hinzu kam, dass gerade 1949 geologische Erfolge gefeiert werden konnten. In diesem Jahr wurden einige neue Goldfelder entdeckt. Vgl. Bacaev, Osobennosti, S. 130. Siehe zur Situation des MVD im Jahr 1949 Ivanova, Istorija, S. 359 sowie Khlevnyuk, Economy of the Gulag, S. 120. Zu den geologischen Erfolgen im Jahr 1949 vgl. Bacaev, Osobennosti, S. 130.

Abb. 22 Abbildungen 22–33: Auszüge aus einem Fotoalbum des NKVD über Dal'stroj in den Jahren 1942–1943. Das Album zeigt auf 150 Seiten Förderanlagen, Infrastrukturen und Siedlungen des Kombinates. Lager oder Häftlinge sind an keiner Stelle zu erkennen. Aus den Beständen des GARF

fußenden Großprojekte zunehmend zu einer ungeheuren Belastung für die gesamte sowjetische Wirtschaft wurden.[53] Valery Lazarev spricht dabei von einem „bankruptcy in the strict economic sense"[54]. In Dal'stroj wurde die extensive, stalinistische Arbeitsweise zu einem Bumerang. Die Prämissen, die bisher die Effektivität des Kombinats ausgemacht hatten, stellten zunehmend seine Leistungsfähigkeit in Frage:

Mit einer erheblichen Verringerung des Metallgehaltes in den Abbaugebieten brach die wichtigste Voraussetzung für den Erfolg des Kombinats weg. Der „räuberische" Abbau zeigte seine verheerenden Folgen. Da in den vergangenen Förderperioden auf eine langfristige und gründliche Produktionsanlage verzichtet worden war, stieß die Kombinatsleitung nun an natürliche Grenzen der Goldvorkommen. Es ließen sich trotz großangelegter Untersuchungen keine weiteren derart reichen Goldlager in gut zugänglichen Erdschichten entdecken.[55] Enthielt 1940 ein Kubikmeter Erde noch 11,1 g chemisch reines Gold (mittlerer Wert), so waren es 1942 noch 10,1 g pro m³, 1950 fiel der Wert auf 4,5 g, 1954 auf 3,98 g und im Jahr 1957 auf nur noch 3,3 g pro m³.

53 Zur ökonomischen Krise des GULAG siehe Ivanova, Istorija, S. 355–385 sowie Borodkin/Gregory/Khlevnjuk, Ėkonomika; Gregory/Lazarev, Forced Labor.
54 Lazarev, Conclusions, S. 196.
55 Vgl. Bacaev, Dinamika, S. 238.

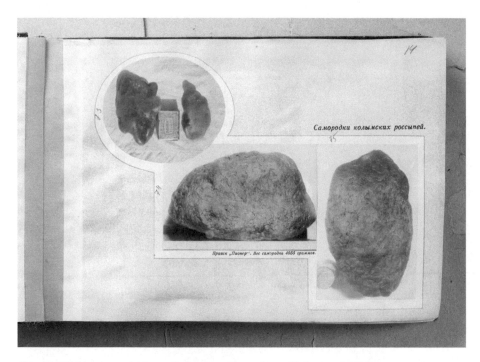

Abb. 23 Goldklumpen mit einem Gewicht von über 4 kg, gefördert an der Kolyma

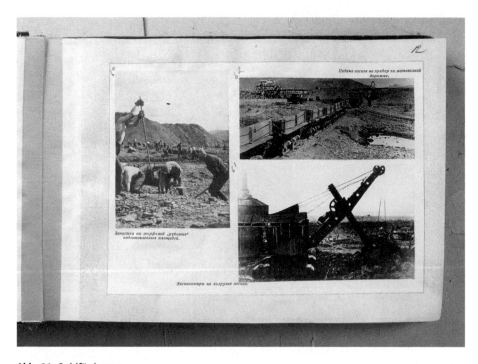

Abb. 24 Goldförderung

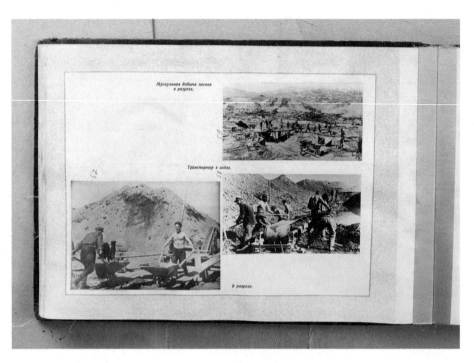

Abb. 25 Goldförderung

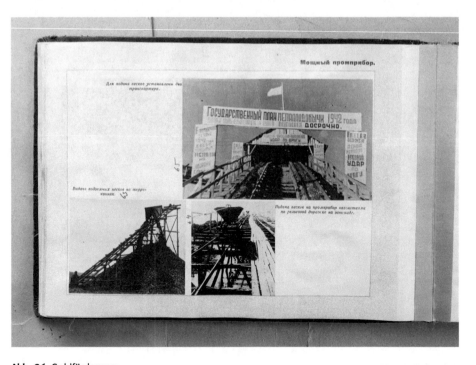

Abb. 26 Goldförderung

Abb. 27 Zinnförderung

Abb. 28 Anlage von Straßen, Brückenbau

Abb. 29 Die Flotte von Dal'stroj

Abb. 30 Transport im Schnee

Abb. 31 Mensa der Dal'stroj-Leitung

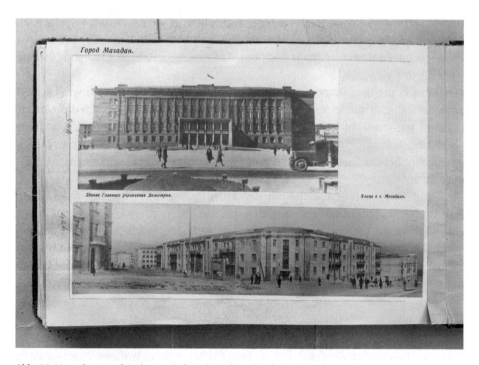

Abb. 32 Verwaltungsgebäude von Dal'stroj, Wohngebäude in Magadan

Abb. 33 Warenlager in Magadan

Dementsprechend musste immer mehr Erdreich bewegt werden. Auf der Suche nach Gold durchpflügte man 1941 21,4 Mio. m³ und 1956 bereits 38,8 Mio. m³ Erde. In der Folge stieg der Selbstkostenpreis des Goldes beständig; zwischen 1940 und 1956 um mehr als das Vierfache.[56]

Dabei drang man immer weiter in den Nordosten der Sowjetunion vor; bis 1953 erreichte Dal'stroj mit 3,5 Mio. km² seine größte Ausdehnung. Zusätzlich dazu kehrte Dal'stroj punktuell auch zu Regionen zurück, die bereits Ende der 1930er Jahre oberflächlich ausgebeutet worden waren. Die mangelnde Technik machte es jedoch unmöglich, bei der Suche nach tiefer liegenden Goldvorkommen nennenswerte Erfolge zu erzielen.

Zehntausende Häftlinge, die mit einfachen Spaten Erde abtrugen, das Gold in Holzwannen wuschen und Schächte mit Ästen stabilisierten, erwiesen sich nur in den ersten Jahren als „billige Arbeitskräfte". Je mehr Boden bearbeitet werden musste, desto weniger konnte aber auf den massenhaften Einsatz von Baggern, LKWs, auf spezielle Sprengtechniken und Förderanlagen verzichtet werden, zumal die Entfernung der Fördergebiete in Tschukotka zu den zentralen Anlagen von Dal'stroj be-

---

56 Zahlenangaben nach einem Bericht des Gebietsparteikomitees an das ZK der KPdSU im Vorfeld der Gründung des Magadaner Volkswirtschaftsrates in GAMO f. R-23, op. 1, d. 6088, l. 1–50, hier l. 11. Im Vergleich dazu umfassten alle Erdarbeiten, die beim Bau des gesamten Weißmeer-Ostsee-Kanals im Laufe von zwei Jahren vorgenommen wurden, lediglich 21 Mio. m³ Erde. Vgl. Ivanova, Istorija, S. 351.

ständig wuchs. Die mangelnde Infrastruktur wurde zu einem riesigen Problem, wenn Anlagen zunächst Hunderte Kilometer weit transportiert werden mussten.[57] Die Suche nach neuen rohstoffreichen Gebieten, der Abbau weiterer Metalle und die seit 1948 betriebene Uranförderung in Dal'stroj machten einen Ausbau wissenschaftlicher Forschung unerlässlich. Der Ministerrat der UdSSR beschloss daher im Mai 1948 die Gründung eines Instituts, bezeichnet als VNII-1 („Vsesojuznyj Naučno-Issledovatel'skij Institut Zolota i Redkich Metallov – Wissenschaftliches Allunionsforschungsinstitut für Gold und seltene Metalle"). Das Institut unterlag völlig den Bedingungen von Dal'stroj, was absolute Geheimhaltung und eine strenge Abkapselung von anderen wissenschaftlichen Einrichtungen mit sich brachte.[58]

Die geänderte Arbeitsweise ließ die Kosten der Metallgewinnung beständig steigen, das Kombinat entwickelte sich für die sowjetische Volkswirtschaft zu einem Fass ohne Boden, während es zugleich immer weniger Erträge lieferte. Da die Sowjetunion jedoch unbedingt auf den Ankauf von Valuta angewiesen war, musste Dal'stroj um fast jeden Preis gestützt werden.[59] Seit Beginn der 1950er Jahre büßte Dal'stroj einen Teil seines exklusiven Status ein. Im Rahmen der großen ökonomischen Krise der sowjetischen Zwangsarbeitswirtschaft spürte auch die Leitung von Dal'stroj eine deutliche Beschneidung ihrer Mittel, die sie z. T. direkt durch eine schlechtere Versorgung an die Lager weitergab.[60] Häufig aber schrieb sie einfach steigende Verluste ab und verschleierte gegenüber der sowjetischen Leitung das wahre Ausmaß ihrer finanziellen Schwierigkeiten.

---

57 Vgl. Zeljak, Osobennosti razvitija, S. 88. Dies gilt in besonderem Maße im Bereich der Zinnförderung. An der Kolyma erwiesen sich die wichtigsten Zinngebiete als erschöpft, seit 1947 fiel auch die Förderung des zweiten Metalls. In Tschukotka gab es allerdings noch reiche Förderstellen, deren Ausbeutung jedoch durch mangelnde Technik, Infrastruktur, Materialien und Arbeitskräfte stark eingeschränkt war. Unter den extremen klimatischen Bedingungen dieser Region am Polarkreis und der nur minimal ausgebauten Infrastruktur erwies sich die große Entfernung von anderen Fördergebieten als besonders nachteilig. Durch neu entdeckte Fundstellen gelang es der Kombinatsleitung, die Zinnförderung 1952 noch einmal anzuheben, so dass in diesem Jahr 5.350 t Zinn gefördert werden konnten. Seit 1953 fiel die Fördermenge jedoch wieder. Zu der Geschichte der Zinnförderung siehe Zeljak, Pjat' metallov, S. 190 ff.

58 Ausführlich zum VNII-1 und dem Nachfolgeinstitut siehe das Kapitel 4.3.3.

59 Im Spätstalinismus machte Dal'stroj einen Verlust von durchschnittlich gut 800 Mio. Rubel im Jahr. Vgl. Bacaev, Formy i Metody, S. 79. Siehe zu den Kosten, die Dal'stroj der sowjetischen Volkswirtschaft verursachte, Ivanova, Istorija, S. 360.

60 Der Leiter des *Sevvostlag*, Generalleutnant G. S. Žukov, kehrte im Februar 1952 von einem Treffen des Innenministers Kruglov mit den Leitern der wichtigsten Lagerverwaltungen nach Dal'stroj zurück und schilderte die Situation des Kombinats im sowjetunionweiten Kontext: „Wir müssen verstehen, dass es gerade zu sehr schwerwiegenden Veränderungen für Dal'stroj kommt. Hatte Dal'stroj früher für eine lange Zeit eine isolierte Stellung und waren nicht alle Anordnungen, Gesetze und Forderungen für seine Wirtschaft bindend, so ist diese Periode jetzt vergangen. [...] Im Ministerium gibt es jetzt Baustellen und Betriebe, die nicht weniger schwierig sind als Dal'stroj." Zitiert nach Bacaev, Osobennosti, S. 157.

Die Ausbeutung des Raumes wurde auch von Seiten des Lagers zunehmend in Frage gestellt. Die beiden Elemente der Einzelleitung – Lager und Industrie – sahen sich mehr und mehr mit unterschiedlichen, mitunter konkurrierenden Aufgaben konfrontiert. Zwar war das *Sevvostlag* nach wie vor für die Bereitstellung von Zwangsarbeitern für das Kombinat verantwortlich, zugleich aber betrachtete der MVD den nordöstlichen Lagerkomplex immer stärker als ein Auffanglager für schwerkriminelle Häftlinge.

„Schwerkriminelle" oder „Berufskriminelle", verurteilt v. a. aufgrund von Mord oder schwerer Körperverletzung, waren Angehörige von Banden, die sich seit dem Zweiten Weltkrieg verstärkt in den Lagern der Sowjetunion gebildet hatten, in streng hierarchisierten Gemeinschaften lebten und ihre Mithäftlinge terrorisierten. Ihre Machtstellung sicherten sie sich meist durch „informelle geschäftliche Arrangements mit Wachleuten und Lagerverwaltern"[61]. In den späten 1940er und zu Beginn der 1950er Jahre drängte die sowjetische Führung darauf, die Lagerkomplexe der zentralen Gebiete der Union von diesen Personen zu „säubern" und sie in weit entfernte Lagergebiete, v. a. in den Nordosten zu überführen.[62] Kriminelle Banden hatte es schon zuvor im *Sevvostlag* gegeben, nun aber stieg ihr Anteil erheblich an.[63] Hinzu kamen ehemalige Wachen, die eine Haftstrafe verbüßen mussten und sich selbstständig organisierten. Diese Gruppierungen waren bestrebt, die gesamte Kontrolle über einen Lagerpunkt oder eine Lagerabteilung an sich zu reißen, die Masse der Häftlinge und die Lagerordnung zu kontrollieren und alle Angelegenheiten des Lagers, bis hin zu Fragen der Produktion, zu diktieren. Immer wieder gab es dabei eine enge Zusammenarbeit zwischen Kriminellen und der oberen Lageradministration.[64] Diverse kriminelle Banden kämpften unter erheblichem Waffeneinsatz äußerst brutal um die Oberhand in den Lagern.[65] Verstärkt wurden die Fehden durch die Anwesenheit verschiedener nationaler Gruppen, die nach Ende des Krieges in das *Sevv-*

---

61 Elie, Verbrecherbanden, S. 493.
62 Vgl. Kozlov, Lagernaja sistema, S. 167. Generell zur Situation in den Lagern Anfang der 1950er Jahre, zu Aufständen und zu Problemen mit schwerkriminellen Häftlingen siehe Gorlizki/Khlevniuk, Cold Peace, S. 124–133.
63 Šalamov hat sich in seinen Erzählungen immer wieder mit den Kriminellen in den Lagern des *Sevvostlag* auseinandergesetzt. Siehe seinen Erzählungen-Block „Skizzen der Verbrecherwelt" in Schalamow, Künstler der Schaufel, S. 391ff. Siehe dazu: Ryklin, Verfluchter Orden sowie die Erinnerungen von Solomon, Magadan und Lipper, Elf Jahre.
64 Vgl. Bacaev, Obostrenie, S. 191 sowie ausführlich zur Veränderung in der Häftlingszusammensetzung Bacaev, Osobennosti, S. 131ff. Siehe zu der Welt der Berufsverbrecher im Gulag und für eine Beschreibung ihrer Distinktionsmerkmale und Fehden Elie, Verbrecherbanden; Putz, Berufsverbrecher; Ivanova, Istorija, S. 318.
65 Siehe dazu diverse Beschreibungen aus verschiedenen Gebieten in Bacaev, Osobennosti, S. 159 sowie bei Kozlov, Lagernaja sistema, S. 171f.

ostlag eingewiesen worden waren und die sich gegenseitig, sowie die bisherigen „Lagerherren" bekämpften.[66]

Im *Sevvostlag* zur Zeit des Spätstalinismus trafen Berufskriminelle und nationale Gruppierungen auf eine große Zahl „politischer Häftlinge"; drei Häftlingsgruppen, die alle zu hohen Freiheitsstrafen verurteilt worden waren und die als Häftlinge „strengen Regimes" fast immer gemeinsam festgehalten wurden (eine Ausnahme stellte lediglich das *Berlag* ausschließlich für politische Häftlinge dar).[67] Diese Konstellation führte – neben den gewalttätigen Bandenkriegen der Berufskriminellen untereinander – zu massiven und extrem brutalen Übergriffen bewaffneter und vollkommen verrohter Krimineller auf ihre Mithäftlinge, v. a. auf die „Politischen".[68] Fluchtversuche häuften sich, bei denen Häftlinge und Wachen zu Tode kamen.[69] In einem Brief an den Chef des MVD, S. N. Kruglov, sprach Mitrakov von einem „faktischen Krieg" mit den Kriminellen und bat um die Erlaubnis der Regierung, „in Form einer Ausnahme auf dem Gebiet von Dal'stroj die Todesstrafe für alle Rückfälligen wiedereinzuführen" – eine Bitte, die ihm jedoch abgeschlagen wurde.[70]

Zur Verstärkung der Wachmannschaften kamen 1951 4.000 zusätzliche Soldaten an die Kolyma, die die Situation jedoch nicht positiv beeinflussen konnten; in einigen Gebieten wagten sich selbst bewaffnete Wachen nicht mehr in die Häftlingsbaracken. Noch immer kamen in den Lagern etwa 33 Häftlinge auf nur eine Wache.[71] Außerdem waren die Sicherheitsvorkehrungen und die Möglichkeiten zur Isolierung bestimmter

---

[66] Diese neuen „nationalen Gruppen" unterschieden sich jedoch deutlich von den Kriminellen. Sie verfügten über ein Netz von Verbindungen zwischen den Lagern und waren auf Widerstandsakte (Flucht, Überfälle auf Wachen) ausgerichtet. Ihr grundsätzliches Ziel bestand in einer massenhaften Befreiung von Häftlingen. Aus der Erfahrung mit diesen Gruppierungen war es offiziell verboten, beispielsweise mehr als eine sehr kleine Zahl von Tschetschenen und Inguschen in einer Lagerabteilung zu inhaftieren. Vgl. Bacaev, Obostrenie, S. 191.

[67] Insgesamt waren mehr als 50 % der Inhaftierten zu mindestens zehn Jahren Haft verurteilt worden. Vgl. Bacaev, Dejatel'nost' organov, S. 217.

[68] Im Jahr 1950 wurden offiziell 313 Fälle von „Lagerbanditentum" registriert, dabei wurden 326 Häftlinge – „Politische" ebenso wie Kriminelle unterschiedlicher Gruppierungen – ermordet. Vgl. Bacaev, Obostrenie, S. 190.

[69] Dabei kam es auch zu Fällen von Kannibalismus, bei denen Kriminelle Mithäftlinge als „lebende Konserven" zur gemeinsamen Flucht zwangen. Vgl. Bacaev, Obostrenie, S. 188. 1951 gab es im *Sevvostlag* 369 Fluchtversuche von Gruppen (insgesamt 1.136 Menschen), 976 Häftlinge versuchten allein zu fliehen. Vgl. Bacaev, Osobennosti, S. 157.

[70] Zitiert nach Kozlov, Lagernaja sistema, S. 174. Die Todesstrafe war in der Sowjetunion am 26. Mai 1947 abgeschafft worden (zur gleichen Zeit wurde die höchste Strafe auf 25 Jahre erhöht). Siehe für eine Darstellung der Umstände dieser Entscheidung Ivanova, Istorija, S. 316. Am 12. Januar 1950 wurde sie für politische Häftlinge wieder eingeführt, im Jahr 1954 dann schließlich auch für Kriminelle. Vgl. Ivanova, Istorija, S. 83.

[71] Vgl. Bacaev, Osobennosti, S. 157. Von den insgesamt gut 18.000 Wachen wurde nur etwa ein Drittel in den Lagern eingesetzt, die übrigen kamen bei der Bewachung von Anlagen, der geförderten Metalle sowie bei Inspektionen zum Einsatz.

Häftlinge gering. In einem Bericht über die Situation in den Lagern aus dem Jahr 1952 heißt es beispielsweise:

> Im Sevvostlag gibt es nach wie vor kein einziges Gefängnis, keinen einzigen steinernen Isolator. Lager strengen Regimes gibt es für etwa 3.000 Häftlinge, wir bräuchten sie aber für mindestens 30.000. 30 % der Wohnzonen [in den Lagerpunkten – M. S.] haben noch immer kein elektrisches Licht, 60 % sind ohne Notsignal und Verbindung zu den Posten, 68 Isolatoren sind in einem solchen Zustand, dass sie mit bloßen Händen zerlegt werden können.[72]

Eine geordnete Trennung der Häftlinge nach unterschiedlichen Haftstrafen und nach Geschlecht war somit schon aus praktischen Gründen flächendeckend nicht möglich. Trotz einer eigens eingerichteten Kommission des MVD und mehrerer strenger Verwarnungen der Leitung von Dal'stroj und *Sevvostlag* änderten sich die Zustände nicht grundlegend. Zwar wurde im Laufe des Jahres 1952 versucht, die Hunderte kleiner Lagerpunkte, die über keine klar erkennbare „Zone" verfügten, in ihrer Zahl zu reduzieren und die „Selbstbewachung" der Häftlinge zu begrenzen. Aufgrund fehlender Maßnahmen in weiterhin bestehenden Lagern führte dies jedoch nur in einzelnen Gebieten zu gewissen Erfolgen. Insgesamt stieg die Kriminalität weiterhin ungebremst an.[73] Gleichzeitig richtete sich die Strategie der Leitung von Dal'stroj auf eine gebietsinterne Verschiebung des Problems. Besonders gefährliche Häftlinge wurden mehr und mehr in die Lager sehr weit im Norden, am Polarkreis verbracht, um die zentralen Produktionsgebiete von ihnen zu „säubern". Die Lagerabteilungen „Saplag", „Janstrojlag", „Indigirlag" u. a. im äußersten Norden wurden damit zu den mit am schlechtesten versorgten und am wenigsten beherrschbaren Lagern im gesamten MVD.[74] Zu Beginn der 1950er Jahre weiteten sich die Übergriffe krimineller Häftlinge auch auf Siedlungen freier Arbeiter aus. Freie Arbeitskräfte waren den Überfällen, zumal in entlegenen Gebieten, schutzlos ausgeliefert.[75]

Diese Verhältnisse waren eine der Ursachen, warum das *Sevvostlag* beständig sinkende Zahlen an Zwangsarbeitern zur Verfügung stellte; ein hoher Prozentsatz der kriminellen Häftlinge verweigerte grundsätzlich die Arbeit. Zugleich wurden kranke Häftlinge nach Dal'stroj verbracht, die kaum ihren Transport dorthin überlebten. Aufgrund der großen Hungersnot in der Sowjetunion, unter der Häftlinge besonders zu leiden hatten, war 1947 bereits die Hälfte der Neuankömmlinge nicht arbeitsfähig.[76] 1953 wurden lediglich etwa 60 % aller Häftlinge des *Sevvostlag* überhaupt zu Arbeiten

---

72 Zitiert nach Bacaev, Osobennosti, S. 157. 1952 war die Zahl der Lagerpunkte, die über keine Notsignale und Verbindungen zu den Posten verfügten, bereits auf über 84 % angestiegen, 60,4 % der Punkte entsprachen nicht den allgemeinen Normen. Vgl. Bacaev, Osobennosti, S. 170.

73 Im Jahr 1952 stieg die Kriminalität im Vergleich zum Vorjahr um 44 % an. Vgl. Bacaev, Dejatel'nost' organov, S. 224.

74 Vgl. Bacaev, Obostrenie, S. 193.

75 Vgl. die Berichte von Betroffenen und Augenzeugen bei Bacaev, Obostrenie, S. 197.

76 Vgl. Kozlov, Lagernaja sistema, S. 154. Allein in den ersten neun Monaten des Jahres 1950 starben 1.351 Häftlinge im *Sevvostlag*. Vgl. ebd., S. 168.

herangezogen, aufgrund von massenhaften Arbeitsverweigerungen gab es Lagerpunkte, in denen die Normerfüllung bei nur 30 % lag.[77]

Dal'stroj selbst erhielt immer weniger Geld für seinen Lagerkomplex und war zudem in abnehmendem Maße dazu bereit, Lager zu finanzieren, die der Produktion nicht zuträglich waren.[78] Die Folgen geringerer Zahlungen wirkten sich wiederum unmittelbar auf die Zwangsarbeiterbasis aus. Wegen der ständig steigenden Häftlingszahlen waren die Lagerpunkte dramatisch unterversorgt, Überbelegungen führten zu katastrophalen hygienischen Zuständen. Dies alles bedingte einen deutlichen Anstieg der Todesrate.[79] Aufgrund der enormen Anforderungen und der miserablen Bedingungen in den Lagern erfüllten durchschnittlich 45 % der Inhaftierten nicht die untersten Arbeitsnormen.[80] Außerdem arbeiteten täglich mehrere Tausend Häftlinge allein deshalb nicht, weil für sie keine ausreichenden Wachen zur Verfügung standen.

Die ökonomische Krise und die Bedrohung, die von der sozialen Lage in den Lagerpunkten ausging, ließen die Region zunehmend als nur noch schwer beherrschbar erscheinen. Der Chef des MVD der UdSSR, S. N. Kruglov, verlangte daher für Dal'stroj, „die Sache vom Kopf auf die Füße zu stellen" und „nicht vom Betrieb, sondern vom Lager auszugehen". Die Erfüllung der Aufgabe des Kombinats sei, so Kruglov, ohne eine Stärkung der Lager absolut undenkbar.[81]

Auch im Verhältnis zu seinen freien Arbeitskräften war das Kombinat nicht bereit, angemessene Lebens- und Arbeitsperspektiven zu schaffen. Zwar waren die im Krieg ausgesetzten Vergünstigungen nach 1945 wieder eingeführt worden, doch konnte dies die katastrophalen Lebensbedingungen nicht ausgleichen.[82] 1949 schilderte der freie Arbeiter S. A. Bugrov in einem Brief an Stalin seine Lage als freier Arbeiter in Dal'stroj:

---

77 Vgl. Bacaev, Amnistija, S. 204.

78 Für den Bau von Gefängnissen und Lagerabteilungen von *Sevvostlag* und *Berlag* wurden lediglich 60 Mio. Rubel zugeteilt, obwohl 650 Mio. benötigt wurden, um die Lager entsprechend der Befehle des MVD auszustatten. Bacaev, Dejatel'nost' organov, S. 225.

79 So fehlte es generell an Medikamenten und warmer Kleidung. Vgl. Kozlov, Lagernaja sistema, S. 158. Siehe ebenso die ausführliche Beschreibung bei Bacaev, Osobennosti, S. 134. Durch die – regelwidrige – Zusammenlegung männlicher und weiblicher Häftlinge nahm die Zahl der Syphilis-Erkrankungen unter den Häftlingen, aber auch unter freien Arbeitskräften dramatisch zu. Vgl. Bacaev, Osobennosti, S. 136.

80 Um die sinkende Produktivität der Zwangsarbeiter zumindest etwas aufzufangen, erließ die sowjetische Führung eine spezifische Sondergenehmigung: Zwar war am 1. April 1948 unionsweit die Anrechenbarkeit von besonderen Arbeitsleistungen auf die Haftzeit (*začety*) abgeschafft worden, auf dem Gebiet von Dal'stroj wurde diese Regelung jedoch im Juni 1948 als eine Ausnahme für die Inhaftierten des *Sevvostlag* und des *Berlag* wieder eingeführt, um ihre Arbeitsproduktion zu stärken. Vgl. Bacaev, Formy i metody, S. 80. Im Folgenden wurde diese Ausnahme auch auf andere Lagersysteme ausgedehnt, deren Produktion eine „besondere staatliche Bedeutung" hatte. Siehe zur Ausweitung dieser Sonderregelung Ivanova, Istorija, S. 363 f.

81 Zitiert nach Bacaev, Osobennosti, S. 156.

82 Der Jahresplan zur Errichtung von Wohnraum wurde beispielsweise 1950 lediglich zu 25 % erfüllt. Die Leitung von Dal'stroj wusch sich regelmäßig von der Verantwortung für die schlimmen Verhältnisse rein, indem sie die Leiter der einzelnen Produktionsstätten für die unzureichenden Baumaß-

Im April 1948 schloss ich einen Vertrag ab und gelangte nach Dal'stroj in die Indigirskoe Berg-
bauabteilung. Seit meinem ersten Arbeitsmonat war ich nur an wenigen Tagen satt, Brot wurde
nie ausgegeben und wird auch jetzt nicht verteilt. Von anderen Produkten oder Fett ganz zu
schweigen. Du sitzt auf der Ration, plus Wasser, aber ohne Gehalt. In drei Monaten habe ich schon
alle meine Kräfte verloren und wie soll ich sie wiedergewinnen? Aber leben will ich doch, verdammt noch mal, noch! Tabak, Tee, das ist in unserem Gebiet eine Seltenheit. Eine Papirossa
kostet 2–3 Rubel. Wäsche [...] und Oberbekleidung ist nicht zu kriegen. Die Leute schlafen auf
dem Boden. Medizinische Hilfe gibt es überhaupt keine.[83]

Unerbittliche Härte und Zwang bestimmten das Verhältnis des Kombinats zur Masse
seiner freien Arbeitskräfte.[84] Auf Proteste antwortete die Kombinatsleitung mit einer
Fülle neuer Regelungen, die Urlaubszeiten und ein Ausscheiden aus dem Kombinat
erheblich erschwerten. Außerdem wurden die Grenzen des Gebietes von Dal'stroj
stärker überwacht, um vertragswidrige Abreisen zu verhindern.[85] Fast 90 % der ehemaligen Häftlinge war es aufgrund von „Produktionsnotwendigkeiten" nicht gestattet,
das Gebiet nach dem Ende ihrer Haftzeit zu verlassen.[86]

In Dal'stroj mangelte es jedoch nicht nur quantitativ an Arbeitskräften, sondern
zu allen Zeiten auch ganz erheblich an gut ausgebildeten Fachleuten. Arbeitskräfte,
die Maschinen bedienen konnten, wurden gebraucht, Technik für die Erschließung
tiefer liegender Goldvorkommen konnte nur mit Fachkräften eingesetzt werden, Infrastrukturprojekte ohne Ingenieure nicht gestemmt werden.[87]

Neben dem Einsatz qualifizierter Zwangsarbeiter wurden auch ausgebildete
Fachkräfte für die Arbeit in Dal'stroj angeworben. 1946 wurde der Anwerbungsplan
von Ingenieuren und Technikern jedoch lediglich zu 58 % erfüllt. 1950 musste die

nahmen verantwortlich machte. Vgl. Zeljak, Pjat' metallov, S. 223–239. Zu der ausgesprochen
schwierigen Versorgungslage siehe Isakov, Istorija torgovli, S. 182 f.

83 Zitiert nach Bacaev, Osobennosti, S. 141. Siehe ausführlich zur Lage der freien Arbeitskräfte im
Spätstalinismus Zeljak, Pjat' metallov, S. 230 ff. sowie 251 ff.

84 Zu den entlassenen Häftlingen und den Personen, die durch organisierte Anwerbung nach Dal'stroj
gekommen waren, kamen im Jahr 1945 noch etwa 2.000 Komsomolzinnen. Von den jungen Frauen
erhoffte man sich auch eine Steigerung der extrem niedrigen Geburtenrate (verursacht durch einen
erheblichen Frauenmangel), um junge Facharbeiter in der Region erziehen zu können. Vgl. Bacaev,
Obostrenie, S. 185.

85 Vgl. Zeljak, Pjat' metallov, S. 228.

86 Zahlenangabe vom Juli 1949, vgl. Širokov, Severo-Vostok, S. 28. Hinzu kam nach 1945 auch eine
Gruppe von Sondersiedlern, die statistisch zu den freien Arbeitskräften gezählt wurde, deren Lebens-
und Arbeitsbedingungen jedoch denen von Häftlingen entsprachen. Vgl. Bacaev, Osobennosti, S. 131.
1949 umfasste die Zahl der Sondersiedler bereits knapp 30.000 Personen. Vgl. Bacaev, Osobennosti,
S. 149. Zu dem Phänomen der Sondersiedler siehe Viola, Unknown Gulag; Zemskov, Specposelency;
Poljan, Ne po svoej vole.

87 In Magadan wurde daher 1948 eine Ausbildungsstätte gegründet, die im Juni 1951 in das Magadaner Bergbau-geologische Technikum (MGGT) umgewandelt wurde. Daneben wurden seit 1952 Mitarbeiter von Dal'stroj in Tomsk, Chabarowsk, in Dnepropetrowsk und in weiteren Städten der Union
ausgebildet. Dennoch konnte auch durch diese Maßnahmen der Bedarf an Fachkräften nicht gedeckt
werden. Vgl. Zeljak, Pjat' metallov, S. 220 f.

Leitung von Dal'stroj konstatieren, dass 60 % der Arbeitsstellen für Ingenieure und Techniker mit Personen besetzt waren, die für diese Arbeit keine Qualifikation vorweisen konnten.[88] Im Juni 1953 wurde sogar offenbar, dass ein großer Teil der Arbeiter auf diesen gut bezahlten Stellen enge Verwandte der jeweiligen Produktionsleiter waren.[89] Angesichts der entsetzlichen Lebens- und Arbeitsbedingungen überraschen diese Zahlen nicht, gut ausgebildetes Personal war eines der wesentlichen Mankos der stalinistischen Produktionsweise, es beruhte auf den Prämissen des Lager-Industriellen Komplexes.

4.2 Entwicklungslinien poststalinistischer Wirtschaft

Zwischen 1953 und 1960 veränderte sich die Wirtschaft des nordöstlichen Raumes erheblich, parallel zu den politischen Entwicklungen. Sie musste von einer quasi-militärischen Kommandowirtschaft mit Zwangsarbeit auf eine zivile Produktion umgestellt werden, mit erheblichen Auswirkungen auf alle Aspekte des gesamten Wirtschaftsraums.[90]

In dieser Zeit setzte sich der rapide Rückgang der Goldförderung fast ungebremst fort. Die spätstalinistische Krise der Lagerwirtschaft weitete sich 1953 zu einer Reorganisationskrise aus. Die Umstellung der Wirtschaft, die hier nun im Folgenden ausführlich betrachtet wird, war jedoch nur eine der Ursachen für die dramatische Verschlechterung der Goldförderung. Denn in diesen Jahren waren auch die geologischen Voraussetzungen in der Region so ungünstig wie noch nie zuvor in der Geschichte des Kombinats.

Die Verringerung des Goldgehaltes in den erforschten Böden und Flüssen der Region, die bereits im Spätstalinismus eingesetzt hatte, nahm seit 1953 dramatische Züge an. Allein zwischen 1953 und 1956 sank der mittlere Goldgehalt in den Gruben von Dal'stroj um 22,6 %.[91] Damit einher ging auch ein immer ungünstigeres Verhältnis zwischen der wegzuschaffenden Erde und dem goldhaltigen Sand – immer mehr Boden musste abgetragen werden, um an immer weniger goldhaltigen Sand zu ge-

---

88 Vgl. Širokov, Severo-Vostok, S. 29.

89 Vgl. Zeljak, Pjat' metallov, S. 221.

90 Der Begriff „Kommandowirtschaft" wird hier als Teil der militärischen Leitung durch den MVD verstanden, nicht in dem generellen Sinn als „administrative Kommandowirtschaft" des Stalinismus. Vgl. Merl, Sowjetische Kommandowirtschaft, S. 656 sowie bei Mercalov, der, wie viele seiner russischen Kollegen und Kolleginnen, den Begriff der administrativen Kommandoverwaltung (der Wirtschaft) für die gesamte sowjetische Periode einsetzt. Mercalov, Reforma chozjajstvennogo upravlenija, S. 221. Zur Entstehung dieser Kommandowirtschaft Ende der 1920er Jahre siehe Easter, Reconstructing, S. 61.

91 Die genauen Zahlen lauten: 1953: 4,29 g pro m³, 1954: 3,98 g pro m³, 1955: 3,79 g pro m³ sowie 1956: 3,32 g pro m³. Vgl. den Bericht des stellv. Leiters von Dal'stroj, Berezin, vom 19. März 1957 in GAMO f. R-23, op. 1, d. 6109, l. 2–12, hier l. 3.

langen.[92] Selbst bei einer realen Verringerung der Goldförderung stieg der Umfang der Bodenbewegungen: „Im Jahr 1956 wurden nur noch 81,6 % der Goldmenge des Jahres 1953 gefördert, im gleichen Zeitraum stieg aber die Menge des geöffneten Torfs [des abgetragenen Erdreiches – M. S.] um 115,4 %; die Menge des Goldsandes, der gewaschen werden musste, um 116,3 %"[93], so der stellvertretende Kombinatsleiter Berezin in seinem Bericht 1957. Angesichts der bereits abgetragenen reichsten Goldfelder, der „Sahnehäubchen", war das Kombinat gezwungen, seine Arbeit auf eine große Zahl von kleinen, nur schwach goldhaltigen oder schon früher einmal oberflächlich ausgebeuteten Goldfeldern auszudehnen.[94]

In absoluten Zahlen sank die Goldförderung zunächst beständig weiter: 1954 lieferte Dal'stroj mit 45,2 Tonnen chemisch reinem Gold bereits 2,4 t weniger als 1953, 1955 sank die Förderung auf 44,1 Tonnen, im Jahr 1956 auf 38,7 t. 1957 wurden im Magadaner Gebiet nur noch 32,4 Tonnen erzielt.[95] Auch die Zinnförderung erlebte einen Einbruch; zwischen 1953 und 1957 sank der Abbau des zweitwichtigsten Metalls um das Zweieinhalbfache.[96] Bei der Förderung von Uran waren erst im Jahre 1952 krisenhafte Erscheinungen erkennbar geworden. Da in diesem Wirtschaftszweig der Anteil der Zwangsarbeiter besonders hoch war und die Förderstellen zu einem großen Teil in einem besonders gering erschlossenen Gebiet in Tschukotka lagen, wirkte sich die Auflösung des Lagersystems besonders negativ auf die Förderung dieses seltenen Metalls aus. Der Uranabbau in Dal'stroj wurde nach sehr schlechten Förderergebnissen und aufgrund zu hoher Selbstkosten im Jahr 1955 ganz eingestellt.[97]

Überraschenderweise hielt die sowjetische Führung auch nach 1954 am Leiter von Dal'stroj, Mitrakov, fest, obwohl er nicht in der Lage war, den Rückgang der Goldförderung oder, in seiner Rolle als Einzelleiter, die Situation im Lagerkomplex positiv zu beeinflussen. Selbst Unterschlagungen und Bilanzfälschungen, die nach der Übergabe an die zivilen Produktionsministerien aufgedeckt worden waren und für die auch Mitrakov als Kombinatsleiter verantwortlich gemacht wurde, zogen zunächst keine personellen Konsequenzen an der Spitze des Kombinats nach sich. Offensichtlich sollten die großen Veränderungen in der Region von Kontinuität beim wirtschaftlichen Führungspersonal begleitet werden. Erst im Feburar 1956 wurde Mitrakov entlassen, Nachfolger wurde sein bisheriger Stellvertreter, Ju. V. Čuguev. Čuguev

92 In den Quellen ist wiederholt von „Torf" die Rede. Gemeint ist dabei jedoch das über den Goldvorkommen liegende Erdreich, das von unterschiedlicher Dicke sein kann und in den meisten Fällen auch gefroren ist.

93 Berezin in einem Bericht vom 19. März 1957 in GAMO f. R-23, op. 1, d. 6109, l. 2–12, hier l. 4.

94 Vgl. GAMO f. R-23, op. 1, d. 6109, l. 4–5.

95 Die Zahl für das Jahr 1957 bezieht sich auf das Magadaner Gebiet, da im Sommer 1957 der Magadaner Volkswirtschaftsrat gegründet wurde, der die bisherigen Anlagen von Dal'stroj auf dem Gebiet der jakutischen ASSR nicht mehr miteinschloss. Zu den Förderzahlen siehe die Tabelle bei Zeljak, Zolotodobyvajuščaja promyšlennost', S. 144 f.

96 Vgl. den Bericht einer Wirtschaftskommission des Büros des ZK der KPdSU für die RSFSR vom 4. März 1958 in RGANI f. 5, op. 32, d. 111, l. 29–31.

97 Die letzten Anlagen schloss man im Jahr 1956. Vgl. Zeljak, Uranodobyvajuščaja otrasl', S. 123.

und seine Stellvertreter (u. a. der hier immer wieder erwähnte V. P. Berezin) wechselten nach Einführung der sowjetischen Wirtschaftsreform im Sommer 1957 in die Leitung des Magadaner Volkswirtschaftsrates.[98] 1959 ernannte die sowjetische Führung den bisherigen Stellvertreter, S. V. Korolev, zum neuen Vorsitzenden des regionalen Volkswirtschaftsrates.

Die Leitung von Dal'stroj bzw. später des Volkswirtschaftsrates stand unter enormem Druck – denn trotz der bestehenden strukturellen Krise hatte die Goldförderung nichts von ihrer Bedeutung für die sowjetische Wirtschaft verloren. Dementsprechend wurde in der Region auch weiterhin aufgebaut, eingerichtet und versorgt, was der Goldförderung nutzte.

Was jedoch tatsächlich einen Nutzen für die Goldförderung bringen könnte – das war der zentralen und der regionalen Leitung selbst nicht immer klar. Unter der Vielzahl von Restrukturierungen und Umstellungen bei der Rohstoffförderung lassen sich drei für die poststalinistische Epoche wesentliche Charakteristika erkennen:

Erstens waren die Forderungen des Zentrums an seine nordöstliche Peripherie die gleichen wie unter stalinistischen Bedingungen – so viel Metall wie möglich sollte aus der Region gepresst werden. Dementsprechend wurde an der Extensivität der Förderung festgehalten.[99] Noch immer ging es darum, durch eine oberflächliche Ausbeutung besonders reicher Goldfelder einen maximalen Ertrag zu erzielen. Zum ersten Mal in seiner Geschichte stützte jedoch das Kombinat während der Entstalinisierung die Förderung auf technische Dokumentationen und ausführliche geologische Karten. Die Arbeiten der einzelnen Anlagen unterlagen nicht mehr nur allgemeinen Zielvorgaben, sondern wurden im Hinblick auf die einzelnen Arbeitsschritte geplant und vorbereitet. Goldfelder wurden nach wie vor extensiv „gestürmt" und der Naturraum gnadenlos ausgebeutet, nun jedoch im Rahmen einer strukturierteren Vorgehensweise, bei der die Rolle von Experten beständig zunahm.

Die Zwangsarbeit verlor *zweitens* in relativ kurzer Zeit ihre Bedeutung für Dal'-stroj. Mit Aufgabe der Lagerwirtschaft brach die enge Verzahnung zwischen Arbeitskräftebasis und Produktion weg: Nach der ersten großen Entlassungswelle im Jahr 1953 stand eine gewaltige Zahl von Förderanlagen still, weil mit der Entlassung der Häftlinge die Arbeitskräfte fehlten. Das Kombinat wurde massiv verkleinert, eine große Zahl von Förderanlagen musste aufgrund von mangelnder Rentabilität geschlossen werden. In den Goldgruben wurde die Zahl der arbeitenden Häftlinge sehr rasch reduziert. Waren Ende 1952 noch 68 % aller Arbeiter in Dal'stroj Häftlinge, so sank ihr Anteil Ende des Jahres 1957 auf weniger als 10 %.[100] Damit war das wichtigste Kennzeichen des Lager-Industriellen Komplexes und der stalinistischen Arbeitsweise

---

98 Zur Einführung der Volkswirtschaftsräte siehe das Kapitel 3.3.4.

99 Dies wurde immer wieder ausdrücklich eingefordert, so z. B. 1959 von der Sektion der Geologen des Ministeriums für Geologie und Bodenschätze der UdSSR, zu der der nordöstliche geologische Schürfdienst zu dieser Zeit gehörte. Vgl. die Stellungnahme des Vorsitzenden der Sektion vom 12. April 1959 in GAMO f. R-137sč, op. 1b, d. 52, l. 47–62, hier l. 48.

100 Vgl. GAMO f. R-23sč, op. 1, d. 503, l. 154 f.

innerhalb von vier Jahren so erheblich reduziert worden, dass das Lager als system-bildendes Element des Kombinats keine Rolle mehr spielte. Der Magadaner Volks-wirtschaftsrat zwang zwar noch immer inhaftierte Menschen zur Arbeit, aber die In-dustrie des Nordostens war keine Lagerwirtschaft mehr.

Für die Region mussten also neue Arbeitskräfte geworben werden. Zu einem großen Teil waren „die Neuen" entlassene Zwangsarbeiter, ehemalige Häftlinge, die aus Mangel an Alternativen Verträge mit Dal'stroj geschlossen hatten. Hinzu kamen freie Vertragsarbeiter und Komsomolzen, die im Rahmen von großen Kampagnen in verschiedenen Gebieten der UdSSR angeworben worden waren. Neben der Rekrutie-rung von Arbeitskräften bestand die Schwierigkeit des Kombinats darin, diese Per-sonen ohne das Raster der Lagerinfrastruktur angemessen über alle Förderanlagen zu verteilen.

Dal'stroj bzw. ab 1957 der Magadaner Volkswirtschaftsrat war darauf angewiesen, den Arbeitskräftebestand über einen längeren Zeitraum zu sichern, das hieß v. a. die Arbeiter in der Region zu halten. Mit einem Mal mussten neue Wirtschaftszweige ausgebildet oder erheblich erweitert werden, die auf die Bedürfnisse einer großen Zahl freier Arbeitskräfte ausgerichtet waren. Dazu zählten die Entwicklung einer rudi-mentären Leichtindustrie, die erhebliche Erweiterung der Bau- und Landwirtschaft ebenso wie die Gestaltung von ziviler Infrastruktur und Handelswegen. Schritt für Schritt entstanden hier Industriefelder, die nach und nach ihren Charakter als reine Hilfsindustrien der Goldförderung verloren und so die Einseitigkeit des nordöstlichen Wirtschaftsraumes aufbrachen; das Gebiet erhielt ein komplexeres industrielles Profil. Zugleich bewirkte die Aufgabe der lagergeprägten Industriestruktur ganz praktische Veränderungen bei der Metallförderung selbst:

In den 1950er Jahren wurde die Rohstoffgewinnung – von Gold ebenso wie von Zinn – im Vergleich zur Zeit des Stalinismus erheblich stärker mechanisiert. Der Einsatz von einfachen Trögen zum Waschen des Goldes wurde innerhalb weniger Jahre ganz aufgegeben, Erdmassen nun fast ausschließlich mit Baggern statt mit Schaufeln bewegt. Dies zog neue Anforderungen an die Versorgung der Anlagen mit Energie und viele technische Baumaßnahmen nach sich. Die Abschaffung der Zwangsarbeit traf dabei auf den beständig sinkenden Goldgehalt in der Region – es gab immer weniger Hände zur Erledigung der Arbeiten und zugleich immer mehr Boden, der durchwühlt werden musste.

Dies veränderte erheblich die Ansprüche an die Arbeitskräftegrundlage. In stei-gendem Maße kam es nicht mehr auf die Quantität der Kräfte, sondern sehr viel mehr auf ihre Qualität, also auf ihre Ausbildung und ihr technisches Wissen an. So stiegen die Anforderungen im Bereich von Qualifizierungsmaßnahmen einfacher Arbeiter ebenso wie bei der Versorgung und angemessenen Ausstattung zuziehender Fach-kräfte.

Drittens schließlich zog das Ende der quasi-militärischen Kommandowirtschaft die Entstehung ziviler Strukturen in der Verwaltung und Versorgung des Kombinats nach sich. Die Auswirkungen waren umfassend, sie lassen sich auf verschiedenen Ebenen des Wirtschaftsraumes erkennen und sind generell Folge der Aufgabe militärischer Privilegien, die die Wirtschaft im Nordosten bis zum März 1953 geprägt hatten. In finanzieller Hinsicht wurden nicht nur die Spielräume erheblich beschnitten, sondern das Kombinat auch in einer bisher nicht bekannten Weise überwacht. Verschiedene staatliche Strukturen verlangten nach einer Finanzaufsicht und nach einer deutlichen Beschneidung des bisherigen Sonderstatus.

Auch Befehlsstrukturen waren durch die Anbindung an ein zivil-industrielles Ministerium unterbrochen worden. Statt einer Kommandowirtschaft im wahrsten Sinne des Wortes – bei der alle technischen Anlagen und eine große Zahl kostengünstiger Zwangsarbeiter den Befehlen militärischer Leiter mit Sondervollmachten unterstanden – kam es nun darauf an, komplexen Strukturen mit verschiedenen bürokratischen Bezugssystemen gerecht zu werden. In den Jahren zwischen 1953 und 1957 wurden eine ganze Reihe wichtiger Dal'stroj-Einrichtungen – bei Infrastruktur, Bau und Energiegewinnung – an zivile Ministerien und die Organe von Partei und Staat in der Region übergeben. Hinzu kam eine lange Liste von Verlagerungen von Gebietszentren und Wirtschaftsstandorten, die für die Industrie von großer Bedeutung waren, wie z. B. geologische Stationen. Immer wieder waren es auch noch bestehende Lagerpunkte, die durch ihre Regelungen bei der Arbeitskräfteverwendung und durch die Fehden krimineller Häftlingsbanden die Produktion negativ beeinflussten. All diese Veränderungen fielen mit Unklarheiten und Strukturproblemen zusammen, die sich aus der Übergabe des Kombinats an ein ziviles Produktionsministerium ergaben. Unmittelbare Folge dieses Reorganisationsprozesses war, dass Leiter einzelner Produktionsstätten, die z. T. nur über eine minimale infrastrukturelle Anbindung an das Zentrum in Magadan verfügten, schlicht nicht mehr wussten, an welche Stelle sie sich mit ihren Fragen wenden sollten.[101]

Die Einführung des Magadaner Volkswirtschaftsrates führte im Sommer 1957 zu gewissen Vereinfachungen durch die weitere Straffung des großen Apparates und die Aufgabe mittlerer Verwaltungsebenen.[102] Die Gliederung der Bergbauindustrie wurde stark zentralisiert; alle Goldförderanlagen unterstanden seitdem unmittelbar einer einheitlichen Leitung – der Bergbauverwaltung, die zugleich von weiteren Verwaltungsaufgaben entlastet wurde. Damit waren die regionalen Industrieverwaltungen abgeschafft worden.[103]

---

101 Verunsicherung herrschte nicht nur in Bezug auf die Entscheidungsstrukturen innerhalb des Kombinats, sondern auch grundsätzlich über die Aufteilung der Verantwortung zwischen wirtschaftlicher und neuer politischer Leitung. Vgl. die vielen Berichte unterschiedlicher Produktionsleiter aus den einzelnen Bezirken auf regionalen Parteikonferenzen in GAMO f. P-21, op. 5, d. 520, l. 64–67 sowie l. 103–115.

102 Zu den Personalkürzungen im Zusammenhang mit der Gründung des Volkswirtschaftsrates siehe die Vorschläge von Ababkov vom 29. April 1957 in seinem Schreiben an das ZK der KPdSU in RGANI f. 5, op. 30, d. 201, l. 185–188. Ababkov sprach von Kürzungen im Umfang von 32 %. Siehe auch den Finanzabschluss der Personalverwaltung von Dal'stroj in GAMO f. R-137, op. 1, d. 1386, l. 23–24, hier l. 23.

103 Lediglich die Bergbauverwaltung von Čaun-Čukotskij wurde aufgrund der großen Entfernung dieses Gebietes zum Zentrum Magadan als Bindeglied zu den einzelnen Produktionsstätten aufrechterhalten. Vgl. die Beschreibung der einzelnen Abteilungen in der Anlage eines Schreibens von

In infrastruktureller Hinsicht hatte das Kombinat mit der Kappung der bisherigen Versorgungs- und Zustellungswege zu kämpfen. Als zivile Einheit war der Wirtschaftskomplex jetzt darauf angewiesen, alle benötigten Materialien, Anlagen und Maschinen einzeln bei den jeweiligen Ministerien zu bestellen. Das Kombinat war zum Aufbau ganz neuer Versorgungswege und Vertragsbeziehungen geradezu verdammt; die Leiter einzelner Wirtschaftsbereiche, Goldgruben und Baustellen wussten nicht mehr, woher sie Benzin, Geräte oder Zement beziehen sollten. Im Laufe der Jahre lässt sich jedoch auch bei Infrastruktur und Versorgung der Förderanlagen eine beständig steigende Differenzierung erkennen. Ganz allmählich verbreiterte sich das Angebot, und die Region wurde besser versorgt.

Die Unterstellung unter ein ziviles Ministerium brachte für die Wirtschaftsleitung ein erheblich gestiegenes Maß an Kontrolle und Kritik mit sich. Moskau überwachte die Arbeit des Kombinats und ab 1957 des Volkswirtschaftsrates auf allen Ebenen, forderte zahllose Berichte sowie die Einsetzung von Sonderkommissionen und eines Beauftragten des Ministeriums für staatliche Kontrolle. Die geologische Schürfverwaltung von Dal'stroj geriet dabei besonders in den Fokus und wurde aufgrund ihrer schlechten Ergebnisse weitgehend dem zentralen Ministerium für Geologie und Bodenschätze unterstellt.

Bei all diesen Prozessen, sei es bei der Mechanisierung, der rationaleren Produktionsplanung oder bei Handel und Versorgung, kam dem Einsatz von Experten eine steigende Bedeutung zu.[104] Von ihnen wurde explizit eine veränderte Einstellung zu der Region und ihrem Wirtschaftsraum verlangt. Ihre Zielvorstellungen sollten sich nicht mehr auf die reine Ausbeutung der Bodenschätze um jeden Preis konzentrieren, vielmehr mussten sie sich den komplexen Anforderungen einer auch ökonomisch effektiven, rationalen und umfassenden Erschließung des Gebietes stellen.

Ganz besonders traf dies auf die Wissenschaft im Nordosten zu, mit der die sowjetische Leitung erhebliche Informationsdefizite über den gesamten Raum des sowjetischen Nordens schließen wollte. Diese Bestrebungen sind historisch nur zu verstehen, wenn man bedenkt, dass weite Teile des Hohen Nordens durch Lager-Industrielle Komplexe beherrscht worden waren, die seit 1953 zerfielen (neben Dal'stroj waren dies v. a. Workuta und Norilsk). Das wichtigste Instrument war dabei die Akademie der Wissenschaften der UdSSR, die ihre Aktivitäten auf den nördlichen Raum ausdehnte und gerade im Magadaner Gebiet eine Vielzahl von Instituten und Forschungseinrichtungen gründete. Zum ersten Mal dienten Wissenschaftszentren nicht allein der Produktion, sondern sollten – in längerer Perspektive – auf der Basis

---

Ababkov zur Gründung des Magadaner Volkswirtschaftsrates an das ZK der KPdSU in RGANI f. 5, op. 30, d. 201, l. 192–194. Diese Gliederung folgte den Wünschen des Magadaner Gebietsparteikomitees. Vgl. den Bericht der regionalen Parteileitung im Vorfeld der Einführung des Magadaner Volkswirtschaftsrates an das ZK der KPdSU in GAMO f. R-23, op. 1, d. 6088, l. 1–50, hier l. 24f. Siehe die Beurteilung Rajzmans in Rajzman, Struktury upravlenija, S. 125.

104 Zur wachsenden Bedeutung von „Experten" (auf den unterschiedlichsten Gebieten) in den Entscheidungsfindungsprozessen der Chruščev-Periode vgl. Gill/Pitty, Power, S. 177.

von Grundlagenforschung das Gebiet in seinen naturwissenschaftlichen, ökonomischen und sozialen Dimensionen erforschen.

Die hier beschriebene Reorganisationsphase war eine der Ursachen für den wirtschaftlichen Niedergang der Jahre 1953 bis 1957; sie verstärkte die enormen Widersprüche, die die strukturelle Krise der Lagerwirtschaft im Spätstalinismus geprägt hatten. Zugleich fielen sie mit besonders ungünstigen geologischen Voraussetzungen zusammen. Dies beschrieb der Leiter des geologischen Schürfdienstes I. E. Drabkin auf einer Parteikonferenz im Jahr 1963, als er sich an die Zeit nach der Gebietsgründung erinnerte:

> Man muss sagen, dass unser Gebiet in der allerschwersten Zeit errichtet wurde, als es die geringsten Kennziffern nicht nur beim Zuwachs neuer Goldvorkommen, sondern auch bei der Förderung gab – in einer depressiven Zeit.[105]

„Depressiv" war die erste Zeit des Magadaner Gebietes für die obersten Leitungskader des Kombinats auf mehreren Ebenen. Die wichtigsten Goldfelder an der Kolyma galten als erschöpft. Es existierte eine „Theorie vom Erlöschen des Goldes", die der Dal'strojer Leitung den Glauben an einen wirtschaftlichen Neubeginn raubte, die aber auch im Verlust des außergewöhnlichen Status der alten Führung selbst begründet war.[106] Mit dem „Versiegen" des Flusses ging zugleich die Zeit der alten Kader zu Ende, der Impetus zu neuen Strategien fehlte.

Die Rechenschaftsberichte des Volkswirtschaftsrates zeigen, dass ab 1958 die größten Umstrukturierungen im Zusammenhang mit der Auflösung der Lager abgeschlossen waren und ganz allmählich positive Effekte aus Mechanisierung, rationaler Arbeitsplanung und Versorgung erkennbar wurden. Diese Reorganisationsmaßnahmen können jedoch nicht allein den deutlichen Umschwung erklären, der sich plötzlich bei den Förderzahlen abzeichnete: Statt der 32,4 Tonnen von 1957 wurden 1958 auf einmal 35,1 und im folgenden Jahr sogar 37,9 Tonnen chemisch reines Gold gefördert, 1960 und 1961 dann schließlich 40,7 bzw. 44 Tonnen. 1962 wurden der Magadaner und der jakutische Volkswirtschaftsrat aufgelöst und zu einem großen „Nordöstlichen Volkswirtschaftsrat" (mit Sitz in Magadan) zusammengefasst.[107] Innerhalb dieser neuen Wirtschaftsstruktur erzielte das Magadaner Gebiet 1962 49,6 Tonnen (insgesamt 66,7) und im Jahr 1963 57,6 Tonnen (insgesamt 72,3).[108]

Die lokale Parteivertretung hat sich später immer wieder bemüht, diese Erfolge auf die Absetzung Ababkovs und die Ernennung Afanas'evs im Jahr 1958 zurückzuführen. Den unmittelbaren Einfluss der Person Afanas'ev hat sie damit weit

---

105 Drabkin zitiert nach Grebenjuk, Kolymskij led, S. 203.

106 Vgl. Afanas'ev, Rossija, S. 55 sowie die Darstellung bei Sergeev, Pervyj predsedatel', S. 26.

107 Dieser hatte bis zur Rücknahme der Chruščev'schen Reformen im Jahr 1964 Bestand. Vgl. Zeljak, Zolotodobyvajuščaja promyšlennost', S. 144 f. Zu den Förderzahlen siehe ebenfalls Rajzman, SNCH MĖAR, S. 161.

108 Zahlen nach einer Tabelle bei Zeljak, Zolotodobyvajuščaja promyšlennost', S. 144 f. sowie für die Zahlen des nordöstlichen Volkswirtschaftsrates Zoloto Rossii, S. 306–310.

übertrieben, um dies propagandistisch für eine politische Stärkung des Ersten Sekretärs nutzen zu können.[109] Denn der entscheidende Schritt war von geologischen Entdeckungen ausgegangen – im westlichen Tschukotka stieß man auf neue große Goldfelder. Die an der Entdeckung beteiligten Geologen wurden besonders vom Moskauer Zentrum, in Gestalt des Ministeriums für Geologie und Bodenschätze, unterstützt; Afanas'ev machte sich anschließend für erhebliche Investitionen im Magadaner Gebiet stark.

„Es gibt wieder Gold" war die erlösende Nachricht, die die seit dem Spätstalinismus andauernde Krise beendete und Afanas'ev in der Folge eine stabile Herrschaft bescherte. Dies erklärt auch, warum die Förderzahlen in den 1960er Jahren weiter nach oben zeigten, obgleich die Struktur der Volkswirtschaftsräte in der Sowjetunion generell zu einem Wirtschaftseinbruch führte.[110] Die neu erschlossenen Lagerstätten bewirkten in den kommenden Jahren, dass sich die positiven Effekte der Umstellung auf eine dauerhaftere, stärker mechanisierte und ökonomisch effektivere Rohstoffgewinnung in steigenden Förderzahlen niederzuschlagen vermochten. Unter diesen Voraussetzungen konnte zugleich auch an der extensiven Ausbeutung besonders reicher Goldfelder in gut zugänglichen Erdschichten festgehalten werden.[111]

Die große Entfernung der neuen Goldfelder von den bisherigen industriellen Zentren erhöhte allerdings die Anforderungen an die dortige Infrastruktur erheblich und vernichtete erneut große Teile bisher vollkommen unberührter Natur.[112] Auch unter den zivilen Bedingungen musste also die Natur ausgleichen, was an Kenntnissen über und Plänen für eine nachhaltigere, humane Rohstoffförderung nur rudimentär umgesetzt wurde.[113]

---

109 So behauptete beispielsweise der Leiter der Wirtschaftsabteilung des Gebietsparteikomitees, Golubev, auf einem Treffen des technisch-wirtschaftlichen Rates des Volkswirtschaftsrates im August 1958, dass die Entlassung Ababkovs und die Einführung der Volkswirtschaftsräte den Umschwung in der Magadaner Wirtschaft herbeigeführt hätten. Vgl. die Mitschrift eines Treffens in GAMO f. R-137, op. 1, d. 59a, l. 51–201, hier l. 51–58. Ähnlich schildert dies auch der damalige Parteisekretär Kaštanov in einem Interview, vgl. Grebenjuk, Kolymskij led, S. 199. Grebenjuk folgt dieser Parteilinie in seiner Darstellung bruchlos. Vgl. Grebenjuk, Kolymskij led, S. 200–203.

110 Zur weiteren positiven Entwicklung der regionalen Goldförderung siehe Gal'ceva, Analiz retrospektivy.

111 Als programmatisch ist dafür ein Ausspruch Afanas'evs aus dem Jahr 1960 anzusehen, der auf einer Versammlung des technisch-ökonomischen Rates des Volkswirtschaftsrates äußerte: „Man muss das Gold heute schnappen. Morgen sollen's die Geologen suchen!" Zitiert nach Zeljak, Osobennosti razvitija, S. 95.

112 Vgl. die Erläuterungen zum Jahresbericht 1959 von Korolev und dem Hauptbuchhalter Gol'dšvend in RGAĖ f. 7733, op. 48, d. 492, l. 1–28, hier l. 3.

113 Die wichtigsten Tendenzen der entstalinisierten Goldförderung setzten sich auch nach Abschaffung der Volkswirtschaftsräte fort. Unter der neuen, im November 1965 geschaffenen Organisationsstruktur *Severovostokzoloto* verfolgte die Wirtschaftspolitik weiterhin einen extensiven Kurs. Sobald es zu Krisenerscheinungen kam (so in der Zeit von 1976 bis 1980) bemühte man sich, die Absenkung des Goldertrages durch die Eröffnung weiterer Goldabbaustätten auszugleichen. Vgl. zur

4.3 Aspekte des zivilen Wirtschaftlebens

Der Anstieg der Förderzahlen seit Ende der 1950er Jahre baute auf neuen Goldfunden im Magadaner Gebiet auf. Ihre Erschließung konnte unter den neuen Verhältnissen jedoch nur gelingen, weil sich grundlegende Bedingungen des Wirtschaftraumes veränderten. Die politische und wirtschaftliche Leitung setzte seit Auflösung des Lager-Industriellen Komplexes auf eine Reihe neuer Strategien – eine zunehmende Kontrolle der finanziellen Lage des Kombinats, neue Produktionsformen, den verstärkten Einbezug von Spezialisten und Wissenschaftlern sowie die Stärkung einer Reihe neuer Industriezweige – die nun im Folgenden näher beleuchtet werden sollen.

4.3.1 Finanzen

Mit der Herauslösung von Dal'stroj aus dem MVD versuchte Berija sein Ministerium von einer gewaltigen finanziellen Belastung zu befreien. Die Kosten des Kombinats wurden durch seine Übergabe an das MMP bzw. das MCM in den zivilen Sektor verlagert. Dieser Schritt hatte entscheidende Konsequenzen für das Kombinat. Der Verlust seines besonderen politischen Status als Lager-Industrieller Komplex führte unmittelbar auch zum Verlust seines herausgehobenen finanzpolitischen Status. Zwar wurden auch weiterhin gigantische Summen in die Metallförderung im Nordosten investiert, zum ersten Mal aber spielte die *Wirtschaftlichkeit* einzelner Maßnahmen eine tragende Rolle bei politischen und ökonomischen Entscheidungen. Außerdem orientierte sich seit 1953 die Mittelvergabe und Rechnungsführung nicht an den Absprachen eines militärischen Leiters mit dem MVD, sondern an allgemein gültigen Regelungen des Finanzministeriums, von *Gosplan* und dem Produktionsministerium für Metalle.

Schon bei der Herauslösung des Kombinats aus dem MVD war der Klärungsbedarf hinsichtlich der tatsächlichen ökonomischen Lage von Dal'stroj sehr hoch. So wurde bereits in dem Übergabeakt des MVD auf die Differenz aus veranschlagten und tatsächlichen Verlusten hingewiesen: „Zum 1. Januar 1953 waren auf der Grundlage der Zahlen von 1952 Verluste von 598,2 Mio. Rubel für das Jahr 1953 veranschlagt worden. Tatsächlich wurde das Jahr 1952 mit Verlusten in Höhe von 1.017 Mio. Rubel abgeschlossen."[114] Zudem meldeten sich einzelne Personen aus dem Kombinat selbst zu

---

Geschichte der Organisation *Severovostokzoloto* Churieva, Struktura Severovostokzolota. Seine Errichtung beruhte auf einem Befehl des MCM vom 25. November 1965.

114 Die Verluste durch Mängel, Unterschlagungen und Diebstähle betrugen insgesamt 21,7 Mio. Rubel. Vgl. den Übergabeakt vom 3. April 1953 in GAMO f. R-23, op. 1, d. 4677, l. 1–28, hier l. 21–22. Der MVD beklagte darin auch die schlechte Qualität der Buchhalter in Dal'stroj, vgl. ebd. l. 24.

Wort, die von enormen wirtschaftlichen Problemen, aber auch von massiven Veruntreuungen und Unterschlagungen berichteten.[115]

Die neuen Verantwortlichen drängten daher auf eine Untersuchung der Lage und auf eine objektive Analyse aller Kostenfaktoren.[116] Schon bald entbrannte zwischen dem MCM, dem Ministerium für staatliche Kontrolle, und Mitrakov, dem Leiter von Dal'stroj, ein heftiger Streit. Es zeigte sich, dass bei einem Kombinat von der Größe und Komplexität Dal'strojs nicht nur die Ursachen der finanziellen Verluste für Diskussionen sorgten, sondern auch die Lage selbst unterschiedlich beurteilt werden konnte.

Die Kommission kam zu dem Ergebnis, dass die Wirtschaftsdaten des Kombinats deutlich schlechter waren als bisher bekannt und dass sie darüber hinaus bisher systematisch von der Kombinatsleitung geschönt worden waren. Mitrakov hingegen stellte die negative Bewertung als Ergebnis einer missgünstigen Präsentation ausgewählter Zahlen dar. In eigenen Berichten, aber auch in persönlichen Schreiben an Chruščev und Bulganin verteidigte er seine bisherige Arbeit und präsentierte von ihm ausgewählte Wirtschaftsdaten.[117]

So schilderte Mitrakov überraschenderweise eine beständige Senkung der Selbstkosten – also der Mittel, die zur Gewinnung eines Gramms chemisch reinen Goldes in Dal'stroj benötigt wurden – im Bereich der „vergleichbaren Güterproduktion", bei einer gewissen Steigung der Bruttoselbstkostenpreise.[118] Die realen Selbst-

---

115 Wichtigster Zuträger war dabei ein Funktionär aus der obersten Leitungsebene des Kombinats, der sich anonym direkt an Chruščev wandte. In seinem Schreiben prangerte er riesige Verluste des Kombinats durch Veruntreuungen, Diebstähle, Abschreibungen und unwirtschaftliches Verhalten an und forderte auch personalpolitische Konsequenzen. Vgl. sein Schreiben in RGAĖ f. 9163, op. 6, d. 14, l. 54–56. Da sich der anonyme Autor als ausgesprochen gut informiert erwies, verlangte das ZK der KPdSU zusätzliche Informationen und den Einsatz einer Kommission bei der Sonderverwaltung des MCM. Vgl. die anschließende Stellungnahme des Leiters der Sonderverwaltung des MCM, M. Konyčev, in RGAĖ f. 9163, op. 6, d. 14, l. 48–50.
116 Zunächst forderte das Ministerium die Umstellung der Abrechnungen auf die Regelungen des Ministeriums und einen stärkeren Einblick in seine Investitionen. Vgl. die Beschwerde über mangelnde Kooperation des Kombinats vom Februar 1954 in RGAĖ f. 9163, op. 6, d. 15, l. 83–85. Parallel dazu entsandte Lomako, der Minister für Buntmetalle, eine breit aufgestellte Kommission in die Hauptverwaltung und an einzelne Produktionsstandorte, dabei sollten auch die in dem anonymen Schreiben genannten Zustände überprüft werden. Vgl. den entsprechenden urschriftlichen Vermerk an Konyčev auf der Stellungnahme der Spezialverwaltung in RGAĖ f. 9163, op. 6, d. 14, l. 48.
117 Vgl. z. B. die ausführlichen Dossiers Mitrakovs über Dal'stroj, die für den Besuch der Brigade des ZK der KPdSU und die Diskussionen im Zusammenhang mit der sich abzeichnenden Gebietsgründung entstanden, sowie das Schreiben Mitrakovs an Bulganin in GAMO f. R-23, op. 1, d. 5610, l. 97–101. Diese Beschreibungen enthalten keinerlei Angaben zur Produktionskrise des Kombinats und den enorm gestiegenen Selbstkosten der Goldförderung seit Anfang der 1950er Jahre. Sie waren vielmehr als reine „Leistungsbilanz" des Kombinats gestaltet. Trotz dieser offensichtlich einseitigen und beschönigenden Darstellung werden sie in Magadan auch heute noch in historischen Abhandlungen zur Beschreibung der tatsächlichen Lage der Region herangezogen, so z. B. in Verkina/Kozlov, K voprosu ob obrazovanii.
118 Vgl. GAMO f. R-23, op. 1, d. 5210, l. 26–33, hier l. 30f. Bei den Kosten für „vergleichbare Güterproduktion" handelt es sich um ein Spezifikum der sowjetischen Planwirtschaft, bei der Kosten un-

kosten des Goldes von Dal'stroj seien von 32,22 Rubel im Jahr 1950 auf 26,73 Rubel in den ersten neun Monaten des Jahres 1954 gesunken.[119] Nach den Angaben des MCM stiegen jedoch die Selbstkosten allein in den ersten neun Monaten des Jahres 1954 um 7,3 %.[120]

Tatsächlich unterlag die Aufstellung von Selbstkosten Produktionsplänen, auf deren Grundlage staatliche Subventionen berechnet wurden. Die Selbstkosten für ein Gramm chemisch reines Gold konnten daher sinken, während zugleich die staatlichen Subventionen zur Stützung des Selbstkostenpreises stiegen.[121] Mitrakov schloss daraus, dass einfach ein neuer Plan aufgestellt werden müsste, der sämtliche Verteuerungen einpreise – und die Bilanz des Kombinats wäre wieder eine erfreuliche.[122] So schrieb er an Chruščev:

> Ausgehend von den hier vorgestellten Daten scheint uns, dass bei einer richtigen Festlegung der geplanten Selbstkosten [...] die Ergebnisse der wirtschaftlichen Tätigkeiten von Dal'stroj bedeutend besser aussehen müssten.[123]

So wichtig die Entwicklung der Selbstkosten für die Beurteilung der Rentabilität von Rohstoffförderung und für eine Darstellung der längerfristigen Entwicklung ist, so begrenzt ist hier ihre Aussagekraft, da in der sowjetischen Planwirtschaft Selbstkosten sinken, tatsächlich aber weniger Gold gefördert werden konnte. Für eine Beurteilung der Kosten, die ein sowjetischer Betrieb dem Staat verursachte, muss also zudem auf die jährlichen Verluste und dabei v. a. auf die „über dem Plan liegenden Verluste" geblickt werden.[124]

---

terschiedlicher Betriebe innerhalb eines Wirtschaftszweiges miteinander verglichen wurden. Bei dieser Form von Berechnung ist die Vergleichbarkeit der einzelnen Betriebe natürlich von großer Bedeutung. Da es sich bei Dal'stroj mit knapp 40 % der gesamten Goldproduktion in der Sowjetunion um den unangefochtenen „leader" der Branche handelte, ist ein realer Vergleich nur schwer möglich. Vgl. zur Rolle des Kombinats für die sowjetische Goldförderung Zeljak, Zolotodobyvajuščaja promyšlennost', S. 145.

119 Vgl. GAMO f. R-23, op. 1, d. 5210, l. 26–33, hier l. 31.

120 Im Bereich des Zinnabbaus waren die Kennzahlen des MCM noch schlechter, hier stiegen die Selbstkosten in bestimmten Wirtschaftsverwaltungen um bis zu 25 %. Vgl. den Bericht vom 25. November 1954 in GAMO f. R-23, op. 1, d. 5610, l. 7–15, hier l. 8.

121 Mitrakov selbst beschwerte sich bei Chruščev über das Gebaren des Finanzministeriums, das das staatliche Budget auf Kosten der Bilanzen von Dal'stroj positiv verzerrt habe: „Während irreale, wirklichkeitsfremde Kennziffern der Wirtschaftstätigkeiten von Dal'stroj festgelegt werden, entsteht der Eindruck von Wohlstand bei der Aufstellung des staatlichen Budgets, aber die riesigen Verluste von Dal'stroj werden am Ende eines Wirtschaftsjahres aufgrund einer speziellen Entscheidung der Regierung gedeckt." Vgl. GAMO f. R-23, op. 1, d. 5210, l. 26–33, hier l. 32. Für die Zahlen der von Mitrakov errechneten Selbstkostenpreise vgl. die Auflistung des Kombinats in GAMO f. R-23, op. 1, d. 5610, l. 138.

122 Vgl. GAMO f. R-23, op. 1, d. 5210, l. 26–33, hier l. 32.

123 Persönlicher Brief von Mitrakov an Chruščev in GAMO f. R-23, op. 1, d. 5210, l. 26–33, hier l. 31f.

124 Dies bestätigte auch Mitrakov, wenn er in einem Bericht vom April 1955 schreibt: „Die Verluste bei der Realisation von Industrieprodukten [d. h. bei der Rohstoffförderung – M. S.] entstanden im Zusammenhang mit der Verteuerung des Selbstkostenpreises und der Übererfüllung des Plans in Be-

Die über dem Plan liegenden Verluste verschwieg auch Mitrakov nicht, er bezifferte sie für das Jahr 1953 auf 731 Mio. Rubel; für ihn spiegelten sie jedoch nicht die eigentliche Leistungsstärke des Kombinats wider.[125] Die steigenden, über dem Plan liegenden Verluste dokumentierten jedoch nicht nur den erhöhten Finanzbedarf des Kombinats, sie können zugleich auch als Ausweis eines geringeren Planungsspielraums angesehen werden. Denn sobald einer Einrichtung weniger Verluste im Plan gestattet wurden, stiegen natürlich die *über dem Plan* liegenden Verluste. Diese Abhängigkeit schilderte anschaulich V. Vasil'ev, der Leiter der Abteilung für perspektivische Planung in Dal'stroj, in einem Bericht an das ZK der KPdSU:

> Die Selbstkosten der Produktion der grundlegenden Metallförderung und die Mehrheit der zuarbeitenden Wirtschaftszweige liegen erheblich über den einheitlichen unionsweiten Preisen für analoge Industrieprodukte. Der Unterschied zwischen den Selbstkosten der Produktion von Dal'stroj und den unionsweiten Preisen wird gewöhnlich im Rahmen des verabschiedeten Planes geschlossen, auf Kosten von Subventionen aus dem staatlichen Budget. Aber das Finanzministerium der UdSSR kürzt von Jahr zu Jahr die Höhe der an Dal'stroj vergebenen Subventionen und als Resultat dessen wird Dal'stroj gezwungen, schon vorhandene Produktionskräfte seiner Wirtschaftseinrichtungen nicht zu nutzen und einige von ihnen überhaupt aufzugeben.[126]

Demnach war also der sowjetische Staat schon seit ein paar Jahren nicht mehr bereit, unbegrenzte Summen in das Kombinat zu pumpen, was sich in der seit dem Spätstalinismus herrschenden ökonomischen Krise spiegelte. Ende des Jahres 1954 ging selbst Mitrakov schon von 1,084 Milliarden über dem Plan liegenden Verlusten für das Jahr 1954 aus, die Kommission des MCM attestierte dem Kombinat Verluste von 1,108 Milliarden Rubel. Daraufhin erhielt Dal'stroj zwei kurzfristige Kredite von insgesamt 853 Mio. Rubel, um seine Bilanz kurzfristig ausgleichen zu können; Teilbereiche von Dal'stroj wurden in der Folge von der weiteren Kreditvergabe ausgeschlossen.[127]

---

trieben, bei denen der Selbstkostenpreis erheblich über dem Durchschnitt des Selbstkostenpreises von Dal'stroj insgesamt liegt." GAMO f. R-23, op. 1, d. 5610, l. 125 – 139, hier l. 126 (Bericht über die Resultate der Wirtschaftstätigkeiten von Dal'stroj im Jahr 1954). Hierbei handelte es sich allerdings um ein Schreiben an das MCM – nicht persönlich an Chruščev – so dass davon ausgegangen werden muss, dass Mitrakov in diesem Schreiben gezwungen war, die Zahlen weitaus präziser zu erläutern. Nach den Angaben der Kommission des MCM waren die Hauptursache der extremen Erhöhung der Verluste die massiv gestiegenen Selbstkosten. Vgl. GAMO f. R-23sč, op. 1, d. 4843, l. 1 – 74, hier l. 67.

125 Für das Jahr 1951 nannte er 260,4 Mio. und für 1952 418,8 Mio. Rubel an über den Plänen liegenden Verlusten. Vgl. GAMO f. R-23, op. 1, d. 5210, l. 26 – 33, hier l. 30.

126 Dossier von Vasil'ev für das ZK der KPdSU über die Lage von Dal'stroj vom 20. Juni 1954. Dieses Dossier kam auf Wunsch von Ababkov zustande, inhaltlich geht es auf ein vertrauliches Gespräch zwischen Ababkov und Vasil'ev mit einem Instrukteur des ZK der KPdSU zurück. Vgl. GAMO f. P-21, op. 5, d. 685, l. 1 – 20, hier l. 7.

127 Vgl. den Bericht von Mitrakov über die Wirtschaftstätigkeiten im Jahr 1954 in GAMO f. R-23, op. 1, d. 5610, l. 133. Laut der Kommission verschlechterte sich die finanzielle Situation des Kombinats im Jahr 1954 noch einmal dadurch, dass die Verwaltung des *Sevvostlag* dem Kombinat 50 Mio. Rubel schuldete. Für die Angaben der Kommission siehe GAMO f. R-23, op. 1, d. 4843, l. 1 – 74, hier l. 66.

Die unterschiedlichen Lagebeurteilungen gingen mit einer stark divergierenden Einschätzung der Ursachen einher. Für Mitrakov waren es an allererster Stelle die Entlassungen der Häftlinge und damit Veränderungen außerhalb des Einflussbereichs des Kombinats, die für die finanziellen Probleme verantwortlich waren. Der Arbeitskräftebestand sei seit der Amnestie im März 1953 vollkommen unzureichend gewesen; durch die massive Reduzierung der Lagerpunkte habe die Produktion einen gewaltigen Aderlass verkraften müssen: „Wegen [...] des Abgangs einer großen Zahl von Häftlingen (mehr als 100.000 Menschen), besonders in den Jahren 1953–1954, im Zusammenhang mit der Amnestie, verringert Dal'stroj die Metallförderung und führt sie nicht zu neuer Stärke"[128], erklärte Mitrakov Bulganin die Lage. Neben der Reduzierung der Häftlinge nannte auch Mitrakov weitere Faktoren, wie eine geringe Mechanisierung und fehlende Infrastruktur, mit den Entlassungen der Häftlinge sei jedoch die Wirtschaft des Komplexes ins Mark getroffen worden.

Wesentlich vielschichtiger sind hingegen die Ursachenanalysen der zivilen Instanzen. In ihren Augen zeigten sich die negativen Auswirkungen der Entlassungen v. a. beim Verlust gut ausgebildeter Häftlinge. Den Schwund an Arbeitskräften beurteilten sie in der breiten Masse jedoch sehr viel weniger dramatisch. Schon für das erste Quartal des Jahres 1954 konstatierte die Kommission des MCM einen Bestand von 75–80 % der benötigten Arbeitskräfte, im zweiten und dritten Quartal habe sich die Versorgung mit Arbeitskräften auf 85–92 % verbessert.[129] Dieser deutliche Unterschied in der Darstellung resultierte aus der Tatsache, dass Mitrakov von „Häftlingen", aber nicht von „arbeitenden Häftlingen" sprach. Tatsächlich war ein Großteil der entlassenen Häftlinge aufgrund von Alter und Krankheit schon seit längerer Zeit nicht mehr arbeitsfähig gewesen oder war wegen produktionsinterner Desorganisation nicht zur Arbeit herangezogen worden; die Gleichsetzung der Entlassungszahlen mit dem Schwund an Arbeitskräften weist so den innenpolitischen Veränderungen die Hauptursache der Krise zu.[130] Die unterschiedliche Beurteilung der Bedeutung der Häftlingsentlassungen ergab sich sicherlich auch aus einer unterschiedlichen Perspektive: Aus Sicht von Mitrakov, vor Ort, fehlten an einem bestimmten neuralgischen Punkt der Rohstoffförderung quasi „über Nacht" die Arbeitskräfte, andere Arbeiter waren Tausende Kilometer weit entfernt und nicht verfügbar. Aus Moskauer Sicht hingegen erschien die prozentuale Verringerung der Arbeitskräfte, die aus den vorgelegten Berichten hervorging, als nicht allzu dramatisch.

---

128 Mitrakov in seinem Schreiben an Bulganin vom 21. April 1955 in GAMO f. R-23, op. 1, d. 5610, l. 97–101, hier l. 98. Siehe auch seine Darstellung der Ursachen in GAMO f. R-23, op. 1, d. 5210, l. 29.

129 Bericht einer Kommission des MCM über die Tätigkeit von Dal'stroj in GAMO f. R-23, op. 1, d. 4843, l. 1–74, hier l. 2–3.

130 Tatsächlich ging Mitrakov von einem ungefähren Bedarf von 132.800 Arbeitern aus, um Dal'stroj langfristig arbeitsfähig halten zu können. Der Bestand sei von 159.500 auf 112.000 Arbeitskräfte gesunken, wobei er hier bereits das Ausscheiden freier Arbeiter miteingerechnet hatte. Vgl. Mitrakov in einem persönlichen Schreiben an Chruščev vom Oktober 1954 in GAMO f. R-23, op. 1, d. 5210, l. 26–33, hier l. 27–28.

Die Staatsbank und die Kommission des Ministeriums verwiesen hingegen noch auf ganz andere Ursachen für die bisher nicht bekannte schlechte finanzielle Lage des Kombinats. Demnach beruhten die bisherigen geschönten Zahlen des Kombinats auf regelrechten Tricksereien in der Buchhaltung von Dal'stroj: So seien etwa die Hälfte der neu dokumentierten über dem Plan liegenden Verluste bereits in den vergangenen Jahren entstanden, aber vom Kombinat bisher einfach nicht eingepreist worden. Faktisch seien die Selbstkosten in den ersten elf Monaten des Jahres 1954 gestiegen, auf dem Papier aber habe das Kombinat die Selbstkosten der Produktion künstlich gesenkt, indem die Fortzahlung der Lohnkosten während der Urlaubszeit von Arbeitern und Angestellten einfach nicht mitgerechnet wurde. Was zunächst wie eine Kleinigkeit erscheint, erweist sich jedoch vor dem Hintergrund der Urlaubsregelung, nach der jeder Arbeiter und Angestellte alle drei Jahre für ein halbes Jahr in einen bezahlten Urlaub (mit Übernahme der Reisekosten) fahren durfte, als eine beträchtliche Summe. Die Ende 1954 durchgeführte Überprüfung habe ergeben, dass 493 Mio. Rubel für Urlaubskosten nicht in die Berechnung der Selbstkosten miteingeflossen seien. „Dadurch wird die Verteuerung der Selbstkosten für die ersten elf Monate des Jahres 1954 und die vorangegangenen Jahre in beträchtlichem Maße über dem liegen, was in den Rechnungsabschlüssen angegeben ist."[131] Statt eine bereits im August erlassene Verordnung des ZK der KPdSU und des Ministerrates der UdSSR zur Senkung der Mehrausgaben im Bereich der Löhne umzusetzen, „benutzen die Leiter von Dal'stroj die Geldmittel für die Löhne gewohnheitsmäßig, um mit ihnen die Mehrausgaben schlecht arbeitender Betriebe zu decken"[132].

An vielen weiteren Stellen deckte das MCM, gemeinsam mit der Staatsbank, erhebliche Bilanzfälschungen auf. Neben diversen Schulden einzelner Wirtschaftseinrichtungen, die nicht in das Bestandsbuch aufgenommen wurden, seien die Bilanzen im Bereich der Zufuhr und Lagerung von technischen Anlagen, Materialien, aber auch Gegenständen des täglichen Gebrauchs deutlich geschönt worden. Als Ergebnis einer „vollkommen unverantwortlichen Politik" seien teuerste technische Anlagen, wertvolle Materialien und Tausende Waren des täglichen Bedarfs ohne Kontrolle der vorhandenen Bestände und ohne eine umfassende Bedarfsanalyse einfach angefordert und in die Region geschafft worden. Da es keine Inventarisierungen der vorhandenen und der angeforderten Wertgegenstände gebe, seien die Verluste des Kombinats in diesem Bereich nicht ausgewiesen worden, obwohl der Ministerrat der UdSSR bereits im September 1953 entsprechende Verordnungen erlassen hatte. Allein

---

131 So der stellv. Minister für Buntmetalle, Šemjakin, in seinem Schreiben an Mitrakov vom 14. März 1955 in GAMO f. R-23, op. 1, d. 5610, l. 41–48, hier l. 42. Siehe dazu auch den Bericht des Ministers Lomako über einen Bericht der Staatsbank der UdSSR an den Ministerrat der UdSSR zu der finanziellen Situation des Kombinats Dal'stroj, in dem all diese Angaben bestätigt wurden. Vgl. GAMO f. R-23, op. 1, d. 5610, l. 49–50. Vor diesem Hintergrund ist nicht verständlich, warum Magadaner Historiker noch immer die Angaben der Selbstkosten von Dal'stroj übernehmen und auch in ihren eigenen Arbeiten von einer fortlaufenden Senkung der Selbstkostenpreise berichten.

132 Šemjakin in seinem Bericht an Mitrakov in GAMO f. R-23, op. 1, d. 5610, l. 43.

im Bereich der Industrieanlagen hätten die Verluste in den ersten zehn Monaten des Jahres 1954 184,7 Mio. Rubel betragen.[133] Dieser sorglose Umgang habe außerdem dazu geführt, dass es zu Diebstählen im Umfang von mehreren Millionen Rubel gekommen sei.[134] Auf der Grundlage dieser Vergehen bat der Vorsitzende der Verwaltung der Staatsbank den Ministerrat der UdSSR darum, die Verantwortlichkeiten für diese Verhältnisse auf der Führungsebene von Dal'stroj zu überprüfen.

Schon vorher hatte auch das Kollegium des MCM (unter dem Vorsitz des Ministers Lomako) die Kombinatsleitung für die schwache Kontrolle der Finanzdisziplin verantwortlich gemacht. Auf ihre mangelnde Aufsicht seien auch die gewaltigen Verluste durch Unterschlagungen und Diebstähle zurückzuführen gewesen. Aufgrund der Häufigkeit und Systematik der nun dokumentierten Vorfälle habe das Ministerium Dal'stroj befohlen, den Hauptbuchhalter von Dal'stroj, Rovnjaličev, zu entlassen:

> Schon seit einigen Jahren präsentiert der Hauptbuchhalter von Dal'stroj irreale Bilanzen, in denen Verluste, Unterschlagungen und Diebstähle nicht richtig ausgewiesen werden. Fehlbeträge, die vom Ministerium für die Buchführung genehmigt wurden, machten am 1. Januar 1953 noch 9,7 Mio. Rubel aus. Am 1. Januar 1954 waren es bereits 53,7 Mio. Rubel. Eigentlich war Dal'stroj verpflichtet, für sämtliche Fehlbeträge eine Genehmigung des Ministers zu beantragen, faktisch konnte er aber nur 36 Mio. Rubel belegen. Das Fehlen dieser Materialien in der Buchhaltung von Dal'stroj bezeugt ein vollkommen unzulängliches Verhältnis der Kombinatsleitung und des ersten Buchhalters Rovnjaličev zu Unterschlagungen und Diebstählen.[135]

Für Lomako, den Minister für Buntmetalle, und für Popov, den Leiter der sowjetischen Staatsbank, waren die hier ausführlich beschriebenen Fälle von Unterschlagungen und Diebstählen, der unverantwortliche Umgang mit Materialien und Waren sowie die vielfältigen Bilanzfälschungen Belege dafür, dass die finanzielle und wirtschaftliche Situation des Kombinats bisher viel zu positiv bewertet und dass das Kombinat in viel zu geringem Maße überwacht worden sei. Neben dem Hauptbuchhalter von Dal'stroj wurden in der Folge weitere 48 Personen wegen Vergehen gegen die „Finanzdisziplin" entlassen, einige von ihnen darüber hinaus gerichtlich zur Verantwortung gezogen.[136]

---

133 Bericht des Ministers Lomako über den Bericht des Vorstandes der Staatsbank zur wirtschaftlichen Lage des Kombinats Dal'stroj vom 8. März 1955 in GAMO f. R-23, op. 1, d. 5610, l. 49–50, hier l. 49.
134 Vgl. GAMO f. R-23, op. 1, d. 5610, l. 46. Nach Angaben des Berichts wurden zu früh gelieferte Waren im Wert von 200 Mio. Rubel (über dem Plan liegende Kosten) in der Bilanz gar nicht ausgewiesen. Entsprechend einer Verordnung des Kollegiums des MCM vom August 1954 begann das Kombinat damit, nicht benötigte Anlagen zu überprüfen, und brachte anschließend überflüssige technische Anlagen und Waren im Wert von etwa 100 Mio. Rubel zu den großen Häfen nach Nachodka und Vanino. Vgl. den Bericht von Mitrakov über die Resultate der Wirtschaftstätigkeiten im Jahr 1954 in GAMO f. R-23, op. 1, d. 5610, l. 125–139, hier l. 133 f. Für die Verordnung des MCM siehe RGAÈ f. 9163, op. 6, d. 13, l. 170–173, hier l. 171 und 172.
135 Vgl. den Bericht des Kollegiums des MCM über die ersten zehn Monate des Jahres 1954 in GAMO f. R-23, op. 1, d. 5610, l. 7–15, l. 11.
136 Vgl. den Bericht einer Kommission des MCM über die Tätigkeit von Dal'stroj in GAMO f. R-23, op. 1, d. 4843, l. 1–74, hier l. 74. Dazu zählte wahrscheinlich auch der in dem anonymen Brief genannte Leiter der Finanzabteilung Mitjušin.

Nicht nur bei der Buchführung, auch bei der Wirtschaftspolitik wurde der Druck auf die Region in der Entstalinisierung noch einmal erhöht. Seit 1954 kam es nicht mehr nur darauf an, möglichst große Mengen Gold aus der Region zu holen, jetzt ging es auch darum, dies mit maximaler ökonomischer Effektivität zu tun. Ein Blick auf die jährlichen Planvorgaben zeigt, dass der Wirtschaft keine Atempause gegönnt wurde. Neben den Forderungen nach großen Infrastrukturprojekten, dem Bau von Wohnungen, der Schaffung von sozialen Einrichtungen und den erhöhten Ausgaben für die Löhne freier Arbeitskräfte sollten Dal'stroj und ab 1957 der Volkswirtschaftsrat auch weiterhin maximale Goldmengen liefern.[137] Die Planvorgaben erwiesen sich unter den Bedingungen der anhaltenden Krise als nahezu unerfüllbar, dennoch wurde unerbittlich an ihnen festgehalten. Immer wieder bemühten sich die Verantwortlichen bei der jeweils übergeordneten Stelle um eine Absenkung der Pläne, um Straßen, Wohnungen und die Energieversorgung errichten zu können.[138] Keine Stelle wollte jedoch die Verantwortung für eine Umstrukturierung der Arbeiten auf Kosten des Planes übernehmen, niemand eine Neuorganisation oder eine Ausbildung der unqualifizierten neuen Arbeitskräfte auch nur in einem Jahr zulassen, wenn dadurch der Plan bedroht worden wäre.

Aus diesem Grund wich das Kombinat auf die bewährte Strategie der Erhöhung der Selbstkosten aus, um durch Mehraufwendungen beim Einsatz von Technik und Energie die angeordnete Goldmenge zu erzielen. Allerdings hatte das Kombinat auf diesem Gebiet einen deutlich kleineren Spielraum. Seit der Umstellung seiner Rechnungsführung im Jahr 1954 kontrollierte man das Finanzgebaren des Kombinats / des Volkswirtschaftsrates streng. Im November 1955 hatten das ZK der KPdSU und der Ministerrat der UdSSR die langfristige Verringerung der Selbstkosten in Dal'stroj eingefordert.[139] Tatsächlich aber lagen sie 1957 noch immer auf dem Niveau des Jahres 1953.[140]

---

137 Die Planerfüllung der Goldförderung lag z. B. noch im Jahr 1956 bei 97,1 % (38,7 Tonnen Gold statt der geplanten 40 Tonnen). Vgl. die Angaben nach dem ausführlichen Bericht von Dal'stroj über das Jahresergebnis 1956 in GAMO f. R-23, op. 1, d. 4897, l. 3–119, hier l. 3. Zu den Mehrkosten für das Kombinat aufgrund der neu entstehenden Lohnkosten vgl. den Bericht des Kombinats vom 19. März 1957 in GAMO f. R-23, op. 1, d. 6109, l. 2–12, hier l. 4.
138 Vgl. z. B. die Bitte des Leiters der Südlichen Verwaltung an Berezin vom 17. September 1956 in GAMO f. R-23, op. 1, d. 6127, l. 5–7. Siehe die Bitte um eine allgemeine Planabsenkung in dem Schreiben von Čuguev an Lomako vom 20. Juli 1956 in GAMO f. R-23sč, op. 1, d. 471, l. 29–30 und die darauf folgende Bitte um Planabsenkungen bei der Wirtschaftskommission des Ministerrates der UdSSR im Schreiben des stellv. Ministers für Buntmetalle, Strigin, vom 9. Oktober 1956 in GAMO f. R-23sč, op. 1, d. 471, l. 54–55.
139 Die Kosten sollten langfristig von 25 Rubel im Jahr 1955 auf 18–20 Rubel im Jahr 1960 sinken. Die Verordnung „Über die weitere Senkung der Selbstkosten für Gold" vom 24. November 1955 richtete sich an das MCM der UdSSR und an das MCM der kasachischen Sowjetrepublik. Entsprechend dieser Verordnung erließ das MCM der UdSSR am 3. Dezember 1955 und dann noch einmal am 17. März 1956 einen ausführlichen Forderungskatalog an Dal'stroj.
140 Vgl. den Bericht von Berezin vom 19. März 1957 in GAMO f. R-23, op. 1, d. 6109, l. 2–12, hier l. 3–4.

Eine Untersuchung des Ministeriums für staatliche Kontrolle der UdSSR vom Frühjahr 1957 ermittelte als wichtigste Ursache für den weiterhin sehr hohen Selbstkostenpreis die Absenkung des mittleren Goldgehaltes. Dal'stroj habe Gold hauptsächlich in vergleichsweise kleinen, weit abgelegenen Gebieten mit einem relativ geringen Goldgehalt gefördert; diese Zersplitterung habe für einen erheblichen Kostenanstieg gesorgt.[141] Noch immer war der Ertrag eines Gebietes fast ausschließlich von seinem Rohstoffreichtum in besonders gut zugänglichen Erdschichten abhängig. Die Tatsache, dass der Selbstkostenpreis trotz beständig sinkendem mittleren Goldgehalt auch in den folgenden Jahren in etwa auf dem Niveau von 1953 gehalten werden konnte, verdankte man, so der stellvertretende Dal'stroj-Leiter Berezin, einer Reihe von Maßnahmen. Dazu habe die nochmalige Erhöhung der Förderung über Tage im Vergleich zu der Arbeit in kostenintensiven Schächten gezählt – ein deutlicher Beleg dafür, dass an der extensiven, oberflächlichen Ausbeutung gut zugänglicher Schichten festgehalten wurde.[142]

Daneben setzte das Kombinat zur Kostensenkung auch auf strukturelle Veränderungen. Eine große Zahl von Betrieben wurden seit 1953 geschlossen oder mehrere Anlagen zu einer größeren Einheit zusammengefasst, um Kosten zu sparen. War dies 1953 noch durch den unmittelbaren Arbeitskräftemangel infolge der Entlassungen nach der Amnestie motiviert, so ging es seit 1954 v. a. darum, Betriebe aufgrund von mangelnder Rentabilität zu schließen. Allein in diesem Jahr sank die Zahl der selbstständigen Einrichtungen um 26 %; 85 Industrieanlagen wurden geschlossen.[143] 1956 wurde noch einmal die Zahl der goldfördernden Betriebe massiv verringert, drei Industrieverwaltungen ganz aufgelöst.[144] Deutliche Kürzungen gab es auch in der Verwaltung. Sie waren Folge der Schließungen und Teil der Dal'stroj auferlegten Einsparbemühungen. Verstärkt wurden sie durch diverse Kampagnen zur Reorganisation und Verkleinerung der überbordenden öffentlichen sowjetischen Verwaltung und ihrer extremen Bürokratie, die unmittelbar nach Stalins Tod einsetzten und die, mit je eigenen Schwerpunkten und Interessen, sowohl von Malenkov als auch von

---

141 Siehe den Bericht Milovidovs an den Minister für staatliche Kontrolle der UdSSR, Molotov, vom 5. April 1957 in GAMO f. R-23ss, op. 1, d. 459, l. 7–8. Molotov hatte diesen Ministerposten bis zum 29. Juni 1957 inne. Anschließend wurde er als sowjetischer Botschafter in die Mongolei verbannt aufgrund seiner Teilnahme an der sogenannten „Antiparteigruppe" gegen Chruščev.

142 Im Jahr 1956 lag die Versorgung mit Arbeitskräften bei 100,8 %, während sie in Dal'stroj insgesamt 96,9 % betrug. So Berezin in seinem Bericht vom 19. März 1957 in GAMO f. R-23, op. 1, d. 6109, l. 2–12, hier l. 6.

143 Die Zahlen beziehen sich auf alle Industrieanlagen, nicht nur auf die Goldförderung. Vgl. den Bericht über die Tätigkeit von Dal'stroj für das Jahr 1954 in GAMO f. R-23, op. 1, d. 4843, l. 1–74, hier l. 38.

144 Vgl. den Bericht von Berezin vom 19. März 1957 in GAMO f. R-23, op. 1, d. 6109, l. 2–12. Siehe als Beispiel die Aufgabe der Goldgrube Utinskij, weil sich der dortige Goldgehalt als zu gering erwiesen hatte; die Selbstkosten für ein Gramm Gold lagen dort bereits bei 40 Rubel. Vgl. die entsprechende Beurteilung des Leiters der Hauptverwaltung der Geologen vom 29. April 1956 in GAMO f. R-23sč, op. 1, d. 456, l. 26–27.

Chruščev vorangetrieben wurden.[145] Allein 1954 wurden daraufhin in Dal'stroj 7.539 Posten für Mitarbeiter in der Verwaltung gestrichen; das waren in vielen Bereichen bis zu 50 % aller Stellen.[146]

Im Sommer 1956 sah sich das MCM schließlich gezwungen, die Finanzen von Dal'stroj zu stützen. Mit Zustimmung der staatlichen Wirtschaftskommission des Ministerrates der UdSSR bat es das Finanzministerium um Sonderzahlungen für das Kombinat.[147] Danach konnten dessen Verluste um 130 Mio. Rubel gesenkt werden[148] und Dal'stroj überzog zum ersten Mal nicht mehr seine Schulden bei der Staatsbank und diversen Lieferanten.[149] Dennoch schnitt das Kombinat auch in diesem Jahr im Vergleich mit anderen Hauptverwaltungen des Ministeriums bei allen wichtigen Kennziffern am schlechtesten ab.[150]

Zur verstärkten Kontrolle des Kombinats wurde im Folgenden die Position des obersten Kontrolleurs für das Magadaner Gebiet und Dal'stroj beim Ministerium für staatliche Kontrolle der UdSSR eingeführt. Dieser Kontrolleur kritisierte auch weiterhin zu hohe Ausgaben für Energie und Materialien, Fehlplanungen, Mängel bei der Mechanisierung und die unorganisierte Verteilung der Arbeitskräfte. Er monierte zudem, dass das Kombinat nicht energisch genug gegen die Unterschlagung von Gold vorging, und insgesamt zu verlustreiche Fördermethoden eingesetzte – in einigen Gebieten hätten diese Verluste 10 % betragen.[151]

Die Entdeckung neuer Goldfelder in Tschukotka 1958 brachte dem Kombinat zwar eine gewisse Entlastung, denn die Steigerung des mittleren Goldgehaltes in den neuen

---

145 Vgl. Gorlizki, Anti-Ministerialism, S. 1291 ff.

146 Vgl. den Bericht über die Tätigkeit von Dal'stroj für das Jahr 1954 in GAMO f. R-23, op. 1, d. 4843, l. 1–74, hier l. 38. Die freigestellten Personen wurden entweder entlassen oder an anderen Stellen eingesetzt. Siehe dazu den Bericht über die Arbeit mit Kadern von Dal'stroj für das Jahr 1954 in GAMO f. R-23, op. 1, d. 5548, l. 1–43, hier l. 5 f.

147 Vgl. die Bitte des Ministers Lomako in GAMO f. R-23sč, op. 1, d. 456, l. 162–164, hier l. 163 f. sowie das Schreiben der Wirtschaftskommission in GAMO f, 23sč, op. 1, d. 456, l. 165–172, hier l. 172.

148 1956 lagen die über dem Plan liegenden Verluste von Dal'stroj noch bei 245,9 Mio. Rubel. Vgl. den Bericht des MCM über das Jahr 1956 in RGAĖ f. 7733, op. 45, d. 1286, l. 1–36, hier l. 29 f.

149 Das Kombinat sah die Ursache für die Verringerung der Schulden nicht nur in den Sonderzahlungen an das Kombinat, sondern auch in eigenen Anstrengungen in der Produktion und Verwaltung. Vgl. den ausführlichen Bericht von Dal'stroj über das Jahresergebnis 1956 in GAMO f. R-23, op. 1, d. 4897, l. 3–119, hier l. 53–54.

150 Bei den über dem Plan liegenden Verlusten lag Dal'stroj mit weitem Abstand an erster Stelle; die Verluste bei Warenlieferungen waren gegenüber dem Kombinat, das in dieser Negativliste nach Dal'stroj an zweiter Stelle stand, etwa zehnmal so hoch. Vgl. den Bericht des MCM über das Jahr 1956 in RGAĖ f. 7733, op. 45, d. 1286, l. 1–36, hier l. 20–21 u. 29 f. sowie den Bericht des stellv. Vorsitzenden der staatlichen Wirtschaftskommission des Ministerrates der UdSSR, Ivanov, vom 9. Juli 1956 in GAMO f. R-23sč, op. 1, d. 456, l. 165–172, hier l. 170. Das MCM forderte daraufhin Čuguev auf, die Verluste in den einzelnen Arbeitsbereichen des Kombinats aufzuklären. Vgl. GAMO f. R-23sč, op. 1, d. 456, l. 162–164, hier l. 163 (Anordnung des Ministers Lomako).

151 Vgl. den Bericht des obersten Kontrolleurs für das Magadaner Gebiet und Dal'stroj, Milovidov, an den Minister für staatliche Kontrolle der UdSSR, Molotov, vom 5. April 1957 in GAMO f. R-23ss, op. 1, d. 459, l. 6–13.

Gebieten führte effektiv zu einer gewissen Absenkung der Selbstkosten.[152] Zugleich aber offenbarte diese Entwicklung das Doppelgesicht aller sowjetischen Investitionen im Nordosten. Denn die Übererfüllung des Produktionsplanes führte automatisch auch zu einer Steigerung der geplanten Verluste.[153] Das neue Gold war zugleich auch ein neuer Kostenfaktor. Dass sich die Sowjetunion Ende der 1950er und zu Beginn der 1960er Jahre zu weiteren Investitionen in der Metallförderung entschied, zeigt, in welchem Maße sie auch weiterhin auf die „Valutazeche" des Nordostens angewiesen war.[154] Um die Kosten der Produktion dennoch so gering wie möglich zu halten, war die sowjetische und regionale Leitung seit 1954 auf der Suche nach Methoden, *vermeidbare* Verluste so gering wie möglich zu halten.

Mit der Offenlegung der Dal'strojer Finanzverhältnisse nach 1953 sollten zum ersten Mal die Kosten aus Unterschlagungen, Misswirtschaft, Fehlplanungen und der Abkapselung des Gebietes in die Bilanzen eingepreist werden. Vor dem Hintergrund dessen, was über Misswirtschaft, Diebstähle und Unterschlagungen in der Wirtschaft des GULAG mittlerweile bekannt ist, überraschen die in Dal'stroj aufgedeckten Vorfälle nicht. Sie zeigen jedoch in bisher unbekannter Deutlichkeit, wie sehr sich die zivile Leitung von den Praktiken des Kombinats abgrenzen wollte und welche ökonomischen Forderungen der Ministerrat an einen ehemaligen Lager-Industriellen Komplex stellte.

Doch auch wenn die strenge Überwachung in der Entstalinisierung aus dem früheren finanziellen Sonderstatus der Region bis 1953 resultierte, war sie dennoch keine isoliert zu betrachtende Erscheinung. Die Kampagnen gegen „Bürokratismus" in der Frühphase der Entstalinisierung, Chruščevs Anstrengungen zur Reorganisation der Ministerien, die Einführung der Volkswirtschaftsräte sowie eine Reihe von Gesetzen, die Ende der 1950er Jahre auf eine Stärkung der Planerfüllung und eine korrekte Rechnungsführung abzielen sollten, zeigen, dass die Kontrolle des Kombinates Dal'stroj und des Volkswirtschaftsrates hier Teil einer größeren Strategie war. Zugleich werfen sie Schlaglichter auf eine Verwaltung, die von extremer Ineffektivität, einem absurden Maß an Bürokratie, einer extremen Zentralisierung und einem grotesken

---

152 Vgl. die Erläuterungen zum Jahresbericht 1959 von Korolev und dem Hauptbuchhalter Gol'dšvend in RGAÈ f. 7733, op. 48, d. 492, l. 1–28, hier l. 19 sowie l. 21.

153 Die Planerfüllung der Produktion lag bei 104,8 %, bei der Goldförderung waren es 103,9 %. Im Jahr 1959 hatten alle Bereiche und Industriezweige des Volkswirtschaftsrats ihre jeweiligen Pläne übererfüllt. Dies bedeutete nicht, dass auch alle einzelnen Betriebe ihre jeweiligen Pläne erreichten, sie konnten jedoch von anderen erfolgreichen Betrieben ihres Industriezweiges aufgefangen werden. Insgesamt verringerte sich die Zahl der Betriebe, die ihre Pläne nicht erfüllten, gegenüber dem Jahr 1958 um die Hälfte; sechs Betriebe blieben 1959 unter den Erwartungen des Planes. Vgl. die Erläuterungen zum Jahresbericht 1959 von Korolev und dem Hauptbuchhalter Gol'dšvend in RGAÈ f. 7733, op. 48, d. 492, l. 1–28, hier l. 1–2.

154 Der Magadaner Historiker Zeljak hat errechnet, dass noch Ende der 1960er Jahre die Kosten für die Goldförderung den Preis des Metalls um das 2 bis 2,5fache überstiegen. Vgl. Zeljak, Zolotodobyvajuščaja promyšlennost', S. 148.

Maß an Parallelstrukturen geprägt war und blieb, auch wenn sich die rhetorischen Angriffe auf die Missstände des Systems deutlich verschärften.[155]

Im Magadaner Gebiet verwiesen die neuen Verantwortlichen dabei bis Ende der 1950er Jahre immer wieder auf unterschiedliche Mentalitäten von „alter" und „neuer" Leitung. Eindrücklich illustriert dies ein Bericht des Leiters des Magadaner Volks- wirtschaftsrates Čuguev aus dem Jahr 1958 über die Tätigkeiten einer Kommission des Ministerrates der RSFSR zu den Verhältnissen im Magadaner Volkswirtschaftsrat. Er schilderte seinen Kollegen im Leitungsgremium des Volkswirtschaftsrates die Beur- teilung des Moskauer Gremiums mündlich mit folgenden Worten:

> Der Genosse Organov [der Leiter der Kommission – M. S.] hat über die Notwendigkeit gesprochen, einen mächtigen Kampf gegen die mangelnde Wirtschaftlichkeit in den Betrieben des Volks- wirtschaftsrates zu führen und unbedingt im Jahr 1958 ganz andere Ergebnisse zu erzielen. Er hat von der Notwendigkeit gesprochen, nicht nur die geplanten Ergebnisse zu erreichen, sondern er hat sogar die Aufmerksamkeit darauf gerichtet, dass wir uns in der nächsten Zeit von den ge- planten Verlusten verabschieden müssen, die wir vom Staat erhalten. Der Genosse Organov sprach davon, dass man die Leute umziehen muss, die früher im System des MVD gearbeitet haben und die die Verluste gar nicht gezählt hätten, weil es dort eine andere Ordnung gab, im Verhältnis zu anderen Organisationen unserer Sowjetischen Union [gemeint ist hier: „weil der MVD gegenüber anderen sowjetischen Einrichtungen unangreifbar war" – M. S.]. Es ist not- wendig, das sowjetische Geld zu sparen, so der Genosse Organov, und er sagte, dass vor uns die wichtige Aufgabe steht, diesen Leuten das Gefühl für die Ökonomie von staatlichem Geld bei- zubringen, die Sorge um die freien Arbeitskräfte, die in unseren Betrieben arbeiten, und das Erreichen guter Kennzahlen bei der Arbeit. Der Genosse Organov sprach über die leitenden Ar- beiter, die diese großen Aufgaben, die vor uns stehen, nicht verstehen. Es ist klar, dass diese Arbeiter ausgetauscht werden müssen. Also, solche Forderungen wurden uns gegenüber erho- ben.[156]

Im Rahmen der neuen Machtverteilung der Volkswirtschaftsräte war hier vor allem das Gebietsparteikomitee in seiner Rolle als kontrollierendes Organ gefragt. Eine wirtschaftlich effektive Arbeitsweise wurde zur wichtigsten Aufgabe erklärt. Der „Wert des sowjetischen Geldes" sollte in allen Industriezweigen des Gebietes geachtet, die Rentabilität einer Maßnahme bei allen Entscheidungen streng untersucht werden. Die politische Leitung war nun das oberste Aufsichtsorgan in dieser Frage.[157]

---

155 1958 und 1961 erließ die Regierung mehrere Gesetze, mit denen Personen für die Nichterfüllung von Plänen und Lieferverträgen sowie für die Verdrehung oder Bereinigung von Rechenschaftsbe- richten juristisch zur Verantwortung gezogen werden konnten. Diese neuen Strafgesetze sind insofern besonders bemerkenswert, da sich die Sowjetunion zwischen 1953 und 1957 von einer Reihe von Strafgesetzen verabschiedet hatte, mit denen Personen für Wirtschaftsvergehen juristisch zur Ver- antwortung gezogen wurden. Vgl. Ivanova, Istorija, S. 88 f.; Filtzer, Soviet Workers, S. 36 – 41. Zu den Reorganisationen in der Verwaltung siehe Gorlizki, Anti-Ministerialism.
156 Čuguev am 19. Mai 1958, Mitschrift des Treffens vom 19. Mai 1958 in GAMO f. R-137, op. 1, d. 57, l. 141 – 145, hier l. 142 – 143.
157 Siehe beispielhaft die Materialien der ersten Wirtschaftskonferenz des neuen Volkswirtschafts- rates, die 1958 unter dem Titel „Für Wirtschaftlichkeit und Sparsamkeit in den Betrieben des Maga-

Das folgende Kapitel wird zeigen, dass sich mit Übergabe an ein ziviles Produktionsministerium nicht nur der Druck auf Finanzabteilungen und Verwaltung erhöhte, sondern auch der Druck bei der Suche nach finanziell effektiveren Produktionsformen.

4.3.2 Neue Industriestrukturen: Mechanisierung und private Goldgräber

Wichtigster Bestandteil einer rationaleren Produktion war die „Mechanisierung" der Magadaner Wirtschaft, also die Umstellung von Handarbeit auf den Einsatz von Maschinen und allgemein die Unterstützung der Arbeiten durch technische Anlagen. In der Entstalinisierung zwang die Entlassung des größten Teils der Häftlinge die Wirtschaftsleitung zu verstärkten Mechanisierungen. Gleichzeitig offenbart sich daran ein langsamer, aber steter Bewusstseinswandel hin zu einer stärker geplanten, rationaleren Form des Wirtschaftens.

Zwar gab es bereits in den 1940er Jahren Bemühungen, die technische und energetische Versorgung der Einrichtungen zu verbessern. Aber gemessen an der Komplexität der Metallförderung in einem so riesigen Gebiet war die Ausstattung der einzelnen Anlagen ausgesprochen kümmerlich. Der Historiker Širokov sieht die Ursache dafür bei den regionalen Versorgungs- und Transportorganisationen, v. a. aber bei den Intentionen der sowjetischen Leitung. Das Gebiet von Dal'stroj hatte die Aufgabe, der Union wertvolle Bodenschätze zu liefern, und sollte nicht zum Empfänger von Hochtechnologie werden.[158] Der Ausbau von Mechanisierung reagierte also auf die Veränderungen im Status der Region, auf ihre allmähliche Umwertung zu einem zivilen Gebiet, in der freie Arbeitskräfte eine industrialisierte Metallförderung organisierten. Auf diesem Wege sollte der rückläufige Trend bei der Goldförderung umgekehrt werden.

In der ersten Zeit nach 1953 waren die Investitionen bei der Mechanisierung und dem Bau neuer Energieanlagen noch vergleichsweise gering, wie Mitrakov und Ababkov in einem gemeinsamen Schreiben an Chruščev und Malenkov betonten.[159] Tatsächlich hatte das MMP bzw. das MCM zunächst eine genauere Planung, eine strukturierte Lieferung, Lagerung und Instandhaltung sowie einen maßvollen Einsatz der tatsächlich benötigten Maschinen und Anlagen verlangt. Dies war nicht nur den Bedingungen des spezialisierten Ministeriums geschuldet, sondern auch der strengen finanziellen Überwachung, die erhebliche Verschwendungen in diesem Bereich aufgedeckt hatte. Dass dies auch mit Bestrebungen einherging, die Metallförderung

---

daner Gebietes" erschienen und in denen v. a. Parteikadern sehr viele lokale Missstände offen angekreidet wurden. Bei den Betrieben der lokalen Industrie sollte diese Aufsichtsfunktion vom Gebietsexekutivkomitee wahrgenommen werden. Vgl. den Entwurf für die Verordnung des Ministerrates der RSFSR in GAMO f. R-146, op. 1, d. 6, l. 110 – 122.

158 Vgl. Širokov, Politika, S. 350.

159 Vgl. das Schreiben vom 18. Februar 1954 in RGANI f. 5, op. 27, d. 233, l. 92 – 99.

insgesamt rationaler zu planen, zeigen u. a. die Untersuchungen des Historikers Zeljak. Demnach gab es bis zur Fördersaison des Jahres 1953 in den jeweiligen Jahresplänen von Dal'stroj keinerlei Konzepte oder technische Vorgaben zur Abarbeitung der Goldfelder. Das bedeutet, dass ohne irgendwelche schriftlichen Planungen die von den Geologen gekennzeichneten Bereiche ausgehoben wurden – fand sich darin zu wenig Gold, verlagerte man die Förderung einfach auf das nächste Stück Erde.[160] Man kann sich vorstellen, dass es nach einer solchen Saison kaum möglich war, den jeweiligen Goldgehalt der einzelnen Gebiete nachzuvollziehen.

Auch nach 1953 wich man während der Förderarbeiten auf andere Gebiete aus, wenn die dem Plan nach vorgesehenen Areale zu wenig Gold enthielten. Aber nun wurden diese Verlagerungen als Veränderungen der Planvorgaben nachvollziehbar dokumentiert. Und seit 1957 waren die Anforderungen des Magadaner Volkswirtschaftsrates an die Dokumentation der Vorgehensweise noch einmal höher als unter dem Kombinat Dal'stroj.[161]

Verbesserte Organisation wurde jedoch nicht nur bei Planungen und Dokumentationen verlangt, sondern auch ganz grundsätzlich bei der jährlichen Einteilung der anstehenden Arbeiten. Eine der Hauptforderungen war dabei, den goldhaltigen Sand für die Fördersaison des nächsten Jahres bereits im alten Jahr vorzubereiten. In der Realität musste lange in den Winter hinein Gold gewaschen werden, um die jeweiligen Jahrespläne noch irgendwie zu erfüllen; für eine Vorbereitung des nächsten Jahres blieben weder Zeit noch Kraft. So hangelte man sich von Jahr zu Jahr durch, ohne die Arbeiten auf eine langfristige Planung auszurichten. Čuguev sah die Ursache für diese Arbeitsweise jedoch nicht in den unerbittlichen Planvorgaben, sondern bei den Leitern der Goldgruben und ihren Einstellungen. Auf einer Versammlung des Volkswirtschaftsrates im August 1958 sagte er:

> Bei uns in den Betrieben, bei einigen Arbeitern, hält sich noch so eine Einstellung – wenn es warm ist, muss man unbedingt Gold waschen; wenn es kalt ist, muss man Erdreich abtragen. Sehr viele sprechen davon, dass die Arbeiter von Dal'stroj nicht daran gewöhnt sind, sich mit mehreren Dingen gleichzeitig zu beschäftigen: Gold fördern heißt Gold fördern, Schürfarbeiten heißt Schürfarbeiten, man kann sich nur mit einer Sache beschäftigen. Diese Einstellung ist in der Bergarbeit völlig falsch und schädlich. Jeder von uns soll sich deutlich vor Augen führen, dass in der Bergindustrie Schürfarbeiten, vorbereitende Maßnahmen und Abtragungsarbeiten sehr eng miteinander verbunden sind. [...] Die alten Einstellungen müssen wir unbedingt überwinden.[162]

Das erste Mal gelang die hier geforderte Parallelität der Arbeiten im Jahr 1959. Sicherlich wurde sie durch die guten Ergebnisse in den neuen Fördergebieten erleichtert; auf einmal gab es Luft für Umstrukturierungen. Aber der Volkswirtschaftsrat hatte

---

160 Dies ist typisch für die wirtschaftliche Vorgehensweise des MVD. Vgl Ivanova, Istorija, S. 355 sowie Khlevnyuk, Economy of the OGPU, S. 64.

161 Vgl. Zeljak, Zolotodobyvajuščaja promyšlennost', S. 148f.

162 Vgl. die Mitschrift des Treffens des technisch-wirtschaftlichen Rates des Volkswirtschaftsrates vom 16. August 1958 in GAMO f. R-137, op. 1, d. 59a, l. 51–201, hier l. 57–58.

auch eine neue Arbeitsorganisation und eine große Zahl von sogenannten „Rationalisatoren" eingeführt (mehr als 3.000 Personen), die die Produktion verbessern und den Einsatz neuer Technik vorbereiten sollten. In wichtigen Fördergebieten wurden Arbeitseinheiten spezialisiert, nun gab es z. B. Einrichtungen, die sich ausschließlich mit den Vorbereitungen zum Waschen des Goldes beschäftigten oder mit notwendigen Arbeiten an den Anlagen.[163]

Verstärkte Anstrengungen zur Steigerung der Mechanisierung in Dal'stroj offenbarten zunächst einmal die enorme Rückständigkeit der bisherigen Goldförderung. So wurde darauf gedrungen endlich alle hölzernen Tröge, in denen das Gold gewaschen wurde, durch metallene zu ersetzen, den Abraum sowie den goldhaltigen Sand per Bagger statt per Hand zu transportieren, die Waschanlagen für das Gold zu elektrifizieren und vermehrt Sprengstoff in den Gruben einzusetzen. Außerdem ging es um den Einsatz von riesigen Schwimmbaggern. Diese ruhen auf einer schwimmenden Plattform und graben mit weit unter die Wasseroberfläche reichenden Armen Kies ab.[164] Der Transport und die Aufstellung dieser Bagger stellte Dal'stroj zwar vor logistische Probleme, ihr Einsatz war jedoch so effektiv, dass selbst das ZK der KPdSU und der Ministerrat der UdSSR das Kombinat zu ihrem verstärkten Einsatz verpflichteten. 1956 waren bereits zehn solcher Bagger im Einsatz, 1962 schon bereits sechzehn.[165]

1958 und 1959 konnte für den Mechanisierungsgrad des Volkswirtschaftsrates ein deutlicher Sprung verzeichnet werden.[166] Abraum und Goldsand wurden jetzt vollständig mit Baggern und Bulldozern transportiert. Bei der Waschung des Goldes stieg die Mechanisierung beständig und erreichte in vielen Gebieten 100 %. Dies ging mit einer genaueren Planung der Arbeiten und einem Ausbau der Reparaturwerkstätten für das schwere Gerät einher, so dass nun auch die Schwimmbagger schneller wieder einsatzfähig waren. Unmittelbare Folge war, dass der Bedarf an Arbeitskräften im Jahr

---

163 Vgl. die Erläuterungen zum Jahresbericht 1959 von Korolev und dem Hauptbuchhalter Gol'dšvend in RGAĖ f. 7733, op. 48, d. 492, l. 1–28, hier l. 3.

164 In Deutschland sind diese Schwimmbagger v. a. durch den Einsatz des gewaltigen Baggers „Rheingold" bekannt, mit dem die Nazis zwischen 1939 und 1943 das angebliche Gold des Rheins abgraben wollten. Erbeutet wurden in all dieser Zeit jedoch lediglich 300 Gramm, von denen sich Reichsmarschall Göring einen Ring anfertigen ließ. Vgl. Lepper, Goldwäscherei, S. 48 f. Generell zur Goldgewinnung und -verarbeitung im Dritten Reich siehe Hayes, Degussa.

165 Vgl. Rajzman, SNCH MĖAR, S. 169, sowie Zeljak, Dražnaja zolotodobyča. Eine stolze Beschreibung dieser neuen Technik stellte der stellvertretende Leiter des Kombinats, M. V. Gruša vor, vgl. K 25-letiju, S. 79–99. Die Selbstkosten bei der Goldförderung mit einem Schwimmbagger lagen 1956 bei nur 15,6/ Rubel (insgesamt betrugen sie ca. 25 Rubel). Demgegenüber stand der erhebliche Aufwand, der mit dem Transport der Bagger aus einem Werk in Irkutsk verbunden war. Zudem fehlte es dem Irkutsker Werk zunächst an Materialien und auch dem MCM an Geld. Siehe den Bericht des obersten Kontrolleurs für das Magadaner Gebiet und Dal'stroj, Milovidov, an den Minister für staatliche Kontrolle der UdSSR, Molotov vom 5. April 1957 in GAMO f. R-23ss, op. 1, d. 459, l. 6–13, hier l. 11.

166 Zu den bisherigen Mechanisierungsbemühungen siehe die ausführlichen Angaben zum Jahresergebnis 1956 von Dal'stroj in GAMO f. R-23, op. 1, d. 4897, l. 3–119, hier l. 18–21.

1959 gegenüber dem Jahr 1955 um 30 % gesenkt wurde; immer stärker rückte nun die Ausbildung der Arbeiter in den Vordergrund.[167]

Außerdem verlangte der neue Mechanisierungsgrad nach einer stärkeren wissenschaftlichen Begleitung vor Ort. Das Magadaner Institut VNII-1 war an der Konstruktion passgenauer metallischer Geräte beteiligt, um ganz auf die Waschung von Hand verzichten zu können, entwarf neue Aggregate für die Förderung unter Tage und arbeitete an einem elektrischen Transportsystem für die Loren. Unbenommen dieser Erfolge waren auch weiterhin die Verluste und Unfälle durch unsachgemäße Verwendung und Lagerung der Maschinen hoch; immer wieder stockte zudem die Produktion, weil es an einfachsten Geräten oder technischem Zubehör wie Kabeln mangelte. Es bewahrheitete sich somit auch Ende der 1950er Jahre, dass die Umstellung der Förderung aufgrund der bisherigen Primitivität der Produktion auch dann einen enormen Effekt vorweisen konnte, wenn sie nur teilweise oder nur in bestimmten Bereichen durchgeführt wurde.[168]

Trotz dieser Einschränkung muss davon gesprochen werden, dass die Rolle der Region in dieser Zeit deutlich umdefiniert wurde: Auf einmal wurde sie zum Empfänger einer großen Zahl teurer sowjetischer und internationaler Technik.[169] Auch in Bezug auf die Metallverarbeitung und den Maschinenbau kam es zu einer Umwertung. Waren Dal'stroj diese Industriezweige bisher untersagt worden, um alle Kräfte auf die Förderung der Metalle konzentrieren zu können, so entstanden allein bis 1957 neun Einrichtungen für Maschinenbau und Metallbearbeitung, die meisten davon in der Nähe von Magadan. Sie dienten der weiteren Aufbereitung der Metalle und der Produktion spezialisierter Maschinen für die Rohstoffförderung.[170]

Ein großer Effekt wurde auch dem Einsatz von Goldgräbern nachgesagt. Im Prinzip wurden damit kapitalistische Bedingungen zugelassen, denn man gestattete Privatpersonen, selbstständig Gold zu schürfen und es an den Staat zu verkaufen.[171] Formal gab es für diesen eigentlich ungeheuerlichen Vorgang strenge Regelungen: Eine offizielle Genehmigung des ZK der KPdSU und des Ministerrates der UdSSR erlaubte es den Leitern der einzelnen Wirtschaftsverwaltungen, Gebiete, in denen die staatliche Förderung bereits eingestellt worden war oder die aufgrund ihrer geringen

---

167 Vgl. die Angabe aus der Abteilung für Löhne des Volkswirtschaftsrates in GAMO f. R-137, op. 1, d. 1007ž, l. 1–11, hier l. 4.

168 Auch die Ergebnisse bei der Erzeugung von elektrischer Energie waren sehr viel besser und unterstützten die Mechanisierungsbestrebungen. Vgl. die Erläuterungen zum Jahresbericht 1959 von Korolev und dem Hauptbuchhalter Gol'dšvend in RGAĖ f. 7733, op. 48, d. 492, l. 1–28, hier l. 3, l. 8 sowie l. 10–13. Siehe die ausführliche Darstellung der Mechanisierung in verschiedenen Industriebereichen bei Rajzman, SNCH MĖAR, S. 167.

169 Vgl. Zeljak, Zolotodobyvajuščaja promyšlennost', S. 143. Ausführlich zur Entwicklung des Energiesektors in dieser Zeit siehe Širokov, Politika, S. 401 f.

170 Vgl. Rajzman, SNCH MĖAR, S. 156 sowie Šilo/Potemkin, Valjutnyj cech, S. 82 f.

171 Goldgräber hatte es in Dal'stroj bis 1933 gegeben, sie wurden dann durch die Häftlingsarbeit ersetzt. Eine weitere Initiative zu ihrer Verwendung im Jahr 1949 wurde von Moskau verboten. Vgl. Zeljak, Zolotodobyvajuščaja promyšlennost', S. 150.

Größe für den Staat nicht rentabel waren, einzelnen Goldgräbern oder ganzen Goldgräberartels zur Verfügung zu stellen. Zudem wurden diese Personen vom Kombinat mit den notwendigen Informationen zu den Gebieten sowie Materialien ausgerüstet.[172]

Die Beurteilung dieser Fördermethode durch die Verantwortlichen war sehr unterschiedlich. Dal'stroj führte immer wieder die sehr niedrigen Selbstkosten an, zudem übertrafen die Ergebnisse die Erwartungen des Kombinats erheblich. Statt der zunächst veranschlagten halben Tonne förderten Goldgräber im Jahr 1956 insgesamt 2,4 Tonnen chemisch reines Gold, das waren 6,2 % der gesamten Fördermenge von Dal'stroj.[173] 1959 lag ihr Anteil bereits bei 13,5 %.[174]

Externe Kontrollen offenbarten aber auch, dass die Arbeit der Goldgräber massive Unterschlagungen und Veruntreuungen ermöglichten und dass die Organisation dieser Förderung nicht immer den Intentionen der Partei- und Staatsführung entsprach: Nach einem Bericht des obersten Kontrolleurs für das Magadaner Gebiet und Dal'stroj des Ministeriums für staatliche Kontrolle der UdSSR, Milovidov, wurden Genehmigungen zu Goldgräber-Einsätzen nie an ganze Artels, sondern nur an Einzelpersonen und dann auch nur in bestimmten Gruben ausgegeben (insgesamt ca. 3.000). Immer wieder kam es vor, dass die Leiter der Gruben sich selbst oder den verantwortlichen Geologen die Genehmigungen erteilten; Berechtigungsscheine erhielten pikanterweise gerade auch die Arbeiter, die bei der Analyse, der Waschung und dem Transport des Goldes eingesetzt waren. Selbst Häftlingen wurde diese Arbeit gestattet. Bei der Festsetzung der Einsatzorte wurden Gebiete für die Goldgräber geöffnet, die noch zur Bilanz der Grube zählten, und Gebiete, die sich in unmittelbarer Nachbarschaft zu staatlichen Förderstellen befanden. Zum Teil hätten die Goldgräber einfach den Sand noch einmal gewaschen, der von der staatlichen Förderung übrig blieb.

Der Kontrolleur Milovidov sprach von enormen Geldzahlungen an Privatleute für Gold von „sehr zweifelhafter Herkunft". 7 bis 10 Rubel pro Gramm sei in Dal'stroj für abgeliefertes Gold gezahlt worden, und trotz dieser geringen Preise hätten einige Goldsucher schier unglaubliche Summen verdient. Die Gattin eines Bergbaumeisters der Grube „Bol'ševik" habe beispielsweise allein in den Monaten August-Oktober des

---

172 Zu der Vorgehensweise siehe das Schreiben des stellv. Ministers für Buntmetalle, Šemjakin, an Čuguev vom 29. Mai 1957 in GAMO f. R-23sč, op. 1, d. 458, l. 47–48, hier l. 48.

173 Für das Jahr 1956 waren die Selbstkosten bei den Goldgräbern erheblich niedriger als die der staatlichen Förderung; sie lagen bei ca. 15 Rubel im Vergleich zu den geplanten knapp 24 Rubel der allgemeinen Arbeiten. Vgl. die Übersicht in einem Bericht von Berezin vom 19. März 1957 in GAMO f. R-23, op. 1, d. 6109, l. 2–12, hier l. 7. Siehe dazu auch den Schriftverkehr des Volkswirtschaftsrates mit dem Finanzministerium vom November 1957 in GAMO f. R-137sč, op. 1b, d. 18, l. 8 sowie GAMO f. R-137sč, op. 1b, d. 20, l. 3–3ob. Vgl. die Übersicht des Kombinats über die Goldgräberarbeit im Jahr 1956 nach den einzelnen Fördergebieten in GAMO f. R-23, op. 1, d. 6109, l. 54.

174 Vgl. Grebenjuk, Kolymskij led, S. 200, der sich bei dieser Angabe auf die Mitschrift der 5. Gebietsparteikonferenz stützt. Im Rahmen des Volkswirtschaftsrates sah man vor, diese Förderweise auf 5 Tonnen im Jahr 1965 und 7,5 Tonnen im Jahr 1970 anzuheben. Siehe die Prognose von Korolev über den Goldabbau bis zum Jahre 1970 vom November 1957 in GAMO f. R-137sč, op. 1b, d. 13, l. 21–23.

Jahres 1956 2.271 g Gold abgeliefert und dafür 22.700 Rubel erhalten. Ein anderer Goldgräber, der früher mit der Erstellung geographischer Karten von goldhaltigen Gebieten betraut gewesen sei, konnte 3.752 g vorweisen und erhielt dafür 37.500 Rubel.[175]

Während also für Dal'stroj diese Vorgehensweise erfolgreich war – schließlich verbesserte sie die Bilanzen des Kombinats erheblich –, verstärkte sie die Möglichkeiten für einzelne Verwaltungsleiter, die Betriebszahlen zu modellieren und sich durch Unterschlagungen zu bereichern. Aufgrund der niedrigeren Selbstkosten wurde jedoch auch im Rahmen des Volkswirtschaftsrates an dieser Fördermethode festgehalten, der Anteil der Goldgräberarbeiten lag im Durchschnitt bei etwa 12 % der jährlichen Fördermenge.[176]

4.3.3 Geologen und Wissenschaften

Die nordöstlichen Geologen trugen zu allen Zeiten eine gewaltige Verantwortung, stellten sie doch die entscheidenden Weichen für die territoriale und inhaltliche Ausrichtung der Arbeit; von ihren Prognosen und Plänen waren alle Investitionen des Zentrums abhängig. Zugleich konnten sie einzelnen Produktionsleitern durch zutreffende Prognosen zu gigantischen Planungserfolgen verhelfen. Staatliche Prämien und Preise, die für die Entdeckung von besonders guten Lagerstätten gezahlt wurden, waren immer wieder Ziel von Unterschlagungen und Korruption, an ihnen wollte sich auch die Kombinatsleitung bereichern. Gleichzeitig drohte den Geologen im Stalinismus ständig die Verhaftung, sollten sich ihre Einschätzungen als nicht zutreffend erweisen.[177] Dementsprechend bestand die erste Erleichterung nach der Verhaftung Berijas darin, dass alle Geologen von juristischen Anklagen freigesprochen wurden. Doch auch nach 1953 standen sie unter besonderer Beobachtung.[178]

In organisatorischer Hinsicht existierte in Dal'stroj seit 1939 eine geologische Schürfverwaltung (GRU), die alle Geologenteams in den einzelnen Abteilungen vereinte.[179] Ihre Arbeiten wurden von der sowjetischen Regierung mit beständig steigenden Zuwendungen bedacht, vor allem in den Kriegsjahren sorgte der hohe Bedarf

---

175 Vgl. den Bericht des obersten Kontrolleurs für das Magadaner Gebiet und Dal'stroj, Milovidov, an den Minister für staatliche Kontrolle der UdSSR, Molotov, vom 5. April 1957 in GAMO f. R-23ss, op. 1, d. 459, l. 6 – 13, hier l. 12. Milovidov verwies auch auf Materialien der Magadaner Verwaltung des MVD, die belegten, dass die Missbrauchsfälle nach Einführung der Goldgräberarbeiten erheblich gestiegen seien.
176 Vgl. Zeljak, Zolotodobyvajuščaja promyšlennost', S. 150 f.
177 Vgl. Mick, Wissenschaft, S. 340.
178 Vgl. die Erinnerungen des damaligen Leiters des lokalen Forschungsinstituts VNII-1, N. A. Šilo. Šilo, Vse zoloto Kolymy, S. 22 und zu den drohenden Verhaftungen im Stalinismus, S. 20.
179 1940 wurde eine erste Forschungsstation in Form eines Labors (CNILDS) gegründet, die grundlegende Fördermöglichkeiten für die konkreten Gegebenheiten in der Region erarbeiten sollte. Vgl. Malagin, Ėkonomičeskij rajon, S. 47.

an Gold und Zinn für große Investitionen und für die Errichtung einzelner wissenschaftlicher Abteilungen. Im Juli 1948 gründete der NKVD im Rahmen seiner eigenen Strukturen ein eigenständiges wissenschaftliches Institut in Magadan, das VNII-1 („Vsesojuznyj Naučno-Issledovatel'skij Institut Zolota i Redkich Metallov – Wissenschaftliches Allunionsforschungsinstitut für Gold und seltene Metalle") unter Leitung des Geologen S. P. Aleksandrov. Es war Teil des streng geheimen Atomprojekts und sollte der Erforschung der Kolymaer Uranvorkommen dienen, dehnte seine Tätigkeit jedoch bald auch auf andere Metalle aus, v. a. auf die Koordination geologischer Untersuchungen zur Goldförderung.[180]

Das größte Problem des Institutes bestand im Mangel an akademischem Personal. Es gab nur sehr wenige freie Angestellte mit einem akademischen Grad, viele hatten nicht einmal eine abgeschlossene höhere Bildung. Vor dem Hintergrund der gewaltigen Aufgaben, vor denen die Magadaner Geologen standen, und angesichts des grundsätzlich hohen Niveaus der geologischen Wissenschaften im zaristischen Russland und in der Sowjetunion war das besonders dramatisch. Geologen profitierten im Allgemeinen von guten Auslandskontakten und einem intensiven Austausch – alles Vorteile, die in Dal'stroj nicht zum Tragen kommen konnten.[181] Gewissermaßen zum Ausgleich wurde eine Reihe bekannter Fachleute, die an der Kolyma in Haft oder als Sondersiedler waren, zur Arbeit im VNII-1 und dabei auch zur Mitarbeit an dem streng geheimen Atomprojekt gezwungen. Sehr viele von ihnen waren einer großangelegten Verfolgung von Geologen im Jahr 1949 zum Opfer gefallen. Bei ihnen muss davon ausgegangen werden, dass sie eigens zur Verwendung in

---

180 Vgl. Žulanova, Akademičeskaja geologija, S. 18. Zum Atomprojekt unter Berija siehe Beyrau, Intelligenz, S. 120. Das bis dahin bestehende Labor wurde damit aufgelöst. Das Institut nahm seine eigentliche Arbeit im Jahr 1949 auf. Vgl. Tolokonceva/Kozlov, U istokov nauki, S. 148 sowie Žulanova, Akademičeskaja geologija, S. 18. Das besondere Profil dieses Institutes wird bereits an der Karriere seines ersten Direktors deutlich. Aleksandrov hatte bereits in den 1930er Jahren an Expertenkommissionen zur Kolyma teilgenommen, 1940 wurde er zum stellv. Leiter der Verwaltung für Bergbau- und Metallindustrie des GULAG ernannt, ein Jahr später zum leitenden Ingenieur der Hauptverwaltung der Lager für Bergbau und Metallförderung. In dieser Zeit erhielt er zahlreiche Auszeichnungen. Seine Ernennung zum Leiter des VNII-1 beruhte somit nicht so sehr auf seinen wissenschaftlichen Erkenntnissen oder Verdiensten, sondern vielmehr auf der Tatsache, dass er seine Karriere im Rahmen des NKVD gemacht hatte. Wie sehr ihm vertraut wurde, zeigt sich an seinen zahlreichen Auslandsaufenthalten, darunter in den USA und in Deutschland. 1946–1947 war er in den USA und nahm dort an den Atombombenversuchen auf den Bikini-Inseln teil. In der Folge war er einer der Leiter des Atomprojektes an der Kolyma. Nachfolger Aleksandrovs wurde N. A. Šilo, der das Institut Anfang der 1950er Jahre schon einmal geleitet hatte. Tolokonceva und Kozlov nennen als Ursache für den Leitungswechsel den schlechten Gesundheitszustand Aleksandrovs. Es ist jedoch auffällig, dass ihm seine Invalidität Ende Dezember 1953 attestiert wurde, nur wenige Wochen nach der Gebietsgründung und dem Verlust des Sonderstatus von Dal'stroj. Vgl. Tolokonceva/Kozlov, U istokov nauki. Siehe auch Vasil'eva, Nauka Dal'nego Vostoka.

181 Vgl. zur Lage der Geologie Mick, Wissenschaft, S. 340.

Dal'stroj oder einem ähnlichen Zwangsarbeiterprojekt verhaftet worden waren. Wissenschaftliche Forschung in Dal'stroj lebte zu großen Teilen von Häftlingen.[182]

Das VNII-1 hatte die Aufgabe, die Arbeiten des Kombinats wissenschaftlich zu begleiten. Es war ausgerichtet auf die Lösung konkreter Fragestellungen und Anforderungen – auf die Arbeit im Permafrostboden, auf die Produktion besonderer technischer Anlagen und Baumaterialien ebenso wie auf die Erforschung der im Kombinat geförderten Metalle. Diesen Zuschnitt behielt das VNII-1 auch in den 1960er und 1970er Jahren bei – die unterschiedlichen Anforderungen an die Metallförderung im Wandel der Zeit lassen sich deshalb auch an den einzelnen Abteilungen des Institutes ablesen: 1959 gründete man eine eigene Abteilung für Mechanisierung und Automatisierung der Produktion, 1962 kam eine Abteilung für ökonomische Forschungen hinzu, die den Forderungen nach sinkenden Selbstkosten und einer steigenden Wirtschaftlichkeit der Produktion gerecht werden sollte.[183]

Der geologische Schürfdienst selbst hatte in der Nachkriegszeit die Untersuchung von Zinnvorkommen massiv ausgebaut.[184] Hinzu kam seit 1948 die neue Suche nach Uranvorkommen, die von der Regierung im beginnenden Kalten Krieg forciert wurde. Diese Neuausrichtung blieb Anfang der 1950er Jahre und im Rahmen der spätstalinistischen Strukturkrise nicht ohne Auswirkung auf die Suche nach Gold.

Zu Beginn der 1950er Jahre sank die finanzielle Ausstattung, Schürfarbeiten für Gold fanden hauptsächlich im Rahmen bereits bestehender Förderanlagen statt, in bisher nicht erschlossenen Gebieten wurde immer weniger gesucht. Diese Orientierung folgte den neuesten Beschlüssen der Regierung, die Schürfarbeiten bewusst an bereits bestehender Infrastruktur ausrichten wollte, um so Kosten zu sparen. Dadurch

---

182 Zur Geschichte des VNII-1 auf der Basis neuer Archivmaterialien siehe Surnina, Iz istorii instituta. Grundsätzlich zu Repressionen gegen Geologen siehe Repressirovannye geologi sowie Mick, Wissenschaft, S. 340–348. Trotz der derartigen Anlage des Instituts bestreitet Šilo die Existenz einer echten „Šaraška" an der Kolyma, einer Lagerabteilung, in der verhaftete Fachleute, z. T. berühmte Koryphäen, zur Arbeit an einem speziellen Projekt gezwungen wurden. Selbst im Jahr 2006 behauptete er noch, Häftlinge wären den freien Mitarbeitern vollkommen gleichgestellt gewesen. Grundsätzlich verharmlost Šilo die Arbeitsbedingungen und den Terror von Dal'stroj in erschreckender Weise. Vgl. Šilo, Vse zoloto Kolymy, S. 22. Siehe zur Geschichte der Wissenschaft unter Dal'stroj auch Simakov/Gončarov, Akademičeskaja nauka. Von einer Gruppe bekannter Geologen, die in Moskau verhaftet und mit einem speziellen Flugzeug an die Kolyma gebracht worden war, handelt auch eine Erzählung Šalamovs, die den Umgang mit den Fachkräften (wahrscheinlich für den Uranabbau) anschaulich schildert. Vgl. Schalamow, Linkes Ufer, S. 26–32. Zur Verhaftung sowjetischer Wissenschaftler und der Ausbeutung ihrer „intellektuellen Zwangsarbeit" siehe Jersak, Rüstungsforschung; Mick, Wissenschaft; Beyrau, Intelligenz, S. 119–122.
183 Vgl. Tolonceva/Kozlov, U istokov nauki, S. 153.
184 Das Gebietsparteikomitee spricht in diesem Zusammenhang von einer „traurigen Erfahrung": Die Schürfverwaltung hätte die Suche nach Zinn massiv ausgebaut und sehr viele neue Vorkommen entdeckt; wegen fehlender Investitionen seien jedoch längst nicht all diese Stellen auch erschlossen worden. Vgl. den Bericht des Gebietsparteikomitees vom April 1957 an das ZK der KPdSU im Vorfeld der Einrichtung des Magadaner Volkswirtschaftsrates in GAMO f. R-23, op. 1, d. 6088, l. 1–50, hier l. 29 f. Zu den Ergebnissen der Zinnförderung siehe Širokov, Politika, S. 348.

ergab sich eine Art von Teufelskreis, da die eingeschränkte Suche nach Gold es immer weniger erlaubte, neue Gebiete zu entdecken – weniger neu nachgewiesene Vorkommen führten wiederum zu einer Beschneidung der Schürfarbeiten nach Gold und zu einer allmählichen Umorientierung auf andere Metalle.[185]

Dieser Rückgang setzte sich nach Gründung des Gebietes fort. Die Suche nach Gold wurde immer schlechter finanziert, und das Gebietsparteikomitee konstatierte einen miserablen Zustand der geologischen Schürfverwaltung. Man zeigte sich entsetzt, wie vernachlässigt die Abteilung des Kombinats wurde, die über die Zukunft des Gebietes entscheiden sollte. Im Rahmen dieser Beurteilung kam auch ein brisanter Fall von persönlicher Bereicherung zutage, der das Verhältnis zwischen dem Gebietsparteikomitee und der Leitung der Schürfverwaltung sicherlich nicht verbesserte.[186] Zudem waren die neuen politisch Verantwortlichen in der ersten Zeit machtlos gegenüber einer allgemeinen Stimmung unter den obersten Leitungskadern, die als „Theorie vom Versiegen der Kolyma" bekannt wurde. Diese Einschätzung verband sich mit dem politischen Umbruch und der Auflösung des Sonderstatus von Dal'stroj – für die alten *Dal'strojevcy* versiegten mit dem Ende der Ära des Kombinats buchstäblich auch die Bodenschätze. Neben dem Fluss Kolyma, auf dessen natürlichen Reichtum sie die Eroberung des Nordostens gebaut hatten, konnte es in ihrer Vorstellung keine weiteren aussichtsreichen Gebiete mehr geben. Umso stärker mag da die Tendenz gewesen sei, auch angesichts der neuen politischen Leitung die letzten „Ressourcen" aus dem alten Projekt Dal'stroj zu holen.[187]

Wegen der sinkenden Goldreserven drang Mitrakov auf eine Stärkung der Zinnförderung, obwohl die Sowjetunion durch die chinesische Produktion immer weniger auf eigenen Zinnabbau angewiesen war.[188] Die Kombinatsleitung hielt sogar an dieser Einschätzung fest, als eine Expedition zum Fluss Anjuj 1955 hohe Goldvorkommen in Tschukotka feststellte. An diesem Punkt schritten jedoch verschiedene unionsweite

---

185 Von allen Schürfparteien, die für die Jahre 1951–1955 geplant wurden (insgesamt 725), wurde nur ein Sechstel in bisher nicht erschlossene, neue Gebiete geschickt. Vgl. Bacaev, Osobennosti, S. 130. Siehe dort auch zu den strukturellen Veränderungen in der geologischen Schürfverwaltung von Dal'stroj in dieser Zeit.

186 Das Gebietsparteikomitee ließ den Schürfdienst zweimal durch den Leiter seiner Wirtschaftsabteilung, Golubev, untersuchen, der sehr umfangreiche Berichte erstellte. In ihnen kritisierte Golubev u. a. eine miserable Arbeitsweise, mangelnde Planerfüllung, eine viel zu geringe Mechanisierung und mangelnde Fürsorge für die Mitarbeiter des Dienstes. Vgl. seinen Bericht vom 12. November 1954 in GAMO f. P-21, op. 5, d. 14, l. 23–42 sowie seine Stellungnahme vom 22. März 1955 in GAMO f. P-21, op. 5, d. 14, l. 43–72. Siehe ausführlich zum Verhältnis zwischen Gebietsparteikomitee und dieser Dal'stroj-Abteilung das Kapitel 3.3.2.

187 Siehe beispielsweise die Erinnerungen bei Drabkin, Razvedčiki nedr, S. 101 sowie das Interview mit dem früheren Parteisekretär Kaštanov in Grebenjuk, Kolymskij led, S. 235.

188 Zum 1. Januar 1955 bezifferte Mitrakov die Zinnvorkommen im Gebiet von Dal'stroj auf 117.000 Tonnen Zinn hoher Qualität. Vgl. die ausführliche Stellungnahme Mitrakovs vom 15. März 1955 an das ZK der KPdSU in GAMO f. R-23, op. 1, d. 5610, l. 55–64, hier l. 57 f. Siehe für eine Beschreibung des Zinnbaus in den 1950er Jahren Šilo/Potemkin, Valjutnyj cech strany, S. 75.

Institutionen ein und machten Einflüsse des machtpolitischen Zentrums in Moskau geltend:

Zunächst war es eine Gruppe von Wissenschaftlern der Akademie der Wissenschaften der UdSSR, die sich im August 1955 unter der Leitung von D. I. Ščerbakov nachdrücklich gegen oberflächliche Untersuchungen und für eine Ausweitung der geologischen Schürfarbeiten in Tschukotka aussprach.[189] Tatsächlich aber wurden 1956 die Investitionen in den Schürfdienst noch nicht erhöht, weiterhin konzentrierte man sich auf bereits erschlossenes Territorium. Ein echtes Umdenken setzte erst im Rahmen der Diskussionen über den großen 15-Jahrplan für Dal'stroj ein, mit dem der Ministerrat der UdSSR das MCM bereits im März 1956 beauftragt hatte.[190]

Ganz im Sinne der Chruščev'schen Anstrengungen, die Bedeutung von Experten und Spezialisten bei wichtigen Sachentscheidungen gegenüber dem Apparat zu stärken, wurde nun eine Kommission eingesetzt, deren Mitglieder zwar aus den staatlichen Strukturen stammten, die aber so breit aufgestellt war, dass sie eine pragmatischere Sicht auf die Region und ihr Entwicklungspotential erhoffen ließ, die nicht von regionalen Machtansprüchen dominiert wurde.[191] Die Kommission von *Gosplan* und der staatlichen Wirtschaftskommission der UdSSR, unter Einbezug von Dal'stroj, allen beteiligten Ministerien und der lokalen Organe von Partei und Staat, überprüfte auf Grundlage dieses Planes im Sommer 1956 ausführlich die Perspektiven der Region und kam zu dem Schluss, dass eine Reihe von Veränderungen bei den Schürfarbeiten dringend erforderlich seien. Die Goldförderung sei gegenüber allen anderen Rohstoffen deutlich zu stärken, die Zinnförderung zu begrenzen und die Suche nach weiteren Metallen, wie z. B. Titan, stark herunterzufahren. Zudem sei die materielle und technische Ausstattung aller geologischen Organisationen in der Region zu verbessern. In struktureller Hinsicht forderte man eine territoriale Aufteilung der geologischen Verwaltung von Dal'stroj, um die Arbeiten besser bewältigen zu können. Die Gebiete des Magadaner Gebietes und der jakutischen ASSR sollten jeweils einer geologischen Verwaltung des Ministeriums für Geologie und Bodenschätze unterstellt werden.[192]

Tatsächlich wurden 1957 zwei neue geologische Organisationen gegründet. Im März 1957 schuf man die vorgeschlagene Nordöstliche geologische Verwaltung (SVGU) des Ministeriums für Geologie und Bodenschätze der UdSSR und im Juli 1957 den geologischen Schürfdienst der Bergbauverwaltung des Volkswirtschaftsrates.[193] Was

---

189 Vgl. Kozlov, Sostojanie geologičeskoj služby, S. 96.

190 Am 16. März 1956 verpflichtete der Ministerrat der UdSSR das MCM, einen Plan über die perspektivische Entwicklung von Dal'stroj in den Jahren 1956 bis 1970 vorzulegen. Vgl. GAMO f. R-23, op. 1, d. 5861, l. 1–71, hier l. 38. Der riesige Plan, bestehend aus sieben Großkapiteln, mit allen Anhängen findet sich in GAMO f. R-23, op. 1, d. 5846–5854, sowie die Anmerkungen in d. 5940.

191 Zur Rolle von Experten unter Chruščev siehe Tompson, Leadership Transition, S. 219.

192 Vgl. Kozlov, Sostojanie geologičeskoj služby, S. 99.

193 Vgl. den Übergabeakt von Dal'stroj an das Ministerium für Geologie und Bodenschätze in GAMO f. R-137, op. 1, d. 726, l. 2–9. In Analogie dazu entstand die jakutische geologische Verwaltung des Mi-

zunächst als Parallelismus erscheint, erweist sich bei näherer Betrachtung jedoch als Versuch des Zentrums, die alltäglichen geologischen Aufgaben bei den einzelnen Goldgruben (dies übernahm der Dienst des Volkswirtschaftsrates) von den Arbeiten zu trennen, die auf langfristige Perspektiven ausgerichtet waren und die so zentral überwacht werden konnten. Obwohl sich das Gebietsparteikomitee selbst gegen diese Aufteilung wehrte und sich bemühte, sie im Rahmen der Einführung des Volkswirtschaftsrates wieder rückgängig zu machen, hielt das Zentrum bewusst an dem großen Einfluss des Ministeriums in der Region fest.[194] Der erste Leiter der geologischen Verwaltung des Ministeriums für Geologie und Bodenschätze, I. E. Drabkin, beschrieb das Profil seiner Organisation im Rückblick folgendermaßen:

> Diese Maßnahme [die Aufteilung der Organisationen – M. S.] schuf die Möglichkeit, die Investitionen, die Masse der Arbeiten und das Tempo der geologischen Untersuchungen unter Einbezug des gesamten Territoriums des Gebietes deutlich zu steigern. Die Geologen bekamen die Chance, in die Weite des Raumes vorzustoßen, die Flanken der goldhaltigen Zonen und bisher nicht erforschte Gebiete zu erfassen. Dies führte zu neuen bedeutenden Entdeckungen. Die Qualität der geologischen Arbeiten stieg erheblich an. Auch in wissenschaftlicher Hinsicht wurde das Arbeitsprofil der Geologen breiter und vielfältiger.[195]

Sowohl diese organisatorischen Veränderungen als auch die steigenden Investitionen zahlten sich in den Augen der Verantwortlichen sehr schnell aus – bereits 1957 konnten die Geologen erste entscheidende Entdeckungen neuer Goldlagerstätten im westlichen Tschukotka (im später entstehenden Bezirk Bilibin) machen, denen in den folgenden Jahren weitere folgten. In seinem Schreiben an das ZK der KPdSU konnte der damalige Erste Parteisekretär verkünden:

> In der Zeit, die seit Erarbeitung des technisch-ökonomischen Vortrags [gemeint ist der 15-Jahrplan von Dal'stroj – M. S.] vergangen ist, infolge der Ausführung von geologischen Schürfarbeiten, haben sich grundlegende Veränderungen bei der Bewertung der Rohstoffbasis des Magadaner Gebietes in Bezug auf Gold ergeben. Ihre prognostizierten Ressourcen liegen jetzt bei 1.996 Tonnen, gegenüber den bisherigen 1.440 Tonnen. Es wurden erhebliche Arbeiten in neuen goldhaltigen Gebieten, Čaunskij und Anjujskij, vorgenommen, sie werden in Zukunft zu den größten der in der UdSSR in den letzten Jahren eröffneten Gebiete gezählt werden können.[196]

---

nisteriums für Geologie und Bodenschätze der UdSSR. Vgl. Rajzman, Geologorazvedočnaja dejatel'nost', S. 178.

194 Zwei Drittel der Geologen im Nordosten unterstanden nun dem Ministerium. Vgl. den Bericht des Gebietsparteikomitees im Vorfeld der Einführung des Magadaner Volkswirtschaftsrates an das ZK der KPdSU in GAMO f. P-23, op. 1, d. 6088, l. 1–50, hier l. 27 f.

195 Drabkin, Razvedčiki nedr, S. 102 f.

196 Diese Veränderungen haben Eingang in den neuen Siebenjahrplan (1958 bis 1965) erhalten. Siehe das Schreiben von Ababkov an das ZK der KPdSU vom 10. November 1957 in GAMO f. R-137sč, op. 1b, d. 11, l. 106–109, hier l. 107 f. Die Prognosen bezogen sich nur auf die bereits durch Schürfarbeiten erkundeten Goldvorkommen. Insgesamt vermutete man 1957 Goldvorkommen in der Region von 2.493 Tonnen. Vgl. den Bericht des Gebietsparteikomitees in GAMO f. R-23, op. 1, d. 6088, l. 1–50, hier l. 13. Siehe die Aufforderung des Leiters der Bergbauverwaltung an Čuguev, die entsprechenden Vorarbeiten

В эти дни молодые сеймчанские геологи заняты обработкой материалов полевых партий.
НА СНИМКЕ (слева направо): комсомольцы — старший коллектор Э. ШЛОТГАУЭР, геолог И. ШАШУРИНА и начальник партии А. РАДЗИ-ВИЛЛ обсуждают геологические данные золотоносного района.
Фото Б. Сергеева.

Abb. 34 Junge Geologen aus dem Bezirk Sejmčan, Magadanskaja Pravda, 29. Oktober 1958

Eine entscheidende Rolle spielte bei diesen Entdeckungen die junge und enthusiastische geologische Schürfabteilung des Bezirkes Sejmčan unter der Leitung von K. A. Ivanov, die sich mit ihren Untersuchungen gegen die vorherrschende Politik der Kombinatsleitung wandte; sie stellte die Suche nach anderen Metallen ein und konzentrierte all ihre Kräfte auf die Entdeckung neuer Goldvorkommen. Zur Finanzierung dieser Arbeiten hatte sie sich, unter Umgehung der Kombinatsleitung, direkt an das Ministerium für Geologie und Bodenschätze gewandt.[197] Hier waren es tatsächlich die „Experten" und „Pragmatiker", die sich im besten Chruščev'schen Sinne über Machtansprüche und die lokalen Animositäten von Dal'stroj hinwegsetzten und allein für „die Sache" kämpften.[198]

In der Folge konnte die Magadaner Parteileitung dem ZK der KPdSU für das Jahr 1965 einen Ertrag von 43 Tonnen und damit fast 40 % mehr Gold als das Jahresergebnis von 1957 versprechen – tatsächlich erreichte man schließlich schon im Jahr 1961 44 Tonnen. Zugleich machte Ababkov bei seiner Prognose auch deutlich, dass diese Rohstoffmengen nur durch erhebliche Investitionen des Zentrums in der Region

und Baumaßnahmen in diesem Gebiet voranzutreiben in GAMO f. R-137sč, op. 1b, d. 34, l. 27–28. Zu den weiteren Plänen des Magadaner Volkswirtschaftsrates siehe die Prognose von Korolev über den Goldabbau bis zum Jahre 1970 vom November 1957 in GAMO f. R-137sč, op. 1b, d. 13, l. 21–23.

197 Vgl. Palymskij, Sejmčanskoe RajGRU.

198 Vgl. Ian Thatchers Beschreibung Chruščevs als „constantly intrigued by real-worl-solutions to real-world-problems". Thatcher, Khrushchev, S. 23.

zu erreichen seien, er sprach von mehr als dem Doppelten der bisher veranschlagten Summen.[199] Das Zentrum entschied sich aufgrund dieser Aussichten für eine massive Ausweitung seiner Investitionen in der Region. Denn eine erfolgreiche „Valutazeche" im Nordosten war für die gesamte Wirtschaft der Sowjetunion von allzu großer Bedeutung – auf das Gold des Magadaner Gebietes war man einfach angewiesen. Die Anstrengungen des Zentrums werteten die beiden geologischen Verwaltungen auch personell auf. 1959 waren 7 % aller Arbeiter des Magadaner Gebietes bei den Schürfabteilungen tätig, zudem waren die finanziellen Investitionen für die Geologen so hoch wie in keinem anderen Gebiet der UdSSR. [200]

Ab Ende der 1950er Jahre wurden die Arbeiten vor Ort in eine neue Perspektive eingebettet, die das Moskauer Zentrum für den gesamten arktischen Raum der Sowjetunion entwickelte.[201] Der Hohe Norden, so Paul Josephson, sollte auf der Grundlage wissenschaftlicher Erkenntnisse und mit erheblichem Technikeinsatz, aber ohne die Struktur von Lager-Industriellen Komplexen, erschlossen und effektiv ausgebeutet werden:

> Engineers began to consider the uniqueness of Arctic climate and resources in a less resolute way only in the Khrushchev era, not the least because of the disbanding of the gulag, but also because of the reforms that led to greater autonomy for specialists and because of the establishment of branch research institutes located in the Arctic and sub-Arctic that focused on local problems.[202]

Bei der Suche nach einer alternativen Eroberungsform stand die sowjetische Führung dabei nicht nur vor großen ökonomischen und infrastrukturellen Problemen – zunächst einmal musste sie ihr Informationsdefizit auf den verschiedenen Gebieten schließen und Kenntnisse über die besonderen wirtschaftlichen Bedingungen und Bedürfnisse des Nordens sammeln; in diesem Stadium spielten die lokalen Leitungen in den einzelnen Regionen eine wichtige Rolle.[203]

---

199 So müssten in dem nächsten Siebenjahrplan etwa die Summen eingesetzt werden (4,9 Milliarden Rubel), die bisher für den gesamten 15-Jahrplan veranschlagt worden waren. Vgl. das Schreiben von Ababkov an das ZK der KPdSU vom 10. November 1957 in GAMO f. R-137sč, op. 1b, d. 11, l. 106–109, hier l. 108.

200 Die Geologen-Sektion des Ministeriums für Geologie und Bodenschätze bezeichnete das Gold für die Sowjetunion als „Valuta-Kraft". Vgl. die Beschreibung des Vorsitzenden der Sektion vom 12. April 1959 in GAMO f. R-137sč, op. 1b, d. 52, l. 47–62, hier l. 62. Auf diesen Umstand verwies Ababkov auch ganz offen in seinem Schreiben an das ZK der KPdSU, vgl. GAMO f. R-137sč, op. 1b, d. 11, l. 108. Siehe zu den Investitionen des Zentrums in den Magadaner Schürfdienst Slavin, Promyšlennoe osvoenie, S. 242. Zugleich gingen mit diesen Investitionen Kürzungen in anderen Bereichen einher, so z. B. bei der Kohleförderung, die zugunsten des Goldes stark reduziert wurde. Vgl. Rajzman, SNCH MĚAR, S. 165.

201 Dieses Gebiet wurde als „Sovetskij Sever" bezeichnet. Zu den verschiedenen Regionen und ihren Bezeichnungen („Ferner und Näherer Norden", „Asiatischer Norden" etc.) siehe Slavin, Promyšlennoe osvoenie, S. 7.

202 Josephson, Soviet Arctic, S. 421. Siehe zur Ausweitung der Institute ebd., S. 426.

203 Siehe die „Beratungen über den Norden" im ZK der KPdSU im Herbst 1956 in RGANI f. 5, op. 32, d. 59, l. 64–67. Damit sollten die bisherigen Anstrengungen des „Komitees des Nordens" beim Ministerrat

Eines der Instrumente, derer sie sich dabei bediente, war die Akademie der Wissenschaften der UdSSR.[204] 1958 organisierte diese eine Konferenz zu den „Produktivkräften des Östlichen Sibiriens", in die die Magadaner Region miteingeschlossen wurde, 1959 dann eine eigene, sehr breit angelegte Konferenz für das Magadaner Gebiet, an der zahlreiche Wissenschaftler aus wissenschaftlichen Zentren der Union teilnahmen. Die Zeitung *Magadanskaja Pravda* begleitete das Ereignis mit einer ausführlichen Berichterstattung.[205] Die Konferenzen hatten die Aufgabe, das vorhandene Wissen über den wirtschaftlichen und sozialen Zustand der Region zu bündeln und Perspektiven für seine Verbesserung aufzuzeigen. Dabei wurde die gesamte Region in den Blick genommen.[206]

Die Anstrengungen der Akademie der Wissenschaften im Magadaner Gebiet dürfen nicht isoliert betrachtet werden. Sie stehen im Zusammenhang mit einer großangelegten Erweiterung der Akademie nach 1953 in den östlichen Teil der Sowjetunion hinein. Am 18. März 1957 beschloss das ZK der KPdSU die Gründung einer Sibirischen Abteilung der Akademie der Wissenschaften, die mit der Gründung einer Wissenschaftsstadt bei Nowosibirsk (*akademgorodok*) sowie einer ganzen Reihe weiterer Institute einhergehen sollte.[207] Dabei handelte es sich um die erste *regionale*

---

der RSFSR verstärkt und die Arbeiten in den einzelnen Regionen zusammengefasst und koordiniert werden. Schon bald beschäftigte sich die Akademie der Wissenschaften mit einzelnen Themengebieten. So wurde 1956 die Leningrader Filiale der Akademie für Bau und Architektur der UdSSR damit beauftragt, sich den Fragen des Baus im Hohen Norden zu widmen. In der Folge entwickelte sie, in Zusammenarbeit mit den wichtigsten Architekten der nördlichen Städte und den Projektorganisationen, eigenständige Baupläne für Arbeiten unter diesen besonderen klimatischen Bedingungen. Siehe für eine Beschreibung ihrer Studien und der von ihnen erstellten wissenschaftlichen Arbeiten Akademija Stroitel'stva i Architektury SSSR, Voprosy stroitel'stva na Krajnem Severe, S. 12–32 (Bericht des stellvertretenden Vorsitzenden) sowie Daniševskij, Akklimatizacija čeloveka.

204 Die Sektion der Geologen des Ministeriums für Geologie und Bodenschätze hatte in ihrer Beratung im März 1959 die geologischen Arbeiten in allen goldhaltigen Gebieten der Sowjetunion stark kritisiert. Im Zentrum stand dabei die Feststellung, dass sie viel zu gering wissenschaftlich untermauert sei, zahlreiche wichtige Untersuchungen überhaupt nicht vorgenommen würden und es keine allgemeine wissenschaftliche Methodik gebe. Sie forderte nachdrücklich die Akademie der Wissenschaften auf, sich diesem Wissenschaftsgebiet zuzuwenden. Vgl. die Stellungnahme des Vorsitzenden der Sektion vom 12. April 1959 in GAMO f. R-137sč, op. 1b, d. 52, l. 47–62, hier l. 50 ff.

205 Vgl. v. a. die Ausgaben der Magadanskaja Pravda vom 11.–13. September 1959.

206 Die Konferenz zu den Produktivkräften des östlichen Sibiriens wurde am 21. August 1957 vom ZK der KPdSU beschlossen; eine ähnliche Konferenz gab es auch im Sommer 1957 in Petropavlovsk (Kamtschatka). Vgl. den Bericht des Leiters der Abteilung für Wissenschaft, Schulen und Kultur des Büros des ZK der KPdSU für die RSFSR vom 30. Dezember 1957 in RGASPI f. 556, op. 16, d. 14, l. 114. Grundlage für die Konferenz war der Rat für die Untersuchung der Produktivkräfte beim Präsidium der Akademie der Wissenschaften. Siehe zu der deutlichen Zunahme derartiger Fachkonferenzen unter Chruščev Schröder, Lebendige Verbindung, S. 539–542.

207 Vgl. den Abdruck der Verordnung des ZK der KPdSU zur Gründung der Sibirischen Abteilung sowie weitere Dokumente in diesem Umfeld in: Afiani, Akademia nauk v rešenijach Politbjuro, S. 751–757. Siehe auch die ausführliche Einleitung des Dokumentenbandes zur Ausweitung der Akademie in

Abteilung / Filiale im Rahmen der Akademie. Die Gründung des Magadaner SVKNII („Severo-Vostočnyj Kompleksnyj Naučno-Issledovatel'skij Institut", Nordöstliches komplexes wissenschaftliches Forschungsinstitut) durch die Akademie der Wissenschaften im Jahr 1960 war eine direkte Folge dieser Entwicklung. Dieses Institut wurde im Bestand der sibirischen Abteilung der Akademie der Wissenschaften als Institut der Grundlagenforschung eingerichtet. N. A. Šilo wechselte von der Leitung des Institutes VNII-1 zu der neuen Einrichtung der Akademie der Wissenschaften, wie beschrieben blieb das VNII-1 als Einrichtung der anwendungsorientierten Forschung bestehen.[208]

Derart von der Akademie der Wissenschaft unterstützt, bot sich für die lokale Wissenschaft die Chance, sich von ihrer unmittelbaren Begrenzung auf die Bedürfnisse der Rohstoffförderung zu lösen und sich dem nordöstlichen Raum in vielen wissenschaftlichen Aspekten zuzuwenden: Das SVKNII arbeitete in den folgenden Jahren an wissenschaftlichen Grundproblemen im Bereich der geologisch-geophysischen, historisch-archäologischen und sozial-ökonomischen Wissenschaften, später dann auch der biologischen und kosmo-physikalischen Wissenschaften des sowjetischen Nordens.[209] Parallel dazu erschienen im Magadaner Verlag eine Reihe populärwissenschaftlicher Schriften, die das interessierte Publikum in die naturräumlichen Besonderheiten des Nordostens einführte.[210]

Das SVKNII galt als „Vorposten der sowjetischen Wissenschaften" und entwickelte sich in den folgenden Jahrzehnten zur Basis einer Reihe weiterer Institute, die sich auf inhaltliche Fragestellungen und einzelne Regionen spezialisierten – 1972 entstand das „Institut für die biologischen Probleme des Nordens", 1987 das „Institut für kosmo-physikalische Forschungen und die Verbreitung von Radiowellen" (in Kamtschatka) sowie 1992 das wissenschaftliche Zentrum „Tschukotka" in Anadyr'.[211]

Nur wenige Jahre nach Auflösung des Lager-Industriellen Komplexes hatte die hohe Bedeutung des Goldes für die Sowjetunion somit zu Entwicklungen in Wissenschaft und Schürfarbeiten geführt, die den Bedingungen der Arbeiten im Stalinismus gera-

---

den Osten der Sowjetunion und zur Rolle der Akademie in der Entstalinisierung. Zum Ausbau höherer Bildungsanstalten in den östlichen Teilen der Sowjetunion siehe Tromly, Soviet Intelligentsia, S. 165.

208 Zur Person Šilo siehe Žulanova, Akademičeskaja geologija, S. 18. Afanas'ev hat den Geologen ganz besonders wertgeschätzt. Vgl. Afanas'ev, Rossija, S. 155. Die beiden Institute existieren noch heute. Vgl. Simakov/Gončarov, Akademičeskaja nauka, S. 26.

209 Vgl. Gel'man, Fundamental'nye problemy.

210 So z. B. der Band von Bulanov über Tschukotka sowie Gromovs Beschreibung der Wrangelinsel im Arktischen Ozean. Vgl. Bulanov, Načinaetsja den' sowie Gromov, Ostrov Vrangelja.

211 1991 entstand außerdem das internationale wissenschaftliche Zentrum „Arktika", als Abspaltung des Instituts für die biologischen Probleme des Nordens. Ein weiteres Beispiel für die Ausweitung der Wissenschaft auf den gesamten nordöstlichen Raum ist die Errichtung eines seismologischen Dienstes. Bis zur Perestrojka wurden insgesamt 19 Stationen errichtet, da das Gebiet seismologisch sehr aktiv ist. Vgl. Simakov/Gončarov, Akademičeskaja nauka, S. 26. Siehe zu der Entwicklung sozialwissenschaftlicher Studien in der Region Šeršakova, Razrabotka planov.

dezu diametral entgegenstanden. Statt geheimer Forschungen, in enger Anlehnung an die unmittelbaren Bedürfnisse der Rohstofffförderung, wandte sich nun ein großes Team unterschiedlicher Wissenschaftler im Rahmen der wichtigsten unionsweiten Einrichtungen für Grundlagenforschung dem ganzen Raum in seinen verschiedenen Facetten zu.[212] Natürlich waren auch diese Arbeiten grundsätzlich einer optimalen Ausbeutung der Region verpflichtet.[213] Doch entwickelte sich das Gebiet – gewissermaßen im Rahmen dieses Utilitarismus – zu einem sowjetischen Wissenschaftsstandort, was erhebliche Auswirkungen auf den gesamten Status der Region hatte. Für die beiden Leiter von Instituten der Akademie der Wissenschaften in Magadan, K. V. Simakov und V. I. Gončarov, waren die Jahre seit Gründung des SVKNII rückblickend „Sternstunden" der nordöstlichen Wissenschaft, die mit einer Reihe von Charakteristika verbunden waren:

Der Mangel an höheren Bildungseinrichtungen führte in den 1960er Jahren dazu, dass das Personal der wissenschaftlichen Institute aus einer für die Wissenschaft sehr fruchtbaren Mischung aus praktisch gebildeten Arbeitern der Produktionseinrichtungen und theoretisch fundierten Absolventen von zentralen Bildungseinrichtungen (v. a. aus Moskau, Leningrad und Nowosibirsk) bestand. Die Magadaner Institute erlangten in der Sowjetunion recht bald große Autorität, ihre Wissenschaftler erhielten viele Preise und Auszeichnungen.[214] Allerdings bedeutete diese Besonderheit auch, dass das Personal der Institute ständig wechselte. Permanent kamen neue junge Leute in das Gebiet, erhielten dort ihre wissenschaftliche Ausbildung, verließen dann aber das Gebiet nach einiger Zeit wieder. Dies sorgte dafür, dass der Anteil wissenschaftlich gebildeter Arbeitskräfte im Magadaner Gebiet im Durchschnitt höher war als in den anderen Gebieten der UdSSR. Zwischen 1960 und dem Ende der Perestrojka legten hier sehr viele Wissenschaftler ihre Promotionen und Habilitationen ab – viele von ihnen verließen das Gebiet jedoch bald wieder.[215]

Die Ausstattung der wissenschaftlichen Einrichtungen war im Hinblick auf Bibliotheken und Labore, aber auch bei den Expeditionen hervorragend. Wissenschaft, und dabei auch die gesamte Grundlagenforschung, wurde seit den 1960er Jahren als Voraussetzung für eine erfolgreiche Metallförderung verstanden. Der Staat investierte in eine ganze Reihe von Programmen, die z. T. international besetzt waren und über

---

212 Zum ersten Mal seit der Gründung von Dal'stroj wurden im Jahr 1963 die Arbeiten der Geologen an der Kolyma in das mehrbändige Werk „Geologie der UdSSR" aufgenommen, vgl. Drabkin, Razvedčiki nedr, S. 108 f.

213 Šilo erinnert sich, dass die Errichtung des Institutes der Akademie der Wissenschaften in der Region vor großen Schwierigkeiten stand, weil alle Forschungen in der Region bisher den Stempel „geheim" getragen hätten. Vgl. Šilo, Interview, S. 22 f.

214 Vgl. zur Entwicklung der Akademie der Wissenschaften in den 1950er Jahren, im Besonderen zur Entwicklung der Filiale von Nowosibirsk, zu der Magadan als Ableger zählte, Beyrau, Intelligenz, S. 152 sowie Krasil'nikov, Fenomen sibirskogo otdelenija AN SSSR.

215 Zwischen 1960 und 1990 wurden in Magadan mehr als 70 Habilitationen und 200 Promotionen vorbereitet, aber vor Ort waren gleichzeitig immer nur etwa 10 – 15 Habilitierte und 30 – 40 Promovierte anwesend.

die Grenzen des Gebietes hinausgingen.[216] Diese Expeditionen zahlten sich immer wieder unmittelbar für die Ausbeutung der Rohstoffe aus – häufig waren akademische Mitarbeiter die ersten Entdecker neuer Fördergebiete. Zudem war die Magadaner Wissenschaft eng mit anderen wissenschaftlichen Einrichtungen der Sowjetunion und weltweit vernetzt. Mehrere internationale Projekte und viele Konferenzen fanden nicht nur vor Ort statt, Magadaner Wissenschaftler waren auch im kapitalistischen Ausland tätig.[217]

Geologen und die Wissenschaften hatten nach der Auflösung des Kombinats Dal'stroj somit eine erhebliche Bedeutung für das Magadaner Gebiet. Sie sicherten nicht nur dauerhaft neue Fördergebiete und deren Ausbeutung, sondern sie schufen auch die Basis für eine ganz neue Bevölkerungsschicht. Junge, gut ausgebildete Menschen kamen in den Nordosten, die hier fortgebildet wurden. Zumindest in der Hauptstadt Magadan beeinflussten sie die soziale und kulturelle Infrastruktur.[218] So erinnern sich heute Intellektuelle, die noch immer in Magadan leben, dass das Leben in ihrer Stadt bis zur Perestrojka keinesfalls mit dem Leben in einer anderen Provinzstadt vergleichbar war. Durch die Anwesenheit so vieler gut ausgebildeter junger Menschen und berühmter Wissenschaftler, aber auch durch die vielen unionsweiten und internationalen Kontakte fühlte man sich im Nordosten vielmehr wie in einem Ableger der großen wissenschaftlichen Zentren in Moskau, Leningrad oder Nowosibirsk.[219] Dietrich Beyrau hat in seiner Studie zu den russischen Bildungsschichten in der Sowjetunion anschaulich beschrieben, dass in den 1960er Jahren gerade in den

---

216 So waren die Magadaner Institute auch auf dem Gebiet von Kamtschatka und verschiedenen Inseln im Nordmeer tätig.

217 Vgl. Simakov/Gončarov, Akademičeskaja nauka, S. 22–24. Zu der generellen Ausweitung wissenschaftlich-technischer Kooperationen mit dem kapitalistischen Ausland seit der Chruščev-Ära siehe Autio-Sarasmo, Challenge, S. 144 f.

218 Zum Aufbau von Kultureinrichtungen im Magadaner Gebiet vgl. den ausführlichen Bericht des Gebietsexekutivkomitees von 1958 in GAMO f. R-146, op. 1, d. 215, l. 38–68. Für die weitere kulturelle Entwicklung bis in die 1970er Jahre siehe Severo-Vostok Rossii s drevnejšich vremen, S. 91. Einen lebendigen Eindruck vom alltäglichen Leben im Magadaner Gebiet der 1960er und 1970er Jahre vermitteln die Erinnerungen Peter Demants, die unter Pseudonym erschienen. Vgl. Kress, Parochoda. Sergej Zhuk hat die kulturellen Folgen der sowjetischen Konsumsteigerungen auf der Grundlage der Betonung eines höheren Lebensstandards als Kennzeichen des entwickelten Sozialismus durch Chruščev in einer ausgesprochen spannenden Regionalstudie untersucht. Am Beispiel der „geschlossenen" ukrainischen Stadt Dnjepropetrovsk beschreibt er die Auswirkungen wachsenden Kulturkonsums auf die Identitätsbildung junger Leute. Vgl. Zhuk, Popular Culture. Siehe dazu auch Varga-Harris, Socialist Contract.

219 In krassem Gegensatz dazu beurteilen die beiden Leiter der Einrichtungen der Akademie der Wissenschaften die Lage der Institute heute. Seit der Perestrojka sei die Wissenschaft strukturell und finanziell ausgeblutet worden. Zum einen werde sie mit sinnlosen bürokratischen Fesseln belegt, zum anderen hätten finanzielle Beschneidungen katastrophale Folgen gezeitigt. Aufgrund der großen Distanz zu anderen Wissenschaftszentren sei die Lage im Nordosten besonders schwer. Eine erfolgreiche wirtschaftliche Ausbeutung des Nordostens sei jedoch auch in der heutigen Zeit ohne eine Förderung der regionalen Wissenschaften undenkbar. Vgl. Simakov/Gončarov, Akademičeskaja nauka, S. 29.

naturwissenschaftlichen Instituten mitunter ein kulturell und gesellschaftlich ausgesprochen aktives Leben geherrscht habe, das die Entstehung „informeller Milieus, die Intensivierung wissenschaftlicher und gesellschaftlicher Kommunikation, die sich der Kontrolle der Partei entzog", begünstigte.[220] In diesem Sinne konnten die Wissenschaftler den Anschluss des Nordostens an die Zentren der Sowjetunion geradezu verkörpern und verliehen dem Gebiet einen Status, der sich nicht allein über seine ökonomische Bedeutung für die Sowjetwirtschaft definierte.[221]

4.3.4 Neue Industriezweige und ihre Repräsentation

Industriezweige abseits der Rohstoffförderung waren im Lager-Industriellen Komplex entweder stark unterentwickelt oder sie wurden vollkommen von Einrichtungen außerhalb des Gebietes übernommen. So war z. B. die Versorgung mit Lebensmitteln und täglichen Gebrauchswaren auf eine winzige lokale Produktion und die Anlieferung einfacher Lebensmittel und von Lagerbedarf sowie eine exklusive Zustellung von Luxusartikeln für die Leitungskader konzentriert. Ebenso die Bauwirtschaft – sie war gänzlich auf die unmittelbaren Bedürfnisse der Metallförderung ausgerichtet, privater Wohnraum wurde im großen Stil fast gar nicht errichtet, auch gab es keine Industrie für Baumaterialien; jeder Sack Zement und jeder Nagel musste aus anderen Teilen der Sowjetunion angeliefert werden.

Die Rolle der Region als ausschließliche Empfängerin von Waren stellten die ersten Maßnahmen der Organe von Partei und Staat nicht in Frage. Sie drängten zwar bereits im Dezember 1953 auf eine Verbesserung der Versorgung (mit Fleisch und Gebrauchsgütern) und der strukturellen Bedingungen (Bau von Wohnungen, Stärkung der Transportorganisationen), allerdings ohne damit den Status anderer Industriezweige grundsätzlich aufzuwerten. Generell galten die Landwirtschaft, die lokale Industrie, das Transportwesen sowie die Bauwirtschaft als Hilfsindustrien, die nicht das industrielle Profil des Gebietes definierten und dadurch auch nicht strukturell gestützt werden sollten.

Seit 1954 sorgten jedoch Entwicklungen in vier Bereichen dafür, dass es zu einer partiellen Neudefinition der wirtschaftlichen Aufgaben des Gebietes kam: Zum einen übten die Entlassung von Häftlingen und die Einstellung von freien Arbeitskräften einen unmittelbaren Druck auf eine bessere Versorgung mit Lebensmitteln, mit Gebrauchsgütern und mit Wohnraum aus. Zweitens mussten durch die Zuordnung einzelner Wirtschaftsbereiche zu zivilen Ministerien, unionsweiten Organisationen oder Einrichtungen der lokalen Exekutivorgane infolge der Verordnungen der Ministerräte vom Mai und Juni 1954 unionsweite Standards schnell umgesetzt werden. In den

---

220 Beyrau, Intelligenz, S. 210.
221 Dementsprechend wurden die Arbeit der Geologen und alle wissenschaftlichen Entwicklungen in der Region ausführlich von der lokalen Presse begleitet. Vgl. zum lokalen Geologen-Kult das Kapitel 5.1.5.

ersten Jahren führte dies zunächst einmal zu ausgesprochen chaotischen Zuständen. So entstanden beispielsweise innerhalb kürzester Zeit dreißig zum Teil winzige Bauorganisationen, die die Hunderte Aufträge der einzelnen Ministerien im zivilen und zivil-industriellen Bereich erfüllen sollten, ohne vor Ort auf Strukturen, Personal und Materialien zurückgreifen zu können. Eine Professionalisierung schien alternativlos. Zumal, drittens, die bisherige Abhängigkeit der Region zu ungeheurer Misswirtschaft und Verschwendung geführt hatte. Die Vernachlässigung von Transport- und Lagerkapazitäten sowie die sorglosen Bestellungen aufgrund des besonderen militärischen Status von Dal'stroj hatten bewirkt, dass selbst den Verantwortlichen der Inhalt vieler Lagergebäude nicht bekannt war.

Viertens schließlich forderte das Moskauer Zentrum eine breiter angelegte Perspektive auf das Potential des Nordostens. Dies muss im Kontext des 20. Parteitages gesehen werden, auf dem grundsätzlich eine Stärkung des industriellen Potentials des Ostens der Union beschlossen worden war.[222] Die bestehenden strukturellen Schwierigkeiten im Magadaner Gebiet wurden bei den Beratungen über die Zukunft der Region, die im Rahmen des 15-Jahrplanes von Dal'stroj geführt wurden, erstmals 1956 grundsätzlich diskutiert.[223] Diagnostiziert wurden große „Disproportionen" in der Entwicklung von Dal'stroj, ein massives Ungleichgewicht zwischen der Metallförderung und ihren Hilfs- und Nebenindustrien.[224]

Daran anschließend forderte die vom Moskauer Zentrum beauftragte Abteilung der Akademie der Wissenschaften, der sogenannte „Sektor für die natürlichen Ressourcen und die Wirtschaft des Nordens des Rates für die Untersuchung der Produktivkräfte" eine „rationalere Erschließung der großen natürlichen Ressourcen" des Gebietes.[225] Die Autoren der Studie unter der Leitung des Professors für Wirtschaftswissenschaften, S. V. Slavin, verstanden darunter nicht nur ein höheres Maß an Effektivität, bessere Planungen und Strukturierungen der Rohstoffförderung, sondern ausdrücklich auch eine Stärkung weiterer Industriezweige. In ihrer Analyse betteten sie die Metallförderung in die Transportwirtschaft, die Kohleförderung, die Industrie für lokale Baumaterialien, die Landwirtschaft, Gebrauchsgüterindustrie u. a. ein. All diese Industriezweige sollten mit dem Ziel gestärkt werden, die Kosten der Metall-

---

222 Vgl. Krasil'nikov, Fenomen sibirskogo otdelenija AN SSSR, S. 517.

223 Am 16. März 1956 verpflichtete der Ministerrat der UdSSR das MCM, einen Plan über die perspektivische Entwicklung von Dal'stroj in den Jahren 1956 bis 1970 vorzulegen. Vgl. GAMO f. R-23, op. 1, d. 5861, l. 1– 71, hier l. 38. Für den Plan siehe GAMO f. R-23sč, op. 1, d. 456. Siehe dort auch die Diskussionen über den Plan und die wirtschaftliche Lage des Gebietes.

224 Vgl. den Bericht in GAMO f. R-146, op. 1, d. 456, l. 6 ff.

225 So die Autoren des breitangelegten Abschlussberichtes, den die Akademie der Wissenschaften 1961 veröffentlichte. Vgl. Slavin, Problemy razvitija, S. 3. Bemerkenswert ist, dass in diesem Band auch die Erfahrungen des amerikanischen Nordens in Bezug auf die besonderen klimatischen Herausforderungen berücksichtigt wurden.

förderung in der Region auf Dauer zu senken, aber auch, um das Wirtschaftsprofil der Region grundsätzlich zu verbreitern.[226]

Die Bedeutung dieser Studie lag in ihrer Sicht auf das Gebiet, das dort den Status einer zu entwickelnden Region erhielt. Um die Ausbeutung des Territoriums zu effektivieren, sollte das Augenmerk langfristig auf die wirtschaftliche Ausgestaltung der Region gelegt und sie an die übrigen Wirtschaftskreise der Sowjetunion angeschlossen werden.

Die industriellen Leistungen des Gebietes spielten bei der Repräsentation der Region eine große Rolle. Eine Vielzahl der Veröffentlichungen Ende der 1950er und zu Beginn der 1960er Jahre war auf die Beschreibung einzelner Industriezweige oder -standorte ausgerichtet.[227] Auch die Zeitschrift *Kolyma*, die sich zur Zeit von Dal'stroj ganz auf technische Fragen der Metallförderung konzentriert hatte, nahm zusehends die gesamte Bandbreite der nordöstlichen Wirtschaft in den Blick.[228] Der Band der Akademie der Wissenschaften ist in dieser Reihe die umfassendste und, da von zentralen Einrichtungen gemeinsam mit den lokalen Experten verfasst, fundierteste Darstellung. Folgt man dieser offiziellen Beschreibung, so war die „Entwicklung der Produktivkräfte" des Magadaner Gebietes zwar vielen Problemen ausgesetzt, lebte aber vor allem von großen Hoffnungen auf zu erschließende Potentiale.

Tatsächlich aber war die Lage in allen Industriezweigen, die in der Region bisher entweder nicht existiert hatten oder lediglich als eine Art von „Hilfsindustrie" geduldet worden waren, dramatisch. Zwischen den Anforderungen, die sich aus der Umstellung der militärischen Lagerwirtschaft auf zivile Bedürfnisse ergaben, und der tatsächlichen Lage in dem Gebiet klaffte eine riesige Lücke. In der Landwirtschaft, bei Verbrauchsgütern, dem Wohnungsbau, den Versorgungseinrichtungen, auf all diesen Gebieten war die Situation im Magadaner Gebiet strukturell schlechter als in den Nachbarregionen Sachalin und Kamtschatka – Gebiete, die auch vor 1953 einer zivilen Herrschaft unterstanden hatten. Ende der 1950er Jahre kann somit zwar in Ansätzen von der Entstehung neuer Industriezweige gesprochen werden, in vielen Bereichen blieb aber die Region noch völlig von Lieferungen aus anderen Gebieten abhängig.

---

226 Ausführlicher zu der Beurteilung der Region durch die Akademie der Wissenschaften siehe das Kapitel „Ausgangslage und grundsätzliche Probleme einer perspektivischen Entwicklung der Produktivkräfte" in Slavin, Problemy razvitija, S. 15 ff. Zum Teil beruhte dies auch auf der Hoffnung auf weitere Bodenschätze wie Gas, wie die Autoren in ihren Schlussbetrachtungen reflektieren, ebd., S. 301.

227 Vgl. Gorochov, Semiletka; Narodnoe Chozjastvo Magadanskoj oblasti; Chodos, Rybnaja promyšlennost'; Slavin, Promyšlennoe osvoenie; Žarkich/Lukin, Vstajut novostrojki; Korobejnikov, Buduščee; Na preobražennoj zemle; Malagin, Ėkonomičeskij rajon.

228 Vgl. Sprau, Magadanskaja pressa, S. 183.

4.3.4.1 Landwirtschaft und lokale Industrie

Die Landwirtschaft war der Wirtschaftsbereich, in dem Eingriffe am dringendsten benötigt wurden, am wenigstens Effekte zeigten, zugleich aber am stärksten propagandistisch beworben wurden.

Bei einer allgemein schlechten Versorgungslage der sowjetischen Bevölkerung Mitte der 1950er Jahre war die Situation im Nordosten besonders verheerend. Die Menschen waren fast zu 100 % auf den Transport von Lebensmitteln in die Region angewiesen. Die Kolchosmärkte, die in den zentralen Gebieten der Sowjetunion für die Versorgung der Bevölkerung so wichtig waren, spielten in Dal'stroj nur eine geringe Rolle. Einen echten „Markt" gab es nur in der Stadt Magadan. Dieser war allerdings in sehr schlechtem Zustand und der Transport der Waren dorthin mit großen Schwierigkeiten verbunden.[229] Zudem hatte kaum jemand eine Datscha oder einen kleinen Garten.[230]

Daher drängte das Zentrum zunächst auf eine strukturelle Angleichung der landwirtschaftlichen Verwaltung. Am 3. Juli 1954 verabschiedete der Ministerrat der UdSSR eine eigene Verordnung „Zur Unterstützung der Landwirtschaft des Magadaner Gebietes" – die die Gründung einer Maschinen-Traktoren-Station (MTS), einer großen landwirtschaftlichen Basis auf der Grundlage der Sovchose Elgen sowie die Gründung von landwirtschaftlichen Instituten zur Ausbildung geeigneter Facharbeiter vorsah. Zudem sollten ehemalige Sondersiedler mit besonderen Boni und Vergünstigungen zur Arbeit in den Kolchosen motiviert werden.[231] In der Stadt Magadan entstand ein überdachter Kolchosmarkt.[232]

Diese Maßnahmen wurden mit Verzögerungen zum Teil auch umgesetzt, sie waren jedoch mitnichten in der Lage, ernsthaft das Ernährungsproblem der Bevölkerung in den Griff zu bekommen. Unter den extremen klimatischen Verhältnissen der Region mutet es bizarr an, wie Gebietspartei- und Gebietsexekutivkomitee immer wieder

---

229 Vgl. Isakov, Istorija torgovli, S. 194.

230 Für einen Überblick über die Landwirtschaft im Rahmen von Dal'stroj siehe Bacaev, Sel'skoe i promyšlovoe chozjajstvo.

231 Vgl. die Verordnung in GAMO f. R-146, op. 1, d. 7, l. 84–87. Die Sovchose hatte als eine große Lagerabteilung, in der auch die sowjetische Schriftstellerin Evgenija Ginzburg zur Arbeit gezwungen wurde, traurige Berühmtheit erlangt. Die Gründung der MTS war mit großen praktischen Schwierigkeiten verbunden, entsprechend der allgemeinen politischen Linie in der Sowjetunion wurde sie 1958 wieder aufgelöst. Vgl. das Schreiben von Afanas'ev an das Ministerium für Landwirtschaft der RSFSR vom 29. März 1955 in GAMO f. R-146, op. 1, d. 107, l. 73–74. Die „Gebietsweite Verwaltung für Sovchosen des Ministeriums der Sovchosen der RSFSR" wurde schließlich im März 1956 gegründet; vgl. die entsprechende Anordnung des Ministerrates der RSFSR vom 7. März 1956 in GAMO f. R-146, op. 1, d. 60, l. 68. Bereits zum 1. Januar 1954 war die Landbevölkerung von der Bezahlung von Steuern auf landwirtschaftliche Produkte befreit worden. Vgl. Bacaev, Agropromyšlennyj kompleks, S. 6.

232 Vgl. das Schreiben von Ferapontov vom 28. Dezember 1954 an den Vorsitzenden des *Gosplan* der RSFSR und den Handelsminister der RSFSR in GAMO f. R-146, op. 1, d. 48, l. 2. In einigen Bezirkszentren wurden bis Ende der 1960er Jahre zusätzlich primitive Märkte (sogenannte „Basare") gegründet. Vgl. Isakov, Istorija torgovli, S. 216.

betonten, die Bedingungen für den Anbau von Kartoffeln und Kohl sowie für Viehzucht und Milchwirtschaft seien im Magadaner Gebiet günstig.[233]

Tatsächlich stellte die Untersuchung der Akademie der Wissenschaften fest, dass der Ertrag bei Kartoffeln und Kohl (durchschnittlich 73 Zentner Kartoffeln und 124 Zentner Kohl pro Hektar Land) seit 1953 zwar erheblich angestiegen sei, dass aber auch 1959 nur 27 % der benötigten Kartoffeln, 40 % der Milch und 20 % des veranschlagten Gemüses im Gebiet produziert wurden. Die Arbeiten waren aufgrund mangelnder Technik und Maschinen noch immer sehr ineffektiv und weit entfernt von Rentabilität – zum Vergleich führte die Akademie der Wissenschaften die Ernteleistungen in Alaska an, hier wurden unter ähnlichen klimatischen Bedingungen durchschnittlich 350 Zentner Kartoffeln pro Hektar Land gewonnen.[234] Aber auch in anderen Gebieten des sowjetischen Fernen Ostens waren die Kosten erheblich geringer als im Magadaner Gebiet. Die regionalen Produkte wurden daher zu Preisen, die weit unter ihren Herstellungskosten lagen, an die lokale Bevölkerung verkauft.[235]

Im krassen Widerspruch zu dem realen Mangel an einfachsten landwirtschaftlichen Erzeugnissen und den extremen klimatischen Bedingungen präsentierte sich das Magadaner Gebiet geradezu als Agrarregion. Gerne wurde die angeblich günstige Lage der Kolchosen dafür herangezogen, so beispielsweise in einer Beschreibung der Ankunft einer jungen Kolchos-Arbeiterin:

> Als Lena Migunova in der Sovchose ‚Dukča' ankam, wollte sie sich als Erstes einmal den großen Wirtschaftsbereich der Sovchose anschauen, in dem sie sich entschlossen hatte zu arbeiten. Die Tierfarmen haben ihr gleich gefallen. Neugierig lugte sie in die Kuhställe. Das erfahrene Auge sah gleich, dass dort alles in Ordnung war. Überall war es trocken, kein Futter lag herum. Die Tiere waren satt. Lena bemerkte, dass es im Stall warm war, dass es ausreichend Licht gab. Mit einem Wort, die Situation auf der Farm war ganz nach ihrem Herzen.[236]

---

233 Vgl. exemplarisch den Brief des Parteisekretärs Timofeev und des stellvertretenden Vorsitzenden des Gebietsexekutivkomitees Ferapontov vom 2. Dezember 1954 in GAMO f. R-146, op. 1, d. 7, l. 163–164. Der Lokalhistoriker Bacaev schildert anschaulich, wie die Losung Chruščevs zur Überholung Amerikas bei der Produktion von Fleisch und Milch in die Propaganda des lokalen Gebietsparteikomitees umgesetzt wurde. Vgl. Bacaev, Agropromyšlennyj kompleks, S. 42. Die neue Leitung bemühte sich immer wieder, die Schwierigkeiten der lokalen landwirtschaftlichen Produktion als Ergebnis der Unfähigkeit einzelner Kader darzustellen. Vgl. z. B. die Diskussionen im Gebietsexekutivkomitee GAMO f. R-146, op. 1, d. 47, l. 94–114, hier l. 110 (Mitschrift). In einzelnen Bereichen konnten jedoch tatsächlich Erfolge erzielt werden. So stieg z. B. die Zahl der in dem Gebiet gezüchteten Hähnchen von 21.000 im Jahr 1953 auf 146.000 im Jahr 1959. Vgl. Slavin, Problemy razvitija, S. 202. Es lässt sich jedoch leicht vorstellen, dass diese Anstrengungen nicht in der Lage gewesen sind, die schwierige Ernährungslage insgesamt zu verbessern.

234 Vgl. Slavin, Problemy razvitija, S. 206 f.

235 Auf produzierte Waren im Wert von einem Rubel kamen noch im Jahr 1958 Verluste von 72 Kopeken, die Produktionskosten waren zweimal bzw. fünfmal so hoch wie in vergleichbaren Gebieten. Vgl. ebd., S. 209 f.

236 Korobejnikov, Buduščee, ohne Seitenangabe.

Der australische Historiker Graeme Gill beschreibt die Darstellung materiellen Überflusses als zentrales Motiv der Chruščev'schen Symbolpolitik, die Landwirtschaft sei dafür besonders häufig als Beispiel angeführt worden.[237] Auch wenn diese Repräsentationsstrategie gerade im sowjetischen Nordosten absurd erscheint, stand Magadan in dieser Hinsicht anderen sowjetischen Gebieten in nichts nach. Fotos von Hühnerfarmen, Aufzuchtstationen begehrter Pelztiere bis hin zu strahlenden Sowchose-Bäuerinnen mit Armen voller Tomaten und sogar Trauben füllten Bildbände über die lokale Wirtschaft.[238]

Rentierhaltung und Fischfang wurden in der lokalen Presse und offiziellen Beschreibungen des Wirtschaftsraums gerne als industrielles und kulturelles Kennzeichen der Region gepriesen[239], nominell waren sie die wichtigsten landwirtschaftlichen Sektoren. Rentier- und Fischwirtschaft beruhten auf der sowjetischen Ausbeutung indigener Wirtschaftsformen. Ende der 1930er und zu Beginn der 1940er Jahren waren im Zuge der wirtschaftlichen Ausbeutung der Bodenschätze die indigenen Bewohner der Region, hauptsächlich Čukčen, aber auch Ėvenen, Yupik u. a., in Kolchosen gedrängt worden, viele Personen als „Kulaken" oder „japanische Spione" verhaftet und verfolgt worden.[240] Die Wirtschaftsergebnisse dieser Kolchosen waren bis 1957 ausgesprochen schlecht, sie erzielten hohe Verluste.[241] Über ein Treffen von Rentierhaltern im Jahr 1957 heißt es:

> Die Leiter verwendeten immer wieder die Worte ‚Katastrophe', ‚Untergang', ‚Fiasko'. Über die Verbesserung der vorhandenen Mängel in der Rentierwirtschaft sind Tonnen an Papier geschrieben worden, von den Schreibtischen in den Arbeitszimmern ergehen eine große Zahl von Ratschlägen und Empfehlungen, aber hinter diesen Worten steht keine lebendige Arbeit.[242]

Erst eine spezielle Verordnung des ZK der KPdSU und des Ministerrates der UdSSR am 16. März 1957 sowie weitere Verordnungen in den Jahren 1958 und 1960 verbesserten allmählich die finanzielle und technische Ausstattung der Kolchosen und damit ihre Ergebnisse.[243] Dennoch hatte die lokale Fischwirtschaft noch 1961 gerade einmal einen Anteil von 1–1,5 % an der gesamten Fischwirtschaft der Union, der Fischfang von

---

237 Vgl. Gill, Symbols, S. 182.

238 Ein besonders leuchtendes Beispiel ist die Darstellung des Bandes Na preobražennoj zemle.

239 Siehe beispielhaft die Darstellung in Guščin/Afanas'ev, Čukotskij okrug, S 37 ff.

240 Vgl. Verkina/Kozlov, Nacional'nye rajony Kolymy, S. 73 – 80; Rajzman, Osobennosti gosudarstvennoj politiki sowie Rajzman, Operativnaja rabota. V. A. Il'ina schildert einen massiven Bevölkerungsverlust als Ergebnis der gnadenlosen Verfolgung Indigener als angebliche „Volksfeinde", da die Rentiere verfolgter Familienangehöriger gänzlich konfisziert wurden. Vgl. Il'nia, Dinamika, S. 51.

241 Vgl. Bacaev, Sostojanie olenevodstva, S. 87 ff.

242 Vgl. den Bericht in GAMO f. R-146, op. 1, d. 177, l. 17, hier zitiert nach Bacaev, Sostojanie olenevodstva, S. 88.

243 Zu den Ergebnissen dieser Verordnung vgl. die Berichte aus den verschiedenen Abteilungen der Exekutiv- und Parteikomitees in GAMO f. R-146, op. 1, d. 356, l. 1– 24 sowie l. 40 – 43.

Kamtschatka war ungefähr zehnmal so ertragreich.[244] Gegen Ende der 1960er Jahre waren die wirtschaftlichen Erträge dieser Kolchosen höher, zugleich blieben jedoch die Lebensbedingungen der Kolchosmitarbeiter ausgesprochen prekär. Die Zerstörung ihrer traditionellen Nomadenwirtschaft hatte die indigene Bevölkerung ihrer kulturellen und wirtschaftlichen Eigenständigkeit beraubt, zugleich unternahm die sowjetische Macht viel zu geringe Anstrengungen, um der Wohnungsnot, den Epidemien und den großen sozialen Problemen in den Kolchosen zu begegnen.[245]

Bei der Produktion von Lebensmitteln und Waren des täglichen Gebrauchs spielte die sogenannte „lokale Industrie" seit Ende der 1950er Jahre eine zumindest wahrnehmbare Rolle.[246] Nach der Gebietsgründung musste sie nahezu von null an aufgebaut werden, da es auf dem riesigen Gebiet lediglich drei Fabriken mit einem derartigen Profil gab. Diese regionalen Anstrengungen wurden durch die unionsweiten Tendenzen zum Ausbau der Leichtindustrie für eine bessere Versorgung der Bevölkerung, die zunächst von Malenkov, später dann von Chruščev vorangetrieben wurden, unterstützt.[247]

Die neue politische Leitung konstatierte im Frühjahr 1954 neben dem grundsätzlichen Mangel ein absolutes Desinteresse der Leitung von Dal'stroj an diesen Industriezweigen.[248] Die wenigen Ausnahmen – so existierte z. B. eine Glasfabrik und eine Ziegelei – produzierten Waren von schlechter Qualität und in sehr geringen Zahlen. Selbst Dal'stroj griff oftmals nicht auf die lokal hergestellten Produkte zurück. Nach Gründung des Gebietes gingen die bestehenden Fabriken der lokalen Industrie in den Zuständigkeitsbereich des Gebietsexekutivkomitees über. Damit waren sie schlagartig von der Versorgung mit Materialien und Rohstoffen abgeschnitten, weil die Handelsorganisation von Dal'stroj sich weigerte, Fabriken des Gebietsexekutivkomitees zu beliefern.[249]

Zur Stärkung dieses Industriezweigs beschloss der Ministerrat der UdSSR schon kurz nach der Gebietsgründung einen Steuererlass für die Dauer von fünf Jahren; auch weiterhin mussten die lokalen Produkte durch staatliche Zuschüsse gestützt wer-

---

244 In der Fischwirtschaft waren lediglich 7,2 % aller Arbeiter des Gebietes beschäftigt. Vgl. ausführlich zur Rolle der Fischerei Slavin, Promyšlennoe osvoenie, S. 242.

245 Zu den Lebens- und Arbeitsbedingungen der Indigenen in dieser Zeit vgl. das Kapitel 5.3.5.

246 In der Sowjetunion fasste man unter dem Begriff „lokale Industrie" alle Produkte zusammen, die aus lokalem Budget finanziert wurden, lokale Ressourcen nutzten und lokale Steuern zahlten. Dazu gehörten klassischerweise Waren des täglichen Bedarfs, Brotfabriken, aber auch Baumaterialien. Vgl. Bol'šaja Sovetskaja Ènciklopedija, Band 16, Moskau 1974, S. 106 f.

247 Vgl. Ivanova, Question of Honour, S. 134 f.; Ivanova, Na poroge, S. 59 f.; Filtzer, Soviet Workers, S. 2.

248 Vgl. das Schreiben des stellvertretenden Vorsitzenden des Gebietsexekutivkomitees, Ferapontov, an den Minister für die Produktion von Waren des täglichen Bedarfs der RSFSR sowie an den Minister für lokale Industrie der RSFSR in GAMO f. R-146, op. 1, d. 49, l. 10–15.

249 Vgl. zur Lage der lokalen Industrie im Jahr 1954 GAMO f. R-146, op. 1, d. 49.

den.[250] Neue Fabriken wurden errichtet oder erweiterten ihr Profil, so dass sie nun auch Nudeln, Schuhe, einfache Möbel oder Kleider aus lokalen Fellen und Leder produzieren konnten.[251] Allerdings waren die Preise der lokalen Waren höher, zugleich war ihre Qualität schlechter als bei den Produkten, die aus den zentralen Versorgungseinrichtungen bezogen wurden.[252] Immer wieder drängte das Gebietsexekutivkomitee den Ministerrat der RSFSR und das MCM, Dal'stroj zur Abnahme dieser Produkte, im Bausektor oder für die Vorräte der Lager, zu zwingen.[253] Vor allem baute man Backhäuser und Fabriken für Brot und Backwaren; im Jahr 1958 musste so zumindest kein Brot mehr in das Gebiet transportiert werden.[254] Durch die Übergabe von Dal'stroj-Einrichtungen an zivile Ministerien veränderten lokale Kombinate ihre Ausrichtung – so wurde zum Beispiel aus einem Kombinat zur Energiegewinnung (Holzschlag) in der Region Jagodnoe ein Kombinat für Waren des täglichen Bedarfs unter der Aufsicht des Exekutivkomitees des Bezirks.[255]

An den Berechnungen der Akademie der Wissenschaften wird grundsätzlich deutlich, dass es aus ökonomischen Gründen keine wirkliche Alternative zu einer wenigstens teilweisen lokalen Produktion von Lebensmitteln und Waren des täglichen Bedarfs gab. Die Kosten der einzelnen Güter lagen unter, zum Teil sehr deutlich unter den Kosten, die der Staat für den Transport der Lebensmittel in die Region aufwenden musste.[256] Tatsächlich verbesserte sich die Versorgung der Bevölkerung aber erst dann grundlegend, als in den folgenden Jahrzehnten neue, günstigere Lieferanten für die

---

250 Dieser Erlass geht zurück auf die Entwürfe des Ministerrates, die im Vorfeld der Verordnungen vom Mai/Juni 1954 entstanden. Vgl. GAMO f. R-146, op. 1, f. 6, l. 33–51, hier l. 48. Erlassen wurde die Streichung der Steuer schließlich im Jahr 1955. Vgl. GAMO f. R-146, op. 1, d. 108, l. 85. Sie erstreckte sich auf die Ministerien für Heizindustrie, für Kommunalwirtschaft, für Lebensmittel und auf die Einrichtungen von Dal'stroj, die Alltagsgegenstände produzierten.

251 1958 existierten schon 21 Fabriken der lokalen Industrie. Vgl. Na preobražennoj zemle, S. 65.

252 Malagin, Ėkonomičeskij rajon, S. 103. Die Zahl der Betriebe für lokale Industrie stieg in der Region von 13 im Jahr 1954 auf 27 im Jahr 1959 an. Vgl. Slavin, Problemy razvitija, S. 181. Allerdings befanden sich fast 70 % dieser Betriebe in der Stadt Magadan, in Tschukotka gab es gerade einmal 6,7 % aller Einrichtungen der lokalen Industrie. Zur Qualität der lokalen Produkte siehe Isakov, Istorija torgovli, S. 206. Zur Unterstützung der lokalen Industrie wollte das Gebietsexekutivkomitee den Volkswirtschaftsrat dazu verpflichten, lokale Produkte einem Ankauf aus anderen sowjetischen Regionen vorzuziehen. Vgl. die Diskussion um die schlechte Qualität des in Magadan produzierten Glases in GAMO f. R-146, op. 1, d. 153, l. 195–196. Vgl. zur Planerfüllung der lokalen Industrie im Vorfeld der Gründung des Volkswirtschaftsrates den Bericht der Staatsbank vom 26. April 1957 in GAMO f. R-146, op. 1, d. 153, l. 135–140.

253 Vgl. den Schriftverkehr in GAMO f. R-146, op. 1, d. 49.

254 Vgl. Slavin, Problemy razvitija, S. 181.

255 Vgl. die Angaben des Jagodninsker Bezirksexekutivkomitees in GAMO f. R-146, op. 1, d. 38, l. 13–15, hier l. 13f. Allgemein zu den Veränderungen dieser Kombinate siehe das Schreiben an den Minister für lokale Industrie der RSFSR in GAMO f. R-146, op. 1, d. 60, l. 53.

256 Vgl. die Berechnungen in Slavin, Problemy razvitija, S. 211. Die Transportkosten waren schon deshalb so hoch, weil viele Güter auf der langen Reise bereits verdarben und sie anschließend abgeschrieben werden mussten.

Region gefunden werden konnten; sehr viele landwirtschaftliche Produkte kamen dann aus China und Korea.

4.3.4.2 Lieferung, Handel und Lagerung

Der Transport von Waren in die Region, ihre Verteilung und Lagerung auf einem Gebiet von gut 1,2 Mio. km², bei weit auseinanderliegenden Lagern, Goldminen und Siedlungen war nicht nur ein infrastrukturelles Problem, sondern v. a. eine Frage der Prioritätensetzung und damit der Machtverteilung.

Für die Lieferung von Rohstoffen, Materialien, Waren des täglichen Bedarfs und Lebensmitteln hatte die Versorgungsorganisation von Dal'stroj, *Kolymsnab*, bis 1954 fast eine Monopolstellung inne. Unterstützt wurde sie von *Dal'strojsnab*, einer Organisation mit Sitz in Moskau, die mit der Lieferung technischer Geräte und Materialien in den Nordosten sowie mit der Entsendung von Fachkräften in das Gebiet betraut war.[257]

Da dem Kombinat bislang eine Zusammenarbeit mit anderen zivilen Organisationen im Fernen Osten verboten war, kontrollierte Dal'stroj durch *Kolymsnab* praktisch den gesamten Warenverkehr in der Region. Die Organe von Partei und Staat mussten somit früh Einfluss auf Lieferungen und Handel gewinnen, um ihre politischen Ziele durchsetzen zu können und um ihre eigene Verwaltung zu versorgen. Ohne eine Kontrolle von Handel und Transport war die neue Leitung praktisch machtlos.

Kolymsnab erhielt zwar bereits im Dezember 1953 vom Ministerrat der UdSSR den Auftrag, alle Organisationen und Einrichtungen des neuen Gebietes mit Waren zu versorgen[258], tatsächlich aber hatte Afanas'ev in der ersten Zeit große Schwierigkeiten, Mitrakov zur Erfüllung dieser Aufgaben zu bewegen. Der Leiter des Kombinats spielte seine Machtposition offen aus und drohte immer wieder mit der Einstellung der Transporte.[259]

Nach der Gebietsgründung begann das Handelsministerium der RSFSR damit, zivile Handels- und Versorgungsorgane aufzubauen, beim Magadaner Gebietsexekutivkomitee wurde eine Handelsabteilung eingerichtet. Das Handelswesen des Gebietes war seitdem von vier verschiedenen Strukturen abhängig: von *Kolymsnab* des MCM,

---

257 Vgl. das Schreiben von Ababkov vom 29. April 1957 an das ZK der KPdSU im Vorfeld der Einführung des Volkswirtschaftsrates in RGANI f. 5, op. 30, d. 201, l. 185–188. Dort werden die vorhandenen Versorgungsorganisationen beschrieben. Verwaltungsabteilungen von *Dal'strojsnab* gab es auch bei den großen Häfen im Chabarowsker und Primorsker Distrikt. *Dal'strojsnab* blieb nach der Auflösung von Dal'stroj und der Einführung des Volkswirtschaftsrates bestehen.

258 Vgl. die Verordnung „Über Maßnahmen in Verbindung mit Gründung des Magadaner Gebietes in der RSFSR" (Nr. 2956) vom 17. Dezember 1953 in GAMO f. R-23, op. 1, d. 6088, l. 59–60.

259 Vgl. das Schreiben von Afanas'ev an Mitrakov vom 24. Mai 1954 in GAMO f. R-146, op. 1, d. 47, l. 17–18 sowie das Schreiben von Mitrakov an Afanas'ev vom April 1954 in GAMO f. R-146, op. 1, d. 47, l. 5–6.

von *Severotorg* des Handelsministeriums der RSFSR (mit der Abteilung *Čukottorg*) und von den Handelseinrichtungen *Glavsevmorput'* und *Rossnabsbyt*.[260]

Formal waren all diese Strukturen dazu verpflichtet, die Region mit Waren zu versorgen. Faktisch aber wurden die Lieferungen maßgeblich von *Kolymsnab* bestimmt, da nur *Kolymsnab* über die notwendigen Arbeiter, Lagerstätten und Transportmittel verfügte. Verträge mit anderen Organisationen waren erst im Entstehen. Die Handelsabteilung des Gebietsexekutivkomitees hatte die Aufgabe, die Arbeit von *Kolymsnab* zu kontrollieren, tatsächlich konnte sie oftmals nur den allgemeinen Mangel beklagen. Ihre Verbesserungsversuche scheiterten an den durch *Kolymsnab* bestimmten Lieferplänen und nicht zuletzt auch an der Unkenntnis über die in der Region vorhandenen Bestände.[261]

Die Quellen zeigen, dass selbst Dal'stroj nicht über den Inhalt seiner Lagerräume informiert war. Bereits im Herbst 1953 war das Kombinat aufgefordert worden, seine Warenbestände genauer zu dokumentieren und vorhandene Lebensmittel und Materialien angemessener unter den einzelnen Verwaltungen aufzuteilen.[262] Doch erst im Laufe der Überprüfungen des Kombinats durch die Ministerien für Buntmetalle und staatliche Kontrolle seit 1954 scheinen die Lagerhallen tatsächlich geöffnet und durchsucht worden zu sein. So ergab eine der vielen Untersuchungen 1955 beispielsweise in der Siedlung Ten'kinsk, dass 7 Tonnen Käse, 10 Tonnen Kaviar, 65 Tonnen Hering und 83 Tonnen Mehl und Graupen abgeschrieben werden mussten.[263] Im Kontor des Čaun-Čukotsker Bezirkes waren die Verluste wegen der „chaotischen Verhältnisse" noch größer, dort gingen 1.050 Tonnen Mehl verloren, 120 Tonnen Sahne, 275 Tonnen Graupen. Der gefangene Fisch wurde einfach im kalten Meerwasser vergessen, die Fischvorräte waren eingefroren – nach Auskunft einer Untersuchungskommission Waren im Wert von 17 Mio. Rubel.[264] Der Anteil der Versor-

---

260 Vgl. die Beschreibung der Handelsstrukturen durch Afanas'ev in seinem Schreiben an den Ministerrat der RSFSR in GAMO f. R-146, op. 1, d. 48, l. 39. Vgl. zur Geschichte von *Glavsevmorput'*, der Hauptverwaltung der Nördlichen Seeroute, Josephson, Soviet Arctic, S. 420 f.

261 Afanas'ev und Ababkov hatten bereits Ende Dezember 1953 den stellv. Vorsitzenden des Ministerrates der UdSSR, Mikojan, um eine verbesserte Lebensmittelversorgung des Gebietes gebeten, worauf Mikojan das Handelsministerium mit einer großen Lieferung von Fleisch, Wurstwaren und Butter an den Hafen Nagaevo beauftragte. Vgl. das Schreiben von Ababkov und Afanas'ev an Mikojan vom 28. Dezember 1953 in GAMO f. R-146, op. 1, d. 47, l. 2. Das Ministerium meldete jedoch wiederum Ababkov und Afanas'ev zurück, dass die Lieferpläne für die Region bereits erschöpft seien, außerdem gebe es in Dal'stroj noch ganz erhebliche Mengen an Lebensmitteln. Vgl. den Brief des stellv. Handelsminister vom 19. Januar 1954 an Afanas'ev und Ababkov in GAMO f. R-146, op. 1, d. 47, l. 1.

262 So die Verordnung des Ministerrates der UdSSR vom 30. September 1953, vgl. GAMO f. R-23, op. 1, d. 5610, l. 41–48, hier l. 46.

263 Vgl. den Bericht des Vertreters aus Ten'kinsk in GAMO f. R-146, op. 1, d. 47, l. 94–14, hier l. 94.

264 Vgl. GAMO f. R-146, op. 1, d. 47, l. 94–14, hier l. 96. Siehe auch den allgemeinen Bericht über die Lage in dem Gebiet vom MCM über die Überprüfung durch die Staatsbank an Mitrakov vom 14. März 1955 in GAMO f. R-23, op. 1, d. 5610, l. 41–48. Die Lagerung war natürlich gerade bei schnell verderblichen Waren eines der größten Probleme. So waren die Fleisch- und Wurstwaren, die Afanas'ev, Ababkov und sogar Mikojan bereits im Dezember 1953 für die neuen Mitarbeiter und die freie Bevöl-

gungseinrichtungen an den Verlusten, die Dal'stroj bzw. später die zivilen Einrichtungen insgesamt machten, war dementsprechend überproportional hoch.[265]

Die Verantwortlichen versuchten, der Probleme auf verschiedenen Ebenen Herr zu werden. In struktureller Hinsicht wurde die bestehende Organisation *Kolymsnab* aufgeteilt – *Kolymtechsnab* war seit dem 1. Juli 1954 für die Versorgung der Industrieanlagen und Baustellen zuständig, *Kolymsnab* für die Versorgung mit Lebensmitteln und Waren des täglichen Bedarfs.[266] Dennoch kam es in der ersten Zeit nach der Übergabe in den zivilen Sektor zu erheblichen Engpässen bei der Belieferung mit Industriewaren: Neue Lieferverträge wurden nicht eingehalten, in mehreren Bereichen wurden nur etwa 25 % der üblichen Mengen in das Gebiet gebracht.[267] Ministerien und unionsweiten Einrichtungen war die Lage des neuen Gebietes häufig vollkommen unbekannt, den lokalen Verantwortlichen fiel es schwer, für die Region und eine angemessene Versorgung zu werben. A. N. Isakov, der die Geschichte des Handels im Nordosten untersucht hat, spricht sogar davon, dass Bestellungen der lokalen Handelsorganisationen ignoriert oder einfach umgewidmet wurden – so wurde z. B. Tschukotka unfreiwilligerweise mit Badeanzügen beliefert, die den Bedarf für die nächsten zwanzig Jahre decken konnten.[268]

---

kerung angefordert hatten, selbst 1956 noch nicht in dem Gebiet eingetroffen, weil es für Magadan – anders als in den unmittelbaren Nachbarregionen Sachalin und Kamtschatka – weder Schiffe mit geeigneten Kühlräumen für den Transport noch große Kühlhäuser in dem Gebiet selbst gab. Afanas'ev bat daher den Vorsitzenden des Ministerrates der RSFSR, Jasnov, für den Transport dieser schnell verderblichen Lebensmittel die Transportbehälter des Ministeriums für Fischwirtschaft zu verwenden und die lokalen Handelsorganisationen außen vor zu lassen. Vgl. den Situationsbericht von Afanas'ev zur Fleisch- und Wurstlieferung in das Gebiet vom 15. Juni 1956 in GAMO f. R-146, op. 1, d. 47, l. 74–75. Insgesamt besaß Dal'stroj im Jahr 1956 nur 60 % der benötigten Lagerflächen. Vgl. den Bericht zur Lage der Versorgung der Bevölkerung von Afanas'ev an den Minister für Metallindustrie, Lomako, vom 25. April 1956 in GAMO f. R-146, op. 1, d. 45, l. 230–232, hier l. 230. Die allermeisten der vorhandenen Lagerhallen stammten zudem aus den Jahren 1936–1938. Vgl. die Situationsbeschreibung aus dem Jahre 1957 in GAMO f. R-137, op. 1, d. 725, l. 1–34, hier l. 5.

265 1954 betrugen allein die über dem Plan liegenden Verluste der Versorgungseinrichtungen 173 Mio. Rubel. Vgl. GAMO f. R-23, op. 1, d. 5610, l. 126.

266 Širokov sieht die Ursache für die Aufteilung von *Kolymsnab* in *Kolymtechsnab* und *Kolymsnab* in den gestiegenen Aufträgen seit Gründung des Gebietes. Vgl. Širokov, Politika, S. 382. Tatsächlich aber reichen die Pläne für eine derartige Umstrukturierung weiter zurück und sind nicht nur lokal zu betrachten. Der Ministerrat der UdSSR hatte in seiner Verordnung vom 5. November 1953 das MMP beauftragt, in Zusammenarbeit mit dem Finanzministerium die bestehenden Organisationen der beiden Hauptverwaltungen „Dal'stroj" und „Enisejstroj" im Hinblick auf den Abbau überflüssiger Strukturen zu überprüfen. Im Zuge dieser Strukturüberprüfung hatte Mitrakov bereits den Vorschlag zur Aufteilung von *Kolymsnab* gemacht. Vgl. ein entsprechendes Schreiben aus der Verwaltung von Dal'stroj an den stellv. Minister für Metallindustrie, Lomako, in RGAÈ f. 9163, op. 6, d. 14, l. 47.

267 Vgl. den Bericht über die Tätigkeit von Dal'stroj für das Jahr 1954 in GAMO f. R-23, op. 1, d. 4843, l. 1–74, hier l. 47–48. Die Probleme hielten auch in den folgenden Jahren an. Vgl. beispielsweise die Schwierigkeiten der Verwaltung *Ènergostroj* aus dem Jahr 1956 in dem Bericht einer Brigade des Gebietsparteikomitees in GAMO f. P-21, op. 5, d. 110, l. 137–147, hier l. 144.

268 Vgl. Isakov, Istorija torgovli, S. 200.

Erst allmählich ersetzten ausführliche Verträge die Willkür der Versorgungsorganisationen.[269] Das Gebietsexekutivkomitee drängte auf eine maßvolle und planmäßige Lieferung und Verteilung der Waren sowie auf eine anständige Lagerung.[270] Der schnell steigende Anteil freier Arbeitskräfte übte zusätzlichen Druck aus. Jetzt kam es nicht nur auf eine bessere Verteilung der Waren, sondern auch auf eine Umstellung des Sortiments an. Afanas'ev und die übrigen Vertreter der Exekutivkomitees drängten deshalb immer mehr auf Veränderungen innerhalb der Organisation *Kolymsnab*:

> Der Handel weitet sich jedes Jahr aus, die Mengen nehmen zu, aber es arbeiten immer noch die alten Kader. [...] Lasst uns doch einmal darüber sprechen, unser gesamtes Handelswesen in die Zuständigkeit des Handelsministeriums zu übertragen (wie dies gerade in Jakutien getan wird). Wir können nicht auf Kader hoffen, die wir nicht haben. Diese Leute [gemeint sind die Vertreter von *Kolymsnab*] haben sich so sehr an einen sorglosen Umgang mit Geld gewöhnt, dass es sehr schwerfällt, sie umzuerziehen.[271]

Für Isakov waren die Einstellungen der alten Kader in den Handelsabteilungen eine der Hauptursachen dafür, dass sich die Bestellungen und Lieferungen erst langsam an die tatsächlichen Bedürfnisse der Bevölkerung anpassten. *Kolymsnab* blieb für Ababkov und Afanas'ev Sinnbild des „Systems Dal'stroj", das „trotz einer breiten materiellen und technischen Basis, Transportmöglichkeiten und angemessener Verbindungen über das Meer nicht gewillt war, die Bürger des Gebietes anständig zu versorgen"[272].

Immer wieder drängte die neue politische Führung daher auf eine stärkere Kontrolle von *Kolymsnab*[273], auf die Einführung einer einheitlichen Handelsorganisation unter der direkten Führung des Gebietsexekutivkomitees und schließlich auf die Auflösung von *Kolymsnab*.[274] Im Januar 1957 wurde *Kolymsnab* in die Hauptverwal-

---

269 Diese Schwierigkeiten bekannte auch der erste Stellvertreter des Vorsitzenden des Ministerrates der RSFSR im Februar 1957 bei einem Treffen mit Afanas'ev. Er sprach von „einem nachlässigen Umgang unserer Ministerien und Einrichtungen" infolge der großen Entfernung zum Nordosten der Union. Zitiert nach Grebenjuk, Kolymskij led, S. 104.

270 Ein Vertreter des Exekutivkomitees, Charitonov, forderte in diesem Zusammenhang, die Verantwortung für den Zustand gelieferter Waren auf die Versorgungseinrichtungen zu übertragen. Vgl. GAMO f. R-146, op. 1, d. 47, l. 94–114, hier l. 100 f.

271 GAMO f. R-146, op. 1, d. 47, l. 94–14, hier l. 105. Immer wieder war auch die Rede davon, Materialien über diese Verschwendungen an die Staatsanwaltschaft zu übergeben; verurteilt wurde jedoch niemand. Vgl. GAMO f. R-146, op. 1, d. 47, l. 94–14, hier l. 100 sowie l. 108.

272 Vgl. die Beschwerde von Ababkov und Afanas'ev über *Kolymsnab* beim ZK der KPdSU vom 2. Februar 1956 in GAMO f. R-146, op. 1, d. 48, l. 70. Siehe ebenso die Beschwerden des stellvertretenden Handelsministers der RSFSR und von Afanas'ev vom 5. August 1957 an den Ministerrat der RSFSR in GAMO f. R-146, op. 1, d. 222, l. 58–66.

273 So Afanas'ev in seinem Schreiben an den Ministerrat der RSFSR vom Mai 1955 in GAMO f. R-146, op. 1, d. 48, l. 39.

274 Zur Bitte um die Einführung einer einheitlichen Handelsorganisation vgl. das Schreiben Afanas'evs an den Ministerrat der RSFSR vom Januar 1956 in GAMO f. R-146, op. 1, d. 60, l. 59–60. Im Mai 1957

tung für die „Arbeiterversorgung des Ministeriums für Buntmetalle" integriert[275], ab November 1957 übernahm seine Position eine entsprechende Gliederung des Volkswirtschaftsrates.[276] Die Versorgung der Bevölkerung verbesserte sich daraufhin allmählich, anhand der Akten der Gebietsabteilung für Handel und Versorgung lässt sich feststellen, wie der Anteil von Waren des täglichen Bedarfs ausgebaut wurde und wie er Stück für Stück mehr den Bedürfnissen der Bevölkerung Rechnung trug: Kinderspielzeug, Damenblusen und Geschirr waren nun Waren, die in steigender, wenn auch noch immer ungenügender Zahl in das Gebiet gebracht wurden.[277] Zugleich blieb die Region auf einem großen Berg von Gütern sitzen, die bisher der Versorgung der Lager gedient hatten. Wattierte Hosen schlechter Qualität, riesige Rollen von Stacheldraht u. ä. verstopften die Lagerräume; trotz Sonderpreisen gab es für diese Waren nun keine Abnehmer mehr.[278]

In der Praxis war die Versorgunglage einer Siedlung jedoch nicht nur von den bürokratischen Planungen der lokalen Leitung, sondern in hohem Maße auch von der vorhandenen Infrastruktur, vom Transport in die Siedlungen und den Lagermöglichkeiten abhängig. Und gerade im Bereich der Transportmöglichkeiten verbesserte sich die Lage erst langsam. Nach wie vor war die Verteilung der Waren innerhalb des Gebietes auf eine begrenzte Zahl von Schiffsverbindungen und Flugzeugen, vor allem aber auf LKWs angewiesen.[279] Aber auch wenn ein Teil der Lebensmittel und Waren des täglichen Bedarfs irgendwann vor Ort eintraf, bedeutete das nicht, dass die Bevölkerung tatsächlich versorgt wurde; Läden und Kantinen waren in den Siedlungen

---

wandte sich Ababkov an das ZK der KPdSU mit der Bitte um Auflösung von *Kolymsnab*. Vgl. GAMO f. R-146, op. 1, d. 47, l. 128–129.

275 Vgl. den Übergabeakt in GAMO f. R-137, op. 1, d. 725, l. 1–34.

276 Vgl. Isakov, Istorija torgovli, S. 201.

277 Siehe den Bericht der Handelsverwaltung vom 15. Oktober 1958 in GAMO f. R-146, op. 1, d. 222, l. 124–141. Die statistische Verwaltung lieferte einen Überblick, welche Waren Ende der 1950er Jahre in dem Gebiet grundsätzlich verfügbar waren. Vgl. den Überblick in Narodnoe chozjajstvo Magadanskoj oblasti, S. 88–90.

278 Bisherige Gegenstände der Lagerpunkte und Waren niedriger Qualität, die nicht mehr benötigt wurden, wurden aussortiert, z. T. verbrannt und z. T. aus dem Gebiet gebracht. Siehe die Beschreibung des Gebietsexekutivkomitees an das Handelsministerium der RSFSR vom 7. März 1958 in GAMO f. R-146, op. 1, d. 222, l. 111–114.

279 Noch 1960 war das Straßennetz des Gebietes, trotz aller Bemühungen um einen Ausbau, dreimal geringer (bezogen auf eine Fläche von 1.000 km²) als im Durchschnitt in der Sowjetunion. Vgl. Slavin, Problemy razvitija, S. 250. Siehe dort die ausführlichen Angaben zur Entwicklung des Transportwesens seit 1954. Die Probleme mit dem Transport von Rentierfleisch veranschaulichen die Schwierigkeiten besonders deutlich. Hier gab es regional produziertes Fleisch, das der Bevölkerung zugutekommen sollte. Die Handelsverwaltung des Gebietsexekutivkomitees schloss mit den Kolchosen einen Vertrag über den Ankauf von 300 Tonnen Fleisch auf Kommission (Vertrag am 24. August 1954). Wegen fehlendem Flugverkehr konnte das Fleisch jedoch nicht geliefert werden, am 25. Januar 1955 erwartete man wenigstens 26 Tonnen, gebracht wurden schließlich 11 Tonnen Fleisch. Vgl. den Bericht des stellv. Leiters der Handelsverwaltung des Gebietsexekutivkomitees vom 28. Januar 1955 an den stellv. Leiter des Gebietsexekutivkomitees in GAMO f. R-146, op. 1, d. 7, l. 135.

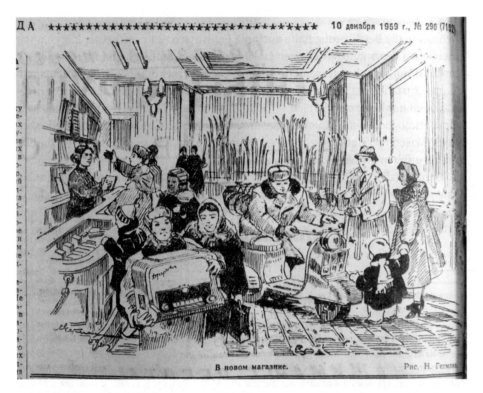

Abb. 35 Offizielle, aber realitätsferne Darstellung des typischen Warenangebots, Magadanskaja
Pravda, 10. Dezember 1959

ausgesprochen seltene Erscheinungen.[280] Viele Waren fanden nie den Weg von einer
Lagerhalle in einen Laden und statistisch gesehen gab es in dem Gebiet für 25 bis 30
Personen einen Platz in einer Kantine – und das obwohl die Wohnheime für Arbeiter
nur sehr selten mit einer Küche ausgestattet waren.[281]

Zu Beginn der 1960er Jahre verbesserte sich die Versorgung der Magadaner Bevölkerung im Rahmen der unionsweiten Steigerung des Konsums weiter. Neben einer
deutlichen Zunahme der Versorgung mit Lebensmitteln waren nun auch Konsumgüter
wie Waschmaschinen, Radios oder Fotoapparate erhältlich.[282]

---

280 Auf der ersten Wirtschaftskonferenz des Gebietes im Jahr 1958 wurden vergleichende Zahlen zu
Verkaufspunkten genannt: In England kämen auf einen Verkaufspunkt 93 Käufer, in Frankreich 59, in
der UdSSR 408 und in Magadan 800. Vgl. Isakov, Istorija torgovli, S. 209.
281 Vgl. den Bericht zur Lage der Versorgung der Bevölkerung von Afanas'ev an den Minister für
Metallindustrie, Lomako, vom 25. April 1956 in GAMO f. R-146, op. 1, d. 45, l. 230–232, hier l. 231. Für die
statistischen Angaben siehe den Bericht zur Lage von *Kolymsnab* vom 1. März 1957 in GAMO f. R-137,
op. 1, d. 725, l. 1–34, hier l. 17.
282 Isakov betrachtet den Zeitraum zwischen 1953 und 1963 und spricht dabei von einer Handels-
steigerung um 50,5 %. Bei einzelnen Waren wie Fleisch, Milch und Kleidungsstücken waren die Zu-

4.3.4.3 Bauwirtschaft

Ebenso wie die Bevölkerung hatte auch die Bauwirtschaft in den ersten Jahren unter erheblichen Versorgungsproblemen zu leiden, obwohl Industrie und Bau theoretisch immer vorrangig beliefert werden sollten.[283] Doch dieser Status war angesichts aufgelöster Zuständigkeiten und Lieferstrukturen sowie der großen Zahl von Bauorganisationen nur begrenzt hilfreich.[284] Nicht eingehaltene Lieferverträge[285], mangelnde Transportmöglichkeiten innerhalb des Gebietes und fehlende Lagerungsmöglichkeiten für Maschinen und Bauteile waren neben dem Mangel an geeigneten Facharbeitern die größten Probleme auf den Baustellen.[286]

Grundsätzlich war für Chruščev die Schaffung von Wohnraum einer der wichtigsten Punkte seiner sozialen, politischen und ideologischen Agenda. Mark Smith bezeichnet in seiner Studie zum Wohnungsbauprogramm der stalinistischen und poststalinistischen Periode diese Reform als „one of the greatest social reforms of

---

nahmen noch deutlich größer. Vgl. Isakov, Istorija torgovli, S. 209 f. Siehe grundsätzlich zur Steigerung des Konsums Merl, Konsum, S. 521 sowie Merl, Anspruch und Realität sowie zur politischen Dimension von Lieferungen in der Sowjetunion Hough; Fainsod, Soviet Union is Governed, S. 508.

283 Ausführlich zur Lage der Bauwirtschaft bei Gründung des Gebietes siehe den Bericht des Leiters der Abteilung für perspektivische Planungen in Dal'stroj, V. Vasil'ev, an das ZK der KPdSU und das Gebietsparteikomitee. Er zeigt ausführlich Beispiele für gigantische Verschwendungen und Planungsfehler auf. Vgl. seinen ausführlichen Bericht in GAMO f. P-21, op. 5, d. 685, l. 1–20 (Bericht vom 20. Juni 1954).

284 Für einen Überblick über die verschiedenen Bauorganisationen siehe den Bericht des Gebietsparteikomitees im Vorfeld der Einführung des Magadaner Volkswirtschaftsrates an das ZK der KPdSU in GAMO f. R-23, op. 1, d. 6088, l. 1–50, hier l. 7.

285 Siehe zu den Lieferausfällen für Dal'stroj Širokov, Politika, S. 383. Nach seinen Angaben verbesserte sich die Situation etwa ab 1956.

286 Zur Lage der technischen Versorgung von Dal'stroj siehe den Bericht für das Jahr 1956 in GAMO f. R-23, op. 1, d. 6011, l. 3–10. Für einen Überblick über die Lage der Bauwirtschaft siehe Žarkich/Lukin, Vstajut novostrojki. Ausführlich schilderte der Leiter der Abteilung für Bauinspektion von Dal'stroj die Schwierigkeiten der lokalen Bauwirtschaft in seinem Schreiben an Afanas'ev und den Leiter der Architekturabteilung des Gebietsexekutivkomitees in GAMO f. R-146, op. 1, d. 45, l. 128–131. Siehe auch die Darstellung der wichtigsten Probleme auf der Grundlage einer Überprüfung der Verwaltung der Magadaner Bank vom 23. Juni 1956 in GAMO f. R-146, op. 1, d. 45, l. 250–260, hier l. 259. Ganz besonders schwierig war die Versorgungslage in Tschukotka. Der Bau des dortigen Iul'tinsker Kombinats lag auf Eis, weil die benötigten Materialien die Baustelle nicht erreichen konnten. Ein vollbeladenes Schiff, das zwischen 50 und 80 % der gesamten jährlichen Materialmenge von Čukotstroj enthielt, war zunächst auf dem Nordmeer unterwegs, musste dann jedoch aufgrund meteorologischer Verhältnisse umdrehen und eine Route im Süden über Gibraltar und den Suezkanal nehmen. Vgl. den Bericht des obersten Kontrolleurs für das Magadaner Gebiet und Dal'stroj, Milovidov, vom 27. Oktober 1956 in GAMO f. R-146, op. 1, d. 45, l. 245–249. Milovidov kritisierte in diesem Bericht deutlich das Desinteresse der Führung von Dal'stroj an der schlechten Versorgungslage und der daraus resultierenden Unterbrechung der Bautätigkeiten. Auch der Wohnungsbau für Arbeiter in Tschukotka kam aufgrund dieser Probleme nicht in Gang, die fertigen Platten für moderne mehrgeschossige Häuer konnten nicht geliefert werden. Vgl. das Schreiben aus dem Handelsministerium der RSFSR vom Juni 1956 in GAMO f. R-146, op. 1, d. 47, l. 70–71.

modern European history"[287]. Die Maßnahmen setzten bereits 1955 ein und kulminierten im Juli 1957 in der Verordnung des ZK der KPdSU und des Ministerrates der UdSSR „Über die Entwicklung des Wohnungsbaus in der UdSSR"; ein gewaltiger Boom des Wohnungsbaus war die Folge.[288] Im Magadaner Gebiet hatten bereits die Verordnungen zur Unterstützung des neuen Gebietes vom Mai/Juni 1954 einen Umschwung herbeiführen sollen; in ihrer Folge ergingen Hunderte Bauaufträge für die Industrie und die soziale Infrastruktur der Bevölkerung.[289] Auch in programmatischer Hinsicht sollte sich einiges ändern – Baustellen, die seit Jahren brachlagen, sollten wieder angegangen, neue Gebäude errichtet und der Wohnungsbau über das Ministerium für den zivilen Wohnungsbau der RSFSR gestärkt werden. Mehr noch, der Ministerrat der UdSSR sah für seine Verordnungen sogar vor, dass im Magadaner Gebiet grundsätzlich keine neuen Anlagen, Betriebe oder Institutionen errichtet werden durften, ohne zugleich die Bedürfnisse der Bevölkerung zu berücksichtigen.[290] Neben der Gründung von Bauorganisationen sollten freien Arbeitern günstige Kredite für den privaten Hausbau gewährt werden. Tatsächlich nahmen jedoch nur sehr wenige freie Arbeitskräfte diese Angebote in Anspruch, da die Kredite im Vergleich zu den enormen Kosten für Baumaterialien viel zu gering waren. Zudem blieben die meisten Arbeiter nur für eine begrenzte Zeit in der Region.[291]

Das MMP verpflichtete Dal'stroj, seine Prioritäten zugunsten größerer Anstrengungen im Bauwesen zu verschieben. Diese inhaltlichen Forderungen gingen jedoch nicht in allen Bereichen mit erhöhten Mittelzuweisungen einher, was viele Projekte von Anfang an verzögerte, z. T. sogar ganz in Frage stellte und gleichzeitig Korruption und die Schattenwirtschaft mit wertvollen Materialien stark begünstigte.[292]

Bei den Versuchen, zusätzliche Gelder für Bauprojekte in die Region zu lenken, arbeiteten der Erste Parteisekretär und der Leiter von Dal'stroj zusammen – schließlich waren ihre jeweiligen Aufgaben von den Aufbauleistungen im Gebiet abhängig.[293]

---

287 Smith, Property, S. 4.

288 Vgl. Davies/Ilic, From Khrushchev to Khrushchev, S. 228.

289 Am 8. Juni 1954 beschloss der Ministerrat der RSFSR die Gründung einer eigenen Bauorganisation für zivilen Wohnungsbau in dem Gebiet – *Magadangraždanstroj*. Vgl. den Bericht von Ababkov und Afanas'ev zu dieser Gründung an das ZK der KPdSU in RGANI f. 5, op. 41, d. 22, l. 74–96, hier l. 74.

290 Vgl. den Entwurf der Verordnung des Ministerrates vom Mai 1954 in GAMO f. R-146, op. 1, f. 6, l. 33–51, hier l. 35.

291 Die Vergabe von Krediten für private Bauaktivitäten war zudem in Siedlungen schwierig, deren Existenz von der Aufrechterhaltung der dortigen Industrie abhängig war. Vgl. zur Problematik der Privatkredite das Schreiben von Čistjakov an den Ministerrat der RSFSR vom Dezember 1956 in GAMO f. R-146, op. 1, d. 45, l. 227–228.

292 Siehe den Bericht der Chabarowsker Kontrollgruppe der Kommission für sowjetische Kontrolle des Ministerrates der RSFSR an Afanas'ev vom 15. Dezember 1959 in GAMO f. R-146, op. 1, d. 221, S. 178–189, hier S. 185.

293 So wandten sie sich schon am 18. Februar 1954 in einem gemeinsamen Schreiben an Chruščev und Malenkov und baten um Mittelerhöhungen von 233 Mio. Rubel für Baumaßnahmen. RGANI f. 5, op. 27, d. 233, l. 92–99, hier l. 99. Siehe auch die genaue Auflistung aller notwendigen Bauarbeiten mit den entsprechenden Kosten ebd., l. 101–103.

Abb. 36 Humoristische Darstellung schlechter Bauplanung in Magadan. Im Bild links, „vormittags", wird der Asphalt planiert, im Bild rechts, „nachmittags", selbiger wieder aufgerissen um Rohre zu verlegen. Magadanskaja Pravda, 25. Juli 1958

Bauarbeiten waren in der Region einfach ungeheuer teuer, wie der Blick auf die Baumaterialien zeigt.[294] So lagen die eingeplanten Kosten für eine Tonne Zement im Jahr 1958 bei 465 Rubel – allerdings nur in der Stadt Magadan. In der Siedlung Jagodnoe kostete die Tonne Zement aufgrund des Transports innerhalb des Gebietes bereits 1.020 Rubel, in Susuman 1.133 Rubel.[295] Gebaut werden sollte jedoch nicht nur in den industriellen Zentren von Jagodnoe und Susuman, sondern eben auch in weit entfernt gelegenen Regionen und dringend auch an den neu erschlossenen Goldförderstellen auf der Halbinsel Tschukotka. Gerade im Bereich des zivilen Wohnungsbaus fehlten Dal'stroj die Erfahrungen und die Beziehungen zu Produzenten geeigneter Materialien.[296] Hinzu kamen erhöhte Personalkosten, da die Bauarbeiter im Hohen Norden Zuschläge erhielten. Dementsprechend gewaltig waren die Ausgaben

---

294 Zur allgemeinen Lage in der Industrie für Baumaterialien siehe den Bericht über die Tätigkeit des Magadaner Volkswirtschaftsrates im Jahr 1958 in RGAĖ f. 7733, op. 47, d. 538, l. 12 bzw. die Erläuterungen zum Jahresbericht 1959 von Korolev und dem Hauptbuchhalter Gol'dšvend in RGAĖ f. 7733, op. 48, d. 492, l. 1–28, hier l. 10.

295 Vgl. Slavin, Problemy razvitija, S. 160.

296 Zum Mangel an Zement und zu seiner sehr ungleichen Verteilung über das gesamte Gebiet von Dal'stroj siehe die Verordnung des Ministeriums für Buntmetalle zur Arbeit von Dal'stroj in GAMO f. 23, op. 1, d. 5610, l. 7–15, hier l. 9. Im Auftrag des Volkswirtschaftsrates und des Gebietsexekutivkomitees soll sich die nordöstliche geologische Verwaltung daher auch um Lagerstätten von Lehm, Kies und Sand bemühen. Vgl. GAMO f. 146, op. 1, d. 153, l. 111–113.

für Investitionsbauten, aber auch beim Wohnungsbau. In den 1950er Jahren war der Bau von einem Quadratmeter Wohnraum im Magadaner Gebiet so teuer wie in keiner anderen sowjetischen Region. Im Jahr 1957 lagen die Kosten für den Bau von einem Quadratmeter Wohnraum im Durchschnitt der RSFSR bei 1.703 Rubel. Zur gleichen Zeit betrugen die Kosten in Murmansk 2.474 Rubel, in Workuta 2.578, in Norilsk 3.691 und in Magadan 5.135 Rubel.[297]

Die Leningrader Filiale der Akademie für Bau und Architektur der UdSSR erarbeitete zahlreiche Vorschläge, wie diese gewaltigen Kosten gesenkt und zugleich ein besseres Leben für die Menschen im Norden ermöglicht werden könnte. Wichtigste Maßnahmen waren für sie ein verstärkter Technikeinsatz, der mit geringeren Arbeitskosten einhergehen sollte, eine bessere Organisation und sinnvolle Projektierung durch eine verkleinerte Zahl geeigneter Institutionen, vor allem aber der Bau von Gebäuden, die den klimatischen Ansprüchen des Permafrostbodens besser gewachsen waren. Denn, so schrieb der stellvertretende Vorsitzende:

> Wegen des geringen technischen Standards der Projekte, die mit veralteten Methoden umgesetzt werden, zwingen wir unsere Nordländer [Bewohner des sowjetischen Nordens] häufig, unter anormalen und mitunter sehr schweren Bedingungen zu leben und zu arbeiten, während dies zugleich dem Staat große Verluste einbringt.[298]

Grundsätzlich müssten sich die Verantwortlichen von ihrer „primitiv-utilitaristischen Herangehensweise an die Erschließung des Nordens"[299] lösen und die Erkenntnisse der sowjetischen und internationalen Wissenschaft auf diesem Gebiet endlich zur Kenntnis nehmen.[300] Ihre Visionen beschrieben die Wissenschaftler folgendermaßen:

> Im Hohen Norden sollte auch die kleinste, unbedeutendste Siedlung Gegenstand der fürsorglichen Aufmerksamkeit von Architekten und Ingenieuren werden, die ihre Aufgabe verstehen und eine große Verantwortung für die ihnen aufgetragene Sache verspüren. [...] Der Bevölkerung sollte der beste Standard geboten werden, um sie dafür zu kompensieren, dass sie unter solch harten klimatischen Bedingungen leben muss, wofür es in den Ortschaften die bestmögliche Versorgung (Wasserleitungen, Kanalisation, Zentralheizung, Heißwasserversorgung, Elektroherde, Müllbeseitigungssysteme) geben muss, unabhängig von der Größe, administrativen und wirtschaftlichen Bedeutung der Stadt oder Siedlung. Zudem sollten die Siedlungen insgesamt durch spezielle Aufbauten vor Wind und Schneefällen geschützt und z. T. in ihnen ein künstliches Klima (z. B. durch atomare Stationen) geschaffen werden.[301]

---

297 Zahlen für mehrstöckige Wohnhäuser nach den Angaben der Zentralen Statistischen Verwaltung der UdSSR; vgl. Akademija Stroitel'stva i Architektury SSSR, Voprosy stroitel'stva na Krajnem Severe, S. 10.

298 Murav'ev, Nasuščnye voprosy, S. 11.

299 Murav'ev, Nasuščnye voprosy, S. 28.

300 Vgl. Murav'ev, Nasuščnye voprosy, S. 11. Ein eigener Beitrag beschäftigte sich dabei mit den Erfahrungen anderer Staaten (Alaska, Grönland, Kanada) bei Baumaßnahmen im Hohen Norden. Vgl. ebd., S. 33 ff.

301 Murav'ev, Nasuščnye voprosy, S. 17. Die Akademie hielt die Stadt Norilsk für ein gelungenes Beispiel für Städtebau im Hohen Norden. Vgl. ebd., S. 13. Siehe auch die Vorschläge der Experten-

Wie weit die tatsächlichen Lebensbedingungen im Magadaner Gebiet von solchen
Vorstellungen entfernt waren, wird das fünfte Kapitel zeigen. Doch machen diese
Konzeptionen deutlich, dass auch die ehemaligen Lagergebiete im Hohen Norden Teil
des hochgradig ideologisch besetzten Wohnungsbauprogramms werden sollten, mit
dessen Verwirklichung für Chruščev zugleich die kommunistische Zukunft erstehen,
die Umgestaltung sowjetischer Städte als Zeichen des epochalen Wandels fungieren
sollte.[302]

So war auch in Magadan der Zuwachs im Vergleich zu der Zeit vor 1954 mehr als
deutlich. Er betrug beim Wohnraum zwischen 1953 und 1959 386 % und lag damit
erheblich über dem unionsweiten Durchschnitt. Der Ausbau von Barackenansamm-
lungen zu ganzen Siedlungen vollzog sich in diesen wenigen Jahren.[303] Eine Gruppe
von Chabarowsker Kontrolleuren der Kommission für die sowjetische Kontrolle des
Ministerrates der RSFSR konnte Ende des Jahrzehnts insgesamt eine allgemeine Verbesserung der Bautätigkeiten und ihrer finanziellen Ausstattung konstatieren.[304]

Der Blick auf die weiteren Industriezweige hat gezeigt, dass in der Konzeption der
Region als stalinistischem Lager-Industriellen Komplex die Förderung eines erweiterten industriellen Profils politisch undenkbar gewesen war. Nach 1953 war es dann
die Abkehr von der strukturell vorherrschenden Zwangsarbeit und des politischen
Sonderstatus, die im Verbund mit der Forderung nach einer rentableren Metallförderung eine weitergehende wirtschaftliche Entwicklung der Region ermöglichte –
auch wenn für die 1950er Jahren hier v. a. Mangel und Schwierigkeiten konstatiert
werden müssen. Die grundsätzliche Neuausrichtung stärkte aber in den Folgejahren
die Bedeutung des Gebietes als zunehmend vollwertiger und gleichberechtigter Teil
der Union. Allerdings war diese Form der „Regionalisierung" als Ergebnis der Entstalinisierung nur denkbar, weil es der politischen und wirtschaftlichen Führung Ende
der 1950er Jahre gelang, die Krise der Goldförderung zu überwinden. Denn nur durch
den Anstieg der Förderzahlen erschien auch die Förderung der regionalen Industrien
wirtschaftlich wie politisch als gerechtfertigt.

---

kommission des Ministeriums für die kommunale Wirtschaft der RSFSR und die Reaktionen aus Magadan vom 2. September 1957 in GAMO f. R-137, op. 1, d. 17a, l. 230–241. Der Leiter der Magadaner
Organisation *Dal'strojproekt*, M. M. Žagullo, berichtete bei dem Treffen von den Magadaner Erfahrungen. Vgl. Akademija Stroitel'stva i Architektury SSSR, Voprosy stroitel'stva na Krajnem Severe,
S. 86–89.

302 Vgl. Smith, Property, S. 102.

303 Vgl. die Zahlen bei Davies/Ilic, From Khrushchev to Khrushchev, S. 214.

304 Seit 1958 sei deutlich mehr Geld in die Bautätigkeiten investiert worden, trotz zahlreicher weiterhin bestehender Probleme seien mehr Gebäude tatsächlich fertiggestellt worden, so die Gruppe der
Kontrolleure. Vgl. den Bericht der Chabarowsker Kontrollgruppe an Afanas'ev vom 15. Dezember 1959
in GAMO f. R-146, op. 1, d. 221, S. 178–189, hier S. 179. Der Magadaner Volkswirtschaftsrat berichtete
zugleich von einer deutlichen Senkung der Kosten im Bereich des Wohnungsbaus. Sie sanken zwischen
1958 und 1959 um 11 %. Vgl. die Erläuterungen zum Jahresbericht 1959 von Korolev und dem Hauptbuchhalter Gol'dšvend in RGAĖ f. 7733, op. 48, d. 492, l. 1–28, hier l. 24.–25.

4.4 Goldförderung vor und nach 1953: Wie effektiv war die Zwangsarbeit?

Der russische Historiker Oleg Chlevnjuk hat Zwangsarbeit als eine Art „Droge" für die sowjetische Wirtschaft bezeichnet, von der sie nur mit großen Schwierigkeiten ablassen konnte.[305] Zu stark waren ganze Wirtschaftsbereiche von Strukturen, Normen und Praxis der erzwungenen Arbeit durchdrungen, als dass man sie einfach in den zivilen Sektor hätte transferieren können. Von den enormen Schwierigkeiten dieser Übergangsperiode im Gebiet Dal'stroj nach Stalins Tod haben die vorangegangenen Kapitel gehandelt.

Warum der stalinistische Staat überhaupt Zwangsarbeit einsetzte, ob er aus politischen oder aus ökonomischen Gründen von ihr abhängig war, diese Frage gilt grundsätzlich als beantwortet. Blickt man auf das gesamte System des GULAG, kann generell nicht von einem Vorrang wirtschaftlicher Motive vor politischen Entscheidungen gesprochen werden. Allein mit der wirtschaftlichen Bedeutung der Zwangsarbeit lassen sich die Verhaftungswellen und die Brutalität, mit der Hunderttausende Menschen zu den körperlich härtesten Arbeiten gezwungen wurden, nicht erklären. So konstatiert auch Chlevnjuk: „politics, as a rule, had priority over economics"[306]. Zugleich war der Einsatz der Zwangsarbeiter einer der wichtigsten und strukturprägendsten Teile der Stalin'schen Industrialisierung; gigantische Projekte sind ohne sie nicht vorstellbar.[307]

Die Frage, ob es auch eine wirtschaftliche Begründung dafür gab, dass die sowjetische Führung im Laufe der Jahre immer weitere Bereiche der Wirtschaft dem NKVD/MVD unterordnete – die Frage also nach dem Nutzen der Zwangsarbeit –, diese Frage wird heute von den wichtigsten Moskauer und westlichen Historikern meist mit dem Hinweis auf ihre extreme Ineffektivität beantwortet. Besonders anschaulich beschreibt Galina Ivanova die „Absurdität" dieses Wirtschaftssystems.[308] Bei Untersuchungen zum Weißmeer-Ostsee-Kanal beispielsweise oder zur Bahnlinie Čum-Salechard-Igarka am Polarkreis steht fast immer die Sinnlosigkeit der Projekte an sich, ihre wirtschaftliche Nutzlosigkeit, die ineffektive Arbeitsweise und ihre Abhängigkeit von den Launen des Diktators im Vordergrund.

---

305 Vgl. Khlevnyuk, Economy of the Gulag, S. 128.
306 Khlevnyuk, Economy of the OGPU, S. 65 f.
307 Vgl. dazu Khlevnyuks Beurteilung „Forced labor was of unique importance in the construction of the largest and most labor-intensive projects". Khlevnyuk, Economy of the OGPU, S. 60. Siehe zur Bedeutung der Zwangsarbeit in stalinistischen Großprojekten ebenso Kraveri/Khlevnyuk, Krizis ėkonomiki MVD; Stettner, Archipel Gulag, S. 340 ff. sowie Merl, Opferzahl.
308 Siehe ihr Kapitel „Lagernaja ėkonomika v poslevoennyj period", in: Ivanova, Istorija, S. 336 – 392, hier S. 341. Allgemein zur Produktivität der stalinistischen Häftlingsarbeit siehe van der Linden, Forced Labour, S. 355 f.; Borodkin/Gregory/Khlevniuk, Ėkonomika; Craveri, Forced Labour; Gregory/Lazarev, Forced Labor.

Anders gelagert ist der Blick Magadaner Historiker auf die ökonomische Effektivität der Zwangsarbeit in Dal'stroj. Sie folgen in ihrer Analyse den Eckdaten der Goldförderung, die nach der Amnestie vom März 1953 und den weiteren Entlassungswellen beständig zurückging. Und sie folgen den historischen Darstellungen der Kombinatsleitung, die als Hauptursache dieser Krise die sinkende Zahl der Arbeitskräfte und dabei v. a. der Zwangsarbeiter identifizierte. Zwar begrüßen sie aus moralischer Perspektive die Zurückdrängung der Zwangsarbeit ausdrücklich, kommen jedoch nicht umhin, die aus ihrer Sicht negativen wirtschaftlichen Folgen zu beschreiben – als hätte das Ende des Stalinismus der Wirtschaft von Dal'stroj den Kopf gekostet.[309]

Diese Sichtweise lässt entscheidende Faktoren einer wirtschaftlichen Beurteilung des Lager-Industriellen Komplexes außer Acht, z. B. seine extreme finanzielle Sonderstellung und die ungeheuren Verluste, die er der sowjetischen Volkswirtschaft brachte. Vor allem aber geht auf diese Weise der Zusammenhang zu der Krise der Lagerwirtschaft, die auch Dal'stroj seit Ende der 1940er / Anfang der 1950er Jahre massiv erfasst hatte, verloren. Die Goldförderung war schließlich schon Jahre zuvor im Fall begriffen, auch wenn die Abschaffung der Zwangsarbeit der Krise eine zunehmende Dynamik bescherte. Die Lage war sozusagen schon schlecht und sie wurde durch das Fehlen Tausender Arbeitskräfte nur noch schlechter, was jedoch nicht als unmittelbares Zeichen einer größeren Effektivität der Zwangsarbeit gewertet werden darf.[310]

Dennoch ist der Blickwinkel der Magadaner Historiker für eine Bewertung von Dal'stroj von Bedeutung. Denn anders als bei Projekten wie der Bahnlinie Čum-Salechard-Igarka war die gesamte sowjetische Wirtschaft auf Dal'stroj angewiesen. Der Außenhandel der Sowjetunion, der Import von Waffen, technischen Anlagen und schweren Geräten für die Industrialisierung beruhte zu einem erheblichen Teil auf dem nordöstlichen Gold, war ohne die Rohstoffe von Dal'stroj nicht denkbar. In diesem Sinne kann von einer grundsätzlichen „Ineffektivität" des Lager-Industriellen Komplexes nicht gesprochen werden. Paul Josephson beschreibt den Einsatz von Zwangsarbeit im gesamten sowjetischen Norden zutreffend, wenn er auf den Zusammenhang zwischen dem krassen Mangel an Technologie und Infrastruktur unter den extremen klimatischen Bedingungen auf der einen und dem „günstigen" Einsatz von Häftlingen auf der anderen Seite aufmerksam macht: „The camps were, in fact, forms of technology: human machines with limited operational capacity and a short of lifetime guarantee."[311] Blendet man alle moralischen Beurteilungen aus, muss sich

---

309 Vgl. Zeljak, Zolotodobyvajuščaja promyšlennost', S. 143 f.; Širokov, Politika, S. 356 sowie Rajzman, SNCH MĚAR, S. 160.

310 Zumal es die Kombinatsleitung schon relativ bald erreichte, dass alle verfügbaren Arbeitskräfte in die Goldförderung geschickt wurden (auf Kosten anderer Industriezweige). Im Jahr 1956 beispielsweise lag die Versorgung mit Arbeitskräften im Gold bei 100,8 %, während sie in Dal'stroj insgesamt 96,9 % betrug. So Berezin in seinem Bericht vom 19. März 1957 in GAMO f. R-23, op. 1, d. 6109, l. 2–12, hier l. 6.

311 Josephson, Soviet Arctic, S. 422.

der Blick daher auf die in Dal'stroj geleistete Arbeit richten, wenn man die Frage nach der wirtschaftlichen Effektivität der Zwangsarbeit stellen will.

Aus dem Kombinat bzw. dem Volkswirtschaftsrat liegen Quellen vor, in denen die Arbeitsproduktivität der in Dal'stroj beschäftigten Menschen zwischen 1947 und 1957 dargestellt wird, wobei keine Unterscheidung zwischen Häftlingen, Sondersiedlern oder freien Vertragsarbeitern getroffen wird – von Interesse ist hier lediglich die durchschnittliche Produktivität menschlicher Arbeitskraft im Laufe der Jahre. Angegeben sind verschiedene Bewertungskriterien. Das erste Kriterium umfasst die in einem Jahr von einem Menschen erzeugte Goldmenge. „Mensch" bezieht sich hier auf einen „Arbeitenden", umfasst also nicht nur die unmittelbar in der Rohstoffförderung Beschäftigten, sondern auch alle Verwaltungsangestellten im Bergbau (ein statistischer Durchschnittswert).[312]

Im Jahr 1947 hatte ein „Arbeitender" in Dal'stroj 702,6 Gramm Gold gefördert, im Jahr 1956 waren es 1.633,2 Gramm. Das bedeutet, innerhalb einer guten Dekade hatte sich die Arbeitsproduktivität der in Dal'stroj Beschäftigten weit mehr als verdoppelt; im Jahr 1956 leistete ein Arbeitender mehr als zwei Arbeitende im Jahr 1947, zugleich sank jedoch der Anteil der Häftlinge. Generell gesprochen war also ein Häftling Mitte der vierziger Jahre deutlich weniger produktiv als eine freie Arbeitskraft Mitte der 1950er Jahre. Nach 1956 nahm die Arbeitsproduktivität sogar noch deutlicher zu.[313]

Blickt man nun genauer auf den Zuwachs innerhalb der Dekade, zeigen sich deutliche Sprünge. Die Zunahme der Arbeitsproduktivität war im Jahr 1948 noch minimal, statt 702,6 Gramm förderte ein Arbeitender im Jahr 1948 704,8 Gramm. 1949 stieg die Produktivität an, nun lag die Fördermenge bereits bei 861,9 Gramm. Dieser Zuwachs verlief analog zu der 1949 sich kurzfristig stabilisierenden Goldförderung

---

312 Siehe die als „geheim" klassifizierte Tabelle des Leiters der Planungsabteilung der Bergbauverwaltung I. Kočin. Diese Tabelle findet sich im Staatlichen Archiv des Magadaner Gebietes (GAMO) in einem Nebenbestand des Bestandes f. R-137 – Volkswirtschaftsrat des Magadaner Gebietes. Dieser Nebenbestand unterlag einer besonderen Geheimhaltungsstufe. Vgl. GAMO f. R-137sč, op. 1b, d. 189, l. 78. Leider fehlt in dieser Tabelle die Bezeichnung der Maßeinheit. Die Angabe lautet lediglich: „Erzeugtes Gold für einen Arbeitenden in der Bergbauverwaltung". Die fehlende Maßeinheit kann jedoch aus anderen Dokumenten übertragen werden. Wann immer von der Menge erzeugten Goldes pro Arbeiter oder Arbeitendem die Rede ist, lautet die Maßeinheit „Gramm". Die dabei genannten Zahlen entsprechen den Angaben in der hier genannten Tabelle oder sind mit ihnen vergleichbar. Vgl. beispielsweise die Angaben in dem Bericht des stellv. Leiters von Dal'stroj, Berezin, vom 19. März 1957 über Maßnahmen zur weiteren Senkung der Selbstkosten der Goldförderung in GAMO f. R-23, op. 1, d. 6109, l. 2–12, hier l. 2. Hier liegen die Zahlen für das Jahr mit 2.006 Gramm etwas über den Angaben in der genannten Tabelle, diese Differenz ergibt sich jedoch daraus, dass hierbei nur die Arbeitsproduktivität der Arbeiter berechnet wurde; eine Einbeziehung aller Arbeitenden senkt natürlich die Arbeitsproduktivität pro Kopf noch einmal ab.

313 Die Arbeitsproduktivität des Volkswirtschaftsrates stieg trotz mangelnder Fachkräfte im Jahr 1958 erheblich an, zum Teil wurden die Pläne um 150 % übererfüllt. Dies führte die Leitung des Volkswirtschaftsrates hauptsächlich auf die fortschreitende Mechanisierung der Arbeit zurück. Vgl. den Bericht von Korolev über die Tätigkeit des Magadaner Volkswirtschaftsrats im Jahr 1958 in RGAĖ f. 7733, op. 47, d. 538, l. 12 sowie l. 26.

durch enorme finanzielle Anstrengungen des MVD; er lässt sich aber auch mit der Einführung einer Verkürzung der Haftzeiten durch gute Arbeitsleistungen und eines kleinen Lohns für Häftlinge (1948 bzw. zum 1. Januar 1949) erklären.[314] 1950 fiel die Arbeitsproduktivität deutlich, von 861,9 auf 774,8 Gramm gefördertes Gold pro Arbeitendem; sie stieg bereits 1951 wieder an und übertraf mit 891,4 Gramm das Ergebnis des Jahres 1949. Seit 1951 nahm die Produktivität in jedem Jahr immer weiter zu, mit größeren und kleineren Sprüngen, in jedem Jahr war jedoch ein sehr deutlicher Zuwachs zu verzeichnen.[315]

Die tatsächliche Produktivität eines Arbeitenden wuchs also trotz des Rückgangs der Goldförderung, des Absinkens des mittleren Goldgehaltes und trotz der ständig steigenden Menge an zu bewegendem Erdreich. Sie war unabhängig vom Anteil der Zwangsarbeit an allen Arbeitenden. Den größten Sprung bei der Steigerung der Arbeitsproduktivität (von 1.253,8 Gramm (1954) auf 1.559,5 Gramm im Jahr 1955) gab es gerade im Jahr 1955, das finanziell wie auch in der Summe des geförderten Goldes ein ausgesprochen schwaches Jahr war.

Ähnlich wie bei der auf die Goldgewinnung bezogenen Arbeitsproduktivität verhielten sich auch die Zuwächse in zwei weiteren Bereichen, wenn man die Bruttoproduktivität eines Arbeitstages, gemittelt für ganz Dal'stroj, betrachtet.[316] Bei der Abtragung des Erdreichs lag die Produktivität eines Arbeitstages im Jahr 1947 bei 11,2 m³, 1956 umfasste sie bereits 47,6 m³ (mit einem gewissen Einbruch im Jahr 1951). Auch die Menge des gewaschenen Sandes wurde betrachtet: 1947 wurden 4,19 m³ goldhaltiger Sand gewaschen, 1956 waren es bereits 26,3 m³. Die Förderung von unter der Erde liegendem goldhaltigen Sand stieg in diesem Zeitraum um das Dreifache.[317]

Diese Zahlen belegen überzeugend, dass die Leistungen des Kombinats in sehr viel höherem Maße als bisher angenommen von der Qualität der Fördergebiete, d. h. vom mittleren Goldgehalt, abhängig waren. Die Zahl der Arbeiter und ihre Zusammensetzung war dabei sehr viel weniger entscheidend. So war z. B. die Goldförderung 1951 auf einen Tiefpunkt gefallen, die Arbeitsproduktivität war jedoch in diesem Jahr im Vergleich zu 1950 besonders hoch. Die Zahl der Häftlinge war zwar 1951 die höchste in der gesamten Nachkriegsepoche, aber im Spätstalinismus erfüllten durchschnittlich 45 % der Inhaftierten die untersten Arbeitsnormen nicht. Dennoch galten auch

---

314 Speziell für die Häftlinge des *Sevvostlag* wurde am 22. Mai 1948 die Möglichkeit der *sačety*, der Haftverkürzung für erbrachte Arbeitsleistung, eingeführt. Löhne für die Arbeit der Häftlinge gab es allgemein in der Sowjetunion seit dem 1. Januar 1949. Vgl. Širokov, Politika, S. 435.

315 In den 1950er Jahren sah die Arbeitsproduktivität folgendermaßen aus: 1951: 891,4 Gramm; 1952: 998,0 Gramm; 1953: 1.143,2 Gramm; 1954: 1.253,8 Gramm; 1955: 1.559,5 Gramm; 1956: 1.633,2 Gramm. Für das Jahr 1957 war zu dieser Zeit eine Produktivität von 1.710,0 Gramm geplant. Vgl. die Tabelle in GAMO f. R-137sč, op. 1b, d. 189, l. 78.

316 Dies gilt hier nun in Bezug auf „Arbeiter", also nur in Bezug auf die tatsächlich in der Produktion tätigen Menschen.

317 Vgl. GAMO f. R-137sč, op. 1b, d. 189, l. 78. Ausführlich zur gestiegenen Arbeitsproduktivität zwischen 1950 und 1955 siehe die Angaben in dem 15-Jahrplan von Dal'stroj in GAMO f. R-23, op. 1, d. 5853, l. 1–25, hier l. 5 ff.

diese Personen als reguläre Arbeitskräfte.[318] Die noch deutlich höheren Werte der Arbeitsproduktivität nach 1954 gingen hingegen mit einem rapide sinkenden Anteil der Zwangsarbeiter einher.

Eine der wichtigsten Ursache für die beständig steigende Arbeitsproduktivität und für ihr hohes Niveau Mitte der 1950er Jahre war die Mechanisierung, die Einführung neuer Technik.[319] Dies sah auch das Gebietsparteikomitee so: Seinen Zahlen zufolge war die Arbeitsproduktivität bei der Abtragung von Torf zwischen 1940 und 1957 um das Fünfzehnfache gestiegen, bei der Goldförderung unter der Erde um das 3,2fache und beim Goldwaschen um das Zwölffache. [320]

Man kann sich vorstellen, welche Wirkung der Einsatz eines einfachen Baggers in einer Grube hatte, in der bisher Häftlinge mit Holzspaten Erde schippten. Oder die Ersetzung einfacher Holztröge zum Waschen des Goldes durch eine elektrische Anlage aus Metall oder der Einsatz von hochwirksamem Sprengstoff im Bergbau. Beispiele gibt es genug, denn auch wenn die Goldförderung in den 1950er Jahren primitiv war, so war sie im Vergleich zu dem kaum vorstellbaren Mangel an schweren Geräten in den 1940er Jahren erheblich fortschrittlicher. Elinor Lipper schildert diesen Umstand in ihren Erinnerungen an ihre Arbeit in der Kohlproduktion in der Kolchose Elgen, dem größten Frauenlager des *Sevvostlag:*

> Unzählige Monate quälten sich die Frauen in den Gräben. Dann kam eines Tages eine Baggermaschine und hob in wenigen Wochen mehr aus, als die Frauen in einem Jahr hatten leisten können. Zwanzigstes Jahrhundert, das du nicht nur das Jahrhundert des Blutes, sondern auch der Technik bist, wann kommst du nach Kolyma, die gefangenen Frauen zu erlösen, die dort mit ihrer Brust die schwerbeladenen Schlitten ziehen, wie einst die Wolgaschlepper den Lastkahn, die die Bäume des Urwalds fällen und auf ihren Schultern hinaustragen müssen, wenn sie auch immer wieder dabei vor Schwäche in die Knie gehen? Wieviel Schneeschipper müssen noch alljährlich erblinden, weil es keine Schneebrillen gibt?[321]

Dieser Tatbestand wirft auch noch einmal ein besonderes Licht auf die Verluste, die das MCM und der Ministerrat 1954 in Dal'stroj beklagten. Denn wenn die Leistungen in diesem Maße von der richtigen Planung der Arbeiten und dem Einsatz von Maschinen abhängig waren, so fallen die Verluste durch Fehllieferungen, Verschrottung durch unsachgemäße Lagerung und Bedienung, der Mangel an Reparaturwerkstätten, organisatorische Defizite bei der Verteilung von Arbeitern und Geräten, falsche geolo-

---

318 Vgl. Bacaev, Formy i metody, S. 80.

319 Diesen Zusammenhang zwischen steigender Mechanisierung, vermehrtem Technikeinsatz und steigender Arbeitsproduktivität beschreiben die Leiter von Dal'stroj bzw. dem Volkswirtschaftsrat immer wieder. Vgl. z. B. den Bericht von Berezin vom 19. März 1957 über Maßnahmen zur weiteren Senkung der Selbstkosten der Goldförderung in GAMO f. R-23, op. 1, d. 6109, l. 2–12, hier l. 2 sowie den Bericht von Korolev über die Tätigkeit des Magadaner Volkswirtschaftsrats im Jahr 1958 in RGAĖ f. 7733, op. 47, d. 538, l. 12 sowie 26.

320 Vgl. den Bericht des Gebietsparteikomitees im Vorfeld der Einführung des Magadaner Volkswirtschaftsrates an das ZK der KPdSU in GAMO f. R-23, op. 1, d. 6088, l. 1–50, hier l. 8.

321 Lipper, Elf Jahre, S. 189.

gische Berechnungen, aber auch der Goldverluste durch einen unzulänglichen Einsatz der Technik bei der Förderung selbst ganz besonders ins Gewicht. Umgekehrt wird deutlich, wie relevant die Steigerung der Mechanisierung, der Ausbau von technischen Anlagen, eine rationale Arbeitsorganisation und Planung sowie wissenschaftliche geologische Untersuchungen für die Steigerung des Ertrages wurden. Eine große Zahl an mobil einsetzbaren Zwangsarbeitern konnte eine industrialisierte Arbeitsweise nicht ersetzen.

Damit ist natürlich noch nichts über die Kosten der jeweiligen Arbeitsweise gesagt. In eine solche Berechnung müssten jedoch nicht nur Faktoren wie die Kosten für Verhaftung, Transport, Bewachung, Unterbringung und Todesfälle gegenüber erhöhten Löhnen, Boni und einer sozialen Infrastruktur für freie Arbeitskräfte eingebracht werden, sondern auch die strukturellen Kosten der Zwangsarbeit. Denn die geringe bis nicht vorhandene Mechanisierung war nicht nur Begleiterscheinung der Zwangsarbeit, sondern eine ihrer Grundprinzipien. Chlevnjuk konstatiert: „The NKVD economy, which was based on hard physical labor, rejected technical progress. [...] Although in many instances NKVD enterprises were technically equipped much better than similar enterprises of other people's commissariats, they made poorer use of this hardware."[322]

Viele Zehntausende Häftlinge, die zur Arbeit gezwungen wurden, waren sehr viel weniger produktiv als freie Arbeitskräfte, die bei sinnvoller Arbeitsplanung die richtigen Maschinen bedienten. Auch die extreme Verschwendung von Ressourcen und die „tufta", die Planerfüllung durch Betrug oder Fälschung, zählten nach Ivanova zu Strukturmerkmalen der Zwangsarbeit.[323] Dies alles sind Kosten, die in eine Bewertung miteinfließen müssen.

Durch den politischen Entwurf des nordöstlichen Raumes als Lager-Industrieller Komplex wurde eine langfristige, effektive und produktive Ausbeutung der Region verhindert. Zu Beginn der Arbeiten in Dal'stroj bildete der Rohstoffreichtum den Ausgleich – durch den enormen Goldgehalt der Erde konnte die reale Ineffektivität der auf Zwangsarbeit beruhenden Goldförderung verschleiert werden. Tatsächlich hat sich noch keiner der Magadaner Historiker an eine Berechnung gewagt, wie hoch denn der Goldertrag zu dieser Zeit unter Einsatz von schwerem Gerät und mit einer effektiven Arbeitsplanung hätte sein können.

Ob die Sowjetunion in der Lage gewesen wäre, seit Anfang der 1930er Jahre eine derartige Fördermethode zu finanzieren, ist eine ganz offene Frage. Sicher ist, dass sie politisch nicht gewollt war. Die Ausbeutung der Goldfelder unterlag einer militärischen Ideologie des beständigen „Stürmens", des „Vorwärtsdrängens", bei der es vom ersten Tag an auf eine maximale Planerfüllung ankam. Im Klima der Repression, der

---

322 Khlevnyuk, Economy of the Gulag, S. 127.
323 Zu diesen Charakteristika siehe Ivanova, Istorija, S. 355 sowie zu dem geringen Mechanisierungsgrad ebd., S. 378. Ivanova kann anhand der Zahlen des Kombinats *Enisejstroj* nachweisen, dass die Selbstkosten der GULAG-Tätigkeiten tatsächlich erheblich über den Kosten der lokalen Industrie lagen. Vgl. ebd., S. 379. Zum Begriff der „tufta" siehe Rossi, Spravočnik po GULagu, S. 414–416.

permanenten Überwachung und Verfolgung hing das Leben eines jeden einzelnen Produktionsleiters von dieser Planerfüllung ab. Häftlinge waren dabei eine „mobile Masse". Sie ermöglichten die blitzartige Verlagerung der Förderstellen, sie konnten ohne weiteres Tausend Kilometer weit zum nächsten Goldfeld verschleppt werden, für sie gab es keinen infrastrukturellen Mindeststandard. Zwangsarbeit suggerierte der Leitung eine grenzenlose Mobilität und Geschwindigkeit, die mit „Effektivität" gleichgesetzt wurde und von der sich der NKVD/MVD zu keinem Zeitpunkt verabschieden wollte.

Als der sinkende Goldgehalt und der erschwerte Zugang zu den Fördergebieten eine Umorientierung notwendig machte, drifteten Lager und Produktion immer weiter auseinander, was zur großen Strukturkrise der Lagerwirtschaft führte.[324] In der beginnenden Entstalinisierung brachen dann schließlich alle wichtigen Koordinaten weg, die die Produktivität von Dal'stroj bisher noch über Wasser gehalten hatten – finanzieller Sonderstatus, exklusive Zulieferbedingungen, militärische Befehlsstrukturen, eine Basis von Zwangsarbeitern (darunter ein paar Tausend wertvolle Fachkräfte). Zudem sank der Goldgehalt in der Region weiter und weiter. An dem „Laboratorium" Lager-Industrieller Komplex durfte jedoch auch dann nicht gerüttelt werden, als sich die Überlegenheit einer stärker mechanisierten Arbeitsweise längst erwiesen hatte – die „Droge Zwangsarbeit" verhinderte eine klare Sicht auf wirtschaftliche Notwendigkeiten. Nach 1953 musste schließlich die Zeche gezahlt werden für ein inhumanes, ineffektives und verschwenderisches Wirtschaftssystem.

---

324 Allgemein zu den Versuchen in der Nachkriegszeit, die Produktivität der Arbeit im GULAG durch Löhne, Mechanisierung u. a. zu heben, siehe Khlevnyuk, Economy of the OGPU, S. 56 f.

5 Beherrschen und Versorgen

Galina Ivanova hat die Mitte der 1950er Jahre einsetzende Sozialpolitik als „Politik des staatlichen Paternalismus"[1] beschrieben. Dieses paternalistische Konzept bezieht sich auf den Begriff des „wohlfahrtstaatlichen Autoritarismus" von George Breslauer. Er geht von einem ungeschriebenen „Gesellschaftsvertrag" aus, in dem ein Mindestmaß an materieller und sozialer Sicherheit, die „väterliche Fürsorge", im Austausch für Loyalität und den Einsatz der Arbeiter garantiert wurde.[2] Dieser Paternalismus zeuge von der Abkehr der obersten staatlichen Leitung von der Politik massenhafter Repression. Sozialpolitik ist für Ivanova ein Kernelement der Entstalinisierung: „At the heart of De-Stalinization stood not only the guarantee of a certain degree of legal certainty, but also a shift in the attention of the state towards the individual citizen, to his / her living conditions and social situation."[3]

Der staatliche Paternalismus der Entstalinisierung, so Ivanova, habe es dem sowjetischen Staat erlaubt, alle Fragen der sozialen Entwicklung auf der Grundlage eigener wirtschaftlicher, ideologischer und politischer Prioritäten zu entscheiden.[4]

Vielleicht ist die Verbindung zwischen der Abkehr von Repression und der Entstehung erster Formen von Sozialpolitik an keinem Ort so deutlich erkennbar wie im Magadaner Gebiet: Nachdem sich die Zwangsarbeit im Spätstalinismus als kostenintensiv und ineffektiv erwiesen hatte, sollten die Arbeiterströme auf paternalistischem Wege in die Region gelenkt werden.

Doch wer waren diese „Arbeiter"? Welche Rolle spielten die Lager, welche Bedeutung hatte die Zwangsarbeit nach Gründung des Magadaner Gebietes? Wer blieb, wer kam in die Region? Und welche praktischen Anstrengungen unternahm die neue Führung, um die Lebens- und Arbeitsbedingungen dieser Menschen zu verbessern? In welchem Verhältnis stand dies zum neuen Kurs der sowjetischen Führung in Moskau?

Diese Fragen bilden die Grundlage des folgenden Einblicks in die sozialen Verhältnisse jener Umbruchjahre. Der hier gewählte Ansatz zielt jedoch nicht nur darauf, die im sozialen Raum Magadan agierenden Personen, den Aufbau sozialpolitischer Leistungen und die Lage der betroffenen Menschen zu beschreiben. Es geht vielmehr darum, durch ein Ausloten der neuen Strategien, der Umstände ihrer Umsetzung und der Grenzen der Veränderung einen Einblick in das Verhältnis zwischen regionaler und sowjetunionweiter Herrschaft auf der einen und der Bevölkerung auf der anderen Seite zu gewinnen.

---

1 Ivanova, Na poroge, S. 99.
2 Vgl. Breslauer, On the Adaptability, S. 221.
3 Ivanova, Question of Honour, S. 133.
4 Vgl. Ivanova, Na poroge, S. 99. Zur systemstabilisierenden Bedeutung der Konsumversprechen vgl. Merl, Konsum, S. 520. Mark Smith argumentiert, dass in den 1950er Jahren die sowjetische Führung ihrer Bevölkerung eine Reihe von sozial-ökonomischen Rechten zugestanden hätte, eine entscheidende Veränderung zwischen Herrschaft und Bevölkerung seit Stalins Tod. Er analysiert den Aufbau von privatem Wohnraum seit 1957 als ein „Bürgerrecht". Vgl. Smith, Khrushchev's Promise.

https://doi.org/10.1515/9783110557879-006

Dazu zählt vor allem eine enorme Spannung zwischen der Präsentation symbolischer Zuschreibungen an das Magadaner Gebiet, der Konstruktion wirklichkeitsferner Bilder und den Realitäten der Arbeits-, Macht- und Lebensbedingungen. Symbolpolitik war im Magadaner Gebiet ein neues Feld, die mentale Besetzung des nordöstlichen Raumes Teil des paternalistischen Herrschaftsverständnisses, das auf eine weitgehende Umschreibung der Repräsentation des von Gewalt und Ausbeutung geprägten Gebietes zielte. Dass der von der Leitung vorgestellte Raum des Magadaner Gebietes nie mit den Realitäten in Deckung gebracht werden konnte, war dabei unbestritten. Kein Arbeiter dachte wohl bei der Beschreibung des „blühenden nördlichen Landes" auf den Seiten der regionalen Zeitung an die Lagerbaracken seiner Siedlung. Dennoch entwickelten diese Zuschreibungen an das Magadaner Gebiet, in Kombination mit den sozialpolitischen Verbesserungen, gerade im Lagergebiet Dal'stroj eine Dynamik, die sich als eine wirkmächtige Strategie zur Herrschaftssicherung der neuen Führung erweisen konnte. Ob dies tatsächlich ein Echo auf Seiten der Bevölkerung hervorrief, ob die neue Repräsentation der poststalinistischen Herrschaft Legitimation verschaffte, ist dabei eine offene Frage.

Zunächst einmal wird ein genauer Blick auf die Bedeutung der Lager in den Jahren nach 1953, auf die diversen Bevölkerungsteile mit ihrem je eigenen arbeitsrechtlichen Status, auf Veränderungen der sozialen Lage, auf Urbanisierungstendenzen und konkrete Lebensbedingungen die Diskussion poststalinistischer Herrschaftsverhältnisse im Magadaner Gebiet empirisch untermauern und eine Gegenüberstellung mit den Repräsentationen der lokalen Leitung ermöglichen.

5.1 Flugsandgesellschaft

Mein Freund ist nach Magadan gefahren
– ziehen Sie den Hut! ziehen Sie den Hut!
Er ist von sich aus gefahren, von sich aus –
nicht als Häftling im Transport ...

Moj drug uechal v Magadan.
– Snimite šljapu! Snimite šljapu!
Uechal sam, uechal sam –
Ne po ėtapu, ne po ėtapu ...

V. Vysockij, 1967[5]

Diese Zeilen eines in den späten 1960er Jahren in der Sowjetunion sehr bekannten Liedes von Vladimir Vysockij spielen ironisch mit der Ungläubigkeit, dass ein Mensch aus freien Stücken in diese Stadt und Region ziehen könnte. Tatsächlich haben dies seit 1953 sehr viele Menschen getan – ob mit oder ohne Kenntnisse über den Charakter der Region als riesiges Lager kamen sie nach Magadan, um in Dal'stroj bzw. im Magadaner Volkswirtschaftsrat zu arbeiten. Tausende ehemalige Häftlinge verblieben in der Region, weil sie nach ihrer Entlassung keine andere Alternative sahen oder weil sich die sofortige Abreise von dieser „Insel" ausgesprochen schwierig gestaltete. Einer

---

5 V. Vysockij hat dieses Lied seinem Freund Kochanovskij gewidmet, der in Magadan lebte. Vysockij selbst war in Magadan ungeheuer populär, vgl. die Erinnerungen bei Pantjuchin, Zapiski, S. 172.

von ihnen war Abrahm Dück, der es nach seiner Haftentlassung im Sommer 1953 ablehnte, die ihm auferlegte Zeit der Verbannung bei seiner Mutter in der Kasachischen SSR zu verbringen. Er beantragte, bei seiner späteren Frau und dem gemeinsamen, im Lager geborenen Kind an der Kolyma zu bleiben. Dück beschreibt die Chancenlosigkeit der Entlassenen und den „freiwilligen Zwang"[6], aufgrund dessen so viele Entlassene in der Region verblieben, in seinen Erinnerungen mit folgenden Worten:

> Aber auf was konnten die politischen Häftlinge, die befreit wurden, nach der Rückkehr in ihre Heimat hoffen? Von Angesicht zu Angesicht ihren Verrätern begegnen, die, wenn auch etwas gedemütigt, keineswegs zur Rechenschaft gezogen wurden. [...] Nein, dann schon besser bleiben, in diesem Stiefmutterland, das sie angenommen und an das sie sich gewöhnt hatten. Wo sie als geschickte Facharbeiter geschätzt und jetzt entlohnt wurden. Sie kannten sich aus wie kein aus den Hauptstädten angeworbener Leiter. Die hatten es ja nur auf die großen Gehälter, einen Karrieresprung oder das Aufpolieren ihrer gesunkenen Autorität abgesehen. Sie kamen und gingen. Im Gegensatz zu den gewesenen Häftlingen und Verbannten, die Jahrzehnte in den Todeslagern zugebracht hatten. Sie waren geblieben und hatten sich mit dieser rauen, ihnen gewaltsam aufgezwungenen zweiten Heimat zufrieden gegeben. Die Hafenstadt Magadan war zu einer kleinen schmucken Hauptstadt dieses Schreckensgebietes geworden.[7]

Selbst nach Aufhebung aller Beschränkungen lebte die Familie bis 1959 im Magadaner Gebiet. Abraham Dück wollte dort seine Ausbildung beenden und Geld verdienen, „aber" – so schreibt er – „wichtiger war das Benehmen und die Gesinnung der Menschen. Fast alle waren sie unsersgleichen, die in den Lagern um das nackte Leben gekämpft hatten, mit allen Wassern gewaschen und allen Hunden gehetzt worden waren"[8].

Auch Personen, die schon unter dem MVD als freie Arbeitskräfte in Dal'stroj gearbeitet hatten, blieben, sie waren an ihre bestehenden Verträge gebunden oder genossen als leitende Funktionäre herausragende Privilegien. Entlassene Häftlinge, ihre bisherigen Bewacher, alte und neue Funktionäre trafen auf den Straßen der Siedlungen, in Behörden, an den Arbeitsplätzen und Schlafstellen aufeinander. Abraham Dück erinnert sich deutlich an zwei ehemalige Offiziere, die ihn noch bis kurz vor seiner Entlassung gequält hatten und die er nun, nachdem sie ihren Dienstgrad und ihre Autorität eingebüßt hatten, auf den Straßen Magadans wiedertraf; ebenso berichtet er von hochgebildeten entlassenen Häftlingen, die, wie Evgenija Ginzburg, nun ihre bisherigen Lageraufseher in den neuen Instituten unterrichteten.[9]

---

6 Diese anschauliche Beschreibung der ambivalenten Lage, in der sich ehemalige Häftlinge befanden, stammt von Wladislaw Hedeler. Hedeler, Rezension zu A. Barenberg: Gulag Town, Company Town, abrufbar unter http://hsozkult.geschichte.hu-berlin.de/rezensionen/2015-1-167 (abgerufen am 6. Februar 2018). Barenberg selbst hat diese Erfahrung beschrieben in Barenberg, Citizen.

7 Dück, Erinnerungen, S. 455.

8 Dück, Erinnerungen, S. 460.

9 Vgl. Dück, Erinnerungen, S. 461; zu Ginzburgs Tätigkeit vgl. Ginsburg, Gratwanderung, S. 438 f. Für die Begegnung mit den beiden ehemaligen Offizieren siehe das Kapitel 3.1.1.

Menschen kamen oder blieben in der Region, viele andere reisten rasch nach dem Ende der Haftzeit, nach der Aufhebung juristischer Beschränkungen oder nach der Erfüllung ihrer Arbeitsverträge ab. Die Migrationsströme im Nordosten der Sowjetunion waren seit Stalins Tod gewaltig, jedes Jahr verließen etwa 20.000 – 40.000 Menschen die Region, ungefähr ebenso viele kamen hinzu – bei einer Gesamtbevölkerungszahl des Gebietes von etwa 260.000 Menschen im Jahr 1954 bzw. 235.000 im Jahr 1959.[10]

Zuzüge und Abreisen prägten das Leben im Gebiet während der gesamten 1950er Jahre. Entlassungen, Aufhebungen von Beschränkungen, Familienvereinigungen, Zuzug neugeworbener Arbeitskräfte, Abzug bewaffneter Truppen, Abreisen durch Stabskürzungen, Ankunft von Dienstreisenden unterschiedlicher Behörden – der politische und wirtschaftliche Umbruch, der die Region seit Stalins Tod erschütterte, spiegelte sich unmittelbar auf den Straßen des Gebietes. Von einer festen Bevölkerungsstruktur kann dabei nur in Ansätzen gesprochen werden, die Lage erinnert immer wieder an Beschreibungen der Sowjetunion nach 1945 als „Flugsandgesellschaft", als eine durch Terror, Deportation und Migration atomisierte Bevölkerung.[11]

Bis auf einen kleinen Personenkreis, der einen Platz im Flugzeug ergattern konnte, waren all diese Menschen auf den Transport per Schiff während weniger Monate im Jahr angewiesen. Die infrastrukturellen Beeinträchtigungen, der nur während weniger Monate eisfreie Hafen und die Tatsache, dass das Gebiet als Grenzregion einer verschärften Überwachung unterlag, machten die Stadt Magadan und die Hafenstädte im Chabarowsker Gebiet (Wanino und Nachodka) zu regelrechten Nadelöhren. Monatelang mussten An- und Abreisewillige in den sogenannten „Transitstädten" ausharren, in denen sie registriert, auf Schiffe bzw. Arbeitsstellen im Magadaner Bezirk verteilt, ihnen die nötigen Papiere ausgestellt und sie nicht zuletzt überwacht wurden.[12] Da die Menschen „im Transit" zwischen dem Festland und der Insel Dal'stroj zwar versorgt werden mussten, aber als Arbeitskräfte nicht mehr oder noch nicht zur Verfügung standen, war das Interesse der Leitung an einer angemessenen Unterbringung minimal:

---

10 Vgl. den Bericht über die Arbeit mit Kadern von Dal'stroj für das Jahr 1954 in GAMO f. R-23, op. 1, d. 5548, l. 1–43 sowie für das Jahr 1955 das Schreiben von Ababkov und Afanas'ev an Bulganin in GAMO f. R-146, op. 1, d. 58, l. 51–52, hier l. 52. Siehe die Angaben des Leiters der Abteilung für Arbeit und Löhne vom 10. April 1956 in GAMO f. R-23sč, op. 1, d. 462, l. 138–141. Für das Jahr 1958 vgl. das Schreiben von Korolev an die Leiter der einzelnen Betriebe des Volkswirtschaftsrates vom 21. August 1958 in GAMO f. R-137, op. 1, d. 54, l. 86–87. Zahlen für das Jahr 1959 in Slavin, Promyšlennoe osvoenie, S. 241. Auch zu Beginn der 1960er Jahre war die Fluktuation der Bevölkerung noch immer sehr hoch. Vgl. Rajzman, SNCH MĖAR, S. 166.
11 Zum Begriff der „Flugsandgesellschaft", der von Moshe Lewin geprägt wurde, siehe Plaggenborg, Lebensverhältnisse, S. 787 sowie Bohn, Minsk, S. 307. Thomas Bohn wendet diesen Begriff auch auf die Verhältnisse im Minsk der 1950er und 1960er Jahre an. Von der Atomisierung der Gesellschaft spricht Filtzer auch für die Chruščev-Periode. Vgl. Filtzer, Soviet Workers, S. 224.
12 Im Schnitt lebten in Magadan 3.000–4.000 Menschen im Transit. Vgl. GAMO f. R-23, op. 1, d. 4804, l. 60–63.

Die Menschen schliefen in kalten, nassen und dunklen Baracken, z. T. wegen fehlender Schlafplätze in mehreren Schichten, es mangelte an sauberem Trinkwasser und Heizmaterial, häufig gab es für viele Hundert Personen keine sanitären Anlagen oder Toiletten, infektiöse Darmkrankheiten brachen aus und verbreiteten sich in den Transitbereichen.[13] Schon unter den Bedingungen des Lager-Industriellen Komplexes hatte Dal'stroj darauf geachtet, An- und Abreisende im Transitbereich streng voneinander zu trennen, um zu vermeiden, dass Einzelheiten über die Arbeits- und Lebensbedingungen an neue Arbeitskräfte weitergegeben werden konnten.[14] Zudem waren diese Sammelplätze kilometerweit von den eigentlichen Städten entfernt. Die Menschen waren abgeschnitten von Informationen, aber auch von der Möglichkeit, benötigte Waren oder zusätzliches Essen zu erwerben.

5.1.1 Arbeitskräftebestand

Der Arbeitskräftebestand des Kombinats war von einer ungeheuren Fluktuation geprägt.[15] Vor allem in den ersten Jahren nach Stalins Tod verließen mehrere Zehntausend Menschen das Kombinat; deutlich weniger Personen wurden eingestellt als entlassen.[16] So sank die Zahl der Arbeitskräfte in Dal'stroj von 207.400 zu Beginn des Jahres 1953 (incl. Häftlinge), auf etwa 129.400 im Jahr 1955.[17]

Der prozentuale Anteil der Häftlinge an der Belegschaft des Kombinats ging in großen Schritten zurück. Ende des Jahres 1952 lag er bei 68 %, im Jahr 1957 waren es bereits weniger als 10 % aller Arbeitskräfte des Kombinats.[18] Sehr viele Entlassene kehrten dabei mit ihrem neuen Status als „Freie" an die gleichen Arbeitsplätze zurück oder sie waren vielfach bis 1955 als „Verbannte" nach dem Ende der Lagerhaft ge-

---

13 Vgl. den Bericht des Kontors der Transitkader in GAMO f. R-146, op. 1, d. 53, l. 1–4. Zur medizinischen Situation im Transitbereich siehe die Angaben der Gesundheitsabteilung des Gebietsexekutivkomitees in GAMO f. R-146, op. 1, d. 105, l. 16–40, hier l. 29. Vgl. daneben Černoluckaja, Tranzitnyj gorodok.

14 Diese Regelung galt seit 1952. Vgl. Zeljak, Pjat' metallov, S. 238.

15 Die Fluktuation der Arbeitskräfte war auch in anderen Gebieten, in denen Zwangsarbeit bis 1953 vorgeherrscht hatte, besonders hoch. So z. B. in der Kasachischen SSR oder in den Betrieben der nickel- und kobaltproduzierenden Industrie. Vgl. die Darstellung des stellv. Vorsitzenden der staatlichen Wirtschaftskommission des Ministerrates der UdSSR, Ivanov, vom 9. Juli 1956 in GAMO f. R-23sč, op. 1, d. 456, l. 165–172, hier l. 167.

16 Vgl. die Angaben des Leiters der Abteilung für Arbeit und Löhne vom 10. April 1956 in GAMO f. R-23sč, op. 1, d. 462, l. 138–141, hier l. 139.

17 Vgl. Širokov, Politika, S. 427. Ausführliche Angaben zur Zahl der Arbeiter (Freie und Zwangsarbeiter zwischen 1952 und 1956), also ohne Angestellte in der Verwaltung, enthält die Tabelle in GAMO f. R-23sč, op. 1, d. 503, l. 154f.

18 Vgl. den ausführlichen Bericht an das ZK der KPdSU und den Ministerrat der UdSSR vom Mai 1957 in GAMO f. R-146, op. 1, d. 58, l. 72–83, hier l. 74. Das Bild wird hier etwas verzerrt, da die Gesamtzahl der Arbeitskräfte parallel zu den Entlassungen sehr schnell abnahm.

zwungen, in der Region zu verbleiben.[19] Die Angaben über den Anteil ehemaliger Häftlinge an den freien Arbeitskräften variieren zum Teil stark, je nachdem, ob auch die Entlassenen miteinbezogen wurden, die sich nur für ein paar Monate an das Kombinat binden ließen. Sicher ist, dass noch Ende der 1950er Jahre gut die Hälfte aller freien Arbeitskräfte frühere Häftlinge des *Sevvostlag* oder des *Berlag* waren.[20]

Das MCM forderte aufgrund der zunehmenden Mechanisierung der Förderung sowie der hohen Kosten für Transport und Unterhalt von neuem Personal, den Bestand an Arbeitskräften insgesamt deutlich zu senken und zugleich den Anteil gut ausgebildeter Spezialisten zu erhöhen.[21] Der geringe Bildungsgrad der Mehrzahl freier Arbeitskräfte war Folge ihrer Anwerbung – junge Männer aus Kolchosen oder ungelernte Industriearbeiter ließen sich am leichtesten von den Vergünstigungen und Boni im Nordosten begeistern. Junge Menschen hingegen, die in dem Gebiet selbst eine weitergehende Ausbildung anstrebten, verließen aufgrund des Mangels an höheren Bildungseinrichtungen häufig die Region. Der typische Arbeiter des Magadaner Gebietes war dabei nicht nur nicht für eine konkrete Tätigkeit oder einen speziellen Beruf qualifiziert, sondern hatte grundsätzlich nur einen geringen Bildungsgrad – und dies selbst dann, wenn er als leitender Arbeiter oder Fachkraft eingestellt wurde. Die statistische Gebietsverwaltung hatte Ende des Jahres 1956 ermittelt, dass von den 23.227 leitenden Arbeitern und Fachkräften 42,5 % keine abgeschlossene mittlere oder höhere Bildung besaßen.[22] Unter diesen war der Anteil der Menschen mit einer nicht abgeschlossenen mittleren Bildung (sieben bis neun Jahren Schulbesuch) oder sogar weniger als sieben Klassen am größten.[23] Besonders krass war der Mangel an Ingenieuren. Selbst in Forschungseinrichtungen oder beim geologischen Schürfdienst arbeiteten nur zu 50 % Leute, die überhaupt irgendeine höhere Bildung hatten.[24] Der Mangel an theoretischer Bildung konnte häufig auch nicht durch eine entsprechende Berufserfahrung ausgeglichen werden, insgesamt verfügten nur 33 % der Arbeiter in den jeweiligen Industriezweigen über mehr als zehn Jahre Arbeitserfahrung. Trotz

---

19 Entlassene aus der Haft und Verbannte machten im Jahr 1954 etwa 60 % des Arbeitskräftebestandes aus. Vgl. den Bericht über die Arbeit mit Kadern von Dal'stroj für das Jahr 1954 in GAMO f. R-23, op. 1, d. 5548, l. 1–43, hier l. 9. Auch im Jahr 1958 machten ehemalige Häftlinge noch die Mehrzahl der Arbeiter des Kombinats (nicht der Angestellten) aus. Vgl. den entsprechenden Bericht von Afanas'ev in RGANI f. 5, op. 32, d. 111, l. 155–158, hier l. 155.

20 Vgl. Nikolaev, K voprosy izučenija, S. 45. 1958 sprach Afanas'ev noch von der Mehrzahl der Arbeiter und einem großen Teil der Angestellten, die früher Häftlinge in Dal'stroj gewesen waren. Vgl. RGANI f. 5, op. 32, d. 111, l. 155–158, hier l. 155.

21 Vgl. die abschließenden Bemerkungen der Organisation „Glavproekt" des MCM über den Vortrag von Dal'stroj zu seinem 15-Jahrplan in GAMO f. R-23, op. 1, d. 5858, l. 3–90, hier l. 8. Zum Mangel an Spezialisten siehe den Bericht von Korolev über die Tätigkeit des Magadaner Volkswirtschaftsrates im Jahr 1958 in RGAĖ f. 7733, op. 47, d. 538, l. 25–27.

22 Vgl. die Angaben aus der statistischen Verwaltung des Magadaner Gebietes vom 18. März 1957 in GAMO f. R-146, op. 1, d. 56, l. 34–41, hier l. 34.

23 Der Anteil betrug 59,5 %. Vgl. GAMO f. R-146, op. 1, d. 56, l. 39.

24 Vgl. GAMO f. R-146, op. 1, d. 56, l. 36.

dieser fehlenden Qualifikation nahm nur ein ganz kleiner Teil der Arbeiter an Fort-
bildungen teil, was sicherlich auch an den geringen Qualifikationsmöglichkeiten lag.[25]
Auffallend war für die Statistiker zugleich, dass Kontore und Verwaltungen sehr viel
besser mit Ingenieuren und Technikern versorgt waren als die eigentliche Produktion.

Diese Zahlen belegen, dass sich gebildete und gut qualifizierte Arbeitskräfte nur
selten zur Arbeitsaufnahme im Magadaner Gebiet bewegen ließen. Wer kam, wurde
eingesetzt, und sei es auch ohne abgeschlossene Schulbildung in leitender Position.
Falls sich Ingenieure für Dal'stroj werben ließen, drängten sie in die Verwaltung, d. h.
an Plätze, wo sie der schweren körperlichen Arbeit unter den extremen klimatischen
Bedingungen entkommen konnten (selbst wenn dort die Vergünstigungen geringer
waren als bei der eigentlichen Produktion). Auf sehr vielen Stellen für ingenieurtechnisches Fachpersonal arbeiteten entlassene Häftlinge und ehemalige Sondersiedler.[26] Diese Personen verfügten zwar meist über keine formale Berufsausbildung,
aber sehr häufig über die geforderte lange und „intensive" Berufserfahrung; sie waren
daher oftmals gefragte Arbeitskräfte. 1955 verlangte der stellvertretende Leiter des
Sevvostlag, Volkov, die produktionsnahe Ausbildung der Häftlinge zu verbessern.
Dabei sollten ausdrücklich junge Häftlinge gefördert werden, um sie nach ihrer Entlassung an das Kombinat zu binden.[27] Trotz seines Status als Verbannter erreichte
Abraham Dück die Aufnahme in das Magadaner Bergbau-Technikum. Er beschreibt
die damals Lernwilligen:

> Das Bergbau-Technikum war die einzige Lehranstalt für das Riesengebiet mit allen Goldfeldern,
> Erzgruben, mit der ganzen Bergbauwirtschaft. Die Fernstudenten waren ein buntes Völkchen:
> Militärs außer Dienst, die nach Schließung der Lager einen Beruf anstrebten, Praktiker-Be-
> triebsleiter auf der Jagd nach einem Diplom, junge Abenteurer, die sich die Kolyma so vorstellten
> wie den Klondike in den Erzählungen von Jack London, und etliche wie ich, die einen langen
> „Lehrgang" in Erzgruben und auf Goldfeldern durchgemacht, die Prüfung bestanden, aber kein
> Diplom dafür bekommen hatten.[28]

Die ausgesprochen schweren Arbeitsbedingungen, die Tatsache, dass viele der vereinbarten Vergünstigungen nicht gewährt wurden sowie die z. T. entsetzlichen
Wohnverhältnisse und die geringe soziale Infrastruktur waren die wichtigsten Grün-

---

25 Vgl. GAMO f. R-146, op. 1, d. 56, l. 39. Die statistische Verwaltung spricht von 7 % der Arbeitskräfte,
die eine Fortbildung machen würden. Vgl. ebd., l. 40. Deutlich positiver stellte der Leiter der Abteilung
für Arbeit und Löhne von Dal'stroj die Weiterbildungen der Arbeiter dar. Zwischen 1951 und 1955 hätten
197.000 Arbeitskräfte irgendeine Form von Fortbildung durchlaufen. Vgl. seine Angaben vom 10. April
1956 in GAMO f. R-23sč, op. 1, d. 462, l. 138–141, hier l. 141. Vgl. zur Entwicklung der Fachausbildung in
der Region (bis in die 1970er Jahre) Grebenjuk, Narodnoe obrazovanie.
26 Vgl. den Bericht über die Arbeit mit Kadern von Dal'stroj für das Jahr 1954 in GAMO f. R-23, op. 1, d.
5548, l. 1–43, hier l. 28.
27 Vgl. GAMO f. R-23, op. 1, d. 5206, l. 67–68ob.
28 Dück, Erinnerungen, S. 467.

de, warum ein hoher Prozentsatz der Arbeitenden ihre Verträge nicht verlängerte.[29] Dal'stroj ging immer wieder mit großer Härte gegen die einseitige Auflösung von Verträgen vor und ließ Personen, die vorzeitig das Kombinat verlassen wollten, als „Bummelanten" juristisch zur Verantwortung ziehen. Lediglich schwere Krankheiten und der Verlust der Arbeitsfähigkeit wurden seit dem März 1956 als Abreisegründe anerkannt. Dennoch versuchten auch weiterhin freie Arbeitskräfte, sich den ausgesprochen harten Bedingungen zu entziehen.[30] Arbeitsverträge wurden in Dal'stroj über die Bewegungsfreiheit von Personen gestellt. Mit juristischen Verfahren zwang das Kombinat seine Arbeiter zum Verbleib, während zur gleichen Zeit in der UdSSR eine ganze Reihe der drakonischen stalinistischen Gesetze aufgehoben wurde, mit denen verspätetes Erscheinen am Arbeitsplatz oder der Arbeitsplatzwechsel massiv kriminalisiert worden war – eine Tendenz, die Donald Filtzer für die Sowjetunion insgesamt als „Demokratisierung der Arbeitsstelle" bezeichnet hat und der die Härte von Dal'stroj zuwiderlief.[31]

Mit zunehmender Mechanisierung war die Wirtschaft der Region in schnell steigendem Maße auf qualifiziertes Personal angewiesen. Vor allem durch eigene Qualifizierungsmaßnahmen konnte der Anteil der ausgebildeten Arbeitskräfte Ende der 1950er Jahre etwas gesteigert werden. 1959 hatten immerhin schon 86 % der Betriebsleiter eine höhere oder mittlere Bildung; viele Arbeiter hatten eine Spezialisierung (z. B. als Maschinist) erhalten.[32] Diese Entwicklung war nicht nur der Gründung des Magadaner Gebietes und dem dortigen Aufbau des Bildungssektors sowie der unionsweiten Tendenz zur Ausweitung des Bildungswesens, zur Abschaffung ihrer Kostenpflicht und zur Steigerung der Qualifizierung der Arbeitskräfte geschuldet.[33] Sie war ebenso auch Teil eines Programms, mit dem die sowjetische Führung seit Mitte der 1950er Jahre die Ausbeutung des sowjetischen Nordens insgesamt durch eine wissenschaftliche Erschließung und damit einhergehend mit einer Professionalisierung und Qualifizierung der Arbeitskräfte vorantreiben wollte.[34]

Dennoch war auch der Magadaner Volkswirtschaftsrat insgesamt nicht in der Lage, eine dauerhafte Arbeitskräftebasis zu schaffen. Noch 1958 wurden auf 67 % aller Arbeitsplätze im Bereich der Industrie neue Leute eingesetzt, weil die bisherigen Arbeiter ihre Verträge nicht verlängert hatten. Der generelle Mangel an Arbeitskräften blieb für die Region eines der beherrschenden Probleme – hier unterschied sich

---

29 Vgl. die Gründe für eine Nichtverlängerung der Arbeitsverträge (mit genauen Zahlenangaben) in den ausführlichen Angaben zum Jahresergebnis 1956 von Dal'stroj in GAMO f. R-23sč, op. 1, d. 4897, l. 3–119, hier l. 31.

30 Vgl. Zeljak, Pjat' metallov, S. 246 f.

31 Vgl. Filtzer, Soviet Workers, S. 232 sowie Sokolov, Soviet Industry, S. 38. Zu weiteren gesetzlichen Neuregelungen in der Arbeitswelt siehe Gregory, Political Economy, S. 259, der von einer „job right-economy" spricht, die in den 1950er Jahren Druck von sowjetischen Arbeitern genommen habe.

32 Vgl. die Erläuterungen zum Jahresbericht des Volkswirtschaftsrates für das Jahr 1959 von Korolev und dem Hauptbuchhalter Gol'dšvend in RGAĖ f. 7733, op. 48, d. 492, l. 1–28, hier l. 17.

33 Vgl. zu dem unionsweiten Reformprogramm zur Bildung Ivanova, Na poroge, S. 77 f.

34 Vgl. Josephson, Soviet Arctic, S. 421.

Magadan nicht von anderen Gebieten in Sibirien und im Fernen Osten, für die das sowjetische Regime in dieser Zeit ebenfalls keine dauerhafte Basis an Industriearbeitern schaffen konnte.[35]

5.1.2 Zwangsarbeiter

Innerhalb weniger Jahre wandelte sich die Rolle der Zwangsarbeiter in Dal'stroj deutlich. Häftlinge verkörperten immer weniger die grundlegende Arbeits- und Wirtschaftsweise im Nordosten, sie wurden zu einer speziellen Kategorie von Arbeitskräften. Dadurch veränderte sich sehr schnell auch die Einstellung des Kombinats zur Zwangsarbeit: Im ersten Jahr nach Stalins Tod hatte Mitrakov noch unbeirrt an Häftlingen als der wichtigsten Arbeitskräftebasis seines Kombinats festgehalten. Die Entscheidung des Ministerrates der UdSSR, die Einzelleitung in Dal'stroj beizubehalten, schien Mitrakov darin zu bestärken. Lager und Produktion sollten wie vor Stalins Tod durch eine Hand geleitet werden und waren dadurch zumindest theoretisch eng aufeinander bezogen. Dementsprechend setzte er ganz auf den Transport neuer Häftlinge, um die Entlassenen zu ersetzen; den Abgang von Zwangsarbeitern beantwortete er mit der „Bestellung" neuer Häftlinge.[36]

Mitrakovs Wünsche wurden jedoch von der Moskauer Führung so nicht bedient, der große Häftlingsstrom an die Kolyma war mit Stalins Tod endgültig versiegt. Die vorhandenen Häftlinge ließen sich zwar theoretisch besser ausbeuten, weil der prozentuale Anteil arbeitsfähiger Häftlinge an der Gesamtzahl der Inhaftierten von 60,8 % im Jahr 1953 auf 86,8 % im Jahr 1955 anstieg.[37] Aber der rasante Rückgang der Häftlingszahlen, verbunden mit dem Auftrag des MCM, die Produktion in Zukunft im Wesentlichen auf der Grundlage freier Arbeitskräfte am Laufen zu halten, schuf große organisatorische Probleme. Lager und Produktion standen sich trotz der Einzelleitung sehr schnell als zwei Einheiten gegenüber, die verschiedenen Zielen verpflichtet waren und die in ihren Entscheidungen unabhängig voneinander agierten:

Lagerpunkte wurden geschlossen, obwohl die zugeordnete Produktionsstätte eigentlich dringend auf die dortigen Zwangsarbeiter angewiesen war, oder die Pro-

---

35 Vgl. den Bericht von Korolev über die Tätigkeit des Magadaner Volkswirtschaftsrates im Jahr 1958 in RGAĖ f. 7733, op. 47, d. 538, l. 27–29. Zur Lage in Sibirien und im Fernen Osten zwischen 1956 und 1960 vgl. Filtzer, From Mobilized to Free, S. 162 sowie Filtzer, Soviet Workers, S. 66–78.

36 Vgl. das Schreiben von Mitrakov an Malenkov und Chruščev in GAMO f. R-23, op. 1, d. 5207, l. 210–214, hier l. 210. Ausführlich dazu das Kapitel 3.1.2.

37 Ursache dafür war die Entlassung einer großen Zahl nichtarbeitsfähiger Häftlinge, aber auch eine bessere Versorgung und Ausstattung der Lager. Vgl. Širokov, Politika, S. 442. Um die Häftlingsverwendung zu steigern, wurde 1954 eine Gruppe nicht mehr arbeitsfähiger Häftlinge aus Dal'stroj in andere Lager in den zentralen Teilen der Union gebracht. D. h., nun beschritt der MVD gerade den umgekehrten Weg im Vergleich zu seiner Politik im Spätstalinismus, als sehr viele arbeitsunfähige Häftlinge in das *Sevvostlag* verlegt wurden, um die zentralen Lager der Sowjetunion von ihnen zu „befreien". Vgl. den Bericht Mitrakovs vom 21. Februar 1955 in GAMO f. R-23, op. 1, d. 5206, l. 8 f.

duktion wechselte ihre Arbeitspläne, so dass die notwendige Trennung von freier und erzwungener Arbeit nicht mehr möglich war.[38] Die Bewachung der Zwangsarbeiter entwickelte sich zu einer der größten Schwierigkeiten, da es sich bei den verbliebenen Häftlingen hauptsächlich um Personen mit hohen Haftstrafen handelte, die einer besonderen Bewachung unterliegen mussten. Zudem wurden Zwangsarbeiter immer schneller zu einer Minderheit inmitten ziviler Betriebe; ihre Wege zu und von der Arbeit mussten genau kontrolliert und ein Kontakt zu freien Arbeitskräften verhindert werden. Das war in der Praxis aber gar nicht möglich, wie eine ganze Reihe von Berichten und Beschwerden zeigen.[39] So schildert der Leiter der Verwaltung des MVD des Magadaner Gebietes am 3. Dezember 1955 dem stellvertretenden Leiter von Dal'stroj, Čuguev, die Situation auf Arbeitsstellen in der Stadt Magadan:

> Auf der Baustelle „Kamenuška" hat im September dieses Jahres der freie Chauffeur Smirnov die dort arbeitenden Häftlinge Čvetkova, Bogačeva und Makeeva regelmäßig mit Benzin versorgt, weshalb alle drei schließlich gemeinsam mit Smirnov in einem Auto fliehen konnten. [...] In der Nacht vom 28. auf den 29. November diesen Jahres kam es in der Magadaner Ziegelfabrik nach einem Trinkgelage zu einer Schlägerei zwischen Häftlingen und freien Arbeitskräften; zwei Häftlinge und eine freie Arbeitskraft wurden dabei erschlagen. Die Tatsache, dass in diesem Betrieb mitten unter den Häftlingen drei Frauen arbeiten, führte zu einer Gruppenvergewaltigung. Das Zusammentreffen von Häftlingen und freien Arbeitskräften verursachte allein in Magadan in den vergangenen elf Monaten 662 Gelage, 260 Mal wurden verbotene Gegenstände in das Lagergebiet gebracht, 182 Fälle von Rowdytum wurden registriert. Ungeachtet der zahlreichen Forderungen der regionalen Verwaltung des MVD und des Sevvostlag zur Verwendung von Häftlingen auf Arbeitsstellen ignorieren die Leiter der Verwaltungen und Betriebe unsere Forderungen. Die regionale Verwaltung des MVD und des Sevvostlag ist der Ansicht, dass die allermeisten Arbeitsstellen eigentlich entweder als Arbeitsplätze für freie Arbeitskräfte oder für Häftlinge deklariert werden könnten.[40]

So weit die Sichtweise der Verwaltung des MVD. Für Dal'stroj, das unter den neuen Bedingungen allein zur Erfüllung seiner Produktionspläne verpflichtet war, kehrte sich die Perspektive rasch um. Nun war es das Kombinat, das selbst auf die Ab-

---

38 Ausführlich zu den Auflösungen von Lagerpunkten, den Veränderungen der Produktionsstandorte und ihren Wechselbeziehungen siehe GAMO f. R-137sč, op. 1b, d. 189, l. 69, l. 79 – 81 sowie l. 93 f. Zu den daraus resultierenden finanziellen Streitigkeiten zwischen einzelnen Lagerpunkten und Produktionsstätten vgl. GAMO f. R-23, op. 1, d. 5844, l. 52–56.

39 Einen praxisnahen Einblick in die Schwierigkeiten bei der Verwendung von Häftlingen vermittelt die ausführliche Mitschrift einer Sitzung aus dem Jahr 1956, die das Gebietsexekutivkomitee einberufen hatte, um Schwierigkeiten auf einer Baustelle zwischen Dal'stroj, dem *Sevvostlag* und dem Auftraggeber, der Verwaltung für die zivile Luftflotte, auszuräumen. Diskutiert wurde die komplizierte Einteilung der Arbeitsbereiche in Zonen für „Freie" und für Häftlinge, fehlende Zugangsberechtigungen für LKWs auf ihrem Weg in Lagerzonen und der ständig drohende Abzug von Zwangsarbeitern durch die plötzliche Auflösung weiterer Lagerpunkte. Freie Arbeitskräfte wurden hingegen händeringend gesucht und man verlangte nach Lösungen, um sie von anderen Baustellen transferieren zu können. Vgl. GAMO f. R-146, op. 1, d. 45, l. 45 – 58.

40 Bericht vom 3. Dezember 1955 in GAMO f. R-23, op. 1, d. 5611, l. 77 f.

schaffung der Zwangsarbeit drängte. Der Leiter der Abteilung für Arbeit und Löhne in Dal'stroj beschrieb den Standpunkt des Kombinats im April 1956 folgendermaßen:

> Der arbeitende Teil eines Lagers ist heute so groß wie der nichtarbeitende (Häftlinge, die die Arbeit verweigern plus Verwaltung plus Wachen). Die Verteilung der Häftlinge über viele verschiedene kleine Produktionsstätten, ihre geringe Arbeitseffektivität, die Kosten für ihre Unterbringung, Versorgung und Bewachung führen zu einer Verteuerung der Produktion. Die Erfahrung der vergangenen Jahre und die durchgeführte Analyse der Produktion von Dal'stroj zeigt die eindeutige Unrentabilität und Sinnlosigkeit einer weiteren Verwendung von Häftlingen, weil dies große über dem Plan liegende Verluste mit sich bringt und die Frage nach der Versorgung der Produktion mit den notwendigen qualifizierten Kadern nicht löst. Dal'stroj plant im Laufe der Jahre 1956 bis 1957 die arbeitenden Häftlinge in den Betrieben vollständig durch freie Arbeitskräfte zu ersetzen.[41]

Innerhalb kurzer Zeit hatten sich Zwangsarbeiter in den Augen des Kombinats von besonders günstigen, immer verfügbaren Arbeitskräften zu einem Faktor entwickelt, der die Produktion erheblich verteuerte und eine sinnvolle perspektivische Entwicklung verhinderte. Zwangsarbeit funktionierte für das Kombinat nur in einem geschlossenen System, das große Industrieanlagen oder Bauprojekte bediente, die vollständig als Lagerraum bewacht werden konnten. Konsequenterweise bat Dal'stroj 1957 den Ministerrat darum, alle Zwangsarbeiter aus der Produktion abzuziehen.[42]

Tatsächlich war das Kombinat zu dieser Zeit schon nicht mehr in der Lage, seine Arbeitskräftebasis durch Wünsche zu beeinflussen. Es war an die Erfüllung von Verträgen gebunden, die es zum Einsatz von Zwangsarbeitern verpflichtete.[43] Das Lager, jetzt als Teil der großen Behörde GULAG, wurde zu einer eigenen Einheit der Baustelle, die ihre Bereiche mit eigener Bürokratie verteidigte. Es entstand eine geradezu paradoxe Situation, in der die bisherige Einzelleitung von Kombinat und Lager mit Nachdruck an die Verträge erinnert werden musste, die sie zum Einsatz von Häftlingen in ihren Betrieben verpflichtete; immer wieder wurde das Kombinat auch

---

41 Vgl. die Angaben des Leiters der Abteilung für Arbeit und Löhne vom 10. April 1956 in GAMO f. R-23sč, op. 1, d. 462, l. 138–141, hier l. 140. Für ähnliche Fälle siehe GAMO f. R-137 šč, op. 1b, d. 57, l. 19.
42 Vgl. den Entwurf zu einer Verordnung des Ministerrates der UdSSR, mit dem der MVD aufgefordert werden sollte, alle Häftlinge aus Dal'stroj abzuziehen. Diesen Entwurf hatte die Kombinatsleitung verfasst und dem Ministerrat zur Verabschiedung vorgeschlagen. Vgl. GAMO f. R-23sč, op. 1, d. 419, l. 2–39, hier l. 37. Zugleich sollte, so die Vorstellung des Kombinats, der MVD verpflichtet werden, die freigesetzten Wachen in den Dienst von Dal'stroj zu überführen. Vgl. den Bericht des Leiters der Verwaltung für Sicherheit in Dal'stroj in GAMO f. R-23, op. 1, d. 5858, l. 79–80, hier l. 79. Marc Elie beschreibt die wachsende Ablehnung von Zwangsarbeitern durch die Leiter großer Industrieprojekte seit 1955 als unionsweites Phänomen, das auf der Umorientierung auf freie Arbeitskräfte beruhte. Vgl. Elie, Khrushchev's Gulag, S. 123.
43 Vgl. den „Vertrag über die Bereitstellung von Arbeitskräften aus der Gruppe der Häftlinge" aus dem Jahr 1956 in GAMO f. R-23, op. 1, d. 5844, l. 20–35 sowie den folgenden Vertrag aus dem Jahr 1962 in GAMO f. R-137sč, op. 1b, d. 152, l. 94–104.

finanziell für die Nichtverwendung von Häftlingen belangt.[44] Vor allem als das *Sevvostlag* im August 1957 aufgelöst und die vorhandenen Lagerabteilungen als sogenannte Kolonien ganz in die Zuständigkeit der regionalen Verwaltung des MVD übergingen[45], häuften sich Beschwerden über die Nichtverwendung von Häftlingen im Volkswirtschaftsrat. Sicher führte gerade die dezentrale Struktur der Haftkolonien dazu, dass der MVD nicht mehr über eine so starke organisatorische Basis verfügte. Die Wirtschaftsleitung versuchte sich jedenfalls mit einem ganzen Bündel an Erklärungen zur Nichtverwendung von Häftlinge zu rechtfertigen.[46] Doch sollten auch nach der Auflösung des GULAG in der Sowjetunion Häftlinge prinzipiell mit Arbeit bestraft und umerzogen werden[47]; 1962 wurden noch immer 3.200 Inhaftierte in den Betrieben des Magadaner Volkswirtschaftsrates eingesetzt.[48] Rein ökonomisch spielte ihre Arbeit aber keine entscheidende Rolle mehr.

Kehrt man zu der prinzipiellen Frage nach der Arbeitskräftebasis des Kombinats seit Stalins Tod zurück, so wird vor diesem Hintergrund verständlich, warum Dal'stroj so daran gelegen war, entlassene Häftlinge unmittelbar an das Kombinat zu binden. Ohne die komplizierten Regelungen mit Zwangsarbeitern beachten zu müssen, war dies schnell verfügbares, bereits eingearbeitetes Personal mit großer „Erfahrung" bezüglich der regionalen Besonderheiten. Dies galt auch für die Gruppe von etwa 15.000 Verbannten, die 1955 ihren besonderen Status verloren und daraufhin die Region verlassen durften.[49] Grundsätzlich wurden auf sie die gleichen Vergünstigungen übertragen, die auch für andere freie Arbeiter in Dal'stroj galten.[50]

---

44 Siehe die Beschwerden des MVD vom 2. April 1954 in GAMO f. R-23, op. 1, d. 5207, l. 110, vom 12. Januar 1956 in GAMO f. R-23sč, op. 1, d. 457, l. 2 sowie vom 10. November 1956 in GAMO f. R-23, op. 1, d. 5844, l. 65 f.

45 Im August 1957 wurde das *Sevvostlag* als Einheit des GULAG aufgelöst; die noch bestehenden Lagerabteilungen unterstanden nun unmittelbar dem MVD der RSFSR. Wie zu dieser Zeit üblich, wurde die neue Struktur als „Verwaltung der nordöstlichen Besserungs- und Arbeitskolonien" bezeichnet und organisatorisch der Verwaltung des MVD des Magadaner Gebietes unterstellt. Vgl. Širokov, Politika, S. 434.

46 Siehe den ausführlichen Schriftverkehr zur Häftlingsverwendung zwischen dem Volkswirtschaftsrat und der regionalen Verwaltung des MVD aus dem Jahr 1959 in GAMO f. R-137sč, op. 1b, d. 58, l. 1–27.

47 Zur weiteren Häftlingsverwendung in der Sowjetunion siehe Hardy, Campaign sowie Elie, Khrushchev's Gulag.

48 Vgl. den Schriftverkehr zwischen dem MVD der RSFSR und dem Magadaner Volkswirtschaftsrat vom 22. Mai 1962 in GAMO f. R-137sč, op. 1b, d. 152, l. 116–118.

49 Vgl. GAMO f. R-137sč, op. 1b, d. 58, l. 11–13.

50 Eine dieser ehemaligen Häftlinge, die nach Ende ihrer Lagerhaft gezwungen worden war, als „Verbannte" in Magadan zu verbleiben, war die Publizistin Evgenija Ginzburg. In ihren Erinnerungen schildert sie anschaulich die Aufhebung der Beschränkungen. Neben besseren Wohnverhältnissen in Magadan wurde ihr, wie allen anderen Arbeitskräften in Magadan, ein regulärer Urlaub auf dem „Kontinent" bewilligt. Vgl. das Kapitel „Vor der Morgendämmerung" in Ginsburg, Gratwanderung, S. 446–460.

Neben entlassenen Häftlingen und Sondersiedlern wurden noch zwei weitere Gruppen unmittelbar vor Ort für die Arbeit in dem Gebiet geworben – Familienangehörige von Personen, die bereits in der Region arbeiteten oder in den Lagern einsaßen, sowie sogenannte „lokale Bewohner". Letztere hatten in arbeitsrechtlicher Hinsicht den schlechtesten Status. Zu dieser Gruppe zählten Personen der „zweiten Generation", also Menschen, deren Eltern bereits als Vertragsarbeiter in die Region gekommen und die dort geboren worden waren, sowie die indigene Bevölkerung. Diese beiden Personengruppen konnten keine besonderen Vergünstigungen in Anspruch nehmen.[51]

5.1.3 Anwerbungskampagnen

Alle weiteren Arbeitskräfte mussten von Industrie und Verwaltung in anderen Regionen der Sowjetunion geworben und nach Magadan gebracht werden. Die wichtigste Rolle spielte dabei die organisierte Sammlung von Arbeitskräften, die sogenannte *orgnabor*, die in den 1950er Jahren mehr und mehr dazu benutzt wurde, Arbeitskräfte in weit entfernte Regionen zu locken.[52] Vertreter von Dal'stroj bzw. des Volkswirtschaftsrates warben in verschiedenen sowjetischen Gebieten um Arbeitskräfte, berichteten von den Aufgaben im Nordosten, versprachen hohe Gehälter und besondere Vergünstigungen. Für Bauern in Kolchosen war diese Sammlung von Arbeitskräften für verschiedene Industriegebiete mitunter die einzige Möglichkeit, den schweren Bedingungen im Kolchos und der rechtlichen Gebundenheit an diese Arbeitsform zu entkommen.[53] Hinzu kamen Soldaten nach Abschluss ihres Wehrdienstes, die auf der Suche nach einer beruflichen Perspektive waren.[54] Daneben wurden auch Facharbeiter durch eigene Anwerbungskampagnen gewonnen.

Etwas besser gestellt als die Masse der *orgnabor*-Kräfte waren Komsomolzen, Mitglieder des Jugendverbandes der Kommunistischen Partei, die gesondert für die Arbeit im Nordosten geworben wurden.[55] Während der 1950er Jahre gab es zwei große Wellen, 1956 kamen 7.500 und 1959 3.251 Komsomolzen.[56] Dal'stroj warb diese jungen

---

51 Vgl. RGASPI f. 556, op. 23, d. 73, l. 20.
52 Vgl. zur Rolle der *orgnabor* in den 1950er Jahren Filtzer, Soviet Workers, S. 70–75; Filtzer, From Mobilized to Free, S. 161.
53 Vgl. Ivanova, Na poroge, S. 139.
54 Siehe zu den Anwerbungen GAMO f. P-21, op. 5, d. 502, l. 31–33.
55 Die offizielle Bezeichnung lautete „junge Arbeiter im Auftrag / mit Marschbefehl des Komsomol". Filtzer beschreibt, wie diese Anwerbekampagnen 1956 auf den Fernen Osten und Hohen Norden ausgeweitet wurden, nachdem sie zunächst eine Arbeitskräftebasis für die sogenannte Neulandkampagne in der Kasachischen SSR schaffen sollten. Vgl. Filtzer, From Mobilized to Free, S. 162. Zu den Kampagnen des Komsomol siehe auch Tromly, Soviet Intelligentsia, S. 176 ff.
56 Für 1956 siehe das Schreiben des stellv. Ministers für Buntmetalle, Strigin, an die Wirtschaftskommission des Ministerrates der UdSSR vom 9. Oktober 1956 in GAMO f. R-23sč, op. 1, d. 471, l. 54–55. Für die Zahl aus 1959 siehe die Erläuterungen zum Jahresbericht des Volkswirtschaftsrates für das Jahr

Leute über diverse Bezirkskomitees des Komsomol, meist handelte es sich um Absolventen technischer Berufsschulen, deren berufliche Perspektiven im Allgemeinen
begrenzt waren. Sehr viele kamen in den 1950er Jahren direkt aus Moskau nach Magadan. Komsomolzen wurden neben den besonderen Angeboten an Boni und hohen
Gehältern gerne mit ideologischen Aufrufen geworben – sie sollten ihre Jugend für die
Erschließung des sowjetischen Nordens und seiner Reichtümer einsetzen, zugleich
versprach ihnen der Komsomol ein abenteuerreiches Leben in einem erstaunlichen
Naturraum, geprägt von Romantik und Freiheit, in dem sie sich beweisen könnten.
Diese Kampagnen unterschieden sich kaum in ihrer Werbung für andere Großprojekte
jener Zeit, wie für die Neulandkampagne, die Arbeiten an der Baikal-Amur-Magistrale
oder anderen Großbaustellen.[57] Zusätzlich zu den Vergünstigungen für Arbeiter in
Dal'stroj erhielten sie bereits bei der Abreise von ihrem bisherigen Wohnort eine
Sonderzahlung.[58]

Für die wirtschaftliche und politische Leitung der Region waren die Komsomolzen
zumeist gern gesehene Arbeitskräfte. Immer wieder verwiesen die Verantwortlichen
auf die Stabilität dieser Arbeitskräftebasis und ihre politische Verlässlichkeit. Noch
1959 waren 70 % der Komsomolzen, die 1956 die Region erreicht hatten, vor Ort, sie
hatten hier eine Ausbildung erhalten und oftmals auch Familien gegründet; gerade in
einer Grenzregion wie in Tschukotka sei auf die Vertreter des Kommunistischen Jugendverbandes Verlass. Der Anteil an Alkoholikern und Arbeitsverweigern sei im
Vergleich zu der Gruppe der *orgnabor* sehr viel geringer.[59]

Zugleich waren die Anforderungen, die die Leitung von Dal'stroj bzw. des
Volkswirtschaftsrates an die einzelnen Wirtschaftsverwaltungen zur Aufnahme von
Komsomolzen stellten, deutlich höher als bei der *orgnabor*. Obwohl hier im Folgenden
gezeigt wird, dass auch Komsomolzen unter den gleichen elenden Lebensbedingun-
gen zu leiden hatten wie die Masse der Arbeiter, wurde für sie zumindest theoretisch
ein höherer Standard gefordert – die Wohnheime sollten mit Lesestoff, Brettspielen,
Radio- und Sportgeräten ausgestattet sein, Sportgruppen, Konzerte und künstlerisch
tätige Gruppen geschaffen werden. Viel Wert wurde auf eine konsequente ideologische
Schulung, eine permanente politische Überwachung und moralische Kontrolle der
Komsomolzen durch Meetings, Vorlesungen und Kameradengerichte gelegt. Aufgrund

---

1959 von Korolev und dem Hauptbuchhalter Gol'dšvend in RGAĖ f. 7733, op. 48, d. 492, l. 1–28, hier l.
16.
57 Vgl. Gestwa, Großbauten, S. 452.
58 Die Einmalzahlung umfasste generell 600 Rubel plus ein Zweimonatsgehalt in Höhe der ersten
Stelle, die in der Region angetreten wurde. Vgl. den Bericht über die Arbeit mit Kadern in der Indigirskoe Bergbauverwaltung für das Jahr 1956 in GAMO f. R-137sč, op. 1b, d. 21, l. 39–100, hier l. 80f.
59 Zu der Beurteilung der Komsomolzen vgl. das Schreiben des Gebietsparteikomitees an das ZK der
KPdSU vom 5. Juli 1961 in GAMO f. P-21, op. 5, d. 502, l. 35. Vgl. den Bericht über die Arbeit mit Kadern in
der Indigirskoe Bergbauverwaltung für das Jahr 1956 in GAMO f. R-137sč, op. 1b, d. 21, l. 39–100, hier l.
82f.

der überwiegend guten Erfahrungen hielten auch in den 1960er Jahren die Werbungen des Gebietsparteikomitees um Komsomolzen an.[60]

5.1.4 Junge Facharbeiter

All die hier vorgestellten freien Arbeitskräfte lassen sich unter eine Gruppe von „Angeworbenen" subsumieren.[61] Anders verhält es sich jedoch mit den sogenannten „jungen Fachkräften / „jungen Spezialisten". Als Abgänger von Hochschulen (mit technischen, pädagogischen, medizinischen u. a. Abschlüssen) waren sie verpflichtet, ihre erste Stelle in einer Region und in einer Einrichtung anzutreten, die ihnen vom Bildungsministerium der RSFSR und *Gosplan* zugewiesen wurde. Ideologisch wurde dies mit ihrer kostenfreien Ausbildung begründet. Die sie aufnehmende Stelle war im Gegenzug dazu verpflichtet, sie entsprechend ihrer Qualifikation einzustellen und zu bezahlen sowie mit angemessenem Wohnraum und einer gewissen sozialen Infrastruktur zu versorgen.[62] Da „junge Facharbeiter" (die ihrem Alter nach nicht zwangsläufig auch „jung" waren) grundsätzlich berechtigt waren, ihren zugewiesenen Arbeitsplatz wieder zu verlassen, wenn die sie aufnehmende Stelle die Bedingungen nicht erfüllte, wurden die Umstände ihrer Arbeits- und Wohnsituation auch von den regionalen Exekutivkomitees überprüft.[63] Dennoch kam es immer wieder vor, dass junge Facharbeiter in ihnen vollkommen fremden Aufgabengebieten arbeiten mussten, nicht die ihnen zustehenden Löhne erhielten und dass ihre Lebensverhältnisse so miserabel waren, dass sie ihre Verträge kündigten und abreisten.[64] Insgesamt kamen jedes Jahr etwa 350 junge Facharbeiter in das Gebiet.[65]

---

60 Vgl. GAMO f. R-137sč, op. 1b, d. 21, l. 39–100, hier l. 83. Zu den Anwerbungen in den 1960er Jahren siehe das Schreiben von Partei, Volkswirtschaftsrat und Komsomol des Gebietes an das ZK der KPdSU vom 4. Januar 1963 in GAMO f. P-21, op. 5, d. 502, l. 41.

61 Ende der 1950er Jahre gab es darüber hinaus eine kleine Gruppe von Personen, die aus eigener Initiative in die Region reisten und sich dort zur Arbeit meldeten (1959 waren dies gut 1.000 Menschen). Man kann davon ausgehen, dass es sich dabei um später nachziehende Familienangehörige oder Freunde von Personen handelte, die bereits in dem Gebiet arbeiteten, und die nicht offiziell als Familienmitglieder mitgereist waren. Vgl. die Erläuterungen zum Jahresbericht 1959 des Volkswirtschaftsrates von Korolev und dem Hauptbuchhalter Gol'dšvend in RGAÈ f. 7733, op. 48, d. 492, l. 1–28, hier l. 16.

62 Vgl. den Bericht über die Arbeit mit Kadern von Dal'stroj im Jahr 1954 in GAMO f. R-23, op. 1, d. 5548, l. 1–43, hier l. 23 f.

63 Ältere Personen hatten den Status „junger Facharbeiter", wenn sie z. B. zunächst den Wehrdienst abgeleistet oder eine zweite Ausbildung erhalten hatten. Vgl. die Darstellung dieser jungen Facharbeiter in der Mitschrift eines Treffens des Volkswirtschaftsrates vom 1. November 1958 in GAMO f. R-137, op. 1, d. 59, l. 122–150, hier l. 132a.

64 Vgl. beispielsweise die Beschwerden in der Mitschrift eines Treffens des Volkswirtschaftsrates vom 1. November 1958 in GAMO f. R-137, op. 1, d. 59, l. 122–150, hier l. 122 f. Zwischen 1957 und 1958 wurden 1.000 junge Facharbeiter vom Magadaner Volkswirtschaftsrat aufgenommen, von denen 1958 noch immer 200 als einfache Arbeiter eingesetzt wurden. Vgl. GAMO f. R-137, op. 1, d. 59, l. 120.

Aufgrund des extremen Fachkräftemangels, besonders in Tschukotka, schickte das Bildungsministerium besonders viele junge Fachleute auf die Halbinsel. Da es sich bei dieser Gruppe um Hochschulabgänger ohne praktische Erfahrungen handelte, war man vor Ort nicht immer begeistert – wie beispielsweise der Leiter des Exekutivkomitees von Anadyr' in seiner Beschwerde vom Juni 1956 schrieb:

> Wer ist denn bei uns in der Lage qualifiziert Leute zu behandeln, wenn die Hälfte der Ärzte überhaupt keine Erfahrungen haben (das sind gestrige Studenten) und die andere Hälfte erst seit sieben Monaten arbeitet? All diese Ärzte kochen im eigenen Saft, sie können niemanden konsultieren, niemanden um Rat fragen. Ganz ähnlich sieht es bei den Pädagogen aus. Bei den kulturellen Einrichtungen (in Klubs, Bibliotheken und Kinos) arbeiten vor allem Mädchen, viele zwischen 17 und 20 Jahren alt – das sind Jugendliche, die überhaupt keine Arbeitserfahrung haben und von denen einige überhaupt nicht arbeiten wollen.[66]

Die enorme Arbeitsbelastung ohne vorherige praktische Erfahrung erlebten junge Facharbeiter selbst als deutliche Überforderung, wie z. B. die junge Facharbeiterin Kirilova, die in der Indigirskoe Bergbauverwaltung eingesetzt wurde:

> Die Arbeiter stellen mir oft Fragen über die Mechanisierung von Arbeitsprozessen, aber ich kann sie ihnen nicht beantworten, weil ich das selbst noch nicht weiß. Einige Worte über die Lebensbedingungen: Man hat mir ein Zimmer gegeben, den Kopf schlage ich mir dort an der Decke an, bei der Versorgung mit Kohle und Lebensmitteln sieht's schlecht aus. Aber darauf blicken wir gar nicht, unsere Arbeit erledigen wir ehrlich. Ich möchte hier nur sagen, dass sie doch bitte die Mädchen, die Bergbaumeister sind, in die Verwaltung schicken sollen, weil das hier doch sehr schwere Arbeit ist.[67]

5.1.5 Die „Magadancy" – Zuschreibungen und Überhöhungen

Thomas Wolfe hat in seiner Untersuchung der sowjetischen Presse eine starke Re-Ideologisierung in der Chruščev-Ära festgestellt, die sich auch deutlich auf die Darstellung sowjetischer Personen auswirkte. Er attestiert der Presse in der Entstalinisierung den Versuch, durch feste Präsentationsformen einen neuen Typus des

---

65 Vgl. das Schreiben von Afanas'ev an *Gosplan* der RSFSR vom 9. April 1956 in GAMO f. R-146, op. 1, d. 56, l. 18 – 20, hier l. 18.

66 Vgl. das Schreiben des Vorsitzenden des Exekutivkomitees von Anadyr' vom 19. Juni 1956 an Afanas'ev in GAMO f. R-146, op. 1, d. 56, l. 24 – 25. Der Leiter der Gebietsverwaltung für Kultur wies diese Vorwürfe von sich, er appellierte an die politische Unterstützung des Exekutivkomitees bei der professionellen Einarbeitung. Vgl. ebd., l. 26. Gegenüber dem ZK der KPdSU berichtete aber auch das Gebietsparteikomitee von Schwierigkeiten aufgrund der fehlenden Erfahrung junger Fachkräfte, v. a. im Bereich der Gesundheitsvorsorge. Vgl. das Schreiben des Sekretärs N. Žicharev an das ZK der KPdSU vom 21. Juli 1956 in RGASPI f. 556, op. 23, d. 13, l. 59 – 60, hier l. 59. Die Antwort aus dem ZK siehe l. 61.

67 Vgl. den Bericht über die Arbeit mit Kadern in der Indigirskoe Bergbauverwaltung für das Jahr 1956 in GAMO f. R-137sč, op. 1b, d. 21, l. 39 – 100, hier l. 73f.

„sowjetischen Menschen" herbeizuschreiben.[68] Diese Typenbildung lässt sich auch regional erkennen. Die Regionalzeitung *Magadanskaja Pravda* und mit ihr weitere Zeitungen, Reisebeschreibungen und Erzählungen gestalteten einen „neuen sowjetischen Magadaner", dem stereotype Eigenschaften zugeschrieben wurden: Der „Magadanec" war in dieser Erzählung jung, schaffensfroh, abenteuerlustig und wagemutig. Er erlebte die klimatischen Härten des Naturraumes, die extreme Kälte als identitätsstiftend, berauschte sich an aufregenden Landschaften voller wilder Tiere, begriff infrastrukturelle Mängel als Herausforderungen, setzte sich mit aller Kraft für seine neue Heimat ein.[69] Das ursowjetische Thema „Jugend" wurde in Magadan immer wieder bis aufs äußerste strapaziert.[70] Alle positiven Zuschreibungen kulminierten in diesem Adjektiv, das der Morgenröte des jüngsten Gebietes der Sowjetunion ein menschliches Gesicht zu verleihen schien und das besonders in Bezug auf neu eintreffende Komsomolzen betont wurde. Die vielen jungen Menschen, Arbeiter, Spezialisten und enthusiastische Komsomolzen, sie alle waren gekommen, um zu bleiben, um als Pioniere das Land zu erschließen, zu bereisen, auszubeuten, das Gebiet zu bevölkern, die neue Zeit zu gestalten. Sie waren die Personifizierung der engen Verbindung zwischen dem Nordosten und den übrigen Gebieten der Sowjetunion:

> [...] Die Jugend reist mit hohen patriotischen Zielen in den äußersten Nordosten – das einmal unerschlossene und finstere Gebiet in die Umgestaltung mit hineinnehmen. Die jungen Neubürger bleiben lange zum Leben und Arbeiten im Fernen Norden, sie werden zu den Alteingesessenen dieses Gebietes werden. [...] Und jedes Jahr treten immer neue Reihen junger Ingenieure, Techniker, Arbeiter, Lehrer, Ärzte, Agronomen aus den Schiffen ans Ufer und verteilen sich in alle Winkel unseres Gebietes.[71]

> Der Parteiorganisator blickte noch einmal auf die jungen Leute. In ihnen sah er nicht nur die Neu-Siedler, sondern starke Leute mit brennenden Herzen, die hierhergekommen waren, um mit ihrem heißen, jungen Atem das ferne nördliche Land zu erwärmen.[72]

Tatsächlich waren die Arbeitskräfte des Gebietes auffällig jung. Mehr als 69 % waren zwischen 20 und 39 Jahre alt, was sich aus den klimatischen Belastungen für ältere Arbeitnehmer und aus den Anwerbungen ergab, die sich zum Großteil an Schulabgänger oder junge Arbeitslose richtete.[73] Junge Leute hoffte man trotz der schweren Lebens- und Arbeitsbedingungen in dem extremen Klima besser einsetzen zu können,

---

68 Vgl. Wolfe, Soviet Journalism.

69 Für eine typische Darstellung des nordöstlichen Naturraums siehe die Reisebeschreibung Danilov, Kraj severnogo sijanija. Die jungen Menschen drängte es in diesen Darstellungen in die härtesten Regionen des Gebietes, in die am wenigsten erschlossenen, in die kältesten und rückständigsten.

70 Siehe zur ideologischen Bedeutung von Jugend in der Chruščev-Ära Fürst, Arrival of Spring; Zhuk, Popular Culture sowie allgemein zum Topos „Jugend" in der Sowjetunion Kuhr-Korolev/Plaggenborg/Wellmann, Sowjetjugend; Kuhr-Korolev, Gezähmte Helden.

71 Klesova, Sever zovet, S. 8 f.

72 Geroi, S. 47.

73 Nach den Angaben von Grebenjuk gab es zweimal so viele junge Arbeitskräfte wie in den zentralen Gebieten der Union. Vgl. Grebenjuk, Kolymskij led, S. 80.

„Мы едем в Магадан!"

Мол...
горячо отк.
Коммунис...

Группа молодых москвичей, получивших комсомольские путевки в Магаданскую область. Слева направо: Михаил АНИШКИН, Александр КОРСАВИН, Тамара ФАДЕЕВА, Виктор ДЬЯКОВ, Николай ТВОРОЖКОВ, Михаил КОРСЕЕВ и Геннадий РУМЯНЦЕВ.

Фото И. Степанова.

Abb. 37 Moskauer Komsomolzen reisen nach Magadan, Magadanskaja Pravda, 7. Juni 1956

zudem waren sie z. T. noch ungebunden. 1954 erlaubte man angeworbenen Arbeitskräften einen Zuzug sogar nur „ohne Familie", was junge, unverheiratete Männer bevorteilte.[74] Der Frauenanteil war in den ersten Jahren extrem gering, stieg jedoch bis Ende der 1950er Jahre deutlich an, nicht zuletzt, weil der Aufbau von Kinderbetreuungseinrichtungen die Einstellung junger Frauen erleichterte. Der Anstieg der weiblichen Arbeitskräfte war aufgrund der bisher so stark männlich dominierten Struktur im Magadaner Gebiet sogar höher als der allgemeine Trend zur Erhöhung des Anteils weiblicher Arbeitskräfte in der Industrie.[75]

1956 erreichten 7.500 junge Menschen den Nordosten, die einem Aufruf des Moskauer Komsomol gefolgt waren. Ihre Ankunft in der Bucht Nagaevo wurde zu einem Volksfest gestaltet, Tausende Magadaner begrüßten die „neuen Mitbürger". Ein Orchester spielte auf, Blumensträuße wurden geworfen, Jubel und Hurra-Rufe ertönten, zahlreiche Reden wurden gehalten. Die Zeitung *Magadanskaja Pravda* wid-

---

74 Vgl. den Bericht über die Arbeit mit Kadern von Dal'stroj für das Jahr 1954 in GAMO f. R-23, op. 1, d. 5548, l. 1–43, hier l. 10.

75 Vgl. zum steigenden Anteil von Frauen an der Volkswirtschaft Ivanova, Na poroge, S. 152. 1959 lag der Anteil weiblicher Arbeitskräfte im Magadaner Gebiet schon bei 35 %. Vgl. den Überblick in Narodnoe chozjajstvo Magadanskoj oblasti, S. 74.

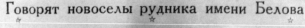

Abb. 38 „Der Ferne Norden wurde für uns nah und heimatlich", Magadanskij Komsomolez, 15. November 1957

mete mehrere Ausgaben der Ankunft der „Neuen", der Erste Sekretär des Komsomol Novokreščenov titelte am 12. Juli 1956: „Herzlich willkommen in unserer Komsomolzen-Familie!"[76] Darstellungen der Neuankommenden und ihrer Biographien erschienen:

> Sie glauben fest an das anbrechende, wunderbare Morgen. Sie gehen darauf zu, hinterlassen ein Denkmal ihrer Hände, ihres schrankenlosen Denkens in der fernen nördlichen Taiga, in den neuen Städten und Siedlungen, neuen Fabriken und Goldminen. Sie erbauen den Kommunismus![77]

Diese Propaganda ist ausgesprochen typisch für sowjetische Mobilisierungskampagnen, zur Erschließung von „Neuland" in der Kasachischen SSR ebenso wie in Sibirien.[78] Magadan war nur ein Ort unter anderen Mobilisierungszielen, er ist aber vielleicht der Ort, an dem der Widerspruch zwischen der angeblichen Geschichtslosigkeit des „jungen Gebietes" und seiner gewaltvollen realen Geschichte am eklatantesten war. Von den Erfahrungen, die „die Jugend" in dieser Inszenierung dabei angeblich machte, erzählten die Legenden, die von der offiziellen Kulturpolitik verbreitet wurden. So heißt es in einer Darstellung Magadaner Komsomolzen mit dem Titel „Der Norden ruft":

> Nicht nur die jungen Bergarbeiter, auch die jungen Geologen, Fahrer, Matrosen antworten auf die Entscheidungen des 20. Parteitages mit Heldentaten der Arbeit. Hier eine Episode aus der Arbeit

---

76 Vgl. die ausführliche Darstellung der Feier in Smolina, Komsomol'cy-Dobrovol'cy, S. 215 f.

77 Geroi, S. 48.

78 Vgl. zur Bedeutung dieser Kampagnen als Mobilisierungsstrategie unter Chruščev Gill, Question of Reformability, S. 134. Detaillierter zur Neulandkampagne siehe Pohl, Tselinograd; Pohl, Virgin Lands, zur Baikal-Amur-Magistrale Grützmacher, Bajkal-Amur-Magistrale.

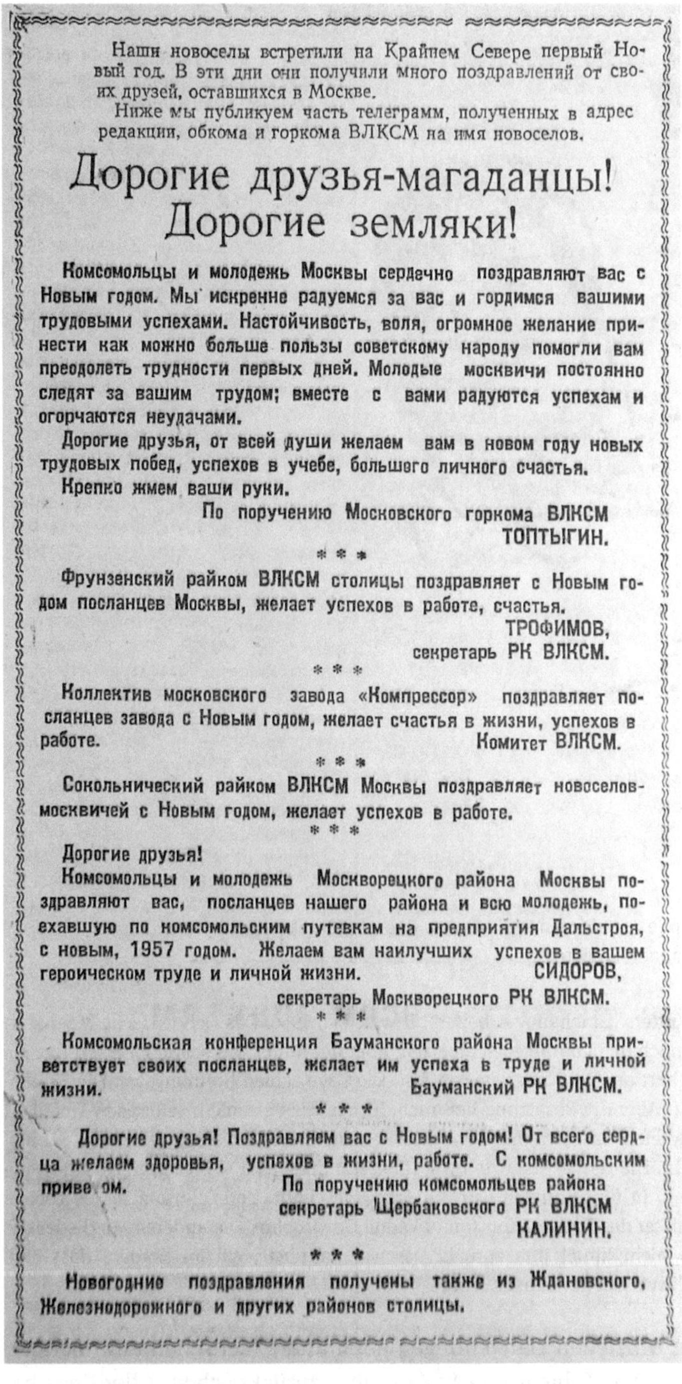

Наши новоселы встретили на Крайнем Севере первый Новый год. В эти дни они получили много поздравлений от своих друзей, оставшихся в Москве.

Ниже мы публикуем часть телеграмм, полученных в адрес редакции, обкома и горкома ВЛКСМ на имя новоселов.

Дорогие друзья-магаданцы! Дорогие земляки!

Комсомольцы и молодежь Москвы сердечно поздравляют вас с Новым годом. Мы искренне радуемся за вас и гордимся вашими трудовыми успехами. Настойчивость, воля, огромное желание принести как можно больше пользы советскому народу помогли вам преодолеть трудности первых дней. Молодые москвичи постоянно следят за вашим трудом; вместе с вами радуются успехам и огорчаются неудачами.

Дорогие друзья, от всей души желаем вам в новом году новых трудовых побед, успехов в учебе, большого личного счастья.

Крепко жмем ваши руки.

По поручению Московского горкома ВЛКСМ
ТОПТЫГИН.

* * *

Фрунзенский райком ВЛКСМ столицы поздравляет с Новым годом посланцев Москвы, желает успехов в работе, счастья.

ТРОФИМОВ,
секретарь РК ВЛКСМ.

* * *

Коллектив московского завода «Компрессор» поздравляет посланцев завода с Новым годом, желает счастья в жизни, успехов в работе. **Комитет ВЛКСМ.**

* * *

Сокольнический райком ВЛКСМ Москвы поздравляет новоселов-москвичей с Новым годом, желает успехов в работе.

* * *

Дорогие друзья!

Комсомольцы и молодежь Москворецкого района Москвы поздравляют вас, посланцев нашего района и всю молодежь, поехавшую по комсомольским путевкам на предприятия Дальстроя, с новым, 1957 годом. Желаем вам наилучших успехов в вашем героическом труде и личной жизни. **СИДОРОВ,**
секретарь Москворецкого РК ВЛКСМ.

* * *

Комсомольская конференция Бауманского района Москвы приветствует своих посланцев, желает им успеха в труде и личной жизни. **Бауманский РК ВЛКСМ.**

* * *

Дорогие друзья! Поздравляем вас с Новым годом! От всего сердца желаем здоровья, успехов в жизни, работе. С комсомольским приве ом. По поручению комсомольцев района
секретарь Щербаковского РК ВЛКСМ
КАЛИНИН.

* * *

Новогодние поздравления получены также из Ждановского, Железнодорожного и других районов столицы.

Abb. 39 Neujahrstelegramme aus den Heimatregionen der Komsomolzen, Magadanskaja Pravda, 5. Januar 1957

Abb. 40 Titelbild des Bandes „Helden nahe bei uns. Reportagen über Komsomolzen des Magadaner Gebietes"

der Besatzung des Kutters „Stachanov-Arbeiter": Es war Mai 1956. Das Ochotskische Meer kalt, rau. Das Eis dachte noch nicht daran zu schmelzen. Aber der Kutter war schon im Meer. Das Eis griff unsere Helden hart an. Der Kutter steckte fest. Die Lage schien hoffnungslos. Die Schiffs-schraube war kaputt. Aber die Besatzung ließ nicht locker. Sie entschied, selbst den Unfall zu beheben. Sie überfluteten das Zwischendeck und begannen im Eiswasser selbst die Schiffs-schraube zu wechseln. Die Hände erstarrten vor Kälte. Am Ende aber war es geglückt, die neue Schraube einzusetzen. In fünf Stunden war die Arbeit geschafft. Unter Einsatz seines Lebens arbeitete der Mechaniker des Kutters, Komsomol Vadim Govoruchin. Die anderen Mitglieder der Mannschaft blieben nicht hinter ihm zurück. Das war das erste Mal im Norden, dass eine Schiffsschraube im Eiswasser gewechselt wurde.[79]

Natürlich tauchten in offiziellen Darstellungen auch ältere Menschen auf. Männer, deren lokale Erfahrungen z. T. bis in die 1930er Jahre zurückreichen. Allerdings be-

---

79 Klesova, Sever zovet, S. 63.

schränkten sich diese Erfahrungen auf den erprobten Umgang mit den harten klimatischen Bedingungen, auf die sicheren Fahrleistungen auf der vereisten Trasse und im Schneesturm, auf das Leben ohne zivilisatorische Annehmlichkeiten und mit einfachsten Mitteln.[80] Erfahrungen anderer Natur wurden nicht thematisiert, Dal'stroj und das Lagersystem spielten keine Rolle; junge wie alte *Magadancy* glichen sich auf diese Weise durch ihre Geschichtslosigkeit.

Objekt dieser realitätsfernen Darstellungsweise waren auch die Indigenen, die als regionale Sehenswürdigkeit bestaunt wurden. Seit 1957 erschien eine historisch-ethnographisch ausgerichtete Zeitschrift, die *Kraevedčeskie Zapiski*, die sich mit den kulturellen Leistungen der Indigenen und ihren Adaptionsbemühungen an das sowjetische System beschäftigte. Indigene Kultur war auch Gegenstand der 1955 gegründeten Zeitschrift *Na Severe Dal'nem*, die den Auftrag erhielt, „das Leben im Hohen Norden schriftstellerisch zu verarbeiten" – so das Gebietsexekutivkomitee. Die Zeitung *Sovetkėn Čukotka* sowie eine ganze Reihe von Büchern erschienen in tschukotkischer Sprache bzw. wurden ins Tschukotkische übersetzt.[81] Die indigene Kultur war dabei gewissermaßen die exotische Würze der Heimatkunde, die die Faszination des Kulturraumes erhöhte und ihn positiv besetzte – ganz im Widerspruch zu den erbärmlichen Bedingungen, unter denen die Völker des Nordostens zu leiden hatten.[82] Ihre kulturelle Vereinnahmung und Überformung durch die Zerstörung ihrer tradierten Lebensweise verstand die regionale Führung ganz bewusst als Beitrag zu einer vollständigen Durchdringung (im Sinne der *osvoenie*) des Territoriums, als Verankerung der sowjetischen Macht im naturräumlichen und kulturellen Raum des Nordostens.[83]

Der indigenen Bevölkerung blieb in diesem Rahmen nur die Rolle des staunenden Bewunderers, des Nutznießers zivilisatorischer Errungenschaften der sowjetischen Macht – darunter der Alphabetisierung – oder die Position des Künstlers, der seine kreativen Potentiale dank sowjetischer Förderung zur Stärkung der kulturellen Eigenart im Rahmen regionaler Identitätsbildung einsetzen durfte.[84] Eine Gruppe junger

---

80 Vgl. die Darstellung des Kolchosvorsitzenden Efim Matveevič Zankin aus der Kolchose „Novyj Put'", dem in der Darstellung „Dort wo es schwieriger ist" ein literarisches Denkmal errichtet wurde. Zankin kam, so die Darstellung, Ende der 1930er Jahre in das Gebiet und hatte sich seitdem für die Arbeit mit Indigenen eingesetzt. Seine Leitung und seine langjährige Erfahrung in dem harten Naturraum habe der brachliegenden Kolchose die Wende gebracht. Diese Darstellung erschien in der literarischen Reihe „Die besten Menschen des Magadaner Gebietes". Kozlov, Tam, gde trudnee. Siehe auch die Beschreibung des tschukotkischen Arztes, L. P. Čaban, in Danilov, Kraj severnogo sijanija, S. 22f. sowie die Darstellung seines Chauffeurs in den Aufzeichnungen Afanas'evs. Vgl. Afanas'ev, Rossija, S. 9.

81 Vgl. den ausführlichen Bericht des Gebietsexekutivkomitees zum Aufbau von Kultureinrichtungen im Magadaner Gebiet aus dem Jahr 1958 in GAMO f. R-146, op. 1, d. 215, l. 38–68.

82 Vgl. zu den realen Arbeits- und Lebensbedingungen der Indigenen das Kapitel 5.3.5.

83 Diesen Prozess der Akkulturation der indigenen Bevölkerung, den die sowjetische Macht in dieser Zeit im gesamten Hohen Norden betrieb, beschreiben anschaulich Slezkine, Arctic Mirrors, S. 330ff. sowie Forsyth, Peoples of Siberia, S. 405f.

84 So z. B. der Künstler Jurij Rytchėc, der in mehreren Büchern die angeblichen Leistungen der sowjetischen Macht für die kulturelle Entwicklung seines Volkes beschrieb. Vgl. Rytchėc, Vremja. In

Abb. 41 Treffen von „Bestarbeitern der Landwirtschaft", Magadan 1957
(RGAKFD Krasnogorsk, 0-37606, Fotograf: A. Solov'ev)

Tschuktschen, die zur Erholung in ein Sanatorium reisten, wurden dementsprechend
auf den Seiten der *Magadanskaja Pravda* porträtiert:

> Besonders freut die jungen Leute, dass sie durch das Gebietszentrum, durch Magadan fahren.
> Miša Ragtugve wird zum ersten Mal in seinem Leben einen echten Baum sehen. Ist das denn nicht
> interessant? Seine Mitreisenden träumen davon, ins Gebietsmuseum zu gehen, ins ‚Haus der
> Pioniere', ins Theater. Die jungen Leute wissen, dass im Sanatorium erfahrene Ärzte auf sie
> warten, eine gute Versorgung, lustige Erholung. Wie viele wunderbare Eindrücke werden ihnen in
> Erinnerung bleiben![85]

Der Berufsgruppe der Geologen kam bei der Darstellung der *Magadancy* eine besondere Rolle zu. Die Abhängigkeit der gesamten Region und der politischen Führung von
ihren Funden produzierte einen regionalen Geologen-Kult, der von der sowjetunionweiten Bedeutung dieser Berufsgruppe getragen wurde.[86] Die Geologen verkörperten

---

dem Reisebericht „Briefe aus einem früheren Nomadenlager" wird der Übergang einer Kolchose zum
„sowjetischen, sesshaften Leben" als Erfolgsgeschichte beschrieben. Vgl. Chakimov, Pis'ma. Vgl. auch
die Darstellung indigener Bewunderung für ein sowjetisches Radiogerät in Danilov, Kraj severnogo
sijanija, S. 12 sowie Menovščikov, Ėskimosy; Bulanov, Načinaetsja den' und Novikova, Fol'klora. Zur
Darstellung tschukotkischer Künstler aus sowjetischer Sicht siehe Guščin/Afanas'ev, Čukotskij okrug,
S. 94 ff.

85 Vgl. Magadanskaja Pravda, 19. Januar 1955, S. 3.

86 Vgl. Mick, Wissenschaft, S. 340 ff.

Abb. 42 Heimtransport nach der Schule, Tschukotka August 1956
(RGAKFD Krasnogorsk, 0-272097, Fotograf: A. L. Less)

das Bild vom tapferen Mann, der dem Klima, der Einsamkeit, dem Hunger und dem allgegenwärtigen Mangel trotzt und der unabhängig von den extremen Härten des Territoriums zu professionellen Höchstleistungen und zu zutreffenden Prognosen in der Lage war, allein durch seine Intuition und intrinsische Motivation. Die Geologen verkörperten so die Chancen des neuen Gebietes, sie standen für den Reichtum, den der Boden bereithielt, ebenso wie für die Möglichkeiten menschlicher / männlicher Existenz, die im Nordosten zutage traten. Zugleich wurden die unmenschlichen Lebens- und Arbeitsbedingungen – die Geologen galten in der Statistik der Arbeitsunfälle als die am gefährdetste Gruppe – auf eine besonders perfide Weise umgewertet. Alle Härten erschienen als Proben echter Männlichkeit, die die Menschen, die sich diesen Herausforderungen stellten, zugleich moralisch veredelten. Schwierigkeiten,

Krankheiten, Hunger und Kälte konnten so zu Zeichen persönlicher Unzulänglichkeiten umgewertet werden.[87]

5.1.6 Arbeitsschutz und die Rolle der Gewerkschaften

Wie viel die Arbeit in der Region den Menschen tatsächlich abverlangte, zeigt sich besonders drastisch an Unfällen und Krankheiten, die die Rohstoffförderung verursachte. Am häufigsten waren Atemwegskrankheiten, die sich durch den langen Aufenthalt im Freien bei extrem niedrigen Temperaturen entwickelten. Während im Jahr 1957 19 von 1.000 Personen in der RSFSR insgesamt an akuter und chronischer Bronchitis litten, waren es im Magadaner Gebiet 33.[88] Noch 1959 lag das Gebiet bei den akuten Entzündungen der oberen Atemwege um 45 % über dem Durchschnitt der RSFSR.[89] Diese Erkrankungen waren so ausgeprägt, weil es in den 1950er Jahren noch keine oder viel zu geringe Maßnahmen für Arbeitsschutz gab. So fehlte es in sehr vielen Betrieben an spezieller Arbeitskleidung und an Trockenräumen, in denen Arbeiter ihre nassen Sachen wechseln konnten. Immer wieder waren sie gezwungen, bei -40 bis -50° C in ihrer feuchten / nassen Arbeitskleidung nach Hause in die Wohnbaracken zu laufen, und selbst dort mangelte es an geeigneten Trockenräumen.[90]

Noch dramatischer als die unter diesen Umständen auftretenden Katarrhe war eine im Deutschen allgemein als „Staublunge" bekannte Berufskrankheit, die Silikose. Sie tritt bei der Metallförderung, v. a. bei Arbeiten im Bergwerk, aber auch auf den Goldfeldern auf. Mineralischer Staub sammelt sich in der Lunge an, verhärtet sie durch Vernarbungen und kann zum Tod durch Ersticken führen. Häufig gehen mit der Silikose tuberkulöse Prozesse einher. Der frühere Häftling Michael Solomon schildert in seinen Erinnerungen die Entstehung der Silikose bei der Goldförderung:

---

87 Der bekannteste regionale Vertreter dieses Genres ist der Roman „Territorija" (deutsche Übersetzung „Goldsucher") von Oleg Kuvaev, erstmals erschienen in Moskau 1975. Kuvaev hatte in den 1950er und 1960er Jahren selbst als Geologe in Tschukotka und in der Geologischen Verwaltung in Magadan gearbeitet, stellenweise liest sich sein Buch wie ein Schlüsselroman über die dortigen Machtverhältnisse. Beginnend bei den Verhältnissen in den 1940er Jahren an der Kolyma schildert der Roman die Entdeckung von Goldvorkommen in Tschukotka und das Ende von Dal'stroj 1957 (im Roman bezeichnet als „Severstroj"), wobei sich zahlreiche historische Persönlichkeiten, wie der Leiter von Dal'stroj, Mitrakov, die Geologen Šilo und Drabkin u. a., in den Charakteren wiedererkennen lassen. „Territorija" erschien in mehreren Auflagen, wurde in zahlreiche Sprachen übersetzt, u. a. verfilmt und für das Theater dramatisiert. Vgl. folgende weitere Geologen-Literatur, die sich auf den nordöstlichen Raum bezieht: Vronskij, Po tropam; Kopteva, Zoloto; Volkov, Veksel' Bilibina; ders., Zolotaja Kolyma; Ustiev, U istokov; Vjatkin, Čelovek; Semenov, Bereg Nadeždy; Caregradskij, Po ėkranu; Novikov, Kolyma ty.
88 Vgl. die Angaben vom 13. April 1959 in GAMO f. R-146, op. 1, d. 220, l. 33 – 37, hier l. 33.
89 Vgl. die Angabe aus der Abteilung für Löhne des Volkswirtschaftsrates in GAMO f. R-137, op. 1, d. 1007ž, l. 1 – 11, hier l. 7.
90 Vgl. die Verordnung des Präsidiums der Magadaner Gewerkschaften vom 13. Mai 1957 in GAMO f. R-146, op. 1, d. 219, l. 29 – 30a.

Die Arbeit in den Gruben war der reinste Alptraum. Keinerlei Sicherheitsmaßnahmen schützten die Bergleute vor Unfällen. Erst nach langem Hin und Her bekamen sie Karbidlampen [...], die Behörden ließen dann auch Frischluft in die Gruben pumpen. Doch weil die Verwaltung möglichst schnell das geplante Produktionsniveau erreichen wollte, wurden einige elementare Sicherheitsmaßnahmen außer acht gelassen, so daß die Luft ständig staubgeschwängert war. Als Folge davon bekamen viele Häftlinge Silkose, d. h. eine Steinstaublunge.[91]

In den 1950er Jahren waren sehr viele Arbeiter des Gebietes an Silikose erkrankt.[92] Bei vielen von ihnen war die Krankheit schon sehr weit fortgeschritten, so dass sie nicht mehr unter Tage oder sogar überhaupt nicht mehr arbeiten konnten.[93] Die eigentlich festgesetzte Norm für die zulässige Staubbelastung in der Sowjetunion wurde z. T. um das 300 – 500fache überschritten.[94]

Allerdings muss bereits das Vorliegen dieser Zahlen als allererste Maßnahme zum Arbeitsschutz und damit als ein kleines Zeichen der Verantwortung des Kombinats gegenüber seinen Arbeitskräften gewertet werden.[95] Denn bis 1953 gab es in Dal'stroj selbst für freie Arbeitskräfte nur vereinzelt Röntgenapparate, mit denen die Silikose festgestellt werden konnte. Ohne jegliche Schutzvorrichtung wurden Arbeiter in die staubhaltige Luft der Bergwerke geschickt, Betriebsärzte zur Überwachung von Arbeitsschutzstandards und zur Aufklärung gab es überhaupt nicht.[96]

Nach der Gebietsgründung drängte die politische Leitung, später auch die Gewerkschaften, auf Maßnahmen im Kampf gegen die Silikose.[97] Zunächst einmal wurden bei einigen Bergwerken Röntgenkabinette eingerichtet, um überhaupt den Krankheitsstand der Arbeiter zu erfassen. Im Jahr 1956 ließ Dal'stroj schließlich generalstabsmäßig die Anti-Silikose-Arbeitsweise als Verfahren der Metallgewinnung einführen. Trotzdem änderten sich in vielen Bergwerken die Bedingungen nicht, in einigen wenigen installierte man Ventilatoren zur besseren Belüftung und setzte Filter ein. Von einer allgemeinen Änderung der Verhältnisse in der Region konnte jedoch

---

91 Solomon, Magadan, S. 173 f.

92 Allein in den Schächten des Bezirkes Susuman gab es im Jahr 1957 157 Fälle von Silikose. Vgl. den Vortrag über die Arbeit der Verwaltung der Magadaner Abteilung der staatlich-technischen Bergbauüberwachung der UdSSR vom Juli 1957 in GAMO f. R-137sč, op. 1b, d. 11, l. 2 – 61, hier l. 18.

93 Siehe zu den Verlegungen von Arbeitskräften aufgrund der Silikose die Verfügung vom 27. April 1955 in GAMO f. R-23, op. 1, d. 5605, l. 65 – 70, hier l. 66.

94 Zahlenangaben sind hier problematisch, da man von einer sehr hohen Dunkelziffer ausgehen muss. Zudem wurde vielen Kranken Tuberkulose attestiert, obwohl sie eigentlich an einer Silikose erkrankt waren. Für die Zahlen für 1955 siehe die Angaben der Gebietsgesundheitsabteilung in GAMO f. R-146, op. 1, d. 105, l. 16 – 40, hier l. 33. Für eine Beschreibung der verschiedenen Diagnosen siehe beispielhaft den Bericht des ersten Ingenieurs der Grube „Pjatiletka" von 1956 in GAMO f. R-137, op. 1, d. 1046, l. 80 – 82.

95 Christopher Burton beschreibt die Diskussion über den Einsatz toxischer Stoffe in der Industrie als Element der Entstalinisierung. Vgl. Burton, Detoxification.

96 Die wichtigsten Bestimmungen der Regierung im Kampf gegen die Silikose wurden in der Region nicht beachtet. Vgl. die Verfügung vom 27. April 1955 in GAMO f. R-23, op. 1, d. 5605, l. 65 – 70, hier l. 65.

97 Zum Stand der Silikose-Aufklärung und Prävention zu Beginn des Jahres 1956 siehe GAMO f. R-146, op. 1, d. 105, l. 33 f.

auch Ende der 1950er Jahre noch keine Rede sein.[98] Beispielhaft äußerte sich der Vertreter des Goldfeldes „im. Belova", Goloulin, gegenüber der obersten Leitung des Magadaner Volkswirtschaftsrates im September 1958:

> Um Maßnahmen im Kampf mit der Silikose durchzuführen, wurden Gelder bereitgestellt, aber einige leitende Arbeiter zeigen in dieser Sache eine vollkommen unverantwortliche Haltung. Drei Jahre haben wir nun schon Gelder für Prophylaxe-Maßnahmen in der Grube im. Belova zur Verfügung gestellt, die Pläne liegen vor, alles ist bereit, aber es wird nichts gebaut. [...] 45 Menschen sind für ihr ganzes Leben gezeichnet, sie wurden zu Invaliden gemacht. Die Frage der zentralen Belüftung muss dringend gelöst werden.[99]

Die lokalen klimatischen Bedingungen erschwerten den Kampf gegen Silikose erheblich. Die übliche Vorgehensweise, bei der der Staub durch das Versprühen von Wasser gebunden wird, ließ sich bei den Arbeiten im ewigen Eis nicht durchführen. Das lokale Forschungsinstitut VNII-1 erarbeitete daher ein Verfahren, mit dem der Staub trocken gebunden werden konnte.[100] Auch mit anderen wissenschaftlichen Institutionen in der Sowjetunion, die Erfahrungen im Kampf gegen die Silikose hatten, wurde eine Zusammenarbeit angestrebt.[101]

Ende der 1950er Jahre kann in Grundsatzbeschlüssen der obersten politischen und wirtschaftlichen Führung der Region zumindest von einer langsam steigenden Sensibilisierung für Berufskrankheiten gesprochen werden. Magadaner Verantwortliche bemühten sich um einen wissenschaftlichen und praktischen Austausch über die Silikose im Rahmen der UdSSR, der Staaten des Warschauer Paktes und international.[102] In der Praxis waren die Verbesserungen für die Arbeitskräfte jedoch minimal.

Ganz ähnlich stellt sich die Lage bei den zahlreichen Unfällen dar, die die Arbeit in der nordöstlichen Metallförderung gefährlich, häufig lebensgefährlich machte.

---

98 Siehe zu den Maßnahmen die Mitschrift des Treffens des technisch-wirtschaftlichen Rates des Volkswirtschaftsrates vom 16. August 1958 in GAMO f. R-137, op. 1, d. 59a, l. 51–201, hier l. 196 sowie den Vortrag über die Arbeit der Verwaltung der Magadaner Abteilung der staatlich-technischen Bergbauüberwachung der UdSSR vom Juli 1957 in GAMO f. R-137sč, op. 1b, d. 11, l. 2–61, hier l. 19. Die Lage Ende des Jahres 1959 schildert der Bericht des leitenden Arztes der Gebietssanitärepidemiestation für das Jahr 1959 in GAMO f. R-146, op. 1, d. 220 l. 48–68, hier l. 61–64.
99 Vgl. die Mitschrift des Leitungsgremiums des Magadaner Volkswirtschaftsrates vom 10. September 1958 in GAMO f. R-137, op. 1, d. 58, l. 270–313, hier l. 311.
100 Vgl. Šilo/Potemkin, Valjutnyj cech, S. 91f.
101 Eine solche Zusammenarbeit gab es z. B. mit dem Hygieneinstitut von Swerdlowsk. Vgl. die Angaben der Abteilung für Gesundheitswesen des Gebietsexekutivkomitees in GAMO f. R-146, op. 1, d. 105, l. 16–40, hier l. 34.
102 Vgl. den Bericht zu den entsprechenden Beratungen in der Mitschrift des Leitungsgremiums des Magadaner Volkswirtschaftsrates vom 10. September 1958 in GAMO f. R-137, op. 1, d. 58, l. 270–313, hier l. 308. Aus Gründen der Geheimhaltung durften die Magadaner Fachleute in den 1950er Jahren nicht im vollen Umfang an diesem wissenschaftlichen Austausch teilnehmen. Vgl. die entsprechende Entscheidung des wissenschaftlich-technischen Komitees des Ministerrates der UdSSR vom 9. Mai 1959 in GAMO f. R-137sč, op. 1b, d. 52, l. 22–23.

Michael Solomon schildert in seinen Erinnerungen die Arbeit unter Tage und die Fahrten mit den Förderkörben im Jahr 1949:

> Kein Tag verging, ohne daß ein Unfall geschah. Entweder versagte die Energieversorgung, und die Häftlinge blieben auf halbem Weg stecken, oder ein Kabel riß und der Förderkorb krachte in die Tiefe. Ständig wurden verstümmelte, schwerverletzte Häftlinge ins Lagerlazarett transportiert. Eine weitere Unfallquelle resultierte aus dem Fehlen geeigneter Kopfbedeckungen. Die Bergleute trugen ihre russischen Fellmützen statt Helmen, und wenn große Steintrümmer oder Felsbrocken einen Mann trafen, war er erledigt.[103]

Der Arbeitsschutz, der in der Entstalinisierung allmählich als prinzipielle Verantwortung der Betriebe gegenüber den Arbeitskräften begriffen wurde, wurde im Nordosten nur sehr schleppend überhaupt ein Thema; eine Besserung der von Solomon geschilderten Verhältnisse trat erst langsam ein:

Im August 1953 hatte der Leiter der bergbautechnischen Inspektion von Dal'stroj, Solomachin, mit seinem seitenlangen Bericht über fehlenden Arbeitsschutz, schwerwiegende Vergehen im Umgang mit Sprengmaterial und der großen Abhängigkeit seiner Inspektion von der Kombinatsleitung eine ausführliche Untersuchung der bergbautechnischen Inspektion des MCM losgetreten.[104] Nach Gebietsgründung wurde die Region dann zum ersten Mal überhaupt der „staatlich-technischen Bergbauüberwachung der UdSSR" (Gostechgornadzor SSSR) unterstellt, die aufgrund des Fehlens minimaler Standards die Beseitigung „langjähriger Verletzungen der Sicherheitstechnik in Betrieben von Dal'stroj" forderte.[105] Bis Ende des Jahrzehnts schlossen sich daran immer wieder Befehle und Anordnungen zur Verbesserung des Arbeitsschutzes an, dennoch blieb die Zahl der Arbeitsunfälle in allen Betrieben von Dal'stroj bzw. des Volkswirtschaftsrates sehr hoch.[106] Viele waren tödlich oder wurden als „schwer" eingestuft – beispielsweise gab es im Januar und Februar 1955 in Dal'stroj 16 Unfälle mit Todesfolge und sechs weitere „schwere Unfälle"[107]. Die in den Berichten genannten Ursachen offenbaren katastrophale Zustände: Schutzvorrichtungen und Schutzkleidung gab es nur in Ausnahmefällen, im Umgang mit Materialien, auch feuergefährlichen wie Benzin, wurden einfachste Sicherheitsregeln nicht eingehalten. Arbeiter wurden durch herabfallende Gesteinsbrocken oder Bauteile verletzt oder erschlagen, Maschinen nicht rechtzeitig abgestellt, die Stromversorgung nicht abge-

---

103 Solomon, Magadan, S. 174.
104 Vgl. RGANI f. 5, op. 27, d. 122, l. 74–84.
105 Die Verordnung erließ das Komitee für die staatlich-technische Bergbauüberwachung am 11. Mai 1956, vgl. den Vortrag über die Arbeit der Verwaltung der Magadaner Abteilung der staatlich-technischen Bergbauüberwachung der UdSSR vom Juli 1957 in GAMO f. R-137sč, op. 1b, d. 11, l. 2–61, hier l. 31. Zu den Unfällen siehe die Angaben der Gebietsgesundheitsabteilung in GAMO f. R-146, op. 1, d. 105, l. 16–40, hier l. 16–17.
106 Siehe zu den Anordnungen der Leitung bezüglich des Arbeitsschutzes GAMO f. R-23, op. 1, d. 5600, l. 185–190 sowie GAMO f. R-23, op. 1, d. 5605, l. 60–64.
107 Vgl. die Anordnung Mitrakovs zur Vermeidung solcher Unfälle vom 2. März 1955 in GAMO f. R-23, op. 1, d. 5605, l. 59.

sichert. Brände brachen aus. Bei der Arbeit unter Tage (beim Gold- und beim Kohleabbau) wurden die Schächte zum Teil mit Stöcken abgestützt, Ein- und Ausstiege aus den Schächten bestanden oft aus einfachen Holzleitern, waren nicht gesichert und drohten abzurutschen.[108] Besonders gefährlich waren auch der Transport von Materialien und der Abtransport von Geröll unter Tage.[109] Erschwert wurde dies durch fehlende Ventilatoren. Der mangelnde Sauerstoff trieb die Arbeiter immer wieder an die Oberfläche, was geregelte Arbeitsabläufe verhinderte.[110] Nach einem Unfall waren die Bergung der Opfer und ihre Erstversorgung durch das Fehlen geeigneter Rettungskräfte oder durch deren mangelnde Ausstattung stark erschwert.[111]

Zu vielen Unfällen kam es außerdem durch den geringen Bildungsgrad der Arbeiter. Sehr vielen wurden schwere Maschinen und Fahrzeuge anvertraut, obwohl sie weder über eine entsprechende theoretische Vorbildung noch über praktische Erfahrungen verfügten. Oft hatten sie nicht einmal eine angemessene Einweisung erhalten.[112]

Ganz besonders dramatisch war dies beim Umgang mit Sprengmaterialien, die für eine große Zahl sehr schwerer Unfälle verantwortlich waren. Sprengmaterialien gab es in Dal'stroj in gewaltiger Menge, sie wurden im Bergbau, beim Abbau über Tage und beim geologischen Schürfdienst eingesetzt. Aufgrund der Einsatzmöglichkeiten als Waffen mussten Sprengmaterialien grundsätzlich beim MVD registriert werden und durften nur mit dessen Genehmigung transportiert und verlagert werden. Tatsächlich aber gab es in Dal'stroj sehr viel mehr als das registrierte Material, einzelne geologische Expeditionen verfügten mitunter über zwei Tonnen Sprengmaterial und acht km Zündschnur.[113] Neben der permanenten Gefahr des Diebstahls kam es durch unsachgemäßen Transport und Lagerung unter freiem Himmel oder in einfachen Zelten zu vielen Unfällen. Sehr viele Menschen wurden auch bei der Anwendung verletzt oder kamen ums Leben, weil das Sprenggebiet nicht abgesperrt wurde, die Wirkung

---

108 Siehe den Bericht des Bezirksexekutivkomitees von Anadyr' vom 11. Juni 1957 in GAMO f. R-146, op. 1, d. 219, l. 55–57. Zu der extrem hohen Zahl von Arbeitsunfällen im Bereich der Uranförderung siehe Zeljak, Uranodobyvajuščaja otrasl', S. 123.

109 Vgl. GAMO f. R-137sč, op. 1b, d. 11, l. 21.

110 Vgl. den Bericht der staatlichen Inspektion für die Aufsicht über Technik und Bergbau des Ministerrates der RSFSR an das Gebietsexekutivkomitee vom 26. August 1957 in GAMO f. R-146, op. 1, d. 153, l. 102–103.

111 Vgl. GAMO f. R-137sč, op. 1b, d. 11, l. 47 f.

112 Vgl. GAMO f. R-137sč, op. 1b, d. 11, l. 38. Dort findet sich eine ausführliche Aufstellung über den Zusammenhang zwischen mangelnder Bildung und Arbeitsunfällen.

113 Vgl. die Mitteilung des *Sevvostlag* an Mitrakov vom 17. August 1955 in GAMO f. R-23, op. 1, d. 5611, l. 69–71. Siehe auch die ausführliche Information über den Umgang mit Sprengmaterialien in der Region vom Leiter der Bergbauinspektion in Dal'stroj, Solomachin, vom 2. August 1953 an Chruščev in RGANI f. 5, op. 27, d. 122, l. 74–79.

falsch berechnet wurde oder sich Arbeiter zu früh nach einer Sprengung dem Gebiet näherten.[114]

Mit Blick auf die Vielzahl und Häufigkeit all dieser Arbeitsunfälle stellte die Wirtschaftsleitung der Region in ihren Anordnungen und Dokumentationen wiederholt fest, dass nur ein Bruchteil der Unfälle vor Ort untersucht und aufgeklärt wurde. Das Verantwortungsgefühl der lokalen Betriebsleitung sei zu gering, selbst vorhandene Gelder für den Arbeitsschutz würden nicht zweckgebunden verwendet werden.[115] Zugleich waren die einzelnen Grubenleiter bei den Schwierigkeiten mit unausgebildetem Personal und beim Materialmangel auf sich gestellt – unter den gegebenen Umständen erschien eine Reihe von Unfällen geradezu als unvermeidlich.[116]

Ende der 1950er Jahre zeichnete sich jedoch auch im Magadaner Gebiet eine Tendenz ab, die Galina Ivanova und die südkoreanische Historikerin Junbae Jo als gewisses Zeichen einer Entstalinisierung der Arbeitswelt in der Sowjetunion werten – die Gewerkschaften lösten sich ein Stück weit von ihrer rein formalen Rolle und begannen, sich in den Betrieben zu engagieren.[117] Im Nordosten stimmten sich einzelne Betriebsleiter in Fragen des Arbeitsschutzes vermehrt mit den Gewerkschaften ab, manchmal wurden auf ihren Druck hin Prophylaxe-Maßnahmen (z. B. gegen die Silikose) eingeführt. In einzelnen Bereichen wurden Gewerkschaften so zu echten Anwälten der Werktätigen.[118]

Im Zusammenhang mit dem Arbeitsschutz standen auch die Pläne des Präsidiums des ZK der KPdSU, bis Ende des Jahres 1960 den allmählichen Übergang zu einem siebenstündigen Arbeitstag (unter Tage sechsstündig) zu erreichen, was in vielen Gruben der Region offiziell bis 1958 umgesetzt wurde.[119] Tatsächlich aber fanden diese

---

114 Vgl. die Direktiven zum Umgang mit Sprengmaterialien von Čuguev vom 27. Januar 1955 in GAMO f. R-23, op. 1, d. 5600, l. 17–23, die Beschwerde des MVD der jakutischen ASSR vom 30. Januar 1957 an Čuguev in GAMO f. R-23sč, op. 1, d. 458, l. 35, den Bericht des Leiters der Bergbauverwaltung an Čuguev vom 2. August 1958 in GAMO f. R-137, op. 1, d. 58, l. 164 f. sowie die vielen Unfallberichte in GAMO f. R-23, op. 1, d. 5600, l. 185–190, hier l. 186.

115 Vgl. die Kritik von Gruša in GAMO f. R-23, op. 1, d. 5605, l. 60–64, hier l. 61 sowie die ausführliche Analyse der Unfallursachen durch den leitenden Ingenieur der Magadaner Vertretung der staatlichtechnischen Bergbauüberwachung der RSFSR, Borisov, für das 1. Halbjahr des Jahres 1958 in GAMO f. R-137, op. 1, d. 54, l. 52–69.

116 Die Rate an Arbeitsunfällen war in der Sowjetunion in den 1950er und 1960er Jahren insgesamt ausgesprochen hoch. Zu den besonders gefährdeten Bereichen zählte grundsätzlich die Arbeit in der Buntmetallwirtschaft und bei den Geologen. Vgl. Ivanova, Na poroge, S. 151.

117 Vgl. Ivanova, Na poroge, S. 52; Jo, Trade Unions. Auf den Zusammenhang zwischen Entstalinisierung und einer partiellen, vorsichtigen Neuausrichtung der Gewerkschaften hat Donald Filtzer bereits zu Beginn der 1990er Jahre hingewiesen. Er bezieht sich dabei u. a. auf das Vetorecht der Gewerkschaften bei Normerhöhungen. Vgl. Filtzer, Soviet Workers, S. 232.

118 Siehe die Mitschrift eines Treffens des Leitungsgremiums des Magadaner Volkswirtschaftsrates vom 10. September 1958 in GAMO f. R-137, op. 1, d. 58, l. 270–313, hier l. 308.

119 Vgl. zu der gesetzlichen Grundlage dieser Arbeitszeitverkürzung Ivanova, Na poroge, S. 90. Hinzu kam eine Regelung, die den Einsatz von Frauen im Bergbau und bei Baumaßnahmen unter Tage nur

Regelungen nur selten dauerhaft Anwendung. Wenn nicht geringe Löhne dafür sorgten, dass Arbeiter von sich aus Mehrarbeit leisteten, um die hohen Lebenshaltungskosten zu decken, so war es die drohende Nichterfüllung des Plansolls, die die Arbeitstage verlängerte. Auf die Arbeiter wurde erheblicher Druck ausgeübt, „freiwillig" Anträge zur Verlängerung ihrer Arbeitszeit zu stellen.[120] Der Arbeitsschutz hatte hier eine klare Grenze – die Planerfüllung stand auch in der Entstalinisierung über der Gesundheit der Arbeitenden.

5.2 Magadaner Mythen und sozialpolitische Anreize

5.2.1 Eine neue Kultur der Beherrschung: die Magadaner Erzählung

Graeme Gill hat in seiner Analyse sowjetischer Metanarrative beschrieben, wie unter Chruščev die charismatische Führungslegitimation, die bislang allein Stalin zugeschrieben worden war, auf die Partei übertragen wurde: „Stalin's leadership was now passed, symbolically, to the party."[121] Auch Yoram Gorlizki konstatiert diese legitimatorische Bedeutung der Partei nach Stalin. Dass diese Partei zugleich den auf dem 20. Parteitag „enttarnten" Personenkult ermöglicht hatte, sei dabei kein ernsthaftes Problem gewesen. Tatsächlich sieht Gorlizki eine zeitliche Koinzidenz zwischen der Kritik am Personenkult und dem Aufbau eines neuen Images: „the incipient criticisms of the ‚cult of personality' were matched by assiduous praise for the leadership role of Communists."[122] Der daraus entstehende Widerspruch habe sich in der Re-Affirmation der leninschen Wurzeln auflösen lassen. Zugleich, so Pavel Kolář in seiner Analyse der poststalinistischen Ideologie, sei damit dezidiert ein Auftrag für die Zukunft verbunden gewesen:

> Trotz ihrer oft vernichtenden Natur war die Kritik am Personenkult nicht antiutopisch, im Gegenteil. [...] Verbreitet war die Wahrnehmung der Entstalinisierungskrise als „Neuanfang" für eine erneuerte Partei, deren Führungsrolle von nun an erst ausgebaut werden sollte. Man betonte immer wieder, dass dieser neue Weg „kompliziert", „dornig" und vor allem lang sein werde. Man dürfe deshalb nicht nur bei der Kritik der Vergangenheit stehen bleiben, sondern müsse auch Vorschläge für die Zukunft machen.[123]

---

mit Sondergenehmigung erlaubte. Diese Regelung beruhte auf einer Verordnung des Ministerrates der UdSSR vom 13. Juli 1957, Ausnahmegenehmigungen wurden am 30. August 1957 erlassen. Vgl. GAMO f. R-137, op. 1, d. 3, l. 298.

120 Vgl. den Überblick über die Ergebnisse der entsprechenden Kampagne im Juni 1961 in GAMO f. R-137, op. 1, d. 1007(ž), l. 39 – 41.

121 Gill, Symbols, S. 166. Siehe zu dieser Rolle der Partei ebenso Thatcher, Khruschchev, S. 20.

122 Gorlizki, Political Reform, S. 265.

123 Kolář, Poststalinismus, S. 105.

So entstand ein Narrativ, in dem die Kommunistische Partei als Vorbedingung einer blühenden Zukunft inszeniert werden konnte.[124] Dieser Mythos entfaltete sich gerade im Magadaner Kontext besonders wirkmächtig, da hier die KPdSU einen echten Neuanfang für sich reklamieren konnte.

Die Repräsentation der neuen Gebietsleitung entwickelte sich parallel zum Neuaufbau einer regionalen „Heimatkunde" (*kraevedenie*). Sie schloss an die sowjetunionweite Aufwertung regionaler Identitätsbildung in den 1950er Jahren an, mit der regionale Strukturen gestärkt werden sollten.[125] In Magadan hatte die Heimatkunde auch die Aufgabe, den institutionellen und infrastrukturellen Aufbau durch eine neue mentale Besetzung zu festigen, zugleich mühte sich die neue Leitung der Partei- und Sowjetorgane darum, sich selbst als legitimen Vertreter der sowjetischen Macht in diese Repräsentation des Territoriums einzuschreiben. Dazu übernahmen sie das bestehende Museum in der Hauptstadt und den bisherigen Verlag „Sovetskaja Kolyma" und bauten diese erheblich aus.[126]

Seit 1954 veröffentlichte der Verlag eine Vielzahl von Reisebeschreibungen, Romanen, Darstellungen von Bezirken und einzelnen Wirtschaftszweigen, regionale historische Abrisse, Fotobände sowie eine eigene Kunst- und Kulturzeitschrift für den nordöstlichen Raum – *Na Severe Dal'nem*.[127] Werbung, Berichte und Rezensionen zu diesen Neuerscheinungen waren fester Bestandteil des Kulturteils der *Magadanskaja Pravda*. Vermischt mit Porträts einzelner Künstler, dem Abdruck von Gedichten sowie Fotos künstlerischer Arbeiten ergab sich so der Eindruck eines reichen kulturellen Lebens, das jedoch stark selbstreferentiell war.[128]

Die neuen Zuschreibungen zielten auf positive Assoziationen, von der Gründung des Gebietes sollte eine besondere Zuversicht, ein „Schwung" ausgehen, in den die neuen Bewohner hineingenommen werden sollten. „Die Zukunft beginnt heute!" – so der Titel eines der Bände, die, mit vielen Fotos unterlegt, die Errungenschaften der

---

124 Siehe zum Chruščev'schen Zeitverständnis Kolář, Poststalinismus, S. 261 ff.

125 Vgl. Johnson, Kraevedenie, S. 221. Siehe zur Bedeutung dieser Form von Regionalgeschichte Evtuhov, Voices; Donovan, Kraevedenie Revival sowie für eine Analyse der Landeskunde in der frühen Sowjetzeit Sobolew, Landeskunde.

126 Der Buchhandel nahm im Rahmen der unionsweiten Organisation „Glavknigotorg" wesentlich zu. 1963 gab es im Gebiet bereits 22 Buchhandlungen. In den ersten zehn Jahren seit 1953 brachte der Magadaner Buchverlag 1.442 Bücher heraus, mit einer Auflage von mehr als 4.590.000 Exemplaren. Vgl. Isakov, Istorija torgovli, S. 214. Konzeption und Exponate des Gebietsmuseums wurden zu seinem 25-jährigen Bestehen im Jahr 1959 in einem Sammelband vorgestellt. Vgl. Izučajte rodnoj kraj. Erst seit Oktober 1957 hatte auch der Komsomol eine eigene Zeitschrift in der Region. Der *Magadanskij Komsomolec* war das Organ des Stadt- und Gebietskomitees des Komsomols, bisher gab es diese in sowjetischen Regionen so übliche Publikation nicht. Vgl. Zlatina, Periodičeskaja pečat', S. 9.

127 Die Zeitschrift *Na Sevre Dal'nem* erschien seit 1955. Vgl. den ausführlichen Bericht des Gebiets-exekutivkomitees zum Aufbau der Kultureinrichtungen im Magadaner Gebiet von 1958 in GAMO f. R-146, op. 1, d. 215, l. 38–68.

128 Siehe beispielsweise den Bericht über die Neuerscheinungen in: Magadanskaja Pravda, 12. Januar 1958, S. 3.

Region in den letzten Jahren dokumentierten.[129] Die Region sollte dabei nicht nur ihr negatives Image ablegen, sondern als ein ebenso aufregendes wie lebenswertes Gebiet inszeniert werden. Mit ihrer offensiv eingesetzten Imagekampagne wollte die neue politische Führung bei freien Arbeitern für die Region werben und sie langfristig an das Gebiet binden und damit zugleich ihren Machtanspruch gegenüber der bisherigen Leitung von Dal'stroj ideologisch untermauern:

Zum fünfjährigen Bestehen des Magadaner Gebietes erschien ein Band mit dem sprechenden Titel „Auf der umgestalteten Erde", der die Erfolge auf der Halbinsel Tschukotka gewissermaßen auf eine mentale Landkarte bannte und alle Entwicklungen an die Struktur des neuen Gebietes knüpfte. Herausgeber war N. A. Žicharev, Sekretär des Gebietsparteikomitees, ein promovierter Historiker, der viele Jahre lang der wichtigste Vertreter der lokalen, parteitreuen Geschichtsschreibung war.[130] Weitere fünf Jahre später kam der Band „10 Jahre [Magadaner Gebiet – M. S.]" heraus, eine Rückschau auf die regionalen Veränderungen seit 1954. Als Herausgeber fungierte I. N. Kaštanov, der – nach einer Unterbrechung durch ein Studium an der obersten Parteischule in Moskau – zunächst wieder Leiter der Abteilung für Agitation und Propaganda war und später Sekretär im Gebietsparteikomitee wurde.

Die beiden Bände sind die wichtigsten einer ganzen Reihe von Publikationen, die sich einzelnen Wirtschaftsbereichen oder besonderen Entwicklungen in der Region widmeten. Angelegt als stolze Leistungsschauen „regionaler Errungenschaften" im industriellen wie auch im sozialen und infrastrukturellen Bereich, sind sie gewissermaßen typisch für die sowjetische Heimatkunde der Zeit. Wie bereits an den Titeln „Auf der umgestalteten Erde" und „10 Jahre Magadaner Gebiet" deutlich wird, wurden jedoch die regionalen Magadaner Entwicklungen nicht einfach an die sowjetische Macht, sondern dezidiert an das Jahr 1954 rückgebunden und alle geschilderten „Erfolge" als Ergebnis der Politik nach der Gebietsgründung präsentiert. So beginnt die Zustandsbeschreibung des Gebietes und seiner Menschen in dem Band „Auf der umgestalteten Erde" mit einem Rückblick auf die Lage unmittelbar nach Gründung des Gebietes:

> Zuerst einmal mussten sich die leitenden Arbeiter mit der Lage vor Ort vertraut machen. [...] Das Erste, was vielen Mitarbeitern des Gebietes ins Auge stach, als sie im Jahr 1954 in den Bezirk Severo-Évenskij kamen, war der verödete Zustand des Bezirkszentrums. Die Siedlung bot einen unansehnlichen Anblick. Man spürte keine Sorge um seine Gestaltung. Es gab keinen Klub. Die Post wurde in Évenks manchmal einen Monat und länger nicht zugestellt. In dem medizinischen Anlaufpunkt, der noch immer „Krankenhaus" hieß, gab es keine medizinischen Geräte. Das Internat bei der Schule war eng, ungemütlich. Man musste dringend mit Bauarbeiten beginnen, aber es gab nichts zum Bauen. Dann wurde beschlossen, im Bezirkszentrum eine Bauabteilung einzurichten, die nach einiger Zeit durch das Gebietsexekutivkomitee eingerichtet wurde.[131]

---

129 Vgl. Korodejnikol, Buduščee.
130 Vgl. Žicharev, Očerki.
131 Na preobražennoj zemle, S. 35 f.

Weitere fünf Jahre später stilisierte Afanas'ev die Gründung des Magadaner Gebietes (im Sammelband „10 Jahre Magadaner Gebiet") zu einem entscheidenden Teil der Entstalinisierung und des Tauwetters. Dabei benutzte er eine Strategie, die Yoram Gorlizki als Kennzeichen der politischen Machtbeziehungen nach Stalins Tod beschrieben hat, die „strategic assignment of blame for Stalin-era repressions"[132]. Afanas'ev schilderte in einem historischen Rückblick offen den besonderen Status von Dal'stroj als strukturelle Einheit des NKVD; in dieser Zeit habe es an der Kolyma viele Menschen gegeben, die „grundlos Repressionen ausgesetzt waren" und die aber, so sein Schluss, dennoch als sowjetische Patrioten an der Aufbauarbeit im Nordosten teilgehabt hätten.

In einem an die Chruščev'sche Geheimrede auf dem 20. Parteitag erinnernden Stil nannte er dabei auch die Namen zweier lokaler Persönlichkeiten, die inhaftiert und von denen einer nun vollständig rehabilitiert worden sei. Afanas'ev erinnerte sodann an die Entstehung des Magadaner Gebietes, die er den Kommunisten des Chabarowsker Distrikts und damit seinem alten Netzwerk zuschrieb. Sie hätten eine stärkere Kontrolle von Dal'stroj gefordert, da „einige der Führer von Dal'stroj die ablehnende Rolle Stalins gegenüber der Gründung eines administrativen Gebietes an der Kolyma" geteilt hätten.[133] Die Gebietsgründung habe dann den Status der Region vollständig verändert und zugleich die Wiederherstellung leninscher Prinzipien ermöglicht:

> Mit diesem Moment begann, so kann man sagen, eine neue Etappe in der Erschließung der Kolyma und von Tschukotka. Denn man musste von Grund auf, vollkommen neu, viele Fragen der industriellen Entwicklung, der Landwirtschaft, von Kultur und Leben, der Erziehung der Menschen lösen. Man musste die dunklen Flecken wegnehmen, die in der Zeit des Personenkultes auf der Kolyma lagen. Vor allem musste man die Verzerrung der sozialistischen Gesetzlichkeit beenden, Kommunisten an wichtige Produktionspunkte setzen, neue Kollektive in der Industrie einsetzen, die Rolle der Parteiorganisationen in der Wirtschaftstätigkeit heben, die politische Erziehung der Arbeiter verbessern. Man musste den Reichtum der Kolyma und von Tschukotka in den Dienst der Heimat stellen, die Kultur heben und das Leben der lokalen Bevölkerung verbessern, damit die Menschen auch in diesem harten Gebiet warm und gemütlich leben können.[134]

Mit Fotografien untermauerte diesen Wandel ein Bildband, der sich der Situation in der Hauptstadt Magadan widmete. Recht plakativ wurden „Vorher-Nachher-Aufnahmen" von Magadaner Straßenzügen einander gegenübergestellt, die die dramatischen Verbesserungen im Wohnungsbau seit der Gebietsgründung belegen sollten.[135]

---

132 Vgl. Gorlizki, Structures of Trust, S. 142.

133 Afanas'ev, Kommunisty, S. 12f. Siehe ebenso die anderen Beiträge dieses Sammelbandes, v. a. Kaštanov, Vse vo imja; Čistjakov, Desjatiletie sowie Žarkich, Vstajut novostrojki.

134 Afanas'ev, Kommunisty, S. 14f.

135 Die Ausgabe der Zeitung *Magadanskij Komsomolec* vom 3. Dezember 1963 schilderte zum zehnjährigen Jubiläum des Gebietes die Veränderungen in der Hauptstadt. In offensichtlich bewusster Verkennung der Tatsache, dass zu dieser Zeit das riesige Gebäude der Hauptverwaltung von Dal'stroj und eine ganze Reihe von Steinhäusern in der Hauptstadt bereits existierten, beschrieb die Redaktion das damalige Magadan als eine Stadt fast gänzlich ohne befestigte Wege oder steinerne Häuser. Auf

тaм, где когда-то стояли
бараки, возвышаются
красивые многоэтаж-
ные дома

Abb. 43 „Dort, wo noch vor kurzem alte Baracken standen, erheben sich nun neue schöne Wohnhäuser", 1939 – 1964, Fotoalbum

Die Darstellungen erinnern an sowjetische Propaganda in westlichen Gebieten der Sowjetunion, die das Bild der „Stunde Null" für die Zeit nach 1945 nicht nur im Hinblick auf den materiellen Wiederaufbau der Städte, sondern auch für den grundsätzlichen Aufbau sowjetischer Strukturen bemühte. Per Brodersen hat diese Repräsentation der Sowjetisierung für das Kaliningrader Gebiet sehr anschaulich beschrieben. Die Parallelen zu den Darstellungen in Magadan sind frappierend – hier

---

diese Verdrehung historischer Tatsachen wies 1963 bereits der Historiker N. V. Kozlov in einem Schreiben an den Parteisekretär Kaštanov hin. Abgedruckt in Grebenjuk, Kolymskij led, S. 257. Siehe auch die entsprechende Darstellungsweise in den Erinnerungen eines der Bauleiter in Magadan, Vospominanija zaslužennogo stroitelja.

Abb. 44 Hier ist der Magadaner Stadtsowjet, das Gebietsparteikomitee und das städtische Komitee der Gewerkschaft untergebracht – und dies ist das alte Gebäude", 1939–1964, Fotoalbum

werden jedoch nicht die Hinterlassenschaften eines feindlichen politischen Systems, sondern verschiedene *inner*sowjetische Herrschaftssysteme miteinander kontrastiert.

Auf unterschiedlichen Ebenen schuf die Parteileitung eine Magadaner Erzählung, deren Aufnahme bei den Adressaten nicht beurteilt werden kann. Dass dieser Text jedoch in seinen unterschiedlichen Formen gelesen und wahrgenommen wurde, davon ist sicherlich auszugehen. Die Verkaufszahlen der Bücher des regionalen Verlages und die hohe Verbreitung der lokalen Zeitungen sind Indizien dafür, aber auch die Wissbegier der ehemaligen Offiziere, die Evgenija Ginzburg nach ihrer Entlassung aus

Дворец спорта - любимое место молодежи.

Abb. 45 „Im Sportpalast – der beliebteste Ort der Jugend", 1939–1964, Fotoalbum

der Haft unterrichten konnte.[136] Der ehemalige Häftling Peter Demant, der nach seiner Entlassung Mitte der 1950er Jahre in dem Bezirkszentrum Jagodnoe lebte, schildert anschaulich die Rolle, die die nach 1954 neu entstandene Bibliothek in seiner Siedlung spielte:

> Die jungen Frauen [Bibliothekarinnen – M. S.] gaben die Bücher und eine Masse an Zeitschriften und Zeitungen in strenger Reihenfolge heraus. Der Lesesaal war bis auf den letzten Platz besetzt, besonders in der arbeitsfreien Zeit. Dort wurden auch Jubiläen begangen. Ich erinnere mich an den hundertsten Todestag von Heine: Der Saal ist so überfüllt, dass Leute weggeschickt werden mussten, der Vortragende liest die Gedichte des Poeten im Original, allerdings mit einem starken Akzent, er hat sein Deutsch, ebenso wie Französisch, unter den Bedingungen des Lagers gelernt. Ich habe in dieser Zeit Bücher des Mechanikers Kudrjavcev gelesen, mich mit den Bibliothekarinnen besprochen, bei ihnen Vorlesungen gehört, im Allgemeinen – ich habe zur ‚Erhöhung meiner Allgemeinbildung' beigetragen. Denn im Lager hatte ich ja praktisch keine einzige Ver-

---

136 Vgl. Ginsburg, Gratwanderung, S. 438 f. Zu den Verkaufszahlen siehe GAMO f. R-146, op. 1, d. 215, l. 61 (für die Verbreitung der Zeitungen) sowie Isakov, Istorija torgovli, S. 214 (zum Buchverkauf).

bindung zur Wissenschaft gehabt, und dabei sind zur gleichen Zeit alle Entdeckungen und Er-
findungen der Mitte des Jahrhunderts gemacht worden.[137]

Auch wenn Peter Demant hier in seinen Erinnerungen vor allem von der großen Be-
geisterung über den Zugang zu literarischen Klassikern und Fachliteratur unter den
gebildeten ehemaligen Häftlingen spricht, muss dennoch davon ausgegangen werden, dass in einer Region, deren kulturelle Möglichkeiten so extrem begrenzt waren,
in denen man sogar für einen Platz in der Bibliothek Schlange stand, auch eine
parteitreue Erzählung, die in verschiedenen publizistischen Medien verbreitet wurde –
in der aktuellen Tageszeitung, in einer Reisebeschreibung, in einer vorgeblich sach-
lichen Beschreibung eines Industriezweiges – einen gewissen Niederschlag in den
Köpfen der Bevölkerung gefunden haben muss.

5.2.2 Aufbau einer sozialpolitischen Infrastruktur – Grundlinien

Die Sorge um die Lebens- und Arbeitsbedingungen der Arbeiter war für die Moskauer
Staats- und Parteiführung eine der neuen Grundvoraussetzungen für eine Stabilisierung der Metallförderung. Der neue Auftrag des ZK der KPdSU, den gewandelten Blick
auf das Gebiet in konkrete Politik umzusetzen, zog ein großes Aufbauprogramm nach
sich, das eine Angleichung an bestehende Institutionen und soziale Standards in
anderen zivilen Teilen der Union ermöglichen sollte. Gleichzeitig verlief diese Angleichung an die zentralen Gebiete der Union nicht im luftleeren Raum, vielmehr
wurde die Region integriert in eine Sowjetunion, die sich auf sozialpolitischem Gebiet
bereits kurz nach Stalins Tod erheblich veränderte. Die Lage in allen Gebieten der
Sowjetunion war vielfach von großer Armut, schlechter Versorgung und mangelndem
Wohnraum geprägt. Schlimm waren die Verhältnisse auch im Nordosten der Sowjetunion. Hier unterschied sich das neue Magadaner Gebiet aber nicht nur graduell
aufgrund der in der Region so schwierigen Versorgungslage, dem Zusammenbruch der
Handelssysteme, dem Mangel an privaten Kleingärten und Kolchosmärkten, sondern
auch in struktureller Hinsicht aufgrund des fast vollständigen Fehlens einer sozialen
Infrastruktur.[138]

Beginnend mit der Forderung nach einer besseren Versorgung der Bevölkerung
unter Malenkov in den Jahren 1954 und 1955, kann seit dem 20. Parteitag von einem
echten sozialpolitischen Programm gesprochen werden. In dessen Zentrum standen
die Einführung der Rentenzahlungen und ein großes Wohnbauprogramm. Es umfasste zudem eine Vielzahl weiterer Maßnahmen, die Chruščev in seiner Geheimrede
auf dem 20. Parteitag folgendermaßen auflistete:

---

137 Kress (Pseudonym Peter Demants), Parochoda, S. 81 f.
138 Vgl. zur allgemeinen sozialen Lage in den 1950er Jahren Ivanova, Sozialpolitik; Smith, Property;
Zubkova, After the War.

Wage increases for low-paid workers, the improvement of the pension system, the expansion of housing construction, the improvement of social food provision programmes, the clear development of a network of institutions for children, reduction in the length of the working day while maintaining the existing salary levels, the development of a network of old people's homes and homes for the disabled, the introduction of free and cheap meals for the children of less well-off parents, the improvement of the national health systems, and several other points.[139]

Als ziviles Gebiet galten diese Leitlinien und die davon tatsächlich umgesetzten Programme auch im bisherigen Lagergebiet Magadan. Die Veränderungen in der Region begannen mit den Verordnungen der Ministerräte von UdSSR und RSFSR vom Mai und Juni 1954. Auf der Grundlage der bisherigen administrativ-zivilen Abteilung von Dal'stroj und durch eigene Erkundigungen hatten Gebietspartei- und Gebietsexekutivkomitee ausführliche Dossiers zur Anzahl und der Situation regionaler Schulen, Kinderheime, Gesundheitsstationen etc. erstellt und den zukünftigen Bedarf abgeschätzt.[140] Diese Dokumente zeugten zum einen von dem realen Abstand, der zwischen der Region und anderen Gebieten der Sowjetunion bestand, zugleich dokumentierten sie das Problembewusstsein der neuen Führung. Ababkov und Afanas'ev setzten sich in einer Weise mit der sozialen Wirklichkeit des Gebietes auseinander, die nicht zur Aufgabe der Leitung von Dal'stroj gehört hatte.

Die Verordnungen der Ministerräte zur Stärkung des Aufbaus im Magadaner Gebiet schufen die institutionellen Voraussetzungen einer Angleichung der Lebensverhältnisse.[141] Bis Ende der 1950er Jahre folgten eine ganze Reihe weiterer Verordnungen in unterschiedlichen sozialen Bereichen. Die Zuwächse in den ersten Jahren seit der Gebietsgründung, also die Größenordnung des zusätzlichen Wohnungsbaus, der neu errichteten Krankenstationen, Kindergärten, Schulen oder Kinos, sind recht einfach zu ermitteln, weil die neue politische Leitung ein großes Interesse daran hatte, die Entwicklung der Region zu überwachen und zu dokumentieren. Immer wieder legten die einzelnen Abteilungen des Exekutivkomitees des Gebietes (für Gesundheitsschutz, für Bildung etc.) Berichte über die Entwicklungen in ihren jeweiligen Bereichen seit Gebietsgründung vor. Das Exekutivkomitee und auch die oberste Parteileitung erstellten auf dieser Grundlage Dokumentationen über die Veränderungen in der Region, die sich auch als Rechenschaftsberichte seit Beginn der zivilen Gestaltung des Gebietes lesen lassen.

---

139 Ivanova, Question of Honour, S. 139. Siehe zu den Reformen im Einzelnen Ivanova, Na poroge; Mücke, Altersrentenversorgung; Zubkova, Marginaly; Bohn, Bevölkerung, S. 621 ff.; Merl, Reformen, S. 203–212; Plaggenborg, Lebensverhältnisse, S. 805 ff.

140 Zur Bestandsaufnahme der Schulen, Kinderbetreuungseinrichtungen und Kinderheime siehe beispielhaft den ausführlichen Bericht des Leiters der Magadaner Gebietsabteilung für Volksbildung vom März 1954 in GAMO f. R-146, op. 1, d. 54, l. 17–27. Zur Einrichtung einer Kommission des Gebietsexekutivkomitees zur Lage elternloser Kinder im Februar 1954 vgl. GAMO f. R-278, op. 1, d. 3, l. 1 f. Zur Lage verwahrloster Kinder siehe den Bericht des MVD an das Gebietsparteikomitee in GAMO f. P-21, op. 5, d. 2, l. 57.

141 Vgl. zu den Verordnungen ausführlich das Kapitel 3.2.4.

Das aussagekräftigste Dokument ist dabei ein ausführlicher Bericht des stellvertretenden Leiters der Finanzabteilung des Magadaner Gebietes, der die Veränderungen in der Region zwischen 1953 und Dezember 1959 anhand der Entwicklung des Budgets des Magadaner Gebietes schildert. Einleitend heißt es:

> Seit Gründung des Gebietes stieg die Zahl der Schulen und die Zahl der in ihnen Lernenden, neun Schulinternate wurden eröffnet, die Zahl der Krankenbetten in den Krankenhäusern stieg, ebenso die Zahl der medizinischen Einrichtungen. In der Stadt Magadan wurde eine pädagogische Fachschule eröffnet, eine medizinische Fachschule in der Siedlung Debin [und in Anadyr' – M. S.], im Gebiet wurden fünf Musikschulen eröffnet, vier Häuser für Volkskunst, das Netz an Bibliotheken und anderen sozial-kulturellen Einrichtungen wurde erweitert. Große Summen wurden in die lokale Leichtindustrie und in die Lebensmittelproduktion investiert, in die Kommunalwirtschaft und in den Wohnungsbau [...].[142]

Der Bericht legte auch eine Reihe absoluter Zahlen vor; so sei das Budget des Magadaner Gebietes zwischen Ende 1953 und 1959 um 203 % gestiegen.[143] In den einzelnen Bereichen stellte sich die Entwicklung der Ausgaben aus dem Budget des Gebietes folgendermaßen dar[144]:

Entwicklung des Budgets des Magadaner Gebietes (in Tausend Rubel)

	1953	1954	1955	1956	1957	1958	1959	Zuwachs zw. 1953 u. 1959 in %
lokale Industrie	528	4.765	19.877	33.398	28.106	43.604	59.119	11.196,8 %
Landwirtschaft	3.762	3.009	6.504	8.000	8.828	8.209	9.940	164,2 %
kommunaler Wohnungsbau	17.618	45.741	38.268	47.693	55.226	57.973	85.697	386,4 %
ziviler Busverkehr	–	310	1.677	1.570	1.916	2.695	4.430	
Volksbildung	53.711	66.622	78.976	96.667	115.131	124.320	141.055	162,6 %
Kultur	5.599	13.629	18.612	21.700	25.575	26.875	29.148	420,6 %
Gesundheitsschutz	73.704	88.252	107.485	132.207	159.687	182.279	194.392	163,7 %

---

142 Vgl. den Bericht vom 14. Dezember 1959 in GAMO f. R-146, op. 1, d. 108, l. 82–90, hier l. 83.
143 Der Anteil der Halbinsel Tschukotka am Gesamtbudget stieg in dieser Zeit sogar um 234,8 %. Vgl. GAMO f. R-146, op. 1, d. 108, l. 82–90, hier l. 83.
144 Vgl. den Bericht vom 14. Dezember 1959 in GAMO f. R-146, op. 1, d. 108, l. 82–90, hier l. 84. Für einen Plan des Zuwachses in den Jahren 1960 bis 1965 siehe GARF f. A-259, op. 42, d. 5281, l. 67–69.

Der Anstieg des Budgets zwischen 1953 und 1959 ist auf den ersten Blick gewaltig, selbst wenn man in dieser Zeit einen deutlichen Zuwachs freier Arbeitskräfte in Rechnung stellt. Neben Bereichen, die bisher kaum wahrnehmbar waren oder die es in Dal'stroj überhaupt nicht gegeben hatte, wie dem zivilen Busverkehr, stiegen die Ausgaben für den kommunalen Wohnungsbau und für Kultur am stärksten. Hier zeigen sich besonders drastisch der bisherige Mangel und das Ausmaß des von der neuen politischen Führung erkannten Handlungsbedarfs. Zugleich wurde damit auch das gewaltige unionsweite Wohnungsbauprogramm Chruščevs seit 1957 umgesetzt.[145] Der Wohnungsbau stieg dementsprechend zwischen 1958 und 1959 noch einmal sprunghaft um 20 % an.[146] In absoluten Zahlen lässt sich in allen Einrichtungen der sozialen Infrastruktur ein deutlicher Zuwachs verzeichnen[147]:

Entwicklung der sozialen Infrastruktur

	1953	1959
Betten in Krankenhäusern	2.505	3.590
Personal in der Gesundheitsvorsorge	3.777	6.525
davon Ärzte	693	1.091
Gesamtzahl aller Schulen	192	201
Plätze in Kindergärten	207	1.390
Plätze in Kinderkrippen	287	1.140
Zahl der Bibliotheken	20	72
Musikschulen	–	5
Pionierhäuser	1	4

145 Zum unionsweiten Wohnungsbauprogramm siehe Smith, Property; Attwood, Housing; Ivanova, Na poroge; Reid, Women in the Home; Harris, Ordinary Russia; Smith, Khrushchev's Promise.
146 Vgl. die Auflistung aller errichteten Wohnhäuser in den Jahren zwischen 1953 und Ende 1959 in Narodnoe chozjajstvo Magadanskoj oblasti, S. 60 f. Siehe zu dem Anstieg zwischen 1958 und 1959 die Angaben des Volkswirtschaftsrates in GAMO f. R-137, op. 1, d. 488, l. 161.
147 Vgl. den Bericht vom 14. Dezember 1959 in GAMO f. R-146, op. 1, d. 108, l. 82–90, hier l. 87 f. Zu den Zuwächsen bei den Kadern im pädagogischen Bereich vgl. den Bericht des Leiters der Magadaner Abteilung für Volksbildung in GAMO f. R-146, op. 1, d. 223, l. 38–50. Für einen Überblick über die Entwicklung auf der Halbinsel Tschukotka siehe die Darstellung der Volkswirtschaft im Čukotsker Kreis für die Jahre 1955–1961 in GAMO f. R-146, op. 1, d. 360, l. 189–190, hier l. 189.

5.2.3 Sozialpolitische Maßnahmen – das Beispiel der Gesundheitsfürsorge

Anhand der Entwicklung der Gesundheitsvorsorge lässt sich exemplarisch zeigen, dass der institutionelle Ausbau in der Region vor allem als eine *strukturelle* Angleichung an unionsweite Verhältnisse verstanden werden muss. Bis 1953 gab es neben den Einrichtungen in den Lagern nur eine produktionsbezogene Gesundheitsfürsorge durch die Sanitätsabteilung von Dal'stroj. Dadurch wurden all die Menschen, die nicht einer Industrieverwaltung zugeordnet waren, nicht vom staatlichen Gesundheitssystem erfasst.[148] Die Region von Dal'stroj war damit von einer Entwicklung abgekoppelt, die in der Sowjetunion 1948 eingesetzt hatte und die der kanadische Historiker Christopher Burton analysiert hat. Seit dieser Zeit orientierte sich, so Burton, die sowjetische Gesundheitsfürsorge nicht mehr an Industrieeinrichtungen, sondern folgte dem Territorialprinzip. Gesundheitseinrichtungen wie Krankenhäuser und Polikliniken versorgten seit 1948 flächendeckend die Bewohner eines bestimmten Bezirkes und nicht mehr nur die Industriearbeiterschaft.[149]

Dieses Territorialprinzip musste im Magadaner Gebiet 1954 von Grund auf aufgebaut werden.[150] Zunächst wurde eine Gebietsabteilung für Gesundheitsschutz unter Leitung von A. S. Denisov gegründet, in den Bezirken entstanden von ihr abhängige Strukturen.[151] Das Exekutivkomitee baute daraufhin in den einzelnen Siedlungen Bezirkskrankenhäuser bzw. Polikliniken auf, wobei bestehende Einrichtungen übernommen und neu definiert wurden. Zwischen 1953 und 1960 stieg die Zahl der Krankenhäuser von 61 auf 106.[152]

Auf Befehl des Gesundheitsministeriums der RSFSR wurde im Oktober 1955 das Magadaner Stadtkrankenhaus in ein Gebietskrankenhaus umgewandelt.[153] Dies darf

---

148 Die medizinischen Einrichtungen der Lager unterstanden der Sanitärabteilung des *Sevvostlag*. Siehe die Beschreibung der vorhandenen Gesundheitseinrichtungen in Dal'stroj im Rahmen des Besuchs der Brigade des ZK der KPdSU vom 31. Juli 1953 in GAMO f. R-23, op. 1, d. 4804, l. 64–73, hier l. 72.
149 Die Ursache dieser Entwicklung sieht Burton im deutlichen Anstieg der Ärztezahlen infolge des Krieges, die in der Nachkriegszeit an neue Institutionen gebunden werden mussten. Burton zufolge lässt sich im Bereich der Gesundheitsvorsorge daher bereits im Spätstalinismus von einer ersten Etappe sowjetischer Sozialpolitik sprechen. Vgl. Barton [Burton], Zdravoochranenie.
150 Der institutionelle Aufbau der Gesundheitseinrichtungen soll hier als Beispiel fungieren. Ähnliche Entwicklungen lassen sich auch in anderen Arbeitsbereichen der Exekutivkomitees und in anderen Gebieten der sozialen Infrastruktur erkennen.
151 Alle Einrichtungen unterstanden seit Gründung des Magadaner Gebietes dem Gesundheitsministerium der RSFSR. Die Gebietsabteilung für Gesundheitsschutz wurde jedoch erst nach und nach mit den notwendigen medizinischen Geräten ausgestattet, ihre Versorgung lag im Jahr 1955 bei 70 %. Es mangelte in den ersten Jahren erheblich an Kühlschränken und Desinfektionseinrichtungen. Vgl. die Angaben der Gebietsgesundheitsabteilung in GAMO f. R-146, op. 1, d. 105, l. 16–40, hier l. 35–37.
152 Vgl. Kruglov/Kozlov, Zdravoochranenie, S. 139.
153 Im Mai 1956 wurde in diesem Krankenhaus eine geschlossene Station, exklusiv für die oberen Mitarbeiter der Partei- und Sowjetorgane, gegründet. Vgl. die erklärenden Angaben zum Bericht des Krankenhauses für das Jahr 1956 in GAMO f. R-307, op. 1, d. 6, l. 30–137, hier l. 30. Unter den Ärzten dieses Krankenhauses waren einige berühmte Koryphäen, die in den 1930er Jahren verhaftet worden

jedoch nicht als eine einfache Umbenennung verstanden werden. Der neue Status des Krankenhauses bewirkte eine Ausweitung seiner Zuständigkeit auf das gesamte Gebiet. Personen mit unklaren Diagnosen, schwierige Fälle oder Patienten, deren Krankheiten besondere Labor- und Diagnoseverfahren erforderten, wurden, entsprechend dem Territorialprinzip, nach Magadan verlegt. Das Magadaner Gebietskrankenhaus renovierte man vollständig, ein eigenes Geburtshaus und ein Kinderkrankenhaus entstanden auf seinem Gelände. Im Jahr 1956 verfügte das Krankenhaus bereits über differenzierte Diagnosemöglichkeiten (z. B. Elektrokardiologie) und Laboratorien (z. B. für Bluttransfusionen), eine Abteilung für Onkologie, für Tuberkulose, Haut- und Geschlechtskrankheiten, spezielle Operationsabteilungen etc.[154] Entsprechend den Bestimmungen des Gesundheitsministeriums der RSFSR entstanden diese Abteilungen zum Teil auch in den Bezirkszentren.[155]

Auch die Prophylaxe war Gegenstand des Aufbaus. Der Ministerrat der UdSSR hatte in seiner Verordnung vom 20. März 1956 eine unionsweite Ausweitung beschlossen; im Magadaner Gebiet entstanden daraufhin fünf neue Sanatorien, in den meisten Fällen für Tuberkulosekranke.[156] Institutionell neu aufgestellt wurde auch das bereits vorhandene, sich aber in erbärmlichem Zustand befindende Haus für Invalide in der Nähe der Stadt Magadan. Es wurde renoviert, technisch und medizinisch neu ausgestattet und besser mit Lebensmitteln und Gebrauchsgegenständen versorgt.[157] Eine weitere derartige Einrichtung in Tschukotka sowie ein Altersheim kamen jedoch nicht über das Planungsstadium hinaus.[158]

Ein großes Problem stellte in den 1950er Jahren die hohe Zahl psychisch kranker Menschen dar, für die es weder genügend geeignete Einrichtungen noch speziell geschultes Personal gab. So litten 11 % der Patienten, die aus den Bezirken in das Gebietskrankenhaus geschickt wurden, an Nervenkrankheiten oder anderen psychi-

---

waren und die bereits in Dal'stroj als Häftlings-Ärzte tätig gewesen waren. So auch der von E. S. Ginzburg in ihren Erinnerungen ausführlich beschriebene Arzt A. Ja. Val'ter. Vgl. Kozlov, Iz istorii zdravoochranenija, S. 110 f.

154 Vgl. GAMO f. R-307, op. 1, d. 6, l. 30–137, hier l. 31 f. Das Gebäude des Krankenhauses wurde weitgehend renoviert, die alten Baracken lediglich als Lagerraum weiterverwendet.

155 Problematisch war dabei, dass die meisten Ärzte keinerlei Erfahrungen z. B. mit onkologischen Erkrankungen hatten und oftmals die Diagnosegeräte nicht benutzen konnten. Vgl. die Angaben der Gebietsgesundheitsabteilung in GAMO f. R-146, op. 1, d. 105, l. 16–40, hier l. 27.

156 Vgl. Kruglov/Kozlov, Zdravoochranenie, S. 139. Zu den unionsweiten Bestimmungen zu Sanatorien siehe Ivanova, Na poroge, S. 91.

157 Zur Lage des „Hauses der Invaliden" zu Beginn des Jahres 1954 siehe den Bericht in GAMO f. R-278, op. 1, d. 7, l. 4–9. Bis 1960 entstanden neue Räumlichkeiten, die mit den entsprechenden Heizsystemen und Hygieneräumen ausgestattet wurden, über getrennte Abteilungen für Frauen, für Tuberkulosekranke und für psychisch kranke Menschen sowie über eine Bibliothek und eine eigene Küche verfügten. Zur Entwicklung des Hauses siehe den Bericht des Leiters der Gebietsabteilung für Sozialfürsorge in GAMO f. R-278, op. 1, d. 7, l. 42–46 (für das Jahr 1958); l. 59–64 (für das Jahr 1959) sowie l. 74–80 (für das Jahr 1960).

158 Vgl. den Bericht des Leiters des Gebietsexekutivkomitees, Afanas'ev, an den Ministerrat der RSFSR in GAMO f. R-146, op. 1, d. 104, l. 1–15, hier l. 13.

schen Erkrankungen – bzw. sie wurden aufgrund der Unkenntnis der lokalen Mediziner mit entsprechenden Diagnosen versehen.[159] Wie hoch der Anteil der Bewohner des Magadaner Gebietes tatsächlich war, die aufgrund der schweren Traumatisierungen, des Hungers und der unmenschlichen Haftbedingungen einer psychiatrischen oder psychotherapeutischen Behandlung bedurft hätten, lässt sich auf Grundlage der vorhandenen Akten nicht einmal abschätzen. Nur Pavel Grebenjuks Analyse der regional extrem hohen Selbstmordrate in den 1950er Jahren erlaubt einen ersten kleinen Einblick in die psychische Verfasstheit der Bevölkerung. Nach den von ihm ausgewerteten statistischen Daten war Selbstmord die zweithäufigste Todesursache im Magadaner Gebiet, das damit weit über dem Unionsdurchschnitt lag.[160]

Die psychiatrische Krankenstation, 23 km von Magadan entfernt, wurde nach Gründung des Gebietes zu einem vollwertigen psychiatrischen Gebietskrankenhaus (nach sowjetischem Standard) ausgebaut. In den 1950er Jahren nahm es sehr viele Alkoholkranke, Patienten mit Schizophrenie, Epilepsie und mit schweren Gehirnverletzungen auf. Bis 1960 entstanden dort eine Reihe spezialisierter Abteilungen, die Zahl der Ärzte stieg zwischen 1953 und 1960 von fünf auf dreizehn.[161] Für den Kampf gegen Alkoholismus leitete die Station eine Reihe besonderer Maßnahmen ein.[162] Diese Krankenstation war im Magadaner Gebiet die einzige Einrichtung für psychisch kranke Menschen, seine Ärzte initiierten daher Schulungen für Allgemeinmediziner, um die Erkennung und Behandlung psychischer Erkrankungen in den einzelnen Bezirken zu ermöglichen.

Der institutionelle Aufbau erstreckte sich auch auf die Apotheken der Region. 1955 wurde die Magadaner Abteilung der Apothekenverwaltung des Gesundheitsministeriums der RSFSR gegründet, sie ersetzte das Kontor für medizinische Versorgung von Dal'stroj. Das Magadaner Exekutivkomitee bemühte sich um die Einrichtung von

---

159 In dem Bericht des Bezirkskrankenhauses werden eine ganze Reihe derartiger Fälle vorgestellt. So wurde ein Mann aus dem Jagodninsker Bezirk nach Magadan geschickt, ohne Diagnose oder Epikrise. Er hatte lediglich einen Fetzen Papier dabei, auf dem als Diagnose stand: „vegetative Neurose, Schizophrenie?" In der Poliklinik erhielt der Mann dann die Diagnose „Epilepsie mit Persönlichkeitsdegeneration". Vgl. GAMO f. R-307, op. 1, d. 6, l. 30 – 137, hier l. 62, zu dem konkreten Fall siehe l. 67.
160 Vgl. Grebenjuk, Samoubijstva, S. 215 f. Diese Tendenz hielt in den 1960er und 1970er Jahren an und wurde seit etwa 1957 aufmerksam von der regionalen Parteileitung beobachtet, freilich ohne eine angemessene Ursachenanalyse. Vgl. Grebenjuk, Kolymskij led, S. 189.
161 Das Krankenhaus war im August 1953 errichtet worden. Vgl. seine Jahresberichte in GAMO f. R-324, op. 1, d. 2, l. 1 – 5 (für das Jahr 1953); GAMO f. R-324, op. 1, d. 3, l. 1 – 2 (für das Jahr 1954); GAMO f. R-324, op. 1, d. 7, l. 1 – 23 (für das Jahr 1958). Ein ausführlicher Bericht aus dem Jahr 1960 zeichnet den Ausbau des Krankenhauses nach. Vgl. GAMO f. R-324, op. 1, d. 9, l. 1 – 34. Zur Weiterentwicklung des Krankenhauses in den 1960er Jahren siehe den Bericht aus dem Jahr 1968 in GAMO f. R-324, op. 1, d. 7, l. 24 – 35. So wie auch alle anderen hier genannten Berichte enthält auch dieser keinerlei Angaben darüber, ob Patienten freiwillig in das psychiatrische Krankenhaus kamen oder ob sie zwangsweise therapiert wurden.
162 Dabei ging es hauptsächlich um Fragen der Betreuung und Isolierung von Alkoholkranken aufgrund ihrer ständig steigenden Zahl. Vgl. GAMO f. R-324, op. 1, d. 7, l. 1 – 23, hier l. 7 f.

Apotheken in den wichtigsten Siedlungen und Bezirkszentren, bis 1958 wurden im Magadaner Gebiet 41 Apotheken eröffnet.[163]

Eine Verbesserung der Hygienesituation konnte die Leitung der Gebietsabteilung für Gesundheitsschutz auch bei der Versorgung von Schwangeren und Wöchnerinnen erreichen. Indem Vorgaben des Gesundheitsministeriums umgesetzt wurden, gingen die Zahlen von Totgeburten und Sepsis-Erkrankungen unter der Geburt durch Reihenuntersuchungen und eine allgemeine Verbesserung der Bedingungen in den Kreißsälen deutlich zurück.[164]

Zur Ausdifferenzierung des gesamten Gesundheitsbereiches gehörte darüber hinaus eine Vernetzung unter den Ärzten. Zu diesem Zweck veranstaltete die Leitung der Gebietsabteilung für Gesundheitsschutz und das Gebietskrankenhaus Konferenzen, Ärzte aus Magadan erteilten Auskünfte oder reisten für Konsultationen selbst in die Bezirke.[165] Neben dieser beruflichen Fortbildung wurden auch neue Kader vor Ort ausgebildet, medizinische Bildungseinrichtungen entstanden 1955 in Debinsk und Anadyr' sowie eine Schule für Krankenschwestern in der Stadt Magadan.[166]

5.2.4 Das Lohn- und Bonussystem

Neben dem Aufbau von sozialer Infrastruktur sollten Arbeiter durch hohe Löhne und Boni in die Region gelockt bzw. zum Bleiben überredet werden. Hierzu existierte im Magadaner Gebiet ein komplexes System, das in den 1950er Jahren einigen Veränderungen unterworfen war. Grundsätzlich waren neben der Arbeitszeit die Löhne der wichtigste Bereich, in dem Chruščev eine Verbesserung der Arbeitsverhältnisse in der sowjetischen Industrie insgesamt erreichen wollte. Vor allem ging es ihm dabei um eine Anhebung der Löhne für Geringverdiener und um eine Neufestsetzung eines Minimallohnes, was mit einer gemeinsamen Verordnung des ZK der KPdSU, des Ministerrates und der Gewerkschaften vom 8. September 1956 erreicht werden sollte.[167] Auch im Magadaner Gebiet stiegen daraufhin die Löhne, in der Metallförderung er-

---

163 Da in einigen Siedlungen keine geeigneten Räume zur Verfügung standen, bat das Exekutivkomitee das Gesundheitsministerium der RSFSR um Gelder für entsprechende Baumaßnahmen. Vgl. die Bitte vom 5. März 1957 in GAMO f. R-146, op. 1, d. 219, l. 3 – 5.
164 Vgl. die Angaben der Gebietsgesundheitsabteilung in GAMO f. R-146, op. 1, d. 105, l. 16 – 40, hier l. 21. Die Versorgung der Neugeborenen mit Tuberkuloseimpfungen verbesserte sich von 64,9 % im Jahr 1954 auf 73 % im Jahr 1955. Vgl. ebd., l. 22.
165 Vgl. GAMO f. R-307, op. 1, d. 6, l. 30 – 137, hier l. 39.
166 Vgl. die Kaderangaben der Gebietsabteilung für Gesundheitsschutz in GAMO f. R-146, op. 1, d. 105, l. 7 – 15, hier l. 12 – 13.
167 Vgl. Ivanova, Na poroge, S. 90. Siehe zu den Lohnsteigerungen ebenso Filtzer, From Mobilized to Free, S. 163 sowie Hanson, Rise and Fall, S. 65 – 67.

höhte sich der durchschnittliche Lohn um 8,2 %, bei den Geringverdienern sogar um 40 – 60 %.[168]

Nach Angaben der zentralen statistischen Verwaltung wurde schon 1956 einem Arbeiter des Magadaner Gebietes so viel Lohn gezahlt wie in keiner anderen Region des Hohen Nordens (z. B. in Murmansk, in der Komi ASSR oder im Krasnojarsker Distrikt). Die zentrale Verwaltung bezifferte den Durchschnittslohn im Magadaner Gebiet auf 1.930 Rubel, regionale Stellen nennen hier für das gleiche Jahr 1.630 Rubel, was allerdings im Vergleich immer noch sehr hoch ist.[169]

Gerade der Durchschnittslohn hat jedoch für die Lage der Arbeitenden in der Region nur eine begrenzte Aussagekraft, da sich der Lohn aus einer Art Grundgehalt, einer Zulage entsprechend regionaler Koeffizienten und bestimmten Vergünstigungen für die Arbeit im Hohen Norden (kostenlose Fahrten in den Urlaub etc.) zusammensetzte. Diese Praxis führte aus mehreren Gründen zu erheblichen Lohnunterschieden:

Grundsätzlich unterstanden alle Arbeiter im Magadaner Gebiet den Lohnregelungen, die bis Ende 1953 nur in Dal'stroj gegolten hatten. Nach der Verordnung des Ministerrates vom 17. Dezember 1953 wurden alle Vergünstigungen des Kombinats auf neu zu gründende Einrichtungen und Betriebe ausgeweitet; in den Einrichtungen, die aus Dal'stroj an die Exekutivkomitees oder verschiedene Ministerien übergeben wurden, behielt man die bestehenden Regelungen bei.[170] Dazu zählten neben besonderen Lohnzuschlägen ein halbjährlicher Urlaub alle drei Jahre, wobei die Fahrt in den Urlaub vom Kombinat bezahlt wurde, sowie eine ganze Reihe von bemerkenswerten Sozialleistungen, wie Rentenzahlungen bei Berufsunfähigkeit, Unterstützung nach der Entlassung aus dem Kombinat oder die Aufnahme von Kindern der Dal'stroj-Kader in alle sowjetischen Bildungseinrichtungen ohne vorhergehende Prüfungen.[171] Diese Bestimmungen boten den Arbeitern grundsätzlich den höchsten Standard im Vergleich zu allen anderen Gebieten des sowjetischen Nordens. Das hohe Niveau zeigt sich auch daran, dass in anderen nördlichen Regionen Mitarbeiter des MVD und des

---

168 Vgl. die Erläuterungen zum Jahresbericht des Volkswirtschaftsrates für das Jahr 1959 von Korolev und dem Hauptbuchhalter Gol'dšvend in RGAĖ f. 7733, op. 48, d. 492, l. 1 – 28, hier l. 14 f.

169 Vgl. die tabellarische Übersicht über alle Durchschnittslöhne der Gebiete des Hohen Nordens in RGANI f. 5, op. 30, d. 217, l. 188. Für die Angaben aus der Region siehe die ausführlichen Angaben zum Jahresergebnis 1956 von Dal'stroj in GAMO f. R-23, op. 1, d. 4897, l. 3 – 119, hier l. 31 sowie den Bericht von Berezin vom 19. März 1957 in GAMO f. R-23, op. 1, d. 6109, l. 2 – 12, hier l. 4.

170 Vgl. die Verordnung „Über Maßnahmen in Verbindung mit Gründung des Magadaner Gebietes in der RSFSR" in GAMO f. R-23, op. 1, d. 6088, l. 59 – 60.

171 Die einzelnen Bestimmungen sind ausgesprochen umfangreich. Die wichtigsten Regelungen, die in den 1950er Jahren in der Region noch in Kraft waren, wurden 1945 erlassen. Siehe die Übersicht in der Anlage zu dem Übergabeakt von Dal'stroj aus dem MVD an das MMP vom 3. April 1953 in GAMO f. R-23, op. 1, d. 4677, l. 105 – 112 sowie die Anlage zu den regionalen Vorschlägen zur Einrichtung der neuen Struktur des Magadaner Volkswirtschaftsrates in GAMO f. R-23, op. 1, d. 6088, l. 54 – 58.

KGB nach den sogenannten „Dal'stroj-Bestimmungen" bezahlt wurden (z. B. in Norilsk) – was über dem ansonst üblichen Standard lag.[172]

Im Magadaner Gebiet waren jedoch eine ganze Reihe von Personen von diesen Dal'strojer Regelungen ausgenommen. Die Gründe dafür waren vielfältig. Die Bestimmungen wurden nicht auf die Beschäftigungsverhältnisse von Personen angewandt, die per Definition keine unmittelbare Bedeutung für die industrielle Entwicklung der Region hatten, so z. B. bei Lehrern, Ärzten, Mitarbeitern von Kultureinrichtungen und in der Landwirtschaft. Auch Personen, die nicht über eine offizielle Anwerbungskampagne einen Vertrag mit Dal'stroj geschlossen hatten, entgingen die üblichen Vergünstigungen.[173] Daneben waren alle Arbeitskräfte aus der Gruppe der Indigenen generell von den Vergünstigungen ausgenommen. Zudem gab es Arbeiter, die – trotz der prinzipiellen Übertragung der Dal'stroj-Bedingungen auf alle Arbeitskräfte – entsprechend ihren jeweiligen Ministerien und deren internen Regelungen entlohnt wurden.[174] An vielen Stellen arbeiteten also Menschen an der gleichen Stelle unter vollkommen verschiedenen Bedingungen. All diese Sonderbestimmungen riefen zahlreiche Beschwerden von Arbeitskollektiven und einzelnen Beschäftigten hervor.[175]

Außerdem waren die Vergünstigungen von Dal'stroj traditionell an die Zahl geleisteter Arbeitsjahre in der Region gebunden; die höchsten Löhne standen nur Per-

---

172 Vgl. die Regelungen von Dal'stroj im Vergleich zu den anderen Vergünstigungen im Hohen Norden in der Beschreibung des Ministerrates der UdSSR an das ZK der KPdSU in RGASPI f. 556, op. 23, d. 16, l. 172–173. Zu der Ausweitung dieser Bestimmungen auf bestimmtes Personal anderer Regionen siehe RGANI f. 5, op. 30, d. 218, l. 57–62.

173 Vgl. die Beschwerde Afanas'evs über diese Praxis vom 5. Juni 1954 an den Ministerrat der UdSSR in GAMO f. R-146, op. 1, d. 58, l. 5–8. Lehrer waren z. B. gezwungen, in Abstimmung mit den Schuljahren jedes Jahr Urlaub zu nehmen. Dadurch wurden ihnen die Reisen in die zentralen Teile der Union nicht gezahlt. Vgl. den Bericht des Leiters der Magadaner Abteilung für Volksbildung in GAMO f. R-146, op. 1, d. 223, l. 38–50, hier l. 49.

174 Die besonderen Regelungen für andere Ministerien betrafen Einrichtungen (z. B. der Gesundheitsfürsorge) in Tschukotka und in den Bezirken (Severo-Èvenskij, Srednekanskij und Ol'skij), die schon vor Gründung des Gebietes als „nationale Bezirke" bestanden hatten. Hier waren die Zuschläge um 50 bis 70 % geringer als in neu gegründeten Einrichtungen und in anderen Bezirken. Vgl. die Beschwerde des Gebietsparteikomitees an *Gosplan* in GAMO f. R-146, op. 1, d. 58, l. 27–28. Im Falle der Bauwirtschaft hatte das ZK der KPdSU und der Ministerrat der UdSSR am 23. August 1955 spezielle Lohnregelungen für alle Bauorganisationen erlassen, die die bisherigen Bestimmungen für Dal'stroj-Arbeiter außer Kraft setzten. Vgl. GAMO f. R-146, op. 1, d. 58, l. 84–86. In der Fischwirtschaft gab es (wie auch in anderen Wirtschaftszweigen) für die gleiche Arbeit zwei verschiedene Gehälter – entsprechend dem Ministerium für Fischwirtschaft und entsprechend Dal'stroj. Vgl. die Darstellung Ababkovs in RGANI f. 5, op. 32, d. 64, l. 182.

175 Siehe zu der Problematik unterschiedlicher Entlohnung bei gleicher Arbeit die kritischen Anmerkungen auf der zweiten Gebietsparteikonferenz in GAMO f. P-21, op. 5, d. 520, l. 108. Diese Ungleichbehandlungen kritisierte auch der oberste Kontrolleur für das Magadaner Gebiet und Dal'stroj des Ministeriums für staatliche Kontrolle der UdSSR, Milovidov, scharf. Vgl. seinen Bericht an den Minister für staatliche Kontrolle der UdSSR, Molotov, vom 5. April 1957 in GAMO f. R-23ss, op. 1, d. 459, l. 10.

sonen zu, die bereits zehn oder mehr Jahre im Nordosten gearbeitet hatten.[176] Leitende Kader von Dal'stroj erhielten darüber hinaus persönliche Gehälter, die auf alten Absprachen beruhten und auch nach 1953 nur z. T. angetastet wurden.[177] Auch die speziellen Dal'strojer Urlaubsregelungen konnten durch informelle Absprachen und Gewohnheiten in besonderem Maße zu ihren Gunsten ausgelegt werden.[178] Dadurch wurden die neu angeworbenen Arbeitskräfte im Vergleich zu den alten Kadern von Dal'stroj erheblich schlechter gestellt. Wenn dann die Berechnung des regionalen Koeffizienten (das Gebiet war auf der Basis der klimatischen Verhältnisse in verschiedene Zonen eingeteilt) erheblich zuungunsten des Arbeiters ausfiel, kam es vor, dass neue Arbeitskräfte sogar weniger verdienten als in den zentralen Gebieten der Sowjetunion. Vor allem Beschäftigte in der Bauwirtschaft waren besonders schlecht gestellt.[179]

Obwohl die Bestrebungen der sowjetischen Führung seit 1956 darauf abzielten, Lohnunterschiede insgesamt in der Sowjetunion abzumildern und das Lohnniveau der Geringverdiener anzuheben, war das Magadaner Gebiet in den 1950er Jahren eine Region mit ganz erheblichem sozialen Gefälle. Die extremen Lohnunterschiede waren ein Erbe des Lager-Industriellen Komplexes, in dem eine kleine Gruppe von Spitzenverdienern der Masse freier Arbeitskräfte und Wachmannschaften gegenüberstanden, sie waren aber auch den Versuchen zahlreicher Ministerien geschuldet, den Kosten des Dal'stroj-Lohnsystems zu entkommen.

Parallel zu den regionalen Diskussionen über Ausweitung oder Beschränkung der Vergünstigungen von Dal'stroj strengte die sowjetische Führung eine Neubeurteilung der regionalen Zulagen für alle Gebiete des „sowjetischen Nordens" an. Dabei war die Karte der Sowjetunion in verschiedene Zonen aufgeteilt, denen bestimmte Koeffizi-

---

176 Hinzu kamen hohe, einmalige Prämienzahlungen bei Dienstjubiläen in der Region. Vgl. RGANI f. 5, op. 32, d. 59, l. 37.

177 Vgl. zu den persönlichen Gehältern Kapitel 3.1.1.

178 Da die Fahrt in den Urlaub noch nicht als Urlaubszeit gewertet, aber bezahlt wurde, weiteten leitende Mitarbeiter des Kombinats die Reise zum Ort des Urlaubs und zurück erheblich aus; statt der vorgesehenen sechs Monate waren sie deshalb meist sieben bis acht Monate nicht an ihrem Arbeitsplatz, was erheblichen Protest auf Seiten der Parteileitung hervorrief. Vgl. das Schreiben des Gebietsparteikomitees an das ZK der KPdSU vom 20. April 1955 in RGANI f. 5, op. 32, d. 28, l. 2 – 3. Für die Mitarbeiter der Parteiorgane legte das ZK der KPdSU fest, dass sie ihren Urlaub einmal im Jahr nehmen durften, dann für jeweils zwei Monate, und dass sie per Flugzeug in den Urlaub geflogen wurden. Vgl. GAMO f. R-146, op. 1, d. 58, l. 25 – 26. Vgl. den Bericht über die Arbeit mit Kadern in der Indigirskoe Bergbauverwaltung für das Jahr 1956 in GAMO f. R-137sč, op. 1b, d. 21, l. 39 – 100, hier l. 85.

179 Vgl. die ausführlichen Angaben zum Jahresergebnis 1956 von Dal'stroj in GAMO f. R-23, op. 1, d. 4897, l. 3 – 119, hier l. 38. Die Tatsache, dass Bauarbeiter z. T. schlechter gestellt waren als in den zentralen Teilen der Union, beruhte auf einer für das Gebiet besonders ungünstigen Einteilung der Lohngruppen für Bauarbeiter nach regionalen Gesichtspunkten, gegen die sich das Gebietsexekutivkomitee seit 1955 heftig zur Wehr setzte. Der Lohnunterschied betrug dabei 12 %. Vgl. das Schreiben von Ababkov und Afanas'ev an Bulganin vom 9. Oktober 1956 in GAMO f. R-146, op. 1, d. 58, l. 45 – 47. Zu den unionsweiten Aufschlägen für Bauarbeiter in den 1950er Jahren siehe Davies/Ilic, From Khrushchev to Khrushchev, S. 227.

enten zugeordnet wurden, um deren Faktor der generelle Lohn in einer Industriebranche erhöht wurde. Die Zuordnung einer Region zu einem bestimmten Koeffizienten (z. B. zu Gebieten nördlich des Polarkreises) entschied somit über das Einkommen der Bevölkerung eines Gebietes.

Das im Mai 1955 gegründete Staatliche Komitee des Ministerrates der UdSSR zu Fragen von Arbeit und Löhnen wurde beauftragt, diese geographische Einteilung einer genauen Überprüfung zu unterziehen.[180] Die Diskussionen zogen sich über mehrere Jahre hin. Dem Magadaner Gebiet drohte demnach für seine südlichen Gebiete und für die Stadt Magadan die Aberkennung seines bisherigen Koeffizienten-Status, was zahlreiche Proteste auf Seiten der Magadaner Führung auslöste.[181] Die erhöhten Löhne waren für die Magadaner Führung nicht nur das wichtigste Argument bei der Anwerbung neuer Kader, das hohe Lohnniveau war unbedingt notwendig, um in der Region den eigenen Lebensunterhalt bestreiten zu können – dem erhöhten Kalorienbedarf, den Mehrausgaben für warme Kleidung und Heizmaterial standen deutlich erhöhte Preise für Lebensmittel und Waren des täglichen Bedarfs gegenüber.[182]

Im April-Mai 1957 wurden die Pläne zur Einschränkung der bestehenden Regelungen in Magadan das erste Mal öffentlich. Arbeiter, Angestellte und das ingenieurtechnische Personal stimmten mit den Füßen ab; es kam zu massenhaften Abreisen, die erst durch eine Versicherung des Vorsitzenden des Staatlichen Komitees für Arbeit und Löhne, es werde nicht zu einer Verschlechterung im Magadaner Gebiet kommen, gestoppt werden konnten.[183]

---

180 Zur Rolle dieses Komitees bei der Entwicklung der Löhne in der Entstalinisierung vgl. Ivanova, Na poroge, S. 75.

181 Ganz besonders erbitterte die Magadaner Führung, dass Teile der Region nach der neuen Koeffizientenregelung schlechter gestellt werden sollten als die Halbinsel Kamtschatka, obwohl die klimatischen Bedingungen der beiden Regionen wohl kaum zu vergleichen seien. Siehe zu den Protesten aus Magadan die Schreiben an Bulganin in GAMO f. R-146, op. 1, d. 58, l. 52–52, den ausführlichen Bericht an das ZK der KPdSU und den Ministerrat vom Mai 1957 in GAMO f. R-146, op. 1, d. 58, l. 72–83 sowie die Darstellung aus Magadan vom 7. August 1957 an das Büro des ZK der KPdSU für die RSFSR in RGASPI f. 556, op. 23, d. 16, l. 135–139. Weitere Proteste und Vorschläge aus dem Jahr 1957 finden sich in RGASPI f. 556, op. 23, d. 16, l. 25, l. 113–139.

182 Zu den erhöhten Preisen vgl. Isakov, Istorija torgovli, S. 215. Zu den Lebenshaltungskosten, aufgeschlüsselt für einzelne Produkte, siehe die Darstellung aus Magadan vom 7. August 1957 an das Büro des ZK der KPdSU für die RSFSR in RGASPI f. 556, op. 23, d. 16, l. 135–139, hier l. 137. Grebenjuk hat errechnet, dass noch im Jahr 1962 35 % aller Arbeitenden einen Lohn erhielten (incl. der Aufschläge für die Arbeit im Hohen Norden), mit dem sie unter dem lokalen Existenzminimum lagen. Vgl. Grebenjuk, Kolymskij led, S. 180.

183 In dieser Zeit wurde der Entwurf zu einem Erlass des Präsidiums des Obersten Sowjets der UdSSR über die Neuregelung der Löhne von Arbeitern im Hohen Norden bekannt. Vgl. den Bericht aus Magadan vom 7. August 1957 an das Büro des ZK der KPdSU für die RSFSR in RGASPI f. 556, op. 23, d. 16, l. 135–139, hier l. 138. Allgemein zu den Diskussionen über die Arbeits- und Lohnbedingungen im Hohen Norden siehe RGANI f. 5, op. 30, d. 218.

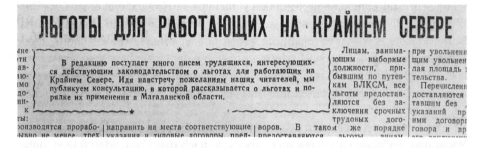

Abb. 46 Bericht über Petitionen zum Lohn- und Bonussystem, Magadanskaja Pravda, 9. Januar 1959

Im September 1957 entschied das Komitee zumindest in Teilen zugunsten der Arbeiter des Magadaner Gebietes, das Staatliche Komitee für Arbeit und Löhne erwartete daraufhin eine Steigerung des Durchschnittslohnes um bis zu 20 %. Allerdings sollten die vereinbarten Zuschläge wie bisher erst nach einem Jahr Arbeit gezahlt werden. Zugleich lehnte das Komitee weitere Vorschläge bezüglich einer Absenkung des Renteneintrittsalters und zur Einführung einer Zahlung bei Berufsunfähigkeit ab.[184]

Dies war jedoch nur ein vorläufiger Sieg; die Diskussionen über Löhne, Boni und bestimmte Vergünstigungen hielten in den nächsten Jahren an. Immer wieder standen einzelne Bestimmungen zur Debatte, die die Magadaner Führung mit immer neuen Argumenten abzuwehren suchte.[185] Begleitet wurde dieser Prozess von vielen privaten und kollektiven Petitionen einzelner Arbeitergruppen, die sich, je nach ihrem rechtlichen Status, z. T. auch gegen hohe Vergünstigungen für einzelne andere Gruppen aussprachen.[186]

Für Chruščev war die Lage viel einfacher. Die Schwierigkeiten des sowjetischen Nordens bei der Werbung und dauerhaften Bindung neuer Arbeitskräfte waren in seinen Augen Ausdruck einer bereits überholten Vorstellung von den Bedingungen sowjetischer Arbeiter. Seine ideologische Revitalisierung des Begriffes „Kommunismus" stützte sich auf extreme Verheißungen einer arbeitsfreien Gesellschaft im Überfluss, die in dem bekannten Ausspruch „Die heutige Generation wird im Kommunismus leben" auf dem 22. Parteitag 1961 gipfelte. In diesem Rahmen waren für Chruščev die Debatten über Koeffizienten, Aufschläge und Boni für die Arbeiter im Hohen Norden umständliche, bürokratische und allzu teure Maßnahmen, die an den

---

184 Der Koeffizient für den Magadaner Bezirk sollte wie zuvor 1,8 betragen, in Tschukotka 2,0. Vgl. das Schreiben über die Neuregelungen vom stellv. Vorsitzenden des Staatlichen Komitees an das ZK der KPdSU in RGASPI f. 556, op. 23, d. 16, l. 172–173.

185 Siehe beispielweise die Ablehnung der Abschaffung von bestehenden Sonderurlaubsregelungen durch Afanas'ev im September 1958 in RGANI f. 5, op. 32, d. 111, l. 155–158.

186 In dieser Zeit gingen aus allen Teilen des Hohen Nordens sehr viele Petitionen einzelner Arbeiter zu diesen Neuregelungen bei der Redaktion der Zeitung *Pravda* ein. Vgl. die für das ZK der KPdSU erstellte Sammlung dieser Briefe in RGASPI f. 556, op. 23, d. 73, l. 15–23.

schon sehr bald eintretenden Realitäten vorbeigingen. 1959 äußerte er sich vor Bürgern in Wladiwostok zur Lage im sowjetischen Fernen Osten und Hohen Norden. Seines Erachtens waren es „nicht die hohen Löhne, sondern die Errichtung guter Lebensbedingungen, die sowjetische Menschen hierher ziehen lassen – der Bau von hochwertigem Wohnraum mit kommunaler Müllabfuhr, Strom- und Wasserversorgung, der Bau von Kindergärten und -krippen, Schulen, Internaten und kulturellen Einrichtungen"[187].

Das folgende Kapitel wird seinen Blick intensiver auf das Verhältnis zwischen Macht und Bevölkerung richten und dabei v. a. nach den Umständen fragen, unter denen Menschen im Nordosten der 1950er Jahre leben mussten. Vorweggenommen sei nur, dass die tatsächlichen Lebensbedingungen der allermeisten Menschen so erbärmlich waren, dass Chruščevs abwertende Äußerung über die Bedeutung von Lohnzuschlägen und Vergünstigungen als ausgesprochen zynisch und von ökonomischen Interessen getrieben erscheint.

5.3 Soziale Realitäten und ihre Repräsentation

Wer in den 1950er Jahren in das Magadaner Gebiet zog oder aus einem der Lager entlassen wurde, konnte sicher sein, irgendeine Art von Arbeitsvertrag zu erhalten, für ein menschenwürdiges Leben gab es jedoch keinerlei Garantie. Große Teile der Bevölkerung waren Leidtragende einer ganzen Reihe von Widersprüchen, die aus der Übergangsphase nach der Auflösung des Lager-Industriellen Komplexes resultierten, die aber auch den neuen Herrschafts- und Wirtschaftsstrukturen als Teil der zivilen Sphäre der Sowjetunion immanent waren. Die reine Implementierung zivil-institutioneller und zivil-infrastruktureller Strukturen war kein Garant für bessere Verhältnisse. Allein die Unterstellung der Schulen unter das Ministerium für Bildung der RSFSR beseitigte noch nicht den dramatischen Lehrermangel, Aufträge des Leiters des Exekutivkomitees bei zivilen Handelsorganisationen für Milchprodukte und Mehl verbesserten nicht flächendeckend die miserable Versorgung. Während in der Übergangsphase viele alte Verbindungen, institutionelle Beziehungen und persönliche Patronagesysteme wegbrachen – die bisher nur einer kleinen Personengruppe gedient hatten –, waren die neu aufgebauten Versorgungskanäle völlig unzureichend und ineffektiv. Das ungerechte Lohn- und Bonussystem belastete die Bevölkerung zusätzlich.

Zugleich erlebte die Sowjetunion in den 1950er Jahren eine Welle von Reformen (so bei der Einführung der Volkswirtschaftsräte und im gesamten Bereich der Sozialpolitik), die Kompetenzüberschneidungen, mangelnde Verantwortlichkeiten und gewaltige Ressourcenprobleme im Nordosten zunächst verschärften.

---

187 Zitiert nach Slavin, Promyšlennoe osvoenie, S. 291.

Obwohl die Verbesserung der Arbeits- und Lebensbedingungen der freien Bevölkerung eine der wichtigsten Aufgaben der neuen Leitung war und als eine der Voraussetzungen für die Stabilisierung der Goldförderung verstanden wurde, war die konkrete Lage der Magadaner nur zu einem Teil von diesem Paradigmenwechsel beeinflusst. Wohnverhältnisse, Gesundheitsversorgung, die Zuteilung von Waren und Lebensmitteln waren nicht nur abhängig von Gehältern, Zuschlägen und dem sozialen Status eines Bewohners, sondern ganz besonders auch von der geographischen Lage seiner Siedlung und vom Umgang der lokalen Funktionäre mit den neuen Verhältnissen.

5.3.1 Leben im Lager-Raum

Die Versuche, freie Arbeitskräfte für das Magadaner Gebiet zu gewinnen, gingen mit der Verkleinerung von *Sevvostlag* und *Berlag* einher. Auch wenn es in den Jahren nach Gründung des Magadaner Gebietes noch immer Häftlingstransporte in den Nordosten gab[188] und es auch weiterhin zu neuen Verhaftungen aus politischen Gründen kam[189], nahm doch die Gesamtzahl aller Inhaftierten rapide ab. Nach der ersten großen Entlassungswelle im Zuge der Amnestie sank die Häftlingszahl des *Sevvostlag* weiter von 88.380 im Sommer 1954 auf etwa 35.400 zu Beginn des Jahres 1956. Gefangene konnten in dieser Zeit die Lager aufgrund einer weiteren Amnestie vom 3. September 1955 verlassen oder kamen frei, weil sie ihre Haftzeit durch die Anrechnung von Arbeitstagen verkürzen konnten.[190] Nach dem 20. Parteitag im Februar 1956 wurde im Magadaner Gebiet eine der Revisionskommissionen eingesetzt, die, in Ausführung eines Erlasses des Präsidiums des Obersten Sowjets, die Urteile der sogenannten „politischen" Häftlinge überprüfte.[191] Im Zuge der Arbeit dieser Kommission kam eine erhebliche Zahl von „politischen Häftlingen" frei, das *Sevvostlag* umfasste Ende des

---

188 So erreichten, auf Befehl des MVD, im Jahr 1955 noch einmal 13.000 Häftlinge die Region. Sie sollten den herrschenden Arbeitskräftemangel ausgleichen, wozu Häftlinge ausgewählt worden waren, die nicht unmittelbar zu entlassen und die „ihrer physischen Konstitution nach für eine Verwendung zur Arbeit im Hohen Norden geeignet" seien. Zitiert nach Kozlov, Sevvostlag, S. 128 f. Nach Angaben von Kozlov wurden außerdem zwischen 1954 und 1957 immer wieder größere und kleinere Häftlingskontingente in die Region verbracht. Vgl. ebd.

189 Peter Demant berichtet in seinen Erinnerungen von Verhaftungen aufgrund des Paragraphen 58 (aufgrund angeblicher „Konterrevolution"), unmittelbar zur Zeit der Revisionskommissionen, die „politische Häftlinge" entlassen sollten. Kress (Pseudonym Peter Demants), Parochoda, S. 82.

190 Vgl. Elic, Khrushchev's Gulag, S. 115.

191 Vgl. zu ihrer Anlage und Vorgehensweise Elie, Revisionskommissionen. Der lokalen Kommission gehörten sechs Personen an – der zweite Sekretär des Gebietsparteikomitees, V. S. Timofeev, der erste Stellvertreter des Staatsanwaltes der RSFSR, G. G. Burimovič, der Militärstaatsanwalt des Fernöstlichen Militärbezirkes, V. V. Danyšin, der leitende Kontrolleur des Ministeriums für staatliche Kontrolle der UdSSR, A. I. Černyšev, der Sekretär des Kreisparteikomitees von Tschukotka, A. N. Grozin, sowie der leitende Ingenieur des Kombinats „Mosgorles", N. K. Dedkov. Vgl. Kozlov, Sevvostlag, S. 129.

Jahres 1956 nur noch ca. 24.000 Häftlinge.[192] Diese Zahl ging bis zur Auflösung des Lagerkomplexes im April 1957 weiter zurück. Die verbliebenen Lagerabteilungen wurden der regionalen Struktur des MVD des Gebietsexekutivkomitees unterstellt, dazu wurde eine lokale „Verwaltung der Besserungs- und Arbeitskolonien" gegründet.[193] Nach dem 20. Parteitag wurden die Beschränkungen für die allermeisten sogenannten „Sondersiedler" und „Verbannten" aufgehoben, die bis dahin gezwungen waren in der Region zu verbleiben. Von über 16.000 Menschen am 1. Januar 1954 sank ihre Zahl auf einige Hundert im Jahr 1957.[194]

Während in den weiter bestehenden Lagern an mancher Stelle Hafterleichterungen spürbar waren, waren die verbliebenen Häftlinge v. a. in den ersten Jahren nach der Gebietsgründung weiterhin der brutalen Gewalt ihrer schwerkriminellen Mithäftlinge und von Wachmannschaften ausgeliefert. Die Reorganisation der Lagerverwaltung, Versorgungsschwierigkeiten sowie die Schließung, Verlagerung und Zusammenlegung von Lagerpunkten verschärften die Zustände an vielen Haftorten zusätzlich.

In der Chandygsker Lagerabteilung herrschten bereits seit Monaten entsetzliche Zustände[195], als es am 20. September 1955 im Lagerpunkt Nr. 3 zu einem Häftlingsaufstand kam. Die Lagerleitung wagte sich zunächst nicht in das Lagerinnere, sie riegelte den Lagerpunkt lediglich von außen ab. Schließlich wurde der Aufstand von Wachmannschaften unter Einsatz schwerer Waffen beendet. Eine Untersuchungskommission sah die Ursache für diesen Aufstand in der Verlegung einer großen Zahl von Häftlingen aus einem anderen, gerade aufgelösten Lagerpunkt in den Lagerpunkt Nr. 3. Diese Verlegung war ohne Vorbereitung vollzogen worden, für die Neuankömmlinge gab es keinerlei Barackenplätze oder Lebensmittel, sie wurden in der Strafabteilung des Lagerpunktes Nr. 3 festgehalten. An diesem Aufstand zeigen sich v. a. die Verwerfungen, die im Zuge der Umstrukturierung des *Sevvostlag* in den Lagern auftraten. Zugleich lässt sich hier ein wachsendes Bewusstsein für die Bedeutung gesetzlicher Verhältnisse in den Lagern ablesen, da die Verantwortlichen von Lager-

---

192 Nach Angabe des stellv. Ministers für Buntmetalle, Strigin, wurden 1956 etwa 7.000 Personen entlassen, die als sogenannte „Konterrevolutionäre" verhaftet worden waren. Vgl. seinen Bericht an die Wirtschaftskommission des Ministerrates der UdSSR vom 9. Oktober 1956 in GAMO f. R-23sč, op. 1, d. 471, l. 54–55. Nach dem 20. Parteitag kam es auch im Magadaner Gebiet zu Rehabilitationen, siehe dazu Rajzman, Process reabilitacii. Peter Demant hat in seinen Erinnerungen (unter dem Pseudonym Vernon Kress) mehrere der Personen vorgestellt, die aufgrund der Kommissionen im Kolymaer Gebiet entlassen wurden. Vgl. Kress, Parochoda, S. 79f.

193 Die Lagerabteilungen des *Sevvostlag*, die auf dem Gebiet der jakutischen ASSR bestanden hatten, wurden den Organen der regionalen Leitung von Jakutien unterstellt. Vgl. Kozlov, Sevvostlag, S. 130. Zur Schließung einzelner Lagerabteilungen vgl. ausführlich Kozlov, Lagernaja sistema, S. 180f. Zur unionsweiten Umstellung auf die Lagerkolonien siehe Elie, Khrushchev's Gulag, S. 116.

194 Vgl. Grebenjuk, Kolymskij led, S. 85 auf der Grundlage einer Statistik über die Lage der „gesellschaftlichen Sicherheit im Magadaner Gebiet" in GAMO f. P-21, op. 5, d. 515, l. 47–48.

195 Vgl. den Befehl des Leiters von *Sevvostlag*, Mitrakov, zur Beseitigung dieser Verhältnisse in GAMO f. R-23, op. 1, d. 5206, l. 51–57.

punkt und -verwaltung später für die unzureichende Versorgung der Häftlinge zur Verantwortung gezogen wurden.[196]

Die regionale Parteileitung hatte sich seit 1954 die Kontrolle der Situation in den Lagern und die Trennung zwischen Lager und dem zivilen Leben der Region zu Eigen gemacht. Bei einem der ersten Treffen im Gebietsparteikomitee, das Fragen des Häftlingsregimes gewidmet war, wurden die schier grenzenlosen Berührungspunkte problematisiert: Häftlinge, die als „Haussklaven" bei Dal'stroj-Offizieren arbeiteten, die parallele Arbeit von freien Männern und inhaftierten Frauen, die zu Übergriffen und zu sexuellen Beziehungen führten, Lager, die sich unmittelbar in der Stadt Magadan befanden und deren Häftlinge mitten durch die Hauptstraße eskortiert wurden, zahllose Häftlinge, die in zivilen Einrichtungen, in Schulen, Krankenhäusern und Bäckereien arbeiteten und die entsprechend bewacht und zur Arbeit begleitet werden mussten. Die Parteileitung konzentrierte sich hier v. a. auf die Situation in der Stadt Magadan, diese Verbindung zwischen Lager und zivilem Leben war aber in der ersten Zeit nach der Gebietsgründung allgegenwärtig.[197] Neben ihren Bemühungen, das neue zivile Leben des Gebietes von Haft und Lager zu trennen, strebte die Parteileitung nach Einblick und Kontrolle in die Verhältnisse der Lager selbst. Sie entsandte Kommissionen, setzte zivile Staatsanwälte zur Inspektion der Lager ein und deckte eine Reihe ungesetzlicher Maßnahmen auf – ohne dabei alle Lagerabteilungen, geschweige denn alle Lagerpunkte, auf dem riesigen Territorium in den Blick nehmen zu können.[198]

Die persönliche Lage der Häftlinge war jedoch weiterhin von ihrem rechtlichen Status und den jeweiligen Wachmannschaften und Lagerfunktionären abhängig. Im Rückblick auf die Jahre 1953 bis 1955 erinnert sich der ehemalige Häftling Michael Solomon einer für ihn fast unerträglichen Spannung zwischen den schrecklichen Haftbedingungen, seiner Hoffnung auf die bereits überfällige Entlassung und permanenten Verlegungen. Als rumänischer Häftling hatte Michael Solomon gemeinsam mit einer Gruppe weiterer Häftlinge aus europäischen Ländern prinzipiell Aussicht auf eine baldige Repatriierung:

> Mit dem Beginn des Jahres 1954 begann eine sanfte Brise der Hoffnung über die Lager zu wehen und gegen die kalten Böen des nördlichen Winterhimmels anzukämpfen. Angeblich war die Regierung wirklich beunruhigt wegen ihrer politischen Häftlinge, und man führte bestimmte Maßnahmen ein, um einige harte Bedingungen des Lagerlebens zu mildern. Vereinzelte Briefe trafen ein, und man erlaubte den Ausländern, unter der Ägide des Internationalen Roten Kreuzes Postkarten nach Hause zu schreiben [...].[199]

Doch tatsächlich wurde Solomon noch im Sommer 1954 Opfer einer brutalen Scheinhinrichtung, in den folgenden Monaten wurde er von Lagerpunkt zu Lager-

---

196 Vgl. den Bericht über den Aufstand in GAMO f. R-23, op. 5600, l. 210–212.
197 Vgl. die Mitschrift in GAMO f. P-21, op. 5, d. 765, l. 1–16.
198 Vgl. Kapitel 3.3.2.
199 Solomon, Magadan, S. 273.

punkt verlegt, musste schwerste Zwangsarbeit leisten, verfolgt von der Angst, in einem Lagerpunkt „vergessen" oder erst nach dem Ende der jeweiligen Fährsaison entlassen zu werden.[200] Ende des Jahres verlegte man eine Gruppe ausländischer Häftlinge, unter ihnen Solomon, nach Magadan. In der enttäuschten Hoffnung auf Entlassung traten sie im Juni 1955 in einen ersten, später dann in einen zweiten Streik:

> Ende Juli hofften wir immer noch auf eine baldige Repatriierung. Ende August, als die Einstellung der Schiffahrt näherrückte, beschlossen wir, etwas zu unternehmen. ‚Handeln oder sterben', das wurde unsere Parole. Wenn wir die erste Septemberhälfte verstreichen ließen, würde das Meer wieder zu sein, und wir mußten bis nächsten Sommer warten. Keiner von uns konnte den Gedanken an einen weiteren Winter ertragen, also traten wir wieder in Streik. Diesmal schlugen die Behörden sofort zurück. Man lud uns mitten in der Nacht auf Lastwagen und fuhr uns in ein weit von der Stadt entferntes, verlassenes Lager mit moderigen, feuchten Baracken, in denen es vor Ratten wimmelte. Unsere kalten Rationen bestanden aus schimmeligem Brot und Getreide, das wir selbst kochen mußten. [...] Mich holte man eines Tages mit dem Wagen ins Zentralgefängnis von Magadan, wo ich drei Tage und drei Nächte verhört wurde.[201]

Die Gewalt der Lager machte auch unter den Bedingungen des Magadaner Gebietes nicht an den Toren der Lagerpunkte halt. Entlassene Häftlinge unterlagen Stigmatisierungen, Diskriminierungen und der fortwährenden Überwachung durch den MVD. In Jagodnoe, der damaligen Heimat des entlassenen Häftlings Peter Demant, habe der dortige Chef des KGB weiterhin Material gegen entlassene Häftlinge gesammelt, „wissend, dass das Tauwetter vergeht, wie jede andere temporäre Kampagne. Die Leitung konnte nicht glauben, dass Chruščev ernsthaft daran denkt, die Willkür zu beenden."[202]

Aber auch durch schwerkriminelle Häftlinge und durch geflohene Häftlinge, die ums Überleben kämpften, dehnte sich die Gewalt des Lagers auf Siedlungen freier Arbeitskräfte aus. Es kam zu Überfällen, schweren Körperverletzungen, Vergewaltigungen, Mord.[203] Besonders gefährlich war die Lage, wenn kriminelle Häftlinge Zugang zu offen gelagertem Sprengmaterial erhielten und sich auf diese Weise eigene Waffen herstellen konnten.[204]

Wie sich die vom Lager ausgehende Kriminalität im Magadaner Gebiet quantitativ entwickelte, lässt sich anhand der vorliegenden Quellen nur schwer beurteilen.[205] Auf

---

200 Vgl. Solomon, Magadan, S. 274–279.

201 Solomon, Magadan, S. 284.

202 Kress (Pseudonym Peter Demants), Parochoda, S. 80.

203 Ausführliche Berichte über brutale kriminelle Vorkommnisse hinter und vor den Lagertoren liegen von der Parteiführung des Gebietes ebenso wie von der Kombinatsleitung vor. Siehe die Berichte in GAMO f. P-21, op. 1, d. 2, l. 253–271 sowie d. 759, l. 1–10. Berichte der Lagerleitung in GAMO f. R-23, op. 1, d. 5206 sowie d. 5600, l. 210–212.

204 Vgl. den Bericht der Politischen Abteilung des *Sevvostlag* an Mitrakov vom 17. August 1955 in GAMO f.23, op. 1, d. 5611, l. 69–71.

205 Der für die Beantwortung dieser Fragen notwendige Zugang zu den Akten des FSB-Archivs blieb der Autorin verwehrt.

Basis der an die Parteileitung gerichteten Berichte kann konstatiert werden, dass die extreme Häufung krimineller Vorkommnisse, wie z. B. im Sommer 1953 nach der großen Amnestie, zurückging. Auch wenn Mitte und Ende der 1950er Jahre noch Berichte über schwere Übergriffe vorgelegt wurden, so nahm doch ihre Zahl insgesamt ab – zeitgleich wurden immer mehr Lagerpunkte geschlossen. Zudem verschoben sich die Gewaltakte zunehmend an die Peripherie des Gebietes – die Kriminalität war dort höher, wo die institutionelle Durchdringung geringer war. Nach offizieller Darstellung – auf den Seiten der regionalen Zeitung *Magadanskaja Pravda* –hatte sich die Sicherheitslage durch einen engeren Kontakt zwischen Miliz und Bevölkerung verbessert. Der Leiter der Gebietsverwaltung des MVD, D. Birjukov, hob dabei besonders die Beteiligung gesellschaftlicher Gruppen hervor. Spezielle Brigaden hätten durch ihre Kontrollen in Wohnheimen, Geschäften und durch Patrouillen auf den Straßen die Arbeit der Miliz maßgeblich unterstützt und kriminelle Aktionen unterbunden.[206]

Erkennbar ist, dass die Lagervergangenheit der Region und die Weiterexistenz von Lagerpunkten bei der Bewertung krimineller Vorkommnisse eine große Rolle spielten. Berichte über Diebstähle, Vergewaltigungen und Einbrüche wurden meist mit einem Verweis auf die Lagervergangenheit der verurteilten Person abgeschlossen oder gleich grundsätzlich ehemaligen Häftlingen zur Last gelegt – wenn man keine konkreten Beweise vorlegen konnte.[207] Selbst bei angeblich „renitenten Kindern" wurden die ihnen zur Last gelegten Vergehen mit der Lagerhaft der Eltern erklärt.[208] Dieses Interpretationsangebot sollte eine Abgrenzung der Vorfälle von zivilen Verhältnissen ermöglichen. Die „Lagervergangenheit" wurde zum Stigma für einzelne Personen, sie betraf weder Struktur noch Vergangenheit des Gebietes.

---

206 Magadanskaja Pravda, 10. Januar 1957, S. 3.

207 Vgl. die Berichte des MVD aus dem Jahr 1954 in den Materialien zu den Sitzungsprotokollen des Gebietsparteikomitees in GAMO f. P-21, op. 5, d. 2, l. 37. Ein breitangelegter kollektiver Brief von 55 Arbeitern des Kombinats Iul'tin in Čukotka an den Obersten Sowjet der UdSSR machte entlassene Häftlinge für sämtliche kriminellen Akte in dem Gebiet, für Raub, Vergewaltigungen, Übergriffe, Morde und Diebstähle verantwortlich. Vgl. ihre Petition vom 18. Januar 1955 in GARF f. R-7523, op. 75, f. 1569, l. 106–108. Der stellvertretende Minister für Buntmetalle machte die Existenz von Lagerpunkten neben Siedlungen von Komsomolzen generell für amoralische Verhaltensweisen verantwortlich. Vgl. sein Schreiben an Dal'stroj vom 5. Januar 1957 in GAMO f. R-137sč, op. 1b, d. 21, l. 120. Derartige Berichte liegen aus vielen Lagergebieten vor, siehe Harry, Campaign, S. 104 f. Zu den Berichten nach der Amnestie vom Frühjahr 1953 siehe Kapitel 3.1.2.

208 Der stellvertretende Leiter der Abteilung für Propaganda und Agitation berichtete der Gebietsparteileitung 1958 ausführlich über „schwere Disziplinverletzungen und amoralisches Verhalten unter Magadaner Schülern". Dazu zählten sexuelle Beziehungen junger Schülerinnen zu älteren Männern, Diebstähle, Trunkenheit und „antisowjetische Handlungen". So habe ein Schüler in betrunkenem Zustand vor einem Porträt Chruščevs gekniet und es in entehrender Weise angebetet. In sehr vielen Fällen wurde dieses als anstößig beurteilte Verhalten mit der Lagervergangenheit der Eltern dieser Kinder erklärt. Vgl. GAMO f. P-21, op. 5, d. 145, l. 141–145. Auch der Direktor der Mittelschule der Siedlung Ust'-Omčug im Bezirk Ten'kinskij, A. I. Gudovič, fürchtete einen negativen Einfluss ehemaliger Häftlinge auf das Verhalten seiner Schüler, wenn sie nicht ausreichend pädagogisch betreut würden. Vgl. GAMO f. R-146, op. 1, d. 54, l. 33–36, hier l. 35.

Doch auch strukturell hatten die „Zonen" weiterhin eine große Bedeutung: Alle größeren Siedlungen waren im Nordosten zunächst einmal Lagerpunkte, alle Kommunikationswege, Straßen, Handelsbeziehungen, die gesamte Infrastruktur der Region war die Infrastruktur der Lager. Die schrittweise Öffnung der Lagertore machte aus dem militärischen Gebiet noch keinen zivilen Bezirk, die Entfernung des Stacheldrahts ließ einen Lagerpunkt nicht zu einer Siedlung freier Sowjetbürger werden, zumal der Aufbau des Gebietes unmittelbar auf den Pfählen der Stacheldrahtzäune ansetzte. Die verlassenen Lagerbaracken waren in vielen Bezirken die einzigen Gebäude, in denen zivile Strukturen entstehen konnten. Verkehrslinien oder Siedlungen außerhalb der Strukturen des bisherigen Lager-Industriellen Komplexes existierten nicht. Straßen führten nicht von einer Siedlung zur Schule oder zu einem Geschäft; sie führten von der Lagerkommandantur zu den Baracken, vom Lager zur Goldgrube, von einer Goldgrube zur nächsten. Der Raum hatte keine zivile Vorgeschichte. Nahezu alles, was in diesem Gebiet an Lebensnotwendigem vorhanden war, der Schutz vor dem extremen Klima, Nahrung, Bekleidung und Trinkwasser, teilte der sowjetische Staat zu. Es gab keine privaten Gärten oder Kleinviehwirtschaft, keine Katen in gewachsenen Dorfstrukturen, keine Brunnen oder alte, unbefestigte Feldwege.

Im Magadaner Gebiet war die Abhängigkeit der freien Bevölkerung von den Zuteilungen des Staates mit der Abhängigkeit der Häftlinge von der Versorgung der Lager vergleichbar. Die Hand des Staates, die bisher Menschen aus ihrer gewohnten Umgebung gerissen, in Lagern im Nordosten zusammengepfercht und zur Arbeit unter unmenschlichen Bedingungen gezwungen hatte, diese Hand sollte nun nicht mehr schlagen, sondern zuteilen und versorgen. Nichtsdestotrotz blieb sie im Nordosten eine fast allmächtige Hand in lebensfeindlicher Umgebung. Gab es in entfernten Gebieten hinter dem Lager nur die Taiga, so gab es in der Entstalinisierung hinter der Arbeiterbaracke nur die Taiga.

In der Region selbst waren die Lager nicht nur nicht zu leugnen, im wörtlichen Sinne „baute" das neue Gebiet auf dem früheren Lagersystem auf, waren zudem ein großer Teil der freien Arbeitskräfte ehemalige Häftlinge. Doch auch in anderen Gebieten der Sowjetunion waren die Vorstellungen von der Kolyma vom Lager bestimmt. Das eingangs dieses Kapitels zitierte Lied von Vladimir Vysockij spielt mit diesem diffusen Wissen, immer wieder berichteten freie Arbeitskräfte, die in die Region kamen, von den Bildern, die sie bis zu ihrer Ankunft mit dem Gebiet verbunden hatten.[209] Genau diese Vorstellungen wollte die Parteileitung mit ihren Repräsentationsstrategien neu besetzen. Es ging ihr um nichts weniger als um eine vollständige Neurepräsentation der Region und ihrer Bewohner. Afanas'ev formulierte dies programmatisch im Vorwort zu seinen „Aufzeichnungen" über das Magadaner Gebiet: „Früher schreckte die Kolyma die Menschen, heute zieht sie an."[210]

---

209 Vgl. den Bericht über die Arbeit mit Kadern in der Indigirskoe Bergbauverwaltung für das Jahr 1956 in GAMO f. R-137sč, op. 1b, d. 21, l. 39 – 100, hier l. 74.
210 Afanas'ev, Rossija, S. 2.

5.3.2 Siedlungsbau und Urbanisierung

Faktisch war das Leben in der Magadaner Region in den 1950er Jahren von drangvoller Enge geprägt – auf dem riesigen Gebiet gab es trotz aller Bemühungen viel zu wenig Wohnraum. Die besondere Wirtschaftsform der Region, die rasche Schließung und Neueröffnung von Gruben und ganzen Standorten verhinderte zudem den Bau kleiner individueller Häuser, die in anderen Regionen eine gewisse Erleichterung schaffen konnten.[211] 1957 stand jedem Bürger im Magadaner Gebiet eine Fläche von 4 m^2 Wohnraum zur Verfügung, in der RSFSR waren dies zur gleichen Zeit 5,4 m^2, in städtischen Siedlungen der gesamten UdSSR lag die durchschnittliche Quadratmeterzahl sogar bei 7,3.[212] So weit die offiziellen Zahlen, in die allerdings auch Wohnflächen eingerechnet wurden, die keineswegs zum Wohnen geeignet waren, wie Keller und geschlossene Industrieanlagen.[213] In der Realität waren die Verhältnisse im Nordosten noch viel beengter. So z. B. im Bezirk Susuman, wo bei einer Industrieanlage 100 Menschen lebten, die insgesamt über 129 m^2 Wohnfläche verfügten.[214]

Wenn aufgrund fehlender Materialien und zu hoher Kosten kein neuer Wohnraum entstand, waren die Menschen des Gebietes auf alle vorhandenen Gebäude angewiesen. Und das waren fast ausschließlich Hinterlassenschaften aufgelöster Lagerpunkte, ehemalige Lagerbaracken.[215] Ehemalige Häftlinge kehrten als freie Bürger in ihre alten Wohnbaracken oder die ehemaligen Verwaltungsgebäude der Lagerpunkte zurück.[216] Statt zu mehreren auf einer Holzpritsche zu liegen, teilten sie die riesigen

---

211 Siehe zu den Möglichkeiten individuellen Hausbesitzes in dieser Zeit Smith, Ownership.

212 Die Werte sind jeweils Durchschnittszahlen. Siehe das Schreiben von Afanas'ev und Korolev an *Gosplan* vom Oktober 1957 in GAMO f. R-146, op. 1, d. 221, l. 68 – 69. Für die Zahl zur RSFSR siehe den Bericht des Leiters der statistischen Verwaltung der RSFSR an das ZK der KPdSU vom Mai 1957 in RGASPI f. 556, op. 21, d. 108, l. 34. Für die Zahl für die städtischen Bewohner siehe Davies/Ilic, From Khrushchev to Khrushchev, S. 214. Tatsächlich stand freien Arbeitskräften 1957 noch weniger Wohnraum zur Verfügung als kurz nach Gründung des Gebietes, weil der Bedarf sehr viel schneller wuchs, als Wohnräume freigegeben oder neu errichtet werden konnten. Im Juli 1954 betrug die Durchschnittsquadratmeterzahl für einen Arbeiter 4,9. Vgl. das Schreiben von Mitrakov an Malenkov und Chruščev in GAMO f. R-23, op. 1, d. 5207, l. 210 – 214, hier l. 212.

213 Vgl. GAMO f. R-146, op. 1, d. 442, l. 17.

214 So die Lage bei der Gasstation Berelechskaja. Vgl. den Bericht des Susumansker Bezirkspartei- und Bezirksexekutivkomitees vom 14. Juli 1960 in GAMO f. R-146, op. 1, d. 442, l. 96 – 97.

215 Im Juli 1954 waren nur 6,5 % des gesamten Wohnraumes Steinhäuser, Holzbaracken machten 75,5 % aus, weitere 18 % aller Häuser waren fast vollständig zerfallen. Vgl. das Schreiben von Mitrakov an Malenkov und Chruščev in GAMO f. R-23, op. 1, d. 5207, l. 210 – 214, hier l. 212.

216 Wohnbaracken wurden ohne großangelegte bauliche Veränderungen als Wohnraum genutzt, andere Lagergebäude einer neuen Nutzung zugeführt. So wurde aus einem Wachturm ein Wohnhaus, aus einem Isolator ein Geschäft, aus einem Klub der Lagerleitung eine Schule etc. Beispielhaft siehe GAMO f. P-21, op. 5, d. 110, l. 181 – 183. Hier wird detailliert beschrieben, wie im Februar 1957 ein ganzer Lagerpunkt zu einer Siedlung freier Arbeitskräfte umgewandelt wurde, welche Lageranlagen auf welche Weise neu genutzt wurden, welche Teile der Wasserversorgung und der elektrischen Leitungen übernommen werden konnten oder neu erstellt werden mussten und wie die baulichen Rekonstruktionen praktisch gestaltet wurden.

Räume nun mit Laken in Verschläge ab, von einem „Wohnraum" im eigentlichen Sinne und von Privatsphäre konnte dabei keine Rede sein.[217] Obwohl Dal'stroj diese Weiterverwendung der Baracken kurz nach Gründung des Gebietes als eine Art „Übergangslösung" betrachtet hatte, lebten noch 1959 60 % der Bürger in früheren Lagerbaracken.[218] Die allermeisten dieser Baracken stammten aus den Jahren 1935 bis 1942, waren ausgesprochen baufällig und während der langen Wintermonate bitterkalt.[219] Epidemien breiteten sich in der Enge besonders einfach aus[220], zumal sich die hygienischen Bedingungen nicht grundsätzlich verbesserten: Noch Ende des Jahres 1959 war der gesamte Wohnbestand des Magadaner Gebietes nur zu einem geringen Teil mit Wasserleitungen, einer Zentralheizung oder Bädern ausgestattet.[221]

Für die überwiegende Mehrheit der Bewohner des Magadaner Gebietes waren die so schlecht ausgestatteten Baracken der einzig vorhandene Rückzugs- und Regenerationsraum. In den ehemaligen Lagerbaracken mussten an Öfen die schwere, nasse Arbeitskleidung getrocknet, Kleidung und Schuhe repariert und die Bewohner immer wieder auch von Ungeziefer und Läusen befreit werden.[222] Die fehlende Infrastruktur setzte sich vor der Barackentür fort, nur in sehr wenigen Siedlungen gab es Trottoirs, ganz selten Mülleimer oder Straßenreinigungen. Sehr viel Abfall wurde einfach vor die

---

217 Zur Gestaltung dieser Wohnräume siehe die ausführlichen Angaben zum Jahresergebnis 1956 von Dal'stroj in GAMO f. R-23, op. 1, d. 4897, l. 3–119, hier l. 35.

218 Vgl. GAMO f. R-146, op. 1, d. 221, l. 73. Zur Weiterverwendung von Lagerbaracken vgl. die Pläne von Dal'stroj aus dem Jahr 1956 in GAMO f. R-23sč, op. 1, d. 462, l. 196. Aufgrund der schlechten Qualität der noch immer benutzten Holzbaracken warnten die Verantwortlichen in Anadyr' vor ihrem Zusammenbruch. Vgl. den Bericht des Kontorleiters für Kommunalwirtschaft in Tschukotka an den Vorsitzenden des Exekutivkomitees von Tschukotka, an den Leiter der Abteilung für Kommunalwirtschaft des Magadaner Exekutivkomitees sowie an Afanas'ev vom 4. März 1957 in GAMO f. R-146, op. 1, d. 50, l. 105–110, hier l. 106.

219 Vgl. das Schreiben des Gebietsexekutivkomitees an den Ministerrat der RSFSR vom 12. August 1959 in GAMO f. R-146, op. 1, d. 50, l. 222. Immer wieder werden vollkommen vereiste Innenwände erwähnt.

220 Siehe die Angaben der Gesundheitsabteilung des Gebietsexekutivkomitees zu den gesundheitlichen Auswirkungen der Wohnsituation in GAMO f. R-146, op. 1, d. 105, l. 16–40, hier l. 34.

221 30 % der Häuser hatten eine Wasserleitung, 55,9 % eine Zentralheizung, lediglich 13,1 % ein Bad. Über einen Anschluss an die Kanalisation verfügten nur 21,6 %. Vgl. den Bericht des Leiters der Statistikverwaltung des Magadaner Gebietes zum 1. Januar 1960 in GAMO f. R-146, op. 1, d. 442, l. 1–5. Beschreibungen der Bauorganisation *Magadanstroj* zeigen, dass auch Mitte der 1950er Jahre noch immer sehr viele Baracken und einfache Holzhäuser, ohne Kanalisation und Bäder, errichtet wurden. Vgl. GAMO f. R-146, op. 1, d. 105, l. 107–111. In den meisten Siedlungen in Tschukotka gab es lange Zeit keinerlei Badehäuser. Vgl. die Angaben der Gebietsgesundheitsabteilung in GAMO f. R-146, op. 1, d. 105, l. 16–40, hier l. 33. Siehe zu den Bedingungen im Susumansker Bezirk (ebenfalls 1956) GAMO f. P-21, op. 5, d. 110, l. 137–147, hier l. 139.

222 Zum noch immer anhaltenden Mangel an Badehäusern und Friseurstuben siehe das Schreiben des Vorsitzenden des Magadaner Exekutivkomitees, Ivanenko, an den Vorsitzenden des Ministerrats der RSFSR vom 25. Juli 1959 in GAMO f. R-146, op. 1, d. 50, l. 213f. Ivanenko bat auch um die Bereitstellung weiterer Gelder, um eine bereits beschlossene Verordnung zum Bau neuer Sanitätseinrichtungen umsetzen zu können.

Tür geworfen, immer wieder beschwerten sich Verantwortliche über offene Müllkippen direkt neben Lebensmittelläden oder Krankenstationen. Die Kantinen der Siedlungen, auf die die Menschen wegen fehlender Küchen unbedingt angewiesen waren, waren oft in einem erbärmlichen hygienischen Zustand.[223] Hygieneprobleme entstanden auch durch das Fehlen einer gesicherten Trinkwasserversorgung, Wassersammelbecken waren oft verschmutzt, Trinkwasser floss direkt durch Abwässer.[224] Erst Ende des Jahres 1959 konnte eine etwas bessere allgemeine Ausstattung der Siedlungen mit Müllcontainern verzeichnet werden, eine reguläre Straßenreinigung gab es noch immer nicht.[225]

Die Lebensbedingungen der Magadaner Bevölkerung waren insgesamt stark von ihrem Wohnort abhängig. Diese Tendenz verstärkte sich im Laufe der Zeit. Die durch gewaltige Migrationsströme, Modernisierungstendenzen und die Entstehung neuer industrieller Zentren ausgelösten Wellen der Urbanisierung, die Thomas Bohn mit Blick auf die gesamte Sowjetunion seit Stalins Tod beschreibt[226], erreichten seit Mitte der 1950er Jahre allmählich auch das Magadaner Gebiet. Nicht nur wurden die Bezirkszentren in städtebaulicher Hinsicht besser ausgestattet, sie erhielten an erster Stelle Kanalisation, Wasserversorgung und z. T. auch Bürgersteige. Durch ihre institutionelle und verwaltungstechnische Rolle wurde auch die soziale Infrastruktur für ihre Bewohner ausgebaut. Krankenhäuser und Polikliniken sollten in den Bezirkszentren eine versorgende Rolle für das Umland übernehmen, ebenso wie Schulen und die Lebensmittelindustrie. All diese Einrichtungen sollten gewissermaßen in die Bezirke ausstrahlen. Dass die Bewohner der Bezirke aufgrund fehlender Straßen, Busverbindungen und Flugzeuge diese Angebote oft überhaupt nicht in Anspruch nehmen konnten, schien die Verantwortlichen dabei weniger zu beunruhigen.

Städten wie Jagodnoe oder Susuman gelang es auf diesem Wege, ihre infrastrukturelle Ausstattung von ihrer industriellen Bedeutung abzukoppeln und als *Bezirkszentren* eine deutlich bessere Infrastruktur zu erhalten. Ende der 1950er Jahre lassen sich tatsächlich einige Ortschaften ausmachen, die annähernd den Vorstel-

---

223 Siehe zu den Verhältnissen bei der Lebensmittelzubereitung und in den Kantinen die Berichte an Afanas'ev in GAMO f. R-146, op. 1, d. 219, l. 48–53 (für 1956) und 32–34 (für 1957) sowie einen mündlichen Bericht in einer Mitschrift eines Treffens des Leitungsgremiums des Magadaner Volkswirtschaftsrates vom 10. September 1958 in GAMO f. R-137, op. 1, d. 58, l. 270–313, hier l. 286.
224 Im Bezirk Anadyr' in Tschukotka gab es große Probleme mit fehlendem Trinkwasser. Die Bevölkerung war im Winter auf aufgetautes Eis angewiesen, im Sommer auf Wasser von sehr schlechter Qualität aus verunreinigten Seen in erheblicher Entfernung zu den Wohngebieten. Vgl. einen entsprechenden Bericht aus dem Jahr 1954 in GAMO f. R 146, op. 1, d. 50, l. 6. Dieses Problem war auch 1957 noch nicht behoben worden, die Bevölkerung war noch immer auf die Seen angewiesen. Vgl. den Bericht des Kontor-Leiters für Kommunalwirtschaft in Tschukotka vom 4. März 1957 in GAMO f. R-146, op. 1, d. 50, l. 105–110, hier l. 106. Siehe zur sowjetischen Trinkwasserversorgung Filtzer, Water Supply.
225 Siehe die Angaben des leitenden Arztes der Gebietssanitärepidemiestation für das Jahr 1959 in GAMO f. R-146, op. 1, d. 220 l. 48–68, hier l. 56.
226 Vgl. Bohn, Minsk, S. 302 sowie für die Städte Osteuropas Bohn, Sozialistische Stadt. Siehe ebenso Ivanova, Na poroge, S. 152.

Abb. 47 Fotoalbum zum 25. Jahrestag der Erhebung Magadans zur Stadt, 1939–1964

lungen von sowjetischen regionalen „Zentren" entsprachen. Die Anwesenheit einer zunehmenden Zahl von Facharbeitern mit ihren Ansprüchen an eine gewisse Infrastruktur sorgte dabei zusätzlich für das Anwachsen eines einigermaßen annehmbaren Wohnungsbestandes. Da der Anteil der Menschen, die im Magadaner Gebiet in Städten oder Arbeitersiedlungen lebten, ausgesprochen hoch war, verbesserten sich dadurch die Lebensverhältnisse einer großen Zahl von Magadanern auf längere Sicht deutlich.[227]

Der Hauptstadt Magadan kam dabei eine besondere Rolle zu. Die Bedingungen waren hier in den ersten Jahren durch die schnell wachsende Bevölkerungszahl und die Masse der Reisenden besonders schlecht, Epidemien verbreiteten sich sehr schnell.[228] Magadan war nach Gründung des Gebietes keine Stadt, die den Vorstellungen von einem zivilen Gebietszentrum entsprach, sie hatte das Erscheinungsbild einer „Lagerhauptstadt", in der der Anteil bewaffneter Personen im Straßenbild sehr

227 Ende der 1950er Jahre lebten ca. 75 % der Magadaner in Städten oder Arbeitersiedlungen, im Unionsdurchschnitt waren es 48 %. In Tschukotka war jedoch der Anteil der Menschen in Dörfern erheblich größer. Vgl. Slavin, Promyšlennoe osvoenie, S. 248. Zur sozialen Lage im Magadaner Gebiet Mitte der 1960er Jahre vgl. den ausführlichen Bericht von Afanas'ev an das ZK der KPdSU in GAMO f. P-21, op. 5, d. 502, l. 58 – 86.
228 Siehe zu den hygienischen Bedingungen in Magadan die Angaben der Gebietsgesundheitsabteilung aus dem Jahr 1955 in GAMO f. R-146, op. 1, d. 105, l. 16 – 40, hier l. 35.

hoch war.[229] So beschreibt sie auch der stellvertretende Vorsitzende des Ministerrates der RSFSR, D. M. Alechin, bei seinem Besuch im Herbst 1955:

> Die Stadt [gemeint ist die Hauptstadt Magadan – M. S.] ruft einen schlechten Eindruck hervor. Sie ist voller Müll. [...] Zum Beispiel wird direkt neben dem Hotel Müll gesammelt und dann von dort aus in der ganzen Stadt verteilt. [...] Auch die Miliz muss die notwendigen Maßnahmen in den Straßen ergreifen, in denen sich Privathäuser befinden. [...] Und mir scheint, die Lager müssen aus der Stadt gebracht werden. Die Sache ist inzwischen so weit, dass sogar Wachtürme in der Stadt stehen. Ihr seid natürlich schon daran gewöhnt. Tja, und die Benennung des Restaurants – ‚Kolyma'! Warum ist das denn notwendig? Im Volk hat die Kolyma eine negative Bedeutung bekommen. Ich will die Kolyma nicht verleumden. Aber dafür gibt es doch keine Notwendigkeit. Die Frage der Lager muss gelöst werden. Nicht in diesem Jahr, aber im nächsten, die Lager müssen unbedingt aus der Stadt gebracht werden.[230]

Tatsächlich gab es seit 1951 ein eigenes Lager für die Stadt Magadan („Maglag") sowie Abteilungen des *Berlag*. Noch 1954 waren in der Stadt 11.000 Menschen inhaftiert, dazu kamen große Abteilungen bewaffneter Lagerwachen.[231] Mit Verweis auf den neuen Status als Gebietshauptstadt wurde schließlich beschlossen, die im Stadtgebiet gelegenen Lagerabteilungen aufzugeben, 1956 wurde das Lager aufgelöst, die Zahl der waffentragenden Personen verringerte sich dementsprechend.[232]

Bis Ende der 1950er Jahre veränderte sich das Gesicht der Stadt deutlich: Breite Straßen mit Bürgersteigen wurden angelegt, für Magadaner Verhältnisse „prächtige Gebäude" und Hotels errichtet. Von 1954 bis 1960 stieg der Bau neuer Wohneinheiten von jährlich 8.000 auf 25.000; aufgrund des enormen Bedarfs in der Gebietshauptstadt war das dennoch zu wenig. Ein großer Sportpalast, weitere Schulen und Hochschulen, Kinos, Klubs, ein Erholungspark sowie spezialisierte Gesundheitseinrichtungen wurden eröffnet. Wie so oft in der sowjetischen Geschichte bediente sich auch die Magadaner Leitung des Topos „Bau", um den sozialen und infrastrukturellen Aufbau zu untermauern. Bilder von der Errichtung neuer Wohnhäuser, wissenschaftlicher Institute, der Anlage von Parks und befestigten Straßen durchzogen die Seiten der *Magadanskaja Pravda* und zahlreicher Publikationen – wie hier in einem Fotoalbum zum 25. Jahrestag der Erhebung Magadans zur Stadt (Abbildung 47).

Sie erweckten den Eindruck einer völlig zivilen Ortschaft und eines urbanen Raumes, der die Möglichkeiten des neuen Gebietes verkörpern und Hoffnungen auf

---

229 In der ersten Zeit waren, so Pantjuchin in seinen Erinnerungen, selbst alle zivilen Staatsanwälte und Mitarbeiter der Miliz zum ständigen Tragen einer Waffe verpflichtet. Vgl. Pantjuchin, Zapiski, S. 86f.

230 Alechin gegenüber Funktionären des Gebietsexekutivkomitees, zitiert nach Grebenjuk, Kolymskij led, S. 85.

231 Zu den Angaben von 1954 siehe Verkina/Kozlov, K voprosu ob obrazovanii, S. 114. Die Häftlinge des „Maglag" – Magadanskij ITL wurden in diversen Fabriken und zum Bau zahlreicher Gebäude eingesetzt. Vgl. Smirnov, Spravočnik, S. 318.

232 Vgl. die Mitschrift eines Treffens im Gebietsparteikomitee zu Fragen einer Verbesserung des Häftlingsregimes in GAMO f. P-21, op. 5, d. 765, l. 1–16, hier l. 4.

СКОРО В МАГАДАНЕ

Перенесемся мыслью на несколько лет вперед, и мы увидим на месте теперешнего пустыря между парком культуры и областной больницей благоустроенную городскую площадь. В самом начале проспекта им. Ленина, где сейчас тянется высокий серый забор у складов Колымснаба, вырастут многоэтажные красные дома. На углу будет один из входов в парк культуры. Но украшением и подлинной новинкой архитектурного ансамбля станет легкая, устремленная к облакам металлическая мачта Магаданского телевизионного центра.

Все это — совсем не фантазия: один дом по правой стороне проспекта уже строится; сооружение мачты также началось, и магаданцы могут видеть вырытые котлованы под фундаменты ее опор.

Мачта нашего будущего телевизионного центра устанавливается на самом высоком месте в городе. При своей пятидесятиметровой высоте, равной высоте 15-этажного дома, мачта будет господствовать над городом, ее увидят отовсюду. Впоследствии у опор мачты разобьют сквер, где в погожие дни будут отдыхать магаданцы.

Мачту телевизионного центра проектировали инженеры Дальстройпроекта тт. Андреев и Бабашинский. Ее сборные стальные конструкции (17 узлов общим весом около 20 тонн) уже изготовляются на Марчеканском заводе. Монтаж и окраску мачты алюминиевой краской, оборудование на ней электрического освещения и телефонной связи — все это предполагается делать на земле. В собранном виде готовая к работе мачта будет поднята и окончательно установлена на месте при помощи электролебедок и подъемного крана.

На мачте намечено оборудовать три площадки, огражденные решетчатыми панелями. На первой площадке, на высоте 13 метров над землей, будет установлено для освещения новой площади и проспекта им. Ленина 8 прожекторов общей мощностью 5,5 киловатт. На высоте 29 метров оборудуется вторая площадка, предназначенная для отдыха обслуживающего персонала. Не легко ведь было бы радистам без передышки подниматься по наружной металлической лестнице на самый верх мачты, на третью площадку, где устанавливаются вибраторы телецентра!

...Сооружение мачты продолжится несколько месяцев, но можно надеяться, что в ночь на 7 ноября 1957 года на ней уже зажгутся огни праздничной иллюминации.

В. СОФРОНОВ,
старший инженер управления «Дальстройпроект».

На рисунке: так будет выглядеть новая площадь.

(Рис. архитектора А. Липковского).

В честь славной годовщины

В начале января, подводя итоги работы за минувший год, коллектив Магаданской автотранспортной конторы решил начать соревнование за достойную встречу 40-й годовщины Великой Октябрьской социалистиче-

Abb. 48 Bericht über die bevorstehende Errichtung des Sendemastes, Magadanskaja Pravda, 31. Januar 1957

eine Verbesserung der allgemeinen Lage wecken sollte. Sinnbild für diese „Leuchtturmpolitik" war das 1957 errichtete Wahrzeichen der Stadt, ein Sendemast des neuen Fernsehstudios, gelegen auf dem höchsten Punkt der Stadt, am Beginn der Leninstraße und der Trasse durch das Magadaner Gebiet. Der Sendemast verkörperte den neuen Status des Gebietes als Kultur- und Wissenschaftsstandort und zugleich die Verbindung mit den übrigen Teilen der Sowjetunion.[233]

---

233 Vgl. den Bericht über den wirtschaftlichen und kulturellen Aufbau der Stadt Magadan von 1959 in GAMO f. R-146, op. 1, d. 344, l. 1–23. Zum Stichtag 1. Januar 1959 liegt ein statistischer Vergleich zwischen dem Stand an sozialer Infrastruktur in der Stadt Magadan und dem Mittelwert der gesamten UdSSR vor. Demnach gab es in der UdSSR für eine Person 5,9 m² Wohnraum, in der Stadt Magadan waren es 3,9 m². Bei der Zahl der Plätze, bezogen auf 1.000 Einwohner, gab es in Schulen in der UdSSR 92, in der Stadt Magadan 44; in Krankenhäusern in der UdSSR 7,4, in der Stadt Magadan 14,9; in Kinos in der UdSSR 18,8 in der Stadt Magadan 10; in Hotels in der Union 2, in der Stadt Magadan hingegen 2,8 (wahrscheinlich aufgrund der Bedeutung der Stadt für Dienstreisende). Bei der Kanalisation hatte die

Abb. 49 Mittelschule Nr. 1, Magadan Dezember 1960 (RGAKFD Krasnogorsk, 0-370739, Fotograf: B.E. Vdovenko)

Abb. 50a und 50b Lenindenkmal vor dem Hauptgebäude von Dal'stroj bzw. dem Volkswirtschaftsrat, Magadan Dezember 1960 (RGAKFD Krasnogorsk, 0-370743, Fotograf: B.E. Vdovenko)

Die Veränderungen waren auch im kulturellen Bereich greifbar. Das „Magadaner Theater" wurde seit dem Frühjahr 1954 nicht mehr über das Dal'strojer Kontor für Filmverleih finanziert. Dieser banale und rein formal erscheinende Akt entzog der Leitung von Dal'stroj schlagartig den Zugriff auf ein Theater, das auch im Rahmen der

---

Stadt Magadan fast den Unionsdurchschnitt erreicht, bei der Wasserversorgung in etwa die Hälfte. Vgl. diese und weitere statistische Angaben in GARF f. A-259, op. 42, d. 5281, l. 73. Zur Darstellung Magadans siehe v. a. Zvik, Magadan sowie Vospominanija zaslužennogo stroitelja.

Abb. 51 Hotel „Magadan", Magadan Dezember 1960 (RGAKFD Krasnogorsk, 0-370741, Fotograf: B.E. Vdovenko)

Abb. 52 Kinotheater „Gornjak", Magadan Dezember 1960 (RGAKFD Krasnogorsk, 0-370740, Fotograf: B.E. Vdovenko)

Abb. 53 Gorki-Theater, Magadan Dezember 1960 (RGAKFD Krasnogorsk, 0-370744, Fotograf: B.E. Vdovenko)

im GULAG üblichen Ausbeutung inhaftierter Künstler einen Sonderstatus innegehabt hatte. Seit seinem Bau im Jahr 1941 hatte der gewaltige Bau einen Klub, eine Bibliothek und einen Theatersaal beherbergt. Schon rein architektonisch war das Haus als Einrichtung der Dal'stroj-Offiziere von weitem erkennbar; die allegorischen Figuren auf dem Dach des Theaters zeigten Offiziere mit Maschinengewehren und eine Bäuerin – plakative Umsetzung der Idee einer militärischen Kultur- und Vergnügungsstätte. Das Theater hatte sich zu einer Art „grausamem Spleen" der obersten Dal'stroj-Führung entwickelt. Berühmte verhaftete sowjetische Künstler, wie Leonid Vegener, der Pianist Ananij Švarcburg und der Regisseur Leonid Varpachovskij, ein früherer Assistent und Freund Mejerchol'ds, wurden in Magadan im Theater zusammengebracht.[234] In ihren Erinnerungen berichtet die Frau von Varpachovskij, die Künstlerin Ida Varpachovskaja, von der erfolgreichen Opernaufführung „Traviata", die in der Zeitung *Sovetskaja Kolyma* frenetisch gefeiert wurde – „nur Namen wurden nicht genannt, nicht der Regisseur, nicht die Künstler – alles Häftlinge!"[235] Den Häftlingen half die gemeinsame künstlerische Arbeit zu überleben, auch wenn diese Arbeit sie sogleich in tödliche Gefahr bringen konnte, wie den Häftling Leonid Vegener beim Zeichnen eines Stalin-Porträts.[236]

---

234 Spielpläne, Ensembles und Häftlingsschicksale hat Inna Klause in ihrer jüngsten Studie anschaulich aufgearbeitet, vgl. Klause, Klang des Gulag.
235 Varpachovskaja, Kolymskoj Traviaty, S. 78.
236 Vgl. Vegener, Vospominanija, S. 188–190.

Abb. 54 Zentrale Leninstraße, Magadan Dezember 1960. Die Leninstraße geht am Ende der Stadt in die „Trasse" des Magadaner Gebietes über (RGAKFD Krasnogorsk, 0-370737, Fotograf: B.E. Vdovenko)

Nach 1954 wurde dieses berühmt-berüchtigte Theater nun zum Gebietstheater, finanziert über das Kulturministerium, und zog in den folgenden Jahren immer wieder bekannte Künstler an, die von Magadan aus zu vielen nationalen und internationalen Gastspielen aufbrachen.[237] Nach seiner Rehabilitation im Jahr 1955 konnte der ehemalige Häftling Vegener als Künstlerischer Leiter selbst die Verantwortung für das Haus übernehmen; er wollte das Magadaner Gebiet in den ersten Jahren nicht verlassen, zu eng waren seine Bindungen an das dortige Theater.[238]

Doch nicht nur in kulturellen, auch in ganz praktischen Fragen erlebte ein Teil der Bewohner der Hauptstadt relativ schnell eine Besserung seiner Lebensbedingungen. So z. B. die Publizistin Evgenija Ginzburg, die, kurz nach dem Ende ihrer Verbannung in Magadan, im Frühjahr 1955 beauftragt wurde, Vorträge am Institut für pädagogische Fortbildung zu halten. Zu ihren Schülern zählten u. a. die Leiter der Abteilung für Volksbildung beim Stadt- und beim Gebietsexekutivkomitee. Für sie und ihre Familie brachte diese unerwartete Aufwertung eine erhebliche Veränderung ihrer Wohnsituation:

---

237 Vgl. Ledovskoj, Melodii, S. 17.
238 Vgl. Vegener, O Leonide Vegenere, S. 427

Abb. 55a und 55b Zentrale Leninstraße, Magadan Dezember 1960 (RGAKFD Krasnogorsk, 0-370738, Fotograf: B.E. Vdovenko)

Nach diesen Besuchen wurden wir plötzlich mit himmlischem Manna überschüttet. Ich wurde ins städtische Wohnungsamt vorgeladen, zu einem Gespräch über ,die Verbesserung der Wohnverhältnisse'. Das einstöckige Holzhaus an der Kommunestraße [...] kam uns vor wie das Schloß von Versailles. Wir bekamen ein Zimmer mit zwanzig Quadratmetern in einer Wohnung, in der außer uns nur noch zwei Familien lebten. Und das nach der Baracke von Nagajewo [die Magadaner Bucht – M. S.] mit ihren neunundzwanzig Mitbewohnern! In der Wohnung befanden sich eine schöne Küche, ein Bad, eine geheizte Toilette. Ungläubig drehten Anton [Ginzburgs Ehemann – M. S.] und ich die Wasserhähne im Bad auf und berührten andächtig die Kacheln des Küchenherdes. Das Geräusch der Wasserspülung in der Toilette schien uns wie ein Zeichen aus einer anderen Welt. Denn eines hatten wir in den letzten zwanzig Jahren ganz gewiß nicht gesehen – ein Wasserklosett. Ein noch größeres Wunder war der Telefonapparat, der plötzlich auf unserem Schreibtisch stand. Man beglückte uns damit, als Anton im Krankenhaus auf die für die Oberen reservierte Station versetzt wurde.[239]

An der Wohnsituation der Familie von Evgenija Ginzburg wird zugleich deutlich, dass die Zuteilungen der neuen Führung zwar nicht mehr den stalinistischen Kategorien folgten, dass sie aber nichtsdestotrotz an bestimmte Bedingungen und an die Bedeutung einzelner Personen geknüpft waren. Zwar unterlag Ginzburg offiziell zu dieser Zeit noch der Verbannung, ihre Rehabilitation als eine alte Parteifunktionärin aus den 1930er Jahren war jedoch schon in Vorbereitung und erfolgte kurz darauf in Moskau, ihr Mann hatte als berühmter Arzt eine hohe Bedeutung für die neue Elite der Stadt. Mit dem neuen Zimmer sollte der Familie wohl auch ein gewichtiges Argument für ein weiteres Verbleiben an der Kolyma geliefert werden.

Neben diesen personenbezogenen Zuteilungen offenbart sich beim Blick auf die gesamte Region ein starkes geographisches Gefälle: Auch wenn die großen Programme zum Aufbau des Magadaner Gebietes auf dem Papier darauf abzielten, allgemeinverbindliche Standards einzuführen und den Aufbau der sozialen Infrastruktur in allen Bezirken vorsahen[240], war die geographische Lage und die industrielle

---

239 Ginsburg, Gratwanderung, S. 457 f.
240 Die Pläne für die Eröffnung neuer Goldförderungsanlagen sahen zu Beginn der 1960er Jahre tatsächlich ganz anders aus als noch unter den Bedingungen des Lager-Industriellen Komplexes. Im

Bedeutung einer Ortschaft noch immer ausschlaggebend für die Lebensbedingungen seiner Bewohner.[241] Ganz besonders problematisch war die Lage in Siedlungen, die von den großen Infrastrukturprogrammen bislang kaum berührt worden waren, zumeist in sehr entlegenen Bezirken des Gebietes.

Im Čaunsker Bezirk des Čukotsker Kreises mit der nördlichsten Stadt der Sowjetunion, Pevek, traten die Probleme besonders geballt auf.[242] Der Čaunsker Bezirk hatte im Spätstalinismus und kurz nach Stalins Tod die Rolle einer Art Auffanglager für besonders schwerkriminelle Häftlinge innerhalb des *Sevvostlag* gespielt.[243] Hier gab es bis zur Gründung des Magadaner Gebietes fast überhaupt keine Infrastruktur für freie Arbeitskräfte. Die große Entfernung des Gebietes, die Kosten für Baumaterialien, fehlende Waren und Bauarbeiter sorgten für einen erheblichen ungestillten Bedarf an Wohnraum. Obwohl in diesem Bezirk die Durchschnittstemperatur selbst in den wärmsten Sommermonaten nur an der Küste knapp über 0 °C liegt, wurden Neuankommende in Zelten untergebracht, in der Grube Komsomol'skij mussten Arbeiter in zwei Schichten in den Wohnheimen schlafen. Hinzu kam ein hohes Maß an Kriminalität durch entlassene kriminelle Häftlinge und große Schwierigkeiten mit Alkoholismus. Neue Arbeitskräfte drängten hier besonders auf eine schnelle Abreise, die Fluktuation betrug selbst im Jahr 1959 noch 47 %.[244] In Regionen wie diesen erlebten die Menschen die Widersprüche zwischen dem Anspruch der neuen Leitung und ihrer realen Lage hautnah als krassen Gegensatz zwischen dem nahezu unendlichen Reichtum des Naturraumes und den eigenen erbärmlichen Lebensverhältnissen, zwischen der schier unendlichen Weite des Territoriums und der Begrenztheit der für sie zugänglichen Räume; im Mangel an Wohn- und Baderäumen, an Räumen zur

---

Čaunsker Bezirk plante das Exekutivkomitee seit 1960 ausführlich die Anlage von Telefonkabeln, den Bau von Schule, Kindergarten, Krankenhaus, Internat, Läden, Kantine etc. für eine Anlage, die 1962 in Betrieb gehen sollte. Was schließlich unter den gegebenen Verhältnissen tatsächlich errichtet wurde, ist allerdings eine ganz andere Frage. Vgl. den Bericht in GAMO f. R-146, op. 1, d. 442, l. 39–40.

241 Siehe beispielsweise den Bericht über die Menschen aus dem Ten'kinsker Bezirk, die zur Arbeit an einer der Trassen herangezogen wurden, in GAMO f. R-146, op. 1, d. 53, l. 8 f. Ebenso den Bericht über die miserable Versorgung der indigenen Bewohner in der Siedlung „Chatyrka" am oberen Verlauf des Flusses „Chatyrka", deren Belieferung per Flugzeug 1956 eingestellt wurde, GAMO f. R-146, op. 1, d. 53, l. 62–63.

242 Aufgrund der extremen Entfernung und der schweren Zugänglichkeit dieses Bezirkes war die Čaun-Čukotsker Bergbauverwaltung das einzige organisatorische Mittelglied, das bei der Einführung des Magadaner Volkswirtschaftsrates erhalten wurde. Siehe dazu Kapitel 3.3.4.

243 In der Region bestand zwischen 1949 und 1957 die Lagerverwaltung „Čaunčukotlag". Siehe zur sozialen Situation in dem Gebiet den Bericht über die Tätigkeit von Dal'stroj für das Jahr 1954 in GAMO f. R-23sč, op. 1, d. 4843, l. 1–74, hier l. 17.

244 Vgl. den Vortrag über die Arbeit mit Kadern im Jahr 1959 in der Čaun-Čukotsker Bergbauverwaltung in GAMO f. R-137, op. 1, d. 996, l. 3–115, hier l. 32. Vgl. zur Lage der gesamten Halbinsel Tschukotka den Bericht der Partei- und Staatsleitung des Kreises an Afanas'ev und Ivanenko vom 19. Januar 1959 in GAMO f. R-146, op. 1, d. 57, l. 89–95.

На северном КУРОРТЕ

Ⱨ ОВЕНЬКИЙ синий автобус въезжает в широкую котло- вину, со всех сторон окружённую | культуры, аптека и специальное детское отделение. Здесь же па- латы на 80 человек. небольшая | лет назад весь посёлок насчиты- вал десяток избушек. Санаторий

Abb. 56 Werbung für den Kurort Talaja, Magadanskaja Pravda, 26. Juni 1957

Ausbildung, an Regenerationsräumen, an geschützten Räumen, v. a. für Frauen und Kinder.[245]

5.3.3 Medizinische Versorgung

Im Laufe der 1950er Jahre verbesserte sich die medizinische Versorgung der Bevölkerung insgesamt in vielen Bereichen, zahlreiche neue Einrichtungen wurden geschaffen. Der Kurort Talaja, der einzige sowjetische Kurort nördlich des Polarkreises, der für die Führung von Dal'stroj geschaffen worden war, stand nun theoretisch allen Bewohnern des Gebietes zur Verfügung.

Doch mit Ausnahme dieser Gebietsattraktivität war auch im Bereich der Krankenversorgung die geographische Lage einer Siedlung von außerordentlicher Bedeutung – nur in der Stadt Magadan waren alle benötigten Fachabteilungen und

---

245 Die Verhältnisse in diesen Gebieten lassen sich in vielem mit den Bedingungen vergleichen, unter denen die Arbeiter in den als „Neuland" bezeichneten Regionen in der Kasachischen SSR leben mussten, die seit Mitte der 1950er Jahre intensiv urbar gemacht und ausgebeutet werden sollten. Vgl. zu den Verhältnissen im „Neuland" ausführlich Kozlov, Mass Uprisings, S. 23 – 85 sowie Mc Cauley, Soviet Agriculture und Pohl, Tselinograd; Pohl, Virgin Lands.

Spezialisten anzutreffen.[246] Der Anteil der Überweisungen aus anderen Bezirken machte im Magadaner Gebietskrankenhaus 13,8 % aus; der tatsächliche Bedarf war jedoch sehr viel höher, sehr viele Patienten mussten abgewiesen werden. Allein auf Operationen warteten im Jahr 1956 300 Menschen. Aus Kapazitätsgründen wurden Kranke häufig unmittelbar nach einer OP wieder entlassen, trotz erheblicher medizinischer Risiken.[247] Zudem profitierten die nördlichen Bezirke aufgrund der schlechten Infrastruktur erheblich weniger von den zentralen Gebietseinrichtungen.[248]

Der allgemeine Trend zum Neuaufbau und zur institutionellen Ausdifferenzierung kann nicht über die harten Realitäten der 1950er Jahre hinwegtäuschen, vor allem nicht über den großen Kadermangel. 1956 waren in medizinischen Berufen 415 Stellen unbesetzt, davon 100 Ärztestellen. Und dies, obwohl allein im Jahr 1955 vom Gesundheitsministerium der RSFSR 89 neue Ärzte und knapp 400 Angehörige des medizinischen Personals in das Gebiet geschickt worden waren.[249] Der Kadermangel innerhalb der neuen Strukturen war besonders bei Spezialisten ausgeprägt. Angesichts der schweren Lebens- und Arbeitsbedingungen hatten die lokalen Stellen die größten Schwierigkeiten, Chirurgen, Gynäkologen, Röntgenärzte etc. anzuwerben und dauerhaft an eine Gesundheitseinrichtung zu binden. Dem zukünftigen Personal konnte einfach kein angemessener Standard geboten werden.[250] Im Bezirk Iul'tinskij

---

246 So war der institutionelle Aufbau im Bereich der Kindermedizin noch immer unzureichend. Spezielle pädiatrische Einrichtungen gab es 1956 lediglich in zwei Bezirken, ansonsten wurden Kinder wie Erwachsene behandelt, was sich sehr negativ auf ihre Genesung auswirkte. Vgl. die Angaben der Gebietsgesundheitsabteilung in GAMO f. R-146, op. 1, d. 105, l. 16–40, hier l. 20.

247 Der Krankenhausleiter sprach für das Jahr 1956 von etwa 1.000 Menschen aus den Bezirken, die trotz dringendem Bedarf nicht in seinem Krankenhaus aufgenommen werden konnten. Bei dieser Angabe handelte es sich um eine Schätzung, da viele Anfragen aus den Bezirken bereits im Vorfeld, per Telefon oder Brief, abgewiesen wurden. Vgl. GAMO f. R-307, op. 1, d. 6, l. 30–137, hier l. 35 f.

248 Ausnahmen waren meist Kader, die eine Dienstreise in die Gebietshauptstadt für einen Arztbesuch nutzen konnten. Ein erhebliches infrastrukturelles Problem waren auch die fehlenden Unterbringungsmöglichkeiten für Patienten aus anderen Bezirken in Magadan. Häufig wurden sie im Gebietskrankenhaus zwar untersucht, aber nicht aufgenommen. Vgl. GAMO f. R-307, op. 1, d. 6, l. 30–137, hier l. 68.

249 Vgl. den Bericht der Gebietsgesundheitsabteilung in GAMO f. R-146, op. 1, d. 105, l. 1–6, hier l. 4 sowie die Kaderangaben der Gebietsgesundheitsabteilung in GAMO f. R-146, op. 1, d. 105, l. 7–15, hier l. 7–8. Der Kadermangel hat die Gebietsabteilung für Gesundheitsschutz seit ihrer Gründung begleitet. Bereits am 4. Februar 1954 hatte Afanas'ev den Vorsitzenden des Ministerrates der RSFSR um medizinisches Personal für das Gebiet gebeten. Vgl. GAMO f. R-146, op. 1, d. 59, l. 10. Weitere Beschwerden und Bitten von Seiten des Exekutivkomitees an den Ministerrat der RSFSR folgten in den nächsten Jahren. Vgl. die Bitte vom 4. Januar 1955 in GAMO f. R-146, op. 1, d. 56, l. 13. Selbst im Gebietskrankenhaus in Magadan waren 1956 noch nicht alle Stellen besetzt, hier fehlten acht Ärzte. Vgl. GAMO f. R-307, op. 1, d. 6, l. 30–137, hier l. 33.

250 Siehe das Schreiben aus Jagodnoe zum dortigen Mangel an medizinischem Personal an Afanas'ev vom 5. Mai 1957 in GAMO f. R-146, op. 1, d. 219, l. 25–26. In vielen Fällen waren die lokalen Behörden gar nicht in der Lage, den Ärzten, Pflegern und Krankenschwestern angemessene Wohnräume zur Verfügung zu stellen. Oft mussten sie direkt in den Wirtschaftsräumen der Gesundheitseinrichtungen

waren selbst im Jahr 1959 von 29 Arztstellen nur 15 besetzt, von den formal vorhandenen Ärzten waren zudem einige im monatelangen Urlaub. Diese extreme Unterversorgung war für die Menschen sehr gefährlich, in dem Bezirkskrankenhaus gab es nicht einmal einen ausgebildeten Chirurgen, seine Stelle hatte eine unerfahrene Gynäkologin übernommen.[251] So scheiterte der Aufbau von sozialer und medizinischer Infrastruktur häufig an der schlechten Infrastruktur des Ortes selbst.

Generell waren die Schwierigkeiten mit Personen, die als „junge Facharbeiter" für die Region geworben worden waren, im medizinischen Bereich besonders groß. Das Gesundheitsministerium der RSFSR schickte sehr viele junge, unerfahrene Kader, die sogenannten „jungen Facharbeiter", die sich gegen eine Zuweisung in den Hohen Norden nicht wehren konnten und die in der Abgeschiedenheit kleiner Krankenhäuser und Polikliniken kaum Chancen auf Hospitation oder Konsultation bei erfahrenen Ärzten hatten.[252]

Viele kleine Einrichtungen waren zudem in einem erbärmlichen Zustand, wie folgende Beispiele illustrieren sollen: So war das Krankenhaus in der Siedlung Orotukan[253], 500 km nördlich von Magadan im Bezirk Jagodnoe, vollkommen heruntergekommen. Es war 1935 erbaut worden und drohte inzwischen zusammenzubrechen. Wärme hielt sich in dem Gebäude nicht, im Winter herrschte in den Krankenzimmern Minusgrade. Seine Einrichtung entsprach nicht annähernd sanitären Standards – funktionierende Toiletten und Waschräume gab es nicht, der Kreißsaal war in einem schrecklichen Zustand, die Kranken wurden mit dem Heizwasser der Siedlung gewaschen.[254]

Sehr schwierig waren auch die Verhältnisse im Bezirk Susumanskij, wo es lediglich eine einzige Poliklinik gab. Aufgrund der beengten Räumlichkeiten konnte der Röntgenapparat nicht abgeschirmt, Chemikalien und Medikamente nicht getrennt gelagert werden. Hochansteckende Patienten wurden auf den allgemeinen Stationen

---

schlafen. Vgl. die Bitte des Gesundheitsministeriums der RSFSR um Wohnungsbau für Ärzte und medizinisches Personal in einem Schreiben an Afanas'ev vom 10. Oktober 1955 in GAMO f. R-146, op. 1, d. 53, l. 21.

251 Vgl. das Schreiben des lokalen Exekutivkomitees vom 14. Februar 1959 in GAMO f. R-146, op. 1, d. 219, l. 114–115.

252 Vgl. das Schreiben des Parteisekretärs N. Žicharev an das ZK der KPdSU vom 21. Juli 1956 in RGASPI f. 556, op. 23, d. 13, l. 59–60, hier l. 59. Das Gesundheitsministerium der RSFSR entschied in Reaktion auf dieses Schreiben, eine erfahrene Gynäkologin und einen erfahrenen Kinderarzt in die Region zu schicken. Vgl. RGASPI f. 556, op. 23, d. 13, l. 59–60, hier l. 61.

253 Den furchtbaren Lagerpunkt von Orotukan hat Solženicyn in „Archipel GULAG" beschrieben. Siehe Solschenizyn, Archipel, S. 350–352.

254 Die regionalen Kader baten Partei- und Staatsorgane sowie den Magadaner Volkswirtschaftsrat um einen Neubau. Vgl. den Brief der lokalen Organe von Partei und Staat vom 16. September 1957 in GAMO f. R-146, op. 1, d. 219, l. 72.

untergebracht. So kam es, dass die Poliklinik selbst die Zahl der Neuerkrankungen in dem Bezirk erheblich erhöhte.[255]

Gefährlich waren auch die Bedingungen in vielen Apotheken, die übereilt in ehemaligen Lagerbaracken eingerichtet worden waren. Labore für die Zubereitung von Medikamenten fehlten, die Desinfektion der Geräte fand in den Fluren statt, wo auch das dreckige Geschirr gespült wurde.[256] Einen Einblick in extreme infrastrukturelle Schwierigkeiten bietet der Susumansker Bezirk: Die epidemiologische Krankenstation, die – entsprechend der neuen institutionellen Vorgaben – im Bezirkszentrum Susuman eingerichtet worden war, benötigte ein Labor. Dies befand sich jedoch in der 23 Kilometer entfernt gelegenen Siedlung Neksikan. Zwischen den beiden Orten gab es keine Busverbindung; alle Patienten der Krankenstation mussten daher für Untersuchungen die Strecke zu Fuß oder per Anhalter bewältigen. Schließlich in Neksikan angekommen, warteten Patienten bei jedem Wetter auf der Straße auf ihre Untersuchung, da das Labor nur aus einem einzigen Raum bestand.[257]

Auch Krankenwagen waren Mangelware: Noch 1959 gab es in Tschukotka keinen einzigen regulären Krankentransport, weil die üblichen Fahrzeuge des Gesundheitsministeriums auf den dortigen Straßen nicht eingesetzt werden konnten; für die Krankentransporte wurden Hundeschlitten, Schiffe und gelegentlich auch Helikopter benutzt.[258]

In einem Schreiben an das ZK der KPdSU urteilte der Sekretär der Magadaner Parteileitung, Žicharev, dass unter diesen geographischen Bedingungen die Anwesenheit aller wichtigen medizinischen Spezialisten in jeder Siedlung, zumindest in jedem Bezirkszentrum unerlässlich sei. Denn im Ernstfall würde das Leben eines sowjetischen Bürgers davon abhängen, ob er über Distanzen von mehreren Hundert Kilometern rechtzeitig eine Klinik erreichen könnte.[259] Tatsächlich aber wurde das Versprechen einer besseren medizinischen Versorgung in den 1950er Jahren nur punktuell eingelöst.

---

255 Wegen dieser schlimmen Verhältnisse wollten Gewerkschaftsvertreter und verschiedene Ärzte der Poliklinik das Krankenhaus schließen lassen. Vgl. den Bericht vom 26. Juni 1957 in GAMO f. R-146, op. 1, d. 219, l. 63–64. Im Anschluss an diese Beschwerde bei der Leitung in Magadan erhielt die Klinik ein zusätzliches Gebäude, vgl. ebd., l. 65.

256 Vgl. das Schreiben der Magadaner Abteilung der Apothekenverwaltung an Afanas'ev und den Leiter der Apothekenverwaltung des Gesundheitsministeriums der RSFSR vom 21. Januar 1958 in GAMO f. R-146, op. 1, d. 219, l. 107–110, Zitat l. 108. In der Antwort aus dem Gesundheitsministerium der RSFSR wurde nur ein sehr kleiner Teil der Wünsche erfüllt, ebd., l. 111.

257 Vgl. das Schreiben Susumaner Ärzte an Afanas'ev vom 5. August 1957 in GAMO f. R-146, op. 1, d. 219, l. 61. Die Ärzte sahen in diesem Fall die Schuld beim lokalen Exekutivkomitee, da es in Susuman sehr wohl geeignete Räumlichkeiten für ein Labor gebe.

258 Čistjakov bat daher *Gosplan* in seinem Schreiben vom 25. April 1959 um die Bereitstellung geeigneter Autos. Vgl. GAMO f. R-146, op. 1, d. 219, l. 124. Die Zahl der Helikopter war für einen effektiven Krankentransport noch vollkommen unzureichend. Vgl. das Schreiben der Magadaner Fluggruppe an Čistjakov vom 30. März 1960 in GAMO f. R-146, op. 1, d. 360, l. 78.

259 Vgl. das Schreiben des Parteisekretärs Žicharev an das ZK der KPdSU vom 21. Juli 1956 in RGASPI f. 556, op. 23, d. 13, l. 59–60, hier l. 59.

Was das neue bürokratische Regime gegenüber seinen Bürgern jedoch erreichte, war eine umfassendere Kontrolle ihres Gesundheitszustandes. Zum einen war diese Kontrolle Teil erster Maßnahmen zum Arbeitsschutz, zum anderen diente sie der Bedarfsermittlung und war ein Gradmesser für die soziale Lage in den einzelnen Bezirken. Die Bevölkerung des Magadaner Gebietes litt an ausgesprochen schweren Krankheiten und war insgesamt sehr viel kränker als die Bewohner anderer Teile der Union. Dies zeigen beispielhaft Untersuchungen zu Tuberkulosefällen in der Region:

Offene Tuberkulose, bezogen auf 1.000 Einwohner[260]

	RSFSR	Magadaner Gebiet	Tschukotka
1954	k. A.	77,7	121,2
1955	19,7	76,8	155,1
1956	17,2	53,3	97,6
1957	16,2	65,8	50,5
1958	k. A.	57,0	102,1

Wie die Tabelle zeigt, war die Lage auf der Halbinsel Tschukotka ganz besonders dramatisch.[261] Indigene waren dort besonders betroffen, noch im Jahr 1959 waren ca. 14 % von ihnen an offener Tuberkulose erkrankt, in einigen Bevölkerungspunkten lag die Tuberkuloserate aller Formen bei 30 %; die Sterberate war besonders bei indigenen Kindern erschreckend hoch.[262]

---

260 Der deutliche Rückgang der Tuberkulose-Fälle in Tschukotka im Jahr 1957 beruhte auf mangelnden Reihenuntersuchungen in diesem Jahr. Vgl. den Bericht des Leiters der Gesundheitsabteilung vom 13. April 1959 in GAMO f. R-146, op. 1, d. 220, l. 33 – 37, hier l. 35. Grundsätzlich müssen Aussagen über die Verbreitung einer Krankheit immer vor dem Hintergrund der institutionellen Erschließung der Region und der Zusammensetzung der Bevölkerung gesehen werden. So waren 1955 fast doppelt so viele Einwohner im Magadaner Gebiet auf Tuberkulose untersucht worden wie noch 1954. Zugleich darf jedoch nicht davon ausgegangen werden, dass die Tuberkuloserate damit zwangsläufig höher liegen musste, da sich die Zusammensetzung der Bevölkerung in diesen beiden Jahren stark veränderte. Vgl. die Angaben der Gebietsgesundheitsabteilung in GAMO f. R-146, op. 1, d. 105, l. 16 – 40, hier l. 18.

261 Vgl. die Bitte um Unterstützung bei der Behandlung der grassierenden Tuberkulose in Tschukotka durch das Gebietsexekutivkomitee und das Gebietspartcikomitee in ihrem Schreiben an das ZK der KPdSU sowie den daraus resultierenden Bericht des Ministeriums für Gesundheit der UdSSR in RGASPI f. 556, op. 23, d. 64, l. 1 – 4, sowie l. 78 – 79.

262 Vgl. das Schreiben des Gebietsexekutivkomitees an *Gosplan* der RSFSR vom 13. Juni 1959 in GAMO f. R-146, op. 1, d. 219, l. 128 – 131, hier l. 128. Hier findet sich auch die Angabe, dass die offene Tuberkulose in Magadan wegen der drangvollen Enge besonders hoch war. Siehe auch das Schreiben des Gebietspartei- und Gebietsexekutivkomitees an das ZK der KPdSU in GAMO f. R-146, op. 1, d. 220, l. 43 – 44.

Insgesamt waren hochinfektiöse Krankheiten weit verbreitet: Im Jahr 1956 überstieg die Zahl der Darminfektionen den Durchschnitt der RSFSR um das 2,5fache, die
Zahl der Ruhr-Erkrankten war im Nordosten fast doppelt so hoch, Hepatitis war eine
sehr weit verbreitete Krankheit. Auch unter den neuen infrastrukturellen Bedingungen nahmen diese Erkrankungen nicht ab, vielmehr stieg die Zahl der Infektionen
Ende der 1950er Jahre sogar an. Alle Verantwortlichen, der leitende Arzt der Gebietsabteilung für Epidemien, der Leiter der Gesundheitsabteilung und das Gesundheitsministerium der RSFSR, betrachteten massive Hygieneprobleme und die extremen Wohnverhältnisse im Nordosten als wichtigste Ursache für die schnelle
Ausbreitung dieser Erkrankungen.[263]

5.3.4 Kinder

Viele Berichte über verheerende Zustände liegen auch aus den Kinderbetreuungseinrichtungen und Schulen, die häufig in zwei Schichten arbeiteten, vor. Überbelegungen und fehlende Toiletten führten zu großen hygienischen Problemen, Heizmaterial und sogar elektrisches Licht fehlten häufig.[264]

Besonders belastend waren die Verhältnisse in den Internaten. Im Magadaner
Gebiet war der Bedarf an dieser Schulform besonders hoch. Zum einen gab es eine
relativ große Zahl von Kindern, deren Eltern noch immer in Haft oder verstorben waren
oder die durch Migration, Verlagerung von Lagereinheiten und Entlassung von ihnen
getrennt worden waren.[265] Zudem waren viele Eltern auf eine Betreuung ihrer Kinder

---

263 Vgl. den Bericht des Gesundheitsministeriums der RSFSR an Afanas'ev vom 25. September 1956 in
GAMO f. R-146, op. 1, d. 219, l. 41. In einigen Siedlungspunkten war die Lage dramatisch. Aufgrund einer
Epidemie stiegen die Fälle von entzündlicher Ruhr in der Region Ol'skij zwischen 1955 und 1956 um
341 %. Vgl. den Bericht des leitenden Arztes der Gebietssanitätsabteilung für Epidemien an Afanas'ev
in GAMO f. R-146, op. 1, d. 219, l. 48 – 53 (für 1956) und l. 32 – 34 (für 1957). Siehe auch den Bericht des
Leiters der Gesundheitsabteilung vom 13. April 1959 in GAMO f. R-146, op. 1, d. 220, l. 33 – 37, hier l. 35.
264 So gab es nach den Angaben des leitenden Arztes der Gebietssanitätsepidemiestation im Jahr
1956 keine einzige Schule, in der die hygienischen Bestimmungen eingehalten wurden. Auf der
Halbinsel Tschukotka wurden zum Unterricht Kerosinlampen eingesetzt, Schüler und Lehrer konnten
vor Kälte ihre Mäntel nicht ablegen. Vgl. den Bericht zu Schulen und Internaten in GAMO f. R-146, op. 1,
d. 54, l. 132 – 137. Ausführlich zu der Lage einzelner Schulen in Tschukotka siehe den Bericht des Leiters
der Bezirksabteilung für Volksbildung vom Januar 1956 in GAMO f. R-146, op. 1, d. 54, l. 105 – 108. Siehe
zu der auch im Jahr 1960 noch immer anhaltenden Enge in den lokalen Krippen und Kindergärten den
Bericht des Vorsitzenden des Exekutivkomitees an den Ministerrat der RSFSR vom Januar 1960 in
GAMO f. R-146, op. 1, d. 362, l. 141 – 142. Aufgrund der beständig steigenden Kinderzahlen in der Region
sagte der Bericht eine weitere Verschärfung der Probleme voraus.
265 Zum Bedarf an Internaten siehe den Bericht des Vorsitzenden der Abteilung für Volksbildung des
Gebietsexekutivkomitees aus dem Jahr 1956 in GAMO f. R-146, op. 1, d. 105, l. 139 – 151, hier l. 141 sowie
das ausführliche Schreiben des Direktors der Mittelschule der Siedlung Ust'-Omčug im Bezirk
Ten'kinskij, A. I. Gudovič, in GAMO f. R-146, op. 1, d. 54, l. 33 – 36. In dem angeschlossenen Internat
waren Kinder untergebracht, deren Eltern an Arbeitsstätten in einer Entfernung von bis zu 300 km

in Internaten angewiesen, da es an ihren Arbeitsplätzen keine Schulen gab. Seit 1958 war der Ausbau von Internaten zudem eine unionsweite Forderung Chruščevs, die staatliche Rundumbetreuung der Kinder war Teil seines ideologischen Konzeptes.[266]

Tatsächlich war jedoch die Betreuung der Kinder außerordentlich schlecht – der Staatsanwalt des Magadaner Gebietes wies in seinem Bericht an Afanas'ev vom Dezember 1956 mit Nachdruck auf die Situation von Waisen und vernachlässigten Kindern hin. Die Exekutivkomitees des Gebietes und der Bezirke kämen ihren Pflichten gegenüber Kindern, deren Eltern in Haft säßen oder die verstorben seien, in keiner Weise nach.[267] Davon zeugt ein Vorfall, der sich im Dezember 1956 im Bezirk Severo-Ėvenskij – auf der Halbinsel Tschukotka – ereignete. Zwei Jungen waren wegen angeblich ungebührlichen Verhaltens, das auf schlechte familiäre Verhältnisse zurückgeführt wurde, von einem anderen Internat in das Internat der Bezirkshauptstadt Ėvensk verlegt worden. Kurze Zeit nach ihrer dortigen Ankunft rissen der elf und der vierzehn Jahre alte Junge aus. Unter den Extrembedingungen des Permafrostgebietes Tschukotka, mitten im Dezember, wurden die beiden erst drei Tage später gefunden, ein Schneesturm hatte inzwischen getobt. Einer der Jungen war bereits tot, der zweite wurde mit schweren Erfrierungen ins Krankenhaus eingeliefert. Das Gebietsexekutivkomitee attestierte der Bezirksverwaltung Gleichgültigkeit gegenüber dem Leben von Kindern in Internaten, die Suche sei nur halbherzig erfolgt und das Verschwinden der Kinder vertuscht worden.[268]

Auch rein materiell waren die Bedingungen, unter denen z. T. kleine Kinder in den Internaten des Magadaner Gebietes hausen mussten, mitunter dramatisch, Infektionen brachen ungehindert aus. Beispielhaft soll hier aus einem Bericht der Gebietssanitärstation für Epidemien zitiert werden, der die Lage in einem Internat in der Siedlung Palatka schildert:

> Im Palatkaer Schulinternat sind die hygienischen Bedingungen der Schüler ausgesprochen schlecht. In den Zimmern herrscht großer Platzmangel, es ist eng, stickig, das Gebäude wird nur schlecht gereinigt. Im Internat der Mädchen gibt es überhaupt keine Toiletten und Waschbecken, weil der bisherige Toilettenraum als Schlafplatz genutzt wird. Deshalb können sich die Kinder nicht waschen, die Füße reinigen, gar nicht zu sprechen von den Hygieneregeln für Mädchen. Die Kinder sind verlaust. [...] Im Internat der Jungs tropft es aus den Rohren, in den Zimmern ist es

---

arbeiteten. Ihre Eltern sahen diese Kinder lediglich in längeren Ferien. Der Magadaner I. A. Davydov hat sich mit den Lebensbedingungen in einem Kinderheim der 1950er Jahre im Ol'sker Bezirk beschäftigt und dabei v. a. statistisches Material ausgewertet. Vgl. Davydov, Rezul'taty vospitanija detej.

266 Zum weiteren Bau von Internaten im Magadaner Gebiet siehe die Angaben aus dem Jahr 1959 in GAMO f. R-146, op. 1, d. 221, l. 172–173. Besonderes Gewicht wurde dabei auf die Unterbringung indigener Kinder in Internaten gelegt, um so eine sowjetische Überformung der traditionellen Lebensweisen, eine unmittelbare politische Indoktrination und eine Beseitigung der noch immer hohen Analphabeten-Quote zu erreichen. 1961 waren schon fast alle indigenen Kinder in Tschukotka in Internaten untergebracht (insgesamt 39 Internate). Vgl. den Bericht aus dem Bezirk Providenskij in GAMO f. R-146, op. 1, d. 362, l. 231–234.

267 Vgl. GAMO f. R-146, op. 1, d. 54, l. 169–170.

268 Vgl. verschiedene Berichte über diesen Vorfall in GAMO f. R-146, op. 1, d. 54, l. 164–168ob.

feucht, der Putz bröckelt. In der Kantine des Internates werden viele Hygieneregeln verletzt: Es gibt zu wenig Sanitätsbekleidung und kein heißes Wasser, infolgedessen wird das Geschirr schlecht abgewaschen. Der Leiter der Gebietsabteilung für Volksbildung hat dennoch Anordnung gegeben, noch mehr Kinder in den Internaten aufzunehmen, in denen schon jetzt sehr viel mehr leben, als es Plätze gibt. In dem Schulinternat in Palatka sind jetzt schon Fälle von Krätze aufgetreten.[269]

Vor dem Hintergrund solcher Berichte verwundert es nicht, dass Kinder im Magadaner Gebiet selbst 1959 noch besonders krank waren. Im Frühling 1959 gab es in der Stadt Magadan, im Magadaner Gebiet und im Vergleich dazu in der gesamten RSFSR bezogen auf 1.000 Kinder jeweils folgende Zahlen für ausgewählte Krankheiten[270]:

Erkrankungen bei Kindern	Magadaner Gebiet	Stadt Magadan	RSFSR
Katarre der oberen Atemwege	873	530,6	240
Katarre der oberen Atemwege bei Kindern bis 1 Jahr	866	1.124	500
Angina	154	162,5	50
Lungenentzündung	50,3	52,7	40,3
Lungenentzündung bei Kindern bis 1 Jahr	203	268	150

Neben den miserablen hygienischen Bedingungen in oftmals nur unzureichend geheizten Räumen wirkte sich eine einseitige, unzureichende Ernährung besonders negativ aus. So war die Rachitis-Rate im Magadaner Gebiet erschreckend hoch, was auf einen eklatanten Vitamin D-Mangel im mütterlichen Organismus zurückgeführt werden muss. Wegen der geringeren Quantität und Qualität der Muttermilch waren in der Region doppelt so viele Kinder auf eine spezielle Beikost angewiesen wie im Durchschnitt der RSFSR.[271] Die Mortalitätsrate bei Kindern lag in dem Gebiet deutlich über dem Unionsniveau, sie war besonders hoch auf der Halbinsel Tschukotka.[272]

---

269 Bericht vom 14. Oktober 1957 in GAMO f. R-146, op. 1, d. 219, l. 82–83, hier l. 82. Siehe auch die Stellungnahme des stellvertretenden Leiters der Gebietsabteilung für Volksbildung vom 18. Oktober 1957, hier l. 84. Ein großes Problem der Internate war auch der extreme Personalmangel, der dazu führte, dass Kinder lange Zeit völlig auf sich gestellt waren. Vgl. das ausführliche Schreiben des Direktors der Mittelschule der Siedlung Ust'-Omčug im Bezirk Ten'kinskij, A. I. Gudovič, in GAMO f. R-146, op. 1, d. 54, l. 33–36.
270 Vgl. die Angaben vom 13. April 1959 in GAMO f. R-146, op. 1, d. 220, l. 33–37, hier l. 35.
271 Im Jahr 1958 waren 12,1 % aller Kinder des Gebietes auf Beikost angewiesen (in der Stadt Magadan 10,3 %). In der RSFSR lag dieser Anteil bei 4,5 %. Im Alter bis zu drei Monaten waren es im Magadaner Gebiet 19 % (in der Gebietshauptstadt 20,4 %) und in der RSFSR 11 %. Vgl. den Bericht an das Gebietsexekutivkomitee vom 13. April 1959 in GAMO f. R-146, op. 1, d. 220, l. 33–37, hier l. 36. Die grundsätzliche Existenz von Beikost war dabei bereits ein großer Erfolg. Noch 1955 gab es nur in Magadan eine einzige Milchküche; alle anderen Mütter, die aufgrund der körperlichen Entbehrungen und der unzureichenden Ernährung nicht genügend Milch hatten, waren auf anderweitige Unterstützungen angewiesen. Vgl. die Angaben der Gebietsgesundheitsabteilung in GAMO f. R-146, op. 1, d. 105, l. 16–40, hier l. 23.

5.3.5 Ausbeutung und Propaganda: die Lage der Indigenen

Die Gründung des Magadaner Gebietes hatte auf die indigene Bevölkerung erhebliche Auswirkungen.[273] Unter den bisherigen Bedingungen der besonderen Raumeroberungsstrategie von Dal'stroj waren die angestammten Bewohner des Gebietes zwar in Kolchosen gezwungen und v. a. Ende der 1930er Jahre auch aus politischen Gründen – als „japanische Spione" oder „Kulaken" – verfolgt worden, anders als in den zentralen und nordwestlichen Teilen der Union waren diese Kollektivierungskampagnen jedoch weder systematisch noch mit dem Ziel einer vollständigen kulturellen Überformung durchgeführt worden – wie es Dietmar Dahlmann beschreibt:

> Noch am Ende der 1930er Jahre waren gerade einmal elf Prozent der Rentierzüchter in die Kollektive eingetreten, während überall sonst in der Sowjetunion der Grad der Kollektivierung über 90 Prozent betrug. Die Čukčen zogen sich mit ihren Herden in immer weiter entfernt liegende Gebiete zurück und suchten so dem sowjetischen System zu entkommen, was bis in die 1950er Jahre hinein sogar teilweise gelang. Die sogenannten Rentierčukčen bewahrten ihren alten Glauben, den Schamanismus, ihre Schamanen besaßen auch weiterhin großen Einfluß.[274]

Nach 1953 richtete die sowjetische Macht, in Gestalt der Organe von Partei und Staat, ihr Augenmerk auf die Situation der Indigenen. Auf Initiative von Afanas'ev hielten sich seit 1954 mehrere Brigaden in den Kolchosen auf, die von den schweren Lebens- und Arbeitsbedingungen der Bewohner und der hohen Sterberate berichteten.[275] Zum einen zielte das Interesse der neuen Leitung auf eine bessere und effektivere Ausbeutung ihrer landwirtschaftlichen Produkte im Zuge einer Intensivierung der Kolchosen, zum anderen aber auch auf eine Verbesserung ihrer sozialen und medizinischen Lage und ihre Erziehung im Sinne sowjetischer Propaganda. Die sowjetische Politik gegenüber der indigenen Bevölkerung des Nordostens zeigt deutlich, dass Johannes Grützmacher in seiner Kritik an Jörg Baberowskis Festlegung einer Zensur von 1953 mit Nachdruck unterstützt werden muss. Baberowski hatte für die Zeit nach 1953 von einem „Ersterben der Zivilisierungsmission" der sowjetischen Macht an ihren Peripherien gesprochen, von einem reinen Verwalten des „Status quo"[276]. Ebenso wie es Dahlmann in seiner Gesamtsicht auf Sibirien und Grützmacher für das Leben der Indigenen mit und durch die Baikal-Amur-Magistrale konstatieren kann, belegt auch der Blick auf das Magadaner Gebiet, dass die sowjetische Herrschaft nach 1953 viel-

---

272 Vgl. die Angaben der Gebietsgesundheitsabteilung in GAMO f. R-146, op. 1, d. 105, l. 16–40, hier l. 19; zu Tschukotka siehe l. 29.

273 Für eine Übersicht über die Bevölkerungszahlen der einzelnen Nationalitäten in den Jahren 1939 und 1959 siehe RGANI f. 5, op. 32, d. 144, l. 4–8.

274 Dahlmann, Sibirien, S. 266. Zur Kollektivierung der übrigen nördlichen Gebiete siehe Josephson, Soviet Arctic, S. 423 f.

275 Vgl. die Berichte der Brigaden in GAMO f. R-146, op. 1, d. 54, l. 121–127. Siehe auch den Bericht von Ababkov und Afanas'ev an Chruščev und Malenkov in RGANI f. 5, op. 32, d. 8, l. 42–45.

276 Baberowski, Suche nach Eindeutigkeit, S. 503.

mehr mit einem neuerstarkten „zivilisatorischen Missionseifer" an ihren inneren Grenzen unterwegs war.[277]

Die ersten Anstrengungen sollten der wirtschaftlichen Effektivierung der Fischzucht, v. a. aber der Rentierhaltung dienen. Dazu wurden viele kleinere Kolchosen zusammengelegt und Überwachung und Kontrolle durch die lokale Parteileitung gestärkt. Russen und Hinzugezogene anderer Nationalitäten ersetzten die früheren indigenen Kolchosleiter. Als Ergebnis dieser Politik wurden sehr viele Menschen zwangsumgesiedelt und aus ihren bisherigen Siedlungsgebieten verdrängt, durch Ignoranz und Unkenntnis der neuen Leitung kamen viele Tausend Rentiere ums Leben – die Lebens- und Arbeitsbedingungen verschlechterten sich noch einmal.[278]

Nach einer Verordnung des ZK der KPdSU und des Ministerrats der UdSSR vom 16. März 1957 und weiteren Verordnungen 1958 und 1960 stiegen zwar die Anstrengungen der sowjetischen Macht, die Indigenen mit Wohnhäusern, Krankenstationen und Schulen zu versorgen, vor dem Hintergrund der enormen Ausdehnung der Siedlungsgebiete konnten jedoch diese Maßnahmen die Situation nicht wirklich verbessern. Das Leben der angestammten Bevölkerung war auch Ende der 1950er Jahre noch geprägt von bitterer Armut aufgrund der ineffektiven Arbeit der Kolchosen sowie der weiten Verbreitung von Alkoholismus und schweren Krankheiten wie Syphilis und Tuberkulose. Maßnahmen zur Alphabetisierung und die Durchsetzung der allgemeinen Schulpflicht gingen mit der Einrichtung von schlecht ausgestatteten Internaten in größeren Siedlungspunkten einher, was indigene Kinder monatelang von ihren Eltern trennte. Neben der großen psychischen Belastung für Eltern und Kinder wurde so auch die Weitergabe von traditionellem Wissen über Fischfang und Rentierzucht verhindert.[279] Zugleich brachten es Umstellungen bei den Löhnen mit sich, dass die indigenen Arbeiter Ende der 1950er Jahre so geringe Gehälter erhielten, dass

---

277 Vgl. Grützmachers vorsichtige Kritik an Baberowskis These in Grützmacher, Baikal-Amur-Magistrale, S. 402f. sowie Dahlmann, Sibirien, S. 295. Zur Lage einer Nomadenethnie im Magadaner Gebiet bis in die 1970er Jahre siehe Grebenjuk, Vovlečenie rassochinskoj kočevoj gruppy.

278 Für Berichte zu diesen Umsiedelungsaktionen siehe GAMO f. R-146, op. 1, d. 56, l. 54–62, allgemein zur Lage der regionalen Landwirtschaft und zur Lage der Indigenen siehe Bacaev, Agropromyšlennyj kompleks, S. 14 ff. sowie Bacaev, Sostojanie olenevodstva.

279 Die Verordnung „Über Maßnahmen für die weitere Entwicklung von Wirtschaft und Kultur der Völker des Nordens" vom 16. März 1957 richtete sich, ebenso wie die kleineren Verordnungen von 1958 und 1960, nicht allein auf die indigene Bevölkerung des Magadaner Gebietes, sondern integrierte das Gebiet in allgemeine Maßnahmen zur Stärkung der indigenen Bevölkerung des sowjetischen Nordens. Für einen Überblick über einzelne Abschnitte der Verordnung und ihre konkrete Umsetzung siehe die Berichte in GAMO f. R-146, op. 1, d. 360, d. 356, l. 40–43, l. 66–69 sowie zu den Berichten aus anderen Regionen des sowjetischen Nordens RGANI f. 5, op. 32, d. 112, l. 1 ff. Zur allgemeinen Bedeutung dieser Verordnung vgl. Slezkine, Arctic Mirrors, S. 339. Zur gesundheitlichen Lage der Indigenen siehe den Bericht des leitenden Gebietsarztes für Geschlechtskrankheiten vom 25. November 1958 in GAMO f. R-146, op. 1, d. 220, l. 21–24, hier l. 22. Zur sozialen Lage der Indigenen in den 1950er und 1960er Jahren siehe Bacaev, Osobennosti sovetskoj social'noj politiki.

sie kaum mehr in der Lage waren, sich das Fleisch der Rentiere, ihre Hauptnahrungsgrundlage, zu kaufen.[280]

In der Landwirtschaft war es die Zerstörung der traditionellen nomadischen Lebensweise, die eine effektive Nutzung der indigenen Arbeitskräfte verhinderte. In der Industrie spielten indigene Arbeitskräfte allerdings kaum eine wahrnehmbare Rolle.

5.3.6 Handel, Alkohol und Gewalt

In der Umbruchsphase zwischen 1953 und 1959 war die Lebensmittelversorgung längst nicht in allen Bezirken gesichert. Und selbst wenn nicht gehungert werden musste, so war die Ernährung sehr einseitig, es mangelte an Vitaminen und Nährstoffen. Der menschliche Organismus war so kaum in der Lage, den extremen Anforderungen durch harte körperliche Arbeit unter den gegebenen klimatischen Bedingungen standzuhalten. Wenn auch die oberen Polit- und Wirtschaftsfunktionäre von diesen Verhältnissen unberührt ihre besonderen Zuteilungen erhielten, so blieb doch die Bevölkerung lange Zeit auf den Transport von Lebensmitteln und Waren des täglichen Bedarfs in das Gebiet angewiesen.[281] Die einfache Bevölkerung war dabei direktes Opfer der Umbruchsphase. So waren beispielsweise entsprechend einer Verordnung des Ministerrates der RSFSR im Juni 1955 7.000 Tonnen Kartoffeln für das Magadaner Gebiet bestellt worden, aufgrund der fehlenden Handelsbeziehungen wurden jedoch tatsächlich nur 2.700 Tonnen geliefert.[282] Dringend benötigte Lebensmittel erreichten in manchen Jahren nicht einmal in einer annähernd angemessenen Größenordnung die Region. Obwohl nach offiziellen Angaben seit 1958 kein Brot mehr in das Gebiet geliefert werden musste, gab es selbst 1959 noch immer Siedlungen, die über keine Bäckerei verfügten.[283]

---

280 Siehe die Berichte von Direktoren verschiedener Kolchosen sowie vom Vorsitzenden des Gebietsexekutivkomitees, Ivanov, in GAMO f. R-146, op. 1, d. 53, l. 91–97.

281 Peter Demant berichtet in seinen Erinnerungen von den speziellen Versorgungsstellen und Lebensmittellieferungen für die Parteileitung in Jagodnoe. Vgl. Kress (Pseudonym Peter Demants), Parochoda, S. 81.

282 Aufgrund dieser Erfahrungen bat Čistjakov, der stellvertretende Vorsitzende des Gebietsexekutivkomitees, den Ministerrat der RSFSR im Jahr 1956 sogleich um erheblich mehr landwirtschaftliche Produkte. Vgl. GAMO f. R-146, op. 1, d. 47, l. 73. Auch die Mengen an Waren des täglichen Bedarfes, die das Handelsministerium in den Jahren 1955 und 1956 für das Gebiet zur Verfügung stellte, waren vollkommen unzureichend. Ganz besonders mangelte es an Lederschuhen für Kinder, an warmer Unterwäsche, an Wintermänteln und Wollpullovern. Vgl. das Schreiben von Afanas'ev, mit Bestellungen für das Jahr 1957, an den Vorsitzenden des Ministerrates der RSFSR vom 2. November 1956 in GAMO f. R-146, op. 1, d. 48, l. 100–101.

283 Dies war v. a. auf der tschukotkischen Halbinsel der Fall. Siehe die Angaben des leitenden Arztes der Gebietssanitärepidemiestation für das Jahr 1959 in GAMO f. R-146, op. 1, d. 220, l. 48–68, hier l. 60. Extremer Mangel herrschte aber auch an Produktionsstandorten weit im Norden des Bezirks Srednekanskij. Siehe die ausführliche Beschreibung der miserablen Lebensbedingungen im Bericht der

Das regionale Gefälle war dabei enorm: In den südlichen Teilen des Gebietes und in den großen Zentren der Bezirke war seit 1957 eine deutliche Verbesserung der Lage spürbar. Neben Grundnahrungsmitteln erweiterte sich das Lebensmittelangebot deutlich, bei den Waren des täglichen Bedarfs lässt sich von einer regelrechten „Zivilisierung" der Handelsgüter sprechen: Kinderspielzeug, Damenblusen, Wecker, Sportgeräte etc. waren nun in längst nicht ausreichender Zahl, aber immerhin in einigen Läden des Gebietes verfügbar.[284] Zwischen 1956 und 1958 betrugen die Zuwächse bei den Lebensmittellieferungen 132 %, bei den Waren des täglichen Bedarfs 136 %.[285]

Sehr viel schlechter war die Lage in weit entfernten Siedlungen und dabei an erster Stelle auf der Halbinsel Tschukotka. Hier waren die strukturellen Probleme der Handelsorganisationen besonders groß, Zuständigkeiten und Verantwortlichkeiten lange Zeit ungeklärt.[286] Fehlende Infrastrukturen und mangelnde Transportmöglichkeiten wirkten sich unter diesen Umständen verheerend aus.[287] Gemüse, frische Kartoffeln, Milchprodukte und Fleisch wurden entweder überhaupt nicht geliefert oder nur in vollkommen unzureichenden Mengen. Auf der Halbinsel gab es Orte, in die drei Jahre lang kein einziger Sack frischer Kartoffeln, Gemüse oder Obst gebracht wurde. Die extensive Rentierzucht wurde durch mangelnde Lieferungen erschwert: Es fehlten Taschenmesser, Lampen, Streichhölzer und eine Art von Kuhglocken, ohne die die Rentiere in den Weiten Tschukotkas und v. a. im dunklen Winter verlorenzugehen drohten.[288]

Partei- und Staatsleitung des Bezirks vom 12. Februar 1959 in GAMO f. R-146, op. 1, d. 53, l. 84–86. Für die offizielle Darstellung zur Brotversorgung siehe Slavin, Problemy razvitija, S. 181.

284 Vgl. beispielsweise den Befehl des Vorsitzenden des Komitees für Körperkultur und Sport beim Ministerrat der RSFSR zur Angleichung der Region an die Gegebenheiten in den zentralen Gebieten der Union durch die Versendung von entsprechender Literatur, von Sportgeräten und Trainern in das Magadaner Gebiet, in GAMO f. R-146, op. 1, d. 52, l. 12–14.

285 Die Zahlenangaben beziehen sich auf die Kolyma, in Tschukotka lagen sie, aufgrund des bisherigen Mangels, sogar etwas darüber. Vgl. den Bericht des Leiters von *Glavseverotorg* an das Büro des ZK der KPdSU für die RSFSR vom 30. Juli 1958 in RGASPI f. 556, op. 23, d. 38, l. 65–67, hier l. 66.

286 Siehe den Bericht von Afanas'ev zur Lage der Handelsorganisationen in Tschukotka vom Dezember 1955 an das ZK der KPdSU. Afanas'ev erhob darin schwere Vorwürfe gegen das Handelsministerium der RSFSR. Vgl. RGANI f. 5, op. 20, d. 154, l. 12–15 sowie die anschließende Rechtfertigung des Handelsministeriums der RSFSR, ebd., l. 16–25.

287 Siehe die Beschreibung des stellv. Leiters der Abteilung für Industrie und Transport des Gebietsparteikomitees, A. Žarkich, über die Lage im Magadaner Gebiet aus dem Jahr 1956 in GAMO f. P-21, op. 5, d. 110, l. 137–147, hier l. 142. Vgl. auch das Schreiben des stellvertretenden Vorsitzenden des Magadaner Exekutivkomitees, B. Rogušin, an den Ministerrat der RSFSR vom 12. August 1959 in GAMO f. R-146, op. 1, d. 153, l. 193 f. Es gab Orte, die ausschließlich im Winter (über vereiste Flüsse) zu erreichen waren, wie die Siedlung Illernej im Bezirk Vostočnaja Tundra. Ihre Bewohner waren besonders auf gute Lagermöglichkeiten angewiesen, da sehr viele Produkte unter den gegebenen klimatischen Bedingungen erfroren. Vgl. die Beschwerden über eine schlechte Versorgung der Siedlung in GAMO f. R-146, op. 1, d. 53, l. 42 und l. 45.

288 Vgl. den Bericht von Afanas'ev zur Lage der Handelsorganisationen in Tschukotka vom Dezember 1955 an das ZK der KPdSU in RGANI f. 5, op. 20, d. 154, l. 12–15.

Was jedoch anscheinend immer vorhanden war, war Alkohol.[289] Selbst im Jahr 1954, das durch extreme Lieferprobleme bei allen Lebensmitteln und Industriewaren hervorsticht, wurden allein in acht Monaten 276 Tonnen Spiritus in die Region gebracht, das waren 20 % sämtlicher Warenlieferungen.[290] Gerade Tschukotka, das so sehr unter mangelnden Lieferungen litt, erhielt sehr viel harten Alkohol; 1954 machte er 30 % aller Lieferungen auf die Halbinsel aus.[291]

Auf Einschränkungen durch Verbote der sowjetischen Regierung reagierte die Bevölkerung mit dem massenhaften Kauf von Eau de Cologne, Brennspiritus, alkoholhaltigen Lacken und Medikamenten sowie flüssiger Teerseife, was zu Erblindungen und Todesfällen führte. Ebenso wurde sehr viel Zucker für das illegale Brennen von Alkohol gekauft.[292] Die lokalen Verantwortlichen griffen dabei vielfach nicht ein und erlaubten den fast uneingeschränkten Alkoholverkauf.[293]

Kuvaev stilisierte in seinem Magadaner Roman „Goldsucher" Alkohol zu einer fast nie erfüllten Sehnsucht der Geologen, zu einer Art moralischen Stütze im Kampf gegen die Naturgewalten, dessen Konsum lediglich bei großen Goldfunden oder hohen Festtagen gestattet wurde. Tatsächlich firmierte Alkohol sogar als eigene „Kolymaer Währung". Peter Demant erzählt in seinen Erinnerungen von einer längeren Fahrt auf der Trasse, für die er dem Fahrer zwei Halbliterflaschen Schnaps organisierte, die – wie er sich ausdrückte – „Standardgebühr für eine Fahrt nach Kolymaer Gewohnheit"[294]. Alkohol prägte das Leben in vielen Siedlungen: Bei seiner Anlieferung bildeten sich lange Schlangen vor den Verkaufsräumen, Schlägereien entbrannten bei Verkauf und Konsum, die Verkaufsbuden wurden zerstört.[295] Berichte über betrunkene Arbeiter und Angestellte liegen aus nahezu allen Wirtschaftsbereichen, selbst aus wissenschaftlichen Instituten, vor. Übermäßiger Alkoholkonsum führte zu vielen Todesfällen, unter seinem Einfluss kam es zu einer gestiegenen Zahl an Selbstmorden.[296] Am 5. April 1955 untersagte Mitrakov der Handelsorganisation

---

289 Zu dem hohen Alkoholkonsum in allen Gebieten des sowjetischen Nordens siehe Mäkinen/Reitan, Alcohol Consumption.

290 Vgl. Širokov, Politika, S. 446.

291 Afanas'ev machte die Handelsorganisationen in Tschukotka selbst für die übermäßigen Alkohollieferungen verantwortlich. Vgl. seinen Bericht vom Dezember 1955 an das ZK der KPdSU in RGANI f. 5, op. 20, d. 154, l. 12–15, hier l. 13.

292 Vgl. den Bericht des Leiter von *Glavseverotorg* an das Büro des ZK der KPdSU für die RSFSR vom 30. Juli 1958 in RGASPI f. 556, op. 23, d. 38, l. 65–67, hier l. 66. Sehr viele Erblindungen und Vergiftungen gab es in kleinen Dörfern Indigener. Vgl. ebd., l. 67.

293 Vgl. den Bericht über Probleme mit Alkohol im Čaunsker Bezirk vom 23. März 1958 in GAMO f. P-21, op. 5, d. 145, l. 26–31, hier l. 28. Hier war Alkohol 14 Stunden am Tag käuflich zu erwerben.

294 Kress (Pseudonym Peter Demants), Parochoda, S. 7.

295 Vgl. den Bericht des Leiters von *Glavseverotorg* an das Büro des ZK der KPdSU für die RSFSR vom 30. Juli 1958 in RGASPI f. 556, op. 23, d. 38, l. 65–67, hier l. 67.

296 Im Jahr 1957 und im ersten Quartal des Jahres 1958 starben im Čaunsker Bezirk 16 Menschen an Alkoholismus, neun Personen erfroren nach übermäßigem Alkoholkonsum, vier Menschen verbrannten, weil sie zu betrunken waren, um sich aus brennenden Gebäuden zu retten, und sechs Personen brachten sich im betrunkenen Zustand um. Vgl. den Bericht über Probleme mit Alkohol im

Kolymsnab den Verkauf von Alkohol in der Nähe von Lagerpunkten, um das Eindringen von Spirituosen in die Zone zu verhindern. In der letzten Zeit hätten Trinkgelage unter Häftlingen massiv zugenommen, die von der Lageradministration nicht verhindert würden. Sie führten zu zahlreichen Gewalttaten mit Todesfolge, zu Übergriffen auf andere Häftlinge und auf Bewohner freier Siedlungen, so Miktrakov.[297]

In den Wohnbaracken, zumal in weit entfernten Gebieten, zerstörte der Alkohol die letzten Rückzugsmöglichkeiten, die für Frauen noch bestanden. Berichte aus verschiedenen Siedlungen offenbaren ein extremes Maß an sexualisierter Gewalt, die durch Alkoholkonsum erheblich verstärkt wurde. Die zum Teil sehr jungen Komsomolzinnen und Vertragsarbeiterinnen waren Vergewaltigungen schutzlos ausgeliefert. Stellvertretend für viele derartige Schilderungen soll hier aus einem Bericht einer Brigade der Gebietsparteileitung, der Gewerkschaft und des Komsomol über einen Besuch in einer Wohnbaracke der Verwaltung „Ėnergostroj" im Bezirk Susumanskij, im Jahr 1956, zitiert werden:

> Bei Besuch des Wohnheims am Samstag, den 12. Januar 1956 wurde die Brigade des Gebietsparteikomitees der KPdSU Zeuge von Schlägereien, Kartenspielen, Trinkgelagen mit Spiritus, des Verprügelns zweier Mädchen. In der einen Hälfte der Baracke Nummer 13 fand gerade eine Hochzeit statt, in der anderen die Vergewaltigung der neunzehnjährigen Komsomolzin I. G. durch zwei betrunkene Männer: Durch den 1929 geborenen P., der als Komsomolze in die Region gekommen war und durch den dreiunddreißigjährigen Chauffeur Z. Auf ihr Schreien hat niemand reagiert, obwohl es im Flur deutlich zu hören war und junge Leute im Flur herumstanden. Als wir begannen an die Tür zu klopfen, hat uns keiner geöffnet. Die Bewohner der Baracke empfahlen uns die Tür einzutreten. [...] Als wir dies taten, sahen wir, wie Z. von dem Bett sprang, auf dem die vollkommen nackte I. G. lag, ihr Kleid war in zwei Teile zerrissen. [...] P. und Z., die in der Siedlung als Rowdys und Trinker bekannt sind, wurden der Miliz übergeben. I. G. hatte bis zum 1. Januar 1956 in einer Autowerkstatt gearbeitet. Seitdem war sie nicht bei ihrer Arbeitsstelle erschienen, aber keiner der Leiter hatte sich für den Grund ihrer Abwesenheit interessiert.[298]

Der Blick der Brigade in die Wohnbaracke scheint eine geradezu „alltägliche Szene" zu offenbaren – menschenverachtende Umstände, Gleichgültigkeit, sexuelle Gewalt. Eine Gruppe junger Frauen aus dieser Industrieverwaltung, in der insgesamt 379 Personen, davon 237 Männer, arbeiteten, schrieb nach dem hier geschilderten Vorfall das ZK der KPdSU, das Gebiets- und das Bezirksparteikomitee an, eine Kopie dieses Briefes sendeten sie zusätzlich an die *Magadanskaja Pravda*. In ihrem Brief schilderten sie offen ihre Lebensbedingungen: Jede von ihnen verdiene zwischen 400 und 500 Rubel, in den Räumen ihrer Baracken sei es 10 °C kalt, es gebe nicht einmal

---

Čaunsker Bezirk vom 23. März 1958 in GAMO f. P-21, op. 5, d. 145, l. 26 – 31, hier l. 26. Über Selbstmorde als Folge massiven Alkoholkonsums berichtet auch der Leiter von Dal'stroj in seinem Schreiben an den Komsomolvorsitzenden und den Vorsitzenden des Gewerkschaftskomitees des Gebietes vom 8. Februar 1957 in GAMO f. R-137sč, op. 1b, d. 21, l. 2f.

297 Vgl. den Befehl Mitrakovs in GAMO f. R-23, op. 1, d. 5206, l. 58 f.

298 Siehe den Bericht der Brigade unter der Leitung des stellv. Leiters der Abteilung für Industrie und Transport des Gebietsparteikomitees, A. Žarkich, in GAMO f. P-21, op. 5, d. 110, l. 137–147, hier l. 140 f.

fließendes Wasser. „Wir leben zu viert in einem Zimmer von 12 m², schlafen je zu zweit auf einer Pritsche. Unter diesen Bedingungen zu leben ist einfach unmöglich, besonders wenn betrunkene Männer und Jungs kommen."[299]

Die politischen Verantwortlichen ignorierten jedoch die greifbaren Ursachen und folgten lieber zwei anderen Deutungsmustern: Zum einen war es der Alkoholkonsum, mit dem derartige Übergriffe erklärt wurden. Vergewaltigungen junger Frauen wurden wie Schlägereien nach Alkoholexzessen als „amoralisches Verhalten" gewertet.[300] Zum anderen wurde das Fehlen von Propagandaarbeit verantwortlich gemacht. Kriminelle Übergriffe nach Alkoholkonsum erklärten sich durch eine mangelnde Durchdringung aller Siedlungen mit Agitatoren (nicht etwa mit dem Fehlen der Miliz) sowie durch fehlende Vorträge zu politischen Vorgängen und richtigen Verhaltensweisen – „Erziehungsmaßnahmen", wie sie in der Entstalinisierung Teil der allgemeinen Propaganda waren.[301] Im Fall des Wohnheims, in dem die Vergewaltigung der neunzehnjährigen Frau stattgefunden hatte, beklagte die Brigade an erster Stelle mangelnde Fortbildungsmöglichkeiten und fehlende kulturelle Angebote.[302]

5.3.7 Repräsentationen: Performanz und Legitimität der neuen Herrschaftsverhältnisse

Die reale Lage einer arbeitenden Person im Magadaner Gebiet war von drei Hauptfaktoren abhängig: Von ihrer persönlichen arbeitsrechtlichen Situation – d. h. ihrem Lohn und den ihr zustehenden Boni –, von der geographischen Lage und der ökonomischen Bedeutung der Siedlung, in der sie lebte, sowie von den Haltungen und Fähigkeiten der zuständigen politischen und wirtschaftlichen Leitung.

Gerade in der Umbruchsphase der 1950er Jahre war das regionale Gefälle enorm. Auch wenn die Bemühungen um eine territorial organisierte, auf die Fläche bezogene soziale Infrastruktur unbestreitbar zu erkennen waren, herrschte an den Rändern des neuen Gebietes ein Elend und ein Maß an Gewalt, das dem Aufbauprogramm Hohn

---

299 GAMO f. P-21, op. 5, d. 110, l. 153 – 162, hier l. 155 f.

300 Die politische Leitung des Čaunsker Bezirks machte im Jahr 1957 und im ersten Quartal des Jahres 1958 Alkoholkonsum für 162 Verbrechen, darunter sieben Morde, sieben Vergewaltigungen und 46 Einbrüche verantwortlich. Vgl. den Bericht über Probleme mit Alkohol im Čaunsker Bezirk vom 23. März 1958 in GAMO f. P-21, op. 5, d. 145, l. 26 – 31, hier l. 26.

301 Susan Reid schildert anschaulich die Re-Ideologisierung der Lebens- und Wohnverhältnisse in der Entstalinisierung. Sie spricht dabei von einer neuen „Front", der „home-front". Vgl. Reid, Utopia.

302 Die Brigade machte dafür die lokalen Vertreter der Partei und des Komsomol verantwortlich. Vgl. GAMO f. P-21, op. 5, d. 110, l. 137 – 147, hier l. 140 f. Ganz ähnlich war auch die Perspektive auf die schwere Lage im Čaunsker Bezirk. Vgl. GAMO f. P-21, op. 5, d. 145, l. 26 – 31, hier l. 28. Mangelnde Bildungsangebote und eine fehlende Erziehungsarbeit waren für Čuguev die Ursache für fehlenden Gemeinschaftssinn auf den Arbeitsstellen, der sich in Diebstählen niederschlug. Vgl. sein Schreiben an den Komsomolvorsitzenden des Gebietes und den Vorsitzenden des Gewerkschaftskomitees vom 8. Februar 1957 in GAMO f. R-137sč, op. 1b, d. 21, l. 2 f.

sprach. Während sich der ehemalige Häftling des *Berlag*, Abraham Dück, in der Hauptstadt Magadan sogar eine Fotokamera anschaffen konnte, gab es in Siedlungen in Tschukotka in den Anfangsjahren nicht genügend Brot, Trinkwasser und einfachste medizinische Einrichtungen.[303] Zudem waren die Bewohner in den Weiten des Gebietes, unter den extremen klimatischen Bedingungen und vor dem Hintergrund des allgemeinen Mangels abhängig von den Fähigkeiten der Verantwortlichen, Waren zu organisieren. Es kam darauf an, offizielle und informelle Kanäle zu nutzen, Absprachen rechtzeitig zu treffen, Mangelware zu beschaffen. Die gesamte Miss- und Mangelwirtschaft der Sowjetunion, Planungsfehler, aber auch Korruption und persönliche Animositäten trafen die Bevölkerung im Magadaner Gebiet mit voller Wucht.[304]

Abhängig war man von der jeweiligen persönlichen Haltung der Funktionäre, von ihrem Interesse und gegebenenfalls ihrem Engagement. Besonders anschaulich illustriert dies eine Schilderung von Bürgern aus der Siedlung Lavrentija, dem Zentrum des nordöstlichsten Zipfels der Sowjetunion auf der Halbinsel Tschukotka. Die Bewohner hatten sich im Februar 1956 mit einer Beschwerde über Kohlenmangel an die Redaktion der Zeitung *Magadanskaja Pravda* gewandt, die diese an die Leitung des Magadaner Gebietsexekutivkomitees weitergab. Um einen Eindruck von den Verhältnissen zu bekommen, wird hier im Folgenden ausführlicher aus ihrem Brief zitiert. Die Gruppe der Lavrentijaer Bürger schrieb:

> Der Winter des Jahres 1956 zeigt sich den Bürgern der Siedlung Lavrentija von seiner kalten Seite, im ganz wörtlichen Sinne. Es gibt schon fast keine Kohle mehr und was das in Tschukotka bedeutet, ist jedem klar. Die Siedlung Lavrentija ist Zentrum des Bezirks und über das Eintreffen der Frachtschiffe waren alle informiert, aber die Leitung war zu dieser Zeit offensichtlich mit wichtigeren Problemen beschäftigt. Diese Sorgen haben sie erst dann vergessen, als das Meer bereits von Eis bedeckt war. Der Staat [gemeint ist wohl eine zentral geleitete Institution, im Gegensatz zu den lokalen Behörden – M. S.] kam uns zügig zu Hilfe. Im Monat November kamen zwei große Eisbrecher und die Kohle wurde auf das Eis der Bucht gezogen. Aber in der Siedlung Lavrentija gibt es zu viel Leitungspersonal und daraus resultiert alles Übel. Wie viel haben sie beraten, wie viel haben sie diskutiert, aber sie konnten nicht entscheiden, wer denn die Kohle herbeischaffen soll. Das ist eine ziemlich unangenehme Sache, wenn man bedenkt, dass sich die Kohle in einer Entfernung von zwei Kilometern vor dem Ufer befand. Der Direktor des čukotkischen Bezirkshandelskontors, der Genosse Gofman, fühlte sich Ende Oktober auf einmal schlecht und flog ganz plötzlich in die Kur, um seine Gesundheit wiederherzustellen. Und so blieb die Kohle auf dem Eis, die Angestellten des Handelskontors waren allein natürlich nicht in der Lage sie ans Ufer zu ziehen. [...] Man kann nicht grundsätzlich sagen, dass sich die politische Leitung von der Führung des Bezirkes entfernt hat. Nein, der Sekretär des Bezirksexekutivkomitees der KPdSU, der Genosse Petuchov, mischt sich in jede Kleinigkeit ein, [..] aber solche Kleinigkeiten wie die Lieferung von

---

303 Vgl. Dück, Erinnerungen, S. 455.
304 Zur Misswirtschaft, der sogenannten „tufta", Tricksereien in der Buchhaltung und ihren Ursachen in der Ära Chruščev siehe Khlevniuk, Economy. Allgemein zur Bedeutung des „blat" – der Ausnutzung eines Systems an informellen Kontakten und Netzwerken zur Erlangung rationierter Waren und Güter und zur Vermeidung formaler Prozeduren – in der sowjetischen Wirtschaft siehe Ledeneva, Blat.

Kohle, Wohnraum für die Arbeiter oder eine Garage für Maschinen, die geraten bei ihm aus dem Blickfeld.[305]

Eine vom Gebietsexekutivkomitee geforderte Überprüfung der Situation durch das Bezirksexekutivkomitee ergab, dass der Gegenstand der Beschwerde der Realität entsprach; der Direktor des Bezirkshandelskontors erhielt eine strenge Rüge. Eine „spezielle Trojka" wurde durch das Bezirksexekutivkomitee eingesetzt, die die Verteilung der Kohle regeln sollte. Bis zur Eisschmelze und damit bis in den Mai des Jahres 1956 blieben jedoch die Bevölkerung, das Krankenhaus, Kinderkrippen, das Bezirkspartei- und das Bezirksexekutivkomitee bei Temperaturen bis -60° C ohne ausreichendes Heizmaterial.[306]

Andere Beispiele zeigen wiederum, dass sich lokale Funktionäre in ihrem Verantwortungsgefühl für die Bevölkerung herausgefordert fühlten. Auch wenn die obere Polit- und Wirtschaftsleitung über ein eigenes Versorgungssystem verfügte und in eigenen Läden einkaufen konnte, vermitteln Mitschriften von Besprechungen und Berichte immer wieder den Eindruck, dass politische Verantwortliche mit Verwunderung, zugleich aber auch mit Bestürzung auf erbärmliche Lebenssituationen reagierten – wenn sie denn einmal unmittelbar damit konfrontiert wurden. So zum Beispiel im Bericht eines Vertreters des Gebietsexekutivkomitees:

> Wir sprechen davon, dass bei uns viele Lebensmittel verderben. Ich möchte aber darüber sprechen, wie wenig Lebensmittel und in was für einem Zustand sie bei uns in weit entfernten Ecken des Gebietes verkauft werden. Im letzten Jahr war ich in der Siedlung Krasnoarmejskij [im Bezirk Čaunskij auf Tschukotka – M. S.], ging in einen Laden und hab mich mal dafür interessiert, was verkauft wird. Hering in einem unansehnlichen Zustand – klein, trocken, schrecklich – wird als Hering aus dem Stillen Ozean verkauft und für einen ziemlich hohen Preis. Öl gibt es dort in der Regel nur bitteres, verdorbenes. Graupen in so einem Zustand, dass es schwerfällt zu glauben, dass das Graupen sind, irgendwelche Klümpchen [...].[307]

Afanas'ev berichtete bei einem Treffen im Gebietsexekutivkomitee über seinen Aufenthalt im Bezirk Jagodninskij:

> Bei einem Aufenthalt im Präsidium bei der Parteikonferenz in Jagodnoe las ich eine Beschwerde der Komsomolzen des Bezirks, die die Konferenz darum baten, sich der Frage der Renovierung des Gebäudes des Debinsker Krankenhauses anzunehmen. [...] Ich war in diesem Krankenhaus und muss sagen, dass die Lage dort tatsächlich katastrophal ist. In das Gebäude wurden schon Leute verlegt, bevor es überhaupt ganz fertiggestellt worden war. Dort herrscht eine schreckliche Kälte, Wasser mit Fäkalien läuft vom 2. Stock herunter. Und an der Renovierung arbeiten nur drei Leute. Unsere Gebietsgesundheitsabteilung hat sich mit diesen schlimmen Zuständen abgefunden.

---

305 GAMO f. R-146, op. 1, d. 53, l. 38 – 41 hier l. 39 f.
306 Vgl. den Bericht des stellvertretenden Sekretärs des Bezirksexekutivkomitees, Eršov, in GAMO f. R-146, op. 1, d. 53, l. 41.
307 GAMO f. R-146, op. 1, d. 47, l. 94 – 114, hier l. 103.

> Genossen, das ist doch ein Verbrechen gegenüber kranken Menschen! Für den Bau dieses Krankenhauses wurden Millionen verschwendet, aber es gibt keinen Nutzen.[308]

Es liegt eine Reihe von Berichten vor, aus denen hervorgeht, das lokale Verantwortliche durch die Gebietsleitung wegen mangelnder Fürsorge für die Bevölkerung gerügt oder auch entlassen wurden.[309] Doch selbst wenn es zu diesen Eingriffen von höherer Stelle kam, war die konkrete Lage vor Ort nur bedingt beeinflussbar; zu gering war der Grad der institutionellen und infrastrukturellen Durchdringung des Gebietes, zu hoch die Abgeschiedenheit einzelner Siedlungen an den Rändern des neuen politischen Raumes.

Blickt man auf die regen publizistischen Tätigkeiten der Leitung, die Darstellungen in der *Magadanskaja Pravda* und die zahlreichen Neuerscheinungen im eigens gegründeten Magadaner Verlag, so ergibt sich schnell der Eindruck, dass der politischen Leitung daran gelegen war, die realen Verhältnisse des Gebietes radikal umzuschreiben. Die Beschreibungen, aber auch die Fotografien angeblicher Alltagsszenen (von Wohnheimen, Transportmitteln, Internaten oder Läden) standen mitunter im grotesken Widerspruch zu den realen Arbeits- und Lebensbedingungen.

Umgeschrieben wurde auch das Verhältnis zwischen Herrschenden und Bevölkerung. Während die Einwohner von Lavrentija aufgrund des Zynismus ihrer lokalen Funktionäre erbärmlich froren, schien sich die sowjetische Leitung auf den Seiten der *Magadanskaja Pravda* ganz der Bevölkerung zuzuwenden:

> In den Jahren nach 1954 wurde die Zeitung durch häufige Reportagen in gut lesbarem Stil deutlich lebendiger. Auffällig ist dabei vor allem der steigende Anteil an Fotografien[310], Karten und graphischen Darstellungen[311]. Der Abdruck von Witzen und Karikaturen, die Veröffentlichung von Gedichten, kurzen Erzählungen, Kinoreklame, die Darstellung neuester Damenmode, auch eine veränderte Aufmachung durch Verzierungen der Seitenränder – all dies sorgte für ein ansprechendes Erscheinungsbild.

Selbst wenn diese Optik im Rahmen sowjetischer Presseerzeugnisse zunächst nicht allzu sehr auffällt, so ist doch der Unterschied zur bisherigen Zeitung *Sovetskaja Kolyma* frappierend. Die *Sovetskaja Kolyma* war bislang fast ohne jedes Foto ausgekommen, sie wurde weitgehend vom Abdruck überregionaler Artikel bzw. von Reden

---

308 GAMO f. R-146, op. 1, d. 47, l. 94–114, hier l. 112f. In der Versammlung berichteten weitere Funktionäre von ihren Beobachtungen im Magadaner Gebiet.
309 Vgl. beispielsweise den Bericht über die Arbeit mit Kadern in der Indigirskoe Bergbauverwaltung für das Jahr 1956 in GAMO f. R-137sč, op. 1b, d. 21, l. 39–100, Berichte über einzelne Kader l. 47–69.
310 Im Durchschnitt gab es in der Zeitung *Sovetskaja Kolyma* etwa drei Bilder pro Ausgabe, schon im Jahr 1955 fanden sich auf jeder Seite der *Magadanskaja Pravda* einige Fotografien (außer beim ganzseitigen Abdruck von Reden).
311 Vgl. z. B. Magadanskaja Pravda, 13. Juni 1957, S. 2.

Abb. 57 Idealisierte Darstellung eines Wohnheimes, Magadanskaja Pravda, 12. Mai 1956

dominiert. Nun erschien eine Zeitung, die den Leser indoktrinieren, aber eindeutig auch unterhalten und umwerben wollte.[312]

Dies konnte die frühere Publizistin Ginzburg, nach langjähriger Lagerhaft an der Kolyma, im Sommer 1954 am eigenen Leib erfahren. Nachdem sich das Gerücht verbreitet hatte, in der Redaktion der Zeitung sei „das Büro zur speziellen Kontrolle der eingehenden Texte aufgelöst worden, da jetzt jeder ehemalige Gefangene oder Verbannte publizieren dürfe"[313], schrieb sie einen Artikel über den spezifischen Dialekt von Kolyma mit ein paar „witzigen Beispielen" und machte sich auf in die Redaktion, aufgeregt, voll Sehnsucht nach ihrem alten Beruf, „schwindlig beim Gedanken an Redaktionskorridore":

---

312 Seit der Übernahme durch die Partei im Jahr 1957 zeigten sich diese Veränderungen auch auf den Seiten der Zeitschrift *Kolyma*. Von einer steifen technischen Zeitschrift entwickelte sie sich zu einem Medium, in dem farbige Beilagen und große Bilder der Arbeitsstätten und von herausragenden Arbeitern von den ökonomischen Leistungen des Gebietes kündeten, technische und ökonomische Themen wurden anschaulich und verständlich dargestellt. Dies zeigt sich vor allem an den breitangelegten Kampagnen zum 21. Parteitag in den Jahren 1958 und 1959.
313 Ginsburg, Gratwanderung, S. 451.

Abb. 58 Magadanskaja Pravda, 6. Mai 1956

Die Zeitung hieß jetzt nicht mehr ‚Sovetskaja Kolyma', sondern ‚Magadanskaja Prawda'. Die Redaktion befand sich auf demselben Platz im Stadtzentrum, wo auch alle wichtigen Ämter lagen. In der Abteilung ‚Kultur' saß ein junges Bürschchen in einem dicken Rollkragenpullover mit einem Muster von springenden Rentieren. [tatsächlich war ein Teil der jungen Redaktion zu Beginn des Jahres unmittelbar aus Moskau nach Magadan gereist – M. S.[314]]. Zwischen den Zähnen hing ihm eine Pfeife, und daran, wie betont er auf ihr herumbiß, sah man, wie jung er war. Nachdem er den Artikel überflogen hatte, rief er freudig aus: ‚Einmal ein neues Thema! Und gut geschrieben. Haben Sie vorher schon einmal geschrieben?'[315]

In Reaktion auf Ginzburgs Schilderung ihrer Biographie und der zweimaligen Verhaftung „fiel [...] dem Jüngelchen die Pfeife aus dem Mund. In einem knappen Jahr hatte er sich an solche Vorkommnisse noch nicht gewöhnen können". Doch nach Rücksprache wurde Ginzburg zum stellvertretenden Chefredakteur bestellt. „Er erhob sich hinter seinem Tisch und streckte mir die Hand entgegen. Wie sich die Zeiten doch

---

314 Vgl. zu den Personalveränderungen das Kapitel 3.2.2.
315 Ginsburg, Gratwanderung, S. 452.

ХАЛАТЫ ИЛИ МЕШКИ?

В середине мая в пошивочной ма-
стерской Промкомбината мы приоб-
рели четыре рабочих халата. Они
оказались весьма странного пошива.
У одного из них огромные карманы
были пришиты на разном уровне, у
другого, вместо трех карманов име-
лось только два. Все халаты пошиты
небрежно. Швы имеют разную шири-
ну, пестрят бахромой.

(Из письма сотрудников лабора-
тории Магаданского авторемонт-
ного завода).

Abb. 59 Humoristische Darstellung schlechter Arbeitskleidung, Magadanskaja Pravda, 4. Juni 1955

СТИХИ МОЛОДЫХ	**НОВОСЕЛКА**	Евгений ВОРОПАНОВ

Ее глаза задумчиво и строго
Глядят на эти новые края.
Тайга, тайга... Проезжая дорога,
Размытая дождями колея...

Во взгляде — грусть по солнечному краю,
Где волны лижут золотой песок,
Разлуки горечь и—я это знаю—
Тревоги неизведанных дорог.

Но в нем не гаснут искорки задора,
Живой огонь нетронутой души.
Что ждет ее на северных просторах?
Какой она здесь подвиг совершит?

И кто она? Быть может, врач, что лечит
Детей и взрослых от лихих хвороб?
Иль, может быть, надев рюкзак на плечи,
Пойдет брать пробы дорогих пород?

Иль, может быть, вот в этот край далекий
Она несет науки яркий свет?..
Не знаю я. Но ясно, что нелегкий
Ей выпал путь до трудовых побед.

И в строгом взгляде, устремленном в дали,
Видна готовность по нему идти.
Нет, никакие бури и печали
Ее не сдвинут с этого пути!

Abb. 60 Abdruck eines Gedichtes, Magadanskaja Pravda, 6. Mai 1957

Abb. 61 Redaktionskollektiv der Magadanskaja Pravda, September 1954 (GAMO f. P-1199 f., op. 1, d. 1)

verändert hatten! Was er mir wohl gesagt hätte, wenn ich vor einem Jahr bei ihm erschienen wäre?"[316]

Ginzburgs Artikel mit den witzigen Beispielen des Kolymaer Dialekts wurde tatsächlich gedruckt; er schien wohl exakt den geforderten Sprachduktus zu treffen. Wann immer auf den Seiten der *Magadanskaja Pravda* das alltägliche Leben im Magadaner Gebiet beschrieben wurde, fällt eine besondere Weichheit der Darstellung auf, ein milder Ton, der häufig durch die bewusste Verwendung von Umgangssprache unterstützt wurde. Solche Artikel tragen Titel wie „Für euch, Magadaner!" oder „Blühe, nördliches Land!". In einem Artikel über langgediente Spezialisten heißt es:

> Wenn sich alte Genossen treffen, die lange und gut miteinander gearbeitet haben, entspinnt sich das Gespräch leicht und einfach, ganz von selbst. Schon eine ganze Ewigkeit sind sie daran gewöhnt, sich mit einem halben Wort zu verständigen. [...] So war es auch dieses Mal, als eine Gruppe von Spezialisten die Redaktion der Magadanskaja Pravda besuchte, Männer, die viele Jahre der Erschließung des Fernen Nordens gewidmet hatten.[317]

Beispiele dieses fast unerträglichen Kitsches gibt es zahlreich. Vor dem Hintergrund der Magadaner Realitäten verstören diese Texte, irritiert ihr platter und allzu offensichtlicher Ansatz, Widersprüche zu überdecken, formalisierte Typen und Bilder statt

---

316 Ginsburg, Gratwanderung, S. 452 f.
317 Magadanskaja Pravda, 13. Juli 1954, S. 3.

Realitäten zu beschreiben.[318] Dennoch wird man den hier repräsentierten Herrschaftsverhältnissen Ende der 1950er und zu Beginn der 1960er Jahre nicht gerecht, wenn man sie als übliche Dichotomie zwischen schweren Lebens- und Arbeitsbedingungen und wirklichkeitsferner Propaganda beschreibt.

Denn trotz aller Klischeehaftigkeit erscheint dieser neue Magadaner Diskurs als elementare Voraussetzung für sich verändernde Herrschaftsverhältnisse. Die Magadaner wurden als wichtige Arbeitskräfte, als enthusiastische Sowjetbürger, die Kader als fürsorgliche Funktionäre *beschrieben*; Sprachduktus und Sprachbilder wurden weicher, milder. Dieses neue Sprechen ging mit den veränderten Verhältnissen unmittelbar einher, begleitete sie, schrieb sich als fester Topos der Magadaner Repräsentation ein.

Alexei Yurchak hat mit seiner aufsehenerregenden These – die reine Teilnahme an Ritualen und die Reproduktion ritualisierter Texte habe das sowjetische System keineswegs unterminiert, sondern es im Gegenteil stabilisiert – die elementare Bedeutung der performativen Dimension des sowjetischen Diskurses seit den 1950er Jahren beschrieben.[319] Überträgt man diesen Ansatz auf die Magadaner Verhältnisse, so fällt auf, dass alle formalen Veränderungen im Magadaner Gebiet an einen performativen Akt geknüpft waren – die Gründung des Magadaner Gebietes. In der offiziellen Darstellung wurde die gesamte Lage des Gebietes an diesen Akt rückgebunden. Alle positiven Entwicklungen gingen, so der offizielle Diskurs, auf diese „zweite Geburt" der Region, auf eine rein performative Handlung zurück.[320]

Dadurch gelang es der regionalen Leitung, die Verbesserung der Verhältnisse gewissermaßen Stück für Stück „herbeizuschreiben". Als entscheidend erschien dann nicht mehr, wie die Verhältnisse tatsächlich waren, wie die Magadaner tatsächlich lebten, sondern welche Möglichkeiten und Optionen sich aus der Gebietsgründung ergaben. Denn die allumfassende Zuständigkeit für alle Lebensbereiche, die die neue regionale Leitung für sich reklamierte und die sie demonstrierte, schloss auch mit ein, dass sie in ihrer Selbstdarstellung einen Weg fand, mit negativen Erscheinungen umzugehen. Im Laufe der Zeit gelang es ihr, einen Raum zu schaffen, in dem scheinbar offen und frei über die bestehenden Unzulänglichkeiten gesprochen werden konnte.

Auf den Seiten der Zeitung wurde kritischen Stimmen zunehmend Platz eingeräumt. Und damit ist hier nicht nur eine quantitative Zunahme gemeint: Kritik in der stalinistischen *Sovetskaja Kolyma* war allein auf mangelnde Leistungen oder einen nicht erfüllten Plan beschränkt geblieben, sie hatte darauf abgezielt, im Gewand einer kritischen Stimme, angebliche „Feinde" der Produktion zu entlarven und damit Druck auf Kader und Arbeiterschaft auszuüben, ohne tatsächlich einen unabhängigen Ge-

---

318 Vgl. zu den stereotypen Darstellungen verschiedener Bevölkerungsgruppen das Kapitel 5.1.5.
319 Yurchak bezieht sich dabei auf die Sprechakttheorie von John L. Austin u. a., die zwischen den „constative acts", die Realität beschreiben, und den „performative acts", die Realität nicht beschreiben und damit auch nicht „wahr" oder „falsch" sein können, unterscheidet. Zu seiner These siehe Yurchak, Was Forever, S. 59 f. sowie seine Schlussbemerkungen.
320 Vgl. dazu Kapitel 3.2.1.

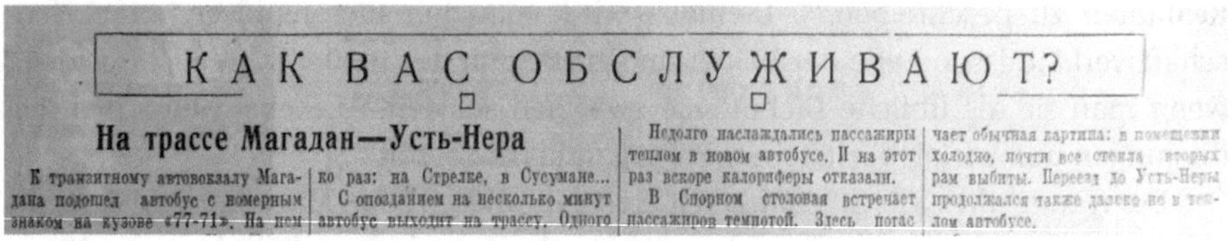

КАК ВАС ОБСЛУЖИВАЮТ?

На трассе Магадан—Усть-Нера

К транзитному автовокзалу Магадана подошел автобус с номерным знаком на кузове «77-71». На нем ко раз: на Стрелке, в Сусумане...

С опозданием на несколько минут автобус выходит на трассу. Одного

Недолго наслаждались пассажиры теплом в новом автобусе. И на этот раз вскоре калориферы отказали.

В Спорном столовая встречает пассажиров темнотой. Здесь погас чает обычная картина: в помещении холодно, почти все стекла вторых рам выбиты. Переезд до Усть-Неры продолжался также далеко не в теплом автобусе.

Abb. 62 „Wie werdet ihr bedient?", Magadanskaja Pravda, 23. Januar 1958

danken zu äußern – wie es Simon Huxtable als Kennzeichen des Journalismus im Spätstalinismus beschreibt.[321] Die *Magadanskaja Pravda* öffnete sich nun den Problemen des Alltags. Die unpersönliche Rede von „Missständen" oder „Defiziten", die Graeme Gill als wesentliches Element der neuen Sprachregelung in der Entstalinisierung diagnostiziert hat und die die stalinistische Hetze gegen individuelle „Volksfeinde" und „Schädlinge" ersetzte[322], prägte auch den offiziellen Diskurs über die Verhältnisse im Magadaner Gebiet.

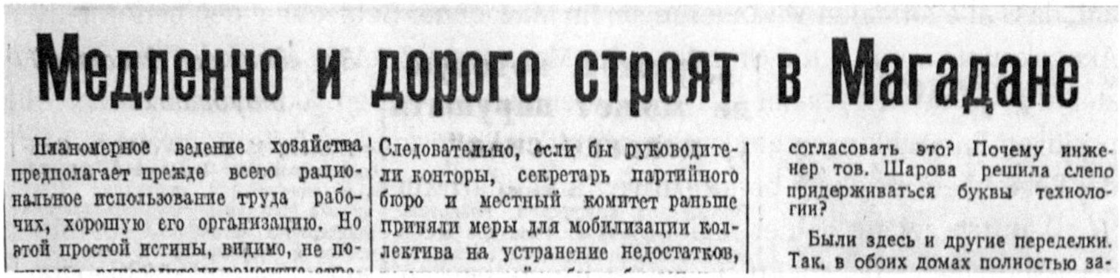

Медленно и дорого строят в Магадане

Планомерное ведение хозяйства предполагает прежде всего рациональное использование труда рабочих, хорошую его организацию. Но этой простой истины, видимо, не по-

Следовательно, если бы руководители конторы, секретарь партийного бюро и местный комитет раньше приняли меры для мобилизации коллектива на устранение недостатков,

согласовать это? Почему инженер тов. Шарова решила слепо придерживаться буквы технологии?

Были здесь и другие переделки. Так, в обоих домах полностью за-

Abb. 63 „Langsam und teuer wird in Magadan gebaut", Magadanskaja Pravda, 28. März 1957

In Reportagen, Berichten, in Karikaturen und durch Briefe an die Redaktion der *Magadanskaja Pravda* wurden immer wieder mangelnder Wohnraum, schlechter öffentlicher Transport, fehlende Geschäfte und Lebensmittel thematisiert. Die folgenden Titel können einen Eindruck von den Themen vermitteln: „Wie werdet ihr bedient?" (eine „Leserbriefserie über Kantinen in der Region), „Langsam und teuer wird in Magadan gebaut" (Bericht über den Baufortgang in Magadan) und „Viele Tonnen wertvollen Korns gehen verloren. Streifzug einer Brigade der Magadanskaja Pravda".[323]

Gerade kleine Zeichnungen waren mitunter recht ironisch und schienen unmittelbar aus dem Magadaner Leben gegriffen zu sein.

---

321 Vgl. Huxtable, Soviet Journalists, S. 210 f.

322 Vgl. Gill, Symbols, S. 172 sowie Kolář, Poststalinismus, S. 203 ff.

323 Vgl. „Viele Tonnen wertvollen Korns gehen verloren. Streifzug einer Brigade der Magadanskaja Pravda", in: Magadanskaja Pravda, 11. Januar 1956, S. 3. „Die Bewohner der Tundra sollen mit allem Notwendigen ausgestattet werden. In Čukotka läuft der Handel weiterhin schlecht", in: Magadanskaja Pravda, 19. Mai 1956, S. 3. Zur Gestaltung von Kritik in Parteizeitungen der Sowjetunion der 1950er Jahre siehe Gill/Pitty, Power, S. 44.

Abb. 64 „47 Kilometer... bis zum Badehaus", Magadanskaja Pravda, 16. Juli 1955

Die humoristische Darstellung machte die schlimmen Zustände – aufgrund eines fehlenden Badehauses war für die Bewohner einer Siedlung das 47 km entfernte Magadan die nächstgelegene Gelegenheit sich zu waschen – öffentlich und setzte die politische Leitung der Kritik aus. Zugleich verniedlichte sie sie dadurch, regte mit ihr lediglich „zum Schmunzeln" an. So wollte sie wohl verhindern, dass Kritik an konkreten Zuständen in Devianz und Dissens umschlug.

Diese „kritischen Stimmen" ließen die mitunter elenden Lebens- und Arbeitsbedingungen in der Region als eine Momentaufnahme, als zu beseitigendes Übel auf dem sicheren Weg in eine bessere Zukunft erscheinen. So konnten die Beschreibungen und Abbildungen idealer Zustände (wie in Abbildung 14, 35 und 57) als greifbare Möglichkeiten gelten, die unter Umständen für manche bereits Realität waren – so wie sich die Kinder des Gebietes in den Erinnerungen Michael Solomons bereits an einer Reklame für Zitrusfrüchte erfreuten, ohne die Früchte jemals real in den Händen zu halten:

> Ende 1955, als wir Kolyma verließen, annoncierten die Lokalzeitungen Bananen und Orangen, die bis aus Sizilien kamen. Natürlich gab es so seltene Früchte nie im Überfluß, sondern sie mußten rationiert werden – und waren teuer. Doch man bekam sie wenigstens hin und wieder zu sehen, und schon das allein war eine große Freude für die Kinder.[324]

---

324 Solomon, Magadan, S. 163.

Aber auch die politische Führung selbst ließ sich zum Gegenstand von Kritik machen – so z. B. in dem Artikel „Ohne Engagement, ohne Initiative ... Das Magadaner Stadtexekutivkomitee kommt Anordnungen nicht nach"[325] – wenn auch mit erheblichen Einschränkungen. Sakrosankt war dabei die oberste Parteileitung selbst. An keiner Stelle wurde die Kritik an einzelnen Missständen auf die oberen Kader des Gebietes übertragen. Zugleich wurden alle heimatkundlich orientierten Artikel, die für die Region warben, sorgsam von kritischen Berichten getrennt. Diese Form der Kritik untergrub dabei nicht die Autorität der neuen Leitung, sondern schien sie im Gegenteil zu stärken. Und dies in einer Region, in der bis 1953 Kritik noch als Verstoß gegen eine militärische Befehlskette gewertet wurde. Auf diese Weise konnte sich die Partei in Chruščevs Metanarrativ einschreiben, das, nach Gill, „auf ein inklusives Modell der politischen Institutionen abzielte"; Kritik in Maßen sollte die Vorstellung von Gestaltbarkeit und politischen Einflussmöglichkeiten vermitteln.[326]

Auffällig ist im Vergleich zu den Tendenzen, die Huxtable in seiner Darstellung der veränderten Rolle einer kritischen Presse beschreibt, dass sich an der Entwicklung der Magadaner Presse zwar eine allmähliche Zunahme kritischer Stimmen seit dem 20. Parteitag erkennen lässt, dass jedoch keineswegs von einem abrupten Umschlag nach dem Februar 1956 gesprochen werden kann. Auf den Seiten der lokalen Zeitung, ebenso wie bei der Zeitung der lokalen Komsomolzen oder dem stärker technisch ausgerichteten Journal *Kolyma* wuchs die Zahl kritischer Stimmen kontinuierlich an. Die Kritik wurde schärfer im Ton, sie griff zusehends auch lokale Autoritäten an und berührte mehr und mehr Fragen des Alltags.

Von einem „immediate transformative effect"[327], den Huxtable auf den Seiten der wichtigsten Moskauer Zeitungen, wie der *Izvestija*, nach dem 20. Parteitag ausmacht, kann im Magadaner Gebiet nicht gesprochen werden. Die Ursachen für diese „Zeitverzögerung" mögen in der prinzipiellen Abhängigkeit lokaler Pressevertreter liegen, die Veränderungen in Moskau zunächst einmal vorsichtig beobachteten, bevor sie sich allzu schnell mit Kritik nach vorne wagten. Zugleich aber sah sich die Presse an der Kolyma anderen Voraussetzungen gegenüber und vor andere Aufgaben gestellt. Seit 1954 wurde sie von der neuen politischen Führung als Element der Machtdemonstration und zur Propagierung ihres neuen Kurses eingesetzt. Die Zunahme kritischer Stimmen folgte dabei nicht nur einer unionsweiten Zunahme von Kritik in der Presse, sondern war zugleich Ausdruck eines wachsenden Selbstbewusstseins und einer sich vergrößernden Unabhängigkeit von Dal'stroj auf Seiten der lokalen Führung. Die Parteileitung benutzte die Zeitung ganz bewusst, um gegen die Kombinatsleitung Stimmung zu machen.[328]

---

325 Vgl. „Ohne Engagement, ohne Initiative ... Das Magadaner Stadtexekutivkomitee kommt Anordnungen nicht nach", in: Magadanskaja Pravda, 14. Dezember 1957, S. 3.
326 Vgl. Gill, Symbols, S. 180.
327 Huxtable, Soviet Journalists, S. 211.
328 Vgl. dazu Kapitel 3.3.4.

In den 1950er und 1960er Jahren entwickelte die neue politische Führung eine Repräsentation des „Nahe-dran-Seins" an den Bedürfnissen und konkreten Lebensumständen der Menschen. Sie inszenierte sich als eine „Herrschaft im Dialog", im offenen Austausch mit den Bürgern – über die Lage des Gebietes und seine Entwicklungsmöglichkeiten, mit einem offenen Ohr für alle Schwierigkeiten. Diese Repräsentationsform war ganz offensichtlich eine regionale Variante des Herrscherbildes, das Chruščev von sich entwarf und das Jan Kusber als ein „ins-Volk-Gehen" des Ersten Sekretärs bezeichnet hat. Kusber beschreibt damit das Bild eines „scheinbar konsensual handelnden" Herrschers, der auf seinen vielen Reisen immer wieder das Gespräch mit „dem Volk" suchte und sich dabei als besonders fürsorglich präsentierte.[329]

Afanas'ev übernahm dieses Bild quasi in den regionalen Kontext. Auch er, der selbst häufig in dem riesigen Gebiet unterwegs war, zeichnete von sich und der lokalen Parteileitung das Bild einer Führung, die aufgrund ihres Einsatzes und ihrer moralischen Integrität Vertrauen verdiente – Vertrauen, das durch bessere Lebensbedingungen belohnt würde. Ihren umfassenden Herrschaftsanspruch inszenierten die neuen Kader, entsprechend der besonderen Bedeutung der Partei, als allumfassende Zuständigkeit und Verantwortung.[330]

Im Gegensatz zu den alten Kadern von Dal'stroj sei die neue Führung dieses Vertrauens würdig, weil sie die Bedürfnisse der Bevölkerung nicht nur ernst nehme, sondern sie auch als gerechtfertigt betrachte. Diese Inszenierung hat Afanas'ev in seinen „Aufzeichnungen" über das Magadaner Gebiet eindrucksvoll vorgeführt. Er schildert einen (fiktiven) Dialog Mitte der 1950er Jahre zwischen einem alten Produktionsleiter und einem neuen Parteivertreter über die Arbeitskräfte des Magadaner Gebietes:

> ‚Mit wem [so der Produktionsleiter – M. S.] soll man denn arbeiten, mit diesen Mädchen und Jungen [gemeint sind junge Vertragsarbeiter und Komsomolzen – M. S.]? Von denen etwas zu fordern ist ja schon verboten. Und die Wohnräume und Kantinen, siehste, gefallen ihnen nicht, und es gibt ja gar keine Tanzgelegenheiten! Und der Plan? Was für einen Plan soll's denn geben, wenn die sich scheuen, auch nur eine Überstunde zu machen?' Dem alten Wirtschaftshasen antworten sie [die Parteivertreter – M. S.]: ‚Versuch doch du mal, die Arbeit so zu organisieren, dass alles in der vorgegebenen Zeit eines Arbeitstages erledigt werden kann; überprüf' mal, wie in den Kantinen gekocht wird und wie die Zustände dort sind.' Aber der andere bleibt stur: ‚Ich bin selbst als Komsomolze hierhergekommen und hab' mich nie über irgendetwas beschwert, nichts gefordert, nur tüchtig geschuftet.' Ich (Afanas'ev) versuche mich einzumischen, erinnere ihn, dass sich die Zeiten geändert haben, dass die Leute mehr Errungenschaften haben wollen, und zwar solche, auf die sie ein volles Anrecht haben. [...]. Der Mann ist beleidigt, geht. Einige Leiter und Direktoren von Unternehmen, in denen die Parteiorganisationen stark waren, haben sich schnell umgestellt. [...] Aber andere

---

329 Kusber, Herrscherbild, S. 753. Siehe zu diesem Porträt Chruščevs ebenso Gill, Symbols, S. 170 sowie Ivanova, Na poroge, S. 53 und Merl, Political Communication, S. 85.
330 Gill beschreibt diese Repräsentation der „Allzuständigkeit" als Stilisierung einer „party of the whole people", auf der Grundlage leninscher Normen der Parteiarbeit. Vgl. Gill, Symbols, S. 168 f.

> Funktionäre aus dem alten Stahl haben's nicht ausgehalten – sie sind abgereist und es ist ihnen bis
> zum Schluss nicht bewusst geworden, was hier geschehen ist.[331]

Unausgesprochen erörtern Afanas'ev und der alte Komsomolze in ihrem Gespräch den Wechsel von Arbeit im Rahmen eines Lager-Industriellen Komplexes in den 1930er Jahren zur Vertragsarbeit in einem zivilen sowjetischen Gebiet nach Stalins Tod. Dabei geht es offensichtlich nicht nur um eine Bewertung „alter" und „neuer" Arbeitsmethoden, sondern vielmehr auch um die Inszenierung unterschiedlicher Mentalitäten. Nicht nur werden in dieser Darstellung die Bedürfnisse der Arbeiter von den „neuen Kadern" als legitim betrachtet, ihre Befriedigung erscheint der neuen Leitung als Frage einer angemessenen Organisation und Kontrolle und damit als ihre ureigene Aufgabe.

Diese Darstellungsweise enthält zugleich eine historische Dimension, die die neue Führung auch in ihrem politischen Machtkampf gegen die Führung von Dal'stroj einsetzte. Durch ihre Rhetorik von der zweiten Geburt der Region konnte sie negative Erscheinungen als historisch zu überwindende Tendenzen abtun; das Gebiet erhielt damit in der sowjetischen Periode eine Art „zweite Chance". Die Partei schuf sich gewissermaßen einen historischen Vorschuss, der noch bestehende Unzulänglichkeiten bei der Versorgung der Bevölkerung als zu überwindendes Erbe einer prinzipiell abgeschlossenen Epoche erscheinen ließ und der zugleich den Eindruck vermittelte, die ganze Region könne seit 1954 einfach mit neuen Assoziationen belegt werden. Recht subtil wurden so aber auch die Gewaltherrschaft von Dal'stroj und die entsetzlichen Erfahrungen ehemaliger Häftlinge, die selbst für Neuankömmlinge den Ruf der Region prägten, lediglich zu einer Art Entwicklungsstufe des Gebietes.

Auch wenn die politischen Verantwortlichen kriminelle Übergriffe, Schlägereien und sogenanntes „amoralisches Verhalten" immer wieder mit der „Lagervergangenheit" einzelner Personen in Verbindung brachten und die Tatsache einer früheren Inhaftierung zur Stigmatisierung benutzten[332], existierten die Lager in der offiziellen Darstellung der historischen Entwicklung nur in Andeutungen, in der Rede von den „alten Zeiten" oder den „dunklen Zeiten", in der Beschreibung von „alten Mentalitäten" bei früheren Dal'stroj-Mitarbeitern.

Auf dem Höhepunkt des Tauwetters, im Jahr 1961, machte der Sekretär der Magadaner Parteileitung Žicharev eine vorsichtige Ausnahme: Er verwies in seinen „Skizzen der Geschichte des Nordostens der RSFSR" zumindest darauf, dass neben Arbeitern und Angestellten in der Region auch „Menschen gearbeitet hatten, die in Lagern eine Haftstrafe absaßen"[333], bezog sich damit jedoch nur auf die Zeit Ende der 1930er Jahre.

---

331 Afanas'ev, Rossija, S. 62.
332 Vgl. das Kapitel 5.3.1.
333 Žicharev, Očerki, S. 207.

Einen weiteren Vorstoß unternahm der bekannte Autor und Publizist Semen Samuilovič Vilenskij, späterer Vorsitzender der Vereinigung ehemaliger Lagerhäftlinge „Vozvraščenie", der im *Berlag* inhaftiert gewesen war. 1962 kehrte er als Korrespondent der Zeitung *Literaturnaja Gazeta* nach Magadan zurück. In seinen Erinnerungen an die Verhältnisse der Zeit schildert er eine Begegnung mit dem Ersten Parteisekretär Afanas'ev. Er habe damals Afanas'ev vorgeworfen, dass in der Zeitung *Magadanskaja Pravda* die Lagervergangenheit des Gebietes keine Erwähnung finde und dass er selbst die lokalen Lager verharmlosend als „Gefängnisabteilungen" bezeichne. Afanas'evs Reaktion auf Vilenskijs Kritik ist bezeichnend für den Kurs der politischen Führung jener Jahre. Afanas'ev war der Ansicht, „dass die Magadaner Literatur nicht die Kraft habe, darüber zu schreiben". Er selbst wolle jedoch ein Buch herausgeben, das den „Mantel des Schweigens über das Vergangene" lüften werde. Vilenskij und Afanas'ev einigten sich daraufhin schnell auf die gemeinsame Publikation eines Sammelbandes mit Werken ehemaliger Kolyma-Häftlinge. Afanas'ev war zunächst sehr entschlossen, dann jedoch um „eine positive" Auswahl der Schriftsteller bemüht, „damit das Buch nicht allzu schwarz"[334] würde. Doch die Zeiten hatten sich bereits geändert. Der von Vilenskij und Afanas'ev geplante Sammelband war zwar schon für die Publikation vorbereitet – Ginzburg, Lev Kopelev, Solženicyn u. a. waren als Autoren gesetzt – Šalamov war zwar angefragt, hatte jedoch seine Teilnahme verweigert, weil ihm die Auswahl der Koautoren missfiel. Doch als das Buch in Magadan tatsächlich in Druck gehen sollte, übte die Abteilung für Ideologie des ZK der KPdSU Druck aus, so dass eine ganze Reihe von Autoren wieder gestrichen wurde. Der Sammelband erschien in einer sehr kleinen Auflage und erfuhr keinerlei Aufmerksamkeit. Erst 1989 gelang es Vilenskij wieder, Lagererinnerungen in der Sowjetunion herauszugeben.[335]

Dennoch war die Lokalgeschichte immer wieder Gegenstand von Darstellungen in der örtlichen Presse und Literatur. Zwei Personen aus der jüngsten Vergangenheit der Kolyma sollten dabei zu positiven Identifikationsfiguren werden: Zum einen war dies der Geologe Ju. A. Bilibin, der als „Entdecker der Goldenen Kolyma" gilt und dem Bemühungen um eine vollständige Erschließung des Gebietes, im Sinne einer „echten osvoenie" nachgesagt wurden. Angeblich hatte sich Bilibin zu Beginn der 1930er Jahre gegen die räuberische stalinistische Ausbeutung gewandt.[336] Über Bilibin und die Arbeit der folgenden Geologengenerationen ließ sich für das neue Gebiet eine zivile, Dal'stroj-unabhängige Geschichte der Region fabrizieren. Bilibin wurde in dieser Darstellung zum sagenhaften Entdecker der Kolyma, zu einer Art „Kolumbus" des

---

334 So Afanas'ev in den Erinnerungen Vilenskijs. Vilenskij, Kak pojavilos', S. 11/f.

335 Vgl. Vilenskij, Kak pojavilos'. Der von Vilenskij und Afanas'ev geplante Band wurde von dem in Magadan sehr bekannten Historiker N. Kozlov redaktionell betreut, das Buch sollte unter dem Titel „Radi žizni na zemle" erscheinen. Nach der Perestrojka konnte Vilenskij eine ganze Reihe sehr bekannter Erinnerungen an die Lager der Kolyma veröffentlichen, darunter „Osvencim bez pečej", „Est' vsjudu svet" sowie „Dodnes' tjagoteet".

336 Vgl. Širokov, Dal'stroj, S. 100. Bilibin zu Ehren wurde 1961 der Bezirk Vostočnaja Tundra in Bilibinsker Bezirk umbenannt, eine Atomstation im Magadaner Gebiet trug seinen Namen.

Nordostens.[337] Neuere Goldfunde wurden zu Etappen sowjetischer Erschließung stilisiert, Geologen zu Pionieren der sowjetischen Kultur.[338]

Zum anderen war dies der legendäre erste Direktor des Kombinats, È. P. Berzin, früherer Sekretär Dzeržinskijs, der im Dezember 1937 verhaftet, einer gemeinsamen Verschwörung mit Jagoda und Rudzutak beschuldigt und im August 1938 erschossen wurde. Nach dem 20. Parteitag wurde Berzin im Jahr 1956 rehabilitiert. Seine soziale Rehabilitierung erfolgte in der Publikation „Skizzen der Geschichte des Nordostens der RSFSR", die der Sekretär der Magadaner Parteileitung, Žicharev, 1961 veröffentlichte. Hier wurde das Wirken Berzins ausführlich dargestellt, seine Verhaftung und Verurteilung aufgrund einer fabrizierten Anklage ebenso wie seine Rehabilitation besprochen.[339] In seinen „Aufzeichnungen" nannte Afanas'ev ihn einen „echten Leninisten" und zeichnete ein stark idealisiertes Bild seiner Person.[340] Dieses Bild wirkte bis in die 2000er Jahre fort. Berzin erhielt vor Ort einen mit Lenin vergleichbaren Status, 1989 wurde in der Magadaner Innenstadt eine Büste Berzins aufgestellt, noch heute ist eine Straße nach dem ersten Direktor benannt.[341]

Die Rehabilitation Berzins, der Verweis auf Bilibin und die „abgewogen-kritische" Sicht auf die Rolle des Kombinats in den vergangenen Jahrzehnten schufen eine eigene, regionale Entstalinisierungs-Erzählung, die sich nahtlos an die Darstellungsweise Chruščevs anpasste. Sie „rettete" gewissermaßen ein positives Erbe der ersten Besiedelungs- und Erschließungsmaßnahmen Ende der 1920er Jahre, das die neue politische Leitung für sich vereinnahmen konnte.

Der Parteileitung gelang mit der geschichtspolitischen Überhöhung ihrer „echten, sowjetischen" Erschließung (im Sinne der *osvoenie*) der Aufbau einer wirkmächtigen Repräsentationsstrategie. Ihre tägliche Arbeit erhielt eine umfassende Legitimation, sie wurde selbst zur historischen Notwendigkeit: Indem sie die Durchdringung der Region mit ihrer eigenen Infrastruktur vorantrieb, wurde sie per se zur zukunftstreibenden, von der Geschichte legitimierten Kraft.

---

337 Zur Bedeutung der ersten Geologengeneration in der offiziellen Geschichtsschreibung der Stadt Magadan siehe Zvik, Magadan, S. 7; Rodin, Iz istorii osvoenija Severo-Vostoka.

338 So z. B. in Malagin, Èkonomičeskij rajon, S. 34 ff. und auch bei Drabkin, Razvedčiki nedr.

339 Zur Biographie Berzins siehe Širokov, Dal'stroj, S. 75 sowie Nordlander, Evolution, S. 655.

340 Der Historiker N. V. Kozlov stellte Berzin ins Zentrum seines Romans „Aufbewahren für alle Zeit", dessen erster Teil 1962 publiziert wurde. Der vollständige erste Band des Romans erschien schließlich 1974, als auch der 80. Geburtstag Berzins gefeiert wurde. Vgl. die Darstellung bei Afanas'ev, Rossija, S. 34.

341 Varlam Šalamov trat in seinen Erzählungen immer wieder der „Berzin-Legende" [W. S.] entgegen. Er schildert schonungslos Berzins Vorgeschichte als Lagerchef auf den Solovkij Ende der 1920er Jahre, seine Beziehungen zu Häftlingen, die Berufung zum Kolyma-Direktor, die regionalen Massenerschießungen der Jahre 1936 bis 1937, für die Berzin die Verantwortung trug, sowie seine Verhaftung und Erschießung. Šalamov lässt seinen Erzähler in der Erzählung „Am Steigbügel" von Berzin als dem „allergewöhnlichste[n] Lagerchef und eifrige[n] Erfüller des Willens seines Entsenders" sprechen. Immer wieder wehrt er sich gegen die Idealisierung des ersten Direktors. Vgl. die Erzählungen „Der grüne Staatsanwalt" in Schalamow, Künstler der Schaufel, die Erzählung „Am Steigbügel" sowie „Khan-Girej" in Schalamow, Auferweckung der Lärche.

Kehrt man nun zu der eingangs zitierten These von Yurchak zurück, nach dem bereits die Reproduktion ritualisierter Texte zur Stabilisierung des sowjetischen Systems beigetragen habe, so erscheint die Überhöhung der Gebietsgründung als eine wirksame Strategie in der performativen Dimension des sowjetischen Diskurses. „Language", so Yurchak, „was not simply fixed in concrete texts, [...], but was normalized across the whole authoritative genre of Soviet discourse."[342] Ebenso wie der formale, institutionelle und infrastrukturelle Anschluss der Region an das Festland hat das Magadaner Gebiet in den 1950er Jahren auch Zugang zu diesem typisierten sowjetischen Diskurs erhalten. Das Gebiet wurde nicht nur als Teil der zivilen sowjetischen Struktur *bezeichnet*, die mentale und sprachliche Besetzung des Gebietes und seiner Bewohner erschien als eine wirkmächtige Zuschreibung. Zumal sich die ritualisierten Texte nicht völlig im luftleeren Raum bewegten. Sie waren nicht nur „performative Akte" im Yurchak'schen Sinne, sondern vielleicht gerade dadurch so besonders wirkmächtig, dass sie durchaus auch Realität abbildeten – schließlich waren Verbesserungen der Arbeits- und Lebensverhältnisse erkennbar.

Die Selbstinszenierung der paternalistischen, hilfreichen Parteileitung, die dem historischen Neuanfang ein Gesicht gab, setzte rhetorisch Standards, sie begleitete die Veränderungen im sozialpolitischen Bereich und schrieb sie zugleich herbei. Denn selbst wenn die Lebens- und Arbeitsverhältnisse eines Arbeiters noch stark von Willkür geprägt und die Bedingungen v. a. an den Rändern des Gebietes elendig waren, schienen sich die publizistischen Verheißungen doch in einigen Bereichen zu erfüllen. Der Aufbau Magadans zu einer echten Gebietshauptstadt mit einer hohen Dichte an medizinischen, pädagogischen und später auch wissenschaftlichen Einrichtungen erfüllte hier eine wichtige Leuchtturm-Funktion. Die publizistische und kulturelle Umschreibung der Region sollte eine positive Aufbruchstimmung konstatieren und evozierte sie zugleich.

Zu fragen wäre, ob diese Zuschreibungen auch bewirkten, dass die *Magadancy* der neuen Herrschaft ein gewisses Maß an Legitimität zugestanden. Die hohe Zahl an Petitionen, die bei Tageszeitungen und der politischen und wirtschaftlichen Leitung eingingen, lassen dies zumindest vermuten. Die Magadaner Bittschriften sind Teil des sowjetischen Petitionswesens, in dem die Hinwendung zu einer konkreten Stelle oder einem bestimmten Funktionär als eine der wenigen aussichtsreichen Möglichkeiten verstanden wurde, willkürlichen Maßnahmen oder ungerechten Entscheidungen zu entgehen bzw. ein persönliches Anliegen außerhalb normierter Strukturen durchzusetzen.[343]

Die Magadaner unterschieden sich von anderen Bevölkerungsteilen der Sowjetunion nicht in dieser Praxis. Sie schrieben an die Leitung von Partei und Staat auf Gebiets- und Bezirksebene, an den Volkswirtschaftsrat und die lokalen Zeitungen,

---

342 Yurchak, Was Forever, S. 53.
343 Das Petitionswesen in der Sowjetunion nach 1953 ist in letzter Zeit vermehrt Gegenstand der Forschung geworden. Vgl. Fitzpatrick, Identity and Imposture, S. 157 ff.; Bittner, Appeals; Dobson, Cold Summer; Sprau, Petitionen.

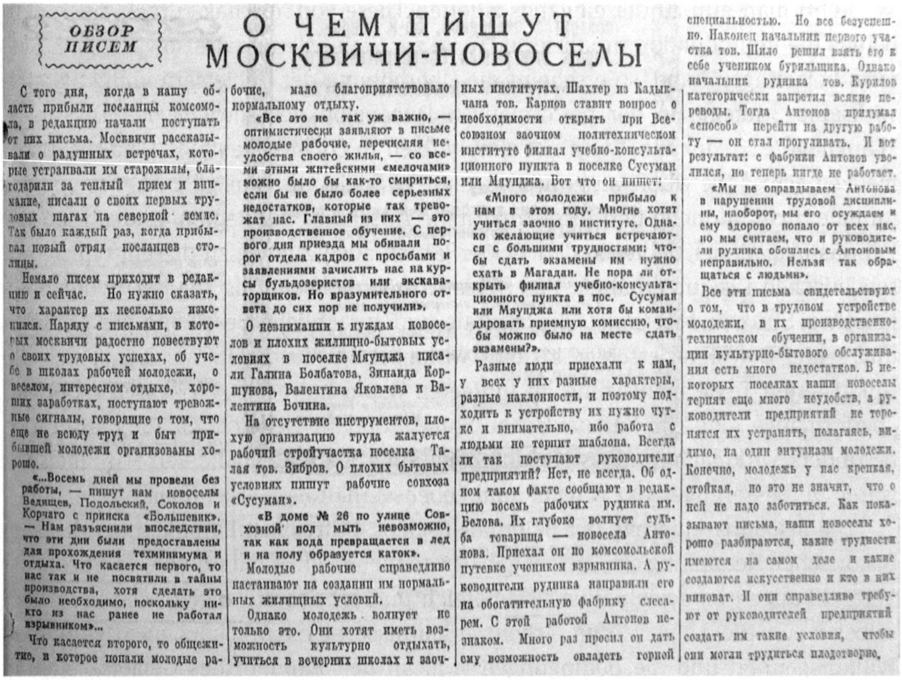

ОБЗОР ПИСЕМ

О ЧЕМ ПИШУТ МОСКВИЧИ-НОВОСЕЛЫ

С того дня, когда в нашу область прибыли посланцы комсомола, в редакцию начали поступать от них письма. Москвичи рассказывали о радушных встречах, которые устраивали им старожилы, благодарили за теплый прием и внимание, писали о своих первых трудовых шагах на северной земле. Так было каждый раз, когда прибывал новый отряд посланцев столицы.

Немало писем приходит в редакцию и сейчас. Но нужно сказать, что характер их несколько изменился. Наряду с письмами, в которых москвичи радостно повествуют о своих трудовых успехах, об учебе в школах рабочей молодежи, о веселом, интересном отдыхе, хороших заработках, поступают тревожные сигналы, говорящие о том, что еще не всюду труд и быт прибывшей молодежи организованы хорошо.

«...Восемь дней мы провели без работы, — пишут нам новоселы Ведищев, Подольский, Соколов и Корчаго с прииска «Большевик». — Нам разъяснили впоследствии, что эти дни были предоставлены для прохождения техминимума и отдыха. Что касается первого, то нас так и не посвятили в тайны производства, хотя сделать это было необходимо, поскольку никто из нас ранее не работал взрывником»...

Что касается второго, то общежитие, в которое попали молодые рабочие, мало благоприятствовало нормальному отдыху.

«Все это не так уж важно, — оптимистически заявляют в письме молодые рабочие, перечисляя неудобства своего жилья, — со всеми этими житейскими «мелочами» можно было бы как-то смириться, если бы не было более серьезных недостатков, которые так тревожат нас. Главный из них — это производственное обучение. С первого дня приезда мы обивали порог отдела кадров с просьбами и заявлениями зачислить нас на курсы бульдозеристов или экскаваторщиков. Но вразумительного ответа до сих пор не получили».

О невнимании к нуждам новоселов и плохих жилищно-бытовых условиях в поселке Мяунджа писали Галина Болбатова, Зинаида Коршунова, Валентина Яковлева и Валентина Бочина.

На отсутствие инструментов, плохую организацию труда жалуется рабочий стройучастка поселка Талая тов. Зибров. О плохих бытовых условиях пишут рабочие совхоза «Сусуман».

«В доме № 26 по улице Совхозной пол мыть невозможно, так как вода превращается в лед и на полу образуется каток».

Молодые рабочие справедливо настаивают на создании им нормальных жилищных условий.

Однако молодежь волнует не только это. Они хотят иметь возможность культурно отдыхать, учиться в вечерних школах и заочных институтах. Шахтер из Кадыкчана тов. Карпов ставит вопрос о необходимости открыть при Всесоюзном заочном политехническом институте филиал учебно-консультационного пункта в поселке Сусуман или Мяунджа. Вот что он пишет:

«Много молодежи прибыло к нам в этом году. Многие хотят учиться заочно в институте. Однако желающие учиться встречаются с большими трудностями: чтобы сдать экзамены им нужно ехать в Магадан. Не пора ли открыть филиал учебно-консультационного пункта в пос. Сусуман или Мяунджа или хотя бы командировать приемную комиссию, чтобы можно было на месте сдать экзамены?».

Разные люди приехали к нам, у всех у них разные характеры, разные наклонности, и поэтому подходить к устройству их нужно чутко и внимательно, ибо работа с людьми не терпит шаблона. Всегда ли так поступают руководители предприятий? Нет, не всегда. Об одном таком факте сообщают в редакцию восемь рабочих рудника им. Белова. Их глубоко волнует судьба товарища — новосела Антонова. Приехал он по комсомольской путевке учеником взрывника. А руководители рудника направили его на обогатительную фабрику слесарем. С этой работой Антонов незнаком. Много раз просил он дать ему возможность овладеть горной специальностью. Но все безуспешно. Наконец начальник первого участка тов. Шило решил взять его к себе учеником бурильщика. Однако начальник рудника тов. Курилов категорически запретил всякие переводы. Тогда Антонов придумал «способ» перейти на другую работу — он стал прогуливать. И вот результат: с фабрики Антонов уволился, но теперь нигде не работает.

«Мы не оправдываем Антонова в нарушении трудовой дисциплины, наоборот, мы его осуждаем и ему здорово попало от всех нас, но мы считаем, что и руководители рудника обошлись с Антоновым неправильно. Нельзя так обращаться с людьми».

Все эти письма свидетельствуют о том, что в трудовом устройстве молодежи, в их производственно-техническом обучении, в организации культурно-бытового обслуживания есть много недостатков. В некоторых поселках наши новоселы терпят еще много неудобств, а руководители предприятий не торопятся их устранять, полагаясь, видимо, на один энтузиазм молодежи. Конечно, молодежь у нас крепкая, стойкая, но это не значит, что о ней не надо заботиться. Как показывают письма, наши новоселы хорошо разбираются, какие трудности имеются на самом деле и какие создаются искусственно и кто в них виноват. И они справедливо требуют от руководителей предприятий создать им такие условия, чтобы они могли трудиться плодотворно.

Abb. 65 Zusammenstellung kritischer Petitionen, Magadanskaja Pravda, 20. Januar 1957

aber auch an unionsweite Stellen. Sie beschwerten sich über ihre Arbeitsbedingungen, das Lohn- und Bonisystem, über ihre Wohnverhältnisse, die Versorgung mit Lebensmitteln und Waren des täglichen Bedarfs, über mangelnde Plätze in Kindereinrichtungen und Internaten – um nur einige der Themen zu nennen. Häufig erhielt die Gebietsleitung erst auf Grundlage von Petitionen Nachricht über die konkrete Lage in einer bestimmten Siedlung oder einer Bevölkerungsgruppe.[344]

So hatte sich auch die eingangs erwähnte frierende Bevölkerung von Lavrentija mit einer Bittschrift an die *Magadanskaja Pravda* gewandt. Wie auch in anderen Fällen geht hier aus den Quellen hervor, dass das Gebietsexekutivkomitee tatsächlich intervenierte. Vermuten lässt sich, dass diese Interventionen zumindest einzelnen Funktionären Legitimität verlieh, dass ein gewisses personales Vertrauen aufgebaut

344 Vgl. beispielsweise GAMO f. R-137, op. 1, d. 58, l. 387–396 (an die Leitung des Volkswirtschaftsrates), GAMO f. R-146, op. 1, d. 348, l. 176–180 (an die Verwaltung des Bezirks Ol'skij), GARF f. R-7523, op. 58, d. 432, l. 2–8 (an den Obersten Sowjet der UdSSR) sowie RGASPI f. 556, op. 23, d. 73, l. 17 ff. (an die unionsweite Tageszeitung *Pravda*). Siehe auch den Brief des Kolchosvorsitzenden N. F. Ryženko aus Tschukotka an die Redaktion der *Pravda*, in der er sich über die schlechte Versorgung und die miserable Infrastruktur der Kolchose beschwerte. Das Schreiben wurde über den Ministerrat der RSFSR und das Gebietsexekutivkomitee an das Gebietsparteikomitee weitergeleitet, das sich in der Folge um eine Verbesserung der Verhältnisse bemühte. Vgl. GAMO f. R-146, op. 1, d. 154, l. 53–57.

werden konnte. Inwieweit daraus institutionelles Vertrauen erwachsen konnte, wäre gerade vor dem Hintergrund des neu gegründeten Magadaner Gebietes eine spannende Forschungsfrage.

Für A. D. Bogdanov, der seit 1955 Erster Sekretär des Gebietskomitees des Komsomol gewesen war und nach einer langen Parteikarriere 1986 den Posten des Ersten Parteisekretärs einnahm, war die Machtübernahme durch die KPdSU nicht nur die historische Voraussetzung für eine Verbesserung der Verhältnisse. Für ihn waren die neuen Kader des Magadaner Gebietes Vorreiter der Entstalinisierung und Pioniere der Perestrojka – mögliche historische Analogien bereits antizipierend.[345] Er äußerte sich 2007 in einem Interview:

> Wir waren doch eigentlich dem Wesen nach in dieser Zeit genau solche Perestrojkaerianer, wie es später Perestrojkaerianer in unserer Zeit gab. Denn wir haben Dal'stroj plattgemacht, haben normale sowjetische Organe und Parteiorgane gegründet. Wie ein Rausch war diese Perestrojka, eine Hinwendung zum Menschen vollzog sich, denn bis dahin hatte man sich mit der sozialen Sphäre überhaupt nicht beschäftigt. Und die Psychologie der Kader – das war eigentlich das allerschwerste Problem. [...] Die alte Psychologie der Kader, hat, denke ich, noch lange überlebt [...].[346]

---

345 Während der Perestrojka stieg allgemein das historische Interesse an der Chruščev-Periode, nachdem Gorbačev positiv auf ihn rekurriert hatte. Vgl. Nordlander, Khrushchev's Image sowie Baberowski, Wege aus der Gewalt.
346 Das Interview führte Grebenjuk. A. D. Bogdanov in Grebenkjuk, Kolymskij led, S. 227–230, hier S. 229 f.

6 Resümee: Entstalinisierung als Sowjetisierung

Die Ergebnisse dieser Arbeit – die Befunde zum Aufbau von Institutionen, sozialer Infrastruktur und Wissenschaftseinrichtungen, zur Mechanisierung, Urbanisierung und Propaganda – lassen sich nur schwer mit unseren Bildern von der Kolyma, dem „Extrempol der Grausamkeit", überein bringen. Wie lässt es sich vorstellen, dass in denselben Baracken, in denen wenige Monate zuvor Häftlinge zu Tode geprügelt wurden, junge Bergbauspezialisten sich auf ihre Facharbeiterprüfung vorbereiten, wie kann man sich ausmalen, dass in den steinernen Isolatoren, in denen Häftlinge gezwungen wurden zur Strafe im eisigen Wasser zu stehen, wenig später Geschäfte untergebracht sind, Schulmaterialien und Kinderbücher verkauft werden?

Doch muss man es sich genau so vorstellen. Im Magadaner Gebiet der Entstalinisierung wurden neue Schilder angebracht, Gebäude umgewidmet, Ausstattungen verbessert. Die Region blieb aus dem Lager geboren und war doch eine Region nach dem GULAG – mit einem anderen Status im Machtgefüge der Sowjetunion, einer anderen Leitung und Wirtschaftsweise und mit einer anderen Sicht auf Arbeitskräfte. Ganz Grundlegendes hatte sich gewandelt, hatte sich unumkehrbar verändert, und gleichzeitig war das Erscheinungsbild der Region merkwürdig banal. Ende der 1950er Jahre war das Magadaner Gebiet fast eine sowjetische Region wie jede andere, hatte sich an eine Sowjetunion angeglichen, die selbst erheblichem Wandel unterlag. Was also zeigt die Banalität der Kolyma nach dem GULAG? Was offenbaren die neuen Erschließungsstrategien im Nordosten für ein allgemeines Verständnis der Jahre nach Stalins Tod?

Wichtigstes Ergebnis ist, dass der genaue Blick auf Magadan unser Verständnis dafür schärfen kann, was die Abschaffung des Terrors bedeutete. Dem Verzicht auf den staatlichen Terror ist zunächst analytisch nicht mit moralischen Kategorien beizukommen. Der 20. Parteitag brachte eine Kehrtwende im Umgang mit politischen Häftlingen, die öffentliche Abrechnung Chruščevs mit Stalin stellte wesentliche ideologische Pfeiler in Frage, Entlassungskommissionen und Rehabilitationen ermöglichten Ansätze von Gerechtigkeit. Jedoch verstellt die Reduzierung der Entstalinisierung auf den 20. Parteitag den Blick auf die fundamentalen Veränderungen, die zur Durchsetzung staatlicher Interessen unmittelbar nach Stalins Tod in Angriff genommen wurden.

Der Blick auf die Kolyma zeigt, dass die Lager aus machtpolitischen, ökonomischen und sicherheitspolitischen Gründen aufgegeben wurden. Im Nordosten ging es der sowjetischen Führung um eine Stärkung ihrer Position und um eine Sicherstellung der Rohstoffförderung. Die Entlassung der Häftlinge und die Auflösung der Lager waren dabei gewissermaßen Nebeneffekte. Die persönliche Freiheit, die ein Entlassener gewinnen konnte, die Chance auf Leben, die das Ende der Zwangsarbeit bedeutete, all das findet keinen Widerhall in den offiziellen Beschreibungen des Magadaner Alltags der späten 1950er Jahre – weil es darum gar nicht ging. Man hat den Eindruck, als sei sich die sowjetische Führung, angefangen bei Berija mit der Am-

https://doi.org/10.1515/9783110557879-007

nestie vom März 1953, nicht bewusst gewesen, welche moralische Leistung die Auflösung von Lagern tatsächlich war. Die Entlassungen waren, so könnte überspitzt formuliert werden, viel größer als die Personen, die sie veranlassten.

Warum sie dann doch veranlasst wurden, lässt sich zeigen, wenn man versteht, inwieweit die strukturelle, nicht die moralische Seite des Terrors zum Problem der sowjetischen Führung geworden war: Das machtpolitische und ökonomische Schwergewicht MVD hatte sich zu einer ungeheuren Belastung entwickelt, die Situation in den Lagern und die unrentable Wirtschaftsweise einen erheblichen Veränderungsdruck aufgebaut. Der militärische Charakter des MVD hatte ein System geschaffen, in das das ZK der KPdSU und seine regionale Nomenklatur keine Einsicht und auf das es keinen Zugriff hatte. Diese Thesen von Yoram Gorlizki und Oleg Chlevnjuk können mit Blick auf eine ganze Region bestätigt werden.

Der Drang nach Einfluss auf das MVD-System wurde zu einem wesentlichen Faktor im Kampf gegen den übermächtig werdenden Berija; die Beschneidung der führenden Rolle der Partei war der Hauptvorwurf, der auf dem Juli-Plenum 1953 gegen ihn erhoben wurde. Die Region Kolyma war eine der Stützen des MVD. Bis 1953 hatte kein einziges ZK-Mitglied jemals die Region besucht; zugleich gab es jahrzehntelang erfolglose Bestrebungen von Parteivertretern, die Einheitsleitung von Dal'stroj zu überwinden. Dementsprechend glichen die Angriffe gegen Berija auf dem Juli-Plenum den Vorwürfen gegen die lokalen Dal'stroj-Vertreter, die in den Diskussionen über die Gründung des Magadaner Gebiets laut wurden.

Nach dem Juli-Plenum reiste eine Brigade des ZK nach Magadan, meldete sich das Netzwerk der Chabarowsker Parteischule mit Ansprüchen aus dem benachbarten Gebiet. Es erscheint als relativ wahrscheinlich, dass Chruščev an der Kolyma eine maßgebliche Rolle spielte, zumindest war er unmittelbar in die Kaderauswahl für Magadan involviert. Der Beschluss über die Gründung des Gebietes und der damit verbundene Aufstieg der Partei zur entscheidenden Macht in der Region fällt in eine Phase, in der Chruščev damit begann, Parteivorsitzende in den einzelnen sowjetischen Regionen auszuwechseln und durch ihm genehme Personen zu ersetzen, wozu er in seiner Funktion als Erster Sekretär des ZK der KPdSU seit September 1953 die Möglichkeiten hatte. Dadurch war er auch mit der besonderen Position Politischer Verwaltungen als der Parteivertretung in militärisch geprägten Herrschaftsformen vertraut.

Die KPdSU benutzte den Aufbau der zivilen staatlichen Strukturen, um über dieses Netz ihren eigenen Machtanspruch durchsetzen zu können. Yoram Gorlizki hat dieses Vorgehen als ein Kennzeichen der Chruščev'schen Politik in den ersten Jahren nach 1953 beschrieben. In der Folge wurde diese Linie durch die Gründung des Büros der RFSRF beim ZK der KPdSU gestärkt. Im äußersten Nordosten wurde somit in Ansätzen verwirklicht, was das ZK der KPdSU auf dem Juli-Plenum in Moskau und regionale Parteiaktive seit 1938 gefordert hatte: Eine Entmilitarisierung des MVD und eine stärkere Kontrolle durch Parteiorgane – strategische Ansätze, die jedoch zu Lebzeiten Stalins niemals möglich gewesen wären.

Wenn in zentralen Gebieten der Union und mit Blick auf bestimmte soziale Entwicklungen der Eindruck entsteht, dass trotz Stalins Tod Kontinuität dominierte, so ist für lagergeprägte Gebiete das Jahr 1953 ein Bruch: Anders als bei früheren Säuberungen schwanden die Privilegien einer ganzen Führungsgruppe, die die Kolyma als ihr ureigenes Herrschaftsgebiet betrachtet hatte. Massenentlassungen und die Freistellung von Lagerbediensteten veränderten die Bevölkerungsstruktur, die Region verlor ihren exklusiven Status als geschlossenes Gebiet.

Das Jahr 1953 brachte die Region gewissermaßen zurück ins Imperium bzw. integrierte sie in der Folge zum ersten Mal in das Herrschaftsgefüge der zivilen Sowjetunion. Die angestoßene Entwicklung, die der Tod des Diktators erst ermöglichte, wurde nicht mehr aufgehalten.

Wenn man die eingangs skizzierten Überlegungen Stolbergs zur Übertragung der Vorstellung von der Binnenkolonisation Sibiriens auf das nordöstliche Territorium aufgreifen will, so kann die poststalinistische Strategie der Angleichung durch den Aufbau ziviler Formen von Administration und Infrastruktur als eine Form des *Frontierismus* verstanden werden. Mit Gründung des Magadaner Gebietes verschob die KPdSU die Grenzlinie der zivilen sowjetischen Struktur bis in den Nordosten. Nach Stalins Tod wurde die Region vollständig in das sowjetische Imperium inkorporiert – sie wurde „sowjetisiert". Als vergleichbar erscheint die Einführung des *Celinnyj kraj*, des Neulanddistriktes im Jahr 1960 und die Rolle, die dieser formale Schritt für das kasachische Gebiet spielte. Nach seiner Gründung, so Michaela Pohl in ihrer Studie, setzten dort eine Phase neuer Investitionen und ein Bauboom ein, Mechanisierung und die Produktivität wurden gesteigert.[1]

Diese auf das Territorium bezogene Perspektive der Moskauer Führung macht den wichtigsten Unterschied zu den „Großbauten des Kommunismus" und der Baikal-Amur-Magistrale aus, die von Klaus Gestwa und Johannes Grützmacher beschrieben wurden. Die lokale Raumeroberung nach 1953 diente der Erschließung des Territoriums, nicht nur der Durchführung eines punktuellen Projektes. Sie zielte, so könnte man argumentieren, tatsächlich auf die Bildung einer „sowjetischen Provinz".

Dennoch blieb das Magadaner Gebiet eine „Insel", hatte es einen Sonderstatus, der den Begriff „Provinz" unpassend erscheinen lässt. Die territoriale Weite des Nordostens war auch für die neue Herrschaft ein entscheidendes Problem. Auch die poststalinistischen Erschließungsstrategien bewältigten diesen riesigen und in weiten Teilen schwer zugänglichen Raum nur teilweise. Die Region ist bis heute ausschließlich per Schiff und Flugzeug erreichbar (wobei der Schiffsverkehr zum Teil eingestellt ist), Pläne für ein ausgebautes Straßennetz bis nach Jakutsk oder für Eisenbahnlinien wurden nie umgesetzt. Zugleich war das Magadaner Gebiet ein exklusiver Raum, dem die permanente Bedeutung der Goldförderung für die Wirtschaft der Sowjetunion und der damit einhergehende Geheimhaltungsgrad eine besondere, zentrale Aufmerksamkeit sicherte.

---

1 Vgl. Pohl, Tselinograd, S. 292f.

Ob sich diese Befunde auch auf die ehemaligen Lagergebiete von Norilsk und Workuta übertragen lassen, müssen weitere Forschungen zeigen. R. V. Pavljukevič hat jüngst die Entwicklungen nach Ende des Industriegiganten *Enisejstroj* in Norilsk nicht im Kontext der Lagerauflösungen, sondern als Folge der Gründung der Volkswirtschaftsräte im Jahr 1957 beschrieben. Inhaltlich kommt er jedoch zu vergleichbaren Ergebnissen, er schildert Phänomene wie an der Kolyma: Die vollständige Abwesenheit einer zivilen, sozialpolitischen und schulischen Infrastruktur, die zu großen Investitionen in den 1950er Jahre führte, sowie die Mechanisierung der bislang auf Handarbeit beruhenden Zwangsarbeit.[2]

Es liegt nahe, daraus zu schließen, dass Reformen der Entstalinisierung nicht nur als Programm im Moskauer Zentrum, quasi von oben, entworfen wurden, sondern dass es gerade auch die so peripher gelegenen Lagergebiete waren, die erheblichen Druck auf unionsweite Veränderungen ausgeübt haben müssen. Denn nur so konnten sie weiterhin ihre volkswirtschaftlich wichtige Rolle spielen. Die Programme zum Wohnungsbau, erste Ansätze zur Verbesserung des Arbeitsschutzes, die Stärkung der Leichtindustrie – all diese Reformen während der Entstalinisierung waren in Lagergebieten für die Stabilisierung der Arbeitskräftezahlen von absoluter Dringlichkeit, zugleich fielen sie aufgrund des bestehenden Mangels dort auf besonders fruchtbaren Boden. Gerade im ehemaligen Lagergebiet war die Parteiführung enorm herausgefordert. Hier mussten neue Konzepte gefunden werde, um freie Arbeitskräfte zum Kommen und zum Bleiben zu bewegen, hier brauchte man eine neue Symbolpolitik, neue Bilder, eine neue Sprache. Einwandfrei belegen lässt sich ein solches reziprokes Verhältnis zwischen Entstalinisierung und EntGULAGisierung mit den vorhandenen Quellen nicht. Aber die Arbeit kann doch zeigen, wie die Einführung gewöhnlicher Beschäftigungsverhältnisse die „kostenlose" Zwangsarbeit als kompliziert, wie Wissenschaft und Mechanisierung die Handarbeit der Häftlinge als ineffektiv erscheinen ließen, wie Ansätze von Sozialpolitik für freie Arbeitskräfte notwendig wurden. Vermuten lässt sich wiederum nur, dass die in zunehmender Zahl präsenten Facharbeiter und Wissenschaftler das kulturelle Leben gefördert und mehr Freiräume in der Gestaltung der persönlichen Lebensumstände gefordert haben müssen.

Für Andreas Hilger rührte das Ende der stalinistischen Strafpolitik in der Entstalinisierung „an den Kern tradierter Herrschaftsausübung. Die zentrale Bedeutung der Strafverfolgung für Selbstverständnis, Sicherung und Arbeitsweise des Systems brachte es mit sich, dass entsprechende Reformen respektive Korrekturen mit zahlreichen nicht-justiziellen Aspekten der sowjetischen Realität in enger Wechselwirkung standen."[3]

Dieser dynamische Charakter der Veränderungen, die nicht-intendierten Folgen politischer und struktureller Entscheidungen in der Entstalinisierung zeigt sich an der Kolyma, wo der Aufbau eines gewöhnlichen sowjetischen Gebietes mit den Verän-

---

2 Vgl. Pavljukevič, Vlijanie.
3 Hilger, Grenzen, S. 253.

derungen des Poststalinismus zusammenfiel. Das Ende des Terrors brachte die institutionelle, infrastrukturelle und soziale Angleichung an den zivilen Sektor der Sowjetunion, sozusagen die „Sowjetisierung der Kolyma". Aus einer Region der stalinistischen Extreme wurde in kurzer Zeit ein Gebiet der entstalinisierten Normalität – wobei man durchaus sagen kann, dass durch die Wechselwirkungen von Entstalinisierung und EntGULAGisierung die Definition von „Normalität" seit 1953 auch von Lagergebieten wie der Kolyma mitbestimmt wurde. Diese „sowjetische Normalität" ruft beim Blick auf weite Teile des Magadaner Lebens 1960 den eingangs geschilderten Eindruck der „Banalität" hervor.

Doch zunächst herrschten in den ersten Jahren des Magadaner Gebietes chaotische Verhältnisse. Die bisherigen militärischen Strukturen waren nicht mehr zuständig, aber der neu gekürte Erste Parteivorsitzende, Tichon Ababkov, und der neue Vorsitzende des Gebietsexekutivkomitees, Pavel Afanas'ev, verfügten ihrerseits noch nicht über eine institutionelle und infrastrukturelle Basis. Zudem war eine große Zahl der Lagerpunkte bereits nach der Amnestie vom März 1953 aufgegeben worden, der Abbau schritt schnell voran. Entlassene Häftlinge drängten darauf abzureisen, eine große Zahl der Produktionsstätten war wegen mangelnder Arbeitskräfte lahmgelegt – die Förderzahlen waren im freien Fall. Die Versorgungslage war sehr schlecht, die Kriminalitätsrate extrem hoch. Auf dem riesigen Territorium wurden Häftlinge nach ihrer Entlassung vielfach einfach ihrem Schicksal überlassen.

In politischer Hinsicht waren mit Einsetzung der neuen Gebietspartei- und Gebietsexekutivleitung die Felle noch lange nicht verteilt. Zwar unterlagen die Kader von Dal'stroj nach der Überführung des Kombinats aus dem MVD in ein gewöhnliches Produktionsministerium erheblichen Verunsicherungen. Die Bedeutung ihrer militärischen Ränge hatte sich vollkommen überlebt, sie kämpften mit dem Verlust ihres Status und erheblicher bisheriger Privilegien. Dennoch blieb der Chef von Dal'stroj, Ivan Mitrakov, Leiter des Kombinats, seine oberste Führungs- und Verwaltungsriege stand allen entscheidenden Infrastruktureinrichtungen und den Produktionsstätten vor. Der Machtanspruch des ZK und der regionalen Parteileitung ließ sich erst Schritt für Schritt durchsetzen; während Ababkov und Afanas'ev mit der Leitung von Dal'stroj in Fragen der Industrie zusammenarbeiteten, lieferten sie sich zugleich in Fragen der politischen Leitung einen veritablen Machtkampf.

Zunächst einmal war jedoch gar nicht eindeutig, was regionale Leitung überhaupt bedeuten sollte. Was waren die Zuständigkeiten der neuen Herren, welche Aufgaben hatten sie, welche Infrastruktur stand ihnen zur Verfügung? Gerungen wurde um eine Definition des „Politischen" in einem Gebiet, das bislang vollkommen von den Bedürfnissen einer maximalen Rohstoffausbeutung beherrscht worden war, dessen Grenzen ökonomisch definiert waren und das nur über eine produktionsbezogene soziale Infrastruktur verfügt hatte. Ababkov und Afanas'ev hatten zunächst nicht einmal Zugriff auf das Straßen- und Wasserstraßennetz, auf die Stromversorgung, auf Waren- und Lagerräume oder auf die nordöstliche Landwirtschaft.

Allmählich setzte sich die neue Leitung gegen Dal'stroj durch, zunächst als Folge eines relativ formalen Prozesses: Alle bisherigen Einrichtungen des Kombinates, die nicht unmittelbar Aufgaben der Produktion erfüllten, wurden in einem gewaltigen bürokratischen Akt inventarisiert, aus Dal'stroj herausgelöst und in die entsprechenden Abteilungen des Gebietsexekutivkomitees aufgenommen bzw. den unionsweiten Ministerien und Behörden unterstellt. Als Teil des zivilen sowjetischen Herrschaftsbereichs erkannten unionsweite Behörden und Ministerien Ababkov und Afanas'ev zunehmend als ihre natürlichen Ansprechpartner an. Die unter Malenkov einsetzende Stärkung der Ministerien in der ersten Phase der Entstalinisierung hat diese regionale Entwicklung gefördert; denkbar ist auch, dass die große Zahl der bisherigen MVD-Verwaltungen, die überall in der Sowjetunion in die Hände ziviler Behörden und Ministerien gelegt wurden, den Druck in Richtung auf eine Stärkung der zivilen sowjetischen Verwaltungsstrukturen erhöhten.

Im Magadaner Fall betraf dies v. a. das Ministerium für Metallwirtschaft / für Buntmetalle, das seit März 1953 für den Giganten Dal'stroj verantwortlich war. Das Finanzministerium verlangte nun zum ersten Mal Einsicht in die ökonomische Lage von Dal'stroj – und das Ergebnis war noch viel verheerender als bislang gemutmaßt worden war. Eine eigene Kontrollinstanz für Dal'stroj wurde geschaffen, die bislang stillschweigend abgeschriebenen Milliardenverluste durch die ineffektive Arbeitsweise, aber auch Unterschlagungen und Bilanzfälschungen wurden einem ganz neuen Kreis der sowjetischen Führung bekannt. Dieser Informationszuwachs betraf auch die einzelnen Infrastrukturbereiche, die medizinische und soziale Versorgung sowie Einrichtungen für Bildung und Kultur, die jeweils an die entsprechenden Ministerien angeschlossen wurden. Die Entstalinisierung brachte durch die Abschaffung des Sonderstatus ein erhebliches Maß an Transparenz und Offenheit – natürlich lediglich im geschlossenen Bereich des ZK und eines wichtigen Teils der obersten sowjetischen Verwaltung. Der Kreis der Personen, die Kenntnisse über Lagergebiete hatten, verbreitete sich erheblich, die Abkapselung löste sich auf formalem Wege. Dies trifft auch auf Miliz und zivile Staatsanwälte zu, die zum ersten Mal überhaupt in die Region gesandt wurden und dort ihre Arbeit aufnahmen. Sie ersetzten die von Willkür geprägte Allmacht der Truppen des MVD und die Militärtribunale als bislang einzige vorhandene Vertreter des sowjetischen Rechtssystems.

Die notwendigen Abstimmungen mit einer großen Vielfalt von Ministerien und Behörden der RSFSR und der UdSSR brachten eine neue politische Kultur in die Region. Die Herrschaftsverhältnisse wurden formalisierter und dadurch leichter berechenbar, sie begrenzten die Möglichkeiten einzelner Kader und einzelner Organisationseinheiten. Die Bedeutung von Experten, die nicht der politischen Führung angehörten und deren wachsender Einfluss als ein Kennzeichen der Entstalinisierung insgesamt gewertet wird, nahm an der Kolyma erheblich zu.

Die neue politische Praxis veränderte auch das alltägliche Gesicht von Herrschaft in der Region. Das Erscheinungsbild Magadans wurde demilitarisiert, Lagerabteilungen aus der Stadt verlegt, die Zahl der waffentragenden Personen ging deutlich zurück. Hotels für die vielen Dienstreisenden aus Moskau mussten errichtet, ein ziviles Verkehrs- und Kommunikationssystem innerhalb des Gebietes ausgebaut werden. Zum ersten Mal gab es an der Kolyma gewöhnliche Briefkästen, ein ziviler Personenbusverkehr wurde eingerichtet. Auch im kulturellen Leben war der Wandel spürbar, die ehemalige Lagerinsassin Evgenija Ginzburg konnte in der nun von der Parteileitung herausgegebenen Tageszeitung *Magadanskaja Pravda* publizieren, der aus der Haft entlassene Künstler Leonid Vegener fungierte als künstlerischer Leiter des Gorkij-Theaters der Stadt.

In der ersten Zeit war das Gebietsexekutivkomitee in seiner koordinierenden Rolle bei der administrativen Strukturierung des Gebietes und in Zusammenarbeit mit den unionsweiten Institutionen von herausragender Bedeutung. Doch schon bald fungierte das Büro des Gebietsparteikomitees als entscheidender Mittler zwischen der Region und dem ZK der KPdSU bzw. dem Büro für die RSFSR des ZK der KPdSU sowie den einzelnen Ministerien. Durch Kommissionen in den einzelnen Bezirken und Lagern sowie durch ihre Präsenz bei lokalen Parteiversammlungen wurde eigenes, internes Wissen über die jeweilige Region generiert. Loyales Personal mit regionalen Kenntnissen für die neuen Strukturen zu gewinnen, war dabei ein gewaltiges Problem, das meist nur durch Übernahme und Schulung der Mitarbeiter von Dal'stroj gelöst werden konnte. An verschiedenen Stellen kämpfte die Partei dabei mit Überbleibseln der militärischen Unterordnung der Parteistrukturen unter die Einheitsleitung von Industrie und Lager, wie z. B. bei den „grundständigen Parteiorganisationen", die die Partei in allen Betrieben, Bergwerken und Fabriken vertrat. Ihre Leitung blieb aufgrund ihrer geringen Größe an der Kolyma häufig der Produktionsführung untergeordnet, wurde von ihr bezahlt und war von ihr abhängig. Auch in den Lagerpunkten des *Sevvostlag* existierten nach wie vor die Politischen Truppenteile als militärische Parteiorganisationen – wie im übergeordneten GULAG üblich.

Diese Schwierigkeiten hielten die regionale Parteileitung nicht davon ab, die Kader von Dal'stroj beständig zu kritisieren. Kritik an der Leitung von Dal'stroj wurde in den 1950er Jahren zu einer Art „common sense" unter den lokalen Vertretern von Partei und Sowjet. Die Vorwürfe an Dal'stroj betrafen wirtschaftliches Fehlverhalten, Desinteresse, aber auch offene Feindseligkeiten gegen die neue Leitung. Selbst die moralische Haltung einzelner Funktionäre und ihre Kaderpolitik wurden debattiert. Die Parteifunktionäre trugen ein kulturelles Überlegenheitsgefühl vor sich her, sie verstanden sich als Vertreter der „reinen sowjetischen Strukturen und Werte".

Von Anfang an führte das Gebietsparteikomitee den Machtkampf mit Dal'stroj nicht nur hinter verschlossenen Türen, sondern besetzte das Feld auch publizistisch. Gegenüber den ehemaligen MVD-Offizieren, aber auch gegenüber der Bevölkerung präsentierte sich die Parteileitung so als die neuen „Herren der Region". Seit 1957 wurde das Kombinat allgemein für die „Rückständigkeit" des Gebietes im sozialen und infrastrukturellen Bereich verantwortlich gemacht, seine Arbeitsweise als „fehlerhaft" und nicht mehr „zeitgemäß" gebrandmarkt. Folgt man der Analyse Graeme Gills, so lassen sich an der Kritik der Magadaner Parteileitung Elemente der neuen Rhetorik der Entstalinisierung erkennen. Nie wurde das Kombinat vollständig diskreditiert, es hatte „Aufbauleistung" in besonders „schweren" oder auch „dunklen" Zeiten vollbracht. Anders im Stalinismus, als personalisierte „innere Feinde" „vernichtet" werden sollten, dominierte nun die unpersönliche Rede von „Missständen" oder „Defiziten", die auszugleichen wären. Die Kombinatsleitung reagierte mit eigenen Darstellungen, stolzen Leistungsbilanzen einer „großen Ära".

Mitrakov selbst wurde am 17. Februar 1956 seines Amtes enthoben, sein bisheriger Stellvertreter Ju. V. Čuguev fungierte fortan als Leiter von Dal'stroj. Die lokalen Produktionsleiter wehrten sich zum Teil ganz offen gegen die angeblichen Zumutungen einer politischen Leitung – wie z.B. im Fall des Leiters der Autostation, der seinen ganzen Fuhrpark vor der Übergabe demontieren ließ, um sie für die neue Leitung unbrauchbar zu machen. Andere verweigerten die Bereitstellung dringend benötigter Infrastrukturen und die Erfüllung von Aufträgen des Gebietsexekutivkomitees, an erster Stelle von Baumaßnahmen. In der Abgeschiedenheit des Nordostens gab es jedoch für die neue Führung keine Alternativen zu den Einrichtungen von Dal'stroj.

Die Rohstoffförderung (neben Gold wurde Zinn, Kobalt, Wolfram und Uran abgebaut) sank in den Umbruchsjahren ab 1953 erheblich. Die spätstalinistische Krise der Goldförderung, die die ökonomische Bilanz von Dal'stroj seit Ende der 1940er Jahre stark belastet hatte, spitzte sich nach Stalins Tod noch einmal dramatisch zu. Dies ist zunächst auf den Abbruch der exklusiven Stellung als Hauptabteilung des MVD zurückzuführen. Finanziell und infrastrukturell war Dal'stroj nun den Bedingungen eines gewöhnlichen Produktionsministeriums, unter besonderer Überwachung durch das Finanzministerium, unterworfen. Das Kombinat musste ganz neue Versorgungswege und Vertragsbeziehungen aufbauen, um Geräte oder Materialien zu beziehen.

Hinzu kam ein Phänomen, das für die Bilanz des sowjetischen Nordostens seit den frühen 1940er Jahren kontinuierlich an Bedeutung gewann: Die reichsten Goldfelder an der Kolyma, in denen das Gold in gut zugänglichen Erdschichten, oder als Waschgold in Flüssen, von Häftlingen in Handarbeit abgebaut werden konnte, waren durch den oberflächlichen Raubbau innerhalb weniger Jahre abgegrast worden. Auf diesen „Erfolgen" hatte die sagenhafte Reputation von Dal'stroj und die Vorstellung von der angeblich kostengünstigen und effektiven Ausbeutung von Zwangsarbeit beruht. Sich auf interne, streng geheime Statistiken stützend, kann die vorliegende Arbeit zeigen, dass die stalinistische, hektische, z.T. grotesk planlose und mit ungeheuren Verlusten einhergehende „Erstürmung" des nordöstlichen Goldes und der weiteren Metalle schlicht von dem bislang unberührten Reichtum des nordöstlichen Raumes profitiert hatte. Es lässt sich nur erahnen, wie produktiv eine strukturierte, mechanisierte und langfristige Arbeitsweise unter den gleichen naturräumlichen Bedingungen hätte sein können. Wenn der Goldgehalt in den 1930er Jahren noch bis zu 36 g Gold pro m^3 Erde betrug, so waren es im Jahr 1957 nur noch 3,3 g pro m^3. Dementsprechend musste immer mehr Erdreich bewegt werden. Auf der Suche nach Gold durchpflügte man im Jahr 1941 21,4 Mio. m^3, im Jahr 1956 dagegen bereits 38,8 Mio. m^3 Erde. In der Folge stieg der Selbstkostenpreis des Goldes beständig. Für die Wirtschaftskader fiel der dramatische Fall der Goldförderung – 1940 hatte Dal'stroj 80 Tonnen chemisch reines Gold gefördert, 1957 waren es noch 32,4 Tonnen – mit den politischen Veränderungen nach 1953 zusammen und erzeugte eine Stimmung, die in der regionalen Literatur als „Depression" beschrieben wurde; die „Theorie vom Versiegen der Kolyma" machte die Runde. Die lokal ohnehin extrem hohe Selbstmordrate stieg noch einmal massiv an.

Neben den infrastrukturellen Schwierigkeiten und dem sinkenden Goldgehalt setzte dem Kombinat seit Stalins Tod vor allem der dramatische Mangel an Arbeitskräften zu. Bereits die große Amnestie vom März 1953 hatte verheerende Auswirkungen auf die nordöstliche Industrie. Dutzende Förderstätten wurden nicht mehr bearbeitet, weil über 80.000 Häftlinge entlassen wurden. Schon im Sommer 1953 standen viele Anlagen still. Innerhalb weniger Jahre reduzierte sich die Zahl ganzer Lagerabteilungen deutlich, Lagerpunkte wurden reihenweise aufgegeben. Zwischen März 1953 und Dezember 1956 sank die Zahl der Häftlinge von ca. 169.000 auf etwa 24.000, 15.000 Personen, die in das Gebiet verbannt worden waren, konnten 1955 die Region verlassen. Auch ein Großteil des Wachpersonals und der Lagerleitung verließ in diesen Jahren die Kolyma.

Hinzu kam, dass die Arbeit mit Zwangsarbeitern für die Produktionsstätten innerhalb kürzester Zeit ineffektiv wurde. Die gleiche Produktionsleitung, die noch vor wenigen Jahren in ihrer Struktur vollständig auf Zwangsarbeit gesetzt hatte, forderte schon Mitte der 1950er Jahre selbst den Einsatz freier Arbeitskräfte. Diese praktischen „Schwierigkeiten", von denen in dieser Arbeit berichtet wird, werfen ein neues Licht auf die Gründe der Aufgabe stalinistischer Zwangsarbeit. Im Nordosten hatte sie sich zu einem regelrechten „Klotz am Bein" der Produktion entwickelt. Die wichtigste Ursache war dabei die Aufgabe der Struktur des Lager-Industriellen Komplexes, die bereits im März 1953 von Berija aufgelöst worden war. Das Kombinat und der Lagerkomplex *Sevvostlag* unterstanden seitdem zwei verschiedenen Ministerien, die jeweils eigene Ansprüche an die regionalen Vertreter formulierten. Auch wenn die sogenannte „Einzelleitung" in der Region noch nach 1953 erhalten blieb und damit eine Person sowohl über die Produktion als auch das dazugehörige Lager einer Industrieeinheit herrschte, so standen sich nun doch zwei unterschiedliche Einrichtungen gegenüber. Häftlinge konnten nur noch auf der Basis von Verträgen an Produktionsstätten verliehen werden. Der GULAG wiederum, als übergeordnete Lagerverwaltung, diktierte den Produktionseinrichtungen seine Vorgaben für die Bereitstellung von Wachen und die Ausstattung der Lager, für die die Produktionseinrichtungen zahlen mussten. Der angeblich einfache, günstige und jederzeit verfügbare Einsatz von Zwangsarbeitern entwickelte sich zu einem höchst bürokratischen Unterfangen. Der Wegfall der militärischen Leitung und die Unterstellung des Kombinates unter das Ministerium für Buntmetalle sorgten zudem für eine Neudefinition der Arbeitsstätten. Bislang waren Goldförderstätten grundsätzlich Zwangsarbeitsprojekte, in denen auch freie Arbeitskräfte tätig waren. Nun waren es Förderstätten freier Arbeitskräfte, in denen auch Zwangsarbeiter eingesetzt wurden. Die parallele Arbeit von Freien und Zwangsarbeitern führte zu vielen Schwierigkeiten, immer wieder kam es zu Übergriffen schwerkrimineller Häftlingen auf freie Arbeitskräfte und zu vielen Fluchtversuchen. Um dies zu vermeiden, begann die Produktionsleitung, einzelne Bereiche als Zwangsarbeitsfelder zu definieren, deren Zugang reglementiert und überwacht werden musste.

Die nach unten taumelnden Förderzahlen wurden schließlich auch dem Ersten Parteisekretär Ababkov zum Verhängnis, die schlechte Wirtschaftsbilanz führte 1958 zu seiner Absetzung. Afanas'ev stieg, wie so häufig in der sowjetischen Geschichte, vom Posten des Vorsitzenden des Gebietsexekutivkomitees zum Leiter des Gebietsparteikomitees auf.

Eines der größten Strukturprobleme des Kombinates betraf die geologische Schürfabteilung, die für die Suche nach neuen Goldfeldern und für die Entwicklung längerfristiger Perspektiven verantwortlich war. Diese Abteilung war besonders eng mit den politischen und finanziellen Interessen der alten Kader verbunden. Unter dem Druck der sinkenden Förderzahlen griff das nun zuständige Ministerium für Geologie und Bodenschätze ein, teilte die Abteilung auf und unterstellte die Einheiten, die neue Perspektiven im Nordosten ermitteln sollten, unmittelbar seiner Leitung. Eine Gruppe lokaler Geologen nutzte ihre Chance, sich auf diesem Wege von den Vorgaben des Kombinates Dal'stroj loszumachen. Sie stellte eigenmächtig die Suche nach anderen Metallen ein und konzentrierte sich ganz auf die Suche nach neuen Goldfeldern in Tschukotka. Unterstützt durch das Ministerium, konnte sie schon bald von einem Gebiet mit erheblichem Goldgehalt im westlichen Teil Tschukotkas berichten.

Das Gebietsparteikomitee begriff schnell die historische Bedeutung dieses Fundes für die weiteren Perspektiven des Gebietes und für die machtpolitische Stabilisierung seiner Position. Dieser neue Goldfund und eine ganze Reihe von Strategien, die bereits im Stalinismus partiell verfolgt, aufgrund zu hoher Kosten jedoch immer wieder verworfen worden waren, steigerten die Förderzahlen: Zunehmend wurden die Kosten einer rationaleren Planung und der massive Ausbau der Mechanisierung als Vorbedingung erfolgreicher Förderung akzeptiert. In diesem Bereich hat der sowjetische Staat erheblich in die Industrie des Nordostens investiert. Zudem wurden Versorgungswege und die Infrastruktur der einzelnen Förderanlagen ausgebaut, man erlaubte den Einsatz von selbstständigen Goldgräbern. Die Förderzahlen bescherten Afanas'ev in der Folge eine stabile Herrschaft.

Die Arbeit in den Goldgruben wurde durch den höheren Mechanisierungsgrad erleichtert, war aber nach wie vor hart und sehr gefährlich. Viele der Arbeiter litten an der Krankheit Silikose, der „Staublunge". Donald Filtzer hat schon früh auf den Zusammenhang zwischen der wachsenden Bedeutung von Gewerkschaften und der Entstalinisierung hingewiesen. Im Nordosten zeigten sich erste Ansätze eines sich entwickelnden Bewusstseins für den Wert von Arbeitsschutz, für vorbeugende Maßnahmen gegen die vielen schweren Unfälle und für Prophylaxe gegen Silikose.

Eine wichtige Rolle spielte zudem der Ausbau von Bildung und Wissenschaft. Neue Institute, Schulen und Weiterbildungseinrichtungen für die stärker mechanisierte Arbeit wurden gegründet, um Ingenieure vor Ort auszubilden. In zunehmendem Maße kam es auf die Qualität der Arbeitskräfte, also auf ihre Ausbildung und ihr technisches Wissen, an. 1960 wurde eine Abteilung der Akademie der Wissenschaften in Magadan eingerichtet, die Stadt zunehmend zu einem Wissenschaftsstandort, mit nationalem und internationalem Austausch, ausgebaut. Hier lässt sich die Bedeutung, die Paul Josephson Wissenschaft und Technik für die Erschließung des sowjetischen Nordens seit den 1960er Jahren zuschreibt, am Magadaner Beispiel veranschaulichen. Im Laufe der folgenden Jahre entstanden eine eigene Universität und mehrere Forschungsstationen in den entfernten Weiten des Territoriums. Dabei ging es nicht mehr nur um die geologische Vorbereitung der Goldförderung, sondern darum, das Territorium, seine naturräumlichen Bedingungen und die Möglichkeiten menschlichen Lebens im Permafrostgebiet zu erforschen.

Wolfgang Kissel hat in seiner literaturwissenschaftlichen Analyse Varlam Šalamovs gezeigt, dass Šalamovs „Erzählungen aus Kolyma" eine menschenverachtende Technik offenbaren. Im Angesicht des Mangels an Maschinen standen „die Lager des GULAG im Dienst eines technischen Experimentes am Menschen, das die Ausbeute an Gold, Zinn und Uran um jeden Preis steigern sollte [...] – ohne Rücksicht auf die Belastbarkeit des ‚Menschenmaterials'"[4].

Nur wenige Jahre nach Stalins Tod waren es nun gerade Wissenschaft und Technik, die dazu benutzt wurden, die Arbeit durch eine durchgreifende Mechanisierung zu humanisieren, den nordöstlichen Raum als Teil des Imperiums anzuerkennen und das ehemalige Lagergebiet zu einem Wissenschaftszentrum auszubauen. Durch Wissenschaft und Technik wurde die Rohstoffausbeutung ohne Zwangsarbeit in der Entstalinisierung nicht nur denkbar, sondern erstrebenswert. Hier wären weitere Forschungen vonnöten, in der Analyse des inneren Zusammenhangs zwischen der Aufgabe der Lagerwirtschaft und der sich enorm dynamisierenden Arktisforschung, die wiederum selbst auch auf kleine, mobile Einheiten setzte – diesmal aber in einer zivilen Variante.

Zu den wirtschaftspolitischen Veränderungen gehörten auch der Aufbau der Leichtindustrie und der Ausbau der Landwirtschaft, zentrale unionsweite Programme seit 1953. Die Umsetzung dieser Vorgaben war im Magadaner Gebiet, angesichts der wachsenden Bevölkerungszahlen, nicht nur eine dringende Notwendigkeit, sie war Teil des politischen Umbruchs. Unter dem Lager-Industriellen Komplex des MVD war eine differenzierte wirtschaftliche Entwicklung der nordöstlichen Region verboten gewesen, das Gebiet lediglich ausgebeutet werden. Nun ging es aber darum, die vielen freien Arbeitskräfte zu versorgen und eine möglichst umfassende Erschließung der Peripherie zu erreichen. Machtpolitisch war dieser Schritt zudem von Bedeutung, weil auf diesem Weg eigenständige Produktionsstätten des Magadaner Gebietes, unabhängig von Dal'stroj, entstanden. Diese Unterscheidung zwischen der Produktion des Kombinats und der lokalen Industrie wurde nach der Auflösung des Kombinats im Juni 1957 ganz aufgegeben. An seine Stelle trat der Magadaner Volkswirtschaftsrat, der faktisch der lokalen Parteileitung unterstand. Er vereinigte alle Industriezweige des Gebietes und brachte die politischen Grenzen des Gebietes mit dem Magadaner Wirtschaftsraum zur Deckung. Die Aufgabe der Bezeichnung „Dal'stroj" war für viele alte Kader ein schwerer Schock, die Einführung des Volkswirtschaftsrates wurde dementsprechend als „Ende einer Ära" wahrgenommen.

---

4 Kissel, Überlebenswissen, S. 186.

Die strukturelle Aufgabe der Häftlingsarbeit bedeutete nicht, dass alle ehemaligen Zwangsarbeiter die Arbeit in den Förderstätten verließen. Die Angaben über den Anteil ehemaliger Häftlinge an den freien Arbeitskräften variieren zum Teil stark, je nachdem, ob auch die Entlassenen miteinbezogen wurden, die sich nur für ein paar Monate an das Kombinat binden ließen. Sicher ist, dass noch Ende der 1950er Jahre gut die Hälfte aller freien Arbeitskräfte frühere Häftlinge des *Sevvostlag* oder des *Berlag* waren. Sie nach ihrer Entlassung anzuwerben war eine der großen Motivationen des Kombinates, aus seiner Sicht handelte es sich um „gut eingearbeitetes" Personal. Ehemalige Häftlinge selbst verblieben oft aus „freiwilligem Zwang" an der Kolyma, aus Mangel an Alternativen oder weiteren Perspektiven. Viele hatten auch den Kontakt zu ihren früheren Familien verloren, neue Bindungen im Nordosten geknüpft. Da freien Arbeitskräften an der Kolyma erheblich höhere Löhne gezahlt wurden als in den zentral gelegenen Teilen der Union, hofften Entlassene auch darauf, durch einen temporären Verbleib ein paar Rücklagen für die Heimkehr zu bilden. Auch nach Auflösung von *Sevvostlag* (im August 1957) und *Berlag* (im Juni 1954) wurden Häftlinge, wie überall in der Sowjetunion, mit Arbeit bestraft. In den Betrieben des Magadaner Volkswirtschaftsrates waren im Jahr 1962 noch 3.200 Inhaftierte eingesetzt, ökonomisch und strukturell spielte diese Arbeit aber keine entscheidende Rolle mehr.

Neben ehemaligen Häftlingen, die aus Mangel an Alternativen Verträge mit Dal'stroj geschlossen hatten, waren die Arbeiter des Gebietes in den 1950er Jahren freie Vertragsarbeiter, „junge Facharbeiter" sowie Komsomolzen. Sie alle wurden im Rahmen von Kampagnen in den westlichen Gebieten der Union angeworben, vergleichbar mit anderen großen Mobilisierungskampagnen dieser Jahre, der Baikal-Amur-Magistrale, dem „Neuland" in Kasachstan oder Großbaustellen. Gelockt wurden sie mit der Aussicht auf hohe Löhne, Vergünstigungen und dem Leben in einer abenteuerreichen Gegend. Jedes Jahr zogen etwa 20.000 Personen in das Gebiet.

Die tatsächlichen Arbeits- und Lebensbedingungen waren in den ersten poststalinistischen Jahren jedoch so schlecht, dass jedes Jahr etwa ebenso viele Menschen die Region verließen. Auf diese „Flugsandgesellschaft", die zwar mit dem Zwang zur Erfüllung von Arbeitsverträgen, nicht aber mit roher Gewalt in der Region gehalten werden konnte, richtete die neue politische Leitung ihre Strategien aus. Es war ihr bewusst, dass sich ohne ein gewisses Maß an Motivation der freien Arbeitskräfte die Bodenschätze nicht fördern ließen.

Im Magadaner Gebiet der 1950er Jahre wird die Verbindung zwischen der Abkehr von Repression und der Entstehung erster Ansätze von Sozialpolitik unmittelbar deutlich: Da der nordöstliche Raum keine zivile Vorgeschichte hatte, war die Abhängigkeit der freien Bevölkerung von den Zuteilungen des sowjetischen Staates dort besonders groß. Nahezu alles, was es in dem Gebiet an Lebensnotwendigem gab, wurde gewährt und verteilt. Die Hand des Staates, die bisher Menschen aus ihrer gewohnten Umgebung gerissen, in Lagern zusammengepfercht und zur Arbeit gezwungen hatte, diese Hand sollte nun nicht mehr schlagen, sondern zuteilen und versorgen. Sie blieb im Nordosten eine fast allmächtige Hand in lebensfeindlicher Umgebung. Der staatliche Paternalismus, den Galina Ivanova als Kern des in den

1950er Jahren entstehenden „sozialistischen Wohlfahrtsstaates" beschrieben hat, erweist sich hier als Strategiewechsel im Verhältnis des Staates zu den Magadaner Arbeitskräften: Nachdem sich die Zwangsarbeit im Spätstalinismus als kostenintensiv und ineffektiv erwiesen hatte, sollten die Arbeiterströme nun auf paternalistischem Wege in die Region gelenkt werden. Die unionsweiten Modernisierungs- und Urbanisierungstendenzen trugen ein Übriges zur Veränderung des Magadaner Gebietes bei.

Im Ergebnis lassen sich im Magadaner Gebiet schon Ende der 1950er Jahre deutliche Veränderungen erkennen: Programme zur Elektrifizierung, zur Trinkwasserversorgung und zum Straßenbau, aber auch der massive Bau von Wohnungen und neuen Baracken, die Einrichtung oder Erweiterung von Krankenstationen, Schulen, Kindergärten, Klubs und Bibliotheken ließen Lagerpunkte zu regulären Siedlungen werden, die allmählich auch mit einem breiteren Warenangebot beliefert wurden.

Die Hauptstadt Magadan nahm dabei eine Sonderrolle ein. Einerseits war sie in den 1950er Jahren ein riesiger Transitraum, die Kriminalitätsrate war hier noch höher als im Magadaner Gebiet insgesamt; aufgrund fehlender Infrastrukturen und Sanitäreinrichtungen stand die Stadt in der Statistik schwerer Infektionskrankheiten unionsweit an der Spitze. Andererseits mühte sich die neue Führung um einen großangelegten Stadtausbau, der ihrem neuen Status als Gebietshauptstadt entsprechen sollte. Bereits Ende der 1950er Jahre wurden auf der Grundlage eines neuen Stadtplans ganze Straßenzüge neu errichtet, die medizinische Versorgung dem Niveau eines regionalen Zentrums angepasst, Bildungsinstitutionen aufgebaut, eine Reihe von Kultur- und Erholungsangeboten geschaffen. Der Sendemast an der Spitze der als „längste Straße der Welt" bekannten Magadaner Trasse, die in Magadan in die Leninstraße mündet, verkörperte die Entwicklung des Gebietes und seine Verbindung zu den zentralen Teilen der Union.

Trotz der punktuellen Verbesserungen herrschten, auch im Verhältnis zu den bereits sehr niedrigen Standards in der Sowjetunion insgesamt, im Magadaner Gebiet extrem beengte Wohnverhältnisse. Die Hinterlassenschaften der Lager waren in vielen Regionen die einzigen Behausungen, die überhaupt existierten. Freie Arbeitskräfte zogen in verlassene Lagerbaracken ein und teilten sich mit Bettlaken private Nischen ab, die Infrastruktur der Lager wurde vielfach einfach umdefiniert: aus Wachtürmen wurden Läden, aus Isolatoren Badehäuser. Private Küchen, Toiletten und Waschräume gab es vielfach gar nicht. Große hygienische Probleme waren die Folge und wurden durch die völlig unzureichende medizinische Versorgung verschärft. Bei vielen Infektionskrankheiten, wie etwa der Ruhr, stand das Magadaner Gebiet lange Zeit an der Spitze geheimer unionsweiter Statistiken.

Leidtragende der schlechten Bedingungen waren vor allem Kinder, von denen viele ohne ihre Eltern in erbärmlichen Internaten untergebracht wurden, und viele junge Frauen. Immer wieder kam es zu alkoholbedingten Exzessen und Gewalttätigkeiten. In einem Gebiet, das bis 1953 von einem stark überproportionalen Anteil an jungen Männern geprägt gewesen war, mangelte es gerade neu ankommenden jungen Frauen an Schutz und Rückzugsmöglichkeiten. Die Gewalt der Lager sickerte in den Alltag des zivilen Gebietes ein, in den Berichten und Statistiken offenbart sie sich in brutalen Übergriffen mitten in den Arbeiterbaracken, in Vergewaltigungen, Morden und einer Selbstmordrate, mit der das Magadaner Gebiet weit über dem Unionsdurchschnitt lag.

Unter diesen Bedingungen musste die Magadaner Führung Vertrauen aufbauen, um Vertrauen werben – sowohl beim ZK und den Moskauer Ministerien, als auch bei den freien Arbeitskräften. In ihrer Repräsentation zeigte sie sich immer wieder als verlässlicher Ansprechpartner für Sorgen und Nöte, als Garant für die Angleichung lokaler Verhältnisse an unionsweite Standards. Afanas'ev warb dabei offen um „personalisiertes Vertrauen". Die Bevölkerung sollte ihm, der starken neuen Parteiführung, statt den sogenannten „alten Kadern" vertrauen, dementsprechend stellte er seine Biographie, seine persönlichen Eindrücke und Kontakte in den Vordergrund.

Bei dieser Analyse bleiben jedoch eine Reihe entscheidender Fragen offen: Entstand denn tatsächlich „Vertrauen" in die neuen Strukturen – um einen Begriff aufzugreifen, der in der Forschung zur poststalinistischen Sowjetunion an Bedeutung gewinnt?[5] Weitete sich denn ein unter Umständen entstandenes personalisiertes Vertrauen zu Afanas'ev zu einer Art von generalisiertem Vertrauen in die neuen lokalen Institutionen aus? Welche Rolle spielte Vertrauen zwischen den Institutionen auf zentraler und lokaler Ebene? Und was geschah dabei mit der Gewalt, die die Beziehungen und Verhältnisse an der Kolyma im Stalinismus bestimmt hatte? Wenn Gewalt als Grundstruktur des Stalinismus beschrieben wurde, welche Rolle spielt sie dann für die poststalinistische Sowjetunion?

Mit den vorliegenden Quellen können diese Fragen nur eingeschränkt beantwortet werden. Bei der Auswertung einer großen Menge an Schriftgut der obersten Leitungsebene von Dal'stroj, aus der zentralen und der lokalen Leitung der Organe von Partei und Sowjet, von zeitgenössischen Publikationen und Erinnerungen hat sich immer deutlicher ein Zusammenhang zwischen dem Institutionenaufbau in Magadan, seiner Sowjetisierung und dem Rückgang offener Formen von Gewalt abgezeichnet. Der Prozess der Angleichung an die institutionellen Gegebenheiten im zivilen Sektor der Sowjetunion ging mit einer allmählichen „Zivilisierung" der Magadaner Verhältnisse einher.[6] Dies entwickelte im Laufe der Zeit eine Eigendynamik, die über das hinausging, was die sowjetische Führung mit ihren Reformen im Jahr 1953 intendiert hatte.

Die erratische Gewalt, die von bewaffneten Wachmannschaften, von schwerkriminellen Häftlingen und Häftlingsbanden ausging und die sich als prägendes Muster der Beziehungen in dieser Region ausgebildet hatte, verschwand nicht urplötzlich mit Gründung des Magadaner Gebietes. Allein im Jahr 1953 und in der ersten Jahreshälfte 1954 starben 107 Häftlinge durch ihre Mithäftlinge, die nun verstärkt auch freie

---

5 Vgl. die Sonderausgabe der SEER von Geoffrey Hosking „Trust and Distrust in the USSR" 91 (2013).
6 Dieser Zusammenhang erinnert an den von Norbert Elias beschriebenen „Prozess der Zivilisation" – hier natürlich in einer sowjetischen Variante. Die von Elias als Folge des Prozesses geschilderte Internalisierung „ziviler Haltungen" lässt sich allerdings mit den vorliegenden Quellen nicht untersuchen. Vgl. Elias, Zivilisation.

Siedlungen überfielen; sehr viele Frauen wurden vergewaltigt. Das staatliche Gewaltmonopol wurde erst dann durchgesetzt, als die zivilen Institutionen und Kontrollen mehr als eine formale Angelegenheit wurden und echte Funktionsteilungen einsetzten.

Das für die Arbeit ausgewertete Verwaltungsschriftgut der regionalen Leitung und die untersuchte Behördenkommunikation zeigt, wie der Einsatz von Verträgen und Verwaltungsabkommen sowie die Zuständigkeit einer großen Zahl unionsweiter Behörden Kontrollen verstärkten, das Aushandeln von Übereinkünften und Kompromissen förderten und auf diesem institutionellen Wege die Macht Einzelner begrenzt wurde. Verträge regelten die Verleihung von Zwangsarbeitern, Verwaltungsabkommen banden die Region in ein Netz der unionsweiten Bürokratie ein. Zuständigkeiten für einzelne Politikfelder wurden geschaffen, die sich nicht allein auf die lokale Einzelleitung, sondern auf die in ihrem jeweiligen Bereich übergeordneten Behörden und Ministerien auf Ebene der RSFSR und der UdSSR ausrichteten. Eine große Anzahl von Experten, Verwaltungsmitarbeitern und Staatsanwälten erhielt Einblick in die einzelnen Verhältnisse im Nordosten – der hermetische Abschluss wurde aufgegeben, sowjetunionweit geltende Standards auf das Magadaner Gebiet übertragen. Die Ausbildung von festen, stabilen Siedlungen, die zur Grundlage von auf Dauer angelegten Bezirken wurden, führte zur Gründung von Einrichtungen, die nicht allein auf die Bedürfnisse der Produktion ausgerichtet waren, sondern die administrative Funktionen innehatten. Eine zivile Miliz wurde aufgebaut, Stationen in den Siedlungen eingerichtet. Je wichtiger die politische Sphäre wurde, je stärker die inter-institutionellen Beziehungen, je effektiver zentrale Strukturen und ihre Überwachungstätigkeit, desto mehr wurde die Willkür der Dal'stroj-Offiziere beschnitten, desto berechenbarer wurden die Herrschaftsverhältnisse, desto geringer die lokale Macht des Einzelleiters in seiner Goldgrube und dem angeschlossenen Lager. Hier kann die Arbeit dazu beitragen, den inneren Mechanismus im Übergang von einer personalen zur institutionellen Diktatur zu verstehen.

Wohl war die neue Parteileitung, die Ende 1953 in Magadan einzog, stolz auf die wirtschaftlichen Leistungen der Sowjetunion und dabei auch auf die des Giganten Dal'stroj, der unter extremen Bedingungen operiert hatte. Ihr eigenes Selbstverständnis gründete aber nicht auf Maschinengewehren, militärischen Befehlen und Sondertribunalen, sondern, um im Bild zu bleiben, auf Aktentaschen, Verträgen und Verordnungen. Für diese Führungsgruppe waren die Lager kein moralisches Problem, aber eine Frage des Prestiges, etwas, das nicht mehr ins poststalinistische Bild passte. Dies verdeutlicht eine Diskussion unter Parteivertretern über die Gebietshauptstadt, unmittelbar nach Gründung des Magadaner Gebietes. Zu dieser Zeit waren dort etwa 11.000 Häftlinge und 4.000 Mann militärische Truppen untergebracht, die Stadt war erfüllt von Struktur und Atmosphäre eines Lager-Industriellen Komplexes. Alle Parteimitglieder sprachen sich dafür aus, die Lager aus der Stadt zu bringen, mit der so sprechenden Begründung, sie seien „einer Gebiets-Hauptstadt nicht angemessen"[7].

Mit Blick auf den Stalinismus ist die Grenzenlosigkeit der Lagerwelt immer wieder als „Gulagisierung" der Lagerumwelt beschrieben worden – das Fehlen einer erkennbaren „Zone", das Fehlen einer permanenten Überwachung, die Vermischung von Freien und Häftlingen. An der Kolyma gab es nur „das Lager", sie war gewissermaßen eine „gulagisierte Region". In der Entstalinisierung wurden nicht nur Lager aufgelöst, sondern auch diese Form gulagisierter Regionen, an der Kolyma wie in Norilsk, Workuta oder Kasachstan, aufgegeben. An ihre Stelle trat nicht der Rechtsstaat, aber immerhin die Verlässlichkeit, sich innerhalb einer bestimmten Norm zu bewegen, innerhalb derer der Einzelne nicht über grenzenlose Macht und Gewalt verfügen konnte. Haft und Lager, das haben Marc Elie, Andreas Hilger und Robert Hornsby anschaulich gezeigt, blieben wesentliche Elemente des sowjetischen Repressionssystems. Aber es gab keine exterritorialen Gebiete mehr; allein die Nennung des Begriffs „Kolyma" konnte nicht mehr als Drohgebärde aufgebaut werden. Es gab danach noch Lager in einem Gebiet, ein ganzes Gebiet aber war nie mehr „das Lager" – und sollte auch nicht mehr diesen Eindruck erwecken.

Leitungs- und Kontrollinstanz des wachsenden Institutionengeflechts war die KPdSU, deren Bedeutung zudem durch den Zuzug freier Arbeitskräfte stieg – sie war für die Versorgung der neuen Bürger des Gebietes verantwortlich. Vor allem in Magadan und in den größeren Siedlungen rückte der sowjetische Staat so tatsächlich näher an die Bevölkerung heran. Auch in der Sowjetunion, so könnte man folgern, ging also ein Mehr an Rechtsstaatlichkeit allmählich mit einem Mehr an sozialpolitischen Maßnahmen einher.[8] Je mehr sich die Region bei gut ausgebildeten freien Arbeitskräften mit anderen Regionen messen lassen musste, je größer der Angleichungsdruck aus den Ministerien wurde, umso größer wurden die sozialen Angebote, desto wichtiger wurde der Arbeitsschutz, das Bonussystem, Versorgungsfragen. An der Kolyma zeigen sich Ansätze, die illustrieren, wie die Reformen der Entstalinisierung in eine stärker auf Normen basierende Herrschaftsform führten.

Zugleich stieß diese spezifisch sowjetische „Zivilisierung" im Magadaner Gebiet an Grenzen, die das System selber schuf. Denn offene Gewalt blieb als Bedrohung stets vorhanden. Dies hatte eine systemerhaltende Funktion – die Angst vor willkürlichen Maßnahmen war auch in der Entstalinisierung Mittel zur Herrschaftssicherung. Ganz konkret zeigt sich das am Umgang des Kombinates mit der Unzufriedenheit über die Lebensbedingungen an den Produktionsstandorten. Eine große Zahl der neu hinzugezogenen Vertragsarbeiter erhob massive Beschwerden und begann, die Auflösung ihrer Arbeitsverträge per Gericht einzuklagen. Die Kombinatsleitung wertete darauf ihre Proteste als Drückebergerei und zog die Arbeiter juristisch zur Verant-

---

7 GAMO f. P-21, op. 5, d. 765, l. 3–4.
8 Dieter Senghaas beschreibt diesen Prozess ausdrücklich als einen „Vorgang wider Willen", in dem den Status-quo-Mächten im Laufe einer Reihe von Konflikten bestimmte Zugeständnisse abgerungen werden. Vgl. Senghaas, Zivilisierung, S. 33 ff.

wortung. Entlassungen wurden nur noch aufgrund schwerer Krankheiten oder Arbeitsinvalidität gestattet. So wurde die Zwangsarbeit der Häftlinge durch den Zwang zur Erfüllung von Arbeitsverträgen ersetzt.

Ungeachtet dessen veränderte die Angleichung an die zivilen sowjetischen Verhältnisse unter der Dynamik der Entstalinisierung auch die Repräsentation der lokalen Herrschaft. Offene Gewalt und ihre Androhung passte als Kommunikationsform nicht mehr in das poststalinistische Bild, selbst wenn sie real noch vorhanden war. Mehr noch, seit Gründung des Magadaner Gebietes setzte die neue politische Leitung auf eine Umschreibung der bisherigen Vorstellungen von der Kolyma und auf eine offensive symbolische Besetzung des Raumes. Eine neu entstehende Heimatkunde entwarf die Geschichte einer großangelegten Umgestaltung. Dabei vereinnahmte die regionale Parteiführung rhetorisch die bisherige Ausbeutung durch das Kombinat als notwendige „Vorgeschichte"; die Gründung des Magadaner Gebietes proklamierte sie als Beginn einer neuen Ära und als deren „zweite Geburt". Sich selbst präsentierte sie als Ausgangspunkt und institutionalisierte Vorbedingung aller Verbesserungen. Im unionsweiten Kontext der Chruščev'schen Re-Ideologisierung, deren Narrativ auf eine Stärkung der Kommunistischen Partei als Vorbedingung einer blühenden Zukunft abzielte, erschien das Magadaner Gebiet so als ein ideales Beispiel. Chruščev soll sich zur Situation an der Kolyma folgendermaßen geäußert haben:

> Man muss die dunklen Flecken von Magadan und der Kolyma nehmen, man muss mit voller Kraft die Linie unserer Partei, ein normales Leben und eine zivile Bevölkerung durchsetzen.[9]

Ebenso wie man Wohnhäuser, Schulen und Krankenhäuser baute, wurde dem Nordosten ein zivilisiertes Image verpasst. Das Gebiet sollte eine gewöhnliche und zugleich eine besondere sowjetische Region werden, aufregend und jugendlich, geprägt von Bildungseinrichtungen und Kultur. Als Gegengewicht zur negativ besetzten Bezeichnung „Kolyma" wurde „Magadan" als neue wesentliche Regionsbezeichnung aufgebaut. Das Gebiet sollte Vorposten im östlichsten Teil der Union sein, ein Aushängeschild, ein Ort, an dem sich der junge Sowjetbürger im harten Klima und schwerer Arbeit beweisen konnte. Ein Ort mit „schwieriger Geschichte" und großer Zukunft.

Es ging um nicht weniger als um die virtuelle Erschaffung einer neuen Heimat „Magadan", um neue Bilder, um die Tilgung alter Vorstellungen, um einen neuen Ton; als regionale Variante einer – wie Pavel Kolář und Graeme Gill untersucht haben – neuen Rhetorik der poststalinistischen Sowjetunion. „Früher schreckte die Kolyma, heute zieht sie an" beschrieb der Erste Parteisekretär das Magadaner Gebiet Anfang der 1960er Jahre. Gerade an der Kolyma war dieser Bruch so elementar wie seine Durchsetzung bizarr erscheint. Die Grenzen dessen, was gesagt werden konnte und sollte, waren klar gesetzt. An keiner Stelle war von Lagern, von Häftlingen oder von Dal'stroj als Teil des MVD die Rede. Die gewaltvolle unmittelbare Vergangenheit

---

9 Zitiert nach Grebenjuk, Kolymskij led, S. 58.

wurde verschwiegen. Nun tat man einfach so, als sei die Region friedfertig und aufregend und lebenswert.

Dem typischen Bewohner dieses Raumes wurde dabei eine ganze Reihe von Eigenschaften zugeschrieben, bei dem das ursowjetische Thema „Jugend" in der Gestalt des jungen, abenteuerlustigen, dem harten Klima trotzenden Geologen eine besondere regionale Variante erhielt. Die indigene Bevölkerung erlebte in dieser Darstellung die sowjetische Erschließung des Raumes als Ankunft der Zivilisation. Während sie tatsächlich mit brutaler Härte zur Aufgabe ihres nomadischen Lebens gezwungen und ihre gesamte Kultur sowjetisch überformt wurde, schilderte die sowjetische Leitung diesen Prozess als eine heilsbringende Verschiebung der *frontier*, die „die Wildnis" gänzlich von der sowjetischen Karte verdrängte.

Der lokalen Parteileitung sollte dabei Legitimität zugeschrieben werden, es ging um ihre Anerkennung als politische Führung. Sie pflegte in ihrer Selbstrepräsentation das Bild einer verständnisvollen paternalistischen Führung der Werktätigen. In dieser Darstellung war sie Kritik gegenüber stets offen, zeigte in den Baracken und Kantinen Präsenz, bemühte sich intensiv um die Befriedigung materieller und kultureller Bedürfnisse.

Es lässt sich nicht belegen, wie sich diese inszenierte Zivilisierung unmittelbar auf das Verhältnis zwischen Herrschaft und Bevölkerung ausgewirkt hat. Aber es kann vermutet werden, dass derartige Inszenierungen die eigene elende Lebens- und Arbeitsrealität als mehr oder minder irreguläre Abweichung einer „eigentlichen" Realität erscheinen ließen, und dass solche Beschreibungen allein bereits eine gewisse Erleichterung oder sogar Freude auslösen konnten. Darüber, welche Rückwirkungen solch ein zivilisiertes Bild der entstalinisierten Kolyma auf die Produzenten dieser Texte selbst hatte, kann nur spekuliert werden. Rekurrierend auf die Thesen zu performativen Sprechakten von Alexei Yurchak erschiene es aussichtsreich, diese Bedeutung der Abbildung einer friedfertigen Region herauszuarbeiten. Doch damit bewegt man sich schon auf ganz anderem historiographischem Terrain, das andere Quellen, andere Fragen und andere methodische Zugänge erfordern würde.

Bis heute ist die Kolyma ein Symbol des stalinistischen GULAG. So entscheidend der GULAG für den Stalinismus war, so wichtig waren die Auflösung des GULAG und ihre Folgen für die Entstalinisierung. Die Entstehung und Entwicklung des Magadaner Gebietes aus den Lagern der Kolyma ist ein besonders schillerndes Beispiel dieser Dynamiken.

Anhang

Abbildungen

Abb. 66 Denkmal für die Opfer von Repression und Gewalt im Kolymaer Lagergebiet: „Maske der Trauer" des Künstlers Ėrnst Neizvestnyj, Fotografin: Mirjam Sprau

https://doi.org/10.1515/9783110557879-008

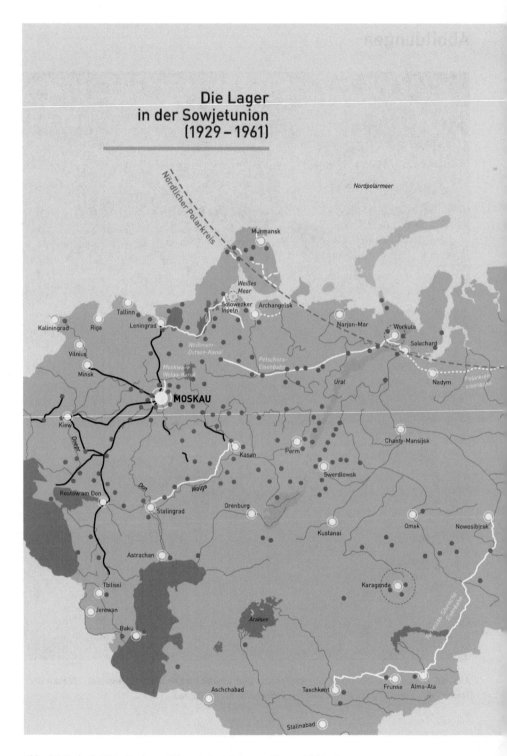

Abb. 67 Gedenkstätte Buchenwald nach Angaben von Memorial Moskau

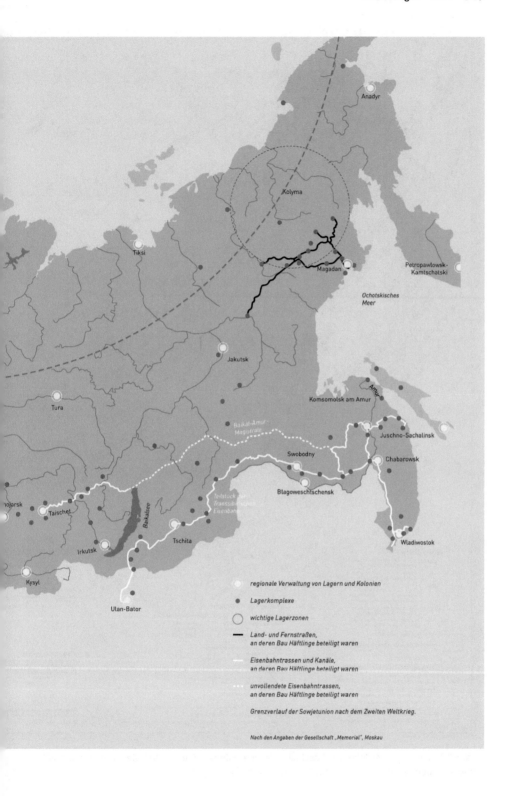

Anadyr

Kolyma

Tiksi

Petropawlowsk-
Kamtschatski

Magadan

Ochotskisches
Meer

Jakutsk

Tura

Komsomolsk am Amur

Amur

Baikal-Amur-
Magistrale

Juschno-Sachalinsk

Swobodny

Chabarowsk

rojarsk

Taischet

Baikalsee

Blagoweschtschensk

Teilstück der
Transsibirischen
Eisenbahn

Irkutsk

Tschita

Wladiwostok

Kysyl

Ulan-Bator

⊚ regionale Verwaltung von Lagern und Kolonien

● Lagerkomplexe

◯ wichtige Lagerzonen

—— Land- und Fernstraßen,
an deren Bau Häftlinge beteiligt waren

—— Eisenbahntrassen und Kanäle,
an deren Bau Häftlinge beteiligt waren

···· unvollendete Eisenbahntrassen,
an deren Bau Häftlinge beteiligt waren

Grenzverlauf der Sowjetunion nach dem Zweiten Weltkrieg.

Nach den Angaben der Gesellschaft „Memorial", Moskau

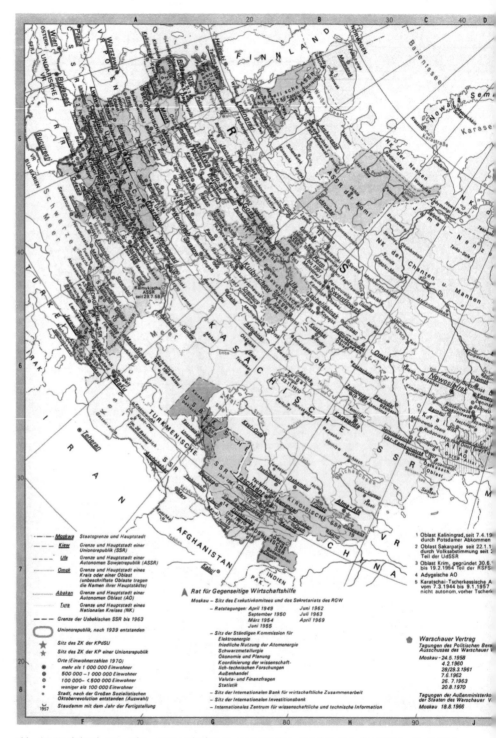

Abb. 68 Nachdruck aus: Atlas zur Geschichte in zwei Bänden. Band 2: Von der Großen Sozialistischen Oktoberrevolution 1917 bis 1972. 1. Aufl. Gotha/Leipzig 1975, © Ernst Klett Verlag GmbH

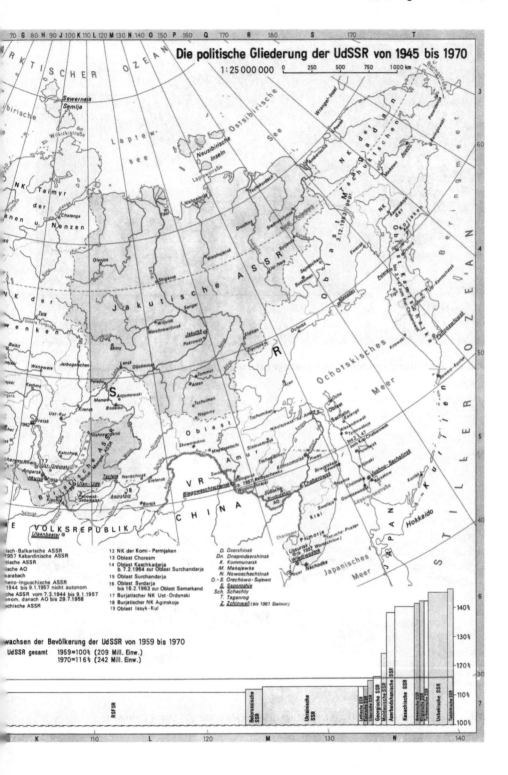

Die politische Gliederung der UdSSR von 1945 bis 1970

1:25 000 000

0 250 500 750 1000 km

isch-Balkarische ASSR
1957 Kabardinische ASSR
tische ASSR
ische AO
carabach
heno-Inguschische ASSR
1944 bis 9.1.1957 nicht autonom
che ASSR vom 7.3.1944 bis 9.1.1957
nom, danach AO bis 29.7.1958
 schische ASSR

12 NK der Komi - Permjaken
13 Oblast Choresm
14 Oblast Kaschkadarja
  b.7.2.1964 zur Oblast Surchandarja
15 Oblast Surchandarja
16 Oblast Syrdarja
  bis 16.2.1963 zur Oblast Samarkand
17 Burjatischer NK Ust-Ordynski
18 Burjatischer NK Aginskoje
19 Oblast Issyk-Kul

D. Dsershinsk
Dn. Dneprodsershinsk
K. Kommunarsk
M. Makejewka
N. Nowoschachtinsk
O.-S. Orechowo-Sujewo
S. Saporoshje
Sch. Schachty
T. Taganrog
Z. Zchinwali (bis 1961 Stalinir)

wachsen der Bevölkerung der UdSSR von 1959 bis 1970

UdSSR gesamt   1959=100% (209 Mill. Einw.)
               1970=116% (242 Mill. Einw.)

Abb. 69 ehemalige Uranaufbearbeitungsanlage nahe des Lagers Butugyčak, ullstein bild – Lieberenz

Abb. 70 alte Schuhe von Häftlingen des Lagers Butugyčak, ullstein bild – Lieberenz

Abkürzungsverzeichnis

AGO — *Administrativno-graždanskij otdel*, Administrativ-zivile Abteilung

ASSR — *Avtonomnaja Sovetskaja Socialističeskaja Respublika*, Autonome Sozialistische Sowjetrepublik

BAM — *Bajkalo-Amurskaja Magistral'*, Baikal-Amur-Magistrale

Berlag — *Beregovoj lager'*, Uferlager

CK — *Central'nyj Komitet*, Zentralkomitee

Čeka — *Črezvyčajnaja Komissija po bor'be s kontrrevoljuciej, spekuljaciej i sabotažem*, Außerordentliche Kommission zur Bekämpfung von Konterrevolution, Spekulation und Sabotage

d. — *delo*, Akte

f. — *fond*, Fond oder Bestand

g. — *god*, Jahr

GARF — *Gosudarstvennyj Archiv Rossijskoj Federacii*, Staatsarchiv der Russischen Föderation

gg. — *gody*, Jahre

Gorkom — *Gorodskoj komitet KPSS*, Stadtkomitee der KPdSU

Gosplan — *Gosudarstvennyj planovyj komitet Soveta Ministrov SSSR*, Staatliches Plankomitee des Ministerrates der UdSSR

GPU — *Gosudarstvennoe Političeskoe Upravlenie*, Staatliche politische Verwaltung

GRU — *Geologorazvedočnoe Upravlenie*, geologische Schürfverwaltung

GULAG — *Glavnoe Upravlenie ispravitel'no-trudovych Lagerej i kolonij*, Hauptverwaltung für Besserungs- und Arbeitslager und Kolonien

GULSDS — *Glavnoe Upravlenie Lagerej i Stroitel'stva Dal'nevo Severa SSSR*, Hauptverwaltung der Lager und für den Bau des Fernen Nordens der UdSSR

GUSDS — *Glavnoe Upravlenie Stroitel'stva Dal'nego Severa SSSR (Dal'stroj)*, Hauptverwaltung für den Bau des Fernen Nordens der UdSSR (Dal'stroj)

GVF — *Graždanskij Vozdušnyj Flot SSSR*, Zivile Luftflotte der UdSSR

INION — *Institut Naučnoj Informacii po Obščestvennym Naukam RAN*, Institut für wissenschaftliche Informationen für Gesellschaftswissenschaften der Russischen Akademie der Wissenschaften

KGB — *Komitet Gosudarstvennoj Bezopasnosti pri Sovete Ministrov SSSR*, Komitee für Staatssicherheit beim Ministerrat der UdSSR

KPdSU — Kommunistische Partei der Sowjetunion

KPSS — *Kommunističeskaja Partija Sovetskogo Sojuza*, Kommunistische Partei der Sowjetunion

l. — *list*, Blatt

Maglag — *Magadanskij ispravitel'no-trudovoj lager'*, Magadaner Besserungs- und Arbeitslager

MCM — *Ministerstvo Cvetnoj Metallurgii*, Ministerium für Buntmetalle

MGB — *Ministerstvo Gosudarstvennoj Bezopasnosti*, Ministerium für die staatliche Sicherheit

MMP — *Ministerstvo Metallurgičeskoj Promyšlennosti*, Ministerium für Metallindustrie

MVD — *Ministerstvo Vnutrennich Del*, Ministerium für Innere Angelegenheiten

NKVD — *Narodnyj Komissariat Vnutrennich Del*, Volkskommissariat für Innere Angelegenheiten

obkom — *oblastnoj komitet KPSS*, Gebietskomitee der KPdSU

oblispolkom — *oblastnoj ispolnitel'nyj komitet*, Gebietsexekutivkomitee

OGPU — *Ob''edinennoe Gosudarstvennoe Političeskoe Upravlenie*, Vereinigte staatliche politische Verwaltung

op. — *opis'*, Verzeichnis

orgnabor — *organizovannyj nabor*, organisierte Arbeitskräfterekrutierung

rajGRU — *rajonnoe Geologorazvedočnoe Upravlenie*, geologische Bezirksschürfverwaltung

https://doi.org/10.1515/9783110557879-009

RAN	*Rossijskaja Akademija Nauk*, Russische Akademie der Wissenschaften
RGAKFD	*Rossijskij Gosudarstvennyj Archiv Kinofotodokumentov*, Russisches Staatsarchiv für Film- und Fotodokumente
RGANI	*Rossijskij Gosudarstvennyj Archiv Novejšej Istorii*, Russisches Staatsarchiv für Neuere Geschichte
RGASPI	*Rossijskij Gosudarstvennyj Archiv Social'no-Političeskoj Istorii*, Russisches Staatsarchiv für Sozialpolitische Geschichte
RGAĖ	*Rossijskij Gosudarstvennyj Archiv Ėkonomiki*, Russisches Staatsarchiv für Wirtschaft
RSFSR	*Rossijskaja Sovetskaja Federativnaja Socialističeskaja Respublika*, Russische Sozialistische Föderative Sowjetrepublik
Sevvostlag	*Severo-vostočnyj ispravitel'no-trudovoj lager'*, Nordöstliches Besserungs- und Arbeitslager
SNK	*Sovet Narodnych Komissarov*, Rat der Volkskommissare
Sovnarchoz	*Sovet narodnogo chozjajstva*, Rat für Volkswirtschaft
SSSR	*Sojuz Sovetskich Socialističeskich Respublik*, Union der Sozialistischen Sowjetrepubliken
STO	*Sovet Truda i Oborony*, Rat für Arbeit und Verteidigung
SVKNII	*Severo-Vostočnyj Kompleksnyj Naučno-Issledovatel'skij Institut*, Nordöstliches komplexes wissenschaftliches Forschungsinstitut
UdSSR	Union der Sozialistischen Sowjetrepubliken
UMVD	*Upravlenie Ministerstva Vnutrennych Del*, Verwaltung des Ministeriums für Innere Angelegenheiten (regionale Abteilung des MVD)
VKP (b)	*Vsesojuznaja Kommunističeskaja Partija (bol'ševikov)*, Kommunistische Allunionspartei (Bolschewiki)
VLKMS	*Vsesojuznyj Leninskij Kommunističeskij Sojuz Molodeži*, Gesamtsowjetischer Leninscher Kommunistischer Jugendverband, Komsomol
VNII-1	*Vsesojuznyj Naučno-Issledovatel'skij Institut zolota i redkich metallov*, Wissenschaftliches Allunionsforschungsinstitut für Gold und seltene Metalle
VČK	*Vserossijskaja Črezvyčajnaja Komissija po bor'be s kontrrevoljuciej, spekuljaciej i sabotažem*, Außerordentliche Allrussische Kommission zur Bekämpfung von Konterrevolution, Spekulation und Sabotage
ZK	Zentralkomitee

Literaturverzeichnis

1 Archivbestände

GAMO – Gosudarstvennyj Archiv Magadanskoj Oblasti (Staatliches Archiv des Magadaner Gebietes)
  f. P-21 – Magadanskij oblastnoj komitet KPSS (obkom) (1953–1991 gg.), Magadaner Gebietskomitee der KPdSU (1953–1991)
  f. R-23 – Glavnoe Upravlenie Stroitel'stva Dal'nego Severa Ministerstva Cvetnoj Metallurgii SSSR (Dal'stroj), Hauptverwaltung für den Bau des Fernen Nordens des Ministeriums für Buntmetalle der UdSSR (Dal'stroj)
  f. R-23ss – Glavnoe Upravlenie Stroitel'stva Dal'nego Severa Ministerstva Cvetnoj Metallurgii SSSR (Dal'stroj), Hauptverwaltung für den Bau des Fernen Nordens des Ministeriums für Buntmetalle der UdSSR (Dal'stroj), ehemals geheimer Bestand
  f. R-23sč – Glavnoe Upravlenie Stroitel'stva Dal'nego Severa Ministerstva Cvetnoj Metallurgii SSSR (Dal'stroj), Hauptverwaltung für den Bau des Fernen Nordens des Ministeriums für Buntmetalle der UdSSR (Dal'stroj), ehemals geheimer Bestand
  f. 38 – Administrativno-graždanskij otdel Glavnogo Upravlenija Stroitel'stva Dal'nego Severa (AGO Dal'stroja), Administrativ-zivile Abteilung der Hauptverwaltung für den Bau des Fernen Nordens
  f. R-146 – Ispolkom Magadanskogo oblastnogo Soveta deputatov trudjaščichsja, Exekutivkomitee des Magadaner Gebietssowjets der Arbeiterdeputierten
  f. R-137 – Sovet narodnogo chozjajstva Severo-Vostočnogo ėkonomičeskogo rajona (Sovnarchoz), Rat für Volkswirtschaft des Nordöstlichen Wirtschaftsbezirkes
  f. R-137sč – Sovet narodnogo chozjajstva Severo-Vostočnogo ėkonomičeskogo rajona (Sovnarchoz), Rat für Volkswirtschaft des Nordöstlichen Wirtschaftsbezirkes, ehemals geheimer Bestand
  f. R-278 – Otdel social'nogo obespečenija Magadanskogo oblispolkoma (oblsobes), Abteilung für soziale Fürsorge des Magadaner Exekutivkomitees
  f. R-307 – Magadanskaja oblastnaja bol'nica, Magadaner Gebietskrankenhaus
  f. R-324 – Magadanskaja oblastnaja psichonevrologičeskaja bol'nica, Magadaner pychiatrisch-neurologisches Gebietskrankenhaus
GARF – Gosudarstvennyj Archiv Rossijskoj Federacii (Staatsarchiv der Russischen Föderation, Moskau)
  f. A-259 – Sovet Ministrov RSFSR (Sovmin RSFSR) 1917–1991, Ministerrat der RSFSR 1917–1991
  f. R-7523 – Verchovnyj Sovet SSSR, Oberster Sowjet der UdSSR
  f. R-9401 – Ministerstvo Vnutrennich Del SSSR, Ministerium für Innere Angelegenheiten der UdSSR
RGAĖ – Rossijskij Gosudarstvennyj Archiv Ėkonomiki (Russisches Staatsarchiv für Wirtschaft, Moskau)
  f. 7733 – Ministerstvo Finansov SSSR, Ministerium für Finanzen der UdSSR
  f. 9163 – Specupravlenie i specotdely Ministerstv Vnutrennich Del, Metallurgičeskoj Promyšlennosti i Metallurgii SSSR 1948–1957, Sonderverwaltung und Sonderabteilungen des Ministeriums für Innere Angelegenheiten, für Metallindustrie und Hüttenindustrie der UdSSR 1948–1957
RGAKFD – Rossijskij Gosudarstvennyj Archiv Kinofotodokumentov (Russisches Staatsarchiv für Film- und Fotodokumente, Krasnogorsk)

https://doi.org/10.1515/9783110557879-010

RGANI – Rossijskij Gosudarstvennyj Archiv Novejšej Istorii (Russisches Staatsarchiv für Neueste Geschichte, Moskau)

f. 5 – Apparat CK KPSS, Apparat des ZK der KPdSU

RGASPI – Rossijskij Gosudarstvennyj Archiv Social'no-Političeskoj Istorii (Russisches Staatsarchiv für sozialpolitische Geschichte, Moskau)

f. 556 – Bjuro CK KPSS po RSFSR, Büro des ZK der KPdSU für die RSFSR

2 Periodika

Al'manach Volja
Archiv pamjati
Bloknot agitatora
Bol'šaja Sovetskaja Ènciklopedija. Moskau 1970 ff.
Izvestija CK KPSS
Kolyma
Kraevedčeskie Zapiski
Magadanskaja Pravda
Magadanskij Komsomolec
Na Severe Dal'nem
Pravda
Sovetkėn Čukotka
Sovetskaja Kolyma
Vremja. Sobytija. Ljudi.

3 Edierte Quellen, Erinnerungen

Abramov, S. V.: Za nami pridut korabli: Spisok reabilitirovannych lic, smertnye prigovory v otnošenii kotorych privedeny v ispolnenie na territorii Magadanskoj oblasti. Magadan 1999 („Za nami pridut korabli").

Adamova-Sliozberg, O. L.: Put'. Moskau 1993 („Put'").

Afanas'ev, E. S. (Hg.): Ideologičeskie komissii CK KPSS: 1958–1964. Moskau 1998 („Ideologičeskie komissii").

Afanas'ev, E. S. (Hg.): Apparat CK KPSS i kul'tura 1953–1958: Dokumenty. Moskau 2001 („Apparat CK KPSS").

Afiani, V. Ju. (Hg.): Apparat CK KPSS i kul'tura 1958–1964: Dokumenty. Moskau 2005 („Apparat CK KPSS i kul'tura").

Afiani, V. Ju. (Hg.): Akademija nauk v rešenijach Politbjuro CK RKP (b) – VKP (b) – KPSS. Tom II: 1952–1958. Moskau 2010 („Akademija nauk v rešenijach Politbjuro").

Ajmermacher, K. u. a. (Hg.): Doklad N. S. Chruščeva o kul'te ličnosti Stalina na XX s"ezde KPSS: Dokumenty. Moskau 2002 („Doklad Chruščeva").

Aliev, I. (Hg.): Reabilitacija narodov i graždan 1954–1994. Dokumenty. Moskau 1994 („Reabilitacija narodov").

Archivnyj Otdel Administracii Magadanskoj oblasti Gosudarstvennyj Archiv Magadanskoj oblasti; Centr Chranenija Sovremennoj Dokumentacii Magadanskoj oblasti: Kalendar' znamenatel'nych i pamjatnych dat Magadanskoj oblasti na 2003 god. Magadan 2003 („Kalendar' 2003").

Archivnyj Otdel Administracii Magadanskoj oblasti Gosudarstvennyj Archiv Magadanskoj oblasti; Centr Chranenija Sovremennoj Dokumentacii Magadanskoj Oblasti: Kalendar' znamenatel'nych i pamjatnych dat Magadanskoj oblasti na 2006 god. Magadan 2006 („Kalendar' 2006").

Artizov, A. N. u. a. (Hg.): Reabilitacija: kak ėto bylo. Dokumenty Prezidiuma CK KPSS i drugie materialy.Tom I. Mart 1953 – fevral' 1956. Moskau 2000 („Reabilitacija Tom I").

Artizov, A. N. u. a. (Hg.): Reabilitacija: kak ėto bylo. Dokumenty Prezidiuma CK KPSS i drugie materialy. Tom II. Fevral' 1956 – načalo 80-ch godov. Moskau 2003 („Reabilitacija Tom II").

Artizov, A. N. u. a. (Hg.): Reabilitacija: kak ėto bylo. Dokumenty Politbjuro CK KPSS, stenogrammy zasedanija Komissii Politbjuro CK KPSS po dopolnitel'nomu izučeniju materialov, svjazannych s repressijami, imevšimi mesto v period 30–40-ch i načala 50-ch gg., i drugie materialy. Tom III. Seredina 80-ch godov – 1991. Moskau 2004 („Reabilitacija Tom III").

Artizov, Andrej N. (Hg.): Nikita Chruščev 1964: Stenogrammy plenuma CK KPSS i drugie dokumenty. Moskau 2007 („Chruščev 1964").

Bardach, Janusz; Gleeson, Kathleen: Man is wolf to man. Surviving the GULAG. Berkeley; Los Angeles 1998 („Wolf").

Bardach, Janusz; Gleeson, Kathleen: Surviving freedom. After the GULAG. Berkeley 2003 („Surviving").

Bezborodov, A. B.; Chrustalev, V. M. (Hg.): Istorija stalinskogo Gulaga. Konec 1920-ch – pervaja polovina 1950-ch godov: Sobranie dokumentov v 7-mi tomach. Tom 4. Naselenie Gulaga: čislennost' i uslovija soderžannija. Moskau 2004 („Naselenie Gulaga").

Caregradskij, V. A.: Po ėkranu pamjati. Magadan 1980 („Po ėkranu").

Carevskaja-Djakina, T. V. (Hg.): Istorija stalinskogo Gulaga. Konec 1920-ch – pervaja polovina 1950-ch godov: Sobranie dokumentov v 7-mi tomach. Tom 5. Specpereselency v SSSR. Moskau 2004 („Specpereselency").

Chilobočenko, A. T. (Hg.): Istoričeskaja chronika Magadanskoj oblasti. Sobytija i fakty. 1917–1972. Magadan 1975 („Istoričeskaja chronika").

Chlevnjuk, O. V. (Hg.): Istorija stalinskogo Gulaga. Konec 1920-ch – pervaja polovina 1950-ch godov: Sobranie dokumentov v 7-mi tomach. Tom 3. Ėkonomika Gulaga. Moskau 2004 („Ėkonomika Gulaga").

Chlevnjuk, Oleg (Hg.): Politbjuro CK VKP (b) i Sovet Ministrov SSSR 1945–1953. Moskau 2002 („Politbjuro CK VKP (b) i Sovet Ministrov").

Chronika Magadanskoj partijnoj organizacii, 1923–1986 gg. Magadan 1987 („Chronika partijnoj organizacii").

Chruschtschow, Sergej: Die Geburt einer Supermacht. Ein Buch über meinen Vater. Klitzschem 2003 („Geburt einer Supermacht").

Chruščev, N. S.: Dva cveta vremeni: Dokumenty iz ličnogo fonda N. S. Chrščeva. V dvuch tomach. Moskau 2009 („Dva cveta").

Der Fall Berija. Protokoll einer Abrechnung. Das Plenum des ZK der KPdSU. Juli 1953. Stenographischer Bericht. Aus dem Russischen von Viktor Knoll und Lothar Kölm. Berlin 1993 („Fall Berija").

Dück, Abraham: Erinnerungen eines Russlanddeutschen. Das Leben zu bestehen ist mehr als übers Feld zu gehen. Lebenschronik in drei Teilen. Neustadt an der Aisch 2005 („Erinnerungen").

Efimov, S. P. (Hg.): Chronika gornodobyvajuščej promyšlennosti Magadanskoj oblasti. Čast' 1: Gornodobyvajuščaja promyšlennost' Dal'stroja (1931–1957). Magadan 2002 („Chronika gornodobyvajuščej promyšlennosti").

Figes, Orlando: The Whisperers: Private Life in Stalin's Russia. London u. a. 2007 („Whisperers").

Figes, Orlando: Schick einen Gruß, zuweilen durch die Sterne. Eine Geschichte von Liebe und Überleben in Zeiten des Terrors. Berlin 2012 („Sterne").

Fursenko, A. A. (Hg.): Prezidium CK KPSS. 1954–1964. Tom I: Černovye protokol'nye zapisi zasedanij. Stenogrammy. Moskau 2003 („Černovye protokol'nye zapisi").

Fursenko, A. A. (Hg.): Prezidium CK KPSS. 1954–1964. Tom II: Postanovlenija. 1954–1958. Moskau 2006 („Postanovlenija 1954–1958").

Fursenko, A. A. (Hg.): Prezidium CK KPSS. 1954–1964. Tom III: Postanovlenija.1959–1964, Moskau 2008 („Postanovlenija 1959–1964").

Ginsburg, Jewgenia: Marschroute eines Lebens. Aus dem Russischen von Swetlana Geier. München 1986 [erster Teil der Erinnerungen; zuerst veröffentlicht als „Krutoj Maršrut I" Frankfurt a. M. 1967] („Marschroute").

Ginsburg, Jewgenia: Gratwanderung. Mit einem Vorwort von Heinrich Böll sowie einem Nachwort von Lew Kopelew und Raisa Orlowa. München 1980 [zweiter Teil der Erinnerungen; zuerst veröffentlicht als „Krutoj Maršrut II" Mailand 1979] („Gratwanderung").

Gorbatov, A. V.: Gody i vojny. Moskau 1965 („Gody").

Hedeler, Wladislaw (Hg.): KARLAG. Das Karagandinsker „Besserungsarbeitslager" 1930–1959. Dokumente zur Geschichte des Lagers. Paderborn u. a. 2008 („KARLAG").

Ioffe, N. A.: Vremja nazad: Moja žizn', moja sud'ba, moja ėpocha. Moskau 1992 („Sud'ba").

Kokurin, A. J.; Morukov, Ju. N. (Hg.): GULAG: Struktura i kadry. Stat'ja dvadcat' vtoraja. In: Svobodnaja Mysl' – XXI, 2001, Nr. 9, S. 97–122 („Struktura i kadry. Stat'ja dvadcat' vtoraja").

Kokurin, A. J.; Morukov, Ju. N. (Hg.): GULAG: Struktura i kadry. Stat'ja dvadcat' tret'ja. In: Svobodnaja Mysl' – XXI, 2001, Nr. 10, S. 104–125 („Struktura i kadry. Stat'ja dvadcat' tret'ja").

Kokurin, A. J.; Morukov, Ju. N. (Hg.): GULAG: Struktura i kadry. Stat'ja dvadcat' četvertaja. In: Svobodnaja Mysl' – XXI, 2001, Nr. 11, S. 99–123 („Struktura i kadry. Stat'ja dvadcat' četvertaja").

Kokurin, A. I; Morukov, Ju. N. (Hg.): Stalinskie strojki GULAGa. 1930–1953. Moskau 2005 („Stalinskie strojki").

Kokurin, A. I.; Petrov, N. V. (Hg.): GULAG: Glavnoe upravlenie lagerej. 1918–1960. Moskau 2002 („GULAG").

Kokurin, A. I.; Pozarov, A. I. (Hg.): „Novyj kurs" L. P. Berii 1953 g. In: Istoričeskij archiv 1996, H. 4, S. 132–164 („Novyj kurs").

Komsomol Magadanskoj oblasti. Magadanskaja oblastnaja organizacija VLKSM v cifrach i faktach, 1954–1984 gg. Magadan 1984 („Komsomol Magadanskoj oblasti").

Kozlov, V. A. (Hg.): Istorija stalinskogo Gulaga. Konec 1920-ch – pervaja polovina 1950-ch godov: Sobranie dokumentov v 7-mi tomach. Tom 6. Vosstanija, bunty i zabastovki zaključennych. Moskau 2004 („Vosstanija").

Kress, Vernon: Moi tri parochoda. Zapiski starogo gruzčika. Moskau 2003 („Parochoda").

Kuz'mina, Marina: Ja pomnju tot Vaninskij port. Komsomol'sk na Amure 2001 („Ja pomnju").

Ledovskoj: Melodii nevoli i svobody. In: Muzykal'nyj žurnal. Ijul' 2013, S. 15–17 („Melodii").

Lipper, Elinor: Elf Jahre in sowjetischen Gefängnissen und Lagern. Zürich 1950 („Elf Jahre").

Meta, V. I.; Digenko, V. V.: Žertvy Kolymy. Magadan: Dokumental'nye očerki i rasskazy. Magadan 2000 („Žertvy Kolymy").

Mochulsky, Fyodor Vasilevich: GULAG Boss. A Soviet Memoir. Translated and Edited by Deborah Kaple. New York 2011 („Gulag Boss").

Naumov, V.; Sigačev, Ju. (Hg.): Lavrentij Berija. 1953. Stenogramma ijul'skogo plenuma CK KPSS i drugie dokumenty. Moskau 1999 („Berija").

Olickaja, E.: Moi vospominanija. Frankfurt a. M. 1971 („Vospominanija").

Osnovnye zakonodatel'nye akty i rešenija pravitel'stva SSSR po voprosam raboty central'nych učreždenij SSSR i sojuznych respublik, sovnarchozov i drugich organizacij (po sostojanij na 1 maja 1960 g.). Moskau 1960 („Osnovnye zakonodatel'nye akty").

Pamjat' Kolymy. Vospominanija, pis'ma, fotodokumenty o godach repressij. Magadan 1990 („Pamjat' Kolymy").

Pantjuchin, I. V.: Zapiski Magadanskogo prokurora. Petrozavodsk 2000 („Zapiski").

Petrov, N. V. (Hg.): Istorija stalinskogo Gulaga. Konec 1920-ch – pervaja polovina 1950-ch godov: Sobranie dokumentov v 7-mi tomach. Tom 2. Karatel'naja sistema: struktura i kadry. Moskau 2004 („Karatel'naja sistema").

Repressirovannye geologi. Biografičeskie materialy. Moskau; St. Petersburg [2]1995 („Repressirovannye geologi").

Sbornik zakonodatel'nych i normativnych aktov o repressijach i reabilitacii žertv političeskich repressij. Moskau 1993 („Sbornik zakonodatel'nych aktov").

Sbornik zakonov SSSR i ukazov Prezidiuma Verchovnogo Soveta SSSR 1938–1967. Tom I. Moskau 1968 („Sbornik zakonov SSSR").

Schalamow, Warlam: Erzählungen aus Kolyma. Band 1: Durch den Schnee. Berlin 2008 („Schnee").

Schalamow, Warlam: Erzählungen aus Kolyma. Band 2: Linkes Ufer. Berlin 2009 („Linkes Ufer").

Schalamow, Warlam: Erzählungen aus Kolyma. Band 3: Künstler der Schaufel. Berlin 2010 („Künstler der Schaufel").

Schalamow, Warlam: Erzählungen aus Kolyma. Band 4: Die Auferweckung der Lärche. Berlin 2011 („Auferweckung der Lärche").

Sergeev, Georgij: Pervyj predsedatel'. In: Vremja. Sobytija. Ljudi. 1957–1970. Magadan 1983 („Pervyj predsedatel'").

Sobolev, Vasilij: 58–10. Pis'ma s Kolymy. Moskau 2000 („Pis'ma").

Solomon, Michael: Magadan. Siebe Jahre in sowjetischen Straflagern. Bayreuth 1974 („Magadan").

Solschenizyn, Alexander: Der Archipel GULAG. Reinbek bei Hamburg [16]2003 („Archipel").

Sovety Severo-Vostoka SSSR (1941–1961). Sbornik dokumentov i materialov. Čast' 2. Magadan 1982 („Sovety").

Steinberger, Nathan; Broggini, Barbara: Berlin – Moskau – Kolyma und zurück. Ein Gespräch über Stalinismus und Antisemitismus. Mit einem Vorwort von Jakob Moneta. Berlin; Amsterdam 1996 („Berlin – Moskau – Kolyma").

Šapiro, Jurij Viktorovič: Vospominanija o prožitoi žizni. Moskau 2006 („Vospominanija").

Šilo, Nikolaj: Vse zoloto Kolymy. In: Nauka i Žizn' 2006, H. 11, S. 16–23 („Vse zoloto Kolymy").

Talbott, Strobe (Hg.): Chruschtschow erinnert sich. Die authentischen Memoiren. Reinbek 1992 („Chruschtschow erinnert").

Varpachovskaja, I.: Iz vospominanij Kolymskoj Traviaty. In: Korallova, M. M. (Hg.): Teatr GULAGA. Vospominanija, očerki. Moskau 1995, S. 64–79 („Kolymskoj Traviaty").

Vegener, K: O chudožnike Leonide Vegener. In: Vilenskij, S. S. (Hg.): Dodnes' tjagoteet: Tom 2: Kolyma. Moskau 2004, S. 421–427 („O Leonide Vegenere").

Vegener, L. V.: Vospominanija. In: Volja: Žurnal uznikov totalitarnogo sistema 2002, H. 8–9, S. 183–192 („Vospominanija").

Vert, N.; Mironenko, S. V. (Hg.): Istorija stalinskogo Gulaga. Konec 1920-ch – pervaja polovina 1950-ch godov: Sobranie dokumentov v 7-mi tomach. Tom 1. Massovye repressii v SSSR. Moskau 2004 („Massovye repressii").

Vilenskij, S. S. (Hg.): Osvencim bez pečej. Is podgotovlennogo k izdaniju sbornika „Dodnes' tjagoteet" Tom II „Kolyma". Moskau 1996 („Osvencim bez pečej").

Vilenskij, S. S.: Kak pojavilos' „Dodnes' tjagoteet". In: Kolyma. Dal'stroj. Gulag. Skorb' i sudy. Materialy naučno-praktičeskoj konferencii. Magadan 1998, S. 117–125 („Kak pojavilos'").

Vilenskij, S. S.: Est' vsjudu svet... Čelovek v totalitarnom obščestve. Moskau 2001 („Est' vsjudu svet").

Vilenskij, S. S. (Hg.): Dodnes' tjagoteet. Tom 2: Kolyma. Moskau 2004 („Dodnes' tjagoteet").

Vjatkin, V.: Čelovek roždaetsja dvašdy. Magadan 1989 („Čelovek").

Volodin, Viktor: Neokončennyj Maršrut. Vospominanija o Kolyme 30–40-ch godov. Magadan 2014 („Neokončennyj Maršrut").

Vospominanija pervogo predsedatelja Magadanskogo oblispolkoma P. Ja. Afanas'eva ob obrazovanii Magadanskoj oblasti. In: Sovety Severo-Vostoka SSSR (1941–1961). Sbornik dokumentov i materialov. Čast' 2. Magadan 1982, S. 223–234 („Vospominanija predsedatelja").

Vospominanija zaslužennogo stroitelja RSFSR I. N. Lukina ob istorii zastrojki goroda. In: Sovety Severo-Vostoka SSSR (1941–1961). Sbornik dokumentov i materialov. Čast' 2. Magadan 1982, S. 297–302 („Vospominanija zaslužennogo stroitelja").

Wallace, Henry A.: Soviet Asia Mission. New York 1945 („Soviet Asia").

4 Zeitgenössische Publikationen

10 let Magadanskoj oblasti. Magadan 1963 („10 let").

1939–1964. Magadan 1964 („1939–1964, Fotoalbum").

70 let Aviacii Severo-Vostoka Rossija. Magadan 2005 („Aviacii Severo-Vostoka").

Afanas'ev, P. Ja.: Kommunisty v bor'be za osvoenie bogatstv Severo-Vostoka. In: 10 let Magadanskoj oblasti. Magadan 1963, S. 13–14 („Kommunisty").

Afanas'ev, P. Ja.: Zdes' načinaetsja Rossija. Zapiski sekretarja obkoma. Moskau 1967 („Rossija").

Akademija Stroitel'stva i Architektury SSSR (Hg.): Voprosy stroitel'stva na Krajnem Severe. Materialy soveščanija po stroitel'stvu na Krajnem Severe, 16–18 dekabrja 1959. Leningrad 1960 („Voprosy stroitel'stva na Krajnem Severe").

Beljaeva, A. V.: Russkie na Krajnem Severe. Magadan 1955 („Russkie").

Bulanov, Vladimir: Zdes' načinaetsja den'. Magadan 1961 („Načinaetsja den'").

Chakimov, K.: Pis'ma iz byvšego stojbišča. Magadan 1959 („Pis'ma").

Chodos, L. A.: Rybnaja promyšlennost' Severo-Vostoka. Kratkij očerk sostojanija i perspektivy razvitija rybnoj promyšlennosti Magadanskoj oblasti. Magadan 1959 („Rybnaja promyšlennost'").

Chrošev, A. F.: Očerki istorii zdravoochranenija Magadanskoj oblasti. Magadan 1959 („Očerki istorii zdravoochranenija").

Čistjakov, I. P.: Desjatiletie mestnych Sovetov. In: 10 let Magadanskoj oblasti. Magadan 1963, S. 36–72 („Desjatiletie").

Dal'stroj. K 25-letiju. Magadan 1956 („K 25-letiju").

Danilov, L. S.: Kraj severnogo sijanija. Zapiski kinorežissera. Magadan 1955 („Kraj severnogo sijanija").

Daniševskij, G. M.: Akklimatizacija čeloveka na Severe. Moskau 1955 („Akklimatizacija čeloveka").

Drabkin, I. E.: Mužestvennye razvedčiki nedr. In: 10 let Magadanskoj oblasti. Magadan 1963, S. 98–110 („Razvedčiki nedr").

Geroi rjadom s nami. Očerki o komsomol'cach Magadanskoj oblasti. Magadan 1959 („Geroi").

Gorochov, N. A.: Semiletka Magadanskoj oblasti. Magadan 1959 („Semiletka").

Gradov, M. N.: Sel'skoe chozjastvo na Severnoj zemle. In: 10 let Magadanskoj oblasti. Magadan 1963, S. 148–186 („Sel'skoe chozjastvo").

Gromov, L.: Ostrov Vrangelja. Naučno-populjarnyj očerk. Magadan 1961 („Ostrov Vrangelja").

Gruša, M. V.: 25 let Dal'stroja. Magadan 1956 („25 let").

Guščin, I. V.; Afanas'ev, A. I.: Čukotskij nacional'nyj okrug. Kratkij istoriko-geografičeskij očerk. Magadan 1956 („Čukotskij okrug").

Izučajte rodnoj kraj. Magadan 1959 („Izučajte rodnoj kraj").

Kaštanov I. N.: Vse vo imja čeloveka. In: 10 let Magadanskoj oblasti. Magadan 1963, S. 187–211 („Vse vo imja").

Klesova, É. V.: Sever zovet! Iz istorii komsomol'skich organizacij Magadanskoj oblasti. Magadan 1956 („Sever zovet").

Kopteva, K.: Zoloto vo l'dach. Magadan 1961 („Zoloto").

Korobejnikov, Boris: Buduščee načinaetsja segodnja. Magadan 1961 („Buduščee").

Kozlov, N. V: Tuda, gde trudnee. Očerk. Magadan 1960 („Tuda, gde trudnee").

Kuwajew, Oleg: Goldsucher. München 1976. [Zuerst veröffentlicht als „Territorija" Moskau 1975] („Goldsucher").

Levčenko, S. V.; Mozeson, D. L.: Zolotaja Kolyma. Iz istorii otkrytija i osvoenija Severo-Vostoka SSSR. Moskau 1963 („Zolotaja Kolyma").

Magadanskaja oblast'. Administrativno-territorial'noe delenie. Magadan 1968 („Administrativno-territorial'noe delenie").

Malagin, A.: Magadanskij ėkonomičeskij rajon. Magadan 1957 („Ėkonomičeskij rajon").

Menovščikov, G. A.: Ėskimosy. Magadan 1959 („Ėskimosy").

Murav'ev, B. V.: Nasuščnye voprosy stroitel'stva v rajonach Krajnego Severa. In: Akademija Stroitel'stva i Architektury SSSR (Hg.): Voprosy stroitel'stva na Krajnem Severe. Materialy soveščanija po stroitel'stvu na Krajnem Severe, 16 – 18 dekabrja 1959. Leningrad 1960, S. 3 – 32 („Nasuščnye voprosy").

My živem na Severe. Sbornik. Magadan 1958 („My živem").

Na preobražennoj zemle. Iz opyta raboty mestnych Sovetov Magadanskoj oblasti. Magadan 1959 („Na preobražennoj zemle").

Narodnoe chozjajstvo Magadanskoj oblasti. Statističeskij sbornik. Magadan 1960 („Narodnoe chozjajstvo Magadanskoj oblasti").

Novikov, Vladimir: Kolyma ty, Kolyma. Rasskazy. Magadan 1960 („Kolyma ty").

Novikova, K. A.: Ėvenskij fol'klor. Magadan 1958 („Fol'klor").

Preobražennyj kraj. Sbornik. Magadan 1956 („Preobražennyj kraj").

Rodin, E. Ď.: Iz istorii osvoenija Severo-Vostoka (k 30-letiju Kolymskoj ėkspedicii I. F. Molodych 1928 – 1929 gg.). Kolyma 1958 („Iz istorii osvoenija Severo-Vostoka").

Rytchėc: Vremja tajanija snegov. Magadan 1960 („Vremja").

Semenov, Andrej: Bereg Nadeždy. Povesť. Magadan 1956 („Bereg Nadeždy").

Slavin, S. V.: Problemy razvitija proizvoditel'nych sil Magadanskoj oblasti. Moskau 1961 („Problemy razvitija").

Slavin, S. V.: Promyšlennoe i transportnoe osvoenie Severa SSSR. Moskau 1961 („Promyšlennoe osvoenie").

Smolina, T. P.: Komsomol'cy-Dobrovol'cy. In: Vremja. Sobytija. Ljudi. 1946 – 1958. Magadan 1973, S. 214 – 227 („Komsomol'cy-Dobrovol'cy").

Šilo, N. A.; Potemkin, S. V.: Valjutnyj cech strany. In: 10 let Magadanskoj oblasti. Magadan 1963, S. 73 – 98 („Valjutnyj cech").

Ustiev, E. K.: U istokov zolotoj reki. Moskau 1977 („U istokov").

Volkov, G. G.: Veksel' Bilibina. Magadan 1977 („Veksel' Bilibina").

Volkov, G. G.: Zolotaja Kolyma. Magadan 1982 („Zolotoja Kolyma").

Vronskij, B.: Po taežnym tropam. Magadan 1960 („Po tropam").

Zlatina, N. S.: Čto čitat' o Magadanskoj oblasti. Rekomendatel'nyj ukazatel' literatury. Magadan 1966 („Čto Čitat'").

Zvik, D.: Magadan. Očerk – chronika. Gorodu 20 let. Magadan 1959 („Magadan").

Žarkich, A. I.; Lukin, I. I.: Vstajut novostrojki... In: 10 let Magadanskoj oblasti. Magadan 1963, S. 111 – 146 („Vstajut novostrojki").

Žicharev, N. A.: V bor'be za Sovety na Čukotke. Očerki istorii bor'by za ustanovlenie Sovetskoj vlasti na Čukotke. Magadan 1958 („V bor'be").

Žicharev, N. A.: Očerki istorii Severo-Vostoka RSFSR (1917 – 1953 gg.). Magadan 1961 („Očerki").

5 Forschungsliteratur

Adler, Nanci: Life in the Big Zone: the Fate of Returnees in the Aftermath of Stalinist Repression. In: Europe-Asia-Studies 51 (1999), S. 5–19 („Life").

Adler, Nanci: The Gulag Survivor. Beyond the Soviet System. New York 2002 („Gulag Survivor").

Adler, Nanci: Enduring Repression: Narratives of Loyalty to the Party before, during, and after the Gulag. In: Europe-Asia Studies 62 (2010), S. 211–234 („Enduring Repression").

Adler, Nanci: Keeping Faith with the Party. Communist Believers Return from the Gulag. Bloomington 2012 („Faith").

Aksjutin, Jurii V.: Chruščevkaja ottepel' i obščestvennye nastroenija v SSSR v 1953–1964 gg. Moskau 2010 („Chruščevkaja ottepel'").

Aksjutin, Jurii V.; Pyšikov, Aleksandr V.: Poststalinskoe obščestvo: Problema liderstva i transformacija vlasti. Moskau 1999 („Poststalinskoe obščestvo").

Alexeyeva, Ludmilla: The Thaw Generation: Growing up in the Post-Stalin Era. Boston 1990 („Thaw").

Alexopoulos, Golfo: A Torture Memo: Reading Violence in the Gulag. In: Alexopoulos, Golfo; Hessler, Julie; Tomoff, Kiril (Hg.): Writing the Stalin Era. Sheila Fitzpatrick and Soviet Historiography. New York 2011, S. 157–176 („Torture Memo").

Antonov-Ovseenko, A.: Put' naverch. In: Nekrasov, Vladimir F. (Hg.): Berija: konec kar'ery. Moskau 1991, S. 4–139 („Put' naverch").

Apor, Balzás; Apor, Péter; Rees, E. A. (Hg.): The Sovietization of Eastern Europe: New Perspectives on the Postwar Period. Washington, DC 2008 („Sovietization").

Applebaum, Anne: Gulag: A history. Armonk, New York 2003 („Gulag").

Applebaum, Anne: Introduction. In: Applebaum, Anne: Gulag Voices. An Anthology. New Haven; London 2011, S. VII-XV („Introduction").

Attwood, Lynne: Housing in the Khrushchev Era. In: Ilic, Melanie; Reid, Susan E.; Attwood, Lynne (Hg.): Women in the Khrushchev Era. Basingstoke; New York 2004, S. 177–202 („Housing").

Autio-Sarasmo, Sari: Khrushchev and the Challenge of Technological Progress. In: Ilic, Melanie; Smith, Jeremy (Hg.): Khrushchev in the Kremlin: Policy and Government in the Soviet Union, 1953–1964. New York 2011, S. 133–145 („Challenge").

Baberowski, Jörg: Auf der Suche nach Eindeutigkeit. Kolonialismus und zivilisatorische Mission im Zarenreich und der Sowjetunion. In: Jahrbücher für Geschichte Osteuropas 47 (1999), S. 482–503 („Suche nach Eindeutigkeit").

Baberowski, Jörg: Wege aus der Gewalt. Nikita Chruschtschow und die Entstalinisierung 1953–1964. In: Bielefeld, Ulrich; Bude, Heinz; Greiner, Bernd (Hg.): Gesellschaft – Gewalt – Vertrauen: Jan Philipp Reemtsma zum 60. Geburtstag. Hamburg 2012, S. 401–436 („Wege aus der Gewalt").

Baberowski, Jörg (Hg.): Was ist Vertrauen? Ein interdisziplinäres Gespräch. Frankfurt a. M.; New York 2014 („Vertrauen").

Baberowski, Jörg: Erwartungssicherheit und Vertrauen: Warum manche Ordnungen stabil sind, und andere nicht. In: Baberowski, Jörg (Hg.): Was ist Vertrauen? Ein interdisziplinäres Gespräch. Frankfurt a. M.; New York 2014, S. 7–29 („Erwartungssicherheit").

Bacaev, I. D.: Kolymskaja grjada Archipelaga GULAg (zaključennye). In: Rossijskaja Akademija Nauk. Dal'nevostočnoe otdelenie. Severo-Vostočnoj Kompleksnyj Naučno-Issledovatel'skij Institut: Istoričeskie aspekty Severo-Vostoka Rossii: Ėkonomika, obrazovanie, Kolymskij GULag. Magadan 1996, S. 46–72 („Kolymskaja grjada").

Bacaev, I. D.: Kolymskij Gulag. In: Dikov, N. N. u. a. (Hg.): Severo-Vostok Rossii s drevnejšich vremen do našich dnej: Novye ėkskursy v istoriju. Magadan 1996, S. 72–78 („Kolymskij Gulag").

Bacaev, I. D.: Sel'skoe i promyšlovoe chozjajstvo Severo-Vostoka Rossii 1929–1953 gg. Magadan 1997 („Sel'skoe i promyšlovoe chozjajstvo").

Bacaev, I. D.: Opyt administrativnogo upravlenija narodnym chozjajstvom Magadanskoj oblasti (1953–1965 gg.). In: Karpenko, N. V. (Hg.): Magadan: Gody, sobytija, ljudi. Magadan 1999, S. 5–6 („Opyt upravlenija").

Bacaev, I. D.: Agropromyšlennyj kompleks Severo-Vostoka Rossii 1954–1991 gg. (Ėtapy razvitija, osobennosti, effektivnost'). Magadan 2001 („Agropromyšlennyj kompleks").

Bacaev, I. D.: Dejatel'nost' organov UNKVD – UMVD – UMGB po Dal'stroju v poslevoennyj period (1946–1953). In: Dikovskie Čtenija. Magadan 2001, S. 216–226 („Dejatel'nost' organov").

Bacaev, I. D.: Dinamika krizisa osnovnogo proizvodstva Dal'stroja (1946–1953). In: Dikovskie Čtenija. Magadan 2001, S. 234–241 („Dinamika").

Bacaev, I. D.: Osobennosti promyšlennogo osvoenija Severo-Vostoka Rossii v period massovych političeskich repressij (1932–1953). Dal'stroj. Magadan 2002 („Osobennosti").

Bacaev, I. D.: Formy i metody povyšenija ėffektivnosti truda zaključennych v Sevvostlage NKVD-MVD SSSR (1932–1953). In: II Dikovskie Čtenija. Magadan 2002, S. 76–81 („Formy i metody").

Bacaev, I. D.: Sostojanie olenevodstva Magadandskoj oblasti v period strukturnoj perestrojki gosudarstvennogo sektora sel'skogo chozjajstva v 50–70-e gg. Xx v. In: II Dikovskie Čtenija. Magadan 2002, S. 87–94 („Sostojanie olenevodstva").

Bacaev, I. D.: Obostrenie kriminal'noj obstanovki v ITL Dal'stroja (seredina 40-ch – načalo 50-ch gg.). In: Materialy po istorii severa Dal'nego Vostoka. Magadan 2004, S. 183–197 („Obostrenie").

Bacaev, I. D.: Amnistija 1953 g. i ee vlijanie na promyšlennyj kompleks Dal'stroja. In: Materialy po istorii Severa Dal'nego Vostoka. Magadan 2004, S. 198–208 („Amnistija").

Bacaev, I. D.: Osobennosti sovetskoj social'noj politiki v nacional'nych okrugach i rajonach Severo-Vostoka Rossii v period reform vtoroj poloviny 1950-ch – serediny 1960-ch gg. In: VI Dikovskie Čtenija. Magadan 2010, S. 198–202 („Osobennosti sovetskoj social'noj politiki").

Bacaev, I. D.; Kozlov, A. G.: Dal'stroj i Sevvostlag NKVD SSSR v cifrach i dokumentach. Čast' 1 i 2. Magadan 2002 („Dal'stroj i Sevvostlag").

Bacon, Edwin: The Gulag at War. Stalin's Forced Labour System in the Light of the Archives. London 1994 („Gulag at War").

Barenberg, Alan: Prisoners without borders. Zazonniki and the Transformation of Vorkuta after Stalin. In: Jahrbücher für Geschichte Osteuropas 57 (2009) [Themenheft: Aufbruch aus dem GULag. Hg. von Klaus Gestwa], S. 513–534 („Vorkuta").

Barenberg, Alan: From Prisoners to Citizens? Ex-Prisoners in Vorkuta during the Thaw. In: Kozlov, Denis; Gilburd, Eleonory: The Thaw: Soviet Society and Culture during the 1950s and 1960s. Toronto 2013, S. 143–175 („Citizens").

Barenberg, Alan: Gulag Town, Company Town. Forced Labor and its Legacy in Vorkuta. New Haven 2014 („Gulag Town").

Barnes, Steven: Soviet Society Confined: The Gulag in the Karaganda region of Kazakhstan, 1930–1950s. Ph.diss. Stanford University 2003 („Gulag in the Karaganda Region").

Barnes, Steven: In a Manner Befitting Soviet Citizens. An Uprising in the post-Stalin Gulag. In: Slavic Review 64 (2005), S. 823–850 („Uprising").

Barnes, Steven: Death and Redemption: The Gulag and the Shaping of Soviet Society. Princeton 2011 („Death and Redemption").

Baron, Nick: New Spatial Histories of Twentieth Century Russia and the Soviet Union: Surveying the Landscape. In: Jahrbücher für Geschichte Osteuropas 55 (2007), S. 374–400 („New Spatial History").

Bassin, Mark: Turner, Solov'ev and the „Frontier Hypothesis": The Nationalist Signification of Open Spaces. In: Journal of Modern History 65 (1993), S. 473–511 („Turner").

Bassin, Mark: Imperialer Raum / Nationaler Raum. Sibirien auf der kognitiven Landkarte Rußlands im 19. Jahrhundert. In: Geschichte und Gesellschaft 28 (2002), H. 3 [Themenheft: Mental Maps. Hg. von Christoph Conrad], S. 378–403 („Imperialer Raum").

Bassin, Mark; Ely, Christopher; Stockdale, Melissa K. (Hg.): Space, Place, and Power in Modern Russia: Essays in the New Spatial History. DeKalb 2010 („Space").

Bassin, Mark; Ely, Christopher; Stockdale, Melissa K.: Russian Space. In: Bassin, Mark; Ely, Christopher; Stockdale, Melissa K. (Hg.): Space, Place, and Power in Modern Russia: Essays in the New Spatial History. DeKalb 2010, S. 3–19 („Russian Space").

Beyrau, Dietrich: Intelligenz und Dissens. Die russischen Bildungsschichten in der Sowjetunion 1917–1985. Göttingen 1993 („Intelligenz").

Beyrau, Dietrich: Dem sowjetischen Brutkasten entwachsen… Sowjetische Hegemonie und sozialistische Staatlichkeit in Ostmitteleuropa. In: Osterkamp, Jana; von Puttkamer, Joachim: Sozialistische Staatlichkeit. München 2012, S. 19–44 („Brutkasten").

Binner, Rolf; Bonwetsch, Bernd; Junge, Marc (Hg.): Stalinismus in der sowjetischen Provinz 1937–1938. Die Massenaktion aufgrund des operativen Befehls № 00447. Berlin 2010 („Stalinismus").

Binner, Rolf; Bonwetsch, Bernd; Junge, Marc: Der operative Befehl № 00447. Sein Schicksal in der Provinz. In: Binner, Rolf; Bonwetsch, Bernd; Junge, Marc (Hg.): Stalinismus in der sowjetischen Provinz 1937–1938. Die Massenaktion aufgrund des operativen Befehls № 00447. Berlin 2010, S. 9–64 („Operativer Befehl").

Bittner, Stephen V.: Local Soviets, Public Order, and Welfare after Stalin: Appeals from Moscow's Kiev Raion. In: The Russian Review 62 (2003), S. 281–293 („Appeals").

Bittner, Stephen V.: The Many Lives of Khrushchev's Thaw. Experience and Memory in Moscow's Arbat. Ithaca; London 2008 („Many Lives").

Bittner, Stephen V.: What's in a Name? De-Stalinization and the End of the Soviet Union. In: Bohn, Thomas M.; Einax, Rayk; Abeßer, Michel (Hg.): De-Stalinization Reconsidered. Persistence and Change in the Soviet Union. Frankfurt a. M.; New York 2014, S. 31–42 („What's in a Name").

Bohn, Thomas: Bevölkerung und Sozialstruktur. In: Plaggenborg, Stefan (Hg.): Handbuch der Geschichte Russlands, Band 5: 1945–1991 – Vom Ende des Zweiten Weltkrieges bis zum Zusammenbruch der Sowjetunion. Stuttgart 2002–2003, S. 596–658 („Bevölkerung").

Bohn, Thomas: Minsk – Musterstadt des Sozialismus. Stadtplanung und Urbanisierung in der Sowjetunion nach 1945. Köln u. a. 2008 („Minsk").

Bohn, Thomas M. (Hg.): Von der „europäischen Stadt" zur „sozialistischen Stadt" und zurück? Urbane Transformationen im östlichen Europa des 20. Jahrhunderts. Vorträge der gemeinsamen Tagung des Collegium Carolinum und des Johann Gottfried Herder-Forschungsrats in Bad Wiessee vom 23. bis 26. November 2006. München 2009 („Europäische Stadt").

Bohn, Thomas M.: Von der „europäischen Stadt" zur „sozialistischen Stadt" und zurück? Zur Einleitung. In: Bohn, Thomas M. (Hg.): Von der „europäischen Stadt" zur „sozialistischen Stadt" und zurück? Urbane Transformationen im östlichen Europa des 20. Jahrhunderts. Vorträge der gemeinsamen Tagung des Collegium Carolinum und des Johann Gottfried Herder-Forschungsrats in Bad Wiessee vom 23. bis 26. November 2006. München 2009, S. 1–20 („Sozialistische Stadt").

Bohn, Thomas M.; Einax, Rayk; Abeßer, Michel (Hg.): De-Stalinization Reconsidered. Persistence and Change in the Soviet Union. Frankfurt a. M.; New York 2014 („De-Stalinization").

Bohn, Thomas M.; Einax, Rayk; Abeßer, Michel: From Stalinist Terror to Collective Constraints. „Homo Sovieticus" and the „Soviet People" after Stalin. In: Bohn, Thomas M.; Einax, Rayk; Abeßer, Michel (Hg.): De-Stalinization Reconsidered. Persistence and Change in the Soviet Union. Frankfurt a. M.; New York 2014, S. 11–27 („Homo Sovieticus").

Borodkin, Leonid; Gregory, Paul R.; Khlevniuk, Oleg (Hg.): GULAG. Ėkonomika prinuditel'nogo truda. Moskau 2005 („Ėkonomika").

Breslauer, George: On the Adaptability of Soviet Welfare-State Authoritarianism. In: Hoffmann, Erik; Laird, Robbin (Hg.): The Soviet Polity in the Modern Era. New York 1984, S. 219–245 („On the Adaptability").

Brodersen, Per: Die Stadt im Westen. Wie Königsberg Kaliningrad wurde. Göttingen 2008 („Stadt im Westen").

Bubnis, G. K.: Iz istorii obrazovanija Magadanskoj oblasti: In: Kraevedčeskie Zapiski 12 (1982), S. 41–49 („Iz istorii obrazovanija").

Barton, K. [Burton, Christopher]: Zdravoochranenie v period pozdnego Stalinizma i duch poslevoennogo gosudarstva blagodenstvija, 1945–1953 gody. In: Žurnal issledovanij social'noj politiki 5 (2007), S. 541–558 („Zdravoochranenie").

Burton, Christopher: Destalinization as Detoxification?-The Expert Debate on Industrial Toxins under Khrushchev. In: Bernstein, Frances L.; Burton, Christopher; Healy, Dan (Hg.): Soviet Medicine. Culture, Practice and Science. DeKalb 2010, S. 237–257 („Detoxification").

Chili, Dėn: Nasledie GULAGa: Prinuditel'nyj trud sovetskoj epochi ka vnutrennaja kolonizacija. In: Ėtkind, A.; Uffellmann, D.; Kukulin, I. (Hg.): Tam, vnutri: Praktiki vnutrennej kolonizacij v kul'turnoj istorii Rossii. Moskau 2012, S. 684–728 („Nasledie GULAGa").

Chlevnjuk, Oleg: Regional'naja vlast' v SSSR v 1953 – konce 1950-ch godov: Ustojčivost' i konflikty. In: Rossiskaja Istorija 6, H. 3 (2007), S. 31–49 („Regional'naja vlast'").

Christova, Christina: Totalitär, modern oder postmodern: Deutungen des poststalinistischen Sowjetsystems im Wandel. Saarbrücken 2007 („Deutungen").

Churieva, L. A.: Organizacionnaja struktura Severovostokzolota v seredine 1960-ch – 1980-e gg. XX stoletija. In: Gorjačev, N. A. u. a. (Hg.): Severo-Vostok Rossii: Prošloe, nastojaščee, buduščee. Materialy II regional'noj naučno-praktičeskoj konferencii. Tom I. Magadan 2004, S. 65–67 („Struktura Severovostokzolota").

Cohen, Stephen F.: The Victims Return: Survivors of the Gulag after Stalin. Exeter 2010 („Victims Return").

Conquest, Robert: Kolyma. The Arctic Death Camps. Oxford u. a. 1979 [Erveröffentlichung London 1978] („Kolyma").

Conquest, Robert: The Great Terror. A Reassessment. New York 1990 („Great Terror").

Conrad, Christoph (Hg.): Mental Maps. Themenheft der Zeitschrift Geschichte und Gesellschaft 28 (2002), H. 3 („Mental Maps").

Conyngham, William J.: Industrial Management in the Soviet Union: The Role of the C.P.S.U. in Industrial Decision-Making 1917–1970. Stanford 1973 („Industrial Management").

Craveri, Marta: Krizis Gulaga: Kengirskoe vosstanie 1954 goda v dokumentach MVD. In: Cahiers du Monde russe 36 (1995), S. 319–344 („Kengirskoe vosstanie").

Craveri, Marta: The Strikes in Norilsk and Vorkuta Camps and their Role in the Breakdown of the Stalinist Forced Labour System. In: van der Linden, Marcel; Brass, T. (Hg.): Free and Unfree Labour. The Debate Continues. Bern 1997, S. 363–378 („Strikes").

Craveri, Marta: Forced Labour in the Soviet Union between 1939 and 1956. In: Fondazione, Giacomo Feltrinelli (Hg.): Reflections on the Gulag. Mailand 2003, S. 25–60 („Forced Labour").

Čajkovskij, R. R. (Hg.): Ė. M. Remark i lagernaja literatura. Magadan 2003 („Remark").

Černoluckaja, E. N.: Tranzitnyj gorodok kak fenomen massovych migracij na Tichookeanskom poberež'e Rossii (seredina 1940-ch – 1950-e gg.). In: Kolymskij gumanitarnyj al'manach 2 (2007), S. 127–138 („Tranzitnyj gorodok").

Dahlmann, Dittmar; Hirschfeld, Gerhard (Hg.): Lager, Zwangsarbeit, Vertreibung und Deportation. Dimensionen der Massenverbrechen in der Sowjetunion und in Deutschland 1933 bis 1945. Essen 1999 („Lager, Zwangsarbeit").

Dahlmann, Dittmar: Sibirien. Vom 16. Jahrhundert bis zur Gegenwart. Paderborn 2009 („Sibirien").

Daly, John C. K.: The „Wild East" Frontier. Russian Expansion into Siberia. In: Journal of the West 34 (1995), S. 32–40 („Wild East").

Damir-Geilsdorf, Sabine; Hartmann, Angelika; Hendrich, Béatrice (Hg.): Mental Maps – Raum – Erinnerung. Kulturwissenschaftliche Zugänge zum Verhältnis von Raum und Erinnerung. Münster 2005 („Mental Maps").

Davies, R. W.; Ilic, Melanie: From Khrushchev (1935–1936) to Khrushchev (1956–1964). Construction Policy Compared. In: Ilic, Melanie; Smith, Jeremy (Hg.): Khrushchev in the Kremlin: Policy and Government in the Soviet Union, 1953–1964. New York 2011, S. 202–231 („From Khrushchev to Khrushchev").

Davydov, I. A.: Otdalennye rezul'taty vospitanija detej v Ol'skom detskom dome Magadanskoj oblasti v 1951–1958 gg. In: VI Dikovskie Čtenija. Magadan 2010, S. 202–206 („Rezul'taty vospitanija detej").

Daycock, Davis: The Pattern of Soviet Leadership Politics: Perestroika, De-Stalinisation and the Cartel of Anxiety. Winnipeg 1989 („Pattern").

Dikov, N. N. u. a.: Severo-Vostok v period ukreplenija gosudarstvennogo komandno-administrativnogo socializma (1953–1985 gg.). In: Dikov, N. N. u. a. (Hg.): Severo-Vostok Rossii s drevnejšich vremen do našich dnej: Novye ėkskursy v istoriju. Magadan 1996, S. 79–93 („Severo-Vostok v period ukreplenija").

Dobrenko, Evgeny; Naiman, Eric (Hg.): The Landscape of Stalinism. The Art and Ideology of Soviet Space. Seattle; London 2003 („Landscape").

Dobson, Miriam: Contesting the Paradigms of De-Stalinization: Readers Responses to One Day in the Life of Ivan Denisovich. In: Slavic Review 64 (2005), S. 580–600 („Contesting the Paradigms").

Dobson, Miriam: „Show the Bandit-Enemies no Mercy!": Amnesty, Criminality and Public Response in 1953. In: Jones, Polly (Hg.): The Dilemmas of De-Stalinization. Negotiating Cultural and Social Change in the Krushchev Era. London u. a. 2006, S. 21–40 („Bandit-Enemies").

Dobson, Miriam: POWs and Purge Victims: Attitudes towards Party Rehabilitation, 1956–75. In: The Slavonic and East European Review 86 (2008) [Themenheft: The Relaunch of the Soviet Project, 1945–1964. Hg. von Juliane Fürst; Polly Jones und Susan Morrisey], S. 328–345 („POWs").

Dobson, Miriam: Khrushchev's Cold Summer: Gulag Returnees, Crime, and the Fate of Reform after Stalin. New York 2009 („Cold Summer").

Dobson, Miriam: ,The Post-Stalin Era. De-Stalinization, Daily Life, and Dissent'. In: Kritika: Explorations in Russian and Eurasian History 12 (2011), S. 905–924 („Post-Stalin Era").

Döring, Jörg; Thielmann, Tristan (Hg.): Spatial Turn. Das Raumparadigma in den Kultur- und Sozialwissenschaften. Bielefeld 2008 („Spatial Turn").

Donovan, Victoria: „How well do you know your krai?" The Kraevedenie Revival and Patriotic Politics in Late Khrushchev-Era Russia. In: Slavic Review 74 (2015), S. 464–483 („Kraevedenie Revival").

Dünne, Jörg: Die Karte als Operations- und Imaginationsmatrix. Zur Geschichte eines Raummediums. In: Döring, Jörg; Thielmann, Tristan (Hg.): Spatial Turn. Das Raumparadigma in den Kultur- und Sozialwissenschaften. Bielefeld 2008, S. 49–69 („Karte").

Easter, Gerald M.: Reconstructing the State: Personal Networks and Elite Identity in Soviet Russia. New York; Cambridge 2000 („Reconstructing").

Einax, Rayk: Entstalinisierung auf Weißrussisch. Krisenbewältigung, sozioökonomische Dynamik und öffentliche Mobilisierung in der Belorussischen Sowjetrepublik 1953–1965. Wiesbaden 2014 („Entstalinisierung auf Weißrussisch").

Elias, Norbert : Über den Prozess der Zivilisation. 2 Bände. Frankfurt a. M. [7]1980 („Zivilisation").

Elie, Marc: Les politiques à l égard des libérés du Goulag: amnistiés et réhabilités dans la region de Novosibirsk, 1953–1960. In: Cahiers du monde russe 47 (2006), S. 327–348 („Amnistiés et réhabilités").

Elie, Marc: Les anciens détenus du Goulag: libérations massives, réinsertion et réhabilitation dans l'URSS poststalinienne, 1953–1964. Paris 2007 („Les anciens détenus du Goulag").

Elie, Marc: Unmögliche Rehabilitation. Die Revisionskommissionen 1956 und die Unsicherheiten des Tauwetters. In: Osteuropa 57 (2007) [Themenheft: Das Lager schreiben. Hg. von Manfred Sapper; Volker Weichsel und Andrea Huterer], S. 369–385 („Revisionskommissionen").

Elie, Marc: Aufstieg und Fall der Verbrecherbanden. Kriminelle Gegenkultur, kriminologische Untersuchungen und Strafpolitik im Tauwetter. In: Jahrbücher für Geschichte Osteuropas 57 (2009) [Themenheft: Aufbruch aus dem GULag. Hg. von Klaus Gestwa], S. 492–512 („Verbrecherbanden").

Elie, Marc: Khrushchev's Gulag: The Soviet Penitentiary System after Stalin's Death, 1953–1964. In: Kozlov, Denis; Gilburd, Eleonory: The Thaw: Soviet Society and Culture during the 1950s and 1960s. Toronto 2013, S. 109–142 („Khrushchev's Gulag").

Elie, Marc: Die „Drehtür" und die Marginalisierungsmaschinerie des stalinistischen Gulag, 1945–1960. In: Landau, Julia; Scherbakowa, Irina (Hg.): GULAG. Texte und Dokumente 1929–1956. Göttingen 2014, S. 106–117 („Drehtür").

Engelmann, Roger; Großbölting, Thomas; Wentker, Hermann (Hg.): Kommunismus in der Krise. Die Entstalinisierung 1956 und die Folgen. Göttingen 2008 („Entstalinisierung 1956").

Ertz, Simon: Lagernaja sistema v 1930-e – 1950-e gg.: Évoljucija struktury i principov upravlenija. In: Borodkin, Leonid; Gregory, Paul R.; Khlevniuk, Oleg (Hg.): GULAG. Ėkonomika prinuditel'nogo truda. Moskau 2005, S. 90–128 („Lagernaja sistema").

Evtuhov, Catherine: Voices from the Regions. Kraevedenie meets the Grand Narrative. In: Kritika: Explorations in Russian and Eurasian History 13 (2012), S. 877–887 („Voices").

Field, Deborah A.: Private life and Communist Morality in Khrushchev's Russia. New York 2007 („Private Life").

Fieseler, Beate: Ende des Gulag-Systems? Amnestien und Rehabilitierungen nach 1953. In: Landau, Julia; Scherbakowa, Irina (Hg.): GULAG. Texte und Dokumente 1929–1956. Göttingen 2014, S. 170–179 („Amnestien").

Filtzer, Donald: Soviet Workers and De-Stalinization. The Consolidation of the Modern System of Soviet Production Relations 1953–1964. Cambridge 1992 („Soviet Workers").

Filtzer, Donald: The Khrushchev Era: De-Stalinisation and the Limits of Reform in the USSR, 1953–1964. London 1993 („Khrushchev Era").

Filtzer, Donald: From Mobilized to Free Labour. De-Stalinization and the Changing Legal Status of Workers. In: Jones, Polly (Hg.): The Dilemmas of De-Stalinization. Negotiating Cultural and Social Change in the Krushchev Era. London u. a. 2006, S. 154–169 („From Mobilized to Free").

Filtzer, Donald: The Political Economy of Water Supply under Late Stalinism. In: Bernstein, Frances L.; Burton, Christopher; Healy, Dan: Soviet Medicine. Culture, Practice and Science. DeKalb 2010, S. 214–236 („Water Supply").

Fitzpatrick, Sheila: Tear off the Masks! Identity and Imposture in Twentieth-Century Russia. Princeton, New Jersey 2005 („Identity and Imposture").

Forsyth, James: A History of the Peoples of Siberia. Russia's North Asian Colony, 1851–1990. Houndsmills 2006 („Peoples of Siberia").

Fraenkel, Ernst: Der Doppelstaat. Frankfurt a. M.; Köln 1974 [Erstveröffentlichung: The Dual State. A Contribution to the Theory of Dictatorship. Aus dem Deutschen übersetzt von E. A. Shils, in Zusammenarbeit mit Edith Lowenstein und Klaus Knorr. New York u. a. 1941] („Doppelstaat").

Frank, Susi: Innere Kolonisation und frontier-Mythos. Räumliche Deutungskonzepte in Rußland und den USA. In: Osteuropa 11 (2003), 1658–1677 („Innere Kolonisation").

Fürst, Juliane: The Arrival of Spring? Changes and Continuities in Soviet Youth Culture and Policy between Stalin and Khrushchev. In: Jones, Polly (Hg.): The Dilemmas of De-Stalinization. Negotiating Cultural and Social Change in the Krushchev Era. London u. a. 2006, S. 135–153 („Arrival of Spring").

Fürst, Juliane; Jones, Polly; Morrisey, Susan (Hg.): The Relaunch of the Soviet Project, 1945–1964. Themenheft der Zeitschrift The Slavonic and East European Review 86 (2008) („Relaunch").

Fürst, Juliane: Stalin's Last Generation: Soviet Post-War Youth and the Emergence of Mature Socialism. Oxford 2010 („Last Generation").

Gal'ceva, N. V.: Analiz retrospektivy zolotodobyči v Magadanskoj oblasti. In: V Dikovskie Čtenija. Magadan 2008, S. 208–210 („Analiz retrospektivy").

Gel'man, M. L.: Fundamental'nye problemy geology Severo-Vostočnoj Sibiri, ich osoznanie i poisk rešenija v trudach SVKNII (1960–2010 gg.). In: VI Dikovskie Čtenija. Magadan 2010, S. 13–16 („Fundamental'nye problemy").

Gestwa, Klaus: Herrschaft und Technik in der spät- und poststalinistischen Sowjetunion. Machtverhältnisse auf den „Großbauten des Kommunismus", 1948–1964. In: Osteuropa 51 (2001), S. 171–197 („Herrschaft und Technik").

Gestwa, Klaus: Das Besitzergreifen von Natur und Gesellschaft im Stalinismus. Enthusiastischer Umgestaltungswille und katastrophischer Fortschritt. In: Saeculum 56 (2005), S. 105–138 („Besitzergreifen").

Gestwa, Klaus: Raum – Macht – Geschichte. Making Sense of Soviet Space. In: Osteuropa 55 (2005), S. 46–69 („Raum – Macht").

Gestwa, Klaus: Technologische Kolonisation und die Konstruktion des Sowjetvolkes. Die Schau- und Bauplätze der stalinistischen Moderne als Zukunftsräume, Erinnerungsorte und Handlungsfelder. In: Damir-Geilsdorf, Sabine; Hartmann, Angelika; Hendrich, Béatrice (Hg.): Mental Maps – Raum – Erinnerung. Kulturwissenschaftliche Zugänge zum Verhältnis von Raum und Erinnerung. Münster 2005, S. 73–115 („Technologische Kolonisation").

Gestwa, Klaus (Hg.): Aufbruch aus dem GULag. Themenheft der Zeitschrift Jahrbücher für Geschichte Osteuropas 57 (2009) („Aufbruch").

Gestwa, Klaus: Aufbruch aus dem GULag? Forschungsstand und Konzeption des Themenheftes. In: Jahrbücher für Geschichte Osteuropas 57 (2009) [Themenheft: Aufbruch aus dem GULag. Hg. von Klaus Gestwa], S. 481–491 („Aufbruch aus dem Gulag?").

Gestwa, Klaus: Die Stalinschen Großbauten des Kommunismus. Sowjetische Technik- und Umweltgeschichte, 1948–1967. München 2010 („Stalinsche Großbauten").

Gestwa, Klaus: Zwischen Erschöpfung und Erschließung. Zur Aneignung von Raum und Macht in der Sowjetunion. In: Schlögel, Karl (Hg.): Mastering Russian Spaces. Raum und Raumbewältigung als Probleme der russischen Geschichte. München 2011, S. 279–311 („Erschöpfung").

Gestwa, Klaus; Grützmacher, Johannes: Infrastrukturen. In: Plaggenborg, Stefan (Hg.): Handbuch der Geschichte Russlands, Band 5: 1945–1991 – Vom Ende des Zweiten Weltkrieges bis zum Zusammenbruch der Sowjetunion. Stuttgart 2002–2003, S. 1089–1152 („Infrastrukturen").

Gill, Graeme: Destalinisation and the Question of the Reformability of the Soviet Union. In: Debatte 18 (2010), H. 2, S. 127–143 („Question of Reformability").

Gill, Graeme: Symbols and Legitimacy in Soviet Politics. Cambridge; New York 2011 („Symbols").

Gill, Graeme; Pitty, Roderic: Power in the Party: the Organization of Power and Central-Republican Relations in the CPSU. New York 1997 („Power").

Giżejewska, Małgorzata: Die Einzigartigkeit und der besondere Charakter der Konzentrationslager in Kolyma und die Möglichkeiten des Überlebens. In: Dahlmann, Dittmar; Hirschfeld, Gerhard (Hg.): Lager, Zwangsarbeit, Vertreibung und Deportation. Dimensionen der Massenverbrechen in der Sowjetunion und in Deutschland 1933 bis 1945. Essen 1999, S. 245–260 („Möglichkeiten des Überlebens").

Gogoleva E. M.: Leksemy „Materik" i „Kolyma" v obščenacional'nom slovare i v regional'noj tradicii. In: Kolymskij gumanitarnyj al'manch 2 (2007), S. 199–208 („Leksemy").

Golovanov, Jaroslav: Korolev. Fakty i Mify. Moskau 1994 („Korolev").

Gorlizki, Yoram: Party Revivalism and the Death of Stalin. In: Slavic Review 54 (1995), S. 1–22 („Party Revivalism").

Gorlizki, Yoram: Anti-Ministerialism and the USSR Ministry of Justice, 1953–56: A Study in Organizational Decline. In: Europe-Asia Studies 48 (1996), S. 1279–1318 („Anti-Ministerialism").

Gorlizki, Yoram: Political Reform and Local Party Interventions under Khrushchev. In: Solomon, Peter (Hg.): Reforming Justice in Russia: Power, Culture, and the Limits of Legal Order. New York 1997, S. 256–281 („Political Reform").

Gorlizki, Yoram: Policing Post-Stalin Society: The *Militsiia* and Public Order under Khrushchev. In: Cahiers du monde russe 44 (2003), S. 465–480 („Militsiia").

Gorlizki, Yoram: Too much Trust: Regional Party Leaders and Local Political Networks under Brezhnev. In: Slavic Review 69 (2010), S. 677–680 („Too much Trust").

Gorlizki, Yoram: Structures of Trust after Stalin. In: The Slavonic and East European Review 91 (2013), S. 119–146 („Structures of Trust").

Gorlizki, Yoram; Khlevniuk, Oleg: Cold Peace. Stalin and the Soviet Ruling Circle, 1945–1953. New York 2004 („Cold Peace").

Grebenjuk, P. S.: Samoubijstva v Magadanskoj oblasti v 1953–1964 gg. In: IV Dikovskie Čtenija. Magadan 2006, S. 214–217 („Samoubijstva").

Grebenjuk, P. S.: Kolymskij led. Sistema upravlenija na Severo-Vostoke Rossii. 1953–1964. Moskau 2007 („Kolymskij led").

Grebenjuk, P. S.: Narodnoe obrazovanie na Severo-Vostoke Rossii v 1950-e – 1960-e gg. In: Gumanitarnye issledovanija v vostočnoj Sibiri i na Dal'nem Vostoke 38 (2016), H. 4, S. 36–46 („Narodnoe obrazovanie").

Grebenjuk, P. S.: Rukovodjaščie kadry Dal'stroja (1938–1945 gody). In: Novyj Istoričeskij Vestnik 49 (2016), H. 3, S. 78–102 („Rukovodjaščie kadry Dal'stroja").

Grebenjuk, P. S.: Vovlečenie rassochinskoj kočevoj gruppy ėvenov v ruslo socialističeskogo razvitija (1950–1970-e gg.). In: Rossija i ATR 94 (2016), H. 4, S. 287–300 („Vovlečenie rassochinskoj kočevoj gruppy").

Grebenjuk, P. S.: Ėkonomičeskaja effektivnost' zolotodobyči Dal'stroja (1932–1956). In: Voprosy istorii 2017, H. 9, S. 48–65 („Ėkonomičeskaja effektivnost'").

Grebenjuk, P. S.: Smechovaja praktika v kontekste gosudarstvennogo upravlenija na Severo-Vostoke SSSR (1940–1950e gg.). In: Dialog so vremenem 58 (2017), S. 318–329 („Smechovaja praktika").

Grebenjuk, P. S.: Faktor „Dal'stroja" I kul'turnaja politika na Sever-Vostoke SSSR v 1953–1960-e gody. In: Novejšaja istorija Rossii 2017, H. 4, S. 115–132 („Kul'turnaja politika")

Gregory, Paul R.: The Institutional Background of the Soviet Enterprise: The Planning Apparatus and the Ministries. With a Comment by László Csaba. Köln 1989 („Institutional Background").

Gregory, Paul R.: An Introduction to the Economics of the Gulag. In: Gregory, Paul R.; Lazarev, Valery (Hg.): The Economics of Forced Labor: The Soviet Gulag. Stanford, Kalifornien 2003, S. 1–22 („Introduction").

Gregory, Paul R.; Lazarev, Valery (Hg.): The Economics of Forced Labor: The Soviet Gulag. Stanford, Kalifornien 2003 („Forced Labor").

Gregory, Paul R.: The Political Economy of Stalinism: Evidence from the Soviet Secret Archives. Cambridge 2004 („Political Economy").

Grützmacher, Johannes: Vielerlei Öffentlichkeiten. Die Bajkal-Amur-Magistrale als Mobilisierungsprojekt der Brežnev-Ära. In: Jahrbücher für Geschichte Osteuropas 50 (2002), S. 204–223 („Vielerlei Öffentlichkeiten").

Grützmacher, Johannes: „Young Men go East!" The BAM Frontier under Brezhnev. In: Stolberg, Eva-Maria (Hg.): The Siberian Saga. A History of Russia's Wild East. Frankfurt a. M. 2005, S. 203–220 („Young Men").

Grützmacher, Johannes: Die Baikal-Amur-Magistrale. Vom stalinistischen Lager zum Mobilisierungsprojekt unter Brežnev. München 2012 („Baikal-Amur-Magistrale").

Gun'ko, S. V.; Galin, A. V.: Iz istorii sozdanija Magadanskoj oblasti. In: Kraevedčeskie Zapiski 10 (1975), S. 17–24 („Iz istorii sozdanija").

Häfner, Lutz: Von der Frontier zum Binnenraum. Visionen und Repräsentationen Sibiriens als innerrussländischer Grenzraum. In: Duhamelle, Christophe; Kossert, Andreas; Struck, Bernhard (Hg.): Grenzregionen. Ein europäischer Vergleich vom 18. bis zum 20. Jahrhundert. Frankfurt a. M.; New York 2007, S. 25–50 („Frontier").

Handley, John R. F.: Historic Overview of the Witwatersrand Goldfields. Howick 2004 („Witwatersrand Goldfields").

Hanson, Philip: The Rise and Fall of the Soviet Economy. An Economic History of the USSR from 1945. New York; London 2003 („Rise and Fall").

Hardy, Jeffrey S.: „The Camp is not a Resort". The Campaign against Privileges in the Soviet Gulag, 1957–61. In: Kritika: Explorations in Russian and Eurasian History 13 (2012), S. 89–122 („Campaign").

Harris, Steven E.: In Search of „Ordinary" Russia. Everyday Life in the NEP, the Thaw, and the Communal Apartment. In: Kritika: Explorations in Russian and Eurasian History 6 (2005), S. 583–614 („Ordinary Russia").

Hartmann, Angelika: Konzepte und Tranformationen der Trias „Mental Maps, Raum und Erinnerung". Einführende Gedanken zum Kolloquium. In: Damir-Geilsdorf, Sabine; Hartmann, Angelika; Hendrich, Béatrice (Hg.): Mental Maps – Raum – Erinnerung. Kulturwissenschaftliche Zugänge zum Verhältnis von Raum und Erinnerung. Münster 2005, S. 3–21 („Konzepte").

Hasanli, Jamil: Khrushchev's Thaw and National Identity in Soviet Azerbaijan, 1954–1959. London 2015 („National Identity").

Hayes, Peter: Die Degussa im Dritten Reich: Von der Zusammenarbeit zur Mittäterschaft. München 2004 („Degussa").

Hedeler, Wladislaw: Widerstand im Gulag. Meuterei, Aufstand, Flucht. In: Osteuropa 57 (2007) [Themenheft: Das Lager schreiben. Hg. von Manfred Sapper; Volker Weichsel und Andrea Huterer], S. 353–368 („Widerstand im Gulag").

Hedeler, Wladislaw: Die Ökonomik des Terrors. Zur Organisationsgeschichte des Gulag 1939 bis 1960. Hannover 2010 („Ökonomik").

Hedeler, Wladislaw; Henning, Horst (Hg.): Schwarze Pyramiden, rote Sklaven. Der Streik in Workuta im Sommer 1953. Leipzip 2007 („Rote Sklaven").

Hedeler, Wladislaw; Stark, Meinhard: Das Grab in der Steppe. Leben im GULAG: Die Geschichte eines sowjetischen Besserungsarbeitslagers 1930–1959. Paderborn u. a. 2009 („Grab in der Steppe").

Hildermeier, Manfred: Geschichte der Sowjetunion 1917–1991. München 1998 („Sowjetunion").

Hilger, Andreas: Grenzen der Entstalinisierung. Sowjetische Politik zwischen Rehabilitierung und Repression 1953–1964. In: Engelmann, Roger; Großbölting, Thomas; Wentker, Hermann (Hg.): Kommunismus in der Krise. Die Entstalinisierung 1956 und die Folgen. Göttingen 2008, S. 253–273 („Grenzen").

Hösler, Joachim: Die sowjetische Geschichtswissenschaft 1953 bis 1991. Studien zur Methodologie- und Organisationsgeschichte. München 1995 („Geschichtswissenschaft").

Hooper, Cynthia: What Can and Cannot Be Said: Between the Stalinist Past and the New Soviet Future. In: The Slavonic and East European Review 86 (2008) [Themenheft: The Relaunch of the Soviet Project, 1945–1964. Hg. von Juliane Fürst; Polly Jones und Susan Morrisey], S. 306–327 („New Soviet Future").

Hoppe, Bert: Auf den Trümmern von Königsberg. Kaliningrad 1946–1970. München 2000 („Königsberg").

Hornsby, Robert: Protest, Reform and Repression in Khrushchev's Soviet Union. Cambridge 2013 („Protest").

Hornsby, Robert: A „Merciless Struggle". De-Stalinisation and the 1957 Clampdown on Dissent. In: Bohn, Thomas M.; Einax, Rayk; Abeßer, Michel (Hg.): De-Stalinization Reconsidered. Persistence and Change in the Soviet Union. Frankfurt a. M.; New York 2014, S. 93–112 („Merciless Struggle").

Hough, Jerry F.; Fainsod, Merle: How the Soviet Union is Governed. Cambridge, Mass. ⁴1980 („Soviet Union is Governed").

Huemer, Ulrich: Doppelstaat DDR? Zur Übertragung der von Ernst Fraenkel geprägten Begriffe „Normenstaat" und „Maßnahmenstaat" auf die DDR. In: Osterkamp, Jana; von Puttkamer, Joachim: Sozialistische Staatlichkeit. München 2012, S. 225–250 („Doppelstaat DDR").

Huhn, Ulrike: Mit Ikonen und Gesang oder: Ein Bischof auf der Flucht vor seinem Kirchenvolk. Massenwallfahrten in Russland unter Stalin und Chruschtschow. In: Jahrbuch für Historische Kommunismusforschung 2012, S. 315–333 („Massenwallfahrten").

Huhn, Ulrike: Glaube und Eigensinn. Volksfrömmigkeit zwischen orthodoxer Kirche und sowjetischem Staat, 1941 bis 1960. Wiesbaden 2014 („Eigensinn").

Huxtable, Simon: Shortcomings. Soviet Journalists and the Changing Role of Press Criticism after the 20th Party Congress. In: Bohn, Thomas M.; Einax, Rayk; Abeßer, Michel (Hg.): De-Stalinization Reconsidered. Persistence and Change in the Soviet Union. Frankfurt a. M.; New York 2014, S. 209–221 („Soviet Journalists").

Ilic, Melanie; Reid, Susan E.; Attwood, Lynne (Hg.): Women in the Khrushchev Era. Basingstoke; New York 2004 („Women").

Ilic, Melanie; Smith, Jeremy (Hg.): Soviet State and Society under Nikita Khrushchev. London 2009 („Soviet State").

Ilic, Melanie; Smith, Jeremy (Hg.): Khrushchev in the Kremlin: Policy and Government in the Soviet Union, 1953–1964. New York 2011 („Khrushchev in the Kremlin").

Il'ina, V. A.: Dinamika čislennosti i nacional'nogo sostava naselenija Kamčatskoj oblasti v 1926–1939 gg. In: Kolymskij gumanitarnyj al'manach 2 (2007), S. 44–53 („Dinamika").

Ioffe, Grigorij; Nesterenko, Aleksandr: Volčij kamen'. Uranovye ostrova archipelago GULAG. St. Petersburg 1998 („Volčij kamen'").

Isakov, A. N.: Istorija torgovli na Severo-Vostoke Rossii (XVII-XX vv.). Magadan 1994 („Istorija torgovli").

Ivanova, G. M.: Gulag v sisteme totalitarnogo gosudarstva. Moskau 1997 („Sistema totalitarnogo gosudarstva").

Ivanova, G. M.: GULAG. Gosudarstvo v gosudarstve. In: Sovetskoe obščestvo: Vozniknovenie, razvitie, istoričeskij final. Tom 2, Moskau 1997, S. 207–272 („Gosudarstvo v gosudarstve").

Ivanova, G. M.: GULAG v sovetskoj gosudarstvennoj sisteme (konec 1920-ch – seredina 1950-ch godov). Moskau 2002 („GULAG").

Ivanova, Galina: Eine unbekannte Seite des GULag: Lagersondergerichte in der UdSSR (1945–1954). In: Jahrbücher für Geschichte Osteuropas 53 (2005), S. 25–41 („Lagersondergerichte").

Ivanova, G. M.: Istorija GULAGa, 1918–1958: Social'no-ėkonomičeskij i politiko-pravovoj aspekty. Moskau 2006 („Istorija").

Ivanova, G. M.: Na poroge „gosudarstva vseobščego blagosostojanija". Social'naja politika v SSSR (seredina 1950-ch – načalo 1970-ch godov). Moskau 2011 [deutsche Fassung: Ivanova, Galina; Plaggenborg, Stefan: Entstalinisierung als Wohlfahrt. Sozialpolitik in der Sowjetunion 1953–1970. Frankfurt a. M.; New York 2015] („Na poroge").

Ivanova, Galina: ‚A Question of Honour'. Socialist Welfare State versus the Stalinist Apparatus of Repression. In: Bohn, Thomas M.; Einax, Rayk; Abeßer, Michel (Hg.): De-Stalinization

Reconsidered. Persistence and Change in the Soviet Union. Frankfurt a. M.; New York 2014, S. 133–143 („Question of Honour").

Jersak, Simon: Rüstungsforschung hinter Stacheldraht: Intellektuelle Zwangsarbeit im Stalinismus. In: von Lingen, Kerstin; Gestwa, Klaus (Hg.): Zwangsarbeit als Kriegsressource in Europa und Asien. Paderborn 2014, S. 171–188 („Rüstungsforschung").

Jo, Junbae: Dismantling Stalin's Fortress. Soviet Trade Unions in the Khrushchev Era. In: Ilic, Melanie; Smith, Jeremy (Hg.): Soviet State and Society under Nikita Khrushchev. London 2009, S. 122–141 („Trade Unions").

Johnson, Emily: How St. Petersburg Learned to Study itself. The Russian Idea of Kraevedenie. Pennsylvania 2006 („Kraevedenie").

Jones, Jeffrey W.: Everyday Life and the „Reconstruction" of Soviet Russia during and after the Great Patriotic War, 1943–1948. Bloomington 2008 („Everyday Life").

Jones, Polly: From Stalinism to Post-Stalinism. De-Mythologising Stalin, 1953–1956. In: Shukman, Harold (Hg.): Redefining Stalinism. London 2003, S. 127–148 („De-Mythologising").

Jones, Polly (Hg.): The Dilemmas of De-Stalinization. Negotiating Cultural and Social Change in the Krushchev Era. London u. a. 2006 („De-Stalinization").

Jones, Polly: Introduction. The Dilemmas of De-Stalinization. In: Jones, Polly (Hg.): The Dilemmas of De-Stalinization. Negotiating Cultural and Social Change in the Krushchev Era. London u. a. 2006, S. 1–18 („Introduction").

Jones, Polly: From Secret Speech to the Burial of Stalin: Real and Ideal Response to De-Stalinization. In: Jones, Polly (Hg.): The Dilemmas of De-Stalinization. Negotiating Cultural and Social Change in the Krushchev Era. London u. a. 2006, S. 41–63 („Secret Speech").

Jones, Polly: Myth, Memory, Trauma. Rethinking the Stalinist Past in the Soviet Union, 1953–70. New Haven, Conn. u. a. 2013 („Myth").

Josephson, Paul: Technology and the Conquest of the Soviet Arctic. In: The Russian Review 70 (2011), S. 419–439 („Soviet Arctic").

Joyce, C. S.: The Gulag 1930–1960: Karelia and the Soviet System of Forced Labor. Birmingham 2001 („Karelia").

Jurgenson, Luba: Spur, Dokument, Prothese. Varlam Šalamovs Erzählungen aus Kolyma. In: Osteuropa 57 (2007) [Themenheft: Das Lager schreiben. Hg. von Manfred Sapper; Volker Weichsel und Andrea Huterer], S. 169–182 („Šalamovs Erzählungen").

Khlevnyuk, Oleg: The Economy of the Gulag. In: Gregory, Paul R. (Hg.): Behind the Façade of Stalin's Command Economy: Evidence from the Soviet State and Party Archives. Stanford 2001, S. 111–129 („Economy of the Gulag").

Khlevnyuk, Oleg: The Economy of the OGPU, NKVD, and MVD of the USSR, 1930–1953. In: Gregory, Paul R.; Lazarev, Valery (Hg.): The Economics of Forced Labor: The Soviet Gulag. Stanford, Kalifornien 2003, S. 43–66 („Economy oft the OGPU").

Khlevniuk, Oleg: The Economy of Illusions. In: Ilic, Melanie; Smith, Jeremy (Hg.): Khrushchev in the Kremlin: Policy and Government in the Soviet Union, 1953–1964. New York 2011, S. 171–189 („Economy").

Khlevniuk, Oleg: The Gulag and the Non-Gulag as One Interrelated Whole. In: Kritika: Explorations in Russian and Eurasian History 16 (2015), S. 479–498 („Gulag and Non-Gulag").

Khodarkovsky, Michael: Russia's Steppe Frontier. The Making of a Colonial Empire, 1500–1800. Bloomington 2002 („Steppe Frontier").

Kibita, Nataliya: Moscow – Kiev Relations and the Sovnarkhoz Reform. In: Ilic, Melanie; Smith, Jeremy (Hg.): Khrushchev in the Kremlin: Policy and Government in the Soviet Union, 1953–1964. New York 2011, S. 94–111 („Moscow – Kiev").

Kibita, Nataliya: Soviet Economic Management under Khrushchev: The Sovnarkhoz Reform. London 2013 („Sovnarkhoz Reform").

Kibita, Nataliya: De-Stalinising Economic Administration. The Alternative Version in Ukraine (1953–1965). In: Bohn, Thomas M.; Einax, Rayk; Abeßer, Michel (Hg.): De-Stalinization Reconsidered. Persistence and Change in the Soviet Union. Frankfurt a. M.; New York 2014, S. 161–173 („Alternative Version").

Kissel, Wolfgang: Pluto, nicht Orpheus": Der Tod des Dichters in Varlam Šalamovs *Erzählungen aus Kolyma*. In: Wiener Slavistischer Almanach 60 (2007), S. 397–419 („Pluto, nicht Orpheus").

Kissel, Wolfgang: Gulag und Autofiktion: Der Fall Varlam Šalamov. In: Grote, Michael; Sandberg, Beatrice (Hg.): Autobiographisches Schreiben in der deutschsprachigen Gegenwartsliteratur. Band 3: Entwicklungen, Kontexte, Grenzgänge. München 2009, S. 49–70 („Gulag und Autofiktion").

Kissel, Wolfgang: Überlebenswissen in Varlam Šalamovs „Erzählungen aus Kolyma": Zur Epistemologie der „Vita minima". In: Poetica 41 (2009), S. 161–187 („Überlebenswissen").

Kissel, Wolfgang: „Sentenz – ein römisches Wort": Antike und kulturelles Gedächtnis in Varlam Šalamovs *Erzählungen aus Kolyma*. In: Brockmann, Agnieszka; Lebedewa, Jekatherina; Smyshliaeva, Maria; Żytyniec, Rafał (Hg.): Kulturelle Grenzgänge. Festschrift für Christa Ebert. Berlin 2012, S. 173–184 („Sentenz").

Klause, Inna: Der Klang des Gulag. Musik und Musiker in den sowjetischen Zwangsarbeitslagern der 1920er- bis 1950er- Jahre. Göttingen 2014 („Klang des Gulag").

Knight, Amy: Beria. Stalin's First Lieutenant. Princeton 1993 („Beria").

Kolář, Pavel: Der Poststalinismus. Ideologie und Utopie einer Epoche. Köln 2016 („Poststalinismus").

Kozlov, A. G.: Svetloe načalo Magadana. In: Reklamnaja gazeta, 7. März 1989, S. 8 („Svetloe načalo").

Kozlov, A. G.: Iz istorii zdravoochranenija Kolymy i Čukotki (1941–1954 gg.). Magadan 1991 („Iz istorii zdravoochranenija").

Kozlov, A. G.: Iz istorii kolymskich lagerej (konec 1937–1938 gg). In: Kraevedčeskie Zapiski (1993), S. 121–138 („Iz istorii kolymskich lagerej").

Kozlov, A. G.: Geologorazvedočnye raboty i staratel'skaja zolotodobyča na Kolyme (1908–1933). In: Dikovskie Čtenija. Magadan 2001, S. 182–190 („Geologorazvedočnye raboty").

Kozlov, A. G.: Čislennosti zaključennych Sevvostlaga: Istoriografija i sovremennost'. In: Dikovskie Čtenija. Magadan 2001, S. 201–207 („Čislennosti zaključennych").

Kozlov, A. G.: Dal'stroj kak „kombinat osobogo tipa" i ego rol' v osvoenii Severo-Vostoka Rossii. In: II Dikovskie Čtenija. Magadan 2002, S. 5–28 („Kombinat osobogo tipa").

Kozlov, A. G.: U istokov Magadanskoj oblasti – k 50-letiju obrazovanija. In: II Dikovskie Čtenija. Magadan 2002, S. 28–45 („U istokov").

Kozlov, A. G.: Reorganizacija gornodobyvajuščej promyšlennosti Dal'stroja v 1931–1957 gg. In: II Dikovskie Čtenija. Magadan 2002, S. 41–46 („Reorganizacija").

Kozlov, A. G.: Osobyj lager' No. 5 MVD SSSR – Beregovoj lager' (Berlag) Dal'stroja: Ot vozniknovenija do reorganizacii. In: II Dikovskie Čtenija. Magadan 2002, S. 87–92 („Osobyj lager'").

Kozlov, A. G.: Sostojanie geologičeskoj služby Dal'stroja (1953–1957). In: II Dikovskie Čtenija. Magadan 2002, S. 94–100 („Sostojanie geologičeskoj služby").

Kozlov, A. G.: Sevvostlag v poslednie periody ego dejatel'nosti (1945–1957). In: II Dikovskie Čtenija. Magadan 2002, S. 124–130 („Sevvostlag").

Kozlov, A. G.: Lagernaja sistema Dal'stroja v period poslevoennoj reorganizacii i posledujuščego raspada (1945–1957). In: Materialy po istorii severa Dal'nego Vostoka. Magadan 2004, S. 151–182 („Lagernaja sistema").

Kozlov, Denis: The Readers of Novyj Mir. Coming to Terms with the Stalinist Past. Cambridge, Ma.; London 2013 („Readers").

Kozlov, Denis; Gilburd, Eleonory (Hg.): The Thaw: Soviet Society and Culture during the 1950s and 1960s. Toronto 2013 („Thaw").

Kozlov, Vladimir: Mass Uprisings in the USSR. Protest and Rebellion in post-Stalin Years. Armonk, New York 2002 („Mass Uprisings").

Kozlov, V. A.: Neizvestnyj SSSR. Protivostojanie naroda i vlast' 1953–1985gg. Moskau 2006 („Neizvestnyj SSSR").

Kozlov, V. A.; Mironenko, S. V. (Hg.): Kramola. Inakomyslie v SSSR pri Chruščeve i Brežneve 1953–1982 gg. Rassekrečennye dokumenty verchovnogo suda i prokuratury SSSR. Moskau 2005 („Kramola").

Kozlov, Vladimir A.; Fitzpatrick, Sheila; Mironenko, Sergei V.: Sedition. Everyday Resistance in the Soviet Union under Khrushchev and Brezhnev. New Haven; London 2011 („Sedition").

Krasil'nikov, S. A.: Fenomen sibirskogo otdelenija AN SSSR v kontekste reformirovanija social'nogo instituta nauki. In: Posle Stalina. Reformy 1950-ch godov v kontekste sovetskoj i postsovetskoj istorii: Materialy VIII meždunarodnoj naučnoj konferencii. Ekaterinburg, 15–17 oktjabrja 2015 g. Moskau 2016, S. 514–523 („Fenomen sibirskogo otdelenija").

Krasnopol'skij, B. Ch.; Piljasov, A. N.: Magadanskaja oblast': Očerk social'no-ėkonomičeskogo razvitija. Magadan 1991 („Očerk social'no-ėkonomičeskogo razvitija").

Kraveri, Marta; Khlevnyuk, Oleg: Krizis ėkonomiki MVD (konec 1940-x – 1950-e gody). In: Cahiers du Monde Russe 36 (1995), S. 179–190 („Krizis ėkonomiki MVD").

Krivoručenko, V. K.; Pyžikov, A. V.; Rogionov, V. A.: Kollizii „Chruščevskoj ottepeli". Stranicy otečestvennoj istorii 1953–1964 godov XX stoletija. Moskau 1998 („Kollizii").

Kruglov, Ju. V.; Kozlov, A.G.: Zdravoochranenie Magadanskoj oblasti (1953–2000). In: III Dikovskie Čtenija. Magadan 2004, S. 138–143 („Zdravoochranenie").

Kruglov, V. N.: Chozjajstvennaja reforma 1957 g. i diskussii o razvitii territorial'nogo ustrojstva SSSR. In: Posle Stalina. Reformy 1950-ch godov v kontekste sovetskoj i postsovetskoj istorii: Materialy VIII meždunarodnoj naučnoj konferencii. Ekaterinburg, 15–17 oktjabrja 2015 g. Moskau 2016, S. 340–348 („Chozjajstvennaja reforma").

Kucher, Katharina: Der Fall Noril'sk. Stadt, Kultur und Geschichte unter Extrembedingungen. In: Schlögel, Karl (Hg.): Mastering Russian Spaces. Raum und Raumbewältigung als Probleme der russischen Geschichte. München 2011, S. 129–148 („Noril'sk").

Kuhr-Korolev, Corinna: Gezähmte Helden. Die Formierung der Sowjetjugend 1917–1932. Essen 2005 („Gezähmte Helden").

Kuhr-Korolev, Corinna; Plaggenborg, Stefan; Wellmann, Monika (Hg.): Sowjetjugend 1917–1941. Generation zwischen Revolution und Resignation. Essen 2001 („Sowjetjugend").

Kulavig, Erik: Dissident in the Years of Khrushchev: Nine Stories about Disobedient Russians. London 2002 („Dissident").

Kur'janova, A. F.; Uškalov, V. A.: Iz istorii profsojuznych organizacij Magadanskoj oblasti. In: Kraevedčeskie Zapiski 12 (1982), S. 49–58 („Iz istorii profsojuznych organizacij").

Kusber, Jan: Gewandeltes Herrscherbild, veränderte Inhalte. Von Stalin zu Chruščev. In: Zeitschrift für Geschichtswissenschaft 56 (2008), S. 743–754 („Herrscherbild").

Kusber, Jan: Mastering the Imperial Space: The Case of Siberia. Theoretical Approaches and Recent Directions of Research. In: Ab Imperio 2008, H. 4, S. 52–74 („Mastering the Imperial Space").

Kuznecov, I. Ju.; Kuznecova, S. A.: Samoopredelenie ličnosti na žiznennom puti. Magadan 2003 („Samoopredelenie ličnosti").

Ladwig-Winters, Simone: Ernst Fraenkel. Ein politisches Leben. Frankfurt a. M. 2003 („Fraenkel").

Langenohl, Andreas: Mental Maps, Raum und Erinnerung. Zur kultursoziologischen Erschließung eines transdisziplinären Konzepts. In: Damir-Geilsdorf, Sabine; Hartmann, Angelika; Hendrich, Béatrice (Hg.): Mental Maps – Raum – Erinnerung. Kulturwissenschaftliche Zugänge zum Verhältnis von Raum und Erinnerung. Münster 2005, S. 51–69 („Mental Maps").

LaPierre, Brian: Hooligans in Khrushchev's Russia: Defining, Policing, and Producing Deviance during the Thaw. Madison 2012 („Devianz").

Lass, Karen: Vom Tauwetter zur Perestrojka: Kulturpolitik in der Sowjetunion, 1953–1991. Köln 2002 („Tauwetter").

Lazarev, Valery: Conclusions. In: Gregory, Paul R.; Lazarev, Valery (Hg.): The Economics of Forced Labor: The Soviet Gulag. Stanford, Kalifornien 2003, S. 189–197 („Conclusions").

Lebina, N. B.: Povsednevnost' ėpochi kosmosa i kukuruzy: Destrukcija bol'šogo stilja: Leningrad, 1950–160-e gody. St. Petersburg 2015 („Povsednevnost'").

Ledeneva, Alena V.: Russia's Economy of Favours: *Blat*, Networking and Informal Exchange. Cambridge 1998 („Blat").

Lejbovič, O. L.: Reforma i modernizacija v 1953–1964 gg. Perm' 1993 („Reforma").

Lejbovič, O. L.: Reformy 1953–1964 gg. v kontekste otečestvennoj modernizacii. Perm' 1995 („Reformy").

Lepper, Carl: Die Goldwäscherei am Rhein. Geschichte und Technik, Münzen und Medaillen aus Rheingold. Heppenheim 1980 („Goldwäscherei").

Levin, B. S.: Lagerja GULAGa (Sevvostlaga) raspolagavšiesja v granicach sovremennoj Magadanskoj oblasti (spisok i karta raspoloženija). In: VI Dikosvkie Čtenija. Magadan 2010, S. 188–193 („Lagerja GULAGa").

Linden, Carl A.: Khrushchev and the Soviet Leadership. Baltimore 1990 („Soviet Leadership").

Ljubavskij, M. K.: Russkaja kolonizacija. Moskau 2014 („Kolonizacija").

Logvinova, I. V.: Osobennosti mestnogo upravlenija na Severo-Vostoke Rossii v uslovijach dejatel'nosti Dal'stroja (1931–1957). In: Dikovskie Čtenija. Magadan 2001, S. 241–247 („Osobennosti mestnogo upravlenija").

Logvinova, I.V.: Pravovoj status Dal'stroja kak organa gosudarstvenno-chozjajstvennogo upravlenija: 1931–1941 gody (istoriko-pravovoj aspekt). Moskau 2001 („Pravovoj status").

Luchterhandt, Otto: Die Justiz. In: Plaggenborg, Stefan (Hg.): Handbuch der Geschichte Russlands, Band 5: 1945–1991 – Vom Ende des Zweiten Weltkrieges bis zum Zusammenbruch der Sowjetunion. Stuttgart 2002–2003, S. 975–1023 („Justiz").

Mäkinen, Ilka Henrik; Reitan, Therese C.: Continuity and Change in Russian Alcohol Consumption from the Tsars to Transition. In: Social History 31 (2006), S. 160–179 („Alcohol Consumption").

Markwick, Roger D.: Thaws and Freezes in Soviet Historiography, 1953–64. In: Jones, Polly (Hg.): The Dilemmas of De-Stalinization. Negotiating Cultural and Social Change in the Krushchev Era. London u. a. 2006, S. 173–192 („Thaws").

Mc Cauley, Martin: Khrushchev and the Development of Soviet Agriculture. The Virgin Lands Programme. 1953–1964. London 1976 („Soviet Agriculture").

Mc Cauley, Martin: The Khrushchev Era: 1953–1964. London 1995 („Khrushchev").

Medwedjew, Roy: Chruschtschow. Eine politische Biographie. Stuttgart 1984 („Politische Biographie").

Medvedev, Žores; Medvedev, Roj: Neizvestnyj Stalin. Moskau 2002 („Neizvestnyj Stalin").

Meissner, Boris: Die Verfassungsentwicklung der Sowjetunion seit dem Tode Stalins. In: Jahrbuch des öffentlichen Rechts 28 (1973), S. 101–202 („Verfassungsentwicklung").

Mel'nikov, S. M.: Dal'stroj: Stranicy istorii (istoriko-sociologičeskij aspect). In: Kolyma 9/10 (1993), S. 44–47 („Stranicy istorii").

Mel'nikov, S. M.: Dal'stroj kak repressivno-proizvodstvennaja struktura NKVD-MVD SSSR (1932–1953 gody). Tomsk 2002 („Repressivno-proizvodstvennaja struktura").

Mercalov, Viktor Ivanovič: Reforma chozjajstvennogo upravlenija 1957–1965 gg.: predposylki, chog, itogi (na materialach Vostočnoj Sibiri). Irkutsk 2000 („Reforma chozjajstvennogo upravlenija").

Merl, Stephan: Das System der Zwangsarbeit und die Opferzahl im Stalinismus. In: Geschichte in Wissenschaft und Unterricht 46 (1995), S. 277–305 („Opferzahl").

Merl, Stephan: „Jeder nach seinen Fähigkeiten, jeder nach seinen Bedürfnissen?" Über Anspruch und Realität von Lebensstandard und Wirtschaftssystem in Russland und der Sowjetunion. In: Fischer, Wolfram (Hg.).: Lebensstandard und Wirtschaftssysteme. Frankfurt a. M. 1995, S. 259 – 306 („Anspruch und Realität").

Merl, Stephan: Berija und Chruščev. Entstalinisierung oder Systemerhalt. Zum Grunddilemma sowjetischer Politik nach Stalins Tod. In: Geschichte in Wissenschaft und Unterricht 49 (2001), S. 484 – 506 („Berija und Chruščev").

Merl, Stephan: Entstalinisierung, Reformen und Wettlauf der Systeme 1953 – 1964. In: Plaggenborg, Stefan (Hg.): Handbuch der Geschichte Russlands, Band 5: 1945 – 1991 – Vom Ende des Zweiten Weltkrieges bis zum Zusammenbruch der Sowjetunion. Stuttgart 2002 – 2003, S. 175 – 318 („Reformen").

Merl, Stephan: Die sowjetische Kommandowirtschaft: Warum scheiterte sie nicht früher? In: Geschichte in Wissenschaft und Unterricht 58 (2007), S. 656 – 675 („Sowjetische Kommandowirtschaft").

Merl, Stephan: Konsum in der Sowjetunion. Element der Systemstabilisierung? In: Geschichte in Wissenschaft und Unterricht 58 (2007), S. 519 – 536 („Konsum").

Merl, Stephan: Political Communication under Khrushchev. Did the Basic Modes Really Change after Stalin's Death? In: Bohn, Thomas M.; Einax, Rayk; Abeßer, Michel (Hg.): De-Stalinization Reconsidered. Persistence and Change in the Soviet Union. Frankfurt a. M.; New York 2014, S. 65 – 92 („Political Communication").

Merridale, Catherine: Night of Stone. Death and Memory in Twentieth Century Russia. New York 2001 („Night of Stone").

Mick, Christoph: Wissenschaft und Wissenschaftler im Stalinismus. In: Plaggenborg, Stefan (Hg.): Stalinismus: Neue Forschungen und Konzepte. Berlin 1998, S. 321 – 361 („Wissenschaft").

Mitrokhin, Nikolai: The Rise of Political Clans in the Era of Nikita Khrushchev. The First Phase, 1953 – 1959. In: Ilic, Melanie; Smith, Jeremy (Hg.): Khrushchev in the Kremlin: Policy and Government in the Soviet Union, 1953 – 1964. New York 2011, S. 26 – 40 („Political Clans").

Mitrochin, N. A.: Ličnye svjasi v apparate ZK KPSS. In: Neprikosnovennyj zapas 2012, H. 3, S. 166 – 175 („Ličnye svjasi").

Mitrochin, N. A.: Kar'era i uspech v 1950-e gg.: Kak včerašnie studenty stanovilis' načal'nikami proizvodstv i partijnymi bjurokratami. In: Posle Stalina. Reformy 1950-ch godov v kontekste sovetskoj i postsovetskoj istorii: Materialy VIII meždunarodnoj naučnoj konferencii. Ekaterinburg, 15 – 17 oktjabrja 2015 g. Moskau 2016, S. 213 – 237 („Kar'era i uspech").

Mücke, Lukas: Die allgemeine Altersrentenversorgung in der UdSSR, 1956 – 1972. Stuttgart 2013 („Altersrentenversorgung").

Naumov, Vladimir: Zur Geschichte der Geheimrede N. S. Chruščevs auf dem XX. Parteitag der KPdSU. In: Forum für osteuropäische Zeit- und Ideengeschichte 1 (1997), S. 137 – 177 („Geschichte").

Navasardov, A. S.: Transportnoe osvoenie Severo-Vostoka Rossii v 1923 – 1936 gg. (morskoj transport). In: Dikovskie Čtenija. Magadan 2001, S. 190 – 195 („Transportnoe osvoenie").

Nefedova, S. D.; Bubnis, G. K.: O podgotovke nacional'nych kadrov na Severo-Vostoke SSSR. In: Kraevedčeskie Zapiski 10 (1975), S. 32 – 41 („O podgotovke nacional'nych kadrov").

Neutatz, Dietmar: Taking Stock of the Khrushchev Era. In: Bohn, Thomas M.; Einax, Rayk; Abeßer, Michel (Hg.): De-Stalinization Reconsidered. Persistence and Change in the Soviet Union. Frankfurt a. M.; New York 2014, S. 251 – 262 („Taking Stock").

Nikolaev, K. B.: K voprosy izučenija istorii Dal'stroja. In: Rossijskaja Akademija Nauk. Dal'nevostočnoe otdelenie. Severo-Vostočnoj kompleksnyj naučno-issledovatel'skij institut: Istoričeskie aspekty Severo-Vostoka Rossii: Ėkonomika, obrazovanie, Kolymskij GULag. Magadan 1996, S. 29 – 46 („K voprosy izučenija").

Nordlander, David: Khrushchev's Image in the Light of Glasnost and Perestroika. In: The Russian Review 52 (1993), S. 248–264 („Khrushchev's Image").

Nordlander, David: Origins of a Gulag Capital: Magadan and Stalinist Control in the early 1930s. In: Slavic Review 57 (1998), S. 791–812 („Gulag Capital").

Nordlander, David: Magadan and the Evolution of the Dalstroi Bosses in the 1930s. In: Cahiers du Monde Russe 42 (2001), S. 649–665 („Evolution").

Nordlander, David: Magadan and the Economic History of Dalstroi in the 1930s. In: Gregory, Paul R.; Lazarev, Valery (Hg.): The Economics of Forced Labor: The Soviet Gulag. Stanford, Kalifornien 2003, S. 105–125 („Magadan").

Nordlander, David: Magadan i stanovlenie ėkonomiki Dal'stroja v 1930-e gg. In: Borodkin, Leonid; Gregory, Paul R.; Khlevniuk, Oleg (Hg.): GULAG. Ėkonomika prinuditel'nogo truda. Moskau 2005, S. 239–254 („Stanovlenie ėkonomiki").

Obertreis, Julia: Infrastrukturen im Sozialismus. Das Beispiel der Bewässerungssysteme im sowjetischen Zentralasien. In: Saeculum 58 (2007), S. 151–182 („Infrastrukturen").

Pallot, Judith: Forced Labour for Forestry: The Twentieth-Century History of Colonisation and Settlement in the North of Perm' Oblast'. In: Europe-Asia Studies 54 (2002), S. 1055–1083 („Forced Labour for Forestry").

Palymskij, B. F.: Sejmčanskoe RajGRU (1955–1961). In: II Dikovskie Čtenija. Magadan 2002, S. 232–236 („Sejmčanskoe RajGRU").

Panikarov, Ivan: Kolyma. Daten und Fakten. In: Osteuropa 57 (2007) [Themenheft: Das Lager schreiben. Hg. von Manfred Sapper; Volker Weichsel und Andrea Huterer], S. 267–283 („Kolyma").

Pauling, Guido: „Wir sind Diener des Plenums…" Chruschtschow und die Partei 1952–1966. In: Geschichte in Wissenschaft und Unterricht 58 (2007), S. 636–655 („Diener des Plenums").

Pavlenko, Ol'ga: The Transformation of the Soviet Myth of Communism in the Era of Nikita Khrushchev (1953–1964). In: Jahrbuch für Historische Kommunismusforschung 2012, S. 63–82 („Soviet Myth").

Pavljukevič, R. V.: Vlijanie reformy upravlenija promyšlennost'ju i stroitel'stvom na razvitie g. Noril'ska. In: Posle Stalina. Reformy 1950-ch godov v kontekste sovetskoj i postsovetskoj istorii: Materialy VIII meždunarodnoj naučnoj konferencii. Ekaterinburg, 15–17 oktjabrja 2015 g. Moskau 2016, S. 360–367 („Vlijanie").

Piljasov, A. N.: Zakonomernosti i osobennosti osvoenija Severo-Vostoka Rossii (retrospektiva i prognoz). Magadan 1996 („Zakonomernosti").

Plaggenborg, Stefan: Lebensverhältnisse und Alltagsprobleme. In: Plaggenborg, Stefan (Hg.): Handbuch der Geschichte Russlands, Band 5: 1945–1991 – Vom Ende des Zweiten Weltkrieges bis zum Zusammenbruch der Sowjetunion. Stuttgart 2002–2003, S. 787–848 („Lebensverhältnisse").

Plaggenborg, Stefan: Experiment Moderne. Der sowjetische Weg. Frankfurt a. M. 2006 („Experiment").

Plaggenborg, Stefan: Soviet History after 1953. Stalinismus under Repair. In: Bohn, Thomas M.; Einax, Rayk; Abeßer, Michel (Hg.): De-Stalinization Reconsidered. Persistence and Change in the Soviet Union. Frankfurt a. M.; New York 2014, S. 43–64 („Under Repair").

Pohl, Michaela: Women and Girls in the Virgin Lands. In: Ilic, Melanie; Reid, Susan E.; Attwood, Lynne (Hg.): Women in the Khrushchev Era. Basingstoke; New York 2004, S. 52–74 („Virgin Lands").

Pohl, Michaela: From White Grave to Tselinograd to Astana: The Virgin Lands Opening, Khrushev's Forgotten First Reform. In: Kozlov, Denis; Gilburd, Eleonory: The Thaw: Soviet Society and Culture during the 1950s and 1960s. Toronto 2013, S. 269–307 („Tselinograd").

Poljan, Pavel: Ne po svoej vole… Istorija i geografia prinuditel'nych migracij v SSSR. Moskau 2001 („Ne po svoej vole").

Posle Stalina. Reformy 1950-ch godov v kontekste sovetskoj i postsovetskoj istorii: Materialy VIII
   meždunarodnoj naučnoj konferencii. Ekaterinburg, 15 – 17 oktjabrja 2015 g. Moskau 2016
   („Posle Stalina").

Pozdnjakov, A. F.: Dal'stroj i razvitie morskich transportnych svjazej na severe Dal'nego Vostoka
   SSSR v 1930 – 1940 gg. In: Kolymskij gumanitarnyj al'manach 2 (2007), S. 68 – 84 („Razvitie
   morskich transportnych svjazej").

Putz, Manuela: Die Herren des Lagers. Berufsverbrecher im Gulag. In: Osteuropa 57 (2007)
   [Themenheft: Das Lager schreiben. Hg. von Manfred Sapper; Volker Weichsel und Andrea
   Huterer], S. 341 – 351 („Berufsverbrecher").

Pyžikov, A. V.: Opyt modernizacii sovetskogo obščestva v 1953 – 1964 godach:
   obščestvenno-političeskij aspekt. Moskau 1998 („Opyt").

Pyžikov, A. V.: Vnutripartinnaja bor'ba i evolucija sistemy vlasti (1953 – 1957). In: Vestnik Rossijskoj
   akademii nauk 71 (2001), S. 246 – 251 („Vnutripartinnaja bor'ba").

Pyžikov, A. V.: Chruščevkaja ottepel', 1953 – 1964. Moskau 2002 („Ottepel'").

Rajzman, D. I.: Operativnaja rabota 61-go Nagaevo-Magadanskogo morpogranotrjada OGPU-NKVD
   (1932 – 1940). In: Dikovskie Čtenija. Magadan 2001, S. 208 – 213 („Operativnaja rabota").

Rajzman, D. I.: Process reabilitacii graždan na territorii Magadanskoj oblasti. In: II Dikovskie
   Čtenija. Magadan 2002, S. 121 – 128 („Process reabilitacii").

Rajzman, D. I.: Osobennosti social'no-ėkonomičeskogo razvitija Severo-Vostoka Rossii v 30 – 50-e
   gody XX veka (ot Dal'stroja – k Magadanskoj oblasti). In: Problemy social'no-ėkonomičeskogo
   razvitija sub"ektov federacii na sovremennom ėtape. Materialy III mežregional'noj
   naučno-praktičeskoj konferencii. Smolensk 2004, S. 165 – 178 („Osobennosti
   social'no-ėkonomičeskogo razvitija").

Rajzman, D. I.: Inostrancy-Nevol'niki Dal'stroja. Inostrannye graždane v ispravitel'no-trudovych
   lagerjach na Kolyme i Čukotke (30 – 50-e gody XX veka). Magadan 2009
   („Inostrancy-Nevol'niki").

Rajzman, D. I.: Osobennosti gosudarstvennoj politiki v otnošenii korennych narodov Severo-Vostoka
   Rossii v 30 – 50-ch gg. XX v. In: VI Dikovskie Čtenija. Magadan 2010, S. 173 – 177 („Osobennosti
   gosudarstvennoj politiki").

Rajzman, S. M.: Rol' organov obrazovanija v formirovanii severnogo mentaliteta (v period
   dejatel'nosti Dal'stroja). In: Karpenko, N. V. (Hg.): Magadan: Gody, sobytija, ljudi. Magadan
   1999, S. 16 – 17 („Rol' organov").

Rajzman, S. M.: Preobrazovanie struktury upravlenija narodno-chozjajstvennym kompleksam pri
   organizacii Magadanskogo Soveta Narodnogo Chozjajstva (1957 g.). In: Kokorev, E. M.;
   Birjukova, L. P. (Hg.): Materialy naučno-praktičeskoj konferencii, posvjaščennoj 40-letiju
   Severnogo Meždunarodnogo Universiteta. Magadan 2001, S. 124 – 126 („Struktury
   upravlenija").

Rajzman, S. M.: Geologorazvedočnaja dejatel'nost' predprijatij Soveta Narodnogo Chozjajstva
   Magadanskogo ėkonomičeskogo administrativnogo rajona (SNCH MĖAR). In: Kokorev, E. M.
   (Hg.): Universitetskij kompleks-strategičeskij faktor social'no-ėkonomičeskogo razvitija
   severnogo regiona. Materialy naučno-praktičeskoj konferencii. Magadan 2003, S. 178 – 180
   („Geologorazvedočnaja dejatel'nost'").

Rajzman, S. M.: Razvitie promyšlenno-proizvodstvennogo kompleksa Soveta Narodnogo Chozjajstva
   Magadanskogo ėkonomičeskogo administrativnogo rajona v 1957 – 1962 gg. In: Gorjačev, N. A.
   u. a. (Hg.): Severo-Vostok Rossii: prošloe, nastojaščee, buduščee. Materialy II regional'noj
   naučno-praktičeskoj konferencii. Tom I. Magadan 2004, S. 50 – 54 („Razvitie
   promyšlenno-proizvodstvennogo kompleksa").

Rajzman, S. M.: Promyšlenno-proizvodstvennyj kompleks SNCH MĖAR v 1957 – 1962 gg. In:
   Kolymskij gumanitarnyj al'manach 2 (2007), S. 154 – 170 („SNCH MĖAR").

Rebrova, M. O.: K voprosu o pričinach obrazovanija Magadanskoj oblasti: istoriografija problemy. In: Gorjačev, N. A. u. a. (Hg.): Severo-Vostok Rossii: prošloe, nastojaščee, buduščee. Materialy II regional'noj naučno-praktičeskoj konferencii. Tom I. Magadan 2004, S. 55–58 („O pričinach obrazovanija Magadanskoj oblasti").

Rees, E. A.: Introduction. The Sovietization of Eastern Europe. In: Apor, Balázs; Apor, Péter; Rees, E. A. (Hg.): The Sovietization of Eastern Europe: New Perspectives on the Postwar Period. Washington, DC 2008, S. 1–27 („Introduction").

Reid, Susan E.: Cold War in the Kitchen: Gender and the De-Stalinization of Consumer Taste in the Soviet Union under Khrushchev. In: Slavic Review 61 (2002), S. 211–252 („Kitchen").

Reid, Susan E.: Women in the Home. In: Ilic, Melanie; Reid, Susan E.; Attwood, Lynne (Hg.): Women in the Khrushchev Era. Basingstoke; New York 2004, S. 149–176 („Women in the Home").

Reid, Susan E.: Building Utopia in the Back Yard. Housing Administration, Participatory Government, and the Cultivation of Socialist Community. In: Schlögel, Karl (Hg.): Mastering Russian Spaces. Raum und Raumbewältigung als Probleme der russischen Geschichte. München 2011, S. 149–185 („Utopia").

Risse, Thomas: Vertrauen in Räumen begrenzter Staatlichkeit – Eine politikwissenschaftliche Analyse. In: Baberowski, Jörg (Hg.): Was ist Vertrauen? Ein interdisziplinäres Gespräch. Frankfurt a. M.; New York 2014, S. 127–145 („Vertrauen in Räumen").

Rogowin, Wadim S.: Die Partei der Hingerichteten. Übers. aus dem Russ. von Hannelore Georgi und Harald Schubärth. Essen 1999 („Partei der Hingerichteten").

Rolf, Malte: Importing the „Spatial Turn" to Russia. Recent Studies on the Spatialization of Russian History. In: Kritika: Explorations in Russian and Eurasian History 11 (2010), S. 359–380 („Spatial Turn").

Rossi, Jacques: Spravočnik po GULagu. Istoričeskij slovar' sovetskich penitenciarnych institucij i terminov, svjazannych s prinuditel'nym trudam. London 1987 („Spravočnik po GULagu").

Roščupkin, G.G.; Bubnis, G. K.: K voprosu ob administrativnom ustrojstve i territorial'nom delenii Kolymy i Čukotki (1917–1967 gg.). In: Kraevedčeskije Zapiski 9 (1972), S. 67–75 („K voprosu ob administrativnom ustrojstve").

Round, John: Marginalised for a Lifetime. The Everyday Experiences of Gulag Survivors in post-Soviet Magadan. In: Geografiska Annaler 87 (2006), S. 15–34 („Marginalised").

Round, John: Surviving the Gulag: the Social and Cultural Legacies of Stalin's Forced Labour System. In: Boren, T. (Hg.): Kring Beringia: Expeditioner Och Folk. Svenska Sällskapet För Anthropologi Och Geografi. Stockholm 2008, S. 42–64 („Surviving the Gulag").

Rupprecht, Tobias: Die sowjetische Gesellschaft in der Welt des Kalten Kriegs. Neue Forschungsperspektiven. In: Jahrbücher für Geschichte Osteuropas 58 (2010), S. 381–399 („Forschungsperspektiven").

Ryklin, Michail: Der „verfluchte Orden". Šalamov, Solčenicyn und die Kriminellen. In: Osteuropa 57 (2007) [Themenheft: Das Lager schreiben. Hg. von Manfred Sapper; Volker Weichsel und Andrea Huterer], S. 107–124 („Verfluchter Orden").

Sapper, Manfred; Weichsel, Volker; Huterer, Andrea (Hg.): Das Lager schreiben. Themenheft der Zeitschrift Osteuropa 57 (2007) („Lager schreiben").

Sapper, Manfred; Weichsel, Volker; Huterer, Andrea: Bollwerk der Hölle. In: Osteuropa 57 (2007) [Themenheft: Das Lager schreiben. Hg. von Manfred Sapper; Volker Weichsel und Andrea Huterer], S. 5–6 („Bollwerk").

Schattenberg, Susanne: „Democracy" or „Despotism". How the Secret Speech was Translated into Everyday Life. In: Jones, Polly (Hg.): The Dilemmas of De-Stalinization. Negotiating Cultural and Social Change in the Krushchev Era. London u. a. 2006, S. 64–78 („Secret Speech").

Schattenberg, Susanne: Die korrupte Provinz? Russische Beamte im 19. Jahrhundert. Frankfurt 2008 („Korrupte Provinz").

Schattenberg, Susanne: Von Chruščev zu Gorbačev – Die Sowjetunion zwischen Reform und Zusammenbruch. In: Neue Politische Literatur 55 (2010), S. 255–284 („Von Chruščev zu Gorbačev").

Schlögel, Karl: Die Wiederkehr des Raums – auch in der Osteuropakunde. In: Osteuropa 55 (2005), S. 5–16 („Wiederkehr des Raums").

Schlögel, Karl (Hg.): Mastering Russian Spaces. Raum und Raumbewältigung als Probleme der russischen Geschichte. München 2011 („Russian Spaces").

Schlögel, Karl: Raum und Raumbewältigung als Probleme der russischen Geschichte. Zur Einführung. In: Schlögel, Karl (Hg.): Mastering Russian Spaces. Raum und Raumbewältigung als Probleme der russischen Geschichte. München 2011, S. 1–25 („Raumbewältigung").

Schmid, Ulrich: Nicht-Literatur ohne Moral. Warum Varlam Šalamov nicht gelesen wurde. In: Osteuropa 57 (2007) [Themenheft: Das Lager schreiben. Hg. von Manfred Sapper; Volker Weichsel und Andrea Huterer], S. 87–106 („Nicht-Literatur").

Schröder, Hans-Henning: „Lebendige Verbindung mit den Massen". Sowjetische Gesellschaftspolitik in der Ära Chruščev. In: Vierteljahrshefte für Zeitgeschichte 34 (1986), S. 523–560 („Lebendige Verbindung").

Senghaas, Dieter: Zivilisierung wider Willen. Der Konflikt der Kulturen mit sich selbst. Frankfurt a. M. 1998 („Zivilisierung").

Service, Robert: Stalinism and the Soviet State Order. In: Shukman, Harold (Hg.): Redefining Stalinism. London 2003, S. 7–22 („Stalinism").

Shearer, David: Mastering the Soviet Frontier: Western Siberia in the 1930s. In: Stolberg, Eva-Maria (Hg.): The Siberian Saga. A History of Russia's Wild East. Frankfurt a. M. 2005, S. 159–172 („Soviet Frontier").

Shearer, David R.: The Soviet Gulag – an Archipelago? In: Kritika: Explorations in Russian and Eurasian History 16 (2015), S. 711–724 („Archipelago").

Shepilov, Dmitrii: The Kremlin's scholar: A Memoir of Soviet politics under Stalin and Khrushchev. Edited by Stephen V. Bittner. New Haven; London 2007 („Kremlin's scholar").

Simakov, K. V.; Gončarov, V.I.: Akademičeskaja nauka Severo-Vostoka Rossii. In: Vestnik Rossijskoj Akademii Nauk 69 (1999), H. 1, S. 21–31 („Akademičeskaja nauka").

Slezkine, Yuri: Arctic Mirrors. Russia and the Small Peoples of the North. Ithaca; London 1994 („Arctic Mirrors").

Smirnov, M. B.: Sistema ispravitel'no-trudovych lagerej v SSSR, 1923–1960. Spravočnik. Moskau 1998 („Sistema lagerej").

Smith, Kathleen E.: Moscow 1956. The silenced spring. Cambridge, MA 2017 („Moscow 1956").

Smith, Mark B.: Individual Forms of Ownership in the Urban Housing Fund of the USSR, 1944–1964. In: The Slavonic and East European Review 86 (2008) [Themenheft: The Relaunch of the Soviet Project, 1945–1964. Hg. von Juliane Fürst; Polly Jones und Susan Morrisey], S. 283–305 („Ownership").

Smith, Mark B.: Property of Communists: The Urban Housing Program from Stalin to Khrushchev. De Kalb 2009 („Property").

Smith, Mark B.: Khrushchev's Promise to Eliminate the Urban Housing Shortage: Rights, Rationality and the Communist Future. In: Ilic, Melanie; Smith, Jeremy (Hg.): Soviet State and Society under Nikita Khrushchev. London 2009, S. 26–45 („Khrushchev's Promise").

Smolina, T. P.: Gazetnoj strokoj... Očerki, stat'i, dokumenty iz istorii oblastnoj gazety „Magadanskaja Pravda". Magadan 1986 („Gazetnoj strokoj").

Sobolew, Wladimir S.: Aufblühen und Untergang der Landeskunde. In: Beyrau, Dietrich (Hg.): Im Dschungel der Macht. Intellektuelle Professionen unter Stalin und Hitler. Göttingen 2000, S. 146–156 („Landeskunde").

Sokolov, Andrei: Forced Labor in Soviet Industry. In: Gregory, Paul R.; Lazarev, Valery (Hg.): The Economics of Forced Labor: The Soviet Gulag. Stanford, Kalifornien 2003, S. 23–42 („Soviet Industry").

Sokolov, A. K.: Prinuždenie k trudu v sovetskoj ėkonomike: 1930-e – seredina 1950-ch gg. In: Borodkin, Leonid; Gregory, Paul R.; Khlevniuk, Oleg (Hg.): GULAG. Ėkonomika prinuditel'nogo truda. Moskau 2005, S. 17–66 („Prinuždenie k trudu").

Solomon Jr., Peter H.: Soviet Politicians and Criminal Prosecutions: The Logic of Party Intervention. In: Millar, James R. (Hg.): Cracks in the Monolith. Armonk, New York 1992, S. 3–34 („Soviet Politicians").

Sperling, Walter: Der Aufbruch der Provinz. Die Eisenbahn und die Neuordnung der Räume im Zarenreich. Frankfurt a. M.; New York 2011 („Provinz").

Sprau, Mirjam: Magadanskaja pressa 1954–1959 gg. kak faktor destalinizacii Severo-Vostočnogo regiona SSSR. In: Kolymskij gumanitarnyj al'manach 2 (2007), S. 171–187 („Magadanskaja pressa").

Sprau, Mirjam: Gold und Zwangsarbeit. Der Lagerkomplex Dal'stroj. In: Osteuropa 58 (2008), H. 2, S. 65–79 („Gold").

Sprau, Mirjam: Entstalinisierung verortet. Die Lagerauflösung an der Kolyma. In: Jahrbücher für Geschichte Osteuropas 57 (2009) [Themenheft: Aufbruch aus dem GULag. Hg. von Klaus Gestwa], S. 535–562 („Entstalinisierung verortet").

Sprau, Mirjam: Diktaturüberwindung in der Diktatur? Auflösung des sowjetischen GULag in der Entstalinisierung. In: Hofmann, Birgit; Wezel, Katja u. a. (Hg.): Diktaturüberwindung in Europa. Neue nationale und transnationale Perspektiven. Heidelberg 2010, S. 180–194 („Diktaturüberwindung").

Sprau, Mirjam: Leben nach dem GULAG. Petitionen ehemaliger sowjetischer Häftlinge als Quelle. In: Vierteljahrshefte für Zeitgeschichte 60 (2012), S. 93–110 („Petitionen").

Sprau, Mirjam: Žizn' posle GULAGa. Molodež' posle lagerej i repressii. In: Neprikosnovennyj zapas 87 (2013), H. 1, http://magazines.russ.ru/nz/2013/1/s14.html (abgerufen am 6. Februar 2018), („Žizn").

Sprau, Mirjam: Kolyma und Magadan. Ökonomie und Lager im Nordosten der Sowjetunion. In: Landau, Julia; Scherbakowa, Irina (Hg.): GULAG. Texte und Dokumente 1929–1956. Göttingen 2014, S. 80–92 („Kolyma und Magadan").

Stark, Meinhardt: Die Gezeichneten. Gulag-Häftlinge nach der Entlassung. Berlin 2010 („Die Gezeichneten").

Städtke, Klaus: Sturz der Idole – Ende des Humanismus? Literaturmodelle der Tauwetterzeit: Solženicyn und Šalamov. In: Osteuropa 57 (2007) [Themenheft: Das Lager schreiben. Hg. von Manfred Sapper; Volker Weichsel und Andrea Huterer], S. 137–155 („Sturz der Idole").

Stettner, Ralf: „Archipel GULag": Stalins Zwangslager – Terrorinstrument und Wirtschaftsgigant. Entstehung, Organisation und Funktion des sowjetischen Lagersystems 1928–1956. Paderborn 1996 („Archipel Gulag").

Stolberg, Eva-Maria: Raumerschließungsprozesse im Sibirien des ausgehenden Zarenreiches: Ein Forschungsdesiderat der Russlandhistoriographie. In: Archiv für Sozialgeschichte 42 (2002), S. 315–334 („Raumerschließungsprozesse").

Stolberg, Eva-Maria (Hg.): The Siberian Saga. A History of Russia's Wild East. Frankfurt a. M. 2005 („Siberian Saga").

Stolberg, Eva-Maria: The Genre of Frontiers and Borderlands: Siberia as a Case Study. In: Stolberg, Eva-Maria (Hg.): The Siberian Saga. A History of Russia's Wild East. Frankfurt a. M. 2005, S. 13–27 („Frontiers").

Stolberg, Eva-Maria: Sibirien: Russlands „Wilder Osten". Mythos und soziale Realität im 19. und 20. Jahrhundert. Stuttgart 2009 („Wilder Osten").

Surnina, M. K.: Iz istorii instituta sistemy „Dal'stroja" (po dokumentan filiala RGANTD). In: Političeskie repressii pervoj poloviny XX veka v sud'bach techničeskoj intelligencii Rossii. Samara 2009, S. 108–121 („Iz istorii instituta").

Šeršakova, E. M.: Osobennosti formirovanija naselenija Magadanskoj oblasti v gody intensivnogo promyšlennogo osvoenija territorii (30–70-e gg. XX v.). In: II Dikovskie Čtenija. Magadan 2002, S. 54–59 („Osobennosti formirovanija naselenija").

Šeršakova, E. M.: Razrabotka planov social'nogo razvitija kollektivov predprijatij Severo-Vostoka v SVKNII (konec 60-ch – 70-e gg. XX v.). In: IV Dikovskie Čtenija. Magadan 2006, S. 51–53 („Razrabotka planov").

Širokov, A. I.: Dal'stroj: Predystorija i pervoe desjatiletie. Magadan 2000 („Dal'stroj").

Širokov, A. I.: K voprosu o konceptual'nych osnovach issledovanija dejatel'nosti Dal'stroja. In: II Dikovskie Čtenija. Magadan 2002, S. 34–36 („O konceptual'nych osnovach issledovanija").

Širokov, A. I.: Osobyj lager' No. 5 MVD SSSR v sisteme Dal'stroja (analiz dokumentov central'nych archivnych chranilišč). In: II Dikovskie Čtenija. Magadan 2002, S. 63–65 („Osobyj lager'").

Širokov, A. I.: Iz istorii železnodorožnogo stroitel'stva na Severo-Vostoke. In: Gorbunov, A. A. u. a. (Hg.): Social'no-ėkonomičeskoe razvitie Severo-Vostoka Rossii: vyzovy XXI veka: Materialy pervoj mežregion. nauč.-prakt. konf., posvjašč. 50-letiju Magadan. obl. Magadan 2003, S. 145–155 („Iz istorii železnodorožnogo stroitel'stva").

Širokov, A. I.: Lagernaja Kolyma v vospominanijach i issledovanijach (istografičeskij ėtjud). In: Čajkovskij, R. R. (Hg.): Ė. M. Remark i lagernaja literatura. Magadan 2003, S. 89–101 („Lagernaja Kolyma v vospominanijach").

Širokov, A. I.: Severo-Vostok v sisteme obščestvennych otnošenij SSSR v 30–50-e gg. XX stoletija (teoretičeskij i praktičeskij aspekty). In: Kolymskij gumanitarnyj al'manach 1 (2006), S. 5–35 („Severo-Vostok").

Širokov, A. I.: Organizacionnye formy kolonizacii Severo-Vostoka Rossii v 1930–1950-ch gg. In: Kolymskij gumanitarnyj al'manach 2 (2007), S. 54–67 („Organizacionnye formy").

Širokov, A. I.: Gosudarstvennaja politika na Severo-Vostoke Rossii v 1920–1950-ch gg. Opyt i uroki istorii. Tomsk 2009 („Politika").

Širokov, A. I.: Dal'stroj v social'no-ėkonomičeskom razvitii Severo-Vostoka SSSR (1930–1950-e gg.). Moskau 2014 („Dal'stroj v social'no-ėkonomičeskom razvitii").

Širokov, A. I.; Ėtlis, M. M.: Sovetskij period istorii Severo-Vostoka Rossii (istoriografija i novye archivnye dannye). Magadan 1993 („Sovetskij period").

Širokov, A. I.; Rajzman, D. I.: Sostojanie zdorov'ja zaključennych v podrazdelenijach Dal'stroja v 1950–1955 gg. (po otčetam medicinskich otdelov Severnogo, Čaun-Čukotskogo i Janskogo ITL). In: Kolymskij gumanitarnyj al'manach 1 (2006), S. 117–131 („Sostojanie zdorov'ja zaključennych").

Širokov, A. I.; Zeljak, V. G.: Metodologičeskie problemy izučenija istorii Severo-Vostoka Rossii XX v. In: Gorjačev, N. A. u. a. (Hg.): Severo-Vostok Rossii: Prošloe, nastojaščee, buduščee. Materialy II regional'noj naučno-praktičeskoj konferencii. Tom I. Magadan 2004, S. 31–35 („Metodologičeskie problemy").

Šulubina, S. A.: Sistemy oplaty truda zaključennych v Dal'stroe (1932–41 gg.). In: Kokorev, E. M.; Birjukova, L. P. (Hg.): Materialy naučno-praktičeskoj konferencii, posvjaščennoj 40-letiju Severnogo Meždunarodnogo Universiteta. Magadan 2001, S. 120–121 („Sistemy oplaty truda zaključennych").

Šulubina, S. A.: Sistema Sevvostlaga. 1932–1957 gg. Avtoreferat dissertacii. Tomsk 2003 („Sistema Sevvostlaga").

Šulubina, S. A.: Osobennosti organizacii Sevvostlaga (1932–1941 gg.). In: Kolymskij gumanitarnyj al'manach 1 (2006), S. 67–84 („Sevvostlaga").

Taubman, William: Khrushchev. The Man and his Era. London ²2004 („Man and Era").

Taubman, William; Khrushchev, Sergei; Gleason, Abbott (Hg.): Nikita Khrushchev. New Haven 2000 („Khrushchev").

Thatcher, Ian D.: Khrushchev as Leader. In: Ilic, Melanie; Smith, Jeremy (Hg.): Khrushchev in the Kremlin: Policy and Government in the Soviet Union, 1953–1964. New York 2011, S. 9–25 („Khrushchev").

Thun-Hohenstein, Franziska: Poetik der Unerbittlichkeit. Varlam Šalamov: Leben und Werk. In: Osteuropa 57 (2007) [Themenheft: Das Lager schreiben. Hg. von Manfred Sapper; Volker Weichsel und Andrea Huterer], S. 35–51 („Poetik der Unerbittlichkeit").

Tikhonov, Aleksei: The End of the Gulag. In: Gregory, Paul R.; Lazarev, Valery (Hg.): The Economics of Forced Labor: The Soviet Gulag. Stanford, Kalifornien 2003, S. 67–73 („The End").

Titov, Alexander: The Central Committee Apparatus under Khrushchev. In: Ilic, Melanie; Smith, Jeremy (Hg.): Khrushchev in the Kremlin: Policy and Government in the Soviet Union, 1953–1964. New York 2011, S. 41–60 („Central Committee").

Toker, Leona: Return from the Archipelago. Narratives of Gulag Survivors. Bloomington 2000 („Return from Archipelago").

Tolokonceva, V. V.; Kozlov, A. G.: U istokov nauki Severo-Vostoka Rossii. Iz istorii VNII-1 (1940–1960). In: II Dikovskie Čtenija. Magadan 2002, S. 148–154 („U istokov nauki").

Tompson, W.: Khrushchev. A Political Life. Basingstoke 1995 („Khrushchev").

Tompson, William: Leadership Transition and Policy Change in the USSR after Stalin. In: Kritika: Explorations in Russian and Eurasian History 15 (2014), S. 217–228 („Leadership Transition").

Tret'jakov, M. V.: Oplata truda i material'noe stimulirovanie rabotnikov aviaotrjada Dal'stroja v 1930-ch gg. In: Kolymskij gumanitarnyj al'manach 2 (2007), S. 94–99 („Oplata truda").

Tromly, Benjamin: Making the Soviet Intelligentsia: Universities and Intellectual Life under Stalin and Khrushchev. Cambridge 2014 („Soviet Intelligentsia").

Tropynina, A. A.: Istorija Kolymskich lagerej na stranicach „Magadanskoj Pravdy" (materialy k bibliografii). In: Čajkovskij, R. R. (Hg.): Ė. M. Remark i lagernaja literatura. Magadan 2003, S. 120–127 („Istorija Kolymskich lagerej na stranicach").

Urbansky, Sören: Auf in die Provinz! Recherchen in Russlands Regionalarchiven. In: Osteuropa 59 (2009), H. 11, S. 121–130 („Auf in die Provinz").

Urbansky, Sören (Hg.): „Unsere Insel". Sowjetische Identitätspolitik auf Sachalin nach 1945. Berlin-Brandenburg 2013 („Unsere Insel").

Urbansky, Sören; Ackermann, Felix (Hg.): Reframing Postwar Sovietization. Power, Conflict, and Accomodation. Themenheft der Zeitschrift Jahrbücher für Geschichte Osteuropas 64 (2016) („Reframing").

Urbansky, Sören; Ackermann, Felix: Introduction. In: Jahrbücher für Geschichte Osteuropas 64 (2016) [Themenheft: Reframing Postwar Sovietization. Power, Conflict, and Accomodation. Hg. von Sören Urbansky und Felix Ackermann], S. 353–362 („Introduction").

Urbansky, Sören; Barop, Helena: Under the Red Star's Faint Light: How Sakhalin Became Soviet. In: Kritika: Explorations in Russian and Eurasian History 18 (2017), S. 283–316 („Faint Light").

Van der Linden, M.: Forced Labour and Non-Capitalist Industrialization: The Case of Stalinism (1929–1956). In: Brass, T.; Van der Linden, M. (Hg.): Free and Unfree Labour. The Debate Continues. New York 1997, S. 351–362 („Forced Labour").

Van Goudoever, Albert P.: The Limits of Destalinization in the Soviet Union. Political Rehabilitations in the Soviet Union since Stalin. London; Sydney 1986 („Limits").

Varga-Harris, Christine: Forging Citizenship on the Home Front: Reviving the Socialist Contract and Constructing Soviet Identity during the Thaw. In: Jones, Polly (Hg.): The Dilemmas of De-Stalinization. Negotiating Cultural and Social Change in the Krushchev Era. London u. a. 2006, S. 101–116 („Socialist Contract").

Vasiliev, Valery: Failings of the Sovnarkhoz Reform: the Ukrainian Experience. In: Ilic, Melanie; Smith, Jeremy (Hg.): Khrushchev in the Kremlin: Policy and Government in the Soviet Union, 1953–1964. New York 2011, S. 112–132 („Failings").

Vasil'eva, E. V.: Nauka Dal'nego Vostoka SSSR v pervoe poslevoennoe desjatiletie. In: Vestnik DVO RAN 1996, S. 109–123 („Nauka Dal'nego Vostoka").

Verkina, T. V.; Kozlov, A. G.: K voprosu ob obrazovanii Magadanskoj oblasti. In: II Dikovskie Čtenija. Magadan 2002, S. 111–116 („K voprosu ob obrazovanii").

Verkina, T. V.; Kozlov, A. G.: Nacional'nye rajony Kolymy nakanune obrazovanija Magadanskoj oblasti. In: II Dikovskie Čtenija. Magadan 2002, S. 73–80 („Nacional'nye rajony Kolymy").

Verkina, T. V.; Kozlov, A. G.: Novye dannye k biografii pervogo direktora Dal'stroja É. P. Berzina. In: II Dikovskie Čtenija. Magadan 2002, S. 105–111 („Novye dannye").

Verkina, T. V.; Kozlov, A. G.: Istoričeskaja spravka ob obrazovanii Magadanskoj oblasti. [unveröff. Beitrag] („Istoričeskaja spravka").

Viola, Lynne: The Unknown Gulag. The Lost World of Stalin's Special Settlements. Oxford u. a. 2007 („Unknown Gulag").

Viola, Lynne: Stalin's Empire: The Gulag and Police Colonization in the Soviet Union in the 1930s. In: Snyder, Timothy; Brandon, Ray: Stalin and Europe: Imitation and Domination, 1928–1953. New York 2014, S. 18–43 („Stalin's Empire").

Weiner, Amir: The Empires Pay a Visit: Gulag Returnees, East European Rebellion, and Soviet Frontier Politics. In: The Journal of Modern History 78 (2006), S. 333–376 („Empires Pay a Visit").

Werth, Nicolas: L'amnistie du 27 mars 1953. La première grande sortie du Goulag. In: Communisme 42 / 43 / 44 (1995), S. 211–223 („L'amnistie").

Widdis, Emma: To Explore or Conquer? Mobile Perspectives on the Soviet Cultural Revolution. In: Dobrenko, Evgeny; Naiman, Eric (Hg.): The Landscape of Stalinism. The Art and Ideology of Soviet Space. Washington 2003, S. 219–240 („Mobile Perspectives").

Wolfe, Thomas C.: Governing Soviet Journalism: the Press and the Socialist Person after Stalin. Bloomington 2005 („Soviet Journalism").

Yurchak, Alexei: Everything Was Forever, Until it Was no More. The Last Soviet Generation. Princeton; New York 2006 („Was Forever").

Zacharčenko, Aleksej V.: Die Aufarbeitung der Geschichte des Gulag in Russland. In: Landau, Julia; Scherbakova, Irina (Hg.): GULAG. Texte und Dokumente 1929–1956. Göttingen 2014, S. 70–79 („Aufarbeitung").

Zacharčenko, A. V.: Ot stalinskogo lagerno-promyšlennogo kompleksa – k raspadu ėkonomiki prinuditel'nogo truda (1953–1956 gg.). In: Posle Stalina. Reformy 1950-ch godov v kontekste sovetskoj i postsovetskoj istorii: Materialy VIII meždunarodnoj naučnoj konferencii. Ekaterinburg, 15–17 oktjabrja 2015 g. Moskau 2016, S. 298–310 („K raspadu ėkonomiki prinuditel'nogo truda").

Zeljak, V. G.: Razvitie social'noj infrastruktury Dal'stroja v gody velikoj otečestvennoj vojny. In: Dikovskie Čtenija. Magadan 2001, S. 213–216 („V gody velikoj otečestvennoj vojny").

Zeljak, V. G.: Uranodobyvajuščaja otrasl' Dal'stroja (1948–1956 gg.). In: Kokorev, E. M.; Birjukova, L. P. (Hg.): Materialy naučno-praktičeskoj konferencii, posvjaščennoj 40-letiju Severnogo Meždunarodnogo Universiteta. Magadan 2001, S. 121–124 („Uranodobyvajuščaja otrasl'").

Zeljak, V. G.: Dražnaja zolotodobyča na Severo-Vostoke Rossii v 50-e gg. XX stoletija. In: II Dikovskie Čtenija. Magadan 2002, S. 47–51 („Dražnaja zolotodobyča").

Zeljak, V. G.: Bilibinskaja atomnaja stancija: Istorija stroitel'stva i sovremennost'. In: Gorbunov, A. A. u. a. (Hg.): Social'no-ėkonomičeskoe razvitie Severo-Vostoka Rossii: vyzovy XXI veka: Materialy pervoj mežregion. nauč.-prakt. konf., posvjašč. 50-letiju Magadan. obl. Magadan 2003, S. 46–51 („Bilibinskaja atomnaja stancija").

Zeljak, V. G.: Pjat' metallov Dal'stroja. Istorija gornodobyvajuščej promyšlennosti Severo-Vostoka Rossii v 30–50-ch gg. XX v. Magadan 2004 („Pjat' metallov").

Zeljak, V. G.: Osobennosti razvitija zolotodobyvajuščej promyšlennosti na Severo-Vostoka Rossii v 30–50-ch gg. XX v. In: Kolymskij gumanitarnyj al'manach 1 (2006), S. 85–102 („Osobennosti razvitija").

Zeljak, V. G.: Zolotodobyvajuščaja promyšlennost' Dal'stroja i Magadanskogo sovnarchoza: sravnitel'no-istoričeskij analiz. In: Kolymskij gumanitarnyj al'manach 2 (2007), S. 139–153 („Zolotodobyvajuščaja promyšlennost'").

Zeljak, V. G.; Širokov, A. I.: Metodologičeskie problemy izučenija istorii Severo-Vostoka Rossii XX v. In: Gorjačev, N. A. u. a. (Hg.): Severo-Vostok Rossii: prošloe, nastojaščee, buduščee: Materialy II. region. nauč.-prakt. konf. Tom I. Magadan 2003, S. 31–35 („Metodologičeskie problemy").

Zemskov, V. N.: Specposelency v SSSR, 1930–1960. Moskau 2003 („Specposelency").

Zhuk, Sergej: Popular Culture, Identity and Soviet Youth in Dniepropetrovsk, 1959–1984. Pittsburgh 2008 („Popular Culture").

Zlatina, N. S.: Periodičeskaja pečat' Magadanskoj oblasti (gazety kraja). Magadan 1967 („Periodičeskaja pečat'").

Zoloto Rossii. Moskau 2002 („Zoloto Rossii").

Zubkova, Elena: Obščestvo i reformy 1945–1964. Moskau 1993 („Obščestvo").

Zubkova, E. Ju.: Malenkov i Chruščev: Ličnyj faktor v politike poslestalinskogo rukovodstva. In: Otečestvennaja Istorija 1995, H. 4, S. 103–115 („Malenkov i Chruščev").

Zubkova, Elena: Russia after the War: Hopes, Illusions, and Disappointments, 1945–1957. Armonk, New York 1998 („After the War").

Zubkova, Elena: Poslevoenne sovetskoe obščestvo: Politika i povsednevnost' 1945–1953. Moskau 1999 („Poslevoenne obščestvo").

Zubkova, Elena: Na „kraju" sovetskogo obščestva. Social'nye marginaly kak ob"ekt gosudarstvennoj politiki 1945–1960-e gg. Moskau 2010 („Marginaly").

Žukov, Ju. N.: Bor'ba za vlast' v partijno-gosudarstvennych verchach SSSR vesnoj 1953 goda. In: Voprosy Istorii 1996, H. 5–6, S. 39–57 („Bor'ba").

Žulanova, I. L.: Akademičeskaja geologija na Severo-Vostoke Rossii: mesto v istoričeskom kontekste, perspektivy. In: VI Dikovskie Čtenija. Magadan 2010, S. 17–19 („Akademičeskaja geologija").

Personenregister